KEY TO WORLD MAP PAGES

— Large scale maps (> 1:2 500 000)
— Medium scale maps (1:2 800 000-1:9 000 000)
— Small scale maps (< 1:10 000 000)

54 · 50-51 · 48-49 · 66-67 · 62-63 · 52-53 · 60-61 · 55 · 68 · 58-59 · 56-57

ASIA
44-69

NORTH AMERICA
94-117

96-97 · 98-99 · 104-105 · 106-107 · 108-109 · 116-117

SOUTH AMERICA
118-128

120-121 · 122-123 · 124-125 · 126-127 · 128

COUN

Afghanistan
Albania
Algeria
Angola
Argentina
Armenia
Australia 88–91
Austria 19, 20–21
Azerbaijan 67

Bahamas 116–117
Bahrain 65
Bangladesh 61
Barbados 117
Belgium 17
Belize 116
Belorussia 40
Benin 79
Bhutan 61
Bolivia 124–125
Bosnia-Herzegovina 21
Botswana 84–85
Brazil 120–127
Brunei 56
Bulgaria 38–39
Burkina Faso 78–79
Burma 61
Burundi 82

Cambodia 58–59
Cameroon 82
Canada 96–101
Central African Republic 82
Chad 73
Chile 126, 128
China 50–54
Colombia 120
Congo 80
Costa Rica 116
Croatia 21
Cuba 116–117
Cyprus 37
Czech Republic 20–21

Denmark 11
Djibouti 68
Dominican Republic 117

Ecuador 120
Egypt 76
El Salvador 116
England 12–13
Equatorial Guinea 80
Eritrea 76–77
Estonia 40
Ethiopia 68, 77

Fiji 87
Finland 8–9
France 24–27
French Guiana 121

Gabon 80
Gambia 78
Georgia 43
Germany 18–19
Ghana 78–79
Greece 39
Greenland 4
Guatemala 116
Guinea 78
Guinea-Bissau 78
Guyana 121

Haiti 117
Honduras 116
Hong Kong 53
Hungary 21

Iceland 8
India 60–63
Indonesia 56–57
Iran 64–65
Iraq 64–65
Irish Republic 15
Israel 69
Italy 32–35
Ivory Coast 78

Jamaica 116
Japan 48–49
Jordan 69

Kazakhstan 44
Kenya 82
Kirghizia 44
Korea, North 51
Korea, South 51

Liberia 78
Libya 73
Lithuania 40
Luxembourg 17

Macedonia 38–39
Madagascar 85
Malawi 83
Malaysia 55–56
Mali 78–79
Malta 37
Mauritania 78
Mauritius 71
Mexico 114–115
Moldavia 42
Mongolia 54
Morocco 74
Mozambique 83

Namibia 84
Nepal 63
Netherlands 16–17
New Zealand 87
Nicaragua 116
Niger 79
Nigeria 79
Northern Ireland 15
Norway 8–9

Oman 68

Pakistan 62
Panama 116
Papua New Guinea 86
Paraguay 126–127
Peru 124
Philippines 55
Poland 20
Portugal 30–31
Puerto Rico 117

Qatar 65

Romania 38
Russia 40–45
Rwanda 82

Saudi Arabia 68
Scotland 14
Senegal 78
Sierra Leone 78
Singapore 59
Slovak Republic 20–21
Slovenia 33
Somali Republic 68
South Africa 84–85
Spain 28–31
Sri Lanka 60
Sudan 77
Surinam 121
Swaziland 85
Sweden 8–9
Switzerland 22–23
Syria 67

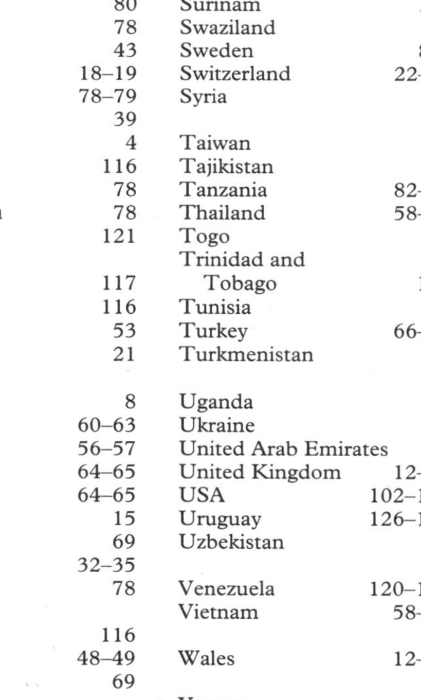

Taiwan 53
Tajikistan 44
Tanzania 82–83
Thailand 58–59
Togo 79
Trinidad and Tobago 117
Tunisia 75
Turkey 66–67
Turkmenistan 44

Uganda 82
Ukraine 42
United Arab Emirates 65
United Kingdom 12–15
USA 102–113
Uruguay 126–127
Uzbekistan 44

Venezuela 120–121
Vietnam 58–59

Wales 12–13

Yemen 68
Yugoslavia 38–39

Zaïre 80–81
Zambia 83
Zimbabwe 83

PHILIP'S

GREAT WORLD ATLAS

Jonathan

Congratulations on the occasion of your Barmitzvah. Now you are a man, you'll want to travel the world.

Regards Geoffrey and Lynn

October 28, 1995

PHILIP'S

GREAT WORLD ATLAS

Published in Great Britain in 1994
by George Philip Limited,
an imprint of Reed Consumer Books Limited,
Michelin House, 81 Fulham Road, London SW3 6RB,
and Auckland, Melbourne, Singapore and Toronto

Cartography by Philip's

Copyright © 1994 Reed International Books Limited

ISBN 0-540-05832-7

A CIP catalogue record for this book is available from the British Library

All rights reserved. Apart from any fair dealing for the purpose of private study, research, criticism or review, as permitted under the Copyright Designs and Patents Act, 1988, no part of this publication may be reproduced, stored in a retrieval system, or transmitted in any form or by any means, electronic, electrical, chemical, mechanical, optical, photocopying, recording, or otherwise, without prior written permission. All enquiries should be addressed to the Publishers.

Printed in Spain

PHILIP'S WORLD MAPS

The reference maps which form the main body of this atlas have been prepared in accordance with the highest standards of international cartography to provide an accurate and detailed representation of the Earth. The scales and projections used have been carefully chosen to give balanced coverage of the world, while emphasizing the most densely populated and economically significant regions. A hallmark of Philip's mapping is the use of hill shading and relief colouring to create a graphic impression of landforms: this makes the maps exceptionally easy to read. However, knowledge of the key features employed in the construction and presentation of the maps will enable the reader to derive the fullest benefit from the atlas.

Map sequence

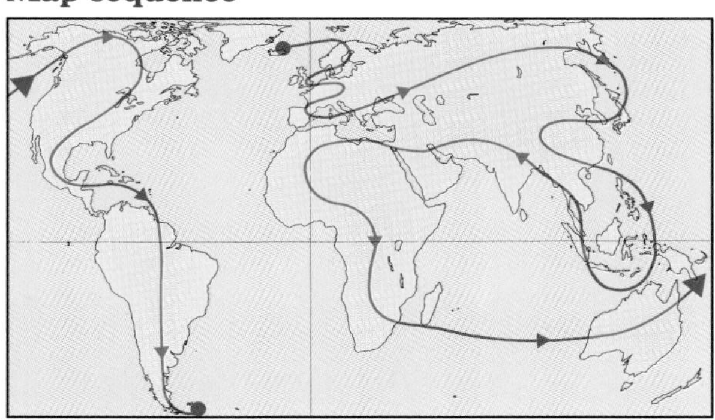

The atlas covers the Earth continent by continent: first Europe; then its land neighbour Asia (mapped north before south, in a clockwise sequence), then Africa, Australia and Oceania, North America and South America. This is the classic arrangement adopted by most cartographers since the 16th century. For each continent, there are maps at a variety of scales. First, physical relief and political maps of the whole continent; then a series of larger-scale maps of the regions within the continent, each followed, where required, by still larger-scale maps of the most important or densely populated areas. The governing principle is that by turning the pages of the atlas, the reader moves steadily from north to south through each continent, with each map overlapping its neighbours. A key map showing this sequence, and the area covered by each map, can be found on the endpapers of the atlas.

Map presentation

With very few exceptions (e.g. for the Arctic and Antarctic), the maps are drawn with north at the top, regardless of whether they are presented upright or sideways on the page. In the borders will be found the map title; a locator diagram showing the area covered and the page numbers for maps of adjacent areas; the scale; the projection used; the degrees of latitude and longitude; and the letters and figures used in the index for locating place names and geographical features. Physical relief maps also have a height reference panel identifying the colours used for each layer of contouring.

Map symbols

Each map contains a vast amount of detail which can only be conveyed clearly and accurately by the use of symbols. Points and circles of varying sizes locate and identify the relative importance of towns and cities; different styles of type are employed for administrative, geographical and regional place names. A variety of pictorial symbols denote landscape features such as glaciers, marshes and reefs, and man-made structures including roads, railways, airports, canals and dams. International borders are shown by red lines. Where neighbouring countries are in dispute, for example in the Middle East, the maps show the *de facto* boundary between nations, regardless of the legal or historical situation. The symbols are explained on the first page of the World Maps section of the atlas.

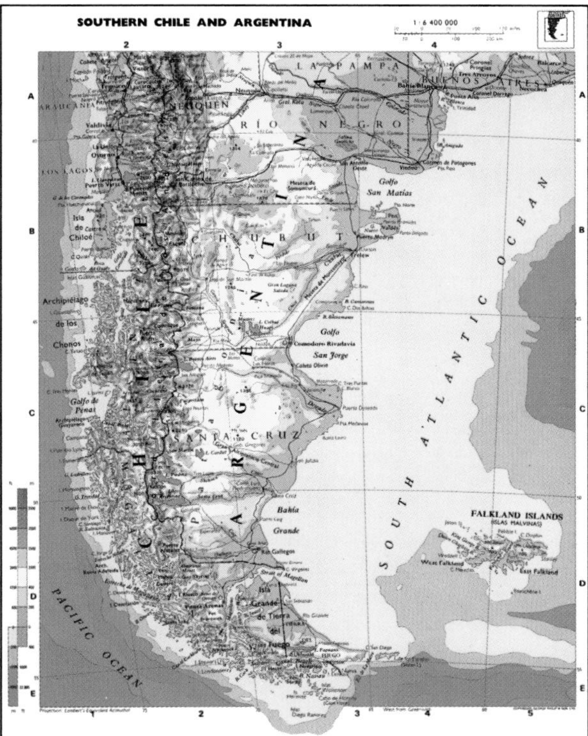
SOUTHERN CHILE AND ARGENTINA
LA PAMPA
RÍO NEGRO
CHUBUT
SANTA CRUZ
FALKLAND ISLANDS
SOUTH ATLANTIC OCEAN
PACIFIC OCEAN
Golfo San Matías
Golfo San Jorge

Map scales

1: 16 000 000
1 inch = 252 statute miles

The scale of each map is given in the numerical form known as the 'representative fraction'. The first figure is always one, signifying one unit of distance on the map; the second figure, usually in millions, is the number by which the map unit must be multiplied to give the equivalent distance on the Earth's surface. Calculations can easily be made in centimetres and kilometres, by dividing the Earth units figure by 100 000 (i.e. deleting the last five 0s). Thus 1:1 000 000 means 1 cm = 10 km. The calculation for inches and miles is more laborious, but 1 000 000 divided by 63 360 (the number of inches in a mile) shows that 1:1 000 000 means approximately 1 inch = 16 miles. The table below provides distance equivalents for scales down to 1:50 000 000.

LARGE SCALE		
1: 1 000 000	1 cm = 10 km	1 inch = 16 miles
1: 2 500 000	1 cm = 25 km	1 inch = 39.5 miles
1: 5 000 000	1 cm = 50 km	1 inch = 79 miles
1: 6 000 000	1 cm = 60 km	1 inch = 95 miles
1: 8 000 000	1 cm = 80 km	1 inch = 126 miles
1: 10 000 000	1 cm = 100 km	1 inch = 158 miles
1: 15 000 000	1 cm = 150 km	1 inch = 237 miles
1: 20 000 000	1 cm = 200 km	1 inch = 316 miles
1: 50 000 000	1 cm = 500 km	1 inch = 790 miles
SMALL SCALE		

Measuring distances

100 0 100 200 300 400 miles
100 0 100 200 300 400 500 600 km

Although each map is accompanied by a scale bar, distances cannot always be measured with confidence because of the distortions involved in portraying the curved surface of the Earth on a flat page. As a general rule, the larger the map scale (i.e. the lower the number of Earth units in the representative fraction), the more accurate and reliable will be the distance measured. On small-scale maps such as those of the world and of entire continents, measurement may only be accurate along the 'standard parallels', or central axes, and should not be attempted without considering the map projection.

Map projections

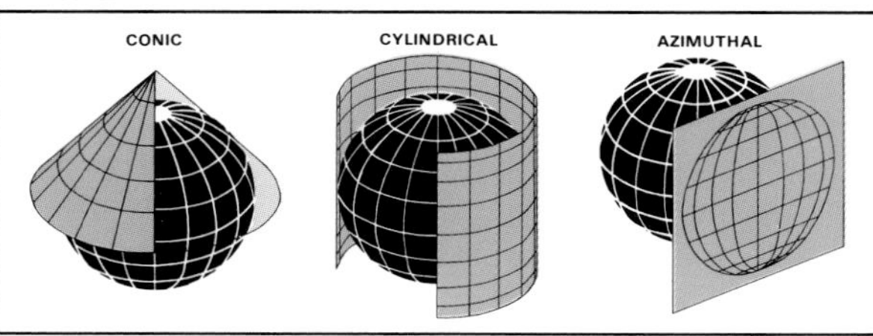
CONIC
CYLINDRICAL
AZIMUTHAL

Unlike a globe, no flat map can give a true scale representation of the world in terms of area, shape and position of every region. Each of the numerous systems that have been devised for projecting the curved surface of the Earth on to a flat page involves the sacrifice of accuracy in one or more of these elements. The variations in shape and position of landmasses such as Alaska, Greenland and Australia, for example, can be quite dramatic when different projections are compared.

For this atlas, the guiding principle has been to select projections that involve the least distortion of size and distance. The projection used for each map is noted in the border. Most fall into one of three categories – conic, cylindrical or azimuthal – whose basic concepts are shown above. Each involves plotting the forms of the Earth's surface on a grid of latitude and longitude lines, which may be shown as parallels, curves or radiating spokes.

Latitude and longitude

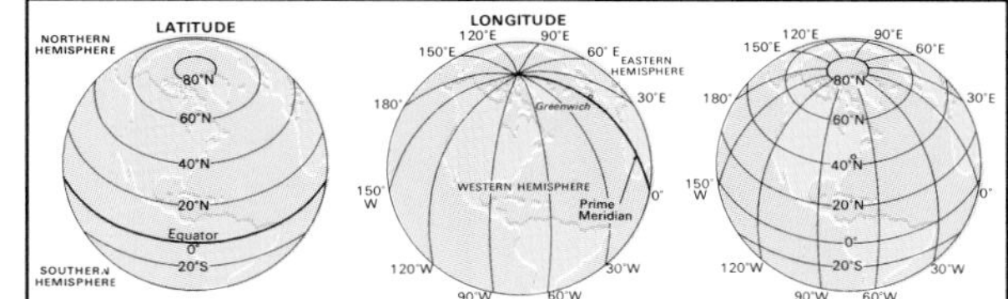
LATITUDE
NORTHERN HEMISPHERE
SOUTHERN HEMISPHERE
Equator
LONGITUDE
EASTERN HEMISPHERE
WESTERN HEMISPHERE
Prime Meridian
Greenwich

Accurate positioning of individual points on the Earth's surface is made possible by reference to the geometrical system of latitude and longitude. Latitude *parallels* are drawn west–east around the Earth and numbered by degrees north and south of the Equator, which is designated 0° of latitude. Longitude *meridians* are drawn north–south and numbered by degrees east and west of the *prime meridian*, 0° of longitude, which passes through Greenwich in England. By referring to these co-ordinates and their subdivisions of minutes (1/60th of a degree) and seconds (1/60th of a minute), any place on Earth can be located to within a few hundred yards. Latitude and longitude are indicated by blue lines on the maps; they are straight or curved according to the projection employed. Reference to these lines is the easiest way of determining the relative positions of places on different maps, and for plotting compass directions.

Name forms

For ease of reference, both English and local name forms appear in the atlas. Oceans, seas and countries are shown in English throughout the atlas; country names may be abbreviated to their commonly accepted form (e.g. Germany, not The Federal Republic of Germany). Conventional English forms are also used for place names on the smaller-scale maps of the continents. However, local name forms are used on all large-scale and regional maps, with the English form given in brackets only for important cities – the large-scale map of Russia and Central Asia thus shows Moskva (Moscow). For countries which do not use a Roman script, place names have been transcribed according to the systems adopted by the British and US Geographic Names Authorities. For China, the Pin Yin system has been used, with some more widely known forms appearing in brackets, as with Beijing (Peking). Both English and local names appear in the index, the English form being cross-referenced to the local form.

Contents

World Statistics

Countries x
Cities xi
Distances xii
Climate xiii
Physical Dimensions xiv–xv

Introduction to World Geography

The Universe 2–3
The Solar System 4–5

The Earth
Time and Motion 6–7
Geology 8–9
Oceans 10–11
Atmosphere 12–13
Climate 14–15
Water and Land Use 16–17
Landscape 18–19
Environment 20–21

People
Demography 22–23
Cities 24–25
The Human Family 26–27
Conflict and Co-operation 28–29

Production
Agriculture 30–31
Energy 32–33
Minerals 34–35
Manufacturing 36–37
Trade 38–39

Quality of Life
Wealth 40–41
Standards 42–43
Health 44–45
Environment 46–47

World Maps 1–128

The World

Map Symbols 1

The World: Political 1:64 000 000 2–3

Arctic Ocean 1:28 000 000 Greenland 4

Antarctica 1:28 000 000 5

NOTE
The titles to the World Maps list the main countries, states and provinces covered by each map. A name given in *italics* indicates that only part of the country is shown on the map.

Europe

Europe: Physical 1:16 000 000 6

Europe: Political 1:16 000 000 7

Scandinavia and the Baltic Lands 1:4 000 000
Norway, Sweden, *Finland*, Iceland

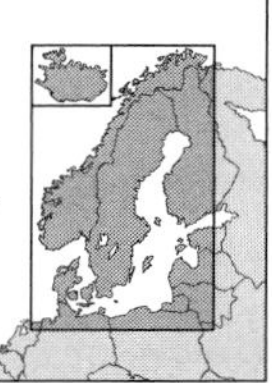

8–9

Denmark and Southern Sweden 1:2 000 000
Denmark, *Norway*, *Sweden*

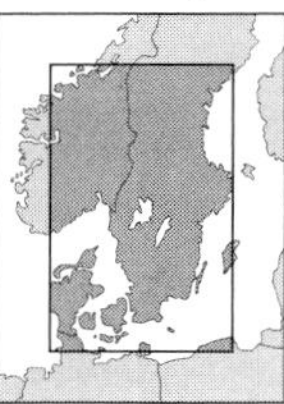

10–11

England and Wales 1:1 600 000
Isle of Man, Channel Islands

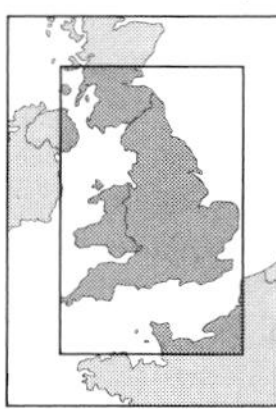

12–13

Scotland 1:1 600 000

14

Ireland 1:1 600 000
Irish Republic, Northern Ireland

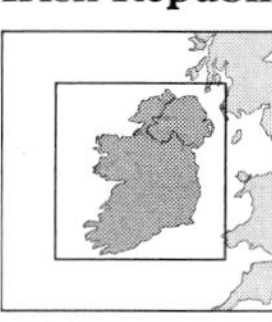

15

Netherlands, Belgium and Luxembourg 1:1 000 000

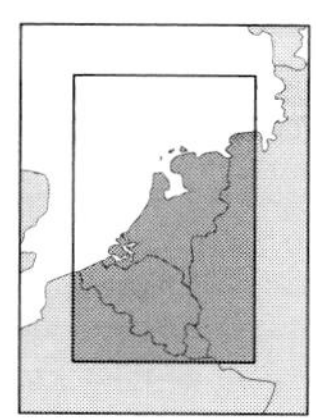

16–17

Germany 1:2 000 000

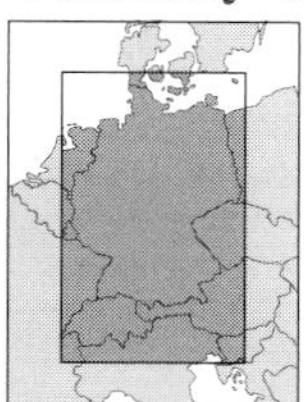

18–19

Middle Europe 1:2 800 000
Austria, Czech Republic, Slovak Republic, Hungary, Poland, Bosnia-Herzegovina, Croatia, Slovenia, Yugoslavia

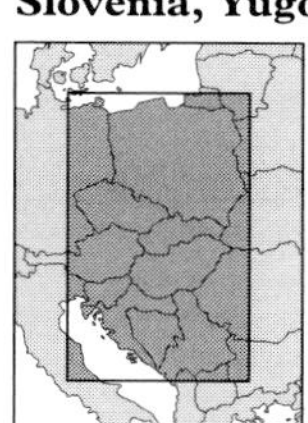

20–21

Switzerland 1:800 000
Liechtenstein

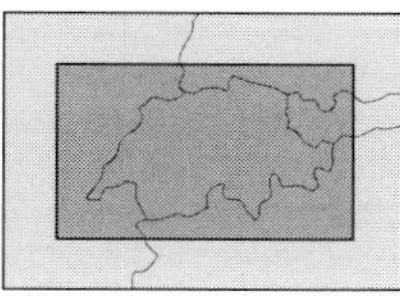

22–23

Northern France 1:2 000 000

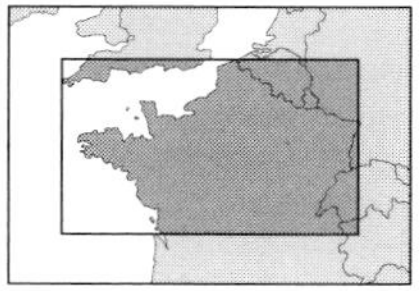

24–25

Southern France 1:2 000 000
Corsica, Monaco

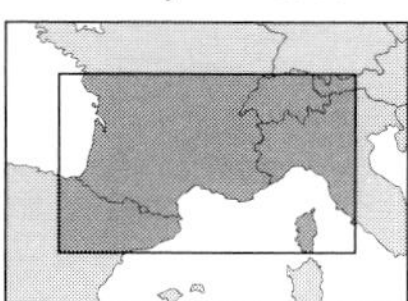

26–27

Eastern Spain 1:2 000 000
Andorra

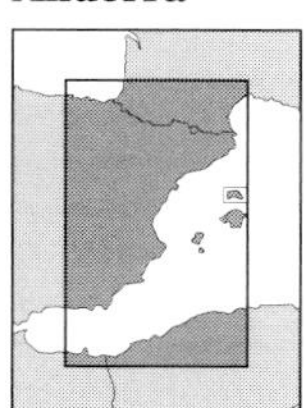

28–29

Western Spain and Portugal 1:2 000 000

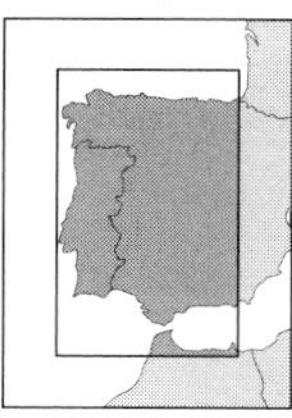

30–31

Northern Italy, Slovenia and Croatia
1:2 000 000
San Marino, Slovenia, *Croatia*

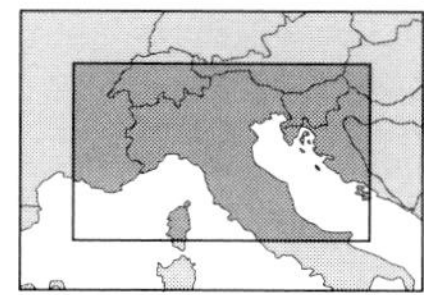

32–33

Southern Italy 1:2 000 000
Sardinia, Sicily

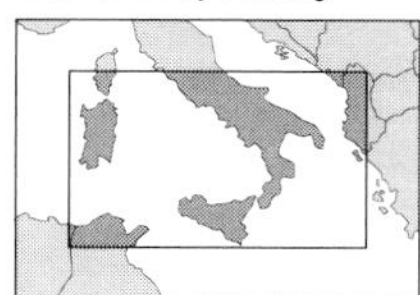

34–35

Balearics, Canaries and Madeira 1:800 000 / 1:1 040 000
Mallorca, Menorca, Ibiza, Tenerife

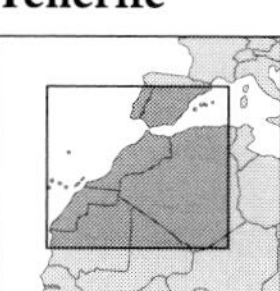

36

Malta, Crete, Corfu, Rhodes and Cyprus
1:800 000 / 1:1 600 000

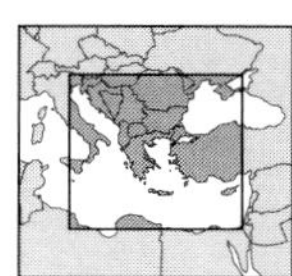

37

The Balkans 1:2 800 000
Yugoslavia, Romania, Bulgaria, Greece, Albania, Macedonia

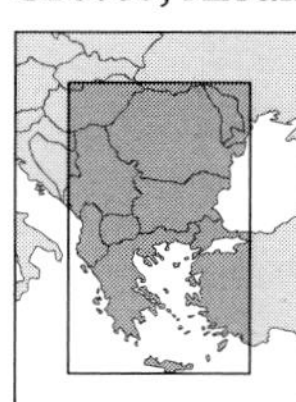

38–39

Western Russia, Belorussia and the Baltic States 1:4 000 000
Russia, Estonia, Latvia, Lithuania, Belorussia, *Ukraine*

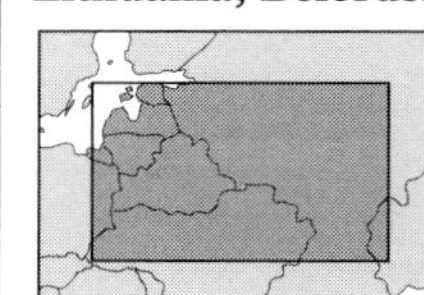

40–41

Ukraine, Moldavia and the Caucasus 1:4 000 000
Russia, Ukraine, Georgia, *Armenia, Azerbaijan,* Moldavia

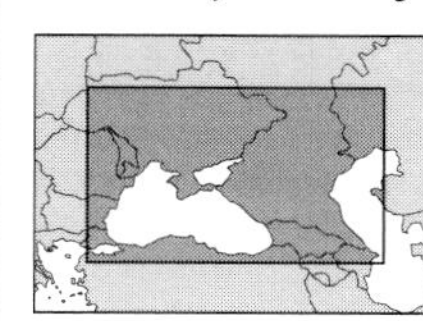

42–43

Asia

Russia and Central Asia
1:16 000 000
Russia, Kazakhstan, Turkmenistan, Uzbekistan

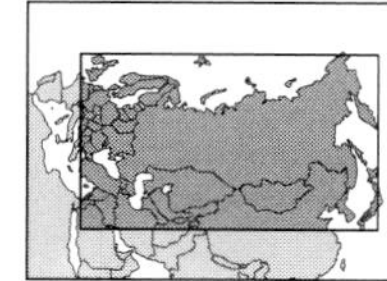

44–45

Asia: Physical
1:40 000 000
46

Asia: Political
1:40 000 000
47

Japan 1:4 000 000
Ryukyu Islands

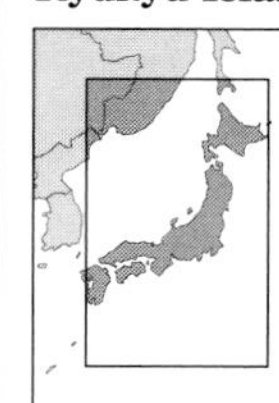

48–49

Northern China and Korea
1:4 800 000
North Korea, South Korea

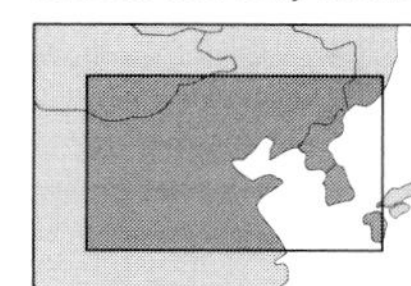

50–51

Southern China 1:4 800 000
Hong Kong, Taiwan, Macau

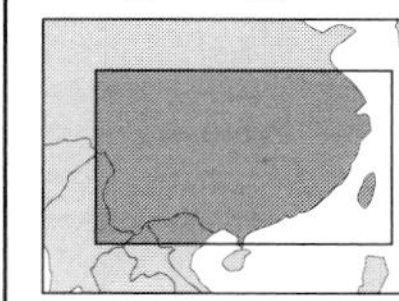

52–53

China 1:16 000 000
Mongolia

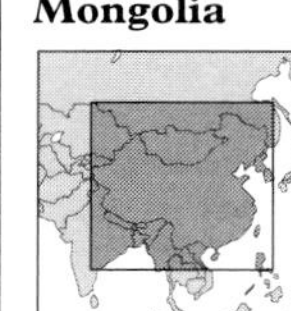

54

Philippines 1:6 000 000

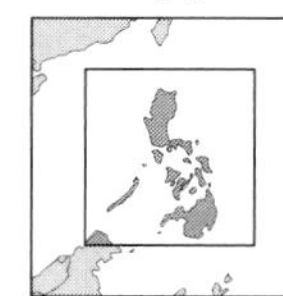

55

Indonesia 1:10 000 000
Malaysia, Singapore, Brunei
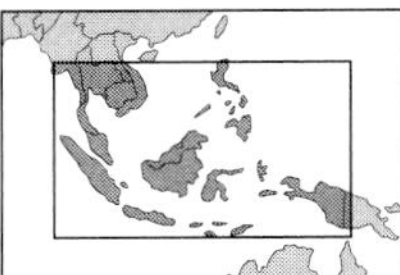
56–57

Mainland South-East Asia
1:4 800 000
Thailand, Vietnam, Cambodia, Laos
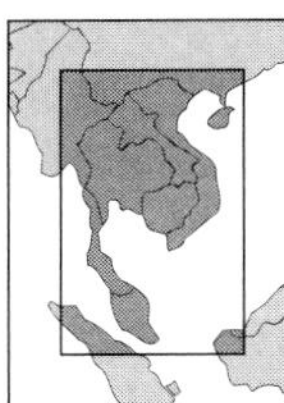
58–59

South Asia 1:8 000 000
India, Pakistan, Bangladesh, Burma, Sri Lanka, Afghanistan
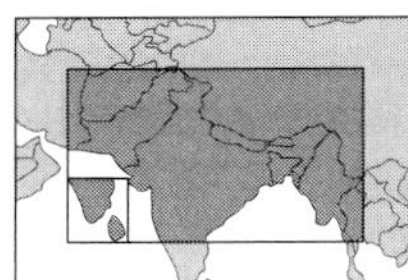
60–61

The Indo-Gangetic Plain
1:4 800 000
India, *Pakistan*, Nepal, Kashmir
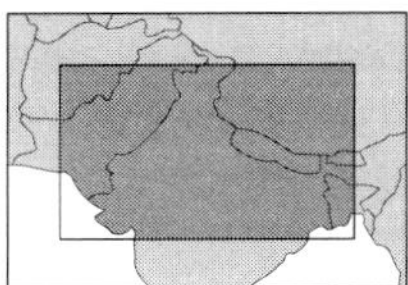
62–63

The Middle East 1:5 600 000
Iran, Iraq, *Saudi Arabia*, United Arab Emirates, Kuwait, Qatar
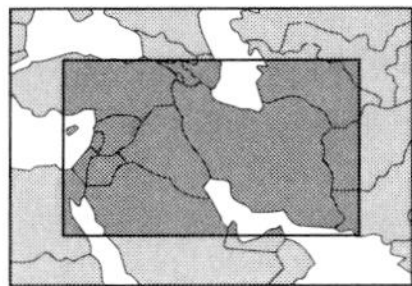
64–65

Turkey 1:4 000 000
Syria
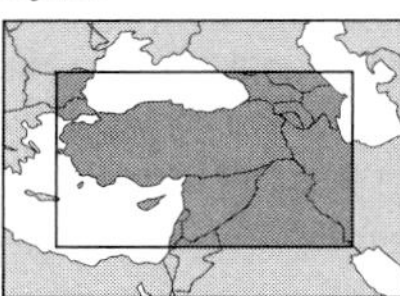
66–67

Arabia and the Horn of Africa 1:12 000 000
Saudi Arabia, Oman, Yemen, *Somalia*, Ethiopia, Eritrea, Djibouti
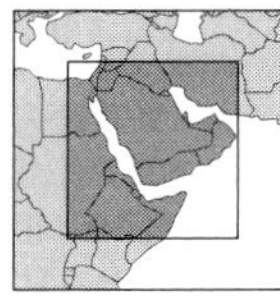
68

The Near East 1:2 000 000
Israel, Lebanon, *Jordan*
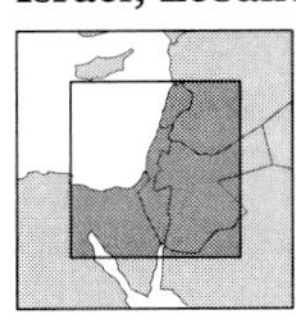
69

AFRICA

Africa: Physical
1:32 000 000
70

Africa: Political
1:32 000 000
71

Northern Africa 1:12 000 000
Libya, Chad, Niger
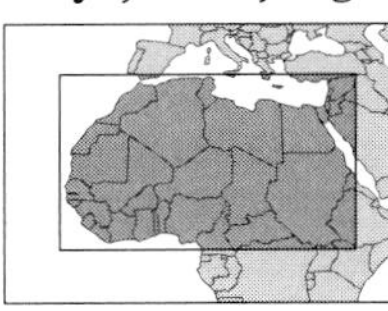
72–73

North-West Africa
1:6 400 000
Algeria, Morocco, Tunisia, *Mauritania*, *Niger*, *Mali*
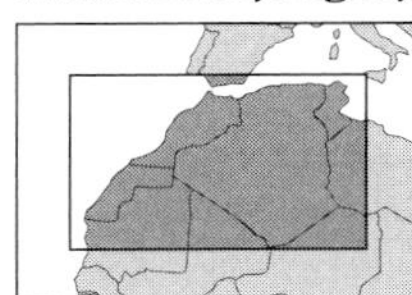
74–75

The Nile Valley 1:6 400 000
Egypt, Sudan, Eritrea, *Ethiopia*
The Nile Delta 1:3 200 000
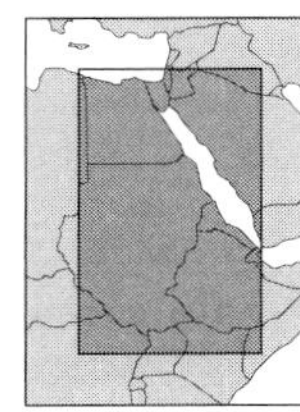
76–77

West Africa 1:6 400 000
Nigeria, Ivory Coast, Ghana, Senegal, Guinea, Burkina Faso
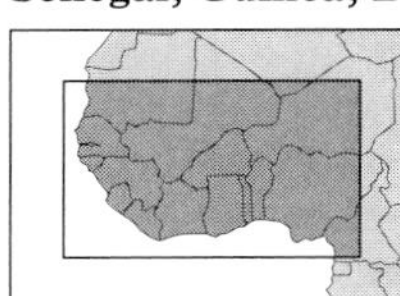
78–79

Central and Southern Africa 1:12 000 000
Zaïre, Angola, Cameroon, Congo, Gabon, Central African Republic
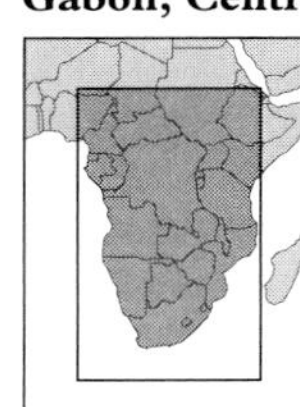
80–81

East Africa 1:6 400 000
Kenya, Tanzania, Zambia, Uganda, Malawi
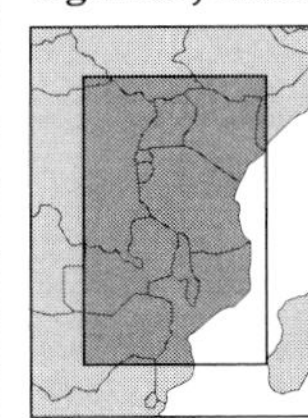
82–83

Southern Africa 1:6 400 000
South Africa, Zimbabwe, Madagascar, *Mozambique*, Botswana, Namibia
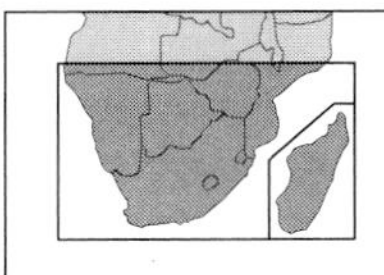
84–85

Australia and Oceania

Australia and Oceania: Physical and Political
1:32 000 000
86

New Zealand 1:4 800 000
Fiji, Tonga, Samoa

87

Western Australia
1:6 400 000
Northern Territory

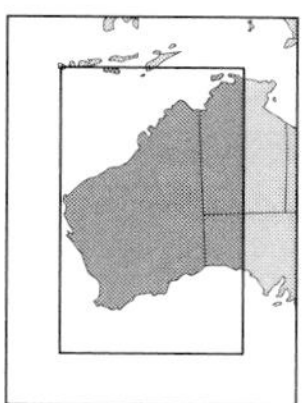

88–89

Eastern Australia 1:6 400 000
New South Wales, Queensland, Victoria, *South Australia*, Tasmania

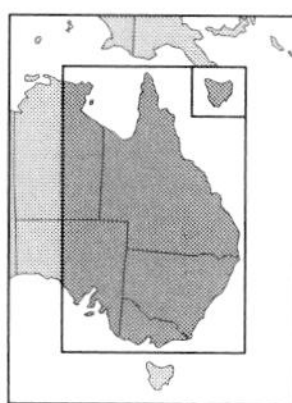

90–91

Pacific Ocean 1:43 200 000
Kiribati, Vanuatu, New Caledonia, Tuvalu, Micronesia, French Polynesia
92–93

North America

North America: Physical
1:28 000 000
94

North America: Political
1:28 000 000
95

Canada 1:12 000 000
Northwest Territories, Yukon
Alaska 1:24 000 000

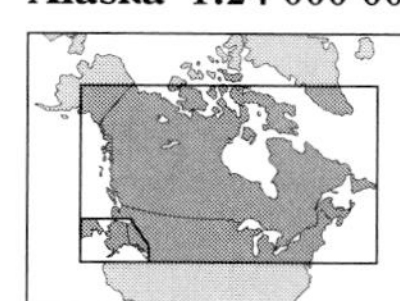

96–97

Eastern Canada 1:5 600 000
Quebec, *Ontario*, Newfoundland

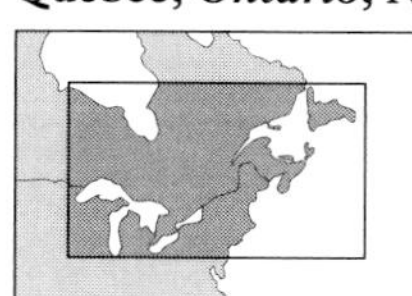

98–99

Western Canada 1:5 600 000
British Columbia, Alberta, Saskatchewan, Manitoba

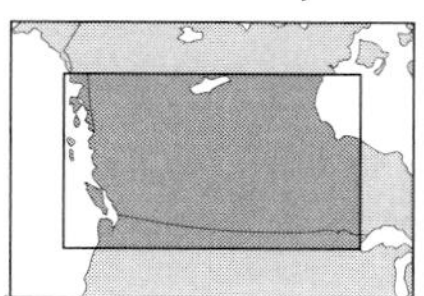

100–101

United States 1:9 600 000
Hawaii 1:8 000 000

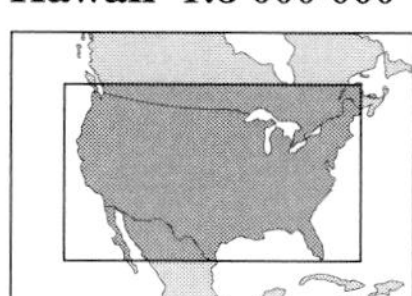

102–103

Eastern United States
1:4 800 000

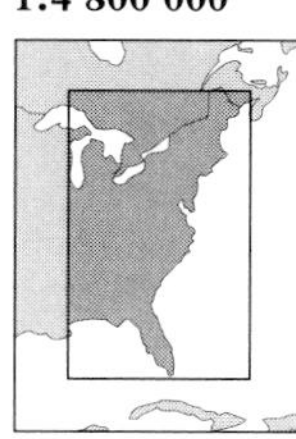

104–105

North-Eastern United States 1:2 000 000
New York, New England, *Pennsylvania*

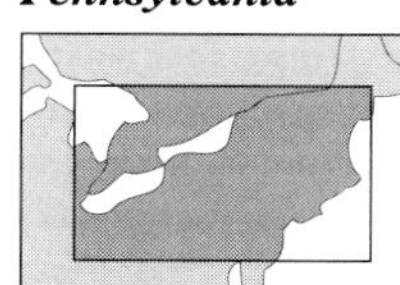

106–107

Middle United States
1:4 800 000

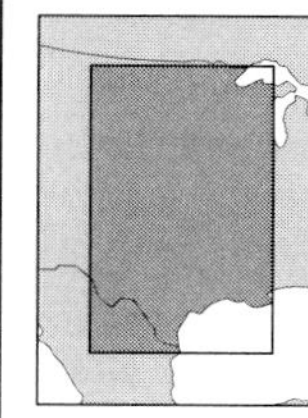

108–109

Western United States
1:4 800 000

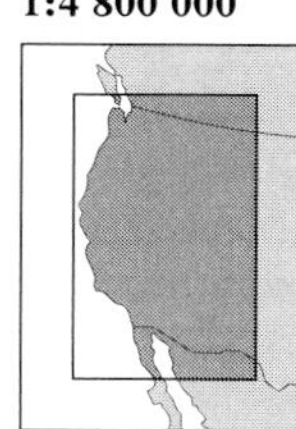

110–111

Central and Southern California and Washington 1:2 000 000

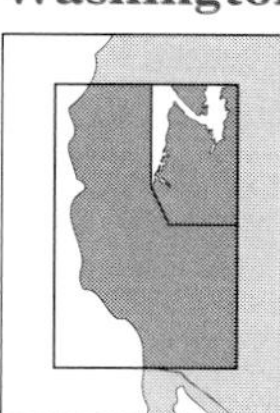

112–113

Mexico 1:6 400 000

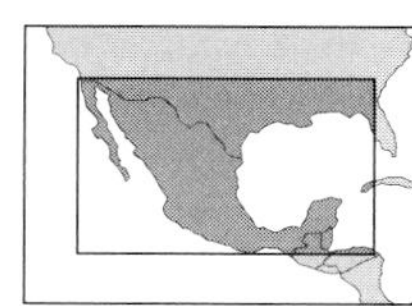

114–115

Central America and the West Indies 1:6 400 000
Guatemala, Nicaragua, Cuba, Jamaica, Panama, Haiti

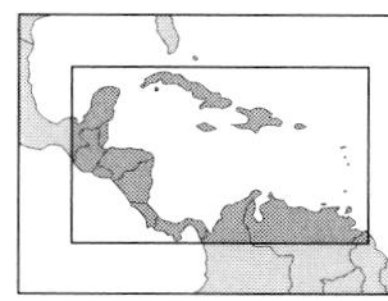

116–117

South America

South America: Physical
1:24 000 000
118

South America: Political
1:24 000 000
119

South America – North-West 1:6 400 000
Colombia, Venezuela, *Brazil*, Ecuador, Guyana

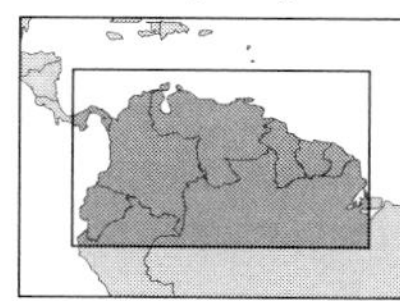

120–121

Eastern Brazil 1:6 400 000

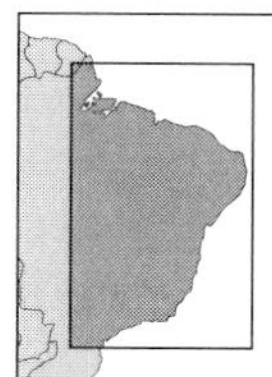

122–123

South America – West
1:6 400 000
Peru, *Brazil*, Bolivia

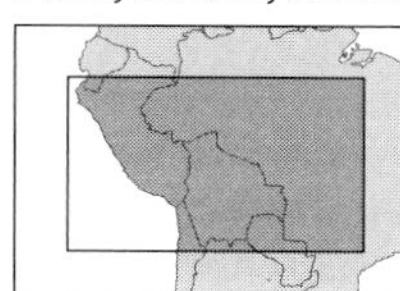

124–125

Central South America
1:6 400 000
Argentina, *Chile*, *Brazil*, Paraguay, Uruguay

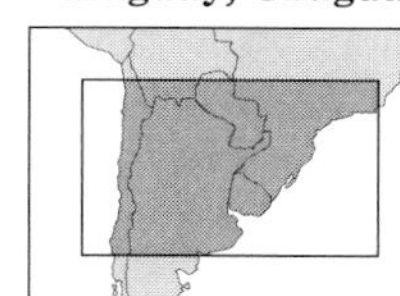

126–127

Southern Chile and Argentina 1:6 400 000

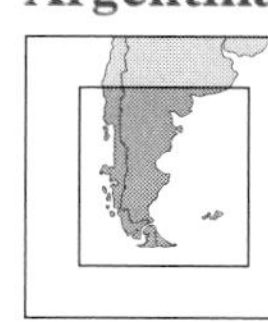

128

Index to World Maps

129–224

World Statistics: Countries

This alphabetical list includes all the countries and territories of the world. If a territory is not completely independent, then the country it is associated with is named. The area figures give the total area of land, inland water and ice. Units for areas and populations are thousands. The annual income is the Gross National Product per capita in US dollars. The figures are the latest available, usually 1993.

Country/Territory	Area km² Thousands	Area miles² Thousands	Population Thousands	Capital	Annual Income US $
Adélie Land (Fr.)	432	167	0.03	–	–
Afghanistan	648	250	19,062	Kabul	450
Albania	28.8	11.1	3,363	Tirana	1,000
Algeria	2,382	920	26,346	Algiers	1,980
American Samoa (US)	0.20	0.08	50	Pago Pago	6,000
Amsterdam Is. (Fr.)	0.05	0.02	0.03	–	–
Andorra	0.45	0.17	58	Andorra la Vella	–
Angola	1,247	481	10,609	Luanda	620
Anguilla (UK)	0.09	0.04	9	The Valley	–
Antigua & Barbuda	0.44	0.17	66	St John's	4,770
Argentina	2,767	1,068	33,101	Buenos Aires	2,790
Armenia	29.8	11.5	3,677	Yerevan	2,150
Aruba (Neths)	0.19	0.07	62	Oranjestad	6,000
Ascension Is. (UK)	0.09	0.03	1.5	Georgetown	–
Australia	7,687	2,968	17,529	Canberra	17,050
Australian Antarctic Territory	6,120	2,363	0	–	–
Austria	83.9	32.4	7,884	Vienna	20,140
Azerbaijan	86.6	33.4	7,398	Baku	1,670
Azores (Port.)	2.2	0.87	260	Ponta Delgada	–
Bahamas	13.9	5.4	262	Nassau	11,750
Bahrain	0.68	0.26	533	Manama	7,130
Bangladesh	144	56	119,288	Dacca	200
Barbados	0.43	0.17	259	Bridgetown	6,630
Belau (US)	0.46	0.18	16	Koror	–
Belgium	30.5	11.8	9,998	Brussels	18,950
Belize	23	8.9	198	Belmopan	2,010
Belorussia	207.6	80.1	10,297	Minsk	3,110
Benin	113	43	4,889	Porto-Novo	380
Bermuda (UK)	0.05	0.02	62	Hamilton	25,000
Bhutan	47	18.1	1,612	Thimphu	180
Bolivia	1,099	424	7,832	La Paz/Sucre	650
Bosnia-Herzegovina	51.2	19.8	4,366	Sarajevo	–
Botswana	582	225	1,373	Gaborone	2,590
Bouvet Is. (Nor.)	0.05	0.02	0.02	–	–
Brazil	8,512	3,286	156,275	Brasilia	2,940
British Antarctic Terr. (UK)	1,709	660	0.3	Stanley	–
British Indian Ocean Terr. (UK)	0.08	0.03	3	–	–
Brunei	5.8	2.2	270	Bandar Seri Begawan	6,000
Bulgaria	111	43	8,963	Sofia	1,840
Burkina Faso	274	106	9,490	Ouagadougou	290
Burma (Myanmar)	679	262	43,668	Rangoon	500
Burundi	27.8	10.7	5,786	Bujumbura	210
Cambodia	181	70	9,054	Phnom Penh	300
Cameroon	475	184	12,198	Yaoundé	850
Canada	9,976	3,852	27,562	Ottawa	20,440
Canary Is. (Spain)	7.3	2.8	1,700	Las Palmas/Santa Cruz	–
Cape Verde Is.	4	1.6	384	Praia	750
Cayman Is. (UK)	0.26	0.10	29	Georgetown	–
Central African Republic	623	241	3,173	Bangui	390
Chad	1,284	496	5,961	Ndjamena	220
Chatham Is. (NZ)	0.96	0.37	0.05	Waitangi	–
Chile	757	292	13,599	Santiago	2,160
China	9,597	3,705	1,187,997	Beijing (Peking)	370
Christmas Is. (Aus.)	0.14	0.05	2.3	The Settlement	–
Cocos (Keeling) Is. (Aus.)	0.01	0.005	0.70	–	–
Colombia	1,139	440	33,424	Bogotá	1,260
Comoros	2.2	0.86	585	Moroni	500
Congo	342	132	2,368	Brazzaville	1,120
Cook Is. (NZ)	0.24	0.09	17	Avarua	900
Costa Rica	51.1	19.7	3,099	San José	1,850
Croatia	56.5	21.8	4,764	Zagreb	1,800
Crozet Is. (Fr.)	0.51	0.19	35	–	–
Cuba	111	43	10,822	Havana	3,000
Cyprus	9.3	3.6	716	Nicosia	8,640
Czech Republic	78.9	30.4	10,299	Prague	2,370
Denmark	43.1	16.6	5,170	Copenhagen	23,700
Djibouti	23.2	9	467	Djibouti	1,000
Dominica	0.75	0.29	72	Roseau	2,440
Dominican Republic	48.7	18.8	7,471	Santo Domingo	950
Ecuador	284	109	10,741	Quito	1,020
Egypt	1,001	387	55,163	Cairo	620
El Salvador	21	8.1	5,396	San Salvador	1,070
Equatorial Guinea	28.1	10.8	369	Malabo	330
Eritrea	94	36	3,500	Asmera	–
Estonia	44.7	17.3	1,542	Tallinn	3,830
Ethiopia	1,128	436	55,117	Addis Ababa	120
Falkland Is. (UK)	12.2	4.7	2	Stanley	–
Faroe Is. (Den.)	1.4	0.54	47	Tórshavn	23,660
Fiji	18.3	7.1	739	Suva	1,930
Finland	338	131	5,042	Helsinki	23,980
France	552	213	57,372	Paris	20,380
French Guiana (Fr.)	90	34.7	104	Cayenne	2,500
French Polynesia (Fr.)	4	1.5	207	Papeete	6,000
Gabon	268	103	1,237	Libreville	3,780
Gambia, The	11.3	4.4	878	Banjul	360
Georgia	69.7	26.9	5,471	Tbilisi	1,640
Germany	357	138	80,569	Berlin	23,650
Ghana	239	92	15,400	Accra	400
Gibraltar (UK)	0.007	0.003	31	–	4,000
Greece	132	51	10,300	Athens	6,340
Greenland (Den.)	2,176	840	57	Godthåb	6,000
Grenada	0.34	0.13	91	St George's	2,180
Guadeloupe (Fr.)	1.7	0.66	400	Basse-Terre	7,000
Guam (US)	0.55	0.21	139	Agana	6,000
Guatemala	109	42	9,745	Guatemala City	930
Guinea	246	95	6,116	Conakry	450
Guinea-Bissau	36.1	13.9	1,006	Bissau	190
Guyana	215	83	808	Georgetown	430
Haiti	27.8	10.7	6,764	Port-au-Prince	370
Honduras	112	43	5,462	Tegucigalpa	570
Hong Kong (UK)	1.1	0.40	5,801	–	13,430
Hungary	93	35.9	10,313	Budapest	2,720
Iceland	103	40	260	Reykjavik	23,170
India	3,288	1,269	879,548	Delhi	330
Indonesia	1,905	735	191,170	Jakarta	610
Iran	1,648	636	56,964	Tehran	2,170
Iraq	438	169	19,290	Baghdad	2,000
Ireland	70.3	27.1	3,547	Dublin	11,120
Israel	27	10.3	4,946	Jerusalem	11,950
Italy	301	116	57,782	Rome	18,580
Ivory Coast	322	125	12,910	Abidjan	690
Jamaica	11	4.2	2,469	Kingston	1,480
Jan Mayen Is. (Nor.)	0.38	0.15	0.06	–	–
Japan	378	146	124,336	Tokyo	26,920
Johnston Is. (US)	0.002	0.0009	0.30	–	–
Jordan	89.2	34.4	4,291	Amman	1,060
Kazakhstan	2,717	1,049	17,038	Alma Ata	7,570
Kenya	580	224	26,985	Nairobi	340
Kerguelen Is. (Fr.)	7.2	2.8	0	–	–
Kermadec Is. (NZ)	0.03	0.01	0	–	–
Kirghizia	198.5	76.6	4,472	Bishkek	4,000
Kiribati	0.72	0.28	74	Tarawa	750
Korea, North	121	47	22,618	Pyongyang	900
Korea, South	99	38.2	43,663	Seoul	6,340
Kuwait	17.8	6.9	1,970	Kuwait City	16,380
Laos	237	91	4,469	Vientiane	230
Latvia	65	25	2,632	Riga	3,410
Lebanon	10.4	4	2,838	Beirut	2,000

Country/Territory	Area km² Thousands	Area miles² Thousands	Population Thousands	Capital	Annual Income US $
Lesotho	30.4	11.7	1,836	Maseru	580
Liberia	111	43	2,580	Monrovia	500
Libya	1,760	679	4,875	Tripoli	5,800
Liechtenstein	0.16	0.06	28	Vaduz	33,000
Lithuania	65.2	25.2	3,759	Vilnius	2,710
Luxembourg	2.6	1	390	Luxembourg	31,780
Macau (Port.)	0.02	0.006	374	–	2,000
Macedonia	25.3	9.8	2,174	Skopje	–
Madagascar	587	227	12,827	Antananarivo	210
Madeira (Port.)	0.81	0.31	280	Funchal	–
Malawi	118	46	8,823	Lilongwe	230
Malaysia	330	127	18,181	Kuala Lumpur	2,520
Maldives	0.30	0.12	231	Malé	460
Mali	1,240	479	9,818	Bamako	280
Malta	0.32	0.12	359	Valletta	6,630
Mariana Is. (US)	0.48	0.18	22	Saipan	–
Marshall Is.	0.18	0.07	49	Dalap-Uliga-Darrit	–
Martinique (Fr.)	1.1	0.42	368	Fort-de-France	4,000
Mauritania	1,025	396	2,143	Nouakchott	510
Mauritius	1.9	0.72	1,084	Port Louis	2,420
Mayotte (Fr.)	0.37	0.14	84	Mamoundzou	–
Mexico	1,958	756	89,538	Mexico City	3,030
Micronesia, Fed. States	0.70	0.27	110	Palikir	–
Midway Is. (US)	0.005	0.002	0.45	–	–
Moldavia	33.7	13	4,458	Kishinev	2,170
Monaco	0.002	0.0001	30	–	20,000
Mongolia	1,567	605	2,310	Ulan Bator	400
Montserrat (UK)	0.10	0.04	11	Plymouth	–
Morocco	447	172	26,318	Rabat	1,030
Mozambique	802	309	14,872	Maputo	80
Namibia	825	318	1,562	Windhoek	1,460
Nauru	0.02	0.008	10	Yaren	–
Nepal	141	54	20,577	Katmandu	180
Netherlands	41.5	16	15,178	Amsterdam	18,780
Neths Antilles (Neths)	0.99	0.38	175	Willemstad	6,000
New Caledonia (Fr.)	19	7.3	173	Nouméa	4,000
New Zealand	269	104	3,414	Wellington	12,350
Nicaragua	130	50	4,130	Managua	460
Niger	1,267	489	8,252	Niamey	300
Nigeria	924	357	88,515	Lagos/Abuja	340
Niue (NZ)	0.26	0.10	2	Alofi	–
Norfolk Is. (Aus.)	0.03	0.01	2	Kingston	–
Norway	324	125	4,286	Oslo	24,220
Oman	212	82	1,637	Muscat	6,120
Pakistan	796	307	115,520	Islamabad	400
Panama	77.1	29.8	2,515	Panama City	2,130
Papua New Guinea	463	179	4,056	Port Moresby	820
Paraguay	407	157	4,519	Asunción	1,270
Peru	1,285	496	22,454	Lima	1,070
Peter 1st Is. (Nor.)	0.18	0.07	0	–	–
Philippines	300	116	64,259	Manila	740
Pitcairn Is. (UK)	0.03	0.01	0.06	Adamstown	–
Poland	313	121	38,356	Warsaw	1,790
Portugal	92.4	35.7	9,846	Lisbon	5,930
Puerto Rico (US)	9	3.5	3,580	San Juan	6,470
Qatar	11	4.2	453	Doha	15,860
Queen Maud Land (Nor.)	2,800	1,081	0	–	–
Réunion (Fr.)	2.5	0.97	624	St-Denis	4,000
Romania	238	92	23,185	Bucharest	1,390
Ross Dependency (NZ)	435	168	0	–	–
Russia	17,075	6,592	149,527	Moscow	3,220
Rwanda	26.3	10.2	7,526	Kigali	260
St Christopher & Nevis	0.36	0.14	42	Basseterre	3,960
St Helena (UK)	0.12	0.05	7	Jamestown	–
St Lucia	0.62	0.24	137	Castries	2,500
St Paul Is. (Fr.)	0.007	0.003	0	–	–
St Pierre & Miquelon (Fr.)	0.24	0.09	6	St-Pierre	–
St Vincent & Grenadines	0.39	0.15	109	Kingstown	1,730
San Marino	0.06	0.02	23	San Marino	–
São Tomé & Príncipe	0.96	0.37	124	São Tomé	350
Saudi Arabia	2,150	830	15,922	Riyadh	7,820
Senegal	197	76	7,736	Dakar	720
Seychelles	0.46	0.18	72	Victoria	5,110
Sierra Leone	71.7	27.7	4,376	Freetown	210
Singapore	0.62	0.24	2,812	Singapore	14,210
Slovak Republic	49	18.9	5,297	Bratislava	1,650
Slovenia	20.3	7.8	1,996	Ljubljana	–
Solomon Is.	28.9	11.2	342	Honiara	690
Somalia	638	246	9,204	Mogadishu	150
South Africa	1,219	471	39,790	Pretoria	2,560
South Georgia (UK)	3.8	1.4	0.05	–	–
South Sandwich Is. (UK)	0.38	0.15	0	–	–
Spain	505	195	39,085	Madrid	12,460
Sri Lanka	65.6	25.3	17,405	Colombo	500
Sudan	2,506	967	26,656	Khartoum	310
Surinam	163	63	438	Paramaribo	3,610
Svalbard (Nor.)	62.9	24.3	4	Longyearbyen	–
Swaziland	17.4	6.7	792	Mbabane	1,060
Sweden	450	174	8,678	Stockholm	25,110
Switzerland	41.3	15.9	6,905	Bern	33,610
Syria	185	71	12,958	Damascus	1,160
Taiwan	36	13.9	20,659	Taipei	6,600
Tajikistan	143.1	55.2	5,465	Dushanbe	2,980
Tanzania	945	365	27,829	Dar es Salaam	100
Thailand	513	198	57,760	Bangkok	1,580
Togo	56.8	21.9	3,763	Lomé	410
Tokelau (NZ)	0.01	0.005	2	Nukunonu	–
Tonga	0.75	0.29	97	Nuku'alofa	1,100
Trinidad & Tobago	5.1	2	1,265	Port of Spain	3,620
Tristan da Cunha (UK)	0.11	0.04	0.33	Edinburgh	–
Tunisia	164	63	8,410	Tunis	1,510
Turkey	779	301	58,775	Ankara	1,820
Turkmenistan	488.1	188.5	3,714	Ashkhabad	1,700
Turks & Caicos Is. (UK)	0.43	0.17	13	Grand Turk	–
Tuvalu	0.03	0.01	12	Funafuti	600
Uganda	236	91	18,674	Kampala	160
Ukraine	603.7	233.1	52,200	Kiev	2,340
United Arab Emirates	83.6	32.3	1,629	Abu Dhabi	20,140
United Kingdom	243.3	94	57,848	London	16,550
United States of America	9,373	3,619	255,020	Washington	22,240
Uruguay	177	68	3,131	Montevideo	2,860
Uzbekistan	447.4	172.7	21,627	Tashkent	1,350
Vanuatu	12.2	4.7	157	Port Vila	1,120
Vatican City	0.0004	0.0002	1	–	–
Venezuela	912	352	20,249	Caracas	2,730
Vietnam	332	127	69,306	Hanoi	200
Virgin Is. (UK)	0.15	0.06	17	Road Town	–
Virgin Is. (US)	0.34	0.13	107	Charlotte Amalie	12,000
Wake Is.	0.008	0.003	0.30	–	–
Wallis & Futuna Is. (Fr.)	0.20	0.08	14	Mata-Utu	–
Western Sahara	266	103	250	El Aaiún	–
Western Samoa	2.8	1.1	161	Apia	960
Yemen	528	204	11,282	Sana	540
Yugoslavia	102.3	39.5	10,469	Belgrade	2,940
Zaire	2,345	906	39,882	Kinshasa	230
Zambia	753	291	8,638	Lusaka	460
Zimbabwe	391	151	10,583	Harare	650

WORLD STATISTICS: CITIES

This list shows the principal cities with more than 500,000 inhabitants (for China only cities with more than 1 million are included). The figures are taken from the most recent census or estimate available, and as far as possible are the population of the metropolitan area, e.g. greater New York, Mexico or London. All the figures are in thousands. The top 20 world cities are indicated with their rank in brackets following the name.

City	Population
Afghanistan	
Kabul	1,424
Algeria	
Algiers	1,722
Oran	664
Angola	
Luanda	1,544
Argentina	
Buenos Aires [7]	11,256
Córdoba	1,198
Rosario	1,096
Mendoza	775
La Plata	640
San Miguel de Tucumán	622
Mar del Plata	520
Armenia	
Yerevan	1,202
Australia	
Sydney	3,657
Melbourne	3,081
Brisbane	1,302
Perth	1,193
Adelaide	1,050
Austria	
Vienna	1,540
Azerbaijan	
Baku	1,149
Bangladesh	
Dacca	6,105
Chittagong	2,041
Khulna	877
Rajshahi	517
Belgium	
Brussels	1,331
Antwerp	668
Belorussia	
Minsk	1,613
Gomel	506
Bolivia	
La Paz	1,126
Santa Cruz	696
Brazil	
São Paulo [11]	9,627
Rio de Janeiro	5,473
Salvador	2,072
Belo Horizonte	2,017
Fortaleza	1,766
Brasília	1,598
Nova Iguaçu	1,512
Curitiba	1,313
Recife	1,297
Pôrto Alegre	1,263
Belém	1,245
Manaus	1,011
Campinas	960
Goiânia	921
Guarulhos	836
São Gonçalo	825
Duque de Caxias	740
São Luís	695
Santo André	691
Osasco	671
São Bernado de Campo	655
Maceió	628
Natal	607
Teresina	598
Campo Grande	525
São João de Meriti	508
Bulgaria	
Sofia	1,141
Burma (Myanmar)	
Rangoon	2,513
Mandalay	533
Cambodia	
Phnom Penh	800
Cameroon	
Douala	884
Yaoundé	750
Canada	
Toronto	3,893
Montréal	3,127
Vancouver	1,603
Ottawa-Hull	921
Edmonton	840
Calgary	754
Winnipeg	652
Québec	646
Hamilton	600
Central African Rep.	
Bangui	597
Chad	
Ndjamena	688
Chile	
Santiago	5,343
China	
Shanghai [5]	12,320
Beijing (Peking)[10]	9,750
Tianjin [18]	7,790
Chongqing [20]	6,511
Wenzhou	5,948
Guangzhou	5,669
Hangzhou	5,234
Shenyang	5,055
Dalian	4,619
Jinzhou	4,448
Wuhan	4,273
Qingdao	4,205
Chengdu	4,025
Jilin	3,974
Nanjing	3,682
Jinan	3,376
Xi'an	2,911
Harbin	2,830
Yingkou	2,789
Dandong	2,574
Anshan	2,517
Nanchang	2,471
Zibo	2,460
Lanzhou	2,340
Lupanshui	2,247
Fushun	2,045
Taiyuan	2,177
Changchun	2,110
Kunming	1,976
Tianshui	1,967
Zhengzhou	1,943
Fuxin	1,693
Zigong	1,673
Fuzhou	1,652
Liaoyang	1,612
Zhaozhuang	1,612
Botou	1,593
Hepei	1,541
Guiyang	1,530
Huainan	1,519
Tangshan	1,500
Linyi	1,385
Qiqihar	1,380
Tai'an	1,370
Changsha	1,330
Shijiazhuang	1,320
Huaibei	1,306
Pingxiang	1,305
Xintao	1,272
Yangcheng	1,265
Yulin	1,255
Dongguang	1,230
Chao'an	1,227
Hohhot	1,206
Baotou	1,200
Suining	1,195
Luoyang	1,190
Macheng	1,190
Xintai	1,167
Yichun	1,167
Ürümqi	1,160
Puyang	1,125
Datong	1,110
Handan	1,110
Shaoxing	1,091
Ningbo	1,090
Zhongshan	1,073
Nanning	1,070
Huangshi	1,069
Laiwu	1,054
Leshan	1,039
Heze	1,017
Linhai	1,012
Changshu	1,004
Colombia	
Bogotá	4,921
Cali	1,624
Medellin	1,581
Barranquilla	1,019
Cartagena	688
Congo	
Brazzaville	938
Pointe-Noire	576
Croatia	
Zagreb	1,175
Cuba	
Havana	2,096
Czech Republic	
Prague	1,216
Denmark	
Copenhagen	1,337
Dominican Rep.	
Santo Domingo	1,601
Ecuador	
Guayaquil	1,508
Quito	1,101
Egypt	
Cairo [19]	6,663
Alexandria	3,295
El Gîza	2,096
Shubra el Kheima	812
El Salvador	
San Salvador	1,522
Ethiopia	
Addis Ababa	1,913
Finland	
Helsinki	929
France	
Paris [12]	9,319
Lyons	1,262
Marseilles	1,087
Lille	959
Bordeaux	696
Toulouse	650
Nice	516
Gabon	
Libreville	830
Georgia	
Tbilisi	1,279
Germany	
Berlin	3,446
Hamburg	1,669
Munich	1,229
Cologne	957
Frankfurt	654
Essen	627
Dortmund	601
Stuttgart	592
Düsseldorf	578
Bremen	553
Duisburg	537
Hanover	517
Leipzig	503
Ghana	
Accra	965
Greece	
Athens	3,097
Guatemala	
Guatemala	2,000
Guinea	
Conakry	705
Haiti	
Port-au-Prince	1,144
Honduras	
Tegucigalpa	679
Hong Kong	
Kowloon	2,031
Hong Kong	1,251
Tsuen Wan	690
Hungary	
Budapest	2,016
India	
Bombay [4]	12,572
Calcutta [8]	10,916
Delhi [14]	8,375
Madras	5,361
Hyderabad	4,280
Bangalore	4,087
Ahmadabad	3,298
Pune	2,485
Kanpur	2,111
Nagpur	1,661
Lucknow	1,642
Surat	1,517
Jaipur	1,514
Kochi	1,140
Coimbatore	1,136
Vadodara	1,115
Indore	1,104
Patna	1,099
Madurai	1,094
Bhopal	1,064
Vishakhapatnam	1,052
Varanasi	1,026
Ludhiana	1,012
Agra	956
Jabalpur	887
Allahabad	858
Meerut	847
Vijayawada	845
Jamshedpur	834
Trivandrum	826
Dhanbad	818
Kozhikode	801
Asansol	764
Nasik	722
Gwalior	720
Tiruchchirappalli	711
Amritsar	709
Durg-Bhilai	689
Mysore	652
Jodhpur	649
Hubli-Dharwad	648
Solapur	621
Faridabad	614
Ranchi	614
Bareilly	608
Srinagar	595
Aurangabad	592
Guwahati	578
Chandigarh	575
Salem	574
Cochin	564
Kota	536
Ghaziabad	520
Jullundur	520
Indonesia	
Jakarta [16]	7,886
Surabaya	2,224
Medan	1,806
Bandung	1,567
Semarang	1,027
Palembang	787
Ujung Pandang	709
Malang	512
Iran	
Tehran	6,476
Mashhad	1,759
Esfahan	1,127
Tabriz	1,089
Shiraz	965
Ahvaz	725
Qom	681
Kermanshah	624
Bakhtaran	561
Iraq	
Baghdad	4,649
Basra	617
Mosul	571
Ireland	
Dublin	1,024
Italy	
Rome	2,791
Milan	1,432
Naples	1,206
Turin	992
Palermo	734
Genoa	701
Ivory Coast	
Abidjan	2,534
Jamaica	
Kingston	588
Japan	
Tokyo [6]	11,936
Yokohama	3,220
Osaka	2,624
Nagoya	2,155
Sapporo	1,672
Kobe	1,477
Kyoto	1,461
Fukuoka	1,237
Kawasaki	1,174
Hiroshima	1,086
Kitakyushu	1,026
Sendai	918
Chiba	829
Sakai	808
Okayama	594
Kumamoto	579
Kagoshima	537
Hamamatsu	535
Funabashi	533
Sagamihara	532
Higashiosaka	518
Jordan	
Amman	1,160
Irbid	680
Kazakhstan	
Alma-Ata	1,147
Karaganda	613
Astrakhan	510
Kenya	
Nairobi	1,429
Kirghizia	
Bishkek	625
Korea, North	
Pyongyang	2,639
Hamhung	775
Chongjin	754
Chinnamp'o	691
Sinuiju	500
Korea, South	
Seoul [9]	10,628
Pusan	3,798
Taegu	2,229
Inchon	1,818
Kwangju	1,145
Taejon	1,062
Ulsan	683
Puch'on	668
Suwon	645
Songnam	541
Chonju	517
Latvia	
Riga	917
Lebanon	
Beirut	1,500
Tripoli	500
Libya	
Tripoli	980
Benghazi	650
Lithuania	
Vilnius	593
Macedonia	
Skopje	563
Madagascar	
Antananarivo	802
Malaysia	
Kuala Lumpur	938
Mali	
Bamako	646
Mexico	
Mexico City [3]	13,636
Guadalajara	2,847
Monterrey	2,522
Puebla	1,055
León	872
Ciudad Juárez	798
Tijuana	743
Culiacán Rosales	602
Mexicali	602
Acapulco	592
Mérida	557
Chihuahua	530
San Luis Potosí	526
Aguascalientés	506
Moldavia	
Kishinev	676
Mongolia	
Ulan Bator	575
Morocco	
Casablanca	2,409
Rabat-Salé	893
Fès	562
Marrakesh	549
Mozambique	
Maputo	1,070
Netherlands	
Amsterdam	1,091
Rotterdam	1,069
's-Gravenhage	694
The Hague	693
Utrecht	543
New Zealand	
Auckland	885
Nicaragua	
Managua	682
Nigeria	
Lagos	1,097
Ibadan	1,060
Ogbomosho	527
Norway	
Oslo	683
Pakistan	
Karachi	5,181
Lahore	2,953
Faisalabad	1,104
Rawalpindi	795
Hyderabad	752
Multan	722
Gujranwala	659
Peshawar	556
Panama	
Panama City	853
Paraguay	
Asunción	729
Peru	
Lima-Callao	6,415
Arequipa	635
Trujillo	532
Callao	515
Philippines	
Manila [17]	7,832
Quezon City	1,587
Davao	844
Cebu	627
Caloocan	616
Poland	
Warsaw	1,655
Lódz	852
Kraków	748
Wroclaw	642
Poznaé	585
Portugal	
Lisbon	1,612
Oporto	1,315
Puerto Rico	
San Juan	1,816
Romania	
Bucharest	2,217
Russia	
Moscow [13]	8,801
St Petersburg	4,467
Nizhniy Novgorod	1,443
Novosibirsk	1,443
Yekaterinburg	1,375
Samara	1,258
Omsk	1,159
Chelyabinsk	1,148
Kazan	1,103
Perm	1,094
Ufa	1,094
Rostov	1,025
Volgograd	1,005
Krasnoyarsk	922
Saratov	909
Voronezh	895
Izhevsk	642
Tolyatti	642
Simbirsk	638
Yaroslavl	636
Irkutsk	635
Vladivostok	634
Krasnodar	627
Khaborovsk	608
Barnaul	603
Barnaul	602
Novokuznetsk	601
Orenburg	552
Penza	548
Tula	543
Ryazan	522
Kemerovo	521
Naberezhnyye-Chelny	507
Tomsk	506
Saudi Arabia	
Riyadh	2,000
Jedda	1,400
Mecca	618
Medina	500
Senegal	
Dakar	1,382
Singapore	
Singapore	3,003
Somali Republic	
Mogadishu	1,000
South Africa	
Cape Town	1,912
Johannesburg	1,726
East Rand	1,038
Durban	982
Pretoria	823
Port Elizabeth	652
West Rand	647
Vereeniging	540
Spain	
Madrid	3,121
Barcelona	1,707
Valencia	753
Seville	659
Zaragoza	586
Málaga	512
Sri Lanka	
Colombo	1,863
Sudan	
Khartoum	561
Omdurman	526
Sweden	
Stockholm	1,503
Gothenburg	734
Switzerland	
Zürich	840
Syria	
Damascus	1,378
Aleppo	1,355
Taiwan	
Taipei	2,718
Kaohsiung	1,396
Taichung	774
Tainan	690
Panchiao	543
Tajikistan	
Dushanbe	582
Tanzania	
Dar es Salaam	1,361
Thailand	
Bangkok	5,876
Tunisia	
Tunis	1,395
Turkey	
Istanbul	6,620
Ankara	2,559
Izmir	1,757
Adana	916
Bursa	835
Uganda	
Kampala	773
Ukraine	
Kiev	2,616
Kharkov	1,618
Dnepropetrovsk	1,187
Donetsk	1,117
Odessa	1,106
Zaporozhye	891
Lvov	798
Krivoy Rog	717
Mariupol	520
Nikolayev	508
Lugansk	501
United Kingdom	
London	6,378
Manchester	1,669
Birmingham	1,400
Liverpool	1,060
Glasgow	730
Newcastle	617
United States	
New York [1]	18,087
Los Angeles [2]	14,532
Chicago [15]	8,066
San Francisco	6,253
Philadelphia	5,899
Detroit	4,665
Boston	4,172
Washington	3,924
Dallas	3,885
Houston	3,711
Miami	3,193
Atlanta	2,834
Cleveland	2,760
Seattle	2,559
San Diego	2,498
Minneapolis-SP.	2,464
St Louis	2,444
Baltimore	2,382
Pittsburgh	2,243
Phoenix	2,122
Tampa	2,098
Denver	1,848
Cincinnati	1,744
Milwaukee	1,607
Kansas City	1,566
Sacramento	1,481
Portland	1,478
Norfolk	1,396
Columbus	1,377
San Antonio	1,303
Indianapolis	1,250
New Orleans	1,239
Buffalo	1,189
Charlotte	1,162
Providence	1,118
Hartford	1,086
Salt Lake City	1,072
San Jose	782
Jacksonville	672
Memphis	610
Uruguay	
Montevideo	1,248
Uzbekistan	
Tashkent	2,094
Venezuela	
Caracas	3,247
Maracaibo	1,295
Valencia	1,135
Maracay	857
Barquisimeto	718
Vietnam	
Ho Chi Minh	3,169
Hanoi	2,571
Haiphong	1,279
Yugoslavia	
Belgrade	1,137
Zaïre	
Kinshasa	2,796
Lubumbashi	795
Zambia	
Lusaka	921
Zimbabwe	
Harare	681
Bulawayo	500

WORLD STATISTICS: DISTANCES

The table shows air distances in miles and kilometres between thirty major cities. Known as 'Great Circle' distances, these measure the shortest routes between the cities, which aircraft use where possible. The maps show the world centred on six individual cities, and illustrate, for example, why direct flights from Japan to northern America and Europe are across the Arctic regions, and Singapore is on the direct line route from Europe to Australia. The maps have been constructed on an Azimuthal Equidistant projection, on which all distances measured through the centre point are true to scale. The circular lines are drawn at 5,000, 10,000 and 15,000 km from the central city.

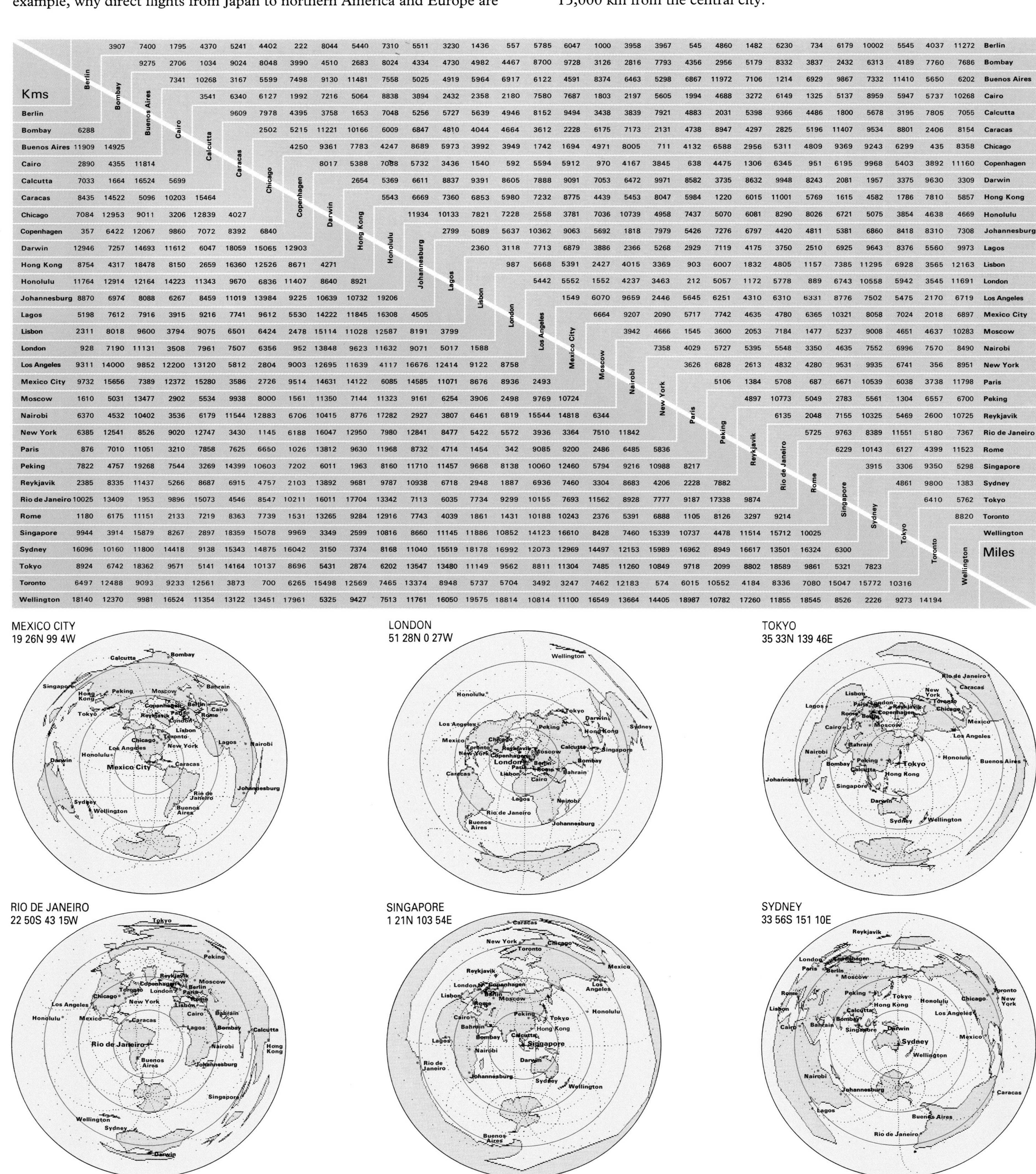

Miles

	Bombay	Buenos Aires	Cairo	Calcutta	Caracas	Chicago	Copenhagen	Darwin	Hong Kong	Honolulu	Johannesburg	Lagos	Lisbon	London	Los Angeles	Mexico City	Moscow	Nairobi	New York	Paris	Peking	Reykjavik	Rio de Janeiro	Rome	Singapore	Sydney	Tokyo	Toronto	Wellington
Berlin	3907	7400	1795	4370	5241	4402	222	8044	5440	7310	5511	3230	1436	557	5785	6047	1000	3958	3967	545	4860	1482	6230	734	6179	10002	5545	4037	11272
Bombay		9275	2706	1034	9024	8048	3990	4510	2683	8024	4334	4730	4982	4467	8700	9728	3126	2816	7793	4356	2956	5179	8332	3837	2432	6313	4189	7760	7686
Buenos Aires			7341	10268	3167	5599	7498	9130	11481	7558	5025	4919	5964	6917	6122	4591	8374	6463	5298	6867	11972	7106	1214	6929	9867	7332	11410	5650	6202
Cairo				3541	6340	6127	1992	7216	5064	8838	3894	2432	2358	2180	7580	7687	1803	2197	5605	1994	4688	3272	6149	1325	5137	8959	5947	5737	10268
Calcutta					9609	7978	4395	3758	1653	7048	5256	5727	5639	4946	8152	9494	3438	3839	7921	4883	2031	5398	9366	4486	1800	5678	3195	7805	7055
Caracas						2502	5215	11221	10166	6009	6847	4810	4044	4664	3612	2228	6175	7173	2131	4738	8947	4297	2825	5196	11407	9534	8801	2406	8154
Chicago							4250	9361	7783	4247	8689	5973	3992	3949	1742	1694	4971	8005	711	4132	6588	2956	5311	4809	9369	9243	6299	435	8358
Copenhagen								8017	5388	7088	5732	3436	1540	592	5594	5912	970	4167	3845	638	4475	1306	6345	951	6195	9968	5403	3892	11160
Darwin									2654	5369	6611	8837	9391	8605	7888	9091	7053	6472	9971	8582	3735	8632	9948	8243	2081	1957	3375	9630	3309
Hong Kong										5543	6669	7360	6853	5980	7232	8775	4439	5453	8047	5984	1220	6015	11001	5769	1615	4582	1786	7810	5857
Honolulu											11934	10133	7821	7228	2558	3781	7036	10739	4958	7437	5070	6081	8290	8026	6721	5075	3854	4638	4669
Johannesburg												2799	5089	5637	10362	9063	5692	1818	7979	5426	7276	6797	4420	4811	5381	6860	8418	8310	7308
Lagos													2360	3118	7713	6879	3886	2366	5268	2929	7119	4175	3750	2510	6925	9643	8376	5560	9973
Lisbon														987	5668	5391	2427	4015	3369	903	6007	1832	4805	1157	7385	11295	6928	3565	12163
London															5442	5552	1552	4237	3463	212	5057	1172	5778	889	6743	10558	5942	3545	11691
Los Angeles																1549	6070	9659	2446	5645	6251	4310	6310	6331	8776	7502	5475	2170	6719
Mexico City																	6664	9207	2090	5717	7742	4635	4780	6365	10321	8058	7024	2018	6897
Moscow																		3942	4666	1545	3600	2053	7184	1477	5237	9008	4651	4637	10283
Nairobi																			7358	4029	5727	5395	5548	3350	4635	7552	6996	7570	8490
New York																				3626	6828	2613	4832	4280	9531	9935	6741	356	8951
Paris																					5106	1384	5708	687	6671	10539	6038	3738	11798
Peking																						4897	10773	5049	2783	5561	1304	6557	6700
Reykjavik																							6135	2048	7155	10325	5469	2600	10725
Rio de Janeiro																								5725	9763	8389	11551	5180	7367
Rome																									6229	10143	6127	4399	11523
Singapore																										3915	3306	9350	5298
Sydney																											4861	9800	1383
Tokyo																												6410	5762
Toronto																													8820

Kms

	Berlin	Bombay	Buenos Aires	Cairo	Calcutta	Caracas	Chicago	Copenhagen	Darwin	Hong Kong	Honolulu	Johannesburg	Lagos	Lisbon	London	Los Angeles	Mexico City	Moscow	Nairobi	New York	Paris	Peking	Reykjavik	Rio de Janeiro	Rome	Singapore	Sydney	Tokyo	Toronto
Bombay	6288																												
Buenos Aires	11909	14925																											
Cairo	2890	4355	11814																										
Calcutta	7033	1664	16524	5699																									
Caracas	8435	14522	5096	10203	15464																								
Chicago	7084	12953	9011	3206	12839	4027																							
Copenhagen	357	6422	12067	9860	7072	8392	6840																						
Darwin	12946	7257	14693	11612	6047	18059	15065	12903																					
Hong Kong	8754	4317	18478	8150	2659	16360	12526	8671	4271																				
Honolulu	11764	12914	12164	14223	11343	9670	6836	11407	8640	8921																			
Johannesburg	8870	6974	8088	6267	8459	11019	13984	9225	10639	10732	19206																		
Lagos	5198	7612	7916	3915	9216	7741	9612	5530	14222	11845	16308	4505																	
Lisbon	2311	8018	9600	3794	9075	6501	6424	2478	15114	11028	12587	8191	3799																
London	928	7190	11131	3508	7961	7507	6356	952	13848	9623	11632	9071	5017	1588															
Los Angeles	9311	14000	9852	12200	13120	5812	2804	9003	12695	11639	4117	16676	12414	9122	8758														
Mexico City	9732	15656	7389	12372	15280	3586	2726	9514	14631	14122	6085	14585	11071	8676	8936	2493													
Moscow	1610	5031	13477	2902	5534	9938	8000	1561	11350	7144	11323	9161	6254	3906	2498	9769	10724												
Nairobi	6370	4532	10402	3536	6179	11544	12883	6706	10415	8776	17282	2927	3807	6461	6819	15544	14818	6344											
New York	6385	12541	8526	9020	12747	3430	1145	6188	16047	12950	7980	12841	8477	5422	5572	3936	3364	7510	11842										
Paris	876	7010	11051	3210	7858	7625	6650	1026	13812	9630	11968	8732	4714	1454	342	9085	9200	2486	6485	5836									
Peking	7822	4757	19268	7544	3269	14399	10603	7202	6011	1963	8160	11710	11457	9668	8138	10060	12460	5794	9216	10988	8217								
Reykjavik	2385	8335	11437	5266	8687	6915	4757	2103	13892	9681	9787	10938	6718	2948	1887	6936	7460	3304	8683	4206	2228	7882							
Rio de Janeiro	10025	13409	1953	9896	15073	4546	8547	10211	16011	17704	13342	7113	6035	7734	9299	10155	7693	11562	8928	7777	9187	17338	9874						
Rome	1180	6175	11151	2133	7219	8363	7739	1531	13265	9284	12916	7743	4039	1861	1431	10188	10243	2376	5391	6888	1105	8126	3297	9214					
Singapore	9944	3914	15879	8267	2897	18359	15078	9969	3349	2599	10816	8660	11145	11886	10852	14123	16610	8428	7460	15339	10737	4478	11514	15712	10025				
Sydney	16096	10160	11800	14418	9138	15343	14875	16042	3150	7374	8168	11040	15519	18178	16992	12073	12969	14497	12153	15989	16962	8949	16617	13501	16324	6300			
Tokyo	8924	6742	18362	9571	5141	14164	10137	8696	5431	2874	6202	13547	13480	11149	9562	8811	11304	7485	11260	10849	9718	2099	8802	18589	9861	5321	7823		
Toronto	6497	12488	9093	9233	12561	3873	700	6265	15498	12569	7465	13374	8948	5737	5704	3492	3247	7462	12183	574	6015	10552	4184	8336	7080	15047	15772	10316	
Wellington	18140	12370	9981	16524	11354	13122	13451	17961	5325	9427	7513	11761	16050	19575	18814	10814	11100	16549	13664	14405	18987	10782	17260	11855	18545	8526	2226	9273	14194

MEXICO CITY
19 26N 99 4W
LONDON
51 28N 0 27W
TOKYO
35 33N 139 46E
RIO DE JANEIRO
22 50S 43 15W
SINGAPORE
1 21N 103 54E
SYDNEY
33 56S 151 10E

World Statistics: Climate

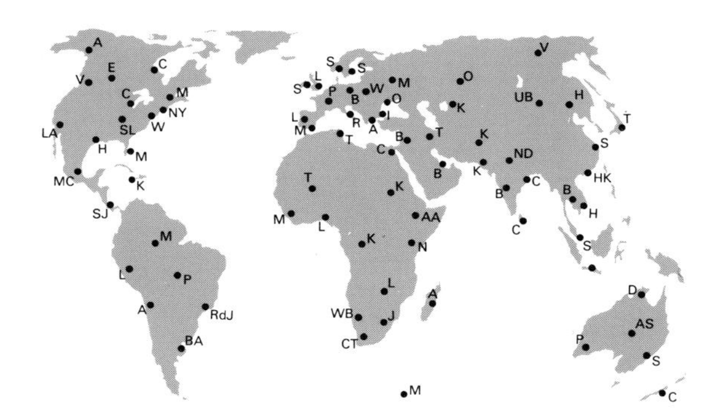

Rainfall and temperature figures are provided for more than 70 cities around the world. As climate is affected by altitude, the height of each city is shown in metres beneath its name. For each month, the figures in red show average temperature in degrees Celsius or centigrade, and in blue the total rainfall or snow in millimetres; the average annual temperature and total annual rainfall are at the end of the rows.

	Jan.	Feb.	Mar.	Apr.	May	June	July	Aug.	Sept.	Oct.	Nov.	Dec.	Year
EUROPE													
Athens, Greece	62	37	37	23	23	14	6	7	15	51	56	71	402
107 m	10	10	12	16	20	25	28	28	24	20	15	11	18
Berlin, Germany	46	40	33	42	49	65	73	69	48	49	46	43	603
55 m	-1	0	4	9	14	17	19	18	15	9	5	1	9
Istanbul, Turkey	109	92	72	46	38	34	34	30	58	81	103	119	816
114 m	5	6	7	11	16	20	23	23	20	16	12	8	14
Lisbon, Portugal	111	76	109	54	44	16	3	4	33	62	93	103	708
77 m	11	12	14	16	17	20	22	23	21	18	14	12	17
London, UK	54	40	37	37	46	45	57	59	49	57	64	48	593
5 m	4	5	7	9	12	16	18	17	15	11	8	5	11
Málaga, Spain	61	51	62	46	26	5	1	3	29	64	64	62	474
33 m	12	13	16	17	19	29	25	26	23	20	16	13	18
Moscow, Russia	39	38	36	37	53	58	88	71	58	45	47	54	624
156 m	-13	-10	-4	6	13	16	18	17	12	6	-1	-7	4
Odessa, Ukraine	57	62	30	21	34	34	42	37	37	13	35	71	473
64 m	-3	-1	2	9	15	20	22	22	18	12	9	1	10
Paris, France	56	46	35	42	57	54	59	64	55	50	51	50	619
75 m	3	4	8	11	15	18	20	19	17	12	7	4	12
Rome, Italy	71	62	57	51	46	37	15	21	63	99	129	93	744
17 m	8	9	11	14	18	22	25	25	22	17	13	10	16
Shannon, Irish Republic	94	67	56	53	61	57	77	79	86	86	96	117	929
2 m	5	5	7	9	12	14	16	16	14	11	8	6	10
Stockholm, Sweden	43	30	25	31	34	45	61	76	60	48	53	48	554
44 m	-3	-3	-1	5	10	15	18	17	12	7	3	0	7
ASIA													
Bahrain	8	18	13	8	<3	0	0	0	0	0	18	18	81
5 m	17	18	21	25	29	32	33	34	31	28	24	19	26
Bangkok, Thailand	8	20	36	58	198	160	160	175	305	206	66	5	1,397
2 m	26	28	29	30	29	29	28	28	28	28	26	25	28
Beirut, Lebanon	191	158	94	53	18	3	<3	<3	5	51	132	185	892
34 m	14	14	16	18	22	24	27	28	26	24	19	16	21
Bombay, India	3	3	3	<3	18	485	617	340	264	64	13	3	1,809
11 m	24	24	26	28	30	29	27	27	27	28	27	26	27
Calcutta, India	10	31	36	43	140	297	325	328	252	114	20	5	1,600
6 m	20	22	27	30	30	30	29	29	29	28	23	19	26
Colombo, Sri Lanka	89	69	147	231	371	224	135	109	160	348	315	147	2,365
7 m	26	26	27	28	28	27	27	27	27	27	26	26	27
Harbin, China	6	5	10	23	43	94	112	104	46	33	8	5	488
160 m	-18	-15	-5	6	13	19	22	21	14	4	-6	-16	3
Ho Chi Minh, Vietnam	15	3	13	43	221	330	315	269	335	269	114	56	1,984
9 m	26	27	29	30	29	28	28	28	27	27	27	26	28
Hong Kong	33	46	74	137	292	394	381	361	257	114	43	31	2,162
33 m	16	15	18	22	26	28	28	28	27	25	21	18	23
Jakarta, Indonesia	300	300	211	147	114	97	64	43	66	112	142	203	1,798
8 m	26	26	27	27	27	27	27	27	27	27	27	26	27
Kabul, Afghanistan	31	36	94	102	20	5	3	3	<3	15	20	10	338
1,815 m	-3	-1	6	13	18	22	25	24	20	14	7	3	12
Karachi, Pakistan	13	10	8	3	3	18	81	41	13	<3	3	5	196
4 m	19	20	24	28	30	31	30	29	28	28	24	20	26
Kazalinsk, Kazakhstan	10	10	13	13	15	5	5	8	8	10	13	15	125
63 m	-12	-11	-3	6	18	23	25	23	16	8	-1	-7	7
New Delhi, India	23	18	13	8	13	74	180	172	117	10	3	10	640
218 m	14	17	23	28	33	34	31	30	29	26	20	15	25
Omsk, Russia	15	8	8	13	31	51	51	51	28	25	18	20	318
85 m	-22	-19	-12	-1	10	16	18	16	10	1	-11	-18	-1
Shanghai, China	48	58	84	94	94	180	147	142	130	71	51	36	1,135
7 m	4	5	9	14	20	24	28	28	23	19	12	7	16
Singapore	252	173	193	188	173	173	170	196	178	208	254	257	2,413
10 m	26	27	28	28	28	28	28	27	27	27	27	27	27
Tehran, Iran	46	38	46	36	13	3	3	3	3	8	20	31	246
1,220 m	2	5	9	16	21	26	30	29	25	18	12	6	17
Tokyo, Japan	48	74	107	135	147	165	142	152	234	208	97	56	1,565
6 m	3	4	7	13	17	21	25	26	23	17	11	6	14
Ulan Bator, Mongolia	<3	<3	3	5	10	28	76	51	23	5	5	3	208
1,325 m	-26	-21	-13	-1	6	14	16	14	8	-1	-13	-22	-3
Verkhoyansk, Russia	5	5	3	5	8	23	28	25	13	8	8	5	134
100 m	-50	-45	-32	-15	0	12	14	9	2	-15	-38	-48	-17
AFRICA													
Addis Ababa, Ethiopia	<3	3	25	135	213	201	206	239	102	28	<3	0	1,151
2,450 m	19	20	20	20	19	18	18	19	21	22	21	20	20
Antananarivo, Madagas.	300	279	178	53	18	8	8	10	18	61	135	287	1,356
1,372 m	21	21	21	19	18	15	14	15	17	19	21	21	19
Cairo, Egypt	5	5	5	3	3	<3	0	0	<3	<3	3	5	28
116 m	13	15	18	21	25	28	28	28	26	24	20	15	22
Cape Town, South Africa	15	8	18	48	79	84	89	66	43	31	18	10	508
17 m	21	21	20	17	14	13	12	13	14	16	18	19	17
Johannesburg, S. Africa	114	109	89	38	25	8	8	8	23	56	107	125	709
1,665 m	20	20	18	16	13	10	11	13	16	18	19	20	16
Khartoum, Sudan	<3	<3	<3	<3	3	8	53	71	18	5	<3	0	158
390 m	24	25	28	31	33	34	32	31	32	32	28	25	29
Kinshasa, Zaïre	135	145	196	196	158	8	3	3	31	119	221	142	1,354
325 m	26	26	27	27	26	24	23	24	25	26	26	26	25
Lagos, Nigeria	28	46	102	150	269	460	279	64	140	206	69	25	1,836
3 m	27	28	29	28	28	26	26	25	26	26	28	28	27
Lusaka, Zambia	231	191	142	18	3	<3	<3	0	<3	10	91	150	836
1,277 m	21	22	21	21	19	16	16	18	22	24	23	22	21
Monrovia, Liberia	31	56	97	216	516	973	996	373	744	772	236	130	5,138
23 m	26	26	27	27	26	25	24	25	25	25	26	26	26
Nairobi, Kenya	38	64	125	211	158	46	15	23	31	53	109	86	958
1,820 m	19	19	19	19	18	16	16	16	18	19	18	18	18
Timbuktu, Mali	<3	<3	3	<3	5	23	79	81	38	3	<3	<3	231
301 m	22	24	28	32	34	35	32	30	32	31	28	23	29
Tunis, Tunisia	64	51	41	36	18	8	3	8	33	51	48	61	419
66 m	10	11	13	16	19	23	26	27	25	20	16	11	18
Walvis Bay, Namibia	<3	5	8	3	3	<3	<3	3	<3	<3	<3	<3	23
7 m	19	19	19	18	17	16	15	14	14	15	17	18	18
AUSTRALIA, NEW ZEALAND AND ANTARCTICA													
Alice Springs, Australia	43	33	28	10	15	13	8	8	8	18	31	38	252
579 m	29	28	25	20	15	12	12	14	18	23	26	28	21
Christchurch, N. Zealand	56	43	48	48	66	66	69	48	46	43	48	56	638
10 m	16	16	14	12	9	6	6	7	9	12	14	16	11
Darwin, Australia	386	312	254	97	15	3	<3	3	13	51	119	239	1,491
30 m	29	29	29	29	28	26	25	26	28	29	30	29	28
Mawson, Antarctica	11	30	20	10	44	180	4	40	3	20	0	0	362
14 m	0	-5	-10	-14	-15	-16	-18	-18	-19	-13	-5	-1	-11
Perth, Australia	8	10	20	43	130	180	170	149	86	56	20	13	881
60 m	23	23	22	19	16	14	13	13	15	16	19	22	18
Sydney, Australia	89	102	127	135	127	117	117	76	73	71	73	73	1,181
42 m	22	22	21	18	15	13	12	13	15	18	19	21	17
NORTH AMERICA													
Anchorage, Alaska, USA	20	18	15	10	13	18	41	66	66	56	25	23	371
40 m	-11	-8	-5	2	7	12	14	13	9	2	-5	-11	2
Chicago, Ill., USA	51	51	66	71	86	89	84	81	79	66	61	51	836
251 m	-4	-3	2	9	14	20	23	22	19	12	5	-1	10
Churchill, Man., Canada	15	13	18	23	32	44	46	58	51	43	39	21	402
13 m	-28	-26	-20	-10	-2	6	12	11	5	-2	-12	-22	-7
Edmonton, Alta., Canada	25	19	19	22	43	77	89	78	39	17	16	25	466
676 m	-15	-10	-5	4	11	15	17	16	11	6	-4	-10	3
Honolulu, Hawaii, USA	104	66	79	48	25	18	23	28	36	48	64	104	643
12 m	23	18	19	20	22	24	25	26	26	24	22	19	22
Houston, Tex., USA	89	76	84	91	119	117	99	99	104	94	89	109	1,171
12 m	12	13	17	21	24	27	28	29	26	22	16	12	21
Kingston, Jamaica	23	15	23	31	102	89	38	91	99	180	74	36	800
34 m	25	25	25	26	26	28	28	28	27	27	26	26	26
Los Angeles, Calif., USA	79	76	71	25	10	3	<3	<3	5	15	31	66	381
95 m	13	14	14	16	17	19	21	22	21	18	16	14	17
Mexico City, Mexico	13	5	10	20	53	119	170	152	130	51	18	8	747
2,309 m	12	13	16	18	19	19	17	18	18	16	14	13	16
Miami, Fla., USA	71	53	64	81	173	178	155	160	203	234	71	51	1,516
8 m	20	20	22	23	25	27	28	28	27	25	22	21	24
Montréal, Que., Canada	72	65	74	74	66	82	90	92	88	76	81	87	946
57 m	-10	-9	-3	-6	13	18	21	20	15	9	2	-7	6
New York, N.Y., USA	94	97	91	81	81	84	107	109	86	89	76	91	1,092
96 m	-1	-1	3	10	16	20	23	23	21	15	7	2	11
St Louis, Mo., USA	58	64	89	97	114	114	89	86	81	74	71	64	1,001
173 m	0	1	7	13	19	24	26	26	22	15	8	2	14
San José, Costa Rica	15	5	20	46	229	241	211	241	305	300	145	41	1,798
1,146 m	19	19	21	21	22	21	21	21	21	20	20	19	20
Vancouver, B.C., Canada	154	115	101	60	52	45	32	41	67	114	150	182	1,113
14 m	3	5	6	9	12	15	17	17	14	10	6	4	10
Washington, D.C., USA	86	76	91	84	94	99	112	109	94	74	66	79	1,064
22 m	1	2	7	12	18	23	25	24	20	14	8	3	13
SOUTH AMERICA													
Antofagasta, Chile	0	0	0	<3	<3	3	5	3	<3	3	<3	0	13
94 m	21	21	20	18	16	15	14	14	15	16	18	19	17
Buenos Aires, Argentina	79	71	109	89	76	61	56	61	79	86	84	99	950
27 m	23	23	21	17	13	9	10	11	13	15	19	22	16
Lima, Peru	3	<3	<3	<3	5	5	8	8	8	3	3	<3	41
120 m	23	24	24	22	19	17	17	16	17	18	19	21	20
Manaus, Brazil	249	231	262	221	170	84	58	38	46	107	142	203	1,811
44 m	28	28	28	27	28	28	28	28	29	29	29	28	28
Paraná, Brazil	287	236	239	102	13	<3	3	5	28	127	231	310	1,582
260 m	23	23	23	23	23	21	21	22	24	24	23	23	23
Rio de Janeiro, Brazil	125	122	130	107	79	53	41	43	66	79	104	137	1,082
61 m	26	26	25	24	22	21	21	21	21	22	23	25	23

World Statistics: Physical Dimensions

Each topic list is divided into continents and within a continent the items are listed in order of size. The order of the continents is as in the atlas, Europe through to South America. Certain lists down to this mark > are complete; below they are selective. The world top ten are shown in square brackets; in the case of mountains this has not been done because the world top 30 are all in Asia. The figures are rounded as appropriate.

World, Continents, Oceans

	km²	miles²	%
The World	509,450,000	196,672,000	–
Land	149,450,000	57,688,000	29.3
Water	360,000,000	138,984,000	70.7
Asia	44,500,000	17,177,000	29.8
Africa	30,302,000	11,697,000	20.3
North America	24,241,000	9,357,000	16.2
South America	17,793,000	6,868,000	11.9
Antarctica	14,100,000	5,443,000	9.4
Europe	9,957,000	3,843,000	6.7
Australia & Oceania	8,557,000	3,303,000	5.7
Pacific Ocean	179,679,000	69,356,000	49.9
Atlantic Ocean	92,373,000	35,657,000	25.7
Indian Ocean	73,917,000	28,532,000	20.5
Arctic Ocean	14,090,000	5,439,000	3.9

Seas

Pacific	km²	miles²
South China Sea	2,974,600	1,148,500
Bering Sea	2,268,000	875,000
Sea of Okhotsk	1,528,000	590,000
East China & Yellow	1,249,000	482,000
Sea of Japan	1,008,000	389,000
Gulf of California	162,000	62,500
Bass Strait	75,000	29,000
Atlantic	**km²**	**miles²**
Caribbean Sea	2,766,000	1,068,000
Mediterranean Sea	2,516,000	971,000
Gulf of Mexico	1,543,000	596,000
Hudson Bay	1,232,000	476,000
North Sea	575,000	223,000
Black Sea	462,000	178,000
Baltic Sea	422,170	163,000
Gulf of St Lawrence	238,000	92,000
Indian	**km²**	**miles²**
Red Sea	438,000	169,000
The Gulf	239,000	92,000

Mountains

Europe		m	ft
Mont Blanc	*France/Italy*	4,807	15,771
Monte Rosa	*Italy/Switzerland*	4,634	15,203
Dom	*Switzerland*	4,545	14,911
Weisshorn	*Switzerland*	4,505	14,780
Matterhorn/Cervino	*Italy/Switzerland*	4,478	14,691
Mt Maudit	*France/Italy*	4,465	14,649
Finsteraarhorn	*Switzerland*	4,274	14,022
Aletschhorn	*Switzerland*	4,182	13,720
Jungfrau	*Switzerland*	4,158	13,642
Barre des Ecrins	*France*	4,103	13,461
Schreckhorn	*Switzerland*	4,078	13,380
Gran Paradiso	*Italy*	4,061	13,323
Piz Bernina	*Italy/Switzerland*	4,049	13,284
Ortles	*Italy*	3,899	12,792
Monte Viso	*Italy*	3,841	12,602
Grossglockner	*Austria*	3,797	12,457
Wildspitze	*Austria*	3,774	12,382
Weisskügel	*Austria/Italy*	3,736	12,257
Balmhorn	*Switzerland*	3,709	12,169
Dammastock	*Switzerland*	3,630	11,909
Tödi	*Switzerland*	3,620	11,877
Presanella	*Italy*	3,556	11,667
Monte Adamello	*Italy*	3,554	11,660
Mulhacén	*Spain*	3,478	11,411
Pico de Aneto	*Spain*	3,404	11,168
Posets	*Spain*	3,375	11,073
Marmolada	*Italy*	3,342	10,964
Etna	*Italy*	3,340	10,958
> Musala	*Bulgaria*	2,925	9,596
Olympus	*Greece*	2,917	9,570
Gerlachovka	*Slovak Republic*	2,655	8,711
Galdhöpiggen	*Norway*	2,469	8,100
Pietrosul	*Romania*	2,305	7,562
Hvannadalshnúkur	*Iceland*	2,119	6,952
Narodnaya	*Russia*	1,894	6,214
Ben Nevis	*UK*	1,343	4,406
Asia		**m**	**ft**
Everest	*China/Nepal*	8,848	29,029
Godwin Austen (K2)	*China/Kashmir*	8,611	28,251
Kanchenjunga	*India/Nepal*	8,598	28,208
Lhotse	*China/Nepal*	8,516	27,939
Makalu	*China/Nepal*	8,481	27,824
Cho Oyu	*China/Nepal*	8,201	26,906
Dhaulagiri	*Nepal*	8,172	26,811
Manaslu	*Nepal*	8,156	26,758
Nanga Parbat	*Kashmir*	8,126	26,660
Annapurna	*Nepal*	8,078	26,502
Gasherbrum	*China/Kashmir*	8,068	26,469
Broad Peak	*India*	8,051	26,414
Gosainthan	*China*	8,012	26,286
Disteghil Sar	*Kashmir*	7,885	25,869
Nuptse	*Nepal*	7,879	25,849
Masherbrum	*Kashmir*	7,821	25,659
Nanda Devi	*India*	7,817	25,646
Rakaposhi	*Kashmir*	7,788	25,551
Kanjut Sar	*India*	7,760	25,459
Kamet	*India*	7,756	25,446
Namcha Barwa	*China*	7,756	25,446
Gurla Mandhata	*China*	7,728	25,354
Muztag	*China*	7,723	25,338
Kongur Shan	*China*	7,719	25,324
Tirich Mir	*Pakistan*	7,690	25,229
Saser	*Kashmir*	7,672	25,170
> K'ula Shan	*Bhutan/China*	7,543	24,747
Pik Kommunizma	*Tajikistan*	7,495	24,590
Aling Gangri	*China*	7,314	23,996
Elbrus	*Russia*	5,633	18,481
Demavend	*Iran*	5,604	18,386
Ararat	*Turkey*	5,165	16,945
Gunong Kinabalu	*Malaysia (Borneo)*	4,101	13,455
Yu Shan	*Taiwan*	3,997	13,113
Fuji-san	*Japan*	3,776	12,388
Rinjani	*Indonesia*	3,726	12,224
Mt Rajang	*Philippines*	3,364	11,037
Pidurutalagala	*Sri Lanka*	2,524	8,281
Africa		**m**	**ft**
Kilimanjaro	*Tanzania*	5,895	19,340
Mt Kenya	*Kenya*	5,199	17,057
Ruwenzori	*Uganda/Zaïre*	5,109	16,762
Ras Dashan	*Ethiopia*	4,620	15,157
Meru	*Tanzania*	4,565	14,977
Karisimbi	*Rwanda/Zaïre*	4,507	14,787
Mt Elgon	*Kenya/Uganda*	4,321	14,176
Batu	*Ethiopia*	4,307	14,130
Guna	*Ethiopia*	4,231	13,882
Toubkal	*Morocco*	4,165	13,665
Irhil Mgoun	*Morocco*	4,071	13,356
Mt Cameroon	*Cameroon*	4,070	13,353
Amba Ferit	*Ethiopia*	3,875	13,042
Teide	*Spain (Tenerife)*	3,718	12,198
Thabana Ntlenyana	*Lesotho*	3,482	11,424
Emi Kussi	*Chad*	3,415	11,204
> Mt aux Sources	*Lesotho/S. Africa*	3,282	10,768
Mt Piton	*Réunion*	3,069	10,069
Oceania		**m**	**ft**
Puncak Jaya	*Indonesia*	5,029	16,499
Puncak Trikora	*Indonesia*	4,750	15,584
Puncak Mandala	*Indonesia*	4,702	15,427
Mt Wilhelm	*Papua New Guinea*	4,508	14,790
> Mauna Kea	*USA (Hawaii)*	4,205	13,796
Mauna Loa	*USA (Hawaii)*	4,170	13,681
Mt Cook	*New Zealand*	3,753	12,313
Mt Balbi	*Solomon Is.*	2,439	8,002
Orohena	*Tahiti*	2,241	7,352
Mt Kosciusko	*Australia*	2,237	7,339
North America		**m**	**ft**
Mt McKinley	*USA (Alaska)*	6,194	20,321
Mt Logan	*Canada*	5,959	19,551
Citlaltepetl	*Mexico*	5,700	18,701
Mt St Elias	*USA/Canada*	5,489	18,008
Popocatepetl	*Mexico*	5,452	17,887
Mt Foraker	*USA (Alaska)*	5,304	17,401
Ixtaccihuatl	*Mexico*	5,286	17,342
Lucania	*Canada*	5,227	17,149
Mt Steele	*Canada*	5,073	16,644
Mt Bona	*USA (Alaska)*	5,005	16,420
Mt Blackburn	*USA (Alaska)*	4,996	16,391
Mt Sanford	*USA (Alaska)*	4,940	16,207
Mt Wood	*Canada*	4,848	15,905
Nevado de Toluca	*Mexico*	4,670	15,321
Mt Fairweather	*USA (Alaska)*	4,663	15,298
Mt Whitney	*USA*	4,418	14,495
Mt Elbert	*USA*	4,399	14,432
Mt Harvard	*USA*	4,395	14,419
Mt Rainier	*USA*	4,392	14,409
Blanca Peak	*USA*	4,372	14,344
Long's Peak	*USA*	4,345	14,255
Nevado de Colima	*Mexico*	4,339	14,235
Mt Shasta	*USA*	4,317	14,163
Tajumulco	*Guatemala*	4,220	13,845
Gannett Peak	*USA*	4,202	13,786
> Mt Waddington	*Canada*	3,994	13,104
Mt Robson	*Canada*	3,954	12,972
Chirripó Grande	*Costa Rica*	3,837	12,589
Pico Duarte	*Dominican Rep.*	3,175	10,417
South America		**m**	**ft**
Aconcagua	*Argentina*	6,960	22,834
Illimani	*Bolivia*	6,882	22,578
Bonete	*Argentina*	6,872	22,546
Ojos del Salado	*Argentina/Chile*	6,863	22,516
Tupungato	*Argentina/Chile*	6,800	22,309
Pissis	*Argentina*	6,779	22,241
Mercedario	*Argentina/Chile*	6,770	22,211
Huascaran	*Peru*	6,768	22,204
Llullaillaco	*Argentina/Chile*	6,723	22,057
Nudo de Cachi	*Argentina*	6,720	22,047
Yerupaja	*Peru*	6,632	21,758
N. de Tres Cruces	*Argentina/Chile*	6,620	21,719
Incahuasi	*Argentina/Chile*	6,600	21,654
Ancohuma	*Bolivia*	6,550	21,489
Sajama	*Bolivia*	6,520	21,391
Coropuna	*Peru*	6,425	21,079
Ausangate	*Peru*	6,384	20,945
Cerro del Toro	*Argentina*	6,380	20,932
Ampato	*Peru*	6,310	20,702
Chimborasso	*Ecuador*	6,267	20,561
> Cotopaxi	*Ecuador*	5,896	19,344
S. Nev. de S. Marta	*Colombia*	5,800	19,029
Cayambe	*Ecuador*	5,796	19,016
Pico Bolivar	*Venezuela*	5,007	16,427
Antarctica		**m**	**ft**
Vinson Massif		4,897	16,066
Mt Kirkpatrick		4,528	14,855
Mt Markham		4,349	14,268

Ocean Depths

Atlantic Ocean	m	ft	
Puerto Rico (Milwaukee) Deep	9,220	30,249	[7]
Cayman Trench	7,680	25,197	[10]
Gulf of Mexico	5,203	17,070	
Mediterranean Sea	5,121	16,801	
Black Sea	2,211	7,254	
North Sea	660	2,165	
Baltic Sea	463	1,519	
Hudson Bay	258	846	
Indian Ocean	**m**	**ft**	
Java Trench	7,450	24,442	
Red Sea	2,635	8,454	
Persian Gulf	73	239	
Pacific Ocean	**m**	**ft**	
Mariana Trench	11,022	36,161	[1]
Tonga Trench	10,882	35,702	[2]
Japan Trench	10,554	34,626	[3]
Kuril Trench	10,542	34,587	[4]
Mindanao Trench	10,497	34,439	[5]
Kermadec Trench	10,047	32,962	[6]
Peru-Chile Trench	8,050	26,410	[8]
Aleutian Trench	7,822	25,662	[9]
Middle American Trench	6,662	21,857	
Arctic Ocean	**m**	**ft**	
Molloy Deep	5,608	18,399	

Land Lows

		m	ft
Caspian Sea	*Europe*	–28	–92
Dead Sea	*Asia*	–400	–1,312
Lake Assal	*Africa*	–156	–512
Lake Eyre North	*Oceania*	–16	–52
Death Valley	*N. America*	–86	–282
Valdés Peninsula	*S. America*	–40	–131

Rivers

Europe		km	miles	
Volga	*Caspian Sea*	3,700	2,300	
Danube	*Black Sea*	2,850	1,770	
Ural	*Caspian Sea*	2,535	1,574	
Dnepr	*Volga*	2,285	1,420	
Kama	*Volga*	2,030	1,260	
Don	*Volga*	1,990	1,240	
Petchora	*Arctic Ocean*	1,790	1,110	
Oka	*Volga*	1,480	920	
Belaya	*Kama*	1,420	880	
Dnestr	*Black Sea*	1,400	870	
Vyatka	*Kama*	1,370	850	
Rhine	*North Sea*	1,320	820	
N. Dvina	*Arctic Ocean*	1,290	800	
Desna	*Dnieper*	1,190	740	
Elbe	*North Sea*	1,145	710	
Vistula	*Baltic Sea*	1,090	675	
Loire	*Atlantic Ocean*	1,020	635	
W. Dvina	*Baltic Sea*	1,019	633	

Asia		km	miles	
Yangtze	*Pacific Ocean*	6,380	3,960	[3]
Yenisey-Angara	*Arctic Ocean*	5,550	3,445	[5]
Huang He	*Pacific Ocean*	5,464	3,395	[6]
Ob-Irtysh	*Arctic Ocean*	5,410	3,360	[7]
Mekong	*Pacific Ocean*	4,500	2,795	[9]
Amur	*Pacific Ocean*	4,400	2,730	[10]
Lena	*Arctic Ocean*	4,400	2,730	
Irtysh	*Ob*	4,250	2,640	
Yenisey	*Arctic Ocean*	4,090	2,540	
Ob	*Arctic Ocean*	3,680	2,285	
Indus	*Indian Ocean*	3,100	1,925	
Brahmaputra	*Indian Ocean*	2,900	1,800	
Syr Darya	*Aral Sea*	2,860	1,775	
Salween	*Indian Ocean*	2,800	1,740	
Euphrates	*Indian Ocean*	2,700	1,675	
Vilyuy	*Lena*	2,650	1,645	
Kolyma	*Arctic Ocean*	2,600	1,615	
Amu Darya	*Aral Sea*	2,540	1,575	
Ural	*Caspian Sea*	2,535	1,575	
Ganges	*Indian Ocean*	2,510	1,560	
Si Kiang	*Pacific Ocean*	2,100	1,305	
Irrawaddy	*Indian Ocean*	2,010	1,250	
Tarim-Yarkand	*Lop Nor*	2,000	1,240	
Tigris	*Indian Ocean*	1,900	1,180	
Angara	*Yenisey*	1,830	1,135	
Godavari	*Indian Ocean*	1,470	915	
Sutlej	*Indian Ocean*	1,450	900	
Yamuna	*Indian Ocean*	1,400	870	

Africa		km	miles	
Nile	*Mediterranean*	6,670	4,140	[1]
Zaïre/Congo	*Atlantic Ocean*	4,670	2,900	[8]
Niger	*Atlantic Ocean*	4,180	2,595	
Zambezi	*Indian Ocean*	3,540	2,200	
Oubangi/Uele	*Zaïre*	2,250	1,400	
Kasai	*Zaïre*	1,950	1,210	
Shaballe	*Indian Ocean*	1,930	1,200	
Orange	*Atlantic Ocean*	1,860	1,155	
Cubango	*Okavango Swamps*	1,800	1,120	
Limpopo	*Indian Ocean*	1,600	995	
Senegal	*Atlantic Ocean*	1,600	995	
Volta	*Atlantic Ocean*	1,500	930	
Benue	*Niger*	1,350	840	

Australia		km	miles
Murray-Darling	*Indian Ocean*	3,750	2,330
Darling	*Murray*	3,070	1,905
Murray	*Indian Ocean*	2,575	1,600
Murrumbidgee	*Murray*	1,690	1,050

North America		km	miles	
Mississippi-Missouri	*Gulf of Mexico*	6,020	3,740	[4]
Mackenzie	*Arctic Ocean*	4,240	2,630	
Mississippi	*Gulf of Mexico*	3,780	2,350	
Missouri	*Mississippi*	3,780	2,350	
Yukon	*Pacific Ocean*	3,185	1,980	
Rio Grande	*Gulf of Mexico*	3,030	1,880	
Arkansas	*Mississippi*	2,340	1,450	
Colorado	*Pacific Ocean*	2,330	1,445	
Red	*Mississippi*	2,040	1,270	
Columbia	*Pacific Ocean*	1,950	1,210	
Saskatchewan	*Lake Winnipeg*	1,940	1,205	
Snake	*Columbia*	1,670	1,040	
Churchill	*Hudson Bay*	1,600	990	
Ohio	*Mississippi*	1,580	980	
Brazos	*Gulf of Mexico*	1,400	870	
St Lawrence	*Atlantic Ocean*	1,170	730	

South America		km	miles	
Amazon	*Atlantic Ocean*	6,450	4,010	[2]
Paraná-Plate	*Atlantic Ocean*	4,500	2,800	
Purus	*Amazon*	3,350	2,080	
Madeira	*Amazon*	3,200	1,990	
São Francisco	*Atlantic Ocean*	2,900	1,800	
Paraná	*Plate*	2,800	1,740	
Tocantins	*Atlantic Ocean*	2,750	1,710	
Paraguay	*Paraná*	2,550	1,580	
Orinoco	*Atlantic Ocean*	2,500	1,550	
Pilcomayo	*Paraná*	2,500	1,550	
Araguaia	*Tocantins*	2,250	1,400	
Juruá	*Amazon*	2,000	1,240	
Xingu	*Amazon*	1,980	1,230	
Ucayali	*Amazon*	1,900	1,180	
Maranón	*Amazon*	1,600	990	
Uruguay	*Plate*	1,600	990	
Magdalena	*Caribbean Sea*	1,540	960	

Lakes

Europe		km^2	$miles^2$
Lake Ladoga	*Russia*	17,700	6,800
Lake Onega	*Russia*	9,700	3,700
Saimaa system	*Finland*	8,000	3,100
Vänern	*Sweden*	5,500	2,100
Rybinsk Res.	*Russia*	4,700	1,800

Asia		km^2	$miles^2$	
Caspian Sea	*Asia*	371,800	143,550	[1]
Aral Sea	*Kazakh./Uzbek.*	36,000	13,900	[6]
Lake Baykal	*Russia*	30,500	11,780	[9]
Tonlé Sap	*Cambodia*	20,000	7,700	
Lake Balkhash	*Kazakhstan*	18,500	7,100	
Dongting Hu	*China*	12,000	4,600	
Issyk Kul	*Kirghizia*	6,200	2,400	
Lake Urmia	*Iran*	5,900	2,300	
Koko Nur	*China*	5,700	2,200	
Poyang Hu	*China*	5,000	1,900	
Lake Khanka	*China/Russia*	4,400	1,700	
Lake Van	*Turkey*	3,500	1,400	
Ubsa Nur	*China*	3,400	1,300	

Africa		km^2	$miles^2$	
Lake Victoria	*E. Africa*	68,000	26,000	[3]
Lake Tanganyika	*C. Africa*	33,000	13,000	[7]
Lake Malawi/Nyasa	*E. Africa*	29,600	11,430	[10]
Lake Chad	*C. Africa*	25,000	9,700	
Lake Turkana	*Ethiopia/Kenya*	8,500	3,300	
Lake Volta	*Ghana*	8,500	3,300	
Lake Bangweulu	*Zambia*	8,000	3,100	
Lake Rukwa	*Tanzania*	7,000	2,700	
Lake Mai-Ndombe	*Zaïre*	6,500	2,500	
Lake Kariba	*Zambia/Zimbabwe*	5,300	2,000	
Lake Mobutu	*Uganda/Zaïre*	5,300	2,000	
Lake Nasser	*Egypt/Sudan*	5,200	2,000	
Lake Mweru	*Zambia/Zaïre*	4,900	1,900	
Lake Cabora Bassa	*South Africa*	4,500	1,700	
Lake Kyoga	*Uganda*	4,400	1,700	
Lake Tana	*Ethiopia*	3,630	1,400	
Lake Kivu	*Rwanda/Zaïre*	2,650	1,000	
Lake Edward	*Uganda/Zaïre*	2,200	850	

Australia		km^2	$miles^2$
Lake Eyre	*Australia*	8,900	3,400
Lake Torrens	*Australia*	5,800	2,200
Lake Gairdner	*Australia*	4,800	1,900

North America		km^2	$miles^2$	
Lake Superior	*Canada/USA*	82,350	31,800	[2]
Lake Huron	*Canada/USA*	59,600	23,010	[4]
Lake Michigan	*USA*	58,000	22,400	[5]
Great Bear Lake	*Canada*	31,800	12,280	[8]
Great Slave Lake	*Canada*	28,500	11,000	
Lake Erie	*Canada/USA*	25,700	9,900	
Lake Winnipeg	*Canada*	24,400	9,400	
Lake Ontario	*Canada/USA*	19,500	7,500	
Lake Nicaragua	*Nicaragua*	8,200	3,200	
Lake Athabasca	*Canada*	8,100	3,100	
Smallwood Res.	*Canada*	6,530	2,520	
Reindeer Lake	*Canada*	6,400	2,500	
Lake Winnipegosis	*Canada*	5,400	2,100	
Nettilling Lake	*Canada*	5,500	2,100	
Lake Nipigon	*Canada*	4,850	1,900	
Lake Manitoba	*Canada*	4,700	1,800	

South America		km^2	$miles^2$
Lake Titicaca	*Bolivia/Peru*	8,300	3,200
Lake Poopo	*Peru*	2,800	1,100

Islands

Europe		km^2	$miles^2$	
Great Britain	*UK*	229,880	88,700	[8]
Iceland	*Atlantic Ocean*	103,000	39,800	
Ireland	*Ireland/UK*	84,400	32,600	
Novaya Zemlya (N.)	*Russia*	48,200	18,600	
W. Spitzbergen	*Norway*	39,000	15,100	
Novaya Zemlya (S.)	*Russia*	33,200	12,800	
Sicily	*Italy*	25,500	9,800	
Sardinia	*Italy*	24,000	9,300	
N. E. Spitzbergen	*Norway*	15,000	5,600	
Corsica	*France*	8,700	3,400	
Crete	*Greece*	8,350	3,200	
Zealand	*Denmark*	6,850	2,600	

Asia		km^2	$miles^2$	
Borneo	*S. E. Asia*	744,360	287,400	[3]
Sumatra	*Indonesia*	473,600	182,860	[6]
Honshu	*Japan*	230,500	88,980	[7]
Celebes	*Indonesia*	189,000	73,000	
Java	*Indonesia*	126,700	48,900	
Luzon	*Philippines*	104,700	40,400	
Mindanao	*Philippines*	101,500	39,200	
Hokkaido	*Japan*	78,400	30,300	
Sakhalin	*Russia*	74,060	28,600	
Sri Lanka	*Indian Ocean*	65,600	25,300	
Taiwan	*Pacific Ocean*	36,000	13,900	
Kyushu	*Japan*	35,700	13,800	
Hainan	*China*	34,000	13,100	
Timor	*Indonesia*	33,600	13,000	
Shikoku	*Japan*	18,800	7,300	
Halmahera	*Indonesia*	18,000	6,900	
Ceram	*Indonesia*	17,150	6,600	
Sumbawa	*Indonesia*	15,450	6,000	
Flores	*Indonesia*	15,200	5,900	
Samar	*Philippines*	13,100	5,100	
Negros	*Philippines*	12,700	4,900	
Bangka	*Indonesia*	12,000	4,600	
Palawan	*Philippines*	12,000	4,600	
Panay	*Philippines*	11,500	4,400	
Sumba	*Indonesia*	11,100	4,300	
Mindoro	*Philippines*	9,750	3,800	
Buru	*Indonesia*	9,500	3,700	
Bali	*Indonesia*	5,600	2,200	
Cyprus	*Mediterranean*	3,570	1,400	
Wrangel Is.	*Russia*	2,800	1,000	

Africa		km^2	$miles^2$	
Madagascar	*Indian Ocean*	587,040	226,660	[4]
Socotra	*Indian Ocean*	3,600	1,400	
Réunion	*Indian Ocean*	2,500	965	
Tenerife	*Atlantic Ocean*	2,350	900	
Mauritius	*Indian Ocean*	1,865	720	

Oceania		km^2	$miles^2$	
New Guinea	*Indon./Pap. NG*	821,030	317,000	[2]
New Zealand (S.)	*New Zealand*	150,500	58,100	
New Zealand (N.)	*New Zealand*	114,700	44,300	
Tasmania	*Australia*	67,800	26,200	
New Britain	*Papua NG*	37,800	14,600	
New Caledonia	*Pacific Ocean*	19,100	7,400	
Viti Levu	*Fiji*	10,500	4,100	
Hawaii	*Pacific Ocean*	10,450	4,000	
Bougainville	*Papua NG*	9,600	3,700	
Guadalcanal	*Solomon Is.*	6,500	2,500	
Vanua Levu	*Fiji*	5,550	2,100	
New Ireland	*Papua NG*	3,200	1,200	

North America		km^2	$miles^2$	
Greenland	*Greenland*	2,175,600	839,800	[1]
Baffin Is.	*Canada*	508,000	196,100	[5]
Victoria Is.	*Canada*	212,200	81,900	[9]
Ellesmere Is.	*Canada*	212,000	81,800	[10]
Cuba	*Cuba*	110,860	42,800	
Newfoundland	*Canada*	110,680	42,700	
Hispaniola	*Atlantic Ocean*	76,200	29,400	
Banks Is.	*Canada*	67,000	25,900	
Devon Is.	*Canada*	54,500	21,000	
Melville Is.	*Canada*	42,400	16,400	
Vancouver Is.	*Canada*	32,150	12,400	
Somerset Is.	*Canada*	24,300	9,400	
Jamaica	*Caribbean Sea*	11,400	4,400	
Puerto Rico	*Atlantic Ocean*	8,900	3,400	
Cape Breton Is.	*Canada*	4,000	1,500	

South America		km^2	$miles^2$
Tierra del Fuego	*Argentina/Chile*	47,000	18,100
Falkland Is. (E.)	*Atlantic Ocean*	6,800	2,600
South Georgia	*Atlantic Ocean*	4,200	1,600
Galapagos (Isabela)	*Pacific Ocean*	2,250	870

INTRODUCTION TO WORLD GEOGRAPHY

The Universe 2,
The Solar System 4,
The Earth: Time and Motion 6, Geology 8, Oceans 10, Atmosphere 12,
Climate 14, Water and Land Use 16, Landscape 18, Environment 20,
People: Demography 22, Cities 24, The Human Family 26,
Conflict and Co-operation 28,
Production: Agriculture 30, Energy 32, Minerals 34,
Manufacturing 36, Trade 38,
Quality of Life: Wealth 40, Standards 42, Health 44, Environment 46

THE UNIVERSE

4: ORBITS OF THE PLANETS
PLANETARY DATA

About 15,000 million years ago, time and space began with the most colossal explosion in cosmic history: the 'Big Bang' that initiated the universe. According to current theory, in the first millionth of a second of its existence it expanded from a dimensionless point of infinite mass and density into a fireball about 30,000 million kilometres across; and it has been expanding ever since.

It took almost a million years for the primal fireball to cool enough for atoms to form. They were mostly hydrogen, still the most abundant material in the universe. But the new matter was not evenly distributed around the young universe, and a few 1,000 million years later atoms in relatively dense regions began to cling together under the influence of gravity, forming distinct masses of gas separated by vast expanses of empty space. To begin with, these first proto-galaxies were dark places: the universe had cooled. But gravitational attraction continued, condensing matter into coherent lumps inside the galactic gas clouds. About 3,000 million years later, some of these masses had contracted so much that internal pressure produced the high temperatures necessary to bring about nuclear fusion: the first stars were born.

There were several generations of stars, each feeding on the wreckage of its extinct predecessors as well as the original galactic gas swirls. With each new generation, progressively larger atoms were forged in stellar furnaces and the galaxy's range of elements, once restricted to hydrogen, grew larger. About 10,000 million years after the Big Bang, a star formed on the outskirts of our galaxy with enough matter left over to create a retinue of planets. Nearly 5,000 million years after that, a few planetary atoms had evolved into structures of complex molecules that lived, breathed and eventually pointed telescopes at the sky.

They found that their Sun is just one of more than 100,000 million stars in the home galaxy alone. Our galaxy, in turn, forms part of a local group of 25 or so similar structures, some much larger than our own; there are at least 100 million other galaxies in the universe as a whole. The most distant ever observed, a highly energetic galactic core known only as Quasar PKS 2000–330, lies about 15,000 million light-years away.

LIFE OF A STAR

For most of its existence, a star produces energy by the nuclear fusion of hydrogen into helium at its core. The duration of this hydrogen-burning period – known as the main sequence – depends on the star's mass; the greater the mass, the higher the core temperatures and the sooner the star's supply of hydrogen is exhausted. Dim, dwarf stars consume their hydrogen slowly, eking it out over 1,000 billion years or more. The Sun, like other stars of its mass, should spend about 10,000 million years on the main sequence; since it was formed less than 5,000 million years ago, it still has half its life left.

Once all a star's core hydrogen has been fused into helium, nuclear activity moves outwards into layers of unconsumed hydrogen. For a time, energy production sharply increases: the star grows hotter and expands enormously, turning into a so-called red giant. Its energy output will increase a thousandfold, and it will swell to a hundred times its present diameter.

After a few hundred million years, helium in the core will become sufficiently compressed to initiate a new cycle of nuclear fusion: from helium to carbon. The star will contract somewhat, before beginning its last expansion, in the Sun's case engulfing the Earth and perhaps Mars. In this bloated condition, the Sun's outer layers will break off into space, leaving a tiny inner core, mainly of carbon, that shrinks progressively under the force of its own gravity: dwarf stars can attain a density more than 10,000 times that of normal matter, with crushing surface gravities to match. Gradually, the nuclear fires will die down, and the Sun will reach its terminal stage: a black dwarf, emitting insignificant amounts of energy.

However, stars more massive than the Sun may undergo another transformation. The additional mass allows gravitational collapse to continue indefinitely: eventually, all the star's remaining matter shrinks to a point, and its density approaches infinity – a state that will not permit even subatomic structures to survive.

The star has become a black hole: an anomalous 'singularity' in the fabric of space and time. Although vast coruscations of radiation will be emitted by any matter falling into its grasp, the singularity itself has an escape velocity that exceeds the speed of light, and nothing can ever be released from it. Within the boundaries of the black hole, the laws of physics are suspended, but no physicist can ever observe the extraordinary events that may occur.

THE END OF THE UNIVERSE

The likely fate of the universe is disputed. One theory (top right) dictates that the expansion begun at the time of the Big Bang will continue 'indefinitely', with ageing galaxies moving further and further apart in an immense, dark graveyard. Alternatively, gravity may overcome the expansion (bottom right). Galaxies will fall back together until everything is again concentrated at a single point, followed by a new Big Bang and a new expansion, in an endlessly repeated cycle. The first theory is supported by the amount of visible matter in the universe; the second assumes there is enough dark material to bring about the gravitational collapse.

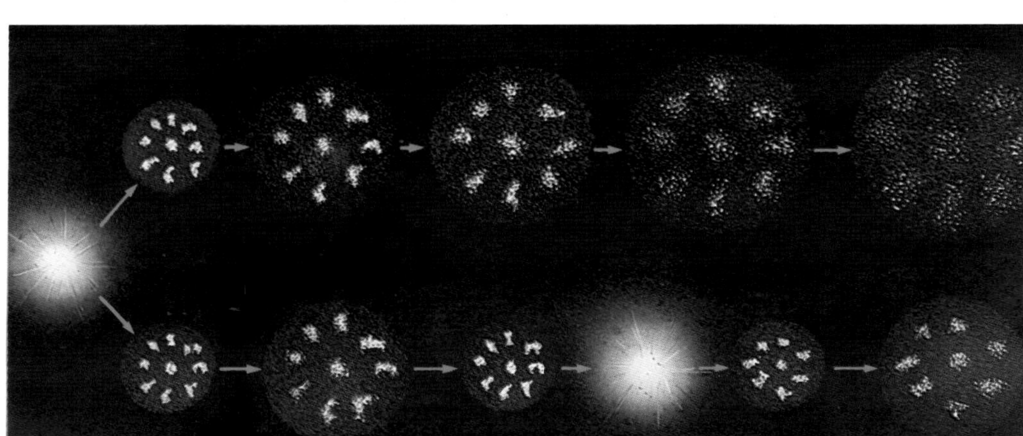

GALACTIC STRUCTURES

The universe's 100 million galaxies show clear structural patterns, originally classified by the American astronomer Edwin Hubble in 1925. Spiral galaxies like our own (top row) have a central, almost spherical bulge and a surrounding disc composed of spiral arms. Barred spirals (bottom row) have a central bar of stars across the nucleus, with spiral arms trailing from the ends of the bar. Elliptical galaxies (far left) have a uniform appearance, ranging from a flattened disc to a near sphere. So-called SO galaxies (left row, right) have a central bulge, but no spiral arms. A few have no discernible structure at all. Galaxies also vary enormously in size, from dwarfs only 2,000 light-years across to great assemblies of stars 80 or more times larger.

THE HOME GALAXY

The Sun and its planets are located in one of the spiral arms, a little less than 30,000 light-years from the galactic centre and orbiting around it in a period of more than 200 million years. The centre is invisible from the Earth, masked by vast, light-absorbing clouds of interstellar dust. The galaxy is probably around 12 billion years old and, like other spiral galaxies, has three distinct regions. The central bulge is about 30,000 light-years in diameter. The disc in which the Sun is located is not much more than 1,000 light-years thick but 100,000 light-years from end to end. Around the galaxy is the halo, a spherical zone 150,000 light-years across, studded with globular star-clusters and sprinkled with individual suns.

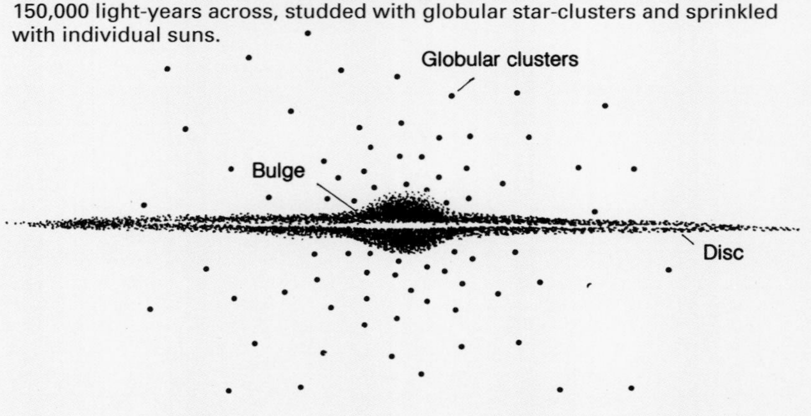
Globular clusters
Bulge
Disc

Solar System

CARTOGRAPHY BY PHILIP'S. COPYRIGHT REED INTERNATIONAL BOOKS LTD

STAR CHARTS

Star charts are drawn as projections of a vast, hollow sphere with the observer in the middle. Each circle below represents one hemisphere, centred on the north and south celestial poles respectively – projections of the Earth's poles in the heavens. At the present era, the north pole is marked by the star Polaris; the south pole has no such convenient reference point. The rectangular map shows the stars immediately above and below the celestial equator.

Astronomical co-ordinates are normally given in terms of 'Right Ascension' for longitude and 'Declination' for latitude or altitude. Since the stars appear to rotate around the Earth once every 24 hours, Right Ascension is measured eastwards – anti-clockwise – in hours and minutes. One hour is equivalent to 15 angular degrees; zero on the scale is the point at which the Sun crosses the celestial equator at the spring equinox, known to astronomers as the First Point in Aries. Unlike the Sun, stars always rise and set at the same point on the horizon. Declination measures (in degrees) a star's angular distance above or below the celestial equator.

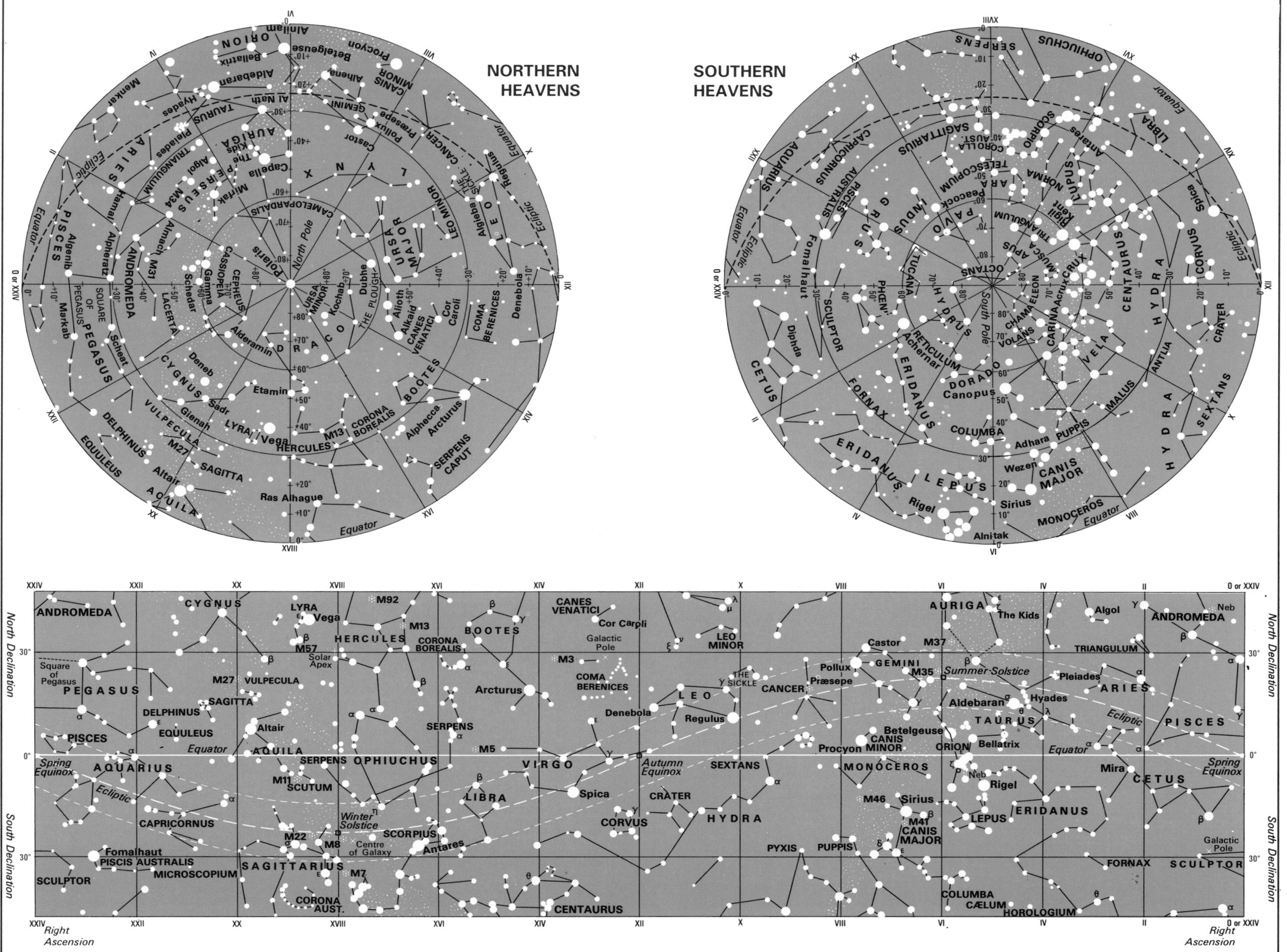
NORTHERN HEAVENS
SOUTHERN HEAVENS
North Pole
South Pole
Equator
Ecliptic
URSA MAJOR
URSA MINOR
Polaris
THE PLOUGH
CASSIOPEIA
CEPHEUS
DRACO
CYGNUS
Deneb
LYRA
Vega
HERCULES
CORONA BOREALIS
BOOTES
Arcturus
AURIGA
Capella
PERSEUS
ANDROMEDA
PEGASUS
ORION
Betelgeuse
Rigel
TAURUS
Aldebaran
GEMINI
Castor
Pollux
LEO
Regulus
CENTAURUS
CRUX
CARINA
Canopus
CANIS MAJOR
Sirius
SCORPIUS
Antares
SAGITTARIUS
Fomalhaut
VIRGO
Spica
OPHIUCHUS
HYDRA
North Declination
South Declination
Right Ascension
Spring Equinox
Autumn Equinox
Summer Solstice
Winter Solstice
Centre of Galaxy
Galactic Pole

THE CONSTELLATIONS

The constellations and their English names

Andromeda	Andromeda
Antila	Air Pump
Apus	Bird of Paradise
Aquarius	Water Carrier
Aquila	Eagle
Ara	Altar
Aries	Ram
Auriga	Charioteer
Boötes	Herdsman
Caelum	Chisel
Camelopardalis	Giraffe
Cancer	Crab
Canes Venatici	Hunting Dogs
Canis Major	Great Dog
Canis Minor	Little Dog
Capricornus	Goat
Carina	Keel
Cassiopeia	Cassiopeia
Centaurus	Centaur
Cepheus	Cepheus
Cetus	Whale
Chamaeleon	Chameleon
Circinus	Compasses
Columba	Dove
Coma Berenices	Berenice's Hair
Corona Australis	Southern Crown
Corona Borealis	Northern Crown
Corvus	Crow
Crater	Cup
Crux	Southern Cross
Cygnus	Swan
Delphinus	Dolphin
Dorado	Swordfish
Draco	Dragon
Equuleus	Little House
Eridanus	Eridanus
Fornax	Furnace
Gemini	Twins
Grus	Crane
Hercules	Hercules
Horologium	Clock
Hydra	Water Snake
Hydrus	Sea Serpent
Indus	Indian
Lacerta	Lizard
Leo	Lion
Leo Minor	Little Lion
Lepus	Hare
Libra	Scales
Lupus	Wolf
Lynx	Lynx
Lyra	Harp
Mensa	Table
Microscopium	Microscope
Monoceros	Unicorn
Musca	Fly
Norma	Level
Octans	Octant
Ophiuchus	Serpent Bearer
Orion	Orion
Pavo	Peacock
Pegasus	Winged Horse
Perseus	Perseus
Phoenix	Phoenix
Pictor	Easel
Pisces	Fishes
Piscis Austrinus	Southern Fish
Puppis	Ship's Stern
Pyxis	Mariner's Compass
Reticulum	Net
Sagitta	Arrow
Sagittarius	Archer
Scorpius	Scorpion
Sculptor	Sculptor
Scutum	Shield
Serpens	Serpent
Sextans	Sextant
Taurus	Bull
Telescopium	Telescope
Triangulum	Triangle
Triangulum Australe	Southern Triangle
Tucana	Toucan
Ursa Major	Great Bear
Ursa Minor	Little Bear
Vela	Sails
Virgo	Virgin
Volans	Flying Fish
Vulpecula	Fox

THE NEAREST STARS

The 20 nearest stars, excluding the Sun, with their distance from Earth in light-years*

Proxima Centauri	4.3
Alpha Centauri A	4.3
Alpha Centauri B	4.3
Barnard's Star	6.0
Wolf 359	8.1
Lal 21185	8.2
Sirius A	8.7
Sirius B	8.7
UV Ceti A	9.0
UV Ceti B	9.0
Ross 154	9.3
Ross 248	10.3
Epsilon Eridani	10.8
L 789-6	11.1
Ross 128	11.1
61 Cygni A	11.2
61 Cygni B	11.2
Procyon A	11.3
Procyon B	11.3
Epsilon Indi	11.4

Many of the nearest stars, like Alpha Centauri A and B, are doubles, orbiting about the common centre of gravity and to all intents and purposes equidistant from Earth. Many of them are dim objects, with no name other than the designation given by the astronomers who investigated them. However, they include Sirius, the brightest star in the sky, and Procyon, the seventh brightest. Both are far larger than the Sun: of the nearest stars, only Epsilon Eridani is similar in size and luminosity.

* A light-year equals approx. 9,500,000,000,000 kilometres

CARTOGRAPHY BY PHILIP'S. COPYRIGHT REED INTERNATIONAL BOOKS LTD

THE SOLAR SYSTEM

2: THE HOME GALAXY
6: THE SEASONS DAY AND NIGHT
7: THE MOON

Lying 27,000 light-years from the centre of one of billions of galaxies that comprise the observable universe, our Solar System contains nine planets and their moons, innumerable asteroids and comets, and a miscellany of dust and gas, all tethered by the immense gravitational field of the Sun, the middling-sized star whose thermonuclear furnaces provide them all with heat and light. The Solar System was formed about 4,600 million years ago, when a spinning cloud of gas, mostly hydrogen but seeded with other, heavier elements, condensed enough to ignite a nuclear reaction and create a star. The Sun still accounts for almost 99.9% of the system's total mass; one planet, Jupiter, contains most of the remainder.

By composition as well as distance, the planetary array divides quite neatly in two: an inner system of four small, solid planets, including the Earth, and an outer system, from Jupiter to Neptune, of four huge gas giants. Between the two groups lies a scattering of asteroids, perhaps as many as 40,000; possibly the remains of a planet destroyed by some unexplained catastrophe, they are more likely to be debris left over from the Solar System's formation, prevented by the gravity of massive Jupiter from coalescing into a larger body. The ninth planet, Pluto, seems to be a world of the inner system type: small, rocky and something of an anomaly.

By the 1990s, however, the Solar System also included some newer anomalies: several thousand spacecraft. Most were in orbit around the Earth, but some had probed far and wide around the system. The valuable information beamed back by these robotic investigators has transformed our knowledge of our celestial environment.

Much of the early history of science is the story of people trying to make sense of the errant points of light that were all they knew of the planets. Now, men have themselves stood on the Earth's Moon; probes have landed on Mars and Venus, and orbiting radars have mapped far distant landscapes with astonishing accuracy. In the 1980s, the US *Voyagers* skimmed all four major planets of the outer system, bringing new revelations with each close approach. Only Pluto, inscrutably distant in an orbit that takes it 50 times the Earth's distance from the Sun, remains unvisited by our messengers.

ORBITS OF THE PLANETS

The solar planets and their orbits, showing the relative position of each planet at the vernal equinox of 1992.

Orbits are drawn to exact scale, but with the Sun and planets greatly enlarged for clarity. The Solar System is shown from the viewpoint of an observer a few light-hours distant in the direction of the constellation Hercules. Seen from such a position, above the plane of the ecliptic, all the planets revolve about the Sun in an anti-clockwise direction. The perspective view exaggerates the elliptical form of all the planetary orbits: only Pluto and Mercury follow paths that deviate noticeably from circularity. Near perihelion – its closest approach to the Sun – Pluto actually passes inside the orbit of Neptune, an event that last occurred in 1983. Pluto will not regain its station as the Sun's outermost planet until February 1999.

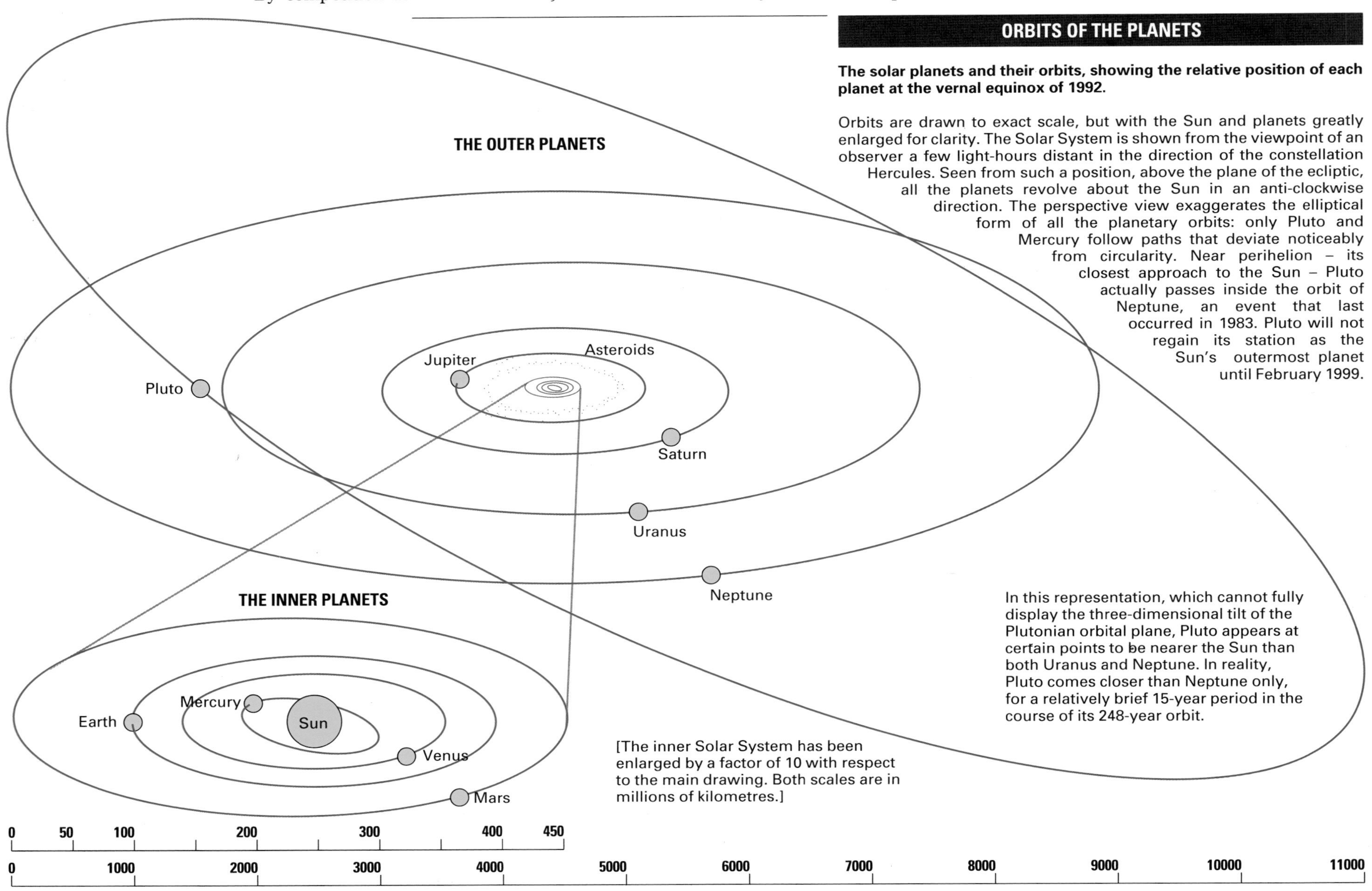
THE OUTER PLANETS
Jupiter
Asteroids
Pluto
Saturn
Uranus
Neptune
THE INNER PLANETS
Mercury
Sun
Earth
Venus
Mars
0 50 100 200 300 400 450
0 1000 2000 3000 4000 5000 6000 7000 8000 9000 10000 11000

In this representation, which cannot fully display the three-dimensional tilt of the Plutonian orbital plane, Pluto appears at certain points to be nearer the Sun than both Uranus and Neptune. In reality, Pluto comes closer than Neptune only, for a relatively brief 15-year period in the course of its 248-year orbit.

[The inner Solar System has been enlarged by a factor of 10 with respect to the main drawing. Both scales are in millions of kilometres.]

PLANETARY DATA

	Mean distance from Sun (million km)	Mass (Earth = 1)	Period of orbit (Earth years)	Period of rotation (Earth days)	Equatorial diameter (km)	Average density (water = 1)	Surface gravity (Earth = 1)	Escape velocity (km/sec)	Number of known satellites
Sun	–	***332,946***	–	***25.38***	***1,392,000***	***1.41***	***27.9***	***617.5***	–
Mercury	58.3	0.06	0.241	58.67	4,878	5.5	0.38	4.27	0
Venus	107.7	0.8	0.615	243.0	12,104	5.25	0.90	10.36	0
Earth	149.6	1.0	1.00	0.99	12,756	5.52	1.00	11.18	1
Mars	227.3	0.1	1.88	1.02	6,794	3.94	0.38	5.03	2
Jupiter	777.9	317.8	11.86	0.41	142,800	1.33	2.64	60.22	16
Saturn	1,427.1	95.2	29.63	0.42	120,000	0.706	1.16	36.25	17
Uranus	2,872.3	14.5	83.97	0.45	52,000	1.70	1.11	22.4	15
Neptune	4,502.7	17.2	164.8	0.67	48,400	1.77	1.21	23.9	8
Pluto	5,894.2	0.002	248.63	6.38	3,000	5.50	0.47	5.1	1

Planetary days are given in sidereal time – that is, with respect to the stars rather than the Sun. Most of the information in the table was confirmed by spacecraft and often obtained from photographs and other data transmitted back to the Earth. In the case of Pluto, however, only earthbound observations have been made, and no spacecraft can hope to encounter it until well into the next century. Given the planet's small size and great distance, figures for its diameter and rotation period cannot be definitive.

Since Pluto does not appear to be massive enough to account for the perturbations in the orbits of Uranus and Neptune that led to its 1930 discovery, it is quite possible that a tenth and even more distant planet may exist. Once Pluto's own 248-year orbit has been observed for long enough, further discrepancies may give a clue as to any tenth planet's whereabouts. Even so, distance alone would make it very difficult to locate, especially since telescopes powerful enough to find it are normally engaged in galactic study.

CARTOGRAPHY BY PHILIP'S. COPYRIGHT REED INTERNATIONAL BOOKS LTD

THE PLANETS

Mercury is the closest planet to the Sun and hence the fastest-moving. It has no significant atmosphere and a cratered, wrinkled surface very similar to that of Earth's moon.

Venus has much the same physical dimensions as Earth. However, its carbon dioxide atmosphere is 90 times as dense, accounting for a runaway greenhouse effect that makes the Venusian surface, at 475°C, the hottest of all the planets in the Solar System. Radar mapping shows relatively level land with volcanic regions whose sulphurous discharges explain the sulphuric acid rains reported by soft-landing space probes before they succumbed to Venus's fierce climate.

Earth seen from space is easily the most beautiful of the inner planets; it is also, and more objectively, the largest, as well the only home of known life. Living things are the main reason why the Earth is able to retain a substantial proportion of corrosive and highly reactive oxygen in its atmosphere, a state of affairs that contradicts the laws of chemical equilibrium; the oxygen in turn supports the life that constantly regenerates it.

Mars was once considered the likeliest of the other planets to share Earth's cargo of life: the seasonal expansion of dark patches strongly suggested vegetation and the planet's apparent ice-caps indicated the vital presence of water. But close inspection by spacecraft brought disappointment: chemical reactions account for the seeming vegetation, the ice-caps are mainly frozen carbon dioxide, and whatever oxygen the planet once possessed is now locked up in the iron-bearing rock that covers its cratered surface and gives it its characteristic red hue.

Jupiter masses almost three times as much as all the other planets combined; had it scooped up a little more matter during its formation, it might have evolved into a small companion star for the Sun. The planet is mostly gas, under intense pressure in the lower atmosphere above a core of fiercely compressed hydrogen and helium. The upper layers form strikingly-coloured rotating belts, the outward sign of the intense storms created by Jupiter's rapid diurnal rotation. Close approaches by spacecraft have shown an orbiting ring system and discovered several previously unknown moons: Jupiter has at least 16 moons.

Saturn is structurally similar to Jupiter, rotating fast enough to produce an obvious bulge at its equator. Ever since the invention of the telescope, however, Saturn's rings have been the feature that has attracted most observers. *Voyager* probes in 1980 and 1981 sent back detailed pictures that showed them to be composed of thousands of separate ringlets, each in turn made up of tiny icy particles, interacting in a complex dance that may serve as a model for the study of galactic and even larger structures.

Uranus was unknown to the ancients. Although it is faintly visible to the naked eye, it was not discovered until 1781. Its composition is broadly similar to Jupiter and Saturn, though its distance from the Sun ensures an even colder surface temperature. Observations in 1977 suggested the presence of a faint ring system, amply confirmed when *Voyager 2* swung past the planet in 1986.

Neptune is always more than 4,000 million kilometres from Earth, and despite its diameter of almost 50,000 km, it can only be seen by telescope. Its 1846 discovery was the result of mathematical predictions by astronomers seeking to explain irregularities in the orbit of Uranus, but until *Voyager 2* closed with the planet in 1989, little was known of it. Like Uranus, it has a ring system; *Voyager's* photographs revealed a total of eight moons.

Pluto is the most mysterious of the solar planets, if only because even the most powerful telescopes can scarcely resolve it from a point of light to a disc. It was discovered as recently as 1930, like Neptune as the result of perturbations in the orbits of the two then outermost planets. Its small size, as well as its eccentric and highly tilted orbit, has led to suggestions that it is a former satellite of Neptune, somehow liberated from its primary. In 1978 Pluto was found to have a moon of its own, Charon, apparently half the size of Pluto itself.

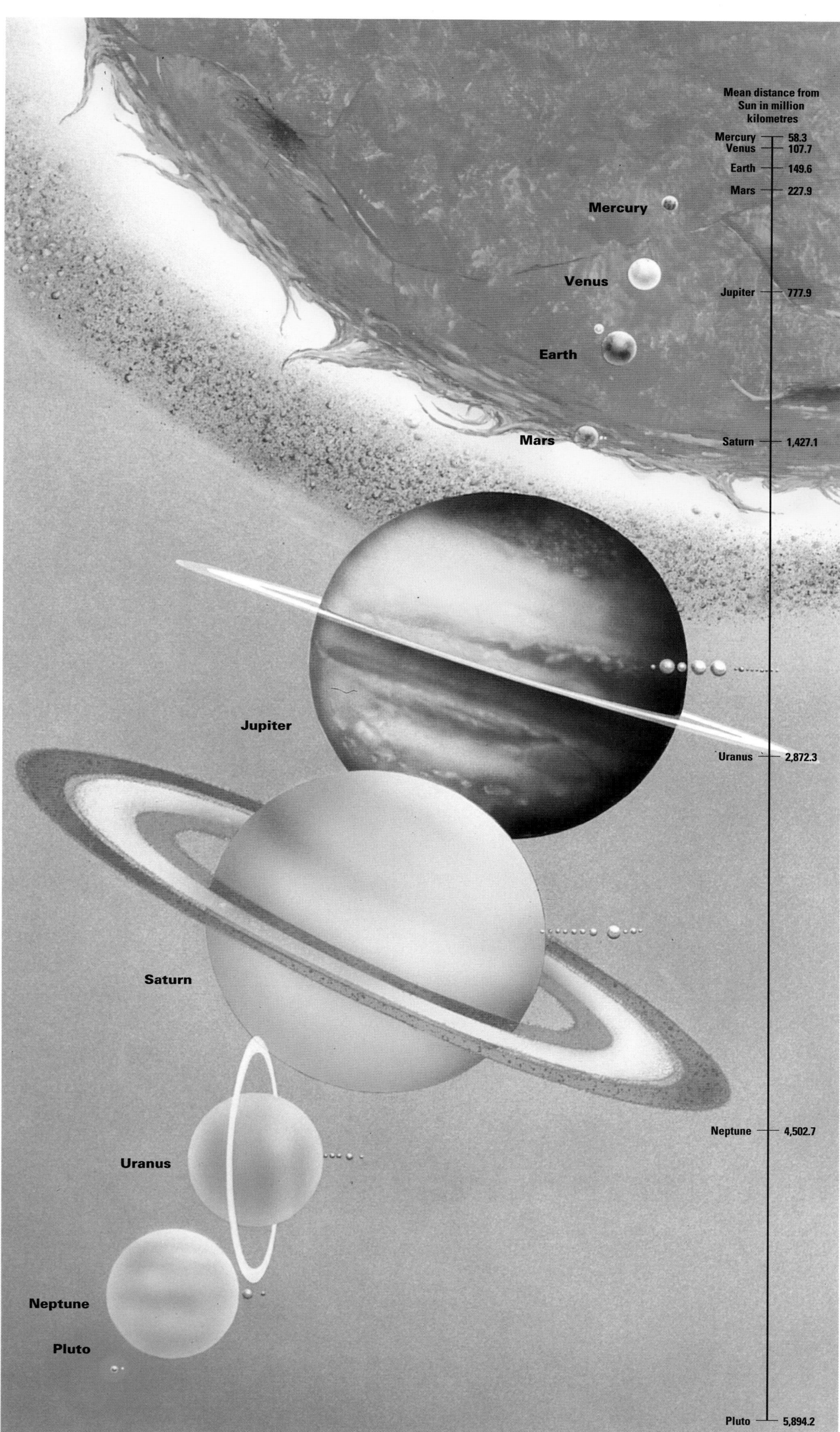
Mean distance from Sun in million kilometres
Mercury 58.3
Venus 107.7
Earth 149.6
Mars 227.9
Jupiter 777.9
Saturn 1,427.1
Uranus 2,872.3
Neptune 4,502.7
Pluto 5,894.2
Mercury
Venus
Earth
Mars
Jupiter
Saturn
Uranus
Neptune
Pluto

CARTOGRAPHY BY PHILIP'S. COPYRIGHT REED INTERNATIONAL BOOKS LTD

THE EARTH: TIME AND MOTION

4: ORBITS OF THE PLANETS
11: OCEAN CURRENTS
12: CIRCULATION OF THE AIR

The basic unit of time measurement is the day, that is, one rotation of the Earth on its axis. The subdivision of the day into hours, minutes and seconds is arbitrary and simply for our convenience. Our present calendar is based on the solar year of 365.24 days, the time taken by the Earth to orbit the Sun. As the Earth rotates from west to east, the Sun appears to rise in the east and set in the west. When the Sun is setting in Shanghai, on the opposite side of the world New York is just emerging into sunlight. Noon, when the Sun is directly overhead, is coincident at all places on the same meridian, with shadows pointing directly towards the poles.

Calendars based on the movements of the Sun and Moon have been used since ancient times. The Julian Calendar, with its leap year, introduced by Julius Caesar, fixed the average length of the year at 365.25 days, which was about 11 minutes too long (the Earth completes its orbit in 365 days, 5 hours, 48 minutes and 46 seconds of mean solar time). The cumulative error was rectified by the Gregorian Calendar, introduced by Pope Gregory XIII in 1582, when he decreed that the day following 4 October was 15 October, and that century years did not count as leap years unless divisible by 400. England did not adopt the reformed calendar until 1752, when the country found itself 11 days behind the continent.

Britain imposed the Gregorian Calendar on all its possessions, including the American colonies. All dates preceding 2 September were marked 'OS', for 'Old Style'.

EARTH DATA

Maximum distance from Sun (Aphelion): 152,007,016 km
Minimum distance from Sun (Perihelion): 147,000,830 km
Obliquity of the ecliptic: 23° 27′ 08″
Length of year – solar tropical (equinox to equinox): 365.24 days
Length of year – sidereal (fixed star to fixed star): 365.26 days
Length of day – mean solar day: 24h, 03m, 56s
Length of day – mean sidereal day: 23h, 56m, 04s

Superficial area: 510,000,000 sq km
Land surface: 149,000,000 sq km (29.2%)
Water surface: 361,000,000 sq km (70.8%)
Equatorial circumference: 40,077 km.
Polar circumference: 40,009 km
Equatorial diameter: 12,756.8 km
Polar diameter: 12,713.8 km
Equatorial radius: 6,378.4 km
Polar radius: 6,356.9 km
Volume of the Earth: 1,083,230 x 10^6 cu km
Mass of the Earth: 5.9 x 10^{21} tonnes

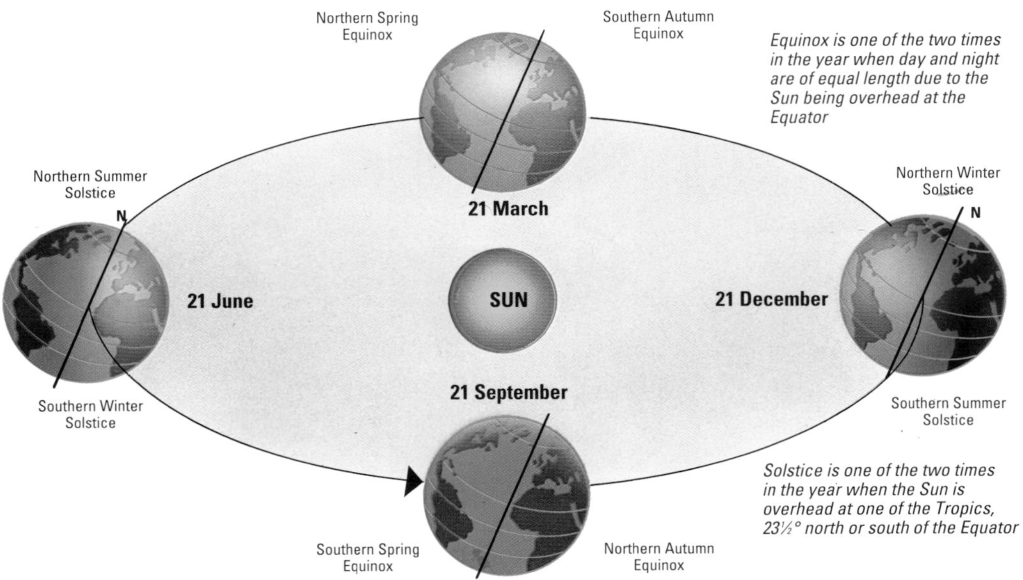
Northern Spring Equinox
Southern Autumn Equinox
Northern Summer Solstice
Southern Winter Solstice
Northern Winter Solstice
Southern Summer Solstice
Southern Spring Equinox
Northern Autumn Equinox
21 March
21 June
SUN
21 December
21 September
N

Equinox is one of the two times in the year when day and night are of equal length due to the Sun being overhead at the Equator

Solstice is one of the two times in the year when the Sun is overhead at one of the Tropics, 23½° north or south of the Equator

THE SEASONS

The Earth revolves around the Sun once a year in an 'anti-clockwise' direction, tilted at a constant angle 66½°. In June, the northern hemisphere is tilted towards the Sun: as a result, it receives more hours of sunshine in a day and therefore has its warmest season, summer. By December, the Earth has rotated halfway round the Sun so that the southern hemisphere is tilted towards the Sun and has its summer; the hemisphere that is tilted away from the Sun has winter. On 21 June the Sun is directly overhead at the Tropic of Cancer (23½° N), and this is midsummer in the northern hemisphere. Midsummer in the southern hemisphere occurs on 21 December, when the Sun is overhead at the Tropic of Capricorn (23½° S).

DAY AND NIGHT

The Sun appears to rise in the east, reach its highest point at noon, and then set in the west, to be followed by night. In reality, it is not the Sun that is moving but the Earth revolving from west to east.

At the summer solstice in the northern hemisphere (21 June), the Arctic has total daylight and the Antarctic total darkness. The opposite occurs at the winter solstice (21 December). At the Equator, the length of day and night are almost equal all year.

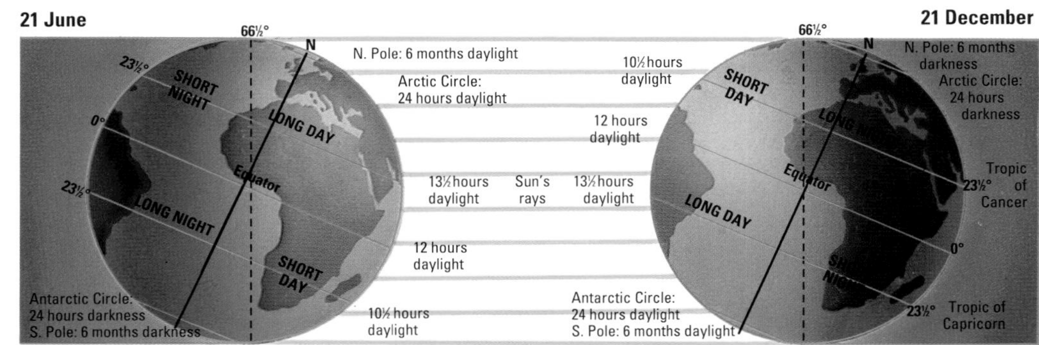
21 June
21 December
66½°
N
N. Pole: 6 months daylight
Arctic Circle: 24 hours daylight
SHORT NIGHT
LONG DAY
Equator
LONG NIGHT
SHORT DAY
Antarctic Circle: 24 hours darkness
S. Pole: 6 months darkness
10½ hours daylight
12 hours daylight
13½ hours daylight
Sun's rays
N. Pole: 6 months darkness
Arctic Circle: 24 hours darkness
Tropic 23½° of Cancer
Tropic of Capricorn
Antarctic Circle: 24 hours daylight
S. Pole: 6 months daylight

(A) **Equator** (B) **45° North** (C) **Arctic Circle** (D) **North Pole**

Zenith, Noon, North star, N, S, E, W, June solstice, Equinox, December solstice

THE SUN'S PATH

The diagrams on the left illustrate the apparent path of the Sun at (A) the Equator, (B) in mid-latitude (45°), (C) at the Arctic Circle (66½°), and (D) at the North Pole, where there are six months of continuous daylight and six months of continuous night.

MEASUREMENTS OF TIME

Astronomers distinguish between solar time and sidereal time. Solar time derives from the period taken by the Earth to rotate on its axis: one rotation defines a solar day. But the speed of the Earth along its orbit around the Sun is not constant. The length of day – or 'apparent solar day', as defined by the apparent successive transits of the Sun – is irregular because the Earth must complete more than one rotation before the Sun returns to the same meridian. The constant sidereal day is defined as the interval between two successive apparent transits of a star, or the first point of Aries, across the same meridian. If the Sun is at the equinox and overhead at a meridian one day, then the next day it will be to the east by approximately 1°. Thus, the Sun will not cross the meridian until four minutes after the sidereal noon.

From the diagrams on the right it is possible to discover the time of sunrise or sunset on a given date and for latitudes between 60°N and 60°S.

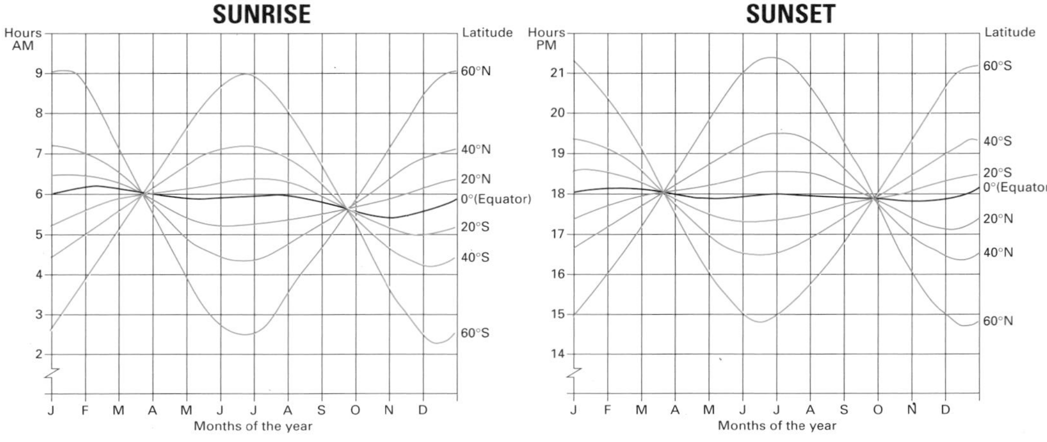
SUNRISE
SUNSET
Hours AM
Hours PM
Latitude
60°N
40°N
20°N
0°(Equator)
20°S
40°S
60°S
J F M A M J J A S O N D
Months of the year

CARTOGRAPHY BY PHILIP'S. COPYRIGHT REED INTERNATIONAL BOOKS LTD

THE MOON

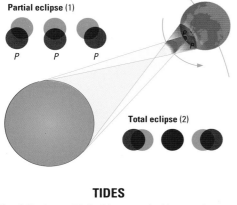

PHASES OF THE MOON

New Moon
Crescent
First quarter
Gibbous
Full Moon
Gibbous
Last quarter
Crescent
New Moon

The Moon rotates more slowly than the Earth, making one complete turn on its axis in just over 27 days. Since this corresponds to its period of revolution around the Earth, the Moon always presents the same hemisphere or face to us, and we never see 'the dark side'. The interval between one Full Moon and the next (and between New Moons) is about $29^{1}/_{2}$ days – a lunar month. The apparent changes in the shape of the Moon are caused by its changing position in relation to the Earth; like the planets, it produces no light of its own and shines only by reflecting the rays of the Sun.

Partial eclipse (1)

P P P

Total eclipse (2)

Lunar eclipse

ECLIPSES

When the Moon passes between the Sun and the Earth, it causes a partial eclipse of the Sun (1) if the Earth passes through the Moon's outer shadow (P), or a total eclipse (2) if the inner cone shadow crosses the Earth's surface. In a lunar eclipse, the Earth's shadow crosses the Moon and, again, provides either a partial or total eclipse. Eclipses of the Sun and the Moon do not occur every month because of the 5° difference between the plane of the Moon's orbit and the plane in which the Earth moves. In the 1990s only 14 lunar eclipses are possible, for example, seven partial and seven total; each is visible only from certain, and variable, parts of the world. The same period witnesses 13 solar eclipses – six partial (or annular) and seven total.

TIDES

The daily rise and fall of the ocean's tides are the result of the gravitational pull of the Moon and that of the Sun, though the effect of the latter is only 46.6% as strong as that of the Moon. This effect is greatest on the hemisphere facing the Moon and causes a tidal 'bulge'. When lunar and solar forces pull together, with Sun, Earth and Moon in line (near New and Full Moons), higher 'spring tides' (and lower low tides) occur; when lunar and solar forces are least coincidental with the Sun and Moon at an angle (near the Moon's first and third quarters), 'neap tides' occur, which have a small tidal range.

Spring tide
New Moon
Last quarter
Neap tide
Spring tide
Full Moon
Neap tide
First quarter
Gravitational pull by Sun and Moon

MOON DATA

Distance from Earth
The Moon orbits at a mean distance of 384,199.1 km, at an average speed of 3,683 km/h in relation to the Earth.

Size and mass
The average diameter of the Moon is 3,475.1 km. It is 400 times smaller than the Sun but is about 400 times closer to the Earth, so we see them as the same size. The Moon has a mass of 7,348 x 10^{19} tonnes, with a density 3.344 times that of water.

Visibility
Only 59% of the Moon's surface is directly visible from Earth. Reflected light takes 1.25 seconds to reach Earth – compared to 8 minutes 27.3 seconds for light to reach us from the Sun.

Temperature
With the Sun overhead, the temperature on the lunar equator can reach 117.2°C [243°F]. At night it can sink to –162.7°C [–261°F].

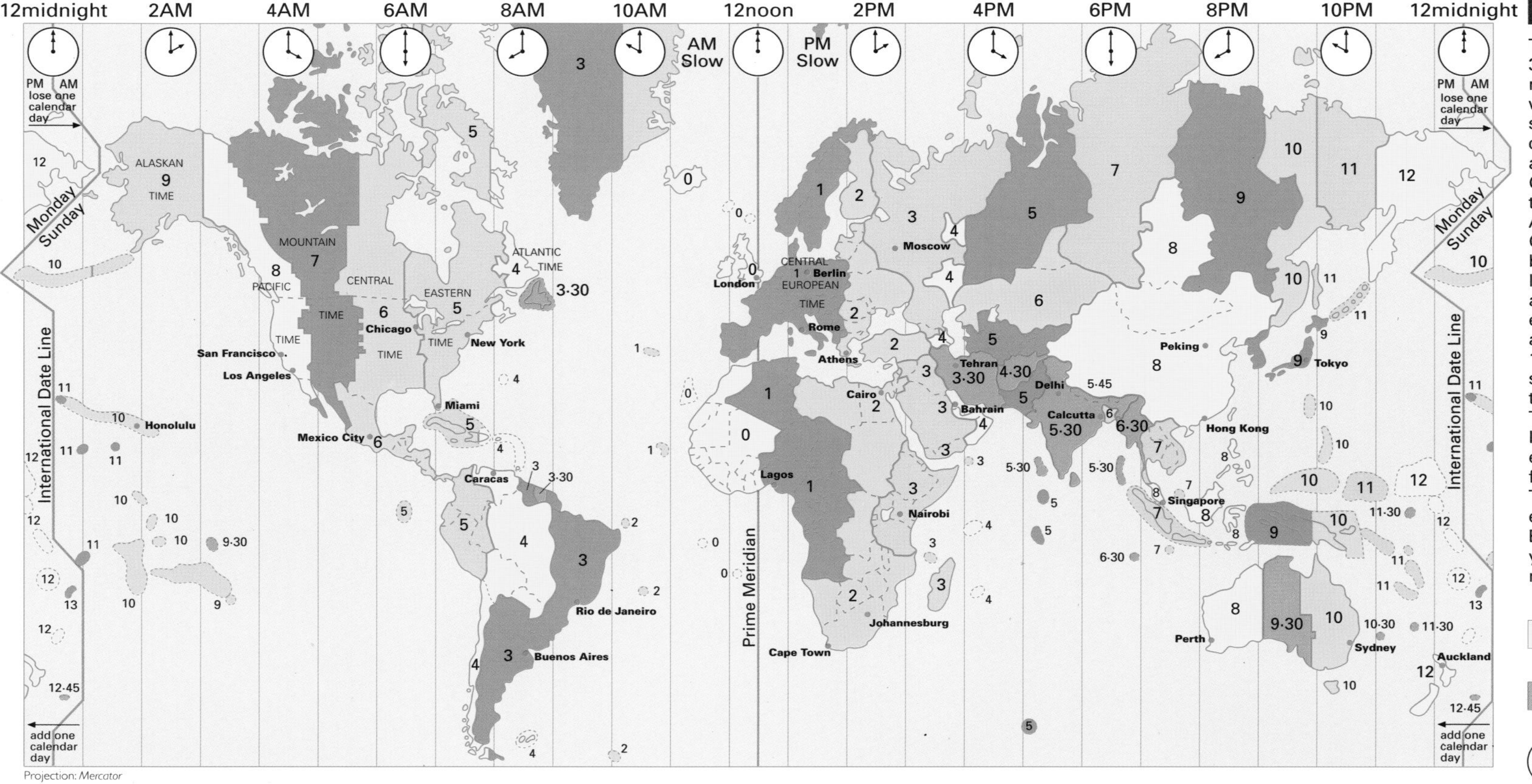
12midnight
2AM
4AM
6AM
8AM
10AM
12noon
2PM
4PM
6PM
8PM
10PM
12midnight
AM Slow
PM Slow
PM AM lose one calendar day
add one calendar day
Monday Sunday
International Date Line
Prime Meridian
ALASKAN 9 TIME
MOUNTAIN 7 TIME
PACIFIC TIME
CENTRAL TIME
EASTERN TIME
ATLANTIC TIME
CENTRAL EUROPEAN TIME
San Francisco
Los Angeles
Chicago
New York
Honolulu
Mexico City
Miami
Caracas
Rio de Janeiro
Buenos Aires
London
Berlin
Rome
Athens
Cairo
Moscow
Lagos
Nairobi
Johannesburg
Cape Town
Tehran
Bahrain
Delhi
Calcutta
Peking
Hong Kong
Singapore
Tokyo
Perth
Sydney
Auckland
Projection: *Mercator*

TIME ZONES

The Earth rotates through 360° in 24 hours, and so moves 15° every hour. The world is divided into 24 standard time zones, each centred on lines of longitude at 15° intervals. The Greenwich meridian lies at the centre of the first zone. All places to the west of Greenwich are one hour behind for every 15° of longitude; places to the east are ahead by one hour for every 15°. When it is 12 noon at the Greenwich meridian, 180° east it is midnight of the same day – while 180° west the day is just beginning. To overcome this, the International Date Line was established, approximately following the 180° meridian. Thus, if you travelled eastwards from Japan (140° East) to Samoa (170° West), you would pass from Sunday night into Sunday morning.

Zones slow or fast of Greenwich Mean Time

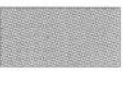
Half-hour zones

The time when it is 12 noon at Greenwich

CARTOGRAPHY BY PHILIP'S. COPYRIGHT REED INTERNATIONAL BOOKS LTD

THE EARTH: GEOLOGY

18: THE SPREADING EARTH
TYPES OF ROCK
MOUNTAIN BUILDING

19: MOULDING THE LAND

21: THE CARBON CYLCE

34: MINERALS

The origin of the Earth is still open to conjecture, although the most widely accepted theory is that it was formed from a solar cloud consisting mainly of hydrogen about 4,600 million years ago. The cloud condensed, forming the planets. The lighter elements floated to the surface of the Earth, where they cooled to form a crust; the inner material remained hot and molten. The first rocks were formed over 3,500 million years ago, but the Earth's surface has since been constantly altered.

The crust consists of a brittle, low-density material, varying from 5 kilometres to 50 kilometres thick beneath the continents, which is predominantly made up of silica and aluminium: hence its name, 'sial'. Below the sial is a basaltic layer known as 'sima', comprising mainly silica and magnesium. The crust accounts for only 1.5% of the Earth's volume.

The mantle lies immediately below the crust, with a distinct change in density and chemical properties. The rock here is rich in iron and magnesium silicates, with temperatures reaching 1,600°C. The rigid upper mantle extends down to a depth of about 1,000 kilometres, below which is a more viscous lower mantle measuring about 1,900 kilometres thick.

The outer core, measuring about 2,310 kilometres thick, consists of molten iron and nickel at temperatures ranging from 2,100°C to 5,000°C, possibly separated from the less dense mantle by an oxidized shell. About 5,000 kilometres below the planetary surface is a liquid transition zone, below which is the solid inner core, a sphere of about 2,700 kilometres diameter, where rock is three times as dense as in the crust. The temperature at the centre of the Earth is probably about 5,000°C.

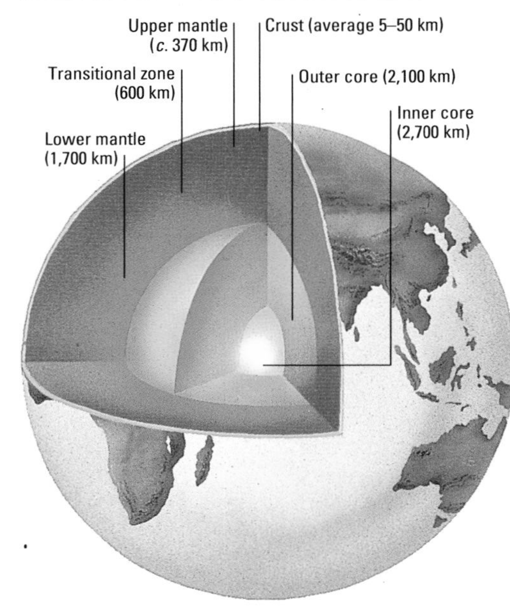
Upper mantle (c. 370 km)
Crust (average 5–50 km)
Transitional zone (600 km)
Outer core (2,100 km)
Inner core (2,700 km)
Lower mantle (1,700 km)

The complementary, almost jigsaw-puzzle fit of the Atlantic coasts led to Alfred Wegener's proposition of continental drift in Germany (1915). His theory suggested that an ancient super-continent, which he called Pangaea, incorporating all the Earth's landmasses, gradually split up to form the continents we know today.

By 180 million years ago, Pangaea had divided into two major groups and the southern part, Gondwanaland, had itself begun to break up with India and Antarctica-Australia becoming isolated.

By 135 million years ago, the widening of the splits in the North Atlantic and Indian Oceans persisted, a South Atlantic gap had appeared, and India continued to move 'north' towards Asia.

By 65 million years ago, South America had completely split from Africa.

To form today's pattern, India 'collided' with Asia (crumpling up sediments to form the Himalayas); South America rotated and moved west to connect with North America; Australia separated from Antarctica and moved north; and the familiar gap developed between Greenland and Europe.

CONTINENTAL DRIFT

About 200 million years ago the original Pangaea landmass began to split into two continental groups, which further separated over time to produce the present-day configuration.

Laurasia

Gondwanaland

180 million years ago

135 million years ago

Present day

Trench
Rift
New ocean floor
Zones of slippage

PLATE TECTONICS

The original debate about the drift theory of Wegener and others formed a long prelude to a more radical idea: plate tectonics. The discovery that the continents are carried along on the top of slowly-moving crustal plates (which float on heavier liquid material – the lower mantle – much as icebergs do on water) provided the mechanism for the drift theories to work. The plates converge and diverge along margins marked by seismic and volcanic activity. Plates diverge from mid-ocean ridges where molten lava pushes up and forces the plates apart at a rate of up to 40 mm a year; converging plates form either a trench (where the oceanic plates sink below the lighter continental rock) or mountain ranges (where two continents collide).

The debate about plate tectonics is not over, however. In addition to abiding questions such as what force actually moves the plates (massive convection currents in the Earth's interior is the most popular explanation), and why so many volcanoes and earthquakes occur in mid-plate (such as Hawaii and central China), evidence began to emerge in the early 1990s that, with more sophisticated equipment and models, the whole theory might be in doubt.

VOLCANOES

Of some 850 volcanoes that have produced recorded eruptions, nearly three-quarters lie in the 'Ring of Fire' that surrounds the Pacific Ocean. The 1980s was a bad decade for loss of life here, with three major eruptions – Mount St Helens, USA, in 1980; El Chichon, Mexico, in 1982; and Nevado del Ruiz, Colombia, in 1985 – killing 25,000 people. This is not because the world is becoming less geologically stable: it is simply that populations are growing fast, with over 350 million people now living in areas vulnerable to seismic activity.

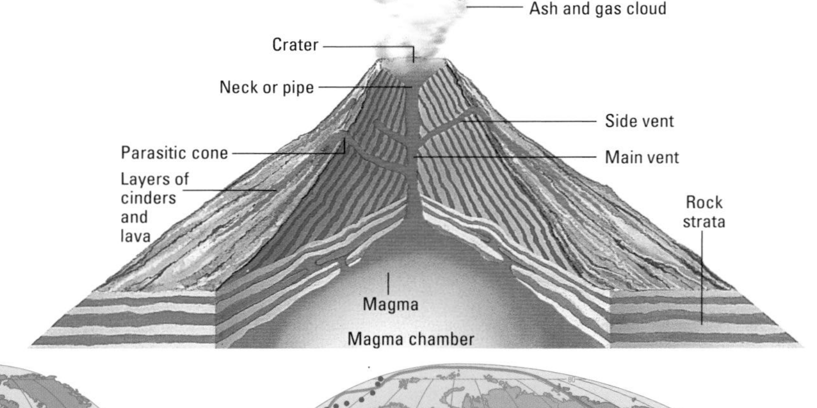
Ash and gas cloud
Crater
Neck or pipe
Side vent
Parasitic cone
Main vent
Layers of cinders and lava
Rock strata
Magma
Magma chamber

Shield cone

Hornit cone

Cinder cone

Caldera

DISTRIBUTION

Land volcanoes active since 1700 ▲

Submarine volcanoes •

Geysers ✚

Boundaries of tectonic plates

Direction of movement along plate boundaries (cm/year) 7.2

Volcanoes can suddenly erupt after lying dormant for centuries: in 1991 Mount Pinatubo, Philippines, burst into life after sleeping for more than 600 years.

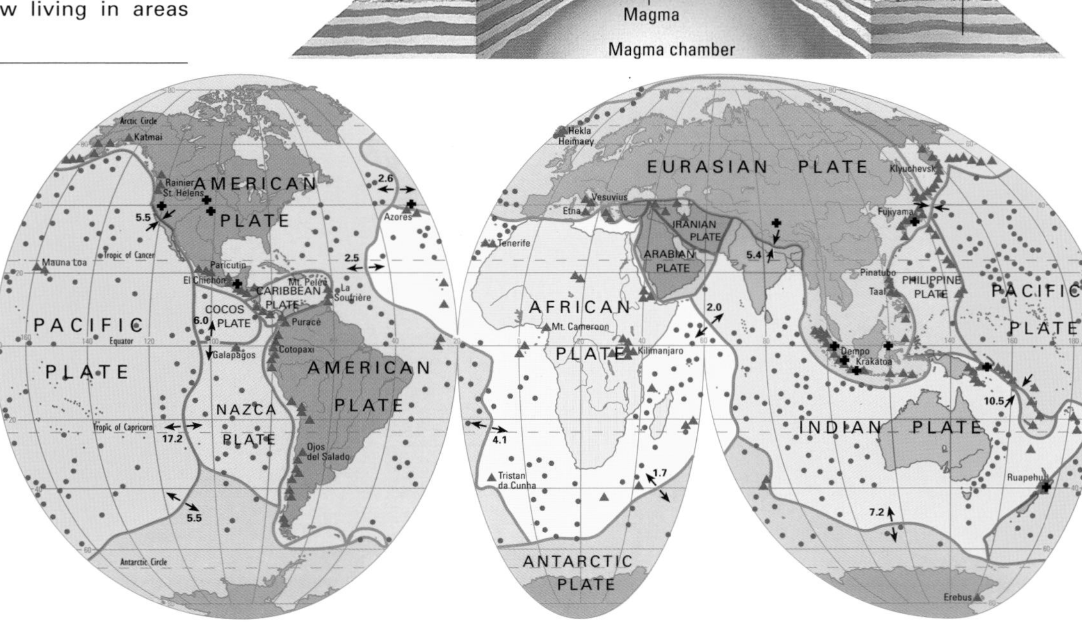
AMERICAN PLATE
PACIFIC PLATE
COCOS PLATE
CARIBBEAN PLATE
NAZCA PLATE
AMERICAN PLATE
EURASIAN PLATE
AFRICAN PLATE
ARABIAN PLATE
IRANIAN PLATE
PHILIPPINE PLATE
PACIFIC PLATE
INDIAN PLATE
ANTARCTIC PLATE
Arctic Circle
Katmai
Rainier
St. Helens
Mauna Loa
El Chichon
Paricutin
Mt. Pelée
Soufrière
Galapagos
Cotopaxi
Ojos del Salado
Azores
Hekla
Heimaey
Vesuvius
Etna
Tenerife
Mt. Cameroon
Kilimanjaro
Tristan da Cunha
Klyuchevsk
Fujiyama
Pinatubo
Taal
Krakatoa
Ruapehu
Erebus
Antarctic Circle
Equator
Tropic of Cancer
Tropic of Capricorn
5.5
2.6
2.5
6.0
17.2
5.5
4.1
1.7
2.0
5.4
10.5
7.2

CARTOGRAPHY BY PHILIP'S. COPYRIGHT REED INTERNATIONAL BOOKS LTD

GEOLOGICAL TIME

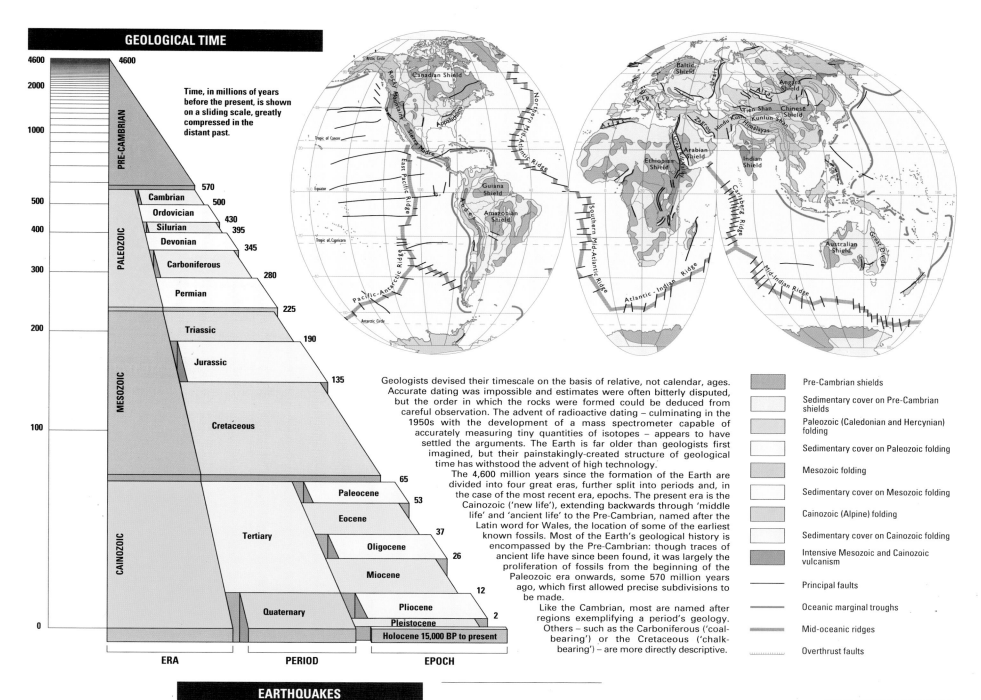

Time, in millions of years before the present, is shown on a sliding scale, greatly compressed in the distant past.

ERA	PERIOD	EPOCH	Millions of years
PRE-CAMBRIAN			4600–570
PALEOZOIC	Cambrian		570–500
	Ordovician		500–430
	Silurian		430–395
	Devonian		395–345
	Carboniferous		345–280
	Permian		280–225
MESOZOIC	Triassic		225–190
	Jurassic		190–135
	Cretaceous		135–65
CAINOZOIC	Tertiary	Paleocene	65–53
		Eocene	53–37
		Oligocene	37–26
		Miocene	26–12
		Pliocene	12–2
	Quaternary	Pleistocene	2
		Holocene 15,000 BP to present	

Geologists devised their timescale on the basis of relative, not calendar, ages. Accurate dating was impossible and estimates were often bitterly disputed, but the order in which the rocks were formed could be deduced from careful observation. The advent of radioactive dating – culminating in the 1950s with the development of a mass spectrometer capable of accurately measuring tiny quantities of isotopes – appears to have settled the arguments. The Earth is far older than geologists first imagined, but their painstakingly-created structure of geological time has withstood the advent of high technology.

The 4,600 million years since the formation of the Earth are divided into four great eras, further split into periods and, in the case of the most recent era, epochs. The present era is the Cainozoic ('new life'), extending backwards through 'middle life' and 'ancient life' to the Pre-Cambrian, named after the Latin word for Wales, the location of some of the earliest known fossils. Most of the Earth's geological history is encompassed by the Pre-Cambrian: though traces of ancient life have since been found, it was largely the proliferation of fossils from the beginning of the Paleozoic era onwards, some 570 million years ago, which first allowed precise subdivisions to be made.

Like the Cambrian, most are named after regions exemplifying a period's geology. Others – such as the Carboniferous ('coal-bearing') or the Cretaceous ('chalk-bearing') – are more directly descriptive.

- Pre-Cambrian shields
- Sedimentary cover on Pre-Cambrian shields
- Paleozoic (Caledonian and Hercynian) folding
- Sedimentary cover on Paleozoic folding
- Mesozoic folding
- Sedimentary cover on Mesozoic folding
- Cainozoic (Alpine) folding
- Sedimentary cover on Cainozoic folding
- Intensive Mesozoic and Cainozoic vulcanism
- Principal faults
- Oceanic marginal troughs
- Mid-oceanic ridges
- Overthrust faults

EARTHQUAKES

Earthquake magnitude is usually rated according to either the Richter or the Modified Mercalli scale, both devised by seismologists in the 1930s. The Richter scale measures absolute earthquake power with mathematical precision: each step upwards represents a ten-fold increase in shockwave amplitude. Theoretically, there is no upper limit, but the largest earthquakes measured have been rated at between 8.8 and 8.9. The 12-point Mercalli scale, based on observed effects, is often more meaningful, ranging from I (earthquakes noticed only by seismographs) to XII (total destruction); intermediate points include V (people awakened at night; unstable objects overturned), VII (collapse of ordinary buildings; chimneys and monuments fall) and IX (conspicuous cracks in ground; serious damage to reservoirs).

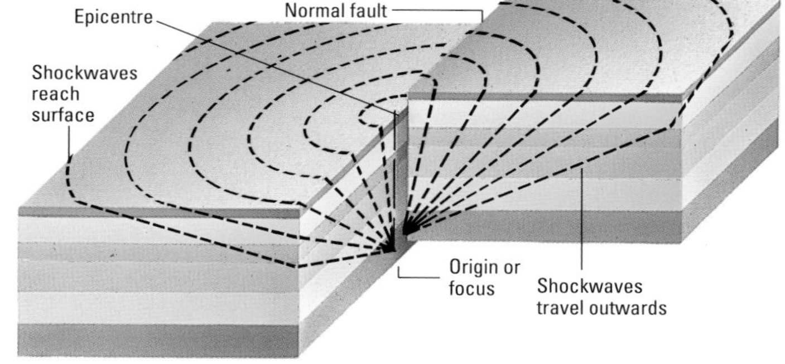
Epicentre
Normal fault
Shockwaves reach surface
Origin or focus
Shockwaves travel outwards

NOTABLE EARTHQUAKES SINCE 1900

Year	Location	Mag.	Deaths
1906	San Francisco, USA	8.3	503
1906	Valparaiso, Chile	8.6	22,000
1908	Messina, Italy	7.5	83,000
1915	Avezzano, Italy	7.5	30,000
1920	Gansu (Kansu), China	8.6	180,000
1923	Yokohama, Japan	8.3	143,000
1927	Nan Shan, China	8.3	200,000
1932	Gansu (Kansu), China	7.6	70,000
1934	Bihar, India/Nepal	8.4	10,700
1935	Quetta, India*	7.5	60,000
1939	Chillan, Chile	8.3	28,000
1939	Erzincan, Turkey	7.9	30,000
1960	Agadir, Morocco	5.8	12,000
1962	Khorasan, Iran	7.1	12,230
1963	Skopje, Yugoslavia**	6.0	1,000
1964	Anchorage, Alaska	8.4	131
1968	N.E. Iran	7.4	12,000
1970	N. Peru	7.7	66,794
1972	Managua, Nicaragua	6.2	5,000
1974	N. Pakistan	6.3	5,200
1976	Guatemala	7.5	22,778
1976	Tangshan, China	8.2	650,000
1978	Tabas, Iran	7.7	25,000
1980	El Asnam, Algeria	7.3	20,000
1980	S. Italy	7.2	4,800
1985	Mexico City, Mexico	8.1	4,200
1988	N.W. Armenia	6.8	55,000
1990	N. Iran	7.7	36,000
1993	Maharashtra, India	6.4	30,000
1994	Los Angeles, USA	6.6	51

The highest magnitude recorded on the Richter scale is 8.9, in Japan on 2 March 1933 (2,990 deaths). The most devastating quake ever was at Shaanxi (Shensi) province, central China, on 24 January 1566, when an estimated 830,000 people were killed.

* now Pakistan
** now Macedonia

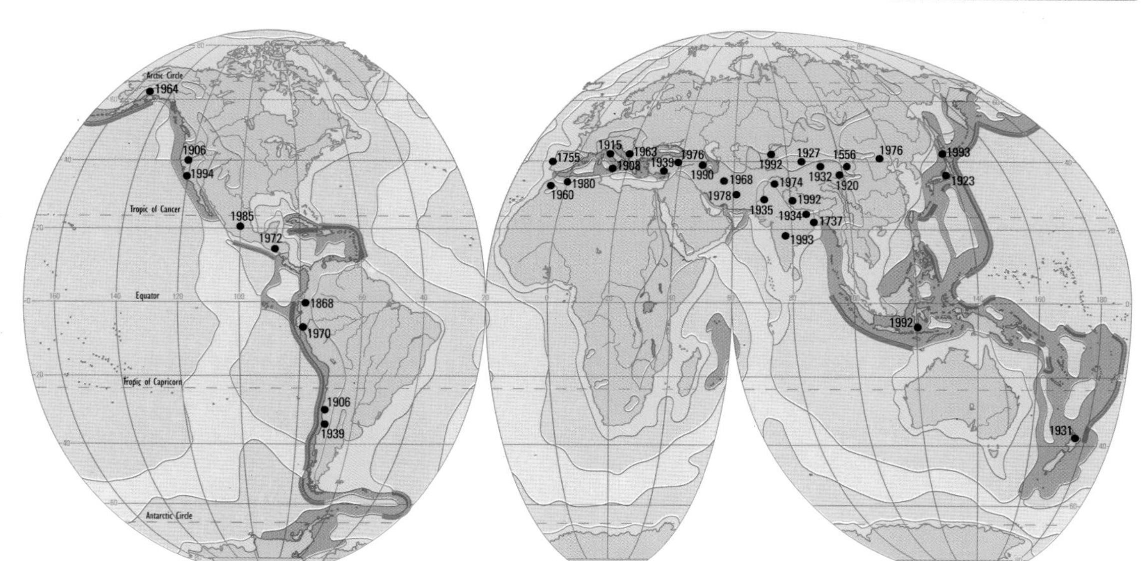
Arctic Circle
Tropic of Cancer
Equator
Tropic of Capricorn
Antarctic Circle
1964
1906
1994
1985
1972
1868
1970
1906
1939
1755
1915
1963
1908
1939
1976
1990
1968
1978
1935
1992
1927
1556
1976
1932
1920
1974
1992
1934
1737
1993
1993
1923
1980
1960
1992
1931

DISTRIBUTION

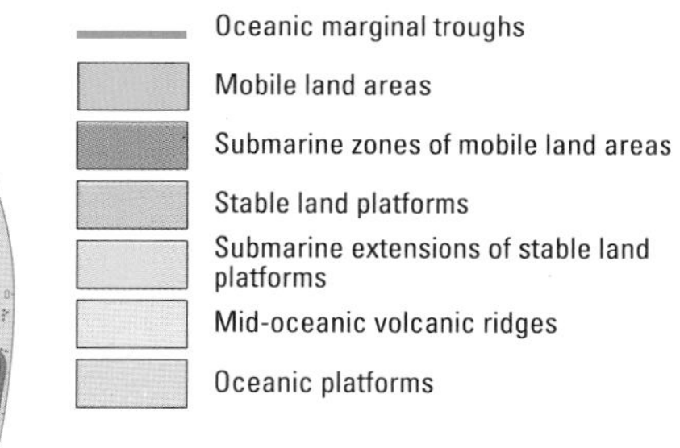
1976 ● Principal earthquakes and dates
Oceanic marginal troughs
Mobile land areas
Submarine zones of mobile land areas
Stable land platforms
Submarine extensions of stable land platforms
Mid-oceanic volcanic ridges
Oceanic platforms

Earthquakes are a series of rapid vibrations originating from the slipping or faulting of parts of the Earth's crust when stresses within build to breaking point, and usually occur at depths between 8 and 30 kilometres.

CARTOGRAPHY BY PHILIP'S. COPYRIGHT REED INTERNATIONAL BOOKS LTD

THE EARTH: OCEANS

7: TIDES

16: HYDROLOGICAL CYCLE WATER DISTRIBUTION

17: WATERSHEDS

18: THE SPREADING EARTH

39: SHIPPING

47: WATER POLLUTION

The Earth is a misnamed planet: more than 70% of its total surface area – 361,740,000 square kilometres – is covered by its oceans and seas. This great cloak of liquid water gives the planet its characteristic blue appearance from space, and is one of two obvious differences between the Earth and its near-neighbours in space, Mars and Venus. The other difference is the presence of life, and the two are closely linked.

In a strict geographical sense, the Earth has only three oceans: the Atlantic, Pacific and Indian Oceans. Subdivided vertically instead of horizontally, however, there are many more. The most active is the sunlit upper layer, home of most sea life and the vital interface between air and water. In this surface zone, huge energies are exchanged between the oceans and the atmosphere above; it is also a kind of membrane through which the ocean breathes, absorbing great quantities of carbon dioxide and partially exchanging them for oxygen, largely through the phytoplankton, tiny plants that photosynthesize solar energy and provide the food base for all other marine life.

As depth increases, so light and colour gradually fade away, the longer wavelengths dying first. At 50 metres, the ocean is a world of green, blue and violet; at 100 metres, only blue remains; by 200 metres, there is only a dim twilight. The temperature falls away with the light, until just before 1,000 metres – the precise depth varies – there occurs a temperature change almost as abrupt as the transition between air and water far above. Below this thermocline, at a near-stable 3°C, the waters are forever unmoved by the winds of the upper world and are stirred only by the slow action of deep ocean currents. The pressure is crushing, reaching 1,000 atmospheres in the deepest trenches: a force of 1 tonne bearing down on every square centimetre.

Yet even here the oceans support life, and not only the handful of strange, deep-sea creatures that find a living in the near-empty abyss. The deep ocean serves as a gigantic storehouse, both for heat and for assorted atmospheric chemicals, regulating and balancing the proportions of various trace compounds and elements, and ensuring a large measure of stability for both the climate and the ecology that depend on it.

Sea level

200 metres

500 metres

1,000 metres

1,500 metres

2,000 metres

6,000 metres

11,000 metres

From the tidal zone at the coastline, the continental shelf, geologically still part of the continental landmass, drops gently to about 200 metres. At the end of the shelf, the seabed falls away in the steeper angle of the continental slope, exaggerated in this drawing, in which the horizontal scale has been greatly compressed. The subsequent descent to the deep ocean floor, known as the continental rise, is more gentle, with gradients between 1 in 100 and 1 in 700 until the abyssal plains, at between 2,500 and 6,000 metres below the surface. Most marine life is confined to the first 200 metres, where sunlight can still penetrate.

For the most part, the sea bottom is flat, seldom descending below 6,000 metres. A few ocean trenches, however, slice almost twice as far into the Earth's crust, especially in the Pacific, where six trenches reach more than 10,000 metres, including the 11,022-metre Mariana Trench. The deepest Atlantic trench is the Puerto Rico trough (Milwaukee Deep), at 9,200 metres. Deep ocean water circulates very slowly, often remaining in place for thousands of years at a time.

Life is very scarce in the deep ocean, but a few organisms have been found even in the abyssal darkness of the great trenches, feeding on the trickle of organic debris that reaches the seafloor from far above.

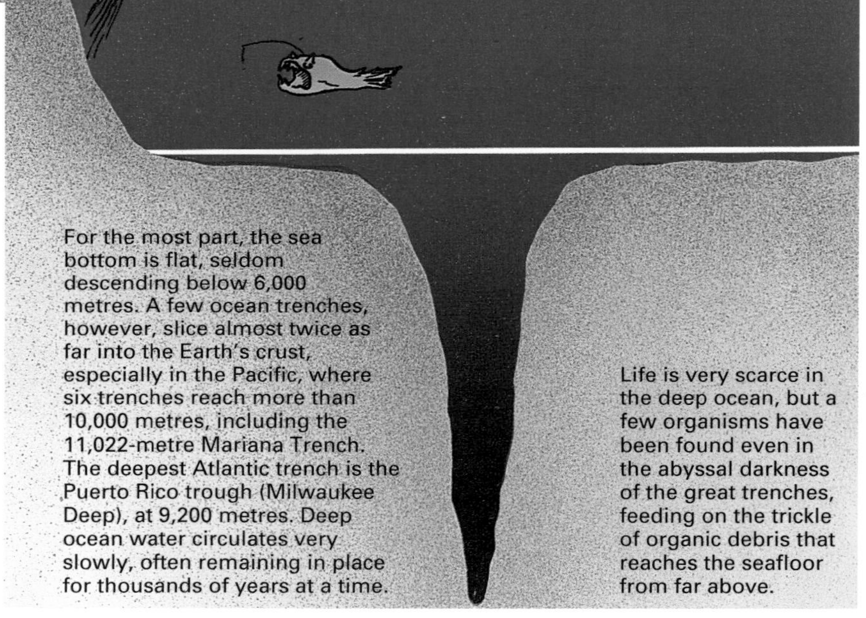

ATOLL BUILDING

A coral atoll begins existence as a bare volcanic peak, thrusting above the ocean surface. A colony of coral – marine organisms called polyps, with skeletons of rigid calcium carbonate – forms itself in the shallow water around the peak. Its seafloor eruption over, the volcano slowly sinks, leaving the coral forming a ring around its remnant. In time, all obvious trace of the volcano vanishes, and the barrier reef of an atoll is all that remains.

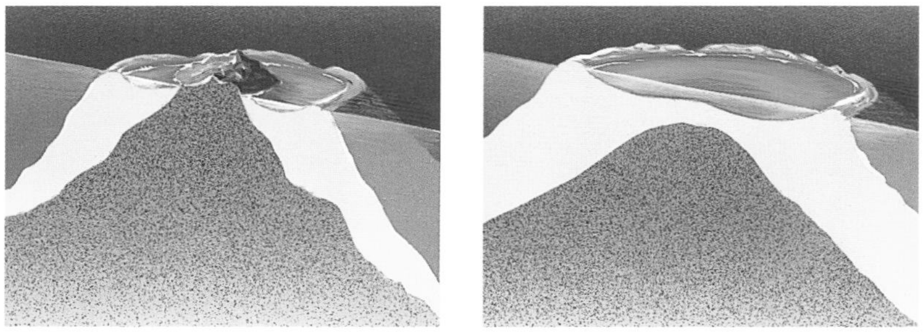

PROFILE OF AN OCEAN

The deep ocean floor is no more uniform than the surface of the continents, although it was not until the development of effective sonar equipment that it was possible to examine submarine contours in detail. The Atlantic (right) and the Pacific show similar patterns. Offshore comes the continental shelf, sliding downwards to the continental slope and the steeper continental rise, after which the seabed rolls onwards into the abyssal plains. In the wide Pacific, these are interrupted by gently-rising abyssal hills; in both oceans, the plains extend all the way to the mid-oceanic ridges, where the upwelling of new crustal material is constantly forcing the oceans wider. Volcanic activity is responsible for the formation of seamounts and tablemounts, or guyots, their flat-topped equivalents. In this cross-section, only the Azores are high enough to break the surface and become islands.

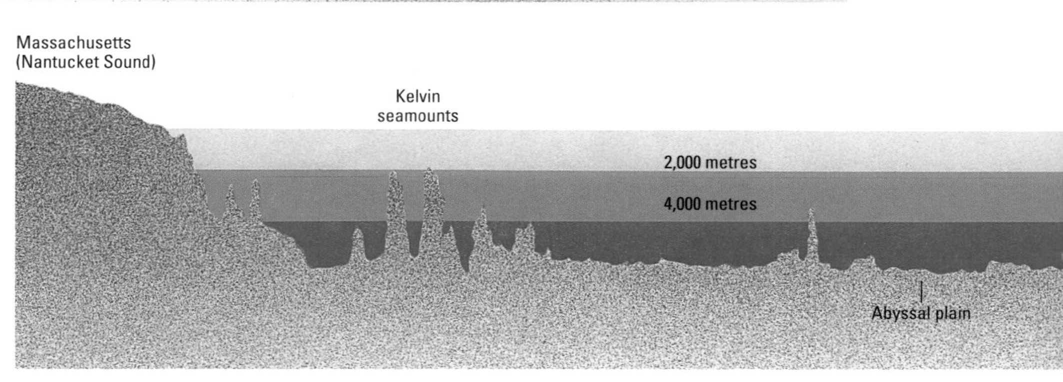
Massachusetts
(Nantucket Sound)
Kelvin
seamounts
2,000 metres
4,000 metres
Abyssal plain

CARTOGRAPHY BY PHILIP'S. COPYRIGHT REED INTERNATIONAL BOOKS LTD

OCEAN CURRENTS

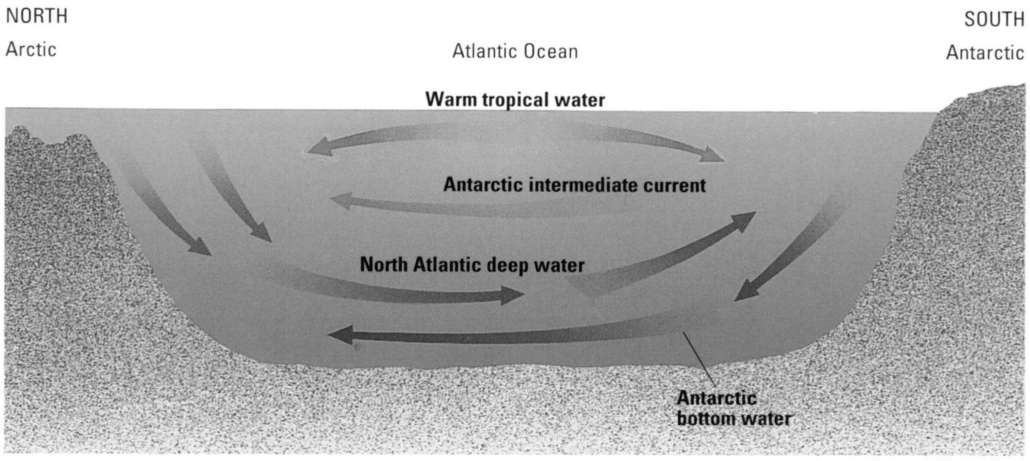

NORTH
Arctic

Atlantic Ocean

SOUTH
Antarctic

Warm tropical water

Antarctic intermediate current

North Atlantic deep water

Antarctic bottom water

Moving immense quantities of energy as well as billions of tonnes of water every hour, the ocean currents are a vital part of the great heat engine that drives the Earth's climate. They themselves are produced by a twofold mechanism. At the surface, winds push huge masses of water before them; in the deep ocean, below an abrupt temperature gradient that separates the churning surface waters from the still depths, density variations cause slow vertical movements.

The pattern of circulation of the great surface currents is determined by the displacement known as the Coriolis effect. As the Earth turns beneath a moving object – whether it is a tennis ball or a vast mass of water – it appears to be deflected to one side. The deflection is most obvious near the Equator, where the Earth's surface is spinning eastwards at 1700 km/h; currents moving polewards are curved clockwise in the northern hemisphere and anti-clockwise in the southern.

The result is a system of spinning circles known as gyres. The Coriolis effect piles up water on the left of each gyre, creating a narrow, fast-moving stream that is matched by a slower, broader returning current on the right. North and south of the Equator, the fastest currents are located in the west and in the east respectively. In each case, warm water moves from the Equator and cold water returns to it. Cold currents often bring an upwelling of nutrients with them, supporting the world's most economically important fisheries.

Depending on the prevailing winds, some currents on or near the Equator may reverse their direction in the course of the year – a seasonal variation on which Asian monsoon rains depend, and whose occasional failure can bring disaster to millions of people.

CURRENTS AND TEMPERATURES

(Northern Hemisphere: winter)

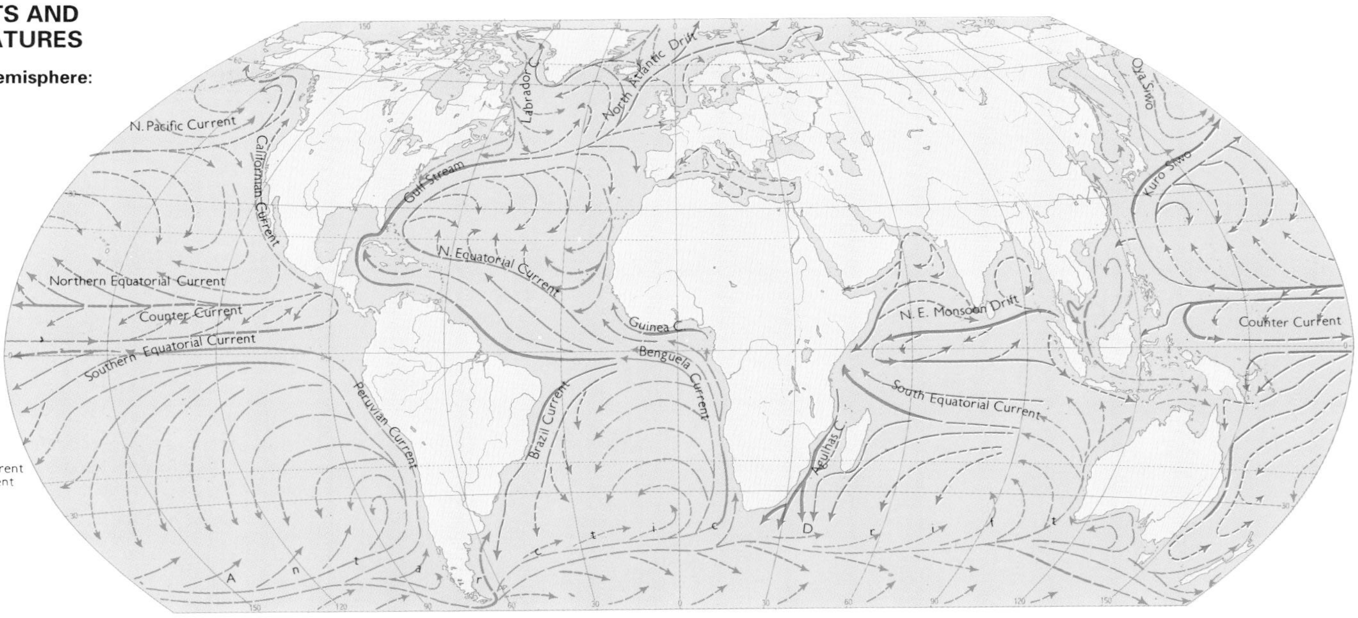

Warm Current
Cold Current

N. Pacific Current
Californian Current
Labrador C.
North Atlantic Drift
Oya Siwo
Kuro Siwo
Gulf Stream
N. Equatorial Current
Northern Equatorial Current
Counter Current
Southern Equatorial Current
Guinea C.
Benguela Current
N. E. Monsoon Drift
Counter Current
South Equatorial Current
Peruvian Current
Brazil Current
Agulhas C.

CURRENTS AND TEMPERATURES

(Northern Hemisphere: summer)

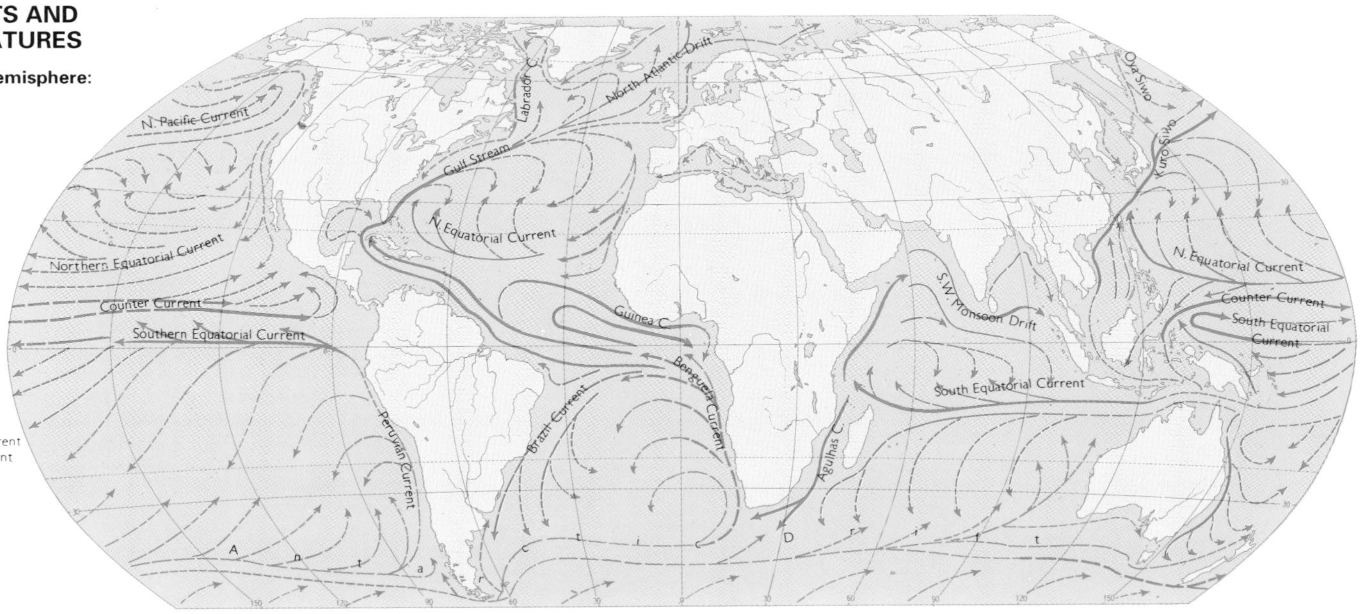

Warm Current
Cold Current

N. Pacific Current
Labrador C.
North Atlantic Drift
Oya Siwo
Kuro Siwo
Gulf Stream
N. Equatorial Current
Northern Equatorial Current
Counter Current
Southern Equatorial Current
Guinea C.
Benguela Current
S.W. Monsoon Drift
N. Equatorial Current
Counter Current
South Equatorial Current
South Equatorial Current
Peruvian Current
Brazil Current
Agulhas C.

SEAWATER

The chemical composition of the sea, in grams per tonne of seawater, excluding the elements of water itself

Chlorine	19,400
Sodium	10,800
Magnesium	1,290
Sulphur	904
Calcium	411
Potassium	392
Bromine	67
Strontium	8.1
Boron	4.5
Fluorine	1.3
Lithium	0.17
Rubidium	0.12
Phosphorus	0.09
Iodine	0.06
Barium	0.02
Arsenic	0.003
Cesium	0.0003

Seawater also contains virtually every other element, although the quantities involved are too small for reliable measurement. In natural conditions, its composition is broadly consistent across the world's seas and oceans; but in coastal areas especially, variations, sometimes substantial, may be caused by the presence of industrial waste and sewage sludge.

Mid-Atlantic Ridge
Atlantic seamount
Azores
Josephine seamounts
Gettysburg seamounts
Gibraltar

CARTOGRAPHY BY PHILIP'S. COPYRIGHT REED INTERNATIONAL BOOKS LTD

THE EARTH: ATMOSPHERE

11: OCEAN CURRENTS

15: BEAUFORT WIND SCALE

21: SOLAR ENERGY GREENHOUSE EFFECT

46: GREENHOUSE POWER

47: ACID RAIN

Extending from the surface far into space, the atmosphere is a meteor shield, a radiation deflector, a thermal blanket and a source of chemical energy for the Earth's diverse inhabitants. Five-sixths of its mass is found in the first 15 kilometres, the troposphere, no thicker in relative terms than the skin of an onion. Clouds, cyclonic winds, precipitation and virtually all the phenomena we call weather occur in this narrow layer. Above, a thin layer of ozone blocks ultra-violet radiation. Beyond 100 kilometres, atmospheric density is lower than most laboratory vacuums, yet these tenuous outer reaches, composed largely of hydrogen and helium, trap cosmic debris and incoming high-energy particles alike.

CIRCULATION OF THE AIR

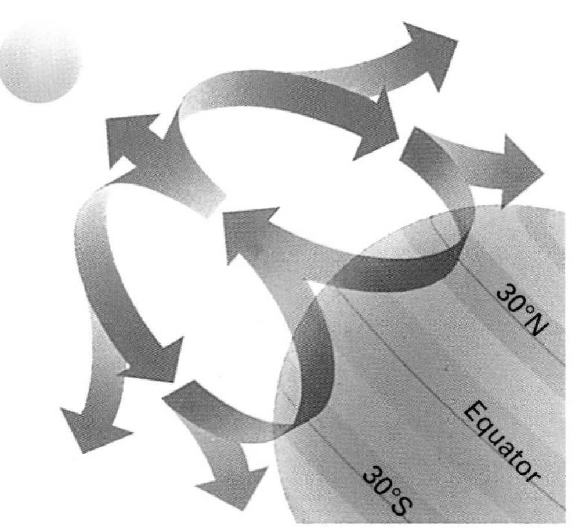

30°N
Equator
30°S

STRUCTURE OF ATMOSPHERE **TEMPERATURE** **PRESSURE**

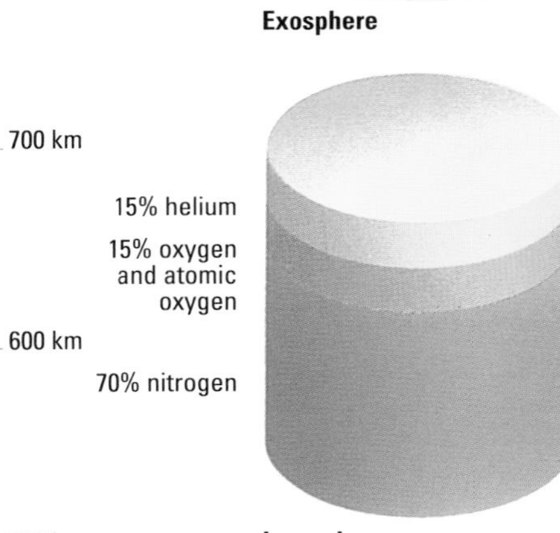

1
2
3
4
F2
F1
E
D
Mesosphere
Ozone layer
Tropopause
ca. 2,200°C
ca. 1,500°C
ca. 750°C
-58°C
-91°C
-93°C
-33°C
-8°C
-12°C
-38°C
-53°C
15°C
10^{-53}mb
10^{-47}mb
10^{-41}mb
10^{-35}mb
10^{-28}mb
10^{-22}mb
10^{-16}mb
10^{-10}mb
10^{-3}mb
10^{3}mb
900 km
800 km
700 km
600 km
500 km
400 km
300 km
200 km
100 km
0

CHEMICAL STRUCTURE

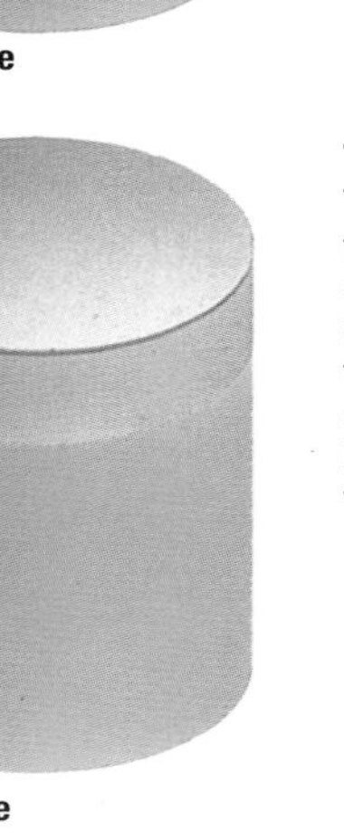

Inner:
50% helium
50% hydrogen
Middle:
25% helium
75% hydrogen
Outer:
100% hydrogen
Exosphere
15% helium
15% oxygen and atomic oxygen
70% nitrogen
Ionosphere
1% ozone
1% argon
18% oxygen
80% nitrogen
Stratosphere
1% argon
21% oxygen
78% nitrogen
Troposphere

Exosphere

The atmosphere's upper layer has no clear outer boundary, merging imperceptibly with interplanetary space. Its lower boundary, at an altitude of approximately 600 kilometres, is almost equally vague. The exosphere is mainly composed of hydrogen and helium in changing proportions, with a small quantity of atomic oxygen up to 600 kilometres. Helium vanishes with increasing altitude, and above 2,400 kilometres the exosphere is almost entirely composed of hydrogen.

Ionosphere

Gas molecules in the ionosphere, mainly helium, oxygen and nitrogen, are electrically charged – ionized – by the Sun's radiation. Within the ionosphere's range of 50 to 600 kilometres in altitude, they group themselves into four layers, known conventionally as D, E, F1 and F2, all of which can reflect radio waves of differing frequencies. The high energy of ionospheric gas gives it a notional temperature of more than 2,000°C, although its density is negligible. The auroras – *aurora borealis* and its southern counterpart, *aurora australis* – occur in the ionosphere when charged particles from the Sun interact with the Earth's magnetic fields, at their strongest near the poles.

Stratosphere

Separated at its upper and lower limits by the distinct thresholds of the stratopause and the tropopause, the stratosphere is a remarkably stable layer between 50 kilometres and about 15 kilometres. Its temperature rises from –55°C at its lower extent to approximately 0°C near the stratopause, where a thin layer of ozone absorbs ultra-violet radiation. 'Mother-of-pearl' or nacreous cloud occurs at about 25 kilometres' altitude. Stratospheric air contains enough ozone to make it poisonous, although it is in any case far too rarified to breathe.

Troposphere

The narrowest of all the atmospheric layers, the troposphere extends up to 15 kilometres at the Equator but only 8 kilometres at the poles. Since this thin region contains about 85% of the atmosphere's total mass and almost all of its water vapour, it is also the realm of the Earth's weather. Temperatures fall steadily with increasing height by about 1°C for every 100 metres above sea level.

CARTOGRAPHY BY PHILIP'S. COPYRIGHT REED INTERNATIONAL BOOKS LTD

Heated by the relatively high surface temperatures near the Earth's Equator, air expands and rises to create a belt of low pressure. Moving northwards towards the poles, it gradually cools, sinking once more and producing high-pressure belts at about latitudes 30° North and South. Water vapour carried with the air falls as rain, releasing vast quantities of energy as well as liquid water when it condenses.

The high- and low-pressure belts are both areas of comparative calm, but between them, blowing from high-pressure to low-pressure areas, are the prevailing winds. The atmospheric circulatory system is enormously complicated by the Coriolis effect brought about by the spinning Earth: winds are deflected to the right in the northern hemisphere and to the left in the southern, giving rise to the typically cyclonic pattern of swirling clouds carried by the moving masses of air.

Although clouds appear in an almost infinite variety of shapes and sizes, there are recognizable features that form the basis of a classification first put forward by Luke Howard, a London chemist, in 1803 and later modified by the World Meteorological Organization. The system is derived from the altitude of clouds and whether they form hairlike filaments ('cirrus'), heaps or piles ('cumulus'), or layers ('stratus'). Each characteristic carries some kind of message – not always a clear one – to forecasters about the weather to come.

CLASSIFICATION OF CLOUDS

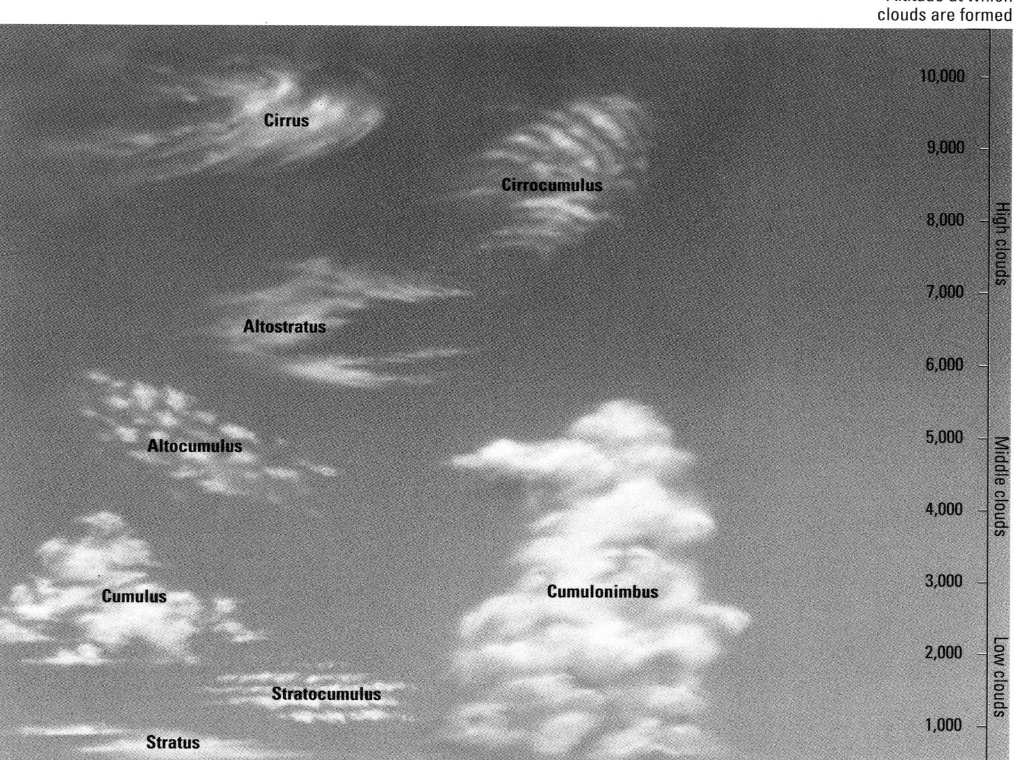
Altitude at which clouds are formed
Cirrus
Cirrocumulus
Altostratus
Altocumulus
Cumulus
Cumulonimbus
Stratocumulus
Stratus
10,000
9,000
8,000
7,000
6,000
5,000
4,000
3,000
2,000
1,000
metres
High clouds
Middle clouds
Low clouds

Clouds form when damp, usually rising, air is cooled. Thus they form when a wind rises to cross hills or mountains; when a mass of air rises over, or is pushed up by, another mass of denser air; or when local heating of the ground causes convection currents.

The types of clouds are classified according to altitude as high, middle or low. The high ones, composed of ice crystals, are cirrus, cirrostratus and cirrocumulus. The middle clouds are altostratus, a grey or bluish striated, fibrous, or uniform sheet producing light drizzle, and altocumulus, a thicker and fluffier version of cirrocumulus.

The low clouds include nimbostratus, a dark grey layer that brings almost continuous rain or snow; cumulus, a detached 'heap' – brilliant white in sunlight but dark and flat at the base; and stratus, which forms dull, overcast skies at low altitudes.

Cumulonimbus, associated with storms and rains, heavy and dense with a flat base and a high, fluffy outline, can be tall enough to occupy middle as well as low altitudes.

PRESSURE AND WINDS

January

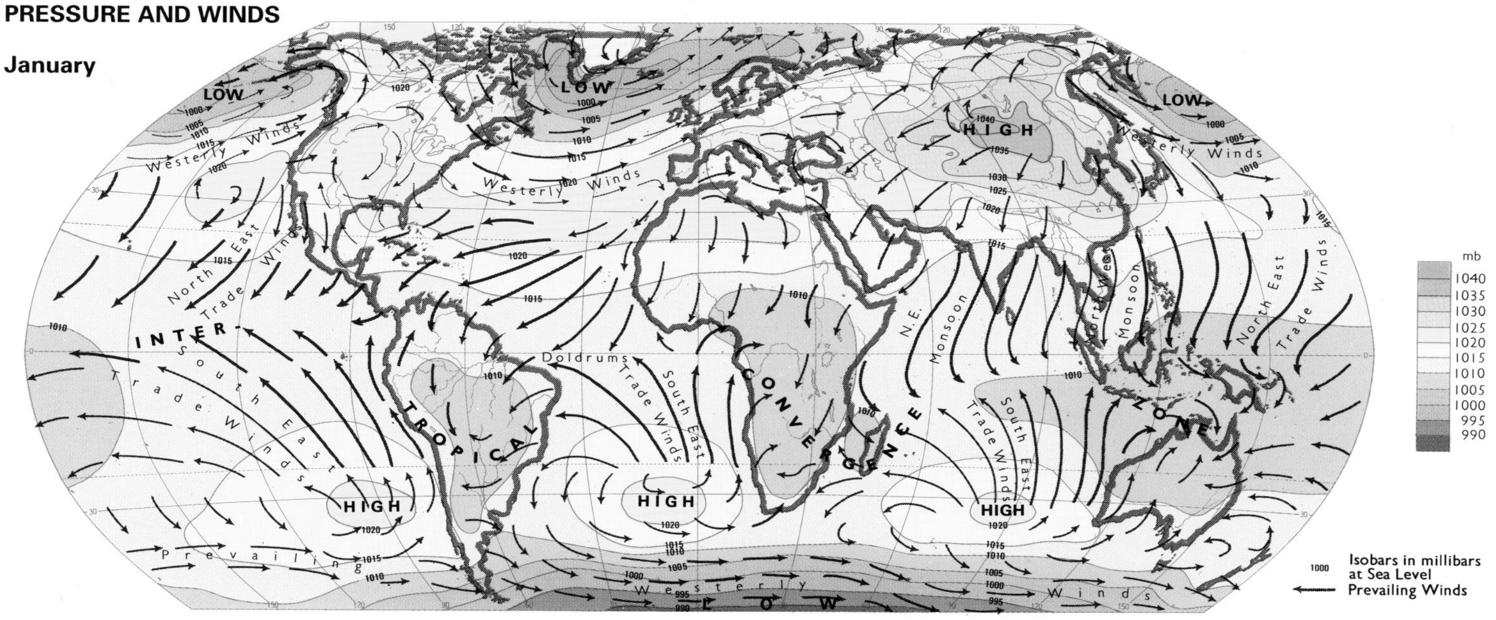

mb: 1040, 1035, 1030, 1025, 1020, 1015, 1010, 1005, 1000, 995, 990

1000 Isobars in millibars at Sea Level

Prevailing Winds

July

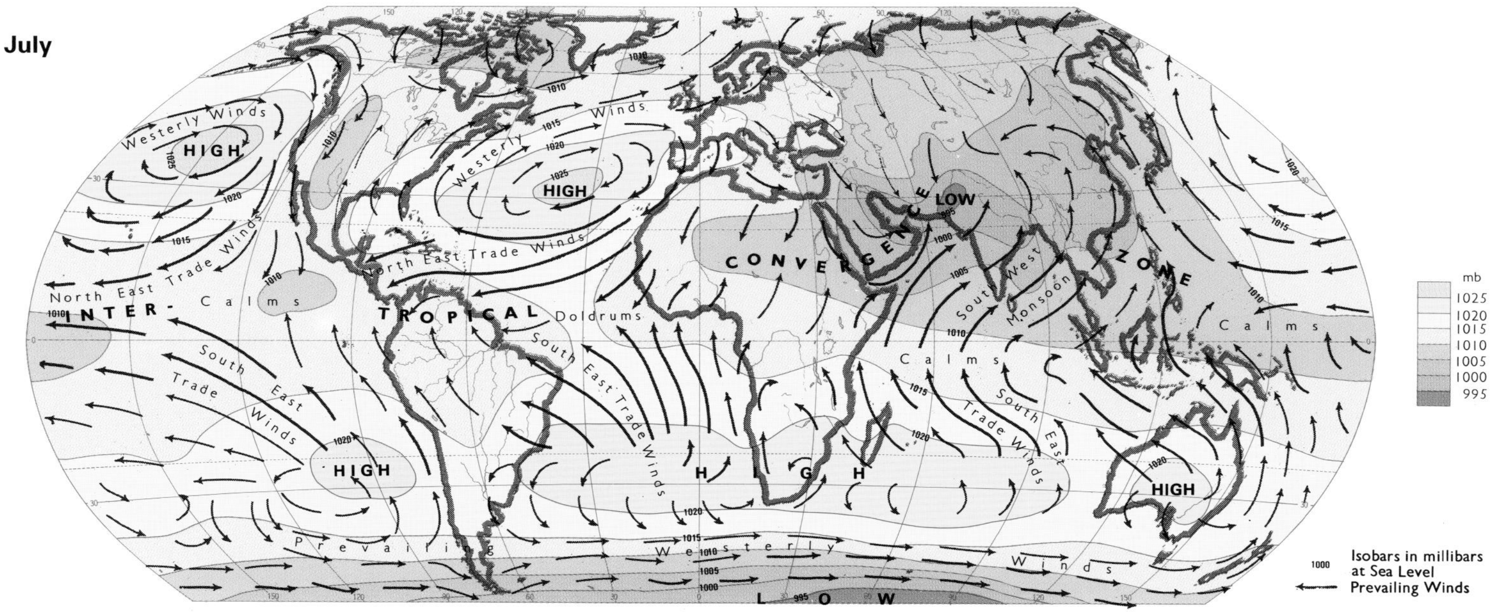

mb: 1025, 1020, 1015, 1010, 1005, 1000, 995

1000 Isobars in millibars at Sea Level

Prevailing Winds

CLIMATE RECORDS

Pressure and winds

Highest barometric pressure: Agata, Siberia, 1,083.8 mb [32 in] at altitude 262 m [862 ft], 31 December 1968.

Lowest barometric pressure: Typhoon Tip, 480 km [300 mls] west of Guam, Pacific Ocean, 870 mb [25.69 in], 12 October 1979.

Highest recorded wind speed: Mt Washington, New Hampshire, USA, 371 km/h [231 mph], 12 April 1934. This is three times as strong as hurricane force on the Beaufort Scale.

Windiest place: Commonwealth Bay, George V Coast, Antarctica, where gales frequently reach over 320 km/h [200 mph].

Worst recorded storm: Bangladesh (then East Pakistan) cyclone*, 13 November 1970 – over 300,000 dead or missing. The 1991 cyclone, Bangladesh's and the world's second worst in terms of loss of life, killed an estimated 138,000 people.

Worst recorded tornado: Missouri/Illinois/Indiana, USA, 18 March 1925 – 792 deaths. The tornado was only 275 m [300 yds] wide.

* Tropical cyclones are known as hurricanes in Central and North America and as typhoons in the Far East.

CARTOGRAPHY BY PHILIP'S. COPYRIGHT REED INTERNATIONAL BOOKS LTD

THE EARTH: CLIMATE

11: OCEAN CURRENTS

12: CIRCULATION OF THE AIR

13: CLASSIFICATION OF CLOUDS PRESSURE AND WINDS

16: HYDROLOGICAL CYCLE

17: NATURAL VEGETATION

21: GREENHOUSE EFFECT

30: LAND USE

46: GLOBAL WARMING

Climate is weather in the long term: the seasonal pattern of hot and cold, wet and dry, averaged over time. At the simplest level, it is caused by the uneven heating of the Earth. Surplus heat at the Equator passes towards the poles, levelling out the energy differential. Its passage is marked by a ceaseless churning of the atmosphere and the oceans, further agitated by the Earth's diurnal spin and the motion it imparts to moving air and water. The heat's means of transport – by winds and ocean currents, by the continual evaporation and recondensation of water molecules – is the weather itself.

There are four basic types of climate, each of which is open to considerable subdivision: tropical, desert, temperate and polar. But although latitude is obviously a critical factor, it is not the only determinant. The differential heating of land and sea, the funnelling and interruption of winds and ocean currents by landmasses and mountain ranges, and the transpiration of vegetation: all these factors combine to add complexity. New York, Naples and the Gobi Desert share almost the same latitude, for example, but their climates are very different. And although the sheer intricacy of the weather system often defies day-to-day prediction in these or any other places – despite the many satellites and number-crunching supercomputers with which present-day meteorologists are now equipped – their climatic patterns retain a year-on-year stability.

They are not indefinitely stable, however. The planet regularly passes through long, cool periods lasting about 100,000 years: these are the Ice Ages, probably caused by recurring long-term oscillations in the Earth's orbital path and fluctuations in the Sun's energy output. In the present era, the Earth is nearest to the Sun in the middle of the northern hemisphere's winter; 11,000 years ago, at the end of the last Ice Age, the northern winter fell with the Sun at its most distant.

Left to its own devices, the climate even now should be drifting towards another glacial period. But global warming caused by increasing carbon dioxide levels in the atmosphere, largely the result of 20th-century fuel-burning and deforestation, may well precipitate change far faster than the great, slow cycles of the Solar System.

Tropical rainy climates
All mean monthly temperatures above 18°C.

Af	Rainforest climate
Am	Monsoon climate
Aw	Savanna climate

Dry climates
Low rainfall combined with a wide range of temperatures

BS	Steppe climate
BW	Desert climate

Warm temperate rainy climates
The mean temperature is below 18°C but above –3°C and that of the warmest month is over 10°C.

Cw	Dry winter climate
Cs	Dry summer climate
Cf	Climate with no dry season

Cold temperate rainy climates
The mean temperature of the coldest month is below –3°C but that of the warmest month is still over 10°C.

Dw	Dry winter climate
Df	Climate with no dry season

Polar climates
The mean temperature of the warmest month is below 10°C, giving permanently frozen subsoil.

ET	Tundra climate

The mean temperature of the warmest month is below 0°C, giving permanent ice and snow.

EF	Polar climate

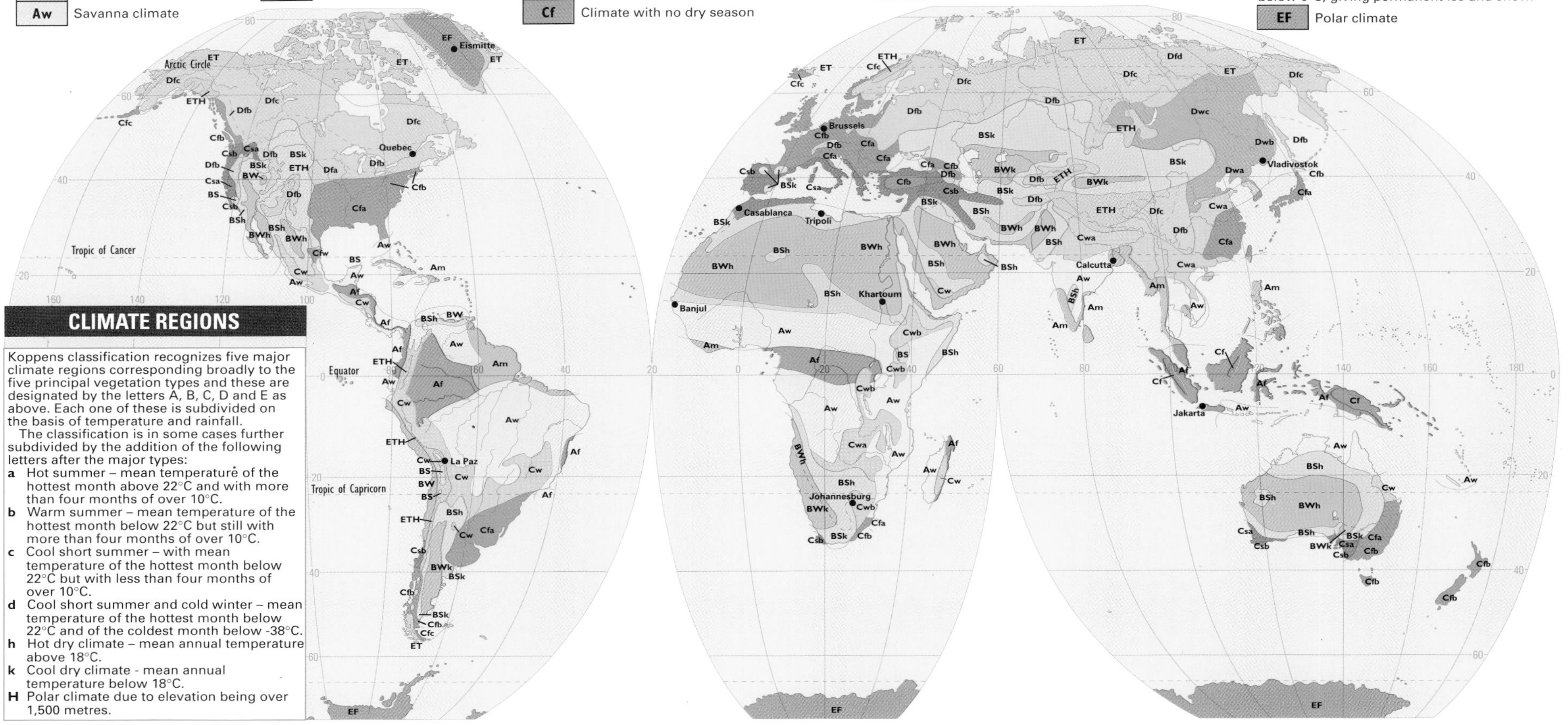

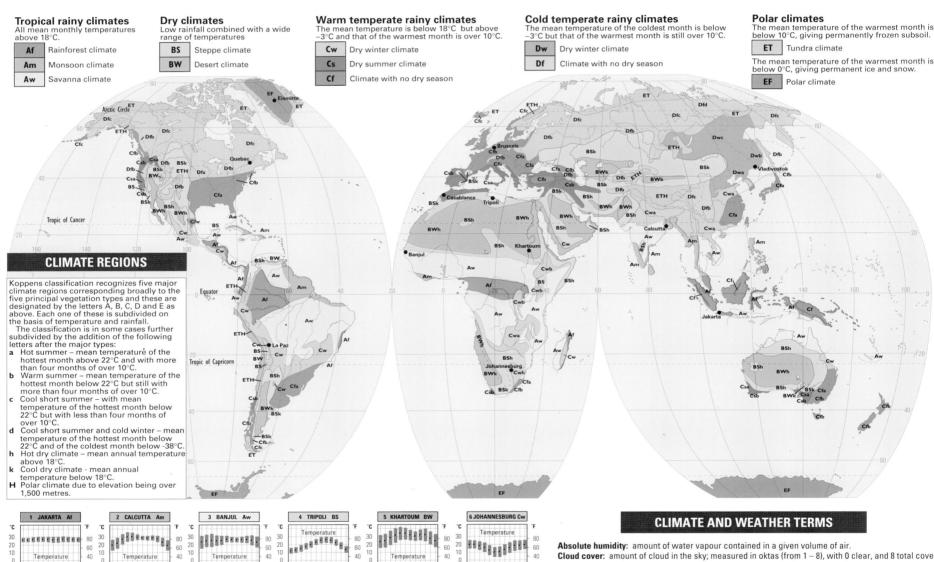

CLIMATE REGIONS

Koppens classification recognizes five major climate regions corresponding broadly to the five principal vegetation types and these are designated by the letters A, B, C, D and E as above. Each one of these is subdivided on the basis of temperature and rainfall.

The classification is in some cases further subdivided by the addition of the following letters after the major types:

- **a** Hot summer – mean temperature of the hottest month above 22°C and with more than four months of over 10°C.
- **b** Warm summer – mean temperature of the hottest month below 22°C but still with more than four months of over 10°C.
- **c** Cool short summer – with mean temperature of the hottest month below 22°C but with less than four months of over 10°C.
- **d** Cool short summer and cold winter – mean temperature of the hottest month below 22°C and of the coldest month below -38°C.
- **h** Hot dry climate – mean annual temperature above 18°C.
- **k** Cool dry climate - mean annual temperature below 18°C.
- **H** Polar climate due to elevation being over 1,500 metres.

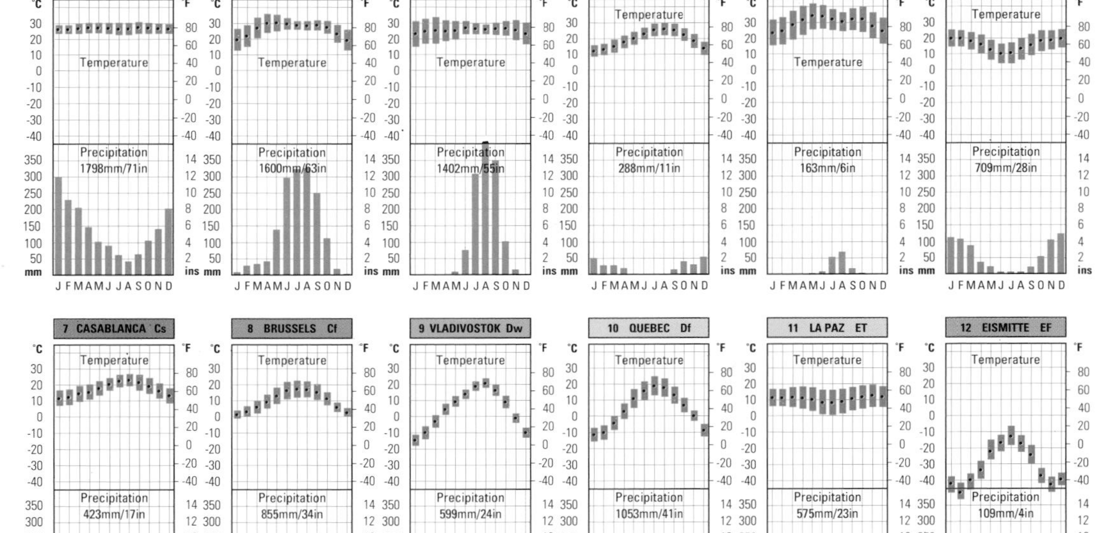

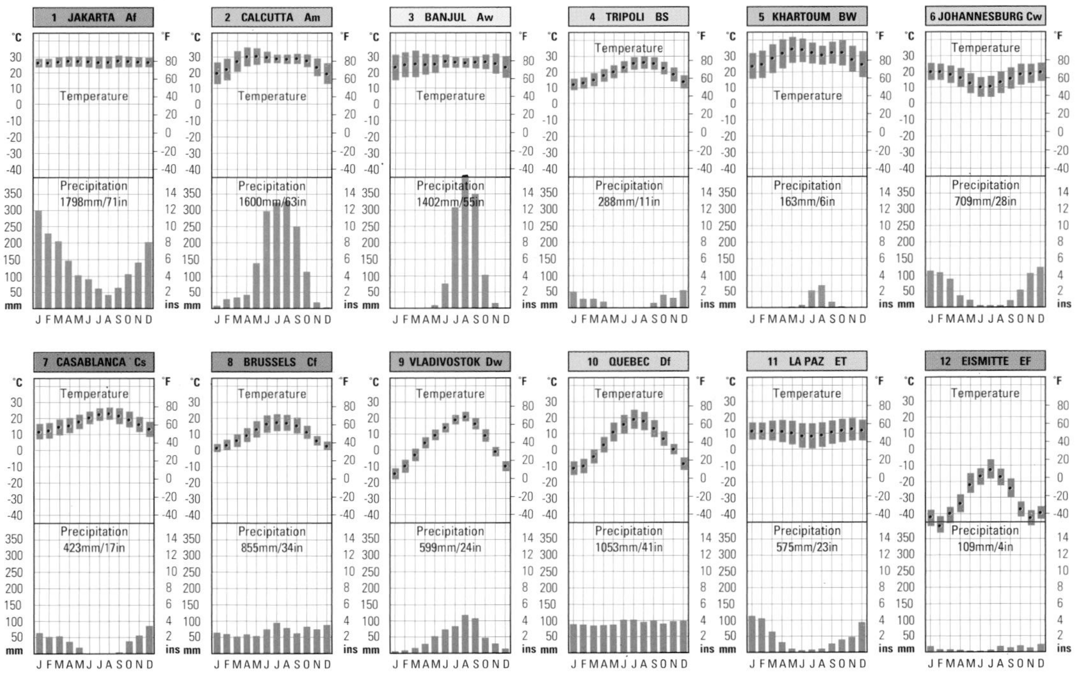

1 JAKARTA Af
Precipitation 1798mm/71in
2 CALCUTTA Am
Precipitation 1600mm/63in
3 BANJUL Aw
Precipitation 1402mm/55in
4 TRIPOLI BS
Precipitation 288mm/11in
5 KHARTOUM BW
Precipitation 163mm/6in
6 JOHANNESBURG Cw
Precipitation 709mm/28in
7 CASABLANCA Cs
Precipitation 423mm/17in
8 BRUSSELS Cf
Precipitation 855mm/34in
9 VLADIVOSTOK Dw
Precipitation 599mm/24in
10 QUEBEC Df
Precipitation 1053mm/41in
11 LA PAZ ET
Precipitation 575mm/23in
12 EISMITTE EF
Precipitation 109mm/4in
Temperature
°C
°F
mm
ins
J F M A M J J A S O N D

CLIMATE AND WEATHER TERMS

Absolute humidity: amount of water vapour contained in a given volume of air.
Cloud cover: amount of cloud in the sky; measured in oktas (from 1 – 8), with 0 clear, and 8 total cover.
Condensation: the conversion of water vapour, or moisture in the air, into liquid.
Cyclone: violent storm resulting from anti-clockwise rotation of winds in the northern hemisphere and clockwise in the southern: called hurricane in N. America, typhoon in the Far East.
Depression: approximately circular area of low pressure.
Dew: water droplets condensed out of the air after the ground has cooled at night.
Dew point: temperature at which air becomes saturated (reaches a relative humidity of 100%) at a constant pressure.
Drizzle: precipitation where drops are less than 0.5 mm [0.02 in] in diameter.
Evaporation: conversion of water from liquid into vapour, or moisture in the air.
Frost: dew that has frozen when the air temperature falls below freezing point.
Hail: frozen rain; small balls of ice, often falling during thunder storms.
Hoar frost: formed on objects when the dew point is below freezing point.
Humidity: amount of moisture in the air.
Isobar: cartographic line connecting places of equal atmospheric pressure.
Isotherm: cartographic line connecting places of equal temperature.
Lightning: massive electrical discharge released in thunderstorm from cloud to cloud or cloud to ground, the result of the tip becoming positively charged and the bottom negatively charged.
Precipitation: measurable rain, snow, sleet or hail.
Prevailing wind: most common direction of wind at a given location.
Rain: precipitation of liquid particles with diameter larger than 0.5 mm [0.02 in].
Relative humidity: amount of water vapour contained in a given volume of air at a given temperature.
Sleet: translucent or transparent ice-pellets (partially melted snow).
Snow: formed when water vapour condenses below freezing point.
Thunder: sound produced by the rapid expansion of air heated by lightning.
Tidal wave: giant ocean wave generated by earthquakes (tsunami) or cyclonic winds.
Tornado: severe funnel-shaped storm that twists as hot air spins vertically (waterspout at sea).
Whirlwind: rapidly rotating column of air, only a few metres across, made visible by dust.

CARTOGRAPHY BY PHILIP'S. COPYRIGHT REED INTERNATIONAL BOOKS LTD

WINDCHILL FACTOR

In sub-zero weather, even moderate winds significantly reduce effective temperatures. The chart below shows the windchill effect across a range of speeds. Figures in the pink zone are not dangerous to well-clad people; in the blue zone, the risk of serious frostbite is acute.

	Wind speed (km/h)				
	16	32	48	64	80
0°C	-8	-14	-17	-19	-20
-5°C	-14	-21	-25	-27	-28
-10°C	-20	-28	-33	-35	-36
-15°C	-26	-36	-40	-43	-44
-20°C	-32	-42	-48	-51	-52
-25°C	-38	-49	-56	-59	-60
-30°C	-44	-57	-63	-66	-68
-35°C	-51	-64	-72	-74	-76
-40°C	-57	-71	-78	-82	-84
-45°C	-63	-78	-86	-90	-92
-50°C	-69	-85	-94	-98	-100

BEAUFORT WIND SCALE

Named for the 19th-century British naval officer who devised it, the Beaufort Scale assesses wind speed according to its effects. It was originally designed as an aid for sailors, but has since been adapted for use on land.

Scale	Wind speed km/h	mph	Effect
0	0-1	0-1	**Calm** Smoke rises vertically
1	1-5	1-3	**Light air** Wind direction shown only by smoke drift
2	6-11	4-7	**Light breeze** Wind felt on face; leaves rustle; vanes moved by wind
3	12-19	8-12	**Gentle breeze** Leaves and small twigs in constant motion; wind extends small flag.
4	20-28	13-18	**Moderate** Raises dust and loose paper; small branches move
5	29-38	19-24	**Fresh** Small trees in leaf sway; crested wavelets on inland waters
6	39-49	25-31	**Strong** Large branches move; difficult to use umbrellas; overhead wires whistle
7	50-61	32-38	**Near gale** Whole trees in motion; difficult to walk against wind
8	62-74	39-46	**Gale** Twigs break from trees; walking very difficult
9	75-88	47-54	**Strong gale** Slight structural damage
10	89-102	55-63	**Storm** Trees uprooted; serious structural damage
11	103-117	64-72	**Violent storm** Widespread damage
12	118+	73+	**Hurricane**

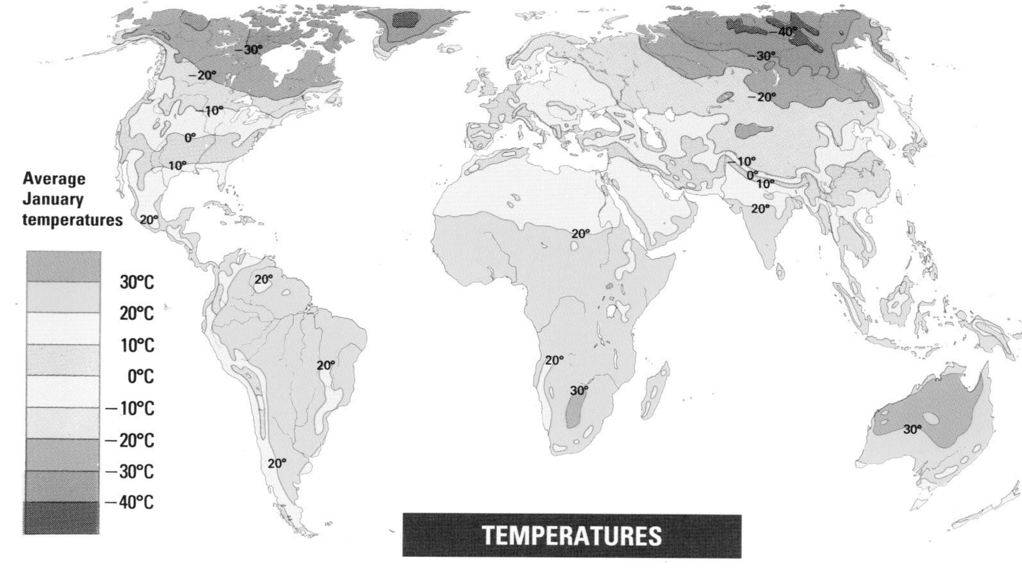
Average January temperatures
30°C
20°C
10°C
0°C
−10°C
−20°C
−30°C
−40°C

TEMPERATURES

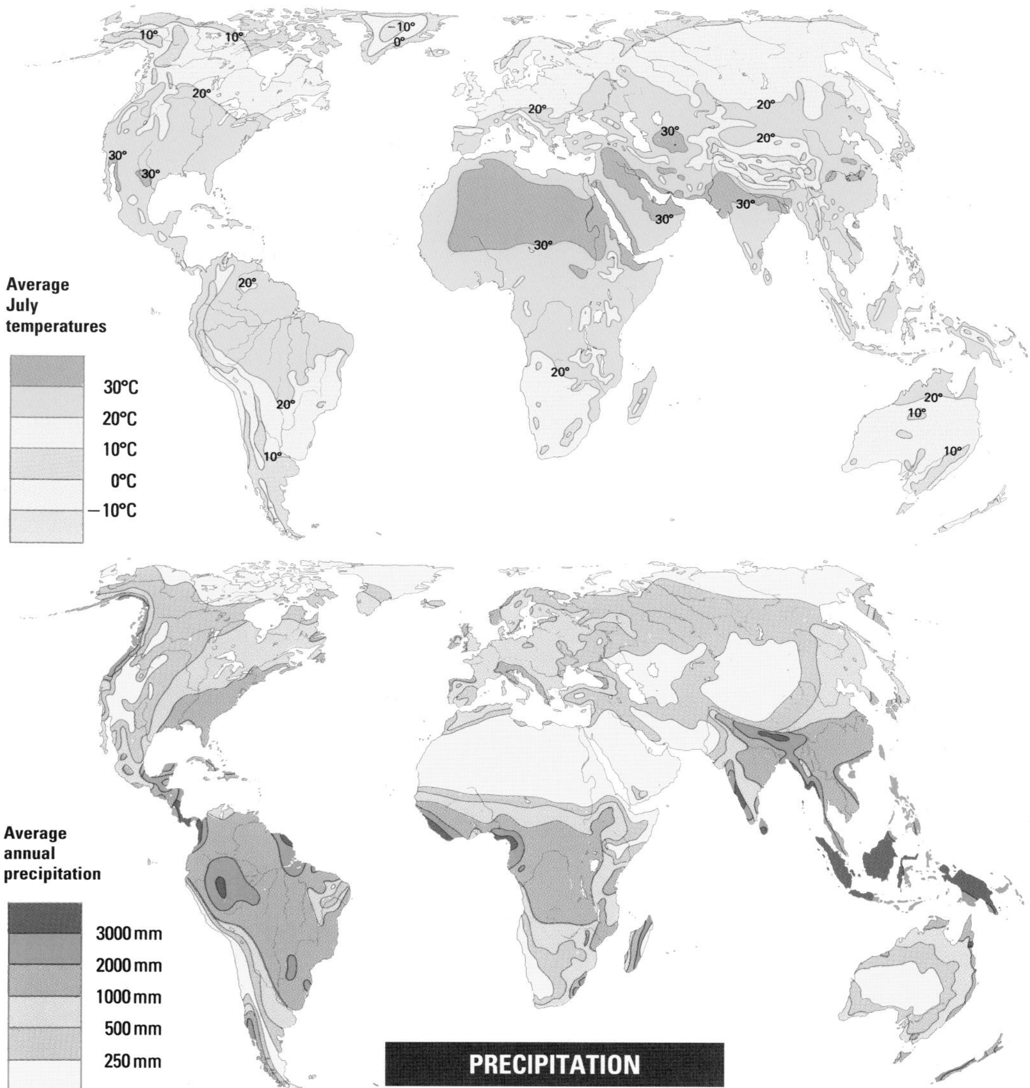
Average July temperatures
30°C
20°C
10°C
0°C
−10°C
Average annual precipitation
3000 mm
2000 mm
1000 mm
500 mm
250 mm

PRECIPITATION

CLIMATE RECORDS

Temperature

Highest recorded temperature: Al Aziziyah, Libya, 58°C [136.4°F], 13 September 1922.

Highest mean annual temperature: Dallol, Ethiopia, 34.4°C [94°F], 1960–66.

Longest heatwave: Marble Bar, W. Australia, 162 days over 38°C [100°F], 23 October 1923 to 7 April 1924.

Lowest recorded temperature (outside poles): Verkhoyansk, Siberia, −68°C [−90°F], 6 February 1933. Verkhoyansk also registered the greatest annual range of temperature: −70°C to 37°C [−94°F to 98°F].

Lowest mean annual temperature: Polus Nedostupnosti, Pole of Cold, Antarctica, −57.8°C [−72°F].

Precipitation

Driest place: Arica, N. Chile, 0.8mm [0.03 in] per year (60-year average).

Longest drought: Calama, N. Chile: no recorded rainfall in 400 years to 1971.

Wettest place (average): Tututendo, Colombia: mean annual rainfall 11,770 mm [463.4 in].

Wettest place (12 months): Cherrapunji, Meghalaya, N.E. India, 26,470 mm [1,040 in], August 1860 to August 1861. Cherrapunji also holds the record for rainfall in one month: 930 mm [37 in], July 1861.

Wettest place (24 hours): Cilaos, Réunion, Indian Ocean, 1,870 mm [73.6 in], 15–16 March 1952.

Heaviest hailstones: Gopalganj, Bangladesh, up to 1.02 kg [2.25 lb], 14 April 1986 (killed 92 people).

Heaviest snowfall (continuous): Bessans, Savoie, France, 1,730 mm [68 in] in 19 hours, 5–6 April 1969.

Heaviest snowfall (season/year): Paradise Ranger Station, Mt Rainier, Washington, USA, 31,102 mm [1,224.5 in], 19 February 1971 to 18 February 1972.

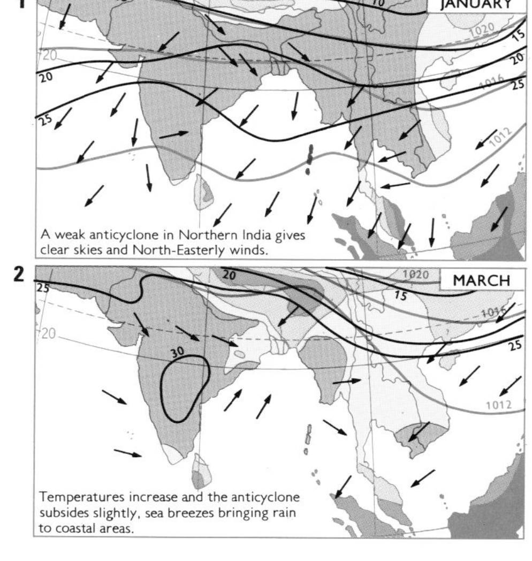
1
JANUARY
2
MARCH

1 A weak anticyclone in Northern India gives clear skies and North-Easterly winds.

2 Temperatures increase and the anticyclone subsides slightly, sea breezes bringing rain to coastal areas.

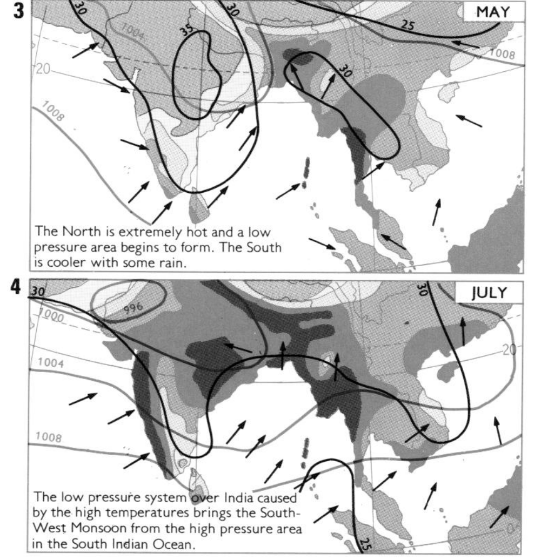
3
MAY
4
JULY

3 The North is extremely hot and a low pressure area begins to form. The South is cooler with some rain.

4 The low pressure system over India caused by the high temperatures brings the South-West Monsoon from the high pressure area in the South Indian Ocean.

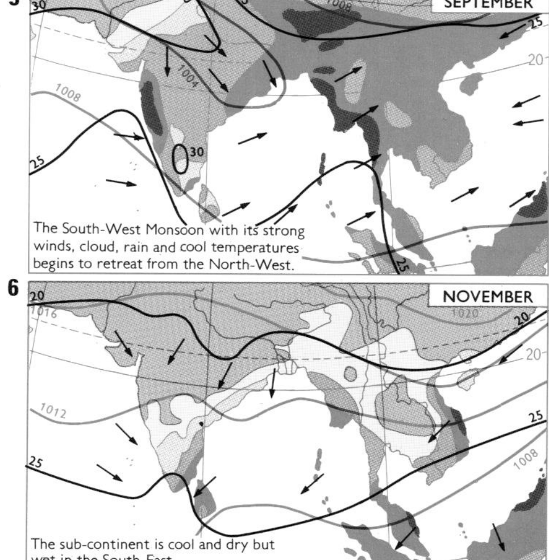
5
SEPTEMBER
6
NOVEMBER

5 The South-West Monsoon with its strong winds, cloud, rain and cool temperatures begins to retreat from the North-West.

6 The sub-continent is cool and dry but wet in the South-East.

COPYRIGHT. GEORGE PHILIP & SON, LTD.

THE MONSOON

While it is crucial to the agriculture of South Asia, the monsoon that follows the dry months is unpredictable – in duration as well as intensity. A season of very heavy rainfall, causing disastrous floods, can be succeeded by years of low precipitation, leading to serious drought.

Monthly rainfall

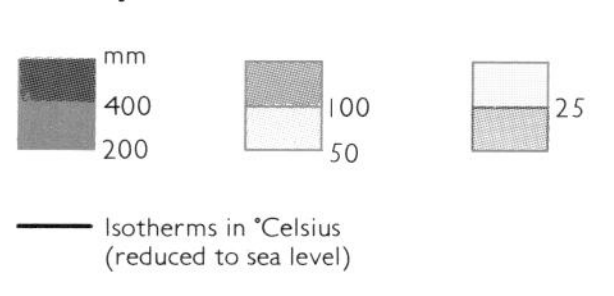
mm
400
200
100
50
25

Isotherms in °Celsius (reduced to sea level)

Isobars in mb

Prevailing winds

CARTOGRAPHY BY PHILIP'S. COPYRIGHT REED INTERNATIONAL BOOKS LTD

THE EARTH: WATER AND LAND USE

14: TYPES OF PRECIPITATION
15: RAINFALL
THE MONSOON
CLIMATE RECORDS
19: SHAPING FORCES: RIVERS AND GLACIERS

Fresh water is essential to all terrestrial life, from the humblest bacterium to the most advanced technological society. Yet freshwater resources form a minute fraction of the Earth's 1.41 billion cubic kilometres of water: most human needs must be met from the 2,000 cubic kilometres circulating in rivers at any one time. Agriculture accounts for huge quantities: without large-scale irrigation, most of the world's people would starve. And since fresh water is just as essential for most industrial processes – smelting a tonne of nickel, for example, requires about 4,000 tonnes of water – the growth of population and advancing industry have together put water supplies under strain.

Fortunately, water is seldom used up: the planet's hydrological cycle circulates it with benign efficiency, at least on a global scale. More locally, though, human activity can cause severe shortages: water for industry and agriculture is being withdrawn from many river basins and underground aquifers faster than natural recirculation can replace it.

THE HYDROLOGICAL CYCLE

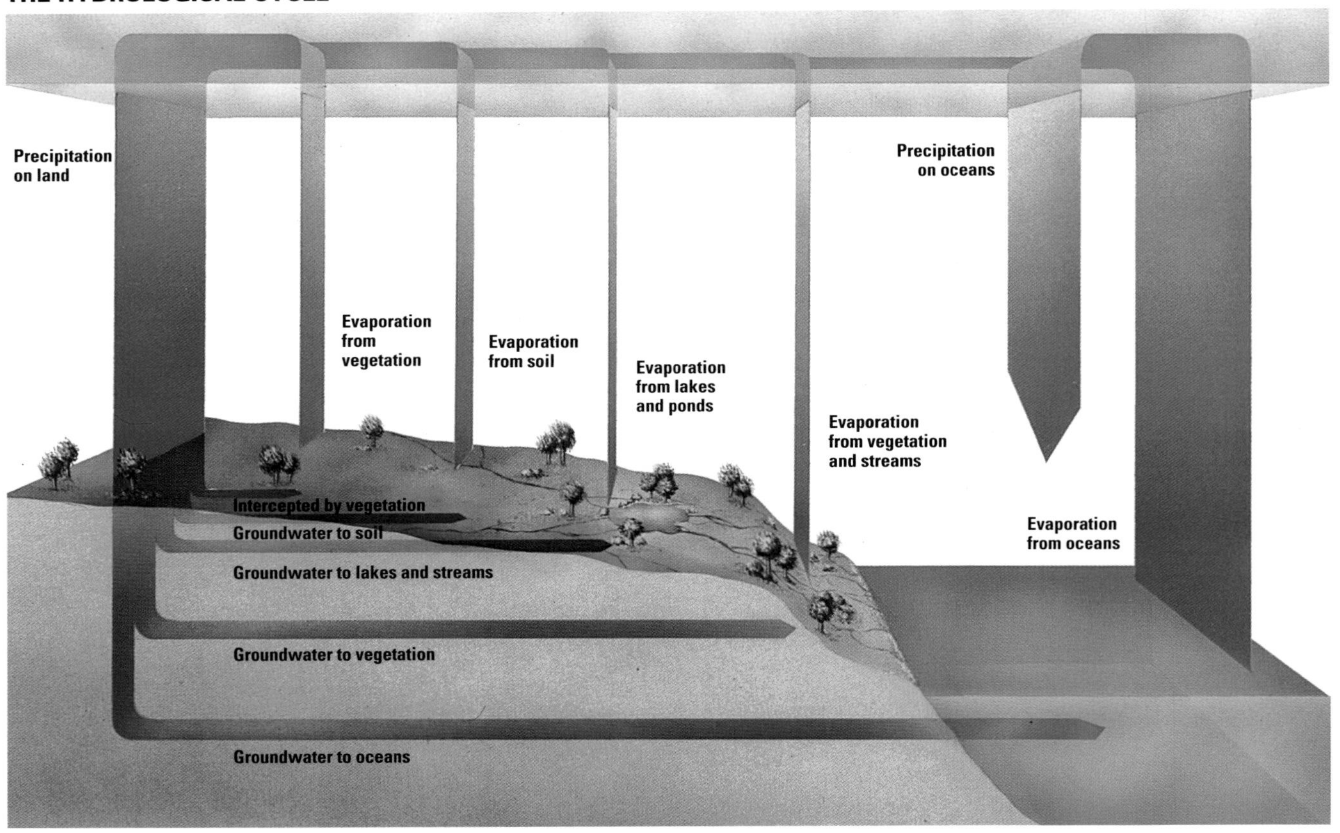

Precipitation on land
Precipitation on oceans
Evaporation from vegetation
Evaporation from soil
Evaporation from lakes and ponds
Evaporation from vegetation and streams
Evaporation from oceans
Intercepted by vegetation
Groundwater to soil
Groundwater to lakes and streams
Groundwater to vegetation
Groundwater to oceans

Water vapour is constantly drawn into the air from the Earth's rivers, lakes, seas and plant transpiration. In the atmosphere, it circulates around the planet, transporting energy as well as water itself. When the vapour cools it falls as rain or snow, and returns to the surface to evaporate once more. The whole cycle is driven by the Sun.

WATER DISTRIBUTION

The distribution of planetary water, by percentage. Oceans and ice-caps together account for more than 99% of the total; the breakdown of the remainder is estimated.

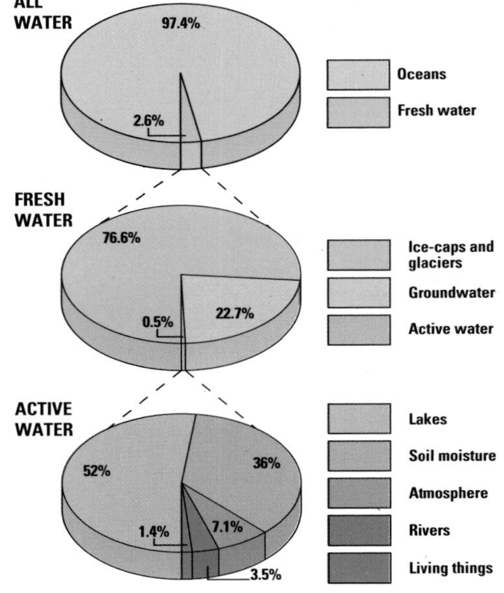

ALL WATER
97.4%
2.6%
Oceans
Fresh water
FRESH WATER
76.6%
22.7%
0.5%
Ice-caps and glaciers
Groundwater
Active water
ACTIVE WATER
52%
36%
1.4%
7.1%
3.5%
Lakes
Soil moisture
Atmosphere
Rivers
Living things

Almost all the world's water is 3,000 million years old, and all of it cycles endlessly through the hydrosphere, though at different rates. Water vapour circulates over days, even hours, deep ocean water circulates over millenia, and ice-cap water remains solid for millions of years.

WATER RUNOFF

Annual freshwater runoff by continent in cubic kilometres

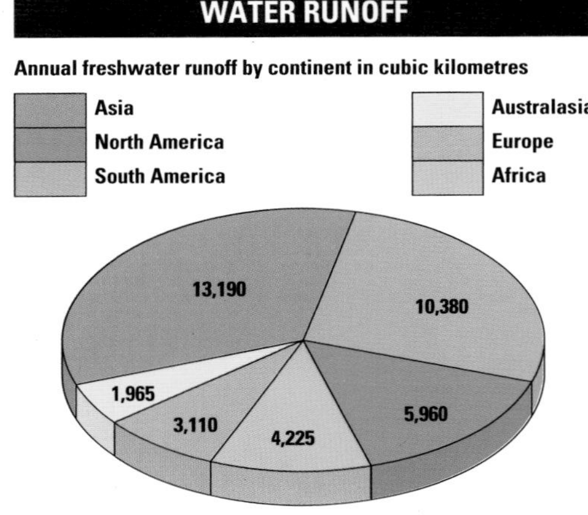

Asia
North America
South America
Australasia
Europe
Africa
13,190
10,380
5,960
4,225
3,110
1,965

WATER UTILIZATION

The percentage breakdown of water usage by sector, selected countries (latest available year)*

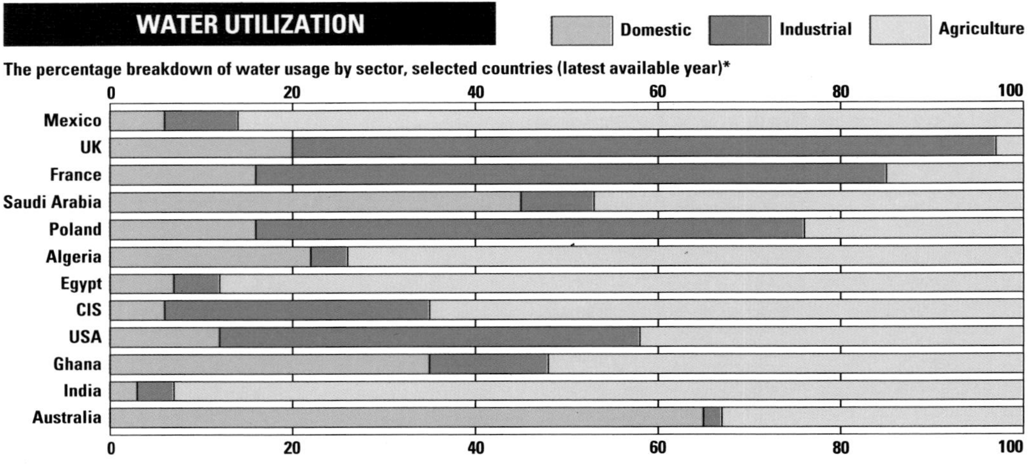

Domestic
Industrial
Agriculture
0
20
40
60
80
100
Mexico
UK
France
Saudi Arabia
Poland
Algeria
Egypt
CIS
USA
Ghana
India
Australia

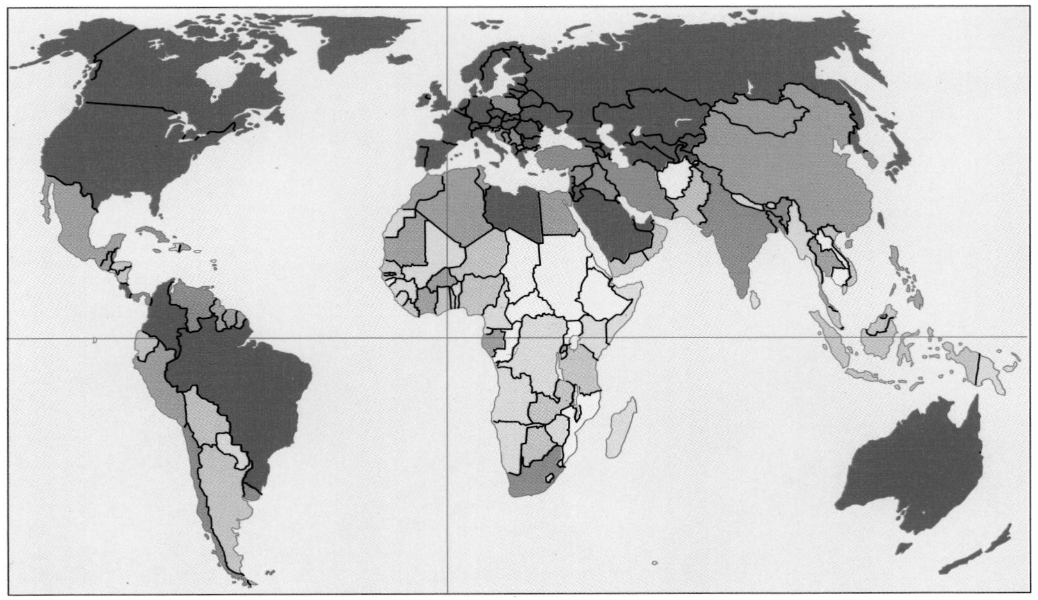

WATER SUPPLY

Percentage of total population with access to safe drinking water (latest available year)*

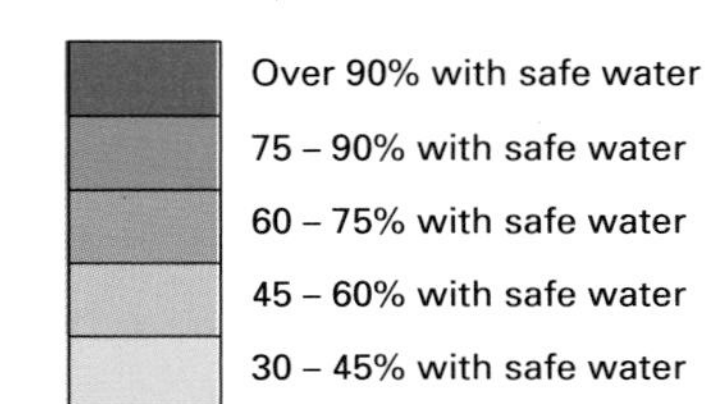

Over 90% with safe water
75 – 90% with safe water
60 – 75% with safe water
45 – 60% with safe water
30 – 45% with safe water
Under 30% with safe water

Least well-provided countries

Cambodia	3%	Afghanistan	21%
Central Africa	12%	Congo	21%
Ethiopia	19%	Guinea-Bissau	21%
Uganda	20%	Sudan	21%

**Statistics for the new republics of the former USSR, Czechoslovakia and Yugoslavia are not yet available. The map shows the statistics for the entire USSR, Czechoslovakia and Yugoslavia.*

CARTOGRAPHY BY PHILIP'S. COPYRIGHT REED INTERNATIONAL BOOKS LTD

WATERSHEDS

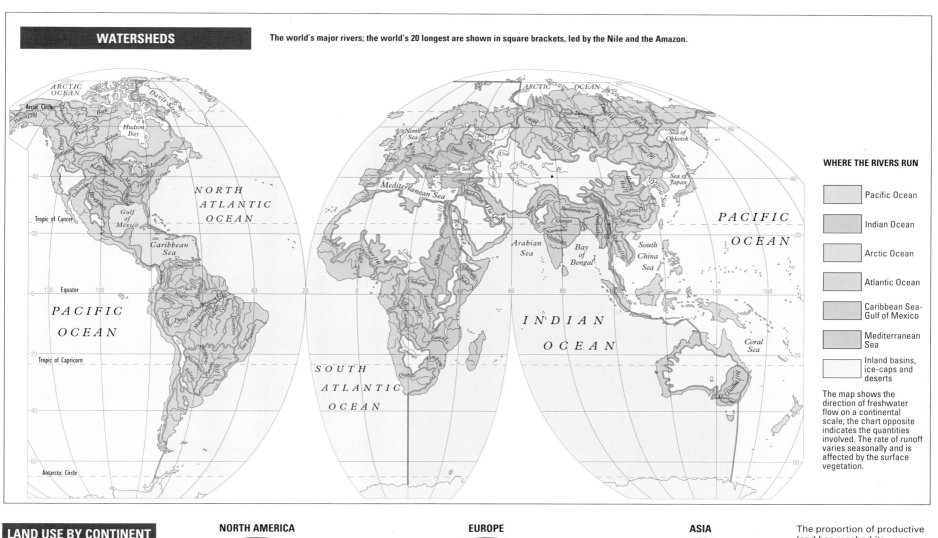

The world's major rivers; the world's 20 longest are shown in square brackets, led by the Nile and the Amazon.

WHERE THE RIVERS RUN

- Pacific Ocean
- Indian Ocean
- Arctic Ocean
- Atlantic Ocean
- Caribbean Sea-Gulf of Mexico
- Mediterranean Sea
- Inland basins, ice-caps and deserts

The map shows the direction of freshwater flow on a continental scale; the chart opposite indicates the quantities involved. The rate of runoff varies seasonally and is affected by the surface vegetation.

LAND USE BY CONTINENT

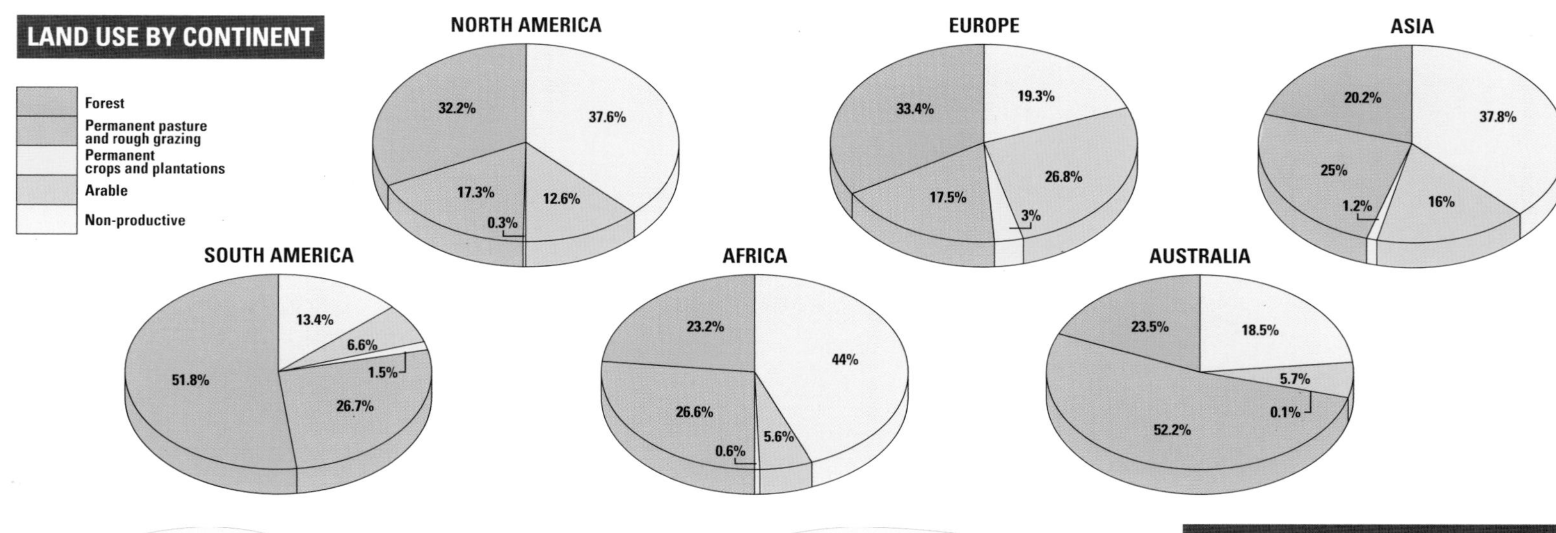

Forest
Permanent pasture and rough grazing
Permanent crops and plantations
Arable
Non-productive
NORTH AMERICA
32.2%
37.6%
17.3%
12.6%
0.3%
EUROPE
33.4%
19.3%
26.8%
17.5%
3%
ASIA
20.2%
37.8%
25%
1.2%
16%
SOUTH AMERICA
13.4%
6.6%
1.5%
51.8%
26.7%
AFRICA
23.2%
44%
26.6%
5.6%
0.6%
AUSTRALIA
23.5%
18.5%
5.7%
0.1%
52.2%

The proportion of productive land has reached its upper limit in Europe, and in Asia more than 80% of potential cropland is already under cultivation. Elsewhere, any increase is often matched by corresponding losses due to desertification and erosion; projections for 2025 show a decline in cropland per capita for all continents, most notably in Africa.

NATURAL VEGETATION

Regional variation in vegetation (after Austin Miller)

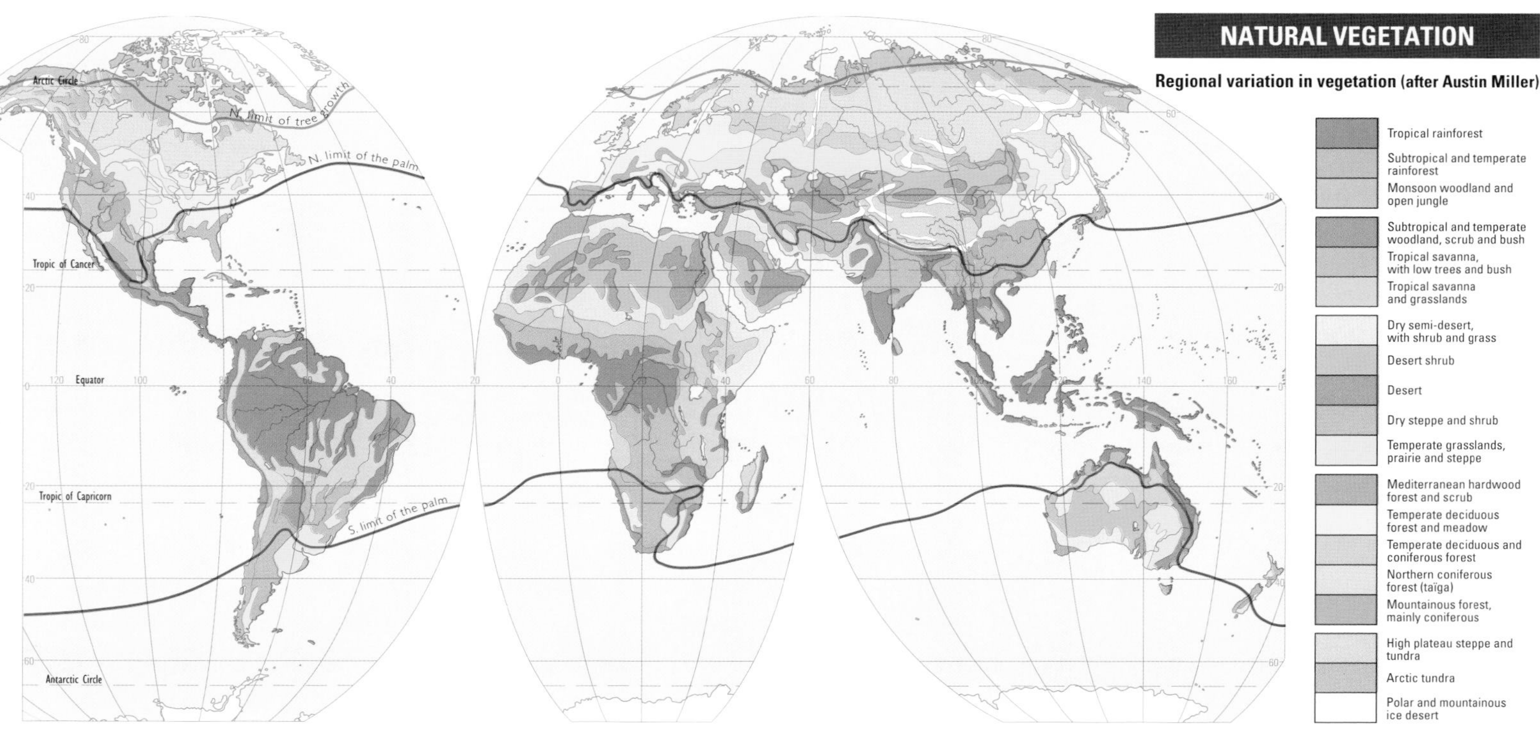

N. limit of tree growth
N. limit of the palm
S. limit of the palm
Arctic Circle
Tropic of Cancer
Equator
Tropic of Capricorn
Antarctic Circle
Tropical rainforest
Subtropical and temperate rainforest
Monsoon woodland and open jungle
Subtropical and temperate woodland, scrub and bush
Tropical savanna, with low trees and bush
Tropical savanna and grasslands
Dry semi-desert, with shrub and grass
Desert shrub
Desert
Dry steppe and shrub
Temperate grasslands, prairie and steppe
Mediterranean hardwood forest and scrub
Temperate deciduous forest and meadow
Temperate deciduous and coniferous forest
Northern coniferous forest (taiga)
Mountainous forest, mainly coniferous
High plateau steppe and tundra
Arctic tundra
Polar and mountainous ice desert

The map illustrates the natural 'climax vegetation' of a region, as dictated by its climate and topography. In most cases, human agricultural activity has drastically altered the vegetation pattern. Western Europe, for example, lost most of its broadleaf forest many centuries ago, while irrigation has turned some natural semi-desert into productive land.

CARTOGRAPHY BY PHILIP'S. COPYRIGHT REED INTERNATIONAL BOOKS LTD

THE EARTH: LANDSCAPE

8: THE EARTH'S STRUCTURE
PLATE TECTONICS
VOLCANOES

9: GEOLOGICAL TIME

10: OCEANS

16: HYDROLOGICAL CYCLE

34: STRUCTURAL REGIONS

Above and below the surface of the oceans, the features of the Earth's crust are constantly changing. The phenomenal forces generated by convection currents in the molten core of our planet carry the vast segments, or 'plates', of the crust across the globe in an endless cycle of creation and destruction. New crust emerges along the central depths of the oceans, where molten magma flows from the margins of neighbouring plates to form the massive mid-ocean ridges. The sea floor spreads, and where ocean plates meet continental plates, they dip back into the Earth's core to melt once again into magma.

Less dense, the continental plates 'float' among the oceans, drifting into and apart from each other at a rate which is almost imperceptibly slow. A continent may travel little more than 25 millimetres each year – in an average lifetime, Europe will move no more than a man's height – yet in the vast span of geological time, this process throws up giant mountain ranges and opens massive rifts in the land's surface.

The world's greatest mountain ranges have been formed in this way: the Himalayas by the collision of the Indo-Australian and Eurasian plates; the Andes by the meeting of the Nazca and South American plates. The Himalayas are a classic example of 'fold mountains', formed by the crumpling of the Earth's surface where two landmasses have been driven together. The coastal range of the Andes, by contrast, was formed by the upsurge of molten volcanic rock created by the friction of the continent 'overriding' the ocean plate.

However, the destruction of the landscape begins as soon as it is formed. Wind, water, ice and sea, the main agents of erosion, mount a constant assault that even the hardest rocks cannot withstand. Mountain peaks may dwindle by as little as a few millimetres each year, but if they are not uplifted by further movements of the crust they will eventually be reduced to rubble. Water is the most powerful destroyer – it has been estimated that 100 billion tonnes of rock is washed into the oceans every year.

When water freezes, its volume increases by about 9%, and no rock is strong enough to resist this pressure. Where water has penetrated tiny fissures or seeped into softer rock, a severe freeze followed by a thaw may result in rockfalls or earthslides, creating major destruction in a few minutes. Over much longer periods, acidity in rainwater breaks down the chemical composition of porous rocks, such as limestone, eating away the rock to form deep caves and tunnels. Chemical decomposition also occurs in riverbeds and glacier valleys, hastening the process of mechanical erosion.

Rivers and glaciers, like the sea itself, generate much of their effect through abrasion – pounding the landscape with the debris they carry with them. But, as well as destroying, they also create new landscapes, many of them spectacular: vast deltas, as seen at the mouth of the Mississippi or the Nile; cliffs, rock arches and stacks, as found along the south coast of Australia; and the fjords cut by long-melted glaciers in British Columbia, Norway and New Zealand.

THE SPREADING EARTH

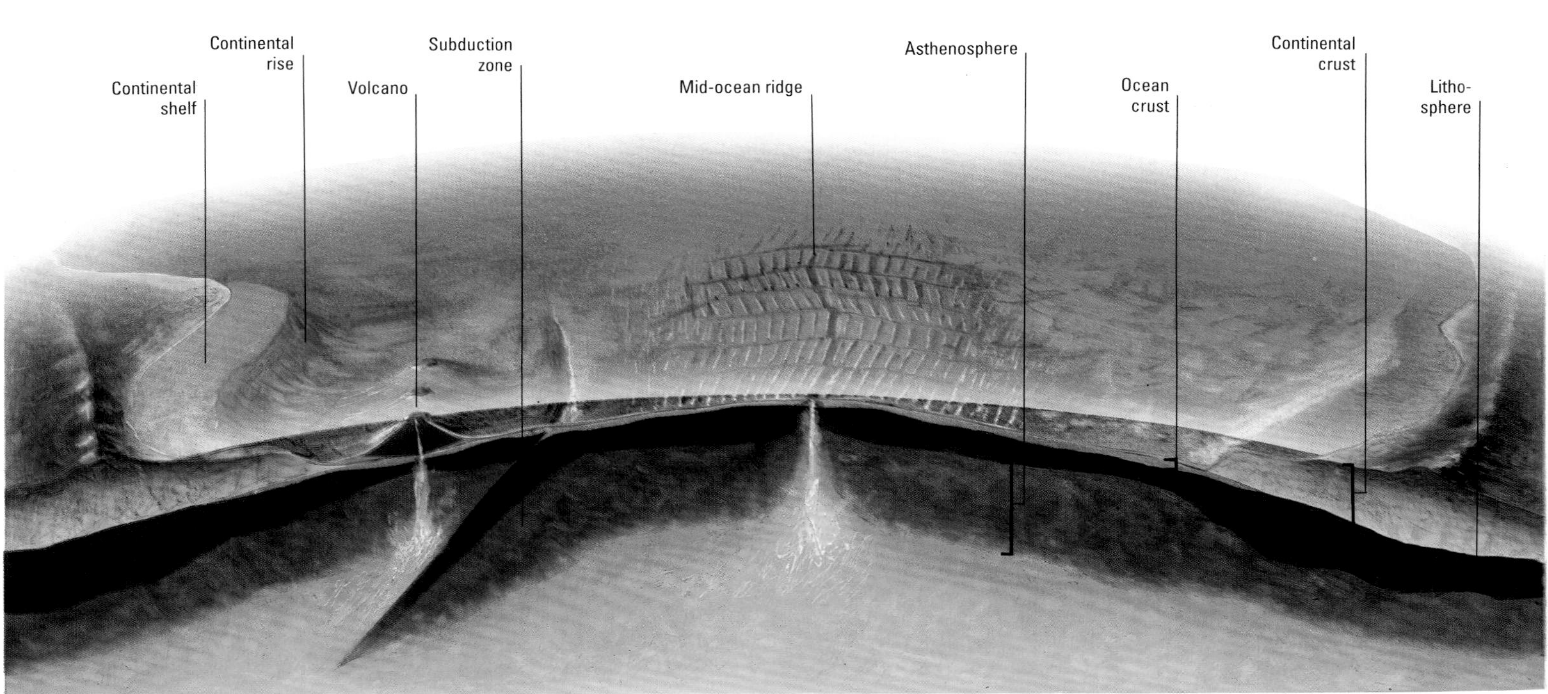
Continental shelf
Continental rise
Volcano
Subduction zone
Mid-ocean ridge
Asthenosphere
Ocean crust
Continental crust
Litho-sphere

The vast ridges that divide the Earth's crust beneath each of the world's major oceans mark the boundaries between tectonic plates which are moving very gradually in opposite directions. As the plates shift apart, molten magma rises from the Earth's core to seal the rift and the sea floor slowly spreads towards the continental landmasses. The rate of sea floor spreading has been calculated by magnetic analysis of the rock – at about 40 mm [1.5 in] a year in the North Atlantic. Near the ocean shore, underwater volcanoes mark the line where the continental rise begins. As the plates meet, much of the denser ocean crust dips beneath the continental plate and melts back into the magma.

TYPES OF ROCK

Rocks are divided into three types, according to the way in which they are formed:

Igneous rocks, including granite and basalt, are formed by the cooling of magma from within the Earth's crust.

Metamorphic rocks, such as slate, marble and quartzite, are formed below the Earth's surface by the compression or baking of existing rocks.

Sedimentary rocks, like sandstone and limestone, are formed on the surface of the Earth from the remains of living organisms and eroded fragments of older rocks.

MOUNTAIN BUILDING

Mountains are formed when pressures on the Earth's crust caused by continental drift become so intense that the surface buckles or cracks. This happens most dramatically where two tectonic plates collide: the Rockies, Andes, Alps, Urals and Himalayas resulted from such impacts. These are all known as fold mountains, because they were formed by the compression of the rocks, forcing the surface to bend and fold like a crumpled rug.

The other main building process occurs when the crust fractures to create faults, allowing rock to be forced upwards in large blocks; or when the pressure of magma within the crust forces the surface to bulge into a dome, or erupts to form a volcano. Large mountain ranges may reveal a combination of those features; the Alps, for example, have been compressed so violently that the folds are fragmented by numerous faults and intrusions of molten rock.

Over millions of years, even the greatest mountain ranges can be reduced by erosion to a rugged landscape known as a peneplain.

Types of fold: Geographers give different names to the degrees of fold that result from continuing pressure on the rock strata. A simple fold may be symmetric, with even slopes on either side, but as the pressure builds up, one slope becomes steeper and the fold becomes asymmetric. Later, the ridge or 'anticline' at the top of the fold may slide over the lower ground or 'syncline' to form a recumbent fold. Eventually, the rock strata may break under the pressure to form an overthrust and finally a nappe fold.

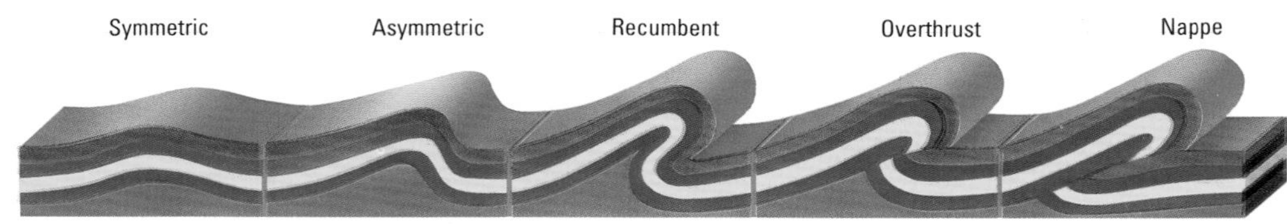
Symmetric
Asymmetric
Recumbent
Overthrust
Nappe

Types of faults: Faults are classified by the direction in which the blocks of rock have moved. A normal fault results when a vertical movement causes the surface to break apart; compression causes a reverse fault. Sideways movement causes shearing, known as a strike-slip fault. When the rock breaks in two places, the central block may be pushed up in a horst fault, or sink in a graben fault.

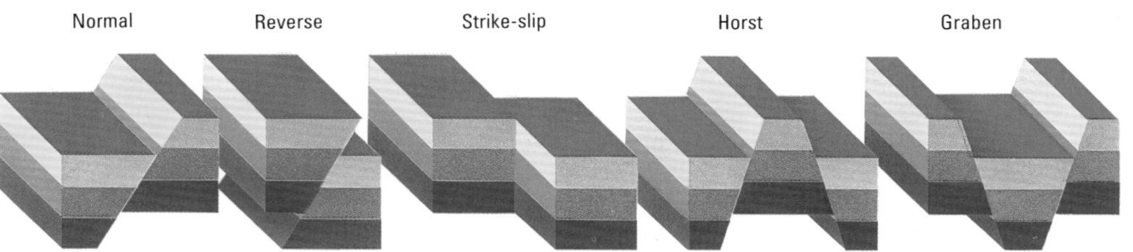
Normal
Reverse
Strike-slip
Horst
Graben

CARTOGRAPHY BY PHILIP'S. COPYRIGHT REED INTERNATIONAL BOOKS LTD

MOULDING THE LAND

While hidden forces of extraordinary power are moving the continents from below the Earth's crust, the more familiar elements of wind, water, heat and cold combine to sculpt the land surface. Erosion by weathering is seen in desert regions, where rocks degrade into sand through the effects of changing temperatures and strong winds.

The power of water is fiercer still. In severe storms, giant waves pound the shoreline with rocks and boulders, and often destroy concrete coastal defences; but even in quieter conditions, the sea steadily erodes cliffs and headlands and creates new land in the form of sand dunes, spits and salt marshes.

Rivers, too, are incessantly at work shaping the landscape on their way to join the sea. In highland regions, where the flow is rapid, they cut deep gorges and V-shaped valleys. As they reach more gentle slopes, rivers release some of the debris they have carried downstream, broadening out and raising levees along their banks by depositing mud and sand. In the lowland plains, they may drift into meanders, depositing more sediment and even building deltas when they finally approach the sea.

Ice has created some of the world's dramatic landscapes. As glaciers move slowly downhill, they scrape away rock from the mountains and valley sides, creating spectacular features.

SHAPING FORCES: THE SEA

In areas of hard rock, waves cut steep cliffs and form underwater platforms; debris is deposited as a terrace. Bays are formed when sections of soft rock are carved away between headlands of harder rock; these are then battered until the headlands are reduced to rock arches and stacks.

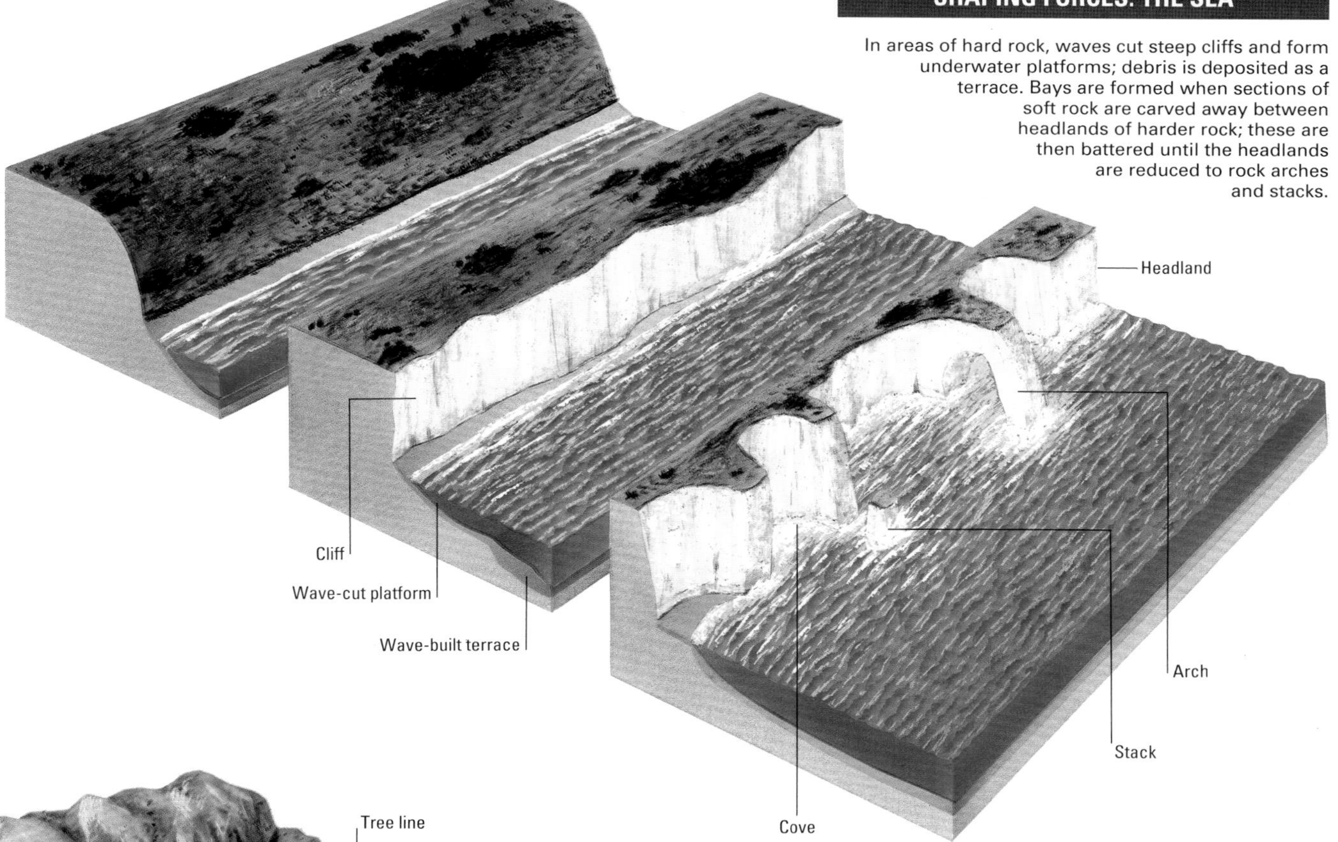

Headland
Cliff
Wave-cut platform
Wave-built terrace
Arch
Stack
Cove

SHAPING FORCES: RIVERS

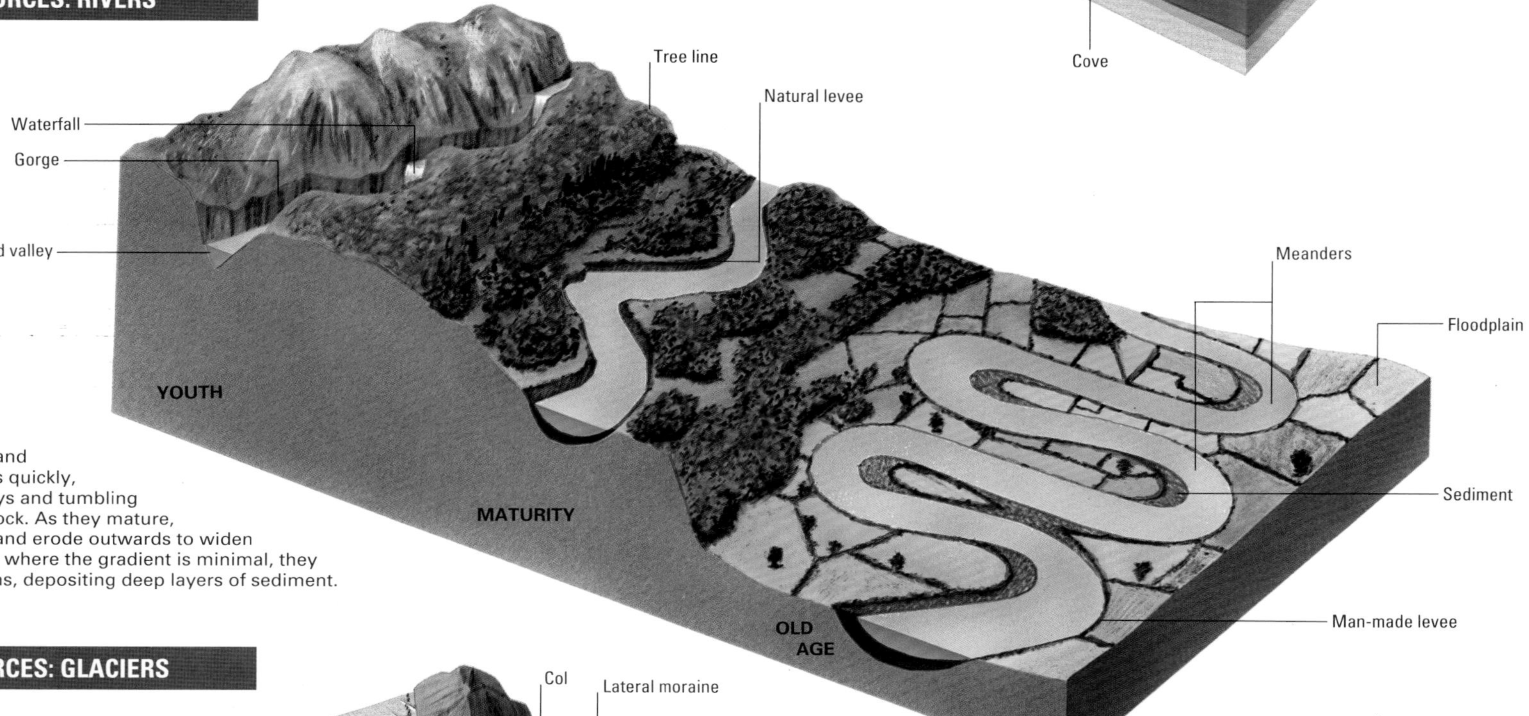

Tree line
Natural levee
Waterfall
Gorge
V-shaped valley
Meanders
Floodplain
YOUTH
MATURITY
Sediment
OLD AGE
Man-made levee

Rivers shape the landscape according to the speed of their flow. In their youthful, upland stage they erode soft rocks quickly, cutting steep narrow valleys and tumbling in waterfalls over harder rock. As they mature, they deposit some debris and erode outwards to widen the valley. In their old age, where the gradient is minimal, they meander across wide plains, depositing deep layers of sediment.

SHAPING FORCES: GLACIERS

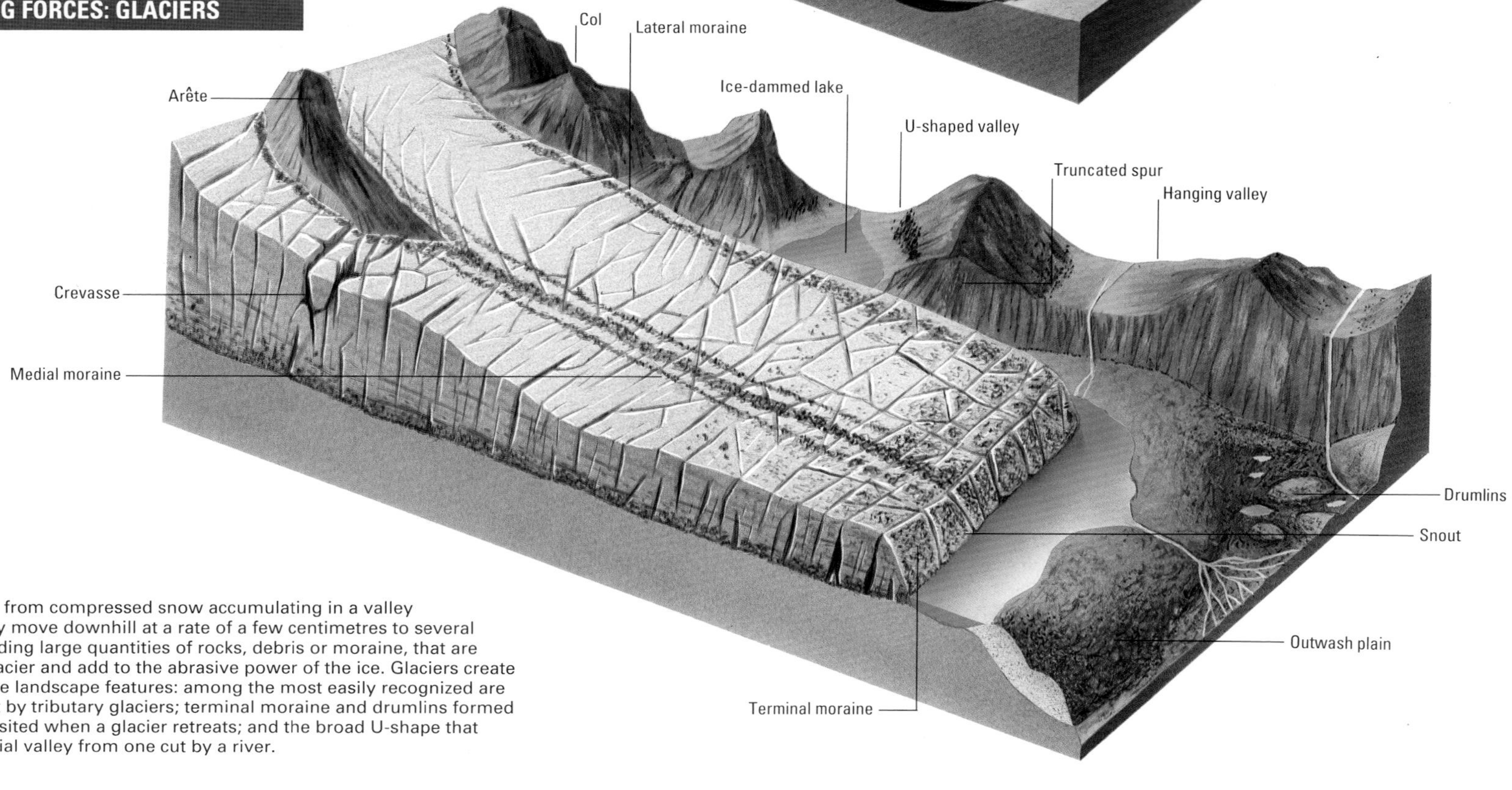

Col
Lateral moraine
Arête
Ice-dammed lake
U-shaped valley
Truncated spur
Hanging valley
Crevasse
Medial moraine
Drumlins
Snout
Outwash plain
Terminal moraine

Glaciers are formed from compressed snow accumulating in a valley head or cirque. They move downhill at a rate of a few centimetres to several metres per day, eroding large quantities of rocks, debris or moraine, that are caught up by the glacier and add to the abrasive power of the ice. Glaciers create numerous distinctive landscape features: among the most easily recognized are hanging valleys, cut by tributary glaciers; terminal moraine and drumlins formed by rock debris deposited when a glacier retreats; and the broad U-shape that distinguishes a glacial valley from one cut by a river.

CARTOGRAPHY BY PHILIP'S. COPYRIGHT REED INTERNATIONAL BOOKS LTD

THE EARTH: ENVIRONMENT

10: OCEANS

12: ATMOSPHERE

17: NATURAL VEGETATION

46: CARBON DIOXIDE
GREENHOUSE POWER
GLOBAL WARMING

47: ACID RAIN
DESERTIFICATION
DEFORESTATION
WATER POLLUTION

Unique among the planets, the Earth has been the home of living creatures for most of its existence. Precisely how these improbable assemblies of self-replicating chemicals ever began remains a matter of conjecture, but the planet and its passengers have matured together for a very long time. Over 3,000 million years, life has not only adapted to its environment, but it has also slowly changed that environment to suit itself.

The planet and its biosphere – the entirety of its living things – function like a single organism. The British scientist James Lovelock, who first stated this 'Gaia hypothesis' in the 1970s, went further: the planet, he declared, actually was a living organism, equipped on a colossal scale with the same sort of stability-seeking mechanisms used by lesser lifeforms like bacteria and humans to keep themselves running at optimum efficiency.

Lovelock's theory was inspired by a study of the Earth's atmosphere whose constituents he noted were very far from the state of chemical equilibrium observed elsewhere in the Solar System. The atmosphere has contained a substantial amount of free oxygen for the last 2,000 million years; yet without constant renewal, the oxygen molecules would soon be locked permanently in oxides. The nitrogen, too, would find chemical stability, probably in nitrates (accounting for some of the oxygen). Without living plants and algae to remove it, carbon dioxide would steadily increase from its present-day 0.03%; in a few million years, it would form a thick blanket similar to the atmosphere of lifeless Venus, where surface temperatures reach 475°C.

It is not enough, however, for the biosphere simply to produce oxygen. While falling concentrations would first be uncomfortable and ultimately prove fatal for most contemporary life, at levels above the current 21% even moist vegetation is highly inflammable, and a massive conflagration becomes almost inevitable – a violent form of negative feedback to set the atmosphere on the path back to sterile equilibrium.

Fortunately, the biosphere has evolved over aeons into a subtle and complex control system, sensing changes and reacting to them quickly but gently, tending always to maintain the balance it has achieved.

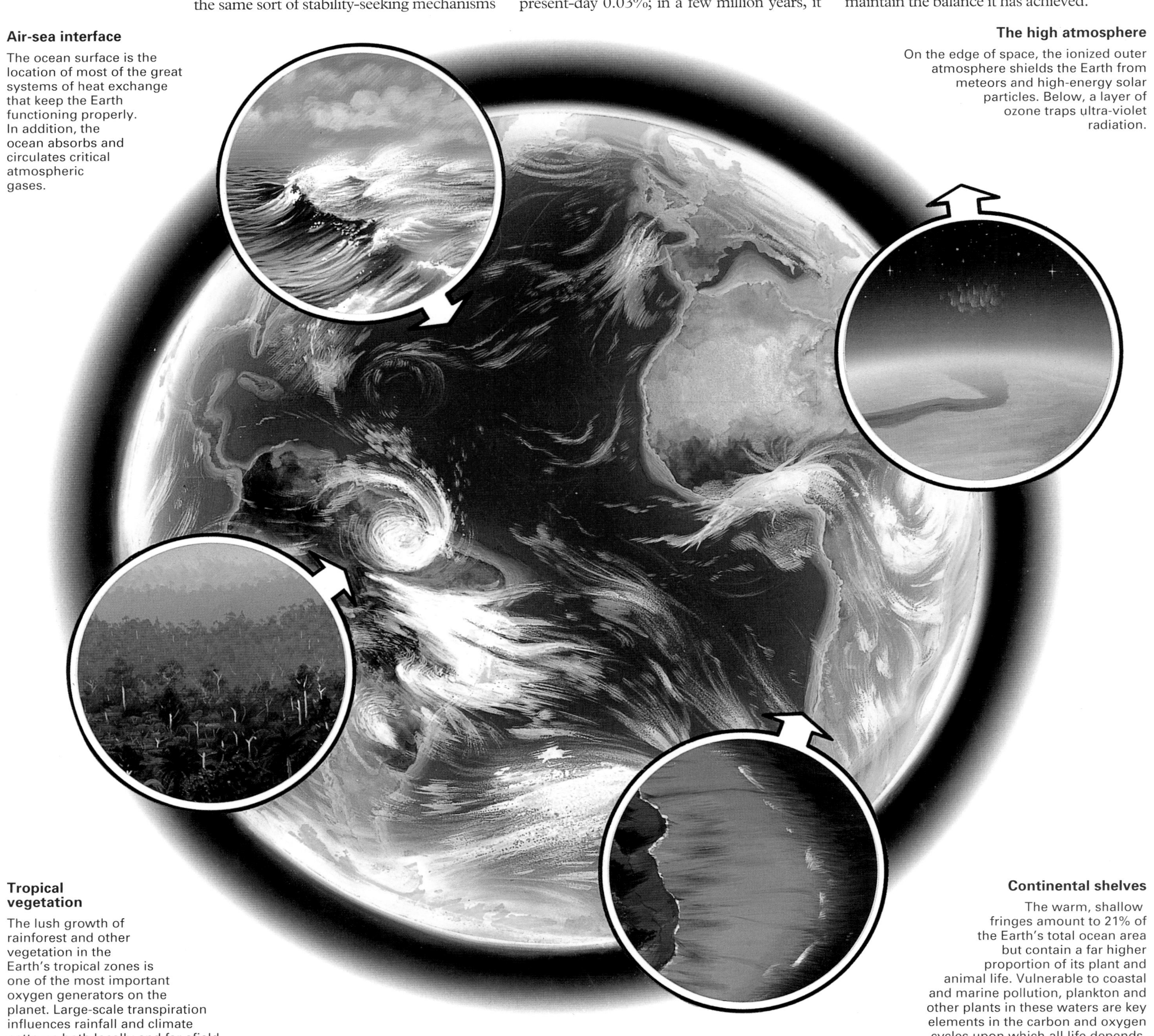

Air-sea interface

The ocean surface is the location of most of the great systems of heat exchange that keep the Earth functioning properly. In addition, the ocean absorbs and circulates critical atmospheric gases.

The high atmosphere

On the edge of space, the ionized outer atmosphere shields the Earth from meteors and high-energy solar particles. Below, a layer of ozone traps ultra-violet radiation.

Tropical vegetation

The lush growth of rainforest and other vegetation in the Earth's tropical zones is one of the most important oxygen generators on the planet. Large-scale transpiration influences rainfall and climate patterns both locally and far afield.

Continental shelves

The warm, shallow fringes amount to 21% of the Earth's total ocean area but contain a far higher proportion of its plant and animal life. Vulnerable to coastal and marine pollution, plankton and other plants in these waters are key elements in the carbon and oxygen cycles upon which all life depends.

CARTOGRAPHY BY PHILIP'S. COPYRIGHT REED INTERNATIONAL BOOKS LTD

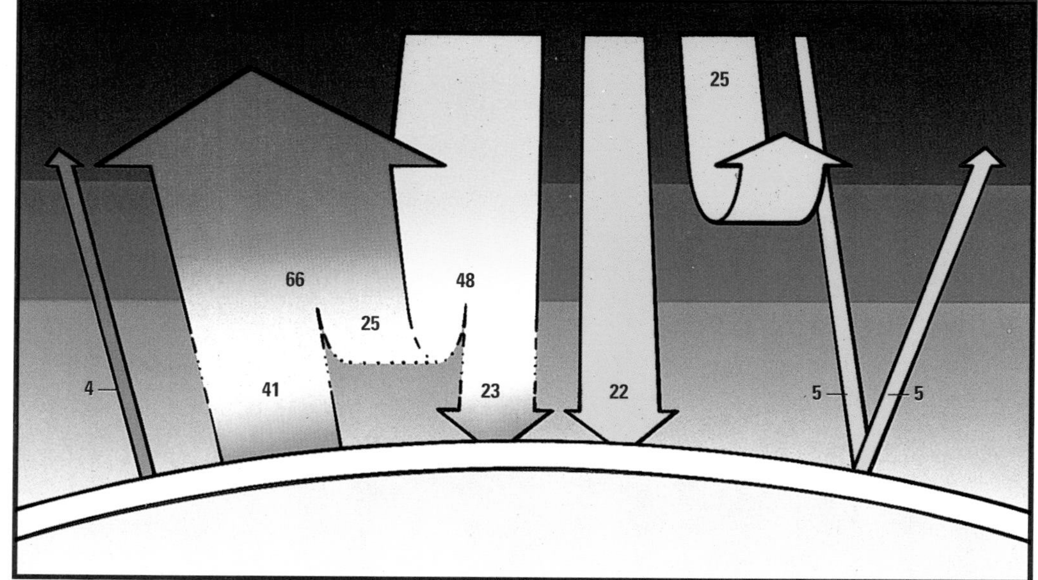
25
66
48
25
4
41
23
22
5
5

THE EARTH'S ENERGY BALANCE

Apart from a modest quantity of internal heat from its molten core, the Earth receives all of its energy from the Sun. If the planet is to remain at a constant temperature, it must reradiate exactly as much energy as it receives. Even a minute surplus would lead to a warmer Earth, a deficit to a cooler one; because the planetary energy budget is constantly audited by the laws of physics, which do not permit juggling, it must balance with absolute precision. The temperature at which thermal equilibrium is reached depends on a multitude of interconnected factors. Two of the most important are the relative brightness of the Earth – its index of reflectivity, called the 'albedo' – and the heat-trapping capacity of the atmosphere – the celebrated 'greenhouse effect'.

Because the Sun is very hot, most of its energy arrives in the form of relatively short-wave radiation: the shorter the waves, the more energy they carry. Some of the incoming energy is reflected straight back into space, exactly as it arrived; some is absorbed by the atmosphere on its way towards the surface; some is absorbed by the Earth itself. Absorbed energy heats the Earth and its atmosphere alike. But since its temperature is very much lower that that of the Sun, outgoing energy is emitted at much longer infra-red wavelengths. Some of the outgoing radiation escapes directly into outer space; some of it is reabsorbed by the atmosphere. Atmospheric energy eventually finds its way back into space, too, after a complex series of interactions. These include the air movements we call the weather and, almost incidentally, the maintenance of life on Earth.

This diagram does not attempt to illustrate the actual mechanisms of heat exchange, but gives a reasonable account (in percentages) of what happens to 100 energy 'units'. Short-wave radiation is shown in yellow, long-wave in red.

THE CARBON CYCLE

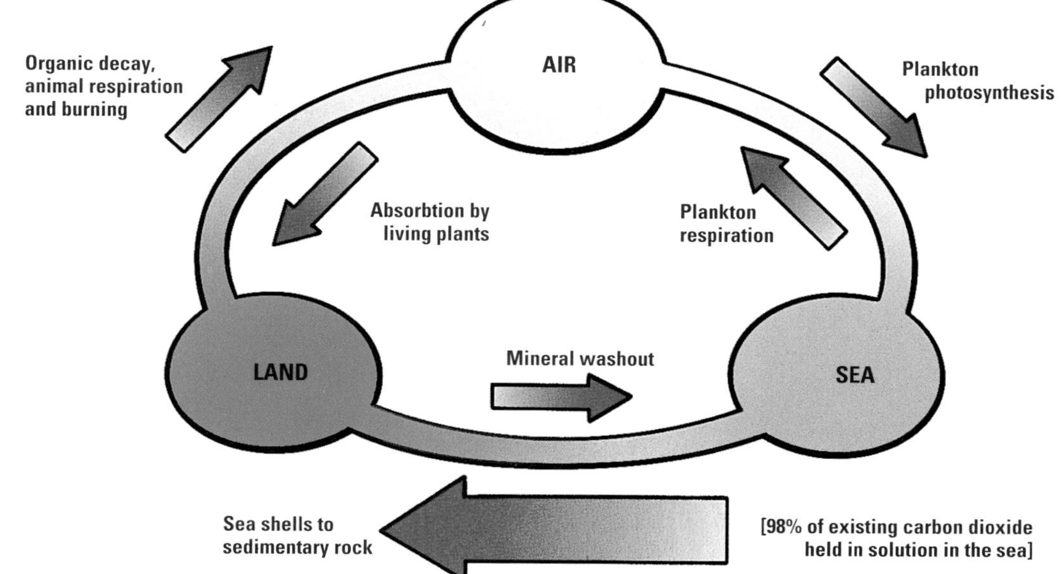
Organic decay, animal respiration and burning
AIR
Plankton photosynthesis
Absorbtion by living plants
Plankton respiration
LAND
Mineral washout
SEA
Sea shells to sedimentary rock
[98% of existing carbon dioxide held in solution in the sea]

Most of the constituents of the atmosphere are kept in constant balance by complex cycles in which life plays an essential and indeed a dominant part. The control of carbon dioxide, which left to its own devices would be the dominant atmospheric gas, is possibly the most important, although since all the Earth's biological and geophysical cycles interact and interlock, it is hard to separate them even in theory and quite impossible in practice.

The Earth has a huge supply of carbon, only a small quantity of which is in the form of carbon dioxide. Of that, around 98% is dissolved in the sea; the fraction circulating in the air amounts to only 340 parts per million of the atmosphere, where its capacity as a greenhouse gas is the key regulator of the planetary temperature. In turn, life regulates the regulator, keeping carbon dioxide concentrations below danger level.

If all life were to vanish tomorrow from the Earth, the atmosphere would begin the process of change immediately, although it might take several million years to achieve a new, inorganic stability. First, the oxygen content would begin to fall away; with no more assistance than a little solar radiation, a few electrical storms and its own high chemical potential, oxygen would steadily combine with atmospheric nitrogen and volcanic outgassing. In doing so, it would yield sufficient acid to react with carbonaceous rocks such as limestone, releasing carbon dioxide. Once carbon dioxide levels exceeded about 1%, its greenhouse power would increase disproportionately. Rising temperatures – well above the boiling point of water – would speed chemical reactions; in time, the Earth's atmosphere would consist of little more than carbon dioxide and superheated water vapour.

Living things, however, circulate carbon. They do so first by simply existing: after all, the carbon atom is the basic building block of living matter. During life, plants absorb atmospheric carbon dioxide, incorporating the carbon itself into their structure – leaves and trunks in the case of land plants, shells in the case of plankton and the tiny creatures that feed on it. The oxygen thereby freed is added to the atmosphere, at least for a time. Most plant carbon is returned to circulation when the plants die and decay, combining once more with the oxygen released during life. However, a small proportion – about one part in 1,000 – is removed almost permanently, buried beneath mud on land, or at sea sinking as dead matter to the ocean floor. In time, it is slowly compressed into sedimentary rocks such as limestone and chalk.

But in the evolution of the Earth, nothing is quite permanent. On an even longer timescale, the planet's crustal movements force new rock upwards in mid-ocean ridges. Limestone deposits are moved, and sea levels change; ancient limestone is exposed to weathering, and a little of its carbon is released to be fixed in turn by the current generation of plants.

The carbon cycle has continued quietly for an immensely long time, and without gross disturbance there is no reason why it would not continue almost indefinitely in the future. However, human beings have found a way to release fixed carbon at a rate far faster than existing global systems can recirculate it. Oil and coal deposits represent the work of millions of years of carbon accumulation; but it has taken only a few human generations of high-energy scavenging to endanger the entire complex regulatory cycle.

THE GREENHOUSE EFFECT

Constituting barely 0.03% of the atmosphere, carbon dioxide has a hugely disproportionate effect on the Earth's climate and even its habitability. Like the glass panes in a greenhouse, it is transparent to most incoming short-wave radiation, which passes freely to heat the planet beneath. But when the warmed Earth retransmits that energy, in the form of longer-wave infra-red radiation, the carbon dioxide functions as an opaque shield, so that the planetary surface (like the interior of a greenhouse) stays relatively hot.

The recent increases in CO_2 levels are causing alarm: global warming associated with a runaway greenhouse effect could bring disaster. But a serious reduction would be just as damaging, with surface temperatures falling dramatically; during the last Ice Age, for example, the carbon dioxide concentration was around 180 parts per million, and a total absence of the gas would likely leave the planet a ball of ice, or at best frozen tundra.

The diagram shows incoming sunlight as yellow; high-energy ultra-violet (blue) is trapped by the ozone layer, while outgoing heat from the warmed Earth (red) is partially retained by carbon dioxide.

CARTOGRAPHY BY PHILIP'S. COPYRIGHT REED INTERNATIONAL BOOKS LTD

PEOPLE: DEMOGRAPHY

24: URBANIZATION OF THE EARTH
URBAN POPULATION

25: LARGEST CITIES

31: FOOD AND POPULATION

40: WEALTH AND POPULATION

46: HUMAN EXPANSION

As the 20th century draws to its close, the Earth's population increases by nearly 10,000 every hour – enough to fill a new major city every week. The growth is almost entirely confined to the developing world, which accounted for 67% of total population in 1950 and is set to reach 84% by 2025. In developed countries, populations are almost static, and in some places, such as Germany, are actually falling. In fact, there is a clear correlation between wealth and low fertility: as incomes rise, reproduction rates drop.

The decline is already apparent. With the exception of Africa, the actual rates of increase are falling nearly everywhere. The population structure, however, ensures that human numbers will continue to rise even as fertility diminishes. Developed nations, like the UK, have an even spread across ages, and usually a growing proportion of elderly people: the over-75s often outnumber the under-5s, and women of child-bearing age form only a small part of the total. Developing nations fall into a pattern somewhere between that of Kenya and Brazil: the great majority of their people are in the younger age groups, about to enter their most fertile years. In time, even Kenya's population profile should resemble the developed model, but the transition will come about only after a few more generations' growth.

It remains to be seen whether the planet will tolerate the population growth that seems inevitable before stability is reached. More people consume more resources, increasing the strain on an already troubled environment. However, more people should mean a greater supply of human ingenuity – the only commodity likely to resolve the crisis.

LARGEST NATIONS

The world's most populous nations, in millions (1993)

1.	China	1,187
2.	India	879
3.	USA	255
4.	Indonesia	191
5.	Brazil	156
6.	Russia	149
7.	Japan	124
8.	Bangladesh	119
9.	Pakistan	115
10.	Mexico	89
11.	Nigeria	88
12.	Germany	80
13.	Vietnam	69
14.	Philippines	64
15.	Turkey	58
16.	Italy	57
17.	UK	57
18.	Thailand	57
19.	France	57
20.	Iran	56
21.	Egypt	55
22.	Ethiopia	55
23.	Ukraine	52
24.	S. Korea	43

CROWDED NATIONS

Population per square kilometre (1993), exc. nations of less than one million.

1.	Hong Kong	5,273.6
2.	Singapore	4,535.5
3.	Bangladesh	828.4
4.	Mauritius	582.8
5.	Taiwan	573.9
6.	S. Korea	441.0
7.	Puerto Rico	397.8
8.	Netherlands	365.7
9.	Japan	329.0
10.	Belgium	327.8
11.	Rwanda	286.2
12.	Lebanon	272.9
13.	India	267.5
14.	Sri Lanka	265.3
15.	El Salvador	257.0
16.	Trinidad & Tobago	248.0
17.	UK	237.8
18.	Germany	225.7
19.	Jamaica	224.7
20.	Israel	183.2

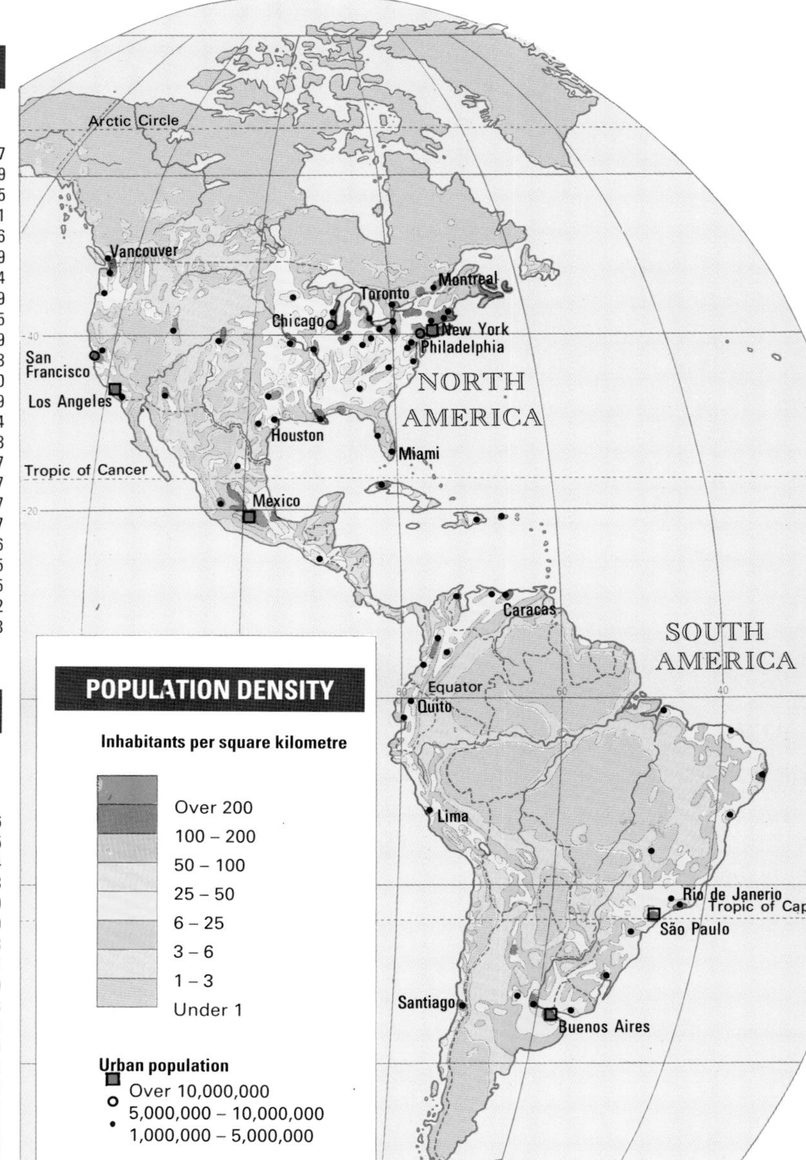

Arctic Circle
Vancouver
Toronto
Montreal
Chicago
New York
Philadelphia
San Francisco
Los Angeles
NORTH AMERICA
Houston
Miami
Tropic of Cancer
Mexico
Caracas
SOUTH AMERICA
Equator
Quito
Lima
Rio de Janerio
Tropic of Capricorn
São Paulo
Santiago
Buenos Aires
POPULATION DENSITY
Inhabitants per square kilometre
Over 200
100 – 200
50 – 100
25 – 50
6 – 25
3 – 6
1 – 3
Under 1
Urban population
Over 10,000,000
5,000,000 – 10,000,000
1,000,000 – 5,000,000
Places marked are conurbations, not city limits; San Francisco itself, for example, has an official population of less than a million.

Projection : Mollweide's Interrupted Homolographic

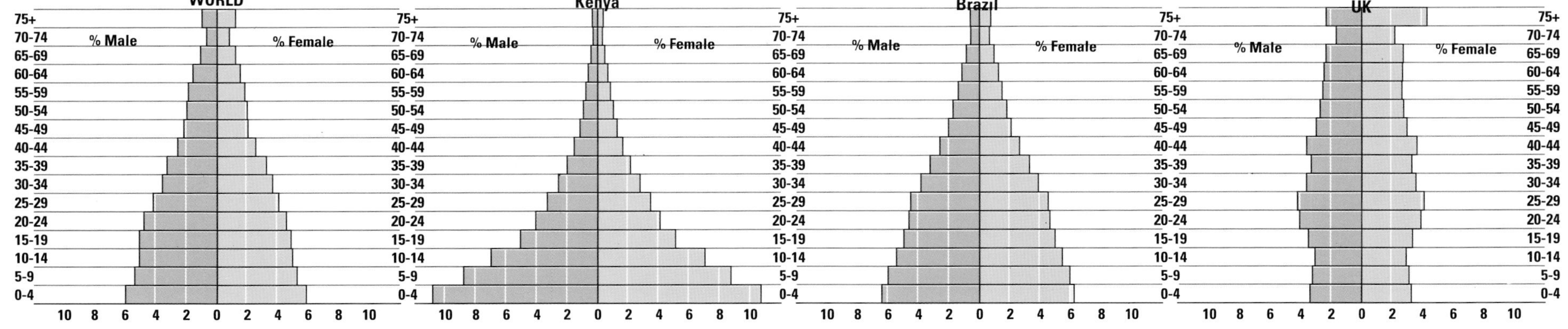

WORLD
Kenya
Brazil
UK
% Male
% Female
75+
70-74
65-69
60-64
55-59
50-54
45-49
40-44
35-39
30-34
25-29
20-24
15-19
10-14
5-9
0-4
10 8 6 4 2 0 2 4 6 8 10

RATES OF GROWTH

Apparently small rates of population growth lead to dramatic increases over two or three generations. The table below translates annual percentage growth into the number of years required to double a population.

% change	Doubling time
0.5	139.0
1.0	69.7
1.5	46.6
2.0	35.0
2.5	28.1
3.0	23.4
3.5	20.1
4.0	17.7

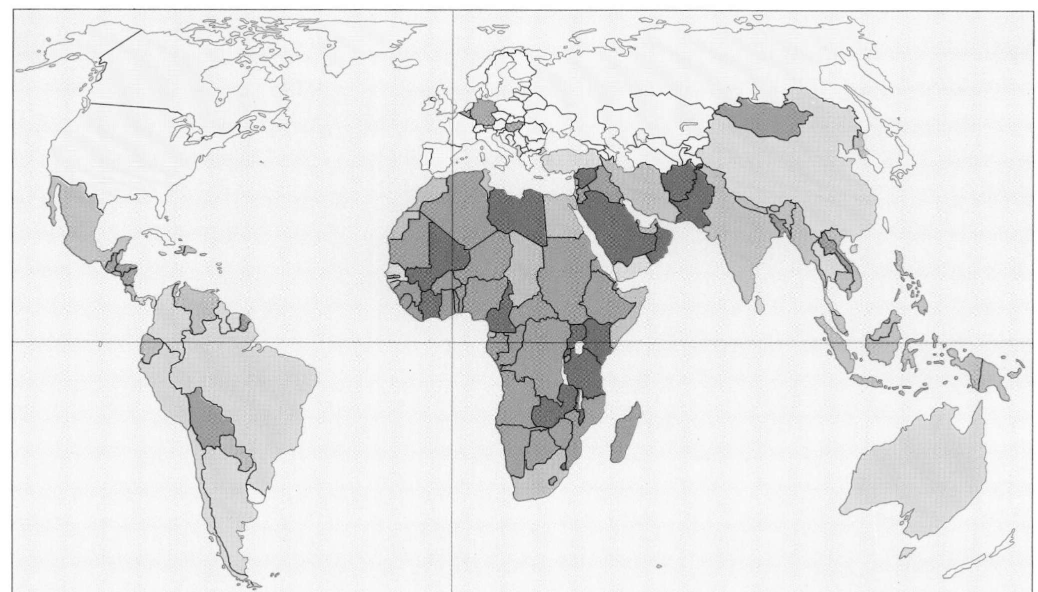

POPULATION CHANGE

Estimated percentage change in total population, between 1990 and 2000

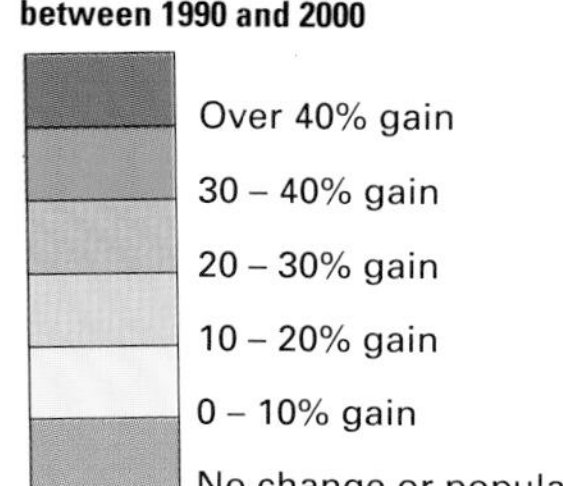

Over 40% gain
30 – 40% gain
20 – 30% gain
10 – 20% gain
0 – 10% gain
No change or population loss

Top 5 countries	
Afghanistan	+60%
Mali	+56%
Tanzania	+55%
Ivory Coast	+47%
Saudi Arabia	+46%

Bottom 5 countries	
Hungary	–0.2%
Singapore	–0.2%
Grenada	–2.4%
Tonga	–3.2%
Germany	–3.2%

CARTOGRAPHY BY PHILIP'S. COPYRIGHT REED INTERNATIONAL BOOKS LTD

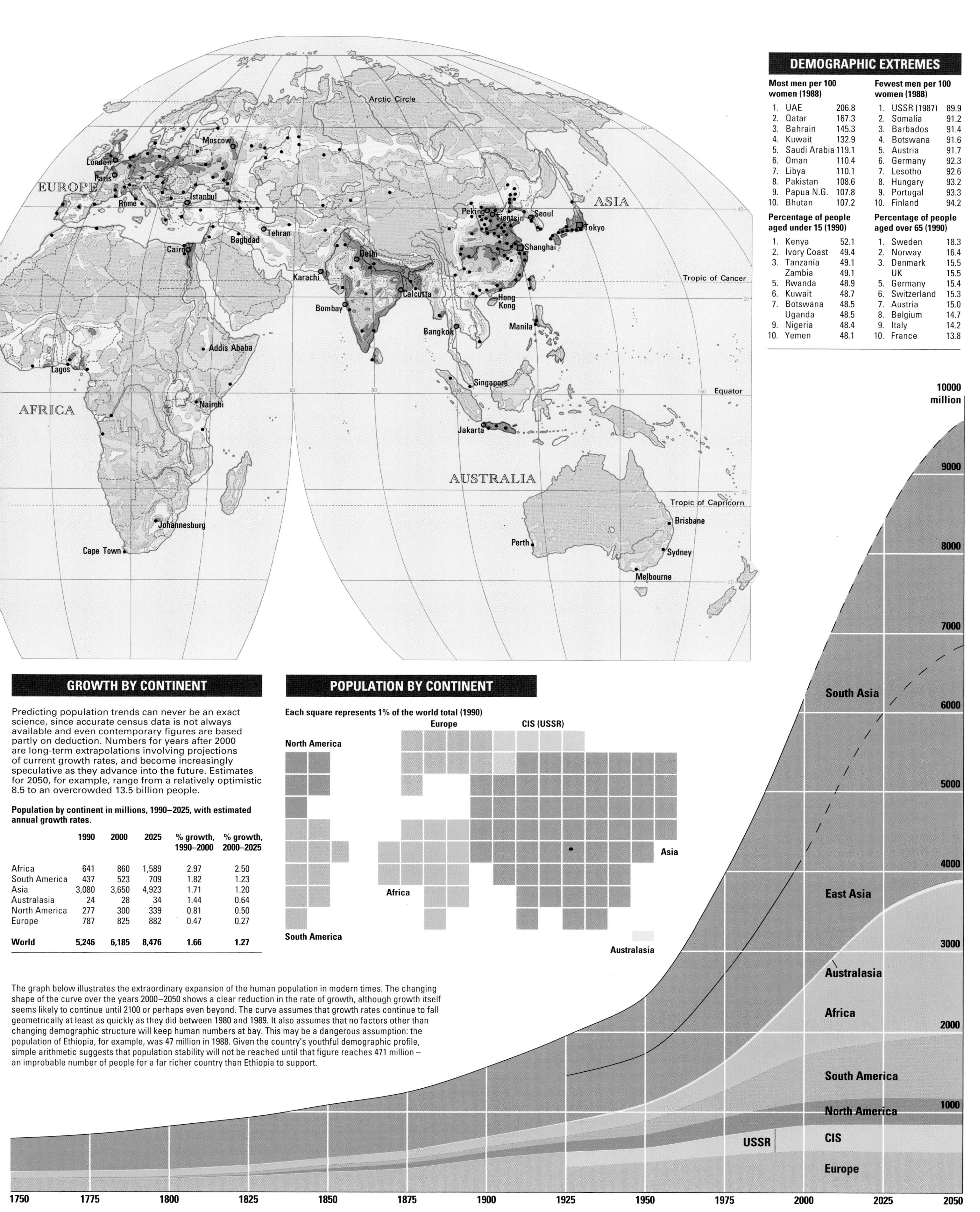

Arctic Circle
Moscow
London
Paris
EUROPE
Rome
Istanbul
Tehran
Baghdad
Cairo
ASIA
Peking
Tientsin
Seoul
Tokyo
Shanghai
Delhi
Karachi
Calcutta
Tropic of Cancer
Hong Kong
Bombay
Manila
Bangkok
Addis Ababa
Lagos
Singapore
Equator
AFRICA
Nairobi
Jakarta
AUSTRALIA
Tropic of Capricorn
Brisbane
Johannesburg
Perth
Sydney
Cape Town
Melbourne
10000 million
9000
8000
7000
6000
5000
4000
3000
2000
1000
South Asia
East Asia
Australasia
Africa
South America
North America
USSR
CIS
Europe
1750
1775
1800
1825
1850
1875
1900
1925
1950
1975
2000
2025
2050

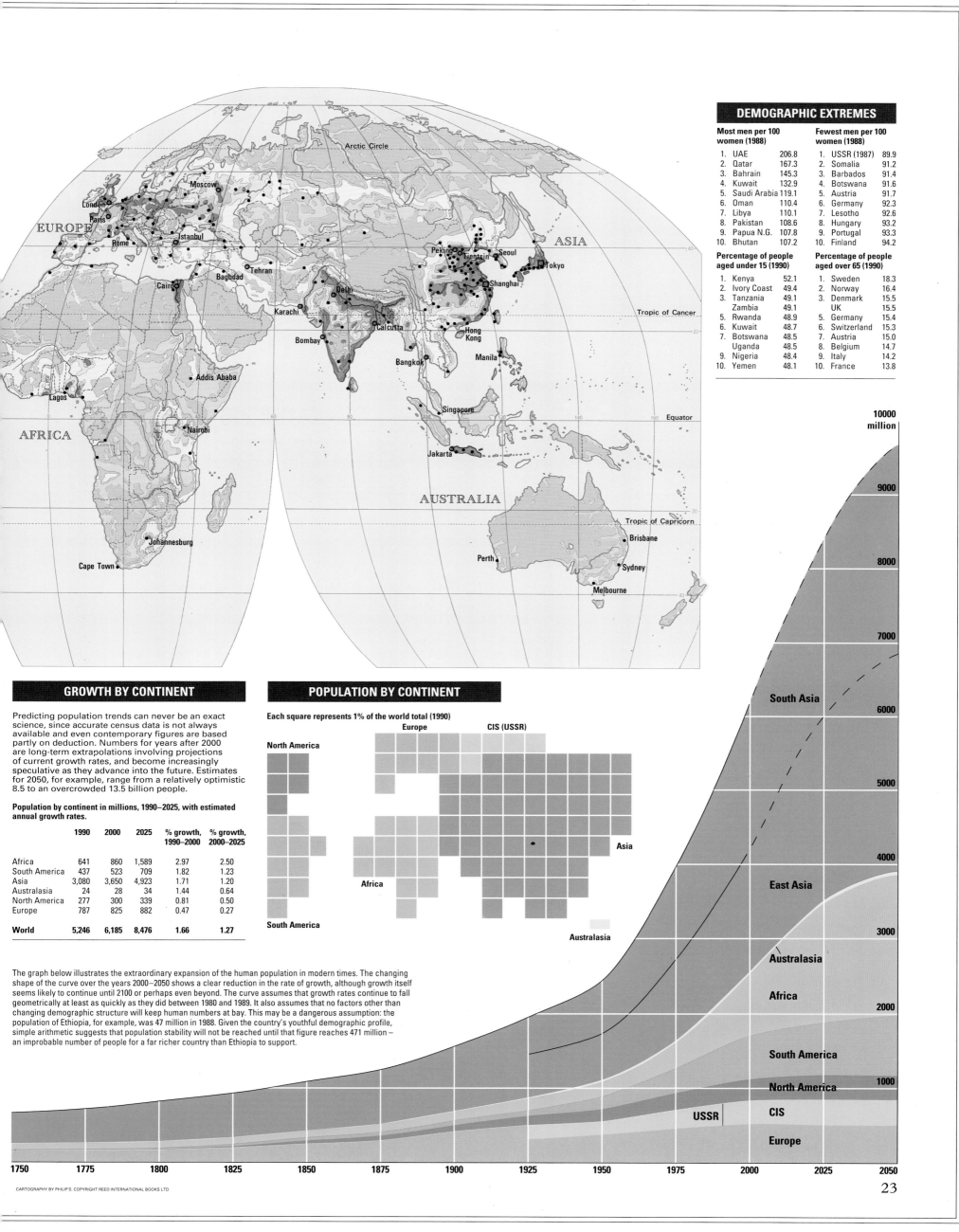

DEMOGRAPHIC EXTREMES

Most men per 100 women (1988)

1.	UAE	206.8
2.	Qatar	167.3
3.	Bahrain	145.3
4.	Kuwait	132.9
5.	Saudi Arabia	119.1
6.	Oman	110.4
7.	Libya	110.1
8.	Pakistan	108.6
9.	Papua N.G.	107.8
10.	Bhutan	107.2

Fewest men per 100 women (1988)

1.	USSR (1987)	89.9
2.	Somalia	91.2
3.	Barbados	91.4
4.	Botswana	91.6
5.	Austria	91.7
6.	Germany	92.3
7.	Lesotho	92.6
8.	Hungary	93.2
9.	Portugal	93.3
10.	Finland	94.2

Percentage of people aged under 15 (1990)

1.	Kenya	52.1
2.	Ivory Coast	49.4
3.	Tanzania	49.1
	Zambia	49.1
5.	Rwanda	48.9
6.	Kuwait	48.7
7.	Botswana	48.5
	Uganda	48.5
9.	Nigeria	48.4
10.	Yemen	48.1

Percentage of people aged over 65 (1990)

1.	Sweden	18.3
2.	Norway	16.4
3.	Denmark	15.5
	UK	15.5
5.	Germany	15.4
6.	Switzerland	15.3
7.	Austria	15.0
8.	Belgium	14.7
9.	Italy	14.2
10.	France	13.8

GROWTH BY CONTINENT

Predicting population trends can never be an exact science, since accurate census data is not always available and even contemporary figures are based partly on deduction. Numbers for years after 2000 are long-term extrapolations involving projections of current growth rates, and become increasingly speculative as they advance into the future. Estimates for 2050, for example, range from a relatively optimistic 8.5 to an overcrowded 13.5 billion people.

Population by continent in millions, 1990–2025, with estimated annual growth rates.

	1990	2000	2025	% growth, 1990–2000	% growth, 2000–2025
Africa	641	860	1,589	2.97	2.50
South America	437	523	709	1.82	1.23
Asia	3,080	3,650	4,923	1.71	1.20
Australasia	24	28	34	1.44	0.64
North America	277	300	339	0.81	0.50
Europe	787	825	882	0.47	0.27
World	**5,246**	**6,185**	**8,476**	**1.66**	**1.27**

POPULATION BY CONTINENT

Each square represents 1% of the world total (1990)

Europe
CIS (USSR)
North America
Asia
Africa
South America
Australasia

The graph below illustrates the extraordinary expansion of the human population in modern times. The changing shape of the curve over the years 2000–2050 shows a clear reduction in the rate of growth, although growth itself seems likely to continue until 2100 or perhaps even beyond. The curve assumes that growth rates continue to fall geometrically at least as quickly as they did between 1980 and 1989. It also assumes that no factors other than changing demographic structure will keep human numbers at bay. This may be a dangerous assumption: the population of Ethiopia, for example, was 47 million in 1988. Given the country's youthful demographic profile, simple arithmetic suggests that population stability will not be reached until that figure reaches 471 million – an improbable number of people for a far richer country than Ethiopia to support.

CARTOGRAPHY BY PHILIP'S. COPYRIGHT REED INTERNATIONAL BOOKS LTD

PEOPLE: CITIES

16: WATER SUPPLY
22: POPULATION DENSITY
39: THE GREAT PORTS

In 1750, barely three humans in every hundred lived in a city; by 2000, more than half the world's population will find a home in some kind of urban area. In 1850, only London and Paris had more than a million inhabitants; by 2000, at least 24 cities will each contain over 10 million people. The increase is concentrated in the Third World, if only because levels of urbanization in most developed countries – more than 90% in the UK and Belgium, and almost 75% in the USA, despite that country's great open spaces – have already reached practical limits.

Such large-scale concentration is relatively new to the human race. Although city life has always attracted country dwellers in search of trade, employment or simply human contact, until modern times they paid a high price. Crowding and poor sanitation ensured high death rates, and until about 1850, most cities needed a steady flow of incomers simply to maintain their population levels: for example, there were 600,000 more deaths than births in 18th-century London, and some other large cities showed an even worse imbalance.

With improved public health, cities could grow from their own human resources, and large-scale urban living became commonplace in the developed world. Since about 1950, the pattern has been global. Like their counterparts in 19th-century Europe and the USA, the great new cities are driven into rapid growth by a kind of push-pull mechanism. The push is generated by agricultural overcrowding: only so many people can live from a single plot of land and population pressure drives many into towns. The pull comes from the possibilities of economic improvement – an irresistible lure to the world's rural hopefuls.

Such improvement is not always obvious: the typical Third World city, with millions of people living (often illegally) in shanty towns and many thousands existing homelessly on the ill-made streets, does not present a great image of prosperity. Yet modern shanty towns are healthier than industrializing Pittsburgh or Manchester in the last century, and these human ant-hills teem with industry as well as squalor: throughout the world, above-average rates of urbanization have gone hand-in-hand with above-average rates of economic growth. Surveys demonstrate that Third World city dwellers are generally better off than their rural counterparts, whose poverty is less concentrated but often more desperate. This only serves to increase the attraction of the city for the rural poor.

However, the sheer speed of the urbanization process threatens to overwhelm the limited abilities of city authorities to provide even rudimentary services. The 24 million people expected to live in Mexico City by 2000, for example, would swamp a more efficient local government than Mexico can provide. Improvements are often swallowed up by the relentless rise in urban population: although safe drinking water should reach 75% of Third World city dwellers by the end of the century – a considerable achievement – population growth will add 100 million to the list of those without it.

THE URBANIZATION OF THE EARTH

City-building, 1850–2000; each white spot represents a city of at least 1 million inhabitants.

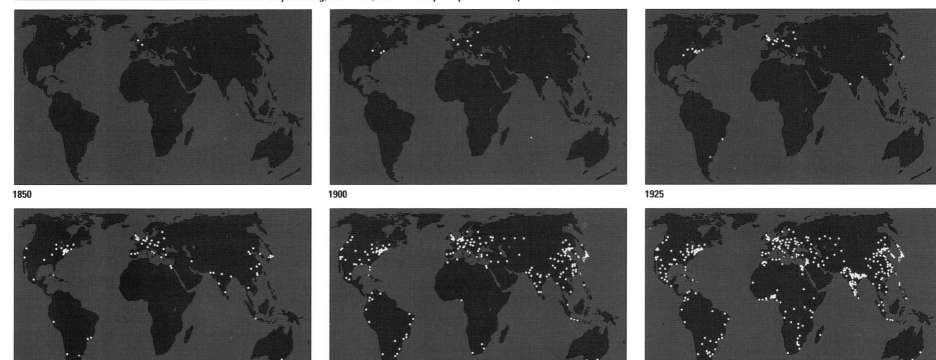

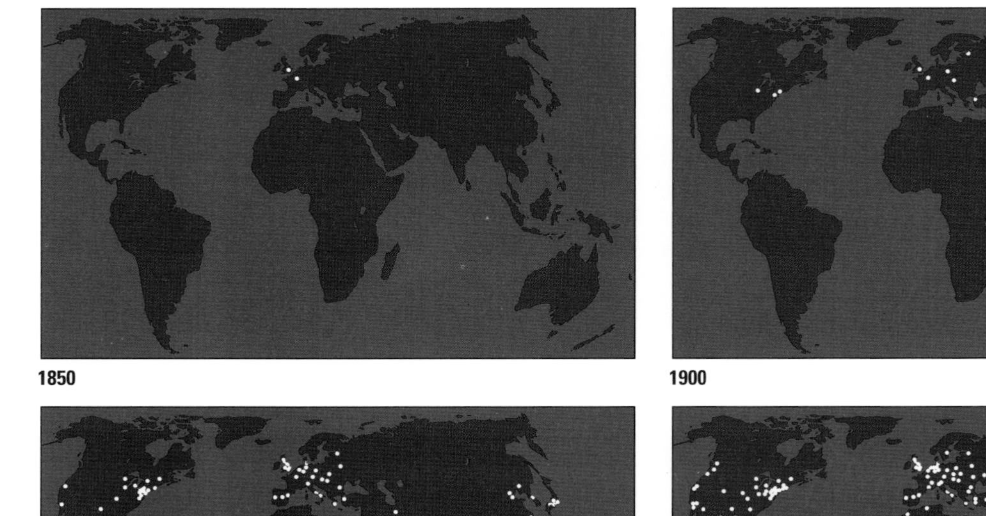

1850

1900

1925

1950

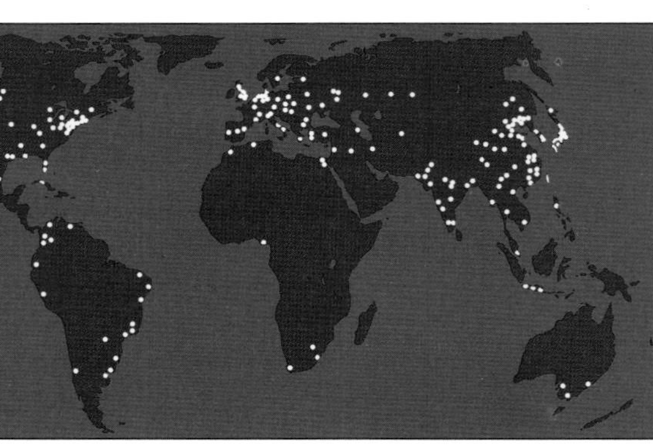

1975

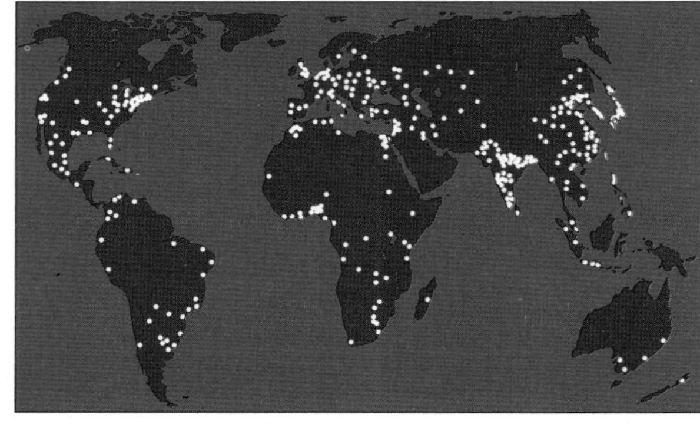

2000

URBAN POPULATION

Percentage of total population living in towns and cities (1990)

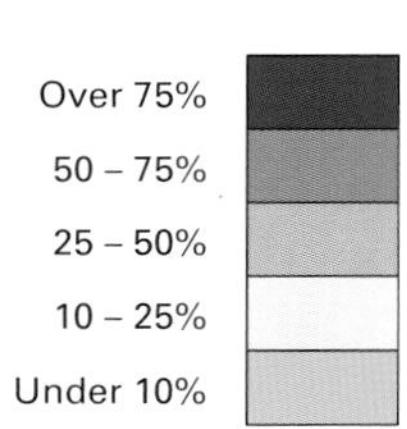
Over 75%
50 – 75%
25 – 50%
10 – 25%
Under 10%

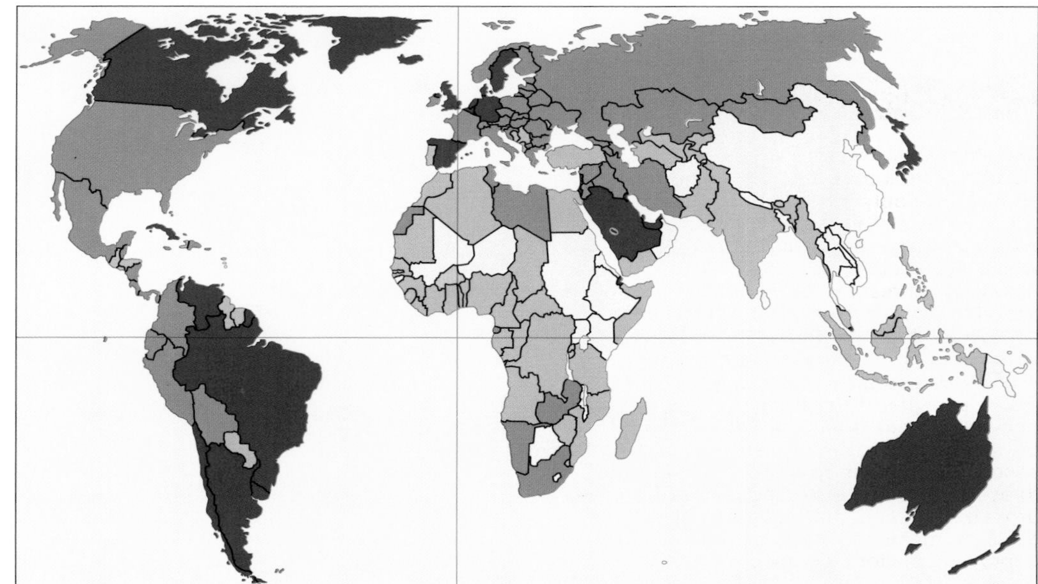

Most urbanized

Singapore	100%
Belgium	97%
Kuwait	96%
Hong Kong	93%
UK	93%

Least urbanized

Bhutan	5%
Burundi	7%
Rwanda	8%
Burkina Faso	9%
Nepal	10%

CARTOGRAPHY BY PHILIP'S. COPYRIGHT REED INTERNATIONAL BOOKS LTD

EXPANDING CITIES

The growth of the world's largest cities, 1950–2000. Intermediate rings indicate relative size in 1970 and 1985.

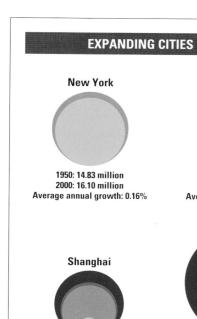

New York
1950: 14.83 million
2000: 16.10 million
Average annual growth: 0.16%

London
1950: 8.35 million
2000: 10.79 million
Average annual growth: 0.51%

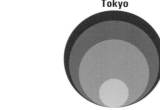

Tokyo
1950: 6.25 million
2000: 21.32 million
Average annual growth: 2.5%

Buenos Aires
1950: 5.25 million
2000: 13.05 million
Average annual growth: 1.8%

Calcutta

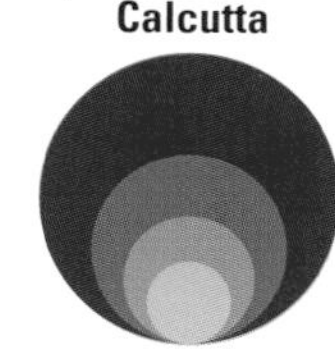

1950: 4.45 million
2000: 15.94 million
Average annual growth: 2.6%

Shanghai
1950: 4.3 million
2000: 14.69 million
Average annual growth: 2.5%

Mexico City

1950: 2.97 million
2000: 24.44 million
Average annual growth: 4.3%

Rio de Janeiro

1950: 2.94 million
2000: 13.0 million
Average annual growth: 3.0%

São Paulo

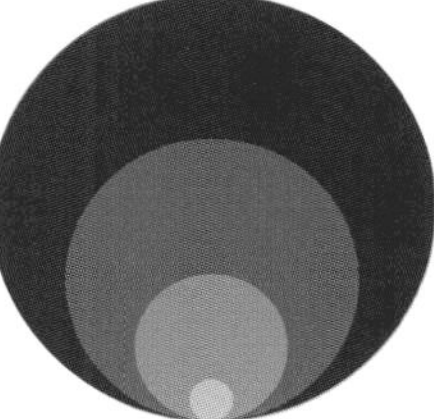

1950: 2.28 million
2000: 23.6 million
Average annual growth: 4.8%

Seoul

1950: 1.45 million
2000: 12.97 million
Average annual growth: 4.5%

Each set of circles illustrates a city's size in 1950, 1970, 1985 and 2000. In most cases, expansion has been steady and, often, explosive. New York and London, however, went through patches of negative growth during the period. In New York, the world's largest city in 1950, population reached a peak around 1970. London shrank slightly between 1970 and 1985 before resuming a very modest rate of increase. In both cases, the divergence from world trends can be explained in part by counting methods: each is at the centre of a great agglomeration, and definitions of where 'city limits' lie may vary over time. But their relative decline also matches a pattern often seen in mature cities in the developed world, where urbanization, already at a very high level, has reached a plateau.

CITIES IN DANGER

As the decade of the 1980s advanced, most industrial countries, alarmed by acid rain and urban smog, took significant steps to limit air pollution. These controls, however, are expensive to install and difficult to enforce, and clean air remains a luxury most developed as well as developing cities must live without.

Those taking part in the United Nations' Global Environment Monitoring System (see right) frequently show dangerous levels of pollutants ranging from soot to sulphur dioxide and photochemical smog; air in the majority of cities without such sampling equipment is likely to be at least as bad.

URBAN AIR POLLUTION

The world's most polluted cities: number of days each year when sulphur dioxide levels exceeded the WHO threshold of 150 micrograms per cubic metre (averaged over 4 to 15 years, 1970s – 1980s)

Sulphur dioxide is the main pollutant associated with industrial cities. According to the World Health Organization, more than seven days in a year above 150 µg per cubic metre bring a serious risk of respiratory disease: at least 600 million people live in urban areas where SO_2 concentrations regularly reach damaging levels.

Manila, Philippines
Calcutta, India
Milan, Italy
Zagreb, Croatia
Guangzhou, China
Madrid, Spain
Peking (Beijing), China
Xian, China
Seoul, South Korea
Tehran, Iran
Shenyang, China
120 90 60 30

INFORMAL CITIZENS

Proportion of population living in squatter settlements, selected cities in the developing world (1980s)

Urbanization in most Third World countries has been coming about far faster than local governments can provide services and accommodation for the new city dwellers. Many – in some cities, most – find their homes in improvised squatter settlements, often unconnected to power, water and sanitation networks. Yet despite their ramshackle housing and marginal legality, these communities are often the most dynamic part of a city economy. They are also growing in size; and given the squatters' reluctance to be counted by tax-demanding authorities, the percentages shown here are likely to be underestimates.

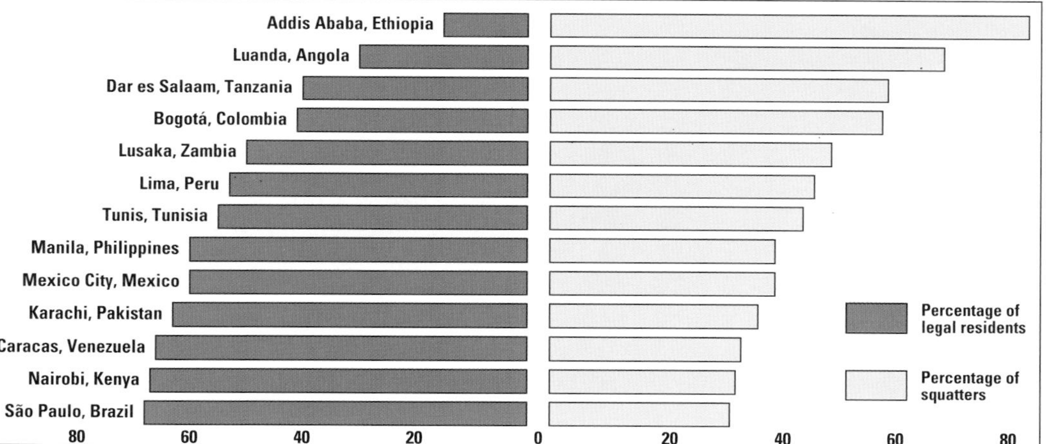

Addis Ababa, Ethiopia
Luanda, Angola
Dar es Salaam, Tanzania
Bogotá, Colombia
Lusaka, Zambia
Lima, Peru
Tunis, Tunisia
Manila, Philippines
Mexico City, Mexico
Karachi, Pakistan
Caracas, Venezuela
Nairobi, Kenya
São Paulo, Brazil
80 60 40 20 0 20 40 60 80
Percentage of legal residents
Percentage of squatters

URBAN ADVANTAGES

Despite overcrowding and poor housing, living standards in the developing world's cities are almost invariably better than in the surrounding countryside. Resources – financial, material and administrative – are concentrated in the towns, which are usually also the centres of political activity and pressure. Governments – frequently unstable, and rarely established on a solid democratic base – are usually more responsive to urban discontent than rural misery.

In many countries, especially in Africa, food prices are often kept artificially low, appeasing underemployed urban masses at the expense of agricultural development. The imbalance encourages further cityward migration, helping to account for the astonishing rate of post-1950 urbanization and putting great strain on the ability of many nations to provide even modest improvements for their people.

RELATIVE MORTALITY

Infant deaths per 1,000 live births in rural and urban areas of selected developing countries (1986–88)

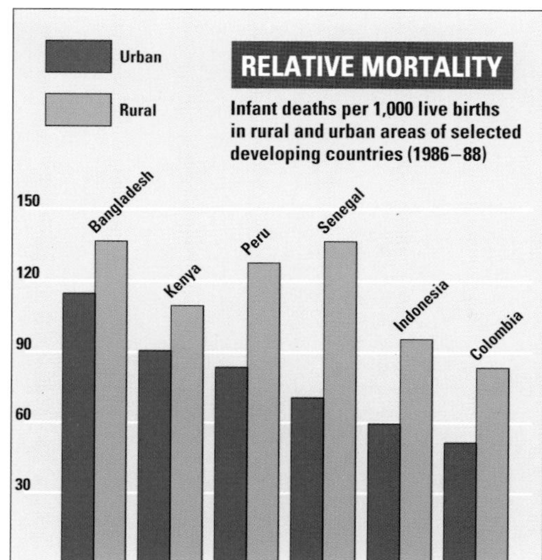

Urban
Rural
150
120
90
60
30
Bangladesh
Kenya
Peru
Senegal
Indonesia
Colombia

RELATIVE LITERACY

Adult literacy rates (%) in urban and rural areas of selected developing countries (1986–88)

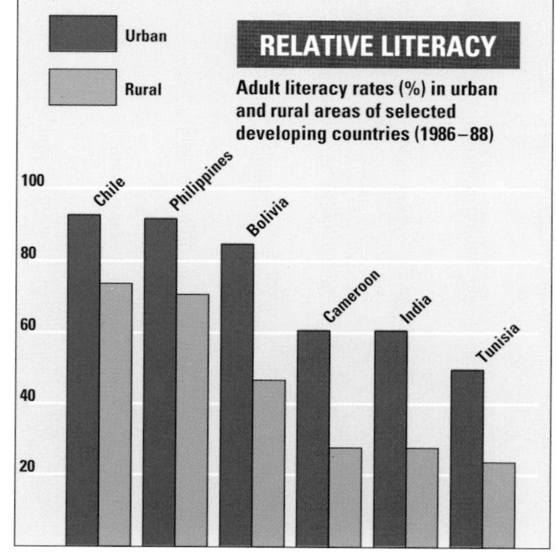

Urban
Rural
100
80
60
40
20
Chile
Philippines
Bolivia
Cameroon
India
Tunisia

LARGEST CITIES

The world's most populous cities, in millions of inhabitants, based on estimates for the year 2000*

City	Population
1. Mexico City	24.4
2. São Paulo	23.6
3. Tokyo-Yokohama	21.3
4. New York	16.1
5. Calcutta	15.9
6. Bombay	15.4
7. Shanghai	14.7
8. Tehran	13.7
9. Jakarta	13.2
10. Buenos Aires	13.1
11. Rio de Janeiro	13.0
12. Seoul	13.0
13. Delhi	12.8
14. Lagos	12.4
15. Cairo-Giza	11.8
16. Karachi	11.6
17. Manila-Quezon	11.5
18. Peking (Beijing)	11.5
19. Dhaka	11.3
20. Osaka-Kobe	11.2
21. Los Angeles	10.9
22. London	10.8
23. Bangkok	10.3
24. Moscow	10.1
25. Tientsin (Tianjin)	10.0
26. Lima-Callao	8.8
27. Paris	8.8
28. Milan	8.7
29. Madras	7.8
30. Baghdad	7.7
31. Chicago	7.0
32. Bogotá	6.9
33. Hong Kong	6.1
34. St Petersburg	5.8
35. Pusan	5.8
36. Santiago	5.6
37. Shenyang	5.5
38. Madrid	5.4
39. Naples	4.5
40. Philadelphia	4.3

[City populations are based on urban agglomerations rather than legal city limits. In some cases, such as Tokyo-Yokohama and Cairo-Giza, where two adjacent cities have merged into one concentration, they have been regarded as a single unit.]

* For list of largest cities in 1993, see page XI

CARTOGRAPHY BY PHILIP'S. COPYRIGHT REED INTERNATIONAL BOOKS LTD

PEOPLE: THE HUMAN FAMILY

20: POPULATION DENSITY

28: THE WORLD'S REFUGEES
WAR SINCE 1945

29: UNITED NATIONS
INTERNATIONAL ORGANIZATIONS

46: THE HISTORY OF HUMAN EXPANSION

Strictly speaking, all human beings belong to a single race – *Homo sapiens* has no subspecies. But although all humans are interfertile, anthropologists and geneticists distinguish three main racial types: Caucasoid, Negroid and Mongoloid. Racial differences reflect not so much evolutionary origin as long periods of separation.

Racial affinities are not always obvious. The Caucasoid group stems from Europe, North Africa and India, but still includes Australian aboriginals within its broad type; Mongoloid peoples comprise American Indians and Eskimos as well as most Chinese, central Asians and Malays; Negroids are mostly of African origin, but also include the Papuan peoples of New Guinea.

Migration in modern times has mingled racial groups to an unprecedented extent, and most nations now have some degree of racially mixed population.

Language is almost the definition of a particular human culture; the world has well over 5,000, most of them with only a few hundred thousand speakers. In one important sense, all languages are equal; although different vocabularies and linguistic structures greatly influence patterns of thought, all true human languages can carry virtually unlimited information. But even if, for example, there is no theoretical difference in the communicative power of English and one of the 500 or more tribal languages of Papua New Guinea, an English speaker has access to much more of the global culture than a Papuan who knows no other tongue.

Like language, religion encourages the internal cohesion of a single human group at the expense of creating gulfs of incomprehension between different groups. All religions satisfy a deep-seated human need, assigning men and women to a comprehensible place in what most of them still consider a divinely ordered world. But religion is also a means by which a culture can assert its individuality; the startling rise of Islam in the late 20th century is partly a response by large sections of the developing world to the secular, Western-inspired world order from which many non-Western peoples feel excluded. Like uncounted millions of human beings before them, they find in their religion not only a personal faith but also a powerful group identity.

WORLD MIGRATION

The greatest voluntary migration was the colonization of North America by 30–35 million European settlers during the 19th century. The greatest forced migration involved 9–11 million Africans taken as slaves to America 1550–1860. The migrations shown on the map are mostly international as population movements within borders are not usually recorded. Many of the statistics are necessarily estimates as so many refugees and migrant workers enter countries illegally and unrecorded. Emigrants may have a variety of motives for leaving, thus making it difficult to distinguish between voluntary and involuntary migrations.

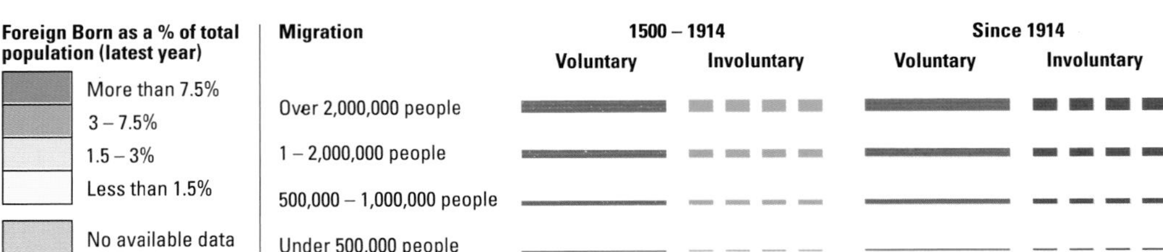

Foreign Born as a % of total population (latest year)
More than 7.5%
3 – 7.5%
1.5 – 3%
Less than 1.5%
No available data
Migration
1500 – 1914
Voluntary
Involuntary
Since 1914
Voluntary
Involuntary
Over 2,000,000 people
1 – 2,000,000 people
500,000 – 1,000,000 people
Under 500,000 people

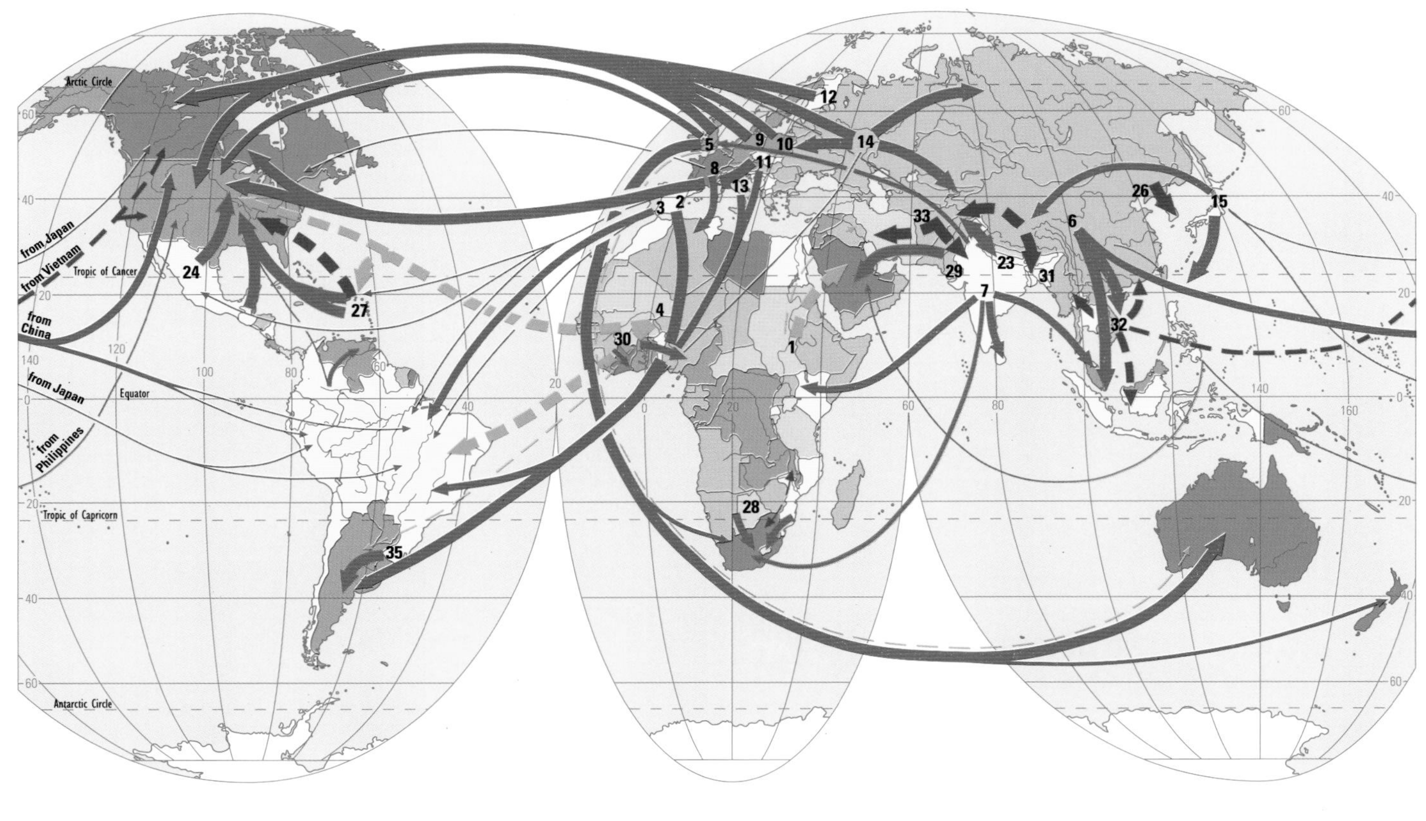

Arctic Circle
Tropic of Cancer
Equator
Tropic of Capricorn
Antarctic Circle
from Japan
from Vietnam
from China
from Japan
from Philippines

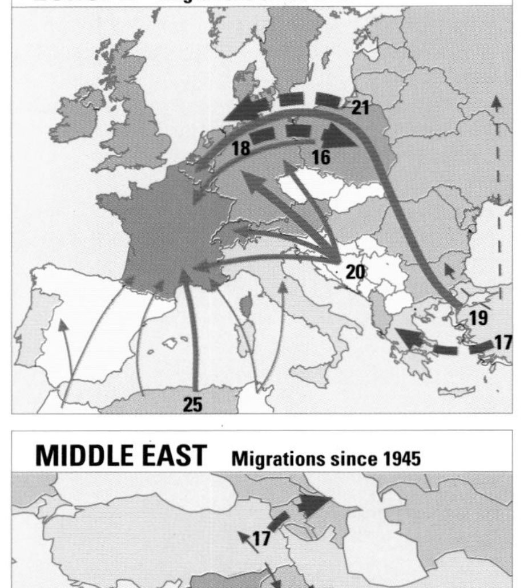

EUROPE Migrations since 1918
MIDDLE EAST Migrations since 1945

BUILDING THE USA

US Immigration 1820–1990

'Give me your tired, your poor/Your huddled masses yearning to breathe free....'

So starts Emma Lazarus's poem *The New Colossus*, inscribed on the Statue of Liberty. For decades the USA was the magnet that attracted millions of immigrants, notably from Central and Eastern Europe, the flow peaking in the early years of this century.

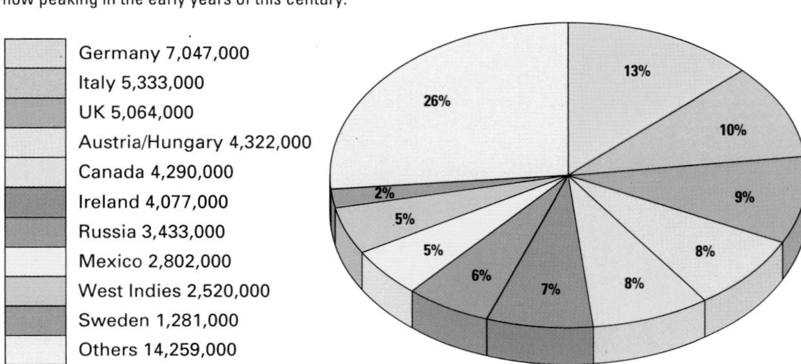

Germany 7,047,000
Italy 5,333,000
UK 5,064,000
Austria/Hungary 4,322,000
Canada 4,290,000
Ireland 4,077,000
Russia 3,433,000
Mexico 2,802,000
West Indies 2,520,000
Sweden 1,281,000
Others 14,259,000
26%
13%
10%
9%
8%
8%
7%
6%
5%
5%
2%

Major world migrations since 1500 (over 1,000,000 people)

1. North African and East African slaves to Arabia (4.3m) 1500–1900
2. Spanish to South and Central America (2.3m) 1530–1914
3. Portuguese to Brazil (1.4m) 1530–1914
4. West African slaves to South America (4.6m) 1550–1860
   to Caribbean (4m) 1580–1860
   to North and Central America (1m) 1650–1820
5. British and Irish to North America (13.5m) 1620–1914
   to Australasia and South Africa (3m) 1790–1914
6. Chinese to South-east Asia (22m) 1820–1914
   to North America (1m) 1880–1914
7. Indian migrant workers (3m) 1850–1914
8. French to North Africa (1.5m) 1850–1914
9. Germans to North America (5m) 1850–1914
10. Poles to North America (3.6m) 1850–1914
11. Austro-Hungarians to North America (3.2m) 1850–1914
    to Western Europe (3.4m) 1850–1914
    to South America (1.8m) 1850–1914
12. Scandinavians to North America (2.7m) 1850–1914
13. Italians to North America (5m) 1860–1914
    to South America (3.7m) 1860–1914
14. Russians to North America (2.2m) 1880–1914
    to Western Europe (2.2m) 1880–1914
    to Siberia (6m) 1880–1914
    to Central Asia (4m) 1880–1914
15. Japanese to Eastern Asia, South-east Asia and America (8m) 1900–1914
16. Poles to Western Europe (1m) 1920–1940
17. Greeks and Armenians from Turkey (1.6m) 1922–1923
18. European Jews to extermination camps (5m) 1940–1944
19. Turks to Western Europe (1.9m) 1940–
20. Yugoslavs to Western Europe (2m) 1940–
21. Germans to Western Europe (9.8m) 1945–1947
22. Palestinian refugees (2m) 1947–
23. Indian and Pakistani refugees (15m) 1947
24. Mexicans to North America (9m) 1950–
25. North Africans to Western Europe (1.1m) 1950–
26. Korean refugees (5m) 1950–1954
27. Latin Americans and West Indians to North America (4.7m) 1960–
28. Migrant workers to South Africa (1.5m) 1960–
29. Indians and Pakistanis to The Gulf (2.4m) 1970–
30. Migrant workers to Nigeria and Ivory Coast (3m) 1970–
31. Bangladeshi and Pakistani refugees (2m) 1972
32. Vietnamese and Cambodian refugees (1.5m) 1975–
33. Afghan refugees (6.1m) 1979–
34. Egyptians to The Gulf and Libya (2.9m) 1980–
35. Migrant workers to Argentina (2m) 1980–

CARTOGRAPHY BY PHILIP'S. COPYRIGHT REED INTERNATIONAL BOOKS LTD

LANGUAGE

INDO-EUROPEAN FAMILY
- 1 Balto-Slavic group (incl. Russian, Ukrainian)
- 2 Germanic group (incl. English, German)
- 3 Celtic group
- 4 Greek
- 5 Albanian
- 6 Iranian group
- 7 Armenian
- 8 Romance group (incl. Spanish, Portuguese, French, Italian)
- 9 Indo-Aryan group (incl. Hindi, Bengali, Urdu, Punjabi, Marathi)

10 CAUCASIAN FAMILY

AFRO-ASIATIC FAMILY
- 11 Semitic group (incl. Arabic)
- 12 Kushitic group
- 13 Berber group

14 KHOISAN FAMILY

15 NIGER-CONGO FAMILY

16 NILO-SAHARAN FAMILY

17 URALIC FAMILY

ALTAIC FAMILY
- 18 Turkic group
- 19 Mongolian group
- 20 Tungus-Manchu group
- 21 Japanese and Korean

SINO-TIBETAN FAMILY
- 22 Sinitic (Chinese) languages
- 23 Tibetic-Burmic languages

24 TAI FAMILY

AUSTRO-ASIATIC FAMILY
- 25 Mon-Khmer group
- 26 Munda group
- 27 Vietnamese

28 DRAVIDIAN FAMILY (incl. Telugu, Tamil)

29 AUSTRONESIAN FAMILY (incl. Malay-Indonesian)

30 OTHER LANGUAGES

OFFICIAL LANGUAGES

Language	Total population	World %
English	1,400m	27.0%
Chinese	1,070m	19.1%
Hindi	700m	13.5%
Spanish	280m	5.4%
Russian	270m	5.2%
French	220m	4.2%
Arabic	170m	3.3%
Portuguese	160m	3.0%
Malay	160m	3.0%
Bengali	150m	2.9%
Japanese	120m	2.3%

Languages form a kind of tree of development, splitting from a few ancient proto-tongues into branches that have grown apart and further divided with the passage of time. English and Hindi, for example, both belong to the great Indo-European family, although the relationship is only apparent after much analysis and comparison with non-Indo-European languages such as Chinese or Arabic; Hindi is part of the Indo-Aryan subgroup, whereas English is a member of Indo-European's Germanic branch; French, another Indo-European tongue, traces its descent through the Latin, or Romance, branch. A few languages – Basque is one example – have no apparent links with any other, living or dead. Most modern languages, of course, have acquired enormous quantities of vocabulary from each other.

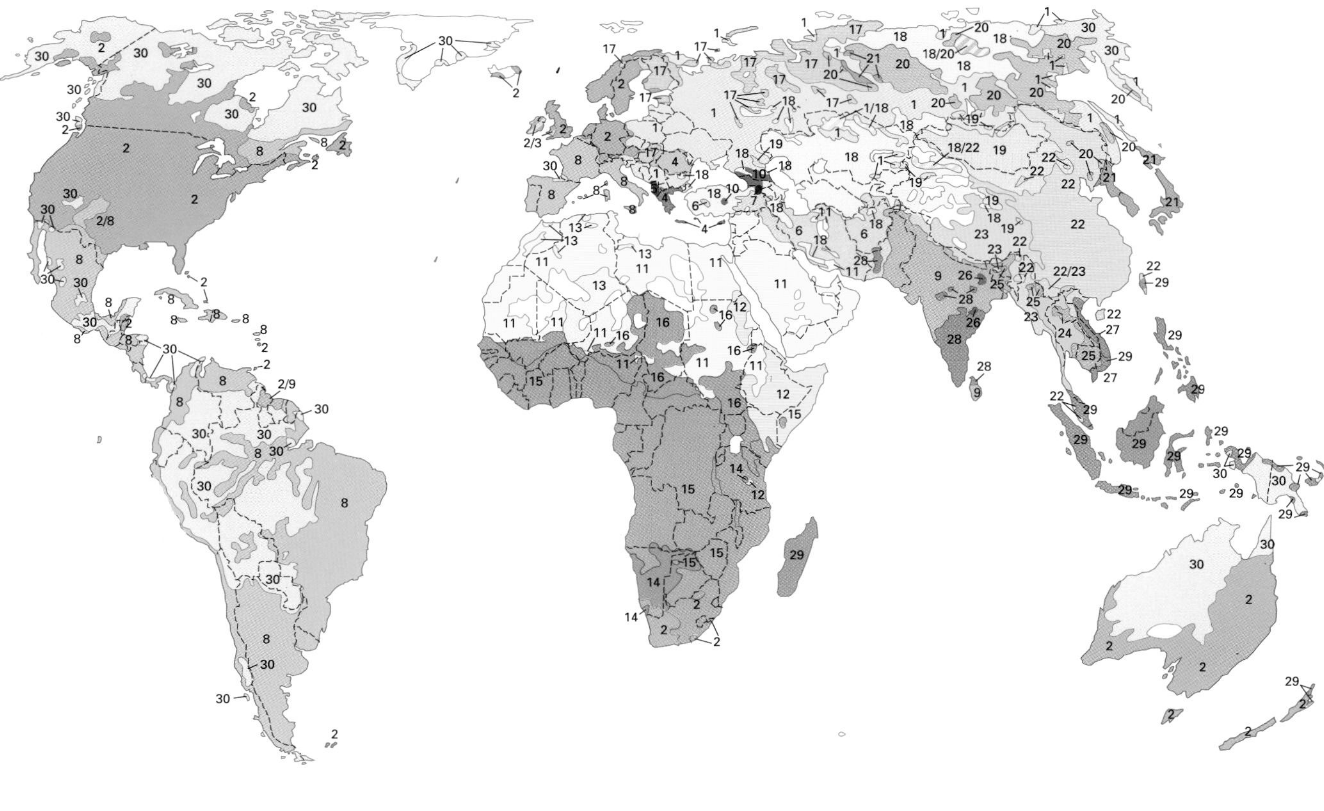

MOTHER TONGUES

Native speakers of the major languages, in millions (1989)

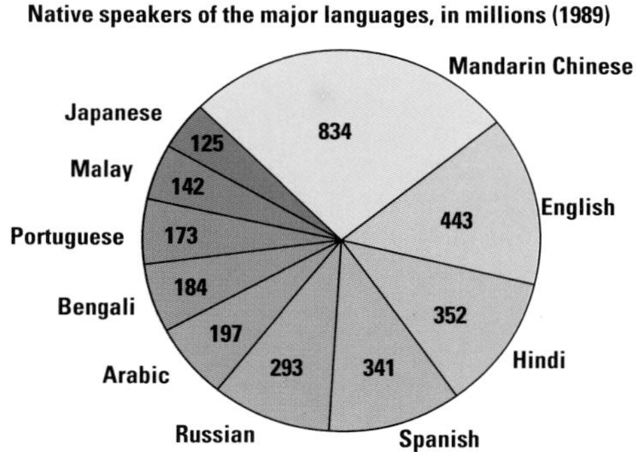

Mandarin Chinese 834
English 443
Hindi 352
Spanish 341
Russian 293
Arabic 197
Bengali 184
Portuguese 173
Malay 142
Japanese 125

RELIGION

- Roman Catholicism
- Orthodox and other Eastern Churches
- Protestantism
- Sunni Islam
- Shia Islam
- Buddhism
- Hinduism
- Confucianism
- Judaism
- Shintoism
- Primitive Religions

Religions are not as easily mapped as the physical contours of landscape. Divisions are often blurred and frequently overlapping: most nations include people of many different faiths – or no faith at all. Some religions, like Islam and Christianity, have proselytes worldwide; others, like Hinduism and Confucianism, are restricted to a particular area, though modern migrations have taken some Indians and Chinese very far from their cultural origins. It is also difficult to show the degree to which religion exercises control over daily life: Christian Western Europe, for example, is nowadays far less dominated by its religion than are the Islamic nations of the Middle East. Similarly, figures for the major faiths' adherents make no distinction between nominal believers enrolled at birth and those for whom religion is a vital part of existence.

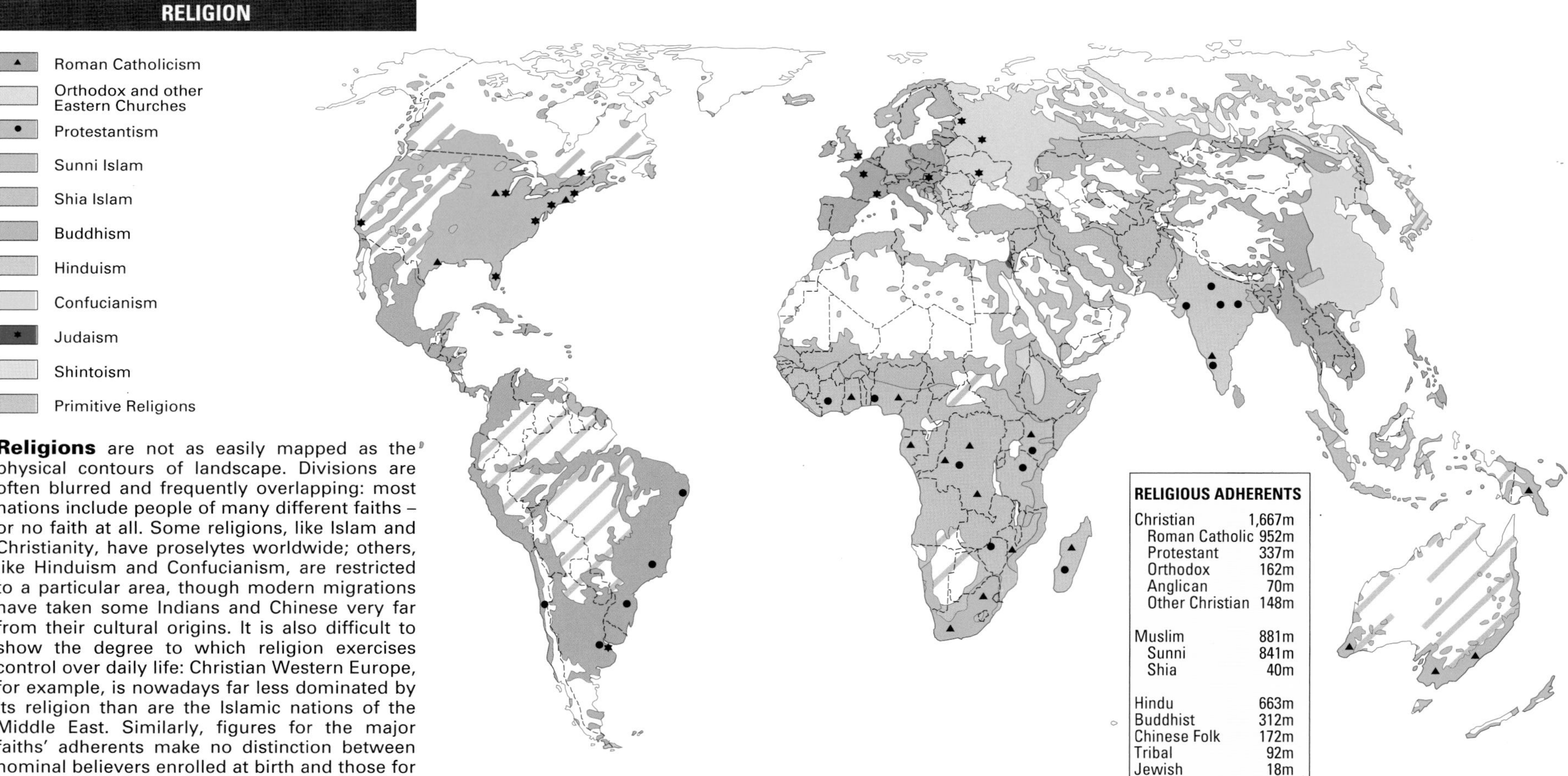

RELIGIOUS ADHERENTS

Christian	1,667m
Roman Catholic	952m
Protestant	337m
Orthodox	162m
Anglican	70m
Other Christian	148m
Muslim	881m
Sunni	841m
Shia	40m
Hindu	663m
Buddhist	312m
Chinese Folk	172m
Tribal	92m
Jewish	18m
Sikhs	17m

CARTOGRAPHY BY PHILIP'S. COPYRIGHT REED INTERNATIONAL BOOKS LTD

PEOPLE: CONFLICT & CO-OPERATION

26: MIGRATION
27: RELIGION
46: HUMAN EXPANSION

Humans are social animals, rarely functioning well except in groups. Evolution has made them so: hunter-gatherers in co-operative bands were far more effective than animals that prowled alone. Agriculture, the building of cities and industrialization are all developments that depended on human co-operative ability – and in turn increased the need for it.

Unfortunately, human groups do not always co-operate so well with other human groups, and friction between them sometimes leads to co-operatively organized violence. War is itself a very human activity, with no real equivalent in any other species. Always murderous, it is sometimes purposeful and may even be very effective. The colonization of the Americas and Australia, for example, was in effect the waging of aggressive war by well-armed Europeans against indigenous peoples incapable of offering a serious defence.

Most often, war achieves little but death and ruin. The great 20th-century wars accomplished nothing for the nations involved in them, although the world paid a price of between 50 and 100 million dead as well as immense material damage. The relative peace in the postwar developed world is at least partly due to the nuclear weapons with which rival powers have armed themselves – weapons so powerful that their use would leave a scarcely habitable planet with no meaningful distinction between victor and vanquished.

Yet warfare remains endemic: the second half of the 20th century was one of the bloodiest periods in history, and death by organized violence remains unhappily common. The map below attempts to show the serious conflicts that have scarred the Earth since 1945. Most are civil wars in poor countries, rather than international conflicts between rich ones; some of them are still unresolved, while others, like apparently extinct volcanoes, may erupt again at intervals, adding to the world's miserable population of refugees.

THE WORLD'S REFUGEES

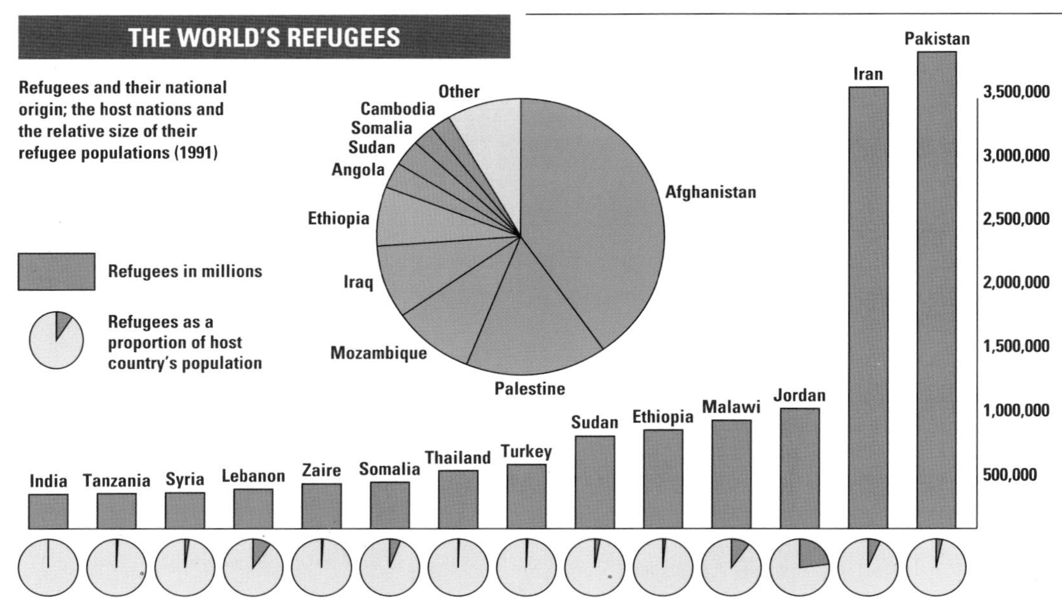
Refugees and their national origin; the host nations and the relative size of their refugee populations (1991)
Refugees in millions
Refugees as a proportion of host country's population
Other
Cambodia
Somalia
Sudan
Angola
Ethiopia
Iraq
Mozambique
Palestine
Afghanistan
India
Tanzania
Syria
Lebanon
Zaire
Somalia
Thailand
Turkey
Sudan
Ethiopia
Malawi
Jordan
Iran
Pakistan
3,500,000
3,000,000
2,500,000
2,000,000
1,500,000
1,000,000
500,000

The pie-chart shows the origins of the world's refugees, while the bar-chart shows their destinations. According to the United Nations High Commissioner for Refugees, in 1990 there were almost 15 million refugees, a number that has continued to increase and is almost certain to be amplified during the decade. Some have fled from climatic change, some from economic disaster and others from political persecution; the great majority, however, are the victims of war.

All but a few who make it overseas seek asylum in neighbouring countries, which are often the least equipped to deal with them and where they are rarely welcome. Lacking any rights or power, they frequently become an embarrassment and a burden to their reluctant hosts.

Usually, the best any refugee can hope for is rudimentary food and shelter in temporary camps that all to often become semi-permanent, with little prospect of assimilation by host populations: many Palestinians, for example, have been forced to live in camps since 1948.

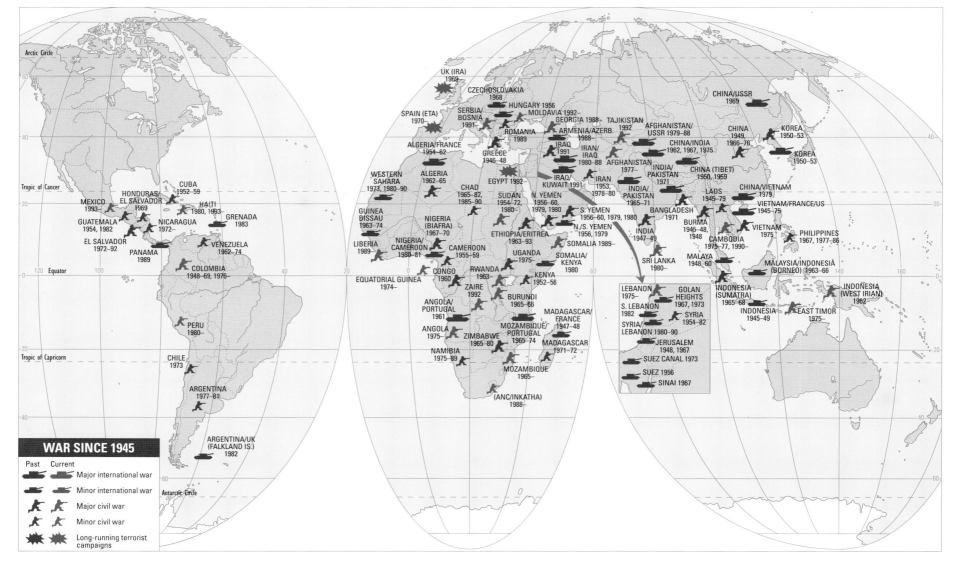

WAR SINCE 1945

Past / Current
Major international war
Minor international war
Major civil war
Minor civil war
Long-running terrorist campaigns

Arctic Circle
Tropic of Cancer
Equator
Tropic of Capricorn
Antarctic Circle

MEXICO 1993–
GUATEMALA 1954, 1982
HONDURAS/EL SALVADOR 1969
EL SALVADOR 1972–92
NICARAGUA 1972–
PANAMA 1989
CUBA 1952–59
HAITI 1980, 1993–
GRENADA 1983
VENEZUELA 1962–74
COLOMBIA 1948–69, 1976–
PERU 1980–
CHILE 1973
ARGENTINA 1977–81
ARGENTINA/UK (FALKLAND IS.) 1982

UK (IRA) 1969–
SPAIN (ETA) 1970–
CZECHOSLOVAKIA 1968
HUNGARY 1956
MOLDAVIA 1992–
SERBIA/BOSNIA 1991–
ROMANIA 1989
GREECE 1946–48
GEORGIA 1988–
ARMENIA/AZERB. 1988–
TAJIKISTAN 1992
AFGHANISTAN/USSR 1979–88
CHINA/USSR 1969
CHINA 1949, 1966–76
KOREA 1950–53
KOREA 1950–53
CHINA/INDIA 1962, 1967, 1975
IRAQ 1991
IRAN/IRAQ 1980–88
AFGHANISTAN 1977–
INDIA/PAKISTAN 1971
CHINA (TIBET) 1950, 1959
IRAQ/KUWAIT 1991
IRAN 1953, 1978–80
INDIA/PAKISTAN 1965–71
LAOS 1945–79
CHINA/VIETNAM 1979
VIETNAM/FRANCE/US 1945–75
ALGERIA/FRANCE 1954–62
WESTERN SAHARA 1973, 1980–90
ALGERIA 1962–65
EGYPT 1992–
CHAD 1965–82, 1985–90
SUDAN 1954–72, 1980–
N. YEMEN 1956–60, 1979, 1980
S. YEMEN 1956–60, 1979, 1980
N./S. YEMEN 1956, 1979
BANGLADESH 1971
BURMA 1945–48, 1948
VIETNAM 1975
PHILIPPINES 1967, 1977–86
INDIA 1947–49
CAMBODIA 1975–77, 1990–
GUINEA BISSAU 1963–74
NIGERIA (BIAFRA) 1967–70
ETHIOPIA/ERITREA 1963–93
SOMALIA 1989–
LIBERIA 1989–
NIGERIA/CAMEROON 1980–81
CAMEROON 1955–59
UGANDA 1975–
SOMALIA/KENYA 1980
SRI LANKA 1980–
MALAYA 1948–60
MALAYSIA/INDONESIA (BORNEO) 1963–66
EQUATORIAL GUINEA 1974–
CONGO 1960
RWANDA 1963–
KENYA 1952–56
INDONESIA (SUMATRA) 1965–68
INDONESIA (WEST IRIAN) 1962
INDONESIA 1945–49
EAST TIMOR 1975–
ZAIRE 1992
BURUNDI 1965–66
ANGOLA/PORTUGAL 1961
MADAGASCAR/FRANCE 1947–48
ANGOLA 1975–
ZIMBABWE 1965–80
MOZAMBIQUE/PORTUGAL 1965–74
MADAGASCAR 1971–72
NAMIBIA 1975–89
MOZAMBIQUE 1965–
(ANC/INKATHA) 1988–

LEBANON 1975–
S. LEBANON 1982
SYRIA/LEBANON 1980–90
GOLAN HEIGHTS 1967, 1973
SYRIA 1954–82
JERUSALEM 1948, 1967
SUEZ CANAL 1973
SUEZ 1956
SINAI 1967

CARTOGRAPHY BY PHILIP'S. COPYRIGHT REED INTERNATIONAL BOOKS LTD

UNITED NATIONS

The United Nations Organization was born as World War II drew to its conclusion. Six years of strife had strengthened the world's desire for peace, but an effective international organization was needed to help achieve it. That body would replace the League of Nations which, since its inception in 1920, had signally failed to curb the aggression of at least some of its member nations. At the United Nations Conference on International Organization held in San Francisco, the United Nations Charter was drawn up. Ratified by the Security Council and signed by the 51 original members, it came into effect on 24 October 1945.

The Charter set out the aims of the organization: to maintain peace and security, and develop friendly relations between nations; to achieve international co-operation in solving economic, social, cultural and humanitarian problems; to promote respect for human rights and fundamental freedoms; and to harmonize the activities of nations in order to achieve these common goals.

By 1993, the UN had expanded to 183 member countries; it is the largest international political organization, employing 23,000 people worldwide; its headquarters in New York accounts for 7,000 staff and it also has major offices in Rome, Geneva and Vienna.

The United Nations has six principal organs:

The General Assembly
The forum at which member nations discuss moral and political issues affecting world development, peace and security meets annually in September, under a newly-elected President whose tenure lasts one year. Any member can bring business to the agenda, and each member nation has one vote. Decisions are made by simple majority, save for matters of very great importance, when a two-thirds majority is required.

The Security Council
A legislative and executive body, the Security Council is the primary instrument for establishing and maintaining international peace by attempting to settle disputes between nations. It has the power to dispatch UN forces to stop aggression, and member nations undertake to make armed forces, assistance and facilities available as required. The Security Council has ten temporary members elected by the General Assembly for two-year terms, and five permanent members – China, France, Russia, UK and USA.

The Economic and Social Council
By far the largest United Nations executive, the Council operates as a conduit between the General Assembly and the many United Nations agencies it instructs to implement Assembly decisions, and whose work it co-ordinates. The Council also sets up commissions to examine economic conditions, collects data and issues studies and reports, and may make recommendations to the Assembly.

The Secretariat
This is the staff of the United Nations, and its task is to administer the policies and programmes of the UN and its organs, and assist and advise the Head of the Secretariat, the Secretary-General – a full-time, non-political, appointment made by the General Assembly.

The Trusteeship Council
The Council administers trust territories with the aim of promoting their advancement. Only one remains – the Trust Territory of the Pacific Is. (Palau), administered by the USA.

The International Court of Justice (the World Court)
The World Court is the judicial organ of the United Nations. It deals only with United Nations disputes and all members are subject to its jurisdiction. There are 15 judges, elected for nine-year terms by the General Assembly and the Security Council. The Court sits in The Hague.

United Nations agencies and programmes, and intergovernmental agencies co-ordinated by the UN, contribute to harmonious world development. Social and humanitarian operations include:

United Nations Development Programme (UNDP) Plans and funds projects to help developing countries make better use of resources.
United Nations International Childrens' Fund (UNICEF) Created at the General Assembly's first session in 1945 to help children in the aftermath of World War II, it now provides basic health care and aid worldwide.
United Nations Fund for Population Activities (UNFPA) Promotes awareness of population issues and family planning, providing appropriate assistance.
Food and Agriculture Organization (FAO) Aims to raise living standards and nutrition levels in rural areas by improving food production and distribution.
United Nations Educational, Scientific and Cultural Organization (UNESCO) Promotes international co-operation through broader and better education.
World Health Organization (WHO) Promotes and provides for better health care, public and environmental health and medical research.

Membership There are seven independent states which are not members of the UN – Kiribati, Nauru, Switzerland, Taiwan, Tonga, Tuvalu and Vatican City. Official languages are Chinese, English, French, Russian, Spanish and Arabic.
Funding The UN budget for 1994–95 is US $2.6 billion. Contributions are assessed by the members' ability to pay, with the maximum 25% of the total, the minimum 0.01%. Contributions for 1992–94 were: USA 25%, Japan 12.45%, Germany 8.93%, Russia 6.71%, France 6%, UK 5.02%, Italy 4.29%, Canada 3.11% (others 28.49%).
Peacekeeping The UN has been involved in 33 peacekeeping operations worldwide since 1948 and there are currently 17 areas of UN patrol. In July 1993 there were 80,146 'blue berets' from 74 countries.

United Nations agencies are involved in many aspects of international trade, safety and security:

General Agreement on Tariffs and Trade (GATT) Sponsors international trade negotiations and advocates a common code of conduct.
International Maritime Organization (IMO) Promotes unity amongst merchant shipping, especially in regard to safety, marine pollution and standardization.
International Labour Organization (ILO) Seeks to improve labour conditions and promote productive employment to raise living standards.
World Meteorological Organization (WMO) Promotes co-operation in weather observation, reporting and forecasting.
World Intellectual Property Organization (WIPO) Seeks to protect intellectual property such as artistic copyright, scientific patents and trademarks.
Disarmament Commission Considers and makes recommendations to the General Assembly on disarmament issues.
International Atomic Energy Agency (IAEA) Fosters development of peaceful uses for nuclear energy, establishes safety standards and monitors the destruction of nuclear material designed for military use.

The World Bank comprises three United Nations agencies:

International Monetary Fund (IMF) Cultivates international monetary co-operation and expansion of trade.
International Bank for Reconstruction and Development (IBRD) Provides funds and technical assistance to developing countries.
International Finance Corporation (IFC) Encourages the growth of productive private enterprise in less developed countries.

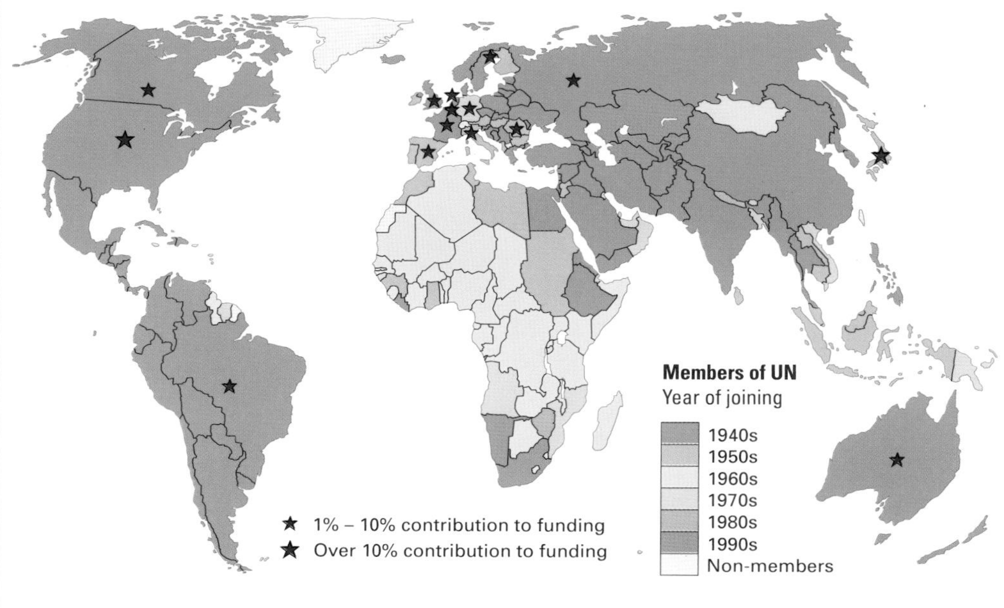

Members of UN
Year of joining
1940s
1950s
1960s
1970s
1980s
1990s
Non-members
★ 1% – 10% contribution to funding
★ Over 10% contribution to funding

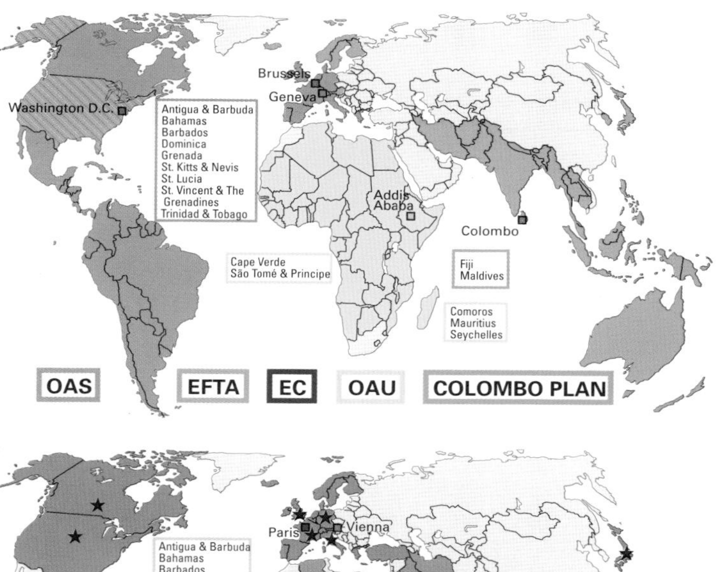

Washington D.C.
Brussels
Geneva
Addis Ababa
Colombo
Antigua & Barbuda
Bahamas
Barbados
Dominica
Grenada
St. Kitts & Nevis
St. Lucia
St. Vincent & The Grenadines
Trinidad & Tobago
Cape Verde
São Tomé & Principe
Fiji
Maldives
Comoros
Mauritius
Seychelles
OAS
EFTA
EC
OAU
COLOMBO PLAN

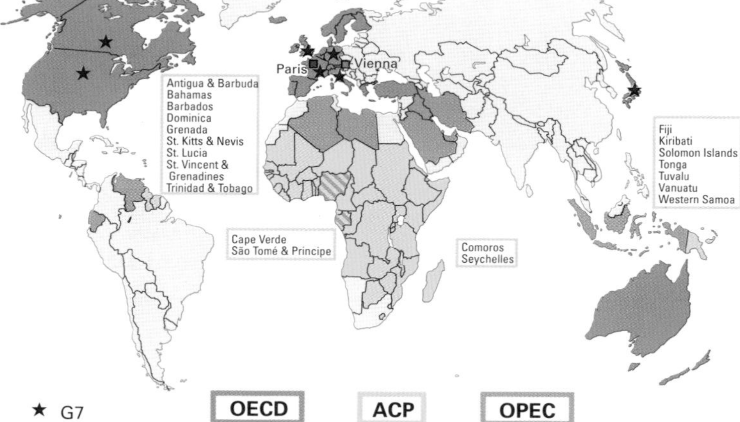

Paris
Vienna
Antigua & Barbuda
Bahamas
Barbados
Dominica
Grenada
St. Kitts & Nevis
St. Lucia
St. Vincent & Grenadines
Trinidad & Tobago
Cape Verde
São Tomé & Principe
Comoros
Seychelles
Fiji
Kiribati
Solomon Islands
Tonga
Tuvalu
Vanuatu
Western Samoa
★ G7
OECD
ACP
OPEC

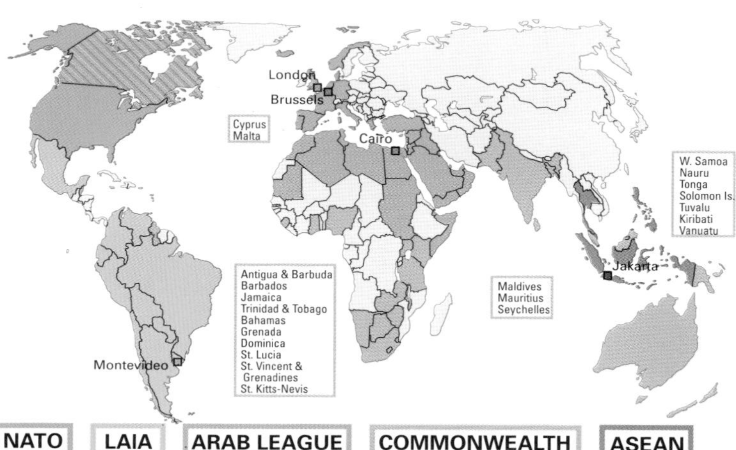

London
Brussels
Cairo
Jakarta
Montevideo
Cyprus
Malta
Antigua & Barbuda
Barbados
Jamaica
Trinidad & Tobago
Bahamas
Grenada
Dominica
St. Lucia
St. Vincent & Grenadines
St. Kitts-Nevis
Maldives
Mauritius
Seychelles
W. Samoa
Nauru
Tonga
Solomon Is.
Tuvalu
Kiribati
Vanuatu
NATO
LAIA
ARAB LEAGUE
COMMONWEALTH
ASEAN

EC As from December 1993 the European Union (EU) refers to matters of foreign policy, security and justice. The European Community (EC) refers to all other matters. The 12 members – Belgium, Denmark, France, Germany, Greece, Ireland, Italy, Luxembourg, Netherlands, Portugal, Spain and the UK – aim to integrate economies, co-ordinate social developments and bring about political union. These members of what is now the world's biggest market share agricultural and industrial policies and tariffs on trade.
EFTA European Free Trade Association (formed in 1960). Portugal left the 'Seven' in 1989 to join the EC.
ACP African-Caribbean-Pacific countries associated with the EC (1963).
NATO North Atlantic Treaty Organization (formed in 1949). It continues after 1991 despite the winding up of the Warsaw Pact.
OAS Organization of American States (1949). It aims to promote social and economic co-operation between developed countries of North America and developing nations of Latin America.
ASEAN Association of South-east Asian Nations (1967).
OAU Organization of African Unity (1963). Its 52 members represent over 90% of Africa's population.
LAIA Latin American Integration Association (1980).
OECD Organization for Economic Co-operation and Development (1961). The 24 major Western free-market economies. 'G7' is its 'inner group' of USA, Canada, Japan, UK, Germany, Italy and France.
COMMONWEALTH The Commonwealth of Nations evolved from the British Empire; it comprises 19 nations recognizing the British monarch as head of state and 32 with their own heads of state.
OPEC Organization of Petroleum Exporting Countries (1960). It controls about three-quarters of the world's oil supply.
ARAB LEAGUE (1945) The League's aim is to promote economic, social, political and military co-operation.
COLOMBO PLAN (1951) Its 26 members aim to promote economic and social development in Asia and the Pacific.

CARTOGRAPHY BY PHILIP'S. COPYRIGHT REED INTERNATIONAL BOOKS LTD

PRODUCTION: AGRICULTURE

14: CLIMATE REGIONS

15: TEMPERATURE AND PRECIPITATION

16: WATER UTILIZATION

17: NATURAL VEGETATION LAND USE BY CONTINENT

36: DIVISION OF EMPLOYMENT

46: HUMAN EXPANSION

The invention of agriculture transformed human existence more than any other development, though it may not have seemed much of an improvement to its first practitioners. Primitive farming require· brutally hard work, and it, tied men and women to a patch of land, highly vulnerable to local weather patterns and to predators, especially human predators – drawbacks still apparent in much of the world today. It is difficult to imagine early humans being interested in such an existence while there were still animals around to hunt and wild seeds and berries to gather. Probably the spur was population pressure, with consequent overhunting and scarcity.

Despite its difficulties, the new life style had a few overwhelming advantages. It supported far larger populations, eventually including substantial cities, with all the varied cultural and economic activities they allowed. Later still, it furnished the surpluses that allowed industrialization – another enormous step in the course of human development. Machines relieved many farmers of their burden of endless toil, and made it possible for relatively small numbers to provide food for more than 5,000 million people.

Now, as in the past, the whole business of farming involves the creation of a severely simplified ecology, under the tutelage and for the benefit of the farmer. Natural plant life is divided into crops, to be protected and nurtured, and weeds, the rest, to be destroyed. From the earliest days, crops were selectively bred to increase their food yield, usually at the expense of their ability to survive, which became the farmer's responsibility; 20th-century plant geneticists have carried the technique to highly productive extremes. Due mainly to new varieties of rice and wheat, world grain production has increased by 70% since 1965, more than doubling in the developing countries, although such high yields demand equally high consumption of fertilizers and pesticides to maintain them. Mechanized farmers in North America and Europe continue to turn out huge surpluses, although not without environmental costs.

Where production is inadequate, the reasons are as likely to be political as agricultural. Africa, the only continent where food production per capita is actually falling, suffers acutely from economic mismanagement, as well as from the perennial problems of war and banditry. Dismal harvests in the USSR, despite its excellent farmland, helped bring about the collapse of the Soviet system.

There are other limits to progress too. Increasing population puts relentless pressure on farmers not only to maintain high yields but also to increase them. Most of the world's potential cropland is already under the plough. The overworking of marginal land is one of the prime causes of desertification; new farmlands burned out of former rainforests are seldom fertile for long. Human numbers may yet outrun the land's ability to feed them, as they did almost 10,000 years ago.

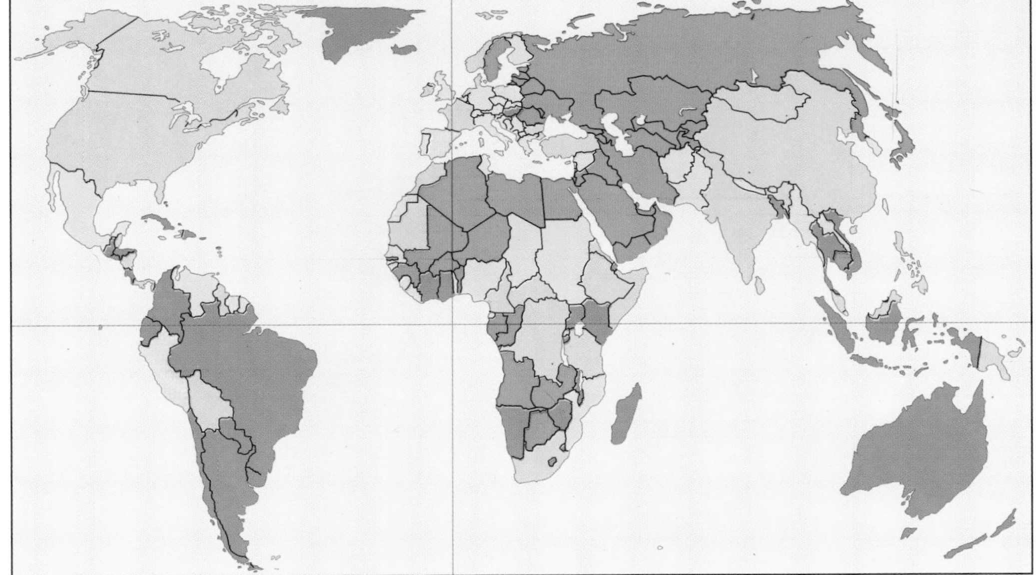

SELF-SUFFICIENCY IN FOOD

Balance of trade in food products as a percentage of total trade in food products (1988)*

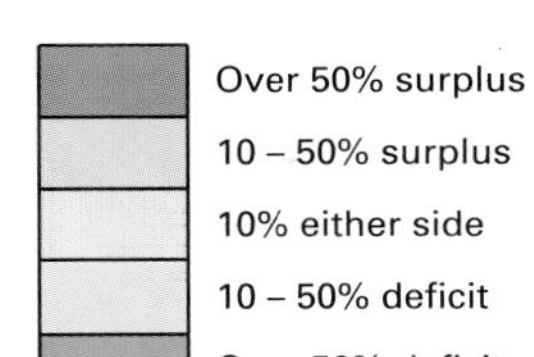

Over 50% surplus
10 – 50% surplus
10% either side
10 – 50% deficit
Over 50% deficit

Most self-sufficient		Least self-sufficient	
Argentina	95%	Algeria	–98%
Zimbabwe	87%	Djibouti	–97%
Honduras	81%	Yemen	–95%
Malawi	81%	Zambia	–95%
Costa Rica	79%	Japan	–91%
Iceland	78%	Gabon	–90%
Chile	75%	Kuwait	–90%
Uruguay	75%	Brunei	–89%
Ecuador	74%	Burkina Faso	–82%

LAND USE

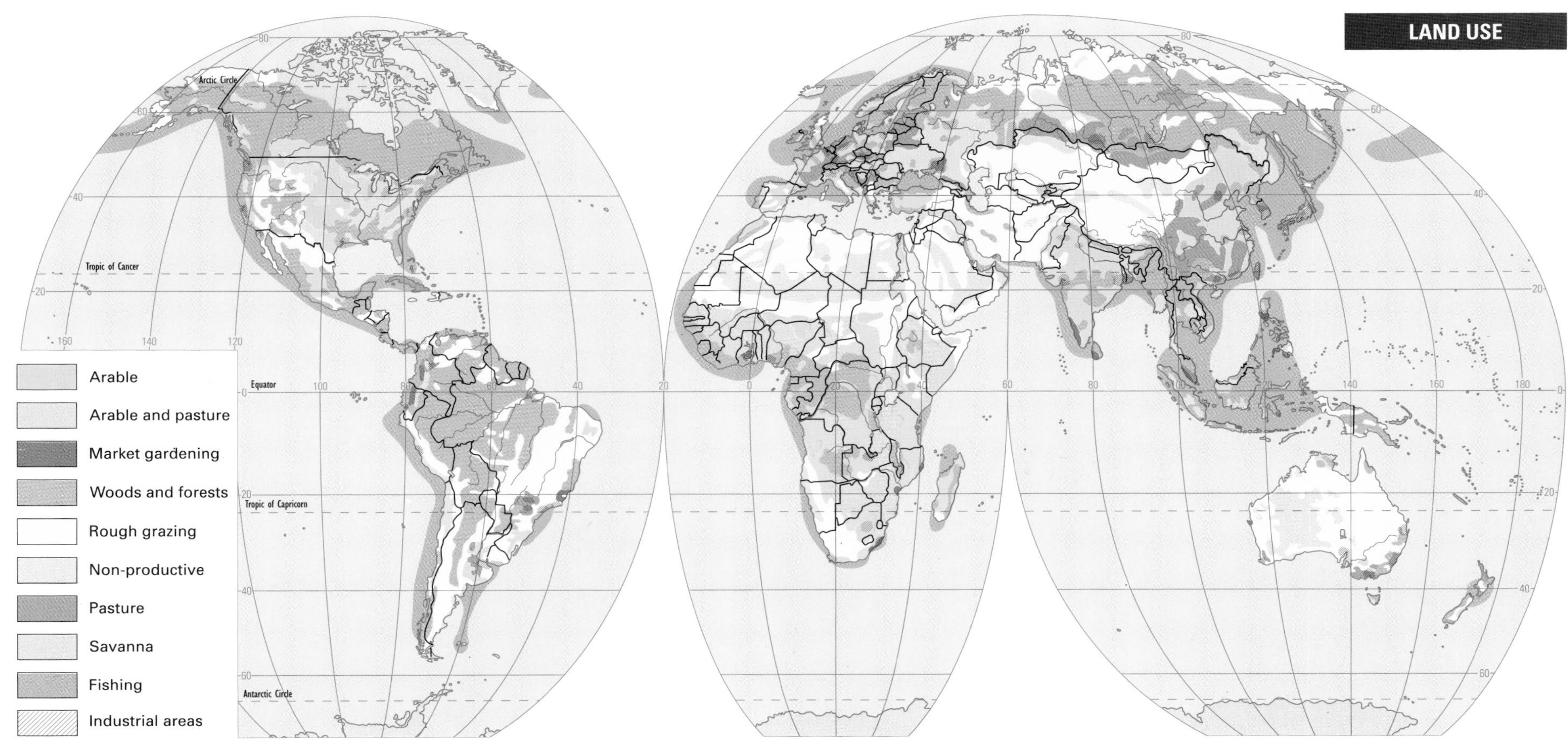

Arctic Circle
Tropic of Cancer
Equator
Tropic of Capricorn
Antarctic Circle
Arable
Arable and pasture
Market gardening
Woods and forests
Rough grazing
Non-productive
Pasture
Savanna
Fishing
Industrial areas

CARTOGRAPHY BY PHILIP'S. COPYRIGHT REED INTERNATIONAL BOOKS LTD

STAPLE CROPS

Separate figures for Russia, Ukraine and the other successors of the former USSR are not yet available

Wheat: Grown in a range of climates, with most varieties – including the highest-quality bread wheats – requiring temperate conditions. Mainly used in baking, it is also used for pasta and breakfast cereals.

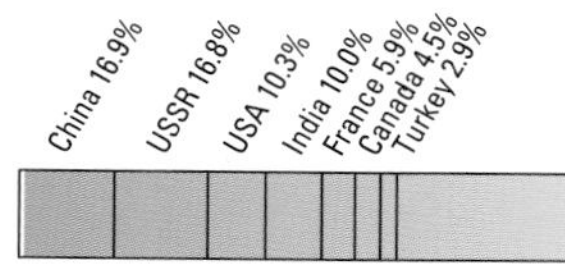

China 16.9%
USSR 16.8%
USA 10.3%
India 10.0%
France 5.9%
Canada 4.5%
Turkey 2.9%

World total (1989): 538,056,000 tonnes

Maize: Originating in the New World and still an important human food in Africa and Latin America, in the developed world it is processed into breakfast cereals, oil, starches and adhesives. It is also used for animal feed.

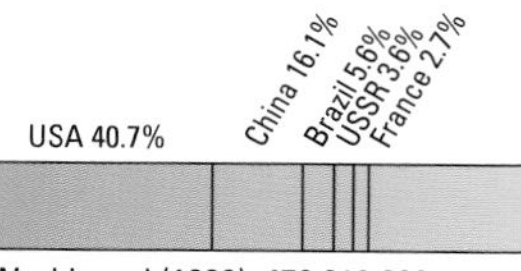

USA 40.7%
China 16.1%
Brazil 5.6%
USSR 3.6%
France 2.7%

World total (1989): 470,318,000 tonnes

Oats: Most widely used to feed livestock, but eaten by humans as oatmeal or porridge. Oats have a beneficial effect on the cardio-vascular system, and human consumption is likely to increase.

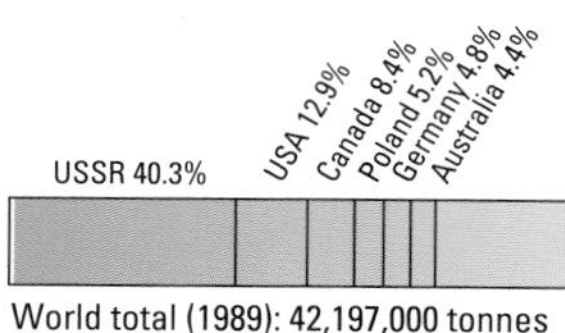

USSR 40.3%
USA 12.9%
Canada 8.4%
Poland 5.2%
Germany 4.8%
Australia 4.4%

World total (1989): 42,197,000 tonnes

Millet: The name covers a number of small grained cereals, members of the grass family with a short growing season. Used to produce flour, meal and animal feed, and fermented to make beer, especially in Africa.

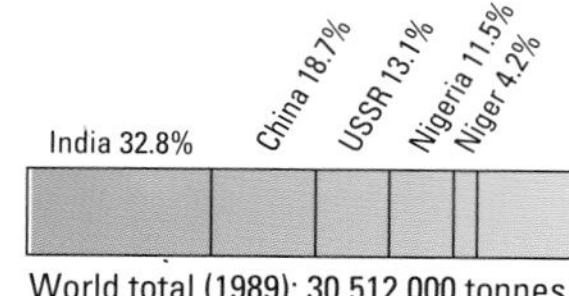

India 32.8%
China 18.7%
USSR 13.1%
Nigeria 11.5%
Niger 4.2%

World total (1989): 30,512,000 tonnes

Cassava: A tropical shrub that needs high rainfall (over 1000 mm annually) and a 10–30 month growing season to produce its large, edible tubers. Used as flour by humans, as cattle feed and in industrial starches.

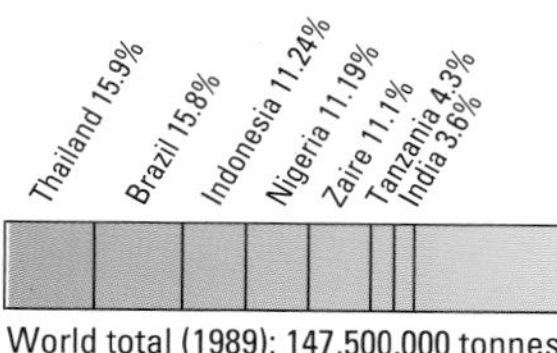

Thailand 15.9%
Brazil 15.8%
Indonesia 11.24%
Nigeria 11.19%
Zaire 11.1%
Tanzania 4.3%
India 3.6%

World total (1989): 147,500,000 tonnes

Rice: Thrives on the high humidity and temperatures of the Far East, where it is the traditional staple food of half the human race. Usually grown standing in water, rice responds well to continuous cultivation, with three or four crops annually.

China 35.4%
India 21.2%
Indonesia 8.6%
Bangladesh 5.2%
Thailand 4.2%
Vietnam 3.6%

World total (1989): 506,291,000 tonnes

Barley: Primarily used as animal feed, but widely eaten by humans in Africa and Asia. Elsewhere, malted barley furnishes beer and spirits. Able to withstand the dry heat of subarid tropics, its growing season is only 80 days.

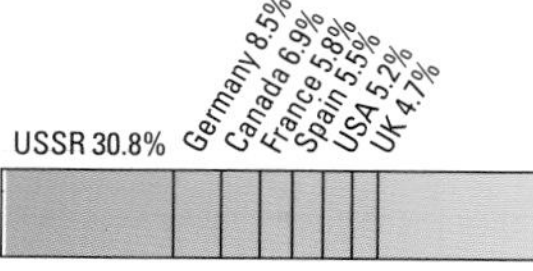

USSR 30.8%
Germany 8.5%
Canada 6.9%
France 5.8%
Spain 5.5%
USA 5.2%
UK 4.7%

World total (1989): 168,964,000 tonnes

Rye: Hardy and tolerant of poor and sandy soils, it is an important foodstuff and animal feed in Central and Eastern Europe. Rye produces a dark, heavy bread as well as alcoholic drinks.

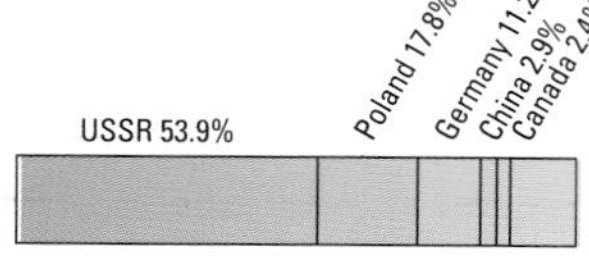

USSR 53.9%
Poland 17.8%
Germany 11.2%
China 2.9%
Canada 2.4%

World total (1989): 34,893,000 tonnes

Potatoes: The most important of the edible tubers, potatoes grow in well-watered, temperate areas. Weight for weight less nutritious than grain, they are a human staple as well as an important animal feed.

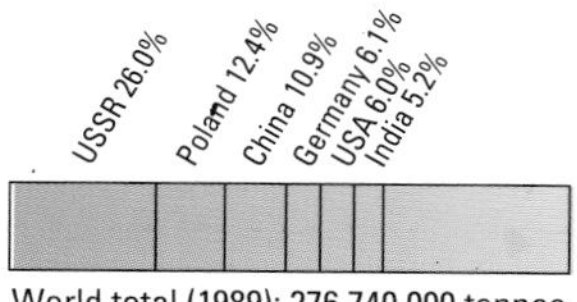

USSR 26.0%
Poland 12.4%
China 10.9%
Germany 6.1%
USA 6.0%
India 5.2%

World total (1989): 276,740,000 tonnes

Soya: Beans from soya bushes are very high (30–40%) in protein. Most are processed into oil and proprietary protein foods. Consumption since 1950 has tripled, mainly due to the health-conscious developed world.

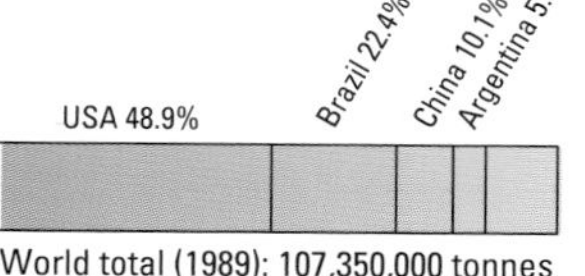

USA 48.9%
Brazil 22.4%
China 10.1%
Argentina 5.8%

World total (1989): 107,350,000 tonnes

Cereals are grasses with starchy, edible seeds; every important civilization has depended on them as a source of food. The major cereal grains contain about 10% protein and 75% carbohydrate; grain is easy to store, handle and transport, and contributes more than any other group of foods to the energy and protein content of human diet. If all the cereals were consumed directly by man, there would be no shortage of food in the world, but a considerable proportion of the total output is used as animal feed.

Starchy tuber crops or root crops, represented here by potatoes and cassava, are second in importance only to cereals as staple foods; easily cultivated, they provide high yields for little effort and store well – potatoes for up to six months, cassava for up to a year in the ground. Protein content is low (2% or less), starch content high, with some minerals and vitamins present, but populations that rely heavily on these crops may suffer from malnutrition.

IMPORTANCE OF AGRICULTURE

Percentage of the total population dependent on agriculture (1991)

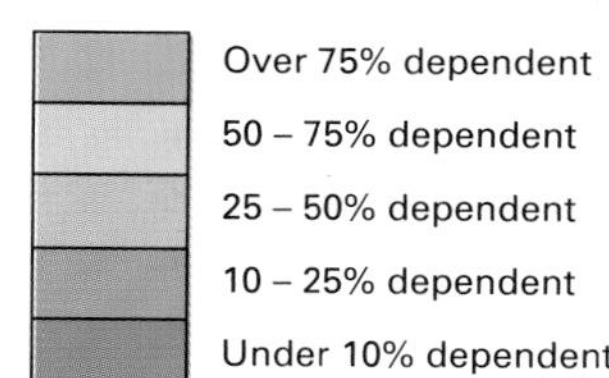

Over 75% dependent
50 – 75% dependent
25 – 50% dependent
10 – 25% dependent
Under 10% dependent

Top 5 countries		Bottom 5 countries	
Nepal	92%	Singapore	0.9%
Rwanda	91%	Hong Kong	1.2%
Burundi	91%	Bahrain	1.7%
Bhutan	91%	Belgium	1.7%
Niger	87%	UK	1.9%

FOOD & POPULATION

Comparison of food production and population by continent (1989). The left column indicates percentage shares of total world food production; the right shows population in proportion.

FOOD		POPULATION
1.2%	Australasia	0.4%
27.6%	Europe	15.5%
44.5%	Asia	58.3%
6.5%	S. America	6.7%
13.8%	N. America	7.1%
6.7%	Africa	12.0%

ANIMAL PRODUCTS

Separate figures for Russia, Ukraine and the other successors of the former USSR are not yet available

Traditionally, food animals subsisted on land unsuitable for cultivation, supporting agricultural production with their fertilizing dung. But free-ranging animals grow slowly and yield less meat than those more intensively reared; the demands of urban markets in the developed world have encouraged the growth of factory-like production methods.

A large proportion of staple crops, especially cereals, are fed to animals, an inefficient way to produce protein but one likely to continue as long as people value meat and dairy products in their diet.

Cheese: Least perishable of all dairy products, cheese is milk fermented with selected bacterial strains to produce a foodstuff with a potentially immense range of flavours and textures. The vast majority of cheeses are made from cow's milk, although sheep and goat cheeses are highly prized.

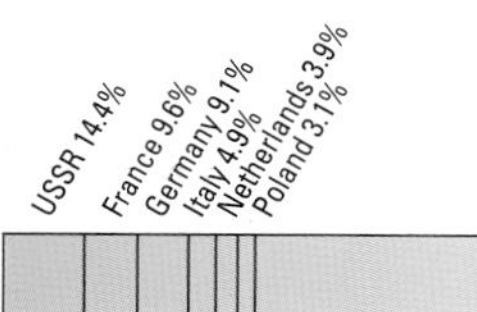

USSR 14.4%
France 9.6%
Germany 9.1%
Italy 4.9%
Netherlands 3.9%
Poland 3.1%

World total (1989): 14,475,276 tonnes

Lamb and Mutton: Sheep are the least demanding of domestic animals. Although unsuited to intensive rearing, they can thrive on marginal pastureland incapable of supporting beef cattle on a commercial scale. Sheep are raised as much for their valuable wool as for the meat that they provide, with Australia the world leader.

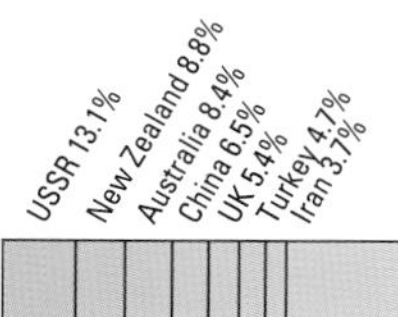

USSR 13.1%
New Zealand 8.8%
Australia 8.4%
China 6.5%
UK 5.4%
Turkey 4.7%
Iran 3.7%

World total (1989): 6,473,000 tonnes

Beef and Veal: Most beef and veal is reared for home markets, and the top five producers are also the biggest consumers. The USA produces nearly a quarter of the world's beef and eats even more. Australia, with its small domestic market, is by far the largest exporter.

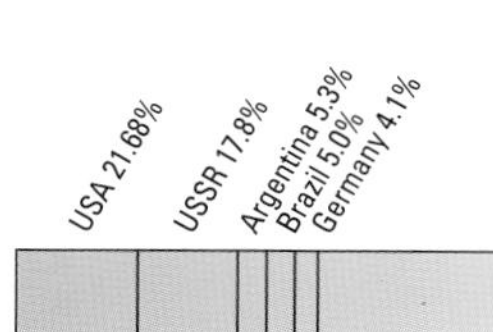

USA 21.68%
USSR 17.8%
Argentina 5.3%
Brazil 5.0%
Germany 4.1%

World total (1989): 49,436,000 tonnes

Milk: Many human groups, including most Asians, find raw milk indigestible after infancy, and it is often only the starting point for other dairy products such as butter, cheese and yoghurt. Most world production comes from cows, but sheep's milk and goats' milk are also important.

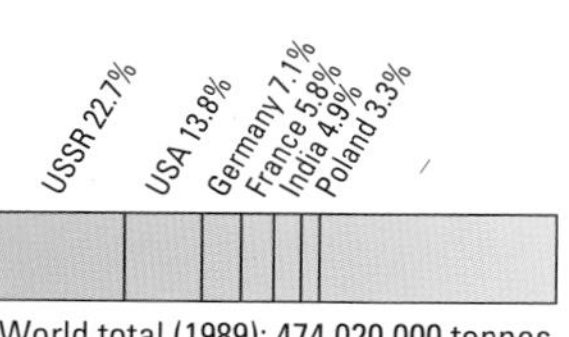

USSR 22.7%
USA 13.8%
Germany 7.1%
France 5.8%
India 4.9%
Poland 3.3%

World total (1989): 474,020,000 tonnes

Butter: A traditional source of vitamin A as well as calories, butter has lost much popularity in the developed world for health reasons, although it remains a valuable food. Most butter from India, the world's second-largest producer, is clarified into ghee, which has religious as well as nutritional importance.

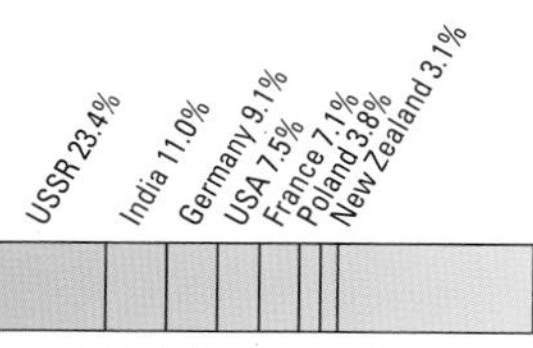

USSR 23.4%
India 11.0%
Germany 9.1%
USA 7.5%
France 7.1%
Poland 3.8%
New Zealand 3.1%

World total (1989): 7,611,826 tonnes

Pork: Although pork is forbidden to many millions, notably Muslims, on religious grounds, more is produced than any other meat in the world, mainly because it is the cheapest. It accounts for about 90% of China's meat output, although per capita meat consumption is relatively low.

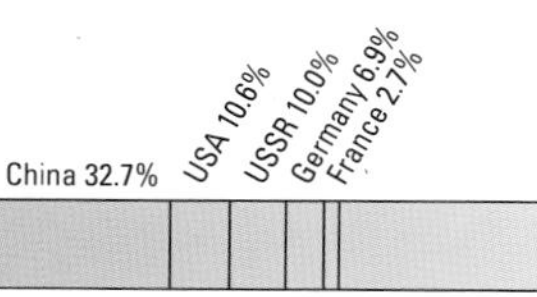

China 32.7%
USA 10.6%
USSR 10.0%
Germany 6.9%
France 2.7%

World total (1989): 67,460,000 tonnes

Fish: Commercial fishing requires large shoals of fish, often of only one species, within easy reach of markets. Although the great majority are caught wild in the sea, fish-farming of both marine and freshwater species is assuming increasing importance, especially as natural stocks become depleted.

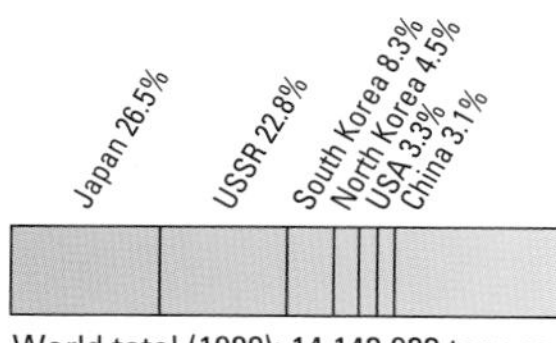

Japan 26.5%
USSR 22.8%
South Korea 8.3%
North Korea 4.5%
USA 3.3%
China 3.1%

World total (1989): 14,143,923 tonnes

SUGARS

Sugar cane: Confined to tropical regions, cane sugar accounts for the bulk of international trade in the commodity. Most is produced as a foodstuff, but some countries, notably Brazil and South Africa, distill sugar cane and use the resulting ethyl alcohol to make motor fuels.

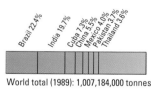

Brazil 22.4%
India 19.7%
Cuba 7.3%
China 5.5%
Mexico 4.0%
Pakistan 3.7%
Thailand 3.6%

World total (1989): 1,007,184,000 tonnes

Sugar beet: A temperate crop closely related to the humble beetroot, sugar beet's yield after processing is indistinguishable from cane sugar. Sugar beet is steadily replacing sugar cane imports in Europe, to the detriment of the developing countries that rely on it as a major cash crop.

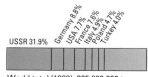

USSR 31.9%
Germany 8.8%
USA 7.7%
France 7.6%
Italy 4.9%
Poland 4.7%
Turkey 4.0%

World total (1989): 305,882,000 tonnes

CARTOGRAPHY BY PHILIP'S. COPYRIGHT REED INTERNATIONAL BOOKS LTD

PRODUCTION: ENERGY

39: WORLD SHIPPING

46: CARBON DIOXIDE
GREENHOUSE POWER
CO_2 PRODUCERS
GLOBAL WARMING

47: MARINE POLLUTION

We live in a high-energy civilization. While vast discrepancies exist between rich and poor – a North American consumes 13 times as much energy as a Chinese, for example – even developing nations have more power at their disposal than was imaginable a century ago. Abundant energy supplies keep us warm or cool, fuel our industries and our transport systems, and even feed us: high-intensity agriculture, with its fertilizers, pesticides and machinery, is heavily energy-dependent.

Unfortunately, most of the world's energy comes from fossil fuels: coal, oil and gas deposits laid down over many millions of years. These are the Earth's capital, not its income, and we are consuming that capital at an alarming rate. New discoveries have persistently extended the known reserves: in 1989, the reserves-to-production ratio for oil assured over 45 years' supply, an improvement of almost a decade on the 1970 situation. But despite the effort and ingenuity of prospectors, stocks are clearly limited. They are also very unequally distributed, with the Middle East accounting for most oil reserves, and the CIS, especially Russia, possessing an even higher proportion of the world's natural gas. Coal reserves are more evenly shared, and also more plentiful: coal will outlast oil and gas by a very wide margin.

It is possible to reduce energy demand by improving efficiency: most industrial nations have dramatically increased output since the 1970s without a matching rise in energy consumption. But as fossil stocks continue to diminish, renewable energy sources – solar, wave and wind power, as well as hydro-electricity – must take on greater importance.

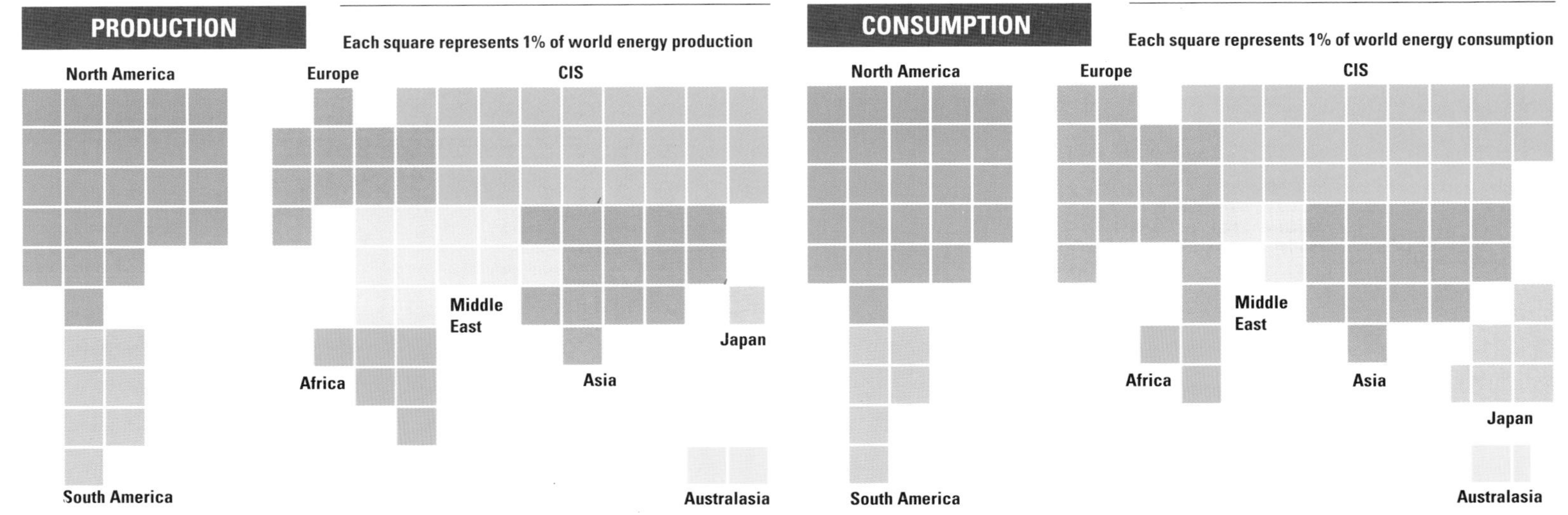

PRODUCTION
Each square represents 1% of world energy production
North America
Europe
CIS
Middle East
Japan
Africa
Asia
South America
Australasia
CONSUMPTION
Each square represents 1% of world energy consumption
North America
Europe
CIS
Middle East
Africa
Asia
Japan
South America
Australasia

CONVERSIONS

For historical reasons, oil is still traded in barrels. The weight and volume equivalents shown below are all based on average density 'Arabian light' crude oil, and should be considered approximate.

The energy equivalents given for a tonne of oil are also somewhat imprecise: oil and coal of different qualities will have varying energy contents, a fact usually reflected in their price on world markets.

1 barrel:
0.136 tonnes
159 litres
35 Imperial gallons
42 US gallons

1 tonne:
7.33 barrels
1185 litres
256 Imperial gallons
261 US gallons

1 tonne oil:
1.5 tonnes hard coal
3.0 tonnes lignite
12,000 kWh

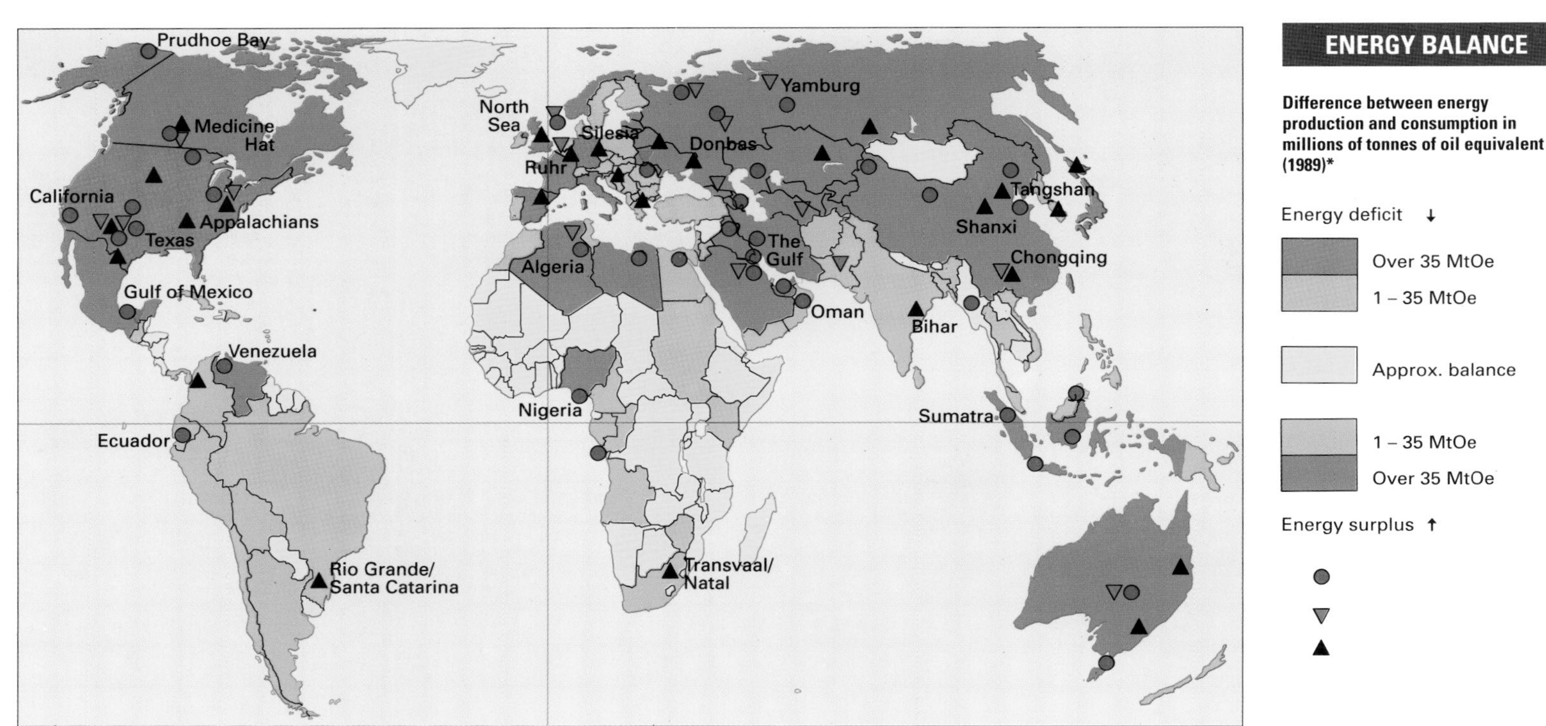

Prudhoe Bay
Medicine Hat
California
Texas
Appalachians
Gulf of Mexico
Venezuela
Ecuador
Rio Grande/ Santa Catarina
North Sea
Ruhr
Silesia
Donbas
Yamburg
Algeria
The Gulf
Oman
Nigeria
Transvaal/ Natal
Tangshan
Shanxi
Chongqing
Bihar
Sumatra

ENERGY BALANCE

Difference between energy production and consumption in millions of tonnes of oil equivalent (1989)*

Energy deficit ↓

Over 35 MtOe

1 – 35 MtOe

Approx. balance

1 – 35 MtOe

Over 35 MtOe

Energy surplus ↑

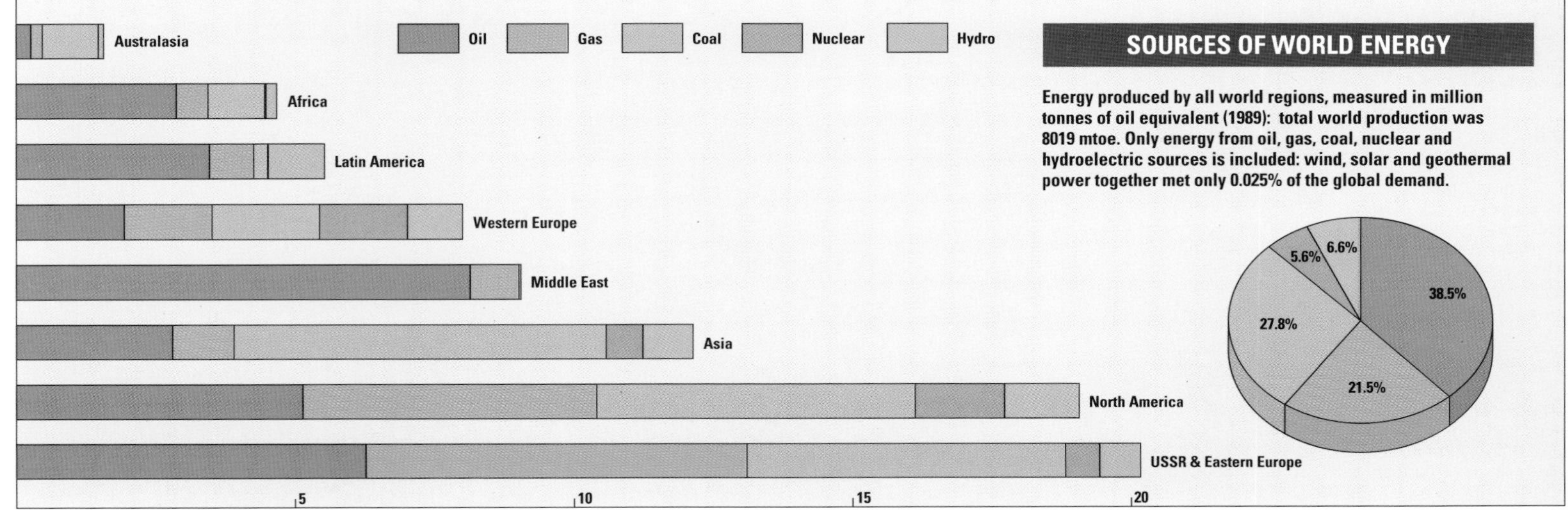

Oil
Gas
Coal
Nuclear
Hydro
Australasia
Africa
Latin America
Western Europe
Middle East
Asia
North America
USSR & Eastern Europe
5
10
15
20
38.5%
21.5%
27.8%
5.6%
6.6%

SOURCES OF WORLD ENERGY

Energy produced by all world regions, measured in million tonnes of oil equivalent (1989): total world production was 8019 mtoe. Only energy from oil, gas, coal, nuclear and hydroelectric sources is included: wind, solar and geothermal power together met only 0.025% of the global demand.

Statistics for the new republics of the former USSR, Czechoslovakia and Yugoslavia are not yet available. The map shows the statistics for the entire USSR, Czechoslovakia and Yugoslavia.

CARTOGRAPHY BY PHILIP'S. COPYRIGHT REED INTERNATIONAL BOOKS LTD

FOSSIL FUEL RESERVES

Known world reserves in years as a multiple of annual production, 1970, 1980 and 1989

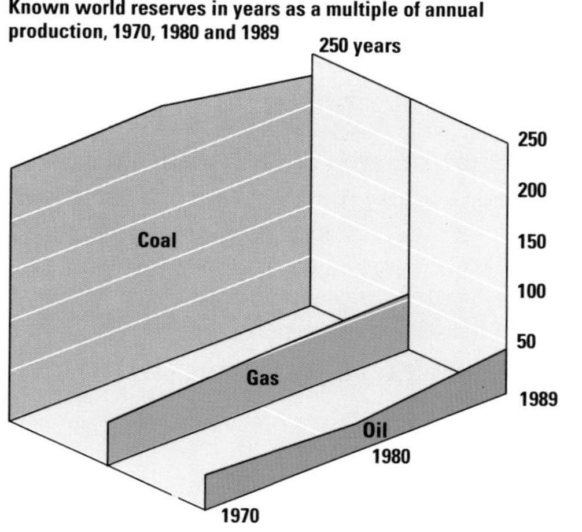

250 years
250
200
150
100
50
Coal
Gas
Oil
1989
1980
1970

ENERGY AND OUTPUT

Tonnes of oil equivalent consumed to produce US $1,000 of GDP, four industrial nations (1973–89)

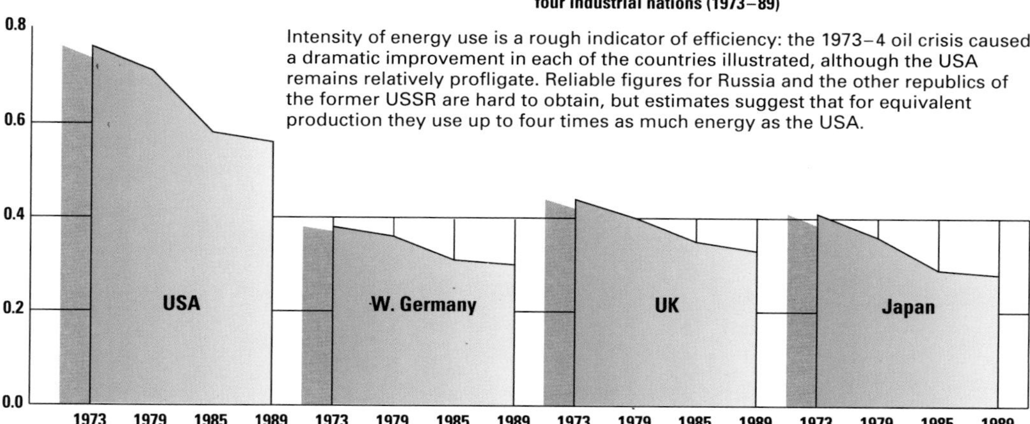

0.8
0.6
0.4
0.2
0.0
USA
W. Germany
UK
Japan
1973
1979
1985
1989

Intensity of energy use is a rough indicator of efficiency: the 1973–4 oil crisis caused a dramatic improvement in each of the countries illustrated, although the USA remains relatively profligate. Reliable figures for Russia and the other republics of the former USSR are hard to obtain, but estimates suggest that for equivalent production they use up to four times as much energy as the USA.

COAL RESERVES

World coal reserves by region and country, thousand million tonnes (1988)

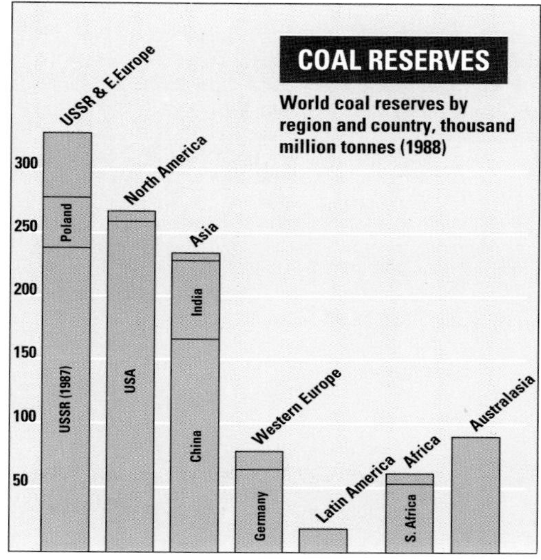

USSR & E.Europe
North America
Asia
Western Europe
Latin America
Africa
Australasia
Poland
USSR (1987)
USA
India
China
Germany
S. Africa
300
250
200
150
100
50

GAS RESERVES

World natural gas reserves by region and country, thousand million tonnes (1988)

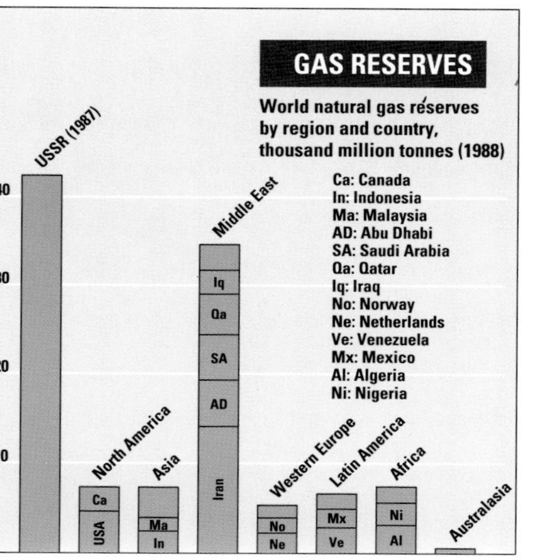

Ca: Canada
In: Indonesia
Ma: Malaysia
AD: Abu Dhabi
SA: Saudi Arabia
Qa: Qatar
Iq: Iraq
No: Norway
Ne: Netherlands
Ve: Venezuela
Mx: Mexico
Al: Algeria
Ni: Nigeria
USSR (1987)
North America
Asia
Middle East
Western Europe
Latin America
Africa
Australasia
Iran
40
30
20
10

OIL RESERVES

World oil reserves by region and country, thousand million tonnes (1988)

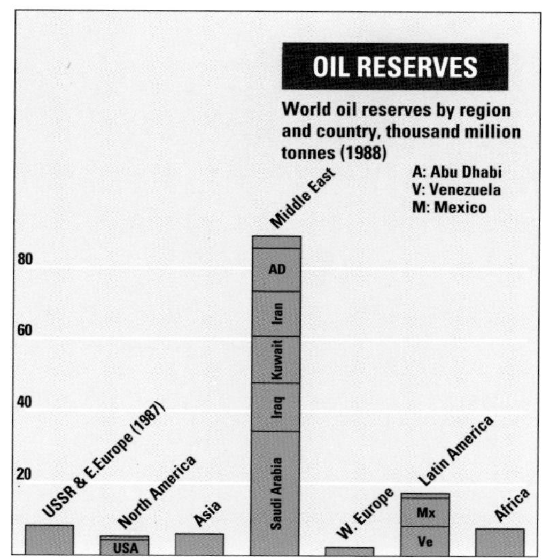

A: Abu Dhabi
V: Venezuela
M: Mexico
Middle East
USSR & E.Europe (1987)
North America
Asia
W. Europe
Latin America
Africa
AD
Iran
Kuwait
Iraq
Saudi Arabia
USA
Mx
Ve
80
60
40
20

OIL MOVEMENTS

Major world movements of oil in millions of tonnes (1989)

Middle East to Western Europe	195.5
Middle East to Japan	150.0
Middle East to Asia (exc. Japan and China)	127.5
Latin America to USA	126.1
Middle East to USA	94.1
USSR to Western Europe	78.1
North Africa to Western Europe	93.5
West Africa to Western Europe	39.6
West Africa to USA	59.8
Canada to USA	45.0
South-east Asia to Japan	42.2
Latin America to Western Europe	28.7
Western Europe to USA	28.7
Middle East to Latin America	20.5

Total world movements: 1,577 million tonnes

Only inter-regional movements in excess of 20 million tonnes are shown. Other Middle Eastern oil shipments throughout the world totalled 47.4 million tonnes; miscellaneous oil exports of the then USSR amounted to 88.8 million tonnes.

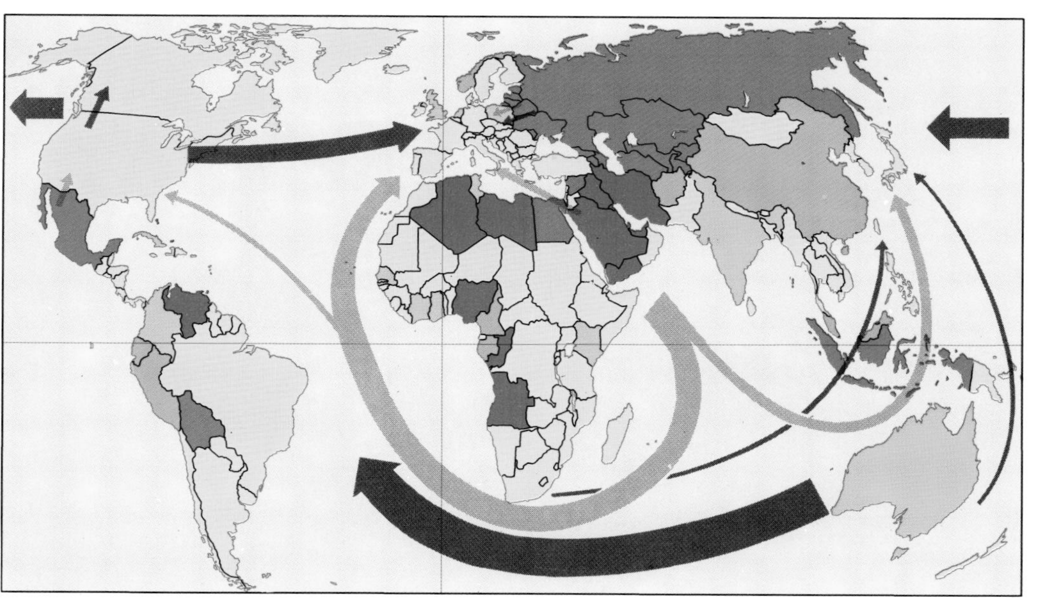

FUEL EXPORTS

Fuels as a percentage of total value of all exports (1986)*

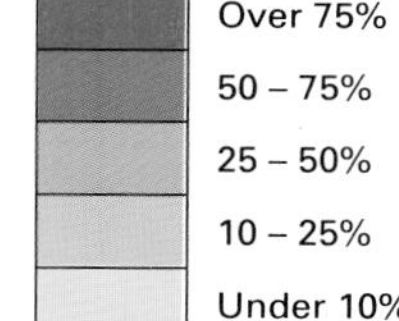

Over 75%
50 – 75%
25 – 50%
10 – 25%
Under 10%

Direction of trade

Coal
Oil

Arrows show the major trade direction of selected fuels, and are proportional to export value.

NUCLEAR POWER

Percentage of electricity generated by nuclear power stations, leading nations (1988)

1. France 70%
2. Belgium 66%
3. Hungary 49%
4. South Korea 47%
5. Sweden 46%
6. Taiwan 41%
7. Switzerland 37%
8. Finland 36%
9. Spain 36%
10. Bulgaria 36%
11. Germany (W) 34%
12. Japan 28%
13. Czechoslovakia 27%
14. UK 18%
15. USA 17%
16. Canada 16%
17. Argentina 12%
18. USSR (1989) 11%
19. Yugoslavia 6%
20. Netherlands 5%

The decade 1980–90 was a bad time for the nuclear power industry. Major projects regularly ran vastly overbudget, and fears of long-term environmental damage were heavily reinforced by the 1986 Soviet disaster at Chernobyl. Although the number of reactors in service continued to increase throughout the period, orders for new plant shrank dramatically, and most countries cut back on their nuclear programmes.

HYDROELECTRICITY

Percentage of electricity generated by hydroelectrical power stations, leading nations (1988)

1. Paraguay 99.9%
2. Zambia 99.6%
3. Norway 99.5%
4. Congo 99.1%
5. Costa Rica 98.3%
6. Uganda 98.3%
7. Rwanda 97.7%
8. Malawi 97.6%
9. Zaïre 97.4%
10. Cameroon 97.2%
11. Laos 95.5%
12. Nepal 95.2%
13. Iceland 94.0%
14. Uruguay 93.0%
15. Brazil 91.7%
16. Albania 87.2%
17. Fiji 81.4%
18. Ecuador 80.7%
19. C. African Rep. 80.4%
20. Sri Lanka 80.4%

Countries heavily reliant on hydroelectricity are usually small and non-industrial: a high proportion of hydroelectric power more often reflects a modest energy budget than vast hydroelectric resources. The USA, for instance, produces only 8% of power requirements from hydroelectricity; yet that 8% amounts to more than three times the hydro-power generated by all of Africa.

ALTERNATIVE ENERGY SOURCES

Solar: Each year the Sun bestows upon the Earth almost a million times as much energy as is locked up in all the planet's oil reserves, but only an insignificant fraction is trapped and used commercially. In some experimental installations, mirrors focus the Sun's rays on to boilers, whose steam generates electricity by spinning turbines. Solar cells turn the sunlight into electricity directly, and although efficiencies are still low, advancing technology offers some prospect of using the Sun as the main world electricity source by 2100.
Wind: Caused by uneven heating of the Earth, winds are themselves a form of solar energy. Windmills have been used for centuries to turn wind power into mechanical work; recent models, often arranged in banks on gust-swept high ground, usually generate electricity.
Tidal: The energy from tides is potentially enormous, although only a few installations have been built to exploit it. In theory at least, waves and currents could also provide almost unimaginable power, and the thermal differences in the ocean depths are another huge well of potential energy. But work on extracting it is still in the experimental stage.
Geothermal: The Earth's temperature rises by 1°C for every 30 metres' descent, with much steeper temperature gradients in geologically active areas. El Salvador, for example, produces 39% of its electricity from geothermal power stations. More than 130 are operating worldwide.
Biomass: The oldest of human fuels ranges from animal dung, still burned in cooking fires in much of North Africa and elsewhere, to sugar cane plantations feeding high-technology distilleries to produce ethanol for motor vehicle engines. In Brazil and South Africa, plant ethanol provides up to 25% of motor fuel. Throughout the developing world, most biomass energy comes from firewood: although accurate figures are impossible to obtain, it may yield as much as 10% of the world's total energy consumption.

**Statistics for the new republics of the former USSR, Czechoslovakia and Yugoslavia are not yet available. The map shows the statistics for the entire USSR, Czechoslovakia and Yugoslavia.*

CARTOGRAPHY BY PHILIP'S. COPYRIGHT REED INTERNATIONAL BOOKS LTD

PRODUCTION: MINERALS

19: GEOLOGY
37: PATTERNS OF PRODUCTION
39: WORLD SHIPPING

Even during the Stone Age, when humans often settled near the outcrops of flint on which their technology depended, mineral resources have attracted human exploiters. Their descendants have learned how to make use of almost every known element. These elements can be found, in one form or another, somewhere in the Earth's bountiful crust. Iron remains the most important, but modern industrial civilization has a voracious appetite for virtually all of them.

Mineral deposits once dictated the site of new industries; today, most industrial countries are heavily dependent on imports for many of their key materials. Most mining, and much refining of raw ores, is done in developing countries, where labour is cheap.

The main map below shows the richest sources of the most important minerals at present; some reserves – lead and mercury, for example – are running very low. The map takes no account of undersea deposits, most of which are considered inaccessible. Growing shortages, though, may encourage submarine mining: plans have already been made to recover the nodules of manganese found widely scattered on ocean floors.

MINERAL EXPORTS

Minerals and metals as a percentage of total exports (1986)

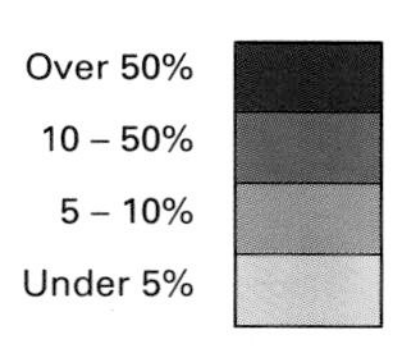
Over 50%
10 – 50%
5 – 10%
Under 5%

Direction of trade

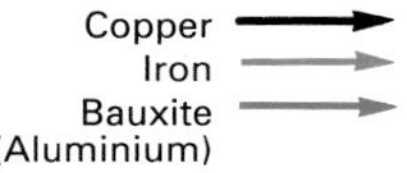
Copper
Iron
Bauxite
(Aluminium)

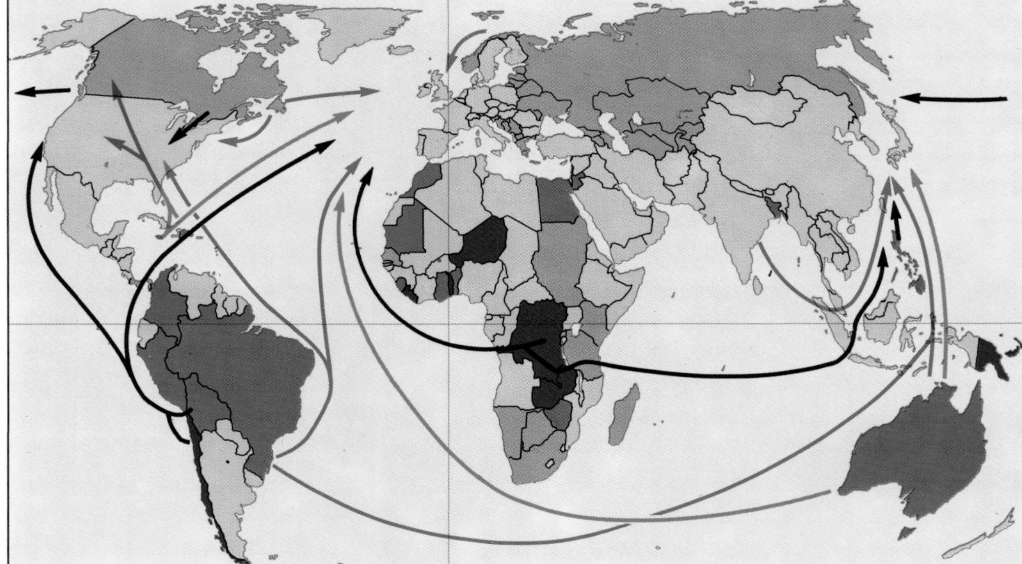

URANIUM

In its pure state, uranium is an immensely heavy, white metal; but although spent uranium is employed as projectiles in anti-missile cannons, where its mass ensures a lethal punch, its main use is as a fuel in nuclear reactors, and in nuclear weaponry. Uranium is very scarce: the main source is the rare ore pitchblende, which itself contains only 0.2% uranium oxide. Only a minute fraction of that is the radioactive U^{235} isotope, though so-called breeder reactors can transmute the more common U^{238} into highly radioactive plutonium.

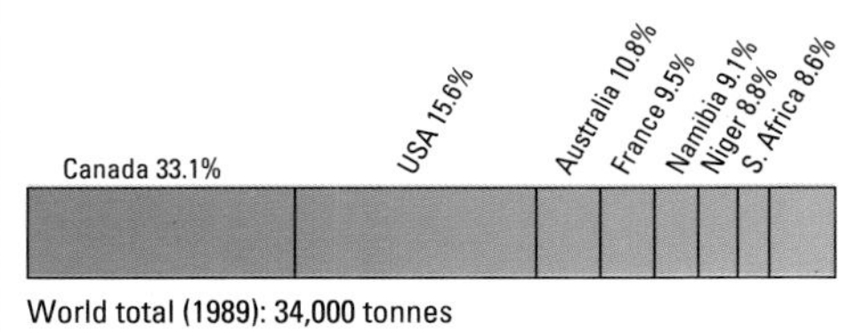
Canada 33.1%
USA 15.6%
Australia 10.8%
France 9.5%
Namibia 9.1%
Niger 8.8%
S. Africa 8.6%

World total (1989): 34,000 tonnes

METALS

Separate figures for Russia, Ukraine and the other successors of the former USSR are not yet available

***Figures for aluminium are for refined metal; all other figures refer to ore production**

Aluminium: Produced mainly from its oxide, bauxite, which yields 25% of its weight in aluminium. The cost of refining and production is often too high for producer-countries to bear, so bauxite is largely exported. Lightweight and corrosion resistant, aluminium alloys are widely used in aircraft, vehicles, cans and packaging.

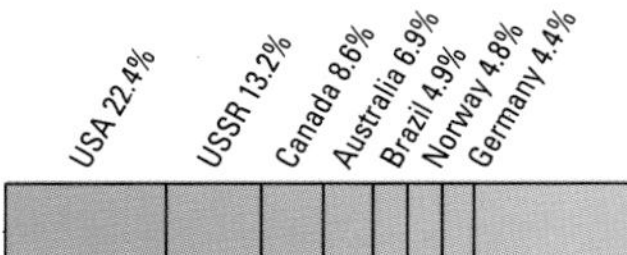
USA 22.4%
USSR 13.2%
Canada 8.6%
Australia 6.9%
Brazil 4.8%
Norway 4.8%
Germany 4.4%

World total (1989): 18,000,000 tonnes*

Copper: Derived from low-yielding sulphide ores, copper is an important export for several developing countries. An excellent conductor of heat and electricity, it forms part of most electrical items, and is used in the manufacture of brass and bronze. Major importers include Japan and Germany.

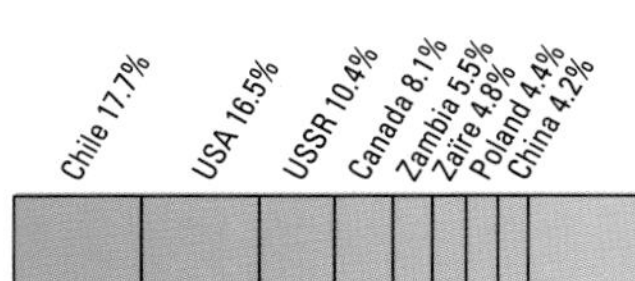
Chile 17.7%
USA 16.5%
USSR 10.4%
Canada 8.1%
Zambia 5.5%
Zaïre 4.8%
Poland 4.4%
China 4.2%

World total (1989): 9,100,000 tonnes*

Lead: A soft metal, obtained mainly from galena (lead sulphide), which occurs in veins associated with iron, zinc and silver sulphides. Its use in vehicle batteries accounts for the USA's prime consumer status; lead is also made into sheeting and piping. Its use as an additive to paints and petrol is decreasing.

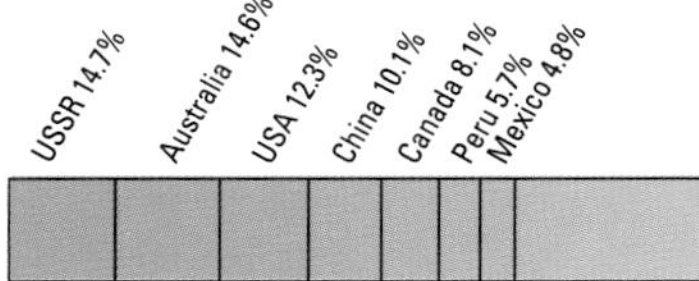
USSR 14.7%
Australia 14.6%
USA 12.3%
China 10.1%
Canada 8.1%
Peru 5.7%
Mexico 4.8%

World total (1989): 3,400,000 tonnes*

Mercury: The only metal that is liquid at normal temperatures, most is derived from its sulphide, cinnabar, found only in small quantities in volcanic areas. Apart from its value in thermometers and other instruments, most mercury production is used in anti-fungal and anti-fouling preparations, and to make detonators.

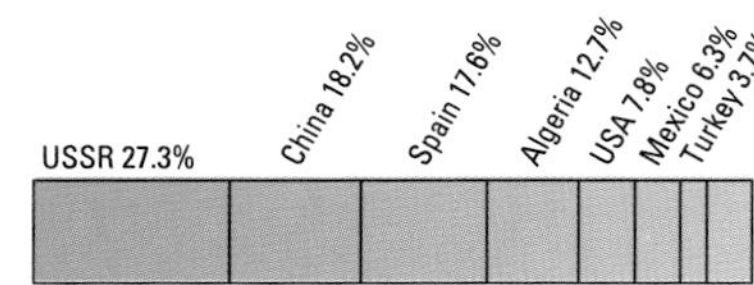
USSR 27.3%
China 18.2%
Spain 17.6%
Algeria 12.7%
USA 7.8%
Mexico 6.3%
Turkey 3.7%

World total (1989): 5,500,000 kilograms*

Tin: Soft, pliable and non-toxic, used to coat 'tin' (tin-plated steel) cans, in the manufacture of foils and in alloys. The principal tin-bearing mineral is cassiterite (SnO_2), found in ore formed from molten rock. Producers and refiners were hit by a price collapse in 1991.

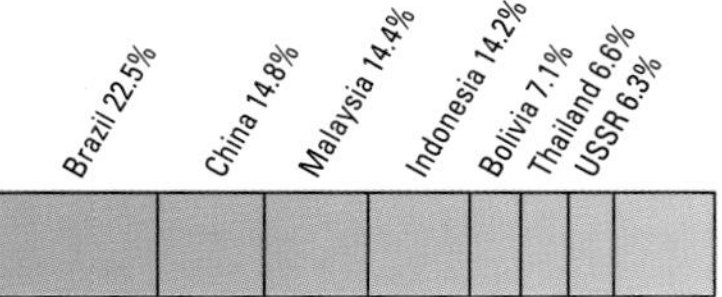
Brazil 22.5%
China 14.8%
Malaysia 14.4%
Indonesia 14.2%
Bolivia 7.1%
Thailand 6.6%
USSR 6.3%

World total (1989): 223,000 tonnes*

Zinc: Often found in association with lead ores, zinc is highly resistant to corrosion, and about 40% of the refined metal is used to plate sheet steel, particularly vehicle bodies – a process known as galvanizing. Zinc is also used in dry batteries, paints and dyes.

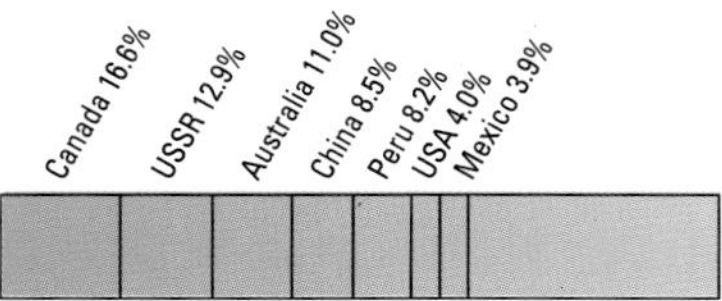
Canada 16.6%
USSR 12.9%
Australia 11.0%
China 8.5%
Peru 8.2%
USA 4.0%
Mexico 3.9%

World total (1989): 7,300,000 tonnes*

Gold: Regarded for centuries as the most valuable metal in the world and used to make coins, gold is still recognized as the monetary standard. A soft metal, it is alloyed to make jewellery; the electronics industry values its corrosion resistance and conductivity.

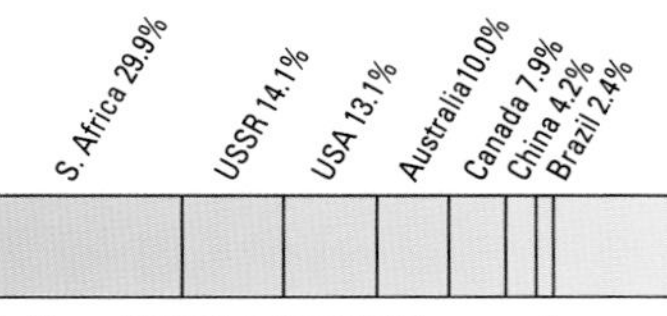
S. Africa 29.9%
USSR 14.1%
USA 13.1%
Australia 10.0%
Canada 7.9%
China 4.2%
Brazil 2.4%

World total (1989): 2,026,000 kilograms*

Silver: Most silver comes from ores mined and processed for other metals (including lead and copper). Pure or alloyed with harder metals, it is used for jewellery and ornaments. Industrial use includes dentistry, electronics, photography and as a chemical catalyst.

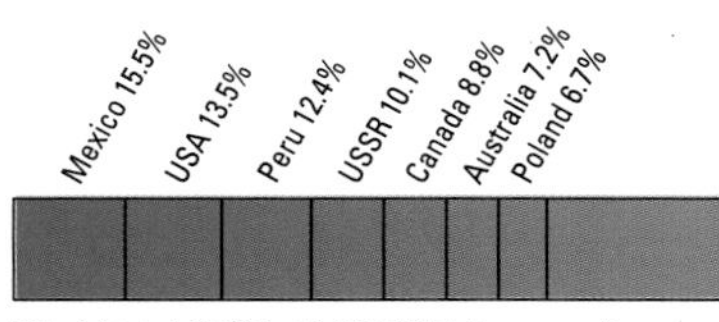
Mexico 15.5%
USA 13.5%
Peru 12.4%
USSR 10.1%
Canada 8.8%
Australia 7.2%
Poland 6.7%

World total (1989): 14,896,000 kilograms*

DIAMOND

Most diamond is found in kimberlite, or 'blue ground', a basic peridotite rock; erosion may wash the diamond from its kimberlite matrix and deposit it with sand or gravel on river beds. Only a small proportion of the world's diamond, the most flawless, is cut into gemstones – 'diamonds'; most is used in industry, where the material's remarkable hardness and abrasion resistance finds a use in cutting tools, drills and dies, as well as in styluses. Australia, not among the top 12 producers at the beginning of the 1980s, had by 1986 become world leader and by 1989 was the source of 37.5% of world production. The other main producers were Zaïre (18.9%), Botswana (16.3%), the then USSR (11.8%) and South Africa (9.7%). Between them, these five nations accounted for over 94% of the world total of 96,600,000 carats – at 0.2 grams per carat, almost one tonne.

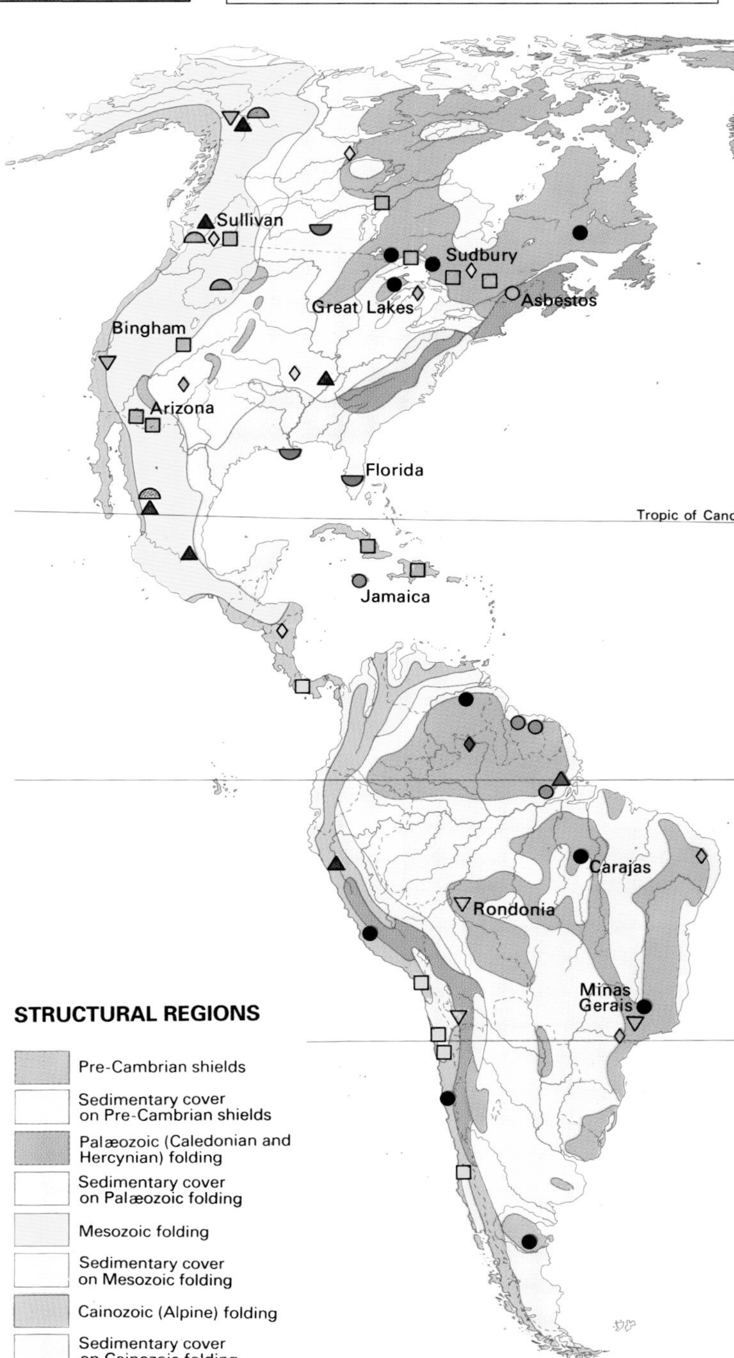
Sullivan
Sudbury
Great Lakes
Asbestos
Bingham
Arizona
Florida
Tropic of Canc
Jamaica
Carajas
Rondonia
Minas Gerais
STRUCTURAL REGIONS
Pre-Cambrian shields
Sedimentary cover on Pre-Cambrian shields
Palæozoic (Caledonian and Hercynian) folding
Sedimentary cover on Palæozoic folding
Mesozoic folding
Sedimentary cover on Mesozoic folding
Cainozoic (Alpine) folding
Sedimentary cover on Cainozoic folding

CARTOGRAPHY BY PHILIP'S. COPYRIGHT REED INTERNATIONAL BOOKS LTD

IRON AND FERRO-ALLOYS

Ever since the art of high-temperature smelting was discovered, some time in the second millennium BC, iron has been by far the most important metal known to man. The earliest iron ploughs transformed primitive agriculture and led to the first human population explosion, while iron weapons – or the lack of them – ensured the rise or fall of entire cultures.

Widely distributed around the world, iron ores usually contain 25–60% iron; blast furnaces process the raw product into pig-iron, which is then alloyed with carbon and other minerals to produce steels of various qualities. From the time of the Industrial Revolution steel has been almost literally the backbone of modern civilization, the prime structural material on which all else is built.

Iron-smelting usually developed close to sources of ore and, later, to the coalfields that fueled the furnaces. Today, most ore comes from a few richly-endowed locations where large-scale mining is possible. Iron and steel plants are generally built at coastal sites so that giant ore carriers, which account for a sizeable proportion of the world's merchant fleet, can easily discharge their cargoes.

World production of pig-iron and ferro-alloys (1988). All countries with an annual output of more than one million tonnes are shown

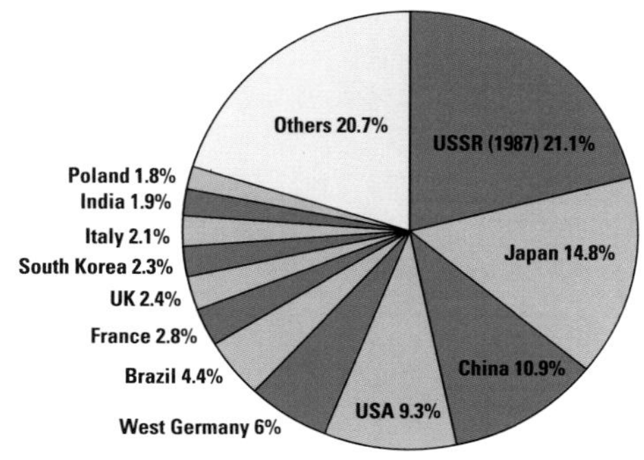
USSR (1987) 21.1%
Japan 14.8%
China 10.9%
USA 9.3%
West Germany 6%
Brazil 4.4%
France 2.8%
UK 2.4%
South Korea 2.3%
Italy 2.1%
India 1.9%
Poland 1.8%
Others 20.7%

Total world production: 545 million tonnes

Development of world production of pig-iron and ferro-alloys (1945–88) in million tonnes

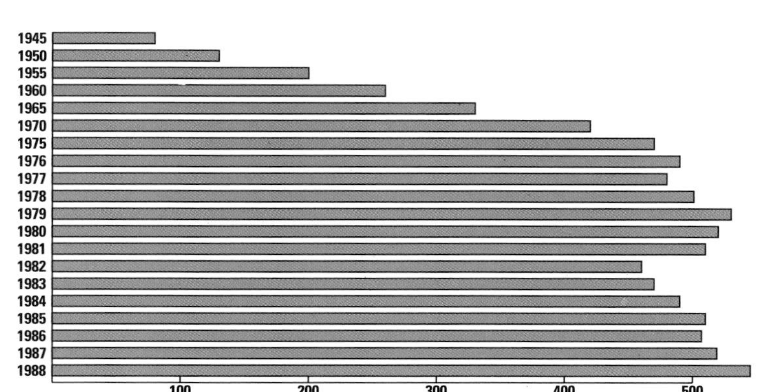
1945
1950
1955
1960
1965
1970
1975
1976
1977
1978
1979
1980
1981
1982
1983
1984
1985
1986
1987
1988
100
200
300
400
500

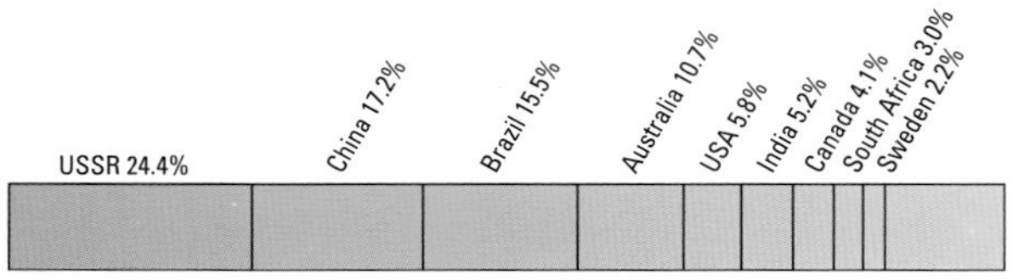

Chromium: Most of the world's chromium production is alloyed with iron and other metals to produce steels with various different properties. Combined with iron, nickel, cobalt and tungsten, chromium produces an exceptionally hard steel, resistant to heat; chrome steels are used for many household items where utility must be matched with appearance – cutlery, for example. Chromium is also used in production of refractory bricks, and its salts for tanning and dyeing leather and cloth.

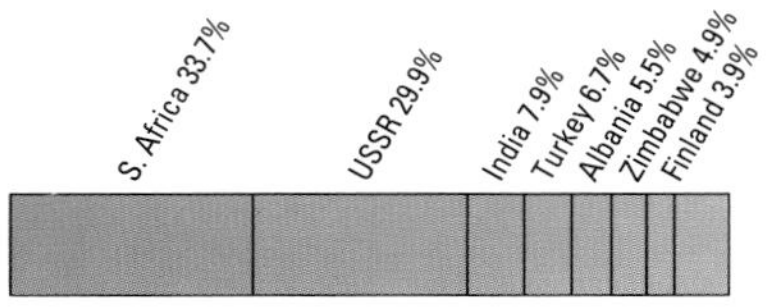

Manganese: In its pure state, manganese is a hard, brittle metal. Alloyed with chrome, iron and nickel, it produces abrasion-resistant steels; manganese-aluminium alloys are light but tough. Found in batteries and inks, manganese is also used in glass production. Manganese ores are frequently found in the same location as sedimentary iron ores. Pyrolusite (MnO_2) and psilomelane are the main economically-exploitable sources.

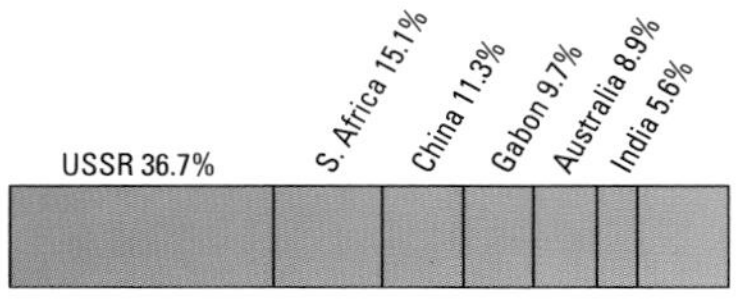

Nickel: Combined with chrome and iron, nickel produces stainless and high-strength steels; similar alloys go to make magnets and electrical heating elements. Nickel combined with copper is widely used to make coins; cupro-nickel alloy is very resistant to corrosion. Its ores yield only modest quantities of nickel – 0.5 to 3.0% – but also contain copper, iron and small amounts of precious metals. Japan, USA, UK, Germany and France are the principal importers.

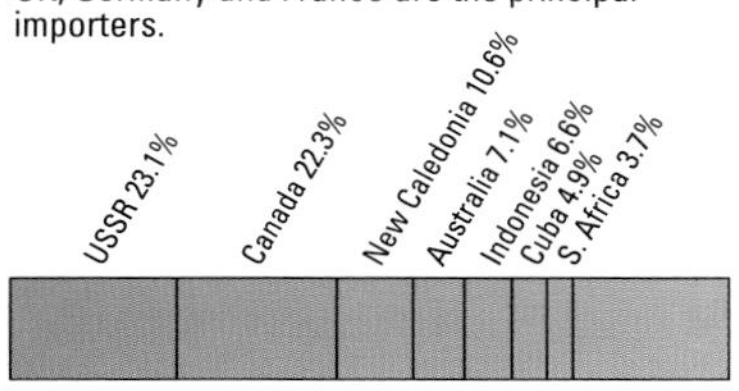

USSR 24.4% · China 17.2% · Brazil 15.5% · Australia 10.7% · USA 5.8% · India 5.2% · Canada 4.1% · South Africa 3.0% · Sweden 2.2%

World total production of iron ore (1989): 989,000,000 tonnes

S. Africa 33.7% · USSR 29.9% · India 7.9% · Turkey 6.7% · Albania 5.5% · Zimbabwe 4.9% · Finland 3.9%

World total (1989): 12,700,000 tonnes

USSR 36.7% · S. Africa 15.1% · China 11.3% · Gabon 9.7% · Australia 8.9% · India 5.6%

World total (1989): 24,000,000 tonnes

USSR 23.1% · Canada 22.3% · New Caledonia 10.6% · Australia 7.1% · Indonesia 6.6% · Cuba 4.9% · S. Africa 3.7%

World total (1989): 910,000 tonnes

DISTRIBUTION

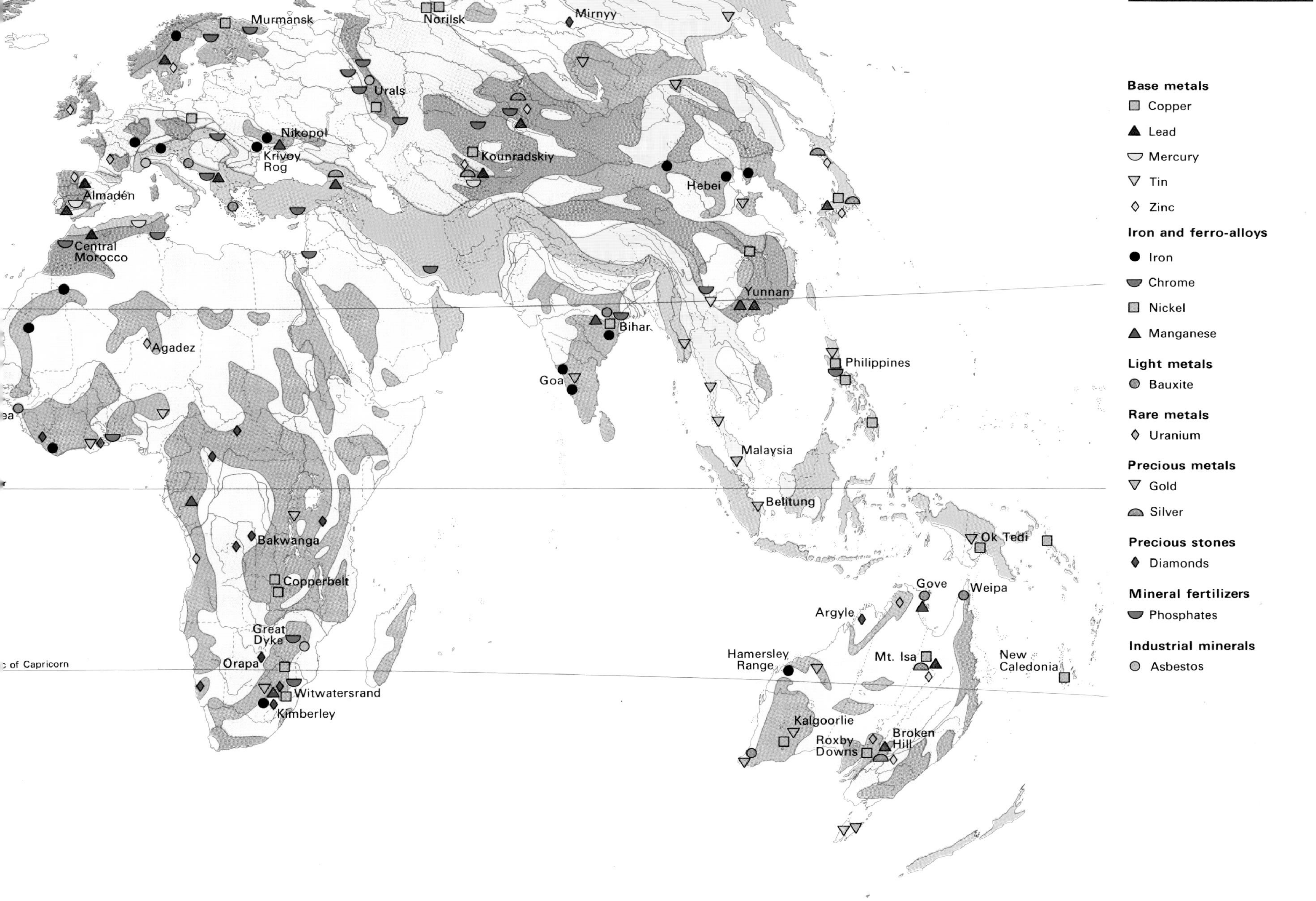

Murmansk · Norilsk · Mirnyy · Urals · Nikopol · Krivoy Rog · Kounradskiy · Hebei · Almadén · Central Morocco · Yunnan · Bihar · Agadez · Goa · Philippines · Malaysia · Belitung · Ok Tedi · Bakwanga · Copperbelt · Great Dyke · Orapa · Witwatersrand · Kimberley · Gove · Weipa · Argyle · Hamersley Range · Mt. Isa · New Caledonia · Kalgoorlie · Roxby Downs · Broken Hill · of Capricorn

Base metals
- Copper
- Lead
- Mercury
- Tin
- Zinc

Iron and ferro-alloys
- Iron
- Chrome
- Nickel
- Manganese

Light metals
- Bauxite

Rare metals
- Uranium

Precious metals
- Gold
- Silver

Precious stones
- Diamonds

Mineral fertilizers
- Phosphates

Industrial minerals
- Asbestos

CARTOGRAPHY BY PHILIP'S. COPYRIGHT REED INTERNATIONAL BOOKS LTD

PRODUCTION: MANUFACTURING

16: WATER UTILIZATION

30: LAND USE AND ECONOMY

34: MINERAL PRODUCTION

35: IRON AND FERRO-ALLOYS

38: TRADING NATIONS MAJOR EXPORTS TRADED PRODUCTS

In its broadest sense, manufacturing is the application of energy, labour and skill to raw materials in order to transform them into finished goods with a higher value than the various elements used in production.

Since the early days of the Industrial Revolution, manufacturing has implied the use of an organized workforce harnessed to some form of machine. The tendency has consistently been for increasingly expensive human labour to be replaced by increasingly complex machinery, which has evolved over time from water-powered looms to fully-integrated robotic plants.

Obviously, not all the world's industries – or manufacturing countries – have reached the same level. Textiles, for example, the foundation of the early Industrial Revolution in the West, can be mass-produced with fairly modest technology; today, they are usually produced in developing countries, mostly in Asia, where the low labour costs compensate for the large workforce that the relatively simple machinery requires. Nevertheless, the trend towards high-technology production, however uneven, seems inexorable. Gains in efficiency make up for the staggering cost of the equipment itself, and the outcome is that fewer and fewer people are employed to produce more and more goods.

One paradoxical result of the increase in industrial efficiency is a relative decline in the importance of the industrial sector of a nation's economy. The economy has already passed through one transition, generations past, when workers were drawn from the land into factories. The second transition releases labour into what is called the service sector of the economy: a diffuse but vital concept that includes not only such obvious services as transport and administration, but also finance, insurance and activities as diverse as fashion design or the writing of computer software.

The process is far advanced in the mature economies of the West, with Japan not far behind. Almost two-thirds of US wealth, for example, is now generated in the service sector, and less than half of Japan's Gross National Product comes from industry. The shrinkage, though, is only relative: between them, these two industrial giants produce almost twice the amount of manufactured goods as the rest of the world put together. And it is on the solid base of production that their general prosperity is founded.

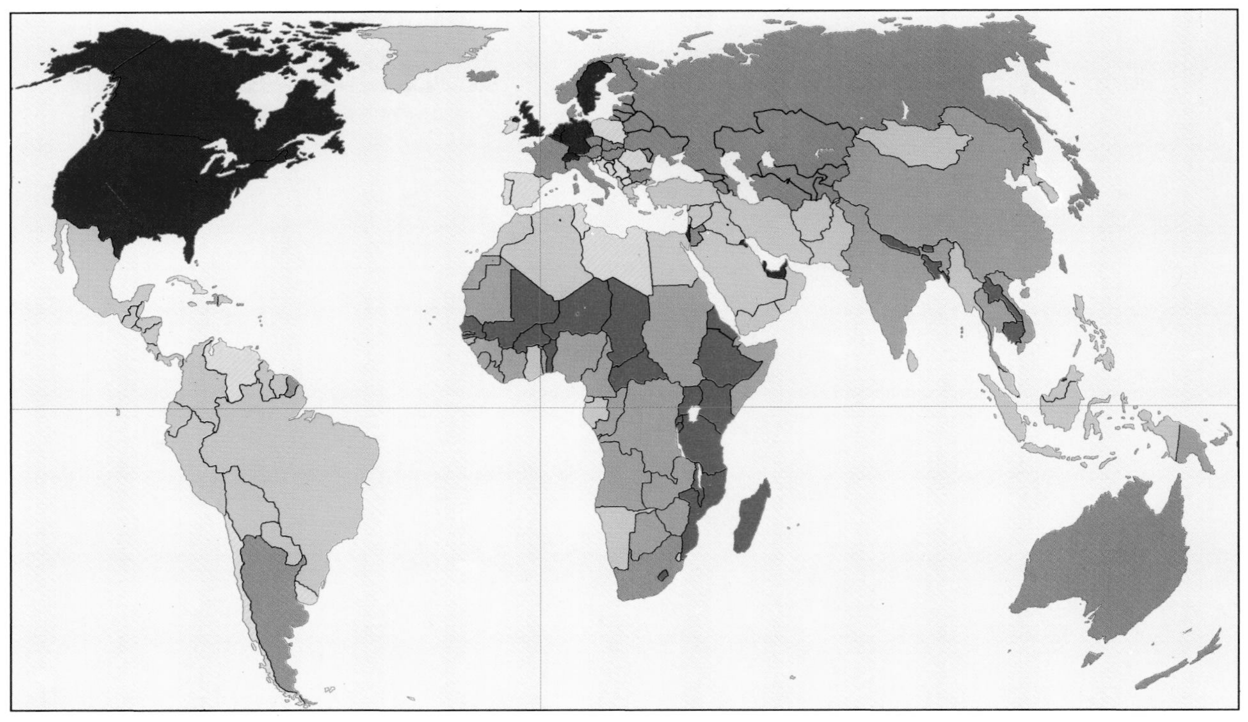

EMPLOYMENT

The number of workers employed in manufacturing for every 100 workers engaged in agriculture

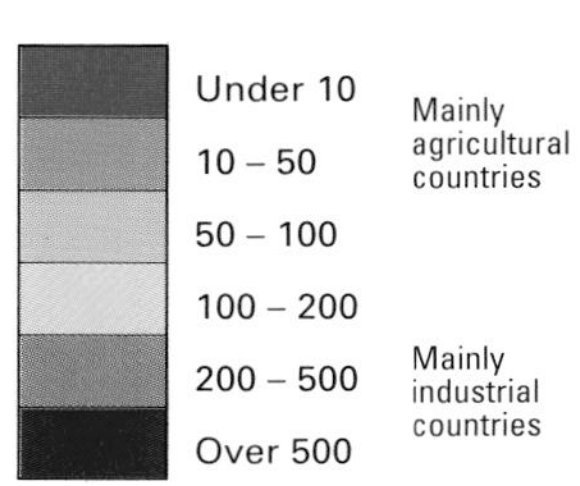

Under 10
10 – 50
50 – 100
100 – 200
200 – 500
Over 500
Mainly agricultural countries
Mainly industrial countries

Selected countries (latest available figures, 1986–89)

Singapore	6,166
Hong Kong	2,632
UK	912
Belgium	751
Germany (W)	749
USA	641
Sweden	615
France	331
Japan	320
Czechoslovakia	286

DIVISION OF EMPLOYMENT

Distribution of workers between agriculture, industry and services, selected countries (late 1980s)

The six countries selected illustrate the usual stages of economic development, from dependence on agriculture through industrial growth to the expansion of the services sector.

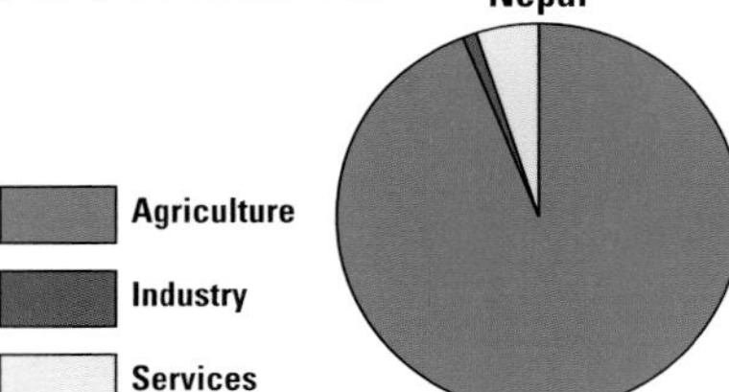

Agriculture
Industry
Services
Nepal

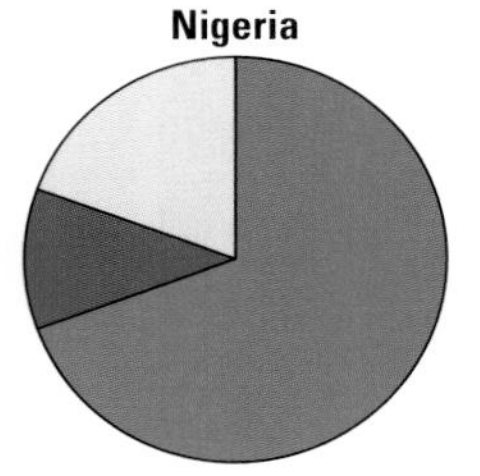

Nigeria

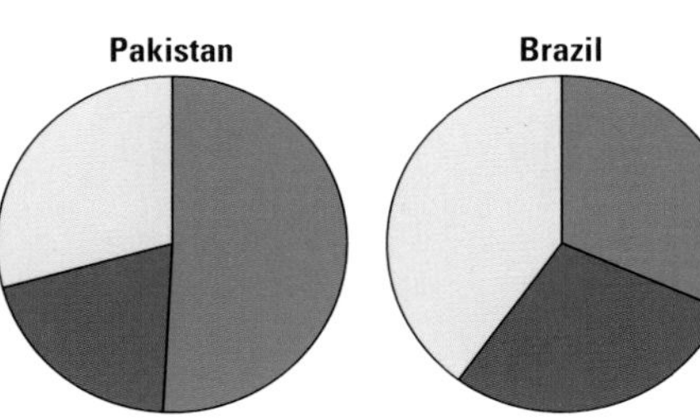

Pakistan
Brazil

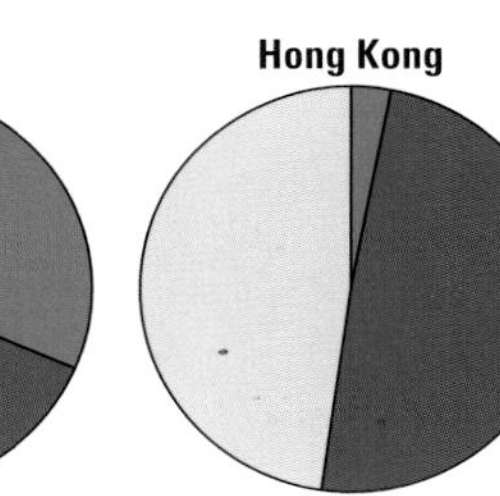

Hong Kong

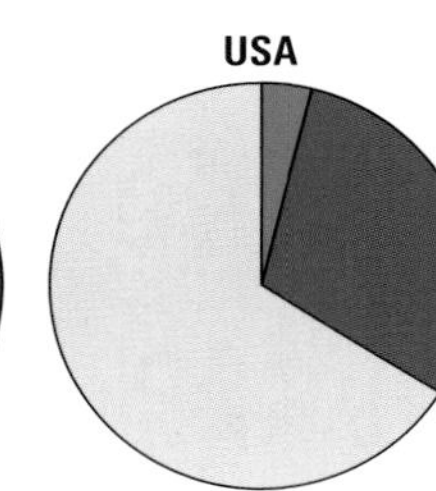

USA

THE WORKFORCE

Percentages of men and women between 15 and 64 in employment, selected countries (late 1980s)

The figures include employees and self-employed, who in developing countries are often subsistence farmers. People in full-time education are excluded. Because of the population age structure in developing countries, the employed population has to support a far larger number of non-workers than its industrial equivalent. For example, more than 52% of Kenya's people are under 15, an age group that makes up less than a tenth of the UK population.

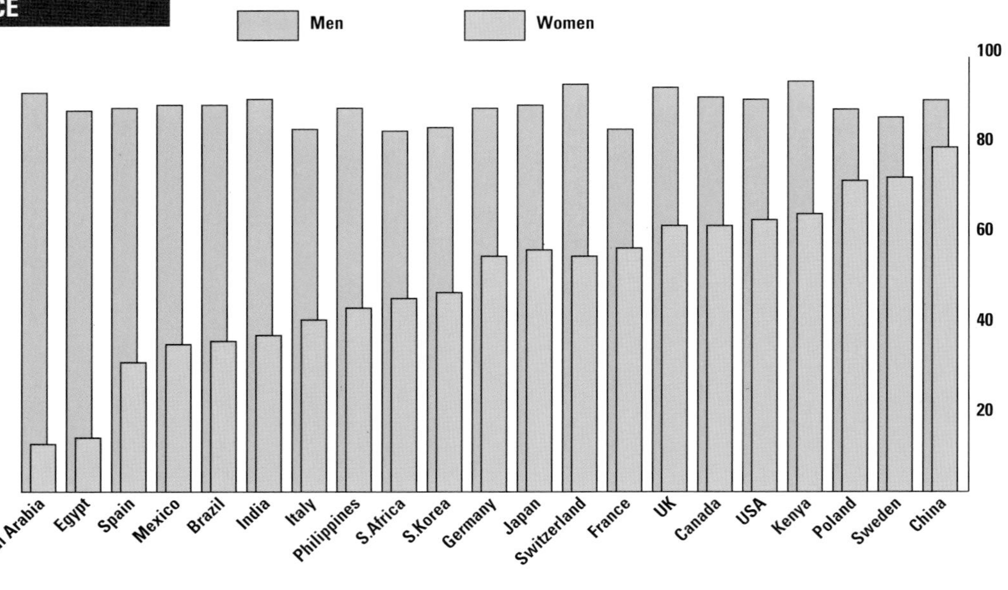

Men
Women
100
80
60
40
20
Saudi Arabia
Egypt
Spain
Mexico
Brazil
India
Italy
Philippines
S.Africa
S.Korea
Germany
Japan
Switzerland
France
UK
Canada
USA
Kenya
Poland
Sweden
China

WEALTH CREATION

The Gross National Product (GNP) of the world's largest economies, US $ billion (1991)

1.	USA	5,686,038	21.	Austria	157,538
2.	Japan	3,337,191	22.	Iran	127,366
3.	Germany	1,516,785	23.	Finland	121,982
4.	France	1,167,749	24.	Denmark	121,695
5.	Italy	1,072,198	25.	Ukraine	121,458
6.	UK	963,696	26.	Indonesia	111,409
7.	Canada	568,765	27.	Saudi Arabia	105,133
8.	Spain	486,614	28.	Turkey	103,388
9.	Russia	479,546	29.	Norway	102,885
10.	Brazil	447,324	30.	Argentina	91,211
11.	China	424,012	31.	South Africa	90,953
12.	Australia	287,765	32.	Thailand	89,548
13.	India	284,668	33.	Hong Kong	77,302
14.	Netherlands	278,839	34.	Poland	70,640
15.	South Korea	274,464	35.	Greece	65,504
16.	Mexico	252,381	36.	Israel	59,128
17.	Switzerland	225,890	37.	Portugal	58,451
18.	Sweden	218,934	38.	Venezuela	52,775
19.	Belgium	192,370	39.	Algeria	52,239
20.	Taiwan	161,000	40.	Pakistan	46,725

CARTOGRAPHY BY PHILIP'S. COPYRIGHT REED INTERNATIONAL BOOKS LTD

PATTERNS OF PRODUCTION

Breakdown of industrial output by value, selected countries (1987)

	Food & agriculture	Textiles & clothing	Machinery & transport	Chemicals	Other
Algeria	26%	20%	11%	1%	41%
Argentina	24%	10%	16%	12%	37%
Australia	18%	7%	21%	8%	45%
Austria	17%	8%	25%	6%	43%
Belgium	19%	8%	23%	13%	36%
Brazil	15%	12%	24%	9%	40%
Burkina Faso	62%	18%	2%	1%	17%
Canada	15%	7%	25%	9%	44%
Denmark	22%	6%	23%	10%	39%
Egypt	20%	27%	13%	10%	31%
Finland	13%	6%	24%	7%	50%
France	18%	7%	33%	9%	33%
Germany	12%	5%	38%	10%	36%
Greece	20%	22%	14%	7%	38%
Hong Kong	6%	40%	20%	2%	33%
Hungary	6%	11%	37%	11%	35%
India	11%	16%	26%	15%	32%
Indonesia	23%	11%	10%	10%	47%
Iran	13%	22%	22%	7%	36%
Israel	13%	10%	28%	8%	42%
Ireland	28%	7%	20%	15%	28%
Italy	7%	13%	32%	10%	38%
Japan	10%	6%	38%	10%	37%
Kenya	35%	12%	14%	9%	29%
Malaysia	21%	5%	23%	14%	37%
Mexico	24%	12%	14%	12%	39%
Netherlands	19%	4%	28%	11%	38%
New Zealand	26%	10%	16%	6%	43%
Norway	21%	3%	26%	7%	44%
Pakistan	34%	21%	8%	12%	25%
Philippines	40%	7%	7%	10%	35%
Poland	15%	16%	30%	6%	33%
Portugal	17%	22%	16%	8%	38%
Singapore	6%	5%	46%	8%	36%
South Africa	14%	8%	17%	11%	49%
South Korea	15%	17%	24%	9%	35%
Spain	17%	9%	22%	9%	43%
Sweden	10%	2%	35%	8%	44%
Thailand	30%	17%	14%	6%	33%
Turkey	20%	14%	15%	8%	43%
UK	14%	6%	32%	11%	36%
USA	12%	5%	35%	10%	38%
Venezuela	23%	8%	9%	11%	49%

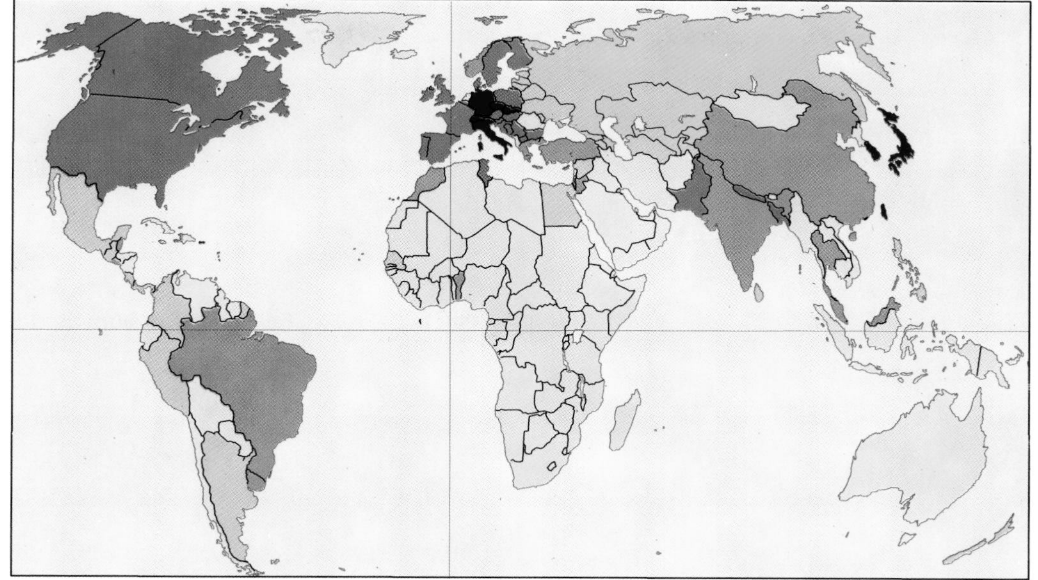

INDUSTRY AND TRADE

Manufactured goods as a percentage of total exports (1989)

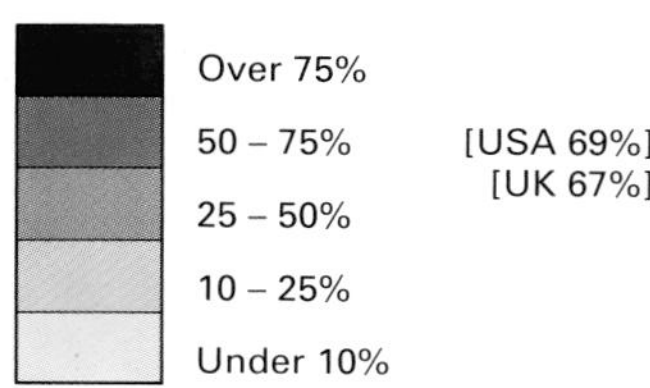

Over 75%
50 – 75%
25 – 50%
10 – 25%
Under 10%
[USA 69%]
[UK 67%]

The Far East and South-east Asia (Japan 99.5%, Macau 98.5%, Taiwan 96.8%, Hong Kong 96.1%, South Korea 95.9%) are most dominant, but many countries in Europe (e.g. Austria 98.4%) are also heavily dependent on manufactured goods.

AUTOMOBILES

Production of passenger cars in thousands (top ten countries, 1988)

COMMERCIAL VEHICLES

Trucks, buses and coaches produced by the top ten manufacturing countries, in thousands (1988)

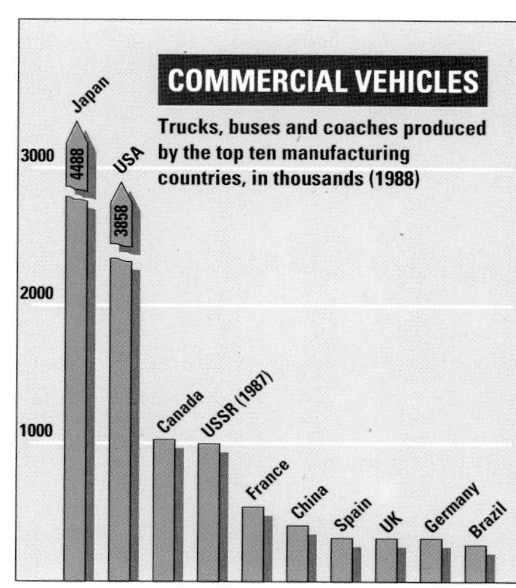
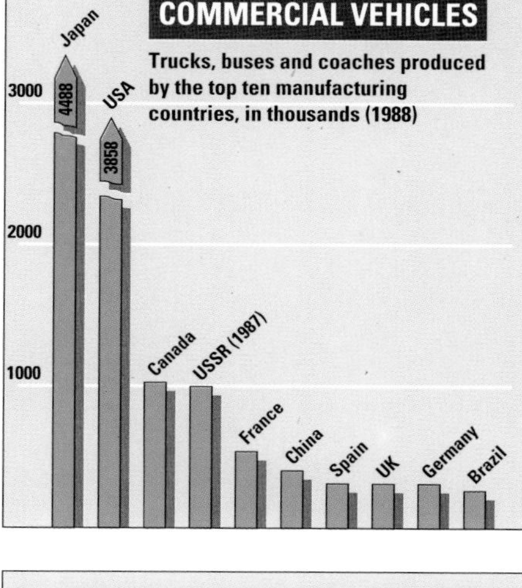

TELEVISION SETS

Production of television receivers in thousands (top ten countries, 1988)

STEEL PRODUCTION

Steel output in thousand tonnes (top ten countries 1989)

SHIPBUILDING

Tonnage produced by top ten shipbuilding countries in thousand tonnes (1989)

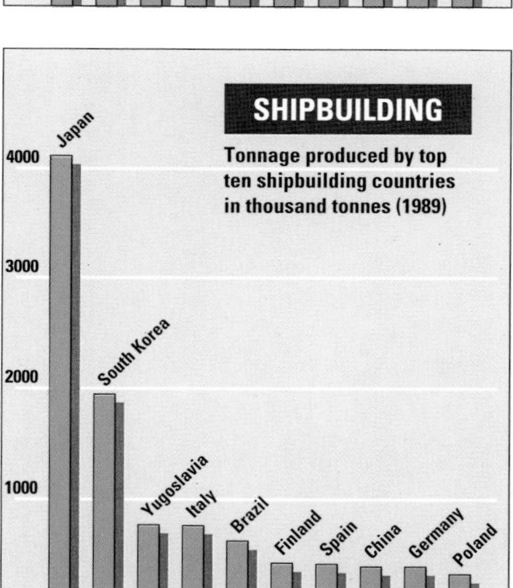

4000
3000
2000
1000
Japan
South Korea
Yugoslavia
Italy
Brazil
Finland
Spain
China
Germany
Poland

NATURAL & SYNTHETIC RUBBER

Rubber produced by top ten manufacturing countries, thousands of tonnes (1988). Natural rubber made up 34% of the total.

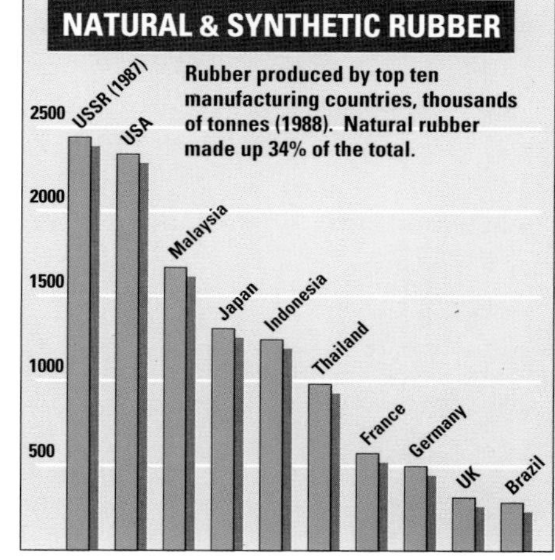

2500
2000
1500
1000
500
USSR (1987)
USA
Malaysia
Japan
Indonesia
Thailand
France
Germany
UK
Brazil

WASHING MACHINES

Production in thousands (top ten countries, 1988)

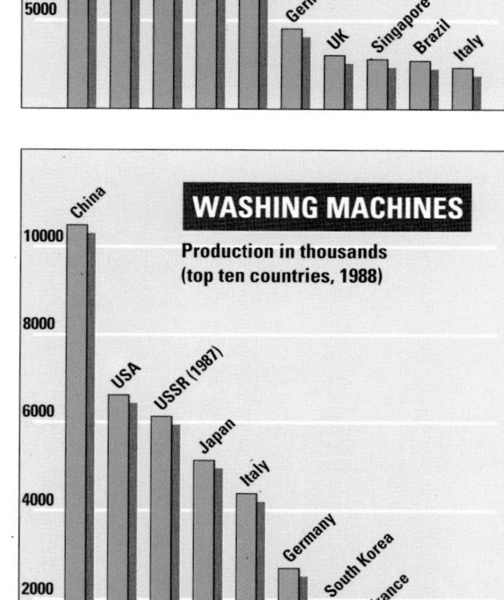

10000
8000
6000
4000
2000
China
USA
USSR (1987)
Japan
Italy
Germany
South Korea
France
UK
Poland

INDUSTRIAL POWER

Industrial output (mining, manufacturing, construction, energy and water production), top 40 nations, US $ billion (1988)

1. USA	1,249.54	21. Austria	50.63
2. Japan	1,155.41	22. Belgium	46.88
3. W. Germany	479.69	23. Poland	39.52
4. USSR (1987)	326.54	24. Finland	35.50
5. France	304.95	25. South Africa	35.46
6. UK	295.00	26. Saudi Arabia	33.36
7. Italy	286.00	27. Denmark	30.79
8. China	174.05	28. Iraq	30.27
9. Canada	171.06	29. Czechoslovakia	30.18
10. Spain	126.60	30. Yugoslavia	29.32
11. Brazil	116.13	31. Indonesia	29.03
12. Netherlands	76.48	32. Norway	28.74
13. Sweden	75.17	33. Argentina	26.27
14. South Korea	74.00	34. Turkey	26.07
15. India	72.69	35. Israel	24.15
16. Australia	72.63	36. Algeria	22.88
17. E. Germany	64.66	37. Venezuela	22.70
18. Switzerland	63.37	38. Romania	22.19
19. Mexico	61.57	39. Iran	19.90
20. Taiwan	54.81	40. Thailand	18.62

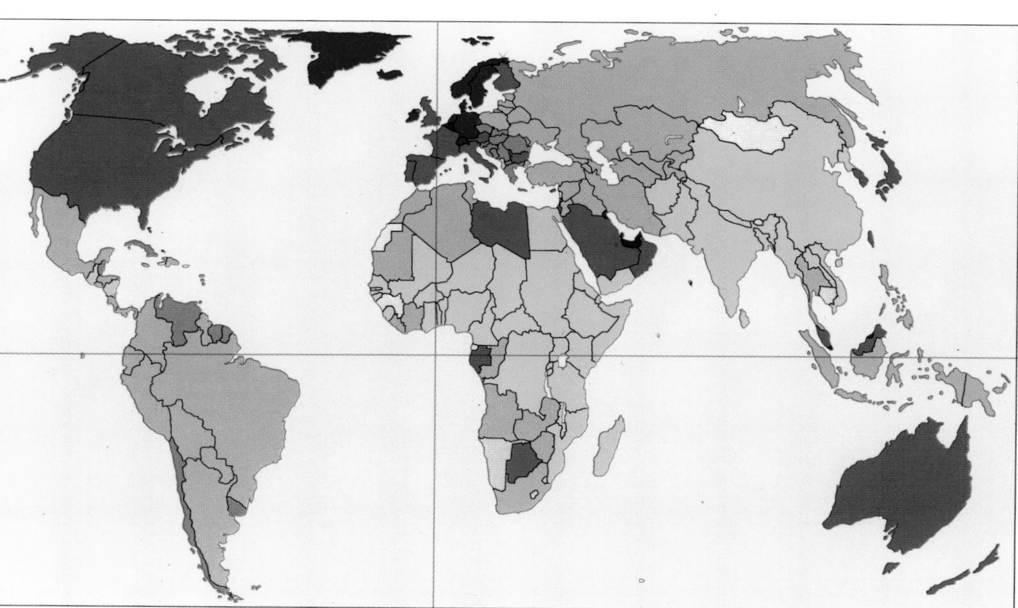

Statistics for the new republics of the former USSR, Czechoslovakia and Yugoslavia are not yet available. The map shows the statistics for the entire USSR, Czechoslovakia and Yugoslavia.

EXPORTS PER CAPITA

Value of exports in US $, divided by total population (1988)

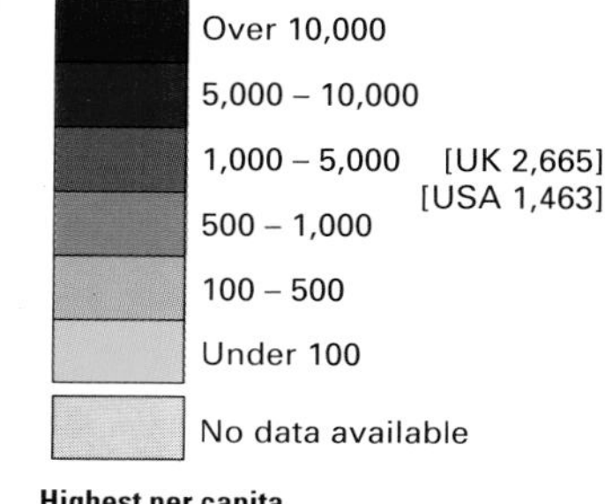

Over 10,000
5,000 – 10,000
1,000 – 5,000
500 – 1,000
100 – 500
Under 100
No data available
[UK 2,665]
[USA 1,463]

Highest per capita

Singapore	16,671
Hong Kong	12,676
UAE	10,217
Belgium	10,200
Bahamas	8,580
Qatar	8,431

CARTOGRAPHY BY PHILIP'S. COPYRIGHT REED INTERNATIONAL BOOKS LTD

PRODUCTION: TRADE

29: INTERNATIONAL ORGANIZATIONS
30: SELF-SUFFICIENCY IN FOOD
33: FUEL EXPORTS MOVEMENTS OF OIL
34: MINERAL EXPORTS
37: INDUSTRY AND TRADE EXPORTS PER CAPITA
43: TOURISM

Thriving international trade is the outward sign of a healthy world economy – the obvious indicator that some countries have goods to sell and others the wherewithal to buy them. Despite local fluctuations, trade throughout the 1980s grew consistently faster than output, increasing in value by almost 50% between 1979–89. It remains dominated by the wealthy, industrialized countries of the Organization for Economic Development: between them, the 24 OECD members account for almost 75% of world imports and exports in most years. OECD dominance is just as marked in the trade in 'invisibles' – a column in the balance sheet that includes, among other headings, the export of services, interest payments on overseas investments, tourism, and even remittances from migrant workers abroad. In the UK, 'invisibles' account for more than half all trading income.

However, the size of these great trading economies means that imports and exports usually comprise a fraction of their total wealth: in the case of the export-conscious Japanese, trade in goods and services amounts to less than 18% of GDP. In poorer countries, trade – often in a single commodity – may amount to 50% of GDP or more. And there are oddities: import-export figures for the entrepôt economy of Singapore, the transit point for much Asian trade, are almost double that small nation's total earnings.

WORLD TRADE

Percentage share of total world exports by value (1990)*

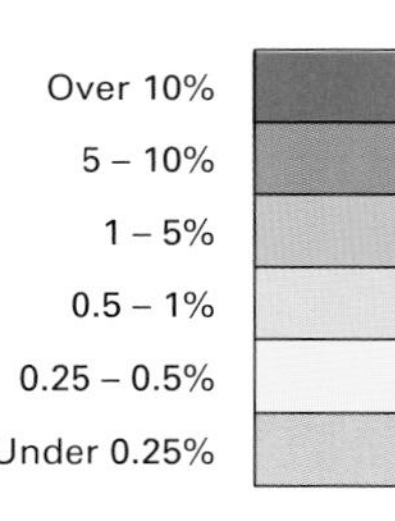
Over 10%
5 – 10%
1 – 5%
0.5 – 1%
0.25 – 0.5%
Under 0.25%

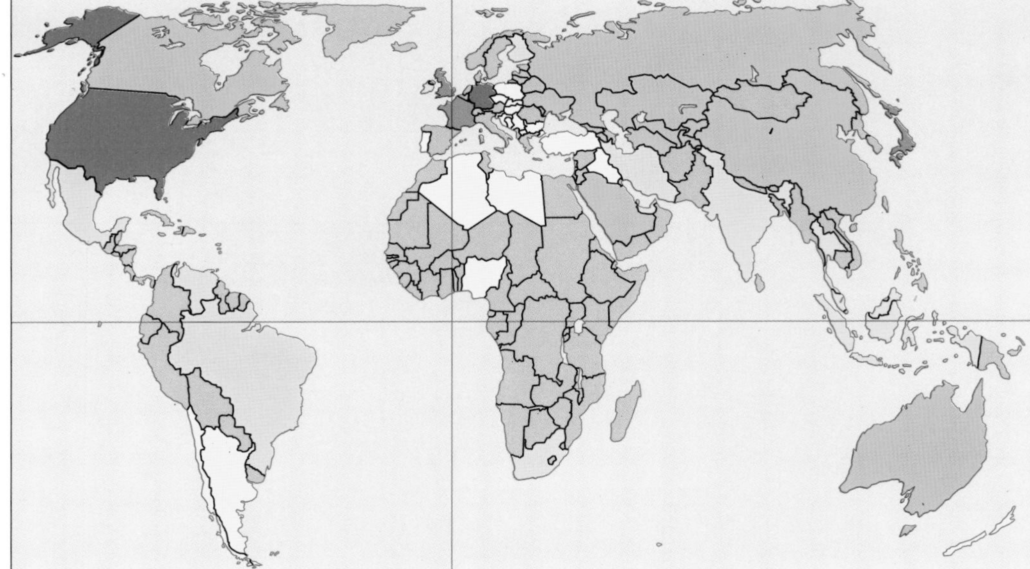

THE GREAT TRADING NATIONS

The imports and exports of the top ten trading nations as a percentage of world trade (latest available year). Each country's trade in manufactured goods is shown in orange.

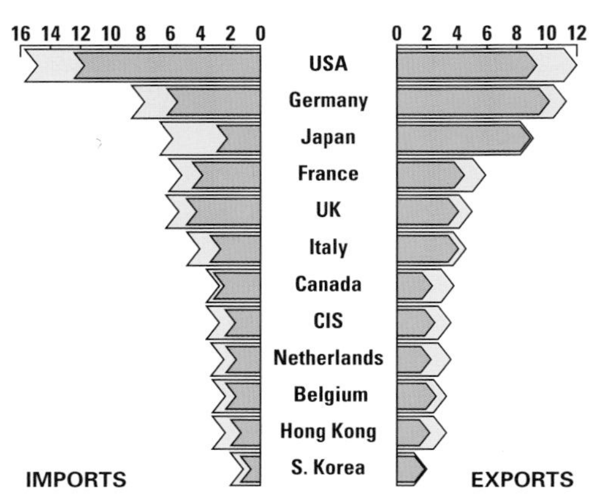
16 14 12 10 8 6 4 2 0
0 2 4 6 8 10 12
USA
Germany
Japan
France
UK
Italy
Canada
CIS
Netherlands
Belgium
Hong Kong
S. Korea
IMPORTS
EXPORTS

MAJOR EXPORTS

Leading manufactured items and their exporters, by percentage of world total in US $ (latest available year)

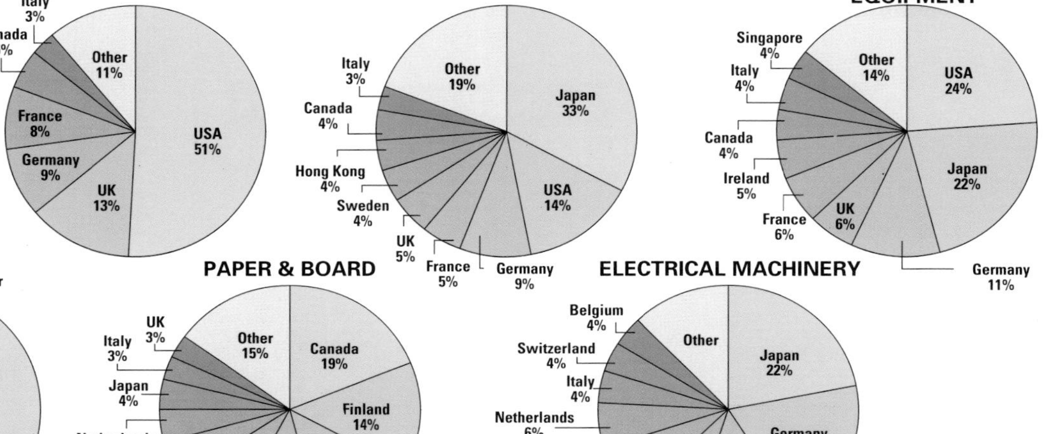
AIRCRAFT
Italy 3%
Canada 5%
Other 11%
France 8%
Germany 9%
UK 13%
USA 51%
TELECOMMUNICATIONS GEAR
Italy 3%
Canada 4%
Other 19%
Japan 33%
Hong Kong 4%
Sweden 4%
UK 5%
France 5%
Germany 9%
USA 14%
DATA PROCESSING EQUIPMENT
Singapore 4%
Italy 4%
Other 14%
USA 24%
Canada 4%
Ireland 5%
France 6%
UK 6%
Japan 22%
Germany 11%
PAPER & BOARD
UK 3%
Italy 3%
Other 15%
Canada 19%
Japan 4%
Finland 14%
Netherlands 4%
France 5%
USA 8%
Sweden 13%
Germany 12%
ELECTRICAL MACHINERY
Belgium 4%
Switzerland 4%
Italy 4%
Other
Japan 22%
Netherlands 6%
France 7%
UK 8%
USA 14%
Germany 19%

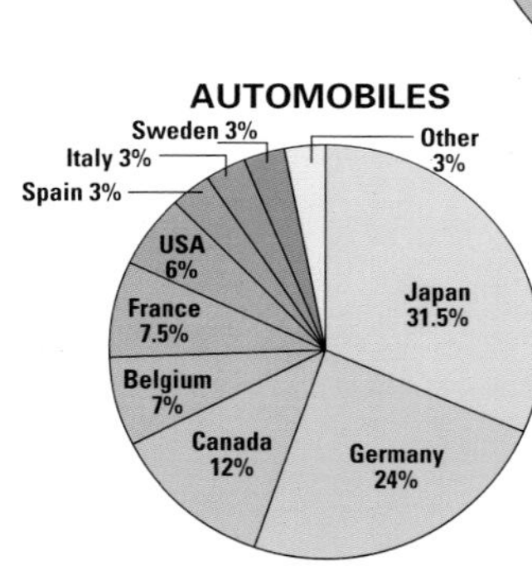
AUTOMOBILES
Sweden 3%
Other 3%
Italy 3%
Spain 3%
USA 6%
France 7.5%
Belgium 7%
Canada 12%
Japan 31.5%
Germany 24%

TRADED PRODUCTS

Top ten manufactures traded, by value in billions of US $ (latest available year)

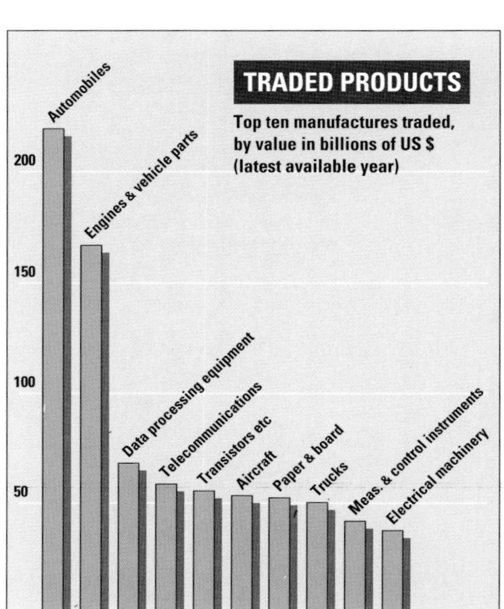
200
150
100
50
Automobiles
Engines & vehicle parts
Data processing equipment
Telecommunications
Transistors etc
Aircraft
Paper & board
Trucks
Meas. & control instruments
Electrical machinery

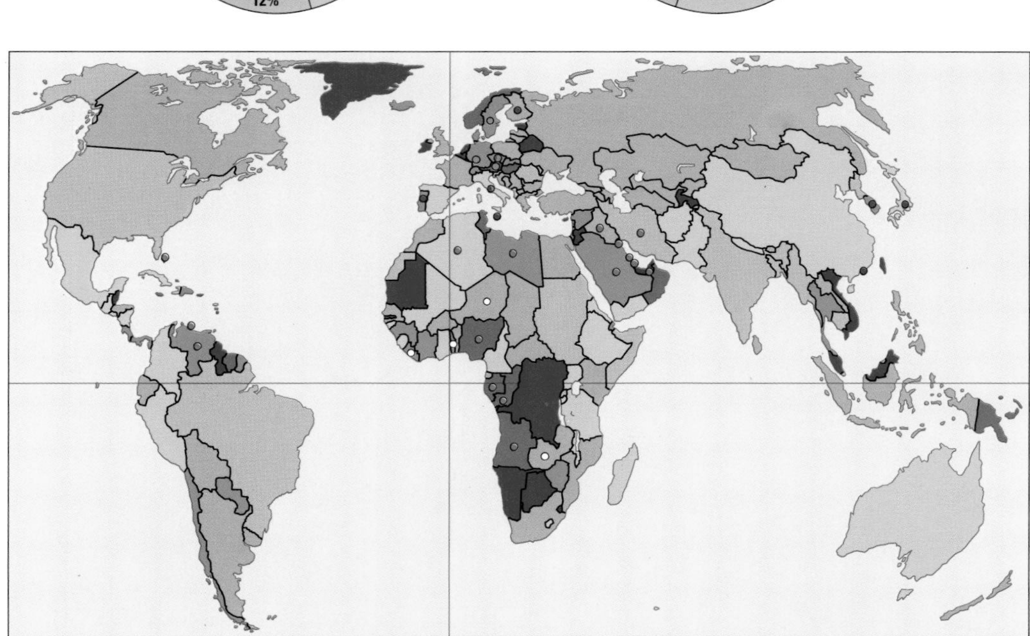

DEPENDENCE ON TRADE

Value of exports as a percentage of Gross Domestic Product (1991)

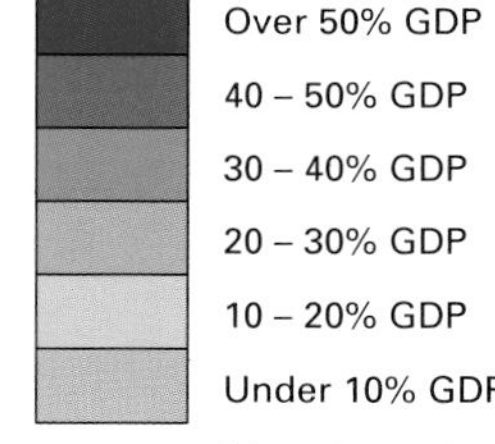
Over 50% GDP
40 – 50% GDP
30 – 40% GDP
20 – 30% GDP
10 – 20% GDP
Under 10% GDP
Most dependent on industrial exports (over 75% of total exports)
Most dependent on fuel exports (over 75% of total exports)
Most dependent on mineral and metal exports (over 75% of total exports)

*Statistics for the new republics of the former USSR, Czechoslovakia and Yugoslavia are not yet available. The map shows the statistics for the entire USSR, Czechoslovakia and Yugoslavia.

CARTOGRAPHY BY PHILIP'S. COPYRIGHT REED INTERNATIONAL BOOKS LTD

WORLD SHIPPING

While ocean passenger traffic is nowadays relatively modest, sea transport still carries most of the world's trade. Oil and bulk carriers make up the majority of the world fleet, although the general cargo category was the fastest growing in 1989, a year in which total tonnage increased by 1.5%.

Almost 30% of world shipping sails under a 'flag of convenience', whereby owners take advantage of low taxes by registering their vessels in a foreign country the ships will never see, notably Panama and Liberia.

MERCHANT FLEETS

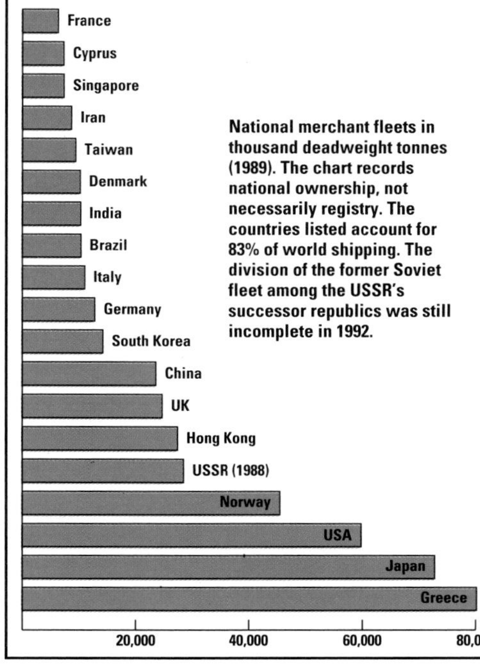
France
Cyprus
Singapore
Iran
Taiwan
Denmark
India
Brazil
Italy
Germany
South Korea
China
UK
Hong Kong
USSR (1988)
Norway
USA
Japan
Greece
20,000
40,000
60,000
80,000

National merchant fleets in thousand deadweight tonnes (1989). The chart records national ownership, not necessarily registry. The countries listed account for 83% of world shipping. The division of the former Soviet fleet among the USSR's successor republics was still incomplete in 1992.

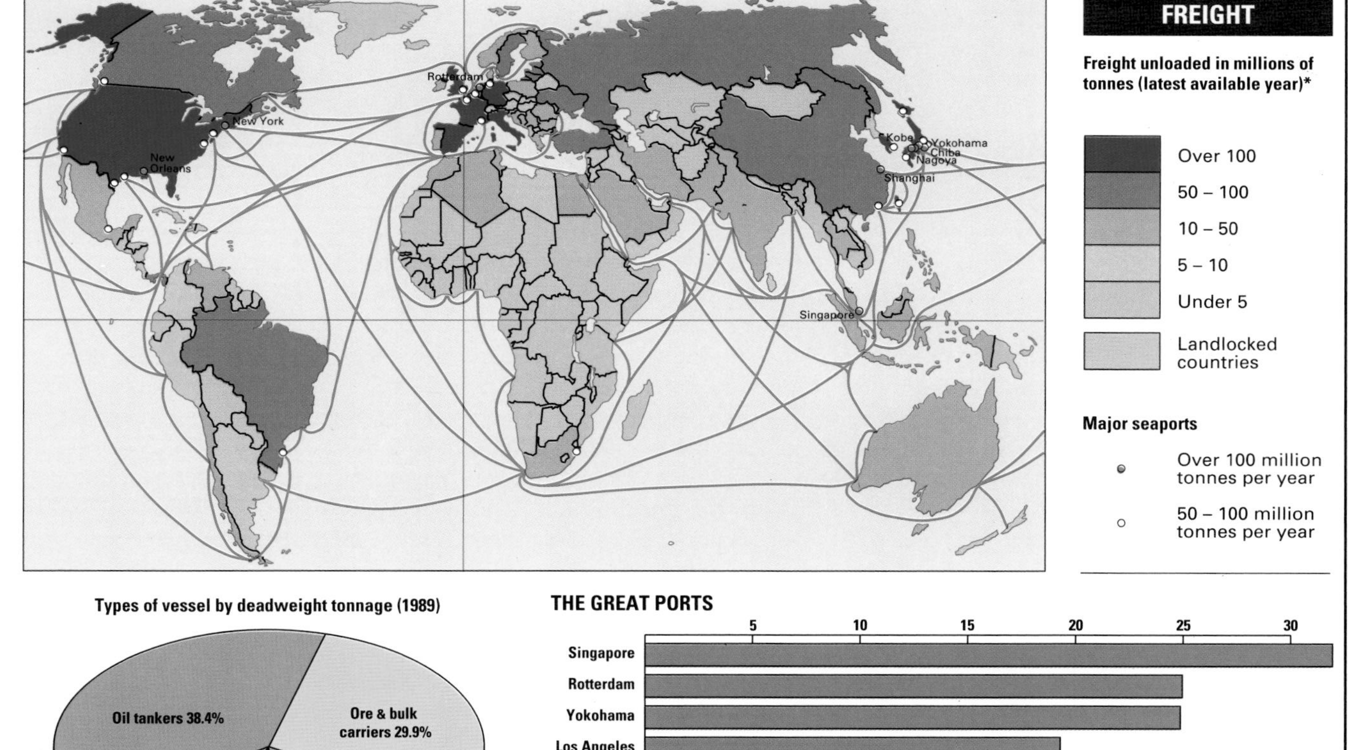
Rotterdam
New York
New Orleans
Kobe
Yokohama
Chiba
Nagoya
Shanghai
Singapore

FREIGHT

Freight unloaded in millions of tonnes (latest available year)*

- Over 100
- 50 – 100
- 10 – 50
- 5 – 10
- Under 5
- Landlocked countries

Major seaports

- Over 100 million tonnes per year
- 50 – 100 million tonnes per year

Types of vessel by deadweight tonnage (1989)

- Oil tankers 38.4%
- Ore & bulk carriers 29.9%
- General cargo 16.1%
- Others 9.7%
- Container ships 3.8%
- Liquid gas carriers 1.6%
- Ferries & passenger ships 0.5%

THE GREAT PORTS

Scale: 5, 10, 15, 20, 25, 30

- Singapore
- Rotterdam
- Yokohama
- Los Angeles
- Antwerp
- Hong Kong
- Europoort
- New Orleans
- Hamburg
- Kobe

The world's ten busiest ports by million tonnes of shipping arrivals (late 1980s)

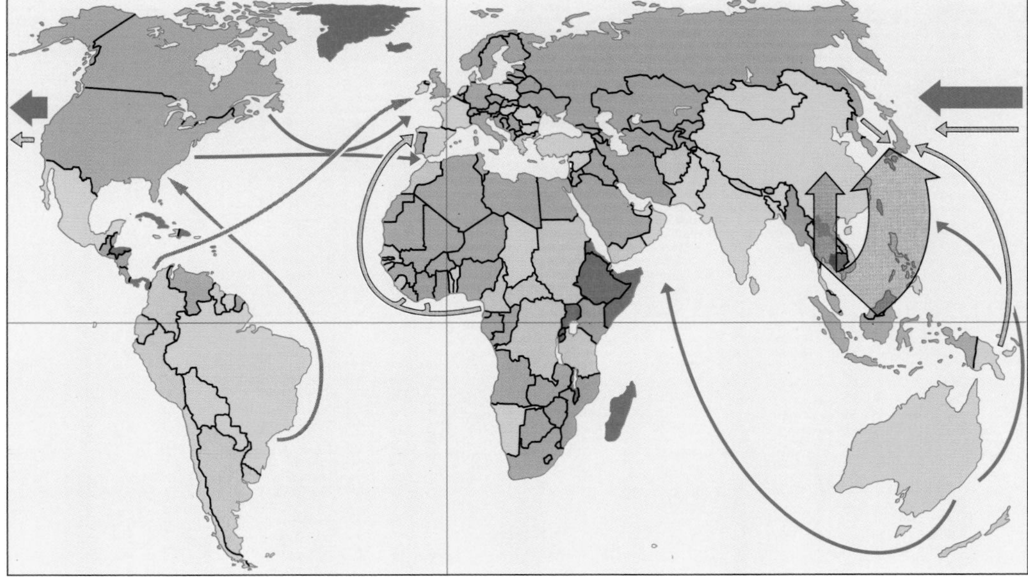

TRADE IN PRIMARY PRODUCTS

Primary products (excluding fuels, minerals and metals) as a percentage of total export value (latest available year)*

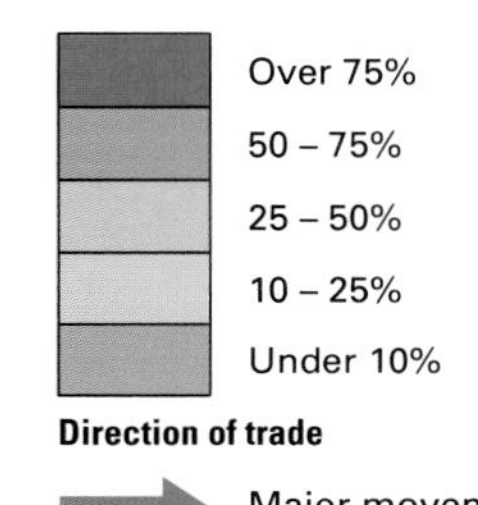
Over 75%
50 – 75%
25 – 50%
10 – 25%
Under 10%

Direction of trade

- Major movements of cereals
- Major movements of coffee
- Major movements of hardwoods

Arrows show the major trade directions of selected primary products, and are proportional to export value.

BALANCE OF TRADE

Value of exports in proportion to the value of imports (latest available year)

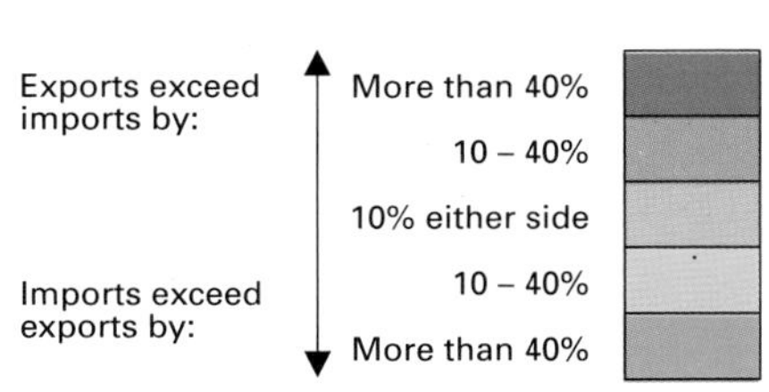
Exports exceed imports by:
More than 40%
10 – 40%
10% either side
Imports exceed exports by:
10 – 40%
More than 40%

The total world trade balance should amount to zero, since exports must equal imports on a global scale. In practice, at least $100 billion in exports go unrecorded, leaving the world with an apparent deficit and many countries in a better position than public accounting reveals. However, a favourable trade balance is not necessarily a sign of prosperity: many poorer countries must maintain a high surplus in order to service debts, and do so by restricting imports below the levels needed to sustain successful economies.

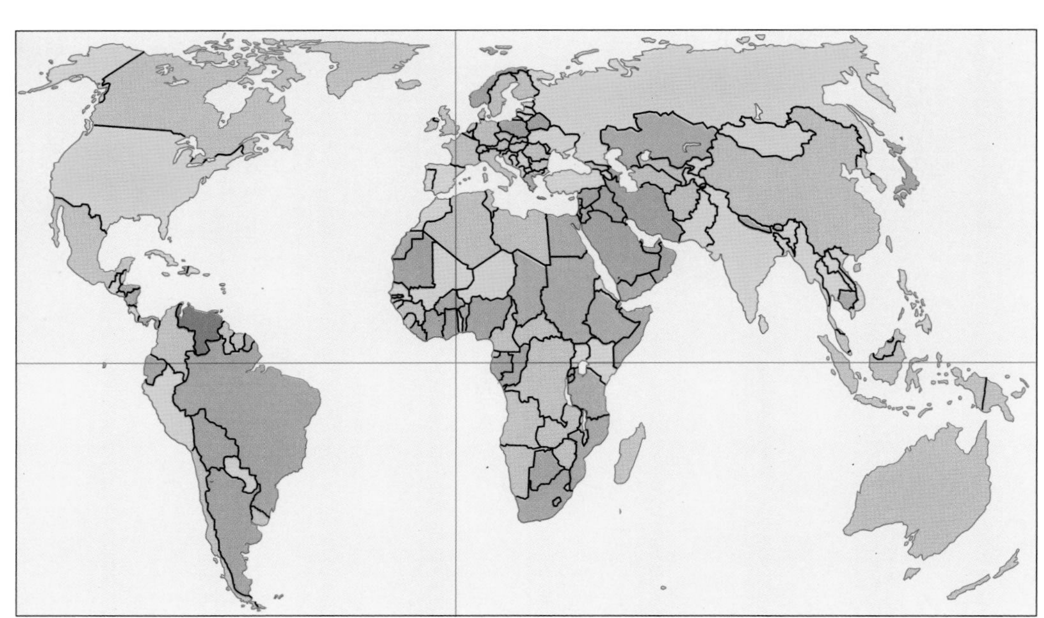

**Statistics for the new republics of the former USSR, Czechoslovakia and Yugoslavia are not yet available. The map shows the statistics for the entire USSR, Czechoslovakia and Yugoslavia.*

CARTOGRAPHY BY PHILIP'S. COPYRIGHT REED INTERNATIONAL BOOKS LTD

QUALITY OF LIFE: WEALTH

36: WEALTH CREATION

37: INDUSTRIAL POWER EXPORT PER CAPITA

38: WORLD TRADE MAJOR EXPORTS

39: BALANCE OF TRADE

43: DISTRIBUTION OF SPENDING DISTRIBUTION OF INCOME

Throughout the 1980s, most of the world became at least slightly richer. There were exceptions: in Africa, the poorest of the continents, many incomes actually fell, and the upheavals in Eastern Europe in 1989 left whole populations awash with political freedom but worse off financially in economies still teetering towards capitalism.

Most of the improvements, however, came to those who were already, in world terms, extremely affluent: the gap between rich and poor grew steadily wider. And in those developing countries that showed significant statistical progress, advances were often confined to a few favoured areas, while conditions in other, usually rural, districts went from bad to worse.

The pattern of world poverty varies from region to region. In most of Asia, the process of recognized development is generally under way, with production increases outpacing population growth. By 2000, less than 10% of the Chinese population should be officially rated 'poor': without the means to buy either adequate food or the basic necessities required to take a full part in everyday life. Even India's lower growth rate should be enough to reduce the burden of poverty for at least some of its people. In Latin America, average per capita production is high enough for most countries to be considered 'middle income' in world rankings. But although adequate resources exist, Latin American wealth is distributed with startling inequality. According to a 1990 World Bank report, a tax of only 2% on the richest fifth would raise enough money to pull every one of the continent's 437 million people above the poverty line.

In Africa, solutions will be much harder to find. The bane of high population growth has often been aggravated by incompetent administration, war and a succession of natural disasters. Population is the crux of the problem: numbers are growing anything up to twice as fast as the economies that try to support them. Aid from the developed world is only a partial solution; although Africa receives more aid than any other continent, much has been wasted on overambitious projects or lost in webs of inexperienced or corrupt bureaucracy. Yet without aid, Africa seems doomed to permanent crisis.

The rich countries can afford to increase their spending. The 24 members of the Organisation for Economic Co-operation and Development comprise only 16% of the world's population, yet between them the nations accounted for almost 80% of total world production in 1988, a share that is likely to increase as the year 2000 approaches.

CONTINENTAL SHARES

Shares of population and of wealth (GNP) by continent

Generalized continental figures show the startling difference between rich and poor, but mask the successes or failures of individual countries. Japan, for example, with less than 4% of Asia's population, produces almost 70% of the continent's output.

POPULATION

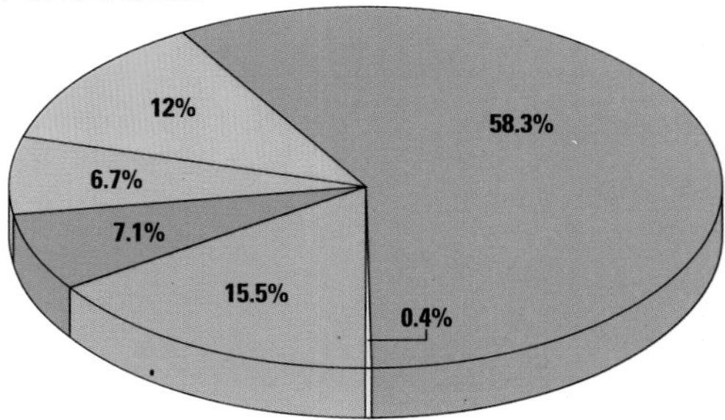
12%
58.3%
6.7%
7.1%
15.5%
0.4%

GNP

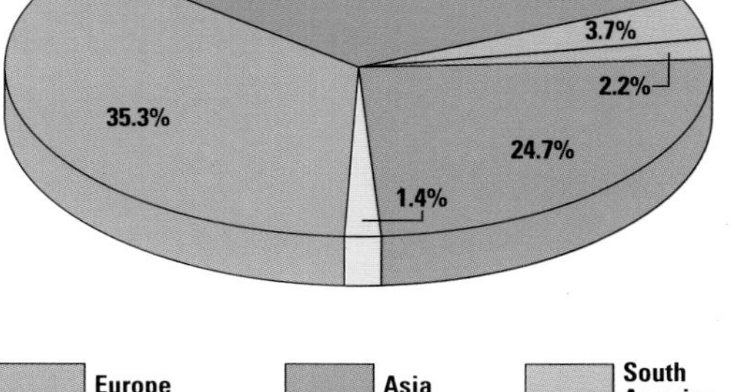
32.6%
3.7%
2.2%
35.3%
24.7%
1.4%

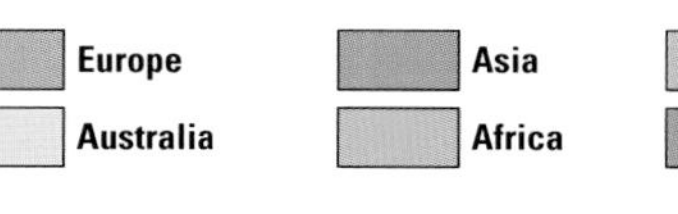
Europe
Asia
South America
Australia
Africa
North America

CURRENCIES

Currency units of the world's most powerful economies

1. USA: US Dollar($, US $) = 100 cents
2. Japan: Yen (Y, ¥) = 100 sen
3. Germany: Deutsche Mark (DM) = 100 Pfennige
4. France: French Franc (Fr) = 100 centimes
5. Italy: Italian Lira (L, £, Lit)
6. UK: Pound Sterling (£) = 100 pence
7. Canada: Canadian Dollar (C$, Can$) = 100 cents
8. China: Renminbi Yuan (RMBY, $, Y) = 10 jiao = 100 fen
9. Brazil: Cruzado (Cr$) = 100 centavos
10. Spain: Peseta (Pta, Pa) = 100 céntimos
11. India: Indian Rupee (Re, Rs) = 100 paisa
12. Australia: Australian Dollar ($A) = 100 cents
13. Netherlands: Guilder, Florin (Gld, f) = 100 centimes
14. Switzerland: Swiss Franc (SFr, SwF) = 100 centimes
15. South Korea: Won (W) = 100 Chon
16. Sweden: Swedish Krona (SKr) = 100 ore
17. Mexico: Mexican Pesos (Mex$) = 100 centavos
18. Belgium: Belgian Franc (BFr) = 100 centimes
19. Austria: Schilling (S, Sch) = 100 groschen
20. Finland: Markka (FMk) = 100 penni
21. Denmark: Danish Krone (DKr) = 100 ore
22. Norway: Norwegian Krone (NKr) = 100 ore
23. Saudi Arabia: Riyal (SAR, SRl$) = 100 halalah
24. Indonesia: Rupiah (Rp) = 100 sen
25. South Africa: Rand (R) = 100 cents

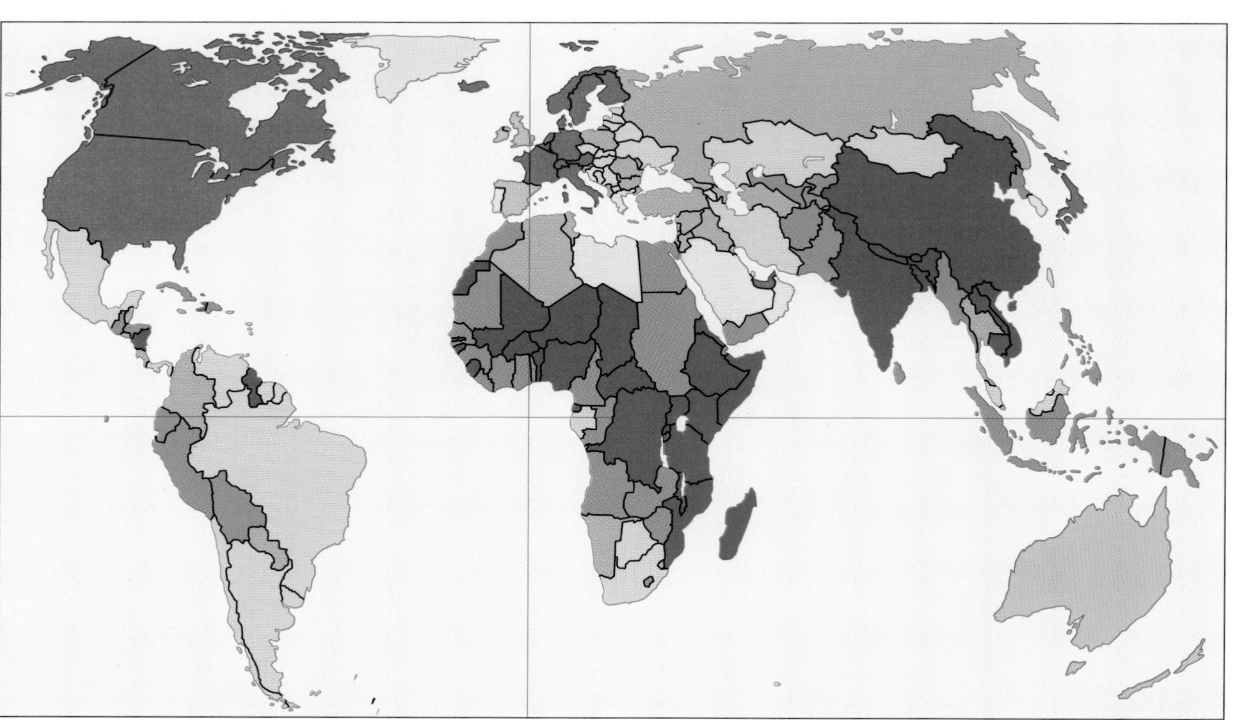

LEVELS OF INCOME

Gross National Product per capita: the value of total production divided by the population (1991)

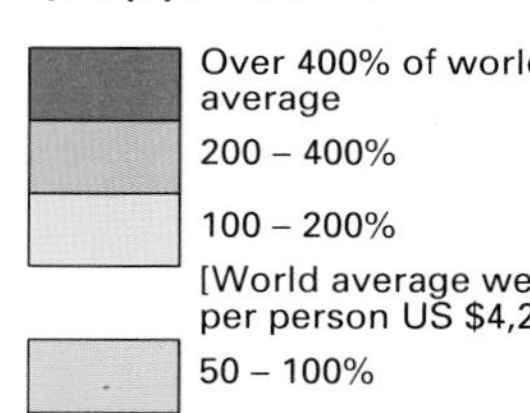
Over 400% of world average
200 – 400%
100 – 200%
[World average wealth per person US $4,210]
50 – 100%
25 – 50%
10 – 25%
Under 10%

Richest countries

Switzerland	$33,510
Luxembourg	$31,080
Japan	$26,920
Sweden	$25,490

Poorest countries

Mozambique	$70
Tanzania	$100
Ethiopia	$120
Somalia	$150

INDICATORS

The gap between the world's rich and poor is now so great that it is difficult to illustrate it on a single graph. Car ownership in the USA, for example, is almost 2,000 times as common as it is in Bangladesh. Within each income group, however, comparisons have some meaning: the affluent Japanese on their overcrowded island have far fewer cars than the Americans; the Chinese, perhaps because of propaganda value, have more television sets than people in India, whose per capita income is similar, while Nigerians prefer to spend their money on vehicles.

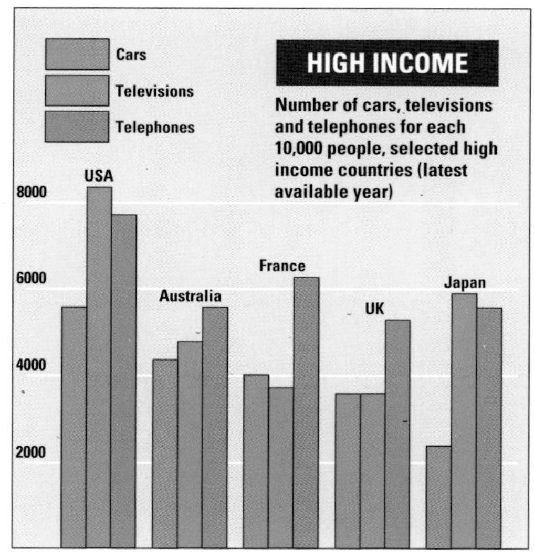
Cars
Televisions
Telephones
HIGH INCOME
Number of cars, televisions and telephones for each 10,000 people, selected high income countries (latest available year)
8000
6000
4000
2000
USA
Australia
France
UK
Japan

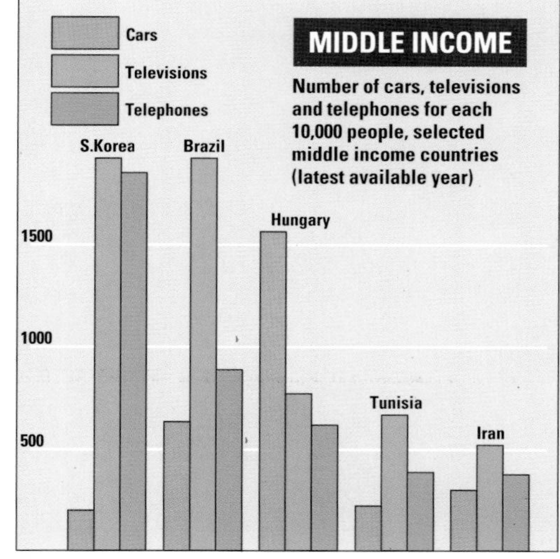
Cars
Televisions
Telephones
MIDDLE INCOME
Number of cars, televisions and telephones for each 10,000 people, selected middle income countries (latest available year)
1500
1000
500
S.Korea
Brazil
Hungary
Tunisia
Iran

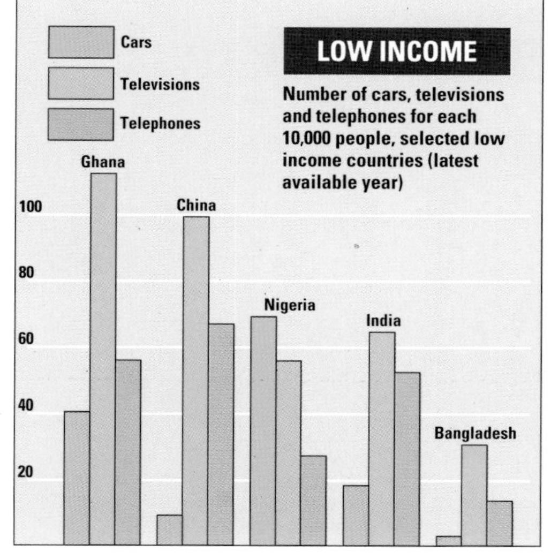
Cars
Televisions
Telephones
LOW INCOME
Number of cars, televisions and telephones for each 10,000 people, selected low income countries (latest available year)
100
80
60
40
20
Ghana
China
Nigeria
India
Bangladesh

CARTOGRAPHY BY PHILIP'S. COPYRIGHT REED INTERNATIONAL BOOKS LTD

DEBT AND AID

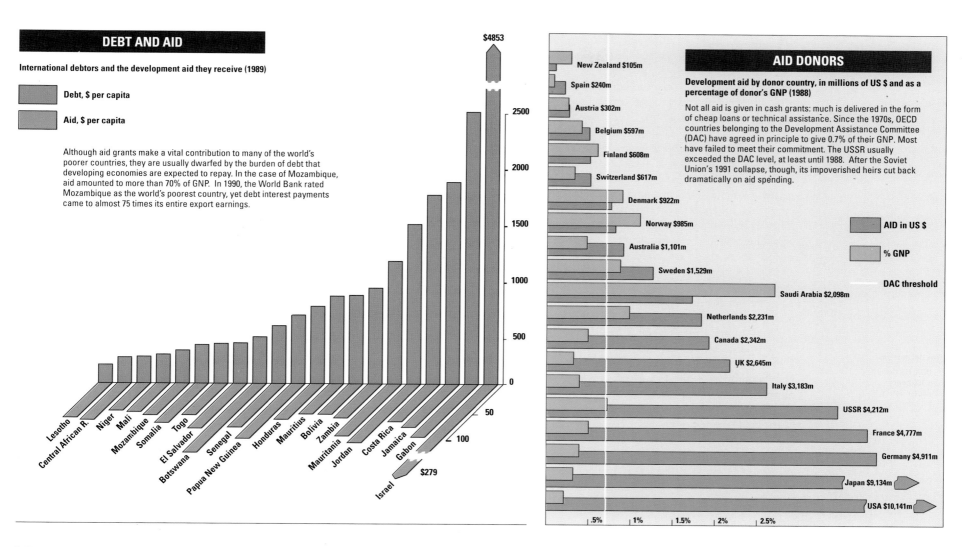

International debtors and the development aid they receive (1989)

Debt, $ per capita

Aid, $ per capita

Although aid grants make a vital contribution to many of the world's poorer countries, they are usually dwarfed by the burden of debt that developing economies are expected to repay. In the case of Mozambique, aid amounted to more than 70% of GNP. In 1990, the World Bank rated Mozambique as the world's poorest country, yet debt interest payments came to almost 75 times its entire export earnings.

$4853

2500
2000
1500
1000
500
0
50
100
$279

Lesotho
Central African R.
Niger
Mali
Mozambique
Somalia
Togo
El Salvador
Botswana
Senegal
Papua New Guinea
Honduras
Mauritius
Bolivia
Zambia
Mauritania
Jordan
Costa Rica
Jamaica
Gabon
Israel

AID DONORS

Development aid by donor country, in millions of US $ and as a percentage of donor's GNP (1988)

Not all aid is given in cash grants: much is delivered in the form of cheap loans or technical assistance. Since the 1970s, OECD countries belonging to the Development Assistance Committee (DAC) have agreed in principle to give 0.7% of their GNP. Most have failed to meet their commitment. The USSR usually exceeded the DAC level, at least until 1988. After the Soviet Union's 1991 collapse, though, its impoverished heirs cut back dramatically on aid spending.

AID in US $

% GNP

DAC threshold

New Zealand $105m
Spain $240m
Austria $302m
Belgium $597m
Finland $608m
Switzerland $617m
Denmark $922m
Norway $985m
Australia $1,101m
Sweden $1,529m
Saudi Arabia $2,098m
Netherlands $2,231m
Canada $2,342m
UK $2,645m
Italy $3,183m
USSR $4,212m
France $4,777m
Germany $4,911m
Japan $9,134m
USA $10,141m

.5% 1% 1.5% 2% 2.5%

Inflation (right) is an excellent index of a country's financial stability, and usually its prosperity or at least its prospects. Inflation rates above 20% are generally matched by slow or even negative growth; above 50%, an economy is left reeling. Most advanced countries during the 1980s had to wrestle with inflation that occasionally touched or even exceeded 10%; in Japan, the growth leader, price increases averaged only 1.8% between 1980 and 1988.

Government spending (below right) is more difficult to interpret. Obviously, very low levels indicate a weak state, and high levels a strong one; but in poor countries, the 10–20% absorbed by the government may well amount to most of the liquid cash available, whereas in rich countries most of the 35–50% typically in government hands is returned in services.

GNP per capita figures (below) should also be compared with caution. They do not reveal the vast differences in living costs between different countries: the equivalent of US $100 is worth considerably more in poorer nations than it is in the USA itself.

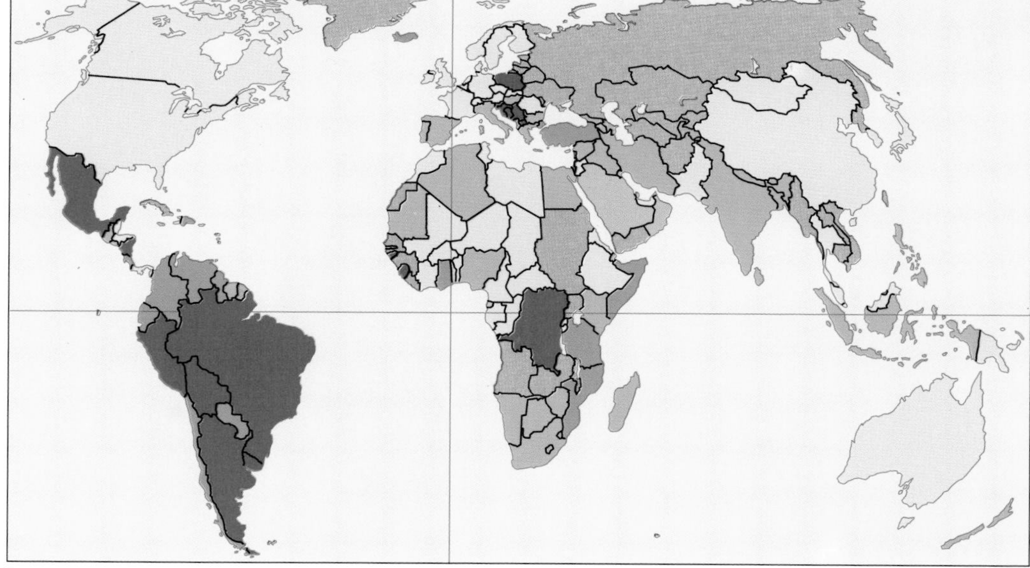

INFLATION

Average annual rate of inflation (1980–91)*

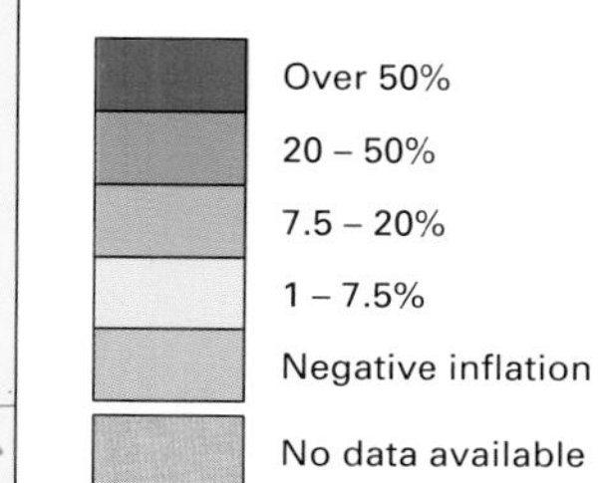

Over 50%
20 – 50%
7.5 – 20%
1 – 7.5%
Negative inflation
No data available

Highest average inflation

Nicaragua	584%
Argentina	417%
Brazil	328%

Lowest average inflation

Oman	–3.1%
Kuwait	–2.7%
Saudi Arabia	–2.4%

THE WEALTH GAP

The world's richest and poorest countries, by Gross National Product per capita in US $ (1991)

Richest	GNP	Poorest	GNP
1. Switzerland	33,510	1. Mozambique	70
2. Liechtenstein	33,000	2. Tanzania	100
3. Luxembourg	31,080	3. Ethiopia	120
4. Japan	26,920	4. Somalia	150
5. Sweden	25,490	5. Uganda	160
6. Bermuda	25,000	6. Bhutan	180
7. Finland	24,400	7. Nepal	180
8. Norway	24,160	8. Guinea-Bissau	190
9. Denmark	23,660	9. Cambodia	200
10. Germany	23,650	10. Burundi	210
11. Iceland	22,580	11. Madagascar	210
12. USA	22,560	12. Sierra Leone	210
13. Canada	21,260	13. Bangladesh	220
14. France	20,600	14. Chad	220
15. Austria	20,380	15. Zaïre	220
16. UAE	19,500	16. Laos	230
17. Belgium	19,300	17. Malawi	230
18. Italy	18,580	18. Rwanda	260
19. Netherlands	18,560	19. Mali	280
20. UK	16,750	20. Guyana	290

GNP per capita is calculated by dividing a country's Gross National Product by its population.

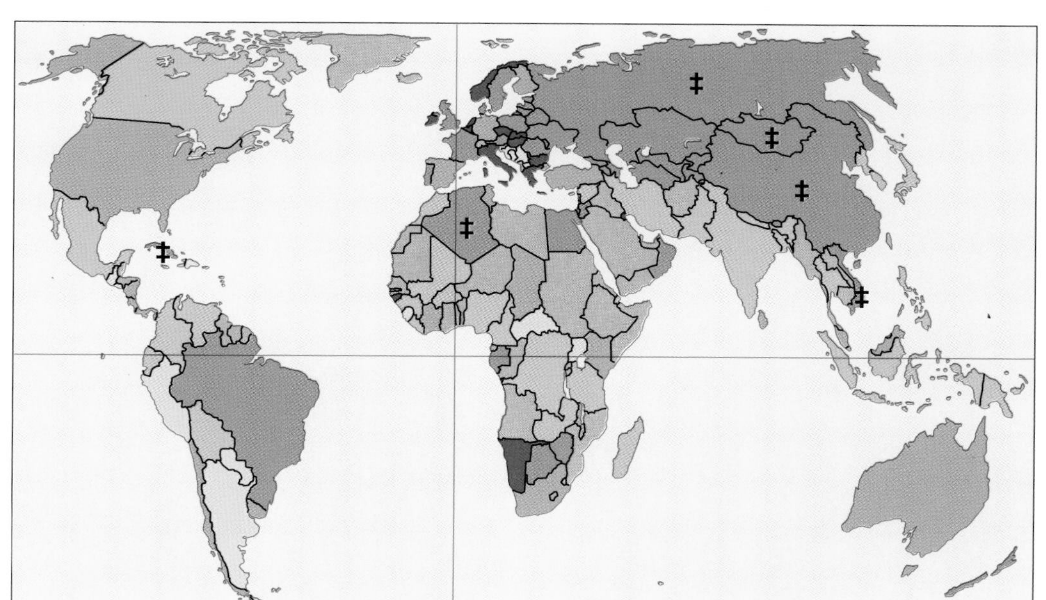

STATE SPENDING

Central government expenditure as a percentage of GNP (latest available year)* [‡ estimate]

Over 45%
35 – 45%
25 – 35%
15 – 25%
0 – 15%
No data available

Top 5 countries

Bulgaria	77.3%
Guinea-Bissau	63.0%
Greece	60.0%
Czechoslovakia	55.6%
Hungary	54.7%

**Statistics for the new republics of the former USSR, Czechoslovakia and Yugoslavia are not yet available. The map shows the statistics for the entire USSR, Czechoslovakia and Yugoslavia.*

CARTOGRAPHY BY PHILIP'S. COPYRIGHT REED INTERNATIONAL BOOKS LTD

QUALITY OF LIFE: STANDARDS

16: WATER SUPPLY
22: POPULATION DENSITY
25: URBAN POLLUTION
INFORMAL CITIZENS
URBAN ADVANTAGES
28: WORLD'S REFUGEES
WAR SINCE 1945
36: EMPLOYMENT
THE WORKFORCE
40: THE WEALTH GAP
41: DEBT AND AID
45: LIFE EXPECTANCY
INFANT MORTALITY
CRIME AND
PUNISHMENT

At first sight, most international contrasts are swamped by differences in wealth. The rich not only have more money, they have more of everything, including years of life. Those with only a little money are obliged to spend most of it on food and clothing, the basic maintenance costs of existence; air travel and tourism are unlikely to feature on the lists of their expenditure. However, poverty and wealth are both relative: slum dwellers living on social security payments in an affluent industrial country have far more resources at their disposal than an average African peasant, but feel their own poverty none the less acutely. A middle-class Indian lawyer cannot command a fraction of the earnings of a counterpart in New York, London or Rome; nevertheless, he rightly sees himself as prosperous.

In 1990 the United Nations Development Programme published its first Human Development Index, an attempt to construct a comparative scale by which at least a simplified form of well-being might be measured. The index, running from 1 to 100, combined figures for life expectancy and literacy with a wealth scale that matched incomes against the official poverty lines of a group of industrialized nations. National scores ranged from a startling 98.7 for Sweden to a miserable 11.6 for Niger, reflecting the all-too-familiar gap between rich and poor.

Comparisons between nations with similar incomes are more interesting, showing the effect of government policies. For example, Sri Lanka was awarded 78.9 against 43.9 for its only slightly poorer neighbour, India; Zimbabwe, at 57.6, had more than double the score of Senegal, despite no apparent disparities in average income. Some development indicators may be interpreted in two ways. There is a very clear correlation, for example, between the wealth of a nation and the level of education that its people enjoy. Education helps create wealth, of course; but are rich countries wealthy because they are educated, or well-educated because they are rich? Women's fertility rates appear to fall almost in direct proportion to the amount of secondary education they receive; but high levels of female education are associated with rich countries, where fertility is already low.

Not everything, though, is married to wealth. The countries cited on these pages have been chosen to give a range covering different cultures as well as different economic power, revealing disparities among rich and among poor as well as between the two obvious groups. Income distribution, for example, shows that in Brazil (following the general pattern of Latin America) most national wealth is concentrated in a few hands; Bangladesh is much poorer, but what little wealth there is, is more evenly spread.

Among the developed countries the USA, with its poorest 20% sharing less than 5% of the national cake, has a noticeably less even distribution than Japan where, despite massive industrialization, traditional values act as a brake against poverty. Hungary, still enmeshed in Communism when these statistics were compiled, shows the most even distribution of all, which certainly matches with Socialist theory. However, the inequalities in Communist societies, a contributing factor in the demise of most of them in the late 1980s, are not easily measured in money terms. Communist élites are less often rewarded with cash than with power and privilege, commodities not easily expressed statistically.

There are other limits to statistical analysis. Even without taking account of such imponderables as personal satisfaction, it will always be more difficult to measure a reasonable standard of living than a nation's income or its productivity. Lack of money certainly brings misery, but its presence does not guarantee contentment.

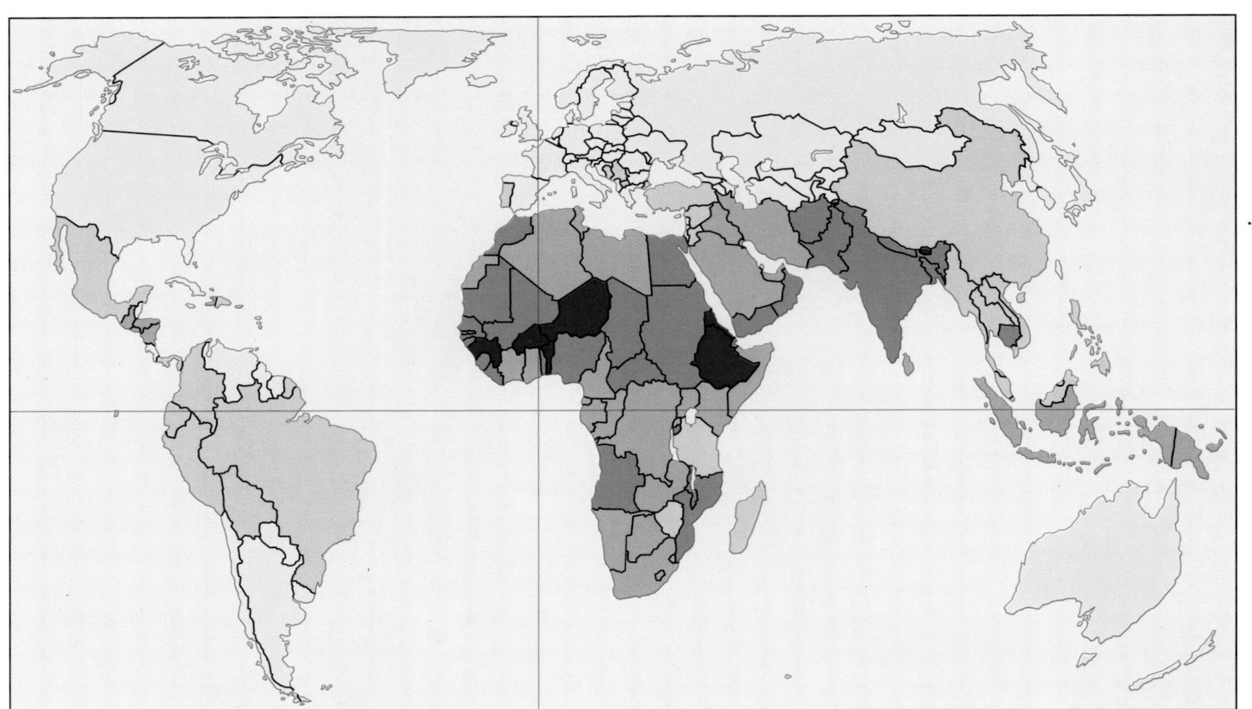

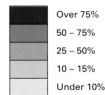

ILLITERACY

Percentage of the total population unable to read or write (latest available year)*

- Over 75%
- 50 – 75%
- 25 – 50%
- 10 – 15%
- Under 10%

Educational expenditure per person (latest available year)

Top 5 countries

Sweden	$997
Qatar	$989
Canada	$983
Norway	$971
Switzerland	$796

Bottom 5 countries

Chad	$2
Bangladesh	$3
Ethiopia	$3
Nepal	$4
Somalia	$4

EDUCATION

The developing countries made great efforts in the 1970s and 1980s to bring at least a basic education to their people. Primary school enrolments rose above 60% in all but the poorest nations. Figures often include teenagers or young adults, however, and there are still an estimated 300 million children worldwide who receive no schooling at all. Secondary and higher education are expanding far more slowly, and the gap between rich and poor is probably even larger than it appears from the charts here, while the bare statistics provide no real reflection of educational quality.

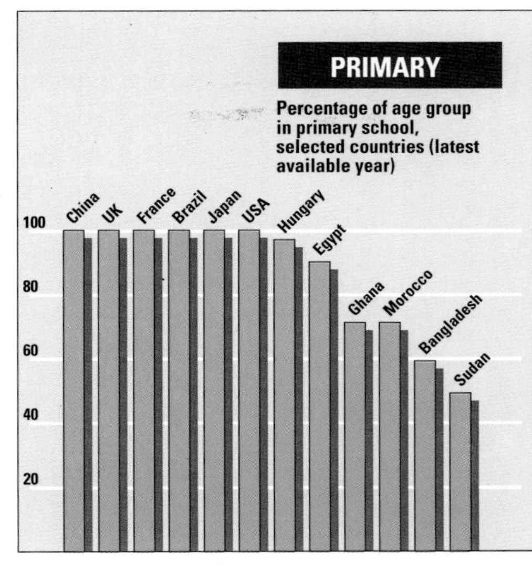
PRIMARY
Percentage of age group in primary school, selected countries (latest available year)
100
80
60
40
20
China
UK
France
Brazil
Japan
USA
Hungary
Egypt
Ghana
Morocco
Bangladesh
Sudan

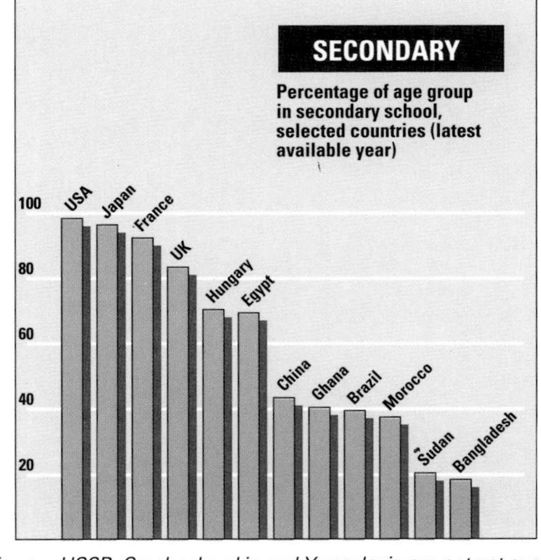
SECONDARY
Percentage of age group in secondary school, selected countries (latest available year)
100
80
60
40
20
USA
Japan
France
UK
Hungary
Egypt
China
Ghana
Brazil
Morocco
Sudan
Bangladesh

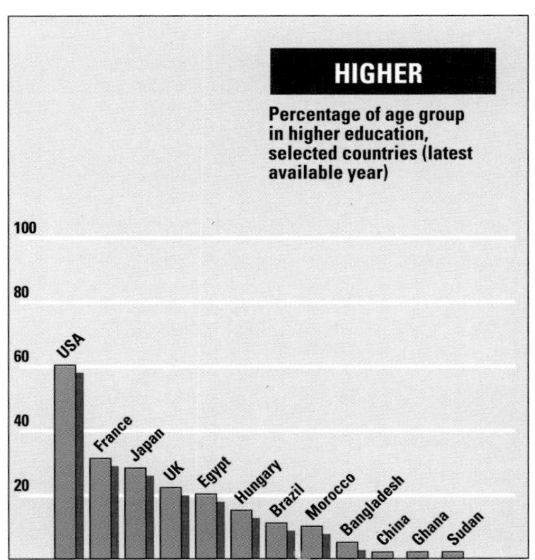
HIGHER
Percentage of age group in higher education, selected countries (latest available year)
100
80
60
40
20
USA
France
Japan
UK
Egypt
Hungary
Brazil
Morocco
Bangladesh
China
Ghana
Sudan

*Statistics for the new republics of the former USSR, Czechoslovakia and Yugoslavia are not yet available.
* The map shows the statistics for the entire USSR, Czechoslovakia and Yugoslavia.

CARTOGRAPHY BY PHILIP'S. COPYRIGHT REED INTERNATIONAL BOOKS LTD

DISTRIBUTION OF SPENDING

Percentage share of household spending (1989)

Food
Clothing
Energy & Housing
Medicine & Education
Transport
Other

100
80
60
40
20

UK
USA
Japan
Hungary
Brazil
Egypt
Nigeria
B'desh

FERTILITY AND EDUCATION

Fertility rates compared with female education, selected countries (latest available year)

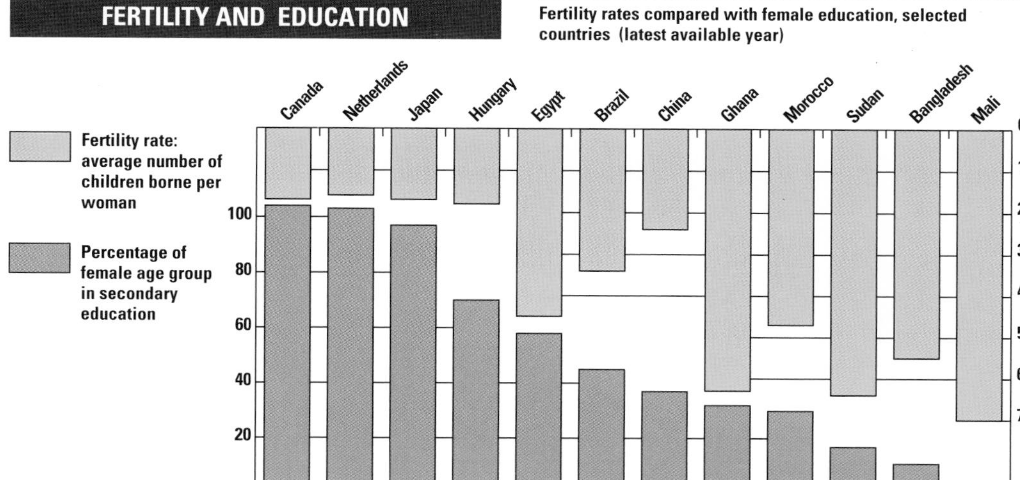

Fertility rate: average number of children borne per woman
Percentage of female age group in secondary education
Canada
Netherlands
Japan
Hungary
Egypt
Brazil
China
Ghana
Morocco
Sudan
Bangladesh
Mali
100
80
60
40
20
0
0
1
2
3
4
5
6
7

Since the age group for secondary schooling is usually defined as 12–17 years, percentages for countries with a significant number of 11- or 18-year-olds in secondary school may actually exceed 100.
A high proportion of employed women may indicate either an advanced, industrial economy where female opportunities are high, or a poor country where many women's lives are dominated by agricultural toil. The lowest rates are found in Islamic nations, whose religious precepts often exclude women even from fieldwork.

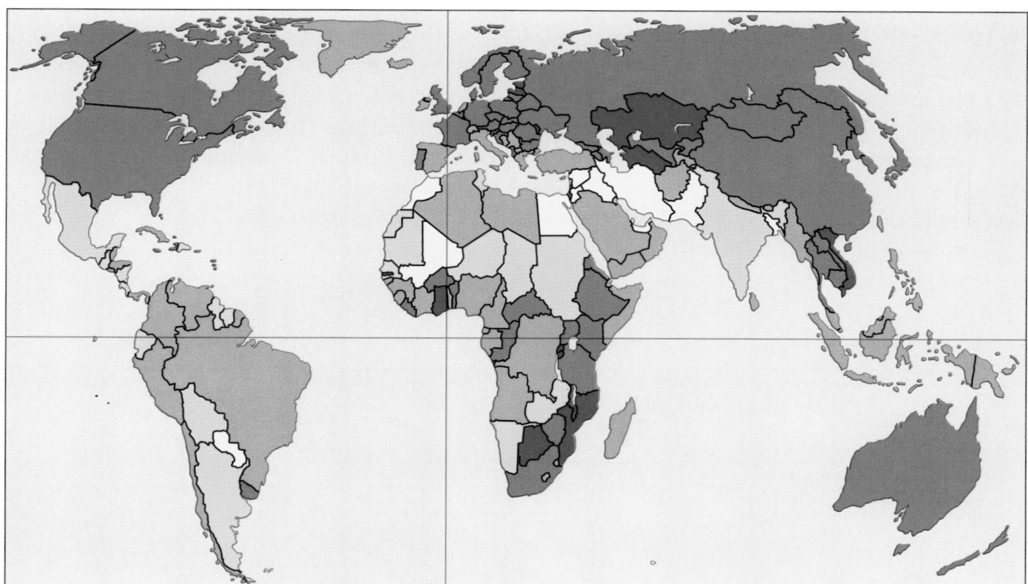

WOMEN AT WORK

Women in paid employment as a percentage of the total workforce (latest available year)

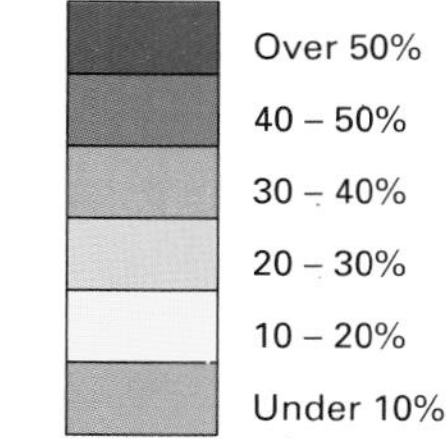

Over 50%
40 – 50%
30 – 40%
20 – 30%
10 – 20%
Under 10%

Most women in work

Kazakhstan 54%
Rwanda 54%
Botswana 53%

Fewest women in work

Guinea-Bissau 3%
Oman 6%
Afghanistan 8%

DISTRIBUTION OF INCOME

Percentage share of household income from poorest fifth to richest fifth, selected countries (1989)

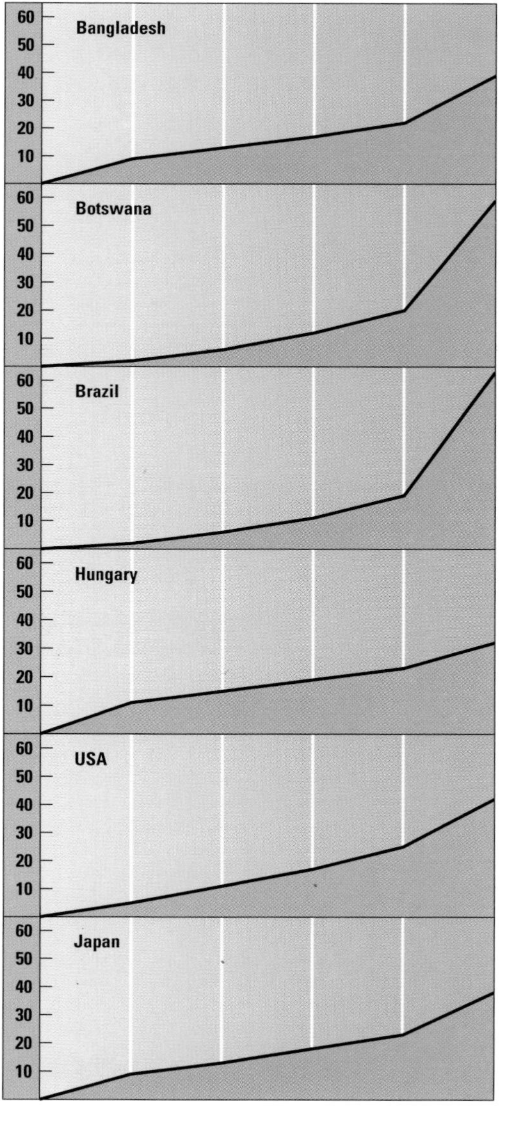

Bangladesh
Botswana
Brazil
Hungary
USA
Japan
60
50
40
30
20
10

TOURIST SPENDING

Nations spending the most on overseas tourism, US $ million (latest available year)

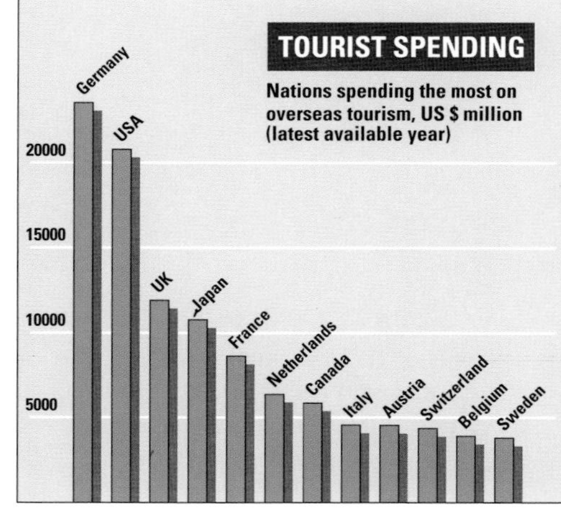

Germany
USA
UK
Japan
France
Netherlands
Canada
Italy
Austria
Switzerland
Belgium
Sweden
20000
15000
10000
5000

TOURIST EARNING

Nations receiving the most from overseas tourism, US $ million (latest available year)

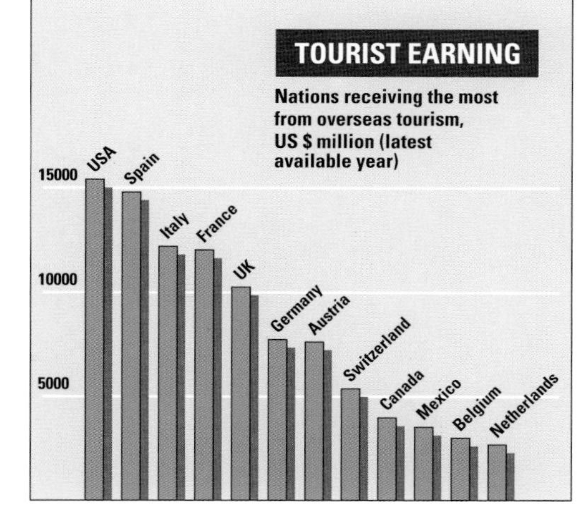

USA
Spain
Italy
France
UK
Germany
Austria
Switzerland
Canada
Mexico
Belgium
Netherlands
15000
10000
5000

Small economies in attractive areas are often completely dominated by tourism: in some West Indian islands, tourist spending provides over 90% of the total income. In cash terms the USA is the world leader: its 1987 earnings exceeded $15 billion, though that sum amounted to only 0.4% of its GDP.

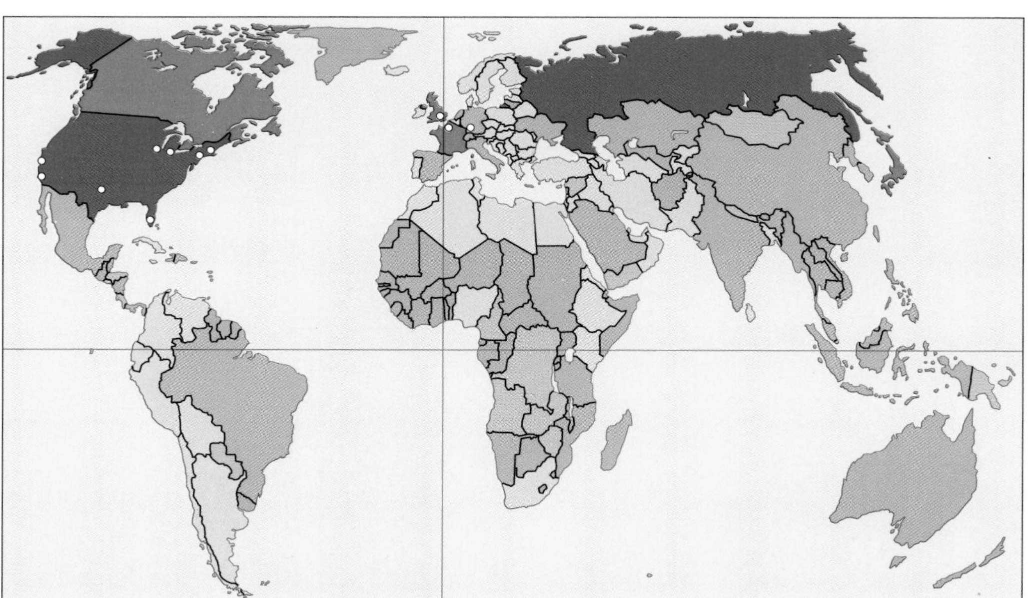

AIR TRAVEL

Millions of passenger km [number carried, international/domestic, multiplied by distance flown from airport of origin] (latest year)

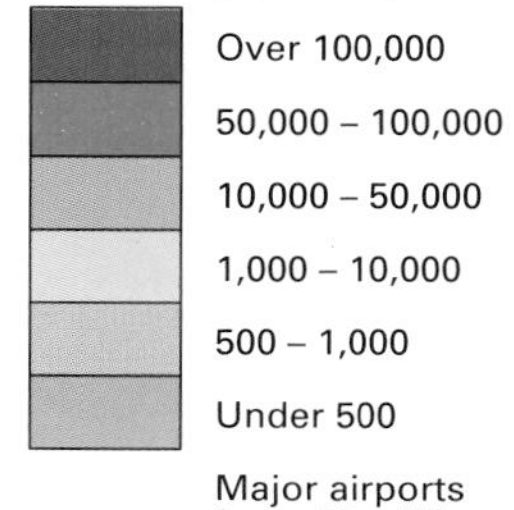

Over 100,000
50,000 – 100,000
10,000 – 50,000
1,000 – 10,000
500 – 1,000
Under 500
Major airports (over 20 million passengers in 1991)

The world's busiest airport in terms of total passengers is Chicago's O'Hare; the busiest international airport is Heathrow, the largest of London's airports

CARTOGRAPHY BY PHILIP'S. COPYRIGHT REED INTERNATIONAL BOOKS LTD

QUALITY OF LIFE: HEALTH

16: WATER SUPPLY

25: URBAN POLLUTION
INFORMAL CITIZENS
URBAN ADVANTAGES

31: FOOD AND POPULATION

43: DISTRIBUTION OF SPENDING

According to statistics gathered in the late 1980s and early 1990s, a third of the world's population has no access to safe drinking water: malaria is on the increase; cholera, thought vanquished, is reappearing in South America; an epidemic of the AIDS virus is gathering force in Africa; and few developing countries can stretch their health care budgets beyond US $2 per person per year.

Yet human beings, by every statistical index, have never been healthier. In the richest nations, where food is plentiful, the demands of daily work are rarely onerous and medical care is both readily available and highly advanced, the average life expectancy is often more than 75 years – approaching the perceived limits for human longevity. In middle-income nations, such as Brazil and the Philippines, life expectancy usually extends at least to the mid-60s; in China, it has already reached 70 years. Even in poverty-stricken Ethiopia and Chad, lifespans are close to 50 years. Despite economic crisis, drought, famine and even war, every country in the world reported an increase between 1965 and 1990.

It was not always so, even in countries then considered rich. By comparison, in 1880 the life expectancy of an average Berliner was under 30 years and infant mortality in the United Kingdom, then the wealthiest nation, stood at 144 per thousand births – a grim toll exceeded today only by three of the poorest African countries (Mali, Sierra Leone and Guinea). Even by 1910, European death rates were almost twice as high as the world average less than 80 years later; infant mortality in Norway, Europe's healthiest country, was then higher than in present-day Indonesia. In far less than a century, human prospects have improved beyond recognition.

In global terms, the transformation is less the result of high-technology medicine – still too expensive for all but a minority, even in rich countries – than of improvements in agriculture and hence nutrition, matched by the widespread diffusion of the basic concepts of disease and public health. One obvious consequence, as death rates everywhere continue to fall, is sustained population growth. Another is the rising expectation of continued improvement felt by both rich and poor nations alike.

In some ways, the task is easier for developing countries, striving with limited resources to attain health levels to which the industrialized world has only recently become accustomed. As the tables below illustrate, infectious disease is rare among the richer nations, while ailments such as cancer, which tend to kill in advanced years, do not seriously impinge on populations with shorter lifespans.

Yet infectious disease is relatively cheap to eliminate, or at least reduce, and it is likely to be easier to raise life expectancy from 60 to 70 years than from 75 to 85 years. The ills of the developed world and its ageing population are more expensive to treat – though most poor countries would be happy to suffer from the problems of the affluent. Western nations regularly spend more money on campaigns to educate their citizens out of overeating and other bad habits than many developing countries can devote to an entire health budget – an irony that marks the dimensions of the rich-poor divide.

Indeed, wealth itself may be the most reliable indicator of longevity. Harmful habits are usually the province of the rich; yet curiously, though the dangerous effects of tobacco have been proved beyond doubt, the affluent Japanese combine very high cigarette consumption with the longest life expectancy of all the major nations. Similarly, heavy alcohol consumption seems to have no effect on longevity: the French, world leaders in 1988 and in most previous surveys, outlive the more moderate British by a year, and the abstemious Indians by almost two decades.

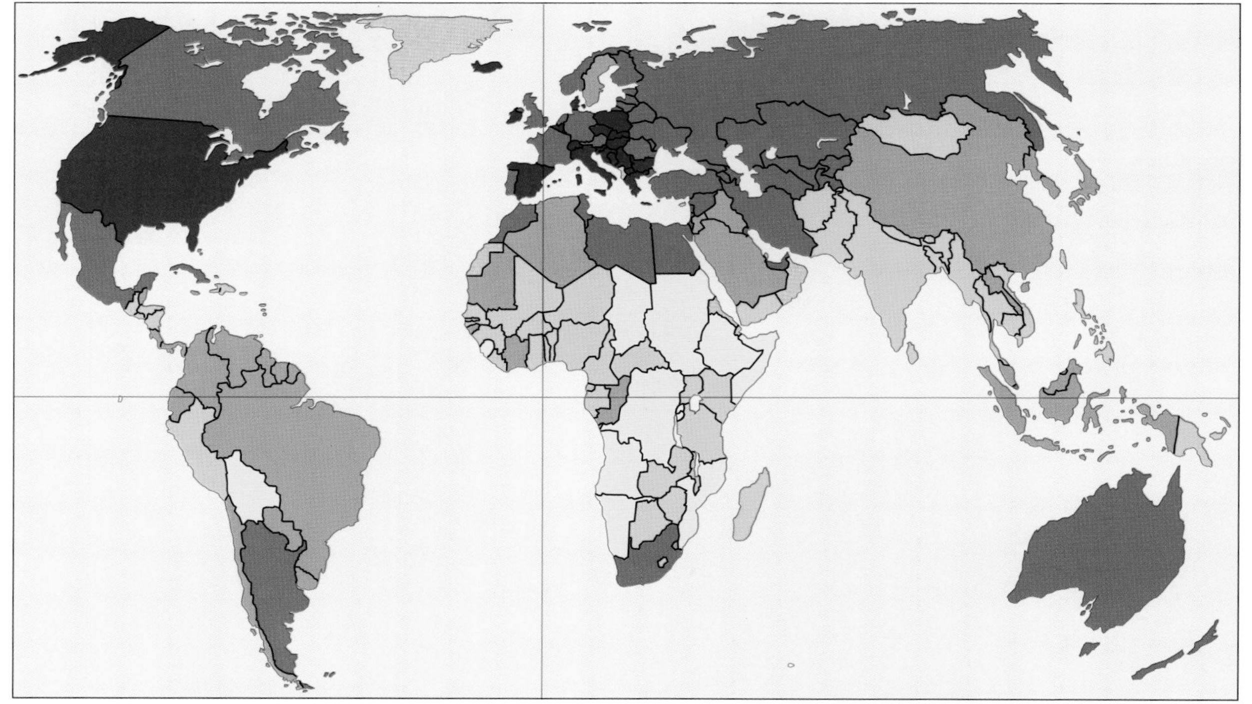

FOOD CONSUMPTION

Average daily food intake in calories per person (1989)*

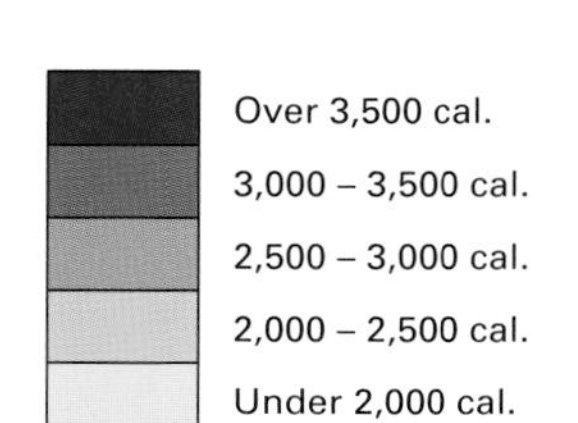
Over 3,500 cal.
3,000 – 3,500 cal.
2,500 – 3,000 cal.
2,000 – 2,500 cal.
Under 2,000 cal.
No available data

Top 5 countries

Belgium	3,902 ca
Greece	3,825 ca
Ireland	3,778 cal.
Bulgaria	3,707 cal.
USA	3,650 cal.

Bottom 5 countries

Ethiopia	1,666 cal.
Mozambique	1,679 cal.
Chad	1,742 cal.
Sierra Leone	1,799 cal.
Angola	1,806 cal.

CAUSES OF DEATH

The rich not only live longer, on average, than the poor; they also die from different causes. Infectious and parasitic diseases, all but eliminated in the developed world, remain a scourge in poorer countries. On the other hand, more than two-thirds of the populations of OECD nations eventually succumb to cancer or circulatory disease; the proportion in Latin America is only about 45%. In addition to the three major diseases shown here, respiratory infection and injury also claim more lives in developing nations, which lack the drugs and medical skills required to treat them.

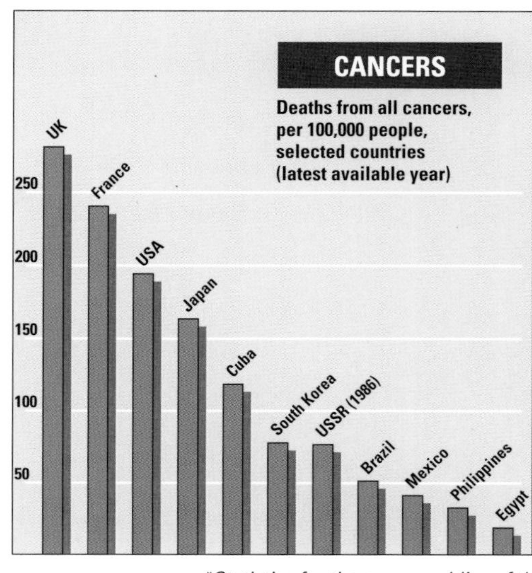
CANCERS
Deaths from all cancers, per 100,000 people, selected countries (latest available year)
250
200
150
100
50
UK
France
USA
Japan
Cuba
South Korea
USSR (1986)
Brazil
Mexico
Philippines
Egypt

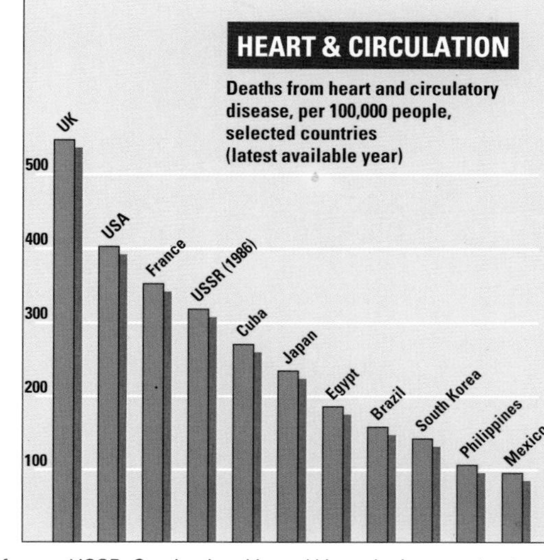
HEART & CIRCULATION
Deaths from heart and circulatory disease, per 100,000 people, selected countries (latest available year)
500
400
300
200
100
UK
USA
France
USSR (1986)
Cuba
Japan
Egypt
Brazil
South Korea
Philippines
Mexico

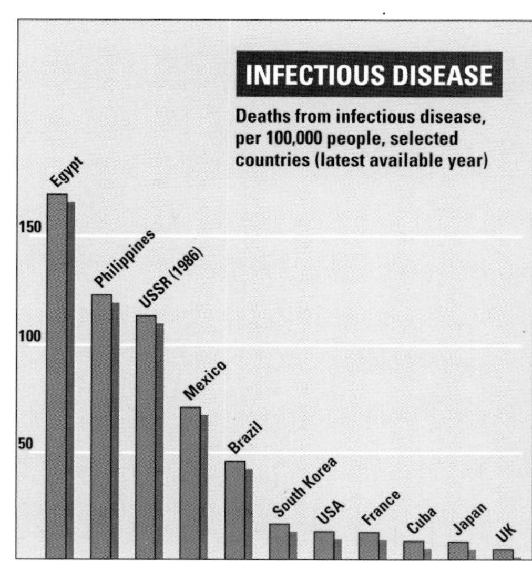
INFECTIOUS DISEASE
Deaths from infectious disease, per 100,000 people, selected countries (latest available year)
150
100
50
Egypt
Philippines
USSR (1986)
Mexico
Brazil
South Korea
USA
France
Cuba
Japan
UK

Statistics for the new republics of the former USSR, Czechoslovakia and Yugoslavia are not yet available. The map shows the statistics for the entire USSR, Czechoslovakia and Yugoslavia.

CARTOGRAPHY BY PHILIP'S. COPYRIGHT REED INTERNATIONAL BOOKS LTD

LIFE EXPECTANCY

Years of life expectancy at birth, selected countries (1988–89)

The chart shows combined data for both sexes. On average, women live longer than men worldwide, even in developing countries with high maternal mortality rates. Overall, life expectancy is steadily rising, though the difference between rich and poor nations remains dramatic.

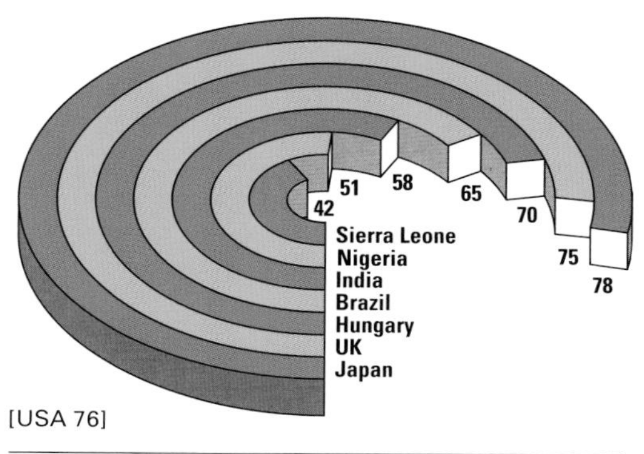

42
51
58
65
70
75
78
Sierra Leone
Nigeria
India
Brazil
Hungary
UK
Japan

[USA 76]

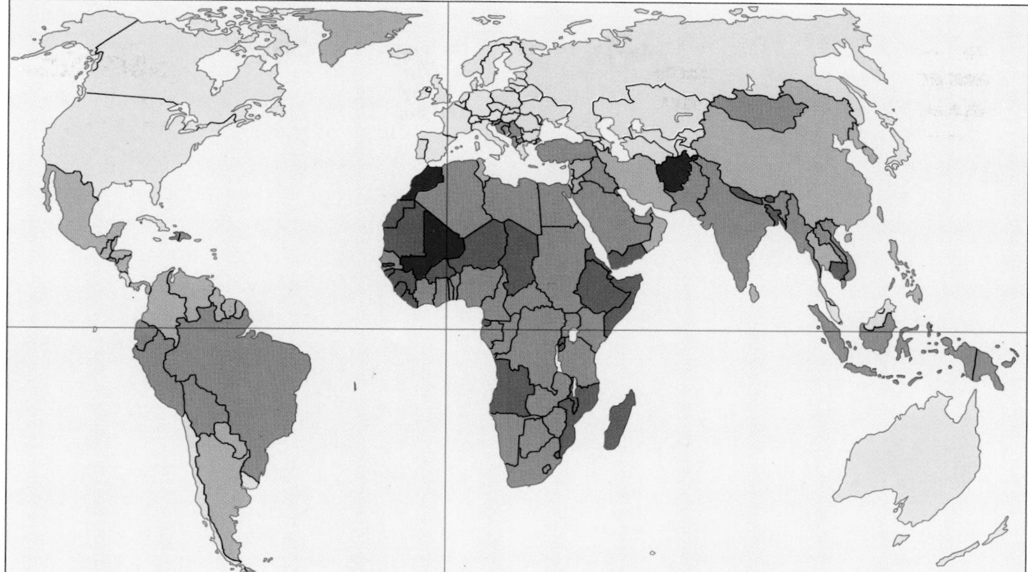

CHILD MORTALITY

Number of babies who will die before the age of one year, per 1,000 live births (average 1990–95)*

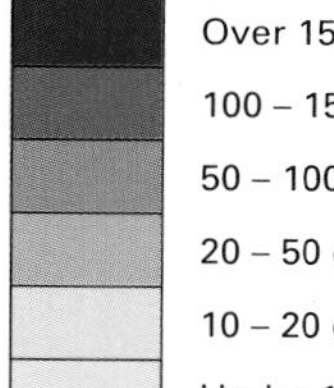

Over 150 deaths
100 – 150 deaths
50 – 100 deaths
20 – 50 deaths
10 – 20 deaths
Under 10 deaths

Highest child mortality

Afghanistan	162
Mali	159

Lowest child mortality

Iceland	5
Finland	5

[USA 9] [UK 8]

HOSPITAL CAPACITY

Hospital beds available for each 1,000 people (latest available year)

Highest capacity		Lowest capacity	
Finland	14.9	Bangladesh	0.2
Sweden	13.2	Nepal	0.2
France	12.9	Ethiopia	0.3
USSR (1986)	12.8	Mauritania	0.4
Netherlands	12.0	Mali	0.5
North Korea	11.7	Burkina Faso	0.6
Switzerland	11.3	Pakistan	0.6
Austria	10.4	Niger	0.7
Czechoslovakia	10.1	Haiti	0.8
Hungary	9.1	Chad	0.8

[UK 8] [USA 5.9]

The availability of a bed can mean anything from a private room in a well-equipped Californian teaching hospital to a place in the overcrowded annexe of a rural African clinic. In the Third World especially, quality of treatment can vary enormously from place to place within the same country.

MEDICAL PROVISION

Doctors per 100,000 population, selected countries (latest available year, 1983–86)

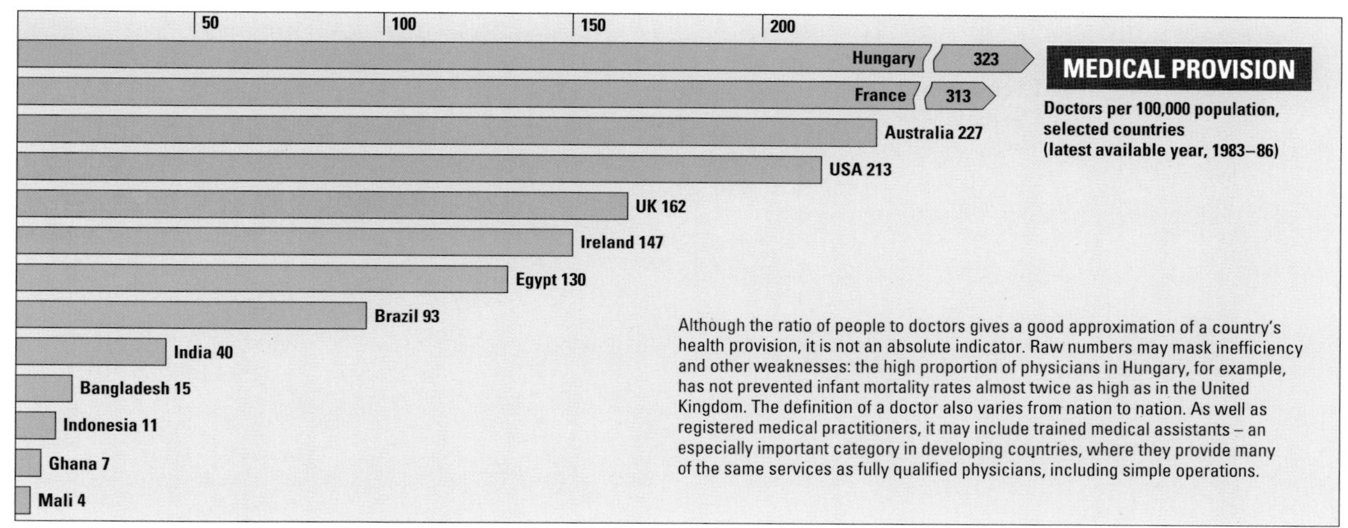

50
100
150
200
Hungary 323
France 313
Australia 227
USA 213
UK 162
Ireland 147
Egypt 130
Brazil 93
India 40
Bangladesh 15
Indonesia 11
Ghana 7
Mali 4

Although the ratio of people to doctors gives a good approximation of a country's health provision, it is not an absolute indicator. Raw numbers may mask inefficiency and other weaknesses: the high proportion of physicians in Hungary, for example, has not prevented infant mortality rates almost twice as high as in the United Kingdom. The definition of a doctor also varies from nation to nation. As well as registered medical practitioners, it may include trained medical assistants – an especially important category in developing countries, where they provide many of the same services as fully qualified physicians, including simple operations.

THE AIDS CRISIS

The Acquired Immune Deficiency Syndrome was first identified in 1981, when American doctors found otherwise healthy young men succumbing to rare infections. By 1984, the cause had been traced to the Human Immunodeficiency Virus (HIV), which can remain dormant for many years and perhaps indefinitely: only half of those known to carry the virus in 1981 had developed AIDS ten years later.

By 1991 the World Health Organization knew of more than 250,000 AIDS cases worldwide and suspected the true number to be at least four times as high. In Western countries in the early 1990s, most AIDS deaths were among male homosexuals or needle-sharing drug-users. However, the disease is spreading fastest among heterosexual men and women, which is its usual vector in the Third World, where most of its victims live. Africa is the most severely hit: a 1992 UN report estimated that 2 million African children will die of AIDS before the year 2000 – and some 10 million will be orphaned.

TOBACCO

Annual consumption of cigarettes per capita (1986–88)

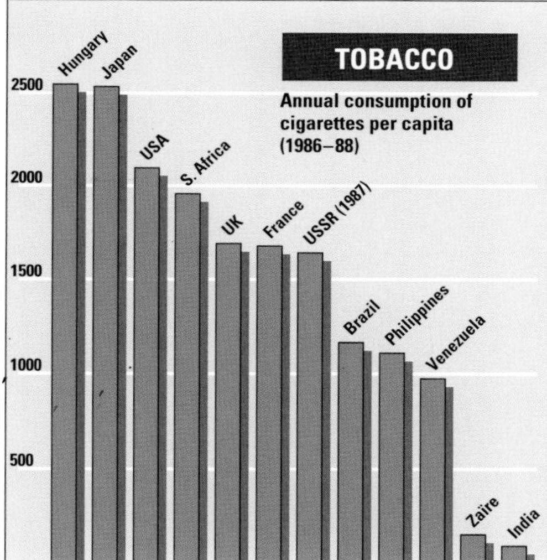

2500
2000
1500
1000
500
Hungary
Japan
USA
S. Africa
UK
France
USSR (1987)
Brazil
Philippines
Venezuela
Zaïre
India

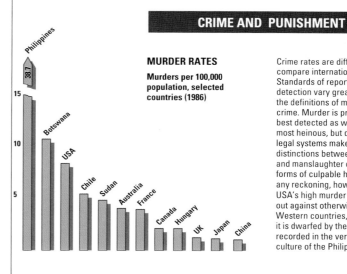

CRIME AND PUNISHMENT

MURDER RATES

Murders per 100,000 population, selected countries (1986)

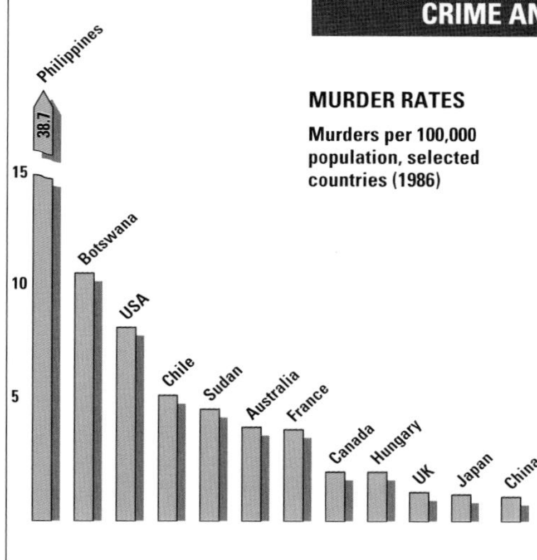

15
10
5
38.7
Philippines
Botswana
USA
Chile
Sudan
Australia
France
Canada
Hungary
UK
Japan
China

Crime rates are difficult to compare internationally. Standards of reporting and detection vary greatly, as do the definitions of many types of crime. Murder is probably the best detected as well as the most heinous, but different legal systems make different distinctions between murder and manslaughter or other forms of culpable homicide. By any reckoning, however, the USA's high murder rate stands out against otherwise similar Western countries, although it is dwarfed by the killings recorded in the very different culture of the Philippines.

AIDS

Cases reported up to 1990, per 100,000 population

[UK 5.7]

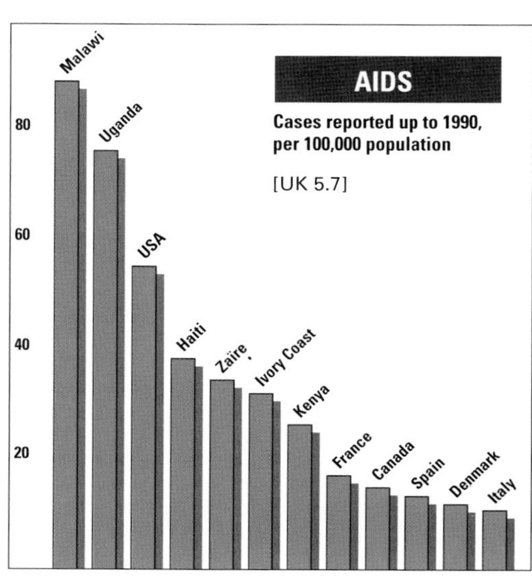

80
60
40
20
Malawi
Uganda
USA
Haiti
Zaïre
Ivory Coast
Kenya
France
Canada
Spain
Denmark
Italy

ALCOHOL

Annual consumption as litres of pure alcohol per capita (1986–88)

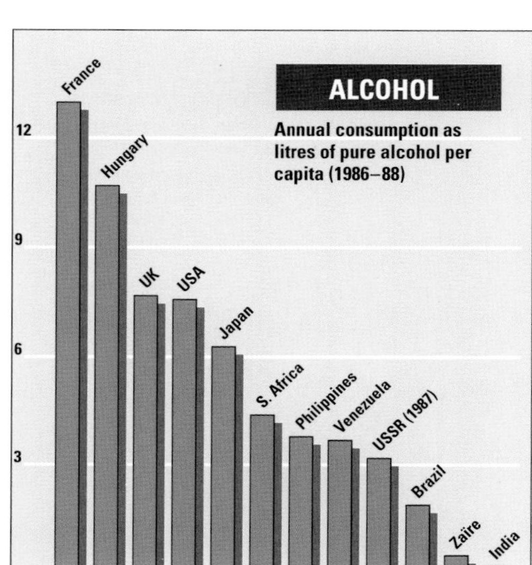

12
9
6
3
France
Hungary
UK
USA
Japan
S. Africa
Philippines
Venezuela
USSR (1987)
Brazil
Zaïre
India

PRISON POPULATIONS

Prisoners per 100,000 population, selected developed countries (1988)

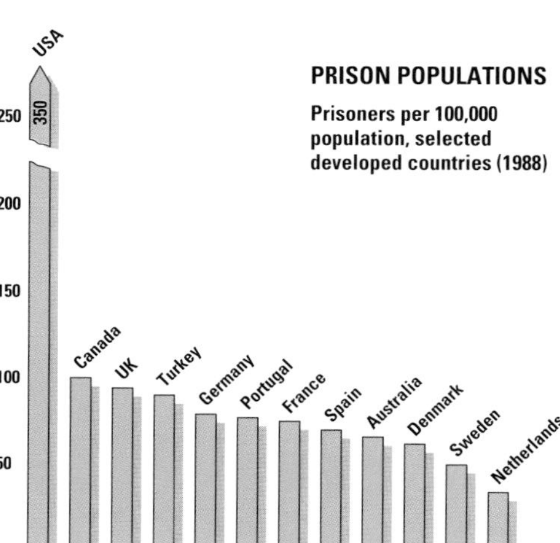

250
200
150
100
50
350
USA
Canada
UK
Turkey
Germany
Portugal
France
Spain
Australia
Denmark
Sweden
Netherlands

Differences in prison population reflect penal policies as much as the relative honesty or otherwise of different nations, and by no means all governments publish accurate figures. In more than 50 countries, people are still regularly imprisoned without trial, in 60 torture is a normal part of interrogation, and some 130 retain the death penalty, often administered for political crimes and in secret. Over 2,000 executions were recorded in 1990 by the civil rights organization Amnesty International; the real figure, as Amnesty itself maintains, was almost certainly much higher.

**Statistics for the new republics of the former USSR, Czechoslovakia and Yugoslavia are not yet available. The map shows the statistics for the entire USSR, Czechoslovakia and Yugoslavia.*

CARTOGRAPHY BY PHILIP'S. COPYRIGHT REED INTERNATIONAL BOOKS LTD

QUALITY OF LIFE: ENVIRONMENT

10: OCEANS

12: ATMOSPHERE

14: CLIMATE

21: GREENHOUSE EFFECT

25: URBAN POLLUTION

Humans have always had a dramatic effect on their environment, at least since the invention of agriculture almost 10,000 years ago. Generally, the Earth has accepted human interference without any obvious ill effects: the complex systems that regulate the global environment have managed to absorb substantial damage while maintaining a stable and comfortable home for the planet's trillions of lifeforms. But advancing human technology and the rapidly expanding populations it supports are now threatening to overwhelm the Earth's ability to cope.

Industrial wastes, acid rainfall, expanding deserts and large-scale deforestation all combine to create environmental change at a rate far faster than the Earth can easily accommodate. Equipped with chain-saws and flame-throwers, humans can now destroy more forest in a day than their ancestors could in a century, upsetting the balance between plant and animal, carbon dioxide and oxygen, on which all life ultimately depends. The fossil fuels that power industrial civilization have pumped enough carbon dioxide and other greenhouse gases into the atmosphere to make climatic change a near-certainty. Chlorofluorocarbons (CFCs) and other man-made chemicals are rapidly eroding the ozone layer, the planet's screen against ultra-violet radiation.

As a result, the Earth's average temperature has risen by about 0.5°C since the beginning of this century. Further rises seem inevitable, with 1990 marked as the hottest year worldwide since records began. A warmer Earth probably means a wetter Earth, with melting ice-caps raising sea levels and causing severe flooding in some of the world's most densely populated regions. Other climatic models suggest an alternative doom: rising temperatures could increase cloud cover, reflecting more solar energy back into space and causing a new Ice Age.

Either way, the consequences for humans could be disastrous – perhaps the Earth's own way of restoring the ecological balance over the next few thousand years. Fortunately, there is a far faster mechanism available. Humans have provoked the present crisis, but human ingenuity can respond to it. CFC production is already almost at a standstill, and the first faltering steps towards stabilization and the reduction of carbon dioxide have been taken, with Denmark pioneering the way by taxing emissions in 1991.

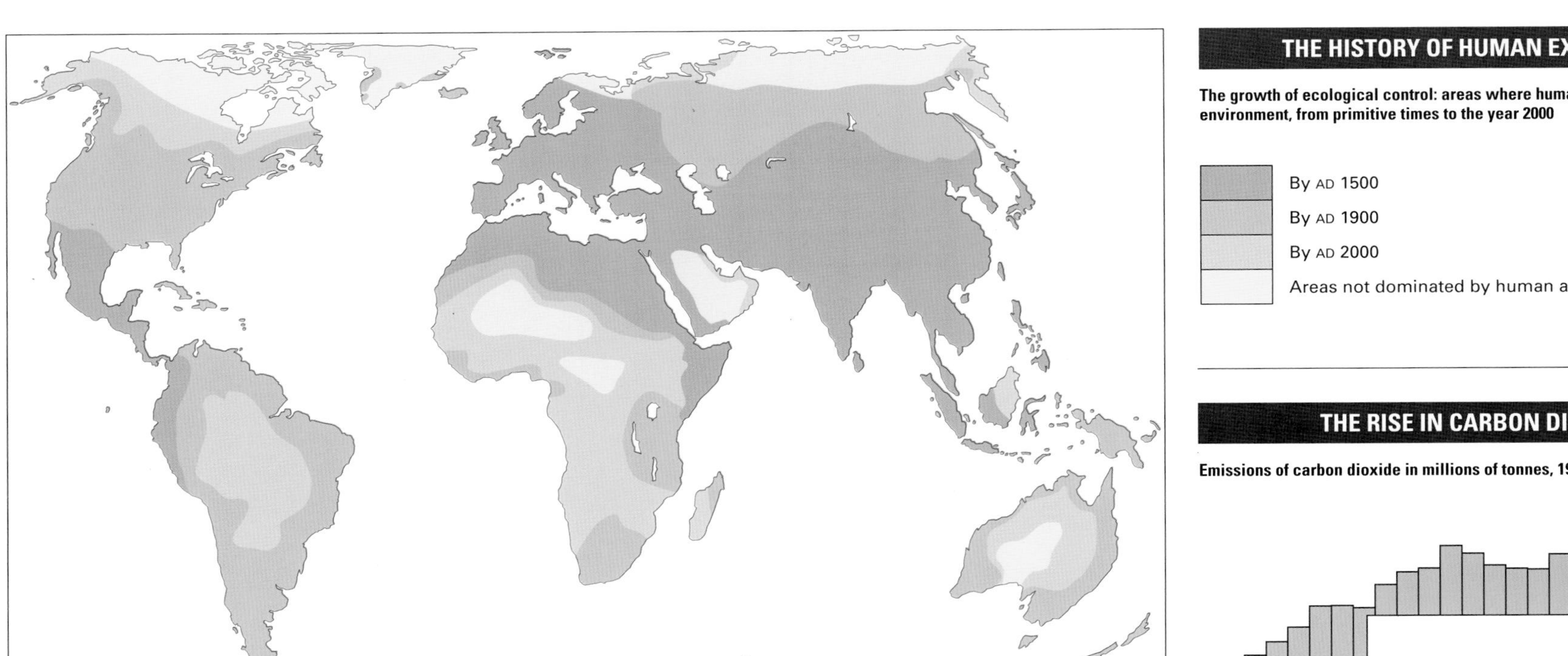

THE HISTORY OF HUMAN EXPANSION

The growth of ecological control: areas where human activity dominates the environment, from primitive times to the year 2000

By AD 1500
By AD 1900
By AD 2000
Areas not dominated by human activity

THE RISE IN CARBON DIOXIDE

Emissions of carbon dioxide in millions of tonnes, 1950–91

6000
5000
4000
3000
2000
1000
1950
1955
1960
1965
1970
1975
1980
1985
1990
400
300
200
100
0
1750
1800
1850
1900
1950
2000

Atmospheric concentration of carbon dioxide, parts per million, 1750–2000. Pre-1950 data were obtained from air samples trapped in Antarctic ice.

Since the beginning of the Industrial Revolution, human activity has pumped steadily more and more carbon dioxide into the atmosphere. Most of it was quietly absorbed by the oceans, whose immense 'sink' capacity meant that 170 years were needed for levels to increase from the pre-industrial 280 parts per million to 300 (inset graph). But the vast increase in fuel-burning since 1950 (main graph) has overwhelmed even the oceanic sink. Atmospheric concentrations are now rising almost as steeply as carbon dioxide emissions themselves.

GREENHOUSE POWER

Relative contributions to the Greenhouse Effect by the major heat-absorbing gases in the atmosphere

The chart combines greenhouse potency and volume. Carbon dioxide has a greenhouse potential of only 1, but its concentration of 350 parts per million makes it predominate. CFC 12, with 25,000 times the absorption capacity of CO_2, is present only as 0.00044 ppm.

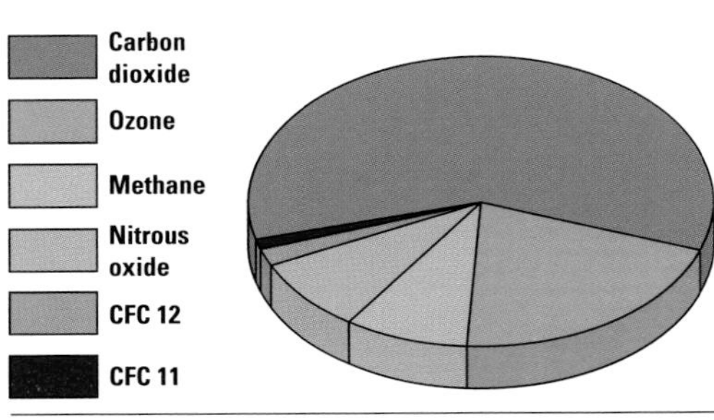

Carbon dioxide
Ozone
Methane
Nitrous oxide
CFC 12
CFC 11

CARBON DIOXIDE

Carbon dioxide released in millions of tonnes (1980s)*

Although most of the net increase in atmospheric carbon dioxide comes from fossil fuel combustion, deforestation and changing land use also contribute.

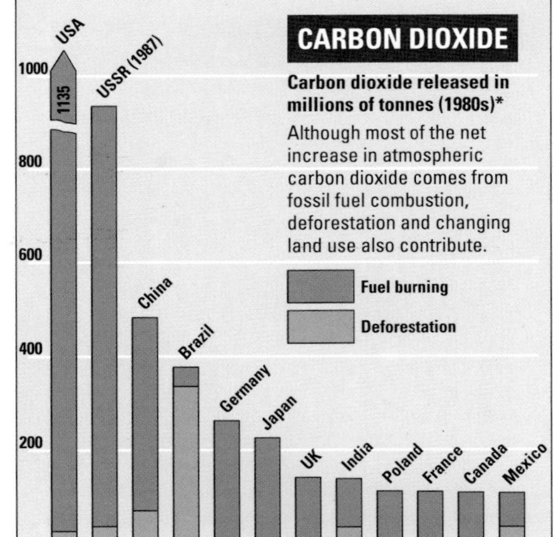

Fuel burning
Deforestation
USA
1135
USSR (1987)
China
Brazil
Germany
Japan
UK
India
Poland
France
Canada
Mexico
1000
800
600
400
200

GLOBAL WARMING

The rise in average temperatures caused by carbon dioxide and other greenhouse gases (1960–2020)

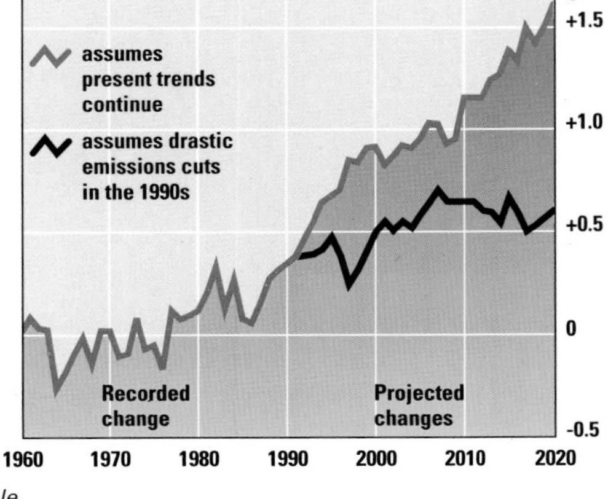

assumes present trends continue
assumes drastic emissions cuts in the 1990s
Recorded change
Projected changes
C°
+1.5
+1.0
+0.5
0
-0.5
1960
1970
1980
1990
2000
2010
2020

**Statistics for the new republics of the former USSR, Czechoslovakia and Yugoslavia are not yet available.*

CARTOGRAPHY BY PHILIP'S. COPYRIGHT REED INTERNATIONAL BOOKS LTD

ACID RAIN

Acid rainfall and sources of acidic emissions (1980s)

Acid rain is caused when sulphur and nitrogen oxides in the air combine with water vapour to form sulphuric, nitric and other acids.

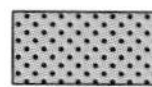

Regions where sulphur and nitrogen oxides are released in high concentrations, mainly from fossil fuel combustion.

Major cities with high levels of air pollution (including nitrogen and sulphur emissions)

Areas of heavy acid deposition

pH numbers indicate acidity, decreasing from a neutral 7. Normal rain, slightly acid from dissolved carbon dioxide, never exceeds a pH of 5.6.

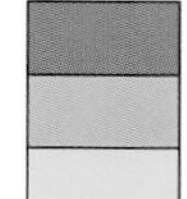

pH less than 4.0 (most acidic)

pH 4.0 to 4.5

pH 4.5 to 5.0

Areas where acid rain is a potential problem

ANTARCTICA

The vast Antarctic ice-sheet, containing some 70% of the Earth's fresh water, plays a crucial role in the circulation of atmosphere and oceans and hence in determining the planetary climate. The frozen southern continent is also the last remaining wilderness – the largest area to remain free from human colonization.

Ever since Amundsen and Scott raced for the South Pole in 1911, various countries have pressed territorial claims over sections of Antarctica, spurred in recent years by its known and suspected mineral wealth: enough iron ore to supply the world at present levels for 200 years, large oil reserves and, probably, the biggest coal deposits on Earth.

However, the 1961 Antarctic Treaty set aside the area for peaceful uses only, guaranteeing freedom of scientific investigation, banning waste disposal and nuclear testing, and suspending the issue of territorial rights. By 1990, the original 12 signatories had grown to 25, with a further 15 nations granted observer status in subsequent deliberations. However, the Treaty itself was threatened by wrangles between different countries, government agencies and international pressure groups.

Finally, in July, 1991, the belated agreement of the UK and the US assured unanimity on a new accord to ban all mineral exploration for a further 50 years. The ban can only be rescinded if all the present signatories, plus a majority of any future adherents, agree. While the treaty has always lacked a formal mechanism for enforcement, it is firmly underwritten by public concern generated by the efforts of environmental pressure groups such as Greenpeace, which has been foremost in the campaign to have Antarctica declared a 'World Park'.

It now seems likely that the virtually uninhabited continent will remain untouched by tourism, staying nuclear-free and dedicated to peaceful scientific research.

DESERTIFICATION

Existing deserts

Areas with a high risk of desertification

Areas with a moderate risk of desertification

Former areas of rainforest

Existing rainforest

DEFORESTATION

Thousands of hectares of forest cleared annually, tropical countries surveyed 1981–85 and 1987–90. Loss as a percentage of remaining stocks is shown in figures on each column.

	1987–90	1981–85
Brazil	1.5	0.4
India	4.1	0.3
Indonesia	0.8	0.5
Burma	2.1	0.3
Thailand	2.5	2.4
Vietnam	2.0	0.7
Philippines	1.5	1.0
Costa Rica	7.6	4.0
Cameroon	0.6	0.4

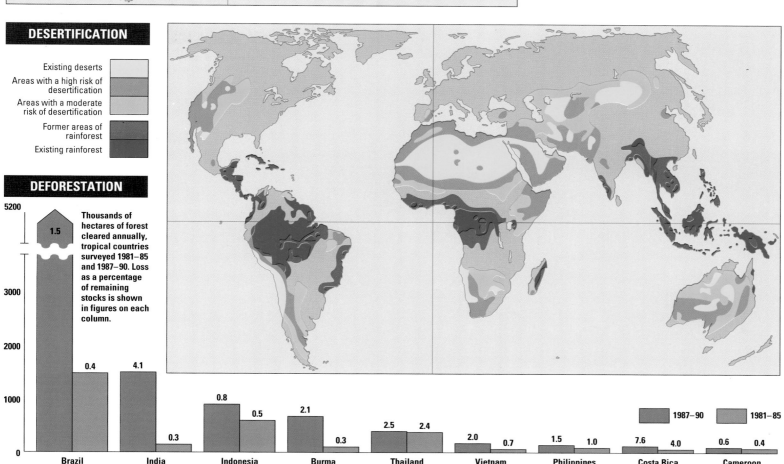

WATER POLLUTION

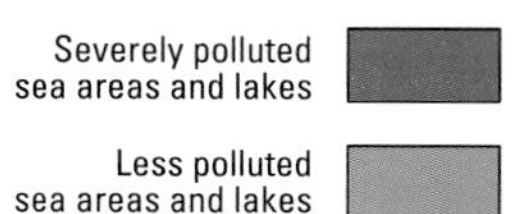

Severely polluted sea areas and lakes

Less polluted sea areas and lakes

Areas of frequent oil pollution by shipping

Major oil tanker spills

Major oil rig blow-outs

Offshore dumpsites for industrial and municipal waste

Severely polluted rivers and estuaries

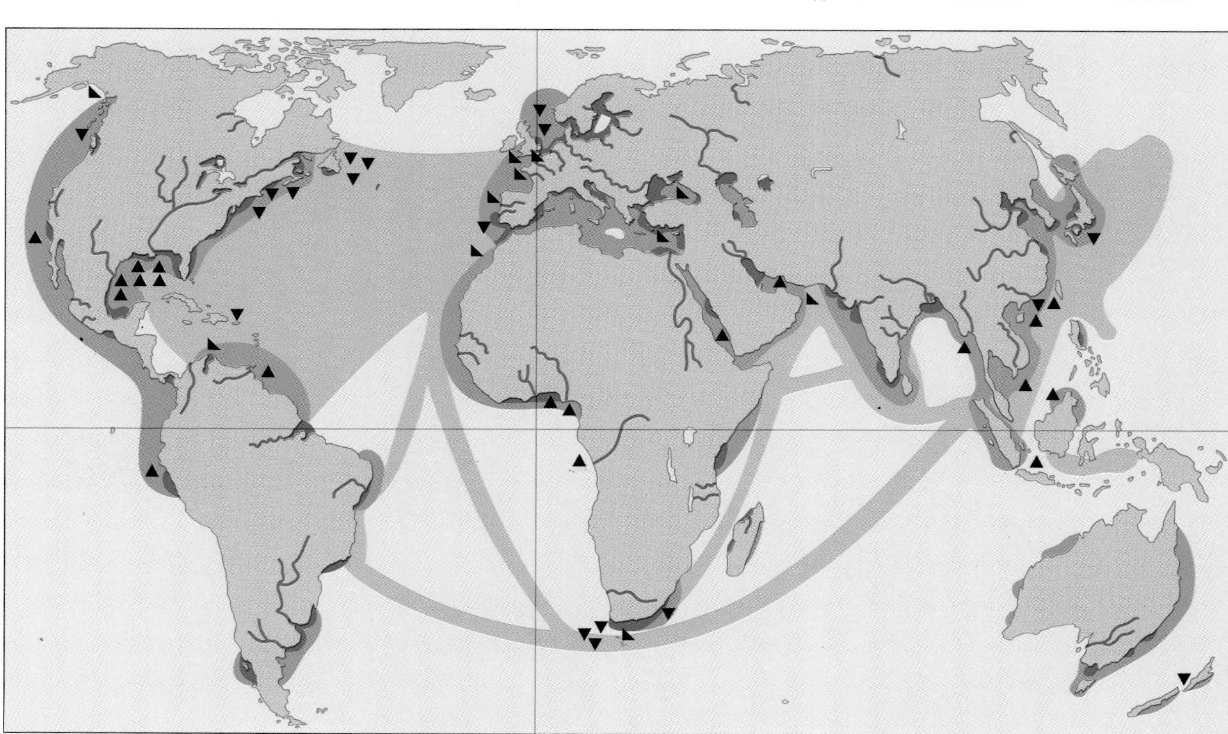

Poisoned rivers, domestic sewage and oil spillage have combined in recent years to reduce the world's oceans to a sorry state of contamination, notably near the crowded coasts of industrialized nations. Shipping routes, too, are constantly affected by tanker discharges. Oil spills of all kinds, however, declined significantly during the 1980s, from a peak of 750,000 tonnes in 1979 to under 50,000 tonnes in 1990. The most notorious tanker spill of that period – when the *Exxon Valdez* (94,999 grt) ran aground in Prince William Sound, Alaska, in March 1989 – released only 267,000 barrels, a relatively small amount compared to the results of blow-outs and war damage. Over 2,500,000 barrels were spilled during the Gulf War of 1991. The worst tanker accident in history occurred in July 1979, when the *Atlantic Empress* and the *Aegean Captain* collided off Trinidad, polluting the Caribbean with 1,890,000 barrels of crude oil.

CARTOGRAPHY BY PHILIP'S. COPYRIGHT REED INTERNATIONAL BOOKS LTD

WORLD MAPS

MAP SYMBOLS

SETTLEMENTS

PARIS   Berne   Livorno   Brugge   *Algeciras*   *Fréjus*   *Oberammergau*   *Thira*

Settlement symbols and type styles vary according to the scale of each map and indicate the importance of towns on the map rather than specific population figures

Ruins or Archæological Sites   Wells in Desert

ADMINISTRATION

International Boundaries

International Boundaries (Undefined or Disputed)

Internal Boundaries

National Parks

Country Names

NICARAGUA

Administrative Area Names

KENT

CALABRIA

International boundaries show the *de facto* situation where there are rival claims to territory

COMMUNICATIONS

Principal Roads

Other Roads

Trails and Seasonal Roads

Passes

Airfields

Principal Railways

Railways Under Construction

Other Railways

Railway Tunnels

Principal Canals

PHYSICAL FEATURES

Perennial Streams

Intermittent Streams

Perennial Lakes

Intermittent Lakes

Swamps and Marshes

Permanent Ice and Glaciers

8848 Elevations in metres

8050 Sea Depths in metres

1134 Height of Lake Surface Above Sea Level in metres

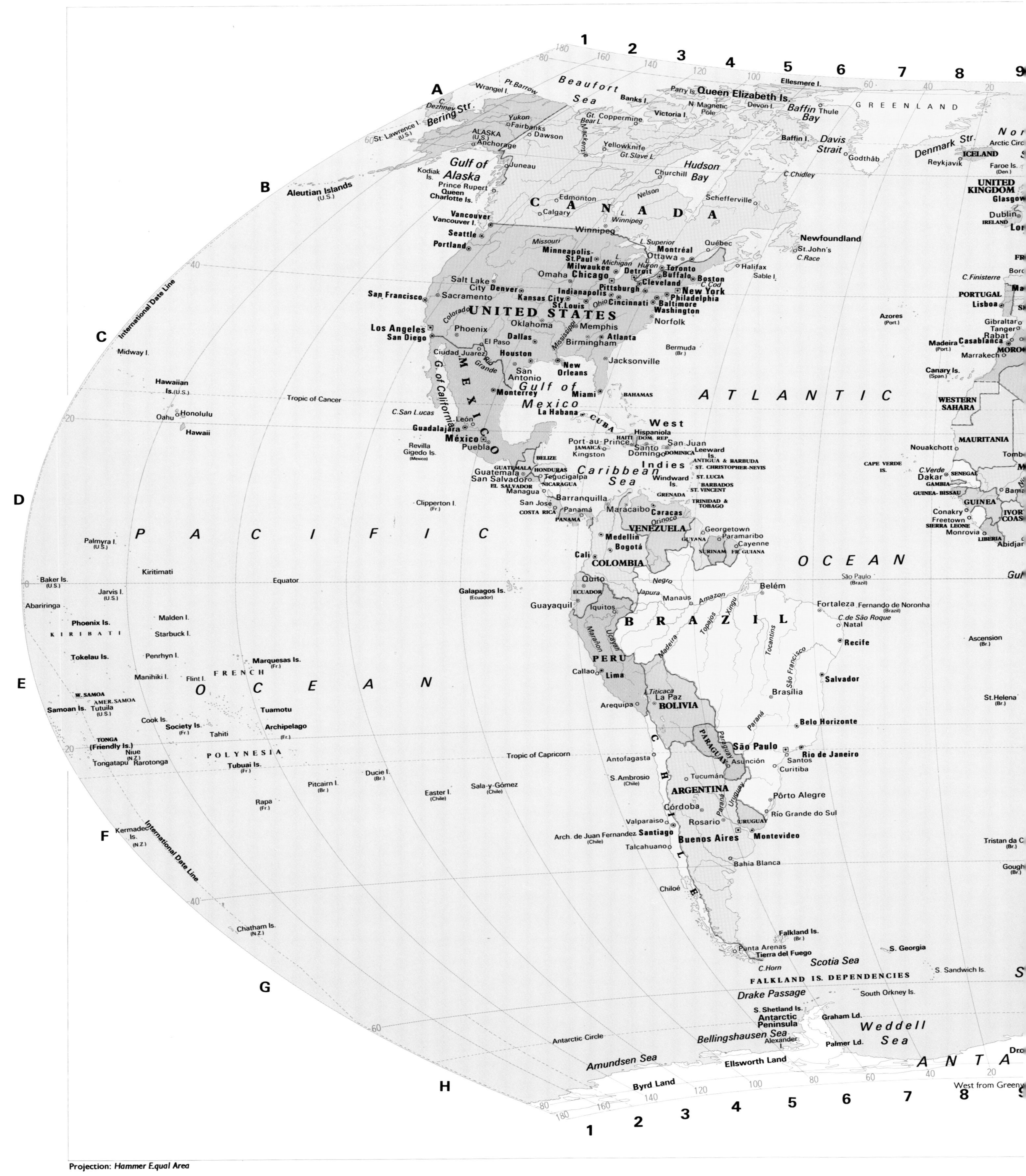

1
2
3
4
5
6
7
8
A
B
C
D
E
F
G
H
Beaufort Sea
Wrangel I.
Pt. Barrow
C. Dezhnev
Bering Str.
St. Lawrence I. (U.S.)
ALASKA (U.S.)
Yukon
Fairbanks
Dawson
Anchorage
Gulf of Alaska
Kodiak Is.
Juneau
Aleutian Islands (U.S.)
Prince Rupert
Queen Charlotte Is.
Banks I.
Parry Is.
Queen Elizabeth Is.
Ellesmere I.
Victoria I.
N. Magnetic Pole
Devon I.
Baffin Bay
Thule
GREENLAND
Gt. Bear L.
Coppermine
Mackenzie
Yellowknife
Gt. Slave L.
Hudson Bay
Churchill
Baffin I.
Davis Strait
Godthåb
C. Chidley
Denmark Str.
ICELAND
Reykjavik
Arctic Circle
Faroe Is. (Den.)
UNITED KINGDOM
Glasgow
Dublin
IRELAND
Edmonton
Calgary
Nelson
CANADA
Schefferville
Vancouver
Vancouver I.
Winnipeg
L. Winnipeg
Seattle
Portland
Missouri
Minneapolis-St. Paul
Milwaukee
L. Michigan
L. Huron
L. Superior
Montréal
Ottawa
Québec
Toronto
Buffalo
Boston
C. Cod
Newfoundland
St. John's
C. Race
Halifax
Sable I.
Salt Lake City
Denver
Omaha
Chicago
Detroit
Cleveland
Pittsburgh
New York
Philadelphia
Baltimore
Washington
San Francisco
Sacramento
Kansas City
Indianapolis
St. Louis
Ohio
Cincinnati
Colorado
UNITED STATES
Oklahoma
Memphis
Norfolk
Los Angeles
San Diego
Phoenix
Dallas
Atlanta
Birmingham
El Paso
Ciudad Juarez
Rio Grande
Houston
Mississippi
New Orleans
Jacksonville
Bermuda (Br.)
San Antonio
Gulf of Mexico
Miami
BAHAMAS
MEXICO
G. of California
Monterrey
C. San Lucas
La Habana
CUBA
León
Guadalajara
México
Puebla
Revilla Gigedo Is. (Mexico)
Hispaniola
HAITI
DOM. REP.
Port-au-Prince
JAMAICA
Kingston
Santo Domingo
San Juan
DOMINICA
Leeward Is.
West Indies
ANTIGUA & BARBUDA
ST. CHRISTOPHER-NEVIS
ST. LUCIA
BARBADOS
ST. VINCENT
GRENADA
Windward Is.
TRINIDAD & TOBAGO
BELIZE
GUATEMALA
HONDURAS
Guatemala
Tegucigalpa
San Salvador
EL SALVADOR
NICARAGUA
Managua
Caribbean Sea
Barranquilla
San José
COSTA RICA
Panamá
PANAMA
Clipperton I. (Fr.)
Maracaibo
Caracas
Orinoco
VENEZUELA
Georgetown
GUYANA
Paramaribo
Cayenne
SURINAM
FR. GUIANA
Medellin
Bogotá
Cali
COLOMBIA
Quito
ECUADOR
Guayaquil
Galapagos Is. (Ecuador)
Iquitos
Negro
Japura
Manaus
Amazon
Belém
Xingu
Tapajós
Madeira
Tocantins
BRAZIL
Fortaleza
Fernando de Noronha (Brazil)
C. de São Roque
Natal
Recife
São Francisco
Salvador
Brasília
Marañon
Ucayali
PERU
Lima
Callao
Titicaca
La Paz
BOLIVIA
Arequipa
Paraná
Belo Horizonte
PARAGUAY
Paraguay
São Paulo
Rio de Janeiro
Asunción
Santos
Curitiba
Antofagasta
S. Ambrosio (Chile)
Tucumán
ARGENTINA
Pôrto Alegre
Uruguay
Córdoba
Rio Grande do Sul
Rosario
URUGUAY
Valparaiso
Santiago
Buenos Aires
Montevideo
Arch. de Juan Fernandez (Chile)
Talcahuano
CHILE
Bahia Blanca
Chiloé
Falkland Is. (Br.)
Punta Arenas
Tierra del Fuego
C. Horn
Scotia Sea
S. Georgia
S. Sandwich Is.
FALKLAND IS. DEPENDENCIES
Drake Passage
South Orkney Is.
S. Shetland Is.
Antarctic Peninsula
Graham Ld.
Weddell Sea
Bellingshausen Sea
Alexander I.
Palmer Ld.
Antarctic Circle
Amundsen Sea
Ellsworth Land
Byrd Land
West from Greenwich
International Date Line
Midway I.
Hawaiian Is. (U.S.)
Tropic of Cancer
Oahu
Honolulu
Hawaii
PACIFIC
OCEAN
Palmyra I. (U.S.)
Kiritimati
Baker Is. (U.S.)
Jarvis I. (U.S.)
Equator
Abariringa
Phoenix Is.
Malden I.
KIRIBATI
Starbuck I.
Tokelau Is.
Penrhyn I.
Marquesas Is. (Fr.)
FRENCH
Manihiki I.
Flint I.
W. SAMOA
AMER. SAMOA
Samoan Is.
Tutuila (U.S.)
Tuamotu Archipelago (Fr.)
Cook Is.
Society Is. (Fr.)
Tahiti
TONGA (Friendly Is.)
Niue (N.Z.)
Tongatapu
Rarotonga
POLYNESIA
Tubuai Is. (Fr.)
Tropic of Capricorn
Ducie I. (Br.)
Pitcairn I. (Br.)
Easter I. (Chile)
Sala-y-Gómez (Chile)
Rapa (Fr.)
Kermadec Is. (N.Z.)
Chatham Is. (N.Z.)
ATLANTIC
OCEAN
Azores (Port.)
C. Finisterre
PORTUGAL
Lisboa
Gibraltar
Tangier
Rabat
Casablanca
Madeira (Port.)
Marrakech
Canary Is. (Span.)
WESTERN SAHARA
MAURITANIA
Nouakchott
CAPE VERDE IS.
C. Verde
Dakar
SENEGAL
GAMBIA
GUINEA-BISSAU
GUINEA
Conakry
Freetown
SIERRA LEONE
Monrovia
LIBERIA
Abidjan
São Paulo (Brazil)
Ascension (Br.)
St. Helena (Br.)
Tristan da C (Br.)
Gough (Br.)

Projection: *Hammer Equal Area*

ARCTIC OCEAN
Zemlya Frantsa Iosifa
Novaya Zemlya
Barents Sea
Nord Kapp
Murmansk
Kara Sea
Severnaya Zemlya
Laptev Sea
New Siberian Is.
East Siberian Sea
Arctic Circle
Ust Port
Yenisey
Tiksi
Verkhoyansk
Nizhne-Kolymsk
Anadyr
Lena
Vilyuysk
Yakutsk
Arkhangelsk
Salekhard
Ob
RUSSIA
Okhotsk
Sea of Okhotsk
Bering Sea
Kamchatka
Petropavlovsk-Kamchatskiy
C. Lopatka
Sakhalin
Komsomolsk
Khabarovsk
Kuril Is.
Amur
Helsinki
St. Peterburg
Oslo
Stockholm
Yaroslavl
Moskva
Perm
Kazan
Yekaterinburg
Novosibirsk
Tomsk
Krasnoyarsk
L. Baykal
Ulan Ude
Omsk
Novokuznetsk
Barnaul
Irkutsk
Ufa
Chelyabinsk
Samara
Orenburg
Minsk
Voronezh
Warszawa
POLAND
Hamburg
Berlin
Praha
Kiyev
Kharkov
UKRAINE
Saratov
Volgograd
Rostov
Astrakhan
Karaganda
Irtysh
Ulaanbaatar
MONGOLIA
KAZAKHSTAN
L. Balkhash
Aral Sea
UZBEKISTAN
Alma Ata
KIRGHIZIA
Tashkent
Dushanbe
TAJ.
Samarkand
TURKMENISTAN
Ashkhabad
Mashhad
Caspian Sea
Baku
Tbilisi
Yerevan
Grozny
Budapest
Wien
Milano
Beograd
ROMANIA
Bucuresti
BULGARIA
Sofiya
Black Sea
Istanbul
Ankara
TURKEY
Odessa
Roma
Napoli
Sardinia
Sicily
Athinai
GREECE
Izmir
Tunis
MALTA
Crete
Mediterranean Sea
CYPRUS
Halab
SYRIA
Dimashq
Bayrut
Tel Aviv-Yafo
Amman
Jerusalem
JORDAN
Baghdad
IRAQ
Tehran
IRAN
Esfahan
Abadan
Shiraz
Tarabulus
Banghazi
El Iskandariya
El Qahira
Bur Said
LIBYA
EGYPT
Nile
Aswan
KUWAIT
The Gulf
BAHRAIN
QATAR
Ar Riyad
U.A.E.
SAUDI ARABIA
Makkah
Red Sea
OMAN
YEMEN
Aden
Gulf of Aden
Socotra (Yemen)
Arabian Sea
AFGHANISTAN
Kabul
Rawalpindi
PAKISTAN
Karachi
Indus
Srinagar
Lahore
XIZANG (TIBET)
Lhasa
Delhi
NEPAL
Katmandu
BHU.
Agra
Kanpur
Lucknow
Ganga
INDIA
BANGLADESH
Dhaka
Calcutta
Ahmadabad
Nagpur
Bombay
Pune
Bay of Bengal
Hyderabad
Bangalore
Madras
Andaman Is. (India)
Lakshadweep Is.
Nicobar Is. (India)
SRI LANKA (CEYLON)
Colombo
Dondra Hd.
MALDIVES
BURMA (MYANMAR)
Mandalay
Rangoon
THAILAND
Bangkok
CAMBODIA
Phnom Penh
Phanh Bho Ho Chi Minh
Vientiane
Hanoi
Hainan
VIETNAM
South China Sea
CHINA
Harbin
Changchun
Shenyang
Beijing
Tianjin
Taiyuan
Dalian
Jinan
Qingdao
Lanzhou
Xi'an
Huang He
Nanjing
Shanghai
Wuhan
Chengdu
Chongqing
Chang Jiang
Changsha
Kunming
Fuzhou
Taibei
TAIWAN
Guangzhou
Hong Kong (Br.)
East China Sea
Ryukyu Is.
Vladivostok
N. KOREA
Pyongyang
Soul
S. KOREA
Pusan
Sea of Japan
JAPAN
Sapporo
Hakodate
Tokyo
Yokohama
Kyoto
Kobe
Nagoya
Osaka
Kitakyushu
PACIFIC OCEAN
Tropic of Cancer
NORTHERN MARIANAS
Wake I. (U.S.)
Manila
PHILIPPINES
Cebu
Guam (U.S.)
Yap
FEDERATED STATES OF MICRONESIA
MARSHALL IS.
Truk
Ponape
BELAU
Caroline Is.
MALAYSIA
BRUNEI
SABAH
SARAWAK
Kuala Lumpur
PEN. MALAYSIA
Kuching
SINGAPORE
Medan
Sumatera
Borneo
Sulawesi
Maluku
Palembang
Banjarmasin
INDONESIA
Ujung Pandang
Jakarta
Bandung
Jawa
Surabaya
Sunda Islands
Irian Jaya
PAPUA NEW GUINEA
Rabaul
New Ireland
New Britain
SOLOMON IS.
Port Moresby
Louisiade Arch.
C. York
Arafura Sea
Timor
Timor Sea
Darwin
Gilbert Is.
NAURU
KIRIBATI
TUVALU
Santa Cruz Is.
VANUATU
Vanua Levu
FIJI
Viti Levu
Suva
New Caledonia (Fr.)
NIGER
CHAD
L. Chad
Ndjamena
Kano
NIGERIA
Ibadan
Lagos
CAMEROON
Douala
Yaounde
CENTRAL AFRICAN REPUBLIC
Bangui
SUDAN
Omdurman
El Khartum
ERITREA
Asmera
DJIBOUTI
Blue Nile
White Nile
Addis Abeba
ETHIOPIA
SOMALI REP.
L. Turkana
Muqdisho
UGANDA
KENYA
Kampala
Kisangani
ZAIRE (CONGO)
Zaire (Congo)
EQUATORIAL GUINEA
Libreville
GABON
CONGO
Brazzaville
Kinshasa
Kasai
CABINDA
Kananga
Victoria
RW.
BUR.
Nairobi
L. Tanganyika
TANZANIA
Mombasa
Zanzibar
Dar es Salaam
Amirante Is.
SEYCHELLES
Aldabra
Luanda
ANGOLA
Benguela
Lubumbashi
ZAMBIA
Lusaka
MALAWI
L. Malawi
Zomba
COMORO IS.
Harare
ZIMBABWE
MOZAMBIQUE
Mozambique Chan.
MADAGASCAR
Antananarivo
Bulawayo
NAMIBIA
BOTSWANA
Windhoek
Gaborone
Pretoria
Johannesburg
SWAZ.
Maputo
SOUTH AFRICA
LES.
Durban
Cape Town
C. of Good Hope
Port Elizabeth
Reunion (Fr.)
MAURITIUS
Rodriguez
INDIAN OCEAN
Equator
Chagos Arch. (Br.)
Diego Garcia (Br.)
Cocos (Keeling Is.) (Australia)
Christmas I. (Australia)
Tropic of Capricorn
North West C.
NORTHERN TERRITORY
Townsville
Cairns
WESTERN AUSTRALIA
QUEENSLAND
Alice Springs
AUSTRALIA
Rockhampton
SOUTH AUSTRALIA
Brisbane
Kalgoorlie-Boulder
Perth
Fremantle
C. Leeuwin
NEW SOUTH WALES
Darling
Great Australian Bight
Adelaide
Newcastle
Sydney
Canberra
VICTORIA
Melbourne
Tasman Sea
TASMANIA
Hobart
Norfolk I. (Australia)
Lord Howe I. (Australia)
North C.
Auckland
North I.
NEW ZEALAND
Wellington
C. Farewell
Christchurch
South I.
Stewart I.
Dunedin
Bounty Is.
Antipodes Is. (N.Z.)
Auckland I. (N.Z.)
Campbell I. (N.Z.)
Macquarie I. (Australia)
Amsterdam (Fr.)
St. Paul (Fr.)
Pr. Edward Is. (South Africa)
Crozet Is. (Fr.)
Kerguelen (Fr.)
McDonald I. (Australia)
Heard I. (Australia)
Bouvet I. (Norway)
SOUTHERN OCEAN
Antarctic Circle
Enderby Land
Wilkes Land
S. Magnetic Pole
Balleny Is.
Ross Sea
ANTARCTICA
East from Greenwich
A
B
C
D
E
F
G
H
10 11 12 13 14 15 16 17 18

COPYRIGHT GEORGE PHILIP & SON, LTD.

ARCTIC OCEAN

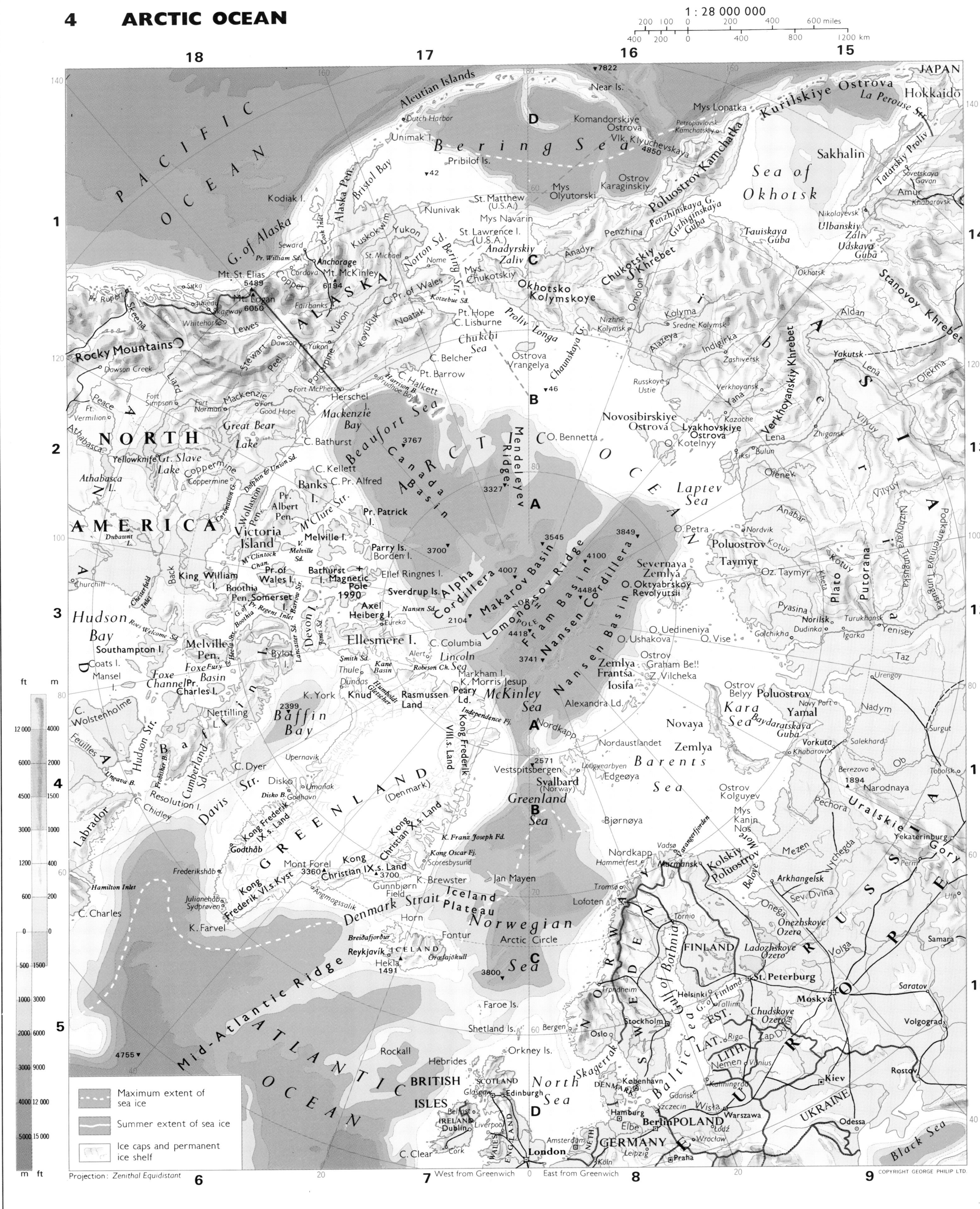
1 : 28 000 000
200 100 0 200 400 600 miles
400 200 0 400 800 1200 km
PACIFIC OCEAN
Bering Sea
Aleutian Islands
Dutch Harbor
Unimak I.
Pribilof Is.
Near Is.
Komandorskiye Ostrova
Vlk. Klyuchevskaya 4850
Petropavlovsk Kamchatskiy
Mys Lopatka
Kurilskiye Ostrova
La Perouse Str.
JAPAN
Hokkaidō
Sakhalin
Tatarskiy Proliv
Sea of Okhotsk
Poluostrov Kamchatka
Ostrov Karaginskiy
Mys Olyutorski
Kodiak I.
Alaska Pen.
Bristol Bay
St. Matthew (U.S.A.)
Nunivak
Mys Navarin
St Lawrence I. (U.S.A.)
Anadyrskiy Zaliv
Anadyr
Penzhina
Penzhinskaya G.
Gizhiginskaya Guba
Tauiskaya Guba
Udskaya Guba
Ulbanskiy Zaliv
G. of Alaska
Anchorage
Mt. McKinley 6194
Mt. St. Elias 5489
Mt. Logan 6050
Seward
Cordova
Juneau
Skagway
Whitehorse
Fairbanks
Kuskokwim
Yukon
Norton Sd.
Nome
Bering Str.
Mys Chukotskiy
C. Pr. of Wales
Kotzebue Sd.
Pt. Hope
C. Lisburne
Chukchi Sea
Ostrova Vrangelya
Chaunskaya G.
Proliv Longa
Okhotsko Kolymskoye
Chukotskiy Khrebet
Omolon
Kolyma
Sredne Kolymsk
Nizhne Kolymsk
Alazeya
Indigirka
Zashiversk
Verkhoyansk
Verkhoyanskiy Khrebet
Yana
Okhotsk
Stanovoy Khrebet
Aldan
Yakutsk
Lena
Olekma
Vilyuy
ALASKA
Rocky Mountains
Dawson Creek
Dawson
Pr. Rupert
Skeena
Lewes
Stewart
Peel
Porcupine
Noatak
Koyukuk
C. Belcher
Pt. Barrow
C. Halkett
Prudhoe Bay
Herschel I.
Mackenzie Bay
Fort McPherson
Fort Good Hope
Fort Norman
Fort Simpson
Mackenzie
Liard
Peace
Ft. Vermilion
Athabasca
Great Bear Lake
Gt. Slave Lake
Yellowknife
Coppermine
Athabasca L.
NORTH AMERICA
Dubawnt L.
Beaufort Sea
C. Bathurst
C. Kellett
Banks I.
C. Pr. Alfred
Pr. Albert Pen.
Wollaston Pen.
Victoria Island
M'Clure Str.
Pr. Patrick I.
Melville I.
Parry Is.
Borden I.
Ellef Ringnes I.
Bathurst I.
Magnetic Pole 1990
Sverdrup Is.
Axel Heiberg I.
Eureka
Nansen Sd.
King William I.
Boothia Pen.
Somerset I.
Pr. of Wales I.
Devon I.
Ellesmere I.
C. Columbia
Alert
Lincoln Sea
Robeson Ch.
Kane Basin
Smith Sd.
Thule
Dundas
Humboldt Gletscher
K. York
Knud Rasmussen Land
Peary Ld.
K. Morris Jesup
Markham I.
Independence Fj.
Kong Frederik VIII.s Land
Baffin Bay 2399
Bylot I.
Baffin I.
Melville Pen.
Foxe Basin
Foxe Channel
Southampton I.
Coats I.
Mansel I.
Pr. Charles I.
Hudson Bay
Churchill
Chesterfield Inlet
Back
Roes Welcome Sd.
C. Wolstenholme
Nettilling L.
Hudson Str.
Cumberland Sd.
Frobisher B.
Ungava B.
Feuilles
Resolution I.
C. Chidley
Labrador
Davis Str.
C. Dyer
Disko
Disko B.
Godhavn
Umanak
Upernavik
GREENLAND (Denmark)
Godthåb
Frederikshåb
Julianehåb
Sydprøven
K. Farvel
C. Charles
Hamilton Inlet
Mont Forel 3360
Kong Christian IX.s Land
Kong Christian X.s Land
Kong Frederik VI.s Kyst
Kong Frederik IX.s Land
Angmagssalik
Gunnbjørn Field 3700
K. Brewster
Scoresbysund
Kong Oscar Fj.
K. Franz Joseph Fd.
Denmark Strait
Iceland Plateau
Jan Mayen
Greenland Sea
Horn
Fontur
Breiđafjörður
Reykjavík
ICELAND
Hekla 1491
Öræfajökull
Norwegian Sea
Arctic Circle
3800
Faroe Is.
Shetland Is.
Orkney Is.
Rockall
Hebrides
BRITISH ISLES
SCOTLAND
Glasgow
Edinburgh
Belfast
IRELAND
Dublin
Liverpool
WALES
ENGLAND
Cork
C. Clear
London
North Sea
Mid-Atlantic Ridge
ATLANTIC OCEAN
4755
ARCTIC OCEAN
Canada Basin 3767
Mendeleyev Ridge 3327
Alpha Cordillera
Makarov Basin 4007
Lomonosov Ridge
NORTH POLE
Fram Basin 4418 4484
Nansen Cordillera 4100
Nansen Basin 3741
3545
3849
3700
2104
O. Bennetta
Novosibirskiye Ostrova
Lyakhovskiye Ostrova
O. Kotelnyy
Russkoye Ustie
Kazache
Laptev Sea
Tiksi
Bulun
Olenek
Anabar
Zhigansk
O. Petra
Nordvik
Poluostrov Taymyr
Oz. Taymyr
Kotuy
Kheta
Plato Putorana
Nizhnaya Tunguska
Podkamennaya Tunguska
Severnaya Zemlya
O. Oktyabrskoy Revolyutsii
O. Uedineniya
O. Ushakova
O. Vise
Golchikha
Pyasina
Norilsk
Dudinka
Turukhansk
Igarka
Yenisey
Taz
Urengoy
Ostrov Graham Bell
Z. Vilcheka
Zemlya Frantsa Iosifa
Alexandra Ld.
McKinley Sea
Nordkapp
Nordaustlandet
Vestspitsbergen 2571
Longyearbyen
Svalbard (Norway)
Edgeøya
Bjørnøya
Barents Sea
Novaya Zemlya
Kara Sea
Ostrov Belyy
Poluostrov Yamal
Novy Port
Baydaratskaya Guba
Nadym
Salekhard
Surgut
Ob
Vorkuta
Khabarova
Berezovo
Narodnaya 1894
Tobolsk
Pechora
Uralskie Gory
Yekaterinburg
Ostrov Kolguyev
Mys Kanin Nos
Mezen
Vychegda
Perm
Ufa
Arkhangelsk
Sev. Dvina
Onega
Onezhskoye Ozero
Ladozhskoye Ozero
Beloye More
Kolskiy Poluostrov
Murmansk
Varangerfjorden
Vadsø
Nordkapp
Hammerfest
Tromsø
Lofoten
Tornio
FINLAND
NORWAY
SWEDEN
Gulf of Bothnia
Trondheim
Bergen
Oslo
Stockholm
Helsinki
G. of Finland
Tallinn
St. Peterburg
EST.
Chudskoye Ozero
Riga
LAT.
LITH.
Vilnius
Nemen
Zap. Dvina
Skagerrak
Baltic Sea
DENMARK
København
Kaliningrad
Gdańsk
Szczecin
Wisła
Warszawa
POLAND
Łódź
Wrocław
Hamburg
Elbe
Berlin
GERMANY
Amsterdam
NETH.
Köln
Leipzig
Praha
Moskva
Volga
Samara
Saratov
Volgograd
Rostov
Kiev
UKRAINE
Odessa
Black Sea
RUSSIA
EUROPE
ASIA
Siberia
Maximum extent of sea ice
Summer extent of sea ice
Ice caps and permanent ice shelf
Projection: Zenithal Equidistant
West from Greenwich
East from Greenwich
ft m
12 000 4000
6000 2000
4500 1500
3000 1000
1200 400
600 200
0 0
500 1500
1000 3000
2000 6000
3000 9000
4000 12 000
5000 15 000
m ft
COPYRIGHT GEORGE PHILIP LTD.

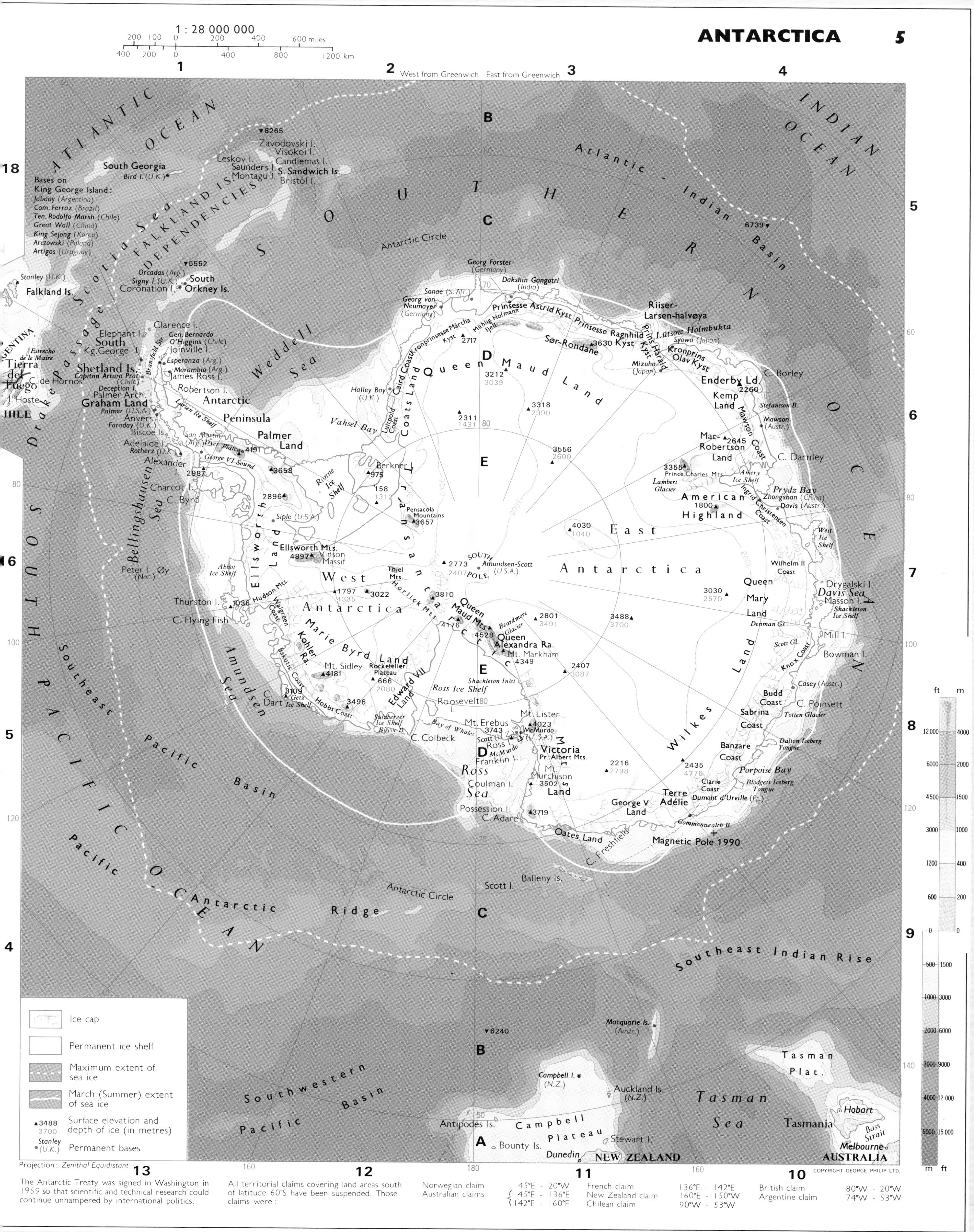
1 : 28 000 000
200 100 0 200 400 600 miles
400 200 0 400 800 1200 km
West from Greenwich East from Greenwich
ATLANTIC OCEAN
INDIAN OCEAN
SOUTHERN OCEAN
SOUTH PACIFIC OCEAN
South Georgia
Bird I. (U.K.)
Bases on King George Island:
Jubany (Argentina)
Com. Ferraz (Brazil)
Ten. Rodolfo Marsh (Chile)
Great Wall (China)
King Sejong (Korea)
Arctowski (Poland)
Artigas (Uruguay)
Zavodovski I.
Visokoi I.
Candlemas I.
Leskov I.
Saunders I.
Montagu I.
S. Sandwich Is.
Bristol I.
FALKLAND IS. DEPENDENCIES
Scotia Sea
Stanley (U.K.)
Falkland Is.
Orcadas (Arg.)
Signy I. (U.K.)
Coronation I.
South Orkney Is.
Clarence I.
Elephant I.
South Shetland Is.
Kg.George I.
Gen. Bernardo O'Higgins (Chile)
Joinville I.
Esperanza (Arg.)
Marambio (Arg.)
James Ross I.
Capitan Arturo Prat (Chile)
Deception I.
Tierra del Fuego
C. de Hornos
Drake Passage
Robertson I.
Antarctic Peninsula
Graham Land
Palmer Arch.
Palmer (U.S.A.)
Anvers I.
Faraday (U.K.)
Biscoe Is.
Adelaide I.
Rotherz (U.K.)
San Martin (Arg.)
Alexander I.
Charcot I.
C. Byrd
Bellingshausen Sea
Peter I Øy (Nor.)
Weddell Sea
Larsen Ice Shelf
Palmer Land
George VI Sound
Ronne Ice Shelf
Berkner I.
Halley Bay (U.K.)
Vahsel Bay
Luitpold Coast
Coats Land
Caird Coast
Atlantic - Indian Basin
Antarctic Circle
Georg Forster (Germany)
Dakshin Gangotri (India)
Sanae (S. Afr.)
Georg von Neumayer (Germany)
Kronprinsesse Martha Kyst
Mühlig Hofmann fjell
Prinsesse Astrid Kyst
Prinsesse Ragnhild Kyst
Sør-Rondane
Riiser-Larsen-halvøya
Lützow Holmbukta
Syowa (Japan)
Prins Harald Kyst
Kronprins Olav Kyst
Mizuho (Japan)
Queen Maud Land
Enderby Ld.
C. Borley
Kemp Land
Stefansson B.
Mawson (Austr.)
Mawson Coast
Mac-Robertson Land
C. Darnley
Prince Charles Mts.
Lambert Glacier
Amery Ice Shelf
American Highland
Prydz Bay
Zhongshan (China)
Davis (Austr.)
Ingrid Christensen Coast
West Ice Shelf
Wilhelm II Coast
East Antarctica
Queen Mary Land
Drygalski I.
Davis Sea
Masson I.
Shackleton Ice Shelf
Denman Gl.
Mill I.
Bowman I.
Scott Gl.
Knox Coast
Casey (Austr.)
Budd Coast
Sabrina Coast
C. Poinsett
Totten Glacier
Banzare Coast
Dalton Iceberg Tongue
Porpoise Bay
Clarie Coast
Blodgett Iceberg Tongue
Terre Adélie
Dumont d'Urville (Fr.)
George V Land
Commonwealth B.
Magnetic Pole 1990
Oates Land
C. Freshfield
Wilkes Land
Balleny Is.
Scott I.
Pensacola Mountains
Transantarctic Mts
Siple (U.S.A.)
Ellsworth Land
Ellsworth Mts.
Vinson Massif
Abbot Ice Shelf
Thurston I.
Hudson Mts.
C. Flying Fish
West Antarctica
Thiel Mts.
Horlick Mts.
SOUTH POLE
Amundsen-Scott (U.S.A.)
Queen Maud Mts.
Beardmore Glacier
Queen Alexandra Ra.
Mt. Markham
Walgreen Coast
Marie Byrd Land
Kohler Ra.
Bakutis Coast
Mt. Sidley
Rockefeller Plateau
Edward VII Land
Amundsen Sea
C. Dart
Getz Ice Shelf
Hobbs Coast
Sulzberger Ice Shelf
Ruppert Coast
Shackleton Inlet
Ross Ice Shelf
Roosevelt I.
Bay of Whales
C. Colbeck
Mt. Erebus
Scott
McMurdo (U.S.A.)
Ross I.
McMurdo Sound
Franklin I.
Mt. Lister
Victoria Land
Pr. Albert Mts.
Mt. Murchison
Ross Sea
Coulman I.
Possession I.
C. Adare
Southeast Pacific Basin
Pacific Antarctic Ridge
Southeast Indian Rise
Macquarie Is. (Austr.)
Campbell I. (N.Z.)
Auckland Is. (N.Z.)
Southwestern Pacific Basin
Antipodes Is.
Bounty Is.
Campbell Plateau
Stewart I.
Dunedin
NEW ZEALAND
Tasman Plat.
Tasman Sea
Hobart
Tasmania
Bass Strait
Melbourne
AUSTRALIA
Ice cap
Permanent ice shelf
Maximum extent of sea ice
March (Summer) extent of sea ice
Surface elevation and depth of ice (in metres)
Permanent bases
Projection: Zenithal Equidistant
ft m
COPYRIGHT GEORGE PHILIP LTD.

The Antarctic Treaty was signed in Washington in 1959 so that scientific and technical research could continue unhampered by international politics.

All territorial claims covering land areas south of latitude 60°S have been suspended. Those claims were:

Norwegian claim	45°E - 20°W
Australian claims	45°E - 136°E; 142°E - 160°E
French claim	136°E - 142°E
New Zealand claim	160°E - 150°W
Chilean claim	90°W - 53°W
British claim	80°W - 20°W
Argentine claim	74°W - 53°W

COPYRIGHT GEORGE PHILIP LTD.

1 : 16 000 000
miles
km
NORWEGIAN SEA
ATLANTIC OCEAN
NORTH SEA
BALTIC SEA
BLACK SEA
CASPIAN SEA
MEDITERRANEAN SEA
ADRIATIC SEA
Ionian Sea
Tyrrhenian Sea
Ligurian Sea
Aegean Sea
Bay of Biscay
English Channel
Irish Sea
White Sea
G. of Bothnia
G. of Finland
G. of Riga
Sea of Azov
Skagerrak
Kattegat
Ural Mountains
Scandinavia
Lapland
Finland
Kola Peninsula
Kanin Peninsula
Tundra
Iceland
British Isles
Great Britain
Ireland
North European Plain
Central Russian Uplands
Volga Uplands
Obshchi Syrt
Ukraine
Pripyat Marshes
Carpathians
Transylvanian Alps
Plain of Hungary
Wallachia
Balkans
Balkan Peninsula
Rhodope
Pindus
Morea
Dinaric Alps
Alps
Apennines
Jura
Vosges
Ardennes
Black For.
Bohemian For.
Erz Geb.
Sudetes
Moravian Heights
Harz
Central Massif
Cevennes
Pyrenees
Cantabrian Mts.
Iberian Peninsula
Old Castile
New Castile
Sierra Morena
Andalusia
Sa. Nevada
Caucasus
Armenia
Kurdistan
Anatolia
Taurus
Maritime Atlas
Plateau of the Shotts
Crimea
Cyprus
Crete
Sicily
Sardinia
Corsica
Balearic Is.
Malta
Shetland Is.
Orkney Is.
Faroe Is.
Hebrides
Fisher Bank
Dogger Bank
Rockall
Heligoland
Netherlands
Brittany
Jutland
Arctic Circle
Projection: Bonne West from Greenwich 0 East from Greenwich
COPYRIGHT, GEORGE PHILIP & SON, LTD.

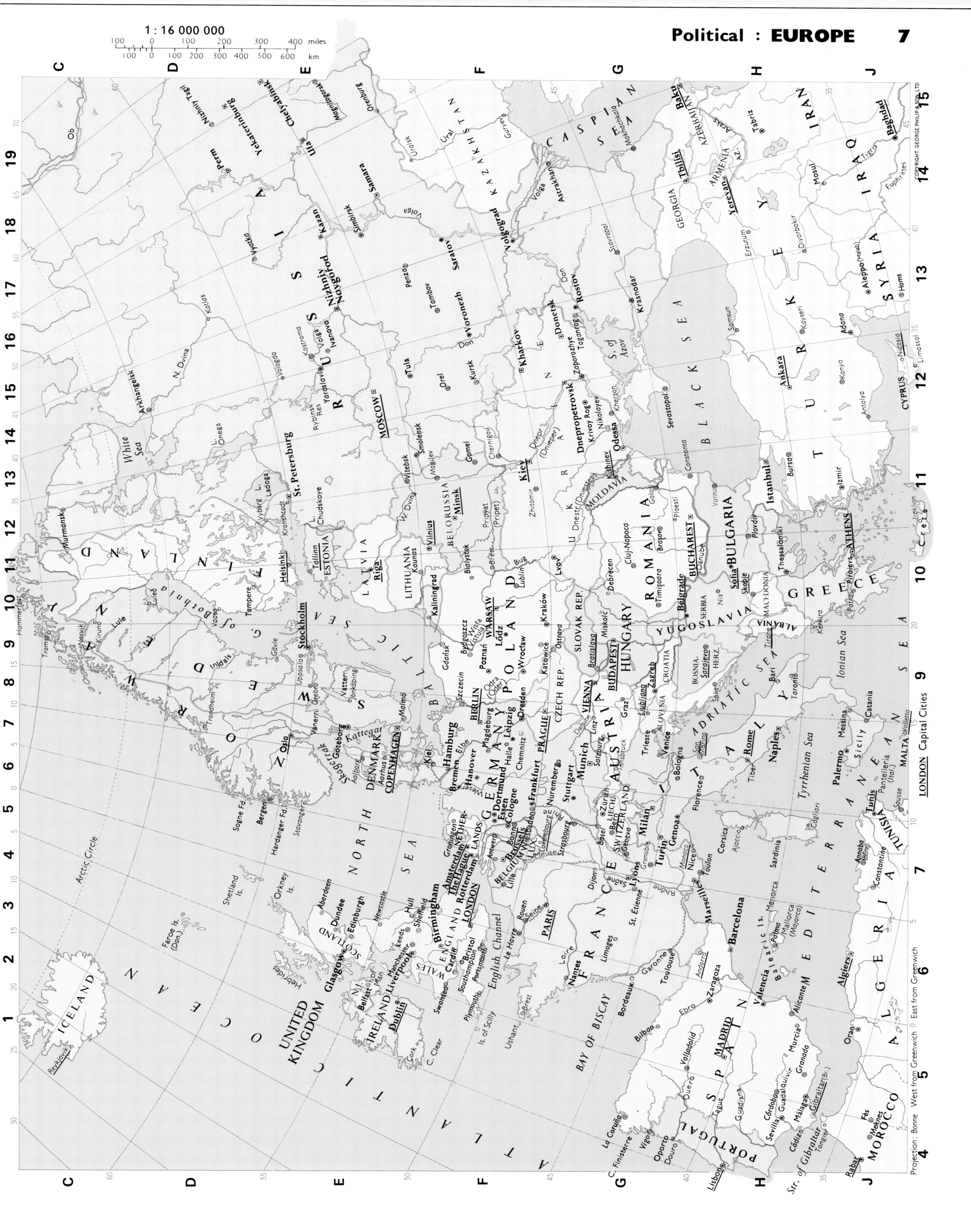
1 : 16 000 000
100 0 100 200 300 400 miles
100 0 100 200 300 400 500 600 km
LONDON Capital Cities
Projection: Bonne West from Greenwich 0 East from Greenwich
COPYRIGHT GEORGE PHILIP & SON LTD
ATLANTIC OCEAN
NORTH SEA
BALTIC SEA
BAY OF BISCAY
MEDITERRANEAN SEA
BLACK SEA
CASPIAN SEA
ADRIATIC SEA
ICELAND
UNITED KINGDOM
IRELAND
NORWAY
SWEDEN
FINLAND
DENMARK
GERMANY
POLAND
FRANCE
SPAIN
PORTUGAL
ITALY
AUSTRIA
HUNGARY
ROMANIA
BULGARIA
GREECE
YUGOSLAVIA
TURKEY
RUSSIA
UKRAINE
KAZAKHSTAN
ESTONIA
LATVIA
LITHUANIA
BELORUSSIA
MOLDAVIA
CZECH REP.
SLOVAK REP.
SWITZERLAND
ALBANIA
MOROCCO
ALGERIA
TUNISIA
SYRIA
IRAQ
IRAN
CYPRUS
GEORGIA
ARMENIA
AZERBAIJAN

ICELAND
on the same scale as general map

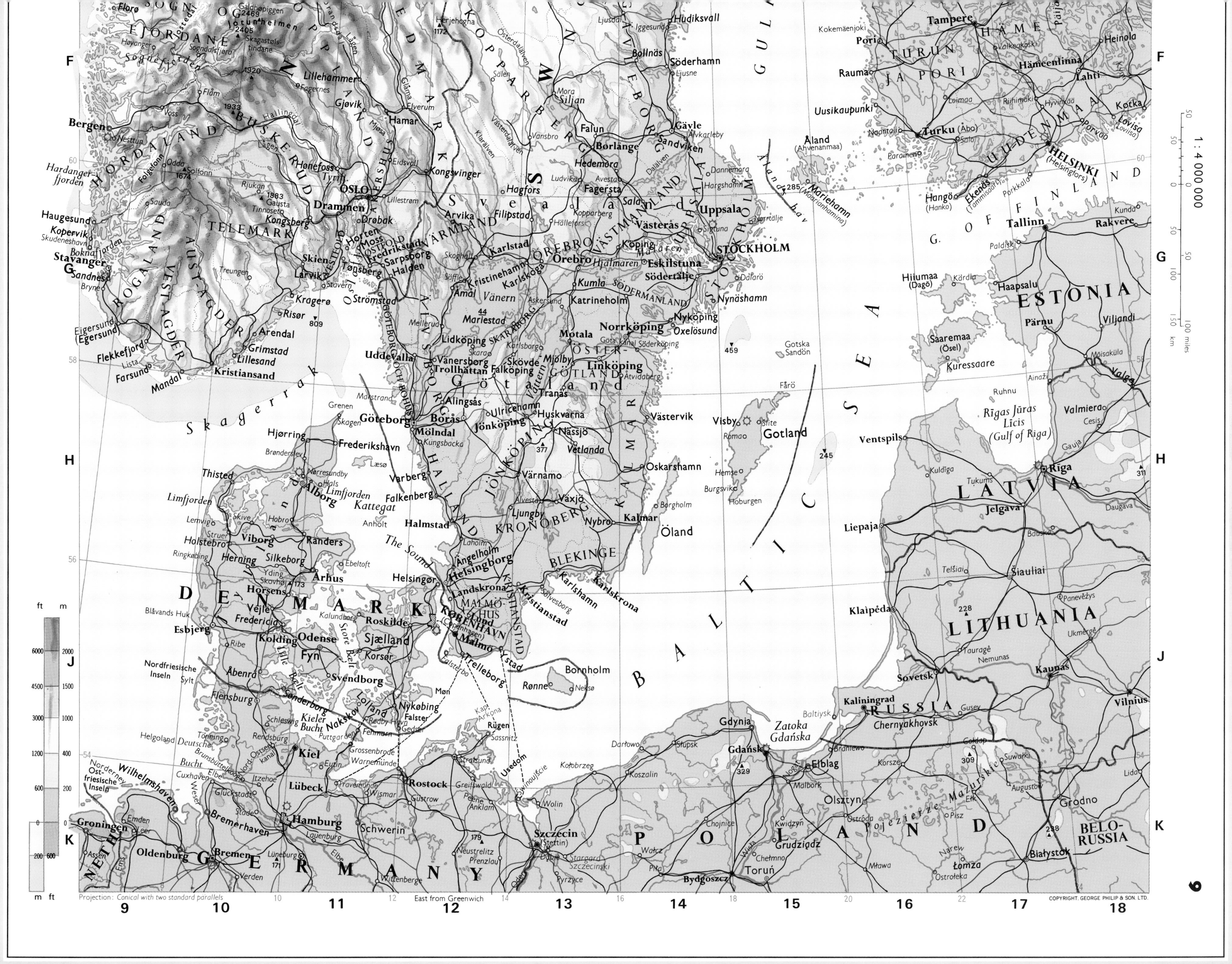

1 : 4 000 000
50 0 50 100 miles
50 0 50 100 150 km
9
NORWAY
SWEDEN
FINLAND
ESTONIA
LATVIA
LITHUANIA
RUSSIA
BELO-RUSSIA
POLAND
GERMANY
DENMARK
BALTIC SEA
GULF OF FINLAND
Rīgas Jūras Līcis (Gulf of Riga)
Skagerrak
Kattegat
The Sound
Zatoka Gdańska
Ålands hav
Svealand
Götaland
Bergen
Stavanger
OSLO
Göteborg
STOCKHOLM
Uppsala
Norrköping
Linköping
Malmö
KØBENHAVN (Copenhagen)
Århus
Odense
Gotland
Öland
Bornholm
HELSINKI (Helsingfors)
Turku (Åbo)
Tampere
Tallinn
Riga
Kaunas
Vilnius
Klaipėda
Kaliningrad
Gdańsk
Gdynia
Szczecin (Stettin)
Hamburg
Kiel
Lübeck
Rostock
Bremen
Groningen
Projection: Conical with two standard parallels
East from Greenwich
COPYRIGHT, GEORGE PHILIP & SON, LTD.

Gulf of Bothnia
JÄMTLANDS LÄN
VÄSTERNORRLANDS LÄN
GÄVLEBORGS LÄN
KOPPARBERGS LÄN
VÄRMLANDS LÄN
VÄSTMANLANDS LÄN
UPPSALA LÄN
STOCKHOLMS LÄN
SÖDERMANLANDS LÄN
ÖREBRO LÄN
SØR TRØNDELAG FYLKE
MØRE OG ROMSDAL FYLKE
HEDMARK FYLKE
OPPLAND FYLKE
BUSKERUD FYLKE
TELEMARK FYLKE
VESTFOLD
ØSTFOLD F.
AKERSHUS FYLKE
Trondheim
Östersund
Sundsvall
Gävle
Uppsala
Västerås
Örebro
Karlstad
Falun
Borlänge
Lillehammer
Hamar
Gjøvik
OSLO
Drammen
Kongsberg
Skien
Larvik
Fredrikstad
STOCKHOLM
Jotunheimen
Rondane
Dovrefjell
Trollheimen
Siljan
Mälaren
Hjälmaren

1 : 2 000 000
10 0 10 20 30 40 50 miles
10 0 10 20 30 40 50 60 70 80 km
Skagerrak
Norskerenna
Kattegat
BALTIC SEA
Kalmarsund
Hanöbukten
Bornholmsgattet
Jammerbugt
Ålborg Bugt
Kieler Bucht
Fehmarn Bælt
Femer Bælt
Store Bælt
Lille Bælt
JYLLAND
SJÆLLAND
FYN
LOLLAND
FALSTER
Bornholm
Öland
Gotland
GERMANY
POLAND
KØBENHAVN (COPENHAGEN)
Göteborg
Malmö
Århus
Odense
Ålborg
Helsingborg
Jönköping
Norrköping
Linköping
Kalmar
Karlskrona
Flensburg
Kiel
Visby
Projection: Conical with two standard parallels
East from Greenwich
COPYRIGHT. GEORGE PHILIP & SON. LTD.

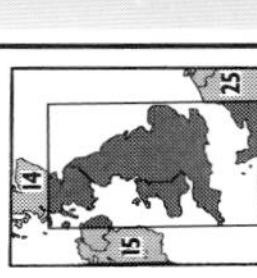

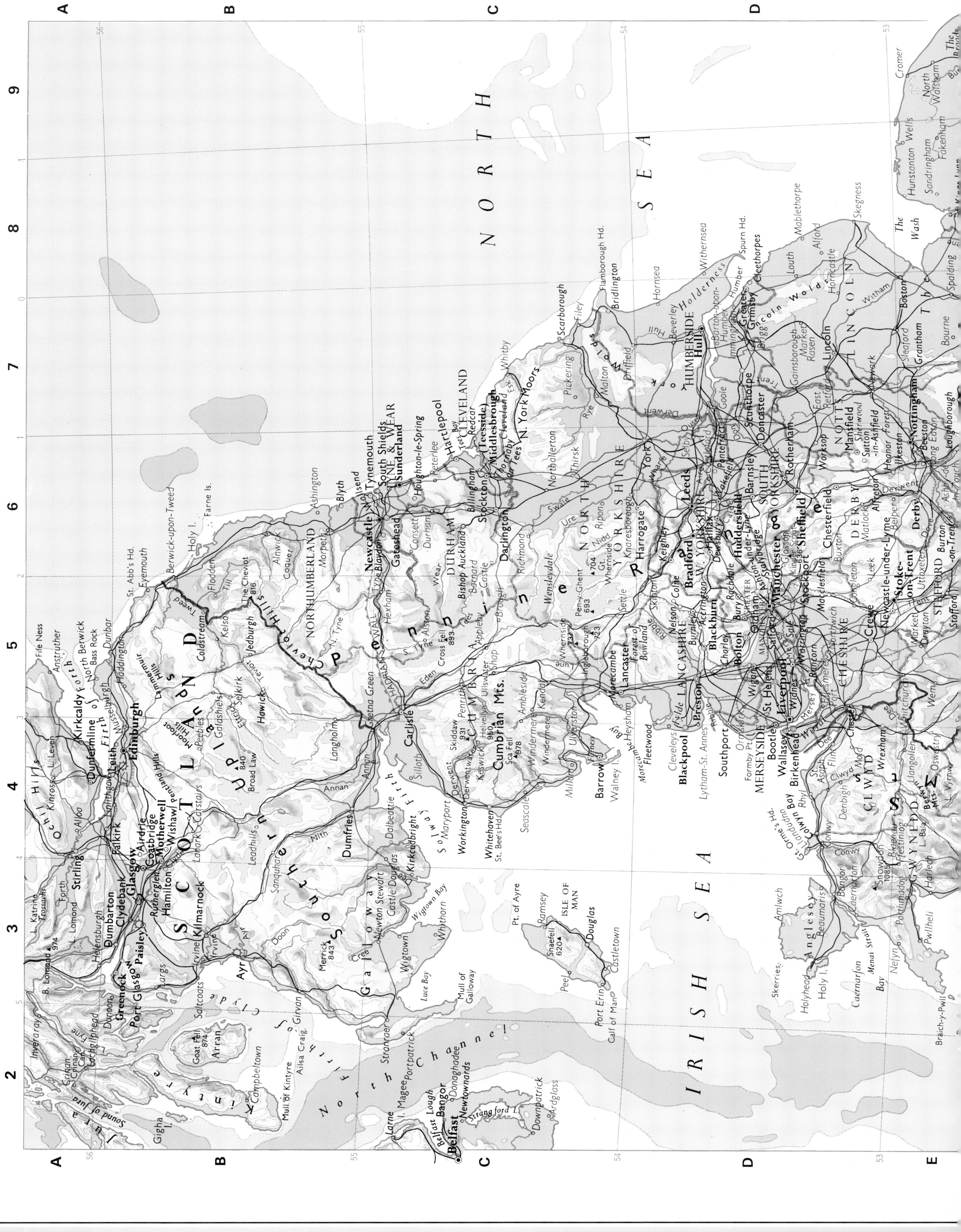
NORTH SEA
IRISH SEA
North Channel
SCOTLAND
Southern Uplands
Pennines
Cumbrian Mts.
Cheviot Hills
NORTHUMBERLAND
DURHAM
CLEVELAND
TYNE & WEAR
CUMBRIA
NORTH YORKSHIRE
W. YORKSHIRE
SOUTH YORKSHIRE
HUMBERSIDE
LANCASHIRE
MERSEYSIDE
GREATER MANCHESTER
CHESHIRE
DERBY
NOTTS
LINCOLN
STAFFORD
CLWYD
GWYNEDD
ISLE OF MAN
Edinburgh
Glasgow
Newcastle
Sunderland
Middlesbrough
Carlisle
Leeds
Bradford
Manchester
Liverpool
Sheffield
Hull
Nottingham
Lincoln
Blackpool
Preston
Stoke-on-Trent
Derby
Douglas
Belfast
Dumfries
Darlington
Lancaster
Scarborough
Doncaster
Birkenhead
Chester

1 : 1 600 000
10 0 10 20 30 40 50 miles
10 0 10 20 30 40 50 60 70 80 km
SCILLY ISLES
On same Scale
Isles of Scilly
St. Mary's
Land's End
Penzance
St. Ives
ENGLISH CHANNEL
Bristol Channel
Channel Islands
Guernsey
St. Peter Port
Sark
Alderney
Jersey
St. Helier
FRANCE
CORNWALL
DEVON
DORSET
SOMERSET
AVON
WILTS
HANTS
BERKS
SURREY
WEST SUSSEX
EAST SUSSEX
KENT
ESSEX
SUFFOLK
HERTFORD
BEDFORD
BUCKS
OXFORD
GLOUCESTER
WORCESTER
HEREFORD & WORCESTER
WARWICK
NORTHAMPTON
CAMBRIDGE
GWENT
WEST GLAMORGAN
MID GLAMORGAN
SOUTH GLAMORGAN
DYFED
POWYS
ISLE OF WIGHT
LONDON
Birmingham
Bristol
Cardiff
Swansea
Newport
Plymouth
Exeter
Southampton
Portsmouth
Bournemouth
Brighton
Reading
Oxford
Cambridge
Ipswich
Colchester
Southend
Canterbury
Dover
Folkestone
Hastings
Eastbourne
Worthing
Weymouth
Poole
Torquay (Torbay)
Gloucester
Cheltenham
Swindon
Northampton
Coventry
Luton
Dieppe
Le Havre
Rouen
Cherbourg
Caen
Lisieux
Bayeux
Projection: Conical with two standard parallels.
West from Greenwich
East from Greenwich
COPYRIGHT, GEORGE PHILIP & SON, LTD.

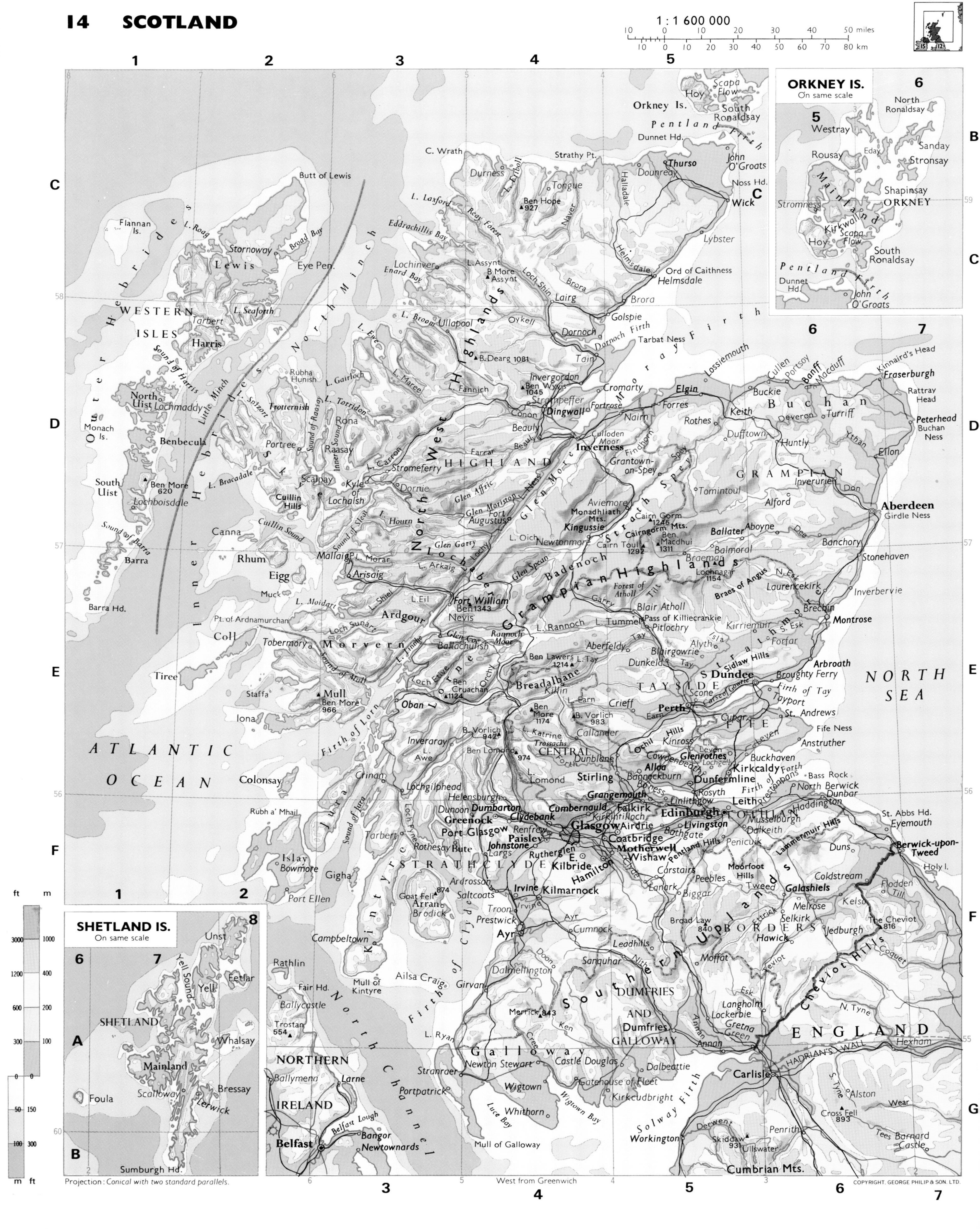

14 SCOTLAND
1 : 1 600 000
50 miles
80 km
ORKNEY IS.
On same scale
SHETLAND IS.
On same scale
Orkney Is.
Pentland Firth
Dunnet Hd.
C. Wrath
Strathy Pt.
Thurso
John O'Groats
Noss Hd.
Wick
Butt of Lewis
Flannan Is.
Stornoway
Lewis
Eye Pen.
Harris
Tarbert
WESTERN ISLES
Outer Hebrides
North Minch
Little Minch
Inner Hebrides
North Uist
Lochmaddy
Monach Is.
Benbecula
South Uist
Ben More 620
Lochboisdale
Sound of Barra
Barra
Barra Hd.
Skye
Portree
Raasay
Rona
Cuillin Hills
Canna
Rhum
Eigg
Muck
Coll
Tiree
Tobermory
Mull
Ben More 966
Staffa
Iona
Colonsay
Jura
Islay
Bowmore
Port Ellen
Gigha
Kintyre
Campbeltown
Mull of Kintyre
Arran
Goat Fell 874
Brodick
Ailsa Craig
Rathlin
ATLANTIC OCEAN
NORTH SEA
Ullapool
Lochinver
B. More Assynt
Ben Hope 927
Lairg
Helmsdale
Ord of Caithness
Lybster
Brora
Golspie
Dornoch
Dornoch Firth
Tarbat Ness
Tain
B. Dearg 1081
Invergordon
Ben Wyvis 1045
Cromarty
Dingwall
Strathpeffer
Beauly
Inverness
Culloden Moor
Nairn
Forres
Elgin
Lossiemouth
Moray Firth
Buckie
Cullen
Portsoy
Banff
Macduff
Fraserburgh
Kinnaird's Head
Rattray Head
Peterhead
Buchan Ness
Buchan
Turriff
Keith
Rothes
Dufftown
Huntly
Ellon
Inverurie
Aberdeen
Girdle Ness
GRAMPIAN
HIGHLAND
North West Highlands
Kyle of Lochalsh
Stromeferry
Fort Augustus
Loch Ness
Glen More
Aviemore
Monadhliath Mts.
Kingussie
Cairn Gorm 1245
Cairngorm Mts.
Ben Macdhui 1311
Cairn Toul 1292
Newtonmore
Badenoch
Grantown-on-Spey
Tomintoul
Alford
Aboyne
Ballater
Balmoral
Banchory
Stonehaven
Lochnagar 1154
Grampian Highlands
Forest of Atholl
Braes of Angus
Laurencekirk
Inverbervie
Brechin
Montrose
Mallaig
Arisaig
Lochaber
Fort William
Ben Nevis 1343
Ardgour
Morvern
Glen Coe
Ballachulish
Rannoch Moor
L. Rannoch
L. Tummel
Blair Atholl
Pass of Killiecrankie
Pitlochry
Kirriemuir
Forfar
Arbroath
Aberfeldy
Ben Lawers 1214
Blairgowrie
Dunkeld
Dundee
Broughty Ferry
Firth of Tay
Tayport
St. Andrews
Fife Ness
Anstruther
TAYSIDE
Breadalbane
Killin
Ben Cruachan 1124
Oban
Firth of Lorn
Inveraray
Crieff
Perth
Scone
FIFE
Cupar
Ochil Hills
Kinross
Glenrothes
Kirkcaldy
Buckhaven
Dunfermline
Rosyth
Callander
Trossachs
L. Katrine
Ben Lomond 974
L. Lomond
CENTRAL
Dunblane
Stirling
Alloa
Bannockburn
Grangemouth
Falkirk
Linlithgow
Bo'ness
Firth of Forth
Bass Rock
North Berwick
Dunbar
Haddington
LOTHIAN
Edinburgh
Leith
Musselburgh
Dalkeith
Livingston
Bathgate
Penicuik
Pentland Hills
Lammermuir Hills
St. Abbs Hd.
Eyemouth
Berwick-upon-Tweed
Holy I.
Duns
Coldstream
Lochgilphead
Helensburgh
Dunoon
Dumbarton
Clydebank
Greenock
Port Glasgow
Renfrew
Paisley
Johnstone
Glasgow
Cumbernauld
Kirkintilloch
Airdrie
Coatbridge
Motherwell
Wishaw
Hamilton
Rutherglen
E. Kilbride
Rothesay
Bute
Largs
STRATHCLYDE
Ardrossan
Saltcoats
Irvine
Kilmarnock
Troon
Prestwick
Ayr
Cumnock
Carstairs
Lanark
Biggar
Peebles
Moorfoot Hills
Galashiels
Melrose
Kelso
Selkirk
Jedburgh
Hawick
BORDERS
Broad Law 840
The Cheviot 816
Cheviot Hills
Southern Uplands
Leadhills
Sanquhar
Moffat
Dalmellington
Girvan
Merrick 843
DUMFRIES AND GALLOWAY
Dumfries
Langholm
Lockerbie
Gretna Green
Annan
Galloway
Newton Stewart
Castle Douglas
Dalbeattie
Gatehouse of Fleet
Kirkcudbright
Wigtown
Wigtown Bay
Whithorn
Luce Bay
Mull of Galloway
Stranraer
Portpatrick
North Channel
Firth of Clyde
Solway Firth
NORTHERN IRELAND
Fair Hd.
Ballycastle
Trostan 554
Ballymena
Larne
Belfast Lough
Belfast
Bangor
Newtownards
ENGLAND
Carlisle
Hadrian's Wall
Hexham
Alston
Cross Fell 893
Barnard Castle
Penrith
Workington
Skiddaw 931
Ullswater
Cumbrian Mts.
Westray
North Ronaldsay
Rousay
Sanday
Stronsay
Mainland
Shapinsay
ORKNEY
Stromness
Kirkwall
Scapa Flow
Hoy
South Ronaldsay
Unst
Yell
Yell Sound
Fetlar
SHETLAND
Whalsay
Mainland
Foula
Scalloway
Lerwick
Bressay
Sumburgh Hd.
Projection: Conical with two standard parallels.
West from Greenwich
COPYRIGHT, GEORGE PHILIP & SON, LTD.

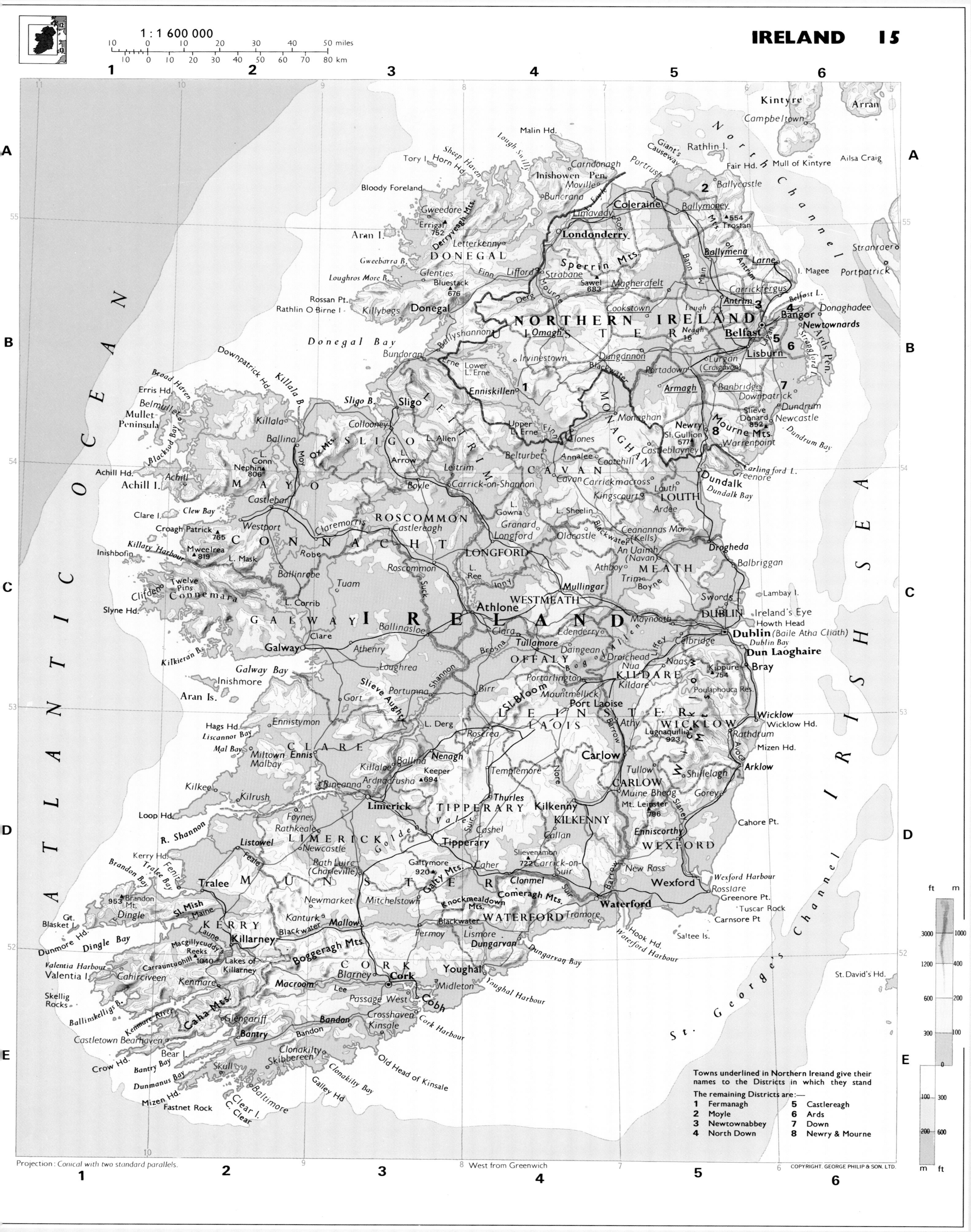

1 : 1 600 000
10 0 10 20 30 40 50 miles
10 0 10 20 30 40 50 60 70 80 km
ATLANTIC OCEAN
IRISH SEA
North Channel
St. George's Channel
IRELAND
NORTHERN IRELAND
ULSTER
CONNACHT
LEINSTER
MUNSTER
DONEGAL
SLIGO
LEITRIM
MAYO
ROSCOMMON
LONGFORD
CAVAN
MONAGHAN
LOUTH
MEATH
WESTMEATH
GALWAY
OFFALY
KILDARE
DUBLIN
WICKLOW
LAOIS
CARLOW
KILKENNY
WEXFORD
TIPPERARY
CLARE
LIMERICK
KERRY
CORK
WATERFORD
Kintyre
Campbeltown
Arran
Ailsa Craig
Mull of Kintyre
Rathlin I.
Fair Hd.
Giant's Causeway
Portrush
Malin Hd.
Lough Swilly
Inishowen Pen.
Carndonagh
Moville
Buncrana
Tory I.
Horn Hd.
Sheep Haven
Bloody Foreland
Gweedore
Errigal 752
Derryveagh Mts.
Aran I.
Letterkenny
Gweebarra B.
Glenties
Loughros More B.
Bluestack 676
Rossan Pt.
Rathlin O Birne I.
Killybegs
Donegal
Donegal Bay
Ballyshannon
Bundoran
Lifford
Strabane
Finn
Derg
Mourne
Londonderry
Limavady
Coleraine
Ballymoney
Ballycastle
Trostan 554
Ballymena
Larne
Carrickfergus
Antrim
Belfast L.
Bangor
Donaghadee
Newtownards
Belfast
Lisburn
Strangford L.
Ards Pen.
Lough Neagh 16
Cookstown
Magherafelt
Sperrin Mts.
Sawel 683
Omagh
Irvinestown
Dungannon
Blackwater
Portadown
Lurgan (Craigavon)
Armagh
Banbridge
Downpatrick
Dundrum
Newcastle
Slieve Donard 852
Mourne Mts.
Dundrum Bay
Newry
Sl. Gullion 577
Warrenpoint
Carlingford L.
Greenore
Enniskillen
Lower L. Erne
Upper L. Erne
Erne
Clones
Monaghan
Castleblayney
Stranraer
Portpatrick
I. Magee
Bann
Main
Mts. of Antrim
Sligo B.
Sligo
Collooney
Ox Mts.
L. Arrow
L. Allen
Leitrim
Boyle
Carrick-on-Shannon
Belturbet
Annalee
Cootehill
Cavan
Carrickmacross
Kingscourt
Louth
Ardee
Dundalk
Dundalk Bay
L. Gowna
L. Sheelin
Granard
Longford
Oldcastle
Ceanannas Mor (Kells)
An Uaimh (Navan)
Drogheda
Balbriggan
Athboy
Trim
Boyne
Mullingar
Inny
L. Ree
Athlone
Lambay I.
Swords
Ireland's Eye
Howth Head
Dublin (Baile Atha Cliath)
Dublin Bay
Dun Laoghaire
Bray
Maynooth
Celbridge
Liffey
Edenderry
Clara
Tullamore
Brosna
Daingean
Bog of Allen
Droichead Nua
Naas
Kippure 754
Kildare
Portarlington
Mountmellick
Port Laoise
Poulaphouca Res.
Wicklow Mts.
Wicklow
Wicklow Hd.
Lugnaquillia 923
Rathdrum
Avoca
Mizen Hd.
Arklow
Shillelagh
Athy
Barrow
Carlow
Tullow
Muine Bheag
Mt. Leinster 796
Gorey
Slaney
Enniscorthy
New Ross
Wexford
Wexford Harbour
Rosslare
Greenore Pt.
Tuscar Rock
Carnsore Pt.
Saltee Is.
Cahore Pt.
Downpatrick Hd.
Killala B.
Broad Haven
Erris Hd.
Belmullet
Mullet Peninsula
Blacksod Bay
Killala
Ballina
Moy
L. Conn
Nephin 806
Achill Hd.
Achill
Achill I.
Castlebar
Clare I.
Clew Bay
Westport
Croagh Patrick 765
Claremorris
Castlereagh
Killary Harbour
Mweelrea 819
Inishbofin
L. Mask
Robe
Ballinrobe
Roscommon
Suck
Tuam
Twelve Pins
Connemara
Clifden
L. Corrib
Slyne Hd.
Ballinasloe
Clare
Athenry
Galway
Kilkieran B.
Galway Bay
Inishmore
Aran Is.
Loughrea
Slieve Aughty
Portumna
Shannon
Birr
Sl. Bloom
Gort
L. Derg
Roscrea
Ennistymon
Hags Hd.
Liscannor Bay
Mal Bay
Miltown Malbay
Ennis
Nenagh
Ballina
Killaloe
Keeper 694
Ardnacrusha
Templemore
Nore
Thurles
Kilkenny
Kilkee
Rineanna
Kilrush
Limerick
Loop Hd.
R. Shannon
Foynes
Rathkeale
Newcastle
Golden Vale
Suir
Cashel
Callan
Tipperary
Listowel
Kerry Hd.
Feale
Fenit
Brandon Bay
Tralee Bay
Tralee
Rath Luirc (Charleville)
Galtymore 920
Galty Mts.
Caher
Slievenamon 722
Carrick-on-Suir
Clonmel
Comeragh Mts.
Waterford
Tramore
Brandon Mt. 953
Dingle
Sl. Mish
Maine
Newmarket
Mitchelstown
Knockmealdown Mts.
Blasket I.
Gt.
Dunmore Hd.
Dingle Bay
Laune
Killarney
Kanturk
Blackwater
Mallow
Fermoy
Lismore
Dungarvan
Dungarvan Bay
Hook Hd.
Waterford Harbour
Valentia Harbour
Valentia I.
Macgillycuddy's Reeks
Carrauntuohill 1040
Lakes of Killarney
Boggeragh Mts.
Cahirciveen
Kenmare
Macroom
Blarney
Cork
Youghal
Youghal Harbour
Midleton
Lee
Passage West
Cobh
Skellig Rocks
Ballinskelligs B.
Kenmare River
Caha Mts.
Glengariff
Bandon
Crosshaven
Kinsale
Cork Harbour
Castletown Bearhaven
Bantry
Bear I.
Clonakilty
Skibbereen
Clonakilty Bay
Old Head of Kinsale
Crow Hd.
Bantry Bay
Skull
Galley Hd
Dunmanus Bay
Mizen Hd.
Fastnet Rock
Baltimore
Clear I.
C. Clear
St. David's Hd.
Towns underlined in Northern Ireland give their names to the Districts in which they stand
The remaining Districts are:—
1 Fermanagh
2 Moyle
3 Newtownabbey
4 North Down
5 Castlereagh
6 Ards
7 Down
8 Newry & Mourne
ft m
3000 1000
1200 400
600 200
300 100
0
100 300
200 600
m ft
Projection: Conical with two standard parallels.
West from Greenwich
COPYRIGHT, GEORGE PHILIP & SON, LTD.
1 2 3 4 5 6
A B C D E

NORTH SEA
WADDENEILANDEN
OSTFRIESISCHE INSELN
WADDENZEE
IJSSELMEER
Markermeer
Texel
Vlieland
Terschelling
Ameland
Schiermonnikoog
Borkum
Groningen
Leeuwarden
Assen
Emmen
Zwolle
Deventer
Apeldoorn
Arnhem
Nijmegen
Amersfoort
Hilversum
Utrecht
AMSTERDAM
Haarlem
Leiden
'S GRAVENHAGE
(DEN HAAG)
(THE HAGUE)
ROTTERDAM
Dordrecht
Den Helder
Alkmaar
Lelystad
Enschede
Hengelo
Almelo
Emden
Noordoostpolder
Oostelijk-Flevoland
Zuidelijk-Flevoland
FRIESLAND
DRENTHE
GELDERLAND
FLEVOLAND
A
B
C
D
E
1
2
3
4
5
6
7
8
9
10

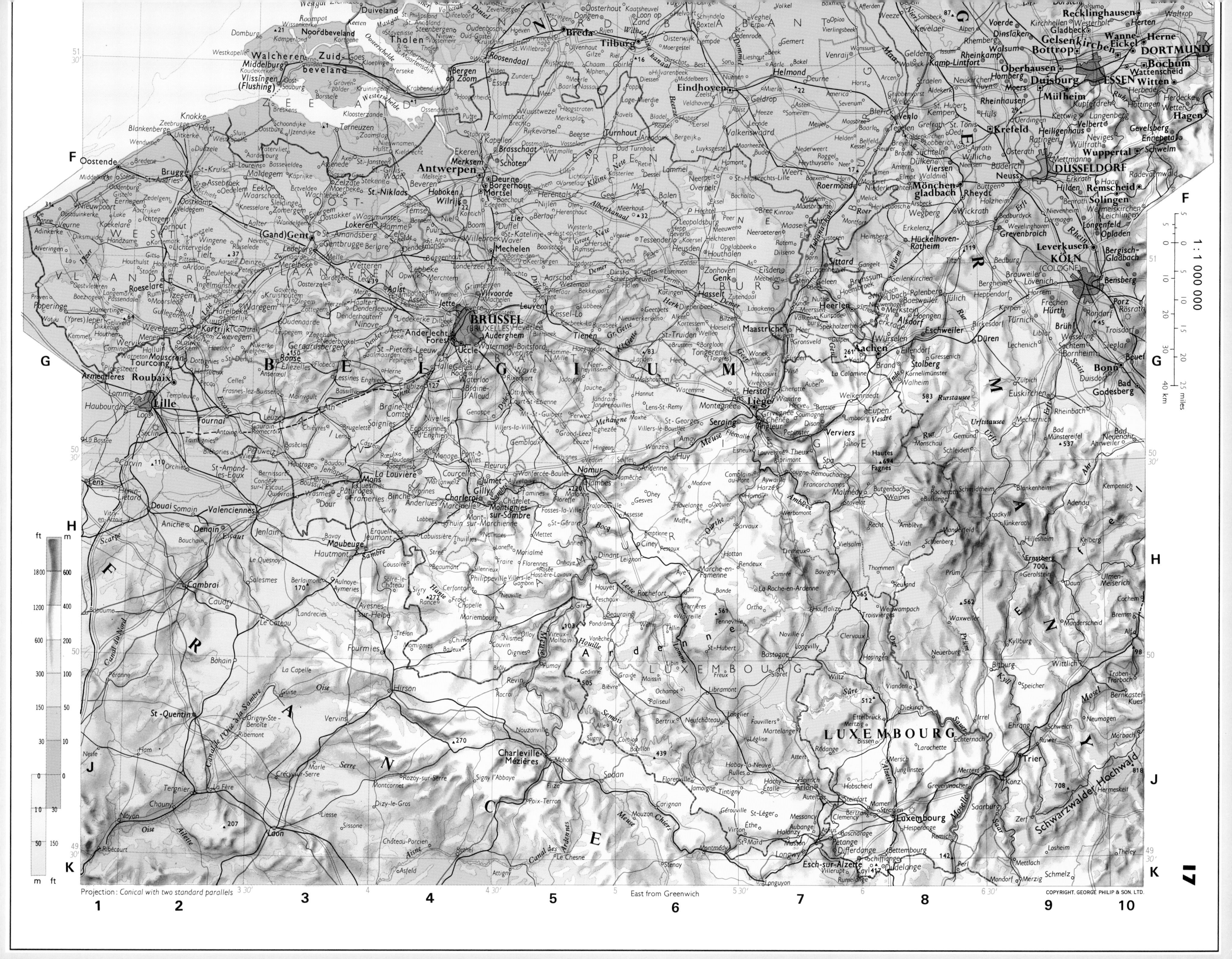

17
1 : 1 000 000
miles
km
Projection: Conical with two standard parallels
East from Greenwich
COPYRIGHT, GEORGE PHILIP & SON, LTD.
BELGIUM
NEDERLAND
GERMANY
FRANCE
LUXEMBOURG
ZEELAND
VLAANDEREN
ANTWERPEN
LIMBURG
Ardennes
BRUSSEL (BRUXELLES)
Antwerpen
(Gand) Gent
Brugge
Oostende
Liège
Namur
Charleroi
Mons
Lille
Roubaix
Tourcoing
Valenciennes
Cambrai
St-Quentin
Laon
Charleville-Mézières
Sedan
Luxembourg
Trier
Aachen
Maastricht
Eindhoven
Tilburg
Breda
KÖLN (COLOGNE)
Bonn
DÜSSELDORF
ESSEN
DORTMUND
Duisburg
Mönchengladbach
Krefeld
Wuppertal
Meuse
Sambre
Escaut
Moselle
Rhein

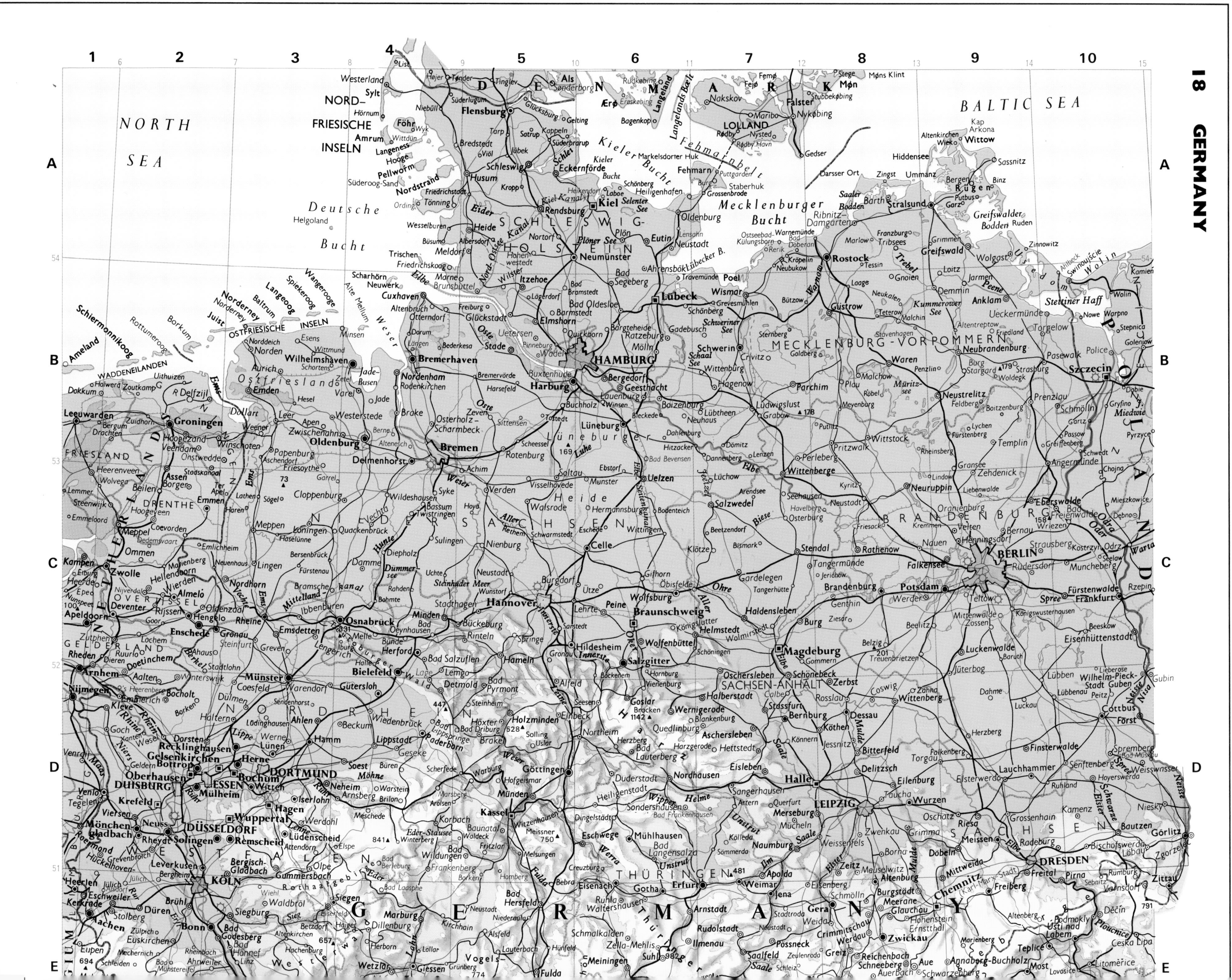
NORTH SEA
BALTIC SEA
DENMARK
POLAND
GERMANY
NETHERLANDS
NORD-FRIESISCHE INSELN
OSTFRIESISCHE INSELN
WADDENEILANDEN
Deutsche Bucht
Kieler Bucht
Mecklenburger Bucht
Fehmarnbelt
SCHLESWIG-HOLSTEIN
MECKLENBURG-VORPOMMERN
NIEDERSACHSEN
BRANDENBURG
SACHSEN-ANHALT
NORDRHEIN-WESTFALEN
THÜRINGEN
SACHSEN
Lüneburger Heide
HAMBURG
BERLIN
Bremen
Hannover
Kiel
Rostock
Lübeck
Schwerin
Magdeburg
LEIPZIG
DRESDEN
Potsdam
Szczecin
KÖLN
DÜSSELDORF
DORTMUND
ESSEN
DUISBURG
Münster
Osnabrück
Bielefeld
Kassel
Göttingen
Braunschweig
Halle
Erfurt
Chemnitz
Groningen
Emden
Wilhelmshaven
Bremerhaven
Cuxhaven
Flensburg
Lolland
Falster
Rügen
Elbe
Weser
Ems
Oder

1 : 2 000 000

10 0 10 20 30 40 50 miles

10 0 10 20 30 40 50 60 70 80 km

F G H J K

2 3 4 5 6 7 8 9

East from Greenwich

Projection: Conical with two standard parallels.

m	ft
4000	12000
3000	9000
2000	6000
1500	4500
1000	3000
400	1200
200	600
0	0

LUXEMBOURG

CZECH REP.

SWITZERLAND

ITALY

AUSTRIA

SLOVENIA

COPYRIGHT GEORGE PHILIP & SON, LTD

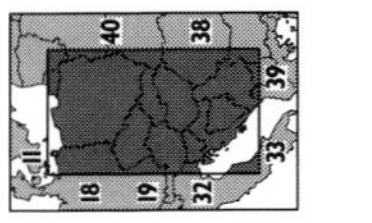

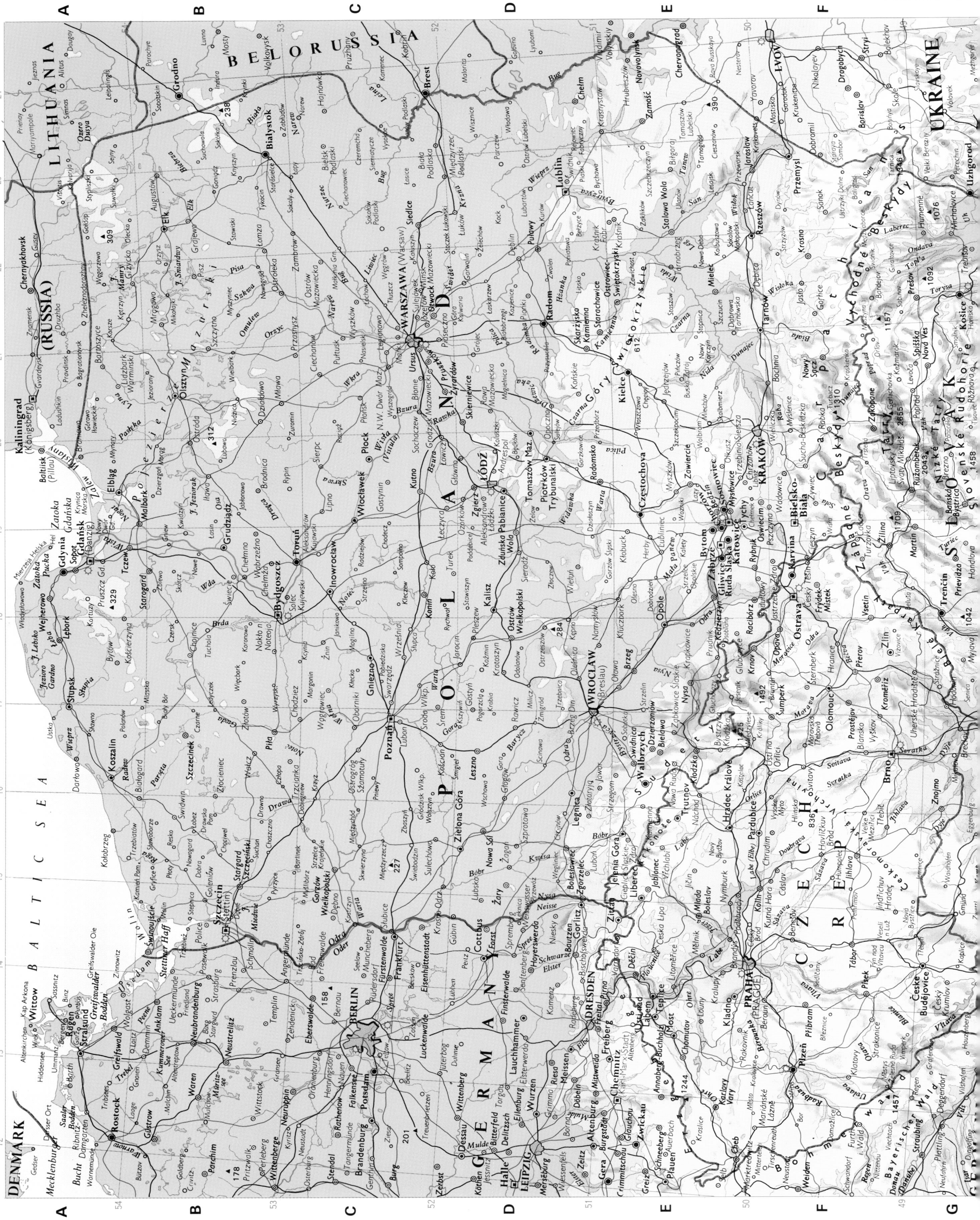

DENMARK
LITHUANIA
(RUSSIA)
BELORUSSIA
UKRAINE
POLAND
GERMANY
CZECH REP.
SLOVAKIA
BALTIC SEA

1 : 2 800 000

10 0 10 20 30 40 50 100 miles

10 0 10 20 30 40 50 100 150 km

H J K L M N

2 3 4 5 6 7 8 9 10 11 12 13

East from Greenwich

Projection: Conical with two standard parallels

m	ft
4000	12,000
3000	9000
2000	6000
1500	4500
1000	3000
400	1200
200	600
0	0
200	600

COPYRIGHT GEORGE PHILIP & SON LTD

1 2 3 4 5 6

A B C D E

HAUTE-SAÔNE
FRANCE
DOUBS
JURA
AIN
HAUTE-SAVOIE
SAVOIE
HAUT-RHIN
Sundgau
BELFORT
Porte de Bourgogne
Ajoie
Montagnes du Lomont
Franches Montagnes
NEUCHÂTEL
VAUD
FRIBOURG
BERN
SOLOTHURN
BASEL LANDSCHAFT
AARGAU
LUZERN
OBWALDEN
VALAIS
VALLE D'AOSTA
Schwarzwald
Mittelland
Jura
Freiburger Alpen
Berner Alpen
Alpi Pennine
Alpi Graie
Chablais
Faucigny
Genevois
Pays de Gex
Gruyère
Emmental
Entlebuch
Valle d'Aosta

Jussey
Vitrey-sur-Mance
Fayl-Billot
Genevrières
Amance
Faverney
Combeaufontaine
Port-s-Saône
Luxeuil-les-Bains
St-Sauveur
Meurcourt
Servance
Plancher-les-Mines
Mélisey
St-Germain
Saulx
Lure
Champagney
Giromagny
Ballon d'Alsace 1247
Masevaux
St-Maurice-s-M.
Thann
Cernay
Wittelsheim
Wittenheim
MULHOUSE
Lutterbach
Brunstatt
Illfurth
Altkirch
Dannemarie
Belfort
Héricourt
Montbéliard
Audincourt
Valentigney
Mandeure
Hérimoncourt
Pont-de-Roide
Delle
Grandvillars
Porrentruy
Delémont
Vesoul
Echenoz-la-Méline
Noroy-le-Bourg
Lavoncourt
Vaite
Dampierre-sur-Salon
Fresne-St.-Mames
Athesans
Villersexel
Rougemont
L'Isle-s.-le Doubs
Baume-les-Dames
Frétigney
Gray
Rioz
Gy
Roulans
Marnay
BESANÇON
Roche-lès-Beaupré
Mamirolle
St.-Vit
Dampierre
Aissey
Valdahon
Ornans
Quingey
Arc-et-Senans
Lods
Amancey
Loue
Mouchard
Mont-sous-Vaudrey
Salins-les-Bains
Levier
Arbois
Poligny
Andelot-en-Montagne
Champagnole
Pont-du-Navoy
Marigny
Conliège
Frasne
Pontarlier
Labergement-Ste-Marie
Mouthe
Foncine-le-Bas
St.-Laurent-en-Grandvaux
Morbier
Morez
Les Rousses
Moirans-en-Montagne
St.-Lupicin
St.-Claude
Dortan
Oyonnax
Chézery-Forens
St. Germain-de-Joux
Châtillon-de-Michaille
Bellegarde-s.-V.
Frangy
Seyssel
Artemare
Culoz
Chazey-Bons
Belley
Albens
Lac du Bourget
Yenne
Aix-les-Bains
Le Bourget-du-Lac
Lescheraines
Le Châtelard
Rumilly
Annecy
Lac d'Annecy
Tournette 2351
St. Jorioz
Faverges
Ugine
Albertville
Beaufort-s-D.
Flumet
Megève
St.-Gervais-les-B.
Sallanches
Thônes
Pte. Percée 2752
Thorens-Glières
Cruseilles
La Roche
Bonneville
Marignier
Cluses
Taninges
St.-Julien-en-Genevois
Veyrier
Annemasse
Chêne-Bourg
Vernier
Lancy
Chancy
GENÈVE (GENEVA)
Versoix
Gex
Divonne-les-Bains
Crêt de la Neige 1718
Nyon
St.-Cergue
Rolle
La Côte
Lac Léman (L. Geneva) 372
310
Thonon-les-Bains
Sciez
Evian-les-Bains
Dranse
Bellevaux
Abondance
2244
2432
St.-Gingolph
Vouvry
Morges
Lutry
Lavaux
LAUSANNE
Bussigny
Vevey
Montreux
Villeneuve
Aigle
Leysin
Les Diablerets
Col des Mosses 1445
Château d'Oex
Gstaad
Lenk
Monthey
Bex
St.-Maurice
Champéry
Dents du Midi 3257
Vernayaz
Col de la Forclaz 1527
Martigny
Le Châtelard
Orsières
Aig. d'Argentière 3896
Chamonix-Mont-Blanc
Mt. Blanc 4807
Courmayeur
Pré S. Didier
Morgex
La Thuile
Col du Petit St. Bernard 2188
3127
3486
Col du Gd. St.-Bernard 2469
3238
Bourg-St. Pierre
Étroubles
Aosta
Dora Baltea
Villeneuve
3559
Verrès
Châtillon
Champoluc
Gressoney S. Jean
Breuil-Cervinia
Matterhorn (Mte. Cervino) 4478
Dufourspitze 4634
Monte Rosa
Alagna Valsesia
Macugnaga
3320
Zermatt
Arolla
Barr. de la Grande Dixence
Saxon
Riddes
Sion
Savièse
Conthey
3051
Sierre
Leuk
Montana
Wildhorn 3248
Wildstrubel 3243
Leukerbad
Visp
Stalden
Visperterminen
St. Niklaus
Zinal
Weisshorn 4505
Dom 4545
Saas Fee
Weissmies 4023
Villadossola
Simplonpass 2005
Simplon
Simplon tunnel
3194
Mte. Leone 3553
Brig
Naters
Lötschbergtunnel
Blatten
Balmhorn 3709
Adelboden
Kandersteg
Blümlisalphorn 3664
Frutigen
Kander
Lauterbrunnen
Wengen
Grindelwald
Schreckhorn 4078
Jungfrau 4158
Finsteraarhorn 4274
Niesen 2362
Reichenbach
Simme
Zweisimmen
Boltigen
Spiez
Interlaken
Thunersee 558
Unterseen
Brienzersee 564
Brienz
Meiringen
Stockhorn 2190
Thun
Steffisburg
Uetendorf
Wattenwil
Münsingen
Konolfingen
Signau
Eggiwil
Schangnau
Sörenberg
Giswil
Escholzmatt
Schüpfheim
Entlebuch
Napf 1408
Langnau i. E.
Sumiswald
Wolhusen
Huttwil
Eriswil
Ruswil
Willisau
Sursee
Burgdorf
Kirchberg
Emme
Worb
Ostermundigen
Köniz
BERN (BERNE)
Zollikofen
Schüpfen
Lyss
Aarberg
Bielersee 429
La Neuveville
Nidau
Brügg
BIEL (BIENNE)
Grenchen
Solothurn
Biberist
Lotzwil
Langenthal
Ober-Aargau
Herzogenbuchsee
Aarwangen
Niederbipp
Murgenthal
Reiden
Rothrist
Zofingen
Aarburg
Olten
Schönenwerd
Aarau
Suhr
Oberentfelden
Balsthal
Passwang 1204
Waldenburg
Laufen
Laufelfingen
Sissach
Liestal
Pratteln
Rheinfelden
Arlesheim
Dornach
Reinach
Aesch
Oberwil
BASEL (BASLE)
Lörrach
B. Rheinfelden
Säckingen
Wehr
Schopfheim
Brombach
Steinen
Zell im Wiesenthal
Schönau im Schwarzwald
Todtnau
Belchen
1415
Badenweiler
Müllheim
Heitersheim
Neuenburg
Kandern
1165
Kembs
Rhein
Wiese
Öflingen
Albbruck
Waldshut
Frick
Brugg
Blotzheim
Ferrette
Pfetterhouse
Waldighofen
Friesen
Bassecourt
Moutier
Tramelan
Tavannes
Saignelégier
Maîche
Le Russey
Les Bois
St.-Imier
Chasseral 1607
La Chaux-de-Fonds
Le Locle
Morteau
Doubs
St. Blaise
Neuchâtel
Peseux
Colombier
Boudry
St. Aubin
1463
Lac de Neuchâtel 429
Couvet
Les Verrières
Fleurier
Chasseron 1607
Ste-Croix
Grandson
Les Hôpitaux-Neufs
Le Mt. d'Or 1461
Vallorbe
Orbe
Yverdon
Le Pont
La Sarraz
Le Sentier
Mt. Tendre 1679
Le Brassus
Echallens
Moudon
Lucens
Broye
Romont
Vaulruz
Bulle
Gruyères
Oron
Moléson 2002
Châtel-St.-Denis
Estavayer-le-Lac
Payerne
Yvonand
Avenches
Murten
Kerzers
Ins
Neuenegg
Düdingen
Fribourg (Freiburg)
Schwarzenburg
Marly le-Grand
Plaffeien
La Roche
Sarine
Sense
Aare
Ognon
Saône
Lanterne
Rhône
Arve
Ain
Vissoie
Dora Baltea

ft m
9000 3000
6000 2000
4500 1500
3000 1000
1200 500
600 200

47°30'
47°
46°30'
46°
6°
6°30'
7°
7°30'
8°

Projection: Conical with two standard parallels

1 2 3 4 5

25 19 25 27 32 32

1 : 800 000

5 0 5 10 15 20 25 miles

5 0 10 20 30 40 km

7 8 9 10 11

A B C D E

East from Greenwich

6 7 8 9 10 11

COPYRIGHT. GEORGE PHILIP & SON. LTD.

NORTHERN FRANCE

DÉPARTEMENTS IN THE PARIS AREA

1 Ville de Paris
2 Seine-St-Denis
3 Val-de-Marne
4 Hauts-de-Seine

ft	m
000	4000
9000	3000
6000	2000
4500	1500
3000	1000
1200	400
600	200
0	0
200	600
2000	6000
m	ft

Projection: *Conical with two standard parallels*

West from Greenwich 0 East from Greenwich

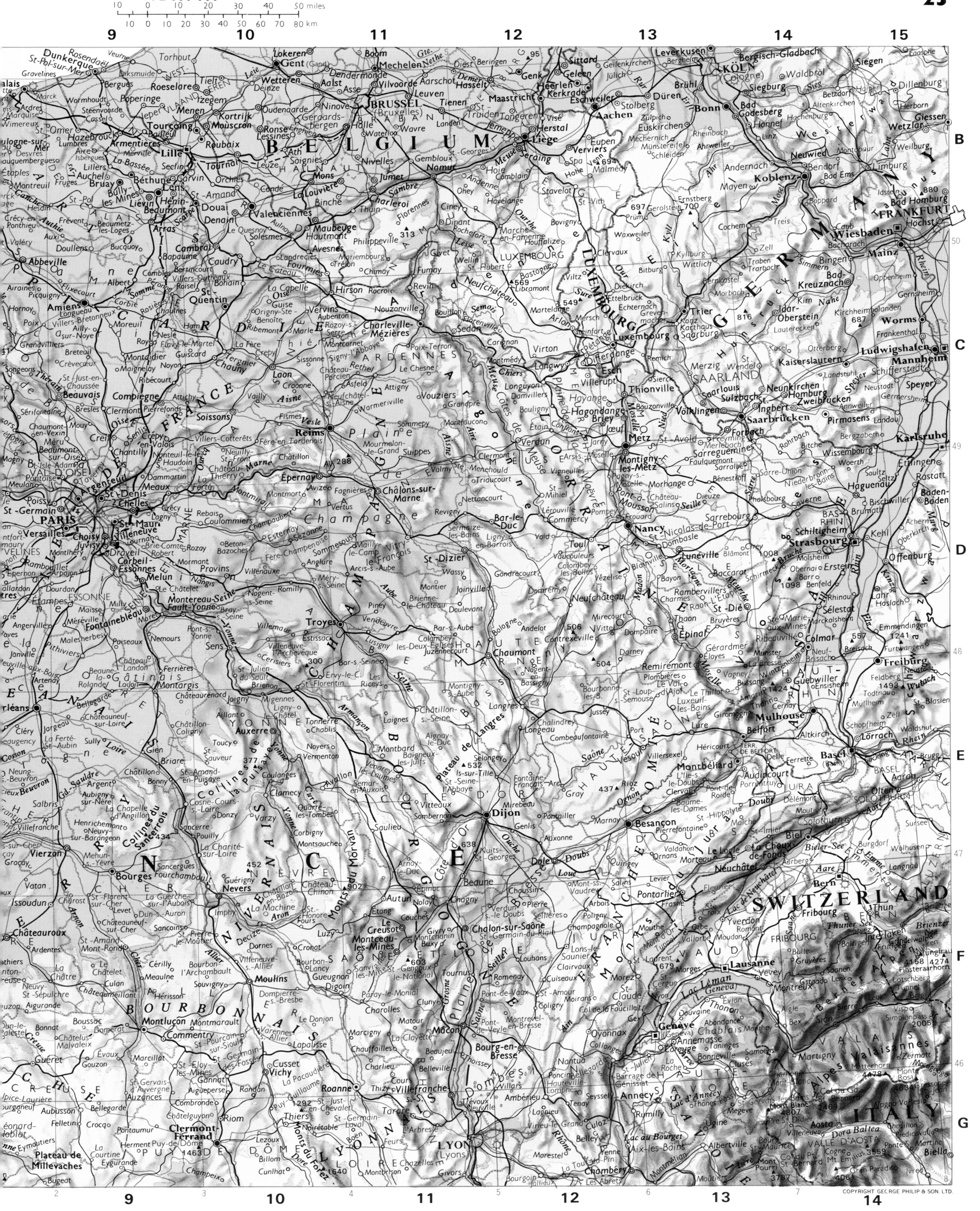
1 : 2 000 000
10 0 10 20 30 40 50 miles
10 0 10 20 30 40 50 60 70 80 km
9 10 11 12 13 14 15
B C D E F G
BELGIUM
LUXEMBOURG
GERMANY
FRANCE
SWITZERLAND
ITALY
SAARLAND
PICARDIE
CHAMPAGNE
LORRAINE
ALSACE
BOURGOGNE
FRANCHE COMTÉ
BOURBONNAIS
SAVOIE
HAUTE-SAVOIE
NIVERNAIS
LYONNAIS
Dunkerque
Lille
Bruxelles
Gent
Liège
Namur
Charleroi
Mons
Aachen
Köln
Bonn
Koblenz
Wiesbaden
Mainz
Frankfurt
Mannheim
Ludwigshafen
Karlsruhe
Saarbrücken
Trier
Luxembourg
Metz
Nancy
Strasbourg
Mulhouse
Basel
Freiburg
Reims
Amiens
Paris
Versailles
St-Denis
Troyes
Dijon
Besançon
Orléans
Bourges
Nevers
Auxerre
Chalon-sur-Saône
Mâcon
Lyon (Lyons)
Genève (Geneva)
Lausanne
Bern
Neuchâtel
Annecy
Chambéry
Clermont-Ferrand
Vichy
Moulins
Montluçon
Roanne
Vierzon
Châteauroux
Lac Léman (L. Geneva)
Plateau de Langres
Plateau de Millevaches
Monts du Morvan
Alpes Valaisannes
COPYRIGHT GEORGE PHILIP & SON, LTD.

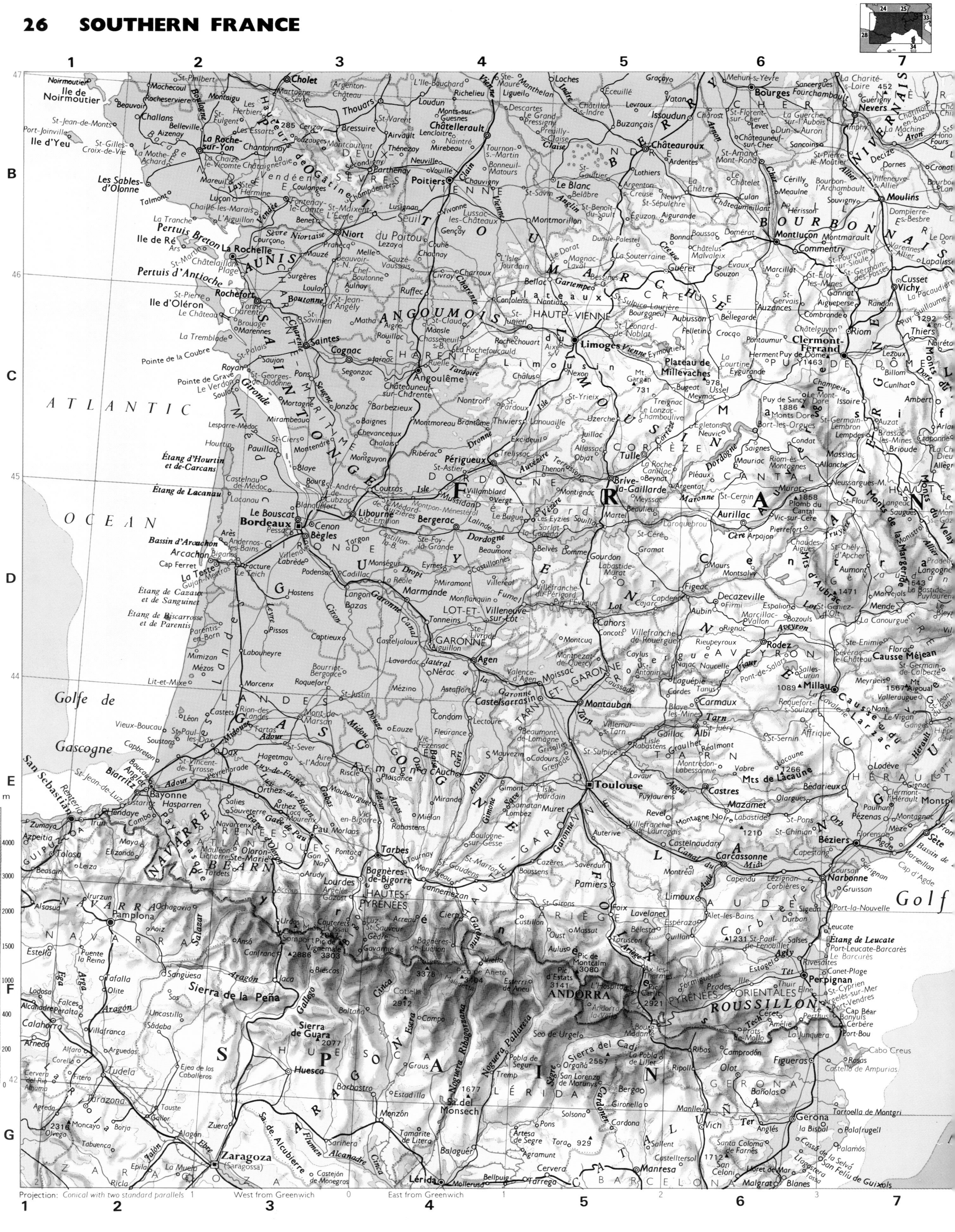

SOUTHERN FRANCE

Projection: Conical with two standard parallels

1 : 2 000 000
10 0 10 20 30 40 50 miles
10 0 10 20 30 40 50 60 70 80 km
SWITZERLAND
ITALY
FRANCE
LYON
MILANO
TORINO
GENÈVE
MARSEILLE
Lausanne
Bern
Grenoble
Nice
Genova
Toulon
Avignon
Aix-en-Provence
Chambéry
Annecy
Valence
Cannes
MONACO
San Remo
La Spezia
Livorno
Bergamo
Brescia
Novara
Vercelli
Asti
Alessàndria
Pavia
Piacenza
Parma
Cremona
Savona
Ajaccio
Bastia
CORSE (CORSICA)
HAUTE-CORSE
CORSE-DU-SUD
Golfo di Génova
LIGURIAN SEA
MEDITERRANEAN SEA
ILES D'HYÈRES
Mont Blanc 4807
Massif du Pelvoux
ALPES-DE-HAUTE-PROVENCE
ALPES-MARITIMES
HAUTE-SAVOIE
SAVOIE
DRÔME
VAUCLUSE
Elba
Capraia
Gorgona
COPYRIGHT. GEORGE PHILIP & SON, LTD.

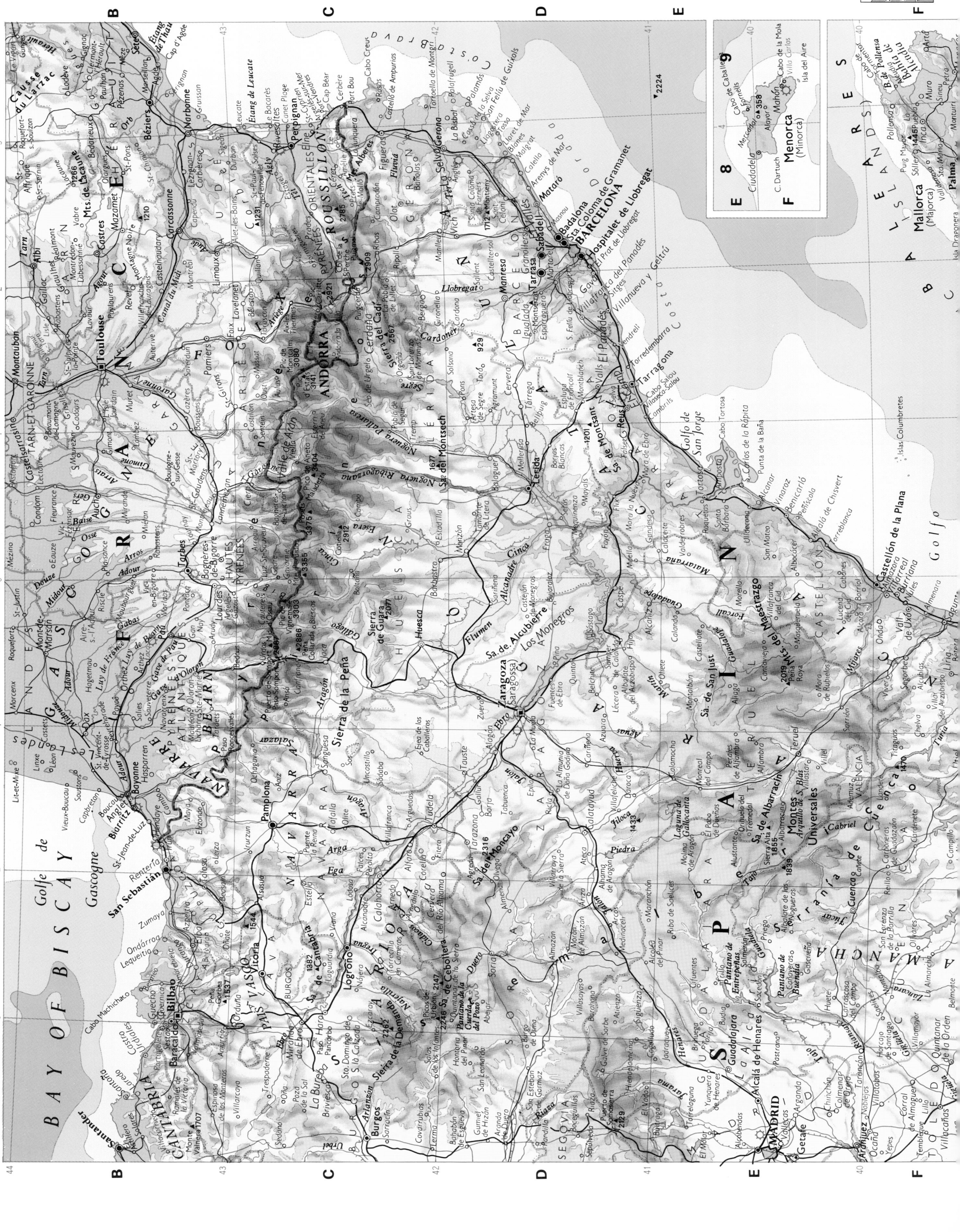
BAY OF BISCAY
Golfe de Gascogne
FRANCE
ANDORRA
PYRENEES
ROUSSILLON
NAVARRA
CATALUÑA
ARAGÓN
BARCELONA
Zaragoza (Saragossa)
Pamplona
Bilbao
San Sebastián
Toulouse
Perpignan
Lérida
Tarragona
Gerona
Huesca
Teruel
Burgos
Logroño
Vitoria
Soria
Guadalajara
MADRID
Castellón de la Plana
VALENCIA
Cuenca
Menorca (Minorca)
Mallorca (Majorca)
Sierra de la Demanda
Sierra de Guara
Los Monegros
Montes Universales
Serranía de Cuenca
Golfo de San Jorge

1: 2 000 000

10 0 10 20 30 40 50 miles

10 0 10 20 30 40 50 60 70 80 km

MEDITERRANEAN SEA
ALGERIA
MOROCCO
ISLAS BALEARES
Valencia
Costa Blanca
Sierra Morena
Sierra Nevada
Sierra de Segura
Sa. de Cazorla
Sa. de los Filabres
Sa. de Almenara
Sa. de Gádor
Sa. Espuña 1584
Sierra de Alcaraz 1790
Sa. de Aitana 1558
Las Alpujarras
Mulhacén 3478
La Veleta 3392
2850
1985
2381
2269
2167
2043
1931
1371
1300
1204
1125
475
192
Golfo de Mazarrón
Golfo de Almería
Mar Menor
Albufera de Valencia
CIUDAD REAL
ALBACETE
MURCIA
ALICANTE
VALENCIA
GRANADA
ALMERÍA
JAÉN
CASTILLA LA MANCHA
Alcázar de San Juan
Daimiel
Manzanares
Tomelloso
Valdepeñas
Linares
Ubeda
Albacete
Hellín
Almansa
Yecla
Jumilla
Villena
Alcoy
Elda
Petrel
Novelda
Alicante
Elche
Orihuela
Murcia
Cartagena
Lorca
Totana
Caravaca
Cieza
Torrevieja
Benidorm
Villajoyosa
Denia
Jávea
Gandía
Oliva
Alcira
Játiva
Sueca
Cullera
Carcagente
Algemesí
Onteniente
Granada
Guadix
Baza
Almería
Motril
Adra
Águilas
Mazarrón
Ibiza (Iviza)
Formentera
Cabrera
Isla Conejera
San Antonio
Sta. Eulalia
Cabo de San Antonio
Cabo de la Nao
Cabo de Palos
Cabo de Gata
Cabo Tiñoso
Cabo Cope
Cabo Sacratif
Alborán (Sp.)
ALGER (Algiers)
Blida
Boufarik
Koléa
Médéa
Miliana
Khemis Miliana
Ech Cheliff
Ténès
Mostaganem
Mohammadia
Ighil Izane
Zemmora
Tiaret
Tissemsilt
Mascara
Sig
ORAN
Arzew
Misserghin
Aïn Témouchent
Beni Saf
Sidi-Bel-Abbès
Nedroma
Ghazaouet
Melilla (Sp.)
Nador
Berkane
C. Tres Forcas
C. del Agua
C. Falcon
C. Caxine
C. Kramis
Ksar el Boukhari
Ksar Chellala
Guelt es Stel
Chabounia
Hamadia
Berrouaghia
Cherchel
Gouraya
Bou Ismael
El Arba

ft	m
9000	3000
6000	2000
4500	1500
3000	1000
1200	400
600	200
0	0
200	600
2000	6000
m	ft

Projection: Conical with two standard parallels

West from Greenwich — East from Greenwich

COPYRIGHT, GEORGE PHILIP & SON, LTD.

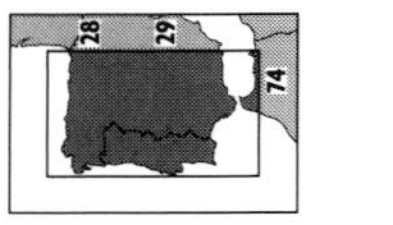

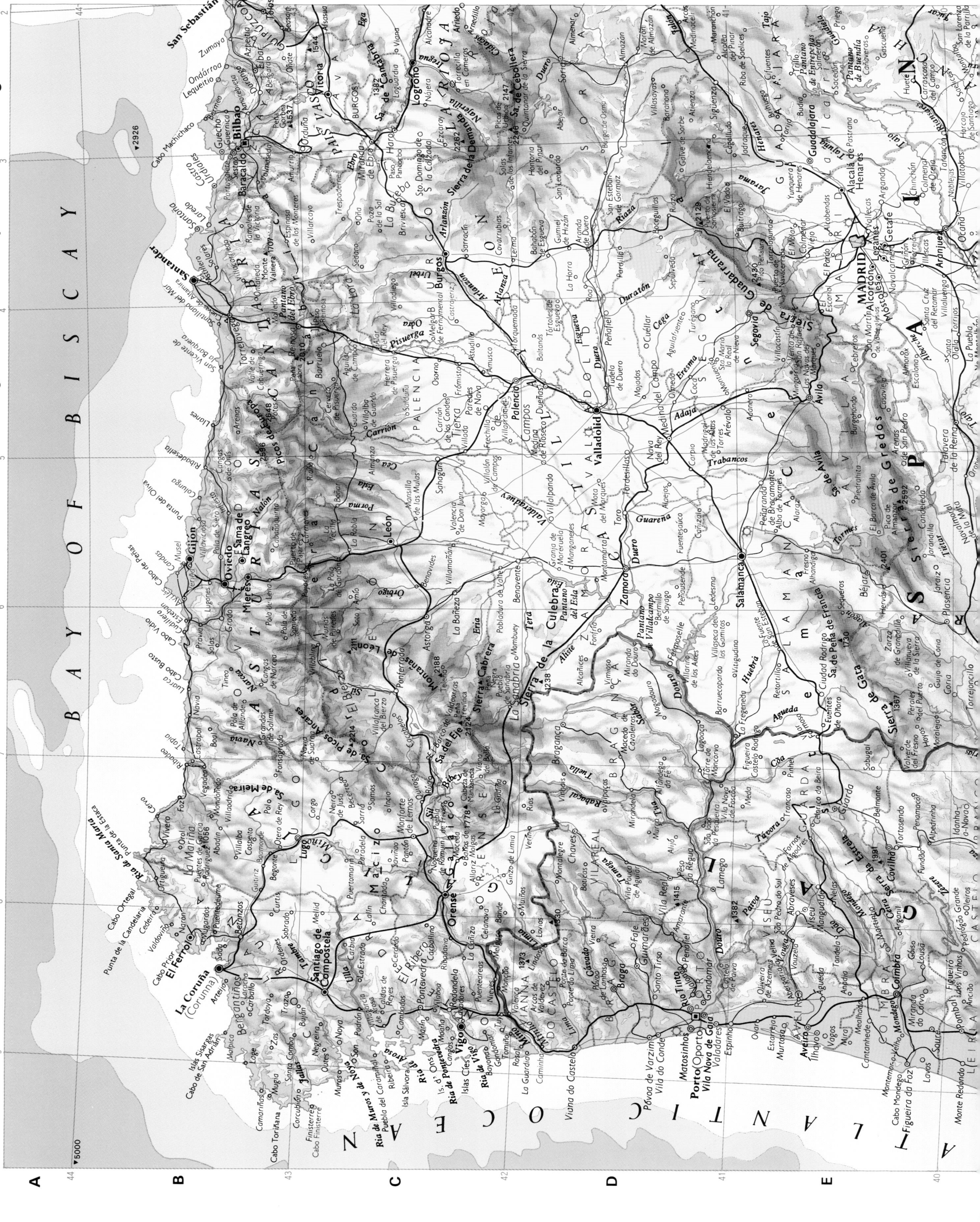
BAY OF BISCAY
ATLANTIC OCEAN
San Sebastián
Bilbao
Santander
Gijón
Oviedo
La Coruña
(Corunna)
El Ferrol
Santiago de Compostela
Lugo
Orense
Vigo
León
Burgos
Logroño
Vitoria
Palencia
Valladolid
Zamora
Salamanca
Segovia
Avila
MADRID
Guadalajara
Braga
Porto (Oporto)
Vila Nova de Gaia
Coimbra
Aveiro
Figueira da Foz
Sierra de Guadarrama
Sierra de Gredos
Picos de Europa
Cabo Finisterre
Cabo Ortegal
Duero
Douro
Tajo
Ebro
Miño

1 : 2 000 000
10 0 10 20 30 40 50 miles
10 0 10 20 30 40 50 60 70 80 km
LISBOA (LISBON)
Setúbal
Évora
Faro
Badajoz
Mérida
Cáceres
Huelva
Sevilla
Cádiz
Córdoba
Jaén
Granada
Málaga
Almería
Ciudad Real
Gibraltar (Br.)
Algeciras
Ceuta (Sp.)
Tanger (Tangier)
Tétouan
Melilla (Sp.)
Strait of Gibraltar
Golfo de Cádiz
MEDITERRANEAN SEA
Costa del Sol
MOROCCO
Sierra Nevada
Sierra Morena
Montes de Toledo
Las Marismas
Playa de Castilla
Algarve
Cabo de São Vicente
Baía de Setúbal
Golfo de Almería
Alborán (Sp.)
C. des Trois Fourches
West from Greenwich
Projection: Conical with two standard parallels
COPYRIGHT. GEORGE PHILIP & SON. LTD.

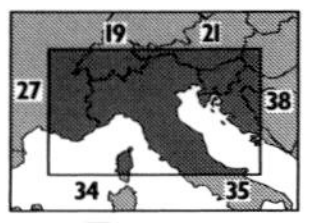

Projection: Conical with two standard parallels

East from Greenwich

1 : 2 000 000

10 0 10 20 30 40 50 miles

10 0 10 20 30 40 50 60 70 80 km

8 9 10 11 12 13 14

A B C D E F G

AUSTRIA

SLOVENIA

CROATIA

HUNGARY

BOSNIA-HERZEGOVINA

ITALY

SAN MARINO

ADRIATIC SEA

Golfo di Venézia

DALMACIJA

Hohe Tauern

Niedere Tauern

Karnische Alpen

Karawanken

Velebit Planina

Dinara Planina

Innsbruck, Bolzano, Graz, Klagenfurt, Villach, Maribor, Ljubljana, Udine, Gorízia, Trieste, Rijeka (Fiume), Zagreb, Karlovac, Banja Luka, Zadar, Šibenik, Split, Venézia (Venice), Pádova (Padua), Vicenza, Treviso, Mestre, Ferrara, Ravenna, Rímini, Pésaro, Ancona, Perúgia, Terni, Pescara, L'Aquila, Chieti, ROMA (ROME), Nagykanizsa, Pula, Nagyatád

8 9 10 11 12 13

COPYRIGHT GEORGE PHILIP & SON, LTD.

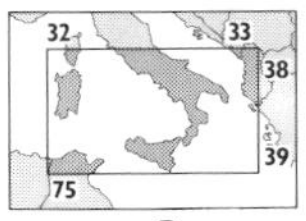

CORSE
CORSICA
SARDEGNA
SARDINIA
TYRRHENIAN SEA
Golfo di Cágliari
Golfo di Oristano
Golfo dell' Asinara
Golfo di Orosei
Golfo di Gaeta
Bouches de Bonifacio
Sicilian Channel
Golfe de Tunis
TUNISIA
ROMA (Rome)
PALERMO
TUNIS
Cagliari
Sássari
Trápani
Marsala
Bizerte (Binzert)
Íschia
Ústica
Pantelleria (It.)
Ísole Égadi
Ísole Ponziane
Iles de la Galite
MEDITE

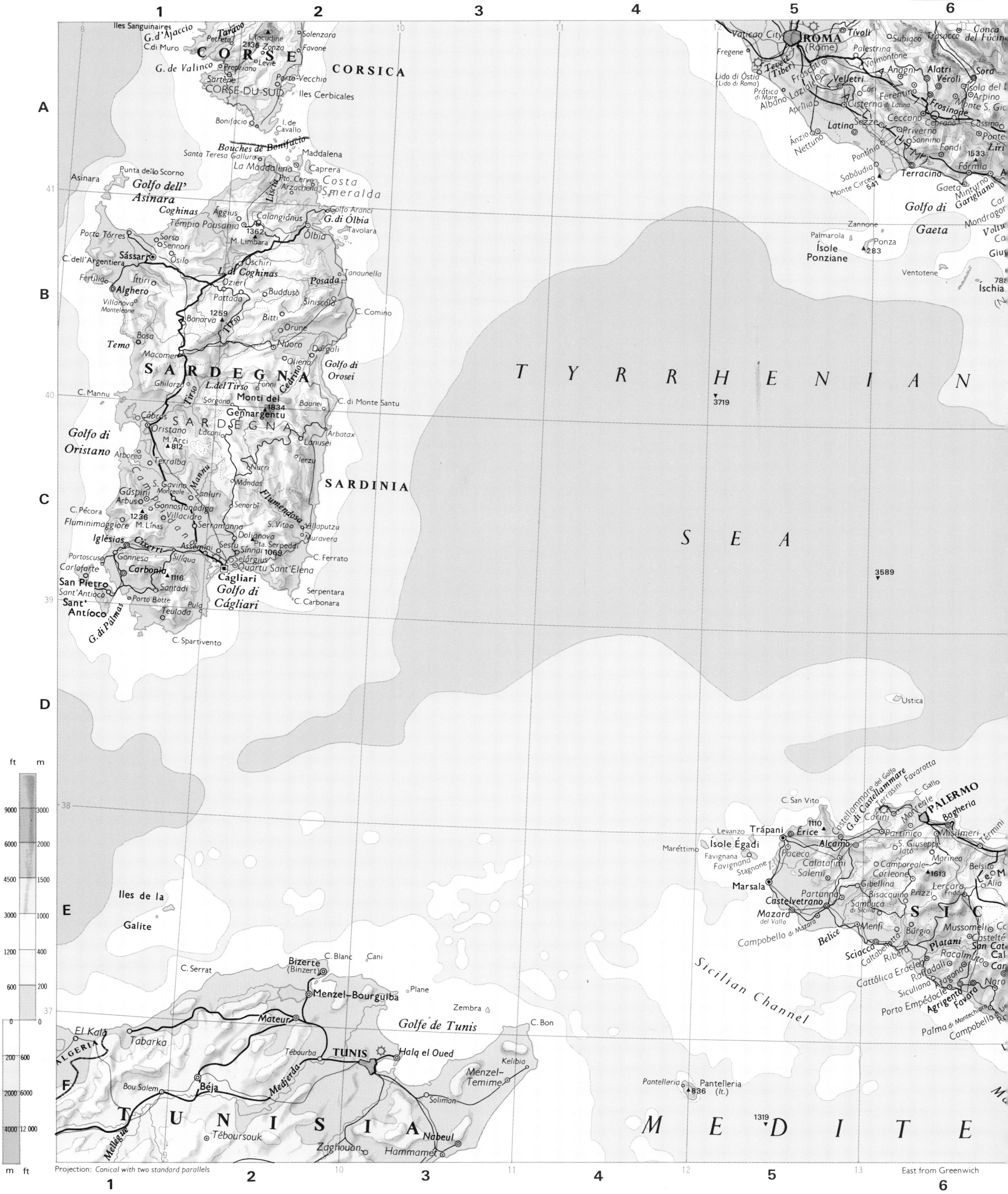

Projection: Conical with two standard parallels

East from Greenwich

1 : 2 000 000
ADRIATIC SEA
IONIAN SEA
Strait of Otranto
Golfo di Táranto
Golfo di Squillace
G. di Manfredónia
G. di Salerno
G. di Policastro
Golfo di Sant'Eufémia
G. di Gióia
Str. di Messina
Isole Eólie o Lípari (Æolian Is.)
BASILICATA
CALABRIA
Bari
Táranto
Bríndisi
Lecce
Fóggia
Potenza
Matera
Salerno
Cosenza
Catanzaro
Crotone
Messina
Réggio
Catánia
Siracusa
Tirana
Durrësi (Durazzo)
Vlorë (Valona)
Kérkira (Corfu)
Otranto
Gallipoli
C. Santa Maria di Leuca
C. Spartivento
Stromboli
Lípari
Vulcano
Etna 3340
Monti Nébrodi
Monte Pollino 2271
3065
4116
COPYRIGHT, GEORGE PHILIP & SON, LTD.

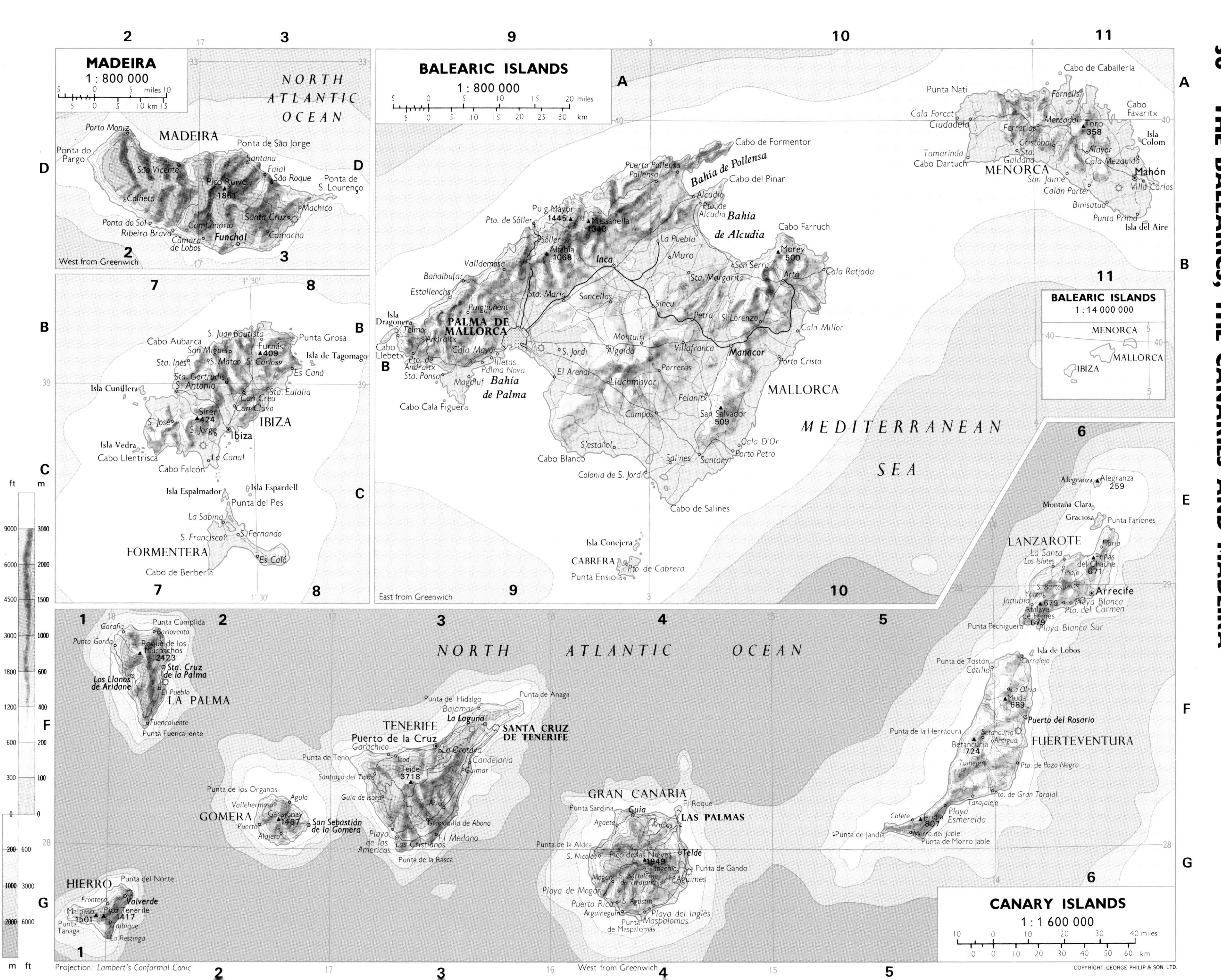
MADEIRA
1 : 800 000
NORTH ATLANTIC OCEAN
Porto Moniz
Ponta do Pargo
Ponta de São Jorge
Santana
Faial
São Roque
Ponta de S. Lourenço
Machico
São Vicente
Pico Ruivo
1861
Calheta
Santa Cruz
Ponta do Sol
Ribeira Brava
Campanário
Câmara de Lobos
Funchal
Camacha
West from Greenwich
BALEARIC ISLANDS
1 : 800 000
Cabo de Formentor
Puerto Pollensa
Pollensa
Bahía de Pollensa
Cabo del Pinar
Alcudia
Pto. de Alcudia
Bahía de Alcudia
Puig Mayor
1445
Massanella
1340
Pto. de Sóller
Sóller
Alfabia
1068
Cabo Farruch
Morey
500
Cala Ratjada
La Puebla
Muro
Inca
San Serra
Artá
Sta. Margarita
Valldemosa
Bañalbufar
Estallenchs
Sta. María
Sancellas
Sineu
Petra
S. Lorenzo
Cala Millor
Puigpuñent
Isla Dragonera
S. Telmo
PALMA DE MALLORCA
Andraitx
Cala Mayor
S. Jordi
Montuiri
Algaida
Villafranca
Manacor
Porto Cristo
Cabo Llebetx
Pto. de Andraitx
Sta. Ponsa
Illetas
Palma Nova
Magaluf
Bahía de Palma
El Arenal
Lluchmayor
Porreras
Felanitx
MALLORCA
Cabo Cala Figuera
Campos
San Salvador
509
MEDITERRANEAN
SEA
S'estañol
Cabo Blanco
Salines
Santanyí
Cala D'Or
Porto Petro
Colonia de S. Jordi
Cabo de Salines
Isla Conejera
CABRERA
Pto. de Cabrera
Punta Ensiola
East from Greenwich
Cabo de Caballería
Punta Nati
Fornells
Cabo Favaritx
Cala Forcat
Ciudadela
Ferrerías
Mercadal
Toro
358
Isla Colom
S. Cristóbal
Sta. Galdana
Alayor
Tamarinda
Cabo Dartuch
Cala Mezquida
MENORCA
Mahón
San Jaime
Villa Carlos
Calán Porter
Binisatua
Punta Prima
Isla del Aire
BALEARIC ISLANDS
1 : 14 000 000
MENORCA
MALLORCA
IBIZA
S. Juan Bautista
Punta Grosa
Cabo Aubarca
San Miguel
Furnás
409
Isla de Tagomago
Sta. Inés
S. Mateo
S. Carlos
Es Caná
Sta. Gertrudis
S. Antonio
Sta. Eulalia
Isla Cunillera
Can Creu
Can Clavo
Sirer
424
S. José
S. Jorge
IBIZA
Ibiza
Isla Vedra
Cabo Llentrisca
La Canal
Cabo Falcón
Isla Espardell
Isla Espalmador
Punta del Pes
La Sabina
S. Francisco
S. Fernando
FORMENTERA
Es Caló
Cabo de Berbería
Garafía
Punta Cumplida
Barlovento
Punta Gorda
Roque de los Muchachos
2423
Sta. Cruz de la Palma
Los Llanos de Aridane
El Pueblo
LA PALMA
Fuencaliente
Punta Fuencaliente
NORTH ATLANTIC OCEAN
Punta del Hidalgo
Punta de Anaga
Bajamar
La Laguna
TENERIFE
SANTA CRUZ DE TENERIFE
Puerto de la Cruz
Garachico
La Orotava
Punta de Teno
Icod
Candelaria
Teide
3718
Güimar
Santiago del Teide
Punta de los Órganos
Agulo
Guía de Isora
Vallehermoso
Garajonay
1487
Arico
GOMERA
San Sebastián de la Gomera
Granadilla de Abona
Puerto
Alajeró
Playa de las Américas
El Médano
Los Cristianos
Punta de la Rasca
GRAN CANARIA
El Roque
Punta Sardina
Guía
LAS PALMAS
Agaete
Arucas
Punta de la Aldea
Telde
S. Nicolás
Pico de las Nieves
1949
Ingenio
Punta de Gando
Mogán
S. Bartolomé de Tirajana
Agüimes
Playa de Mogán
S. Agustín
Puerto Rico
Arguineguín
Playa del Inglés
Punta Maspalomas
de Maspalomas
HIERRO
Punta del Norte
Frontera
Valverde
Malpaso
1501
Pico Tenerife
1417
Taibique
Punta Tanaga
La Restinga
Alegranza
259
Montaña Clara
Graciosa
Punta Fariones
LANZAROTE
Haría
La Santa
Los Islotes
Peñas del Chache
671
Tinajo
S. Bartolomé
Yaiza
Janubio
679
Arrecife
Atalaya de Femes
679
Playa Blanca
Pto. del Carmen
Punta Pechiguera
Playa Blanca Sur
Isla de Lobos
Corralejo
Punta de Tostón
Cotillo
La Oliva
Muda
689
Puerto del Rosario
Punta de la Herradura
Betancuria
Antigua
Betancuria
724
FUERTEVENTURA
Tuineje
Pto. de Pozo Negro
Pto. de Gran Tarajal
Tarajalejo
Cofete
Jandía
807
Playa Esmerelda
Punta de Jandía
Morro del Jable
Punta de Morro Jable
CANARY ISLANDS
1 : 1 600 000
Projection: Lambert's Conformal Conic
West from Greenwich
COPYRIGHT, GEORGE PHILIP & SON, LTD.

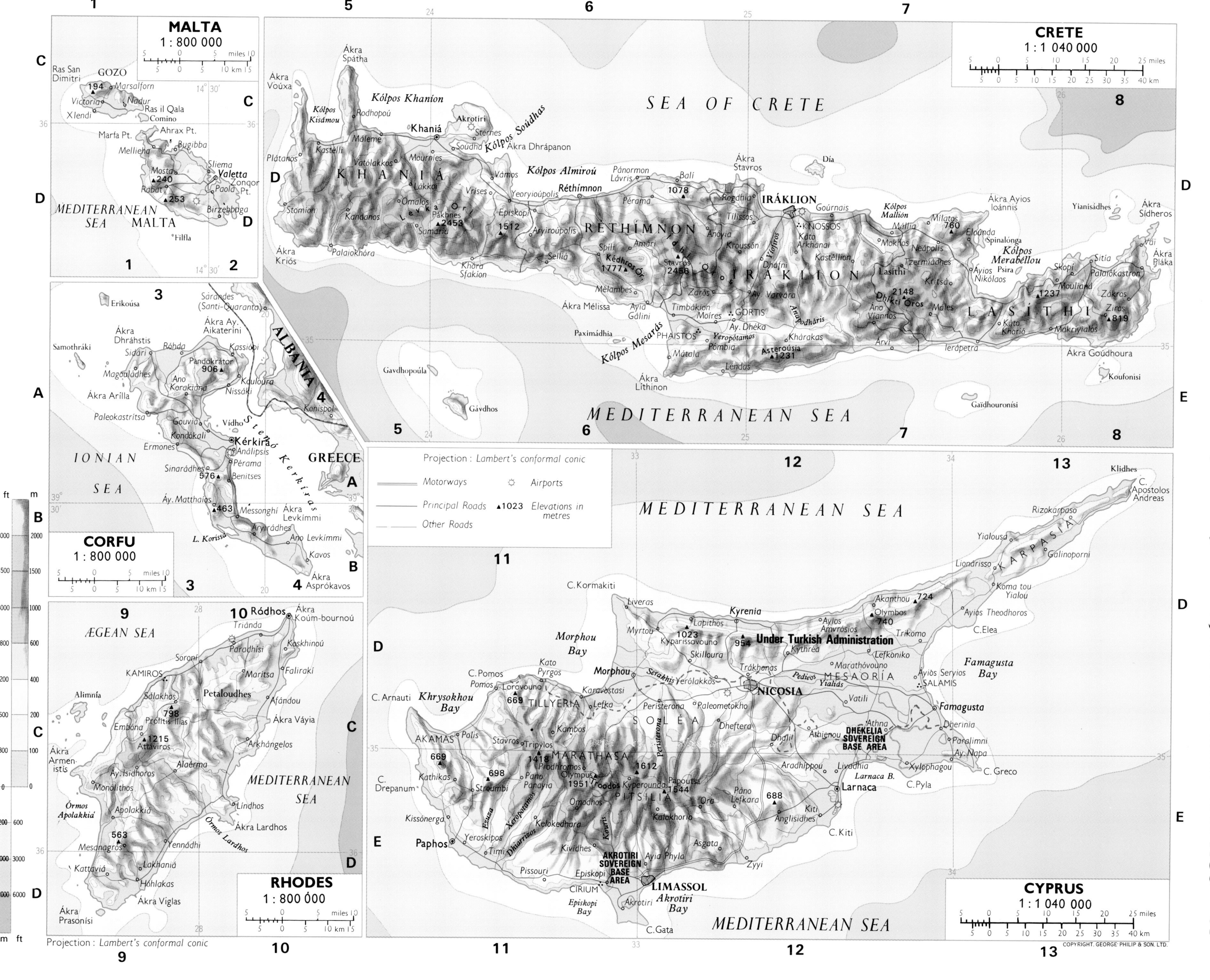
MALTA
1 : 800 000
GOZO
Victoria
Valletta
MEDITERRANEAN SEA
MALTA
CRETE
1 : 1 040 000
SEA OF CRETE
MEDITERRANEAN SEA
KHANIÁ
RÉTHIMNON
IRÁKLION
LASÍTHI
Khaniá
Réthimnon
IRÁKLION
KNOSSOS
Gávdhos
Dia
CORFU
1 : 800 000
ALBANIA
GREECE
IONIAN SEA
Kérkira
RHODES
1 : 800 000
Ródhos
ÆGEAN SEA
MEDITERRANEAN SEA
CYPRUS
1 : 1 040 000
MEDITERRANEAN SEA
NICOSIA
Under Turkish Administration
Kyrenia
Famagusta
Famagusta Bay
Larnaca
LIMASSOL
Paphos
Morphou Bay
Khrysokhou Bay
Akrotiri Bay
DHEKELIA SOVEREIGN BASE AREA
AKROTIRI SOVEREIGN BASE AREA
MESAORIA
Troodos
KARPASIA
Projection : Lambert's conformal conic
Motorways
Principal Roads
Other Roads
Airports
Elevations in metres
COPYRIGHT GEORGE PHILIP & SON LTD.

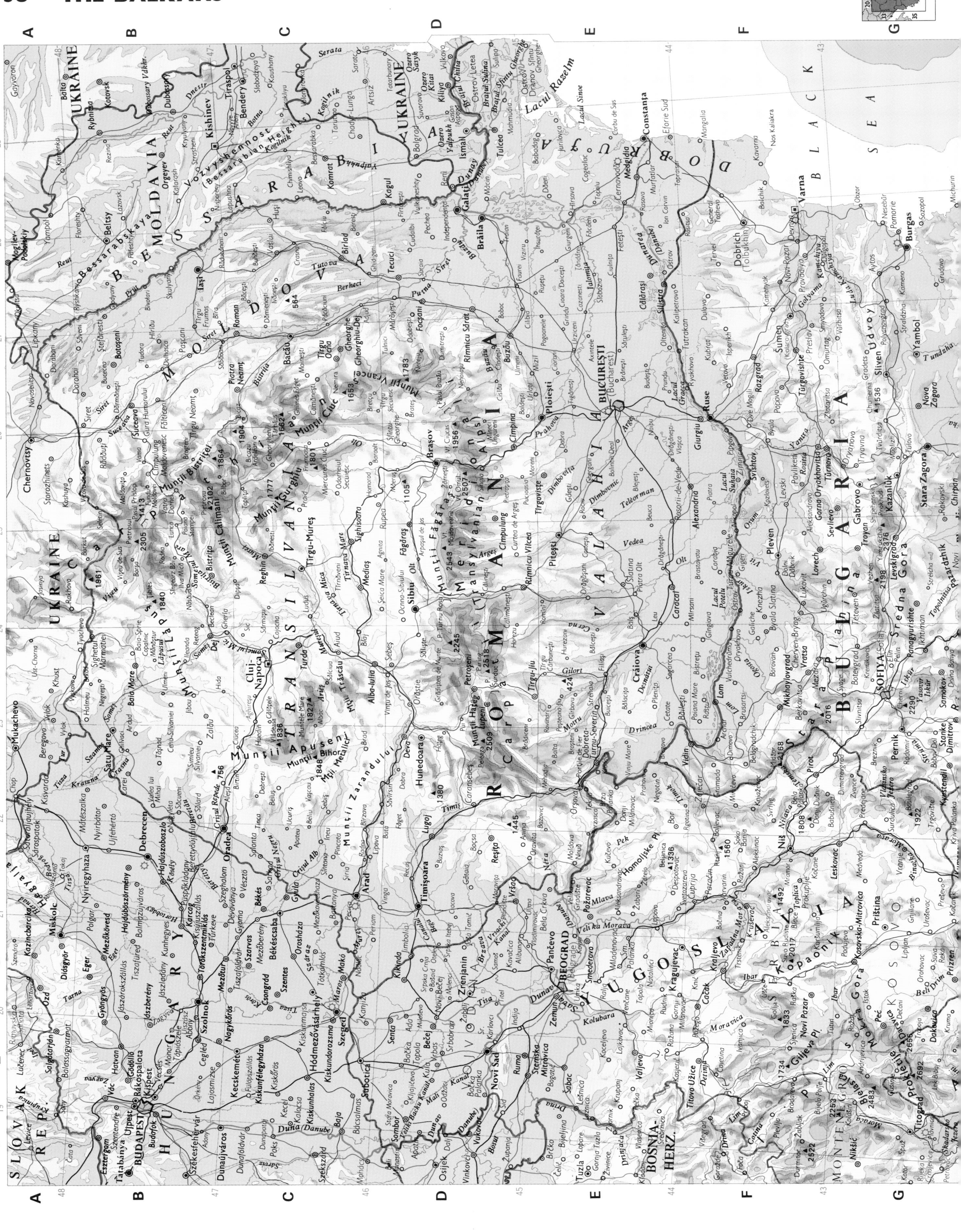

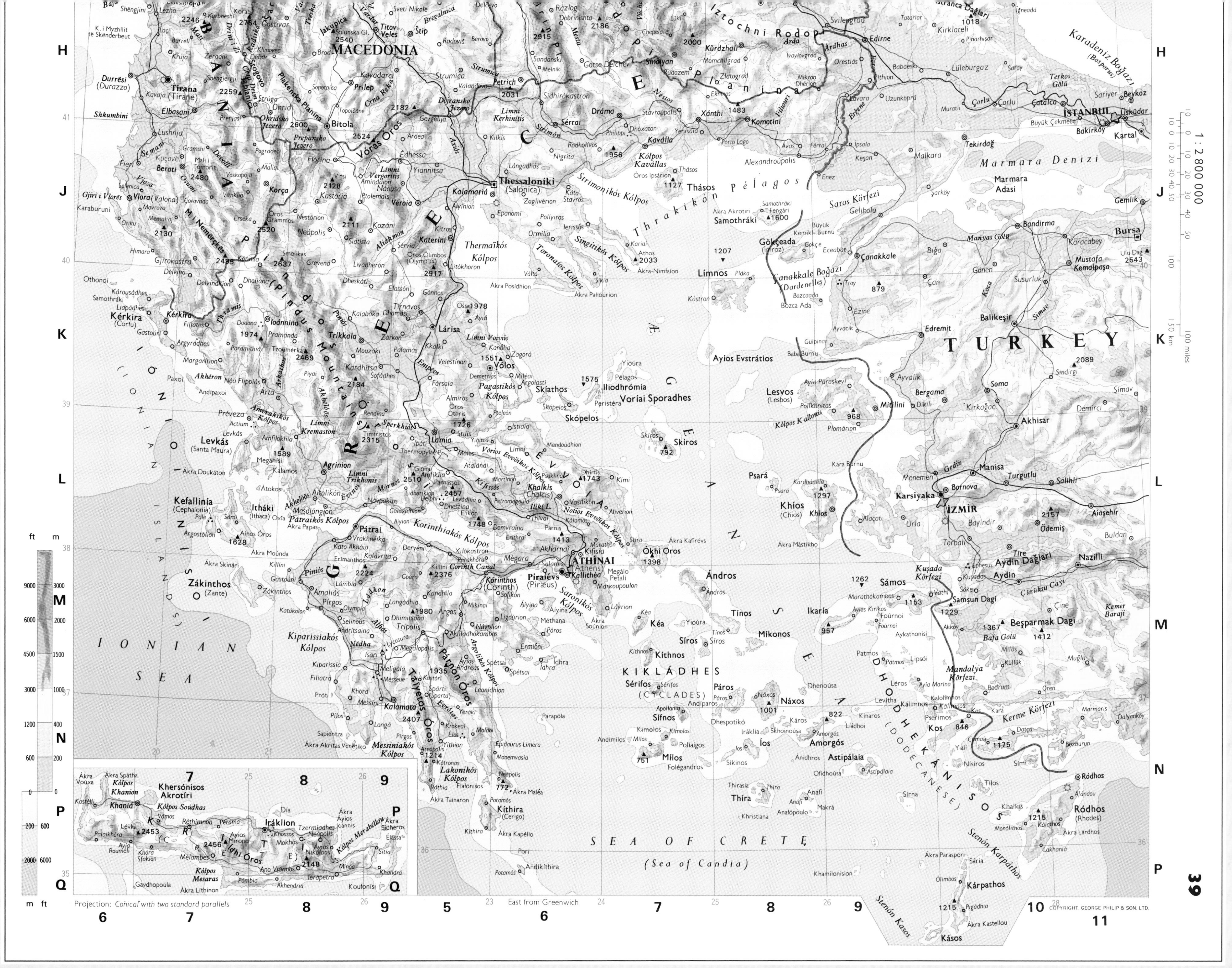
1 : 2 800 000
100 miles
150 km
TURKEY
MACEDONIA
IONIAN SEA
SEA OF CRETE
(Sea of Candia)
KIKLÁDHES
(CYCLADES)
DHODHEKÁNISOS
(DODECANESE)
Marmara Denizi
Karadeniz Boğazı (Bosporus)
Çanakkale Boğazı (Dardanelles)
Thrakikón Pélagos
Thessaloníki (Salonica)
ATHÍNAI
Piraiévs (Piraeus)
İSTANBUL
İZMIR
Bursa
Kérkira (Corfu)
Kefallinía (Cephalonia)
Zákinthos (Zante)
Levkás (Santa Maura)
Lesvos (Lesbos)
Khíos (Chios)
Sámos
Náxos
Ródhos (Rhodes)
Kárpathos
Kíthira (Cerigo)
Pátrai
Kalamata
Iráklion
Khaniá
Projection: Conical with two standard parallels
East from Greenwich
COPYRIGHT GEORGE PHILIP & SON, LTD.

WESTERN RUSSIA, BELORUSSIA AND THE BALTIC STATES

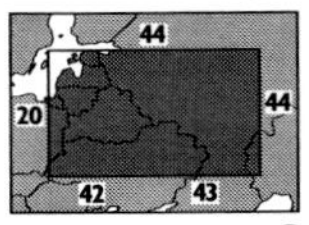

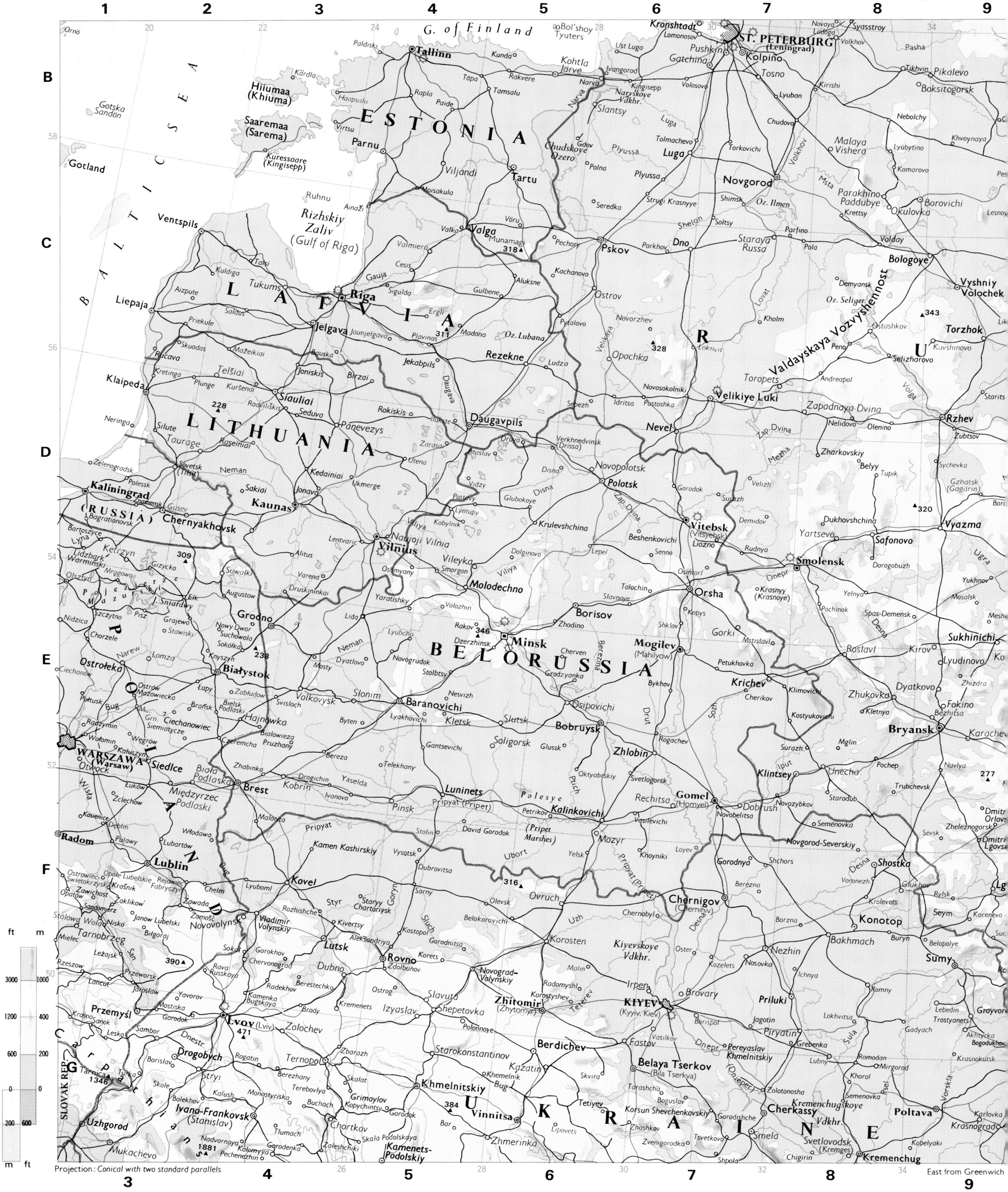

ft	m
3000	1000
1200	400
600	200
0	0
200	600
m	ft

Projection: Conical with two standard parallels

East from Greenwich

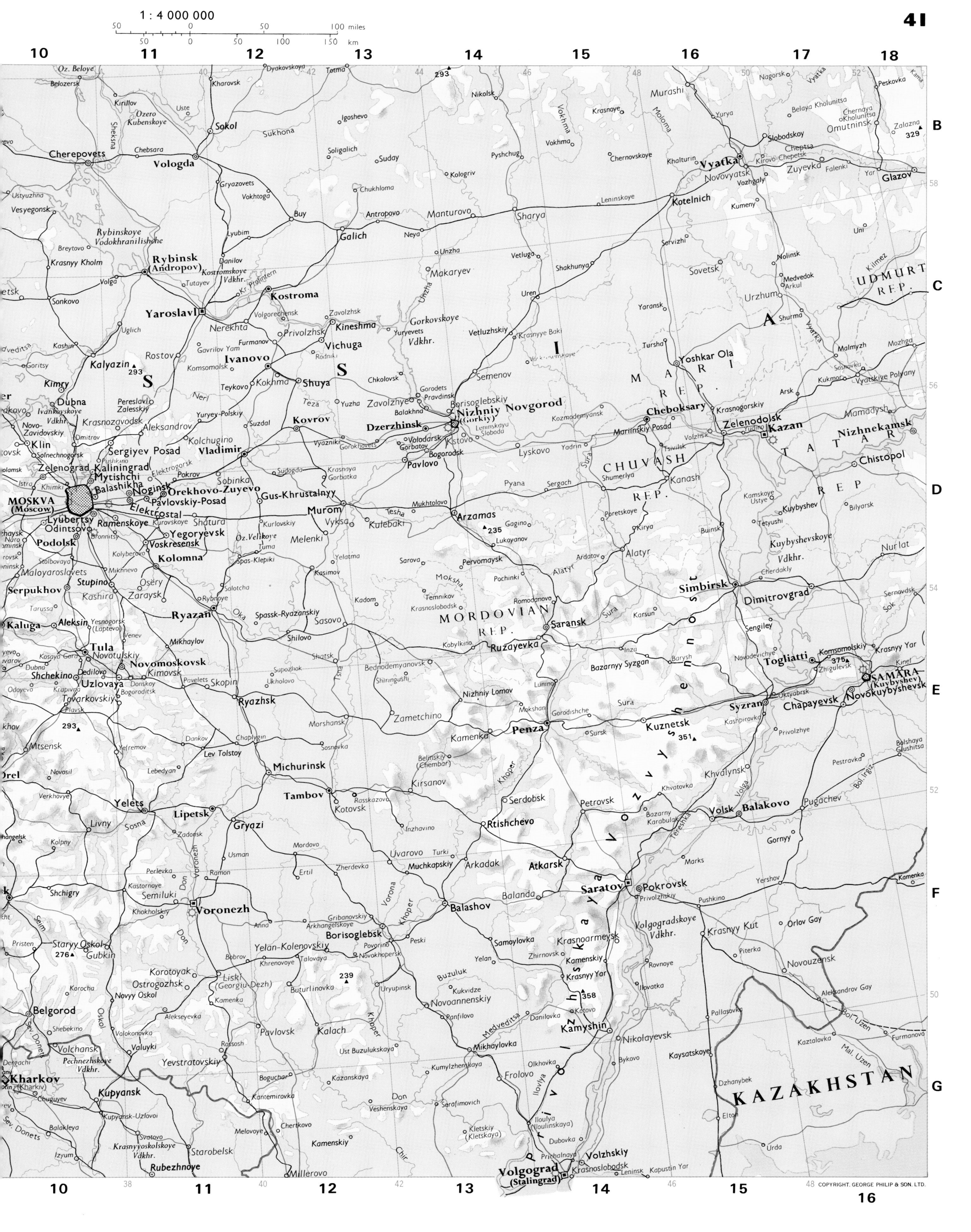
1 : 4 000 000
50 0 50 100 miles
50 0 50 100 150 km
10
11
12
13
14
15
16
17
18
B
C
D
E
F
G
Cherepovets
Vologda
Sokol
Rybinsk (Andropov)
Rybinskoye Vodokhranilishche
Yaroslavl
Kostroma
Galich
Buy
Manturovo
Sharya
Kotelnich
Vyatka
Glazov
Kineshma
Ivanovo
Shuya
Vichuga
Kovrov
Vladimir
Sergiyev Posad
Dzerzhinsk
Nizhniy Novgorod (Gorkiy)
Gorkovskoye Vdkhr.
Cheboksary
Yoshkar Ola
Zelenodolsk
Kazan
Nizhnekamsk
Chistopol
MARI REP.
CHUVASH REP.
TATAR REP.
UDMURT REP.
MOSKVA (Moscow)
Mytishchi
Balashikha
Noginsk
Orekhovo-Zuyevo
Pavlovskiy-Posad
Elektrostal
Lyubertsy
Odintsovo
Ramenskoye
Yegoryevsk
Voskresensk
Kolomna
Podolsk
Serpukhov
Kaluga
Aleksin
Tula
Novomoskovsk
Shchekino
Uzlovaya
Ryazan
Gus-Khrustalnyy
Murom
Arzamas
Saransk
Ruzayevka
MORDOVIAN REP.
Simbirsk
Dimitrovgrad
Togliatti
SAMARA (Kuybyshev)
Novokuybyshevsk
Syzran
Chapayevsk
Penza
Kuznetsk
Michurinsk
Tambov
Lipetsk
Yelets
Gryazi
Voronezh
Borisoglebsk
Balashov
Rtishchevo
Atkarsk
Saratov
Pokrovsk
Volsk
Balakovo
Kamyshin
Volgograd (Stalingrad)
Volzhskiy
Volgogradskoye Vdkhr.
Privolzhskaya Vozvyshennost
Belgorod
Kharkov
Staryy Oskol
Kupyansk
KAZAKHSTAN
COPYRIGHT, GEORGE PHILIP & SON, LTD.

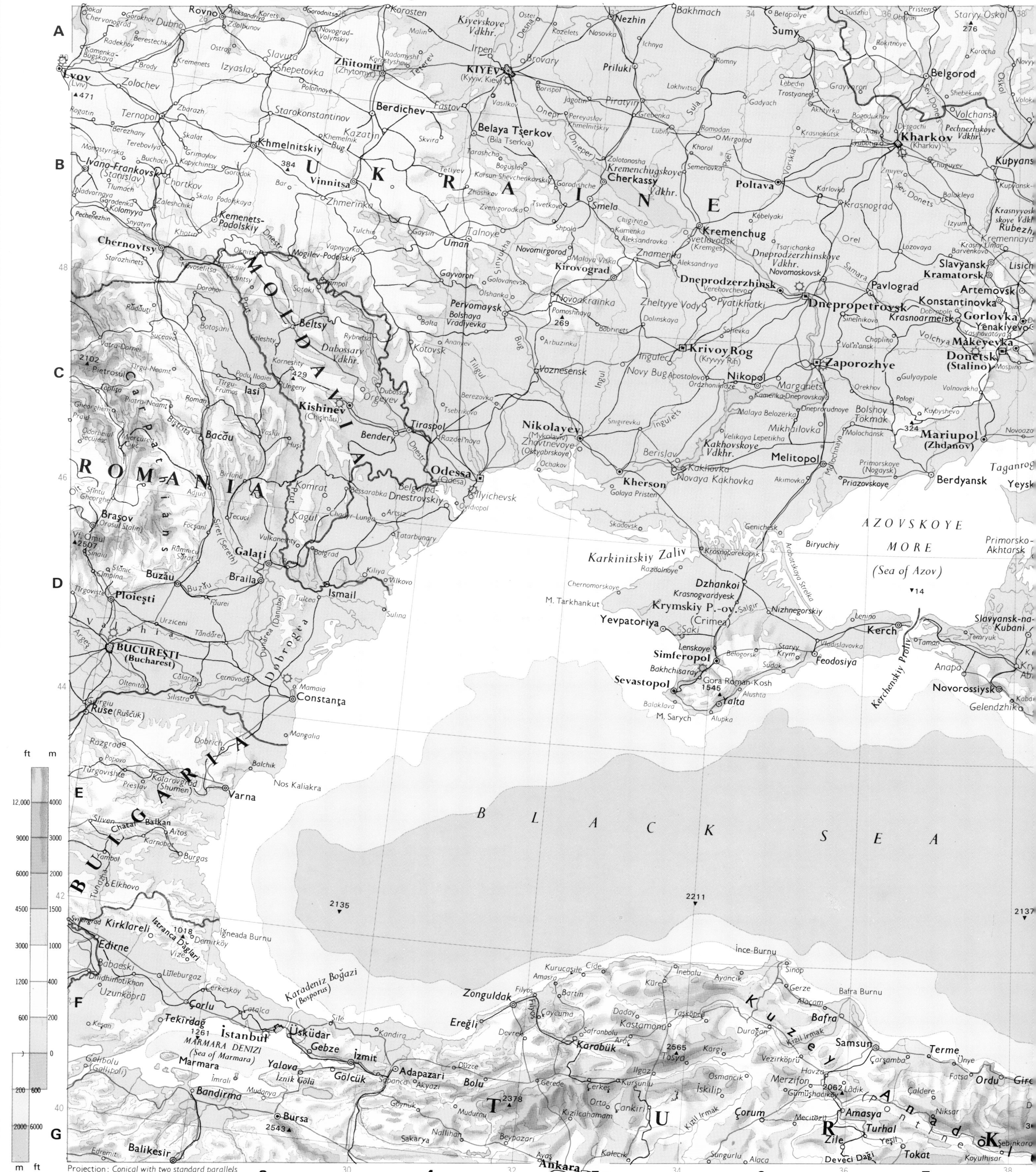

UKRAINE, MOLDAVIA AND THE CAUCASUS

1 2 3 4 5 6 7

A B C D E F G

UKRAINE
MOLDAVIA
ROMANIA
BULGARIA
TURKEY

Sokal, Chervonograd, Gorokhov, Dubno, Rovno, Aleksandriya, Korets, Gorodnitsa, Korosten, Zdolbunov, Novograd-Volynskiy, Malin, Kiyevskoye Vdkhr., Oster, Desna, Nezhin, Bakhmach, Belopolye, Sudzha, Oboyan, Pristen, Staryy Oskol, 276, Radekhov, Berestechko, Ostrog, Kozelets, Nosovka, Ichnya, Sumy, Rokitnoye, Korocha, Kamenka-Bugskaya, Kremenets, Slavuta, Izyaslav, Shepetovka, Zhitomir (Zhytomyr), Korostyshev, Radomyshl, Teterev, Irpen, KIYEV (Kyyiv, Kiev), Brovary, Priluki, Romny, Belgorod, Lvov (Lviv), Brody, Zolochev, 471, Polonnoye, Borispol, Lokhvitsa, Lebedin, Trostyanets, Grayvoron, Shebekino, Volchansk, Rogatin, Ternopol, Zbarazh, Starokonstantinov, Berdichev, Fastov, Vasilkov, Jagotin, Pereyaslav-Khmelnitskiy, Piryatin, Grebenka, Sula, Gadyach, Akhtyrka, Bogodukhov, Olshany, Dergachi, Pechenezhskoye Vdkhr., Berezhany, Terebovlya, Skalat, Grimaylov, Khmelnitskiy, Khmelnik, Kazatin, Skvira, Belaya Tserkov (Bila Tserkva), Dnepr (Dnieper), Lubny, Romodan, Mirgorod, Krasnokutsk, Lyubotin, Kharkov (Kharkiv), Monastyriska, Buchach, Kopychintsy, Ivano-Frankovsk (Stanislav), 384, Bug, Tetiyev, Tarashcha, Boguslav, Korsun-Shevchenkovskiy, Zolotonosha, Kremenchugskoye Vdkhr., Khorol, Semenovka, Psel, Vorskla, Chuguyev, Kupyansk, Tlumach, Nadvornaya, Gorodenka, Kolomyya, Chortkov, Gorodok, Zaleshchiki, Bar, Vinnitsa, Zhmerinka, Zhashkov, Gorodishche, Cherkassy, Smela, Poltava, Karlovka, Zmiyev, Sev. Donets, Balakleya, Kupyansk-Uzlovoy, Pechenezhin, Snyatyn, Skala Podolskaya, Kamenets-Podolskiy, Khotin, Dnestr, Tulchin, Gaysin, Talnoye, Uman, Zvenigorodka, Tsvetkovo, Shpola, Chigirin, Kamenka, Aleksandrovka, Kremenchug, Svetlovodsk (Kremges), Kobelyaki, Krasnograd, Izyum, Krasnyy Oskol skoye Vdkhr., Rubezhnoye, Kremennaya, Chernovtsy, Storozhinets, Novoselitsa, Lipkany, Okniţa, Mogilev-Podolskiy, Vapnyarka, Sinyukha, Novomirgorod, Malaya Viska, Kirovograd, Znamenka, Aleksandriya, Dneprodzerzhinskoye Vdkhr., Tsarichanka, Novomoskovsk, Orel, Samara, Lozovaya, Krasnyy Liman, Barvenkovo, Slavyansk, Kramatorsk, Lisichansk, Edintsy, Soroki, Gayvoron, Golovanevsk, Dondyushany, Dneprodzerzhinsk, Verkhnedneprovsk, Pavlograd, Artemovsk, Dorohoi, Rădăuţi, Botoşani, Olshanka, Pervomaysk, Novoarkhangelsk, Novoukrainka, Zheltyye Vody, Pyatikhatki, Dnepropetrovsk, Sinelnikovo, Krasnoarmeisk, Dobropolye, Konstantinovka, Gorlovka, Yenakiyevo, Beltsy, Rybnitsa, Balta, Bolshaya Vradiyevka, Pomoshnaya, 269, Bobrinets, Dolinskaya, Sofievka, Chaplino, Volchya, Makeyevka, Yasinovataya, Suceava, Faleshty, Dubossary Vdkhr., Kotovsk, Ananyev, Arbuzinka, Ingulets, Krivoy Rog (Kryvyy Rih), Vol'n'ansk, Donetsk (Stalino), Vatra Dornei, 2102, Pietrosul, Tirgu-Neamt, Podu Iloaiei, Korneshty, 429, Ungeny, Tirgu-Frumos, Iasi, Tiligul, Voznesensk, Ingul, Novy Bug, Apostolovo, Ordzhonikidze, Nikopol, Marganets, Zaporozhye, Gulyaypole, Mospino, Toplita, Piatra-Neamţ, Roman, Kishinev (Chişinău), Orgeyev, Dubossary, Berezovka, Kamenka-Dneprovskaya, Orekhov, Volnovakha, Gheorgheni, Praid, Bistriţa, Vaslui, Huşi, Tsebrikovo, Snigirevka, Malaya Belozerka, Dneprorudnoye, Bolshoy Tokmak, Pologi, Kuybyshevo, Odorheiul Secuiesc, Miercurea Ciuc, Bacău, Bendery, Tiraspol, Razdel'naya, Nikolayev (Mykolayiv), Zhovtnevoye (Oktyabrskoye), Velikaya Lepetikha, Mikhaylovka, Molochansk, 324, Mariupol (Zhdanov), Novoazovsk, Ochakov, Berislav, Kakhovskoye Vdkhr., Melitopol, Molochnaya, Primorskoye (Nogaysk), Taganrog, Odessa, Kakhovka, Novaya Kakhovka, Kherson, Golaya Pristen, Akimovka, Priazovskoye, Berdyansk, Yeysk, Olt, Sfintu Gheorghe, Adjud, Bîrlad, Komrat, Bessarabka, Belgorod-Dnestrovskiy, Ilyichevsk, Ovidiopol, Braşov (Orasul Stalin), Vi. Omul, 2507, Sinaia, Focşani, Tecuci, Kagul, Chadyr-Lunga, Artsiz, Tatarbunary, Skadovsk, Genichesk, AZOVSKOYE MORE (Sea of Azov), Primorsko-Akhtarsk, Rîmnicu Sărat, Siret (Sereth), Vulkaneshty, Bolgrad, Galaţi, Braila, Buzău, Slănic, Cimpina, Ploieşti, Tîrgovişte, Kiliya, Vilkovo, Ismail, Tulcea, Sulina, Karkinitskiy Zaliv, Razdolnoye, Krasnoperekopsk, Arabatskaya Strelka, Biryuchiy, Chernomorskoye, M. Tarkhankut, Dzhankoi, Krasnogvardeysk, Krymskiy P.-ov. (Crimea), Salgir, Nizhnegorskiy, 14, Urziceni, Ţăndărei, Fauréi, Dunărea (Danube), Dobrogea, Yevpatoriya, Saki, Lenino, Kerch, Slavyansk-na-Kubani, Taman, Temryuk, BUCUREŞTI (Bucharest), Argeş, Olteniţa, Călăraşi, Cernavodă, Mamaia, Constanţa, Lenskoye, Simferopol, Belogorsk, Staryy Krym, Sudak, Feodosiya, Vladislavovka, Kerchenskiy Proliv, Anapa, Bakhchisaray, Sevastopol, Gora Roman-Kosh, 1545, Yalta, Alushta, Alupka, Balaklava, M. Sarych, Novorossiysk, Gelendzhik, Giurgiu, Ruse (Ruščuk), Silistra, Mangalia, Dobrich, Razgrad, Popovo, Balchik, Turgovishte, Preslav, Kolarovgrad (Shumen), Varna, Nos Kaliakra

B L A C K   S E A

Sliven, Chatal, Balkan, Aitos, Karnobat, Burgas, Yambol, Tundzha, Elkhovo, 2135, 2211, 2137, Svilengrad, Kirklareli, Istranca Dağlari, 1018, Demirköy, İğneada Burnu, Edirne, Babaeski, Vize, Didimhotikhon, Lüleburgaz, Uzunköprü, Çerkeskoy, Karadeniz Boğazi (Bosporus), İnce-Burnu, Kurucaşile, Cide, Amasra, İnebolu, Ayancık, Sinop, Gerze, Bafra Burnu, Zonguldak, Filyos, Bartın, Küre, Çorlu, Çatalca, Çaycuma, Daday, Kastamonu, Taşköprü, Alaçam, Bafra, Kuzey Anadolu Dağları, Keşan, Tekirdağ, İstanbul, Üsküdar, Şile, Kandıra, Ereğli, Devrek, Safranbolu, Araç, Duragan, Kızıl Irmak, Samsun, Terme, 1261, MARMARA DENIZI (Sea of Marmara), Gebze, İzmit, Karabük, 2565, Tosya, Kargı, Vezirköprü, Çarşamba, Ünye, Gelibolu (Gallipoli), Marmara, Yalova, İznik Gölü, Gölcük, Sapanca, Adapazari, Düzce, Bolu, Gerede, Kurşunlu, Ilgaz, Osmancık, Havza, Merzifon, Fatsa, Ordu, Giresun, İmralı, Mudanya, Akyazi, Çerkeş, Orta, Çankiri, İskilip, Gümüşhacıköy, 2062, Ladik, Çaldere, Bandırma, Geyve, Mudurnu, 2378, Kızılcahamam, Çorum, Mecitözü, Amasya, Niksar, Bursa, 2543, Nallıhan, Turhal, Zile, Yeşil, Edremit, Balikesir, Sakarya, Beypazarı, Ayaş, Kalecik, Sungurlu, Alaca, Deveci Dağı, Tokat, Şebinkarahisar, Koyulhisar, Ankara

30, 32, 34, 36, 38, 40, 42, 44, 46, 48

ft m
12,000 4000
9000 3000
6000 2000
4500 1500
3000 1000
1200 400
600 200
0
200 600
2000 6000
m ft

Projection: Conical with two standard parallels

2 3 4 5 6 7

1 : 4 000 000

50 0 50 100 miles

50 0 50 100 150 km

8 9 10 11 12 13 14 15

A B C D E F G

Yelan-Kolenovskiy
Povorino
Peski
Bobrov
Khrenovoye
Talovaya
Novokhopersk
Samoylovka
Krasnoarmeysk
Zhirnovsk
Krasnyy Kut
Orlov Gay
Oz. Chalkar
Chalkar
Liski (Georgiu-Dezh)
Yelan
Kamenskiy
Rovnoye
Piterka
Dzhambeyty
Ostrogozhsk
Buturlinovka
239
Uryupinsk
Buzuluk
Kukvidze
Krasnyy Yar
358
Ilovatka
Volgogradskoye
Novouzensk
Kushum
Chapayev
Kamenka
Novoannenskiy
Vozyshennost
Vdkhr.
Aleksandrov Gay
Panfilovo
Kotovo
Danilovka
Pallasovka
Mergenevskiy
Karsha
Pavlovsk
Kalach
Khoper
Medveditsa
Rossosh
Kamyshin
Nikolayevsk
Bol. Uzen
Ural
Ust Buzulukskaya
Mikhaylovka
Kaysatskoye
Furmanovo
Bazartobe
Kaztalovka
Mal. Uzen
Antonovo
Boguchar
Kumylzhenskaya
Olkhovka
Bykovo
Kazanskaya
Frolovo
Kalmykovo
Kantemirovka
Don
Ilovlya
Dzhanybek
Veshenskaya
Serafimovich
Privolzhskaya
Melovoye
Chertkovo
Kletskiy (Kletskaya)
Ilovlya (Iloulinskaya)
Elton
KAZAKHSTAN
Inderborskiy
Kamenskiy
Dubovka
Starobelsk
Chir
Sovetskaya
Prichalnaya
Volzhskiy
Urda
Leninsk
Millerovo
Volgograd (Stalingrad)
Krasnoslobodsk
Kapustin Yar
Shungay
Zelënyy
Kalach na Donu
Lugansk (Voroshilovgrad)
Glubokiy
Surovikino
Krasnoarmeysk
Vladimirovka
Topoli
Chernyshkovskiy
Volga
Verkhniy Baskunchak
Kamensk-Shakhtinskiy
Morozovsk
Akhtubinsk (Petropavlovsk)
Makhambet (Yamankhalinka)
Krasnodon
Lenin
Tsimlyanskoye Vdkhr.
Krasnyy Luch
Sverdlovsk
Belaya Kalitva
Likhovskoi
Rovenki
Gukovo
Krasnodonetskaya
RUSSIA
Novobogatinskoye
Sinegorski
Krasny Sulin
Tsimlyansk
Kotelnikovo
Guryev
Artemovski
Novoshakhtinsk
Shakhty
Ust-Donetskiy
Kamenolomini
Obilnoye
Kopanovka
-28
Konstantinovski
Volgodonsk
Matveyev Kurgan
Dubovskoye
Yenotayevka
Tuzlov
Novocherkassk
Zavetnoye
Bolshaya Martynovka
Taganrog
Rostov
Zimovniki
KALMYK REP.
Ganyushkino
Azov
Bataysk
Manych
Krasnyy Yar
Veselovskoye Vdkhr.
Kuberle
Mechetinskaya
Port Katon
Zernograd
Ergeni Vozyshennost
Astrakhan
Proletarskaya
Remontnoye
Yeya
Kushchevskaya
Yegorlykskaya
Kamyzyak
Stara-minskaya
Gigant
Oz. Manych-Gudilo
Krasnoye
-28
Salsk
Elista (Stepnoi)
Peschanokopskoye
Prikaspiyskaya Nizmennost
Kirovski
Leninsk
Priyutnoye
Yegorlyk
Pavlovskaya
Mumra
Liman
Kultay
Kanevskaya
Belaya Glina
Krasnogvardeyskoye
Divnoye
Kalaus
Tikhoretsk
Ipatovo
CASPIAN SEA
Kaspiyskiy
Timashevsk
Novaleksandrovskaya
Kulaly
Mangyshlakskiy Zaliv
Kropotkin
Arzgir
Korenovsk
Izobil'nyy
Svetlograd (Petrovskoye)
Beloye Ozero
M. Tyub Karagan
Blagodarnoye
Kuma
Fort Shevchenko
P-ov. Mangyshlak
Ust-Labinsk
Starya Biryuzyak
Krasnodar
Armavir
Stavropol
Budennovsk
Neftekumsk
Kuban
Tyuleniy
Kurganinsk (Kurgannaya)
831
Vladimirovka
Maykop
Labinsk
Nevinnomyssk
Zelenokumsk (Vorontsovo-Aleksandrovskoye)
Bryanskoye
Khadyzhensk
Urup
Kursavka
Apsheronsk
Laba
O. Chechen
Aktau
Neftegorsk
Mineralnyye Vody
Cherkessk
Georgievsk
Aleksandriyskaya
Lopatin
Dakhovskaya
Yessentuki
Pyatigorsk
Kislovodsk
Prokhladnyy
Mozdok
CHECHENO-INGUSH REP.
Kizlyar
Terek
Karachayevsk
Mayskiy
Nartkala
Malgobek
Gudermes
Sulak
Kizil Yurt
Sochi
Krasnaya Polyana
Teberda
Nalchik
Grozny
Khasavyurt
Matsesta
Elbrus
5633
Tyrnyauz
KABARDINO-BALKAR REP.
Elkhotovo
Beslan
Makhachkala
Adler
Gagra
ABKHAZ REP.
Kodori
5203
Vladikavkaz (Ordzhonikidze)
Kumtorkala
Kaspiysk
Inguri
N. OSSETIAN REP.
Sayasan
Buynaksk
Gudata
Novyy Afon
Sadon
Balta
Izberbash
Sukhumi
Tkvarcheli
Kazbek
5047
Tebulos
4492
Khunzakh
DAGESTAN REP.
Novokayakent
Gali
Dzhvari
Tsageri
Rioni
Oni
Agvali
Kakhib
Akusha
Ochamchire
Zugdidi
Dagestanskiye Ogni
800
Anaklia
GEORGIA
Sachkhere
Tskhinvali
Tlyarata
Madzhalis
Derbent
Tkibuli
Chiatura
Kuli
Senaki
Kutaisi
Zestafoni
Dusheti
Kasumkent
Poti
Samtredia
Khashuri
Gori
Telavi
Kvareli
Lagodekhi
Mikhaylovka
Kobuleti
Ozurgety
Kaspi
Mtskheta
Gurdzhaani
Zakataly
Samur
Khachmas
Batumi
Khulo
Borzhomi
Tbilisi
Signakhi
Citeli Ckaro
Alazan
Akhty
Kuba
Divichi
ADZHAR REP.
Akhaltsikhe
Khrami
Mirzaani
Vale
Marneuli
Rustavi
Iori
Sheki (Nukha)
Bazar Dyuzi
4466
Siazan
Akhalkalaki
Shaumyani
Mingechaurskoye Vdkhr.
Baba dag 3629
Hopa
Borcka
Kutkashen
Akstafa
Kura
Pazar
Ardahan
Çildir
Alaverdi
Tauz
Mingechaur
Agdash
Shemakha
Mashtaga
Artvin
Shamkhor
Geokchay
Sumgait
Surakhany
Artem
Zyrya
Görele
Akçaabat
Ardanuç
Kisir 3192
Gyandzha (Kirovabad)
Yevlakh
Tirebolu
Trabzon
Rize
Kumayri
Karakalis
Chanlar
AZERBAIJAN
Lyaki
BAKU (Baky)
Kaçkar 3937
Dilizhan
Kyurdamir
Sürmene
Sevan
Dashkesan
Harşit
Çakirgöl 3063
Oltu
Şelim
Kars
Artik
Aragats 4090
Ozero Sevan
Mir-Bashir
Barda
Kazi Magomed
Gümüşane
Ispir
Narman
Sarikamiş
Digor
ARMENIA
Kamo
Terter
NAGORNO-KARABAKH
Sabirabad
Alyata
Çoruh
Agdzhabedi
Ali-Bayramly
Tortum
Kağizman
Echmiadzin
Yerevan
Martuni
Agdam
Imishly
Karachala
Bayburt
Aras
M. Byandovan
Alucra
Doğu Karadeniz Dağlari
Bolshoy Kavkaz

40 42 44 46 48 50

East from Greenwich

COPYRIGHT. GEORGE PHILIP & SON. LTD.

D
C
B
RUSSIA
1. Daghestan Rep.
2. Kabardino–Balkar Rep.
3. Mari Rep.
4. Mordovian Rep.
5. North Ossetian Rep.
6. Tatar Rep.
7. Udmurt Rep.
8. Chuvash Rep.
9. Checheno–Ingush Rep.
AZERBAIJAN
10. Nakhichevan Rep.
GEORGIA
11. Abkhaz Rep.
12. Adzhar Rep.
North Sea
DENMARK
København
Skagerrak
Kattegat
NORWAY
SWEDEN
Oslo
Bergen
Trondheim
Stockholm
Göteborg
Gulf of Bothnia
Helsinki
FINLAND
Tampere
Barents Sea
Murmansk
Zemlya Frantsa Iosifa
Ostrov Rudolph
Zemlya Georga
Novaya Zemlya
Kara Sea
Poluostrov Kolskiy
Beloye More
Arkhangelsk
Arctic Circle
Ostrov Kolguyev
Cheshskaya Guba
Pechorskaya Guba
Ostrov Vaygach
Amderma
Poluostrov Yamal
Gydanskiy Poluostrov
Obskaya Guba
Yeniseyskiy Zaliv
Hamburg
Bremen
Hannover
Berlin
Leipzig
Dresden
Szczecin
Gdansk
Kaliningrad
POLAND
Warszawa
Wrocław
Łódź
Kraków
Riga
Tallinn
ESTONIA
LATVIA
LITHUANIA
Vilnius
Kaunas
Minsk
BELORUSSIA
St. Petersburg
Novgorod
Petrozavodsk
Cherepovets
Vologda
Tver
Moskva
Yaroslavl
Kostroma
Ivanovo
Vladimir
Nizhniy Novgorod
Smolensk
Tula
Kaluga
Orel
Kursk
Bryansk
Ryazan
Lipetsk
Tambov
Penza
Saransk
Cheboksary
Kazan
Izhevsk
Perm
Kirov
Syktyvkar
Kotlas
Vorkuta
Yekaterinburg
Nizhniy Tagil
Serov
Chelyabinsk
Magnitogorsk
Ufa
Samara
Togliatti
Saratov
Volgograd
Astrakhan
Rostov
Krasnodar
Stavropol
Orenburg
Orsk
Kurgan
Tyumen
Tobolsk
Omsk
Novosibirsk
Tomsk
Barnaul
Surgut
Nizhnevartovsk
UKRAINE
Kiyev
Kharkov
Dnepropetrovsk
Donetsk
Zaporozhye
Odessa
Simferopol
Sevastopol
MOLDAVIA
Kishinev
ROMANIA
Black Sea
TURKEY
Tbilisi
GEORGIA
ARMENIA
Yerevan
AZERBAIJAN
Baku
Grozny
Makhachkala
Caspian Sea
RUSSIA
KOMI REP.
KARELIAN REP.
BASHKIR REP.
KALMYK REP.
Ural
Guryev
Aktyubinsk
Kustanay
Kokchetav
Petropavlovsk
Tselinograd
Karaganda
Pavlodar
Semipalatinsk
Ust Kamenogorsk
KAZAKHSTAN
Aralskoye More
Ozero Balkhash
Kzyl-Orda
Dzhambul
Chimkent
Tashkent
Alma Ata
Bishkek
KIRGHIZIA
UZBEKISTAN
TURKMENISTAN
Ashkhabad
Krasnovodsk
Nukus
Urgench
Bukhara
Samarkand
Dushanbe
TAJIKISTAN
Pamirs
AFGHANISTAN
Herat
Mashhad
Tehrān
IRAN
IRAQ
Baghdad
Tabrīz
Esfahan
Dasht-e-Kavir
Junggar
Ürümqi
CHINA
Projection: Conical Orthomorphic with two standard parallels
East from Greenwich
E
F
G
6
7
8
9
ft
m
12000
6000
3000
1200
600
200
4000
2000
1000
400
200
0
600

1 : 16 000 000
miles
km
Sea of Okhotsk
Sea of JAPAN
Bering Sea
East Siberian Sea
Laptev Sea
Yakutsk
Irkutsk
Ulaanbaatar
Beijing
Harbin
Vladivostok
Sapporo
Boundaries of Autonomous Republics

COPYRIGHT. GEORGE PHILIP & SON, LTD.

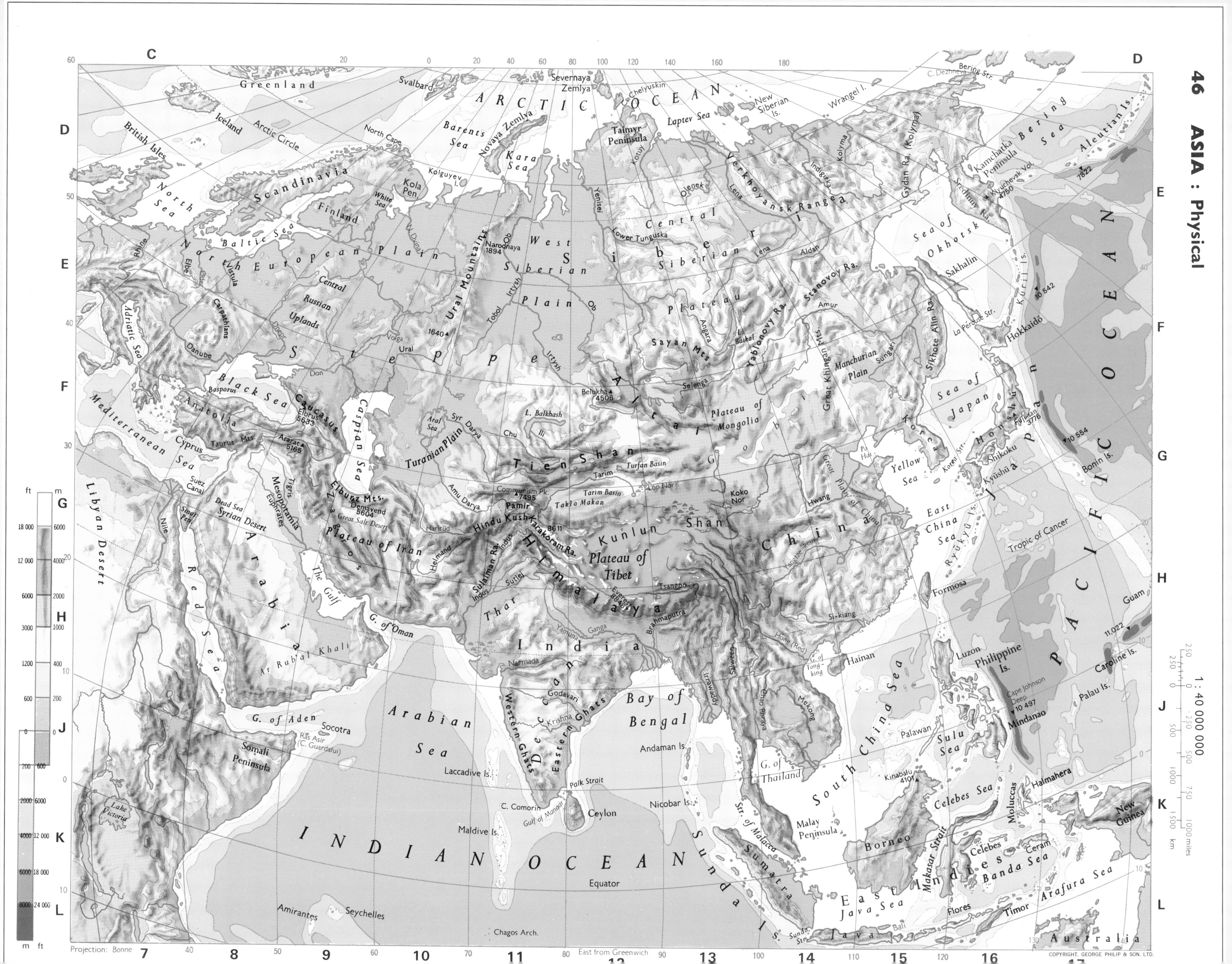
1 : 40 000 000
250 0 250 500 750 1000 miles
250 0 500 1000 1500 km
PACIFIC OCEAN
ARCTIC OCEAN
INDIAN OCEAN
Aleutian Is.
Bering Sea
Bering Str.
C. Dezhneva
Kamchatka Peninsula
Sredinny Ra.
Sea of Okhotsk
Kuril Is.
Hokkaido
La Perouse Str.
Sakhalin
Sea of Japan
Japan
Honshu
Kyushu
Shikoku
Bonin Is.
Ryukyu Is.
Tropic of Cancer
Guam
Caroline Is.
Palau Is.
Philippine Is.
Luzon
Mindanao
Cape Johnson Deep
Formosa
East China Sea
Yellow Sea
Korea
Sikhote Alin Ra.
Gydan Ra. (Kolyma)
Wrangel I.
New Siberian Is.
Verkhoyansk Range
Kolyma
Indigirka
Lena
Olenek
Aldan
Stanovoy Ra.
Yablonovy Ra.
Amur
Sungari
Great Khingan Mts.
Manchurian Plain
Great Plain of China
Hwang
Si-kiang
Hong (Red)
G. of Tongking
Hainan
South China Sea
Palawan
Kinabalu 4101
Sulu Sea
Celebes Sea
Celebes
Borneo
Makasar Strait
Moluccas
Halmahera
Ceram
Banda Sea
East Indies
Arafura Sea
Timor
Flores
Java Sea
Java
Bali
Sunda Str.
Sumatra
Str. of Malacca
Malay Peninsula
G. of Thailand
Mekong
Chao Phraya
Salween
Irrawaddy
Sunda Is.
New Guinea
Australia
Laptev Sea
Chelyuskin
Taimyr Peninsula
Central Siberian Plateau
Lower Tunguska
Yenisei
Angara
Baikal
Selenga
Sayan Mts.
Plateau of Mongolia
Altai
Gobi
Belukha 4506
Koko Nor
Lop Nor
Turfan Basin
Tarim
Tarim Basin
Takla Makan
Tien Shan
Kunlun Shan
China
Plateau of Tibet
Himalaya
Everest
Tsangpo
Brahmaputra
Karakoram Ra.
Communism Pk. 7495
Pamir
Hindu Kush
Sulaiman Ra.
Indus
Sutlej
Thar
India
Ganga
Yamuna
Narmada
Godavari
Krishna
Deccan
Western Ghats
Eastern Ghats
Bay of Bengal
Andaman Is.
Nicobar Is.
Ceylon
Palk Strait
Gulf of Mannar
C. Comorin
Laccadive Is.
Maldive Is.
Chagos Arch.
Equator
Arabian Sea
G. of Oman
The Gulf
Zagros
Plateau of Iran
Great Salt Desert
Helmand
Harirud
Elburz Mts.
Demavend 5604
Caspian Sea
Aral Sea
Turanian Plain
Amu Darya
Syr Darya
Chu
Ili
L. Balkhash
Irtysh
Ob
Tobol
West Siberian Plain
Steppe
Ural Mountains
Narodnaya 1894
1640
Ural
Volga
Kara Sea
Novaya Zemlya
Severnaya Zemlya
Barents Sea
Kolguyev I.
Kola Pen.
White Sea
N. Dvina
Svalbard
North Cape
North European Plain
Central Russian Uplands
Don
Dnepr
Finland
Scandinavia
Baltic Sea
Vistula
Carpathians
Danube
Oder
Elbe
Rhine
North Sea
British Isles
Iceland
Greenland
Arctic Circle
Black Sea
Caucasus
Elbrus 5633
Ararat 5165
Bosporus
Anatolia
Taurus Mts.
Cyprus
Mesopotamia
Tigris
Euphrates
Syrian Desert
Dead Sea
Arabia
Ar Rub al Khali
Red Sea
Sinai Pen.
Suez Canal
Nile
Mediterranean Sea
Adriatic Sea
Libyan Desert
Lake Victoria
Somali Peninsula
Ras Asir (C. Guardafui)
G. of Aden
Socotra
Amirantes
Seychelles
East from Greenwich
Projection: Bonne
COPYRIGHT, GEORGE PHILIP & SON, LTD.
m ft
6000 18 000
4000 12 000
2000 6000
1000 3000
400 1200
200 600
0 0

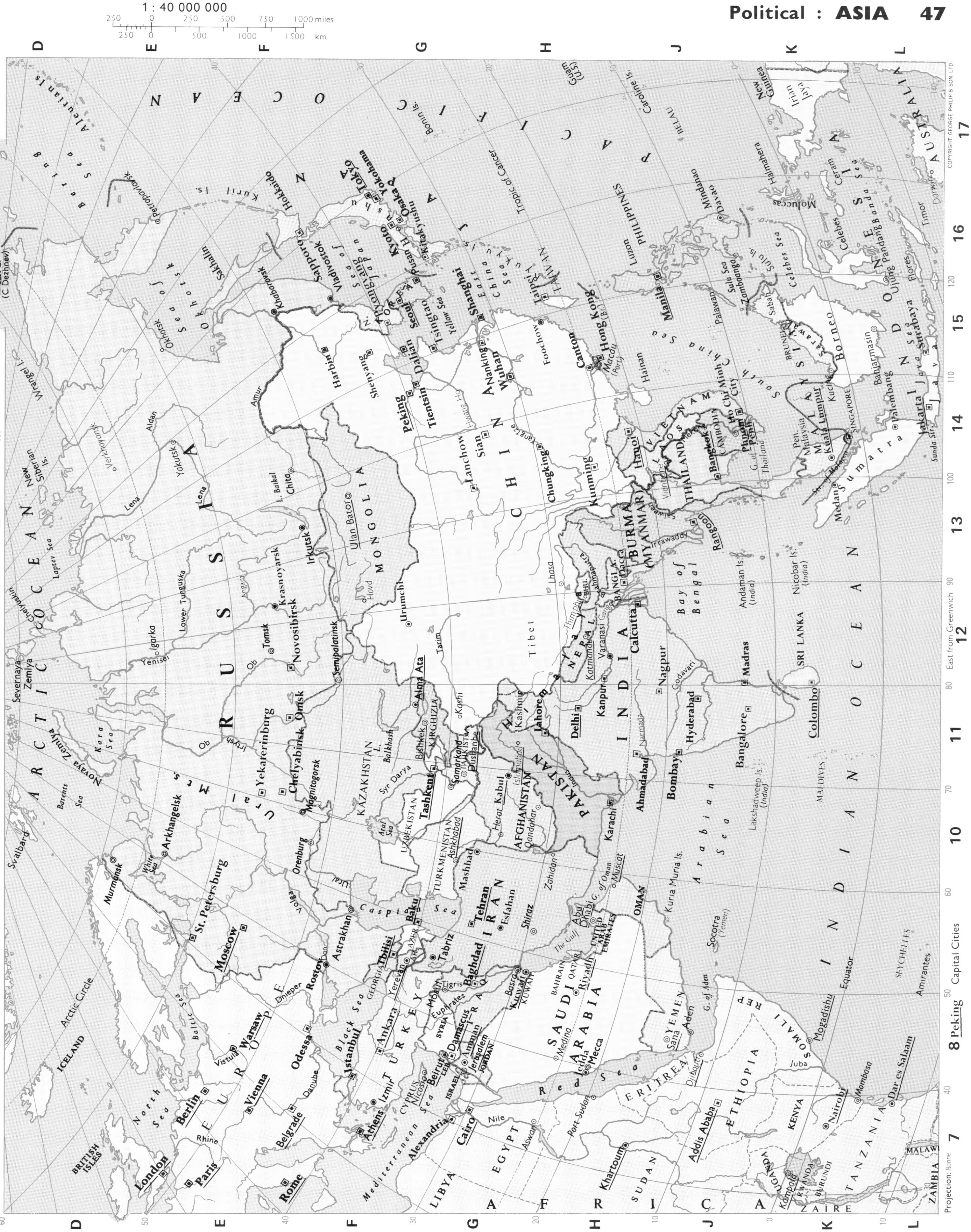

1 : 40 000 000

250 0 250 500 750 1000 miles

250 0 500 1000 1500 km

ARCTIC OCEAN

PACIFIC OCEAN

INDIAN OCEAN

RUSSIA

CHINA

MONGOLIA

KAZAKHSTAN

INDIA

PAKISTAN

AFGHANISTAN

IRAN

TURKEY

SAUDI ARABIA

BURMA (MYANMAR)

THAILAND

INDONESIA

JAPAN

PHILIPPINES

Moscow, St. Petersburg, Peking, Tokyo, Delhi, Calcutta, Bombay, Madras, Karachi, Tehran, Baghdad, Ankara, Istanbul, Shanghai, Hong Kong, Manila, Jakarta, Bangkok, Rangoon, Colombo, Kabul, Tashkent, Alma Ata, Ulan Bator, Seoul, Hanoi, Singapore, Novosibirsk, Irkutsk, Vladivostok, Khabarovsk

Projection: Bonne

East from Greenwich

Capital Cities: 8 Peking

COPYRIGHT GEORGE PHILIP & SON LTD

SEA OF OKHOTSK
SEA OF JAPAN
RUSSIA
CHINA
NORTH KOREA
HOKKAIDŌ
HOKKAIDO
TŌHOKU
Sakhalin
La Pérouse Strait
(Sōya-Kaikyō)
Tsugaru-Kaikyō
Nemuro-Kaikyō
Ostrov Kunashir
Abashiri-Wan
Ishikari-Wan
(Otaru-Wan)
Uchiura-Wan
Mutsu-Wan
Sendai-Wan
Zaliv Petra Velikogo
Ozero Khanka
Sikhote Alin
Khrebet
Hidaka-Sammyaku
Kitami
Wakkanai
Rishiri-Tō
Rebun-Tō
Okushiri-Tō
Sado
SAPPORO
Otaru
Asahigawa
Kushiro
Obihiro
Tomakomai
Muroran
Hakodate
Aomori
Hachinohe
Hirosaki
Noshiro
Akita
Morioka
Miyako
Kamaishi
Kesennuma
Ishinomaki
Shiogama
Sendai
Yamagata
Sakata
Tsuruoka
Niigata
Shibata
Yonezawa
Fukushima
Vladivostok
Nakhodka
Ussuriysk
Artem
Dalnerechensk
Lesozavodsk
Spassk-Dalniy
Dalnegorsk
Kavalerovo
Bikin
Preobrazheniye
Chongjin
Najin
Jiamusi
Shuangyashan
Baoqing
Jixi
Linkou
Boli
Khasan
Kraskino
Slavyanka
Pogranichnyy
Terney
Plastun
Amgu
Svetlaya
Olga

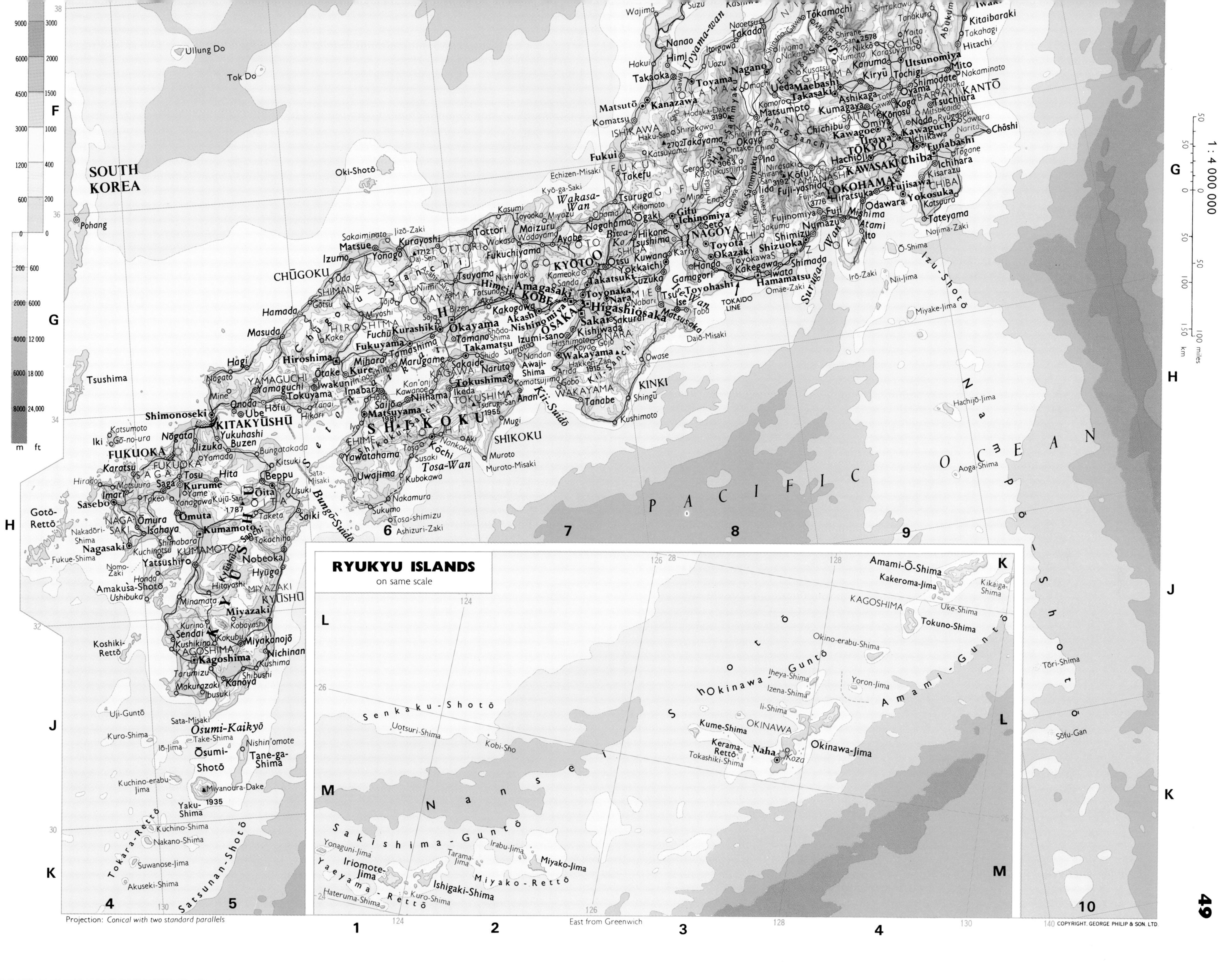
1 : 4 000 000
50 0 50 100 miles
50 0 50 100 150 km
RYUKYU ISLANDS
on same scale
SOUTH KOREA
PACIFIC OCEAN
Nampō-Shotō
Izu-Shotō
Hachijō-Jima
Miyake-Jima
Ō-Shima
Aoga-Shima
Oki-Shotō
Tsushima
Iki
Ullung Do
Tok Do
Pohang
Gotō-Rettō
Koshiki-Rettō
Ōsumi-Shotō
Ōsumi-Kaikyō
Tane-ga-Shima
Yaku-Shima
Tokara-Rettō
Satsunan-Shotō
Amami-Ō-Shima
Tokuno-Shima
Amami-Guntō
Okinawa-Jima
Okinawa-Guntō
Naha
Kume-Shima
Kerama-Rettō
Miyako-Jima
Miyako-Rettō
Ishigaki-Shima
Iriomote-Jima
Yaeyama-Rettō
Sakishima-Guntō
Senkaku-Shotō
Nansei-Shotō
KYŪSHŪ
SHIKOKU
CHŪGOKU
KINKI
KANTŌ
FUKUOKA
KITAKYŪSHŪ
Shimonoseki
Nagasaki
Sasebo
Kumamoto
Kagoshima
Miyazaki
Ōita
Beppu
Hiroshima
Okayama
Matsuyama
Kōchi
Takamatsu
Tokushima
KŌBE
ŌSAKA
KYŌTO
Nara
Wakayama
NAGOYA
Gifu
Shizuoka
Hamamatsu
Kanazawa
Toyama
Nagano
Matsumoto
Kōfu
YOKOHAMA
KAWASAKI
TŌKYŌ
Chiba
Utsunomiya
Mito
Maebashi
Fukui
Tottori
Matsue
Izumo
Bungo-Suidō
Kii-Suidō
Tosa-Wan
Ise-Wan
Suruga-Wan
Wakasa-Wan
Toyama-wan
East from Greenwich
Projection: Conical with two standard parallels

© COPYRIGHT GEORGE PHILIP & SON LTD.

NORTHERN CHINA AND KOREA

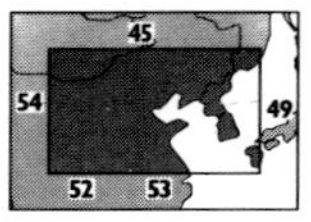

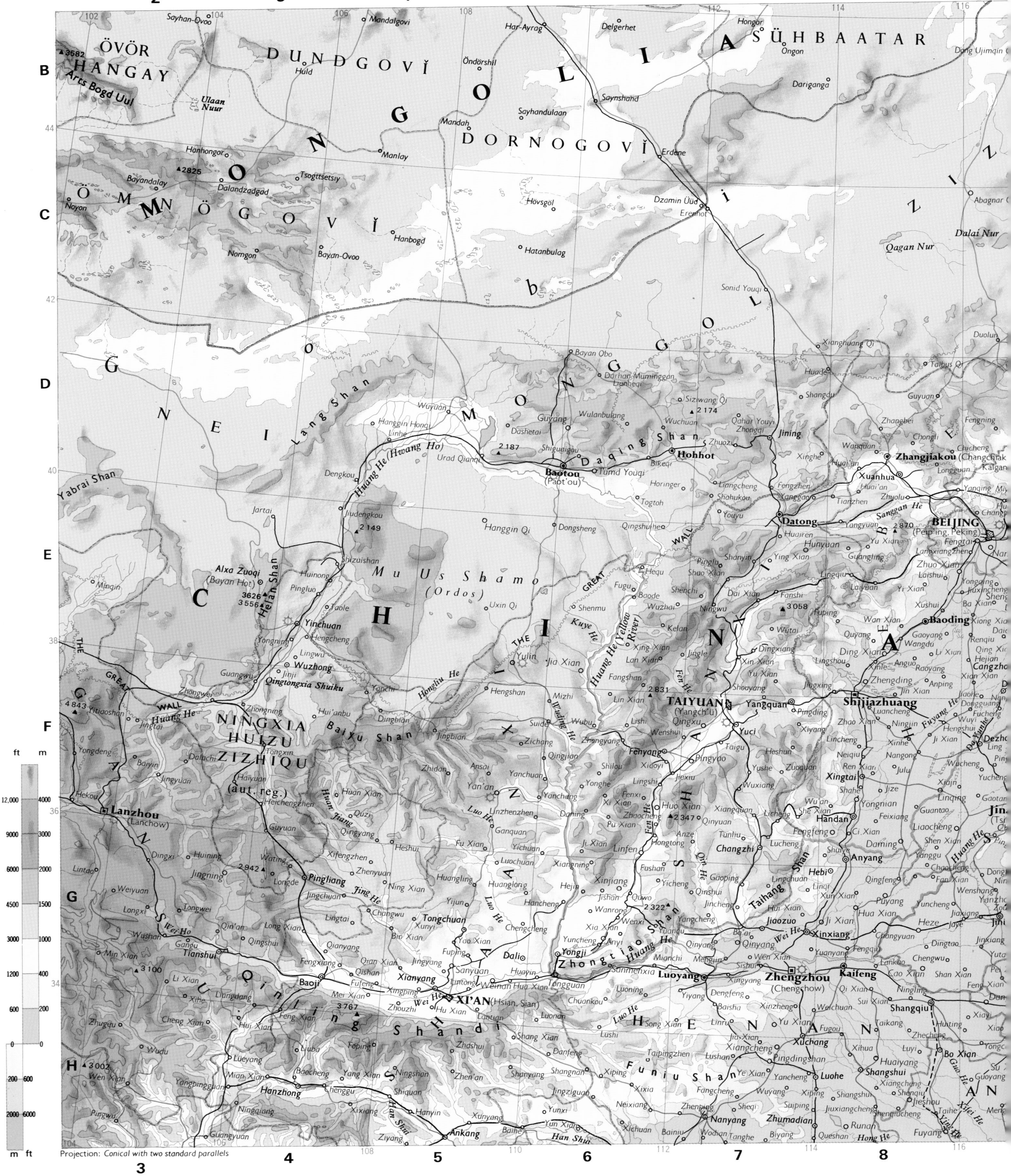

Projection: Conical with two standard parallels

1 : 4 800 000

50 0 50 100 150 miles

50 0 50 100 150 200 km

9 10 11 12 13 14 15 16

B C D E F G H

HEILONGJIANG

JILIN (Manchuria)

LIAONING

RUSSIA

NORTH KOREA

SOUTH KOREA

JAPAN

SEA OF JAPAN

HUANG HAI (Yellow Sea)

Bo Hai (Gulf of Chihli)

Korea Bay

Liaodong Wan

Liaodong Bandao

Shandong Bandao

Laizhou Wan

Haizhou Wan

Tongjosŏn Man

Korea Strait

Tsushima-kaikyō

Cease Fire Line

WILLOW THE WALL

Changbai Shan

Zhangguangcai Ling

HARBIN (Haerhpin)

Changchun

Jilin (Kirin)

SHENYANG (Mukden)

Fushun

Anshan

Benxi

Liaoyang

Jinzhou

Dandong

DALIAN (Lüda)

Lüshun

Qinhuangdao

Tangshan

TIANJIN (Tientsin, T'ienching)

Yantai

Weihai

Weifang

Zibo

QINGDAO (Ch'ingtao)

Lianyungang (Hsinhailien)

Huai'an

Bengbu

Mudanjiang

Vladivostok

Ussuriysk (Voroshilov)

Yanji

Chongjin

Kimchaek (Songjin)

Hamhung

Hŭngnam

Wŏnsan

P'YŎNGYANG

Sinŭiju

Kaesŏng

SŎUL (Seoul)

INCH'ŎN

Chunchŏn

Wŏnju

Taejŏn

Chŏnju

Kwangju

TAEGU

PUSAN

Ulsan

Pohang

Mokpo

Masan

Cheju-do

Cheju

Tsushima

Iki

Sasebo

Nagasaki

Fukue-jima

Nakadōri-jima

Karatsu

East from Greenwich

118 120 122 124 126 128

COPYRIGHT, GEORGE PHILIP & SON, LTD.

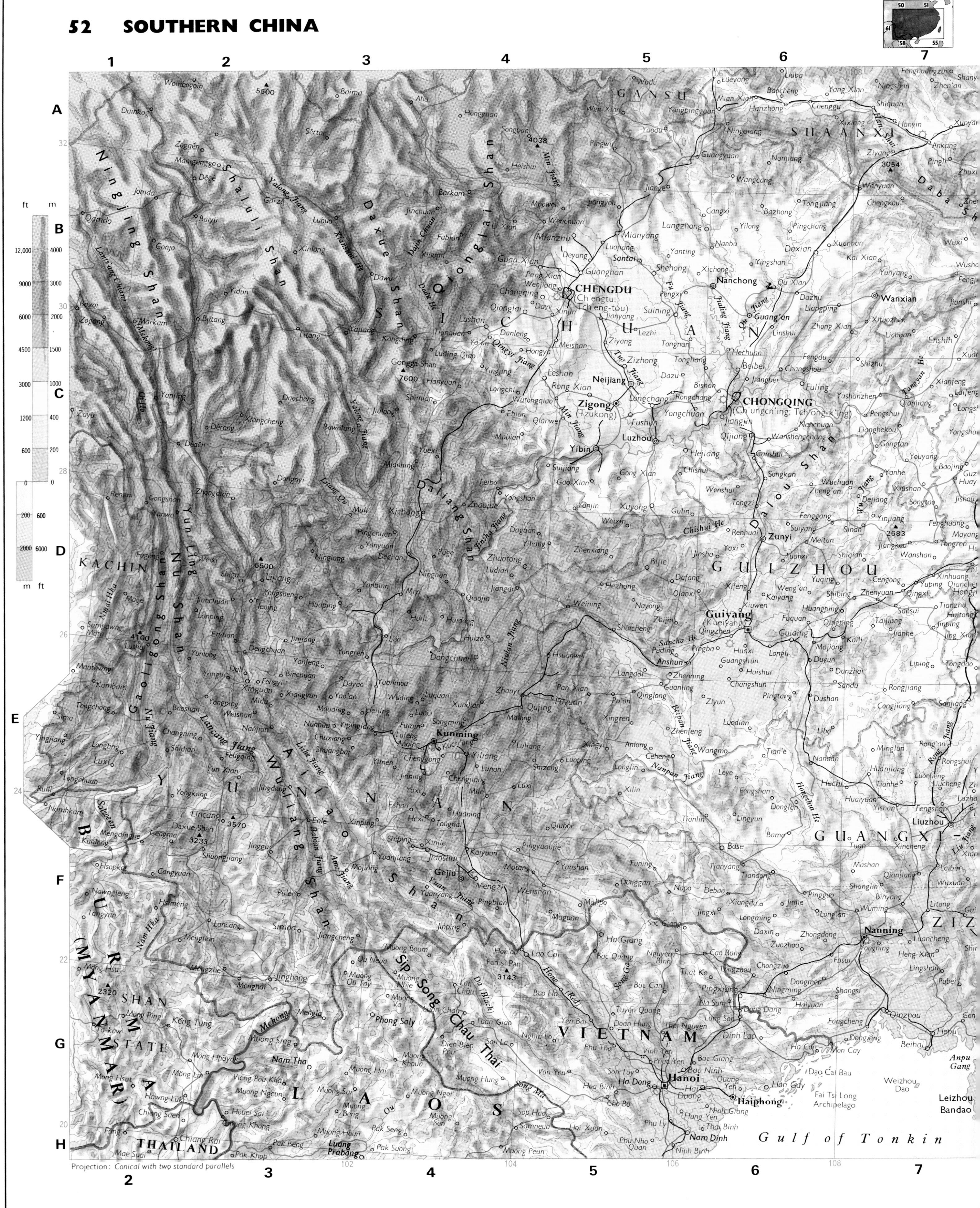
1
2
3
4
5
6
7
A
B
C
D
E
F
G
H
ft
m
12,000
9000
6000
4500
3000
1200
600
4000
3000
2000
1500
1000
400
200
0
200
2000
600
6000
GANSU
SHAANXI
SICHUAN
GUIZHOU
YUNNAN
GUANGXI
KACHIN
BURMA (MYANMAR)
SHAN STATE
LAOS
VIETNAM
THAILAND
Gulf of Tonkin
CHENGDU
(Ch'engtu; Tch'eng-tou)
CHONGQING
(Ch'ungch'ing; Tch'ong-k'ing)
Kunming
Guiyang
Nanning
Hanoi
Haiphong
Zigong
(Tzukong)
Neijiang
Luzhou
Yibin
Nanchong
Wanxian
Zunyi
Liuzhou
Ningjing Shan
Shaluli Shan
Daxue Shan
Qionglai Shan
Min Shan
Daba Shan
Daliang Shan
Dalou Shan
Yun Ling
Nu Shan
Gaoligong Shan
Ailao Shan
Wuliang Shan
Sip Song Chau Thai
Gongga Shan
7600
5500
4038
3054
4100
3570
3233
3143
2683
2320
Mekong
Lancang Jiang
Nu Jiang
Jinsha Jiang
Yalong Jiang
Min Jiang
Tuo Jiang
Jialing Jiang
Wu Jiang
Hong (Red)
Da (Black)
Leizhou Bandao
Weizhou Dao
Fai Tsi Long Archipelago
Luang Prabang
Projection: Conical with two standard parallels

1 : 4 800 000

50 0 50 100 150 miles

50 0 50 100 150 200 km

8 9 10 11 12 13 14

A B C D E F G H

Shangnan Xiping Xixia Fangcheng Wuyang Xiping Xiangcheng Shenqiu Jieshou Guo He Mengcheng Guzhen Hongze Hu Wuhe Xinghua Dongtai
Jingziguan Neixiang Nanyang Sheqi Suiping Shangcai Jiuxiangcheng T'aiho Xifei He Huaiyuan Bengbu Fengyang Gaoyou Hu Gaoyou
Yunxi Xichuan Zhenping Zhumadian Runan Linquan Ying He Madian Jiashan Tianchang JIANGSU Hai'an
Yun Xian Han Shui Deng Xian Wodian Tanghe Biyang Queshan Hong He Fuyang Fengtai Huainan Lai'an Yangzhou Taizhou Tai Xian Rugao Rudong
Shiyan Baihiu HENAN Minggang Zhengyang Xincai Yingshang Zhengyangguan Shou Xian Dingyuan Luhe Yizheng Guazhou Taixing
Zhushan Guanghua Xinye Tongbai Huai He Xi Xian Huoqiu Changfeng Chu Xian Zhenjiang (Chenchiang) Jingjiang Nantong Haimen Qidong
Fang Xian Xiangfan Zaoyang Luoshan Gushi Chengyi Hu Chengdong Hu Wabu Hu Pukou NANJING (Nanking; Nanching) Jurong Danyang Jiangyin Chang Jiang (Yangtze)
Baokang Dongjinwan Xinyang Huangchuan Hefei Zhegao Changzhou (Ch'angchou) Changshu Chongming Chongming Dao
Shennongjia Nanzhang Sui Xian Shangcheng Lu'an Chao Hu Ma'anshan Wuxi (Wuhsi) Kunshan Jiading Baoshan SHANGHAI (Changhai) Nanhui
Jiejiping Xiemahe Yicheng Dahong Shan Maping Jinzhai Huoshan Chao Xian He Xian Lishui Shijiu Hu Liyang Suzhou (Suchou) Qingpu Songjiang Fengxian
Jing Shan Han Shui Yingshan Shucheng Wuwei Wuhu Nanyi Hu Yixing Changxing Wujiang
Xingshan Fengle Anlu Hong'an Dabie Shan ANHUI Lujiang Fanchang Langxi Wuxing Jinshan Jiaxing Pinghu
Yangping Zhongxiang Yunmeng Macheng 1834 Tongcheng Tongling Nanling Guangde Haining Hangzhou Wan
Zigui Yuan'an Jingshan Xiaogan Huangpi Yuexi Gurchi Datong Xuancheng Xiaofeng Da Yunhe Chongde Haiyan Dai Shan Daqu Shan
HUBEI Jingmen Tianmen Yingcheng Hankou Xinzhou Luotian Gaohebu Qianshan Qingyang Jing Xian Ningguo Hangzhou (Hangchou; Hangchow) Dinghai Zhoushan Dao
Yichang (Ich'ang) Dangyang Hanchuan WUHAN (Wou-han) Tuanfeng Yingshan Anqing Taiping Lin'an Xiaoshan Putuo
Changyang Zhijiang Jiangling Hanyang Jinkou Xishui Taihu Huaining Jingde 1810 Qianyang Fuyang Shaoxing Yuyao Ningbo (Ningpo) Zhenhai Taohua Dao
Yidu Shashi Qianjiang Mianyang Huangshi Huangmei Wangjiang Dongliu Shitai Changhua Jiuyuhang Fuchun Jiang Zhuji Liuheng Dao
393 Wufeng Songzi Gong'an Paizhou Echeng Qichun Susong Dongzhi Yi Xian She Xian Tonglu Sheng Xian Xinchang Fenghua Xiangshan
Nanping Hooxue Daye Meichuan Guangji Pengze Qimen Tunxi Chun'an Meicheng ZHEJIANG Ninghai Niutou Shan
Shimen Jinshi Jianli Jiayu Yangxin Ruichang Hukou Suian Jiande Sanmen
Linli Li Xian Shishou Honghu Xianning Jiujiang Shimenjie Jingdezhen Shouchang Lanxi Yiwu Dongyang Tiantai
Sangzhi Cili Anxiang Huarong Linxiang Pugi Mufu Shan De'an Duchang Wuyuan Kaihua Longyou Jinhua Tangxi Yongkang Xianju Linhai
Li Shui Changde Nan Xian Yueyang Dongting Hu Tongcheng Hsiu Shui Xiushui Wuning Poyang Hu Yongxiu Leping Changshan Qu Xian Wuyi Haimen Taizhou Liedao
Dayong Yuan Jiang Hanshou Yuanjiang Pingjiang Jiuling Shan Jing'an Anyi Gan Jiang Nanchang Dexing Yushan Jiangshan Jinyun Huangyan Wenling
Taoyuan Xiangyin Fengxin Yugan Wannian Hengfeng Shangrao Suichang Lishui Qingtian Yuhuan
Zi Shui Yiyang Xiang Jiang Liuyang Tonggu Jin Jiang Go'an Jinxian Yiyang Xin Jiang Guangfeng 1725 Xiping Yueqing Yuhuan Dao
Yuanling Anhua Changsha Shanggao Fengcheng Dongxiang Guixi Yanshan Longquan Yunhe Wenzhou (Wenchow) Yueqing Wan
Chenxi Meichengzhen Ningxiang Wanzai Qingjiang Linchuan Yujiang Pucheng Hexi Wencheng Rui'an
Xupu Xiangtan Zhuzhou Yichun Xinyu Chongren Jinxi 2120 Chong'an Qingyuan Pingyang Nanji Shan
Xinhua Loudi Xiangxiang Liling Fenyi Xingan Zixi Guangze Songxi Shouning Taishun
HUNAN Lianyuan Pingxiang JIANGXI Gaokeng Yihuang Nancheng Shuiji Zhenghe Zherong Fuding
Qianyang Xinshao Shuangfeng Anfu Xiajiang Yongfeng Le'an Shaowu Lichuan Jianyang Zhouning Fu'an Sansha
Longhui Shaoyang Hengshan Wugong Shan Gujiang Ji'an Jishui Nanfeng Taining Jian'ou Pingnan Xiapu
Xuefeng Shan Shaoyang Hengyang You Xian Lienhua Xinfeng Jiangle Shunchang 1629 Ningde
Wugang Qidong Hengyang Anren Chaling Yongxin Taihe Guangchang Wuyi Shan Nanping Gutian Fuying Dao
Hengyangsi Lei Shui Ling Xian Xincheng Ninggang Wan'an Ningdu Jianning Mingxi Sha Xi Sha Xian Min Jiang Minqing Luoyuan Lianjiang Mazu Dao
Xinning Qiyang Suichuan Xingguo Qin Jiang Shicheng Qingliu Sanming Youxi Fuzhou (Foochow; Fuchou) Minhou Changle
Dong'an Changning Leiyang 2164 Ninghua FUJIAN
Lingling Yongxing Guidong Shadi Yudu Longkou Yong'an Yongtai Fuqing
Quanzhou Xintian Zixing Ganzhou Ruijin Changting Datian Pingtan
Xing'an Guiyang Chen Xian Chongyi Shangyou Huichang Liancheng Maiyuan Dehua Xianyou Hanjiang Xinghua Wan Danshui Jilong
Lingchuan Ningyuan Jiahe Yizhang Rucheng Nankang Ting Jiang Zhangping Yongchun Putian Taoyuan TAIBEI (T'aipei)
Guanyang Dao Xian Xinfeng Dayu Nanri Dao Daxi Yilan
Guilin Jiangyong Lanshan Linwu Lechang Renhua Nanxiong Anyuan Wuping Shanghang Hud'an Anxi Nan'an Hui'an Quanzhou (Ch'uanchou) Jinjiang Xinzhu Luodong
Gongcheng Zizhixian Lian Xian Shixing Longnan Xunwu Yongding Tong'an Formosa Strait Tuchang Miaoli Xue Shan 3931
Pingle Fuchuan Lianshan Ruyuan Shaoguan Quannan Dingnan Jiaoling Changtai Zhangzhou Xiamen Jinmen Dao Yuanli Dajia Dongshi
Lipu Zhaoshan He Xian Yangshan Wengcheng Heping Pingyuan Mei Xian Mei Jiang Nanjing Longhai (Hsiamen; Amoy) Taizhong (T'aichung) Zhanghua
Xiuren Zhaoping Yingde Wengyuan Lianping Dabu Pinghe Lugang Yuanlin Hualian
ZHUANGZU Gui Jiang Huaiji Bei Jiang Xinfeng Longchuan Xingning Han Jiang Yunxiao Zhangpu Erlin Yunlin
Nanfeng Qingyuan Fogang Heyuan Wuhua Zhao'an TAIWAN (FORMOSA) Dounan Jiayi Yu Shan
Xun Jiang Guangning Longmen Zijin Chao'an Dongshan Tropic of Cancer Beigang Puzi Baihe 3997 Taiwan Shan
Wuzhou Fengkai Sihui GUANGDONG Dong Jiang Jieyang Nan'ao Tainan
Teng Xian Deqing Xi Jiang Hekou GUANGZHOU (Kuangchou; Canton) Zengcheng Boluo Puning Chaoyang Shantou (Swatow) Haimen Jiali Tainan Qishan Taidong
QU Yunan Zhaoqing Sanshui Foshan Shilong Dongguan Huizhou Haifeng Lufeng Huilai Gaoxiong (Kaohsiung) Pingdong Huoshao Dao
Yunfu Jiujiang Panyu Shunde Honghai Wan Fangliao
Rong Xian Beiliu Luoding Xinxing Gaohe Xiaolan Shenzhen
Jiangmen Zhongshan HONG KONG (U.K.) Kowloon Lan Yu
Luchuan Kaiping Xinhui Zhuhai Eluanbi
Xinyi 1703 Enping Taishan Macau (Macao) (Port.) Dangan Liedao
Yangchun Chixi Gaolan Dao
Gaozhou Yangjiang
Huazhou Maoming Xiachuan Dao Shangchuan Dao Luzon Strait
Lianjiang Dianbai Diancheng Hailing Dao
Suixi Wuchuan
Zhanjiang
Donghai Dao Naozhou Dao
Leizhou Wan Tungsha Tao
SOUTH CHINA SEA
Xuwen Xu'an

112 114 116 118 120 122 32 30 28 26 24 22 20

8 9 10 11 12 13

COPYRIGHT. GEORGE PHILIP & SON. LTD.

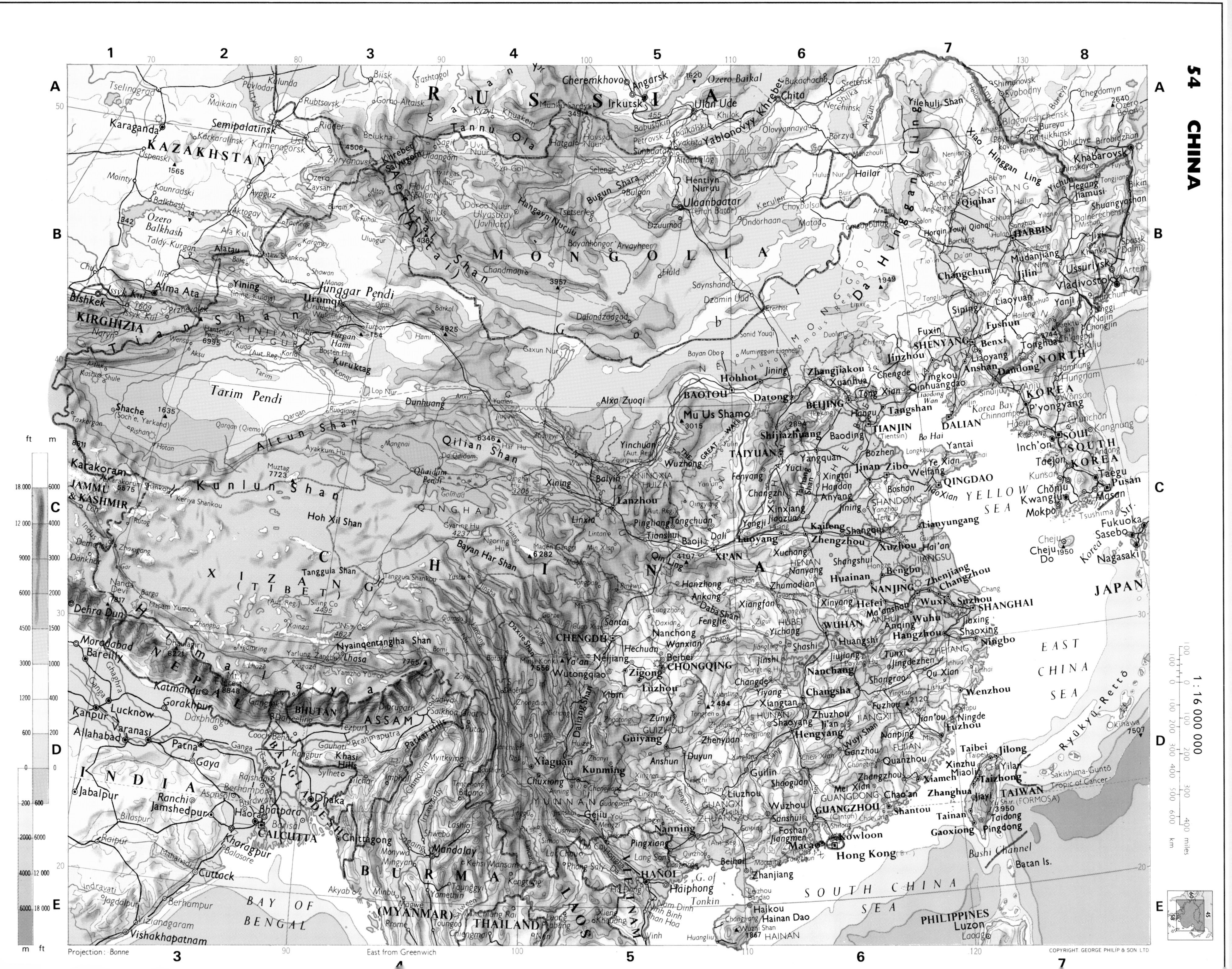
1 : 16 000 000
miles
km
RUSSIA
MONGOLIA
CHINA
KAZAKHSTAN
KIRGHIZIA
JAMMU & KASHMIR
XIZANG (TIBET)
NEPAL
BHUTAN
ASSAM
BANGLADESH
INDIA
BURMA (MYANMAR)
THAILAND
LAOS
VIETNAM
NORTH KOREA
SOUTH KOREA
JAPAN
TAIWAN (FORMOSA)
PHILIPPINES
YELLOW SEA
EAST CHINA SEA
SOUTH CHINA SEA
BAY OF BENGAL
Projection: Bonne
East from Greenwich
COPYRIGHT GEORGE PHILIP & SON LTD

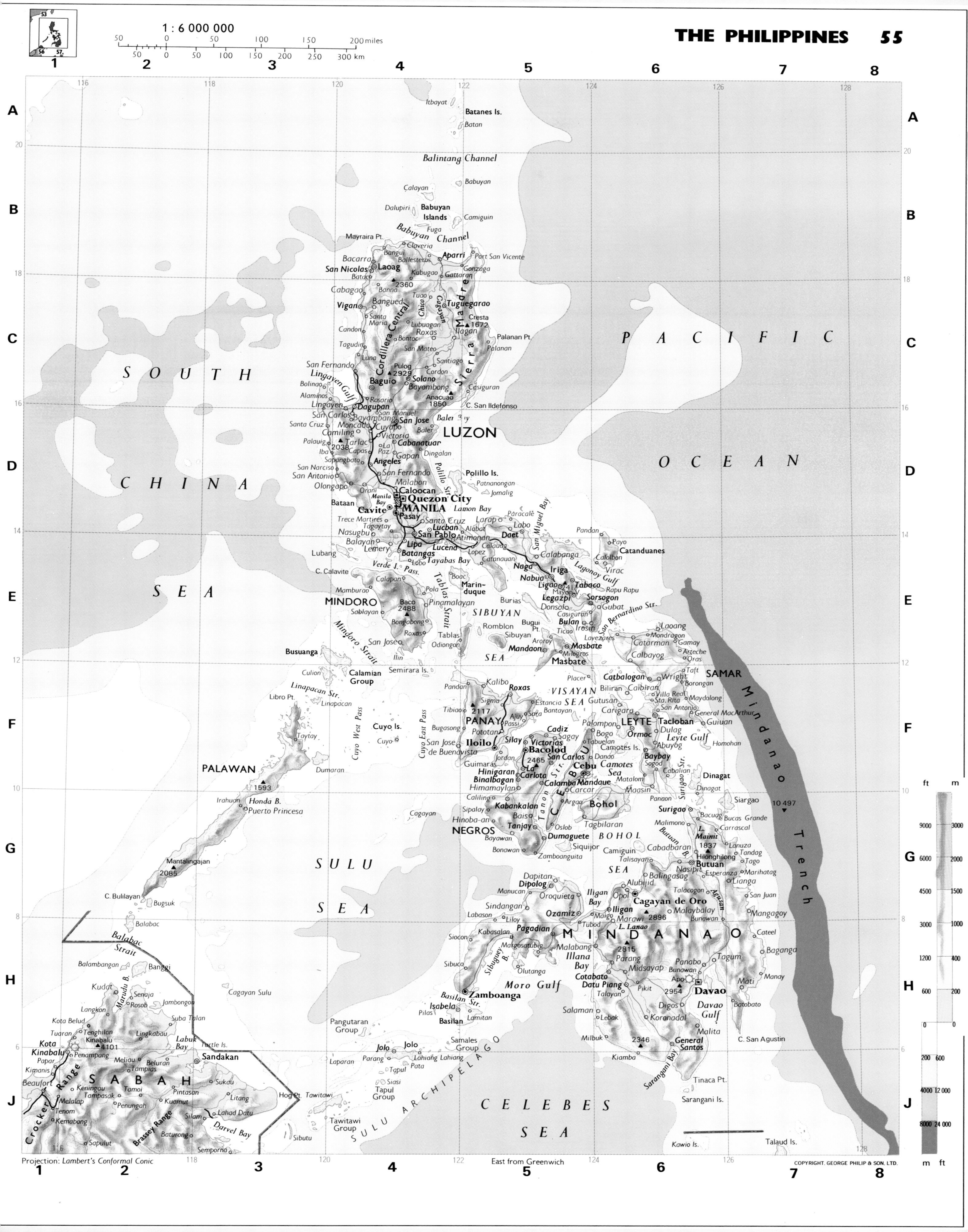
1 : 6 000 000
50 0 50 100 150 200 miles
50 0 50 100 150 200 250 300 km
Batanes Is.
Itbayat
Batan
Balintang Channel
Babuyan
Calayan
Dalupiri
Babuyan Islands
Camiguin
Fuga
Babuyan Channel
Mayraira Pt.
Claveria
Aparri
Port San Vicente
Laoag
San Nicolas
Bacarra
Batac
2360
Gonzaga
Gattaran
Vigan
Bangued
Tuguegarao
Cordillera Central
Sierra Madre
Cresta 1672
Ilagan
Palanan Pt.
Palanan
San Fernando
Lingayen Gulf
Baguio
Pulog 2929
Solano
Bayombong
Anacuao 1850
Casiguran
C. San Ildefonso
Dagupan
Lingayen
San Jose
Baler Bay
LUZON
Cabanatuan
Tarlac
Angeles
San Fernando
Polillo Is.
Olongapo
Bataan
Caloocan
Quezon City
MANILA
Cavite
Pasay
Lamon Bay
San Pablo
Lucena
Batangas
Lipa
Daet
San Miguel Bay
Catanduanes
Virac
Naga
Iriga
Lagonoy Gulf
Legazpi
Tabaco
Sorsogon
San Bernardino Str.
Mindoro Strait
MINDORO
Calapan
Baco 2488
Marinduque
Tablas Strait
SIBUYAN SEA
Romblon
Tablas
Masbate
Busuanga
Calamian Group
Linapacan Str.
Cuyo Is.
Cuyo West Pass
Cuyo East Pass
PALAWAN
1593
Puerto Princesa
Honda B.
Mantalingajan 2085
C. Bulilayan
Balabac
Balabac Strait
PANAY
Roxas
Kalibo
Iloilo
2117
VISAYAN SEA
Catbalogan
SAMAR
LEYTE
Tacloban
Ormoc
Leyte Gulf
Bacolod
2465
La Carlota
CEBU
Cebu
Mandaue
Camotes Sea
Tañon Str.
Bohol
NEGROS
Dumaguete
Kabankalan
BOHOL SEA
Siquijor
Camiguin
Surigao
Surigao Str.
Dinagat
Siargao
Mindanao Trench
10 497
Butuan
L. Mainit
1837
Cagayan de Oro
Iligan
Iligan Bay
Ozamiz
Dipolog
2896
L. Lanao
2815
MINDANAO
Pagadian
Sibuguey B.
Illana Bay
Moro Gulf
Cotabato
Zamboanga
Basilan Str.
Isabela
Basilan
Jolo
Sulu Archipelago
Tawitawi Group
Apo 2954
Davao
Davao Gulf
2346
General Santos
Sarangani Is.
C. San Agustin
Talaud Is.
SULU SEA
CELEBES SEA
SOUTH CHINA SEA
PACIFIC OCEAN
SABAH
Kota Kinabalu
Kinabalu 4101
Sandakan
Crocker Range
Brassey Range
Darvel Bay
Marudu B.
Banggi
Kudat
Labuk Bay
Tenom
Beaufort
Lahad Datu
Projection: Lambert's Conformal Conic
East from Greenwich
COPYRIGHT, GEORGE PHILIP & SON, LTD.

THAILAND

CAMBODIA

LAOS

VIET-NAM

BURMA (MYANMAR)

PENINSULAR MALAYSIA

MALAYSIA

SOUTH CHINA SEA

ANDAMAN SEA

Gulf of Thailand

Strait of Malacca

SUMATERA

BORNEO

KALIMANTAN

INDONESIA

Greater Sunda Islands

JAVA SEA

JAWA (JAVA)

INDIAN OCEAN

Java Trench

ft m

12 000 4000

9000 3000

6000 2000

4500 1500

3000 1000

1200 400

600 200

0 0

200 600

2000 6000

4000 12 000

6000 18 000

8000 24 000

m ft

Projection: Mercator

East from Greenwich

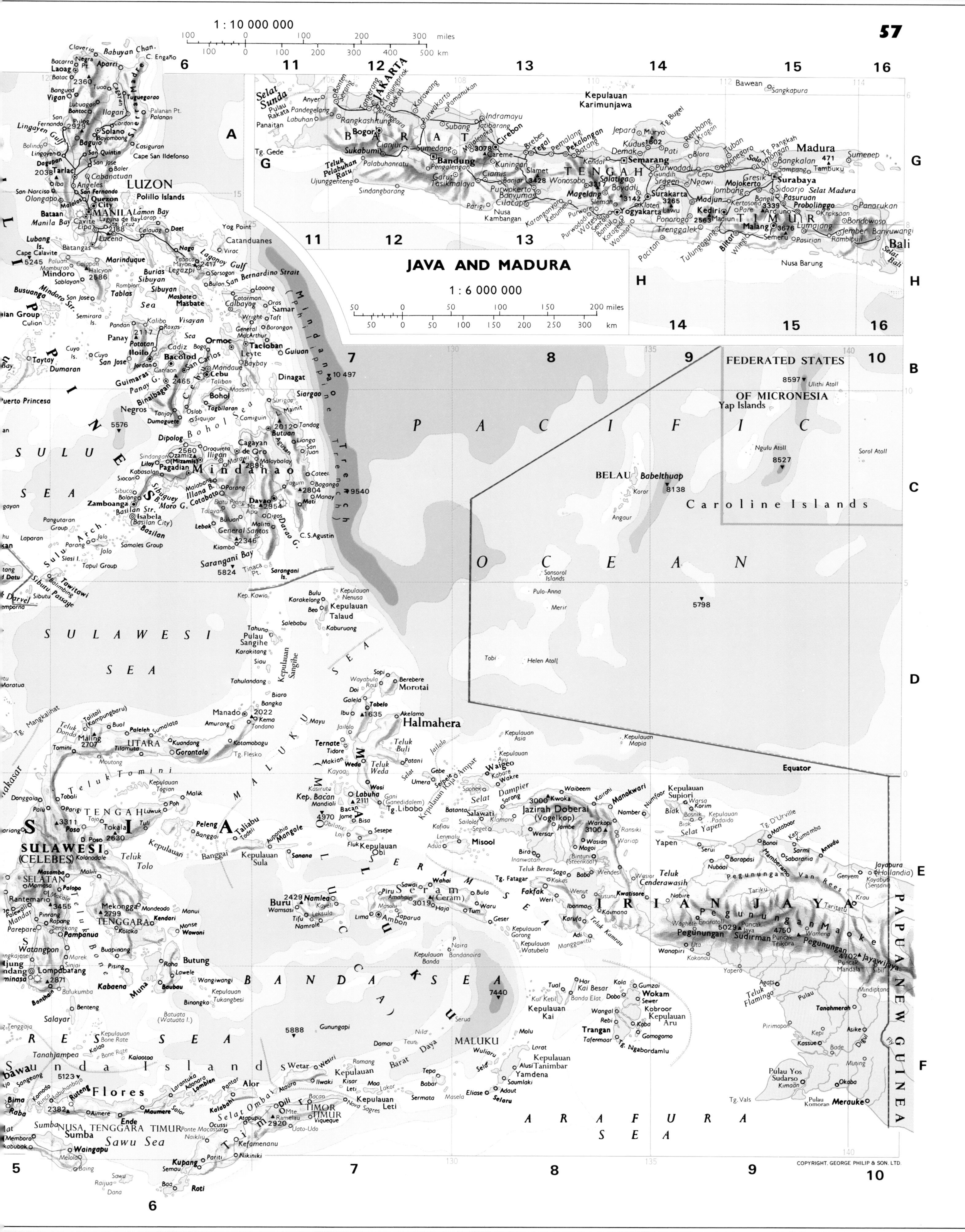
1 : 10 000 000
miles
km
LUZON
Polillo Islands
MANILA
Quezon City
Mindoro
Busuanga
Panay
Negros
Cebu
Bohol
Leyte
Samar
Mindanao
Zamboanga
Davao
General Santos
Sarangani Bay
SULU SEA
Sulu Arch.
SULAWESI SEA
PHILIPPINES
Mindanao Trench (Philippine Trench)
10 497
9540
JAVA AND MADURA
1 : 6 000 000
Selat Sunda
JAKARTA
Bogor
Bandung
Cirebon
Semarang
Yogyakarta
Surakarta
Surabaya
Madura
Malang
Bali
Kepulauan Karimunjawa
BARAT
TENGAH
TIMUR
Nusa Barung
PACIFIC OCEAN
FEDERATED STATES OF MICRONESIA
Yap Islands
Ulithi Atoll
Ngulu Atoll
Sorol Atoll
BELAU
Babelthuap
Koror
Angaur
Caroline Islands
Sonsorol Islands
Pulo-Anna
Merir
Tobi
Helen Atoll
5798
Equator
Kepulauan Talaud
Kepulauan Sangihe
Morotai
Halmahera
Ternate
Tidore
MALUKU SEA
Manado
Gorontalo
Teluk Tomini
UTARA
TENGAH
SULAWESI (CELEBES)
SELATAN
TENGGARA
Kepulauan Banggai
Kepulauan Sula
Buru
Seram (Ceram)
Ambon
SERAM SEA
Misool
Waigeo
Salawati
Jazirah Doberai (Vogelkop)
Manokwari
Kepulauan Supiori
Yapen
Teluk Cenderawasih
IRIAN JAYA
Pegunungan Sudirman
Pegunungan Maoke
Puncak Jaya
5029
4750
Jayapura (Hollandia)
PAPUA NEW GUINEA
Butung
Muna
BANDA SEA
7440
Kepulauan Kai
Kepulauan Aru
Kepulauan Tanimbar
Yamdena
MALUKU
Merauke
Pulau Yos Sudarso
ARAFURA SEA
FLORES SEA
Lesser Sunda Islands
Flores
Sumba
Sawu Sea
NUSA TENGGARA TIMUR
TIMUR
Timor
Dili
Kupang
Roti
Wetar
Alor
Kepulauan Leti
Selat Ombai
COPYRIGHT, GEORGE PHILIP & SON, LTD.

BURMA (MYANMAR)
THAILAND
LAOS
CAMBODIA
VIETNAM
YUNNAN
GUANGXI ZHUANGZU ZIZHIQU AUTONOMOUS REGION
HAINAN
Gulf of Tonkin
Gulf of Martaban
HANOI
Haiphong
Vientiane
BANGKOK (Krung Thep)
Rangoon
Mandalay
Moulmein
Da Nang (Tourane)
Hue
Luang Prabang
Chiang Mai
Nakhon Ratchasima (Khorat)
Ubon Ratchathani
Battambang
Haikou
Zhanjiang
Nanning
Mekong
Salween
Red River Delta
Phnom Dangrek
Khorat
Tran Ninh
Cao Nguyen
Central Highlands
Dawna Range
Taunggyi
Inle Lake

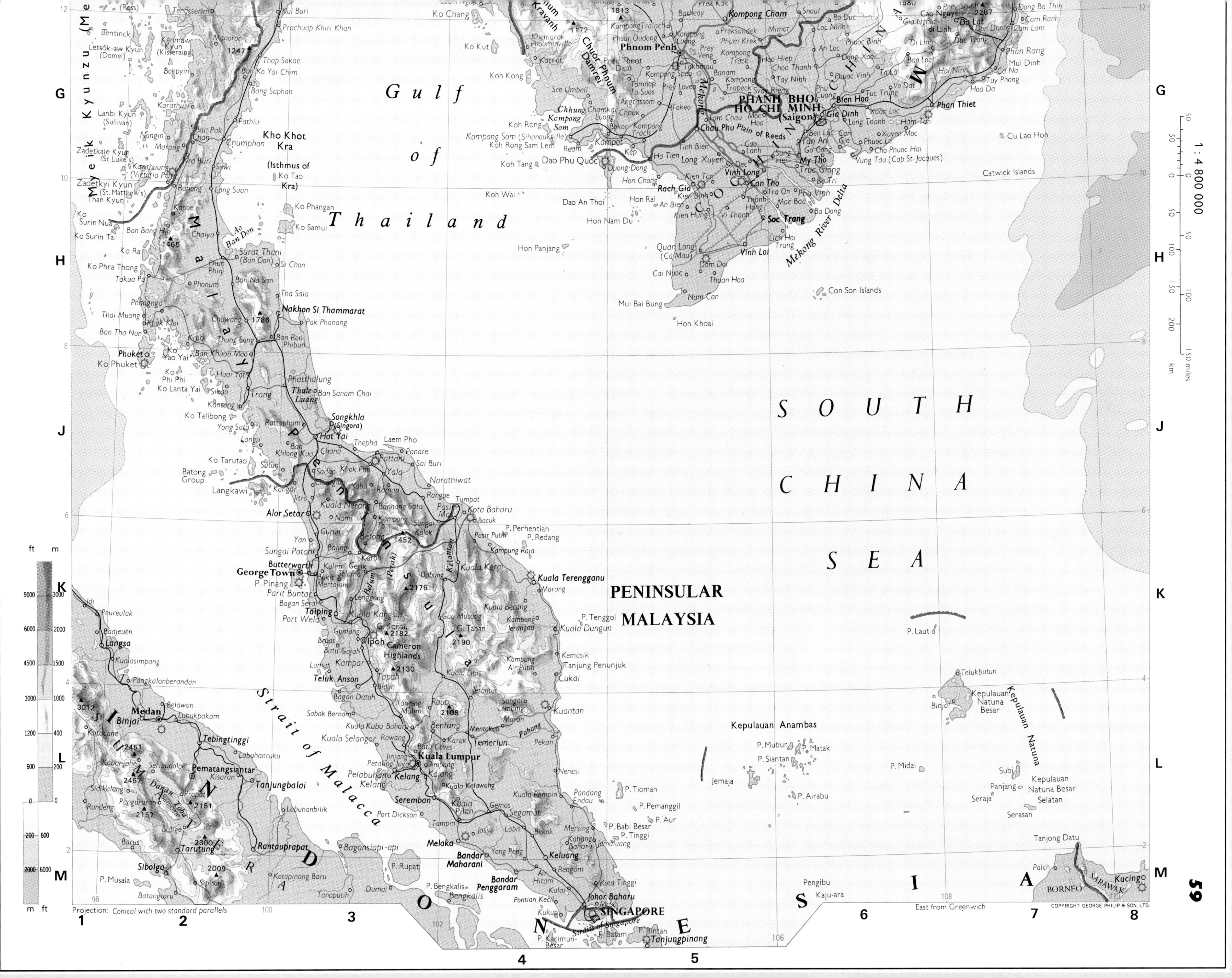
1 : 4 800 000
50 0 50 100 150 miles
50 0 50 100 150 200 km
Gulf of Thailand
SOUTH CHINA SEA
PENINSULAR MALAYSIA
INDONESIA
Strait of Malacca
Mekong River Delta
Kepulauan Natuna
Kepulauan Anambas
SINGAPORE
Kuala Lumpur
George Town
Phnom Penh
PHANH BHO HO CHI MINH (Saigon)
Phuket
Medan
Nakhon Si Thammarat
Songkhla
Kuala Terengganu
Kota Baharu
Johor Baharu
Melaka
Kucing
SARAWAK
BORNEO
Kho Khot Kra
(Isthmus of Kra)
Projection: Conical with two standard parallels
East from Greenwich
COPYRIGHT GEORGE PHILIP & SON LTD.

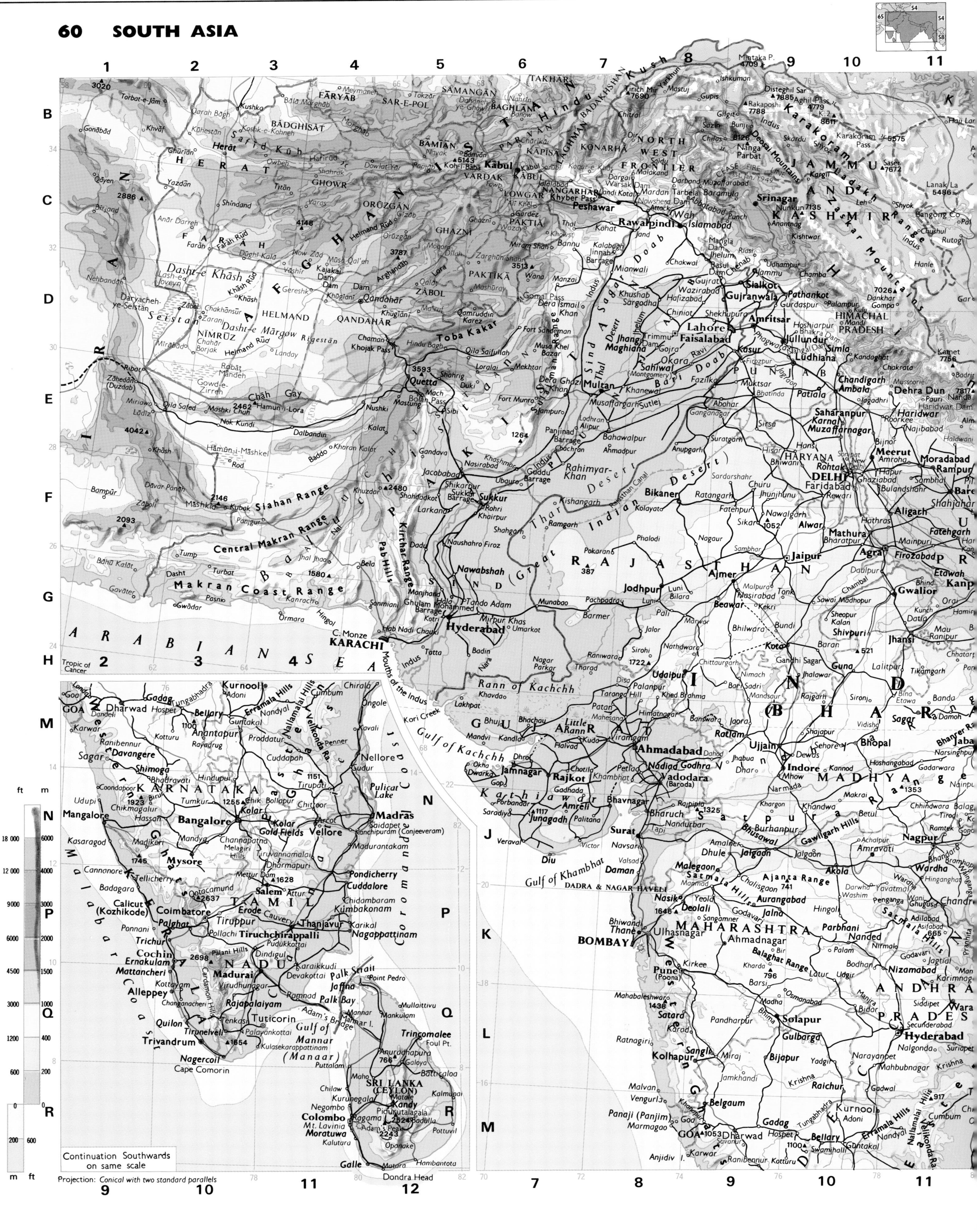
ARABIAN SEA
Tropic of Cancer
Gulf of Kachchh
Gulf of Khambhat
Rann of Kachchh
Mouths of the Indus
Kori Creek
C. Monze
KARACHI
Hyderabad
Sukkur
Nawabshah
Larkana
Jacobabad
Quetta
Multan
Lahore
Faisalabad
Rawalpindi
Islamabad
Peshawar
Sialkot
Gujranwala
Sargodha
Bahawalpur
Kabul
Herāt
Qandahār
Farāh
Shīndand
Kushka
Dasht-e Khāsh
Dasht-e Mārgow
Rigestān
Hindu Kush
Safīd Kūh
Toba Kakar
Siahan Range
Central Makran Range
Makran Coast Range
Kirthar Range
Pab Hills
Thar or Great Indian Desert
Sind Sagar Doab
Bari Doab
Thal Desert
Karakoram
Zaskar Mountains
Deosai Mountains
Ladakh Range
Nanga Parbat
Srinagar
Leh
Jammu
Amritsar
Jullundur
Ludhiana
Simla
Chandigarh
Ambala
Dehra Dun
Patiala
Saharanpur
Meerut
Moradabad
DELHI
Rohtak
Aligarh
Agra
Mathura
Jaipur
Ajmer
Jodhpur
Bikaner
Gwalior
Jhansi
Kota
Udaipur
Ahmadabad
Vadodara (Baroda)
Rajkot
Jamnagar
Bhavnagar
Junagadh
Surat
Daman
Diu
DADRA & NAGAR HAVELI
BOMBAY
Nasik
Pune (Poona)
Aurangabad
Ajanta Range
Satmala Hills
Balaghat Range
Solapur
Kolhapur
Belgaum
Panaji (Panjim)
GOA
Hyderabad
Nizamabad
Gulbarga
Bijapur
Raichur
Indore
Bhopal
Ujjain
Ratlam
Jabalpur
Nagpur
Akola
Amravati
Wardha
Kathiawar
Satpura Range
MAHARASHTRA
MADHYA PRADESH
ANDHRA PRADESH
RAJASTHAN
PUNJAB
HARYANA
HIMACHAL PRADESH
JAMMU AND KASHMIR
NORTH WEST FRONTIER
AFGHANISTAN
PAKISTAN
INDIA
BHARAT
SIND
BALUCHISTAN
IRAN
KARNATAKA
TAMIL NADU
KERALA
Western Ghats
Malabar Coast
Coromandel Coast
Eastern Ghats
Mangalore
Bangalore
Mysore
Madras
Vellore
Pondicherry
Cuddalore
Salem
Coimbatore
Calicut (Kozhikode)
Cochin
Ernakulam
Alleppey
Quilon
Trivandrum
Nagercoil
Cape Comorin
Madurai
Tiruchchirappalli
Thanjavur
Tuticorin
Palk Strait
Palk Bay
Gulf of Mannar
SRI LANKA (CEYLON)
Jaffna
Trincomalee
Anuradhapura
Kandy
Colombo
Galle
Dondra Head
Continuation Southwards on same scale
Projection: Conical with two standard parallels

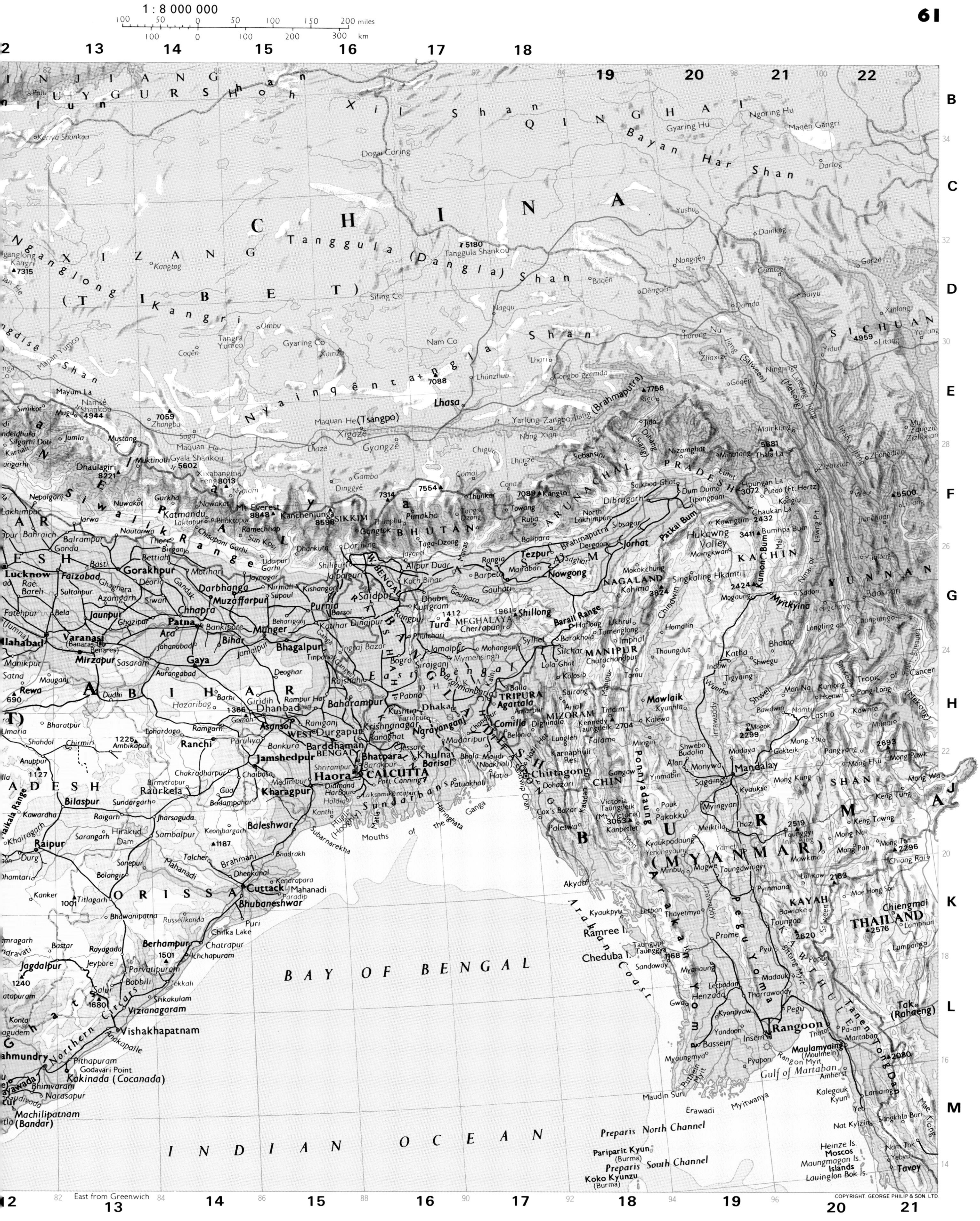

1 : 8 000 000

100 50 0 50 100 150 200 miles

100 0 100 200 300 km

CHINA

XIZANG (TIBET)

QINGHAI

SICHUAN

YUNNAN

Xinjiang Uygur

Xil Shan

Tanggula (Dangla) Shan

Nyainqêntanglha Shan

Bayan Har Shan

Ngangla Ringco

Kangtog

Dogai Coring

Tangra Yumco

Gyaring Co

Nam Co

Siling Co

Lhasa

Maquan He (Tsangpo)

Yarlung Zangbo Jiang (Brahmaputra)

Xigazê

Gyangzê

Mt. Everest 8848

Kanchenjunga 8598

SIKKIM

BHUTAN

Thimphu

Punakha

Gangtok

Darjiling

Katmandu

NEPAL

Siwalik Range

Dhaulagiri 8221

ARUNACHAL PRADESH

ASSAM

NAGALAND

MANIPUR

MIZORAM

TRIPURA

MEGHALAYA

Shillong

Cherrapunji

Tezpur

Jorhat

Dibrugarh

Nowgong

Gauhati

Imphal

Kohima

Agartala

BANGLADESH

Dhaka

Chittagong

Comilla

Khulna

Barisal

Rajshahi

Mymensingh

Sylhet

WEST BENGAL

CALCUTTA

Haora

Sundarbans

Mouths of the Ganga

BIHAR

Patna

Gaya

Ranchi

Jamshedpur

Dhanbad

Bhagalpur

Munger

Muzaffarpur

Darbhanga

Purnia

Asansol

Durgapur

Barddhaman

UTTAR PRADESH

Lucknow

Faizabad

Gorakhpur

Varanasi (Banaras)

Allahabad

Mirzapur

ORISSA

Cuttack

Bhubaneshwar

Puri

Chilka Lake

Berhampur

Sambalpur

Raurkela

Baleshwar

Kharagpur

MADHYA PRADESH

Bilaspur

Raipur

Jagdalpur

Vizianagaram

Vishakhapatnam

Kakinada (Cocanada)

Machilipatnam (Bandar)

Northern Circars

BAY OF BENGAL

INDIAN OCEAN

BURMA (MYANMAR)

CHIN

KACHIN

SHAN

KAYAH

KAWTHULEI

Arakan Yoma

Arakan Coast

Pegu Yoma

Irrawaddy

Chindwin

Salween

Mandalay

Sagaing

Myitkyina

Bhamo

Lashio

Akyab

Ramree I.

Cheduba I.

Prome

Henzada

Bassein

Pegu

Rangoon

Moulmeingyaing (Moulmein)

Martaban

Gulf of Martaban

Thaton

Tavoy

Preparis North Channel

Preparis South Channel

Coco Kyunzu (Burma)

Paripari Kyun (Burma)

Moscos Islands

THAILAND

Chiengmai

Tak (Rahaeng)

Tropic of Cancer

Mekong (Lancang Jiang)

Salween (Nu Jiang)

Tanen Tong Dan

COPYRIGHT, GEORGE PHILIP & SON, LTD

East from Greenwich

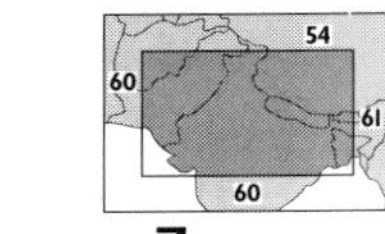
54
60
61
60

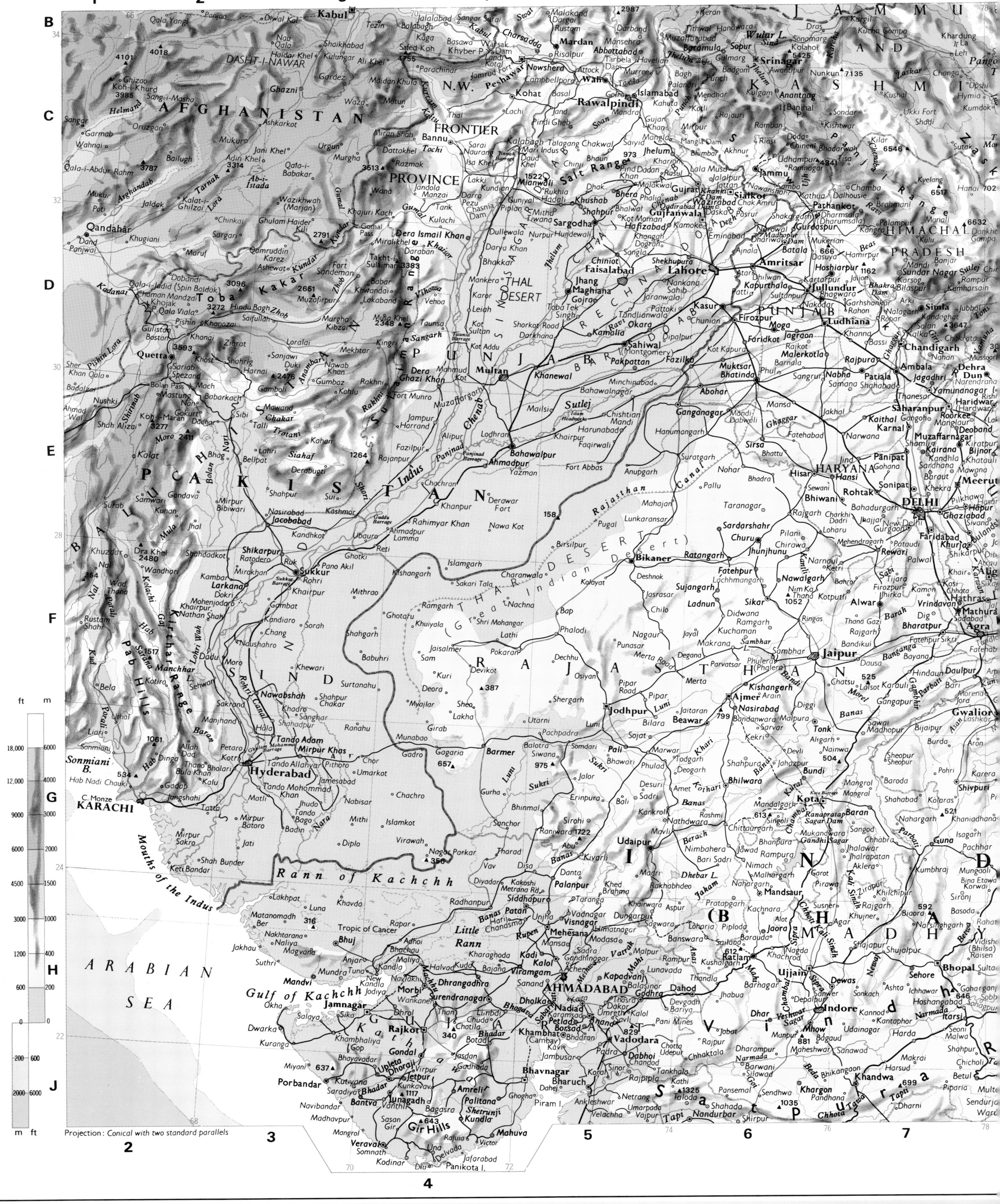

Projection: Conical with two standard parallels

1 : 4 800 000

50 0 50 100 miles

50 0 50 100 150 km

JAMMU AND KASHMIR

On same scale as Main Map

East from Greenwich

COPYRIGHT. GEORGE PHILIP & SON. LTD.

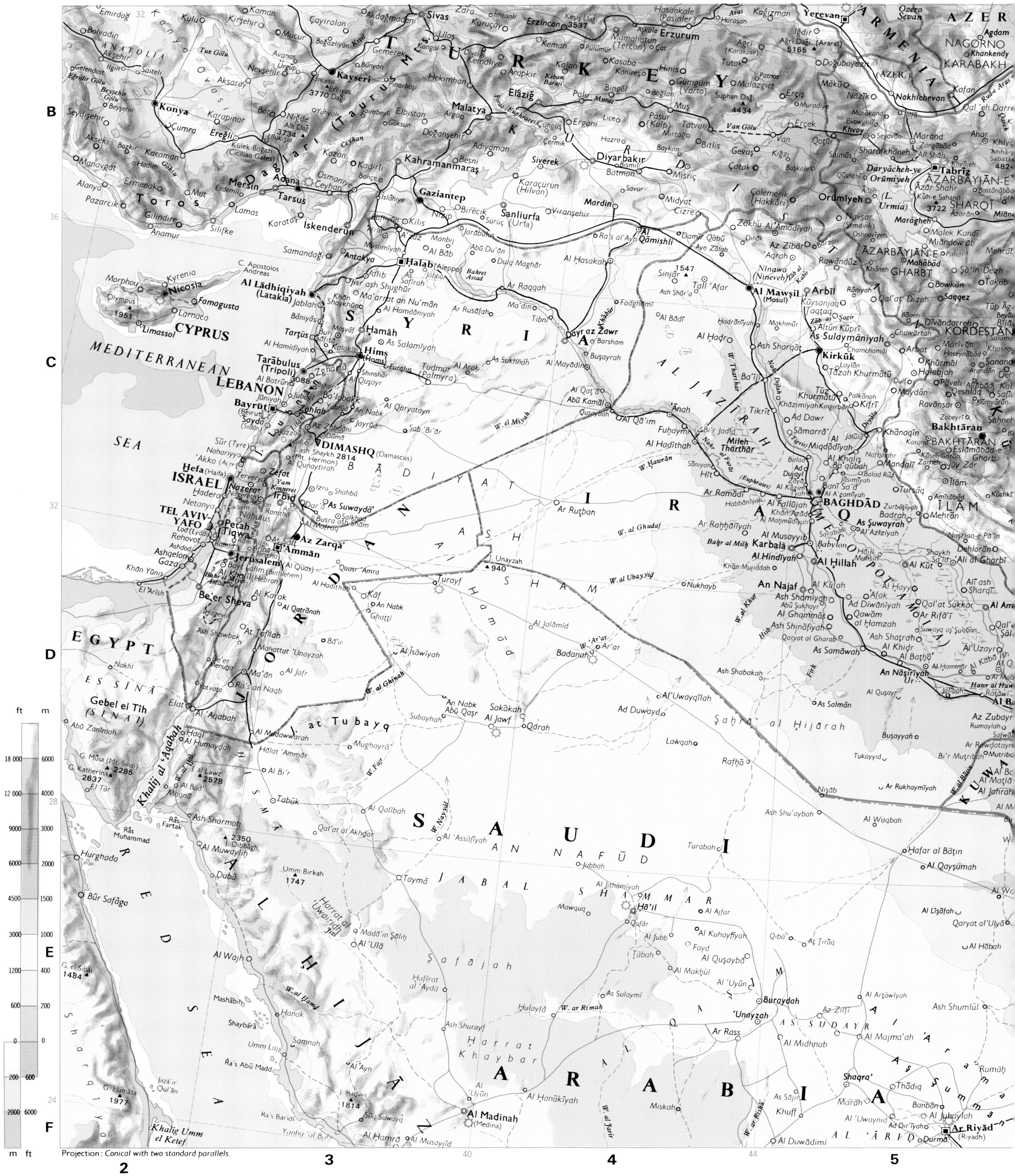

1 2 3 4 5

TURKEY

ARMENIA

AZER.

CYPRUS

MEDITERRANEAN SEA

LEBANON

SYRIA

ISRAEL

JORDAN

IRAQ

AL JAZĪRAH

MESOPOTAMIA

BĀDIYAT ASH SHAM

EGYPT

SAUDI ARABIA

AN NAFŪD

AL HIJĀZ

RED SEA

Projection: Conical with two standard parallels

2 3 4 5

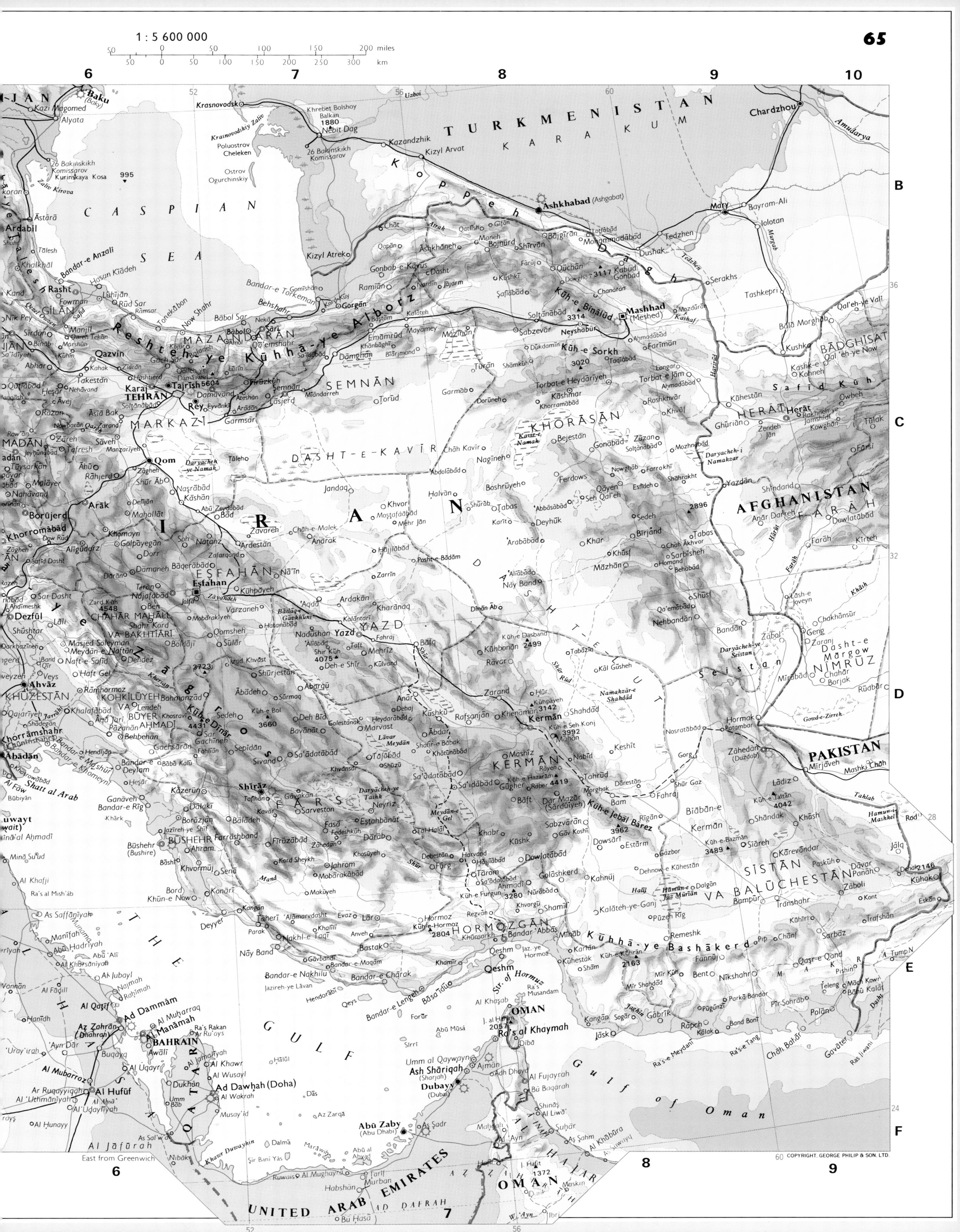
1 : 5 600 000
50 0 50 100 150 200 miles
50 0 50 100 150 200 250 300 km
6
7
8
9
10
B
C
D
E
F
T U R K M E N I S T A N
K A R A K U M
C A S P I A N S E A
Krasnovodsk
Khrebet Bolshoy Balkan 1880
Nebit Dag
Kazandzhik
Kizyl Arvat
Kizyl Atreko
Chardzhou
Amudarya
Ashkhabad (Ashgabat)
Mary
Bayram-Ali
Iolotan
Tedzhen
Dushak
Serakhs
Tashkepri
Kushka
Baku (Baky)
Alyata
Kazi Magomed
26 Bakinskikh Komissarov
Kurinskaya Kosa
Poluostrov Cheleken
Ostrov Ogurchinskiy
995
Āstārā
Ardabil
Tālesh
Bandar-e Anzalī
Rasht
GĪLĀN
Lāhījān
Rūd Sar
Rāmsar
Tonekābon
Now Shahr
Bābol Sar
Bābol
Sārī
Behshahr
Gorgān
Gonbad-e Kāvūs
Bandar-e Torkeman
MĀZANDARĀN
Reshteh-ye Kūhhā-ye Alborz
Qazvīn
Karaj
Tajrīsh
TEHRĀN
Rey
Damāvand 5604
Semnān
Dāmghān
Shāhrūd
Emāmrūd
Sabzevār
Neyshābūr
Mashhad (Meshed)
Kūh-e Bīnālūd 3314
Kūh-e Sorkh 3020
Qūchān
Bojnūrd
Shīrvān
Kopet Dagh
Torbat-e Heydarīyeh
Torbat-e Jām
Kāshmar
KHORĀSĀN
SEMNĀN
MARKAZĪ
Qom
Kāshān
Arāk
Sāveh
Hamadān
DASHT-E-KAVĪR
Daryācheh-ye Namak
I R A N
DASHT-E-LŪT
Tabas
Ferdows
Gonābād
Qāyen
Bīrjand
Nehbandān
Zābol
Daryācheh-ye Sīstān
Sīstān
Zāhedān (Duzdāb)
Hormak
Mīrjāveh
PAKISTAN
AFGHANISTAN
FARĀH
Farāh
HERĀT
Herāt
Safīd Kūh
BĀDGHĪSĀT
Shīndand
NĪMRŪZ
Dasht-e Mārgow
Chakhānsūr
Eşfahān
ESFAHĀN
Nā'īn
Ardestān
Natanz
Najafābād
Zāyandeh
CHAHĀR MAHĀLL VA BAKHTĪĀRĪ
Shahr Kord
Zard Kūh 4548
Borūjerd
Khorramābād
Dezfūl
Shūshtar
Ahvāz
KHŪZESTĀN
Khorramshahr
Ābādān
Shatt al Arab
Behbehān
KOHKĪLŪYEH VA BŪYER AHMADĪ
Kūh-e Dīnār 4431
Zāgros
Yazd
YAZD
Ardakān
Bāfq
Shīr Kūh 4075
Kermān
KERMĀN
Rafsanjān
Sīrjān
Bam
Kūh-e Hazārān 4419
Kūh-e Jebāl Bārez
Shīrāz
FĀRS
Neyrīz
Fasā
Jahrom
Kāzerūn
Būshehr (Bushire)
BŪSHEHR
Bandar-e Deylam
Ganāveh
Bandar-e Rīg
Khārk
Bandar 'Abbās
HORMOZGĀN
Mīnāb
Qeshm
Bandar-e Lengeh
Bandar-e Chārak
Kūhhā-ye Bashākerd
SĪSTĀN VA BALŪCHESTĀN
Īrānshahr
Chāh Bahār
Jāsk
Hamun-i Mashkel
Gulf of Oman
Str. of Hormuz
THE GULF
OMAN
Ra's al Khaymah
Ash Shāriqah (Sharjah)
Dubayy (Dubai)
Abū Zaby (Abu Dhabi)
Al Fujayrah
UNITED ARAB EMIRATES
QATAR
Ad Dawhah (Doha)
BAHRAIN
Al Manāmah
Ad Dammām
Al Hufūf
Al Mubarraz
Az Zahrān (Dhahran)
Kuwayt (Kuwait)
Mīnā' al Ahmadī
Al Jāfūrah
East from Greenwich
52
56
60
36
32
28
24
COPYRIGHT, GEORGE PHILIP & SON, LTD.

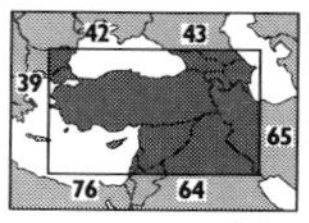

Projection: *Conical with two standard parallels*

Provinces in Turkey are named after the chief towns which are underlined.

Division between Greeks and Turks in Cyprus; Turks to the North.

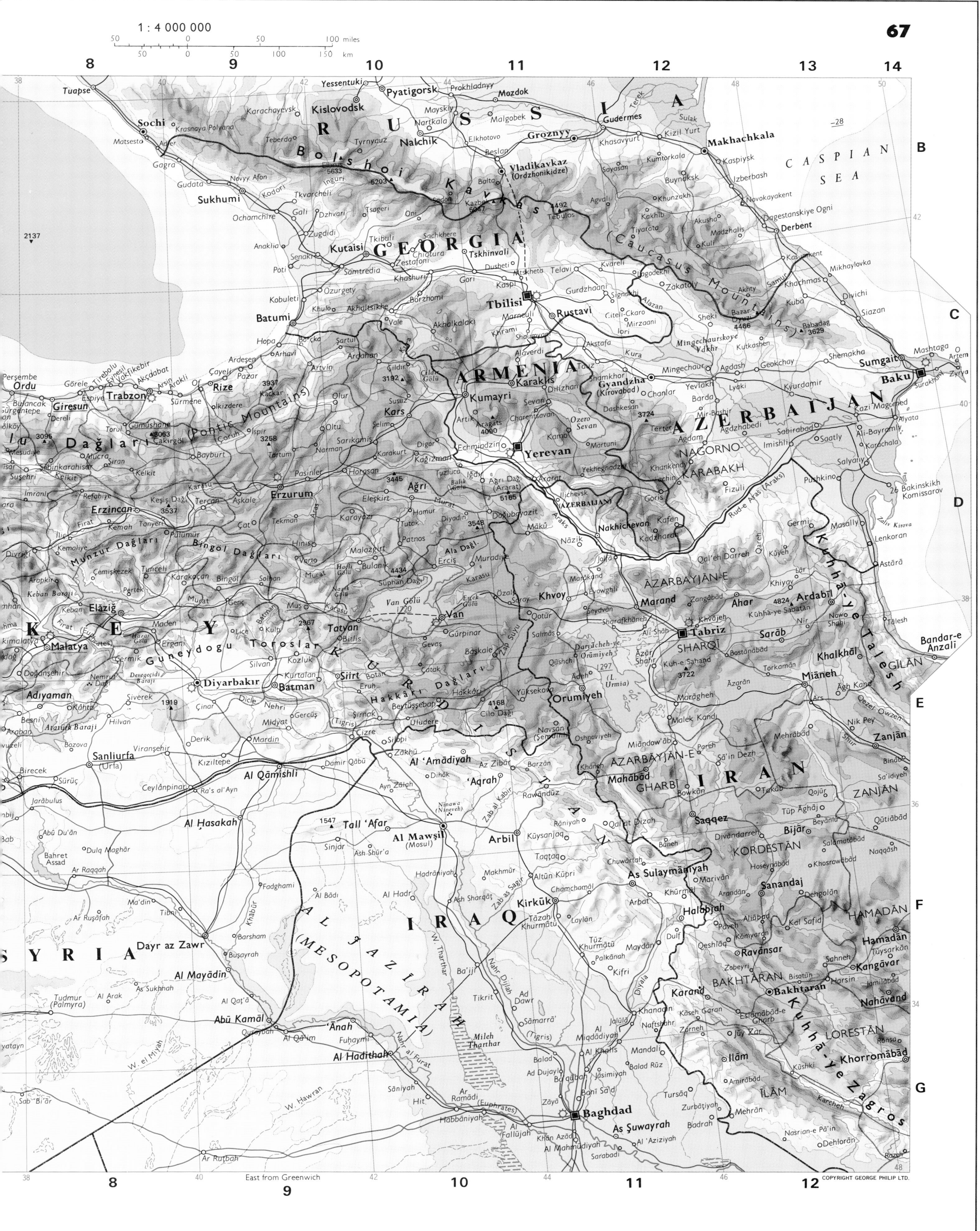
1 : 4 000 000
50 0 50 100 miles
50 0 50 100 150 km
8
9
10
11
12
13
14
B
C
D
E
F
G
RUSSIA
GEORGIA
ARMENIA
AZERBAIJAN
IRAN
IRAQ
SYRIA
CASPIAN SEA
Bolshoi Kavkas
Caucasus Mountains
Pontic Mountains
Toroslar
Güneydoğu
KURDISTAN
Hakkari Dağları
Munzut Dağları
Bingöl Dağları
Kuhhā-ye Talesh
Kuhhā-ye Zagros
AL JAZIRAH (MESOPOTAMIA)
NAGORNO-KARABAKH
Tuapse
Sochi
Sukhumi
Kislovodsk
Pyatigorsk
Yessentuki
Nalchik
Mozdok
Groznyy
Gudermes
Makhachkala
Vladikavkaz (Ordzhonikidze)
Derbent
Kutaisi
Batumi
Tbilisi
Rustavi
Kumayri
Yerevan
Gyandzha (Kirovabad)
Sumgait
Baku
Stepanakert
Nakhichevan
Trabzon
Rize
Giresun
Ordu
Erzurum
Erzincan
Kars
Ağrı
Elâzığ
Malatya
Van
Van Gölü
Diyarbakır
Batman
Siirt
Adıyaman
Sanliurfa (Urfa)
Mardin
Al Qāmishlī
Al Ḥasakah
Dayr az Zawr
Al Mayādīn
Abū Kamāl
Tall 'Afar
Al Mawşil (Mosul)
Arbīl
Kirkūk
As Sulaymānīyah
Tikrīt
Baghdad
As Şuwayrah
Al Ḥadīthah
Tabrīz
Orūmīyeh
Daryācheh-ye Orūmīyeh (L. Urmia)
Khvoy
Marand
Ardabīl
Mīāneh
Zanjān
Mahābād
Saqqez
Sanandaj
Hamadān
Bakhtarān
Khorramābād
Īlām
Bandar-e Anzali
Lenkoran
ĀZARBAYJĀN-E SHARQĪ
ĀZARBAYJĀN-E GHARBĪ
ZANJĀN
KORDESTĀN
HAMADĀN
BAKHTARĀN
LORESTĀN
ĪLĀM
GĪLĀN
Agri Daği (Ararat) 5165
Elbrus 5633
5203
Kazbek 5047
4492
Bazar Dyuzi 4466
Babadag 3629
3937
3063
Keban Baraji
Atatürk Baraji
East from Greenwich
COPYRIGHT GEORGE PHILIP LTD.

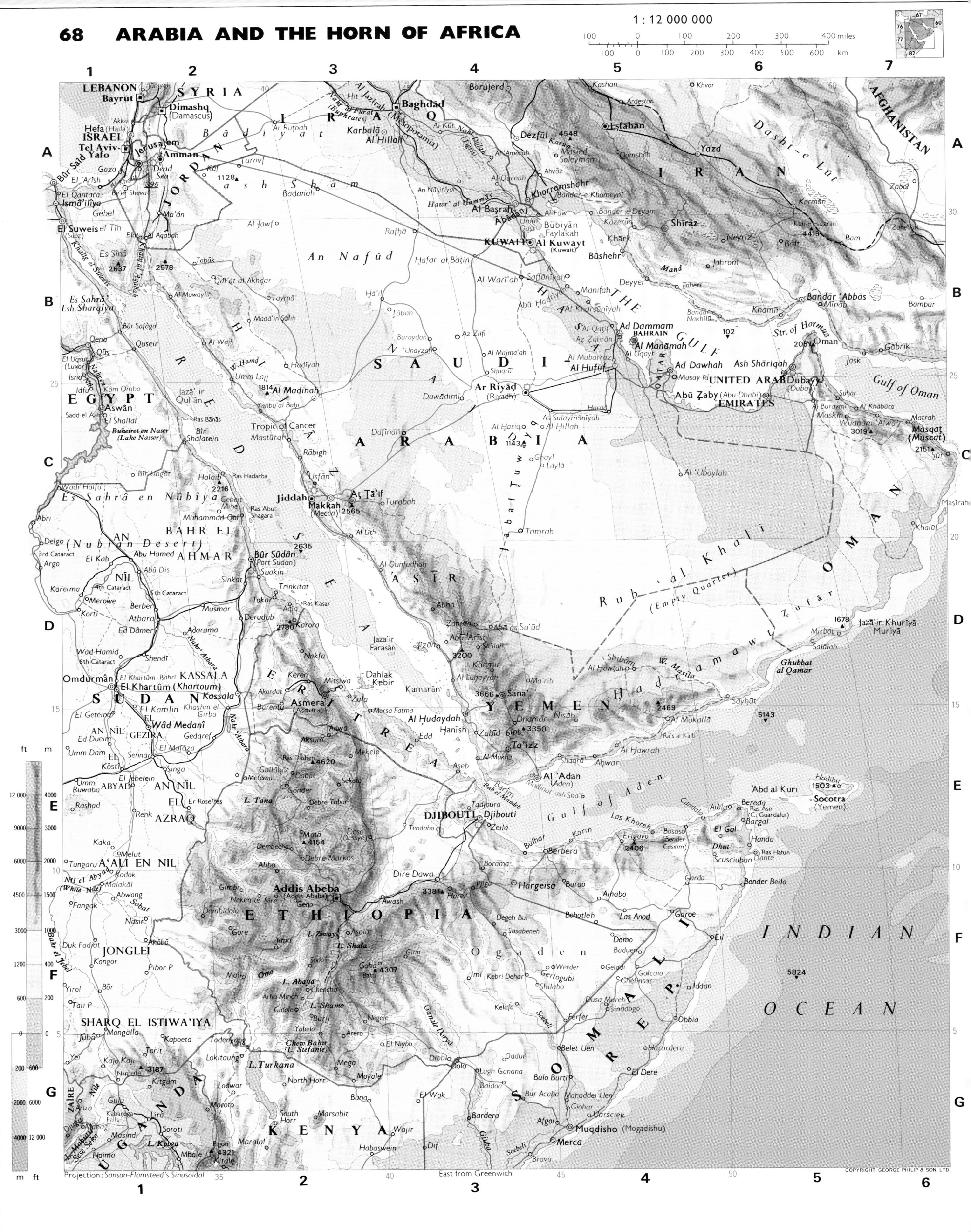
1 : 12 000 000
400 miles
km
LEBANON
Bayrūt
SYRIA
Dimashq
(Damascus)
ISRAEL
Tel Aviv-Yafo
Jerusalem
Amman
JORDAN
Bādiyat ash Shām
IRAQ
Baghdād
Karbalā
Al Hillah
Mesopotamia
Al Başrah
Ābādān
KUWAIT
Al Kuwayt
IRAN
Eşfahān
Yazd
Dasht-e Lūt
Shīrāz
Kermān
Bandar 'Abbās
AFGHANISTAN
An Nafūd
SAUDI ARABIA
Ar Riyāḑ
Al Madīnah
Makkah
(Mecca)
Jiddah
Aţ Ţā'if
Tropic of Cancer
THE GULF
Ad Dammam
BAHRAIN
Al Manāmah
QATAR
Ad Dawhah
UNITED ARAB EMIRATES
Abū Ẓaby
Dubayy
Str. of Hormuz
Gulf of Oman
Masqaţ
(Muscat)
OMAN
Rub 'al Khali
(Empty Quarter)
Ẓufār
Ḩaḑramawt
YEMEN
Sana'
Al Ḩudaydah
Ta'izz
Al 'Adan
(Aden)
Gulf of Aden
Socotra
(Yemen)
EGYPT
Aswân
Buheiret en Naser
(Lake Nasser)
Bûr Sa'îd
El Suweis
RED SEA
BAHR EL AHMAR
Bûr Sûdân
(Port Sudan)
Es Sahrâ en Nûbîya
(Nubian Desert)
SUDAN
Omdurmân
El Khartûm (Khartoum)
Kassala
Wâd Medanî
ERITREA
Asmera
(Asmara)
DJIBOUTI
Djibouti
Bab el Mandeb
ETHIOPIA
Addis Abeba
L. Tana
Dire Dawa
Hargeisa
Ogaden
SOMALI REP.
Muqdisho (Mogadishu)
Merca
L. Turkana
KENYA
UGANDA
ZAIRE
INDIAN OCEAN
Projection: Sanson-Flamsteed's Sinusoidal
East from Greenwich
COPYRIGHT. GEORGE PHILIP & SON. LTD.

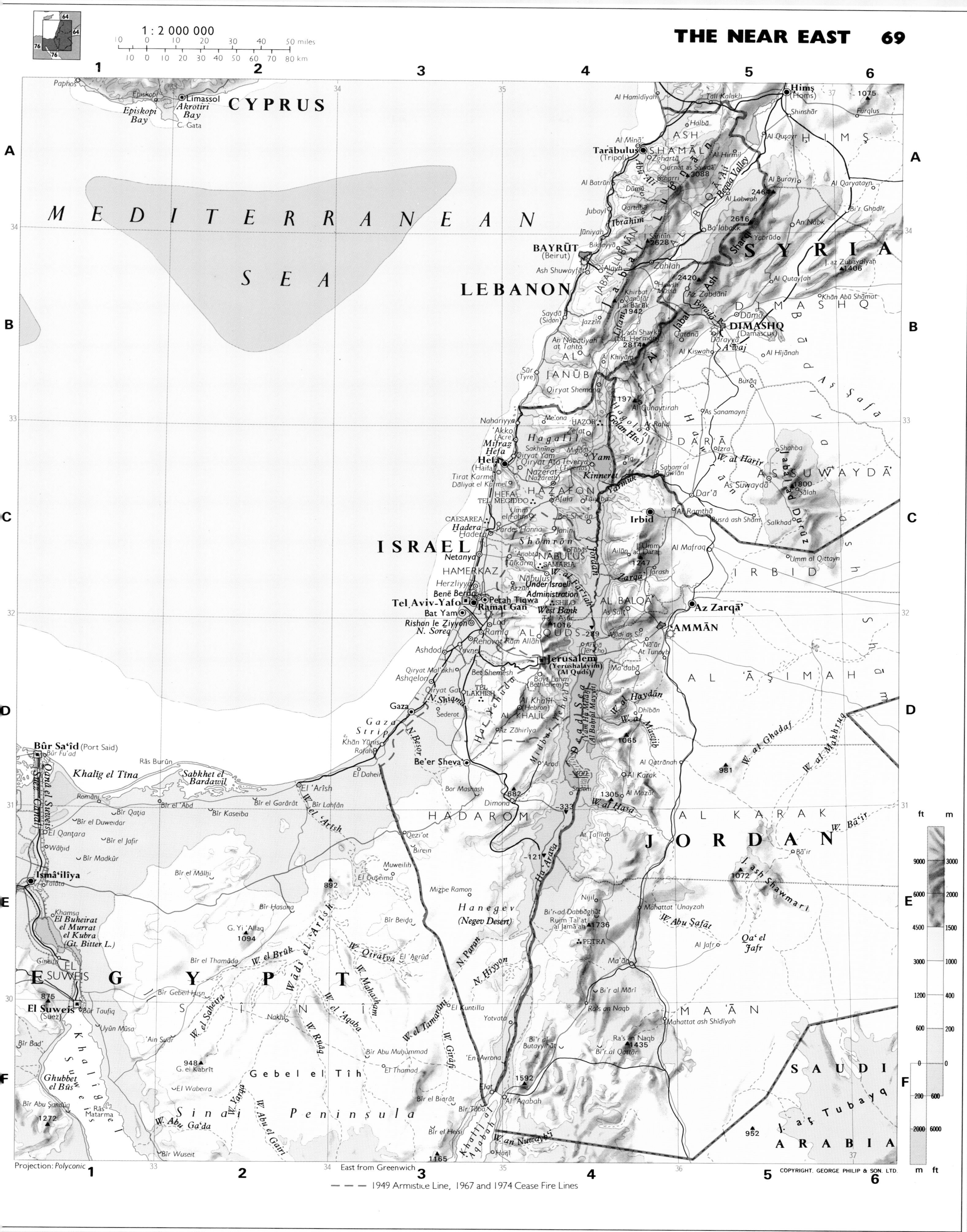
1 : 2 000 000
10 0 10 20 30 40 50 miles
10 0 10 20 30 40 50 60 70 80 km
CYPRUS
Paphos
Episkopi
Limassol
Episkopi Bay
Akrotiri Bay
C. Gata
MEDITERRANEAN
SEA
LEBANON
ISRAEL
SYRIA
JORDAN
EGYPT
SAUDI ARABIA
Ḩimş (Homs)
Ţarābulus (Tripoli)
BAYRŪT (Beirut)
Şaydā (Sidon)
Şūr (Tyre)
DIMASHQ (Damascus)
Nahariyya
'Akko (Acre)
Hefa (Haifa)
Tiberias
Kinneret
Yam Kinneret
Netanya
Herzliyya
Tel Aviv-Yafo
Petah Tiqwa
Ramat Gan
Bat Yam
Rishon le Ziyyon
Ashdod
Ashqelon
Gaza
Gaza Strip
Khān Yūnis
Rafah
Be'er Sheva
Dimona
Jerusalem (Yerushalayim) (Al Quds)
Bayt Lahm (Bethlehem)
Al Khalīl (Hebron)
Nābulus
Under Israeli Administration
West Bank
Jordan
Dead Sea
Irbid
Az Zarqā'
AMMĀN
Ma'dabā
Al Karak
Aţ Ţafīlah
PETRA
Ma'ān
Al 'Aqabah
Elat
Bûr Sa'îd (Port Said)
Ismâ'ilîya
El Suweis (Suez)
Suez Canal
El Buheirat el Murrat el Kubra (Gt. Bitter L.)
Khalîg el Tîna
Sabkhet el Bardawîl
El 'Arîsh
Hanegev (Negev Desert)
Gebel el Tîh
Sinai Peninsula
Khalîg el Suweis
Khalīj al 'Aqabah
Golan Hts.
Nahr al Litani
Jabal Lubnān
Jabal ash Sharqī
Jabal ad Durūz
Projection: Polyconic
East from Greenwich
— — — 1949 Armistice Line, 1967 and 1974 Cease Fire Lines
COPYRIGHT. GEORGE PHILIP & SON. LTD.

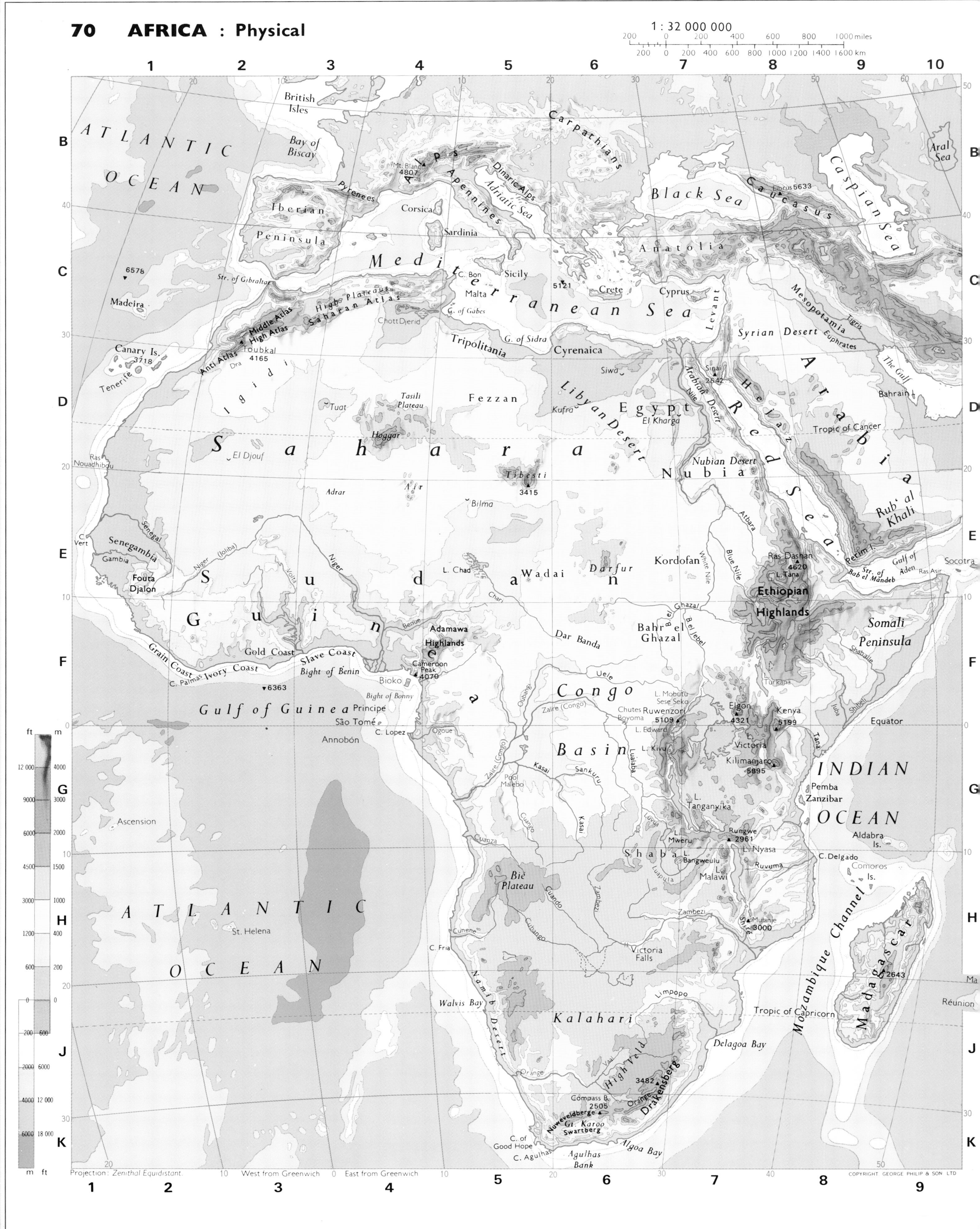
1 : 32 000 000
ATLANTIC OCEAN
British Isles
Bay of Biscay
Carpathians
Aral Sea
Caspian Sea
Mt. Blanc 4807
Alps
Dinaric Alps
Apennines
Adriatic Sea
Black Sea
Elbrus 5633
Caucasus
Pyrenees
Iberian Peninsula
Corsica
Sardinia
Anatolia
Mediterranean Sea
6576
Madeira
Str. of Gibraltar
High Plateaus
Saharan Atlas
Middle Atlas
High Atlas
Anti Atlas
Toubkal 4165
C. Bon
Sicily
Malta
5121
Crete
Cyprus
Levant
Mesopotamia
Tigris
Euphrates
G. of Gabes
Chott Djerid
G. of Sidra
Tripolitania
Cyrenaica
Syrian Desert
Canary Is.
3718
Tenerife
Dra
Igidi
Siwa
Sinai 2642
Arabian Desert
Nile
Hejaz
Arabia
The Gulf
Bahrain
Tuat
Tasili Plateau
Fezzan
Libyan Desert
Egypt
Kufra
El Kharga
Red Sea
Tropic of Cancer
Hoggar
Sahara
El Djouf
Ras Nouadhibou
Tibesti 3415
Nubian Desert
Nubia
Adrar
Air
Bilma
Rub' al Khali
Atbara
C. Vert
Senegal
Senegambia
Gambia
Fouta Djalon
Niger (Joliba)
Volta
Niger
L. Chad
Wadai
Darfur
Kordofan
White Nile
Blue Nile
Ras Dashan 4620
L. Tana
Ethiopian Highlands
Perim I.
Str. of Bab el Mandeb
Gulf of Aden
Socotra
Ras Asir
Sudan
Guinea
Chari
Benue
Adamawa Highlands
Bel Ghazal
Bahr el Ghazal
Bel Jebel
Dar Banda
Somali Peninsula
Shabelle
Grain Coast
Gold Coast
Slave Coast
Ivory Coast
C. Palmas
Bight of Benin
Cameroon Peak 4070
Bioko
6363
Bight of Bonny
Uele
Congo
L. Mobutu Sese Seko
Turkana
Gulf of Guinea
Principe
São Tomé
Annobón
C. Lopez
Ogoue
Oubangi
Zaire (Congo)
Chutes Boyoma
Ruwenzori 5109
L. Edward
Elgon 4321
Kenya 5199
Juba
Equator
Basin
Lualaba
L. Kivu
Victoria
Kilimanjaro 5895
Tana
INDIAN OCEAN
Kasai
Sankuru
Pool Malebo
Zaire (Congo)
L. Tanganyika
Pemba
Zanzibar
Ascension
Cuango
Luvua
Rungwe 2961
L. Mweru
Aldabra Is.
Cuanza
Shaba
L. Bangweulu
L. Nyasa
L. Malawi
Luapula
Ruvuma
C. Delgado
Comoros Is.
Bié Plateau
Cuando
Zambezi
Mozambique Channel
Madagascar
ATLANTIC OCEAN
St. Helena
Cunene
Cubango
Zambezi
Mulanje 3000
C. Fria
Victoria Falls
2643
Namib Desert
Walvis Bay
Limpopo
Kalahari
Tropic of Capricorn
Réunion
Delagoa Bay
Vaal
Highveld
Drakensberg
3482
Orange
Compass B. 2505
Nuweveldberge
Gt. Karoo
Swartberg
C. of Good Hope
C. Agulhas
Agulhas Bank
Algoa Bay
Projection: Zenithal Equidistant.
West from Greenwich
East from Greenwich
COPYRIGHT GEORGE PHILIP & SON LTD

1 : 32 000 000

200 0 200 400 600 800 1000 miles

200 0 200 400 600 800 1000 1200 1400 1600 km

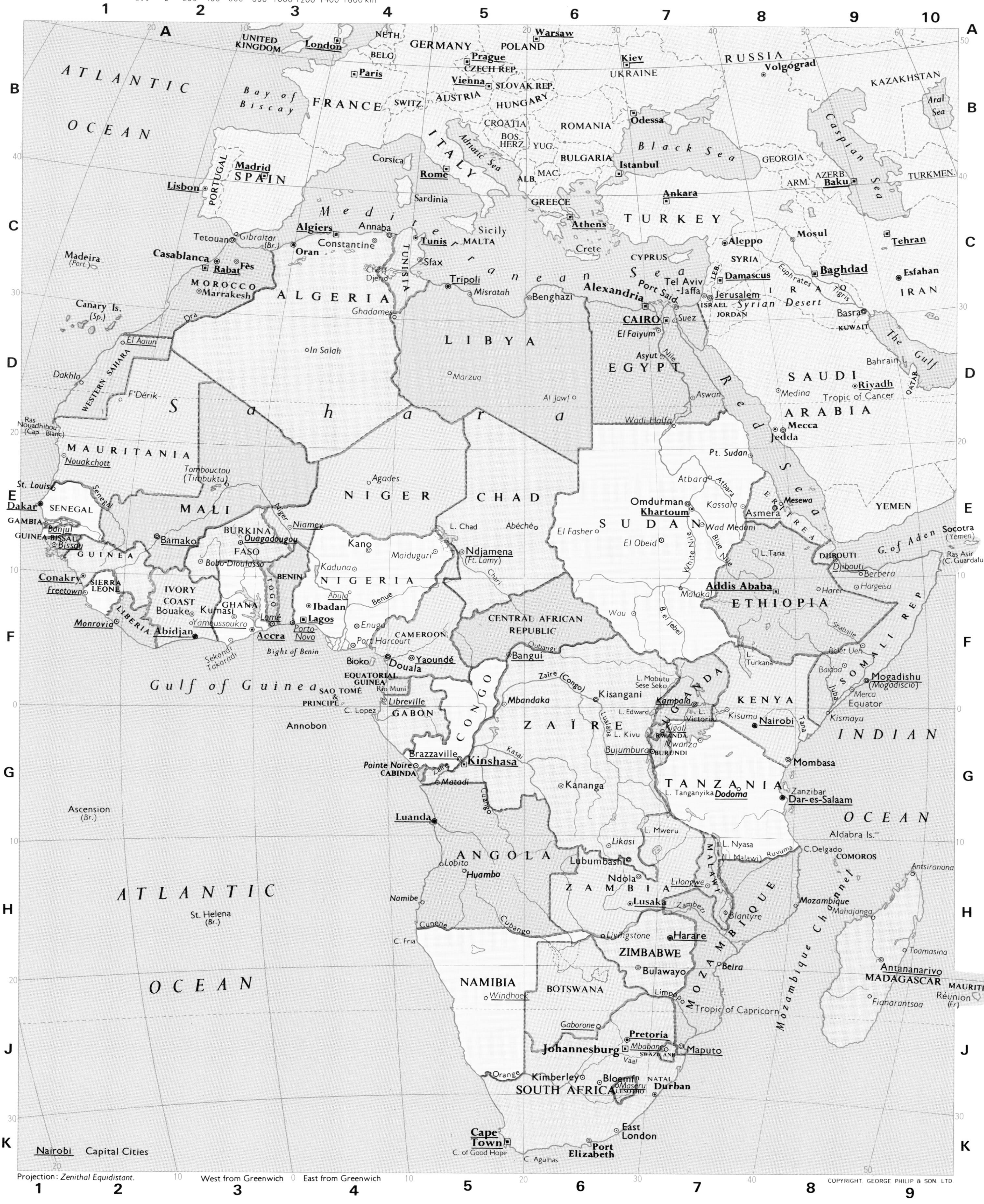

ATLANTIC OCEAN
Bay of Biscay
UNITED KINGDOM
London
NETH.
BELG.
Paris
FRANCE
GERMANY
POLAND
Warsaw
Prague
CZECH REP.
Vienna
SLOVAK REP.
AUSTRIA
SWITZ.
HUNGARY
Kiev
UKRAINE
RUSSIA
Volgograd
KAZAKHSTAN
Aral Sea
Caspian Sea
Odessa
ROMANIA
CROATIA
BOS.-HERZ.
YUG.
BULGARIA
Black Sea
Istanbul
GEORGIA
ARM.
AZERB.
Baku
TURKMEN.
ITALY
Adriatic Sea
Corsica
Rome
Sardinia
ALB.
MAC.
GREECE
Athens
Ankara
TURKEY
Madrid
SPAIN
PORTUGAL
Lisbon
Mediterranean Sea
Sicily
MALTA
Crete
CYPRUS
LEB.
SYRIA
Aleppo
Mosul
Tehran
Damascus
Baghdad
Esfahan
IRAN
Tel Aviv-Jaffa
Jerusalem
ISRAEL
JORDAN
Syrian Desert
IRAQ
Euphrates
Tigris
Basra
KUWAIT
The Gulf
Bahrain I.
QATAR
Riyadh
SAUDI ARABIA
Medina
Tropic of Cancer
Mecca
Jedda
YEMEN
Red Sea
Madeira (Port.)
Canary Is. (Sp.)
Tetouan
Gibraltar (Br.)
Algiers
Annaba
Tunis
Oran
Constantine
Casablanca
Rabat
Fès
MOROCCO
Marrakesh
Sfax
Chott Djerid
TUNISIA
Tripoli
Misratah
Benghazi
Alexandria
Port Said
Suez
CAIRO
El Faiyum
Asyut
Nile
ALGERIA
Ghadames
Dra
El Aaiun
In Salah
LIBYA
EGYPT
Dakhla
WESTERN SAHARA
F'Dérik
Marzuq
Al Jawf
Aswan
Wadi-Halfa
Sahara
Ras Nouadhibou (Cap Blanc)
MAURITANIA
Nouakchott
Tombouctou (Timbuktu)
Agades
Pt. Sudan
Atbara
Atbara
Kassala
Mesewa
ERITREA
Asmera
St. Louis
Senegal
Dakar
SENEGAL
GAMBIA
Banjul
GUINEA-BISSAU
Bissau
GUINEA
MALI
Niger
Niamey
NIGER
CHAD
Omdurman
Khartoum
SUDAN
Wad Medani
El Fasher
El Obeid
Abéché
L. Chad
Blue Nile
White Nile
L. Tana
DJIBOUTI
Djibouti
G. of Aden
Socotra (Yemen)
Ras Asir (C. Guardafui)
Berbera
Hargeisa
Harer
BURKINA FASO
Ouagadougou
Bamako
Bobo-Dioulasso
Kano
Maiduguri
Ndjamena (Ft. Lamy)
Chari
Kaduna
NIGERIA
BENIN
TOGO
Conakry
Freetown
SIERRA LEONE
IVORY COAST
Bouake
Kumasi
GHANA
Abuja
Benue
Ibadan
Lagos
Porto Novo
Lomé
Accra
Yamoussoukro
Abidjan
LIBERIA
Monrovia
Sekondi Takoradi
Bight of Benin
Enugu
Port Harcourt
CAMEROON
Malakal
Addis Ababa
ETHIOPIA
Wau
Bei Jebel
CENTRAL AFRICAN REPUBLIC
Ubangi
Bangui
Shaballe
SOMALI REP.
Belet Uen
Baidoa
Juba
Mogadishu (Mogadiscio)
Merca
Gulf of Guinea
Bioko
Douala
Yaoundé
EQUATORIAL GUINEA
Rio Muni
SAO TOMÉ & PRINCIPE
Libreville
GABON
C. Lopez
Annobon
CONGO
Mbandaka
Zaire (Congo)
Kisangani
L. Mobutu Sese Seko
L. Turkana
UGANDA
Kampala
L. Edward
L. Victoria
KENYA
Kisumu
Nairobi
Tana
Equator
Kismayu
INDIAN OCEAN
ZAÏRE
Lualaba
L. Kivu
Kigali
RWANDA
Mwanza
Bujumbura
BURUNDI
Kasai
Brazzaville
Kinshasa
Pointe Noire
CABINDA
Zaire
Matadi
Kananga
Cuango
Mombasa
TANZANIA
L. Tanganyika
Dodoma
Zanzibar
Dar-es-Salaam
Luanda
Ascension (Br.)
L. Mweru
Likasi
Lubumbashi
L. Nyasa (L. Malawi)
Ruvuma
MALAWI
C. Delgado
COMOROS
Aldabra Is.
Antsiranana
ANGOLA
Lobito
Huambo
Ndola
ZAMBIA
Lilongwe
Lusaka
Zambezi
Blantyre
MOZAMBIQUE
Mozambique
Mahajanga
Mozambique Channel
ATLANTIC OCEAN
Namibe
St. Helena (Br.)
Cunene
Cubango
Livingstone
Harare
C. Fria
ZIMBABWE
Bulawayo
Beira
Toamasina
Antananarivo
MADAGASCAR
MAURITIUS
Réunion (Fr.)
Fianarantsoa
NAMIBIA
Windhoek
BOTSWANA
Limpopo
Tropic of Capricorn
Gaborone
Pretoria
Johannesburg
Mbabane
SWAZILAND
Maputo
Vaal
Orange
Kimberley
Bloemfn
Maseru
LESOTHO
NATAL
Durban
SOUTH AFRICA
East London
Cape Town
C. of Good Hope
C. Agulhas
Port Elizabeth

Nairobi Capital Cities

Projection: *Zenithal Equidistant.*

West from Greenwich East from Greenwich

COPYRIGHT. GEORGE PHILIP & SON. LTD

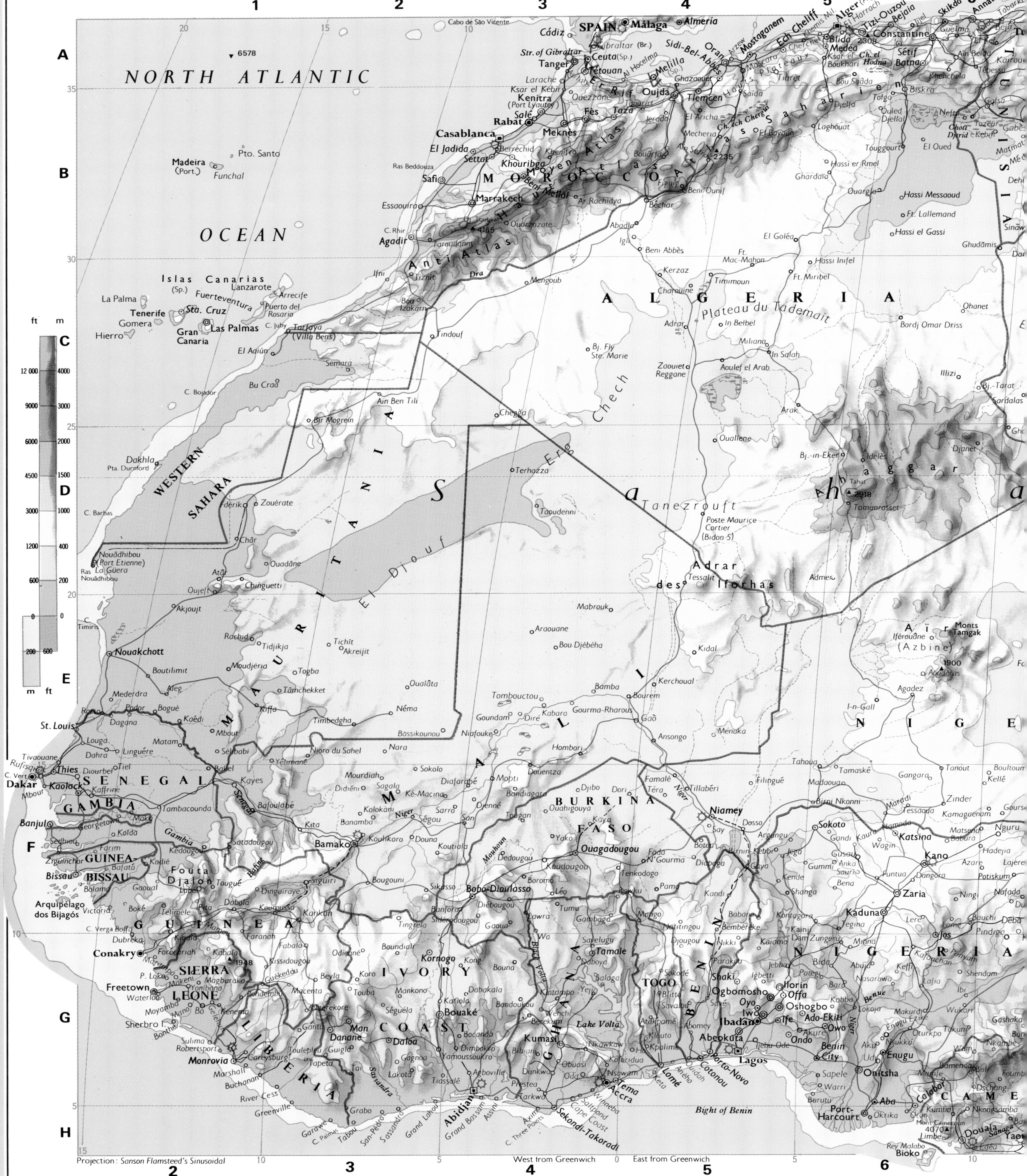

NORTH ATLANTIC OCEAN

Madeira (Port.)
Pto. Santo
Funchal
Islas Canarias (Sp.)
Lanzarote
Fuerteventura
La Palma
Tenerife
Gomera
Hierro
Sta. Cruz
Gran Canaria
Las Palmas
Arrecife
Puerto del Rosario

SPAIN
Málaga
Almería
Cádiz
Str. of Gibraltar
Gibraltar (Br.)
Ceuta (Sp.)
Melilla (Sp.)
Tanger
Tétouan
Larache
Ksar el Kebir
Kenitra (Port Lyautey)
Salé
Rabat
Casablanca
El Jadida
Settat
Safi
Essaouira
Marrakech
Agadir
Fès
Meknès
Taza
Oujda
Khouribga
Beni Mellal
Ar Rachidiya
Tiznit
Ifni
Tarfaya (Villa Bens)
El Aaiún
Semara
Bu Craa
C. Bojador
Dakhla
WESTERN SAHARA
C. Barbas
MOROCCO
Er Rif
Moyen Atlas
Haut Atlas
Anti Atlas

ALGERIA
Oran
Mostaganem
Ech Cheliff
Alger (Algiers)
Blida
Médéa
Tizi-Ouzou
Bejaia
Skikda
Annaba
Constantine
Sétif
Batna
Biskra
Sidi-Bel-Abbès
Tlemcen
Saïda
Tiaret
Laghouat
Ghardaïa
Ouargla
Touggourt
El Oued
Hassi Messaoud
Béchar
Beni Abbès
El Goléa
Timimoun
Adrar
In Salah
Reggane
Tindouf
Plateau du Tademait
Hoggar
Tamanrasset
Djanet
Illizi
Tanezrouft
Erg Chech
Bordj Omar Driss

MAURITANIA
Nouâdhibou (Port Etienne)
Atâr
Chinguetti
Akjoujt
Nouakchott
Rosso
Kiffa
Tidjikja
Néma
Zouérate
Fdérik
El Djouf

MALI
Taoudenni
Tombouctou
Gao
Kidal
Adrar des Iforhas
Mopti
Ségou
Bamako
Kayes
Sikasso

NIGER
Agadez
Aïr
Niamey
Zinder
Maradi
Tahoua

SENEGAL
St. Louis
Dakar
Thies
Kaolack
Tambacounda
GAMBIA
Banjul
GUINEA-BISSAU
Bissau
Arquipélago dos Bijagós
GUINEA
Conakry
Fouta Djalon
SIERRA LEONE
Freetown
LIBERIA
Monrovia
IVORY COAST
Abidjan
Bouaké
BURKINA FASO
Ouagadougou
Bobo-Dioulasso
GHANA
Kumasi
Lake Volta
Accra
Sekondi-Takoradi
TOGO
Lomé
BENIN
Cotonou
Porto-Novo
NIGERIA
Lagos
Ibadan
Kano
Kaduna
Zaria
Jos
Enugu
Port-Harcourt
Bight of Benin
CAMEROON
Douala
Bioko
TUNISIA

Projection: Sanson Flamsteed's Sinusoidal
West from Greenwich
East from Greenwich

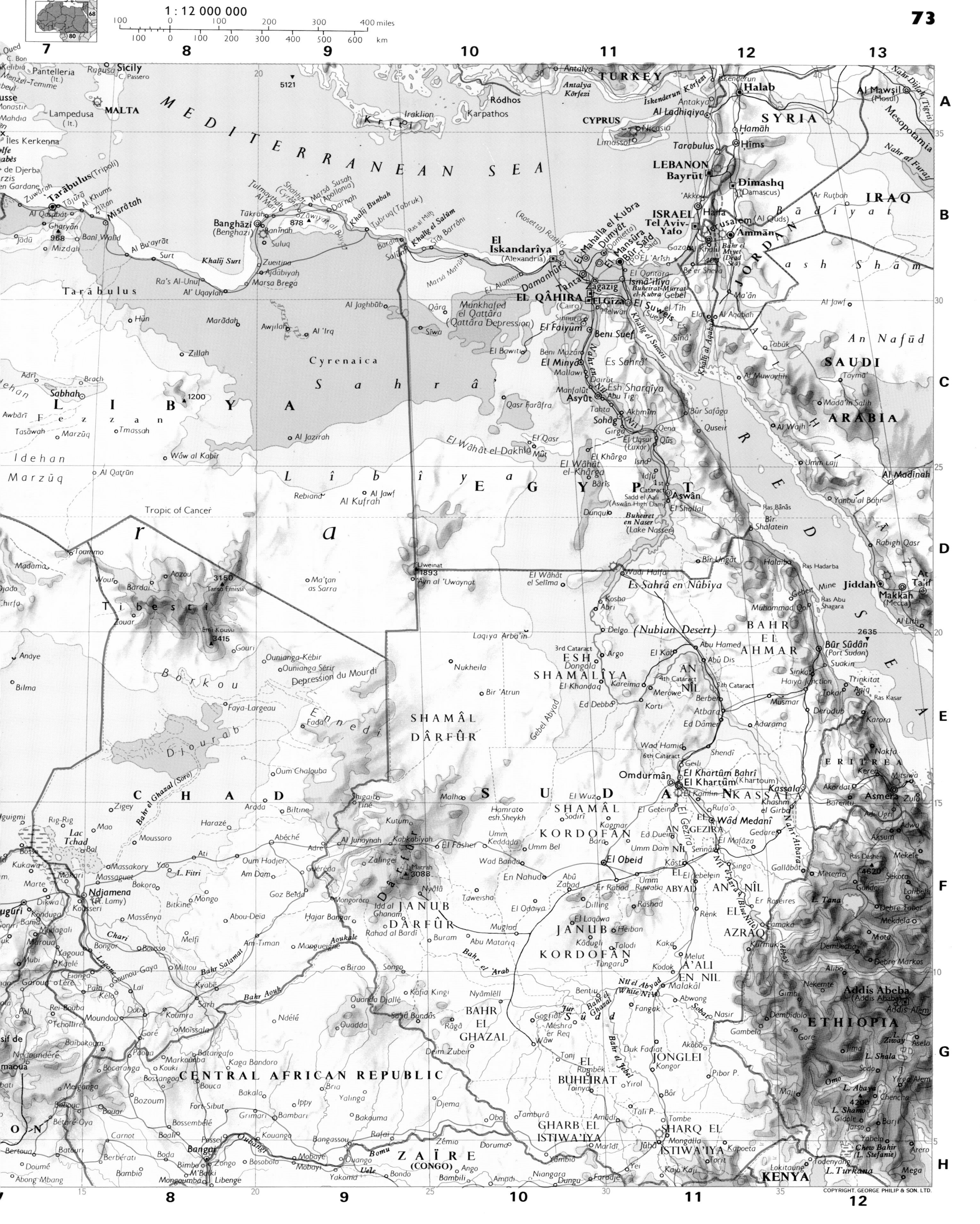
1 : 12 000 000
100 0 100 200 300 400 miles
100 0 100 200 300 400 500 600 km
7
8
9
10
11
12
13
A
B
C
D
E
F
G
H
MEDITERRANEAN SEA
TURKEY
CYPRUS
SYRIA
LEBANON
ISRAEL
JORDAN
IRAQ
SAUDI ARABIA
MALTA
LIBYA
EGYPT
SUDAN
CHAD
CENTRAL AFRICAN REPUBLIC
ZAÏRE (CONGO)
ETHIOPIA
ERITREA
KENYA
RED SEA
Sicily
Pantelleria (It.)
Lampedusa (It.)
Rhodos
Kriti
Iraklion
Karpathos
Antalya
Antalya Körfezi
Iskenderun Körfezi
Iskenderun
Antakya
Halab
Al Ladhiqiya
Hamāh
Hims
Tarabulus
Nicosia
Limassol
Bayrūt
Dimashq (Damascus)
'Akko
Haifa
Tel Aviv-Yafo
Jerusalem (Al Quds)
'Ammān
Al Mawsil (Mosul)
Mesopotamia
Nahr Dijlah (Tigris)
Nahr al Furat
Bādiyat ash Shām
Ar Rutbah
Al Jawf
An Nafūd
Tabūk
Taymā'
Al Muwaylih
Madā'in Salih
Al Wajh
Umm Lajj
Al Madinah
Yanbu' al Bahr
Rabigh
Qasr
Jiddah
Makkah (Mecca)
At Ta'if
Al Lith
Tarābulus (Tripoli)
Misrātah
Al Khums
Zuwārah
Gharyān
Mizdah
Banī Walīd
Khalīj Surt
Surt
Al Bu'ayrāt
Ra's Al-Unuf
Al' Uqaylah
Marsa Brega
Ajdābiyah
Zueitina
Suluq
Banghāzī (Benghazi)
Tulmaythah
Al Marj
Shahhāt (Cyrene)
Marsá Susah (Apollonia)
Darnah
Tubruq (Tobruk)
Khalīj Bunbah
Tūkrah
Bardia
Salûm
Khalîg el Salûm
Sîdi Barrâni
Marsa Matrûh
El Alamein
El Iskandarîya (Alexandria)
Damanhûr
Tanta
El Mahalla el Kubra
Dumyât (Damietta)
El Mansûra
Bûr Sa'îd (Port Said)
El 'Arîsh
Ismâ'iliya
Zagazig
EL QÂHIRA (Cairo)
El Gîza
Helwân
El Suweis (Suez)
El Faiyûm
Beni Suef
El Minya
Mallawi
Asyût
Sohâg
Qena
Luxor
Aswân
Sadd el Aali (Aswân High Dam)
Buheiret en Naser (Lake Nasser)
Wadi Halfa
Es Sahrâ en Nûbiya
Es Sahrâ Esh Sharqîya
Sînâ'
Gulf of Aqaba
Al 'Aqabah
Ma'ān
Munkhafed el Qattâra (Qattâra Depression)
Sîwa
Qâra
Al Jaghbūb
El Bawiti
Qasr Farâfra
El Wâhât el-Dakhla
Mût
El Khârga
El Wâhât el-Khârga
Bârîs
Dunqul
Cyrenaica
Sahrâ' Lîbîya
Al Jawf
Al Kufrah
Rebiana
Uweinat 1893
'Ayn al 'Uwaynat
Tropic of Cancer
Sahara
Ma'tan as Sarra
Marādah
Awjilah
Al 'Irq
Hūn
Zillah
Sabhah
Fezzan
Ubari
Tasāwah
Marzūq
Tmassah
Al Jazirah
Wāw al Kabīr
Al Qatrūn
Idehan Marzūq
Tibesti
Aozou
Tarso Emissi 3150
Emi Koussi 3415
Bardai
Zouar
Gouri
Tummo
Madama
Borkou
Ounianga-Kébir
Ounianga Sérir
Depression du Mourdi
Faya-Largeau
Ennedi
Fada
Djourab
Oum Chalouba
Biltine
Arada
Abéché
Adré
Am Dam
Oum Hadjer
Lac Tchad
Ndjamena (Ft. Lamy)
Massakory
Massaguet
Bol
Mao
Moussoro
L. Fitri
Bokoro
Mongo
Bitkine
Abou-Deia
Am-Timan
Melfi
Goz Beïda
Chari
Bousso
Sarh
Koumra
Moïssala
Doba
Moundou
Laï
Kélo
Bahr Salamat
Bahr Aouk
Kyabé
Logone
Ndélé
Ouanda Djallé
Birao
Kaga Bandoro
Batangafo
Bouca
Bossangoa
Bozoum
Bouar
Bambari
Bakala
Ippy
Grimari
Fort Sibut
Bossembélé
Bangui
Mbaïki
Zongo
Kouango
Bangassou
Oubangi
Bomu
Uele
Bondo
Ango
Bambili
Mobaye
Rafai
Zémio
Obo
Doruma
Djema
Yalinga
Bakouma
Bria
Laqiya Arba'in
Nukheila
Bir 'Atrun
Delgo
(Nubian Desert)
ESH SHAMALÎYA
Dongola
Kareima
Merowe
Abu Hamed
Berber
Atbara
Ed Dâmer
Shendî
Ed Debba
Korti
El Khandaq
Gebel Abyad
SHAMÂL DÂRFÛR
Kutum
Kabkabiyah
El Fâsher
Jebel Marra 3088
Zalingei
Nyala
JANUB DÂRFÛR
Buram
Muglad
Abu Matariq
Bahr el 'Arab
SHAMÂL KORDOFÂN
El Obeid
Umm Ruwaba
Er Rahad
Dilling
Kâdugli
Talodi
JANUB KORDOFÂN
Tonga
Kodok
Malakâl
A'ALI EN NÎL
Nîl el Abyad (White Nile)
Kosti
Ed Dueim
El Gezira
Wad Medanî
Sennâr
Singa
Er Roseires
Kurmuk
Omdurmân
El Khartûm (Khartoum)
El Khartûm Bahrî
KASSALA
Kassala
El Girba
Nahr Atbara
BAHR EL AHMAR
Bûr Sûdân (Port Sudan)
Suakin
Tokar
Haiya Junction
Derudeb
Musmar
Sinkat
BAHR EL GHAZAL
Wâw
Rumbek
Deim Zubeir
Bahr el Jebel
JONGLEI
Bor
Akobo
Pibor P.
Sobat
Nasir
Fangak
EL BUHEIRAT
Yirol
GHARB EL ISTIWA'IYA
Tambura
Yambio
Maridi
SHARQ EL ISTIWA'IYA
Juba
Kapoeta
Torit
Kaja Kaji
Sudd
Asmera
Mitsiwa
Keren
Akordat
Adigrat
Aksum
Mekele
Gonder
L. Tana
Debre Tabor
Dessie
Debre Markos
Nekemte
Addis Abeba
Gimbi
Gambela
Gore
Jima
L. Ziway
L. Shala
L. Abaya
L. Shamo
Omo
Chew Bahir (L. Stefanie)
L. Turkana
Mega
Lokitaung
Ras Dashen 4620
4200
2635
Ras Kasar
Ras Abu Shagara
Ras Banâs
Bir Shalatein
Halaib
Gebeit Mine
Muhammad Qol

COPYRIGHT, GEORGE PHILIP & SON, LTD.

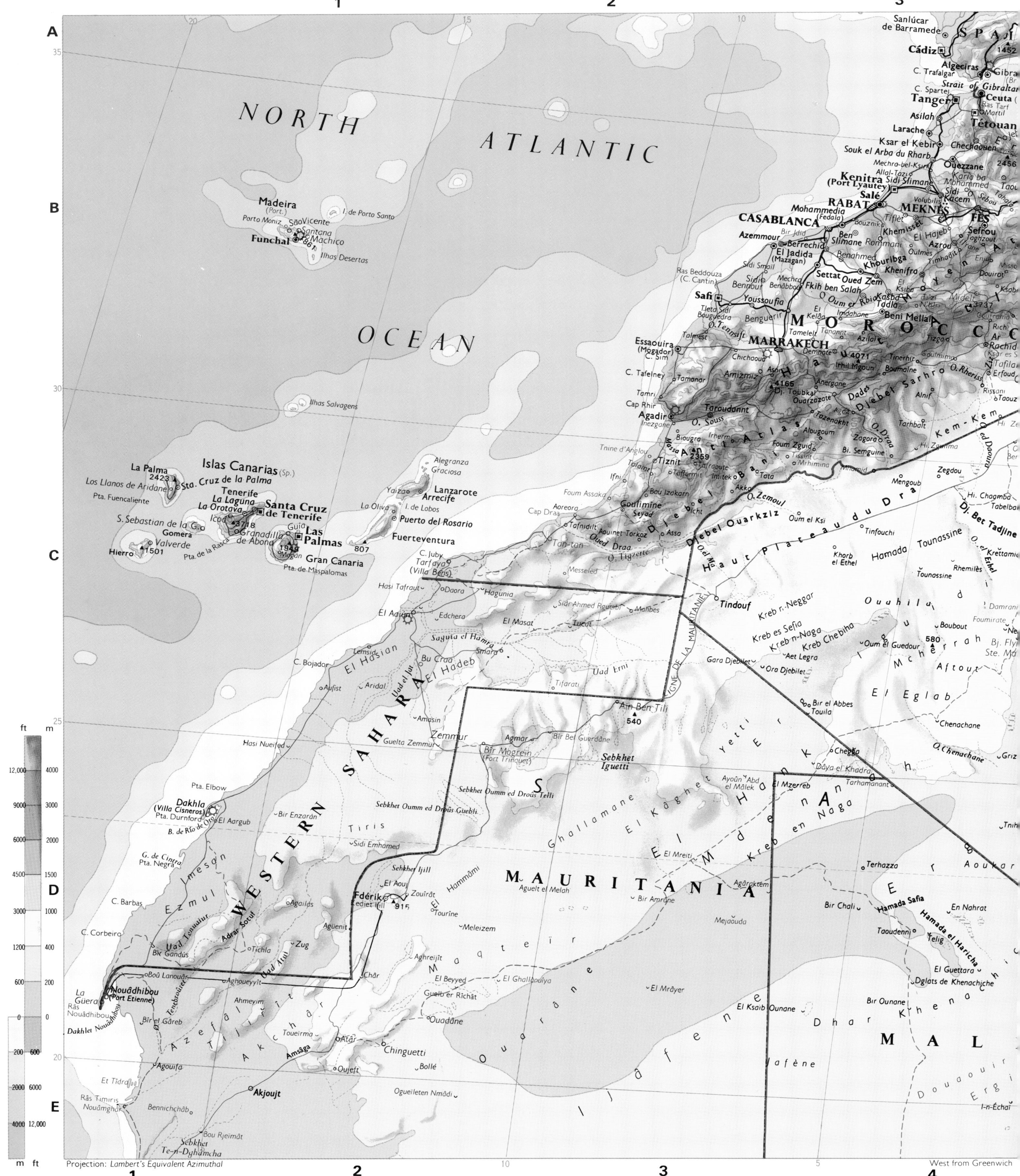
NORTH ATLANTIC
OCEAN
Madeira
(Port.)
Funchal
Islas Canarias (Sp.)
La Palma
Tenerife
Santa Cruz de Tenerife
Las Palmas
Gran Canaria
Gomera
Hierro
Lanzarote
Fuerteventura
Ilhas Salvagens
SPAIN
Cádiz
Tanger
Ceuta
Tétouan
Kenitra (Port Lyautey)
RABAT
Salé
CASABLANCA
MEKNES
FES
Safi
MARRAKECH
Essaouira (Mogador)
Agadir
MOROCCO
Tindouf
WESTERN SAHARA
El Aaiún
Dakhla (Villa Cisneros)
Nouâdhibou (Port Etienne)
MAURITANIA
Akjoujt
Atâr
Chinguetti
Fdérik
MALI
Taoudenni
Projection: Lambert's Equivalent Azimuthal
West from Greenwich

1 : 6 400 000

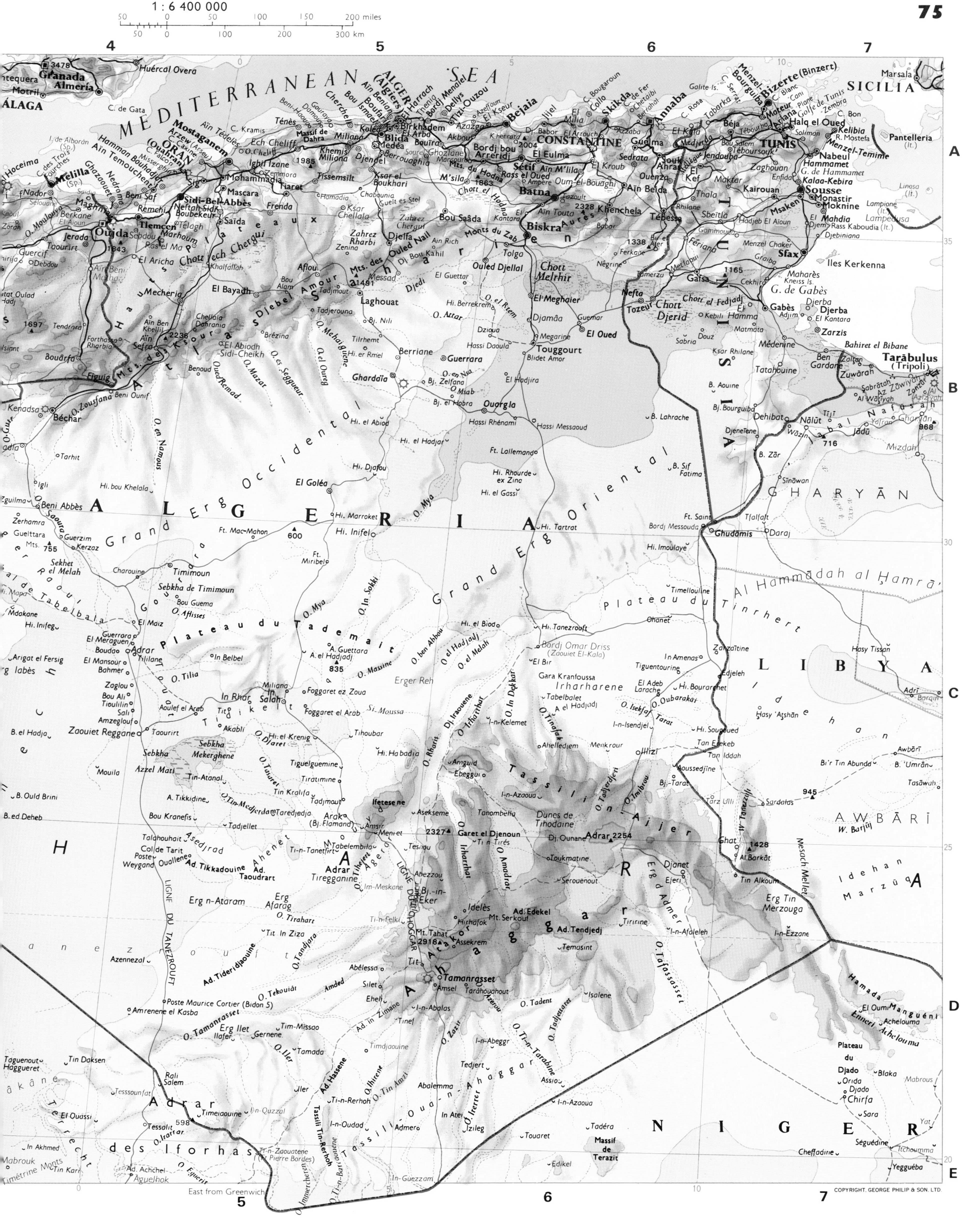
50 0 50 100 150 200 miles
50 0 100 200 300 km
4
5
6
7
A
B
C
D
E
MEDITERRANEAN SEA
SICILIA
ALGER (Algiers)
ORAN (Ouahran)
CONSTANTINE
TUNIS
Bizerte (Binzert)
Annaba
Skikda
Bejaia
Sétif
Batna
Biskra
Blida
Médéa
Mostaganem
Sidi-Bel-Abbès
Tlemcen
Oujda
Melilla
Granada
Almería
MÁLAGA
Sousse
Sfax
Gabès
Djerba
Kairouan
Tébessa
Gafsa
Tozeur
Nefta
Chott Djerid
Chott Melrhir
El Oued
Touggourt
Ouargla
Ghardaïa
Laghouat
El Goléa
Béchar
Timimoun
Adrar
In Salah
Tamanrasset
Djanet
Ghat
Ghudāmis
Ṭarābulus (Tripoli)
Zuwārah
Pantelleria
Iles Kerkenna
G. de Gabès
Hauts Plateaux
Atlas Saharien
Djebel Amour
Monts du Zab
Aurès
Grand Erg Occidental
Grand Erg Oriental
Plateau du Tademait
Plateau du Tinrhert
Al Ḥammādah al Ḥamrā'
Tassili n' Ajjer
Ahaggar
Erg Admer
Tanezrouft
Adrar des Iforhas
Tassili-Oua-n-Ahaggar
ALGERIA
TUNISIA
LIBYA
NIGER
GHARYĀN
AWBĀRĪ
Idehan Marzūq
Hamada Manguéni
Plateau du Djado
Massif de Terazit
Mt. Tahat 2918
Assekrem
Erg Tin Merzouga
LIGNE DU TANEZROUFT
LIGNE DU HOGGAR
East from Greenwich
COPYRIGHT. GEORGE PHILIP & SON. LTD.

1 : 6 400 000

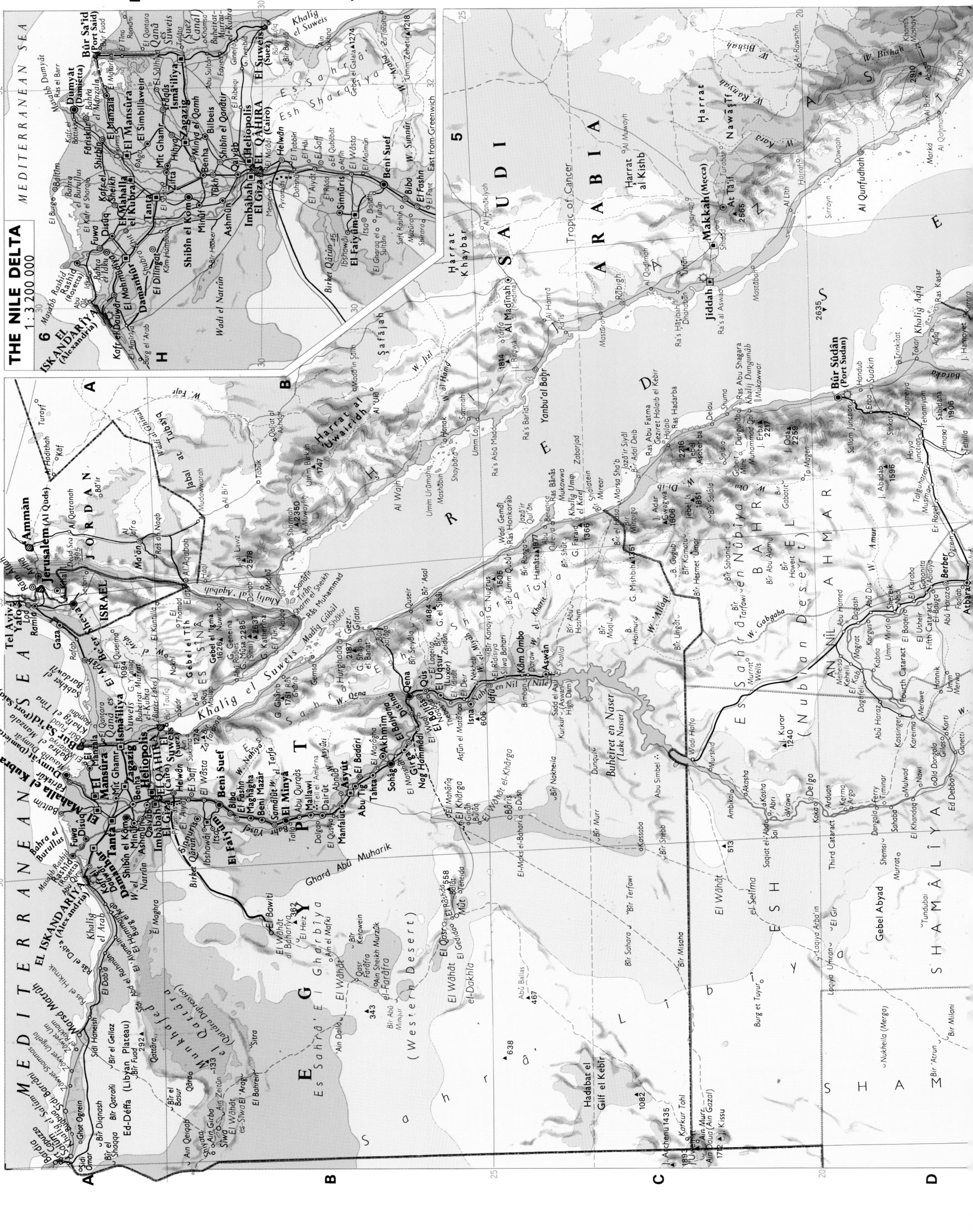

50 0 50 100 150 200 miles

50 0 100 200 300 km

THE NILE DELTA
1 : 3 200 000

East from Greenwich

SUDAN

ETHIOPIA

ERITREA

DJIBOUTI

KENYA

UGANDA

ZAÏRE

CENTRAL AFRICAN REPUBLIC

SOMALI REP.

YEMEN

SHAMÂL KORDOFÂN

JANUB KORDOFÂN

SHAMÂL DÂRFÛR

JANUB DÂRFÛR

KASSALÂ

EL KHARTÛM

EL GEZIRA

AN NIL EL AZRAQ

AN NIL EL ABYAD

A'ALI EN NIL

JONGLEI

BAHR EL GHAZAL

EL BUHEIRAT

GHARB EL ISTIWA'IYA

SHARQ EL ISTIWA'IYA

Sûdd

GONDER

GOJAM

WELEGA

SHEWA

WELO

TIGRAY

ILUBABOR

KEFA

ARSI

BALE

SIDAMO

GAMO GOFA

HARERGE

Danakil Desert

ADDIS ABEBA (Addis Ababa)

El Khartûm (Khartoum)

Omdurmân

ASMERA (Asmara)

Djibouti

L. Tana

L. Turkana (L. Rudolf)

ft	m
12,000	4000
9000	3000
6000	2000
4500	1500
3000	1000
1200	400
600	200
0	0
200	600
ft	m

Projection: Lambert's Equivalent Azimuthal

East from Greenwich

1 2 3 4 5

E F G

COPYRIGHT GEORGE PHILIP & SON LTD

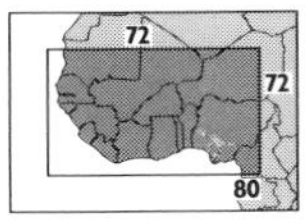

MAURITANIA

SENEGAL

GAMBIA

GUINEA-BISSAU

GUINEA

SIERRA LEONE

LIBERIA

IVORY COAST

Nouakchott

Akjoujt

St. Louis

DAKAR

Thiès

Kaolack

Banjul

Ziguinchor

Bissau

Arquipélago dos Bijagós

Conakry

Îles de Los

Freetown

Monrovia

Bamako

Ségou

Mopti

Tombouctou (Timbuktu)

Kayes

Kankan

Bouaké

Abidjan

Bobo-Dioulasso

Grain Coast

Ivory Coast

ft	m
12 000	4000
9000	3000
6000	2000
4500	1500
3000	1000
1200	400
600	200
0	0
600	200
6000	2000
12 000	4000
18 000	6000

Projection: Lambert's Equivalent Azimuthal

West from Gre[enwich]

1 : 6 400 000

50 0 50 100 150 200 miles

50 0 100 200 300 km

4 5 6 7

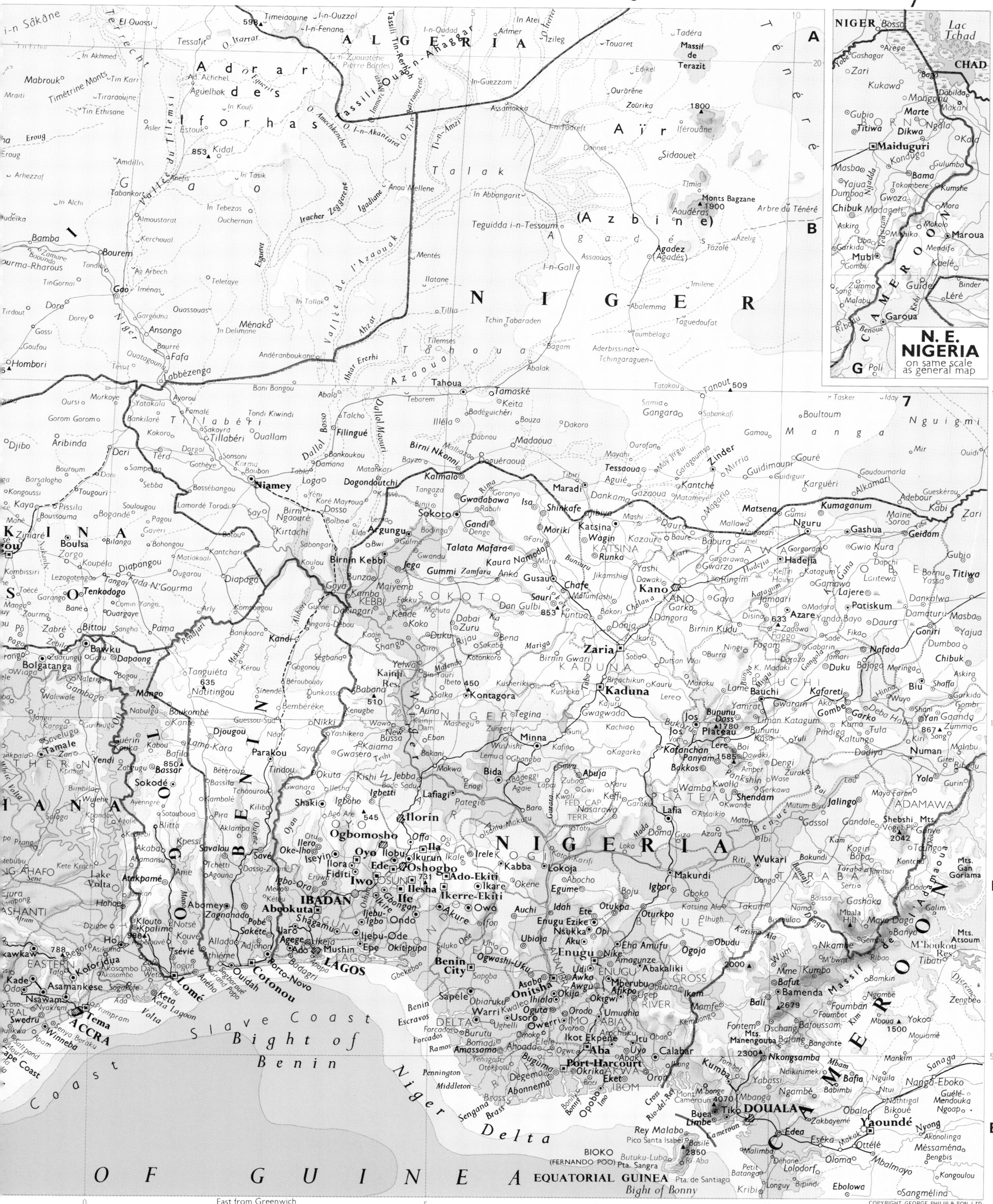

ALGERIA

NIGER

NIGERIA

CAMEROON

CHAD

Adrar des Iforhas

Aïr (Azbine)

Ténéré

Slave Coast

Bight of Benin

Niger Delta

GULF OF GUINEA

EQUATORIAL GUINEA

Bight of Bonny

BIOKO (FERNANDO POO)

N. E. NIGERIA

on same scale as general map

East from Greenwich

COPYRIGHT, GEORGE PHILIP & SON, LTD.

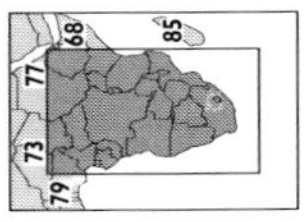

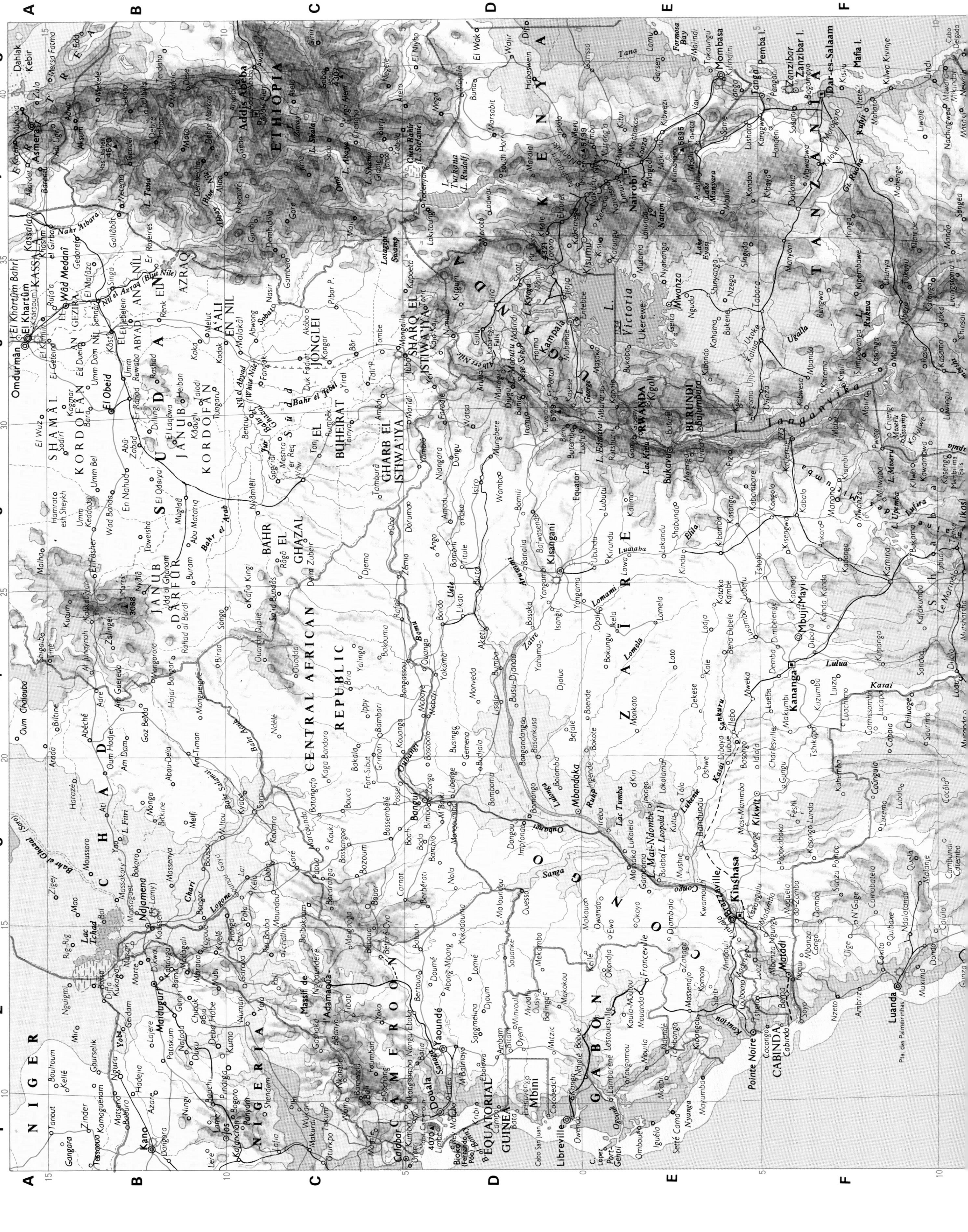

ETHIOPIA
Addis Abeba
Asmera
El Khartûm
Omdurmân
Kassala
Nairobi
Mombasa
Dar-es-Salaam
Kampala
Kigali
Bujumbura
Kinshasa
Brazzaville
Luanda
Libreville
Yaoundé
Douala
Bangui
Ndjamena
Kano
Maiduguri
Kisangani
Mbandaka
Kananga
Mbuji-Mayi
Pointe Noire
CABINDA
EQUATORIAL GUINEA
CENTRAL AFRICAN REPUBLIC
RWANDA
BURUNDI
L. Victoria
L. Tanganyika
Lac Tchad

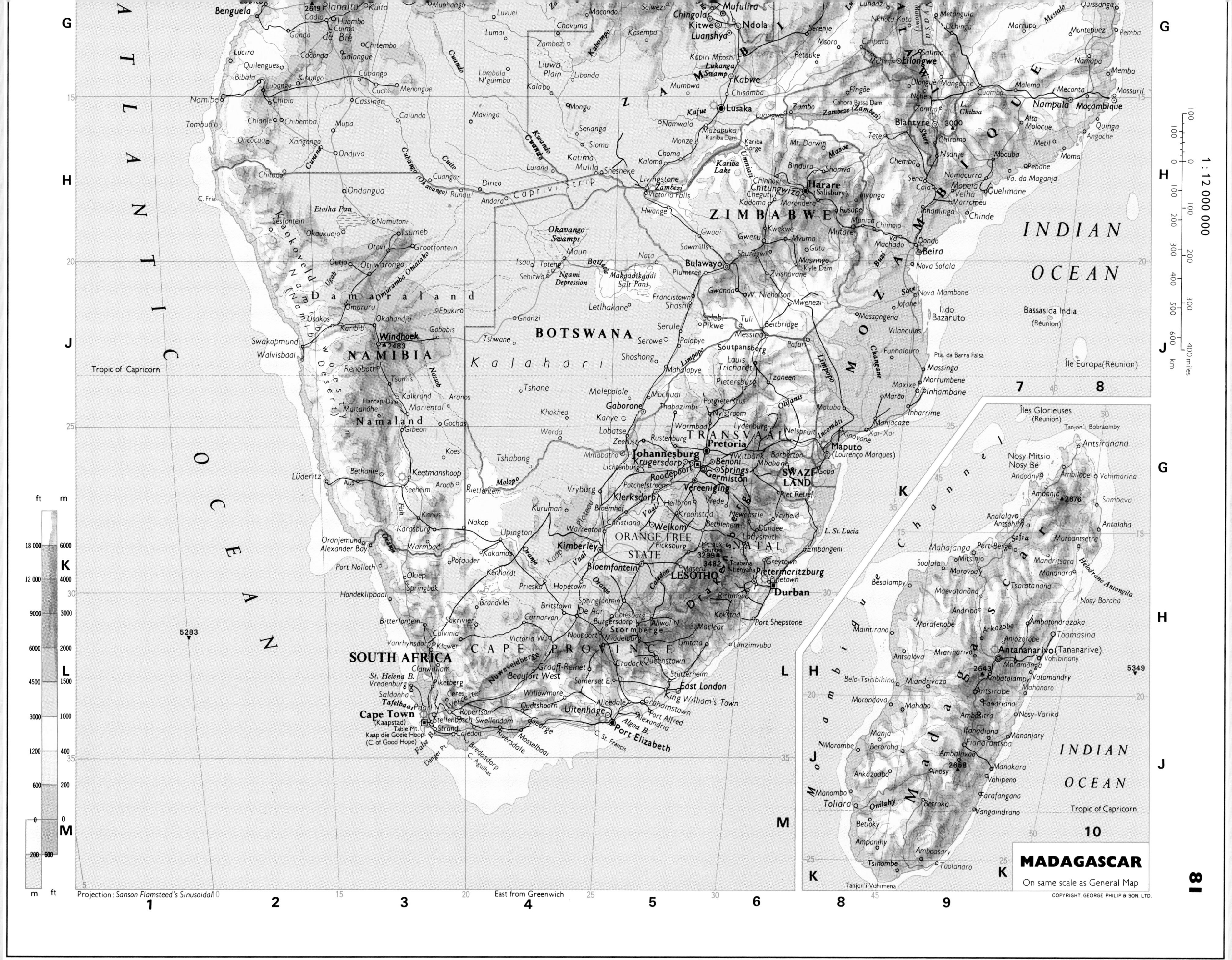

1 : 12 000 000
ATLANTIC OCEAN
INDIAN OCEAN
ZAMBIA
ZIMBABWE
MOZAMBIQUE
MALAWI
BOTSWANA
NAMIBIA
SOUTH AFRICA
TRANSVAAL
ORANGE FREE STATE
NATAL
LESOTHO
SWAZILAND
CAPE PROVINCE
Kalahari
Damaraland
Namaland
Caprivi Strip
Okavango Swamps
Makgadikgadi Salt Pans
Ngami Depression
Etosha Pan
Kaokoveld
Namib Desert
Mozambique Channel
Tropic of Capricorn
Lusaka
Harare (Salisbury)
Bulawayo
Gaborone
Windhoek
Pretoria
Johannesburg
Bloemfontein
Kimberley
Durban
Pietermaritzburg
Maputo (Lourenço Marques)
Beira
Blantyre
Lilongwe
Ndola
Kitwe
Cape Town (Kapstad)
Port Elizabeth
East London
Walvisbaai
Swakopmund
Lüderitz
Benguela
Bassas da India (Réunion)
Île Europa (Réunion)
Îles Glorieuses (Réunion)
Antananarivo (Tananarive)
Toamasina
Mahajanga
Antsiranana
Toliara
Taolanaro
MADAGASCAR
On same scale as General Map
Projection: Sanson Flamsteed's Sinusoidal
East from Greenwich
COPYRIGHT. GEORGE PHILIP & SON, LTD.

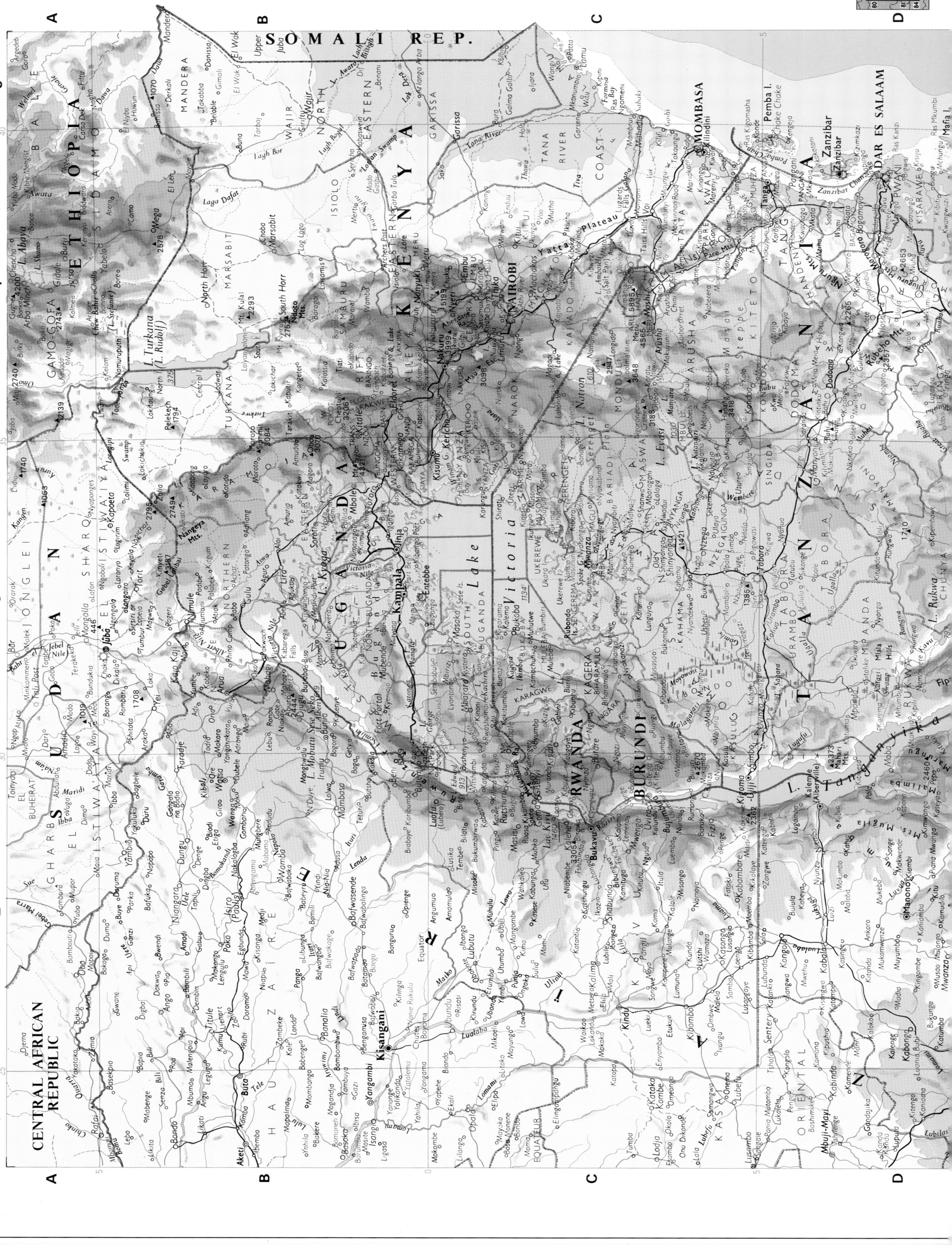

SOMALI REP.

ETHIOPIA

KENYA

UGANDA

SUDAN

TANZANIA

RWANDA

BURUNDI

CENTRAL AFRICAN REPUBLIC

NAIROBI

MOMBASA

DAR ES SALAAM

KAMPALA

Kisangani

L. Victoria

L. Tanganyika

L. Turkana (L. Rudolf)

1 : 6 400 000

50 0 50 100 150 200 miles

50 0 100 200 300 km

E F G

1 2 3 4 5

ZAMBIA

MALAWI

MOZAMBIQUE

ZIMBABWE

BOTSWANA

SOUTH AFRICA

ANGOLA

INDIAN OCEAN

Lusaka

HARARE (Salisbury)

Bulawayo

Lilongwe

Blantyre

Beira

Moçambique (Mozambique)

Ndola

Kitwe

Lubumbashi

Likasi

Livingstone

Gweru

Kabwe

Quelimane

Chipata

Lindi

Mtwara-Mikindani

Pemba

Angoche

Zambezi

Lake Kariba

NORTHERN

CENTRAL

SOUTHERN

WESTERN

NORTH WESTERN

COPPERBELT

EASTERN

MASHONALAND

MATABELELAND

MASVINGO

CABO DELGADO

NIASSA

NAMPULA

ZAMBEZIA

TETE

SOFALA

MANICA

INHAMBANE

GAZA

Île Juan de Nova (Réunion)

Projection: Lambert's Equivalent Azimuthal

East from Greenwich

COPYRIGHT GEORGE PHILIP & SON, LTD.

ft	m
18 000	6000
12 000	4000
9000	3000
6000	2000
4500	1500
3000	1000
1200	400
600	200
0	0
200	600
2000	6000
m	ft

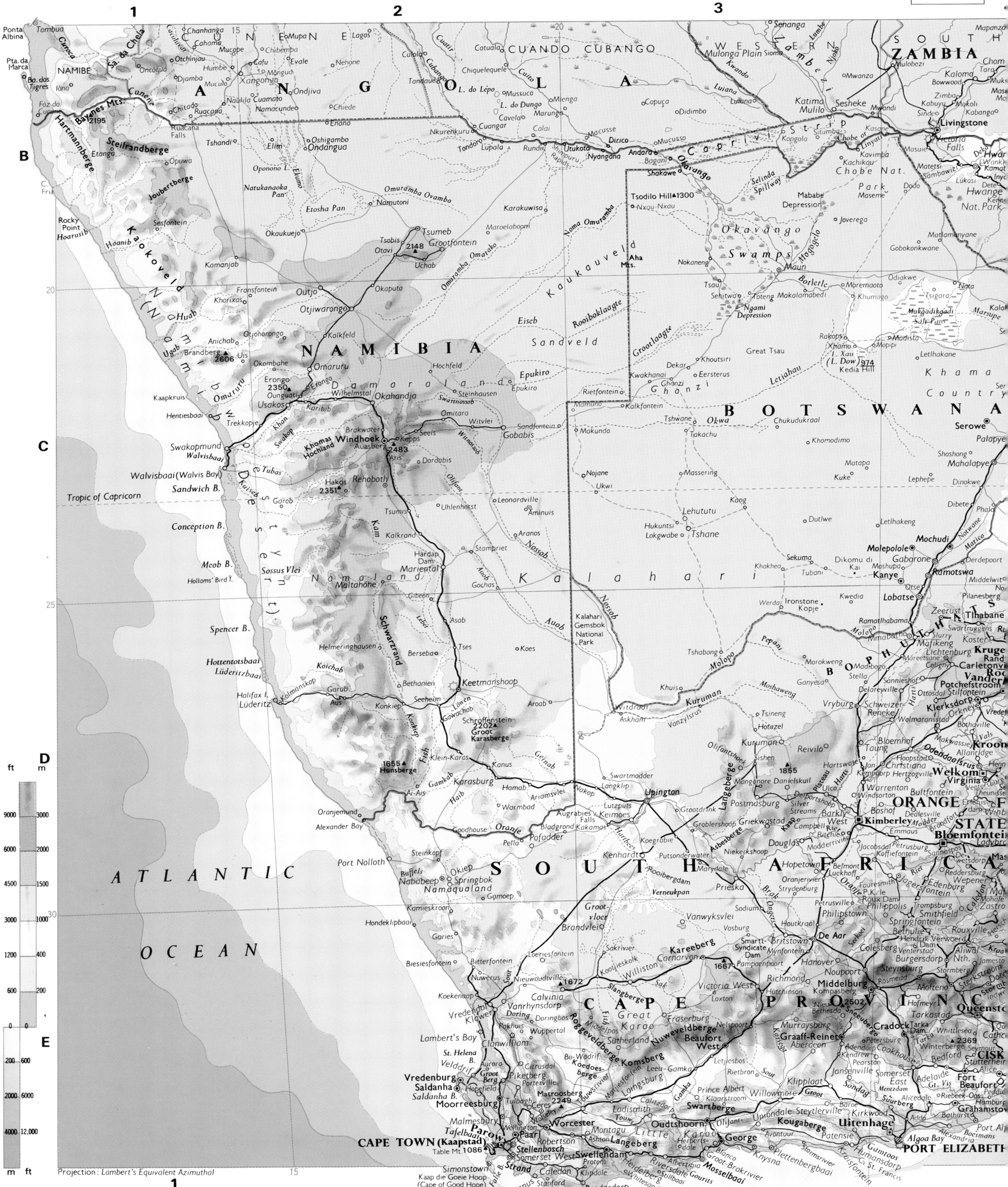

Projection: *Lambert's Equivalent Azimuthal*

This map shows the four provinces in South Africa prior to the April 1994 elections. A map at the end of the index shows the proposed nine new provinces.

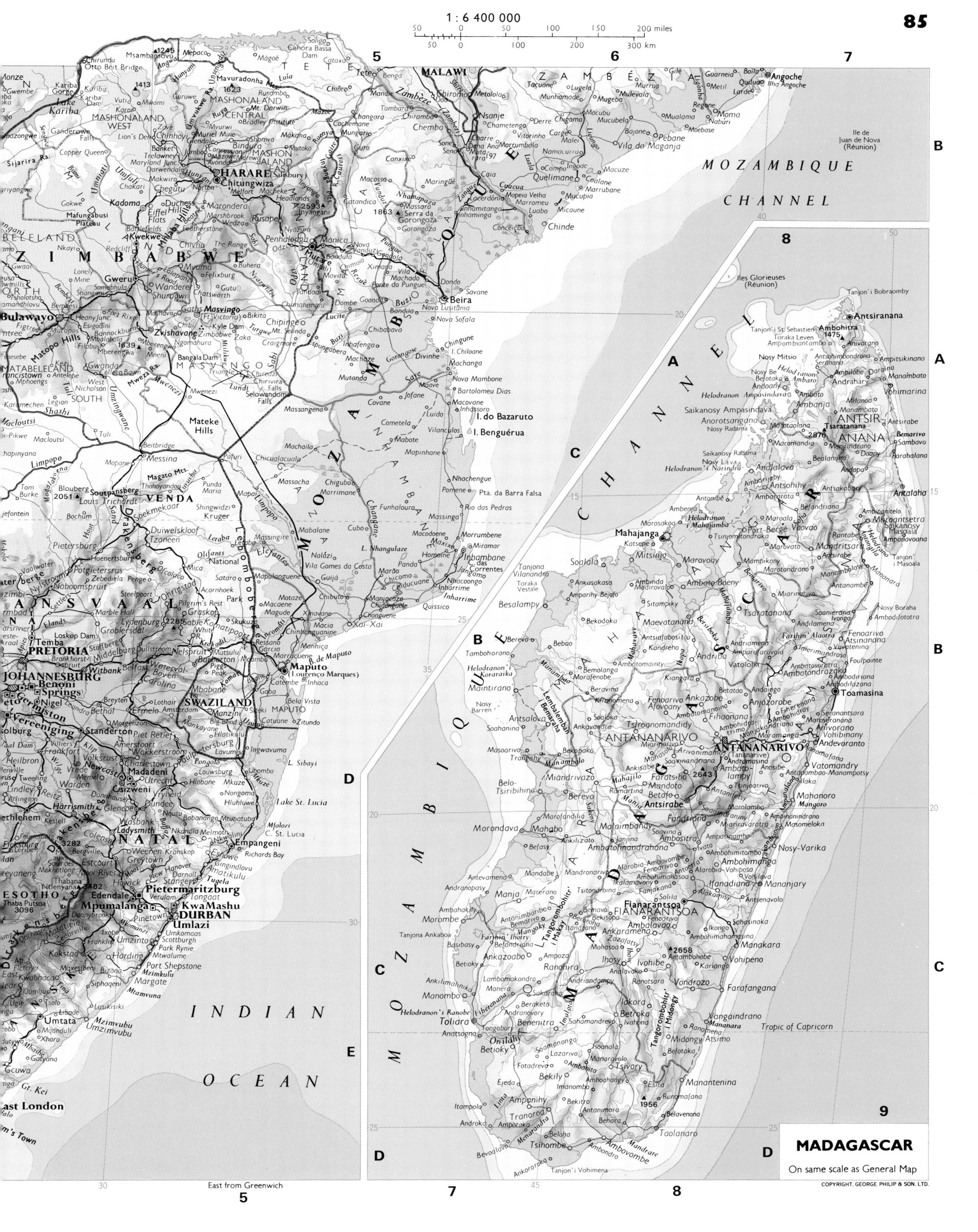
1 : 6 400 000
50 0 50 100 150 200 miles
50 0 100 200 300 km
ZIMBABWE
MOZAMBIQUE
MALAWI
SWAZILAND
MAPUTO
TRANSVAAL
NATAL
LESOTHO
VENDA
MASHONALAND CENTRAL
MASHONALAND WEST
MASHONALAND EAST
MASVINGO
MANICA
SOFALA
TETE
ZAMBÉZIA
GAZA
INHAMBANE
HARARE (Salisbury)
Chitungwiza
Bulawayo
Gweru
Kwekwe
Kadoma
Masvingo
Mutare
Beira
Maputo (Lourenço Marques)
Xai-Xai
Inhambane
Quelimane
Chinde
Angoche
Tete
PRETORIA
JOHANNESBURG
Benoni
Springs
Germiston
Vereeniging
Pietersburg
Soutpansberg
Messina
Beitbridge
Newcastle
Madadeni
Osizweni
Ladysmith
Pietermaritzburg
Edendale
Mpumalanga
KwaMashu
DURBAN
Umlazi
Empangeni
Richards Bay
Lake St. Lucia
Port Shepstone
Umtata
East London
Harrismith
Kruger National Park
Lebombo
Drakensberg
Limpopo
Zambeze
Save
Buzi
I. do Bazaruto
I. Benguérua
Pta. da Barra Falsa
Ile de Juan de Nova (Réunion)
MOZAMBIQUE CHANNEL
INDIAN OCEAN
East from Greenwich
MADAGASCAR
On same scale as General Map
MOZAMBIQUE CHANNEL
Iles Glorieuses (Réunion)
Antsiranana
ANTSIRANANA
Mahajanga
MAHAJANGA
ANTANANARIVO
Antananarivo (Tananarive)
Toamasina
TOAMASINA
Antsirabe
FIANARANTSOA
Fianarantsoa
TOLIARA
Toliara
Morondava
Maintirano
Besalampy
Manakara
Farafangana
Mananjary
Taolanaro
Ambovombe
Tsihombe
Tropic of Capricorn
Tanjon' i Bobraomby
Tanjon' i Vohimena
Nosy Be
Sainte Marie
COPYRIGHT, GEORGE PHILIP & SON, LTD.

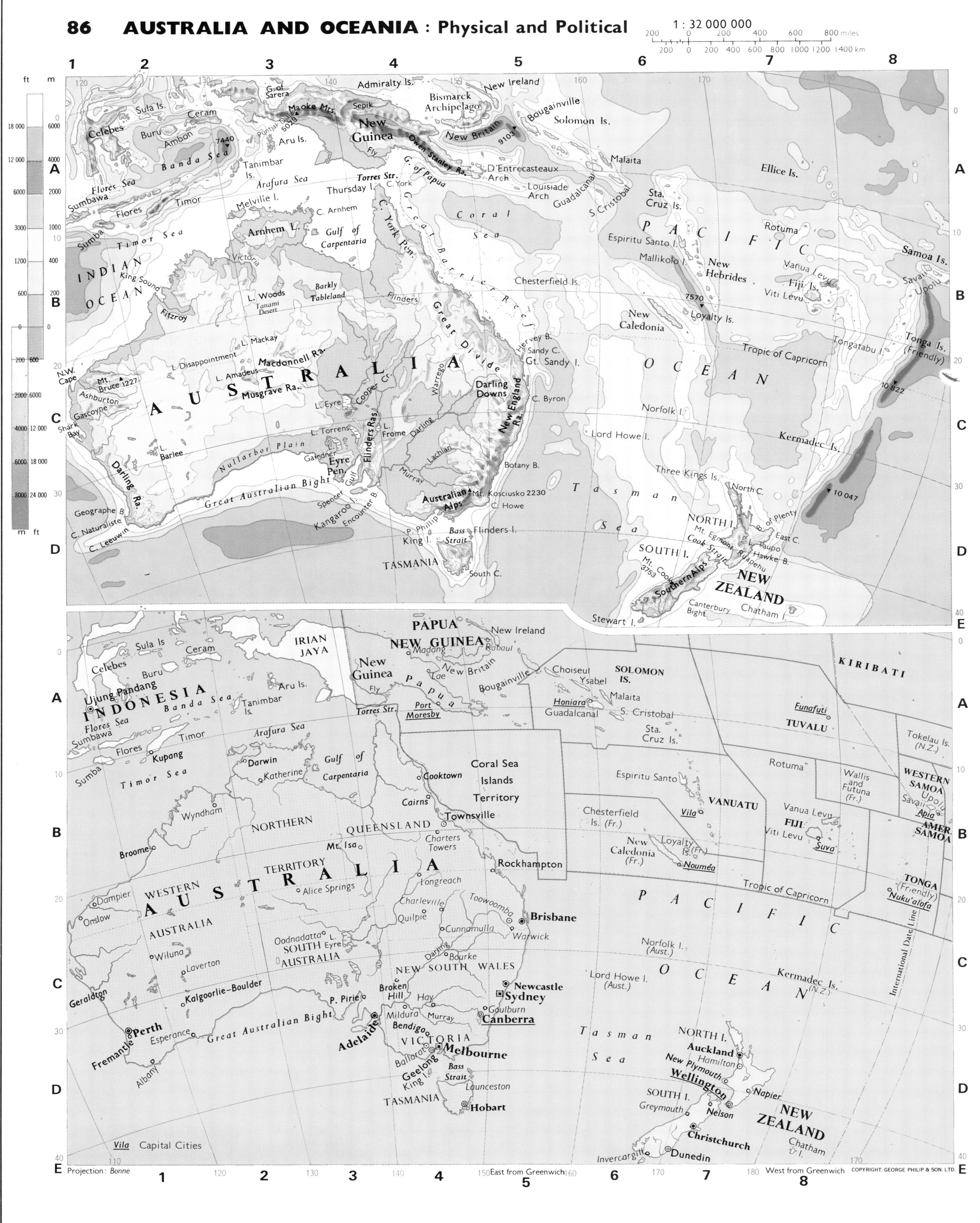

1 : 32 000 000
200 0 200 400 600 800 miles
200 0 200 400 600 800 1000 1200 1400 km
Admiralty Is.
New Ireland
G. of Sarera
Bismarck Archipelago
Bougainville
Solomon Is.
Celebes
Sula Is.
Ceram
Buru
Ambon
Maoke Mts.
Puntjak Djaja 5029
Sepik
New Guinea
New Britain
9103
Aru Is.
Banda Sea
7440
Fly
Owen Stanley Ra.
Malaita
Tanimbar Is.
D'Entrecasteaux Arch
Ellice Is.
Flores Sea
Arafura Sea
Torres Str.
G. of Papua
Louisiade Arch
Guadalcanal
S. Cristobal
Sumbawa
Thursday I.
C. York
Sta. Cruz Is.
Flores
Timor
Melville I.
C. Arnhem
Coral Sea
Rotuma
Sumba
Timor Sea
Arnhem L.
Gulf of Carpentaria
C. York Pen.
Great Barrier Reef
PACIFIC
Espiritu Santo I.
Victoria
Mallikolo I.
New Hebrides
Vanua Levu
Samoa Is.
INDIAN OCEAN
King Sound
Barkly Tableland
Chesterfield Is.
Fiji Is.
Savaii
Upolu
Viti Levu
L. Woods
Tanami Desert
Flinders
7570
Fitzroy
Great Divide
New Caledonia
Loyalty Is.
L. Mackay
Hervey B.
Sandy C.
Tonga Is. (Friendly)
Tongatabu I.
L. Disappointment
Macdonnell Ra.
Gt. Sandy I.
Tropic of Capricorn
N.W. Cape
Mt. Bruce 1227
L. Amadeus
AUSTRALIA
Warrego
OCEAN
Darling Downs
Ashburton
Musgrave Ra.
L. Eyre
Cooper Cr.
New England Ra.
C. Byron
10 822
Gascoyne
Shark Bay
Norfolk I.
L. Torrens
Flinders Ras
L. Frome
Darling
Lord Howe I.
Kermadec Is.
L. Barlee
Nullarbor Plain
Gairdner
Lachlan
Eyre Pen.
Botany B.
Three Kings Is.
Darling Ra.
Murray
Spencer Gulf
North C.
Great Australian Bight
Australian Alps
Mt. Kosciusko 2230
Tasman
10 047
Geographe B.
C. Howe
C. Naturaliste
Kangaroo I.
Encounter B.
P. Phillip
Bass Strait
Flinders I.
NORTH I.
B. of Plenty
C. Leeuwin
Sea
Mt. Egmont
East C.
King I.
Cook Strait
Taupo
Ruapehu
SOUTH I.
Hawke B.
TASMANIA
Mt. Cook 3753
South C.
Southern Alps
NEW ZEALAND
Canterbury Bight
Chatham I.
Stewart I.
PAPUA NEW GUINEA
New Ireland
IRIAN JAYA
Rabaul
Madang
Sula Is
Ceram
New Britain
KIRIBATI
New Guinea
Lae
Choiseul
SOLOMON IS.
Celebes
Buru
Papua
Bougainville
Ysabel
Aru Is.
Fly
Malaita
Ujung Pandang
INDONESIA
Banda Sea
Tanimbar Is.
Honiara
Guadalcanal
Funafuti
Torres Str.
Port Moresby
S. Cristobal
Flores Sea
TUVALU
Sumbawa
Arafura Sea
Sta. Cruz Is.
Timor
Tokelau Is. (N.Z.)
Flores
Kupang
Coral Sea Islands Territory
Darwin
Gulf of Carpentaria
Rotuma
Sumba
Timor Sea
Katherine
Cooktown
Espiritu Santo
Wallis and Futuna (Fr.)
WESTERN SAMOA
Upolu
Savaii
Apia
Cairns
Chesterfield Is. (Fr.)
VANUATU
Wyndham
Townsville
Vila
Vanua Levu
AMER. SAMOA
NORTHERN
QUEENSLAND
FIJI
Viti Levu
Charters Towers
New Caledonia (Fr.)
Loyalty Is. (Fr.)
Broome
Mt. Isa
Suva
TERRITORY
Rockhampton
Nouméa
Longreach
Tropic of Capricorn
TONGA (Friendly)
Nuku'alofa
Dampier
WESTERN
Alice Springs
Toowoomba
Charleville
Onslow
Quilpie
Brisbane
PACIFIC
AUSTRALIA
Cunnamulla
Warwick
Oodnadatta
L. Eyre
SOUTH AUSTRALIA
Norfolk I. (Aust.)
Wiluna
Bourke
International Date Line
Laverton
NEW SOUTH WALES
OCEAN
Kermadec Is. (N.Z.)
Lord Howe I. (Aust.)
Kalgoorlie-Boulder
Broken Hill
Newcastle
Geraldton
P. Pirie
Hay
Sydney
Mildura
Murray
Goulburn
Canberra
Perth
Adelaide
Bendigo
Tasman
NORTH I.
Fremantle
Esperance
VICTORIA
Melbourne
Auckland
Hamilton
Ballarat
Geelong
Sea
New Plymouth
Albany
King I.
Bass Strait
Wellington
Napier
Launceston
SOUTH I.
Nelson
NEW ZEALAND
TASMANIA
Greymouth
Hobart
Christchurch
Vila Capital Cities
Chatham I.
Invercargill
Dunedin
Projection: Bonne
East from Greenwich
West from Greenwich

COPYRIGHT. GEORGE PHILIP & SON. LTD.

1 : 4 800 000

NEW ZEALAND & S.W. PACIFIC

1 : 48 000 000

SAMOA ISLANDS

1 : 9 600 000

FIJI AND TONGA ISLANDS

1 : 9 600 000

Projection: *Conical with two standard parallels*

COPYRIGHT, GEORGE PHILIP & SON, LTD.

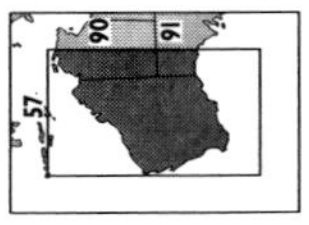

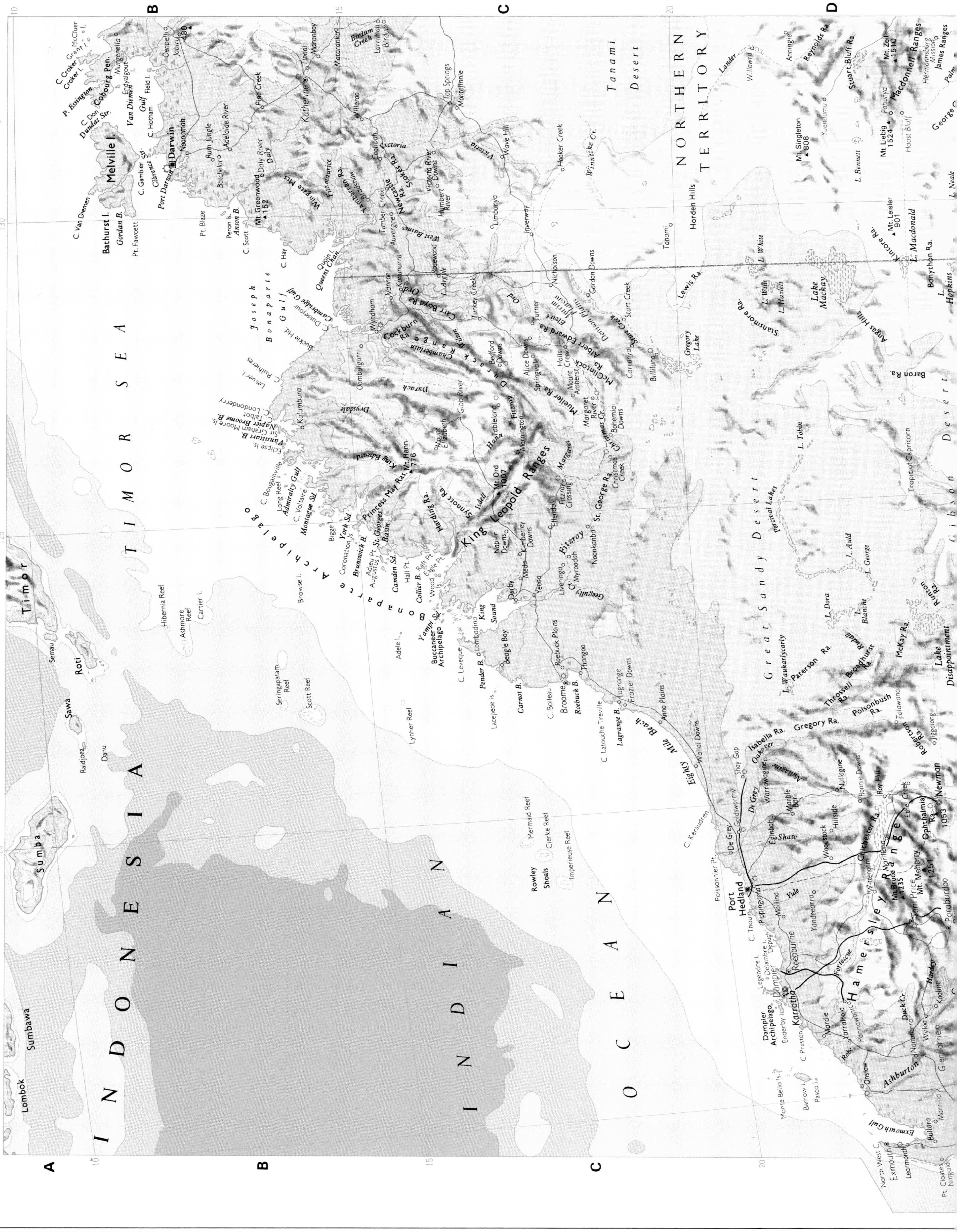

TIMOR SEA
INDIAN OCEAN
INDONESIA
NORTHERN TERRITORY
Tanami Desert
Great Sandy Desert
Gibson Desert
Bonaparte Archipelago
King Leopold Ranges
Hamersley Range
Timor
Sumba
Sumbawa
Lombok
Roti
Sawa
Melville I.
Bathurst I.
Darwin
Port Hedland
Broome
Eighty Mile Beach
Joseph Bonaparte Gulf

1 : 6 400 000
50 0 50 100 150 200 miles
50 0 100 200 300 km
WESTERN
SOUTH AUSTRALIA
Great Victoria Desert
Nullarbor Plain
Hampton Tableland
Great Australian Bight
SOUTHERN OCEAN
PERTH
Fremantle
New Town
Rockingham
Kwinana
Mandurah
Kalgoorlie-Boulder
Geraldton
Carnarvon
Bunbury
Busselton
Albany
Esperance
Norseman
Northam
Eucla Motel
Mt. Olga 1069
Ayers Rock 868
Archipelago of the Recherche
Shark Bay
Dirk Hartog I.
Houtman Abrolhos
Projection: Bonne
East from Greenwich
COPYRIGHT GEORGE PHILIP & SON LTD

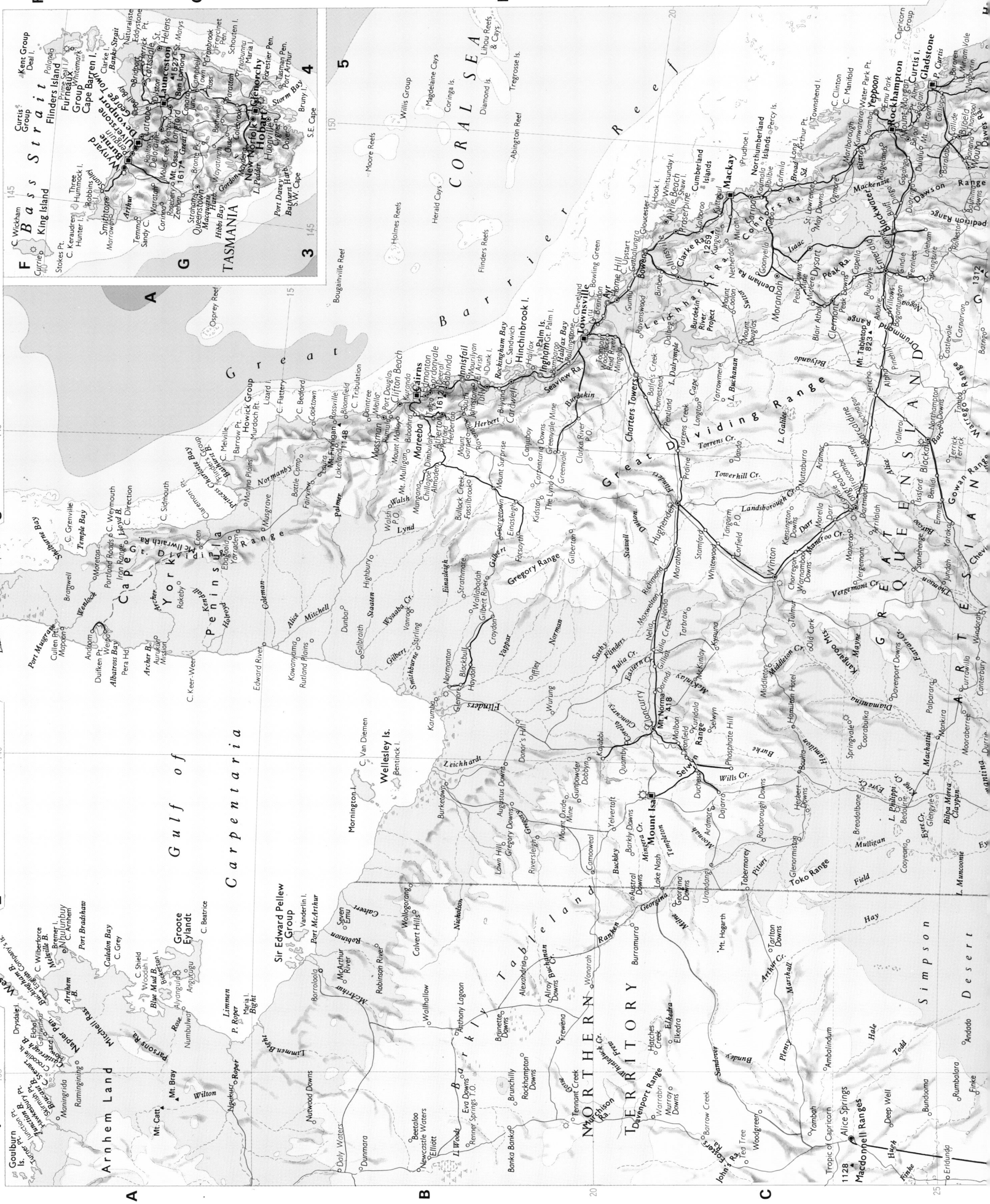

EASTERN AUSTRALIA

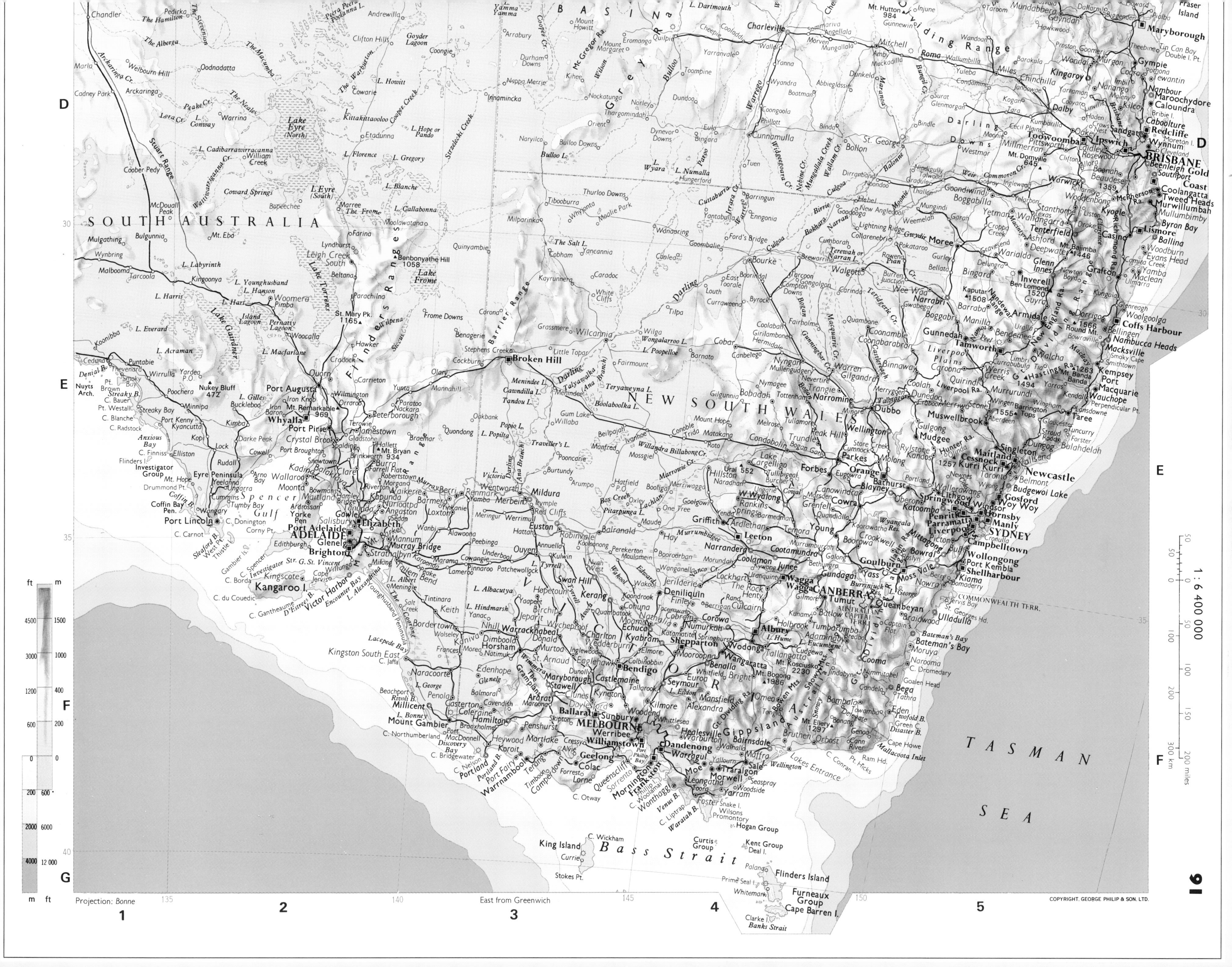

91
1 : 6 400 000
SOUTH AUSTRALIA
NEW SOUTH WALES
VICTORIA
TASMAN SEA
Bass Strait
Spencer Gulf
Kangaroo I.
Flinders Ranges
Lake Eyre (North)
Lake Torrens
Lake Gairdner
Lake Frome
Barrier Range
Grey Range
Darling Downs
Great Dividing Range
SYDNEY
MELBOURNE
ADELAIDE
BRISBANE
CANBERRA
Broken Hill
Newcastle
Port Augusta
Port Pirie
Whyalla
Port Lincoln
Mildura
Geelong
Ballarat
Bendigo
Wollongong
Toowoomba
Dubbo
Wagga Wagga
Albury
Tamworth
Armidale
King Island
Flinders Island
Furneaux Group
Cape Barren I.
Projection: Bonne
East from Greenwich
COPYRIGHT, GEORGE PHILIP & SON, LTD.

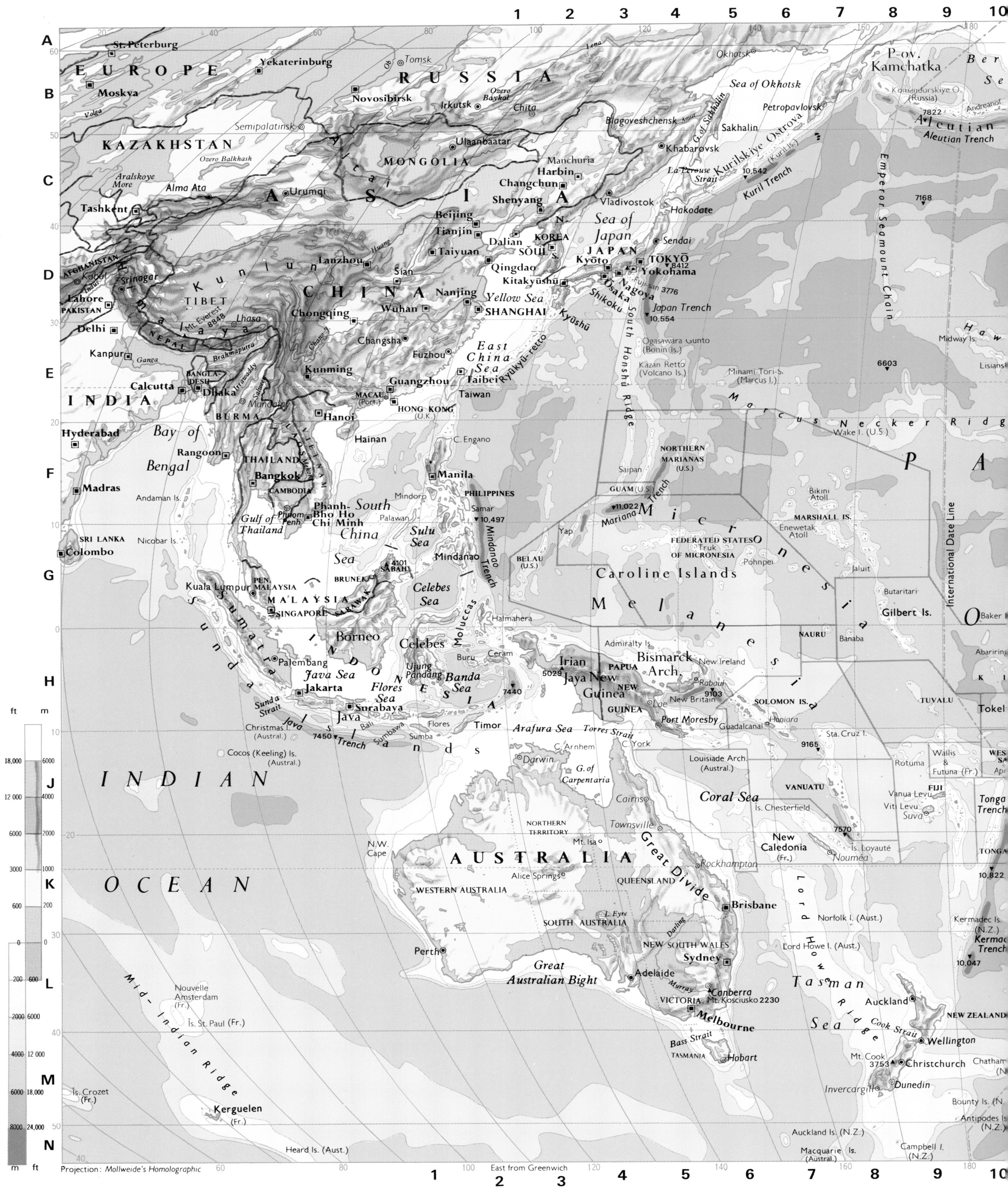
EUROPE
RUSSIA
KAZAKHSTAN
MONGOLIA
ASIA
CHINA
TIBET
INDIA
PAKISTAN
NEPAL
BURMA
THAILAND
CAMBODIA
KOREA
JAPAN
PHILIPPINES
MALAYSIA
INDONESIA
AUSTRALIA
NEW ZEALAND
INDIAN OCEAN
Bay of Bengal
South China Sea
East China Sea
Sea of Japan
Sea of Okhotsk
Yellow Sea
Coral Sea
Tasman Sea
Arafura Sea
Great Australian Bight
Micronesia
Melanesia
Caroline Islands
Mariana Trench
Japan Trench
Kuril Trench
Aleutian Trench
Emperor Seamount Chain
Marcus Necker Ridge
Mid-Indian Ridge
Lord Howe Rise
Great Divide
International Date Line
Moskva
St. Peterburg
Yekaterinburg
Novosibirsk
Irkutsk
Ulaanbaatar
Beijing
Tianjin
Shanghai
Tōkyō
Yokohama
Manila
Bangkok
Jakarta
Singapore
Sydney
Melbourne
Brisbane
Perth
Adelaide
Canberra
Hobart
Auckland
Wellington
Christchurch
Dunedin
Projection: Mollweide's Homolographic
East from Greenwich

ALASKA (U.S.)
Bristol Bay
Gulf of Alaska
Juneau
5959
Prince of Wales I.
Prince Rupert
Kitimat
Queen Charlotte Is.
Vancouver
Vancouver I.
Victoria
Seattle
Portland
Edmonton
Calgary
Regina
Winnipeg
L. Winnipeg
Hudson Bay
GREENLAND
C. Farewell
U.K.
C A N A D A
NORTH AMERICA
Labrador
Newfoundland
St. Lawrence
Quebec
Montreal
Ottawa
L. Superior
L. Huron
Michigan
Toronto
L. Ontario
L. Erie
Buffalo
Pittsburgh
Detroit
Pr. Edward I.
Saint John
Boston
C. Sable
NEW YORK
Philadelphia
Baltimore
Washington
Cincinnati
Minneapolis
CHICAGO
Missouri
Rocky Mountains
Boise
Snake
Salt Lake City
Colorado
Denver
Kansas City
St. Louis
C. Mendocino
San Francisco
4418
UNITED STATES
Oklahoma
Memphis
Mississippi
Appalachian Mts.
Atlanta
C. Hatteras
ATLANTIC
OCEAN
Bermuda (U.K.)
Jacksonville
Los Angeles
San Diego
Dallas
Ciudad Juarez
6741
6225
Houston
San Antonio
New Orleans
Gulf of Mexico
Miami
Florida Strait
BAHAMAS
MEXICO
Sierra Madre
Gulf of California
Monterrey
Hawaiian Is. (U.S.)
Oahu
Honolulu
Hawaii
Tropic of Cancer
La Habana
CUBA
Yucatan Channel
Mérida
West Indies
Hispaniola
9200
DOM. REP.
HAITI
7680
JAMAICA
Kingston
PUERTO RICO (U.S.)
Leeward Is.
Is. Revilla Gigedo (Mexico)
Guadalajara
México
Puebla
5700
Acapulco
BELIZE
Caribbean Sea
GUATEMALA
Guatemala
HONDURAS
San Salvador
EL SALVADOR
NICARAGUA
Managua
CENTRAL AMERICA
Windward Is.
BARBADOS
TRINIDAD & TOBAGO
Barranquilla
Maracaibo
Caracas
Orinoco
VENEZUELA
I. Clipperton (Fr.)
San José
COSTA RICA
Colón
Panama
PANAMA
Canal
P A C I F I C
OCEAN
Palmyra Is. (U.S.)
Christmas Island Ridge
Teraina
Tabuaeran
Kiritimati
Jarvis I. (U.S.)
I. del Coco (Costa Rica)
Medellín
Bogota
Cali
COLOMBIA
Equator
Galápagos (Ecuador)
Quito
ECUADOR
Guayaquil
Manaus
Amazonas
Iquitos
C. Pariñas
BRAZIL
SOUTH AMERICA
Malden I.
Starbuck I.
Îs. Marquises
Tongareva
Penrhyn Is.
Caroline I.
Vostok I.
Flint I.
Manihiki
Suwarrow Is.
Trujillo
PERU
Lima
6369
Cuzco
Andes
L. Titicaca
Illampu & Ancohuma 6550
La Paz
BOLIVIA
Arequipa
6866
Peru-Chile Trench
Cook Islands (N.Z.)
Îs. de la Société
Îs. Tuamotu
Tuamotu Ridge
Tahiti
Manuae
FRENCH POLYNESIA
Austral Seamount Chain
Rarotonga
Iquique
East Pacific Ridge
Pitcairn I. (U.K.)
Ducie I (U.K.)
Tropic of Capricorn
PARAGUAY
8050
Antofagasta
Îs. Tubuai (Îs. Australes)
Rapa
I. de Pascua (Easter I.) (Chile)
Sala-y-Gomez (Chile)
San Félix (Chile)
San Ambrosio (Chile)
Asunción
Tucumán
Pto. Alegre
Córdoba
Rosario
URUGUAY
Montevideo
6960
Arch. de Juan Fernández (Chile)
Valparaíso
Santiago
Buenos Aires
Río de la Plata
Concepción
ARGENTINA
Pacific-Antarctic Ridge
Chile Rise
Patagonia
SOUTH ATLANTIC OCEAN
6212
Falkland Is. (U.K.)
Punta Arenas
Str. of Magellan
Tierra del Fuego
C. Horn
South Georgia
West from Greenwich
COPYRIGHT. GEORGE PHILIP & SON. LTD.

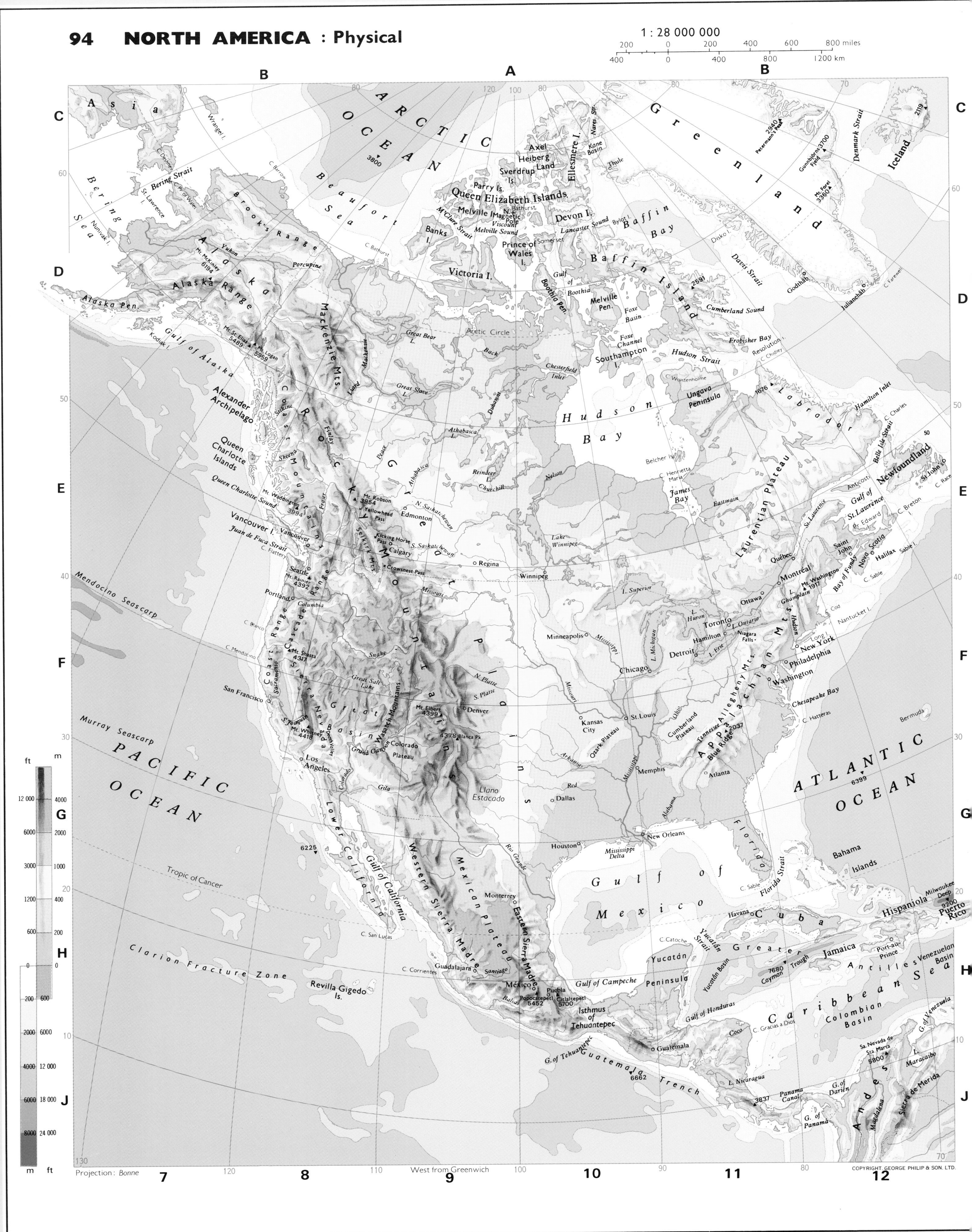
1 : 28 000 000
200 0 200 400 600 800 miles
400 0 400 800 1200 km
ARCTIC OCEAN
Beaufort Sea
Greenland
Bering Sea
Bering Strait
Asia
Queen Elizabeth Islands
Axel Heiberg Land
Sverdrup Is.
Parry Is.
Ellesmere I.
Melville I.
Devon I.
Banks I.
Victoria I.
Prince of Wales I.
Baffin Bay
Baffin Island
Davis Strait
Denmark Strait
Iceland
Brook's Range
Alaska
Alaska Range
Mt. McKinley 6194
Alaska Pen.
Gulf of Alaska
Mackenzie Mts.
Great Bear L.
Great Slave L.
Arctic Circle
Foxe Basin
Southampton I.
Hudson Strait
Hudson Bay
James Bay
Ungava Peninsula
Labrador
Laurentian Plateau
Newfoundland
Gulf of St. Lawrence
Alexander Archipelago
Queen Charlotte Islands
Coast Mountains
Rocky Mountains
Great Plains
Vancouver I.
Edmonton
Calgary
Regina
Winnipeg
Lake Winnipeg
L. Superior
L. Michigan
L. Huron
L. Erie
L. Ontario
Québec
Montreal
Ottawa
Toronto
Detroit
Chicago
Minneapolis
New York
Philadelphia
Washington
Appalachian Mts.
Seattle
Portland
Cascade Range
Coast Range
San Francisco
Sierra Nevada
Great Basin
Great Salt Lake
Denver
Mt. Elbert 4399
Colorado Plateau
Los Angeles
Kansas City
St. Louis
Memphis
Atlanta
Dallas
Houston
New Orleans
PACIFIC OCEAN
ATLANTIC OCEAN
Gulf of Mexico
Gulf of California
Lower California
Western Sierra Madre
Eastern Sierra Madre
Mexican Plateau
Monterrey
Guadalajara
México
Isthmus of Tehuantepec
Yucatán Peninsula
Cuba
Havana
Jamaica
Hispaniola
Puerto Rico
Bahama Islands
Florida
Caribbean Sea
Greater Antilles
Guatemala
Panama Canal
Andes
Tropic of Cancer
Clarion Fracture Zone
Murray Seascarp
Mendocino Seascarp
Projection: Bonne
West from Greenwich
COPYRIGHT, GEORGE PHILIP & SON, LTD.

1 : 28 000 000

200 0 200 400 600 800 miles

400 0 400 800 1200 km

Washington Capital Cities

U.S. State Capitals and Canadian Provincial Capitals

C	CONNECTICUT	N.H.	NEW HAMPSHIRE
D.	DELAWARE	N.J.	NEW JERSEY
D.C.	DISTRICT OF COLUMBIA	R.I.	RHODE ISLAND
M.	MARYLAND	VER.	VERMONT
MASS.	MASSACHUSETTS	SPM	ST. PIERRE ET MIQUELON

Projection: Bonne

West from Greenwich

COPYRIGHT, GEORGE PHILIP & SON, LTD.

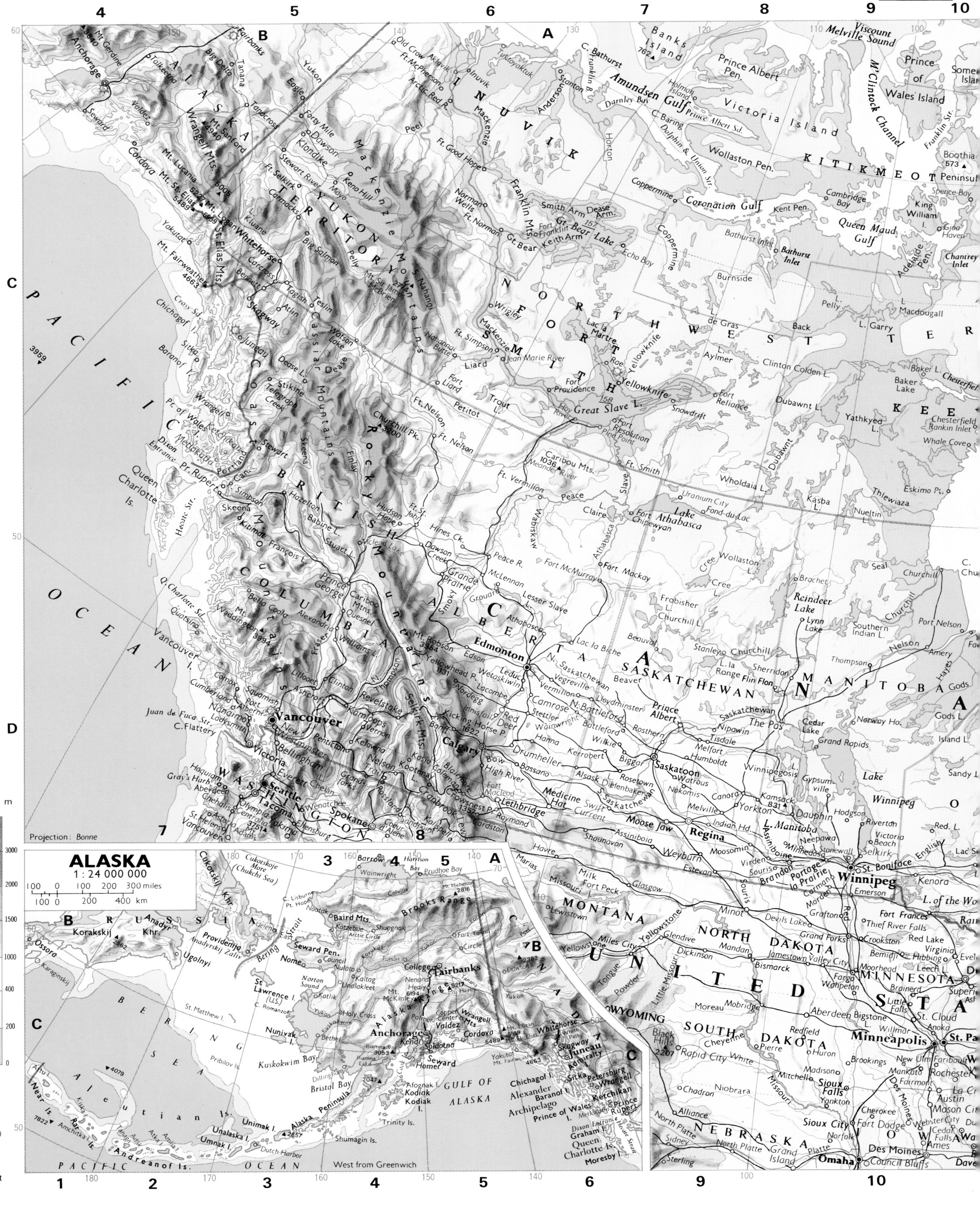

ALASKA
1 : 24 000 000

Projection: Bonne

West from Greenwich

4 5 6 7 8 9 10

YUKON TERRITORY
NORTH WEST TERRITORIES
BRITISH COLUMBIA
ALBERTA
SASKATCHEWAN
MANITOBA
PACIFIC OCEAN
KITIKMEOT
INUVIK
KEEWATIN

Banks Island
Victoria Island
Prince of Wales Island
Amundsen Gulf
Coronation Gulf
Queen Maud Gulf
M'Clintock Channel
Viscount Melville Sound
Prince Albert Pen.
Boothia Peninsula

Rocky Mountains
Mackenzie Mountains
Coast Mountains
Cassiar Mountains
Selkirk Mts.
Cariboo Mts.

Gt. Bear Lake
Gt. Slave L.
Lake Athabasca
Reindeer Lake
Lake Winnipeg
L. Manitoba
L. Winnipegosis

Anchorage
Fairbanks
Whitehorse
Juneau
Skagway
Vancouver
Victoria
Seattle
Tacoma
Spokane
Edmonton
Calgary
Lethbridge
Medicine Hat
Saskatoon
Regina
Moose Jaw
Winnipeg
Yellowknife

Queen Charlotte Is.
Vancouver I.
Juan de Fuca Str.
Dixon Entrance
Hecate Str.

100 0 100 200 300 miles
100 200 400 km

RUSSIA
BERING SEA
Anadyr
Nome
Barrow
Prudhoe Bay
Brooks Range
Seward Pen.
Fairbanks
College
Anchorage
Valdez
Cordova
Homer
Kodiak
Aleutian Is.
Alaska Peninsula
Bristol Bay
Kuskokwim Bay
Norton Sound
St. Lawrence I. (U.S.)
Nunivak
Pribilof Is.
Unimak I.
Dutch Harbor
GULF OF ALASKA
Arctic Circle
PACIFIC OCEAN

UNITED STATES
MONTANA
NORTH DAKOTA
SOUTH DAKOTA
WYOMING
NEBRASKA
MINNESOTA
IOWA

Minneapolis
St. Paul
Winnipeg
Omaha
Des Moines
Sioux Falls
Fargo
Bismarck
Rapid City
Pierre
Aberdeen

ft m
9000 3000
6000 2000
4500 1500
3000 1000
1200 400
600 200
0 0
200 600
2000 6000
m ft

1 2 3 4 5 6 9 10

1 : 12 000 000
100 0 100 200 300 400 miles
100 0 100 200 300 400 500 600 km
11
12
13
14
15
16
B
C
D
E
Devon Island
Lancaster Sound
Bylot I.
Pond Inlet
Brodeur Peninsula
Milne Inlet
Baffin Bay
Svartenhuk Halvø
Disko
Disko B.
Angmagssalik
GREENLAND
Søndre Strømfjord
Kong Frederik VI Kyst
Holsteinsborg
Sukkertoppen
Godthåb
Frederikshåb
Ivigtut
Kap Farvel
C. Hewett
Clyde
Scott I.
Home B.
Davis Strait
Broughton Island
C. Dyer
Cape Dyer
Cumberland Peninsula
Pangnirtung
Hoare B.
C. Mercy
Cumberland Sd.
Fury & Hecla Str.
Igloolik Island
Hall Lake
Melville Peninsula
Pelly Bay
Committee B.
Prince Charles I.
Foxe Basin
Nettilling L.
BAFFIN
Rae Isthmus
Repulse Bay
Wager B.
C. Dorchester
Foxe Channel
Foxe Penin.
Amadjuak L.
Amadjuak
Cape Dorset
Southampton I.
Coral Harbour
Bell Pen.
Roes Welcome Sd.
Frobisher Bay
Lake Harbour
Resolution I.
Hudson Strait
C. Chidley
Digges Is.
Coats I.
Mansel I.
Ivujivik
Saglouc (Sugluk)
Maricourt (Wakeham)
Koartac (Notre Dame de Koartac)
Akpatok I.
Arnaud (Payne Bay)
Bellin
Ungava Bay
Ungava Peninsula
Payne L.
Port Nouveau Quebec
Hebron
Nutak
Nain
Hopedale
C. Harrison
Indian Harbour
Rigolet
Cartwright
L. Melville
Belle Isle
Battle Harb.
Ottawa Is.
Portland Promontory
Inoucdjouac (Port Harrison)
Feuilles
Koksoak
Kaniapiskau
Whale
George
Hudson Bay
King George Is.
Sleeper Is.
Baker's Dozen Is.
L. Minto
Mélèze
L. à l'Eau Claire
Lac Bienville
Schefferville
Petitsikapau L.
COAST OF LABRADOR
NEWFOUNDLAND
Churchill Falls
Churchill
North West R.
Goose Bay
Belcher Is.
Grand Baleine
Poste-de-la-Baleine (Great Whale River)
Kanaaupscow
La Grande
C. Henrietta Maria
Pte. Louis-XIV
Ft. George
Kaniapiskau L.
Ashuanipi
Natashquan
St-Augustin
Saguenay
Str. of Belle Isle
Romaine
Notashquan
Mingan
Moisie
James Bay
Akimiski I.
Nouveau Comptoir (Paint Hills)
Eastmain
Charlton I.
Ft. Albany
Albany
Fort Rupert (Rupert House)
Rupert
Nottaway
Moosonee
Mistassini
L. Albanel
Péribonca
Manicouagan
Gagnon
Sept Îles
Port-Cartier
I. d'Anticosti
Gulf of St. Lawrence
C. de Gaspé
Gaspé
Pen. de Gaspé
Matane
Rimouski
Campbellton
Dalhousie
Bathurst
Baie-Comeau
Betsiamites
R. St. Lawrence
Chibougamau
Harricana
Missinaibi
Kenogami
Nakina
Longlac
Hearst
Cochrane
L. Abitibi
Matagami
Mattagami
Timmins
Rouyn
Noranda
Val d'Or
Toschereau
Senneterre
Rés. de Gouin
Roberval
Dolbeau
L. St-Jean
Saguenay
Jonquière
Chicoutimi
Tadoussac
Rivière-du-Loup
Edmundston
Newcastle
Chatham
NEW BRUNSWICK
Moncton
Amherst
Springhill
Fredericton
Saint John
Woodstock
Quebec
Lévis
Thetford Mines
La Tuque
Shawinigan
Trois-Rivières
Joliette
St-Hyacinthe
Sherbrooke
MONTRÉAL
Lachine
Granby
Hull
Ottawa
Arnprior
Pembroke
North Bay
Sudbury
Haileybury
Témiscamingue
Kirkland Lake
Cobalt
Thunder Bay
Nipigon
Heron Bay
Oba
Franz
Michipicoten
Lake Superior
Sault Ste. Marie
Copper Cliff
Parry Sound
Georgian Bay
Orillia
Peterborough
Belleville
Kingston
Cornwall
Burlington
L. Champlain
Lake Huron
Owen Sound
Oshawa
TORONTO
Guelph
Kitchener
Stratford
London
Brantford
Hamilton
St. Catharines
Niagara Falls
L. Ontario
Buffalo
Rochester
Syracuse
Utica
Watertown
Albany
Springfield
Worcester
Boston
Lowell
Manchester
Concord
NEW HAMPSHIRE
VERMONT
MAINE
Bangor
Augusta
Lewiston
Portland
C. Cod
Providence
New Haven
Waterbury
Bridgeport
NEW YORK
Newark
Jersey City
Trenton
NEW JERSEY
Reading
Allentown
Scranton
Binghamton
Elmira
Jamestown
Erie
Williamsport
Youngstown
PENNSYLVANIA
Cleveland
Akron
Toledo
OHIO
Detroit
Windsor
Chatham
Sarnia
Lake Erie
South Bend
INDIANA
Gary
CHICAGO
Evanston
Kenosha
Racine
Milwaukee
Sheboygan
Manitowoc
Appleton
Green Bay
Kalamazoo
Grand Rapids
Muskegon
Saginaw
Ludington
Cadillac
Traverse City
Petoskey
Cheboygan
Manistique
Escanaba
Menominee
Marquette
Ironwood
Wausau
Antigo
Iron Mt.
L. Michigan
Sault Ste. Marie
Anticosti
Cabot Str.
C. North
Cape Breton I.
Glace Bay
Sydney
Port Hawkesbury
Mulgrave
Îs. de la Madeleine
PR. EDWARD I.
Charlottetown
Summerside
Northumberland Str.
Pictou
New Glasgow
Truro
Windsor
Kentville
Dartmouth
Halifax
NOVA SCOTIA
Bridgewater
Liverpool
Shelburne
C. Sable
Yarmouth
Digby
B. of Fundy
Sable I. (Nova Scotia)
ST. PIERRE et MIQUELON (Fr.)
St. John's
C. Race
Trepassey
Placentia
Carbonear
Harbour Grace
Bonavista
Trinity B.
Gander
Grand Falls
Lewisporte
Twillingate
Notre Dame B.
Corner Brook
P. aux Basques
Ray C.
ATLANTIC OCEAN
Big Trout L.
Attawapiskat
Winisk
Severn
Ft. Severn
Albany
St. Joseph
ONTARIO
QUEBEC
2136
1890
2850
2591
3809
1676
1128
1190
1917
814
6309
257
West from Greenwich
COPYRIGHT, GEORGE PHILIP & SON, LTD.
11
12
13
14

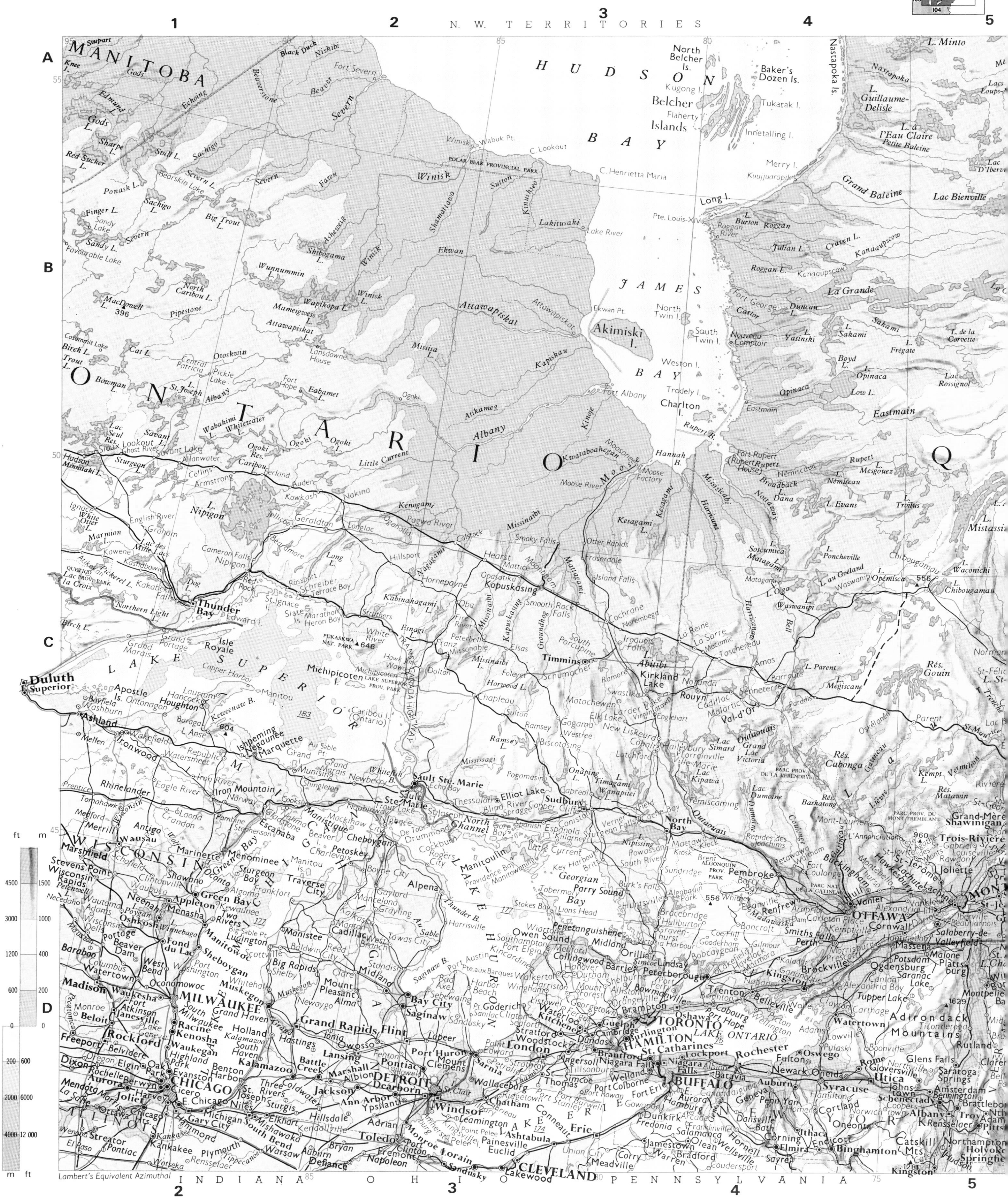

N.W. TERRITORIES

MANITOBA

HUDSON BAY

North Belcher Is.
Baker's Dozen Is.
Kugong I.
Tukarak I.
Belcher Islands
Flaherty I.
Innetalling I.
Nastapoka Is.

L. Minto
L. Guillaume-Delisle
L. à l'Eau Claire
Lac Bienville
Petite Baleine
Grand Baleine

Knee
Stupart
Gods
Edmund
Black Duck
Niskibi
Fort Severn
Beaverstone
Beaver
Severn

Winisk
Wabuk Pt.
C. Lookout
Polar Bear Provincial Park
C. Henrietta Maria

Kuujjuarapik
Merry I.
Pte. Louis-XIV

L. D'Iberville

ONTARIO

JAMES BAY

Burton L.
Roggan River
Roggan L.
Julian L.
Craven L.
Kanaaupscow
Kanaaupscow
Fort George
Castor
Duncan
La Grande
Sakami
Yasinski

Attawapiskat
Ekwan Pt.
North Twin I.
South Twin I.
Akimiski I.
Weston I.
Tradely I.
Charlton
Fort Albany
Rupert B.
Eastmain
Charlton
Hannah B.
Moose Factory
Moosonee
Rupert
Némiscau
Eastmain

LAKE SUPERIOR

Thunder Bay
Isle Royale
Duluth
Superior

WISCONSIN

MICHIGAN

LAKE MICHIGAN

LAKE HURON

LAKE ONTARIO

LAKE ERIE

MILWAUKEE
CHICAGO
Madison
Rockford
Green Bay
Grand Rapids
Flint
DETROIT
Windsor
TORONTO
HAMILTON
OTTAWA
London
BUFFALO
CLEVELAND
Toledo
Kingston
Rochester

ILLINOIS
INDIANA
OHIO
PENNSYLVANIA
NEW YORK

Sault Ste. Marie
Sudbury
North Bay
Timmins
Kirkland Lake
Rouyn
Val-d'Or

Adirondack Mountains

Thunder Bay
Georgian Bay
Parry Sound

ft m
4500 1500
3000 1000
1200 400
600 200
0 0
200 600
2000 6000
4000 12000
m ft

Lambert's Equivalent Azimuthal

1 : 5 600 000
miles
km
COAST OF
LABRADOR
NEWFOUNDLAND
QUEBEC
GULF OF ST. LAWRENCE
ATLANTIC OCEAN
Cabot Strait
Str. of Belle Isle
Bay of Fundy
NEW BRUNSWICK
PRINCE EDWARD ISLAND
NOVA SCOTIA
MAINE
Cape Breton Island
Avalon Peninsula
SAINT-PIERRE ET MIQUELON (Fr.)
Î. d'Anticosti
Îs. de la Madeleine (Quebec)
Sable I. (Nova Scotia)
Smallwood Res.
Rés. Manicouagan
Kaniapiskau Lake
Mealy Mts.
Long Range Mts.
Mts. Chic-Chocs
Pén. de Gaspé
St. Lawrence
Labrador City
Schefferville
Happy Valley-Goose Bay
North West River
Churchill Falls
Hopedale
Nain
Rigolet
Cartwright
Battle Harbour
Belle I.
St. Anthony
Sept-Îles
Clarke City
Port-Cartier
Havre-St-Pierre
Natashquan
Corner Brook
Stephenville
Grand Falls
Gander
Lewisporte
Botwood
Bonavista
Twillingate
Fogo I.
Channel-Port aux Basques
St. John's
Placentia
Marystown
Grand Bank
Miquelon
Langlade
St. Pierre
Rimouski
Matane
Gaspé
Chandler
Percé
Dalhousie
Campbellton
Bathurst
Chatham
Newcastle
Moncton
Saint John
Fredericton
Edmundston
St. Leonard
Grand Falls
Summerside
Charlottetown
Amherst
Truro
New Glasgow
Halifax
Dartmouth
Sydney
Glace Bay
Sydney Mines
New Waterford
Louisbourg
Yarmouth
Digby
Liverpool
Bridgewater
Lunenburg
Kentville
Windsor
Chicoutimi
Jonquière
Alma
Arvida
Rivière-du-Loup
Lévis
Lauzon
Montmagny
Thetford Mines
Sherbrooke
Magog
Coaticook
Lac-Mégantic
Asbestos
Presque Isle
Caribou
Houlton
Millinocket
Bangor
Old Town
Brewer
Augusta
Waterville
Skowhegan
Rumford
Auburn
Lewiston
Bath
Brunswick
Portland
Saco
Biddeford
Sanford
Rochester
Concord
Dover
Portsmouth
Manchester
Nashua
Haverhill
Lawrence
Lowell
Lynn
Gloucester
Waltham
BOSTON
Brockton
Bar Harbor
Mt. Desert I.
Rockland
Belfast
Camden
Berlin
GULF OF
West from Greenwich
COPYRIGHT, GEORGE PHILIP & SON, LTD.

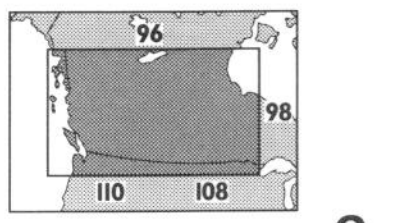

ft	m
12 000	4000
9000	3000
6000	2000
4500	1500
3000	1000
1200	400
600	200
0	0
200	600
2000	6000
m	ft

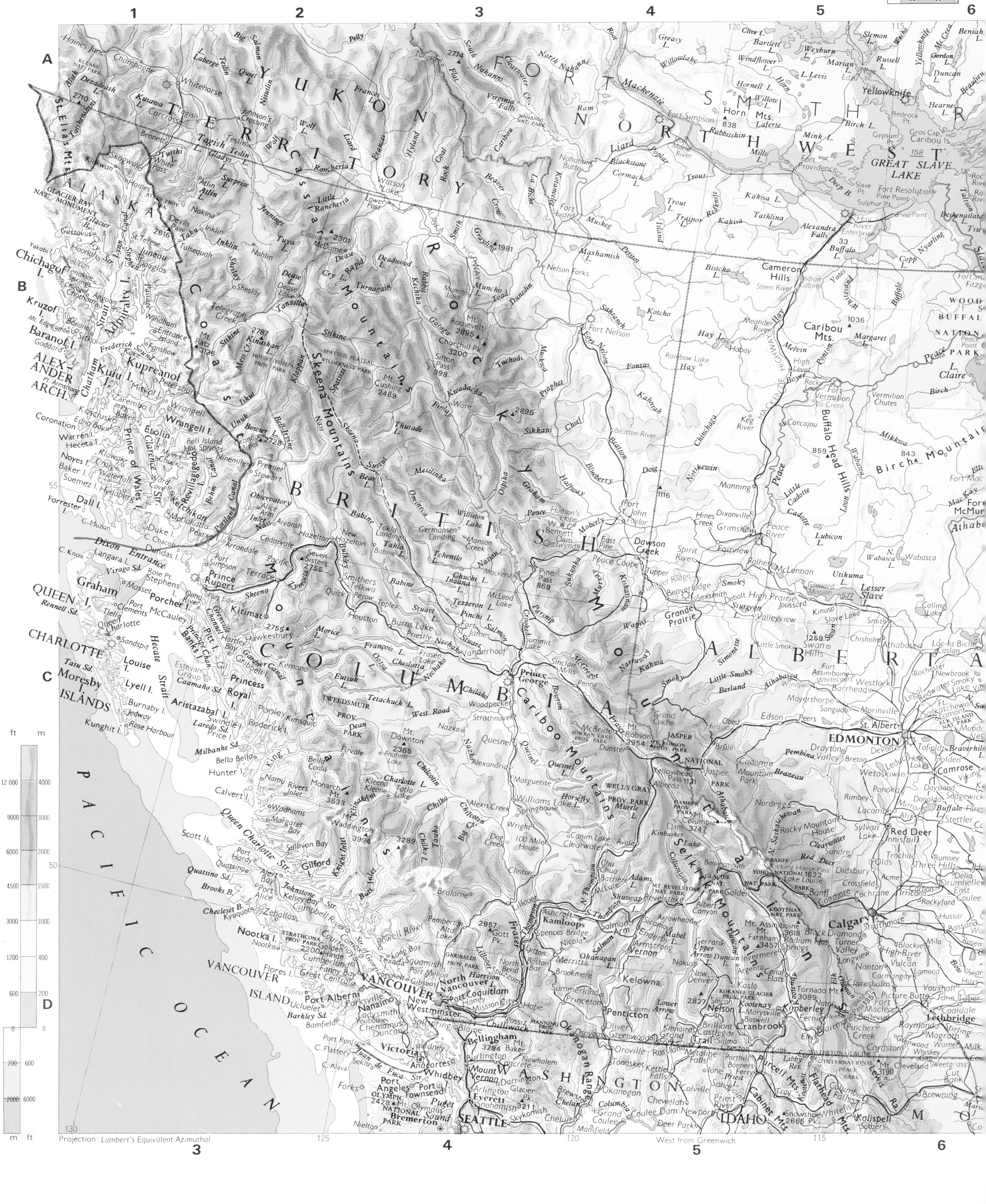

PACIFIC OCEAN

Projection: Lambert's Equivalent Azimuthal

West from Greenwich

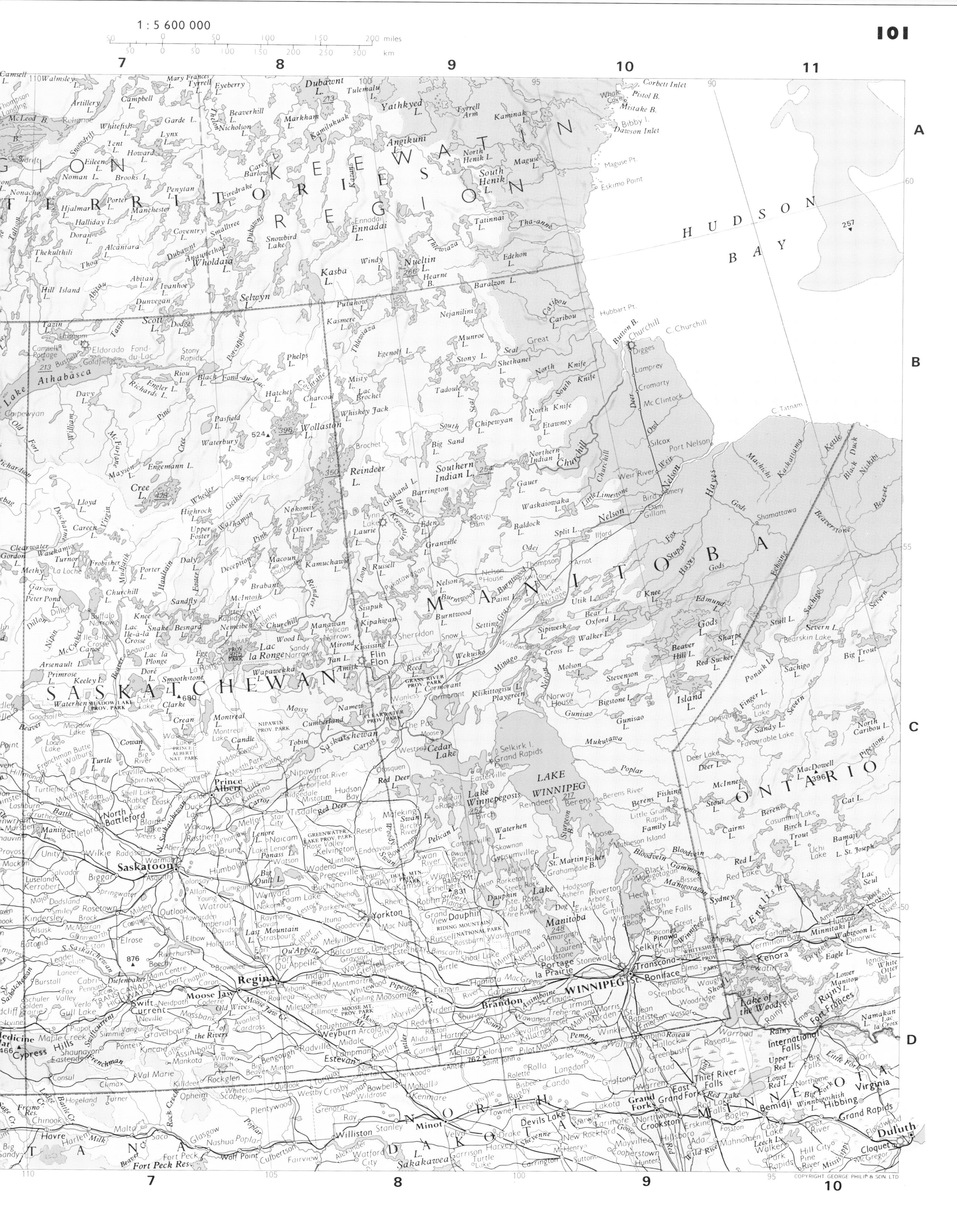
1 : 5 600 000
miles
km
7
8
9
10
11
A
B
C
D
KEEWATIN
REGION
HUDSON BAY
SASKATCHEWAN
MANITOBA
ONTARIO
NORTH DAKOTA
MINNESOTA
Lake Athabasca
Wollaston L.
Reindeer L.
Southern Indian L.
Nueltin L.
Dubawnt L.
Yathkyed L.
Kaminak L.
Angikuni L.
Kasba L.
Selwyn L.
Scott L.
Lac la Ronge
Cree L.
Churchill
C. Churchill
Port Nelson
Nelson
Hayes
Gods
Island L.
Sandy L.
Red Lake
Lake of the Woods
Rainy L.
Lac Seul
LAKE WINNIPEG
Lake Winnipegosis
Lake Manitoba
Cedar Lake
Flin Flon
The Pas
Thompson
Prince Albert
North Battleford
Saskatoon
Regina
Moose Jaw
Swift Current
Medicine Hat
Yorkton
Brandon
Portage la Prairie
WINNIPEG
St. Boniface
Kenora
Fort Frances
International Falls
Minot
Williston
Devils Lake
Grand Forks
Bemidji
Duluth
Hibbing
Virginia
Grand Rapids
Estevan
Weyburn
Dauphin
Selkirk
Steinbach
Thief River Falls
Crookston
Havre
Fort Peck Res.
Sakakawea
Cypress Hills
Riding Mountain National Park
COPYRIGHT GEORGE PHILIP & SON LTD

HAWAII

1 : 8 000 000

20 0 20 40 60 80 miles

20 0 40 80 120 km

Projection: Albers Equal Area

West from Greenwich

PACIFIC OCEAN

Kauai, Lihue, Niihau, Kaula, Kauai Channel, Oahu, Kahana, Wahiawa, Pearl City, Honolulu, Pearl Harbor, Kaiwi Channel, Molokai, Kalaupapa, Lanai, Paia, Maui, Hana, Lahaina, Makena, Haleakala 3056, Kahoolawe, Hawaiian Islands, Alenuihaha Channel, Mahukona, Kawaihae, 4205, Mauna Kea, Mauna Loa, 4170, Hilo, Keaau, Hawaii, Kailua, Glenwood, Kilauea Crater, 1247, Pahala

ft	m
12 000	4000
9000	3000
6000	2000
4500	1500
3000	1000
1200	400
600	200
0	0
200	600
2000	6000
m	ft

1 : 9 600 000
GULF OF MEXICO
ATLANTIC OCEAN
CHICAGO
NEW YORK
PHILADELPHIA
DETROIT
TORONTO
MONTREAL
BAHAMAS
COPYRIGHT. GEORGE PHILIP & SON. LTD

1 : 4 800 000
miles
km
Continuation Eastwards On same scale.
TENNESSEE
NORTH CAROLINA
SOUTH CAROLINA
GEORGIA
ALABAMA
MISSISSIPPI
FLORIDA
MAINE
NEW HAMPSHIRE
CANADA
BAHAMAS
ATLANTIC OCEAN
GULF OF MEXICO
NASHVILLE
ATLANTA
Birmingham
JACKSONVILLE
Montgomery
Tallahassee
Columbia
Raleigh
Charleston
Savannah
Augusta
Macon
Chattanooga
Knoxville
Charlotte
Wilmington
Orlando
Tampa
St. Petersburg
Miami
Ft. Lauderdale
West Palm Beach
Pensacola
Mobile
Portland
Bangor
Augusta
Freeport
Grand Bahama I.
Great Abaco I.
EVERGLADES NAT. PARK
West from Greenwich
Projection: Alber's Equal Area with two standard parallels
COPYRIGHT GEORGE PHILIP & SON, LTD

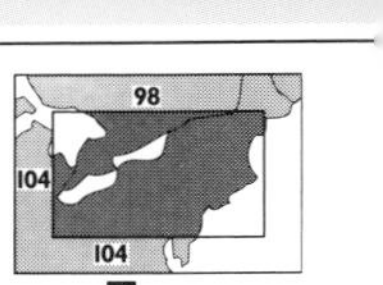

LAKE HURON

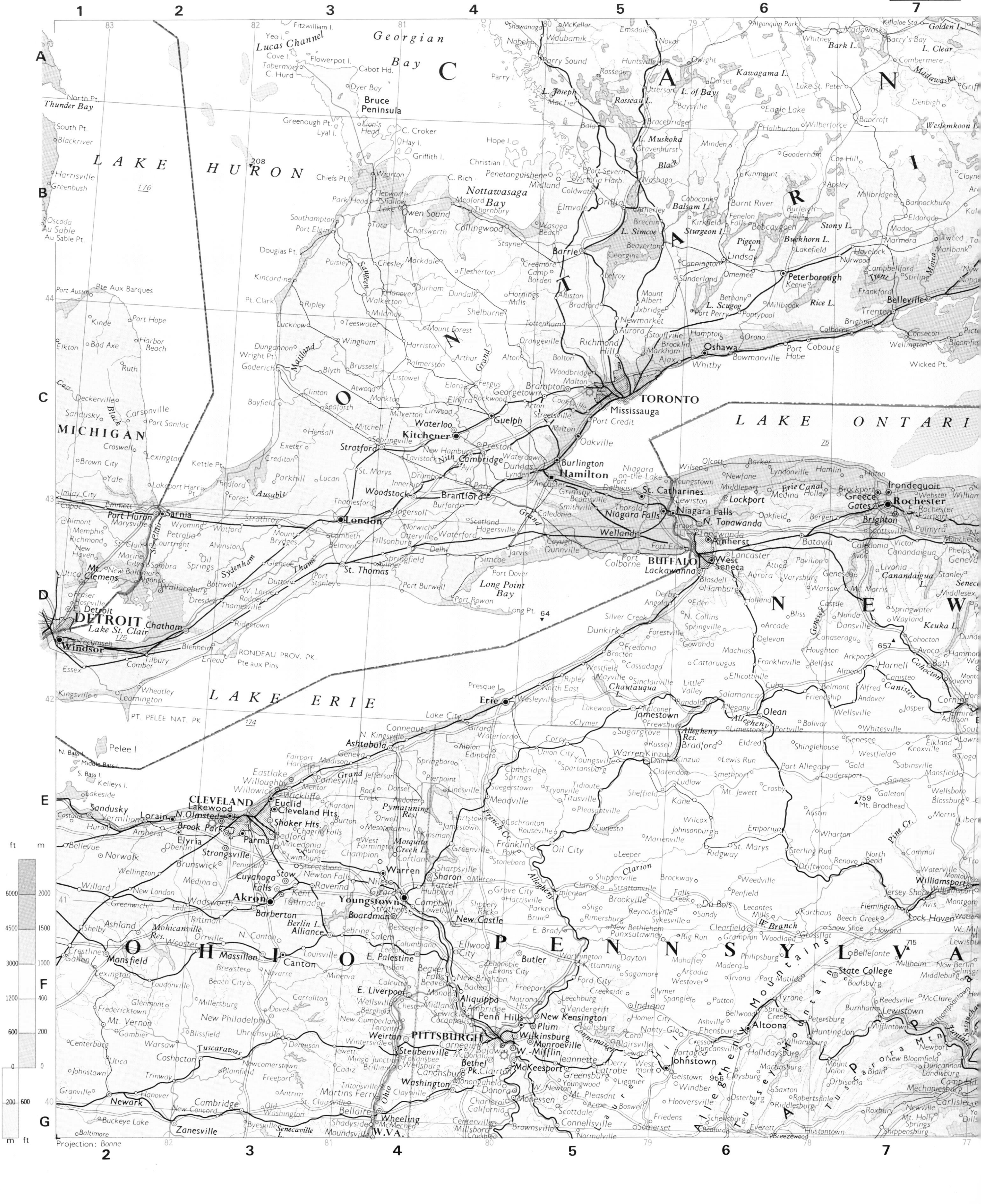

LAKE ERIE

LAKE ONTARIO

Georgian Bay

CANADA ONTARIO

MICHIGAN

OHIO

PENNSYLVANIA

NEW YORK

TORONTO

DETROIT

CLEVELAND

PITTSBURGH

BUFFALO

Projection: Bonne

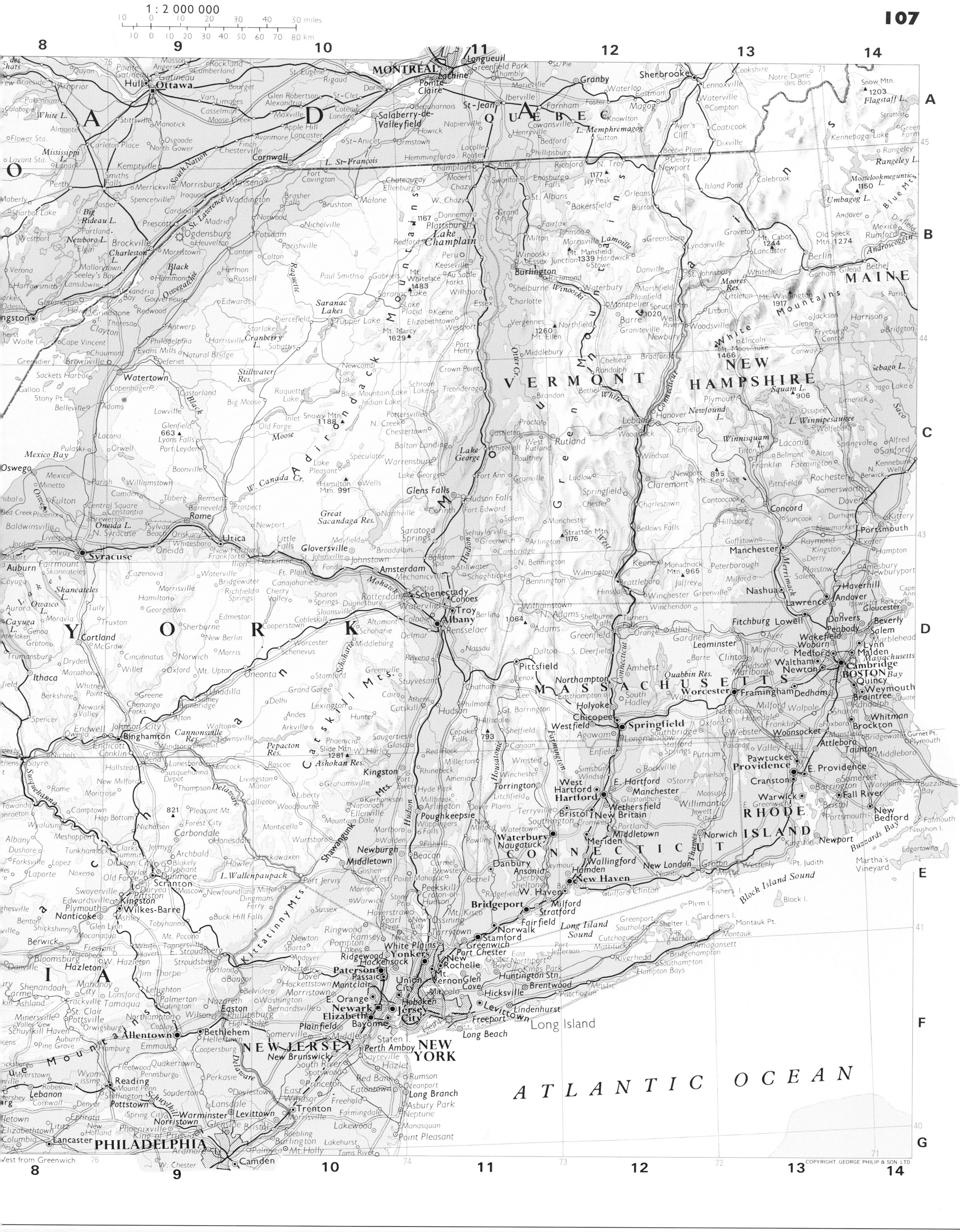

1 : 2 000 000

10 0 10 20 30 40 50 miles

10 0 10 20 30 40 50 60 70 80 km

8 9 10 11 12 13 14

A B C D E F G

QUEBEC

CANADA

ONTARIO

NEW YORK

PENNSYLVANIA

VERMONT

NEW HAMPSHIRE

MAINE

MASSACHUSETTS

CONNECTICUT

RHODE ISLAND

NEW JERSEY

ATLANTIC OCEAN

Long Island

Long Island Sound

Block Island Sound

Buzzards Bay

Lake Champlain

Adirondack Mountains

Green Mountains

White Mountains

Catskill Mts.

MONTREAL · Ottawa · Sherbrooke · Syracuse · Utica · Schenectady · Albany · Troy · Burlington · Concord · Manchester · Portsmouth · Lowell · Lawrence · BOSTON · Cambridge · Worcester · Springfield · Hartford · New Haven · Providence · Bridgeport · Stamford · Yonkers · Paterson · Newark · Jersey City · NEW YORK · Trenton · Allentown · Reading · Scranton · Wilkes-Barre · Binghamton · PHILADELPHIA · Camden

West from Greenwich 76 74 73 72 71

COPYRIGHT. GEORGE PHILIP & SON. LTD.

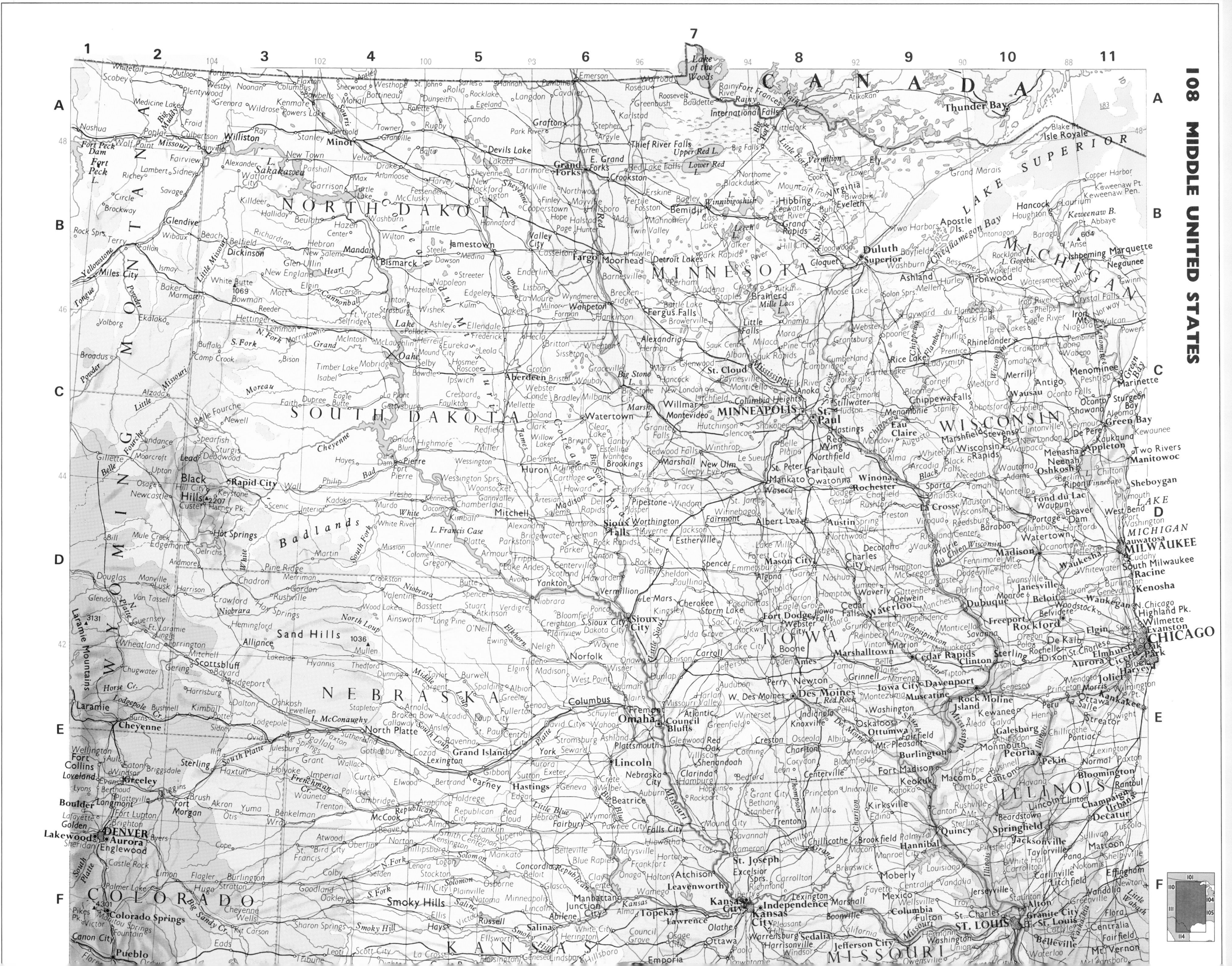
CANADA
LAKE SUPERIOR
LAKE MICHIGAN
MICHIGAN
MINNESOTA
WISCONSIN
NORTH DAKOTA
SOUTH DAKOTA
IOWA
ILLINOIS
NEBRASKA
MISSOURI
KANSAS
COLORADO
WYOMING
MONTANA
CHICAGO
MILWAUKEE
MINNEAPOLIS
St. Paul
Des Moines
Omaha
DENVER
ST. LOUIS
Kansas City
Duluth
Thunder Bay
Sand Hills
Badlands
Smoky Hills
Laramie Mountains
Lake of the Woods

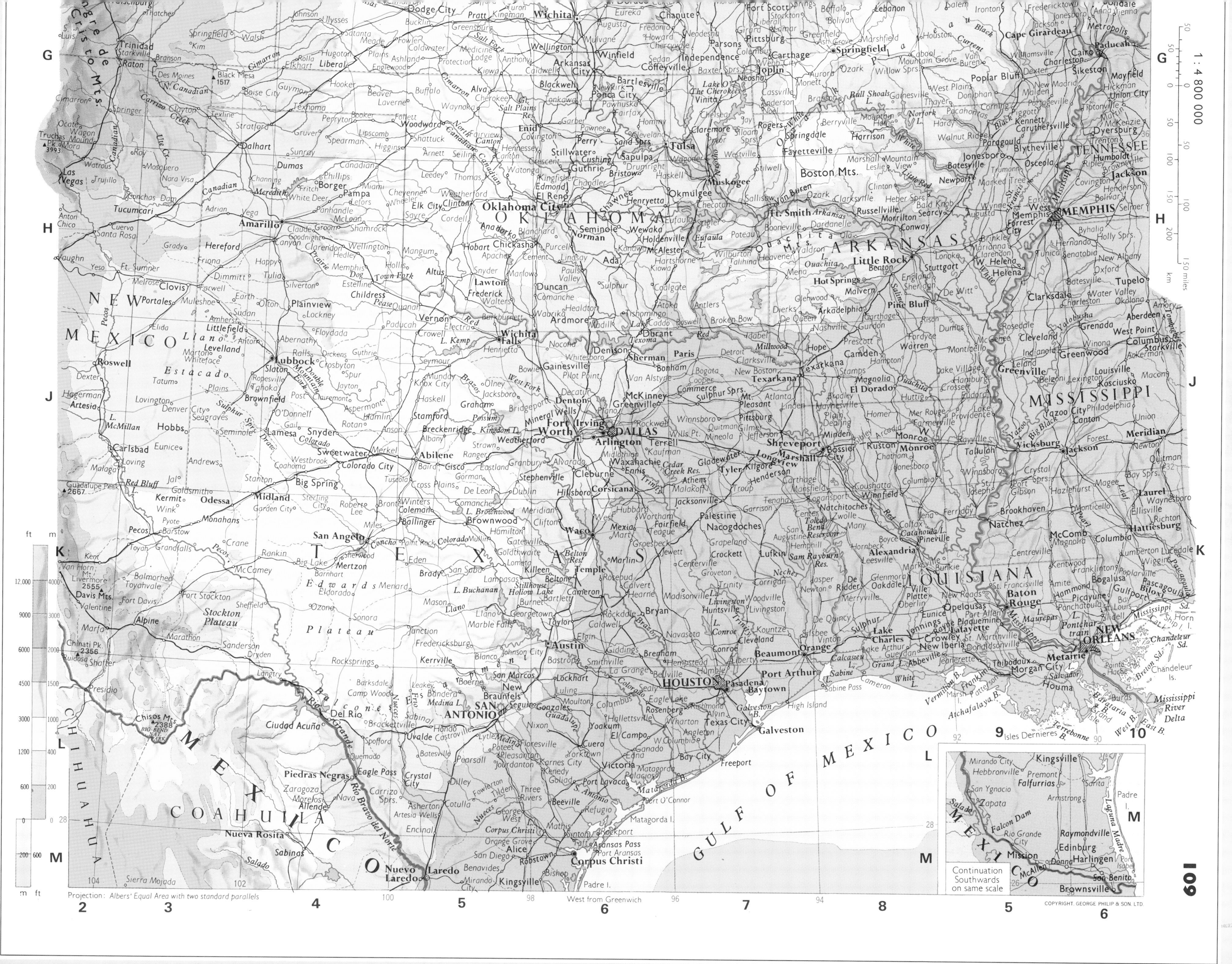
1 : 4 800 000
150 miles
km
GULF OF MEXICO
TEXAS
OKLAHOMA
ARKANSAS
LOUISIANA
MISSISSIPPI
TENNESSEE
NEW MEXICO
MEXICO
COAHUILA
CHIHUAHUA
Continuation Southwards on same scale
West from Greenwich
Projection: Albers' Equal Area with two standard parallels
COPYRIGHT GEORGE PHILIP & SON LTD

1 : 4 800 000
50 0 50 100 miles
50 0 50 100 150 km
WASHINGTON
OREGON
IDAHO
MONTANA
WYOMING
NEVADA
BRITISH COLUMBIA
ALBERTA
SASKATCHEWAN
CANADA
Seattle
Portland
Spokane
Boise
Salt Lake City
Great Salt Lake
Great Basin
Great Sandy Desert
Bighorn Mountains
Salmon River Mountains
Blue Mountains
Olympic Mts.
Wind River Range
Uinta Mountains
Sacramento
Reno

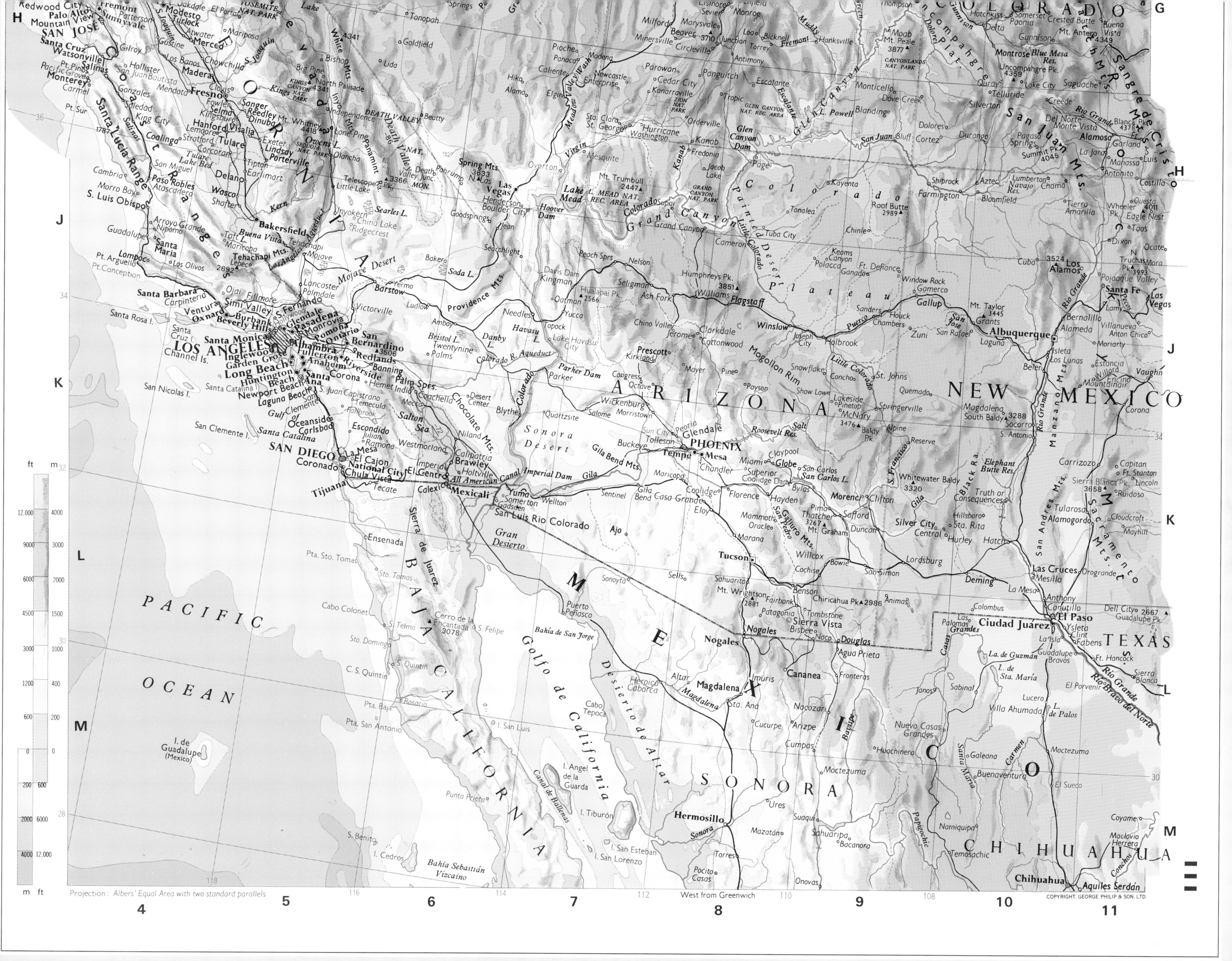

COLORADO
NEW MEXICO
ARIZONA
TEXAS
MEXICO
SONORA
CHIHUAHUA
BAJA CALIFORNIA
PACIFIC OCEAN
Golfo de California
Desierto de Altar
Gran Desierto
Sonora Desert
Mojave Desert
Painted Desert
Colorado Plateau
Grand Canyon
Sierra Nevada
Coast Ranges
Santa Lucia Range
San Juan Mts.
Sangre de Cristo Mts.
Sacramento Mts.
Mogollon Rim
LOS ANGELES
SAN DIEGO
SAN JOSE
PHOENIX
Albuquerque
Tucson
El Paso
Ciudad Juárez
Las Vegas
Santa Fe
Flagstaff
Bakersfield
Fresno
Santa Barbara
Tijuana
Mexicali
Hermosillo
Chihuahua
Nogales
Death Valley
Salton Sea
Lake Mead
Hoover Dam
Rio Grande
Projection: Albers' Equal Area with two standard parallels
West from Greenwich
COPYRIGHT. GEORGE PHILIP & SON, LTD.

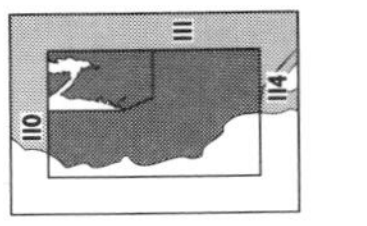

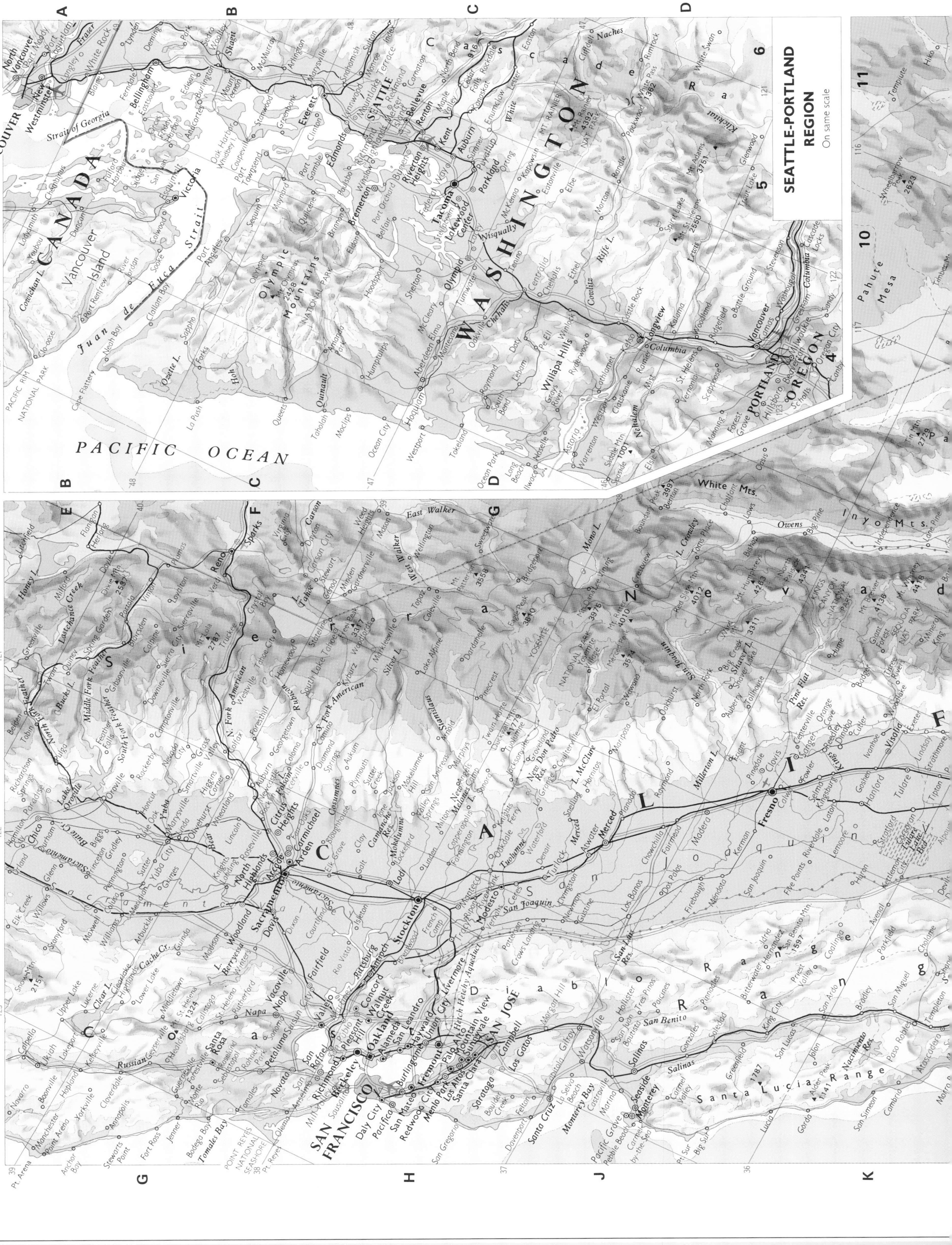

SEATTLE-PORTLAND REGION
On same scale

PACIFIC OCEAN

CANADA

WASHINGTON

OREGON

CALIFORNIA

Sierra Nevada

San Joaquin

Coast Ranges

Santa Lucia Range

Inyo Mts.

White Mts.

Pahute Mesa

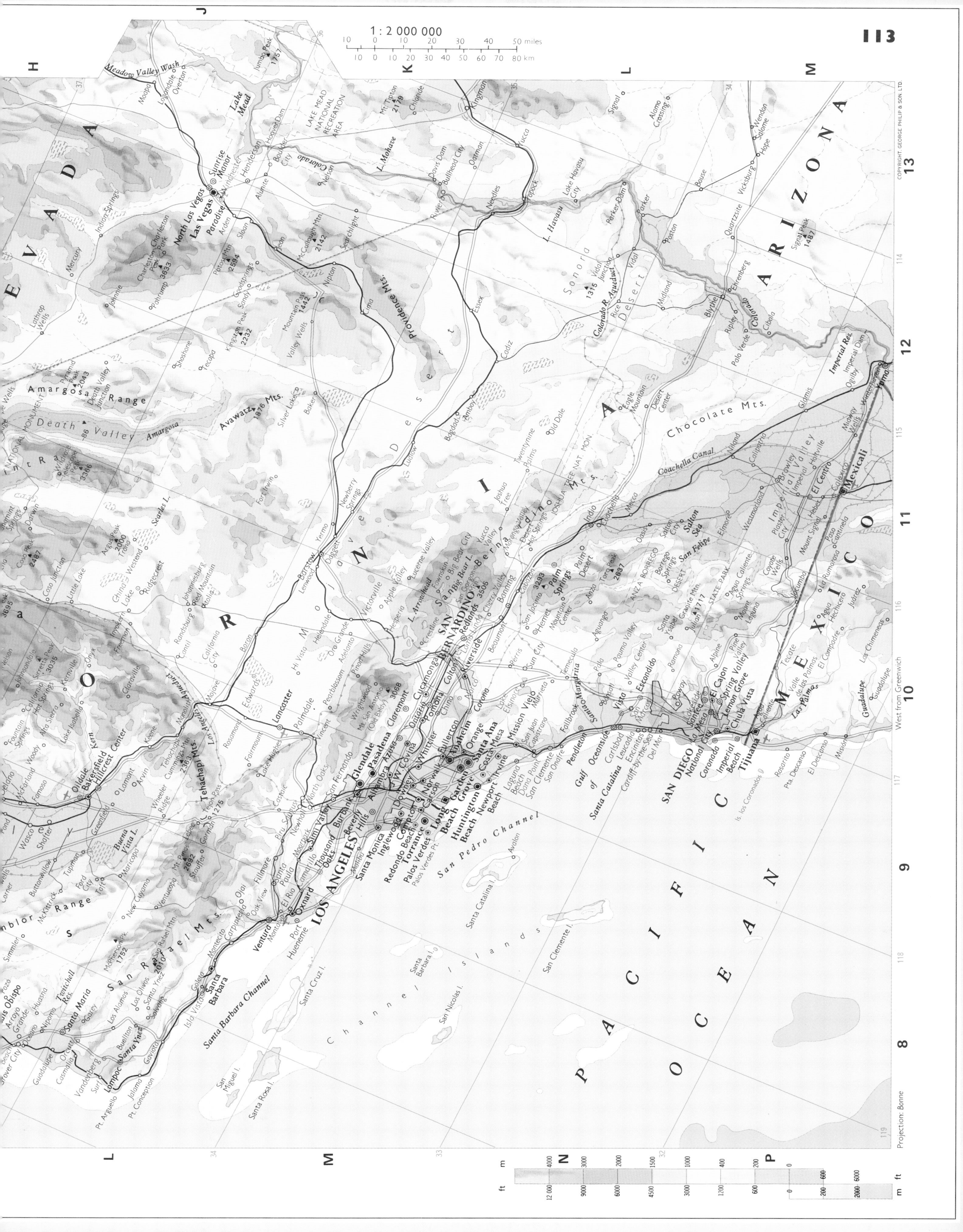
1 : 2 000 000
NEVADA
ARIZONA
CALIFORNIA
MEXICO
PACIFIC OCEAN
LOS ANGELES
SAN DIEGO
SAN BERNARDINO
Las Vegas
North Las Vegas
Lake Mead
LAKE MEAD NATIONAL RECREATION AREA
L. Mohave
L. Havasu
Mojave Desert
Sonora Desert
Colorado R. Aqueduct
Chocolate Mts.
Coachella Canal
Salton Sea
Imperial Valley
Mexicali
Tijuana
Death Valley
Amargosa Range
Avawatz Mts.
Providence Mts.
Tehachapi Mts.
Santa Barbara Channel
San Pedro Channel
Channel Islands
Gulf of Santa Catalina
Santa Catalina I.
San Clemente I.
Bakersfield
Lancaster
Palmdale
Barstow
Victorville
Palm Springs
Riverside
Pasadena
Glendale
Long Beach
Santa Ana
Anaheim
Oxnard
Ventura
Santa Barbara
Santa Maria
Escondido
Chula Vista
Yuma
Kingman
Needles
Blythe
Projection: Bonne
West from Greenwich
COPYRIGHT, GEORGE PHILIP & SON, LTD.

ft m

12 000 4000

9000 3000

6000 2000

4500 1500

3000 1000

1200 400

600 200

0 0

200 600

2000 6000

4000 12 000

m ft

REFERENCE TO NUMBERS

1	Federal District	5	México
2	Aguascalientes	6	Morelos
3	Guanajuato	7	Querétaro
4	Hidalgo	8	Tlaxcala

Projection: *Bi-polar oblique Conical Orthomorphic*

West from Greenwich

1 : 6 400 000
50 0 50 100 150 200 miles
50 0 100 200 300 km
5
6
7
8
A
B
C
D
E
GULF OF MEXICO
Golfo de Campeche
Canal de Yucatán
Tropic of Cancer
Wichita Falls
Denison
Sherman
Paris
Texarkana
Hope
Camden
El Dorado
Greenville
ARKANSAS
MISSISSIPPI
Tuscaloosa
Opelika
Columbus
Selma
Phenix City
Montgomery
ALABAMA
GEORGIA
Americus
Cordele
Albany
Tifton
Waycross
McRae
Denton
FORT WORTH
DALLAS
Marshall
Longview
Tyler
Monroe
Shreveport
Vicksburg
Meridian
Jackson
Tallulah
Natchez
Laurel
Hattiesburg
Dothan
Troy
Flomaton
Valdosta
Tallahassee
Lake City
Cleburne
Hillsboro
Corsicana
Palestine
Nacogdoches
Lufkin
Alexandria
McComb
Bogalusa
Hammond
Baton Rouge
Biloxi
MOBILE
Pensacola
Panama City
FLORIDA
Apalachee Bay
C. San Blas
Suwannee
Brownwood
Waco
Temple
Huntsville
Bryan
Austin
Navasota
Lake Charles
Lafayette
Beaumont
Port Arthur
NEW ORLEANS
Gulfport
Breton Sound
Mobile Bay
Mississippi Delta
Atchafalaya Bay
Terrebonne B.
HOUSTON
Rosenberg
Galveston
SAN ANTONIO
Victoria
Dilley
Clearwater
Alice
Corpus Christi
Laredo
Kingsville
Nuevo Laredo
Zapata
Camargo
Mc Allen
Harlingen
Brownsville
Laguna Madre
Reynosa
Matamoros
Valle Hermoso
Montemorelos
Mendez
San Fernando
Linares
Villagrán
Santander-Jiménez
La Pesca
Soto la Marina
Ciudad Victoria
Sierra de Tamaulipas
TAMAULIPAS
Aldama
Pta. Jerez
Ciudad Mante
Ciudad Madero
Tampico
Ciudad de Valles
Pánuco
Laguna de Tamiahua
Ozuluama
C. Rojo
Tempoal
Tantoyuca
Tamazunchale
Tuxpan
Poza Rica
Papantla
Nautla
Pachuca
Huauchinango
Tulancingo
Teziutlán
Jalapa Enríquez
Zempoala
MÉXICO
Tlaxcala
Apizaco
PUEBLA
Coatepec
Veracruz Llave
Amecameca
Orizaba
Córdoba
Alvarado
Tlacotalpan
Cuernavaca
Tehuacán
Cosamaloapan
San Andrés Tuxtla
Coatzacoalcos
Acayucan
Minatitlán
Iguala
Chilpancingo
Oaxaca
Ocotlán
Acapulco
Ometepec
Jamiltepec
Puerto Escondido
Puerto Ángel
Miahuatlán
Pochutla
Tehuantepec
Juchitán
Salina Cruz
Golfo de Tehuantepec
Ixtepec
Matías Romero
Istmo de Tehuantepec
Tonalá
Arriaga
Tuxtla Gutiérrez
San Cristóbal de las Casas
Comitán
CHIAPAS
Tapachula
Huixtla
Motozintla
Frontera
Ciudad del Carmen
Laguna de Términos
Villahermosa
Cárdenas
TABASCO
CAMPECHE
Champotón
Campeche
Hopelchén
Mérida
Progreso
Motul
Izamal
Tizimín
Valladolid
Ticul
Tekax
Peto
YUCATÁN
Cancun
Pto. Juárez
Isla Cozumel
C. Catoche
Isla Desterrada
Isla Pérez
QUINTANA ROO
Felipe Carrillo Puerto
Chetumal
B. de Chetumal
Ambergris Cay
Turneffe Is.
Belize City
BELIZE
Belmopan
Dangriga
Banco Chinchorro
Golfo de Honduras
Islas de la Bahía
Puerto Barrios
Puerto Cortés
Tela
La Ceiba
San Pedro Sula
HONDURAS
Tegucigalpa
GUATEMALA
Cobán
Huehuetenango
Quezaltenango
Antigua
Zacapa
Chiquimula
Flores
L. Petén Itzá
Tikal
CUBA
Guane
C. San Antonio
C. Corrientes
La Esperanza
COPYRIGHT. GEORGE PHILIP & SON, LTD.

GULF OF MEXICO
Isla Desterrada
Isla Pérez
Canal de Yucatán
U.S.A.
Fort Myers
Fort Lauderdale
West Palm Beach
Boca Raton
L. Okeechobee
Naples
C. Romano
Everglades
Hialeah
MIAMI
Florida City
C. Sable
Florida Bay
Key West
Florida Keys
Straits of Florida
Dry Tortugas
Grand Bahama I.
Little Abaco I.
Great Abaco I.
West End
Freeport
Northwest Providence Channel
Northeast Providence Channel
Bimini Is.
Berry Is.
Nassau
New Providence I.
Eleuthera I.
Andros Island
Andros Town
Nicolls Town
Great Guana Cay
Great Exuma I.
GREAT BAHAMA BANK
Santaren Channel
Cay Sal Bank
Canal Nicolás
Canal Viejo de Bahama
(Havana) LA HABANA
MARIANAO
Guanabacoa
Matanzas
San Antonio de los Baños
Guanajay
Bahía Honda
La Esperanza
Pinar del Río
San Luis
Los Palacios
Güines
Batabanó
Jagüey Grande
Playa Larga
Cárdenas
Colón
Jovellanos
Sagua la Grande
Santa Clara
Caibarién
Placetas
Cienfuegos
Trinidad
Sancti-Spíritus
Morón
Ciego de Avila
Nuevitas
Florida
Camagüey
Victoria de las Tunas
Santa Cruz del Sur
Golfo de Guacanayabo
Manzanillo
Sierra Maestra
C. Cruz
Nueva Gerona
Isla de la Juventud
Archipiélago de los Canarreos
C. San Antonio
C. Corrientes
Guane
Arch. de los Jardines de la Reina
CUBA
GREATER
Cayman Islands (Br.)
Cayman Brac
Little Cayman
Georgetown
Grand Cayman
7680
Montego Bay
Falmouth
St. Ann's Bay
Lucea
South Negril Pt.
Savanna la Mar
Black River
Mandeville
May Pen
Spanish Town
JAMAICA
KINGSTON
Pedro Cays (Jamaica)
Swan Islands (U.S.A. & Honduras)
Bajo Nuevo (Colombia)
CARIBBEAN
Cayos Roncador (U.S.A. & Colombia)
I. de Providencia (Colombia)
I. de San Andrés (Colombia)
Cayos de Albuquerque (Colombia)
Islas del Maíz (Nicaragua, U.S.A.)
Progreso
Mérida
Motul
Izamal
Tizimín
Valladolid
Espita
YUCATÁN
Ticul
Tekax
Peto
Maxcanú
Calkiní
Tenabo
Campeche
Champotón
Hopelchén
Ciudad del Carmen
Laguna de Términos
CAMPECHE
Escárcega
QUINTANA ROO
Chetumal
Corozal
B. de Chetumal
Isla Cozumel
Puerto Morelos
Cancún
C. Catoche
B. de la Ascensión
B. del Espíritu Santo
Banco Chinchorro
Ambergris Cay
Turneffe Is.
BELIZE
Belize City
Belmopan
Orange Walk
Maya Mts.
Dangriga
Punta Gorda
Golfo de Honduras
Islas de la Bahía
Roatán
Puerto Barrios
Puerto Cortés
Tela
La Ceiba
Trujillo
San Pedro Sula
HONDURAS
Tegucigalpa
Comayagua
Juticalpa
Catacamas
Laguna Caratasca
C. Camarón
C. Falso
C. Gracias á Dios
Mosquitia
Kisalaya
Cayos Miskitos (Nicaragua)
Pta. Gorda
Puerto Cabezas
Prinzapolca
Río Grande
GUATEMALA
Cobán
Huehuetenango
Quezaltenango
San Marcos
Totonicapán
Sololá
Antigua
Escuintla
Amatitlán
Jalapa
Zacapa
Chiquimula
L. de Izabal
L. Petén Itzá
Flores
Tikal
Palenque
Comitán
Tenosique
Ocosingo
Usumacinta
Coatepeque
Mazatenango
Retalhuleu
Ahuachapán
Santa Ana
Sonsonate
Suchitoto
Cojutepeque
Zacatecoluca
SAN SALVADOR
EL SALVADOR
Usulután
San Miguel
Golfo de Fonseca
Choluteca
Estelí
Matagalpa
NICARAGUA
Chinandega
León
Corinto
Boaco
Juigalpa
MANAGUA
Masaya
Granada
Diriamba
Lago de Nicaragua
Isla de Ometepe
Rivas
San Juan del Sur
Bluefields
Rama
El Bluff
Bahía de San Juan del Norte
San Juan del Norte
San Carlos
San Juan
Golfo de Papagayo
C. Velas
Santa Cruz
Liberia
COSTA RICA
Puntarenas
Alajuela
San José
Cartago
Limón
Pen. de Nicoya
Golfo de Nicoya
C. Blanco
Puerto Quepos
Chirripó Grande
3837
Cord. de Talamanca
Bahía de Coronado
Pen. de Osa
Golfo Dulce
Puerto Armuelles
Pta. Burica
Volcán Barú
3374
David
Golfo de Chiriquí
Laguna de Chiriquí
Bocas del Toro
Golfo de los Mosquitos
Serranía de Tabasará
Santiago
Chitré
Pen. de Azuero
Las Tablas
I. de Coiba
I. de Cebaco
Colón
Portobelo
Nombre de Dios
Archipiélago de San Blas
Balboa
PANAMÁ
La Chorrera
Golfo de Panamá
Arch. de las Perlas
Golfo del Darién
Serranía del Darién
La Palma
CARTAGENA

Projection: Bi-polar oblique Conical Orthomorphic

1 : 6 400 000
50 0 50 100 150 200 miles
50 0 100 200 300 km
ATLANTIC OCEAN
Tropic of Cancer
Puerto Rico Trench
Milwaukee Deep 9200
CARIBBEAN SEA
ANTILLES
LESSER ANTILLES
LEEWARD ISLANDS
WINDWARD ISLANDS
HISPANIOLA
HAITI
DOMINICAN REP.
PUERTO RICO (U.S.A.)
SAN JUAN
PORT-AU-PRINCE
SANTO DOMINGO
Cap-Haïtien
Port-de-Paix
Gonaïves
Hinche
Jacmel
Les Cayes
Jérémie
Santiago de los Caballeros
Puerto Plata
San Francisco de Macorís
La Vega
San Pedro de Macorís
La Romana
Barahona
Higüey
Hato Mayor
Mayagüez
Ponce
Arecibo
Bayamón
Caguas
Carolina
Fajardo
Guayama
Isla Mona (U.S.A.)
Canal de la Mona
Caicos Islands (Br.)
Turks Islands (Br.)
Great Inagua I.
Little Inagua I.
Crooked I.
Acklins I.
Long I.
Cat I.
San Salvador (Watling I., Guanahani)
Mayaguana I.
Rum Cay
Baracoa
Guantánamo
Paso de los Vientos (Windward Passage)
Virgin Is. (Br.)
Virgin Is. (U.S.A.)
Road Town
Charlotte Amalie
St. Croix
Christiansted
Frederiksted
Anegada
Anegada Passage
Anguilla (Br.)
St.-Martin (Guad.)
St. Maarten (Neth.)
St.-Barthélemy (Fr.)
Saba (Neth.)
St. Eustatius (Neth.)
ST. CHRISTOPHER-NEVIS
Basseterre
Barbuda
ANTIGUA & BARBUDA
St. Johns
Montserrat
Redonda
Guadeloupe Passage
GUADELOUPE (Fr.)
Pointe-a-Pitre
Basse-Terre
Marie-Galante (Fr.)
Désirade
Dominica Passage
DOMINICA
Roseau
Portsmouth
I. de Aves (Bird I.) (Venezuela)
Martinique Passage
MARTINIQUE
Fort-de-France
Mt. Pelée 1397
St. Lucia Channel
ST. LUCIA
Castries
Soufrière
St. Vincent Passage
ST. VINCENT
Kingstown
Soufrière 1234
BARBADOS
Bridgetown
Speightstown
THE GRENADINES
GRENADINES
Hillsborough
GRENADA
St. George's
Aruba (Neth.)
Curaçao
Bonaire
NETH. ANTILLES
Willemstad
Is. de Aves (Ven.)
Is. Los Roques (Ven.)
I. Orchila (Ven.)
I. Blanquilla (Ven.)
I. Los Hermanos (Ven.)
Is. Los Testigos (Ven.)
I. La Tortuga (Ven.)
I. Margarita
La Asunción
Porlamar
NUEVA ESPARTA
Tobago
Scarborough
TRINIDAD & TOBAGO
Port of Spain
Arima
San Fernando
Dragon's Mouth
Serpent's Mouth
Golfo de Paria
Pen. de Paria
Carúpano
Cumaná
SUCRE
Caripito
Barcelona
Puerto La Cruz
Maturín
MONAGAS
ANZOÁTEGUI
El Tigre
Anaco
DELTA AMACURO
Tucupita
Ciudad Guayana
Ciudad Bolívar
Upata
El Callao
Tumeremo
Sierra Imataca
CARACAS
DISTRITO FEDERAL
La Guaira
Maiquetía
Maracay
Los Teques
Valencia
Puerto Cabello
CARABOBO
ARAGUA
MIRANDA
San Felipe
YARACUY
Barquisimeto
LARA
Carora
Coro
FALCÓN
Punto Fijo
Pen. de Paraguaná
Golfo de Venezuela
Pen. de la Guajira
GUAJIRA
Maracaibo
Lago de Maracaibo
ZULIA
Cabimas
Santa Rita
Ciudad Ojeda
Mene Grande
Machiques
TRUJILLO
Valera
Trujillo
MÉRIDA
Mérida
Cord. de Mérida
TÁCHIRA
San Cristóbal
Barinas
BARINAS
PORTUGUESA
Guanare
Acarigua
COJEDES
San Carlos
GUÁRICO
Calabozo
Valle de la Pascua
San Fernando de Apure
Orinoco
VENEZUELA
Riohacha
Santa Marta
Ciénaga
Valledupar
Barranquilla
Soledad
Sabanalarga
Fundación
MAGDALENA
CÉSAR
Plato
Magangué
Mompós
El Banco
NORTE DE SANTANDER
Cúcuta
Ocaña
BOLÍVAR
Serranía de los Motilones
West from Greenwich

COPYRIGHT. GEORGE PHILIP & SON. LTD.

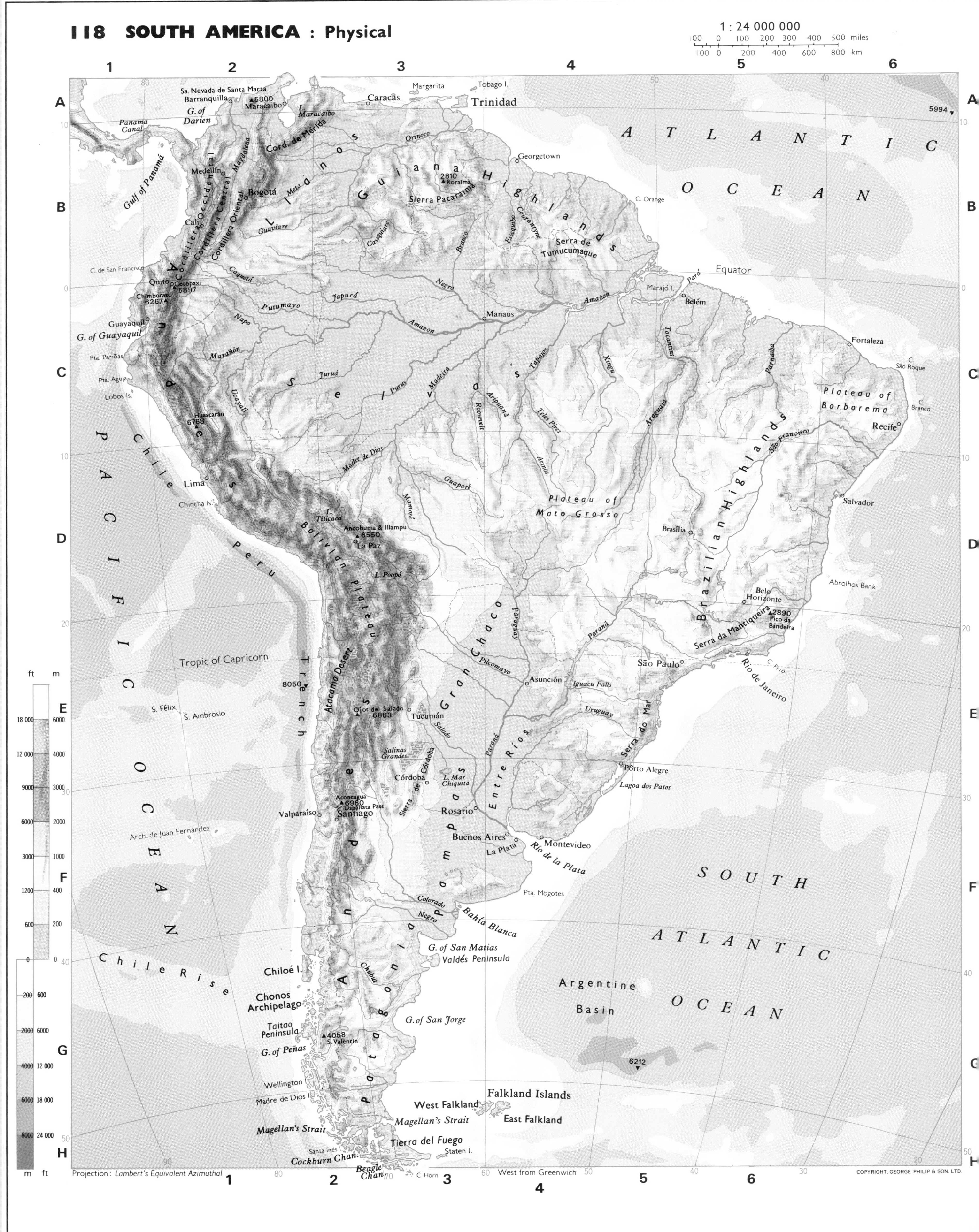
1 : 24 000 000
100 0 100 200 300 400 500 miles
100 0 200 400 600 800 km
ATLANTIC OCEAN
PACIFIC OCEAN
SOUTH ATLANTIC OCEAN
Sa. Nevada de Santa Marta
Barranquilla
Maracaibo
5800
G. of Darien
Panama Canal
Caracas
Margarita
Tobago I.
Trinidad
L. Maracaibo
Cord. de Mérida
Llanos
Orinoco
Georgetown
Guiana Highlands
2810 Roraima
Sierra Pacaraima
Gulf of Panamá
Medellín
Cordillera Occidental
Cordillera Central
Cordillera Oriental
Magdalena
Bogotá
Meta
Cali
Guaviare
Casiquiare
Branco
Essequibo
Courantyne
C. Orange
Serra de Tumucumaque
C. de San Francisco
Quito
Cotopaxi 5897
Chimborazo 6267
Caquetá
Negro
Equator
Pará
Marajó I.
Belém
Amazon
Putumayo
Japurá
Manaus
Guayaquil
G. of Guayaquil
Napo
Pta. Pariñas
Pta. Aguja
Lobos Is.
Marañón
Juruá
Purus
Madeira
Tapajós
Xingu
Tocantins
Parnaíba
Fortaleza
C. São Roque
Plateau of Borborema
C. Branco
Recife
Ucayali
Huascarán 6768
Aripuanã
Roosevelt
Teles Pires
Araguaia
São Francisco
Madre de Dios
Arinos
Guaporé
Andes
Selvas
Chile Peru Trench
Lima
Chincha Is.
Mamoré
Plateau of Mato Grosso
Salvador
L. Titicaca
Ancohuma & Illampu 6550
La Paz
Bolivian Plateau
L. Poopó
Brasília
Brazilian Highlands
Abrolhos Bank
Belo Horizonte
2890 Pico da Bandeira
Serra da Mantiqueira
Paraguay
Paraná
Gran Chaco
Tropic of Capricorn
Atacama Desert
8050
Pilcomayo
Asunción
São Paulo
C. Frio
Rio de Janeiro
Iguaçu Falls
S. Félix
S. Ambrosio
Ojos del Salado 6863
Tucumán
Salado
Uruguay
Serra do Mar
Salinas Grandes
Sierra de Córdoba
Córdoba
L. Mar Chiquita
Entre Ríos
Porto Alegre
Lagoa dos Patos
Aconcagua 6960
Uspallata Pass
Santiago
Valparaíso
Rosario
Arch. de Juan Fernández
Pampas
Buenos Aires
La Plata
Montevideo
Río de la Plata
Pta. Mogotes
Colorado
Negro
Bahía Blanca
G. of San Matias
Valdés Peninsula
Chile Rise
Chiloé I.
Chubut
Patagonia
Chonos Archipelago
Argentine Basin
G. of San Jorge
Taitao Peninsula
4058 S. Valentín
G. of Peñas
6212
Wellington I.
Madre de Dios I.
Falkland Islands
West Falkland
East Falkland
Magellan's Strait
Tierra del Fuego
Staten I.
Santa Inés I.
Cockburn Chan.
Beagle Chan.
C. Horn
5994
ft m
18 000 6000
12 000 4000
9000 3000
6000 2000
3000 1000
1200 400
600 200
0 0
200 600
2000 6000
4000 12 000
6000 18 000
8000 24 000
m ft
Projection: Lambert's Equivalent Azimuthal
West from Greenwich

COPYRIGHT, GEORGE PHILIP & SON, LTD.

1 : 24 000 000

100 0 100 200 300 400 500 miles

100 0 200 400 600 800 km

NORTH ATLANTIC OCEAN

SOUTH ATLANTIC OCEAN

PACIFIC OCEAN

COSTA RICA
San José
PANAMA
Panamá
Colón
Golfo de Panamá
Golfo de Darién
Barranquilla
Cartagena
Maracaibo
Barquisimeto
Caracas
Valencia
TRINIDAD AND TOBAGO
Port of Spain
Ciudad Guayana
Orinoco
VENEZUELA
Cúcuta
San Cristóbal
Bucaramanga
Medellín
Bogotá
Cali
COLOMBIA
Magdalena
Meta
Georgetown
Paramaribo
Cayenne
GUYANA
SURINAM
FRENCH GUIANA
C. Orange
Essequibo
Corantijn
Maroni
Branco
Negro
Caquetá
C. de San Francisco
Quito
ECUADOR
Guayaquil
G. de Guayaquil
Putumayo
Napo
Iquitos
Marañón
Japurá
Manaus
Amazonas (Amazon)
Santarem
Ilha de Marajó
Belém
Equator
São Luís
Fortaleza (Ceara)
Teresina
C. de São Roque
Natal
João Pessoa
Recife (Pernambuco)
Maceió
Aracaju
Salvador
Tocantins
Xingu
Tapajós
Madeira
Juruá
Purus
Aripuanã
Pôrto Velho
Araguaia
Parnaíba
São Francisco
Pta. Aguja
Chiclayo
Trujillo
Chimbote
Ucayali
PERU
Callao
Lima
Cuzco
Madre de Dios
Guaporé
Mamoré
BRAZIL
L. Titicaca
BOLIVIA
Arequipa
La Paz
Cochabamba
Santa Cruz
Sucre
Cuiabá
Brasília
Goiânia
Belo Horizonte
Campo Grande
Iquique
Ribeirão Prêto
Vitória
Juiz de Fora
Campos
Paraná
PARAGUAY
Paraguay
Pilcomayo
Londrina
Campinas
Niterói
SÃO PAULO
Santos
RIO DE JANEIRO
Tropic of Capricorn
Antofagasta
Asunción
Curitiba
Salta
San Miguel de Tucumán
Isla San Felix (Chile)
Isla San Ambrosio (Chile)
Resistencia
Corrientes
Uruguay
Salado
ARGENTINA
Córdoba
San Juan
Santa Fe
Paraná
Pôrto Alegre
Lagoa dos Patos
Pelotas
CHILE
Mendoza
Rosario
URUGUAY
Viña del Mar
Valparaíso
Arch de Juan Fernández (Chile)
Santiago
BUENOS AIRES
La Plata
Rio de la Plata
Montevideo
Talca
Concepción
Mar del Plata
Bahia Blanca
Colorado
Negro
Valdivia
Viedma
Puerto Montt
Chubut
Golfo San Jorge
Comodoro Rivadavia
G. de Penas
FALKLAND ISLANDS (U.K.)
West Falkland
Stanley
East Falkland
Strait of Magellan
Punta Arenas
Tierra del Fuego
Cape Horn

Projection: Lambert's Equivalent Azimuthal

West from Greenwich

COPYRIGHT, GEORGE PHILIP & SON, LTD

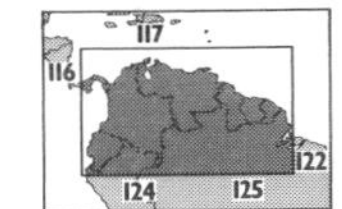
117
116
124
125
122

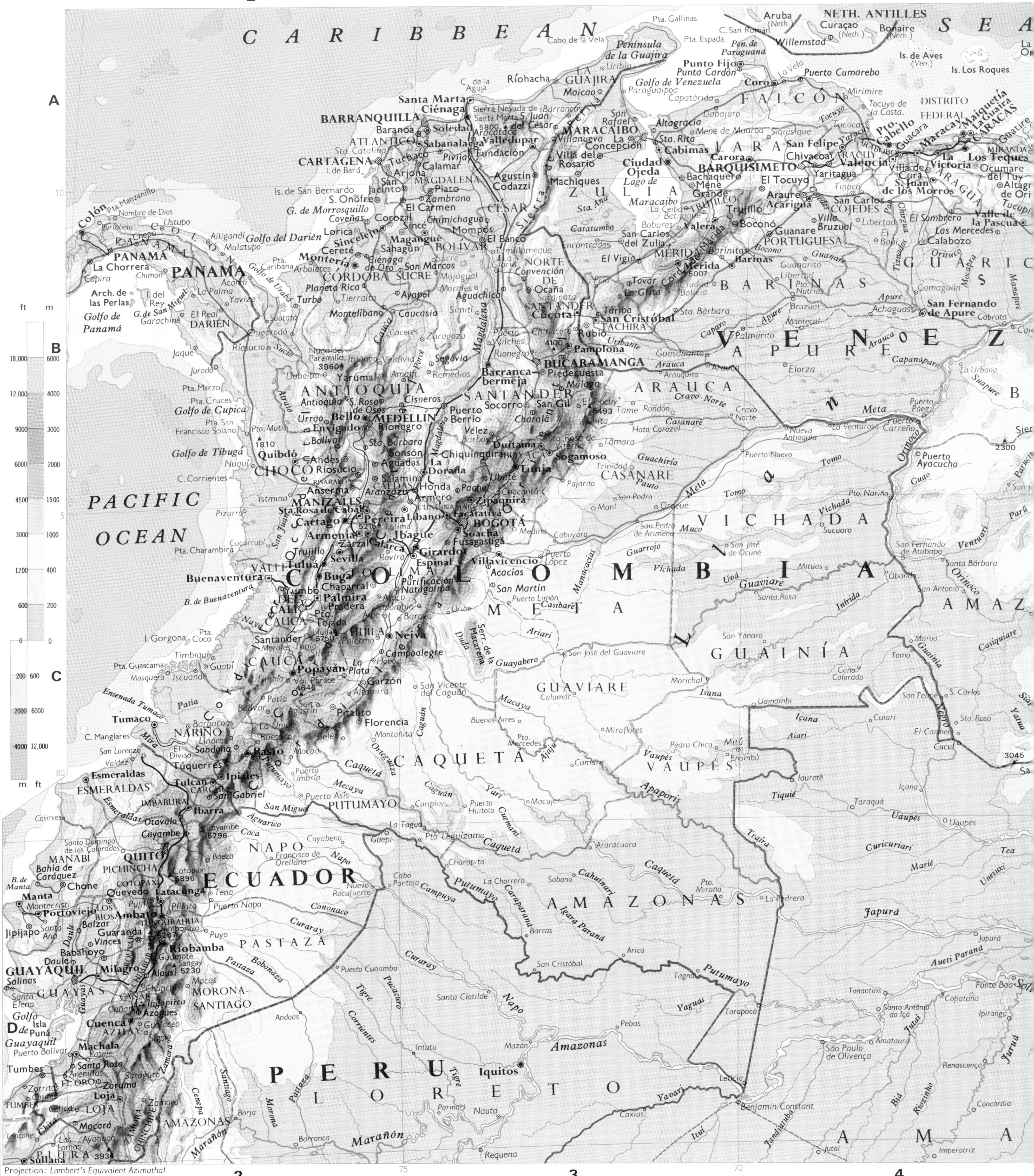

Projection: *Lambert's Equivalent Azimuthal*

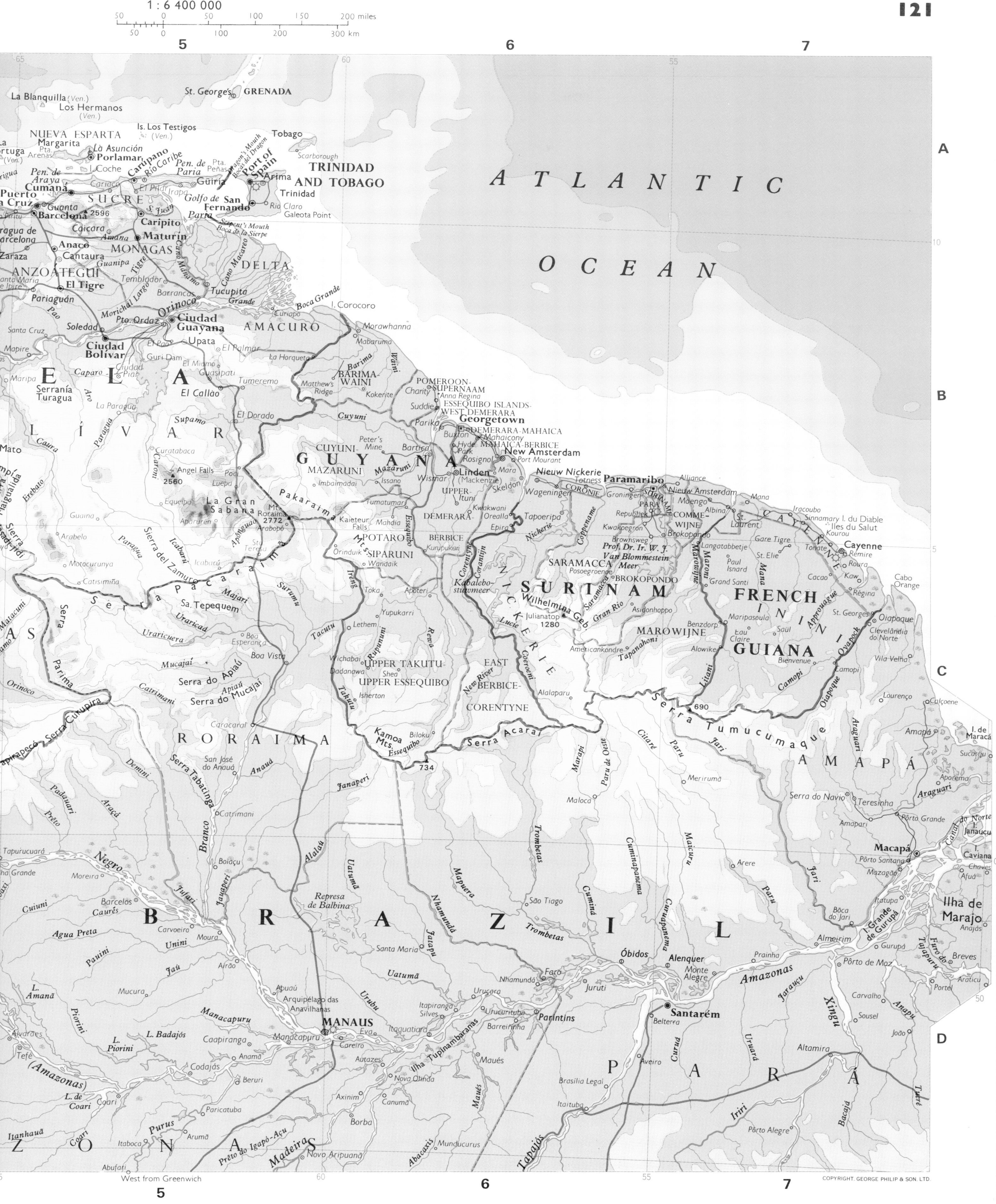
1 : 6 400 000
50 0 50 100 150 200 miles
50 0 100 200 300 km
5
6
7
A
B
C
D
ATLANTIC
OCEAN
St. George's
GRENADA
La Blanquilla (Ven.)
Los Hermanos (Ven.)
Is. Los Testigos (Ven.)
NUEVA ESPARTA
Margarita
La Asunción
Porlamar
I. Coche
Tobago
Scarborough
TRINIDAD AND TOBAGO
Port of Spain
Arima
Trinidad
San Fernando
Galeota Point
Carúpano
Río Caribe
Pen. de Paria
Güiria
Golfo de Paria
Serpent's Mouth
Boca de la Sierpe
Cumaná
Puerto la Cruz
Barcelona
SUCRE
Caripito
Maturín
MONAGAS
Anaco
Cantaura
ANZOATEGUI
El Tigre
Pariaguán
Soledad
Ciudad Bolívar
DELTA
Tucupita
Orinoco
Pto. Ordaz
Ciudad Guayana
Upata
AMACURO
Boca Grande
I. Corocoro
Guri Dam
El Callao
Tumeremo
El Dorado
Serranía Turagua
Angel Falls
2560
La Gran Sabana
Mt. Roraima
2772
Sa. Tepequem
Boa Vista
Serra do Apiaú
Serra do Mucajaí
Caracaraí
RORAIMA
Serra Pacaraima
Pakaraima Mts.
GUYANA
BARIMA-WAINI
POMEROON-SUPERNAAM
ESSEQUIBO ISLANDS-WEST DEMERARA
Georgetown
DEMERARA-MAHAICA
MAHAICA-BERBICE
New Amsterdam
CUYUNI-MAZARUNI
Linden
UPPER-DEMERARA-BERBICE
POTARO-SIPARUNI
Kaieteur Falls
UPPER TAKUTU-UPPER ESSEQUIBO
EAST BERBICE-CORENTYNE
Lethem
Kamoa Mts.
Serra Acaraí
734
Nieuw Nickerie
Paramaribo
Nieuw Amsterdam
Moengo
SURINAM
SARAMACCA
BROKOPONDO
NICKERIE
MAROWIJNE
CORONIE
COMMEWIJNE
Prof. Dr. Ir. W. J. Van Blommestein Meer
Wilhelmina Geb.
Julianatop 1280
FRENCH GUIANA
INNINI
CAYENNE
Cayenne
St. Laurent
Iles du Salut
Oiapoque
Cabo Orange
Serra Tumucumaque
690
AMAPÁ
Macapá
Ilha de Marajó
B R A Z I L
MANAUS
Santarém
Óbidos
Alenquer
Monte Alegre
Parintins
Amazonas
Negro
Trombetas
Xingu
Tapajós
Madeira
Represa de Balbina
P A R Á
A M A Z O N A S
West from Greenwich
65
60
55
50
10
5
0

COPYRIGHT. GEORGE PHILIP & SON. LTD.

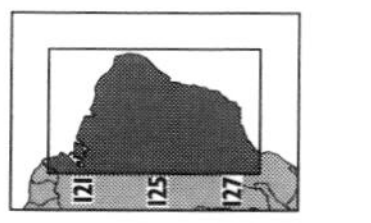

121
125
127

A
B
C
1
2
3
4
5
ATLANTIC OCEAN
FORTALEZA (Ceará)
NATAL
RIO GRANDE DO NORTE
João Pessoa (Paraíba)
RECIFE (Pernambuco)
MACEIÓ
SÃO LUÍS (Maranhão)
BELÉM (Pará)
Teresina
CEARÁ
MARANHÃO
PIAUÍ
PERNAMBUCO
TOCANTINS
PARÁ
AMAPÁ
Macapá
Ilha de Marajó
Sobral
Parnaíba
Caxias
Codó
Bacabal
Imperatriz
Marabá
Petrolina
Juazeiro
Floriano
Campina Grande
Caruaru
Mossoró
Serra do Gurupi
Serra dos Carajás
Serra do Estrondo
Serra do Penitente
Chapada das Mangabeiras
Tocantins
Xingu

1 : 6 400 000
50 0 50 100 150 200 miles
50 0 100 200 300 km
ATLANTIC OCEAN
ESPIRITO SANTO
BAHIA
GOIÁS
MINAS GERAIS
SÃO PAULO
PARANÁ
RIO DE JANEIRO
DISTRITO FEDERAL
SALVADOR (Bahia)
Baía de Todos os Santos
BRASÍLIA
BELO HORIZONTE
RIO DE JANEIRO
NITERÓI
SÃO PAULO
SANTOS
SANTO ANDRÉ
CURITIBA
GOIÂNIA
CAMPOS
Vitória
Serra Geral de Goiás
Serra do Espinhaço
Cabo Frio
Cabo de São Tomé
Banka Abrolhos
Ilha de São Sebastião
Tropic of Capricorn
West from Greenwich
Projection: Lambert's Equivalent Azimuthal
COPYRIGHT, GEORGE PHILIP & SON, LTD.
ft m
6000 2000
4500 1500
3000 1000
1200 400
600 200
0 0
200 600
2000 6000
4000 12 000

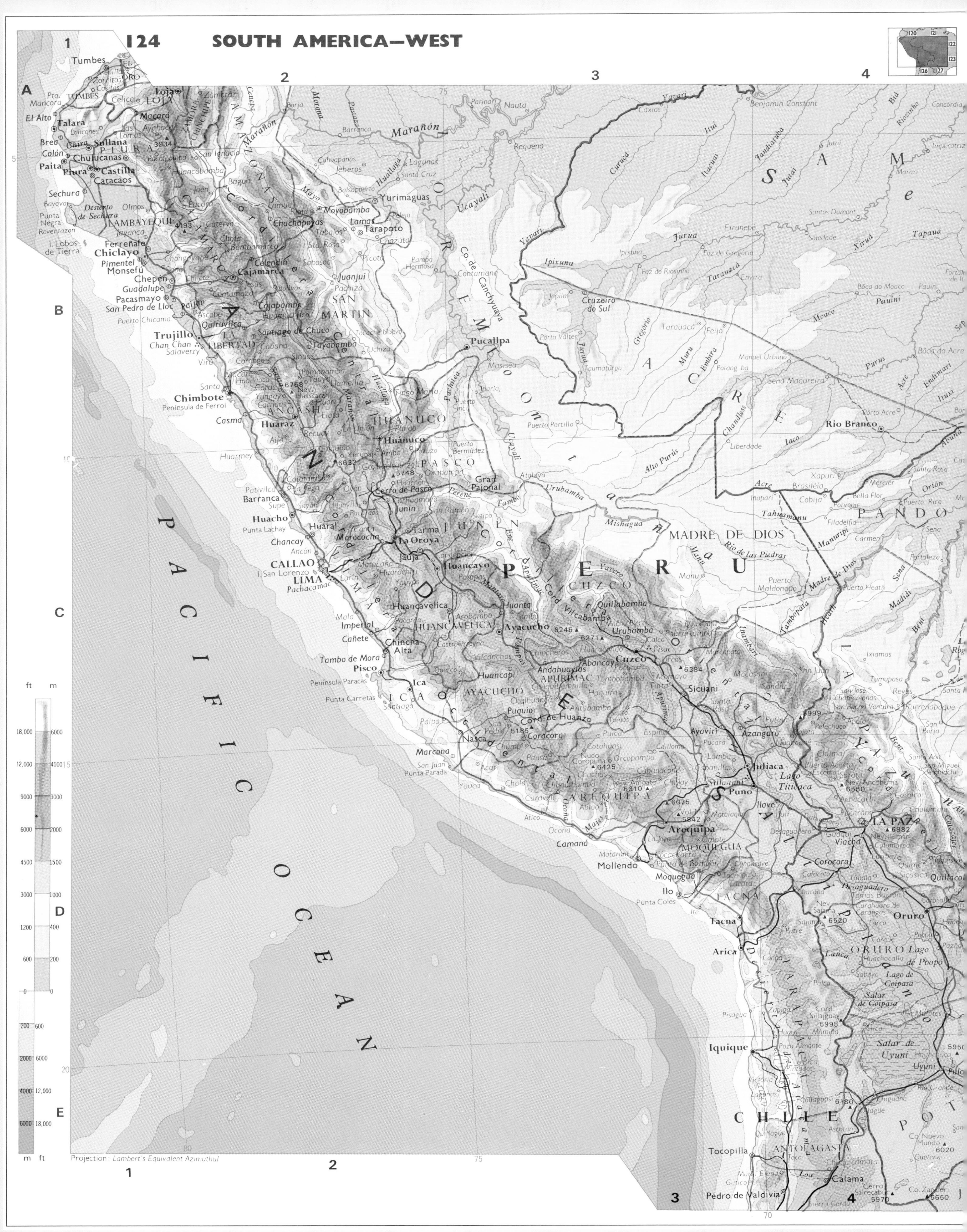
PACIFIC OCEAN
PERU
ANDES
Cordillera Central
Cordillera Occidental
Cordillera Oriental
Lima
Callao
Trujillo
Chiclayo
Piura
Arequipa
Cuzco
Huancayo
Pucallpa
Iquique
Arica
Tacna
La Paz
Oruro
Rio Branco
Lago Titicaca
Salar de Uyuni
CHILE
ACRE
MADRE DE DIOS
PANDO
Projection: Lambert's Equivalent Azimuthal

1 : 6 400 000

50 0 50 100 150 200 miles

50 0 100 200 300 km

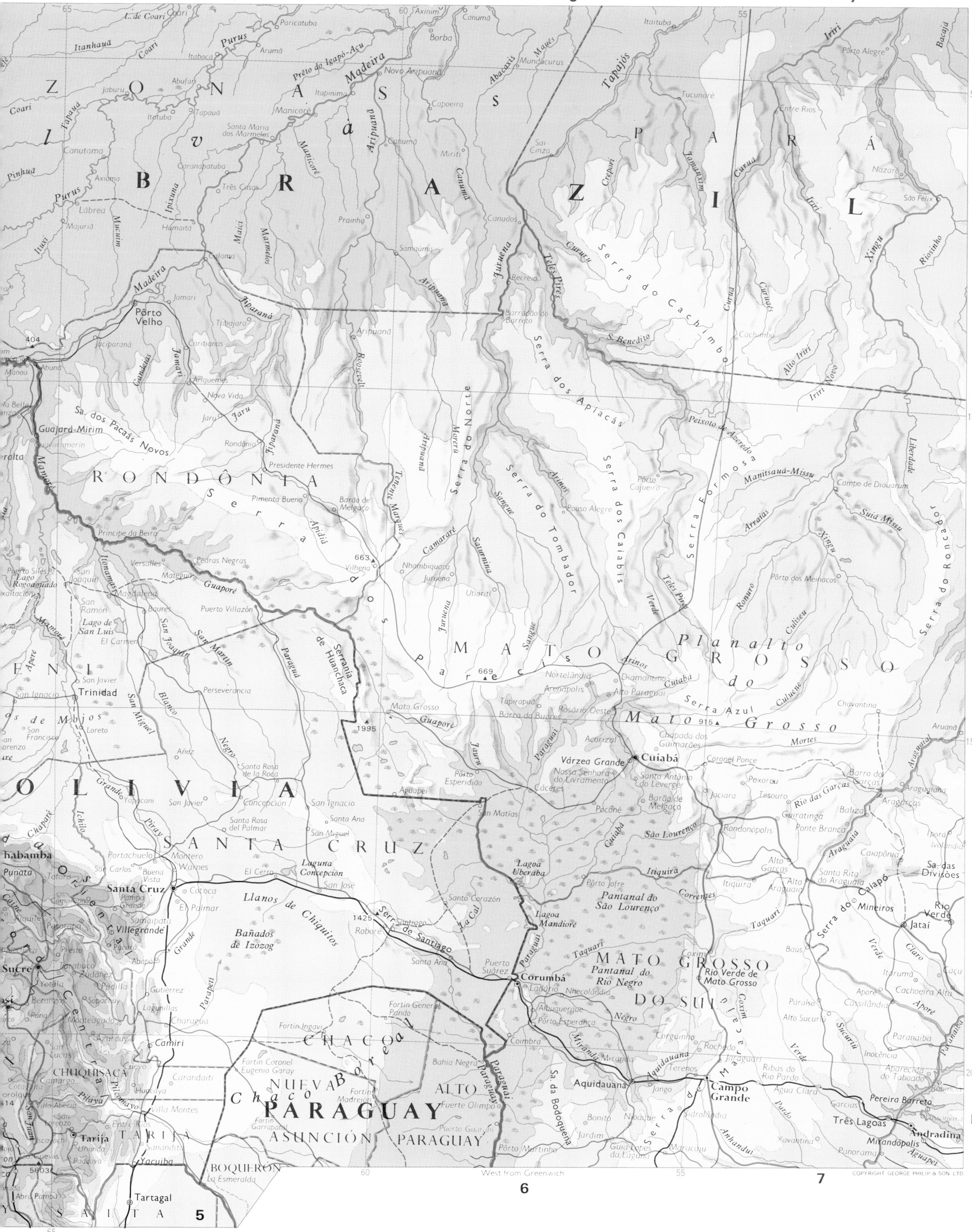

5 6 7

A B C D E

BRAZIL

AMAZONAS

PARÁ

RONDÔNIA

MATO GROSSO

MATO GROSSO DO SUL

BOLIVIA

BENI

SANTA CRUZ

CHUQUISACA

TARIJA

SALTA

PARAGUAY

NUEVA ASUNCIÓN

CHACO

ALTO PARAGUAY

BOQUERON

Chaco Boreal

Planalto do Mato Grosso

Serra dos Pacaás Novos

Serra dos Parecis

Serra do Norte

Serra do Tombador

Serra dos Caiabis

Serra dos Apiacás

Serra do Cachimbo

Serra Formosa

Serra Azul

Serra do Roncador

Serra do Caiapó

Serra de Maracaju

Sa. da Bodoquena

Sa. das Divisões

Serranía de Huanchaca

Serra de Santiago

Chapada dos Guimarães

Llanos de Chiquitos

Bañados de Izozog

Pantanal do São Lourenço

Pantanal do Rio Negro

Madeira, Purus, Coari, Tapauá, Itanhauã, Ituxi, Mucuim, Ipixuna, Marmelos, Maici, Manicoré, Aripuanã, Roosevelt, Camararé, Juruena, Arinos, Sangue, Teles Pires, Tapajós, Crepori, Jamanxim, Curuá, Curuaés, Iriri, Xingu, Riosinho, Bacajá, Liberdade, Culuene, Suiá Missu, Manitsauá-Missu, Ronuro, Culiseu, Arraias, Jamari, Jiparaná, Guaporé, Mamoré, Itonamas, San Miguel, Blanco, Paraguá, Negro, Grande, Piray, Ichilo, Chaparé, Parapetí, Pilcomayo, Paraguai, Jauru, Cuiabá, São Lourenço, Itiquira, Correntes, Taquari, Coxim, Negro, Miranda, Aquidauana, Anhanduí, Pardo, Verde, Sucuriú, Aporé, Araguaia, Rio das Garças, Mortes, Paranaíba, Claro, Caçu

Coari, Tapauá, Canutama, Lábrea, Humaitá, Manicoré, Borba, Novo Aripuanã, Prainha, Canudos, Itaituba, Tucunaré, Sai Cinza, Porto Alegre, Nazaré, São Félix, Entre Rios, Cachimbo, Pôrto Velho, Jaciparaná, Abunã, Guajará-Mirim, Ariquemes, Jaru, Rondônia, Presidente Hermes, Pimenta Bueno, Vilhena, Barão de Melgaço, Príncipe da Beira, Pedras Negras, Versalles, Principe da Beira, Aripuanã, Barradão do Barreto, Porto Cajueiro, Pouso Alegre, Utiariti, Nortelândia, Arenápolis, Diamantino, Alto Paraguai, Rosário Oeste, Tapirapuã, Barra do Bugres, Mato Grosso, Acorizal, Várzea Grande, Cuiabá, Nossa Senhora do Livramento, Santo Antônio do Leverger, Cáceres, Pôrto Esperidião, Poconé, Barão de Melgaço, Rondonópolis, Jaciara, Poxoréu, Tesouro, Guiratinga, Coronel Ponce, Ponte Branca, Barra do Garças, Aragarças, Chavantina, Aruanã, Alto Garças, Alto Araguaia, Santa Rita do Araguaia, Mineiros, Jataí, Rio Verde, Caiapônia, Porto dos Meinacos, Campo de Diauarum, Peixoto de Azeredo, Pôrto Jofre, Corumbá, Ladário, Albuquerque, Pôrto Esperança, Coimbra, Aquidauana, Miranda, Campo Grande, Coxim, Rio Verde de Mato Grosso, Corguinho, Rochedo, Jaraguari, Terenos, Jango, Sidrolândia, Nioaque, Bonito, Jardim, Guia Lopes da Laguna, Maracaju, Ribas do Rio Pardo, Agua Clara, Três Lagoas, Andradina, Mirandópolis, Pereira Barreto, Paranaíba, Inocência, Cassilândia, Aporé, Cachoeira Alta, Itarumã, Baús, Paraíso, Alto Sucuriú, Xavantina, Panorama

Trinidad, San Javier, San Ignacio, Loreto, San Joaquín, Magdalena, Baures, San Ramón, El Carmen, Puerto Villazón, Mategua, Puerto Siles, Concepción, San Javier, Yotaú, Santa Rosa de la Roca, Perseverancia, Añez, San Ignacio, Santa Ana, San Miguel, Santa Rosa del Palmar, San Matías, Santa Cruz, Montero, Warnes, Portachuelo, Buena Vista, El Cerro, Laguna Concepción, San José, Cotoca, El Palmar, Santa Corazón, Roboré, Santiago, Puerto Suárez, Santa Ana, Lagoa Uberaba, Lagoa Mandioré, Vallegrande, Samaipata, Abapó, Gutiérrez, Lagunillas, Charagua, Camiri, Sucre, Zudáñez, Padilla, Monteagudo, Azurduy, Cuevo, Huacaya, Villa Montes, Tarija, Entre Ríos, Yacuiba, Tartagal, Carandaití, Fortín Ingavi, Fortín General Pando, Fortín Coronel Eugenio Garay, Bahía Negra, Fuerte Olimpo, Puerto Guaraní, Pôrto Murtinho, La Esmeralda, Fortín Garrapatal

404 663 669 1995 915 1425 5603

60 55 65

5 10 15 20

West from Greenwich

COPYRIGHT GEORGE PHILIP & SON LTD

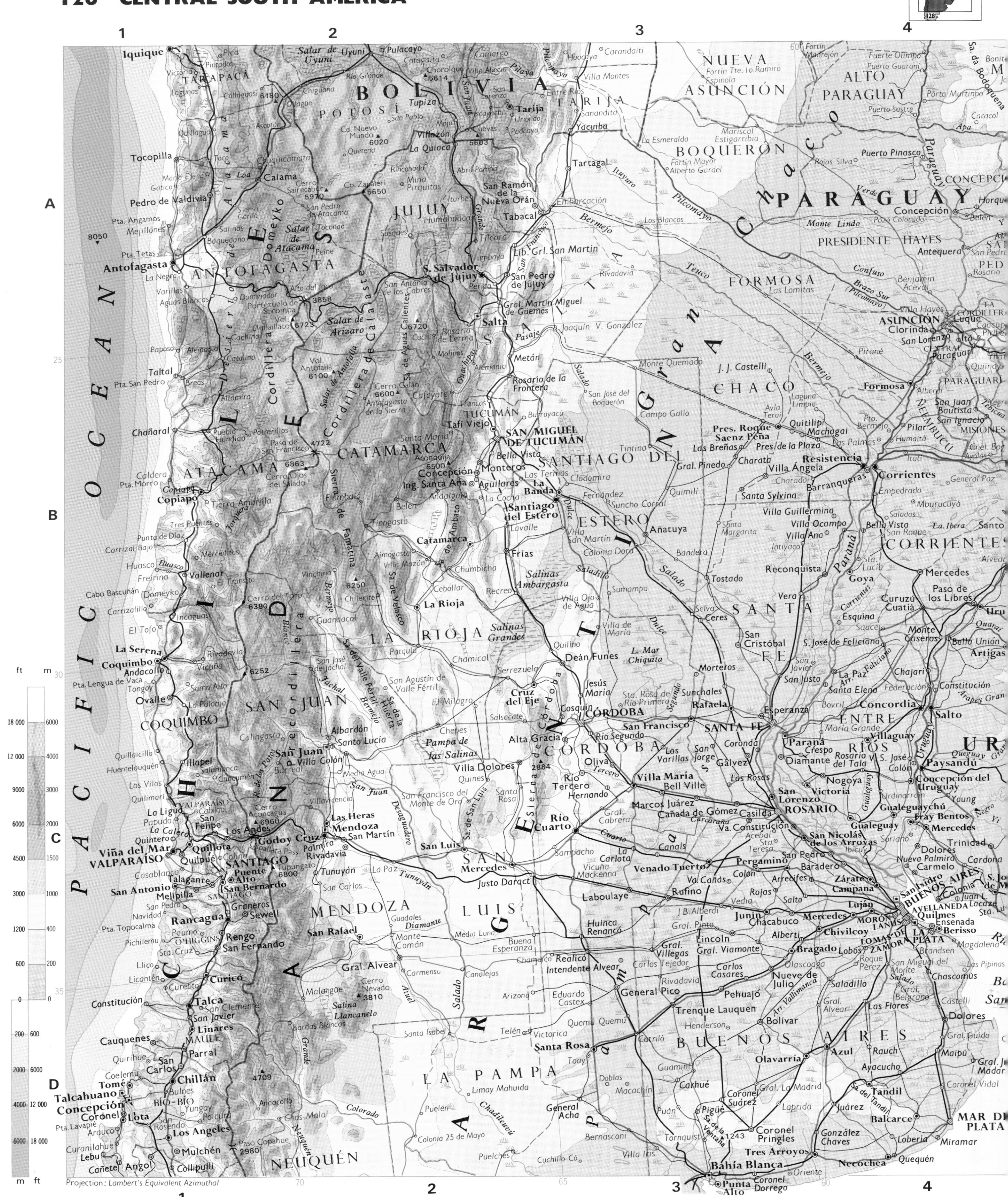
PACIFIC OCEAN
BOLIVIA
PARAGUAY
ARGENTINA
CHILE
ANDES
Gran Chaco
Iquique
Tarapacá
Salar de Uyuni
Uyuni
Pulacayo
Potosí
Tupiza
Villazón
La Quiaca
Tarija
Yacuiba
Tocopilla
Calama
Pedro de Valdivia
Mejillones
Antofagasta
Desierto de Atacama
Cordillera Domeyko
Salar de Atacama
San Pedro de Atacama
Jujuy
S. Salvador de Jujuy
San Pedro de Jujuy
Salta
Tartagal
Tabacal
San Ramón de la Nueva Orán
Lib. Grl. San Martín
Gral. Martín Miguel de Güemes
Joaquín V. González
Metán
Rosario de la Frontera
Nueva Asunción
Alto Paraguay
Boquerón
Presidente Hayes
Concepción
Formosa
Asunción
Luque
Clorinda
San Lorenzo
Chaco
Pres. Roque Sáenz Peña
Resistencia
Corrientes
Barranqueras
Taltal
Chañaral
Copiapó
Caldera
Atacama
Catamarca
Tucumán
San Miguel de Tucumán
Tafí Viejo
Santiago del Estero
La Banda
Añatuya
Frías
Salinas Grandes
Vallenar
Huasco
La Serena
Coquimbo
Ovalle
La Rioja
Chilecito
Reconquista
Goya
Santa Fe
Esperanza
Rafaela
San Juan
Albardón
Córdoba
Cosquín
Cruz del Eje
Deán Funes
Villa María
Bell Ville
Río Cuarto
Río Tercero
San Francisco
Paraná
Entre Ríos
Concordia
Salto
Paysandú
Rosario
San Lorenzo
San Nicolás de los Arroyos
Illapel
Los Andes
Valparaíso
Viña del Mar
Quillota
Santiago
Puente Alto
San Bernardo
San Antonio
Mendoza
Godoy Cruz
Las Heras
San Martín
San Luis
Villa Mercedes
San Rafael
Rancagua
Rengo
San Fernando
Curicó
Talca
Linares
Cauquenes
Chillán
Talcahuano
Concepción
Tomé
Lota
Coronel
Los Angeles
Angol
Mulchén
Collipulli
Neuquén
La Pampa
Santa Rosa
General Acha
General Pico
Buenos Aires
La Plata
Quilmes
Avellaneda
Luján
Mercedes
Junín
Pergamino
Zárate
Campana
Chivilcoy
Bragado
Olavarría
Azul
Tandil
Mar del Plata
Necochea
Tres Arroyos
Bahía Blanca
Punta Alto
Coronel Pringles
Coronel Suárez
Dolores
Balcarce
Projection: Lambert's Equivalent Azimuthal

1 : 6 400 000
ATLANTIC OCEAN
BRAZIL
West from Greenwich
Tropic of Capricorn

COPYRIGHT. GEORGE PHILIP & SON. LTD

SOUTHERN CHILE AND ARGENTINA

1 : 6 400 000
50 0 50 100 150 200 miles
50 0 100 200 300 km
LA PAMPA
BUENOS AIRES
NEUQUÉN
ARAUCANIA
RÍO NEGRO
LOS LAGOS
CHUBUT
SANTA CRUZ
MAGALLANES
TIERRA DEL FUEGO
CHILE
ARGENTINA
Patagonia
Angol
Mulchén
Victoria
Temuco
Lautaro
Neuquén
Zapala
Cipolletti
Gral. Roca
Choele Choel
Valdivia
La Unión
Osorno
Puerto Varas
Puerto Montt
San Carlos de Bariloche
Ancud
Isla de Chiloé
Castro
Esquel
Trelew
Rawson
Puerto Madryn
Bahía Blanca
Punta Alta
Coronel Pringles
Tres Arroyos
Necochea
Coronel Dorrego
Balcarce
Carmen de Patagones
Viedma
San Antonio Oeste
Golfo San Matías
Pen. Valdés
Meseta de Somuncurá
Archipiélago de los Chonos
Coihaique
Puerto Aisén
Comodoro Rivadavia
Golfo San Jorge
Caleta Olivia
Puerto Deseado
Golfo de Penas
Mte. San Valentín 4058
San Julián
Santa Cruz
Bahía Grande
Puerto Natales
Río Gallegos
Strait of Magellan
Punta Arenas
Isla Grande de Tierra del Fuego
Río Grande
Ushuaia
Canal Beagle
I. de los Estados (Staten I.)
Islas Wollaston
Cabo de Hornos (Cape Horn)
Islas Diego Ramirez
PACIFIC OCEAN
SOUTH ATLANTIC OCEAN
FALKLAND ISLANDS (ISLAS MALVINAS)
West Falkland
East Falkland
Stanley
Beauchêne I.
Projection: Lambert's Equivalent Azimuthal
West from Greenwich
COPYRIGHT, GEORGE PHILIP & SON, LTD.

INDEX

The index contains the names of all the principal places and features shown on the World Maps. Each name is followed by an additional entry in italics giving the country or region within which it is located. The alphabetical order of names composed of two or more words is governed primarily by the first word and then by the second. This is an example of the rule:

Mīr Kūh, *Iran* 65 **E8**
Mīr Shahdād, *Iran* 65 **E8**
Miraj, *India* 60 **L9**
Miram Shah, *Pakistan* 62 **C4**
Miramar, *Mozam.* 126 **D4**

Physical features composed of a proper name (Erie) and a description (Lake) are positioned alphabetically by the proper name. The description is positioned after the proper name and is usually abbreviated:

Erie, L., *N. Amer.* 106 **D4**

Where a description forms part of a settlement or administrative name however, it is always written in full and put in its true alphabetic position:

Mount Morris, *U.S.A.* 106 **D7**

Names beginning with M' and Mc are indexed as if they were spelt Mac. Names beginning St. are alphabetised under Saint, but Sankt, Sint, Sant', Santa and San are all spelt in full and are alphabetised accordingly. If the same place name occurs two or more times in the index and all are in the same country, each is followed by the name of the administrative subdivision in which it is located. The names are placed in the alphabetical order of the subdivisions. For example:

Jackson, *Ky., U.S.A.* 104 **G4**
Jackson, *Mich., U.S.A.* 104 **D3**
Jackson, *Minn., U.S.A.* 108 **D7**

The number in bold type which follows each name in the index refers to the number of the map page where that feature or place will be found. This is usually the largest scale at which the place or feature appears. The letter and figure which are in bold type immediately after the page number give the grid square on the map page, within which the feature is situated. The letter represents the latitude and the figure the longitude.

In some cases the feature itself may fall within the specified square, while the name is outside. This is usually the case only with features which are larger than a grid square. Rivers are indexed to their mouths or confluences, and carry the symbol → after their names. A solid square ■ follows the name of a country while, an open square □ refers to a first order administrative area.

ABBREVIATIONS USED IN THE INDEX

A.C.T. — Australian Capital Territory
Afghan. — Afghanistan
Ala. — Alabama
Alta. — Alberta
Amer. — America(n)
Arch. — Archipelago
Ariz. — Arizona
Ark. — Arkansas
Atl. Oc. — Atlantic Ocean
B. — Baie, Bahía, Bay, Bucht, Bugt
B.C. — British Columbia
Bangla. — Bangladesh
Barr. — Barrage
Bos.-H. — Bosnia-Herzegovina
C. — Cabo, Cap, Cape, Coast
C.A.R. — Central African Republic
C. Prov. — Cape Province
Calif. — California
Cent. — Central
Chan. — Channel
Colo. — Colorado
Conn. — Connecticut
Cord. — Cordillera
Cr. — Creek
D.C. — District of Columbia
Del. — Delaware
Dep. — Dependency
Des. — Desert
Dist. — District
Dj. — Djebel
Domin. — Dominica
Dom. Rep. — Dominican Republic
E. — East
El Salv. — El Salvador
Eq. Guin. — Equatorial Guinea
Fla. — Florida
Falk. Is. — Falkland Is.
G. — Golfe, Golfo, Gulf, Guba, Gebel
Ga. — Georgia
Gt. — Great, Greater
Guinea-Biss. — Guinea-Bissau
H.K. — Hong Kong
H.P. — Himachal Pradesh
Hants. — Hampshire
Harb. — Harbor, Harbour
Hd. — Head
Hts. — Heights
I.(s). — Île, Ilha, Insel, Isla, Island, Isle
Ill. — Illinois
Ind. — Indiana
Ind. Oc. — Indian Ocean
Ivory C. — Ivory Coast
J. — Jabal, Jebel, Jazira
Junc. — Junction
K. — Kap, Kapp
Kans. — Kansas
Kep. — Kepulauan
Ky. — Kentucky
L. — Lac, Lacul, Lago, Lagoa, Lake, Limni, Loch, Lough
La. — Louisiana
Liech. — Liechtenstein
Lux. — Luxembourg
Mad. P. — Madhya Pradesh
Madag. — Madagascar
Man. — Manitoba
Mass. — Massachusetts
Md. — Maryland
Me. — Maine
Medit. S. — Mediterranean Sea
Mich. — Michigan
Minn. — Minnesota
Miss. — Mississippi
Mo. — Missouri
Mont. — Montana
Moza. — Mozambique
Mt.(e). — Mont, Monte, Monti, Montaña, Mountain
N. — Nord, Norte, North, Northern, Nouveau
N.B. — New Brunswick
N.C. — North Carolina
N. Cal. — New Caledonia
N. Dak. — North Dakota
N.H. — New Hampshire
N.I. — North Island
N.J. — New Jersey
N. Mex. — New Mexico
N.S. — Nova Scotia
N.S.W. — New South Wales
N.W.T. — North West Territory
N.Y. — New York
N.Z. — New Zealand
Nebr. — Nebraska
Neths. — Netherlands
Nev. — Nevada
Nfld. — Newfoundland
Nic. — Nicaragua
O. — Oued, Ouadi
Occ. — Occidentale
O.F.S. — Orange Free State
Okla. — Oklahoma
Ont. — Ontario
Or. — Orientale
Oreg. — Oregon
Os. — Ostrov
Oz. — Ozero
P. — Pass, Passo, Pasul, Pulau
P.E.I. — Prince Edward Island
Pa. — Pennsylvania
Pac. Oc. — Pacific Ocean
Papua N.G. — Papua New Guinea
Pass. — Passage
Pen. — Peninsula, Péninsule
Phil. — Philippines
Pk. — Park, Peak
Plat. — Plateau
P-ov. — Poluostrov
Prov. — Province, Provincial
Pt. — Point
Pta. — Ponta, Punta
Pte. — Pointe
Qué. — Québec
Queens. — Queensland
R. — Rio, River
R.I. — Rhode Island
Ra.(s). — Range(s)
Raj. — Rajasthan
Reg. — Region
Rep. — Republic
Res. — Reserve, Reservoir
S. — San, South, Sea
Si. Arabia — Saudi Arabia
S.C. — South Carolina
S. Dak. — South Dakota
S.I. — South Island
S. Leone — Sierra Leone
Sa. — Serra, Sierra
Sask. — Saskatchewan
Scot. — Scotland
Sd. — Sound
Sev. — Severnaya
Sib. — Siberia
Sprs. — Springs
St. — Saint, Sankt, Sint
Sta. — Santa, Station
Ste. — Sainte
Sto. — Santo
Str. — Strait, Stretto
Switz. — Switzerland
Tas. — Tasmania
Tenn. — Tennessee
Tex. — Texas
Tg. — Tanjung
Trin. & Tob. — Trinidad & Tobago
U.A.E. — United Arab Emirates
U.K. — United Kingdom
U.S.A. — United States of America
Ut. P. — Uttar Pradesh
Va. — Virginia
Vdkhr. — Vodokhranilishche
Vf. — Vîrful
Vic. — Victoria
Vol. — Volcano
Vt. — Vermont
W. — Wadi, West
W. Va. — West Virginia
Wash. — Washington
Wis. — Wisconsin
Wlkp. — Wielkopolski
Wyo. — Wyoming
Yorks. — Yorkshire
Yug. — Yugoslavia

A

A Coruña = La Coruña, *Spain* 30 B2
Aachen, *Germany* 18 E2
Aadorf, *Switz.* 23 B7
Aalborg = Ålborg, *Denmark* 11 G3
Aalen, *Germany* 19 G6
A'âli en Nîl □, *Sudan* 77 F3
Aalsmeer, *Neths.* 16 D5
Aalst, *Belgium* 17 G4
Aalst, *Neths.* 17 F6
Aalten, *Neths.* 16 E9
Aalter, *Belgium* 17 F2
Aarau, *Switz.* 22 B6
Aarberg, *Switz.* 22 B4
Aardenburg, *Belgium* 17 F2
Aare →, *Switz.* 22 A6
Aargau □, *Switz.* 22 B6
Aarhus = Århus, *Denmark* 11 H4
Aarle, *Neths.* 17 E7
Aarschot, *Belgium* 17 G5
Aarsele, *Belgium* 17 G2
Aartrijke, *Belgium* 17 F2
Aarwangen, *Switz.* 22 B5
Aba, *China* 52 A3
Aba, *Nigeria* 79 D6
Aba, *Zaïre* 82 B3
Âbâ, Jazîrat, *Sudan* 77 E3
Abacaxis →, *Brazil* 121 D6
Ābādān, *Iran* 65 D6
Abade, *Ethiopia* 77 F4
Ābādeh, *Iran* 65 D7
Abadin, *Spain* 30 B3
Abadla, *Algeria* 75 B4
Abaeté, *Brazil* 123 E2
Abaeté →, *Brazil* 123 E2
Abaetetuba, *Brazil* 122 B2
Abagnar Qi, *China* 50 C9
Abai, *Paraguay* 127 B4
Abak, *Nigeria* 79 E6
Abakaliki, *Nigeria* 79 D6
Abakan, *Russia* 45 D10
Abalemma, *Niger* 79 B6
Abana, *Turkey* 66 C6
Abancay, *Peru* 124 C3
Abanilla, *Spain* 29 G3
Abano Terme, *Italy* 33 C8
Abapó, *Bolivia* 125 D5
Abarán, *Spain* 29 G3
Abariringa, *Kiribati* 92 H10
Abarqū, *Iran* 65 D7
Abashiri, *Japan* 48 B12
Abashiri-Wan, *Japan* 48 B12
Abaújszántó, *Hungary* 21 G11
Abay, *Kazakhstan* 44 E8
Abaya, L., *Ethiopia* 77 F4
Abaza, *Russia* 44 D10
Abbadia San Salvatore, *Italy* 33 F8
'Abbāsābād, *Iran* 65 C8
Abbay = Nîl el Azraq →, *Sudan* 77 D3
Abbaye, Pt., *U.S.A.* 104 B1
Abbé, L., *Ethiopia* 77 E5
Abbeville, *France* 25 B8
Abbeville, *La., U.S.A.* 109 K8
Abbeville, *S.C., U.S.A.* 105 H4
Abbiategrasso, *Italy* 32 C5
Abbieglassie, *Australia* 91 D4
Abbot Ice Shelf, *Antarctica* 5 D16
Abbotsford, *Canada* 100 D4
Abbotsford, *U.S.A.* 108 C9
Abbottabad, *Pakistan* 62 B5
Abcoude, *Neths.* 16 D5
Abd al Kūrī, *Ind. Oc.* 68 E5
Ābdar, *Iran* 65 D7
'Abdolābād, *Iran* 65 C8
Abéché, *Chad* 73 F9
Abejar, *Spain* 28 D2
Abekr, *Sudan* 77 E2
Abêlessa, *Algeria* 75 D5
Abengourou, *Ivory C.* 78 D4
Åbenrå, *Denmark* 11 J3
Abensberg, *Germany* 19 G7
Abeokuta, *Nigeria* 79 D5
Aber, *Uganda* 82 B3
Aberaeron, *U.K.* 13 E3
Aberayron = Aberaeron, *U.K.* 13 E3
Abercorn = Mbala, *Zambia* 83 D3
Abercorn, *Australia* 91 D5
Aberdare, *U.K.* 13 F4
Aberdare Ra., *Kenya* 82 C4
Aberdeen, *Australia* 91 E5
Aberdeen, *Canada* 101 C7
Aberdeen, *S. Africa* 84 E3
Aberdeen, *U.K.* 14 D6
Aberdeen, *Ala., U.S.A.* 105 J1
Aberdeen, *Idaho, U.S.A.* 110 E7
Aberdeen, *S. Dak., U.S.A.* 108 C5
Aberdeen, *Wash., U.S.A.* 112 D3
Aberdovey = Aberdyfi, *U.K.* 13 E3
Aberdyfi, *U.K.* 13 E3
Aberfeldy, *U.K.* 14 E5
Abergaria-a-Velha, *Portugal* 30 E2
Abergavenny, *U.K.* 13 F4
Abernathy, *U.S.A.* 109 J4
Abert, L., *U.S.A.* 110 E3
Aberystwyth, *U.K.* 13 E3
Abha, *Si. Arabia* 76 D5
Abhar, *Iran* 65 B6
Abhayapuri, *India* 63 F14
Abia □, *Nigeria* 79 D6
Abidiya, *Sudan* 76 D3
Abidjan, *Ivory C.* 78 D4
Abilene, *Kans., U.S.A.* 108 F6
Abilene, *Tex., U.S.A.* 109 J5
Abingdon, *U.K.* 13 F6
Abingdon, *Ill., U.S.A.* 108 E9
Abingdon, *Va., U.S.A.* 105 G5
Abington Reef, *Australia* 90 B4
Abitau →, *Canada* 101 B7
Abitau L., *Canada* 101 A7
Abitibi L., *Canada* 98 C4
Abiy Adi, *Ethiopia* 77 E4
Abkhaz Republic □, *Georgia* 43 E9
Abkit, *Russia* 45 C16
Abminga, *Australia* 91 D1
Abnûb, *Egypt* 76 B3
Abocho, *Nigeria* 79 D6
Abohar, *India* 62 D6
Aboisso, *Ivory C.* 78 D4
Abomey, *Benin* 79 D5
Abondance, *France* 27 B10
Abong-Mbang, *Cameroon* 80 D2
Abonnema, *Nigeria* 79 E6
Abony, *Hungary* 21 H10
Aboso, *Ghana* 78 D4
Abou-Deïa, *Chad* 73 F8
Aboyne, *U.K.* 14 D6
Abra Pampa, *Argentina* 126 A2
Abrantes, *Portugal* 31 F2
Abraveses, *Portugal* 30 E3
Abreojos, Pta., *Mexico* 114 B2
Abreschviller, *France* 25 D14
Abri, *Esh Shamâliya, Sudan* 76 C3
Abri, *Janub Kordofân, Sudan* 77 E3
Abrolhos, Banka, *Brazil* 123 E4
Abruzzi □, *Italy* 33 F10
Absaroka Range, *U.S.A.* 110 D9
Abū al Khaṣīb, *Iraq* 65 D6
Abū 'Alī, *Si. Arabia* 65 E6
Abū 'Alī →, *Lebanon* 69 A4
Abu 'Arīsh, *Si. Arabia* 68 D3
Abû Ballas, *Egypt* 76 C2
Abu Deleiq, *Sudan* 77 D3
Abu Dhabi = Abū Ẓāby, *U.A.E.* 65 E7
Abû Dis, *Sudan* 76 D3
Abû Dom, *Sudan* 77 D3
Abū Du'ān, *Syria* 64 B3
Abu el Gairi, W. →, *Egypt* 69 F2
Abû Gabra, *Sudan* 77 E2
Abu Ga'da, W. →, *Egypt* 69 F1
Abû Gubeiha, *Sudan* 77 E3
Abu Habl, Khawr →, *Sudan* 77 E3
Abū Ḥadrīyah, *Si. Arabia* 65 E6
Abu Hamed, *Sudan* 76 D3
Abu Haraz, *An Nîl el Azraq, Sudan* 77 E3
Abû Haraz, *Esh Shamâliya, Sudan* 76 D3
Abû Higar, *Sudan* 77 E3
Abū Kamāl, *Syria* 64 C4
Abū Madd, Ra's, *Si. Arabia* 64 E3
Abu Matariq, *Sudan* 77 E2
Abu Qir, *Egypt* 76 H7
Abu Qireiya, *Egypt* 76 C4
Abu Qurqâs, *Egypt* 76 J7
Abu Ṣafāt, W. →, *Jordan* 69 E5
Abû Simbel, *Egypt* 76 C3
Abū Ṣukhayr, *Iraq* 64 D5
Abu Tig, *Egypt* 76 B3
Abu Tiga, *Sudan* 77 E3
Abû Zabad, *Sudan* 77 E2
Abū Ẓāby, *U.A.E.* 65 E7
Abū Zeydābād, *Iran* 65 C6
Abufari, *Brazil* 125 B5
Abuja, *Nigeria* 79 D6
Abukuma-Gawa →, *Japan* 48 E10
Abukuma-Sammyaku, *Japan* 48 F10
Abunã, *Brazil* 125 B4
Abunã →, *Brazil* 125 B4
Aburo, *Zaïre* 82 B3
Abut Hd., *N.Z.* 87 K3
Abwong, *Sudan* 77 F3
Åby, *Sweden* 11 F10
Aby, Lagune, *Ivory C.* 78 D4
Acacías, *Colombia* 120 C3
Acajutla, *El Salv.* 116 D2
Açailândia, *Brazil* 122 C2
Acámbaro, *Mexico* 114 C4
Acaponeta, *Mexico* 114 C3
Acapulco, *Mexico* 115 D5
Acarai, Serra, *Brazil* 121 C6
Acaraú, *Brazil* 122 B3
Acari, *Brazil* 122 C4
Acarí, *Peru* 124 D3
Acarigua, *Venezuela* 120 B4
Acatlán, *Mexico* 115 D5
Acayucan, *Mexico* 115 D6
Accéglio, *Italy* 32 D3
Accomac, *U.S.A.* 104 G8
Accous, *France* 26 E3
Accra, *Ghana* 79 D4
Accrington, *U.K.* 12 D5
Acebal, *Argentina* 126 C3
Aceh □, *Indonesia* 56 D1
Acerenza, *Italy* 35 B8
Acerra, *Italy* 35 B7
Aceuchal, *Spain* 31 G4
Achacachi, *Bolivia* 124 D4
Achaguas, *Venezuela* 120 B4
Achalpur, *India* 60 J10
Achao, *Chile* 128 B2
Achel, *Belgium* 17 F6
Acheng, *China* 51 B14
Achenkirch, *Austria* 19 H7
Achensee, *Austria* 19 H7
Acher, *India* 62 H5
Achern, *Germany* 19 G4
Achill, *Ireland* 15 C2
Achill Hd., *Ireland* 15 C1
Achill I., *Ireland* 15 C1
Achill Sd., *Ireland* 15 C2
Achim, *Germany* 18 B5
Achinsk, *Russia* 45 D10
Achol, *Sudan* 77 F3
Acıgöl, *Turkey* 66 E3
Acireale, *Italy* 35 E8
Ackerman, *U.S.A.* 109 J10
Acklins I., *Bahamas* 117 B5
Acme, *Canada* 100 C6
Acobamba, *Peru* 124 C3
Acomayo, *Peru* 124 C3
Aconcagua □, *Chile* 126 C1
Aconcagua, Cerro, *Argentina* 126 C2
Aconquija, Mt., *Argentina* 126 B2
Acopiara, *Brazil* 122 C4
Açores, Is. dos = Azores, *Atl. Oc.* 2 C8
Acorizal, *Brazil* 125 D6
Acquapendente, *Italy* 33 F8
Acquasanta, *Italy* 33 F10
Acquaviva delle Fonti, *Italy* 35 B9
Acqui, *Italy* 32 D5
Acraman, L., *Australia* 91 E2
Acre = 'Akko, *Israel* 69 C4
Acre □, *Brazil* 124 B3
Acre →, *Brazil* 124 B4
Acri, *Italy* 35 C9
Acs, *Hungary* 21 H8
Acton, *Canada* 106 C4
Açu, *Brazil* 122 C4
Ad Dammām, *Si. Arabia* 65 E6
Ad Dawhah, *Qatar* 65 E6
Ad Dawr, *Iraq* 64 C4
Ad Dir'īyah, *Si. Arabia* 64 E5
Ad Dīwānīyah, *Iraq* 64 D5
Ad Dujayl, *Iraq* 64 C5
Ad Durūz, J., *Jordan* 69 C5
Ada, *Ghana* 79 D5
Ada, *Serbia* 21 K10
Ada, *Minn., U.S.A.* 108 B6
Ada, *Okla., U.S.A.* 109 H6
Adaja →, *Spain* 30 D6
Ådalslinden, *Sweden* 10 A10
Adam, Mt., *Falk. Is.* 128 D4
Adamantina, *Brazil* 123 F1
Adamaoua, Massif de l', *Cameroon* 79 D7
Adamawa □, *Nigeria* 79 D7
Adamawa Highlands = Adamaoua, Massif de l', *Cameroon* 79 D7
Adamello, Mt., *Italy* 32 B7
Adami Tulu, *Ethiopia* 77 F4
Adaminaby, *Australia* 91 F4
Adams, *Mass., U.S.A.* 107 D11
Adams, *N.Y., U.S.A.* 107 C8
Adams, *Wis., U.S.A.* 108 D10
Adam's Bridge, *Sri Lanka* 60 Q11
Adams L., *Canada* 100 C5
Adams Mt., *U.S.A.* 112 D5
Adam's Peak, *Sri Lanka* 60 R12
Adamuz, *Spain* 31 G6
Adana, *Turkey* 66 E6
Adana □, *Turkey* 66 E6
Adanero, *Spain* 30 E6
Adapazarı, *Turkey* 66 C4
Adarama, *Sudan* 77 D3
Adare, C., *Antarctica* 5 D11
Adaut, *Indonesia* 57 F8
Adavale, *Australia* 91 D3
Adda →, *Italy* 32 C6
Addis Ababa = Addis Abeba, *Ethiopia* 77 F4
Addis Abeba, *Ethiopia* 77 F4
Addis Alem, *Ethiopia* 77 F4
Addison, *U.S.A.* 106 D7
Addo, *S. Africa* 84 E4
Adebour, *Niger* 79 C7
Ādeh, *Iran* 64 B5
Adel, *U.S.A.* 105 K4
Adelaide, *Australia* 91 E2
Adelaide, *Bahamas* 116 A4
Adelaide, *S. Africa* 84 E4
Adelaide I., *Antarctica* 5 C17
Adelaide Pen., *Canada* 96 B10
Adelaide River, *Australia* 88 B5
Adelanto, *U.S.A.* 113 L9
Adelboden, *Switz.* 22 D5
Adele I., *Australia* 88 C3
Adélie, Terre, *Antarctica* 5 C10
Adélie Land = Adélie, Terre, *Antarctica* 5 C10
Ademuz, *Spain* 28 E3
Aden = Al 'Adan, *Yemen* 68 E4
Aden, G. of, *Asia* 68 E4
Adendorp, *S. Africa* 84 E3
Adh Dhayd, *U.A.E.* 65 E7
Adhoi, *India* 62 H4
Adi, *Indonesia* 57 E8
Adi Daro, *Ethiopia* 77 E4
Adi Keyih, *Eritrea* 77 E4
Adi Kwala, *Eritrea* 77 E4
Adi Ugri, *Eritrea* 77 E4
Adieu, C., *Australia* 89 F5
Adieu Pt., *Australia* 88 C3
Adigala, *Ethiopia* 77 E5
Adige →, *Italy* 33 C9
Adigrat, *Ethiopia* 77 E4
Adilabad, *India* 60 K11
Adin, *U.S.A.* 110 F3
Adin Khel, *Afghan.* 60 C6
Adinkerke, *Belgium* 17 F1
Adirondack Mts., *U.S.A.* 107 C10
Adıyaman, *Turkey* 67 E8
Adıyaman □, *Turkey* 67 E8
Adjim, *Tunisia* 75 B7
Adjohon, *Benin* 79 D5
Adjud, *Romania* 38 C10
Adjumani, *Uganda* 82 B3
Adlavik Is., *Canada* 99 B8
Adler, *Russia* 43 E8
Adliswil, *Switz.* 23 B7
Admer, *Algeria* 75 D6
Admer, Erg d', *Algeria* 75 D6
Admiralty G., *Australia* 88 B4
Admiralty I., *U.S.A.* 96 C6
Admiralty Inlet, *U.S.A.* 110 C2
Admiralty Is., *Papua N. G.* 92 H6
Ado, *Nigeria* 79 D5
Ado Ekiti, *Nigeria* 79 D6
Adok, *Sudan* 77 F3
Adola, *Ethiopia* 77 E5
Adonara, *Indonesia* 57 F6
Adoni, *India* 60 M10
Adony, *Hungary* 21 H8
Adour →, *France* 26 E2
Adra, *India* 63 H12
Adra, *Spain* 29 J1
Adrano, *Italy* 35 E7
Adrar, *Algeria* 75 C4
Adré, *Chad* 73 F9
Adrī, *Libya* 75 C7
Ádria, *Italy* 33 C9
Adrian, *Mich., U.S.A.* 104 E3
Adrian, *Tex., U.S.A.* 109 H3
Adriatic Sea, *Europe* 6 G9
Adua, *Indonesia* 57 E7
Adula, *Switz.* 23 D8
Adwa, *Ethiopia* 77 E4
Adzhar Republic □, *Georgia* 43 F10
Adzopé, *Ivory C.* 78 D4
Ægean Sea, *Europe* 39 L8
Æolian Is. = Eólie, Is., *Italy* 35 D7
Aerhtai Shan, *Mongolia* 54 B4
Ærø, *Denmark* 11 K4
Ærøskøbing, *Denmark* 11 K4
Aesch, *Switz.* 22 B5
'Afak, *Iraq* 64 C5
Afándou, *Greece* 37 C10
Afarag, Erg, *Algeria* 75 D5
Afars & Issas, Terr. of = Djibouti ■, *Africa* 68 E3
Affreville = Khemis Miliana, *Algeria* 75 A5
Afghanistan ■, *Asia* 60 C4
Afgoi, *Somali Rep.* 68 G3
Afikpo, *Nigeria* 79 D6
Aflou, *Algeria* 75 B5
Afogados da Ingàzeira, *Brazil* 122 C4
Afognak I., *U.S.A.* 96 C4
Afragola, *Italy* 35 B7
Afrera, *Ethiopia* 77 E5
Africa 70 E6
'Afrīn, *Syria* 64 B3
Afşin, *Turkey* 66 D7
Afton, *U.S.A.* 107 D9
Aftout, *Algeria* 74 C4
Afuá, *Brazil* 121 D7
Afula, *Israel* 69 C4
Afyonkarahisar, *Turkey* 66 D4
Afyonkarahisar □, *Turkey* 66 D4
Aga, *Egypt* 76 H7
Agadès = Agadez, *Niger* 79 B6
Agadez, *Niger* 79 B6
Agadir, *Morocco* 74 B3
Agaete, *Canary Is.* 36 F4
Agailás, *Mauritania* 74 D2
Agapa, *Russia* 45 B9
Agar, *India* 62 H7
Agaro, *Ethiopia* 77 F4
Agartala, *India* 61 H17
Agassiz, *Canada* 100 D4
Agats, *Indonesia* 57 F9
Agbélouvé, *Togo* 79 D5
Agboville, *Ivory C.* 78 D4
Agdam, *Azerbaijan* 43 G12
Agdash, *Azerbaijan* 43 F12
Agde, *France* 26 E7
Agde, C. d', *France* 26 E7
Agdz, *Morocco* 74 B3
Agdzhabedi, *Azerbaijan* 43 F12
Agen, *France* 26 D4
Agersø, *Denmark* 11 J5
Ageyevo, *Russia* 41 D10
Agger, *Denmark* 11 H2
Ággius, *Italy* 34 B2
Āgh Kand, *Iran* 65 B6
Aghoueyyît, *Mauritania* 74 D1
Aginskoye, *Russia* 45 D12
Agira, *Italy* 35 E7
Ağlasun, *Turkey* 66 E4
Agly →, *France* 26 F7
Agnibilékrou, *Ivory C.* 78 D4
Agnita, *Romania* 38 D7
Agnone, *Italy* 35 A7
Agofie, *Ghana* 79 D5
Agogna →, *Italy* 32 C5
Agogo, *Sudan* 77 F2
Agon, *France* 24 C5
Agön, *Sweden* 10 C11
Ágordo, *Italy* 33 B9
Agout →, *France* 26 E5
Agra, *India* 62 F7
Agramunt, *Spain* 28 D6
Agreda, *Spain* 28 D3
Ağri, *Turkey* 67 D10
Ağri □, *Turkey* 67 D10
Agri →, *Italy* 35 B9
Ağrı Dağı, *Turkey* 67 D11
Ağrı Karakose, *Turkey* 67 D10
Agrigento, *Italy* 34 E6
Agrinion, *Greece* 39 L4
Agrópoli, *Italy* 35 B7
Água Branca, *Brazil* 122 C3
Agua Caliente, *Baja Calif. N., Mexico* 113 N10
Agua Caliente, *Sinaloa, Mexico* 114 B3
Agua Caliente Springs, *U.S.A.* 113 N10
Água Clara, *Brazil* 125 E7
Agua Hechicero, *Mexico* 113 N10
Agua Preta →, *Brazil* 121 D5
Agua Prieta, *Mexico* 114 A3
Aguachica, *Colombia* 120 B3
Aguada Cecilio, *Argentina* 128 B3
Aguadas, *Colombia* 120 B2
Aguadilla, *Puerto Rico* 117 C6
Aguadulce, *Panama* 116 E3
Aguanga, *U.S.A.* 113 M10
Aguanish, *Canada* 99 B7
Aguanus →, *Canada* 99 B7
Aguapeí, *Brazil* 125 D6
Aguapeí →, *Brazil* 123 F1
Aguapey →, *Argentina* 126 B4
Aguaray Guazú →, *Paraguay* 126 A4
Aguarico →, *Ecuador* 120 D2
Aguas →, *Spain* 28 D4
Aguas Blancas, *Chile* 126 A2
Aguas Calientes, Sierra de, *Argentina* 126 B2
Águas Formosas, *Brazil* 123 E3
Aguascalientes, *Mexico* 114 C4
Aguascalientes □, *Mexico* 114 C4
Agudo, *Spain* 31 G6
Águeda, *Portugal* 30 E2
Agueda →, *Spain* 30 D4
Aguié, *Niger* 79 C6
Aguilafuente, *Spain* 30 D6
Aguilar, *Spain* 31 H6
Aguilar de Campóo, *Spain* 30 C6
Aguilares, *Argentina* 126 B2
Aguilas, *Spain* 29 H3
Agüimes, *Canary Is.* 36 G4
Aguja, C. de la, *Colombia* 120 A3
Agulaa, *Ethiopia* 77 E4
Agulhas, C., *S. Africa* 84 E3
Agulo, *Canary Is.* 36 F2
Agung, *Indonesia* 56 F5
Agur, *Uganda* 82 B3
Agusan →, *Phil.* 55 G6
Agustín Codazzi, *Colombia* 120 A3
Agvali, *Russia* 43 E12
Aha Mts., *Botswana* 84 B3
Ahaggar, *Algeria* 75 D6
Ahamansu, *Ghana* 79 D5
Ahar, *Iran* 64 B5
Ahaus, *Germany* 18 C3
Ahelledjem, *Algeria* 75 C6
Ahipara B., *N.Z.* 87 F4
Ahiri, *India* 60 K12
Ahlen, *Germany* 18 D3
Ahmad Wal, *Pakistan* 62 E1
Ahmadabad, *India* 62 H5
Aḥmadābād, *Khorāsān, Iran* 65 C9
Aḥmadābād, *Khorāsān, Iran* 65 C8
Aḥmadī, *Iran* 65 E8
Ahmadnagar, *India* 60 K9
Ahmadpur, *Pakistan* 62 E4
Ahmar, *Ethiopia* 77 F5
Ahmedabad = Ahmadabad, *India* 62 H5
Ahmednagar = Ahmadnagar, *India* 60 K9
Ahoada, *Nigeria* 79 D6
Ahome, *Mexico* 114 B3
Ahr →, *Germany* 18 E3
Ahram, *Iran* 65 D6
Ahrax Pt., *Malta* 37 D1
Ahrensbök, *Germany* 18 A6
Ahrweiler, *Germany* 18 E3
Āhū, *Iran* 65 C6
Ahuachapán, *El Salv.* 116 D2
Ahvāz, *Iran* 65 D6
Ahvenanmaa = Åland, *Finland* 9 F16
Aḥwar, *Yemen* 68 E4
Ahzar, *Mali* 79 B5
Aiari →, *Brazil* 120 C4
Aichach, *Germany* 19 G7
Aichi □, *Japan* 49 G8

Aidone, *Italy* 35 E7
Aiello Cálabro, *Italy* 35 C9
Aigle, *Switz.* 22 D3
Aignay-le-Duc, *France* 25 E11
Aigoual, Mt., *France* 26 D7
Aigre, *France* 26 C4
Aigua, *Uruguay* 127 C5
Aigueperse, *France* 26 B7
Aigues →, *France* 27 D8
Aigues-Mortes, *France* 27 E8
Aigues-Mortes, G. d', *France* 27 E8
Aiguilles, *France* 27 D10
Aiguillon, *France* 26 D4
Aigurande, *France* 26 B5
Aihui, *China* 54 A7
Aija, *Peru* 124 B2
Aikawa, *Japan* 48 E9
Aiken, *U.S.A.* 105 J5
Ailao Shan, *China* 52 F3
Aillant-sur-Tholon, *France* 25 E10
Aillik, *Canada* 99 A8
Ailly-sur-Noye, *France* 25 C9
Ailsa Craig, *U.K.* 14 F3
'Ailūn, *Jordan* 69 C4
Aim, *Russia* 45 D14
Aimere, *Indonesia* 57 F6
Aimogasta, *Argentina* 126 B2
Aimorés, *Brazil* 123 E3
Ain □, *France* 27 B9
Ain →, *France* 27 C9
Aïn Beïda, *Algeria* 75 A6
Aïn Ben Khellil, *Algeria* 75 B4
Aïn Ben Tili, *Mauritania* 74 C3
Aïn Beni Mathar, *Morocco* 75 B4
Aïn Benian, *Algeria* 75 A5
Ain Dalla, *Egypt* 76 B2
Ain el Mafki, *Egypt* 76 B2
Ain Girba, *Egypt* 76 B2
Aïn M'lila, *Algeria* 75 A6
Ain Qeiqab, *Egypt* 76 B1
Aïn-Sefra, *Algeria* 75 B4
Ain Sheikh Murzûk, *Egypt* 76 B2
'Ain Sudr, *Egypt* 69 F2
Ain Sukhna, *Egypt* 76 J8
Aïn Tédelès, *Algeria* 75 A5
Aïn-Témouchent, *Algeria* 75 A4
Aïn Touta, *Algeria* 75 A6
Ain Zeitûn, *Egypt* 76 B2
Aïn Zorah, *Morocco* 75 B4
Ainabo, *Somali Rep.* 68 F4
Ainaži, *Latvia* 40 C4
Aínos Óros, *Greece* 39 L3
Ainsworth, *U.S.A.* 108 D5
Aipe, *Colombia* 120 C2
Aiquile, *Bolivia* 125 D4
Aïr, *Niger* 79 B6
Air Hitam, *Malaysia* 59 M4
Airaines, *France* 25 C8
Airão, *Brazil* 121 D5
Airdrie, *U.K.* 14 F5
Aire →, *France* 25 C11
Aire →, *U.K.* 12 D7
Aire, I. del, *Spain* 36 B11
Aire-sur-la-Lys, *France* 25 B9
Aire-sur-l'Adour, *France* 26 E3
Airlie Beach, *Australia* 90 C4
Airolo, *Switz.* 23 C7
Airvault, *France* 24 F6
Aisch →, *Germany* 19 F7
Aisen □, *Chile* 128 C2
Aisne □, *France* 25 C10
Aisne →, *France* 25 C9
Aitana, Sierra de, *Spain* 29 G4
Aitkin, *U.S.A.* 108 B8
Aitolikón, *Greece* 39 L4
Aiuaba, *Brazil* 122 C3
Aiud, *Romania* 38 C6
Aix-en-Provence, *France* 27 E9
Aix-la-Chapelle = Aachen, *Germany* 18 E2
Aix-les-Bains, *France* 27 C9
Aixe-sur-Vienne, *France* 26 C5
Aiyansh, *Canada* 100 B3
Aíyina, *Greece* 39 M6
Aiyínion, *Greece* 39 J5
Aiyion, *Greece* 39 L5
Aizawl, *India* 61 H18
Aizenay, *France* 24 F5
Aizpute, *Latvia* 40 C2
Aizuwakamatsu, *Japan* 48 F9
Ajaccio, *France* 27 G12
Ajaccio, G. d', *France* 27 G12
Ajaju →, *Colombia* 120 C3
Ajalpan, *Mexico* 115 D5
Ajanta Ra., *India* 60 J9
Ajari Rep. = Adzhar Republic □, *Georgia* 43 F10
Ajax, *Canada* 106 C5
Ajdâbiyah, *Libya* 73 B9
Ajdovščina, *Slovenia* 33 C10
Ajibar, *Ethiopia* 77 E4
Ajka, *Hungary* 21 H7
'Ajmān, *U.A.E.* 65 E7
Ajmer, *India* 62 F6
Ajo, *U.S.A.* 111 K7
Ajoie, *Switz.* 22 B4
Ajok, *Sudan* 77 F2
Ajuy, *Phil.* 55 F5
Ak Dağ, *Antalya, Turkey* 66 E3
Ak Dağ, *Sivas, Turkey* 66 D7
Akaba, *Togo* 79 D5
Akabira, *Japan* 48 C11
Akabli, *Algeria* 75 C5
Akaki Beseka, *Ethiopia* 77 F4
Akala, *Sudan* 77 D4
Akamas □, *Cyprus* 37 D11
Akanthou, *Cyprus* 37 D12
Akaroa, *N.Z.* 87 K4
Akasha, *Sudan* 76 C3
Akashi, *Japan* 49 G7
Akbou, *Algeria* 75 A5
Akçaabat, *Turkey* 67 C8
Akçakoca, *Turkey* 66 C4
Akchâr, *Mauritania* 74 D2
Akdağmadeni, *Turkey* 66 D6
Akelamo, *Indonesia* 57 D7
Akershus fylke □, *Norway* 10 E5
Aketi, *Zaïre* 80 D4
Akhalkalaki, *Georgia* 43 F10
Akhaltsikhe, *Georgia* 43 F10
Akharnaí, *Greece* 39 L6
Akhelóös →, *Greece* 39 L4
Akhendria, *Greece* 39 Q8
Akhéron →, *Greece* 39 K3
Akhladhókambos, *Greece* 39 M5
Akhmîm, *Egypt* 76 B3
Akhnur, *India* 63 C6
Akhtubinsk, *Russia* 43 B12
Akhty, *Russia* 43 F12
Akhtyrka, *Ukraine* 40 F9
Aki, *Japan* 49 H6
Akimiski I., *Canada* 98 B3
Akimovka, *Ukraine* 42 C6
Akita, *Japan* 48 E10
Akita □, *Japan* 48 E10
Akjoujt, *Mauritania* 78 B2
Akka, *Morocco* 74 C3
Akkeshi, *Japan* 48 C12
'Akko, *Israel* 69 C4
Akkol, *Kazakhstan* 44 E8
Akkrum, *Neths.* 16 B7
Aklampa, *Benin* 79 D5
Aklavik, *Canada* 96 B6
Akmolinsk = Tselinograd, *Kazakhstan* 44 D8
Akmonte, *Spain* 31 H4
Aknoul, *Morocco* 75 B4
Akō, *Japan* 49 G7
Ako, *Nigeria* 79 C7
Akobo →, *Ethiopia* 77 F3
Akola, *India* 60 J10
Akonolinga, *Cameroon* 79 E7
Akordat, *Eritrea* 77 D4
Akosombo Dam, *Ghana* 79 D5
Akot, *Sudan* 77 F3
Akpatok I., *Canada* 97 B13
Akranes, *Iceland* 8 D3
Akreïjit, *Mauritania* 78 B3
Akrítas Venétiko, Ákra, *Greece* 39 N4
Akron, *Colo., U.S.A.* 108 E3
Akron, *Ohio, U.S.A.* 106 E3
Akrotiri, *Cyprus* 37 E11
Akrotíri, Ákra, *Greece* 39 J8
Akrotiri Bay, *Cyprus* 37 E12
Aksai Chih, *India* 63 B8
Aksaray, *Turkey* 66 D6
Aksarka, *Russia* 44 C7
Aksay, *Kazakhstan* 44 D6
Akşehir, *Turkey* 66 D4
Akşehir Gölü, *Turkey* 66 D4
Aksenovo Zilovskoye, *Russia* 45 D12
Akstafa, *Azerbaijan* 43 F11
Aksu, *China* 54 B3
Aksu →, *Turkey* 66 E4
Aksum, *Ethiopia* 77 E4
Aktogay, *Kazakhstan* 44 E8
Aktyubinsk, *Kazakhstan* 44 D6
Aku, *Nigeria* 79 D6
Akure, *Nigeria* 79 D6
Akureyri, *Iceland* 8 D4
Akuseki-Shima, *Japan* 49 K4
Akusha, *Russia* 43 E12
Akwa-Ibom □, *Nigeria* 79 E6
Akyab = Sittwe, *Burma* 61 J18
Akyazı, *Turkey* 66 C4
Al 'Adan, *Yemen* 68 E4
Al Aḩsā, *Si. Arabia* 65 E6
Al Ajfar, *Si. Arabia* 64 E4
Al Amādīyah, *Iraq* 64 B4
Al Amārah, *Iraq* 64 D5
Al 'Aqabah, *Jordan* 69 F4
Al Arak, *Syria* 64 C3
Al 'Aramah, *Si. Arabia* 64 E5
Al Arţāwīyah, *Si. Arabia* 64 E5
Al 'Āşimah □, *Jordan* 69 D5
Al' Assāfīyah, *Si. Arabia* 64 D3
Al 'Ayn, *Oman* 65 E7
Al 'Ayn, *Si. Arabia* 64 E3
Al A'ẓamīyah, *Iraq* 64 C5
Al 'Azīzīyah, *Iraq* 64 C5
Al 'Azīzīyah, *Libya* 75 B7
Al Bāb, *Syria* 64 B3
Al Bad', *Si. Arabia* 64 D2
Al Bādī, *Iraq* 64 C4
Al Baḩrah, *Kuwait* 64 D5
Al Balqā' □, *Jordan* 69 C4
Al Barkāt, *Libya* 75 D7
Al Bārūk, J., *Lebanon* 69 B4
Al Başrah, *Iraq* 64 D5
Al Baţḩā, *Iraq* 64 D5
Al Batrūn, *Lebanon* 69 A4
Al Bi'r, *Si. Arabia* 64 D3
Al Bu'ayrāt, *Libya* 73 B8
Al Burayj, *Syria* 69 A5
Al Fallūjah, *Iraq* 64 C4
Al Fāw, *Iraq* 65 D6
Al Fujayrah, *U.A.E.* 65 E8
Al Ghadaf, W. →, *Jordan* 69 D5
Al Ghammās, *Iraq* 64 D5
Al Ḩābah, *Si. Arabia* 64 E5
Al Ḩadīthah, *Iraq* 64 C4
Al Ḩadīthah, *Si. Arabia* 64 D3
Al Ḩājānah, *Syria* 69 B5
Al Ḩāmad, *Si. Arabia* 64 D3
Al Hamdānīyah, *Syria* 64 C3
Al Ḩamīdīyah, *Syria* 69 A4
Al Hammādah al Ḩamrā', *Libya* 75 C7
Al Ḩammār, *Iraq* 64 D5
Al Ḩarīr, W. →, *Syria* 69 C4
Al Ḩasā, W. →, *Jordan* 69 D4
Al Ḩasakah, *Syria* 64 B4
Al Ḩawrah, *Yemen* 68 E4
Al Ḩaydān, W. →, *Jordan* 69 D4
Al Ḩayy, *Iraq* 64 C5
Al Ḩijāz, *Si. Arabia* 68 B2
Al Ḩillah, *Iraq* 64 C5
Al Ḩillah, *Si. Arabia* 68 C4
Al Hirmil, *Lebanon* 69 A5
Al Hoceïma, *Morocco* 74 A4
Al Ḩudaydah, *Yemen* 68 E3
Al Hufūf, *Si. Arabia* 65 E6
Al Ḩumaydah, *Si. Arabia* 64 D2
Al Ḩunayy, *Si. Arabia* 65 E6
Al Irq, *Libya* 73 C9
Al 'Īsāwīyah, *Si. Arabia* 64 D3
Al Ittihad = Madīnat ash Sha'b, *Yemen* 68 E3
Al Jafr, *Jordan* 69 E5
Al Jaghbūb, *Libya* 73 C9
Al Jahrah, *Kuwait* 64 D5
Al Jalāmīd, *Si. Arabia* 64 D3
Al Jamalīyah, *Qatar* 65 E6
Al Janūb □, *Lebanon* 69 B4
Al Jawf, *Libya* 73 D9
Al Jawf, *Si. Arabia* 64 D3
Al Jazirah, *Iraq* 64 C5
Al Jazirah, *Libya* 73 C9
Al Jithāmīyah, *Si. Arabia* 64 E4
Al Jubayl, *Si. Arabia* 65 E6
Al Jubaylah, *Si. Arabia* 64 E5
Al Jubb, *Si. Arabia* 64 E4
Al Junaynah, *Sudan* 73 F9
Al Kabā'ish, *Iraq* 64 D5
Al Karak, *Jordan* 69 D4
Al Karak □, *Jordan* 69 E5
Al Kāzim Tyah, *Iraq* 64 C5
Al Khalīl, *Jordan* 69 D4
Al Khalīl □, *Jordan* 69 D4
Al Khawr, *Qatar* 65 E6
Al Khiḑr, *Iraq* 64 D5
Al Khiyām, *Lebanon* 69 B4
Al Kiswah, *Syria* 69 B5
Al Kufrah, *Libya* 73 D9
Al Kuhayfīyah, *Si. Arabia* 64 E4
Al Kūt, *Iraq* 64 C5
Al Kuwayt, *Kuwait* 64 D5
Al Labwah, *Lebanon* 69 A5
Al Lādhiqīyah, *Syria* 64 C2
Al Līth, *Si. Arabia* 76 C5
Al Liwā', *Oman* 65 E8
Al Luḩayyah, *Yemen* 68 D3
Al Madīnah, *Iraq* 64 D5
Al Madīnah, *Si. Arabia* 64 E3
Al-Mafraq, *Jordan* 69 C5
Al Maḩmūdīyah, *Iraq* 64 C5
Al Majma'ah, *Si. Arabia* 64 E5
Al Makhruq, W. →, *Jordan* 69 D6
Al Makḩūl, *Si. Arabia* 64 E4
Al Manāmah, *Bahrain* 65 E6
Al Maqwa', *Kuwait* 64 D5
Al Marj, *Libya* 73 B9
Al Maţlā, *Kuwait* 64 D5
Al Mawjib, W. →, *Jordan* 69 D4
Al Mawşil, *Iraq* 64 B4
Al Mayādin, *Syria* 64 C4
Al Mazār, *Jordan* 69 D4
Al Midhnab, *Si. Arabia* 64 E5
Al Minā', *Lebanon* 69 A4
Al Miqdādīyah, *Iraq* 64 C5
Al Mubarraz, *Si. Arabia* 65 E6
Al Mughayrā', *U.A.E.* 65 E7
Al Muḩarraq, *Bahrain* 65 E6
Al Mukallā, *Yemen* 68 E4
Al Mukhā, *Yemen* 68 E3
Al Musayjīd, *Si. Arabia* 64 E3
Al Musayyib, *Iraq* 64 C5
Al Muwayliḩ, *Si. Arabia* 64 E2
Al Owuho = Otukpa, *Nigeria* 79 D6
Al Qā'im, *Iraq* 64 C4
Al Qalībah, *Si. Arabia* 64 D3
Al Qaryatayn, *Syria* 69 A6
Al Qaşabát, *Libya* 73 B7
Al Qaţ'ā, *Syria* 64 C4
Al Qaţīf, *Si. Arabia* 65 E6
Al Qatrānah, *Jordan* 69 D5
Al Qaţrūn, *Libya* 73 D8
Al Qayşūmah, *Si. Arabia* 64 D5
Al Quds = Jerusalem, *Israel* 69 D4
Al Quds □, *Jordan* 69 D4
Al Qunaytirah, *Syria* 69 C4
Al Qunfudhah, *Si. Arabia* 76 D5
Al Qurnah, *Iraq* 64 D5
Al Quşayr, *Iraq* 64 D5
Al Quşayr, *Syria* 69 A5
Al Qutayfah, *Syria* 69 B5
Al' Uḑaylīyah, *Si. Arabia* 65 E6
Al 'Ulā, *Si. Arabia* 64 E3
Al Uqaylah ash Sharqīgah, *Libya* 73 B8
Al Uqayr, *Si. Arabia* 65 E6
Al 'Uwaynid, *Si. Arabia* 64 E5
Al' 'Uwayqīlah, *Si. Arabia* 64 D4
Al 'Uyūn, *Si. Arabia* 64 E4
Al 'Uyūn, *Si. Arabia* 64 E3
Al Wajh, *Si. Arabia* 64 E3
Al Wakrah, *Qatar* 65 E6
Al Wannān, *Si. Arabia* 65 E6
Al Waqbah, *Si. Arabia* 64 D5
Al Wari'āh, *Si. Arabia* 64 E5
Al Wātīyah, *Libya* 75 B7
Al Wusayl, *Qatar* 65 E6
Ala, *Italy* 32 C8
Ala Dağları, *Turkey* 67 D10
Alabama □, *U.S.A.* 105 J2
Alabama →, *U.S.A.* 105 K2
Alaca, *Turkey* 66 C6
Alaçam, *Turkey* 66 C6
Alaçam Dağları, *Turkey* 66 D3
Alaejos, *Spain* 30 D5
Alaérma, *Greece* 37 C9
Alagna Valsésia, *Italy* 32 C4
Alagoa Grande, *Brazil* 122 C4
Alagoas □, *Brazil* 122 C4
Alagoinhas, *Brazil* 123 D4
Alagón, *Spain* 28 D3
Alagón →, *Spain* 31 F4
Alajero, *Canary Is.* 36 F2
Alajuela, *Costa Rica* 116 D3
Alakamisy, *Madag.* 85 C8
Alalapura, *Surinam* 121 C6
Alalaú →, *Brazil* 121 D5
Alameda, *Spain* 31 H6
Alameda, *Calif., U.S.A.* 112 H4
Alameda, *N. Mex., U.S.A.* 111 J10
Alaminos, *Phil.* 55 C3
Alamo, *U.S.A.* 113 J11
Alamo Crossing, *U.S.A.* 113 L13
Alamogordo, *U.S.A.* 111 K11
Alamos, *Mexico* 114 B3
Alamosa, *U.S.A.* 111 H11
Åland, *Finland* 9 F16
Alandroal, *Portugal* 31 G3
Ålands hav, *Sweden* 9 G15
Alandur, *India* 60 N12
Alange, Presa de, *Spain* 31 G4
Alanis, *Spain* 31 G5
Alanya, *Turkey* 66 E4
Alaotra, Farihin', *Madag.* 85 B8
Alapayevsk, *Russia* 44 D7
Alar del Rey, *Spain* 30 C6
Alaraz, *Spain* 30 E5
Alaşehir, *Turkey* 66 D3
Alaska □, *U.S.A.* 96 B5
Alaska, G. of, *Pac. Oc.* 96 C5
Alaska Highway, *Canada* 100 B3
Alaska Peninsula, *U.S.A.* 96 C4
Alaska Range, *U.S.A.* 96 B4
Alássio, *Italy* 32 D5
Alataw Shankou, *China* 54 B3
Alatri, *Italy* 34 A6
Alatyr, *Russia* 41 D15
Alatyr →, *Russia* 41 D15
Alausi, *Ecuador* 120 D2
Álava □, *Spain* 28 C2
Alava, C., *U.S.A.* 110 B1
Alaverdi, *Armenia* 43 F11
Alawoona, *Australia* 91 E3
'Alayh, *Lebanon* 69 B4
Alayor, *Spain* 36 B11
Alazan →, *Azerbaijan* 43 F12
Alba, *Italy* 32 D5
Alba de Tormes, *Spain* 30 E5
Alba Iulia, *Romania* 38 C6
Albac, *Romania* 38 C6
Albacete, *Spain* 29 G3
Albacete □, *Spain* 29 G3
Albacutya, L., *Australia* 91 F3
Ålbæk, *Denmark* 11 G4
Ålbæk Bugt, *Denmark* 11 G4
Albaida, *Spain* 29 G4
Albalate de las Nogueras, *Spain* 28 E2
Albalate del Arzobispo, *Spain* 28 D4
Albania ■, *Europe* 39 J3
Albano Laziale, *Italy* 34 A5
Albany, *Australia* 89 G2
Albany, *Ga., U.S.A.* 105 K3
Albany, *Minn., U.S.A.* 108 C7
Albany, *N.Y., U.S.A.* 107 D11
Albany, *Oreg., U.S.A.* 110 D2
Albany, *Tex., U.S.A.* 109 J5
Albany →, *Canada* 98 B3
Albardón, *Argentina* 126 C2
Albarracín, *Spain* 28 E3
Albarracín, Sierra de, *Spain* 28 E3
Albatross B., *Australia* 90 A3
Albegna →, *Italy* 33 F8
Albemarle, *U.S.A.* 105 H5
Albemarle Sd., *U.S.A.* 105 H7
Albenga, *Italy* 32 D5
Alberche →, *Spain* 30 F6
Alberdi, *Paraguay* 126 B4
Alberes, Mts., *Spain* 28 C7
Alberique, *Spain* 29 F4
Albersdorf, *Germany* 18 A5
Albert, *France* 25 B9
Albert, L. = Mobutu Sese Seko, L., *Africa* 82 B3
Albert, L., *Australia* 91 F2
Albert Canyon, *Canada* 100 C5
Albert Edward Ra., *Australia* 88 C4
Albert Lea, *U.S.A.* 108 D8
Albert Nile →, *Uganda* 82 B3
Albert Town, *Bahamas* 117 B5
Alberta □, *Canada* 100 C6
Alberti, *Argentina* 126 D3
Albertinia, *S. Africa* 84 E3
Albertkanaal →, *Belgium* 17 F4
Alberton, *Canada* 99 C7
Albertville = Kalemie, *Zaïre* 82 D2
Albertville, *France* 27 C10
Albi, *France* 26 E6
Albia, *U.S.A.* 108 E8
Albina, *Surinam* 121 B7
Albina, Ponta, *Angola* 84 B1
Albino, *Italy* 32 C6
Albion, *Idaho, U.S.A.* 110 E7
Albion, *Mich., U.S.A.* 104 D3
Albion, *Nebr., U.S.A.* 108 E5
Albion, *Pa., U.S.A.* 106 E4
Alblasserdam, *Neths.* 16 E5
Albocácer, *Spain* 28 E5
Alborán, *Medit. S.* 31 K7
Alborea, *Spain* 29 F3
Ålborg, *Denmark* 11 G3
Ålborg Bugt, *Denmark* 11 H4
Alborz, Reshteh-ye Kūhhā-ye, *Iran* 65 C7
Albox, *Spain* 29 H2
Albreda, *Canada* 100 C5
Albufeira, *Portugal* 31 H2
Albula →, *Switz.* 23 C8
Albuñol, *Spain* 29 J1
Albuquerque, *Brazil* 125 D6
Albuquerque, *U.S.A.* 111 J10
Albuquerque, Cayos de, *Caribbean* 116 D3
Alburg, *U.S.A.* 107 B11
Alburno, Mte., *Italy* 35 B8
Alburquerque, *Spain* 31 F4
Albury, *Australia* 91 F4
Alby, *Sweden* 10 B9
Alcácer do Sal, *Portugal* 31 G2
Alcaçovas, *Portugal* 31 G2
Alcalá de Chisvert, *Spain* 28 E5
Alcalá de Guadaira, *Spain* 31 H5
Alcalá de Henares, *Spain* 28 E1
Alcalá de los Gazules, *Spain* 31 J5
Alcalá la Real, *Spain* 31 H7
Alcamo, *Italy* 34 E5
Alcanadre, *Spain* 28 C2
Alcanadre →, *Spain* 28 D4
Alcanar, *Spain* 28 E5
Alcanede, *Portugal* 31 F2
Alcanena, *Portugal* 31 F2
Alcañices, *Spain* 30 D4
Alcaníz, *Spain* 28 D4
Alcântara, *Brazil* 122 B3
Alcántara, *Spain* 31 F4
Alcantara L., *Canada* 101 A7
Alcantarilla, *Spain* 29 H3
Alcaracejos, *Spain* 31 G6
Alcaraz, *Spain* 29 G2
Alcaraz, Sierra de, *Spain* 29 G2
Alcaudete, *Spain* 31 H6
Alcázar de San Juan, *Spain* 29 F1
Alchevsk = Kommunarsk, *Ukraine* 43 B8
Alcira, *Spain* 29 F4
Alcoa, *U.S.A.* 105 H4
Alcobaça, *Portugal* 31 F2
Alcobendas, *Spain* 28 E1
Alcolea del Pinar, *Spain* 28 D2
Alcora, *Spain* 28 E4
Alcorcón, *Spain* 30 E7
Alcoutim, *Portugal* 31 H3
Alcova, *U.S.A.* 110 E10
Alcoy, *Spain* 29 G4
Alcubierre, Sierra de, *Spain* 28 D4
Alcublas, *Spain* 28 F4
Alcudia, *Spain* 36 B10
Alcudia, B. de, *Spain* 36 B10
Alcudia, Sierra de la, *Spain* 31 G6
Aldabra Is., *Seychelles* 71 G8
Aldama, *Mexico* 115 C5
Aldan, *Russia* 45 D13
Aldan →, *Russia* 45 C13
Aldea, Pta. de la, *Canary Is.* 36 G4
Aldeburgh, *U.K.* 13 E9
Aldeia Nova, *Portugal* 31 H3
Alder, *U.S.A.* 110 D7
Alder Pk., *U.S.A.* 112 K5
Alderney, *Chan. Is.* 13 H5
Aldershot, *U.K.* 13 F7
Aledo, *U.S.A.* 108 E9
Alefa, *Ethiopia* 77 E4
Aleg, *Mauritania* 78 B2
Alegranza, *Canary Is.* 36 E6
Alegranza, I., *Canary Is.* 36 E6
Alegre, *Brazil* 123 F3
Alegrete, *Brazil* 127 B4
Aleisk, *Russia* 44 D9
Aleksandriya, *Ukraine* 40 F5
Aleksandriya, *Ukraine* 42 B5
Aleksandriyskaya, *Russia* 43 E12
Aleksandrov, *Russia* 41 C11
Aleksandrovac, *Serbia* 21 L11
Aleksandrovka, *Ukraine* 42 B5
Aleksandrovo, *Bulgaria* 38 F7
Aleksandrovsk-Sakhalinskiy, *Russia* 45 D15
Aleksandrovskiy Zavod, *Russia* 45 D12

Aleksandrovskoye, *Russia* 44 C8
Aleksandrów Kujawski, *Poland* 20 C8
Aleksandrów Łódźki, *Poland* 20 D9
Alekseyevka, *Russia* 41 F11
Aleksin, *Russia* 41 D10
Aleksinac, *Serbia, Yug.* 21 M11
Além Paraíba, *Brazil* 123 F3
Alemania, *Argentina* 126 B2
Alemania, *Chile* 126 B2
Ålen, *Norway* 10 B5
Alençon, *France* 24 D7
Alenuihaha Channel, *U.S.A.* 102 H17
Aleppo = Ḥalab, *Syria* 64 B3
Aléria, *France* 27 F13
Alert Bay, *Canada* 100 C3
Alès, *France* 27 D8
Aleşd, *Romania* 38 B5
Alessándria, *Italy* 32 D5
Ålestrup, *Denmark* 11 H3
Ålesund, *Norway* 8 E9
Alet-les-Bains, *France* 26 F6
Aletschhorn, *Switz.* 22 D6
Aleutian Is., *Pac. Oc.* 96 C2
Aleutian Trench, *Pac. Oc.* 92 B10
Alexander, *U.S.A.* 108 B3
Alexander, Mt., *Australia* 89 E3
Alexander Arch., *U.S.A.* 100 B2
Alexander B., *S. Africa* 84 D2
Alexander Bay, *S. Africa* 84 D2
Alexander City, *U.S.A.* 105 J3
Alexander I., *Antarctica* 5 C17
Alexandra, *Australia* 91 F4
Alexandra, *N.Z.* 87 L2
Alexandra Falls, *Canada* 100 A5
Alexandretta = İskenderun, *Turkey* 66 E7
Alexandria = El Iskandarîya, *Egypt* 76 H6
Alexandria, *Australia* 90 B2
Alexandria, *B.C., Canada* 100 C4
Alexandria, *Ont., Canada* 98 C5
Alexandria, *Romania* 38 F8
Alexandria, *S. Africa* 84 E4
Alexandria, *Ind., U.S.A.* 104 E3
Alexandria, *La., U.S.A.* 109 K8
Alexandria, *Minn., U.S.A.* 108 C7
Alexandria, *S. Dak., U.S.A.* 108 D6
Alexandria, *Va., U.S.A.* 104 F7
Alexandria Bay, *U.S.A.* 107 B9
Alexandrina, L., *Australia* 91 F2
Alexandroúpolis, *Greece* 39 J8
Alexis →, *Canada* 99 B8
Alexis Creek, *Canada* 100 C4
Alfabia, *Spain* 36 B9
Alfambra, *Spain* 28 E3
Alfândega da Fé, *Portugal* 30 D4
Alfaro, *Spain* 28 C3
Alfeld, *Germany* 18 D5
Alfenas, *Brazil* 127 A6
Alfiós →, *Greece* 39 M4
Alfonsine, *Italy* 33 D9
Alford, *U.K.* 14 D6
Alfred, *Maine, U.S.A.* 107 C14
Alfred, *N.Y., U.S.A.* 106 D7
Alfreton, *U.K.* 12 D6
Alga, *Kazakhstan* 44 E6
Algaida, *Spain* 36 B9
Algar, *Spain* 31 J5
Algarinejo, *Spain* 31 H6
Algarve, *Portugal* 31 J2
Algeciras, *Spain* 31 J5
Algemesí, *Spain* 29 F4
Alger, *Algeria* 75 A5
Algeria ■, *Africa* 75 C5
Alghero, *Italy* 34 B1
Algiers = Alger, *Algeria* 75 A5
Algoa B., *S. Africa* 84 E4
Algodonales, *Spain* 31 J5
Algodor →, *Spain* 30 F7
Algoma, *U.S.A.* 104 C2
Algona, *U.S.A.* 108 D7
Algonac, *U.S.A.* 106 D2
Alhama de Almería, *Spain* 29 J2
Alhama de Aragón, *Spain* 28 D3
Alhama de Granada, *Spain* 31 J7
Alhama de Murcia, *Spain* 29 H3
Alhambra, *Spain* 29 G1
Alhambra, *U.S.A.* 113 L8
Alhaurín el Grande, *Spain* 31 J6
Alhucemas = Al Hoceïma, *Morocco* 74 A4
'Alī al Gharbī, *Iraq* 64 C5
Alī ash Sharqī, *Iraq* 64 C5
Ali Bayramly, *Azerbaijan* 43 G13
'Alī Khēl, *Afghan.* 62 C3
Ali Sahîh, *Djibouti* 77 E5
Alī Shāh, *Iran* 64 B5
Ália, *Italy* 34 E6
'Alīābād, *Khorāsān, Iran* 65 C8
Alīābād, *Kordestān, Iran* 64 C5
'Alīābād, *Yazd, Iran* 65 D7
Aliaga, *Spain* 28 E4
Aliağa, *Turkey* 66 D2
Aliákmon →, *Greece* 39 J5
Alibo, *Ethiopia* 77 F4
Alibunar, *Serbia, Yug.* 21 K10
Alicante, *Spain* 29 G4
Alicante □, *Spain* 29 G4
Alice, *S. Africa* 84 E4
Alice, *U.S.A.* 109 M5
Alice →, *Queens., Australia* 90 C3
Alice →, *Queens., Australia* 90 B3
Alice, Punta dell', *Italy* 35 C10
Alice Arm, *Canada* 100 B3
Alice Downs, *Australia* 88 C4
Alice Springs, *Australia* 90 C1
Alicedale, *S. Africa* 84 E4
Aliceville, *U.S.A.* 105 J1
Alick Cr. →, *Australia* 90 C3
Alicudi, I., *Italy* 35 D7
Alida, *Canada* 101 D8
Aligarh, *Raj., India* 62 G7
Aligarh, *Ut. P., India* 62 F8
Alīgūdarz, *Iran* 65 C6
Alijó, *Portugal* 30 D3
Alimena, *Italy* 35 E7
Alimnía, *Greece* 37 C9
Alingsås, *Sweden* 11 G6
Alipur, *Pakistan* 62 E4
Alipur Duar, *India* 61 F16
Aliquippa, *U.S.A.* 106 F4
Aliste →, *Spain* 30 D5
Alitus, *Lithuania* 40 D4
Alivérion, *Greece* 39 L7
Aliwal North, *S. Africa* 84 E4
Alix, *Canada* 100 C6
Aljezur, *Portugal* 31 H2
Aljustrel, *Portugal* 31 H2
Alkamari, *Niger* 79 C7
Alken, *Belgium* 17 G6
Alkmaar, *Neths.* 16 C5
All American Canal, *U.S.A.* 111 K6
Allada, *Benin* 79 D5
Allah Dad, *Pakistan* 62 G2
Allahabad, *India* 63 G9
Allakh-Yun, *Russia* 45 C14
Allal Tazi, *Morocco* 74 B3
Allan, *Canada* 101 C7
Allanche, *France* 26 C6
Allanmyo, *Burma* 61 K19
Allanridge, *S. Africa* 84 D4
Allanwater, *Canada* 98 B1
Allaqi, Wadi →, *Egypt* 76 C3
Allariz, *Spain* 30 C3
Allassac, *France* 26 C5
Alle, *Belgium* 17 J5
Allegan, *U.S.A.* 104 D3
Allegany, *U.S.A.* 106 D6
Allegheny →, *U.S.A.* 106 F5
Allegheny Plateau, *U.S.A.* 104 G6
Allegheny Reservoir, *U.S.A.* 106 E6
Allègre, *France* 26 C7
Allen, *Argentina* 128 A3
Allen, Bog of, *Ireland* 15 C4
Allen, L., *Ireland* 15 B3
Allende, *Mexico* 114 B4
Allentown, *U.S.A.* 107 F9
Alleppey, *India* 60 Q10
Aller →, *Germany* 18 C5
Alleur, *Belgium* 17 G7
Allevard, *France* 27 C10
Alliance, *Surinam* 121 B7
Alliance, *Nebr., U.S.A.* 108 D3
Alliance, *Ohio, U.S.A.* 106 F3
Allier □, *France* 26 B6
Allier →, *France* 25 F10
Allingåbro, *Denmark* 11 H4
Alliston, *Canada* 98 D4
Alloa, *U.K.* 14 E5
Allora, *Australia* 91 D5
Allos, *France* 27 D10
Alluitsup Paa = Sydprøven, *Greenland* 4 C5
Alma, *Canada* 99 C5
Alma, *Ga., U.S.A.* 105 K4
Alma, *Kans., U.S.A.* 108 F6
Alma, *Mich., U.S.A.* 104 D3
Alma, *Nebr., U.S.A.* 108 E5
Alma, *Wis., U.S.A.* 108 C9
Alma Ata, *Kazakhstan* 44 E8
Almada, *Portugal* 31 G1
Almaden, *Australia* 90 B3
Almadén, *Spain* 31 G6
Almagro, *Spain* 31 G7
Almanor, L., *U.S.A.* 110 F3
Almansa, *Spain* 29 G3
Almanza, *Spain* 30 C5
Almanzor, Pico de, *Spain* 30 E5
Almanzora →, *Spain* 29 H3
Almas, *Brazil* 123 D2
Almaty = Alma Ata, *Kazakhstan* 44 E8
Almazán, *Spain* 28 D2
Almazora, *Spain* 28 F4
Almeirim, *Brazil* 121 D7
Almeirim, *Portugal* 31 F2
Almelo, *Neths.* 16 D9
Almenar, *Spain* 28 D2
Almenara, *Brazil* 123 E3
Almenara, *Spain* 28 F4
Almenara, Sierra de, *Spain* 29 H3
Almendralejo, *Spain* 31 G4
Almería, *Spain* 29 J2
Almería □, *Spain* 29 H2
Almería, G. de, *Spain* 29 J2
Almirante, *Panama* 116 E3
Almirante Montt, G., *Chile* 128 D2
Almirós, *Greece* 39 K5
Almiroú, Kólpos, *Greece* 37 D6
Almodôvar, *Portugal* 31 H2
Almodóvar del Campo, *Spain* 31 G6
Almogia, *Spain* 31 J6
Almonaster la Real, *Spain* 31 H4
Almont, *U.S.A.* 106 D1
Almonte, *Canada* 107 A8
Almonte →, *Spain* 31 F4
Almora, *India* 63 E8
Almoradi, *Spain* 29 G4
Almorox, *Spain* 30 E6
Almoustarat, *Mali* 79 B5
Almuñécar, *Spain* 31 J7
Alnif, *Morocco* 74 B3
Alnwick, *U.K.* 12 B6
Aloi, *Uganda* 82 B3
Alon, *Burma* 61 H19
Alor, *Indonesia* 57 F6
Alor Setar, *Malaysia* 59 J3
Alora, *Spain* 31 J6
Alosno, *Spain* 31 H3
Alougoum, *Morocco* 74 B3
Aloysius, Mt., *Australia* 89 E4
Alpaugh, *U.S.A.* 112 K7
Alpedrinha, *Portugal* 30 E3
Alpena, *U.S.A.* 104 C4
Alpercatas →, *Brazil* 122 C3
Alpes-de-Haute-Provence □, *France* 27 D10
Alpes-Maritimes □, *France* 27 E11
Alpha, *Australia* 90 C4
Alphen, *Neths.* 17 F5
Alphen aan den Rijn, *Neths.* 16 D5
Alpiarça, *Portugal* 31 F2
Alpine, *Ariz., U.S.A.* 111 K9
Alpine, *Calif., U.S.A.* 113 N10
Alpine, *Tex., U.S.A.* 109 K3
Alpnach, *Switz.* 23 C6
Alps, *Europe* 6 F7
Alpu, *Turkey* 66 D4
Alrø, *Denmark* 11 J4
Alroy Downs, *Australia* 90 B2
Alsace, *France* 25 D14
Alsask, *Canada* 101 C7
Alsásua, *Spain* 28 C2
Alsen, *Sweden* 10 A7
Alsfeld, *Germany* 18 E5
Alsten, *Norway* 8 D12
Alta, *Norway* 8 B17
Alta, Sierra, *Spain* 28 E3
Alta Gracia, *Argentina* 126 C3
Alta Lake, *Canada* 100 C4
Alta Sierra, *U.S.A.* 113 K8
Altaelva →, *Norway* 8 B17
Altafjorden, *Norway* 8 A17
Altagracia, *Venezuela* 120 A3
Altagracia de Orituco, *Venezuela* 120 B4
Altai = Aerhtai Shan, *Mongolia* 54 B4
Altai = Aerhtai Shan, *Mongolia* 54 B4
Altamachi →, *Bolivia* 124 D4
Altamaha →, *U.S.A.* 105 K5
Altamira, *Brazil* 121 D7
Altamira, *Chile* 126 B2
Altamira, *Colombia* 120 C2
Altamira, *Mexico* 115 C5
Altamira, Cuevas de, *Spain* 30 B6
Altamont, *U.S.A.* 107 D10
Altamura, *Italy* 35 B9
Altanbulag, *Mongolia* 54 A5
Altar, *Mexico* 114 A2
Altata, *Mexico* 114 C3
Altavista, *U.S.A.* 104 G6
Altay, *China* 54 B3
Altdorf, *Switz.* 23 C7
Alte Mellum, *Germany* 18 B4
Altea, *Spain* 29 G4
Altenberg, *Germany* 18 E9
Altenbruch, *Germany* 18 B4
Altenburg, *Germany* 18 E8
Altenkirchen, *Mecklenburg-Vorpommern, Germany* 18 A9
Altenkirchen, *Rhld-Pfz., Germany* 18 E3
Altenteptow, *Germany* 18 B9
Alter do Chão, *Portugal* 31 F3
Altıntas, *Turkey* 66 D4
Altiplano, *Bolivia* 124 D4
Altkirch, *France* 25 E14
Altmühl →, *Germany* 19 G7
Alto Adige = Trentino-Alto Adige □, *Italy* 32 B8
Alto Araguaia, *Brazil* 125 D7
Alto Cuchumatanes = Cuchumatanes, Sierra de los, *Guatemala* 116 C1
Alto del Inca, *Chile* 126 A2
Alto Garças, *Brazil* 125 D7
Alto Iriri →, *Brazil* 125 B7
Alto Ligonha, *Mozam.* 83 F4
Alto Molocue, *Mozam.* 83 F4
Alto Paraguai, *Brazil* 125 C6
Alto Paraguay □, *Paraguay* 126 A4
Alto Paraná □, *Paraguay* 127 B5
Alto Parnaíba, *Brazil* 122 C2
Alto Purús →, *Peru* 124 B3
Alto Río Senguerr, *Argentina* 128 C2
Alto Santo, *Brazil* 122 C4
Alto Sucuriú, *Brazil* 125 D7
Alto Turi, *Brazil* 122 B2
Alton, *Canada* 106 C4
Alton, *U.S.A.* 108 F9
Alton Downs, *Australia* 91 D2
Altoona, *U.S.A.* 106 F6
Altopáscio, *Italy* 32 E7
Altos, *Brazil* 122 C3
Altötting, *Germany* 19 G8
Altstätten, *Switz.* 23 B9
Altūn Kūprī, *Iraq* 64 C5
Altun Shan, *China* 54 C3
Alturas, *U.S.A.* 110 F3
Altus, *U.S.A.* 109 H5
Alubijid, *Phil.* 55 G6
Alucra, *Turkey* 43 F8
Alūksne, *Latvia* 40 C5
Alùla, *Somali Rep.* 68 E5
Alunite, *U.S.A.* 113 K12
Alupka, *Ukraine* 42 D6
Alushta, *Ukraine* 42 D6
Alusi, *Indonesia* 57 F8
Alustante, *Spain* 28 E3
Al'Uzayr, *Iraq* 64 D5
Alva, *U.S.A.* 109 G5
Alvaiázere, *Portugal* 30 F2
Älvängen, *Sweden* 11 G6
Alvarado, *Mexico* 115 D5
Alvarado, *U.S.A.* 109 J6
Alvarães, *Brazil* 121 D5
Alvaro Obregón, Presa, *Mexico* 114 B3
Alvdal, *Norway* 10 B4
Alvear, *Argentina* 126 B4
Alverca, *Portugal* 31 G1
Alveringen, *Belgium* 17 F1
Alvesta, *Sweden* 9 H13
Alvie, *Australia* 91 F3
Alvin, *U.S.A.* 109 L7
Alvinston, *Canada* 106 D3
Alvito, *Portugal* 31 G3
Älvkarleby, *Sweden* 9 F14
Älvros, *Sweden* 10 B8
Älvsborgs län □, *Sweden* 11 F6
Älvsbyn, *Sweden* 8 D16
Älvsered, *Sweden* 11 G6
Alwar, *India* 62 F7
Alxa Zuoqi, *China* 50 E3
Alyaskitovyy, *Russia* 45 C15
Alyata, *Azerbaijan* 43 G13
Alyth, *U.K.* 14 E5
Alzada, *U.S.A.* 108 C2
Alzano Lombardo, *Italy* 32 C6
Alzette →, *Lux.* 17 J8
Alzey, *Germany* 19 F4
Am Dam, *Chad* 73 F9
Am-Timan, *Chad* 73 F9
Amacuro □, *Venezuela* 121 B5
Amadeus, L., *Australia* 89 D5
Amâdi, *Sudan* 77 F3
Amadi, *Zaïre* 82 B2
Amadjuak, *Canada* 97 B12
Amadjuak L., *Canada* 97 B12
Amadora, *Portugal* 31 G1
Amagasaki, *Japan* 49 G7
Amager, *Denmark* 11 J6
Amakusa-Shotō, *Japan* 49 H5
Amalfi, *Colombia* 120 B2
Amalfi, *Italy* 35 B7
Amaliás, *Greece* 39 M4
Amalner, *India* 60 J9
Amambaí, *Brazil* 127 A4
Amambaí →, *Brazil* 127 A5
Amambay □, *Paraguay* 127 A4
Amambay, Cordillera de, *S. Amer.* 127 A4
Amami-Guntō, *Japan* 49 L4
Amami-Ō-Shima, *Japan* 49 L4
Amana →, *Venezuela* 121 B5
Amaná, L., *Brazil* 121 D5
Amanda Park, *U.S.A.* 112 C3
Amándola, *Italy* 33 F10
Amangeldy, *Kazakhstan* 44 D7
Amantea, *Italy* 35 C9
Amapá, *Brazil* 121 C7
Amapá □, *Brazil* 121 C7
Amapari, *Brazil* 121 C7
Amara, *Sudan* 77 E3
Amarante, *Brazil* 122 C3
Amarante, *Portugal* 30 D2
Amarante do Maranhão, *Brazil* 122 C2
Amaranth, *Canada* 101 C9
Amareleja, *Portugal* 31 G3
Amargosa, *Brazil* 123 D4
Amargosa →, *U.S.A.* 113 J10
Amargosa Range, *U.S.A.* 113 J10
Amári, *Greece* 37 D6
Amarillo, *U.S.A.* 109 H4
Amaro, Mt., *Italy* 33 F11
Amaro Leite, *Brazil* 123 D2
Amarpur, *India* 63 G12
Amasra, *Turkey* 66 C5
Amassama, *Nigeria* 79 D6
Amasya, *Turkey* 66 C6
Amasya □, *Turkey* 66 C6
Amatauá, *Brazil* 120 D4
Amatikulu, *S. Africa* 85 D5
Amatitlán, *Guatemala* 116 D1
Amatrice, *Italy* 33 F10
Amay, *Belgium* 17 G6
Amazon = Amazonas →, *S. Amer.* 121 D7
Amazonas □, *Brazil* 125 B5
Amazonas □, *Peru* 124 B2
Amazonas □, *Venezuela* 120 C4
Amazonas →, *S. Amer.* 121 D7
Ambahakily, *Madag.* 85 C7
Ambala, *India* 62 D7
Ambalavao, *Madag.* 85 C8
Ambalindum, *Australia* 90 C2
Ambam, *Cameroon* 80 D2
Ambanja, *Madag.* 85 A8
Ambarchik, *Russia* 45 C17
Ambarijeby, *Madag.* 85 A8
Ambaro, Helodranon', *Madag.* 85 A8
Ambartsevo, *Russia* 44 D9
Ambato, *Ecuador* 120 D2
Ambato, Sierra de, *Argentina* 126 B2
Ambato Boeny, *Madag.* 85 B8
Ambatofinandrahana, *Madag.* 85 C8
Ambatolampy, *Madag.* 85 B8
Ambatondrazaka, *Madag.* 85 B8
Ambatosoratra, *Madag.* 85 B8
Ambenja, *Madag.* 85 B8
Amberg, *Germany* 19 F7
Ambergris Cay, *Belize* 115 D7
Ambérieu-en-Bugey, *France* 27 C9
Amberley, *N.Z.* 87 K4
Ambert, *France* 26 C7
Ambidédi, *Mali* 78 C2
Ambikapur, *India* 63 H10
Ambikol, *Sudan* 76 C3
Ambilobé, *Madag.* 85 A8
Ambinanindrano, *Madag.* 85 C8
Ambjörnarp, *Sweden* 11 G7
Ambleside, *U.K.* 12 C5
Amblève, *Belgium* 17 H8
Amblève →, *Belgium* 17 H7
Ambo, *Ethiopia* 77 E4
Ambo, *Peru* 124 C2
Ambodifototra, *Madag.* 85 B8
Ambodilazana, *Madag.* 85 B8
Ambohimahasoa, *Madag.* 85 C8
Ambohimanga, *Madag.* 85 C8
Ambohitra, *Madag.* 85 A8
Ambon, *Indonesia* 57 E7
Amboseli L., *Kenya* 82 C4
Ambositra, *Madag.* 85 C8
Ambovombé, *Madag.* 85 D8
Amboy, *U.S.A.* 113 L11
Amboyna I., *S. China Sea* 56 C4
Ambridge, *U.S.A.* 106 F4
Ambriz, *Angola* 80 F2
Amby, *Australia* 91 D4
Amchitka I., *U.S.A.* 96 C1
Amderma, *Russia* 44 C7
Ameca, *Mexico* 114 C4
Ameca →, *Mexico* 114 C3
Amecameca, *Mexico* 115 D5
Ameland, *Neths.* 16 B7
Amélia, *Italy* 33 F9
Amélie-les-Bains-Palalda, *France* 26 F6
Amen, *Russia* 45 C18
Amendolaro, *Italy* 35 C9
America, *Neths.* 17 F7
American Falls, *U.S.A.* 110 E7
American Falls Reservoir, *U.S.A.* 110 E7
American Highland, *Antarctica* 5 D6
American Samoa ■, *Pac. Oc.* 87 B13
Americana, *Brazil* 127 A6
Americus, *U.S.A.* 105 J3
Amersfoort, *Neths.* 16 D6
Amersfoort, *S. Africa* 85 D4
Amery, *Australia* 89 F2
Amery, *Canada* 101 B10
Amery Ice Shelf, *Antarctica* 5 C6
Ames, *U.S.A.* 108 E8
Amesbury, *U.S.A.* 107 D14
Amfíklia, *Greece* 39 L5
Amfilokhía, *Greece* 39 L4
Amga, *Russia* 45 C14
Amga →, *Russia* 45 C14
Amgu, *Russia* 45 E14
Amgun →, *Russia* 45 D14
Amherst, *Burma* 61 L20
Amherst, *Canada* 99 C7
Amherst, *Mass., U.S.A.* 107 D12
Amherst, *N.Y., U.S.A.* 106 D6
Amherst, *Ohio, U.S.A.* 106 E2
Amherst, *Tex., U.S.A.* 109 H3
Amherst I., *Canada* 107 B8
Amherstburg, *Canada* 98 D3
Amiata, Mte., *Italy* 33 F8
Amiens, *France* 25 C9
Amindaion, *Greece* 39 J4
Amīrābād, *Iran* 64 C5
Amirante Is., *Seychelles* 3 E12
Amisk L., *Canada* 101 C8
Amistad, Presa de la, *Mexico* 114 B4
Amite, *U.S.A.* 109 K9
Amizmiz, *Morocco* 74 B3
Åmli, *Norway* 11 F2
Amlwch, *U.K.* 12 D3
Amm Adam, *Sudan* 77 D4
'Ammān, *Jordan* 69 D4
Ammanford, *U.K.* 13 F3
Ammassalik = Angmagssalik, *Greenland* 4 C6
Ammerån, *Sweden* 10 A10
Ammerån →, *Sweden* 10 A10
Ammersee, *Germany* 19 G7
Ammerzoden, *Neths.* 16 E6
Amnat Charoen, *Thailand* 58 E5
Amo Jiang →, *China* 52 F3
Āmol, *Iran* 65 B7
Amorebieta, *Spain* 28 B2

Amorgós, *Greece* 39 N8
Amory, *U.S.A.* 105 J1
Amos, *Canada* 98 C4
Åmot, *Buskerud, Norway* 10 E3
Åmot, *Telemark, Norway* 10 E2
Åmotsdal, *Norway* 10 E2
Amour, Djebel, *Algeria* 75 B5
Amoy = Xiamen, *China* 53 E12
Ampang, *Malaysia* 59 L3
Ampanihy, *Madag.* 85 C7
Ampasindava, Helodranon', *Madag.* 85 A8
Ampasindava, Saikanosy, *Madag.* 85 A8
Ampato, Nevado, *Peru* 124 D3
Ampenan, *Indonesia* 56 F5
Amper, *Nigeria* 79 D6
Amper →, *Germany* 19 G7
Ampère, *Algeria* 75 A6
Ampezzo, *Italy* 33 B9
Amposta, *Spain* 28 E5
Ampotaka, *Madag.* 85 D7
Ampoza, *Madag.* 85 C7
Amqui, *Canada* 99 C6
Amravati, *India* 60 J10
Amreli, *India* 62 J4
Amrenene el Kasba, *Algeria* 75 D5
Amriswil, *Switz.* 23 A8
Amritsar, *India* 62 D6
Amroha, *India* 63 E8
Amrum, *Germany* 18 A4
Amsel, *Algeria* 75 D6
Amsterdam, *Neths.* 16 D5
Amsterdam, *U.S.A.* 107 D10
Amsterdam, I., *Ind. Oc.* 3 F13
Amstetten, *Austria* 21 G4
Amudarya →, *Uzbekistan* 44 E6
Amundsen Gulf, *Canada* 96 A7
Amundsen Sea, *Antarctica* 5 D15
Amuntai, *Indonesia* 56 E5
Amur →, *Russia* 45 D15
Amurang, *Indonesia* 57 D6
Amuri Pass, *N.Z.* 87 K4
Amurrio, *Spain* 28 B1
Amursk, *Russia* 45 D14
Amurzet, *Russia* 45 E14
Amusco, *Spain* 30 C6
Amvrakikós Kólpos, *Greece* 39 L4
Amvrosiyevka, *Ukraine* 43 C8
Amyderya = Amudarya →, *Uzbekistan* 44 E6
Amzeglouf, *Algeria* 75 C5
An Bien, *Vietnam* 59 H5
An Hoa, *Vietnam* 58 E7
An Khe, *Vietnam* 58 F7
An Nabatīyah at Tahta, *Lebanon* 69 B4
An Nabk, *Si. Arabia* 64 D3
An Nabk, *Syria* 69 A5
An Nabk Abū Qaşr, *Si. Arabia* 64 D3
An Nafūd, *Si. Arabia* 64 D4
An Najaf, *Iraq* 64 C5
An Nāşirīyah, *Iraq* 64 D5
An Nhon, *Vietnam* 58 F7
An Nîl □, *Sudan* 76 D3
An Nîl el Abyad □, *Sudan* 77 E3
An Nîl el Azraq □, *Sudan* 77 E3
An Nu'ayrīyah, *Si. Arabia* 65 E6
An Nuwayb'ī, W. →, *Si. Arabia* 69 F3
An Thoi, Dao, *Vietnam* 59 H4
An Uaimh, *Ireland* 15 C5
Anabar →, *Russia* 45 B12
'Anabtā, *Jordan* 69 C4
Anaco, *Venezuela* 121 B5
Anaconda, *U.S.A.* 110 C7
Anacortes, *U.S.A.* 112 B4
Anacuao, Mt., *Phil.* 55 C4
Anadarko, *U.S.A.* 109 H5
Anadia, *Brazil* 122 C4
Anadia, *Portugal* 30 E2
Anadolu, *Turkey* 66 D4
Anadyr, *Russia* 45 C18
Anadyr →, *Russia* 45 C18
Anadyrskiy Zaliv, *Russia* 45 C19
Anáfi, *Greece* 39 N8
Anafópoulo, *Greece* 39 N8
Anaga, Pta. de, *Canary Is.* 36 F3
Anagni, *Italy* 34 A6
'Ānah, *Iraq* 64 C4
Anaheim, *U.S.A.* 113 M9
Anahim Lake, *Canada* 100 C3
Anáhuac, *Mexico* 114 B4
Anajás, *Brazil* 122 B2
Anajatuba, *Brazil* 122 B3
Anakapalle, *India* 61 L13
Anakie, *Australia* 90 C4
Anaklia, *Georgia* 43 E9
Analalava, *Madag.* 85 A8
Análipsis, *Greece* 37 A3
Anamã, *Brazil* 121 D5
Anambar →, *Pakistan* 62 D3
Anambas, Kepulauan, *Indonesia* 56 D3
Anambas Is. = Anambas, Kepulauan, *Indonesia* 56 D3
Anambra □, *Nigeria* 79 D6
Anamoose, *U.S.A.* 108 B4
Anamosa, *U.S.A.* 108 D9
Anamur, *Turkey* 66 E5
Anamur Burnu, *Turkey* 66 E5
Anan, *Japan* 49 H7
Anand, *India* 62 H5
Anantnag, *India* 63 C6
Ananyev, *Ukraine* 42 C3
Anapa, *Russia* 42 D7
Anapodháris →, *Greece* 37 E7
Anápolis, *Brazil* 123 E2
Anapu →, *Brazil* 121 D7
Anār, *Iran* 65 D7
Anārak, *Iran* 65 C7
Anatolia = Anadolu, *Turkey* 66 D4
Anatone, *U.S.A.* 110 C5
Anatsogno, *Madag.* 85 C7
Añatuya, *Argentina* 126 B3
Anauá →, *Brazil* 121 C5
Anaunethad L., *Canada* 101 A8
Anavilhanas, Arquipélago das, *Brazil* 121 D5
Anaye, *Niger* 73 E7
Anbyŏn, *N. Korea* 51 E14
Ancash □, *Peru* 124 B2
Ancenis, *France* 24 E5
Ancho, Canal, *Chile* 128 D2
Anchor Bay, *U.S.A.* 112 G3
Anchorage, *U.S.A.* 96 B5
Anci, *China* 50 E9
Ancohuma, Nevada, *Bolivia* 124 D4
Ancón, *Peru* 124 C2
Ancona, *Italy* 33 E10
Ancud, *Chile* 128 B2
Ancud, G. de, *Chile* 128 B2
Andacollo, *Argentina* 126 D1
Andacollo, *Chile* 126 C1
Andado, *Australia* 90 D2
Andahuaylas, *Peru* 124 C3
Andalgalá, *Argentina* 126 B2
Åndalsnes, *Norway* 10 B1
Andalucía □, *Spain* 31 H6
Andalusia, *U.S.A.* 105 K2
Andalusia □ = Andalucía □, *Spain* 31 H6
Andaman Is., *Ind. Oc.* 46 H13
Andaman Sea, *Ind. Oc.* 56 B1
Andara, *Namibia* 84 B3
Andaraí, *Brazil* 123 D3
Andeer, *Switz.* 23 C8
Andelfingen, *Switz.* 23 A7
Andelot, *France* 25 D12
Andenne, *Belgium* 17 H6
Andéranboukane, *Mali* 79 B5
Anderlecht, *Belgium* 17 G4
Anderlues, *Belgium* 17 H4
Andermatt, *Switz.* 23 C7
Andernach, *Germany* 18 E3
Andernos-les-Bains, *France* 26 D2
Anderslöv, *Sweden* 11 J7
Anderson, *Calif., U.S.A.* 110 F2
Anderson, *Ind., U.S.A.* 104 E3
Anderson, *Mo., U.S.A.* 109 G7
Anderson, *S.C., U.S.A.* 105 H4
Anderson →, *Canada* 96 B7
Anderson, Mt., *S. Africa* 85 D5
Andes = Andes, Cord. de los, *S. Amer.* 124 C3
Andes, *S. Amer.* 124 C2
Andes, Cord. de los, *S. Amer.* 124 C3
Andfjorden, *Norway* 8 B14
Andhra Pradesh □, *India* 60 L11
Andijon = Andizhan, *Uzbekistan* 44 E8
Andikíthira, *Greece* 39 P6
Andīmeshk, *Iran* 65 C6
Andímilos, *Greece* 39 N7
Andípaxoi, *Greece* 39 K3
Andizhan, *Uzbekistan* 44 E8
Andoany, *Madag.* 85 A8
Andoas, *Peru* 120 D2
Andong, *S. Korea* 51 F15
Andongwei, *China* 51 G10
Andorra ■, *Europe* 28 C6
Andorra La Vella, *Andorra* 28 C6
Andover, *U.K.* 13 F6
Andover, *Mass., U.S.A.* 107 D13
Andover, *N.Y., U.S.A.* 106 D7
Andover, *Ohio, U.S.A.* 106 E4
Andradina, *Brazil* 123 F1
Andrahary, Mt., *Madag.* 85 A8
Andraitx, *Spain* 36 B9
Andramasina, *Madag.* 85 B8
Andranopasy, *Madag.* 85 C7
Andreanof Is., *U.S.A.* 96 C2
Andreapol, *Russia* 40 C8
Andrespol, *Poland* 20 D9
Andrewilla, *Australia* 91 D2
Andrews, *S.C., U.S.A.* 105 J6
Andrews, *Tex., U.S.A.* 109 J3
Ándria, *Italy* 35 A9
Andriba, *Madag.* 85 B8
Andrijevica, *Montenegro* 21 N9
Andrítsaina, *Greece* 39 M4
Androka, *Madag.* 85 C7
Andropov = Rybinsk, *Russia* 41 B11
Ándros, *Greece* 39 M7
Andros I., *Bahamas* 116 B4
Andros Town, *Bahamas* 116 B4
Andújar, *Spain* 31 G6
Andulo, *Angola* 80 G3
Anegada, B., *Argentina* 128 B4
Anegada I., *Virgin Is.* 117 C7
Anegada Passage, *W. Indies* 117 C7
Aného, *Togo* 79 D5
Añelo, *Argentina* 128 A3
Anergane, *Morocco* 74 B3
Aneto, Pico de, *Spain* 28 C5
Añez, *Bolivia* 125 D5
Anfu, *China* 53 D10
Ang Thong, *Thailand* 58 E3
Angamos, Punta, *Chile* 126 A1
Ang'angxi, *China* 54 B7
Angara →, *Russia* 45 D10
Angarab, *Ethiopia* 77 E4
Angarsk, *Russia* 45 D11
Angas Downs, *Australia* 89 E5
Angas Hills, *Australia* 88 D4
Angaston, *Australia* 91 E2
Ånge, *Sweden* 10 B9
Ángel de la Guarda, I., *Mexico* 114 B2
Angel Falls, *Venezuela* 121 B5
Angeles, *Phil.* 55 D4
Ängelholm, *Sweden* 11 H6
Angellala, *Australia* 91 D4
Angels Camp, *U.S.A.* 111 G3
Anger →, *Ethiopia* 77 F4
Angereb →, *Ethiopia* 77 E4
Ångermanälven →, *Sweden* 10 B12
Angermünde, *Germany* 18 B10
Angers, *Canada* 107 A9
Angers, *France* 24 E6
Angerville, *France* 25 D8
Ångesån →, *Sweden* 8 C17
Anghiari, *Italy* 33 E9
Angical, *Brazil* 123 D3
Angikuni L., *Canada* 101 A9
Angkor, *Cambodia* 58 F4
Anglés, *Spain* 28 D7
Anglesey, *U.K.* 12 D3
Anglet, *France* 26 E2
Angleton, *U.S.A.* 109 L7
Angleur, *Belgium* 17 G7
Anglin →, *France* 26 B4
Anglisidhes, *Cyprus* 37 E12
Anglure, *France* 25 D10
Angmagssalik, *Greenland* 4 C6
Ango, *Zaïre* 82 B2
Angoche, *Mozam.* 83 F4
Angoche, I., *Mozam.* 83 F4
Angol, *Chile* 126 D1
Angola, *Ind., U.S.A.* 104 E3
Angola, *N.Y., U.S.A.* 106 D5
Angola ■, *Africa* 81 G3
Angoon, *U.S.A.* 100 B2
Angoulême, *France* 26 C4
Angoumois, *France* 26 C4
Angra dos Reis, *Brazil* 127 A7
Angren, *Uzbekistan* 44 E8
Angtassom, *Cambodia* 59 G5
Angu, *Zaïre* 82 B1
Anguang, *China* 51 B12
Anguilla ■, *W. Indies* 117 C7
Anguo, *China* 50 E8
Angurugu, *Australia* 90 A2
Angus, Braes of, *U.K.* 14 E5
Anhanduí →, *Brazil* 127 A5
Anhée, *Belgium* 17 H5
Anholt, *Denmark* 11 H5
Anhua, *China* 53 C8
Anhui □, *China* 53 B11
Anhwei □ = Anhui □, *China* 53 B11
Anichab, *Namibia* 84 C1
Anicuns, *Brazil* 123 E2
Ánidhros, *Greece* 39 N8
Anie, *Togo* 79 D5
Animas, *U.S.A.* 111 L9
Ånimskog, *Sweden* 11 F6
Anina, *Romania* 38 D4
Anivorano, *Madag.* 85 B8
Anjar, *India* 62 H4
Anjidiv I., *India* 60 M9
Anjou, *France* 24 E6
Anjozorobe, *Madag.* 85 B8
Anju, *N. Korea* 51 E13
Anka, *Nigeria* 79 C6
Ankaboa, Tanjona, *Madag.* 85 C7
Ankang, *China* 50 H5
Ankara, *Turkey* 66 D5
Ankara □, *Turkey* 66 D5
Ankaramena, *Madag.* 85 C8
Ankazoabo, *Madag.* 85 C7
Ankazobe, *Madag.* 85 B8
Ankisabe, *Madag.* 85 B8
Anklam, *Germany* 18 B9
Ankober, *Ethiopia* 77 F4
Ankoro, *Zaïre* 82 D2
Anlong, *China* 52 E5
Anlu, *China* 53 B9
Anmyŏn-do, *S. Korea* 51 F14
Ånn, *Sweden* 10 A6
Ann, C., *U.S.A.* 107 D14
Ann Arbor, *U.S.A.* 104 D4
Anna, *Russia* 41 F12
Anna, *U.S.A.* 109 G10
Anna Plains, *Australia* 88 C3
Anna Regina, *Guyana* 121 B6
Annaba, *Algeria* 75 A6
Annaberg-Buchholz, *Germany* 18 E8
Annalee →, *Ireland* 15 B4
Annam = Trung-Phan, *Vietnam* 58 E7
Annamitique, Chaîne, *Asia* 58 D6
Annan, *U.K.* 14 G5
Annan →, *U.K.* 14 G5
Annapolis, *U.S.A.* 104 F7
Annapolis Royal, *Canada* 99 D6
Annapurna, *Nepal* 63 E10
Annean, L., *Australia* 89 E2
Anneberg, *Sweden* 11 G6
Annecy, *France* 27 C10
Annecy, L. d', *France* 27 C10
Annemasse, *France* 27 B10
Anning, *China* 52 E4
Anningie, *Australia* 88 D5
Anniston, *U.S.A.* 105 J3
Annobón, *Atl. Oc.* 71 G4
Annonay, *France* 27 C8
Annot, *France* 27 E10
Annotto Bay, *Jamaica* 116 C4
Annuello, *Australia* 91 E3
Annville, *U.S.A.* 107 F8
Annweiler, *Germany* 19 F3
Áno Viánnos, *Greece* 37 D7
Anoka, *U.S.A.* 108 C8
Anorotsangana, *Madag.* 85 A8
Anóyia, *Greece* 37 D6
Anping, *Hebei, China* 50 E8
Anping, *Liaoning, China* 51 D12
Anpu Gang, *China* 52 G7
Anqing, *China* 53 B11
Anqiu, *China* 51 F10
Anren, *China* 53 D9
Ans, *Belgium* 17 G7
Ansai, *China* 50 F5
Ansbach, *Germany* 19 F6
Anseba →, *Eritrea* 77 D4
Anserma, *Colombia* 120 B2
Anseroeul, *Belgium* 17 G3
Anshan, *China* 54 B7
Anshan, *Liaoning, China* 51 D12
Anshun, *China* 52 D5
Ansião, *Portugal* 30 F2
Ansirabe, *Madag.* 85 B8
Ansley, *U.S.A.* 108 E5
Ansó, *Spain* 28 C4
Anson, *U.S.A.* 109 J5
Anson B., *Australia* 88 B5
Ansongo, *Mali* 79 B5
Ansonia, *U.S.A.* 107 E11
Anstruther, *U.K.* 14 E6
Ansudu, *Indonesia* 57 E9
Antabamba, *Peru* 124 C3
Antakya, *Turkey* 66 E7
Antalaha, *Madag.* 85 A9
Antalya, *Turkey* 66 E4
Antalya □, *Turkey* 66 E4
Antalya Körfezi, *Turkey* 66 E4
Antananarivo, *Madag.* 85 B8
Antananarivo □, *Madag.* 85 B8
Antanimbaribe, *Madag.* 85 C7
Antarctic Pen., *Antarctica* 5 C18
Antarctica 5 E3
Antelope, *Zimbabwe* 83 G2
Antenor Navarro, *Brazil* 122 C4
Antequera, *Paraguay* 126 A4
Antequera, *Spain* 31 H6
Antero, Mt., *U.S.A.* 111 G10
Anthony, *Kans., U.S.A.* 109 G5
Anthony, *N. Mex., U.S.A.* 111 K10
Anthony Lagoon, *Australia* 90 B2
Anti Atlas, *Morocco* 74 C2
Anti-Lebanon = Ash Sharqi, Al Jabal, *Lebanon* 69 B5
Antibes, *France* 27 E11
Antibes, C. d', *France* 27 E11
Anticosti, I. d', *Canada* 99 C7
Antifer, C. d', *France* 24 C7
Antigo, *U.S.A.* 108 C10
Antigonish, *Canada* 99 C7
Antigua, *Canary Is.* 36 F5
Antigua, *Guatemala* 116 D1
Antigua, *W. Indies* 117 C7
Antigua & Barbuda ■, *W. Indies* 117 C7
Antilla, *Cuba* 116 B4
Antimony, *U.S.A.* 111 G8
Antioch, *U.S.A.* 112 G5
Antioche, Pertuis d', *France* 26 B2
Antioquia, *Colombia* 120 B2
Antioquia □, *Colombia* 120 B2
Antipodes Is., *Pac. Oc.* 92 M9
Antler, *U.S.A.* 108 A4
Antler →, *Canada* 101 D8
Antlers, *U.S.A.* 109 H7
Antofagasta, *Chile* 126 A1
Antofagasta □, *Chile* 126 A2
Antofagasta de la Sierra, *Argentina* 126 B2
Antofalla, *Argentina* 126 B2
Antofalla, Salar de, *Argentina* 126 B2
Antoing, *Belgium* 17 G2
Anton, *U.S.A.* 109 J3
Anton Chico, *U.S.A.* 111 J11
Antongila, Helodrano, *Madag.* 85 B8
Antonibé, *Madag.* 85 B8
Antonibé, Presqu'île d', *Madag.* 85 A8
Antonina, *Brazil* 127 B6
Antonito, *U.S.A.* 111 H10
Antonovo, *Kazakhstan* 43 B14
Antrain, *France* 24 D5
Antrim, *U.K.* 15 B5
Antrim □, *U.K.* 15 B5
Antrim, Mts. of, *U.K.* 15 B5
Antrim Plateau, *Australia* 88 C4
Antrodoco, *Italy* 33 F10
Antropovo, *Russia* 41 B13
Antsalova, *Madag.* 85 B7
Antsiranana, *Madag.* 85 A8
Antsohihy, *Madag.* 85 A8
Antsohimbondrona Seranana, *Madag.* 85 A8
Antu, *China* 51 C15
Antwerp = Antwerpen, *Belgium* 17 F4
Antwerp, *U.S.A.* 107 B9
Antwerpen, *Belgium* 17 F4
Antwerpen □, *Belgium* 17 F5
Anupgarh, *India* 62 E5
Anuradhapura, *Sri Lanka* 60 Q12
Anveh, *Iran* 65 E7
Anvers = Antwerpen, *Belgium* 17 F4
Anvers I., *Antarctica* 5 C17
Anxi, *Fujian, China* 53 E12
Anxi, *Gansu, China* 54 B4
Anxiang, *China* 53 C9
Anxious B., *Australia* 91 E1
Anyama, *Ivory C.* 78 D4
Anyang, *China* 50 F8
Anyi, *Jiangxi, China* 53 C10
Anyi, *Shanxi, China* 50 G6
Anyuan, *China* 53 E10
Anza, *U.S.A.* 113 M10
Anze, *China* 50 F7
Anzhero-Sudzhensk, *Russia* 44 D9
Ánzio, *Italy* 34 A5
Anzoátegui □, *Venezuela* 121 B5
Aoga-Shima, *Japan* 49 H9
Aoiz, *Spain* 28 C3
Aomori, *Japan* 48 D10
Aomori □, *Japan* 48 D10
Aonla, *India* 63 E8
Aosta, *Italy* 32 C4
Aoudéras, *Niger* 79 B6
Aouinet Torkoz, *Morocco* 74 C3
Aoukar, *Mali* 74 D4
Aouker, *Mauritania* 78 B3
Aoulef el Arab, *Algeria* 75 C5
Apa →, *S. Amer.* 126 A4
Apache, *U.S.A.* 109 H5
Apalachee B., *U.S.A.* 105 L3
Apalachicola, *U.S.A.* 105 L3
Apalachicola →, *U.S.A.* 105 L3
Apapa, *Nigeria* 79 D5
Apaporis →, *Colombia* 120 D4
Aparecida do Taboado, *Brazil* 123 F1
Aparri, *Phil.* 55 B4
Aparurén, *Venezuela* 121 B5
Apateu, *Romania* 38 C4
Apatin, *Serbia* 21 K8
Apatzingán, *Mexico* 114 D4
Apeldoorn, *Neths.* 16 D7
Apeldoornsch Kanal →, *Neths.* 16 D8
Apen, *Germany* 18 B3
Apennines = Appennini, *Italy* 32 D7
Apere →, *Bolivia* 125 C4
Apia, *W. Samoa* 87 A13
Apiacás, Serra dos, *Brazil* 125 B6
Apiaú →, *Brazil* 121 C5
Apiaú, Serra do, *Brazil* 121 C5
Apidiá →, *Brazil* 125 C5
Apinajé, *Brazil* 123 D2
Apizaco, *Mexico* 115 D5
Aplao, *Peru* 124 D3
Apo, Mt., *Phil.* 57 C7
Apodi, *Brazil* 122 C4
Apolakkiá, *Greece* 37 C9
Apolakkiá, Órmos, *Greece* 37 C9
Apolda, *Germany* 18 D7
Apollonia = Marsá Susah, *Libya* 73 B9
Apollonia, *Greece* 39 N7
Apolo, *Bolivia* 124 C4
Apónguao →, *Venezuela* 121 C5
Aporé, *Brazil* 125 D7
Aporé →, *Brazil* 123 E1
Aporema, *Brazil* 122 A1
Apostle Is., *U.S.A.* 108 B9
Apóstoles, *Argentina* 127 B4
Apostolos Andreas, C., *Cyprus* 37 D13
Apostolovo, *Ukraine* 42 C5
Apoteri, *Guyana* 121 C6
Appalachian Mts., *U.S.A.* 104 G6
Appelscha, *Neths.* 16 C8
Appennini, *Italy* 32 D7
Appennino Ligure, *Italy* 32 D5
Appenzell, *Switz.* 23 B8
Appenzell-Ausser Rhoden □, *Switz.* 23 B8
Appenzell-Inner Rhoden □, *Switz.* 23 B8
Appiano, *Italy* 33 B8
Appingedam, *Neths.* 16 B9
Apple Hill, *Canada* 107 A10
Apple Valley, *U.S.A.* 113 L9
Appleby, *U.K.* 12 C5
Appleton, *U.S.A.* 104 C1
Approuague, *Fr. Guiana* 121 C7
Approuague →, *Fr. Guiana* 121 C7
Apricena, *Italy* 35 A8
Aprigliano, *Italy* 35 C9
Aprília, *Italy* 34 A5
Apsheronsk, *Russia* 43 D8
Apt, *France* 27 E9

Apuane, Alpi, *Italy* 32 D7
Apuaú, *Brazil* 121 D5
Apucarana, *Brazil* 127 A5
Apulia = Púglia □, *Italy* 35 B9
Apure □, *Venezuela* 120 B4
Apure →, *Venezuela* 120 B4
Apurímac □, *Peru* 124 C3
Apurimac →, *Peru* 124 C3
Apuseni, Munţii, *Romania* 38 C5
Aqabah = Al 'Aqabah, *Jordan* 69 F4
'Aqabah, Khalīj al, *Red Sea* 64 D2
'Aqdā, *Iran* 65 C7
Aqîq, *Sudan* 76 D4
Aqîq, Khalîg, *Sudan* 76 D4
Aqmola = Tselinograd, *Kazakhstan* 44 D8
Aqrah, *Iraq* 64 B4
Aqtöbe = Aktyubinsk, *Kazakhstan* 44 D6
Aquidauana, *Brazil* 125 E6
Aquidauana →, *Brazil* 125 D6
Aquiles Serdán, *Mexico* 114 B3
Aquin, *Haiti* 117 C5
Ar Rachidiya, *Morocco* 74 B4
Ar Rafīd, *Syria* 69 C4
Ar Raḩḩālīyah, *Iraq* 64 C4
Ar Ramādī, *Iraq* 64 C4
Ar Ramthā, *Jordan* 69 C5
Ar Raqqah, *Syria* 64 C3
Ar Rass, *Si. Arabia* 64 E4
Ar Rifā'ī, *Si. Arabia* 64 D5
Ar Riyāḑ, *Si. Arabia* 64 E5
Ar Ru'ays, *Qatar* 65 E6
Ar Rukhaymīyah, *Iraq* 64 D5
Ar Ruqayyidah, *Si. Arabia* 65 E6
Ar Ruşāfah, *Syria* 64 C3
Ar Ruţbah, *Iraq* 64 C4
Ara, *India* 63 G11
'Arab, Bahr el →, *Sudan* 77 F2
Arab, Khalîg el, *Egypt* 76 H6
'Arabābād, *Iran* 65 C8
Araban, *Turkey* 67 E7
Arabatskaya Strelka, *Ukraine* 42 D6
Arabba, *Italy* 33 B8
Arabelo, *Venezuela* 121 C5
Arabia, *Asia* 68 C4
Arabian Desert = Es Sahrâ' Esh Sharqîya, *Egypt* 76 B3
Arabian Gulf = Gulf, The, *Asia* 65 E6
Arabian Sea, *Ind. Oc.* 46 H10
Araç, *Turkey* 66 C5
Aracaju, *Brazil* 122 D4
Aracataca, *Colombia* 120 A3
Aracati, *Brazil* 122 B4
Araçatuba, *Brazil* 127 A5
Aracena, *Spain* 31 H4
Aracena, Sierra de, *Spain* 31 H4
Araçuaí, *Brazil* 123 E3
Araçuaí →, *Brazil* 123 E3
'Arad, *Israel* 69 D4
Arad, *Romania* 38 C4
Arada, *Chad* 73 F9
Aradhippou, *Cyprus* 37 E12
Arafura Sea, *E. Indies* 57 F8
Aragarças, *Brazil* 125 D7
Aragats, *Armenia* 43 F11
Aragón □, *Spain* 28 D4
Aragón →, *Spain* 28 C3
Aragona, *Italy* 34 E6
Aragua □, *Venezuela* 120 B4
Aragua de Barcelona, *Venezuela* 121 B5
Araguacema, *Brazil* 122 C2
Araguaçu, *Brazil* 123 D2
Araguaia →, *Brazil* 122 C2
Araguaiana, *Brazil* 125 D7
Araguaína, *Brazil* 122 C2
Araguari, *Brazil* 123 E2
Araguari →, *Brazil* 121 C8
Araguatins, *Brazil* 122 C2
Araioses, *Brazil* 122 B3
Arak, *Algeria* 75 C5
Arāk, *Iran* 65 C6
Arakan Coast, *Burma* 61 K19
Arakan Yoma, *Burma* 61 K19
Arakli, *Turkey* 67 C9
Araks = Aras, Rūd-e →, *Iran* 64 B5
Aral Sea = Aralskoye More, *Asia* 44 E7
Aralsk, *Kazakhstan* 44 E7
Aralskoye More, *Asia* 44 E7
Aramac, *Australia* 90 C4
Arambag, *India* 63 H12
Aran I., *Ireland* 15 B3
Aran Is., *Ireland* 15 C2
Aranda de Duero, *Spain* 28 D1
Arandān, *Iran* 64 C5
Aranjuez, *Spain* 30 E7
Aranos, *Namibia* 84 C2
Aransas Pass, *U.S.A.* 109 M6
Aranzazu, *Colombia* 120 B2
Araouane, *Mali* 78 B4
Arapahoe, *U.S.A.* 108 E5
Arapari, *Brazil* 122 C2
Arapey Grande →, *Uruguay* 126 C4
Arapiraca, *Brazil* 122 C4
Arapkir, *Turkey* 67 D8
Arapongas, *Brazil* 127 A5
Ar'ar, *Si. Arabia* 64 D4
Araracuara, *Colombia* 120 D3
Araranguá, *Brazil* 127 B6
Araraquara, *Brazil* 123 F2
Ararás, Serra das, *Brazil* 127 B5
Ararat, *Australia* 91 F3
Ararat, Mt. = Ağrı Dağı, *Turkey* 67 D11
Arari, *Brazil* 122 B3
Araria, *India* 63 F12
Araripe, Chapada do, *Brazil* 122 C3
Araripina, *Brazil* 122 C3
Araruama, L. de, *Brazil* 123 F3
Araruna, *Brazil* 122 C4
Aras, Rūd-e →, *Iran* 64 B5
Araticu, *Brazil* 122 B2
Arauca, *Colombia* 120 B3
Arauca □, *Colombia* 120 B3
Arauca →, *Venezuela* 120 B4
Arauco, *Chile* 126 D1
Arauco □, *Chile* 126 D1
Araújos, *Brazil* 123 E2
Arauquita, *Colombia* 120 B3
Araure, *Venezuela* 120 B4
Arawa, *Ethiopia* 77 F5
Araxá, *Brazil* 123 E2
Araya, Pen. de, *Venezuela* 121 A5
Arba Minch, *Ethiopia* 77 F4
Arbat, *Iraq* 64 C5
Arbatax, *Italy* 34 C2
Arbaza, *Russia* 45 D10
Arbedo, *Switz.* 23 D8
Arbīl, *Iraq* 64 B5
Arbois, *France* 25 F12
Arboletes, *Colombia* 120 B2
Arbon, *Switz.* 23 A8
Arbore, *Ethiopia* 77 F4
Arborea, *Italy* 34 C1
Arborfield, *Canada* 101 C8
Arborg, *Canada* 101 C9
Arbrå, *Sweden* 10 C10
Arbroath, *U.K.* 14 E6
Arbuckle, *U.S.A.* 112 F4
Arbus, *Italy* 34 C1
Arbuzinka, *Ukraine* 42 C4
Arc, *France* 25 E12
Arc →, *France* 27 C10
Arcachon, *France* 26 D2
Arcachon, Bassin d', *France* 26 D2
Arcade, *U.S.A.* 106 D6
Arcadia, *Fla., U.S.A.* 105 M5
Arcadia, *La., U.S.A.* 109 J8
Arcadia, *Nebr., U.S.A.* 108 E5
Arcadia, *Pa., U.S.A.* 106 F6
Arcadia, *Wis., U.S.A.* 108 C9
Arcata, *U.S.A.* 110 F1
Arcévia, *Italy* 33 E9
Archangel = Arkhangelsk, *Russia* 44 C5
Archar, *Bulgaria* 38 F5
Archbald, *U.S.A.* 107 E9
Archena, *Spain* 29 G3
Archer →, *Australia* 90 A3
Archer B., *Australia* 90 A3
Archers Post, *Kenya* 82 B4
Archidona, *Spain* 31 H6
Arci, Monte, *Italy* 34 C1
Arcidosso, *Italy* 33 F8
Arcila = Asilah, *Morocco* 74 A3
Arcis-sur-Aube, *France* 25 D11
Arckaringa, *Australia* 91 D1
Arckaringa Cr. →, *Australia* 91 D2
Arco, *Italy* 32 C7
Arco, *U.S.A.* 110 E7
Arcola, *Canada* 101 D8
Arcos, *Spain* 28 D2
Arcos de los Frontera, *Spain* 31 J5
Arcos de Valdevez, *Portugal* 30 D2
Arcot, *India* 60 N11
Arcoverde, *Brazil* 122 C4
Arctic Bay, *Canada* 97 A11
Arctic Ocean, *Arctic* 4 B18
Arctic Red River, *Canada* 96 B6
Arda →, *Bulgaria* 39 H9
Arda →, *Italy* 32 D6
Ardabīl, *Iran* 65 B6
Ardahan, *Turkey* 67 C10
Ardakān = Sepīdān, *Iran* 65 D7
Ardales, *Spain* 31 J6
Årdalstangen, *Norway* 10 C1
Ardatov, *Russia* 41 D15
Ardea, *Greece* 39 J5
Ardèche □, *France* 27 D8
Ardèche →, *France* 27 D8
Ardee, *Ireland* 15 C5
Arden, *Canada* 106 B8
Arden, *Denmark* 11 H3
Arden, *Calif., U.S.A.* 112 G5
Arden, *Nev., U.S.A.* 113 J11
Ardenne, *Belgium* 25 C12
Ardennes = Ardenne, *Belgium* 25 C12
Ardennes □, *France* 25 C11
Ardentes, *France* 25 F8
Ardeşen, *Turkey* 67 C9
Ardestān, *Iran* 65 C7
Ardgour, *U.K.* 14 E3
Árdhas →, *Greece* 39 H9
Ardila →, *Portugal* 31 G3
Ardlethan, *Australia* 91 E4
Ardmore, *Australia* 90 C2
Ardmore, *Okla., U.S.A.* 109 H6
Ardmore, *Pa., U.S.A.* 107 G9
Ardmore, *S. Dak., U.S.A.* 108 D3
Ardnacrusha, *Ireland* 15 D3
Ardnamurchan, Pt. of, *U.K.* 14 E2
Ardooie, *Belgium* 17 G2
Ardore Marina, *Italy* 35 D9
Ardres, *France* 25 B8
Ardrossan, *Australia* 91 E2
Ardrossan, *U.K.* 14 F4
Ards □, *U.K.* 15 B6
Ards Pen., *U.K.* 15 B6
Ardud, *Romania* 38 B5
Ardunac, *Turkey* 43 F10
Åre, *Sweden* 10 A7
Arecibo, *Puerto Rico* 117 C6
Areia Branca, *Brazil* 122 B4
Arena, Pt., *U.S.A.* 112 G3
Arenales, Cerro, *Chile* 128 C2
Arenápolis, *Brazil* 125 C6
Arenas, *Spain* 30 B6
Arenas de San Pedro, *Spain* 30 E5
Arendal, *Norway* 11 F2
Arendonk, *Belgium* 17 F6
Arendsee, *Germany* 18 C7
Arenillas, *Ecuador* 120 D1
Arenys de Mar, *Spain* 28 D7
Arenzano, *Italy* 32 D5
Areópolis, *Greece* 39 N5
Arequipa, *Peru* 124 D3
Arequipa □, *Peru* 124 D3
Arere, *Brazil* 121 D7
Arero, *Ethiopia* 77 G4
Arès, *France* 26 D2
Arévalo, *Spain* 30 D6
Arezzo, *Italy* 33 E8
Arga →, *Spain* 28 C3
Argalastí, *Greece* 39 K6
Argamakmur, *Indonesia* 56 E2
Argamasilla de Alba, *Spain* 29 F1
Arganda, *Spain* 28 E1
Arganil, *Portugal* 30 E2
Argelès-Gazost, *France* 26 F3
Argelès-sur-Mer, *France* 26 F7
Argens →, *France* 27 E10
Argent-sur-Sauldre, *France* 25 E9
Argenta, *Italy* 33 D8
Argentan, *France* 24 D6
Argentário, Mte., *Italy* 33 F8
Argentat, *France* 26 C5
Argentera, *Italy* 32 D3
Argentera, Monte del, *Italy* 32 D4
Argenteuil, *France* 25 D9
Argentia, *Canada* 99 C9
Argentiera, C. dell', *Italy* 34 B1
Argentière, Aiguilles d', *Switz.* 22 E4
Argentina ■, *S. Amer.* 128 B3
Argentina Is., *Antarctica* 5 C17
Argentino, L., *Argentina* 128 D2
Argenton-Château, *France* 24 F6
Argenton-sur-Creuse, *France* 26 B5
Argeş →, *Romania* 38 E9
Arghandab →, *Afghan.* 62 D1
Argo, *Sudan* 76 D3
Argolikós Kólpos, *Greece* 39 M5
Argonne, *France* 25 C12
Árgos, *Greece* 39 M5
Argostólion, *Greece* 39 L3
Arguedas, *Spain* 28 C3
Arguello, Pt., *U.S.A.* 113 L6
Arguineguín, *Canary Is.* 36 G4
Argun →, *Russia* 45 D13
Argungu, *Nigeria* 79 C5
Argus Pk., *U.S.A.* 113 K9
Argyle, *U.S.A.* 108 A6
Argyle, L., *Australia* 88 C4
Arhavi, *Turkey* 67 C9
Århus, *Denmark* 11 H4
Århus Amtskommune □, *Denmark* 11 H4
Ariadnoye, *Russia* 48 B7
Ariamsvlei, *Namibia* 84 D2
Ariana, *Tunisia* 75 A7
Ariano Irpino, *Italy* 35 A8
Ariano nel Polèsine, *Italy* 33 D9
Ariari →, *Colombia* 120 C3
Aribinda, *Burkina Faso* 79 C4
Arica, *Chile* 124 D3
Arica, *Colombia* 120 D3
Arico, *Canary Is.* 36 F3
Arid, C., *Australia* 89 F3
Arida, *Japan* 49 G7
Ariège □, *France* 26 F5
Ariège →, *France* 26 E5
Arieş →, *Romania* 38 C6
Arīḩā, *Syria* 64 C3
Arílla, Ákra, *Greece* 37 A3
Arima, *Trin. & Tob.* 117 D7
Arinos →, *Brazil* 125 C6
Ario de Rosales, *Mexico* 114 D4
Aripuanã, *Brazil* 125 B5
Aripuanã →, *Brazil* 125 B5
Ariquemes, *Brazil* 125 B5
Arisaig, *U.K.* 14 E3
Arîsh, W. el →, *Egypt* 76 H8
Arismendi, *Venezuela* 120 B4
Arissa, *Ethiopia* 77 E5
Aristazabal I., *Canada* 100 C3
Arivaca, *U.S.A.* 111 L8
Arivonimamo, *Madag.* 85 B8
Ariza, *Spain* 28 D2
Arizaro, Salar de, *Argentina* 126 A2
Arizona, *Argentina* 126 D2
Arizona □, *U.S.A.* 111 J8
Arizpe, *Mexico* 114 A2
Arjeplog, *Sweden* 8 C15
Arjona, *Colombia* 120 A2
Arjona, *Spain* 31 H6
Arjuno, *Indonesia* 57 G15
Arka, *Russia* 45 C15
Arkadak, *Russia* 41 F13
Arkadelphia, *U.S.A.* 109 H8
Arkaig, L., *U.K.* 14 E3
Arkalyk, *Kazakhstan* 44 D7
Arkansas □, *U.S.A.* 109 H8
Arkansas →, *U.S.A.* 109 J9
Arkansas City, *U.S.A.* 109 G6
Árkathos →, *Greece* 39 K4
Arkhángelos, *Greece* 37 C10
Arkhangelsk, *Russia* 44 C5
Arkhangelskoye, *Russia* 41 F12
Arkiko, *Eritrea* 77 D4
Arklow, *Ireland* 15 D5
Arkona, Kap, *Germany* 18 A9
Arkösund, *Sweden* 11 F10
Arkticheskiy, Mys, *Russia* 45 A10
Arkul, *Russia* 41 C17
Arlanc, *France* 26 C7
Arlanza →, *Spain* 30 C6
Arlanzón →, *Spain* 30 C6
Arlberg Pass, *Austria* 19 H6
Arlee, *U.S.A.* 110 C6
Arles, *France* 27 E8
Arlesheim, *Switz.* 22 B5
Arlington, *S. Africa* 85 D4
Arlington, *Oreg., U.S.A.* 110 D3
Arlington, *S. Dak., U.S.A.* 108 C6
Arlington, *Va., U.S.A.* 104 F7
Arlington, *Wash., U.S.A.* 112 B4
Arlon, *Belgium* 17 J7
Arlöv, *Sweden* 11 J7
Arly, *Burkina Faso* 79 C5
Armagh, *U.K.* 15 B5
Armagh □, *U.K.* 15 B5
Armagnac, *France* 26 E4
Armançon →, *France* 25 E10
Armavir, *Russia* 43 D9
Armenia, *Colombia* 120 C2
Armenia ■, *Asia* 43 F11
Armenistís, Ákra, *Greece* 37 C9
Armentières, *France* 25 B9
Armidale, *Australia* 91 E5
Armour, *U.S.A.* 108 D5
Armstrong, *B.C., Canada* 100 C5
Armstrong, *Ont., Canada* 98 B2
Armstrong, *U.S.A.* 109 M6
Armstrong →, *Australia* 88 C5
Arnarfjörður, *Iceland* 8 D2
Arnaud →, *Canada* 97 B12
Arnauti, C., *Cyprus* 37 D11
Arnay-le-Duc, *France* 25 E11
Arnedillo, *Spain* 28 C2
Arnedo, *Spain* 28 C2
Arnemuiden, *Neths.* 17 F3
Árnes, *Iceland* 8 C3
Årnes, *Norway* 10 D5
Arnett, *U.S.A.* 109 G5
Arnhem, *Neths.* 16 E7
Arnhem, C., *Australia* 90 A2
Arnhem B., *Australia* 90 A2
Arnhem Land, *Australia* 90 A1
Arno →, *Italy* 32 E7
Arno Bay, *Australia* 91 E2
Arnold, *Calif., U.S.A.* 112 G6
Arnold, *Nebr., U.S.A.* 108 E4
Arnoldstein, *Austria* 21 J3
Arnon →, *France* 25 E9
Arnot, *Canada* 101 B9
Arnøy, *Norway* 8 A16
Arnprior, *Canada* 98 C4
Arnsberg, *Germany* 18 D4
Arnstadt, *Germany* 18 E6
Aro →, *Venezuela* 121 B5
Aroab, *Namibia* 84 D2
Aroche, *Spain* 31 H4
Aroeiras, *Brazil* 122 C4
Arolla, *Switz.* 22 D4
Arolsen, *Germany* 18 D5
Aron →, *France* 26 B7
Arona, *Italy* 32 C5
Aroroy, *Phil.* 55 E5
Arosa, *Switz.* 23 C9
Arosa, Ria de, *Spain* 30 C2
Arpajon, *France* 25 D9
Arpajon-sur-Cère, *France* 26 D6
Arpino, *Italy* 34 A6
Arque, *Bolivia* 124 D4
Arrabury, *Australia* 91 D3
Arrah = Ara, *India* 63 G11
Arraias, *Brazil* 123 D2
Arraias →, *Mato Grosso, Brazil* 125 C7
Arraias →, *Pará, Brazil* 122 C2
Arraiolos, *Portugal* 31 G3
Arran, *U.K.* 14 F3
Arrandale, *Canada* 100 C3
Arras, *France* 25 B9
Arrats →, *France* 26 D4
Arreau, *France* 26 F4
Arrecife, *Canary Is.* 36 F6
Arrecifes, *Argentina* 126 C3
Arrée, Mts. d', *France* 24 D3
Arriaga, *Chiapas, Mexico* 115 D6
Arriaga, *San Luis Potosí, Mexico* 114 C4
Arrilalah P.O., *Australia* 90 C3
Arrino, *Australia* 89 E2
Arrojado →, *Brazil* 123 D3
Arromanches-les-Bains, *France* 24 C6
Arronches, *Portugal* 31 F3
Arros →, *France* 26 E3
Arrou, *France* 24 D8
Arrow, L., *Ireland* 15 B3
Arrow Rock Res., *U.S.A.* 110 E6
Arrowhead, *Canada* 100 C5
Arrowhead, L., *U.S.A.* 113 L9
Arrowtown, *N.Z.* 87 L2
Arroyo de la Luz, *Spain* 31 F4
Arroyo Grande, *U.S.A.* 113 K6
Års, *Denmark* 11 H3
Ars, *Iran* 64 B5
Ars-en-Ré, *France* 26 B2
Ars-sur-Moselle, *France* 25 C13
Arsenault L., *Canada* 101 B7
Arsenev, *Russia* 48 B6
Arsi □, *Ethiopia* 77 F4
Arsiero, *Italy* 33 C8
Arsin, *Turkey* 67 C8
Arsk, *Russia* 41 C16
Árta, *Greece* 39 K4
Artá, *Spain* 36 B10
Arteaga, *Mexico* 114 D4
Arteche, *Phil.* 55 E6
Arteijo, *Spain* 30 B2
Artem, *Russia* 48 C6
Artem, Ostrov, *Azerbaijan* 43 F14
Artemovsk, *Russia* 45 D10
Artemovsk, *Ukraine* 42 B8
Artemovskiy, *Russia* 43 C9
Artenay, *France* 25 D8
Artern, *Germany* 18 D7
Artesa de Segre, *Spain* 28 D6
Artesia = Mosomane, *Botswana* 84 C4
Artesia, *U.S.A.* 109 J2
Artesia Wells, *U.S.A.* 109 L5
Artesian, *U.S.A.* 108 C6
Arth, *Switz.* 23 B7
Arthez-de-Béarn, *France* 26 E3
Arthington, *Liberia* 78 D2
Arthur →, *Australia* 90 G3
Arthur Cr. →, *Australia* 90 C2
Arthur Pt., *Australia* 90 C5
Arthur's Pass, *N.Z.* 87 K3
Arthur's Town, *Bahamas* 117 B4
Artigas, *Uruguay* 126 C4
Artik, *Armenia* 43 F10
Artillery L., *Canada* 101 A7
Artois, *France* 25 B9
Artsiz, *Ukraine* 42 C3
Artvin, *Turkey* 43 F9
Artvin □, *Turkey* 67 C9
Aru, Kepulauan, *Indonesia* 57 F8
Aru Is. = Aru, Kepulauan, *Indonesia* 57 F8
Aru Meru □, *Tanzania* 82 C4
Arua, *Uganda* 82 B3
Aruanã, *Brazil* 123 D1
Aruba ■, *W. Indies* 117 D6
Arucas, *Canary Is.* 36 F4
Arudy, *France* 26 E3
Arumã, *Brazil* 121 D5
Arumpo, *Australia* 91 E3
Arun →, *Nepal* 63 F12
Arunachal Pradesh □, *India* 61 E19
Arusha, *Tanzania* 82 C4
Arusha □, *Tanzania* 82 C4
Arusha Chini, *Tanzania* 82 C4
Aruwimi →, *Zaïre* 82 B1
Arvada, *U.S.A.* 110 D10
Arvayheer, *Mongolia* 54 B5
Arve →, *France* 27 B10
Árvi, *Greece* 37 E7
Arvida, *Canada* 99 C5
Arvidsjaur, *Sweden* 8 D15
Arvika, *Sweden* 9 G12
Arvin, *U.S.A.* 113 K8
Arxan, *China* 54 B6
Aryirádhes, *Greece* 37 B3
Aryiroúpolis, *Greece* 37 D6
Arys, *Kazakhstan* 44 E7
Arzachena, *Italy* 34 A2
Arzamas, *Russia* 41 D13
Arzew, *Algeria* 75 A4
Arzgir, *Russia* 43 D11
Arzignano, *Italy* 33 C8
As, *Belgium* 17 F7
Aş Şadr, *U.A.E.* 65 E7
Aş Şafā, *Syria* 69 B6
'As Saffānīyah, *Si. Arabia* 65 D6
As Safīrah, *Syria* 64 B3
Aş Şahm, *Oman* 65 E8
As Sājir, *Si. Arabia* 64 E5
As Salamīyah, *Syria* 64 C3
As Salt, *Jordan* 69 C4
As Sal'w'a, *Qatar* 65 E6
As Samāwah, *Iraq* 64 D5
As Sanamayn, *Syria* 69 B5
As Sukhnąh, *Syria* 64 C3
As Sulaymānīyah, *Iraq* 64 C5
As Sulaymī, *Si. Arabia* 64 E4
As Summān, *Si. Arabia* 64 E5
As Suwaydā', *Syria* 69 C5
As Suwaydā' □, *Syria* 69 C5
As Şuwayrah, *Iraq* 64 C5
Asab, *Namibia* 84 D2
Asaba, *Nigeria* 79 D6
Asafo, *Ghana* 78 D4

Asahi-Gawa →, *Japan* 49 G6
Asahigawa, *Japan* 48 C11
Asale, L., *Ethiopia* 77 E5
Asamankese, *Ghana* 79 D4
Asansol, *India* 63 H12
Åsarna, *Sweden* 10 B8
Asbe Teferi, *Ethiopia* 77 F5
Asbesberge, *S. Africa* 84 D3
Asbestos, *Canada* 99 C5
Asbury Park, *U.S.A.* 107 F10
Ascensión, *Mexico* 114 A3
Ascensión, B. de la, *Mexico* 115 D7
Ascension I., *Atl. Oc.* 2 E9
Aschaffenburg, *Germany* 19 F5
Aschendorf, *Germany* 18 B3
Aschersleben, *Germany* 18 D7
Asciano, *Italy* 33 E8
Áscoli Piceno, *Italy* 33 F10
Áscoli Satriano, *Italy* 35 A8
Ascona, *Switz.* 23 D7
Ascope, *Peru* 124 B2
Ascotán, *Chile* 126 A2
Aseb, *Eritrea* 68 E3
Asedjrad, *Algeria* 75 D5
Asela, *Ethiopia* 77 F4
Asenovgrad, *Bulgaria* 39 G7
Asfeld, *France* 25 C11
Asfûn el Matâ'na, *Egypt* 76 B3
Åsgårdstrand, *Norway* 10 E4
Asgata, *Cyprus* 37 E12
Ash Fork, *U.S.A.* 111 J7
Ash Grove, *U.S.A.* 109 G8
Ash Shamāl □, *Lebanon* 69 A5
Ash Shāmīyah, *Iraq* 64 D5
Ash Shāriqah, *U.A.E.* 65 E7
Ash Sharmah, *Si. Arabia* 64 D2
Ash Sharqāt, *Iraq* 64 C4
Ash Sharqi, Al Jabal, *Lebanon* 69 B5
Ash Shaṭrah, *Iraq* 64 D5
Ash Shawbak, *Jordan* 64 D2
Ash Shawmari, J., *Jordan* 69 E5
Ash Shaykh, J., *Lebanon* 69 B4
Ash Shināfīyah, *Iraq* 64 D5
Ash Shu'aybah, *Si. Arabia* 64 E5
Ash Shumlūl, *Si. Arabia* 64 E5
Ash Shūr'a, *Iraq* 64 C4
Ash Shurayf, *Si. Arabia* 64 E3
Ash Shuwayfāt, *Lebanon* 69 B4
Ashanti □, *Ghana* 79 D4
Ashau, *Vietnam* 58 D6
Ashburn, *U.S.A.* 105 K4
Ashburton, *N.Z.* 87 K3
Ashburton →, *Australia* 88 D1
Ashburton Downs, *Australia* 88 D2
Ashby de la Zouch, *U.K.* 12 E6
Ashcroft, *Canada* 100 C4
Ashdod, *Israel* 69 D3
Asheboro, *U.S.A.* 105 H6
Asherton, *U.S.A.* 109 L5
Asheville, *U.S.A.* 105 H4
Asheweig →, *Canada* 98 B2
Ashford, *Australia* 91 D5
Ashford, *U.K.* 13 F8
Ashford, *U.S.A.* 110 C2
Ashgabat = Ashkhabad, *Turkmenistan* 44 F6
Ashibetsu, *Japan* 48 C11
Ashikaga, *Japan* 49 F9
Ashizuri-Zaki, *Japan* 49 H6
Ashkarkot, *Afghan.* 62 C2
Ashkhabad, *Turkmenistan* 44 F6
Ashland, *Kans., U.S.A.* 109 G5
Ashland, *Ky., U.S.A.* 104 F4
Ashland, *Maine, U.S.A.* 99 C6
Ashland, *Mont., U.S.A.* 110 D10
Ashland, *Nebr., U.S.A.* 108 E6
Ashland, *Ohio, U.S.A.* 106 F2
Ashland, *Oreg., U.S.A.* 110 E2
Ashland, *Pa., U.S.A.* 107 F8
Ashland, *Va., U.S.A.* 104 G7
Ashland, *Wis., U.S.A.* 108 B9
Ashley, *N. Dak., U.S.A.* 108 B5
Ashley, *Pa., U.S.A.* 107 E9
Ashmont, *Canada* 100 C6
Ashmore Reef, *Australia* 88 B3
Ashmûn, *Egypt* 76 H7
Ashq'elon, *Israel* 69 D3
Ashtabula, *U.S.A.* 106 E4
Ashton, *S. Africa* 84 E3
Ashton, *U.S.A.* 110 D8
Ashton under Lyne, *U.K.* 12 D5
Ashuanipi, L., *Canada* 99 B6
Asia 46 E11
Asia, Kepulauan, *Indonesia* 57 D8
Āsīā Bak, *Iran* 65 C6
Asiago, *Italy* 33 C8
Asidonhoppo, *Surinam* 121 C6
Asifabad, *India* 60 K11
Asike, *Indonesia* 57 F10
Asilah, *Morocco* 74 A3
Asinara, *Italy* 34 A1
Asinara, G. dell', *Italy* 34 B1
Asino, *Russia* 44 D9
'Asīr □, *Si. Arabia* 68 D3
Asir, Ras, *Somali Rep.* 68 E5
Aşkale, *Turkey* 67 D9
Asker, *Norway* 10 E4
Askersund, *Sweden* 11 F8
Askham, *S. Africa* 84 D3
Askim, *Norway* 10 E5
Askja, *Iceland* 8 D5
Asl, *Egypt* 76 J8
Asmara = Asmera, *Eritrea* 77 D4
Asmera, *Eritrea* 77 D4
Asnæs, *Denmark* 11 J5
Asni, *Morocco* 74 B3
Ásola, *Italy* 32 C7
Asoteriba, Jebel, *Sudan* 76 C4
Asotin, *U.S.A.* 110 C5
Aspe, *Spain* 29 G4
Aspen, *U.S.A.* 111 G10
Aspendos, *Turkey* 66 E4
Aspermont, *U.S.A.* 109 J4
Aspiring, Mt., *N.Z.* 87 L2
Aspres-sur-Buëch, *France* 27 D9
Asprókavos, Ákra, *Greece* 37 B4
Aspromonte, *Italy* 35 D8
Aspur, *India* 62 H6
Asquith, *Canada* 101 C7
Assa, *Morocco* 74 C3
Assâba, *Mauritania* 78 B2
Assam □, *India* 61 F18
Assamakka, *Niger* 79 B6
Asse, *Belgium* 17 H4
Assebroek, *Belgium* 17 F2
Assekrem, *Algeria* 75 D6
Assémini, *Italy* 34 C2
Assen, *Neths.* 16 C9
Assendelft, *Neths.* 16 D5
Assenede, *Belgium* 17 F3
Assens, *Århus, Denmark* 11 H4
Assens, *Fyn, Denmark* 11 J3
Assesse, *Belgium* 17 H6
Assini, *Ivory C.* 78 D4
Assiniboia, *Canada* 101 D7
Assiniboine →, *Canada* 101 D9
Assis, *Brazil* 127 A5
Assisi, *Italy* 33 E9
Assynt, L., *U.K.* 14 C3
Astaffort, *France* 26 D4
Astara, *Azerbaijan* 43 D13
Asten, *Neths.* 17 F7
Asteroúsia, *Greece* 37 E7
Asti, *Italy* 32 D5
Astipálaia, *Greece* 39 N9
Astorga, *Spain* 30 C4
Astoria, *U.S.A.* 112 D3
Åstorp, *Sweden* 11 H6
Astrakhan, *Russia* 43 C13
Astudillo, *Spain* 30 C6
Asturias □, *Spain* 30 B5
Asunción, *Paraguay* 126 B4
Asunción Nochixtlán, *Mexico* 115 D5
Asutri, *Sudan* 77 D4
Aswa →, *Uganda* 82 B3
Aswad, Ras al, *Si. Arabia* 76 C4
Aswân, *Egypt* 76 C3
Aswân High Dam = Sadd el Aali, *Egypt* 76 C3
Asyût, *Egypt* 76 B3
Asyûti, Wadi →, *Egypt* 76 B3
Aszód, *Hungary* 21 H9
At Ṭafīlah, *Jordan* 69 E4
At Tā'if, *Si. Arabia* 68 C3
Aṭ Ṭirāq, *Si. Arabia* 64 E5
Atacama □, *Chile* 126 B2
Atacama, Desierto de, *Chile* 126 A2
Atacama, Salar de, *Chile* 126 A2
Ataco, *Colombia* 120 C2
Atakor, *Algeria* 75 D6
Atakpamé, *Togo* 79 D5
Atalándi, *Greece* 39 L5
Atalaya, *Peru* 124 C3
Atalaya de Femes, *Canary Is.* 36 F6
Ataléia, *Brazil* 123 E3
Atami, *Japan* 49 G9
Atapupu, *Indonesia* 57 F6
Atâr, *Mauritania* 74 D2
Atara, *Russia* 45 C13
Ataram, Erg n-, *Algeria* 75 D5
Atarfe, *Spain* 31 H7
Atascadero, *Calif., U.S.A.* 111 J3
Atascadero, *Calif., U.S.A.* 112 K6
Atasu, *Kazakhstan* 44 E8
Atauro, *Indonesia* 57 F7
Atbara, *Sudan* 76 D3
'Atbara →, *Sudan* 76 D3
Atbasar, *Kazakhstan* 44 D7
Atchafalaya B., *U.S.A.* 109 L9
Atchison, *U.S.A.* 108 F7
Atebubu, *Ghana* 79 D4
Ateca, *Spain* 28 D3
Aterno →, *Italy* 33 F10
Atesine, Alpi, *Italy* 32 B8
Atessa, *Italy* 33 F11
Ath, *Belgium* 17 G3
Athabasca, *Canada* 100 C6
Athabasca →, *Canada* 101 B6
Athabasca, L., *Canada* 101 B7
Athboy, *Ireland* 15 C5
Athenry, *Ireland* 15 C3
Athens = Athínai, *Greece* 39 M6
Athens, *Ala., U.S.A.* 105 H2
Athens, *Ga., U.S.A.* 105 J4
Athens, *N.Y., U.S.A.* 107 D11
Athens, *Ohio, U.S.A.* 104 F4
Athens, *Pa., U.S.A.* 107 E8
Athens, *Tenn., U.S.A.* 105 H3
Athens, *Tex., U.S.A.* 109 J7
Atherley, *Canada* 106 B5
Atherton, *Australia* 90 B4
Athiéme, *Benin* 79 D5
Athienou, *Cyprus* 37 D12
Athínai, *Greece* 39 M6
Athlone, *Ireland* 15 C4
Athna, *Cyprus* 37 D12
Atholl, Forest of, *U.K.* 14 E5
Atholville, *Canada* 99 C6
Áthos, *Greece* 39 J7
Athus, *Belgium* 17 J7
Athy, *Ireland* 15 D5
Ati, *Chad* 73 F8
Ati, *Sudan* 77 E2
Atiak, *Uganda* 82 B3
Atico, *Peru* 124 D3
Atienza, *Spain* 28 D2
Atikokan, *Canada* 98 C1
Atikonak L., *Canada* 99 B7
Atimonan, *Phil.* 55 E4
Atka, *Russia* 45 C16
Atkarsk, *Russia* 41 F14
Atkinson, *U.S.A.* 108 D5
Atlanta, *Ga., U.S.A.* 105 J3
Atlanta, *Tex., U.S.A.* 109 J7
Atlantic, *U.S.A.* 108 E7
Atlantic City, *U.S.A.* 104 F8
Atlantic Ocean 2 E9
Atlántico □, *Colombia* 120 A2
Atlas Mts. = Haut Atlas, *Morocco* 74 B3
Atlin, *Canada* 100 B2
Atlin, L., *Canada* 100 B2
Atmore, *U.S.A.* 105 K2
Atoka, *U.S.A.* 109 H6
Átokos, *Greece* 39 L3
Atolia, *U.S.A.* 113 K9
Atouguia, *Portugal* 31 F1
Atoyac →, *Mexico* 115 D5
Atrak →, *Iran* 65 B8
Ätran, *Sweden* 11 G6
Atrato →, *Colombia* 120 B2
Atrauli, *India* 62 E8
Atri, *Italy* 33 F10
Atsbi, *Ethiopia* 77 E4
Atsoum, Mts., *Cameroon* 79 D7
Atsuta, *Japan* 48 C10
Attalla, *U.S.A.* 105 H2
Attáviros, *Greece* 37 C9
Attawapiskat, *Canada* 98 B3
Attawapiskat →, *Canada* 98 B3
Attawapiskat, L., *Canada* 98 B2
Attendorn, *Germany* 18 D3
Attert, *Belgium* 17 J7
Attica, *U.S.A.* 104 E2
Attichy, *France* 25 C10
Attigny, *France* 25 C11
Attikamagen L., *Canada* 99 A6
Attleboro, *U.S.A.* 107 E13
Attock, *Pakistan* 62 C5
Attopeu, *Laos* 58 E6
Attur, *India* 60 P11
Atuel →, *Argentina* 126 D2
Atvacik, *Turkey* 66 D2
Åtvidaberg, *Sweden* 11 F10
Atwater, *U.S.A.* 111 H3
Atwood, *Canada* 106 C3
Atwood, *U.S.A.* 108 F4
Atyrau, *Kazakhstan* 43 C14
Au Sable →, *U.S.A.* 104 C4
Au Sable Pt., *U.S.A.* 98 C2
Aubagne, *France* 27 E9
Aubange, *Belgium* 17 J7
Aubarca, C., *Spain* 36 B7
Aube □, *France* 25 D11
Aube →, *France* 25 D10
Aubel, *Belgium* 17 G7
Aubenas, *France* 27 D8
Aubenton, *France* 25 C11
Auberry, *U.S.A.* 112 H7
Aubigny-sur-Nère, *France* 25 E9
Aubin, *France* 26 D6
Aubrac, Mts. d', *France* 26 D7
Auburn, *Ala., U.S.A.* 105 J3
Auburn, *Calif., U.S.A.* 112 G5
Auburn, *Ind., U.S.A.* 104 E3
Auburn, *N.Y., U.S.A.* 107 D8
Auburn, *Nebr., U.S.A.* 108 E7
Auburn, *Wash., U.S.A.* 112 C4
Auburn Ra., *Australia* 91 D5
Auburndale, *U.S.A.* 105 L5
Aubusson, *France* 26 C6
Auch, *France* 26 E4
Auchel, *France* 25 B9
Auchi, *Nigeria* 79 D6
Auckland, *N.Z.* 87 G5
Auckland Is., *Pac. Oc.* 92 N8
Aude □, *France* 26 E6
Aude →, *France* 26 E7
Auden, *Canada* 98 B2
Auderghem, *Belgium* 17 G4
Auderville, *France* 24 C5
Audierne, *France* 24 D2
Audincourt, *France* 25 E13
Audo, *Ethiopia* 77 F5
Audubon, *U.S.A.* 108 E7
Aue, *Germany* 18 E8
Auerbach, *Germany* 18 E8
Aueti Paraná →, *Brazil* 120 D4
Aufist, *W. Sahara* 74 C2
Augathella, *Australia* 91 D4
Augrabies Falls, *S. Africa* 84 D3
Augsburg, *Germany* 19 G6
Augusta, *Italy* 35 E8
Augusta, *Ark., U.S.A.* 109 H9
Augusta, *Ga., U.S.A.* 105 J5
Augusta, *Kans., U.S.A.* 109 G6
Augusta, *Maine, U.S.A.* 99 D6
Augusta, *Mont., U.S.A.* 110 C7
Augusta, *Wis., U.S.A.* 108 C9
Augustenborg, *Denmark* 11 K3
Augustów, *Poland* 20 B12
Augustus, Mt., *Australia* 88 D2
Augustus Downs, *Australia* 90 B2
Augustus I., *Australia* 88 C3
Aukan, *Eritrea* 77 D5
Aukum, *U.S.A.* 112 G6
Auld, L., *Australia* 88 D3
Aulla, *Italy* 32 D6
Aulnay, *France* 26 B3
Aulne →, *France* 24 D2
Aulnoye-Aymeries, *France* 25 B10
Ault, *France* 24 B8
Ault, *U.S.A.* 108 E2
Aulus-les-Bains, *France* 26 F5
Aumale, *France* 25 C8
Aumont-Aubrac, *France* 26 D7
Auna, *Nigeria* 79 C5
Aunis, *France* 26 B3
Auponhia, *Indonesia* 57 E7
Aups, *France* 27 E10
Aur, P., *Malaysia* 59 L5
Auraiya, *India* 63 F8
Aurangabad, *Bihar, India* 63 G11
Aurangabad, *Maharashtra, India* 60 K9
Auray, *France* 24 E4
Aurès, *Algeria* 75 A6
Aurich, *Germany* 18 B3
Aurilândia, *Brazil* 123 E1
Aurillac, *France* 26 D6
Auronza, *Italy* 33 B9
Aurora, *Canada* 106 C5
Aurora, *S. Africa* 84 E2
Aurora, *Colo., U.S.A.* 108 F2
Aurora, *Ill., U.S.A.* 104 E1
Aurora, *Mo., U.S.A.* 109 G8
Aurora, *Nebr., U.S.A.* 108 E6
Aurora, *Ohio, U.S.A.* 106 E3
Aursmoen, *Norway* 10 E5
Aurukun Mission, *Australia* 90 A3
Aus, *Namibia* 84 D2
Auschwitz = Oświecim, *Poland* 20 E9
Aust-Agder fylke □, *Norway* 9 G9
Austin, *Minn., U.S.A.* 108 D8
Austin, *Nev., U.S.A.* 110 G5
Austin, *Pa., U.S.A.* 106 E6
Austin, *Tex., U.S.A.* 109 K6
Austin, L., *Australia* 89 E2
Austral Downs, *Australia* 90 C2
Austral Is. = Tubuai Is., *Pac. Oc.* 93 K12
Austral Seamount Chain, *Pac. Oc.* 93 K13
Australia ■, *Oceania* 92 K5
Australian Alps, *Australia* 91 F4
Australian Capital Territory □, *Australia* 91 F4
Austria ■, *Europe* 21 H4
Austvågøy, *Norway* 8 B13
Autazes, *Brazil* 121 D6
Autelbas, *Belgium* 17 J7
Auterive, *France* 26 E5
Authie →, *France* 25 B8
Authon-du-Perche, *France* 24 D7
Autlán, *Mexico* 114 D4
Autun, *France* 25 F11
Auvelais, *Belgium* 17 H5
Auvergne, *Australia* 88 C5
Auvergne, *France* 26 C7
Auvergne, Mts. d', *France* 26 C6
Auvézère →, *France* 26 C4
Auxerre, *France* 25 E10
Auxi-le-Château, *France* 25 B9
Auxonne, *France* 25 E12
Auzances, *France* 26 B6
Auzat-sur-Allier, *France* 26 C7
Avallon, *France* 25 E10
Avalon, *U.S.A.* 113 M8
Avalon Pen., *Canada* 99 C9
Avaré, *Brazil* 127 A6
Ávas, *Greece* 39 J8
Avawatz Mts., *U.S.A.* 113 K10
Aveiro, *Brazil* 121 D6
Aveiro, *Portugal* 30 E2
Aveiro □, *Portugal* 30 E2
Āvej, *Iran* 65 C6
Avelgem, *Belgium* 17 G2
Avellaneda, *Argentina* 126 C4
Avellino, *Italy* 35 B7
Avenal, *U.S.A.* 112 K6
Avenches, *Switz.* 22 C4
Averøya, *Norway* 10 A1
Aversa, *Italy* 35 B7
Avery, *U.S.A.* 110 C6
Aves, I. de, *W. Indies* 117 C7
Aves, Is. de, *Venezuela* 117 D6
Avesnes-sur-Helpe, *France* 25 B10
Avesta, *Sweden* 9 F14
Aveyron □, *France* 26 D6
Aveyron →, *France* 26 D5
Avezzano, *Italy* 33 F10
Aviá Terai, *Argentina* 126 B3
Aviano, *Italy* 33 B9
Avigliana, *Italy* 32 C4
Avigliano, *Italy* 35 B8
Avignon, *France* 27 E8
Ávila, *Spain* 30 E6
Ávila □, *Spain* 30 E6
Ávila, Sierra de, *Spain* 30 E5
Avila Beach, *U.S.A.* 113 K6
Avilés, *Spain* 30 B5
Avisio →, *Italy* 33 B8
Aviz, *Portugal* 31 F3
Avize, *France* 25 D11
Avoca, *Ireland* 15 D5
Avoca, *U.S.A.* 106 D7
Avoca →, *Australia* 91 F3
Avola, *Canada* 100 C5
Avola, *Italy* 35 F8
Avon, *N.Y., U.S.A.* 106 D7
Avon, *S. Dak., U.S.A.* 108 D5
Avon □, *U.K.* 13 F5
Avon →, *Australia* 89 F2
Avon →, *Avon, U.K.* 13 F5
Avon →, *Hants., U.K.* 13 G6
Avon →, *Warks., U.K.* 13 F5
Avondale, *Zimbabwe* 83 F3
Avonlea, *Canada* 101 D7
Avonmore, *Canada* 107 A10
Avonmouth, *U.K.* 13 F5
Avranches, *France* 24 D5
Avre →, *France* 24 D8
Awag el Baqar, *Sudan* 77 E3
A'waj →, *Syria* 69 B5
Awaji-Shima, *Japan* 49 G7
'Awālī, *Bahrain* 65 E6
Awantipur, *India* 63 C6
Awasa, L., *Ethiopia* 77 F4
Awash, *Ethiopia* 68 F3
Awash →, *Ethiopia* 77 E5
Awaso, *Ghana* 78 D4
Awatere →, *N.Z.* 87 J5
Awbārī, *Libya* 75 C7
Awbārī □, *Libya* 75 C7
Awe, L., *U.K.* 14 E3
Aweil, *Sudan* 77 F2
Awgu, *Nigeria* 79 D6
Awjilah, *Libya* 73 C9
Ax-les-Thermes, *France* 26 F5
Axarfjörður, *Iceland* 8 C5
Axel, *Neths.* 17 F3
Axel Heiberg I., *Canada* 4 B3
Axim, *Ghana* 78 E4
Axinim, *Brazil* 121 D6
Axintele, *Romania* 38 E9
Axioma, *Brazil* 125 B5
Axiós →, *Greece* 39 J5
Axminster, *U.K.* 13 G4
Axvall, *Sweden* 11 F7
Aÿ, *France* 25 C11
Ayabaca, *Peru* 124 A2
Ayabe, *Japan* 49 G7
Ayacucho, *Argentina* 126 D4
Ayacucho, *Peru* 124 C3
Ayaguz, *Kazakhstan* 44 E9
Ayamonte, *Spain* 31 H3
Ayan, *Russia* 45 D14
Ayancık, *Turkey* 42 F6
Ayapel, *Colombia* 120 B2
Ayas, *Turkey* 42 F5
Ayaviri, *Peru* 124 C3
Aybastı, *Turkey* 66 C7
Aydın, *Turkey* 66 E2
Aydin □, *Turkey* 66 E2
Aye, *Belgium* 17 H6
Ayenngré, *Togo* 79 D5
Ayer's Cliff, *Canada* 107 A12
Ayers Rock, *Australia* 89 E5
Ayiá, *Greece* 39 K5
Ayía Aikateríni, Ákra, *Greece* 37 A3
Ayia Dhéka, *Greece* 37 D6
Ayia Gálini, *Greece* 37 D6
Ayía Marína, *Greece* 39 M9
Ayia Napa, *Cyprus* 37 E13
Ayía Paraskeví, *Greece* 39 K9
Áyia Phyla, *Cyprus* 37 E12
Ayía Rouméli, *Greece* 39 P6
Ayia Varvára, *Greece* 37 D7
Áyios Amvrósios, *Cyprus* 37 D12
Áyios Andréas, *Greece* 39 M5
Ayíos Evstrátios, *Greece* 39 K7
Áyios Ioánnis, Ákra, *Greece* 37 D7
Áyios Isidhoros, *Greece* 37 C9
Áyios Kiríkos, *Greece* 39 M9
Áyios Matthaíos, *Greece* 37 B3
Áyios Mírono, *Greece* 39 P8
Áyios Nikólaos, *Greece* 37 D7
Áyios Seryios, *Cyprus* 37 D12
Ayios Theodhoros, *Cyprus* 37 D13
Aykathonisi, *Greece* 39 M9
Aylesbury, *U.K.* 13 F7
Aylmer, *Canada* 106 D4
Aylmer, L., *Canada* 96 B8
Ayna, *Spain* 29 G2
Ayolas, *Paraguay* 126 B4
Ayom, *Sudan* 77 F2
Ayon, Ostrov, *Russia* 45 C17
Ayora, *Spain* 29 F3
Ayr, *Australia* 90 B4
Ayr, *U.K.* 14 F4
Ayr →, *U.K.* 14 F4
Ayrancı, *Turkey* 66 E5
Ayre, Pt. of, *U.K.* 12 C3
Aysha, *Ethiopia* 77 E5
Aytos, *Bulgaria* 38 G10
Ayu, Kepulauan, *Indonesia* 57 D8
Ayutla, *Guatemala* 116 D1
Ayutla, *Mexico* 115 D5
Ayvacık, *Turkey* 66 C7
Ayvalık, *Turkey* 66 D2
Aywaille, *Belgium* 17 H7
Az Zabdānī, *Syria* 69 B5
Aẓ Ẓāhirīyah, *Jordan* 69 D3
Aẓ Ẓahrān, *Si. Arabia* 65 E6

Az Zarqā, Jordan 69 C5
Az Zāwiyah, Libya 75 B7
Az Zībār, Iraq 64 B5
Az-Zilfī, Si. Arabia 64 E5
Az Zubayr, Iraq 64 D5
Azambuja, Portugal 31 F2
Azamgarh, India 63 F10
Azangaro, Peru 124 C3
Azaouak, Vallée de l', Mali 79 B5
Āzār Shahr, Iran 64 B5
Azārbayjan = Azerbaijan ■, Asia 43 F12
Āzarbāyjān-e Gharbī □, Iran 64 B5
Āzarbāyjān-e Sharqī □, Iran 64 B5
Azare, Nigeria 79 C7
Azay-le-Rideau, France 24 E7
A'zāz, Syria 64 B3
Azazga, Algeria 75 A5
Azbine = Aïr, Niger 79 B6
Azefal, Mauritania 74 D2
Azeffoun, Algeria 75 A5
Azemmour, Morocco 74 B3
Azerbaijan ■, Asia 43 F12
Azerbaijchan = Azerbaijan ■, Asia 43 F12
Azezo, Ethiopia 77 E4
Azimganj, India 63 G13
Aznalcóllar, Spain 31 H4
Azogues, Ecuador 120 D2
Azores, Atl. Oc. 2 C8
Azov, Russia 43 C8
Azov, Sea of = Azovskoye More, Europe 42 C7
Azovskoye More, Europe 42 C7
Azovy, Russia 44 C7
Azpeitia, Spain 28 B2
Azrou, Morocco 74 B3
Aztec, U.S.A. 111 H10
Azúa, Dom. Rep. 117 C5
Azuaga, Spain 31 G5
Azuara, Spain 28 D4
Azuay □, Ecuador 120 D2
Azuer →, Spain 31 F7
Azuero, Pen. de, Panama 116 E3
Azul, Argentina 126 D4
Azul, Serra, Brazil 125 C7
Azurduy, Bolivia 125 D5
Azusa, U.S.A. 113 L9
Azzaba, Algeria 75 A6
Azzano Décimo, Italy 33 C9
'Azzūn, Jordan 69 C4

B

Ba Don, Vietnam 58 D6
Ba Dong, Vietnam 59 H6
Ba Ngoi = Cam Lam, Vietnam 59 G7
Ba Ria, Vietnam 59 G6
Ba Tri, Vietnam 59 G6
Ba Xian, China 50 E9
Baa, Indonesia 57 F6
Baamonde, Spain 30 B3
Baar, Switz. 23 B7
Baarle Nassau, Belgium 17 F5
Baarlo, Neths. 17 F8
Baarn, Neths. 16 D6
Bab el Mandeb, Red Sea 68 E3
Baba Burnu, Turkey 66 D2
Baba dag, Azerbaijan 43 F13
Bābā Kalū, Iran 65 D6
Babaçulândia, Brazil 122 C2
Babadag, Romania 38 E11
Babadayhan = Kirovsk, Turkmenistan 44 F7
Babaeski, Turkey 66 C2
Babahoyo, Ecuador 120 D2
Babakin, Australia 89 F2
Babana, Nigeria 79 C5
Babar, Algeria 75 A6
Babar, Indonesia 57 F7
Babar, Pakistan 62 D3
Babarkach, Pakistan 62 E2
Babayevo, Russia 41 B9
Babb, U.S.A. 110 B7
Babenhausen, Germany 19 F4
Babi Besar, P., Malaysia 59 L4
Babian Jiang →, China 52 F3
Babile, Ethiopia 77 F5
Babinda, Australia 90 B4
Babine, Canada 100 B3
Babine →, Canada 100 B3
Babine L., Canada 100 C3
Babo, Indonesia 57 E8
Bābol, Iran 65 B7
Bābol Sar, Iran 65 B7
Baboua, C.A.R. 80 C2
Babruysk = Bobruysk, Belorussia 40 E6
Babura, Nigeria 79 C6
Babusar Pass, Pakistan 63 B5
Babušnica, Serbia, Yug. 21 M12
Babuyan Chan., Phil. 55 B4
Babuyan Is., Phil. 55 B4
Babylon, Iraq 64 C5
Bac Can, Vietnam 58 A5
Bac Giang, Vietnam 58 B6
Bac Ninh, Vietnam 58 B6
Bac Phan, Vietnam 58 B5
Bac Quang, Vietnam 58 A5
Bacabal, Brazil 122 B3
Bacajá →, Brazil 121 D7
Bacalar, Mexico 115 D7
Bacan, Indonesia 57 F7
Bacan, Kepulauan, Indonesia 57 E7
Bacan, Pulau, Indonesia 57 E7
Bacarra, Phil. 55 B4
Bacău, Romania 38 C9
Baccarat, France 25 D13
Bacerac, Mexico 114 A3
Băceşti, Romania 38 C10
Bach Long Vi, Dao, Vietnam 58 B6
Bachaquero, Venezuela 120 B3
Bacharach, Germany 19 E3
Bachelina, Russia 44 D7
Bachuma, Ethiopia 77 F4
Bačina, Serbia, Yug. 21 M11
Back →, Canada 96 B9
Bačka Palanka, Serbia, Yug. 21 K9
Bačka Topola, Serbia, Yug. 21 K9
Bäckefors, Sweden 11 F6
Backnang, Germany 19 G5
Backstairs Passage, Australia 91 F2
Baco, Mt., Phil. 55 E4
Bacolod, Phil. 55 F5
Bacqueville-en-Caux, France 24 C8
Bácsalmás, Hungary 21 J9
Bacuag, Phil. 55 G6
Bacuk, Malaysia 59 J4
Bād, Iran 65 C7
Bad →, U.S.A. 108 C4
Bad Axe, U.S.A. 106 C2
Bad Bergzabern, Germany 19 F4
Bad Berleburg, Germany 18 D4
Bad Bevensen, Germany 18 B6
Bad Bramstedt, Germany 18 B5
Bad Brückenau, Germany 19 E5
Bad Doberan, Germany 18 A7
Bad Driburg, Germany 18 D5
Bad Ems, Germany 19 E3
Bad Frankenhausen, Germany 18 D7
Bad Freienwalde, Germany 18 C10
Bad Godesberg, Germany 18 E3
Bad Hersfeld, Germany 18 E5
Bad Hofgastein, Austria 21 H3
Bad Homburg, Germany 19 E4
Bad Honnef, Germany 18 E3
Bad Ischl, Austria 21 H3
Bad Kissingen, Germany 19 E6
Bad Königshofen, Germany 19 E6
Bad Kreuznach, Germany 19 F3
Bad Laasphe, Germany 18 E4
Bad Lands, U.S.A. 108 D3
Bad Langensalza, Germany 18 D6
Bad Lauterberg, Germany 18 D6
Bad Lippspringe, Germany 18 D4
Bad Mergentheim, Germany 19 F5
Bad Münstereifel, Germany 18 E2
Bad Muskau, Germany 18 D10
Bad Nauheim, Germany 19 E4
Bad Oeynhausen, Germany 18 C4
Bad Oldesloe, Germany 18 B6
Bad Orb, Germany 19 E5
Bad Pyrmont, Germany 18 D5
Bad Ragaz, Switz. 23 B9
Bad Reichenhall, Germany 19 H8
Bad Säckingen, Germany 19 H3
Bad Salzuflen, Germany 18 C4
Bad Segeberg, Germany 18 B6
Bad Tölz, Germany 19 H7
Bad Urach, Germany 19 G5
Bad Waldsee, Germany 19 H5
Bad Wildungen, Germany 18 D5
Bad Wimpfen, Germany 19 F5
Bad Windsheim, Germany 19 F6
Badagara, India 60 P9
Badagri, Nigeria 79 D5
Badajós, L., Brazil 121 D5
Badajoz, Spain 31 G4
Badajoz □, Spain 31 G4
Badalona, Spain 28 D7
Badalzai, Afghan. 60 E1
Badampahar, India 61 H15
Badanah, Si. Arabia 64 D4
Badarinath, India 63 D8
Badas, Brunei 56 D4
Badas, Kepulauan, Indonesia 56 D3
Baddo →, Pakistan 60 F4
Bade, Indonesia 57 F9
Baden, Austria 21 G6
Baden, Switz. 23 B6
Baden-Baden, Germany 19 G4
Baden-Württemberg □, Germany 19 G5
Badenoch, U.K. 14 E4
Badger, Canada 99 C8
Badger, U.S.A. 112 J7
Bādghīsāt □, Afghan. 60 B3
Badgom, India 63 B6
Badhoevedorp, Neths. 16 D5
Badia Polèsine, Italy 33 C8
Badin, Pakistan 62 G3
Badogo, Mali 78 C3
Badong, China 53 B8
Baduen, Somali Rep. 68 F4
Badulla, Sri Lanka 60 R12
Baena, Spain 31 H6
Baexem, Neths. 17 F7
Baeza, Ecuador 120 D2
Baeza, Spain 29 H1
Bafa Gölü, Turkey 66 E2
Bafang, Cameroon 79 D7
Bafatá, Guinea-Biss. 78 C2
Baffin B., Canada 4 B4
Baffin I., Canada 97 B12
Bafia, Cameroon 79 E7
Bafilo, Togo 79 D5
Bafing →, Mali 78 C2
Bafliyūn, Syria 64 B3
Baflo, Neths. 16 B9
Bafoulabé, Mali 78 C2
Bafoussam, Cameroon 79 D7
Bāfq, Iran 65 D7
Bafra, Turkey 42 F6
Bafra Burnu, Turkey 42 F6
Bāft, Iran 65 D8
Bafut, Cameroon 79 D7
Bafwasende, Zaïre 82 B2
Bagamoyo, Tanzania 82 D4
Bagamoyo □, Tanzania 82 D4
Bagan Datoh, Malaysia 59 L3
Bagan Serai, Malaysia 59 K3
Baganga, Phil. 55 H7
Bagani, Namibia 84 B3
Bagansiapiapi, Indonesia 56 D2
Bagasra, India 62 J4
Bagawi, Sudan 77 E3
Bagdad, U.S.A. 113 L11
Bagdarin, Russia 45 D12
Bagé, Brazil 127 C5
Bagenalstown = Muine Bheag, Ireland 15 D5
Baggs, U.S.A. 110 F10
Bagh, Pakistan 63 C5
Baghdād, Iraq 64 C5
Bagheria, Italy 34 D6
Baghlān, Afghan. 60 A6
Bagley, U.S.A. 108 B7
Bagnacavallo, Italy 33 D8
Bagnara Cálabra, Italy 35 D8
Bagnères-de-Bigorre, France 26 E4
Bagnères-de-Luchon, France 26 F4
Bagni di Lucca, Italy 32 D7
Bagno di Romagna, Italy 33 E8
Bagnoles-de-l'Orne, France 24 D6
Bagnoli di Sopra, Italy 33 C8
Bagnolo Mella, Italy 32 C7
Bagnols-sur-Cèze, France 27 D8
Bagnorégio, Italy 33 F9
Bagolino, Italy 32 C7
Bagotville, Canada 99 C5
Bagua, Peru 124 B2
Baguio, Phil. 55 C4
Bahabón de Esgueva, Spain 28 D1
Bahadurgarh, India 62 E7
Bahama, Canal Viejo de, W. Indies 116 B4
Bahamas ■, N. Amer. 117 B5
Baharampur, India 63 G13
Baharîya, El Wâhât al, Egypt 76 J6
Bahau, Malaysia 59 L4
Bahawalnagar, Pakistan 62 D5
Bahawalpur, Pakistan 62 E4
Bahçe, Turkey 66 E7
Baheri, India 63 E8
Bahi, Tanzania 82 D4
Bahi Swamp, Tanzania 82 D4
Bahía = Salvador, Brazil 123 D4
Bahía □, Brazil 123 D3
Bahía, Is. de la, Honduras 116 C2
Bahía Blanca, Argentina 126 D3
Bahía de Caráquez, Ecuador 120 D1
Bahía Honda, Cuba 116 B3
Bahía Laura, Argentina 128 C3
Bahía Negra, Paraguay 125 E6
Bahir Dar, Ethiopia 77 E4
Bahmanzād, Iran 65 D6
Bahmer, Algeria 75 C4
Bahönye, Hungary 21 J7
Bahr Aouk →, C.A.R. 80 C3
Bahr el Ahmar □, Sudan 76 C3
Bahr el Ghazâl □, Sudan 77 F2
Bahr Salamat →, Chad 73 G8
Bahr Yûsef →, Egypt 76 J7
Bahra el Burullus, Egypt 76 H7
Bahraich, India 63 F9
Bahrain ■, Asia 65 E6
Bahret Assad, Syria 64 C3
Bahror, India 62 F7
Bāhū Kalāt, Iran 65 E9
Bai, Mali 78 C4
Bai Bung, Mui, Vietnam 59 H5
Bai Duc, Vietnam 58 C5
Bai Thuong, Vietnam 58 C5
Baia Mare, Romania 38 B6
Baia-Sprie, Romania 38 B6
Baião, Brazil 122 B2
Baïbokoum, Chad 73 G8
Baicheng, China 51 B12
Baidoa, Somali Rep. 68 G3
Baie Comeau, Canada 99 C6
Baie-St-Paul, Canada 99 C5
Baie Trinité, Canada 99 C6
Baie Verte, Canada 99 C8
Baignes-Ste.-Radegonde, France 26 C3
Baigneux-les-Juifs, France 25 E11
Baihe, China 50 H6
Baihe, Taiwan 53 F13
Ba'ījī, Iraq 64 C4
Baikal, L. = Baykal, Oz., Russia 45 D11
Baile Atha Cliath = Dublin, Ireland 15 C5
Bailei, Ethiopia 77 F5
Bailén, Spain 31 G7
Băileşti, Romania 38 E6
Baileux, Belgium 17 H4
Bailique, Ilha, Brazil 122 A2
Bailleul, France 25 B9
Bailundo, Angola 81 G3
Baima, China 52 A3
Bain-de-Bretagne, France 24 E5
Bainbridge, Ga., U.S.A. 105 K3
Bainbridge, N.Y., U.S.A. 107 D9
Baing, Indonesia 57 F6
Bainiu, China 50 H7
Bainville, U.S.A. 108 A2
Bā'ir, Jordan 69 E5
Baird, U.S.A. 109 J5
Baird Mts., U.S.A. 96 B3
Bairin Youqi, China 51 C10
Bairin Zuoqi, China 51 C10
Bairnsdale, Australia 91 F4
Bais, Phil. 55 G5
Baisha, China 50 G7
Baïsole →, France 26 E4
Baissa, Nigeria 79 D7
Baitadi, Nepal 63 E9
Baixa Grande, Brazil 123 D3
Baiyin, China 50 F3
Baiyü, China 52 B2
Baiyu Shan, China 50 F4
Baiyuda, Sudan 76 D3
Baj Baj, India 63 H13
Baja, Hungary 21 J8
Baja, Pta., Mexico 114 B1
Baja California, Mexico 114 A1
Bajamar, Canary Is. 36 F3
Bajana, India 62 H4
Bājgīrān, Iran 65 B8
Bajimba, Mt., Australia 91 D5
Bajo Nuevo, Caribbean 116 C4
Bajoga, Nigeria 79 C7
Bajool, Australia 90 C5
Bakala, C.A.R. 73 G9
Bakar, Croatia 33 C11
Bakchar, Russia 44 D9
Bakel, Neths. 17 E7
Bakel, Senegal 78 C2
Baker, Calif., U.S.A. 113 K10
Baker, Mont., U.S.A. 108 B2
Baker, Oreg., U.S.A. 110 D5
Baker, Canal, Chile 128 C2
Baker, L., Canada 96 B10
Baker I., Pac. Oc. 92 G10
Baker L., Australia 89 E4
Baker Lake, Canada 96 B10
Baker Mt., U.S.A. 110 B3
Bakers Creek, Australia 90 C4
Baker's Dozen Is., Canada 98 A4
Bakersfield, Calif., U.S.A. 113 K7
Bakersfield, Vt., U.S.A. 107 B12
Bakhchisaray, Ukraine 42 D5
Bakhmach, Ukraine 40 F8
Bākhtarān, Iran 64 C5
Bākhtarān □, Iran 64 C5
Bakırdaği, Turkey 66 D6
Bakırköy, Turkey 39 H11
Bakkafjörður, Iceland 8 C6
Bakkagerði, Iceland 8 D7
Bakony →, Hungary 21 H7
Bakony Forest = Bakony Hegyseg, Hungary 21 H7
Bakony Hegyseg, Hungary 21 H7
Bakori, Nigeria 79 C6
Bakouma, C.A.R. 73 G9
Baku, Azerbaijan 43 F13
Bakutis Coast, Antarctica 5 D15
Baky = Baku, Azerbaijan 43 F13
Bala, Canada 106 A5
Bâlâ, Turkey 66 D5
Bala, L., U.K. 12 E4
Balabac I., Phil. 55 H2
Balabac Str., E. Indies 56 C5
Balabagh, Afghan. 62 B4
Balabakk, Lebanon 69 A5
Balabalangan, Kepulauan, Indonesia 56 E5
Bălăciţa, Romania 38 E6
Balad, Iraq 64 C5
Balad Rūz, Iraq 64 C5
Bālādeh, Fārs, Iran 65 D6
Bālādeh, Māzandaran, Iran 65 B6
Balaghat, India 60 J12
Balaghat Ra., India 60 K10
Balaguer, Spain 28 D5
Balakhna, Russia 41 C13
Balaklava, Australia 91 E2
Balaklava, Ukraine 42 D5
Balakleya, Ukraine 42 B7
Balakovo, Russia 41 E15
Balancán, Mexico 115 D6
Balanda, Russia 41 F14
Balashikha, Russia 41 D10
Balashov, Russia 41 F13
Balasinor, India 62 H5
Balasore = Baleshwar, India 61 J15
Balassagyarmat, Hungary 21 G9
Balât, Egypt 76 B2
Balaton, Hungary 21 J7
Balayan, Phil. 55 E4
Balazote, Spain 29 G2
Balboa, Panama 116 E4
Balbriggan, Ireland 15 C5
Balcarce, Argentina 126 D4
Balcarres, Canada 101 C8
Balchik, Bulgaria 38 F11
Balclutha, N.Z. 87 M2
Bald Hd., Australia 89 G2
Bald I., Australia 89 F2
Bald Knob, U.S.A. 109 H9
Baldock L., Canada 101 B9
Baldwin, Fla., U.S.A. 105 K4
Baldwin, Mich., U.S.A. 104 D3
Baldwinsville, U.S.A. 107 C8
Baldy Peak, U.S.A. 111 K9
Bale, Croatia 33 C10
Bale □, Ethiopia 77 F5
Baleares □, Spain 28 F7
Baleares, Is., Spain 36 B10
Balearic Is. = Baleares, Is., Spain 36 B10
Baleia, Pta. da, Brazil 123 E4
Balen, Belgium 17 F6
Baler, Phil. 55 D4
Baler Bay, Phil. 55 D4
Balerna, Switz. 23 E8
Baleshwar, India 61 J15
Balfate, Honduras 116 C2
Balfe's Creek, Australia 90 C4
Balfour, S. Africa 85 D4
Bali, Cameroon 79 D6
Balí, Greece 37 D6
Bali, Indonesia 56 F5
Bali □, Indonesia 56 F5
Bali, Selat, Indonesia 57 H16
Baligród, Poland 20 F12
Balık Gölü, Turkey 67 D10
Balikeşir, Turkey 66 D2
Balikeşir □, Turkey 66 D2
Balikpapan, Indonesia 56 E5
Balimbing, Phil. 57 C5
Baling, Malaysia 59 K3
Balintang Channel, Phil. 55 B4
Balipara, India 61 F18
Baliza, Brazil 125 D7
Balk, Neths. 16 C7
Balkan Mts. = Stara Planina, Bulgaria 38 F6
Balkan Peninsula, Europe 6 G10
Balkhash, Kazakhstan 44 E8
Balkhash, Ozero, Kazakhstan 44 E8
Balla, Bangla. 61 G17
Ballachulish, U.K. 14 E3
Balladonia, Australia 89 F3
Ballarat, Australia 91 F3
Ballard, L., Australia 89 E3
Ballater, U.K. 14 D5
Ballenas, Canal de, Mexico 114 B2
Balleny Is., Antarctica 5 C11
Ballesteros, Phil. 55 B4
Ballia, India 63 G11
Ballidu, Australia 89 F2
Ballina, Australia 91 D5
Ballina, Mayo, Ireland 15 B2
Ballina, Tipp., Ireland 15 D3
Ballinasloe, Ireland 15 C3
Ballinger, U.S.A. 109 K5
Ballinrobe, Ireland 15 C2
Ballinskelligs B., Ireland 15 E1
Ballon, France 24 D7
Ballycastle, U.K. 15 A5
Ballymena, U.K. 15 B5
Ballymena □, U.K. 15 B5
Ballymoney, U.K. 15 A5
Ballymoney □, U.K. 15 A5
Ballyshannon, Ireland 15 B3
Balmaceda, Chile 128 C2
Balmazújváros, Hungary 21 H11
Balmhorn, Switz. 22 D5
Balmoral, Australia 91 F3
Balmoral, U.K. 14 D5
Balmorhea, U.S.A. 109 K3
Balonne →, Australia 91 D4
Balqash Kol = Balkhash, Ozero, Kazakhstan 44 E8
Balrampur, India 63 F10
Balranald, Australia 91 E3
Balş, Romania 38 E7
Balsapuerto, Peru 124 B2
Balsas, Mexico 115 D5
Balsas →, Goiás, Brazil 122 C2
Balsas →, Maranhão, Brazil 122 C3
Balsas →, Mexico 114 D4
Bålsta, Sweden 10 E11
Balsthal, Switz. 22 B5
Balston Spa, U.S.A. 107 D11
Balta, Romania 38 E5
Balta, Russia 43 E11
Balta, Ukraine 42 B3
Balta, U.S.A. 108 A4
Baltanás, Spain 30 D6
Bălţi = Beltsy, Moldavia 42 C3
Baltic Sea, Europe 9 H15
Baltîm, Egypt 76 H7
Baltimore, Ireland 15 E2
Baltimore, U.S.A. 104 F7
Baltit, Pakistan 63 A6
Baltrum, Germany 18 B3
Baluchistan □, Pakistan 60 F4
Balurghat, India 63 G13
Balya, Turkey 66 D2
Balygychan, Russia 45 C16
Balzar, Ecuador 120 D2

Bam, *Iran* 65 D8
Bama, *China* 52 E6
Bama, *Nigeria* 79 C7
Bamako, *Mali* 78 C3
Bamba, *Mali* 79 B4
Bambamarca, *Peru* 124 B2
Bambari, *C.A.R.* 73 G9
Bambaroo, *Australia* 90 B4
Bamberg, *Germany* 19 F6
Bamberg, *U.S.A.* 105 J5
Bambesi, *Ethiopia* 77 F3
Bambey, *Senegal* 78 C1
Bambili, *Zaïre* 82 B2
Bambuí, *Brazil* 123 F2
Bamenda, *Cameroon* 79 D7
Bamfield, *Canada* 100 D3
Bāmīān □, *Afghan.* 60 B5
Bamiancheng, *China* 51 C13
Bamkin, *Cameroon* 79 D7
Bampūr, *Iran* 65 E9
Ban Aranyaprathet, *Thailand* 58 F4
Ban Ban, *Laos* 58 C4
Ban Bang Hin, *Thailand* 59 H2
Ban Chiang Klang, *Thailand* 58 C3
Ban Chik, *Laos* 58 D4
Ban Choho, *Thailand* 58 E4
Ban Dan Lan Hoi, *Thailand* 58 D2
Ban Don = Surat Thani, *Thailand* 59 H2
Ban Don, *Vietnam* 58 F6
Ban Don, Ao, *Thailand* 59 H2
Ban Dong, *Thailand* 58 C3
Ban Hong, *Thailand* 58 C2
Ban Kaeng, *Thailand* 58 D3
Ban Keun, *Laos* 58 C4
Ban Khai, *Thailand* 58 F3
Ban Kheun, *Laos* 58 B3
Ban Khlong Kua, *Thailand* 59 J3
Ban Khuan Mao, *Thailand* 59 J2
Ban Khun Yuam, *Thailand* 58 C1
Ban Ko Yai Chim, *Thailand* 59 G2
Ban Kok, *Thailand* 58 D4
Ban Laem, *Thailand* 58 F2
Ban Lao Ngam, *Laos* 58 E6
Ban Le Kathe, *Thailand* 58 E2
Ban Mae Chedi, *Thailand* 58 C2
Ban Mae Laeng, *Thailand* 58 B2
Ban Mae Sariang, *Thailand* 58 C1
Ban Mê Thuôt = Buon Me Thuot, *Vietnam* 58 F7
Ban Mi, *Thailand* 58 E3
Ban Muong Mo, *Laos* 58 C4
Ban Na Mo, *Laos* 58 D5
Ban Na San, *Thailand* 59 H2
Ban Na Tong, *Laos* 58 B3
Ban Nam Bac, *Laos* 58 B4
Ban Nam Ma, *Laos* 58 A3
Ban Ngang, *Laos* 58 E6
Ban Nong Bok, *Laos* 58 D5
Ban Nong Boua, *Laos* 58 E6
Ban Nong Pling, *Thailand* 58 E3
Ban Pak Chan, *Thailand* 59 G2
Ban Phai, *Thailand* 58 D4
Ban Pong, *Thailand* 58 F2
Ban Ron Phibun, *Thailand* 59 H2
Ban Sanam Chai, *Thailand* 59 J3
Ban Sangkha, *Thailand* 58 E4
Ban Tak, *Thailand* 58 D2
Ban Tako, *Thailand* 58 E4
Ban Tha Dua, *Thailand* 58 D2
Ban Tha Li, *Thailand* 58 D3
Ban Tha Nun, *Thailand* 59 H2
Ban Thahine, *Laos* 58 E5
Ban Xien Kok, *Laos* 58 B3
Ban Yen Nhan, *Vietnam* 58 B6
Baña, Punta de la, *Spain* 28 E5
Banaba, *Kiribati* 92 H8
Bañalbufar, *Spain* 36 B9
Banalia, *Zaïre* 82 B2
Banam, *Cambodia* 59 G5
Banamba, *Mali* 78 C3
Banana, *Australia* 90 C5
Bananal, I. do, *Brazil* 123 D1
Banaras = Varanasi, *India* 63 G10
Banas →, *Gujarat, India* 62 H4
Banas →, *Mad. P., India* 63 G9
Bânâs, Ras, *Egypt* 76 C4
Banaz, *Turkey* 66 D3
Banbān, *Si. Arabia* 64 E5
Banbridge, *U.K.* 15 B5
Banbridge □, *U.K.* 15 B5
Banbury, *U.K.* 13 E6
Banchory, *U.K.* 14 D6
Bancroft, *Canada* 98 C4
Band Bonī, *Iran* 65 E8
Band Qīr, *Iran* 65 D6
Banda, *India* 63 G9
Banda, Kepulauan, *Indonesia* 57 E7
Banda Aceh, *Indonesia* 56 C1
Banda Banda, Mt., *Australia* 91 E5
Banda Elat, *Indonesia* 57 F8
Banda Is. = Banda, Kepulauan, *Indonesia* 57 E7
Banda Sea, *Indonesia* 57 F7
Bandai-San, *Japan* 48 F10
Bandama →, *Ivory C.* 78 D3
Bandān, *Iran* 65 D9
Bandanaira, *Indonesia* 57 E7
Bandanwara, *India* 62 F6
Bandar = Machilipatnam, *India* 61 L12
Bandār 'Abbās, *Iran* 65 E8
Bandar-e Anzalī, *Iran* 65 B6
Bandar-e Chārak, *Iran* 65 E7
Bandar-e Deylam, *Iran* 65 D6
Bandar-e Khomeyni, *Iran* 65 D6
Bandar-e Lengeh, *Iran* 65 E7
Bandar-e Maqām, *Iran* 65 E7
Bandar-e Ma'shur, *Iran* 65 D6
Bandar-e Nakhīlū, *Iran* 65 E7
Bandar-e Rīg, *Iran* 65 D6
Bandar-e Torkeman, *Iran* 65 B7
Bandar Maharani = Muar, *Malaysia* 59 L4
Bandar Penggaram = Batu Pahat, *Malaysia* 59 M4
Bandar Seri Begawan, *Brunei* 56 C4
Bandawe, *Malawi* 83 E3
Bande, *Belgium* 17 H6
Bande, *Spain* 30 C3
Bandeira, Pico da, *Brazil* 123 F3
Bandeirante, *Brazil* 123 D1
Bandera, *Argentina* 126 B3
Bandera, *U.S.A.* 109 L5
Banderas, B. de, *Mexico* 114 C3
Bandiagara, *Mali* 78 C4
Bandırma, *Turkey* 66 C3
Bandon, *Ireland* 15 E3
Bandon →, *Ireland* 15 E3
Bandula, *Mozam.* 83 F3
Bandundu, *Zaïre* 80 E3
Bandung, *Indonesia* 57 G12
Bandya, *Australia* 89 E3
Bāneh, *Iran* 64 C5
Bañeres, *Spain* 29 G4
Banes, *Cuba* 117 B4
Banff, *Canada* 100 C5
Banff, *U.K.* 14 D6
Banff Nat. Park, *Canada* 100 C5
Banfora, *Burkina Faso* 78 C4
Bang Fai →, *Laos* 58 D5
Bang Hieng →, *Laos* 58 D5
Bang Krathum, *Thailand* 58 D3
Bang Lamung, *Thailand* 58 F3
Bang Mun Nak, *Thailand* 58 D3
Bang Pa In, *Thailand* 58 E3
Bang Rakam, *Thailand* 58 D3
Bang Saphan, *Thailand* 59 G2
Bangala Dam, *Zimbabwe* 83 G3
Bangalore, *India* 60 N10
Bangante, *Cameroon* 79 D7
Bangaon, *India* 63 H13
Bangassou, *C.A.R.* 80 D4
Banggai, Kepulauan, *Indonesia* 57 E6
Banggi, P., *Malaysia* 56 C5
Banghāzī, *Libya* 73 B9
Bangil, *Indonesia* 57 G15
Bangjang, *Sudan* 77 E3
Bangka, P., *Sulawesi, Indonesia* 57 D7
Bangka, P., *Sumatera, Indonesia* 56 E3
Bangka, Selat, *Indonesia* 56 E3
Bangkalan, *Indonesia* 57 G15
Bangkinang, *Indonesia* 56 D2
Bangko, *Indonesia* 56 E2
Bangkok, *Thailand* 58 F3
Bangladesh ■, *Asia* 61 H17
Bangolo, *Ivory C.* 78 D3
Bangong Co, *India* 63 B8
Bangor, *Down, U.K.* 15 B6
Bangor, *Gwynedd, U.K.* 12 D3
Bangor, *Maine, U.S.A.* 99 D6
Bangor, *Pa., U.S.A.* 107 F9
Bangued, *Phil.* 55 C4
Bangui, *C.A.R.* 80 D3
Bangui, *Phil.* 55 B4
Banguru, *Zaïre* 82 B2
Bangweulu, L., *Zambia* 83 E3
Bangweulu Swamp, *Zambia* 83 E3
Bani, *Dom. Rep.* 117 C5
Bani →, *Mali* 78 C4
Bani, Djebel, *Morocco* 74 C3
Bani Bangou, *Niger* 79 B5
Banī Sa'd, *Iraq* 64 C5
Banī Walīd, *Libya* 73 B7
Bania, *Ivory C.* 78 D4
Banihal Pass, *India* 63 C6
Banīnah, *Libya* 73 B9
Bāniyās, *Syria* 64 C3
Banja Luka, *Bos.-H.* 21 L7
Banjar, *Indonesia* 57 G13
Banjarmasin, *Indonesia* 56 E4
Banjarnegara, *Indonesia* 57 G13
Banjul, *Gambia* 78 C1
Banka Banka, *Australia* 90 B1
Banket, *Zimbabwe* 83 F3
Bankilaré, *Niger* 79 C5
Bankipore, *India* 63 G11
Banks I., *B.C., Canada* 100 C3
Banks I., *N.W.T., Canada* 96 A7
Banks Pen., *N.Z.* 87 K4
Banks Str., *Australia* 90 G4
Bankura, *India* 63 H12
Bann →, *Down, U.K.* 15 B5
Bann →, *L'derry., U.K.* 15 A5
Banna, *Phil.* 55 C4
Bannalec, *France* 24 E3
Bannang Sata, *Thailand* 59 J3
Banning, *U.S.A.* 113 M10
Banningville = Bandundu, *Zaïre* 80 E3
Bannockburn, *Canada* 106 B7
Bannockburn, *U.K.* 14 E5
Bannockburn, *Zimbabwe* 83 G2
Bannu, *Pakistan* 60 C7
Bañolas, *Spain* 28 C7
Banon, *France* 27 D9
Baños de la Encina, *Spain* 31 G7
Baños de Molgas, *Spain* 30 C3
Banská Bystrica, *Slovak Rep.* 20 G9
Banská Štiavnica, *Slovak Rep.* 21 G8
Banswara, *India* 62 H6
Bantayan, *Phil.* 55 F5
Banten, *Indonesia* 57 G12
Bantry, *Ireland* 15 E2
Bantry B., *Ireland* 15 E2
Bantul, *Indonesia* 57 G14
Bantva, *India* 62 J4
Banu, *Afghan.* 60 B6
Banyak, Kepulauan, *Indonesia* 56 D1
Banyo, *Cameroon* 79 D7
Banyuls-sur-Mer, *France* 26 F7
Banyumas, *Indonesia* 57 G13
Banyuwangi, *Indonesia* 57 H16
Banzare Coast, *Antarctica* 5 C9
Banzyville = Mobayi, *Zaïre* 80 D4
Bao Ha, *Vietnam* 58 A5
Bao Lac, *Vietnam* 58 A5
Bao Loc, *Vietnam* 59 G6
Bao'an, *China* 53 F10
Baocheng, *China* 50 H4
Baode, *China* 50 E6
Baodi, *China* 51 E9
Baoding, *China* 50 E8
Baoji, *China* 50 G4
Baojing, *China* 52 C7
Baokang, *China* 53 B8
Baoshan, *Shanghai, China* 53 B13
Baoshan, *Yunnan, China* 52 E2
Baotou, *China* 50 D6
Baoying, *China* 51 H10
Bap, *India* 62 F5
Bapatla, *India* 61 M12
Bapaume, *France* 25 B9
Bāqerābād, *Iran* 65 C6
Ba'qūbah, *Iraq* 64 C5
Baquedano, *Chile* 126 A2
Bar, *Montenegro* 21 N9
Bar, *Ukraine* 42 B2
Bar Bigha, *India* 63 G11
Bar Harbor, *U.S.A.* 99 D6
Bar-le-Duc, *France* 25 D12
Bar-sur-Aube, *France* 25 D11
Bar-sur-Seine, *France* 25 D11
Barabai, *Indonesia* 56 E5
Barabinsk, *Russia* 44 D8
Baraboo, *U.S.A.* 108 D10
Baracaldo, *Spain* 28 B2
Baracoa, *Cuba* 117 B5
Baradero, *Argentina* 126 C4
Baraga, *U.S.A.* 108 B10
Barahona, *Dom. Rep.* 117 C5
Barahona, *Spain* 28 D2
Barail Range, *India* 61 G18
Baraka →, *Sudan* 76 D4
Barakhola, *India* 61 G18
Barakot, *India* 63 J11
Barakpur, *India* 63 H13
Barakula, *Australia* 91 D5
Baralaba, *Australia* 90 C4
Baralzon L., *Canada* 101 B9
Barameiya, *Sudan* 76 D4
Baramula, *India* 63 B6
Baran, *India* 62 G7
Baranavichy = Baranovichi, *Belorussia* 40 E5
Baranoa, *Colombia* 120 A3
Baranof I., *U.S.A.* 100 B1
Baranovichi, *Belorussia* 40 E5
Barão de Cocais, *Brazil* 123 E3
Barão de Grajaú, *Brazil* 122 C3
Barão de Melgaço, *Mato Grosso, Brazil* 125 D6
Barão de Melgaço, *Rondônia, Brazil* 125 C5
Baraolt, *Romania* 38 C8
Barapasi, *Indonesia* 57 E9
Barasat, *India* 63 H13
Barat Daya, Kepulauan, *Indonesia* 57 F7
Barataria B., *U.S.A.* 109 L10
Baraut, *India* 62 E7
Baraya, *Colombia* 120 C2
Barbacena, *Brazil* 123 F3
Barbacoas, *Colombia* 120 C2
Barbacoas, *Venezuela* 120 B4
Barbados ■, *W. Indies* 117 D8
Barbalha, *Brazil* 122 C4
Barban, *Croatia* 33 C11
Barbastro, *Spain* 28 C5
Barbate, *Spain* 31 J5
Barberino di Mugello, *Italy* 33 D8
Barberton, *S. Africa* 85 D5
Barberton, *U.S.A.* 106 E3
Barbezieux, *France* 26 C3
Barbosa, *Colombia* 120 B3
Barbourville, *U.S.A.* 105 G4
Barbuda, *W. Indies* 117 C7
Barcaldine, *Australia* 90 C4
Barcarrota, *Spain* 31 G4
Barcellona Pozzo di Gotto, *Italy* 35 D8
Barcelona, *Spain* 28 D7
Barcelona, *Venezuela* 121 A5
Barcelona □, *Spain* 28 D7
Barcelonette, *France* 27 D10
Barcelos, *Brazil* 121 D5
Barcoo →, *Australia* 90 D3
Barcs, *Hungary* 21 K7
Barda, *Azerbaijan* 43 F12
Barda del Medio, *Argentina* 128 A3
Bardai, *Chad* 73 D8
Bardas Blancas, *Argentina* 126 D2
Barddhaman, *India* 63 H12
Bardejov, *Slovak Rep.* 20 F11
Bardera, *Somali Rep.* 68 G3
Bardi, *Italy* 32 D6
Bardia, *Libya* 73 B9
Bardolino, *Italy* 32 C7
Bardsey I., *U.K.* 12 E3
Bardstown, *U.S.A.* 104 G3
Bareilly, *India* 63 E8
Barentin, *France* 24 C7
Barenton, *France* 24 D6
Barents Sea, *Arctic* 4 B9
Barentu, *Eritrea* 77 D4
Barfleur, *France* 24 C5
Barfleur, Pte. de, *France* 24 C5
Barga, *China* 54 C3
Barga, *Italy* 32 D7
Bargal, *Somali Rep.* 68 E5
Bargara, *Australia* 90 C5
Barge, *Italy* 32 D4
Bargnop, *Sudan* 77 F2
Bargteheide, *Germany* 18 B6
Barguzin, *Russia* 45 D11
Barh, *India* 63 G11
Barhaj, *India* 63 F10
Barhi, *India* 63 G11
Bari, *India* 62 F7
Bari, *Italy* 35 A9
Bari Doab, *Pakistan* 62 D5
Bariadi □, *Tanzania* 82 C3
Barīm, *Yemen* 68 E3
Barima →, *Guyana* 121 B5
Barinas, *Venezuela* 120 B3
Barinas □, *Venezuela* 120 B4
Baring, C., *Canada* 96 B8
Baringo, *Kenya* 82 B4
Baringo □, *Kenya* 82 B4
Baringo, L., *Kenya* 82 B4
Barinitas, *Venezuela* 120 B3
Bariri, *Brazil* 123 F2
Bârîs, *Egypt* 76 C3
Barisal, *Bangla.* 61 H17
Barisan, Bukit, *Indonesia* 56 E2
Barito →, *Indonesia* 56 E4
Barjac, *France* 27 D8
Barjols, *France* 27 E10
Barjūj, Wadi →, *Libya* 75 C7
Bark L., *Canada* 106 A7
Barka = Baraka →, *Sudan* 76 D4
Barkam, *China* 52 B4
Barker, *U.S.A.* 106 C6
Barkley Sound, *Canada* 100 D3
Barkly Downs, *Australia* 90 C2
Barkly East, *S. Africa* 84 E4
Barkly Tableland, *Australia* 90 B2
Barkly West, *S. Africa* 84 D3
Barkol, Wadi →, *Sudan* 76 D3
Barksdale, *U.S.A.* 109 L4
Barlee, L., *Australia* 89 E2
Barlee, Mt., *Australia* 89 D4
Barletta, *Italy* 35 A9
Barlinek, *Poland* 20 C5
Barlovento, *Canary Is.* 36 F2
Barlow L., *Canada* 101 A8
Barmedman, *Australia* 91 E4
Barmer, *India* 62 G4
Barmera, *Australia* 91 E3
Barmouth, *U.K.* 12 E3
Barmstedt, *Germany* 18 B5
Barnagar, *India* 62 H6
Barnard Castle, *U.K.* 12 C6
Barnato, *Australia* 91 E3
Barnaul, *Russia* 44 D9
Barnesville, *U.S.A.* 105 J3
Barnet, *U.K.* 13 F7
Barneveld, *Neths.* 16 D7
Barneveld, *U.S.A.* 107 C9
Barneville-Cartevert, *France* 24 C5
Barngo, *Australia* 90 D4
Barnhart, *U.S.A.* 109 K4
Barnsley, *U.K.* 12 D6
Barnstaple, *U.K.* 13 F3
Barnsville, *U.S.A.* 108 B6
Baro, *Nigeria* 79 D6
Baro →, *Ethiopia* 77 F3
Baroda = Vadodara, *India* 62 H5
Baroda, *India* 62 G7
Baroe, *S. Africa* 84 E3
Baron Ra., *Australia* 88 D4
Barpeta, *India* 61 F17
Barques, Pt. Aux, *U.S.A.* 104 C4
Barquinha, *Portugal* 31 F2
Barquísimeto, *Venezuela* 120 A4
Barr, *France* 25 D14
Barra, *Brazil* 122 D3
Barra, *U.K.* 14 E1
Barra, Sd. of, *U.K.* 14 D1
Barra da Estiva, *Brazil* 123 D3
Barra de Navidad, *Mexico* 114 D4
Barra do Corda, *Brazil* 122 C2
Barra do Mendes, *Brazil* 123 D3
Barra do Piraí, *Brazil* 123 F3
Barra Falsa, Pta. da, *Mozam.* 85 C6
Barra Hd., *U.K.* 14 E1
Barra Mansa, *Brazil* 123 F3
Barraba, *Australia* 91 E5
Barracão do Barreto, *Brazil* 125 B6
Barrackpur = Barakpur, *India* 63 H13
Barrafranca, *Italy* 35 E7
Barranca, *Lima, Peru* 124 C2
Barranca, *Loreto, Peru* 120 D2
Barrancabermeja, *Colombia* 120 B3
Barrancas, *Colombia* 120 A3
Barrancas, *Venezuela* 121 B5
Barrancos, *Portugal* 31 G4
Barranqueras, *Argentina* 126 B4
Barranquilla, *Colombia* 120 A3
Barras, *Brazil* 122 B3
Barras, *Colombia* 120 D3
Barraute, *Canada* 98 C4
Barre, *Mass., U.S.A.* 107 D12
Barre, *Vt., U.S.A.* 107 B12
Barre do Bugres, *Brazil* 125 C6
Barreal, *Argentina* 126 C2
Barreiras, *Brazil* 123 D3
Barreirinha, *Brazil* 121 D6
Barreirinhas, *Brazil* 122 B3
Barreiro, *Portugal* 31 G1
Barreiros, *Brazil* 122 C4
Barrême, *France* 27 E10
Barren, Nosy, *Madag.* 85 B7
Barretos, *Brazil* 123 F2
Barrhead, *Canada* 100 C6
Barrie, *Canada* 98 D4
Barrier Ra., *Australia* 91 E3
Barrière, *Canada* 100 C4
Barrington, *U.S.A.* 107 E13
Barrington L., *Canada* 101 B8
Barrington Tops, *Australia* 91 E5
Barringun, *Australia* 91 D4
Barro do Garças, *Brazil* 125 D7
Barrow, *U.S.A.* 96 A4
Barrow →, *Ireland* 15 D4
Barrow, C., *U.S.A.* 94 B4
Barrow Creek, *Australia* 90 C1
Barrow I., *Australia* 88 D2
Barrow-in-Furness, *U.K.* 12 C4
Barrow Pt., *Australia* 90 A3
Barrow Ra., *Australia* 89 E4
Barrow Str., *Canada* 4 B3
Barruecopardo, *Spain* 30 D4
Barruelo, *Spain* 30 C6
Barry, *U.K.* 13 F4
Barry's Bay, *Canada* 98 C4
Barsalogho, *Burkina Faso* 79 C4
Barsat, *Pakistan* 63 A5
Barsham, *Syria* 64 C4
Barsi, *India* 60 K9
Barsø, *Denmark* 11 J3
Barsoi, *India* 61 G15
Barstow, *Calif., U.S.A.* 113 L9
Barstow, *Tex., U.S.A.* 109 K3
Barth, *Germany* 18 A8
Barthélemy, Col, *Vietnam* 58 C5
Bartica, *Guyana* 121 B6
Bartin, *Turkey* 66 C5
Bartlesville, *U.S.A.* 109 G7
Bartlett, *Calif., U.S.A.* 112 J8
Bartlett, *Tex., U.S.A.* 109 K6
Bartlett, L., *Canada* 100 A5
Bartolomeu Dias, *Mozam.* 83 G4
Barton, *Australia* 89 F5
Barton upon Humber, *U.K.* 12 D7
Bartoszyce, *Poland* 20 A10
Bartow, *U.S.A.* 105 M5
Barú, I. de, *Colombia* 120 A2
Barú, Volcan, *Panama* 116 E3
Barumba, *Zaïre* 82 B1
Baruth, *Germany* 18 C9
Barvaux, *Belgium* 17 H6
Barvenkovo, *Ukraine* 42 B7
Barwani, *India* 62 H6
Barysaw = Borisov, *Belorussia* 40 D6
Barysh, *Russia* 41 E15
Barzān, *Iraq* 64 B5
Bas-Rhin □, *France* 25 D14
Bašaid, *Serbia* 21 K10
Bāsa'idū, *Iran* 65 E7
Basal, *Pakistan* 62 C5
Basankusa, *Zaïre* 80 D3
Basawa, *Afghan.* 62 B4
Bascharage, *Lux.* 17 J7
Bascuñán, C., *Chile* 126 B1
Basècles, *Belgium* 17 G3
Basel, *Switz.* 22 A5
Basel-Stadt □, *Switz.* 22 A5
Baselland □, *Switz.* 22 B5
Basento →, *Italy* 35 B9
Bāshī, *Iran* 65 D6
Bashi Channel, *Phil.* 54 D7
Bashkir Republic □, *Russia* 44 D6
Bashkortostan = Bashkir Republic □, *Russia* 44 D6
Basilan, *Phil.* 55 H5
Basilan Str., *Phil.* 55 H5
Basildon, *U.K.* 13 F8
Basilicata □, *Italy* 35 B9
Basim = Washim, *India* 60 J10
Basin, *U.S.A.* 110 D9
Basingstoke, *U.K.* 13 F6
Baška, *Croatia* 33 D11
Başkale, *Turkey* 67 D10
Baskatong, Rés., *Canada* 98 C4
Basle = Basel, *Switz.* 22 A5
Basoda, *India* 62 H7
Basodino, *Switz.* 23 D6
Basoka, *Zaïre* 82 B1
Basongo, *Zaïre* 80 E4

Basque, Pays, France 26 E2
Basque Provinces = País Vasco □, Spain 28 C2
Basra = Al Başrah, Iraq 64 D5
Bass Rock, U.K. 14 E6
Bass Str., Australia 90 F4
Bassano, Canada 100 C6
Bassano del Grappa, Italy 33 C8
Bassar, Togo 79 D5
Bassas da India, Ind. Oc. 81 J7
Basse Santa-Su, Gambia 78 C2
Basse-Terre, Guadeloupe 117 C7
Bassecourt, Switz. 22 B4
Bassein, Burma 61 L19
Basseterre, St. Christopher-Nevis 117 C7
Bassett, Nebr., U.S.A. 108 D5
Bassett, Va., U.S.A. 105 G6
Bassevelde, Belgium 17 F3
Bassi, India 62 D7
Bassigny, France 25 E12
Bassikounou, Mauritania 78 B3
Bassilly, Belgium 17 G3
Bassum, Germany 18 C4
Båstad, Sweden 11 H6
Bastak, Iran 65 E7
Baştām, Iran 65 B7
Bastar, India 61 K12
Bastelica, France 27 F13
Basti, India 63 F10
Bastia, France 27 F13
Bastia Umbra, Italy 33 E9
Bastogne, Belgium 17 H7
Bastrop, U.S.A. 109 K6
Bat Yam, Israel 69 C3
Bata, Eq. Guin. 80 D1
Bata, Romania 38 C5
Bataan, Phil. 55 D4
Batabanó, Cuba 116 B3
Batabanó, G. de, Cuba 116 B3
Batac, Phil. 55 B4
Batagoy, Russia 45 C14
Batak, Bulgaria 39 H7
Batalha, Portugal 31 F2
Batama, Zaïre 82 B2
Batamay, Russia 45 C13
Batan I., Phil. 55 A4
Batanes Is., Phil. 55 A4
Batang, China 52 B2
Batang, Indonesia 57 G13
Batangafo, C.A.R. 73 G8
Batangas, Phil. 55 E4
Batanta, Indonesia 57 E8
Batatais, Brazil 127 A6
Batavia, U.S.A. 106 D6
Bataysk, Russia 43 C8
Batchelor, Australia 88 B5
Bateman's B., Australia 91 F5
Batemans Bay, Australia 91 F5
Bates Ra., Australia 89 E3
Batesburg, U.S.A. 105 J5
Batesville, Ark., U.S.A. 109 H9
Batesville, Miss., U.S.A. 109 H10
Batesville, Tex., U.S.A. 109 L5
Bath, U.K. 13 F5
Bath, Maine, U.S.A. 99 D6
Bath, N.Y., U.S.A. 106 D7
Batheay, Cambodia 59 G5
Bathgate, U.K. 14 F5
Bathmen, Neths. 16 D8
Bathurst = Banjul, Gambia 78 C1
Bathurst, Australia 91 E4
Bathurst, Canada 99 C6
Bathurst, S. Africa 84 E4
Bathurst, C., Canada 96 A7
Bathurst B., Australia 90 A3
Bathurst Harb., Australia 90 G4
Bathurst I., Australia 88 B5
Bathurst I., Canada 4 B2
Bathurst Inlet, Canada 96 B9
Batie, Burkina Faso 78 D4
Batlow, Australia 91 F4
Batman, Turkey 67 E9
Batna, Algeria 75 A6
Batobato, Phil. 55 H7
Batoka, Zambia 83 F2
Baton Rouge, U.S.A. 109 K9
Batong, Ko, Thailand 59 J2
Batopilas, Mexico 114 B3
Batouri, Cameroon 80 D2
Battambang, Cambodia 58 F4
Batticaloa, Sri Lanka 60 R12
Battice, Belgium 17 G7
Battipáglia, Italy 35 B7
Battle, U.K. 13 G8
Battle →, Canada 101 C7
Battle Camp, Australia 90 B3
Battle Creek, U.S.A. 104 D3
Battle Ground, U.S.A. 112 E4
Battle Harbour, Canada 99 B8
Battle Lake, U.S.A. 108 B7
Battle Mountain, U.S.A. 110 F5
Battlefields, Zimbabwe 83 F2
Battleford, Canada 101 C7
Battonya, Hungary 21 J11
Batu, Ethiopia 68 F2
Batu, Kepulauan, Indonesia 56 E1
Batu Caves, Malaysia 59 L3
Batu Gajah, Malaysia 59 K3
Batu Is. = Batu, Kepulauan, Indonesia 56 E1
Batu Pahat, Malaysia 59 M4
Batuata, Indonesia 57 F6
Batumi, Georgia 43 F9
Baturaja, Indonesia 56 E2
Baturité, Brazil 122 B4
Bau, Malaysia 56 D4
Baubau, Indonesia 57 F6
Bauchi, Nigeria 79 C6
Bauchi □, Nigeria 79 C6
Baud, France 24 E3
Baudette, U.S.A. 108 A7
Baudour, Belgium 17 H3
Bauer, C., Australia 91 E1
Baugé, France 24 E6
Bauhinia Downs, Australia 90 C4
Bauma, Switz. 23 B7
Baume-les-Dames, France 25 E13
Baunatal, Germany 18 D5
Baunei, Italy 34 B2
Baures, Bolivia 125 C5
Bauru, Brazil 127 A6
Baús, Brazil 125 D7
Bauska, Latvia 40 C4
Bautzen, Germany 18 D10
Bavānāt, Iran 65 D7
Bavaria = Bayern □, Germany 19 F7
Båven, Sweden 10 F10
Bavi Sadri, India 62 G6
Bavispe →, Mexico 114 B3
Bawdwin, Burma 61 H20
Bawean, Indonesia 56 F4
Bawku, Ghana 79 C4
Bawlake, Burma 61 K20
Bawolung, China 52 C3
Baxley, U.S.A. 105 K4
Baxoi, China 52 B1
Baxter Springs, U.S.A. 109 G7
Bay, L. de, Phil. 57 B6
Bay Bulls, Canada 99 C9
Bay City, Mich., U.S.A. 104 D4
Bay City, Oreg., U.S.A. 110 D2
Bay City, Tex., U.S.A. 109 L7
Bay de Verde, Canada 99 C9
Bay Minette, U.S.A. 105 K2
Bay St. Louis, U.S.A. 109 K10
Bay Springs, U.S.A. 109 K10
Bay View, N.Z. 87 H6
Baya, Zaïre 83 E2
Bayamo, Cuba 116 B4
Bayamón, Puerto Rico 117 C6
Bayan Har Shan, China 54 C4
Bayan Hot = Alxa Zuoqi, China 50 E3
Bayan Obo, China 50 D5
Bayan-Ovoo, Mongolia 50 C4
Bayana, India 62 F7
Bayanaul, Kazakhstan 44 D8
Bayandalay, Mongolia 50 C2
Bayanhongor, Mongolia 54 B5
Bayard, U.S.A. 108 E3
Bayawan, Phil. 55 G5
Baybay, Phil. 55 F6
Bayburt, Turkey 67 C9
Bayerischer Wald, Germany 19 F8
Bayern □, Germany 19 F7
Bayeux, France 24 C6
Bayfield, Canada 106 C3
Bayfield, U.S.A. 108 B9
Bayındır, Turkey 66 D2
Baykal, Oz., Russia 45 D11
Baykit, Russia 45 C10
Baykonur, Kazakhstan 44 E7
Baynes Mts., Namibia 84 B1
Bayombong, Phil. 55 C4
Bayon, France 25 D13
Bayona, Spain 30 C2
Bayonne, France 26 E2
Bayonne, U.S.A. 107 F10
Bayovar, Peru 124 B1
Bayram-Ali, Turkmenistan 44 F7
Bayramiç, Turkey 66 D2
Bayreuth, Germany 19 F7
Bayrischzell, Germany 19 H8
Bayrūt, Lebanon 69 B4
Bayt Lahm, Jordan 69 D4
Baytown, U.S.A. 109 L7
Bayzo, Niger 79 C5
Baza, Spain 29 H2
Bazar Dyuzi, Russia 43 F12
Bazarny Karabulak, Russia 41 E15
Bazarnyy Syzgan, Russia 41 E15
Bazartobe, Kazakhstan 43 B14
Bazaruto, I. do, Mozam. 85 C6
Bazas, France 26 D3
Bazhong, China 52 B6
Bazmān, Kūh-e, Iran 65 D9
Beach, U.S.A. 108 B3
Beach City, U.S.A. 106 F3
Beachport, Australia 91 F2
Beachy Hd., U.K. 13 G8
Beacon, Australia 89 F2
Beacon, U.S.A. 107 E11
Beaconia, Canada 101 C9
Beagle, Canal, S. Amer. 128 E3
Beagle Bay, Australia 88 C3
Bealanana, Madag. 85 A8
Beamsville, Canada 106 C5
Bear →, U.S.A. 112 G5
Béar, C., France 26 F7
Bear I., Ireland 15 E2
Bear L., B.C., Canada 100 B3
Bear L., Man., Canada 101 B9
Bear L., U.S.A. 110 E8
Bearcreek, U.S.A. 110 D9
Beardmore, Canada 98 C2
Beardmore Glacier, Antarctica 5 E11
Beardstown, U.S.A. 108 F9
Béarn, France 26 E3
Bearpaw Mts., U.S.A. 110 B9
Bearskin Lake, Canada 98 B1
Beas de Segura, Spain 29 G2
Beasain, Spain 28 B2
Beata, C., Dom. Rep. 117 C5
Beata, I., Dom. Rep. 117 C5
Beatrice, U.S.A. 108 E6
Beatrice, Zimbabwe 83 F3
Beatrice, C., Australia 90 A2
Beatton →, Canada 100 B4
Beatton River, Canada 100 B4
Beatty, U.S.A. 111 H5
Beaucaire, France 27 E8
Beauce, Plaine de la, France 25 D8
Beauceville, Canada 99 C5
Beauchêne, I., Falk. Is. 128 D5
Beaudesert, Australia 91 D5
Beaufort, Malaysia 56 C5
Beaufort, N.C., U.S.A. 105 H7
Beaufort, S.C., U.S.A. 105 J5
Beaufort Sea, Arctic 4 B1
Beaufort West, S. Africa 84 E3
Beaugency, France 25 E8
Beauharnois, Canada 98 C5
Beaujeu, France 27 B8
Beaulieu →, Canada 100 A6
Beaulieu-sur-Dordogne, France 26 D5
Beaulieu-sur-Mer, France 27 E11
Beauly, U.K. 14 D4
Beauly →, U.K. 14 D4
Beaumaris, U.K. 12 D3
Beaumetz-lès-Loges, France 25 B9
Beaumont, Belgium 17 H4
Beaumont, France 26 D4
Beaumont, Calif., U.S.A. 113 M10
Beaumont, Tex., U.S.A. 109 K7
Beaumont-de-Lomagne, France 26 E4
Beaumont-le-Roger, France 24 C7
Beaumont-sur-Oise, France 25 C9
Beaumont-sur-Sarthe, France 24 D7
Beaune, France 25 E11
Beaune-la-Rolande, France 25 D9
Beaupréau, France 24 E6
Beauraing, Belgium 17 H5
Beauséjour, Canada 101 C9
Beauvais, France 25 C9
Beauval, Canada 101 B7
Beauvoir-sur-Mer, France 24 F4
Beauvoir-sur-Niort, France 26 B3
Beaver, Alaska, U.S.A. 96 B5
Beaver, Okla., U.S.A. 109 G4
Beaver, Pa., U.S.A. 106 F4
Beaver, Utah, U.S.A. 111 G7
Beaver →, B.C., Canada 100 B4
Beaver →, Ont., Canada 98 A2
Beaver →, Sask., Canada 101 B7
Beaver City, U.S.A. 108 E5
Beaver Dam, U.S.A. 108 D10
Beaver Falls, U.S.A. 106 F4
Beaver Hill L., Canada 101 C10
Beaver I., U.S.A. 104 C3
Beaverhill L., Alta., Canada 100 C6
Beaverhill L., N.W.T., Canada 101 A8
Beaverlodge, Canada 100 B5
Beavermouth, Canada 100 C5
Beaverstone →, Canada 98 B2
Beaverton, Canada 106 B5
Beaverton, U.S.A. 112 E4
Beawar, India 62 F6
Bebedouro, Brazil 127 A6
Beboa, Madag. 85 B7
Bebra, Germany 18 E5
Beccles, U.K. 13 E9
Bečej, Serbia 21 K10
Becerreá, Spain 30 C3
Béchar, Algeria 75 B4
Beckley, U.S.A. 104 G5
Beckum, Germany 18 D4
Bečva →, Czech. 20 F7
Bédar, Spain 29 H3
Bédarieux, France 26 E7
Bédarrides, France 27 D8
Beddouza, Ras, Morocco 74 B3
Bedele, Ethiopia 77 F4
Bederkesa, Germany 18 B4
Bedeso, Ethiopia 77 F5
Bedford, Canada 98 C5
Bedford, S. Africa 84 E4
Bedford, U.K. 13 E7
Bedford, Ind., U.S.A. 104 F2
Bedford, Iowa, U.S.A. 108 E7
Bedford, Ohio, U.S.A. 106 E3
Bedford, Pa., U.S.A. 106 F6
Bedford, Va., U.S.A. 104 G6
Bedford, C., Australia 90 B4
Bedford Downs, Australia 88 C4
Bedfordshire □, U.K. 13 E7
Będków, Poland 20 D9
Bednja →, Croatia 33 B13
Bednodemyanovsk, Russia 41 E13
Bedónia, Italy 32 D6
Bedourie, Australia 90 C2
Bedretto, Switz. 23 C7
Bedum, Neths. 16 B9
Będzin, Poland 20 E9
Beech Grove, U.S.A. 104 F2
Beechy, Canada 101 C7
Beek, Gelderland, Neths. 16 E8
Beek, Limburg, Neths. 17 G7
Beek, Noord-Brabant, Neths. 17 E7
Beekbergen, Neths. 16 D7
Beelitz, Germany 18 C8
Beenleigh, Australia 91 D5
Be'er Menuḥa, Israel 64 D2
Be'er Sheva', Israel 69 D3
Beersheba = Be'er Sheva', Israel 69 D3
Beerta, Neths. 16 B10
Beerze →, Neths. 16 E6
Beesd, Neths. 16 E6
Beeskow, Germany 18 C10
Beeston, U.K. 12 E6
Beetaloo, Australia 90 B1
Beetsterzwaag, Neths. 16 B8
Beetzendorf, Germany 18 C7
Beeville, U.S.A. 109 L6
Befale, Zaïre 80 D4
Befandriana, Madag. 85 C7
Befotaka, Madag. 85 C8
Bega, Australia 91 F4
Bega, Canalul, Romania 38 D3
Bégard, France 24 D3
Bègles, France 26 D3
Begna →, Norway 10 D4
Begonte, Spain 30 B3
Begusarai, India 63 G12
Behābād, Iran 65 C8
Behara, Madag. 85 C8
Behbehān, Iran 65 D6
Behshahr, Iran 65 B7
Bei Jiang →, China 53 F9
Bei'an, China 54 B7
Beibei, China 54 D5
Beigang, Taiwan 53 F13
Beihai, China 52 G7
Beijing, China 50 E9
Beijing □, China 50 E9
Beilen, Neths. 16 C8
Beiliu, China 53 F8
Beilngries, Germany 19 F7
Beilpajah, Australia 91 E3
Beilul, Eritrea 77 E5
Beipiao, China 51 D11
Beira, Mozam. 83 F3
Beirut = Bayrūt, Lebanon 69 B4
Beitaolaizhao, China 51 B13
Beitbridge, Zimbabwe 83 G3
Beiuş, Romania 38 C5
Beizhen, Liaoning, China 51 D11
Beizhen, Shandong, China 51 F10
Beizhengzhen, China 51 B12
Beja, Portugal 31 G3
Béja, Tunisia 75 A6
Beja □, Portugal 31 H3
Bejaia, Algeria 75 A6
Béjar, Spain 30 E5
Bejestān, Iran 65 C8
Bekasi, Indonesia 57 G12
Békés, Hungary 21 J11
Békéscsaba, Hungary 21 J11
Bekily, Madag. 85 C8
Bekkevoort, Belgium 17 G5
Bekoji, Ethiopia 77 F4
Bekok, Malaysia 59 L4
Bekwai, Ghana 79 D4
Bela, India 63 G9
Bela, Pakistan 62 F2
Bela Crkva, Serbia 21 L11
Bela Palanka, Serbia 21 M12
Bela Vista, Brazil 126 A4
Bela Vista, Mozam. 85 D5
Bélâbre, France 26 B5
Belalcázar, Spain 31 G5
Belarus = Belorussia ■, Europe 40 E5
Belau ■, Pac. Oc. 92 G5
Belavenona, Madag. 85 C8
Belawan, Indonesia 56 D1
Belaya, Ethiopia 77 E4
Belaya Glina, Russia 43 C9
Belaya Kalitva, Russia 43 B9
Belaya Kholunitsa, Russia 41 B17
Belaya Tserkov, Ukraine 40 G7
Belcher Is., Canada 97 C12
Belchite, Spain 28 D4
Belden, U.S.A. 112 E5
Belém, Brazil 122 B2
Belém de São Francisco, Brazil 122 C4
Belén, Argentina 126 B2
Belén, Colombia 120 C2
Belén, Paraguay 126 A4
Belen, U.S.A. 111 J10
Bélesta, France 26 F5
Belet Uen, Somali Rep. 68 G4
Belev, Russia 41 E10
Belfair, U.S.A. 112 C4
Belfast, S. Africa 85 D5
Belfast, U.K. 15 B6
Belfast, Maine, U.S.A. 99 D6
Belfast, N.Y., U.S.A. 106 D6
Belfast □, U.K. 15 B6
Belfast L., U.K. 15 B6
Belfeld, Neths. 17 F8
Belfield, U.S.A. 108 B3
Belfort, France 25 E13
Belfort, Territoire de □, France 25 E13
Belfry, U.S.A. 110 D9
Belgaum, India 60 M9
Belgioioso, Italy 32 C6
Belgium ■, Europe 17 G5
Belgorod, Russia 41 F10
Belgorod-Dnestrovskiy, Ukraine 42 C4
Belgrade = Beograd, Serbia 21 L10
Belgrade, U.S.A. 110 D8
Belhaven, U.S.A. 105 H7
Beli Drim →, Europe 21 N10
Beli Manastir, Croatia 21 K8
Belice →, Italy 34 E5
Belin-Béliet, France 26 D3
Belinga, Gabon 80 D2
Belinskiy, Russia 41 E13
Belinyu, Indonesia 56 E3
Beliton Is. = Belitung, Indonesia 56 E3
Belitung, Indonesia 56 E3
Beliu, Romania 38 C5
Belize ■, Cent. Amer. 115 D7
Belize City, Belize 115 D7
Beljanica, Serbia 21 L11
Belkovskiy, Ostrov, Russia 45 B14
Bell →, Canada 98 C4
Bell Bay, Australia 90 G4
Bell I., Canada 99 B8
Bell-Irving →, Canada 100 B3
Bell Peninsula, Canada 97 B11
Bell Ville, Argentina 126 C3
Bella Bella, Canada 100 C3
Bella Coola, Canada 100 C3
Bella Flor, Bolivia 124 C4
Bella Unión, Uruguay 126 C4
Bella Vista, Corrientes, Argentina 126 B4
Bella Vista, Tucuman, Argentina 126 B2
Bellac, France 26 B5
Bellágio, Italy 32 C6
Bellaire, U.S.A. 106 F4
Bellary, India 60 M10
Bellata, Australia 91 D4
Belle Fourche, U.S.A. 108 C3
Belle Fourche →, U.S.A. 108 C3
Belle Glade, U.S.A. 105 M5
Belle-Ile, France 24 E3
Belle Isle, Canada 99 B8
Belle Isle, Str. of, Canada 99 B8
Belle-Isle-en-Terre, France 24 D3
Belle Plaine, Iowa, U.S.A. 108 E8
Belle Plaine, Minn., U.S.A. 108 C8
Belle Yella, Liberia 78 D3
Belledonne, Chaîne de, France 27 C10
Belledune, Canada 99 C6
Bellefontaine, U.S.A. 104 E4
Bellefonte, U.S.A. 106 F7
Bellegarde, France 25 E9
Bellegarde-en-Marche, France 26 C6
Bellegarde-sur-Valserine, France 27 B9
Bellême, France 24 D7
Belleoram, Canada 99 C8
Belleville, Canada 98 D4
Belleville, France 27 B8
Belleville, Ill., U.S.A. 108 F10
Belleville, Kans., U.S.A. 108 F6
Belleville, N.Y., U.S.A. 107 C8
Belleville-sur-Vie, France 24 F5
Bellevue, Canada 100 D6
Bellevue, Idaho, U.S.A. 110 E6
Bellevue, Ohio, U.S.A. 106 E2
Bellevue, Wash., U.S.A. 112 C4
Belley, France 27 C9
Bellin, Canada 97 B13
Bellingen, Australia 91 E5
Bellingham, U.S.A. 112 B4
Bellingshausen Sea, Antarctica 5 C17
Bellinzona, Switz. 23 D8
Bello, Colombia 120 B2
Bellows Falls, U.S.A. 107 C12
Bellpat, Pakistan 62 E3
Bellpuig, Spain 28 D6
Belluno, Italy 33 B9
Bellville, U.S.A. 109 L6
Bellwood, U.S.A. 106 F6
Bélmez, Spain 31 G5
Belmont, Australia 91 E5
Belmont, Canada 106 D3
Belmont, S. Africa 84 D3
Belmont, U.S.A. 106 D6
Belmonte, Brazil 123 E4
Belmonte, Portugal 30 E3
Belmonte, Spain 28 F2
Belmopan, Belize 115 D7
Belmullet, Ireland 15 B2
Belo Horizonte, Brazil 123 E3
Belo Jardim, Brazil 122 C4
Belo-sur-Mer, Madag. 85 C7
Belo-Tsiribihina, Madag. 85 B7
Belogorsk, Russia 45 D13
Belogorsk, Ukraine 42 D6
Belogradchik, Bulgaria 38 F5
Beloha, Madag. 85 D8
Beloit, Kans., U.S.A. 108 F5
Beloit, Wis., U.S.A. 108 D10
Belokorovichi, Ukraine 40 F6
Belomorsk, Russia 44 C4
Belonia, India 61 H17
Belopolye, Ukraine 40 F9
Belorussia ■, Europe 40 E5
Belovo, Russia 44 D9
Beloye More, Russia 44 C4

Beloye Ozero, *Russia* 43 D12
Belozersk, *Russia* 41 A10
Belpasso, *Italy* 35 E7
Belsele, *Belgium* 17 F4
Belsito, *Italy* 34 E6
Beltana, *Australia* 91 E2
Belterra, *Brazil* 121 D7
Beltinci, *Slovenia* 33 B13
Belton, *S.C., U.S.A.* 105 H4
Belton, *Tex., U.S.A.* 109 K6
Belton Res., *U.S.A.* 109 K6
Beltsy, *Moldavia* 42 C3
Belturbet, *Ireland* 15 B4
Belukha, *Russia* 44 E9
Beluran, *Malaysia* 56 C5
Belvedere Marittimo, *Italy* 35 C8
Belvès, *France* 26 D5
Belvidere, *Ill., U.S.A.* 108 D10
Belvidere, *N.J., U.S.A.* 107 F9
Belvis de la Jara, *Spain* 31 F6
Belyando →, *Australia* 90 C4
Belyy, *Russia* 40 D8
Belyy, Ostrov, *Russia* 44 B8
Belyy Yar, *Russia* 44 D9
Belzig, *Germany* 18 C8
Belzoni, *U.S.A.* 109 J9
Bemaraha, Lembalemban' i, *Madag.* 85 B7
Bemarivo, *Madag.* 85 C7
Bemarivo →, *Madag.* 85 B8
Bemavo, *Madag.* 85 C8
Bembéréke, *Benin* 79 C5
Bembesi, *Zimbabwe* 83 F2
Bembesi →, *Zimbabwe* 83 F2
Bembézar →, *Spain* 31 H5
Bemidji, *U.S.A.* 108 B7
Bemmel, *Neths.* 16 E7
Ben, *Iran* 65 C6
Ben Cruachan, *U.K.* 14 E3
Ben Dearg, *U.K.* 14 D4
Ben Gardane, *Tunisia* 75 B7
Ben Hope, *U.K.* 14 C4
Ben Lawers, *U.K.* 14 E4
Ben Lomond, *N.S.W., Australia* 91 E5
Ben Lomond, *Tas., Australia* 90 G4
Ben Lomond, *U.K.* 14 E4
Ben Luc, *Vietnam* 59 G6
Ben Macdhui, *U.K.* 14 D5
Ben Mhor, *U.K.* 14 D1
Ben More, *Central, U.K.* 14 E4
Ben More, *Strath., U.K.* 14 E2
Ben More Assynt, *U.K.* 14 C4
Ben Nevis, *U.K.* 14 E4
Ben Quang, *Vietnam* 58 D6
Ben Slimane, *Morocco* 74 B3
Ben Tre, *Vietnam* 59 G6
Ben Vorlich, *U.K.* 14 E4
Ben Wyvis, *U.K.* 14 D4
Bena, *Nigeria* 79 C6
Bena Dibele, *Zaïre* 80 E4
Benagalbón, *Spain* 31 J6
Benagerie, *Australia* 91 E3
Benahmed, *Morocco* 74 B3
Benalla, *Australia* 91 F4
Benambra, Mt., *Australia* 91 F4
Benamejí, *Spain* 31 H6
Benares = Varanasi, *India* 63 G10
Bénat, C., *France* 27 E10
Benavente, *Portugal* 31 G2
Benavente, *Spain* 30 C5
Benavides, *Spain* 30 C5
Benavides, *U.S.A.* 109 M5
Benbecula, *U.K.* 14 D1
Benbonyathe, *Australia* 91 E2
Bencubbin, *Australia* 89 F2
Bend, *U.S.A.* 110 D3
Bender Beila, *Somali Rep.* 68 F5
Bendering, *Australia* 89 F2
Bendery, *Moldavia* 42 C3
Bendigo, *Australia* 91 F3
Bendorf, *Germany* 18 E3
Benē Beraq, *Israel* 69 C3
Beneden Knijpe, *Neths.* 16 C7
Beneditinos, *Brazil* 122 C3
Benedito Leite, *Brazil* 122 C3
Bénéna, *Mali* 78 C4
Benenitra, *Madag.* 85 C8
Benešŏv, *Czech.* 20 F4
Bénestroff, *France* 25 D13
Benet, *France* 26 B3
Benevento, *Italy* 35 A7
Benfeld, *France* 25 D14
Benga, *Mozam.* 83 F3
Bengal, Bay of, *Ind. Oc.* 61 K16
Bengbu, *China* 51 H9
Benghazi = Banghāzī, *Libya* 73 B9
Bengkalis, *Indonesia* 56 D2
Bengkulu, *Indonesia* 56 E2
Bengkulu □, *Indonesia* 56 E2
Bengough, *Canada* 101 D7
Benguela, *Angola* 81 G2
Benguerir, *Morocco* 74 B3
Benguérua, I., *Mozam.* 85 C6
Benha, *Egypt* 76 H7
Beni, *Zaïre* 82 B2
Beni □, *Bolivia* 125 C4
Beni →, *Bolivia* 125 C4
Beni Abbès, *Algeria* 75 B4
Beni-Haoua, *Algeria* 75 A5
Beni Mazâr, *Egypt* 76 J7
Beni Mellal, *Morocco* 74 B3
Beni Ounif, *Algeria* 75 B4
Beni Saf, *Algeria* 75 A4
Beni Suef, *Egypt* 76 J7
Beniah L., *Canada* 100 A6
Benicarló, *Spain* 28 E5
Benicia, *U.S.A.* 112 G4
Benidorm, *Spain* 29 G4
Benidorm, Islote de, *Spain* 29 G4
Benin ■, *Africa* 79 D5
Benin, Bight of, *W. Afr.* 79 D5
Benin City, *Nigeria* 79 D6
Benisa, *Spain* 29 G5
Benitses, *Greece* 37 A3
Benjamin Aceval, *Paraguay* 126 A4
Benjamin Constant, *Brazil* 120 D3
Benjamin Hill, *Mexico* 114 A2
Benkelman, *U.S.A.* 108 E4
Benkovac, *Croatia* 33 D12
Benlidi, *Australia* 90 C3
Bennebroek, *Neths.* 16 D5
Bennekom, *Neths.* 16 D7
Bennett, *Canada* 100 B2
Bennett, L., *Australia* 88 D5
Bennett, Ostrov, *Russia* 45 B15
Bennettsville, *U.S.A.* 105 H6
Bennington, *U.S.A.* 107 D11
Bénodet, *France* 24 E2
Benoni, *S. Africa* 85 D4
Benoud, *Algeria* 75 B5
Benque Viejo, *Belize* 115 D7
Bensheim, *Germany* 19 F4
Benson, *U.S.A.* 111 L8
Bent, *Iran* 65 E8
Benteng, *Indonesia* 57 F6
Bentinck I., *Australia* 90 B2
Bentiu, *Sudan* 77 F2
Bento Gonçalves, *Brazil* 127 B5
Benton, *Ark., U.S.A.* 109 H8
Benton, *Calif., U.S.A.* 112 H8
Benton, *Ill., U.S.A.* 108 F10
Benton Harbor, *U.S.A.* 104 D2
Bentu Liben, *Ethiopia* 77 F4
Bentung, *Malaysia* 59 L3
Benue □, *Nigeria* 79 D6
Benue →, *Nigeria* 79 D6
Benxi, *China* 51 D12
Benzdorp, *Surinam* 121 C7
Beo, *Indonesia* 57 D7
Beograd, *Serbia, Yug.* 21 L10
Beowawe, *U.S.A.* 110 F5
Bepan Jiang →, *China* 52 E6
Beppu, *Japan* 49 H5
Berati, *Albania* 39 J2
Berau, Teluk, *Indonesia* 57 E8
Berber, *Sudan* 76 D3
Berbera, *Somali Rep.* 68 E4
Berbérati, *C.A.R.* 80 D3
Berberia, C. del, *Spain* 36 C7
Berbice →, *Guyana* 121 B6
Berceto, *Italy* 32 D7
Berchtesgaden, *Germany* 19 H8
Berdichev, *Ukraine* 42 B3
Berdsk, *Russia* 44 D9
Berdyansk, *Ukraine* 42 C7
Berdychiv = Berdichev, *Ukraine* 42 B3
Berea, *U.S.A.* 104 G3
Berebere, *Indonesia* 57 D7
Bereda, *Somali Rep.* 68 E5
Berekum, *Ghana* 78 D4
Berenice, *Egypt* 76 C4
Berens →, *Canada* 101 C9
Berens I., *Canada* 101 C9
Berens River, *Canada* 101 C9
Berestechko, *Ukraine* 40 F4
Bereşti, *Romania* 38 C10
Beretău →, *Romania* 38 B4
Berettyo →, *Hungary* 21 J11
Berettyóújfalu, *Hungary* 21 H11
Berevo, *Mahajanga, Madag.* 85 B7
Berevo, *Toliara, Madag.* 85 B7
Bereza, *Belorussia* 40 E4
Berezhany, *Ukraine* 40 G4
Berezina →, *Belorussia* 40 E7
Berezna, *Ukraine* 40 F7
Berezniki, *Russia* 44 D6
Berezovka, *Ukraine* 42 C4
Berezovo, *Russia* 44 C7
Berga, *Spain* 28 C6
Bergama, *Turkey* 66 D2
Bergambacht, *Neths.* 16 E5
Bérgamo, *Italy* 32 C6
Bergantiños, *Spain* 30 B2
Bergara, *Spain* 28 B2
Bergedorf, *Germany* 18 B6
Bergeijk, *Neths.* 17 F6
Bergen, *Germany* 18 A9
Bergen, *Neths.* 16 C5
Bergen, *Norway* 9 F8
Bergen, *U.S.A.* 106 C7
Bergen-op-Zoom, *Neths.* 17 F4
Bergerac, *France* 26 D4
Bergheim, *Germany* 18 E2
Berghem, *Neths.* 16 E7
Bergisch-Gladbach, *Germany* 18 E3
Bergschenhoek, *Neths.* 16 E5
Bergsjö, *Sweden* 10 C11
Bergues, *France* 25 B9
Bergum, *Neths.* 16 B7
Bergville, *S. Africa* 85 D4
Berhala, Selat, *Indonesia* 56 E2
Berhampore = Baharampur, *India* 63 G13
Berhampur, *India* 61 K14
Berheci →, *Romania* 38 C10
Bering Sea, *Pac. Oc.* 96 C1
Bering Strait, *U.S.A.* 96 B3
Beringen, *Belgium* 17 F6
Beringen, *Switz.* 23 A7
Beringovskiy, *Russia* 45 C18
Berislav, *Ukraine* 42 C5
Berisso, *Argentina* 126 C4
Berja, *Spain* 29 J2
Berkane, *Morocco* 75 B4
Berkel →, *Neths.* 16 D8
Berkeley, *U.K.* 13 F5
Berkeley, *U.S.A.* 112 H4
Berkeley Springs, *U.S.A.* 104 F6
Berkhout, *Neths.* 16 C5
Berkner I., *Antarctica* 5 D18
Berkovitsa, *Bulgaria* 38 F6
Berkshire □, *U.K.* 13 F6
Berlaar, *Belgium* 17 F5
Berland →, *Canada* 100 C5
Berlanga, *Spain* 31 G5
Berlare, *Belgium* 17 F4
Berlenga, I., *Portugal* 31 F1
Berlin, *Germany* 18 C9
Berlin, *Md., U.S.A.* 104 F8
Berlin, *N.H., U.S.A.* 107 B13
Berlin, *Wis., U.S.A.* 104 D1
Bermeja, Sierra, *Spain* 31 J5
Bermejo →, *Formosa, Argentina* 126 B4
Bermejo →, *San Juan, Argentina* 126 C2
Bermeo, *Spain* 28 B2
Bermillo de Sayago, *Spain* 30 D4
Bermuda ■, *Atl. Oc.* 2 C6
Bern, *Switz.* 22 C4
Bern □, *Switz.* 22 C5
Bernado, *U.S.A.* 111 J10
Bernalda, *Italy* 35 B9
Bernalillo, *U.S.A.* 111 J10
Bernardo de Irigoyen, *Argentina* 127 B5
Bernardo O'Higgins □, *Chile* 126 C1
Bernasconi, *Argentina* 126 D3
Bernau, *Bayern, Germany* 19 H8
Bernau, *Brandenburg, Germany* 18 C9
Bernay, *France* 24 C7
Bernburg, *Germany* 18 D7
Berne = Bern, *Switz.* 22 C4
Berne = Bern □, *Switz.* 22 C5
Berner Alpen, *Switz.* 22 D5
Bernese Oberland = Oberland, *Switz.* 22 C5
Bernier I., *Australia* 89 D1
Bernina, Piz, *Switz.* 23 D9
Bernina, Pizzo, *Switz.* 23 D9
Bernissart, *Belgium* 17 H3
Bernkastel-Kues, *Germany* 19 F3
Beroroha, *Madag.* 85 C8
Béroubouay, *Benin* 79 C5
Beroun, *Czech.* 20 F4
Berounka →, *Czech.* 20 F4
Berovo, *Macedonia* 39 H5
Berrahal, *Algeria* 75 A6
Berre, Étang de, *France* 27 E9
Berrechid, *Morocco* 74 B3
Berri, *Australia* 91 E3
Berriane, *Algeria* 75 B5
Berrouaghia, *Algeria* 75 A5
Berry, *Australia* 91 E5
Berry, *France* 25 F8
Berry Is., *Bahamas* 116 A4
Berryessa L., *U.S.A.* 112 G4
Berryville, *U.S.A.* 109 G8
Bersenbrück, *Germany* 18 C3
Berthold, *U.S.A.* 108 A4
Berthoud, *U.S.A.* 108 E2
Bertincourt, *France* 25 B9
Bertoua, *Cameroon* 80 D2
Bertrand, *U.S.A.* 108 E5
Bertrange, *Lux.* 17 J8
Bertrix, *Belgium* 17 J6
Berufjörður, *Iceland* 8 D6
Beruri, *Brazil* 121 D5
Berwick, *U.S.A.* 107 E8
Berwick-upon-Tweed, *U.K.* 12 B5
Berwyn Mts., *U.K.* 12 E4
Berzasca, *Romania* 38 E4
Besal, *Pakistan* 63 B5
Besalampy, *Madag.* 85 B7
Besançon, *France* 25 E13
Besar, *Indonesia* 56 E5
Beshenkovichi, *Belorussia* 40 D6
Beslan, *Russia* 43 E11
Besnard L., *Canada* 101 B7
Besni, *Turkey* 67 E7
Besor, N. →, *Egypt* 69 D3
Bessarabiya, *Moldavia* 38 B11
Bessarabka, *Moldavia* 42 C3
Bessèges, *France* 27 D8
Bessemer, *Ala., U.S.A.* 105 J2
Bessemer, *Mich., U.S.A.* 108 B9
Bessin, *France* 24 C5
Bessines-sur-Gartempe, *France* 26 B5
Best, *Neths.* 17 E6
Bet She'an, *Israel* 69 C4
Bet Shemesh, *Israel* 69 D3
Bet Tadjine, Djebel, *Algeria* 74 C4
Betafo, *Madag.* 85 B8
Betancuria, *Canary Is.* 36 F5
Betanzos, *Bolivia* 125 D4
Betanzos, *Spain* 30 B2
Bétaré Oya, *Cameroon* 80 C2
Betera, *Spain* 28 F4
Bethal, *S. Africa* 85 D4
Bethanien, *Namibia* 84 D2
Bethany, *S. Africa* 84 D4
Bethany, *U.S.A.* 108 E7
Bethel, *Alaska, U.S.A.* 96 B3
Bethel, *Vt., U.S.A.* 107 C12
Bethel Park, *U.S.A.* 106 F4
Bethlehem = Bayt Lahm, *Jordan* 69 D4
Bethlehem, *S. Africa* 85 D4
Bethlehem, *U.S.A.* 107 F9
Bethulie, *S. Africa* 84 E4
Béthune, *France* 25 B9
Béthune →, *France* 24 C8
Bethungra, *Australia* 91 E4
Betijoque, *Venezuela* 120 B3
Betim, *Brazil* 123 E3
Betioky, *Madag.* 85 C7
Beton-Bazoches, *France* 25 D10
Betong, *Thailand* 59 K3
Betoota, *Australia* 90 D3
Betroka, *Madag.* 85 C8
Betsiamites, *Canada* 99 C6
Betsiamites →, *Canada* 99 C6
Betsiboka →, *Madag.* 85 B8
Betsjoeanaland, *S. Africa* 84 D3
Bettembourg, *Lux.* 17 J8
Bettiah, *India* 63 F11
Béttola, *Italy* 32 D6
Betul, *India* 60 J10
Betung, *Malaysia* 56 D4
Betzdorf, *Germany* 18 E3
Beuca, *Romania* 38 E7
Beuil, *France* 27 D10
Beulah, *U.S.A.* 108 B4
Beuvron →, *France* 24 E8
Beveren, *Belgium* 17 F4
Beverley, *Australia* 89 F2
Beverley, *U.K.* 12 D7
Beverlo, *Belgium* 17 F6
Beverly, *Mass., U.S.A.* 107 D14
Beverly, *Wash., U.S.A.* 110 C4
Beverly Hills, *U.S.A.* 113 L8
Beverwijk, *Neths.* 16 D5
Bex, *Switz.* 22 D4
Bey Dağları, *Turkey* 66 E4
Beyānlū, *Iran* 64 C5
Beyin, *Ghana* 78 D4
Beyla, *Guinea* 78 D3
Beynat, *France* 26 C5
Beyneu, *Kazakhstan* 44 E6
Beypazarı, *Turkey* 66 C4
Beyşehir Gölü, *Turkey* 66 E4
Beytüşşebap, *Turkey* 67 E10
Bezhetsk, *Russia* 41 C10
Bezhitsa, *Russia* 40 E9
Béziers, *France* 26 E7
Bezwada = Vijayawada, *India* 61 L12
Bhachau, *India* 60 H7
Bhadarwah, *India* 63 C6
Bhadrakh, *India* 61 J15
Bhadravati, *India* 60 N9
Bhagalpur, *India* 63 G12
Bhakkar, *Pakistan* 62 D4
Bhakra Dam, *India* 62 D7
Bhamo, *Burma* 61 G20
Bhandara, *India* 60 J11
Bhanrer Ra., *India* 62 H8
Bharat = India ■, *Asia* 60 K11
Bharatpur, *India* 62 F7
Bhatinda, *India* 62 D6
Bhatpara, *India* 63 H13
Bhaun, *Pakistan* 62 C5
Bhaunagar = Bhavnagar, *India* 62 J5
Bhavnagar, *India* 62 J5
Bhawanipatna, *India* 61 K12
Bhera, *Pakistan* 62 C5
Bhilsa = Vidisha, *India* 62 H7
Bhilwara, *India* 62 G6
Bhima →, *India* 60 L10
Bhimavaram, *India* 61 L12
Bhimbar, *Pakistan* 63 C6
Bhind, *India* 63 F8
Bhiwandi, *India* 60 K8
Bhiwani, *India* 62 E7
Bhola, *Bangla.* 61 H17
Bhopal, *India* 62 H7
Bhubaneshwar, *India* 61 J14
Bhuj, *India* 62 H3
Bhumiphol Dam = Phumiphon, Khuan, *Thailand* 58 D2
Bhusaval, *India* 60 J9
Bhutan ■, *Asia* 61 F17
Biá →, *Brazil* 120 D4
Biafra, B. of = Bonny, Bight of, *Africa* 79 E6
Biak, *Indonesia* 57 E9
Biała →, *Poland* 20 E10
Biała Podlaska, *Poland* 20 C13
Białogard, *Poland* 20 A5
Białystok, *Poland* 20 B13
Biancavilla, *Italy* 35 E7
Bīārjmand, *Iran* 65 B7
Biaro, *Indonesia* 57 D7
Biarritz, *France* 26 E2
Biasca, *Switz.* 23 D7
Biba, *Egypt* 76 J7
Bibai, *Japan* 48 C10
Bibala, *Angola* 81 G2
Bibane, Bahiret el, *Tunisia* 75 B7
Bibbiena, *Italy* 33 E8
Bibby I., *Canada* 101 A10
Biberach, *Germany* 19 G5
Biberist, *Switz.* 22 B5
Bibey →, *Spain* 30 C3
Bibiani, *Ghana* 78 D4
Biboohra, *Australia* 90 B4
Bibungwa, *Zaïre* 82 C2
Bic, *Canada* 99 C6
Bicaz, *Romania* 38 C9
Biccari, *Italy* 35 A8
Bichena, *Ethiopia* 77 E4
Bickerton I., *Australia* 90 A2
Bicknell, *Ind., U.S.A.* 104 F2
Bicknell, *Utah, U.S.A.* 111 G8
Bida, *Nigeria* 79 D6
Bidar, *India* 60 L10
Biddeford, *U.S.A.* 99 D5
Biddwara, *Ethiopia* 77 F4
Bideford, *U.K.* 13 F3
Bidon 5 = Poste Maurice Cortier, *Algeria* 75 D5
Bidor, *Malaysia* 59 K3
Bié, Planalto de, *Angola* 81 G3
Bieber, *U.S.A.* 110 F3
Biel, *Switz.* 22 B4
Bielawa, *Poland* 20 E6
Bielé Karpaty, *Europe* 20 F7
Bielefeld, *Germany* 18 C4
Bielersee, *Switz.* 22 B4
Biella, *Italy* 32 C5
Bielsk Podlaski, *Poland* 20 C13
Bielsko-Biała, *Poland* 20 F9
Bien Hoa, *Vietnam* 59 G6
Bienfait, *Canada* 101 D8
Bienne = Biel, *Switz.* 22 B4
Bienvenida, *Spain* 31 G4
Bienvenue, *Fr. Guiana* 121 C7
Bienville, L., *Canada* 98 A5
Biescas, *Spain* 28 C4
Biese →, *Germany* 18 C7
Biesiesfontein, *S. Africa* 84 E2
Bietigheim, *Germany* 19 G5
Bievre, *Belgium* 17 J6
Biferno →, *Italy* 35 A8
Big →, *Canada* 99 B8
Big B., *Canada* 99 A7
Big Bear City, *U.S.A.* 113 L10
Big Bear Lake, *U.S.A.* 113 L10
Big Beaver, *Canada* 101 D7
Big Belt Mts., *U.S.A.* 110 C8
Big Bend, *Swaziland* 85 D5
Big Bend National Park, *U.S.A.* 109 L3
Big Black →, *U.S.A.* 109 J9
Big Blue →, *U.S.A.* 108 F6
Big Cr. →, *Canada* 100 C4
Big Creek, *U.S.A.* 112 H7
Big Cypress Swamp, *U.S.A.* 105 M5
Big Falls, *U.S.A.* 108 A8
Big Fork →, *U.S.A.* 108 A8
Big Horn Mts. = Bighorn Mts., *U.S.A.* 110 D10
Big Lake, *U.S.A.* 109 K4
Big Moose, *U.S.A.* 107 C10
Big Muddy Cr. →, *U.S.A.* 108 A2
Big Pine, *U.S.A.* 111 H4
Big Piney, *U.S.A.* 110 E8
Big Quill L., *Canada* 101 C8
Big Rapids, *U.S.A.* 104 D3
Big River, *Canada* 101 C7
Big Run, *U.S.A.* 106 F6
Big Sable Pt., *U.S.A.* 104 C2
Big Sand L., *Canada* 101 B9
Big Sandy, *U.S.A.* 110 B8
Big Sandy Cr. →, *U.S.A.* 108 F3
Big Sioux →, *U.S.A.* 108 D6
Big Spring, *U.S.A.* 109 J4
Big Springs, *U.S.A.* 108 E3
Big Stone City, *U.S.A.* 108 C6
Big Stone Gap, *U.S.A.* 105 G4
Big Stone L., *U.S.A.* 108 C6
Big Sur, *U.S.A.* 112 J5
Big Timber, *U.S.A.* 110 D9
Big Trout L., *Canada* 98 B1
Biğa, *Turkey* 66 C2
Bigadiç, *Turkey* 66 D3
Biganos, *France* 26 D3
Bigfork, *U.S.A.* 110 B6
Biggar, *Canada* 101 C7
Biggar, *U.K.* 14 F5
Bigge I., *Australia* 88 B4
Biggenden, *Australia* 91 D5
Biggs, *U.S.A.* 112 F5
Bighorn, *U.S.A.* 110 C10
Bighorn →, *U.S.A.* 110 C10
Bighorn Mts., *U.S.A.* 110 D10
Bignona, *Senegal* 78 C1
Bigorre, *France* 26 E4
Bigstone L., *Canada* 101 C9
Bigwa, *Tanzania* 82 D4
Bihać, *Bos.-H.* 33 D12
Bihar, *India* 63 G11
Bihar □, *India* 63 G11
Biharamulo, *Tanzania* 82 C3
Biharamulo □, *Tanzania* 82 C3
Bihor, Munţii, *Romania* 38 C5
Bijagós, Arquipélago dos, *Guinea-Biss.* 78 C1
Bijaipur, *India* 62 F7
Bijapur, *Karnataka, India* 60 L9
Bijapur, *Mad. P., India* 61 K12
Bījār, *Iran* 64 C5

Bijeljina, *Bos.-H.* 21 L9
Bijelo Polje, *Montenegro* 21 M9
Bijie, *China* 52 D5
Bijnor, *India* 62 E8
Bikaner, *India* 62 E5
Bikapur, *India* 63 F10
Bikeqi, *China* 50 D6
Bikfayyā, *Lebanon* 69 B4
Bikin, *Russia* 45 E14
Bikin →, *Russia* 48 A7
Bikini Atoll, *Pac. Oc.* 92 F8
Bikoué, *Cameroon* 79 E7
Bila Tserkva = Belaya Tserkov, *Ukraine* 40 G7
Bilara, *India* 62 F5
Bilaspur, *Mad. P., India* 63 H10
Bilaspur, *Punjab, India* 62 D7
Bilauk Taungdan, *Thailand* 58 F2
Bilbao, *Spain* 28 B2
Bilbeis, *Egypt* 76 H7
Bilbo = Bilbao, *Spain* 28 B2
Bilbor, *Romania* 38 B8
Bíldudalur, *Iceland* 8 D2
Bileća, *Bos.-H.* 21 N8
Bilecik, *Turkey* 66 C4
Bilecik □, *Turkey* 66 C4
Biłgoraj, *Poland* 20 E12
Bilibino, *Russia* 45 C17
Bilibiza, *Mozam.* 83 E5
Bilir, *Russia* 45 C14
Biliran I., *Phil.* 55 F6
Bill, *U.S.A.* 108 D2
Billabalong, *Australia* 89 E2
Billiluna, *Australia* 88 C4
Billingham, *U.K.* 12 C6
Billings, *U.S.A.* 110 D9
Billiton Is. = Belitung, *Indonesia* 56 E3
Billom, *France* 26 C7
Bilma, *Niger* 73 E7
Bilo Gora, *Croatia* 21 K7
Biloela, *Australia* 90 C5
Biloku, *Guyana* 121 C6
Biloxi, *U.S.A.* 109 K10
Bilpa Morea Claypan, *Australia* 90 D2
Bilthoven, *Neths.* 16 D6
Biltine, *Chad* 73 F9
Bilyana, *Australia* 90 B4
Bilyarsk, *Russia* 41 D17
Bilzen, *Belgium* 17 G7
Bima, *Indonesia* 57 F5
Bimban, *Egypt* 76 C3
Bimbila, *Ghana* 79 D5
Bimbo, *C.A.R.* 80 D3
Bimini Is., *Bahamas* 116 A4
Bin Xian, *Heilongjiang, China* 51 B14
Bin Xian, *Shaanxi, China* 50 G5
Bina-Etawah, *India* 62 G8
Bināb, *Iran* 65 B6
Binalbagan, *Phil.* 55 F5
Binalong, *Australia* 91 E4
Bīnālūd, Kūh-e, *Iran* 65 B8
Binatang, *Malaysia* 56 D4
Binbee, *Australia* 90 C4
Binche, *Belgium* 17 H4
Binchuan, *China* 52 E3
Binda, *Australia* 91 D4
Bindle, *Australia* 91 D4
Bindura, *Zimbabwe* 83 F3
Bingara, *N.S.W., Australia* 91 D5
Bingara, *Queens., Australia* 91 D3
Bingen, *Germany* 19 F3
Bingerville, *Ivory C.* 78 D4
Bingham, *U.S.A.* 99 C6
Bingham Canyon, *U.S.A.* 110 F7
Binghamton, *U.S.A.* 107 D9
Bingöl, *Turkey* 67 D9
Bingöl □, *Turkey* 67 D9
Bingöl Dağları, *Turkey* 67 D9
Binh Dinh = An Nhon, *Vietnam* 58 F7
Binh Khe, *Vietnam* 58 F7
Binh Son, *Vietnam* 58 E7
Binhai, *China* 51 G10
Binisatua, *Spain* 36 B11
Binjai, *Indonesia* 56 D1
Binnaway, *Australia* 91 E4
Binongko, *Indonesia* 57 F6
Binscarth, *Canada* 101 C8
Bintan, *Indonesia* 56 D2
Bintulu, *Malaysia* 56 D4
Bintuni, *Indonesia* 57 E8
Binyang, *China* 52 F7
Binz, *Germany* 18 A9
Binzert = Bizerte, *Tunisia* 75 A6
Bío Bío □, *Chile* 126 D1
Biograd, *Croatia* 33 E12
Bioko, *Eq. Guin.* 79 E6
Biougra, *Morocco* 74 B3
Bir, *India* 60 K9
Bir, Ras, *Djibouti* 77 E5
Bîr Abu Hashim, *Egypt* 76 C3
Bîr Abu M'nqar, *Egypt* 76 B2
Bîr Abu Muḥammad, *Egypt* 69 F3
Bi'r ad Dabbāghāt, *Jordan* 69 E4
Bîr Adal Deib, *Sudan* 76 C4
Bi'r al Butayyihāt, *Jordan* 69 F4
Bi'r al Mārī, *Jordan* 69 E4
Bi'r al Qattār, *Jordan* 69 F4
Bir Aouine, *Tunisia* 75 B6
Bîr 'Asal, *Egypt* 76 B3
Bir Autrun, *Sudan* 76 D2
Bîr Beiḍa, *Egypt* 69 E3
Bîr Diqnash, *Egypt* 76 A2
Bir el Abbes, *Algeria* 74 C3
Bîr el 'Abd, *Egypt* 69 D2
Bir el Ater, *Algeria* 75 B6
Bîr el Basur, *Egypt* 76 B2
Bîr el Biarât, *Egypt* 69 F3
Bîr el Duweidar, *Egypt* 69 E1
Bîr el Garârât, *Egypt* 69 D2
Bîr el Gellaz, *Egypt* 76 A2
Bîr el Heisi, *Egypt* 69 F3
Bîr el Jafir, *Egypt* 69 E1
Bîr el Mâlḥi, *Egypt* 69 E2
Bîr el Shaqqa, *Egypt* 76 A2
Bîr el Thamâda, *Egypt* 69 E2
Bîr Fuad, *Egypt* 76 A2
Bîr Gebeil Ḥiṣn, *Egypt* 69 E2
Bi'r Ghadīr, *Syria* 69 A6
Bîr Haimur, *Egypt* 76 C3
Bîr Ḥasana, *Egypt* 69 E2
Bi'r Jadīd, *Iraq* 64 C4
Bir Jdid, *Morocco* 74 B3
Bîr Kanayis, *Egypt* 76 C3
Bîr Kaseiba, *Egypt* 69 E2
Bîr Kerawein, *Egypt* 76 B2
Bîr Lahfân, *Egypt* 69 D2
Bir Lahrache, *Algeria* 75 B6
Bîr Madkûr, *Egypt* 69 E1
Bîr Maql, *Egypt* 76 C3
Bîr Misaha, *Egypt* 76 C2
Bir Mogrein, *Mauritania* 74 C2
Bîr Murr, *Egypt* 76 C3
Bi'r Muṭribah, *Kuwait* 64 D5
Bîr Nakheila, *Egypt* 76 C3
Bîr Qaṭia, *Egypt* 69 E1
Bîr Qatrani, *Egypt* 76 A2
Bîr Ranga, *Egypt* 76 C4
Bîr Sahara, *Egypt* 76 C2
Bîr Seiyâla, *Egypt* 76 B3
Bir Semguine, *Morocco* 74 B3
Bîr Shalatein, *Egypt* 76 C4
Bîr Shebb, *Egypt* 76 C2
Bîr Shût, *Egypt* 76 C4
Bîr Terfawi, *Egypt* 76 C2
Bîr Umm Qubûr, *Egypt* 76 C3
Bîr Ungât, *Egypt* 76 C3
Bîr Za'farâna, *Egypt* 76 J8
Bîr Zeidûn, *Egypt* 76 B3
Bira, *Indonesia* 57 E8
Bîra, *Romania* 38 B10
Biramféro, *Guinea* 78 C3
Birao, *C.A.R.* 73 F9
Birawa, *Zaïre* 82 C2
Bîrca, *Romania* 38 F6
Birch Hills, *Canada* 101 C7
Birch I., *Canada* 101 C9
Birch L., *N.W.T., Canada* 100 A5
Birch L., *Ont., Canada* 98 B1
Birch L., *U.S.A.* 98 C1
Birch Mts., *Canada* 100 B6
Birch River, *Canada* 101 C8
Birchip, *Australia* 91 F3
Bird, *Canada* 101 B10
Bird City, *U.S.A.* 108 F4
Bird I. = Aves, I. de, *W. Indies* 117 C7
Bird I., *S. Africa* 84 E2
Birdaard, *Neths.* 16 B7
Birdlip, *U.K.* 13 F5
Birdsville, *Australia* 90 D2
Birdum, *Australia* 88 C5
Birein, *Israel* 69 E3
Bireuen, *Indonesia* 56 C1
Birifo, *Gambia* 78 C2
Birigui, *Brazil* 127 A5
Birkenfeld, *Germany* 19 F3
Birkenhead, *U.K.* 12 D4
Birket Qârûn, *Egypt* 76 J7
Birkhadem, *Algeria* 75 A5
Bîrlad, *Romania* 38 C10
Birmingham, *U.K.* 13 E6
Birmingham, *U.S.A.* 105 J2
Birmitrapur, *India* 61 H14
Birni Ngaouré, *Niger* 79 C5
Birni Nkonni, *Niger* 79 C6
Birnin Gwari, *Nigeria* 79 C6
Birnin Kebbi, *Nigeria* 79 C5
Birnin Kudu, *Nigeria* 79 C6
Birobidzhan, *Russia* 45 E14
Birr, *Ireland* 15 C4
Birrie →, *Australia* 91 D4
Birs →, *Switz.* 22 B5
Birsilpur, *India* 62 E5
Birsk, *Russia* 44 D6
Birtin, *Romania* 38 C5
Birtle, *Canada* 101 C8
Birur, *India* 60 N9
Biryuchiy, *Ukraine* 42 C6
Biržai, *Lithuania* 40 C4
Bîrzava, *Romania* 38 C4
Birzebugga, *Malta* 37 D2
Bisa, *Indonesia* 57 E7
Bisáccia, *Italy* 35 A8
Bisacquino, *Italy* 34 E6
Bisalpur, *India* 63 E8
Bisbee, *U.S.A.* 111 L9
Biscarrosse et de Parentis, Étang de, *France* 26 D2
Biscay, B. of, *Atl. Oc.* 6 F5
Biscayne B., *U.S.A.* 105 N5
Biscéglie, *Italy* 35 A9
Bischofshofen, *Austria* 21 H3
Bischofswerda, *Germany* 18 D10
Bischofszell, *Switz.* 23 B8
Bischwiller, *France* 25 D14
Biscoe Bay, *Antarctica* 5 D13
Biscoe Is., *Antarctica* 5 C17
Biscostasing, *Canada* 98 C3
Biscucuy, *Venezuela* 120 B4
Biševo, *Croatia* 33 F13
Bisha, *Eritrea* 77 D4
Bishah, W. →, *Si. Arabia* 76 C5
Bishan, *China* 52 C6
Bishkek, *Kirghizia* 44 E8
Bishnupur, *India* 63 H12
Bisho, *S. Africa* 85 E4
Bishop, *Calif., U.S.A.* 111 H4
Bishop, *Tex., U.S.A.* 109 M6
Bishop Auckland, *U.K.* 12 C6
Bishop's Falls, *Canada* 99 C8
Bishop's Stortford, *U.K.* 13 F8
Bisignano, *Italy* 35 C9
Bisina, L., *Uganda* 82 B3
Biskra, *Algeria* 75 B6
Bislig, *Phil.* 57 C7
Bismarck, *U.S.A.* 108 B4
Bismarck Arch., *Papua N. G.* 92 H6
Bismark, *Germany* 18 C7
Biso, *Uganda* 82 B3
Bison, *U.S.A.* 108 C3
Bīsotūn, *Iran* 64 C5
Bispfors, *Sweden* 8 E14
Bispgården, *Sweden* 10 A10
Bissagos = Bijagós, Arquipélago dos, *Guinea-Biss.* 78 C1
Bissau, *Guinea-Biss.* 78 C1
Bissett, *Canada* 101 C9
Bissikrima, *Guinea* 78 C2
Bistcho L., *Canada* 100 B5
Bistreţu, *Romania* 38 F6
Bistrica = Ilirska-Bistrica, *Slovenia* 33 C11
Bistriţa, *Romania* 38 B7
Bistriţa →, *Romania* 38 C9
Bistriţei, Munţii, *Romania* 38 B8
Biswan, *India* 63 F9
Bitam, *Gabon* 80 D2
Bitburg, *Germany* 19 F2
Bitche, *France* 25 C14
Bithynia, *Turkey* 66 C4
Bitkine, *Chad* 73 F8
Bitlis, *Turkey* 67 D10
Bitlis □, *Turkey* 67 D10
Bitola, *Macedonia* 39 H4
Bitolj = Bitola, *Macedonia* 39 H4
Bitonto, *Italy* 35 A9
Bitter Creek, *U.S.A.* 110 F9
Bitter L. = Buheirat-Murrat-el-Kubra, *Egypt* 76 H8
Bitterfeld, *Germany* 18 D8
Bitterfontein, *S. Africa* 84 E2
Bitterroot →, *U.S.A.* 110 C6
Bitterroot Range, *U.S.A.* 110 D6
Bitterwater, *U.S.A.* 112 J6
Bitti, *Italy* 34 B2
Bittou, *Burkina Faso* 79 C4
Biu, *Nigeria* 79 C7
Bivolari, *Romania* 38 B10
Biwa-Ko, *Japan* 49 G8
Biwabik, *U.S.A.* 108 B8
Bixad, *Romania* 38 B6
Biyang, *China* 50 H7
Biysk, *Russia* 44 D9
Bizana, *S. Africa* 85 E4
Bizen, *Japan* 49 G7
Bizerte, *Tunisia* 75 A6
Bjargtangar, *Iceland* 8 D1
Bjelasica, *Montenegro* 21 N9
Bjelovar, *Croatia* 21 K6
Bjerringbro, *Denmark* 11 H3
Bjørnøya, *Arctic* 4 B8
Bjuv, *Sweden* 11 H6
Blace, *Serbia* 21 M11
Black = Da →, *Vietnam* 58 B5
Black →, *Canada* 106 B5
Black →, *Ark., U.S.A.* 109 H9
Black →, *N.Y., U.S.A.* 107 C8
Black →, *Wis., U.S.A.* 108 D9
Black Diamond, *Canada* 100 C6
Black Forest = Schwarzwald, *Germany* 19 H4
Black Hills, *U.S.A.* 108 C3
Black I., *Canada* 101 C9
Black L., *Canada* 101 B7
Black L., *U.S.A.* 104 C3
Black Mesa, *U.S.A.* 109 G3
Black Mt. = Mynydd Du, *U.K.* 13 F4
Black Mts., *U.K.* 13 F4
Black Range, *U.S.A.* 111 K10
Black River, *Jamaica* 116 C4
Black River Falls, *U.S.A.* 108 C9
Black Sea, *Europe* 42 E6
Black Volta →, *Africa* 78 D4
Black Warrior →, *U.S.A.* 105 J2
Blackall, *Australia* 90 C4
Blackball, *N.Z.* 87 K3
Blackbull, *Australia* 90 B3
Blackburn, *U.K.* 12 D5
Blackduck, *U.S.A.* 108 B7
Blackfoot, *U.S.A.* 110 E7
Blackfoot →, *U.S.A.* 110 C7
Blackfoot River Reservoir, *U.S.A.* 110 E8
Blackie, *Canada* 100 C6
Blackpool, *U.K.* 12 D4
Blackriver, *U.S.A.* 106 B1
Blacks Harbour, *Canada* 99 C6
Blacksburg, *U.S.A.* 104 G5
Blacksod B., *Ireland* 15 B2
Blackstone, *U.S.A.* 104 G6
Blackstone →, *Canada* 100 A4
Blackstone Ra., *Australia* 89 E4
Blackville, *Canada* 99 C6
Blackwater, *Australia* 90 C4
Blackwater →, *Ireland* 15 E4
Blackwater →, *U.K.* 15 B5
Blackwater Cr. →, *Australia* 91 D3
Blackwell, *U.S.A.* 109 G6
Blackwells Corner, *U.S.A.* 113 K7
Bladel, *Neths.* 17 F6
Blaenau Ffestiniog, *U.K.* 12 E4
Blagodarnoye, *Russia* 43 D10
Blagoevgrad, *Bulgaria* 39 G6
Blagoveshchensk, *Russia* 45 D13
Blain, *France* 24 E5
Blaine, *U.S.A.* 112 B4
Blaine Lake, *Canada* 101 C7
Blainville-sur-l'Eau, *France* 25 D13
Blair, *U.S.A.* 108 E6
Blair Athol, *Australia* 90 C4
Blair Atholl, *U.K.* 14 E5
Blairgowrie, *U.K.* 14 E5
Blairmore, *Canada* 100 D6
Blairsden, *U.S.A.* 112 F6
Blairsville, *U.S.A.* 106 F5
Blaj, *Romania* 38 C6
Blake Pt., *U.S.A.* 108 A10
Blakely, *U.S.A.* 105 K3
Blâmont, *France* 25 D13
Blanc, C., *Tunisia* 75 A6
Blanc, Mont, *Alps* 27 C10
Blanca, B., *Argentina* 128 A4
Blanca Peak, *U.S.A.* 111 H11
Blanchard, *U.S.A.* 109 H6
Blanche, C., *Australia* 91 E1
Blanche, L., *S. Austral., Australia* 91 D2
Blanche, L., *W. Austral., Australia* 88 D3
Blanco, *S. Africa* 84 E3
Blanco, *U.S.A.* 109 K5
Blanco →, *Argentina* 126 C2
Blanco, C., *U.S.A.* 110 E1
Blanco, C., *Costa Rica* 116 E2
Blanco, C., *Spain* 36 B9
Blanda →, *Iceland* 8 D4
Blandford Forum, *U.K.* 13 G5
Blanding, *U.S.A.* 111 H9
Blanes, *Spain* 28 D7
Blangy-sur-Bresle, *France* 25 C8
Blanice →, *Czech.* 20 F4
Blankenberge, *Belgium* 17 F2
Blankenburg, *Germany* 18 D6
Blanquefort, *France* 26 D3
Blanquillo, *Uruguay* 127 C4
Blansko, *Czech.* 20 F6
Blantyre, *Malawi* 83 F4
Blaricum, *Neths.* 16 D6
Blarney, *Ireland* 15 E3
Blato, *Croatia* 33 F13
Blatten, *Switz.* 22 D5
Blaubeuren, *Germany* 19 G5
Blåvands Huk, *Denmark* 9 J10
Blaydon, *U.K.* 12 C6
Blaye, *France* 26 C3
Blaye-les-Mines, *France* 26 D6
Blayney, *Australia* 91 E4
Blaze, Pt., *Australia* 88 B5
Bleckede, *Germany* 18 B6
Bled, *Slovenia* 33 B11
Blednaya, Gora, *Russia* 44 B7
Bléharis, *Belgium* 17 G2
Blejeşti, *Romania* 38 E8
Blekinge län □, *Sweden* 9 H13
Blenheim, *Canada* 106 D2
Blenheim, *N.Z.* 87 J4
Bléone →, *France* 27 D10
Blerick, *Neths.* 17 F8
Bletchley, *U.K.* 13 F7
Blida, *Algeria* 75 A5
Blidet Amor, *Algeria* 75 B6
Blidö, *Sweden* 10 E12
Bligh Sound, *N.Z.* 87 L1
Blind River, *Canada* 98 C3
Blinnenhorn, *Switz.* 23 D6
Blitar, *Indonesia* 57 H15
Blitta, *Togo* 79 D5
Block I., *U.S.A.* 107 E13
Block Island Sd., *U.S.A.* 107 E13
Blodgett Iceberg Tongue, *Antarctica* 5 C9
Bloemendaal, *Neths.* 16 D5
Bloemfontein, *S. Africa* 84 D4
Bloemhof, *S. Africa* 84 D4
Blois, *France* 24 E8
Blokziji, *Neths.* 16 C7
Blönduós, *Iceland* 8 D3
Bloodvein →, *Canada* 101 C9
Bloody Foreland, *Ireland* 15 A3
Bloomer, *U.S.A.* 108 C9
Bloomfield, *Australia* 90 B4
Bloomfield, *Canada* 106 C7
Bloomfield, *Iowa, U.S.A.* 108 E8
Bloomfield, *N. Mex., U.S.A.* 111 H10
Bloomfield, *Nebr., U.S.A.* 108 D6
Bloomington, *Ill., U.S.A.* 108 E10
Bloomington, *Ind., U.S.A.* 104 F2
Bloomsburg, *U.S.A.* 107 F8
Blora, *Indonesia* 57 G14
Blossburg, *U.S.A.* 106 E7
Blouberg, *S. Africa* 85 C4
Blountstown, *U.S.A.* 105 K3
Bludenz, *Austria* 19 H5
Blue Island, *U.S.A.* 104 E2
Blue Lake, *U.S.A.* 110 F2
Blue Mesa Reservoir, *U.S.A.* 111 G10
Blue Mts., *Oreg., U.S.A.* 110 D4
Blue Mts., *Pa., U.S.A.* 107 F8
Blue Mud B., *Australia* 90 A2
Blue Nile = An Nîl el Azraq □, *Sudan* 77 E3
Blue Nile = Nîl el Azraq →, *Sudan* 77 D3
Blue Rapids, *U.S.A.* 108 F6
Blue Ridge Mts., *U.S.A.* 105 G5
Blue Stack Mts., *Ireland* 15 B3
Blueberry →, *Canada* 100 B4
Bluefield, *U.S.A.* 104 G5
Bluefields, *Nic.* 116 D3
Bluff, *Australia* 90 C4
Bluff, *N.Z.* 87 M2
Bluff, *U.S.A.* 111 H9
Bluff Knoll, *Australia* 89 F2
Bluff Pt., *Australia* 89 E1
Bluffton, *U.S.A.* 104 E3
Blumenau, *Brazil* 127 B6
Blümisalphorn, *Switz.* 22 D5
Blunt, *U.S.A.* 108 C4
Bly, *U.S.A.* 110 E3
Blyth, *Canada* 106 C3
Blyth, *U.K.* 12 B6
Blyth Bridge, *U.K.* 12 E5
Blythe, *U.S.A.* 113 M12
Bø, *Norway* 10 E3
Bo, *S. Leone* 78 D2
Bo Duc, *Vietnam* 59 G6
Bo Hai, *China* 51 E10
Bo Xian, *China* 50 H8
Boa Esperança, *Brazil* 121 C5
Boa Nova, *Brazil* 123 D3
Boa Viagem, *Brazil* 122 C4
Boa Vista, *Brazil* 121 C5
Boac, *Phil.* 55 E4
Boaco, *Nic.* 116 D2
Bo'ai, *China* 50 G7
Boal, *Spain* 30 B4
Boardman, *U.S.A.* 106 E4
Boatman, *Australia* 91 D4
Bobadah, *Australia* 91 E4
Bobai, *China* 52 F7
Bobbili, *India* 61 K13
Bóbbio, *Italy* 32 D6
Bobcaygeon, *Canada* 98 D4
Böblingen, *Germany* 19 G5
Bobo-Dioulasso, *Burkina Faso* 78 C4
Boboc, *Romania* 38 D9
Bobonaza →, *Ecuador* 120 D2
Bobov Dol, *Bulgaria* 38 G5
Bóbr →, *Poland* 20 C5
Bobraomby, Tanjon' i, *Madag.* 85 A8
Bobrinets, *Ukraine* 42 B5
Bobrov, *Russia* 41 F12
Bobruysk, *Belorussia* 40 E6
Bobures, *Venezuela* 120 B3
Boca de Drago, *Venezuela* 121 A5
Bôca do Acre, *Brazil* 124 B4
Bôca do Jari, *Brazil* 121 D7
Bôca do Moaco, *Brazil* 124 B4
Boca Grande, *Venezuela* 121 B5
Boca Raton, *U.S.A.* 105 M5
Bocaiúva, *Brazil* 123 E3
Bocanda, *Ivory C.* 78 D4
Bocaranga, *C.A.R.* 73 G8
Bocas del Toro, *Panama* 116 E3
Boceguillas, *Spain* 28 D1
Bochnia, *Poland* 20 F10
Bocholt, *Belgium* 17 F7
Bocholt, *Germany* 18 D2
Bochum, *Germany* 18 D3
Bockenem, *Germany* 18 C6
Bocognano, *France* 27 F13
Boconó, *Venezuela* 120 B3
Boconó →, *Venezuela* 120 B4
Bocoyna, *Mexico* 114 B3
Bocq →, *Belgium* 17 H5
Boda, *C.A.R.* 80 D3
Bodaybo, *Russia* 45 D12
Boddington, *Australia* 89 F2
Bodega Bay, *U.S.A.* 112 G3
Bodegraven, *Neths.* 16 D5
Boden, *Sweden* 8 D16
Bodensee, *Europe* 23 A8
Bodenteich, *Germany* 18 C6
Bodhan, *India* 60 K10
Bodinga, *Nigeria* 79 C6
Bodio, *Switz.* 23 D7
Bodmin, *U.K.* 13 G3
Bodmin Moor, *U.K.* 13 G3
Bodoquena, Serra da, *Brazil* 125 E6
Bodrog →, *Hungary* 21 G11
Bodrum, *Turkey* 66 E2
Boechout, *Belgium* 17 F5
Boegoebergdam, *S. Africa* 84 D3
Boekelo, *Neths.* 16 D9
Boelenslaan, *Neths.* 16 B8
Boën, *France* 27 C8
Boende, *Zaïre* 80 E4
Boerne, *U.S.A.* 109 L5
Boertange, *Neths.* 16 B10

Boezinge, *Belgium* 17 G1
Boffa, *Guinea* 78 C2
Bogalusa, *U.S.A.* 109 K10
Bogan Gate, *Australia* 91 E4
Bogantungan, *Australia* 90 C4
Bogata, *U.S.A.* 109 J7
Bogatić, *Serbia, Yug.* 21 L9
Boğazlıyan, *Turkey* 66 D6
Bogense, *Denmark* 11 J4
Boggabilla, *Australia* 91 D5
Boggabri, *Australia* 91 E5
Boggeragh Mts., *Ireland* 15 D3
Bognor Regis, *U.K.* 13 G7
Bogø, *Denmark* 11 K6
Bogo, *Phil.* 55 F6
Bogodukhov, *Ukraine* 42 A6
Bogong, Mt., *Australia* 91 F4
Bogor, *Indonesia* 57 G12
Bogoroditsk, *Russia* 41 E11
Bogorodsk, *Russia* 41 C13
Bogorodskoye, *Russia* 45 D15
Bogoso, *Ghana* 78 D4
Bogotá, *Colombia* 120 C3
Bogotol, *Russia* 44 D9
Bogra, *Bangla.* 61 G16
Boguchany, *Russia* 45 D10
Boguchar, *Russia* 43 B9
Bogué, *Mauritania* 78 B2
Boguslav, *Ukraine* 42 B4
Bohain-en-Vermandois, *France* 25 C10
Bohemia Downs, *Australia* 88 C4
Bohemian Forest = Böhmerwald, *Germany* 19 F8
Bohena Cr. →, *Australia* 91 E4
Bohinjska Bistrica, *Slovenia* 33 B11
Böhmerwald, *Germany* 19 F8
Bohmte, *Germany* 18 C4
Bohol, *Phil.* 55 G6
Bohol Sea, *Phil.* 57 C6
Bohotleh, *Somali Rep.* 68 F4
Boi, *Nigeria* 79 D6
Boi, Pta. de, *Brazil* 127 A6
Boiaçu, *Brazil* 121 D5
Boiano, *Italy* 35 A7
Boileau, C., *Australia* 88 C3
Boipeba, I. de, *Brazil* 123 D4
Bois →, *Brazil* 123 E1
Boischot, *Belgium* 17 F5
Boise, *U.S.A.* 110 E5
Boise City, *U.S.A.* 109 G3
Boissevain, *Canada* 101 D8
Boite →, *Italy* 33 B9
Boitzenburg, *Germany* 18 B9
Boizenburg, *Germany* 18 B6
Bojador C., *W. Sahara* 74 C2
Bojnūrd, *Iran* 65 B8
Bojonegoro, *Indonesia* 57 G14
Boju, *Nigeria* 79 D6
Boka Kotorska, *Montenegro, Yug.* 21 N8
Bokala, *Ivory C.* 78 D4
Boké, *Guinea* 78 C2
Bokhara →, *Australia* 91 D4
Bokkos, *Nigeria* 79 D6
Boknafjorden, *Norway* 9 G8
Bokoro, *Chad* 73 F8
Bokote, *Zaïre* 80 E4
Boksitogorsk, *Russia* 40 B8
Bokungu, *Zaïre* 80 E4
Bol, *Chad* 73 F7
Bol, *Croatia* 33 E13
Bolama, *Guinea-Biss.* 78 C1
Bolan Pass, *Pakistan* 60 E5
Bolaños →, *Mexico* 114 C4
Bolbec, *France* 24 C7
Boldājī, *Iran* 65 D6
Boldeşti, *Romania* 38 D9
Bole, *China* 54 B3
Bole, *Ethiopia* 77 F4
Bolekhov, *Ukraine* 40 G3
Bolesławiec, *Poland* 20 D5
Bolgatanga, *Ghana* 79 C4
Bolgrad, *Ukraine* 42 D3
Boli, *Sudan* 77 F2
Bolinao, *Phil.* 55 C3
Bolinao C., *Phil.* 57 A5
Bolívar, *Argentina* 126 D3
Bolívar, *Antioquía, Colombia* 120 B2
Bolívar, *Cauca, Colombia* 120 C2
Bolívar, *Peru* 124 B2
Bolivar, *Mo., U.S.A.* 109 G8
Bolivar, *Tenn., U.S.A.* 109 H10
Bolívar □, *Colombia* 120 B3
Bolívar □, *Ecuador* 120 D2
Bolívar □, *Venezuela* 121 B5
Bolivia ■, *S. Amer.* 125 D5
Bolivian Plateau, *S. Amer.* 118 D3
Bolkhov, *Russia* 41 E10
Bollène, *France* 27 D8
Bollnäs, *Sweden* 10 C10
Bollon, *Australia* 91 D4
Bollstabruk, *Sweden* 10 A11
Bollullos, *Spain* 31 H4
Bolobo, *Zaïre* 80 E3
Bologna, *Italy* 33 D8
Bologne, *France* 25 D12
Bologoye, *Russia* 40 C9
Bolomba, *Zaïre* 80 D3
Bolonchenticul, *Mexico* 115 D7
Bolong, *Phil.* 57 C6
Boloven, Cao Nguyen, *Laos* 58 E6
Bolpur, *India* 63 H12
Bolsena, *Italy* 33 F8
Bolsena, L. di, *Italy* 33 F8
Bolshaya Glushitsa, *Russia* 41 E17
Bolshaya Martynovka, *Russia* 43 C9
Bolshaya Vradiyevka, *Ukraine* 42 C4
Bolshereche, *Russia* 44 D8
Bolshevik, Ostrov, *Russia* 45 B11
Bolshoi Kavkas, *Asia* 43 E11
Bolshoy Anyuy →, *Russia* 45 C17
Bolshoy Atlym, *Russia* 44 C7
Bolshoy Begichev, Ostrov, *Russia* 45 B12
Bolshoy Lyakhovskiy, Ostrov, *Russia* 45 B15
Bolshoy Tokmak, *Ukraine* 42 C6
Bol'shoy Tyuters, *Estonia* 40 B5
Bolsward, *Neths.* 16 B7
Boltaña, *Spain* 28 C5
Boltigen, *Switz.* 22 C4
Bolton, *Canada* 106 C5
Bolton, *U.K.* 12 D5
Bolu, *Turkey* 66 C4
Bolu □, *Turkey* 66 C4
Boluo, *China* 53 F10
Bolvadin, *Turkey* 66 D4
Bolzano, *Italy* 33 B8
Bom Comércio, *Brazil* 125 B4
Bom Conselho, *Brazil* 122 C4
Bom Despacho, *Brazil* 123 E2
Bom Jesus, *Brazil* 122 C3
Bom Jesus da Gurguéia, Serra, *Brazil* 122 C3
Bom Jesus da Lapa, *Brazil* 123 D3
Boma, *Zaïre* 80 F2
Bomaderry, *Australia* 91 E5
Bombala, *Australia* 91 F4
Bombarral, *Portugal* 31 F1
Bombay, *India* 60 K8
Bomboma, *Zaïre* 80 D3
Bombombwa, *Zaïre* 82 B2
Bomi Hills, *Liberia* 78 D2
Bomili, *Zaïre* 82 B2
Bommel, *Neths.* 16 E4
Bomokandi →, *Zaïre* 82 B2
Bomongo, *Zaïre* 80 D3
Bomu →, *C.A.R.* 80 D4
Bon, C., *Tunisia* 75 A7
Bon Sar Pa, *Vietnam* 58 F6
Bonaduz, *Switz.* 23 C8
Bonaire, *Neth. Ant.* 117 D6
Bonang, *Australia* 91 F4
Bonanza, *Nic.* 116 D3
Bonaparte Arch., *Australia* 88 B3
Boñar, *Spain* 30 C5
Bonaventure, *Canada* 99 C6
Bonavista, *Canada* 99 C9
Bonavista, C., *Canada* 99 C9
Bonawan, *Phil.* 55 G5
Bondeno, *Italy* 33 D8
Bondo, *Zaïre* 82 B1
Bondoukou, *Ivory C.* 78 D4
Bondowoso, *Indonesia* 57 G15
Bone, Teluk, *Indonesia* 57 E6
Bone Rate, *Indonesia* 57 F6
Bone Rate, Kepulauan, *Indonesia* 57 F6
Bonefro, *Italy* 35 A7
Bo'ness, *U.K.* 14 E5
Bong Son = Hoai Nhon, *Vietnam* 58 E7
Bongabong, *Phil.* 55 E4
Bongandanga, *Zaïre* 80 D4
Bongor, *Chad* 73 F8
Bongouanou, *Ivory C.* 78 D4
Bonham, *U.S.A.* 109 J6
Bonheiden, *Belgium* 17 F5
Bonifacio, *France* 27 G13
Bonifacio, Bouches de, *Medit. S.* 34 A2
Bonin Is. = Ogasawara Gunto, *Pac. Oc.* 92 E6
Bonke, *Ethiopia* 77 F4
Bonn, *Germany* 18 E3
Bonnat, *France* 26 B5
Bonne Terre, *U.S.A.* 109 G9
Bonners Ferry, *U.S.A.* 110 B5
Bonnétable, *France* 24 D7
Bonneuil-Matours, *France* 24 F7
Bonneval, *France* 24 D8
Bonneville, *France* 27 B10
Bonney, L., *Australia* 91 F3
Bonnie Downs, *Australia* 90 C3
Bonnie Rock, *Australia* 89 F2
Bonny, *Nigeria* 79 E6
Bonny →, *Nigeria* 79 E6
Bonny, Bight of, *Africa* 79 E6
Bonny-sur-Loire, *France* 25 E9
Bonnyville, *Canada* 101 C6
Bonoi, *Indonesia* 57 E9
Bonorva, *Italy* 34 B1
Bonsall, *U.S.A.* 113 M9
Bontang, *Indonesia* 56 D5
Bonthain, *Indonesia* 57 F5
Bonthe, *S. Leone* 78 D2
Bontoc, *Phil.* 55 C4
Bonyeri, *Ghana* 78 D4
Bonython Ra., *Australia* 88 D4
Bookabie, *Australia* 89 F5
Booker, *U.S.A.* 109 G4
Boolaboolka L., *Australia* 91 E3
Booligal, *Australia* 91 E3
Boom, *Belgium* 17 F4
Boonah, *Australia* 91 D5
Boone, *Iowa, U.S.A.* 108 D8
Boone, *N.C., U.S.A.* 105 G5
Booneville, *Ark., U.S.A.* 109 H8
Booneville, *Miss., U.S.A.* 105 H1
Boonville, *Calif., U.S.A.* 112 F3
Boonville, *Ind., U.S.A.* 104 F2
Boonville, *Mo., U.S.A.* 108 F8
Boonville, *N.Y., U.S.A.* 107 C9
Boorindal, *Australia* 91 E4
Boorowa, *Australia* 91 E4
Boothia, Gulf of, *Canada* 97 A11
Boothia Pen., *Canada* 96 A10
Bootle, *Cumb., U.K.* 12 C4
Bootle, *Mersey., U.K.* 12 D4
Booué, *Gabon* 80 E2
Bophuthatswana □, *S. Africa* 84 D4
Boppard, *Germany* 19 E3
Boquerón □, *Paraguay* 125 E5
Boquete, *Panama* 116 E3
Boquilla, Presa de la, *Mexico* 114 B3
Boquillas del Carmen, *Mexico* 114 B4
Bor, *Czech.* 20 F2
Bor, *Serbia, Yug.* 21 L12
Bôr, *Sudan* 77 F3
Bor, *Turkey* 66 E6
Bor Mashash, *Israel* 69 D3
Boradā →, *Syria* 69 B5
Borah Peak, *U.S.A.* 110 D7
Borama, *Somali Rep.* 68 F3
Borang, *Sudan* 77 G3
Borås, *Sweden* 11 G6
Borāzjān, *Iran* 65 D6
Borba, *Brazil* 121 D6
Borba, *Portugal* 31 G3
Borborema, Planalto da, *Brazil* 122 C4
Borçka, *Turkey* 43 F9
Borculo, *Neths.* 16 D9
Bord Khūn-e Now, *Iran* 65 D6
Borda, C., *Australia* 91 F2
Bordeaux, *France* 26 D3
Borden, *Australia* 89 F2
Borden, *Canada* 99 C7
Borden I., *Canada* 4 B2
Borders □, *U.K.* 14 F6
Bordertown, *Australia* 91 F3
Borðeyri, *Iceland* 8 D3
Bordighera, *Italy* 32 E4
Bordj bou Arreridj, *Algeria* 75 A5
Bordj Bourguiba, *Tunisia* 75 B7
Bordj el Hobra, *Algeria* 75 B5
Bordj Fly Ste. Marie, *Algeria* 74 C4
Bordj-in-Eker, *Algeria* 75 D6
Bordj Menaiel, *Algeria* 75 A5
Bordj Messouda, *Algeria* 75 B6
Bordj Nili, *Algeria* 75 B5
Bordj Omar Driss, *Algeria* 75 C6
Bordj-Tarat, *Algeria* 75 C6
Bordj Zelfana, *Algeria* 75 B5
Borensberg, *Sweden* 11 F9
Borgå, *Finland* 9 F18
Borgarnes, *Iceland* 8 D3
Børgefjellet, *Norway* 8 D12
Borger, *Neths.* 16 C9
Borger, *U.S.A.* 109 H4
Borgerhout, *Belgium* 17 F4
Borghamn, *Sweden* 11 F8
Borgholm, *Sweden* 9 H14
Bórgia, *Italy* 35 D9
Borgloon, *Belgium* 17 G6
Borgo San Dalmazzo, *Italy* 32 D4
Borgo San Lorenzo, *Italy* 33 E8
Borgo Valsugano, *Italy* 33 B8
Borgomanero, *Italy* 32 C5
Borgonovo Val Tidone, *Italy* 32 C6
Borgorose, *Italy* 33 F10
Borgosésia, *Italy* 32 C5
Borgvattnet, *Sweden* 10 A9
Borikhane, *Laos* 58 C4
Borislav, *Ukraine* 40 G3
Borisoglebsk, *Russia* 41 F13
Borisoglebskiy, *Russia* 41 C13
Borisov, *Belorussia* 40 D6
Borispol, *Ukraine* 40 F7
Borja, *Peru* 120 D2
Borja, *Spain* 28 D3
Borjas Blancas, *Spain* 28 D5
Borken, *Germany* 18 D2
Borkou, *Chad* 73 E8
Borkum, *Germany* 18 B2
Borlänge, *Sweden* 9 F13
Borley, C., *Antarctica* 5 C5
Bormida →, *Italy* 32 D5
Bórmio, *Italy* 32 B7
Born, *Neths.* 17 F7
Borna, *Germany* 18 D8
Borndiep, *Neths.* 16 B7
Borne, *Neths.* 16 D9
Bornem, *Belgium* 17 F4
Borneo, *E. Indies* 56 D5
Bornholm, *Denmark* 9 J13
Borno □, *Nigeria* 79 C7
Bornos, *Spain* 31 J5
Bornu Yassa, *Nigeria* 79 C7
Borobudur, *Indonesia* 57 G14
Borodino, *Russia* 40 D9
Borogontsy, *Russia* 45 C14
Boromo, *Burkina Faso* 78 C4
Boron, *U.S.A.* 113 L9
Borongan, *Phil.* 55 F6
Bororen, *Australia* 90 C5
Borotangba Mts., *C.A.R.* 77 F1
Borovan, *Bulgaria* 38 F6
Borovichi, *Russia* 40 B8
Borovsk, *Russia* 41 D10
Borrego Springs, *U.S.A.* 113 M10
Borriol, *Spain* 28 E4
Borroloola, *Australia* 90 B2
Borşa, *Romania* 38 B7
Borssele, *Neths.* 17 F3
Bort-les-Orgues, *France* 26 C6
Borth, *U.K.* 13 E3
Borujerd, *Iran* 65 C6
Borzhomi, *Georgia* 43 F10
Borzna, *Ukraine* 40 F8
Borzya, *Russia* 45 D12
Bosa, *Italy* 34 B1
Bosanska Dubica, *Bos.-H.* 33 C13
Bosanska Gradiška, *Bos.-H.* 21 K7
Bosanska Kostajnica, *Bos.-H.* 33 C13
Bosanska Krupa, *Bos.-H.* 33 D13
Bosanski Novi, *Bos.-H.* 33 C13
Bosanski Šamac, *Bos.-H.* 21 K8
Bosansko Grahovo, *Bos.-H.* 33 D13
Bosansko Petrovac, *Bos.-H.* 33 D13
Bosaso, *Somali Rep.* 68 E4
Boscastle, *U.K.* 13 G3
Boscotrecase, *Italy* 35 B7
Bose, *China* 52 F6
Boshan, *China* 51 F9
Boshoek, *S. Africa* 84 D4
Boshof, *S. Africa* 84 D4
Boshrūyeh, *Iran* 65 C8
Bosilegrad, *Serbia, Yug.* 21 N12
Boskoop, *Neths.* 16 D5
Bosna →, *Bos.-H.* 21 K8
Bosna i Hercegovina = Bosnia-Herzegovina ■, *Europe* 21 L7
Bosnia-Herzegovina ■, *Europe* 21 L7
Bosnik, *Indonesia* 57 E9
Bosobolo, *Zaïre* 80 D3
Bosporus = Karadeniz Boğazı, *Turkey* 66 C3
Bossangoa, *C.A.R.* 73 G8
Bossekop, *Norway* 8 B17
Bossembélé, *C.A.R.* 73 G8
Bossier City, *U.S.A.* 109 J8
Bosso, *Niger* 79 C7
Bostānābād, *Iran* 64 B5
Bosten Hu, *China* 54 B3
Boston, *U.K.* 12 E7
Boston, *U.S.A.* 107 D13
Boston Bar, *Canada* 100 D4
Bosut →, *Croatia* 21 K8
Boswell, *Canada* 100 D5
Boswell, *Okla., U.S.A.* 109 H7
Boswell, *Pa., U.S.A.* 106 F5
Botad, *India* 62 H4
Botan →, *Turkey* 67 E9
Botany B., *Australia* 91 E5
Botene, *Laos* 58 D3
Botevgrad, *Bulgaria* 38 G6
Bothaville, *S. Africa* 84 D4
Bothnia, G. of, *Europe* 8 E16
Bothwell, *Australia* 90 G4
Bothwell, *Canada* 106 D3
Boticas, *Portugal* 30 D3
Botletle →, *Botswana* 84 C3
Botoşani, *Romania* 38 B9
Botro, *Ivory C.* 78 D3
Botswana ■, *Africa* 84 C3
Bottineau, *U.S.A.* 108 A4
Bottrop, *Germany* 17 E9
Botucatu, *Brazil* 127 A6
Botwood, *Canada* 99 C8
Bou Alam, *Algeria* 75 B5
Bou Ali, *Algeria* 75 C4
Bou Djébéha, *Mali* 78 B4
Bou Guema, *Algeria* 75 C5
Bou Ismael, *Algeria* 75 A5
Bou Izakarn, *Morocco* 74 C3
Boû Lanouâr, *Mauritania* 74 D1
Bou Saâda, *Algeria* 75 A5
Bou Salem, *Tunisia* 75 A6
Bouaké, *Ivory C.* 78 D3
Bouar, *C.A.R.* 80 C3
Bouârfa, *Morocco* 75 B4
Bouca, *C.A.R.* 73 G8
Boucau, *France* 26 E2
Boucaut B., *Australia* 90 A1
Bouches-du-Rhône □, *France* 27 E9
Bouda, *Algeria* 75 C4
Boudenib, *Morocco* 74 B4
Boudry, *Switz.* 22 C3
Boufarik, *Algeria* 75 A5
Bougainville, C., *Australia* 88 B4
Bougainville Reef, *Australia* 90 B4
Bougaroun, C., *Algeria* 75 A6
Bougie = Bejaia, *Algeria* 75 A6
Bougouni, *Mali* 78 C3
Bouillon, *Belgium* 17 J6
Bouïra, *Algeria* 75 A5
Boulder, *Colo., U.S.A.* 108 E2
Boulder, *Mont., U.S.A.* 110 C7
Boulder City, *U.S.A.* 113 K12
Boulder Creek, *U.S.A.* 112 H4
Boulder Dam = Hoover Dam, *U.S.A.* 113 K12
Bouli, *Mauritania* 78 B2
Boulia, *Australia* 90 C2
Bouligny, *France* 25 C12
Boulogne →, *France* 24 E5
Boulogne-sur-Gesse, *France* 26 E4
Boulogne-sur-Mer, *France* 25 B8
Bouloire, *France* 24 E7
Boulsa, *Burkina Faso* 79 C4
Boultoum, *Niger* 79 C7
Boumalne, *Morocco* 74 B3
Boun Neua, *Laos* 58 B3
Boun Tai, *Laos* 58 B3
Bouna, *Ivory C.* 78 D4
Boundary Peak, *U.S.A.* 112 H8
Boundiali, *Ivory C.* 78 D3
Bountiful, *U.S.A.* 110 F8
Bounty Is., *Pac. Oc.* 92 M9
Bourbon-Lancy, *France* 26 B7
Bourbon-l'Archambault, *France* 26 B7
Bourbonnais, *France* 26 B7
Bourbonne-les-Bains, *France* 25 E12
Bourem, *Mali* 79 B4
Bourg, *France* 26 C3
Bourg-Argental, *France* 27 C8
Bourg-de-Péage, *France* 27 C9
Bourg-en-Bresse, *France* 27 B9
Bourg-St.-Andéol, *France* 27 D8
Bourg-St.-Maurice, *France* 27 C10
Bourg-St.-Pierre, *Switz.* 22 E4
Bourganeuf, *France* 26 C5
Bourges, *France* 25 E9
Bourget, *Canada* 107 A9
Bourget, L. du, *France* 27 C9
Bourgneuf, B. de, *France* 24 E4
Bourgneuf-en-Retz, *France* 24 E5
Bourgogne, *France* 25 F11
Bourgoin-Jallieu, *France* 27 C9
Bourgueil, *France* 24 E7
Bourke, *Australia* 91 E4
Bournemouth, *U.K.* 13 G6
Bourriot-Bergonce, *France* 26 D3
Bouse, *U.S.A.* 113 M13
Boussac, *France* 26 B6
Boussens, *France* 26 E4
Bousso, *Chad* 73 F8
Boussu, *Belgium* 17 H3
Boutilimit, *Mauritania* 78 B2
Bouvet I. = Bouvetøya, *Antarctica* 3 G10
Bouvetøya, *Antarctica* 3 G10
Bouznika, *Morocco* 74 B3
Bouzonville, *France* 25 C13
Bova Marina, *Italy* 35 E8
Bovalino Marina, *Italy* 35 D9
Bovec, *Slovenia* 33 B10
Bovenkarspel, *Neths.* 16 C6
Bovigny, *Belgium* 17 H7
Bovill, *U.S.A.* 110 C5
Bovino, *Italy* 35 A8
Bow Island, *Canada* 100 D6
Bowbells, *U.S.A.* 108 A3
Bowdle, *U.S.A.* 108 C5
Bowelling, *Australia* 89 F2
Bowen, *Australia* 90 C4
Bowen Mts., *Australia* 91 F4
Bowie, *Ariz., U.S.A.* 111 K9
Bowie, *Tex., U.S.A.* 109 J6
Bowkān, *Iran* 64 B5
Bowland, Forest of, *U.K.* 12 D5
Bowling Green, *Ky., U.S.A.* 104 G2
Bowling Green, *Ohio, U.S.A.* 104 E4
Bowling Green, C., *Australia* 90 B4
Bowman, *U.S.A.* 108 B3
Bowman I., *Antarctica* 5 C8
Bowmans, *Australia* 91 E2
Bowmanville, *Canada* 98 D4
Bowmore, *U.K.* 14 F2
Bowral, *Australia* 91 E5
Bowraville, *Australia* 91 E5
Bowron →, *Canada* 100 C4
Bowser L., *Canada* 100 B3
Bowsman, *Canada* 101 C8
Bowwood, *Zambia* 83 F2
Boxholm, *Sweden* 11 F9
Boxmeer, *Neths.* 17 E7
Boxtel, *Neths.* 17 E6
Boyabat, *Turkey* 42 F6
Boyaca = Casanare □, *Colombia* 120 B3
Boyce, *U.S.A.* 109 K8
Boyer →, *Canada* 100 B5
Boyle, *Ireland* 15 C3
Boyne →, *Ireland* 15 C5
Boyne City, *U.S.A.* 104 C3
Boynton Beach, *U.S.A.* 105 M5
Boyoma, Chutes, *Zaïre* 82 B2
Boyup Brook, *Australia* 89 F2
Boz Dağ, *Turkey* 66 E3
Boz Dağları, *Turkey* 66 D3
Bozburun, *Turkey* 66 E3
Bozdoğan, *Turkey* 66 E3
Bozeman, *U.S.A.* 110 D8
Bozen = Bolzano, *Italy* 33 B8
Bozkır, *Turkey* 66 E5
Bozouls, *France* 26 D6

Bozoum, *C.A.R.* 73 G8
Bozova, *Turkey* 67 E8
Bozovici, *Romania* 38 E5
Bozüyük, *Turkey* 66 D4
Bra, *Italy* 32 D4
Brabant □, *Belgium* 17 G5
Brabant L., *Canada* 101 B8
Brabrand, *Denmark* 11 H4
Brač, *Croatia* 33 E13
Bracadale, L., *U.K.* 14 D2
Bracciano, *Italy* 33 F9
Bracciano, L. di, *Italy* 33 F9
Bracebridge, *Canada* 98 C4
Brach, *Libya* 73 C7
Bracieux, *France* 25 E8
Bräcke, *Sweden* 10 B9
Brackettville, *U.S.A.* 109 L4
Brački Kanal, *Croatia* 33 E13
Brad, *Romania* 38 C5
Brádano →, *Italy* 35 B9
Bradenton, *U.S.A.* 105 M4
Bradford, *Canada* 106 B5
Bradford, *U.K.* 12 D6
Bradford, *Pa., U.S.A.* 106 E6
Bradford, *Vt., U.S.A.* 107 C12
Brădiceni, *Romania* 38 D6
Bradley, *Ark., U.S.A.* 109 J8
Bradley, *Calif., U.S.A.* 112 K6
Bradley, *S. Dak., U.S.A.* 108 C6
Bradley Institute, *Zimbabwe* 83 F3
Bradore Bay, *Canada* 99 B8
Bradshaw, *Australia* 88 C5
Brady, *U.S.A.* 109 K5
Brædstrup, *Denmark* 11 J3
Braemar, *Australia* 91 E2
Braeside, *Canada* 107 A8
Braga, *Portugal* 30 D2
Braga □, *Portugal* 30 D2
Bragado, *Argentina* 126 D3
Bragança, *Brazil* 122 B2
Bragança, *Portugal* 30 D4
Bragança □, *Portugal* 30 D4
Bragança Paulista, *Brazil* 127 A6
Brahmanbaria, *Bangla.* 61 H17
Brahmani →, *India* 61 J15
Brahmaputra →, *India* 63 G13
Braich-y-pwll, *U.K.* 12 E3
Braidwood, *Australia* 91 F4
Brăila, *Romania* 38 D10
Braine-l'Alleud, *Belgium* 17 G4
Braine-le-Comte, *Belgium* 17 G4
Brainerd, *U.S.A.* 108 B7
Braintree, *U.K.* 13 F8
Braintree, *U.S.A.* 107 D14
Brak →, *S. Africa* 84 D3
Brake, *Niedersachsen, Germany* 18 B4
Brake, *Nordrhein-Westfalen, Germany* 18 D5
Brakel, *Neths.* 16 E6
Brakwater, *Namibia* 84 C2
Brålanda, *Sweden* 11 F6
Bralorne, *Canada* 100 C4
Bramberg, *Germany* 19 E6
Bramminge, *Denmark* 11 J2
Brämön, *Sweden* 10 B11
Brampton, *Canada* 98 D4
Bramsche, *Germany* 18 C3
Bramwell, *Australia* 90 A3
Branco →, *Brazil* 121 D5
Branco, C., *Brazil* 122 C5
Brande, *Denmark* 11 J3
Brandenburg = Neubrandenburg, *Germany* 18 B9
Brandenburg, *Germany* 18 C8
Brandenburg □, *Germany* 18 C9
Brandfort, *S. Africa* 84 D4
Brandon, *Canada* 101 D9
Brandon, *U.S.A.* 107 C11
Brandon B., *Ireland* 15 D1
Brandon Mt., *Ireland* 15 D1
Brandsen, *Argentina* 126 D4
Brandval, *Norway* 10 D6
Brandvlei, *S. Africa* 84 E3
Brandýs, *Czech.* 20 E4
Branford, *U.S.A.* 107 E12
Braniewo, *Poland* 20 A9
Bransfield Str., *Antarctica* 5 C18
Branson, *Colo., U.S.A.* 109 G3
Branson, *Mo., U.S.A.* 109 G8
Brantford, *Canada* 98 D3
Brantôme, *France* 26 C4
Branxholme, *Australia* 91 F3
Branzi, *Italy* 32 B6
Bras d'Or, L., *Canada* 99 C7
Brasiléia, *Brazil* 124 C4
Brasília, *Brazil* 123 E2
Brasília Legal, *Brazil* 121 D6
Braslav, *Belorussia* 40 D5
Braslovce, *Slovenia* 33 B12
Braşov, *Romania* 38 D8
Brass, *Nigeria* 79 E6
Brass →, *Nigeria* 79 E6
Brassac-les-Mines, *France* 26 C7
Brasschaat, *Belgium* 17 F4
Brassey, Banjaran, *Malaysia* 56 D5
Brassey Ra., *Australia* 89 E3
Brasstown Bald, *U.S.A.* 105 H4
Bratislava, *Slovakia* 21 G7
Bratsk, *Russia* 45 D11
Brattleboro, *U.S.A.* 107 D12
Braunau, *Austria* 21 G3
Braunschweig, *Germany* 18 C6
Braunton, *U.K.* 13 F3
Brava, *Somali Rep.* 68 G3
Bråviken, *Sweden* 10 F10
Bravo del Norte →, *Mexico* 114 B5
Brawley, *U.S.A.* 113 N11
Bray, *Ireland* 15 C5
Bray, Mt., *Australia* 90 A1
Bray, Pays de, *France* 25 C8
Bray-sur-Seine, *France* 25 D10
Brazeau →, *Canada* 100 C5
Brazil, *U.S.A.* 104 F2
Brazil ■, *S. Amer.* 123 D2
Brazo Sur →, *S. Amer.* 126 B4
Brazos →, *U.S.A.* 109 L7
Brazzaville, *Congo* 80 E3
Brčko, *Bos.-H.* 21 L8
Brea, *Peru* 124 A1
Breadalbane, *Australia* 90 C2
Breadalbane, *U.K.* 14 E4
Breaden, L., *Australia* 89 E4
Breaksea Sd., *N.Z.* 87 L1
Bream B., *N.Z.* 87 F5
Bream Hd., *N.Z.* 87 F5
Breas, *Chile* 126 B1
Brebes, *Indonesia* 57 G13
Brechin, *Canada* 106 B5
Brechin, *U.K.* 14 E6
Brecht, *Belgium* 17 F5
Breckenridge, *Colo., U.S.A.* 110 G10
Breckenridge, *Minn., U.S.A.* 108 B6
Breckenridge, *Tex., U.S.A.* 109 J5
Breckland, *U.K.* 13 E8
Brecknock, Pen., *Chile* 128 D2
Břeclav, *Czech.* 20 G6
Brecon, *U.K.* 13 F4
Brecon Beacons, *U.K.* 13 F4
Breda, *Neths.* 17 E5
Bredasdorp, *S. Africa* 84 E3
Bredbo, *Australia* 91 F4
Bredene, *Belgium* 17 F1
Bredstedt, *Germany* 18 A4
Bree, *Belgium* 17 F7
Breezand, *Neths.* 16 C5
Bregalnica →, *Macedonia* 39 H5
Bregenz, *Austria* 19 H5
Bréhal, *France* 24 D5
Bréhat, I. de, *France* 24 D4
Breiðafjörður, *Iceland* 8 D2
Breil-sur-Roya, *France* 27 E11
Breisach, *Germany* 19 G3
Brejinho de Nazaré, *Brazil* 122 D2
Brejo, *Brazil* 122 B3
Bremen, *Germany* 18 B4
Bremen □, *Germany* 18 B4
Bremer I., *Australia* 90 A2
Bremerhaven, *Germany* 18 B4
Bremerton, *U.S.A.* 112 C4
Bremervörde, *Germany* 18 B5
Bremsnes, *Norway* 10 A1
Brenes, *Spain* 31 H5
Brenham, *U.S.A.* 109 K6
Brenner Pass, *Austria* 19 H7
Breno, *Italy* 32 C7
Brent, *Canada* 98 C4
Brent, *U.K.* 13 F7
Brenta →, *Italy* 33 C9
Brentwood, *U.K.* 13 F8
Brentwood, *U.S.A.* 107 F11
Bréscia, *Italy* 32 C7
Breskens, *Neths.* 17 F3
Breslau = Wrocław, *Poland* 20 D7
Bresle →, *France* 24 B8
Bresles, *France* 25 C9
Bressanone, *Italy* 33 B8
Bressay, *U.K.* 14 A7
Bresse, *France* 25 F12
Bressuire, *France* 24 F6
Brest, *Belorussia* 40 E3
Brest, *France* 24 D2
Brest-Litovsk = Brest, *Belorussia* 40 E3
Bretagne, *France* 24 D4
Bretçu, *Romania* 38 C9
Breteuil, *Eure, France* 24 D7
Breteuil, *Oise, France* 25 C9
Breton, *Canada* 100 C6
Breton, Pertuis, *France* 26 B2
Breton Sd., *U.S.A.* 109 L10
Brett, C., *N.Z.* 87 F5
Bretten, *Germany* 19 F4
Breukelen, *Neths.* 16 D6
Brevard, *U.S.A.* 105 H4
Breves, *Brazil* 122 B1
Brevik, *Norway* 10 E3
Brewarrina, *Australia* 91 D4
Brewer, *U.S.A.* 99 D6
Brewer, Mt., *U.S.A.* 112 J8
Brewster, *N.Y., U.S.A.* 107 E11
Brewster, *Wash., U.S.A.* 110 B4
Brewster, Kap, *Greenland* 4 B6
Brewton, *U.S.A.* 105 K2
Breyten, *S. Africa* 85 D4
Breytovo, *Russia* 41 B10
Brezhnev = Naberezhnyye Chelny, *Russia* 44 D6
Brežice, *Slovenia* 33 C12
Brézina, *Algeria* 75 B5
Březnice, *Czech.* 20 F3
Breznik, *Bulgaria* 38 G5
Brezno, *Slovakia* 20 G9
Bria, *C.A.R.* 73 G9
Briançon, *France* 27 D10
Briare, *France* 25 E9
Bribie I., *Australia* 91 D5
Bricquebec, *France* 24 C5
Bridgehampton, *U.S.A.* 107 F12
Bridgend, *U.K.* 13 F4
Bridgeport, *Calif., U.S.A.* 111 G4
Bridgeport, *Conn., U.S.A.* 107 E11
Bridgeport, *Nebr., U.S.A.* 108 E3
Bridgeport, *Tex., U.S.A.* 109 J6
Bridger, *U.S.A.* 110 D9
Bridgeton, *U.S.A.* 104 F8
Bridgetown, *Australia* 89 F2
Bridgetown, *Barbados* 117 D8
Bridgetown, *Canada* 99 D6
Bridgewater, *Canada* 99 D7
Bridgewater, *Mass., U.S.A.* 107 E14
Bridgewater, *S. Dak., U.S.A.* 108 D6
Bridgewater, C., *Australia* 91 F3
Bridgnorth, *U.K.* 13 E5
Bridgton, *U.S.A.* 107 B14
Bridgwater, *U.K.* 13 F4
Bridlington, *U.K.* 12 C7
Bridport, *Australia* 90 G4
Bridport, *U.K.* 13 G5
Brie, Plaine de la, *France* 25 D10
Brie-Comte-Robert, *France* 25 D9
Briec, *France* 24 D2
Brielle, *Neths.* 16 E4
Brienne-le-Château, *France* 25 D11
Brienon-sur-Armançon, *France* 25 E10
Brienz, *Switz.* 22 C6
Brienzersee, *Switz.* 22 C5
Brig, *Switz.* 22 D5
Brigg, *U.K.* 12 D7
Briggsdale, *U.S.A.* 108 E2
Brigham City, *U.S.A.* 110 F7
Bright, *Australia* 91 F4
Brighton, *Australia* 91 F2
Brighton, *Canada* 98 D4
Brighton, *U.K.* 13 G7
Brighton, *U.S.A.* 108 F2
Brignogan-Plage, *France* 24 D2
Brignoles, *France* 27 E10
Brihuega, *Spain* 28 E2
Brikama, *Gambia* 78 C1
Brilliant, *Canada* 100 D5
Brilliant, *U.S.A.* 106 F4
Brilon, *Germany* 18 D4
Bríndisi, *Italy* 35 B10
Brinje, *Croatia* 33 D12
Brinkley, *U.S.A.* 109 H9
Brinkworth, *Australia* 91 E2
Brinnon, *U.S.A.* 112 C4
Brion, I., *Canada* 99 C7
Brionne, *France* 24 C7
Brionski, *Croatia* 33 D10
Brioude, *France* 26 C7
Briouze, *France* 24 D6
Brisbane, *Australia* 91 D5
Brisbane →, *Australia* 91 D5
Brisighella, *Italy* 33 D8
Bristol, *U.K.* 13 F5
Bristol, *Conn., U.S.A.* 107 E12
Bristol, *Pa., U.S.A.* 107 F10
Bristol, *R.I., U.S.A.* 107 E13
Bristol, *S. Dak., U.S.A.* 108 C6
Bristol, *Tenn., U.S.A.* 105 G4
Bristol B., *U.S.A.* 96 C4
Bristol Channel, *U.K.* 13 F3
Bristol I., *Antarctica* 5 B1
Bristol L., *U.S.A.* 111 J5
Bristow, *U.S.A.* 109 H6
British Columbia □, *Canada* 100 C3
British Guiana = Guyana ■, *S. Amer.* 121 B6
British Honduras = Belize ■, *Cent. Amer.* 115 D7
British Isles, *Europe* 6 E5
Brits, *S. Africa* 85 D4
Britstown, *S. Africa* 84 E3
Britt, *Canada* 98 C3
Brittany = Bretagne, *France* 24 D4
Britton, *U.S.A.* 108 C6
Brive-la-Gaillarde, *France* 26 C5
Briviesca, *Spain* 28 C1
Brixton, *Australia* 90 C3
Brlik, *Kazakhstan* 44 E8
Brno, *Czech.* 20 F6
Bro, *Sweden* 10 E11
Broad →, *U.S.A.* 105 J5
Broad Arrow, *Australia* 89 F3
Broad B., *U.K.* 14 C2
Broad Haven, *Ireland* 15 B2
Broad Law, *U.K.* 14 F5
Broad Sd., *Australia* 90 C4
Broadhurst Ra., *Australia* 88 D3
Broads, The, *U.K.* 12 E9
Broadus, *U.S.A.* 108 C2
Broadview, *Canada* 101 C8
Broager, *Denmark* 11 K3
Broaryd, *Sweden* 11 G7
Brochet, *Canada* 101 B8
Brochet, L., *Canada* 101 B8
Brock, *Canada* 101 C7
Brocken, *Germany* 18 D6
Brockport, *U.S.A.* 106 C7
Brockton, *U.S.A.* 107 D13
Brockville, *Canada* 98 D4
Brockway, *Mont., U.S.A.* 108 B2
Brockway, *Pa., U.S.A.* 106 E6
Brocton, *U.S.A.* 106 D5
Brod, *Macedonia* 39 H4
Brodarevo, *Serbia, Yug.* 21 M9
Brodeur Pen., *Canada* 97 A11
Brodick, *U.K.* 14 F3
Brodnica, *Poland* 20 B9
Brody, *Ukraine* 40 F4
Broechem, *Belgium* 17 F5
Broek, *Neths.* 16 D6
Broek op Langedijk, *Neths.* 16 C5
Brogan, *U.S.A.* 110 D5
Broglie, *France* 24 C7
Broken Bow, *Nebr., U.S.A.* 108 E5
Broken Bow, *Okla., U.S.A.* 109 H7
Broken Hill = Kabwe, *Zambia* 83 E2
Broken Hill, *Australia* 91 E3
Brokind, *Sweden* 11 F9
Brokopondo, *Surinam* 121 B7
Brokopondo □, *Surinam* 121 C6
Bromfield, *U.K.* 13 E5
Bromley, *U.K.* 13 F8
Brønderslev, *Denmark* 11 G3
Brong-Ahafo □, *Ghana* 78 D4
Bronkhorstspruit, *S. Africa* 85 D4
Bronnitsy, *Russia* 41 D11
Bronte, *Italy* 35 E7
Bronte, *U.S.A.* 109 K4
Bronte Park, *Australia* 90 G4
Brook Park, *U.S.A.* 106 E4
Brookfield, *U.S.A.* 108 F8
Brookhaven, *U.S.A.* 109 K9
Brookings, *Oreg., U.S.A.* 110 E1
Brookings, *S. Dak., U.S.A.* 108 C6
Brooklin, *Canada* 106 C6
Brookmere, *Canada* 100 D4
Brooks, *Canada* 100 C6
Brooks B., *Canada* 100 C3
Brooks L., *Canada* 101 A7
Brooks Ra., *U.S.A.* 96 B5
Brooksville, *U.S.A.* 105 L4
Brookville, *U.S.A.* 104 F3
Brooloo, *Australia* 91 D5
Broom, L., *U.K.* 14 D3
Broome, *Australia* 88 C3
Broomehill, *Australia* 89 F2
Broons, *France* 24 D4
Brora, *U.K.* 14 C5
Brora →, *U.K.* 14 C5
Brosna →, *Ireland* 15 C4
Broşteni, *Romania* 38 B8
Brotas de Macaúbas, *Brazil* 123 D3
Brothers, *U.S.A.* 110 E3
Brøttum, *Norway* 10 C4
Brou, *France* 24 D8
Brough, *U.K.* 12 C5
Broughton Island, *Canada* 97 B13
Broughty Ferry, *U.K.* 14 E6
Brouwershaven, *Neths.* 16 E3
Brouwershavensche Gat, *Neths.* 16 E3
Brovary, *Ukraine* 40 F7
Brovst, *Denmark* 11 G3
Browerville, *U.S.A.* 108 B7
Brown, Pt., *Australia* 91 E1
Brown Willy, *U.K.* 13 G3
Brownfield, *U.S.A.* 109 J3
Browning, *U.S.A.* 110 B7
Brownlee, *Canada* 101 C7
Brownsville, *Oreg., U.S.A.* 110 D2
Brownsville, *Tenn., U.S.A.* 109 H10
Brownsville, *Tex., U.S.A.* 109 N6
Brownsweg, *Surinam* 121 B6
Brownwood, *U.S.A.* 109 K5
Brownwood, L., *U.S.A.* 109 K5
Browse I., *Australia* 88 B3
Broye →, *Switz.* 22 C3
Brozas, *Spain* 31 F4
Bruas, *Malaysia* 59 K3
Bruay-en-Artois, *France* 25 B9
Bruce, Mt., *Australia* 88 D2
Bruce Pen., *Canada* 106 A3
Bruce Rock, *Australia* 89 F2
Bruche →, *France* 25 D14
Bruchsal, *Germany* 19 F4
Bruck an der Leitha, *Austria* 21 G6
Bruck an der Mur, *Austria* 21 H5
Brue →, *U.K.* 13 F5
Brugelette, *Belgium* 17 G3
Bruges = Brugge, *Belgium* 17 F2
Brugg, *Switz.* 22 B6
Brugge, *Belgium* 17 F2
Brühl, *Germany* 18 E2
Bruinisse, *Neths.* 17 E4
Brûlé, *Canada* 100 C5
Brûlon, *France* 24 E6
Brûly, *Belgium* 17 J5
Brumado, *Brazil* 123 D3
Brumado →, *Brazil* 123 D3
Brumath, *France* 25 D14
Brummen, *Neths.* 16 D8
Brumunddal, *Norway* 10 D4
Brunchilly, *Australia* 90 B1
Brundidge, *U.S.A.* 105 K3
Bruneau, *U.S.A.* 110 E6
Bruneau →, *U.S.A.* 110 E6
Brunei = Bandar Seri Begawan, *Brunei* 56 C4
Brunei ■, *Asia* 56 D4
Brunette Downs, *Australia* 90 B2
Brunflo, *Sweden* 10 A8
Brunico, *Italy* 33 B8
Brünig, P., *Switz.* 22 C6
Brunkeberg, *Norway* 10 E2
Brunna, *Sweden* 10 E11
Brunnen, *Switz.* 23 C7
Brunner, L., *N.Z.* 87 K3
Bruno, *Canada* 101 C7
Brunsbüttel, *Germany* 18 B5
Brunssum, *Neths.* 17 G7
Brunswick = Braunschweig, *Germany* 18 C6
Brunswick, *Ga., U.S.A.* 105 K5
Brunswick, *Maine, U.S.A.* 99 D6
Brunswick, *Md., U.S.A.* 104 F7
Brunswick, *Mo., U.S.A.* 108 F8
Brunswick, *Ohio, U.S.A.* 106 E3
Brunswick, Pen. de, *Chile* 128 D2
Brunswick B., *Australia* 88 C3
Brunswick Junction, *Australia* 89 F2
Bruntál, *Czech.* 20 F7
Bruny I., *Australia* 90 G4
Brus Laguna, *Honduras* 116 C3
Brusartsi, *Bulgaria* 38 F6
Brush, *U.S.A.* 108 E3
Brushton, *U.S.A.* 107 B10
Brusio, *Switz.* 23 D10
Brusque, *Brazil* 127 B6
Brussel, *Belgium* 17 G4
Brussels = Brussel, *Belgium* 17 G4
Brussels, *Canada* 106 C3
Brustem, *Belgium* 17 G6
Bruthen, *Australia* 91 F4
Bruxelles = Brussel, *Belgium* 17 G4
Bruyères, *France* 25 D13
Bryan, *Ohio, U.S.A.* 104 E3
Bryan, *Tex., U.S.A.* 109 K6
Bryan, Mt., *Australia* 91 E2
Bryanka, *Ukraine* 43 B8
Bryansk, *Russia* 40 E9
Bryanskoye, *Russia* 43 D12
Bryant, *U.S.A.* 108 C6
Bryne, *Norway* 9 G8
Bryson City, *U.S.A.* 105 H4
Brza Palanka, *Serbia, Yug.* 21 L12
Brzava →, *Serbia, Yug.* 21 K10
Brzeg, *Poland* 20 E7
Brzeg Din, *Poland* 20 D6
Bsharri, *Lebanon* 69 A5
Bū Baqarah, *U.A.E.* 65 E8
Bu Craa, *W. Sahara* 74 C2
Bū Ḩasā, *U.A.E.* 65 F7
Bua Yai, *Thailand* 58 E4
Buapinang, *Indonesia* 57 E6
Buayan, *Phil.* 57 C7
Buba, *Guinea-Biss.* 78 C2
Bubanza, *Burundi* 82 C2
Būbiyān, *Kuwait* 65 D6
Bucak, *Turkey* 66 E4
Bucaramanga, *Colombia* 120 B3
Bucas Grande I., *Phil.* 55 G6
Buccaneer Arch., *Australia* 88 C3
Bucchiánico, *Italy* 33 F11
Bucecea, *Romania* 38 B9
Buchach, *Ukraine* 40 G4
Buchan, *U.K.* 14 D6
Buchan Ness, *U.K.* 14 D7
Buchanan, *Canada* 101 C8
Buchanan, *Liberia* 78 D2
Buchanan, L., *Queens., Australia* 90 C4
Buchanan, L., *W. Austral., Australia* 89 E3
Buchanan, L., *U.S.A.* 109 K5
Buchanan Cr. →, *Australia* 90 B2
Buchans, *Canada* 99 C8
Bucharest = Bucureşti, *Romania* 38 E9
Buchholz, *Germany* 18 B5
Buchloe, *Germany* 19 G6
Buchon, Pt., *U.S.A.* 112 K6
Buchs, *Switz.* 23 B8
Bückeburg, *Germany* 18 C5
Buckeye, *U.S.A.* 111 K7
Buckhannon, *U.S.A.* 104 F5
Buckhaven, *U.K.* 14 E5
Buckie, *U.K.* 14 D6
Buckingham, *Canada* 98 C4
Buckingham, *U.K.* 13 F7
Buckingham B., *Australia* 90 A2
Buckinghamshire □, *U.K.* 13 F7
Buckle Hd., *Australia* 88 B4
Buckleboo, *Australia* 91 E2
Buckley, *U.S.A.* 110 C2
Buckley →, *Australia* 90 C2
Bucklin, *U.S.A.* 109 G5
Bucks L., *U.S.A.* 112 F5
Bucquoy, *France* 25 B9
Buctouche, *Canada* 99 C7
Bucureşti, *Romania* 38 E9
Bucyrus, *U.S.A.* 104 E4
Budafok, *Hungary* 21 H9
Budalin, *Burma* 61 H19
Budapest, *Hungary* 21 H9
Budaun, *India* 63 E8
Budd Coast, *Antarctica* 5 C8
Buddusò, *Italy* 34 B2
Bude, *U.K.* 13 G3
Budel, *Neths.* 17 F7
Budennovsk, *Russia* 43 D11
Budeşti, *Romania* 38 E9
Budge Budge = Baj Baj, *India* 63 H13

Budgewoi, *Australia* 91 E5
Búðareyri, *Iceland* 8 D6
Búðir, *Iceland* 8 D2
Budia, *Spain* 28 E2
Budjala, *Zaïre* 80 D3
Búdrio, *Italy* 33 D8
Buea, *Cameroon* 79 E6
Buellton, *U.S.A.* 113 L6
Buena Vista, *Bolivia* 125 D5
Buena Vista, *Colo., U.S.A.* 111 G10
Buena Vista, *Va., U.S.A.* 104 G6
Buena Vista L., *U.S.A.* 113 K7
Buenaventura, *Colombia* 120 C2
Buenaventura, *Mexico* 114 B3
Buenaventura, B. de, *Colombia* 120 C2
Buendía, Pantano de, *Spain* 28 E2
Buenópolis, *Brazil* 123 E3
Buenos Aires, *Argentina* 126 C4
Buenos Aires, *Colombia* 120 C3
Buenos Aires, *Costa Rica* 116 E3
Buenos Aires □, *Argentina* 126 D4
Buenos Aires, L., *Chile* 128 C2
Buesaco, *Colombia* 120 C2
Buffalo, *Mo., U.S.A.* 109 G8
Buffalo, *N.Y., U.S.A.* 106 D6
Buffalo, *Okla., U.S.A.* 109 G5
Buffalo, *S. Dak., U.S.A.* 108 C3
Buffalo, *Wyo., U.S.A.* 110 D10
Buffalo →, *Canada* 100 A5
Buffalo Head Hills, *Canada* 100 B5
Buffalo L., *Canada* 100 C6
Buffalo Narrows, *Canada* 101 B7
Buffels →, *S. Africa* 84 D2
Buford, *U.S.A.* 105 H4
Bug →, *Poland* 20 C11
Bug →, *Ukraine* 42 C4
Buga, *Colombia* 120 C2
Buganda, *Uganda* 82 C3
Buganga, *Uganda* 82 C3
Bugasong, *Phil.* 55 F5
Bugeat, *France* 26 C5
Bugel, Tanjung, *Indonesia* 56 F4
Buggenhout, *Belgium* 17 F4
Bugibba, *Malta* 37 D1
Bugsuk, *Phil.* 55 G2
Buguma, *Nigeria* 79 E6
Bugun Shara, *Mongolia* 54 B5
Buguruslan, *Russia* 44 D6
Buhăeşti, *Romania* 38 C10
Buheirat-Murrat-el-Kubra, *Egypt* 76 H8
Buhl, *Idaho, U.S.A.* 110 E6
Buhl, *Minn., U.S.A.* 108 B8
Buick, *U.S.A.* 109 G9
Builth Wells, *U.K.* 13 E4
Buinsk, *Russia* 41 D16
Buíque, *Brazil* 122 C4
Buir Nur, *Mongolia* 54 B6
Buis-les-Baronnies, *France* 27 D9
Buitenpost, *Neths.* 16 B8
Buitrago, *Spain* 30 E7
Bujalance, *Spain* 31 H6
Buján, *Spain* 30 C2
Bujaraloz, *Spain* 28 D4
Buje, *Croatia* 33 C10
Bujumbura, *Burundi* 82 C2
Bukachacha, *Russia* 45 D12
Bukama, *Zaïre* 83 D2
Bukavu, *Zaïre* 82 C2
Bukene, *Tanzania* 82 C3
Bukhara, *Uzbekistan* 44 F7
Bukhoro = Bukhara, *Uzbekistan* 44 F7
Bukima, *Tanzania* 82 C3
Bukit Mertajam, *Malaysia* 59 K3
Bukittinggi, *Indonesia* 56 E2
Bukoba, *Tanzania* 82 C3
Bukoba □, *Tanzania* 82 C3
Bukuru, *Nigeria* 79 D6
Bukuya, *Uganda* 82 B3
Bula, *Guinea-Biss.* 78 C1
Bula, *Indonesia* 57 E8
Bülach, *Switz.* 23 A7
Bulahdelah, *Australia* 91 E5
Bulan, *Phil.* 55 E5
Bulancak, *Turkey* 67 C8
Bulandshahr, *India* 62 E7
Bulanık, *Turkey* 67 D10
Bûlâq, *Egypt* 76 B3
Bulawayo, *Zimbabwe* 83 G2
Buldan, *Turkey* 66 D3
Bulgan, *Mongolia* 54 B5
Bulgaria ■, *Europe* 38 G8
Bulgroo, *Australia* 91 D3
Bulgunnia, *Australia* 91 E1
Bulhar, *Somali Rep.* 68 E3
Buli, Teluk, *Indonesia* 57 D7
Buliluyan, C., *Phil.* 55 G2
Bulki, *Ethiopia* 77 F4
Bulkley →, *Canada* 100 B3
Bull Shoals L., *U.S.A.* 109 G8
Bullange, *Belgium* 17 H8
Bullaque →, *Spain* 31 G6
Bullara, *Australia* 88 D1
Bullaring, *Australia* 89 F2
Bullas, *Spain* 29 G3
Bulle, *Switz.* 22 C4
Bulli, *Australia* 91 E5
Bullock Creek, *Australia* 90 B3
Bulloo →, *Australia* 91 D3
Bulloo Downs, *Queens., Australia* 91 D3
Bulloo Downs, *W. Austral., Australia* 88 D2
Bulloo L., *Australia* 91 D3
Bulls, *N.Z.* 87 J5
Bully-les-Mines, *France* 25 B9
Bulnes, *Chile* 126 D1
Bulo Burti, *Somali Rep.* 68 G4
Bulsar = Valsad, *India* 60 J8
Bultfontein, *S. Africa* 84 D4
Bulu Karakelong, *Indonesia* 57 D7
Bulukumba, *Indonesia* 57 F6
Bulun, *Russia* 45 B13
Bumba, *Zaïre* 80 D4
Bumbiri I., *Tanzania* 82 C3
Bumhpa Bum, *Burma* 61 F20
Bumi →, *Zimbabwe* 83 F2
Buna, *Kenya* 82 B4
Bunawan, *Agusan del S., Phil.* 55 G6
Bunawan, *Davao del S., Phil.* 55 H6
Bunazi, *Tanzania* 82 C3
Bunbah, Khalīj, *Libya* 73 B9
Bunbury, *Australia* 89 F2
Buncrana, *Ireland* 15 A4
Bundaberg, *Australia* 91 C5
Bünde, *Germany* 18 C4
Bundey →, *Australia* 90 C2
Bundi, *India* 62 G6
Bundooma, *Australia* 90 C1
Bundoran, *Ireland* 15 B3
Bundukia, *Sudan* 77 F3
Bung Kan, *Thailand* 58 C4
Bungatakada, *Japan* 49 H5
Bungil Cr. →, *Australia* 90 D4
Bungo-Suidō, *Japan* 49 H6
Bungoma, *Kenya* 82 B3
Bungu, *Tanzania* 82 D4
Bunia, *Zaïre* 82 B3
Bunji, *Pakistan* 63 B6
Bunkie, *U.S.A.* 109 K8
Bunnell, *U.S.A.* 105 L5
Bunnik, *Neths.* 16 D6
Buñol, *Spain* 29 F4
Bunsbeek, *Belgium* 17 G5
Bunschoten, *Neths.* 16 D6
Buntok, *Indonesia* 56 E4
Bununu, *Nigeria* 79 D6
Bununu Dass, *Nigeria* 79 C6
Bünyan, *Turkey* 66 D6
Bunyu, *Indonesia* 56 D5
Bunza, *Nigeria* 79 C5
Buol, *Indonesia* 57 D6
Buon Brieng, *Vietnam* 58 F7
Buon Me Thuot, *Vietnam* 58 F7
Buong Long, *Cambodia* 58 F6
Buorkhaya, Mys, *Russia* 45 B14
Buqayq, *Si. Arabia* 65 E6
Buqbua, *Egypt* 76 A2
Bur Acaba, *Somali Rep.* 68 G3
Bûr Fuad, *Egypt* 76 H8
Bûr Safâga, *Egypt* 76 B3
Bûr Sa'îd, *Egypt* 76 H8
Bûr Sûdân, *Sudan* 76 D4
Bûr Taufiq, *Egypt* 76 J8
Bura, *Kenya* 82 C4
Burao, *Somali Rep.* 68 F4
Burāq, *Syria* 69 B5
Buras, *U.S.A.* 109 L10
Buraydah, *Si. Arabia* 64 E5
Burbank, *U.S.A.* 113 L8
Burcher, *Australia* 91 E4
Burdekin →, *Australia* 90 B4
Burdett, *Canada* 100 D6
Burdur, *Turkey* 66 E4
Burdur □, *Turkey* 66 E4
Burdur Gölü, *Turkey* 66 E4
Burdwan = Barddhaman, *India* 63 H12
Bure, *Ethiopia* 77 E4
Bure →, *U.K.* 12 E9
Büren, *Germany* 18 D4
Buren, *Neths.* 16 E6
Bureya →, *Russia* 45 E13
Burford, *Canada* 106 C4
Burg, *Sachsen-Anhalt, Germany* 18 C7
Burg, *Schleswig-Holstein, Germany* 18 A7
Burg el Arab, *Egypt* 76 H6
Burg et Tuyur, *Sudan* 76 C2
Burg Stargard, *Germany* 18 B9
Burgas, *Bulgaria* 38 G10
Burgdorf, *Germany* 18 C5
Burgdorf, *Switz.* 22 B5
Burgeo, *Canada* 99 C8
Burgersdorp, *S. Africa* 84 E4
Burges, Mt., *Australia* 89 F3
Burghausen, *Germany* 19 G8
Búrgio, *Italy* 34 E6
Bürglen, *Switz.* 23 C7
Burglengenfeld, *Germany* 19 F8
Burgo de Osma, *Spain* 28 D1
Burgohondo, *Spain* 30 E6
Burgos, *Spain* 28 C1
Burgos □, *Spain* 28 C1
Burgstädt, *Germany* 18 E8
Burgsvik, *Sweden* 9 H15
Burguillos del Cerro, *Spain* 31 G4
Burgundy = Bourgogne, *France* 25 F11
Burhanpur, *India* 60 J10
Burhou, *U.K.* 24 C4
Buri Pen., *Eritrea* 77 D4
Burias, *Phil.* 55 E5
Burica, Pta., *Costa Rica* 116 E3
Burigi, L., *Tanzania* 82 C3
Burin, *Canada* 99 C8
Buriram, *Thailand* 58 E4
Buriti Alegre, *Brazil* 123 E2
Buriti Bravo, *Brazil* 122 C3
Buriti dos Lopes, *Brazil* 122 B3
Burj Sāfitā, *Syria* 64 C3
Burji, *Ethiopia* 77 F4
Burkburnett, *U.S.A.* 109 H5
Burke, *U.S.A.* 110 C6
Burke →, *Australia* 90 C2
Burketown, *Australia* 90 B2
Burkina Faso ■, *Africa* 78 C4
Burk's Falls, *Canada* 98 C4
Burley, *U.S.A.* 110 E7
Burlingame, *U.S.A.* 112 H4
Burlington, *Canada* 106 C5
Burlington, *Colo., U.S.A.* 108 F3
Burlington, *Iowa, U.S.A.* 108 E9
Burlington, *Kans., U.S.A.* 108 F7
Burlington, *N.C., U.S.A.* 105 G6
Burlington, *N.J., U.S.A.* 107 F10
Burlington, *Vt., U.S.A.* 107 B11
Burlington, *Wash., U.S.A.* 112 B4
Burlington, *Wis., U.S.A.* 104 D1
Burlyu-Tyube, *Kazakhstan* 44 E8
Burma ■, *Asia* 61 J20
Burnaby I., *Canada* 100 C2
Burnet, *U.S.A.* 109 K5
Burney, *U.S.A.* 110 F3
Burngup, *Australia* 89 F2
Burnham, *U.S.A.* 106 F7
Burnie, *Australia* 90 G4
Burnley, *U.K.* 12 D5
Burns, *Oreg., U.S.A.* 110 E4
Burns, *Wyo., U.S.A.* 108 E2
Burns Lake, *Canada* 100 C3
Burnside →, *Canada* 96 B9
Burnside, L., *Australia* 89 E3
Burnt River, *Canada* 106 B6
Burntwood →, *Canada* 101 B9
Burntwood L., *Canada* 101 B8
Burqān, *Kuwait* 64 D5
Burqin, *China* 54 B3
Burra, *Australia* 91 E2
Burramurra, *Australia* 90 C2
Burreli, *Albania* 39 H3
Burren Junction, *Australia* 91 E4
Burrendong Dam, *Australia* 91 E4
Burriana, *Spain* 28 F4
Burrinjuck Res., *Australia* 91 F4
Burro, Serranías del, *Mexico* 114 B4
Burruyacú, *Argentina* 126 B3
Burry Port, *U.K.* 13 F3
Bursa, *Turkey* 66 C3
Bursa □, *Turkey* 66 C3
Burseryd, *Sweden* 11 G7
Burstall, *Canada* 101 C7
Burton L., *Canada* 98 B4
Burton upon Trent, *U.K.* 12 E6
Burtundy, *Australia* 91 E3
Buru, *Indonesia* 57 E7
Burullus, Bahra el, *Egypt* 76 H7
Burûn, Râs, *Egypt* 69 D2
Burundi ■, *Africa* 82 C3
Bururi, *Burundi* 82 C2
Burutu, *Nigeria* 79 D6
Burwell, *U.S.A.* 108 E5
Bury, *U.K.* 12 D5
Bury St. Edmunds, *U.K.* 13 E8
Buryat Republic □, *Russia* 45 D11
Buryn, *Ukraine* 40 F8
Busalla, *Italy* 32 D5
Busango Swamp, *Zambia* 83 E2
Buşayrah, *Syria* 64 C4
Buşayyah, *Iraq* 64 D5
Busca, *Italy* 32 D4
Būshehr, *Iran* 65 D6
Būshehr □, *Iran* 65 D6
Bushell, *Canada* 101 B7
Bushenyi, *Uganda* 82 C3
Bushire = Būshehr, *Iran* 65 D6
Bushnell, *Ill., U.S.A.* 108 E9
Bushnell, *Nebr., U.S.A.* 108 E3
Busia □, *Kenya* 82 B3
Busie, *Ghana* 78 C4
Businga, *Zaïre* 80 D4
Buskerud fylke □, *Norway* 10 D3
Busko Zdrój, *Poland* 20 E10
Busoga □, *Uganda* 82 B3
Busovača, *Bos.-H.* 21 L7
Busra ash Shām, *Syria* 69 C5
Bussang, *France* 25 E13
Busselton, *Australia* 89 F2
Busseto, *Italy* 32 D7
Bussigny, *Switz.* 22 C3
Bussum, *Neths.* 16 D6
Bustamante, B., *Argentina* 128 C3
Busto, C., *Spain* 30 B4
Busto Arsizio, *Italy* 32 C5
Busu-Djanoa, *Zaïre* 80 D4
Busuanga, *Phil.* 55 E3
Büsum, *Germany* 18 A4
Buta, *Zaïre* 82 B1
Butare, *Rwanda* 82 C2
Butaritari, *Kiribati* 92 G9
Bute, *U.K.* 14 F3
Bute Inlet, *Canada* 100 C4
Butemba, *Uganda* 82 B3
Butembo, *Zaïre* 82 B2
Butera, *Italy* 35 E7
Bütgenbach, *Belgium* 17 H8
Butha Qi, *China* 54 B7
Butiaba, *Uganda* 82 B3
Butler, *Mo., U.S.A.* 108 F7
Butler, *Pa., U.S.A.* 106 F5
Bütschwil, *Switz.* 23 B8
Butte, *Mont., U.S.A.* 110 C7
Butte, *Nebr., U.S.A.* 108 D5
Butte Creek →, *U.S.A.* 112 F5
Butterworth = Gcuwa, *S. Africa* 85 E4
Butterworth, *Malaysia* 59 K3
Buttfield, Mt., *Australia* 89 D4
Button B., *Canada* 101 B10
Buttonwillow, *U.S.A.* 113 K7
Butty Hd., *Australia* 89 F3
Butuan, *Phil.* 55 G6
Butuku-Luba, *Eq. Guin.* 79 E6
Butung, *Indonesia* 57 E6
Buturlinovka, *Russia* 41 F12
Butzbach, *Germany* 18 E4
Bützow, *Germany* 18 B7
Buxar, *India* 63 G10
Buxton, *Guyana* 121 B6
Buxton, *S. Africa* 84 D3
Buxton, *U.K.* 12 D6
Buxy, *France* 25 F11
Buy, *Russia* 41 B12
Buyaga, *Russia* 45 D13
Buynaksk, *Russia* 43 E12
Büyük Menderes →, *Turkey* 66 E2
Büyükçekmece, *Turkey* 39 H11
Buzançais, *France* 24 F8
Buzău, *Romania* 38 D9
Buzău →, *Romania* 38 D10
Buzău, Pasul, *Romania* 38 D9
Buzen, *Japan* 49 H5
Buzet, *Croatia* 33 C10
Buzi →, *Mozam.* 83 F3
Buziaş, *Romania* 38 D4
Buzuluk, *Russia* 44 D6
Buzuluk →, *Russia* 41 F13
Buzzards Bay, *U.S.A.* 107 E14
Bwana Mkubwe, *Zaïre* 83 E2
Byala, *Bulgaria* 38 F8
Byala Slatina, *Bulgaria* 38 F6
Byandovan, Mys, *Azerbaijan* 43 G13
Bychawa, *Poland* 20 D12
Bydgoszcz, *Poland* 20 B8
Byelarus = Belorussia ■, *Europe* 40 E5
Byelorussia = Belorussia ■, *Europe* 40 E5
Byers, *U.S.A.* 108 F2
Byesville, *U.S.A.* 106 G3
Byhalia, *U.S.A.* 109 H10
Bykhov, *Belorussia* 40 E7
Bykovo, *Russia* 43 B11
Bylas, *U.S.A.* 111 K8
Bylderup, *Denmark* 11 K3
Bylot I., *Canada* 97 A12
Byrd, C., *Antarctica* 5 C17
Byro, *Australia* 89 E2
Byrock, *Australia* 91 E4
Byron Bay, *Australia* 91 D5
Byrranga, Gory, *Russia* 45 B11
Byrranga Mts. = Byrranga, Gory, *Russia* 45 B11
Byrum, *Denmark* 11 G5
Byske, *Sweden* 8 D16
Byske älv →, *Sweden* 8 D16
Bystrzyca Kłodzka, *Poland* 20 E6
Byten, *Belorussia* 40 E4
Bytom, *Poland* 20 E8
Bytów, *Poland* 20 A7
Byumba, *Rwanda* 82 C3

C

C.I.S. = Commonwealth of Independent States ■, *Eurasia* 45 D11
Ca →, *Vietnam* 58 C5
Ca Mau = Quan Long, *Vietnam* 59 H5
Ca Mau, Mui = Bai Bung, Mui, *Vietnam* 59 H5
Ca Na, *Vietnam* 59 G7
Caacupé, *Paraguay* 126 B4
Caála, *Angola* 81 G3
Caamano Sd., *Canada* 100 C3
Caapiranga, *Brazil* 121 D5
Caazapá, *Paraguay* 126 B4
Caazapá □, *Paraguay* 127 B4
Cabadbaran, *Phil.* 55 G6
Cabalian, *Phil.* 55 F6
Caballeria, C. de, *Spain* 36 A11
Cabana, *Peru* 124 B2
Cabanaconde, *Peru* 124 D3
Cabañaquinta, *Spain* 30 B5
Cabanatuan, *Phil.* 55 D4
Cabanes, *Spain* 28 E5
Cabanillas, *Peru* 124 D3
Cabano, *Canada* 99 C6
Čabar, *Croatia* 33 C11
Cabazon, *U.S.A.* 113 M10
Cabedelo, *Brazil* 122 C5
Cabeza del Buey, *Spain* 31 G5
Cabildo, *Chile* 126 C1
Cabimas, *Venezuela* 120 A3
Cabinda, *Angola* 80 F2
Cabinda □, *Angola* 80 F2
Cabinet Mts., *U.S.A.* 110 C6
Cabo Blanco, *Argentina* 128 C3
Cabo Frio, *Brazil* 123 F3
Cabo Pantoja, *Peru* 120 D2
Cabo Raso, *Argentina* 128 B3
Cabonga, Réservoir, *Canada* 98 C4
Cabool, *U.S.A.* 109 G8
Caboolture, *Australia* 91 D5
Cabora Bassa Dam = Cahora Bassa Dam, *Mozam.* 83 F3
Caborca, *Mexico* 114 A2
Cabot, Mt., *U.S.A.* 107 B13
Cabot Str., *Canada* 99 C8
Cabra, *Spain* 31 H6
Cabra del Santo Cristo, *Spain* 29 H1
Cábras, *Italy* 34 C1
Cabrera, I., *Spain* 36 B9
Cabrera, Sierra, *Spain* 30 C4
Cabri, *Canada* 101 C7
Cabriel →, *Spain* 29 F3
Cabruta, *Venezuela* 120 B4
Cabugao, *Phil.* 55 C4
Cabuyaro, *Colombia* 120 C3
Cacabelos, *Spain* 30 C4
Čačak, *Serbia* 21 M10
Cacao, *Fr. Guiana* 121 C7
Cáceres, *Brazil* 125 D6
Cáceres, *Colombia* 120 B2
Cáceres, *Spain* 31 F4
Cáceres □, *Spain* 31 F4
Cache Bay, *Canada* 98 C4
Cache Cr. →, *U.S.A.* 112 G5
Cachepo, *Portugal* 31 H3
Cachéu, *Guinea-Biss.* 78 C1
Cachi, *Argentina* 126 B2
Cachimbo, *Brazil* 125 B7
Cachimbo, Serra do, *Brazil* 125 B6
Cachoeira, *Brazil* 123 D4
Cachoeira Alta, *Brazil* 123 E1
Cachoeira de Itapemirim, *Brazil* 123 F3
Cachoeira do Sul, *Brazil* 127 C5
Cachoeiro do Arari, *Brazil* 122 B2
Cachopo, *Portugal* 31 H3
Cachuela Esperanza, *Bolivia* 125 C4
Cacólo, *Angola* 80 G3
Caconda, *Angola* 81 G3
Cacongo, *Angola* 80 F2
Caçu, *Brazil* 123 E1
Caculé, *Brazil* 123 D3
Cadarache, *France* 27 E9
Čadca, *Slovak Rep.* 20 F8
Caddo, *U.S.A.* 109 H6
Cadell Cr. →, *Australia* 90 C3
Cadenazzo, *Switz.* 23 D7
Cader Idris, *U.K.* 12 E4
Cadí, Sierra del, *Spain* 28 C6
Cadibarrawirracanna, L., *Australia* 91 D2
Cadillac, *Canada* 98 C4
Cadillac, *France* 26 D3
Cadillac, *U.S.A.* 104 C3
Cadiz, *Phil.* 55 F5
Cádiz, *Spain* 31 J4
Cadiz, *U.S.A.* 106 F4
Cádiz □, *Spain* 31 J5
Cádiz, G. de, *Spain* 31 J4
Cadney Park, *Australia* 91 D1
Cadomin, *Canada* 100 C5
Cadotte →, *Canada* 100 B5
Cadours, *France* 26 E5
Cadoux, *Australia* 89 F2
Caen, *France* 24 C6
Caernarfon, *U.K.* 12 D3
Caernarfon B., *U.K.* 12 D3
Caernarvon = Caernarfon, *U.K.* 12 D3
Caerphilly, *U.K.* 13 F4
Caesarea, *Israel* 69 C3
Caeté, *Brazil* 123 E3
Caetité, *Brazil* 123 D3
Cafayate, *Argentina* 126 B2
Cafifi, *Colombia* 120 B3
Cafu, *Angola* 84 B2
Cagayan →, *Phil.* 55 B4
Cagayan de Oro, *Phil.* 55 G6
Cagayan Is., *Phil.* 55 G4
Cagayan Sulu I., *Phil.* 55 H3
Cagli, *Italy* 33 E9
Cágliari, *Italy* 34 C2
Cágliari, G. di, *Italy* 34 C2
Cagnano Varano, *Italy* 35 A8
Cagnes-sur-Mer, *France* 27 E11
Caguán →, *Colombia* 120 D3
Caguas, *Puerto Rico* 117 C6
Caha Mts., *Ireland* 15 E2
Cahama, *Angola* 84 B1
Caher, *Ireland* 15 D4
Cahersiveen, *Ireland* 15 E1
Cahora Bassa Dam, *Mozam.* 83 F3
Cahore Pt., *Ireland* 15 D5
Cahors, *France* 26 D5
Cahuapanas, *Peru* 124 B2
Cahuinari →, *Colombia* 120 D3
Cai Bau, Dao, *Vietnam* 58 B6
Cai Nuoc, *Vietnam* 59 H5
Caia, *Mozam.* 83 F4
Caiabis, Serra dos, *Brazil* 125 C6
Caianda, *Angola* 83 E1
Caiapó, Serra do, *Brazil* 125 D7
Caiapônia, *Brazil* 125 D7
Caibarién, *Cuba* 116 B4

Caibiran, *Phil.* 55 F6
Caicara, *Bolívar, Venezuela* 120 B4
Caicara, *Monagas, Venezuela* 121 B5
Caicó, *Brazil* 122 C4
Caicos Is., *W. Indies* 117 B5
Caicos Passage, *W. Indies* 117 B5
Cailloma, *Peru* 124 D3
Caine →, *Bolivia* 125 D4
Caird Coast, *Antarctica* 5 D1
Cairn Gorm, *U.K.* 14 D5
Cairn Toul, *U.K.* 14 D5
Cairngorm Mts., *U.K.* 14 D5
Cairns, *Australia* 90 B4
Cairo = El Qâhira, *Egypt* 76 H7
Cairo, *Ga., U.S.A.* 105 K3
Cairo, *Ill., U.S.A.* 109 G10
Cairo Montenotte, *Italy* 32 D5
Caithness, Ord of, *U.K.* 14 C5
Caiundo, *Angola* 81 H3
Caiza, *Bolivia* 125 E4
Cajabamba, *Peru* 124 B2
Cajamarca, *Peru* 124 B2
Cajamarca □, *Peru* 124 B2
Cajapió, *Brazil* 122 B3
Cajarc, *France* 26 D5
Cajatambo, *Peru* 124 C2
Cajàzeiras, *Brazil* 122 C4
Čajetina, *Serbia, Yug.* 21 M9
Çakirgol, *Turkey* 43 F8
Čakovec, *Croatia* 33 B13
Çal, *Turkey* 66 D3
Cala, *Spain* 31 H4
Cala →, *Spain* 31 H4
Cala Cadolar, Punta de, *Spain* 29 G6
Cala d'Or, *Spain* 36 B10
Cala Figuera, C., *Spain* 36 B9
Cala Forcat, *Spain* 36 A10
Cala Mayor, *Spain* 36 B9
Cala Mezquida, *Spain* 36 B11
Cala Millor, *Spain* 36 B10
Cala Ratjada, *Spain* 36 B10
Calabanga, *Phil.* 55 E5
Calabar, *Nigeria* 79 E6
Calabozo, *Venezuela* 120 B4
Calábria □, *Italy* 35 C9
Calaburras, Pta. de, *Spain* 31 J6
Calaceite, *Spain* 28 D5
Calacota, *Bolivia* 124 D4
Calafate, *Argentina* 128 D2
Calahorra, *Spain* 28 C3
Calais, *France* 25 B8
Calais, *U.S.A.* 99 C6
Calais, Pas de, *France* 25 B8
Calalaste, Cord. de, *Argentina* 126 B2
Calama, *Brazil* 125 B5
Calama, *Chile* 126 A2
Calamar, *Bolívar, Colombia* 120 A3
Calamar, *Vaupés, Colombia* 120 C3
Calamarca, *Bolivia* 124 D4
Calamba, *Phil.* 55 F5
Calamian Group, *Phil.* 55 F3
Calamocha, *Spain* 28 E3
Calán Porter, *Spain* 36 B11
Calañas, *Spain* 31 H4
Calanda, *Spain* 28 E4
Calang, *Indonesia* 56 D1
Calangiánus, *Italy* 34 B2
Calapan, *Phil.* 55 E4
Călăraşi, *Romania* 38 E10
Calasparra, *Spain* 29 G3
Calatafimi, *Italy* 34 E5
Calatayud, *Spain* 28 D3
Calato = Kálathos, *Greece* 39 N11
Calauag, *Phil.* 55 E5
Calavà, C., *Italy* 35 D7
Calavite, C., *Phil.* 55 E4
Calayan, *Phil.* 55 B4
Calbayog, *Phil.* 55 E6
Calbe, *Germany* 18 D7
Calca, *Peru* 124 C3
Calcasieu L., *U.S.A.* 109 L8
Calci, *Italy* 32 E7
Calcutta, *India* 63 H13
Caldaro, *Italy* 33 B8
Caldas □, *Colombia* 120 B2
Caldas da Rainha, *Portugal* 31 F1
Caldas de Reyes, *Spain* 30 C2
Caldas Novas, *Brazil* 123 E2
Calder →, *U.K.* 12 D6
Caldera, *Chile* 126 B1
Caldwell, *Idaho, U.S.A.* 110 E5
Caldwell, *Kans., U.S.A.* 109 G6
Caldwell, *Tex., U.S.A.* 109 K6
Caledon, *S. Africa* 84 E2
Caledon →, *S. Africa* 84 E4
Caledon B., *Australia* 90 A2
Caledonia, *Canada* 106 C5
Caledonia, *U.S.A.* 106 D7
Calella, *Spain* 28 D7
Calemba, *Angola* 84 B2
Calenzana, *France* 27 F12
Caleta Olivia, *Argentina* 128 C3
Calexico, *U.S.A.* 113 N11
Calf of Man, *U.K.* 12 C3
Calgary, *Canada* 100 C6
Calheta, *Madeira* 36 D2
Calhoun, *U.S.A.* 105 H3
Cali, *Colombia* 120 C2
Calicut, *India* 60 P9
Caliente, *U.S.A.* 111 H6
California, *Mo., U.S.A.* 108 F8
California, *Pa., U.S.A.* 106 F5
California □, *U.S.A.* 111 H4
California, Baja, *Mexico* 114 A1
California, Baja, T.N. □, *Mexico* 114 B2
California, Baja, T.S. □, *Mexico* 114 B2
California, G. de, *Mexico* 114 B2
California City, *U.S.A.* 113 K9
California Hot Springs, *U.S.A.* 113 K8
Călimăneşti, *Romania* 38 D7
Călimani, Munţii, *Romania* 38 B8
Călineşti, *Romania* 38 D7
Calingasta, *Argentina* 126 C2
Calipatria, *U.S.A.* 113 M11
Calistoga, *U.S.A.* 112 G4
Calitri, *Italy* 35 B8
Calitzdorp, *S. Africa* 84 E3
Callabonna, L., *Australia* 91 D3
Callac, *France* 24 D3
Callan, *Ireland* 15 D4
Callander, *U.K.* 14 E4
Callantsoog, *Neths.* 16 C5
Callao, *Peru* 124 C2
Callaway, *U.S.A.* 108 E5
Calles, *Mexico* 115 C5
Callide, *Australia* 90 C5
Calling Lake, *Canada* 100 B6
Calliope, *Australia* 90 C5
Callosa de Ensarriá, *Spain* 29 G4
Callosa de Segura, *Spain* 29 G4
Calola, *Angola* 84 B2
Calolbon, *Phil.* 55 E6
Caloocan, *Phil.* 55 D4
Calore →, *Italy* 35 A7
Caloundra, *Australia* 91 D5
Calpe, *Spain* 29 G5
Calpella, *U.S.A.* 112 F3
Calpine, *U.S.A.* 112 F6
Calstock, *Canada* 98 C3
Caltabellotta, *Italy* 34 E6
Caltagirone, *Italy* 35 E7
Caltanissetta, *Italy* 35 E7
Calulo, *Angola* 80 G2
Calumet, *U.S.A.* 104 B1
Calunda, *Angola* 81 G4
Caluso, *Italy* 32 C4
Calvados □, *France* 24 C6
Calvert, *U.S.A.* 109 K6
Calvert →, *Australia* 90 B2
Calvert Hills, *Australia* 90 B2
Calvert I., *Canada* 100 C3
Calvert Ra., *Australia* 88 D3
Calvi, *France* 27 F12
Calvillo, *Mexico* 114 C4
Calvinia, *S. Africa* 84 E2
Calw, *Germany* 19 G4
Calwa, *U.S.A.* 112 J7
Calzada Almuradiel, *Spain* 29 G1
Calzada de Calatrava, *Spain* 31 G7
Cam →, *U.K.* 13 E8
Cam Lam, *Vietnam* 59 G7
Cam Pha, *Vietnam* 58 B6
Cam Ranh, *Vietnam* 59 G7
Cam Xuyen, *Vietnam* 58 C6
Camabatela, *Angola* 80 F3
Camacã, *Brazil* 123 E4
Camaçari, *Brazil* 123 D4
Camacha, *Madeira* 36 D3
Camacho, *Mexico* 114 C4
Camacupa, *Angola* 81 G3
Camaguán, *Venezuela* 120 B4
Camagüey, *Cuba* 116 B4
Camaiore, *Italy* 32 E7
Camamu, *Brazil* 123 D4
Camaná, *Peru* 124 D3
Camanche Reservoir, *U.S.A.* 112 G6
Camaquã →, *Brazil* 127 C5
Câmara de Lobos, *Madeira* 36 D3
Camararé →, *Brazil* 125 C6
Camarat, C., *France* 27 E10
Camaret, *France* 24 D2
Camargo, *Bolivia* 125 E4
Camargue, *France* 27 E8
Camarillo, *U.S.A.* 113 L7
Camariñas, *Spain* 30 B1
Camarón, C., *Honduras* 116 C2
Camarones, *Argentina* 128 B3
Camarones, B., *Argentina* 128 B3
Camas, *U.S.A.* 112 E4
Camas Valley, *U.S.A.* 110 E2
Cambados, *Spain* 30 C2
Cambará, *Brazil* 127 A5
Cambay = Khambhat, *India* 62 H5
Cambay, G. of = Khambat, G. of, *India* 62 J5
Cambil, *Spain* 29 H1
Cambo-les-Bains, *France* 26 E2
Cambodia ■, *Asia* 58 F5
Camborne, *U.K.* 13 G2
Cambrai, *France* 25 B10
Cambria, *U.S.A.* 111 J3
Cambrian Mts., *U.K.* 13 E4
Cambridge, *Canada* 98 D3
Cambridge, *Jamaica* 116 C4
Cambridge, *N.Z.* 87 G5
Cambridge, *U.K.* 13 E8
Cambridge, *Idaho, U.S.A.* 110 D5
Cambridge, *Mass., U.S.A.* 107 D13
Cambridge, *Md., U.S.A.* 104 F7
Cambridge, *Minn., U.S.A.* 108 C8
Cambridge, *N.Y., U.S.A.* 107 C11
Cambridge, *Nebr., U.S.A.* 108 E4
Cambridge, *Ohio, U.S.A.* 106 F3
Cambridge Bay, *Canada* 96 B9
Cambridge G., *Australia* 88 B4
Cambridge Springs, *U.S.A.* 106 E4
Cambridgeshire □, *U.K.* 13 E8
Cambrils, *Spain* 28 D6
Cambuci, *Brazil* 123 F3
Cambundi-Catembo, *Angola* 80 G3
Camden, *Ala., U.S.A.* 105 K2
Camden, *Ark., U.S.A.* 109 J8
Camden, *Maine, U.S.A.* 99 D6
Camden, *N.J., U.S.A.* 107 G9
Camden, *S.C., U.S.A.* 105 H5
Camden Sd., *Australia* 88 C3
Camdenton, *U.S.A.* 109 F8
Çameli, *Turkey* 66 E3
Camembert, *France* 24 D7
Cámeri, *Italy* 32 C5
Camerino, *Italy* 33 E10
Cameron, *Ariz., U.S.A.* 111 J8
Cameron, *La., U.S.A.* 109 L8
Cameron, *Mo., U.S.A.* 108 F7
Cameron, *Tex., U.S.A.* 109 K6
Cameron Falls, *Canada* 98 C2
Cameron Highlands, *Malaysia* 59 K3
Cameron Hills, *Canada* 100 B5
Cameroon ■, *Africa* 73 G7
Camerota, *Italy* 35 B8
Cameroun →, *Cameroon* 79 E6
Cameroun, Mt., *Cameroon* 79 E6
Cametá, *Brazil* 122 B2
Camiguin □, *Phil.* 55 G6
Camiguin I., *Phil.* 55 B4
Camiling, *Phil.* 55 D4
Caminha, *Portugal* 30 D2
Camino, *U.S.A.* 112 G6
Camira Creek, *Australia* 91 D5
Camiranga, *Brazil* 122 B2
Camiri, *Bolivia* 125 E5
Camissombo, *Angola* 80 F4
Cammal, *U.S.A.* 106 E7
Camocim, *Brazil* 122 B3
Camogli, *Italy* 32 D6
Camooweal, *Australia* 90 B2
Camopi, *Fr. Guiana* 121 C7
Camopi →, *Fr. Guiana* 121 C7
Camotes Is., *Phil.* 55 F6
Camotes Sea, *Phil.* 55 F6
Camp Crook, *U.S.A.* 108 C3
Camp Nelson, *U.S.A.* 113 J8
Camp Wood, *U.S.A.* 109 L4
Campagna, *Italy* 35 B8
Campana, *Argentina* 126 C4
Campana, I., *Chile* 128 C1
Campanário, *Madeira* 36 D2
Campanario, *Spain* 31 G5
Campania □, *Italy* 35 B7
Campbell, *S. Africa* 84 D3
Campbell, *Calif., U.S.A.* 112 H5
Campbell, *Ohio, U.S.A.* 106 E4
Campbell I., *Pac. Oc.* 92 N8
Campbell L., *Canada* 101 A7
Campbell River, *Canada* 100 C3
Campbell Town, *Australia* 90 G4
Campbellford, *Canada* 106 B7
Campbellpur, *Pakistan* 62 C5
Campbellsville, *U.S.A.* 104 G3
Campbellton, *Canada* 99 C6
Campbelltown, *Australia* 91 E5
Campbeltown, *U.K.* 14 F3
Campeche, *Mexico* 115 D6
Campeche □, *Mexico* 115 D6
Campeche, B. de, *Mexico* 115 D6
Camperdown, *Australia* 91 F3
Camperville, *Canada* 101 C8
Campi Salentina, *Italy* 35 B11
Campidano, *Italy* 34 C1
Campíglia Maríttima, *Italy* 32 E7
Campillo de Altobuey, *Spain* 28 F3
Campillo de Llerena, *Spain* 31 G5
Campillos, *Spain* 31 H6
Campina Grande, *Brazil* 122 C4
Campina Verde, *Brazil* 123 E2
Campinas, *Brazil* 127 A6
Campine, *Belgium* 17 F6
Campli, *Italy* 33 F10
Campo, *Cameroon* 80 D1
Campo, *Spain* 28 C5
Campo Belo, *Brazil* 123 F2
Campo de Criptana, *Spain* 29 F1
Campo de Diauarum, *Brazil* 125 C7
Campo de Gibraltar, *Spain* 31 J5
Campo Flórido, *Brazil* 123 E2
Campo Formoso, *Brazil* 122 D3
Campo Grande, *Brazil* 125 E7
Campo Maíor, *Brazil* 122 B3
Campo Maior, *Portugal* 31 G3
Campo Mourão, *Brazil* 127 A5
Campo Tencia, *Switz.* 23 D7
Campo Túres, *Italy* 33 B8
Campoalegre, *Colombia* 120 C2
Campobasso, *Italy* 35 A7
Campobello di Licata, *Italy* 34 E6
Campobello di Mazara, *Italy* 34 E5
Campofelice, *Italy* 34 E6
Camporeale, *Italy* 34 E6
Campos, *Brazil* 123 F3
Campos Altos, *Brazil* 123 E2
Campos Belos, *Brazil* 123 D2
Campos del Puerto, *Spain* 36 B10
Campos Novos, *Brazil* 127 B5
Campos Sales, *Brazil* 122 C3
Camprodón, *Spain* 28 C7
Camptonville, *U.S.A.* 112 F5
Campuya →, *Peru* 120 D3
Camrose, *Canada* 100 C6
Camsell Portage, *Canada* 101 B7
Çan, *Turkey* 66 C2
Can Clavo, *Spain* 36 C7
Can Creu, *Spain* 36 C7
Can Gio, *Vietnam* 59 G6
Can Tho, *Vietnam* 59 G5
Canaan, *U.S.A.* 107 D11
Canada ■, *N. Amer.* 96 C10
Cañada de Gómez, *Argentina* 126 C3
Canadian, *U.S.A.* 109 H4
Canadian →, *U.S.A.* 109 H7
Canadian Shield, *Canada* 97 C10
Çanakkale, *Turkey* 39 J9
Çanakkale □, *Turkey* 66 C2
Çanakkale Boğazı, *Turkey* 66 C2
Canal Flats, *Canada* 100 C5
Canalejas, *Argentina* 126 D2
Canals, *Argentina* 126 C3
Canals, *Spain* 29 G4
Canandaigua, *U.S.A.* 106 D7
Cananea, *Mexico* 114 A2
Cañar, *Ecuador* 120 D2
Cañar □, *Ecuador* 120 D2
Canarias, Is., *Atl. Oc.* 36 F4
Canarreos, Arch. de los, *Cuba* 116 B3
Canary Is. = Canarias, Is., *Atl. Oc.* 36 F4
Canastra, Serra da, *Brazil* 123 F2
Canatlán, *Mexico* 114 C4
Canaveral, C., *U.S.A.* 105 L5
Cañaveras, *Spain* 28 E2
Canavieiras, *Brazil* 123 E4
Canbelego, *Australia* 91 E4
Canberra, *Australia* 91 F4
Canby, *Calif., U.S.A.* 110 F3
Canby, *Minn., U.S.A.* 108 C6
Canby, *Oreg., U.S.A.* 112 E4
Cancale, *France* 24 D5
Canche →, *France* 25 B8
Canchyuaya, Cordillera de, *Peru* 124 B3
Cancún, *Mexico* 115 C7
Candala, *Somali Rep.* 68 E4
Candarave, *Peru* 124 D3
Candas, *Spain* 30 B5
Candé, *France* 24 E5
Candeias →, *Brazil* 125 B5
Candela, *Italy* 35 A8
Candelaria, *Argentina* 127 B4
Candelaria, *Canary Is.* 36 F3
Candelaria, Pta. de la, *Spain* 30 B2
Candeleda, *Spain* 30 E5
Candelo, *Australia* 91 F4
Candia = Iráklion, *Greece* 37 D7
Candia, Sea of = Crete, Sea of, *Greece* 39 N8
Cândido de Abreu, *Brazil* 123 F1
Cândido Mendes, *Brazil* 122 B2
Candle L., *Canada* 101 C7
Candlemas I., *Antarctica* 5 B1
Cando, *U.S.A.* 108 A5
Candon, *Phil.* 55 C4
Canea = Khaniá, *Greece* 37 D6
Canela, *Brazil* 122 D2
Canelli, *Italy* 32 D5
Canelones, *Uruguay* 127 C4
Canet-Plage, *France* 26 F7
Cañete, *Chile* 126 D1
Cañete, *Peru* 124 C2
Cañete, *Spain* 28 E3
Cañete de las Torres, *Spain* 31 H6
Canfranc, *Spain* 28 C4
Cangas, *Spain* 30 C2
Cangas de Narcea, *Spain* 30 B4
Cangas de Onís, *Spain* 30 B5
Canguaretama, *Brazil* 122 C4
Canguçu, *Brazil* 127 C5
Cangxi, *China* 52 B5
Cangyuan, *China* 52 F2
Cangzhou, *China* 50 E9
Cani, I., *Tunisia* 75 A7
Canicattì, *Italy* 34 E6
Canicattini, *Italy* 35 E8
Canim Lake, *Canada* 100 C4
Canindé, *Brazil* 122 B4
Canindé →, *Brazil* 122 C3
Canindeyu □, *Paraguay* 127 A4
Canipaan, *Phil.* 56 C5
Canisteo, *U.S.A.* 106 D7
Canisteo →, *U.S.A.* 106 D7
Cañitas, *Mexico* 114 C4
Cañizal, *Spain* 30 D5
Canjáyar, *Spain* 29 H2
Çankırı, *Turkey* 66 C5
Çankırı □, *Turkey* 66 C5
Cankuzo, *Burundi* 82 C3
Canmore, *Canada* 100 C5
Cann River, *Australia* 91 F4
Canna, *U.K.* 14 D2
Cannanore, *India* 60 P9
Cannes, *France* 27 E11
Canning Town = Port Canning, *India* 63 H13
Cannington, *Canada* 106 B5
Cannock, *U.K.* 12 E5
Cannon Ball →, *U.S.A.* 108 B4
Cannondale Mt., *Australia* 90 D4
Caño Colorado, *Colombia* 120 C4
Canoas, *Brazil* 127 B5
Canoe L., *Canada* 101 B7
Canon City, *U.S.A.* 108 F2
Canora, *Canada* 101 C8
Canosa di Púglia, *Italy* 35 A9
Canowindra, *Australia* 91 E4
Canso, *Canada* 99 C7
Canta, *Peru* 124 C2
Cantabria □, *Spain* 30 B6
Cantabria, Sierra de, *Spain* 28 C2
Cantabrian Mts. = Cantábrica, Cordillera, *Spain* 30 C5
Cantábrica, Cordillera, *Spain* 30 C5
Cantal □, *France* 26 C6
Cantal, Plomb du, *France* 26 C6
Cantanhede, *Portugal* 30 E2
Cantaura, *Venezuela* 121 B5
Cantavieja, *Spain* 28 E4
Canterbury, *Australia* 90 D3
Canterbury, *U.K.* 13 F9
Canterbury □, *N.Z.* 87 K3
Canterbury Bight, *N.Z.* 87 L3
Canterbury Plains, *N.Z.* 87 K3
Cantil, *U.S.A.* 113 K9
Cantillana, *Spain* 31 H5
Canto do Buriti, *Brazil* 122 C3
Canton = Guangzhou, *Guangdong, China* 53 F9
Canton = Guangzhou, *Guangdong, China* 53 F9
Canton, *Ga., U.S.A.* 105 H3
Canton, *Ill., U.S.A.* 108 E9
Canton, *Miss., U.S.A.* 109 J9
Canton, *Mo., U.S.A.* 108 E9
Canton, *N.Y., U.S.A.* 107 B9
Canton, *Ohio, U.S.A.* 106 F3
Canton, *Okla., U.S.A.* 109 G5
Canton, *S. Dak., U.S.A.* 108 D6
Canton L., *U.S.A.* 109 G5
Cantù, *Italy* 32 C6
Canudos, *Brazil* 125 B6
Canumã, *Amazonas, Brazil* 121 D6
Canumã, *Amazonas, Brazil* 125 B5
Canumã →, *Brazil* 125 A6
Canutama, *Brazil* 125 B5
Canutillo, *U.S.A.* 111 L10
Canyon, *Tex., U.S.A.* 109 H4
Canyon, *Wyo., U.S.A.* 110 D8
Canyonlands National Park, *U.S.A.* 111 G9
Canyonville, *U.S.A.* 110 E2
Canzo, *Italy* 32 C6
Cao Bang, *Vietnam* 58 A6
Cao He →, *China* 51 D13
Cao Lanh, *Vietnam* 59 G5
Cao Xian, *China* 50 G8
Cáorle, *Italy* 33 C9
Cap-aux-Meules, *Canada* 99 C7
Cap-Chat, *Canada* 99 C6
Cap-de-la-Madeleine, *Canada* 98 C5
Cap-Haïtien, *Haiti* 117 C5
Cap St.-Jacques = Vung Tau, *Vietnam* 59 G6
Capa, *Vietnam* 58 A4
Capa Stilo, *Italy* 35 D9
Capáccio, *Italy* 35 B8
Capaia, *Angola* 80 F4
Capanaparo →, *Venezuela* 120 B4
Capanema, *Brazil* 122 B2
Caparo →, *Barinas, Venezuela* 120 B3
Caparo →, *Bolívar, Venezuela* 121 B5
Capatárida, *Venezuela* 120 A3
Capbreton, *France* 26 E2
Capdenac, *France* 26 D6
Cape →, *Australia* 90 C4
Cape Barren I., *Australia* 90 G4
Cape Breton Highlands Nat. Park, *Canada* 99 C7
Cape Breton I., *Canada* 99 C7
Cape Charles, *U.S.A.* 104 G8
Cape Coast, *Ghana* 79 D4
Cape Dorset, *Canada* 97 B12
Cape Dyer, *Canada* 97 B13
Cape Fear →, *U.S.A.* 105 H6
Cape Girardeau, *U.S.A.* 109 G10
Cape Jervis, *Australia* 91 F2
Cape May, *U.S.A.* 104 F8
Cape May Point, *U.S.A.* 103 C12
Cape Palmas, *Liberia* 78 E3
Cape Province □, *S. Africa* 84 E3
Cape Tormentine, *Canada* 99 C7
Cape Town, *S. Africa* 84 E2
Cape Verde Is. ■, *Atl. Oc.* 2 D8
Cape Vincent, *U.S.A.* 107 B8
Cape York Peninsula, *Australia* 90 A3
Capela, *Brazil* 122 D4
Capela de Campo, *Brazil* 122 B3
Capelinha, *Brazil* 123 E3
Capella, *Australia* 90 C4
Capendu, *France* 26 E6
Capestang, *France* 26 E7
Capim, *Brazil* 122 B2
Capim →, *Brazil* 122 B2
Capinópolis, *Brazil* 123 E2
Capinota, *Bolivia* 124 D4

Capitan, *U.S.A.* 111 K11
Capitán Aracena, I., *Chile* 128 D2
Capitán Pastene, *Chile* 128 A2
Capitola, *U.S.A.* 112 J5
Capivara, Serra da, *Brazil* 123 D3
Capizzi, *Italy* 35 E7
Čapljina, *Bos.-H.* 21 M7
Capoche →, *Mozam.* 83 F3
Capoeira, *Brazil* 125 B6
Cappadocia, *Turkey* 66 D6
Capraia, *Italy* 32 E6
Caprarola, *Italy* 33 F9
Capreol, *Canada* 98 C3
Caprera, *Italy* 34 A2
Capri, *Italy* 35 B7
Capricorn Group, *Australia* 90 C5
Capricorn Ra., *Australia* 88 D2
Caprino Veronese, *Italy* 32 C7
Caprivi Strip, *Namibia* 84 B3
Captainganj, *India* 63 F10
Captain's Flat, *Australia* 91 F4
Captieux, *France* 26 D3
Cápua, *Italy* 35 A7
Caquetá □, *Colombia* 120 C3
Caquetá →, *Colombia* 120 D4
Carabobo, *Venezuela* 120 A4
Carabobo □, *Venezuela* 120 A4
Caracal, *Romania* 38 E7
Caracaraí, *Brazil* 121 C5
Caracas, *Venezuela* 120 A4
Caracol, *Brazil* 122 C3
Caracollo, *Bolivia* 124 D4
Caradoc, *Australia* 91 E3
Caráglio, *Italy* 32 D4
Carahue, *Chile* 128 A2
Caraí, *Brazil* 123 E3
Carajás, Serra dos, *Brazil* 122 C1
Caranapatuba, *Brazil* 125 B5
Carandaiti, *Bolivia* 125 E5
Carangola, *Brazil* 123 F3
Carani, *Australia* 89 F2
Caransebeş, *Romania* 38 D5
Carantec, *France* 24 D3
Caraparaná →, *Colombia* 120 D3
Carapelle →, *Italy* 35 A8
Caras, *Peru* 124 B2
Caratasca, L., *Honduras* 116 C3
Caratinga, *Brazil* 123 E3
Caraúbas, *Brazil* 122 C4
Caravaca, *Spain* 29 G3
Caravággio, *Italy* 32 C6
Caravelas, *Brazil* 123 E4
Caraveli, *Peru* 124 D3
Caràzinho, *Brazil* 127 B5
Carballino, *Spain* 30 C2
Carballo, *Spain* 30 B2
Carberry, *Canada* 101 D9
Carbia, *Spain* 30 C2
Carbó, *Mexico* 114 B2
Carbon, *Canada* 100 C6
Carbonara, C., *Italy* 34 C2
Carbondale, *Colo., U.S.A.* 110 G10
Carbondale, *Ill., U.S.A.* 109 G10
Carbondale, *Pa., U.S.A.* 107 E9
Carbonear, *Canada* 99 C9
Carboneras, *Spain* 29 J3
Carboneras de Guadazaón, *Spain* 28 F3
Carbonia, *Italy* 34 C1
Carcabuey, *Spain* 31 H6
Carcagente, *Spain* 29 F4
Carcajou, *Canada* 100 B5
Carcar, *Phil.* 55 F5
Carcasse, C., *Haiti* 117 C5
Carcassonne, *France* 26 E6
Carche, *Spain* 29 G3
Carchi □, *Ecuador* 120 C2
Carcross, *Canada* 96 B6
Cardabia, *Australia* 88 D1
Çardak, *Turkey* 66 E3
Cardamon Hills, *India* 60 Q10
Cárdenas, *Cuba* 116 B3
Cárdenas, *San Luis Potosí, Mexico* 115 C5
Cárdenas, *Tabasco, Mexico* 115 D6
Cardenete, *Spain* 28 F3
Cardiel, L., *Argentina* 128 C2
Cardiff, *U.K.* 13 F4
Cardiff-by-the-Sea, *U.S.A.* 113 M9
Cardigan, *U.K.* 13 E3
Cardigan B., *U.K.* 13 E3
Cardinal, *Canada* 107 B9
Cardón, Punta, *Venezuela* 120 A3
Cardona, *Spain* 28 D6
Cardona, *Uruguay* 126 C4
Cardoner →, *Spain* 28 D6
Cardross, *Canada* 101 D7
Cardston, *Canada* 100 D6
Cardwell, *Australia* 90 B4
Careen L., *Canada* 101 B7
Carei, *Romania* 38 B5
Careiro, *Brazil* 121 D6
Careme, *Indonesia* 57 G13
Carentan, *France* 24 C5
Carey, *Idaho, U.S.A.* 110 E7
Carey, *Ohio, U.S.A.* 104 E4
Carey, L., *Australia* 89 E3
Carey L., *Canada* 101 A8
Careysburg, *Liberia* 78 D2
Cargèse, *France* 27 F12
Carhaix-Plouguer, *France* 24 D3
Carhuamayo, *Peru* 124 C2
Carhuas, *Peru* 124 B2
Carhué, *Argentina* 126 D3
Caria, *Turkey* 66 E3
Cariacica, *Brazil* 123 F3
Caribbean Sea, *W. Indies* 117 C5
Cariboo Mts., *Canada* 100 C4
Caribou, *U.S.A.* 99 C6
Caribou →, *Man., Canada* 101 B10
Caribou →, *N.W.T., Canada* 100 A3
Caribou I., *Canada* 98 C2
Caribou Is., *Canada* 100 A6
Caribou L., *Man., Canada* 101 B9
Caribou L., *Ont., Canada* 98 B2
Caribou Mts., *Canada* 100 B5
Carichic, *Mexico* 114 B3
Carigara, *Phil.* 55 F6
Carignan, *France* 25 C12
Carignano, *Italy* 32 D4
Carillo, *Mexico* 114 B4
Carinda, *Australia* 91 E4
Cariñena, *Spain* 28 D3
Carinhanha, *Brazil* 123 D3
Carinhanha →, *Brazil* 123 D3
Carini, *Italy* 34 D6
Carinola, *Italy* 34 A6
Caripito, *Venezuela* 121 A5
Caritianas, *Brazil* 125 B5
Carlbrod = Dimitrovgrad, *Serbia, Yug.* 21 M12
Carlentini, *Italy* 35 E8
Carleton Place, *Canada* 98 C4
Carletonville, *S. Africa* 84 D4
Carlin, *U.S.A.* 110 F5
Carlingford, L., *Ireland* 15 B5
Carlinville, *U.S.A.* 108 F10
Carlisle, *U.K.* 12 C5
Carlisle, *U.S.A.* 106 F7
Carlit, Pic, *France* 26 F5
Carloforte, *Italy* 34 C1
Carlos Casares, *Argentina* 126 D3
Carlos Chagas, *Brazil* 123 E3
Carlos Tejedor, *Argentina* 126 D3
Carlow, *Ireland* 15 D5
Carlow □, *Ireland* 15 D5
Carlsbad, *Calif., U.S.A.* 113 M9
Carlsbad, *N. Mex., U.S.A.* 109 J2
Carlyle, *Canada* 101 D8
Carlyle, *U.S.A.* 108 F10
Carmacks, *Canada* 96 B6
Carmagnola, *Italy* 32 D4
Carman, *Canada* 101 D9
Carmangay, *Canada* 100 C6
Carmanville, *Canada* 99 C9
Carmarthen, *U.K.* 13 F3
Carmarthen B., *U.K.* 13 F3
Carmaux, *France* 26 D6
Carmel, *U.S.A.* 107 E11
Carmel-by-the-Sea, *U.S.A.* 111 H3
Carmel Valley, *U.S.A.* 112 J5
Carmelo, *Uruguay* 126 C4
Carmen, *Bolivia* 124 C4
Carmen, *Colombia* 120 B2
Carmen, *Paraguay* 127 B4
Carmen →, *Mexico* 114 A3
Carmen, I., *Mexico* 114 B2
Carmen de Patagones, *Argentina* 128 B4
Cármenes, *Spain* 30 C5
Carmensa, *Argentina* 126 D2
Carmi, *U.S.A.* 104 F1
Carmichael, *U.S.A.* 112 G5
Carmila, *Australia* 90 C4
Carmona, *Spain* 31 H5
Carnarvon, *Queens., Australia* 90 C4
Carnarvon, *W. Austral., Australia* 89 D1
Carnarvon, *S. Africa* 84 E3
Carnarvon Ra., *Queens., Australia* 90 D4
Carnarvon Ra., *W. Austral., Australia* 89 E3
Carnation, *U.S.A.* 112 C5
Carnaxide, *Portugal* 31 G1
Carndonagh, *Ireland* 15 A4
Carnduff, *Canada* 101 D8
Carnegie, *U.S.A.* 106 F4
Carnegie, L., *Australia* 89 E3
Carnic Alps = Karnische Alpen, *Europe* 21 J3
Carniche Alpi = Karnische Alpen, *Europe* 21 J3
Carnot, *C.A.R.* 80 D3
Carnot, C., *Australia* 91 E2
Carnot B., *Australia* 88 C3
Carnsore Pt., *Ireland* 15 D5
Caro, *U.S.A.* 104 D4
Carol City, *U.S.A.* 105 N5
Carolina, *Brazil* 122 C2
Carolina, *Puerto Rico* 117 C6
Carolina, *S. Africa* 85 D5
Caroline I., *Kiribati* 93 H12
Caroline Is., *Pac. Oc.* 92 G6
Caron, *Canada* 101 C7
Caroni →, *Venezuela* 121 B5
Caroona, *Australia* 91 E5
Carora, *Venezuela* 120 A3
Carovigno, *Italy* 35 B10
Carpathians, *Europe* 20 F11
Carpaţii Meridionali, *Romania* 38 D8
Carpenédolo, *Italy* 32 C7
Carpentaria, G. of, *Australia* 90 A2
Carpentaria Downs, *Australia* 90 B3
Carpentras, *France* 27 D9
Carpi, *Italy* 32 D7
Carpina, *Brazil* 122 C4
Carpino, *Italy* 35 A8
Carpinteria, *U.S.A.* 113 L7
Carpio, *Spain* 30 D5
Carpolac = Morea, *Australia* 91 F3
Carr Boyd Ra., *Australia* 88 C4
Carrabelle, *U.S.A.* 105 L3
Carranya, *Australia* 88 C4
Carrara, *Italy* 32 D7
Carrascal, *Phil.* 55 G6
Carrascosa del Campo, *Spain* 28 E2
Carrauntoohill, *Ireland* 15 E2
Carretas, Punta, *Peru* 124 C2
Carrick-on-Shannon, *Ireland* 15 C3
Carrick-on-Suir, *Ireland* 15 D4
Carrickfergus, *U.K.* 15 B6
Carrickfergus □, *U.K.* 15 B6
Carrickmacross, *Ireland* 15 C5
Carrieton, *Australia* 91 E2
Carrington, *U.S.A.* 108 B5
Carrión →, *Spain* 30 D6
Carrión de los Condes, *Spain* 30 C6
Carrizal Bajo, *Chile* 126 B1
Carrizalillo, *Chile* 126 B1
Carrizo Cr. →, *U.S.A.* 109 G3
Carrizo Springs, *U.S.A.* 109 L5
Carrizozo, *U.S.A.* 111 K11
Carroll, *U.S.A.* 108 D7
Carrollton, *Ga., U.S.A.* 105 J3
Carrollton, *Ill., U.S.A.* 108 F9
Carrollton, *Ky., U.S.A.* 104 F3
Carrollton, *Mo., U.S.A.* 108 F8
Carrollton, *Ohio, U.S.A.* 106 F3
Carron →, *U.K.* 14 D3
Carron, L., *U.K.* 14 D3
Carrot →, *Canada* 101 C8
Carrot River, *Canada* 101 C8
Carrouges, *France* 24 D6
Carruthers, *Canada* 101 C7
Çarşamba, *Turkey* 66 C7
Carse of Gowrie, *U.K.* 14 E5
Carsoli, *Italy* 33 F10
Carson, *Calif., U.S.A.* 113 M8
Carson, *N. Dak., U.S.A.* 108 B4
Carson →, *U.S.A.* 112 F8
Carson City, *U.S.A.* 112 F7
Carson Sink, *U.S.A.* 110 G4
Carstairs, *U.K.* 14 F5
Cartagena, *Colombia* 120 A2
Cartagena, *Spain* 29 H4
Cartago, *Colombia* 120 C2
Cartago, *Costa Rica* 116 E3
Cartaxo, *Portugal* 31 F2
Cartaya, *Spain* 31 H3
Carteret, *France* 24 C5
Cartersville, *U.S.A.* 105 H3
Carterton, *N.Z.* 87 J5
Carthage, *Ark., U.S.A.* 109 H8
Carthage, *Ill., U.S.A.* 108 E9
Carthage, *Mo., U.S.A.* 109 G7
Carthage, *S. Dak., U.S.A.* 108 C6
Carthage, *Tex., U.S.A.* 109 J7
Cartier I., *Australia* 88 B3
Cartwright, *Canada* 99 B8
Caruaru, *Brazil* 122 C4
Carúpano, *Venezuela* 121 A5
Carutapera, *Brazil* 122 B2
Caruthersville, *U.S.A.* 109 G10
Carvalho, *Brazil* 121 D7
Carvin, *France* 25 B9
Carvoeiro, *Brazil* 121 D5
Carvoeiro, C., *Portugal* 31 F1
Casa Branca, *Brazil* 123 F2
Casa Branca, *Portugal* 31 G2
Casa Grande, *U.S.A.* 111 K8
Casablanca, *Chile* 126 C1
Casablanca, *Morocco* 74 B3
Casacalenda, *Italy* 35 A7
Casal di Principe, *Italy* 35 B7
Casalbordino, *Italy* 33 F11
Casale Monferrato, *Italy* 32 C5
Casalmaggiore, *Italy* 32 D7
Casalpusterlengo, *Italy* 32 C6
Casamance →, *Senegal* 78 C1
Casamássima, *Italy* 35 B9
Casanare □, *Colombia* 120 B3
Casanare □, *Colombia* 120 B3
Casanare →, *Colombia* 120 B4
Casarano, *Italy* 35 B11
Casares, *Spain* 31 J5
Casas Grandes, *Mexico* 114 A3
Casas Ibañez, *Spain* 29 F3
Casasimarro, *Spain* 29 F2
Casatejada, *Spain* 30 F5
Casavieja, *Spain* 30 E6
Cascade, *Idaho, U.S.A.* 110 D5
Cascade, *Mont., U.S.A.* 110 C8
Cascade Locks, *U.S.A.* 112 E5
Cascade Ra., *U.S.A.* 112 D5
Cascais, *Portugal* 31 G1
Cascavel, *Brazil* 127 A5
Cáscina, *Italy* 32 E7
Caselle Torinese, *Italy* 32 C4
Caserta, *Italy* 35 A7
Cashel, *Ireland* 15 D4
Cashmere, *U.S.A.* 110 C3
Cashmere Downs, *Australia* 89 E2
Casibare →, *Colombia* 120 C3
Casiguran, *Phil.* 55 C5
Casilda, *Argentina* 126 C3
Casino, *Australia* 91 D5
Casiquiare →, *Venezuela* 120 C4
Casitas, *Peru* 124 A1
Caslan, *Canada* 100 C6
Čáslav, *Czech.* 20 F5
Casma, *Peru* 124 B2
Casmalia, *U.S.A.* 113 L6
Casola Valsenio, *Italy* 33 D8
Cásoli, *Italy* 33 F11
Caspe, *Spain* 28 D4
Casper, *U.S.A.* 110 E10
Caspian Sea, *Asia* 44 E6
Casquets, *Chan. Is.* 24 C4
Cass City, *U.S.A.* 104 D4
Cass Lake, *U.S.A.* 108 B7
Cassá de la Selva, *Spain* 28 D7
Cassano Iónio, *Italy* 35 C9
Cassel, *France* 25 B9
Casselman, *Canada* 107 A9
Casselton, *U.S.A.* 108 B6
Cassiar, *Canada* 100 B3
Cassiar Mts., *Canada* 100 B2
Cassilândia, *Brazil* 125 D7
Cassinga, *Angola* 81 H3
Cassino, *Italy* 34 A6
Cassis, *France* 27 E9
Cassville, *U.S.A.* 109 G8
Cástagneto Carducci, *Italy* 32 E7
Castaic, *U.S.A.* 113 L8
Castanhal, *Brazil* 122 B2
Casteau, *Belgium* 17 G4
Castéggio, *Italy* 32 C6
Castejón de Monegros, *Spain* 28 D4
Castel di Sangro, *Italy* 33 G11
Castel San Giovanni, *Italy* 32 C6
Castel San Pietro, *Italy* 33 D8
Castelbuono, *Italy* 35 E7
Casteldelfino, *Italy* 32 D4
Castelfiorentino, *Italy* 32 E7
Castelfranco Emília, *Italy* 32 D8
Castelfranco Véneto, *Italy* 33 C8
Casteljaloux, *France* 26 D4
Castellabate, *Italy* 35 B7
Castellammare, G. di, *Italy* 34 D5
Castellammare del Golfo, *Italy* 34 D5
Castellammare di Stábia, *Italy* 35 B7
Castellamonte, *Italy* 32 C4
Castellana Grotte, *Italy* 35 B10
Castellane, *France* 27 E10
Castellaneta, *Italy* 35 B9
Castellar de Santisteban, *Spain* 29 G1
Castelleone, *Italy* 32 C6
Castelli, *Argentina* 126 D4
Castelló de Ampurias, *Spain* 28 C8
Castellón □, *Spain* 28 E4
Castellón de la Plana, *Spain* 28 F4
Castellote, *Spain* 28 E4
Castelltersol, *Spain* 28 D7
Castelmáuro, *Italy* 35 A7
Castelnau-de-Médoc, *France* 26 C3
Castelnaudary, *France* 26 E5
Castelnovo ne' Monti, *Italy* 32 D7
Castelnuovo di Val di Cécina, *Italy* 32 E7
Castelo, *Brazil* 123 F3
Castelo Branco, *Portugal* 30 F3
Castelo Branco □, *Portugal* 30 F3
Castelo de Paiva, *Portugal* 30 D2
Castelo de Vide, *Portugal* 31 F3
Castelo do Piauí, *Brazil* 122 C3
Castelsarrasin, *France* 26 D5
Casteltérmini, *Italy* 34 E6
Castelvetrano, *Italy* 34 E5
Casterton, *Australia* 91 F3
Castets, *France* 26 E2
Castiglione del Lago, *Italy* 33 E9
Castiglione della Pescáia, *Italy* 32 F7
Castiglione della Stiviere, *Italy* 32 C7
Castiglione Fiorentino, *Italy* 33 E8
Castilblanco, *Spain* 31 F5
Castilla, *Peru* 124 B1
Castilla, Playa de, *Spain* 31 H4
Castilla La Mancha □, *Spain* 31 F7
Castilla La Nueva = Castilla La Mancha □, *Spain* 31 F7
Castilla La Vieja = Castilla y Leon □, *Spain* 30 D6
Castilla y Leon □, *Spain* 30 D6
Castillon, Barr. de, *France* 27 E10
Castillon-en-Couserans, *France* 26 F5
Castillon-la-Bataille, *France* 26 D3
Castillonès, *France* 26 D4
Castillos, *Uruguay* 127 C5
Castle Dale, *U.S.A.* 110 G8
Castle Douglas, *U.K.* 14 G5
Castle Rock, *Colo., U.S.A.* 108 F2
Castle Rock, *Wash., U.S.A.* 112 D4
Castlebar, *Ireland* 15 C2
Castleblaney, *Ireland* 15 B5
Castlegar, *Canada* 100 D5
Castlemaine, *Australia* 91 F3
Castlereagh, *Ireland* 15 C3
Castlereagh □, *U.K.* 15 B6
Castlereagh →, *Australia* 91 E4
Castlereagh B., *Australia* 90 A2
Castletown, *I. of Man* 12 C3
Castletown Bearhaven, *Ireland* 15 E2
Castlevale, *Australia* 90 C4
Castor, *Canada* 100 C6
Castres, *France* 26 E6
Castricum, *Neths.* 16 C5
Castries, *St. Lucia* 117 D7
Castril, *Spain* 29 H2
Castro, *Brazil* 127 A5
Castro, *Chile* 128 B2
Castro Alves, *Brazil* 123 D4
Castro del Río, *Spain* 31 H6
Castro Marim, *Portugal* 31 H3
Castro Urdiales, *Spain* 28 B1
Castro Verde, *Portugal* 31 H2
Castrojeriz, *Spain* 30 C6
Castropol, *Spain* 30 B3
Castroreale, *Italy* 35 D8
Castrovíllari, *Italy* 35 C9
Castroville, *Calif., U.S.A.* 112 J5
Castroville, *Tex., U.S.A.* 109 L5
Castrovirreyna, *Peru* 124 C2
Castuera, *Spain* 31 G5
Casummit Lake, *Canada* 98 B1
Çat, *Turkey* 67 D9
Cat Ba, Dao, *Vietnam* 58 B6
Cat I., *Bahamas* 117 B4
Cat I., *U.S.A.* 109 K10
Cat L., *Canada* 98 B1
Catacamas, *Honduras* 116 D2
Catacáos, *Peru* 124 B1
Cataguases, *Brazil* 123 F3
Catahoula L., *U.S.A.* 109 K8
Çatak, *Turkey* 67 D10
Catalão, *Brazil* 123 E2
Çatalca, *Turkey* 66 C3
Catalina, *Canada* 99 C9
Catalonia = Cataluña □, *Spain* 28 D6
Cataluña □, *Spain* 28 D6
Çatalzeytin, *Turkey* 66 C6
Catamarca, *Argentina* 126 B2
Catamarca □, *Argentina* 126 B2
Catanauan, *Phil.* 55 E5
Catanduanes, *Phil.* 55 E6
Catanduva, *Brazil* 127 A6
Catánia, *Italy* 35 E8
Catánia, G. di, *Italy* 35 E8
Catanzaro, *Italy* 35 D9
Cataonia, *Turkey* 66 E6
Catarman, *Phil.* 55 E6
Catbalogan, *Phil.* 55 F6
Cateel, *Phil.* 55 H7
Catende, *Brazil* 122 C4
Cathcart, *S. Africa* 84 E4
Cathlamet, *U.S.A.* 112 D3
Catio, *Guinea-Biss.* 78 C1
Catismiña, *Venezuela* 121 C5
Catita, *Brazil* 122 C3
Catlettsburg, *U.S.A.* 104 F4
Catoche, C., *Mexico* 115 C7
Catolé do Rocha, *Brazil* 122 C4
Catral, *Spain* 29 G4
Catria, Mt., *Italy* 33 E9
Catrimani, *Brazil* 121 C5
Catrimani →, *Brazil* 121 C5
Catskill, *U.S.A.* 107 D11
Catskill Mts., *U.S.A.* 107 D10
Catt, Mt., *Australia* 90 A1
Cattaraugus, *U.S.A.* 106 D6
Cattólica, *Italy* 33 E9
Cattólica Eraclea, *Italy* 34 E6
Catu, *Brazil* 123 D4
Catuala, *Angola* 84 B2
Catur, *Mozam.* 83 E4
Catwick Is., *Vietnam* 59 G7
Cauca □, *Colombia* 120 C2
Cauca →, *Colombia* 120 B3
Caucaia, *Brazil* 122 B4
Caucasia, *Colombia* 120 B2
Caucasus = Bolshoi Kavkas, *Asia* 43 E11
Caudebec-en-Caux, *France* 24 C7
Caudete, *Spain* 29 G3
Caudry, *France* 25 B10
Caulnes, *France* 24 D4
Caulónia, *Italy* 35 D9
Caúngula, *Angola* 80 F3
Cauquenes, *Chile* 126 D1
Caura →, *Venezuela* 121 B5
Caurés →, *Brazil* 121 D5
Cauresi →, *Mozam.* 83 F3
Causapscal, *Canada* 99 C6
Caussade, *France* 26 D5
Causse-Méjean, *France* 26 D7
Cauterets, *France* 26 F3
Cautín □, *Chile* 128 A2
Cauvery →, *India* 60 P11
Caux, Pays de, *France* 24 C7
Cava dei Tirreni, *Italy* 35 B7
Cávado →, *Portugal* 30 D2
Cavaillon, *France* 27 E9
Cavalaire-sur-Mer, *France* 27 E10
Cavalcante, *Brazil* 123 D2
Cavalese, *Italy* 33 B8
Cavalier, *U.S.A.* 108 A6
Cavalla = Cavally →, *Africa* 78 E3
Cavallo, I. de, *France* 27 G13
Cavally →, *Africa* 78 E3
Cavan, *Ireland* 15 C4
Cavan □, *Ireland* 15 C4

Cavárzere, *Italy* 33 C9
Cave City, *U.S.A.* 104 G3
Cavenagh Ra., *Australia* 89 E4
Cavendish, *Australia* 91 F3
Caviana, I., *Brazil* 121 C7
Cavite, *Phil.* 55 D4
Cavour, *Italy* 32 D4
Cavtat, *Croatia* 21 N8
Cavuşcu Gölü, *Turkey* 66 D4
Cawndilla L., *Australia* 91 E3
Cawnpore = Kanpur, *India* 63 F9
Caxias, *Brazil* 122 B3
Caxias do Sul, *Brazil* 127 B5
Caxine, C., *Algeria* 75 A4
Caxito, *Angola* 80 F2
Çay, *Turkey* 66 D4
Cay Sal Bank, *Bahamas* 116 B3
Cayambe, *Ecuador* 120 C2
Cayambe, *Ecuador* 120 C2
Çaycuma, *Turkey* 66 C5
Çayeli, *Turkey* 67 C9
Cayenne, *Fr. Guiana* 121 B7
Cayenne □, *Fr. Guiana* 121 C7
Cayeux-sur-Mer, *France* 25 B8
Cayiralan, *Turkey* 66 D6
Caylus, *France* 26 D5
Cayman Brac, *Cayman Is.* 116 C4
Cayman Is. ■, *W. Indies* 116 C3
Cayo Romano, *Cuba* 117 B4
Cayuga, *Canada* 106 D5
Cayuga, *U.S.A.* 107 D8
Cayuga L., *U.S.A.* 107 D8
Cazalla de la Sierra, *Spain* 31 H5
Căzăneşti, *Romania* 38 E10
Cazaux et de Sanguinet, Étang de, *France* 26 D2
Cazères, *France* 26 E5
Cazin, *Bos.-H.* 33 D12
Čazma, *Croatia* 33 C13
Čazma →, *Croatia* 33 C13
Cazombo, *Angola* 81 G4
Cazorla, *Spain* 29 H1
Cazorla, *Venezuela* 120 B4
Cazorla, Sierra de, *Spain* 29 G2
Cea →, *Spain* 30 C5
Ceanannus Mor, *Ireland* 15 C5
Ceará = Fortaleza, *Brazil* 122 B4
Ceará □, *Brazil* 122 C4
Ceará Mirim, *Brazil* 122 C4
Cebaco, I. de, *Panama* 116 E3
Cebollar, *Argentina* 126 B2
Cebollera, Sierra de, *Spain* 28 D2
Cebreros, *Spain* 30 E6
Cebu, *Phil.* 55 F5
Ceccano, *Italy* 34 A6
Čechi, *Ivory C.* 78 D4
Čechy, *Czech.* 19 F9
Cecil Plains, *Australia* 91 D5
Cécina, *Italy* 32 E7
Cécina →, *Italy* 32 E7
Ceclavin, *Spain* 30 F4
Cedar →, *U.S.A.* 108 E9
Cedar City, *U.S.A.* 111 H7
Cedar Creek Reservoir, *U.S.A.* 109 J6
Cedar Falls, *Iowa, U.S.A.* 108 D8
Cedar Falls, *Wash., U.S.A.* 112 C5
Cedar Key, *U.S.A.* 105 L4
Cedar L., *Canada* 101 C8
Cedar Rapids, *U.S.A.* 108 E9
Cedartown, *U.S.A.* 105 H3
Cedarvale, *Canada* 100 B3
Cedarville, *S. Africa* 85 E4
Cedarville, *U.S.A.* 110 F3
Cedeira, *Spain* 30 B2
Cedral, *Mexico* 114 C4
Cedrino →, *Italy* 34 B2
Cedro, *Brazil* 122 C4
Cedros, I. de, *Mexico* 114 B1
Ceduna, *Australia* 91 E1
Cefalù, *Italy* 35 D7
Cega →, *Spain* 30 D6
Cegléd, *Hungary* 21 H9
Céglie Messápico, *Italy* 35 B10
Cehegín, *Spain* 29 G3
Ceheng, *China* 52 E5
Cehu-Silvaniei, *Romania* 38 B6
Ceira →, *Portugal* 30 E2
Cekhira, *Tunisia* 75 B7
Celano, *Italy* 33 F10
Celanova, *Spain* 30 C3
Celaya, *Mexico* 114 C4
Celbridge, *Ireland* 15 C5
Celebes = Sulawesi □, *Indonesia* 57 E6
Celebes Sea = Sulawesi Sea, *Indonesia* 57 D6
Celendín, *Peru* 124 B2
Čelić, *Bos.-H., Yug.* 21 L8
Celica, *Ecuador* 120 D2
Celina, *U.S.A.* 104 E3
Celje, *Slovenia* 33 B12
Celle, *Germany* 18 C6
Celles, *Belgium* 17 G2
Celorico da Beira, *Portugal* 30 E3
Cement, *U.S.A.* 109 H5
Çemişgezek, *Turkey* 67 D8
Cenepa →, *Peru* 120 D2
Cengong, *China* 52 D7
Ceno →, *Italy* 32 D7
Centallo, *Italy* 32 D4
Centenário do Sul, *Brazil* 123 F1
Center, *N. Dak., U.S.A.* 108 B4
Center, *Tex., U.S.A.* 109 K7
Centerfield, *U.S.A.* 111 G8
Centerville, *Calif., U.S.A.* 112 J7
Centerville, *Iowa, U.S.A.* 108 E8
Centerville, *Pa., U.S.A.* 106 F5
Centerville, *S. Dak., U.S.A.* 108 D6
Centerville, *Tenn., U.S.A.* 105 H2
Centerville, *Tex., U.S.A.* 109 K7
Cento, *Italy* 33 D8
Central, *Brazil* 122 D3
Central, *U.S.A.* 111 K9
Central □, *Kenya* 82 C4
Central □, *Malawi* 83 E3
Central □, *U.K.* 14 E4
Central □, *Zambia* 83 E2
Central, Cordillera, *Bolivia* 125 D5
Central, Cordillera, *Colombia* 120 C2
Central, Cordillera, *Costa Rica* 116 D3
Central, Cordillera, *Dom. Rep.* 117 C5
Central, Cordillera, *Peru* 124 B2
Central, Cordillera, *Phil.* 55 C4
Central, Sistema, *Spain* 30 E5
Central African Rep. ■, *Africa* 73 G9
Central City, *Ky., U.S.A.* 104 G2
Central City, *Nebr., U.S.A.* 108 E5
Central I., *Kenya* 82 B4
Central Makran Range, *Pakistan* 60 F4
Central Patricia, *Canada* 98 B1
Central Russian Uplands, *Europe* 6 E13
Central Siberian Plateau, *Russia* 46 C14
Centralia, *Ill., U.S.A.* 108 F10
Centralia, *Mo., U.S.A.* 108 F8
Centralia, *Wash., U.S.A.* 112 D4
Centreville, *Ala., U.S.A.* 105 J2
Centreville, *Miss., U.S.A.* 109 K9
Centúripe, *Italy* 35 E7
Cephalonia = Kefallinía, *Greece* 39 L3
Ceprano, *Italy* 34 A6
Cepu, *Indonesia* 57 G14
Ceram = Seram, *Indonesia* 57 E7
Ceram Sea = Seram Sea, *Indonesia* 57 E7
Cerbère, *France* 26 F7
Cerbicales, Is., *France* 27 G13
Cercal, *Portugal* 31 H2
Cercemaggiore, *Italy* 35 A7
Cerdaña, *Spain* 28 C6
Cerdedo, *Spain* 30 C2
Cère →, *France* 26 D5
Cerea, *Italy* 33 C8
Ceres, *Argentina* 126 B3
Ceres, *Brazil* 123 E2
Ceres, *Italy* 32 C4
Ceres, *S. Africa* 84 E2
Ceres, *U.S.A.* 112 H6
Céret, *France* 26 F6
Cereté, *Colombia* 120 B2
Cerfontaine, *Belgium* 17 H4
Cerignola, *Italy* 35 A8
Cerigo = Kíthira, *Greece* 39 N7
Cérilly, *France* 26 B6
Cerisiers, *France* 25 D10
Cerizay, *France* 24 F6
Çerkeş, *Turkey* 66 C5
Çerkezköy, *Turkey* 66 C2
Cerknica, *Slovenia* 33 C11
Çermik, *Turkey* 67 D8
Cerna →, *Romania* 38 E7
Cernavodă, *Romania* 38 E11
Cernay, *France* 25 E14
Cernik, *Croatia* 21 K7
Cerralvo, I., *Mexico* 114 C3
Cerreto Sannita, *Italy* 35 A7
Cerritos, *Mexico* 114 C4
Cerro Sombrero, *Chile* 128 D3
Certaldo, *Italy* 32 E8
Cervaro →, *Italy* 35 A8
Cervera, *Spain* 28 D6
Cervera de Pisuerga, *Spain* 30 C6
Cervera del Río Alhama, *Spain* 28 C3
Cérvia, *Italy* 33 D9
Cervignano del Friuli, *Italy* 33 C10
Cervinara, *Italy* 35 A7
Cervione, *France* 27 F13
Cervo, *Spain* 30 B3
César □, *Colombia* 120 B3
Cesaro, *Italy* 35 E7
Cesena, *Italy* 33 D9
Cesenático, *Italy* 33 D9
Cēsis, *Latvia* 40 C4
Česká Lípa, *Czech.* 20 E4
České Budějovice, *Czech.* 20 G4
Ceskomoravská Vrchovina, *Czech.* 20 F5
Český Brod, *Czech.* 20 E4
Český Krumlov, *Czech.* 20 G4
Český Těšin, *Czech.* 20 F8
Çeşme, *Turkey* 66 D2
Cessnock, *Australia* 91 E5
Cestos →, *Liberia* 78 D3
Cétin Grad, *Croatia* 33 C12
Cetina →, *Croatia* 33 E13
Cetraro, *Italy* 35 C8
Ceuta, *Morocco* 74 A3
Ceva, *Italy* 32 D5
Cévennes, *France* 26 D7
Ceyhan, *Turkey* 66 E6
Ceyhan →, *Turkey* 66 E6
Ceylânpınar, *Turkey* 67 E9
Ceylon = Sri Lanka ■, *Asia* 60 R12
Cèze →, *France* 27 D8
Cha-am, *Thailand* 58 F2
Chaam, *Neths.* 17 E5
Chabeuil, *France* 27 D9
Chablais, *France* 27 B10
Chablis, *France* 25 E10
Chabounia, *Algeria* 75 A5
Chacabuco, *Argentina* 126 C3
Chachapoyas, *Peru* 124 B2
Chachasp, *Peru* 124 D3
Chachoengsao, *Thailand* 58 F3
Chachran, *Pakistan* 60 E7
Chachro, *Pakistan* 62 G4
Chaco □, *Argentina* 126 B3
Chaco □, *Paraguay* 126 B3
Chad ■, *Africa* 73 E8
Chad, L. = Tchad, L., *Chad* 73 F7
Chadan, *Russia* 45 D10
Chadileuvú →, *Argentina* 126 D2
Chadiza, *Zambia* 83 E3
Chadron, *U.S.A.* 108 D3
Chadyr-Lunga, *Moldavia* 42 C3
Chae Hom, *Thailand* 58 C2
Chaem →, *Thailand* 58 C2
Chaeryŏng, *N. Korea* 51 E13
Chagai Hills, *Afghan.* 60 E3
Chagda, *Russia* 45 D14
Chagny, *France* 25 F11
Chagoda, *Russia* 40 B9
Chagos Arch., *Ind. Oc.* 46 K11
Chāh Ākhvor, *Iran* 65 C8
Chāh Bahār, *Iran* 65 E9
Chāh-e-Malek, *Iran* 65 D8
Chāh Kavīr, *Iran* 65 D7
Chahar Burjak, *Afghan.* 60 D3
Chaibasa, *India* 61 H14
Chaillé-les-Marais, *France* 26 B2
Chainat, *Thailand* 58 E3
Chaitén, *Chile* 128 B2
Chaiya, *Thailand* 59 H2
Chaj Doab, *Pakistan* 62 C5
Chajari, *Argentina* 126 C4
Chake Chake, *Tanzania* 82 D4
Chakhānsūr, *Afghan.* 60 D3
Chakonipau, L., *Canada* 99 A6
Chakradharpur, *India* 63 H11
Chakwal, *Pakistan* 62 C5
Chala, *Peru* 124 D3
Chalais, *France* 26 C4
Chalchihuites, *Mexico* 114 C4
Chalcis = Khalkís, *Greece* 39 L6
Chaleur B., *Canada* 99 C6
Chalfant, *U.S.A.* 112 H8
Chalhuanca, *Peru* 124 C3
Chalindrey, *France* 25 E12
Chaling, *China* 53 D9
Chalisgaon, *India* 60 J9
Chalkar, *Kazakhstan* 43 A14
Chalkar, Ozero, *Kazakhstan* 43 A14
Chalky Inlet, *N.Z.* 87 M1
Challans, *France* 24 F5
Challapata, *Bolivia* 124 D4
Challis, *U.S.A.* 110 D6
Chalna, *India* 63 H13
Chalon-sur-Saône, *France* 25 F11
Chalonnes-sur-Loire, *France* 24 E6
Châlons-sur-Marne, *France* 25 D11
Châlus, *France* 26 C4
Chalyaphum, *Thailand* 58 E4
Cham, *Germany* 19 F8
Cham, *Switz.* 23 B6
Cham, Cu Lao, *Vietnam* 58 E7
Chama, *U.S.A.* 111 H10
Chaman, *Pakistan* 60 D5
Chamba, *India* 62 C7
Chamba, *Tanzania* 83 E4
Chambal →, *India* 63 F8
Chamberlain, *U.S.A.* 108 D5
Chamberlain →, *Australia* 88 C4
Chambers, *U.S.A.* 111 J9
Chambersburg, *U.S.A.* 104 F7
Chambéry, *France* 27 C9
Chambly, *Canada* 107 A11
Chambord, *Canada* 99 C5
Chamchamal, *Iraq* 64 C5
Chamela, *Mexico* 114 D3
Chamical, *Argentina* 126 C2
Chamkar Luong, *Cambodia* 59 G4
Chamonix-Mont-Blanc, *France* 27 C10
Champa, *India* 63 H10
Champagne, *Canada* 100 A1
Champagne, *France* 25 D11
Champagne, Plaine de, *France* 25 D11
Champagnole, *France* 25 F12
Champaign, *U.S.A.* 104 E1
Champassak, *Laos* 58 E5
Champaubert, *France* 25 D10
Champdeniers, *France* 26 B3
Champeix, *France* 26 C7
Champlain, *Canada* 104 B9
Champlain, *U.S.A.* 107 B11
Champlain, L., *U.S.A.* 107 B11
Champotón, *Mexico* 115 D6
Chamusca, *Portugal* 31 F2
Chan Chan, *Peru* 124 B2
Chana, *Thailand* 59 J3
Chañaral, *Chile* 126 B1
Chanārān, *Iran* 65 B8
Chanasma, *India* 62 H5
Chancay, *Peru* 124 C2
Chancy, *Switz.* 22 D1
Chandannagar, *India* 63 H13
Chandausi, *India* 63 E8
Chandeleur Is., *U.S.A.* 109 L10
Chandeleur Sd., *U.S.A.* 109 L10
Chandigarh, *India* 62 D7
Chandler, *Australia* 91 D1
Chandler, *Canada* 99 C7
Chandler, *Ariz., U.S.A.* 111 K8
Chandler, *Okla., U.S.A.* 109 H6
Chandless →, *Brazil* 124 B4
Chandmani, *Mongolia* 54 B4
Chandpur, *Bangla.* 61 H17
Chandpur, *India* 62 E8
Chandrapur, *India* 60 K11
Chānf, *Iran* 65 E9
Chang, *Pakistan* 62 F3
Chang, Ko, *Thailand* 59 F4
Ch'ang Chiang = Chang Jiang →, *China* 53 B13
Chang Jiang →, *China* 53 B13
Changa, *India* 63 C7
Changanacheri, *India* 60 Q10
Changane →, *Mozam.* 85 C5
Changbai, *China* 51 D15
Changbai Shan, *China* 51 C15
Changchiak'ou = Zhangjiakou, *China* 50 D8
Ch'angchou = Changzhou, *China* 53 B12
Changchun, *China* 51 C13
Changchunling, *China* 51 B13
Changde, *China* 53 C8
Changdo-ri, *N. Korea* 51 E14
Changfeng, *China* 53 A11
Changhai = Shanghai, *China* 53 B13
Changhua, *China* 53 B12
Changhŭng, *S. Korea* 51 G14
Changhŭngni, *N. Korea* 51 D15
Changjiang, *China* 54 E5
Changjin, *N. Korea* 51 D14
Changjin-chŏsuji, *N. Korea* 51 D14
Changle, *China* 53 E12
Changli, *China* 51 E10
Changling, *China* 51 B12
Changlun, *Malaysia* 59 J3
Changning, *Hunan, China* 53 D9
Changning, *Yunnan, China* 52 E2
Changping, *China* 50 D9
Changsha, *China* 53 C9
Changshan, *China* 53 C12
Changshou, *China* 52 C6
Changshu, *China* 53 B13
Changshun, *China* 52 D6
Changtai, *China* 53 E11
Changting, *China* 53 E11
Changwu, *China* 50 G4
Changxing, *China* 53 B12
Changyang, *China* 53 B8
Changyi, *China* 51 F10
Changyŏn, *N. Korea* 51 E13
Changyuan, *China* 50 G8
Changzhi, *China* 50 F7
Changzhou, *China* 53 B12
Chanhanga, *Angola* 84 B1
Chanlar, *Azerbaijan* 43 F12
Channapatna, *India* 60 N10
Channel Is., *U.K.* 13 H5
Channel Is., *U.S.A.* 113 M7
Channel-Port aux Basques, *Canada* 99 C8
Channing, *Mich., U.S.A.* 104 B1
Channing, *Tex., U.S.A.* 109 H3
Chantada, *Spain* 30 C3
Chanthaburi, *Thailand* 58 F4
Chantilly, *France* 25 C9
Chantonnay, *France* 24 F5
Chantrey Inlet, *Canada* 96 B10
Chanute, *U.S.A.* 109 G7
Chanza →, *Spain* 31 H3
Chao Hu, *China* 53 B11
Chao Phraya →, *Thailand* 58 F3
Chao Phraya Lowlands, *Thailand* 58 E3
Chao Xian, *China* 53 B11
Chao'an, *China* 53 F11
Chaocheng, *China* 50 F8
Chaoyang, *Guangdong, China* 53 F11
Chaoyang, *Liaoning, China* 51 D11
Chapada dos Guimarães, *Brazil* 125 D6
Chapala, *Mozam.* 83 F4
Chapala, L. de, *Mexico* 114 C4
Chaparé →, *Bolivia* 125 D5
Chaparral, *Colombia* 120 C2
Chapayevo, *Kazakhstan* 43 A14
Chapayevsk, *Russia* 41 E16
Chapecó, *Brazil* 127 B5
Chapel Hill, *U.S.A.* 105 H6
Chapleau, *Canada* 98 C3
Chaplin, *Canada* 101 C7
Chaplino, *Ukraine* 42 B7
Chaplygin, *Russia* 41 E12
Chapra = Chhapra, *India* 63 G11
Châr, *Mauritania* 74 D2
Chara, *Russia* 45 D12
Charadai, *Argentina* 126 B4
Charagua, *Bolivia* 125 D5
Charalá, *Colombia* 120 B3
Charambirá, Punta, *Colombia* 120 C2
Charaña, *Bolivia* 124 D4
Charapita, *Colombia* 120 D3
Charata, *Argentina* 126 B3
Charcas, *Mexico* 114 C4
Charcoal L., *Canada* 101 B8
Chard, *U.K.* 13 G5
Chardara, *Kazakhstan* 44 E7
Chardon, *U.S.A.* 106 E3
Chardzhou, *Turkmenistan* 44 F7
Charente □, *France* 26 C4
Charente →, *France* 26 C2
Charente-Maritime □, *France* 26 C3
Charentsavan, *Armenia* 43 F11
Chari →, *Chad* 73 F7
Chārīkār, *Afghan.* 60 B6
Chariton →, *U.S.A.* 108 F8
Charity, *Guyana* 121 B6
Chärjew = Chardzhou, *Turkmenistan* 44 F7
Charkhari, *India* 63 G8
Charkhi Dadri, *India* 62 E7
Charleroi, *Belgium* 17 H4
Charleroi, *U.S.A.* 106 F5
Charles, C., *U.S.A.* 104 G8
Charles City, *U.S.A.* 108 D8
Charles L., *Canada* 101 B6
Charles Town, *U.S.A.* 104 F7
Charleston, *Ill., U.S.A.* 104 F1
Charleston, *Miss., U.S.A.* 109 H9
Charleston, *Mo., U.S.A.* 109 G10
Charleston, *S.C., U.S.A.* 105 J6
Charleston, *W. Va., U.S.A.* 104 F5
Charleston Peak, *U.S.A.* 113 J11
Charlestown, *S. Africa* 85 D4
Charlestown, *U.S.A.* 104 F3
Charlesville, *Zaïre* 80 F4
Charleville = Rath Luirc, *Ireland* 15 D3
Charleville, *Australia* 91 D4
Charleville-Mézières, *France* 25 C11
Charlevoix, *U.S.A.* 104 C3
Charlieu, *France* 27 B8
Charlotte, *Mich., U.S.A.* 104 D3
Charlotte, *N.C., U.S.A.* 105 H5
Charlotte Amalie, *Virgin Is.* 117 C7
Charlotte Harbor, *U.S.A.* 105 M4
Charlottesville, *U.S.A.* 104 F6
Charlottetown, *Canada* 99 C7
Charlton, *Australia* 91 F3
Charlton, *U.S.A.* 108 E8
Charlton I., *Canada* 98 B4
Charmes, *France* 25 D13
Charny, *Canada* 99 C5
Charolles, *France* 27 B8
Chârost, *France* 25 F9
Charouine, *Algeria* 75 C4
Charre, *Mozam.* 83 F4
Charroux, *France* 26 B4
Charsadda, *Pakistan* 62 B4
Charters Towers, *Australia* 90 C4
Chartres, *France* 24 D8
Chascomús, *Argentina* 126 D4
Chasefu, *Zambia* 83 E3
Chasovnya-Uchurskaya, *Russia* 45 D14
Chasseneuil-sur-Bonnieure, *France* 26 C4
Chāt, *Iran* 65 B7
Chatal Balkan = Udvoy Balkan, *Bulgaria* 38 G9
Château-Arnoux, *France* 27 D10
Château-Chinon, *France* 25 E10
Château d'Oex, *Switz.* 22 D4
Château-du-Loir, *France* 24 E7
Château-Gontier, *France* 24 E6
Château-la-Vallière, *France* 24 E7
Château-Landon, *France* 25 D9
Château-Porcien, *France* 25 C11
Château-Renault, *France* 24 E7
Château-Salins, *France* 25 D13
Château-Thierry, *France* 25 C10
Châteaubourg, *France* 24 D5
Châteaubriant, *France* 24 E5
Châteaudun, *France* 24 D8
Châteaugiron, *France* 24 D5
Châteaulin, *France* 24 D2
Châteaumeillant, *France* 26 B6
Châteauneuf-du-Faou, *France* 24 D3
Châteauneuf-en-Thymerais, *France* 24 D8
Châteauneuf-sur-Charente, *France* 26 C3
Châteauneuf-sur-Cher, *France* 25 F9
Châteauneuf-sur-Loire, *France* 25 E9
Châteaurenard, *Bouches-du-Rhône, France* 27 E8
Châteaurenard, *Loiret, France* 25 E9
Châteauroux, *France* 25 F8
Châtel-St.-Denis, *Switz.* 22 C3
Châtelaillon-Plage, *France* 26 B2
Châtelaudren, *France* 24 D4
Chatelet, *Belgium* 17 H5
Châtelguyon, *France* 26 C7
Châtellerault, *France* 24 F7
Châtelus-Malvaleix, *France* 26 B6

Chatfield, U.S.A. 108 D9
Chatham, N.B., Canada 99 C6
Chatham, Ont., Canada 98 D3
Chatham, U.K. 13 F8
Chatham, La., U.S.A. 109 J8
Chatham, N.Y., U.S.A. 107 D11
Chatham, I., Chile 128 D2
Chatham Is., Pac. Oc. 92 M10
Chatham Str., U.S.A. 100 B2
Chatillon, Italy 32 C4
Châtillon-Coligny, France 25 E9
Châtillon-en-Bazois, France 25 E10
Châtillon-en-Diois, France 27 D9
Châtillon-sur-Indre, France 24 F8
Châtillon-sur-Loire, France 25 E9
Châtillon-sur-Marne, France 25 C10
Châtillon-sur-Seine, France 25 E11
Chatmohar, Bangla. 63 G13
Chatra, India 63 G11
Chatrapur, India 61 K14
Chats, L. des, Canada 107 A8
Chatsworth, Canada 106 B4
Chatsworth, Zimbabwe 83 F3
Chattahoochee →, U.S.A. 105 K3
Chattanooga, U.S.A. 105 H3
Chaturat, Thailand 58 E3
Chau Doc, Vietnam 59 G5
Chaudanne, Barr. de, France 27 E10
Chaudes-Aigues, France 26 D7
Chauffailles, France 27 B8
Chauk, Burma 61 J19
Chaukan La, Burma 61 F20
Chaulnes, France 25 C9
Chaumont, France 25 D12
Chaumont, U.S.A. 107 B8
Chaumont-en-Vexin, France 25 C8
Chaumont-sur-Loire, France 24 E8
Chaunay, France 26 B4
Chauny, France 25 C10
Chausey, Is., France 24 D5
Chaussin, France 25 F12
Chautauqua L., U.S.A. 106 D5
Chauvigny, France 24 F7
Chauvin, Canada 101 C6
Chavantina, Brazil 125 C7
Chaves, Brazil 122 B2
Chaves, Portugal 30 D3
Chavuma, Zambia 81 G4
Chawang, Thailand 59 H2
Chazelles-sur-Lyon, France 27 C8
Chazuta, Peru 124 B2
Chazy, U.S.A. 107 B11
Cheb, Czech. 20 E2
Cheboksary, Russia 41 C15
Cheboygan, U.S.A. 104 C3
Chebsara, Russia 41 B11
Chech, Erg, Africa 74 D4
Chechaouen, Morocco 74 A3
Chechen, Os., Russia 43 E12
Checheno-Ingush Republic □, Russia 43 E11
Chechon, S. Korea 51 F15
Chęciny, Poland 20 E10
Checleset B., Canada 100 C3
Checotah, U.S.A. 109 H7
Chedabucto B., Canada 99 C7
Cheduba I., Burma 61 K18
Cheepie, Australia 91 D4
Chef-Boutonne, France 26 B3
Chegdomyn, Russia 45 D14
Chegga, Mauritania 74 C3
Chegutu, Zimbabwe 83 F3
Chehalis, U.S.A. 112 D4
Cheiron, Mt., France 27 E10
Cheju Do, S. Korea 51 H14
Chekalin, Russia 41 D10
Chekiang = Zhejiang □, China 53 C13
Chel = Kuru, Bahr el →, Sudan 77 F2
Chela, Sa. da, Angola 84 B1
Chelan, U.S.A. 110 C4
Chelan, L., U.S.A. 110 C3
Cheleken, Turkmenistan 44 F6
Chelforó, Argentina 128 A3
Chéliff, O. →, Algeria 75 A5
Chelkar, Kazakhstan 44 E6
Chelkar Tengiz, Solonchak, Kazakhstan 44 E7
Chellala Dahrania, Algeria 75 B5
Chelles, France 25 D9
Chełm, Poland 20 D13
Chełmek, Poland 20 E9
Chełmno, Poland 20 B8
Chelmsford, U.K. 13 F8
Chelmsford Dam, S. Africa 85 D4
Chełmża, Poland 20 B8
Chelsea, Okla., U.S.A. 109 G7
Chelsea, Vt., U.S.A. 107 C12
Cheltenham, U.K. 13 F5
Chelva, Spain 28 F4
Chelyabinsk, Russia 44 D7
Chelyuskin, C., Russia 46 B14
Chemainus, Canada 100 D4
Chembar = Belinskiy, Russia 41 E13
Chemillé, France 24 E6
Chemnitz, Germany 18 E8
Chemult, U.S.A. 110 E3
Chen, Gora, Russia 45 C15
Chen Xian, China 53 E9
Chenab →, Pakistan 62 D4
Chenachane, O. →, Algeria 74 C4
Chenango Forks, U.S.A. 107 D9
Chencha, Ethiopia 77 F4
Chenchiang = Zhenjiang, China 53 A12
Chênée, Belgium 17 G7
Cheney, U.S.A. 110 C5
Cheng Xian, China 50 H3
Chengbu, China 53 D8
Chengcheng, China 50 G5
Chengchou = Zhengzhou, China 50 G7
Chengde, China 51 D9
Chengdong Hu, China 53 A11
Chengdu, China 52 B5
Chenggong, China 52 E4
Chenggu, China 50 H4
Chengjiang, China 52 E4
Chengkou, China 52 B7
Ch'engtu = Chengdu, China 52 B5
Chengwu, China 50 G8
Chengxi Hu, China 53 A11
Chengyang, China 51 F11
Chenjiagang, China 51 G10
Chenkán, Mexico 115 D6
Chenxi, China 53 C8
Cheo Reo, Vietnam 58 F7
Cheom Ksan, Cambodia 58 E5
Chepelare, Bulgaria 39 H7
Chepén, Peru 124 B2
Chepes, Argentina 126 C2
Chepo, Panama 116 E4
Cheptsa →, Russia 41 B17
Cheptulil, Mt., Kenya 82 B4
Chequamegon B., U.S.A. 108 B9
Cher □, France 25 E9
Cher →, France 24 E7
Cherasco, Italy 32 D4
Cheratte, Belgium 17 G7
Cheraw, U.S.A. 105 H6
Cherbourg, France 24 C5
Cherchell, Algeria 75 A5
Cherdakly, Russia 41 D16
Cherdyn, Russia 44 C6
Cheremkhovo, Russia 45 D11
Cherepanovo, Russia 44 D9
Cherepovets, Russia 41 B10
Chergui, Chott ech, Algeria 75 B5
Cherikov, Belorussia 40 E7
Cherkassy, Ukraine 42 B5
Cherkasy = Cherkassy, Ukraine 42 B5
Cherkessk, Russia 43 D10
Cherlak, Russia 44 D8
Chernaya Kholunitsa, Russia 41 B17
Cherni, Bulgaria 38 G6
Chernigov, Ukraine 40 F7
Chernihiv = Chernigov, Ukraine 40 F7
Chernivtsi = Chernovtsy, Ukraine 42 B1
Chernobyl, Ukraine 40 F7
Chernogorsk, Russia 45 D10
Chernomorskoye, Ukraine 42 D5
Chernovskoye, Russia 41 B15
Chernovtsy, Ukraine 42 B1
Chernoye, Russia 45 B9
Chernyakhovsk, Russia 40 D2
Chernyshkovskiy, Russia 43 B10
Chernyshovskiy, Russia 45 C12
Cherokee, Iowa, U.S.A. 108 D7
Cherokee, Okla., U.S.A. 109 G5
Cherokees, Lake O' The, U.S.A. 109 G7
Cherquenco, Chile 128 A2
Cherrapunji, India 61 G17
Cherry Creek, U.S.A. 110 G6
Cherry Valley, U.S.A. 113 M10
Cherryvale, U.S.A. 109 G7
Cherskiy, Russia 45 C17
Cherskogo Khrebet, Russia 45 C15
Chertkovo, Russia 43 B9
Cherven, Belorussia 40 E6
Cherven-Bryag, Bulgaria 38 F7
Chervonograd, Ukraine 40 F4
Cherwell →, U.K. 13 F6
Chesapeake, U.S.A. 104 G7
Chesapeake B., U.S.A. 104 F7
Cheshire □, U.K. 12 D5
Cheshskaya Guba, Russia 44 C5
Cheslatta L., Canada 100 C3
Chesley, Canada 106 B3
Cheste, Spain 29 F4
Chester, U.K. 12 D5
Chester, Calif., U.S.A. 110 F3
Chester, Ill., U.S.A. 109 G10
Chester, Mont., U.S.A. 110 B8
Chester, Pa., U.S.A. 104 F8
Chester, S.C., U.S.A. 105 H5
Chesterfield, U.K. 12 D6
Chesterfield, Is., N. Cal. 92 J7
Chesterfield Inlet, Canada 96 B10
Chesterton Ra., Australia 91 D4
Chesterville, Canada 107 A9
Chesuncook L., U.S.A. 99 C6
Chetaibi, Algeria 75 A6
Chéticamp, Canada 99 C7
Chetumal, B. de, Mexico 115 D7
Chetwynd, Canada 100 B4
Chevanceaux, France 26 C3
Cheviot, The, U.K. 12 B5
Cheviot Hills, U.K. 12 B5
Cheviot Ra., Australia 90 D3
Chew Bahir, Ethiopia 77 G4
Chewelah, U.S.A. 110 B5
Cheyenne, Okla., U.S.A. 109 H5
Cheyenne, Wyo., U.S.A. 108 E2
Cheyenne →, U.S.A. 108 C4
Cheyenne Wells, U.S.A. 108 F3
Cheyne B., Australia 89 F2
Chhabra, India 62 G7
Chhapra, India 63 G11
Chhata, India 62 F7
Chhatarpur, India 63 G8
Chhep, Cambodia 58 F5
Chhindwara, India 63 H8
Chhlong, Cambodia 59 F5
Chhuk, Cambodia 59 G5
Chi →, Thailand 58 E5
Chiamis, Indonesia 57 G13
Chiamussu = Jiamusi, China 54 B8
Chiang Dao, Thailand 58 C2
Chiang Kham, Thailand 58 C3
Chiang Khan, Thailand 58 D3
Chiang Khong, Thailand 58 B3
Chiang Mai, Thailand 58 C2
Chiang Saen, Thailand 58 B3
Chiange, Angola 81 H2
Chiapa →, Mexico 115 D6
Chiapa de Corzo, Mexico 115 D6
Chiapas □, Mexico 115 D6
Chiaramonte Gulfi, Italy 35 E7
Chiaravalle, Italy 33 E10
Chiaravalle Centrale, Italy 35 D9
Chiari, Italy 32 C6
Chiasso, Switz. 23 E8
Chiatura, Georgia 43 E10
Chiautla, Mexico 115 D5
Chiávari, Italy 32 D6
Chiavenna, Italy 32 B6
Chiba, Japan 49 G10
Chibabava, Mozam. 85 C5
Chibatu, Indonesia 57 G12
Chibemba, Cunene, Angola 81 H2
Chibemba, Huila, Angola 84 B2
Chibia, Angola 81 H2
Chibougamau, Canada 98 C5
Chibougamau L., Canada 98 C5
Chibuk, Nigeria 79 C7
Chic-Chocs, Mts., Canada 99 C6
Chicacole = Srikakulam, India 61 K13
Chicago, U.S.A. 104 E2
Chicago Heights, U.S.A. 104 E2
Chichagof I., U.S.A. 100 B1
Chichaoua, Morocco 74 B3
Chicheng, China 50 D8
Chichester, U.K. 13 G7
Chichibu, Japan 49 F9
Ch'ich'ihaerh = Qiqihar, China 45 E13
Chickasha, U.S.A. 109 H5
Chiclana de la Frontera, Spain 31 J4
Chiclayo, Peru 124 B2
Chico, U.S.A. 112 F5
Chico →, Chubut, Argentina 128 B3
Chico →, Santa Cruz, Argentina 128 C3
Chicomo, Mozam. 85 C5
Chicontepec, Mexico 115 C5
Chicopee, U.S.A. 107 D12
Chicoutimi, Canada 99 C5
Chicualacuala, Mozam. 85 C5
Chidambaram, India 60 P11
Chidenguele, Mozam. 85 C5
Chidley, C., Canada 97 B13
Chiede, Angola 84 B2
Chiefs Pt., Canada 106 B3
Chiem Hoa, Vietnam 58 A5
Chiemsee, Germany 19 H8
Chiengi, Zambia 83 D2
Chiengmai = Chiang Mai, Thailand 58 C2
Chienti →, Italy 33 E10
Chieri, Italy 32 D4
Chiers →, France 25 C11
Chiese →, Italy 32 C7
Chieti, Italy 33 F11
Chièvres, Belgium 17 G3
Chifeng, China 51 C10
Chigirin, Ukraine 42 B5
Chignecto B., Canada 99 C7
Chigorodó, Colombia 120 B2
Chiguana, Bolivia 126 A2
Chiha-ri, N. Korea 51 E14
Chihli, G. of = Bo Hai, China 51 E10
Chihuahua, Mexico 114 B3
Chihuahua □, Mexico 114 B3
Chiili, Kazakhstan 44 E7
Chik Bollapur, India 60 N10
Chikmagalur, India 60 N9
Chikwawa, Malawi 83 F3
Chilac, Mexico 115 D5
Chilako →, Canada 100 C4
Chilam Chavki, Pakistan 63 B6
Chilanga, Zambia 83 F2
Chilapa, Mexico 115 D5
Chilas, Pakistan 63 B6
Chilaw, Sri Lanka 60 R11
Chilcotin →, Canada 100 C4
Childers, Australia 91 D5
Childress, U.S.A. 109 H4
Chile ■, S. Amer. 128 B2
Chile Chico, Chile 128 C2
Chile Rise, Pac. Oc. 93 L18
Chilecito, Argentina 126 B2
Chilete, Peru 124 B2
Chilia, Braţul →, Romania 38 D12
Chililabombwe, Zambia 83 E2
Chilin = Jilin, China 51 C14
Chilka L., India 61 K14
Chilko →, Canada 100 C4
Chilko, L., Canada 100 C4
Chillagoe, Australia 90 B3
Chillán, Chile 126 D1
Chillicothe, Ill., U.S.A. 108 E10
Chillicothe, Mo., U.S.A. 108 F8
Chillicothe, Ohio, U.S.A. 104 F4
Chilliwack, Canada 100 D4
Chilo, India 62 F5
Chiloane, I., Mozam. 85 C5
Chiloé □, Chile 128 B2
Chiloé, I. de, Chile 128 B2
Chilpancingo, Mexico 115 D5
Chiltern Hills, U.K. 13 F7
Chilton, U.S.A. 104 C1
Chiluage, Angola 80 F4
Chilubi, Zambia 83 E2
Chilubula, Zambia 83 E3
Chilumba, Malawi 83 E3
Chilwa, L., Malawi 83 F4
Chimaltitán, Mexico 114 C4
Chimán, Panama 116 E4
Chimay, Belgium 17 H4
Chimbay, Uzbekistan 44 E6
Chimborazo, Ecuador 120 D2
Chimborazo □, Ecuador 120 D2
Chimbote, Peru 124 B2
Chimkent, Kazakhstan 44 E7
Chimoio, Mozam. 83 F3
Chimpembe, Zambia 83 D2
Chin □, Burma 61 J18
Chin Ling Shan = Qinling Shandi, China 50 H5
China, Mexico 115 B5
China ■, Asia 50 E3
China Lake, U.S.A. 113 K9
Chinacota, Colombia 120 B3
Chinan = Jinan, China 50 F9
Chinandega, Nic. 116 D2
Chinati Peak, U.S.A. 109 K2
Chincha Alta, Peru 124 C2
Chinchilla, Australia 91 D5
Chinchilla de Monte Aragón, Spain 29 G3
Chinchón, Spain 28 E1
Chinchorro, Banco, Mexico 115 D7
Chinchou = Jinzhou, China 51 D11
Chincoteague, U.S.A. 104 G8
Chinde, Mozam. 83 F4
Chindo, S. Korea 51 G14
Chindwin →, Burma 61 J19
Chineni, India 63 C6
Chinga, Mozam. 83 F4
Chingola, Zambia 83 E2
Chingole, Malawi 83 E3
Ch'ingtao = Qingdao, China 51 F11
Chinguetti, Mauritania 74 D2
Chingune, Mozam. 85 C5
Chinhae, S. Korea 51 G15
Chinhanguanine, Mozam. 85 D5
Chinhoyi, Zimbabwe 83 F3
Chiniot, Pakistan 62 D5
Chínipas, Mexico 114 B3
Chinju, S. Korea 51 G15
Chinle, U.S.A. 111 H9
Chinnampo, N. Korea 51 E13
Chino, Japan 49 G9
Chino, U.S.A. 113 L9
Chino Valley, U.S.A. 111 J7
Chinon, France 24 E7
Chinook, Canada 101 C6
Chinook, U.S.A. 110 B9
Chinsali, Zambia 83 E3
Chióggia, Italy 33 C9
Chíos = Khíos, Greece 39 L9
Chipata, Zambia 83 E3
Chipewyan L., Canada 101 B9
Chipinge, Zimbabwe 83 G3
Chipiona, Spain 31 J4
Chipley, U.S.A. 105 K3
Chipman, Canada 99 C6
Chipoka, Malawi 83 E3
Chippenham, U.K. 13 F5
Chippewa →, U.S.A. 108 C8
Chippewa Falls, U.S.A. 108 C9
Chiquián, Peru 124 C2
Chiquimula, Guatemala 116 D2
Chiquinquira, Colombia 120 B3
Chiquitos, Llanos de, Bolivia 125 D5
Chir →, Russia 43 B10
Chirala, India 60 M12
Chiramba, Mozam. 83 F3
Chirawa, India 62 E6
Chirchik, Uzbekistan 44 E7
Chirgua →, Venezuela 120 B4
Chiricahua Peak, U.S.A. 111 L9
Chiriquí, G. de, Panama 116 E3
Chiriquí, L. de, Panama 116 E3
Chirivira Falls, Zimbabwe 83 G3
Chirmiri, India 61 H13
Chiromo, Malawi 81 H7
Chirpan, Bulgaria 38 G8
Chirripó Grande, Cerro, Costa Rica 116 E3
Chisamba, Zambia 83 E2
Chisapani Garhi, Nepal 61 F14
Chisholm, Canada 100 C6
Chishtian Mandi, Pakistan 62 E5
Chishui, China 52 C5
Chishui He →, China 52 C5
Chisimba Falls, Zambia 83 E3
Chişinău = Kishinev, Moldavia 42 C3
Chisone →, Italy 32 D4
Chisos Mts., U.S.A. 109 L3
Chistopol, Russia 41 D17
Chita, Colombia 120 B3
Chita, Russia 45 D12
Chitado, Angola 81 H2
Chitembo, Angola 81 G3
Chitipa, Malawi 83 D3
Chitose, Japan 48 C10
Chitral, Pakistan 60 B7
Chitré, Panama 116 E3
Chittagong, Bangla. 61 H17
Chittagong □, Bangla. 61 G17
Chittaurgarh, India 62 G6
Chittoor, India 60 N11
Chitungwiza, Zimbabwe 83 F3
Chiusa, Italy 33 B8
Chiusi, Italy 33 E8
Chiva, Spain 29 F4
Chivacoa, Venezuela 120 A4
Chivasso, Italy 32 C4
Chivay, Peru 124 D3
Chivhu, Zimbabwe 83 F3
Chivilcoy, Argentina 126 C4
Chiwanda, Tanzania 83 E3
Chixi, China 53 G9
Chizera, Zambia 83 E1
Chkalov = Orenburg, Russia 44 D6
Chkolovsk, Russia 41 C13
Chloride, U.S.A. 113 K12
Cho Bo, Vietnam 58 B5
Cho-do, N. Korea 51 E13
Cho Phuoc Hai, Vietnam 59 G6
Choba, Kenya 82 B4
Chobe National Park, Botswana 84 B3
Chochiwŏn, S. Korea 51 F14
Chociwel, Poland 20 B5
Chocó □, Colombia 120 B2
Chocontá, Colombia 120 B3
Choctawhatchee B., U.S.A. 103 D9
Chodecz, Poland 20 C9
Chodziez, Poland 20 C6
Choele Choel, Argentina 128 A3
Choisy-le-Roi, France 25 D9
Choix, Mexico 114 B3
Chojnice, Poland 20 B7
Chojnów, Poland 20 D5
Chōkai-San, Japan 48 E10
Choke, Ethiopia 77 E4
Chokurdakh, Russia 45 B15
Cholame, U.S.A. 112 K6
Cholet, France 24 E6
Choluteca, Honduras 116 D2
Choluteca →, Honduras 116 D2
Chom Bung, Thailand 58 F2
Chom Thong, Thailand 58 C2
Choma, Zambia 83 F2
Chomen Swamp, Ethiopia 77 F4
Chomun, India 62 F6
Chomutov, Czech. 20 E3
Chon Buri, Thailand 58 F3
Chon Thanh, Vietnam 59 G6
Chonan, S. Korea 51 F14
Chone, Ecuador 120 D2
Chong Kai, Cambodia 58 F4
Chong Mek, Thailand 58 E5
Chong'an, China 53 D12
Chongde, China 53 B13
Chŏngdo, S. Korea 51 G15
Chŏngha, S. Korea 51 F15
Chongjin, N. Korea 51 D15
Chŏngju, N. Korea 51 E13
Chŏngju, S. Korea 51 F14
Chongli, China 50 D8
Chongming, China 53 B13
Chongming Dao, China 53 B13
Chongoyape, Peru 124 B2
Chongqing, Sichuan, China 52 C6
Chongqing, Sichuan, China 52 B4
Chongren, China 53 D11
Chŏngŭp, S. Korea 51 G14
Chongzuo, China 52 F6
Chŏnju, S. Korea 51 G14
Chonos, Arch. de los, Chile 128 C2
Chopim →, Brazil 127 B5
Chorbat La, India 63 B7
Chorley, U.K. 12 D5
Chornobyl = Chernobyl, Ukraine 40 F7
Chorolque, Cerro, Bolivia 126 A2
Chorregon, Australia 90 C3
Chortkov, Ukraine 40 G4
Chŏrwŏn, S. Korea 51 E14
Chorzów, Poland 20 E8
Chos-Malal, Argentina 126 D1
Chosan, N. Korea 51 D13
Choszczno, Poland 20 B5
Chota, Peru 124 B2
Choteau, U.S.A. 110 C7
Chotila, India 62 H4
Chowchilla, U.S.A. 111 H3
Choybalsan, Mongolia 54 B6
Christchurch, N.Z. 87 K4
Christchurch, U.K. 13 G6

Christian I., Canada 106 B4
Christiana, S. Africa 84 D4
Christiansfeld, Denmark 11 J3
Christiansted, Virgin Is. 117 C7
Christie B., Canada 101 A6
Christina →, Canada 101 B6
Christmas Cr. →, Australia 88 C4
Christmas Creek, Australia 88 C4
Christmas I. = Kiritimati, Kiribati 93 G12
Christmas I., Ind. Oc. 92 J2
Christopher L., Australia 89 D4
Chrudim, Czech. 20 F5
Chrzanów, Poland 20 E9
Chtimba, Malawi 83 E3
Chu, Kazakhstan 44 E8
Chu →, Vietnam 58 C5
Chu Chua, Canada 100 C4
Chu Lai, Vietnam 58 E7
Chu Xian, China 53 A12
Ch'uanchou = Quanzhou, China 53 E12
Chuankou, China 50 G6
Chūbu □, Japan 49 F8
Chubut □, Argentina 128 B3
Chubut →, Argentina 128 B3
Chuchi L., Canada 100 B4
Chudovo, Russia 40 B7
Chudskoye, Oz., Estonia 40 B5
Chūgoku □, Japan 49 G6
Chūgoku-Sanchi, Japan 49 G6
Chuguyev, Ukraine 42 B7
Chugwater, U.S.A. 108 E2
Chukhloma, Russia 41 B13
Chukotskiy Khrebet, Russia 45 C18
Chukotskoye More, Russia 45 C19
Chula Vista, U.S.A. 113 N9
Chulman, Russia 45 D13
Chulucanas, Peru 124 B1
Chulumani, Bolivia 124 D4
Chulym →, Russia 44 D9
Chum Phae, Thailand 58 D4
Chum Saeng, Thailand 58 E3
Chuma, Bolivia 124 D4
Chumar, India 63 C8
Chumbicha, Argentina 126 B2
Chumerna, Bulgaria 38 G8
Chumikan, Russia 45 D14
Chumphon, Thailand 59 G2
Chumpi, Peru 124 D3
Chumuare, Mozam. 83 E3
Chumunjin, S. Korea 51 F15
Chuna →, Russia 45 D10
Chun'an, China 53 C12
Chunchŏn, S. Korea 51 F14
Chunchura, India 63 H13
Chunga, Zambia 83 F2
Chunggang-ŭp, N. Korea 51 D14
Chunghwa, N. Korea 51 E13
Chungju, S. Korea 51 F14
Chungking = Chongqing, China 52 C6
Chungmu, S. Korea 51 G15
Chungt'iaoshan = Zhongtiao Shan, China 50 G6
Chunian, Pakistan 62 D6
Chunya, Tanzania 83 D3
Chunya □, Tanzania 82 D3
Chunyang, China 51 C15
Chuquibamba, Peru 124 D3
Chuquibambilla, Peru 124 C3
Chuquicamata, Chile 126 A2
Chuquisaca □, Bolivia 125 E5
Chur, Switz. 23 C9
Churachandpur, India 61 G18
Churchill, Canada 101 B10
Churchill →, Man., Canada 101 B10
Churchill →, Nfld., Canada 99 B7
Churchill, C., Canada 101 B10
Churchill Falls, Canada 99 B7
Churchill L., Canada 101 B7
Churchill Pk., Canada 100 B3
Churfisten, Switz. 23 B8
Churu, India 62 E6
Churwalden, Switz. 23 C9
Chushal, India 63 C8
Chusovoy, Russia 44 D6
Chuuronjang, N. Korea 51 D15
Chuvash Republic □, Russia 41 D15
Chuwārtah, Iraq 64 C5
Chuxiong, China 52 E3
Ci Xian, China 50 F8
Ciacova, Romania 38 D4
Cianjur, Indonesia 57 G12
Cibadok, Indonesia 57 G12
Cibatu, Indonesia 57 G12
Cibola, U.S.A. 113 M12
Cicero, U.S.A. 104 E2
Cícero Dantas, Brazil 122 D4
Cidacos →, Spain 28 C3
Cide, Turkey 42 F5
Ciechanów, Poland 20 C10
Ciego de Avila, Cuba 116 B4
Ciénaga, Colombia 120 A3
Ciénaga de Oro, Colombia 120 B2
Cienfuegos, Cuba 116 B3
Cieplice Śląskie Zdrój, Poland 20 E5
Cierp, France 26 F4
Cíes, Is., Spain 30 C2
Cieszyn, Poland 20 F8
Cieza, Spain 29 G3
Çifteler, Turkey 66 D4
Cifuentes, Spain 28 E2
Cihanbeyli, Turkey 66 D5
Cihuatlán, Mexico 114 D4
Cijara, Pantano de, Spain 31 F6
Cijulang, Indonesia 57 G13
Cikajang, Indonesia 57 G12
Cikampek, Indonesia 57 G12
Cilacap, Indonesia 57 G13
Çıldır, Turkey 43 F10
Çıldır Gölü, Turkey 67 C10
Cili, China 53 C8
Cilicia, Turkey 66 E5
Cilo Dağı, Turkey 67 E10
Cima, U.S.A. 113 K11
Cimahi, Indonesia 57 G12
Cimarron, Kans., U.S.A. 109 G4
Cimarron, N. Mex., U.S.A. 109 G2
Cimarron →, U.S.A. 109 G6
Cimone, Mte., Italy 32 D7
Cîmpina, Romania 38 D8
Cîmpulung, Argeş, Romania 38 D8
Cîmpulung, Suceava, Romania 38 B8
Çinar, Turkey 67 E9
Cinca →, Spain 28 D5
Cincinnati, U.S.A. 104 F3
Cîndeşti, Romania 38 D9
Çine, Turkey 66 E3
Ciney, Belgium 17 H6
Cíngoli, Italy 33 E10
Cinigiano, Italy 33 F8
Cinto, Mte., France 27 F12
Çiorani, Romania 38 E9
Čiovo, Croatia 33 E13
Cipó, Brazil 122 D4
Circeo, Monte, Italy 34 A6
Çirçir, Turkey 66 C7
Circle, Alaska, U.S.A. 96 B5
Circle, Mont., U.S.A. 108 B2
Circleville, Ohio, U.S.A. 104 F4
Circleville, Utah, U.S.A. 111 G7
Cirebon, Indonesia 57 G13
Cirencester, U.K. 13 F6
Cirey-sur-Vezouze, France 25 D13
Ciriè, Italy 32 C4
Cirium, Cyprus 37 E11
Cirò, Italy 35 C10
Ciron →, France 26 D3
Cisco, U.S.A. 109 J5
Ciskei □, S. Africa 85 E4
Cislău, Romania 38 D9
Cisneros, Colombia 120 B2
Cisterna di Latina, Italy 34 A5
Cisternino, Italy 35 B10
Citaré →, Brazil 121 C7
Citeli-Ckaro, Georgia 43 F12
Citlaltépetl, Mexico 115 D5
Citrus Heights, U.S.A. 112 G5
Citrusdal, S. Africa 84 E2
Città della Pieve, Italy 33 F9
Città di Castello, Italy 33 E9
Città Sant' Angelo, Italy 33 F11
Cittadella, Italy 33 C8
Cittaducale, Italy 33 F9
Cittanova, Italy 35 D9
Ciucaş, Romania 38 D8
Ciudad Altamirano, Mexico 114 D4
Ciudad Bolívar, Venezuela 121 B5
Ciudad Camargo, Mexico 114 B3
Ciudad Chetumal, Mexico 115 D7
Ciudad de Valles, Mexico 115 C5
Ciudad del Carmen, Mexico 115 D6
Ciudad Delicias = Delicias, Mexico 114 B3
Ciudad Guayana, Venezuela 121 B5
Ciudad Guerrero, Mexico 114 B3
Ciudad Guzmán, Mexico 114 D4
Ciudad Juárez, Mexico 114 A3
Ciudad Madero, Mexico 115 C5
Ciudad Mante, Mexico 115 C5
Ciudad Obregón, Mexico 114 B3
Ciudad Ojeda, Venezuela 120 A3
Ciudad Real, Spain 31 G7
Ciudad Real □, Spain 31 G7
Ciudad Rodrigo, Spain 30 E4
Ciudad Trujillo = Santo Domingo, Dom. Rep. 117 C6
Ciudad Victoria, Mexico 115 C5
Ciudadela, Spain 36 B10
Ciulniţa, Romania 38 E10
Civa Burnu, Turkey 66 C7
Cividale del Friuli, Italy 33 B10
Cívita Castellana, Italy 33 F9
Civitanova Marche, Italy 33 E10
Civitavécchia, Italy 33 F8
Civitella del Tronto, Italy 33 F10
Civray, France 26 B4
Çivril, Turkey 66 D3
Cixerri →, Italy 34 C1
Cizre, Turkey 67 E10
Clacton-on-Sea, U.K. 13 F9
Clain →, France 24 F7
Claire, L., Canada 100 B6
Clairemont, U.S.A. 109 J4
Clairton, U.S.A. 106 F5
Clairvaux-les-Lacs, France 27 B9
Clallam Bay, U.S.A. 112 B2
Clamecy, France 25 E10
Clanton, U.S.A. 105 J2
Clanwilliam, S. Africa 84 E2
Clara, Ireland 15 C4
Clara →, Australia 90 B3
Claraville, U.S.A. 113 K8
Clare, Australia 91 E2
Clare, U.S.A. 104 D3
Clare □, Ireland 15 D3
Clare →, Ireland 15 C2
Clare I., Ireland 15 C2
Claremont, Calif., U.S.A. 113 L9
Claremont, N.H., U.S.A. 107 C12
Claremont Pt., Australia 90 A3
Claremore, U.S.A. 109 G7
Claremorris, Ireland 15 C3
Clarence →, Australia 91 D5
Clarence →, N.Z. 87 K4
Clarence, I., Chile 128 D2
Clarence I., Antarctica 5 C18
Clarence Str., Australia 88 B5
Clarence Str., U.S.A. 100 B2
Clarence Town, Bahamas 117 B5
Clarendon, Ark., U.S.A. 109 H9
Clarendon, Tex., U.S.A. 109 H4
Clarenville, Canada 99 C9
Claresholm, Canada 100 C6
Clarie Coast, Antarctica 5 C9
Clarinda, U.S.A. 108 E7
Clarion, Iowa, U.S.A. 108 D8
Clarion, Pa., U.S.A. 106 E5
Clarion →, U.S.A. 106 E5
Clark, U.S.A. 108 C6
Clark, Pt., Canada 106 B3
Clark Fork, U.S.A. 110 B5
Clark Fork →, U.S.A. 110 B5
Clark Hill Res., U.S.A. 105 J4
Clarkdale, U.S.A. 111 J7
Clarke City, Canada 99 B6
Clarke I., Australia 90 G4
Clarke L., Canada 101 C7
Clarke Ra., Australia 90 C4
Clark's Fork →, U.S.A. 110 D9
Clark's Harbour, Canada 99 D6
Clarks Summit, U.S.A. 107 E9
Clarksburg, U.S.A. 104 F5
Clarksdale, U.S.A. 109 H9
Clarkston, U.S.A. 110 C5
Clarksville, Ark., U.S.A. 109 H8
Clarksville, Tenn., U.S.A. 105 G2
Clarksville, Tex., U.S.A. 109 J7
Claro →, Brazil 123 E1
Clatskanie, U.S.A. 112 D3
Claude, U.S.A. 109 H4
Claveria, Phil. 55 B4
Clay, U.S.A. 112 G5
Clay Center, U.S.A. 108 F6
Claypool, U.S.A. 111 K8
Claysville, U.S.A. 106 F4
Clayton, Idaho, U.S.A. 110 D6
Clayton, N. Mex., U.S.A. 109 G3
Cle Elum, U.S.A. 110 C3
Clear, C., Ireland 15 E2
Clear I., Ireland 15 E2
Clear L., U.S.A. 112 F4
Clear Lake, S. Dak., U.S.A. 108 C6
Clear Lake, Wash., U.S.A. 110 B2
Clear Lake Reservoir, U.S.A. 110 F3
Clearfield, Pa., U.S.A. 104 E6
Clearfield, Utah, U.S.A. 110 F7
Clearlake Highlands, U.S.A. 112 G4
Clearmont, U.S.A. 110 D10
Clearwater, Canada 100 C4
Clearwater, U.S.A. 105 M4
Clearwater →, Alta., Canada 100 C6
Clearwater →, Alta., Canada 101 B6
Clearwater Cr. →, Canada 100 A3
Clearwater Mts., U.S.A. 110 C6
Clearwater Prov. Park, Canada 101 C8
Cleburne, U.S.A. 109 J6
Cleethorpes, U.K. 12 D7
Cleeve Hill, U.K. 13 F6
Clelles, France 27 D9
Clemency, Lux. 17 J7
Clerke Reef, Australia 88 C2
Clermont, Australia 90 C4
Clermont, France 25 C9
Clermont-en-Argonne, France 25 C12
Clermont-Ferrand, France 26 C7
Clermont-l'Hérault, France 26 E7
Clerval, France 25 E13
Clervaux, Lux. 17 H8
Cléry-St.-André, France 25 E8
Cles, Italy 32 B8
Cleveland, Australia 91 D5
Cleveland, Miss., U.S.A. 109 J9
Cleveland, Ohio, U.S.A. 106 E3
Cleveland, Okla., U.S.A. 109 G6
Cleveland, Tenn., U.S.A. 105 H3
Cleveland, Tex., U.S.A. 109 K7
Cleveland □, U.K. 12 C9
Cleveland, C., Australia 90 B4
Cleveland Heights, U.S.A. 106 E3
Clevelândia, Brazil 127 B5
Clevelândia do Norte, Brazil 121 C7
Clew B., Ireland 15 C2
Clewiston, U.S.A. 105 M5
Clifden, Ireland 15 C1
Clifden, N.Z. 87 M1
Cliffdell, U.S.A. 112 D5
Clifton, Australia 91 D5
Clifton, Ariz., U.S.A. 111 K9
Clifton, Tex., U.S.A. 109 K6
Clifton Beach, Australia 90 B4
Clifton Forge, U.S.A. 104 G6
Clifton Hills, Australia 91 D2
Climax, Canada 101 D7
Clinch →, U.S.A. 105 H3
Clingmans Dome, U.S.A. 105 H4
Clint, U.S.A. 111 L10
Clinton, B.C., Canada 100 C4
Clinton, Ont., Canada 98 D3
Clinton, N.Z. 87 M2
Clinton, Ark., U.S.A. 109 H8
Clinton, Ill., U.S.A. 108 E10
Clinton, Ind., U.S.A. 104 F2
Clinton, Iowa, U.S.A. 108 E9
Clinton, Mass., U.S.A. 107 D13
Clinton, Mo., U.S.A. 108 F8
Clinton, N.C., U.S.A. 105 H6
Clinton, Okla., U.S.A. 109 H5
Clinton, S.C., U.S.A. 105 H5
Clinton, Tenn., U.S.A. 105 G3
Clinton, Wash., U.S.A. 112 C4
Clinton C., Australia 90 C5
Clinton Colden L., Canada 96 B9
Clintonville, U.S.A. 108 C10
Clipperton, I., Pac. Oc. 93 F17
Clisson, France 24 E5
Clive L., Canada 100 A5
Cliza, Bolivia 125 D4
Cloates, Pt., Australia 88 D1
Clocolan, S. Africa 85 D4
Clodomira, Argentina 126 B3
Clonakilty, Ireland 15 E3
Clonakilty B., Ireland 15 E3
Cloncurry, Australia 90 C3
Cloncurry →, Australia 90 B3
Clones, Ireland 15 B4
Clonmel, Ireland 15 D4
Cloppenburg, Germany 18 C4
Cloquet, U.S.A. 108 B8
Clorinda, Argentina 126 B4
Cloud Peak, U.S.A. 110 D10
Cloudcroft, U.S.A. 111 K11
Cloverdale, U.S.A. 112 G4
Clovis, Calif., U.S.A. 111 H4
Clovis, N. Mex., U.S.A. 109 H3
Cloyes-sur-le-Loir, France 24 E8
Cluj-Napoca, Romania 38 C6
Clunes, Australia 91 F3
Cluny, France 27 B8
Cluses, France 27 B10
Clusone, Italy 32 C6
Clutha →, N.Z. 87 M2
Clwyd □, U.K. 12 D4
Clwyd →, U.K. 12 D4
Clyde, N.Z. 87 L2
Clyde, U.S.A. 106 C8
Clyde →, U.K. 14 F4
Clyde, Firth of, U.K. 14 F4
Clyde River, Canada 97 A13
Clydebank, U.K. 14 F4
Clymer, U.S.A. 106 D5
Côa →, Portugal 30 D3
Coachella, U.S.A. 113 M10
Coachella Canal, U.S.A. 113 N12
Coahoma, U.S.A. 109 J4
Coahuayana →, Mexico 114 D4
Coahuayutla, Mexico 114 D4
Coahuila □, Mexico 114 B4
Coal →, Canada 100 B3
Coalane, Mozam. 83 F4
Coalcomán, Mexico 114 D4
Coaldale, Canada 100 D6
Coalgate, U.S.A. 109 H6
Coalinga, U.S.A. 111 H3
Coalville, U.K. 12 E6
Coalville, U.S.A. 110 F8
Coaraci, Brazil 123 D4
Coari, Brazil 121 D5
Coari →, Brazil 121 D5
Coari, L. de, Brazil 121 D5
Coast □, Kenya 82 C4
Coast Mts., Canada 100 C3
Coast Ranges, U.S.A. 112 E4
Coatbridge, U.K. 14 F4
Coatepec, Mexico 115 D5
Coatepeque, Guatemala 116 D1
Coatesville, U.S.A. 104 F8
Coaticook, Canada 99 C5
Coats I., Canada 97 B11
Coats Land, Antarctica 5 D1
Coatzacoalcos, Mexico 115 D6
Cobalt, Canada 98 C4
Cobán, Guatemala 116 C1
Cobar, Australia 91 E4
Cóbh, Ireland 15 E3
Cobham, Australia 91 E3
Cobija, Bolivia 124 C4
Cobleskill, U.S.A. 107 D10
Coboconk, Canada 106 B6
Cobourg, Canada 98 D4
Cobourg Pen., Australia 88 B5
Cobram, Australia 91 F4
Cobre, U.S.A. 110 F6
Cóbué, Mozam. 83 E3
Coburg, Germany 19 E6
Coca, Spain 30 D6
Coca →, Ecuador 120 D2
Cocachacra, Peru 124 D3
Cocal, Brazil 122 B3
Cocanada = Kakinada, India 61 L13
Cocentaina, Spain 29 G4
Cochabamba, Bolivia 125 D4
Coche, I., Venezuela 121 A5
Cochem, Germany 19 E3
Cochemane, Mozam. 83 F3
Cochin, India 60 Q10
Cochin China = Nam-Phan, Vietnam 59 G6
Cochise, U.S.A. 111 K9
Cochran, U.S.A. 105 J4
Cochrane, Alta., Canada 100 C6
Cochrane, Ont., Canada 98 C3
Cochrane →, Canada 101 B8
Cochrane, L., Chile 128 C2
Cockburn, Australia 91 E3
Cockburn, Canal, Chile 128 D2
Cockburn I., Canada 98 C3
Cockburn Ra., Australia 88 C4
Cocklebiddy Motel, Australia 89 F4
Coco →, Cent. Amer. 116 D3
Coco, Pta., Colombia 120 C2
Cocoa, U.S.A. 105 L5
Cocobeach, Gabon 80 D1
Côcos, Brazil 123 D3
Côcos →, Brazil 123 D3
Cocos, I. del, Pac. Oc. 93 G19
Cocos Is., Ind. Oc. 92 J1
Cod, C., U.S.A. 103 B13
Codajás, Brazil 121 D5
Codera, C., Venezuela 120 A4
Coderre, Canada 101 C7
Codigoro, Italy 33 D9
Codó, Brazil 122 B3
Codogno, Italy 32 C6
Codpa, Chile 124 D4
Codróipo, Italy 33 C10
Cody, U.S.A. 110 D9
Coe Hill, Canada 98 D4
Coelemu, Chile 126 D1
Coelho Neto, Brazil 122 B3
Coen, Australia 90 A3
Coeroeni →, Surinam 121 C6
Coesfeld, Germany 18 D3
Cœur d'Alene, U.S.A. 110 C5
Cœur d'Alene L., U.S.A. 110 C5
Coevorden, Neths. 16 C9
Cofete, Canary Is. 36 F5
Coffeyville, U.S.A. 109 G7
Coffin B., Australia 91 E2
Coffin Bay Peninsula, Australia 91 E2
Coffs Harbour, Australia 91 E5
Cofrentes, Spain 29 F3
Cogealac, Romania 38 E11
Coghinas →, Italy 34 B1
Coghinas, L. di, Italy 34 B2
Cognac, France 26 C3
Cogne, Italy 32 C4
Cogolludo, Spain 28 E1
Cohagen, U.S.A. 110 C10
Cohoes, U.S.A. 107 D11
Cohuna, Australia 91 F3
Coiba, I., Panama 116 E3
Coig →, Argentina 128 D3
Coihaique, Chile 128 C2
Coimbatore, India 60 P10
Coimbra, Brazil 125 D6
Coimbra, Portugal 30 E2
Coimbra □, Portugal 30 E2
Coín, Spain 31 J6
Coipasa, L. de, Bolivia 124 D4
Coipasa, Salar de, Bolivia 124 D4
Cojata, Peru 124 D4
Cojedes □, Venezuela 120 B4
Cojedes →, Venezuela 120 B4
Cojimies, Ecuador 120 C1
Cojocna, Romania 38 C6
Cojutepequé, El Salv. 116 D2
Cokeville, U.S.A. 110 E8
Colac, Australia 91 F3
Colares, Portugal 31 G1
Colatina, Brazil 123 E3
Colbeck, C., Antarctica 5 D13
Colbinabbin, Australia 91 F3
Colborne, Canada 106 B7
Colby, U.S.A. 108 F4
Colchagua □, Chile 126 C1
Colchester, U.K. 13 F8
Coldstream, U.K. 14 F6
Coldwater, Canada 106 B5
Coldwater, U.S.A. 109 G5
Colebrook, Australia 90 G4
Colebrook, U.S.A. 107 B13
Coleman, Canada 100 D6
Coleman, U.S.A. 109 K5
Coleman →, Australia 90 B3
Colenso, S. Africa 85 D4
Coleraine, Australia 91 F3
Coleraine, U.K. 15 A5
Coleraine □, U.K. 15 A5
Coleridge, L., N.Z. 87 K3
Colesberg, S. Africa 84 E4
Coleville, U.S.A. 112 G7
Colfax, Calif., U.S.A. 112 F6
Colfax, La., U.S.A. 109 K8
Colfax, Wash., U.S.A. 110 C5
Colhué Huapi, L., Argentina 128 C3
Cólico, Italy 32 B6
Coligny, France 27 B9
Coligny, S. Africa 85 D4
Colima, Mexico 114 D4
Colima □, Mexico 114 D4
Colima, Nevado de, Mexico 114 D4
Colina, Chile 126 C1
Colina do Norte, Guinea-Biss. 78 C2

Colinas, *Goiás, Brazil* 123 D2
Colinas, *Maranhão, Brazil* 122 C3
Coll, *U.K.* 14 E2
Collaguasi, *Chile* 126 A2
Collarada, Peña, *Spain* 28 C4
Collarenebri, *Australia* 91 D4
Collbran, *U.S.A.* 111 G10
Colle di Val d'Elsa, *Italy* 33 E8
Colle Salvetti, *Italy* 32 E7
Colle Sannita, *Italy* 35 A7
Collécchio, *Italy* 32 D7
Colleen Bawn, *Zimbabwe* 83 G2
College Park, *U.S.A.* 105 J3
Collette, *Canada* 99 C6
Collie, *Australia* 89 F2
Collier B., *Australia* 88 C3
Collier Ra., *Australia* 88 D2
Colline Metallifere, *Italy* 32 E7
Collingwood, *Canada* 98 D3
Collingwood, *N.Z.* 87 J4
Collins, *Canada* 98 B2
Collinsville, *Australia* 90 C4
Collipulli, *Chile* 126 D1
Collo, *Algeria* 75 A6
Collonges, *France* 27 B9
Collooney, *Ireland* 15 B3
Colmar, *France* 25 D14
Colmars, *France* 27 D10
Colmenar, *Spain* 31 J6
Colmenar de Oreja, *Spain* 28 E1
Colmenar Viejo, *Spain* 30 E7
Colne, *U.K.* 12 D5
Colo →, *Australia* 91 E5
Cologna Véneta, *Italy* 33 C8
Cologne = Köln, *Germany* 18 E2
Colom, I., *Spain* 36 B11
Coloma, *U.S.A.* 112 G6
Colomb-Béchar = Béchar, *Algeria* 75 B4
Colombey-les-Belles, *France* 25 D12
Colombey-les-Deux-Églises, *France* 25 D11
Colômbia, *Brazil* 123 F2
Colombia ■, *S. Amer.* 120 C3
Colombier, *Switz.* 22 C3
Colombo, *Sri Lanka* 60 R11
Colome, *U.S.A.* 108 D5
Colón, *Argentina* 126 C4
Colón, *Cuba* 116 B3
Colón, *Panama* 116 E4
Colón, *Peru* 124 A1
Colona, *Australia* 89 F5
Colonella, *Italy* 33 F10
Colonia, *Uruguay* 126 C4
Colonia de San Jordi, *Spain* 36 B9
Colonia Dora, *Argentina* 126 B3
Colonial Heights, *U.S.A.* 104 G7
Colonne, C. delle, *Italy* 35 C10
Colonsay, *Canada* 101 C7
Colonsay, *U.K.* 14 E2
Colorado □, *U.S.A.* 111
Colorado →, *Argentina* 128 A4
Colorado →, *N. Amer.* 111 L6
Colorado →, *U.S.A.* 109 L7
Colorado City, *U.S.A.* 109 J4
Colorado Desert, *U.S.A.* 102 D3
Colorado Plateau, *U.S.A.* 111 H8
Colorado River Aqueduct, *U.S.A.* 113 L12
Colorado Springs, *U.S.A.* 108 F2
Colorno, *Italy* 32 D7
Colotlán, *Mexico* 114 C4
Colquechaca, *Bolivia* 125 D4
Colton, *Calif., U.S.A.* 113 L9
Colton, *N.Y., U.S.A.* 107 B10
Colton, *Wash., U.S.A.* 110 C5
Columbia, *La., U.S.A.* 109 J8
Columbia, *Miss., U.S.A.* 109 K10
Columbia, *Mo., U.S.A.* 108 F8
Columbia, *Pa., U.S.A.* 107 F8
Columbia, *S.C., U.S.A.* 105 H5
Columbia, *Tenn., U.S.A.* 105 H2
Columbia →, *U.S.A.* 110 C1
Columbia, C., *Canada* 4 A4
Columbia, District of □, *U.S.A.* 104 F7
Columbia, Mt., *Canada* 100 C5
Columbia Basin, *U.S.A.* 110 C4
Columbia Falls, *U.S.A.* 110 B6
Columbia Heights, *U.S.A.* 108 C8
Columbiana, *U.S.A.* 106 F4
Columbretes, Is., *Spain* 28 F5
Columbus, *Ga., U.S.A.* 105 J3
Columbus, *Ind., U.S.A.* 104 F3
Columbus, *Kans., U.S.A.* 109 G7
Columbus, *Miss., U.S.A.* 105 J1
Columbus, *Mont., U.S.A.* 110 D9
Columbus, *N. Dak., U.S.A.* 108 A3
Columbus, *N. Mex., U.S.A.* 111 L10
Columbus, *Nebr., U.S.A.* 108 E6
Columbus, *Ohio, U.S.A.* 104 F4
Columbus, *Tex., U.S.A.* 109 L6
Columbus, *Wis., U.S.A.* 108 D10
Colunga, *Spain* 30 B5
Colusa, *U.S.A.* 112 F4
Colville, *U.S.A.* 110 B5
Colville →, *U.S.A.* 96 A4
Colville, C., *N.Z.* 87 G5
Colwyn Bay, *U.K.* 12 D4
Coma, *Ethiopia* 77 F4
Comácchio, *Italy* 33 D9
Comalcalco, *Mexico* 115 D6
Comallo, *Argentina* 128 B2
Comanche, *Okla., U.S.A.* 109 H6
Comanche, *Tex., U.S.A.* 109 K5
Comandante Luis Piedrabuena, *Argentina* 128 C3
Comănești, *Romania* 38 C9
Comarapa, *Bolivia* 125 D5
Comayagua, *Honduras* 116 D2
Combahee →, *U.S.A.* 105 J5
Combeaufontaine, *France* 25 E12
Comber, *Canada* 106 D2
Comblain-au-Pont, *Belgium* 17 H7
Combles, *France* 25 B9
Combourg, *France* 24 D5
Combronde, *France* 26 C7
Comeragh Mts., *Ireland* 15 D4
Comet, *Australia* 90 C4
Comilla, *Bangla.* 61 H17
Comines, *Belgium* 17 G1
Comino, *Malta* 37 C1
Comino, C., *Italy* 34 B2
Cómiso, *Italy* 35 F7
Comitán, *Mexico* 115 D6
Commentry, *France* 26 B6
Commerce, *Ga., U.S.A.* 105 H4
Commerce, *Tex., U.S.A.* 109 J7
Commercy, *France* 25 D12
Commewijne □, *Surinam* 121 B7
Committee B., *Canada* 97 B11
Commonwealth B., *Antarctica* 5 C10
Commonwealth of Independent States ■, *Eurasia* 45 D11
Commoron Cr. →, *Australia* 91 D5
Communism Pk. = Kommunizma, Pik, *Tajikistan* 44 F8
Como, *Italy* 32 C6
Como, L. di, *Italy* 32 B6
Comodoro Rivadavia, *Argentina* 128 C3
Comorin, C., *India* 60 Q10
Comoro Is. = Comoros ■, *Ind. Oc.* 71 H8
Comoros ■, *Ind. Oc.* 71 H8
Comox, *Canada* 100 D4
Compiègne, *France* 25 C9
Comporta, *Portugal* 31 G2
Compostela, *Mexico* 114 C4
Comprida, I., *Brazil* 127 A6
Compton, *U.S.A.* 113 M8
Compton Downs, *Australia* 91 E4
Con Cuong, *Vietnam* 58 C5
Con Son, Is., *Vietnam* 59 H6
Cona Niyeu, *Argentina* 128 B3
Conakry, *Guinea* 78 D2
Conara Junction, *Australia* 90 G4
Concarneau, *France* 24 E3
Conceição, *Brazil* 122 C4
Conceição, *Mozam.* 83 F4
Conceição da Barra, *Brazil* 123 E4
Conceição do Araguaia, *Brazil* 122 C2
Conceição do Canindé, *Brazil* 122 C3
Concepción, *Argentina* 126 B2
Concepción, *Bolivia* 125 D5
Concepción, *Chile* 126 D1
Concepción, *Mexico* 115 D6
Concepción, *Paraguay* 126 A4
Concepción, *Peru* 124 C2
Concepción □, *Chile* 126 D1
Concepción →, *Mexico* 114 A2
Concepción, Est. de, *Chile* 128 D2
Concepción, L., *Bolivia* 125 D5
Concepción, Punta, *Mexico* 114 B2
Concepción del Oro, *Mexico* 114 C4
Concepción del Uruguay, *Argentina* 126 C4
Conception, Pt., *U.S.A.* 113 L6
Conception B., *Namibia* 84 C1
Conception I., *Bahamas* 117 B4
Concession, *Zimbabwe* 83 F3
Conchas Dam, *U.S.A.* 109 H2
Conche, *Canada* 99 B8
Concho, *U.S.A.* 111 J9
Concho →, *U.S.A.* 109 K5
Conchos →, *Chihuahua, Mexico* 114 B4
Conchos →, *Tamaulipas, Mexico* 115 B5
Concord, *Calif., U.S.A.* 112 H4
Concord, *N.C., U.S.A.* 105 H5
Concord, *N.H., U.S.A.* 107 C13
Concordia, *Argentina* 126 C4
Concórdia, *Brazil* 120 D4
Concordia, *Mexico* 114 C3
Concordia, *U.S.A.* 108 F6
Concots, *France* 26 D5
Concrete, *U.S.A.* 110 B3
Condamine, *Australia* 91 D5
Condat, *France* 26 C6
Conde, *Brazil* 123 D4
Conde, *U.S.A.* 108 C5
Condé-sur-l'Escaut, *France* 25 B10
Condé-sur-Noireau, *France* 24 D6
Condeúba, *Brazil* 123 D3
Condobolin, *Australia* 91 E4
Condom, *France* 26 E4
Condon, *U.S.A.* 110 D3
Condove, *Italy* 32 C4
Conegliano, *Italy* 33 C9
Conejera, I., *Spain* 36 B9
Conejos, *Mexico* 114 B4
Conflans-en-Jarnisy, *France* 25 C12
Confolens, *France* 26 B4
Confuso →, *Paraguay* 126 B4
Congjiang, *China* 52 E7
Congleton, *U.K.* 12 D5
Congo = Zaïre →, *Africa* 80 F2
Congo, *Brazil* 122 C4
Congo (Kinshasa) = Zaïre ■, *Africa* 80 E4
Congo ■, *Africa* 80 E3
Congo Basin, *Africa* 70 G6
Congonhas, *Brazil* 123 F3
Congress, *U.S.A.* 111 J7
Conil, *Spain* 31 J4
Coniston, *Canada* 98 C3
Conjeeveram = Kanchipuram, *India* 60 N11
Conjuboy, *Australia* 90 B3
Conklin, *Canada* 101 B6
Conlea, *Australia* 91 E3
Conn, L., *Ireland* 15 B2
Connacht, *Ireland* 15 C3
Conneaut, *U.S.A.* 106 E4
Connecticut □, *U.S.A.* 107 E12
Connecticut →, *U.S.A.* 107 E12
Connell, *U.S.A.* 110 C4
Connellsville, *U.S.A.* 106 F5
Connemara, *Ireland* 15 C2
Connemaugh →, *U.S.A.* 106 F5
Connerré, *France* 24 D7
Connersville, *U.S.A.* 104 F3
Connors Ra., *Australia* 90 C4
Conoble, *Australia* 91 E3
Cononaco →, *Ecuador* 120 D2
Cononbridge, *U.K.* 14 D4
Conquest, *Canada* 101 C7
Conrad, *U.S.A.* 110 B8
Conran, C., *Australia* 91 F4
Conroe, *U.S.A.* 109 K7
Conselheiro Lafaiete, *Brazil* 123 F3
Conselheiro Pena, *Brazil* 123 E3
Consort, *Canada* 101 C6
Constance = Konstanz, *Germany* 19 H5
Constance, L. = Bodensee, *Europe* 23 A8
Constanța, *Romania* 38 E11
Constantina, *Spain* 31 H5
Constantine, *Algeria* 75 A6
Constitución, *Chile* 126 D1
Constitución, *Uruguay* 126 C4
Consuegra, *Spain* 31 F7
Consul, *Canada* 101 D7
Contact, *U.S.A.* 110 F6
Contai, *India* 63 J12
Contamana, *Peru* 124 B3
Contarina, *Italy* 33 C9
Contas →, *Brazil* 123 D4
Contes, *France* 27 E11
Conthey, *Switz.* 22 D4
Contoocook, *U.S.A.* 107 C13
Contra Costa, *Mozam.* 85 D5
Contres, *France* 24 E8
Contrexéville, *France* 25 D12
Contumaza, *Peru* 124 B2
Convención, *Colombia* 120 B3
Conversano, *Italy* 35 B10
Conway = Conwy, *U.K.* 12 D4
Conway = Conwy →, *U.K.* 12 D4
Conway, *Ark., U.S.A.* 109 H8
Conway, *N.H., U.S.A.* 107 C13
Conway, *S.C., U.S.A.* 105 J6
Conway, L., *Australia* 91 D2
Conwy, *U.K.* 12 D4
Conwy →, *U.K.* 12 D4
Coober Pedy, *Australia* 91 D1
Cooch Behar = Koch Bihar, *India* 61 F16
Coodardy, *Australia* 89 E2
Cook, *Australia* 89 F5
Cook, *U.S.A.* 108 B8
Cook, B., *Chile* 128 E2
Cook, Mt., *N.Z.* 87 K3
Cook Inlet, *U.S.A.* 96 C4
Cook Is., *Pac. Oc.* 93 J11
Cook Strait, *N.Z.* 87 J5
Cookeville, *U.S.A.* 105 G3
Cookhouse, *S. Africa* 84 E4
Cookshire, *Canada* 107 A13
Cookstown, *U.K.* 15 B5
Cookstown □, *U.K.* 15 B5
Cooksville, *Canada* 106 C5
Cooktown, *Australia* 90 B4
Coolabah, *Australia* 91 E4
Cooladdi, *Australia* 91 D4
Coolah, *Australia* 91 E4
Coolamon, *Australia* 91 E4
Coolangatta, *Australia* 91 D5
Coolgardie, *Australia* 89 F3
Coolibah, *Australia* 88 C5
Coolidge, *U.S.A.* 111 K8
Coolidge Dam, *U.S.A.* 111 K8
Cooma, *Australia* 91 F4
Coonabarabran, *Australia* 91 E4
Coonamble, *Australia* 91 E4
Coonana, *Australia* 89 F3
Coondapoor, *India* 60 N9
Coongie, *Australia* 91 D3
Coongoola, *Australia* 91 D4
Cooninie, L., *Australia* 91 D2
Cooper, *U.S.A.* 109 J7
Cooper →, *U.S.A.* 105 J6
Cooper Cr. →, *Australia* 91 D2
Cooperstown, *N. Dak., U.S.A.* 108 B5
Cooperstown, *N.Y., U.S.A.* 107 D10
Coorabie, *Australia* 89 F5
Coorabulka, *Australia* 90 C3
Coorow, *Australia* 89 E2
Cooroy, *Australia* 91 D5
Coos Bay, *U.S.A.* 110 E1
Cootamundra, *Australia* 91 E4
Cootehill, *Ireland* 15 B4
Cooyar, *Australia* 91 D5
Cooyeana, *Australia* 90 C2
Copahue Paso, *Argentina* 126 D1
Copainalá, *Mexico* 115 D6
Copán, *Honduras* 116 D2
Copatana, *Brazil* 120 D4
Cope, *U.S.A.* 108 F3
Cope, C., *Spain* 29 H3
Copenhagen = København, *Denmark* 11 J6
Copertino, *Italy* 35 B11
Copiapó, *Chile* 126 B1
Copiapó →, *Chile* 126 B1
Copley, *Australia* 91 E2
Copp L., *Canada* 100 A6
Copparo, *Italy* 33 D8
Coppename →, *Surinam* 121 B6
Copper Center, *U.S.A.* 96 B5
Copper Cliff, *Canada* 98 C3
Copper Harbor, *U.S.A.* 104 B2
Copper Queen, *Zimbabwe* 83 F2
Copperbelt □, *Zambia* 83 E2
Coppermine, *Canada* 96 B8
Coppermine →, *Canada* 96 B8
Copperopolis, *U.S.A.* 112 H6
Coquet →, *U.K.* 12 B6
Coquilhatville = Mbandaka, *Zaïre* 80 D3
Coquille, *U.S.A.* 110 E1
Coquimbo, *Chile* 126 B1
Coquimbo □, *Chile* 126 C1
Corabia, *Romania* 38 F7
Coração de Jesus, *Brazil* 123 E3
Coracora, *Peru* 124 D3
Coradi, Is., *Italy* 35 B10
Coral Gables, *U.S.A.* 105 N5
Coral Harbour, *Canada* 97 B11
Coral Sea, *Pac. Oc.* 92 J7
Corantijn →, *Surinam* 121 B6
Coraopolis, *U.S.A.* 106 F4
Corato, *Italy* 35 A9
Corbeil-Essonnes, *France* 25 D9
Corbie, *France* 25 C9
Corbières, *France* 26 F6
Corbigny, *France* 25 E10
Corbin, *U.S.A.* 104 G3
Corbion, *Belgium* 17 J6
Corbones →, *Spain* 31 H5
Corby, *U.K.* 13 E7
Corby Glen, *U.K.* 13 E7
Corcoles →, *Spain* 29 F1
Corcoran, *U.S.A.* 111 H4
Corcubión, *Spain* 30 C1
Cordele, *U.S.A.* 105 K4
Cordell, *U.S.A.* 109 H5
Cordenons, *Italy* 33 C9
Cordes, *France* 26 D5
Cordisburgo, *Brazil* 123 E3
Córdoba, *Argentina* 126 C3
Córdoba, *Mexico* 115 D5
Córdoba, *Spain* 31 H6
Córdoba □, *Argentina* 126 C3
Córdoba □, *Colombia* 120 B2
Córdoba □, *Spain* 31 G6
Córdoba, Sierra de, *Argentina* 126 C3
Cordon, *Phil.* 55 C4
Cordova, *Ala., U.S.A.* 105 J2
Cordova, *Alaska, U.S.A.* 96 B5
Corella, *Spain* 28 C3
Corella →, *Australia* 90 B3
Coremas, *Brazil* 122 C4
Corentyne →, *Guyana* 121 B6
Corfield, *Australia* 90 C3
Corfu = Kérkira, *Greece* 37 A3
Corfu, Str of, *Greece* 37 A4
Corgo, *Spain* 30 C3
Corguinho, *Brazil* 125 D7
Cori, *Italy* 34 A5
Coria, *Spain* 30 F4
Corigliano Cálabro, *Italy* 35 C9
Coringa Is., *Australia* 90 B4
Corinna, *Australia* 90 G4
Corinth = Kórinthos, *Greece* 39 M5
Corinth, *Miss., U.S.A.* 105 H1
Corinth, *N.Y., U.S.A.* 107 C11
Corinth, G. of = Korinthiakós Kólpos, *Greece* 39 L5
Corinth Canal, *Greece* 39 M6
Corinto, *Brazil* 123 E3
Corinto, *Nic.* 116 D2
Cork, *Ireland* 15 E3
Cork □, *Ireland* 15 E3
Cork Harbour, *Ireland* 15 E3
Corlay, *France* 24 D3
Corleone, *Italy* 34 E6
Corleto Perticara, *Italy* 35 B9
Çorlu, *Turkey* 39 H10
Cormack L., *Canada* 100 A4
Cormóns, *Italy* 33 C10
Cormorant, *Canada* 101 C8
Cormorant L., *Canada* 101 C8
Corn Is. = Maiz, Is. del, *Nic.* 116 D3
Cornélio Procópio, *Brazil* 127 A5
Cornell, *U.S.A.* 108 C9
Corner Brook, *Canada* 99 C8
Corníglio, *Italy* 32 D7
Corning, *Ark., U.S.A.* 109 G9
Corning, *Calif., U.S.A.* 110 G2
Corning, *Iowa, U.S.A.* 108 E7
Corning, *N.Y., U.S.A.* 106 D7
Corno, Monte, *Italy* 33 F10
Cornwall, *Canada* 98 C5
Cornwall □, *U.K.* 13 G3
Corny Pt., *Australia* 91 E2
Coro, *Venezuela* 120 A4
Coroaci, *Brazil* 123 E3
Coroatá, *Brazil* 122 B3
Corocoro, *Bolivia* 124 D4
Corocoro, I., *Venezuela* 121 B5
Coroico, *Bolivia* 124 D4
Coromandel, *Brazil* 123 E2
Coromandel, *N.Z.* 87 G5
Coromandel Coast, *India* 60 N12
Corona, *Australia* 91 E3
Corona, *Calif., U.S.A.* 113 M9
Corona, *N. Mex., U.S.A.* 111 J11
Coronado, *U.S.A.* 113 N9
Coronado, B. de, *Costa Rica* 116 E3
Coronados, G. de los, *Chile* 128 B2
Coronados, Is. los, *U.S.A.* 113 N9
Coronation, *Canada* 100 C6
Coronation Gulf, *Canada* 96 B8
Coronation I., *Antarctica* 5 C18
Coronation I., *U.S.A.* 100 B2
Coronation Is., *Australia* 88 B3
Coronda, *Argentina* 126 C3
Coronel, *Chile* 126 D1
Coronel Bogado, *Paraguay* 126 B4
Coronel Dorrego, *Argentina* 126 D3
Coronel Fabriciano, *Brazil* 123 E3
Coronel Murta, *Brazil* 123 E3
Coronel Oviedo, *Paraguay* 126 B4
Coronel Ponce, *Brazil* 125 D6
Coronel Pringles, *Argentina* 126 D3
Coronel Suárez, *Argentina* 126 D3
Coronel Vidal, *Argentina* 126 D4
Corongo, *Peru* 124 B2
Coronie □, *Surinam* 121 B6
Coropuna, Nevado, *Peru* 124 D3
Çorovoda, *Albania* 39 J3
Corowa, *Australia* 91 F4
Corozal, *Belize* 115 D7
Corozal, *Colombia* 120 B2
Corps, *France* 27 D9
Corpus, *Argentina* 127 B4
Corpus Christi, *U.S.A.* 109 M6
Corpus Christi, L., *U.S.A.* 109 L6
Corque, *Bolivia* 124 D4
Corral, *Chile* 128 A2
Corral de Almaguer, *Spain* 28 F1
Corralejo, *Canary Is.* 36 F6
Corréggio, *Italy* 32 D7
Corrente, *Brazil* 122 D2
Corrente →, *Brazil* 123 D3
Correntes →, *Brazil* 125 D6
Correntes, C. das, *Mozam.* 85 C6
Correntina, *Brazil* 123 D3
Corrèze □, *France* 26 C5
Corrèze →, *France* 26 C5
Corrib, L., *Ireland* 15 C2
Corrientes, *Argentina* 126 B4
Corrientes □, *Argentina* 126 B4
Corrientes →, *Argentina* 126 C4
Corrientes →, *Peru* 120 D3
Corrientes, C., *Colombia* 120 B2
Corrientes, C., *Cuba* 116 B3
Corrientes, C., *Mexico* 114 C3
Corrigan, *U.S.A.* 109 K7
Corrigin, *Australia* 89 F2
Corry, *U.S.A.* 106 E5
Corse, *France* 27 F13
Corse, C., *France* 27 E13
Corse-du-Sud □, *France* 27 G13
Corsica = Corse, *France* 27 F13
Corsicana, *U.S.A.* 109 J6
Corte, *France* 27 F13
Corte do Pinto, *Portugal* 31 H3
Cortegana, *Spain* 31 H4
Cortez, *U.S.A.* 111 H9
Cortina d'Ampezzo, *Italy* 33 B9
Cortland, *U.S.A.* 107 D8
Cortona, *Italy* 33 E8
Coruche, *Portugal* 31 G2
Çoruh →, *Turkey* 67 C9
Çorum, *Turkey* 66 C6
Çorum □, *Turkey* 66 C6
Corumbá, *Brazil* 125 D6
Corumbá →, *Brazil* 123 E2
Corumbá de Goiás, *Brazil* 123 E2
Corumbaíba, *Brazil* 123 E2
Corunna = La Coruña, *Spain* 30 B2
Corvallis, *U.S.A.* 110 D2
Corvette, L. de la, *Canada* 98 B5
Corydon, *U.S.A.* 108 E8
Cosalá, *Mexico* 114 C3
Cosamaloapan, *Mexico* 115 D5
Cosenza, *Italy* 35 C9
Coshocton, *U.S.A.* 106 F3
Cosmo Newberry, *Australia* 89 E3
Cosne-sur-Loire, *France* 25 E9
Coso Junction, *U.S.A.* 113 J9

Coso Pk., *U.S.A.* 113 J9
Cospeito, *Spain* 30 B3
Cosquín, *Argentina* 126 C3
Cossato, *Italy* 32 C5
Cossé-le-Vivien, *France* 24 E6
Cosson →, *France* 24 E8
Costa Blanca, *Spain* 29 G4
Costa Brava, *Spain* 28 D8
Costa del Sol, *Spain* 31 J6
Costa Dorada, *Spain* 28 E6
Costa Mesa, *U.S.A.* 113 M9
Costa Rica ■, *Cent. Amer.* 116 D3
Costa Smeralda, *Italy* 34 A2
Costigliole d'Asti, *Italy* 32 D5
Costilla, *U.S.A.* 111 H11
Cosumnes →, *U.S.A.* 112 G5
Coswig, *Germany* 18 D8
Cotabato, *Phil.* 55 H6
Cotacajes →, *Bolivia* 124 D4
Cotagaita, *Bolivia* 126 A2
Cotahuasi, *Peru* 124 D3
Côte d'Azur, *France* 27 E11
Côte-d'Ivoire ■ = Ivory Coast ■, *Africa* 78 D3
Côte d'Or, *France* 25 E11
Côte-d'Or □, *France* 25 E11
Coteau des Prairies, *U.S.A.* 108 C6
Coteau du Missouri, *U.S.A.* 108 B4
Coteau Landing, *Canada* 107 A10
Cotegipe, *Brazil* 123 D3
Cotentin, *France* 24 C5
Côtes-d'Armor □, *France* 24 D4
Côtes de Meuse, *France* 25 C12
Côtes-du-Nord = Côtes-d'Armor □, *France* 24 D4
Cotiella, *Spain* 28 C5
Cotillo, *Canary Is.* 36 F5
Cotina →, *Bos.-H.* 21 M8
Cotoca, *Bolivia* 125 D5
Cotonou, *Benin* 79 D5
Cotopaxi, *Ecuador* 120 D2
Cotopaxi □, *Ecuador* 120 D2
Cotronei, *Italy* 35 C9
Cotswold Hills, *U.K.* 13 F5
Cottage Grove, *U.S.A.* 110 E2
Cottbus, *Germany* 18 D10
Cottingham, *U.K.* 12 C5
Cottonwood, *U.S.A.* 111 J7
Cotulla, *U.S.A.* 109 L5
Coubre, Pte. de la, *France* 26 C2
Couches, *France* 25 F11
Couço, *Portugal* 31 G2
Coudersport, *U.S.A.* 106 E6
Couedic, C. du, *Australia* 91 F2
Couëron, *France* 24 E5
Couesnon →, *France* 24 D5
Couhé, *France* 26 B4
Coulanges-sur-Yonne, *France* 25 E10
Coulee City, *U.S.A.* 110 C4
Coulman I., *Antarctica* 5 D11
Coulommiers, *France* 25 D10
Coulonge →, *Canada* 98 C4
Coulonges-sur-l'Autize, *France* 26 B3
Coulterville, *U.S.A.* 112 H6
Council, *Alaska, U.S.A.* 96 B3
Council, *Idaho, U.S.A.* 110 D5
Council Bluffs, *U.S.A.* 108 E7
Council Grove, *U.S.A.* 108 F6
Coupeville, *U.S.A.* 112 B4
Courantyne →, *S. Amer.* 121 B6
Courcelles, *Belgium* 17 H4
Courçon, *France* 26 B3
Couronne, C., *France* 27 E9
Cours-la-Ville, *France* 27 B8
Coursan, *France* 26 E7
Courseulles-sur-Mer, *France* 24 C6
Court-St.-Etienne, *Belgium* 17 G5
Courtenay, *Canada* 100 D3
Courtland, *U.S.A.* 112 G5
Courtrai = Kortrijk, *Belgium* 17 G2
Courtright, *Canada* 106 D2
Courville-sur-Eure, *France* 24 D8
Coushatta, *U.S.A.* 109 J8
Coutances, *France* 24 C5
Couterne, *France* 24 D6
Coutras, *France* 26 C3
Coutts, *Canada* 100 D6
Couvet, *Switz.* 22 C3
Couvin, *Belgium* 17 H4
Covarrubias, *Spain* 28 C1
Coveñas, *Colombia* 120 B2
Coventry, *U.K.* 13 E6
Coventry L., *Canada* 101 A7
Covilhã, *Portugal* 30 E3
Covington, *Ga., U.S.A.* 105 J4
Covington, *Ky., U.S.A.* 104 F3
Covington, *Okla., U.S.A.* 109 G6
Covington, *Tenn., U.S.A.* 109 H10
Cowal, L., *Australia* 91 E4
Cowan, *Canada* 101 C8
Cowan, L., *Australia* 89 F3
Cowan L., *Canada* 101 C7
Cowangie, *Australia* 91 F3
Cowansville, *Canada* 107 A12
Cowarie, *Australia* 91 D2
Cowcowing Lakes, *Australia* 89 F2
Cowdenbeath, *U.K.* 14 E5
Cowell, *Australia* 91 E2
Cowes, *U.K.* 13 G6
Cowlitz →, *U.S.A.* 112 D4
Cowra, *Australia* 91 E4
Coxilha Grande, *Brazil* 127 B5
Coxim, *Brazil* 125 D7
Coxim →, *Brazil* 125 D7
Cox's Bazar, *Bangla.* 61 J17
Cox's Cove, *Canada* 99 C8
Coyame, *Mexico* 114 B3
Coyote Wells, *U.S.A.* 113 N11
Coyuca de Benítez, *Mexico* 115 D4
Coyuca de Catalan, *Mexico* 114 D4
Cozad, *U.S.A.* 108 E5
Cozumel, *Mexico* 115 C7
Cozumel, I. de, *Mexico* 115 C7
Craboon, *Australia* 91 E4
Cracow = Kraków, *Poland* 20 E9
Cracow, *Australia* 91 D5
Cradock, *S. Africa* 84 E4
Craig, *Alaska, U.S.A.* 100 B2
Craig, *Colo., U.S.A.* 110 F10
Craigavon = Lurgan, *U.K.* 15 B5
Craigmore, *Zimbabwe* 83 G3
Crailsheim, *Germany* 19 F6
Craiova, *Romania* 38 E6
Cramsie, *Australia* 90 C3
Cranberry Portage, *Canada* 101 C8
Cranbrook, *Tas., Australia* 90 G4
Cranbrook, *W. Austral., Australia* 89 F2
Cranbrook, *Canada* 100 D5
Crandon, *U.S.A.* 108 C10
Crane, *Oreg., U.S.A.* 110 E4
Crane, *Tex., U.S.A.* 109 K3
Cranston, *U.S.A.* 107 E13
Craon, *France* 24 E6
Craonne, *France* 25 C10
Craponne-sur-Arzon, *France* 26 C7
Crasna, *Romania* 38 C10
Crater L., *U.S.A.* 110 E2
Crateús, *Brazil* 122 C3
Crati →, *Italy* 35 C9
Crato, *Brazil* 122 C4
Crato, *Portugal* 31 F3
Cravo Norte, *Colombia* 120 B3
Cravo Norte →, *Colombia* 120 B3
Crawford, *U.S.A.* 108 D3
Crawfordsville, *U.S.A.* 104 E2
Crawley, *U.K.* 13 F7
Crazy Mts., *U.S.A.* 110 C8
Crean L., *Canada* 101 C7
Crécy-en-Brie, *France* 25 D9
Crécy-en-Ponthieu, *France* 25 B8
Crediton, *Canada* 106 C3
Credo, *Australia* 89 F3
Cree →, *Canada* 101 B7
Cree →, *U.K.* 14 G4
Cree L., *Canada* 101 B7
Creede, *U.S.A.* 111 H10
Creel, *Mexico* 114 B3
Creighton, *U.S.A.* 108 D6
Creil, *France* 25 C9
Crema, *Italy* 32 C6
Cremona, *Italy* 32 C7
Crepori →, *Brazil* 125 B6
Crépy, *France* 25 C10
Crépy-en-Valois, *France* 25 C9
Cres, *Croatia* 33 D11
Cresbard, *U.S.A.* 108 C5
Crescent, *Okla., U.S.A.* 109 H6
Crescent, *Oreg., U.S.A.* 110 E3
Crescent City, *U.S.A.* 110 F1
Crescentino, *Italy* 32 C5
Crespino, *Italy* 33 D8
Crespo, *Argentina* 126 C3
Cressy, *Australia* 91 F3
Crest, *France* 27 D9
Cresta, Mt., *Phil.* 55 C5
Crested Butte, *U.S.A.* 111 G10
Crestline, *Calif., U.S.A.* 113 L9
Crestline, *Ohio, U.S.A.* 106 F2
Creston, *Canada* 100 D5
Creston, *Calif., U.S.A.* 112 K6
Creston, *Iowa, U.S.A.* 108 E7
Creston, *Wash., U.S.A.* 110 C4
Crestview, *Calif., U.S.A.* 112 H8
Crestview, *Fla., U.S.A.* 105 K2
Crete = Kríti, *Greece* 37 D7
Crete, *U.S.A.* 108 E6
Crete, Sea of, *Greece* 39 N8
Creus, C., *Spain* 28 C8
Creuse □, *France* 26 B6
Creuse →, *France* 26 B4
Creuzburg, *Germany* 18 D6
Crevalcore, *Italy* 33 D8
Crèvecœur-le-Grand, *France* 25 C9
Crevillente, *Spain* 29 G4
Crewe, *U.K.* 12 D5
Criciúma, *Brazil* 127 B6
Crieff, *U.K.* 14 E5
Crikvenica, *Croatia* 33 C11
Crimea = Krymskiy Poluostrov, *Ukraine* 42 D5
Crimmitschau, *Germany* 18 E8
Cristalândia, *Brazil* 122 D2
Cristino Castro, *Brazil* 122 C3
Crişul Alb →, *Romania* 38 C4
Crişul Negru →, *Romania* 38 C4
Crişul Repede →, *Romania* 38 C3
Crivitz, *Germany* 18 B7
Crixás, *Brazil* 123 D2
Crna Gora = Montenegro □, *Montenegro, Yug.* 21 N9
Crni Drim →, *Macedonia* 39 H3
Črnomelj, *Slovenia* 33 C12
Croaghpatrick, *Ireland* 15 C2
Croatia ■, *Europe* 33 C13
Crocker, Banjaran, *Malaysia* 56 C5
Crockett, *U.S.A.* 109 K7
Crocodile = Krokodil →, *Mozam.* 85 D5
Crocodile Is., *Australia* 90 A1
Crocq, *France* 26 C6
Croisette, C., *France* 27 E9
Croisic, Pte. du, *France* 24 E4
Croix, L. La, *Canada* 98 C1
Croker, C., *Australia* 88 B5
Croker I., *Australia* 88 B5
Cromarty, *Canada* 101 B10
Cromarty, *U.K.* 14 D4
Cromer, *U.K.* 12 E9
Cromwell, *N.Z.* 87 L2
Cronat, *France* 25 F10
Cronulla, *Australia* 91 E5
Crooked →, *Canada* 100 C4
Crooked →, *U.S.A.* 110 D3
Crooked I., *Bahamas* 117 B5
Crooked Island Passage, *Bahamas* 117 B5
Crookston, *Minn., U.S.A.* 108 B6
Crookston, *Nebr., U.S.A.* 108 D4
Crooksville, *U.S.A.* 104 F4
Crookwell, *Australia* 91 E4
Crosby, *Minn., U.S.A.* 108 B8
Crosby, *N. Dak., U.S.A.* 101 D8
Crosby, *Pa., U.S.A.* 106 E6
Crosbyton, *U.S.A.* 109 J4
Cross →, *Nigeria* 79 E6
Cross City, *U.S.A.* 105 L4
Cross Fell, *U.K.* 12 C5
Cross L., *Canada* 101 C9
Cross Plains, *U.S.A.* 109 J5
Cross River □, *Nigeria* 79 D6
Cross Sound, *U.S.A.* 96 C6
Crossett, *U.S.A.* 109 J9
Crossfield, *Canada* 100 C6
Crosshaven, *Ireland* 15 E3
Croton-on-Hudson, *U.S.A.* 107 E11
Crotone, *Italy* 35 C10
Crow →, *Canada* 100 B4
Crow Agency, *U.S.A.* 110 D10
Crow Hd., *Ireland* 15 E1
Crowell, *U.S.A.* 109 J5
Crowley, *U.S.A.* 109 K8
Crowley, L., *U.S.A.* 112 H8
Crown Point, *U.S.A.* 104 E2
Crows Landing, *U.S.A.* 112 H5
Crows Nest, *Australia* 91 D5
Crowsnest Pass, *Canada* 100 D6
Croydon, *Australia* 90 B3
Croydon, *U.K.* 13 F7
Crozet Is., *Ind. Oc.* 3 G12
Crozon, *France* 24 D2
Cruz, C., *Cuba* 116 C4
Cruz Alta, *Brazil* 127 B5
Cruz das Almas, *Brazil* 123 D4
Cruz de Malta, *Brazil* 122 C3
Cruz del Eje, *Argentina* 126 C3
Cruzeiro, *Brazil* 123 F2
Cruzeiro do Oeste, *Brazil* 127 A5
Cruzeiro do Sul, *Brazil* 124 B3
Cry L., *Canada* 100 B3
Crystal Bay, *U.S.A.* 112 F7
Crystal Brook, *Australia* 91 E2
Crystal City, *Mo., U.S.A.* 108 F9
Crystal City, *Tex., U.S.A.* 109 L5
Crystal Falls, *U.S.A.* 104 B1
Crystal River, *U.S.A.* 105 L4
Crystal Springs, *U.S.A.* 109 K9
Csongrád, *Hungary* 21 J10
Csorna, *Hungary* 21 H7
Csurgo, *Hungary* 21 J7
Cu Lao Hon, *Vietnam* 59 G7
Cua Rao, *Vietnam* 58 C5
Cuácua →, *Mozam.* 83 F4
Cuamato, *Angola* 84 B2
Cuamba, *Mozam.* 83 E4
Cuando →, *Angola* 81 H4
Cuando Cubango □, *Angola* 84 B3
Cuangar, *Angola* 84 B2
Cuanza →, *Angola* 70 G5
Cuarto →, *Argentina* 126 C3
Cuatrociénegas, *Mexico* 114 B4
Cuauhtémoc, *Mexico* 114 B3
Cuba, *Portugal* 31 G3
Cuba, *N. Mex., U.S.A.* 111 J10
Cuba, *N.Y., U.S.A.* 106 D6
Cuba ■, *W. Indies* 116 B4
Cuballing, *Australia* 89 F2
Cubango →, *Africa* 84 B3
Çubuk, *Turkey* 66 C5
Cucamonga, *U.S.A.* 113 L9
Cuchi, *Angola* 81 G3
Cuchillo-Có, *Argentina* 128 A4
Cuchivero →, *Venezuela* 120 B4
Cuchumatanes, Sierra de los, *Guatemala* 116 C1
Cucuí, *Brazil* 120 C4
Cucurpe, *Mexico* 114 A2
Cucurrupí, *Colombia* 120 C2
Cúcuta, *Colombia* 120 B3
Cudahy, *U.S.A.* 104 D2
Cudalbi, *Romania* 38 D10
Cuddalore, *India* 60 P11
Cuddapah, *India* 60 M11
Cuddapan, L., *Australia* 90 D3
Cudgewa, *Australia* 91 F4
Cudillero, *Spain* 30 B4
Cue, *Australia* 89 E2
Cuéllar, *Spain* 30 D6
Cuenca, *Ecuador* 120 D2
Cuenca, *Spain* 28 E2
Cuenca □, *Spain* 28 F2
Cuenca, Serranía de, *Spain* 28 F3
Cuerdo del Pozo, Pantano de la, *Spain* 28 D2
Cuernavaca, *Mexico* 115 D5
Cuero, *U.S.A.* 109 L6
Cuers, *France* 27 E10
Cuervo, *U.S.A.* 109 H2
Cuesmes, *Belgium* 17 H3
Cuevas, Cerro, *Bolivia* 125 E4
Cuevas del Almanzora, *Spain* 29 H3
Cuevo, *Bolivia* 125 E5
Cuiabá, *Brazil* 125 D6
Cuiabá →, *Brazil* 125 D6
Cuilco, *Guatemala* 116 C1
Cuillin Hills, *U.K.* 14 D2
Cuillin Sd., *U.K.* 14 D2
Cuima, *Angola* 81 G3
Cuiseaux, *France* 27 B9
Cuité, *Brazil* 122 C4
Cuito →, *Angola* 84 B3
Cuitzeo, L. de, *Mexico* 114 D4
Cuiuni →, *Brazil* 121 D5
Cukai, *Malaysia* 59 K4
Culan, *France* 26 B6
Culbertson, *U.S.A.* 108 A2
Culcairn, *Australia* 91 F4
Culebra, Sierra de la, *Spain* 30 D4
Culemborg, *Neths.* 16 E6
Culgoa →, *Australia* 91 D4
Culiacán, *Mexico* 114 C3
Culiacán →, *Mexico* 114 C3
Culion, *Phil.* 55 F4
Culiseu →, *Brazil* 125 C7
Cúllar de Baza, *Spain* 29 H2
Cullarin Ra., *Australia* 91 E4
Cullen, *U.K.* 14 D6
Cullen Pt., *Australia* 90 A3
Cullera, *Spain* 29 F4
Cullman, *U.S.A.* 105 H2
Culloden Moor, *U.K.* 14 D4
Culoz, *France* 27 C9
Culpeper, *U.S.A.* 104 F7
Culuene →, *Brazil* 125 C7
Culver, Pt., *Australia* 89 F3
Culverden, *N.Z.* 87 K4
Cumaná, *Venezuela* 121 A5
Cumare, *Colombia* 120 C3
Cumari, *Brazil* 123 E2
Cumberland, *Canada* 100 D3
Cumberland, *Md., U.S.A.* 104 F6
Cumberland, *Wis., U.S.A.* 108 C8
Cumberland →, *U.S.A.* 105 G2
Cumberland I., *U.S.A.* 105 K5
Cumberland Is., *Australia* 90 C4
Cumberland L., *Canada* 101 C8
Cumberland Pen., *Canada* 97 B13
Cumberland Plateau, *U.S.A.* 105 H3
Cumberland Sd., *Canada* 97 B13
Cumborah, *Australia* 91 D4
Cumbres Mayores, *Spain* 31 G4
Cumbria □, *U.K.* 12 C5
Cumbrian Mts., *U.K.* 12 C4
Cumbum, *India* 60 M11
Cuminá →, *Brazil* 121 D6
Cuminapanema →, *Brazil* 121 D7
Cummings Mt., *U.S.A.* 113 K8
Cummins, *Australia* 91 E2
Cumnock, *Australia* 91 E4
Cumnock, *U.K.* 14 F4
Cumpas, *Mexico* 114 A3
Cumplida, Pta., *Canary Is.* 36 F2
Çumra, *Turkey* 66 E5
Cuncumén, *Chile* 126 C1
Cundeelee, *Australia* 89 F3
Cunderdin, *Australia* 89 F2
Cundinamarca □, *Colombia* 120 C3
Cunene →, *Angola* 84 B1
Cúneo, *Italy* 32 D4
Cunillera, I., *Spain* 36 C7
Cunlhat, *France* 26 C7
Cunnamulla, *Australia* 91 D4
Cuorgnè, *Italy* 32 C4
Cupar, *Canada* 101 C8
Cupar, *U.K.* 14 E5
Cupica, G. de, *Colombia* 120 B2
Ćuprija, *Serbia, Yug.* 21 M11
Curaçá, *Brazil* 122 C4
Curaçao, *Neth. Ant.* 117 D6
Curacautín, *Chile* 128 A2
Curahuara de Carangas, *Bolivia* 124 D4
Curanilahue, *Chile* 126 D1
Curaray →, *Peru* 120 D3
Curatabaca, *Venezuela* 121 B5
Cure →, *France* 25 E10
Curepto, *Chile* 126 D1
Curiapo, *Venezuela* 121 B5
Curicó, *Chile* 126 C1
Curicó □, *Chile* 126 C1
Curicuriari →, *Brazil* 120 D4
Curimatá, *Brazil* 122 D3
Curiplaya, *Colombia* 120 C3
Curitiba, *Brazil* 127 B6
Currabubula, *Australia* 91 E5
Currais Novos, *Brazil* 122 C4
Curralinho, *Brazil* 122 B2
Currant, *U.S.A.* 110 G6
Curraweena, *Australia* 91 E4
Currawilla, *Australia* 90 D3
Current →, *U.S.A.* 109 G9
Currie, *Australia* 90 F3
Currie, *U.S.A.* 110 F6
Currie, Mt., *S. Africa* 85 E4
Currituck Sd., *U.S.A.* 105 G8
Curtea de Argeş, *Romania* 38 D7
Curtis, *Spain* 30 B2
Curtis, *U.S.A.* 108 E4
Curtis Group, *Australia* 90 F4
Curtis I., *Australia* 90 C5
Curuá →, *Pará, Brazil* 121 D7
Curuá →, *Pará, Brazil* 125 B7
Curuá, I., *Brazil* 122 A1
Curuaés →, *Brazil* 125 B7
Curuápanema →, *Brazil* 121 D6
Curuçá, *Brazil* 122 B2
Curuguaty, *Paraguay* 127 A4
Curup, *Indonesia* 56 E2
Curupira, Serra, *S. Amer.* 121 C5
Cururu →, *Brazil* 125 B6
Cururupu, *Brazil* 122 B3
Curuzú Cuatiá, *Argentina* 126 B4
Curvelo, *Brazil* 123 E3
Cushing, *U.S.A.* 109 H6
Cushing, Mt., *Canada* 100 B3
Cusihuiriáchic, *Mexico* 114 B3
Cusna, Monte, *Italy* 32 D7
Cusset, *France* 26 B7
Custer, *U.S.A.* 108 D3
Cut Bank, *U.S.A.* 110 B7
Cutervo, *Peru* 124 B2
Cuthbert, *U.S.A.* 105 K3
Cutler, *U.S.A.* 112 J7
Cutral-Có, *Argentina* 128 A3
Cutro, *Italy* 35 C9
Cuttaburra →, *Australia* 91 D3
Cuttack, *India* 61 J14
Cuvier, C., *Australia* 89 D1
Cuvier I., *N.Z.* 87 G5
Cuxhaven, *Germany* 18 B4
Cuyabeno, *Ecuador* 120 D2
Cuyahoga Falls, *U.S.A.* 106 E3
Cuyapo, *Phil.* 55 D4
Cuyo, *Phil.* 55 F4
Cuyo East Pass, *Phil.* 55 F4
Cuyo West Pass, *Phil.* 55 F4
Cuyuni →, *Guyana* 121 B6
Cuzco, *Bolivia* 124 E4
Cuzco, *Peru* 124 C3
Cuzco □, *Peru* 124 C3
Cwmbran, *U.K.* 13 F4
Cyangugu, *Rwanda* 82 C2
Cyclades = Kikládhes, *Greece* 39 M7
Cygnet, *Australia* 90 G4
Cynthiana, *U.S.A.* 104 F3
Cypress Hills, *Canada* 101 D7
Cyprus ■, *Asia* 37 E12
Cyrenaica, *Libya* 70 C6
Cyrene = Shaḩḩāt, *Libya* 73 B9
Czar, *Canada* 101 C6
Czarne, *Poland* 20 B6
Czech Rep. ■, *Europe* 20 F4
Czersk, *Poland* 20 B7
Częstochowa, *Poland* 20 E9

D

Da →, *Vietnam* 58 B5
Da Hinggan Ling, *China* 54 B7
Da Lat, *Vietnam* 59 G7
Da Nang, *Vietnam* 58 D7
Da Qaidam, *China* 54 C4
Da Yunhe →, *China* 51 G11
Da'an, *China* 51 B13
Daarlerveen, *Neths.* 16 D9
Dab'a, Râs el, *Egypt* 76 H6
Daba Shan, *China* 52 B7
Dabai, *Nigeria* 79 C6
Dabajuro, *Venezuela* 120 A3
Dabakala, *Ivory C.* 78 D4
Dabeiba, *Colombia* 120 B2
Dabhoi, *India* 62 H5
Dąbie, *Poland* 20 B4
Dabie Shan, *China* 53 B10
Dabo, *Indonesia* 56 E2
Dabola, *Guinea* 78 C2
Dabou, *Ivory C.* 78 D4
Daboya, *Ghana* 79 D4
Dabrowa Tarnówska, *Poland* 20 E10
Dabu, *China* 53 E11
Dabung, *Malaysia* 59 K4
Dabus →, *Ethiopia* 77 E4
Dacato →, *Ethiopia* 77 F5
Dacca = Dhaka, *Bangla.* 63 H14
Dacca = Dhaka □, *Bangla.* 63 G14
Dachau, *Germany* 19 G7
Dadanawa, *Guyana* 121 C6
Daday, *Turkey* 42 F5
Dade City, *U.S.A.* 105 L4
Dades, Oued →, *Morocco* 74 B3
Dadiya, *Nigeria* 79 D7
Dadra and Nagar Haveli □, *India* 60 J8
Dadri = Charkhi Dadri, *India* 62 E7
Dadu, *Pakistan* 62 F2

Dadu He →, China 52 C4
Dăeni, Romania 38 E11
Daet, Phil. 55 D5
Dafang, China 52 D5
Dagana, Senegal 78 B1
Dagash, Sudan 76 D3
Dagestanskiye Ogni, Russia 43 E13
Daggett, U.S.A. 113 L10
Daghestan Republic □, Russia 43 E12
Daghfeli, Sudan 76 D3
Dagö = Hiiumaa, Estonia 40 B3
Dagu, China 51 E9
Daguan, China 52 D4
Dagupan, Phil. 55 C4
Dahab, Egypt 76 B3
Dahlak Kebir, Eritrea 68 D3
Dahlenburg, Germany 18 B6
Dahlonega, U.S.A. 105 H4
Dahme, Germany 18 D9
Dahod, India 62 H6
Dahomey = Benin ■, Africa 79 D5
Dahong Shan, China 53 B9
Dahra, Senegal 78 B1
Dahra, Massif de, Algeria 75 A5
Dai Hao, Vietnam 58 C6
Dai-Sen, Japan 49 G6
Dai Shan, China 53 B14
Dai Xian, China 50 E7
Daicheng, China 50 E9
Daimiel, Spain 29 F1
Daingean, Ireland 15 C4
Dainkog, China 52 A1
Daintree, Australia 90 B4
Daiō-Misaki, Japan 49 G8
Dairût, Egypt 76 B3
Daisetsu-Zan, Japan 48 C11
Dajarra, Australia 90 C2
Dajia, Taiwan 53 E13
Dajin Chuan →, China 52 B3
Dak Dam, Cambodia 58 F6
Dak Nhe, Vietnam 58 E6
Dak Pek, Vietnam 58 E6
Dak Song, Vietnam 59 F6
Dak Sui, Vietnam 58 E6
Dakar, Senegal 78 C1
Dakhla, W. Sahara 74 D1
Dakhla, El Wâhât el-, Egypt 76 B2
Dakhovskaya, Russia 43 D9
Dakingari, Nigeria 79 C5
Dakor, India 62 H5
Dakoro, Niger 79 C6
Dakota City, U.S.A. 108 D6
Đakovica, Serbia 21 N10
Đakovo, Croatia 21 K8
Dalaba, Guinea 78 C2
Dalachi, China 50 F3
Dalai Nur, China 50 C9
Dālakī, Iran 65 D6
Dalälven, Sweden 9 F14
Dalaman, Turkey 66 E3
Dalaman →, Turkey 66 E3
Dalandzadgad, Mongolia 50 C3
Dalarö, Sweden 9 G15
Dālbandīn, Pakistan 60 E4
Dalbeattie, U.K. 14 G5
Dalbosjön, Sweden 11 F6
Dalby, Australia 91 D5
Dalby, Sweden 11 J7
Dalen, Neths. 16 C9
Dalen, Norway 10 E2
Dalfsen, Neths. 16 C8
Dalga, Egypt 76 B3
Dalgān, Iran 65 E8
Dalhart, U.S.A. 109 G3
Dalhousie, Canada 99 C6
Dalhousie, India 62 C6
Dali, Shaanxi, China 50 G5
Dali, Yunnan, China 52 E3
Dalian, China 51 E11
Daliang Shan, China 52 D4
Dalias, Spain 29 J2
Daling He →, China 51 D11
Dāliyat el Karmel, Israel 69 C4
Dalkeith, U.K. 14 F5
Dall I., U.S.A. 100 C2
Dallarnil, Australia 91 D5
Dallas, Oreg., U.S.A. 110 D2
Dallas, Tex., U.S.A. 109 J6
Dallol, Ethiopia 77 E5
Dalmacija = Dalmatia □, Croatia 21 M7
Dalmatia □, Croatia 21 M7
Dalmellington, U.K. 14 F4
Dalnegorsk, Russia 45 E14
Dalnerechensk, Russia 45 E14
Daloa, Ivory C. 78 D3
Dalou Shan, China 52 C6
Dalsjöfors, Sweden 11 G7
Dalskog, Sweden 11 F6
Daltenganj, India 63 G11
Dalton, Canada 98 C3
Dalton, Ga., U.S.A. 105 H3
Dalton, Mass., U.S.A. 107 D11
Dalton, Nebr., U.S.A. 108 E3
Dalton Iceberg Tongue, Antarctica 5 C9
Dalupiri I., Phil. 55 B4
Dalvík, Iceland 8 D4
Daly →, Australia 88 B5
Daly City, U.S.A. 112 H4
Daly L., Canada 101 B7
Daly Waters, Australia 90 B1
Dam Doi, Vietnam 59 H5
Dam Ha, Vietnam 58 B6
Daman, India 60 J8
Dāmaneh, Iran 65 C6
Damanhûr, Egypt 76 H7
Damanzhuang, China 50 E9
Damar, Indonesia 57 F7
Damaraland, Namibia 84 C2
Damascus = Dimashq, Syria 69 B5
Damaturu, Nigeria 79 C7
Damāvand, Iran 65 C7
Damāvand, Qolleh-ye, Iran 65 C7
Damba, Angola 80 F3
Dame Marie, Haiti 117 C5
Dāmghān, Iran 65 B7
Dămienesti, Romania 38 C10
Damietta = Dumyât, Egypt 76 H7
Daming, China 50 F8
Damīr Qābū, Syria 64 B4
Dammam = Ad Dammām, Si. Arabia 65 E6
Dammarie, France 24 D8
Dammartin-en-Goële, France 25 C9
Dammastock, Switz. 23 C6
Damme, Germany 18 C4
Damodar →, India 63 H12
Damoh, India 63 H8
Damous, Algeria 75 A5
Dampier, Australia 88 D2
Dampier, Selat, Indonesia 57 E8
Dampier Arch., Australia 88 D2
Damrei, Chuor Phnum, Cambodia 59 G4
Damville, France 24 D8
Damvillers, France 25 C12
Dan-Gulbi, Nigeria 79 C6
Dana, Indonesia 57 F6
Dana, L., Canada 98 B4
Dana, Mt., U.S.A. 112 H7
Danakil Depression, Ethiopia 77 E5
Danao, Phil. 55 F6
Danbury, U.S.A. 107 E11
Danby L., U.S.A. 111 J6
Dand, Afghan. 62 D1
Dandaragan, Australia 89 F2
Dandeldhura, Nepal 63 E9
Dandeli, India 60 M9
Dandenong, Australia 91 F4
Dandong, China 51 D13
Danfeng, China 50 H6
Danforth, U.S.A. 99 C6
Dangan Liedao, China 53 F10
Danger Is. = Pukapuka, Cook Is. 93 J11
Danger Pt., S. Africa 84 E2
Dangla, Ethiopia 77 E4
Dangora, Nigeria 79 C6
Dangrek, Phnom, Thailand 58 E5
Dangriga, Belize 115 D7
Dangshan, China 50 G9
Dangtu, China 53 B12
Dangyang, China 53 B8
Daniel, U.S.A. 110 E8
Daniel's Harbour, Canada 99 B8
Danielskuil, S. Africa 84 D3
Danielson, U.S.A. 107 E13
Danilov, Russia 41 B12
Danilovka, Russia 41 F14
Daning, China 50 F6
Danissa, Kenya 82 B5
Danja, Nigeria 79 C6
Dankalwa, Nigeria 79 C7
Dankama, Nigeria 79 C6
Dankhar Gompa, India 60 C11
Dankov, Russia 41 E11
Danleng, China 52 B4
Danlí, Honduras 116 D2
Dannemora, Sweden 9 F14
Dannemora, U.S.A. 107 B11
Dannenberg, Germany 18 B7
Dannevirke, N.Z. 87 J6
Dannhauser, S. Africa 85 D5
Danshui, Taiwan 53 E13
Dansville, U.S.A. 106 D7
Dantan, India 63 J12
Dante, Somali Rep. 68 E5
Danvers, U.S.A. 107 D14
Danville, Ill., U.S.A. 104 E2
Danville, Ky., U.S.A. 104 G3
Danville, Va., U.S.A. 105 G6
Danyang, China 53 B12
Danzhai, China 52 D6
Danzig = Gdańsk, Poland 20 A8
Dao, Phil. 57 B6
Dão →, Portugal 30 E2
Dao Xian, China 53 E8
Daocheng, China 52 C3
Daora, W. Sahara 74 C2
Daoud = Aïn Beïda, Algeria 75 A6
Daoulas, France 24 D2
Dapitan, Phil. 55 G5
Dapong, Togo 79 C5
Daqing Shan, China 50 D6
Daqu Shan, China 53 B14
Dar es Salaam, Tanzania 82 D4
Dar Mazār, Iran 65 D8
Dar'ā, Syria 69 C5
Dar'ā □, Syria 69 C5
Dārāb, Iran 65 D7
Daraj, Libya 75 B7
Dārān, Iran 65 C6
Daravica, Serbia 21 N10
Daraw, Egypt 76 C3
Dārayyā, Syria 69 B5
Darazo, Nigeria 79 C7
Darband, Pakistan 62 B5
Darband, Kūh-e, Iran 65 D8
Darbhanga, India 63 F11
Darby, U.S.A. 110 C6
Dardanelle, Ark., U.S.A. 109 H8
Dardanelle, Calif., U.S.A. 112 G7
Dardanelles = Çanakkale Boğazı, Turkey 66 C2
Darende, Turkey 66 D7
Dārestān, Iran 65 D8
Darfo, Italy 32 C7
Dârfûr, Sudan 70 E6
Dargai, Pakistan 62 B4
Dargan Ata, Uzbekistan 44 E7
Dargaville, N.Z. 87 F4
Darhan Muminggan Lianheqi, China 50 D6
Dari, Sudan 77 F3
Darién, G. del, Colombia 120 B2
Darién, Serranía del, Colombia 120 B2
Dariganga, Mongolia 50 B7
Darjeeling = Darjiling, India 63 F13
Darjiling, India 63 F13
Dark Cove, Canada 99 C9
Darkan, Australia 89 F2
Darkhazīneh, Iran 65 D6
Darkot Pass, Pakistan 63 A5
Darling →, Australia 91 E3
Darling Downs, Australia 91 D5
Darling Ra., Australia 89 F2
Darlington, U.K. 12 C6
Darlington, S.C., U.S.A. 105 H6
Darlington, Wis., U.S.A. 108 D9
Darlot, L., Australia 89 E3
Darłowo, Poland 20 A6
Darmstadt, Germany 19 F4
Darnah, Libya 73 B9
Darnall, S. Africa 85 D5
Darnétal, France 24 C8
Darney, France 25 D13
Darnley, C., Antarctica 5 C6
Darnley B., Canada 96 B7
Daroca, Spain 28 D3
Darr, Australia 90 C3
Darr →, Australia 90 C3
Darrington, U.S.A. 110 B3
Darsser Ort, Germany 18 A8
Dart →, U.K. 13 G4
Dart, C., Antarctica 5 D14
Dartmoor, U.K. 13 G4
Dartmouth, Australia 90 C3
Dartmouth, Canada 99 D7
Dartmouth, U.K. 13 G4
Dartmouth, L., Australia 91 D4
Dartuch, C., Spain 36 B10
Darvaza, Turkmenistan 44 E6
Darvel, Teluk, Malaysia 57 D5
Darwha, India 60 J10
Darwin, Australia 88 B5
Darwin, U.S.A. 113 J9
Darwin, Mt., Chile 128 D3
Darwin River, Australia 88 B5
Daryoi Amu = Amudarya →, Uzbekistan 44 E6
Dās, U.A.E. 65 E7
Dashetai, China 50 D5
Dashkesan, Azerbaijan 43 F12
Dasht, Iran 65 B8
Dasht →, Pakistan 60 G2
Dasht-e Mārgow, Afghan. 60 D3
Dasht-i-Nawar, Afghan. 62 C3
Daska, Pakistan 62 C6
Dassa-Zoume, Benin 79 D5
Dasseneiland, S. Africa 84 E2
Datça, Turkey 66 E2
Datia, India 63 G8
Datian, China 53 E11
Datong, Anhui, China 53 B11
Datong, Shanxi, China 50 D7
Datu, Tanjung, Indonesia 56 D3
Datu Piang, Phil. 55 H6
Daugava →, Latvia 40 C4
Daugavpils, Latvia 40 D5
Daule, Ecuador 120 D2
Daule →, Ecuador 120 D2
Daulpur, India 62 F7
Daun, Germany 19 E2
Dauphin, Canada 101 C8
Dauphin I., U.S.A. 105 K1
Dauphin L., Canada 101 C9
Dauphiné, France 27 C9
Daura, Borno, Nigeria 79 C7
Daura, Kaduna, Nigeria 79 C6
Dausa, India 62 F7
Davangere, India 60 M9
Davao, Phil. 55 H6
Davao, G. of, Phil. 55 H6
Dāvar Panāh, Iran 65 E9
Davenport, Calif., U.S.A. 112 H4
Davenport, Iowa, U.S.A. 108 E9
Davenport, Wash., U.S.A. 110 C4
Davenport Downs, Australia 90 C3
Davenport Ra., Australia 90 C1
David, Panama 116 E3
David City, U.S.A. 108 E6
David Gorodok, Belorussia 40 E5
Davidson, Canada 101 C7
Davis, U.S.A. 112 G5
Davis Dam, U.S.A. 113 K12
Davis Inlet, Canada 99 A7
Davis Mts., U.S.A. 109 K2
Davis Sea, Antarctica 5 C7
Davis Str., N. Amer. 97 B14
Davos, Switz. 23 C9
Davy L., Canada 101 B7
Dawa →, Ethiopia 77 G5
Dawaki, Bauchi, Nigeria 79 D6
Dawaki, Kano, Nigeria 79 C6
Dawes Ra., Australia 90 C5
Dawson, Canada 96 B6
Dawson, Ga., U.S.A. 105 K3
Dawson, N. Dak., U.S.A. 108 B5
Dawson, I., Chile 128 D2
Dawson Creek, Canada 100 B4
Dawson Inlet, Canada 101 A10
Dawson Ra., Australia 90 C4
Dawu, China 52 B3
Dax, France 26 E2
Daxi, Taiwan 53 E13
Daxian, China 52 B6
Daxin, China 52 F6
Daxindian, China 51 F11
Daxinggou, China 51 C15
Daxue Shan, Sichuan, China 52 B3
Daxue Shan, Yunnan, China 52 F2
Dayao, China 52 E3
Daye, China 53 B10
Dayi, China 52 B4
Daylesford, Australia 91 F3
Dayong, China 53 C8
Dayr az Zawr, Syria 64 C4
Daysland, Canada 100 C6
Dayton, Nev., U.S.A. 112 F7
Dayton, Ohio, U.S.A. 104 F3
Dayton, Pa., U.S.A. 106 F5
Dayton, Tenn., U.S.A. 105 H3
Dayton, Wash., U.S.A. 110 C4
Daytona Beach, U.S.A. 105 L5
Dayu, China 53 E10
Dayville, U.S.A. 110 D4
Dazhu, China 52 B6
Dazu, China 52 C5
De Aar, S. Africa 84 E3
De Bilt, Neths. 16 D6
De Funiak Springs, U.S.A. 105 K2
De Grey, Australia 88 D2
De Grey →, Australia 88 D2
De Kalb, U.S.A. 108 E10
De Koog, Neths. 16 B5
De Land, U.S.A. 105 L5
De Leon, U.S.A. 109 J5
De Panne, Belgium 17 F1
De Pere, U.S.A. 104 C1
De Queen, U.S.A. 109 H7
De Quincy, U.S.A. 109 K8
De Ridder, U.S.A. 109 K8
De Rijp, Neths. 16 C5
De Smet, U.S.A. 108 C6
De Soto, U.S.A. 108 F9
De Tour Village, U.S.A. 104 C4
De Witt, U.S.A. 109 H9
Dead Sea, Asia 69 D4
Deadwood, U.S.A. 108 C3
Deadwood L., Canada 100 B3
Deakin, Australia 89 F4
Deal, U.K. 13 F9
Deal I., Australia 90 F4
Dealesville, S. Africa 84 D4
De'an, China 53 C10
Dean, Forest of, U.K. 13 F5
Deán Funes, Argentina 126 C3
Dearborn, U.S.A. 98 D3
Dease →, Canada 100 B3
Dease L., Canada 100 B2
Dease Lake, Canada 100 B2
Death Valley, U.S.A. 113 J10
Death Valley Junction, U.S.A. 113 J10
Death Valley National Monument, U.S.A. 113 J10
Deauville, France 24 C7
Deba Habe, Nigeria 79 C7
Debaltsevo, Ukraine 42 B8
Debao, China 52 F6
Debar, Macedonia 39 H3
Debden, Canada 101 C7
Debdou, Morocco 75 B4
Dębica, Poland 20 E11
Dęblin, Poland 20 D11
Débo, L., Mali 78 B4
Debolt, Canada 100 B5
Deborah East, L., Australia 89 F2
Deborah West, L., Australia 89 F2
Debre Birhan, Ethiopia 77 F4
Debre Markos, Ethiopia 77 E4
Debre May, Ethiopia 77 E4
Debre Sina, Ethiopia 77 F4
Debre Tabor, Ethiopia 77 E4
Debre Zebit, Ethiopia 77 E4
Debrecen, Hungary 21 H11
Dečani, Serbia 21 N10
Decatur, Ala., U.S.A. 105 H2
Decatur, Ga., U.S.A. 105 J3
Decatur, Ill., U.S.A. 108 F10
Decatur, Ind., U.S.A. 104 E3
Decatur, Tex., U.S.A. 109 J6
Decazeville, France 26 D6
Deccan, India 60 M10
Deception L., Canada 101 B8
Dechang, China 52 D4
Děčín, Czech. 20 E4
Decize, France 25 F10
Deckerville, U.S.A. 106 C2
Decollatura, Italy 35 C9
Decorah, U.S.A. 108 D9
Dedéagach = Alexandroúpolis, Greece 39 J8
Dedegöl Dağları, Turkey 66 E4
Dedemsvaart, Neths. 16 C8
Dedham, U.S.A. 107 D13
Dedilovo, Russia 41 E10
Dédougou, Burkina Faso 78 C4
Dedza, Malawi 83 E3
Dee →, Clwyd, U.K. 12 D4
Dee →, Gramp., U.K. 14 D6
Deep B., Canada 100 A5
Deep Well, Australia 90 C1
Deepwater, Australia 91 D5
Deer →, Canada 101 B10
Deer Lake, Nfld., Canada 99 C8
Deer Lake, Ont., Canada 101 C10
Deer Lodge, U.S.A. 110 C7
Deer Park, U.S.A. 110 C5
Deer River, U.S.A. 108 B8
Deeral, Australia 90 B4
Deerdepoort, S. Africa 84 C4
Deerlijk, Belgium 17 G2
Deferiet, U.S.A. 107 B9
Defiance, U.S.A. 104 E3
Dêgê, China 52 B2
Degebe →, Portugal 31 G3
Degeh Bur, Ethiopia 68 F3
Degema, Nigeria 79 E6
Degersheim, Switz. 23 B8
Deggendorf, Germany 19 G8
Deh Bīd, Iran 65 D7
Deh-e Shīr, Iran 65 D7
Dehaj, Iran 65 D7
Dehdez, Iran 65 D6
Dehestān, Iran 65 D7
Dehgolān, Iran 64 C5
Dehi Titan, Afghan. 60 C3
Dehibat, Tunisia 75 B7
Dehlorān, Iran 64 C5
Dehnow-e Kūhestān, Iran 65 E8
Dehra Dun, India 62 D8
Dehri, India 63 G11
Dehua, China 53 E12
Dehui, China 51 B13
Deinze, Belgium 17 G3
Dej, Romania 38 B6
Dejiang, China 52 C7
Dekemhare, Eritrea 77 D4
Dekese, Zaïre 80 E4
Del Mar, U.S.A. 113 N9
Del Norte, U.S.A. 111 H10
Del Rio, U.S.A. 109 L4
Delai, Sudan 76 D4
Delano, U.S.A. 113 K7
Delareyville, S. Africa 84 D4
Delavan, U.S.A. 108 D10
Delaware, U.S.A. 104 E4
Delaware □, U.S.A. 104 F8
Delaware →, U.S.A. 104 F8
Delaware B., U.S.A. 103 C12
Delegate, Australia 91 F4
Delémont, Switz. 22 B4
Delft, Neths. 16 D4
Delfzijl, Neths. 16 B9
Delgado, C., Mozam. 83 E5
Delgerhet, Mongolia 50 B6
Delgo, Sudan 76 C3
Delhi, Canada 106 D4
Delhi, India 62 E7
Delhi, U.S.A. 107 D10
Delia, Canada 100 C6
Delice, Turkey 66 D6
Delice →, Turkey 66 D6
Delicias, Mexico 114 B3
Delījān, Iran 65 C6
Delitzsch, Germany 18 D8
Dell City, U.S.A. 111 L11
Dell Rapids, U.S.A. 108 D6
Delle, France 25 E14
Dellys, Algeria 75 A5
Delmar, U.S.A. 107 D11
Delmenhorst, Germany 18 B4
Delmiro Gouveia, Brazil 122 C4
Delnice, Croatia 33 C11
Delong, Ostrova, Russia 45 B15
Deloraine, Australia 90 G4
Deloraine, Canada 101 D8
Delphi, U.S.A. 104 E2
Delphos, U.S.A. 104 E3
Delportshoop, S. Africa 84 D3
Delray Beach, U.S.A. 105 M5
Delsbo, Sweden 10 C10
Delta, Colo., U.S.A. 111 G9
Delta, Utah, U.S.A. 110 G7
Delta □, Nigeria 79 D6
Delta Amacuro □, Venezuela 121 B5
Delungra, Australia 91 D5
Delvina, Albania 39 K3
Delvinákion, Greece 39 K3
Demanda, Sierra de la, Spain 28 C1
Demavand = Damāvand, Iran 65 C7
Demba, Zaïre 80 F4
Dembecha, Ethiopia 77 E4
Dembi, Ethiopia 77 F4
Dembia, Zaïre 82 B2
Dembidolo, Ethiopia 77 F3

Demer →, Belgium 17 G5
Demidov, Russia 40 D7
Deming, N. Mex., U.S.A. 111 K10
Deming, Wash., U.S.A. 112 B4
Demini →, Brazil 121 D5
Demirci, Turkey 66 D3
Demirköy, Turkey 66 C2
Demmin, Germany 18 B9
Demnate, Morocco 74 B3
Demonte, Italy 32 D4
Demopolis, U.S.A. 105 J2
Dempo, Indonesia 56 E2
Demyansk, Russia 40 C8
Den Burg, Neths. 16 B5
Den Chai, Thailand 58 D3
Den Dungen, Neths. 17 E6
Den Haag = 's-Gravenhage, Neths. 16 D4
Den Ham, Neths. 16 D8
Den Helder, Neths. 16 C5
Den Hulst, Neths. 16 C8
Den Oever, Neths. 16 C6
Denain, France 25 B10
Denair, U.S.A. 112 H6
Denau, Uzbekistan 44 F7
Denbigh, U.K. 12 D4
Dendang, Indonesia 56 E3
Dender →, Belgium 17 F4
Denderhoutem, Belgium 17 G4
Denderleeuw, Belgium 17 G4
Dendermonde, Belgium 17 F4
Deneba, Ethiopia 77 F4
Denekamp, Neths. 16 D10
Deng Xian, China 53 A9
Dengchuan, China 52 E3
Denge, Nigeria 79 C6
Dengfeng, China 50 G7
Dengi, Nigeria 79 D6
Dengkou, China 50 D4
Denham, Australia 89 E1
Denham Ra., Australia 90 C4
Denham Sd., Australia 89 E1
Denia, Spain 29 G5
Denial B., Australia 91 E1
Deniliquin, Australia 91 F3
Denison, Iowa, U.S.A. 108 D7
Denison, Tex., U.S.A. 109 J6
Denison Plains, Australia 88 C4
Denizli, Turkey 66 E3
Denizli □, Turkey 66 E3
Denman Glacier, Antarctica 5 C7
Denmark, Australia 89 F2
Denmark ■, Europe 11 J3
Denmark Str., Atl. Oc. 4 C6
Dennison, U.S.A. 106 F3
Denpasar, Indonesia 56 F5
Denton, Mont., U.S.A. 110 C9
Denton, Tex., U.S.A. 109 J6
D'Entrecasteaux, Pt., Australia 89 F2
Dents du Midi, Switz. 22 D3
Denu, Ghana 79 D5
Denver, U.S.A. 108 F2
Denver City, U.S.A. 109 J3
Deoband, India 62 E7
Deoghar, India 63 G12
Deolali, India 60 K8
Deoli = Devli, India 62 G6
Deoria, India 63 F10
Deosai Mts., Pakistan 63 B6
Deping, China 51 F9
Deposit, U.S.A. 107 D9
Depot Springs, Australia 89 E3
Deputatskiy, Russia 45 C14
Dêqên, China 52 C2
Deqing, China 53 F8
Dera Ghazi Khan, Pakistan 62 D4
Dera Ismail Khan, Pakistan 62 D4
Derbent, Russia 43 E13
Derby, Australia 88 C3
Derby, U.K. 12 E6
Derby, Conn., U.S.A. 107 E11
Derby, N.Y., U.S.A. 106 D6
Derbyshire □, U.K. 12 E6
Dereli, Turkey 67 C8
Derg →, U.K. 15 B4
Derg, L., Ireland 15 D3
Dergachi, Ukraine 42 A7
Dergaon, India 61 F19
Derik, Turkey 67 E9
Derinkuyu, Turkey 66 D6
Dernieres, Isles, U.S.A. 109 L9
Dêrong, China 52 C2
Derry = Londonderry, U.K. 15 B4
Derryveagh Mts., Ireland 15 B3
Derudub, Sudan 76 D4
Derval, France 24 E5
Dervéni, Greece 39 L5
Derwent, Canada 101 C6
Derwent →, Derby, U.K. 12 E6
Derwent →, N. Yorks., U.K. 12 D7
Derwent Water, U.K. 12 C4
Des Moines, Iowa, U.S.A. 108 E8
Des Moines, N. Mex., U.S.A. 109 G3
Des Moines →, U.S.A. 108 E9
Desaguadero →, Argentina 126 C2
Desaguadero →, Bolivia 124 D4
Descanso, Pta., Mexico 113 N9
Descartes, France 26 B4
Deschaillons, Canada 99 C5
Descharme →, Canada 101 B7
Deschutes →, U.S.A. 110 D3
Dese, Ethiopia 68 E2
Deseado, C., Chile 128 D2
Desenzano del Gardo, Italy 32 C7
Desert Center, U.S.A. 113 M11
Desert Hot Springs, U.S.A. 113 M10
Désirade, I., Guadeloupe 117 C7
Deskenatlata L., Canada 100 A6
Desna →, Ukraine 40 F7
Desnătui →, Romania 38 E6
Desolación, I., Chile 128 D2
Despeñaperros, Paso, Spain 29 G1
Despotovac, Serbia, Yug. 21 L11
Dessau, Germany 18 D8
Dessel, Belgium 17 F6
Dessye = Dese, Ethiopia 68 E2
D'Estrees B., Australia 91 F2
Desuri, India 62 G5
Desvres, France 25 B8
Det Udom, Thailand 58 E5
Dete, Zimbabwe 83 F2
Detinja →, Serbia, Yug. 21 M9
Detmold, Germany 18 D4
Detour, Pt., U.S.A. 104 C2
Detroit, Mich., U.S.A. 98 D3
Detroit, Tex., U.S.A. 109 J7
Detroit Lakes, U.S.A. 108 B7
Deurne, Belgium 17 F4
Deurne, Neths. 17 F7
Deutsche Bucht, Germany 18 A4
Deutschlandsberg, Austria 21 J5
Deux-Sèvres □, France 24 F6
Deva, Romania 38 D5
Devakottai, India 60 Q11
Devaprayag, India 63 D8
Dévaványa, Hungary 21 H10
Deveci Daği, Turkey 42 F7
Deveci Dağları, Turkey 66 C6
Develi, Turkey 66 D6
Deventer, Neths. 16 D8
Deveron →, U.K. 14 D6
Devgadh Bariya, India 62 H5
Devils Den, U.S.A. 112 K7
Devils Lake, U.S.A. 108 A5
Devils Paw, Canada 100 B2
Devizes, U.K. 13 F6
Devli, India 62 G6
Devnya, Bulgaria 38 F10
Devolii →, Albania 39 J3
Devon, Canada 100 C6
Devon □, U.K. 13 G4
Devon I., Canada 4 B3
Devonport, Australia 90 G4
Devonport, N.Z. 87 G5
Devonport, U.K. 13 G3
Devrek, Turkey 66 C4
Devrekâni, Turkey 66 C5
Devrez →, Turkey 66 C6
Dewas, India 62 H7
Dewetsdorp, S. Africa 84 D4
Dewsbury, U.K. 12 D6
Dexing, China 53 C11
Dexter, Mo., U.S.A. 109 G9
Dexter, N. Mex., U.S.A. 109 J2
Dey-Dey, L., Australia 89 E5
Deyang, China 52 B5
Deyhūk, Iran 65 C8
Deyyer, Iran 65 E6
Dezadeash L., Canada 100 A1
Dezfūl, Iran 65 C6
Dezhneva, Mys, Russia 45 C19
Dezhou, China 50 F9
Dháfni, Greece 37 D7
Dhahaban, Si. Arabia 76 C4
Dhahiriya = Az Zāhirīyah, Jordan 69 D3
Dhahran = Az Zahrān, Si. Arabia 65 E6
Dhaka, Bangla. 63 H14
Dhaka □, Bangla. 63 G14
Dhali, Cyprus 37 D12
Dhamar, Yemen 68 E3
Dhamási, Greece 39 K5
Dhampur, India 63 E8
Dhamtari, India 61 J12
Dhanbad, India 63 H12
Dhangarhi, Nepal 61 E12
Dhankuta, Nepal 63 F12
Dhar, India 62 H6
Dharampur, India 62 H6
Dharamsala = Dharmsala, India 62 C7
Dharmapuri, India 60 N11
Dharmsala, India 62 C7
Dharwad, India 60 M9
Dharwar, India 60 M9
Dhaulagiri, Nepal 63 E10
Dhebar, L., India 62 G6
Dheftera, Cyprus 37 D12
Dhenkanal, India 61 J14
Dhenoúsa, Greece 39 M8
Dherinia, Cyprus 37 D12
Dheskáti, Greece 39 K4
Dhespotikó, Greece 39 N7
Dhestina, Greece 39 L5
Dhiarrizos →, Cyprus 37 E11
Dhībān, Jordan 69 D4
Dhíkti Óros, Greece 37 D7
Dhimitsána, Greece 39 M5
Dhírfis, Greece 39 L6
Dhodhekánisos, Greece 39 N10
Dholiana, Greece 39 K3
Dholka, India 62 H5
Dhoraji, India 62 J4
Dhoxáton, Greece 39 H7
Dhráhstis, Ákra, Greece 37 A3
Dhrangadhra, India 62 H4
Dhrápanon, Ákra, Greece 37 D6
Dhrol, India 62 H4
Dhuburi, India 61 F16
Dhule, India 60 J9
Dhut →, Somali Rep. 68 E5
Di Linh, Vietnam 59 G7
Di Linh, Cao Nguyen, Vietnam 59 G7
Día, Greece 37 D7
Diablo, Mt., U.S.A. 112 H5
Diablo Range, U.S.A. 112 J5
Diafarabé, Mali 78 C4
Diala, Mali 78 C3
Dialakoro, Mali 78 C3
Diallassagou, Mali 78 C4
Diamante, Argentina 126 C3
Diamante →, Argentina 126 C2
Diamantina, Brazil 123 E3
Diamantina →, Australia 91 D2
Diamantino, Brazil 125 C6
Diamond Harbour, India 63 H13
Diamond Is., Australia 90 B5
Diamond Mts., U.S.A. 110 G6
Diamond Springs, U.S.A. 112 G6
Diamondville, U.S.A. 110 F8
Dianbai, China 53 G8
Diancheng, China 53 G8
Diano Marina, Italy 32 E5
Dianópolis, Brazil 123 D2
Dianra, Ivory C. 78 D3
Diapaga, Burkina Faso 79 C5
Diapangou, Burkina Faso 79 C5
Diariguila, Guinea 78 C2
Dībā, Oman 65 E8
Dibaya, Zaïre 80 F4
Dibaya-Lubue, Zaïre 80 E3
Dibbi, Ethiopia 68 G3
Dibete, Botswana 84 C4
Dibrugarh, India 61 F19
Dickinson, U.S.A. 108 B3
Dickson, U.S.A. 105 G2
Dickson City, U.S.A. 107 E9
Dicomano, Italy 33 E8
Didam, Neths. 16 E8
Didesa, W. →, Ethiopia 77 E4
Didiéni, Mali 78 C3
Didsbury, Canada 100 C6
Didwana, India 62 F6
Die, France 27 D9
Diébougou, Burkina Faso 78 C4
Diefenbaker L., Canada 101 C7
Diego Garcia, Ind. Oc. 3 E13
Diekirch, Lux. 17 J8
Diélette, France 24 C5
Diéma, Mali 78 C3
Diémbéring, Senegal 78 C1
Diemen, Neths. 16 D5
Dien Ban, Vietnam 58 E7
Dien Bien, Vietnam 58 B4
Dien Khanh, Vietnam 59 F7
Diepenbeek, Belgium 17 G6
Diepenheim, Neths. 16 D9
Diepenveen, Neths. 16 D8
Diepholz, Germany 18 C4
Diepoldsau, Switz. 23 B9
Dieppe, France 24 C8
Dieren, Neths. 16 D8
Dierks, U.S.A. 109 H7
Diessen, Neths. 17 F6
Diessenhofen, Switz. 23 A7
Diest, Belgium 17 G6
Dietikon, Switz. 23 B6
Dieulefit, France 27 D9
Dieuze, France 25 D13
Diever, Neths. 16 C8
Differdange, Lux. 17 J7
Dig, India 62 F7
Digba, Zaïre 82 B2
Digby, Canada 99 D6
Digges, Canada 101 B10
Digges Is., Canada 97 B12
Dighinala, Bangla. 61 H18
Dighton, U.S.A. 108 F4
Digne, France 27 D10
Digoin, France 26 B7
Digor, Turkey 67 C10
Digos, Phil. 55 H6
Digranes, Iceland 8 C6
Digul →, Indonesia 57 F9
Dihang →, India 61 F19
Dīhōk, Iraq 64 B3
Dijlah, Nahr →, Asia 64 D5
Dijle →, Belgium 17 G5
Dijon, France 25 E12
Dikala, Sudan 77 G3
Dikkil, Djibouti 77 E5
Dikomu di Kai, Botswana 84 C3
Diksmuide, Belgium 17 F1
Dikson, Russia 44 B9
Dikwa, Nigeria 79 C7
Dila, Ethiopia 77 F4
Dilbeek, Belgium 17 G4
Dili, Indonesia 57 F7
Dilizhan, Armenia 43 F11
Dillenburg, Germany 18 E4
Dilley, U.S.A. 109 L5
Dilling, Sudan 77 E2
Dillingen, Germany 19 G6
Dillingham, U.S.A. 96 C4
Dillon, Canada 101 B7
Dillon, Mont., U.S.A. 110 D7
Dillon, S.C., U.S.A. 105 H6
Dillon →, Canada 101 B7
Dilolo, Zaïre 80 G4
Dilsen, Belgium 17 F7
Dilston, Australia 90 G4
Dimas, Mexico 114 C3
Dimashq, Syria 69 B5
Dimashq □, Syria 69 B5
Dimbaza, S. Africa 85 E4
Dimbokro, Ivory C. 78 D4
Dimboola, Australia 91 F3
Dîmboviţa →, Romania 38 E9
Dîmbovnic →, Romania 38 E8
Dimbulah, Australia 90 B4
Dimitrovgrad, Bulgaria 39 G8
Dimitrovgrad, Russia 41 D16
Dimitrovgrad, Serbia, Yug. 21 M12
Dimitrovo = Pernik, Bulgaria 38 G6
Dimmitt, U.S.A. 109 H3
Dimo, Sudan 77 F2
Dimona, Israel 69 D4
Dimovo, Bulgaria 38 F5
Dinagat, Phil. 55 F6
Dinajpur, Bangla. 61 G16
Dinan, France 24 D4
Dīnān Āb, Iran 65 C8
Dinant, Belgium 17 H5
Dinapur, India 63 G11
Dinar, Turkey 66 D4
Dinara Planina, Croatia 33 E13
Dinard, France 24 D4
Dinaric Alps = Dinara Planina, Croatia 33 E13
Dinder, Nahr ed →, Sudan 77 E3
Dindigul, India 60 P11
Ding Xian, China 50 E8
Dingalan, Phil. 55 D4
Dingbian, China 50 F4
Dingelstädt, Germany 18 D6
Dinghai, China 53 B14
Dingle, Ireland 15 D1
Dingle B., Ireland 15 D1
Dingmans Ferry, U.S.A. 107 E10
Dingnan, China 53 E10
Dingo, Australia 90 C4
Dingolfing, Germany 19 G8
Dingtao, China 50 G8
Dinguiraye, Guinea 78 C2
Dingwall, U.K. 14 D4
Dingxi, China 50 G3
Dingxiang, China 50 E7
Dingyuan, China 53 A11
Dinh, Mui, Vietnam 59 G7
Dinh Lap, Vietnam 58 B6
Dinkel →, Neths. 16 D9
Dinokwe, Botswana 84 C4
Dinosaur National Monument, U.S.A. 110 F9
Dinslaken, Germany 17 E9
Dintel →, Neths. 17 E4
Dinteloord, Neths. 17 E4
Dinuba, U.S.A. 111 H4
Dinxperlo, Neths. 16 E9
Diósgyör, Hungary 21 G10
Diourbel, Senegal 78 C1
Diplo, Pakistan 62 G3
Dipolog, Phil. 55 G5
Dipşa, Romania 38 C7
Dir, Pakistan 60 B7
Diré, Mali 78 B4
Dire Dawa, Ethiopia 68 F3
Diriamba, Nic. 116 D2
Dirico, Angola 81 H4
Dirk Hartog I., Australia 89 E1
Dirranbandi, Australia 91 D4
Disa, India 62 G5
Disa, Sudan 77 E3
Disappointment, C., U.S.A. 110 C1
Disappointment, L., Australia 88 D3
Disaster B., Australia 91 F4
Discovery B., Australia 91 F3
Disentis, Switz. 23 C7
Dishna, Egypt 76 B3
Disina, Nigeria 79 C6
Disko, Greenland 4 C5
Disko Bugt, Greenland 4 C5
Disna →, Belorussia 40 D6
Dison, Belgium 17 G7
Disteghil Sar, Pakistan 63 A6
Distrito Federal □, Brazil 123 E2
Distrito Federal □, Venezuela 120 A4
Disûq, Egypt 76 H7
Diu, India 62 J4
Dīvāndarreh, Iran 64 C5
Dives →, France 24 C6
Dives-sur-Mer, France 24 C6
Divichi, Azerbaijan 43 F13
Divide, U.S.A. 110 D7
Dividing Ra., Australia 89 E2
Divinópolis, Brazil 123 F3
Divisões, Serra dos, Brazil 123 E1
Divnoye, Russia 43 D10
Divo, Ivory C. 78 D3
Divriği, Turkey 67 D8
Dīwāl Kol, Afghan. 62 B2
Dixie Mt., U.S.A. 112 F6
Dixon, Calif., U.S.A. 112 G5
Dixon, Ill., U.S.A. 108 E10
Dixon, Mont., U.S.A. 110 C6
Dixon, N. Mex., U.S.A. 111 H11
Dixon Entrance, U.S.A. 100 C2
Dixonville, Canada 100 B5
Diyadin, Turkey 67 D10
Diyarbakır, Turkey 67 E9
Diyarbakir □, Turkey 67 E9
Djado, Niger 73 D7
Djakarta = Jakarta, Indonesia 57 G12
Djamâa, Algeria 75 B6
Djamba, Angola 84 B1
Djambala, Congo 80 E2
Djanet, Algeria 75 D6
Djawa = Jawa, Indonesia 57 G14
Djebiniana, Tunisia 75 A7
Djelfa, Algeria 75 B5
Djema, C.A.R. 82 A2
Djendel, Algeria 75 A5
Djeneïene, Tunisia 75 B7
Djenné, Mali 78 C4
Djenoun, Garet el, Algeria 75 C6
Djerba, Tunisia 75 B7
Djerba, I. de, Tunisia 73 B7
Djerid, Chott, Tunisia 75 B6
Djibo, Burkina Faso 79 C4
Djibouti, Djibouti 68 E3
Djibouti ■, Africa 68 E3
Djolu, Zaïre 80 D4
Djougou, Benin 79 D5
Djoum, Cameroon 80 D2
Djourab, Chad 73 E8
Djugu, Zaïre 82 B3
Djúpivogur, Iceland 8 D6
Djursholm, Sweden 10 E12
Djursland, Denmark 11 H4
Dmitriev-Lgovskiy, Russia 40 E9
Dmitriya Lapteva, Proliv, Russia 45 B15
Dmitrov, Russia 41 C10
Dmitrovsk-Orlovskiy, Russia 40 E9
Dnepr →, Ukraine 42 C5
Dneprodzerzhinsk, Ukraine 42 B6
Dneprodzerzhinskoye Vdkhr., Ukraine 42 B6
Dnepropetrovsk, Ukraine 42 B6
Dneprorudnoye, Ukraine 42 C6
Dnestr →, Europe 42 C4
Dnestrovski = Belgorod, Russia 41 F10
Dnieper = Dnepr →, Ukraine 42 C5
Dniester = Dnestr →, Europe 42 C4
Dnipro = Dnepr →, Ukraine 42 C5
Dniprodzerzhynsk = Dneprodzerzhinsk, Ukraine 42 B6
Dnipropetrovsk = Dnepropetrovsk, Ukraine 42 B6
Dno, Russia 40 C6
Dnyapro = Dnepr →, Ukraine 42 C5
Doan Hung, Vietnam 58 B5
Doba, Chad 73 G8
Dobbiaco, Italy 33 B9
Dobbyn, Australia 90 B3
Döbeln, Germany 18 D9
Doberai, Jazirah, Indonesia 57 E8
Dobiegniew, Poland 20 C5
Doblas, Argentina 126 D3
Dobo, Indonesia 57 F8
Doboj, Bos.-H. 21 L8
Dobra, Dîmbovita, Romania 38 E8
Dobra, Hunedoara, Romania 38 D5
Dobreta-Turnu-Severin, Romania 38 E5
Dobrinishta, Bulgaria 39 H6
Dobrodzień, Poland 20 E8
Dobropole, Ukraine 42 B7
Dobruja, Romania 38 E11
Dobrush, Belorussia 40 E7
Dobtong, Sudan 77 F3
Doc, Mui, Vietnam 58 D6
Doce →, Brazil 123 E4
Doda, India 63 C6
Dodecanese = Dhodhekánisos, Greece 39 N10
Dodewaard, Neths. 16 E7
Dodge Center, U.S.A. 108 C8
Dodge City, U.S.A. 109 G5
Dodge L., Canada 101 B7
Dodgeville, U.S.A. 108 D9
Dodo, Sudan 77 F2
Dodola, Ethiopia 77 F4
Dodoma, Tanzania 82 D4
Dodoma □, Tanzania 82 D4
Dodsland, Canada 101 C7
Dodson, U.S.A. 110 B9
Doesburg, Neths. 16 D8
Doetinchem, Neths. 16 E8
Dog Creek, Canada 100 C4
Dog L., Man., Canada 101 C9
Dog L., Ont., Canada 98 C2
Doğanşehir, Turkey 67 D7
Dogger Bank, N. Sea 6 E6
Dogi, Afghan. 60 C3
Dogliani, Italy 32 D4
Dogondoutchi, Niger 79 C5
Dogran, Pakistan 62 D5
Doğubayazıt, Turkey 67 D11
Doguéraoua, Niger 79 C6
Doha = Ad Dawhah, Qatar 65 E6
Dohazari, Bangla. 61 H18
Doi, Indonesia 57 D7
Doi Luang, Thailand 58 C3
Doi Saket, Thailand 58 C2

Doig →, Canada 100 B4
Dois Irmãos, Sa., Brazil 122 C3
Dokka, Norway 9 F11
Dokka →, Norway 10 D4
Dokkum, Neths. 16 B7
Dokkumer Ee →, Neths. 16 B7
Dokri, Pakistan 62 F3
Dol-de-Bretagne, France 24 D5
Doland, U.S.A. 108 C5
Dolbeau, Canada 99 C5
Dole, France 25 E12
Doleib, Wadi →, Sudan 77 E3
Dolgellau, U.K. 12 E4
Dolgelley = Dolgellau, U.K. 12 E4
Dolginovo, Belorussia 40 D5
Dolianova, Italy 34 C2
Dolinskaya, Ukraine 42 B5
Dollart, Neths. 16 B10
Dolna Banya, Bulgaria 38 G6
Dolni Dŭbnik, Bulgaria 38 F7
Dolo, Ethiopia 77 G5
Dolo, Italy 33 C9
Dolomites = Dolomiti, Italy 33 B8
Dolomiti, Italy 33 B8
Dolores, Argentina 126 D4
Dolores, Uruguay 126 C4
Dolores, U.S.A. 111 H9
Dolores →, U.S.A. 111 G9
Dolphin, C., Falk. Is. 128 D5
Dolphin and Union Str., Canada 96 B8
Dom, Switz. 22 D5
Dom Joaquim, Brazil 123 E3
Dom Pedrito, Brazil 127 C5
Dom Pedro, Brazil 122 B3
Doma, Nigeria 79 D6
Domaniç, Turkey 66 D3
Domasi, Malawi 83 F4
Domat Ems, Switz. 23 C8
Domazlice, Czech. 20 F2
Dombarovskiy, Russia 44 D6
Dombås, Norway 9 E10
Dombasle-sur-Meurthe, France 25 D13
Dombes, France 27 B8
Dombóvár, Hungary 21 J8
Domburg, Neths. 17 E3
Domérat, France 26 B6
Domeyko, Chile 126 B1
Domeyko, Cordillera, Chile 126 A2
Domfront, France 24 D6
Dominador, Chile 126 A2
Dominica ■, W. Indies 117 C7
Dominica Passage, W. Indies 117 C7
Dominican Rep. ■, W. Indies 117 C5
Dömitz, Germany 18 B7
Domme, France 26 D5
Dommel →, Neths. 17 E6
Domo, Ethiopia 68 F4
Domodóssola, Italy 32 B5
Dompaire, France 25 D13
Dompierre-sur-Besbre, France 26 B7
Dompim, Ghana 78 D4
Domrémy-la-Pucelle, France 25 D12
Domsjö, Sweden 10 A12
Domville, Mt., Australia 91 D5
Domvraína, Greece 39 L5
Domžale, Slovenia 33 B11
Don →, Russia 43 C8
Don →, Gramp., U.K. 14 D6
Don →, S. Yorks., U.K. 12 D7
Don, C., Australia 88 B5
Don Benito, Spain 31 G5
Don Duong, Vietnam 59 G7
Don Martín, Presa de, Mexico 114 B4
Dona Ana = Nhamaabué, Mozam. 83 F4
Donaghadee, U.K. 15 B6
Donald, Australia 91 F3
Donalda, Canada 100 C6
Donaldsonville, U.S.A. 109 K9
Donalsonville, U.S.A. 105 K3
Donau →, Austria 21 G7
Donaueschingen, Germany 19 H4
Donauwörth, Germany 19 G6
Doncaster, U.K. 12 D6
Dondo, Angola 80 F2
Dondo, Mozam. 83 F3
Dondo, Teluk, Indonesia 57 D6
Dondra Head, Sri Lanka 60 S12
Donegal, Ireland 15 B3
Donegal □, Ireland 15 B4
Donegal B., Ireland 15 B3
Donets →, Russia 43 C9
Donetsk, Ukraine 42 C7
Dong Ba Thin, Vietnam 59 F7
Dong Dang, Vietnam 58 B6
Dong Giam, Vietnam 58 C5
Dong Ha, Vietnam 58 D6
Dong Hene, Laos 58 D5
Dong Hoi, Vietnam 58 D6
Dong Jiang →, China 53 F10
Dong Khe, Vietnam 58 A6
Dong Ujimqin Qi, China 50 B9
Dong Van, Vietnam 58 A5
Dong Xoai, Vietnam 59 G6
Donga, Nigeria 79 D7
Dong'an, China 53 D8
Dongara, Australia 89 E1
Dongbei, China 51 D13
Dongchuan, China 52 D4
Dongen, Neths. 17 E5
Donges, France 24 E4
Dongfang, China 58 C7
Dongfeng, China 51 C13
Donggala, Indonesia 57 E5
Donggan, China 52 F5
Donggou, China 51 E13
Dongguan, China 53 F9
Dongguang, China 50 F9
Donghai Dao, China 53 G8
Dongjingcheng, China 51 B15
Donglan, China 52 E6
Dongliu, China 53 B11
Dongmen, China 52 F6
Dongning, China 51 B16
Dongnyi, China 52 C3
Dongola, Sudan 76 D3
Dongou, Congo 80 D3
Dongping, China 50 G9
Dongshan, China 53 F11
Dongsheng, China 50 E6
Dongshi, Taiwan 53 E13
Dongtai, China 51 H11
Dongting Hu, China 53 C9
Dongxiang, China 53 C11
Dongxing, China 52 G7
Dongyang, China 53 C13
Dongzhi, China 53 B11
Donington, C., Australia 91 E2
Doniphan, U.S.A. 109 G9
Donja Stubica, Croatia 33 C13
Donji Dušnik, Serbia 21 M12
Donji Miholjac, Croatia 21 K8
Donji Milanovac, Serbia 21 L12
Donji Vakuf, Bos.-H. 21 L7
Dønna, Norway 8 C12
Donna, U.S.A. 109 M5
Donnaconna, Canada 99 C5
Donnelly's Crossing, N.Z. 87 F4
Donnybrook, Australia 89 F2
Donnybrook, S. Africa 85 D4
Donora, U.S.A. 106 F5
Donor's Hill, Australia 90 B3
Donostia = San Sebastián, Spain 28 B3
Donskoy, Russia 41 E11
Donsol, Phil. 55 E5
Donya Lendava, Slovenia 33 B13
Donzère, France 27 D8
Donzère-Mondragon, Barr. de, France 27 D8
Donzy, France 25 E10
Doon →, U.K. 14 F4
Doorn, Neths. 16 D6
Dora, L., Australia 88 D3
Dora Báltea →, Italy 32 C5
Dora Riparia →, Italy 32 C4
Doran L., Canada 101 A7
Dorchester, U.K. 13 G5
Dorchester, C., Canada 97 B12
Dordogne □, France 26 C4
Dordogne →, France 26 C3
Dordrecht, Neths. 16 E5
Dordrecht, S. Africa 84 E4
Dore →, France 26 C7
Dore, Mts., France 26 C6
Doré L., Canada 101 C7
Doré Lake, Canada 101 C7
Dores do Indaiá, Brazil 123 E2
Dorfen, Germany 19 G8
Dorgali, Italy 34 B2
Dori, Burkina Faso 79 C4
Doring →, S. Africa 84 E2
Doringbos, S. Africa 84 E2
Dorion, Canada 98 C5
Dormaa-Ahenkro, Ghana 78 D4
Dormo, Ras, Eritrea 77 E5
Dornach, Switz. 22 B5
Dornberg, Slovenia 33 C10
Dornbirn, Austria 19 H5
Dornes, France 25 F10
Dornoch, U.K. 14 D4
Dornoch Firth, U.K. 14 D4
Dornogovĭ □, Mongolia 50 B6
Doro, Mali 79 B4
Dorogobuzh, Russia 40 D8
Dorohoi, Romania 38 B9
Döröö Nuur, Mongolia 54 B4
Dorr, Iran 65 C6
Dorre I., Australia 89 E1
Dorrigo, Australia 91 E5
Dorris, U.S.A. 110 F3
Dorset, Canada 106 A6
Dorset, U.S.A. 106 E4
Dorset □, U.K. 13 G5
Dorsten, Germany 18 D2
Dortmund, Germany 18 D3
Dörtyol, Turkey 66 E7
Dorum, Germany 18 B4
Doruma, Zaïre 82 B2
Dorūneh, Iran 65 C8
Dos Bahías, C., Argentina 128 B3
Dos Hermanas, Spain 31 H5
Dos Palos, U.S.A. 112 J6
Dosso, Niger 79 C5
Dothan, U.S.A. 105 K3
Dottignies, Belgium 17 G2
Doty, U.S.A. 112 D3
Douai, France 25 B10
Douala, Cameroon 79 E6
Douarnenez, France 24 D2
Double Island Pt., Australia 91 D5
Doubrava →, Czech. 20 F5
Doubs □, France 25 E13
Doubs →, France 25 F12
Doubtful Sd., N.Z. 87 L1
Doubtless B., N.Z. 87 F4
Doudeville, France 24 C7
Doué-la-Fontaine, France 24 E6
Douentza, Mali 78 C4
Douglas, S. Africa 84 D3
Douglas, U.K. 12 C3
Douglas, Alaska, U.S.A. 100 B2
Douglas, Ariz., U.S.A. 111 L9
Douglas, Ga., U.S.A. 105 K4
Douglas, Wyo., U.S.A. 108 D2
Douglastown, Canada 99 C7
Douglasville, U.S.A. 105 J3
Douirat, Morocco 74 B4
Doukáton, Ákra, Greece 39 L3
Doulevant-le-Château, France 25 D11
Doullens, France 25 B9
Doumé, Cameroon 80 D2
Douna, Mali 78 C3
Dounan, Taiwan 53 F13
Dounreay, U.K. 14 C5
Dour, Belgium 17 H3
Dourada, Serra, Brazil 123 D2
Dourados, Brazil 127 A5
Dourados →, Brazil 127 A5
Dourdan, France 25 D9
Douro →, Europe 30 D2
Douvaine, France 27 B10
Douz, Tunisia 75 B6
Douze →, France 26 E3
Dove →, U.K. 12 E6
Dove Creek, U.S.A. 111 H9
Dover, Australia 90 G4
Dover, U.K. 13 F9
Dover, Del., U.S.A. 104 F8
Dover, N.H., U.S.A. 107 C14
Dover, N.J., U.S.A. 107 F10
Dover, Ohio, U.S.A. 106 F3
Dover, Pt., Australia 89 F4
Dover, Str. of, Europe 24 B8
Dover-Foxcroft, U.S.A. 99 C6
Dover Plains, U.S.A. 107 E11
Dovey = Dyfi →, U.K. 13 E4
Dovrefjell, Norway 10 B3
Dow Rūd, Iran 65 C6
Dowa, Malawi 83 E3
Dowagiac, U.S.A. 104 E2
Dowgha'i, Iran 65 B8
Dowlatābād, Iran 65 D8
Down □, U.K. 15 B6
Downey, Calif., U.S.A. 113 M8
Downey, Idaho, U.S.A. 110 E7
Downham Market, U.K. 13 E8
Downieville, U.S.A. 112 F6
Downpatrick, U.K. 15 B6
Downpatrick Hd., Ireland 15 B2
Dowsārī, Iran 65 D8
Doyle, U.S.A. 112 E6
Doylestown, U.S.A. 107 F9
Draa, C., Morocco 74 C2
Draa, Oued →, Morocco 74 C2
Drac →, France 27 C9
Drachten, Neths. 16 B8
Drăgănești, Romania 38 E7
Drăgănești-Viașca, Romania 38 E8
Dragaš, Serbia 21 N10
Drăgăsani, Romania 38 E7
Dragonera, I., Spain 36 B9
Draguignan, France 27 E10
Drain, U.S.A. 110 E2
Drake, Australia 91 D5
Drake, U.S.A. 108 B4
Drake Passage, S. Ocean 5 B17
Drakensberg, S. Africa 85 E4
Dráma, Greece 39 H7
Drammen, Norway 10 E4
Drangajökull, Iceland 8 C2
Drangedal, Norway 10 E3
Dranov, Ostrov, Romania 38 E12
Dras, India 63 B6
Drau = Drava →, Croatia 21 K8
Drava →, Croatia 21 K8
Draveil, France 25 D9
Dravograd, Slovenia 33 B12
Drawa →, Poland 20 C5
Drawno, Poland 20 B5
Drayton Valley, Canada 100 C6
Dreibergen, Neths. 16 D6
Drenthe □, Neths. 16 C9
Drentsche Hoofdvaart, Neths. 16 C8
Drepanum, C., Cyprus 37 E11
Dresden, Canada 106 D2
Dresden, Germany 18 D9
Dreux, France 24 D8
Driel, Neths. 16 E7
Driffield = Great Driffield, U.K. 12 C7
Driftwood, U.S.A. 106 E6
Driggs, U.S.A. 110 E8
Drin i zi →, Albania 39 H3
Drina →, Bos.-H. 21 L9
Drincea →, Romania 38 E5
Drini →, Albania 38 G3
Drinjača →, Bos.-H. 21 L9
Drissa = Verkhnedvinsk, Belorussia 40 D5
Drivstua, Norway 10 B3
Drniš, Croatia 33 E13
Drøbak, Norway 10 E4
Drogheda, Ireland 15 C5
Drogichin, Belorussia 40 E4
Drogobych, Ukraine 40 G3
Drohobych = Drogobych, Ukraine 40 G3
Droichead Nua, Ireland 15 C5
Droitwich, U.K. 13 E5
Drôme □, France 27 D9
Drôme →, France 27 D8
Dromedary, C., Australia 91 F5
Dronero, Italy 32 D4
Dronfield, Australia 90 C3
Dronne →, France 26 C3
Dronninglund, Denmark 11 G4
Dronrijp, Neths. 16 B7
Dropt →, France 26 D3
Drumbo, Canada 106 C4
Drumheller, Canada 100 C6
Drummond, U.S.A. 110 C7
Drummond I., U.S.A. 98 C3
Drummond Pt., Australia 91 E2
Drummond Ra., Australia 90 C4
Drummondville, Canada 98 C5
Drumright, U.S.A. 109 H6
Drunen, Neths. 17 E6
Druskininkai, Lithuania 40 D3
Drut →, Belorussia 40 E7
Druten, Neths. 16 E7
Druya, Latvia 40 D5
Druzhina, Russia 45 C15
Drvar, Bos.-H. 33 D13
Drvenik, Croatia 33 E13
Dry Tortugas, U.S.A. 116 B3
Dryanovo, Bulgaria 38 G8
Dryden, Canada 101 D10
Dryden, U.S.A. 109 K3
Drygalski I., Antarctica 5 C7
Drysdale →, Australia 88 B4
Drysdale I., Australia 90 A2
Dschang, Cameroon 79 D7
Du Bois, U.S.A. 106 E6
Du Quoin, U.S.A. 108 G10
Duanesburg, U.S.A. 107 D10
Duaringa, Australia 90 C4
Ḍubā, Si. Arabia 64 E2
Dubai = Dubayy, U.A.E. 65 E7
Dubawnt →, Canada 101 A8
Dubawnt, L., Canada 101 A8
Dubayy, U.A.E. 65 E7
Dubbeldam, Neths. 16 E5
Dubbo, Australia 91 E4
Dubele, Zaïre 82 B2
Dübendorf, Switz. 23 B7
Dubica, Croatia 33 C13
Dublin, Ireland 15 C5
Dublin, Ga., U.S.A. 105 J4
Dublin, Tex., U.S.A. 109 J5
Dublin □, Ireland 15 C5
Dublin B., Ireland 15 C5
Dubna, Russia 41 C10
Dubna, Russia 41 D10
Dubno, Ukraine 40 F4
Dubois, U.S.A. 110 D7
Dubossary, Moldavia 42 C3
Dubossary Vdkhr., Moldavia 42 C3
Dubovka, Russia 43 B11
Dubovskoye, Russia 43 C10
Dubrajpur, India 63 H12
Dubréka, Guinea 78 D2
Dubrovitsa, Ukraine 40 F5
Dubrovnik, Croatia 21 N8
Dubrovskoye, Russia 45 D12
Dubuque, U.S.A. 108 D9
Duchang, China 53 C11
Duchesne, U.S.A. 110 F8
Duchess, Australia 90 C2
Ducie I., Pac. Oc. 93 K15
Duck Cr. →, Australia 88 D2
Duck Lake, Canada 101 C7
Duck Mountain Prov. Park, Canada 101 C8
Duckwall, Mt., U.S.A. 112 H6
Düdelange, Lux. 17 K8
Duderstadt, Germany 18 D6
Dudhi, India 61 G13
Düdingen, Switz. 22 C4
Dudinka, Russia 45 C9
Dudley, U.K. 13 E5
Dueñas, Spain 30 D6
Dueré, Brazil 123 D2
Duero = Douro →, Europe 30 D2
Duffel, Belgium 17 F5
Dufftown, U.K. 14 D5
Dufourspitz, Switz. 22 E5
Dugi Otok, Croatia 33 E12
Dugo Selo, Croatia 33 C13
Duifken Pt., Australia 90 A3
Duisburg, Germany 18 D2
Duitama, Colombia 120 B3
Duiveland, Neths. 17 E4
Duiwelskloof, S. Africa 85 C5
Dŭkdamīn, Iran 65 C8
Duke I., U.S.A. 100 C2
Dukhān, Qatar 65 E6
Dukhovshchina, Russia 40 D8
Duki, Pakistan 60 D6
Duku, Bauchi, Nigeria 79 C7
Duku, Sokoto, Nigeria 79 C5
Dulag, Phil. 55 F6
Dulce →, Argentina 126 C3
Dulce, G., Costa Rica 116 E3
Dulf, Iraq 64 C5
Dŭlgopol, Bulgaria 38 F10
Dulit, Banjaran, Malaysia 56 D4
Duliu, China 50 E9
Dullewala, Pakistan 62 D4
Dülmen, Germany 18 D3
Dulovo, Bulgaria 38 F10
Dulq Maghār, Syria 64 B3
Dululu, Australia 90 C5
Duluth, U.S.A. 108 B8
Dum Dum, India 63 H13
Dum Duma, India 61 F19
Dum Hadjer, Chad 73 F8
Dūmā, Lebanon 69 A4
Dūmā, Syria 69 B5
Dumaguete, Phil. 55 G5
Dumai, Indonesia 56 D2
Dumaran, Phil. 55 F3
Dumas, Ark., U.S.A. 109 J9
Dumas, Tex., U.S.A. 109 H4
Dumbarton, U.K. 14 F4
Dumbleyung, Australia 89 F2
Dumfries, U.K. 14 F5
Dumfries & Galloway □, U.K. 14 F5
Dumka, India 63 G12
Dümmersee, Germany 18 C4
Dumoine →, Canada 98 C4
Dumoine L., Canada 98 C4
Dumraon, India 63 G11
Dumyât, Egypt 76 H7
Dumyât, Masabb, Egypt 76 H7
Dun Laoghaire, Ireland 15 C5
Dun-le-Palestel, France 26 B5
Dun-sur-Auron, France 25 F9
Duna →, Hungary 21 K8
Dunaföldvár, Hungary 21 J8
Dunaj →, Slovak Rep. 21 H8
Dunajec →, Poland 20 E10
Dunajska Streda, Slovak Rep. 21 H7
Dunapatai, Hungary 21 J9
Dunărea →, Romania 38 D12
Dunaújváros, Hungary 21 J8
Dunav →, Serbia 21 L11
Dunay, Russia 48 C6
Dunback, N.Z. 87 L3
Dunbar, Australia 90 B3
Dunbar, U.K. 14 E6
Dunblane, U.K. 14 E5
Duncan, Canada 100 D4
Duncan, Ariz., U.S.A. 111 K9
Duncan, Okla., U.S.A. 109 H6
Duncan, L., Canada 98 B4
Duncan L., Canada 100 A6
Duncan Town, Bahamas 116 B4
Duncannon, U.S.A. 106 F7
Dundalk, Canada 106 B4
Dundalk, Ireland 15 B5
Dundalk Bay, Ireland 15 C5
Dundas, Canada 98 D4
Dundas, L., Australia 89 F3
Dundas I., Canada 100 C2
Dundas Str., Australia 88 B5
Dundee, S. Africa 85 D5
Dundee, U.K. 14 E6
Dundgovĭ □, Mongolia 50 B4
Dundoo, Australia 91 D3
Dundrum, U.K. 15 B6
Dundrum B., U.K. 15 B6
Dundwara, India 63 F8
Dunedin, N.Z. 87 L3
Dunedin, U.S.A. 105 L4
Dunedin →, Canada 100 B4
Dunfermline, U.K. 14 E5
Dungannon, Canada 106 C3
Dungannon, U.K. 15 B5
Dungannon □, U.K. 15 B5
Dungarpur, India 62 H5
Dungarvan, Ireland 15 D4
Dungarvan Bay, Ireland 15 D4
Dungeness, U.K. 13 G8
Dungo, L. do, Angola 84 B2
Dungog, Australia 91 E5
Dungu, Zaïre 82 B2
Dungunâb, Sudan 76 C4
Dungunâb, Khalij, Sudan 76 C4
Dunhua, China 51 C15
Dunhuang, China 54 B4
Dunières, France 27 C8
Dunk I., Australia 90 B4
Dunkeld, U.K. 14 E5
Dunkerque, France 25 A9
Dunkery Beacon, U.K. 13 F4
Dunkirk = Dunkerque, France 25 A9
Dunkirk, U.S.A. 106 D5
Dunkuj, Sudan 77 E3
Dunkwa, Central, Ghana 78 D4
Dunkwa, Central, Ghana 79 D4
Dunlap, U.S.A. 108 E7
Dúnleary = Dun Laoghaire, Ireland 15 C5
Dunmanus B., Ireland 15 E2
Dunmara, Australia 90 B1
Dunmore, U.S.A. 107 E9
Dunmore Hd., Ireland 15 D1
Dunmore Town, Bahamas 116 A4
Dunn, U.S.A. 105 H6
Dunnellon, U.S.A. 105 L4
Dunnet Hd., U.K. 14 C5
Dunning, U.S.A. 108 E4
Dunnville, Canada 106 D5
Dunolly, Australia 91 F3
Dunoon, U.K. 14 F4
Dunqul, Egypt 76 C3
Duns, U.K. 14 F6
Dunseith, U.S.A. 108 A4
Dunsmuir, U.S.A. 110 F2
Dunstable, U.K. 13 F7
Dunstan Mts., N.Z. 87 L2
Dunster, Canada 100 C5

Dunvegan L., *Canada* 101 A7
Duolun, *China* 50 C9
Duong Dong, *Vietnam* 59 G4
Dupree, *U.S.A.* 108 C4
Dupuyer, *U.S.A.* 110 B7
Duque de Caxias, *Brazil* 123 F3
Duque de York, I., *Chile* 128 D1
Durack →, *Australia* 88 C4
Durack Ra., *Australia* 88 C4
Durağan, *Turkey* 66 C6
Durance →, *France* 27 E8
Durand, *U.S.A.* 104 D4
Durango = Victoria de Durango, *Mexico* 114 C4
Durango, *Spain* 28 B2
Durango, *U.S.A.* 111 H10
Durango □, *Mexico* 114 C4
Duranillin, *Australia* 89 F2
Durant, *U.S.A.* 109 J6
Duratón →, *Spain* 30 D6
Durazno, *Uruguay* 126 C4
Durazzo = Durrësi, *Albania* 39 H2
Durban, *France* 26 F6
Durban, *S. Africa* 85 D5
Dúrcal, *Spain* 31 J7
Düren, *Germany* 18 E2
Durg, *India* 61 J12
Durgapur, *India* 63 H12
Durham, *Canada* 98 D3
Durham, *U.K.* 12 C6
Durham, *Calif., U.S.A.* 112 F5
Durham, *N.C., U.S.A.* 105 G6
Durham □, *U.K.* 12 C6
Durham Downs, *Australia* 91 D4
Durmitor, *Montenegro* 21 M9
Durness, *U.K.* 14 C4
Durrësi, *Albania* 39 H2
Durrie, *Australia* 90 D3
Dursunbey, *Turkey* 66 D3
Durtal, *France* 24 E6
Duru, *Zaïre* 82 B2
D'Urville, Tanjung, *Indonesia* 57 E9
D'Urville I., *N.Z.* 87 J4
Duryea, *U.S.A.* 107 E9
Dusa Mareb, *Somali Rep.* 68 F4
Dûsh, *Egypt* 76 C3
Dushak, *Turkmenistan* 44 F7
Dushan, *China* 52 E6
Dushanbe, *Tajikistan* 44 F7
Dusheti, *Georgia* 43 E11
Dusky Sd., *N.Z.* 87 L1
Dussejour, C., *Australia* 88 B4
Düsseldorf, *Germany* 18 D2
Dussen, *Neths.* 16 E5
Dutch Harbor, *U.S.A.* 96 C3
Dutlwe, *Botswana* 84 C3
Dutsan Wai, *Nigeria* 79 C6
Dutton, *Canada* 106 D3
Dutton →, *Australia* 90 C3
Duved, *Sweden* 10 A6
Duvno, *Bos.-H.* 21 M7
Duyun, *China* 52 D6
Düzce, *Turkey* 66 C4
Duzdab = Zāhedān, *Iran* 65 D9
Dvina, Sev. →, *Russia* 44 C5
Dvinsk = Daugavpils, *Latvia* 40 D5
Dvor, *Croatia* 33 C13
Dwarka, *India* 62 H3
Dwellingup, *Australia* 89 F2
Dwight, *Canada* 106 A5
Dwight, *U.S.A.* 104 E1
Dyakovskoya, *Russia* 41 A12
Dyatkovo, *Russia* 40 E9
Dyatlovo, *Belorussia* 40 E4
Dyer, C., *Canada* 97 B13
Dyer Plateau, *Antarctica* 5 D17
Dyersburg, *U.S.A.* 109 G10
Dyfed □, *U.K.* 13 E3
Dyfi →, *U.K.* 13 E4
Dyje →, *Czech.* 20 G6
Dyle →, *Belgium* 17 G5
Dynevor Downs, *Australia* 91 D3
Dynów, *Poland* 20 F12
Dysart, *Canada* 101 C8
Dzamin Üüd, *Mongolia* 50 C6
Dzerzhinsk, *Belorussia* 40 E5
Dzerzhinsk, *Russia* 41 C13
Dzhalinda, *Russia* 45 D13
Dzhambeyty, *Kazakhstan* 43 A15
Dzhambul, *Kazakhstan* 44 E8
Dzhankoi, *Ukraine* 42 D6
Dzhanybek, *Kazakhstan* 43 B12
Dzhardzhan, *Russia* 45 C13
Dzhelinde, *Russia* 45 C12
Dzhetygara, *Kazakhstan* 44 D7
Dzhezkazgan, *Kazakhstan* 44 E7
Dzhikimde, *Russia* 45 D13
Dzhizak, *Uzbekistan* 44 E7
Dzhugdzur, Khrebet, *Russia* 45 D14
Dzhvari, *Georgia* 43 E10
Działdowo, *Poland* 20 B10
Działoszyn, *Poland* 20 D8
Dzierzgoń, *Poland* 20 B9
Dzierzoniów, *Poland* 20 E6
Dzilam de Bravo, *Mexico* 115 C7
Dzioua, *Algeria* 75 B6
Dzungaria = Junggar Pendi, *China* 54 B3
Dzungarian Gate = Alataw Shankou, *China* 54 B3
Dzuumod, *Mongolia* 54 B5

E

Eabamet, L., *Canada* 98 B2
Eads, *U.S.A.* 108 F3
Eagle, *U.S.A.* 110 G10
Eagle →, *Canada* 99 B8
Eagle Butte, *U.S.A.* 108 C4
Eagle Grove, *U.S.A.* 108 D8
Eagle L., *Calif., U.S.A.* 110 F3
Eagle L., *Maine, U.S.A.* 99 C6
Eagle Lake, *U.S.A.* 109 L6
Eagle Mountain, *U.S.A.* 113 M11
Eagle Nest, *U.S.A.* 111 H11
Eagle Pass, *U.S.A.* 109 L4
Eagle Pk., *U.S.A.* 112 G7
Eagle Pt., *Australia* 88 C3
Eagle River, *U.S.A.* 108 C10
Ealing, *U.K.* 13 F7
Earaheedy, *Australia* 89 E3
Earl Grey, *Canada* 101 C8
Earle, *U.S.A.* 109 H9
Earlimart, *U.S.A.* 113 K7
Earn →, *U.K.* 14 E5
Earn, L., *U.K.* 14 E4
Earnslaw, Mt., *N.Z.* 87 L2
Earth, *U.S.A.* 109 H3
Easley, *U.S.A.* 105 H4
East Angus, *Canada* 99 C5
East Aurora, *U.S.A.* 106 D6
East B., *U.S.A.* 109 L10
East Bengal, *Bangla.* 61 G17
East Beskids = Vychodné Beskydy, *Europe* 20 F11
East Brady, *U.S.A.* 106 F5
East C., *N.Z.* 87 G7
East Chicago, *U.S.A.* 104 E2
East China Sea, *Asia* 54 C7
East Coulee, *Canada* 100 C6
East Falkland, *Falk. Is.* 128 D5
East Grand Forks, *U.S.A.* 108 B6
East Greenwich, *U.S.A.* 107 E13
East Hartford, *U.S.A.* 107 E12
East Helena, *U.S.A.* 110 C8
East Indies, *Asia* 57 E6
East Jordan, *U.S.A.* 104 C3
East Lansing, *U.S.A.* 104 D3
East Liverpool, *U.S.A.* 106 F4
East London, *S. Africa* 85 E4
East Main = Eastmain, *Canada* 98 B4
East Orange, *U.S.A.* 107 F10
East Pacific Ridge, *Pac. Oc.* 93 J17
East Pakistan = Bangladesh ■, *Asia* 61 H17
East Palestine, *U.S.A.* 106 F4
East Pine, *Canada* 100 B4
East Pt., *Canada* 99 C7
East Point, *U.S.A.* 105 J3
East Providence, *U.S.A.* 107 E13
East Retford, *U.K.* 12 D7
East St. Louis, *U.S.A.* 108 F9
East Schelde → = Oosterschelde, *Neths.* 17 E4
East Siberian Sea, *Russia* 45 B17
East Stroudsburg, *U.S.A.* 107 E9
East Sussex □, *U.K.* 13 G8
East Tawas, *U.S.A.* 104 C4
East Toorale, *Australia* 91 E4
East Walker →, *U.S.A.* 112 G7
Eastbourne, *N.Z.* 87 J5
Eastbourne, *U.K.* 13 G8
Eastend, *Canada* 101 D7
Easter Dal = Österdalälven →, *Sweden* 9 F12
Easter Islands = Pascua, I. de, *Pac. Oc.* 93 K17
Eastern □, *Kenya* 82 B4
Eastern □, *Uganda* 82 B3
Eastern Cr. →, *Australia* 90 C3
Eastern Ghats, *India* 60 N11
Eastern Group = Lau Group, *Fiji* 87 C9
Eastern Group, *Australia* 89 F3
Eastern Province □, *S. Leone* 78 D2
Easterville, *Canada* 101 C9
Easthampton, *U.S.A.* 107 D12
Eastland, *U.S.A.* 109 J5
Eastleigh, *U.K.* 13 G6
Eastmain, *Canada* 98 B4
Eastmain →, *Canada* 98 B4
Eastman, *Canada* 107 A12
Eastman, *U.S.A.* 105 J4
Easton, *Md., U.S.A.* 104 F7
Easton, *Pa., U.S.A.* 107 F9
Easton, *Wash., U.S.A.* 112 C5
Eastport, *U.S.A.* 99 D6
Eastsound, *U.S.A.* 112 B4
Eaton, *U.S.A.* 108 E2
Eatonia, *Canada* 101 C7
Eatonton, *U.S.A.* 105 J4
Eatontown, *U.S.A.* 107 F10
Eatonville, *U.S.A.* 112 D4
Eau Claire, *Fr. Guiana* 121 C7
Eau Claire, *U.S.A.* 108 C9
Eauze, *France* 26 E4
Ebagoola, *Australia* 90 A3
Eban, *Nigeria* 79 D5
Ebbw Vale, *U.K.* 13 F4
Ebeggui, *Algeria* 75 C6
Ebeltoft, *Denmark* 9 H11
Ebensburg, *U.S.A.* 106 F6
Ebensee, *Austria* 21 H3
Eber Gölü, *Turkey* 66 D4
Eberbach, *Germany* 19 F4
Eberswalde, *Germany* 18 C9
Ebetsu, *Japan* 48 C10
Ebian, *China* 52 C4
Ebikon, *Switz.* 23 B6
Ebingen, *Germany* 19 G5
Ebnat-Kappel, *Switz.* 23 B8
Eboli, *Italy* 35 B8
Ebolowa, *Cameroon* 79 E7
Ebrach, *Germany* 19 F6
Ébrié, Lagune, *Ivory C.* 78 D4
Ebro →, *Spain* 28 E5
Ebro, Pantano del, *Spain* 30 B7
Ebstorf, *Germany* 18 B6
Ecaussines-d' Enghien, *Belgium* 17 G4
Eceabat, *Turkey* 66 C2
Ech Cheliff, *Algeria* 75 A5
Echallens, *Switz.* 22 C3
Echeng, *China* 53 B10
Echigo-Sammyaku, *Japan* 49 F9
Echizen-Misaki, *Japan* 49 G7
Echmiadzin, *Armenia* 43 F11
Echo Bay, *N.W.T., Canada* 96 B8
Echo Bay, *Ont., Canada* 98 C3
Echoing →, *Canada* 101 B10
Echt, *Neths.* 17 F7
Echternach, *Lux.* 17 J8
Echuca, *Australia* 91 F3
Ecija, *Spain* 31 H5
Eckernförde, *Germany* 18 A5
Eclipse Is., *Australia* 88 B4
Écommoy, *France* 24 E7
Ecoporanga, *Brazil* 123 E3
Écos, *France* 25 C8
Écouché, *France* 24 D6
Ecuador ■, *S. Amer.* 120 D2
Écueillé, *France* 24 E8
Ed, *Sweden* 11 F5
Ed Dabbura, *Sudan* 76 D3
Ed Dâmer, *Sudan* 76 D3
Ed Debba, *Sudan* 76 D3
Ed-Déffa, *Egypt* 76 A2
Ed Deim, *Sudan* 77 E2
Ed Dueim, *Sudan* 77 E3
Edah, *Australia* 89 E2
Edam, *Canada* 101 C7
Edam, *Neths.* 16 C6
Eday, *U.K.* 14 B6
Edd, *Eritrea* 68 E3
Eddrachillis B., *U.K.* 14 C3
Eddystone, *U.K.* 13 G3
Eddystone Pt., *Australia* 90 G4
Ede, *Neths.* 16 D7
Ede, *Nigeria* 79 D5
Édea, *Cameroon* 79 E7
Edegem, *Belgium* 17 F4
Edehon L., *Canada* 101 A9
Edekel, Adrar, *Algeria* 75 D6
Eden, *Australia* 91 F4
Eden, *N.C., U.S.A.* 105 G6
Eden, *N.Y., U.S.A.* 106 D6
Eden, *Tex., U.S.A.* 109 K5
Eden, *Wyo., U.S.A.* 110 E9
Eden →, *U.K.* 12 C4
Eden L., *Canada* 101 B8
Edenburg, *S. Africa* 84 D4
Edendale, *S. Africa* 85 D5
Edenderry, *Ireland* 15 C4
Edenton, *U.S.A.* 105 G7
Edenville, *S. Africa* 85 D4
Eder →, *Germany* 18 D5
Ederstausee, *Germany* 18 D4
Edgar, *U.S.A.* 108 E5
Edgartown, *U.S.A.* 107 E14
Edge Hill, *U.K.* 13 E6
Edgefield, *U.S.A.* 105 J5
Edgeley, *U.S.A.* 108 B5
Edgemont, *U.S.A.* 108 D3
Edgeøya, *Svalbard* 4 B9
Édhessa, *Greece* 39 J5
Edievale, *N.Z.* 87 L2
Edina, *Liberia* 78 D2
Edina, *U.S.A.* 108 E8
Edinburg, *U.S.A.* 109 M5
Edinburgh, *U.K.* 14 F5
Edirne, *Turkey* 39 H9
Edirne □, *Turkey* 66 C2
Edison, *U.S.A.* 112 B4
Edithburgh, *Australia* 91 F2
Edjeleh, *Algeria* 75 C6
Edjudina, *Australia* 89 E3
Edmeston, *U.S.A.* 107 D9
Edmond, *U.S.A.* 109 H6
Edmonds, *U.S.A.* 112 C4
Edmonton, *Australia* 90 B4
Edmonton, *Canada* 100 C6
Edmund L., *Canada* 101 C10
Edmundston, *Canada* 99 C6
Edna, *U.S.A.* 109 L6
Edna Bay, *U.S.A.* 100 B2
Edo □, *Nigeria* 79 D6
Edolo, *Italy* 32 B7
Edremit, *Turkey* 66 D2
Edremit Körfezi, *Turkey* 66 D2
Edsbyn, *Sweden* 10 C9
Edsele, *Sweden* 10 A10
Edson, *Canada* 100 C5
Eduardo Castex, *Argentina* 126 D3
Edward →, *Australia* 91 F3
Edward, L., *Africa* 82 C2
Edward I., *Canada* 98 C2
Edward River, *Australia* 90 A3
Edward VII Land, *Antarctica* 5 E13
Edwards, *U.S.A.* 113 L9
Edwards Plateau, *U.S.A.* 109 K4
Edwardsville, *U.S.A.* 107 E9
Edzo, *Canada* 100 A5
Eefde, *Neths.* 16 D8
Eekloo, *Belgium* 17 F3
Eelde, *Neths.* 16 B9
Eem →, *Neths.* 16 D6
Eems →, *Neths.* 16 B9
Eems Kanaal, *Neths.* 16 B9
Eenrum, *Neths.* 16 B8
Eernegem, *Belgium* 17 F2
Eerste Valthermond, *Neths.* 16 C9
Eferi, *Algeria* 75 D6
Effingham, *U.S.A.* 104 F1
Effretikon, *Switz.* 23 B7
Eforie Sud, *Romania* 38 E11
Ega →, *Spain* 28 C3
Égadi, Ísole, *Italy* 34 E5
Eganville, *Canada* 98 C4
Egeland, *U.S.A.* 108 A5
Egenolf L., *Canada* 101 B9
Eger = Cheb, *Czech.* 20 E2
Eger, *Hungary* 21 H10
Eger →, *Hungary* 21 H10
Egersund, *Norway* 9 G9
Egg L., *Canada* 101 B7
Eggenburg, *Austria* 20 G5
Eggenfelden, *Germany* 19 G8
Eggiwil, *Switz.* 22 C5
Éghezée, *Belgium* 17 G5
Eginbah, *Australia* 88 D2
Égletons, *France* 26 C6
Eglisau, *Switz.* 23 A7
Egmond-aan-Zee, *Neths.* 16 C5
Egmont, C., *N.Z.* 87 H4
Egmont, Mt., *N.Z.* 87 H5
Eğridir, *Turkey* 66 E4
Eğridir Gölü, *Turkey* 66 E4
Egtved, *Denmark* 11 J3
Éguas →, *Brazil* 123 D3
Egume, *Nigeria* 79 D6
Éguzon, *France* 26 B5
Egvekinot, *Russia* 45 C19
Egypt ■, *Africa* 76 J7
Eha Amufu, *Nigeria* 79 D6
Ehime □, *Japan* 49 H6
Ehingen, *Germany* 19 G5
Ehrenberg, *U.S.A.* 113 M12
Ehrwald, *Austria* 19 H6
Eibar, *Spain* 28 B2
Eibergen, *Neths.* 16 D9
Eichstatt, *Germany* 19 G7
Eider →, *Germany* 18 A4
Eidsvold, *Australia* 91 D5
Eidsvoll, *Norway* 9 F11
Eifel, *Germany* 19 E2
Eiffel Flats, *Zimbabwe* 83 F3
Eigg, *U.K.* 14 E2
Eighty Mile Beach, *Australia* 88 C3
Eil, *Somali Rep.* 68 F4
Eil, L., *U.K.* 14 E3
Eildon, L., *Australia* 91 F4
Eileen L., *Canada* 101 A7
Eilenburg, *Germany* 18 D8
Ein el Luweiqa, *Sudan* 77 E3
Einasleigh, *Australia* 90 B3
Einasleigh →, *Australia* 90 B3
Einbeck, *Germany* 18 D5
Eindhoven, *Neths.* 17 F6
Einsiedeln, *Switz.* 23 B7
Eire ■ = Ireland ■, *Europe* 15 D4
Eiríksjökull, *Iceland* 8 D3
Eirlandsche Gat, *Neths.* 16 B5
Eirunepé, *Brazil* 124 B4
Eisden, *Belgium* 17 G7
Eisenach, *Germany* 18 E6
Eisenberg, *Germany* 18 E7
Eisenerz, *Austria* 21 H4
Eisenhüttenstadt, *Germany* 18 C10
Eisenstadt, *Austria* 21 H6
Eiserfeld, *Germany* 18 E3
Eisfeld, *Germany* 18 E6
Eisleben, *Germany* 18 D7
Eivissa = Ibiza, *Spain* 36 C7
Ejby, *Denmark* 11 J3
Eje, Sierra del, *Spain* 30 C4
Ejea de los Caballeros, *Spain* 28 C3
Ejutla, *Mexico* 115 D5
Ekalaka, *U.S.A.* 108 C2
Ekeren, *Belgium* 17 F4
Eket, *Nigeria* 79 E6
Eketahuna, *N.Z.* 87 J5
Ekhínos, *Greece* 39 H8
Ekibastuz, *Kazakhstan* 44 D8
Ekimchan, *Russia* 45 D14
Ekoli, *Zaïre* 82 C1
Eksel, *Belgium* 17 F6
Ekwan →, *Canada* 98 B3
Ekwan Pt., *Canada* 98 B3
El Aaiún, *W. Sahara* 74 C2
El Aargub, *Mauritania* 74 D1
El Abiodh-Sidi-Cheikh, *Algeria* 75 B5
El 'Agrûd, *Egypt* 69 E3
El Aïoun, *Morocco* 75 B4
El 'Aiyat, *Egypt* 76 J7
El Alamein, *Egypt* 76 H6
El Alto, *Peru* 124 A1
El 'Aqaba, W. →, *Egypt* 69 E2
El 'Arag, *Egypt* 76 B2
El Arahal, *Spain* 31 H5
El Arenal, *Spain* 36 B9
El Aricha, *Algeria* 75 B4
El Arīhā, *Jordan* 69 D4
El Arish, *Australia* 90 B4
El 'Arîsh, *Egypt* 69 D2
El 'Arîsh, W. →, *Egypt* 69 D2
El Arrouch, *Algeria* 75 A6
El Asnam = Ech Cheliff, *Algeria* 75 A5
El Astillero, *Spain* 30 B7
El Badâri, *Egypt* 76 B3
El Bahrein, *Egypt* 76 B2
El Ballâs, *Egypt* 76 B3
El Balyana, *Egypt* 76 B3
El Banco, *Colombia* 120 B3
El Baqeir, *Sudan* 76 D3
El Barco de Ávila, *Spain* 30 E5
El Barco de Valdeorras, *Spain* 30 C4
El Bauga, *Sudan* 76 D3
El Baúl, *Venezuela* 120 B4
El Bawiti, *Egypt* 76 J6
El Bayadh, *Algeria* 75 B5
El Bierzo, *Spain* 30 C4
El Bluff, *Nic.* 116 D3
El Bolsón, *Argentina* 128 B2
El Bonillo, *Spain* 29 G2
El Brûk, W. →, *Egypt* 69 E2
El Buheirat □, *Sudan* 77 F2
El Caín, *Argentina* 128 B3
El Cajon, *U.S.A.* 113 N10
El Callao, *Venezuela* 121 B5
El Camp, *Spain* 28 D6
El Campo, *U.S.A.* 109 L6
El Carmen, *Bolivia* 125 C5
El Carmen, *Venezuela* 120 C4
El Castillo, *Spain* 31 H4
El Centro, *U.S.A.* 113 N11
El Cerro, *Bolivia* 125 D5
El Cerro, *Spain* 31 H4
El Cocuy, *Colombia* 120 B3
El Compadre, *Mexico* 113 N10
El Corcovado, *Argentina* 128 B2
El Coronil, *Spain* 31 H5
El Cuy, *Argentina* 128 A3
El Cuyo, *Mexico* 115 C7
El Dab'a, *Egypt* 76 H6
El Daheir, *Egypt* 69 D3
El Deir, *Egypt* 76 B3
El Dere, *Somali Rep.* 68 G4
El Descanso, *Mexico* 113 N10
El Desemboque, *Mexico* 114 A2
El Dilingat, *Egypt* 76 H7
El Diviso, *Colombia* 120 C2
El Djem, *Tunisia* 75 A7
El Djouf, *Mauritania* 70 D3
El Dorado, *Ark., U.S.A.* 109 J8
El Dorado, *Kans., U.S.A.* 109 G6
El Dorado, *Venezuela* 121 B5
El Eglab, *Algeria* 74 C4
El Escorial, *Spain* 30 E6
El Eulma, *Algeria* 75 A6
El Faiyûm, *Egypt* 76 J7
El Fâsher, *Sudan* 77 E2
El Fashn, *Egypt* 76 J7
El Ferrol, *Spain* 30 B2
El Fifi, *Sudan* 77 E1
El Fuerte, *Mexico* 114 B3
El Gal, *Somali Rep.* 68 E5
El Gebir, *Sudan* 77 E2
El Gedida, *Egypt* 76 B2
El Geteina, *Sudan* 77 E3
El Gezira □, *Sudan* 77 E3
El Gîza, *Egypt* 76 H7
El Goléa, *Algeria* 75 B5
El Guettar, *Algeria* 75 B5
El Hadeb, *W. Sahara* 74 C2
El Hadjira, *Algeria* 75 B6
El Hagiz, *Sudan* 77 D4
El Hajeb, *Morocco* 74 B3
El Hammam, *Egypt* 76 H6
El Hammâmi, *Mauritania* 74 D2
El Hank, *Mauritania* 74 D3
El Harrach, *Algeria* 75 A5
El Hasian, *W. Sahara* 74 C2
El Hawata, *Sudan* 77 E3
El Heiz, *Egypt* 76 B2
El 'Idisât, *Egypt* 76 B3
El Iskandarîya, *Egypt* 76 H6
El Jadida, *Morocco* 74 B3
El Jebelein, *Sudan* 77 E3
El Kab, *Sudan* 76 D3
El Kabrît, G., *Egypt* 69 F2
El Kala, *Algeria* 75 A6
El Kalâa, *Morocco* 74 B3
El Kamlin, *Sudan* 77 D3
El Kantara, *Algeria* 75 A6
El Kantara, *Tunisia* 75 B7
El Karaba, *Sudan* 76 D3
El Kef, *Tunisia* 75 A6
El Khandaq, *Sudan* 76 D3
El Khârga, *Egypt* 76 B3
El Khartûm, *Sudan* 77 D3
El Khartûm □, *Sudan* 77 D3
El Khartûm Bahrî, *Sudan* 77 D3
El Khroub, *Algeria* 75 A6
El Kseur, *Algeria* 75 A5
El Ksiba, *Morocco* 74 B3
El Kuntilla, *Egypt* 69 E3
El Laqâwa, *Sudan* 77 E2
El Laqeita, *Egypt* 76 B3
El Leiya, *Sudan* 77 D4
El Mafâza, *Sudan* 77 E3

El Mahalla el Kubra, Egypt 76 H7
El Mahârîq, Egypt 76 B3
El Mahmûdîya, Egypt 76 H7
El Maitén, Argentina 128 B2
El Maiz, Algeria 75 C4
El-Maks el-Bahari, Egypt 76 C3
El Manshâh, Egypt 76 B3
El Mansour, Algeria 75 C4
El Mansûra, Egypt 76 H7
El Mantico, Venezuela 121 B5
El Manzala, Egypt 76 H7
El Marâgha, Egypt 76 B3
El Masid, Sudan 77 D3
El Matariya, Egypt 76 H8
El Medano, Canary Is. 36 F3
El Meghaier, Algeria 75 B6
El Meraguen, Algeria 75 C4
El Metemma, Sudan 77 D3
El Miamo, Venezuela 121 B5
El Milagro, Argentina 126 C2
El Milia, Algeria 75 A6
El Minyâ, Egypt 76 J7
El Molar, Spain 28 E1
El Mreyye, Mauritania 78 B3
El Obeid, Sudan 77 E3
El Odaiya, Sudan 77 E2
El Oro, Mexico 115 D4
El Oro □, Ecuador 120 D2
El Oued, Algeria 75 B6
El Palmar, Bolivia 125 D5
El Palmar, Venezuela 121 B5
El Palmito, Presa, Mexico 114 B3
El Panadés, Spain 28 D6
El Pardo, Spain 30 E7
El Paso, U.S.A. 111 L10
El Paso Robles, U.S.A. 112 K6
El Pedernoso, Spain 29 F2
El Pedroso, Spain 31 H5
El Pobo de Dueñas, Spain 28 E3
El Portal, U.S.A. 111 H4
El Porvenir, Mexico 114 A3
El Prat de Llobregat, Spain 28 D7
El Progreso, Honduras 116 C2
El Provencío, Spain 29 F2
El Pueblito, Mexico 114 B3
El Pueblo, Canary Is. 36 F2
El Qâhira, Egypt 76 H7
El Qantara, Egypt 69 E1
El Qasr, Egypt 76 B2
El Quseima, Egypt 69 E3
El Qusîya, Egypt 76 B3
El Râshda, Egypt 76 B2
El Reno, U.S.A. 109 H6
El Ribero, Spain 30 C2
El Rîdisiya, Egypt 76 C3
El Rio, U.S.A. 113 L7
El Ronquillo, Spain 31 H4
El Roque, Pta., Canary Is. 36 F4
El Rosarito, Mexico 114 B2
El Rubio, Spain 31 H5
El Saff, Egypt 76 J7
El Saheira, W. →, Egypt 69 E2
El Salto, Mexico 114 C3
El Salvador ■, Cent. Amer. 116 D2
El Sancejo, Spain 31 H5
El Sauce, Nic. 116 D2
El Shallal, Egypt 76 C3
El Simbillawein, Egypt 76 H7
El Sombrero, Venezuela 120 B4
El Suweis, Egypt 76 J8
El Tamarâni, W. →, Egypt 69 E3
El Thamad, Egypt 69 F3
El Tigre, Venezuela 121 B5
El Tîh, G., Egypt 69 F2
El Tîna, Khalîg, Egypt 69 D1
El Tocuyo, Venezuela 120 B4
El Tofo, Chile 126 B1
El Tránsito, Chile 126 B1
El Tûr, Egypt 76 J8
El Turbio, Argentina 128 D2
El Uqsur, Egypt 76 B3
El Vado, Spain 28 D1
El Vallés, Spain 28 D7
El Venado, Mexico 114 C4
El Vigía, Venezuela 120 B3
El Wabeira, Egypt 69 F2
El Wak, Kenya 82 B5
El Waqf, Egypt 76 B3
El Wâsta, Egypt 76 J7
El Weguet, Ethiopia 77 F5
El Wuz, Sudan 77 D3
Elafónisos, Greece 39 N5
Elandsvlei, S. Africa 84 E2
Élassa, Greece 39 P9
Elassón, Greece 39 K5
Elat, Israel 69 F3
Elâzığ, Turkey 67 D8
Elâzığ □, Turkey 67 D8
Elba, Italy 32 F7
Elba, U.S.A. 105 K2
Elbasani, Albania 39 H3
Elbe, U.S.A. 112 D4
Elbe →, Europe 18 B4
Elbe-Seiten Kanal, Germany 18 C6
Elbert, Mt., U.S.A. 111 G10
Elberta, U.S.A. 104 C2
Elberton, U.S.A. 105 H4
Elbeuf, France 24 C8
Elbing = Elbląg, Poland 20 A9
Elbistan, Turkey 66 D7
Elbląg, Poland 20 A9
Elbow, Canada 101 C7
Elbrus, Asia 43 E10
Elburg, Neths. 16 D7
Elburz Mts. = Alborz, Reshteh-ye Kūhhā-ye, Iran 65 C7
Elche, Spain 29 G4
Elche de la Sierra, Spain 29 G2
Elcho I., Australia 90 A2
Elda, Spain 29 G4
Eldon, Mo., U.S.A. 108 F8
Eldon, Wash., U.S.A. 112 C3
Eldora, U.S.A. 108 D8
Eldorado, Argentina 127 B5
Eldorado, Canada 101 B7
Eldorado, Mexico 114 C3
Eldorado, Ill., U.S.A. 104 G1
Eldorado, Tex., U.S.A. 109 K4
Eldorado Springs, U.S.A. 109 G8
Eldoret, Kenya 82 B4
Eldred, U.S.A. 106 E6
Elea, C., Cyprus 37 D13
Electra, U.S.A. 109 H5
Elefantes →, Mozam. 85 C5
Elefantes, G., Chile 128 C2
Elektrogorsk, Russia 41 D11
Elektrostal, Russia 41 D11
Elele, Nigeria 79 D6
Elephant Butte Reservoir, U.S.A. 111 K10
Elephant I., Antarctica 5 C18
Elesbão Veloso, Brazil 122 C3
Eleşkirt, Turkey 67 D10
Eleuthera, Bahamas 116 A4
Elgepiggen, Norway 10 B5
Elgeyo-Marakwet □, Kenya 82 B4
Elgg, Switz. 23 B7
Elgin, N.B., Canada 99 C6
Elgin, Ont., Canada 107 B8
Elgin, U.K. 14 D5
Elgin, Ill., U.S.A. 104 D1
Elgin, N. Dak., U.S.A. 108 B4
Elgin, Nebr., U.S.A. 108 E5
Elgin, Nev., U.S.A. 111 H6
Elgin, Oreg., U.S.A. 110 D5
Elgin, Tex., U.S.A. 109 K6
Elgon, Mt., Africa 82 B3
Eliase, Indonesia 57 F8
Elida, U.S.A. 109 J3
Elikón, Greece 39 L5
Elim, S. Africa 84 E2
Elisabethville = Lubumbashi, Zaïre 83 E2
Eliseu Martins, Brazil 122 C3
Elista, Russia 43 C11
Elizabeth, Australia 91 E2
Elizabeth, U.S.A. 107 F10
Elizabeth City, U.S.A. 105 G7
Elizabethton, U.S.A. 105 G4
Elizabethtown, Ky., U.S.A. 104 G3
Elizabethtown, N.Y., U.S.A. 107 B11
Elizabethtown, Pa., U.S.A. 107 F8
Elizondo, Spain 28 B3
Ełk, Poland 20 B12
Elk City, U.S.A. 109 H5
Elk Creek, U.S.A. 112 F4
Elk Grove, U.S.A. 112 G5
Elk Island Nat. Park, Canada 100 C6
Elk Lake, Canada 98 C3
Elk Point, Canada 101 C6
Elk River, Idaho, U.S.A. 110 C5
Elk River, Minn., U.S.A. 108 C8
Elkedra, Australia 90 C2
Elkedra →, Australia 90 C2
Elkhart, Ind., U.S.A. 104 E3
Elkhart, Kans., U.S.A. 109 G4
Elkhorn, Canada 101 D8
Elkhorn →, U.S.A. 108 E6
Elkhotovo, Russia 43 E11
Elkhovo, Bulgaria 38 G9
Elkin, U.S.A. 105 G5
Elkins, U.S.A. 104 F6
Elko, Canada 100 D5
Elko, U.S.A. 110 F6
Ell, L., Australia 89 E4
Ellecom, Neths. 16 D8
Ellef Ringnes I., Canada 4 B2
Ellendale, Australia 88 C3
Ellendale, U.S.A. 108 B5
Ellensburg, U.S.A. 110 C3
Ellenville, U.S.A. 107 E10
Ellery, Mt., Australia 91 F4
Ellesmere, L., N.Z. 87 M4
Ellesmere I., Canada 4 B4
Ellesmere Port, U.K. 12 D5
Ellezelles, Belgium 17 G3
Ellice Is. = Tuvalu ■, Pac. Oc. 92 H9
Ellinwood, U.S.A. 108 F5
Elliot, Australia 90 B1
Elliot, S. Africa 85 E4
Elliot Lake, Canada 98 C3
Elliotdale = Xhora, S. Africa 85 E4
Ellis, U.S.A. 108 F5
Elliston, Australia 91 E1
Ellisville, U.S.A. 109 K10
Ellon, U.K. 14 D6
Ellore = Eluru, India 61 L12
Ells →, Canada 100 B6
Ellsworth, U.S.A. 108 F5
Ellsworth Land, Antarctica 5 D16
Ellsworth Mts., Antarctica 5 D16
Ellwangen, Germany 19 G6
Ellwood City, U.S.A. 106 F4
Elm, Switz. 23 C8
Elma, Canada 101 D9
Elma, U.S.A. 112 D3
Elmadağ, Turkey 66 D5
Elmalı, Turkey 66 E3
Elmhurst, U.S.A. 104 E2
Elmina, Ghana 79 D4
Elmira, Canada 106 C4
Elmira, U.S.A. 106 D8
Elmore, Australia 91 F3
Elmore, U.S.A. 113 M11
Elmshorn, Germany 18 B5
Elmvale, Canada 106 B5
Elne, France 26 F6
Elora, Canada 106 C4
Elorza, Venezuela 120 B4
Eloúnda, Greece 37 D7
Eloy, U.S.A. 111 K8
Éloyes, France 25 D13
Elrose, Canada 101 C7
Elsas, Canada 98 C3
Elsie, U.S.A. 112 E3
Elsinore = Helsingør, Denmark 11 H6
Elsinore, U.S.A. 111 G7
Elspe, Germany 18 D4
Elspeet, Neths. 16 D7
Elst, Neths. 16 E7
Elster →, Germany 18 D7
Elsterwerda, Germany 18 D9
Elten, Neths. 16 E8
Eltham, N.Z. 87 H5
Elton, Russia 43 B12
Eluanbi, Taiwan 53 G13
Eluru, India 61 L12
Elvas, Portugal 31 G3
Elven, France 24 E4
Elverum, Norway 10 D5
Elvire →, Australia 88 C4
Elvo →, Italy 32 C5
Elvran, Norway 10 A5
Elwood, Ind., U.S.A. 104 E3
Elwood, Nebr., U.S.A. 108 E5
Elx = Elche, Spain 29 G4
Ely, U.K. 13 E8
Ely, Minn., U.S.A. 108 B9
Ely, Nev., U.S.A. 110 G6
Elyria, U.S.A. 106 E2
Elz →, Germany 19 G3
Emāmrūd, Iran 65 B7
Emba, Kazakhstan 44 E6
Emba →, Kazakhstan 44 E6
Embarcación, Argentina 126 A3
Embarras Portage, Canada 101 B6
Embetsu, Japan 48 B10
Embira →, Brazil 124 B3
Embóna, Greece 37 C9
Embrach, Switz. 23 A7
Embrun, France 27 D10
Embu, Kenya 82 C4
Embu □, Kenya 82 C4
Emden, Germany 18 B3
Emerald, Australia 90 C4
Emerson, Canada 101 D9
Emery, U.S.A. 111 G8
Emet, Turkey 66 D3
Emi Koussi, Chad 73 E8
Emilia-Romagna □, Italy 32 D7
Emilius, Mte., Italy 32 C4
Eminabad, Pakistan 62 C6
Emirdağ, Turkey 66 D4
Emlenton, U.S.A. 106 E5
Emlichheim, Germany 18 C2
Emme →, Switz. 22 B5
Emmeloord, Neths. 16 C7
Emmen, Neths. 16 C9
Emmendingen, Germany 19 G3
Emmental, Switz. 22 C4
Emmer-Compascuum, Neths. 16 C10
Emmerich, Germany 18 D2
Emmet, Australia 90 C3
Emmetsburg, U.S.A. 108 D7
Emmett, U.S.A. 110 E5
Empalme, Mexico 114 B2
Empangeni, S. Africa 85 D5
Empedrado, Argentina 126 B4
Emperor Seamount Chain, Pac. Oc. 92 D9
Empoli, Italy 32 E7
Emporia, Kans., U.S.A. 108 F6
Emporia, Va., U.S.A. 105 G7
Emporium, U.S.A. 106 E6
Empress, Canada 101 C6
Emptinne, Belgium 17 H6
Empty Quarter = Rub' al Khali, Si. Arabia 68 D4
Ems →, Germany 18 B3
Emsdale, Canada 106 A5
Emsdetten, Germany 18 C3
Emu, China 51 C15
Emu Park, Australia 90 C5
'En 'Avrona, Israel 69 F3
En Nahud, Sudan 77 E2
Ena, Japan 49 G8
Enafors, Sweden 10 A6
Enambú, Colombia 120 C3
Enana, Namibia 84 B2
Enånger, Sweden 10 C11
Enaratoli, Indonesia 57 E9
Enard B., U.K. 14 C3
Enare = Inarijärvi, Finland 8 B19
Encantadas, Serra, Brazil 127 C5
Encanto, C., Phil. 57 A6
Encarnación, Paraguay 127 B4
Encarnación de Diaz, Mexico 114 C4
Enchi, Ghana 78 D4
Encinal, U.S.A. 109 L5
Encinitas, U.S.A. 113 M9
Encino, U.S.A. 111 J11
Encontrados, Venezuela 120 B3
Encounter B., Australia 91 F2
Encruzilhada, Brazil 123 E3
Ende, Indonesia 57 F6
Endeavour, Canada 101 C8
Endeavour Str., Australia 90 A3
Endelave, Denmark 11 J4
Enderbury I., Kiribati 92 H10
Enderby, Canada 100 C5
Enderby I., Australia 88 D2
Enderby Land, Antarctica 5 C5
Enderlin, U.S.A. 108 B6
Endicott, N.Y., U.S.A. 107 D8
Endicott, Wash., U.S.A. 110 C5
Endimari →, Brazil 124 B4
Endyalgout I., Australia 88 B5
Ene →, Peru 124 C3
Enewetak Atoll, Pac. Oc. 92 F8
Enez, Turkey 66 C2
Enfida, Tunisia 75 A7
Enfield, U.K. 13 F7
Engadin, Switz. 19 J6
Engaño, C., Dom. Rep. 117 C6
Engaño, C., Phil. 57 A6
Engcobo, S. Africa 85 E4
Engelberg, Switz. 23 C6
Engels = Pokrovsk, Russia 41 F15
Engemann L., Canada 101 B7
Enger, Norway 10 D4
Enggano, Indonesia 56 F2
Enghien, Belgium 17 G4
Engil, Morocco 74 B4
Engkilili, Malaysia 56 D4
England, U.S.A. 109 H9
England □, U.K. 7 E5
Englee, Canada 99 B8
Englehart, Canada 98 C4
Engler L., Canada 101 B7
Englewood, Colo., U.S.A. 108 F2
Englewood, Kans., U.S.A. 109 G5
English →, Canada 101 C10
English Bazar = Ingraj Bazar, India 63 G13
English Channel, Europe 13 G6
English River, Canada 98 C1
Enid, U.S.A. 109 G6
Enipévs →, Greece 39 K5
Enkhuizen, Neths. 16 C6
Enköping, Sweden 10 E11
Enle, China 52 E3
Enna, Italy 35 E7
Ennadai, Canada 101 A8
Ennadai L., Canada 101 A8
Ennedi, Chad 73 E9
Enngonia, Australia 91 D4
Ennis, Ireland 15 D3
Ennis, Mont., U.S.A. 110 D8
Ennis, Tex., U.S.A. 109 J6
Enniscorthy, Ireland 15 D5
Enniskillen, U.K. 15 B4
Ennistimon, Ireland 15 D2
Enns →, Austria 21 G4
Enontekiö, Finland 8 B17
Enping, China 53 F9
Enriquillo, L., Dom. Rep. 117 C5
Ens, Neths. 16 C7
Enschede, Neths. 16 D9
Ensenada, Argentina 126 C4
Ensenada, Mexico 114 A1
Enshi, China 52 B7
Ensiola, Pta., Spain 36 B9
Ensisheim, France 25 E14
Entebbe, Uganda 82 B3
Enter, Neths. 16 D9
Enterprise, Canada 100 A5
Enterprise, Oreg., U.S.A. 110 D5
Enterprise, Utah, U.S.A. 111 H7
Entlebuch, Switz. 22 C6
Entre Ríos, Bolivia 126 A3
Entre Rios, Bahia, Brazil 123 D4
Entre Rios, Pará, Brazil 125 B7
Entre Ríos □, Argentina 126 C4
Entrepeñas, Pantano de, Spain 28 E2
Enugu, Nigeria 79 D6
Enugu □, Nigeria 79 D6
Enugu Ezike, Nigeria 79 D6
Enumclaw, U.S.A. 112 C5
Envermeu, France 24 C8
Envigado, Colombia 120 B2
Envira, Brazil 124 B3
Enz →, Germany 19 F5
Enza →, Italy 32 D7
Eólie, Is., Italy 35 D7
Epanomí, Greece 39 J5
Epe, Neths. 16 D7
Epe, Nigeria 79 D5
Épernay, France 25 C10
Épernon, France 25 D8
Ephesus, Turkey 66 E2
Ephraim, U.S.A. 110 G8
Ephrata, U.S.A. 110 C4
Epila, Spain 28 D3
Épinac-les-Mines, France 25 F11
Épinal, France 25 D13
Epira, Guyana 121 B6
Episkopi, Cyprus 37 E11
Episkopí, Greece 37 D6
Episkopi Bay, Cyprus 37 E11
Epping, U.K. 13 F8
Epukiro, Namibia 84 C2
Equatorial Guinea ■, Africa 80 D1
Equeipa, Venezuela 121 B5
Er Rahad, Sudan 77 E3
Er Rif, Morocco 75 A4
Er Roseires, Sudan 77 E3
Erāwadī Myit = Irrawaddy →, Burma 61 M19
Erba, Italy 32 C6
Erba, Sudan 76 D4
Erbaa, Turkey 66 C7
Erbil = Arbīl, Iraq 64 B5
Erçek Gölü, Turkey 67 D10
Ercha, Russia 45 C15
Erçiş, Turkey 67 D10
Erciyaş Dağı, Turkey 66 D6
Erdao Jiang →, China 51 C14
Erdek, Turkey 66 C2
Erdemli, Turkey 66 E6
Erdene, Mongolia 50 B6
Erding, Germany 19 G7
Erdre →, France 24 E5
Erebato →, Venezuela 121 B5
Erebus, Mt., Antarctica 5 D11
Erechim, Brazil 127 B5
Ereğli, Konya, Turkey 66 E6
Ereğli, Zonguldak, Turkey 66 C4
Erei, Monti, Italy 35 E7
Erembodegem, Belgium 17 G4
Erenhot, China 50 C7
Eresma →, Spain 30 D6
Erewadi Myitwanya, Burma 61 M19
Erfenisdam, S. Africa 84 D4
Erfoud, Morocco 74 B4
Erft →, Germany 18 D2
Erfurt, Germany 18 E7
Ergani, Turkey 67 D8
Ergeni Vozvyshennost, Russia 43 C11
Ērgli, Latvia 40 C4
Eria →, Spain 30 C5
Eriba, Sudan 77 D4
Eriboll, L., U.K. 14 C4
Erica, Neths. 16 C9
Érice, Italy 34 D5
Erie, U.S.A. 106 D4
Erie, L., N. Amer. 106 D3
Erie Canal, U.S.A. 106 C6
Erieau, Canada 106 D3
Erigavo, Somali Rep. 68 E4
Erikoúsa, Greece 37 A3
Eriksdale, Canada 101 C9
Erikslund, Sweden 10 B9
Erímanthos, Greece 39 M4
Erimo-misaki, Japan 48 D11
Eriswil, Switz. 22 B5
Erithraí, Greece 39 L6
Eritrea ■, Africa 77 E4
Erjas →, Portugal 31 F3
Erlangen, Germany 19 F7
Erldunda, Australia 90 D1
Erlin, Taiwan 53 F13
Ermelo, Neths. 16 D7
Ermelo, S. Africa 85 D4
Ermenak, Turkey 66 E5
Ermióni, Greece 39 M6
Ermones, Greece 37 A3
Ermoúpolis = Síros, Greece 39 M7
Ernakulam = Cochin, India 60 Q10
Erne →, Ireland 15 B3
Erne, Lower L., U.K. 15 B4
Erne, Upper L., U.K. 15 B4
Ernée, France 24 D6
Ernest Giles Ra., Australia 89 E3
Ernstberg, Germany 19 E2
Erode, India 60 P10
Eromanga, Australia 91 D3
Erongo, Namibia 84 C2
Erp, Neths. 17 E7
Erquelinnes, Belgium 17 H4
Erquy, France 24 D4
Erquy, C. d', France 24 D4
Err, Piz d', Switz. 23 C9
Errabiddy, Australia 89 E2
Erramala Hills, India 60 M11
Errer →, Ethiopia 77 F5
Errigal, Ireland 15 A3
Erris Hd., Ireland 15 B1
Erseka, Albania 39 J3
Erskine, U.S.A. 108 B7
Erstein, France 25 D14
Erstfeld, Switz. 23 C7
Ertil, Russia 41 F12
Ertis = Irtysh →, Russia 44 C7
Ertvelde, Belgium 17 F3
Eruh, Turkey 67 E10
Eruwa, Nigeria 79 D5
Ervy-le-Châtel, France 25 D10
Erwin, U.S.A. 105 G4
Eryuan, China 52 D2
Erzgebirge, Germany 18 E9
Erzin, Russia 45 D10
Erzincan, Turkey 67 D8
Erzincan □, Turkey 67 D8
Erzurum, Turkey 67 D9
Erzurum □, Turkey 67 D9
Es Caló, Spain 36 C8
Es Caná, Spain 36 B8
Es Sahrâ' Esh Sharqîya, Egypt 76 B3
Es Sînâ', Egypt 76 J8
Es Sûkî, Sudan 77 E3
Esambo, Zaïre 82 C1
Esan-Misaki, Japan 48 D10
Esashi, Hokkaidō, Japan 48 B11

Esashi, Hokkaidō, Japan 48 D10
Esbjerg, Denmark 11 J2
Escada, Brazil 122 C4
Escalante, U.S.A. 111 H8
Escalante →, U.S.A. 111 H8
Escalón, Mexico 114 B4
Escalona, Spain 30 E6
Escambia →, U.S.A. 105 K2
Escanaba, U.S.A. 104 C2
Escaut →, Belgium 17 F3
Esch-sur-Alzette, Lux. 17 J7
Eschede, Germany 18 C6
Escholzmatt, Switz. 22 C5
Eschwege, Germany 18 D6
Eschweiler, Germany 18 E2
Escoma, Bolivia 124 D4
Escondido, U.S.A. 113 M9
Escuinapa, Mexico 114 C3
Escuintla, Guatemala 116 D1
Eséka, Cameroon 79 E7
Esens, Germany 18 B3
Esera →, Spain 28 C5
Eşfahān, Iran 65 C6
Esfīdeh, Iran 65 C8
Esgueva →, Spain 30 D6
Esh Sham = Dimashq, Syria 69 B5
Esh Shamâlîya □, Sudan 76 D2
Eshan, China 52 E4
Eshowe, S. Africa 85 D5
Esiama, Ghana 78 E4
Esil = Ishim →, Russia 44 D8
Esino →, Italy 33 E10
Esk →, Dumf. & Gall., U.K. 14 G5
Esk →, N. Yorks., U.K. 12 C7
Eskifjörður, Iceland 8 D7
Eskilstuna, Sweden 10 E10
Eskimalatya, Turkey 67 D8
Eskimo Pt., Canada 101 A10
Eskişehir, Turkey 66 D4
Eskişehir □, Turkey 66 D4
Esla →, Spain 30 D4
Esla, Pantano del, Spain 30 D4
Eslāmābād-e Gharb, Iran 64 C5
Eslöv, Sweden 11 J7
Eşme, Turkey 66 D3
Esmeralda, I., Chile 128 C1
Esmeraldas, Ecuador 120 C2
Esmeraldas □, Ecuador 120 C2
Esmeraldas →, Ecuador 120 C2
Esneux, Belgium 17 G7
Espada, Pta., Colombia 120 A3
Espalion, France 26 D6
Espalmador, I., Spain 36 C7
Espanola, Canada 98 C3
Espardell, I. del, Spain 36 C7
Esparraguera, Spain 28 D6
Esparta, Costa Rica 116 E3
Espejo, Spain 31 H6
Esperança, Brazil 122 C4
Esperance, Australia 89 F3
Esperance B., Australia 89 F3
Esperantinópolis, Brazil 122 B3
Esperanza, Santa Cruz, Argentina 128 D2
Esperanza, Santa Fe, Argentina 126 C3
Esperanza, Phil. 55 G6
Espéraza, France 26 F6
Espichel, C., Portugal 31 G1
Espiel, Spain 31 G5
Espigão, Serra do, Brazil 127 B5
Espinal, Colombia 120 C3
Espinar, Peru 124 C3
Espinazo, Sierra del = Espinhaço, Serra do, Brazil 123 E3
Espinhaço, Serra do, Brazil 123 E3
Espinho, Portugal 30 D2
Espinilho, Serra do, Brazil 127 B5
Espino, Venezuela 120 B4
Espinosa de los Monteros, Spain 30 B7
Espírito Santo □, Brazil 123 F3
Espíritu Santo, B. del, Mexico 115 D7
Espíritu Santo, I., Mexico 114 C2
Espita, Mexico 115 C7
Espiye, Turkey 67 C8
Esplanada, Brazil 123 D4
Espluga de Francolí, Spain 28 D6
Espuña, Sierra, Spain 29 H3
Espungabera, Mozam. 85 C5
Esquel, Argentina 128 B2
Esquina, Argentina 126 B4
Essaouira, Morocco 74 B3
Essebie, Zaïre 82 B3
Essen, Belgium 17 F4
Essen, Germany 18 D2
Essendon, Mt., Australia 89 E3
Essequibo →, Guyana 121 B6
Essex, Canada 106 D2
Essex, Calif., U.S.A. 113 L11
Essex, N.Y., U.S.A. 107 B11
Essex □, U.K. 13 F8
Esslingen, Germany 19 G5
Essonne □, France 25 D9
Essvik, Sweden 10 B11
Estaca, Pta. del, Spain 30 B3
Estadilla, Spain 28 C5
Estados, I. de Los, Argentina 128 D4
Estagel, France 26 F6
Eşţahbānāt, Iran 65 D7
Estallenchs, Spain 36 B9
Estância, Brazil 122 D4
Estancia, U.S.A. 111 J10
Estārm, Iran 65 D8
Estarreja, Portugal 30 E2
Estats, Pic d', Spain 28 C6
Estavayer-le-Lac, Switz. 22 C3
Estcourt, S. Africa 85 D4
Este, Italy 33 C8
Esteban, Spain 30 B4
Estelí, Nic. 116 D2
Estella, Spain 28 C2
Estelline, S. Dak., U.S.A. 108 C6
Estelline, Tex., U.S.A. 109 H4
Estena →, Spain 31 F6
Estepa, Spain 31 H6
Estepona, Spain 31 J5
Esterhazy, Canada 101 C8
Esternay, France 25 D10
Esterri de Aneu, Spain 28 C6
Estevan, Canada 101 D8
Estevan Group, Canada 100 C3
Estherville, U.S.A. 108 D7
Estissac, France 25 D10
Eston, Canada 101 C7
Estonia ■, Europe 40 B4
Estoril, Portugal 31 G1
Estouk, Mali 79 B5
Estrêla, Serra da, Portugal 30 E3
Estrella, Spain 29 G1
Estremoz, Portugal 31 G3
Estrondo, Serra do, Brazil 122 C2
Esztergom, Hungary 21 H8
Et Tîdra, Mauritania 78 B1
Étables-sur-Mer, France 24 D4
Etadunna, Australia 91 D2
Etah, India 63 F8
Étain, France 25 C12
Etalle, Belgium 17 J7
Etamamu, Canada 99 B8
Étampes, France 25 D9
Étang-sur-Arroux, France 27 B8
Etanga, Namibia 84 B1
Étaples, France 25 B8
Etawah, India 63 F8
Etawah →, U.S.A. 105 H3
Etawney L., Canada 101 B9
Ete, Nigeria 79 D6
Éthe, Belgium 17 J7
Ethel, U.S.A. 112 D4
Ethel, Oued el →, Algeria 74 C4
Ethel Creek, Australia 88 D3
Ethelbert, Canada 101 C8
Ethiopia ■, Africa 68 F3
Ethiopian Highlands, Ethiopia 70 E7
Etive, L., U.K. 14 E3
Etna, Italy 35 E8
Etoile, Zaïre 83 E2
Etolin I., U.S.A. 100 B2
Etosha Pan, Namibia 84 B2
Etowah, U.S.A. 105 H3
Étrépagny, France 25 C8
Étretat, France 24 C7
Ettelbruck, Lux. 17 J8
Etten, Neths. 17 E5
Ettlingen, Germany 19 G4
Ettrick Water →, U.K. 14 F6
Etuku, Zaïre 82 C2
Etzatlán, Mexico 114 C4
Eu, France 24 B8
Euboea = Évvoia, Greece 39 L7
Eucla Motel, Australia 89 F4
Euclid, U.S.A. 106 E3
Euclides da Cunha, Brazil 122 D4
Eucumbene, L., Australia 91 F4
Eudora, U.S.A. 109 J9
Eufaula, Ala., U.S.A. 105 K3
Eufaula, Okla., U.S.A. 109 H7
Eufaula L., U.S.A. 109 H7
Eugene, U.S.A. 110 E2
Eugowra, Australia 91 E4
Eulo, Australia 91 D4
Eunice, La., U.S.A. 109 K8
Eunice, N. Mex., U.S.A. 109 J3
Eupen, Belgium 17 G8
Euphrates = Furāt, Nahr al →, Asia 64 D5
Eure □, France 24 C8
Eure →, France 24 C8
Eure-et-Loir □, France 24 D8
Eureka, Canada 4 B3
Eureka, Calif., U.S.A. 110 F1
Eureka, Kans., U.S.A. 109 G6
Eureka, Mont., U.S.A. 110 B6
Eureka, Nev., U.S.A. 110 G5
Eureka, S. Dak., U.S.A. 108 C5
Eureka, Utah, U.S.A. 110 G7
Eureka, Mt., Australia 89 E3
Euroa, Australia 91 F4
Europa, I., Ind. Oc. 81 J8
Europa, Picos de, Spain 30 B6
Europa, Pta. de, Gib. 31 J5
Europa Pt. = Europa, Pta. de, Gib. 31 J5
Europe 6 F10
Europoort, Neths. 16 E4
Euskirchen, Germany 18 E2
Eustis, U.S.A. 105 L5
Eutin, Germany 18 A6
Eutsuk L., Canada 100 C3
Eva, Brazil 121 D6
Eva Downs, Australia 90 B1
Evale, Angola 84 B2
Evans, U.S.A. 108 E2
Evans Head, Australia 91 D5
Evans L., Canada 98 B4
Evans Mills, U.S.A. 107 B9
Evanston, Ill., U.S.A. 104 D2
Evanston, Wyo., U.S.A. 110 F8
Evansville, Ind., U.S.A. 104 F2
Evansville, Wis., U.S.A. 108 D10
Évaux-les-Bains, France 26 B6
Evaz, Iran 65 E7
Eveleth, U.S.A. 108 B8
Evensk, Russia 45 C16
Evenstad, Norway 10 C5
Everard, L., Australia 91 E1
Everard Park, Australia 89 E5
Everard Ras., Australia 89 E5
Evere, Belgium 17 G4
Everest, Mt., Nepal 63 E12
Everett, Pa., U.S.A. 106 F6
Everett, Wash., U.S.A. 112 C4
Evergem, Belgium 17 F3
Everglades, The, U.S.A. 105 N5
Everglades City, U.S.A. 105 N5
Everglades National Park, U.S.A. 105 N5
Evergreen, U.S.A. 105 K2
Everson, U.S.A. 110 B2
Evesham, U.K. 13 E6
Évian-les-Bains, France 27 B10
Evinayong, Eq. Guin. 80 D2
Évinos →, Greece 39 L4
Évisa, France 27 F12
Évora, Portugal 31 G3
Évora □, Portugal 31 G3
Evowghlī, Iran 64 B5
Évreux, France 24 C8
Évron, France 24 D6
Evrótas →, Greece 39 N5
Évvoia, Greece 39 L7
Évvoia □, Greece 39 L6
Ewe, L., U.K. 14 D3
Ewing, U.S.A. 108 D5
Ewo, Congo 80 E2
Exaltación, Bolivia 125 C4
Excelsior Springs, U.S.A. 108 F7
Excideuil, France 26 C5
Exe →, U.K. 13 G4
Exeter, Canada 106 C3
Exeter, U.K. 13 G4
Exeter, Calif., U.S.A. 111 H4
Exeter, N.H., U.S.A. 107 D14
Exeter, Nebr., U.S.A. 108 E6
Exloo, Neths. 16 C9
Exmes, France 24 D7
Exmoor, U.K. 13 F4
Exmouth, Australia 88 D1
Exmouth, U.K. 13 G4
Exmouth G., Australia 88 D1
Expedition Ra., Australia 90 C4
Extremadura □, Spain 31 F4
Exuma Sound, Bahamas 116 B4
Eyasi, L., Tanzania 82 C4
Eyeberry L., Canada 101 A8
Eyemouth, U.K. 14 F6
Eygurande, France 26 C6
Eyjafjörður, Iceland 8 C4
Eymet, France 26 D4
Eymoutiers, France 26 C5
Eynesil, Turkey 67 C8
Eyrarbakki, Iceland 8 E3
Eyre, Australia 89 F4
Eyre (North), L., Australia 91 D2
Eyre (South), L., Australia 91 D2
Eyre Cr. →, Australia 91 D2
Eyre Mts., N.Z. 87 L2
Eyre Pen., Australia 91 E2
Eyvānkī, Iran 65 C6
Ez Zeidab, Sudan 76 D3
Ezcaray, Spain 28 C2
Ezine, Turkey 66 D2
Ezmul, Mauritania 74 D1
Ezouza →, Cyprus 37 E11

F

Fabens, U.S.A. 111 L10
Fåborg, Denmark 11 J4
Fabriano, Italy 33 E9
Făcăeni, Romania 38 E10
Facatativá, Colombia 120 C3
Fachi, Niger 72 E7
Facture, France 26 D3
Fada, Chad 73 E9
Fada-n-Gourma, Burkina Faso 79 C5
Faddeyevskiy, Ostrov, Russia 45 B15
Fadghāmī, Syria 64 C4
Fadlab, Sudan 76 D3
Faenza, Italy 33 D8
Fafa, Mali 79 B5
Fafe, Portugal 30 D2
Fagam, Nigeria 79 C7
Făgăras, Romania 38 D7
Făgăras, Munţii, Romania 38 D7
Fågelsjö, Sweden 10 C8
Fagernes, Norway 9 F10
Fagersta, Sweden 9 F13
Făget, Romania 38 D5
Fagnano, L., Argentina 128 D3
Fagnano Castello, Italy 35 C9
Fagnières, France 25 D11
Fahlīān, Iran 65 D6
Fahraj, Kermān, Iran 65 D8
Fahraj, Yazd, Iran 65 D7
Faial, Madeira 36 D3
Faido, Switz. 23 D7
Fair Hd., U.K. 15 A5
Fair Oaks, U.S.A. 112 G5
Fairbank, U.S.A. 111 L8
Fairbanks, U.S.A. 96 B5
Fairbury, U.S.A. 108 E6
Fairfax, U.S.A. 109 G6
Fairfield, Ala., U.S.A. 105 J2
Fairfield, Calif., U.S.A. 112 G4
Fairfield, Conn., U.S.A. 107 E11
Fairfield, Idaho, U.S.A. 110 E6
Fairfield, Ill., U.S.A. 104 F1
Fairfield, Iowa, U.S.A. 108 E9
Fairfield, Mont., U.S.A. 110 C8
Fairfield, Tex., U.S.A. 109 K7
Fairford, Canada 101 C9
Fairhope, U.S.A. 105 K2
Fairlie, N.Z. 87 L3
Fairmead, U.S.A. 112 H6
Fairmont, Minn., U.S.A. 108 D7
Fairmont, W. Va., U.S.A. 104 F5
Fairmount, U.S.A. 113 L8
Fairplay, U.S.A. 111 G11
Fairport, U.S.A. 106 C7
Fairport Harbor, U.S.A. 106 E3
Fairview, Australia 90 B3
Fairview, Canada 100 B5
Fairview, Mont., U.S.A. 108 B2
Fairview, Okla., U.S.A. 109 G5
Fairview, Utah, U.S.A. 110 G8
Fairweather, Mt., U.S.A. 96 C6
Faisalabad, Pakistan 62 D5
Faith, U.S.A. 108 C3
Faizabad, India 63 F10
Fajardo, Puerto Rico 117 C6
Fakfak, Indonesia 57 E8
Fakobli, Ivory C. 78 D3
Fakse, Denmark 11 J6
Fakse B., Denmark 11 J6
Fakse Ladeplads, Denmark 11 J6
Faku, China 51 C12
Falaise, France 24 D6
Falaise, Mui, Vietnam 58 C5
Falam, Burma 61 H18
Falces, Spain 28 C3
Fălciu, Romania 38 C11
Falcón □, Venezuela 120 A4
Falcón, C., Spain 36 C7
Falcon, C., Algeria 75 A4
Falcon Dam, U.S.A. 109 M5
Falconara Marittima, Italy 33 E10
Falconer, U.S.A. 106 D5
Faléa, Mali 78 C2
Falenki, Russia 41 B17
Faleshty, Moldavia 42 C2
Falfurrias, U.S.A. 109 M5
Falher, Canada 100 B5
Falirakí, Greece 37 C10
Falkenberg, Germany 18 D9
Falkenberg, Sweden 11 H6
Falkensee, Germany 18 C9
Falkenstein, Germany 18 E8
Falkirk, U.K. 14 F5
Falkland, East, I., Falk. Is. 128 D5
Falkland, West, I., Falk. Is. 128 D4
Falkland Is. ■, Atl. Oc. 128 D5
Falkland Is. Dependency □, Atl. Oc. 5 B1
Falkland Sd., Falk. Is. 128 D5
Falköping, Sweden 11 F7
Fall River, U.S.A. 107 E13
Fall River Mills, U.S.A. 110 F3
Fallbrook, U.S.A. 111 K5
Fallbrook, Calif., U.S.A. 113 M9
Fallon, Mont., U.S.A. 108 B2
Fallon, Nev., U.S.A. 110 G4
Falls City, Nebr., U.S.A. 108 E7
Falls City, Oreg., U.S.A. 110 D2
Falls Creek, U.S.A. 106 E6
Falmouth, Jamaica 116 C4
Falmouth, U.K. 13 G2
Falmouth, U.S.A. 104 F3
False B., S. Africa 84 E2
Falset, Spain 28 D5
Falso, C., Honduras 116 C3
Falster, Denmark 11 K5
Falsterbo, Sweden 11 J6
Fălticeni, Romania 38 B9
Falun, Sweden 9 F13
Famagusta, Cyprus 37 D12
Famagusta Bay, Cyprus 37 D13
Famatina, Sierra de, Argentina 126 B2
Family L., Canada 101 C9
Famoso, U.S.A. 113 K7
Fan Xian, China 50 G8
Fana, Mali 78 C3
Fandriana, Madag. 85 C8
Fang, Thailand 58 C2
Fang Xian, China 53 A8
Fangchang, China 53 B12
Fangcheng, Guangxi Zhuangzu, China 52 G7
Fangcheng, Henan, China 50 H7
Fangliao, Taiwan 53 F13
Fangshan, China 50 E6
Fangzi, China 51 F10
Fani i Madh →, Albania 39 H3
Fanjiatun, China 51 C13
Fannich, L., U.K. 14 D4
Fannūj, Iran 65 E8
Fanny Bay, Canada 100 D4
Fanø, Denmark 11 J2
Fano, Italy 33 E10
Fanshaw, U.S.A. 100 B2
Fanshi, China 50 E7
Fao = Al Fāw, Iraq 65 D6
Faqirwali, Pakistan 62 E5
Fara in Sabina, Italy 33 F9
Faradje, Zaïre 82 B2
Farafangana, Madag. 85 C8
Farâfra, El Wâhât el-, Egypt 76 B2
Farāh, Afghan. 60 C3
Farāh □, Afghan. 60 C3
Farahalana, Madag. 85 A9
Faraid, Gebel, Egypt 76 C4
Faramana, Burkina Faso 78 C4
Faranah, Guinea 78 C2
Farasān, Jazā'ir, Si. Arabia 68 D3
Farasan Is. = Farasān, Jazā'ir, Si. Arabia 68 D3
Faratsiho, Madag. 85 B8
Fardes →, Spain 29 H1
Fareham, U.K. 13 G6
Farewell, C., N.Z. 87 J4
Farewell C. = Farvel, Kap, Greenland 4 D5
Farghona = Fergana, Uzbekistan 44 E8
Fargo, U.S.A. 108 B6
Fari'a →, Jordan 69 C4
Faribault, U.S.A. 108 C8
Faridkot, India 62 D6
Faridpur, Bangla. 63 H13
Färila, Sweden 10 C9
Farim, Guinea-Biss. 78 C1
Farīmān, Iran 65 C8
Farina, Australia 91 E2
Farinha →, Brazil 122 C2
Fariones, Pta., Canary Is. 36 E6
Fâriskûr, Egypt 76 H7
Farmerville, U.S.A. 109 J8
Farmington, Calif., U.S.A. 112 H6
Farmington, N.H., U.S.A. 107 C13
Farmington, N. Mex., U.S.A. 111 H9
Farmington, Utah, U.S.A. 110 F8
Farmington →, U.S.A. 107 E12
Farmville, U.S.A. 104 G6
Farnborough, U.K. 13 F7
Farne Is., U.K. 12 B6
Farnham, Canada 107 A12
Faro, Brazil 121 D6
Faro, Portugal 31 H3
Fårö, Sweden 9 H15
Faro □, Portugal 31 H2
Faroe Is. = Føroyar, Atl. Oc. 7 C4
Farquhar, C., Australia 89 D1
Farrars Cr. →, Australia 90 D3
Farrāshband, Iran 65 D7
Farrell, U.S.A. 106 E4
Farrell Flat, Australia 91 E2
Farrokhī, Iran 65 C8
Farruch, C., Spain 36 B10
Farrukhabad-cum-Fatehgarh, India 63 F8
Fārs □, Iran 65 D7
Fársala, Greece 39 K5
Farsø, Denmark 11 H3
Farsund, Norway 9 G9
Fartak, Râs, Si. Arabia 64 D2
Fartura, Serra da, Brazil 127 B5
Faru, Nigeria 79 C6
Fārūj, Iran 65 B8
Farum, Denmark 11 J6
Farvel, Kap, Greenland 4 D5
Farwell, U.S.A. 109 H3
Fasā, Iran 65 D7
Fasano, Italy 35 B10
Fashoda, Sudan 77 F3
Fastnet Rock, Ireland 15 E2
Fastov, Ukraine 40 F6
Fatagar, Tanjung, Indonesia 57 E8
Fatehgarh, India 63 F8
Fatehpur, Raj., India 62 F6
Fatehpur, Ut. P., India 63 G9
Fatesh, Russia 41 E9
Fatick, Senegal 78 C1
Fatima, Canada 99 C7
Fátima, Portugal 31 F2
Fatoya, Guinea 78 C3
Faucille, Col de la, France 27 B10
Faulkton, U.S.A. 108 C5
Faulquemont, France 25 C13
Fauquembergues, France 25 B9
Faure I., Australia 89 E1
Făurei, Romania 38 D10
Fauresmith, S. Africa 84 D4
Fauske, Norway 8 C13
Fauvillers, Belgium 17 J7
Favara, Italy 34 E6
Favaritx, C., Spain 36 A11
Favignana, Italy 34 E5
Favignana, I., Italy 34 E5
Favourable Lake, Canada 98 B1
Fawn →, Canada 98 A2
Fawnskin, U.S.A. 113 L10
Faxaflói, Iceland 8 D2
Faya-Largeau, Chad 73 E8
Fayd, Si. Arabia 64 E4
Fayence, France 27 E10
Fayette, Ala., U.S.A. 105 J2
Fayette, Mo., U.S.A. 108 F8
Fayetteville, Ark., U.S.A. 109 G7

Fayetteville, N.C., U.S.A. 105 H6
Fayetteville, Tenn., U.S.A. 105 H2
Fayón, Spain 28 D5
Fazenda Nova, Brazil 123 E1
Fazilka, India 62 D6
Fazilpur, Pakistan 62 E4
Fdérik, Mauritania 74 D2
Feale →, Ireland 15 D2
Fear, C., U.S.A. 105 J7
Feather →, U.S.A. 110 G3
Feather Falls, U.S.A. 112 F5
Featherston, N.Z. 87 J5
Featherstone, Zimbabwe 83 F3
Fécamp, France 24 C7
Fedala = Mohammedia, Morocco 74 B3
Federación, Argentina 126 C4
Fedeshkūh, Iran 65 D7
Fedjadj, Chott el, Tunisia 75 B6
Fehmarn, Germany 18 A7
Fehmarn Bælt, Denmark 18 A7
Fei Xian, China 51 G9
Feijó, Brazil 124 B3
Feilding, N.Z. 87 J5
Feira de Santana, Brazil 123 D4
Feixiang, China 50 F8
Fejø, Denmark 11 K5
Feke, Turkey 66 E6
Felanitx, Spain 36 B10
Feldberg, Baden-W., Germany 19 H3
Feldberg, Mecklenburg-Vorpommern, Germany 18 B9
Feldkirch, Austria 19 H5
Felipe Carrillo Puerto, Mexico 115 D7
Felixlândia, Brazil 123 E3
Felixstowe, U.K. 13 F9
Felletin, France 26 C6
Felton, U.K. 12 B6
Felton, U.S.A. 112 H4
Feltre, Italy 33 B8
Femø, Denmark 11 K5
Femunden, Norway 10 B5
Fen He →, China 50 G6
Fenelon Falls, Canada 106 B6
Feneroa, Ethiopia 77 E4
Feng Xian, Jiangsu, China 50 G9
Feng Xian, Shaanxi, China 50 H4
Fengári, Greece 39 J8
Fengcheng, Jiangxi, China 53 C10
Fengcheng, Liaoning, China 51 D13
Fengdu, China 52 C6
Fengfeng, China 50 F8
Fenggang, China 52 D6
Fenghua, China 53 C13
Fenghuang, China 52 D7
Fenghuangzui, China 52 A7
Fengjie, China 52 B7
Fengkai, China 53 F8
Fengle, China 53 B9
Fengning, China 50 D9
Fengqing, China 52 E2
Fengqiu, China 50 G8
Fengrun, China 51 E10
Fengshan, Guangxi Zhuangzu, China 52 E7
Fengshan, Guangxi Zhuangzu, China 52 E6
Fengtai, Anhui, China 53 A11
Fengtai, Beijing, China 50 E9
Fengxian, China 53 B13
Fengxiang, China 50 G4
Fengxin, China 53 C10
Fengyang, China 51 H9
Fengyi, China 52 E3
Fengzhen, China 50 D7
Fenit, Ireland 15 D2
Fennimore, U.S.A. 108 D9
Feno, C. de, France 27 G12
Fenoarivo Afovoany, Madag. 85 B8
Fenoarivo Atsinanana, Madag. 85 B8
Fens, The, U.K. 12 E8
Fenton, U.S.A. 104 D4
Fenxi, China 50 F6
Fenyang, China 54 C6
Fenyang, Shanxi, China 50 F6
Fenyi, China 53 D10
Feodosiya, Ukraine 42 D6
Fer, C. de, Algeria 75 A6
Ferdows, Iran 65 C8
Fère-Champenoise, France 25 D10
Fère-en-Tardenois, France 25 C10
Ferentino, Italy 34 A6
Ferfer, Somali Rep. 68 F4
Fergana, Uzbekistan 44 E8
Fergus, Canada 98 D3
Fergus Falls, U.S.A. 108 B6
Fériana, Tunisia 75 B6
Feričanci, Croatia 21 K8
Ferkane, Algeria 75 B6
Ferkéssédougou, Ivory C. 78 D3
Ferlach, Austria 21 J4
Ferland, Canada 98 B2
Ferlo, Vallée du, Senegal 78 B2
Fermanagh □, U.K. 15 B4
Fermo, Italy 33 E10
Fermoselle, Spain 30 D4
Fermoy, Ireland 15 D3
Fernán Nuñéz, Spain 31 H6
Fernández, Argentina 126 B3
Fernandina Beach, U.S.A. 105 K5
Fernando de Noronha, Brazil 122 B5
Fernando Póo = Bioko, Eq. Guin. 79 E6
Fernandópolis, Brazil 123 F1
Ferndale, Calif., U.S.A. 110 F1
Ferndale, Wash., U.S.A. 112 B4
Fernie, Canada 100 D5
Fernlees, Australia 90 C4
Fernley, U.S.A. 110 G4
Ferozepore = Firozpur, India 62 D6
Férrai, Greece 39 J9
Ferrandina, Italy 35 B9
Ferrara, Italy 33 D8
Ferrato, C., Italy 34 C2
Ferreira do Alentejo, Portugal 31 G2
Ferreñafe, Peru 124 B2
Ferrerías, Spain 36 B11
Ferret, C., France 26 D2
Ferrette, France 25 E14
Ferriday, U.S.A. 109 K9
Ferrières, France 25 D9
Ferriete, Italy 32 D6
Ferrol = El Ferrol, Spain 30 B2
Ferrol, Pen. de, Peru 124 B2
Ferron, U.S.A. 111 G8
Ferros, Brazil 123 E3
Ferryland, Canada 99 C9
Fertile, U.S.A. 108 B6
Fertília, Italy 34 B1
Fès, Morocco 74 B4
Feschaux, Belgium 17 H5
Feshi, Zaïre 80 F3
Fessenden, U.S.A. 108 B5
Feteşti, Romania 38 E10
Fethiye, Turkey 66 E3
Fetlar, U.K. 14 A8
Feuerthalen, Switz. 23 A7
Feuilles →, Canada 97 C12
Feurs, France 27 C8
Fezzan, Libya 70 D5
Ffestiniog, U.K. 12 E4
Fiambalá, Argentina 126 B2
Fianarantsoa, Madag. 85 C8
Fianarantsoa □, Madag. 85 B8
Fianga, Cameroon 73 G8
Fichtelgebirge, Germany 19 E7
Ficksburg, S. Africa 85 D4
Fidenza, Italy 32 D7
Fiditi, Nigeria 79 D5
Field, Canada 98 C3
Field →, Australia 90 C2
Field I., Australia 88 B5
Fieri, Albania 39 J2
Fiesch, Switz. 22 D6
Fife □, U.K. 14 E5
Fife Ness, U.K. 14 E6
Fifth Cataract, Sudan 76 D3
Figeac, France 26 D6
Figline Valdarno, Italy 33 E8
Figtree, Zimbabwe 83 G2
Figueira Castelo Rodrigo, Portugal 30 E4
Figueira da Foz, Portugal 30 E2
Figueiró dos Vinhos, Portugal 30 F2
Figueras, Spain 28 C7
Figuig, Morocco 75 B4
Fihaonana, Madag. 85 B8
Fiherenana, Madag. 85 B8
Fiherenana →, Madag. 85 C7
Fiji ■, Pac. Oc. 87 C8
Fika, Nigeria 79 C7
Filabres, Sierra de los, Spain 29 H2
Filadelfia, Bolivia 124 C4
Filadélfia, Brazil 122 C2
Filadélfia, Italy 35 D9
Filer, U.S.A. 110 E6
Filey, U.K. 12 C7
Filfla, Malta 37 D1
Filiaşi, Romania 38 E6
Filiátes, Greece 39 K3
Filiatrá, Greece 39 M4
Filicudi, Italy 35 D7
Filiourí →, Greece 39 H8
Filipstad, Sweden 9 G13
Filisur, Switz. 23 C9
Fillmore, Canada 101 D8
Fillmore, Calif., U.S.A. 113 L8
Fillmore, Utah, U.S.A. 111 G7
Filottrano, Italy 33 E10
Filyos, Turkey 42 F5
Finale Lígure, Italy 32 D5
Finale nell' Emília, Italy 33 D8
Fiñana, Spain 29 H2
Finch, Canada 107 A9
Findhorn →, U.K. 14 D5
Findlay, U.S.A. 104 E4
Finger L., Canada 101 C10
Fíngõe, Mozam. 83 E3
Finike, Turkey 66 E4
Finistère □, France 24 D2
Finisterre, Spain 30 C1
Finisterre, C., Spain 30 C1
Finke, Australia 90 D1
Finke →, Australia 91 D2
Finland ■, Europe 9 E19
Finland, G. of, Europe 9 G19
Finlay →, Canada 100 B3
Finley, Australia 91 F4
Finley, U.S.A. 108 B6
Finn →, Ireland 15 B4
Finnigan, Mt., Australia 90 B4
Finniss, C., Australia 91 E1
Finnmark fylke □, Norway 8 B18
Finsteraarhorn, Switz. 22 C6
Finsterwalde, Germany 18 D9
Finsterwolde, Neths. 16 B10
Fiora →, Italy 33 F8
Fiorenzuola d'Arda, Italy 32 D6
Fīq, Syria 69 C4
Firat = Furāt, Nahr al →, Asia 64 D5
Fire River, Canada 98 C3
Firebag →, Canada 101 B6
Firebaugh, U.S.A. 112 J6
Firedrake L., Canada 101 A8
Firenze, Italy 33 E8
Firk →, Iraq 64 D5
Firmi, France 26 D6
Firminy, France 27 C8
Firozabad, India 63 F8
Firozpur, India 62 D6
Fīrūzābād, Iran 65 D7
Fīrūzkūh, Iran 65 C7
Firvale, Canada 100 C3
Fish →, Namibia 84 D2
Fish →, S. Africa 84 E3
Fisher, Australia 89 F5
Fisher B., Canada 101 C9
Fishguard, U.K. 13 F3
Fishing L., Canada 101 C9
Fismes, France 25 C10
Fitchburg, U.S.A. 107 D13
Fitero, Spain 28 C3
Fitri, L., Chad 73 F8
Fitz Roy, Argentina 128 C3
Fitzgerald, Canada 100 B6
Fitzgerald, U.S.A. 105 K4
Fitzmaurice →, Australia 88 B5
Fitzroy →, Queens., Australia 90 C5
Fitzroy →, W. Austral., Australia 88 C3
Fitzroy Crossing, Australia 88 C4
Fitzwilliam I., Canada 106 A3
Fiume = Rijeka, Croatia 33 C11
Fiumefreddo Brúzio, Italy 35 C9
Five Points, U.S.A. 112 J6
Fivizzano, Italy 32 D7
Fizi, Zaïre 82 C2
Fjellerup, Denmark 11 H4
Fjerritslev, Denmark 11 G3
Fkih ben Salah, Morocco 74 B3
Flå, Norway 10 A4
Flagler, U.S.A. 108 F3
Flagstaff, U.S.A. 111 J8
Flaherty I., Canada 98 A4
Flåm, Norway 9 F9
Flambeau →, U.S.A. 108 C9
Flamborough Hd., U.K. 12 C7
Flaming Gorge Dam, U.S.A. 110 F9
Flaming Gorge Reservoir, U.S.A. 110 F9
Flamingo, Teluk, Indonesia 57 F9
Flanders = West-Vlaanderen □, Belgium 17 G2
Flanders = West-Vlaanderen □, Belgium 17 G2
Flandre Occidentale = West-Vlaanderen □, Belgium 17 G2
Flandre Orientale = Oost-Vlaanderen □, Belgium 17 F3
Flandreau, U.S.A. 108 C6
Flanigan, U.S.A. 112 E7
Flannan Is., U.K. 14 C1
Flåsjön, Sweden 8 D13
Flat →, Canada 100 A3
Flat River, U.S.A. 109 G9
Flatey, Barðastrandarsýsla, Iceland 8 C5
Flatey, Suður-þingeyjarsýsla, Iceland 8 D2
Flathead L., U.S.A. 110 C6
Flattery, C., U.S.A. 112 B2
Flattery, C., Australia 90 A4
Flavy-le-Martel, France 25 C10
Flawil, Switz. 23 B8
Flaxton, U.S.A. 108 A3
Fleetwood, U.K. 12 D4
Flekkefjord, Norway 9 G9
Flémalle, Belgium 17 G6
Flemington, U.S.A. 106 E7
Flensborg Fjord, Germany 11 K3
Flensburg, Germany 18 A5
Flers, France 24 D6
Flesherton, Canada 106 B4
Flesko, Tanjung, Indonesia 57 D6
Fleurance, France 26 E4
Fleurier, Switz. 22 C3
Fleurus, Belgium 17 H5
Flevoland □, Neths. 16 C7
Flims, Switz. 23 C8
Flin Flon, Canada 101 C8
Flinders →, Australia 90 B3
Flinders B., Australia 89 F2
Flinders Group, Australia 90 A3
Flinders I., Australia 90 F4
Flinders Ras., Australia 91 E2
Flinders Reefs, Australia 90 B4
Flint, U.K. 12 D4
Flint, U.S.A. 104 D4
Flint →, U.S.A. 105 K3
Flint I., Kiribati 93 J12
Flinton, Australia 91 D4
Flix, Spain 28 D5
Flixecourt, France 25 B9
Flobecq, Belgium 17 G3
Flodden, U.K. 12 B5
Floodwood, U.S.A. 108 B8
Flora, Norway 10 A5
Flora, U.S.A. 104 F1
Florac, France 26 D7
Florala, U.S.A. 105 K2
Florânia, Brazil 122 C4
Floreffe, Belgium 17 H5
Florence = Firenze, Italy 33 E8
Florence, Ala., U.S.A. 105 H2
Florence, Ariz., U.S.A. 111 K8
Florence, Colo., U.S.A. 108 F2
Florence, Oreg., U.S.A. 110 E1
Florence, S.C., U.S.A. 105 H6
Florence, L., Australia 91 D2
Florennes, Belgium 17 H5
Florensac, France 26 E7
Florenville, Belgium 17 J6
Flores, Brazil 122 C4
Flores, Guatemala 116 C2
Flores, Indonesia 57 F6
Flores I., Canada 100 D3
Flores Sea, Indonesia 57 F6
Floresta, Brazil 122 C4
Floresville, U.S.A. 109 L5
Floriano, Brazil 122 C3
Florianópolis, Brazil 127 B6
Florida, Cuba 116 B4
Florida, Uruguay 127 C4
Florida □, U.S.A. 105 L5
Florida, Straits of, U.S.A. 116 B3
Florida B., U.S.A. 116 A3
Florida Keys, U.S.A. 103 F10
Florídia, Italy 35 E8
Floridsdorf, Austria 21 G6
Flórina, Greece 39 J4
Florø, Norway 9 F8
Flower Station, Canada 107 A8
Flower's Cove, Canada 99 B8
Floydada, U.S.A. 109 J4
Fluk, Indonesia 57 E7
Flumen →, Spain 28 D4
Flumendosa →, Italy 34 C2
Fluminimaggiore, Italy 34 C1
Flushing = Vlissingen, Neths. 17 F3
Fluviá →, Spain 28 C8
Flying Fish, C., Antarctica 5 D15
Foam Lake, Canada 101 C8
Foča, Bos.-H. 21 M8
Foça, Turkey 66 D2
Focşani, Romania 38 D10
Fogang, China 53 F9
Foggaret el Arab, Algeria 75 C5
Foggaret ez Zoua, Algeria 75 C5
Fóggia, Italy 35 A8
Foggo, Nigeria 79 C6
Foglia →, Italy 33 E9
Fogo, Canada 99 C9
Fogo I., Canada 99 C9
Fohnsdorf, Austria 21 H4
Föhr, Germany 18 A4
Foia, Portugal 31 H2
Foix, France 26 F5
Fokino, Russia 40 E9
Folda, Nord-Trøndelag, Norway 8 D11
Folda, Nordland, Norway 8 C13
Foleyet, Canada 98 C3
Folgefonn, Norway 9 F9
Foligno, Italy 33 F9
Folkestone, U.K. 13 F9
Folkston, U.S.A. 105 K5
Follett, U.S.A. 109 G4
Follónica, Italy 32 F7
Follónica, G. di, Italy 32 F7
Folsom Res., U.S.A. 112 G5
Fond-du-Lac, Canada 101 B7
Fond du Lac, U.S.A. 108 D10
Fond-du-Lac →, Canada 101 B7
Fonda, U.S.A. 107 D10
Fondi, Italy 34 A6
Fonfría, Spain 30 D4
Fongen, Norway 10 A5
Fonni, Italy 34 B2
Fonsagrada, Spain 30 B3
Fonseca, G. de, Cent. Amer. 116 D2
Fontaine-Française, France 25 E12
Fontainebleau, France 25 D9
Fontana, L., Argentina 128 B2
Fontas →, Canada 100 B4
Fonte Boa, Brazil 120 D4
Fontem, Cameroon 79 D6
Fontenay-le-Comte, France 26 B3
Fontur, Iceland 8 C6
Fonyód, Hungary 21 J7
Foochow = Fuzhou, China 53 D12
Foping, China 50 H4
Foppiano, Italy 32 B5
Forbach, France 25 C13
Forbes, Australia 91 E4
Forbesganj, India 63 F12
Forcados, Nigeria 79 D6
Forcados →, Nigeria 79 D6
Forcall →, Spain 28 E4
Forcalquier, France 27 E9
Forchheim, Germany 19 F7
Forclaz, Col de la, Switz. 22 D4
Ford City, Calif., U.S.A. 113 K7
Ford City, Pa., U.S.A. 106 F5
Ford's Bridge, Australia 91 D4
Fordyce, U.S.A. 109 J8
Forécariah, Guinea 78 D2
Forel, Mt., Greenland 4 C6
Foremost, Canada 100 D6
Forenza, Italy 35 B8
Forest, Belgium 17 G4
Forest, Canada 106 C3
Forest, U.S.A. 109 J10
Forest City, Iowa, U.S.A. 108 D8
Forest City, N.C., U.S.A. 105 H5
Forest City, Pa., U.S.A. 107 E9
Forest Grove, U.S.A. 112 E3
Forestburg, Canada 100 C6
Foresthill, U.S.A. 112 F6
Forestier Pen., Australia 90 G4
Forestville, Canada 99 C6
Forestville, Calif., U.S.A. 112 G4
Forestville, Wis., U.S.A. 104 C2
Forez, Mts. du, France 26 C7
Forfar, U.K. 14 E6
Forges-les-Eaux, France 25 C8
Forks, U.S.A. 112 C2
Forlì, Italy 33 D9
Forman, U.S.A. 108 B6
Formazza, Italy 32 B5
Formby Pt., U.K. 12 D4
Formentera, Spain 36 C7
Formentor, C. de, Spain 36 B10
Fórmia, Italy 34 A6
Formiga, Brazil 123 F2
Formigine, Italy 32 D7
Formiguères, France 26 F6
Formosa = Taiwan ■, Asia 53 F13
Formosa, Argentina 126 B4
Formosa, Brazil 123 E2
Formosa □, Argentina 126 B3
Formosa, Serra, Brazil 125 C6
Formosa Bay, Kenya 82 C5
Formosa Strait, Asia 53
Formoso →, Brazil 123 D2
Fornells, Spain 36 A11
Fornos de Algodres, Portugal 30 E3
Fornovo di Taro, Italy 32 D7
Føroyar, Atl. Oc. 7 C4
Forres, U.K. 14 D5
Forrest, Vic., Australia 91 F3
Forrest, W. Austral., Australia 89 F4
Forrest, Mt., Australia 89 D4
Forrest City, U.S.A. 109 H9
Forrières, Belgium 17 H6
Forsa, Sweden 10 C10
Forsayth, Australia 90 B3
Forsmo, Sweden 10 A11
Forst, Germany 18 D10
Forster, Australia 91 E5
Forsyth, Ga., U.S.A. 105 J4
Forsyth, Mont., U.S.A. 110 C10
Fort Albany, Canada 98 B3
Fort Apache, U.S.A. 111 K9
Fort Assiniboine, Canada 100 C6
Fort Augustus, U.K. 14 D4
Fort Beaufort, S. Africa 84 E4
Fort Benton, U.S.A. 110 C8
Fort Bragg, U.S.A. 110 G2
Fort Bridger, U.S.A. 110 F8
Fort Chipewyan, Canada 101 B6
Fort Collins, U.S.A. 108 E2
Fort-Coulonge, Canada 98 C4
Fort Davis, U.S.A. 109 K3
Fort-de-France, Martinique 117 D7
Fort de Possel = Possel, C.A.R. 80 C3
Fort Defiance, U.S.A. 111 J9
Fort Dodge, U.S.A. 108 D7
Fort Edward, U.S.A. 107 C11
Fort Frances, Canada 101 D10
Fort Franklin, Canada 96 B7
Fort Garland, U.S.A. 111 H11
Fort George, Canada 98 B4
Fort Good-Hope, Canada 96 B7
Fort Hancock, U.S.A. 111 L11
Fort Hertz = Putao, Burma 61 F20
Fort Hope, Canada 98 B2
Fort Irwin, U.S.A. 113 K10
Fort Jameson = Chipata, Zambia 83 E3
Fort Kent, U.S.A. 99 C6
Fort Klamath, U.S.A. 110 E3
Fort Lallemand, Algeria 75 B6
Fort-Lamy = Ndjamena, Chad 73 F7
Fort Laramie, U.S.A. 108 D2
Fort Lauderdale, U.S.A. 105 M5
Fort Liard, Canada 100 A4
Fort Liberté, Haiti 117 C5
Fort Lupton, U.S.A. 108 E2
Fort Mackay, Canada 100 B6
Fort McKenzie, Canada 99 A6
Fort Macleod, Canada 100 D6
Fort MacMahon, Algeria 75 C5
Fort McMurray, Canada 100 B6
Fort McPherson, Canada 96 B6
Fort Madison, U.S.A. 108 E9
Fort Meade, U.S.A. 105 M5
Fort Miribel, Algeria 75 C5
Fort Morgan, U.S.A. 108 E3
Fort Myers, U.S.A. 105 M5
Fort Nelson, Canada 100 B4
Fort Nelson →, Canada 100 B4

Fort Norman, *Canada* 96 B7
Fort Payne, *U.S.A.* 105 H3
Fort Peck, *U.S.A.* 110 B10
Fort Peck Dam, *U.S.A.* 110 C10
Fort Peck L., *U.S.A.* 110 C10
Fort Pierce, *U.S.A.* 105 M5
Fort Pierre, *U.S.A.* 108 C4
Fort Pierre Bordes = Ti-n-Zaouaténe, *Algeria* 75 E5
Fort Plain, *U.S.A.* 107 D10
Fort Portal, *Uganda* 82 B3
Fort Providence, *Canada* 100 A5
Fort Qu'Appelle, *Canada* 101 C8
Fort Resolution, *Canada* 100 A6
Fort Rixon, *Zimbabwe* 83 G2
Fort Rosebery = Mansa, *Zambia* 83 E2
Fort Ross, *U.S.A.* 112 G3
Fort Rupert, *Canada* 98 B4
Fort Saint, *Tunisia* 75 B6
Fort St. James, *Canada* 100 C4
Fort St. John, *Canada* 100 B4
Fort Sandeman, *Pakistan* 62 D3
Fort Saskatchewan, *Canada* 100 C6
Fort Scott, *U.S.A.* 109 G7
Fort Severn, *Canada* 98 A2
Fort Shevchenko, *Kazakhstan* 43 E14
Fort-Sibut, *C.A.R.* 73 G8
Fort Simpson, *Canada* 100 A4
Fort Smith, *Canada* 100 B6
Fort Smith, *U.S.A.* 109 H7
Fort Stanton, *U.S.A.* 111 K11
Fort Stockton, *U.S.A.* 109 K3
Fort Sumner, *U.S.A.* 109 H2
Fort Trinquet = Bir Mogrein, *Mauritania* 74 C2
Fort Valley, *U.S.A.* 105 J4
Fort Vermilion, *Canada* 100 B5
Fort Walton Beach, *U.S.A.* 105 K2
Fort Wayne, *U.S.A.* 104 E3
Fort William, *U.K.* 14 E3
Fort Worth, *U.S.A.* 109 J6
Fort Yates, *U.S.A.* 108 B4
Fort Yukon, *U.S.A.* 96 B5
Fortaleza, *Bolivia* 124 C4
Fortaleza, *Brazil* 122 B4
Forteau, *Canada* 99 B8
Forth →, *U.K.* 14 E5
Forth, Firth of, *U.K.* 14 E6
Forthassa Rharbia, *Algeria* 75 B4
Fortín Coronel Eugenio Garay, *Paraguay* 125 E5
Fortín Garrapatal, *Paraguay* 125 E5
Fortín General Pando, *Paraguay* 125 D6
Fortín Madrejón, *Paraguay* 125 E6
Fortín Uno, *Argentina* 128 A3
Fortore →, *Italy* 33 G12
Fortrose, *U.K.* 14 D4
Fortuna, *Spain* 29 G3
Fortuna, *Calif., U.S.A.* 110 F1
Fortuna, *N. Dak., U.S.A.* 108 A3
Fortune B., *Canada* 99 C8
Fos-sur-Mer, *France* 27 E8
Foshan, *China* 53 F9
Fossacesia, *Italy* 33 F11
Fossano, *Italy* 32 D4
Fosses-la-Ville, *Belgium* 17 H5
Fossil, *U.S.A.* 110 D3
Fossilbrook, *Australia* 90 B3
Fossombrone, *Italy* 33 E9
Fosston, *U.S.A.* 108 B7
Foster, *Canada* 107 A12
Foster →, *Canada* 101 B7
Fosters Ra., *Australia* 90 C1
Fostoria, *U.S.A.* 104 E4
Fougamou, *Gabon* 80 E2
Fougères, *France* 24 D5
Foul Pt., *Sri Lanka* 60 Q12
Foula, *U.K.* 14 A6
Foulness I., *U.K.* 13 F8
Foulpointe, *Madag.* 85 B8
Foum Assaka, *Morocco* 74 C2
Foum Zguid, *Morocco* 74 B3
Foumban, *Cameroon* 79 D7
Foundiougne, *Senegal* 78 C1
Fountain, *Colo., U.S.A.* 108 F2
Fountain, *Utah, U.S.A.* 110 G8
Fountain Springs, *U.S.A.* 113 K8
Fourchambault, *France* 25 E10
Fourchu, *Canada* 99 C7
Fouriesburg, *S. Africa* 84 D4
Fourmies, *France* 25 B11
Foúrnoi, *Greece* 39 M9
Fours, *France* 25 F10
Fouta Djalon, *Guinea* 78 C2
Foux, Cap-à-, *Haiti* 117 C5
Foveaux Str., *N.Z.* 87 M2
Fowey, *U.K.* 13 G3
Fowler, *Calif., U.S.A.* 111 H4
Fowler, *Colo., U.S.A.* 108 F2
Fowler, *Kans., U.S.A.* 109 G4
Fowlers B., *Australia* 89 F5
Fowlerton, *U.S.A.* 109 L5
Fox →, *Canada* 101 B10
Fox Valley, *Canada* 101 C7
Foxe Basin, *Canada* 97 B12
Foxe Chan., *Canada* 97 B11
Foxe Pen., *Canada* 97 B12
Foxhol, *Neths.* 16 B9
Foxpark, *U.S.A.* 110 F10
Foxton, *N.Z.* 87 J5
Foyle, Lough, *U.K.* 15 A4
Foynes, *Ireland* 15 D2
Foz, *Spain* 30 B3
Fóz do Cunene, *Angola* 84 B1
Foz do Gregório, *Brazil* 124 B3
Foz do Iguaçu, *Brazil* 127 B5
Foz do Riosinho, *Brazil* 124 B3
Frackville, *U.S.A.* 107 F8
Fraga, *Spain* 28 D5
Fraire, *Belgium* 17 H5
Frameries, *Belgium* 17 H3
Framingham, *U.S.A.* 107 D13
Franca, *Brazil* 123 F2
Francavilla al Mare, *Italy* 33 F11
Francavilla Fontana, *Italy* 35 B10
France ■, *Europe* 7 F6
Frances, *Australia* 91 F3
Frances →, *Canada* 100 A3
Frances L., *Canada* 100 A3
Francés Viejo, C., *Dom. Rep.* 117 C6
Franceville, *Gabon* 80 E2
Franche-Comté, *France* 25 F12
Franches Montagnes, *Switz.* 22 B4
Francisco de Orellana, *Ecuador* 120 D2
Francisco I. Madero, *Coahuila, Mexico* 114 B4
Francisco I. Madero, *Durango, Mexico* 114 C4
Francisco Sá, *Brazil* 123 E3
Francistown, *Botswana* 85 C4
Francofonte, *Italy* 35 E7
François, *Canada* 99 C8
François L., *Canada* 100 C3
Francorchamps, *Belgium* 17 H7
Franeker, *Neths.* 16 B7
Frankado, *Djibouti* 77 E5
Frankenberg, *Germany* 18 D4
Frankenthal, *Germany* 19 F4
Frankenwald, *Germany* 19 E7
Frankfort, *S. Africa* 85 D4
Frankfort, *Ind., U.S.A.* 104 E2
Frankfort, *Kans., U.S.A.* 108 F6
Frankfort, *Ky., U.S.A.* 104 F3
Frankfort, *Mich., U.S.A.* 104 C2
Frankfurt am Main, *Germany* 19 E4
Frankfurt an der Oder, *Germany* 18 C10
Fränkische Alb, *Germany* 19 F7
Fränkische Rezal →, *Germany* 19 F7
Fränkische Saale →, *Germany* 19 E5
Fränkische Schweiz, *Germany* 19 F7
Frankland →, *Australia* 89 G2
Franklin, *Ky., U.S.A.* 105 G2
Franklin, *La., U.S.A.* 109 L9
Franklin, *Mass., U.S.A.* 107 D13
Franklin, *N.H., U.S.A.* 107 C13
Franklin, *Nebr., U.S.A.* 108 E5
Franklin, *Pa., U.S.A.* 106 E5
Franklin, *Tenn., U.S.A.* 105 H2
Franklin, *Va., U.S.A.* 105 G7
Franklin, *W. Va., U.S.A.* 104 F6
Franklin B., *Canada* 96 B7
Franklin D. Roosevelt L., *U.S.A.* 110 B4
Franklin I., *Antarctica* 5 D11
Franklin L., *U.S.A.* 110 F6
Franklin Mts., *Canada* 96 B7
Franklin Str., *Canada* 96 A10
Franklinton, *U.S.A.* 109 K9
Franklinville, *U.S.A.* 106 D6
Franks Pk., *U.S.A.* 110 E9
Frankston, *Australia* 91 F4
Fränsta, *Sweden* 10 B10
Frantsa Iosifa, Zemlya, *Russia* 44 A6
Franz, *Canada* 98 C3
Franz Josef Land = Frantsa Iosifa, Zemlya, *Russia* 44 A6
Franzburg, *Germany* 18 A8
Frascati, *Italy* 34 A5
Fraser →, *B.C., Canada* 100 D4
Fraser →, *Nfld., Canada* 99 A7
Fraser, Mt., *Australia* 89 E2
Fraser I., *Australia* 91 D5
Fraser Lake, *Canada* 100 C4
Fraserburg, *S. Africa* 84 E3
Fraserburgh, *U.K.* 14 D6
Fraserdale, *Canada* 98 C3
Frasne, *France* 25 F13
Frauenfeld, *Switz.* 23 A7
Fray Bentos, *Uruguay* 126 C4
Frazier Downs, *Australia* 88 C3
Frechilla, *Spain* 30 C6
Fredericia, *Denmark* 11 J3
Frederick, *Md., U.S.A.* 104 F7
Frederick, *Okla., U.S.A.* 109 H5
Frederick, *S. Dak., U.S.A.* 108 C5
Frederick Sd., *U.S.A.* 100 B2
Fredericksburg, *Tex., U.S.A.* 109 K5
Fredericksburg, *Va., U.S.A.* 104 F7
Fredericktown, *U.S.A.* 109 G9
Frederico I. Madero, Presa, *Mexico* 114 B3
Fredericton, *Canada* 99 C6
Fredericton Junc., *Canada* 99 C6
Frederikshåb, *Greenland* 4 C5
Frederikshavn, *Denmark* 11 G4
Frederikssund, *Denmark* 11 J6
Frederiksted, *Virgin Is.* 117 C7
Fredonia, *Ariz., U.S.A.* 111 H7
Fredonia, *Kans., U.S.A.* 109 G7
Fredonia, *N.Y., U.S.A.* 106 D5
Fredrikstad, *Norway* 10 E4
Freehold, *U.S.A.* 107 F10
Freel Peak, *U.S.A.* 112 G7
Freeland, *U.S.A.* 107 E9
Freels, C., *Canada* 99 C9
Freeman, *Calif., U.S.A.* 113 K9
Freeman, *S. Dak., U.S.A.* 108 D6
Freeport, *Bahamas* 116 A4
Freeport, *Canada* 99 D6
Freeport, *Ill., U.S.A.* 108 D10
Freeport, *N.Y., U.S.A.* 107 F11
Freeport, *Tex., U.S.A.* 109 L7
Freetown, *S. Leone* 78 D2
Frégate, L., *Canada* 98 B5
Fregenal de la Sierra, *Spain* 31 G4
Fregene, *Italy* 34 A5
Fréhel, C., *France* 24 D4
Freiberg, *Germany* 18 E9
Freibourg = Fribourg, *Switz.* 22 C4
Freiburg, *Baden-W., Germany* 19 H3
Freiburg, *Niedersachsen, Germany* 18 B5
Freiburger Alpen, *Switz.* 22 C4
Freire, *Chile* 128 A2
Freirina, *Chile* 126 B1
Freising, *Germany* 19 G7
Freistadt, *Austria* 20 G4
Freital, *Germany* 18 E9
Fréjus, *France* 27 E10
Fremantle, *Australia* 89 F2
Fremont, *Calif., U.S.A.* 111 H2
Fremont, *Mich., U.S.A.* 104 D3
Fremont, *Nebr., U.S.A.* 108 E6
Fremont, *Ohio, U.S.A.* 104 E4
Fremont →, *U.S.A.* 111 G8
Fremont L., *U.S.A.* 110 E9
French Camp, *U.S.A.* 112 H5
French Creek →, *U.S.A.* 106 E5
French Guiana ■, *S. Amer.* 121 C7
French Pass, *N.Z.* 87 J4
French Polynesia ■, *Pac. Oc.* 93 J13
French Terr. of Afars & Issas = Djibouti ■, *Africa* 68 E3
Frenchglen, *U.S.A.* 110 E4
Frenchman Butte, *Canada* 101 C7
Frenchman Cr. →, *Mont., U.S.A.* 110 B10
Frenchman Cr. →, *Nebr., U.S.A.* 108 E4
Frenda, *Algeria* 75 A5
Fresco →, *Brazil* 125 B7
Freshfield, C., *Antarctica* 5 C10
Fresnay-sur-Sarthe, *France* 24 D7
Fresnillo, *Mexico* 114 C4
Fresno, *U.S.A.* 111 H4
Fresno Alhandiga, *Spain* 30 E5
Fresno Reservoir, *U.S.A.* 110 B9
Freudenstadt, *Germany* 19 G4
Freux, *Belgium* 17 J6
Frévent, *France* 25 B9
Frew →, *Australia* 90 C2
Frewena, *Australia* 90 B2
Freycinet Pen., *Australia* 90 G4
Freyming-Merlebach, *France* 25 C13
Freyung, *Germany* 19 G9
Fria, *Guinea* 78 C2
Fria, C., *Namibia* 84 B1
Friant, *U.S.A.* 112 J7
Frías, *Argentina* 126 B2
Fribourg, *Switz.* 22 C4
Fribourg □, *Switz.* 22 C4
Frick, *Switz.* 22 A6
Friday Harbor, *U.S.A.* 112 B3
Friedberg, *Bayern, Germany* 19 G6
Friedberg, *Hessen, Germany* 19 E4
Friedland, *Germany* 18 B9
Friedrichshafen, *Germany* 19 H5
Friedrichskoog, *Germany* 18 A4
Friedrichstadt, *Germany* 18 A5
Friendly Is. = Tonga ■, *Pac. Oc.* 87 D11
Friesack, *Germany* 18 C8
Friesche Wad, *Neths.* 16 B7
Friesland □, *Neths.* 16 B7
Friesoythe, *Germany* 18 B3
Frillesås, *Sweden* 11 G6
Frio →, *U.S.A.* 109 L5
Friona, *U.S.A.* 109 H3
Frisian Is., *Europe* 18 B2
Fristad, *Sweden* 11 G7
Fritch, *U.S.A.* 109 H4
Fritsla, *Sweden* 11 G6
Fritzlar, *Germany* 18 D5
Friuli-Venezia Giulia □, *Italy* 33 B10
Frobisher B., *Canada* 97 B13
Frobisher Bay = Iqaluit, *Canada* 97 B13
Frobisher L., *Canada* 101 B7
Frohavet, *Norway* 8 E10
Froid, *U.S.A.* 108 A2
Froid-Chapelle, *Belgium* 17 H4
Frolovo, *Russia* 43 B10
Fromberg, *U.S.A.* 110 D9
Frome, *U.K.* 13 F5
Frome, L., *Australia* 91 E2
Frome Downs, *Australia* 91 E2
Frómista, *Spain* 30 C6
Front Range, *U.S.A.* 110 G11
Front Royal, *U.S.A.* 104 F6
Fronteira, *Portugal* 31 F3
Fronteiras, *Brazil* 122 C3
Frontera, *Canary Is.* 36 G2
Frontera, *Mexico* 115 D6
Frontignan, *France* 26 E7
Frosinone, *Italy* 34 A6
Frosolone, *Italy* 35 A7
Frostburg, *U.S.A.* 104 F6
Frostisen, *Norway* 8 B14
Frouard, *France* 25 D13
Frøya, *Norway* 8 E10
Fruges, *France* 25 B9
Frumoasa, *Romania* 38 C8
Frunze = Bishkek, *Kirghizia* 44 E8
Frutal, *Brazil* 123 F2
Frutigen, *Switz.* 22 C5
Frýdek-Místek, *Czech.* 20 F8
Frýdlant, *Czech.* 20 E5
Fu Jiang →, *China* 52 C6
Fu Xian, *Liaoning, China* 51 E11
Fu Xian, *Shaanxi, China* 50 F5
Fu'an, *China* 53 D12
Fubian, *China* 52 B4
Fucécchio, *Italy* 32 E7
Fucheng, *China* 50 F9
Fuchou = Fuzhou, *China* 53 D12
Fuchū, *Japan* 49 G6
Fuchuan, *China* 53 E8
Fuchun Jiang →, *China* 53 B13
Fúcino, Conca del, *Italy* 33 F10
Fuding, *China* 53 D13
Fuencaliente, *Canary Is.* 36 F2
Fuencaliente, *Spain* 31 G6
Fuencaliente, Pta., *Canary Is.* 36 F2
Fuengirola, *Spain* 31 J6
Fuente Alamo, *Albacete, Spain* 29 G3
Fuente Álamo, *Murcia, Spain* 29 H3
Fuente de Cantos, *Spain* 31 G4
Fuente del Maestre, *Spain* 31 G4
Fuente el Fresno, *Spain* 31 F7
Fuente Ovejuna, *Spain* 31 G5
Fuentes de Andalucía, *Spain* 31 H5
Fuentes de Ebro, *Spain* 28 D4
Fuentes de León, *Spain* 31 G4
Fuentes de Oñoro, *Spain* 30 E4
Fuentesaúco, *Spain* 30 D5
Fuerte →, *Mexico* 114 B3
Fuerte Olimpo, *Paraguay* 126 A4
Fuerteventura, *Canary Is.* 36 F6
Fufeng, *China* 50 G4
Fuga I., *Phil.* 55 B4
Fugløysund, *Norway* 8 A16
Fugong, *China* 52 D2
Fugou, *China* 50 G8
Fugu, *China* 50 E6
Fuhai, *China* 54 B3
Fuḥaymī, *Iraq* 64 C4
Fuji, *Japan* 49 G9
Fuji-San, *Japan* 49 G9
Fuji-yoshida, *Japan* 49 G9
Fujian □, *China* 53 E12
Fujinomiya, *Japan* 49 G9
Fujisawa, *Japan* 49 G9
Fukien = Fujian □, *China* 53 E12
Fukuchiyama, *Japan* 49 G7
Fukue-Shima, *Japan* 49 H4
Fukui, *Japan* 49 F8
Fukui □, *Japan* 49 G8
Fukuoka, *Japan* 49 H5
Fukuoka □, *Japan* 49 H5
Fukushima, *Japan* 48 F10
Fukushima □, *Japan* 48 F10
Fukuyama, *Japan* 49 G6
Fulda, *Germany* 18 E5
Fulda →, *Germany* 18 D5
Fuling, *China* 52 C6
Fullerton, *Calif., U.S.A.* 113 M9
Fullerton, *Nebr., U.S.A.* 108 E5
Fulongquan, *China* 51 B13
Fulton, *Mo., U.S.A.* 108 F9
Fulton, *N.Y., U.S.A.* 107 C8
Fulton, *Tenn., U.S.A.* 105 G1
Fuluälven →, *Sweden* 10 C7
Fulufjället, *Sweden* 10 C6
Fumay, *France* 25 C11
Fumel, *France* 26 D4
Fumin, *China* 52 E4
Funabashi, *Japan* 49 G10
Funchal, *Madeira* 36 D3
Fundación, *Colombia* 120 A3
Fundão, *Brazil* 123 E3
Fundão, *Portugal* 30 E3
Fundy, B. of, *Canada* 99 D6
Funing, *Hebei, China* 51 E10
Funing, *Jiangsu, China* 51 H10
Funing, *Yunnan, China* 52 F5
Funiu Shan, *China* 50 H7
Funsi, *Ghana* 78 C4
Funtua, *Nigeria* 79 C6
Fuping, *Hebei, China* 50 E8
Fuping, *Shaanxi, China* 50 G5
Fuqing, *China* 53 E12
Fuquan, *China* 52 D6
Fur, *Denmark* 11 H3
Furano, *Japan* 48 C11
Furāt, Nahr al →, *Asia* 64 D5
Fūrg, *Iran* 65 D7
Furkapass, *Switz.* 23 C7
Furmanov, *Russia* 41 C12
Furmanovo, *Kazakhstan* 43 B13
Furnás, *Spain* 36 B8
Furnas, Reprêsa de, *Brazil* 123 F2
Furneaux Group, *Australia* 90 G4
Furness, *U.K.* 12 C4
Furqlus, *Syria* 69 A6
Fürstenau, *Germany* 18 C3
Fürstenberg, *Germany* 18 B9
Fürstenfeld, *Austria* 21 H6
Fürstenfeldbruck, *Germany* 19 G7
Fürstenwalde, *Germany* 18 C10
Fürth, *Germany* 19 F6
Furth im Wald, *Germany* 19 F8
Furtwangen, *Germany* 19 G4
Furukawa, *Japan* 48 E10
Furusund, *Sweden* 10 E12
Fury and Hecla Str., *Canada* 97 B11
Fusagasuga, *Colombia* 120 C3
Fuscaldo, *Italy* 35 C9
Fushan, *Shandong, China* 51 F11
Fushan, *Shanxi, China* 50 G6
Fushun, *Liaoning, China* 51 D12
Fushun, *Sichuan, China* 52 C5
Fusio, *Switz.* 23 D7
Fusong, *China* 51 C14
Füssen, *Germany* 19 H6
Fusui, *China* 52 F6
Futrono, *Chile* 128 B2
Futuna, *Wall. & F. Is.* 87 B8
Fuwa, *Egypt* 76 H7
Fuxin, *China* 51 C11
Fuyang, *Anhui, China* 50 H8
Fuyang, *Zhejiang, China* 53 B12
Fuyang He →, *China* 50 E9
Fuying Dao, *China* 53 D13
Fuyu, *China* 51 B13
Fuyuan, *Heilongjiang, China* 54 B8
Fuyuan, *Yunnan, China* 52 E5
Fuzhou, *China* 53 D12
Fylde, *U.K.* 12 D5
Fyn, *Denmark* 11 J4
Fyne, L., *U.K.* 14 F3
Fyns Amtskommune □, *Denmark* 11 J4
Fyresvatn, *Norway* 10 E2

G

Gaanda, *Nigeria* 79 C7
Gabarin, *Nigeria* 79 C7
Gabas →, *France* 26 E3
Gabela, *Angola* 80 G2
Gabès, *Tunisia* 75 B7
Gabès, G. de, *Tunisia* 75 B7
Gabgaba, W. →, *Egypt* 76 C3
Gabon ■, *Africa* 80 E2
Gaborone, *Botswana* 84 C4
Gabriels, *U.S.A.* 107 B10
Gābrīk, *Iran* 65 E8
Gabrovo, *Bulgaria* 38 G8
Gacé, *France* 24 D7
Gāch Sār, *Iran* 65 B6
Gachsārān, *Iran* 65 D6
Gacko, *Bos.-H.* 21 M8
Gadag, *India* 60 M9
Gadamai, *Sudan* 77 D4
Gadap, *Pakistan* 62 G2
Gadarwara, *India* 63 H8
Gadebusch, *Germany* 18 B7
Gadein, *Sudan* 77 F2
Gadhada, *India* 62 J4
Gadmen, *Switz.* 23 C6
Gádor, Sierra de, *Spain* 29 J2
Gadsden, *Ala., U.S.A.* 105 H2
Gadsden, *Ariz., U.S.A.* 111 K6
Gadwal, *India* 60 L10
Gadyach, *Ukraine* 40 F9
Găeşti, *Romania* 38 E8
Gaeta, *Italy* 34 A6
Gaeta, G. di, *Italy* 34 A6
Gaffney, *U.S.A.* 105 H5
Gafsa, *Tunisia* 75 B6
Gagarin = Gzhatsk, *Russia* 40 D9
Gagetown, *Canada* 99 C6
Gagino, *Russia* 41 D14
Gagliano del Capo, *Italy* 35 C11
Gagnoa, *Ivory C.* 78 D3
Gagnon, *Canada* 99 B6
Gagnon, L., *Canada* 101 A6
Gagra, *Georgia* 43 E9
Gahini, *Rwanda* 82 C3
Gahmar, *India* 63 G10
Gai Xian, *China* 51 D12
Gaïdhouronísi, *Greece* 37 E7
Gail, *U.S.A.* 109 J4
Gail →, *Austria* 21 J3
Gaillac, *France* 26 E5
Gaillon, *France* 24 C8
Gaimán, *Argentina* 128 B3
Gaines, *U.S.A.* 106 E7
Gainesville, *Fla., U.S.A.* 105 L4
Gainesville, *Ga., U.S.A.* 105 H4
Gainesville, *Mo., U.S.A.* 109 G8
Gainesville, *Tex., U.S.A.* 109 J6
Gainsborough, *U.K.* 12 D7

Gairdner, L., *Australia* 91 E2
Gairloch, L., *U.K.* 14 D3
Gais, *Switz.* 23 B8
Gakuch, *Pakistan* 63 A5
Galán, Cerro, *Argentina* 126 B2
Galana →, *Kenya* 82 C5
Galangue, *Angola* 81 G3
Galápagos, *Pac. Oc.* 93 H18
Galashiels, *U.K.* 14 F6
Galaţi, *Romania* 38 D11
Galatia, *Turkey* 66 D5
Galatina, *Italy* 35 B11
Galátone, *Italy* 35 B11
Galax, *U.S.A.* 105 G5
Galaxídhion, *Greece* 39 L5
Galbraith, *Australia* 90 B3
Galcaio, *Somali Rep.* 68 F4
Galdhøpiggen, *Norway* 10 C2
Galeana, *Mexico* 114 C4
Galela, *Indonesia* 57 D7
Galera, *Spain* 29 H2
Galera, Pta., *Chile* 128 A2
Galera Point, *Trin. & Tob.* 117 D7
Galesburg, *U.S.A.* 108 E9
Galeton, *U.S.A.* 106 E7
Galheirão →, *Brazil* 123 D2
Galheiros, *Brazil* 123 D2
Gali, *Georgia* 43 E9
Galich, *Russia* 41 B13
Galiche, *Bulgaria* 38 F6
Galicia □, *Spain* 30 C3
Galilee = Hagalil, *Israel* 69 C4
Galilee, L., *Australia* 90 C4
Galilee, Sea of = Yam Kinneret, *Israel* 69 C4
Galinoporni, *Cyprus* 37 D13
Galion, *U.S.A.* 106 F2
Galite, Is. de la, *Tunisia* 75 A6
Galiuro Mts., *U.S.A.* 111 K8
Gallabat, *Sudan* 77 E4
Gallardon, *France* 25 D8
Gallarte, *Italy* 32 C5
Gallatin, *U.S.A.* 105 G2
Galle, *Sri Lanka* 60 R12
Gállego →, *Spain* 28 D4
Gallegos →, *Argentina* 128 D3
Galley Hd., *Ireland* 15 E3
Galliate, *Italy* 32 C5
Gallinas, Pta., *Colombia* 120 A3
Gallipoli = Gelibolu, *Turkey* 39 J9
Gallípoli, *Italy* 35 B11
Gallipolis, *U.S.A.* 104 F4
Gällivare, *Sweden* 8 C16
Gallo, C., *Italy* 34 D6
Gallocanta, L. de, *Spain* 28 E3
Galloway, *U.K.* 14 G4
Galloway, Mull of, *U.K.* 14 G4
Gallup, *U.S.A.* 111 J9
Gallur, *Spain* 28 D3
Galong, *Australia* 91 E4
Galoya, *Sri Lanka* 60 Q12
Galt, *U.S.A.* 112 G5
Galtström, *Sweden* 10 B11
Galtür, *Austria* 19 J6
Galty Mts., *Ireland* 15 D3
Galtymore, *Ireland* 15 D3
Galva, *U.S.A.* 108 E9
Galvarino, *Chile* 128 A2
Galve de Sorbe, *Spain* 28 D1
Galveston, *U.S.A.* 109 L7
Galveston B., *U.S.A.* 109 L7
Gálvez, *Argentina* 126 C3
Gálvez, *Spain* 31 F6
Galway, *Ireland* 15 C2
Galway □, *Ireland* 15 C2
Galway B., *Ireland* 15 C2
Gam →, *Vietnam* 58 B5
Gamagori, *Japan* 49 G8
Gamari, L., *Ethiopia* 77 E5
Gamawa, *Nigeria* 79 C7
Gamay, *Phil.* 55 E6
Gambaga, *Ghana* 79 C4
Gambat, *Pakistan* 62 F3
Gambela, *Ethiopia* 77 F3
Gambia ■, *W. Afr.* 78 C1
Gambia →, *W. Afr.* 78 C1
Gambier, C., *Australia* 88 B5
Gambier Is., *Australia* 91 F2
Gamboli, *Pakistan* 62 E3
Gamboma, *Congo* 80 E3
Gamerco, *U.S.A.* 111 J9
Gamlakarleby = Kokkola, *Finland* 8 E17
Gammon →, *Canada* 101 C9
Gammouda, *Tunisia* 75 A6
Gamu-Gofa □, *Ethiopia* 77 F4
Gan, *France* 26 E3
Gan Gan, *Argentina* 128 B3
Gan Goriama, Mts., *Cameroon* 79 D7
Gan Jiang →, *China* 53 C10
Ganado, *Ariz., U.S.A.* 111 J9
Ganado, *Tex., U.S.A.* 109 L6
Gananoque, *Canada* 98 D4
Ganaveh, *Iran* 65 D6
Gäncä = Gyandzha, *Azerbaijan* 43 F12
Gand = Gent, *Belgium* 17 F3
Ganda, *Angola* 81 G2
Gandak →, *India* 63 G11
Gandava, *Pakistan* 62 E2
Gander, *Canada* 99 C9
Gander L., *Canada* 99 C9
Ganderowe Falls, *Zimbabwe* 83 F2
Gandesa, *Spain* 28 D5
Gandhi Sagar, *India* 62 G6
Gandi, *Nigeria* 79 C6
Gandía, *Spain* 29 G4
Gandino, *Italy* 32 C6
Gando, Pta., *Canary Is.* 36 G4
Gandole, *Nigeria* 79 D7
Gandu, *Brazil* 123 D4
Ganedidalem = Gani, *Indonesia* 57 E7
Ganetti, *Sudan* 76 D3
Ganga →, *India* 63 H14
Ganga, Mouths of the, *India* 63 J13
Ganganagar, *India* 62 E5
Gangapur, *India* 62 F7
Gangara, *Niger* 79 C6
Gangaw, *Burma* 61 H19
Gangdisê Shan, *China* 61 D12
Ganges = Ganga →, *India* 63 H14
Ganges, *France* 26 E7
Gangoh, *India* 62 E7
Gangtok, *India* 61 F16
Gangu, *China* 50 G3
Gangyao, *China* 51 B14
Gani, *Indonesia* 57 E7
Ganj, *India* 63 F8
Gannat, *France* 26 B7
Gannett Peak, *U.S.A.* 110 E9
Gannvalley, *U.S.A.* 108 C5
Ganquan, *China* 50 F5
Gänserdorf, *Austria* 21 G6
Ganshui, *China* 52 C6
Gansu □, *China* 50 G3
Ganta, *Liberia* 78 D3
Gantheaume, C., *Australia* 91 F2
Gantheaume B., *Australia* 89 E1
Gantsevichi, *Belorussia* 40 E5
Ganyem, *Indonesia* 57 E10
Ganyu, *China* 51 G10
Ganyushkino, *Kazakhstan* 43 C13
Ganzhou, *China* 53 E10
Gao, *Mali* 79 B5
Gao Xian, *China* 52 C5
Gao'an, *China* 53 C10
Gaohe, *China* 53 F9
Gaohebu, *China* 53 B11
Gaokeng, *China* 53 D9
Gaolan Dao, *China* 53 G9
Gaoligong Shan, *China* 52 E2
Gaomi, *China* 51 F10
Gaoping, *China* 50 G7
Gaotang, *China* 50 F9
Gaoua, *Burkina Faso* 78 C4
Gaoual, *Guinea* 78 C2
Gaoxiong, *Taiwan* 53 F13
Gaoyang, *China* 50 E8
Gaoyou, *China* 53 A12
Gaoyou Hu, *China* 51 H10
Gaoyuan, *China* 51 F9
Gaozhou, *China* 53 G8
Gap, *France* 27 D10
Gapan, *Phil.* 55 D4
Gar, *China* 54 C2
Garabogazkol Aylagy = Kara Bogaz Gol, Zaliv, *Turkmenistan* 44 E6
Garachico, *Canary Is.* 36 F3
Garachiné, *Panama* 116 E4
Garafia, *Canary Is.* 36 F2
Garajonay, *Canary Is.* 36 F2
Garanhuns, *Brazil* 122 C4
Garawe, *Liberia* 78 E3
Garba Tula, *Kenya* 82 B4
Garber, *U.S.A.* 109 G6
Garberville, *U.S.A.* 110 F2
Garça, *Brazil* 123 F2
Garças →, *Mato Grosso, Brazil* 125 D7
Garças →, *Pernambuco, Brazil* 122 C4
Garcias, *Brazil* 125 E7
Gard, *Somali Rep.* 68 F4
Gard □, *France* 27 D8
Gard →, *France* 27 E8
Garda, L. di, *Italy* 32 C7
Gardanne, *France* 27 E9
Garde L., *Canada* 101 A7
Gardelegen, *Germany* 18 C7
Garden City, *Kans., U.S.A.* 109 G4
Garden City, *Tex., U.S.A.* 109 K4
Garden Grove, *U.S.A.* 113 M9
Gardēz, *Afghan.* 62 C3
Gardiner, *U.S.A.* 110 D8
Gardiners I., *U.S.A.* 107 E12
Gardner, *U.S.A.* 107 D13
Gardner Canal, *Canada* 100 C3
Gardnerville, *U.S.A.* 112 G7
Gare Tigre, *Fr. Guiana* 121 C7
Garéssio, *Italy* 32 D5
Garey, *U.S.A.* 113 L6
Garfield, *U.S.A.* 110 C5
Gargan, Mt., *France* 26 C5
Gargano, Mte., *Italy* 35 A8
Gargouna, *Mali* 79 B5
Garhshankar, *India* 62 D7
Garibaldi Prov. Park, *Canada* 100 D4
Garies, *S. Africa* 84 E2
Garigliano →, *Italy* 34 A6
Garissa, *Kenya* 82 C4
Garissa □, *Kenya* 82 C5
Garkida, *Nigeria* 79 C7
Garko, *Nigeria* 79 C6
Garland, *U.S.A.* 110 F7
Garlasco, *Italy* 32 C5
Garm, *Tajikistan* 44 F8
Garmāb, *Iran* 65 C8
Garmisch-Partenkirchen, *Germany* 19 H7
Garmsār, *Iran* 65 C7
Garner, *U.S.A.* 108 D8
Garnett, *U.S.A.* 108 F7
Garo Hills, *India* 63 G14
Garoe, *Somali Rep.* 68 F4
Garonne →, *France* 26 C3
Garonne, Canal Latéral à la →, *France* 26 D4
Garoua, *Cameroon* 79 D7
Garrel, *Germany* 18 C3
Garrigue, *France* 26 E7
Garrison, *Mont., U.S.A.* 110 C7
Garrison, *N. Dak., U.S.A.* 108 B4
Garrison, *Tex., U.S.A.* 109 K7
Garrison Res. = Sakakawea, L., *U.S.A.* 108 B3
Garrovillas, *Spain* 31 F4
Garrucha, *Spain* 29 H3
Garry →, *U.K.* 14 E5
Garry, L., *Canada* 96 B9
Garsen, *Kenya* 82 C5
Garson L., *Canada* 101 B6
Gartempe →, *France* 26 B4
Gartz, *Germany* 18 B10
Garu, *Ghana* 79 C4
Garub, *Namibia* 84 D2
Garut, *Indonesia* 57 G12
Garvão, *Portugal* 31 H2
Garvie Mts., *N.Z.* 87 L2
Garwa = Garoua, *Cameroon* 79 D7
Garwa, *India* 63 G10
Garwolin, *Poland* 20 D11
Gary, *U.S.A.* 104 E2
Garz, *Germany* 18 A9
Garzê, *China* 52 B3
Garzón, *Colombia* 120 C2
Gas-San, *Japan* 48 E10
Gasan Kuli, *Turkmenistan* 44 F6
Gascogne, *France* 26 E4
Gascogne, G. de, *Europe* 28 B2
Gascony = Gascogne, *France* 26 E4
Gascoyne →, *Australia* 89 D1
Gascoyne Junc. T.O., *Australia* 89 E2
Gascueña, *Spain* 28 E2
Gash, Wadi →, *Ethiopia* 77 D4
Gashaka, *Nigeria* 79 D7
Gasherbrum, *Pakistan* 63 B7
Gashua, *Nigeria* 79 C7
Gaspé, *Canada* 99 C7
Gaspé, C. de, *Canada* 99 C7
Gaspé, Pén. de, *Canada* 99 C6
Gaspésie, Parc Prov. de la, *Canada* 99 C6
Gassaway, *U.S.A.* 104 F5
Gasselte, *Neths.* 16 C9
Gasselternijveen, *Neths.* 16 C9
Gássino Torinese, *Italy* 32 C4
Gassol, *Nigeria* 79 D7
Gasteiz = Vitoria, *Spain* 28 C2
Gastonia, *U.S.A.* 105 H5
Gastoúni, *Greece* 39 M4
Gastoúri, *Greece* 39 K2
Gastre, *Argentina* 128 B3
Gata, C., *Cyprus* 37 E12
Gata, C. de, *Spain* 29 J2
Gata, Sierra de, *Spain* 30 E4
Gataga →, *Canada* 100 B3
Gătaia, *Romania* 38 D4
Gatchina, *Russia* 40 B7
Gates, *U.S.A.* 106 C7
Gateshead, *U.K.* 12 C6
Gatesville, *U.S.A.* 109 K6
Gaths, *Zimbabwe* 83 G3
Gatico, *Chile* 126 A1
Gâtinais, *France* 25 D9
Gâtine, Hauteurs de, *France* 26 B3
Gatineau →, *Canada* 98 C4
Gatineau, Parc de la, *Canada* 98 C4
Gattaran, *Phil.* 55 B4
Gattinara, *Italy* 32 C5
Gatun, L., *Panama* 116 E4
Gatyana, *S. Africa* 85 E4
Gau, *Fiji* 87 D8
Gaucín, *Spain* 31 J5
Gauer L., *Canada* 101 B9
Gauhati, *India* 63 F14
Gauja →, *Latvia* 40 C4
Gaula →, *Norway* 8 E11
Gaurain-Ramecroix, *Belgium* 17 G3
Gausta, *Norway* 10 E2
Gāv Koshī, *Iran* 65 D8
Gavá, *Spain* 28 D6
Gāvakān, *Iran* 65 D7
Gavarnie, *France* 26 F3
Gavāter, *Iran* 65 E9
Gāvbandī, *Iran* 65 E7
Gavdhopoúla, *Greece* 37 E6
Gávdhos, *Greece* 37 E6
Gavere, *Belgium* 17 G3
Gavião, *Portugal* 31 F3
Gaviota, *U.S.A.* 113 L6
Gävleborgs län □, *Sweden* 10 C10
Gavorrano, *Italy* 32 F7
Gavray, *France* 24 D5
Gavrilov Yam, *Russia* 41 C11
Gawachab, *Namibia* 84 D2
Gawilgarh Hills, *India* 60 J10
Gawler, *Australia* 91 E2
Gaxun Nur, *China* 54 B5
Gaya, *India* 63 G11
Gaya, *Niger* 79 C5
Gaya, *Nigeria* 79 C6
Gaylord, *U.S.A.* 104 C3
Gayndah, *Australia* 91 D5
Gaysin, *Ukraine* 42 B3
Gayvoron, *Ukraine* 42 B3
Gaza, *Egypt* 69 D3
Gaza □, *Mozam.* 85 C5
Gaza Strip, *Egypt* 69 D3
Gazaoua, *Niger* 79 C6
Gāzbor, *Iran* 65 D8
Gazi, *Zaïre* 82 B1
Gaziantep, *Turkey* 66 E7
Gaziantep □, *Turkey* 66 E7
Gazipaşa, *Turkey* 66 E5
Gazli, *Uzbekistan* 44 E7
Gbarnga, *Liberia* 78 D3
Gbekebo, *Nigeria* 79 D5
Gboko, *Nigeria* 79 D6
Gbongan, *Nigeria* 79 D5
Gcuwa, *S. Africa* 85 E4
Gdańsk, *Poland* 20 A8
Gdańska, Zatoka, *Poland* 20 A9
Gdov, *Russia* 40 B5
Gdynia, *Poland* 20 A8
Gebe, *Indonesia* 57 D7
Gebeit Mine, *Sudan* 76 C4
Gebel Mûsa, *Egypt* 76 J8
Gebze, *Turkey* 66 C3
Gecha, *Ethiopia* 77 F4
Gedaref, *Sudan* 77 E4
Gede, Tanjung, *Indonesia* 56 F3
Gedinne, *Belgium* 17 J5
Gediz, *Turkey* 66 D3
Gediz →, *Turkey* 66 D2
Gedo, *Ethiopia* 77 F4
Gèdre, *France* 26 F4
Gedser, *Denmark* 11 K5
Gedser Odde, *Denmark* 11 K5
Geegully Cr. →, *Australia* 88 C3
Geel, *Belgium* 17 F5
Geelong, *Australia* 91 F3
Geelvink Chan., *Australia* 89 E1
Geer →, *Belgium* 17 G7
Geesthacht, *Germany* 18 B6
Geffen, *Neths.* 16 E6
Geidam, *Nigeria* 79 C7
Geikie →, *Canada* 101 B8
Geili, *Sudan* 77 D3
Geilo, *Norway* 10 D2
Geisingen, *Germany* 19 H4
Geislingen, *Germany* 19 G5
Geita, *Tanzania* 82 C3
Geita □, *Tanzania* 82 C3
Gejiu, *China* 52 F4
Gel →, *Sudan* 77 F2
Gel River, *Sudan* 77 F2
Gela, *Italy* 35 E7
Gela, G. di, *Italy* 35 F7
Geladi, *Ethiopia* 68 F4
Gelderland □, *Neths.* 16 D8
Geldermalsen, *Neths.* 16 E6
Geldern, *Germany* 18 D2
Geldrop, *Neths.* 17 F7
Geleen, *Neths.* 17 G7
Gelehun, *S. Leone* 78 D2
Gelendost, *Turkey* 66 D4
Gelendzhik, *Russia* 42 D8
Gelibolu, *Turkey* 39 J9
Gelidonya Burnu, *Turkey* 66 E4
Gelnhausen, *Germany* 19 E5
Gelsenkirchen, *Germany* 18 D3
Gelting, *Germany* 18 A5
Gemas, *Malaysia* 59 L4
Gembloux, *Belgium* 17 G5
Gemena, *Zaïre* 80 D3
Gemerek, *Turkey* 66 D7
Gemert, *Neths.* 17 E7
Gemlik, *Turkey* 66 C3
Gemona del Friuli, *Italy* 33 B10
Gemsa, *Egypt* 76 B3
Gemünden, *Germany* 19 E5
Genale, *Ethiopia* 77 F4
Genappe, *Belgium* 17 G4
Genç, *Turkey* 67 D9
Gençay, *France* 26 B4
Gendringen, *Neths.* 16 E8
Gendt, *Neths.* 16 E7
Geneina, Gebel, *Egypt* 76 J8
Genemuiden, *Neths.* 16 C8
General Acha, *Argentina* 126 D3
General Alvear, *Buenos Aires, Argentina* 126 D3
General Alvear, *Mendoza, Argentina* 126 D2
General Artigas, *Paraguay* 126 B4
General Belgrano, *Argentina* 126 D4
General Cabrera, *Argentina* 126 C3
General Carrera, L., *Chile* 128 C2
General Cepeda, *Mexico* 114 B4
General Conesa, *Argentina* 128 B4
General Guido, *Argentina* 126 D4
General Juan Madariaga, *Argentina* 126 D4
General La Madrid, *Argentina* 126 D3
General Lorenzo Vintter, *Argentina* 128 B4
General MacArthur, *Phil.* 55 F6
General Martin Miguel de Güemes, *Argentina* 126 A3
General Paz, *Argentina* 126 B4
General Pico, *Argentina* 126 D3
General Pinedo, *Argentina* 126 B3
General Pinto, *Argentina* 126 C3
General Sampaio, *Brazil* 122 B4
General Santos, *Phil.* 55 H6
General Toshevo, *Bulgaria* 38 F11
General Trevino, *Mexico* 115 B5
General Trías, *Mexico* 114 B3
General Viamonte, *Argentina* 126 D3
General Villegas, *Argentina* 126 D3
General Vintter, L., *Argentina* 128 B2
Generoso, Mte., *Switz.* 23 E8
Genesee, *Idaho, U.S.A.* 110 C5
Genesee, *Pa., U.S.A.* 106 E7
Genesee →, *U.S.A.* 106 C7
Geneseo, *Ill., U.S.A.* 108 E9
Geneseo, *Kans., U.S.A.* 108 F5
Geneseo, *N.Y., U.S.A.* 106 D7
Geneva = Genève, *Switz.* 22 D2
Geneva, *Ala., U.S.A.* 105 K3
Geneva, *N.Y., U.S.A.* 106 D7
Geneva, *Nebr., U.S.A.* 108 E6
Geneva, *Ohio, U.S.A.* 106 E4
Geneva, L. = Léman, Lac, *Switz.* 22 D3
Geneva, L., *U.S.A.* 104 D1
Genève, *Switz.* 22 D2
Genève □, *Switz.* 22 D2
Gengenbach, *Germany* 19 G4
Gengma, *China* 52 F2
Genichesk, *Ukraine* 42 C6
Genil →, *Spain* 31 H5
Génissiat, Barr. de, *France* 27 B9
Genk, *Belgium* 17 G7
Genlis, *France* 25 E12
Gennargentu, Mti. del, *Italy* 34 C2
Gennep, *Neths.* 17 E7
Gennes, *France* 24 E6
Genoa = Génova, *Italy* 32 D5
Genoa, *Australia* 91 F4
Genoa, *N.Y., U.S.A.* 107 D8
Genoa, *Nebr., U.S.A.* 108 E6
Genoa, *Nev., U.S.A.* 112 F7
Genoa →, *Argentina* 128 B2
Génova, *Italy* 32 D5
Génova, G. di, *Italy* 32 E6
Gent, *Belgium* 17 F3
Gentbrugge, *Belgium* 17 F3
Genthin, *Germany* 18 C8
Gentio do Ouro, *Brazil* 122 D3
Geographe B., *Australia* 89 F2
Geographe Chan., *Australia* 89 D1
Geokchay, *Azerbaijan* 43 F12
Georga, Zemlya, *Russia* 44 A5
George, *S. Africa* 84 E3
George →, *Canada* 99 A6
George, L., *N.S.W., Australia* 91 F4
George, L., *S. Austral., Australia* 91 F3
George, L., *W. Austral., Australia* 88 D3
George, L., *Uganda* 82 B3
George, L., *Fla., U.S.A.* 105 L5
George, L., *N.Y., U.S.A.* 107 C11
George Gill Ra., *Australia* 88 D5
George River = Port Nouveau-Québec, *Canada* 97 C13
George Sound, *N.Z.* 87 L1
George Town, *Bahamas* 116 B4
George Town, *Malaysia* 59 K3
George V Land, *Antarctica* 5 C10
George VI Sound, *Antarctica* 5 D17
George West, *U.S.A.* 109 L5
Georgetown, *Australia* 90 B3
Georgetown, *Ont., Canada* 98 D4
Georgetown, *P.E.I., Canada* 99 C7
Georgetown, *Cayman Is.* 116 C3
Georgetown, *Gambia* 78 C2
Georgetown, *Guyana* 121 B6
Georgetown, *Calif., U.S.A.* 112 G6
Georgetown, *Colo., U.S.A.* 110 G11
Georgetown, *Ky., U.S.A.* 104 F3
Georgetown, *S.C., U.S.A.* 105 J6
Georgetown, *Tex., U.S.A.* 109 K6
Georgia □, *U.S.A.* 105 J4
Georgia ■, *Asia* 43 E10
Georgia, Str. of, *Canada* 100 D4
Georgian B., *Canada* 98 C3
Georgievsk, *Russia* 43 D10
Georgina →, *Australia* 90 C2
Georgina Downs, Australia 90 C2
Georgiu-Dezh = Liski, *Russia* 41 F11
Gera, *Germany* 18 E8
Geraardsbergen, *Belgium* 17 G3
Geral, Serra, *Bahia, Brazil* 123 D3
Geral, Serra, *Goiás, Brazil* 122 D2
Geral, Serra, *Sta. Catarina, Brazil* 127 B6
Geral de Goiás, Serra, *Brazil* 123 D2
Geral do Paranã Serra, *Brazil* 123 E2
Geraldine, *U.S.A.* 110 C8

Geraldton, *Australia* 89 E1
Geraldton, *Canada* 98 C2
Gérardmer, *France* 25 D13
Gercüş, *Turkey* 67 E9
Gerede, *Turkey* 42 F5
Gereshk, *Afghan.* 60 D4
Gérgal, *Spain* 29 H2
Gerik, *Malaysia* 59 K3
Gering, *U.S.A.* 108 E3
Gerlach, *U.S.A.* 110 F4
Gerlachovka, *Slovakia* 20 F10
Gerlogubi, *Ethiopia* 68 F4
Germansen Landing, *Canada* 100 B4
Germany ■, *Europe* 18 E6
Germersheim, *Germany* 19 F4
Germiston, *S. Africa* 85 D4
Gernsheim, *Germany* 19 F4
Gero, *Japan* 49 G8
Gerolstein, *Germany* 19 E2
Gerolzhofen, *Germany* 19 F6
Gerona, *Spain* 28 D7
Gerona □, *Spain* 28 C7
Gérouville, *Belgium* 17 J6
Gerrard, *Canada* 100 C5
Gers □, *France* 26 E4
Gers →, *France* 26 D4
Gersfeld, *Germany* 18 E5
Gerze, *Turkey* 66 C6
Geseke, *Germany* 18 D4
Geser, *Indonesia* 57 E8
Gesso →, *Italy* 32 D4
Gestro, Wabi →, *Ethiopia* 77 G5
Gesves, *Belgium* 17 H6
Getafe, *Spain* 30 E7
Gethsémani, *Canada* 99 B7
Gettysburg, *Pa., U.S.A.* 104 F7
Gettysburg, *S. Dak., U.S.A.* 108 C5
Getz Ice Shelf, *Antarctica* 5 D14
Geul →, *Neths.* 17 G7
Gevaş, *Turkey* 67 D10
Gévaudan, *France* 26 D7
Gevgelija, *Macedonia* 39 H5
Gévora →, *Spain* 31 G4
Gex, *France* 27 B10
Geyser, *U.S.A.* 110 C8
Geyserville, *U.S.A.* 112 G4
Geysir, *Iceland* 8 D3
Geyve, *Turkey* 66 C4
Ghâbat el Arab = Wang Kai, *Sudan* 77 F2
Ghaghara →, *India* 63 G11
Ghalla, Wadi el →, *Sudan* 77 E2
Ghallamane, *Mauritania* 74 D3
Ghana ■, *W. Afr.* 79 D4
Ghansor, *India* 63 H9
Ghanzi, *Botswana* 84 C3
Ghanzi □, *Botswana* 84 C3
Gharb el Istiwa'iya □, *Sudan* 77 F2
Gharbîya, Es Sahrâ el, *Egypt* 76 B2
Ghard Abû Muharik, *Egypt* 76 B2
Ghardaïa, *Algeria* 75 B5
Ghârib, G., *Egypt* 76 J8
Ghârib, Râs, *Egypt* 76 J8
Gharyān, *Libya* 75 B7
Gharyān □, *Libya* 75 B7
Ghat, *Libya* 75 D7
Ghatal, *India* 63 H12
Ghatampur, *India* 63 F9
Ghaṭṭī, *Si. Arabia* 64 D3
Ghawdex = Gozo, *Malta* 37 C1
Ghazal, Bahr el →, *Chad* 73 F8
Ghazâl, Bahr el →, *Sudan* 77 F3
Ghazaouet, *Algeria* 75 A4
Ghaziabad, *India* 62 E7
Ghazipur, *India* 63 G10
Ghaznī, *Afghan.* 62 C3
Ghaznī □, *Afghan.* 60 C6
Ghedi, *Italy* 32 C7
Ghèlinsor, *Somali Rep.* 68 F4
Ghent = Gent, *Belgium* 17 F3
Gheorghe Gheorghiu-Dej, *Romania* 38 C9
Gheorgheni, *Romania* 38 C8
Ghergani, *Romania* 38 E8
Gherla, *Romania* 38 B6
Ghilarza, *Italy* 34 B1
Ghisonaccia, *France* 27 F13
Ghisoni, *France* 27 F13
Ghizao, *Afghan.* 62 C1
Ghizar →, *Pakistan* 63 A5
Ghogha, *India* 62 J5
Ghot Ogrein, *Egypt* 76 A2
Ghotaru, *India* 62 F4
Ghotki, *Pakistan* 62 E3
Ghowr □, *Afghan.* 60 C4
Ghudaf, W. al →, *Iraq* 64 C4
Ghudāmis, *Libya* 75 B6
Ghughri, *India* 63 H9
Ghugus, *India* 60 K11
Ghulam Mohammad Barrage, *Pakistan* 62 G3
Ghūrīān, *Afghan.* 60 B2
Gia Dinh, *Vietnam* 59 G6
Gia Lai = Pleiku, *Vietnam* 58 F7
Gia Nghia, *Vietnam* 59 G6
Gia Ngoc, *Vietnam* 58 E7
Gia Vuc, *Vietnam* 58 E7
Gian, *Phil.* 57 C7
Giannutri, *Italy* 32 F8
Giant Forest, *U.S.A.* 112 J8
Giant Mts. = Krkonoše, *Czech.* 20 E5
Giants Causeway, *U.K.* 15 A5
Giarabub = Al Jaghbūb, *Libya* 73 C9
Giarre, *Italy* 35 E8
Giaveno, *Italy* 32 C4
Gibara, *Cuba* 116 B4
Gibb River, *Australia* 88 C4
Gibbon, *U.S.A.* 108 E5
Gibe →, *Ethiopia* 77 F4
Gibellina, *Italy* 34 E6
Gibraléon, *Spain* 31 H4
Gibraltar ■, *Europe* 31 J5
Gibraltar, Str. of, *Medit. S.* 31 K5
Gibson Desert, *Australia* 88 D4
Gibsons, *Canada* 100 D4
Gibsonville, *U.S.A.* 112 F6
Giddings, *U.S.A.* 109 K6
Gidole, *Ethiopia* 77 F4
Gien, *France* 25 E9
Giessen, *Germany* 18 E4
Gieten, *Neths.* 16 B9
Gīfān, *Iran* 65 B8
Gifatin, Geziret, *Egypt* 76 B3
Gifford Creek, *Australia* 88 D2
Gifhorn, *Germany* 18 C6
Gifu, *Japan* 49 G8
Gifu □, *Japan* 49 G8
Gigant, *Russia* 43 C9
Giganta, Sa. de la, *Mexico* 114 B2
Gigen, *Bulgaria* 38 F7
Gigha, *U.K.* 14 F3
Giglio, *Italy* 32 F7
Gignac, *France* 26 E7
Gigüela →, *Spain* 29 F1
Gijón, *Spain* 30 B5
Gil I., *Canada* 100 C3
Gila →, *U.S.A.* 111 K6
Gila Bend, *U.S.A.* 111 K7
Gila Bend Mts., *U.S.A.* 111 K7
Gīlān □, *Iran* 65 B6
Gilbert →, *Australia* 90 B3
Gilbert Is., *Kiribati* 92 G9
Gilbert Plains, *Canada* 101 C8
Gilbert River, *Australia* 90 B3
Gilberton, *Australia* 90 B3
Gilbués, *Brazil* 122 C2
Gilf el Kebîr, Hadabat el, *Egypt* 76 C2
Gilford I., *Canada* 100 C3
Gilgandra, *Australia* 91 E4
Gilgil, *Kenya* 82 C4
Gilgit, *India* 63 B6
Gilgit →, *Pakistan* 63 B6
Giljeva Planina, *Serbia, Yug.* 21 M10
Gillam, *Canada* 101 B10
Gilleleje, *Denmark* 11 H6
Gillen, L., *Australia* 89 E3
Gilles, L., *Australia* 91 E2
Gillette, *U.S.A.* 108 C2
Gilliat, *Australia* 90 C3
Gillingham, *U.K.* 13 F8
Gilly, *Belgium* 17 H4
Gilmer, *U.S.A.* 109 J7
Gilmore, *Australia* 91 F4
Gilmore, L., *Australia* 89 F3
Gilmour, *Canada* 98 D4
Gilo →, *Ethiopia* 77 F3
Gilort →, *Romania* 38 E6
Gilroy, *U.S.A.* 111 H3
Gilze, *Neths.* 17 E5
Gimbi, *Ethiopia* 77 F4
Gimigliano, *Italy* 35 D9
Gimli, *Canada* 101 C9
Gimone →, *France* 26 E5
Gimont, *France* 26 E4
Gin Gin, *Australia* 91 D5
Ginâh, *Egypt* 76 B3
Gindie, *Australia* 90 C4
Gingin, *Australia* 89 F2
Gîngiova, *Romania* 38 F6
Ginir, *Ethiopia* 68 F3
Ginosa, *Italy* 35 B9
Ginzo de Limia, *Spain* 30 C3
Giohar, *Somali Rep.* 68 G4
Gióia, G. di, *Italy* 35 D8
Gióia del Colle, *Italy* 35 B9
Gióia Táuro, *Italy* 35 D8
Gioiosa Iónica, *Italy* 35 D9
Gióna, Óros, *Greece* 39 L5
Giovi, Passo dei, *Italy* 32 D5
Giovinazzo, *Italy* 35 A9
Gir Hills, *India* 62 J4
Girab, *India* 62 F4
Girâfi, W. →, *Egypt* 69 F3
Giraltovce, *Slovakia* 20 F11
Girard, *Kans., U.S.A.* 109 G7
Girard, *Ohio, U.S.A.* 106 E4
Girard, *Pa., U.S.A.* 106 D4
Girardot, *Colombia* 120 C3
Girdle Ness, *U.K.* 14 D6
Giresun, *Turkey* 67 C8
Giresun □, *Turkey* 67 C8
Girga, *Egypt* 76 B3
Giridih, *India* 63 G12
Girifalco, *Italy* 35 D9
Girilambone, *Australia* 91 E4
Giro, *Nigeria* 79 C5
Giromagny, *France* 25 E13
Girona = Gerona, *Spain* 28 D7
Gironde □, *France* 26 D3
Gironde →, *France* 26 C2
Gironella, *Spain* 28 C6
Giru, *Australia* 90 B4
Girvan, *U.K.* 14 F4
Gisborne, *N.Z.* 87 H7
Gisenyi, *Rwanda* 82 C2
Gisors, *France* 25 C8
Gistel, *Belgium* 17 F1
Giswil, *Switz.* 22 C6
Gitega, *Burundi* 82 C2
Gits, *Belgium* 17 F2
Giuba →, *Somali Rep.* 68 G3
Giubiasco, *Switz.* 23 D8
Giugliano in Campania, *Italy* 35 B7
Giulianova, *Italy* 33 F10
Giurgeni, *Romania* 38 E10
Giurgiu, *Romania* 38 F8
Give, *Denmark* 11 J3
Givet, *France* 25 B11
Givors, *France* 27 C8
Givry, *Belgium* 17 H4
Givry, *France* 25 F11
Giyon, *Ethiopia* 77 F4
Giza = El Gîza, *Egypt* 76 H7
Gizhiga, *Russia* 45 C17
Gizhiginskaya Guba, *Russia* 45 C16
Giżycko, *Poland* 20 A11
Gizzeria, *Italy* 35 D9
Gjegjan, *Albania* 39 H3
Gjerstad, *Norway* 10 F3
Gjirokastra, *Albania* 39 J3
Gjoa Haven, *Canada* 96 B10
Gjøl, *Denmark* 11 G3
Gjøvik, *Norway* 10 D4
Glace Bay, *Canada* 99 C8
Glacier Bay, *U.S.A.* 100 B1
Glacier Nat. Park, *Canada* 100 C5
Glacier Park, *U.S.A.* 110 B7
Glacier Peak, *U.S.A.* 110 B3
Gladewater, *U.S.A.* 109 J7
Gladstone, *Queens., Australia* 90 C5
Gladstone, *S. Austral., Australia* 91 E2
Gladstone, *W. Austral., Australia* 89 E1
Gladstone, *Canada* 101 C9
Gladstone, *U.S.A.* 104 C2
Gladwin, *U.S.A.* 104 D3
Gladys L., *Canada* 100 B2
Gláma, *Iceland* 8 D2
Glåma →, *Norway* 10 E4
Glamis, *U.S.A.* 113 N11
Glamoč, *Bos.-H.* 33 D13
Glan, *Sweden* 11 F10
Glanerbrug, *Neths.* 16 D9
Glarner Alpen, *Switz.* 23 C8
Glärnisch, *Switz.* 23 C7
Glarus, *Switz.* 23 B8
Glarus □, *Switz.* 23 C8
Glasco, *Kans., U.S.A.* 108 F6
Glasco, *N.Y., U.S.A.* 107 D11
Glasgow, *U.K.* 14 F4
Glasgow, *Ky., U.S.A.* 104 G3
Glasgow, *Mont., U.S.A.* 110 B10
Glastonbury, *U.K.* 13 F5
Glastonbury, *U.S.A.* 107 E12
Glatt →, *Switz.* 23 B7
Glattfelden, *Switz.* 23 A7
Glauchau, *Germany* 18 E8
Glazov, *Russia* 41 B18
Gleiwitz = Gliwice, *Poland* 20 E8
Glen, *U.S.A.* 107 B13
Glen Affric, *U.K.* 14 D4
Glen Canyon Dam, *U.S.A.* 111 H8
Glen Canyon National Recreation Area, *U.S.A.* 111 H8
Glen Coe, *U.K.* 14 E4
Glen Cove, *U.S.A.* 107 F11
Glen Garry, *U.K.* 14 D3
Glen Innes, *Australia* 91 D5
Glen Lyon, *U.S.A.* 107 E8
Glen Mor, *U.K.* 14 D4
Glen Moriston, *U.K.* 14 D4
Glen Orchy, *U.K.* 14 E4
Glen Spean, *U.K.* 14 E4
Glen Ullin, *U.S.A.* 108 B4
Glénan, Is. de, *France* 24 E2
Glenburgh, *Australia* 89 E2
Glencoe, *Canada* 106 D3
Glencoe, *S. Africa* 85 D5
Glencoe, *U.S.A.* 108 C7
Glendale, *Ariz., U.S.A.* 111 K7
Glendale, *Calif., U.S.A.* 113 L8
Glendale, *Oreg., U.S.A.* 110 E2
Glendale, *Zimbabwe* 83 F3
Glendive, *U.S.A.* 108 B2
Glendo, *U.S.A.* 108 D2
Glenelg, *Australia* 91 E2
Glenelg →, *Australia* 91 F3
Glenflorrie, *Australia* 88 D2
Glengarriff, *Ireland* 15 E2
Glengyle, *Australia* 90 C2
Glenmora, *U.S.A.* 109 K8
Glenmorgan, *Australia* 91 D4
Glenn, *U.S.A.* 112 F4
Glenns Ferry, *U.S.A.* 110 E6
Glenorchy, *Australia* 90 G4
Glenore, *Australia* 90 B3
Glenormiston, *Australia* 90 C2
Glenreagh, *Australia* 91 E5
Glenrock, *U.S.A.* 110 E11
Glenrothes, *U.K.* 14 E5
Glens Falls, *U.S.A.* 107 C11
Glenties, *Ireland* 15 B3
Glenville, *U.S.A.* 104 F5
Glenwood, *Alta., Canada* 100 D6
Glenwood, *Nfld., Canada* 99 C9
Glenwood, *Ark., U.S.A.* 109 H8
Glenwood, *Hawaii, U.S.A.* 102 J17
Glenwood, *Iowa, U.S.A.* 108 E7
Glenwood, *Minn., U.S.A.* 108 C7
Glenwood, *Wash., U.S.A.* 112 D5
Glenwood Springs, *U.S.A.* 110 G10
Gletsch, *Switz.* 23 C6
Glina, *Croatia* 33 C13
Glittertind, *Norway* 10 C2
Gliwice, *Poland* 20 E8
Globe, *U.S.A.* 111 K8
Glödnitz, *Austria* 21 J4
Głogów, *Poland* 20 D6
Glorieuses, Is., *Ind. Oc.* 85 A8
Glossop, *U.K.* 12 D6
Gloucester, *Australia* 91 E5
Gloucester, *U.K.* 13 F5
Gloucester, *U.S.A.* 107 D14
Gloucester I., *Australia* 90 B4
Gloucestershire □, *U.K.* 13 F5
Gloversville, *U.S.A.* 107 C10
Glovertown, *Canada* 99 C9
Głowno, *Poland* 20 D9
Głubczyce, *Poland* 20 E7
Glubokiy, *Russia* 43 B9
Glubokoye, *Belorussia* 40 D5
Głuchołazy, *Poland* 20 E7
Glücksburg, *Germany* 18 A5
Glückstadt, *Germany* 18 B5
Glukhov, *Ukraine* 40 F8
Glusk, *Belorussia* 40 E6
Glyngøre, *Denmark* 11 H2
Gmünd, *Kärnten, Austria* 21 J3
Gmünd, *Niederösterreich, Austria* 20 G5
Gnarp, *Sweden* 10 B11
Gnesta, *Sweden* 10 E11
Gniew, *Poland* 20 B8
Gniezno, *Poland* 20 C7
Gnoien, *Germany* 18 B8
Gnowangerup, *Australia* 89 F2
Go Cong, *Vietnam* 59 G6
Gō-no-ura, *Japan* 49 H4
Go Quao, *Vietnam* 59 H5
Goa, *India* 60 M8
Goa □, *India* 60 M8
Goalen Hd., *Australia* 91 F5
Goalpara, *India* 61 F17
Goalundo Ghat, *Bangla.* 63 H13
Goaso, *Ghana* 78 D4
Goat Fell, *U.K.* 14 F3
Goba, *Ethiopia* 68 F2
Goba, *Mozam.* 85 D5
Gobabis, *Namibia* 84 C2
Gobernador Gregores, *Argentina* 128 C2
Gobi, *Asia* 50 C5
Gobō, *Japan* 49 H7
Gobo, *Sudan* 77 F3
Goch, *Germany* 18 D2
Gochas, *Namibia* 84 C2
Godavari →, *India* 61 L13
Godavari Point, *India* 61 L13
Godbout, *Canada* 99 C6
Godda, *India* 63 G12
Godegård, *Sweden* 11 F9
Goderich, *Canada* 98 D3
Goderville, *France* 24 C7
Godhavn, *Greenland* 4 C5
Godhra, *India* 62 H5
Gödöllö, *Hungary* 21 H9
Godoy Cruz, *Argentina* 126 C2
Gods →, *Canada* 101 B10
Gods L., *Canada* 101 C10
Godthåb, *Greenland* 97 B14
Godwin Austen = K2, Mt., *Pakistan* 63 B7
Goeie Hoop, Kaap die = Good Hope, C. of, *S. Africa* 84 E2
Goéland, L. au, *Canada* 98 C4
Goeree, *Neths.* 16 E4
Goes, *Neths.* 17 F3
Gogama, *Canada* 98 C3
Gogango, *Australia* 90 C5
Gogebic, L., *U.S.A.* 108 B10
Gogra = Ghaghara →, *India* 63 G11
Gogriâl, *Sudan* 77 F2
Goiana, *Brazil* 122 C5
Goianésia, *Brazil* 123 E2
Goiânia, *Brazil* 123 E2
Goiás, *Brazil* 123 E1
Goiás □, *Brazil* 122 D2
Goiatuba, *Brazil* 123 E2
Goio-Ere, *Brazil* 127 A5
Goirle, *Neths.* 17 E6
Góis, *Portugal* 30 E2
Gojam □, *Ethiopia* 77 E4
Gojeb, Wabi →, *Ethiopia* 77 F4
Gojō, *Japan* 49 G7
Gojra, *Pakistan* 62 D5
Gokarannath, *India* 63 F9
Gökçeada, *Turkey* 39 J8
Gökırmak →, *Turkey* 66 C6
Göksu →, *Turkey* 66 E6
Göksun, *Turkey* 66 D7
Gokteik, *Burma* 61 H20
Gokurt, *Pakistan* 62 E2
Gola, *India* 63 E9
Golakganj, *India* 63 F13
Golan Heights = Hagolan, *Syria* 69 B4
Golāshkerd, *Iran* 65 E8
Golaya Pristen, *Ukraine* 42 C5
Gölbaşı, *Adiyaman, Turkey* 67 E7
Gölbaşı, *Ankara, Turkey* 66 D5
Golchikha, *Russia* 4 B12
Golconda, *U.S.A.* 110 F5
Gölcük, *Kocaeli, Turkey* 66 C3
Gölcük, *Niğde, Turkey* 66 D6
Gold Beach, *U.S.A.* 110 E1
Gold Coast, *Australia* 91 D5
Gold Coast, *W. Afr.* 70 F3
Gold Hill, *U.S.A.* 110 E2
Goldach, *Switz.* 23 B8
Goldau, *Switz.* 23 B7
Goldberg, *Germany* 18 B8
Golden, *Canada* 100 C5
Golden, *U.S.A.* 108 F2
Golden B., *N.Z.* 87 J4
Golden Gate, *U.S.A.* 110 H2
Golden Hinde, *Canada* 100 D3
Golden Lake, *Canada* 106 A7
Golden Prairie, *Canada* 101 C7
Golden Vale, *Ireland* 15 D3
Goldendale, *U.S.A.* 110 D3
Goldfield, *U.S.A.* 111 H5
Goldfields, *Canada* 101 B7
Goldsand L., *Canada* 101 B8
Goldsboro, *U.S.A.* 105 H7
Goldsmith, *U.S.A.* 109 K3
Goldsworthy, *Australia* 88 D2
Goldthwaite, *U.S.A.* 109 K5
Golegã, *Portugal* 31 F2
Goleniów, *Poland* 20 B4
Golestānak, *Iran* 65 D7
Goleta, *U.S.A.* 113 L7
Golfito, *Costa Rica* 116 E3
Golfo Aranci, *Italy* 34 B2
Gölgeli Dağları, *Turkey* 66 E3
Goliad, *U.S.A.* 109 L6
Golija, *Serbia, Yug.* 21 M10
Gölköy, *Turkey* 67 C7
Golo →, *France* 27 F13
Golovanevsk, *Ukraine* 42 B4
Golpāyegān, *Iran* 65 C6
Gölpazarı, *Turkey* 66 C4
Golra, *Pakistan* 62 C5
Golspie, *U.K.* 14 D5
Golyama Kamchiya →, *Bulgaria* 38 F10
Goma, *Rwanda* 82 C2
Goma, *Zaïre* 82 C2
Gomati →, *India* 63 G10
Gombari, *Zaïre* 82 B2
Gombe, *Nigeria* 79 C7
Gombe →, *Tanzania* 82 C3
Gombi, *Nigeria* 79 C7
Gomel, *Belorussia* 40 E7
Gomera, *Canary Is.* 36 F2
Gómez Palacio, *Mexico* 114 B4
Gomīshān, *Iran* 65 B7
Gommern, *Germany* 18 C7
Gomogomo, *Indonesia* 57 F8
Gomoh, *India* 61 H15
Gompa = Ganta, *Liberia* 78 D3
Goms, *Switz.* 22 D6
Gonābād, *Iran* 65 C8
Gonaïves, *Haiti* 117 C5
Gonâve, G. de la, *Haiti* 117 C5
Gonâve, I. de la, *Haiti* 117 C5
Gonbab-e Kāvūs, *Iran* 65 B7
Gonda, *India* 63 F9
Gondal, *India* 62 J4
Gonder, *Ethiopia* 77 E4
Gonder □, *Ethiopia* 77 E4
Gondia, *India* 60 J12
Gondola, *Mozam.* 83 F3
Gondomar, *Portugal* 30 D2
Gondomar, *Spain* 30 C2
Gondrecourt-le-Château, *France* 25 D12
Gönen, *Turkey* 66 C2
Gong Xian, *China* 52 C5
Gong'an, *China* 53 B9
Gongcheng, *China* 53 E8
Gongga Shan, *China* 52 C3
Gongguan, *China* 52 G7
Gonghe, *China* 54 C5
Gongola →, *Nigeria* 79 D7
Gongolgon, *Australia* 91 E4
Gongshan, *China* 52 D2
Gongtan, *China* 52 C7
Goniadz, *Poland* 20 B12
Goniri, *Nigeria* 79 C7
Gonjo, *China* 52 B2
Gonnesa, *Italy* 34 C1
Gónnos, *Greece* 39 K5
Gonnosfanadiga, *Italy* 34 C1
Gonzaga, *Phil.* 55 B5
Gonzales, *Calif., U.S.A.* 111 H3
Gonzales, *Tex., U.S.A.* 109 L6
González Chaves, *Argentina* 126 D3
Good Hope, C. of, *S. Africa* 84 E2
Gooderham, *Canada* 98 D4
Goodeve, *Canada* 101 C8
Gooding, *U.S.A.* 110 E6
Goodland, *U.S.A.* 108 F4
Goodnight, *U.S.A.* 109 H4
Goodooga, *Australia* 91 D4
Goodsoil, *Canada* 101 C7
Goodsprings, *U.S.A.* 111 J6
Goole, *U.K.* 12 D7
Goolgowi, *Australia* 91 E4
Goomalling, *Australia* 89 F2
Goombalie, *Australia* 91 D4
Goonda, *Mozam.* 83 F3

Goondiwindi, *Australia* 91 D5
Goongarrie, L., *Australia* 89 F3
Goonyella, *Australia* 90 C4
Goor, *Neths.* 16 D9
Gooray, *Australia* 91 D5
Goose →, *Canada* 99 B7
Goose L., *U.S.A.* 110 F3
Gop, *India* 60 H6
Gopalganj, *India* 63 F11
Goppenstein, *Switz.* 22 D5
Göppingen, *Germany* 19 G5
Gor, *Spain* 29 H2
Góra, *Poland* 20 D6
Gorakhpur, *India* 63 F10
Gorbatov, *Russia* 41 C13
Gorbea, Peña, *Spain* 28 B2
Gorda, *U.S.A.* 112 K5
Gorda, Pta., *Nic.* 116 D3
Gorda, Pta., *Canary Is.* 36 F2
Gordan B., *Australia* 88 B5
Gordon, *U.S.A.* 108 D3
Gordon →, *Australia* 90 G4
Gordon, I., *Chile* 128 D3
Gordon Downs, *Australia* 88 C4
Gordon L., *Alta., Canada* 101 B6
Gordon L., *N.W.T., Canada* 100 A6
Gordonia, *S. Africa* 84 D3
Gordonvale, *Australia* 90 B4
Gore, *Australia* 91 D5
Goré, *Chad* 73 G8
Gore, *Ethiopia* 77 F4
Gore, *N.Z.* 87 M2
Gore Bay, *Canada* 98 C3
Görele, *Turkey* 67 C8
Gorey, *Ireland* 15 D5
Gorg, *Iran* 65 D8
Gorgān, *Iran* 65 B7
Gorgona, *Italy* 32 E6
Gorgora, *Ethiopia* 77 E4
Gorham, *U.S.A.* 107 B13
Gori, *Georgia* 43 E11
Gorinchem, *Neths.* 16 E5
Gorinhatã, *Brazil* 123 E2
Goritsy, *Russia* 41 C10
Gorízia, *Italy* 33 C10
Gorki = Nizhniy Novgorod, *Russia* 41 C14
Gorki, *Belorussia* 40 D7
Gorkiy = Nizhniy Novgorod, *Russia* 41 C14
Gorkovskoye Vdkhr., *Russia* 41 C13
Gørlev, *Denmark* 11 J5
Gorlice, *Poland* 20 F11
Görlitz, *Germany* 18 D10
Gorlovka, *Ukraine* 42 B8
Gorman, *Calif., U.S.A.* 113 L8
Gorman, *Tex., U.S.A.* 109 J5
Gorna Dzhumayo = Blagoevgrad, *Bulgaria* 39 G6
Gorna Oryakhovitsa, *Bulgaria* 38 F8
Gornja Radgona, *Slovenia* 33 B13
Gornja Tuzla, *Bos.-H.* 21 L8
Gornji Grad, *Slovenia* 33 B11
Gornji Milanovac, *Serbia, Yug.* 21 M10
Gornji Vakuf, *Bos.-H.* 21 M7
Gorno-Altaysk, *Russia* 44 D9
Gorno Slinkino, *Russia* 44 C8
Gornyi, *Russia* 48 B6
Gornyy, *Russia* 41 F16
Gorodenka, *Ukraine* 42 B1
Gorodets, *Russia* 41 C13
Gorodishche, *Russia* 41 E14
Gorodishche, *Ukraine* 42 B4
Gorodnitsa, *Ukraine* 40 F5
Gorodnya, *Ukraine* 40 F7
Gorodok, *Belorussia* 40 D7
Gorodok, *Ukraine* 40 G3
Gorokhov, *Ukraine* 40 F4
Gorokhovets, *Russia* 41 C13
Gorom Gorom, *Burkina Faso* 79 C4
Goromonzi, *Zimbabwe* 83 F3
Gorongose →, *Mozam.* 85 C5
Gorongoza, *Mozam.* 83 F3
Gorongoza, Sa. da, *Mozam.* 83 F3
Gorontalo, *Indonesia* 57 D6
Goronyo, *Nigeria* 79 C6
Gorredijk, *Neths.* 16 C8
Gorron, *France* 24 D6
Gorssel, *Neths.* 16 D8
Gort, *Ireland* 15 C3
Gortis, *Greece* 37 D6
Gorzkowice, *Poland* 20 D9
Gorzów Śląski, *Poland* 20 D8
Gorzów Wielkopolski, *Poland* 20 C5
Göschenen, *Switz.* 23 C7
Gosford, *Australia* 91 E5
Goshen, *Calif., U.S.A.* 112 J7
Goshen, *Ind., U.S.A.* 104 E3
Goshen, *N.Y., U.S.A.* 107 E10
Goshogawara, *Japan* 48 D10
Goslar, *Germany* 18 D6
Gospič, *Croatia* 33 D12
Gosport, *U.K.* 13 G6
Gossau, *Switz.* 23 B8
Gosse →, *Australia* 90 B1
Gostivar, *Macedonia, Yug.* 39 H3
Gostyń, *Poland* 20 D7
Gostynin, *Poland* 20 C9
Göta älv →, *Sweden* 11 G5
Göta kanal, *Sweden* 9 G12
Göteborg, *Sweden* 11 G5
Göteborgs och Bohus län □, *Sweden* 9 G11
Götene, *Sweden* 11 F7
Gotha, *Germany* 18 E6
Gothenburg, *U.S.A.* 108 E4
Gotland, *Sweden* 9 H15
Gotse Delchev, *Bulgaria* 39 H6
Gotska Sandön, *Sweden* 9 G15
Gōtsu, *Japan* 49 G6
Göttingen, *Germany* 18 D5
Gottwald = Zmiyev, *Ukraine* 42 B7
Gottwaldov = Zlin, *Czech.* 20 F7
Goubangzi, *China* 51 D11
Gouda, *Neths.* 16 D5
Goúdhoura, Ákra, *Greece* 37 E8
Goudiry, *Senegal* 78 C2
Gough I., *Atl. Oc.* 2 G9
Gouin, Rés., *Canada* 98 C5
Gouitafla, *Ivory C.* 78 D3
Goulburn, *Australia* 91 E4
Goulburn Is., *Australia* 90 A1
Goulia, *Ivory C.* 78 C3
Goulimine, *Morocco* 74 C3
Goulmina, *Morocco* 74 B4
Gounou-Gaya, *Chad* 73 G8
Goúra, *Greece* 39 M5
Gouraya, *Algeria* 75 A5
Gourdon, *France* 26 D5
Gouré, *Niger* 79 C7
Gouri, *Chad* 73 E8
Gourits →, *S. Africa* 84 E3
Gourma Rharous, *Mali* 79 B4
Goúrnais, *Greece* 37 D7
Gournay-en-Bray, *France* 25 C8
Gourock Ra., *Australia* 91 F4
Goursi, *Burkina Faso* 78 C4
Gouvêa, *Brazil* 123 E3
Gouverneur, *U.S.A.* 107 B9
Gouviá, *Greece* 37 A3
Gouzon, *France* 26 B6
Govan, *Canada* 101 C8
Governador Valadares, *Brazil* 123 E3
Governor's Harbour, *Bahamas* 116 A4
Gowan Ra., *Australia* 90 C4
Gowanda, *U.S.A.* 106 D6
Gowd-e Zirreh, *Afghan.* 60 E3
Gower, *U.K.* 13 F3
Gowna, L., *Ireland* 15 C4
Goya, *Argentina* 126 B4
Goyder Lagoon, *Australia* 91 D2
Goyllarisquisga, *Peru* 124 C2
Göynük, *Turkey* 66 C4
Goz Beïda, *Chad* 73 F9
Goz Regeb, *Sudan* 77 D4
Gozo, *Malta* 37 C1
Graaff-Reinet, *S. Africa* 84 E3
Grabow, *Germany* 18 B7
Grabs, *Switz.* 23 B8
Gračac, *Croatia* 33 D12
Gračanica, *Bos.-H.* 21 L8
Graçay, *France* 25 E8
Grace, *U.S.A.* 110 E8
Graceville, *U.S.A.* 108 C6
Gracias a Dios, C., *Honduras* 116 C3
Graciosa, I., *Canary Is.* 36 E6
Gradaús, *Brazil* 122 C1
Gradaús, Serra dos, *Brazil* 122 C1
Gradets, *Bulgaria* 38 G9
Grado, *Italy* 33 C10
Grado, *Spain* 30 B4
Gradule, *Australia* 91 D4
Grady, *U.S.A.* 109 H3
Graeca, Lacul, *Romania* 38 E9
Graénalon, L., *Iceland* 8 D5
Grafenau, *Germany* 19 G9
Gräfenberg, *Germany* 19 F7
Grafton, *Australia* 91 D5
Grafton, *U.S.A.* 108 A6
Gragnano, *Italy* 35 B7
Graham, *Canada* 98 C1
Graham, *N.C., U.S.A.* 105 G6
Graham, *Tex., U.S.A.* 109 J5
Graham →, *Canada* 100 B4
Graham, Mt., *U.S.A.* 111 K9
Graham Bell, Os., *Russia* 44 A7
Graham I., *Canada* 100 C2
Graham Land, *Antarctica* 5 C17
Grahamdale, *Canada* 101 C9
Grahamstown, *S. Africa* 84 E4
Graïba, *Tunisia* 75 B7
Graide, *Belgium* 17 J6
Graie, Alpi, *Europe* 32 C4
Grain Coast, *W. Afr.* 70 F2
Grajaú, *Brazil* 122 C2
Grajaú →, *Brazil* 122 B3
Grajewo, *Poland* 20 B12
Gramada, *Bulgaria* 38 F5
Gramat, *France* 26 D5
Grammichele, *Italy* 35 E7
Grampian □, *U.K.* 14 D6
Grampian Highlands = Grampian Mts., *U.K.* 14 E5
Grampian Mts., *U.K.* 14 E5
Gran →, *Surinam* 121 C6
Gran Altiplanicie Central, *Argentina* 128 C3
Gran Canaria, *Canary Is.* 36 F4
Gran Chaco, *S. Amer.* 126 B3
Gran Paradiso, *Italy* 32 C4
Gran Sasso d'Italia, *Italy* 33 F10
Granada, *Nic.* 116 D2
Granada, *Spain* 29 H1
Granada, *U.S.A.* 109 F3
Granada □, *Spain* 31 H7
Granadilla de Abona, *Canary Is.* 36 F3
Granard, *Ireland* 15 C4
Granbury, *U.S.A.* 109 J6
Granby, *Canada* 98 C5
Grand →, *Mo., U.S.A.* 108 F8
Grand →, *S. Dak., U.S.A.* 108 C4
Grand Bahama, *Bahamas* 116 A4
Grand Bank, *Canada* 99 C8
Grand Bassam, *Ivory C.* 78 D4
Grand Béréby, *Ivory C.* 78 E3
Grand-Bourg, *Guadeloupe* 117 C7
Grand Canal = Yun Ho →, *China* 51 E9
Grand Canyon, *U.S.A.* 111 H7
Grand Canyon National Park, *U.S.A.* 111 H7
Grand Cayman, *Cayman Is.* 116 C3
Grand Cess, *Liberia* 78 E3
Grand Coulee, *U.S.A.* 110 C4
Grand Coulee Dam, *U.S.A.* 110 C4
Grand Erg Occidental, *Algeria* 75 B5
Grand Erg Oriental, *Algeria* 75 C6
Grand Falls, *Canada* 99 C8
Grand Forks, *Canada* 100 D5
Grand Forks, *U.S.A.* 108 B6
Grand-Fougeray, *France* 24 E5
Grand Haven, *U.S.A.* 104 D2
Grand I., *U.S.A.* 104 B2
Grand Island, *U.S.A.* 108 E5
Grand Isle, *U.S.A.* 109 L10
Grand Junction, *U.S.A.* 111 G9
Grand L., *U.S.A.* 109 L8
Grand Lac Victoria, *Canada* 98 C4
Grand Lahou, *Ivory C.* 78 D3
Grand L., *N.B., Canada* 99 C6
Grand L., *Nfld., Canada* 99 C8
Grand L., *Nfld., Canada* 99 B7
Grand Lake, *U.S.A.* 110 F11
Grand-Leez, *Belgium* 17 G5
Grand-Lieu, L. de, *France* 24 E5
Grand Manan I., *Canada* 99 D6
Grand Marais, *Canada* 108 B9
Grand Marais, *U.S.A.* 104 B3
Grand-Mère, *Canada* 98 C5
Grand Popo, *Benin* 79 D5
Grand Portage, *U.S.A.* 98 C2
Grand Rapids, *Canada* 101 C9
Grand Rapids, *Mich., U.S.A.* 104 D2
Grand Rapids, *Minn., U.S.A.* 108 B8
Grand St-Bernard, Col du, *Switz.* 22 E4
Grand Santi, *Fr. Guiana* 121 C7
Grand Teton, *U.S.A.* 110 E8
Grand Valley, *U.S.A.* 110 G9
Grand View, *Canada* 101 C8
Grandas de Salime, *Spain* 30 B4
Grande →, *Jujuy, Argentina* 126 A2
Grande →, *Mendoza, Argentina* 126 D2
Grande →, *Bolivia* 125 D5
Grande →, *Bahia, Brazil* 122 D3
Grande →, *Minas Gerais, Brazil* 123 F1
Grande →, *Spain* 29 F4
Grande →, *Venezuela* 121 B5
Grande, B., *Argentina* 128 D3
Grande, I., *Brazil* 123 F3
Grande, Rio →, *U.S.A.* 109 N6
Grande, Serra, *Goiás, Brazil* 122 D2
Grande, Serra, *Piauí, Brazil* 122 C2
Grande Baie, *Canada* 99 C5
Grande Baleine, R. de la →, *Canada* 98 A4
Grande Cache, *Canada* 100 C5
Grande de Santiago →, *Mexico* 114 C3
Grande Dixence, Barr. de la, *Switz.* 22 D4
Grande-Entrée, *Canada* 99 C7
Grande Prairie, *Canada* 100 B5
Grande-Rivière, *Canada* 99 C7
Grande Sauldre →, *France* 25 E9
Grande-Vallée, *Canada* 99 C6
Grandes-Bergeronnes, *Canada* 99 C6
Grandfalls, *U.S.A.* 109 K3
Grandoe Mines, *Canada* 100 B3
Grândola, *Portugal* 31 G2
Grandpré, *France* 25 C11
Grandson, *Switz.* 22 C3
Grandview, *U.S.A.* 110 C4
Grandvilliers, *France* 25 C8
Graneros, *Chile* 126 C1
Grangemouth, *U.K.* 14 E5
Granger, *Wash., U.S.A.* 110 C3
Granger, *Wyo., U.S.A.* 110 F9
Grangeville, *U.S.A.* 110 D5
Granite City, *U.S.A.* 108 F9
Granite Falls, *U.S.A.* 108 C7
Granite Mt., *U.S.A.* 113 M10
Granite Peak, *Australia* 89 E3
Granite Peak, *U.S.A.* 110 D9
Granity, *N.Z.* 87 J3
Granja, *Brazil* 122 B3
Granja de Moreruela, *Spain* 30 D5
Granja de Torrehermosa, *Spain* 31 G5
Granollers, *Spain* 28 D7
Gransee, *Germany* 18 B9
Grant, *U.S.A.* 108 E4
Grant, Mt., *U.S.A.* 110 G4
Grant City, *U.S.A.* 108 E7
Grant I., *Australia* 88 B5
Grant Range, *U.S.A.* 111 G6
Grantham, *U.K.* 12 E7
Grantown-on-Spey, *U.K.* 14 D5
Grants, *U.S.A.* 111 J10
Grants Pass, *U.S.A.* 110 E2
Grantsburg, *U.S.A.* 108 C8
Grantsville, *U.S.A.* 110 F7
Granville, *France* 24 D5
Granville, *N. Dak., U.S.A.* 108 A4
Granville, *N.Y., U.S.A.* 104 D9
Granville L., *Canada* 101 B8
Grao de Gandía, *Spain* 29 F4
Grapeland, *U.S.A.* 109 K7
Gras, L. de, *Canada* 96 B8
Graskop, *S. Africa* 85 C5
Grass →, *Canada* 101 B9
Grass Range, *U.S.A.* 110 C9
Grass River Prov. Park, *Canada* 101 C8
Grass Valley, *Calif., U.S.A.* 112 F6
Grass Valley, *Oreg., U.S.A.* 110 D3
Grassano, *Italy* 35 B9
Grasse, *France* 27 E10
Grassmere, *Australia* 91 E3
Graubünden □, *Switz.* 23 C9
Graulhet, *France* 26 E5
Graus, *Spain* 28 C5
Gravatá, *Brazil* 122 C4
Grave, *Neths.* 16 E7
Grave, Pte. de, *France* 26 C2
's-Graveland, *Neths.* 16 D6
Gravelbourg, *Canada* 101 D7
Gravelines, *France* 25 B9
's-Gravendeel, *Neths.* 16 E5
's-Gravenhage, *Neths.* 16 D4
Gravenhurst, *Canada* 106 B5
's-Gravenpolder, *Neths.* 17 F3
's-Gravensande, *Neths.* 16 D4
Gravesend, *Australia* 91 D5
Gravesend, *U.K.* 13 F8
Gravina di Púglia, *Italy* 35 B9
Gravois, Pointe-à-, *Haiti* 117 C5
Gravone →, *France* 27 G12
Gray, *France* 25 E12
Grayling, *U.S.A.* 104 C3
Grayling →, *Canada* 100 B3
Grays Harbor, *U.S.A.* 110 C1
Grays L., *U.S.A.* 110 E8
Grays River, *U.S.A.* 112 D3
Grayson, *Canada* 101 C8
Graz, *Austria* 21 H5
Grazalema, *Spain* 31 J5
Greasy L., *Canada* 100 A4
Great Abaco I., *Bahamas* 116 A4
Great Artesian Basin, *Australia* 90 C3
Great Australian Bight, *Australia* 89 F5
Great Bahama Bank, *Bahamas* 116 B4
Great Barrier I., *N.Z.* 87 G5
Great Barrier Reef, *Australia* 90 B4
Great Barrington, *U.S.A.* 107 D11
Great Basin, *U.S.A.* 110 G5
Great Bear →, *Canada* 96 B7
Great Bear L., *Canada* 96 B7
Great Belt = Store Bælt, *Denmark* 11 J5
Great Bend, *Kans., U.S.A.* 108 F5
Great Bend, *Pa., U.S.A.* 107 E9
Great Blasket I., *Ireland* 15 D1
Great Britain, *Europe* 6 E5
Great Central, *Canada* 100 D3
Great Dividing Ra., *Australia* 90 C4
Great Driffield, *U.K.* 12 C7
Great Exuma I., *Bahamas* 116 B4
Great Falls, *Canada* 101 C9
Great Falls, *U.S.A.* 110 C8
Great Fish = Groot Vis →, *S. Africa* 84 E4
Great Guana Cay, *Bahamas* 116 B4
Great Harbour Deep, *Canada* 99 B8
Great Inagua I., *Bahamas* 117 B5
Great Indian Desert = Thar Desert, *India* 62 F4
Great I., *Canada* 101 B9
Great Karoo, *S. Africa* 84 E3
Great Lake, *Australia* 90 G4
Great Ormes Head, *U.K.* 12 D4
Great Ouse →, *U.K.* 12 E8
Great Palm I., *Australia* 90 B4
Great Plains, *N. Amer.* 102 A6
Great Ruaha →, *Tanzania* 82 D4
Great Saint Bernard P. = Grand St-Bernard, Col du, *Switz.* 22 E4
Great Salt L., *U.S.A.* 110 F7
Great Salt Lake Desert, *U.S.A.* 110 F7
Great Salt Plains L., *U.S.A.* 109 G5
Great Sandy Desert, *Australia* 88 D3
Great Sangi = Sangihe, P., *Indonesia* 57 D7
Great Scarcies →, *S. Leone* 78 D2
Great Slave L., *Canada* 100 A5
Great Smoky Mts. Nat. Pk., *U.S.A.* 105 H4
Great Stour = Stour →, *U.K.* 13 F9
Great Victoria Desert, *Australia* 89 E4
Great Wall, *China* 50 E5
Great Whernside, *U.K.* 12 C6
Great Yarmouth, *U.K.* 12 E9
Greater Antilles, *W. Indies* 117 C5
Greater London □, *U.K.* 13 F7
Greater Manchester □, *U.K.* 12 D5
Greater Sunda Is., *Indonesia* 56 F4
Grebbestad, *Sweden* 11 F5
Grebenka, *Ukraine* 40 F8
Greco, C., *Cyprus* 37 E13
Greco, Mte., *Italy* 34 A6
Gredos, Sierra de, *Spain* 30 E5
Greece, *U.S.A.* 106 C7
Greece ■, *Europe* 39 K6
Greeley, *Colo., U.S.A.* 108 E2
Greeley, *Nebr., U.S.A.* 108 E5
Green →, *Ky., U.S.A.* 104 G2
Green →, *Utah, U.S.A.* 111 G9
Green B., *U.S.A.* 104 C2
Green Bay, *U.S.A.* 104 C2
Green C., *Australia* 91 F5
Green Cove Springs, *U.S.A.* 105 L5
Green River, *U.S.A.* 111 G8
Greenbank, *U.S.A.* 112 B4
Greenbush, *Mich., U.S.A.* 106 B1
Greenbush, *Minn., U.S.A.* 108 A6
Greencastle, *U.S.A.* 104 F2
Greene, *U.S.A.* 107 D9
Greenfield, *Calif., U.S.A.* 112 J5
Greenfield, *Calif., U.S.A.* 113 K8
Greenfield, *Ind., U.S.A.* 104 F3
Greenfield, *Iowa, U.S.A.* 108 E7
Greenfield, *Mass., U.S.A.* 107 D12
Greenfield, *Mo., U.S.A.* 109 G8
Greenfield Park, *Canada* 107 A11
Greenland ■, *N. Amer.* 4 C5
Greenland Sea, *Arctic* 4 B7
Greenock, *U.K.* 14 F4
Greenore, *Ireland* 15 B5
Greenore Pt., *Ireland* 15 D5
Greenough →, *Australia* 89 E1
Greenport, *U.S.A.* 107 E12
Greensboro, *Ga., U.S.A.* 105 J4
Greensboro, *N.C., U.S.A.* 105 G6
Greensburg, *Ind., U.S.A.* 104 F3
Greensburg, *Kans., U.S.A.* 109 G5
Greensburg, *Pa., U.S.A.* 106 F5
Greenville, *Liberia* 78 D3
Greenville, *Ala., U.S.A.* 105 K2
Greenville, *Calif., U.S.A.* 112 E6
Greenville, *Ill., U.S.A.* 108 F10
Greenville, *Maine, U.S.A.* 99 C6
Greenville, *Mich., U.S.A.* 104 D3
Greenville, *Miss., U.S.A.* 109 J9
Greenville, *N.C., U.S.A.* 105 H7
Greenville, *Ohio, U.S.A.* 104 E3
Greenville, *Pa., U.S.A.* 106 E4
Greenville, *S.C., U.S.A.* 105 H4
Greenville, *Tenn., U.S.A.* 105 G4
Greenville, *Tex., U.S.A.* 109 J6
Greenwater Lake Prov. Park, *Canada* 101 C8
Greenwich, *U.K.* 13 F8
Greenwich, *Conn., U.S.A.* 107 E11
Greenwich, *N.Y., U.S.A.* 107 C11
Greenwich, *Ohio, U.S.A.* 106 E2
Greenwood, *Canada* 100 D5
Greenwood, *Miss., U.S.A.* 109 J9
Greenwood, *S.C., U.S.A.* 105 H4
Greenwood, Mt., *Australia* 88 B5
Gregório →, *Brazil* 124 B3
Gregory, *U.S.A.* 108 D5
Gregory →, *Australia* 90 B2
Gregory, L., *S. Austral., Australia* 91 D2
Gregory, L., *W. Austral., Australia* 89 E2
Gregory Downs, *Australia* 90 B2
Gregory L., *Australia* 88 D4
Gregory Ra., *Queens., Australia* 90 B3
Gregory Ra., *W. Austral., Australia* 88 D3
Greiffenberg, *Germany* 18 B9
Greifswald, *Germany* 18 A9
Greifswalder Bodden, *Germany* 18 A9
Grein, *Austria* 21 G4
Greiz, *Germany* 18 E8
Gremikha, *Russia* 44 C4
Grenå, *Denmark* 11 H4

Grenada, *U.S.A.* 109 J10
Grenada ■, *W. Indies* 117 D7
Grenade, *France* 26 E5
Grenadines, *W. Indies* 117 D7
Grenchen, *Switz.* 22 B4
Grenen, *Denmark* 11 G4
Grenfell, *Australia* 91 E4
Grenfell, *Canada* 101 C8
Grenoble, *France* 27 C9
Grenora, *U.S.A.* 108 A3
Grenville, C., *Australia* 90 A3
Grenville Chan., *Canada* 100 C3
Gréoux-les-Bains, *France* 27 E9
Gresham, *U.S.A.* 112 E4
Gresik, *Indonesia* 57 G15
Grèssoney St. Jean, *Italy* 32 C4
Gretna Green, *U.K.* 14 F5
Grevelingen Krammer, *Neths.* 16 E4
Greven, *Germany* 18 C3
Grevená, *Greece* 39 J4
Grevenbroich, *Germany* 18 D2
Grevenmacher, *Lux.* 17 J8
Grevesmühlen, *Germany* 18 B7
Grevie, *Sweden* 11 H6
Grey →, *N.Z.* 87 K3
Grey, C., *Australia* 90 A2
Grey Ra., *Australia* 91 D3
Grey Res., *Canada* 99 C8
Greybull, *U.S.A.* 110 D9
Greymouth, *N.Z.* 87 K3
Greytown, *N.Z.* 87 J5
Greytown, *S. Africa* 85 D5
Gribanovskiy, *Russia* 41 F12
Gribbell I., *Canada* 100 C3
Gridley, *U.S.A.* 112 F5
Griekwastad, *S. Africa* 84 D3
Griffin, *U.S.A.* 105 J3
Griffith, *Australia* 91 E4
Grijpskerk, *Neths.* 16 B8
Grillby, *Sweden* 10 E11
Grimari, *C.A.R.* 73 G9
Grimaylov, *Ukraine* 40 G5
Grimbergen, *Belgium* 17 G4
Grimes, *U.S.A.* 112 F5
Grimma, *Germany* 18 D8
Grimmen, *Germany* 18 A9
Grimsby, *Canada* 106 C5
Grimsby, *U.K.* 12 D7
Grimselpass, *Switz.* 23 C6
Grímsey, *Iceland* 8 C5
Grimshaw, *Canada* 100 B5
Grimstad, *Norway* 11 F2
Grindelwald, *Switz.* 22 C6
Grindsted, *Denmark* 11 J2
Grindu, *Romania* 38 E9
Grinnell, *U.S.A.* 108 E8
Griñón, *Spain* 30 E7
Grintavec, *Slovenia* 33 B11
Grip, *Norway* 10 A1
Gris-Nez, C., *France* 25 B8
Grisolles, *France* 26 E5
Grisons = Graubünden □, *Switz.* 23 C9
Grivegnée, *Belgium* 17 G7
Grmeč Planina, *Bos.-H.* 33 D13
Groais I., *Canada* 99 B8
Groblersdal, *S. Africa* 85 D4
Grobming, *Austria* 21 H3
Grodno, *Belorussia* 40 E3
Grodzisk Mázowiecki, *Poland* 20 C10
Grodzisk Wielkopolski, *Poland* 20 C6
Grodzyanka, *Belorussia* 40 E6
Groenlo, *Neths.* 16 D9
Groesbeck, *U.S.A.* 109 K6
Groesbeek, *Neths.* 16 E7
Groix, *France* 24 E3
Groix, I. de, *France* 24 E3
Grójec, *Poland* 20 D10
Grolloo, *Neths.* 16 C9
Gronau, *Niedersachsen, Germany* 18 C5
Gronau, *Nordrhein-Westfalen, Germany* 18 C3
Grong, *Norway* 8 D12
Groningen, *Neths.* 16 B9
Groningen, *Surinam* 121 B6
Groningen □, *Neths.* 16 B9
Groninger Wad, *Neths.* 16 B9
Gronsveld, *Neths.* 17 G7
Groom, *U.S.A.* 109 H4
Groot →, *S. Africa* 84 E3
Groot Berg →, *S. Africa* 84 E2
Groot-Brakrivier, *S. Africa* 84 E3
Groot-Kei →, *S. Africa* 85 E4
Groot Vis →, *S. Africa* 84 E4
Groote Eylandt, *Australia* 90 A2
Grootebroek, *Neths.* 16 C6
Grootfontein, *Namibia* 84 B2
Grootlaagte →, *Africa* 84 C3
Grootvloer, *S. Africa* 84 E3
Gros C., *Canada* 100 A6
Grosa, Pta., *Spain* 36 B8
Grósio, *Italy* 32 B7
Grosne →, *France* 27 B8
Gross Glockner, *Austria* 21 H2
Grossenbrode, *Germany* 18 A7
Grossenhain, *Germany* 18 D9
Grosseto, *Italy* 32 F8
Groswater B., *Canada* 99 B8
Grote Gette →, *Neths.* 17 G6
Grote Nete →, *Belgium* 17 F5
Groton, *Conn., U.S.A.* 107 E12
Groton, *S. Dak., U.S.A.* 108 C5
Grottáglie, *Italy* 35 B10
Grottaminarda, *Italy* 35 A8
Grottammare, *Italy* 33 F10
Grouard Mission, *Canada* 100 B5
Grouin, Pte. du, *France* 24 D5
Groundhog →, *Canada* 98 C3
Grouse Creek, *U.S.A.* 110 F7
Grouw, *Neths.* 16 B7
Grove City, *U.S.A.* 106 E4
Groveland, *U.S.A.* 112 H6
Grover City, *U.S.A.* 113 K6
Groveton, *N.H., U.S.A.* 107 B13
Groveton, *Tex., U.S.A.* 109 K7
Grožnjan, *Croatia* 33 C10
Groznyy, *Russia* 43 E11
Grubbenvorst, *Neths.* 17 F8
Grudziądz, *Poland* 20 B8
Gruissan, *France* 26 E7
Grumo Áppula, *Italy* 35 A9
Grünberg, *Germany* 18 E4
Grundy Center, *U.S.A.* 108 D8
Gruver, *U.S.A.* 109 G4
Gruyères, *Switz.* 22 C4
Gryazi, *Russia* 41 E11
Gryazovets, *Russia* 41 B12
Gstaad, *Switz.* 22 D4
Gua, *India* 61 H14
Gua Musang, *Malaysia* 59 K3
Guacanayabo, G. de, *Cuba* 116 B4
Guacara, *Venezuela* 120 A4
Guachípas →, *Argentina* 126 B2
Guachiría →, *Colombia* 120 B3
Guadajoz →, *Spain* 31 H6
Guadalajara, *Mexico* 114 C4
Guadalajara, *Spain* 28 E1
Guadalajara □, *Spain* 28 E2
Guadalcanal, *Solomon Is.* 92 H8
Guadalcanal, *Spain* 31 G5
Guadalén →, *Spain* 31 G7
Guadales, *Argentina* 126 C2
Guadalete →, *Spain* 31 J4
Guadalhorce →, *Spain* 31 J6
Guadalimar →, *Spain* 29 G1
Guadalmena →, *Spain* 29 G2
Guadalmez →, *Spain* 31 G5
Guadalope →, *Spain* 28 D4
Guadalquivir →, *Spain* 31 J4
Guadalupe = Guadeloupe ■, *W. Indies* 117 C7
Guadalupe, *Brazil* 122 C3
Guadalupe, *Mexico* 113 N10
Guadalupe, *Spain* 31 F5
Guadalupe, *U.S.A.* 113 L6
Guadalupe →, *Mexico* 113 N10
Guadalupe →, *U.S.A.* 109 L6
Guadalupe, Sierra de, *Spain* 31 F5
Guadalupe Bravos, *Mexico* 114 A3
Guadalupe Peak, *U.S.A.* 111 L11
Guadalupe y Calvo, *Mexico* 114 B3
Guadarrama, Sierra de, *Spain* 30 E6
Guadeloupe ■, *W. Indies* 117 C7
Guadeloupe Passage, *W. Indies* 117 C7
Guadiamar →, *Spain* 31 J4
Guadiana →, *Portugal* 31 H3
Guadiana Menor →, *Spain* 29 H1
Guadiaro →, *Spain* 31 J5
Guadiato →, *Spain* 31 H5
Guadiela →, *Spain* 28 E2
Guadix, *Spain* 29 H1
Guafo, Boca del, *Chile* 128 B2
Guafo, I., *Chile* 128 B2
Guainía □, *Colombia* 120 C4
Guainía →, *Colombia* 120 C4
Guaíra, *Brazil* 127 A5
Guaitecas, Is., *Chile* 128 B2
Guajará-Mirim, *Brazil* 125 C4
Guajira □, *Colombia* 120 A3
Guajira, Pen. de la, *Colombia* 120 A3
Gualaceo, *Ecuador* 120 D2
Gualán, *Guatemala* 116 C2
Gualdo Tadino, *Italy* 33 E9
Gualeguay, *Argentina* 126 C4
Gualeguaychú, *Argentina* 126 C4
Gualicho, Salina, *Argentina* 128 B3
Gualjaina, *Argentina* 128 B2
Guam ■, *Pac. Oc.* 92 F6
Guamá, *Brazil* 122 B2
Guamá →, *Brazil* 122 B2
Guamblin, I., *Chile* 128 B1
Guaminí, *Argentina* 126 D3
Guamote, *Ecuador* 120 D2
Guampí, Sierra de, *Venezuela* 121 B4
Guamúchil, *Mexico* 114 B3
Guan Xian, *China* 52 B4
Guanabacoa, *Cuba* 116 B3
Guanacaste, Cordillera del, *Costa Rica* 116 D2
Guanaceví, *Mexico* 114 B3
Guanahani = San Salvador, *Bahamas* 117 B5
Guanajay, *Cuba* 116 B3
Guanajuato, *Mexico* 114 C4
Guanajuato □, *Mexico* 114 C4
Guanambi, *Brazil* 123 D3
Guanare, *Venezuela* 120 B4
Guanare →, *Venezuela* 120 B4
Guandacol, *Argentina* 126 B2
Guane, *Cuba* 116 B3
Guang'an, *China* 52 B6
Guangchang, *China* 53 D11
Guangde, *China* 53 B12
Guangdong □, *China* 53 F9
Guangfeng, *China* 53 C12
Guanghan, *China* 52 B5
Guanghua, *China* 53 A8
Guangji, *China* 53 C10
Guangling, *China* 50 E8
Guangning, *China* 53 F9
Guangrao, *China* 51 F10
Guangshun, *China* 52 D6
Guangwu, *China* 50 F3
Guangxi Zhuangzu Zizhiqu □, *China* 52 E7
Guangyuan, *China* 52 A5
Guangze, *China* 53 D11
Guangzhou, *China* 53 F9
Guanhães, *Brazil* 123 E3
Guanipa →, *Venezuela* 121 B5
Guanling, *China* 52 E5
Guannan, *China* 51 G10
Guanta, *Venezuela* 121 A5
Guantánamo, *Cuba* 117 B4
Guantao, *China* 50 F8
Guanyang, *China* 53 E8
Guanyun, *China* 51 G10
Guapí, *Colombia* 120 C2
Guápiles, *Costa Rica* 116 D3
Guaporé →, *Brazil* 125 C4
Guaqui, *Bolivia* 124 D4
Guara, Sierra de, *Spain* 28 C4
Guarabira, *Brazil* 122 C4
Guaranda, *Ecuador* 120 D2
Guarapari, *Brazil* 123 F3
Guarapuava, *Brazil* 123 G1
Guaratinguetá, *Brazil* 127 A6
Guaratuba, *Brazil* 127 B6
Guarda, *Portugal* 30 E3
Guarda □, *Portugal* 30 E3
Guardafui, C. = Asir, Ras, *Somali Rep.* 68 E5
Guardamar del Segura, *Spain* 29 G4
Guardavalle, *Italy* 35 D9
Guardiagrele, *Italy* 33 F11
Guardo, *Spain* 30 C6
Guareña, *Spain* 31 G4
Guareña →, *Spain* 30 D5
Guaria □, *Paraguay* 126 B4
Guárico □, *Venezuela* 120 B4
Guarrojo →, *Colombia* 120 C3
Guarujá, *Brazil* 127 A6
Guarus, *Brazil* 123 F3
Guasave, *Mexico* 114 B3
Guascama, Pta., *Colombia* 120 C2
Guasdualito, *Venezuela* 120 B3
Guasipati, *Venezuela* 121 B5
Guastalla, *Italy* 32 D7
Guatemala, *Guatemala* 116 D1
Guatemala ■, *Cent. Amer.* 116 C1
Guatire, *Venezuela* 120 A4
Guaviare □, *Colombia* 120 C3
Guaviare →, *Colombia* 120 C4
Guaxupé, *Brazil* 127 A6
Guayabero →, *Colombia* 120 C3
Guayama, *Puerto Rico* 117 C6
Guayaneco, Arch., *Chile* 128 C1
Guayaquil, *Ecuador* 120 D2
Guayaquil, G. de, *Ecuador* 120 D1
Guayaramerín, *Bolivia* 125 C4
Guayas →, *Ecuador* 120 D2
Guaymas, *Mexico* 114 B2
Guazhou, *China* 53 A12
Guba, *Zaïre* 83 E2
Gûbâl, Madîq, *Egypt* 76 B3
Gubat, *Phil.* 55 E6
Gúbbio, *Italy* 33 E9
Gubio, *Nigeria* 79 C7
Gubkin, *Russia* 41 F10
Gudata, *Georgia* 43 E9
Gudbrandsdalen, *Norway* 9 F10
Guddu Barrage, *Pakistan* 60 E6
Gudenå, *Denmark* 11 H3
Gudermes, *Russia* 43 E12
Gudivada, *India* 61 L12
Gudur, *India* 60 M11
Guebwiller, *France* 25 E14
Guecho, *Spain* 28 B2
Guékédou, *Guinea* 78 D2
Guelma, *Algeria* 75 A6
Guelph, *Canada* 98 D3
Guelt es Stel, *Algeria* 75 A5
Guelttara, *Algeria* 75 C4
Guemar, *Algeria* 75 B6
Guéméné-Penfao, *France* 24 E5
Guéméné-sur-Scorff, *France* 24 D3
Guéné, *Benin* 79 C5
Güepi, *Peru* 120 D2
Guer, *France* 24 E4
Güer Aike, *Argentina* 128 D3
Guérande, *France* 24 E4
Guercif, *Morocco* 75 B4
Guéréda, *Chad* 73 F9
Guéret, *France* 26 B5
Guérigny, *France* 25 E10
Guerneville, *U.S.A.* 112 G4
Guernica, *Spain* 28 B2
Guernsey, *U.K.* 13 H5
Guernsey, *U.S.A.* 108 D2
Guerrara, *Oasis, Algeria* 75 B5
Guerrara, *Saoura, Algeria* 75 C4
Guerrero □, *Mexico* 115 D5
Guerzim, *Algeria* 75 C4
Gueugnon, *France* 27 B8
Gueydan, *U.S.A.* 109 K8
Gügher, *Iran* 65 D8
Guglionesi, *Italy* 35 A7
Gui Jiang →, *China* 53 F8
Gui Xian, *China* 52 F7
Guia, *Canary Is.* 36 F4
Guia de Isora, *Canary Is.* 36 F3
Guia Lopes da Laguna, *Brazil* 127 A4
Guichi, *China* 53 B11
Guider, *Cameroon* 79 D7
Guidimouni, *Niger* 79 C6
Guiding, *China* 52 D6
Guidong, *China* 53 D9
Guiglo, *Ivory C.* 78 D3
Guijá, *Mozam.* 85 C5
Guijo de Coria, *Spain* 30 E4
Guildford, *U.K.* 13 F7
Guilford, *U.S.A.* 99 C6
Guilin, *China* 53 E8
Guillaumes, *France* 27 D10
Guillestre, *France* 27 D10
Guilvinec, *France* 24 E2
Güimar, *Canary Is.* 36 F3
Guimarães, *Brazil* 122 B3
Guimarães, *Portugal* 30 D2
Guimaras, *Phil.* 55 F5
Guinda, *U.S.A.* 112 G4
Guinea ■, *W. Afr.* 78 C2
Guinea, Gulf of, *Atl. Oc.* 70 F3
Guinea-Bissau ■, *Africa* 78 C2
Güines, *Cuba* 116 B3
Guingamp, *France* 24 D3
Guipavas, *France* 24 D2
Guiping, *China* 53 F8
Guipúzcoa □, *Spain* 28 B2
Guir, O. →, *Algeria* 75 B4
Guiratinga, *Brazil* 125 D7
Güiria, *Venezuela* 121 A5
Guiscard, *France* 25 C10
Guise, *France* 25 C10
Guitiriz, *Spain* 30 B3
Guiuan, *Phil.* 55 F6
Guixi, *China* 53 C11
Guiyang, *Guizhou, China* 52 D6
Guiyang, *Hunan, China* 53 E9
Guizhou □, *China* 52 D6
Gujan-Mestras, *France* 26 D2
Gujarat □, *India* 62 H4
Gujiang, *China* 53 D10
Gujranwala, *Pakistan* 62 C6
Gujrat, *Pakistan* 62 C6
Gukovo, *Russia* 43 B8
Gulbarga, *India* 60 L10
Gulbene, *Latvia* 40 C5
Gulf, The, *Asia* 65 E6
Gulfport, *U.S.A.* 109 K10
Gulgong, *Australia* 91 E4
Gulin, *China* 52 C5
Gulistan, *Pakistan* 62 D2
Gull Lake, *Canada* 101 C7
Gullegem, *Belgium* 17 G2
Güllük, *Turkey* 66 E2
Gulma, *Nigeria* 79 C5
Gulmarg, *India* 63 B6
Gülnar, *Turkey* 66 E5
Gulpen, *Neths.* 17 G7
Gülşehir, *Turkey* 66 D6
Gulshad, *Kazakhstan* 44 E8
Gulsvik, *Norway* 10 D3
Gulu, *Uganda* 82 B3
Gulwe, *Tanzania* 82 D4
Gulyaypole, *Ukraine* 42 C7
Gum Lake, *Australia* 91 E3
Gumal →, *Pakistan* 62 D4
Gumbaz, *Pakistan* 62 D3
Gumel, *Nigeria* 79 C6
Gumiel de Hizán, *Spain* 28 D1
Gumlu, *Australia* 90 B4
Gumma □, *Japan* 49 F9
Gummersbach, *Germany* 18 D3
Gummi, *Nigeria* 79 C6
Gümüşhaciköy, *Turkey* 42 F6
Gümüşhane, *Turkey* 67 C8
Gümüşhane □, *Turkey* 67 C8
Gumzai, *Indonesia* 57 F8
Guna, *Ethiopia* 77 E4
Guna, *India* 62 G7
Gundagai, *Australia* 91 F4
Gundelfingen, *Germany* 19 G6
Gundih, *Indonesia* 57 G14
Guneydogu Toroslar, *Turkey* 67 D9
Gungu, *Zaïre* 80 F3
Gunisao →, *Canada* 101 C9
Gunisao L., *Canada* 101 C9
Gunnbjørn Fjeld, *Greenland* 4 C6
Gunnedah, *Australia* 91 E5
Gunningbar Cr. →, *Australia* 91 E4
Gunnison, *Colo., U.S.A.* 111 G10
Gunnison, *Utah, U.S.A.* 110 G8
Gunnison →, *U.S.A.* 111 G9
Gunpowder, *Australia* 90 B2
Guntakal, *India* 60 M10
Guntersville, *U.S.A.* 105 H2
Guntong, *Malaysia* 59 K3
Guntur, *India* 61 L12
Gunungapi, *Indonesia* 57 F7
Gunungsitoli, *Indonesia* 56 D1
Günz →, *Germany* 19 G6
Gunza, *Angola* 80 G2
Günzburg, *Germany* 19 G6
Gunzenhausen, *Germany* 19 F6
Guo He →, *China* 51 H9
Guoyang, *China* 50 H9
Gupis, *Pakistan* 63 A5
Gura Humorului, *Romania* 38 B8
Gurag, *Ethiopia* 77 F4
Gurdaspur, *India* 62 C6
Gurdon, *U.S.A.* 109 J8
Gurdzhaani, *Georgia* 43 F11
Gurgaon, *India* 62 E7
Gürgentepe, *Turkey* 67 C8
Gurguéia →, *Brazil* 122 C3
Gurha, *India* 62 G4
Guri, Embalse de, *Venezuela* 121 B5
Gurk →, *Austria* 21 J4
Gurkha, *Nepal* 63 E11
Gurley, *Australia* 91 D4
Gurué, *Mozam.* 83 F4
Gurun, *Malaysia* 59 K3
Gürün, *Turkey* 66 D7
Gurupá, *Brazil* 121 D7
Gurupá, I. Grande de, *Brazil* 121 D7
Gurupi, *Brazil* 123 D2
Gurupi →, *Brazil* 122 B2
Gurupi, Serra do, *Brazil* 122 C2
Guryev = Atyrau, *Kazakhstan* 43 C14
Gus-Khrustalnyy, *Russia* 41 D12
Gusau, *Nigeria* 79 C6
Gusev, *Russia* 40 D3
Gushan, *China* 51 E12
Gushi, *China* 53 A10
Gushiago, *Ghana* 79 D4
Gusinje, *Montenegro, Yug.* 21 N9
Gusinoozersk, *Russia* 45 D11
Gúspini, *Italy* 34 C1
Gustanj, *Slovenia* 33 B11
Gustine, *U.S.A.* 111 H3
Güstrow, *Germany* 18 B8
Gusum, *Sweden* 11 F10
Guta = Kalárovo, *Slovakia* 21 H7
Gütersloh, *Germany* 18 D4
Gutha, *Australia* 89 E2
Guthalongra, *Australia* 90 B4
Guthrie, *U.S.A.* 109 H6
Gutian, *China* 53 D12
Gutiérrez, *Bolivia* 125 D5
Guttannen, *Switz.* 23 C6
Guttenberg, *U.S.A.* 108 D9
Guyana ■, *S. Amer.* 121 B6
Guyane française ■ = French Guiana ■, *S. Amer.* 121 C7
Guyang, *China* 50 D6
Guyenne, *France* 26 D4
Guymon, *U.S.A.* 109 G4
Guyra, *Australia* 91 E5
Guyuan, *Hebei, China* 50 D8
Guyuan, *Ningxia Huizu, China* 50 F4
Guzhang, *China* 52 C7
Guzhen, *China* 51 H9
Guzmán, L. de, *Mexico* 114 A3
Gwa, *Burma* 61 L19
Gwaai, *Zimbabwe* 83 F2
Gwabegar, *Australia* 91 E4
Gwadabawa, *Nigeria* 79 C6
Gwādar, *Pakistan* 60 G3
Gwagwada, *Nigeria* 79 C6
Gwalia, *Australia* 89 E3
Gwalior, *India* 62 F8
Gwanda, *Zimbabwe* 83 G2
Gwandu, *Nigeria* 79 C5
Gwane, *Zaïre* 82 B2
Gwaram, *Nigeria* 79 C7
Gwarzo, *Nigeria* 79 C6
Gweebarra B., *Ireland* 15 B3
Gweedore, *Ireland* 15 A3
Gwent □, *U.K.* 13 F5
Gweru, *Zimbabwe* 83 F2
Gwi, *Nigeria* 79 D6
Gwinn, *U.S.A.* 104 B2
Gwio Kura, *Nigeria* 79 C7
Gwol, *Ghana* 78 C4
Gwoza, *Nigeria* 79 C7
Gwydir →, *Australia* 91 D4
Gwynedd □, *U.K.* 12 E4
Gyandzha, *Azerbaijan* 43 F12
Gyaring Hu, *China* 54 C4
Gydanskiy P-ov., *Russia* 44 C8
Gympie, *Australia* 91 D5
Gyoma, *Hungary* 21 J10
Gyöngyös, *Hungary* 21 H9
Györ, *Hungary* 21 H7
Gypsum Pt., *Canada* 100 A6
Gypsumville, *Canada* 101 C9
Gyula, *Hungary* 21 J11
Gyumri = Kumayri, *Armenia* 43 F10
Gzhatsk, *Russia* 40 D9

H

Ha 'Arava →, *Israel* 69 E4
Ha Coi, *Vietnam* 58 B6
Ha Dong, *Vietnam* 58 B5
Ha Giang, *Vietnam* 58 A5
Ha Tien, *Vietnam* 59 G5
Ha Tinh, *Vietnam* 58 C5
Ha Trung, *Vietnam* 58 C5

Haacht, *Belgium* 17 G5
Haag, *Germany* 19 G8
Haaksbergen, *Neths.* 16 D9
Haaltert, *Belgium* 17 G4
Haamstede, *Neths.* 17 E3
Haapamäki, *Finland* 8 E18
Haapsalu, *Estonia* 40 B3
Haarlem, *Neths.* 16 D5
Haast →, *N.Z.* 87 K2
Haast Bluff, *Australia* 88 D5
Haastrecht, *Neths.* 16 E5
Hab Nadi Chauki, *Pakistan* 62 G2
Habaswein, *Kenya* 82 B4
Habay, *Canada* 100 B5
Habay-la-Neuve, *Belgium* 17 J7
Habbānīyah, *Iraq* 64 C4
Haboro, *Japan* 48 B10
Haccourt, *Belgium* 17 G7
Hachenburg, *Germany* 18 E3
Hachijō-Jima, *Japan* 49 H9
Hachinohe, *Japan* 48 D10
Hachiōji, *Japan* 49 G9
Hachŏn, *N. Korea* 51 D15
Hachy, *Belgium* 17 J7
Hacıbektaş, *Turkey* 66 D6
Hacılar, *Turkey* 66 D6
Hackensack, *U.S.A.* 107 F10
Haçli Gölü, *Turkey* 67 D10
Hadali, *Pakistan* 62 C5
Hadarba, Ras, *Sudan* 76 C4
Hadarom □, *Israel* 69 E3
Haddington, *U.K.* 14 F6
Hadejia, *Nigeria* 79 C7
Hadejia →, *Nigeria* 79 C7
Haden, *Australia* 91 D5
Ḥadera, *Israel* 69 C3
Ḥadera, N. →, *Israel* 69 C3
Haderslev, *Denmark* 11 J3
Hadhramaut = Ḥaḍramawt, *Yemen* 68 D4
Hadım, *Turkey* 66 E5
Hadjeb El Aïoun, *Tunisia* 75 A6
Hadong, *S. Korea* 51 G14
Ḥaḍramawt, *Yemen* 68 D4
Ḥadrānīyah, *Iraq* 64 C4
Hadrian's Wall, *U.K.* 12 C5
Hadsten, *Denmark* 11 H4
Hadsund, *Denmark* 11 H4
Haeju, *N. Korea* 51 E13
Haenam, *S. Korea* 51 G14
Haerhpin = Harbin, *China* 51 B14
Hafar al Bāṭin, *Si. Arabia* 64 D5
Hafik, *Turkey* 66 D7
Ḥafīrat al 'Aydā, *Si. Arabia* 64 E3
Hafizabad, *Pakistan* 62 C5
Haflong, *India* 61 G18
Hafnarfjörður, *Iceland* 8 D3
Hafun, Ras, *Somali Rep.* 68 E5
Hagalil, *Israel* 69 C4
Hagen, *Germany* 18 D3
Hagenow, *Germany* 18 B7
Hagerman, *U.S.A.* 109 J2
Hagerstown, *U.S.A.* 104 F7
Hagetmau, *France* 26 E3
Hagfors, *Sweden* 9 F12
Häggenås, *Sweden* 10 A8
Hagi, *Iceland* 8 D2
Hagi, *Japan* 49 G5
Hagolan, *Syria* 69 B4
Hagondange-Briey, *France* 25 C13
Hags Hd., *Ireland* 15 D2
Hague, C. de la, *France* 24 C5
Hague, The = 's-Gravenhage, *Neths.* 16 D4
Haguenau, *France* 25 D14
Hai □, *Tanzania* 82 C4
Hai Duong, *Vietnam* 58 B6
Hai'an, *Guangdong, China* 53 G8
Hai'an, *Jiangsu, China* 53 A13
Haicheng, *Fujian, China* 53 E11
Haicheng, *Liaoning, China* 51 D12
Haidar Khel, *Afghan.* 62 C3
Haifa = Ḥefa, *Israel* 69 C3
Haifeng, *China* 53 F10
Haig, *Australia* 89 F4
Haiger, *Germany* 18 E4
Haikang, *China* 53 G8
Haikou, *China* 54 D6
Ḥā'il, *Si. Arabia* 64 E4
Hailar, *China* 54 B6
Hailey, *U.S.A.* 110 E6
Haileybury, *Canada* 98 C4
Hailin, *China* 51 B15
Hailing Dao, *China* 53 G8
Hailong, *China* 51 C13
Hailun, *China* 54 B7
Hailuoto, *Finland* 8 D18
Haimen, *Guangdong, China* 53 F11
Haimen, *Jiangsu, China* 53 B13
Haimen, *Zhejiang, China* 53 C13
Hainan □, *China* 54 E5
Hainaut □, *Belgium* 17 H4
Haines, *U.S.A.* 110 D5
Haines City, *U.S.A.* 105 L5
Haines Junction, *Canada* 100 A1
Haining, *China* 53 B13
Haiphong, *Vietnam* 54 D5
Haiti ■, *W. Indies* 117 C5
Haiya Junction, *Sudan* 76 D4
Haiyan, *China* 53 B13
Haiyang, *China* 51 F11
Haiyuan, *Guangxi Zhuangzu, China* 52 F6
Haiyuan, *Ningxia Huizu, China* 50 F3
Haizhou, *China* 51 G10
Haizhou Wan, *China* 51 G10
Haja, *Indonesia* 57 E7
Hajar Bangar, *Sudan* 73 F9
Hajdúböszörmény, *Hungary* 21 H11
Hajdúszobaszló, *Hungary* 21 H11
Hajipur, *India* 63 G11
Ḥājjī Muḥsin, *Iraq* 64 C5
Ḥājjīābād, *Eşfahan, Iran* 65 C7
Ḥājjīābād, *Hormozgān, Iran* 65 D7
Hakansson, Mts., *Zaïre* 83 D2
Håkantorp, *Sweden* 11 F6
Hakkâri, *Turkey* 67 E10
Hakkâri □, *Turkey* 67 E10
Hakkâri Dağları, *Turkey* 67 E10
Hakken-Zan, *Japan* 49 G7
Hakodate, *Japan* 48 D10
Haku-San, *Japan* 49 F8
Hakui, *Japan* 49 F8
Hala, *Pakistan* 60 G6
Ḥalab, *Syria* 64 B3
Ḥalabjah, *Iraq* 64 C5
Halaib, *Sudan* 76 C4
Halanzy, *Belgium* 17 J7
Hālat' Ammār, *Si. Arabia* 64 D3
Halbā, *Lebanon* 69 A5
Halberstadt, *Germany* 18 D7
Halcombe, *N.Z.* 87 J5
Halcon, Mt., *Phil.* 57 B6
Halden, *Norway* 10 E5
Haldensleben, *Germany* 18 C7
Haldia, *India* 61 H16
Haldwani, *India* 63 E8
Hale →, *Australia* 90 C2
Haleakala Crater, *U.S.A.* 102 H16
Halen, *Belgium* 17 G6
Haleyville, *U.S.A.* 105 H2
Half Assini, *Ghana* 78 D4
Halfway →, *Canada* 100 B4
Haliburton, *Canada* 98 C4
Halifax, *Australia* 90 B4
Halifax, *Canada* 99 D7
Halifax, *U.K.* 12 D6
Halifax B., *Australia* 90 B4
Halifax I., *Namibia* 84 D2
Halīl →, *Iran* 65 E8
Hall, *Austria* 19 H7
Hall Beach, *Canada* 97 B11
Hall Pt., *Australia* 88 C3
Hallands län □, *Sweden* 11 H6
Hallands Väderö, *Sweden* 11 H6
Hallandsås, *Sweden* 11 H7
Halle, *Belgium* 17 G4
Halle, *Nordrhein-Westfalen, Germany* 18 C4
Halle, *Sachsen-Anhalt, Germany* 18 D7
Hällefors, *Sweden* 9 G13
Hallein, *Austria* 21 H3
Hällekis, *Sweden* 11 F7
Hallett, *Australia* 91 E2
Hallettsville, *U.S.A.* 109 L6
Hällevadsholm, *Sweden* 11 F5
Halliday, *U.S.A.* 108 B3
Halliday L., *Canada* 101 A7
Hallim, *S. Korea* 51 H14
Hallingdal →, *Norway* 9 F10
Hällnäs, *Sweden* 8 D15
Hallock, *U.S.A.* 101 D9
Halls Creek, *Australia* 88 C4
Hallstahammar, *Sweden* 10 E10
Hallstead, *U.S.A.* 107 E9
Halmahera, *Indonesia* 57 D7
Halmeu, *Romania* 38 B6
Halmstad, *Sweden* 11 H6
Halq el Oued, *Tunisia* 75 A7
Hals, *Denmark* 11 H4
Halsafjorden, *Norway* 10 A2
Hälsingborg = Helsingborg, *Sweden* 11 H6
Halstad, *U.S.A.* 108 B6
Haltdalen, *Norway* 10 B5
Haltern, *Germany* 18 D3
Halul, *Qatar* 65 E7
Ḥalvān, *Iran* 65 C8
Ham, *France* 25 C10
Ham Tan, *Vietnam* 59 G6
Ham Yen, *Vietnam* 58 A5
Hamab, *Namibia* 84 D2
Hamad, *Sudan* 77 D3
Hamada, *Japan* 49 G6
Hamadān, *Iran* 65 C6
Hamadān □, *Iran* 65 C6
Hamadia, *Algeria* 75 A5
Hamāh, *Syria* 64 C3
Hamamatsu, *Japan* 49 G8
Hamar, *Norway* 10 D5
Hamarøy, *Norway* 8 B13
Hamâta, Gebel, *Egypt* 76 C3
Hambantota, *Sri Lanka* 60 R12
Hamber Prov. Park, *Canada* 100 C5
Hamburg, *Germany* 18 B5
Hamburg, *Ark., U.S.A.* 109 J9
Hamburg, *Iowa, U.S.A.* 108 E7
Hamburg, *N.Y., U.S.A.* 106 D6
Hamburg, *Pa., U.S.A.* 107 F9
Hamburg □, *Germany* 18 B6
Ḥamḍ, W. al →, *Si. Arabia* 64 E3
Hamden, *U.S.A.* 107 E12
Hame □ = Hämeen lääni □, *Finland* 9 F18
Hämeen lääni □, *Finland* 9 F18
Hämeenlinna, *Finland* 9 F18
Hamélé, *Ghana* 78 C4
Hamelin Pool, *Australia* 89 E1
Hameln, *Germany* 18 C5
Hamer Koke, *Ethiopia* 77 F4
Hamerkaz □, *Israel* 69 C3
Hamersley Ra., *Australia* 88 D2
Hamhung, *N. Korea* 51 E14
Hami, *China* 54 B4
Hamilton, *Australia* 91 F3
Hamilton, *Canada* 98 D4
Hamilton, *N.Z.* 87 G5
Hamilton, *U.K.* 14 F4
Hamilton, *Mo., U.S.A.* 108 F8
Hamilton, *Mont., U.S.A.* 110 C6
Hamilton, *N.Y., U.S.A.* 107 D9
Hamilton, *Ohio, U.S.A.* 104 F3
Hamilton, *Tex., U.S.A.* 109 K5
Hamilton →, *Australia* 90 C2
Hamilton City, *U.S.A.* 112 F4
Hamilton Hotel, *Australia* 90 C3
Hamilton Inlet, *Canada* 99 B8
Hamiota, *Canada* 101 C8
Hamlet, *U.S.A.* 105 H6
Hamley Bridge, *Australia* 91 E2
Hamlin = Hameln, *Germany* 18 C5
Hamlin, *N.Y., U.S.A.* 106 C7
Hamlin, *Tex., U.S.A.* 109 J4
Hamm, *Germany* 18 D3
Hammam Bouhadjar, *Algeria* 75 A4
Hammamet, *Tunisia* 75 A7
Hammamet, G. de, *Tunisia* 75 A7
Hammarstrand, *Sweden* 10 A10
Hamme, *Belgium* 17 F4
Hamme-Mille, *Belgium* 17 G5
Hammel, *Denmark* 11 H3
Hammelburg, *Germany* 19 E5
Hammerfest, *Norway* 8 A17
Hammond, *Ind., U.S.A.* 104 E2
Hammond, *La., U.S.A.* 109 K9
Hammonton, *U.S.A.* 104 F8
Hamoir, *Belgium* 17 H7
Hamont, *Belgium* 17 F7
Hamoyet, Jebel, *Sudan* 76 D4
Hampden, *N.Z.* 87 L3
Hampshire □, *U.K.* 13 F6
Hampshire Downs, *U.K.* 13 F6
Hampton, *Ark., U.S.A.* 109 J8
Hampton, *Iowa, U.S.A.* 108 D8
Hampton, *N.H., U.S.A.* 107 D14
Hampton, *S.C., U.S.A.* 105 J5
Hampton, *Va., U.S.A.* 104 G7
Hampton Tableland, *Australia* 89 F4
Hamrat esh Sheykh, *Sudan* 77 E2
Hamur, *Turkey* 67 D10
Hamyang, *S. Korea* 51 G14
Han Jiang →, *China* 53 F11
Han Shui →, *China* 53 B10
Hana, *U.S.A.* 102 H17
Hanak, *Si. Arabia* 64 E3
Hanamaki, *Japan* 48 E10
Hanang, *Tanzania* 82 C4
Hanau, *Germany* 19 E4
Hanbogd, *Mongolia* 50 C4
Hancheng, *China* 50 G6
Hanchuan, *China* 53 B9
Hancock, *Mich., U.S.A.* 108 B10
Hancock, *Minn., U.S.A.* 108 C7
Hancock, *N.Y., U.S.A.* 107 E9
Handa, *Japan* 49 G8
Handa, *Somali Rep.* 68 E5
Handan, *China* 50 F8
Handen, *Sweden* 10 E12
Handeni, *Tanzania* 82 D4
Handeni □, *Tanzania* 82 D4
Handub, *Sudan* 76 D4
Handwara, *India* 63 B6
Handzame, *Belgium* 17 F2
Hanegev, *Israel* 69 E3
Haney, *Canada* 100 D4
Hanford, *U.S.A.* 111 H4
Hang Chat, *Thailand* 58 C2
Hang Dong, *Thailand* 58 C2
Hangang →, *S. Korea* 51 F14
Hangayn Nuruu, *Mongolia* 54 B4
Hangchou = Hangzhou, *China* 53 B13
Hanggin Houqi, *China* 50 D4
Hanggin Qi, *China* 50 E5
Hangö, *Finland* 9 G17
Hangu, *China* 51 E9
Hangzhou, *China* 53 B13
Hangzhou Wan, *China* 53 B13
Hanhongor, *Mongolia* 50 C3
Ḥanīdh, *Si. Arabia* 65 E6
Ḥanīsh, *Yemen* 68 E3
Hanjiang, *China* 53 E12
Hankinson, *U.S.A.* 108 B6
Hanko = Hangö, *Finland* 9 G17
Hanko, *Finland* 9 G17
Hankou, *China* 53 B10
Hanksville, *U.S.A.* 111 G8
Hanle, *India* 63 C8
Hanmer Springs, *N.Z.* 87 K4
Hann →, *Australia* 88 C4
Hann, Mt., *Australia* 88 C4
Hanna, *Canada* 100 C6
Hannaford, *U.S.A.* 108 B5
Hannah, *U.S.A.* 108 A5
Hannah B., *Canada* 98 B4
Hannibal, *U.S.A.* 108 F9
Hannik, *Sudan* 76 D3
Hannover, *Germany* 18 C5
Hannut, *Belgium* 17 G6
Hanoi, *Vietnam* 54 D5
Hanover = Hannover, *Germany* 18 C5
Hanover, *Canada* 106 B3
Hanover, *S. Africa* 84 E3
Hanover, *N.H., U.S.A.* 107 C12
Hanover, *Ohio, U.S.A.* 106 F2
Hanover, *Pa., U.S.A.* 104 F7
Hanover, I., *Chile* 128 D2
Hanshou, *China* 53 C8
Hansi, *India* 62 E6
Hanson, L., *Australia* 91 E2
Hanyang, *China* 53 B10
Hanyin, *China* 52 A7
Hanyuan, *China* 52 C4
Hanzhong, *China* 50 H4
Hanzhuang, *China* 51 G9
Haora, *India* 63 H13
Haoxue, *China* 53 B9
Haparanda, *Sweden* 8 D18
Hapert, *Neths.* 17 F6
Happy, *U.S.A.* 109 H4
Happy Camp, *U.S.A.* 110 F2
Happy Valley-Goose Bay, *Canada* 99 B7
Hapsu, *N. Korea* 51 D15
Hapur, *India* 62 E7
Ḥaql, *Si. Arabia* 69 F3
Haquira, *Peru* 124 C3
Har, *Indonesia* 57 F8
Har-Ayrag, *Mongolia* 50 B5
Har Hu, *China* 54 C4
Har Us Nuur, *Mongolia* 54 B4
Har Yehuda, *Israel* 69 D3
Ḥaraḍ, *Si. Arabia* 68 C4
Haranomachi, *Japan* 48 F10
Harardera, *Somali Rep.* 68 G4
Harare, *Zimbabwe* 83 F3
Harat, *Eritrea* 77 D4
Harazé, *Chad* 73 F8
Harbin, *China* 51 B14
Harbiye, *Turkey* 66 E7
Harboør, *Denmark* 11 H2
Harbor Beach, *U.S.A.* 104 D4
Harbor Springs, *U.S.A.* 104 C3
Harbour Breton, *Canada* 99 C8
Harbour Grace, *Canada* 99 C9
Harburg, *Germany* 18 B5
Hårby, *Denmark* 11 J4
Harda, *India* 62 H7
Hardangerfjorden, *Norway* 9 F8
Hardap Dam, *Namibia* 84 C2
Hardegarijp, *Neths.* 16 B7
Hardenberg, *Neths.* 16 C9
Harderwijk, *Neths.* 16 D7
Hardey →, *Australia* 88 D2
Hardin, *U.S.A.* 110 D10
Harding, *S. Africa* 85 E4
Harding Ra., *Australia* 88 C3
Hardisty, *Canada* 100 C6
Hardman, *U.S.A.* 110 D4
Hardoi, *India* 63 F9
Hardwar = Haridwar, *India* 62 E8
Hardwick, *U.S.A.* 107 B12
Hardy, *U.S.A.* 109 G9
Hardy, Pen., *Chile* 128 E3
Hare B., *Canada* 99 B8
Harelbeke, *Belgium* 17 G2
Haren, *Germany* 18 C3
Haren, *Neths.* 16 B9
Harer, *Ethiopia* 68 F3
Harerge □, *Ethiopia* 77 F5
Hareto, *Ethiopia* 77 F4
Harfleur, *France* 24 C7
Hargeisa, *Somali Rep.* 68 F3
Hargshamn, *Sweden* 9 F15
Hari →, *Indonesia* 56 E2
Haria, *Canary Is.* 36 E6
Haricha, Hamada el, *Mali* 74 D4
Haridwar, *India* 62 E8
Haringhata →, *Bangla.* 61 J16
Haringvliet, *Neths.* 16 E4
Harīrūd →, *Asia* 60 A2
Harlan, *Iowa, U.S.A.* 108 E7
Harlan, *Ky., U.S.A.* 105 G4
Harlech, *U.K.* 12 E3
Harlem, *U.S.A.* 110 B9
Harlingen, *Neths.* 16 B6
Harlingen, *U.S.A.* 109 M6
Harlowton, *U.S.A.* 110 C9
Harmånger, *Sweden* 10 C11
Harmil, *Eritrea* 77 D5
Harney Basin, *U.S.A.* 110 E4
Harney L., *U.S.A.* 110 E4
Harney Peak, *U.S.A.* 108 D3
Härnön, *Sweden* 10 B12
Härnösand, *Sweden* 10 B11
Haro, *Spain* 28 C2
Harp L., *Canada* 99 A7
Harper, *Liberia* 78 E3
Harplinge, *Sweden* 11 H6
Harrand, *Pakistan* 62 E4
Harriman, *U.S.A.* 105 H3
Harrington Harbour, *Canada* 99 B8
Harris, *U.K.* 14 D2
Harris, Sd. of, *U.K.* 14 D1
Harris L., *Australia* 91 E2
Harrisburg, *Ill., U.S.A.* 109 G10
Harrisburg, *Nebr., U.S.A.* 108 E3
Harrisburg, *Oreg., U.S.A.* 110 D2
Harrisburg, *Pa., U.S.A.* 106 F8
Harrismith, *S. Africa* 85 D4
Harrison, *Ark., U.S.A.* 109 G8
Harrison, *Idaho, U.S.A.* 110 C5
Harrison, *Nebr., U.S.A.* 108 D3
Harrison, C., *Canada* 99 B8
Harrison Bay, *U.S.A.* 96 A4
Harrison L., *Canada* 100 D4
Harrisonburg, *U.S.A.* 104 F6
Harrisonville, *U.S.A.* 108 F7
Harriston, *Canada* 98 D3
Harrisville, *U.S.A.* 106 B1
Harrogate, *U.K.* 12 D6
Harrow, *U.K.* 13 F7
Harsefeld, *Germany* 18 B5
Harsīn, *Iran* 64 C5
Harskamp, *Neths.* 16 D7
Harstad, *Norway* 8 B14
Hart, *U.S.A.* 104 D2
Hart, L., *Australia* 91 E2
Hartbees →, *S. Africa* 84 D3
Hartberg, *Austria* 21 H5
Hartford, *Conn., U.S.A.* 107 E12
Hartford, *Ky., U.S.A.* 104 G2
Hartford, *S. Dak., U.S.A.* 108 D6
Hartford, *Wis., U.S.A.* 108 D10
Hartford City, *U.S.A.* 104 E3
Hartland, *Canada* 99 C6
Hartland Pt., *U.K.* 13 F3
Hartlepool, *U.K.* 12 C6
Hartley Bay, *Canada* 100 C3
Hartmannberge, *Namibia* 84 B1
Hartney, *Canada* 101 D8
Harts →, *S. Africa* 84 D3
Hartselle, *U.S.A.* 105 H2
Hartshorne, *U.S.A.* 109 H7
Hartsville, *U.S.A.* 105 H5
Hartwell, *U.S.A.* 105 H4
Harunabad, *Pakistan* 62 E5
Harvand, *Iran* 65 D7
Harvey, *Australia* 89 F2
Harvey, *Ill., U.S.A.* 104 E2
Harvey, *N. Dak., U.S.A.* 108 B5
Harwich, *U.K.* 13 F9
Haryana □, *India* 62 E7
Harz, *Germany* 18 D6
Harzé, *Belgium* 17 H7
Harzgerode, *Germany* 18 D7
Hasaheisa, *Sudan* 77 E3
Hasan Kīādeh, *Iran* 65 B6
Ḥasanābād, *Iran* 65 C7
Hasanpur, *India* 62 E8
Haselünne, *Germany* 18 C3
Hashimoto, *Japan* 49 G7
Hashtjerd, *Iran* 65 C6
Håsjö, *Sweden* 10 A10
Haskell, *Okla., U.S.A.* 109 H7
Haskell, *Tex., U.S.A.* 109 J5
Haslach, *Germany* 19 G4
Haslev, *Denmark* 11 J5
Hasparren, *France* 26 E2
Hassa, *Turkey* 66 E7
Hasselt, *Belgium* 17 G6
Hasselt, *Neths.* 16 C8
Hassene, Adrar, *Algeria* 75 D5
Hassfurt, *Germany* 19 E6
Hassi Berrekrem, *Algeria* 75 B6
Hassi bou Khelala, *Algeria* 75 B4
Hassi Daoula, *Algeria* 75 B6
Hassi Djafou, *Algeria* 75 B5
Hassi el Abiod, *Algeria* 75 B5
Hassi el Biod, *Algeria* 75 C6
Hassi el Gassi, *Algeria* 75 B6
Hassi el Hadjar, *Algeria* 75 B5
Hassi er Rmel, *Algeria* 75 B5
Hassi Imoulaye, *Algeria* 75 C6
Hassi Inifel, *Algeria* 75 C5
Hassi Messaoud, *Algeria* 75 B6
Hassi Rhénami, *Algeria* 75 B6
Hassi Tartrat, *Algeria* 75 B6
Hassi Zerzour, *Morocco* 74 B4
Hastière-Lavaux, *Belgium* 17 H5
Hastings, *N.Z.* 87 H6
Hastings, *U.K.* 13 G8
Hastings, *Mich., U.S.A.* 104 D3
Hastings, *Minn., U.S.A.* 108 C8
Hastings, *Nebr., U.S.A.* 108 E5
Hastings Ra., *Australia* 91 E5
Hat Yai, *Thailand* 59 J3
Hatanbulag, *Mongolia* 50 C5
Hatay = Antalya, *Turkey* 66 E4
Hatay □, *Turkey* 66 E7
Hatch, *U.S.A.* 111 K10
Hatches Creek, *Australia* 90 C2
Hatchet L., *Canada* 101 B8
Haţeg, *Romania* 38 D5
Haţeg, Mţii., *Romania* 38 D6
Hatert, *Neths.* 16 E7
Hateruma-Shima, *Japan* 49 M1
Hatfield P.O., *Australia* 91 E3
Hatgal, *Mongolia* 54 A5
Hathras, *India* 62 F8
Hatia, *Bangla.* 61 H17
Hato de Corozal, *Colombia* 120 B3
Hato Mayor, *Dom. Rep.* 117 C6
Hattah, *Australia* 91 E3
Hattem, *Neths.* 16 D8
Hatteras, C., *U.S.A.* 105 H8
Hattiesburg, *U.S.A.* 109 K10
Hatvan, *Hungary* 21 H9
Hau Bon = Cheo Reo, *Vietnam* 58 F7
Hau Duc, *Vietnam* 58 E7
Haug, *Norway* 10 D4
Haugastøl, *Norway* 10 D1
Haugesund, *Norway* 9 G8

Haulerwijk, *Neths.* 16 B8
Haultain →, *Canada* 101 B7
Hauraki G., *N.Z.* 87 G5
Haut Atlas, *Morocco* 74 B3
Haut-Rhin □, *France* 25 E14
Haut Zaïre □, *Zaïre* 82 B2
Haute-Corse □, *France* 27 F13
Haute-Garonne □, *France* 26 E5
Haute-Loire □, *France* 26 C7
Haute-Marne □, *France* 25 D12
Haute-Saône □, *France* 25 E13
Haute-Savoie □, *France* 27 C10
Haute-Vienne □, *France* 26 C5
Hauterive, *Canada* 99 C6
Hautes-Alpes □, *France* 27 D10
Hautes Fagnes = Hohe Venn, *Belgium* 17 H8
Hautes Fagnes, *Belgium* 17 G8
Hautes-Pyrénées □, *France* 26 F4
Hauteville-Lompnès, *France* 27 C9
Hautmont, *France* 25 B10
Hautrage, *Belgium* 17 H3
Hauts-de-Seine □, *France* 25 D9
Hauts Plateaux, *Algeria* 75 B4
Hauzenberg, *Germany* 19 G9
Havana = La Habana, *Cuba* 116 B3
Havana, *U.S.A.* 108 E9
Havant, *U.K.* 13 G7
Havasu, L., *U.S.A.* 113 L12
Havel →, *Germany* 18 C8
Havelange, *Belgium* 17 H6
Havelian, *Pakistan* 62 B5
Havelock, *N.B., Canada* 99 C6
Havelock, *Ont., Canada* 98 D4
Havelock, *N.Z.* 87 J4
Havelte, *Neths.* 16 C8
Haverfordwest, *U.K.* 13 F3
Haverhill, *U.S.A.* 107 D13
Havering, *U.K.* 13 F8
Haverstraw, *U.S.A.* 107 E11
Håverud, *Sweden* 11 F6
Havlíčkův Brod, *Czech.* 20 F5
Havneby, *Denmark* 11 J2
Havre, *U.S.A.* 110 B9
Havre-Aubert, *Canada* 99 C7
Havre-St.-Pierre, *Canada* 99 B7
Havza, *Turkey* 66 C6
Haw →, *U.S.A.* 105 H6
Hawaii □, *U.S.A.* 102 H16
Hawaii I., *Pac. Oc.* 102 J17
Hawaiian Is., *Pac. Oc.* 102 H17
Hawaiian Ridge, *Pac. Oc.* 93 E11
Hawarden, *Canada* 101 C7
Hawarden, *U.S.A.* 108 D6
Hawea, L., *N.Z.* 87 L2
Hawera, *N.Z.* 87 H5
Hawick, *U.K.* 14 F6
Hawk Junction, *Canada* 98 C3
Hawke B., *N.Z.* 87 H6
Hawker, *Australia* 91 E2
Hawkesbury, *Canada* 98 C5
Hawkesbury I., *Canada* 100 C3
Hawkesbury Pt., *Australia* 90 A1
Hawkinsville, *U.S.A.* 105 J4
Hawkwood, *Australia* 91 D5
Hawley, *U.S.A.* 108 B6
Hawrān, *Syria* 69 C5
Hawsh Mūssá, *Lebanon* 69 B4
Hawthorne, *U.S.A.* 110 G4
Hawzen, *Ethiopia* 77 E4
Haxtun, *U.S.A.* 108 E3
Hay, *Australia* 91 E3
Hay →, *Australia* 90 C2
Hay →, *Canada* 100 A5
Hay, C., *Australia* 88 B4
Hay L., *Canada* 100 B5
Hay Lakes, *Canada* 100 C6
Hay-on-Wye, *U.K.* 13 E4
Hay River, *Canada* 100 A5
Hay Springs, *U.S.A.* 108 D3
Hayachine-San, *Japan* 48 E10
Hayange, *France* 25 C13
Hayden, *Ariz., U.S.A.* 111 K8
Hayden, *Colo., U.S.A.* 110 F10
Haydon, *Australia* 90 B3
Hayes, *U.S.A.* 108 C4
Hayes →, *Canada* 101 B10
Haymana, *Turkey* 66 D5
Haynesville, *U.S.A.* 109 J8
Hayrabolu, *Turkey* 66 C2
Hays, *Canada* 100 C6
Hays, *U.S.A.* 108 F5
Hayward, *Calif., U.S.A.* 112 H4
Hayward, *Wis., U.S.A.* 108 B9
Haywards Heath, *U.K.* 13 F7
Hazafon □, *Israel* 69 C4
Hazar Gölü, *Turkey* 67 D8
Hazarām, Kūh-e, *Iran* 65 D8
Hazard, *U.S.A.* 104 G4
Hazaribag, *India* 63 H11
Hazaribag Road, *India* 63 G11
Hazebrouck, *France* 25 B9
Hazelton, *Canada* 100 B3
Hazelton, *U.S.A.* 108 B4
Hazen, *N. Dak., U.S.A.* 108 B4
Hazen, *Nev., U.S.A.* 110 G4
Hazerswoude, *Neths.* 16 D5
Hazlehurst, *Ga., U.S.A.* 105 K4
Hazlehurst, *Miss., U.S.A.* 109 K9
Hazleton, *U.S.A.* 107 F9
Hazlett, L., *Australia* 88 D4
Ḩazor, *Israel* 69 B4
He Xian, *Anhui, China* 53 B12
He Xian, *Guangxi Zhuangzu, China* 53 E8
Head of Bight, *Australia* 89 F5
Headlands, *Zimbabwe* 83 F3
Healdsburg, *U.S.A.* 112 G4
Healdton, *U.S.A.* 109 H6
Healesville, *Australia* 91 F4
Heanor, *U.K.* 12 D6
Heard I., *Ind. Oc.* 3 G13
Hearne, *U.S.A.* 109 K6
Hearne B., *Canada* 101 A9
Hearne L., *Canada* 100 A6
Hearst, *Canada* 98 C3
Heart →, *U.S.A.* 108 B4
Heart's Content, *Canada* 99 C9
Heath →, *Bolivia* 124 C4
Heath Pt., *Canada* 99 C7
Heath Steele, *Canada* 99 C6
Heavener, *U.S.A.* 109 H7
Hebbronville, *U.S.A.* 109 M5
Hebei □, *China* 50 E9
Hebel, *Australia* 91 D4
Heber, *U.S.A.* 113 N11
Heber Springs, *U.S.A.* 109 H9
Hebert, *Canada* 101 C7
Hebgen L., *U.S.A.* 110 D8
Hebi, *China* 50 G8
Hebrides, *U.K.* 14 D1
Hebron = Al Khalīl, *Jordan* 69 D4
Hebron, *Canada* 97 C13
Hebron, *N. Dak., U.S.A.* 108 B3
Hebron, *Nebr., U.S.A.* 108 E6
Hecate Str., *Canada* 100 C2
Hechi, *China* 52 E7
Hechingen, *Germany* 19 G4
Hechtel, *Belgium* 17 F6
Hechuan, *China* 52 B6
Hecla, *U.S.A.* 108 C5
Hecla I., *Canada* 101 C9
Heddal, *Norway* 10 E3
Hédé, *France* 24 D5
Hede, *Sweden* 10 B7
Hedemora, *Sweden* 9 F13
Hedley, *U.S.A.* 109 H4
Hedmark fylke □, *Norway* 10 C5
Hedrum, *Norway* 10 E4
Heeg, *Neths.* 16 C7
Heegermeer, *Neths.* 16 C7
Heemskerk, *Neths.* 16 C5
Heemstede, *Neths.* 16 D5
Heer, *Neths.* 17 G7
Heerde, *Neths.* 16 D8
's Heerenburg, *Neths.* 16 E8
Heerenveen, *Neths.* 16 C7
Heerhugowaard, *Neths.* 16 C5
Heerlen, *Neths.* 17 G7
Heers, *Belgium* 17 G6
Heesch, *Neths.* 16 E7
Heestert, *Belgium* 17 G2
Heeze, *Neths.* 17 F7
Ḩefa, *Israel* 69 C3
Ḩefa □, *Israel* 69 C4
Hefei, *China* 53 B11
Hegang, *China* 54 B8
Hegyalja, *Hungary* 21 G11
Heichengzhen, *China* 50 F4
Heide, *Germany* 18 A5
Heidelberg, *Germany* 19 F4
Heidelberg, *C. Prov., S. Africa* 84 E3
Heidelberg, *Trans., S. Africa* 85 D4
Heidenheim, *Germany* 19 G6
Heijing, *China* 52 E3
Heilbron, *S. Africa* 85 D4
Heilbronn, *Germany* 19 F5
Heiligenblut, *Austria* 21 H2
Heiligenhafen, *Germany* 18 A6
Heiligenstadt, *Germany* 18 D6
Heilongjiang □, *China* 51 B14
Heilunkiang = Heilongjiang □, *China* 51 B14
Heino, *Neths.* 16 D8
Heinola, *Finland* 9 F19
Heinsch, *Belgium* 17 J7
Heinze Is., *Burma* 61 M20
Heishan, *China* 51 D12
Heishui, *Liaoning, China* 51 C10
Heishui, *Sichuan, China* 52 A4
Heist, *Belgium* 17 F2
Heist-op-den-Berg, *Belgium* 17 F5
Hejaz = Al Ḩijāz, *Si. Arabia* 68 B2
Hejian, *China* 50 E9
Hejiang, *China* 52 C5
Hejin, *China* 50 G6
Hekelgem, *Belgium* 17 G4
Hekimhan, *Turkey* 67 D7
Hekla, *Iceland* 8 E4
Hekou, *Gansu, China* 50 F2
Hekou, *Guangdong, China* 53 F9
Hekou, *Yunnan, China* 54 D5
Helagsfjället, *Sweden* 10 B6
Helan Shan, *China* 50 E3
Helchteren, *Belgium* 17 F6
Helden, *Neths.* 17 F7
Helechosa, *Spain* 31 F6
Helena, *Ark., U.S.A.* 109 H9
Helena, *Mont., U.S.A.* 110 C7
Helendale, *U.S.A.* 113 L9
Helensburgh, *U.K.* 14 E4
Helensville, *N.Z.* 87 G5
Helgeroa, *Norway* 10 F3
Helgoland, *Germany* 18 A3
Heligoland = Helgoland, *Germany* 18 A3
Heligoland B. = Deutsche Bucht, *Germany* 18 A4
Heliopolis, *Egypt* 76 H7
Hellebæk, *Denmark* 11 H6
Hellendoorn, *Neths.* 16 D8
Hellevoetsluis, *Neths.* 16 E4
Hellín, *Spain* 29 G3
Helmand □, *Afghan.* 60 D4
Helmand →, *Afghan.* 60 D2
Helme →, *Germany* 18 D7
Helmond, *Neths.* 17 F7
Helmsdale, *U.K.* 14 C5
Helmstedt, *Germany* 18 C7
Helnæs, *Denmark* 11 J4
Helong, *China* 51 C15
Helper, *U.S.A.* 110 G8
Helsingborg, *Sweden* 11 H6
Helsinge, *Denmark* 11 H6
Helsingfors, *Finland* 9 F18
Helsingør, *Denmark* 11 H6
Helsinki, *Finland* 9 F18
Helston, *U.K.* 13 G2
Helvellyn, *U.K.* 12 C4
Helvoirt, *Neths.* 17 E6
Helwân, *Egypt* 76 J7
Hemet, *U.S.A.* 113 M10
Hemingford, *U.S.A.* 108 D3
Hemphill, *U.S.A.* 109 K8
Hempstead, *U.S.A.* 109 K6
Hemse, *Sweden* 9 H15
Hemsö, *Sweden* 10 B12
Henan □, *China* 50 G8
Henares →, *Spain* 28 E1
Henashi-Misaki, *Japan* 48 D9
Hendaye, *France* 26 E2
Hendek, *Turkey* 66 C4
Henderson, *Argentina* 126 D3
Henderson, *Ky., U.S.A.* 104 G2
Henderson, *N.C., U.S.A.* 105 G6
Henderson, *Nev., U.S.A.* 113 J12
Henderson, *Tenn., U.S.A.* 105 H1
Henderson, *Tex., U.S.A.* 109 J7
Hendersonville, *U.S.A.* 105 H4
Hendījān, *Iran* 65 D6
Hendon, *Australia* 91 D5
Heng Xian, *China* 52 F7
Hengcheng, *China* 50 E4
Hengdaohezi, *China* 51 B15
Hengelo, *Gelderland, Neths.* 16 D8
Hengelo, *Overijssel, Neths.* 16 D9
Hengfeng, *China* 53 C10
Hengshan, *Hunan, China* 53 D9
Hengshan, *Shaanxi, China* 50 F5
Hengshui, *China* 50 F8
Hengyang, *Hunan, China* 53 D9
Hengyang, *Hunan, China* 53 D9
Hénin-Beaumont, *France* 25 B9
Henlopen, C., *U.S.A.* 104 F8
Hennan, *Sweden* 10 B9
Hennebont, *France* 24 E3
Hennenman, *S. Africa* 84 D4
Hennessey, *U.S.A.* 109 G6
Hennigsdorf, *Germany* 18 C9
Henrichemont, *France* 25 E9
Henrietta, *U.S.A.* 109 J5
Henrietta, Ostrov, *Russia* 45 B16
Henrietta Maria C., *Canada* 98 A3
Henry, *U.S.A.* 108 E10
Henryetta, *U.S.A.* 109 H6
Hensall, *Canada* 106 C3
Hentiyn Nuruu, *Mongolia* 54 B5
Henty, *Australia* 91 F4
Henzada, *Burma* 61 L19
Heping, *China* 53 E10
Heppner, *U.S.A.* 110 D4
Hepu, *China* 52 G7
Hepworth, *Canada* 106 B3
Heqing, *China* 52 D3
Hequ, *China* 50 E6
Héraðsflói, *Iceland* 8 D6
Héraðsvötn →, *Iceland* 8 D4
Herald Cays, *Australia* 90 B4
Herāt, *Afghan.* 60 B3
Herāt □, *Afghan.* 60 B3
Hérault □, *France* 26 E7
Hérault →, *France* 26 E7
Herbault, *France* 24 E8
Herbert →, *Australia* 90 B4
Herbert Downs, *Australia* 90 C2
Herberton, *Australia* 90 B4
Herbignac, *France* 24 E4
Herborn, *Germany* 18 E4
Herby, *Poland* 20 E8
Hercegnovi, *Montenegro, Yug.* 21 N8
Herðubreið, *Iceland* 8 D5
Hereford, *U.K.* 13 E5
Hereford, *U.S.A.* 109 H3
Hereford and Worcester □, *U.K.* 13 E5
Herefoss, *Norway* 11 F2
Herent, *Belgium* 17 G5
Herentals, *Belgium* 17 F5
Herenthout, *Belgium* 17 F5
Herfølge, *Denmark* 11 J6
Herford, *Germany* 18 C4
Héricourt, *France* 25 E13
Herington, *U.S.A.* 108 F6
Herisau, *Switz.* 23 B8
Hérisson, *France* 26 B6
Herjehogna, *Norway* 9 F12
Herk →, *Belgium* 17 G6
Herkenbosch, *Neths.* 17 F8
Herkimer, *U.S.A.* 107 D10
Herlong, *U.S.A.* 112 E6
Herm, *Chan. Is.* 24 C4
Hermagor-Pressegger See, *Austria* 21 J3
Herman, *U.S.A.* 108 C6
Hermann, *U.S.A.* 108 F9
Hermannsburg, *Germany* 18 C6
Hermannsburg Mission, *Australia* 88 D5
Hermanus, *S. Africa* 84 E2
Herment, *France* 26 C6
Hermidale, *Australia* 91 E4
Hermiston, *U.S.A.* 110 D4
Hermitage, *N.Z.* 87 K3
Hermite, I., *Chile* 128 E3
Hermon, Mt. = Ash Shaykh, J., *Lebanon* 69 B4
Hermosillo, *Mexico* 114 B2
Hernád →, *Hungary* 21 H11
Hernandarias, *Paraguay* 127 B5
Hernandez, *U.S.A.* 112 J6
Hernando, *Argentina* 126 C3
Hernando, *U.S.A.* 109 H10
Herne, *Belgium* 17 G4
Herne, *Germany* 17 E10
Herne Bay, *U.K.* 13 F9
Herning, *Denmark* 11 H2
Heroica = Caborca, *Mexico* 114 A2
Heroica Nogales = Nogales, *Mexico* 114 A2
Heron Bay, *Canada* 98 C2
Herradura, Pta. de la, *Canary Is.* 36 F5
Herreid, *U.S.A.* 108 C4
Herrera, *Spain* 31 H6
Herrera de Alcántar, *Spain* 31 F3
Herrera de Pisuerga, *Spain* 30 C6
Herrera del Duque, *Spain* 31 F5
Herrick, *Australia* 90 G4
Herrin, *U.S.A.* 109 G10
Herrljunga, *Sweden* 11 F7
Hersbruck, *Germany* 19 F7
Herseaux, *Belgium* 17 G2
Herselt, *Belgium* 17 F5
Hersonissos, *Greece* 37 D7
Herstal, *Belgium* 17 G7
Hertford, *U.K.* 13 F7
Hertfordshire □, *U.K.* 13 F7
's-Hertogenbosch, *Neths.* 17 E6
Hertzogville, *S. Africa* 84 D4
Hervás, *Spain* 30 E5
Herve, *Belgium* 17 G7
Herwijnen, *Neths.* 16 E6
Herzberg, *Brandenburg, Germany* 18 D9
Herzberg, *Niedersachsen, Germany* 18 D6
Herzele, *Belgium* 17 G3
Herzliyya, *Israel* 69 C3
Herzogenbuchsee, *Switz.* 22 B5
Ḩeşār, *Fārs, Iran* 65 D6
Ḩeşār, *Markazī, Iran* 65 C6
Hesdin, *France* 25 B9
Hesel, *Germany* 18 B3
Heshui, *China* 50 G5
Heshun, *China* 50 F7
Hesperange, *Lux.* 17 J8
Hesperia, *U.S.A.* 113 L9
Hesse = Hessen □, *Germany* 18 E5
Hessen □, *Germany* 18 E5
Hetch Hetchy Aqueduct, *U.S.A.* 112 H5
Hettinger, *U.S.A.* 108 C3
Hettstedt, *Germany* 18 D7
Heugem, *Neths.* 17 G7
Heule, *Belgium* 17 G2
Heusden, *Belgium* 17 F6
Heusden, *Neths.* 16 E6
Hève, C. de la, *France* 24 C7
Heverlee, *Belgium* 17 G5
Hewett, C., *Canada* 97 A13
Hexham, *U.K.* 12 C5
Hexi, *Yunnan, China* 52 E4
Hexi, *Zhejiang, China* 53 D12
Hexigten Qi, *China* 51 C9
Hexrivier, *S. Africa* 84 E2
Ḩeydarābād, *Iran* 65 D7
Heyfield, *Australia* 91 F4
Heysham, *U.K.* 12 C5
Heythuysen, *Neths.* 17 F7
Heyuan, *China* 53 F10
Heywood, *Australia* 91 F3
Heze, *China* 50 G8
Hezhang, *China* 52 D5
Hi Vista, *U.S.A.* 113 L9
Hialeah, *U.S.A.* 105 N5
Hiawatha, *Kans., U.S.A.* 108 F7
Hiawatha, *Utah, U.S.A.* 110 G8
Hibbing, *U.S.A.* 108 B8
Hibbs B., *Australia* 90 G4
Hibernia Reef, *Australia* 88 B3
Hickory, *U.S.A.* 105 H5
Hicks, Pt., *Australia* 91 F4
Hicksville, *U.S.A.* 107 F11
Hida, *Romania* 38 B6
Hida-Gawa →, *Japan* 49 G8
Hida-Sammyaku, *Japan* 49 F8
Hidaka-Sammyaku, *Japan* 48 C11
Hidalgo, *Mexico* 115 C5
Hidalgo □, *Mexico* 115 C5
Hidalgo, Presa M., *Mexico* 114 B3
Hidalgo, Pta. del, *Canary Is.* 36 F3
Hidalgo del Parral, *Mexico* 114 B3
Hiddensee, *Germany* 18 A9
Hidrolândia, *Brazil* 123 E2
Hieflau, *Austria* 21 H4
Hiendelaencina, *Spain* 28 D1
Hierapolis, *Turkey* 66 E3
Hierro, *Canary Is.* 36 G1
Higashiajima-San, *Japan* 48 F10
Higashiōsaka, *Japan* 49 G7
Higgins, *U.S.A.* 109 G4
Higgins Corner, *U.S.A.* 112 F5
Higginsville, *Australia* 89 F3
High Atlas = Haut Atlas, *Morocco* 74 B3
High I., *Canada* 99 A7
High Island, *U.S.A.* 109 L7
High Level, *Canada* 100 B5
High Point, *U.S.A.* 105 H6
High Prairie, *Canada* 100 B5
High River, *Canada* 100 C6
High Springs, *U.S.A.* 105 L4
High Tatra = Tatry, *Slovakia* 20 F9
High Wycombe, *U.K.* 13 F7
Highbury, *Australia* 90 B3
Highland □, *U.K.* 14 D4
Highland Park, *U.S.A.* 104 D2
Highmore, *U.S.A.* 108 C5
Highrock L., *Canada* 101 B7
Higüay, *Dom. Rep.* 117 C6
Hihya, *Egypt* 76 H7
Hiiumaa, *Estonia* 40 B3
Híjar, *Spain* 28 D4
Ḩijāz □, *Si. Arabia* 68 C2
Hijken, *Neths.* 16 C8
Hijo = Tagum, *Phil.* 55 H6
Hikari, *Japan* 49 H5
Hiko, *U.S.A.* 111 H6
Hikone, *Japan* 49 G8
Hikurangi, *N.Z.* 87 F5
Hikurangi, Mt., *N.Z.* 87 H6
Hildburghhausen, *Germany* 19 E6
Hildesheim, *Germany* 18 C5
Hill →, *Australia* 89 F2
Hill City, *Idaho, U.S.A.* 110 E6
Hill City, *Kans., U.S.A.* 108 F5
Hill City, *Minn., U.S.A.* 108 B8
Hill City, *S. Dak., U.S.A.* 108 D3
Hill Island L., *Canada* 101 A7
Hillared, *Sweden* 11 G7
Hillcrest Center, *U.S.A.* 113 K8
Hillegom, *Neths.* 16 D5
Hillerød, *Denmark* 11 J6
Hillingdon, *U.K.* 13 F7
Hillman, *U.S.A.* 104 C4
Hillmond, *Canada* 101 C7
Hillsboro, *Kans., U.S.A.* 108 F6
Hillsboro, *N. Dak., U.S.A.* 108 B6
Hillsboro, *N.H., U.S.A.* 107 C13
Hillsboro, *N. Mex., U.S.A.* 111 K10
Hillsboro, *Oreg., U.S.A.* 112 E4
Hillsboro, *Tex., U.S.A.* 109 J6
Hillsborough, *Grenada* 117 D7
Hillsdale, *Mich., U.S.A.* 104 E3
Hillsdale, *N.Y., U.S.A.* 107 D11
Hillside, *Australia* 88 D2
Hillsport, *Canada* 98 C2
Hillston, *Australia* 91 E4
Hilo, *U.S.A.* 102 J17
Hilton, *U.S.A.* 106 C7
Hilvan, *Turkey* 67 E8
Hilvarenbeek, *Neths.* 17 F6
Hilversum, *Neths.* 16 D6
Himachal Pradesh □, *India* 62 D7
Himalaya, *Asia* 63 E11
Himamaylan, *Phil.* 55 F5
Himara, *Albania* 39 J2
Himatnagar, *India* 60 H8
Himeji, *Japan* 49 G7
Himi, *Japan* 49 F8
Himmerland, *Denmark* 11 H3
Ḩimş, *Syria* 69 A5
Ḩims □, *Syria* 69 A5
Hinche, *Haiti* 117 C5
Hinchinbrook I., *Australia* 90 B4
Hinckley, *U.K.* 13 E6
Hinckley, *U.S.A.* 110 G7
Hindås, *Sweden* 11 G6
Hindaun, *India* 62 F7
Hindmarsh, L., *Australia* 91 F3
Hindsholm, *Denmark* 11 J4
Hindu Bagh, *Pakistan* 62 D2
Hindu Kush, *Asia* 60 B7
Hindubagh, *Pakistan* 60 D5
Hindupur, *India* 60 N10
Hines Creek, *Canada* 100 B5
Hinganghat, *India* 60 J11
Hingeon, *Belgium* 17 G5
Hingham, *U.S.A.* 110 B8
Hingoli, *India* 60 K10
Hinigaran, *Phil.* 55 F5
Hinis, *Turkey* 67 D9
Hinna = Imi, *Ethiopia* 68 F3
Hinna, *Nigeria* 79 C7
Hinojosa del Duque, *Spain* 31 G5
Hinsdale, *U.S.A.* 110 B10
Hinterrhein →, *Switz.* 23 C8
Hinton, *Canada* 100 C5
Hinton, *U.S.A.* 104 G5
Hinwil, *Switz.* 23 B7
Hınzır Burnu, *Turkey* 66 E6
Hippolytushoef, *Neths.* 16 C5
Hirado, *Japan* 49 H4
Hirakud Dam, *India* 61 J13

Hiratsuka, *Japan* 49 G9
Hirfanlı Baraji, *Turkey* 66 D5
Hirhafok, *Algeria* 75 D6
Hîrlău, *Romania* 38 B9
Hiroo, *Japan* 48 C11
Hirosaki, *Japan* 48 D10
Hiroshima, *Japan* 49 G6
Hiroshima □, *Japan* 49 G6
Hirsholmene, *Denmark* 11 G4
Hirson, *France* 25 C11
Hîrşova, *Romania* 38 E10
Hirtshals, *Denmark* 11 G3
Hisar, *India* 62 E6
Hisb →, *Iraq* 64 D5
Ḥismá, *Si. Arabia* 64 D3
Hispaniola, *W. Indies* 117 C5
Hīt, *Iraq* 64 C4
Hita, *Japan* 49 H5
Hitachi, *Japan* 49 F10
Hitchin, *U.K.* 13 F7
Hitoyoshi, *Japan* 49 H5
Hitra, *Norway* 8 E10
Hitzacker, *Germany* 18 B7
Ḥiyyon, N. →, *Israel* 69 E4
Hjalmar L., *Canada* 101 A7
Hjälmare kanal, *Sweden* 10 E9
Hjälmaren, *Sweden* 10 E9
Hjartdal, *Norway* 10 E2
Hjerkinn, *Norway* 10 B3
Hjørring, *Denmark* 11 G3
Hjortkvarn, *Sweden* 11 F9
Hlinsko, *Czech.* 20 F5
Hluhluwe, *S. Africa* 85 D5
Ho, *Ghana* 79 D5
Ho Chi Minh City = Phanh Bho Ho Chi Minh, *Vietnam* 59 G6
Ho Thuong, *Vietnam* 58 C5
Hoa Binh, *Vietnam* 58 B5
Hoa Da, *Vietnam* 59 G7
Hoa Hiep, *Vietnam* 59 G5
Hoai Nhon, *Vietnam* 58 E7
Hoare B., *Canada* 97 B13
Hobart, *Australia* 90 G4
Hobart, *U.S.A.* 109 H5
Hobbs, *U.S.A.* 109 J3
Hobbs Coast, *Antarctica* 5 D14
Hobo, *Colombia* 120 C2
Hoboken, *Belgium* 17 F4
Hoboken, *U.S.A.* 107 F10
Hobro, *Denmark* 11 H3
Hobscheid, *Lux.* 17 J7
Hoburgen, *Sweden* 9 H15
Hochdorf, *Switz.* 23 B6
Hochschwab, *Austria* 21 H5
Höchstadt, *Germany* 19 F6
Hockenheim, *Germany* 19 F4
Hodaka-Dake, *Japan* 49 F8
Hodgson, *Canada* 101 C9
Hódmezővásárhely, *Hungary* 21 J10
Hodna, Chott el, *Algeria* 75 A5
Hodna, Monts du, *Algeria* 75 A5
Hodonín, *Czech.* 20 G7
Hoeamdong, *N. Korea* 51 C16
Hœdic, I. de, *France* 24 E4
Hoegaarden, *Belgium* 17 G5
Hoek van Holland, *Neths.* 16 E4
Hoeksche Waard, *Neths.* 16 F4
Hoenderloo, *Neths.* 16 D7
Hoengsŏng, *S. Korea* 51 F14
Hoensbroek, *Neths.* 17 G7
Hoeryong, *N. Korea* 51 C15
Hoeselt, *Belgium* 17 G6
Hoeven, *Neths.* 17 E5
Hoeyang, *N. Korea* 51 E14
Hof, *Germany* 19 E7
Hof, *Iceland* 8 D6
Höfðakaupstaður, *Iceland* 8 D3
Hofgeismar, *Germany* 18 D5
Hofmeyr, *S. Africa* 84 E4
Hofsjökull, *Iceland* 8 D4
Hofsós, *Iceland* 8 D4
Hōfu, *Japan* 49 G5
Hogan Group, *Australia* 90 F4
Hogansville, *U.S.A.* 105 J3
Hogeland, *U.S.A.* 110 B9
Hoggar = Ahaggar, *Algeria* 75 D6
Högsäter, *Sweden* 11 F6
Hogsty Reef, *Bahamas* 117 B5
Hoh →, *U.S.A.* 112 C2
Hoh Xil Shan, *China* 54 C3
Hohe Rhön, *Germany* 19 E5
Hohe Tauern, *Austria* 21 H2
Hohe Venn, *Belgium* 17 H8
Hohenau, *Austria* 20 G6
Hohenems, *Austria* 19 H5
Hohenstein-Ernstthal, *Germany* 18 E8
Hohenwald, *U.S.A.* 105 H2
Hohenwestedt, *Germany* 18 A5
Hohhot, *China* 50 D6
Hóhlakas, *Greece* 37 D9
Hohoe, *Ghana* 79 D5
Hoi An, *Vietnam* 58 E7
Hoi Xuan, *Vietnam* 58 B5
Hoisington, *U.S.A.* 108 F5
Højer, *Denmark* 11 K2
Hōjō, *Japan* 49 H6
Hökerum, *Sweden* 11 G7
Hokianga Harbour, *N.Z.* 87 F4
Hokitika, *N.Z.* 87 K3
Hokkaidō □, *Japan* 48 C11
Hokksund, *Norway* 10 E3
Hol-Hol, *Djibouti* 77 E5
Holbæk, *Denmark* 11 J5
Holbrook, *Australia* 91 F4
Holbrook, *U.S.A.* 111 J8
Holden, *Canada* 100 C6
Holden, *U.S.A.* 110 G7
Holdenville, *U.S.A.* 109 H6
Holderness, *U.K.* 12 D7
Holdfast, *Canada* 101 C7
Holdich, *Argentina* 128 C3
Holdrege, *U.S.A.* 108 E5
Holguín, *Cuba* 116 B4
Hollabrunn, *Austria* 20 G6
Hollams Bird I., *Namibia* 84 C1
Holland, *U.S.A.* 104 D2
Hollandia = Jayapura, *Indonesia* 57 E10
Hollandsch Diep, *Neths.* 17 E5
Hollandsch IJssel →, *Neths.* 16 E5
Hollfeld, *Germany* 19 F7
Hollidaysburg, *U.S.A.* 106 F6
Hollis, *U.S.A.* 109 H5
Hollister, *Calif., U.S.A.* 111 H3
Hollister, *Idaho, U.S.A.* 110 E6
Hollum, *Neths.* 16 B7
Holly, *U.S.A.* 108 F3
Holly Hill, *U.S.A.* 105 L5
Holly Springs, *U.S.A.* 109 H10
Hollywood, *Calif., U.S.A.* 111 J4
Hollywood, *Fla., U.S.A.* 105 N5
Holm, *Sweden* 10 B10
Holman Island, *Canada* 96 A8
Hólmavík, *Iceland* 8 D3
Holmes Reefs, *Australia* 90 B4
Holmestrand, *Norway* 10 E4
Holmsbu, *Norway* 10 E4
Holmsjön, *Sweden* 10 B9
Holmsland Klit, *Denmark* 11 J2
Holmsund, *Sweden* 8 E16
Holroyd →, *Australia* 90 A3
Holstebro, *Denmark* 11 H2
Holsworthy, *U.K.* 13 G3
Holt, *Iceland* 8 E4
Holte, *Denmark* 11 J6
Holten, *Neths.* 16 D8
Holton, *Canada* 99 B8
Holton, *U.S.A.* 108 F7
Holtville, *U.S.A.* 113 N11
Holwerd, *Neths.* 16 B7
Holy Cross, *U.S.A.* 96 B4
Holy I., *Gwynedd, U.K.* 12 D3
Holy I., *Northumb., U.K.* 12 B6
Holyhead, *U.K.* 12 D3
Holyoke, *Colo., U.S.A.* 108 E3
Holyoke, *Mass., U.S.A.* 107 D12
Holyrood, *Canada* 99 C9
Holzkirchen, *Germany* 19 H7
Holzminden, *Germany* 18 D5
Homa Bay, *Kenya* 82 C3
Homa Bay □, *Kenya* 82 C3
Homalin, *Burma* 61 G19
Homand, *Iran* 65 C8
Homberg, *Germany* 18 D5
Hombori, *Mali* 79 B4
Homburg, *Germany* 19 F3
Home B., *Canada* 97 B13
Home Hill, *Australia* 90 B4
Homedale, *U.S.A.* 110 E5
Homer, *Alaska, U.S.A.* 96 C4
Homer, *La., U.S.A.* 109 J8
Homestead, *Australia* 90 C4
Homestead, *Fla., U.S.A.* 105 N5
Homestead, *Oreg., U.S.A.* 110 D5
Homewood, *U.S.A.* 112 F6
Hominy, *U.S.A.* 109 G6
Homoine, *Mozam.* 85 C6
Homoljske Planina, *Serbia* 21 L11
Homorod, *Romania* 38 C8
Homs = Ḥimş, *Syria* 69 A5
Homyel = Gomel, *Belorussia* 40 E7
Hon Chong, *Vietnam* 59 G5
Hon Me, *Vietnam* 58 C5
Hon Quan, *Vietnam* 59 G6
Honan = Henan □, *China* 50 G8
Honbetsu, *Japan* 48 C11
Honcut, *U.S.A.* 112 F5
Honda, *Colombia* 120 B3
Honda Bay, *Phil.* 55 G3
Hondeklipbaai, *S. Africa* 84 E2
Hondo, *Japan* 49 H5
Hondo, *U.S.A.* 109 L5
Hondo →, *Belize* 115 D7
Honduras ■, *Cent. Amer.* 116 D2
Honduras, G. de, *Caribbean* 116 C2
Hønefoss, *Norway* 9 F11
Honesdale, *U.S.A.* 107 E9
Honey L., *U.S.A.* 112 E6
Honfleur, *France* 24 C7
Hong Gai, *Vietnam* 58 B6
Hong He →, *China* 50 H8
Hong Kong ■, *Asia* 53 F10
Hong'an, *China* 53 B10
Hongchŏn, *S. Korea* 51 F14
Honghai Wan, *China* 53 F10
Honghu, *China* 53 C9
Hongjiang, *China* 52 D7
Hongliu He →, *China* 50 F5
Hongor, *Mongolia* 50 B7
Hongsa, *Laos* 58 C3
Hongshui He →, *China* 52 F7
Hongsŏng, *S. Korea* 51 F14
Hongtong, *China* 50 F6
Honguedo, Détroit d', *Canada* 99 C7
Hongwon, *N. Korea* 51 E14
Hongya, *China* 52 C4
Hongyuan, *China* 52 A4
Hongze Hu, *China* 51 H10
Honiara, *Solomon Is.* 92 H7
Honiton, *U.K.* 13 G4
Honjō, *Japan* 48 E10
Honkorâb, Ras, *Egypt* 76 C4
Honolulu, *U.S.A.* 102 H16
Honshū, *Japan* 49 G9
Hontoria del Pinar, *Spain* 28 D1
Hood, Mt., *U.S.A.* 110 D3
Hood, Pt., *Australia* 89 F2
Hood River, *U.S.A.* 110 D3
Hoodsport, *U.S.A.* 112 C3
Hooge, *Germany* 18 A4
Hoogerheide, *Neths.* 17 F4
Hoogeveen, *Neths.* 16 C8
Hoogeveensche Vaart, *Neths.* 16 C8
Hoogezand, *Neths.* 16 B9
Hooghly → = Hughli →, *India* 63 J13
Hooghly-Chinsura = Chunchura, *India* 63 H13
Hoogkerk, *Neths.* 16 B9
Hooglede, *Belgium* 17 G2
Hoogstraten, *Belgium* 17 F5
Hoogvliet, *Neths.* 16 E4
Hook Hd., *Ireland* 15 D5
Hook I., *Australia* 90 C4
Hook of Holland = Hoek van Holland, *Neths.* 16 E4
Hooker, *U.S.A.* 109 G4
Hooker Creek, *Australia* 88 C5
Hoopeston, *U.S.A.* 104 E2
Hoopstad, *S. Africa* 84 D4
Hoorn, *Neths.* 16 C6
Hoover Dam, *U.S.A.* 113 K12
Hooversville, *U.S.A.* 106 F6
Hop Bottom, *U.S.A.* 107 E9
Hopa, *Turkey* 43 F9
Hope, *Canada* 100 D4
Hope, *Ariz., U.S.A.* 113 M13
Hope, *Ark., U.S.A.* 109 J8
Hope, *N. Dak., U.S.A.* 108 B6
Hope, L., *Australia* 91 D2
Hope, Pt., *U.S.A.* 96 B3
Hope Town, *Bahamas* 116 A4
Hopedale, *Canada* 99 A7
Hopefield, *S. Africa* 84 E2
Hopei = Hebei □, *China* 50 E9
Hopelchén, *Mexico* 115 D7
Hopetoun, *Vic., Australia* 91 F3
Hopetoun, *W. Austral., Australia* 89 F3
Hopetown, *S. Africa* 84 D3
Hopkins, *U.S.A.* 108 E7
Hopkins, L., *Australia* 88 D4
Hopkinsville, *U.S.A.* 105 G2
Hopland, *U.S.A.* 112 G3
Hoptrup, *Denmark* 11 J3
Hoquiam, *U.S.A.* 112 D3
Horasan, *Turkey* 67 C10
Horcajo de Santiago, *Spain* 28 F1
Hordaland fylke □, *Norway* 9 F9
Horden Hills, *Australia* 88 D5
Horezu, *Romania* 38 D6
Horgen, *Switz.* 23 B7
Horinger, *China* 50 D6
Horlick Mts., *Antarctica* 5 E15
Horlivka = Gorlovka, *Ukraine* 42 B8
Hormoz, *Iran* 65 E7
Hormoz, Jaz. ye, *Iran* 65 E8
Hormuz Str. of, *The Gulf* 65 E8
Horn, *Ísafjarðarsýsla, Iceland* 8 C2
Horn, *Suður-Múlasýsla, Iceland* 8 D7
Horn, *Neths.* 17 F7
Horn →, *Canada* 100 A5
Horn, Cape = Hornos, C. de, *Chile* 128 E3
Horn Head, *Ireland* 15 A3
Horn I., *Australia* 90 A3
Horn I., *U.S.A.* 105 K1
Horn Mts., *Canada* 100 A5
Hornachuelos, *Spain* 31 H5
Hornavan, *Sweden* 8 C14
Hornbæk, *Denmark* 11 H6
Hornbeck, *U.S.A.* 109 K8
Hornbrook, *U.S.A.* 110 F2
Hornburg, *Germany* 18 C6
Horncastle, *U.K.* 12 D7
Hornell, *U.S.A.* 106 D7
Hornell L., *Canada* 100 A5
Hornepayne, *Canada* 98 C3
Hornitos, *U.S.A.* 112 H6
Hornos, C. de, *Chile* 128 E3
Hornoy, *France* 25 C8
Hornsby, *Australia* 91 E5
Hornsea, *U.K.* 12 D7
Hornslandet, *Sweden* 10 C11
Hornslet, *Denmark* 11 H4
Hornu, *Belgium* 17 H3
Hörnum, *Germany* 18 A4
Horobetsu, *Japan* 48 C10
Horqin Youyi Qianqi, *China* 51 A12
Horqueta, *Paraguay* 126 A4
Horred, *Sweden* 11 G6
Horse Creek, *U.S.A.* 108 E3
Horse Is., *Canada* 99 B8
Horsefly L., *Canada* 100 C4
Horsens, *Denmark* 11 J3
Horsens Fjord, *Denmark* 11 J4
Horsham, *Australia* 91 F3
Horsham, *U.K.* 13 F7
Horst, *Neths.* 17 F8
Horten, *Norway* 10 E4
Hortobágy →, *Hungary* 21 H11
Horton, *U.S.A.* 108 F7
Horton →, *Canada* 96 B7
Horw, *Switz.* 23 B6
Horwood, L., *Canada* 98 C3
Hosaina, *Ethiopia* 77 F4
Hose, Gunung-Gunung, *Malaysia* 56 D4
Ḥoseynābād, *Khuzestān, Iran* 65 C6
Ḥoseynābād, *Kordestān, Iran* 64 C5
Hoshangabad, *India* 62 H7
Hoshiarpur, *India* 62 D6
Hosingen, *Lux.* 17 H8
Hosmer, *U.S.A.* 108 C5
Hospental, *Switz.* 23 C7
Hospet, *India* 60 M10
Hospitalet de Llobregat, *Spain* 28 D7
Hoste, I., *Chile* 128 E3
Hostens, *France* 26 D3
Hot, *Thailand* 58 C2
Hot Creek Range, *U.S.A.* 110 G5
Hot Springs, *Ark., U.S.A.* 109 H8
Hot Springs, *S. Dak., U.S.A.* 108 D3
Hotagen, *Sweden* 8 E13
Hotan, *China* 54 C2
Hotazel, *S. Africa* 84 D3
Hotchkiss, *U.S.A.* 111 G10
Hotham, C., *Australia* 88 B5
Hoting, *Sweden* 8 D14
Hotte, Massif de la, *Haiti* 117 C5
Hottentotsbaai, *Namibia* 84 D1
Hotton, *Belgium* 17 H6
Houat, I. de, *France* 24 E4
Houck, *U.S.A.* 111 J9
Houdan, *France* 25 D8
Houdeng-Goegnies, *Belgium* 17 H4
Houei Sai, *Laos* 58 B3
Houffalize, *Belgium* 17 H7
Houghton, *U.S.A.* 108 B10
Houghton L., *U.S.A.* 104 C3
Houghton-le-Spring, *U.K.* 12 C6
Houhora Heads, *N.Z.* 87 F4
Houille →, *Belgium* 17 H5
Houlton, *U.S.A.* 99 C6
Houma, *U.S.A.* 109 L9
Houndé, *Burkina Faso* 78 C4
Hourtin, *France* 26 C2
Hourtin-Carcans, Étang d', *France* 26 C2
Houston, *Canada* 100 C3
Houston, *Mo., U.S.A.* 109 G9
Houston, *Tex., U.S.A.* 109 L7
Houten, *Neths.* 16 D6
Houthalen, *Belgium* 17 F6
Houthem, *Belgium* 17 G1
Houthulst, *Belgium* 17 G2
Houtman Abrolhos, *Australia* 89 E1
Houyet, *Belgium* 17 H6
Hov, *Denmark* 11 J4
Hova, *Sweden* 11 F8
Høvåg, *Norway* 11 F2
Hovd, *Mongolia* 54 B4
Hove, *U.K.* 13 G7
Hoveyzeh, *Iran* 65 D6
Hövsgöl, *Mongolia* 50 C5
Hövsgöl Nuur, *Mongolia* 54 A5
Howakil, *Eritrea* 77 D5
Howar, Wadi →, *Sudan* 77 D2
Howard, *Australia* 91 D5
Howard, *Kans., U.S.A.* 109 G6
Howard, *Pa., U.S.A.* 106 E7
Howard, *S. Dak., U.S.A.* 108 C6
Howard I., *Australia* 90 A2
Howard L., *Canada* 101 A7
Howe, *U.S.A.* 110 E7
Howe, C., *Australia* 91 F5
Howell, *U.S.A.* 104 D4
Howick, *Canada* 107 A11
Howick, *S. Africa* 85 D5
Howick Group, *Australia* 90 A4
Howitt, L., *Australia* 91 D2
Howley, *Canada* 99 C8
Howrah = Haora, *India* 63 H13
Howth Hd., *Ireland* 15 C5
Höxter, *Germany* 18 D5
Hoy, *U.K.* 14 C5
Hoya, *Germany* 18 C5
Høyanger, *Norway* 9 F9
Hoyerswerda, *Germany* 18 D10
Hoyos, *Spain* 30 E4
Hpungan Pass, *Burma* 61 F20
Hradec Králové, *Czech.* 20 E5
Hranice, *Czech.* 20 F7
Hrodna = Grodno, *Belorussia* 40 E3
Hron →, *Slovak Rep.* 21 H8
Hrubieszów, *Poland* 20 E13
Hrvatska = Croatia ■, *Europe* 33 C13
Hsenwi, *Burma* 61 H20
Hsiamen = Xiamen, *China* 53 E12
Hsian = Xi'an, *China* 50 G5
Hsinhailien = Lianyungang, *China* 51 G10
Hsisha Chuntao, *Pac. Oc.* 56 A4
Hsüchou = Xuzhou, *China* 51 G9
Hu Xian, *China* 50 G5
Hua Hin, *Thailand* 58 F2
Hua Xian, *Henan, China* 50 G8
Hua Xian, *Shaanxi, China* 50 G5
Hua'an, *China* 53 E11
Huacaya, *Bolivia* 125 E5
Huacheng, *China* 53 E10
Huachinera, *Mexico* 114 A3
Huacho, *Peru* 124 C2
Huachón, *Peru* 124 C2
Huade, *China* 50 D7
Huadian, *China* 51 C14
Huai He →, *China* 53 A12
Huai Yot, *Thailand* 59 J2
Huai'an, *Hebei, China* 50 D8
Huai'an, *Jiangsu, China* 51 H10
Huaide, *China* 51 C13
Huaidezhen, *China* 51 C13
Huaihua, *China* 52 D7
Huaiji, *China* 53 F9
Huainan, *China* 53 A11
Huaining, *China* 53 B11
Huairen, *China* 50 E7
Huairou, *China* 50 D9
Huaiyang, *China* 50 H8
Huaiyuan, *Anhui, China* 51 H9
Huaiyuan, *Guangxi Zhuangzu, China* 52 E7
Huajianzi, *China* 51 D13
Huajuapan de Leon, *Mexico* 115 D5
Hualapai Peak, *U.S.A.* 111 J7
Hualian, *Taiwan* 53 F13
Huallaga →, *Peru* 124 B2
Huallanca, *Peru* 124 B2
Huamachuco, *Peru* 124 B2
Huambo, *Angola* 81 G3
Huan Jiang →, *China* 50 G5
Huan Xian, *China* 50 F4
Huancabamba, *Peru* 124 B2
Huancane, *Peru* 124 D4
Huancapi, *Peru* 124 C3
Huancavelica, *Peru* 124 C2
Huancavelica □, *Peru* 124 C3
Huancayo, *Peru* 124 C2
Huanchaca, *Bolivia* 124 E4
Huanchaca, Serranía de, *Bolivia* 125 C5
Huang Hai = Yellow Sea, *China* 51 G12
Huang He →, *China* 51 F10
Huang Xian, *China* 51 F11
Huangchuan, *China* 53 A10
Huanggang, *China* 53 B10
Huangling, *China* 50 G5
Huangliu, *China* 54 E5
Huanglong, *China* 50 G5
Huanglongtan, *China* 53 A8
Huangmei, *China* 53 B10
Huangpi, *China* 53 B10
Huangping, *China* 52 D6
Huangshi, *China* 53 B10
Huangsongdian, *China* 51 C14
Huangyan, *China* 53 C13
Huangyangsi, *China* 53 D8
Huaning, *China* 52 E4
Huanjiang, *China* 52 E7
Huanta, *Peru* 124 C3
Huantai, *China* 51 F9
Huánuco, *Peru* 124 B2
Huánuco □, *Peru* 124 B2
Huanuni, *Bolivia* 124 D4
Huanzo, Cordillera de, *Peru* 124 C3
Huaping, *China* 52 D3
Huaral, *Peru* 124 C2
Huaraz, *Peru* 124 B2
Huari, *Peru* 124 B2
Huarmey, *Peru* 124 C2
Huarochiri, *Peru* 124 C2
Huarocondo, *Peru* 124 C3
Huarong, *China* 53 C9
Huascarán, *Peru* 124 B2
Huascarán, Nevado, *Peru* 124 B2
Huasco, *Chile* 126 B1
Huasco →, *Chile* 126 B1
Huasna, *U.S.A.* 113 K6
Huatabampo, *Mexico* 114 B3
Huauchinango, *Mexico* 115 C5
Huautla de Jiménez, *Mexico* 115 D5
Huaxi, *China* 52 D6
Huay Namota, *Mexico* 114 C4
Huayin, *China* 50 G6
Huayllay, *Peru* 124 C2
Huayuan, *China* 52 C7
Huazhou, *China* 53 G8
Hubbard, *U.S.A.* 109 K6
Hubbart Pt., *Canada* 101 B10
Hubei □, *China* 53 B9
Hubli-Dharwad = Dharwad, *India* 60 M9
Huchang, *N. Korea* 51 D14
Hückelhoven, *Germany* 18 D2
Huddersfield, *U.K.* 12 D6
Hudi, *Sudan* 76 D3
Hudiksvall, *Sweden* 10 C11
Hudson, *Canada* 101 C10
Hudson, *Mass., U.S.A.* 107 D13
Hudson, *Mich., U.S.A.* 104 E3
Hudson, *N.Y., U.S.A.* 107 D11
Hudson, *Wis., U.S.A.* 108 C8
Hudson, *Wyo., U.S.A.* 110 E9
Hudson →, *U.S.A.* 107 F10

Hudson Bay, N.W.T., Canada 97 C11
Hudson Bay, Sask., Canada 101 C8
Hudson Falls, U.S.A. 107 C11
Hudson Mts., Antarctica 5 D16
Hudson Str., Canada 97 B13
Hudson's Hope, Canada 100 B4
Hue, Vietnam 58 D6
Huebra →, Spain 30 D4
Huechucuicui, Pta., Chile 128 B2
Huedin, Romania 38 C6
Huehuetenango, Guatemala 116 C1
Huejúcar, Mexico 114 C4
Huelgoat, France 24 D3
Huelma, Spain 29 H1
Huelva, Spain 31 H4
Huelva □, Spain 31 H4
Huelva →, Spain 31 H5
Huentelauquén, Chile 126 C1
Huércal Overa, Spain 29 H3
Huerta, Sa. de la, Argentina 126 C2
Huertas, C. de las, Spain 29 G4
Huerva →, Spain 28 D4
Huesca, Spain 28 C4
Huesca □, Spain 28 C5
Huéscar, Spain 29 H2
Huetamo, Mexico 114 D4
Huete, Spain 28 E2
Hugh →, Australia 90 D1
Hughenden, Australia 90 C3
Hughes, Australia 89 F4
Hughli →, India 63 J13
Hugo, U.S.A. 108 F3
Hugoton, U.S.A. 109 G4
Hui Xian, Gansu, China 50 H4
Hui Xian, Henan, China 50 G7
Hui'an, China 53 E12
Hui'anbu, China 50 F4
Huichang, China 53 E10
Huichapán, Mexico 115 C5
Huidong, China 52 D4
Huifa He →, China 51 C14
Huila □, Colombia 120 C2
Huila, Nevado del, Colombia 120 C2
Huilai, China 53 F11
Huili, China 52 D4
Huimin, China 51 F9
Huinan, China 51 C14
Huinca Renancó, Argentina 126 C3
Huining, China 50 G3
Huinong, China 50 E4
Huise, Belgium 17 G3
Huishui, China 52 D6
Huisne →, France 24 E7
Huissen, Neths. 16 E7
Huiting, China 50 G9
Huitong, China 52 D7
Huixtla, Mexico 115 D6
Huize, China 52 D4
Huizen, Neths. 16 D6
Huizhou, China 53 F10
Hukawng Valley, Burma 61 F20
Hukou, China 53 C11
Hukuntsi, Botswana 84 C3
Hula, Ethiopia 77 F4
Hulan, China 54 B7
Ḥulayfā', Si. Arabia 64 E4
Huld, Mongolia 50 B3
Hulin He →, China 51 B12
Hull = Kingston upon Hull, U.K. 12 D7
Hull, Canada 98 C4
Hull →, U.K. 12 D7
Hulst, Neths. 17 F4
Hulun Nur, China 54 B6
Humahuaca, Argentina 126 A2
Humaitá, Brazil 125 B5
Humaitá, Paraguay 126 B4
Humansdorp, S. Africa 84 E3
Humbe, Angola 84 B1
Humber →, U.K. 12 D7
Humberside □, U.K. 12 D7
Humbert River, Australia 88 C5
Humble, U.S.A. 109 L8
Humboldt, Canada 101 C7
Humboldt, Iowa, U.S.A. 108 D7
Humboldt, Tenn., U.S.A. 109 H10
Humboldt →, U.S.A. 110 F4
Humboldt Gletscher, Greenland 4 B4
Hume, U.S.A. 112 J8
Hume, L., Australia 91 F4
Humenné, Slovakia 20 G11
Humphreys, Mt., U.S.A. 112 H8
Humphreys Peak, U.S.A. 111 J8
Humpolec, Czech. 20 F5
Humptulips, U.S.A. 112 C3
Hūn, Libya 73 C8
Hun Jiang →, China 51 D13
Húnaflói, Iceland 8 D3
Hunan □, China 53 D9
Hunchun, China 51 C16
Hundested, Denmark 11 J5
Hundred Mile House, Canada 100 C4
Hunedoara, Romania 38 D5
Hünfeld, Germany 18 E5
Hung Yen, Vietnam 58 B6
Hungary ■, Europe 21 H9
Hungary, Plain of, Europe 6 F9
Hungerford, Australia 91 D3
Hŭngnam, N. Korea 51 E14
Huni Valley, Ghana 78 D4
Hunsberge, Namibia 84 D2
Hunsrück, Germany 19 F3
Hunstanton, U.K. 12 E8
Hunte →, Germany 18 C4
Hunter, N. Dak., U.S.A. 108 B6
Hunter, N.Y., U.S.A. 107 D10
Hunter I., Australia 90 G3
Hunter I., Canada 100 C3
Hunter Ra., Australia 91 E5
Hunters Road, Zimbabwe 83 F2
Hunterville, N.Z. 87 H5
Huntingburg, U.S.A. 104 F2
Huntingdon, Canada 98 C5
Huntingdon, U.K. 13 E7
Huntingdon, U.S.A. 106 F6
Huntington, Ind., U.S.A. 104 E3
Huntington, N.Y., U.S.A. 107 F11
Huntington, Oreg., U.S.A. 110 D5
Huntington, Utah, U.S.A. 110 G8
Huntington, W. Va., U.S.A. 104 F4
Huntington Beach, U.S.A. 113 M8
Huntington Park, U.S.A. 111 K4
Huntly, N.Z. 87 G5
Huntly, U.K. 14 D6
Huntsville, Canada 98 C4
Huntsville, Ala., U.S.A. 105 H2
Huntsville, Tex., U.S.A. 109 K7
Hunyani →, Zimbabwe 83 F3
Hunyuan, China 50 E7
Hunza →, India 63 B6
Huo Xian, China 50 F6
Huong Hoa, Vietnam 58 D6
Huong Khe, Vietnam 58 C5
Huonville, Australia 90 G4
Huoqiu, China 53 A11
Huoshan, Anhui, China 53 A12
Huoshan, Anhui, China 53 B11
Huoshao Dao, Taiwan 53 F13
Hupeh = Hubei □, China 53 B9
Ḥūr, Iran 65 D8
Hure Qi, China 51 C11
Hurezani, Romania 38 E6
Hurghada, Egypt 76 B3
Hurley, N. Mex., U.S.A. 111 K9
Hurley, Wis., U.S.A. 108 B9
Huron, Calif., U.S.A. 112 J6
Huron, Ohio, U.S.A. 106 E2
Huron, S. Dak., U.S.A. 108 C5
Huron, L., U.S.A. 106 B2
Hurricane, U.S.A. 111 H7
Hurso, Ethiopia 77 F5
Hurum, Norway 10 C2
Hurunui →, N.Z. 87 K4
Hurup, Denmark 11 H2
Húsavík, Iceland 8 C5
Huşi, Romania 38 C11
Huskvarna, Sweden 9 H13
Hussar, Canada 100 C6
Husum, Germany 18 A5
Husum, Sweden 10 A13
Hutchinson, Kans., U.S.A. 109 F6
Hutchinson, Minn., U.S.A. 108 C7
Huttig, U.S.A. 109 J8
Hutton, Mt., Australia 91 D4
Huttwil, Switz. 22 B5
Huwun, Ethiopia 77 G5
Huy, Belgium 17 G6
Hvammur, Iceland 8 D3
Hvar, Croatia 33 E13
Hvarski Kanal, Croatia 33 E13
Hvítá, Iceland 8 D3
Hvítá →, Iceland 8 D3
Hvítárvatn, Iceland 8 D4
Hwachon-chosuji, S. Korea 51 E14
Hwang Ho = Huang He →, China 51 F10
Hwange, Zimbabwe 83 F2
Hwange Nat. Park, Zimbabwe 84 B4
Hyannis, U.S.A. 108 E4
Hyargas Nuur, Mongolia 54 B4
Hybo, Sweden 10 C10
Hyde Park, Guyana 121 B6
Hyden, Australia 89 F2
Hyderabad, India 60 L11
Hyderabad, Pakistan 62 G3
Hyères, France 27 E10
Hyères, Is. d', France 27 F10
Hyesan, N. Korea 51 D15
Hyland →, Canada 100 B3
Hyltebruk, Sweden 11 H7
Hymia, India 63 C8
Hyndman Peak, U.S.A. 110 E6
Hyōgo □, Japan 49 G7
Hyrum, U.S.A. 110 F8
Hysham, U.S.A. 110 C10
Hythe, U.K. 13 F9
Hyūga, Japan 49 H5
Hyvinge = Hyvinkää, Finland 9 F18
Hyvinkää, Finland 9 F18

I

I-n-Échaï, Mali 74 D4
I-n-Gall, Niger 79 B6
Iabès, Erg, Algeria 75 C4
Iaco →, Brazil 124 B4
Iaçu, Brazil 123 D3
Iakora, Madag. 85 C8
Iaşi, Romania 38 B10
Iauaretê, Colombia 120 C4
Iba, Phil. 55 D3
Ibadan, Nigeria 79 D5
Ibagué, Colombia 120 C2
Ibaiti, Brazil 123 F1
Iballja, Albania 38 G3
Ibăneşti, Romania 38 C7
Ibar →, Serbia, Yug. 21 M10
Ibaraki □, Japan 49 F10
Ibarra, Ecuador 120 C2
Ibba, Sudan 77 G2
Ibba, Bahr el →, Sudan 77 F2
Ibbenbüren, Germany 18 C3
Ibembo, Zaïre 82 B1
Ibera, L., Argentina 126 B4
Iberian Peninsula, Europe 6 G5
Iberico, Sistema, Spain 28 E2
Iberville, Canada 98 C5
Iberville, Lac d', Canada 98 A5
Ibi, Nigeria 79 D6
Ibiá, Brazil 123 E2
Ibicaraí, Brazil 123 D4
Ibicuí, Brazil 123 D4
Ibicuy, Argentina 126 C4
Ibioapaba, Sa. da, Brazil 122 B3
Ibipetuba, Brazil 122 D3
Ibitiara, Brazil 123 D3
Ibiza, Spain 36 C7
Íblei, Monti, Italy 35 E7
Ibo, Mozam. 83 E5
Ibonma, Indonesia 57 E8
Ibotirama, Brazil 123 D3
Ibrāhīm →, Lebanon 69 A4
Ibshawâi, Egypt 76 J7
Ibu, Indonesia 57 D7
Iburg, Germany 18 C4
Ibusuki, Japan 49 J5
Icá, Peru 124 C2
Ica □, Peru 124 C2
Iça →, Brazil 124 A4
Icabarú, Venezuela 121 C5
Icabarú →, Venezuela 121 C5
Içana, Brazil 120 C4
Içana →, Brazil 120 C4
Icatu, Brazil 122 B3
İçel = Mersin, Turkey 66 E6
İçel □, Turkey 66 E6
Iceland ■, Europe 8 D4
Icha, Russia 45 D16
Ich'ang = Yichang, China 53 B8
Ichchapuram, India 61 K14
Ichihara, Japan 49 G10
Ichikawa, Japan 49 G9
Ichilo →, Bolivia 125 D5
Ichinohe, Japan 48 D10
Ichinomiya, Japan 49 G8
Ichinoseki, Japan 48 E10
Ichnya, Ukraine 40 F8
Ichŏn, S. Korea 51 F14
Icht, Morocco 74 C3
Ichtegem, Belgium 17 F2
Icó, Brazil 122 C4
Icod, Canary Is. 36 F3
Icoraci, Brazil 122 B2
Icy Str., U.S.A. 100 B1
Ida Grove, U.S.A. 108 D7
Ida Valley, Australia 89 E3
Idabel, U.S.A. 109 J7
Idaga Hamus, Ethiopia 77 E4
Idah, Nigeria 79 D6
Idaho □, U.S.A. 110 D6
Idaho City, U.S.A. 110 E6
Idaho Falls, U.S.A. 110 E7
Idaho Springs, U.S.A. 110 G11
Idanha-a-Nova, Portugal 30 F3
Idar-Oberstein, Germany 19 F3
Idd el Ghanam, Sudan 73 F9
Iddan, Somali Rep. 68 F4
Idehan, Libya 75 C7
Idehan Marzūq, Libya 73 D7
Idelès, Algeria 75 D6
Idfû, Egypt 76 C3
Ídhi Óros, Greece 37 D6
Ídhra, Greece 39 M6
Idi, Indonesia 56 C1
Idiofa, Zaïre 80 E3
Idku, Bahra el, Egypt 76 H7
Idlib, Syria 64 C3
Idria, U.S.A. 112 J6
Idrija, Slovenia 33 B11
Idritsa, Russia 40 C6
Idstein, Germany 19 E4
Idutywa, S. Africa 85 E4
Ieper, Belgium 17 G1
Ierápetra, Greece 37 E7
Ierissós, Greece 39 J6
Ierzu, Italy 34 C2
Iesi, Italy 33 E10
Ifach, Punta, Spain 29 G5
'Ifāl, W. al →, Si. Arabia 64 D2
Ifanadiana, Madag. 85 C8
Ife, Nigeria 79 D5
Iférouâne, Niger 79 B6
Iffley, Australia 90 B3
Ifni, Morocco 74 C2
Ifon, Nigeria 79 D6
Iforas, Adrar des, Mali 79 B5
Ifould, L., Australia 89 F5
Ifrane, Morocco 74 B3
Iganga, Uganda 82 B3
Igara Paraná →, Colombia 120 D3
Igarapava, Brazil 123 F2
Igarapé Açu, Brazil 122 B2
Igarapé-Mirim, Brazil 122 B2
Igarka, Russia 44 C9
Igatimi, Paraguay 127 A4
Igbetti, Nigeria 79 D5
Igbo-Ora, Nigeria 79 D5
Igboho, Nigeria 79 D5
Iğdır, Turkey 67 D11
Iggesund, Sweden 10 C11
Ighil Izane, Algeria 75 A5
Iglésias, Italy 34 C1
Igli, Algeria 75 B4
Igloolik, Canada 97 B11
Igma, Gebel el, Egypt 76 J8
Ignace, Canada 98 C1
İğneada Burnu, Turkey 66 C3
Igoshevo, Russia 41 B13
Iguaçu →, Brazil 127 B5
Iguaçu, Cat. del, Brazil 127 B5
Iguaçu Falls = Iguaçu, Cat. del, Brazil 127 B5
Iguala, Mexico 115 D5
Igualada, Spain 28 D6
Iguape, Brazil 123 F2
Iguassu = Iguaçu →, Brazil 127 B5
Iguatu, Brazil 122 C4
Iguéla, Gabon 80 E1
Igunga □, Tanzania 82 C3
Iheya-Shima, Japan 49 L3
Ihiala, Nigeria 79 D6
Ihosy, Madag. 85 C8
Ihotry, L., Madag. 85 C7
Ii, Finland 8 D18
Ii-Shima, Japan 49 L3
Iida, Japan 49 G8
Iijoki →, Finland 8 D18
Iisalmi, Finland 8 E19
Iiyama, Japan 49 F9
Iizuka, Japan 49 H5
Ijâfene, Mauritania 74 D3
Ijebu-Igbo, Nigeria 79 D5
Ijebu-Ode, Nigeria 79 D5
IJmuiden, Neths. 16 D5
IJssel →, Neths. 16 C7
IJsselmeer, Neths. 16 C6
IJsselmuiden, Neths. 16 C7
IJsselstein, Neths. 16 D6
Ijuí →, Brazil 127 B4
IJzendijke, Neths. 17 F3
IJzer →, Belgium 17 F1
Ikale, Nigeria 79 D6
Ikare, Nigeria 79 D6
Ikaría, Greece 39 M9
Ikast, Denmark 11 H3
Ikeda, Japan 49 G6
Ikeja, Nigeria 79 D5
Ikela, Zaïre 80 E4
Ikerre-Ekiti, Nigeria 79 D6
Ikhtiman, Bulgaria 38 G6
Iki, Japan 49 H4
Ikimba L., Tanzania 82 C3
Ikire, Nigeria 79 D5
İkizdere, Turkey 67 C9
Ikom, Nigeria 79 D6
Ikopa →, Madag. 85 B8
Ikot Ekpene, Nigeria 79 D6
Ikungu, Tanzania 82 C3
Ikurun, Nigeria 79 D5
Ila, Nigeria 79 D5
Ilagan, Phil. 55 C4
Īlām, Iran 64 C5
Ilam, Nepal 63 F12
Ilanskiy, Russia 45 D10
Ilanz, Switz. 23 C8
Ilaro, Nigeria 79 D5
Iława, Poland 20 B9
Ilbilbie, Australia 90 C4
Ile-à-la-Crosse, Canada 101 B7
Ile-à-la-Crosse, Lac, Canada 101 B7
Île-de-France, France 25 D9
Ilebo, Zaïre 80 E4
Ileje □, Tanzania 83 D3
Ilek, Russia 44 D6
Ilek →, Russia 44 D6
Ilero, Nigeria 79 D5
Ilesha, Kwara, Nigeria 79 D5
Ilesha, Oyo, Nigeria 79 D5
Ilford, Canada 101 B9
Ilfracombe, Australia 90 C3
Ilfracombe, U.K. 13 F3
Ilgaz, Turkey 66 C5
Ilgaz Dağları, Turkey 66 C5
Ilgın, Turkey 66 D4
Ilha Grande, Brazil 121 D4
Ilha Grande, B. da, Brazil 123 F3
Ílhavo, Portugal 30 E2
Ilhéus, Brazil 123 D4
Ili →, Kazakhstan 44 E8
Iliç, Turkey 67 D8
Ilich, Kazakhstan 44 E7
Iliff, U.S.A. 108 E3
Iligan, Phil. 55 G6
Iligan Bay, Phil. 55 G6
Ilíki, L., Greece 39 L6
Ilin I., Phil. 55 E4
Iliodhrómia, Greece 39 K6
Ilion, U.S.A. 107 D9
Ilirska-Bistrica, Slovenia 33 C11
Ilkeston, U.K. 12 E6
Illampu = Ancohuma, Nevada, Bolivia 124 D4
Illana B., Phil. 55 H5
Illapel, Chile 126 C1
Ille-et-Vilaine □, France 24 D5
Ille-sur-Têt, France 26 F6
Iller →, Germany 19 G5
Illescas, Spain 30 E7
Illetas, Spain 36 B9
Illiers-Combray, France 24 D8
Illimani, Bolivia 124 D4
Illinois □, U.S.A. 103 C9
Illinois →, U.S.A. 103 C8
Illium = Troy, Turkey 66 D2
Illizi, Algeria 75 C6
Illora, Spain 31 H7
Ilm →, Germany 18 D7
Ilmen, Oz., Russia 40 B7
Ilmenau, Germany 18 E6
Ilo, Peru 124 D3
Ilobu, Nigeria 79 D5
Iloilo, Phil. 55 F5
Ilora, Nigeria 79 D5
Ilorin, Nigeria 79 D5
Iloulya, Russia 43 B11
Ilovatka, Russia 41 F14
Ilovlya →, Russia 43 B10
Ilubabor □, Ethiopia 77 F3
Ilūkste, Latvia 40 D5
Ilva Mică, Romania 38 B7
Ilwaco, U.S.A. 112 D2
Ilwaki, Indonesia 57 F7
Ilyichevsk, Ukraine 42 C4
Imabari, Japan 49 G6
Imaloto →, Madag. 85 C8
İmamoğlu, Turkey 66 E6
Imandra, Oz., Russia 44 C4
Imari, Japan 49 H4
Imasa, Sudan 76 D4
Imbâbah, Egypt 76 H7
Imbabura □, Ecuador 120 C2
Imbaimadai, Guyana 121 B5
Imbler, U.S.A. 110 D5
Imdahane, Morocco 74 B3
imeni 26 Bakinskikh Komissarov, Azerbaijan 67 D13
Imeni Poliny Osipenko, Russia 45 D14
Imeri, Serra, Brazil 120 C4
Imerimandroso, Madag. 85 B8
Imesan, Mauritania 74 D1
Imi, Ethiopia 68 F3
Imishly, Azerbaijan 43 G13
Imitek, Morocco 74 C3
Imlay, U.S.A. 110 F4
Imlay City, U.S.A. 106 C1
Immenstadt, Germany 19 H6
Immingham, U.K. 12 D7
Immokalee, U.S.A. 105 M5
Imo □, Nigeria 79 D6
Imola, Italy 33 D8
Imotski, Croatia 21 M7
Imperatriz, Amazonas, Brazil 124 B4
Imperatriz, Maranhão, Brazil 122 C2
Impéria, Italy 32 E5
Imperial, Canada 101 C7
Imperial, Peru 124 C2
Imperial, Calif., U.S.A. 113 N11
Imperial, Nebr., U.S.A. 108 E4
Imperial Beach, U.S.A. 113 N9
Imperial Dam, U.S.A. 113 N12
Imperial Reservoir, U.S.A. 113 N12
Imperial Valley, U.S.A. 113 N11
Imperieuse Reef, Australia 88 C2
Impfondo, Congo 80 D3
Imphal, India 61 G18
Imphy, France 26 B7
İmralı, Turkey 66 C3
Imranlı, Turkey 67 D8
İmroz = Gökçeada, Turkey 39 J8
Imst, Austria 19 H6
Imuruan B., Phil. 57 B5
In Belbel, Algeria 75 C5
In Delimane, Mali 79 B5
In Rhar, Algeria 75 C5
In Salah, Algeria 75 C5
In Tallak, Mali 79 B5
Ina, Japan 49 G8
Inajá, Brazil 122 C4
Inangahua Junction, N.Z. 87 J3
Inanwatan, Indonesia 57 E8
Iñapari, Peru 124 C4
Inari, Finland 8 B19
Inarijärvi, Finland 8 B19
Inawashiro-Ko, Japan 48 F10
Inca, Spain 36 B9
Incaguasi, Chile 126 B1
İnce-Burnu, Turkey 42 E6
İncekum Burnu, Turkey 66 E5
Inchon, S. Korea 51 F14
Incio, Spain 30 C3
İncirliova, Turkey 66 E2
Incomáti →, Mozam. 85 D5
Inda Silase, Ethiopia 77 E4
Indalsälven →, Sweden 10 B11
Indaw, Burma 61 G20
Indbir, Ethiopia 77 F4
Independence, Calif., U.S.A. 111 H4
Independence, Iowa, U.S.A. 108 D9
Independence, Kans., U.S.A. 109 G7
Independence, Mo., U.S.A. 108 F7
Independence, Oreg., U.S.A. 110 D2
Independence Fjord, Greenland 4 A6
Independence Mts., U.S.A. 110 F5
Independência, Brazil 122 C3
Independenţa, Romania 38 D10

Inderborskiy, *Kazakhstan* 43 B14
Index, *U.S.A.* 112 C5
India ■, *Asia* 60 K11
Indian →, *U.S.A.* 105 M5
Indian Cabins, *Canada* 100 B5
Indian Harbour, *Canada* 99 B8
Indian Head, *Canada* 101 C8
Indian Ocean 46 K11
Indian Springs, *U.S.A.* 113 J11
Indiana, *U.S.A.* 106 F5
Indiana □, *U.S.A.* 104 E3
Indianapolis, *U.S.A.* 104 F2
Indianola, *Iowa, U.S.A.* 108 E8
Indianola, *Miss., U.S.A.* 109 J9
Indiapora, *Brazil* 123 E1
Indiga, *Russia* 44 C5
Indigirka →, *Russia* 45 B15
Inđija, *Serbia, Yug.* 21 K10
Indio, *U.S.A.* 113 M10
Indonesia ■, *Asia* 56 F5
Indore, *India* 62 H6
Indramayu, *Indonesia* 57 G13
Indravati →, *India* 61 K12
Indre □, *France* 25 F8
Indre →, *France* 24 E7
Indre-et-Loire □, *France* 24 E7
Indus →, *Pakistan* 62 G2
Indus, Mouth of the, *Pakistan* 62 H2
İnebolu, *Turkey* 66 C5
İnegöl, *Turkey* 66 C3
Inés, Mt., *Argentina* 128 C3
Ineu, *Romania* 38 C4
Inezgane, *Morocco* 74 B3
Infantes, *Spain* 29 G1
Infiernillo, Presa del, *Mexico* 114 D4
Infiesto, *Spain* 30 B5
Ingapirca, *Ecuador* 120 D2
Ingelmunster, *Belgium* 17 G2
Ingende, *Zaïre* 80 E3
Ingeniero Jacobacci, *Argentina* 128 B3
Ingenio, *Canary Is.* 36 G4
Ingenio Santa Ana, *Argentina* 126 B2
Ingersoll, *Canada* 106 C4
Ingham, *Australia* 90 B4
Ingleborough, *U.K.* 12 C5
Inglewood, *Queens., Australia* 91 D5
Inglewood, *Vic., Australia* 91 F3
Inglewood, *N.Z.* 87 H5
Inglewood, *U.S.A.* 113 M8
Ingólfshöfði, *Iceland* 8 E5
Ingolstadt, *Germany* 19 G7
Ingomar, *U.S.A.* 110 C10
Ingonish, *Canada* 99 C7
Ingore, *Guinea-Biss.* 78 C1
Ingraj Bazar, *India* 63 G13
Ingrid Christensen Coast, *Antarctica* 5 C6
Ingul →, *Ukraine* 42 C5
Ingulec, *Ukraine* 42 C5
Ingulets →, *Ukraine* 42 C5
Inguri →, *Georgia* 43 E9
Ingwavuma, *S. Africa* 85 D5
Inhaca, I., *Mozam.* 85 D5
Inhafenga, *Mozam.* 85 C5
Inhambane, *Mozam.* 85 C6
Inhambane □, *Mozam.* 85 C5
Inhambupe, *Brazil* 123 D4
Inhaminga, *Mozam.* 83 F4
Inharrime, *Mozam.* 85 C6
Inharrime →, *Mozam.* 85 C6
Inhuma, *Brazil* 122 C3
Inhumas, *Brazil* 123 E2
Iniesta, *Spain* 29 F3
Ining = Yining, *China* 44 E9
Inini □, *Fr. Guiana* 121 C7
Inírida →, *Colombia* 120 C4
Inishbofin, *Ireland* 15 C1
Inishmore, *Ireland* 15 C2
Inishowen, *Ireland* 15 A4
Injune, *Australia* 91 D4
Inklin, *Canada* 100 B2
Inklin →, *Canada* 100 B2
Inkom, *U.S.A.* 110 E7
Inle L., *Burma* 61 J20
Inn →, *Austria* 19 G9
Innamincka, *Australia* 91 D3
Inner Hebrides, *U.K.* 14 D2
Inner Mongolia = Nei Monggol Zizhiqu □, *China* 50 C6
Inner Sound, *U.K.* 14 D3
Innerkip, *Canada* 106 C4
Innerkirchen, *Switz.* 22 C6
Innerste →, *Germany* 18 C5
Innetalling I., *Canada* 98 A4
Innisfail, *Australia* 90 B4
Innisfail, *Canada* 100 C6
In'no-shima, *Japan* 49 G6
Innsbruck, *Austria* 19 H7
Inny →, *Ireland* 15 C4
Inocência, *Brazil* 123 E1
Inongo, *Zaïre* 80 E3
Inoucdjouac, *Canada* 97 C12
Inowrocław, *Poland* 20 C8
Inpundong, *N. Korea* 51 D14
Inquisivi, *Bolivia* 124 D4
Ins, *Switz.* 22 B4
Inscription, C., *Australia* 89 E1
Insein, *Burma* 61 L20
Însurăţei, *Romania* 38 E10
Intendente Alvear, *Argentina* 126 D3
Interior, *U.S.A.* 108 D4
Interlaken, *Switz.* 25 F14
International Falls, *U.S.A.* 108 A8
Intiyaco, *Argentina* 126 B3
Intragna, *Switz.* 23 D7
Intutu, *Peru* 120 D3
Inútil, B., *Chile* 128 D2
Inuvik, *Canada* 96 B6
Inveraray, *U.K.* 14 E3
Inverbervie, *U.K.* 14 E6
Invercargill, *N.Z.* 87 M2
Inverell, *Australia* 91 D5
Invergordon, *U.K.* 14 D4
Invermere, *Canada* 100 C5
Inverness, *Canada* 99 C7
Inverness, *U.K.* 14 D4
Inverness, *U.S.A.* 105 L4
Inverurie, *U.K.* 14 D6
Inverway, *Australia* 88 C4
Investigator Group, *Australia* 91 E1
Investigator Str., *Australia* 91 F2
Inya, *Russia* 44 D9
Inyanga, *Zimbabwe* 83 F3
Inyangani, *Zimbabwe* 83 F3
Inyantue, *Zimbabwe* 83 F2
Inyo Mts., *U.S.A.* 111 H5
Inyokern, *U.S.A.* 113 K9
Inza, *Russia* 41 E15
Inzhavino, *Russia* 41 E13
Iō-Jima, *Japan* 49 J5
Ioánnina, *Greece* 39 K3
Iola, *U.S.A.* 109 G7
Ion Corvin, *Romania* 38 E10
Iona, *U.K.* 14 E2
Ione, *Calif., U.S.A.* 112 G6
Ione, *Wash., U.S.A.* 110 B5
Ionia, *U.S.A.* 104 D3
Ionian Is. = Iónioi Nísoi, *Greece* 39 L3
Ionian Sea, *Europe* 6 H9
Iónioi Nísoi, *Greece* 39 L3
Iori →, *Azerbaijan* 43 F12
Íos, *Greece* 39 N8
Iowa □, *U.S.A.* 108 D8
Iowa City, *U.S.A.* 108 E9
Iowa Falls, *U.S.A.* 108 D8
Ipala, *Tanzania* 82 C3
Ipameri, *Brazil* 123 E2
Iparía, *Peru* 124 B3
Ipáti, *Greece* 39 L5
Ipatinga, *Brazil* 123 E3
Ipatovo, *Russia* 43 D10
Ipel →, *Europe* 21 G9
Ipiales, *Colombia* 120 C2
Ipiaú, *Brazil* 123 D4
Ipin = Yibin, *China* 52 C5
Ipirá, *Brazil* 123 D4
Ipiranga, *Brazil* 120 D4
Ipixuna, *Brazil* 124 B3
Ipixuna →, *Amazonas, Brazil* 124 B3
Ipixuna →, *Amazonas, Brazil* 125 B5
Ipoh, *Malaysia* 59 K3
Iporá, *Brazil* 123 D1
Ippy, *C.A.R.* 73 G9
Ipsala, *Turkey* 66 C2
Ipsárion Óros, *Greece* 39 J7
Ipswich, *Australia* 91 D5
Ipswich, *U.K.* 13 E9
Ipswich, *Mass., U.S.A.* 107 D14
Ipswich, *S. Dak., U.S.A.* 108 C5
Ipu, *Brazil* 122 B3
Ipueiras, *Brazil* 122 B3
Ipupiara, *Brazil* 123 D3
Iput →, *Belorussia* 40 E7
Iqaluit, *Canada* 97 B13
Iquique, *Chile* 124 E3
Iquitos, *Peru* 120 D3
Irabu-Jima, *Japan* 49 M2
Iracoubo, *Fr. Guiana* 121 B7
Īrafshān, *Iran* 65 E9
Irahuan, *Phil.* 55 G3
Iráklia, *Greece* 39 N8
Iráklion, *Greece* 37 D7
Iráklion □, *Greece* 37 D7
Irala, *Paraguay* 127 B5
Iramba □, *Tanzania* 82 C3
Iran ■, *Asia* 65 C7
Iran, Gunung-Gunung, *Malaysia* 56 D4
Iran Ra. = Iran, Gunung-Gunung, *Malaysia* 56 D4
Īrānshahr, *Iran* 65 E9
Irapa, *Venezuela* 121 A5
Irapuato, *Mexico* 114 C4
Iraq ■, *Asia* 64 C5
Irarrar, O. →, *Mali* 75 D5
Irati, *Brazil* 127 B5
Irbid, *Jordan* 69 C4
Irbid □, *Jordan* 69 C5
Irebu, *Zaïre* 80 E3
Irecê, *Brazil* 122 D3
Iregua →, *Spain* 28 C7
Ireland ■, *Europe* 15 D4
Ireland's Eye, *Ireland* 15 C5
Irele, *Nigeria* 79 D6
Ireng →, *Brazil* 121 C6
Iret, *Russia* 45 C16
Irgiz, Bolshaya →, *Russia* 41 E16
Irhârharene, *Algeria* 75 C6
Irharrhar, O. →, *Algeria* 75 C6
Irherm, *Morocco* 74 B3
Irhil Mgoun, *Morocco* 74 B3
Irhyangdong, *N. Korea* 51 D15
Iri, *S. Korea* 51 G14
Irian Jaya □, *Indonesia* 57 E9
Irié, *Guinea* 78 D3
Iriga, *Phil.* 55 E5
Iringa, *Tanzania* 82 D4
Iringa □, *Tanzania* 82 D4
Iriomote-Jima, *Japan* 49 M1
Iriona, *Honduras* 116 C2
Iriri →, *Brazil* 121 D7
Iriri Novo →, *Brazil* 125 B7
Irish Republic ■, *Europe* 15 D4
Irish Sea, *Europe* 12 D3
Irkineyeva, *Russia* 45 D10
Irkutsk, *Russia* 45 D11
Irma, *Canada* 101 C6
Irō-Zaki, *Japan* 49 G9
Iroise, Mer d', *France* 24 D2
Iron Baron, *Australia* 91 E2
Iron Gate = Portile de Fier, *Europe* 38 E5
Iron Knob, *Australia* 91 E2
Iron Mountain, *U.S.A.* 104 C1
Iron Ra., *Australia* 90 A3
Iron River, *U.S.A.* 108 B10
Ironbridge, *U.K.* 13 E5
Irondequoit, *U.S.A.* 106 C7
Ironstone Kopje, *Botswana* 84 D3
Ironton, *Mo., U.S.A.* 109 G9
Ironton, *Ohio, U.S.A.* 104 F4
Ironwood, *U.S.A.* 108 B9
Iroquois Falls, *Canada* 98 C3
Irosin, *Phil.* 55 E6
Irpen, *Ukraine* 40 F7
Irrara Cr. →, *Australia* 91 D4
Irrawaddy □, *Burma* 61 L19
Irrawaddy →, *Burma* 61 M19
Irsina, *Italy* 35 B9
Irtysh →, *Russia* 44 C7
Irumu, *Zaïre* 82 B2
Irún, *Spain* 28 B3
Irunea = Pamplona, *Spain* 28 C3
Irurzun, *Spain* 28 C3
Irvine, *Canada* 101 D6
Irvine, *U.K.* 14 F4
Irvine, *Calif., U.S.A.* 113 M9
Irvine, *Ky., U.S.A.* 104 G4
Irvinestown, *U.K.* 15 B4
Irving, *U.S.A.* 109
Irvona, *U.S.A.* 106 F6
Irwin →, *Australia* 89 E1
Irymple, *Australia* 91 E3
Is-sur-Tille, *France* 25 E12
Isa, *Nigeria* 79 C6
Isaac →, *Australia* 90 C4
Isabel, *U.S.A.* 108 C4
Isabela, I., *Mexico* 114 C3
Isabella, *Phil.* 55 H5
Isabella, Cord., *Nic.* 116 D2
Isabella Ra., *Australia* 88 D3
Ísafjarðardjúp, *Iceland* 8 C2
Ísafjörður, *Iceland* 8 C2
Isagarh, *India* 62 G7
Isahaya, *Japan* 49 H5
Isaka, *Tanzania* 82 C3
Isana = Içana →, *Brazil* 120 C4
Isangi, *Zaïre* 80 D4
Isar →, *Germany* 19 G8
Isarco →, *Italy* 33 B8
Ísari, *Greece* 39 M5
Isbergues, *France* 25 B9
Iscayachi, *Bolivia* 125 E4
Íschia, *Italy* 34 B6
Iscuandé, *Colombia* 120 C2
Isdell →, *Australia* 88 C3
Ise, *Japan* 49 G8
Ise-Wan, *Japan* 49 G8
Isefjord, *Denmark* 11 J5
Iseltwald, *Switz.* 22 C5
Isenthal, *Switz.* 23 C7
Iseo, *Italy* 32 C7
Iseo, L. d', *Italy* 32 C7
Iseramagazi, *Tanzania* 82 C3
Isère □, *France* 27 C9
Isère →, *France* 27 D8
Iserlohn, *Germany* 18 D3
Isérnia, *Italy* 35 A7
Iseyin, *Nigeria* 79 D5
Isherton, *Guyana* 121 C6
Ishigaki-Shima, *Japan* 49 M2
Ishikari-Gawa →, *Japan* 48 C10
Ishikari-Sammyaku, *Japan* 48 C11
Ishikari-Wan, *Japan* 48 C10
Ishikawa □, *Japan* 49 F8
Ishim, *Russia* 44 D7
Ishim →, *Russia* 44 D8
Ishinomaki, *Japan* 48 E10
Ishioka, *Japan* 49 F10
Ishkuman, *Pakistan* 63 A5
Ishpeming, *U.S.A.* 104 B2
Isigny-sur-Mer, *France* 24 C5
Isil Kul, *Russia* 44 D8
Isiolo, *Kenya* 82 B4
Isiolo □, *Kenya* 82 B4
Isipingo Beach, *S. Africa* 85 E5
Isiro, *Zaïre* 82 B2
Isisford, *Australia* 90 C3
İskederun, *Turkey* 66 E7
İskenderun, *Turkey* 66 E7
İskenderun Körfezi, *Turkey* 66 E6
İskilip, *Turkey* 42 F6
Iskŭr →, *Bulgaria* 38 F7
Iskut →, *Canada* 100 B2
Isla →, *U.K.* 14 E5
Isla Cristina, *Spain* 31 H3
Isla Vista, *U.S.A.* 113 L7
İslâhiye, *Turkey* 66 E7
Islamabad, *Pakistan* 62 C5
Islamkot, *Pakistan* 62 G4
Island →, *Canada* 100 A4
Island Falls, *Canada* 98 C3
Island Falls, *U.S.A.* 99 C6
Island L., *Canada* 101 C10
Island Lagoon, *Australia* 91 E2
Island Pond, *U.S.A.* 107 B13
Islands, B. of, *Canada* 99 C8
Islay, *U.K.* 14 F2
Isle →, *France* 26 D3
Isle aux Morts, *Canada* 99 C8
Isle of Wight □, *U.K.* 13 G6
Isle Royale, *U.S.A.* 108 A10
Isleta, *U.S.A.* 111 J10
Isleton, *U.S.A.* 112 G5
Ismail, *Ukraine* 42 D3
Ismâ'ilîya, *Egypt* 76 H8
Ismaning, *Germany* 19 G7
Ismay, *U.S.A.* 108 B2
Isna, *Egypt* 76 B3
Isogstalo, *India* 63 B8
Isola del Gran Sasso d'Italia, *Italy* 33 F10
Ísola del Liri, *Italy* 34 A6
Ísola della Scala, *Italy* 32 C8
Ísola di Capo Rizzuto, *Italy* 35 D10
Isparta, *Turkey* 66 E4
Isparta □, *Turkey* 66 E4
Isperikh, *Bulgaria* 38 F9
Íspica, *Italy* 35 F7
İspir, *Turkey* 43 F9
Israel ■, *Asia* 69 D3
Issano, *Guyana* 121 B6
Issia, *Ivory C.* 78 D3
Issoire, *France* 26 C7
Issoudun, *France* 25 F8
Issyk-Kul, Ozero, *Kirghizia* 44 E8
Ist, *Croatia* 33 D11
Istaihah, *U.A.E.* 65 F7
İstanbul, *Turkey* 66 C3
İstanbul □, *Turkey* 66 C3
Istmina, *Colombia* 120 B2
Istok, *Serbia, Yug.* 21 N10
Istokpoga, L., *U.S.A.* 105 M5
Istra, *Croatia* 33 C11
Istra, *Russia* 41 D10
İstranca Dağları, *Turkey* 39 H10
Istres, *France* 27 E8
Istria = Istra, *Croatia* 33 C11
Itá, *Paraguay* 126 B4
Itabaiana, *Paraíba, Brazil* 122 C4
Itabaiana, *Sergipe, Brazil* 122 D4
Itabaianinha, *Brazil* 122 D4
Itaberaba, *Brazil* 123 D3
Itaberaí, *Brazil* 123 E2
Itabira, *Brazil* 123 E3
Itabirito, *Brazil* 123 F3
Itaboca, *Brazil* 121 D5
Itabuna, *Brazil* 123 D4
Itacajá, *Brazil* 122 C2
Itacaunas →, *Brazil* 122 C2
Itacoatiara, *Brazil* 121 D6
Itacuaí →, *Brazil* 124 A3
Itaguaçu, *Brazil* 123 E3
Itaguari →, *Brazil* 123 D3
Itaguatins, *Brazil* 122 C2
Itaim →, *Brazil* 122 C3
Itainópolis, *Brazil* 122 C3
Itaipu Dam, *Brazil* 127 B5
Itaituba, *Brazil* 121 D6
Itajaí, *Brazil* 127 B6
Itajubá, *Brazil* 123 F2
Itajuípe, *Brazil* 123 D4
Itaka, *Tanzania* 83 D3
Italy ■, *Europe* 7 G8
Itamaraté, *Brazil* 122 B2
Itambacuri, *Brazil* 123 E3
Itambé, *Brazil* 123 E3
Itampolo, *Madag.* 85 C7
Itanhauã →, *Brazil* 121 D5
Itanhém, *Brazil* 123 E3
Itapaci, *Brazil* 123 D2
Itapagé, *Brazil* 122 B4
Itaparica, I. de, *Brazil* 123 D4
Itapebi, *Brazil* 123 E4
Itapecuru-Mirim, *Brazil* 122 B3
Itaperuna, *Brazil* 123 F3
Itapetinga, *Brazil* 123 E3
Itapetininga, *Brazil* 127 A6
Itapeva, *Brazil* 127 A6
Itapicuru →, *Bahia, Brazil* 122 D4
Itapicuru →, *Maranhão, Brazil* 122 B3
Itapinima, *Brazil* 125 B5
Itapipoca, *Brazil* 122 B4
Itapiranga, *Brazil* 121 D6
Itapiúna, *Brazil* 122 B4
Itaporanga, *Brazil* 122 C4
Itapuá □, *Paraguay* 127 B4
Itapuranga, *Brazil* 123 E2
Itaquari, *Brazil* 123 F3
Itaquatiara, *Brazil* 121 D6
Itaquí, *Brazil* 126 B4
Itararé, *Brazil* 127 A6
Itarsi, *India* 62 H7
Itarumã, *Brazil* 123 E1
Itatí, *Argentina* 126 B4
Itatira, *Brazil* 122 B4
Itatuba, *Brazil* 125 B5
Itatupa, *Brazil* 121 D7
Itaueira, *Brazil* 122 C3
Itaueira →, *Brazil* 122 C3
Itaúna, *Brazil* 123 F3
Itbayat, *Phil.* 55 A4
Itchen →, *U.K.* 13 G6
Ite, *Peru* 124 D3
Itezhi Tezhi, L., *Zambia* 83 F2
Ithaca = Itháki, *Greece* 39 L3
Ithaca, *U.S.A.* 107 D8
Itháki, *Greece* 39 L3
Itinga, *Brazil* 123 E3
Itiquira, *Brazil* 125 D7
Itiquira →, *Brazil* 125 D6
Itiruçu, *Brazil* 123 D3
Itiúba, *Brazil* 122 D4
Ito, *Japan* 49 G9
Itoigawa, *Japan* 49 F8
Iton →, *France* 24 C8
Itonamas →, *Bolivia* 125 C5
Itsa, *Egypt* 76 J7
Ittiri, *Italy* 34 B1
Ittoqqortoormiit = Scoresbysund, *Greenland* 4 B6
Itu, *Brazil* 127 A6
Itu, *Nigeria* 79 D6
Ituaçu, *Brazil* 123 D3
Ituango, *Colombia* 120 B2
Ituiutaba, *Brazil* 123 E2
Itumbiara, *Brazil* 123 E2
Ituna, *Canada* 101 C8
Itunge Port, *Tanzania* 83 D3
Ituni, *Guyana* 121 B6
Itupiranga, *Brazil* 122 C2
Iturama, *Brazil* 123 E1
Iturbe, *Argentina* 126 A2
Ituri →, *Zaïre* 82 B2
Iturup, Ostrov, *Russia* 45 E15
Ituverava, *Brazil* 123 F2
Ituxi →, *Brazil* 125 B5
Ituyuro →, *Argentina* 126 A3
Itzehoe, *Germany* 18 B5
Ivaí →, *Brazil* 127 A5
Ivalo, *Finland* 8 B19
Ivalojoki →, *Finland* 8 B19
Ivangorod, *Russia* 40 B6
Ivanhoe, *N.S.W., Australia* 91 E3
Ivanhoe, *W. Austral., Australia* 88 C4
Ivanhoe, *U.S.A.* 112 J7
Ivanhoe L., *Canada* 101 A7
Ivanić Grad, *Croatia* 33 C13
Ivanjica, *Serbia, Yug.* 21 M10
Ivanjšcice, *Croatia* 33 B13
Ivankoyskoye Vdkhr., *Russia* 41 C10
Ivano-Frankivsk = Ivano-Frankovsk, *Ukraine* 40 G4
Ivano-Frankovsk, *Ukraine* 40 G4
Ivanovo, *Belorussia* 40 E4
Ivanovo, *Russia* 41 C12
Ivato, *Madag.* 85 C8
Ivaylovgrad, *Bulgaria* 39 H9
Ivinheima →, *Brazil* 127 A5
Iviza = Ibiza, *Spain* 36 C7
Ivohibe, *Madag.* 85 C8
Ivolândia, *Brazil* 123 E1
Ivory Coast ■, *Africa* 78 D3
Ivrea, *Italy* 32 C4
Ivugivik, *Canada* 97 B12
Iwahig, *Phil.* 56 C5
Iwaizumi, *Japan* 48 E10
Iwaki, *Japan* 49 F10
Iwakuni, *Japan* 49 G6
Iwamizawa, *Japan* 48 C10
Iwanai, *Japan* 48 C10
Iwata, *Japan* 49 G8
Iwate □, *Japan* 48 E10
Iwate-San, *Japan* 48 E10
Iwo, *Nigeria* 79 D5
Ixiamas, *Bolivia* 124 C4
Ixopo, *S. Africa* 85 E5
Ixtepec, *Mexico* 115 D5
Ixtlán del Río, *Mexico* 114 C4
Iyo, *Japan* 49 H6
Izabal, L. de, *Guatemala* 116 C2
Izamal, *Mexico* 115 C7
Izberbash, *Russia* 43 E12
Izegem, *Belgium* 17 G2
Izena-Shima, *Japan* 49 L3
Izhevsk, *Russia* 44 D6
Izmayil = Ismail, *Ukraine* 42 D3
İzmir, *Turkey* 66 D2
İzmir □, *Turkey* 66 D2
İzmit, *Turkey* 66 C3
Iznajar, *Spain* 31 H6
Iznalloz, *Spain* 29 H1
İznik Gölü, *Turkey* 66 C3
Izobil'nyy, *Russia* 43 D9
Izola, *Slovenia* 33 C10
Izozog, Bañados de, *Bolivia* 125 D5
Izra, *Syria* 69 C5
Iztochni Rodopi, *Bulgaria* 39 H8
Izu-Shotō, *Japan* 49 G10
Izumi-sano, *Japan* 49 G7
Izumo, *Japan* 49 G6
Izyaslav, *Ukraine* 40 F5
Izyum, *Ukraine* 42 B7

J

J.F. Rodrigues, *Brazil* 122 B1
Jaba, *Ethiopia* 77 F4
Jabal el Awlîya, *Sudan* 77 D3
Jabal Lubnān, *Lebanon* 69 B4
Jabalón →, *Spain* 31 G6
Jabalpur, *India* 63 H8

Jabbūl, *Syria* 64 B3
Jablah, *Syria* 64 C3
Jablanac, *Croatia* 33 D11
Jablonec, *Czech.* 20 E5
Jabłonowo, *Poland* 20 B9
Jaboatão, *Brazil* 122 C4
Jaboticabal, *Brazil* 127 A6
Jaburu, *Brazil* 125 B5
Jaca, *Spain* 28 C4
Jacaré →, *Brazil* 122 D3
Jacareí, *Brazil* 127 A6
Jacarèzinho, *Brazil* 127 A6
Jaciara, *Brazil* 125 D7
Jacinto, *Brazil* 123 E3
Jaciparaná, *Brazil* 125 B5
Jackman, *U.S.A.* 99 C5
Jacksboro, *U.S.A.* 109 J5
Jackson, *Australia* 91 D4
Jackson, *Ala., U.S.A.* 105 K2
Jackson, *Calif., U.S.A.* 112 G6
Jackson, *Ky., U.S.A.* 104 G4
Jackson, *Mich., U.S.A.* 104 D3
Jackson, *Minn., U.S.A.* 108 D7
Jackson, *Miss., U.S.A.* 109 J9
Jackson, *Mo., U.S.A.* 109 G10
Jackson, *Ohio, U.S.A.* 104 F4
Jackson, *Tenn., U.S.A.* 105 H1
Jackson, *Wyo., U.S.A.* 110 E8
Jackson B., *N.Z.* 87 K2
Jackson L., *U.S.A.* 110 E8
Jacksons, *N.Z.* 87 K3
Jacksonville, *Ala., U.S.A.* 105 J3
Jacksonville, *Calif., U.S.A.* 112 H6
Jacksonville, *Fla., U.S.A.* 105 K5
Jacksonville, *Ill., U.S.A.* 108 F9
Jacksonville, *N.C., U.S.A.* 105 H7
Jacksonville, *Oreg., U.S.A.* 110 E2
Jacksonville, *Tex., U.S.A.* 109 K7
Jacksonville Beach, *U.S.A.* 105 K5
Jacmel, *Haiti* 117 C5
Jacob Lake, *U.S.A.* 111 H7
Jacobabad, *Pakistan* 62 E3
Jacobina, *Brazil* 122 D3
Jacques-Cartier, Mt., *Canada* 99 C6
Jacqueville, *Ivory C.* 78 D4
Jacuí →, *Brazil* 127 C5
Jacumba, *U.S.A.* 113 N10
Jacundá →, *Brazil* 122 B1
Jade, *Germany* 18 B4
Jadebusen, *Germany* 18 B4
Jadoigne, *Belgium* 17 G5
Jadotville = Likasi, *Zaïre* 83 E2
Jadraque, *Spain* 28 E2
Jādū, *Libya* 75 B7
Jaén, *Peru* 124 B2
Jaén, *Spain* 31 H7
Jaén □, *Spain* 31 H7
Jafène, *Africa* 74 D3
Jaffa = Tel Aviv-Yafo, *Israel* 69 C3
Jaffa, C., *Australia* 91 F2
Jaffna, *Sri Lanka* 60 Q12
Jagadhri, *India* 62 D7
Jagadishpur, *India* 63 G11
Jagdalpur, *India* 61 K12
Jagersfontein, *S. Africa* 84 D4
Jagraon, *India* 60 D9
Jagst →, *Germany* 19 F5
Jagtial, *India* 60 K11
Jaguaquara, *Brazil* 123 D4
Jaguariaíva, *Brazil* 127 A6
Jaguaribe, *Brazil* 122 C4
Jaguaribe →, *Brazil* 122 B4
Jaguaruana, *Brazil* 122 B4
Jagüey Grande, *Cuba* 116 B3
Jahangirabad, *India* 62 E8
Jahrom, *Iran* 65 D7
Jaicós, *Brazil* 122 C3
Jailolo, *Indonesia* 57 D7
Jailolo, Selat, *Indonesia* 57 D7
Jaipur, *India* 62 F6
Jājarm, *Iran* 65 B8
Jajce, *Bos.-H.* 21 L7
Jakarta, *Indonesia* 57 G12
Jakobstad, *Finland* 8 E17
Jakupica, *Macedonia* 39 H4
Jal, *U.S.A.* 109 J3
Jalalabad, *Afghan.* 62 B4
Jalalabad, *India* 63 F8
Jalalpur Jattan, *Pakistan* 62 C6
Jalama, *U.S.A.* 113 L6
Jalapa, *Guatemala* 116 D2
Jalapa Enríquez, *Mexico* 115 D5
Jalaun, *India* 63 F8
Jales, *Brazil* 123 F1
Jaleswar, *Nepal* 63 F11
Jalgaon, *Maharashtra, India* 60 J10
Jalgaon, *Maharashtra, India* 60 J9
Jalhay, *Belgium* 17 G7
Jalībah, *Iraq* 64 D5
Jalingo, *Nigeria* 79 D7
Jalisco □, *Mexico* 114 C4
Jalkot, *Pakistan* 63 B5
Jallas →, *Spain* 30 C1
Jalna, *India* 60 K9
Jalón →, *Spain* 28 D3
Jalpa, *Mexico* 114 C4
Jalpaiguri, *India* 61 F16
Jaluit I., *Pac. Oc.* 92 G8
Jalūlā, *Iraq* 64 C5
Jamaari, *Nigeria* 79 C6
Jamaica ■, *W. Indies* 116 C4
Jamalpur, *Bangla.* 61 G16
Jamalpur, *India* 63 G12
Jamalpurganj, *India* 63 H13
Jamanxim →, *Brazil* 125 A6
Jamari, *Brazil* 125 B5
Jamari →, *Brazil* 125 B5
Jambe, *Indonesia* 57 E8
Jambes, *Belgium* 17 H5
Jambi, *Indonesia* 56 E2
Jambi □, *Indonesia* 56 E2
Jambusar, *India* 62 H5
James →, *U.S.A.* 108 D6
James B., *Canada* 97 C11
James Ras., *Australia* 88 D5
James Ross I., *Antarctica* 5 C18
Jamestown, *Australia* 91 E2
Jamestown, *S. Africa* 84 E4
Jamestown, *Ky., U.S.A.* 104 G3
Jamestown, *N. Dak., U.S.A.* 108 B5
Jamestown, *N.Y., U.S.A.* 106 D5
Jamestown, *Pa., U.S.A.* 106 E4
Jamestown, *Tenn., U.S.A.* 105 G3
Jamīlābād, *Iran* 65 C6
Jamiltepec, *Mexico* 115 D5
Jamkhandi, *India* 60 L9
Jammerbugt, *Denmark* 11 G3
Jammu, *India* 62 C6
Jammu & Kashmir □, *India* 63 B7
Jamnagar, *India* 62 H4
Jamoigne, *Belgium* 17 J6
Jampur, *Pakistan* 62 E4
Jamrud, *Pakistan* 62 C4
Jamshedpur, *India* 63 H12
Jamtara, *India* 63 H12
Jämtlands län □, *Sweden* 10 B7
Jan Kempdorp, *S. Africa* 84 D3
Jan L., *Canada* 101 C8
Jan Mayen, *Arctic* 4 B7
Janaúba, *Brazil* 123 E3
Janaucu, I., *Brazil* 122 A1
Jand, *Pakistan* 62 C5
Janda, L. de la, *Spain* 31 J5
Jandaia, *Brazil* 123 E1
Jandaq, *Iran* 65 C7
Jandia, *Canary Is.* 36 F5
Jandia, Pta. de, *Canary Is.* 36 F5
Jandiatuba →, *Brazil* 120 D4
Jandola, *Pakistan* 62 C4
Jandowae, *Australia* 91 D5
Jandrain-Jandrenouilles, *Belgium* 17 G5
Jándula →, *Spain* 31 G6
Janesville, *U.S.A.* 108 D10
Janga, *Ghana* 79 C4
Jango, *Brazil* 125 E6
Janīn, *Jordan* 69 C4
Janjina, *Croatia* 21 N7
Janos, *Mexico* 114 A3
Jánosháza, *Hungary* 21 H7
Janów Podlaski, *Poland* 20 C13
Januária, *Brazil* 123 E3
Janub Dârfûr □, *Sudan* 77 E2
Janub Kordofân □, *Sudan* 77 E3
Janubio, *Canary Is.* 36 F6
Janville, *France* 25 D8
Janzé, *France* 24 E5
Jaora, *India* 62 H6
Japan ■, *Asia* 49 G8
Japan, Sea of, *Asia* 48 E7
Japan Trench, *Pac. Oc.* 92 D6
Japen = Yapen, *Indonesia* 57 E9
Japurá →, *Brazil* 120 D4
Jaque, *Panama* 120 B2
Jarābulus, *Syria* 64 B3
Jaraguá, *Brazil* 123 E2
Jaraguari, *Brazil* 125 E7
Jaraicejo, *Spain* 31 F5
Jaraiz, *Spain* 30 E5
Jarama →, *Spain* 28 E1
Jaramillo, *Argentina* 128 C3
Jarandilla, *Spain* 30 E5
Jaranwala, *Pakistan* 62 D5
Jarash, *Jordan* 69 C4
Jarauçu →, *Brazil* 121 D7
Jardim, *Brazil* 126 A4
Jardín →, *Spain* 29 G2
Jardines de la Reina, Is., *Cuba* 116 B4
Jargalang, *China* 51 C12
Jargalant = Hovd, *Mongolia* 54 B4
Jargeau, *France* 25 E9
Jari →, *Brazil* 121 D7
Jarīr, W. al →, *Si. Arabia* 64 E4
Jarmen, *Germany* 18 B9
Jarnac, *France* 26 C3
Jarny, *France* 25 C12
Jarocin, *Poland* 20 D7
Jarosław, *Poland* 20 E12
Järpås, *Sweden* 11 F6
Järpen, *Sweden* 10 A7
Jarrahdale, *Australia* 89 F2
Jarres, Plaine des, *Laos* 58 C4
Jarso, *Ethiopia* 77 F4
Jartai, *China* 50 E3
Jaru, *Brazil* 125 C5
Jaru →, *Brazil* 125 C5
Jarud Qi, *China* 51 B11
Jarvis, *Canada* 106 D4
Jarvis I., *Pac. Oc.* 93 H12
Jarwa, *India* 63 F10
Jaša Tomić, *Serbia, Yug.* 21 K10
Jāsimīyah, *Iraq* 64 C5
Jasin, *Malaysia* 59 L4
Jāsk, *Iran* 65 E8
Jasło, *Poland* 20 F11
Jason, Is., *Falk. Is.* 128 D4
Jasper, *Alta., Canada* 100 C5
Jasper, *Ont., Canada* 107 B9
Jasper, *Ala., U.S.A.* 105 J2
Jasper, *Fla., U.S.A.* 105 K4
Jasper, *Minn., U.S.A.* 108 D6
Jasper, *Tex., U.S.A.* 109 K8
Jasper Nat. Park, *Canada* 100 C5
Jassy = Iaşi, *Romania* 38 B10
Jastrebarsko, *Croatia* 33 C12
Jastrzębie Zdrój, *Poland* 20 F8
Jászárokszállás, *Hungary* 21 H10
Jászberény, *Hungary* 21 H9
Jászladány, *Hungary* 21 H10
Jataí, *Brazil* 123 E1
Jatapu →, *Brazil* 121 D6
Jati, *Pakistan* 62 G3
Jatibarang, *Indonesia* 57 G13
Jatinegara, *Indonesia* 57 G12
Játiva, *Spain* 29 G4
Jatobal, *Brazil* 122 B2
Jaú, *Brazil* 127 A6
Jaú →, *Brazil* 121 D5
Jauaperí →, *Brazil* 121 D5
Jauche, *Belgium* 17 G5
Jauja, *Peru* 124 C2
Jaunjelgava, *Latvia* 40 C4
Jaunpur, *India* 63 G10
Jauru →, *Brazil* 125 D6
Java = Jawa, *Indonesia* 57 G14
Java Sea, *Indonesia* 56 E3
Java Trench, *Ind. Oc.* 92 H2
Jávea, *Spain* 29 G5
Javhlant = Ulyasutay, *Mongolia* 54 B4
Javier, I., *Chile* 128 C2
Javron, *France* 24 D6
Jawa, *Indonesia* 57 G14
Jawor, *Poland* 20 D6
Jaworzno, *Poland* 20 E9
Jay, *U.S.A.* 109 G7
Jaya, Puncak, *Indonesia* 57 E9
Jayanca, *Peru* 124 B2
Jayanti, *India* 61 F16
Jayapura, *Indonesia* 57 E10
Jayawijaya, Pegunungan, *Indonesia* 57 E9
Jaynagar, *India* 61 F15
Jayrūd, *Syria* 64 C3
Jayton, *U.S.A.* 109 J4
Jazīreh-ye Shīf, *Iran* 65 D6
Jazminal, *Mexico* 114 C4
Jazzīn, *Lebanon* 69 B4
Jean, *U.S.A.* 113 K11
Jean Marie River, *Canada* 100 A4
Jean Rabel, *Haiti* 117 C5
Jeanerette, *U.S.A.* 109 L9
Jeanette, Ostrov, *Russia* 45 B16
Jeannette, *U.S.A.* 106 F5
Jebba, *Morocco* 74 A4
Jebba, *Nigeria* 79 D5
Jebel, Bahr el →, *Sudan* 77 F3
Jebel Qerri, *Sudan* 77 D3
Jeberos, *Peru* 124 B2
Jedburgh, *U.K.* 14 F6
Jedda = Jiddah, *Si. Arabia* 68 C2
Jędrzejów, *Poland* 20 E10
Jedway, *Canada* 100 C2
Jeetzel →, *Germany* 18 B7
Jefferson, *Iowa, U.S.A.* 108 D7
Jefferson, *Ohio, U.S.A.* 106 E4
Jefferson, *Tex., U.S.A.* 109 J7
Jefferson, *Wis., U.S.A.* 108 D10
Jefferson, Mt., *Nev., U.S.A.* 110 G5
Jefferson, Mt., *Oreg., U.S.A.* 110 D3
Jefferson City, *Mo., U.S.A.* 108 F8
Jefferson City, *Tenn., U.S.A.* 105 G4
Jeffersonville, *U.S.A.* 104 F3
Jega, *Nigeria* 79 C5
Jēkabpils, *Latvia* 40 C4
Jelenia Góra, *Poland* 20 E5
Jelgava, *Latvia* 9 H17
Jelli, *Sudan* 77 F3
Jellicoe, *Canada* 98 C2
Jemaja, *Indonesia* 56 D3
Jemaluang, *Malaysia* 59 L4
Jemappes, *Belgium* 17 H3
Jember, *Indonesia* 57 H15
Jembongan, *Malaysia* 56 C5
Jemeppe, *Belgium* 17 G7
Jemnice, *Czech.* 20 F5
Jena, *Germany* 18 E7
Jena, *U.S.A.* 109 K8
Jendouba, *Tunisia* 75 A6
Jenkins, *U.S.A.* 104 G4
Jenner, *U.S.A.* 112 G3
Jennings, *U.S.A.* 109 K8
Jennings →, *Canada* 100 B2
Jeparit, *Australia* 91 F3
Jequié, *Brazil* 123 D3
Jequitaí →, *Brazil* 123 E3
Jequitinhonha, *Brazil* 123 E3
Jequitinhonha →, *Brazil* 123 E4
Jerada, *Morocco* 75 B4
Jerantut, *Malaysia* 59 L4
Jérémie, *Haiti* 117 C5
Jeremoabo, *Brazil* 122 D4
Jerez, Punta, *Mexico* 115 C5
Jerez de García Salinas, *Mexico* 114 C4
Jerez de la Frontera, *Spain* 31 J4
Jerez de los Caballeros, *Spain* 31 G4
Jericho = Arīḩā, *Syria* 64 C3
Jericho = El Arīḩā, *Jordan* 69 D4
Jericho, *Australia* 90 C4
Jerichow, *Germany* 18 C8
Jerilderie, *Australia* 91 F4
Jermyn, *U.S.A.* 107 E9
Jerome, *U.S.A.* 111 J8
Jersey, *Chan. Is.* 13 H5
Jersey City, *U.S.A.* 107 F10
Jersey Shore, *U.S.A.* 106 E7
Jerseyville, *U.S.A.* 108 F9
Jerusalem, *Israel* 69 D4
Jervis B., *Australia* 91 F5
Jesenice, *Slovenia* 33 B11
Jesenké, *Slovakia* 21 G10
Jesselton = Kota Kinabalu, *Malaysia* 56 C5
Jessnitz, *Germany* 18 D8
Jessore, *Bangla.* 61 H16
Jesup, *U.S.A.* 105 K5
Jesús, *Peru* 124 B2
Jesús Carranza, *Mexico* 115 D5
Jesús María, *Argentina* 126 C3
Jetmore, *U.S.A.* 109 F5
Jetpur, *India* 62 J4
Jette, *Belgium* 17 G4
Jevnaker, *Norway* 10 D4
Jewett, *Ohio, U.S.A.* 106 F3
Jewett, *Tex., U.S.A.* 109 K6
Jewett City, *U.S.A.* 107 E13
Jeyḩūnābād, *Iran* 65 C6
Jeypore, *India* 61 K13
Jeziorany, *Poland* 20 B10
Jhajjar, *India* 62 E7
Jhal Jhao, *Pakistan* 60 F4
Jhalawar, *India* 62 G7
Jhang Maghiana, *Pakistan* 62 D5
Jhansi, *India* 63 G8
Jharia, *India* 63 H12
Jharsaguda, *India* 61 J14
Jhelum, *Pakistan* 62 C5
Jhelum →, *Pakistan* 62 D5
Jhunjhunu, *India* 62 E6
Ji Xian, *Hebei, China* 50 F8
Ji Xian, *Henan, China* 50 G8
Ji Xian, *Shanxi, China* 50 F6
Jia Xian, *Henan, China* 50 H7
Jia Xian, *Shaanxi, China* 50 E6
Jiading, *China* 53 B13
Jiahe, *China* 53 E9
Jiali, *Taiwan* 53 F13
Jialing Jiang →, *China* 52 C6
Jiamusi, *China* 54 B8
Ji'an, *Jiangxi, China* 53 D10
Ji'an, *Jilin, China* 51 D14
Jianchang, *China* 51 D11
Jianchangying, *China* 51 D10
Jianchuan, *China* 52 D2
Jiande, *China* 53 C12
Jiangbei, *China* 52 C6
Jiangcheng, *China* 52 F3
Jiangdi, *China* 52 D4
Jiange, *China* 52 A5
Jiangjin, *China* 52 C6
Jiangkou, *China* 52 D7
Jiangle, *China* 53 D11
Jiangling, *China* 53 B9
Jiangmen, *China* 53 F9
Jiangshan, *China* 53 C12
Jiangsu □, *China* 51 H10
Jiangxi □, *China* 53 D10
Jiangyin, *China* 53 B13
Jiangyong, *China* 53 E8
Jiangyou, *China* 52 B5
Jianhe, *China* 52 D7
Jianli, *China* 53 C9
Jianning, *China* 53 D11
Jian'ou, *China* 53 D12
Jianshi, *China* 52 B7
Jianshui, *China* 52 F4
Jianyang, *Fujian, China* 53 D12
Jianyang, *Sichuan, China* 52 B5
Jiao Xian, *China* 51 F11
Jiaohe, *Hebei, China* 50 E9
Jiaohe, *Jilin, China* 51 C14
Jiaoling, *China* 53 E11
Jiaozhou Wan, *China* 51 F11
Jiaozuo, *China* 50 G7
Jiashan, *China* 53 A11
Jiawang, *China* 51 G9
Jiaxiang, *China* 50 G9
Jiaxing, *China* 53 B13
Jiayi, *Taiwan* 53 F13
Jiayu, *China* 53 C9
Jibão, Serra do, *Brazil* 123 D3
Jibiya, *Nigeria* 79 C6
Jibou, *Romania* 38 B6
Jibuti = Djibouti ■, *Africa* 68 E3
Jicarón, I., *Panama* 116 E3
Jičín, *Czech.* 20 E5
Jiddah, *Si. Arabia* 68 C2
Jido, *India* 61 E19
Jieshou, *China* 50 H8
Jiexiu, *China* 50 F6
Jieyang, *China* 53 F11
Jigawa □, *Nigeria* 79 C6
Jiggalong, *Australia* 88 D3
Jihlava, *Czech.* 20 F5
Jijel, *Algeria* 75 A6
Jijiga, *Ethiopia* 68 F3
Jijona, *Spain* 29 G4
Jikamshi, *Nigeria* 79 C6
Jilin, *China* 51 C14
Jilin □, *China* 51 C13
Jiloca →, *Spain* 28 D3
Jilong, *Taiwan* 53 E13
Jima, *Ethiopia* 77 F4
Jimbolia, *Romania* 38 D3
Jimena de la Frontera, *Spain* 31 J5
Jiménez, *Mexico* 114 B4
Jimo, *China* 51 F11
Jin Jiang →, *China* 53 C10
Jin Xian, *Hebei, China* 50 E8
Jin Xian, *Liaoning, China* 51 E11
Jinan, *China* 50 F9
Jincheng, *China* 50 G7
Jinchuan, *China* 52 B4
Jind, *India* 62 E7
Jindabyne, *Australia* 91 F4
Jindrichuv Hradeç, *Czech.* 20 F5
Jing He →, *China* 50 G5
Jing Shan, *China* 53 B8
Jing Xian, *Anhui, China* 53 B12
Jing Xian, *Hunan, China* 52 D7
Jing'an, *China* 53 C10
Jingbian, *China* 50 F5
Jingchuan, *China* 50 G4
Jingde, *China* 53 B12
Jingdezhen, *China* 53 C11
Jingdong, *China* 52 E3
Jinggu, *China* 52 F3
Jinghai, *China* 50 E9
Jinghong, *China* 52 F3
Jingjiang, *China* 53 A13
Jingle, *China* 50 E6
Jingmen, *China* 53 B9
Jingning, *China* 50 G3
Jingpo Hu, *China* 51 C15
Jingshan, *China* 53 B9
Jingtai, *China* 50 F3
Jingxi, *China* 52 F6
Jingxing, *China* 50 E8
Jingyang, *China* 50 G5
Jingyu, *China* 51 C14
Jingyuan, *China* 50 F3
Jingziguan, *China* 50 H6
Jinhua, *China* 53 C12
Jining, *Nei Mongol Zizhiqu, China* 50 D7
Jining, *Shandong, China* 50 G9
Jinja, *Uganda* 82 B3
Jinjang, *Malaysia* 59 L3
Jinji, *China* 50 F4
Jinjiang, *Fujian, China* 53 E12
Jinjiang, *Yunnan, China* 52 D3
Jinjie, *China* 52 F6
Jinjini, *Ghana* 78 D4
Jinkou, *China* 53 B10
Jinmen Dao, *China* 53 E12
Jinnah Barrage, *Pakistan* 60 C7
Jinning, *China* 52 E4
Jinotega, *Nic.* 116 D2
Jinotepe, *Nic.* 116 D2
Jinping, *Guizhou, China* 52 D7
Jinping, *Yunnan, China* 52 F4
Jinsha, *China* 52 D6
Jinsha Jiang →, *China* 52 C5
Jinshan, *China* 53 B13
Jinshi, *China* 53 C8
Jintan, *China* 53 B12
Jinxi, *Jiangxi, China* 53 D11
Jinxi, *Liaoning, China* 51 D11
Jinxian, *China* 53 C11
Jinxiang, *China* 50 G9
Jinyun, *China* 53 C13
Jinzhai, *China* 53 B10
Jinzhou, *China* 51 D11
Jiparaná →, *Brazil* 125 B5
Jipijapa, *Ecuador* 120 D1
Jiquilpan, *Mexico* 114 D4
Jishan, *China* 50 G6
Jishou, *China* 52 C7
Jishui, *China* 53 D10
Jisr ash Shughūr, *Syria* 64 C3
Jitarning, *Australia* 89 F2
Jitra, *Malaysia* 59 J3
Jiu →, *Romania* 38 F6
Jiudengkou, *China* 50 E4
Jiujiang, *Guangdong, China* 53 F9
Jiujiang, *Jiangxi, China* 53 C10
Jiuling Shan, *China* 53 C10
Jiulong, *China* 52 C3
Jiuquan, *China* 54 C4
Jiutai, *China* 51 B13
Jiuxiangcheng, *China* 50 H8
Jiuxincheng, *China* 50 E8
Jiuyuhang, *China* 53 B12
Jixi, *Anhui, China* 53 B12
Jixi, *Heilongjiang, China* 51 B16
Jiyang, *China* 51 F9
Jīzān, *Si. Arabia* 68 D3
Jize, *China* 50 F8
Jizera →, *Czech.* 20 E4
Jizō-Zaki, *Japan* 49 G6
Joaçaba, *Brazil* 127 B5
Joaíma, *Brazil* 123 E3
João, *Brazil* 122 B1
João Amaro, *Brazil* 123 D3
João Câmara, *Brazil* 122 C4
João Pessoa, *Brazil* 122 C5
João Pinheiro, *Brazil* 123 E2
Joaquim Távora, *Brazil* 123 F2
Joaquín V. González, *Argentina* 126 B3
Jobourg, Nez de, *France* 24 C5
Jódar, *Spain* 29 H1
Jodhpur, *India* 62 F5
Jœuf, *France* 25 C13
Jofane, *Mozam.* 85 C5
Joggins, *Canada* 99 C7

Jogjakarta = Yogyakarta, *Indonesia* 57 G14
Johannesburg, *S. Africa* 85 D4
Johannesburg, *U.S.A.* 113 K9
John Day, *U.S.A.* 110 D4
John Day →, *U.S.A.* 110 D3
John H. Kerr Reservoir, *U.S.A.* 105 G6
John o' Groats, *U.K.* 14 C5
Johnnie, *U.S.A.* 113 J10
John's Ra., *Australia* 90 C1
Johnson, *U.S.A.* 109 G4
Johnson City, *N.Y., U.S.A.* 107 D9
Johnson City, *Tenn., U.S.A.* 105 G4
Johnson City, *Tex., U.S.A.* 109 K5
Johnsonburg, *U.S.A.* 106 E6
Johnsondale, *U.S.A.* 113 K8
Johnson's Crossing, *Canada* 100 A2
Johnston, L., *Australia* 89 F3
Johnston Falls = Mambilima Falls, *Zambia* 83 E2
Johnston I., *Pac. Oc.* 93 F11
Johnstone Str., *Canada* 100 C3
Johnstown, *N.Y., U.S.A.* 107 C10
Johnstown, *Pa., U.S.A.* 106 F6
Johor Baharu, *Malaysia* 59 M4
Joigny, *France* 25 E10
Joinvile, *Brazil* 127 B6
Joinville, *France* 25 D12
Joinville I., *Antarctica* 5 C18
Jojutla, *Mexico* 115 D5
Jokkmokk, *Sweden* 8 C15
Jökulsá á Bru →, *Iceland* 8 D6
Jökulsá á Fjöllum →, *Iceland* 8 C5
Jolfā, *Āzarbājān-e Sharqī, Iran* 64 B5
Jolfā, *Eşfahan, Iran* 65 C6
Joliet, *U.S.A.* 104 E1
Joliette, *Canada* 98 C5
Jolo, *Phil.* 55 J4
Jolon, *U.S.A.* 112 K5
Jomalig, *Phil.* 55 D5
Jombang, *Indonesia* 57 G15
Jomda, *China* 52 B2
Jome, *Indonesia* 57 E7
Jomfruland, *Norway* 11 F3
Jönåker, *Sweden* 11 F10
Jonava, *Lithuania* 40 D4
Jones Sound, *Canada* 4 B3
Jonesboro, *Ark., U.S.A.* 109 H9
Jonesboro, *Ill., U.S.A.* 109 G10
Jonesboro, *La., U.S.A.* 109 J8
Jonesport, *U.S.A.* 99 D6
Jonglei, *Sudan* 77 F3
Jonglei □, *Sudan* 77 F3
Joniškis, *Lithuania* 40 C3
Jönköping, *Sweden* 9 H13
Jönköpings län □, *Sweden* 9 H13
Jonquière, *Canada* 99 C5
Jonsberg, *Sweden* 11 F10
Jonsered, *Sweden* 11 G6
Jonzac, *France* 26 C3
Joplin, *U.S.A.* 109 G7
Jordan, *U.S.A.* 110 C10
Jordan ■, *Asia* 69 E5
Jordan →, *Asia* 69 D4
Jordan Valley, *U.S.A.* 110 E5
Jordânia, *Brazil* 123 E3
Jorge, C., *Chile* 128 D1
Jorhat, *India* 61 F19
Jörn, *Sweden* 8 D16
Jorong, *Indonesia* 56 E4
Jorquera →, *Chile* 126 B2
Jos, *Nigeria* 79 D6
José Batlle y Ordóñez, *Uruguay* 127 C4
José de San Martín, *Argentina* 128 B2
Joseph, *U.S.A.* 110 D5
Joseph, L., *Nfld., Canada* 99 B6
Joseph, L., *Ont., Canada* 106 A5
Joseph Bonaparte G., *Australia* 88 B4
Joseph City, *U.S.A.* 111 J8
Joshua Tree, *U.S.A.* 113 L10
Joshua Tree National Monument, *U.S.A.* 113 M10
Josselin, *France* 24 E4
Jostedal, *Norway* 9 F9
Jotunheimen, *Norway* 10 C2
Jourdanton, *U.S.A.* 109 L5
Joure, *Neths.* 16 C7
Joussard, *Canada* 100 B5
Jovellanos, *Cuba* 116 B3
Joyeuse, *France* 27 D8
Józefów, *Poland* 20 C11
Ju Xian, *China* 51 F10
Juan Aldama, *Mexico* 114 C4
Juan Bautista Alberdi, *Argentina* 126 C3
Juan de Fuca Str., *Canada* 112 B2
Juan de Nova, *Ind. Oc.* 85 B7
Juan Fernández, Arch. de, *Pac. Oc.* 93 L20
Juan José Castelli, *Argentina* 126 B3
Juan L. Lacaze, *Uruguay* 126 C4
Juanjuí, *Peru* 124 B2
Juárez, *Argentina* 126 D4
Juárez, *Mexico* 113 N11
Juárez, Sierra de, *Mexico* 114 A1
Juatinga, Ponta de, *Brazil* 123 F3
Juàzeiro, *Brazil* 122 C3
Juàzeiro do Norte, *Brazil* 122 C4
Jubayl, *Lebanon* 69 A4
Jubbah, *Si. Arabia* 64 D4
Jubbulpore = Jabalpur, *India* 63 H8
Jübek, *Germany* 18 A5
Jubga, *Russia* 43 D8
Jubilee L., *Australia* 89 E4
Juby, C., *Morocco* 72 C2
Júcar →, *Spain* 29 F4
Júcaro, *Cuba* 116 B4
Juchitán, *Mexico* 115 D5
Judaea = Har Yehuda, *Israel* 69 D3
Judenburg, *Austria* 21 H4
Judith →, *U.S.A.* 110 C9
Judith, Pt., *U.S.A.* 107 E13
Judith Gap, *U.S.A.* 110 C9
Jufari →, *Brazil* 121 D5
Jugoslavia = Yugoslavia ■, *Europe* 21 M10
Juigalpa, *Nic.* 116 D2
Juillac, *France* 26 C5
Juist, *Germany* 18 B2
Juiz de Fora, *Brazil* 123 F3
Jujuy □, *Argentina* 126 A2
Julesburg, *U.S.A.* 108 E3
Juli, *Peru* 124 D4
Julia Cr. →, *Australia* 90 C3
Julia Creek, *Australia* 90 C3
Juliaca, *Peru* 124 D3
Julian, *U.S.A.* 113 M10
Julian Alps = Julijske Alpe, *Slovenia* 33 B11
Julianakanaal, *Neths.* 17 F7
Julianatop, *Surinam* 121 C6
Julianehåb, *Greenland* 4 C5
Jülich, *Germany* 18 E2
Julierpass, *Switz.* 23 D9
Julijske Alpe, *Slovenia* 33 B11
Julimes, *Mexico* 114 B3
Jullundur, *India* 62 D6
Julu, *China* 50 F8
Jumbo, *Zimbabwe* 83 F3
Jumbo Pk., *U.S.A.* 113 J12
Jumentos Cays, *Bahamas* 117 B4
Jumet, *Belgium* 17 H4
Jumilla, *Spain* 29 G3
Jumla, *Nepal* 63 E10
Jumna = Yamuna →, *India* 63 G9
Junagadh, *India* 62 J4
Junction, *Tex., U.S.A.* 109 K5
Junction, *Utah, U.S.A.* 111 G7
Junction B., *Australia* 90 A1
Junction City, *Kans., U.S.A.* 108 F6
Junction City, *Oreg., U.S.A.* 110 D2
Junction Pt., *Australia* 90 A1
Jundah, *Australia* 90 C3
Jundiaí, *Brazil* 127 A6
Juneau, *U.S.A.* 96 C6
Junee, *Australia* 91 E4
Jungfrau, *Switz.* 22 C5
Junggar Pendi, *China* 54 B3
Junglinster, *Lux.* 17 J8
Jungshahi, *Pakistan* 62 G2
Juniata →, *U.S.A.* 106 F7
Junín, *Argentina* 126 C3
Junín, *Peru* 124 C2
Junín □, *Peru* 124 C3
Junín de los Andes, *Argentina* 128 A2
Jūniyah, *Lebanon* 69 B4
Juntura, *U.S.A.* 110 E4
Juparanã, L., *Brazil* 123 E3
Jupiter →, *Canada* 99 C7
Juquiá, *Brazil* 123 F2
Jur, Nahr el →, *Sudan* 77 F2
Jura = Jura, Mts. du, *Europe* 27 B10
Jura = Schwäbische Alb, *Germany* 19 G5
Jura, *Europe* 25 F13
Jura, *U.K.* 14 F3
Jura □, *France* 25 F12
Jura, Mts. du, *Europe* 27 B10
Jura, Sd. of, *U.K.* 14 F3
Jura Suisse, *Switz.* 22 B3
Jurado, *Colombia* 120 B2
Jurilovca, *Romania* 38 E11
Jurong, *China* 53 B12
Juruá →, *Brazil* 120 D4
Juruena, *Brazil* 125 C6
Juruena →, *Brazil* 125 B6
Juruti, *Brazil* 121 D6
Jussey, *France* 25 E12
Justo Daract, *Argentina* 126 C2
Jutaí, *Brazil* 124 B4
Jutaí →, *Brazil* 120 D4
Jüterbog, *Germany* 18 D9
Juticalpa, *Honduras* 116 D2
Jutland = Jylland, *Denmark* 11 H3
Jutphaas, *Neths.* 16 D6
Juventud, I. de la, *Cuba* 116 B3
Juvigny-sous-Andaine, *France* 24 D6
Juvisy-sur-Orge, *France* 25 D9
Juwain, *Afghan.* 60 D2
Jūy Zar, *Iran* 64 C5
Juye, *China* 50 G9
Juzennecourt, *France* 25 D11
Jylland, *Denmark* 11 H3
Jyväskylä, *Finland* 8 E18

K

K2, Mt., *Pakistan* 63 B7
Kaap Plateau, *S. Africa* 84 D3
Kaapkruis, *Namibia* 84 C1
Kaapstad = Cape Town, *S. Africa* 84 E2
Kaatsheuvel, *Neths.* 17 E6
Kabaena, *Indonesia* 57 F6
Kabala, *S. Leone* 78 D2
Kabale, *Uganda* 82 C3
Kabalo, *Zaïre* 82 D2
Kabambare, *Zaïre* 82 C2
Kabango, *Zaïre* 83 D2
Kabanjahe, *Indonesia* 56 D1
Kabankalan, *Phil.* 55 G5
Kabara, *Mali* 78 B4
Kabardinka, *Russia* 42 D7
Kabardino-Balkar Republic □, *Russia* 43 E10
Kabare, *Indonesia* 57 E8
Kabarega Falls, *Uganda* 82 B3
Kabasalan, *Phil.* 55 H5
Kabba, *Nigeria* 79 D6
Kabin Buri, *Thailand* 58 F3
Kabinakagami L., *Canada* 98 C3
Kabīr, Zab al →, *Iraq* 64 C4
Kabkabīyah, *Sudan* 73 F9
Kabna, *Sudan* 76 D3
Kabompo, *Zambia* 83 E1
Kabompo →, *Zambia* 81 G4
Kabondo, *Zaïre* 83 D2
Kabongo, *Zaïre* 82 D2
Kabou, *Togo* 79 D5
Kaboudia, Rass, *Tunisia* 75 A7
Kabra, *Australia* 90 C5
Kabūd Gonbad, *Iran* 65 B8
Kabugao, *Phil.* 55 B4
Kābul, *Afghan.* 62 B3
Kābul □, *Afghan.* 60 B6
Kabul →, *Pakistan* 62 C5
Kabunga, *Zaïre* 82 C2
Kaburuang, *Indonesia* 57 D7
Kabushiya, *Sudan* 77 D3
Kabwe, *Zambia* 83 E2
Kačanik, *Serbia, Yug.* 21 N11
Kachanovo, *Russia* 40 C5
Kachchh, Gulf of, *India* 62 H3
Kachchh, Rann of, *India* 62 G4
Kachebera, *Zambia* 83 E3
Kachin □, *Burma* 61 F20
Kachira, L., *Uganda* 82 C3
Kachiry, *Kazakhstan* 44 D8
Kachisi, *Ethiopia* 77 F4
Kachot, *Cambodia* 59 G4
Kackar, *Turkey* 43 F9
Kadan Kyun, *Burma* 56 B1
Kadanai →, *Afghan.* 62 D1
Kadarkút, *Hungary* 21 J7
Kade, *Ghana* 79 D4
Kadi, *India* 62 H5
Kadina, *Australia* 91 E2
Kadınhanı, *Turkey* 66 D5
Kadirli, *Turkey* 66 E7
Kadiyevka, *Ukraine* 43 B8
Kadoka, *U.S.A.* 108 D4
Kadom, *Russia* 41 D13
Kadoma, *Zimbabwe* 83 F2
Kâdugli, *Sudan* 77 E2
Kaduna, *Nigeria* 79 C6
Kaduna □, *Nigeria* 79 C6
Kaédi, *Mauritania* 78 B2
Kaelé, *Cameroon* 79 C7
Kaeng Khoï, *Thailand* 58 E3
Kaesŏng, *N. Korea* 51 F14
Kāf, *Si. Arabia* 64 D3
Kafakumba, *Zaïre* 80 F4
Kafan, *Armenia* 67 D12
Kafanchan, *Nigeria* 79 D6
Kafareti, *Nigeria* 79 C7
Kaffrine, *Senegal* 78 C1
Kafia Kingi, *Sudan* 73 G9
Kafinda, *Zambia* 83 E3
Kafirévs, Ákra, *Greece* 39 L7
Kafr el Dauwâr, *Egypt* 76 H7
Kafr el Sheikh, *Egypt* 76 H7
Kafue, *Zambia* 83 F2
Kafue →, *Zambia* 81 H5
Kafue Flats, *Zambia* 83 F2
Kafue Nat. Park, *Zambia* 83 F2
Kafulwe, *Zambia* 83 D2
Kaga, *Afghan.* 62 B4
Kaga Bandoro, *C.A.R.* 73 G8
Kagan, *Uzbekistan* 44 F7
Kagawa □, *Japan* 49 G6
Kagera □, *Tanzania* 82 C3
Kagera →, *Uganda* 82 C3
Kağizman, *Turkey* 67 C10
Kagoshima, *Japan* 49 J5
Kagoshima □, *Japan* 49 J5
Kagul, *Moldavia* 42 D3
Kahak, *Iran* 65 B6
Kahama, *Tanzania* 82 C3
Kahama □, *Tanzania* 82 C3
Kahang, *Malaysia* 59 L4
Kahayan →, *Indonesia* 56 E4
Kahe, *Tanzania* 82 C4
Kahemba, *Zaïre* 80 F3
Kahil, Djebel bou, *Algeria* 75 B5
Kahniah →, *Canada* 100 B4
Kahnūj, *Iran* 65 E8
Kahoka, *U.S.A.* 108 E9
Kahoolawe, *U.S.A.* 102 H16
Kahramanmaraş, *Turkey* 66 E7
Kahramanmaraş □, *Turkey* 66 E7
Kâhta, *Turkey* 67 E8
Kahuta, *Pakistan* 62 C5
Kai, Kepulauan, *Indonesia* 57 F8
Kai Besar, *Indonesia* 57 F8
Kai Is. = Kai, Kepulauan, *Indonesia* 57 F8
Kai-Ketil, *Indonesia* 57 F8
Kai Xian, *China* 52 B7
Kaiama, *Nigeria* 79 D5
Kaiapoi, *N.Z.* 87 K4
Kaieteur Falls, *Guyana* 121 B6
Kaifeng, *China* 50 G8
Kaihua, *China* 53 C12
Kaikohe, *N.Z.* 87 F4
Kaikoura, *N.Z.* 87 K4
Kaikoura Ra., *N.Z.* 87 J4
Kailahun, *S. Leone* 78 D2
Kaili, *China* 52 D6
Kailu, *China* 51 C11
Kailua Kona, *U.S.A.* 102 J17
Kaimana, *Indonesia* 57 E8
Kaimanawa Mts., *N.Z.* 87 H5
Kaimganj, *India* 63 F8
Kaimur Hills, *India* 63 G9
Kaingaroa Forest, *N.Z.* 87 H6
Kainji Res., *Nigeria* 79 C5
Kaipara Harbour, *N.Z.* 87 G5
Kaiping, *China* 53 F9
Kaipokok B., *Canada* 99 B8
Kairana, *India* 62 E7
Kaironi, *Indonesia* 57 E8
Kairouan, *Tunisia* 75 A7
Kaiserslautern, *Germany* 19 F3
Kaitaia, *N.Z.* 87 F4
Kaitangata, *N.Z.* 87 M2
Kaithal, *India* 62 E7
Kaitu →, *Pakistan* 62 C4
Kaiwi Channel, *U.S.A.* 102 H16
Kaiyang, *China* 52 D6
Kaiyuan, *Liaoning, China* 51 C13
Kaiyuan, *Yunnan, China* 52 F4
Kajaani, *Finland* 8 D19
Kajabbi, *Australia* 90 B3
Kajana = Kajaani, *Finland* 8 D19
Kajang, *Malaysia* 59 L3
Kajiado, *Kenya* 82 C4
Kajiado □, *Kenya* 82 C4
Kajo Kaji, *Sudan* 77 G3
Kaka, *Sudan* 77 E3
Kakabeka Falls, *Canada* 98 C2
Kakamas, *S. Africa* 84 D3
Kakamega, *Kenya* 82 B3
Kakamega □, *Kenya* 82 B3
Kakanj, *Bos.-H.* 21 L8
Kakanui Mts., *N.Z.* 87 L3
Kake, *Japan* 49 G6
Kakegawa, *Japan* 49 G9
Kakeroma-Jima, *Japan* 49 K4
Kakhib, *Russia* 43 E12
Kakhovka, *Ukraine* 42 C5
Kakhovskoye Vdkhr., *Ukraine* 42 C6
Kakinada, *India* 61 L13
Kakisa →, *Canada* 100 A5
Kakisa L., *Canada* 100 A5
Kakogawa, *Japan* 49 G7
Kakwa →, *Canada* 100 C5
Kāl Gūsheh, *Iran* 65 D8
Kal Safīd, *Iran* 64 C5
Kala, *Nigeria* 79 C7
Kalaa-Kebira, *Tunisia* 75 A7
Kalabagh, *Pakistan* 62 C4
Kalabahi, *Indonesia* 57 F6
Kalabáka, *Greece* 39 K4
Kalabo, *Zambia* 81 G4
Kalach, *Russia* 41 F12
Kalach na Donu, *Russia* 43 B10
Kaladan →, *Burma* 61 J18
Kaladar, *Canada* 106 B7
Kalahari, *Africa* 84 C3
Kalahari Gemsbok Nat. Park, *S. Africa* 84 D3
Kālak, *Iran* 65 E8
Kalakamati, *Botswana* 85 C4
Kalakan, *Russia* 45 D12
Kalakh, *Syria* 64 C3
K'alak'unlun Shank'ou, *Pakistan* 63 B7
Kalam, *Pakistan* 63 B5
Kalama, *U.S.A.* 112 E4
Kalama, *Zaïre* 82 C2
Kalamariá, *Greece* 39 J5
Kalamata, *Greece* 39 M5
Kalamazoo, *U.S.A.* 104 D3
Kalamazoo →, *U.S.A.* 104 D2
Kalambo Falls, *Tanzania* 83 D3
Kálamos, *Greece* 39 L3
Kalannie, *Australia* 89 F2
Kalāntarī, *Iran* 65 C7
Kalao, *Indonesia* 57 F6
Kalaotoa, *Indonesia* 57 F6
Kälarne, *Sweden* 10 B10
Kalárovo, *Slovakia* 21 H7
Kalasin, *Thailand* 58 D4
Kalat, *Pakistan* 60 E5
Kalāteh, *Iran* 65 B7
Kalāteh-ye-Ganj, *Iran* 65 E8
Kálathos, *Greece* 39 N11
Kalaus →, *Russia* 43 D11
Kalávrita, *Greece* 39 L5
Kalbarri, *Australia* 89 E1
Kale, *Turkey* 66 E3
Kalecik, *Turkey* 42 F5
Kalegauk Kyun, *Burma* 61 M20
Kalehe, *Zaïre* 82 C2
Kalema, *Tanzania* 82 C3
Kalemie, *Zaïre* 82 D2
Kalety, *Poland* 20 E8
Kalewa, *Burma* 61 H19
Kálfafellsstaður, *Iceland* 8 D6
Kalgan = Zhangjiakou, *China* 50 D8
Kalgoorlie-Boulder, *Australia* 89 F3
Kaliakra, Nos, *Bulgaria* 38 F11
Kalianda, *Indonesia* 56 F3
Kalibo, *Phil.* 55 F5
Kaliganj, *Bangla.* 63 H13
Kalima, *Zaïre* 82 C2
Kalimantan, *Indonesia* 56 E4
Kalimantan Barat □, *Indonesia* 56 E4
Kalimantan Selatan □, *Indonesia* 56 E5
Kalimantan Tengah □, *Indonesia* 56 E4
Kalimantan Timur □, *Indonesia* 56 D5
Kálimnos, *Greece* 39 N10
Kalimpong, *India* 63 F13
Kalinin = Tver, *Russia* 41 C9
Kaliningrad, *Russia* 40 D2
Kalinkavichy = Kalinkovichi, *Belorussia* 40 E6
Kalinkovichi, *Belorussia* 40 E6
Kalinovik, *Bos.-H.* 21 M8
Kalipetrovo, *Bulgaria* 38 E10
Kaliro, *Uganda* 82 B3
Kalispell, *U.S.A.* 110 B6
Kalisz, *Poland* 20 D8
Kaliua, *Tanzania* 82 D3
Kalix →, *Sweden* 8 D17
Kalka, *India* 62 D7
Kalkan, *Turkey* 66 E3
Kalkaska, *U.S.A.* 104 C3
Kalkfeld, *Namibia* 84 C2
Kalkfontein, *Botswana* 84 C3
Kalkrand, *Namibia* 84 C2
Kållandsö, *Sweden* 11 F7
Kallithéa, *Greece* 39 M6
Kallonís, Kólpos, *Greece* 39 K9
Kallsjön, *Sweden* 8 E12
Kalmalo, *Nigeria* 79 C6
Kalmar, *Sweden* 9 H14
Kalmthout, *Belgium* 17 F4
Kalmyk Republic □, *Russia* 43 C12
Kalmykovo, *Kazakhstan* 43 B14
Kalna, *India* 63 H13
Kalocsa, *Hungary* 21 J9
Kalokhorio, *Cyprus* 37 E12
Kaloko, *Zaïre* 82 D2
Kalol, *Gujarat, India* 62 H5
Kalol, *Gujarat, India* 62 H5
Kalolímnos, *Greece* 39 M10
Kalomo, *Zambia* 83 F2
Kalpi, *India* 63 F8
Kaltbrunn, *Switz.* 23 B8
Kaltungo, *Nigeria* 79 D7
Kalu, *Pakistan* 62 G2
Kaluga, *Russia* 41 D10
Kalulushi, *Zambia* 83 E2
Kalundborg, *Denmark* 11 J5
Kalush, *Ukraine* 40 G4
Kałuszyn, *Poland* 20 C11
Kalutara, *Sri Lanka* 60 R11
Kalyazin, *Russia* 41 C10
Kama, *Zaïre* 82 C2
Kama →, *Russia* 44 D6
Kamachumu, *Tanzania* 82 C3
Kamaishi, *Japan* 48 E10
Kamalia, *Pakistan* 62 D5
Kamapanda, *Zambia* 83 E1
Kamaran, *Yemen* 68 D3
Kamativi, *Zimbabwe* 83 F2
Kamba, *Nigeria* 79 C5
Kambalda, *Australia* 89 F3
Kambar, *Pakistan* 62 F3
Kambia, *S. Leone* 78 D2
Kambolé, *Zambia* 83 D3
Kambos, *Cyprus* 37 D11
Kambove, *Zaïre* 83 E2
Kamchatka, P-ov., *Russia* 45 D16
Kamchatka Pen. = Kamchatka, P-ov., *Russia* 45 D16
Kamen, *Russia* 44 D9
Kamen Kashirskiy, *Ukraine* 40 F4
Kamen-Rybolov, *Russia* 48 B6
Kamenets-Podolskiy, *Ukraine* 42 B2
Kamenjak, Rt., *Croatia* 33 D10
Kamenka, *Russia* 41 E14
Kamenka, *Russia* 41 F11
Kamenka, *Ukraine* 42 B5
Kamenka Bugskaya, *Ukraine* 40 F4
Kamenka Dneprovskaya, *Ukraine* 42 C6
Kamenolomini, *Russia* 43 C9
Kamensk-Shakhtinskiy, *Russia* 43 B9
Kamensk Uralskiy, *Russia* 44 D7
Kamenskiy, *Russia* 41 F14
Kamenskiy, *Russia* 43 B9
Kamenskoye, *Russia* 45 C17
Kamenyak, *Bulgaria* 38 F9
Kamenz, *Germany* 18 D10
Kameoka, *Japan* 49 G7
Kamiah, *U.S.A.* 110 C5
Kamień Pomorski, *Poland* 20 B4

Kamieskroon, *S. Africa* 84 E2
Kamilukuak, L., *Canada* 101 A8
Kamina, *Zaïre* 83 D1
Kaminak L., *Canada* 101 A9
Kaminoyama, *Japan* 48 E10
Kamiros, *Greece* 37 C9
Kamituga, *Zaïre* 82 C2
Kamloops, *Canada* 100 C4
Kamnik, *Slovenia* 33 B11
Kamo, *Armenia* 43 F11
Kamo, *Japan* 48 F9
Kamoa Mts., *Guyana* 121 C6
Kamoke, *Pakistan* 62 C6
Kamp →, *Austria* 21 G5
Kampala, *Uganda* 82 B3
Kampar, *Malaysia* 59 K3
Kampar →, *Indonesia* 56 D2
Kampen, *Neths.* 16 C7
Kamperland, *Neths.* 17 E3
Kamphaeng Phet, *Thailand* 58 D2
Kampolombo, L., *Zambia* 83 E2
Kampong To, *Thailand* 59 J3
Kampot, *Cambodia* 59 G5
Kampti, *Burkina Faso* 78 C4
Kampuchea = Cambodia ■, *Asia* 58 F5
Kampung →, *Indonesia* 57 F9
Kampung Air Putih, *Malaysia* 59 K4
Kampung Jerangau, *Malaysia* 59 K4
Kampung Raja, *Malaysia* 59 K4
Kampungbaru = Tolitoli, *Indonesia* 57 D6
Kamrau, Teluk, *Indonesia* 57 E8
Kamsack, *Canada* 101 C8
Kamskoye Ustye, *Russia* 41 D16
Kamuchawie L., *Canada* 101 B8
Kamui-Misaki, *Japan* 48 C10
Kamyanets-Podilskyy = Kamenets-Podolskiy, *Ukraine* 42 B2
Kāmyārān, *Iran* 64 C5
Kamyshin, *Russia* 41 F14
Kamyzyak, *Russia* 43 C13
Kanaaupscow, *Canada* 98 B4
Kanab, *U.S.A.* 111 H7
Kanab →, *U.S.A.* 111 H7
Kanagi, *Japan* 48 D10
Kanairiktok →, *Canada* 99 A7
Kanália, *Greece* 39 K5
Kananga, *Zaïre* 80 F4
Kanarraville, *U.S.A.* 111 H7
Kanash, *Russia* 41 D15
Kanaskat, *U.S.A.* 112 C5
Kanawha →, *U.S.A.* 104 F4
Kanazawa, *Japan* 49 F8
Kanchanaburi, *Thailand* 58 E2
Kanchenjunga, *Nepal* 63 F13
Kanchipuram, *India* 60 N11
Kanda Kanda, *Zaïre* 80 F4
Kandahar = Qandahār, *Afghan.* 60 D4
Kandalaksha, *Russia* 44 C4
Kandalu, *Afghan.* 60 E3
Kandangan, *Indonesia* 56 E5
Kandanos, *Greece* 37 D5
Kander →, *Switz.* 22 C5
Kandersteg, *Switz.* 22 D5
Kandhíla, *Greece* 39 M5
Kandhkot, *Pakistan* 62 E3
Kandhla, *India* 62 E7
Kandi, *Benin* 79 C5
Kandi, *India* 63 H13
Kandıra, *Turkey* 66 C4
Kandla, *India* 62 H4
Kandos, *Australia* 91 E4
Kandy, *Sri Lanka* 60 R12
Kane, *U.S.A.* 106 E6
Kane Basin, *Greenland* 4 B4
Kanevskaya, *Russia* 43 C8
Kanfanar, *Croatia* 33 C10
Kangaba, *Mali* 78 C3
Kangal, *Turkey* 66 D7
Kangān, *Fārs, Iran* 65 E7
Kangān, *Hormozgān, Iran* 65 E8
Kangar, *Malaysia* 59 J3
Kangaroo I., *Australia* 91 F2
Kangavar, *Iran* 65 C6
Kangding, *China* 52 B3
Kăngdong, *N. Korea* 51 E14
Kangean, Kepulauan, *Indonesia* 56 F5
Kangean Is. = Kangean, Kepulauan, *Indonesia* 56 F5
Kanggye, *N. Korea* 51 D14
Kanggyŏng, *S. Korea* 51 F14
Kanghwa, *S. Korea* 51 F14
Kangnŭng, *S. Korea* 51 F15
Kango, *Gabon* 80 D2
Kangping, *China* 51 C12
Kangto, *India* 61 F18
Kani, *Ivory C.* 78 D3
Kaniama, *Zaïre* 82 D1
Kaniapiskau →, *Canada* 99 A6
Kaniapiskau L., *Canada* 99 B6
Kanin, P-ov., *Russia* 44 C5
Kanin Nos, Mys, *Russia* 44 C5
Kanin Pen. = Kanin, P-ov., *Russia* 44 C5
Kaniva, *Australia* 91 F3
Kanjiža, *Serbia, Yug.* 21 J10
Kanjut Sar, *Pakistan* 63 A6
Kankakee, *U.S.A.* 104 E2
Kankakee →, *U.S.A.* 104 E1
Kankan, *Guinea* 78 C3
Kanker, *India* 61 J12
Kankunskiy, *Russia* 45 D13
Kannapolis, *U.S.A.* 105 H5
Kannauj, *India* 63 F8
Kannod, *India* 60 H10
Kano, *Nigeria* 79 C6
Kano □, *Nigeria* 79 C6
Kan'onji, *Japan* 49 G6
Kanoroba, *Ivory C.* 78 D3
Kanowit, *Malaysia* 56 D4
Kanowna, *Australia* 89 F3
Kanoya, *Japan* 49 J5
Kanpetlet, *Burma* 61 J18
Kanpur, *India* 63 F9
Kansas □, *U.S.A.* 108 F6
Kansas →, *U.S.A.* 108 F7
Kansas City, *Kans., U.S.A.* 108 F7
Kansas City, *Mo., U.S.A.* 108 F7
Kansenia, *Zaïre* 83 E2
Kansk, *Russia* 45 D10
Kansŏng, *S. Korea* 51 E15
Kansu = Gansu □, *China* 50 G3
Kantang, *Thailand* 59 J2
Kantché, *Niger* 79 C6
Kanté, *Togo* 79 D5
Kantemirovka, *Russia* 43 B8
Kantharalak, *Thailand* 58 E5
Kantō □, *Japan* 49 F9
Kantō-Sanchi, *Japan* 49 G9
Kanturk, *Ireland* 15 D3
Kanuma, *Japan* 49 F9
Kanus, *Namibia* 84 D2
Kanye, *Botswana* 84 C4
Kanzenze, *Zaïre* 83 E2
Kanzi, Ras, *Tanzania* 82 D4
Kaohsiung = Gaoxiong, *Taiwan* 53 F13
Kaokoveld, *Namibia* 84 B1
Kaolack, *Senegal* 78 C1
Kaoshan, *China* 51 B13
Kapadvanj, *India* 62 H5
Kapanga, *Zaïre* 80 F4
Kapchagai, *Kazakhstan* 44 E8
Kapellen, *Belgium* 17 F4
Kapéllo, Ákra, *Greece* 39 N6
Kapema, *Zaïre* 83 E2
Kapfenberg, *Austria* 21 H5
Kapiri Mposhi, *Zambia* 83 E2
Kapiskau →, *Canada* 98 B3
Kapit, *Malaysia* 56 D4
Kapiti I., *N.Z.* 87 J5
Kaplice, *Czech.* 20 G4
Kapoe, *Thailand* 59 H2
Kapoeta, *Sudan* 77 G3
Kapos →, *Hungary* 21 J8
Kaposvár, *Hungary* 21 J7
Kapowsin, *U.S.A.* 112 D4
Kappeln, *Germany* 18 A5
Kapps, *Namibia* 84 C2
Kaprije, *Croatia* 33 E12
Kaprijke, *Belgium* 17 F3
Kapsan, *N. Korea* 51 D15
Kapsukas = Mariyampol, *Lithuania* 40 D3
Kapuas →, *Indonesia* 56 E3
Kapuas Hulu, Pegunungan, *Malaysia* 56 D4
Kapuas Hulu Ra. = Kapuas Hulu, Pegunungan, *Malaysia* 56 D4
Kapulo, *Zaïre* 83 D2
Kapunda, *Australia* 91 E2
Kapuni, *N.Z.* 87 H5
Kapurthala, *India* 62 D6
Kapuskasing, *Canada* 98 C3
Kapuskasing →, *Canada* 98 C3
Kapustin Yar, *Russia* 43 B11
Kaputar, *Australia* 91 E5
Kaputir, *Kenya* 82 B4
Kapuvár, *Hungary* 21 H7
Kara, *Russia* 44 C7
Kara Bogaz Gol, Zaliv, *Turkmenistan* 44 E6
Kara Kalpak Republic □, *Uzbekistan* 44 E6
Kara Kum = Karakum, Peski, *Turkmenistan* 44 F6
Kara Sea, *Russia* 44 B7
Karabük, *Turkey* 42 F5
Karaburun, *Turkey* 66 D2
Karaburuni, *Albania* 39 J2
Karabutak, *Kazakhstan* 44 E7
Karacabey, *Turkey* 66 C3
Karacasu, *Turkey* 66 E3
Karachala, *Azerbaijan* 43 G13
Karachayevsk, *Russia* 43 E9
Karachev, *Russia* 40 E9
Karachi, *Pakistan* 62 G2
Karad, *India* 60 L9
Karadeniz Boğazı, *Turkey* 66 C3
Karaga, *Ghana* 79 D4
Karaganda, *Kazakhstan* 44 E8
Karagayly, *Kazakhstan* 44 E8
Karaginskiy, Ostrov, *Russia* 45 D17
Karagüney Dağları, *Turkey* 66 C6
Karagwe □, *Tanzania* 82 C3
Karaikal, *India* 60 P11
Karaikkudi, *India* 60 P11
Karaisali, *Turkey* 66 E6
Karaj, *Iran* 65 C6
Karak, *Malaysia* 59 L4
Karakas, *Kazakhstan* 44 E9
Karakitang, *Indonesia* 57 D7
Karaklis, *Armenia* 43 F11
Karakoçan, *Turkey* 67 D9
Karakoram Pass, *Pakistan* 63 B7
Karakoram Ra., *Pakistan* 63 B7
Karakum, Peski, *Turkmenistan* 44 F6
Karakurt, *Turkey* 67 C10
Karalon, *Russia* 45 D12
Karaman, *Turkey* 66 E5
Karamay, *China* 54 B3
Karambu, *Indonesia* 56 E5
Karamea Bight, *N.Z.* 87 J3
Karamoja □, *Uganda* 82 B3
Karamsad, *India* 62 H5
Karand, *Iran* 64 C5
Karanganyar, *Indonesia* 57 G13
Karapınar, *Turkey* 66 E5
Karasburg, *Namibia* 84 D2
Karasino, *Russia* 44 C9
Karasjok, *Norway* 8 B18
Karasu, *Turkey* 66 C4
Karasu →, *Turkey* 67 D8
Karasuk, *Russia* 44 D8
Karasuyama, *Japan* 49 F10
Karataş Burnu, *Turkey* 66 E6
Karatau, *Kazakhstan* 44 E8
Karatau, Khrebet, *Kazakhstan* 44 E7
Karatepe, *Turkey* 66 E7
Karauli, *India* 62 F7
Karavostasi, *Cyprus* 37 D11
Karawang, *Indonesia* 57 G12
Karawanken, *Europe* 21 J4
Karayazı, *Turkey* 67 D10
Karazhal, *Kazakhstan* 44 E8
Karbalā, *Iraq* 64 C5
Kårböle, *Sweden* 10 C9
Karcag, *Hungary* 21 H10
Karcha →, *Pakistan* 63 B7
Karda, *Russia* 45 D11
Kardhámila, *Greece* 39 L9
Kardhítsa, *Greece* 39 K4
Kärdla, *Estonia* 40 B3
Kareeberge, *S. Africa* 84 E3
Kareima, *Sudan* 76 D3
Karelian Republic □, *Russia* 44 C4
Kārevāndar, *Iran* 65 E9
Kargasok, *Russia* 44 D9
Kargat, *Russia* 44 D9
Kargı, *Turkey* 42 F6
Kargil, *India* 63 B7
Karguéri, *Niger* 79 C7
Karia ba Mohammed, *Morocco* 74 B3
Karīān, *Iran* 65 E8
Kariba, *Zimbabwe* 83 F2
Kariba, L., *Zimbabwe* 83 F2
Kariba Dam, *Zimbabwe* 83 F2
Kariba Gorge, *Zambia* 83 F2
Karibib, *Namibia* 84 C2
Karimata, Kepulauan, *Indonesia* 56 E3
Karimata, Selat, *Indonesia* 56 E3
Karimata Is. = Karimata, Kepulauan, *Indonesia* 56 E3
Karimnagar, *India* 60 K11
Karimunjawa, Kepulauan, *Indonesia* 56 F4
Karin, *Somali Rep.* 68 E4
Karīt, *Iran* 65 C8
Kariya, *Japan* 49 G8
Karkaralinsk, *Kazakhstan* 44 E8
Karkinitskiy Zaliv, *Ukraine* 42 D5
Karkur Tohl, *Egypt* 76 C2
Karl Libknekht, *Russia* 40 F9
Karl-Marx-Stadt = Chemnitz, *Germany* 18 E8
Karla, L. = Voiviïs Límni, *Greece* 39 K5
Karlobag, *Croatia* 33 D12
Karlovac, *Croatia* 33 C12
Karlovka, *Ukraine* 42 B6
Karlovy Vary, *Czech.* 20 E2
Karlsbad = Karlovy Vary, *Czech.* 20 E2
Karlsborg, *Sweden* 11 F8
Karlshamn, *Sweden* 9 H13
Karlskoga, *Sweden* 9 G13
Karlskrona, *Sweden* 9 H13
Karlsruhe, *Germany* 19 F4
Karlstad, *Sweden* 9 G12
Karlstad, *U.S.A.* 108 A6
Karlstadt, *Germany* 19 F5
Karnal, *India* 62 E7
Karnali →, *Nepal* 63 E9
Karnaphuli Res., *Bangla.* 61 H18
Karnataka □, *India* 60 N10
Karnes City, *U.S.A.* 109 L6
Karnische Alpen, *Europe* 21 J3
Karo, *Mali* 78 C4
Karoi, *Zimbabwe* 83 F2
Karonga, *Malawi* 83 D3
Karoonda, *Australia* 91 F2
Karora, *Sudan* 76 D4
Káros, *Greece* 39 N8
Karousádhes, *Greece* 39 K2
Karpasia □, *Cyprus* 37 D13
Kárpathos, *Greece* 39 P10
Kárpathos, Stenón, *Greece* 39 P10
Karrebæk, *Denmark* 11 J5
Kars, *Turkey* 43 F10
Kars □, *Turkey* 67 C10
Karsakpay, *Kazakhstan* 44 E7
Karsha, *Kazakhstan* 43 B14
Karshi, *Uzbekistan* 44 F7
Karsiyang, *India* 63 F13
Karst, *Croatia* 33 C11
Karsun, *Russia* 41 D15
Kartaly, *Russia* 44 D7
Kartapur, *India* 62 D6
Karthaus, *U.S.A.* 106 E6
Kartuzy, *Poland* 20 A8
Karufa, *Indonesia* 57 E8
Karumba, *Australia* 90 B3
Karumo, *Tanzania* 82 C3
Karumwa, *Tanzania* 82 C3
Karungu, *Kenya* 82 C3
Karup, *Denmark* 11 H3
Karviná, *Czech.* 20 F8
Karwar, *India* 60 M9
Karwi, *India* 63 G9
Kaş, *Turkey* 66 E3
Kasache, *Malawi* 83 E3
Kasai →, *Zaïre* 80 E3
Kasai Oriental □, *Zaïre* 82 C1
Kasaji, *Zaïre* 83 E1
Kasama, *Zambia* 83 E3
Kasan-dong, *N. Korea* 51 D14
Kasane, *Namibia* 84 B3
Kasanga, *Tanzania* 83 D3
Kasangulu, *Zaïre* 80 E3
Kasaragod, *India* 60 N9
Kasba L., *Canada* 101 A8
Kasba Tadla, *Morocco* 74 B3
Kāseh Garān, *Iran* 64 C5
Kasempa, *Zambia* 83 E2
Kasenga, *Zaïre* 83 E2
Kasese, *Uganda* 82 B3
Kasewa, *Zambia* 83 E2
Kasganj, *India* 63 F8
Kashabowie, *Canada* 98 C1
Kāshān, *Iran* 65 C6
Kashi, *China* 54 C2
Kashimbo, *Zaïre* 83 E2
Kashin, *Russia* 41 C10
Kashipur, *India* 63 E8
Kashira, *Russia* 41 D11
Kashiwazaki, *Japan* 49 F9
Kashk-e Kohneh, *Afghan.* 60 B3
Kāshmar, *Iran* 65 C8
Kashmir, *Asia* 63 C7
Kashmor, *Pakistan* 62 E3
Kashpirovka, *Russia* 41 E16
Kashun Noerh = Gaxun Nur, *China* 54 B5
Kasimov, *Russia* 41 D12
Kasinge, *Zaïre* 82 D2
Kasiruta, *Indonesia* 57 E7
Kaskaskia →, *U.S.A.* 108 G10
Kaskattama →, *Canada* 101 B10
Kaskinen, *Finland* 8 E16
Kaskö, *Finland* 8 E16
Kaslo, *Canada* 100 D5
Kasmere L., *Canada* 101 B8
Kasongo, *Zaïre* 82 C2
Kasongo Lunda, *Zaïre* 80 F3
Kásos, *Greece* 39 P9
Kásos, Stenón, *Greece* 39 P9
Kaspi, *Georgia* 43 F11
Kaspiysk, *Russia* 43 E12
Kaspiyskiy, *Russia* 43 D12
Kassab ed Doleib, *Sudan* 77 E3
Kassaba, *Egypt* 76 C2
Kassala, *Sudan* 77 D4
Kassalâ □, *Sudan* 77 D4
Kassel, *Germany* 18 D5
Kassinger, *Sudan* 76 D3
Kassiópi, *Greece* 37 A3
Kassue, *Indonesia* 57 F9
Kastamonu, *Turkey* 66 C5
Kastamonu □, *Turkey* 66 C5
Kastav, *Croatia* 33 C11
Kastélli, *Greece* 37 D5
Kastéllion, *Greece* 37 D7
Kastellou, Ákra, *Greece* 39 P10
Kasterlee, *Belgium* 17 F5
Kastóri, *Greece* 39 M5
Kastoría, *Greece* 39 J4
Kastornoye, *Russia* 41 F11
Kástron, *Greece* 39 K8
Kasulu, *Tanzania* 82 C3
Kasulu □, *Tanzania* 82 C3
Kasumi, *Japan* 49 G7
Kasumkent, *Azerbaijan* 43 F13
Kasungu, *Malawi* 83 E3
Kasur, *Pakistan* 62 D6
Kata, *Russia* 45 D11
Kataba, *Zambia* 83 F2
Katako Kombe, *Zaïre* 82 C1
Katákolon, *Greece* 39 M4
Katale, *Tanzania* 82 C3
Katamatite, *Australia* 91 F4
Katanda, *Kivu, Zaïre* 82 C2
Katanda, *Shaba, Zaïre* 82 D1
Katangi, *India* 60 J11
Katangli, *Russia* 45 D15
Katavi Swamp, *Tanzania* 82 D3
Kateríni, *Greece* 39 J5
Katha, *Burma* 61 G20
Katherîna, Gebel, *Egypt* 76 J8
Katherine, *Australia* 88 B5
Kathiawar, *India* 62 H4
Kathikas, *Cyprus* 37 E11
Kati, *Mali* 78 C3
Katihar, *India* 63 G12
Katima Mulilo, *Zambia* 84 B3
Katimbira, *Malawi* 83 E3
Katingan = Mendawai →, *Indonesia* 56 E4
Katiola, *Ivory C.* 78 D3
Katmandu, *Nepal* 63 F11
Kato Akhaïa, *Greece* 39 L4
Káto Arkhánai, *Greece* 37 D7
Káto Khorió, *Greece* 37 D7
Kato Pyrgos, *Cyprus* 37 D11
Káto Stavros, *Greece* 39 J6
Katompe, *Zaïre* 82 D2
Katonga →, *Uganda* 82 B3
Katoomba, *Australia* 91 E5
Katowice, *Poland* 20 E9
Katrine, L., *U.K.* 14 E4
Katrineholm, *Sweden* 10 E10
Katsepe, *Madag.* 85 B8
Katsina, *Nigeria* 79 C6
Katsina □, *Nigeria* 79 C6
Katsina Ala →, *Nigeria* 79 D6
Katsumoto, *Japan* 49 H4
Katsuura, *Japan* 49 G10
Katsuyama, *Japan* 49 F8
Kattaviá, *Greece* 37 D9
Kattegatt, *Denmark* 11 H5
Katumba, *Zaïre* 82 D2
Katungu, *Kenya* 82 C5
Katwa, *India* 63 H13
Katwijk-aan-Zee, *Neths.* 16 D4
Kauai, *U.S.A.* 102 H15
Kauai Channel, *U.S.A.* 102 H15
Kaub, *Germany* 19 E3
Kaufbeuren, *Germany* 19 H6
Kaufman, *U.S.A.* 109 J6
Kaukauna, *U.S.A.* 104 C1
Kaukauveld, *Namibia* 84 C3
Kaukonen, *Finland* 8 C18
Kauliranta, *Finland* 8 C17
Kaunas, *Lithuania* 40 D3
Kaura Namoda, *Nigeria* 79 C6
Kautokeino, *Norway* 8 B17
Kavacha, *Russia* 45 C17
Kavadarci, *Macedonia* 39 H5
Kavaja, *Albania* 39 H2
Kavak, *Turkey* 66 C7
Kavalerovo, *Russia* 48 B7
Kavali, *India* 60 M12
Kavála, *Greece* 39 J7
Kavār, *Iran* 65 D7
Kavarna, *Bulgaria* 38 F11
Kavos, *Greece* 37 B4
Kaw, *Fr. Guiana* 121 C7
Kawa, *Sudan* 77 E3
Kawagama L., *Canada* 106 A6
Kawagoe, *Japan* 49 G9
Kawaguchi, *Japan* 49 G9
Kawaihae, *U.S.A.* 102 H17
Kawambwa, *Zambia* 83 D2
Kawanoe, *Japan* 49 G6
Kawardha, *India* 63 J9
Kawasaki, *Japan* 49 G9
Kawene, *Canada* 98 C1
Kawerau, *N.Z.* 87 H6
Kawhia Harbour, *N.Z.* 87 H5
Kawio, Kepulauan, *Indonesia* 57 D7
Kawnro, *Burma* 61 H21
Kawthoolei = Kawthule □, *Burma* 61 L20
Kawthule □, *Burma* 61 L20
Kaya, *Burkina Faso* 79 C4
Kayah □, *Burma* 61 K20
Kayan →, *Indonesia* 56 D5
Kaycee, *U.S.A.* 110 E10
Kayeli, *Indonesia* 57 E7
Kayenta, *U.S.A.* 111 H8
Kayes, *Mali* 78 C2
Kayima, *S. Leone* 78 D2
Kayl, *Lux.* 17 K8
Kayoa, *Indonesia* 57 D7
Kayomba, *Zambia* 83 E1
Kayoro, *Ghana* 79 C4
Kayrunnera, *Australia* 91 E3
Kaysatskoye, *Russia* 43 B12
Kayseri, *Turkey* 66 D6
Kayseri □, *Turkey* 66 D6
Kaysville, *U.S.A.* 110 F8
Kayuagung, *Indonesia* 56 E2
Kazachinskoye, *Russia* 45 D11
Kazachye, *Russia* 45 B14
Kazakhstan ■, *Asia* 44 E7
Kazan, *Russia* 41 D16
Kazan-Rettō, *Pac. Oc.* 92 E6
Kazanlúk, *Bulgaria* 38 G8
Kazanskaya, *Russia* 43 B9
Kazatin, *Ukraine* 42 B3
Kazbek, *Georgia* 43 E11
Kāzerūn, *Iran* 65 D6
Kazi Magomed, *Azerbaijan* 43 F13
Kazincbarcika, *Hungary* 21 G10
Kaztalovka, *Kazakhstan* 43 B13
Kazumba, *Zaïre* 80 F4
Kazuno, *Japan* 48 D10
Kazym →, *Russia* 44 C7
Kcynia, *Poland* 20 C7
Ké-Macina, *Mali* 78 C3
Kéa, *Greece* 39 M7
Keams Canyon, *U.S.A.* 111 J8
Kearney, *U.S.A.* 108 E5
Keban, *Turkey* 67 D8
Keban Baraji, *Turkey* 67 D8
Kebbje □, *Nigeria* 79 C6
Kébi, *Ivory C.* 78 D3
Kebili, *Tunisia* 75 B6
Kebnekaise, *Sweden* 8 C15
Kebri Dehar, *Ethiopia* 68 F3
Kebumen, *Indonesia* 57 G13
Kecel, *Hungary* 21 J9

Kechika →, *Canada* 100 B3
Kecskemét, *Hungary* 21 J9
Kedada, *Ethiopia* 77 F4
Kedgwick, *Canada* 99 C6
Kédhros Óros, *Greece* 37 D6
Kedia Hill, *Botswana* 84 C3
Kediniai, *Lithuania* 40 D4
Kediri, *Indonesia* 57 G15
Kédougou, *Senegal* 78 C2
Kedzierzyn, *Poland* 20 E8
Keeler, *U.S.A.* 112 J9
Keeley L., *Canada* 101 C7
Keeling Is. = Cocos Is., *Ind. Oc.* 92 J1
Keene, *Calif., U.S.A.* 113 K8
Keene, *N.H., U.S.A.* 107 D12
Keeper Hill, *Ireland* 15 D3
Keer-Weer, C., *Australia* 90 A3
Keerbergen, *Belgium* 17 F5
Keeseville, *U.S.A.* 107 B11
Keeten Mastgat, *Neths.* 17 E4
Keetmanshoop, *Namibia* 84 D2
Keewatin, *U.S.A.* 108 B8
Keewatin □, *Canada* 101 A9
Keewatin →, *Canada* 101 B8
Kefa □, *Ethiopia* 77 F4
Kefallinía, *Greece* 39 L3
Kefamenanu, *Indonesia* 57 F6
Keffi, *Nigeria* 79 D6
Kefken, *Turkey* 66 C4
Keflavík, *Iceland* 8 D2
Keg River, *Canada* 100 B5
Kegaska, *Canada* 99 B7
Kehl, *Germany* 19 G3
Keighley, *U.K.* 12 D6
Keimoes, *S. Africa* 84 D3
Keita, *Niger* 79 C6
Keith, *Australia* 91 F3
Keith, *U.K.* 14 D6
Keith Arm, *Canada* 96 B7
Kejser Franz Joseph Fjord = Kong Franz Joseph Fd., *Greenland* 4 B6
Kekri, *India* 62 G6
Kël, *Russia* 45 C13
Kelamet, *Eritrea* 77 D4
Kelan, *China* 50 E6
Kelang, *Malaysia* 59 L3
Kelantan →, *Malaysia* 59 J4
Kelheim, *Germany* 19 G7
Kelibia, *Tunisia* 75 A7
Kelkit, *Turkey* 67 C8
Kelkit →, *Turkey* 66 C7
Kellé, *Congo* 80 E2
Keller, *U.S.A.* 110 B4
Kellerberrin, *Australia* 89 F2
Kellett, C., *Canada* 4 B1
Kelleys I., *U.S.A.* 106 E2
Kellogg, *U.S.A.* 110 C5
Kelloselkä, *Finland* 8 C20
Kells = Ceanannus Mor, *Ireland* 15 C5
Kélo, *Chad* 73 G8
Kelokedhara, *Cyprus* 37 E11
Kelowna, *Canada* 100 D5
Kelsey Bay, *Canada* 100 C3
Kelseyville, *U.S.A.* 112 G4
Kelso, *N.Z.* 87 L2
Kelso, *U.K.* 14 F6
Kelso, *U.S.A.* 112 D4
Keluang, *Malaysia* 59 L4
Kelvington, *Canada* 101 C8
Kem, *Russia* 44 C4
Kem-Kem, *Morocco* 74 B4
Kema, *Indonesia* 57 D7
Kemah, *Turkey* 67 D8
Kemaliye, *Turkey* 67 D8
Kemano, *Canada* 100 C3
Kemasik, *Malaysia* 59 K4
Kembolcha, *Ethiopia* 77 E4
Kemer, *Turkey* 66 E4
Kemerovo, *Russia* 44 D9
Kemi, *Finland* 8 D18
Kemi älv = Kemijoki →, *Finland* 8 D18
Kemijärvi, *Finland* 8 C19
Kemijoki →, *Finland* 8 D18
Kemmel, *Belgium* 17 G1
Kemmerer, *U.S.A.* 110 F8
Kemmuna = Comino, *Malta* 37 C1
Kemp, L., *U.S.A.* 109 J5
Kemp Land, *Antarctica* 5 C5
Kempsey, *Australia* 91 E5
Kempt, L., *Canada* 98 C5
Kempten, *Germany* 19 H6
Kemptville, *Canada* 98 C4
Kenadsa, *Algeria* 75 B4
Kendal, *Indonesia* 56 F4
Kendal, *U.K.* 12 C5
Kendall, *Australia* 91 E5
Kendall →, *Australia* 90 A3
Kendallville, *U.S.A.* 104 E3
Kendari, *Indonesia* 57 E6
Kendawangan, *Indonesia* 56 E4
Kende, *Nigeria* 79 C5
Kendenup, *Australia* 89 F2
Kendrapara, *India* 61 J15
Kendrew, *S. Africa* 84 E3
Kendrick, *U.S.A.* 110 C5
Kene Thao, *Laos* 58 D3
Kenedy, *U.S.A.* 109 L6
Kenema, *S. Leone* 78 D2
Keng Kok, *Laos* 58 D5
Keng Tawng, *Burma* 61 J21
Keng Tung, *Burma* 61 J21
Kenge, *Zaïre* 80 E3
Kengeja, *Tanzania* 82 D4
Kenhardt, *S. Africa* 84 D3
Kenitra, *Morocco* 74 B3
Kenli, *China* 51 F10
Kenmare, *Ireland* 15 E2
Kenmare, *U.S.A.* 108 A3
Kenmare →, *Ireland* 15 E2
Kennebec, *U.S.A.* 108 D5
Kennedy, *Zimbabwe* 83 F2
Kennedy Ra., *Australia* 89 D2
Kennedy Taungdeik, *Burma* 61 H18
Kennet →, *U.K.* 13 F7
Kenneth Ra., *Australia* 88 D2
Kennett, *U.S.A.* 109 G9
Kennewick, *U.S.A.* 110 C4
Kénogami, *Canada* 99 C5
Kenogami →, *Canada* 98 B3
Kenora, *Canada* 101 D10
Kenosha, *U.S.A.* 104 D2
Kensington, *Canada* 99 C7
Kensington, *U.S.A.* 108 F5
Kensington Downs, *Australia* 90 C3
Kent, *Ohio, U.S.A.* 106 E3
Kent, *Oreg., U.S.A.* 110 D3
Kent, *Tex., U.S.A.* 109 K2
Kent, *Wash., U.S.A.* 112 C4
Kent □, *U.K.* 13 F8
Kent Group, *Australia* 90 F4
Kent Pen., *Canada* 96 B9
Kentau, *Kazakhstan* 44 E7
Kentland, *U.S.A.* 104 E2
Kenton, *U.S.A.* 104 E4
Kentucky □, *U.S.A.* 104 G3
Kentucky →, *U.S.A.* 104 F3
Kentucky L., *U.S.A.* 105 G2
Kentville, *Canada* 99 C7
Kentwood, *La., U.S.A.* 109 K9
Kentwood, *La., U.S.A.* 109 K9
Kenya ■, *Africa* 82 B4
Kenya, Mt., *Kenya* 82 C4
Keo Neua, Deo, *Vietnam* 58 C5
Keokuk, *U.S.A.* 108 E9
Kep, *Cambodia* 59 G5
Kep, *Vietnam* 58 B6
Kepi, *Indonesia* 57 F9
Kępno, *Poland* 20 D7
Kepsut, *Turkey* 66 D3
Kerala □, *India* 60 P10
Kerama-Rettō, *Japan* 49 L3
Keran, *Pakistan* 63 B5
Kerang, *Australia* 91 F3
Keraudren, C., *Australia* 88 C2
Kerch, *Ukraine* 42 D7
Kerchenskiy Proliv, *Black Sea* 42 D7
Kerchoual, *Mali* 79 B5
Kerempe Burnu, *Turkey* 66 B5
Keren, *Eritrea* 77 D4
Kerewan, *Gambia* 78 C1
Kerguelen, *Ind. Oc.* 3 G13
Keri Kera, *Sudan* 77 E3
Kericho, *Kenya* 82 C4
Kericho □, *Kenya* 82 C4
Kerinci, *Indonesia* 56 E2
Kerkdriel, *Neths.* 16 E6
Kerkenna, Is., *Tunisia* 75 B7
Kerki, *Turkmenistan* 44 F7
Kérkira, *Greece* 37 A3
Kerkrade, *Neths.* 17 G8
Kerma, *Sudan* 76 D3
Kermadec Is., *Pac. Oc.* 92 K10
Kermadec Trench, *Pac. Oc.* 92 L10
Kermān, *Iran* 65 D8
Kerman, *U.S.A.* 112 J6
Kermān □, *Iran* 65 D8
Kermānshāh = Bākhtarān, *Iran* 64 C5
Kerme Körfezi, *Turkey* 66 E2
Kermit, *U.S.A.* 109 K3
Kern →, *U.S.A.* 113 K7
Kerns, *Switz.* 23 C6
Kernville, *U.S.A.* 113 K8
Keroh, *Malaysia* 59 K3
Kerrobert, *Canada* 101 C7
Kerrville, *U.S.A.* 109 K5
Kerry □, *Ireland* 15 D2
Kerry Hd., *Ireland* 15 D2
Kersa, *Ethiopia* 77 F5
Kerteminde, *Denmark* 11 J4
Kertosono, *Indonesia* 57 G15
Kerulen →, *Asia* 54 B6
Kerzaz, *Algeria* 75 C4
Kerzers, *Switz.* 22 C4
Kesagami →, *Canada* 98 B4
Kesagami L., *Canada* 98 B3
Keşan, *Turkey* 66 C2
Kesch, Piz, *Switz.* 23 C9
Kesennuma, *Japan* 48 E10
Keshit, *Iran* 65 D8
Keşiş Dağ, *Turkey* 67 D8
Keski-Suomen lääni □, *Finland* 8 E18
Keskin, *Turkey* 66 D5
Kessel, *Belgium* 17 F5
Kessel, *Neths.* 17 F8
Kessel-Lo, *Belgium* 17 G5
Kestell, *S. Africa* 85 D4
Kestenga, *Russia* 44 C4
Kesteren, *Neths.* 16 E7
Keswick, *U.K.* 12 C4
Keszthely, *Hungary* 21 J7
Ket →, *Russia* 44 D9
Keta, *Ghana* 79 D5
Ketapang, *Indonesia* 56 E4
Ketchikan, *U.S.A.* 96 C6
Ketchum, *U.S.A.* 110 E6
Kete Krachi, *Ghana* 79 D4
Ketef, Khalîg Umm el, *Egypt* 76 C4
Ketelmeer, *Neths.* 16 C7
Keti Bandar, *Pakistan* 62 G2
Ketri, *India* 62 E6
Kętrzyn, *Poland* 20 A11
Kettering, *U.K.* 13 E7
Kettle →, *Canada* 101 B11
Kettle Falls, *U.S.A.* 110 B4
Kettleman City, *U.S.A.* 112 J7
Kevin, *U.S.A.* 110 B8
Kewanee, *U.S.A.* 108 E10
Kewaunee, *U.S.A.* 104 C2
Keweenaw B., *U.S.A.* 104 B1
Keweenaw Pen., *U.S.A.* 104 B2
Keweenaw Pt., *U.S.A.* 104 B2
Key Harbour, *Canada* 98 C3
Key West, *U.S.A.* 103 F10
Keyser, *U.S.A.* 104 F6
Keystone, *U.S.A.* 108 D3
Kezhma, *Russia* 45 D11
Kežmarok, *Slovak Rep.* 20 F10
Khabarovo, *Russia* 44 C7
Khabarovsk, *Russia* 45 E14
Khabr, *Iran* 65 D8
Khābūr →, *Syria* 64 C4
Khachmas, *Azerbaijan* 43 F13
Khachrod, *India* 62 H6
Khadari, W. el →, *Sudan* 77 E2
Khadro, *Pakistan* 62 F3
Khadyzhensk, *Russia* 43 D8
Khadzhilyangar, *India* 63 B8
Khagaria, *India* 63 G12
Khaipur, *Bahawalpur, Pakistan* 62 E5
Khaipur, *Hyderabad, Pakistan* 62 F3
Khair, *India* 62 F7
Khairabad, *India* 63 F9
Khairagarh, *India* 63 J9
Khairpur, *Pakistan* 60 F6
Khakhea, *Botswana* 84 C3
Khalafābād, *Iran* 65 D6
Khalfallah, *Algeria* 75 B5
Khalilabad, *India* 63 F10
Khalīlī, *Iran* 65 E7
Khalkhāl, *Iran* 65 B6
Khálki, *Greece* 39 K5
Khalkís, *Greece* 39 L6
Khalmer-Sede = Tazovskiy, *Russia* 44 C8
Khalmer Yu, *Russia* 44 C7
Khalturin, *Russia* 41 B16
Khalūf, *Oman* 68 C6
Kham Keut, *Laos* 58 C5
Khamas Country, *Botswana* 84 C4
Khambat, G. of, *India* 62 J5
Khambhaliya, *India* 62 H3
Khambhat, *India* 62 H5
Khamilonísion, *Greece* 39 P9
Khamīr, *Iran* 65 E7
Khamir, *Yemen* 68 D3
Khamsa, *Egypt* 69 E1
Khān Abū Shāmat, *Syria* 69 B5
Khān Azād, *Iraq* 64 C5
Khān Mujiddah, *Iraq* 64 C4
Khān Shaykhūn, *Syria* 64 C3
Khān Yūnis, *Egypt* 69 D3
Khānaqīn, *Iraq* 64 C5
Khānbāghī, *Iran* 65 B7
Khandrá, *Greece* 39 P9
Khandwa, *India* 60 J10
Khandyga, *Russia* 45 C14
Khāneh, *Iran* 64 B5
Khanewal, *Pakistan* 62 D4
Khanh Duong, *Vietnam* 58 F7
Khaniá, *Greece* 37 D6
Khaniá □, *Greece* 37 D6
Khaníon, Kólpos, *Greece* 37 D5
Khanka, Ozero, *Asia* 45 E14
Khankendy, *Azerbaijan* 67 D12
Khanna, *India* 62 D7
Khanpur, *Pakistan* 62 E4
Khanty-Mansiysk, *Russia* 44 C7
Khapalu, *Pakistan* 63 B7
Khapcheranga, *Russia* 45 E12
Kharagpur, *India* 63 H12
Khárakas, *Greece* 37 D7
Kharan Kalat, *Pakistan* 60 E4
Kharānaq, *Iran* 65 C7
Kharda, *India* 60 K9
Khardung La, *India* 63 B7
Khârga, El Wâhât el, *Egypt* 76 B3
Khargon, *India* 60 J9
Kharit, Wadi el →, *Egypt* 76 C3
Khārk, Jazireh, *Iran* 65 D6
Kharkiv = Kharkov, *Ukraine* 42 B7
Kharkov, *Ukraine* 42 B7
Kharmanli, *Bulgaria* 39 H8
Kharovsk, *Russia* 41 B12
Khartoum = El Khartûm, *Sudan* 77 D3
Khasan, *Russia* 48 C5
Khasavyurt, *Russia* 43 E12
Khāsh, *Iran* 60 E2
Khashm el Girba, *Sudan* 77 E4
Khashuri, *Georgia* 43 F10
Khaskovo, *Bulgaria* 39 H8
Khatanga, *Russia* 45 B11
Khatanga →, *Russia* 45 B11
Khatauli, *India* 62 E7
Khātūnābād, *Iran* 65 C6
Khatyrka, *Russia* 45 C18
Khaybar, Harrat, *Si. Arabia* 64 E4
Khāzimiyah, *Iraq* 64 C4
Khazzân Jabal el Awliyâ, *Sudan* 77 D3
Khe Bo, *Vietnam* 58 C5
Khe Long, *Vietnam* 58 B5
Khed Brahma, *India* 60 G8
Khekra, *India* 62 E7
Khemarak Phouminville, *Cambodia* 59 G4
Khemelnik, *Ukraine* 42 B2
Khemis Miliana, *Algeria* 75 A5
Khemissèt, *Morocco* 74 B3
Khemmarat, *Thailand* 58 D5
Khenāmān, *Iran* 65 D8
Khenchela, *Algeria* 75 A6
Khenifra, *Morocco* 74 B3
Kherrata, *Algeria* 75 A6
Kherson, *Ukraine* 42 C5
Khersónisos Akrotíri, *Greece* 37 D6
Kheta →, *Russia* 45 B11
Khilok, *Russia* 45 D12
Khimki, *Russia* 41 D10
Khíos, *Greece* 39 L9
Khirbat Qanāfār, *Lebanon* 69 B4
Khiuma = Hiiumaa, *Estonia* 40 B3
Khiva, *Uzbekistan* 44 E7
Khīyāv, *Iran* 64 B5
Khlong Khlung, *Thailand* 58 D2
Khmelnitskiy, *Ukraine* 40 G5
Khmelnytskyy = Khmelnitskiy, *Ukraine* 40 G5
Khmer Rep. = Cambodia ■, *Asia* 58 F5
Khoai, Hon, *Vietnam* 59 H5
Khodzent, *Tajikistan* 44 E7
Khojak P., *Afghan.* 60 D5
Khok Kloi, *Thailand* 59 H2
Khok Pho, *Thailand* 59 J3
Khokholskiy, *Russia* 41 F11
Kholm, *Russia* 40 C7
Kholmsk, *Russia* 45 E15
Khomas Hochland, *Namibia* 84 C2
Khomayn, *Iran* 65 C6
Khon Kaen, *Thailand* 58 D4
Khong, *Laos* 58 E5
Khong Sedone, *Laos* 58 E5
Khonu, *Russia* 45 C15
Khoper →, *Russia* 41 G13
Khor el 'Atash, *Sudan* 77 E3
Khóra, *Greece* 39 M4
Khóra Sfakíon, *Greece* 37 D6
Khorāsān □, *Iran* 65 C8
Khorat = Nakhon Ratchasima, *Thailand* 58 E4
Khorat, Cao Nguyen, *Thailand* 58 E4
Khorb el Ethel, *Algeria* 74 C3
Khorixas, *Namibia* 84 C1
Khorog, *Tajikistan* 44 F8
Khorol, *Ukraine* 42 B5
Khorramābād, *Khorāsān, Iran* 65 C8
Khorramābād, *Lorestān, Iran* 65 C6
Khorrāmshahr, *Iran* 65 D6
Khosravī, *Iran* 65 D6
Khosrowābād, *Khuzestān, Iran* 65 D6
Khosrowābād, *Kordestān, Iran* 64 C5
Khosūyeh, *Iran* 65 D7
Khotin, *Ukraine* 42 B2
Khouribga, *Morocco* 74 B3
Khowai, *Bangla.* 61 G17
Khoyniki, *Belorussia* 40 F6
Khrami →, *Azerbaijan* 43 F11
Khrenovoye, *Russia* 41 F12
Khristianá, *Greece* 39 N8
Khrysokhou B., *Cyprus* 37 D11
Khu Khan, *Thailand* 58 E5
Khuff, *Si. Arabia* 64 E5
Khūgīānī, *Afghan.* 62 D1
Khulna, *Bangla.* 61 H16
Khulna □, *Bangla.* 61 H16
Khulo, *Georgia* 43 F10
Khumago, *Botswana* 84 C3
Khūnsorkh, *Iran* 65 E8
Khunzakh, *Russia* 43 E12
Khūr, *Iran* 65 C8
Khurai, *India* 62 G8
Khurayş, *Si. Arabia* 65 E6
Khūrīyā Mūrīyā, Jazā 'ir, *Oman* 68 D6
Khurja, *India* 62 E7
Khūsf, *Iran* 65 C8
Khush, *Afghan.* 60 C3
Khushab, *Pakistan* 62 C5
Khuzdar, *Pakistan* 62 F2
Khūzestān □, *Iran* 65 D6
Khvājeh, *Iran* 64 B5
Khvalynsk, *Russia* 41 E16
Khvānsār, *Iran* 65 D7
Khvatovka, *Russia* 41 E15
Khvor, *Iran* 65 C7
Khvorgū, *Iran* 65 E8
Khvormūj, *Iran* 65 D6
Khvoy, *Iran* 64 B5
Khvoynaya, *Russia* 40 B9
Khyber Pass, *Afghan.* 62 B4
Kiabukwa, *Zaïre* 83 D1
Kiama, *Australia* 91 E5
Kiamba, *Phil.* 55 H6
Kiambi, *Zaïre* 82 D2
Kiambu, *Kenya* 82 C4
Kiangsi = Jiangxi □, *China* 53 D10
Kiangsu = Jiangsu □, *China* 51 H10
Kibæk, *Denmark* 11 H2
Kibanga Port, *Uganda* 82 B3
Kibangou, *Congo* 80 E2
Kibara, *Tanzania* 82 C3
Kibare, Mts., *Zaïre* 82 D2
Kibombo, *Zaïre* 82 C2
Kibondo, *Tanzania* 82 C3
Kibondo □, *Tanzania* 82 C3
Kibumbu, *Burundi* 82 C2
Kibungu, *Rwanda* 82 C3
Kibuye, *Burundi* 82 C2
Kibuye, *Rwanda* 82 C2
Kibwesa, *Tanzania* 82 D2
Kibwezi, *Kenya* 82 C4
Kichiga, *Russia* 45 D17
Kicking Horse Pass, *Canada* 100 C5
Kidal, *Mali* 79 B5
Kidderminster, *U.K.* 13 E5
Kidete, *Tanzania* 82 D4
Kidira, *Senegal* 78 C2
Kidnappers, C., *N.Z.* 87 H6
Kidston, *Australia* 90 B3
Kidugallo, *Tanzania* 82 D4
Kiel, *Germany* 18 A6
Kiel Kanal = Nord-Ostsee Kanal, *Germany* 18 A5
Kielce, *Poland* 20 E10
Kieldrecht, *Belgium* 17 F4
Kieler Bucht, *Germany* 18 A6
Kien Binh, *Vietnam* 59 H5
Kien Tan, *Vietnam* 59 G5
Kienge, *Zaïre* 83 E2
Kiessé, *Niger* 79 C5
Kiev = Kiyev, *Ukraine* 40 F7
Kiffa, *Mauritania* 78 B2
Kifisiá, *Greece* 39 L6
Kifissós →, *Greece* 39 L6
Kifrī, *Iraq* 64 C5
Kigali, *Rwanda* 82 C3
Kigarama, *Tanzania* 82 C3
Kigoma □, *Tanzania* 82 D2
Kigoma-Ujiji, *Tanzania* 82 C2
Kigomasha, Ras, *Tanzania* 82 C4
Kihee, *Australia* 91 D3
Kii-Sanchi, *Japan* 49 G7
Kii-Suidō, *Japan* 49 H7
Kikaiga-Shima, *Japan* 49 K4
Kikinda, *Serbia* 21 K10
Kikládhes, *Greece* 39 M7
Kikwit, *Zaïre* 80 E3
Kílalki, *Greece* 39 N10
Kilauea Crater, *U.S.A.* 102 J17
Kilchberg, *Switz.* 23 B7
Kilcoy, *Australia* 91 D5
Kildare, *Ireland* 15 C5
Kildare □, *Ireland* 15 C5
Kilgore, *U.S.A.* 109 J7
Kilifi, *Kenya* 82 C4
Kilifi □, *Kenya* 82 C4
Kilimanjaro, *Tanzania* 82 C4
Kilimanjaro □, *Tanzania* 82 C4
Kilindini, *Kenya* 82 C4
Kilis, *Turkey* 66 E7
Kiliya, *Ukraine* 42 D3
Kilju, *N. Korea* 51 D15
Kilkee, *Ireland* 15 D2
Kilkenny, *Ireland* 15 D4
Kilkenny □, *Ireland* 15 D4
Kilkieran B., *Ireland* 15 C2
Kilkís, *Greece* 39 J5
Killala, *Ireland* 15 B2
Killala B., *Ireland* 15 B2
Killaloe, *Ireland* 15 D3
Killaloe Sta., *Canada* 106 A7
Killam, *Canada* 100 C6
Killarney, *Australia* 91 D5
Killarney, *Canada* 98 C3
Killarney, *Ireland* 15 D2
Killarney, Lakes of, *Ireland* 15 E2
Killary Harbour, *Ireland* 15 C2
Killdeer, *Canada* 101 D7
Killdeer, *U.S.A.* 108 B3
Killeen, *U.S.A.* 109 K6
Killiecrankie, Pass of, *U.K.* 14 E5
Killin, *U.K.* 14 E4
Killíni, *Ilía, Greece* 39 M4
Killíni, *Korinthía, Greece* 39 M5
Killybegs, *Ireland* 15 B3
Kilmarnock, *U.K.* 14 F4
Kilmez, *Russia* 41 C17
Kilmez →, *Russia* 41 C17
Kilmore, *Australia* 91 F3
Kilondo, *Tanzania* 83 D3
Kilosa, *Tanzania* 82 D4
Kilosa □, *Tanzania* 82 D4
Kilrush, *Ireland* 15 D2
Kilwa □, *Tanzania* 83 D4
Kilwa Kisiwani, *Tanzania* 83 D4
Kilwa Kivinje, *Tanzania* 83 D4
Kilwa Masoko, *Tanzania* 83 D4
Kim, *U.S.A.* 109 G3
Kimaam, *Indonesia* 57 F9

Kimamba, *Tanzania* 82 D4
Kimba, *Australia* 91 E2
Kimball, *Nebr., U.S.A.* 108 E3
Kimball, *S. Dak., U.S.A.* 108 D5
Kimberley, *Canada* 100 D5
Kimberley, *S. Africa* 84 D3
Kimberley Downs, *Australia* 88 C3
Kimberly, *U.S.A.* 110 E6
Kimchaek, *N. Korea* 51 D15
Kimchŏn, *S. Korea* 51 F15
Kími, *Greece* 39 L7
Kimje, *S. Korea* 51 G14
Kímolos, *Greece* 39 N7
Kimovsk, *Russia* 41 D11
Kimparana, *Mali* 78 C4
Kimry, *Russia* 41 C10
Kimsquit, *Canada* 100 C3
Kimstad, *Sweden* 11 F9
Kinabalu, Gunong, *Malaysia* 56 C5
Kínaros, *Greece* 39 N9
Kinaskan L., *Canada* 100 B2
Kinbasket L., *Canada* 100 C5
Kincaid, *Canada* 101 D7
Kincardine, *Canada* 98 D3
Kinda, *Zaïre* 83 D2
Kinder Scout, *U.K.* 12 D6
Kindersley, *Canada* 101 C7
Kindia, *Guinea* 78 C2
Kindu, *Zaïre* 82 C2
Kinel, *Russia* 41 E17
Kineshma, *Russia* 41 C13
Kinesi, *Tanzania* 82 C3
King, L., *Australia* 89 F2
King, Mt., *Australia* 90 D4
King City, *U.S.A.* 111 H3
King Cr. →, *Australia* 90 C2
King Edward →, *Australia* 88 B4
King Frederick VI Land = Kong Frederik VI.s Kyst, *Greenland* 4 C5
King George B., *Falk. Is.* 128 D4
King George I., *Antarctica* 5 C18
King George Is., *Canada* 97 C11
King I. = Kadan Kyun, *Burma* 56 B1
King I., *Australia* 90 F3
King I., *Canada* 100 C3
King Leopold Ras., *Australia* 88 C4
King Sd., *Australia* 88 C3
King William I., *Canada* 96 B10
King William's Town, *S. Africa* 84 E4
Kingaroy, *Australia* 91 D5
Kingfisher, *U.S.A.* 109 H6
Kingirbān, *Iraq* 64 C5
Kingisepp = Kuressaare, *Estonia* 40 B3
Kingisepp, *Russia* 40 B6
Kingman, *Ariz., U.S.A.* 113 K12
Kingman, *Kans., U.S.A.* 109 G5
Kingoonya, *Australia* 91 E2
Kings →, *U.S.A.* 111 H4
Kings Canyon National Park, *U.S.A.* 111 H4
King's Lynn, *U.K.* 12 E8
Kings Mountain, *U.S.A.* 105 H5
King's Peak, *U.S.A.* 110 F8
Kingsbridge, *U.K.* 13 G4
Kingsburg, *U.S.A.* 111 H4
Kingscote, *Australia* 91 F2
Kingscourt, *Ireland* 15 C5
Kingsley, *U.S.A.* 108 D7
Kingsport, *U.S.A.* 105 G4
Kingston, *Canada* 98 D4
Kingston, *Jamaica* 116 C4
Kingston, *N.Z.* 87 L2
Kingston, *N.Y., U.S.A.* 107 E10
Kingston, *Pa., U.S.A.* 107 E9
Kingston, *R.I., U.S.A.* 107 E13
Kingston Pk., *U.S.A.* 113 K11
Kingston South East, *Australia* 91 F2
Kingston upon Hull, *U.K.* 12 D7
Kingston-upon-Thames, *U.K.* 13 F7
Kingstown, *St. Vincent* 117 D7
Kingstree, *U.S.A.* 105 J6
Kingsville, *Canada* 98 D3
Kingsville, *U.S.A.* 109 M6
Kingussie, *U.K.* 14 D4
Kinistino, *Canada* 101 C7
Kinkala, *Congo* 80 E2
Kinki □, *Japan* 49 H8
Kinleith, *N.Z.* 87 H5
Kinmount, *Canada* 106 B6
Kinna, *Sweden* 11 G6
Kinnaird, *Canada* 100 D5
Kinnairds Hd., *U.K.* 14 D7
Kinnared, *Sweden* 11 G7
Kinnarodden, *Norway* 6 A11
Kino, *Mexico* 114 B2
Kinoje →, *Canada* 98 B3
Kinomoto, *Japan* 49 G8
Kinoni, *Uganda* 82 C3
Kinrooi, *Belgium* 17 F7
Kinross, *U.K.* 14 E5
Kinsale, *Ireland* 15 E3
Kinsale, Old Hd. of, *Ireland* 15 E3
Kinsha = Chang Jiang →, *China* 53 B13
Kinshasa, *Zaïre* 80 E3
Kinsley, *U.S.A.* 109 G5
Kinston, *U.S.A.* 105 H7
Kintampo, *Ghana* 79 D4
Kintap, *Indonesia* 56 E5
Kintore Ra., *Australia* 88 D4
Kintyre, *U.K.* 14 F3
Kintyre, Mull of, *U.K.* 14 F3
Kinushseo →, *Canada* 98 A3
Kinuso, *Canada* 100 B5
Kinyangiri, *Tanzania* 82 C3
Kinzig →, *Germany* 19 G3
Kinzua, *U.S.A.* 106 E6
Kinzua Dam, *U.S.A.* 106 E5
Kiosk, *Canada* 98 C4
Kiowa, *Kans., U.S.A.* 109 G5
Kiowa, *Okla., U.S.A.* 109 H7
Kipahigan L., *Canada* 101 B8
Kipanga, *Tanzania* 82 D4
Kiparissía, *Greece* 39 M4
Kiparissiakós Kólpos, *Greece* 39 M4
Kipembawe, *Tanzania* 82 D3
Kipengere Ra., *Tanzania* 83 D3
Kipili, *Tanzania* 82 D3
Kipini, *Kenya* 82 C5
Kipling, *Canada* 101 C8
Kippure, *Ireland* 15 C5
Kipushi, *Zaïre* 83 E2
Kiratpur, *India* 62 E8
Kirchberg, *Switz.* 22 B5
Kirchhain, *Germany* 18 E4
Kirchheim, *Germany* 19 G5
Kirchheim-Bolanden, *Germany* 19 F4
Kirensk, *Russia* 45 D11
Kirgella Rocks, *Australia* 89 F3
Kirghizia ■, *Asia* 44 E8
Kirghizstan = Kirghizia ■, *Asia* 44 E8
Kirgizia = Kirghizia ■, *Asia* 44 E8
Kiri, *Zaïre* 80 E3
Kiribati ■, *Pac. Oc.* 92 H10
Kırıkhan, *Turkey* 66 E7
Kırıkkale, *Turkey* 66 D5
Kirillov, *Russia* 41 B11
Kirin = Jilin, *China* 51 C14
Kirin = Jilin □, *China* 51 C13
Kirishi, *Russia* 40 B7
Kiritimati, *Kiribati* 93 G12
Kırka, *Turkey* 66 D4
Kirkcaldy, *U.K.* 14 E5
Kirkcudbright, *U.K.* 14 G4
Kirkee, *India* 60 K8
Kirkenær, *Norway* 10 D6
Kirkenes, *Norway* 8 B21
Kirkintilloch, *U.K.* 14 F4
Kirkjubæjarklaustur, *Iceland* 8 E4
Kirkland, *U.S.A.* 111 J7
Kirkland Lake, *Canada* 98 C3
Kırklareli, *Turkey* 39 H10
Kırklareli □, *Turkey* 66 C2
Kirksville, *U.S.A.* 108 E8
Kirkūk, *Iraq* 64 C5
Kirkwall, *U.K.* 14 C6
Kirkwood, *S. Africa* 84 E4
Kirn, *Germany* 19 F3
Kirov = Vyatka, *Russia* 41 B16
Kirov, *Russia* 40 D9
Kirovabad = Gyandzha, *Azerbaijan* 43 F12
Kirovakan = Karaklis, *Armenia* 43 F11
Kirovo-Chepetsk, *Russia* 41 B17
Kirovograd, *Ukraine* 42 B5
Kirovohrad = Kirovograd, *Ukraine* 42 B5
Kirovsk, *Russia* 44 C4
Kirovsk, *Turkmenistan* 44 F7
Kirovsk, *Ukraine* 43 B8
Kirovskiy, *Russia* 43 D13
Kirovskiy, *Russia* 45 D16
Kirovskiy, *Russia* 48 B6
Kirriemuir, *U.K.* 14 E6
Kirsanov, *Russia* 41 E13
Kırşehir, *Turkey* 66 D6
Kırşehir □, *Turkey* 66 D6
Kirstonia, *S. Africa* 84 D3
Kirtachi, *Niger* 79 C5
Kirthar Range, *Pakistan* 62 F2
Kiruna, *Sweden* 8 C16
Kirundu, *Zaïre* 82 C2
Kirup, *Australia* 89 F2
Kirya, *Russia* 41 D15
Kiryū, *Japan* 49 F9
Kisaga, *Tanzania* 82 C3
Kisalaya, *Nic.* 116 D3
Kisámou, Kólpos, *Greece* 37 D5
Kisanga, *Zaïre* 82 B2
Kisangani, *Zaïre* 82 B2
Kisar, *Indonesia* 57 F7
Kisaran, *Indonesia* 56 D1
Kisarawe, *Tanzania* 82 D4
Kisarawe □, *Tanzania* 82 D4
Kisarazu, *Japan* 49 G9
Kisbér, *Hungary* 21 H8
Kiselevsk, *Russia* 44 D9
Kishanganga →, *Pakistan* 63 B5
Kishanganj, *India* 63 F13
Kishangarh, *India* 62 F4
Kishi, *Nigeria* 79 D5
Kishinev, *Moldavia* 42 C3
Kishiwada, *Japan* 49 G7
Kishtwar, *India* 63 C6
Kisii, *Kenya* 82 C3
Kisii □, *Kenya* 82 C3
Kisiju, *Tanzania* 82 D4
Kısır Dağ, *Turkey* 43 F10
Kisizi, *Uganda* 82 C2
Kiska I., *U.S.A.* 96 C1
Kiskatinaw →, *Canada* 100 B4
Kiskittogisu L., *Canada* 101 C9
Kiskörös, *Hungary* 21 J9
Kiskundorozsma, *Hungary* 21 J10
Kiskunfélegyháza, *Hungary* 21 J9
Kiskunhalas, *Hungary* 21 J9
Kiskunmajsa, *Hungary* 21 J9
Kislovodsk, *Russia* 43 E10
Kiso-Gawa →, *Japan* 49 G8
Kiso-Sammyaku, *Japan* 49 G8
Kisofukushima, *Japan* 49 G8
Kisoro, *Uganda* 82 C2
Kispest, *Hungary* 21 H9
Kissidougou, *Guinea* 78 D2
Kissimmee, *U.S.A.* 105 L5
Kissimmee →, *U.S.A.* 105 M5
Kississing L., *Canada* 101 B8
Kissónerga, *Cyprus* 37 E11
Kistanje, *Croatia* 33 E12
Kisújszállás, *Hungary* 21 H10
Kisumu, *Kenya* 82 C3
Kisvárda, *Hungary* 21 G12
Kiswani, *Tanzania* 82 C4
Kiswere, *Tanzania* 83 D4
Kit Carson, *U.S.A.* 108 F3
Kita, *Mali* 78 C3
Kitab, *Uzbekistan* 44 F7
Kitaibaraki, *Japan* 49 F10
Kitakami, *Japan* 48 E10
Kitakami-Gawa →, *Japan* 48 E10
Kitakami-Sammyaku, *Japan* 48 E10
Kitakata, *Japan* 48 F9
Kitakyūshū, *Japan* 49 H5
Kitale, *Kenya* 82 B4
Kitami, *Japan* 48 C11
Kitami-Sammyaku, *Japan* 48 B11
Kitangiri, L., *Tanzania* 82 C3
Kitaya, *Tanzania* 83 E5
Kitchener, *Australia* 89 F3
Kitchener, *Canada* 98 D3
Kitega = Gitega, *Burundi* 82 C2
Kitengo, *Zaïre* 82 D1
Kiteto □, *Tanzania* 82 C4
Kitgum, *Uganda* 82 B3
Kíthira, *Greece* 39 N7
Kíthnos, *Greece* 39 M7
Kiti, *Cyprus* 37 E12
Kiti, C., *Cyprus* 37 E12
Kitikmeot □, *Canada* 96 A9
Kitimat, *Canada* 100 C3
Kitinen →, *Finland* 8 C19
Kitiyab, *Sudan* 77 D3
Kítros, *Greece* 39 J5
Kitsuki, *Japan* 49 H5
Kittakittaooloo, L., *Australia* 91 D2
Kittanning, *U.S.A.* 106 F5
Kittatinny Mts., *U.S.A.* 107 E10
Kittery, *U.S.A.* 105 D10
Kitui, *Kenya* 82 C4
Kitui □, *Kenya* 82 C4
Kitwe, *Zambia* 83 E2
Kitzbühel, *Austria* 19 H8
Kitzingen, *Germany* 19 F6
Kivalo, *Finland* 8 C19
Kivarli, *India* 62 G5
Kividhes, *Cyprus* 37 E11
Kivu □, *Zaïre* 82 C2
Kivu, L., *Zaïre* 82 C2
Kiyev, *Ukraine* 40 F7
Kiyevskoye Vdkhr., *Ukraine* 40 F7
Kiziguru, *Rwanda* 82 C3
Kızıl Irmak →, *Turkey* 42 F6
Kizil Jilga, *India* 63 B8
Kizil Yurt, *Russia* 43 E12
Kızılcahamam, *Turkey* 42 F5
Kızılhisar, *Turkey* 66 E3
Kızılırmak, *Turkey* 66 C5
Kızıltepe, *Turkey* 67 E9
Kizimkazi, *Tanzania* 82 D4
Kizlyar, *Russia* 43 E12
Kizyl-Arvat, *Turkmenistan* 44 F6
Kjellerup, *Denmark* 11 H3
Kladanj, *Bos.-H.* 21 L8
Kladno, *Czech.* 20 E4
Kladovo, *Serbia, Yug.* 21 L12
Klaeng, *Thailand* 58 F3
Klagenfurt, *Austria* 21 J4
Klagshamn, *Sweden* 11 J6
Klagstorp, *Sweden* 11 J7
Klaipėda, *Lithuania* 40 D2
Klamath →, *U.S.A.* 110 F1
Klamath Falls, *U.S.A.* 110 E3
Klamath Mts., *U.S.A.* 110 F2
Klanjec, *Croatia* 33 B12
Klappan →, *Canada* 100 B3
Klarälven →, *Sweden* 9 G12
Klaten, *Indonesia* 57 G14
Klatovy, *Czech.* 20 F3
Klawer, *S. Africa* 84 E2
Klawock, *U.S.A.* 100 B2
Klazienaveen, *Neths.* 16 C10
Kleczew, *Poland* 20 C8
Kleena Kleene, *Canada* 100 C4
Klein, *U.S.A.* 110 C9
Klein-Karas, *Namibia* 84 D2
Kleine Gette →, *Belgium* 17 G6
Kleine Nete →, *Belgium* 17 F5
Klekovača, *Bos.-H.* 33 D13
Klenovec, *Macedonia* 39 H3
Klenovec, *Slovakia* 20 G9
Klerksdorp, *S. Africa* 84 D4
Kletnya, *Russia* 40 E8
Kletsk, *Belorussia* 40 E5
Kletskiy, *Russia* 43 B10
Kleve, *Germany* 18 D2
Klickitat, *U.S.A.* 110 D3
Klickitat →, *U.S.A.* 112 E5
Klidhes, *Cyprus* 37 D13
Klimovichi, *Belorussia* 40 E8
Klin, *Russia* 41 C10
Klinaklini →, *Canada* 100 C3
Klintsey, *Russia* 40 E8
Klipdale, *S. Africa* 84 E2
Klipplaat, *S. Africa* 84 E3
Klitmøller, *Denmark* 11 G2
Kljajićevo, *Serbia, Yug.* 21 K9
Ključ, *Bos.-H.* 33 D13
Kłobuck, *Poland* 20 E8
Kłodzko, *Poland* 20 E6
Kloetinge, *Neths.* 17 F3
Klondike, *Canada* 96 B6
Kloosterzande, *Neths.* 17 F4
Klosterneuburg, *Austria* 21 G6
Klosters, *Switz.* 23 C9
Kloten, *Switz.* 23 B7
Klötze, *Germany* 18 C7
Klouto, *Togo* 79 D5
Kluane L., *Canada* 96 B6
Kluczbork, *Poland* 20 E8
Klundert, *Neths.* 17 E5
Klyuchevskaya, Gora, *Russia* 45 D17
Knaresborough, *U.K.* 12 C6
Knee L., *Man., Canada* 101 B10
Knee L., *Sask., Canada* 101 B7
Kneïss, Is., *Tunisia* 75 B7
Knesselare, *Belgium* 17 F2
Knezha, *Bulgaria* 38 F7
Knić, *Serbia, Yug.* 21 M10
Knight Inlet, *Canada* 100 C3
Knighton, *U.K.* 13 E4
Knights Ferry, *U.S.A.* 112 H6
Knights Landing, *U.S.A.* 112 G5
Knin, *Croatia* 33 D13
Knittelfeld, *Austria* 21 H4
Knjaževac, *Serbia, Yug.* 21 M12
Knob, C., *Australia* 89 F2
Knockmealdown Mts., *Ireland* 15 D4
Knokke, *Belgium* 17 F2
Knossós, *Greece* 37 D7
Knox, *U.S.A.* 104 E2
Knox, C., *Canada* 100 C2
Knox City, *U.S.A.* 109 J5
Knox Coast, *Antarctica* 5 C8
Knoxville, *Iowa, U.S.A.* 108 E8
Knoxville, *Tenn., U.S.A.* 105 H4
Knutshø, *Norway* 10 B3
Knysna, *S. Africa* 84 E3
Knyszyn, *Poland* 20 B12
Ko Kha, *Thailand* 58 C2
Ko Tao, *Thailand* 59 G2
Koartac, *Canada* 97 B13
Koba, *Aru, Indonesia* 57 F8
Koba, *Bangka, Indonesia* 56 E3
Kobarid, *Slovenia* 33 B10
Kobayashi, *Japan* 49 J5
Kobdo = Hovd, *Mongolia* 54 B4
Kōbe, *Japan* 49 G7
Kobelyaki, *Ukraine* 42 B6
København, *Denmark* 11 J6
Kōbi-Sho, *Japan* 49 M1
Koblenz, *Germany* 19 E3
Koblenz, *Switz.* 22 A6
Kobo, *Ethiopia* 77 E4
Kobrin, *Belorussia* 40 E4
Kobroor, Kepulauan, *Indonesia* 57 F8
Kobuleti, *Georgia* 43 F9
Kobyłka, *Poland* 20 C11
Kobylkino, *Russia* 41 D13
Kobylnik, *Belorussia* 40 D5
Kocaeli = İzmit, *Turkey* 66 C3
Kocaeli □, *Turkey* 66 C3
Kočani, *Macedonia* 39 H5
Koceljevo, *Serbia, Yug.* 21 L9
Kočevje, *Slovenia* 33 C11
Koch Bihar, *India* 61 F16
Kochang, *S. Korea* 51 G14
Kochas, *India* 63 G10
Kocher →, *Germany* 19 F5
Kocheya, *Russia* 45 D13
Kōchi, *Japan* 49 H6
Kōchi □, *Japan* 49 H6
Kochiu = Gejiu, *China* 52 F4
Kodiak, *U.S.A.* 96 C4
Kodiak I., *U.S.A.* 96 C4
Kodinar, *India* 62 J4
Kodori →, *Georgia* 43 E9
Koekelare, *Belgium* 17 F1
Koersel, *Belgium* 17 F6
Koes, *Namibia* 84 D2
Koffiefontein, *S. Africa* 84 D4
Kofiau, *Indonesia* 57 E7
Koforidua, *Ghana* 79 D4
Kōfu, *Japan* 49 G9
Koga, *Japan* 49 F9
Kogaluk →, *Canada* 99 A7
Kogan, *Australia* 91 D5
Kogi □, *Nigeria* 79 D6
Kogin Baba, *Nigeria* 79 D7
Koh-i-Bābā, *Afghan.* 60 B5
Koh-i-Khurd, *Afghan.* 62 C1
Kohat, *Pakistan* 62 C4
Kohima, *India* 61 G19
Kohkīlūyeh va Būyer Aḥmadi □, *Iran* 65 D6
Kohler Ra., *Antarctica* 5 D15
Kohtla-Järve, *Estonia* 40 B5
Koin-dong, *N. Korea* 51 D14
Kojŏ, *N. Korea* 51 E14
Kojonup, *Australia* 89 F2
Kojūr, *Iran* 65 B6
Koka, *Sudan* 76 C3
Kokand, *Uzbekistan* 44 E8
Kokanee Glacier Prov. Park, *Canada* 100 D5
Kokas, *Indonesia* 57 E8
Kokchetav, *Kazakhstan* 44 D7
Kokemäenjoki, *Finland* 9 F16
Kokerite, *Guyana* 121 B6
Kokhma, *Russia* 41 C12
Kokkola, *Finland* 8 E17
Koko, *Nigeria* 79 C5
Koko Kyunzu, *Burma* 61 M18
Kokolopozo, *Ivory C.* 78 D3
Kokomo, *U.S.A.* 104 E2
Kokonau, *Indonesia* 57 E9
Kokoro, *Niger* 79 C5
Koksan, *N. Korea* 51 E14
Koksoak →, *Canada* 97 C13
Kokstad, *S. Africa* 85 E4
Kokubu, *Japan* 49 J5
Kokuora, *Russia* 45 B15
Kola, *Indonesia* 57 F8
Kola, *Russia* 44 C4
Kola Pen. = Kolskiy Poluostrov, *Russia* 44 C4
Kolahoi, *India* 63 B6
Kolahun, *Liberia* 78 D2
Kolaka, *Indonesia* 57 E6
Kolar, *India* 60 N11
Kolar Gold Fields, *India* 60 N11
Kolari, *Finland* 8 C17
Kolayat, *India* 60 F8
Kolby Kås, *Denmark* 11 J4
Kolchugino = Leninsk-Kuznetskiy, *Russia* 44 D9
Kolchugino, *Russia* 41 C11
Kolda, *Senegal* 78 C2
Kolding, *Denmark* 11 J3
Kole, *Zaïre* 80 E4
Koléa, *Algeria* 75 A5
Kolepom = Yos Sudarso, Pulau, *Indonesia* 57 F9
Kolguyev, Ostrov, *Russia* 44 C5
Kolham, *Neths.* 16 B9
Kolhapur, *India* 60 L9
Kolia, *Ivory C.* 78 D3
Kolín, *Czech.* 20 E5
Kolind, *Denmark* 11 H4
Kölleda, *Germany* 18 D7
Kollum, *Neths.* 16 B8
Kolmanskop, *Namibia* 84 D2
Köln, *Germany* 18 E2
Koło, *Poland* 20 C8
Kołobrzeg, *Poland* 20 A5
Kologriv, *Russia* 41 B14
Kolokani, *Mali* 78 C3
Kolomna, *Russia* 41 D11
Kolomyya, *Ukraine* 42 B1
Kolondiéba, *Mali* 78 C3
Kolonodale, *Indonesia* 57 E6
Kolosib, *India* 61 G18
Kolpashevo, *Russia* 44 D9
Kolpino, *Russia* 40 B7
Kolpny, *Russia* 41 E10
Kolskiy Poluostrov, *Russia* 44 C4
Kolubara →, *Serbia, Yug.* 21 L10
Koluszki, *Poland* 20 D9
Kolwezi, *Zaïre* 83 E2
Kolyberovo, *Russia* 41 D11
Kolyma →, *Russia* 45 C17
Kolymskoye, Okhotsko, *Russia* 45 C16
Kôm Ombo, *Egypt* 76 C3
Komandorskiye Is. = Komandorskiye Ostrova, *Russia* 45 D17
Komandorskiye Ostrova, *Russia* 45 D17
Komárno, *Slovakia* 21 H8
Komárom, *Hungary* 21 H8
Komarovo, *Russia* 40 B8
Komatipoort, *S. Africa* 85 D5
Komatou Yialou, *Cyprus* 37 D13
Komatsu, *Japan* 49 F8
Komatsujima, *Japan* 49 H7
Kombissiri, *Burkina Faso* 79 C4
Kombori, *Burkina Faso* 78 C4
Komen, *Slovenia* 33 C10
Komenda, *Ghana* 79 D4
Komi Republic □, *Russia* 44 C6
Komiža, *Croatia* 33 E13
Komló, *Hungary* 21 J8
Kommunarsk, *Ukraine* 43 B8
Kommunizma, Pik, *Tajikistan* 44 F8
Komodo, *Indonesia* 57 F5
Komoé, *Ivory C.* 78 D4
Komono, *Congo* 80 E2
Komoran, Pulau, *Indonesia* 57 F9
Komoro, *Japan* 49 F9
Komotini, *Greece* 39 H8
Kompasberg, *S. Africa* 84 E3
Kompong Bang, *Cambodia* 59 F5
Kompong Cham, *Cambodia* 59 F5

Kompong Chhnang, Cambodia 59 F5
Kompong Chikreng, Cambodia 58 F5
Kompong Kleang, Cambodia 58 F5
Kompong Luong, Cambodia 59 G5
Kompong Pranak, Cambodia 58 F5
Kompong Som, Cambodia 59 G4
Kompong Som, Chhung, Cambodia 59 G4
Kompong Speu, Cambodia 59 G5
Kompong Sralao, Cambodia 58 E5
Kompong Thom, Cambodia 58 F5
Kompong Trabeck, Cambodia 58 F5
Kompong Trabeck, Cambodia 59 G5
Kompong Trach, Cambodia 59 G5
Kompong Tralach, Cambodia 59 G5
Komrat, Moldavia 42 C3
Komsberg, S. Africa 84 E3
Komsomolets, Ostrov, Russia 45 A10
Komsomolsk, Russia 41 C12
Komsomolsk, Russia 45 D14
Komsomolskiy, Russia 41 E16
Konakovo, Russia 41 C10
Konarhá □, Afghan. 60 B7
Konārī, Iran 65 D6
Konawa, U.S.A. 109 H6
Konch, India 63 G8
Kondakovo, Russia 45 C16
Konde, Tanzania 82 C4
Kondinin, Australia 89 F2
Kondoa, Tanzania 82 C4
Kondoa □, Tanzania 82 D4
Kondókali, Greece 37 A3
Kondratyevo, Russia 45 D10
Konduga, Nigeria 79 C7
Kong, Ivory C. 78 D4
Kong →, Cambodia 58 F5
Kong, Koh, Cambodia 59 G4
Kong Christian IX.s Land, Greenland 4 C6
Kong Christian X.s Land, Greenland 4 B6
Kong Franz Joseph Fd., Greenland 4 B6
Kong Frederik IX.s Land, Greenland 4 C5
Kong Frederik VI.s Kyst, Greenland 4 C5
Kong Frederik VIII.s Land, Greenland 4 B6
Kong Oscar Fjord, Greenland 4 B6
Kongeå →, Denmark 11 J3
Kongju, S. Korea 51 F14
Konglu, Burma 61 F20
Kongolo, Kasai Or., Zaïre 82 D1
Kongolo, Shaba, Zaïre 82 D2
Kongor, Sudan 77 F3
Kongoussi, Burkina Faso 79 C4
Kongsberg, Norway 10 E3
Kongsvinger, Norway 10 D6
Kongwa, Tanzania 82 D4
Koni, Zaïre 83 E2
Koni, Mts., Zaïre 83 E2
Königsberg = Kaliningrad, Russia 40 D2
Königslutter, Germany 18 C6
Königswusterhausen, Germany 18 C9
Konin, Poland 20 C8
Kónitsa, Greece 39 J3
Köniz, Switz. 22 C4
Konjice, Slovenia 33 B12
Konkiep, Namibia 84 D2
Konkouré →, Guinea 78 D2
Könnern, Germany 18 D7
Kono, S. Leone 78 D2
Konolfingen, Switz. 22 C5
Konongo, Ghana 79 D4
Konosha, Russia 44 C5
Kōnosu, Japan 49 F9
Konotop, Ukraine 40 F8
Konqi He →, China 54 B4
Końskie, Poland 20 D10
Konstantinovka, Ukraine 42 B7
Konstantinovski, Russia 43 C9
Konstanz, Germany 19 H5
Kont, Iran 65 E9
Kontagora, Nigeria 79 C6
Kontich, Belgium 17 F4
Kontum, Vietnam 58 E7
Kontum, Plateau du, Vietnam 58 E7
Konya, Turkey 66 E5
Konya □, Turkey 66 E5
Konya Ovasi, Turkey 66 D5
Konz, Germany 19 F2
Konza, Kenya 82 C4
Kookynie, Australia 89 E3
Kooline, Australia 88 D2
Kooloonong, Australia 91 E3
Koolyanobbing, Australia 89 F2
Koondrook, Australia 91 F3
Koonibba, Australia 91 E1
Koorawatha, Australia 91 E4
Koorda, Australia 89 F2
Kooskia, U.S.A. 110 C6
Kootenai →, Canada 110 B5
Kootenay L., Canada 100 D5
Kootenay Nat. Park, Canada 100 C5
Kootjieskolk, S. Africa 84 E3
Kopanovka, Russia 43 C12
Kopaonik, Serbia, Yug. 21 M11
Kópavogur, Iceland 8 D3
Koper, Slovenia 33 C10
Kopervik, Norway 9 G8
Kopeysk, Russia 44 D7
Kopi, Australia 91 E2
Köping, Sweden 10 E10
Kopiste, Croatia 33 F13
Köpmanholmen, Sweden 10 A12
Koppang, Norway 10 C5
Kopparberg, Sweden 9 G13
Kopparbergs län □, Sweden 9 F13
Kopperå, Norway 10 A5
Koppies, S. Africa 85 D4
Koprivnica, Croatia 33 B13
Kopychintsy, Ukraine 40 G4
Kopys, Belorussia 40 D7
Korab, Macedonia 39 H3
Korakiána, Greece 37 A3
Korba, India 63 H10
Korbach, Germany 18 D4
Korbu, G., Malaysia 59 K3
Korça, Albania 39 J3
Korce = Korça, Albania 39 J3
Korčula, Croatia 33 F14
Korčulanski Kanal, Croatia 33 E13
Kord Kūy, Iran 65 B7
Kord Sheykh, Iran 65 D7
Kordestān □, Iran 64 C5
Korea, North ■, Asia 51 E14
Korea, South ■, Asia 51 F15
Korea Bay, Korea 51 E13
Korea Strait, Asia 51 G15
Korenevo, Russia 40 F9
Korenovsk, Russia 43 D8
Korets, Ukraine 40 F5
Korgan, Turkey 67 C7
Korgus, Sudan 76 D3
Korhogo, Ivory C. 78 D3
Koribundu, S. Leone 78 D2
Korim, Indonesia 57 E9
Korinthiakós Kólpos, Greece 39 L5
Kórinthos, Greece 39 M5
Korioumé, Mali 78 B4
Koríssa, Límni, Greece 37 B3
Kōriyama, Japan 48 F10
Korkuteli, Turkey 66 E4
Kormakiti, C., Cyprus 37 D11
Körmend, Hungary 21 H6
Kornat, Croatia 33 E12
Korneshty, Moldavia 42 C3
Kornsjø, Norway 10 F5
Kornstad, Norway 10 B1
Koro, Fiji 87 C8
Koro, Ivory C. 78 D3
Koro, Mali 78 C4
Koro Sea, Fiji 87 C9
Korocha, Russia 41 F10
Köroğlu Dağları, Turkey 66 C4
Korogwe, Tanzania 82 D4
Korogwe □, Tanzania 82 D4
Koroit, Australia 91 F3
Koronadal, Phil. 55 H6
Koronowo, Poland 20 B7
Koror, Pac. Oc. 57 C8
Körös →, Hungary 21 J10
Korosten, Ukraine 40 F6
Korotoyak, Russia 41 F11
Korraraika, Helodranon' i, Madag. 85 B7
Korsakov, Russia 45 E15
Korshunovo, Russia 45 D12
Korsør, Denmark 9 J11
Korsun Shevchenkovskiy, Ukraine 42 B4
Korsze, Poland 20 A11
Kortemark, Belgium 17 F2
Kortessem, Belgium 17 G6
Korti, Sudan 76 D3
Kortrijk, Belgium 17 G2
Korwai, India 62 G8
Koryakskiy Khrebet, Russia 45 C18
Koryŏng, S. Korea 51 G15
Kos, Greece 39 N10
Kosa, Ethiopia 77 F4
Kosaya Gora, Russia 41 D10
Kościan, Poland 20 C6
Kościerzyna, Poland 20 A7
Kosciusko, U.S.A. 109 J10
Kosciusko, Mt., Australia 91 F4
Kosciusko I., U.S.A. 100 B2
Kösély →, Hungary 21 H11
Kosha, Sudan 76 C3
Köshetau = Kokchetav, Kazakhstan 44 D7
K'oshih = Kashi, China 54 C2
Koshiki-Rettō, Japan 49 J4
Kosi, India 62 F7
Kosi-meer, S. Africa 85 D5
Košice, Slovakia 20 G11
Kosjerić, Serbia, Yug. 21 M9
Koskhinoú, Greece 37 C10
Kosŏng, N. Korea 51 E15
Kosovska-Mitrovica, Serbia, Yug. 21 N10
Kostajnica, Croatia 33 C13
Kostanjevica, Slovenia 33 C12
Kostelec, Czech. 20 E6
Koster, S. Africa 84 D4
Kôstî, Sudan 77 E3
Kostopol, Ukraine 40 F5
Kostroma, Russia 41 C12
Kostromskoye Vdkhr., Russia 41 C12
Kostyantynivka = Konstantinovka, Ukraine 42 B7
Kostyukovichi, Belorussia 40 E8
Koszalin, Poland 20 A6
Köszeg, Hungary 21 H6
Kot Addu, Pakistan 62 D4
Kot Moman, Pakistan 62 C5
Kota, India 62 G6
Kota Baharu, Malaysia 59 J4
Kota Belud, Malaysia 56 C5
Kota Kinabalu, Malaysia 56 C5
Kota Tinggi, Malaysia 59 M4
Kotaagung, Indonesia 56 F2
Kotabaru, Indonesia 56 E5
Kotabumi, Indonesia 56 E2
Kotagede, Indonesia 57 G14
Kotamobagu, Indonesia 57 D6
Kotaneelee →, Canada 100 A4
Kotawaringin, Indonesia 56 E4
Kotcho L., Canada 100 B4
Kotelnich, Russia 41 B16
Kotelnikovo, Russia 43 C10
Kotelnyy, Ostrov, Russia 45 B14
Köthen, Germany 18 D7
Kothi, India 63 G9
Kotiro, Pakistan 62 F2
Kotka, Finland 9 F19
Kotlas, Russia 44 C5
Kotli, Pakistan 62 C5
Kotmul, Pakistan 63 B6
Kotonkoro, Nigeria 79 C6
Kotor, Montenegro, Yug. 21 N8
Kotoriba, Croatia 33 B13
Kotovo, Russia 41 F14
Kotovsk, Ukraine 42 C3
Kotputli, India 62 F7
Kotri, Pakistan 62 G3
Kótronas, Greece 39 N5
Kottayam, India 60 Q10
Kotturu, India 60 M10
Kotuy →, Russia 45 B11
Kotzebue, U.S.A. 96 B3
Kouango, C.A.R. 80 C4
Koudekerke, Neths. 17 F3
Koudougou, Burkina Faso 78 C4
Koufonísi, Greece 37 E8
Kougaberge, S. Africa 84 E3
Kouibli, Ivory C. 78 D3
Kouilou →, Congo 80 E2
Kouki, C.A.R. 80 C3
Koula Moutou, Gabon 80 E2
Koulen, Cambodia 58 F5
Koulikoro, Mali 78 C3
Kouloúra, Greece 37 A3
Koúm-bournoú, Ákra, Greece 37 C10
Koumala, Australia 90 C4
Koumankou, Mali 78 C3
Koumbia, Burkina Faso 78 C4
Koumbia, Guinea 78 C2
Koumboum, Guinea 78 C2
Koumpenntoum, Senegal 78 C2
Koumra, Chad 73 G8
Koundara, Guinea 78 C2
Kounradskiy, Kazakhstan 44 E8
Kountze, U.S.A. 109 K7
Koupéla, Burkina Faso 79 C4
Kouris →, Cyprus 37 E11
Kourou, Fr. Guiana 121 B7
Kouroussa, Guinea 78 C3
Koussané, Mali 78 C2
Kousseri, Cameroon 73 F7
Koutiala, Mali 78 C3
Kouto, Ivory C. 78 D3
Kouvé, Togo 79 D5
Kovačica, Serbia, Yug. 21 K10
Kovel, Ukraine 40 F4
Kovin, Serbia, Yug. 21 L10
Kovrov, Russia 41 C12
Kowanyama, Australia 90 B3
Kowkash, Canada 98 B2
Kowloon, H.K. 53 F10
Kowŏn, N. Korea 51 E14
Koyabuti, Indonesia 57 E10
Köyceğiz, Turkey 66 E3
Koyuk, U.S.A. 96 B3
Koyukuk →, U.S.A. 96 B4
Koyulhisar, Turkey 42 F7
Koza, Japan 49 L3
Kozan, Turkey 66 E6
Kozáni, Greece 39 J4
Kozara, Bos.-H. 33 D14
Kozarac, Bos.-H. 33 D13
Kozelsk, Russia 40 D9
Kozhikode = Calicut, India 60 P9
Kozje, Slovenia 33 B12
Kozlovets, Bulgaria 38 F8
Kozlu, Turkey 66 C4
Kozluk, Turkey 67 D9
Koźmin, Poland 20 D7
Kozmodemyansk, Russia 41 C15
Kpabia, Ghana 79 D4
Kpalimé, Togo 79 D5
Kpandae, Ghana 79 D4
Kpessi, Togo 79 D5
Kra, Isthmus of = Kra, Kho Khot, Thailand 59 G2
Kra, Kho Khot, Thailand 59 G2
Kra Buri, Thailand 59 G2
Krabbendijke, Neths. 17 F4
Krabi, Thailand 59 H2
Kragan, Indonesia 57 G14
Kragerø, Norway 10 F3
Kragujevac, Serbia, Yug. 21 L10
Krajina, Bos.-H. 33 D13
Krakatau = Rakata, Pulau, Indonesia 56 F3
Krakor, Cambodia 58 F5
Kraków, Poland 20 E9
Kraksaan, Indonesia 57 G15
Kråkstad, Norway 10 E4
Kralanh, Cambodia 58 F4
Králiky, Czech. 20 E6
Kraljevo, Serbia, Yug. 21 M10
Kralovice, Czech. 20 F3
Kralupy, Czech. 20 E4
Kramatorsk, Ukraine 42 B7
Kramfors, Sweden 10 B11
Kramis, C., Algeria 75 A5
Krångede, Sweden 10 A10
Kranj, Slovenia 33 B11
Kranjska Gora, Slovenia 33 B10
Krankskop, S. Africa 85 D5
Krapina, Croatia 33 B12
Krapina →, Croatia 33 C12
Krapivna, Russia 41 E10
Krapkowice, Poland 20 E7
Kraskino, Russia 45 E14
Kraslice, Czech. 20 E2
Krasnaya Gorbatka, Russia 41 D12
Krasnaya Polyana, Russia 43 E9
Kraśnik, Poland 20 E12
Kraśnik Fabryczny, Poland 20 E12
Krasnoarmeisk, Ukraine 42 B7
Krasnoarmeysk, Russia 41 F14
Krasnoarmeysk, Russia 43 B11
Krasnodar, Russia 43 D8
Krasnodon, Ukraine 43 B8
Krasnodonetskaya, Russia 43 B9
Krasnogorskiy, Russia 41 C16
Krasnograd, Ukraine 42 B6
Krasnogvardeyskoye, Russia 43 D9
Krasnogvardyesk, Ukraine 42 D6
Krasnokutsk, Ukraine 40 F9
Krasnoperekopsk, Ukraine 42 D5
Krasnorechenskiy, Russia 48 B7
Krasnoselkupsk, Russia 44 C9
Krasnoslobodsk, Russia 41 D13
Krasnoslobodsk, Russia 43 B11
Krasnoturinsk, Russia 44 D7
Krasnoufimsk, Russia 44 D6
Krasnouralsk, Russia 44 D7
Krasnovodsk, Turkmenistan 44 E6
Krasnoyarsk, Russia 45 D10
Krasnoye = Krasnyy, Russia 40 D7
Krasnoye, Russia 41 B15
Krasnoye, Russia 43 C11
Krasnozavodsk, Russia 41 C11
Krasny Liman, Ukraine 42 B7
Krasny Sulin, Russia 43 C9
Krasnystaw, Poland 20 E13
Krasnyy, Russia 40 D7
Krasnyy Kholm, Russia 41 B10
Krasnyy Kut, Russia 41 F15
Krasnyy Luch, Ukraine 43 B8
Krasnyy Profintern, Russia 41 C12
Krasnyy Yar, Russia 41 E17
Krasnyy Yar, Russia 41 F14
Krasnyy Yar, Russia 43 C13
Krasnyye Baki, Russia 41 C14
Krasnyyoskolskoye Vdkhr., Ukraine 42 B7
Kraszna →, Hungary 21 G12
Kratie, Cambodia 58 F6
Krau, Indonesia 57 E10
Kravanh, Chuor Phnum, Cambodia 59 G4
Krefeld, Germany 18 D2
Krémaston, Límni, Greece 39 L4
Kremenchug, Ukraine 42 B5
Kremenchugskoye Vdkhr., Ukraine 42 B5
Kremenchuk = Kremenchug, Ukraine 42 B5
Kremenets, Ukraine 42 A1
Kremennaya, Ukraine 42 B8
Kremges = Svetlovodsk, Ukraine 40 G8
Kremikovtsi, Bulgaria 38 G6
Kremmen, Germany 18 C9
Kremmling, U.S.A. 110 F10
Krems, Austria 21 G5
Kremsmünster, Austria 21 G4
Kretinga, Lithuania 40 D2
Krettamia, Algeria 74 C4
Krettsy, Russia 40 B8
Kreuzberg, Germany 19 E5
Kreuzlingen, Switz. 23 A8
Kribi, Cameroon 79 E6
Krichem, Bulgaria 38 G7
Krichev, Belorussia 40 E7
Krim, Slovenia 33 C11
Krimpen, Neths. 16 E5
Kriós, Ákra, Greece 37 D5
Krishna →, India 61 M12
Krishnanagar, India 63 H13
Kristiansand, Norway 9 G10
Kristianstad, Sweden 9 H13
Kristianstads län □, Sweden 9 H13
Kristiansund, Norway 10 A1
Kristiinankaupunki, Finland 8 E16
Kristinehamn, Sweden 9 G13
Kristinestad, Finland 8 E16
Kríti, Greece 37 D7
Kritsá, Greece 37 D7
Kriva →, Macedonia 38 G4
Kriva Palanka, Macedonia 38 G5
Krivaja →, Bos.-H. 21 L8
Krivoy Rog, Ukraine 42 C5
Križevci, Croatia 33 B13
Krk, Croatia 33 C11
Krka →, Slovenia 33 C12
Krkonoše, Czech. 20 E5
Krnov, Czech. 20 E7
Krobia, Poland 20 D6
Krokeaí, Greece 39 N5
Krokodil →, Mozam. 85 D5
Krokom, Sweden 10 A8
Krolevets, Ukraine 40 F8
Kroměříz, Czech. 20 F7
Krommenie, Neths. 16 D5
Kromy, Russia 40 E9
Kronach, Germany 19 E7
Kronobergs län □, Sweden 9 H13
Kronprins Olav Kyst, Antarctica 5 C5
Kronshtadt, Russia 40 A6
Kroonstad, S. Africa 84 D4
Kröpelin, Germany 18 A7
Kropotkin, Russia 43 D9
Kropotkin, Russia 45 D12
Kropp, Germany 18 A5
Krościenko, Poland 20 F10
Krosno, Poland 20 F11
Krosno Odrzańskie, Poland 20 C5
Krotoszyn, Poland 20 D7
Kroussón, Greece 37 D6
Krško, Slovenia 33 C12
Kruger Nat. Park, S. Africa 85 C5
Krugersdorp, S. Africa 85 D4
Kruiningen, Neths. 17 F4
Kruisfontein, S. Africa 84 E3
Kruishoutem, Belgium 17 G3
Kruisland, Neths. 17 E4
Kruja, Albania 39 H2
Krulevshchina, Belorussia 40 D5
Kruma, Albania 38 G3
Krumbach, Germany 19 G6
Krung Thep = Bangkok, Thailand 58 F3
Krupanj, Serbia, Yug. 21 L9
Krupinica →, Slovakia 21 G8
Kruševac, Serbia, Yug. 21 M11
Kruzof I., U.S.A. 100 B1
Krychaw = Krichev, Belorussia 40 E7
Krymsk Abinsk, Russia 42 D8
Krymskiy Poluostrov, Ukraine 42 D5
Krynica Morska, Poland 20 A9
Krynki, Poland 20 B13
Kryvyy Rih = Krivoy Rog, Ukraine 42 C5
Krzywiń, Poland 20 D6
Krzyz, Poland 20 C6
Ksabi, Morocco 74 B4
Ksar Chellala, Algeria 75 A5
Ksar el Boukhari, Algeria 75 A5
Ksar el Kebir, Morocco 74 B3
Ksar es Souk = Ar Rachidiya, Morocco 74 B4
Ksar Rhilane, Tunisia 75 B6
Ksour, Mts. des, Algeria 75 B4
Kstovo, Russia 41 C14
Kuala, Indonesia 56 D3
Kuala Berang, Malaysia 59 K4
Kuala Dungun, Malaysia 59 K4
Kuala Kangsar, Malaysia 59 K3
Kuala Kelawang, Malaysia 59 L4
Kuala Kerai, Malaysia 59 K4
Kuala Kubu Baharu, Malaysia 59 L3
Kuala Lipis, Malaysia 59 K4
Kuala Lumpur, Malaysia 59 L3
Kuala Nerang, Malaysia 59 J3
Kuala Pilah, Malaysia 59 L4
Kuala Rompin, Malaysia 59 L4
Kuala Selangor, Malaysia 59 L3
Kuala Terengganu, Malaysia 59 K4
Kualajelai, Indonesia 56 E4
Kualakapuas, Indonesia 56 E4
Kualakurun, Indonesia 56 E4
Kualapembuang, Indonesia 56 E4
Kualasimpang, Indonesia 56 D1
Kuancheng, China 51 D10
Kuandang, Indonesia 57 D6
Kuandian, China 51 D13
Kuangchou = Guangzhou, China 53 F9
Kuantan, Malaysia 59 L4
Kuba, Azerbaijan 43 F13
Kuban →, Russia 42 D7
Kubenskoye, Oz., Russia 41 B11
Kuberle, Russia 43 C10
Kubokawa, Japan 49 H6
Kubrat, Bulgaria 38 F9
Kučevo, Serbia, Yug. 21 L11
Kucha Gompa, India 63 B7
Kuchaman, India 62 F6
Kuchino-eruba-Jima, Japan 49 J5
Kuchino-Shima, Japan 49 K4
Kuchinotsu, Japan 49 H5
Kucing, Malaysia 56 D4
Kuçove = Qytet Stalin, Albania 39 J2

Kud →, *Pakistan* 62 F2
Kuda, *India* 60 H7
Kudat, *Malaysia* 56 C5
Kudus, *Indonesia* 57 G14
Kudymkar, *Russia* 44 D6
Kueiyang = Guiyang, *China* 52 D6
Kufstein, *Austria* 19 H8
Kugong I., *Canada* 98 A4
Kūh-e Dīnār, *Iran* 65 D6
Kūh-e-Hazārām, *Iran* 65 D8
Kūhak, *Iran* 60 F3
Kūhbonān, *Iran* 65 D8
Kūhestak, *Iran* 65 E8
Kūhīn, *Iran* 65 C6
Kūhīrī, *Iran* 65 E9
Kuhnsdorf, *Austria* 21 J4
Kūhpāyeh, *Eşfahan, Iran* 65 C7
Kūhpāyeh, *Kermān, Iran* 65 D8
Kui Buri, *Thailand* 59 F2
Kuinre, *Neths.* 16 C7
Kuito, *Angola* 81 G3
Kujang, *N. Korea* 51 E14
Kuji, *Japan* 48 D10
Kujū-San, *Japan* 49 H5
Kukawa, *Nigeria* 79 C7
Kukerin, *Australia* 89 F2
Kukmor, *Russia* 41 C17
Kukup, *Malaysia* 59 M4
Kukvidze, *Russia* 41 F13
Kula, *Serbia, Yug.* 21 K9
Kulai, *Malaysia* 59 M4
Kulal, Mt., *Kenya* 82 B4
Kulaly, Os., *Kazakhstan* 43 D14
Kulasekarappattinam, *India* 60 Q11
Kuldiga, *Latvia* 40 C2
Kuldja = Yining, *China* 44 E9
Kuldu, *Sudan* 77 E2
Kulebaki, *Russia* 41 D13
Kulen Vakuf, *Bos.-H.* 33 D13
Kulgam, *India* 63 C6
Kuli, *Russia* 43 E12
Kulim, *Malaysia* 59 K3
Kulin, *Australia* 89 F2
Kulja, *Australia* 89 F2
Kulm, *U.S.A.* 108 B5
Kulmbach, *Germany* 19 E7
Kulp, *Turkey* 67 D9
Kulsary, *Kazakhstan* 44 E6
Kultay, *Kazakhstan* 43 D14
Kulti, *India* 63 H12
Kulu, *Turkey* 66 D5
Kulumbura, *Australia* 88 B4
Kulunda, *Russia* 44 D8
Kulungar, *Afghan.* 62 C3
Kūlvand, *Iran* 65 D7
Kulwin, *Australia* 91 F3
Kulyab, *Tajikistan* 44 F7
Kum Tekei, *Kazakhstan* 44 E8
Kuma →, *Russia* 43 D12
Kumaganum, *Nigeria* 79 C7
Kumagaya, *Japan* 49 F9
Kumai, *Indonesia* 56 E4
Kumamba, Kepulauan, *Indonesia* 57 E9
Kumamoto, *Japan* 49 H5
Kumamoto □, *Japan* 49 H5
Kumanovo, *Macedonia* 38 G4
Kumara, *N.Z.* 87 K3
Kumarl, *Australia* 89 F3
Kumasi, *Ghana* 78 D4
Kumayri, *Armenia* 43 F10
Kumba, *Cameroon* 79 E6
Kumbakonam, *India* 60 P11
Kumbarilla, *Australia* 91 D5
Kumbo, *Cameroon* 79 D7
Kūmchŏn, *N. Korea* 51 E14
Kumdok, *India* 63 C8
Kume-Shima, *Japan* 49 L3
Kumeny, *Russia* 41 B16
Kūmhwa, *S. Korea* 51 E14
Kumi, *Uganda* 82 B3
Kumla, *Sweden* 9 G13
Kumluca, *Turkey* 66 E4
Kummerower See, *Germany* 18 B8
Kumo, *Nigeria* 79 C7
Kumon Bum, *Burma* 61 F20
Kumtorkala, *Russia* 43 E12
Kumylzhenskaya, *Russia* 43 B10
Kunama, *Australia* 91 F4
Kunashir, Ostrov, *Russia* 45 E15
Kunda, *Estonia* 40 B5
Kundla, *India* 62 J4
Kungala, *Australia* 91 D5
Kungälv, *Sweden* 11 G5
Kunghit I., *Canada* 100 C2
Kungrad, *Uzbekistan* 44 E6
Kungsbacka, *Sweden* 11 G6
Kungur, *Russia* 44 D6
Kungurri, *Australia* 90 C4
Kunhar →, *Pakistan* 63 B5
Kunhegyes, *Hungary* 21 H10
Kuningan, *Indonesia* 57 G13
Kunlong, *Burma* 61 H21
Kunlun Shan, *Asia* 54 C3
Kunming, *China* 52 E4
Kunrade, *Neths.* 17 G7
Kunsan, *S. Korea* 51 G14
Kunshan, *China* 53 B13
Kununurra, *Australia* 88 C4
Kunwarara, *Australia* 90 C5
Kunya-Urgench, *Turkmenistan* 44 E6
Künzelsau, *Germany* 19 F5
Kuopio, *Finland* 8 E19
Kuopion lääni □, *Finland* 8 E19
Kupa →, *Croatia* 33 C13
Kupang, *Indonesia* 57 F6
Kupres, *Bos.-H.* 21 L7
Kupyansk, *Ukraine* 42 B7
Kupyansk-Uzlovoi, *Ukraine* 42 B7
Kuqa, *China* 54 B3
Kuranda, *Australia* 90 B4
Kurashiki, *Japan* 49 G6
Kurayoshi, *Japan* 49 G6
Kurdistan, *Asia* 67 E10
Kūrdzhali, *Bulgaria* 39 H8
Kure, *Japan* 49 G6
Küre, *Turkey* 66 C5
Küre Dağları, *Turkey* 66 C6
Kuressaare, *Estonia* 40 B3
Kurgaldzhino, *Kazakhstan* 44 D8
Kurgan, *Russia* 44 D7
Kurganinsk, *Russia* 43 D9
Kurgannaya = Kurganinsk, *Russia* 43 D9
Kuria Maria Is. = Khūrīyā Mūrīyā, Jazā 'ir, *Oman* 68 D6
Kuridala, *Australia* 90 C3
Kurigram, *Bangla.* 61 G16
Kuril Is. = Kurilskiye Ostrova, *Russia* 45 E15
Kuril Trench, *Pac. Oc.* 92 C7
Kurilsk, *Russia* 45 E15
Kurilskiye Ostrova, *Russia* 45 E15
Kuringen, *Belgium* 17 G6
Kurino, *Japan* 49 J5
Kurkur, *Egypt* 76 C3
Kurlovskiy, *Russia* 41 D12
Kurmuk, *Sudan* 77 E3
Kurnool, *India* 60 M10
Kuro-Shima, *Kagoshima, Japan* 49 J4
Kuro-Shima, *Okinawa, Japan* 49 M2
Kurovskoye, *Russia* 41 D11
Kurow, *N.Z.* 87 L3
Kurrajong, *Australia* 91 E5
Kurram →, *Pakistan* 62 C4
Kurri Kurri, *Australia* 91 E5
Kursavka, *Russia* 43 D10
Kuršėnai, *Lithuania* 40 C3
Kursk, *Russia* 41 F10
Kuršumlija, *Serbia, Yug.* 21 M11
Kurşunlu, *Turkey* 66 C5
Kurtalan, *Turkey* 67 E9
Kuru, Bahr el →, *Sudan* 77 F2
Kurucaşile, *Turkey* 66 C5
Kuruktag, *China* 54 B3
Kuruman, *S. Africa* 84 D3
Kuruman →, *S. Africa* 84 D3
Kurume, *Japan* 49 H5
Kurunegala, *Sri Lanka* 60 R12
Kurupukari, *Guyana* 121 C6
Kurya, *Russia* 45 C11
Kus Gölü, *Turkey* 66 C2
Kuşadası, *Turkey* 66 E2
Kusatsu, *Japan* 49 F9
Kusawa L., *Canada* 100 A1
Kusel, *Germany* 19 F3
Kushchevskaya, *Russia* 43 C8
Kushikino, *Japan* 49 J5
Kushima, *Japan* 49 J5
Kushimoto, *Japan* 49 H7
Kushiro, *Japan* 48 C12
Kushiro →, *Japan* 48 C12
Kūshk, *Iran* 65 D8
Kushka, *Turkmenistan* 44 F7
Kūshkī, *Īlām, Iran* 64 C5
Kūshkī, *Khorāsān, Iran* 65 B8
Kūshkū, *Iran* 65 E7
Kushol, *India* 63 C7
Kushtia, *Bangla.* 61 H16
Kushum →, *Kazakhstan* 43 B14
Kuskokwim →, *U.S.A.* 96 B3
Kuskokwim B., *U.S.A.* 96 C3
Küsnacht, *Switz.* 23 B7
Kussharo-Ko, *Japan* 48 C12
Küssnacht, *Switz.* 23 B6
Kustanay, *Kazakhstan* 44 D7
Kut, Ko, *Thailand* 59 G4
Kütahya, *Turkey* 66 D4
Kütahya □, *Turkey* 66 D3
Kutaisi, *Georgia* 43 E10
Kutaraja = Banda Aceh, *Indonesia* 56 C1
Kutch, Gulf of = Kachchh, Gulf of, *India* 62 H3
Kutch, Rann of = Kachchh, Rann of, *India* 62 G4
Kutina, *Croatia* 33 C13
Kutiyana, *India* 62 J4
Kutkashen, *Azerbaijan* 43 F12
Kutná Hora, *Czech.* 20 F5
Kutno, *Poland* 20 C9
Kuttabul, *Australia* 90 C4
Kutu, *Zaïre* 80 E3
Kutum, *Sudan* 77 E1
Kuujjuaq, *Canada* 97 C13
Kuŭp-tong, *N. Korea* 51 D14
Kuurne, *Belgium* 17 G2
Kuvshinovo, *Russia* 40 C9
Kuwait = Al Kuwayt, *Kuwait* 64 D5
Kuwait ■, *Asia* 64 D5
Kuwana, *Japan* 49 G8
Kuybyshev = Samara, *Russia* 41 E17
Kuybyshev, *Russia* 44 D8
Kuybyshevo, *Ukraine* 42 C7
Kuybyshevskoye Vdkhr., *Russia* 41 D16
Kuye He →, *China* 50 E6
Kūyeh, *Iran* 64 B5
Kūysanjaq, *Iraq* 64 B5
Kuyumba, *Russia* 45 C10
Kuzey Anadolu Dağları, *Turkey* 66 C6
Kuznetsk, *Russia* 41 E15
Kvænangen, *Norway* 8 A16
Kvam, *Norway* 10 C3
Kvareli, *Georgia* 43 F11
Kvarner, *Croatia* 33 D11
Kvarnerič, *Croatia* 33 D11
Kviteseid, *Norway* 10 E2
Kwabhaca, *S. Africa* 85 E4
Kwadacha →, *Canada* 100 B3
Kwakhanai, *Botswana* 84 C3
Kwakoegron, *Surinam* 121 B6
Kwale, *Kenya* 82 C4
Kwale, *Nigeria* 79 D6
Kwale □, *Kenya* 82 C4
KwaMashu, *S. Africa* 85 D5
Kwamouth, *Zaïre* 80 E3
Kwando →, *Africa* 84 B3
Kwangdaeri, *N. Korea* 51 D14
Kwangju, *S. Korea* 51 G14
Kwangsi-Chuang = Guangxi Zhuangzu Zizhiqu □, *China* 52 E7
Kwangtung = Guangdong □, *China* 53 F9
Kwara □, *Nigeria* 79 D5
Kwataboahegan →, *Canada* 98 B3
Kwatisore, *Indonesia* 57 E8
Kweichow = Guizhou □, *China* 52 D6
Kwekwe, *Zimbabwe* 83 F2
Kwimba □, *Tanzania* 82 C3
Kwinana New Town, *Australia* 89 F2
Kwoka, *Indonesia* 57 E8
Kyabé, *Chad* 73 G8
Kyabra Cr. →, *Australia* 91 D3
Kyabram, *Australia* 91 F4
Kyaikto, *Burma* 58 D1
Kyakhta, *Russia* 45 D11
Kyancutta, *Australia* 91 E2
Kyangin, *Burma* 61 K19
Kyaukpadaung, *Burma* 61 J19
Kyaukpyu, *Burma* 61 K18
Kyaukse, *Burma* 61 J20
Kyburz, *U.S.A.* 112 G6
Kycen, *Russia* 45 D11
Kyenjojo, *Uganda* 82 B3
Kyle Dam, *Zimbabwe* 83 G3
Kyle of Lochalsh, *U.K.* 14 D3
Kyll →, *Germany* 19 F2
Kyllburg, *Germany* 19 E2
Kyneton, *Australia* 91 F3
Kynuna, *Australia* 90 C3
Kyō-ga-Saki, *Japan* 49 G7
Kyoga, L., *Uganda* 82 B3
Kyogle, *Australia* 91 D5
Kyongju, *S. Korea* 51 G15
Kyongpyaw, *Burma* 61 L19
Kyŏngsŏng, *N. Korea* 51 D15
Kyōto, *Japan* 49 G7
Kyōto □, *Japan* 49 G7
Kyparissovouno, *Cyprus* 37 D12
Kyperounda, *Cyprus* 37 E11
Kyrenia, *Cyprus* 37 D12
Kyrgystan = Kirghizia ■, *Asia* 44 E8
Kyritz, *Germany* 18 C8
Kystatyam, *Russia* 45 C13
Kytal Ktakh, *Russia* 45 C13
Kythréa, *Cyprus* 37 D12
Kyulyunken, *Russia* 45 C14
Kyunhla, *Burma* 61 H19
Kyuquot, *Canada* 100 C3
Kyurdamir, *Azerbaijan* 43 F13
Kyūshū, *Japan* 49 H5
Kyūshū □, *Japan* 49 H5
Kyūshū-Sanchi, *Japan* 49 H5
Kyustendil, *Bulgaria* 38 G5
Kyusyur, *Russia* 45 B13
Kywong, *Australia* 91 E4
Kyyiv = Kiyev, *Ukraine* 40 F7
Kyzyl, *Russia* 45 D10
Kyzyl-Kiya, *Kirghizia* 44 E8
Kyzylkum, Peski, *Uzbekistan* 44 E7
Kzyl-Orda, *Kazakhstan* 44 E7

L

La Albuera, *Spain* 31 G4
La Alcarria, *Spain* 28 E2
La Algaba, *Spain* 31 H4
La Almarcha, *Spain* 28 F2
La Almunia de Doña Godina, *Spain* 28 D3
La Asunción, *Venezuela* 121 A5
La Banda, *Argentina* 126 B3
La Bañeza, *Spain* 30 C5
La Barca, *Mexico* 114 C4
La Barge, *U.S.A.* 110 E8
La Bassée, *France* 25 B9
La Bastide-Puylaurent, *France* 26 D7
La Baule, *France* 24 E4
La Belle, *U.S.A.* 105 M5
La Biche →, *Canada* 100 B4
La Bisbal, *Spain* 28 D8
La Blanquilla, *Venezuela* 121 A5
La Bomba, *Mexico* 114 A1
La Bresse, *France* 25 D13
La Bureba, *Spain* 28 C1
La Cal →, *Bolivia* 125 D6
La Calera, *Chile* 126 C1
La Campiña, *Spain* 31 H6
La Canal, *Spain* 36 C7
La Cañiza, *Spain* 30 C2
La Capelle, *France* 25 C10
La Carlota, *Argentina* 126 C3
La Carlota, *Phil.* 55 F5
La Carolina, *Spain* 31 G7
La Cavalerie, *France* 26 D7
La Ceiba, *Honduras* 116 C2
La Chaise-Dieu, *France* 26 C7
La Chaize-le-Vicomte, *France* 24 F5
La Chapelle d'Angillon, *France* 25 E9
La Chapelle-Glain, *France* 24 E5
La Charité-sur-Loire, *France* 25 E10
La Chartre-sur-le-Loir, *France* 24 E7
La Châtaigneraie, *France* 26 B3
La Châtre, *France* 26 B5
La Chaux de Fonds, *Switz.* 22 B3
La Chorrera, *Colombia* 120 D3
La Ciotat, *France* 27 E9
La Clayette, *France* 27 B8
La Cocha, *Argentina* 126 B2
La Concepción = Ri-Aba, *Eq. Guin.* 79 E6
La Concepción, *Venezuela* 120 A3
La Concordia, *Mexico* 115 D6
La Conner, *U.S.A.* 110 B2
La Coruña, *Spain* 30 B2
La Coruña □, *Spain* 30 B2
La Côte, *Switz.* 22 D2
La Côte-St.-André, *France* 27 C9
La Courtine-le-Trucq, *France* 26 C6
La Crau, *France* 27 E8
La Crete, *Canada* 100 B5
La Crosse, *Kans., U.S.A.* 108 F5
La Crosse, *Wis., U.S.A.* 108 D9
La Cruz, *Costa Rica* 116 D2
La Cruz, *Mexico* 114 C3
La Dorada, *Colombia* 120 B3
La Ensenada, *Chile* 128 B2
La Escondida, *Mexico* 114 C5
La Esmeralda, *Paraguay* 126 A3
La Esperanza, *Argentina* 128 B3
La Esperanza, *Cuba* 116 B3
La Esperanza, *Honduras* 116 D2
La Estrada, *Spain* 30 C2
La Fayette, *U.S.A.* 105 H3
La Fé, *Cuba* 116 B3
La Fère, *France* 25 C10
La Ferté-Bernard, *France* 24 D7
La Ferté-Macé, *France* 24 D6
La Ferté-St.-Aubin, *France* 25 E8
La Ferté-sous-Jouarre, *France* 25 D10
La Ferté-Vidame, *France* 24 D7
La Flèche, *France* 24 E6
La Follette, *U.S.A.* 105 G3
La Fregeneda, *Spain* 30 E4
La Fría, *Venezuela* 120 B3
La Fuente de San Esteban, *Spain* 30 E4
La Gineta, *Spain* 29 F2
La Gloria, *Colombia* 120 B3
La Gran Sabana, *Venezuela* 121 B5
La Grand-Combe, *France* 27 D8
La Grande, *U.S.A.* 110 D4
La Grande-Motte, *France* 27 E8
La Grange, *U.S.A.* 112 H6
La Grange, *Ga., U.S.A.* 105 J3
La Grange, *Ky., U.S.A.* 104 F3
La Grange, *Tex., U.S.A.* 109 L6
La Grita, *Venezuela* 120 B3
La Guaira, *Venezuela* 120 A4
La Guardia, *Spain* 30 D2
La Gudiña, *Spain* 30 C3
La Güera, *Mauritania* 74 D1
La Guerche-de-Bretagne, *France* 24 E5
La Guerche-sur-l'Aubois, *France* 25 F9
La Habana, *Cuba* 116 B3
La Harpe, *U.S.A.* 108 E9
La Haye-du-Puits, *France* 24 C5
La Horqueta, *Venezuela* 121 B5
La Horra, *Spain* 30 D7
La Independencia, *Mexico* 115 D6
La Isabela, *Dom. Rep.* 117 C5
La Jara, *U.S.A.* 111 H11
La Joya, *Peru* 124 D3
La Junquera, *Spain* 28 C7
La Junta, *U.S.A.* 109 F3
La Laguna, *Canary Is.* 36 F3
La Libertad, *Guatemala* 116 C1
La Libertad, *Mexico* 114 B2
La Libertad □, *Peru* 124 B2
La Ligua, *Chile* 126 C1
La Línea de la Concepción, *Spain* 31 J5
La Loche, *Canada* 101 B7
La Londe-les-Maures, *France* 27 E10
La Lora, *Spain* 30 C7
La Loupe, *France* 24 D8
La Louvière, *Belgium* 17 H4
La Machine, *France* 25 F10
La Maddalena, *Italy* 34 A2
La Malbaie, *Canada* 99 C5
La Mancha, *Spain* 29 F2
La Mariña, *Spain* 30 B3
La Mesa, *Calif., U.S.A.* 113 N9
La Mesa, *N. Mex., U.S.A.* 111 K10
La Misión, *Mexico* 114 A1
La Mothe-Achard, *France* 24 F5
La Motte, *France* 27 D10
La Motte-Chalançon, *France* 27 D9
La Moure, *U.S.A.* 108 B5
La Muela, *Spain* 28 D3
La Mure, *France* 27 D9
La Negra, *Chile* 126 A1
La Neuveville, *Switz.* 22 B4
La Oliva, *Canary Is.* 36 F6
La Oraya, *Peru* 124 C2
La Orotava, *Canary Is.* 36 F3
La Pacaudière, *France* 26 B7
La Palma, *Canary Is.* 36 F2
La Palma, *Panama* 116 E4
La Palma, *Spain* 31 H4
La Paloma, *Chile* 126 C1
La Pampa □, *Argentina* 126 D2
La Paragua, *Venezuela* 121 B5
La Paz, *Entre Ríos, Argentina* 126 C4
La Paz, *San Luis, Argentina* 126 C2
La Paz, *Bolivia* 124 D4
La Paz, *Honduras* 116 D2
La Paz, *Mexico* 114 C2
La Paz, *Phil.* 55 D4
La Paz □, *Bolivia* 124 D4
La Paz Centro, *Nic.* 116 D2
La Pedrera, *Colombia* 120 D4
La Perouse Str., *Asia* 48 B11
La Pesca, *Mexico* 115 C5
La Piedad, *Mexico* 114 C4
La Pine, *U.S.A.* 110 E3
La Plant, *U.S.A.* 108 C4
La Plata, *Argentina* 126 D4
La Plata, *Colombia* 120 C2
La Plata, L., *Argentina* 128 B2
La Pobla de Lillet, *Spain* 28 C6
La Pola de Gordón, *Spain* 30 C5
La Porte, *U.S.A.* 104 E2
La Puebla, *Spain* 28 F8
La Puebla de Cazalla, *Spain* 31 H5
La Puebla de los Infantes, *Spain* 31 H5
La Puebla de Montalbán, *Spain* 30 F6
La Puerta, *Spain* 29 G2
La Punt, *Switz.* 23 C9
La Purísima, *Mexico* 114 B2
La Push, *U.S.A.* 112 C2
La Quiaca, *Argentina* 126 A2
La Rambla, *Spain* 31 H6
La Reine, *Canada* 98 C4
La Réole, *France* 26 D3
La Restinga, *Canary Is.* 36 G2
La Rioja, *Argentina* 126 B2
La Rioja □, *Argentina* 126 B2
La Rioja □, *Spain* 28 C2
La Robla, *Spain* 30 C5
La Roche, *Switz.* 22 C4
La Roche-Bernard, *France* 24 E4
La Roche-Canillac, *France* 26 C5
La Roche-en-Ardenne, *Belgium* 17 H7
La Roche-sur-Yon, *France* 24 F5
La Rochefoucauld, *France* 26 C4
La Rochelle, *France* 26 B2
La Roda, *Albacete, Spain* 29 F2
La Roda, *Sevilla, Spain* 31 H6
La Romana, *Dom. Rep.* 117 C6
La Ronge, *Canada* 101 B7
La Rumorosa, *Mexico* 113 N10
La Sabina, *Spain* 36 C7
La Sagra, *Spain* 29 H2
La Salle, *U.S.A.* 108 E10
La Sanabria, *Spain* 30 C4
La Santa, *Canary Is.* 36 E6
La Sarraz, *Switz.* 22 C3
La Sarre, *Canada* 98 C4
La Scie, *Canada* 99 C8
La Selva, *Spain* 28 D7
La Selva Beach, *U.S.A.* 112 J5
La Serena, *Chile* 126 B1
La Serena, *Spain* 31 G5
La Seyne, *France* 27 E9
La Sila, *Italy* 35 C9
La Solana, *Spain* 29 G1
La Souterraine, *France* 26 B5
La Spézia, *Italy* 32 D6
La Suze-sur-Sarthe, *France* 24 E7
La Tagua, *Colombia* 120 C3
La Teste, *France* 26 D2
La Tortuga, *Venezuela* 117 D6
La Tour-du-Pin, *France* 27 C9
La Tranche-sur-Mer, *France* 24 F5
La Tremblade, *France* 26 C2
La Tuque, *Canada* 98 C5
La Unión, *Chile* 128 B2

La Unión, *Colombia* 120 C2
La Unión, *El Salv.* 116 D2
La Unión, *Mexico* 114 D4
La Unión, *Peru* 124 B2
La Unión, *Spain* 29 H4
La Urbana, *Venezuela* 120 B4
La Vecilla, *Spain* 30 C5
La Vega, *Dom. Rep.* 117 C5
La Vega, *Peru* 124 C2
La Vela, *Venezuela* 120 A4
La Veleta, *Spain* 31 H7
La Venta, *Mexico* 115 D6
La Ventura, *Mexico* 114 C4
La Venturosa, *Colombia* 120 B4
La Victoria, *Venezuela* 120 A4
La Voulte-sur-Rhône, *France* 27 D8
La Zarza, *Spain* 31 H4
Laaber →, *Germany* 19 G8
Laage, *Germany* 18 B8
Laba →, *Russia* 43 D8
Labason, *Phil.* 55 G5
Labastide-Murat, *France* 26 D5
Labastide-Rouairoux, *France* 26 E6
Labbézenga, *Mali* 79 B5
Labe = Elbe →, *Europe* 18 B4
Labé, *Guinea* 78 C2
Laberec →, *Slovakia* 20 G11
Laberge, L., *Canada* 100 A1
Labin, *Croatia* 33 C11
Labinsk, *Russia* 43 D9
Labis, *Malaysia* 59 L4
Labo, *Phil.* 55 D5
Laboe, *Germany* 18 A6
Labouheyre, *France* 26 D3
Laboulaye, *Argentina* 126 C3
Labra, Peña, *Spain* 30 B6
Labrador, Coast of □, *Canada* 99 B7
Labrador City, *Canada* 99 B6
Lábrea, *Brazil* 125 B5
Labrède, *France* 26 D3
Labuan, Pulau, *Malaysia* 56 C5
Labuha, *Indonesia* 57 E7
Labuhan, *Indonesia* 57 G11
Labuhanbajo, *Indonesia* 57 F6
Labuissière, *Belgium* 17 H4
Labuk, Telok, *Malaysia* 56 C5
Labyrinth, L., *Australia* 91 E2
Labytnangi, *Russia* 44 C7
Lac Allard, *Canada* 99 B7
Lac Bouchette, *Canada* 99 C5
Lac du Flambeau, *U.S.A.* 108 B10
Lac Édouard, *Canada* 98 C5
Lac La Biche, *Canada* 100 C6
Lac la Martre, *Canada* 96 B8
Lac-Mégantic, *Canada* 99 C5
Lac Seul, Res., *Canada* 98 B1
Lac Thien, *Vietnam* 58 F7
Lacanau, *France* 26 D2
Lacanau, Étang de, *France* 26 D2
Lacantúm →, *Mexico* 115 D6
Lacara →, *Spain* 31 G4
Lacaune, *France* 26 E6
Lacaune, Mts. de, *France* 26 E6
Laccadive Is. = Lakshadweep Is., *Ind. Oc.* 46 J11
Lacepede B., *Australia* 91 F2
Lacepede Is., *Australia* 88 C3
Lacerdónia, *Mozam.* 83 F4
Lacey, *U.S.A.* 112 C4
Lachay, Pta., *Peru* 124 C2
Lachen, *Switz.* 23 B7
Lachhmangarh, *India* 62 F6
Lachi, *Pakistan* 62 C4
Lachine, *Canada* 98 C5
Lachlan →, *Australia* 91 E3
Lachute, *Canada* 98 C5
Lackawanna, *U.S.A.* 106 D6
Lacolle, *Canada* 107 A11
Lacombe, *Canada* 100 C6
Lacona, *U.S.A.* 107 C8
Láconi, *Italy* 34 C2
Laconia, *U.S.A.* 107 C13
Lacq, *France* 26 E3
Lacrosse, *U.S.A.* 110 C5
Ladakh Ra., *India* 63 B8
Ladário, *Brazil* 125 D6
Ládhon →, *Greece* 39 M4
Lâdik, *Turkey* 42 F6
Ladismith, *S. Africa* 84 E3
Lādīz, *Iran* 65 D9
Ladnun, *India* 62 F6
Ladoga, L. = Ladozhskoye Ozero, *Russia* 44 C4
Ladon, *France* 25 D9
Ladozhskoye Ozero, *Russia* 44 C4
Ladrillero, G., *Chile* 128 C1
Lady Grey, *S. Africa* 84 E4
Ladybrand, *S. Africa* 84 D4
Ladysmith, *Canada* 100 D4
Ladysmith, *S. Africa* 85 D4
Ladysmith, *U.S.A.* 108 C9
Lae, *Papua N. G.* 92 H6
Laem Ngop, *Thailand* 59 F4
Laem Pho, *Thailand* 59 J3
Læsø, *Denmark* 11 G4
Læsø Rende, *Denmark* 11 G4
Lafayette, *Colo., U.S.A.* 108 F2
Lafayette, *Ind., U.S.A.* 104 E2
Lafayette, *La., U.S.A.* 109 K9
Lafayette, *Tenn., U.S.A.* 105 G3
Laferte →, *Canada* 100 A5
Lafia, *Nigeria* 79 D6
Lafiagi, *Nigeria* 79 D6
Lafleche, *Canada* 101 D7
Lafon, *Sudan* 77 F3
Laforsen, *Sweden* 10 C9
Lagan →, *Sweden* 11 H7
Lagan →, *U.K.* 15 B6
Lagarfljót →, *Iceland* 8 D6
Lagarto, *Brazil* 122 D4
Lage, *Germany* 18 D4
Lage, *Spain* 30 B2
Lage-Mierde, *Neths.* 17 F6
Lågen →, *Norway* 9 F11
Lägerdorf, *Germany* 18 B5
Laghouat, *Algeria* 75 B5
Lagnieu, *France* 27 C9
Lagny, *France* 25 D9
Lago, *Italy* 35 C9
Lago Posadas, *Argentina* 128 C2
Lago Ranco, *Chile* 128 B2
Lagôa, *Portugal* 31 H2
Lagoaça, *Portugal* 30 D4
Lagodekhi, *Georgia* 43 F12
Lagónegro, *Italy* 35 B8
Lagonoy Gulf, *Phil.* 55 E5
Lagos, *Nigeria* 79 D5
Lagos, *Portugal* 31 H2
Lagos de Moreno, *Mexico* 114 C4
Lagrange, *Australia* 88 C3
Lagrange B., *Australia* 88 C3
Laguardia, *Spain* 28 C2
Laguépie, *France* 26 D5
Laguna, *Brazil* 127 B6
Laguna, *U.S.A.* 111 J10
Laguna Beach, *U.S.A.* 113 M9
Laguna de la Janda, *Spain* 31 J5
Laguna Limpia, *Argentina* 126 B4
Laguna Madre, *U.S.A.* 115 B5
Lagunas, *Chile* 126 A2
Lagunas, *Peru* 124 B2
Lagunillas, *Bolivia* 125 D5
Lahad Datu, *Malaysia* 57 C5
Lahan Sai, *Thailand* 58 E4
Lahanam, *Laos* 58 D5
Laharpur, *India* 63 F9
Lahat, *Indonesia* 56 E2
Lahewa, *Indonesia* 56 D1
Lahiang Lahiang, *Phil.* 55 H4
Lahijan, *Iran* 65 B6
Lahn →, *Germany* 19 E3
Laholm, *Sweden* 11 H7
Laholmsbukten, *Sweden* 11 H6
Lahontan Reservoir, *U.S.A.* 110 G4
Lahore, *Pakistan* 62 D6
Lahr, *Germany* 19 G3
Lahti, *Finland* 9 F18
Lahtis = Lahti, *Finland* 9 F18
Laï, *Chad* 73 G8
Lai Chau, *Vietnam* 58 A4
Lai'an, *China* 53 A12
Laibin, *China* 52 F7
Laidley, *Australia* 91 D5
Laifeng, *China* 52 C7
L'Aigle, *France* 24 D7
Laignes, *France* 25 E11
L'Aiguillon-sur-Mer, *France* 26 B2
Laikipia □, *Kenya* 82 B4
Laingsburg, *S. Africa* 84 E3
Lairg, *U.K.* 14 C4
Laishui, *China* 50 E8
Laiwu, *China* 51 F9
Laixi, *China* 51 F11
Laiyang, *China* 51 F11
Laiyuan, *China* 50 E8
Laizhou Wan, *China* 51 F10
Laja →, *Mexico* 114 C4
Lajere, *Nigeria* 79 C7
Lajes, *Rio Grande do N., Brazil* 122 C4
Lajes, *Sta. Catarina, Brazil* 127 B5
Lajinha, *Brazil* 123 F3
Lajkovac, *Serbia, Yug.* 21 L10
Lajosmizse, *Hungary* 21 H9
Lak Sao, *Laos* 58 C5
Lakaband, *Pakistan* 62 D3
Lakar, *Indonesia* 57 F7
Lake Alpine, *U.S.A.* 112 G7
Lake Andes, *U.S.A.* 108 D5
Lake Anse, *U.S.A.* 104 B1
Lake Arthur, *U.S.A.* 109 K8
Lake Cargelligo, *Australia* 91 E4
Lake Charles, *U.S.A.* 109 K8
Lake City, *Colo., U.S.A.* 111 G10
Lake City, *Fla., U.S.A.* 105 K4
Lake City, *Iowa, U.S.A.* 108 D7
Lake City, *Mich., U.S.A.* 104 C3
Lake City, *Minn., U.S.A.* 108 C8
Lake City, *Pa., U.S.A.* 106 D4
Lake City, *S.C., U.S.A.* 105 J6
Lake George, *U.S.A.* 107 C11
Lake Grace, *Australia* 89 F2
Lake Harbour, *Canada* 97 B13
Lake Havasu City, *U.S.A.* 113 L12
Lake Hughes, *U.S.A.* 113 L8
Lake Isabella, *U.S.A.* 113 K8
Lake King, *Australia* 89 F2
Lake Lenore, *Canada* 101 C8
Lake Louise, *Canada* 100 C5
Lake Mead National Recreation Area, *U.S.A.* 113 K12
Lake Mills, *U.S.A.* 108 D8
Lake Nash, *Australia* 90 C2
Lake Providence, *U.S.A.* 109 J9
Lake River, *Canada* 98 B3
Lake Superior Prov. Park, *Canada* 98 C3
Lake Village, *U.S.A.* 109 J9
Lake Wales, *U.S.A.* 105 M5
Lake Worth, *U.S.A.* 105 M5
Lakefield, *Canada* 98 D4
Lakeland, *Australia* 90 B3
Lakeland, *U.S.A.* 105 L5
Lakemba, *Fiji* 87 D9
Lakeport, *U.S.A.* 112 F4
Lakes Entrance, *Australia* 91 F4
Lakeside, *Ariz., U.S.A.* 111 J9
Lakeside, *Calif., U.S.A.* 113 N10
Lakeside, *Nebr., U.S.A.* 108 D3
Lakeview, *U.S.A.* 110 E3
Lakewood, *Colo., U.S.A.* 108 F2
Lakewood, *N.J., U.S.A.* 107 F10
Lakewood, *Ohio, U.S.A.* 106 E3
Lakewood Center, *U.S.A.* 112 C4
Lakhaniá, *Greece* 37 D9
Lakhonpheng, *Laos* 58 E5
Lakhpat, *India* 62 H3
Laki, *Iceland* 8 D4
Lakin, *U.S.A.* 109 G4
Lakitusaki →, *Canada* 98 B3
Lákkoi, *Greece* 37 D5
Lakonikós Kólpos, *Greece* 39 N5
Lakota, *Ivory C.* 78 D3
Lakota, *U.S.A.* 108 A5
Laksefjorden, *Norway* 8 A19
Lakselv, *Norway* 8 A18
Lakshadweep Is., *Ind. Oc.* 46 J11
Lakshmikantapur, *India* 63 H13
Lala Ghat, *India* 61 G18
Lala Musa, *Pakistan* 62 C5
Lalago, *Tanzania* 82 C3
Lalapanzi, *Zimbabwe* 83 F3
Lalganj, *India* 63 G11
Lalibela, *Ethiopia* 77 E4
Lalin, *China* 51 B14
Lalín, *Spain* 30 C2
Lalin He →, *China* 51 B13
Lalinde, *France* 26 D4
Lalitapur = Patan, *Nepal* 61 F14
Lalitpur, *India* 63 G8
Lam, *Vietnam* 58 B6
Lam Pao Res., *Thailand* 58 D4
Lama Kara, *Togo* 79 D5
Lamaing, *Burma* 61 M20
Lamar, *Colo., U.S.A.* 108 F3
Lamar, *Mo., U.S.A.* 109 G7
Lamarque, *Argentina* 128 A3
Lamas, *Peru* 124 B2
Lamastre, *France* 27 D8
Lamballe, *France* 24 D4
Lambaréné, *Gabon* 80 E2
Lambasa, *Fiji* 87 C8
Lambay I., *Ireland* 15 C5
Lambayeque □, *Peru* 124 B2
Lambert, *U.S.A.* 108 B2
Lambert Glacier, *Antarctica* 5 D6
Lamberts Bay, *S. Africa* 84 E2
Lambesc, *France* 27 E9
Lámbia, *Greece* 39 M4
Lambro →, *Italy* 32 C6
Lame, *Nigeria* 79 C6
Lame Deer, *U.S.A.* 110 D10
Lamego, *Portugal* 30 D3
Lamèque, *Canada* 99 C7
Lameroo, *Australia* 91 F3
Lamesa, *U.S.A.* 109 J4
Lamía, *Greece* 39 L5
Lamitan, *Phil.* 55 H5
Lammermuir Hills, *U.K.* 14 F6
Lamon Bay, *Phil.* 55 D5
Lamont, *Canada* 100 C6
Lamont, *U.S.A.* 113 K8
Lampa, *Peru* 124 D3
Lampang, *Thailand* 58 C2
Lampasas, *U.S.A.* 109 K5
Lampaul, *France* 24 D1
Lampazos de Naranjo, *Mexico* 114 B4
Lampeter, *U.K.* 13 E3
Lampione, *Medit. S.* 75 A7
Lampman, *Canada* 101 D8
Lamprey, *Canada* 101 B10
Lampung □, *Indonesia* 56 F2
Lamu, *Kenya* 82 C5
Lamu □, *Kenya* 82 C5
Lamud, *Peru* 124 B2
Lamy, *U.S.A.* 111 J11
Lan Xian, *China* 50 E6
Lan Yu, *Taiwan* 53 F13
Lanai I., *U.S.A.* 102 H16
Lanak La, *India* 63 B8
Lanaken, *Belgium* 17 G7
Lanak'o Shank'ou = Lanak La, *India* 63 B8
Lanao, L., *Phil.* 55 H6
Lanark, *Canada* 107 A8
Lanark, *U.K.* 14 F5
Lancang, *China* 52 F2
Lancang Jiang →, *China* 52 G3
Lancashire □, *U.K.* 12 D5
Lancaster, *Canada* 107 A10
Lancaster, *U.K.* 12 C5
Lancaster, *Calif., U.S.A.* 113 L8
Lancaster, *Ky., U.S.A.* 104 G3
Lancaster, *N.H., U.S.A.* 107 B13
Lancaster, *N.Y., U.S.A.* 106 D6
Lancaster, *Pa., U.S.A.* 107 F8
Lancaster, *S.C., U.S.A.* 105 H5
Lancaster, *Wis., U.S.A.* 108 D9
Lancaster Sd., *Canada* 97 A11
Lancer, *Canada* 101 C7
Lanchow = Lanzhou, *China* 50 F2
Lanciano, *Italy* 33 F11
Lanco, *Chile* 128 A2
Lancones, *Peru* 124 A1
Lancun, *China* 51 F11
Łańcut, *Poland* 20 E12
Lancy, *Switz.* 22 D2
Landau, *Bayern, Germany* 19 G8
Landau, *Rhld-Pfz., Germany* 19 F4
Landeck, *Austria* 19 H6
Landen, *Belgium* 17 G6
Lander, *U.S.A.* 110 E9
Lander →, *Australia* 88 D5
Landerneau, *France* 24 D2
Landeryd, *Sweden* 11 G7
Landes, *France* 26 D3
Landes □, *France* 26 E3
Landete, *Spain* 28 F3
Landi Kotal, *Pakistan* 62 B4
Landivisiau, *France* 24 D2
Landor, *Australia* 89 E2
Landquart, *Switz.* 23 C9
Landquart →, *Switz.* 23 C9
Landrecies, *France* 25 B10
Land's End, *U.K.* 13 G2
Landsberg, *Germany* 19 G6
Landsborough Cr. →, *Australia* 90 C3
Landshut, *Germany* 19 G8
Landskrona, *Sweden* 11 J6
Landstuhl, *Germany* 19 F3
Landvetter, *Sweden* 11 G6
Laneffe, *Belgium* 17 H5
Lanesboro, *U.S.A.* 107 E9
Lanett, *U.S.A.* 105 J3
Lang Bay, *Canada* 100 D4
Lang Qua, *Vietnam* 58 A5
Lang Shan, *China* 50 D4
Lang Son, *Vietnam* 58 B6
Lang Suan, *Thailand* 59 H2
La'nga Co, *China* 61 D12
Lángadhás, *Greece* 39 J6
Langádhia, *Greece* 39 M5
Långan →, *Sweden* 10 A8
Langar, *Iran* 65 C9
Langara I., *Canada* 100 C2
Langatabbetje, *Surinam* 121 C7
Langdai, *China* 52 D5
Langdon, *U.S.A.* 108 A5
Langdorp, *Belgium* 17 G5
Langeac, *France* 26 C7
Langeais, *France* 24 E7
Langeb Baraka →, *Sudan* 76 D4
Langeberg, *S. Africa* 84 E3
Langeberge, *S. Africa* 84 D3
Langeland, *Denmark* 11 K4
Langemark, *Belgium* 17 G1
Langen, *Germany* 19 F4
Langenburg, *Canada* 101 C8
Langeness, *Germany* 18 A4
Langenthal, *Switz.* 22 B5
Langeoog, *Germany* 18 B3
Langeskov, *Denmark* 11 J4
Langesund, *Norway* 10 F3
Länghem, *Sweden* 11 G7
Langhirano, *Italy* 32 D7
Langholm, *U.K.* 14 F6
Langhus, *Norway* 10 E4
Langjökull, *Iceland* 8 D3
Langkawi, P., *Malaysia* 59 J2
Langklip, *S. Africa* 84 D3
Langkon, *Malaysia* 56 C5
Langlade, *St- P. & M.* 99 C8
Langlois, *U.S.A.* 110 E1
Langnau, *Switz.* 22 C5
Langogne, *France* 26 D7
Langon, *France* 26 D3
Langøya, *Norway* 8 B13
Langres, *France* 25 E12
Langres, Plateau de, *France* 25 E12
Langsa, *Indonesia* 56 D1
Långsele, *Sweden* 10 A11
Langtry, *U.S.A.* 109 L4
Langu, *Thailand* 59 J2
Languedoc, *France* 26 E7
Langwies, *Switz.* 23 C9
Langxi, *China* 53 B12
Langxiangzhen, *China* 50 E9
Langzhong, *China* 52 B5
Lanigan, *Canada* 101 C7
Lankao, *China* 50 G8
Lannemezan, *France* 26 E4
Lannilis, *France* 24 D2
Lannion, *France* 24 D3
L'Annonciation, *Canada* 98 C5
Lanouaille, *France* 26 C5
Lanping, *China* 52 D2
Lansdale, *U.S.A.* 107 F9
Lansdowne, *Australia* 91 E5
Lansdowne, *Canada* 107 B8
Lansdowne House, *Canada* 98 B2
L'Anse, *U.S.A.* 98 C2
L'Anse au Loup, *Canada* 99 B8
Lansford, *U.S.A.* 107 F9
Lanshan, *China* 53 E9
Lansing, *U.S.A.* 104 D3
Lanslebourg-Mont-Cenis, *France* 27 C10
Lanta Yai, Ko, *Thailand* 59 J2
Lantian, *China* 50 G5
Lanus, *Argentina* 126 C4
Lanusei, *Italy* 34 C2
Lanuza, *Phil.* 55 G7
Lanxi, *China* 53 C12
Lanzarote, *Canary Is.* 36 E6
Lanzhou, *China* 50 F2
Lanzo Torinese, *Italy* 32 C4
Lao →, *Italy* 35 C8
Lao Bao, *Laos* 58 D6
Lao Cai, *Vietnam* 58 A4
Laoag, *Phil.* 55 B4
Laoang, *Phil.* 55 E6
Laoha He →, *China* 51 C11
Laois □, *Ireland* 15 D4
Laon, *France* 25 C10
Laona, *U.S.A.* 104 C1
Laos ■, *Asia* 58 D5
Lapa, *Brazil* 127 B6
Lapalisse, *France* 26 B7
Laparan, *Phil.* 57 C6
Lapeer, *U.S.A.* 104 D4
Lapi □ = Lapin lääni □, *Finland* 8 C19
Lapin lääni □, *Finland* 8 C19
Lapithos, *Cyprus* 37 D12
Lapland = Lappland, *Europe* 8 B18
Laporte, *U.S.A.* 107 E8
Lapovo, *Serbia, Yug.* 21 L11
Lappland, *Europe* 8 B18
Laprida, *Argentina* 126 D3
Laptev Sea, *Russia* 45 B13
Lăpuşul →, *Romania* 38 B6
L'Áquila, *Italy* 33 F10
Lār, *Āzarbājān-e Sharqī, Iran* 64 B5
Lār, *Fārs, Iran* 65 E7
Lara □, *Venezuela* 120 A4
Larabanga, *Ghana* 78 D4
Laracha, *Spain* 30 B2
Larache, *Morocco* 74 A3
Laragne-Montéglin, *France* 27 D9
Laramie, *U.S.A.* 108 E2
Laramie Mts., *U.S.A.* 108 E2
Laranjeiras, *Brazil* 122 D4
Laranjeiras do Sul, *Brazil* 127 B5
Larantuka, *Indonesia* 57 F6
Larap, *Phil.* 55 D5
Larat, *Indonesia* 57 F8
L'Arbresle, *France* 27 C8
Larde, *Mozam.* 83 F4
Larder Lake, *Canada* 98 C4
Lardhos, Ákra, *Greece* 37 C10
Lardhos, Órmos, *Greece* 37 C10
Laredo, *Spain* 28 B1
Laredo, *U.S.A.* 109 M5
Laredo Sd., *Canada* 100 C3
Laren, *Neths.* 16 D6
Largentière, *France* 27 D8
L'Argentière-la-Bessée, *France* 27 D10
Largs, *U.K.* 14 F4
Lari, *Italy* 32 E7
Lariang, *Indonesia* 57 E5
Larimore, *U.S.A.* 108 B6
Lārīn, *Iran* 65 C7
Larino, *Italy* 35 A7
Lárisa, *Greece* 39 K5
Larkana, *Pakistan* 62 F3
Larnaca, *Cyprus* 37 E12
Larnaca Bay, *Cyprus* 37 E12
Larne, *U.K.* 15 B6
Larned, *U.S.A.* 108 F5
Larochette, *Belgium* 17 J8
Laroquebrou, *France* 26 D6
Larrimah, *Australia* 88 C5
Larsen Ice Shelf, *Antarctica* 5 C17
Larvik, *Norway* 10 E4
Laryak, *Russia* 44 C8
Larzac, Causse du, *France* 26 E7
Las Alpujarras, *Spain* 29 J1
Las Animas, *U.S.A.* 108 F3
Las Anod, *Somali Rep.* 68 F4
Las Blancos, *Spain* 29 H4
Las Brenãs, *Argentina* 126 B3
Las Cabezas de San Juan, *Spain* 31 J5
Las Chimeneas, *Mexico* 113 N10
Las Coloradas, *Argentina* 128 A2
Las Cruces, *U.S.A.* 111 K10
Las Flores, *Argentina* 126 D4
Las Heras, *Argentina* 126 C2
Las Horquetas, *Argentina* 128 C2
Las Khoreh, *Somali Rep.* 68 E4
Las Lajas, *Argentina* 128 A2
Las Lomas, *Peru* 124 A1
Las Lomitas, *Argentina* 126 A3
Las Marismas, *Spain* 31 H4
Las Mercedes, *Venezuela* 120 B4
Las Navas de la Concepción, *Spain* 31 H5
Las Navas de Tolosa, *Spain* 31 G7
Las Navas del Marqués, *Spain* 30 E6
Las Palmas, *Argentina* 126 B4
Las Palmas, *Canary Is.* 36 F4
Las Palmas →, *Mexico* 113 N10
Las Piedras, *Uruguay* 127 C4
Las Pipinas, *Argentina* 126 D4
Las Plumas, *Argentina* 128 B3
Las Rosas, *Argentina* 126 C3
Las Tablas, *Panama* 116 E3
Las Termas, *Argentina* 126 B3
Las Truchas, *Mexico* 114 D4
Las Varillas, *Argentina* 126 C3
Las Vegas, *N. Mex., U.S.A.* 111 J11

Las Vegas, *Nev., U.S.A.* 113 J11
Lascano, *Uruguay* 127 C5
Lashburn, *Canada* 101 C7
Lashio, *Burma* 61 H20
Lashkar, *India* 62 F8
Łasin, *Poland* 20 B9
Lasíthi, *Greece* 37 D7
Lasíthi □, *Greece* 37 D7
Laško, *Slovenia* 33 B12
Lassance, *Brazil* 123 E3
Lassay, *France* 24 D6
Lassen Pk., *U.S.A.* 110 F3
Last Mountain L., *Canada* 101 C7
Lastchance Cr. →, *U.S.A.* 112 E5
Lastoursville, *Gabon* 80 E2
Lastovo, *Croatia* 33 F13
Lastovski Kanal, *Croatia* 33 F13
Lat Yao, *Thailand* 58 E2
Latacunga, *Ecuador* 120 D2
Latakia = Al Lādhiqīyah, *Syria* 64 C2
Latchford, *Canada* 98 C4
Laterza, *Italy* 35 B9
Latham, *Australia* 89 E2
Lathen, *Germany* 18 C3
Lathrop Wells, *U.S.A.* 113 J10
Latiano, *Italy* 35 B10
Latina, *Italy* 34 A5
Latisana, *Italy* 33 C10
Latium = Lazio □, *Italy* 33 F9
Laton, *U.S.A.* 112 J7
Latorica →, *Slovakia* 21 G11
Latouche Treville, C., *Australia* 88 C3
Latrobe, *Australia* 90 G4
Latrobe, *U.S.A.* 106 F5
Latrónico, *Italy* 35 B9
Latvia ■, *Europe* 40 C3
Lau Group, *Fiji* 87 C9
Lauca →, *Bolivia* 124 D4
Lauchhammer, *Germany* 18 D9
Lauenburg, *Germany* 18 B6
Läufelfingen, *Switz.* 22 B5
Laufen, *Switz.* 22 B5
Lauffen, *Germany* 19 F5
Laugarbakki, *Iceland* 8 D3
Laujar, *Spain* 29 J2
Launceston, *Australia* 90 G4
Launceston, *U.K.* 13 G3
Laune →, *Ireland* 15 D2
Laupheim, *Germany* 19 G5
Laura, *Australia* 90 B3
Laureana di Borrello, *Italy* 35 D9
Laurel, *Miss., U.S.A.* 109 K10
Laurel, *Mont., U.S.A.* 110 D9
Laurencekirk, *U.K.* 14 E6
Laurens, *U.S.A.* 105 H4
Laurentian Plateau, *Canada* 99 B6
Laurentides, Parc Prov. des, *Canada* 99 C5
Lauria, *Italy* 35 B8
Laurie L., *Canada* 101 B8
Laurinburg, *U.S.A.* 105 H6
Laurium, *U.S.A.* 104 B1
Lausanne, *Switz.* 22 C3
Laut, *Indonesia* 56 D3
Laut Ketil, Kepulauan, *Indonesia* 56 E5
Lautaro, *Chile* 128 A2
Lauterbach, *Germany* 18 E5
Lauterbrunnen, *Switz.* 22 C5
Lauterecken, *Germany* 19 F3
Lautoka, *Fiji* 87 C7
Lauwe, *Belgium* 17 G2
Lauwers, *Neths.* 16 A8
Lauwers Zee, *Neths.* 16 B8
Lauzon, *Canada* 99 C5
Lava Hot Springs, *U.S.A.* 110 E7
Lavadores, *Spain* 30 C2
Lavagna, *Italy* 32 D6
Laval, *France* 24 D6
Lavalle, *Argentina* 126 B2
Lávara, *Greece* 39 H9
Lavardac, *France* 26 D4
Lavaur, *France* 26 E5
Lavaux, *Switz.* 22 D3
Lavelanet, *France* 26 F5
Lavello, *Italy* 35 A8
Laverne, *U.S.A.* 109 G5
Laverton, *Australia* 89 E3
Lavos, *Portugal* 30 E2
Lavras, *Brazil* 123 F3
Lavre, *Portugal* 31 G2
Lavrentiya, *Russia* 45 C19
Lávrion, *Greece* 39 M7
Lávris, *Greece* 37 D6
Lavumisa, *Swaziland* 85 D5
Lawas, *Malaysia* 56 D5
Lawele, *Indonesia* 57 F6
Lawn Hill, *Australia* 90 B2
Lawng Pit, *Burma* 61 G20
Lawqar, *Si. Arabia* 64 D4
Lawra, *Ghana* 78 C4
Lawrence, *N.Z.* 87 L2
Lawrence, *Kans., U.S.A.* 108 F7
Lawrence, *Mass., U.S.A.* 107 D13
Lawrenceburg, *Ind., U.S.A.* 104 F3
Lawrenceburg, *Tenn., U.S.A.* 105 H2
Lawrenceville, *U.S.A.* 105 J4
Laws, *U.S.A.* 112 H8
Lawton, *U.S.A.* 109 H5
Lawu, *Indonesia* 57 G14
Laxford, L., *U.K.* 14 C3
Laylān, *Iraq* 64 C5
Layon →, *France* 24 E6
Laysan I., *Pac. Oc.* 93 E11
Laytonville, *U.S.A.* 110 G2
Lazio □, *Italy* 33 F9
Lazo, *Russia* 48 C6
Le Barcarès, *France* 26 F7
Le Beausset, *France* 27 E9
Le Blanc, *France* 26 B5
Le Bleymard, *France* 26 D7
Le Bourgneuf-la-Fôret, *France* 24 D6
Le Bouscat, *France* 26 D3
Le Brassus, *Switz.* 22 C2
Le Bugue, *France* 26 D4
Le Canourgue, *France* 26 D7
Le Cateau, *France* 25 B10
Le Chambon-Feugerolles, *France* 27 C8
Le Château-d'Oléron, *France* 26 C2
Le Châtelard, *Switz.* 22 D3
Le Châtelet, *France* 26 B6
Le Châtelet-en-Brie, *France* 25 D9
Le Chesne, *France* 25 C11
Le Cheylard, *France* 27 D8
Le Conquet, *France* 24 D2
Le Creusot, *France* 25 F11
Le Croisic, *France* 24 E4
Le Donjon, *France* 26 B7
Le Dorat, *France* 26 B5
Le François, *Martinique* 117 D7
Le Grand-Lucé, *France* 24 E7
Le Grand-Pressigny, *France* 24 F7
Le Havre, *France* 24 C7
Le Lavandou, *France* 27 E10
Le Lion-d'Angers, *France* 24 E6
Le Locle, *Switz.* 22 B3
Le Louroux-Béconnais, *France* 24 E6
Le Luc, *France* 27 E10
Le Madonie, *Italy* 34 E6
Le Maire, Est. de, *Argentina* 128 D4
Le Mans, *France* 24 E7
Le Marinel, *Zaïre* 83 E2
Le Mars, *U.S.A.* 108 D6
Le Mêle-sur-Sarthe, *France* 24 D7
Le Merlerault, *France* 24 D7
Le Monastier-sur-Gazeille, *France* 26 D7
Le Monêtier-les-Bains, *France* 27 D10
Le Mont d'Or, *France* 25 F13
Le Mont-Dore, *France* 26 C6
Le Mont-St.-Michel, *France* 24 D5
Le Moule, *Guadeloupe* 117 C7
Le Muy, *France* 27 E10
Le Palais, *France* 24 E3
Le Perthus, *France* 26 F6
Le Pont, *Switz.* 22 C2
Le Pouldu, *France* 24 E3
Le Puy, *France* 26 C7
Le Quesnoy, *France* 25 B10
Le Roy, *U.S.A.* 109 F7
Le Sentier, *Switz.* 22 C2
Le Sueur, *U.S.A.* 108 C8
Le Teil, *France* 27 D8
Le Teilleul, *France* 24 D6
Le Theil, *France* 24 D7
Le Thillot, *France* 25 E13
Le Thuy, *Vietnam* 58 D6
Le Touquet-Paris-Plage, *France* 25 B8
Le Tréport, *France* 24 B8
Le Val-d'Ajol, *France* 25 E13
Le Verdon-sur-Mer, *France* 26 C2
Le Vigan, *France* 26 E7
Lea →, *U.K.* 13 F7
Leach, *Cambodia* 59 F4
Lead, *U.S.A.* 108 C3
Leader, *Canada* 101 C7
Leadhills, *U.K.* 14 F5
Leadville, *U.S.A.* 111 G10
Leaf →, *U.S.A.* 109 K10
Leakey, *U.S.A.* 109 L5
Leamington, *Canada* 98 D3
Leamington, *U.S.A.* 110 G7
Leamington Spa = Royal Leamington Spa, *U.K.* 13 E6
Le'an, *China* 53 D10
Leandro Norte Alem, *Argentina* 127 B4
Learmonth, *Australia* 88 D1
Leask, *Canada* 101 C7
Leavenworth, *Kans., U.S.A.* 108 F7
Leavenworth, *Wash., U.S.A.* 110 C3
Łeba, *Poland* 20 A7
Lebak, *Phil.* 55 H6
Lebam, *U.S.A.* 112 D3
Lebanon, *Ind., U.S.A.* 104 E2
Lebanon, *Kans., U.S.A.* 108 F5
Lebanon, *Ky., U.S.A.* 104 G3
Lebanon, *Mo., U.S.A.* 109 G8
Lebanon, *Oreg., U.S.A.* 110 D2
Lebanon, *Pa., U.S.A.* 107 F8
Lebanon, *Tenn., U.S.A.* 105 G2
Lebanon ■, *Asia* 69 B4
Lebbeke, *Belgium* 17 G4
Lebec, *U.S.A.* 113 L8
Lebedin, *Ukraine* 40 F9
Lebedyan, *Russia* 41 E11
Lebomboberge, *S. Africa* 85 C5
Lębork, *Poland* 20 A7
Lebrija, *Spain* 31 J4
Lebu, *Chile* 126 D1
Lecce, *Italy* 35 B11
Lecco, *Italy* 32 C6
Lecco, L. di, *Italy* 32 C6
Lécera, *Spain* 28 D4
Lech, *Austria* 19 H6
Lech →, *Germany* 19 G6
Lechang, *China* 53 E9
Lechtaler Alpen, *Austria* 19 H6
Lectoure, *France* 26 E4
Łęczyca, *Poland* 20 C9
Ledbury, *U.K.* 13 E5
Lede, *Belgium* 17 G3
Ledeberg, *Belgium* 17 F3
Ledesma, *Spain* 30 D5
Ledong, *China* 58 C7
Leduc, *Canada* 100 C6
Ledyczek, *Poland* 20 B6
Lee, *U.S.A.* 107 D11
Lee →, *Ireland* 15 E3
Lee Vining, *U.S.A.* 112 H7
Leech L., *U.S.A.* 108 B7
Leedey, *U.S.A.* 109 H5
Leeds, *U.K.* 12 D6
Leeds, *U.S.A.* 105 J2
Leek, *Neths.* 16 B8
Leek, *U.K.* 12 D5
Leende, *Neths.* 17 F7
Leer, *Germany* 18 B3
Leerdam, *Neths.* 16 E6
Leersum, *Neths.* 16 E6
Leesburg, *U.S.A.* 105 L5
Leesville, *U.S.A.* 109 K8
Leeton, *Australia* 91 E4
Leetonia, *U.S.A.* 106 F4
Leeu Gamka, *S. Africa* 84 E3
Leeuwarden, *Neths.* 16 B7
Leeuwin, C., *Australia* 89 F2
Leeward Is., *Atl. Oc.* 117 C7
Lefka, *Cyprus* 37 D11
Lefkoniko, *Cyprus* 37 D12
Lefors, *U.S.A.* 109 H4
Lefroy, L., *Australia* 89 F3
Legal, *Canada* 100 C6
Leganés, *Spain* 30 E7
Legazpi, *Phil.* 55 E5
Legendre I., *Australia* 88 D2
Leghorn = Livorno, *Italy* 32 E7
Legionowo, *Poland* 20 C10
Léglise, *Belgium* 17 J7
Legnago, *Italy* 33 C8
Legnano, *Italy* 32 C5
Legnica, *Poland* 20 D6
Legrad, *Croatia* 33 B13
Legume, *Australia* 91 D5
Leh, *India* 63 B7
Lehi, *U.S.A.* 110 F8
Lehighton, *U.S.A.* 107 F9
Lehrte, *Germany* 18 C5
Lehututu, *Botswana* 84 C3
Lei Shui →, *China* 53 D9
Leiah, *Pakistan* 62 D4
Leibnitz, *Austria* 21 J5
Leibo, *China* 52 C4
Leicester, *U.K.* 13 E6
Leicestershire □, *U.K.* 13 E6
Leichhardt →, *Australia* 90 B2
Leichhardt Ra., *Australia* 90 C4
Leiden, *Neths.* 16 D5
Leiderdorp, *Neths.* 16 D5
Leidschendam, *Neths.* 16 D4
Leie →, *Belgium* 25 A10
Leignon, *Belgium* 17 H6
Leine →, *Germany* 18 C5
Leinster, *Australia* 89 E3
Leinster □, *Ireland* 15 C4
Leinster, Mt., *Ireland* 15 D5
Leipzig, *Germany* 18 D8
Leiria, *Portugal* 31 F2
Leiria □, *Portugal* 31 F2
Leisler, Mt., *Australia* 88 D4
Leith, *U.K.* 14 F5
Leith Hill, *U.K.* 13 F7
Leitha →, *Europe* 21 H7
Leitrim, *Ireland* 15 B3
Leitrim □, *Ireland* 15 B3
Leiyang, *China* 53 D9
Leiza, *Spain* 28 B3
Leizhou Bandao, *China* 54 D6
Leizhou Wan, *China* 53 G8
Lek →, *Neths.* 16 E5
Leke, *Belgium* 17 F1
Lekkerkerk, *Neths.* 16 E5
Leksula, *Indonesia* 57 E7
Leland, *U.S.A.* 109 J9
Leland Lakes, *Canada* 101 A6
Leleque, *Argentina* 128 B2
Lelystad, *Neths.* 16 D6
Lema, *Nigeria* 79 C5
Léman, Lac, *Switz.* 22 D3
Lemelerveld, *Neths.* 16 D8
Lemera, *Zaïre* 82 C2
Lemery, *Phil.* 55 E4
Lemgo, *Germany* 18 C4
Lemhi Ra., *U.S.A.* 110 D7
Lemmer, *Neths.* 16 C7
Lemmon, *U.S.A.* 108 C3
Lemon Grove, *U.S.A.* 113 N9
Lemoore, *U.S.A.* 111 H4
Lempdes, *France* 26 C7
Lemsid, *W. Sahara* 74 C2
Lemvig, *Denmark* 11 H2
Lena →, *Russia* 45 B13
Lencloître, *France* 24 F7
Lençóis, *Brazil* 123 D3
Léndas, *Greece* 37 E6
Lendeh, *Iran* 65 D6
Lendelede, *Belgium* 17 G2
Lendinara, *Italy* 33 C8
Lengerich, *Germany* 18 C3
Lenggong, *Malaysia* 59 K3
Lenggries, *Germany* 19 H7
Lengua de Vaca, Pta., *Chile* 126 C1
Lenin, *Russia* 43 B9
Leninabad = Khodzent, *Tajikistan* 44 E7
Leninakan = Kumayri, *Armenia* 43 F10
Leningrad = Sankt-Peterburg, *Russia* 40 B7
Lenino, *Ukraine* 42 D6
Leninogorsk = Ridder, *Kazakhstan* 44 D9
Leninsk, *Russia* 43 B11
Leninsk, *Russia* 43 C10
Leninsk-Kuznetskiy, *Russia* 44 D9
Leninskaya Sloboda, *Russia* 41 C14
Leninskoye, *Russia* 41 B15
Leninskoye, *Russia* 45 E14
Lenk, *Switz.* 22 D4
Lenkoran, *Azerbaijan* 67 D13
Lenmalu, *Indonesia* 57 E8
Lenne →, *Germany* 18 D3
Lennox, I., *Chile* 128 E3
Lennoxville, *Canada* 107 A13
Leno, *Italy* 32 C7
Lenoir, *U.S.A.* 105 H5
Lenoir City, *U.S.A.* 105 H3
Lenora, *U.S.A.* 108 F4
Lenore L., *Canada* 101 C8
Lenox, *U.S.A.* 107 D11
Lens, *Belgium* 17 G3
Lens, *France* 25 B9
Lens St. Remy, *Belgium* 17 G6
Lensk, *Russia* 45 C12
Lenskoye, *Ukraine* 42 D6
Lent, *Neths.* 16 E7
Lentini, *Italy* 35 E8
Lentvaric, *Lithuania* 40 D4
Lenwood, *U.S.A.* 113 L9
Lenzburg, *Switz.* 22 B6
Lenzen, *Germany* 18 B7
Lenzerheide, *Switz.* 23 C9
Léo, *Burkina Faso* 78 C4
Leoben, *Austria* 21 H5
Leola, *U.S.A.* 108 C5
Leominster, *U.K.* 13 E5
Leominster, *U.S.A.* 107 D13
Léon, *France* 26 E2
León, *Mexico* 114 C4
León, *Nic.* 116 D2
León, *Spain* 30 C5
Leon, *U.S.A.* 108 E8
León □, *Spain* 30 C5
León, Montañas de, *Spain* 30 C4
Leonardtown, *U.S.A.* 104 F7
Leone, Mte., *Switz.* 22 D6
Leonforte, *Italy* 35 E7
Leongatha, *Australia* 91 F4
Leonídhion, *Greece* 39 M5
Leonora, *Australia* 89 E3
Léopold II, Lac = Mai-Ndombe, L., *Zaïre* 80 E3
Leopoldina, *Brazil* 123 F3
Leopoldo Bulhões, *Brazil* 123 E2
Leopoldsburg, *Belgium* 17 F6
Léopoldville = Kinshasa, *Zaïre* 80 E3
Leoti, *U.S.A.* 108 F4
Leoville, *Canada* 101 C7
Lépa, L. do, *Angola* 84 B2
Lepe, *Spain* 31 H3
Lepel, *Belorussia* 40 D6
Lepikha, *Russia* 45 C13
Leping, *China* 53 C11
Lepontine, Alpi, *Italy* 23 D6
Lequeitio, *Spain* 28 B2
Lercara Friddi, *Italy* 34 E6
Lerdo, *Mexico* 114 B4
Léré, *Chad* 73 G7
Lere, *Nigeria* 79 D6
Leribe, *Lesotho* 85 D4
Lérici, *Italy* 32 D6
Lérida, *Spain* 28 D5
Lérida □, *Spain* 28 C6
Lérins, Is. de, *France* 27 E11
Lerma, *Spain* 30 C7
Léros, *Greece* 39 M9
Lérouville, *France* 25 D12
Lerwick, *U.K.* 14 A7
Les Abrets, *France* 27 C9
Les Andelys, *France* 24 C8
Les Arcs, *France* 27 E10
Les Baux-de-Provence, *France* 27 E8
Les Bois, *Switz.* 22 B3
Les Cayes, *Haiti* 117 C5
Les Diablerets, *Switz.* 22 D4
Les Échelles, *France* 27 C9
Les Essarts, *France* 24 F5
Les Étroits, *Canada* 99 C6
Les Eyzies-de-Tayac-Sireuil, *France* 26 D5
Les Herbiers, *France* 24 F5
Les Minquiers, *Chan. Is.* 24 D4
Les Ponts-de-Cé, *France* 24 E6
Les Riceys, *France* 25 E11
Les Sables-d'Olonne, *France* 26 B2
Les Vans, *France* 27 D8
Les Verrières, *Switz.* 22 C2
Lesbos = Lésvos, *Greece* 39 K9
Leshan, *China* 52 C4
Lésina, L. di, *Italy* 33 G12
Lesja, *Norway* 10 B2
Lesjaverk, *Norway* 10 B2
Leskov I., *Antarctica* 5 B1
Leskovac, *Serbia, Yug.* 21 M11
Leslie, *U.S.A.* 109 H8
Lesneven, *France* 24 D2
Lešnica, *Serbia, Yug.* 21 L9
Lesnoye, *Russia* 40 B9
Lesopilnoye, *Russia* 48 A7
Lesotho ■, *Africa* 85 D4
Lesozavodsk, *Russia* 45 E14
Lesparre-Médoc, *France* 26 C3
Lessay, *France* 24 C5
Lesse →, *Belgium* 17 H5
Lesser Antilles, *W. Indies* 117 C7
Lesser Slave L., *Canada* 100 B5
Lesser Sunda Is., *Indonesia* 57 F6
Lessines, *Belgium* 17 G3
Lester, *U.S.A.* 112 C5
Lestock, *Canada* 101 C8
Lesuer I., *Australia* 88 B4
Lésvos, *Greece* 39 K9
Leszno, *Poland* 20 D6
Letchworth, *U.K.* 13 F7
Letea, Ostrov, *Romania* 38 D12
Lethbridge, *Canada* 100 D6
Lethem, *Guyana* 121 C6
Leti, Kepulauan, *Indonesia* 57 F7
Leti Is. = Leti, Kepulauan, *Indonesia* 57 F7
Letiahau →, *Botswana* 84 C3
Leticia, *Colombia* 120 D4
Leting, *China* 51 E10
Letjiesbos, *S. Africa* 84 E3
Letlhakeng, *Botswana* 84 C3
Letpadan, *Burma* 61 L19
Letpan, *Burma* 61 K19
Letterkenny, *Ireland* 15 B4
Leu, *Romania* 38 E7
Leucadia, *U.S.A.* 113 M9
Leucate, *France* 26 F7
Leucate, Étang de, *France* 26 F7
Leuk, *Switz.* 22 D5
Leukerbad, *Switz.* 22 D5
Leupegem, *Belgium* 17 G3
Leuser, G., *Indonesia* 56 D1
Leutkirch, *Germany* 19 H6
Leuven, *Belgium* 17 G5
Leuze, *Hainaut, Belgium* 17 G3
Leuze, *Namur, Belgium* 17 G5
Lev Tolstoy, *Russia* 41 E11
Levádhia, *Greece* 39 L5
Levan, *U.S.A.* 110 G8
Levanger, *Norway* 8 E11
Levant, I. du, *France* 27 E10
Lévanto, *Italy* 32 D6
Levanzo, *Italy* 34 E5
Levelland, *U.S.A.* 109 J3
Leven, *U.K.* 14 E6
Leven, L., *U.K.* 14 E5
Leven, Toraka, *Madag.* 85 A8
Levens, *France* 27 E11
Leveque C., *Australia* 88 C3
Leverano, *Italy* 35 B10
Leverkusen, *Germany* 18 D2
Levet, *France* 25 F9
Levice, *Slovakia* 21 G8
Levico, *Italy* 33 C8
Levie, *France* 27 G13
Levier, *France* 25 F13
Levin, *N.Z.* 87 J5
Lévis, *Canada* 99 C5
Levis, L., *Canada* 100 A5
Levítha, *Greece* 39 M9
Levittown, *N.Y., U.S.A.* 107 F11
Levittown, *Pa., U.S.A.* 107 F10
Levka Óri, *Greece* 37 D6
Levkás, *Greece* 39 L3
Levkímmi, *Greece* 37 B4
Levkímmi, Ákra, *Greece* 37 B4
Levkôsia = Nicosia, *Cyprus* 37 D12
Levoča, *Slovakia* 20 F10
Levroux, *France* 25 F8
Levski, *Bulgaria* 38 F8
Levskigrad, *Bulgaria* 38 G7
Lewellen, *U.S.A.* 108 E3
Lewes, *U.K.* 13 G8
Lewes, *U.S.A.* 104 F8
Lewis, *U.K.* 14 C2
Lewis →, *U.S.A.* 112 E4
Lewis, Butt of, *U.K.* 14 C2
Lewis Ra., *Australia* 88 D4
Lewis Range, *U.S.A.* 110 C7
Lewisburg, *Pa., U.S.A.* 106 F8
Lewisburg, *Tenn., U.S.A.* 105 H2
Lewisporte, *Canada* 99 C8
Lewiston, *Idaho, U.S.A.* 110 C5
Lewiston, *Maine, U.S.A.* 105 C11
Lewistown, *Mont., U.S.A.* 110 C9
Lewistown, *Pa., U.S.A.* 106 F7
Lexington, *Ill., U.S.A.* 108 E10
Lexington, *Ky., U.S.A.* 104 F3
Lexington, *Miss., U.S.A.* 109 J9
Lexington, *Mo., U.S.A.* 108 F8
Lexington, *N.C., U.S.A.* 105 H5
Lexington, *Nebr., U.S.A.* 108 E5
Lexington, *Ohio, U.S.A.* 106 F2
Lexington, *Oreg., U.S.A.* 110 D4

Lexington, *Tenn., U.S.A.* . 105 H1
Lexington Park, *U.S.A.* .. 104 F7
Leye, *China* 52 E6
Leyre →, *France* 26 D2
Leysin, *Switz.* 22 D4
Leyte, *Phil.* 55 F6
Leyte Gulf, *Phil.* 55 F6
Lezay, *France* 26 B4
Lezha, *Albania* 39 H2
Lezhi, *China* 52 B5
Lézignan-Corbières, *France* 26 E6
Lezoux, *France* 26 C7
Lgov, *Russia* 40 F9
Lhasa, *China* 54 D4
Lhazê, *China* 54 D3
Lhokkruet, *Indonesia* 56 D1
Lhokseumawe, *Indonesia* . 56 C1
Lhuntsi Dzong, *India* 61 F17
Li, *Thailand* 58 D2
Li Shui →, *China* 53 C9
Li Xian, *Gansu, China* 50 G3
Li Xian, *Hebei, China* 50 E8
Li Xian, *Hunan, China* ... 53 C8
Li Xian, *Sichuan, China* .. 52 B4
Liádhoi, *Greece* 39 N9
Lian Xian, *China* 53 E9
Liancheng, *China* 53 E11
Lianga, *Phil.* 55 G7
Liangcheng,
Nei Mongol Zizhiqu, China 50 D7
Liangcheng, *Shandong, China* 51 G10
Liangdang, *China* 50 H4
Lianghekou, *China* 52 C7
Liangping, *China* 52 B6
Lianhua, *China* 53 D9
Lianjiang, *Fujian, China* .. 53 D12
Lianjiang, *Guangdong, China* 53 G8
Lianping, *China* 53 E10
Lianshan, *China* 53 E9
Lianshanguan, *China* 51 D12
Lianshui, *China* 51 H10
Lianyuan, *China* 53 D8
Lianyungang, *China* 51 G10
Liao He →, *China* 51 D11
Liaocheng, *China* 50 F8
Liaodong Bandao, *China* . 51 E12
Liaodong Wan, *China* 51 D11
Liaoning □, *China* 54 B7
Liaoning □, *Liaoning, China* 51 D12
Liaoyang, *China* 51 D12
Liaoyuan, *China* 51 C13
Liaozhong, *China* 51 D12
Liapádhes, *Greece* 39 K2
Liard →, *Canada* 100 A4
Liari, *Pakistan* 62 G2
Líbano, *Colombia* 120 C2
Libau = Liepāja, *Latvia* .. 40 C2
Libby, *U.S.A.* 110 B6
Libenge, *Zaïre* 80 D3
Liberal, *Kans., U.S.A.* ... 109 G4
Liberal, *Mo., U.S.A.* 109 G7
Liberdade, *Brazil* 124 C3
Liberdade →, *Brazil* 125 B7
Liberec, *Czech.* 20 E5
Liberia, *Costa Rica* 116 D2
Liberia ■, *W. Afr.* 78 D3
Libertad, *Venezuela* 120 B4
Liberty, *Mo., U.S.A.* 108 F7
Liberty, *Tex., U.S.A.* 109 K7
Libin, *Belgium* 17 J6
Lîbîya, Sahrâ', *Africa* 73 C9
Libo, *China* 52 E6
Libobo, Tanjung, *Indonesia* 57 E7
Libode, *S. Africa* 85 E4
Libonda, *Zambia* 81 G4
Libourne, *France* 26 D3
Libramont, *Belgium* 17 J6
Libreville, *Gabon* 80 D1
Libya ■, *N. Afr.* 73 C8
Libyan Desert = Lîbîya, Sahrâ', *Africa* 73 C9
Libyan Plateau = Ed-Déffa, *Egypt* 76 A2
Licantén, *Chile* 126 D1
Licata, *Italy* 34 E6
Lice, *Turkey* 67 D9
Licheng, *China* 50 F7
Lichfield, *U.K.* 12 E6
Lichinga, *Mozam.* 83 E4
Lichtaart, *Belgium* 17 F5
Lichtenburg, *S. Africa* 84 D4
Lichtenfels, *Germany* 19 E7
Lichtenvoorde, *Neths.* 16 E9
Lichtervelde, *Belgium* 17 F2
Lichuan, *Hubei, China* 52 B7
Lichuan, *Jiangxi, China* .. 53 D11
Licosa, Punta, *Italy* 35 B7
Lida, *Belorussia* 40 E4
Lida, *U.S.A.* 111 H5
Lidingö, *Sweden* 10 E12
Lidköping, *Sweden* 11 F7
Lido, *Italy* 33 C9
Lido, *Niger* 79 C5
Lido di Roma = Óstia, Lido di, *Italy* 34 A5
Lidzbark Warminski, *Poland* 20 A10
Liebenwalde, *Germany* ... 18 C9
Lieberose, *Germany* 18 D10
Liebig, Mt., *Australia* 88 D5
Liechtenstein ■, *Europe* .. 23 B9
Liederkerke, *Belgium* 17 G4
Liège, *Belgium* 17 G7
Liège □, *Belgium* 17 G7
Liegnitz = Legnica, *Poland* 20 D6
Liempde, *Neths.* 17 E6
Lienart, *Zaïre* 82 B2
Lienyünchiangshih = Lianyungang, *China* 51 G10
Lienz, *Austria* 21 J2
Liepāja, *Latvia* 40 C2
Lier, *Belgium* 17 F5
Lierneux, *Belgium* 17 H7
Lieshout, *Neths.* 17 E7
Liestal, *Switz.* 22 B5
Liévin, *France* 25 B9
Lièvre →, *Canada* 98 C4
Liezen, *Austria* 21 H4
Liffey →, *Ireland* 15 C5
Lifford, *Ireland* 15 B4
Liffré, *France* 24 D5
Lifjell, *Norway* 10 E2
Lifudzin, *Russia* 48 B7
Ligao, *Phil.* 55 E5
Lightning Ridge, *Australia* 91 D4
Lignano, *Italy* 33 C10
Ligny-en-Barrois, *France* . 25 D12
Ligny-le-Châtel, *France* .. 25 E10
Ligoúrion, *Greece* 39 M6
Ligueil, *France* 24 E7
Liguria □, *Italy* 32 D6
Ligurian Sea, *Italy* 32 E5
Lihou Reefs and Cays, *Australia* 90 B5
Lihue, *U.S.A.* 102 H15
Lijiang, *China* 52 D3
Likasi, *Zaïre* 83 E2
Likati, *Zaïre* 80 D4
Likhoslavl, *Russia* 40 C9
Likhovski, *Russia* 43 B9
Likoma I., *Malawi* 83 E3
Likumburu, *Tanzania* 83 D4
L'Île-Bouchard, *France* ... 24 E7
L'Ile-Rousse, *France* 27 F12
Liling, *China* 53 D9
Lille, *Belgium* 17 F5
Lille, *France* 25 B10
Lille Bælt, *Denmark* 11 J3
Lillebonne, *France* 24 C7
Lillehammer, *Norway* 10 C4
Lillers, *France* 25 B9
Lillesand, *Norway* 11 F2
Lilleshall, *U.K.* 13 E5
Lillestrøm, *Norway* 10 E5
Lillian Point, Mt., *Australia* 89 E4
Lillo, *Spain* 28 F1
Lillooet →, *Canada* 100 D4
Lilongwe, *Malawi* 83 E3
Liloy, *Phil.* 57 C6
Lim →, *Bos.-H.* 21 M9
Lima, *Indonesia* 57 E7
Lima, *Peru* 124 C2
Lima, *Mont., U.S.A.* 110 D7
Lima, *Ohio, U.S.A.* 104 E3
Lima □, *Peru* 124 C2
Lima →, *Portugal* 30 D2
Limages, *Canada* 107 A9
Liman, *Russia* 43 D12
Limassol, *Cyprus* 37 E12
Limavady, *U.K.* 15 A5
Limavady □, *U.K.* 15 B5
Limay →, *Argentina* 128 A3
Limay Mahuida, *Argentina* 126 D2
Limbang, *Brunei* 56 D5
Limbara, Monti, *Italy* 34 B2
Limbdi, *India* 62 H4
Limbe, *Cameroon* 79 E6
Limbourg, *Belgium* 17 G7
Limbri, *Australia* 91 E5
Limbunya, *Australia* 88 C4
Limburg, *Germany* 19 E4
Limburg □, *Belgium* 17 F6
Limburg □, *Neths.* 17 F7
Limeira, *Brazil* 127 A6
Limerick, *Ireland* 15 D3
Limerick □, *Ireland* 15 D3
Limestone, *U.S.A.* 106 D6
Limestone →, *Canada* ... 101 B10
Limfjorden, *Denmark* 11 H3
Limia = Lima →, *Portugal* 30 D2
Limmared, *Sweden* 11 G7
Limmat →, *Switz.* 23 B6
Limmen, *Neths.* 16 C5
Limmen Bight, *Australia* .. 90 A2
Limmen Bight →, *Australia* 90 B2
Límni, *Greece* 39 L6
Límnos, *Greece* 39 K8
Limoeiro, *Brazil* 122 C4
Limoeiro do Norte, *Brazil* 122 C4
Limoges, *France* 26 C5
Limón, *Costa Rica* 116 D3
Limon, *U.S.A.* 108 F3
Limone Piemonte, *Italy* ... 32 D4
Limousin, *France* 26 C5
Limousin, Plateaux du, *France* 26 C5
Limoux, *France* 26 E6
Limpopo →, *Africa* 85 D5
Limuru, *Kenya* 82 C4
Lin Xian, *China* 50 F6
Lin'an, *China* 53 B12
Linapacan I., *Phil.* 55 F3
Linapacan Str., *Phil.* 55 F3
Linares, *Chile* 126 D1
Linares, *Colombia* 120 C2
Linares, *Mexico* 115 C5
Linares, *Spain* 29 G1
Linares □, *Chile* 126 D1
Línas Mte., *Italy* 34 C1
Lincang, *China* 52 F3
Lincheng, *China* 50 F8
Linchuan, *China* 53 D11
Lincoln, *Argentina* 126 C3
Lincoln, *N.Z.* 87 K4
Lincoln, *U.K.* 12 D7
Lincoln, *Calif., U.S.A.* ... 112 G5
Lincoln, *Ill., U.S.A.* 108 E10
Lincoln, *Kans., U.S.A.* ... 108 F5
Lincoln, *Maine, U.S.A.* ... 99 C6
Lincoln, *N.H., U.S.A.* ... 107 B13
Lincoln, *N. Mex., U.S.A.* . 111 K11
Lincoln, *Nebr., U.S.A.* ... 108 E6
Lincoln Hav = Lincoln Sea, *Arctic* 4 A5
Lincoln Sea, *Arctic* 4 A5
Lincoln Wolds, *U.K.* 12 D7
Lincolnshire □, *U.K.* 12 D7
Lincolnton, *U.S.A.* 105 H5
L'Incudine, *France* 27 G13
Lind, *U.S.A.* 110 C4
Linda, *U.S.A.* 112 F5
Lindau, *Germany* 19 H5
Linde →, *Neths.* 16 C7
Linden, *Guyana* 121 B6
Linden, *Calif., U.S.A.* 112 G5
Linden, *Tex., U.S.A.* 109 J7
Lindenheuvel, *Neths.* 17 G7
Lindenhurst, *U.S.A.* 107 F11
Linderöd, *Sweden* 11 J7
Linderödsåsen, *Sweden* ... 11 J7
Lindesnes, *Norway* 6 D7
Líndhos, *Greece* 37 C10
Lindi, *Tanzania* 83 D4
Lindi □, *Tanzania* 83 D4
Lindi →, *Zaïre* 82 B2
Lindoso, *Portugal* 30 D2
Lindow, *Germany* 18 C8
Lindsay, *Canada* 98 D4
Lindsay, *Calif., U.S.A.* ... 111 H4
Lindsay, *Okla., U.S.A.* ... 109 H6
Lindsborg, *U.S.A.* 108 F6
Linfen, *China* 50 F6
Ling Xian, *Hunan, China* . 53 D9
Ling Xian, *Shandong, China* 50 F9
Lingao, *China* 58 C7
Lingayen, *Phil.* 57 A6
Lingayen G., *Phil.* 55 C4
Lingbi, *China* 51 H9
Lingchuan, *Guangxi Zhuangzu, China* 53 E8
Lingchuan, *Shanxi, China* . 50 G7
Lingen, *Germany* 18 C3
Lingga, *Indonesia* 56 E2
Lingga, Kepulauan, *Indonesia* 56 E2
Lingga Arch. = Lingga, Kepulauan, *Indonesia* .. 56 E2
Lingle, *U.S.A.* 108 D2
Lingling, *China* 53 D8
Lingqiu, *China* 50 E8
Lingshan, *China* 52 F7
Lingshi, *China* 50 F6
Lingshou, *China* 50 E8
Lingshui, *China* 58 C8
Lingtai, *China* 50 G4
Linguéré, *Senegal* 78 B1
Lingwu, *China* 50 E4
Lingyuan, *China* 51 D10
Lingyun, *China* 52 E6
Linh Cam, *Vietnam* 58 C5
Linhai, *China* 53 C13
Linhares, *Brazil* 123 E3
Linhe, *China* 50 D4
Linjiang, *China* 51 D14
Linköping, *Sweden* 11 F9
Linkou, *China* 51 B16
Linli, *China* 53 C8
Linlithgow, *U.K.* 14 F5
Linnhe, L., *U.K.* 14 E3
Linosa, I., *Medit. S.* 75 A7
Linqi, *China* 50 G7
Linqing, *China* 50 F8
Linqu, *China* 51 F10
Linru, *China* 50 G7
Lins, *Brazil* 127 A6
Linshui, *China* 52 B6
Lintao, *China* 50 G2
Linth →, *Switz.* 19 H5
Linthal, *Switz.* 23 C8
Lintlaw, *Canada* 101 C8
Linton, *Canada* 99 C5
Linton, *Ind., U.S.A.* 104 F2
Linton, *N. Dak., U.S.A.* . 108 B4
Lintong, *China* 50 G5
Linville, *Australia* 91 D5
Linwood, *Canada* 106 C4
Linwu, *China* 53 E9
Linxi, *China* 51 C10
Linxia, *China* 54 C5
Linxiang, *China* 53 C9
Linyanti →, *Africa* 84 B4
Linyi, *China* 51 G10
Linz, *Austria* 21 G4
Linz, *Germany* 18 E3
Linzhenzhen, *China* 50 F5
Linzi, *China* 51 F10
Lion, G. du, *France* 27 E8
Lionárisso, *Cyprus* 37 D13
Lioni, *Italy* 35 B8
Lions, G. of = Lion, G. du, *France* 27 E8
Lion's Den, *Zimbabwe* ... 83 F3
Lion's Head, *Canada* 98 D3
Liozno, *Belorussia* 40 D7
Lipa, *Phil.* 55 E4
Lipali, *Mozam.* 83 F4
Lípari, *Italy* 35 D7
Lípari, Is., *Italy* 35 D7
Lipetsk, *Russia* 41 E11
Liping, *China* 52 D7
Lipkany, *Moldavia* 42 B2
Lipljan, *Serbia, Yug.* 21 N11
Lipno, *Poland* 20 C9
Lipova, *Romania* 38 C4
Lipovcy Manzovka, *Russia* 48 B6
Lipovets, *Ukraine* 42 B3
Lippe →, *Germany* 18 D2
Lippstadt, *Germany* 18 D4
Lipscomb, *U.S.A.* 109 G4
Lipsko, *Poland* 20 D11
Lipsói, *Greece* 39 M9
Liptovsky Svaty Milkulaš, *Slovakia* 20 F9
Liptrap C., *Australia* 91 F4
Lipu, *China* 53 E8
Lira, *Uganda* 82 B3
Liri →, *Italy* 34 A6
Liria, *Spain* 28 F4
Lisala, *Zaïre* 80 D4
Lisboa, *Portugal* 31 G1
Lisboa □, *Portugal* 31 G1
Lisbon = Lisboa, *Portugal* 31 G1
Lisbon, *N. Dak., U.S.A.* . 108 B6
Lisbon, *N.H., U.S.A.* ... 107 B13
Lisbon, *Ohio, U.S.A.* 106 F4
Lisburn, *U.K.* 15 B5
Lisburne, C., *U.S.A.* 96 B3
Liscannor, B., *Ireland* 15 D2
Liscia →, *Italy* 34 A2
Lishe Jiang →, *China* 52 E3
Lishi, *China* 50 F6
Lishu, *China* 51 C13
Lishui, *Jiangsu, China* ... 53 B12
Lishui, *Zhejiang, China* .. 53 C12
Lisianski I., *Pac. Oc.* 92 E10
Lisichansk, *Ukraine* 42 B8
Lisieux, *France* 24 C7
Liski, *Russia* 41 F11
L'Isle-Adam, *France* 25 C9
L'Isle-Jourdain, *Gers, France* 26 E5
L'Isle-Jourdain, *Vienne, France* 26 B4
L'Isle-sur-le-Doubs, *France* 25 E13
Lisle-sur-Tarn, *France* 26 E5
Lismore, *Australia* 91 D5
Lismore, *Ireland* 15 D4
Lisse, *Neths.* 16 D5
List, *Germany* 18 A4
Lista, *Norway* 9 G9
Lista, *Sweden* 9 G14
Lister, Mt., *Antarctica* 5 D11
Liston, *Australia* 91 D5
Listowel, *Canada* 98 D3
Listowel, *Ireland* 15 D2
Lit-et-Mixe, *France* 26 D2
Litang, *Guangxi Zhuangzu, China* 52 F7
Litang, *Sichuan, China* ... 52 B3
Litang, *Malaysia* 57 C5
Litang Qu →, *China* 52 C3
Litani →, *Lebanon* 69 B4
Litchfield, *Calif., U.S.A.* . 112 E6
Litchfield, *Conn., U.S.A.* . 107 E11
Litchfield, *Ill., U.S.A.* 108 F10
Litchfield, *Minn., U.S.A.* . 108 C7
Lithgow, *Australia* 91 E5
Líthinon, Ákra, *Greece* ... 37 E6
Lithuania ■, *Europe* 40 D3
Litija, *Slovenia* 33 B11
Litókhoron, *Greece* 39 J5
Litoměřice, *Czech.* 20 E4
Little Abaco I., *Bahamas* . 116 A4
Little Barrier I., *N.Z.* ... 87 G5
Little Belt Mts., *U.S.A.* ... 110 C8
Little Blue →, *U.S.A.* .. 108 F6
Little Bushman Land, *S. Africa* 84 D2
Little Cadotte →, *Canada* 100 B5
Little Cayman, I., *Cayman Is.* 116 C3
Little Churchill →, *Canada* 101 B9
Little Colorado →, *U.S.A.* 111 H8
Little Current, *Canada* ... 98 C3
Little Current →, *Canada* 98 B3
Little Falls, *Minn., U.S.A.* 108 C7
Little Falls, *N.Y., U.S.A.* . 107 C10
Little Fork →, *U.S.A.* 108 A8
Little Grand Rapids, *Canada* 101 C9
Little Humboldt →, *U.S.A.* 110 F5
Little Inagua I., *Bahamas* . 117 B5
Little Karoo, *S. Africa* ... 84 E3
Little Lake, *U.S.A.* 113 K9
Little Laut Is. = Laut Ketil, Kepulauan, *Indonesia* 56 E5
Little Minch, *U.K.* 14 D2
Little Missouri →, *U.S.A.* 108 B3
Little Namaqualand, *S. Africa* 84 D2
Little Ouse →, *U.K.* 13 E8
Little Rann, *India* 62 H4
Little Red →, *U.S.A.* 109 H9
Little River, *N.Z.* 87 K4
Little Rock, *U.S.A.* 109 H8
Little Ruaha →, *Tanzania* 82 D4
Little Sable Pt., *U.S.A.* ... 104 D2
Little Sioux →, *U.S.A.* .. 108 E6
Little Smoky →, *Canada* . 100 C5
Little Snake →, *U.S.A.* .. 110 F9
Little Valley, *U.S.A.* 106 D6
Little Wabash →, *U.S.A.* 104 G1
Littlefield, *U.S.A.* 109 J3
Littlefork, *U.S.A.* 108 A8
Littlehampton, *U.K.* 13 G7
Littleton, *U.S.A.* 107 B13
Liu He →, *China* 51 D11
Liu Jiang →, *China* 52 F7
Liuba, *China* 50 H4
Liucheng, *China* 52 E7
Liugou, *China* 51 D10
Liuhe, *China* 51 C13
Liuheng Dao, *China* 53 C14
Liukang Tenggaja, *Indonesia* 57 F5
Liuli, *Tanzania* 83 E3
Liuwa Plain, *Zambia* 81 G4
Liuyang, *China* 53 C9
Liuzhou, *China* 52 E7
Liuzhuang, *China* 51 H11
Livadherón, *Greece* 39 J4
Livadhia, *Cyprus* 37 E12
Livarot, *France* 24 D7
Live Oak, *Calif., U.S.A.* . 112 F5
Live Oak, *Fla., U.S.A.* ... 105 K4
Liveras, *Cyprus* 37 D11
Liveringa, *Australia* 88 C3
Livermore, *U.S.A.* 112 H5
Livermore, Mt., *U.S.A.* .. 109 K2
Liverpool, *Australia* 91 E5
Liverpool, *Canada* 99 D7
Liverpool, *U.K.* 12 D5
Liverpool Plains, *Australia* 91 E5
Liverpool Ra., *Australia* .. 91 E5
Livingston, *Guatemala* 116 C2
Livingston, *Calif., U.S.A.* . 112 H6
Livingston, *Mont., U.S.A.* 110 D8
Livingston, *Tex., U.S.A.* .. 109 K7
Livingstone, *Zambia* 83 F2
Livingstone Mts., *Tanzania* 83 D3
Livingstonia, *Malawi* 83 E3
Livny, *Russia* 41 E10
Livonia, *U.S.A.* 104 D4
Livorno, *Italy* 32 E7
Livramento, *Brazil* 127 C4
Livramento do Brumado, *Brazil* 123 D3
Livron-sur-Drôme, *France* 27 D8
Liwale, *Tanzania* 83 D4
Liwale □, *Tanzania* 83 D4
Lixi, *China* 52 D3
Liyang, *China* 53 B12
Lizard I., *Australia* 90 A4
Lizard Pt., *U.K.* 13 H2
Lizarda, *Brazil* 122 C2
Lizzano, *Italy* 35 B10
Ljubija, *Bos.-H.* 33 D13
Ljubljana, *Slovenia* 33 B11
Ljubno, *Slovenia* 33 B11
Ljubuški, *Bos.-H.* 21 M7
Ljung, *Sweden* 11 F7
Ljungan →, *Sweden* 10 B11
Ljungaverk, *Sweden* 10 B10
Ljungby, *Sweden* 9 H12
Ljusdal, *Sweden* 10 C10
Ljusnan = Ljungan →, *Sweden* 10 B11
Ljusnan →, *Sweden* 9 F14
Ljusne, *Sweden* 9 F14
Ljutomer, *Slovenia* 33 B13
Llagostera, *Spain* 28 D7
Llamellín, *Peru* 124 B2
Llancanelo, Salina, *Argentina* 126 D2
Llandeilo, *U.K.* 13 F3
Llandovery, *U.K.* 13 F4
Llandrindod Wells, *U.K.* . 13 E4
Llandudno, *U.K.* 12 D4
Llanelli, *U.K.* 13 F3
Llanes, *Spain* 30 B6
Llangollen, *U.K.* 12 E4
Llanidloes, *U.K.* 13 E4
Llano, *U.S.A.* 109 K5
Llano →, *U.S.A.* 109 K5
Llano Estacado, *U.S.A.* ... 109 J3
Llanos, *S. Amer.* 118 B2
Llanquihue □, *Chile* 128 B2
Llanquihue, L., *Chile* 128 B1
Llebetx, C., *Spain* 36 B9
Lleida = Lérida, *Spain* ... 28 D5
Llentrisca, C., *Spain* 36 C7
Llera, *Mexico* 115 C5
Llerena, *Spain* 31 G4
Llica, *Bolivia* 124 D4
Llico, *Chile* 126 C1
Llobregat →, *Spain* 28 D7
Lloret de Mar, *Spain* 28 D7
Lloyd B., *Australia* 90 A3
Lloyd L., *Canada* 101 B7
Lloydminster, *Canada* 101 C6
Lluchmayor, *Spain* 36 B9
Llullaillaco, Volcán, *S. Amer.* 126 A2
Lo, *Belgium* 17 G1
Lo →, *Vietnam* 58 B5
Loa, *U.S.A.* 111 G8

Loa →, *Chile* **126 A1**
Loano, *Italy* **32 D5**
Lobatse, *Botswana* **84 D4**
Löbau, *Germany* **18 D10**
Lobbes, *Belgium* **17 H4**
Lobenstein, *Germany* **18 E7**
Lobería, *Argentina* **126 D4**
Lobito, *Angola* **81 G2**
Lobón, Canal de, *Spain* **31 G4**
Lobos, *Argentina* **126 D4**
Lobos, I., *Mexico* **114 B2**
Lobos, Is., *Peru* **118 C1**
Lobos, I. de, *Canary Is.* **36 F6**
Lobos de Tierra, I., *Peru* **124 B1**
Loc Binh, *Vietnam* **58 B6**
Loc Ninh, *Vietnam* **59 G6**
Locarno, *Switz.* **23 D7**
Lochaber, *U.K.* **14 E4**
Lochcarron, *U.K.* **14 D3**
Lochem, *Neths.* **16 D8**
Loches, *France* **24 E8**
Lochgelly, *U.K.* **14 E5**
Lochgilphead, *U.K.* **14 E3**
Lochinver, *U.K.* **14 C3**
Lochnagar, *Australia* **90 C4**
Lochnagar, *U.K.* **14 E5**
Łochów, *Poland* **20 C11**
Lochy →, *U.K.* **14 E3**
Lock, *Australia* **91 E2**
Lock Haven, *U.S.A.* **106 E7**
Lockeford, *U.S.A.* **112 G5**
Lockeport, *Canada* **99 D6**
Lockerbie, *U.K.* **14 F5**
Lockhart, *U.S.A.* **109 L6**
Lockhart, L., *Australia* **89 F2**
Lockney, *U.S.A.* **109 H4**
Lockport, *U.S.A.* **106 C6**
Locminé, *France* **24 E4**
Locri, *Italy* **35 D9**
Locronan, *France* **24 D2**
Loctudy, *France* **24 E2**
Lod, *Israel* **69 D3**
Lodève, *France* **26 E7**
Lodge Grass, *U.S.A.* **110 D10**
Lodgepole, *U.S.A.* **108 E3**
Lodgepole Cr. →, *U.S.A.* **108 E2**
Lodhran, *Pakistan* **62 E4**
Lodi, *Italy* **32 C6**
Lodi, *U.S.A.* **112 G5**
Lodja, *Zaïre* **82 C1**
Lodosa, *Spain* **28 C2**
Lödöse, *Sweden* **11 F6**
Lodwar, *Kenya* **82 B4**
Łódź, *Poland* **20 D9**
Loei, *Thailand* **58 D3**
Loenen, *Neths.* **16 D8**
Loengo, *Zaïre* **82 C2**
Loeriesfontein, *S. Africa* **84 E2**
Lofoten, *Norway* **8 B13**
Lofsdalen, *Sweden* **10 B7**
Lofsen →, *Sweden* **10 B7**
Logan, *Kans., U.S.A.* **108 F5**
Logan, *Ohio, U.S.A.* **104 F4**
Logan, *Utah, U.S.A.* **110 F8**
Logan, *W. Va., U.S.A.* **104 G5**
Logan, Mt., *Canada* **96 B5**
Logan Pass, *U.S.A.* **100 D6**
Logandale, *U.S.A.* **113 J12**
Logansport, *Ind., U.S.A.* **104 E2**
Logansport, *La., U.S.A.* **109 K8**
Logo, *Sudan* **77 F3**
Logone →, *Chad* **73 F8**
Logroño, *Spain* **28 C2**
Logrosán, *Spain* **31 F5**
Løgstør, *Denmark* **11 H3**
Lohardaga, *India* **63 H11**
Lohr, *Germany* **19 F5**
Loi-kaw, *Burma* **61 K20**
Loimaa, *Finland* **9 F17**
Loir →, *France* **24 E6**
Loir-et-Cher □, *France* **24 E8**
Loire □, *France* **27 C8**
Loire →, *France* **24 E4**
Loire-Atlantique □, *France* **24 E5**
Loiret □, *France* **25 E9**
Loitz, *Germany* **18 B9**
Loja, *Ecuador* **124 A2**
Loja, *Spain* **31 H6**
Loja □, *Ecuador* **120 D2**
Loji, *Indonesia* **57 E7**
Loka, *Sudan* **77 G3**
Lokandu, *Zaïre* **82 C2**
Løken, *Norway* **10 E5**
Lokeren, *Belgium* **17 F3**
Lokhvitsa, *Ukraine* **40 F8**
Lokichokio, *Kenya* **82 B3**
Lokitaung, *Kenya* **82 B4**
Lokka, *Finland* **8 C19**
Løkken, *Denmark* **11 G3**
Løkken Verk, *Norway* **10 A3**
Loknya, *Russia* **40 C7**
Lokoja, *Nigeria* **79 D6**
Lokolama, *Zaïre* **80 E3**
Lol →, *Sudan* **77 F2**
Lola, *Guinea* **78 D3**
Lola, Mt., *U.S.A.* **112 F6**
Lolibai, Gebel, *Sudan* **77 G3**
Lolimi, *Sudan* **77 G3**
Loliondo, *Tanzania* **82 C4**
Lolland, *Denmark* **11 K5**
Lollar, *Germany* **18 E4**
Lolo, *U.S.A.* **110 C6**
Lolodorf, *Cameroon* **79 E7**
Lom, *Bulgaria* **38 F6**
Lom →, *Bulgaria* **38 F6**
Lom Kao, *Thailand* **58 D3**
Lom Sak, *Thailand* **58 D3**
Loma, *U.S.A.* **110 C8**
Loma Linda, *U.S.A.* **113 L9**
Lomami →, *Zaïre* **82 B1**
Lomas de Zamóra, *Argentina* **126 C4**
Lombadina, *Australia* **88 C3**
Lombardia □, *Italy* **32 C6**
Lombardy = Lombardia □, *Italy* **32 C6**
Lombez, *France* **26 E4**
Lomblen, *Indonesia* **57 F6**
Lombok, *Indonesia* **56 F5**
Lomé, *Togo* **79 D5**
Lomela, *Zaïre* **80 E4**
Lomela →, *Zaïre* **80 E4**
Lomello, *Italy* **32 C5**
Lometa, *U.S.A.* **109 K5**
Lomié, *Cameroon* **80 D2**
Lomma, *Sweden* **11 J7**
Lomme →, *Belgium* **17 H6**
Lommel, *Belgium* **17 F6**
Lomond, *Canada* **100 C6**
Lomond, L., *U.K.* **14 E4**
Lomonosov, *Russia* **40 B6**
Lomphat, *Cambodia* **58 F6**
Lompobatang, *Indonesia* **57 F5**
Lompoc, *U.S.A.* **113 L6**
Lomsegga, *Norway* **10 C2**
Łomża, *Poland* **20 B12**
Loncoche, *Chile* **128 A2**
Loncopuè, *Argentina* **128 A2**
Londa, *India* **60 M9**
Londerzeel, *Belgium* **17 G4**
Londiani, *Kenya* **82 C4**
Londinières, *France* **24 C8**
London, *Canada* **98 D3**
London, *U.K.* **13 F7**
London, *Ky., U.S.A.* **104 G3**
London, *Ohio, U.S.A.* **104 F4**
London, Greater □, *U.K.* **13 F7**
Londonderry, *U.K.* **15 B4**
Londonderry □, *U.K.* **15 B4**
Londonderry, C., *Australia* **88 B4**
Londonderry, I., *Chile* **128 E2**
Londrina, *Brazil* **127 A5**
Lone Pine, *U.S.A.* **111 H4**
Long Beach, *Calif., U.S.A.* **113 M8**
Long Beach, *N.Y., U.S.A.* **107 F11**
Long Beach, *Wash., U.S.A.* **112 D2**
Long Branch, *U.S.A.* **107 F11**
Long Creek, *U.S.A.* **110 D4**
Long Eaton, *U.K.* **12 E6**
Long I., *Australia* **90 C4**
Long I., *Bahamas* **117 B4**
Long I., *U.S.A.* **107 F11**
Long Island Sd., *U.S.A.* **107 E12**
Long L., *Canada* **98 C2**
Long Lake, *U.S.A.* **107 C10**
Long Pine, *U.S.A.* **108 D5**
Long Pt., *Nfld., Canada* **99 C8**
Long Pt., *Ont., Canada* **106 D4**
Long Point B., *Canada* **106 D4**
Long Range Mts., *Canada* **99 C8**
Long Reef, *Australia* **88 B4**
Long Str. = Longa, Proliv, *Russia* **4 C16**
Long Thanh, *Vietnam* **59 G6**
Long Xian, *China* **50 G4**
Long Xuyen, *Vietnam* **59 G5**
Longá, *Greece* **39 N4**
Longa, Proliv, *Russia* **4 C16**
Long'an, *China* **52 F6**
Longarone, *Italy* **33 B9**
Longchang, *China* **52 C5**
Longchi, *China* **52 C4**
Longchuan, *Guangdong, China* **53 E10**
Longchuan, *Yunnan, China* **52 E1**
Longde, *China* **50 G4**
Longeau, *France* **25 E12**
Longford, *Australia* **90 G4**
Longford, *Ireland* **15 C4**
Longford □, *Ireland* **15 C4**
Longguan, *China* **50 D8**
Longhua, *China* **51 D9**
Longhui, *China* **53 D8**
Longido, *Tanzania* **82 C4**
Longiram, *Indonesia* **56 E5**
Longkou, *Jiangxi, China* **53 D10**
Longkou, *Shandong, China* **51 F11**
Longlac, *Canada* **98 C2**
Longli, *China* **52 D6**
Longlier, *Belgium* **17 J6**
Longlin, *China* **52 E5**
Longling, *China* **52 E2**
Longmen, *China* **53 F10**
Longming, *China* **52 F6**
Longmont, *U.S.A.* **108 E2**
Longnan, *China* **53 E10**
Longnawan, *Indonesia* **56 D4**
Longobucco, *Italy* **35 C9**
Longquan, *China* **53 C12**
Longreach, *Australia* **90 C3**
Longshan, *China* **52 C7**
Longsheng, *China* **53 E8**
Longton, *Australia* **90 C4**
Longtown, *U.K.* **13 F5**
Longué-Jumelles, *France* **24 E6**
Longueau, *France* **25 C9**
Longueuil, *Canada* **107 A11**
Longuyon, *France* **25 C12**
Longview, *Canada* **100 C6**
Longview, *Tex., U.S.A.* **109 J7**
Longview, *Wash., U.S.A.* **112 D4**
Longvilly, *Belgium* **17 H7**
Longwy, *France* **25 C12**
Longxi, *China* **50 G3**
Longyou, *China* **53 C12**
Longzhou, *China* **52 F6**
Lonigo, *Italy* **33 C8**
Löningen, *Germany* **18 C3**
Lonja →, *Croatia* **33 C13**
Lonoke, *U.S.A.* **109 H9**
Lonquimay, *Chile* **128 A2**
Lons-le-Saunier, *France* **25 F12**
Lønstrup, *Denmark* **11 G3**
Lookout, C., *U.S.A.* **105 H7**
Lookout, C., *Canada* **98 A3**
Loolmalasin, *Tanzania* **82 C4**
Loon →, *Alta., Canada* **100 B5**
Loon →, *Man., Canada* **101 B8**
Loon Lake, *Canada* **101 C7**
Loon-op-Zand, *Neths.* **17 E6**
Loongana, *Australia* **89 F4**
Loop Hd., *Ireland* **15 D2**
Loosduinen, *Neths.* **16 D4**
Lop Buri, *Thailand* **58 E3**
Lop Nor = Lop Nur, *China* **54 B4**
Lop Nur, *China* **54 B4**
Lopare, *Bos.-H.* **21 L8**
Lopatin, *Russia* **43 E12**
Lopatina, G., *Russia* **45 D15**
Lopaye, *Sudan* **77 F3**
Lopera, *Spain* **31 H6**
Lopez, *Phil.* **55 E5**
Lopez, C., *Gabon* **80 E1**
Loppersum, *Neths.* **16 B9**
Lopphavet, *Norway* **8 A16**
Lora →, *Afghan.* **60 D4**
Lora, Hamun-i-, *Pakistan* **60 E4**
Lora Cr. →, *Australia* **91 D2**
Lora del Río, *Spain* **31 H5**
Lorain, *U.S.A.* **106 E2**
Loralai, *Pakistan* **62 D3**
Lorca, *Spain* **29 H3**
Lord Howe I., *Pac. Oc.* **92 L7**
Lord Howe Ridge, *Pac. Oc.* **92 L8**
Lordsburg, *U.S.A.* **111 K9**
Loreto, *Bolivia* **125 D5**
Loreto, *Brazil* **122 C2**
Loreto, *Italy* **33 E10**
Loreto, *Mexico* **114 B2**
Loreto □, *Peru* **120 D3**
Loreto Aprutina, *Italy* **33 F10**
Lorgues, *France* **27 E10**
Lorica, *Colombia* **120 B2**
Lorient, *France* **24 E3**
Lorn, *U.K.* **14 E3**
Lorn, Firth of, *U.K.* **14 E3**
Lorne, *Australia* **91 F3**
Lorovouno, *Cyprus* **37 D11**
Lörrach, *Germany* **19 H3**
Lorraine, *France* **25 D12**
Lorrainville, *Canada* **98 C4**
Los, Îles de, *Guinea* **78 D2**
Los Alamos, *Calif., U.S.A.* **113 L6**
Los Alamos, *N. Mex., U.S.A.* **111 J10**
Los Altos, *U.S.A.* **112 H4**
Los Andes, *Chile* **126 C1**
Los Angeles, *Chile* **126 D1**
Los Angeles, *U.S.A.* **113 L8**
Los Angeles Aqueduct, *U.S.A.* **113 K9**
Los Antiguos, *Argentina* **128 C2**
Los Banos, *U.S.A.* **111 H3**
Los Barrios, *Spain* **31 J5**
Los Blancos, *Argentina* **126 A3**
Los Cristianos, *Canary Is.* **36 F3**
Los Gatos, *U.S.A.* **112 H5**
Los Hermanos, *Venezuela* **117 D7**
Los Islotes, *Canary Is.* **36 E6**
Los Lagos, *Chile* **128 A2**
Los Llanos de Aridane, *Canary Is.* **36 F2**
Los Lomas, *Peru* **124 A1**
Los Lunas, *U.S.A.* **111 J10**
Los Menucos, *Argentina* **128 B3**
Los Mochis, *Mexico* **114 B3**
Los Monegros, *Spain* **28 D4**
Los Monos, *Argentina* **128 C3**
Los Olivos, *U.S.A.* **113 L6**
Los Palacios, *Cuba* **116 B3**
Los Palacios y Villafranca, *Spain* **31 H5**
Los Reyes, *Mexico* **114 D4**
Los Ríos □, *Ecuador* **120 D2**
Los Roques, *Venezuela* **120 A4**
Los Santos de Maimona, *Spain* **31 G4**
Los Teques, *Venezuela* **120 A4**
Los Testigos, *Venezuela* **121 A5**
Los Vilos, *Chile* **126 C1**
Los Yébenes, *Spain* **31 F7**
Losada →, *Colombia* **120 C3**
Loshkalakh, *Russia* **45 C15**
Lošinj, *Croatia* **33 D11**
Losser, *Neths.* **16 D10**
Lossiemouth, *U.K.* **14 D5**
Lot □, *France* **26 D5**
Lot →, *France* **26 D4**
Lot-et-Garonne □, *France* **26 D4**
Lota, *Chile* **126 D1**
Løten, *Norway* **10 D5**
Lotfābād, *Iran* **65 B8**
Lothair, *S. Africa* **85 D5**
Lothian □, *U.K.* **14 F5**
Lothiers, *France* **25 F8**
Lötschbergtunnel, *Switz.* **22 D5**
Lottefors, *Sweden* **10 C10**
Lotzwil, *Switz.* **22 B5**
Loubomo, *Congo* **80 E2**
Loudéac, *France* **24 D4**
Loudi, *China* **53 D8**
Loudon, *U.S.A.* **105 H3**
Loudonville, *U.S.A.* **106 F2**
Loudun, *France* **24 E7**
Loué, *France* **24 E6**
Loue →, *France* **25 E12**
Louga, *Senegal* **78 B1**
Loughborough, *U.K.* **12 E6**
Loughrea, *Ireland* **15 C3**
Loughros More B., *Ireland* **15 B3**
Louhans, *France* **27 B9**
Louis Trichardt, *S. Africa* **85 C4**
Louis XIV, Pte., *Canada* **98 B4**
Louisa, *U.S.A.* **104 F4**
Louisbourg, *Canada* **99 C8**
Louise I., *Canada* **100 C2**
Louiseville, *Canada* **98 C5**
Louisiade Arch., *Papua N. G.* **92 J7**
Louisiana, *U.S.A.* **108 F9**
Louisiana □, *U.S.A.* **109 K9**
Louisville, *Ky., U.S.A.* **104 F3**
Louisville, *Miss., U.S.A.* **109 J10**
Loulay, *France* **26 B3**
Loulé, *Portugal* **31 H2**
Louny, *Czech.* **20 E3**
Loup City, *U.S.A.* **108 E5**
Lourdes, *France* **26 E3**
Lourdes-du-Blanc-Sablon, *Canada* **99 B8**
Lourenço, *Brazil* **121 C7**
Lourenço-Marques = Maputo, *Mozam.* **85 D5**
Loures, *Portugal* **31 G1**
Lourinhã, *Portugal* **31 F1**
Lousã, *Portugal* **30 E2**
Louth, *Australia* **91 E4**
Louth, *Ireland* **15 C5**
Louth, *U.K.* **12 D7**
Louth □, *Ireland* **15 C5**
Louvain = Leuven, *Belgium* **17 G5**
Louveigné, *Belgium* **17 G7**
Louviers, *France* **24 C8**
Louwsburg, *S. Africa* **85 D5**
Lovat →, *Russia* **40 B7**
Love, *Canada* **101 C8**
Lovech, *Bulgaria* **38 F7**
Loveland, *U.S.A.* **108 E2**
Lovell, *U.S.A.* **110 D9**
Lovelock, *U.S.A.* **110 F4**
Lóvere, *Italy* **32 C7**
Loviisa = Lovisa, *Finland* **9 F19**
Loving, *U.S.A.* **109 J2**
Lovington, *U.S.A.* **109 J3**
Lovios, *Spain* **30 D2**
Lovisa, *Finland* **9 F19**
Lovran, *Croatia* **33 C11**
Low Pt., *Australia* **89 F4**
Low Tatra = Nízké Tatry, *Slovakia* **20 G9**
Lowa, *Zaïre* **82 C2**
Lowa →, *Zaïre* **82 C2**
Lowell, *U.S.A.* **107 D13**
Lower Arrow L., *Canada* **100 D5**
Lower California = Baja California, *Mexico* **114 A1**
Lower California = California, Baja, *Mexico* **114 A1**
Lower Hutt, *N.Z.* **87 J5**
Lower L., *U.S.A.* **110 F3**
Lower Lake, *U.S.A.* **112 G4**
Lower Post, *Canada* **100 B3**
Lower Red L., *U.S.A.* **108 B7**
Lower Saxony = Niedersachsen □, *Germany* **18 C5**
Lower Tunguska = Tunguska, Nizhnyaya →, *Russia* **45 C9**
Lowestoft, *U.K.* **13 E9**
Łowicz, *Poland* **20 C9**
Lowville, *U.S.A.* **107 C9**
Loxton, *Australia* **91 E3**
Loxton, *S. Africa* **84 E3**
Loyalton, *U.S.A.* **112 F6**
Loyalty Is. = Loyauté, Is., *N. Cal.* **92 K8**
Loyang = Luoyang, *China* **50 G7**
Loyauté, Is., *N. Cal.* **92 K8**
Loyev, *Belorussia* **40 F7**
Loyoro, *Uganda* **82 B3**
Lož, *Slovenia* **33 C11**
Lozère □, *France* **26 D7**
Loznica, *Serbia, Yug.* **21 L9**
Lozovaya, *Ukraine* **42 B7**
Luachimo, *Angola* **80 F4**
Luacono, *Angola* **80 G4**
Lualaba →, *Zaïre* **82 B5**
Luampa, *Zambia* **83 F1**
Lu'an, *China* **53 B11**
Luan Chau, *Vietnam* **58 B4**
Luan He →, *China* **51 E10**
Luan Xian, *China* **51 E10**
Luancheng, *Guangxi Zhuangzu, China* **52 F7**
Luancheng, *Hebei, China* **50 F8**
Luanda, *Angola* **80 F2**
Luang Prabang, *Laos* **58 C4**
Luang Thale, *Thailand* **59 J3**
Luangwa, *Zambia* **83 F3**
Luangwa →, *Zambia* **83 E3**
Luangwa Valley, *Zambia* **83 E3**
Luanne, *China* **51 D9**
Luanping, *China* **51 D9**
Luanshya, *Zambia* **83 E2**
Luapula □, *Zambia* **83 E2**
Luapula →, *Africa* **83 D2**
Luarca, *Spain* **30 B4**
Luashi, *Zaïre* **83 E1**
Luau, *Angola* **80 G4**
Lubalo, *Angola* **80 F3**
Lubań, *Poland* **20 D5**
Lubana, Ozero, *Latvia* **40 C5**
Lubang, *Phil.* **55 E4**
Lubang Is., *Phil.* **57 B6**
Lubartów, *Poland* **20 D12**
Lubawa, *Poland* **20 B9**
Lubbeek, *Belgium* **17 G5**
Lübben, *Germany* **18 D9**
Lübbenau, *Germany* **18 D9**
Lubbock, *U.S.A.* **109 J4**
Lübeck, *Germany* **18 B6**
Lübecker Bucht, *Germany* **18 A7**
Lubefu, *Zaïre* **82 C1**
Lubefu →, *Zaïre* **82 C1**
Lubero = Luofu, *Zaïre* **82 C2**
Lubicon L., *Canada* **100 B5**
Lublin, *Poland* **20 D12**
Lubliniec, *Poland* **20 E8**
Lubnān, J., *Lebanon* **69 B4**
Lubny, *Ukraine* **40 F8**
Lubon, *Poland* **20 C6**
Lubongola, *Zaïre* **82 C2**
Lubsko, *Poland* **20 D4**
Lübtheen, *Germany* **18 B7**
Lubuagan, *Phil.* **55 C4**
Lubudi →, *Zaïre* **83 D2**
Lubuk Antu, *Malaysia* **56 D4**
Lubuklinggau, *Indonesia* **56 E2**
Lubuksikaping, *Indonesia* **56 D2**
Lubumbashi, *Zaïre* **83 E2**
Lubunda, *Zaïre* **82 D2**
Lubungu, *Zambia* **83 E2**
Lubutu, *Zaïre* **82 C2**
Luc An Chau, *Vietnam* **58 A5**
Luc-en-Diois, *France* **27 D9**
Lucan, *Canada* **106 C3**
Lucban, *Phil.* **55 D4**
Lucca, *Italy* **32 E7**
Luce Bay, *U.K.* **14 G4**
Lucea, *Jamaica* **116 C4**
Lucedale, *U.S.A.* **105 K1**
Lucena, *Phil.* **55 E4**
Lucena, *Spain* **31 H6**
Lucena del Cid, *Spain* **28 E4**
Lučenec, *Slovakia* **21 G9**
Lucens, *Switz.* **22 C3**
Lucera, *Italy* **35 A8**
Lucerne = Luzern, *Switz.* **23 B6**
Lucerne, *U.S.A.* **112 F4**
Lucerne Valley, *U.S.A.* **113 L10**
Lucero, *Mexico* **114 A3**
Luchena →, *Spain* **29 H3**
Lucheng, *China* **50 F7**
Lucheringo →, *Mozam.* **83 E4**
Lüchow, *Germany* **18 C7**
Luchuan, *China* **53 F8**
Lucie →, *Surinam* **121 C6**
Lucira, *Angola* **81 G2**
Luckau, *Germany* **18 D9**
Luckenwalde, *Germany* **18 C9**
Lucknow, *India* **63 F9**
Luçon, *France* **26 B2**
Lüda = Dalian, *China* **51 E11**
Luda Kamchiya →, *Bulgaria* **38 F10**
Ludbreg, *Croatia* **33 B13**
Lüdenscheid, *Germany* **18 D3**
Lüderitz, *Namibia* **84 D2**
Ludewe □, *Tanzania* **83 D3**
Ludhiana, *India* **62 D6**
Ludian, *China* **52 D4**
Luding Qiao, *China* **52 C4**
Lüdinghausen, *Germany* **18 D3**
Ludington, *U.S.A.* **104 D2**
Ludlow, *U.K.* **13 E5**
Ludlow, *Calif., U.S.A.* **113 L10**
Ludlow, *Vt., U.S.A.* **107 C12**
Ludus, *Romania* **38 C7**
Ludvika, *Sweden* **9 F13**
Ludwigsburg, *Germany* **19 G5**
Ludwigshafen, *Germany* **19 F4**
Ludwigslust, *Germany* **18 B7**
Ludza, *Latvia* **40 C5**
Luebo, *Zaïre* **80 F4**
Lueki, *Zaïre* **82 C2**
Luena, *Zaïre* **83 D2**
Luena, *Zambia* **83 E3**
Luepa, *Venezuela* **121 B5**
Lüeyang, *China* **50 H4**
Lufeng, *Guangdong, China* **53 F10**
Lufeng, *Yunnan, China* **52 E4**
Lufira →, *Zaïre* **83 D2**
Lufkin, *U.S.A.* **109 K7**
Lufupa, *Zaïre* **83 E1**
Luga, *Russia* **40 B6**
Luga →, *Russia* **40 B6**
Lugang, *Taiwan* **53 E13**
Lugano, *Switz.* **23 D7**
Lugano, L. di, *Switz.* **23 E8**
Lugansk, *Ukraine* **43 B8**
Lugard's Falls, *Kenya* **82 C4**

Lugela, *Mozam.* 83 F4
Lugenda →, *Mozam.* 83 E4
Lugh Ganana, *Somali Rep.* 68 G3
Lugnaquilla, *Ireland* 15 D5
Lugnvik, *Sweden* 10 B11
Lugo, *Italy* 33 D8
Lugo, *Spain* 30 B3
Lugo □, *Spain* 30 C3
Lugoj, *Romania* 38 D4
Lugones, *Spain* 30 B5
Lugovoye, *Kazakhstan* 44 E8
Luhansk = Lugansk, *Ukraine* 43 B8
Luhe, *China* 53 A12
Luhe →, *Germany* 18 B6
Luhuo, *China* 52 B3
Luiana, *Angola* 84 B3
Luino, *Italy* 32 C5
Luís Correia, *Brazil* 122 B3
Luís Gonçalves, *Brazil* 122 C1
Luitpold Coast, *Antarctica* 5 D1
Luiza, *Zaïre* 80 F4
Luizi, *Zaïre* 82 D2
Luján, *Argentina* 126 C4
Lujiang, *China* 53 B11
Lukanga Swamp, *Zambia* 83 E2
Lukenie →, *Zaïre* 80 E3
Lukhisaral, *India* 63 G12
Lŭki, *Bulgaria* 39 H7
Lukolela, *Equateur, Zaïre* 80 E3
Lukolela, *Kasai Or., Zaïre* 82 D1
Lukosi, *Zimbabwe* 83 F2
Lukovit, *Bulgaria* 38 F7
Łuków, *Poland* 20 D12
Lukoyanov, *Russia* 41 D14
Lule älv →, *Sweden* 8 D17
Luleå, *Sweden* 8 D17
Lüleburgaz, *Turkey* 39 H10
Luliang, *China* 52 E4
Luling, *U.S.A.* 109 L6
Lulong, *China* 51 E10
Lulonga →, *Zaïre* 80 D3
Lulua →, *Zaïre* 80 E4
Luluabourg = Kananga, *Zaïre* 80 F4
Lumai, *Angola* 81 G4
Lumajang, *Indonesia* 57 H15
Lumbala N'guimbo, *Angola* 81 G4
Lumberton, *Miss., U.S.A.* 109 K10
Lumberton, *N.C., U.S.A.* 105 H6
Lumberton, *N. Mex., U.S.A.* 111 H10
Lumbres, *France* 25 B9
Lumbwa, *Kenya* 82 C4
Lummen, *Belgium* 17 G6
Lumsden, *N.Z.* 87 L2
Lumut, *Malaysia* 59 K3
Lumut, Tg., *Indonesia* 56 E3
Luna, *Phil.* 55 C4
Lunan, *China* 52 E4
Lunavada, *India* 62 H5
Lunca, *Romania* 38 B8
Lund, *Sweden* 11 J7
Lund, *U.S.A.* 110 G6
Lundazi, *Zambia* 83 E3
Lunde, *Norway* 10 E3
Lunderskov, *Denmark* 11 J3
Lundi →, *Zimbabwe* 83 G3
Lundu, *Malaysia* 56 D3
Lundy, *U.K.* 13 F3
Lune →, *U.K.* 12 C5
Lüneburg, *Germany* 18 B6
Lüneburg Heath = Lüneburger Heide, *Germany* 18 C6
Lüneburger Heide, *Germany* 18 C6
Lunel, *France* 27 E8
Lünen, *Germany* 18 D3
Lunenburg, *Canada* 99 D7
Lunéville, *France* 25 D13
Lunga →, *Zambia* 83 E2
Lungern, *Switz.* 22 C6
Lungi Airport, *S. Leone* 78 D2
Lunglei, *India* 61 H18
Luni, *India* 62 F5
Luni →, *India* 62 G4
Luninets, *Belorussia* 40 E5
Luning, *U.S.A.* 110 G4
Lunino, *Russia* 41 E14
Luninyets = Luninets, *Belorussia* 40 E5
Lunner, *Norway* 10 D4
Lunsemfwa →, *Zambia* 83 E3
Lunsemfwa Falls, *Zambia* 83 E2
Lunteren, *Neths.* 16 D7
Luo He →, *China* 50 G6
Luocheng, *China* 52 E7
Luochuan, *China* 50 G5
Luoci, *China* 52 E4
Luodian, *China* 52 E6
Luoding, *China* 53 F8
Luodong, *Taiwan* 53 E13
Luofu, *Zaïre* 82 C2
Luohe, *China* 50 H8
Luojiang, *China* 52 B5
Luonan, *China* 50 G6
Luoning, *China* 50 G6
Luoshan, *China* 53 A10
Luotian, *China* 53 B10
Luoyang, *China* 50 G7
Luoyuan, *China* 53 D12
Luozi, *Zaïre* 80 E2
Luozigou, *China* 51 C16
Lupeni, *Romania* 38 D6
Lupilichi, *Mozam.* 83 E4
Lupoing, *China* 52 E5
Luquan, *China* 52 E4
Luque, *Paraguay* 126 B4
Luque, *Spain* 31 H6
Luray, *U.S.A.* 104 F6
Lure, *France* 25 E13
Luremo, *Angola* 80 F3
Lurgan, *U.K.* 15 B5
Luribay, *Bolivia* 124 D4
Lurin, *Peru* 124 C2
Lusaka, *Zambia* 83 F2
Lusambo, *Zaïre* 82 C1
Lusangaye, *Zaïre* 82 C2
Luseland, *Canada* 101 C7
Lushan, *Henan, China* 50 H7
Lushan, *Sichuan, China* 52 B4
Lushi, *China* 50 G6
Lushnja, *Albania* 39 J2
Lushoto, *Tanzania* 82 C4
Lushoto □, *Tanzania* 82 C4
Lushui, *China* 52 E2
Lüshun, *China* 51 E11
Lusignan, *France* 26 B4
Lusigny-sur-Barse, *France* 25 D11
Lusk, *U.S.A.* 108 D2
Lussac-les-Châteaux, *France* 26 B4
Lussanvira, *Brazil* 123 F1
Luta = Dalian, *China* 51 E11
Luton, *U.K.* 13 F7
Lutong, *Malaysia* 56 D4
Lutry, *Switz.* 22 C3
Lutsk, *Ukraine* 40 F4
Lützow Holmbukta, *Antarctica* 5 C4
Lutzputs, *S. Africa* 84 D3
Luverne, *U.S.A.* 108 D6
Luvua, *Zaïre* 83 D2
Luvua →, *Zaïre* 82 D2
Luwegu →, *Tanzania* 83 D4
Luwuk, *Indonesia* 57 E6
Luxembourg, *Lux.* 17 J8
Luxembourg □, *Belgium* 17 J7
Luxembourg ■, *Europe* 17 J8
Luxeuil-les-Bains, *France* 25 E13
Luxi, *Hunan, China* 53 C8
Luxi, *Yunnan, China* 52 E4
Luxi, *Yunnan, China* 52 E2
Luxor = El Uqsur, *Egypt* 76 B3
Luy →, *France* 26 E2
Luy-de-Béarn →, *France* 26 E3
Luy-de-France →, *France* 26 E3
Luyi, *China* 50 H8
Luyksgestel, *Neths.* 17 F6
Luz-St.-Sauveur, *France* 26 F4
Luzern, *Switz.* 23 B6
Luzern □, *Switz.* 22 B5
Luzhai, *China* 52 E7
Luzhou, *China* 52 C5
Luziânia, *Brazil* 123 E2
Luzilândia, *Brazil* 122 B3
Luzon, *Phil.* 55 D4
Luzy, *France* 25 F10
Luzzi, *Italy* 35 C9
Lviv = Lvov, *Ukraine* 40 G4
Lvov, *Ukraine* 40 G4
Lyakhovichi, *Belorussia* 40 E5
Lyakhovskiye, Ostrova, *Russia* 45 B15
Lyaki, *Azerbaijan* 43 F12
Lyallpur = Faisalabad, *Pakistan* 62 D5
Lycaonia, *Turkey* 66 D5
Lychen, *Germany* 18 B9
Lycia, *Turkey* 66 E3
Lycksele, *Sweden* 8 D15
Lydda = Lod, *Israel* 69 D3
Lydenburg, *S. Africa* 85 D5
Lydia, *Turkey* 66 D3
Lyell, *N.Z.* 87 J4
Lyell I., *Canada* 100 C2
Lygnern, *Sweden* 11 G6
Lyman, *U.S.A.* 110 F8
Lyme Regis, *U.K.* 13 G5
Lymington, *U.K.* 13 G6
Lynchburg, *U.S.A.* 104 G6
Lynd →, *Australia* 90 B3
Lynd Ra., *Australia* 91 D4
Lynden, *Canada* 106 C4
Lynden, *U.S.A.* 112 B4
Lyndhurst, *Queens., Australia* 90 B3
Lyndhurst, *S. Austral., Australia* 91 E2
Lyndon →, *Australia* 89 D1
Lyndonville, *N.Y., U.S.A.* 106 C6
Lyndonville, *Vt., U.S.A.* 107 B12
Lyngdal, *Norway* 10 E3
Lynher Reef, *Australia* 88 C3
Lynn, *U.S.A.* 107 D14
Lynn Canal, *U.S.A.* 100 B1
Lynn Lake, *Canada* 101 B8
Lynnwood, *U.S.A.* 112 C4
Lynton, *U.K.* 13 F4
Lyntupy, *Belorussia* 40 D5
Lynx L., *Canada* 101 A7
Lyø, *Denmark* 11 J4
Lyon, *France* 27 C8
Lyonnais, *France* 27 C8
Lyons = Lyon, *France* 27 C8
Lyons, *Colo., U.S.A.* 108 E2
Lyons, *Ga., U.S.A.* 105 J4
Lyons, *Kans., U.S.A.* 108 F5
Lyons, *N.Y., U.S.A.* 106 C8
Lyrestad, *Sweden* 11 F8
Lys = Leie →, *Belgium* 25 A10
Lysekil, *Sweden* 11 F5
Lyskovo, *Russia* 41 D14
Lyss, *Switz.* 22 B4
Lytle, *U.S.A.* 109 L5
Lyttelton, *N.Z.* 87 K4
Lytton, *Canada* 100 C4
Lyuban, *Russia* 40 B7
Lyubcha, *Belorussia* 40 E5
Lyubertsy, *Russia* 41 D10
Lyubim, *Russia* 41 B12
Lyuboml, *Ukraine* 40 F4
Lyubotin, *Ukraine* 42 B6
Lyubytino, *Russia* 40 B8
Lyudinovo, *Russia* 40 E9

M

Ma →, *Vietnam* 58 C5
Ma'adaba, *Jordan* 69 E4
Maamba, *Zambia* 84 B4
Ma'ān, *Jordan* 69 E4
Ma'ān □, *Jordan* 69 F5
Ma'anshan, *China* 53 B12
Maarheeze, *Neths.* 17 F7
Maarianhamina, *Finland* 9 F15
Maarn, *Neths.* 16 D6
Ma'arrat an Nu'mān, *Syria* 64 C3
Maarssen, *Neths.* 16 D6
Maartensdijk, *Neths.* 16 D6
Maas →, *Neths.* 16 E5
Maasbracht, *Belgium* 17 F7
Maasbree, *Neths.* 17 F8
Maasdam, *Neths.* 16 E5
Maasdijk, *Neths.* 16 E4
Maaseik, *Belgium* 17 F7
Maasland, *Neths.* 16 E4
Maasniel, *Neths.* 17 F8
Maassluis, *Neths.* 16 E4
Maastricht, *Neths.* 17 G7
Maave, *Mozam.* 85 C5
Mabaruma, *Guyana* 121 B6
Mabel L., *Canada* 100 C5
Mabenge, *Zaïre* 82 B1
Mabian, *China* 52 C4
Mablethorpe, *U.K.* 12 D8
Maboma, *Zaïre* 82 B2
Mabrouk, *Mali* 79 B4
Mabton, *U.S.A.* 110 C3
Mac Bac, *Vietnam* 59 H6
Macachín, *Argentina* 126 D3
Macaé, *Brazil* 123 F3
Macaíba, *Brazil* 122 C4
Macajuba, *Brazil* 123 D3
McAlester, *U.S.A.* 109 H7
McAllen, *U.S.A.* 109 M5
Macamic, *Canada* 98 C4
Macao = Macau ■, *China* 53 F9
Macão, *Portugal* 31 F3
Macapá, *Brazil* 121 C7
Macará, *Ecuador* 120 D2
Macarani, *Brazil* 123 E3
Macarena, Serranía de la, *Colombia* 120 C3
McArthur →, *Australia* 90 B2
McArthur, Port, *Australia* 90 B2
McArthur River, *Australia* 90 B2
Macas, *Ecuador* 120 D2
Macate, *Peru* 124 B2
Macau, *Brazil* 122 C4
Macau ■, *China* 53 F9
Macaúbas, *Brazil* 123 D3
Macaya →, *Colombia* 120 C3
McBride, *Canada* 100 C4
McCall, *U.S.A.* 110 D5
McCamey, *U.S.A.* 109 K3
McCammon, *U.S.A.* 110 E7
McCauley I., *Canada* 100 C2
McCleary, *U.S.A.* 112 C3
Macclesfield, *U.K.* 12 D5
McClintock, *Canada* 101 B10
McClintock Ra., *Australia* 88 C4
McCloud, *U.S.A.* 110 F2
McCluer I., *Australia* 88 B5
McClure, *U.S.A.* 106 F7
McClure, L., *U.S.A.* 112 H6
M'Clure Str., *Canada* 4 B2
McClusky, *U.S.A.* 108 B4
McComb, *U.S.A.* 109 K9
McConaughy, L., *U.S.A.* 108 E4
McCook, *U.S.A.* 108 E4
McCullough Mt., *U.S.A.* 113 K11
McCusker →, *Canada* 101 B7
McDame, *Canada* 100 B3
McDermitt, *U.S.A.* 110 F5
Macdonald, L., *Australia* 88 D4
McDonald Is., *Ind. Oc.* 3 G13
Macdonnell Ras., *Australia* 88 D5
McDouall Peak, *Australia* 91 D1
Macdougall L., *Canada* 96 B10
MacDowell L., *Canada* 98 B1
Macduff, *U.K.* 14 D6
Maceda, *Spain* 30 C3
Macedonia ■, *Europe* 39 H4
Maceió, *Brazil* 122 C4
Maceira, *Portugal* 31 F2
Macenta, *Guinea* 78 D3
Macerata, *Italy* 33 E10
McFarland, *U.S.A.* 113 K7
McFarlane →, *Canada* 101 B7
Macfarlane, L., *Australia* 91 E2
McGehee, *U.S.A.* 109 J9
McGill, *U.S.A.* 110 G6
Macgillycuddy's Reeks, *Ireland* 15 D2
MacGregor, *Canada* 101 D9
McGregor, *U.S.A.* 108 D9
McGregor →, *Canada* 100 B4
McGregor Ra., *Australia* 91 D3
Mach, *Pakistan* 60 E5
Māch Kowr, *Iran* 65 E9
Machacalis, *Brazil* 123 E3
Machado = Jiparaná →, *Brazil* 125 B5
Machagai, *Argentina* 126 B3
Machakos, *Kenya* 82 C4
Machakos □, *Kenya* 82 C4
Machala, *Ecuador* 120 D2
Machanga, *Mozam.* 85 C6
Machattie, L., *Australia* 90 C2
Machava, *Mozam.* 85 D5
Machece, *Mozam.* 83 F4
Machecoul, *France* 24 F5
Machelen, *Belgium* 17 G4
Macheng, *China* 53 B10
Machevna, *Russia* 45 C18
Machezo, *Spain* 31 F6
Machias, *U.S.A.* 99 D6
Machichaco, C., *Spain* 28 B2
Machichi →, *Canada* 101 B10
Machico, *Madeira* 36 D3
Machilipatnam, *India* 61 L12
Machiques, *Venezuela* 120 A3
Machupicchu, *Peru* 124 C3
Machynlleth, *U.K.* 13 E4
McIlwraith Ra., *Australia* 90 A3
Măcin, *Romania* 38 D11
Macina, *Mali* 78 C4
McIntosh, *U.S.A.* 108 C4
McIntosh L., *Canada* 101 B8
Macintosh Ra., *Australia* 89 E4
Macintyre →, *Australia* 91 D5
Macizo Galaico, *Spain* 30 C3
Mackay, *Australia* 90 C4
Mackay, *U.S.A.* 110 E7
MacKay →, *Canada* 100 B6
Mackay, L., *Australia* 88 D4
McKay Ra., *Australia* 88 D3
McKeesport, *U.S.A.* 106 F5
McKenna, *U.S.A.* 112 D4
Mackenzie, *Canada* 100 B4
Mackenzie, *Guyana* 121 B6
McKenzie, *U.S.A.* 105 G1
Mackenzie →, *Australia* 90 C4
Mackenzie →, *Canada* 96 B6
McKenzie →, *U.S.A.* 110 D2
Mackenzie Bay, *Canada* 4 B1
Mackenzie City = Linden, *Guyana* 121 B6
Mackenzie Highway, *Canada* 100 B5
Mackenzie Mts., *Canada* 96 B6
Mackinaw City, *U.S.A.* 104 C3
McKinlay, *Australia* 90 C3
McKinlay →, *Australia* 90 C3
McKinley, Mt., *U.S.A.* 96 B4
McKinley Sea, *Arctic* 4 A7
McKinney, *U.S.A.* 109 J6
Mackinnon Road, *Kenya* 82 C4
Macksville, *Australia* 91 E5
McLaughlin, *U.S.A.* 108 C4
Maclean, *Australia* 91 D5
McLean, *U.S.A.* 109 H4
McLeansboro, *U.S.A.* 108 F10
Maclear, *S. Africa* 85 E4
Macleay →, *Australia* 91 E5
McLennan, *Canada* 100 B5
MacLeod, B., *Canada* 101 A7
McLeod, L., *Australia* 89 D1
MacLeod Lake, *Canada* 100 C4
M'Clintock Chan., *Canada* 96 A9
McLoughlin, Mt., *U.S.A.* 110 E2
McLure, *Canada* 100 C4
McMechen, *U.S.A.* 106 G4
McMillan, L., *U.S.A.* 109 J2
McMinnville, *Oreg., U.S.A.* 110 D2
McMinnville, *Tenn., U.S.A.* 105 H3
McMorran, *Canada* 101 C7
McMurdo Sd., *Antarctica* 5 D11
McMurray = Fort McMurray, *Canada* 100 B6
McMurray, *U.S.A.* 112 B4
McNary, *U.S.A.* 111 J9
MacNutt, *Canada* 101 C8
Macodoene, *Mozam.* 85 C6
Macomb, *U.S.A.* 108 E9
Macomer, *Italy* 34 B1
Mâcon, *France* 27 B8
Macon, *Ga., U.S.A.* 105 J4
Macon, *Miss., U.S.A.* 105 J1
Macon, *Mo., U.S.A.* 108 F8
Macondo, *Angola* 81 G4
Macossa, *Mozam.* 83 F3
Macoun L., *Canada* 101 B8
Macovane, *Mozam.* 85 C6
McPherson, *U.S.A.* 108 F6
McPherson Pk., *U.S.A.* 113 L7
McPherson Ra., *Australia* 91 D5
Macquarie Harbour, *Australia* 90 G4
Macquarie Is., *Pac. Oc.* 92 N7
MacRobertson Land, *Antarctica* 5 D6
Macroom, *Ireland* 15 E3
Macroy, *Australia* 88 D2
MacTier, *Canada* 106 A5
Macubela, *Mozam.* 83 F4
Macugnaga, *Italy* 32 C4
Macuiza, *Mozam.* 83 F3
Macujer, *Colombia* 120 C3
Macusani, *Peru* 124 C3
Macuse, *Mozam.* 83 F4
Macuspana, *Mexico* 115 D6
Macusse, *Angola* 84 B3
McVille, *U.S.A.* 108 B5
Madadeni, *S. Africa* 85 D5
Madagali, *Nigeria* 79 C7
Madagascar ■, *Africa* 85 C8
Madā'in Sālih, *Si. Arabia* 64 E3
Madama, *Niger* 73 D7
Madame I., *Canada* 99 C7
Madaoua, *Niger* 79 C6
Madara, *Nigeria* 79 C7
Madaripur, *Bangla.* 61 H17
Madauk, *Burma* 61 L20
Madawaska, *Canada* 106 A7
Madawaska →, *Canada* 98 C4
Madaya, *Burma* 61 H20
Madbar, *Sudan* 77 F3
Maddaloni, *Italy* 35 A7
Made, *Neths.* 17 E5
Madeira, *Atl. Oc.* 36 D3
Madeira →, *Brazil* 121 D6
Madeleine, Is. de la, *Canada* 99 C7
Maden, *Turkey* 67 D8
Madera, *U.S.A.* 111 H3
Madha, *India* 60 L9
Madhubani, *India* 63 F12
Madhya Pradesh □, *India* 62 J7
Madian, *China* 53 A11
Madidi →, *Bolivia* 124 C4
Madikeri, *India* 60 N9
Madill, *U.S.A.* 109 H6
Madimba, *Zaïre* 80 E3
Ma'din, *Syria* 64 C3
Madīnat ash Sha'b, *Yemen* 68 E3
Madingou, *Congo* 80 E2
Madirovalo, *Madag.* 85 B8
Madison, *Calif., U.S.A.* 112 G5
Madison, *Fla., U.S.A.* 105 K4
Madison, *Ind., U.S.A.* 104 F3
Madison, *Nebr., U.S.A.* 108 E6
Madison, *Ohio, U.S.A.* 106 E3
Madison, *S. Dak., U.S.A.* 108 D6
Madison, *Wis., U.S.A.* 108 D10
Madison →, *U.S.A.* 110 D8
Madisonville, *Ky., U.S.A.* 104 G2
Madisonville, *Tex., U.S.A.* 109 K7
Madista, *Botswana* 84 C4
Madiun, *Indonesia* 57 G14
Madley, *U.K.* 13 E5
Madol, *Sudan* 77 F2
Madon →, *France* 25 D13
Madona, *Latvia* 40 C5
Madras = Tamil Nadu □, *India* 60 P10
Madras, *India* 60 N12
Madras, *U.S.A.* 110 D3
Madre, L., *Mexico* 115 B5
Madre, Laguna, *U.S.A.* 109 M6
Madre, Sierra, *Phil.* 55 C5
Madre de Dios □, *Peru* 124 C3
Madre de Dios →, *Bolivia* 124 C4
Madre de Dios, I., *Chile* 128 D1
Madre del Sur, Sierra, *Mexico* 115 D5
Madre Occidental, Sierra, *Mexico* 114 B3
Madre Oriental, Sierra, *Mexico* 114 C4
Madri, *India* 62 G5
Madrid, *Spain* 30 E7
Madrid □, *Spain* 30 E7
Madridejos, *Spain* 31 F7
Madrigal de las Altas Torres, *Spain* 30 D6
Madrona, Sierra, *Spain* 31 G6
Madroñera, *Spain* 31 F5
Madu, *Sudan* 77 E2
Madura, Selat, *Indonesia* 57 G15
Madura Motel, *Australia* 89 F4
Madurai, *India* 60 Q11
Madurantakam, *India* 60 N11
Madzhalis, *Russia* 43 E12
Mae Chan, *Thailand* 58 B2
Mae Hong Son, *Thailand* 58 C2
Mae Khlong →, *Thailand* 58 F3
Mae Phrik, *Thailand* 58 D2
Mae Ramat, *Thailand* 58 D2
Mae Rim, *Thailand* 58 C2
Mae Sot, *Thailand* 58 D2
Mae Suai, *Thailand* 58 C2
Mae Tha, *Thailand* 58 C2
Maebashi, *Japan* 49 F9
Maella, *Spain* 28 D5
Măeruş, *Romania* 38 D8
Maesteg, *U.K.* 13 F4
Maestra, Sierra, *Cuba* 116 B4
Maestrazgo, Mts. del, *Spain* 28 E4
Maevatanana, *Madag.* 85 B8
Mafeking = Mafikeng, *S. Africa* 84 D4
Mafeking, *Canada* 101 C8
Maféré, *Ivory C.* 78 D4
Mafeteng, *Lesotho* 84 D4
Maffe, *Belgium* 17 H6
Maffra, *Australia* 91 F4
Mafia I., *Tanzania* 82 D4
Mafikeng, *S. Africa* 84 D4

Mafra, *Brazil* 127 B6
Mafra, *Portugal* 31 G1
Mafungabusi Plateau, *Zimbabwe* 83 F2
Magadan, *Russia* 45 D16
Magadi, *Kenya* 82 C4
Magadi, L., *Kenya* 82 C4
Magaliesburg, *S. Africa* 85 D4
Magallanes □, *Chile* 128 D2
Magallanes, Estrecho de, *Chile* 128 D2
Magangué, *Colombia* 120 B3
Magaria, *Niger* 79 C6
Magburaka, *S. Leone* 78 D2
Magdalen Is. = Madeleine, Is. de la, *Canada* 99 C7
Magdalena, *Argentina* 126 D4
Magdalena, *Bolivia* 125 C5
Magdalena, *Malaysia* 56 D5
Magdalena, *Mexico* 114 A2
Magdalena, *U.S.A.* 111 J10
Magdalena □, *Colombia* 120 A3
Magdalena →, *Colombia* 120 A3
Magdalena →, *Mexico* 114 A2
Magdalena, B., *Mexico* 114 C2
Magdalena, I., *Chile* 128 B2
Magdalena, Llano de la, *Mexico* 114 C2
Magdeburg, *Germany* 18 C7
Magdelaine Cays, *Australia* 90 B5
Magdub, *Sudan* 77 E2
Magee, *U.S.A.* 109 K10
Magee, I., *U.K.* 15 B6
Magelang, *Indonesia* 57 G14
Magellan's Str. = Magallanes, Estrecho de, *Chile* 128 D2
Magenta, *Italy* 32 C5
Magenta, L., *Australia* 89 F2
Maggia, *Switz.* 23 D7
Maggia →, *Switz.* 23 D7
Maggiorasca, Mte., *Italy* 32 D6
Maggiore, L., *Italy* 32 C5
Maghama, *Mauritania* 78 B2
Magherafelt, *U.K.* 15 B5
Maghnia, *Algeria* 75 B4
Magione, *Italy* 33 E9
Magliano in Toscana, *Italy* 33 F8
Máglie, *Italy* 35 B11
Magnac-Laval, *France* 26 B5
Magnetic Pole (North) = North Magnetic Pole, *Canada* 4 B2
Magnetic Pole (South) = South Magnetic Pole, *Antarctica* 5 C9
Magnitogorsk, *Russia* 44 D6
Magnolia, *Ark., U.S.A.* 109 J8
Magnolia, *Miss., U.S.A.* 109 K9
Magnor, *Norway* 10 E6
Magny-en-Vexin, *France* 25 C8
Magog, *Canada* 99 C5
Magoro, *Uganda* 82 B3
Magosa = Famagusta, *Cyprus* 37 D12
Magouládhes, *Greece* 37 A3
Magoye, *Zambia* 83 F2
Magpie L., *Canada* 99 B7
Magrath, *Canada* 100 D6
Magro →, *Spain* 29 F4
Magrur, Wadi →, *Sudan* 77 D2
Magu □, *Tanzania* 82 C3
Maguan, *China* 52 F5
Maguarinho, C., *Brazil* 122 B2
Maguse L., *Canada* 101 A9
Maguse Pt., *Canada* 101 A10
Magwe, *Burma* 61 J19
Maha Sarakham, *Thailand* 58 D4
Mahābād, *Iran* 64 B5
Mahabharat Lekh, *Nepal* 63 E9
Mahabo, *Madag.* 85 C7
Mahadeo Hills, *India* 62 H8
Mahagi, *Zaïre* 82 B3
Mahaicony, *Guyana* 121 B6
Mahajamba →, *Madag.* 85 B8
Mahajamba, Helodranon' i, *Madag.* 85 B8
Mahajan, *India* 62 E5
Mahajanga, *Madag.* 85 B8
Mahajanga □, *Madag.* 85 B8
Mahajilo →, *Madag.* 85 B8
Mahakam →, *Indonesia* 56 E5
Mahalapye, *Botswana* 84 C4
Maḩallāt, *Iran* 65 C6
Māhān, *Iran* 65 D8
Mahanadi →, *India* 61 J15
Mahanoro, *Madag.* 85 B8
Mahanoy City, *U.S.A.* 107 F8
Maharashtra □, *India* 60 J9
Maharès, *Tunisia* 75 B7
Mahari Mts., *Tanzania* 82 D2
Mahasham, W. →, *Egypt* 69 E3
Mahasolo, *Madag.* 85 B8
Mahattat ash Shīdīyah, *Jordan* 69 F4
Mahattat 'Unayzah, *Jordan* 69 E4
Mahaxay, *Laos* 58 D5
Mahbes, *W. Sahara* 74 C3
Mahbubnagar, *India* 60 L10
Maḩḑah, *Oman* 65 E7
Mahdia, *Guyana* 121 B6
Mahdia, *Tunisia* 75 A7
Mahe, *India* 63 C8
Mahenge, *Tanzania* 83 D4
Maheno, *N.Z.* 87 L3
Mahesana, *India* 62 H5
Mahia Pen., *N.Z.* 87 H6
Mahilyow = Mogilev, *Belorussia* 40 E7
Mahirija, *Morocco* 75 B4
Mahmiya, *Sudan* 77 D3
Mahmud Kot, *Pakistan* 62 D4
Mahmudia, *Romania* 38 D12
Mahnomen, *U.S.A.* 108 B7
Mahoba, *India* 63 G8
Mahón, *Spain* 36 B11
Mahone Bay, *Canada* 99 D7
Mahuta, *Nigeria* 79 C5
Mai-Ndombe, L., *Zaïre* 80 E3
Mai-Sai, *Thailand* 58 B2
Maicao, *Colombia* 120 A3
Maîche, *France* 25 E13
Maici →, *Brazil* 125 B5
Maicurú →, *Brazil* 121 D7
Máida, *Italy* 35 D9
Maidan Khula, *Afghan.* 62 C3
Maidenhead, *U.K.* 13 F7
Maidi, *Yemen* 77 D5
Maidstone, *Canada* 101 C7
Maidstone, *U.K.* 13 F8
Maiduguri, *Nigeria* 79 C7
Maignelay, *France* 25 C9
Maigo, *Phil.* 55 G5
Maigualida, Sierra, *Venezuela* 121 B4
Maigudo, *Ethiopia* 77 F4
Maijdi, *Bangla.* 61 H17
Maikala Ra., *India* 61 J12
Mailly-le-Camp, *France* 25 D11
Mailsi, *Pakistan* 62 E5
Main →, *Germany* 19 F4
Main →, *U.K.* 15 B5
Main Centre, *Canada* 101 C7
Mainburg, *Germany* 19 G7
Maine, *France* 24 E6
Maine □, *U.S.A.* 99 C6
Maine →, *Ireland* 15 D2
Maine-et-Loire □, *France* 24 E6
Maïne-Soroa, *Niger* 79 C7
Maingkwan, *Burma* 61 F20
Mainit, L., *Phil.* 55 G6
Mainland, *Orkney, U.K.* 14 C5
Mainland, *Shet., U.K.* 14 A7
Mainpuri, *India* 63 F8
Maintenon, *France* 25 D8
Maintirano, *Madag.* 85 B7
Mainvault, *Belgium* 17 G3
Mainz, *Germany* 19 F4
Maipú, *Argentina* 126 D4
Maiquetía, *Venezuela* 120 A4
Maira →, *Italy* 32 D4
Mairabari, *India* 61 F18
Mairipotaba, *Brazil* 123 E2
Maisí, *Cuba* 117 B5
Maisi, Pta. de, *Cuba* 117 B5
Maisse, *France* 25 D9
Maissin, *Belgium* 17 J6
Maitland, *N.S.W., Australia* 91 E5
Maitland, *S. Austral., Australia* 91 E2
Maitland →, *Canada* 106 C3
Maiyema, *Nigeria* 79 C5
Maiyuan, *China* 53 E11
Maiz, Is. del, *Nic.* 116 D3
Maizuru, *Japan* 49 G7
Majagual, *Colombia* 120 B3
Majalengka, *Indonesia* 57 G13
Majari →, *Brazil* 121 C5
Majene, *Indonesia* 57 E5
Majes →, *Peru* 124 D3
Maji, *Ethiopia* 77 F4
Majiang, *China* 52 D6
Major, *Canada* 101 C7
Majorca = Mallorca, *Spain* 36 B10
Majuriã, *Brazil* 125 B5
Maka, *Senegal* 78 C2
Makak, *Cameroon* 79 E7
Makale, *Indonesia* 57 E5
Makamba, *Burundi* 82 C2
Makari, *Cameroon* 80 B2
Makarikari = Makgadikgadi Salt Pans, *Botswana* 84 C4
Makarovo, *Russia* 45 D11
Makarska, *Croatia* 21 M7
Makaryev, *Russia* 41 C13
Makasar = Ujung Pandang, *Indonesia* 57 F5
Makasar, Selat, *Indonesia* 57 E5
Makasar, Str. of = Makasar, Selat, *Indonesia* 57 E5
Makat, *Kazakhstan* 44 E6
Makedonija = Macedonia ■, *Europe* 39 H4
Makena, *U.S.A.* 102 H16
Makeni, *S. Leone* 78 D2
Makeyevka, *Ukraine* 42 B7
Makgadikgadi Salt Pans, *Botswana* 84 C4
Makhachkala, *Russia* 43 E12
Makhambet, *Kazakhstan* 43 C14
Makharadze = Ozurgety, *Georgia* 43 F10
Makhmūr, *Iraq* 64 C4
Makian, *Indonesia* 57 D7
Makindu, *Kenya* 82 C4
Makinsk, *Kazakhstan* 44 D8
Makiyivka = Makeyevka, *Ukraine* 42 B7
Makkah, *Si. Arabia* 68 C2
Makkovik, *Canada* 99 A8
Makkum, *Neths.* 16 B6
Makó, *Hungary* 21 J10
Makokou, *Gabon* 80 D2
Makongo, *Zaïre* 82 B2
Makoro, *Zaïre* 82 B2
Makoua, *Congo* 80 E3
Makrá, *Greece* 39 N8
Makrai, *India* 60 H10
Makran Coast Range, *Pakistan* 60 G4
Makrana, *India* 62 F6
Makriyialos, *Greece* 37 D7
Maksimkin Yar, *Russia* 44 D9
Maktar, *Tunisia* 75 A6
Mākū, *Iran* 64 B5
Makumbi, *Zaïre* 80 F4
Makunda, *Botswana* 84 C3
Makurazaki, *Japan* 49 J5
Makurdi, *Nigeria* 79 D6
Makūyeh, *Iran* 65 D7
Makwassie, *S. Africa* 84 D4
Mal B., *Ireland* 15 D2
Mal i Nemërçkës, *Albania* 39 J3
Mal i Tomorit, *Albania* 39 J3
Mala, *Peru* 124 C2
Mala, Pta., *Panama* 116 E3
Mala Kapela, *Croatia* 33 D12
Malabang, *Phil.* 55 H6
Malabar Coast, *India* 60 P9
Malabo = Rey Malabo, *Eq. Guin.* 79 E6
Malabon, *Phil.* 55 D4
Malacca, Str. of, *Indonesia* 59 L3
Malacky, *Slovakia* 21 G7
Malad City, *U.S.A.* 110 E7
Maladzyechna = Molodechno, *Belorussia* 40 D5
Málaga, *Colombia* 120 B3
Málaga, *Spain* 31 J6
Malaga, *U.S.A.* 109 J2
Málaga □, *Spain* 31 J6
Malagarasi, *Tanzania* 82 D3
Malagarasi →, *Tanzania* 82 D2
Malagón, *Spain* 31 F7
Malagón →, *Spain* 31 H3
Malaimbandy, *Madag.* 85 C8
Malakâl, *Sudan* 77 F3
Malakand, *Pakistan* 62 B4
Malakoff, *U.S.A.* 109 J7
Malamyzh, *Russia* 45 E14
Malang, *Indonesia* 57 G15
Malanje, *Angola* 80 F3
Mälaren, *Sweden* 10 E11
Malargüe, *Argentina* 126 D2
Malartic, *Canada* 98 C4
Malatya, *Turkey* 67 D8
Malatya □, *Turkey* 67 D8
Malawi ■, *Africa* 83 E3
Malawi, L., *Africa* 83 E3
Malay Pen., *Asia* 59 J3
Malaya Belozërka, *Ukraine* 42 C6
Malaya Vishera, *Russia* 40 B8
Malaya Viska, *Ukraine* 42 B4
Malaybalay, *Phil.* 55 G6
Malāyer, *Iran* 65 C6
Malaysia ■, *Asia* 56 D4
Malazgirt, *Turkey* 67 D10
Malbon, *Australia* 90 C3
Malbooma, *Australia* 91 E1
Malbork, *Poland* 20 A9
Malcésine, *Italy* 32 C7
Malchin, *Germany* 18 B8
Malchow, *Germany* 18 B8
Malcolm, *Australia* 89 E3
Malcolm, Pt., *Australia* 89 F3
Maldegem, *Belgium* 17 F2
Malden, *Mass., U.S.A.* 107 D13
Malden, *Mo., U.S.A.* 109 G10
Malden I., *Kiribati* 93 H12
Maldives ■, *Ind. Oc.* 47 J11
Maldonado, *Uruguay* 127 C5
Maldonado, Punta, *Mexico* 115 D5
Malé, *Italy* 32 B7
Maléa, Ákra, *Greece* 39 N6
Malebo, Pool, *Africa* 70 G5
Malegaon, *India* 60 J9
Malei, *Mozam.* 83 F4
Malek Kandī, *Iran* 64 B5
Malela, *Zaïre* 82 C2
Malema, *Mozam.* 83 E4
Máleme, *Greece* 37 D5
Malerkotla, *India* 62 D6
Máles, *Greece* 37 D7
Malesherbes, *France* 25 D9
Malestroit, *France* 24 E4
Malfa, *Italy* 35 D7
Malgobek, *Russia* 43 E11
Malgomaj, *Sweden* 8 D14
Malgrat, *Spain* 28 D7
Malha, *Sudan* 77 D2
Malheur →, *U.S.A.* 110 D5
Malheur L., *U.S.A.* 110 E4
Mali, *Guinea* 78 C2
Mali ■, *Africa* 78 B4
Mali →, *Burma* 61 G20
Mali Kanal, *Serbia, Yug.* 21 K9
Malibu, *U.S.A.* 113 L8
Malik, *Indonesia* 57 E6
Malili, *Indonesia* 57 E6
Malimba, Mts., *Zaïre* 82 D2
Malin, *Ukraine* 40 F6
Malin Hd., *Ireland* 15 A4
Malindi, *Kenya* 82 C5
Malines = Mechelen, *Belgium* 17 F4
Maling, *Indonesia* 57 D6
Malinyi, *Tanzania* 83 D4
Malipo, *China* 52 F5
Maliqi, *Albania* 39 J3
Malita, *Phil.* 57 C7
Malkara, *Turkey* 66 C2
Małkinia Górna, *Poland* 20 C12
Malko Tŭrnovo, *Bulgaria* 39 H10
Mallacoota, *Australia* 91 F4
Mallacoota Inlet, *Australia* 91 F4
Mallaig, *U.K.* 14 E3
Mallawan, *India* 63 F9
Mallawi, *Egypt* 76 B3
Malleco □, *Chile* 128 A2
Mallemort, *France* 27 E9
Málles Venosta, *Italy* 32 B7
Mállia, *Greece* 37 D7
Mallión, Kólpos, *Greece* 37 D7
Mallorca, *Spain* 36 B10
Mallorytown, *Canada* 107 B9
Mallow, *Ireland* 15 D3
Malmberget, *Sweden* 8 C16
Malmédy, *Belgium* 17 H8
Malmesbury, *S. Africa* 84 E2
Malmö, *Sweden* 11 J6
Malmöhus län □, *Sweden* 11 J7
Malmslätt, *Sweden* 11 F9
Malmyzh, *Russia* 41 C17
Maloarkhangelsk, *Russia* 41 E10
Maloca, *Brazil* 121 C6
Maloja, *Switz.* 23 D9
Maloja, P., *Switz.* 23 D9
Malolos, *Phil.* 57 B6
Malombe L., *Malawi* 83 E4
Malone, *U.S.A.* 107 B10
Malong, *China* 52 E4
Malorita, *Belorussia* 40 F4
Maloyaroslovets, *Russia* 41 D10
Malpartida, *Spain* 31 F4
Malpaso, *Canary Is.* 36 G1
Malpica, *Spain* 30 B2
Malta, *Brazil* 122 C4
Malta, *Idaho, U.S.A.* 110 E7
Malta, *Mont., U.S.A.* 110 B10
Malta ■, *Europe* 37 D1
Malta Channel, *Medit. S.* 34 F6
Maltahöhe, *Namibia* 84 C2
Malters, *Switz.* 22 B6
Malton, *Canada* 106 C5
Malton, *U.K.* 12 C7
Maluku, *Indonesia* 57 E7
Maluku □, *Indonesia* 57 E7
Maluku Sea, *Indonesia* 57 E6
Malumfashi, *Nigeria* 79 C6
Malvan, *India* 60 L8
Malvern, *U.S.A.* 109 H8
Malvern Hills, *U.K.* 13 E5
Malvik, *Norway* 10 A4
Malvinas, Is. = Falkland Is. ■, *Atl. Oc.* 128 D5
Malya, *Tanzania* 82 C3
Malyy Lyakhovskiy, Ostrov, *Russia* 45 B15
Mama, *Russia* 45 D12
Mamadysh, *Russia* 41 D17
Mamanguape, *Brazil* 122 C4
Mamasa, *Indonesia* 57 E5
Mambasa, *Zaïre* 82 B2
Mamberamo →, *Indonesia* 57 E9
Mambilima Falls, *Zambia* 83 E2
Mambirima, *Zaïre* 83 E2
Mambo, *Tanzania* 82 C4
Mambrui, *Kenya* 82 C5
Mamburao, *Phil.* 55 E4
Mameigwess L., *Canada* 98 B2
Mamer, *Lux.* 17 J8
Mamers, *France* 24 D7
Mamfe, *Cameroon* 79 D6
Mamiña, *Chile* 124 E4
Mámmola, *Italy* 35 D9
Mammoth, *U.S.A.* 111 K8
Mamoré →, *Bolivia* 125 C4
Mamou, *Guinea* 78 C2
Mampatá, *Guinea-Biss.* 78 C2
Mampong, *Ghana* 79 D4
Mamuil Malal, Paso, *S. Amer.* 128 A2
Mamuju, *Indonesia* 57 E5
Man, *Ivory C.* 78 D3
Man, I. of, *U.K.* 12 C3
Man Na, *Burma* 61 H20
Mana, *Fr. Guiana* 121 B7
Mana →, *Fr. Guiana* 121 B7
Måna →, *Norway* 10 E2
Manaar, G. of = Mannar, G. of, *Asia* 60 Q11
Manabí □, *Ecuador* 120 D1
Manacacías →, *Colombia* 120 C3
Manacapuru, *Brazil* 121 D5
Manacapuru →, *Brazil* 121 D5
Manacor, *Spain* 36 B10
Manado, *Indonesia* 57 D6
Manage, *Belgium* 17 G4
Managua, *Nic.* 116 D2
Managua, L., *Nic.* 116 D2
Manakara, *Madag.* 85 C8
Manama = Al Manāmah, *Bahrain* 65 E6
Manambao →, *Madag.* 85 B7
Manambato, *Madag.* 85 A8
Manambolo →, *Madag.* 85 B7
Manambolosy, *Madag.* 85 B8
Mananara, *Madag.* 85 B8
Mananara →, *Madag.* 85 C8
Mananjary, *Madag.* 85 C8
Manantenina, *Madag.* 85 C8
Manaos = Manaus, *Brazil* 121 D6
Manapire →, *Venezuela* 120 B4
Manapouri, *N.Z.* 87 L1
Manapouri, L., *N.Z.* 87 L1
Manas, *China* 54 B3
Manas →, *India* 61 F17
Manaslu, *Nepal* 63 E11
Manasquan, *U.S.A.* 107 F10
Manassa, *U.S.A.* 111 H11
Manaung, *Burma* 61 K18
Manaus, *Brazil* 121 D6
Manavgat, *Turkey* 66 E4
Manawan L., *Canada* 101 B8
Manay, *Phil.* 55 H7
Manbij, *Syria* 64 B3
Mancelona, *U.S.A.* 104 C3
Mancha Real, *Spain* 31 H7
Manche □, *France* 24 C5
Manchester, *U.K.* 12 D5
Manchester, *Calif., U.S.A.* 112 G3
Manchester, *Conn., U.S.A.* 107 E12
Manchester, *Ga., U.S.A.* 105 J3
Manchester, *Iowa, U.S.A.* 108 D9
Manchester, *Ky., U.S.A.* 104 G4
Manchester, *N.H., U.S.A.* 107 D13
Manchester, *N.Y., U.S.A.* 106 D7
Manchester, *Vt., U.S.A.* 107 C11
Manchester L., *Canada* 101 A7
Manchuria = Dongbei, *China* 51 D13
Manciano, *Italy* 33 F8
Mancifa, *Ethiopia* 77 F5
Mancora, Pta., *Peru* 124 A1
Mand →, *Iran* 65 D7
Manda, *Chunya, Tanzania* 82 D3
Manda, *Ludewe, Tanzania* 83 E3
Mandabé, *Madag.* 85 C7
Mandaguari, *Brazil* 127 A5
Mandah, *Mongolia* 50 B5
Mandal, *Norway* 9 G9
Mandalay, *Burma* 61 J20
Mandale = Mandalay, *Burma* 61 J20
Mandalgovi, *Mongolia* 50 B4
Mandalī, *Iraq* 64 C5
Mandan, *U.S.A.* 108 B4
Mandaon, *Phil.* 55 E5
Mandar, Teluk, *Indonesia* 57 E5
Mandas, *Italy* 34 C2
Mandasor = Mandsaur, *India* 62 G6
Mandaue, *Phil.* 55 F5
Mandelieu-la-Napoule, *France* 27 E10
Mandera, *Kenya* 82 B5
Mandera □, *Kenya* 82 B5
Manderfeld, *Belgium* 17 H8
Mandi, *India* 62 D7
Mandimba, *Mozam.* 83 E4
Mandioli, *Indonesia* 57 E7
Mandioré, L., *S. Amer.* 125 D6
Mandla, *India* 63 H9
Mandø, *Denmark* 11 J2
Mandoto, *Madag.* 85 B8
Mandoúdhion, *Greece* 39 L6
Mandra, *Pakistan* 62 C5
Mandrare →, *Madag.* 85 D8
Mandritsara, *Madag.* 85 B8
Mandsaur, *India* 62 G6
Mandurah, *Australia* 89 F2
Mandúria, *Italy* 35 B10
Mandvi, *India* 62 H3
Mandya, *India* 60 N10
Mandzai, *Pakistan* 62 D2
Mané, *Burkina Faso* 79 C4
Maneh, *Iran* 65 B8
Manengouba, Mts., *Cameroon* 79 D6
Maneroo, *Australia* 90 C3
Maneroo Cr. →, *Australia* 90 C3
Manfalût, *Egypt* 76 B3
Manfred, *Australia* 91 E3
Manfredónia, *Italy* 35 A8
Manfredónia, G. di, *Italy* 35 A9
Manga, *Brazil* 123 D3
Manga, *Burkina Faso* 79 C4
Manga, *Niger* 79 C7
Mangabeiras, Chapada das, *Brazil* 122 D2
Mangalia, *Romania* 38 F11
Mangalore, *India* 60 N9
Manganeses, *Spain* 30 D5
Mangaweka, *N.Z.* 87 H5
Manggar, *Indonesia* 56 E3
Manggawitu, *Indonesia* 57 E8
Mangkalihat, Tanjung, *Indonesia* 57 D5
Mangla Dam, *Pakistan* 63 C5
Manglares, C., *Colombia* 120 C2
Manglaur, *India* 62 E7
Mangnai, *China* 54 C4
Mango, *Togo* 79 C5
Mangoche, *Malawi* 83 E4
Mangoky →, *Madag.* 85 C7
Mangole, *Indonesia* 57 E7
Mangombe, *Zaïre* 82 C2
Mangonui, *N.Z.* 87 F4
Mangualde, *Portugal* 30 E3
Mangueigne, *Chad* 73 F9
Mangueira, L. da, *Brazil* 127 C5
Manguéni, Hamada, *Niger* 75 D7
Mangum, *U.S.A.* 109 H5
Mangyshlak Poluostrov, *Kazakhstan* 43 D15

Mangyshlakskiy Zaliv, *Kazakhstan* 43 D14
Manhattan, *U.S.A.* 108 F6
Manhiça, *Mozam.* 85 D5
Manhuaçu, *Brazil* 123 F3
Manhumirim, *Brazil* 123 F3
Maní, *Colombia* 120 C3
Mania →, *Madag.* 85 B8
Maniago, *Italy* 33 B9
Manica, *Mozam.* 85 B5
Manica e Sofala □, *Mozam.* 85 B5
Manicaland □, *Zimbabwe* 83 F3
Manicoré, *Brazil* 125 B5
Manicoré →, *Brazil* 125 B5
Manicouagan →, *Canada* 99 C6
Manīfah, *Si. Arabia* 65 E6
Manifold, *Australia* 90 C5
Manifold, C., *Australia* 90 C5
Maniganggo, *China* 52 B2
Manigotagan, *Canada* 101 C9
Manihiki, *Cook Is.* 93 J11
Manika, Plateau de la, *Zaïre* 83 E2
Manila, *Phil.* 55 D4
Manila, *U.S.A.* 110 F9
Manila B., *Phil.* 55 D4
Manilla, *Australia* 91 E5
Manimpé, *Mali* 78 C3
Maningrida, *Australia* 90 A1
Manipur □, *India* 61 G18
Manipur →, *Burma* 61 H19
Manisa, *Turkey* 66 D2
Manisa □, *Turkey* 66 D2
Manistee, *U.S.A.* 104 C2
Manistee →, *U.S.A.* 104 C2
Manistique, *U.S.A.* 104 C2
Manito L., *Canada* 101 C7
Manitoba □, *Canada* 101 B9
Manitoba, L., *Canada* 101 C9
Manitou, *Canada* 101 D9
Manitou I., *U.S.A.* 98 C2
Manitou Is., *U.S.A.* 104 C2
Manitou L., *Canada* 99 B6
Manitou Springs, *U.S.A.* 108 F2
Manitoulin I., *Canada* 98 C3
Manitowaning, *Canada* 98 C3
Manitowoc, *U.S.A.* 104 C2
Manitsauá-Missu →, *Brazil* 125 C7
Manizales, *Colombia* 120 B2
Manja, *Madag.* 85 C7
Manjacaze, *Mozam.* 85 C5
Manjakandriana, *Madag.* 85 B8
Manjhand, *Pakistan* 62 G3
Manjil, *Iran* 65 B6
Manjimup, *Australia* 89 F2
Manjra →, *India* 60 K10
Mankato, *Kans., U.S.A.* 108 F5
Mankato, *Minn., U.S.A.* 108 C8
Mankayane, *Swaziland* 85 D5
Mankono, *Ivory C.* 78 D3
Mankota, *Canada* 101 D7
Manlay, *Mongolia* 50 B4
Manlleu, *Spain* 28 C7
Manly, *Australia* 91 E5
Manmad, *India* 60 J9
Mann Ras., *Australia* 89 E5
Manna, *Indonesia* 56 E2
Mannahill, *Australia* 91 E3
Mannar, *Sri Lanka* 60 Q11
Mannar, G. of, *Asia* 60 Q11
Mannar I., *Sri Lanka* 60 Q11
Männedorf, *Switz.* 23 B7
Mannheim, *Germany* 19 F4
Manning, *Canada* 100 B5
Manning, *Oreg., U.S.A.* 112 E3
Manning, *S.C., U.S.A.* 105 J5
Manning Prov. Park, *Canada* 100 D4
Mannington, *U.S.A.* 104 F5
Mannu →, *Italy* 34 C2
Mannu, C., *Italy* 34 B1
Mannum, *Australia* 91 E2
Mano, *S. Leone* 78 D2
Manoa, *Bolivia* 125 B4
Manokwari, *Indonesia* 57 E8
Manombo, *Madag.* 85 C7
Manono, *Zaïre* 82 D2
Manosque, *France* 27 E9
Manouane, L., *Canada* 99 B5
Manpojin, *N. Korea* 51 D14
Manresa, *Spain* 28 D6
Mansa, *Gujarat, India* 62 H5
Mansa, *Punjab, India* 62 E6
Mansa, *Zambia* 83 E2
Mansehra, *Pakistan* 62 B5
Mansel I., *Canada* 97 B11
Mansfield, *Australia* 91 F4
Mansfield, *U.K.* 12 D6
Mansfield, *La., U.S.A.* 109 J8
Mansfield, *Mass., U.S.A.* 107 D13
Mansfield, *Ohio, U.S.A.* 106 F2
Mansfield, *Pa., U.S.A.* 106 E7
Mansfield, *Wash., U.S.A.* 110 C4
Mansidão, *Brazil* 122 D3
Mansilla de las Mulas, *Spain* 30 C5
Mansle, *France* 26 C4
Manso →, *Brazil* 123 D2
Mansoa, *Guinea-Biss.* 78 C1
Manson Creek, *Canada* 100 B4
Mansoura, *Algeria* 75 A5
Manta, *Ecuador* 120 D1
Manta, B. de, *Ecuador* 120 D1
Mantalingajan, Mt., *Phil.* 55 G2
Mantare, *Tanzania* 82 C3
Manteca, *U.S.A.* 111 H3
Mantecal, *Venezuela* 120 B4
Mantena, *Brazil* 123 E3
Manteo, *U.S.A.* 105 H8
Mantes-la-Jolie, *France* 25 D8
Manthani, *India* 60 K11
Manthelan, *France* 24 E7
Manti, *U.S.A.* 110 G8
Mantiqueira, Serra da, *Brazil* 123 F3
Manton, *U.S.A.* 104 C3
Mantorp, *Sweden* 11 F9
Mántova, *Italy* 32 C7
Mänttä, *Finland* 8 E18
Mantua = Mántova, *Italy* 32 C7
Manturovo, *Russia* 41 B14
Manu, *Peru* 124 C3
Manu →, *Peru* 124 C3
Manua Is., *Amer. Samoa* 87 B14
Manuae, *Cook Is.* 93 J12
Manuel Alves →, *Brazil* 123 D2
Manuel Alves Grande →, *Brazil* 122 C2
Manuel Urbano, *Brazil* 124 B4
Manui, *Indonesia* 57 E6
Manuripi →, *Bolivia* 124 C4
Manville, *U.S.A.* 108 D2
Many, *U.S.A.* 109 K8
Manyara, L., *Tanzania* 82 C4
Manych →, *Russia* 43 C8
Manych-Gudilo, Oz., *Russia* 43 C10
Manyonga →, *Tanzania* 82 C3
Manyoni, *Tanzania* 82 D3
Manyoni □, *Tanzania* 82 D3
Manzai, *Pakistan* 62 C4
Manzala, Bahra el, *Egypt* 76 H7
Manzanares, *Spain* 29 F1
Manzaneda, Cabeza de, *Spain* 30 C3
Manzanillo, *Cuba* 116 B4
Manzanillo, *Mexico* 114 D4
Manzanillo, Pta., *Panama* 116 E4
Manzano Mts., *U.S.A.* 111 J10
Manzarīyeh, *Iran* 65 C6
Manzhouli, *China* 54 B6
Manzini, *Swaziland* 85 D5
Mao, *Chad* 73 F8
Maoke, Pegunungan, *Indonesia* 57 E9
Maolin, *China* 51 C12
Maoming, *China* 53 G8
Maowen, *China* 52 B4
Maoxing, *China* 51 B13
Mapam Yumco, *China* 54 C3
Mapastepec, *Mexico* 115 D6
Mapia, Kepulauan, *Indonesia* 57 D8
Mapimí, *Mexico* 114 B4
Mapimí, Bolsón de, *Mexico* 114 B4
Maping, *China* 53 B9
Mapinga, *Tanzania* 82 D4
Mapinhane, *Mozam.* 85 C6
Mapire, *Venezuela* 121 B5
Maple Creek, *Canada* 101 D7
Maple Valley, *U.S.A.* 112 C4
Mapleton, *U.S.A.* 110 D2
Mapuera →, *Brazil* 121 D6
Maputo, *Mozam.* 85 D5
Maputo, B. de, *Mozam.* 85 D5
Maqiaohe, *China* 51 B16
Maqnā, *Si. Arabia* 64 D2
Maqteïr, *Mauritania* 74 D2
Maquela do Zombo, *Angola* 80 F3
Maquinchao, *Argentina* 128 B3
Maquoketa, *U.S.A.* 108 D9
Mar, Serra do, *Brazil* 127 B6
Mar Chiquita, L., *Argentina* 126 C3
Mar del Plata, *Argentina* 126 D4
Mar Menor, L., *Spain* 29 H4
Mara, *Guyana* 121 B6
Mara, *Tanzania* 82 C3
Mara □, *Tanzania* 82 C3
Maraã, *Brazil* 120 D4
Marabá, *Brazil* 122 C2
Maracá, I. de, *Brazil* 121 C7
Maracaibo, *Venezuela* 120 A3
Maracaibo, L. de, *Venezuela* 120 B3
Maracaju, *Brazil* 127 A4
Maracajú, Serra de, *Brazil* 125 E6
Maracanã, *Brazil* 122 B2
Maracás, *Brazil* 123 D3
Maracay, *Venezuela* 120 A4
Marādah, *Libya* 73 C8
Maradi, *Niger* 79 C6
Maradun, *Nigeria* 79 C6
Marāgheh, *Iran* 64 B5
Maragogipe, *Brazil* 123 D4
Marāh, *Si. Arabia* 64 E5
Marajó, B. de, *Brazil* 122 B2
Marajó, I. de, *Brazil* 122 B2
Marākand, *Iran* 64 B5
Maralal, *Kenya* 82 B4
Maralinga, *Australia* 89 F5
Marama, *Australia* 91 F3
Marampa, *S. Leone* 78 D2
Maran, *Malaysia* 59 L4
Marana, *U.S.A.* 111 K8
Maranboy, *Australia* 88 B5
Maranchón, *Spain* 28 D2
Marand, *Iran* 64 B5
Marang, *Malaysia* 59 K4
Maranguape, *Brazil* 122 B4
Maranhão = São Luís, *Brazil* 122 B3
Maranhão □, *Brazil* 122 B2
Marano, L. di, *Italy* 33 C10
Maranoa →, *Australia* 91 D4
Marañón →, *Peru* 124 A3
Marão, *Mozam.* 85 C5
Marapi →, *Brazil* 121 C6
Marari, *Brazil* 124 B4
Maraş = Kahramanmaraş, *Turkey* 66 E7
Mărăşeşti, *Romania* 38 D10
Maratea, *Italy* 35 C8
Marateca, *Portugal* 31 G2
Marathasa □, *Cyprus* 37 E11
Marathókambos, *Greece* 39 M9
Marathon, *Australia* 90 C3
Marathon, *Canada* 98 C2
Marathón, *Greece* 39 L6
Marathon, *N.Y., U.S.A.* 107 D8
Marathon, *Tex., U.S.A.* 109 K3
Marathóvouno, *Cyprus* 37 D12
Maratua, *Indonesia* 57 D5
Maraú, *Brazil* 123 D4
Maravatío, *Mexico* 114 D4
Marawi City, *Phil.* 55 G6
Marāwih, *U.A.E.* 65 E7
Marbella, *Spain* 31 J6
Marble Bar, *Australia* 88 D2
Marble Falls, *U.S.A.* 109 K5
Marblehead, *U.S.A.* 107 D14
Marburg, *Germany* 18 E4
Marby, *Sweden* 10 A8
Marcal →, *Hungary* 21 H7
Marcapata, *Peru* 124 C3
Marcaria, *Italy* 32 C7
March, *U.K.* 13 E8
Marchand = Rommani, *Morocco* 74 B3
Marche, *France* 26 B5
Marche □, *Italy* 33 E10
Marche-en-Famenne, *Belgium* 17 H6
Marchena, *Spain* 31 H5
Marches = Marche □, *Italy* 33 E10
Marciana Marina, *Italy* 32 F7
Marcianise, *Italy* 35 A7
Marcigny, *France* 27 B8
Marcillat-en-Combraille, *France* 26 B6
Marcinelle, *Belgium* 17 H4
Marck, *France* 25 B8
Marckolsheim, *France* 25 D14
Marcona, *Peru* 124 D2
Marcos Juárez, *Argentina* 126 C3
Marcus I. = Minami-Tori-Shima, *Pac. Oc.* 92 E7
Marcus Necker Ridge, *Pac. Oc.* 92 F9
Marcy, Mt., *U.S.A.* 107 B11
Mardan, *Pakistan* 62 B5
Mardie, *Australia* 88 D2
Mardin, *Turkey* 67 E9
Marechal Deodoro, *Brazil* 122 C4
Maree L., *U.K.* 14 D3
Mareeba, *Australia* 90 B4
Marek = Stanke Dimitrov, *Bulgaria* 38 G6
Marek, *Indonesia* 57 E6
Maremma, *Italy* 32 F8
Maréna, *Mali* 78 C3
Marenberg, *Slovenia* 33 B12
Marengo, *U.S.A.* 108 E8
Marennes, *France* 26 C2
Marenyi, *Kenya* 82 C4
Marerano, *Madag.* 85 C7
Marettimo, *Italy* 34 E5
Mareuil-sur-Lay, *France* 26 B2
Marfa, *U.S.A.* 109 K2
Marfa Pt., *Malta* 37 D1
Marganets, *Ukraine* 42 C6
Margaret →, *Australia* 88 C4
Margaret Bay, *Canada* 100 C3
Margaret L., *Canada* 100 B5
Margaret River, *Australia* 88 C4
Margarita, I. de, *Venezuela* 121 A5
Margarítion, *Greece* 39 K3
Margaritovo, *Russia* 48 C7
Margate, *S. Africa* 85 E5
Margate, *U.K.* 13 F9
Margelan, *Uzbekistan* 44 E8
Margeride, Mts. de la, *France* 26 D7
Margherita di Savola, *Italy* 35 A9
Margosatubig, *Phil.* 55 H5
Marguerite, *Canada* 100 C4
Marhoum, *Algeria* 75 B4
Mari Republic □, *Russia* 41 C16
María Elena, *Chile* 126 A2
María Grande, *Argentina* 126 C4
Maria I., *N. Terr., Australia* 90 A2
Maria I., *Tas., Australia* 90 G4
Maria van Diemen, C., *N.Z.* 87 F4
Mariager, *Denmark* 11 H4
Mariager Fjord, *Denmark* 11 H4
Mariakani, *Kenya* 82 C4
Marian L., *Canada* 100 A5
Mariana Trench, *Pac. Oc.* 92 F6
Marianao, *Cuba* 116 B3
Marianna, *Ark., U.S.A.* 109 H9
Marianna, *Fla., U.S.A.* 105 K3
Mariánské Lázně, *Czech.* 20 F2
Marias →, *U.S.A.* 110 C8
Mariato, Punta, *Panama* 116 E3
Mariazell, *Austria* 21 H5
Ma'rib, *Yemen* 68 D4
Maribo, *Denmark* 11 K5
Maribor, *Slovenia* 33 B12
Marico →, *Africa* 84 C4
Maricopa, *Ariz., U.S.A.* 111 K7
Maricopa, *Calif., U.S.A.* 113 K7
Maricourt, *Canada* 97 C12
Marīdī, *Sudan* 77 G2
Maridi, Wadi →, *Sudan* 77 F2
Marié →, *Brazil* 120 D4
Marie Byrd Land, *Antarctica* 5 D14
Marie-Galante, *Guadeloupe* 117 C7
Mariecourt, *Canada* 97 B12
Mariefred, *Sweden* 10 E11
Mariehamn, *Finland* 9 F15
Marienbad = Mariánské Lázně, *Czech.* 20 F2
Marienberg, *Germany* 18 E9
Marienberg, *Neths.* 16 D9
Marienbourg, *Belgium* 17 H5
Mariental, *Namibia* 84 C2
Marienville, *U.S.A.* 106 E5
Mariestad, *Sweden* 11 F7
Marietta, *Ga., U.S.A.* 105 J3
Marietta, *Ohio, U.S.A.* 104 F5
Marieville, *Canada* 107 A11
Marignane, *France* 27 E9
Marihatag, *Phil.* 55 G7
Mariinsk, *Russia* 44 D9
Mariinskiy Posad, *Russia* 41 C15
Marília, *Brazil* 127 A5
Marillana, *Australia* 88 D2
Marín, *Spain* 30 C2
Marina, *U.S.A.* 112 J5
Marina di Cirò, *Italy* 35 C10
Marina Plains, *Australia* 90 A3
Marinduque, *Phil.* 55 E5
Marine City, *U.S.A.* 104 D4
Marineo, *Italy* 34 E6
Marinette, *U.S.A.* 104 C2
Maringá, *Brazil* 127 A5
Marinha Grande, *Portugal* 31 F2
Marion, *Ala., U.S.A.* 105 J2
Marion, *Ill., U.S.A.* 109 G10
Marion, *Ind., U.S.A.* 104 E3
Marion, *Iowa, U.S.A.* 108 D9
Marion, *Kans., U.S.A.* 108 F6
Marion, *Mich., U.S.A.* 104 C3
Marion, *N.C., U.S.A.* 105 H4
Marion, *Ohio, U.S.A.* 104 E4
Marion, *S.C., U.S.A.* 105 H6
Marion, *Va., U.S.A.* 105 G5
Marion, L., *U.S.A.* 105 J5
Maripa, *Venezuela* 121 B4
Maripasoula, *Fr. Guiana* 121 C7
Mariposa, *U.S.A.* 111 H4
Mariscal Estigarribia, *Paraguay* 126 A3
Maritime Alps = Maritimes, Alpes, *Europe* 27 D11
Maritimes, Alpes, *Europe* 27 D11
Maritsa, *Greece* 37 C10
Mariupol, *Ukraine* 42 C7
Marīvān, *Iran* 64 C5
Mariyampol, *Lithuania* 40 D3
Markam, *China* 52 C2
Markazī □, *Iran* 65 C6
Markdale, *Canada* 106 B4
Marke, *Belgium* 17 G2
Marked Tree, *U.S.A.* 109 H9
Markelsdorfer Huk, *Germany* 18 A6
Marken, *Neths.* 16 D6
Markermeer, *Neths.* 16 C6
Market Drayton, *U.K.* 12 E5
Market Harborough, *U.K.* 13 E7
Markham, *Canada* 106 C5
Markham, Mt., *Antarctica* 5 E11
Markham L., *Canada* 101 A8
Marki, *Poland* 20 C11
Markleeville, *U.S.A.* 112 G7
Markoupoulon, *Greece* 39 M6
Markovo, *Russia* 45 C17
Markoye, *Burkina Faso* 79 C5
Marks, *Russia* 41 F15
Marksville, *U.S.A.* 109 K8
Markt Schwaben, *Germany* 19 G7
Marktredwitz, *Germany* 19 E8
Marla, *Australia* 91 D1
Marlboro, *U.S.A.* 107 D13
Marlborough, *Australia* 90 C4
Marlborough Downs, *U.K.* 13 F6
Marle, *France* 25 C10
Marlin, *U.S.A.* 109 K6
Marlow, *Germany* 18 A8
Marlow, *U.S.A.* 109 H6
Marly-le-Grand, *Switz.* 22 C4
Marmagao, *India* 60 M8
Marmande, *France* 26 D4
Marmara, *Turkey* 42 F2
Marmara, Sea of = Marmara Denizi, *Turkey* 66 C3
Marmara Denizi, *Turkey* 66 C3
Marmara Gölü, *Turkey* 66 D3
Marmaris, *Turkey* 66 E3
Marmarth, *U.S.A.* 108 B3
Marmelos →, *Brazil* 125 B5
Marmion, Mt., *Australia* 89 E2
Marmion L., *Canada* 98 C1
Marmolada, Mte., *Italy* 33 B8
Marmolejo, *Spain* 31 G6
Marmora, *Canada* 98 D4
Marnay, *France* 25 E12
Marne, *Germany* 18 B5
Marne □, *France* 25 D11
Marne →, *France* 25 D9
Marneuli, *Georgia* 43 F11
Maroa, *Venezuela* 120 C4
Maroala, *Madag.* 85 B8
Maroantsetra, *Madag.* 85 B8
Maromandia, *Madag.* 85 A8
Marondera, *Zimbabwe* 83 F3
Maroni →, *Fr. Guiana* 121 B7
Maronne →, *France* 26 C5
Maroochydore, *Australia* 91 D5
Maroona, *Australia* 91 F3
Maros →, *Hungary* 21 J10
Marosakoa, *Madag.* 85 B8
Marostica, *Italy* 33 C8
Maroua, *Cameroon* 79 C7
Marovoay, *Madag.* 85 B8
Marowijne □, *Surinam* 121 C7
Marowijne →, *Surinam* 121 B7
Marquard, *S. Africa* 84 D4
Marqueira, *Portugal* 31 G1
Marquesas Is. = Marquises, Is., *Pac. Oc.* 93 H14
Marquette, *U.S.A.* 104 B2
Marquise, *France* 25 B8
Marquises, Is., *Pac. Oc.* 93 H14
Marra, Gebel, *Sudan* 77 F2
Marracuene, *Mozam.* 85 D5
Marradi, *Italy* 33 D8
Marrakech, *Morocco* 74 B3
Marrawah, *Australia* 90 G3
Marrecas, Serra das, *Brazil* 122 C3
Marree, *Australia* 91 D2
Marrilla, *Australia* 88 D1
Marrimane, *Mozam.* 85 C5
Marromeu, *Mozam.* 85 B6
Marroquí, Punta, *Spain* 31 K5
Marrowie Cr. →, *Australia* 91 E4
Marrubane, *Mozam.* 83 F4
Marrum, *Neths.* 16 B7
Marrupa, *Mozam.* 83 E4
Marsá Matrûh, *Egypt* 76 A2
Marsá Susah, *Libya* 73 B9
Marsabit, *Kenya* 82 B4
Marsabit □, *Kenya* 82 B4
Marsala, *Italy* 34 E5
Marsalforn, *Malta* 37 C1
Marsberg, *Germany* 18 D4
Marsciano, *Italy* 33 F9
Marsden, *Australia* 91 E4
Marsdiep, *Neths.* 16 C5
Marseillan, *France* 26 E7
Marseille, *France* 27 E9
Marseilles = Marseille, *France* 27 E9
Marsh I., *U.S.A.* 109 L9
Marsh L., *U.S.A.* 108 C6
Marshall, *Liberia* 78 D2
Marshall, *Ark., U.S.A.* 109 H8
Marshall, *Mich., U.S.A.* 104 D3
Marshall, *Minn., U.S.A.* 108 C7
Marshall, *Mo., U.S.A.* 108 F8
Marshall, *Tex., U.S.A.* 109 J7
Marshall →, *Australia* 90 C2
Marshall Is. ■, *Pac. Oc.* 92 G9
Marshalltown, *U.S.A.* 108 D8
Marshfield, *Mo., U.S.A.* 109 G8
Marshfield, *Wis., U.S.A.* 108 C9
Marshūn, *Iran* 65 B6
Mársico Nuovo, *Italy* 35 B8
Märsta, *Sweden* 10 E11
Marstal, *Denmark* 11 K4
Marstrand, *Sweden* 11 G5
Mart, *U.S.A.* 109 K6
Marta →, *Italy* 33 F8
Martaban, *Burma* 61 L20
Martaban, G. of, *Burma* 61 L20
Martano, *Italy* 35 B11
Martapura, *Kalimantan, Indonesia* 56 E4
Martapura, *Sumatera, Indonesia* 56 E2
Marte, *Nigeria* 79 C7
Martel, *France* 26 D5
Martelange, *Belgium* 17 J7
Martés, Sierra, *Spain* 29 F4
Martha's Vineyard, *U.S.A.* 107 E14
Martigné-Ferchaud, *France* 24 E5
Martigny, *Switz.* 22 D4
Martigues, *France* 27 E9
Martil, *Morocco* 74 A3
Martin, *Slovakia* 20 F8
Martin, *S. Dak., U.S.A.* 108 D4
Martin, *Tenn., U.S.A.* 109 G10
Martín →, *Spain* 28 D4
Martin L., *U.S.A.* 105 J3
Martina, *Switz.* 23 C10
Martina Franca, *Italy* 35 B10
Martinborough, *N.Z.* 87 J5
Martinez, *U.S.A.* 112 G4
Martinho Campos, *Brazil* 123 E2
Martinique ■, *W. Indies* 117 D7
Martinique Passage, *W. Indies* 117 C7
Martínon, *Greece* 39 L6
Martinópolis, *Brazil* 127 A5
Martins Ferry, *U.S.A.* 106 F4
Martinsburg, *Pa., U.S.A.* 106 F6
Martinsburg, *W. Va., U.S.A.* 104 F7

Martinsville, *Ind., U.S.A.* 104 F2
Martinsville, *Va., U.S.A.* 105 G6
Marton, *N.Z.* 87 J5
Martorell, *Spain* 28 D6
Martos, *Spain* 31 H7
Martuni, *Armenia* 43 F11
Maru, *Nigeria* 79 C6
Marudi, *Malaysia* 56 D4
Ma'ruf, *Afghan.* 60 D5
Marugame, *Japan* 49 G6
Marúggio, *Italy* 35 B10
Maruim, *Brazil* 122 D4
Marulan, *Australia* 91 E5
Marum, *Neths.* 16 B8
Marunga, *Angola* 84 B3
Marungu, Mts., *Zaïre* 82 D2
Marvast, *Iran* 65 D7
Marvejols, *France* 26 D7
Marwar, *India* 62 G5
Mary, *Turkmenistan* 44 F7
Mary Frances L., *Canada* 101 A7
Mary Kathleen, *Australia* 90 C2
Maryborough = Port Laoise, *Ireland* 15 C4
Maryborough, *Queens., Australia* 91 D5
Maryborough, *Vic., Australia* 91 F3
Maryfield, *Canada* 101 D8
Maryland □, *U.S.A.* 104 F7
Maryland Junction, *Zimbabwe* 83 F3
Maryport, *U.K.* 12 C4
Mary's Harbour, *Canada* 99 B8
Marystown, *Canada* 99 C8
Marysvale, *U.S.A.* 111 G7
Marysville, *Canada* 100 D5
Marysville, *Calif., U.S.A.* 112 F5
Marysville, *Kans., U.S.A.* 108 F6
Marysville, *Mich., U.S.A.* 106 D2
Marysville, *Ohio, U.S.A.* 104 E4
Marysville, *Wash., U.S.A.* 112 B4
Maryvale, *Australia* 91 D5
Maryville, *U.S.A.* 105 H4
Marzo, Punta, *Colombia* 120 B2
Marzūq, *Libya* 73 C7
Masahunga, *Tanzania* 82 C3
Masai, *Malaysia* 59 M4
Masai Steppe, *Tanzania* 82 C4
Masaka, *Uganda* 82 C3
Masalembo, Kepulauan, *Indonesia* 56 F4
Masalima, Kepulauan, *Indonesia* 56 F5
Masamba, *Indonesia* 57 E6
Masan, *S. Korea* 51 G15
Masanasa, *Spain* 29 F4
Masasi, *Tanzania* 83 E4
Masasi □, *Tanzania* 83 E4
Masaya, *Nic.* 116 D2
Masba, *Nigeria* 79 C7
Masbate, *Phil.* 55 E5
Mascara, *Algeria* 75 A5
Mascota, *Mexico* 114 C4
Masela, *Indonesia* 57 F7
Maseru, *Lesotho* 84 D4
Mashaba, *Zimbabwe* 83 G3
Mashābih, *Si. Arabia* 64 E3
Mashan, *China* 52 F7
Masherbrum, *Pakistan* 63 B7
Mashhad, *Iran* 65 B8
Mashi, *Nigeria* 79 C6
Mashīz, *Iran* 65 D8
Mashkel, Hamun-i-, *Pakistan* 60 E3
Mashki Chāh, *Pakistan* 60 E3
Mashonaland Central □, *Zimbabwe* 85 B5
Mashonaland East □, *Zimbabwe* 85 B5
Mashonaland West □, *Zimbabwe* 85 B4
Mashtaga, *Azerbaijan* 43 F13
Masi, *Norway* 8 B17
Masi Manimba, *Zaïre* 80 E3
Masindi, *Uganda* 82 B3
Masindi Port, *Uganda* 82 B3
Masisea, *Peru* 124 B3
Masisi, *Zaïre* 82 C2
Masjed Soleyman, *Iran* 65 D6
Mask, L., *Ireland* 15 C2
Maslinica, *Croatia* 33 E13
Masnou, *Spain* 28 D7
Masoala, Tanjon' i, *Madag.* 85 B9
Masoarivo, *Madag.* 85 B7
Masohi, *Indonesia* 57 E7
Masomeloka, *Madag.* 85 C8
Mason, *Nev., U.S.A.* 112 G7
Mason, *Tex., U.S.A.* 109 K5
Mason City, *U.S.A.* 108 D8
Maspalomas, *Canary Is.* 36 G4
Maspalomas, Pta., *Canary Is.* 36 G4
Masqat, *Oman* 68 C6
Massa, *Italy* 32 D7
Massa, O. →, *Morocco* 74 B3
Massa Maríttima, *Italy* 32 E7
Massachusetts □, *U.S.A.* 107 D12
Massachusetts B., *U.S.A.* 107 D14
Massafra, *Italy* 35 B10
Massaguet, *Chad* 73 F8
Massakory, *Chad* 73 F8
Massanella, *Spain* 36 B9
Massangena, *Mozam.* 85 C5
Massapê, *Brazil* 122 B3
Massarosa, *Italy* 32 E7
Massat, *France* 26 F5
Massawa = Mitsiwa, *Eritrea* 77 D4
Massena, *U.S.A.* 107 B10
Massénya, *Chad* 73 F8
Masset, *Canada* 100 C2
Massiac, *France* 26 C7
Massif Central, *France* 26 D7
Massillon, *U.S.A.* 106 F3
Massinga, *Mozam.* 85 C6
Masson, *Canada* 107 A9
Masson I., *Antarctica* 5 C7
Mastanli = Momchilgrad, *Bulgaria* 39 H8
Masterton, *N.Z.* 87 J5
Mástikho, Ákra, *Greece* 39 L9
Mastuj, *Pakistan* 63 A5
Mastung, *Pakistan* 60 E5
Mastūrah, *Si. Arabia* 76 C4
Masuda, *Japan* 49 G5
Masvingo, *Zimbabwe* 83 G3
Masvingo □, *Zimbabwe* 83 G3
Maswa □, *Tanzania* 82 C3
Maşyāf, *Syria* 64 C3
Mata de São João, *Brazil* 123 D4
Matabeleland North □, *Zimbabwe* 83 F2
Matabeleland South □, *Zimbabwe* 83 G2
Mataboor, *Indonesia* 57 E9
Matachel →, *Spain* 31 G4
Matachewan, *Canada* 98 C3
Matacuni →, *Venezuela* 121 C4
Matad, *Mongolia* 54 B6
Matadi, *Zaïre* 80 F2
Matagalpa, *Nic.* 116 D2
Matagami, *Canada* 98 C4
Matagami, L., *Canada* 98 C4
Matagorda, *U.S.A.* 109 L7
Matagorda B., *U.S.A.* 109 L6
Matagorda I., *U.S.A.* 109 L6
Matak, P., *Indonesia* 59 L6
Matakana, *Australia* 91 E4
Mátala, *Greece* 37 E6
Matalaque, *Peru* 124 D3
Matam, *Senegal* 78 B2
Matameye, *Niger* 79 C6
Matamoros, *Campeche, Mexico* 115 D6
Matamoros, *Coahuila, Mexico* 114 B4
Matamoros, *Puebla, Mexico* 115 D5
Matamoros, *Tamaulipas, Mexico* 115 B5
Ma'ţan as Sarra, *Libya* 73 D9
Matandu →, *Tanzania* 83 D3
Matane, *Canada* 99 C6
Matang, *China* 52 F5
Matankari, *Niger* 79 C5
Matanzas, *Cuba* 116 B3
Matapan, C. = Taínaron, Ákra, *Greece* 39 N5
Matapédia, *Canada* 99 C6
Matara, *Sri Lanka* 60 S12
Mataram, *Indonesia* 56 F5
Matarani, *Peru* 124 D3
Mataranka, *Australia* 88 B5
Matarma, Râs, *Egypt* 69 E1
Mataró, *Spain* 28 D7
Matarraña →, *Spain* 28 D5
Matatiele, *S. Africa* 85 E4
Mataura, *N.Z.* 87 M2
Mategua, *Bolivia* 125 C5
Matehuala, *Mexico* 114 C4
Mateira, *Brazil* 123 E1
Mateke Hills, *Zimbabwe* 83 G3
Matélica, *Italy* 33 E10
Matera, *Italy* 35 B9
Mátészalka, *Hungary* 21 H12
Matetsi, *Zimbabwe* 83 F2
Mateur, *Tunisia* 75 A6
Matfors, *Sweden* 10 B11
Matha, *France* 26 C3
Matheson Island, *Canada* 101 C9
Mathis, *U.S.A.* 109 L6
Mathura, *India* 62 F7
Mati, *Phil.* 55 H7
Mati →, *Albania* 39 H2
Matías Romero, *Mexico* 115 D5
Matibane, *Mozam.* 83 E5
Matima, *Botswana* 84 C3
Matiri Ra., *N.Z.* 87 J4
Matlock, *U.K.* 12 D6
Matmata, *Tunisia* 75 B6
Matna, *Sudan* 77 E4
Mato →, *Venezuela* 121 B4
Mato, Serrania de, *Venezuela* 120 B4
Mato Grosso □, *Brazil* 125 C6
Mato Grosso, Planalto do, *Brazil* 125 C7
Mato Grosso do Sul □, *Brazil* 125 D7
Matochkin Shar, *Russia* 44 B6
Matopo Hills, *Zimbabwe* 83 G2
Matopos, *Zimbabwe* 83 G2
Matosinhos, *Portugal* 30 D2
Matour, *France* 27 B8
Matsena, *Nigeria* 79 C7
Matsesta, *Russia* 43 E8
Matsue, *Japan* 49 G6
Matsumae, *Japan* 48 D10
Matsumoto, *Japan* 49 F9
Matsusaka, *Japan* 49 G8
Matsuura, *Japan* 49 H4
Matsuyama, *Japan* 49 H6
Mattagami →, *Canada* 98 B3
Mattancheri, *India* 60 Q10
Mattawa, *Canada* 98 C4
Mattawamkeag, *U.S.A.* 99 C6
Matterhorn, *Switz.* 22 E5
Matthew Town, *Bahamas* 117 B5
Matthew's Ridge, *Guyana* 121 B5
Mattice, *Canada* 98 C3
Mattituck, *U.S.A.* 107 F12
Mattmar, *Sweden* 10 A7
Matuba, *Mozam.* 85 C5
Matucana, *Peru* 124 C2
Matun, *Afghan.* 62 C3
Maturín, *Venezuela* 121 B5
Matveyev Kurgan, *Russia* 43 C8
Mau, *India* 63 G10
Mau Escarpment, *Kenya* 82 C4
Mau Ranipur, *India* 63 G8
Maubeuge, *France* 25 B10
Maubourguet, *France* 26 E4
Maud, Pt., *Australia* 88 D1
Maude, *Australia* 91 E3
Maudin Sun, *Burma* 61 M19
Maués, *Brazil* 121 D6
Mauganj, *India* 61 G12
Maui, *U.S.A.* 102 H16
Maulamyaing = Moulmein, *Burma* 61 L20
Maule □, *Chile* 126 D1
Mauléon-Licharre, *France* 26 E3
Maullín, *Chile* 128 B2
Maumee, *U.S.A.* 104 E4
Maumee →, *U.S.A.* 104 E4
Maumere, *Indonesia* 57 F6
Maun, *Botswana* 84 B3
Mauna Kea, *U.S.A.* 102 J17
Mauna Loa, *U.S.A.* 102 J17
Maungmagan Kyunzu, *Burma* 61 M20
Maupin, *U.S.A.* 110 D3
Maure-de-Bretagne, *France* 24 E5
Maurepas, L., *U.S.A.* 109 K9
Maures, *France* 27 E10
Mauriac, *France* 26 C6
Maurice, L., *Australia* 89 E5
Mauritania ■, *Africa* 74 D3
Mauritius ■, *Ind. Oc.* 71 J9
Mauron, *France* 24 D4
Maurs, *France* 26 D6
Mauston, *U.S.A.* 108 D9
Mauterndorf, *Austria* 21 H3
Mauvezin, *France* 26 E4
Mauzé-sur-le-Mignon, *France* 26 B3
Mavaca →, *Venezuela* 121 C4
Mavinga, *Angola* 81 H4
Mavli, *India* 62 G5
Mavrova, *Albania* 39 J2
Mavuradonha Mts., *Zimbabwe* 83 F3
Mawa, *Zaïre* 82 B2
Mawana, *India* 62 E7
Mawand, *Pakistan* 62 E3
Mawk Mai, *Burma* 61 J20
Mawlaik, *Burma* 61 H19
Mawquq, *Si. Arabia* 64 E4
Mawson Coast, *Antarctica* 5 C6
Max, *U.S.A.* 108 B4
Maxcanú, *Mexico* 115 C6
Maxesibeni, *S. Africa* 85 E4
Maxhamish L., *Canada* 100 B4
Maxixe, *Mozam.* 85 C6
Maxville, *Canada* 107 A10
Maxwell, *U.S.A.* 112 F4
Maxwelton, *Australia* 90 C3
May Downs, *Australia* 90 C4
May Pen, *Jamaica* 116 C4
Maya, *Spain* 28 B3
Maya →, *Russia* 45 D14
Maya Mts., *Belize* 115 D7
Mayaguana, *Bahamas* 117 B5
Mayagüez, *Puerto Rico* 117 C6
Mayahi, *Niger* 79 C6
Mayals, *Spain* 28 D5
Mayāmey, *Iran* 65 B7
Mayang, *China* 52 D7
Mayarí, *Cuba* 117 B4
Maybell, *U.S.A.* 110 F9
Maychew, *Ethiopia* 77 E4
Maydān, *Iraq* 64 C5
Maydena, *Australia* 90 G4
Mayen, *Germany* 19 E3
Mayenne, *France* 24 D6
Mayenne □, *France* 24 D6
Mayenne →, *France* 24 E6
Mayer, *U.S.A.* 111 J7
Mayerthorpe, *Canada* 100 C5
Mayfield, *U.S.A.* 105 G1
Mayhill, *U.S.A.* 111 K11
Maykop, *Russia* 43 D9
Maymyo, *Burma* 58 A1
Maynard, *U.S.A.* 112 C4
Maynard Hills, *Australia* 89 E2
Mayne →, *Australia* 90 C3
Maynooth, *Ireland* 15 C5
Mayo, *Canada* 96 B6
Mayo □, *Ireland* 15 C2
Mayo →, *Argentina* 128 C3
Mayo →, *Peru* 124 B2
Mayo L., *Canada* 96 B6
Mayon Volcano, *Phil.* 55 E5
Mayor I., *N.Z.* 87 G6
Mayorga, *Spain* 30 C5
Mayraira Pt., *Phil.* 55 B4
Mayskiy, *Russia* 43 E11
Mayson L., *Canada* 101 B7
Maysville, *U.S.A.* 104 F4
Mayu, *Indonesia* 57 D7
Mayville, *N. Dak., U.S.A.* 108 B6
Mayville, *N.Y., U.S.A.* 106 D5
Mayya, *Russia* 45 C14
Mazabuka, *Zambia* 83 F2
Mazagán = El Jadida, *Morocco* 74 B3
Mazagão, *Brazil* 121 D7
Mazamet, *France* 26 E6
Mazán, *Peru* 120 D3
Māzandarān □, *Iran* 65 B7
Mazapil, *Mexico* 114 C4
Mazar, O. →, *Algeria* 75 B5
Mazara del Vallo, *Italy* 34 E5
Mazarredo, *Argentina* 128 C3
Mazarrón, *Spain* 29 H3
Mazarrón, G. de, *Spain* 29 H3
Mazaruni →, *Guyana* 121 B6
Mazatán, *Mexico* 114 B2
Mazatenango, *Guatemala* 116 D1
Mazatlán, *Mexico* 114 C3
Mažeikiai, *Lithuania* 40 C3
Māzhān, *Iran* 65 C8
Mazīnān, *Iran* 65 B8
Mazoe, *Mozam.* 83 F3
Mazoe →, *Mozam.* 83 F3
Mazowe, *Zimbabwe* 83 F3
Mazrûb, *Sudan* 77 E2
Mazu Dao, *China* 53 D12
Mazurian Lakes = Mazurski, Pojezierze, *Poland* 20 B10
Mazurski, Pojezierze, *Poland* 20 B10
Mazzarino, *Italy* 35 E7
Mbaba, *Senegal* 78 C1
Mbabane, *Swaziland* 85 D5
Mbagne, *Mauritania* 78 B2
M'bahiakro, *Ivory C.* 78 D4
Mbaïki, *C.A.R.* 80 D3
Mbala, *Zambia* 83 D3
Mbale, *Uganda* 82 B3
Mbalmayo, *Cameroon* 79 E7
Mbamba Bay, *Tanzania* 83 E3
Mbandaka, *Zaïre* 80 D3
Mbanga, *Cameroon* 79 E6
Mbanza Congo, *Angola* 80 F2
Mbanza Ngungu, *Zaïre* 80 F2
Mbarara, *Uganda* 82 C3
Mbashe →, *S. Africa* 85 E4
Mbatto, *Ivory C.* 78 D4
Mbenkuru →, *Tanzania* 83 D4
Mberengwa, *Zimbabwe* 83 G2
Mberengwa, Mt., *Zimbabwe* 83 G2
Mberubu, *Nigeria* 79 D6
Mbesuma, *Zambia* 83 D3
Mbeya, *Tanzania* 83 D3
Mbeya □, *Tanzania* 82 D3
Mbinga, *Tanzania* 83 E4
Mbinga □, *Tanzania* 83 E3
Mbini □, *Eq. Guin.* 80 D2
Mboki, *C.A.R.* 77 F2
Mboro, *Senegal* 78 B1
Mboune, *Senegal* 78 C2
Mbour, *Senegal* 78 C1
Mbout, *Mauritania* 78 B2
Mbozi □, *Tanzania* 83 D3
Mbuji-Mayi, *Zaïre* 82 D1
Mbulu, *Tanzania* 82 C4
Mbulu □, *Tanzania* 82 C4
Mburucuyá, *Argentina* 126 B4
Mcherrah, *Algeria* 74 C4
Mchinja, *Tanzania* 83 D4
Mchinji, *Malawi* 83 E3
Mdennah, *Mauritania* 74 D3
Mead, L., *U.S.A.* 113 J12
Meade, *U.S.A.* 109 G4
Meadow, *Australia* 89 E1
Meadow Lake, *Canada* 101 C7
Meadow Lake Prov. Park, *Canada* 101 C7
Meadow Valley Wash →, *U.S.A.* 113 J12
Meadville, *U.S.A.* 106 E4
Meaford, *Canada* 98 D3
Mealhada, *Portugal* 30 E2
Mealy Mts., *Canada* 99 B8
Meander River, *Canada* 100 B5
Meares, C., *U.S.A.* 110 D2
Mearim →, *Brazil* 122 B3
Meath □, *Ireland* 15 C5
Meath Park, *Canada* 101 C7
Meaulne, *France* 26 B6
Meaux, *France* 25 D9
Mebechi-Gawa →, *Japan* 48 D10
Mecanhelas, *Mozam.* 83 F4
Mecaya →, *Colombia* 120 C2
Mecca = Makkah, *Si. Arabia* 68 C2
Mecca, *U.S.A.* 113 M10
Mechanicsburg, *U.S.A.* 106 F8
Mechanicville, *U.S.A.* 107 D11
Mechara, *Ethiopia* 77 F5
Mechelen, *Antwerpen, Belgium* 17 F4
Mechelen, *Limburg, Belgium* 17 G7
Mecheria, *Algeria* 75 B4
Mechernich, *Germany* 18 E2
Mechetinskaya, *Russia* 43 C9
Mechra Benâbbou, *Morocco* 74 B3
Mecitözü, *Turkey* 42 F6
Mecklenburg-Vorpommern □, *Germany* 18 B8
Mecklenburger Bucht, *Germany* 18 A7
Meconta, *Mozam.* 83 E4
Meda, *Australia* 88 C3
Meda, *Portugal* 30 E3
Medan, *Indonesia* 56 D1
Médanos, *Argentina* 128 A4
Medanosa, Pta., *Argentina* 128 C3
Medéa, *Algeria* 75 A5
Medeiros Neto, *Brazil* 123 E3
Medel, Pic, *Switz.* 23 C7
Medellín, *Colombia* 120 B2
Medemblik, *Neths.* 16 C6
Médenine, *Tunisia* 75 B7
Mederdra, *Mauritania* 78 B1
Medford, *Mass., U.S.A.* 107 D13
Medford, *Oreg., U.S.A.* 110 E2
Medford, *Wis., U.S.A.* 108 C9
Medgidia, *Romania* 38 E11
Medi, *Sudan* 77 F3
Media Agua, *Argentina* 126 C2
Media Luna, *Argentina* 126 C2
Mediaş, *Romania* 38 C7
Medical Lake, *U.S.A.* 110 C5
Medicina, *Italy* 33 D8
Medicine Bow, *U.S.A.* 110 F10
Medicine Bow Pk., *U.S.A.* 110 F10
Medicine Bow Ra., *U.S.A.* 110 F10
Medicine Hat, *Canada* 101 D6
Medicine Lake, *U.S.A.* 108 A2
Medicine Lodge, *U.S.A.* 109 G5
Medina = Al Madīnah, *Si. Arabia* 64 E3
Medina, *Brazil* 123 E3
Medina, *Colombia* 120 C3
Medina, *N. Dak., U.S.A.* 108 B5
Medina, *N.Y., U.S.A.* 106 C6
Medina, *Ohio, U.S.A.* 106 E3
Medina →, *U.S.A.* 109 L5
Medina de Ríoseco, *Spain* 30 D5
Medina del Campo, *Spain* 30 D6
Medina L., *U.S.A.* 109 L5
Medina-Sidonia, *Spain* 31 J5
Medinaceli, *Spain* 28 D2
Medinipur, *India* 63 H12
Mediterranean Sea, *Europe* 70 C5
Medjerda, O. →, *Tunisia* 75 A7
Medley, *Canada* 101 C6
Médoc, *France* 26 C3
Medstead, *Canada* 101 C7
Medulin, *Croatia* 33 D10
Medveda, *Serbia* 21 N11
Medveditsa →, *Russia* 41 G13
Medveditsa →, *Russia* 41 C10
Medvedok, *Russia* 41 C17
Medvezhi, Ostrava, *Russia* 45 B17
Medvezhyegorsk, *Russia* 44 C4
Medway →, *U.K.* 13 F8
Medyn, *Russia* 41 D9
Medzilaborce, *Slovak Rep.* 20 F11
Meeberrie, *Australia* 89 E2
Meekatharra, *Australia* 89 E2
Meeker, *U.S.A.* 110 F10
Meer, *Belgium* 17 F5
Meerane, *Germany* 18 E8
Meerbeke, *Belgium* 17 G4
Meerhout, *Belgium* 17 F6
Meerle, *Belgium* 17 F5
Meersburg, *Germany* 19 H5
Meerssen, *Neths.* 17 G7
Meerut, *India* 62 E7
Meeteetse, *U.S.A.* 110 D9
Meeuwen, *Belgium* 17 F7
Mega, *Ethiopia* 77 G4
Megálo Petalí, *Greece* 39 M7
Megalópolis, *Greece* 39 M5
Meganísi, *Greece* 39 L3
Mégara, *Greece* 39 M6
Megarine, *Algeria* 75 B6
Megève, *France* 27 C10
Meghalaya □, *India* 61 G17
Meghezez, *Ethiopia* 77 F4
Mégiscane, L., *Canada* 98 C4
Mehadia, *Romania* 38 E5
Mehaigne →, *Belgium* 17 G6
Mehaïguene, O. →, *Algeria* 75 B5
Meheisa, *Sudan* 76 D3
Mehndawal, *India* 63 F10
Mehr Jān, *Iran* 65 C7
Mehrābād, *Iran* 64 B5
Mehrān, *Iran* 64 C5
Mehrīz, *Iran* 65 D7
Mehun-sur-Yèvre, *France* 25 E9
Mei Jiang →, *China* 53 E11
Mei Xian, *Guangdong, China* 53 E11
Mei Xian, *Shaanxi, China* 50 G4
Meia Ponte →, *Brazil* 123 E2
Meicheng, *China* 53 C12
Meichengzhen, *China* 53 C8
Meichuan, *China* 53 B10
Meiganga, *Cameroon* 80 C2
Meijel, *Neths.* 17 F7
Meiktila, *Burma* 61 J19
Meilen, *Switz.* 23 B7
Meiningen, *Germany* 18 E6
Meio →, *Brazil* 123 D3
Meira, Sierra de, *Spain* 30 B3

Meiringen, *Switz.* 22 C6
Meishan, *China* 52 B4
Meissen, *Germany* 18 D9
Meissner, *Germany* 18 D5
Meitan, *China* 52 D6
Mejillones, *Chile* 126 A1
Meka, *Australia* 89 E2
Mékambo, *Gabon* 80 D2
Mekdela, *Ethiopia* 77 E4
Mekele, *Ethiopia* 77 E4
Mekhtar, *Pakistan* 60 D6
Meknès, *Morocco* 74 B3
Meko, *Nigeria* 79 D5
Mekong →, *Asia* 59 H6
Mekongga, *Indonesia* 57 E6
Melagiri Hills, *India* 60 N10
Melah, Sebkhet el, *Algeria* 75 C4
Melaka, *Malaysia* 59 L4
Melalap, *Malaysia* 56 C5
Mélambes, *Greece* 37 D6
Melanesia, *Pac. Oc.* 92 H7
Melbourne, *Australia* 91 F3
Melbourne, *U.S.A.* 105 L5
Melchor Múzquiz, *Mexico* 114 B4
Melchor Ocampo, *Mexico* 114 C4
Méldola, *Italy* 33 D9
Meldorf, *Germany* 18 A5
Melegnano, *Italy* 32 C6
Melenci, *Serbia* 21 K10
Melenki, *Russia* 41 D12
Mélèzes →, *Canada* 97 C12
Melfi, *Chad* 73 F8
Melfi, *Italy* 35 B8
Melfort, *Canada* 101 C8
Melfort, *Zimbabwe* 83 F3
Melgaço, *Madeira* 30 C2
Melgar de Fernamental, *Spain* 30 C6
Melhus, *Norway* 10 A4
Melick, *Neths.* 17 F8
Melide, *Switz.* 23 E7
Meligalá, *Greece* 39 M4
Melilla, *Morocco* 75 A4
Melipilla, *Chile* 126 C1
Mélissa, Ákra, *Greece* 37 D6
Melita, *Canada* 101 D8
Mélito di Porto Salvo, *Italy* 35 E8
Melitopol, *Ukraine* 42 C6
Melk, *Austria* 21 G5
Mellansel, *Sweden* 8 E15
Melle, *Belgium* 17 G3
Melle, *France* 26 B3
Melle, *Germany* 18 C4
Mellégue, O. →, *Tunisia* 75 A6
Mellen, *U.S.A.* 108 B9
Mellerud, *Sweden* 11 F6
Mellette, *U.S.A.* 108 C5
Mellid, *Spain* 30 C2
Mellieha, *Malta* 37 D1
Mellit, *Sudan* 77 E2
Mellizo Sur, Cerro, *Chile* 128 C2
Mellrichstadt, *Germany* 19 E6
Melnik, *Bulgaria* 39 H6
Mělník, *Czech.* 20 E4
Melo, *Uruguay* 127 C5
Melolo, *Indonesia* 57 F6
Melouprey, *Cambodia* 58 F5
Melovoye, *Ukraine* 43 B9
Melrhir, Chott, *Algeria* 75 B6
Melrose, *N.S.W., Australia* 91 E4
Melrose, *W. Austral., Australia* 89 E3
Melrose, *U.K.* 14 F6
Melrose, *U.S.A.* 109 H3
Mels, *Switz.* 23 B8
Melsele, *Belgium* 17 F4
Melstone, *U.S.A.* 110 C10
Melsungen, *Germany* 18 D5
Melton Mowbray, *U.K.* 12 E7
Melun, *France* 25 D9
Melut, *Sudan* 77 E3
Melville, *Canada* 101 C8
Melville, C., *Australia* 90 A3
Melville, L., *Canada* 99 B8
Melville B., *Australia* 90 A2
Melville I., *Australia* 88 B5
Melville I., *Canada* 4 B2
Melville Pen., *Canada* 97 B11
Melvin →, *Canada* 100 B5
Memaliaj, *Albania* 39 J2
Memba, *Mozam.* 83 E5
Memboro, *Indonesia* 57 F5
Membrilla, *Spain* 29 G1
Memel = Klaìpéda, *Lithuania* 40 D2
Memel, *S. Africa* 85 D4
Memmingen, *Germany* 19 H6
Mempawah, *Indonesia* 56 D3
Memphis, *Tenn., U.S.A.* 109 H10
Memphis, *Tex., U.S.A.* 109 H4
Mena, *U.S.A.* 109 H7
Mena →, *Ethiopia* 77 F5
Menai Strait, *U.K.* 12 D3
Ménaka, *Mali* 79 B5
Menaldum, *Neths.* 16 B7
Menan = Chao Phraya →, *Thailand* 58 F3
Menarandra →, *Madag.* 85 D7
Menard, *U.S.A.* 109 K5
Menasha, *U.S.A.* 104 C1
Menate, *Indonesia* 56 E4
Mendawai →, *Indonesia* 56 E4
Mende, *France* 26 D7
Mendebo, *Ethiopia* 77 F4
Mendez, *Mexico* 115 B5
Mendhar, *India* 63 C6
Mendi, *Ethiopia* 77 F4
Mendip Hills, *U.K.* 13 F5
Mendocino, *U.S.A.* 110 G2
Mendocino, C., *U.S.A.* 110 F1
Mendota, *Calif., U.S.A.* 111 H3
Mendota, *Ill., U.S.A.* 108 E10
Mendoza, *Argentina* 126 C2
Mendoza □, *Argentina* 126 C2
Mendrisio, *Switz.* 23 E7
Mene Grande, *Venezuela* 120 B3
Menemen, *Turkey* 66 D2
Menen, *Belgium* 17 G2
Menéndez, L., *Argentina* 128 B2
Menfi, *Italy* 34 E5
Mengcheng, *China* 53 A11
Mengdingjie, *China* 52 F2
Mengeš, *Slovenia* 33 B11
Menggala, *Indonesia* 56 E3
Menghai, *China* 52 G3
Mengíbar, *Spain* 31 H7
Mengjin, *China* 50 G7
Mengla, *China* 52 G3
Menglian, *China* 52 F2
Mengoub, *Algeria* 74 C3
Mengshan, *China* 53 E8
Mengyin, *China* 51 G9
Mengzhe, *China* 52 F3
Mengzi, *China* 52 F4
Menihek L., *Canada* 99 B6
Menin = Menen, *Belgium* 17 G2
Menindee, *Australia* 91 E3
Menindee L., *Australia* 91 E3
Meningie, *Australia* 91 F2
Menlo Park, *U.S.A.* 112 H4
Menominee, *U.S.A.* 104 C2
Menominee →, *U.S.A.* 104 C2
Menomonie, *U.S.A.* 108 C9
Menongue, *Angola* 81 G3
Menorca, *Spain* 36 B11
Mentakab, *Malaysia* 59 L4
Mentawai, Kepulauan, *Indonesia* 56 E1
Menton, *France* 27 E11
Mentor, *U.S.A.* 106 E3
Mentz Dam, *S. Africa* 84 E4
Menzel-Bourguiba, *Tunisia* 75 A6
Menzel Chaker, *Tunisia* 75 B7
Menzel-Temime, *Tunisia* 75 A7
Menzies, *Australia* 89 E3
Me'ona, *Israel* 69 B4
Meoqui, *Mexico* 114 B3
Mepaco, *Mozam.* 83 F3
Meppel, *Neths.* 16 C8
Meppen, *Germany* 18 C3
Mequinenza, *Spain* 28 D5
Mer Rouge, *U.S.A.* 109 J9
Merabéllou, Kólpos, *Greece* 37 D7
Meramangye, L., *Australia* 89 E5
Meran = Merano, *Italy* 33 B8
Merano, *Italy* 33 B8
Merate, *Italy* 32 C6
Merauke, *Indonesia* 57 F10
Merbabu, *Indonesia* 57 G14
Merbein, *Australia* 91 E3
Merca, *Somali Rep.* 68 G3
Mercadal, *Spain* 36 B11
Mercato Saraceno, *Italy* 33 E9
Merced, *U.S.A.* 111 H3
Merced Pk., *U.S.A.* 112 H7
Mercedes, *Buenos Aires, Argentina* 126 C4
Mercedes, *Corrientes, Argentina* 126 B4
Mercedes, *San Luis, Argentina* 126 C2
Mercedes, *Uruguay* 126 C4
Merceditas, *Chile* 126 B1
Mercer, *N.Z.* 87 G5
Mercer, *U.S.A.* 106 E4
Merchtem, *Belgium* 17 G4
Mercier, *Bolivia* 124 C4
Mercury, *U.S.A.* 113 J11
Mercy C., *Canada* 97 B13
Merdrignac, *France* 24 D4
Mere, *Belgium* 17 G3
Meredith, C., *Falk. Is.* 128 D4
Meredith, L., *U.S.A.* 109 H4
Merelbeke, *Belgium* 17 G3
Méréville, *France* 25 D9
Merga = Nukheila, *Sudan* 76 D2
Mergenevsky, *Kazakhstan* 43 B14
Mergui Arch. = Myeik Kyunzu, *Burma* 59 G1
Mérida, *Mexico* 115 C7
Mérida, *Spain* 31 G4
Mérida, *Venezuela* 120 B3
Mérida □, *Venezuela* 120 B3
Mérida, Cord. de, *Venezuela* 118 B2
Meriden, *U.S.A.* 107 E12
Meridian, *Calif., U.S.A.* 112 F5
Meridian, *Idaho, U.S.A.* 110 E5
Meridian, *Miss., U.S.A.* 105 J1
Meridian, *Tex., U.S.A.* 109 K6
Mering, *Germany* 19 G7
Meriruma, *Brazil* 121 C7
Merkel, *U.S.A.* 109 J4
Merksem, *Belgium* 17 F4
Merksplas, *Belgium* 17 F5
Mermaid Reef, *Australia* 88 C2
Mern, *Denmark* 11 J6
Merowe, *Sudan* 76 D3
Merredin, *Australia* 89 F2
Merrick, *U.K.* 14 F4
Merrickville, *Canada* 107 B9
Merrill, *Oreg., U.S.A.* 110 E3
Merrill, *Wis., U.S.A.* 108 C10
Merriman, *U.S.A.* 108 D4
Merritt, *Canada* 100 C4
Merriwa, *Australia* 91 E5
Merriwagga, *Australia* 91 E4
Merry I., *Canada* 98 A4
Merrygoen, *Australia* 91 E4
Merryville, *U.S.A.* 109 K8
Mersa Fatma, *Eritrea* 68 E3
Mersch, *Lux.* 17 J8
Merseburg, *Germany* 18 D7
Mersey →, *U.K.* 12 D5
Merseyside □, *U.K.* 12 D5
Mersin, *Turkey* 66 E6
Mersing, *Malaysia* 59 L4
Merta, *India* 62 F6
Mertert, *Lux.* 17 J8
Merthyr Tydfil, *U.K.* 13 F4
Mértola, *Portugal* 31 H3
Mertzig, *Lux.* 17 J8
Mertzon, *U.S.A.* 109 K4
Méru, *France* 25 C9
Meru, *Kenya* 82 B4
Meru, *Tanzania* 82 C4
Meru □, *Kenya* 82 B4
Merville, *France* 25 B9
Méry-sur-Seine, *France* 25 D10
Merzifon, *Turkey* 42 F6
Merzig, *Germany* 19 F2
Merzouga, Erg Tin, *Algeria* 75 D7
Mesa, *U.S.A.* 111 K8
Mesach Mellet, *Libya* 75 D7
Mesagne, *Italy* 35 B10
Mesanagrós, *Greece* 37 C9
Mesaoría □, *Cyprus* 37 D12
Mesarás, Kólpos, *Greece* 37 D6
Meschede, *Germany* 18 D4
Mesfinto, *Ethiopia* 77 E4
Mesgouez, L., *Canada* 98 B4
Meshchovsk, *Russia* 40 D9
Meshed = Mashhad, *Iran* 65 B8
Meshoppen, *U.S.A.* 107 E8
Meshra er Req, *Sudan* 77 F2
Mesick, *U.S.A.* 104 C3
Mesilinka →, *Canada* 100 B4
Mesilla, *U.S.A.* 111 K10
Meslay-du-Maine, *France* 24 E6
Mesocco, *Switz.* 23 D8
Mesolóngion, *Greece* 39 L4
Mesopotamia = Al Jazirah, *Iraq* 64 C5
Mesoraca, *Italy* 35 C9
Mesquite, *U.S.A.* 111 H6
Mess Cr. →, *Canada* 100 B2
Messac, *France* 24 E5
Messad, *Algeria* 75 B5
Messalo →, *Mozam.* 83 E4
Méssaména, *Cameroon* 79 E7
Messancy, *Belgium* 17 J7
Messier, Canal, *Chile* 128 C2
Messina, *Italy* 35 D8
Messina, *S. Africa* 85 C5
Messina, Str. di, *Italy* 35 D8
Messíni, *Greece* 39 M5
Messiniakós Kólpos, *Greece* 39 N5
Messkirch, *Germany* 19 H5
Messonghi, *Greece* 37 B3
Mesta →, *Bulgaria* 39 H7
Mestanza, *Spain* 31 G6
Mestre, *Italy* 33 C9
Mestre, Espigão, *Brazil* 123 D2
Městys Zelezná Ruda, *Czech.* 20 F3
Meta □, *Colombia* 120 C3
Meta →, *S. Amer.* 120 B4
Metairie, *U.S.A.* 109 L9
Metaline Falls, *U.S.A.* 110 B5
Metán, *Argentina* 126 B3
Metangula, *Mozam.* 83 E3
Metauro →, *Italy* 33 E10
Metema, *Ethiopia* 77 E4
Metengobalame, *Mozam.* 83 E3
Méthana, *Greece* 39 M6
Methven, *N.Z.* 87 K3
Methy L., *Canada* 101 B7
Metil, *Mozam.* 83 F4
Metlakatla, *U.S.A.* 100 B2
Metlaoui, *Tunisia* 75 B6
Metlika, *Slovenia* 33 C12
Metropolis, *U.S.A.* 109 G10
Mettet, *Belgium* 17 H5
Mettur Dam, *India* 60 P10
Metz, *France* 25 C13
Meulaboh, *Indonesia* 56 D1
Meulan, *France* 25 C8
Meung-sur-Loire, *France* 25 E8
Meureudu, *Indonesia* 56 C1
Meurthe →, *France* 25 D13
Meurthe-et-Moselle □, *France* 25 D13
Meuse □, *France* 25 C12
Meuse →, *Europe* 17 G7
Meuselwitz, *Germany* 18 D8
Mexborough, *U.K.* 12 D6
Mexia, *U.S.A.* 109 K6
Mexiana, I., *Brazil* 122 A2
Mexicali, *Mexico* 114 A1
México, *Mexico* 115 D5
Mexico, *Maine, U.S.A.* 107 B14
Mexico, *Mo., U.S.A.* 108 F9
México □, *Mexico* 114 D5
Mexico ■, *Cent. Amer.* 114 C4
Mexico, G. of, *Cent. Amer.* 115 C7
Meyenburg, *Germany* 18 B8
Meymac, *France* 26 C6
Meymaneh, *Afghan.* 60 B4
Meyrargues, *France* 27 E9
Meyrueis, *France* 26 D7
Meyssac, *France* 26 C5
Mezdra, *Bulgaria* 38 F6
Mèze, *France* 26 E7
Mezen, *Russia* 44 C5
Mezen →, *Russia* 44 C5
Mézenc, Mt., *France* 27 D8
Mezha →, *Russia* 40 D7
Mézidon, *France* 24 C6
Mézilhac, *France* 27 D8
Mézin, *France* 26 D4
Mezőberény, *Hungary* 21 J11
Mezőkövácsháza, *Hungary* 21 J10
Mezőkövesd, *Hungary* 21 H10
Mézos, *France* 26 D2
Mezőtúr, *Hungary* 21 J10
Mezquital, *Mexico* 114 C4
Mezzolombardo, *Italy* 32 B8
Mgeta, *Tanzania* 83 D4
Mglin, *Russia* 40 E8
Mhlaba Hills, *Zimbabwe* 83 F3
Mhow, *India* 62 H6
Miahuatlán, *Mexico* 115 D5
Miajadas, *Spain* 31 F5
Miallo, *Australia* 90 B4
Miami, *Ariz., U.S.A.* 111 K8
Miami, *Fla., U.S.A.* 105 N5
Miami, *Tex., U.S.A.* 109 H4
Miami →, *U.S.A.* 104 F3
Miami Beach, *U.S.A.* 105 N5
Miamisburg, *U.S.A.* 104 F3
Mian Xian, *China* 50 H4
Mianchi, *China* 50 G6
Mīāndowāb, *Iran* 64 B5
Miandrivazo, *Madag.* 85 B8
Mīāneh, *Iran* 64 B5
Mianning, *China* 52 C4
Mianwali, *Pakistan* 62 C4
Mianyang, *Hubei, China* 53 B9
Mianyang, *Sichuan, China* 52 B5
Mianzhu, *China* 52 B5
Miaoli, *Taiwan* 53 E13
Miarinarivo, *Madag.* 85 B8
Miass, *Russia* 44 D7
Miastko, *Poland* 20 A6
Michelstadt, *Germany* 19 F5
Michigan □, *U.S.A.* 104 C3
Michigan, L., *U.S.A.* 104 C2
Michigan City, *U.S.A.* 104 E2
Michikamau L., *Canada* 99 B7
Michipicoten, *Canada* 98 C3
Michipicoten I., *Canada* 98 C2
Michoacan □, *Mexico* 114 D4
Michurin, *Bulgaria* 38 G10
Michurinsk, *Russia* 41 E12
Miclere, *Australia* 90 C4
Mico, Pta., *Nic.* 116 D3
Micronesia, Federated States of ■, *Pac. Oc.* 92 G7
Mid Glamorgan □, *U.K.* 13 F4
Midai, P., *Indonesia* 59 L6
Midale, *Canada* 101 D8
Middagsfjället, *Sweden* 10 A6
Middelbeers, *Neths.* 17 F6
Middelburg, *Neths.* 17 F3
Middelburg, *C. Prov., S. Africa* 84 E3
Middelburg, *Trans., S. Africa* 85 D4
Middelfart, *Denmark* 11 J3
Middelharnis, *Neths.* 16 E4
Middelkerke, *Belgium* 17 F1
Middelrode, *Neths.* 17 E6
Middelwit, *S. Africa* 84 C4
Middle Alkali L., *U.S.A.* 110 F3
Middle Fork Feather →, *U.S.A.* 112 F5
Middle I., *Australia* 89 F3
Middle Loup →, *U.S.A.* 108 E5
Middleboro, *U.S.A.* 107 E14
Middleburg, *N.Y., U.S.A.* 107 D10
Middleburg, *Pa., U.S.A.* 106 F7
Middlebury, *U.S.A.* 107 B11
Middleport, *U.S.A.* 104 F4
Middlesboro, *Ky., U.S.A.* 103 C10
Middlesboro, *Ky., U.S.A.* 105 G4
Middlesbrough, *U.K.* 12 C6
Middlesex, *Belize* 116 C2
Middlesex, *U.S.A.* 107 F10
Middleton, *Australia* 90 C3
Middleton, *Canada* 99 D6
Middletown, *Calif., U.S.A.* 112 G4
Middletown, *Conn., U.S.A.* 107 E12
Middletown, *N.Y., U.S.A.* 107 E10
Middletown, *Ohio, U.S.A.* 104 F3
Middletown, *Pa., U.S.A.* 107 F8
Midelt, *Morocco* 74 B4
Midi, Canal du →, *France* 26 E5
Midi d'Ossau, Pic du, *France* 26 F3
Midland, *Canada* 98 D4
Midland, *Calif., U.S.A.* 113 M12
Midland, *Mich., U.S.A.* 104 D3
Midland, *Pa., U.S.A.* 106 F4
Midland, *Tex., U.S.A.* 109 K3
Midlands □, *Zimbabwe* 83 F2
Midleton, *Ireland* 15 E3
Midlothian, *U.S.A.* 109 J6
Midongy, Tangorombohitr' i, *Madag.* 85 C8
Midongy Atsimo, *Madag.* 85 C8
Midou →, *France* 26 E3
Midouze →, *France* 26 E3
Midsayap, *Phil.* 55 H6
Midu, *China* 52 E3
Midway Is., *Pac. Oc.* 92 E10
Midway Wells, *U.S.A.* 113 N11
Midwest, *U.S.A.* 103 B9
Midwest, *Wyo., U.S.A.* 110 E10
Midwolda, *Neths.* 16 B9
Midyat, *Turkey* 67 E9
Mie □, *Japan* 49 G8
Miechów, *Poland* 20 E10
Międzychód, *Poland* 20 C5
Międzyrzec Podlaski, *Poland* 20 D12
Międzyrzecz, *Poland* 20 C5
Miélan, *France* 26 E4
Mielec, *Poland* 20 E11
Mienga, *Angola* 84 B2
Miercurea Ciuc, *Romania* 38 C8
Mieres, *Spain* 30 B5
Mierlo, *Neths.* 17 F7
Mieso, *Ethiopia* 77 F5
Mifflintown, *U.S.A.* 106 F7
Mifraz Hefa, *Israel* 69 C4
Migdāl, *Israel* 69 C4
Migennes, *France* 25 E10
Migliarino, *Italy* 33 D8
Miguel Alemán, Presa, *Mexico* 115 D5
Miguel Alves, *Brazil* 122 B3
Miguel Calmon, *Brazil* 122 D3
Mihaliççık, *Turkey* 66 D4
Mihara, *Japan* 49 G6
Mijares →, *Spain* 28 F4
Mijas, *Spain* 31 J6
Mikese, *Tanzania* 82 D4
Mikha-Tskhakaya = Senaki, *Georgia* 43 E10
Mikhailovka, *Ukraine* 42 C6
Mikhaylovgrad, *Bulgaria* 38 F6
Mikhaylovka, *Azerbaijan* 43 F13
Mikhaylovka, *Russia* 41 D11
Mikhaylovka, *Russia* 41 F13
Mikhnevo, *Russia* 41 D10
Mikínai, *Greece* 39 M5
Mikkeli, *Finland* 9 F19
Mikkeli □ = Mikkelin lääni □, *Finland* 8 F20
Mikkelin lääni □, *Finland* 8 F20
Mikkwa →, *Canada* 100 B6
Mikniya, *Sudan* 77 D3
Mikołajki, *Poland* 20 B11
Míkonos, *Greece* 39 M8
Mikrón Dhérion, *Greece* 39 H9
Mikulov, *Czech.* 20 G6
Mikumi, *Tanzania* 82 D4
Milaca, *U.S.A.* 108 C8
Milagro, *Ecuador* 120 D2
Milagros, *Phil.* 55 E5
Milan = Milano, *Italy* 32 C6
Milan, *Mo., U.S.A.* 108 E8
Milan, *Tenn., U.S.A.* 105 H1
Milang, *Australia* 91 E2
Milange, *Mozam.* 83 F4
Milano, *Italy* 32 C6
Milâs, *Turkey* 66 E2
Mílatos, *Greece* 37 D7
Milazzo, *Italy* 35 D8
Milbank, *U.S.A.* 108 C6
Milden, *Canada* 101 C7
Mildmay, *Canada* 106 B3
Mildura, *Australia* 91 E3
Mile, *China* 52 E4
Miléai, *Greece* 39 K6
Mileh Tharthār, *Iraq* 64 C4
Miles, *Australia* 91 D5
Miles, *U.S.A.* 109 K4
Miles City, *U.S.A.* 108 B2
Milestone, *Canada* 101 D8
Mileto, *Italy* 35 D9
Miletto, Mte., *Italy* 35 A7
Miletus, *Turkey* 66 E2
Mileura, *Australia* 89 E2
Milford, *Calif., U.S.A.* 112 E6
Milford, *Conn., U.S.A.* 107 E11
Milford, *Del., U.S.A.* 104 F8
Milford, *Mass., U.S.A.* 107 D13
Milford, *Pa., U.S.A.* 107 E10
Milford, *Utah, U.S.A.* 111 G7
Milford Haven, *U.K.* 13 F2
Milford Sd., *N.Z.* 87 L1
Milgun, *Australia* 89 D2
Milh, Baḩr al, *Iraq* 64 C4
Miliana, *Aïn Salah, Algeria* 75 C5
Miliana, *Médéa, Algeria* 75 A5
Miling, *Australia* 89 F2
Militello in Val di Catánia, *Italy* 35 E7
Milk →, *U.S.A.* 110 B10
Milk, Wadi el →, *Sudan* 76 D3
Milk River, *Canada* 100 D6
Mill, *Neths.* 17 E7
Mill City, *U.S.A.* 110 D2
Mill I., *Antarctica* 5 C8
Mill Valley, *U.S.A.* 112 H4
Millau, *France* 26 D7
Millbridge, *Canada* 106 B7
Millbrook, *Canada* 106 B6
Mille Lacs, L. des, *Canada* 98 C1
Mille Lacs L., *U.S.A.* 108 B8
Milledgeville, *U.S.A.* 105 J4
Millen, *U.S.A.* 105 J5
Miller, *U.S.A.* 108 C5
Millerovo, *Russia* 43 B9

Millersburg, *Ohio, U.S.A.* 106 F3
Millersburg, *Pa., U.S.A.* 106 F8
Millerton, *U.S.A.* 107 E11
Millerton L., *U.S.A.* 112 J7
Millevaches, Plateau de, *France* 26 C6
Millicent, *Australia* 91 F3
Millingen, *Neths.* 16 E8
Millinocket, *U.S.A.* 99 C6
Millmerran, *Australia* 91 D5
Mills L., *Canada* 100 A5
Millsboro, *U.S.A.* 106 G4
Milltown Malbay, *Ireland* 15 D2
Millville, *U.S.A.* 104 F8
Millwood L., *U.S.A.* 109 J8
Milly-la-Forêt, *France* 25 D9
Milna, *Croatia* 33 E13
Milne →, *Australia* 90 C2
Milne Inlet, *Canada* 97 A11
Milnor, *U.S.A.* 108 B6
Milo, *Canada* 100 C6
Mílos, *Greece* 39 N7
Miloševo, *Serbia* 21 K10
Milparinka P.O., *Australia* 91 D3
Miltenberg, *Germany* 19 F5
Milton, *Canada* 106 C5
Milton, *N.Z.* 87 M2
Milton, *U.K.* 14 D4
Milton, *Calif., U.S.A.* 112 G6
Milton, *Fla., U.S.A.* 105 K2
Milton, *Pa., U.S.A.* 106 F8
Milton-Freewater, *U.S.A.* 110 D4
Milton Keynes, *U.K.* 13 E7
Miltou, *Chad* 73 F8
Milverton, *Canada* 106 C4
Milwaukee, *U.S.A.* 104 D2
Milwaukee Deep, *Atl. Oc.* 117 C6
Milwaukie, *U.S.A.* 112 E4
Mim, *Ghana* 78 D4
Mimizan, *France* 26 D2
Mimoso, *Brazil* 123 E2
Min Chiang →, *China* 53 E12
Min Jiang →, *China* 52 C5
Min Xian, *China* 50 G3
Mina, *U.S.A.* 111 G4
Mina Pirquitas, *Argentina* 126 A2
Mīnā Su'ud, *Si. Arabia* 65 D6
Mīnā'al Aḥmadī, *Kuwait* 65 D6
Mīnāb, *Iran* 65 E8
Minago →, *Canada* 101 C9
Minaki, *Canada* 101 D10
Minamata, *Japan* 49 H5
Minami-Tori-Shima, *Pac. Oc.* 92 E7
Minas, *Uruguay* 127 C4
Minas, Sierra de las, *Guatemala* 116 C2
Minas Basin, *Canada* 99 C7
Minas de Rio Tinto, *Spain* 31 H4
Minas de San Quintín, *Spain* 31 G6
Minas Gerais □, *Brazil* 123 E2
Minas Novas, *Brazil* 123 E3
Minatitlán, *Mexico* 115 D6
Minbu, *Burma* 61 J19
Mincio →, *Italy* 32 C7
Mindanao, *Phil.* 55 H6
Mindanao Sea = Bohol Sea, *Phil.* 57 C6
Mindanao Trench, *Pac. Oc.* 55 F7
Mindel →, *Germany* 19 G6
Mindelheim, *Germany* 19 G6
Minden, *Canada* 106 B6
Minden, *Germany* 18 C4
Minden, *La., U.S.A.* 109 J8
Minden, *Nev., U.S.A.* 112 G7
Mindiptana, *Indonesia* 57 F10
Mindoro, *Phil.* 55 E4
Mindoro Str., *Phil.* 55 E4
Mindouli, *Congo* 80 E2
Mine, *Japan* 49 G5
Minehead, *U.K.* 13 F4
Mineiros, *Brazil* 125 D7
Mineola, *U.S.A.* 109 J7
Mineral King, *U.S.A.* 112 J8
Mineral Wells, *U.S.A.* 109 J5
Mineralnyye Vody, *Russia* 43 D10
Minersville, *Pa., U.S.A.* 107 F8
Minersville, *Utah, U.S.A.* 111 G7
Minerva, *U.S.A.* 106 F3
Minervino Murge, *Italy* 35 A9
Minetto, *U.S.A.* 107 C8
Mingan, *Canada* 99 B7
Mingechaur, *Azerbaijan* 43 F12
Mingechaurskoye Vdkhr., *Azerbaijan* 43 F12
Mingela, *Australia* 90 B4
Mingenew, *Australia* 89 E2
Mingera Cr. →, *Australia* 90 C2
Minggang, *China* 53 A10
Mingin, *Burma* 61 H19
Minglanilla, *Spain* 28 F3
Minglun, *China* 52 E7
Mingorria, *Spain* 30 E6
Mingt'iehkaitafan = Mintaka Pass, *Pakistan* 63 A6
Mingxi, *China* 53 D11
Mingyuegue, *China* 51 C15
Minhou, *China* 53 E12
Minićevo, *Serbia* 21 M12
Minidoka, *U.S.A.* 110 E7
Minigwal, L., *Australia* 89 E3
Minilya, *Australia* 89 D1
Minilya →, *Australia* 89 D1
Minipi, L., *Canada* 99 B7
Mink L., *Canada* 100 A5
Minna, *Nigeria* 79 D6
Minneapolis, *Kans., U.S.A.* 108 F6
Minneapolis, *Minn., U.S.A.* 108 C8
Minnedosa, *Canada* 101 C9
Minnesota □, *U.S.A.* 108 B7
Minnesund, *Norway* 10 D5
Minnie Creek, *Australia* 89 D2
Minnipa, *Australia* 91 E2
Minnitaki L., *Canada* 98 C1
Mino, *Japan* 49 G8
Miño →, *Spain* 30 D2
Minorca = Menorca, *Spain* 36 B11
Minore, *Australia* 91 E4
Minot, *U.S.A.* 108 A4
Minqin, *China* 50 E2
Minqing, *China* 53 D12
Minsen, *Germany* 18 B3
Minsk, *Belorussia* 40 E5
Mińsk Mazowiecki, *Poland* 20 C11
Mintaka Pass, *Pakistan* 63 A6
Minto, *U.S.A.* 96 B5
Minton, *Canada* 101 D8
Minturn, *U.S.A.* 110 G10
Minturno, *Italy* 34 A6
Minûf, *Egypt* 76 H7
Minusinsk, *Russia* 45 D10
Minutang, *India* 61 E20
Minvoul, *Gabon* 80 D2
Minya el Qamh, *Egypt* 76 H7
Mionica, *Serbia* 21 L10
Mir, *Niger* 79 C7
Mir-Bashir, *Azerbaijan* 43 F12
Mīr Kūh, *Iran* 65 E8
Mīr Shahdād, *Iran* 65 E8
Mira, *Italy* 33 C9
Mira, *Portugal* 30 E2
Mira →, *Colombia* 120 C2
Mira →, *Portugal* 31 H2
Mira por vos Cay, *Bahamas* 117 B5
Mirabella Eclano, *Italy* 35 A7
Miracema do Norte, *Brazil* 122 C2
Mirador, *Brazil* 122 C3
Miraflores, *Colombia* 120 C3
Miraj, *India* 60 L9
Miram Shah, *Pakistan* 62 C4
Miramar, *Argentina* 126 D4
Miramar, *Mozam.* 85 C6
Miramas, *France* 27 E8
Mirambeau, *France* 26 C3
Miramichi B., *Canada* 99 C7
Miramont-de-Guyenne, *France* 26 D4
Miranda, *Brazil* 125 E6
Miranda □, *Venezuela* 120 A4
Miranda →, *Brazil* 125 D6
Miranda de Ebro, *Spain* 28 C2
Miranda do Corvo, *Spain* 30 E2
Miranda do Douro, *Portugal* 30 D4
Mirande, *France* 26 E4
Mirandela, *Portugal* 30 D3
Mirando City, *U.S.A.* 109 M5
Mirandola, *Italy* 32 D8
Mirandópolis, *Brazil* 127 A5
Mirango, *Malawi* 83 E3
Mirani, *Australia* 90 C4
Mirano, *Italy* 33 C9
Mirassol, *Brazil* 127 A6
Mirbāṭ, *Oman* 68 D5
Mirear, *Egypt* 76 C4
Mirebeau, *Côte-d'Or, France* 25 E12
Mirebeau, *Vienne, France* 24 F7
Mirecourt, *France* 25 D13
Mirgorod, *Ukraine* 40 G8
Miri, *Malaysia* 56 D4
Miriam Vale, *Australia* 90 C5
Mirim, L., *S. Amer.* 127 C5
Mirimire, *Venezuela* 120 A4
Miriti, *Brazil* 125 B6
Mirnyy, *Russia* 45 C12
Mirond L., *Canada* 101 B8
Mirpur, *Pakistan* 63 C5
Mirpur Bibiwari, *Pakistan* 62 E2
Mirpur Khas, *Pakistan* 62 G3
Mirpur Sakro, *Pakistan* 62 G2
Mirria, *Niger* 79 C6
Mirror, *Canada* 100 C6
Mîrşani, *Romania* 38 E6
Miryang, *S. Korea* 51 G15
Mirzaani, *Georgia* 43 F12
Mirzapur, *India* 63 G10
Mirzapur-cum-Vindhyachal = Mirzapur, *India* 63 G10
Misantla, *Mexico* 115 D5
Misawa, *Japan* 48 D10
Miscou I., *Canada* 99 C7
Mish'āb, Ra'as al, *Si. Arabia* 65 D6
Mishagua →, *Peru* 124 C3
Mishan, *China* 54 B8
Mishawaka, *U.S.A.* 104 E2
Mishbih, Gebel, *Egypt* 76 C3
Mishima, *Japan* 49 G9
Misilmeri, *Italy* 34 D6
Misión, *Mexico* 113 N10
Misión Fagnano, *Argentina* 128 D3
Misiones □, *Argentina* 127 B5
Misiones □, *Paraguay* 126 B4
Miskah, *Si. Arabia* 64 E4
Miskitos, Cayos, *Nic.* 116 D3
Miskolc, *Hungary* 21 G10
Misoke, *Zaïre* 82 C2
Misool, *Indonesia* 57 E8
Misrātah, *Libya* 73 B8
Missanabie, *Canada* 98 C3
Missão Velha, *Brazil* 122 C4
Missinaibi →, *Canada* 98 B3
Missinaibi L., *Canada* 98 C3
Mission, *S. Dak., U.S.A.* 108 D4
Mission, *Tex., U.S.A.* 109 M5
Mission City, *Canada* 100 D4
Mission Viejo, *U.S.A.* 113 M9
Missisa L., *Canada* 98 B2
Missisagi →, *Canada* 98 C3
Mississippi □, *U.S.A.* 109 J10
Mississippi →, *U.S.A.* 109 L10
Mississippi L., *Canada* 107 A8
Mississippi River Delta, *U.S.A.* 109 L9
Mississippi Sd., *U.S.A.* 109 K10
Missoula, *U.S.A.* 110 C6
Missour, *Morocco* 74 B4
Missouri □, *U.S.A.* 108 F8
Missouri →, *U.S.A.* 108 F9
Missouri Valley, *U.S.A.* 108 E7
Mist, *U.S.A.* 112 E3
Mistake B., *Canada* 101 A10
Mistassini →, *Canada* 99 C5
Mistassini L., *Canada* 98 B5
Mistastin L., *Canada* 99 A7
Mistatim, *Canada* 101 C8
Mistelbach, *Austria* 20 G6
Misterbianco, *Italy* 35 E8
Mistretta, *Italy* 35 E7
Misty L., *Canada* 101 B8
Misurata = Misrātah, *Libya* 73 B8
Mît Ghamr, *Egypt* 76 H7
Mitatib, *Sudan* 77 D4
Mitchell, *Australia* 91 D4
Mitchell, *Canada* 106 C3
Mitchell, *Ind., U.S.A.* 104 F2
Mitchell, *Nebr., U.S.A.* 108 E3
Mitchell, *Oreg., U.S.A.* 110 D3
Mitchell, *S. Dak., U.S.A.* 108 D5
Mitchell →, *Australia* 90 B3
Mitchell, Mt., *U.S.A.* 105 H4
Mitchell Ras., *Australia* 90 A2
Mitchelstown, *Ireland* 15 D3
Mitha Tiwana, *Pakistan* 62 C5
Mitilíni, *Greece* 39 K9
Mito, *Japan* 49 F10
Mitsinjo, *Madag.* 85 B8
Mitsiwa, *Eritrea* 77 D4
Mitsiwa Channel, *Eritrea* 77 D5
Mitsukaidō, *Japan* 49 F9
Mittagong, *Australia* 91 E5
Mittelland, *Switz.* 22 C4
Mittelland Kanal, *Germany* 18 C3
Mittenwalde, *Germany* 18 C9
Mitterteich, *Germany* 19 F8
Mittweida, *Germany* 18 E8
Mitú, *Colombia* 120 C3
Mituas, *Colombia* 120 C4
Mitumba, *Tanzania* 82 D3
Mitumba, Chaîne des, *Zaïre* 82 D2
Mitumba Mts. = Mitumba, Chaîne des, *Zaïre* 82 D2
Mitwaba, *Zaïre* 83 D2
Mityana, *Uganda* 82 B3
Mitzic, *Gabon* 80 D2
Mixteco →, *Mexico* 115 D5
Miyagi □, *Japan* 48 E10
Miyâh, W. el →, *Egypt* 76 B3
Miyah, W. el →, *Syria* 64 C3
Miyake-Jima, *Japan* 49 G9
Miyako, *Japan* 48 E10
Miyako-Jima, *Japan* 49 M2
Miyako-Rettō, *Japan* 49 M2
Miyakonojō, *Japan* 49 J5
Miyanoura-Dake, *Japan* 49 J5
Miyazaki, *Japan* 49 J5
Miyazaki □, *Japan* 49 H5
Miyazu, *Japan* 49 G7
Miyet, Bahr el = Dead Sea, *Asia* 69 D4
Miyi, *China* 52 D4
Miyoshi, *Japan* 49 G6
Miyun, *China* 50 D9
Miyun Shuiku, *China* 51 D9
Mizamis = Ozamiz, *Phil.* 55 G5
Mizdah, *Libya* 75 B7
Mizen Hd., *Cork, Ireland* 15 E2
Mizen Hd., *Wick., Ireland* 15 D5
Mizhi, *China* 50 F6
Mizil, *Romania* 38 E9
Mizoram □, *India* 61 H18
Mizpe Ramon, *Israel* 69 E3
Mizusawa, *Japan* 48 E10
Mjöbäck, *Sweden* 11 G6
Mjölby, *Sweden* 11 F9
Mjörn, *Sweden* 11 G6
Mjøsa, *Norway* 10 D5
Mkata, *Tanzania* 82 D4
Mkokotoni, *Tanzania* 82 D4
Mkomazi, *Tanzania* 82 C4
Mkomazi →, *S. Africa* 85 E5
Mkulwe, *Tanzania* 83 D3
Mkumbi, Ras, *Tanzania* 82 D4
Mkushi, *Zambia* 83 E2
Mkushi River, *Zambia* 83 E2
Mkuze, *S. Africa* 85 D5
Mkuze →, *S. Africa* 85 D5
Mladá Boleslav, *Czech.* 20 E4
Mladenovac, *Serbia* 21 L10
Mlala Hills, *Tanzania* 82 D3
Mlange, *Malawi* 83 F4
Mlava →, *Serbia* 21 L11
Mława, *Poland* 20 B10
Mlinište, *Bos.-H.* 33 D13
Mljet, *Croatia* 21 N7
Młynary, *Poland* 20 A9
Mmabatho, *S. Africa* 84 D4
Mme, *Cameroon* 79 D7
Mo i Rana, *Norway* 8 C13
Moa, *Indonesia* 57 F7
Moa →, *S. Leone* 78 D2
Moab, *U.S.A.* 111 G9
Moabi, *Gabon* 80 E2
Moaco →, *Brazil* 124 B4
Moala, *Fiji* 87 D8
Moalie Park, *Australia* 91 D3
Moaña, *Spain* 30 C2
Moba, *Zaïre* 82 D2
Mobārakābād, *Iran* 65 D7
Mobārakīyeh, *Iran* 65 C6
Mobaye, *C.A.R.* 80 D4
Mobayi, *Zaïre* 80 D4
Moberly, *U.S.A.* 108 F8
Moberly →, *Canada* 100 B4
Mobile, *U.S.A.* 105 K1
Mobile B., *U.S.A.* 105 K2
Mobridge, *U.S.A.* 108 C4
Mobutu Sese Seko, L., *Africa* 82 B3
Moc Chau, *Vietnam* 58 B5
Moc Hoa, *Vietnam* 59 G5
Mocabe Kasari, *Zaïre* 83 D2
Mocajuba, *Brazil* 122 B2
Moçambique, *Mozam.* 83 F5
Moçâmedes = Namibe, *Angola* 81 H2
Mocapra →, *Venezuela* 120 B4
Mocha, I., *Chile* 128 A2
Mochudi, *Botswana* 84 C4
Mocimboa da Praia, *Mozam.* 83 E5
Moclips, *U.S.A.* 112 C2
Mocoa, *Colombia* 120 C2
Mococa, *Brazil* 127 A6
Mocorito, *Mexico* 114 B3
Moctezuma, *Mexico* 114 B3
Moctezuma →, *Mexico* 115 C5
Mocuba, *Mozam.* 83 F4
Mocúzari, Presa, *Mexico* 114 B3
Modane, *France* 27 C10
Modasa, *India* 62 H5
Modave, *Belgium* 17 H6
Modder →, *S. Africa* 84 D3
Modderrivier, *S. Africa* 84 D3
Módena, *Italy* 32 D7
Modena, *U.S.A.* 111 H7
Modesto, *U.S.A.* 111 H3
Módica, *Italy* 35 F7
Modigliana, *Italy* 33 D8
Modo, *Sudan* 77 F3
Modra, *Slovak Rep.* 21 G7
Moe, *Australia* 91 F4
Moebase, *Mozam.* 83 F4
Moëlan-sur-Mer, *France* 24 E3
Moengo, *Surinam* 121 B7
Moergestel, *Neths.* 17 E6
Moers, *Germany* 17 F9
Moësa →, *Switz.* 23 D8
Moffat, *U.K.* 14 F5
Moga, *India* 62 D6
Mogadishu = Muqdisho, *Somali Rep.* 68 G4
Mogador = Essaouira, *Morocco* 74 B3
Mogadouro, *Portugal* 30 D4
Mogalakwena →, *S. Africa* 85 C4
Mogami →, *Japan* 48 E10
Mogán, *Canary Is.* 36 G4
Mogaung, *Burma* 61 G20
Møgeltønder, *Denmark* 11 K2
Mogente, *Spain* 29 G4
Mogho, *Ethiopia* 77 G5
Mogi das Cruzes, *Brazil* 127 A6
Mogi-Guaçu →, *Brazil* 127 A6
Mogi-Mirim, *Brazil* 127 A6
Mogielnica, *Poland* 20 D10
Mogilev, *Belorussia* 40 E7
Mogilev-Podolskiy, *Moldavia* 42 B2
Mogilno, *Poland* 20 C7
Mogincual, *Mozam.* 83 F5
Mogliano Véneto, *Italy* 33 C9
Mogocha, *Russia* 45 D12
Mogoi, *Indonesia* 57 E8
Mogok, *Burma* 61 H20
Moguer, *Spain* 31 H4
Mogumber, *Australia* 89 F2
Mohács, *Hungary* 21 K8
Mohales Hoek, *Lesotho* 84 E4
Mohall, *U.S.A.* 108 A4
Moḥammadābād, *Iran* 65 B8
Mohammadia, *Algeria* 75 A5
Mohammedia, *Morocco* 74 B3
Mohave, L., *U.S.A.* 113 K12
Mohawk →, *U.S.A.* 107 D11
Möhne →, *Germany* 18 D3
Moholm, *Sweden* 11 F8
Mohoro, *Tanzania* 82 D4
Moia, *Sudan* 77 F2
Moidart, L., *U.K.* 14 E3
Moineşti, *Romania* 38 C9
Mointy, *Kazakhstan* 44 E8
Moirans, *France* 27 C9
Moirans-en-Montagne, *France* 27 B9
Moíres, *Greece* 37 D6
Moisaküla, *Estonia* 40 B4
Moisie, *Canada* 99 B6
Moisie →, *Canada* 99 B6
Moissac, *France* 26 D5
Moïssala, *Chad* 73 G8
Moita, *Portugal* 31 G2
Mojácar, *Spain* 29 H3
Mojados, *Spain* 30 D6
Mojave, *U.S.A.* 113 K8
Mojave Desert, *U.S.A.* 113 L10
Mojiang, *China* 52 F3
Mojo, *Bolivia* 126 A2
Mojo, *Ethiopia* 77 F4
Mojokerto, *Indonesia* 57 G15
Mojos, Llanos de, *Bolivia* 125 D5
Moju →, *Brazil* 122 B2
Mokai, *N.Z.* 87 H5
Mokambo, *Zaïre* 83 E2
Mokameh, *India* 63 G11
Mokelumne →, *U.S.A.* 112 G5
Mokelumne Hill, *U.S.A.* 112 G6
Mokhós, *Greece* 37 D7
Mokhotlong, *Lesotho* 85 D4
Moknine, *Tunisia* 75 A7
Mokokchung, *India* 61 F19
Mokra Gora, *Serbia* 21 N10
Mokronog, *Slovenia* 33 C12
Moksha →, *Russia* 41 D12
Mokshan, *Russia* 41 E14
Mol, *Belgium* 17 F6
Mola, C. de la, *Spain* 28 F9
Mola di Bari, *Italy* 35 A10
Moláoi, *Greece* 39 N5
Molat, *Croatia* 33 D11
Molchanovo, *Russia* 44 D9
Mold, *U.K.* 12 D4
Moldavia = Moldova, *Romania* 38 C10
Moldavia ■, *Europe* 42 C3
Molde, *Norway* 8 E9
Moldova, *Romania* 38 C10
Moldova ■ = Moldavia ■, *Europe* 42 C3
Moldova Nouă, *Romania* 38 E4
Moldoveanu, *Romania* 38 D7
Molepolole, *Botswana* 84 C4
Moléson, *Switz.* 22 C4
Molfetta, *Italy* 35 A9
Molina de Aragón, *Spain* 28 E3
Moline, *U.S.A.* 108 E9
Molinella, *Italy* 33 D8
Molinos, *Argentina* 126 B2
Moliro, *Zaïre* 82 D3
Molise □, *Italy* 33 G11
Moliterno, *Italy* 35 B8
Mollahat, *Bangla.* 63 H13
Mölle, *Sweden* 11 H6
Molledo, *Spain* 30 B6
Mollendo, *Peru* 124 D3
Mollerin, L., *Australia* 89 F2
Mollerusa, *Spain* 28 D5
Mollina, *Spain* 31 H6
Mölln, *Germany* 18 B6
Mölltorp, *Sweden* 11 F8
Mölndal, *Sweden* 11 G6
Molochansk, *Ukraine* 42 C6
Molochnaya →, *Ukraine* 42 C6
Molodechno, *Belorussia* 40 D5
Molokai, *U.S.A.* 102 H16
Moloma →, *Russia* 41 B16
Molong, *Australia* 91 E4
Molopo →, *Africa* 84 D3
Mólos, *Greece* 39 L5
Molotov = Perm, *Russia* 44 D6
Moloundou, *Cameroon* 80 D3
Molsheim, *France* 25 D14
Molson L., *Canada* 101 C9
Molteno, *S. Africa* 84 E4
Molu, *Indonesia* 57 F8
Molucca Sea = Maluku Sea, *Indonesia* 57 E6
Moluccas = Maluku, *Indonesia* 57 E7
Moma, *Mozam.* 83 F4
Moma, *Zaïre* 82 C1
Mombaça, *Brazil* 122 C4
Mombasa, *Kenya* 82 C4
Mombetsu, *Japan* 48 B11
Mombuey, *Spain* 30 C4
Momchilgrad, *Bulgaria* 39 H8
Momi, *Zaïre* 82 C2
Momignies, *Belgium* 17 H4
Mompós, *Colombia* 120 B3
Møn, *Denmark* 11 K6
Mon →, *Burma* 61 J19
Mona, Canal de la, *W. Indies* 117 C6
Mona, Isla, *Puerto Rico* 117 C6
Mona, Pta., *Costa Rica* 116 E3
Mona, Pta., *Spain* 31 J7
Monach Is., *U.K.* 14 D1
Monaco ■, *Europe* 27 E11
Monadhliath Mts., *U.K.* 14 D4
Monagas □, *Venezuela* 121 B5
Monaghan, *Ireland* 15 B5
Monaghan □, *Ireland* 15 B5
Monahans, *U.S.A.* 109 K3
Monapo, *Mozam.* 83 E5
Monarch Mt., *Canada* 100 C3
Monastir = Bitola, *Macedonia* 39 H4
Monastir, *Tunisia* 75 A7
Monastyriska, *Ukraine* 40 G4
Moncada, *Phil.* 55 D4
Moncada, *Spain* 28 F4

Moncalieri, *Italy* 32 D4
Moncalvo, *Italy* 32 C5
Moncão, *Portugal* 30 C2
Moncarapacho, *Portugal* 31 H3
Moncayo, Sierra del, *Spain* 28 D3
Mönchengladbach, *Germany* 18 D2
Monchique, *Portugal* 31 H2
Monclova, *Mexico* 114 B4
Moncontour, *France* 24 D4
Moncoutant, *France* 26 B3
Moncton, *Canada* 99 C7
Mondego →, *Portugal* 30 E2
Mondego, C., *Portugal* 30 E2
Mondeodo, *Indonesia* 57 E6
Mondolfo, *Italy* 33 E10
Mondoñedo, *Spain* 30 B3
Mondoví, *Italy* 32 D4
Mondovi, *U.S.A.* 108 C9
Mondragon, *France* 27 D8
Mondragon, *Phil.* 55 E6
Mondragone, *Italy* 34 A6
Mondrain I., *Australia* 89 F3
Monduli □, *Tanzania* 82 C4
Monemvasía, *Greece* 39 N6
Monessen, *U.S.A.* 106 F5
Monesterio, *Spain* 31 G4
Monestier-de-Clermont, *France* 27 D9
Monett, *U.S.A.* 109 G8
Monfalcone, *Italy* 33 C10
Monflanquin, *France* 26 D4
Monforte, *Portugal* 31 F3
Monforte de Lemos, *Spain* 30 C3
Mong Hsu, *Burma* 61 J21
Mong Kung, *Burma* 61 J20
Mong Nai, *Burma* 61 J20
Mong Pawk, *Burma* 61 H21
Mong Ton, *Burma* 61 J21
Mong Wa, *Burma* 61 J22
Mong Yai, *Burma* 61 H21
Mongalla, *Sudan* 77 F3
Mongers, L., *Australia* 89 E2
Monghyr = Munger, *India* 63 G12
Mongo, *Chad* 73 F8
Mongolia ■, *Asia* 45 E10
Mongonu, *Nigeria* 79 C7
Mongororo, *Chad* 73 F9
Mongu, *Zambia* 81 H4
Mônguà, *Angola* 84 B2
Monistrol-d'Allier, *France* 26 D7
Monistrol-sur-Loire, *France* 27 C8
Monkey Bay, *Malawi* 83 E4
Monkey River, *Belize* 115 D7
Monkira, *Australia* 90 C3
Monkoto, *Zaïre* 80 E4
Monmouth, *U.K.* 13 F5
Monmouth, *U.S.A.* 108 E9
Mono L., *U.S.A.* 111 H4
Monolith, *U.S.A.* 113 K8
Monólithos, *Greece* 37 C9
Monongahela, *U.S.A.* 106 F5
Monópoli, *Italy* 35 B10
Monor, *Hungary* 21 H9
Monóvar, *Spain* 29 G4
Monqoumba, *C.A.R.* 80 D3
Monreal del Campo, *Spain* 28 E3
Monreale, *Italy* 34 D6
Monroe, *Ga., U.S.A.* 105 J4
Monroe, *La., U.S.A.* 109 J8
Monroe, *Mich., U.S.A.* 104 E4
Monroe, *N.C., U.S.A.* 105 H5
Monroe, *N.Y., U.S.A.* 107 E10
Monroe, *Utah, U.S.A.* 111 G7
Monroe, *Wash., U.S.A.* 112 C5
Monroe, *Wis., U.S.A.* 108 D10
Monroe City, *U.S.A.* 108 F9
Monroeville, *Ala., U.S.A.* 105 K2
Monroeville, *Pa., U.S.A.* 106 F5
Monrovia, *Liberia* 78 D2
Monrovia, *U.S.A.* 111 J4
Mons, *Belgium* 17 H3
Monsaraz, *Portugal* 31 G3
Monse, *Indonesia* 57 E6
Monsefú, *Peru* 124 B2
Monségur, *France* 26 D4
Monsélice, *Italy* 33 C8
Monster, *Neths.* 16 D4
Mont Cenis, Col du, *France* 27 C10
Mont-de-Marsan, *France* 26 E3
Mont-Joli, *Canada* 99 C6
Mont-Laurier, *Canada* 98 C4
Mont-St.-Michel, Le = Le Mont-St.-Michel, *France* 24 D5
Mont-sous-Vaudrey, *France* 25 F12
Mont-sur-Marchienne, *Belgium* 17 H4
Mont Tremblant Prov. Park, *Canada* 98 C5
Montabaur, *Germany* 18 E3
Montagnac, *France* 26 E7
Montagnana, *Italy* 33 C8
Montagu, *S. Africa* 84 E3
Montagu I., *Antarctica* 5 B1
Montague, *Canada* 99 C7
Montague, *U.S.A.* 110 F2
Montague, I., *Mexico* 114 A2
Montague Ra., *Australia* 89 E2
Montague Sd., *Australia* 88 B4
Montaigu, *France* 24 F5
Montalbán, *Spain* 28 E4
Montalbano di Elicona, *Italy* 35 D8
Montalbano Iónico, *Italy* 35 B9
Montalbo, *Spain* 28 F2
Montalcino, *Italy* 33 E8
Montalegre, *Portugal* 30 D3
Montalto di Castro, *Italy* 33 F8
Montalto Uffugo, *Italy* 35 C9
Montalvo, *U.S.A.* 113 L7
Montamarta, *Spain* 30 D5
Montaña, *Peru* 124 B3
Montana, *Switz.* 22 D4
Montana □, *U.S.A.* 110
Montaña Clara, I., *Canary Is.* 36 E6
Montánchez, *Spain* 31 F4
Montañita, *Colombia* 120 C2
Montargis, *France* 25 E9
Montauban, *France* 26 D5
Montauk, *U.S.A.* 107 E13
Montauk Pt., *U.S.A.* 107 E13
Montbard, *France* 25 E11
Montbéliard, *France* 25 E13
Montblanch, *Spain* 28 D6
Montbrison, *France* 27 C8
Montcalm, Pic de, *France* 26 F5
Montceau-les-Mines, *France* 25 F11
Montchanin, *France* 27 B8
Montclair, *U.S.A.* 107 F10
Montcornet, *France* 25 C11
Montcuq, *France* 26 D5
Montdidier, *France* 25 C9
Monte Albán, *Mexico* 115 D5
Monte Alegre, *Brazil* 121 D7
Monte Alegre de Goiás, *Brazil* 123 D2
Monte Alegre de Minas, *Brazil* 123 E2
Monte Azul, *Brazil* 123 E3
Monte Bello Is., *Australia* 88 D2
Monte-Carlo, *Monaco* 27 E11
Monte Carmelo, *Brazil* 123 E2
Monte Caseros, *Argentina* 126 C4
Monte Comán, *Argentina* 126 C2
Monte Cristi, *Dom. Rep.* 117 C5
Monte Dinero, *Argentina* 128 D3
Monte Lindo →, *Paraguay* 126 A4
Monte Quemado, *Argentina* 126 B3
Monte Redondo, *Portugal* 30 F2
Monte Rio, *U.S.A.* 112 G4
Monte San Giovanni, *Italy* 34 A6
Monte San Savino, *Italy* 33 E8
Monte Sant' Ángelo, *Italy* 35 A8
Monte Santu, C. di, *Italy* 34 B2
Monte Vista, *U.S.A.* 111 H10
Monteagudo, *Argentina* 127 B5
Monteagudo, *Bolivia* 125 D5
Montealegre, *Spain* 29 G3
Montebello, *Canada* 98 C5
Montebelluna, *Italy* 33 C9
Montebourg, *France* 24 C5
Montecastrilli, *Italy* 33 F9
Montecatini Terme, *Italy* 32 E7
Montecito, *U.S.A.* 113 L7
Montecristi, *Ecuador* 120 D1
Montecristo, *Italy* 32 F7
Montefalco, *Italy* 33 F9
Montefiascone, *Italy* 33 F9
Montefrío, *Spain* 31 H6
Montegnée, *Belgium* 17 G7
Montego Bay, *Jamaica* 116 C4
Montegranaro, *Italy* 33 E10
Monteiro, *Brazil* 122 C4
Montejicar, *Spain* 29 H1
Montejinnie, *Australia* 88 C5
Montelíbano, *Colombia* 120 B2
Montélimar, *France* 27 D8
Montella, *Italy* 35 B8
Montellano, *Spain* 31 J5
Montello, *U.S.A.* 108 D10
Montelupo Fiorentino, *Italy* 32 E8
Montemor-o-Novo, *Portugal* 31 G2
Montemor-o-Velho, *Portugal* 30 E2
Montemorelos, *Mexico* 115 B5
Montendre, *France* 26 C3
Montenegro, *Brazil* 127 B5
Montenegro □, *Montenegro, Yug.* 21 N9
Montenero di Bisaccia, *Italy* 33 G11
Montepuez, *Mozam.* 83 E4
Montepuez →, *Mozam.* 83 E5
Montepulciano, *Italy* 33 E8
Montereale, *Italy* 33 F10
Montereau-Fault-Yonne, *France* 25 D9
Monterey, *U.S.A.* 111 H3
Monterey B., *U.S.A.* 112 J5
Montería, *Colombia* 120 B2
Montero, *Bolivia* 125 D5
Monteros, *Argentina* 126 B2
Monterotondo, *Italy* 33 F9
Monterrey, *Mexico* 114 B4
Montes Altos, *Brazil* 122 C2
Montes Claros, *Brazil* 123 E3
Montesano, *U.S.A.* 112 D3
Montesárchio, *Italy* 35 A7
Montescaglioso, *Italy* 35 B9
Montesilvano, *Italy* 33 F11
Montevarchi, *Italy* 33 E8
Montevideo, *Uruguay* 127 C4
Montevideo, *U.S.A.* 108 C7
Montezuma, *U.S.A.* 108 E8
Montfaucon, *France* 25 C12
Montfaucon-en-Velay, *France* 27 C8
Montfort, *France* 24 D5
Montfort, *Neths.* 17 F7
Montfort-l'Amaury, *France* 25 D8
Montgenèvre, *France* 27 D10
Montgomery = Sahiwal, *Pakistan* 62 D5
Montgomery, *U.K.* 13 E4
Montgomery, *Ala., U.S.A.* 105 J2
Montgomery, *W. Va., U.S.A.* 104 F5
Montguyon, *France* 26 C3
Monthey, *Switz.* 22 D3
Monticelli d'Ongina, *Italy* 32 C6
Monticello, *Ark., U.S.A.* 109 J9
Monticello, *Fla., U.S.A.* 105 K4
Monticello, *Ind., U.S.A.* 104 E2
Monticello, *Iowa, U.S.A.* 108 D9
Monticello, *Ky., U.S.A.* 105 G3
Monticello, *Minn., U.S.A.* 108 C8
Monticello, *Miss., U.S.A.* 109 K9
Monticello, *N.Y., U.S.A.* 107 E10
Monticello, *Utah, U.S.A.* 111 H9
Montichiari, *Italy* 32 C7
Montier-en-Der, *France* 25 D11
Montignac, *France* 26 C5
Montignies-sur-Sambre, *Belgium* 17 H4
Montigny, *France* 25 C13
Montigny-sur-Aube, *France* 25 E11
Montijo, *Spain* 31 G4
Montijo, Presa de, *Spain* 31 G4
Montilla, *Spain* 31 H6
Montlhéry, *France* 25 D9
Montluçon, *France* 26 B6
Montmagny, *Canada* 99 C5
Montmarault, *France* 26 B6
Montmartre, *Canada* 101 C8
Montmédy, *France* 25 C12
Montmélian, *France* 27 C10
Montmirail, *France* 25 D10
Montmoreau-St.-Cybard, *France* 26 C4
Montmorency, *Canada* 99 C5
Montmorillon, *France* 26 B4
Montmort, *France* 25 D10
Monto, *Australia* 90 C5
Montoir-sur-le-Loir, *France* 24 E7
Montório al Vomano, *Italy* 33 F10
Montoro, *Spain* 31 G6
Montour Falls, *U.S.A.* 106 D8
Montpelier, *Idaho, U.S.A.* 110 E8
Montpelier, *Ohio, U.S.A.* 104 E3
Montpelier, *Vt., U.S.A.* 107 B12
Montpellier, *France* 26 E7
Montpezat-de-Quercy, *France* 26 D5
Montpon-Ménestérol, *France* 26 D4
Montréal, *Canada* 98 C5
Montréal, *France* 26 E6
Montreal L., *Canada* 101 C7
Montreal Lake, *Canada* 101 C7
Montredon-Labessonnié, *France* 26 E6
Montréjeau, *France* 26 E4
Montrésor, *France* 24 E8
Montreuil, *France* 25 B8
Montreuil-Bellay, *France* 24 E6
Montreux, *Switz.* 22 D3
Montrevault, *France* 24 E5
Montrevel-en-Bresse, *France* 27 B9
Montrichard, *France* 24 E8
Montrose, *U.K.* 14 E6
Montrose, *Colo., U.S.A.* 111 G10
Montrose, *Pa., U.S.A.* 107 E9
Monts, Pte. des, *Canada* 99 C6
Monts-sur-Guesnes, *France* 24 F7
Montsalvy, *France* 26 D6
Montsant, Sierra de, *Spain* 28 D5
Montsauche, *France* 25 E11
Montsech, Sierra del, *Spain* 28 C5
Montseny, *Spain* 28 D2
Montserrat, *Spain* 28 D6
Montserrat ■, *W. Indies* 117 C7
Montuenga, *Spain* 30 D6
Montuiri, *Spain* 36 B9
Monveda, *Zaïre* 80 D4
Monywa, *Burma* 61 H19
Monza, *Italy* 32 C6
Monze, *Zambia* 83 F2
Monze, C., *Pakistan* 62 G2
Monzón, *Spain* 28 D5
Mooi River, *S. Africa* 85 D4
Mook, *Neths.* 16 E7
Moolawatana, *Australia* 91 D2
Mooliabeenee, *Australia* 89 F2
Mooloogool, *Australia* 89 E2
Moomin Cr. →, *Australia* 91 D4
Moonah →, *Australia* 90 C2
Moonbeam, *Canada* 98 C3
Moonda, L., *Australia* 90 D3
Moonie, *Australia* 91 D5
Moonie →, *Australia* 91 D4
Moonta, *Australia* 91 E2
Moora, *Australia* 89 F2
Mooraberree, *Australia* 90 D3
Moorarie, *Australia* 89 E2
Moorcroft, *U.S.A.* 108 C2
Moore →, *Australia* 89 F2
Moore, L., *Australia* 89 E2
Moore Reefs, *Australia* 90 B4
Moorefield, *U.S.A.* 104 F6
Moores Res., *U.S.A.* 107 B13
Mooresville, *U.S.A.* 105 H5
Moorfoot Hills, *U.K.* 14 F5
Moorhead, *U.S.A.* 108 B6
Mooroopna, *Australia* 91 F4
Moorpark, *U.S.A.* 113 L8
Moorreesburg, *S. Africa* 84 E2
Moorslede, *Belgium* 17 G2
Moosburg, *Germany* 19 G7
Moose →, *Canada* 98 B3
Moose Factory, *Canada* 98 B3
Moose I., *Canada* 101 C9
Moose Jaw, *Canada* 101 C7
Moose Jaw →, *Canada* 101 C7
Moose Lake, *Canada* 101 C8
Moose Lake, *U.S.A.* 108 B8
Moose Mountain Cr. →, *Canada* 101 D8
Moose Mountain Prov. Park, *Canada* 101 D8
Moose River, *Canada* 98 B3
Moosehead L., *U.S.A.* 99 C6
Moosomin, *Canada* 101 C8
Moosonee, *Canada* 98 B3
Moosup, *U.S.A.* 107 E13
Mopeia Velha, *Mozam.* 83 F4
Mopipi, *Botswana* 84 C3
Mopoi, *C.A.R.* 82 A2
Mopti, *Mali* 78 C4
Moqatta, *Sudan* 77 E4
Moquegua, *Peru* 124 D3
Moquegua □, *Peru* 124 D3
Mór, *Hungary* 21 H8
Móra, *Portugal* 31 G2
Mora, *Sweden* 9 F13
Mora, *Minn., U.S.A.* 108 C8
Mora, *N. Mex., U.S.A.* 111 J11
Mora de Ebro, *Spain* 28 D5
Mora de Rubielos, *Spain* 28 E4
Mora la Nueva, *Spain* 28 D5
Morača →, *Montenegro, Yug.* 21 N9
Morada Nova, *Brazil* 122 C4
Morada Nova de Minas, *Brazil* 123 E2
Moradabad, *India* 63 E8
Morafenobe, *Madag.* 85 B7
Morąg, *Poland* 20 B9
Moral de Calatrava, *Spain* 29 G1
Moraleja, *Spain* 30 E4
Morales, *Colombia* 120 C2
Moramanga, *Madag.* 85 B8
Moran, *Kans., U.S.A.* 109 G7
Moran, *Wyo., U.S.A.* 110 E8
Moranbah, *Australia* 90 C4
Morano Cálabro, *Italy* 35 C9
Morant Cays, *Jamaica* 116 C4
Morant Pt., *Jamaica* 116 C4
Morar, L., *U.K.* 14 E3
Moratalla, *Spain* 29 G3
Moratuwa, *Sri Lanka* 60 R11
Morava →, *Europe* 20 G6
Moravia, *U.S.A.* 108 E8
Moravian Hts. = Ceskomoravská Vrchovina, *Czech.* 20 F5
Moravica →, *Serbia, Yug.* 21 M10
Moravice →, *Czech.* 20 F7
Moraviţa, *Romania* 21 K11
Moravská Třebová, *Czech.* 20 F6
Morawa, *Australia* 89 E2
Morawhanna, *Guyana* 121 B6
Moray Firth, *U.K.* 14 D5
Morbach, *Germany* 19 F3
Morbegno, *Italy* 32 B6
Morbi, *India* 62 H4
Morbihan □, *France* 24 E4
Morcenx, *France* 26 D3
Mordelles, *France* 24 D5
Morden, *Canada* 101 D9
Mordovian Republic □, *Russia* 41 D14
Mordovo, *Russia* 41 E12
Mordvinia = Mordovian Republic □, *Russia* 41 D14
Møre og Romsdal fylke □, *Norway* 10 B2
Morea, *Australia* 91 F3
Morea, *Greece* 6 H10
Moreau →, *U.S.A.* 108 C4
Morecambe, *U.K.* 12 C5
Morecambe B., *U.K.* 12 C5
Moree, *Australia* 91 D4
Morehead, *U.S.A.* 104 F4
Morehead City, *U.S.A.* 105 H7
Morelia, *Mexico* 114 D4
Morella, *Australia* 90 C3
Morella, *Spain* 28 E4
Morelos, *Mexico* 114 B3
Morelos □, *Mexico* 115 D5
Morena, Sierra, *Spain* 31 G7
Morenci, *U.S.A.* 111 K9
Moreni, *Romania* 38 E8
Morero, *Bolivia* 125 C4
Moreru →, *Brazil* 125 C6
Moresby I., *Canada* 100 C2
Morestel, *France* 27 C9
Moret-sur-Loing, *France* 25 D9
Moreton, *Australia* 90 A3
Moreton I., *Australia* 91 D5
Moreuil, *France* 25 C9
Morey, *Spain* 36 B10
Morez, *France* 27 B10
Morgan, *Australia* 91 E2
Morgan, *U.S.A.* 110 F8
Morgan City, *U.S.A.* 109 L9
Morgan Hill, *U.S.A.* 112 H5
Morganfield, *U.S.A.* 104 G2
Morganton, *U.S.A.* 105 H5
Morgantown, *U.S.A.* 104 F6
Morgat, *France* 24 D2
Morgenzon, *S. Africa* 85 D4
Morges, *Switz.* 22 C2
Morghak, *Iran* 65 D8
Morhange, *France* 25 D13
Mori, *Italy* 32 C7
Morialmée, *Belgium* 17 H5
Morice L., *Canada* 100 C3
Morichal, *Colombia* 120 C3
Morichal Largo →, *Venezuela* 121 B5
Moriki, *Nigeria* 79 C6
Morinville, *Canada* 100 C6
Morioka, *Japan* 48 E10
Moris, *Mexico* 114 B3
Morlaàs, *France* 26 E3
Morlaix, *France* 24 D3
Morlanwelz, *Belgium* 17 H4
Mormanno, *Italy* 35 C8
Mormant, *France* 25 D9
Mornington, *Vic., Australia* 91 F4
Mornington, *W. Austral., Australia* 88 C4
Mornington, I., *Chile* 128 C1
Mornington I., *Australia* 90 B2
Mórnos →, *Greece* 39 L4
Moro, *Sudan* 77 E3
Moro G., *Phil.* 55 H5
Morocco ■, *N. Afr.* 74 B3
Morococha, *Peru* 124 C2
Morogoro, *Tanzania* 82 D4
Morogoro □, *Tanzania* 82 D4
Moroleón, *Mexico* 114 C4
Morombe, *Madag.* 85 C7
Moron, *Argentina* 126 C4
Morón, *Cuba* 116 B4
Mörön →, *Mongolia* 54 B6
Morón de Almazán, *Spain* 28 D2
Morón de la Frontera, *Spain* 31 H5
Morona →, *Peru* 120 D2
Morona-Santiago □, *Ecuador* 120 D2
Morondava, *Madag.* 85 C7
Morondo, *Ivory C.* 78 D3
Morongo Valley, *U.S.A.* 113 L10
Moronou, *Ivory C.* 78 D4
Morotai, *Indonesia* 57 D7
Moroto, *Uganda* 82 B3
Moroto Summit, *Kenya* 82 B3
Morozovsk, *Russia* 43 B9
Morpeth, *U.K.* 12 B6
Morphou, *Cyprus* 37 D11
Morphou Bay, *Cyprus* 37 D11
Morrilton, *U.S.A.* 109 H8
Morrinhos, *Ceara, Brazil* 122 B3
Morrinhos, *Minas Gerais, Brazil* 123 E2
Morrinsville, *N.Z.* 87 G5
Morris, *Canada* 101 D9
Morris, *Ill., U.S.A.* 104 E1
Morris, *Minn., U.S.A.* 108 C7
Morris, Mt., *Australia* 89 E5
Morrisburg, *Canada* 98 D4
Morrison, *U.S.A.* 108 E10
Morristown, *Ariz., U.S.A.* 111 K7
Morristown, *N.J., U.S.A.* 107 F10
Morristown, *S. Dak., U.S.A.* 108 C4
Morristown, *Tenn., U.S.A.* 105 G4
Morro, Pta., *Chile* 126 B1
Morro Bay, *U.S.A.* 111 J3
Morro del Jable, *Canary Is.* 36 F5
Morro do Chapéu, *Brazil* 123 D3
Morro Jable, Pta. de, *Canary Is.* 36 F5
Morros, *Brazil* 122 B3
Morrosquillo, G. de, *Colombia* 116 E4
Morrumbene, *Mozam.* 85 C6
Mors, *Denmark* 11 H2
Morshansk, *Russia* 41 E12
Mörsil, *Sweden* 10 A7
Mortagne →, *France* 25 D13
Mortagne-au-Perche, *France* 24 D7
Mortagne-sur-Gironde, *France* 26 C3
Mortagne-sur-Sèvre, *France* 24 F6
Mortain, *France* 24 D6
Mortara, *Italy* 32 C5
Morteau, *France* 25 E13
Morteros, *Argentina* 126 C3
Mortes, R. das →, *Brazil* 123 D1
Mortlake, *Australia* 91 F3
Morton, *Tex., U.S.A.* 109 J3
Morton, *Wash., U.S.A.* 112 D4
Mortsel, *Belgium* 17 F4
Morundah, *Australia* 91 E4
Moruya, *Australia* 91 F5
Morvan, *France* 25 E11
Morven, *Australia* 91 D4
Morvern, *U.K.* 14 E3
Morwell, *Australia* 91 F4
Mosalsk, *Russia* 40 D9
Mosbach, *Germany* 19 F5
Moščenice, *Croatia* 33 C11
Mosciano Sant' Ángelo, *Italy* 33 F10
Moscos Is., *Burma* 58 E1
Moscow = Moskva, *Russia* 41 D10
Moscow, *U.S.A.* 110 C5
Mosel →, *Europe* 19 E3

Moselle = Mosel →, *Europe* 19 E3
Moselle □, *France* 25 D13
Moses Lake, *U.S.A.* 110 C4
Mosgiel, *N.Z.* 87 L3
Moshi, *Tanzania* 82 C4
Moshi □, *Tanzania* 82 C4
Moshupa, *Botswana* 84 C4
Mosjøen, *Norway* 8 D12
Moskenesøya, *Norway* 8 C12
Moskenstraumen, *Norway* 8 C12
Moskva, *Russia* 41 D10
Moskva →, *Russia* 41 D11
Moslavačka Gora, *Croatia* 33 C13
Mosomane, *Botswana* 84 C4
Mosonmagyaróvár, *Hungary* 21 H7
Mospino, *Ukraine* 42 C7
Mosquera, *Colombia* 120 C2
Mosquero, *U.S.A.* 109 H3
Mosqueruela, *Spain* 28 E4
Mosquitia, *Honduras* 116 C3
Mosquitos, G. de los, *Panama* 116 E3
Moss, *Norway* 10 E4
Moss Vale, *Australia* 91 E5
Mossaka, *Congo* 80 E3
Mossâmedes, *Brazil* 123 E1
Mossbank, *Canada* 101 D7
Mossburn, *N.Z.* 87 L2
Mosselbaai, *S. Africa* 84 E3
Mossendjo, *Congo* 80 E2
Mosses, Col des, *Switz.* 22 D4
Mossgiel, *Australia* 91 E3
Mossman, *Australia* 90 B4
Mossoró, *Brazil* 122 C4
Mossuril, *Mozam.* 83 E5
Mossy →, *Canada* 101 C8
Most, *Czech.* 20 E3
Mosta, *Malta* 37 D1
Moşţafáābād, *Iran* 65 C7
Mostaganem, *Algeria* 75 A5
Mostar, *Bos.-H.* 21 M7
Mostardas, *Brazil* 127 C5
Mostefa, Rass, *Tunisia* 75 A7
Mostiska, *Ukraine* 40 G3
Móstoles, *Spain* 30 E7
Mosty, *Belorussia* 40 E4
Mosul = Al Mawşil, *Iraq* 64 B4
Mosulpo, *S. Korea* 51 H14
Mota del Cuervo, *Spain* 28 F2
Mota del Marqués, *Spain* 30 D5
Motagua →, *Guatemala* 116 C2
Motala, *Sweden* 11 F9
Motherwell, *U.K.* 14 F5
Motihari, *India* 63 F11
Motilla del Palancar, *Spain* 28 F3
Motnik, *Slovenia* 33 B11
Motocurunya, *Venezuela* 121 C5
Motovun, *Croatia* 33 C10
Motozintla de Mendoza, *Mexico* 115 D6
Motril, *Spain* 29 J1
Motru →, *Romania* 38 E6
Mott, *U.S.A.* 108 B3
Móttola, *Italy* 35 B10
Motueka, *N.Z.* 87 J4
Motueka →, *N.Z.* 87 J4
Motul, *Mexico* 115 C7
Mouanda, *Gabon* 80 E2
Mouchalagane →, *Canada* 99 B6
Mouding, *China* 52 E3
Moudjeria, *Mauritania* 78 B2
Moudon, *Switz.* 22 C3
Mouila, *Gabon* 80 E2
Moulamein, *Australia* 91 F3
Moulianá, *Greece* 37 D7
Moulins, *France* 26 B7
Moulmein, *Burma* 61 L20
Moulouya, O. →, *Morocco* 75 A4
Moulton, *U.S.A.* 109 L6
Moultrie, *U.S.A.* 105 K4
Moultrie, L., *U.S.A.* 105 J5
Mound City, *Mo., U.S.A.* 108 E7
Mound City, *S. Dak., U.S.A.* 108 C4
Moúnda, Ákra, *Greece* 39 L3
Moundou, *Chad* 73 G8
Moundsville, *U.S.A.* 106 G4
Moung, *Cambodia* 58 F4
Mount Airy, *U.S.A.* 105 G5
Mount Albert, *Canada* 106 B5
Mount Amherst, *Australia* 88 C4
Mount Angel, *U.S.A.* 110 D2
Mount Augustus, *Australia* 88 D2
Mount Barker, *S. Austral., Australia* 91 F2
Mount Barker, *W. Austral., Australia* 89 F2
Mount Carmel, *U.S.A.* 104 F2
Mount Clemens, *U.S.A.* 98 D3
Mount Coolon, *Australia* 90 C4
Mount Darwin, *Zimbabwe* 83 F3
Mount Desert I., *U.S.A.* 99 D6
Mount Dora, *U.S.A.* 105 L5
Mount Douglas, *Australia* 90 C4
Mount Eba, *Australia* 91 E2
Mount Edgecumbe, *U.S.A.* 100 B1
Mount Elizabeth, *Australia* 88 C4
Mount Fletcher, *S. Africa* 85 E4
Mount Forest, *Canada* 98 D3
Mount Gambier, *Australia* 91 F3
Mount Garnet, *Australia* 90 B4
Mount Hope, *N.S.W., Australia* 91 E4
Mount Hope, *S. Austral., Australia* 91 E2
Mount Hope, *U.S.A.* 104 G5
Mount Horeb, *U.S.A.* 108 D10
Mount Howitt, *Australia* 91 D3
Mount Isa, *Australia* 90 C2
Mount Keith, *Australia* 89 E3
Mount Laguna, *U.S.A.* 113 N10
Mount Larcom, *Australia* 90 C5
Mount Lofty Ra., *Australia* 91 E2
Mount McKinley National Park, *U.S.A.* 96 B5
Mount Magnet, *Australia* 89 E2
Mount Margaret, *Australia* 91 D3
Mount Maunganui, *N.Z.* 87 G6
Mount Molloy, *Australia* 90 B4
Mount Monger, *Australia* 89 F3
Mount Morgan, *Australia* 90 C5
Mount Morris, *U.S.A.* 106 D7
Mount Mulligan, *Australia* 90 B3
Mount Narryer, *Australia* 89 E2
Mount Olympus = Uludağ, *Turkey* 66 C3
Mount Oxide Mine, *Australia* 90 B2
Mount Pearl, *Canada* 99 C9
Mount Perry, *Australia* 91 D5
Mount Phillips, *Australia* 88 D2
Mount Pleasant, *Iowa, U.S.A.* 108 E9
Mount Pleasant, *Mich., U.S.A.* 104 D3
Mount Pleasant, *Pa., U.S.A.* 106 F5
Mount Pleasant, *S.C., U.S.A.* 105 J6
Mount Pleasant, *Tenn., U.S.A.* 105 H2
Mount Pleasant, *Tex., U.S.A.* 109 J7
Mount Pleasant, *Utah, U.S.A.* 110 G8
Mount Pocono, *U.S.A.* 107 E9
Mount Rainier National Park, *U.S.A.* 112 D5
Mount Revelstoke Nat. Park, *Canada* 100 C5
Mount Robson Prov. Park, *Canada* 100 C5
Mount Sandiman, *Australia* 89 D2
Mount Shasta, *U.S.A.* 110 F2
Mount Signal, *U.S.A.* 113 N11
Mount Sterling, *Ill., U.S.A.* 108 F9
Mount Sterling, *Ky., U.S.A.* 104 F4
Mount Surprise, *Australia* 90 B3
Mount Union, *U.S.A.* 106 F7
Mount Vernon, *Australia* 88 D2
Mount Vernon, *Ind., U.S.A.* 108 F10
Mount Vernon, *N.Y., U.S.A.* 107 F11
Mount Vernon, *Ohio, U.S.A.* 106 F2
Mount Vernon, *Wash., U.S.A.* 112 B4
Mountain Center, *U.S.A.* 113 M10
Mountain City, *Nev., U.S.A.* 110 F6
Mountain City, *Tenn., U.S.A.* 105 G5
Mountain Grove, *U.S.A.* 109 G8
Mountain Home, *Ark., U.S.A.* 109 G8
Mountain Home, *Idaho, U.S.A.* 110 E6
Mountain Iron, *U.S.A.* 108 B8
Mountain Park, *Canada* 100 C5
Mountain Pass, *U.S.A.* 113 K11
Mountain View, *Ark., U.S.A.* 109 H8
Mountain View, *Calif., U.S.A.* 111 H2
Mountainair, *U.S.A.* 111 J10
Mountmellick, *Ireland* 15 C4
Moura, *Australia* 90 C4
Moura, *Brazil* 121 D5
Moura, *Portugal* 31 G3
Mourão, *Portugal* 31 G3
Mourdi, Dépression du, *Chad* 73 E9
Mourdiah, *Mali* 78 C3
Mourenx-Ville-Nouvelle, *France* 26 E3
Mouri, *Ghana* 79 D4
Mourilyan, *Australia* 90 B4
Mourmelon-le-Grand, *France* 25 C11
Mourne →, *U.K.* 15 B4
Mourne Mts., *U.K.* 15 B5
Mournies, *Greece* 37 D6
Mouscron, *Belgium* 17 G2
Moussoro, *Chad* 73 F8
Mouthe, *France* 25 F13
Moutier, *Switz.* 22 B4
Moûtiers, *France* 27 C10
Moutohara, *N.Z.* 87 H6
Moutong, *Indonesia* 57 D6
Mouy, *France* 25 C9
Mouzáki, *Greece* 39 K4
Movas, *Mexico* 114 B3
Moville, *Ireland* 15 A4
Moxhe, *Belgium* 17 G6
Moxotó →, *Brazil* 122 C4
Moy →, *Ireland* 15 B3
Moyale, *Kenya* 68 G2
Moyamba, *S. Leone* 78 D2
Moyen Atlas, *Morocco* 74 B3
Moyle □, *U.K.* 15 A5
Moyo, *Indonesia* 56 F5
Moyobamba, *Peru* 124 B2
Moyyero →, *Russia* 45 C11
Mozambique = Moçambique, *Mozam.* 83 F5
Mozambique ■, *Africa* 83 F4
Mozambique Chan., *Africa* 85 B7
Mozdok, *Russia* 43 E11
Mozdūrān, *Iran* 65 B9
Mozhaysk, *Russia* 41 D10
Mozhga, *Russia* 41 C18
Mozhnābād, *Iran* 65 C9
Mozirje, *Slovenia* 33 B11
Mozyr, *Belorussia* 40 E6
Mpanda, *Tanzania* 82 D3
Mpanda □, *Tanzania* 82 D3
Mpésoba, *Mali* 78 C3
Mpika, *Zambia* 83 E3
Mpulungu, *Zambia* 83 D3
Mpumalanga, *S. Africa* 85 D5
Mpwapwa, *Tanzania* 82 D4
Mpwapwa □, *Tanzania* 82 D4
Mrągowo, *Poland* 20 B11
Mramor, *Serbia, Yug.* 21 M11
Mrimina, *Morocco* 74 C3
Mrkonjić Grad, *Bos.-H.* 21 L7
Mrkopalj, *Croatia* 33 C11
Msab, Oued en →, *Algeria* 75 B6
Msaken, *Tunisia* 75 A7
Msambansovu, *Zimbabwe* 83 F3
M'sila, *Algeria* 75 A5
Msoro, *Zambia* 83 E3
Msta →, *Russia* 40 B7
Mstislavl, *Belorussia* 40 E7
Mtama, *Tanzania* 83 E4
Mtilikwe →, *Zimbabwe* 83 G3
Mtsensk, *Russia* 41 E10
Mtskheta, *Georgia* 43 F11
Mtubatuba, *S. Africa* 85 D5
Mtwara-Mikindani, *Tanzania* 83 E5
Mu Gia, Deo, *Vietnam* 58 D5
Mu Us Shamo, *China* 50 E5
Muaná, *Brazil* 122 B2
Muang Chiang Rai, *Thailand* 58 C2
Muang Lamphun, *Thailand* 58 C2
Muang Pak Beng, *Laos* 58 C3
Muar, *Malaysia* 59 L4
Muarabungo, *Indonesia* 56 E2
Muaraenim, *Indonesia* 56 E2
Muarajuloi, *Indonesia* 56 E4
Muarakaman, *Indonesia* 56 E5
Muaratebo, *Indonesia* 56 E2
Muaratembesi, *Indonesia* 56 E2
Muaratewe, *Indonesia* 56 E4
Mubarakpur, *India* 63 F10
Mubarraz = Al Mubarraz, *Si. Arabia* 65 E6
Mubende, *Uganda* 82 B3
Mubi, *Nigeria* 79 C7
Mubur, P., *Indonesia* 59 L6
Mucajaí →, *Brazil* 121 C5
Mucajaí, Serra do, *Brazil* 121 C5
Muchachos, Roque de los, *Canary Is.* 36 F2
Mücheln, *Germany* 18 D7
Muchinga Mts., *Zambia* 83 E3
Muchkapskiy, *Russia* 41 F13
Muck, *U.K.* 14 E2
Muckadilla, *Australia* 91 D4
Muco →, *Colombia* 120 C3
Muconda, *Angola* 80 G4
Mucuim →, *Brazil* 125 B5
Mucur, *Turkey* 66 D6
Mucura, *Brazil* 121 D5
Mucuri, *Brazil* 123 E4
Mucurici, *Brazil* 123 E3
Mucusso, *Angola* 84 B3
Muda, *Canary Is.* 36 F6
Mudan Jiang →, *China* 51 A15
Mudanjiang, *China* 51 B15
Mudanya, *Turkey* 42 F3
Muddy Cr. →, *U.S.A.* 111 H8
Mudgee, *Australia* 91 E4
Mudjatik →, *Canada* 101 B7
Mudurnu, *Turkey* 66 C4
Muecate, *Mozam.* 83 E4
Muêda, *Mozam.* 83 E4
Mueller Ra., *Australia* 88 C4
Muende, *Mozam.* 83 E3
Muerto, Mar, *Mexico* 115 D6
Muertos, Punta de los, *Spain* 29 J3
Mufindi □, *Tanzania* 83 D4
Mufu Shan, *China* 53 C10
Mufulira, *Zambia* 83 E2
Mufumbiro Range, *Africa* 82 C2
Mugardos, *Spain* 30 B2
Muge, *Portugal* 31 F2
Muge →, *Portugal* 31 F2
Múggia, *Italy* 33 C10
Mughayrā', *Si. Arabia* 64 D3
Mugi, *Japan* 49 H7
Mugia, *Spain* 30 B1
Mugila, Mts., *Zaïre* 82 D2
Muğla, *Turkey* 66 E3
Muğla □, *Turkey* 66 E3
Müglizh, *Bulgaria* 38 G8
Mugu, *Nepal* 63 E10
Muhammad, Râs, *Egypt* 76 B3
Muhammad Qol, *Sudan* 76 C4
Muhammadabad, *India* 63 F10
Muhesi →, *Tanzania* 82 D4
Muheza □, *Tanzania* 82 C4
Mühldorf, *Germany* 19 G8
Mühlhausen, *Germany* 18 D6
Mühlig Hofmann fjella, *Antarctica* 5 D3
Muhutwe, *Tanzania* 82 C3
Muiden, *Neths.* 16 D6
Muikamachi, *Japan* 49 F9
Muine Bheag, *Ireland* 15 D5
Muiños, *Spain* 30 D3
Muir, L., *Australia* 89 F2
Mukachevo, *Ukraine* 40 G3
Mukah, *Malaysia* 56 D4
Mukawwa, Geziret, *Egypt* 76 C4
Mukdahan, *Thailand* 58 D5
Mukden = Shenyang, *China* 51 D12
Mukhtolovo, *Russia* 41 D13
Mukhtuya = Lensk, *Russia* 45 C12
Mukinbudin, *Australia* 89 F2
Mukishi, *Zaïre* 83 D1
Mukomuko, *Indonesia* 56 E2
Mukomwenze, *Zaïre* 82 D2
Muktsar, *India* 62 D6
Mukur, *Afghan.* 62 C2
Mukutawa →, *Canada* 101 C9
Mukwela, *Zambia* 83 F2
Mula, *Spain* 29 G3
Mulange, *Zaïre* 82 C2
Mulchén, *Chile* 126 D1
Mulde →, *Germany* 18 D8
Mule Creek, *U.S.A.* 108 D2
Muleba, *Tanzania* 82 C3
Muleba □, *Tanzania* 82 C3
Mulegns, *Switz.* 23 C9
Muleshoe, *U.S.A.* 109 H3
Mulgathing, *Australia* 91 E1
Mulgrave, *Canada* 99 C7
Mulhacén, *Spain* 29 H1
Mülheim, *Germany* 18 D2
Mulhouse, *France* 25 E14
Muli, *China* 52 D3
Muling, *China* 51 B16
Mull, *U.K.* 14 E3
Mullaittvu, *Sri Lanka* 60 Q12
Mullen, *U.S.A.* 108 D4
Mullengudgery, *Australia* 91 E4
Mullens, *U.S.A.* 104 G5
Muller, Pegunungan, *Indonesia* 56 D4
Mullet Pen., *Ireland* 15 B1
Mullewa, *Australia* 89 E2
Müllheim, *Germany* 19 H3
Mulligan →, *Australia* 90 C2
Mullin, *U.S.A.* 109 K5
Mullingar, *Ireland* 15 C4
Mullins, *U.S.A.* 105 H6
Mullumbimby, *Australia* 91 D5
Mulobezi, *Zambia* 83 F2
Multan, *Pakistan* 62 D4
Multrå, *Sweden* 10 A11
Mulumbe, Mts., *Zaïre* 83 D2
Mulungushi Dam, *Zambia* 83 E2
Mulvane, *U.S.A.* 109 G6
Mulwad, *Sudan* 76 D3
Mulwala, *Australia* 91 F4
Mumbwa, *Zambia* 83 E2
Mumra, *Russia* 43 D12
Mun →, *Thailand* 58 E5
Muna, *Indonesia* 57 F6
Munamagi, *Estonia* 40 C5
Münchberg, *Germany* 19 E7
Müncheberg, *Germany* 18 C10
München, *Germany* 19 G7
Munchen-Gladbach = Mönchengladbach, *Germany* 18 D2
Muncho Lake, *Canada* 100 B3
Munchŏn, *N. Korea* 51 E14
Münchwilen, *Switz.* 23 B7
Muncie, *U.S.A.* 104 E3
Muncoonie, L., *Australia* 90 D2
Mundala, *Indonesia* 57 E10
Mundare, *Canada* 100 C6
Munday, *U.S.A.* 109 J5
Münden, *Germany* 18 D5
Mundiwindi, *Australia* 88 D3
Mundo →, *Spain* 29 G2
Mundo Novo, *Brazil* 123 D3
Mundra, *India* 62 H3
Mundrabilla, *Australia* 89 F4
Munducurus, *Brazil* 121 D6
Munera, *Spain* 29 F2
Mungallala, *Australia* 91 D4
Mungallala Cr. →, *Australia* 91 D4
Mungana, *Australia* 90 B3
Mungaoli, *India* 62 G8
Mungari, *Mozam.* 83 F3
Mungbere, *Zaïre* 82 B2
Munger, *India* 63 G12
Mungindi, *Australia* 91 D4
Munhango, *Angola* 81 G3
Munich = München, *Germany* 19 G7
Munising, *U.S.A.* 104 B2
Munka-Ljungby, *Sweden* 11 H6
Munkedal, *Sweden* 11 F5
Munku-Sardyk, *Russia* 45 D11
Münnerstadt, *Germany* 19 E6
Muñoz Gamero, Pen., *Chile* 128 D2
Munroe L., *Canada* 101 B9
Munsan, *S. Korea* 51 F14
Münsingen, *Switz.* 22 C5
Munster, *France* 25 D14
Munster, *Niedersachsen, Germany* 18 C6
Münster, *Nordrhein-Westfalen, Germany* 18 D3
Münster, *Switz.* 23 D6
Munster □, *Ireland* 15 D3
Muntadgin, *Australia* 89 F2
Muntele Mare, *Romania* 38 C6
Muntok, *Indonesia* 56 E3
Munyak, *Uzbekistan* 44 E6
Munyama, *Zambia* 83 F2
Muong Beng, *Laos* 58 B3
Muong Boum, *Vietnam* 58 A4
Muong Et, *Laos* 58 B5
Muong Hai, *Laos* 58 B3
Muong Hiem, *Laos* 58 B4
Muong Houn, *Laos* 58 B3
Muong Hung, *Vietnam* 58 B4
Muong Kau, *Laos* 58 E5
Muong Khao, *Laos* 58 C4
Muong Khoua, *Laos* 58 B4
Muong Liep, *Laos* 58 C3
Muong May, *Laos* 58 E6
Muong Ngeun, *Laos* 58 B3
Muong Ngoi, *Laos* 58 B4
Muong Nhie, *Vietnam* 58 A4
Muong Nong, *Laos* 58 D6
Muong Ou Tay, *Laos* 58 A3
Muong Oua, *Laos* 58 C3
Muong Peun, *Laos* 58 B4
Muong Phalane, *Laos* 58 D5
Muong Phieng, *Laos* 58 C3
Muong Phine, *Laos* 58 D6
Muong Sai, *Laos* 58 B3
Muong Saiapoun, *Laos* 58 C3
Muong Sen, *Vietnam* 58 C5
Muong Sing, *Laos* 58 B3
Muong Son, *Laos* 58 B4
Muong Soui, *Laos* 58 C4
Muong Va, *Laos* 58 B4
Muong Xia, *Vietnam* 58 B5
Muonio, *Finland* 8 C17
Muotathal, *Switz.* 23 C7
Mupa, *Angola* 81 H3
Muping, *China* 51 F11
Muqaddam, Wadi →, *Sudan* 76 D3
Muqdisho, *Somali Rep.* 68 G4
Mur-de-Bretagne, *France* 24 D4
Mura →, *Slovenia* 33 B13
Muradiye, *Turkey* 67 D10
Murakami, *Japan* 48 E9
Murallón, Cuerro, *Chile* 128 C2
Muralto, *Switz.* 23 D7
Muranda, *Rwanda* 82 C2
Murang'a, *Kenya* 82 C4
Murashi, *Russia* 41 B16
Murat, *France* 26 C6
Murat →, *Turkey* 67 D8
Muratlı, *Turkey* 66 C2
Muravera, *Italy* 34 C2
Murayama, *Japan* 48 E10
Murban, *U.A.E.* 65 F7
Murça, *Portugal* 30 D3
Murchison →, *Australia* 89 E1
Murchison, Mt., *Antarctica* 5 D11
Murchison Falls = Kabarega Falls, *Uganda* 82 B3
Murchison House, *Australia* 89 E1
Murchison Ra., *Australia* 90 C1
Murchison Rapids, *Malawi* 83 F3
Murcia, *Spain* 29 G3
Murcia □, *Spain* 29 H3
Murdo, *U.S.A.* 108 D4
Murdoch Pt., *Australia* 90 A3
Mureş →, *Romania* 38 C3
Mureşul = Mureş →, *Romania* 38 C3
Muret, *France* 26 E5
Murfatlar, *Romania* 38 E11
Murfreesboro, *U.S.A.* 105 H2
Murg, *Switz.* 23 B8
Murg →, *Germany* 19 G4
Murgab, *Tajikistan* 44 F8
Murgenthal, *Switz.* 22 B5
Murgon, *Australia* 91 D5
Murgoo, *Australia* 89 E2
Muri, *Switz.* 23 B6
Muria, *Indonesia* 57 G14
Muriaé, *Brazil* 123 F3
Murias de Paredes, *Spain* 30 C4
Murici, *Brazil* 122 C4
Muriel Mine, *Zimbabwe* 83 F3
Müritz See, *Germany* 18 B8
Murka, *Kenya* 82 C4
Murmansk, *Russia* 44 C4
Murmerwoude, *Neths.* 16 B8
Murnau, *Germany* 19 H7
Muro, *France* 27 F12
Muro, *Spain* 36 B10
Muro, C. de, *France* 27 G12
Muro Lucano, *Italy* 35 B8
Murom, *Russia* 41 D13
Muroran, *Japan* 48 C10
Muros, *Spain* 30 C1
Muros y de Noya, Ría de, *Spain* 30 C2
Muroto, *Japan* 49 H7
Muroto-Misaki, *Japan* 49 H7
Murphy, *U.S.A.* 110 E5

Murphys, *U.S.A.* 112 G6
Murphysboro, *U.S.A.* 109 G10
Murrat, *Sudan* 76 D2
Murray, *Ky., U.S.A.* 105 G1
Murray, *Utah, U.S.A.* 110 F8
Murray →, *Australia* 91 F2
Murray →, *Canada* 100 B4
Murray, L., *U.S.A.* 105 H5
Murray Bridge, *Australia* 91 F2
Murray Downs, *Australia* 90 C1
Murray Harbour, *Canada* 99 C7
Murraysburg, *S. Africa* 84 E3
Murree, *Pakistan* 62 C5
Murrieta, *U.S.A.* 113 M9
Murrin Murrin, *Australia* 89 E3
Murrumbidgee →, *Australia* 91 E3
Murrumburrah, *Australia* 91 E4
Murrurundi, *Australia* 91 E5
Mursala, *Indonesia* 56 D1
Murshid, *Sudan* 76 C3
Murshidabad, *India* 63 G13
Murska Sobota, *Slovenia* 33 B13
Murten, *Switz.* 22 C4
Murtensee, *Switz.* 22 C4
Murtle L., *Canada* 100 C5
Murtoa, *Australia* 91 F3
Murtosa, *Portugal* 30 E2
Muru →, *Brazil* 124 B3
Murungu, *Tanzania* 82 C3
Murwara, *India* 63 H9
Murwillumbah, *Australia* 91 D5
Mürz →, *Austria* 21 H5
Mürzzuschlag, *Austria* 21 H5
Muş, *Turkey* 67 D9
Muş □, *Turkey* 67 D9
Mûsa, G., *Egypt* 76 J8
Musa Khel, *Pakistan* 62 D3
Mūsá Qal'eh, *Afghan.* 60 C4
Musaffargarh, *Pakistan* 60 D7
Musala, *Bulgaria* 38 G6
Musan, *N. Korea* 51 C15
Musangu, *Zaïre* 83 E1
Musasa, *Tanzania* 82 C3
Musay'īd, *Qatar* 65 E6
Muscat = Masqat, *Oman* 68 C6
Muscat & Oman = Oman ■, *Asia* 68 C6
Muscatine, *U.S.A.* 108 E9
Musel, *Spain* 30 B5
Musgrave, *Australia* 90 A3
Musgrave Ras., *Australia* 89 E5
Mushie, *Zaïre* 80 E3
Mushin, *Nigeria* 79 D5
Musi →, *Indonesia* 56 E2
Muskeg →, *Canada* 100 A4
Muskegon, *U.S.A.* 104 D2
Muskegon →, *U.S.A.* 104 D2
Muskegon Heights, *U.S.A.* 104 D2
Muskogee, *U.S.A.* 109 H7
Muskwa →, *Canada* 100 B4
Muslīmiyah, *Syria* 64 B3
Musmar, *Sudan* 76 D4
Musofu, *Zambia* 83 E2
Musoma, *Tanzania* 82 C3
Musoma □, *Tanzania* 82 C3
Musquaro, L., *Canada* 99 B7
Musquodoboit Harbour, *Canada* 99 D7
Musselburgh, *U.K.* 14 F5
Musselkanaal, *Neths.* 16 C10
Musselshell →, *U.S.A.* 110 C10
Mussidan, *France* 26 C4
Mussomeli, *Italy* 34 E6
Musson, *Belgium* 17 J7
Mussoorie, *India* 62 D8
Mussuco, *Angola* 84 B2
Mustafakemalpaşa, *Turkey* 66 C3
Mustang, *Nepal* 63 E10
Musters, L., *Argentina* 128 C3
Musudan, *N. Korea* 51 D15
Muswellbrook, *Australia* 91 E5
Mût, *Egypt* 76 B2
Mut, *Turkey* 66 E5
Mutanda, *Mozam.* 85 C5
Mutanda, *Zambia* 83 E2
Mutaray, *Russia* 45 C11
Mutare, *Zimbabwe* 83 F3
Muting, *Indonesia* 57 F10
Mutshatsha, *Zaïre* 83 E1
Mutsu, *Japan* 48 D10
Mutsu-Wan, *Japan* 48 D10
Muttaburra, *Australia* 90 C3
Mutuáli, *Mozam.* 83 E4
Mutunópolis, *Brazil* 123 D2
Muweilih, *Egypt* 69 E3
Muxima, *Angola* 80 F2
Muy Muy, *Nic.* 116 D2
Muya, *Russia* 45 D12
Muyinga, *Burundi* 82 C3
Muzaffarabad, *Pakistan* 63 B5
Muzaffargarh, *Pakistan* 62 D4
Muzaffarnagar, *India* 62 E7
Muzaffarpur, *India* 63 F11
Muzhi, *Russia* 44 C7
Muzillac, *France* 24 E4
Muzon, C., *U.S.A.* 100 C2
Muztag, *China* 54 C3
Mvôlô, *Sudan* 77 F2
Mvuma, *Zimbabwe* 83 F3
Mvurwi, *Zimbabwe* 83 F3
Mwadui, *Tanzania* 82 C3
Mwambo, *Tanzania* 83 E5
Mwandi, *Zambia* 83 F1
Mwanza, *Tanzania* 82 C3
Mwanza, *Zaïre* 82 D2
Mwanza, *Zambia* 83 F1
Mwanza □, *Tanzania* 82 C3
Mwaya, *Tanzania* 83 D3
Mweelrea, *Ireland* 15 C2
Mweka, *Zaïre* 80 E4
Mwenezi, *Zimbabwe* 83 G3
Mwenezi →, *Mozam.* 83 G3
Mwenga, *Zaïre* 82 C2
Mweru, L., *Zambia* 83 D2
Mweza Range, *Zimbabwe* 83 G3
Mwilambwe, *Zaïre* 82 D5
Mwimbi, *Tanzania* 83 D3
Mwinilunga, *Zambia* 83 E1
My Tho, *Vietnam* 59 G6
Mya, O. →, *Algeria* 75 B5
Myajlar, *India* 62 F4
Myanaung, *Burma* 61 K19
Myanmar = Burma ■, *Asia* 61 J20
Myaungmya, *Burma* 61 L19
Mycenae = Mikínai, *Greece* 39 M5
Myeik Kyunzu, *Burma* 59 G1
Myerstown, *U.S.A.* 107 F8
Myingyan, *Burma* 61 J19
Myitkyina, *Burma* 61 G20
Myjava, *Slovak Rep.* 20 G7
Mykolayiv = Nikolayev, *Ukraine* 42 C4
Mymensingh, *Bangla.* 61 G17
Mynydd Du, *U.K.* 13 F4
Mýrdalsjökull, *Iceland* 8 E4
Myroodah, *Australia* 88 C3
Myrtle Beach, *U.S.A.* 105 J6
Myrtle Creek, *U.S.A.* 110 E2
Myrtle Point, *U.S.A.* 110 E1
Myrtou, *Cyprus* 37 D12
Mysen, *Norway* 10 E5
Mysia, *Turkey* 66 D2
Myslenice, *Poland* 20 F9
Myślibórz, *Poland* 20 C4
Mysłowice, *Poland* 20 E9
Mysore = Karnataka □, *India* 60 N10
Mysore, *India* 60 N10
Mystic, *U.S.A.* 107 E13
Myszków, *Poland* 20 E9
Mythen, *Switz.* 23 B7
Mytishchi, *Russia* 41 D10
Myton, *U.S.A.* 110 F8
Mývatn, *Iceland* 8 D5
Mzimba, *Malawi* 83 E3
Mzimkulu →, *S. Africa* 85 E5
Mzimvubu →, *S. Africa* 85 E4
Mzuzu, *Malawi* 83 E3

N

N' Dioum, *Senegal* 78 B2
Na Noi, *Thailand* 58 C3
Na Phao, *Laos* 58 D5
Na Sam, *Vietnam* 58 A6
Na San, *Vietnam* 58 B5
Naab →, *Germany* 19 F8
Naaldwijk, *Neths.* 16 E4
Na'am, *Sudan* 77 F2
Naantali, *Finland* 9 F17
Naarden, *Neths.* 16 D6
Naas, *Ireland* 15 C5
Nababiep, *S. Africa* 84 D2
Nabadwip = Navadwip, *India* 63 H13
Nabari, *Japan* 49 G8
Nabawa, *Australia* 89 E1
Nabberu, L., *Australia* 89 E3
Nabburg, *Germany* 19 F8
Naberezhnyye Chelny, *Russia* 44 D6
Nabeul, *Tunisia* 75 A7
Nabha, *India* 62 D7
Nabīd, *Iran* 65 D8
Nabire, *Indonesia* 57 E9
Nabisar, *Pakistan* 62 G3
Nabisipi →, *Canada* 99 B7
Nabiswera, *Uganda* 82 B3
Nablus = Nābulus, *Jordan* 69 C4
Naboomspruit, *S. Africa* 85 C4
Nabua, *Phil.* 55 E5
Nābulus, *Jordan* 69 C4
Nābulus □, *Jordan* 69 C4
Nacala, *Mozam.* 83 E5
Nacala-Velha, *Mozam.* 83 E5
Nacaome, *Honduras* 116 D2
Nacaroa, *Mozam.* 83 E4
Naches, *U.S.A.* 110 C3
Naches →, *U.S.A.* 112 D6
Nachingwea, *Tanzania* 83 E4
Nachingwea □, *Tanzania* 83 E4
Nachna, *India* 62 F4
Náchod, *Czech.* 20 E6
Nacimiento Reservoir, *U.S.A.* 112 K6
Nacka, *Sweden* 10 E12
Nackara, *Australia* 91 E2
Naco, *Mexico* 114 A3
Naco, *U.S.A.* 111 L9
Nacogdoches, *U.S.A.* 109 K7
Nácori Chico, *Mexico* 114 B3
Nacozari, *Mexico* 114 A3
Nadi, *Sudan* 76 D3
Nadiad, *India* 62 H5
Nădlac, *Romania* 38 C3
Nador, *Morocco* 75 A4
Nadur, *Malta* 37 C1
Nadūshan, *Iran* 65 C7
Nadvornaya, *Ukraine* 42 B1
Nadym, *Russia* 44 C8
Nadym →, *Russia* 44 C8
Næstved, *Denmark* 11 J5
Nafada, *Nigeria* 79 C7
Näfels, *Switz.* 23 B8
Naftshahr, *Iran* 64 C5
Nafud Desert = An Nafūd, *Si. Arabia* 64 D4
Nafūsah, Jabal, *Libya* 75 B7
Nag Hammâdi, *Egypt* 76 B3
Naga, *Phil.* 55 E5
Naga, Kreb en, *Africa* 74 D3
Nagagami →, *Canada* 98 C3
Nagahama, *Japan* 49 G8
Nagai, *Japan* 48 E10
Nagaland □, *India* 61 F19
Nagano, *Japan* 49 F9
Nagano □, *Japan* 49 F9
Nagaoka, *Japan* 49 F9
Nagappattinam, *India* 60 P11
Nagar Parkar, *Pakistan* 62 G4
Nagasaki, *Japan* 49 H4
Nagasaki □, *Japan* 49 H4
Nagato, *Japan* 49 G5
Nagaur, *India* 62 F5
Nagercoil, *India* 60 Q10
Nagina, *India* 63 E8
Nagīneh, *Iran* 65 C8
Nagir, *Pakistan* 63 A6
Nagold, *Germany* 19 G4
Nagold →, *Germany* 19 G4
Nagoorin, *Australia* 90 C5
Nagornyy, *Russia* 45 D13
Nagorsk, *Russia* 41 B17
Nagoya, *Japan* 49 G8
Nagpur, *India* 60 J11
Nagua, *Dom. Rep.* 117 C6
Nagykanizsa, *Hungary* 21 J7
Nagykörös, *Hungary* 21 H9
Nagyléta, *Hungary* 21 H11
Naha, *Japan* 49 L3
Nahanni Butte, *Canada* 100 A4
Nahanni Nat. Park, *Canada* 100 A3
Nahariyya, *Israel* 64 C2
Nahāvand, *Iran* 65 C6
Nahe →, *Germany* 19 F3
Nahîya, Wadi →, *Egypt* 76 J7
Nahlin, *Canada* 100 B2
Nahuel Huapi, L., *Argentina* 128 B2
Naicá, *Mexico* 114 B3
Naicam, *Canada* 101 C8
Nā'ifah, *Si. Arabia* 68 D5
Naila, *Germany* 19 E7
Nain, *Canada* 99 A7
Nā'īn, *Iran* 65 C7
Naini Tal, *India* 63 E8
Nainpur, *India* 60 H12
Naintré, *France* 24 F7
Naipu, *Romania* 38 E8
Naira, *Indonesia* 57 E7
Nairn, *U.K.* 14 D5
Nairobi, *Kenya* 82 C4
Naivasha, *Kenya* 82 C4
Naivasha, L., *Kenya* 82 C4
Najac, *France* 26 D5
Najafābād, *Iran* 65 C6
Nájera, *Spain* 28 C2
Najerilla →, *Spain* 28 C2
Najibabad, *India* 62 E8
Najin, *N. Korea* 51 C16
Najmah, *Si. Arabia* 65 E6
Naju, *S. Korea* 51 G14
Nakadōri-Shima, *Japan* 49 H4
Nakalagba, *Zaïre* 82 B2
Nakaminato, *Japan* 49 F10
Nakamura, *Japan* 49 H6
Nakano, *Japan* 49 F9
Nakano-Shima, *Japan* 49 K4
Nakashibetsu, *Japan* 48 C12
Nakfa, *Eritrea* 77 D4
Nakhichevan, *Azerbaijan* 67 D11
Nakhichevan Republic □, *Azerbaijan* 44 F5
Nakhl, *Egypt* 69 F2
Nakhl-e Taqī, *Iran* 65 E7
Nakhodka, *Russia* 45 E14
Nakhon Nayok, *Thailand* 58 E3
Nakhon Pathom, *Thailand* 58 F3
Nakhon Phanom, *Thailand* 58 D5
Nakhon Ratchasima, *Thailand* 58 E4
Nakhon Sawan, *Thailand* 58 E3
Nakhon Si Thammarat, *Thailand* 59 H3
Nakhon Thai, *Thailand* 58 D3
Nakina, *B.C., Canada* 100 B2
Nakina, *Ont., Canada* 98 B2
Nakło nad Notecią, *Poland* 20 B7
Nakodar, *India* 62 D6
Nakskov, *Denmark* 11 K5
Näkten, *Sweden* 10 B8
Naktong →, *S. Korea* 51 G15
Nakuru, *Kenya* 82 C4
Nakuru □, *Kenya* 82 C4
Nakuru, L., *Kenya* 82 C4
Nakusp, *Canada* 100 C5
Nal →, *Pakistan* 62 G1
Nalchik, *Russia* 43 E10
Nälden, *Sweden* 10 A8
Näldsjön, *Sweden* 10 A8
Nalerigu, *Ghana* 79 C4
Nalgonda, *India* 60 L11
Nalhati, *India* 63 G12
Nalinnes, *Belgium* 17 H4
Nallamalai Hills, *India* 60 M11
Nallıhan, *Turkey* 66 C4
Nalón →, *Spain* 30 B4
Nālūt, *Libya* 75 B7
Nam Can, *Vietnam* 59 H5
Nam Co, *China* 54 C4
Nam Dinh, *Vietnam* 58 B6
Nam Du, Hon, *Vietnam* 59 H5
Nam Ngum Dam, *Laos* 58 C4
Nam-Phan, *Vietnam* 59 G6
Nam Phong, *Thailand* 58 D4
Nam Tha, *Laos* 58 B3
Nam Tok, *Thailand* 58 E2
Namacunde, *Angola* 84 B2
Namacurra, *Mozam.* 85 B6
Namak, Daryācheh-ye, *Iran* 65 C7
Namak, Kavir-e, *Iran* 65 C8
Namaland, *Namibia* 84 C2
Namangan, *Uzbekistan* 44 E8
Namapa, *Mozam.* 83 E4
Namaqualand, *S. Africa* 84 D2
Namasagali, *Uganda* 82 B3
Namber, *Indonesia* 57 E8
Nambour, *Australia* 91 D5
Nambucca Heads, *Australia* 91 E5
Namche Bazar, *Nepal* 63 F12
Namchonjŏm, *N. Korea* 51 E14
Namêche, *Belgium* 17 H6
Namecunda, *Mozam.* 83 E4
Nameh, *Indonesia* 56 D5
Nameponda, *Mozam.* 83 F4
Nametil, *Mozam.* 83 F4
Namew L., *Canada* 101 C8
Namib Desert = Namibwoestyn, *Namibia* 84 C2
Namibe, *Angola* 81 H2
Namibe □, *Angola* 84 B1
Namibia ■, *Africa* 84 C2
Namibwoestyn, *Namibia* 84 C2
Namlea, *Indonesia* 57 E7
Namoi →, *Australia* 91 E4
Namous, O. en →, *Algeria* 75 B4
Nampa, *U.S.A.* 110 E5
Nampō-Shotō, *Japan* 49 J10
Nampula, *Mozam.* 83 F4
Namrole, *Indonesia* 57 E7
Namse Shankou, *China* 61 E13
Namsen →, *Norway* 8 D11
Namsos, *Norway* 8 D11
Namtay, *Russia* 45 C13
Namtu, *Burma* 61 H20
Namtumbo, *Tanzania* 83 E4
Namu, *Canada* 100 C3
Namur, *Belgium* 17 H5
Namur □, *Belgium* 17 H6
Namutoni, *Namibia* 84 B2
Namwala, *Zambia* 83 F2
Namwŏn, *S. Korea* 51 G14
Namysłów, *Poland* 20 D7
Nan, *Thailand* 58 C3
Nan →, *Thailand* 58 E3
Nan Xian, *China* 53 C9
Nanaimo, *Canada* 100 D4
Nanam, *N. Korea* 51 D15
Nanan, *China* 53 E12
Nanango, *Australia* 91 D5
Nan'ao, *China* 53 F11
Nanao, *Japan* 49 F8
Nanbu, *China* 52 B6
Nanchang, *China* 53 C10
Nancheng, *China* 53 D11
Nanching = Nanjing, *China* 53 A12
Nanchong, *China* 52 B6
Nanchuan, *China* 52 C6
Nancy, *France* 25 D13
Nanda Devi, *India* 63 D8
Nandan, *China* 52 E6
Nandan, *Japan* 49 G7
Nanded, *India* 60 K10
Nandewar Ra., *Australia* 91 E5
Nandi, *Fiji* 87 C7
Nandi □, *Kenya* 82 B4
Nandurbar, *India* 60 J9
Nandyal, *India* 60 M11
Nanfeng, *Guangdong, China* 53 F8
Nanfeng, *Jiangxi, China* 53 D11
Nanga, *Australia* 89 E1
Nanga-Eboko, *Cameroon* 79 E7
Nanga Parbat, *Pakistan* 63 B6
Nangade, *Mozam.* 83 E4
Nangapinoh, *Indonesia* 56 E4
Nangarhár □, *Afghan.* 60 B7
Nangatayap, *Indonesia* 56 E4
Nangeya Mts., *Uganda* 82 B3
Nangis, *France* 25 D10
Nangong, *China* 50 F8
Nanhua, *China* 52 E3
Nanhuang, *China* 51 F11
Nanhui, *China* 53 B13
Nanjeko, *Zambia* 83 F1
Nanji Shan, *China* 53 D13
Nanjian, *China* 52 E3
Nanjiang, *China* 52 A6
Nanjing, *Fujian, China* 53 E11
Nanjing, *Jiangsu, China* 53 A12
Nanjirinji, *Tanzania* 83 D4
Nankana Sahib, *Pakistan* 62 D5
Nankang, *China* 53 E10
Nanking = Nanjing, *China* 53 A12
Nankoku, *Japan* 49 H6
Nanling, *China* 53 B12
Nanning, *China* 52 F7
Nannup, *Australia* 89 F2
Nanpan Jiang →, *China* 52 E6
Nanpara, *India* 63 F9
Nanpi, *China* 50 E9
Nanping, *Fujian, China* 53 D12
Nanping, *Henan, China* 53 C9
Nanri Dao, *China* 53 E12
Nanripe, *Mozam.* 83 E4
Nansei-Shotō = Ryūkyū-rettō, *Japan* 49 M2
Nansen Sd., *Canada* 4 A3
Nansio, *Tanzania* 82 C3
Nant, *France* 26 D7
Nantes, *France* 24 E5
Nanteuil-le-Haudouin, *France* 25 C9
Nantiat, *France* 26 B5
Nanticoke, *U.S.A.* 107 E8
Nanton, *Canada* 100 C6
Nantong, *China* 53 A13
Nantua, *France* 27 B9
Nantucket I., *U.S.A.* 94 E12
Nanuque, *Brazil* 123 E3
Nanutarra, *Australia* 88 D2
Nanxiong, *China* 53 E10
Nanyang, *China* 50 H7
Nanyi Hu, *China* 53 B12
Nanyuan, *China* 50 E9
Nanyuki, *Kenya* 82 B4
Nanzhang, *China* 53 B8
Náo, C. de la, *Spain* 29 G5
Naococane L., *Canada* 99 B5
Naoetsu, *Japan* 49 F9
Náousa, *Greece* 39 J5
Naozhou Dao, *China* 53 G8
Napa, *U.S.A.* 112 G4
Napa →, *U.S.A.* 112 G4
Napanee, *Canada* 98 D4
Napanoch, *U.S.A.* 107 E10
Nape, *Laos* 58 C5
Nape Pass = Keo Neua, Deo, *Vietnam* 58 C5
Napf, *Switz.* 22 B5
Napier, *N.Z.* 87 H6
Napier Broome B., *Australia* 88 B4
Napier Downs, *Australia* 88 C3
Napier Pen., *Australia* 90 A2
Naples = Nápoli, *Italy* 35 B7
Naples, *U.S.A.* 105 M5
Napo, *China* 52 F5
Napo □, *Ecuador* 120 D2
Napo →, *Peru* 120 D3
Napoleon, *N. Dak., U.S.A.* 108 B5
Napoleon, *Ohio, U.S.A.* 104 E3
Nápoli, *Italy* 35 B7
Nápoli, G. di, *Italy* 35 B7
Napopo, *Zaïre* 82 B2
Nappa Merrie, *Australia* 91 D3
Naqâda, *Egypt* 76 B3
Naqqāsh, *Iran* 65 C6
Nara, *Japan* 49 G7
Nara, *Mali* 78 B3
Nara □, *Japan* 49 G8
Nara Canal, *Pakistan* 62 G3
Nara Visa, *U.S.A.* 109 H3
Naracoorte, *Australia* 91 F3
Naradhan, *Australia* 91 E4
Narasapur, *India* 61 L12
Narathiwat, *Thailand* 59 J3
Narayanganj, *Bangla.* 61 H17
Narayanpet, *India* 60 L10
Narbonne, *France* 26 E7
Narcea →, *Spain* 30 B4
Nardīn, *Iran* 65 B7
Nardò, *Italy* 35 B11
Narembeen, *Australia* 89 F2
Nares Str., *Arctic* 94 B13
Naretha, *Australia* 89 F3
Narew →, *Poland* 20 C10
Nari →, *Pakistan* 62 E2
Narin, *Afghan.* 60 A6
Narindra, Helodranon' i, *Madag.* 85 A8
Narino □, *Colombia* 120 C2
Narita, *Japan* 49 G10
Narmada →, *India* 62 J5
Narman, *Turkey* 67 C9
Narnaul, *India* 62 E7
Narni, *Italy* 33 F9
Naro, *Ghana* 78 C4
Naro, *Italy* 34 E6
Naro Fominsk, *Russia* 41 D10
Narodnaya, *Russia* 6 B17
Narok, *Kenya* 82 C4
Narok □, *Kenya* 82 C4
Narón, *Spain* 30 B2
Narooma, *Australia* 91 F5
Narowal, *Pakistan* 62 C6
Narrabri, *Australia* 91 E4
Narran →, *Australia* 91 D4
Narrandera, *Australia* 91 E4
Narraway →, *Canada* 100 B5
Narrogin, *Australia* 89 F2
Narromine, *Australia* 91 E4
Narsimhapur, *India* 63 H8
Nartkala, *Russia* 43 E10
Naruto, *Japan* 49 G7
Narva, *Estonia* 40 B6
Narva →, *Russia* 40 B6
Narvik, *Norway* 8 B14
Narvskoye Vdkhr., *Russia* 40 B6

Narwana, *India* 62 **E7**
Naryan-Mar, *Russia* 44 **C6**
Naryilco, *Australia* 91 **D3**
Narym, *Russia* 44 **D9**
Narymskoye, *Kazakhstan* 44 **E9**
Naryn, *Kirghizia* 44 **E8**
Nasa, *Norway* 8 **C13**
Nasarawa, *Nigeria* 79 **D6**
Năsăud, *Romania* 38 **B7**
Naseby, *N.Z.* 87 **L3**
Naselle, *U.S.A.* 112 **D3**
Naser, Buheirat en, *Egypt* 76 **C3**
Nashua, *Iowa, U.S.A.* 108 **D8**
Nashua, *Mont., U.S.A.* 110 **B10**
Nashua, *N.H., U.S.A.* 107 **D13**
Nashville, *Ark., U.S.A.* 109 **J8**
Nashville, *Ga., U.S.A.* 105 **K4**
Nashville, *Tenn., U.S.A.* 105 **G2**
Našice, *Croatia* 21 **K8**
Nasielsk, *Poland* 20 **C10**
Nasik, *India* 60 **K8**
Nasipit, *Phil.* 55 **G6**
Nasirabad, *India* 62 **F6**
Naskaupi →, *Canada* 99 **B7**
Naso, *Italy* 35 **D7**
Naṣriān-e Pā'īn, *Iran* 64 **C5**
Nass →, *Canada* 100 **B3**
Nassau, *Bahamas* 116 **A4**
Nassau, *U.S.A.* 107 **D11**
Nassau, B., *Chile* 128 **E3**
Nasser, L. = Naser, Buheirat en, *Egypt* 76 **C3**
Nasser City = Kôm Ombo, *Egypt* 76 **C3**
Nassian, *Ivory C.* 78 **D4**
Nässjö, *Sweden* 9 **H13**
Nasugbu, *Phil.* 55 **D4**
Näsviken, *Sweden* 10 **C10**
Nat Kyizin, *Burma* 61 **M20**
Nata, *Botswana* 84 **C4**
Natagaima, *Colombia* 120 **C2**
Natal, *Brazil* 122 **C4**
Natal, *Canada* 100 **D6**
Natal, *Indonesia* 56 **D1**
Natal □, *S. Africa* 85 **D5**
Natalinci, *Serbia, Yug.* 21 **L10**
Naṭanz, *Iran* 65 **C6**
Natashquan, *Canada* 99 **B7**
Natashquan →, *Canada* 99 **B7**
Natchez, *U.S.A.* 109 **K9**
Natchitoches, *U.S.A.* 109 **K8**
Naters, *Switz.* 22 **D5**
Nathalia, *Australia* 91 **F4**
Nathdwara, *India* 62 **G5**
Nati, Pta., *Spain* 36 **A10**
Natimuk, *Australia* 91 **F3**
Nation →, *Canada* 100 **B4**
National City, *U.S.A.* 113 **N9**
Natitingou, *Benin* 79 **C5**
Natividad, I., *Mexico* 114 **B1**
Natoma, *U.S.A.* 108 **F5**
Natron, L., *Tanzania* 82 **C4**
Natrona Heights, *U.S.A.* 106 **F5**
Natrûn, W. el →, *Egypt* 76 **H7**
Natuna Besar, Kepulauan, *Indonesia* 59 **L7**
Natuna Is. = Natuna Besar, Kepulauan, *Indonesia* 59 **L7**
Natuna Selatan, Kepulauan, *Indonesia* 59 **L7**
Natural Bridge, *U.S.A.* 107 **B9**
Naturaliste, C., *Australia* 90 **G4**
Nau Qala, *Afghan.* 62 **B3**
Naubinway, *U.S.A.* 98 **C2**
Naucelle, *France* 26 **D6**
Nauders, *Austria* 19 **J6**
Nauen, *Germany* 18 **C8**
Naugatuck, *U.S.A.* 107 **E11**
Naujoji Vilnia, *Lithuania* 40 **D4**
Naumburg, *Germany* 18 **D7**
Nā'ūr at Tunayb, *Jordan* 69 **D4**
Nauru ■, *Pac. Oc.* 92 **H8**
Naushahra = Nowshera, *Pakistan* 60 **B8**
Nauta, *Peru* 120 **D3**
Nautanwa, *India* 61 **F13**
Nautla, *Mexico* 115 **C5**
Nava, *Mexico* 114 **B4**
Nava del Rey, *Spain* 30 **D5**
Navacerrada, Puerto de, *Spain* 30 **E7**
Navadwip, *India* 63 **H13**
Navahermosa, *Spain* 31 **F6**
Navajo Reservoir, *U.S.A.* 111 **H10**
Navalcarnero, *Spain* 30 **E6**
Navalmoral de la Mata, *Spain* 30 **F5**
Navalvillar de Pela, *Spain* 31 **F5**
Navan = An Uaimh, *Ireland* 15 **C5**
Navarino, I., *Chile* 128 **E3**
Navarra □, *Spain* 28 **C3**
Navarre, *U.S.A.* 106 **F3**
Navarrenx, *France* 26 **E3**
Navarro →, *U.S.A.* 112 **F3**
Navasota, *U.S.A.* 109 **K6**
Navassa, *W. Indies* 117 **C4**
Nave, *Italy* 32 **C7**
Naver →, *U.K.* 14 **C4**
Navia, *Spain* 30 **B4**
Navia →, *Spain* 30 **B4**
Navia de Suarna, *Spain* 30 **C4**
Navidad, *Chile* 126 **C1**
Navlya, *Russia* 40 **E9**
Navoi, *Uzbekistan* 44 **E7**
Navojoa, *Mexico* 114 **B3**
Navolato, *Mexico* 114 **C3**
Návpaktos, *Greece* 39 **L4**
Návplion, *Greece* 39 **M5**
Navrongo, *Ghana* 79 **C4**
Navsari, *India* 60 **J8**
Nawa Kot, *Pakistan* 62 **E4**
Nawabganj, *Ut. P., India* 63 **F9**
Nawabganj, *Ut. P., India* 63 **E8**
Nawabshah, *Pakistan* 62 **F3**
Nawada, *India* 63 **G11**
Nawakot, *Nepal* 63 **F11**
Nawalgarh, *India* 62 **F6**
Nawanshahr, *India* 63 **C6**
Nawi, *Sudan* 76 **D3**
Náxos, *Greece* 39 **M8**
Nay, *France* 26 **E3**
Nāy Band, *Iran* 65 **E7**
Naya →, *Colombia* 120 **C2**
Nayakhan, *Russia* 45 **C16**
Nayarit □, *Mexico* 114 **C4**
Nayé, *Senegal* 78 **C2**
Nayong, *China* 52 **D5**
Nayoro, *Japan* 48 **B11**
Nayyāl, W. →, *Si. Arabia* 64 **D3**
Nazaré, *Bahia, Brazil* 123 **D4**
Nazaré, *Goiás, Brazil* 122 **C2**
Nazaré, *Pará, Brazil* 125 **B7**
Nazaré, *Portugal* 31 **F1**
Nazareth = Nazerat, *Israel* 69 **C4**
Nazas, *Mexico* 114 **B4**
Nazas →, *Mexico* 114 **B4**
Naze, The, *U.K.* 13 **F9**
Nazerat, *Israel* 69 **C4**
Nāzīk, *Iran* 64 **B5**
Nazik Gölü, *Turkey* 67 **D10**
Nazilli, *Turkey* 66 **E3**
Nazir Hat, *Bangla.* 61 **H17**
Nazko, *Canada* 100 **C4**
Nazko →, *Canada* 100 **C4**
Nazret, *Ethiopia* 77 **F4**
Nchanga, *Zambia* 83 **E2**
Ncheu, *Malawi* 83 **E3**
Ndala, *Tanzania* 82 **C3**
Ndalatando, *Angola* 80 **F2**
Ndali, *Benin* 79 **D5**
Ndareda, *Tanzania* 82 **C4**
Ndélé, *C.A.R.* 73 **G9**
Ndendé, *Gabon* 80 **E2**
Ndjamena, *Chad* 73 **F7**
Ndjolé, *Gabon* 80 **E2**
Ndola, *Zambia* 83 **E2**
Ndoto Mts., *Kenya* 82 **B4**
Nduguti, *Tanzania* 82 **C3**
Nea →, *Norway* 10 **A5**
Néa Flippiás, *Greece* 39 **K3**
Neagh, Lough, *U.K.* 15 **B5**
Neah Bay, *U.S.A.* 112 **B2**
Neale, L., *Australia* 88 **D5**
Neápolis, *Kozan, Greece* 39 **J4**
Neápolis, *Kríti, Greece* 37 **D7**
Neápolis, *Lakonia, Greece* 39 **N6**
Near Is., *U.S.A.* 96 **C1**
Neath, *U.K.* 13 **F4**
Nebbou, *Burkina Faso* 79 **C4**
Nebine Cr. →, *Australia* 91 **D4**
Nebit Dag, *Turkmenistan* 44 **F6**
Nebolchy, *Russia* 40 **B8**
Nebraska □, *U.S.A.* 108 **E5**
Nebraska City, *U.S.A.* 108 **E7**
Nébrodi, Monti, *Italy* 35 **E7**
Necedah, *U.S.A.* 108 **C9**
Nechako →, *Canada* 100 **C4**
Neches →, *U.S.A.* 109 **L8**
Neckar →, *Germany* 19 **F4**
Necochea, *Argentina* 126 **D4**
Nedelišće, *Croatia* 33 **B13**
Neder Rijn →, *Neths.* 16 **E8**
Nederbrakel, *Belgium* 17 **G3**
Nederweert, *Neths.* 17 **F7**
Nédha →, *Greece* 39 **M4**
Nedroma, *Algeria* 75 **A4**
Neede, *Neths.* 16 **D9**
Needles, *U.S.A.* 113 **L12**
Needles, The, *U.K.* 13 **G6**
Ñeembucú □, *Paraguay* 126 **B4**
Neemuch = Nimach, *India* 62 **G6**
Neenah, *U.S.A.* 104 **C1**
Neepawa, *Canada* 101 **C9**
Neer, *Neths.* 17 **F7**
Neerpelt, *Belgium* 17 **F6**
Neft-chala = imeni 26 Bakinskikh Komissarov, *Azerbaijan* 67 **D13**
Nefta, *Tunisia* 75 **B6**
Neftah Sidi Boubekeur, *Algeria* 75 **A5**
Neftegorsk, *Russia* 43 **D8**
Neftekumsk, *Russia* 43 **D11**
Neftenbach, *Switz.* 23 **A7**
Negapatam = Nagappattinam, *India* 60 **P11**
Negaunee, *U.S.A.* 104 **B2**
Negele, *Ethiopia* 68 **F2**
Negev Desert = Hanegev, *Israel* 69 **E3**
Negombo, *Sri Lanka* 60 **R11**
Negotin, *Serbia, Yug.* 21 **L12**
Negra, Peña, *Spain* 30 **C4**
Negra, Pta., *Mauritania* 74 **D1**
Negra, Pta., *Peru* 124 **B1**
Negra Pt., *Phil.* 57 **A6**
Negrais, C. = Maudin Sun, *Burma* 61 **M19**
Negreira, *Spain* 30 **C2**
Négrine, *Algeria* 75 **B6**
Negro →, *Argentina* 128 **B4**
Negro →, *Bolivia* 125 **C5**
Negro →, *Brazil* 121 **D6**
Negro →, *Uruguay* 127 **C4**
Negros, *Phil.* 55 **G5**
Nehalem →, *U.S.A.* 112 **E3**
Nehāvand, *Iran* 65 **C6**
Nehbandān, *Iran* 65 **D9**
Neheim, *Germany* 18 **D3**
Nehoiaşu, *Romania* 38 **D9**
Nei Monggol Zizhiqu □, *China* 50 **C6**
Neidpath, *Canada* 101 **C7**
Neihart, *U.S.A.* 110 **C8**
Neijiang, *China* 52 **C5**
Neilton, *U.S.A.* 110 **C2**
Neiqiu, *China* 50 **F8**
Neira de Jusá, *Spain* 30 **C3**
Neiva, *Colombia* 120 **C2**
Neixiang, *China* 50 **H6**
Nejanilini L., *Canada* 101 **B9**
Nejo, *Ethiopia* 77 **F4**
Nekā, *Iran* 65 **B7**
Nekemte, *Ethiopia* 77 **F4**
Nêkheb, *Egypt* 76 **B3**
Neksø, *Denmark* 9 **J13**
Nelas, *Portugal* 30 **E3**
Nelia, *Australia* 90 **C3**
Nelidovo, *Russia* 40 **C8**
Neligh, *U.S.A.* 108 **D5**
Nelkan, *Russia* 45 **D14**
Nellore, *India* 60 **M11**
Nelma, *Russia* 45 **E14**
Nelson, *Canada* 100 **D5**
Nelson, *N.Z.* 87 **J4**
Nelson, *U.K.* 12 **D5**
Nelson, *U.S.A.* 111 **J7**
Nelson →, *Canada* 101 **C9**
Nelson, C., *Australia* 91 **F3**
Nelson, Estrecho, *Chile* 128 **D2**
Nelson Forks, *Canada* 100 **B4**
Nelson House, *Canada* 101 **B9**
Nelson L., *Canada* 101 **B8**
Nelspoort, *S. Africa* 84 **E3**
Nelspruit, *S. Africa* 85 **D5**
Néma, *Mauritania* 78 **B3**
Neman →, *Lithuania* 40 **D2**
Nemeiben L., *Canada* 101 **B7**
Nemira, *Romania* 38 **C9**
Nemours, *France* 25 **D9**
Nemunas = Neman →, *Lithuania* 40 **D2**
Nemuro, *Japan* 48 **C12**
Nemuro-Kaikyō, *Japan* 48 **C12**
Nemuy, *Russia* 45 **D14**
Nen Jiang →, *China* 51 **B13**
Nenagh, *Ireland* 15 **D3**
Nenana, *U.S.A.* 96 **B5**
Nenasi, *Malaysia* 59 **L4**
Nene →, *U.K.* 12 **E8**
Nenjiang, *China* 54 **B7**
Neno, *Malawi* 83 **F3**
Nenusa, Kepulauan, *Indonesia* 57 **D7**
Neodesha, *U.S.A.* 109 **G7**
Neópolis, *Brazil* 122 **D4**
Neosho, *U.S.A.* 109 **G7**
Neosho →, *U.S.A.* 109 **H7**
Nepal ■, *Asia* 63 **F11**
Nepalganj, *Nepal* 63 **E9**
Nephi, *U.S.A.* 110 **G8**
Nephin, *Ireland* 15 **B2**
Neptune, *U.S.A.* 107 **F10**
Néra →, *Romania* 38 **E4**
Nérac, *France* 26 **D4**
Nerchinsk, *Russia* 45 **D12**
Nerchinskiy Zavod, *Russia* 45 **D12**
Nereju, *Romania* 38 **D9**
Nerekhta, *Russia* 41 **C12**
Néret L., *Canada* 99 **B5**
Neringa, *Lithuania* 40 **D2**
Nerja, *Spain* 31 **J7**
Nerl →, *Russia* 41 **C12**
Nerpio, *Spain* 29 **G2**
Nerva, *Spain* 31 **H4**
Nes, *Iceland* 8 **D5**
Nes, *Neths.* 16 **B7**
Nesbyen, *Norway* 10 **D3**
Nesebŭr, *Bulgaria* 38 **G10**
Neskaupstaður, *Iceland* 8 **D7**
Nesland, *Norway* 10 **E1**
Neslandsvatn, *Norway* 10 **F3**
Nesle, *France* 25 **C9**
Nesodden, *Norway* 10 **E4**
Nesque →, *France* 27 **E8**
Ness, L., *U.K.* 14 **D4**
Nesslau, *Switz.* 23 **B8**
Néstos →, *Greece* 39 **H7**
Nesttun, *Norway* 9 **F8**
Nesvizh, *Belorussia* 40 **E5**
Netanya, *Israel* 69 **C3**
Nète →, *Belgium* 17 **F4**
Netherdale, *Australia* 90 **C4**
Netherlands ■, *Europe* 16 **E6**
Netherlands Antilles ■, *W. Indies* 120 **A4**
Neto →, *Italy* 35 **C10**
Nettancourt, *France* 25 **D11**
Nettilling L., *Canada* 97 **B12**
Nettuno, *Italy* 34 **A5**
Netzahualcoyotl, Presa, *Mexico* 115 **D6**
Neu-Isenburg, *Germany* 19 **E4**
Neu-Ulm, *Germany* 19 **G6**
Neubrandenburg, *Germany* 18 **B9**
Neubukow, *Germany* 18 **A7**
Neuburg, *Germany* 19 **G7**
Neuchâtel, *Switz.* 22 **C3**
Neuchâtel □, *Switz.* 22 **C3**
Neuchâtel, Lac de, *Switz.* 22 **C3**
Neudau, *Austria* 21 **H6**
Neuenegg, *Switz.* 22 **C4**
Neuenhaus, *Germany* 18 **C2**
Neuf-Brisach, *France* 25 **D14**
Neufahrn, *Germany* 19 **G8**
Neufchâteau, *Belgium* 17 **J6**
Neufchâteau, *France* 25 **D12**
Neufchâtel-en-Bray, *France* 24 **C8**
Neufchâtel-sur-Aisne, *France* 25 **C11**
Neuhaus, *Germany* 18 **B6**
Neuhausen, *Switz.* 23 **A7**
Neuillé-Pont-Pierre, *France* 24 **E7**
Neuilly-St.-Front, *France* 25 **C10**
Neukalen, *Germany* 18 **B8**
Neumarkt, *Germany* 19 **F7**
Neumarkt-Sankt Veit, *Germany* 19 **G8**
Neumünster, *Germany* 18 **A5**
Neung-sur-Beuvron, *France* 25 **E8**
Neunkirchen, *Austria* 21 **H6**
Neunkirchen, *Germany* 19 **F3**
Neuquén, *Argentina* 128 **A3**
Neuquén □, *Argentina* 126 **D2**
Neuquén →, *Argentina* 128 **A3**
Neuruppin, *Germany* 18 **C8**
Neuse →, *U.S.A.* 105 **H7**
Neusiedler See, *Austria* 21 **H6**
Neuss, *Germany* 17 **F9**
Neussargues-Moissac, *France* 26 **C7**
Neustadt, *Baden-W., Germany* 19 **H4**
Neustadt, *Bayern, Germany* 19 **F8**
Neustadt, *Bayern, Germany* 19 **G7**
Neustadt, *Bayern, Germany* 19 **F6**
Neustadt, *Bayern, Germany* 19 **E7**
Neustadt, *Brandenburg, Germany* 18 **C8**
Neustadt, *Hessen, Germany* 18 **E5**
Neustadt, *Niedersachsen, Germany* 18 **C5**
Neustadt, *Rhld-Pfz., Germany* 19 **F4**
Neustadt, *Schleswig-Holstein, Germany* 18 **A6**
Neustadt, *Thüringen, Germany* 18 **E7**
Neustrelitz, *Germany* 18 **B9**
Neuvic, *France* 26 **C6**
Neuville, *Belgium* 17 **H5**
Neuville-aux-Bois, *France* 25 **D9**
Neuville-de-Poitou, *France* 26 **B4**
Neuville-sur-Saône, *France* 27 **C8**
Neuvy-le-Roi, *France* 24 **E7**
Neuvy-St.-Sépulchre, *France* 26 **B5**
Neuvy-sur-Barangeon, *France* 25 **E9**
Neuwerk, *Germany* 18 **B4**
Neuwied, *Germany* 18 **E3**
Neva →, *Russia* 6 **D12**
Nevada, *U.S.A.* 109 **G7**
Nevada □, *U.S.A.* 110 **G5**
Nevada, Sierra, *Spain* 29 **H1**
Nevada, Sierra, *U.S.A.* 110 **G3**
Nevada City, *U.S.A.* 112 **F6**
Nevado, Cerro, *Argentina* 126 **D2**
Nevanka, *Russia* 45 **D10**
Nevel, *Russia* 40 **D6**
Nevele, *Belgium* 17 **F3**
Nevers, *France* 25 **F10**
Nevertire, *Australia* 91 **E4**
Neville, *Canada* 101 **D7**
Nevinnomyssk, *Russia* 43 **D9**
Nevis, *W. Indies* 117 **C7**
Nevrokop = Gotse Delchev, *Bulgaria* 39 **H6**
Nevşehir, *Turkey* 66 **D6**
Nevşehir □, *Turkey* 66 **D6**
New →, *Guyana* 121 **C6**
New Albany, *Ind., U.S.A.* 104 **F3**
New Albany, *Miss., U.S.A.* 109 **H10**
New Albany, *Pa., U.S.A.* 107 **E8**
New Amsterdam, *Guyana* 121 **B6**
New Angledool, *Australia* 91 **D4**
New Bedford, *U.S.A.* 107 **E14**
New Bern, *U.S.A.* 105 **H7**
New Bethlehem, *U.S.A.* 106 **E5**
New Bloomfield, *U.S.A.* 106 **F7**
New Boston, *U.S.A.* 109 **J7**
New Braunfels, *U.S.A.* 109 **L5**
New Brighton, *N.Z.* 87 **K4**
New Brighton, *U.S.A.* 106 **F4**
New Britain, *Papua N. G.* 92 **H7**
New Britain, *U.S.A.* 107 **E12**
New Brunswick, *U.S.A.* 107 **F10**
New Brunswick □, *Canada* 99 **C6**
New Bussa, *Nigeria* 79 **D5**
New Caledonia, *Pac. Oc.* 92 **K8**
New Castile = Castilla La Mancha □, *Spain* 31 **F7**
New Castle, *Ind., U.S.A.* 104 **F3**
New Castle, *Pa., U.S.A.* 106 **E4**
New City, *U.S.A.* 107 **E11**
New Cumberland, *U.S.A.* 106 **F4**
New Cuyama, *U.S.A.* 113 **L7**
New Delhi, *India* 62 **E7**
New Denver, *Canada* 100 **D5**
New Don Pedro Reservoir, *U.S.A.* 112 **H6**
New England, *U.S.A.* 108 **B3**
New England Ra., *Australia* 91 **E5**
New Forest, *U.K.* 13 **G6**
New Glasgow, *Canada* 99 **C7**
New Guinea, *Oceania* 92 **H5**
New Hamburg, *Canada* 106 **C4**
New Hampshire □, *U.S.A.* 107 **C13**
New Hampton, *U.S.A.* 108 **D8**
New Hanover, *S. Africa* 85 **D5**
New Haven, *Conn., U.S.A.* 107 **E12**
New Haven, *Mich., U.S.A.* 106 **D2**
New Hazelton, *Canada* 100 **B3**
New Hebrides = Vanuatu ■, *Pac. Oc.* 92 **J8**
New Iberia, *U.S.A.* 109 **K9**
New Ireland, *Papua N. G.* 92 **H7**
New Jersey □, *U.S.A.* 107 **F10**
New Kensington, *U.S.A.* 106 **F5**
New Lexington, *U.S.A.* 104 **F4**
New Liskeard, *Canada* 98 **C4**
New London, *Conn., U.S.A.* 107 **E12**
New London, *Minn., U.S.A.* 108 **C7**
New London, *Ohio, U.S.A.* 106 **E2**
New London, *Wis., U.S.A.* 108 **C10**
New Madrid, *U.S.A.* 109 **G10**
New Meadows, *U.S.A.* 110 **D5**
New Melones L., *U.S.A.* 112 **H6**
New Mexico □, *U.S.A.* 111
New Milford, *Conn., U.S.A.* 107 **E11**
New Milford, *Pa., U.S.A.* 107 **E9**
New Norcia, *Australia* 89 **F2**
New Norfolk, *Australia* 90 **G4**
New Orleans, *U.S.A.* 109 **K9**
New Philadelphia, *U.S.A.* 106 **F3**
New Plymouth, *N.Z.* 87 **H5**
New Plymouth, *U.S.A.* 110 **E5**
New Providence, *Bahamas* 116 **A4**
New Radnor, *U.K.* 13 **E4**
New Richmond, *U.S.A.* 108 **C8**
New Roads, *U.S.A.* 109 **K9**
New Rochelle, *U.S.A.* 107 **F11**
New Rockford, *U.S.A.* 108 **B5**
New Ross, *Ireland* 15 **D5**
New Salem, *U.S.A.* 108 **B4**
New Scone, *U.K.* 14 **E5**
New Siberian Is. = Novaya Sibir, Ostrov, *Russia* 45 **B16**
New Siberian Is. = Novosibirskiye Ostrova, *Russia* 45 **B15**
New Smyrna Beach, *U.S.A.* 105 **L5**
New South Wales □, *Australia* 91 **E4**
New Springs, *Australia* 89 **E3**
New Town, *U.S.A.* 108 **A3**
New Ulm, *U.S.A.* 108 **C7**
New Waterford, *Canada* 99 **C7**
New Westminster, *Canada* 100 **D4**
New York □, *U.S.A.* 107 **D9**
New York City, *U.S.A.* 107 **F11**
New Zealand ■, *Oceania* 87 **J5**
Newala, *Tanzania* 83 **E4**
Newala □, *Tanzania* 83 **E4**
Newark, *Del., U.S.A.* 104 **F8**
Newark, *N.J., U.S.A.* 107 **F10**
Newark, *N.Y., U.S.A.* 106 **C7**
Newark, *Ohio, U.S.A.* 106 **F2**
Newark-on-Trent, *U.K.* 12 **D7**
Newaygo, *U.S.A.* 104 **D3**
Newberg, *U.S.A.* 110 **D2**
Newberry, *Mich., U.S.A.* 104 **B3**
Newberry, *S.C., U.S.A.* 105 **H5**
Newberry Springs, *U.S.A.* 113 **L10**
Newbrook, *Canada* 100 **C6**
Newburgh, *U.S.A.* 107 **E10**
Newbury, *U.K.* 13 **F6**
Newbury, *U.S.A.* 107 **B12**
Newburyport, *U.S.A.* 107 **D14**
Newcastle, *Australia* 91 **E5**
Newcastle, *Canada* 99 **C6**
Newcastle, *S. Africa* 85 **D4**
Newcastle, *U.K.* 15 **B6**
Newcastle, *Calif., U.S.A.* 112 **G5**
Newcastle, *Wyo., U.S.A.* 108 **D2**
Newcastle Emlyn, *U.K.* 13 **E3**
Newcastle Ra., *Australia* 88 **C5**
Newcastle-under-Lyme, *U.K.* 12 **D5**
Newcastle-upon-Tyne, *U.K.* 12 **C6**
Newcastle Waters, *Australia* 90 **B1**
Newdegate, *Australia* 89 **F2**
Newell, *U.S.A.* 108 **C3**
Newfoundland □, *Canada* 99 **B8**
Newhalem, *U.S.A.* 100 **D4**
Newhall, *U.S.A.* 113 **L8**
Newham, *U.K.* 13 **F8**
Newhaven, *U.K.* 13 **G8**
Newkirk, *U.S.A.* 109 **G6**
Newman, *Australia* 88 **D2**
Newman, *U.S.A.* 112 **H5**
Newmarket, *Canada* 106 **B5**
Newmarket, *Ireland* 15 **D3**
Newmarket, *U.K.* 13 **E8**
Newmarket, *U.S.A.* 107 **C14**
Newnan, *U.S.A.* 105 **J3**
Newport, *Gwent, U.K.* 13 **F5**
Newport, *I. of W., U.K.* 13 **G6**

Newport, Shrops., U.K. 13 E5
Newport, Ark., U.S.A. 109 H9
Newport, Ky., U.S.A. 104 F3
Newport, N.H., U.S.A. 107 C12
Newport, Oreg., U.S.A. 110 D1
Newport, Pa., U.S.A. 106 F7
Newport, R.I., U.S.A. 107 E13
Newport, Tenn., U.S.A. 105 H4
Newport, Vt., U.S.A. 107 B12
Newport, Wash., U.S.A. 110 B5
Newport Beach, U.S.A. 113 M9
Newport News, U.S.A. 104 G7
Newquay, U.K. 13 G2
Newry, U.K. 15 B5
Newry & Mourne □, U.K. 15 B5
Newton, Iowa, U.S.A. 108 E8
Newton, Mass., U.S.A. 107 D13
Newton, Miss., U.S.A. 109 J10
Newton, N.C., U.S.A. 105 H5
Newton, N.J., U.S.A. 107 E10
Newton, Tex., U.S.A. 109 K8
Newton Abbot, U.K. 13 G4
Newton Boyd, Australia 91 D5
Newton Stewart, U.K. 14 G4
Newtonmore, U.K. 14 D4
Newtown, U.K. 13 E4
Newtownabbey □, U.K. 15 B6
Newtownards, U.K. 15 B6
Newville, U.S.A. 106 F7
Nexon, France 26 C5
Neya, Russia 41 B13
Neyrīz, Iran 65 D7
Neyshābūr, Iran 65 B8
Nezhin, Ukraine 40 F7
Nezperce, U.S.A. 110 C5
Ngabang, Indonesia 56 D3
Ngabordamlu, Tanjung, Indonesia 57 F8
Ngambé, Cameroon 79 D7
Ngami Depression, Botswana 84 C3
Ngamo, Zimbabwe 83 F2
Nganglong Kangri, China 61 C12
Nganjuk, Indonesia 57 G14
Ngao, Thailand 58 C2
Ngaoundéré, Cameroon 80 C2
Ngapara, N.Z. 87 L3
Ngara, Tanzania 82 C3
Ngara □, Tanzania 82 C3
Ngawi, Indonesia 57 G14
Nghia Lo, Vietnam 58 B5
Ngoma, Malawi 83 E3
Ngomahura, Zimbabwe 83 G3
Ngomba, Tanzania 83 D3
Ngop, Sudan 77 F3
Ngoring Hu, China 54 C4
Ngorkou, Mali 78 B4
Ngorongoro, Tanzania 82 C4
Ngozi, Burundi 82 C2
Ngudu, Tanzania 82 C3
Nguigmi, Niger 73 F7
Ngukurr, Australia 90 A1
Ngunga, Tanzania 82 C3
Nguru, Nigeria 79 C7
Nguru Mts., Tanzania 82 D4
Nguyen Binh, Vietnam 58 A5
Nha Trang, Vietnam 59 F7
Nhacoongo, Mozam. 85 C6
Nhamaabué, Mozam. 83 F4
Nhambiquara, Brazil 125 C6
Nhamundá, Brazil 121 D6
Nhamundá →, Brazil 121 D6
Nhangutazi, L., Mozam. 85 C5
Nhecolândia, Brazil 125 D6
Nhill, Australia 91 F3
Nho Quan, Vietnam 58 B5
Nhulunbuy, Australia 90 A2
Nia-nia, Zaïre 82 B2
Niafounké, Mali 78 B4
Niagara, U.S.A. 104 C1
Niagara Falls, Canada 98 D4
Niagara Falls, U.S.A. 106 C6
Niagara-on-the-Lake, Canada 106 C5
Niah, Malaysia 56 D4
Niamey, Niger 79 C5
Nianforando, Guinea 78 D2
Nianfors, Sweden 10 C10
Niangara, Zaïre 82 B2
Nias, Indonesia 56 D1
Niassa □, Mozam. 83 E4
Nibbiano, Italy 32 D6
Nibe, Denmark 11 H3
Nicaragua ■, Cent. Amer. 116 D2
Nicaragua, L. de, Nic. 116 D2
Nicastro, Italy 35 D9
Nice, France 27 E11
Niceville, U.S.A. 105 K2
Nichinan, Japan 49 J5
Nicholás, Canal, W. Indies 116 B3
Nicholasville, U.S.A. 104 G3
Nichols, U.S.A. 107 D8
Nicholson, Australia 88 C4
Nicholson, U.S.A. 107 E9
Nicholson →, Australia 90 B2
Nicholson Ra., Australia 89 E2
Nickerie □, Surinam 121 C6
Nickerie →, Surinam 121 B6
Nicobar Is., Ind. Oc. 46 J13
Nicoclí, Colombia 120 B2
Nicola, Canada 100 C4
Nicolet, Canada 98 C5
Nicolls Town, Bahamas 116 A4
Nicosia, Cyprus 37 D12
Nicosia, Italy 35 E7
Nicótera, Italy 35 D8
Nicoya, Costa Rica 116 D2
Nicoya, G. de, Costa Rica 116 E3
Nicoya, Pen. de, Costa Rica 116 E2
Nidau, Switz. 22 B4
Nidd →, U.K. 12 C6
Nidda, Germany 18 E5
Nidda →, Germany 19 E4
Nidwalden □, Switz. 23 C6
Nidzica, Poland 20 B10
Niebüll, Germany 18 A4
Nied →, Germany 25 C13
Niederaula, Germany 18 E5
Niederbipp, Switz. 22 B5
Niederbronn-les-Bains, France 25 D14
Niedere Tauern, Austria 21 H4
Niedersachsen □, Germany 18 C5
Niekerkshoop, S. Africa 84 D3
Niel, Belgium 17 F4
Niellé, Ivory C. 78 C3
Niemba, Zaïre 82 D2
Niemen = Neman →, Lithuania 40 D2
Nienburg, Germany 18 C5
Niers →, Germany 18 D2
Niesen, Switz. 22 C5
Niesky, Germany 18 D10
Nieu Bethesda, S. Africa 84 E3
Nieuw-Amsterdam, Neths. 16 C9
Nieuw Amsterdam, Surinam 121 B6
Nieuw Beijerland, Neths. 16 E4
Nieuw-Dordrecht, Neths. 16 C9
Nieuw Loosdrecht, Neths. 16 D6
Nieuw Nickerie, Surinam 121 B6
Nieuw-Schoonebeek, Neths. 16 C10
Nieuw-Vennep, Neths. 16 D5
Nieuw-Vossemeer, Neths. 17 E4
Nieuwe-Niedorp, Neths. 16 C5
Nieuwe-Pekela, Neths. 16 B9
Nieuwe-Schans, Neths. 16 B10
Nieuwendijk, Neths. 16 E5
Nieuwerkerken, Belgium 17 G6
Nieuwkoop, Neths. 16 D5
Nieuwleusen, Neths. 16 C8
Nieuwnamen, Neths. 17 F4
Nieuwolda, Neths. 16 B9
Nieuwoudtville, S. Africa 84 E2
Nieuwpoort, Belgium 17 F1
Nieuwveen, Neths. 16 D5
Nieves, Spain 30 C2
Nieves, Pico de las, Canary Is. 36 G4
Nièvre □, France 25 E10
Niğde, Turkey 66 E6
Niğde □, Turkey 66 E6
Nigel, S. Africa 85 D4
Niger □, Nigeria 79 C6
Niger ■, W. Afr. 79 B6
Niger →, W. Afr. 79 D6
Nigeria ■, W. Afr. 79 D6
Nightcaps, N.Z. 87 L2
Nigríta, Greece 39 J6
Nihtaur, India 63 E8
Nii-Jima, Japan 49 G9
Niigata, Japan 48 F9
Niigata □, Japan 49 F9
Niihama, Japan 49 H6
Niihau, U.S.A. 102 H14
Niimi, Japan 49 G6
Niitsu, Japan 48 F9
Níjar, Spain 29 J2
Nijil, Jordan 69 E4
Nijkerk, Neths. 16 D7
Nijlen, Belgium 17 F5
Nijmegen, Neths. 16 E7
Nijverdal, Neths. 16 D8
Nīk Pey, Iran 65 B6
Nike, Nigeria 79 D6
Nikel, Russia 8 B21
Nikiniki, Indonesia 57 F6
Nikki, Benin 79 D5
Nikkō, Japan 49 F9
Nikolayev, Ukraine 42 C4
Nikolayevsk, Russia 41 G14
Nikolayevsk-na-Amur, Russia 45 D15
Nikolsk, Russia 41 B14
Nikolskoye, Russia 45 D17
Nikopol, Bulgaria 38 F7
Nikopol, Ukraine 42 C6
Niksar, Turkey 42 F7
Nīkshahr, Iran 65 E9
Nikšić, Montenegro 21 N8
Nîl, Nahr en →, Africa 76 H7
Nîl el Abyad →, Sudan 77 D3
Nîl el Azraq →, Sudan 77 D3
Niland, U.S.A. 113 M11
Nile = Nîl, Nahr en →, Africa 76 H7
Nile □, Uganda 82 B3
Nile Delta, Egypt 76 H7
Niles, U.S.A. 106 E4
Nilo Peçanha, Brazil 123 D4
Nimach, India 62 G6
Nimbahera, India 62 G6
Nîmes, France 27 E8
Nimfaíon, Ákra-, Greece 39 J7
Nimmitabel, Australia 91 F4
Nimneryskiy, Russia 45 D13
Nimule, Sudan 77 G3
Nin, Croatia 33 D12
Nīnawá, Iraq 64 B4
Nindigully, Australia 91 D4
Ninemile, U.S.A. 100 B2
Nineveh = Nīnawá, Iraq 64 B4
Ning Xian, China 50 G4
Ningaloo, Australia 88 D1
Ning'an, China 51 B15
Ningbo, China 53 C13
Ningcheng, China 51 D10
Ningde, China 53 D12
Ningdu, China 53 D10
Ninggang, China 53 D9
Ningguo, China 53 B12
Ninghai, China 53 C13
Ninghua, China 53 D11
Ningjin, China 50 F8
Ningjing Shan, China 52 B2
Ninglang, China 52 D3
Ningling, China 50 G8
Ningming, China 52 F6
Ningnan, China 52 D4
Ningpo = Ningbo, China 53 C13
Ningqiang, China 50 H4
Ningshan, China 50 H5
Ningsia Hui A.R. = Ningxia Huizu Zizhiqu □, China 50 E3
Ningwu, China 50 E7
Ningxia Huizu Zizhiqu □, China 50 E3
Ningxiang, China 53 C9
Ningyang, China 50 G9
Ningyuan, China 53 E8
Ninh Binh, Vietnam 58 B5
Ninh Giang, Vietnam 58 B6
Ninh Hoa, Vietnam 58 F7
Ninh Ma, Vietnam 58 F7
Ninove, Belgium 17 G4
Nioaque, Brazil 127 A4
Niobrara, U.S.A. 108 D6
Niobrara →, U.S.A. 108 D6
Niono, Mali 78 C3
Nioro du Rip, Senegal 78 C1
Nioro du Sahel, Mali 78 B3
Niort, France 26 B3
Nipawin, Canada 101 C8
Nipawin Prov. Park, Canada 101 C8
Nipigon, Canada 98 C2
Nipigon, L., Canada 98 C2
Nipin →, Canada 101 B7
Nipishish L., Canada 99 B7
Nipissing L., Canada 98 C4
Nipomo, U.S.A. 113 K6
Nipton, U.S.A. 113 K11
Niquelândia, Brazil 123 D2
Nīr, Iran 64 B5
Nirasaki, Japan 49 G9
Nirmal, India 60 K11
Nirmali, India 63 F12
Niš, Serbia 21 M11
Nisa, Portugal 31 F3
Nişāb, Yemen 68 E4
Nišava →, Serbia 21 M11
Niscemi, Italy 35 E7
Nishinomiya, Japan 49 G7
Nishin'omote, Japan 49 J5
Nishiwaki, Japan 49 G7
Nísíros, Greece 39 N10
Niskibi →, Canada 98 A2
Nispen, Neths. 17 F4
Nisqually →, U.S.A. 112 C4
Nissáki, Greece 37 A3
Nissan →, Sweden 11 H6
Nissedal, Norway 10 E2
Nisser, Norway 10 E2
Nissum Fjord, Denmark 11 H2
Nistelrode, Neths. 17 E7
Nisutlin →, Canada 100 A2
Nitchequon, Canada 99 B5
Niterói, Brazil 123 F3
Nith →, U.K. 14 F5
Nitra, Slovak Rep. 21 G8
Nittedal, Norway 10 D4
Nittendau, Germany 19 F8
Niuafo'ou, Tonga 87 B11
Niue, Cook Is. 93 J11
Niulan Jiang →, China 52 D4
Niut, Indonesia 56 D4
Niutou Shan, China 53 C13
Niuzhuang, China 51 D12
Nivelles, Belgium 17 G4
Nivernais, France 25 E10
Nixon, U.S.A. 109 L6
Nizamabad, India 60 K11
Nizamghat, India 61 E19
Nizhne Kolymsk, Russia 45 C17
Nizhne-Vartovsk, Russia 44 C8
Nizhneangarsk, Russia 45 D11
Nizhnegorskiy, Ukraine 42 D6
Nizhnekamsk, Russia 41 D17
Nizhneudinsk, Russia 45 D10
Nizhneyansk, Russia 45 B14
Nizhniy Lomov, Russia 41 E13
Nizhniy Novgorod, Russia 41 C14
Nizhniy Tagil, Russia 44 D6
Nizip, Turkey 67 E7
Nizké Tatry, Slovak Rep. 20 G9
Nizza Monferrato, Italy 32 D5
Njakwa, Malawi 83 E3
Njanji, Zambia 83 E3
Njinjo, Tanzania 83 D4
Njombe, Tanzania 83 D3
Njombe □, Tanzania 83 D3
Njombe →, Tanzania 82 D4
Nkambe, Cameroon 79 D7
Nkana, Zambia 83 E2
Nkawkaw, Ghana 79 D4
Nkayi, Zimbabwe 83 F2
Nkhata Bay, Malawi 80 G6
Nkhota Kota, Malawi 83 E3
Nkongsamba, Cameroon 79 E6
Nkurenkuru, Namibia 84 B2
Nkwanta, Ghana 78 D4
Nmai →, Burma 61 G20
Noakhali = Maijdi, Bangla. 61 H17
Noatak, U.S.A. 96 B3
Nobel, Canada 106 A4
Nobeoka, Japan 49 H5
Noblejas, Spain 28 F1
Noblesville, U.S.A. 104 E3
Noce →, Italy 32 B8
Nocera Inferiore, Italy 35 B7
Nocera Terinese, Italy 35 C9
Nocera Umbra, Italy 33 E9
Noci, Italy 35 B10
Nockatunga, Australia 91 D3
Nocona, U.S.A. 109 J6
Noda, Japan 49 G9
Noel, U.S.A. 109 G7
Nogales, Mexico 114 A2
Nogales, U.S.A. 111 L8
Nōgata, Japan 49 H5
Nogent-en-Bassigny, France 25 D12
Nogent-le-Rotrou, France 24 D7
Nogent-sur-Seine, France 25 D10
Noggerup, Australia 89 F2
Noginsk, Russia 41 D11
Noginsk, Sib., Russia 45 C10
Nogoa →, Australia 90 C4
Nogoyá, Argentina 126 C4
Nogueira de Ramuin, Spain 30 C3
Noguera Pallaresa →, Spain 28 D5
Noguera Ribagorzana →, Spain 28 D5
Nohar, India 62 E6
Noire, Mt., France 24 D3
Noirétable, France 26 C7
Noirmoutier, I. de, France 24 F4
Noirmoutier-en-l'Île, France 24 F4
Nojane, Botswana 84 C3
Nojima-Zaki, Japan 49 G9
Nok Kundi, Pakistan 60 E3
Nokaneng, Botswana 84 B3
Nokhtuysk, Russia 45 C12
Nokomis, Canada 101 C8
Nokomis L., Canada 101 B8
Nol, Sweden 11 G6
Nola, C.A.R. 80 D3
Nola, Italy 35 B7
Nolay, France 25 F11
Noli, C. di, Italy 32 D5
Nolinsk, Russia 41 C16
Noma Omuramba →, Namibia 84 B3
Noman L., Canada 101 A7
Nombre de Dios, Panama 116 E4
Nome, U.S.A. 96 B3
Nomo-Zaki, Japan 49 H4
Nonacho L., Canada 101 A7
Nonancourt, France 24 D8
Nonant-le-Pin, France 24 D7
Nonda, Australia 90 C3
Nong Chang, Thailand 58 E2
Nong Het, Laos 58 C4
Nong Khai, Thailand 58 D4
Nong'an, China 51 B13
Nongoma, S. Africa 85 D5
Nonoava, Mexico 114 B3
Nonthaburi, Thailand 58 F3
Nontron, France 26 C4
Nonza, France 27 F13
Noonamah, Australia 88 B5
Noonan, U.S.A. 108 A3
Noondoo, Australia 91 D4
Noonkanbah, Australia 88 C3
Noord-Bergum, Neths. 16 B8
Noord Brabant □, Neths. 17 E6
Noord Holland □, Neths. 16 D5
Noordbeveland, Neths. 17 E3
Noordeloos, Neths. 16 E5
Noordhollandsch Kanaal, Neths. 16 C5
Noordhorn, Neths. 16 B8
Noordoostpolder, Neths. 16 C7
Noordwijk aan Zee, Neths. 16 D4
Noordwijk-Binnen, Neths. 16 D4
Noordwijkerhout, Neths. 16 D5
Noordzee Kanaal, Neths. 16 D5
Noorwolde, Neths. 16 C8
Nootka, Canada 100 D3
Nootka I., Canada 100 D3
Nóqui, Angola 80 F2
Nora, Eritrea 77 D5
Noranda, Canada 98 C4
Nórcia, Italy 33 F10
Norco, U.S.A. 113 M9
Nord □, France 25 B10
Nord-Ostsee Kanal, Germany 18 A5
Nord-Trøndelag fylke □, Norway 8 D12
Nordagutu, Norway 10 E3
Nordaustlandet, Svalbard 4 B9
Nordborg, Denmark 11 J3
Nordby, Århus, Denmark 11 J4
Nordby, Ribe, Denmark 11 J2
Norddeich, Germany 18 B3
Nordegg, Canada 100 C5
Norden, Germany 18 B3
Nordenham, Germany 18 B4
Norderhov, Norway 10 D4
Norderney, Germany 18 B3
Nordfriesische Inseln, Germany 18 A4
Nordhausen, Germany 18 D6
Nordhorn, Germany 18 C3
Nordjyllands Amtskommune □, Denmark 11 H4
Nordkapp, Norway 8 A18
Nordkapp, Svalbard 4 A9
Nordkinn = Kinnarodden, Norway 6 A11
Nordland fylke □, Norway 8 D12
Nördlingen, Germany 19 G6
Nordrhein-Westfalen □, Germany 18 D3
Nordstrand, Germany 18 A4
Nordvik, Russia 45 B12
Nore, Norway 10 D3
Norefjell, Norway 10 D3
Norembega, Canada 98 C3
Noresund, Norway 10 D3
Norfolk, Nebr., U.S.A. 108 D6
Norfolk, Va., U.S.A. 104 G7
Norfolk □, U.K. 12 E9
Norfolk Broads, U.K. 12 E9
Norfolk I., Pac. Oc. 92 K8
Norfork Res., U.S.A. 109 G8
Norg, Neths. 16 B8
Norilsk, Russia 45 C9
Norley, Australia 91 D3
Norma, Mt., Australia 90 C3
Normal, U.S.A. 108 E10
Norman, U.S.A. 109 H6
Norman →, Australia 90 B3
Norman Wells, Canada 96 B7
Normanby →, Australia 90 A3
Normandie, France 24 D7
Normandie, Collines de, France 24 D6
Normandin, Canada 98 C5
Normandy = Normandie, France 24 D7
Normanhurst, Mt., Australia 89 E3
Normanton, Australia 90 B3
Norquay, Canada 101 C8
Norquinco, Argentina 128 B2
Norrbotten □, Sweden 8 C17
Norrby, Sweden 8 D15
Nørre Åby, Denmark 11 J3
Nørre Nebel, Denmark 11 J2
Nørresundby, Denmark 11 G3
Norris, U.S.A. 110 D8
Norristown, U.S.A. 107 F9
Norrköping, Sweden 11 F10
Norrland, Sweden 8 E13
Norrtälje, Sweden 10 E12
Norseman, Australia 89 F3
Norsholm, Sweden 11 F9
Norsk, Russia 45 D14
Norte, Pta., Argentina 128 B4
Norte, Pta. del, Canary Is. 36 G2
Norte de Santander □, Colombia 120 B3
Nortelândia, Brazil 125 C6
North Adams, U.S.A. 107 D11
North America 94 F10
North Battleford, Canada 101 C7
North Bay, Canada 98 C4
North Belcher Is., Canada 98 A4
North Bend, Canada 100 D4
North Bend, Oreg., U.S.A. 110 E1
North Bend, Pa., U.S.A. 106 E7
North Bend, Wash., U.S.A. 112 C5
North Berwick, U.K. 14 E6
North Berwick, U.S.A. 107 C14
North Buganda □, Uganda 82 B3
North Canadian →, U.S.A. 109 H7
North Cape = Nordkapp, Norway 8 A18
North Cape = Nordkapp, Svalbard 4 A9
North C., Canada 99 C7
North C., N.Z. 87 F4
North Caribou L., Canada 98 B1
North Carolina □, U.S.A. 105 H5
North Channel, Canada 98 C3
North Channel, U.K. 14 G3
North Chicago, U.S.A. 104 D2
North Dakota □, U.S.A. 108 B5
North Dandalup, Australia 89 F2
North Down □, U.K. 15 B6
North Downs, U.K. 13 F8
North East, U.S.A. 106 D5
North East Frontier Agency = Arunachal Pradesh □, India 61 E19
North East Providence Chan., W. Indies 116 A4
North Eastern □, Kenya 82 B5
North Esk →, U.K. 14 E6
North European Plain, Europe 6 D11
North Foreland, U.K. 13 F9
North Fork, U.S.A. 112 H7
North Fork American →, U.S.A. 112 G5
North Fork Feather →, U.S.A. 112 F5
North Frisian Is. = Nordfriesische Inseln, Germany 18 A4

North Henik L., *Canada* 101 A9
North Highlands, *U.S.A.* 112 G5
North Horr, *Kenya* 82 B4
North I., *Kenya* 82 B4
North I., *N.Z.* 87 H5
North Kingsville, *U.S.A.* 106 E4
North Knife →, *Canada* 101 B10
North Koel →, *India* 63 G10
North Korea ■, *Asia* 51 E14
North Lakhimpur, *India* 61 F19
North Las Vegas, *U.S.A.* 113 J11
North Loup →, *U.S.A.* 108 E5
North Magnetic Pole, *Canada* 4 B2
North Minch, *U.K.* 14 C3
North Nahanni →, *Canada* 100 A4
North Olmsted, *U.S.A.* 106 E3
North Ossetian Republic □, *Russia* 43 E11
North Pagai, I. = Pagai Utara, *Indonesia* 56 E2
North Palisade, *U.S.A.* 111 H4
North Platte, *U.S.A.* 108 E4
North Platte →, *U.S.A.* 108 E4
North Pt., *Canada* 99 C7
North Pole, *Arctic* 4 A
North Portal, *Canada* 101 D8
North Powder, *U.S.A.* 110 D5
North Rhine Westphalia □ = Nordrhein-Westfalen □, *Germany* 18 D3
North Ronaldsay, *U.K.* 14 B6
North Saskatchewan →, *Canada* 101 C7
North Sea, *Europe* 6 D6
North Sporades = Voríai Sporádhes, *Greece* 39 K6
North Sydney, *Canada* 99 C7
North Taranaki Bight, *N.Z.* 87 H5
North Thompson →, *Canada* 100 C4
North Tonawanda, *U.S.A.* 106 C6
North Troy, *U.S.A.* 107 B12
North Truchas Pk., *U.S.A.* 111 J11
North Twin I., *Canada* 98 B3
North Tyne →, *U.K.* 12 C5
North Uist, *U.K.* 14 D1
North Vancouver, *Canada* 100 D4
North Vernon, *U.S.A.* 104 F3
North Wabasca L., *Canada* 100 B6
North Walsham, *U.K.* 12 E9
North West C., *Australia* 88 D1
North West Christmas I. Ridge, *Pac. Oc.* 93 G11
North West Frontier □, *Pakistan* 62 C4
North West Highlands, *U.K.* 14 D3
North West Providence Channel, *W. Indies* 116 A4
North West River, *Canada* 99 B7
North West Territories □, *Canada* 96 B9
North Western □, *Zambia* 83 E2
North York Moors, *U.K.* 12 C7
North Yorkshire □, *U.K.* 12 C6
Northallerton, *U.K.* 12 C6
Northam, *S. Africa* 84 C4
Northampton, *Australia* 89 E1
Northampton, *U.K.* 13 E7
Northampton, *Mass., U.S.A.* 107 D12
Northampton, *Pa., U.S.A.* 107 F9
Northampton Downs, *Australia* 90 C4
Northamptonshire □, *U.K.* 13 E7
Northbridge, *U.S.A.* 107 D13
Northcliffe, *Australia* 89 F2
Northeim, *Germany* 18 D6
Northern □, *Malawi* 83 E3
Northern □, *Uganda* 82 B3
Northern □, *Zambia* 83 E3
Northern Circars, *India* 61 L13
Northern Indian L., *Canada* 101 B9
Northern Ireland □, *U.K.* 15 B5
Northern Light, L., *Canada* 98 C1
Northern Marianas ■, *Pac. Oc.* 92 F6
Northern Province □, *S. Leone* 78 D2
Northern Territory □, *Australia* 88 D5
Northfield, *U.S.A.* 108 C8
Northland □, *N.Z.* 87 F4
Northome, *U.S.A.* 108 B7
Northport, *Ala., U.S.A.* 105 J2
Northport, *Mich., U.S.A.* 104 C3
Northport, *Wash., U.S.A.* 110 B5
Northumberland □, *U.K.* 12 B5
Northumberland, C., *Australia* 91 F3
Northumberland Is., *Australia* 90 C4
Northumberland Str., *Canada* 99 C7
Northwich, *U.K.* 12 D5
Northwood, *Iowa, U.S.A.* 108 D8
Northwood, *N. Dak., U.S.A.* 108 B6
Norton, *U.S.A.* 108 F5
Norton, *Zimbabwe* 83 F3
Norton Sd., *U.S.A.* 96 B3
Nortorf, *Germany* 18 A5
Norwalk, *Calif., U.S.A.* 113 M8
Norwalk, *Conn., U.S.A.* 107 E11
Norwalk, *Ohio, U.S.A.* 106 E2
Norway, *U.S.A.* 104 C2
Norway ■, *Europe* 8 E11
Norway House, *Canada* 101 C9
Norwegian Sea, *Atl. Oc.* 4 C8
Norwich, *Canada* 106 D4
Norwich, *U.K.* 12 E9
Norwich, *Conn., U.S.A.* 107 E12
Norwich, *N.Y., U.S.A.* 107 D9
Norwood, *Canada* 106 B7
Noshiro, *Japan* 48 D10
Nosok, *Russia* 44 B9
Nosovka, *Ukraine* 40 F7
Noss Hd., *U.K.* 14 C5
Nossa Senhora da Glória, *Brazil* 122 D4
Nossa Senhora das Dores, *Brazil* 122 D4
Nossa Senhora do Livramento, *Brazil* 125 D6
Nossebro, *Sweden* 11 F6
Nossob →, *S. Africa* 84 D3
Nosy Bé, *Madag.* 81 G9
Nosy Boraha, *Madag.* 85 B8
Nosy Mitsio, *Madag.* 81 G9
Nosy Varika, *Madag.* 85 C8
Noteć →, *Poland* 20 C5
Notigi Dam, *Canada* 101 B9
Notikewin →, *Canada* 100 B5
Notios Evvoïkos Kólpos, *Greece* 39 L7
Noto, *Italy* 35 F8
Noto, G. di, *Italy* 35 F8
Notodden, *Norway* 10 E3
Notre-Dame, *Canada* 99 C7
Notre Dame B., *Canada* 99 C8
Notre Dame de Koartac = Koartac, *Canada* 97 B13
Notre Dame d'Ivugivic = Ivujivik, *Canada* 97 B12
Notsé, *Togo* 79 D5
Nottaway →, *Canada* 98 B4
Nøtterøy, *Norway* 10 E4
Nottingham, *U.K.* 12 E6
Nottinghamshire □, *U.K.* 12 D7
Nottoway →, *U.S.A.* 104 G7
Notwane →, *Botswana* 84 C4
Nouâdhibou, *Mauritania* 74 D1
Nouâdhibou, Ras, *Mauritania* 74 D1
Nouakchott, *Mauritania* 78 B1
Nouméa, *N. Cal.* 92 K8
Noupoort, *S. Africa* 84 E3
Nouveau Comptoir, *Canada* 98 B4
Nouvelle-Calédonie = New Caledonia, *Pac. Oc.* 92 K8
Nouzonville, *France* 25 C11
Nová Baňa, *Slovakia* 21 G8
Nová Bystřice, *Czech.* 20 F5
Nova Casa Nova, *Brazil* 122 C3
Nova Cruz, *Brazil* 122 C4
Nova Era, *Brazil* 123 E3
Nova Esperança, *Brazil* 127 A5
Nova Friburgo, *Brazil* 123 F3
Nova Gaia = Cambundi-Catembo, *Angola* 80 G3
Nova Gradiška, *Croatia* 21 K7
Nova Granada, *Brazil* 123 F2
Nova Iguaçu, *Brazil* 123 F3
Nova Iorque, *Brazil* 122 C3
Nova Lamego, *Guinea-Biss.* 78 C2
Nova Lima, *Brazil* 127 A7
Nova Lisboa = Huambo, *Angola* 81 G3
Nova Lusitânia, *Mozam.* 83 F3
Nova Mambone, *Mozam.* 85 C6
Nova Mesto, *Slovenia* 33 C12
Nova Ponte, *Brazil* 123 E2
Nova Scotia □, *Canada* 99 C7
Nova Sofala, *Mozam.* 85 C5
Nova Venécia, *Brazil* 123 E3
Nova Vida, *Brazil* 125 C5
Nova Zagora, *Bulgaria* 38 G8
Novaleksandrovskaya, *Russia* 43 D9
Novannenskiy, *Russia* 41 F13
Novara, *Italy* 32 C5
Novato, *U.S.A.* 112 G4
Novaya Kakhovka, *Ukraine* 42 C5
Novaya Lyalya, *Russia* 44 D7
Novaya Sibir, Ostrov, *Russia* 45 B16
Novaya Zemlya, *Russia* 44 B6
Novelda, *Spain* 29 G4
Novellara, *Italy* 32 D7
Noventa Vicentina, *Italy* 33 C8
Novgorod, *Russia* 40 B7
Novgorod-Severskiy, *Ukraine* 40 E8
Novi Bečej, *Serbia, Yug.* 21 K10
Novi Grad, *Croatia* 33 C10
Novi Krichim, *Bulgaria* 38 G7
Novi Lígure, *Italy* 32 D5
Novi Pazar, *Bulgaria* 38 F10
Novi Pazar, *Serbia, Yug.* 21 M10
Novi Sad, *Serbia, Yug.* 21 K9
Novi Vinodolski, *Croatia* 33 C11
Novigrad, *Croatia* 33 D12
Noville, *Belgium* 17 H7
Novo Acôrdo, *Brazil* 122 D2
Novo Aripuanã, *Brazil* 121 E5
Nôvo Cruzeiro, *Brazil* 123 E3
Nôvo Hamburgo, *Brazil* 127 B5
Novo Horizonte, *Brazil* 123 F2
Novo Remanso, *Brazil* 122 C3
Novo-Zavidovskiy, *Russia* 41 C10
Novoakrainka, *Ukraine* 42 B4
Novoataysk, *Russia* 44 D9
Novoazovsk, *Ukraine* 42 C8
Novobelitsa, *Belorussia* 40 E7
Novobogatinskoye, *Kazakhstan* 43 C14
Novocherkassk, *Russia* 43 C9
Novodevichye, *Russia* 41 E16
Novograd-Volynskiy, *Ukraine* 40 F5
Novogrudok, *Belorussia* 40 E4
Novokachalinsk, *Russia* 48 B6
Novokayakent, *Russia* 43 E12
Novokazalinsk, *Kazakhstan* 44 E7
Novokhopersk, *Russia* 41 F12
Novokuybyshevsk, *Russia* 41 E16
Novokuznetsk, *Russia* 44 D9
Novomirgorod, *Ukraine* 42 B4
Novomoskovsk, *Russia* 41 D11
Novomoskovsk, *Ukraine* 42 B6
Novopolotsk, *Belorussia* 40 D6
Novorossiysk, *Russia* 42 D7
Novorybnoye, *Russia* 45 B11
Novorzhev, *Russia* 40 C6
Novoselitsa, *Ukraine* 42 B2
Novoshakhtinsk, *Russia* 43 C8
Novosibirsk, *Russia* 44 D9
Novosibirskiye Ostrova, *Russia* 45 B15
Novosil, *Russia* 41 E10
Novosokolniki, *Russia* 40 C7
Novotroitsk, *Russia* 44 D6
Novotulskiy, *Russia* 41 D10
Novouzensk, *Russia* 41 F16
Novovolynsk, *Ukraine* 40 F4
Novovyatsk, *Russia* 41 B16
Novozybkov, *Russia* 40 E8
Novska, *Croatia* 21 K6
Novvy Port, *Russia* 44 C8
Novy Bug, *Ukraine* 42 C5
Nový Bydzov, *Czech.* 20 E5
Novy Dwór Mazowiecki, *Poland* 20 C10
Novyy Afon, *Georgia* 43 E9
Novyy Oskol, *Russia* 41 F10
Now Shahr, *Iran* 65 B6
Nowa Deba, *Poland* 20 E11
Nowa Ruda, *Poland* 20 E6
Nowa Sól, *Poland* 20 D5
Nowbarān, *Iran* 65 C6
Nowe, *Poland* 20 B8
Nowghāb, *Iran* 65 C8
Nowgong, *India* 61 F18
Nowogard, *Poland* 20 B5
Nowogród, *Poland* 20 B11
Nowra, *Australia* 91 E5
Nowshera, *Pakistan* 60 B8
Nowy Korczyn, *Poland* 20 E10
Nowy Sącz, *Poland* 20 F10
Noxen, *U.S.A.* 107 E8
Noxon, *U.S.A.* 110 C6
Noya, *Spain* 30 C2
Noyant, *France* 24 E7
Noyers, *France* 25 E10
Noyes I., *U.S.A.* 100 B2
Noyon, *France* 25 C9
Noyon, *Mongolia* 50 C2
Nozay, *France* 24 E5
Nsa, O. en →, *Algeria* 75 B6
Nsanje, *Malawi* 83 F4
Nsawam, *Ghana* 79 D4
Nsomba, *Zambia* 83 E2
Nsukka, *Nigeria* 79 D6
Nu Jiang →, *China* 52 C1
Nu Shan, *China* 52 D2
Nuba Mts. = Nubah, Jibalan, *Sudan* 77 E3
Nubah, Jibalan, *Sudan* 77 E3
Nubian Desert = Nûbîya, Es Sahrâ En, *Sudan* 76 C3
Nûbîya, Es Sahrâ En, *Sudan* 76 C3
Ñuble □, *Chile* 126 D1
Nuboai, *Indonesia* 57 E9
Nubra →, *India* 63 B7
Nueces →, *U.S.A.* 109 M6
Nueltin L., *Canada* 101 A9
Nuenen, *Neths.* 17 F7
Nueva, I., *Chile* 128 E3
Nueva Antioquia, *Colombia* 120 B4
Nueva Asunción □, *Paraguay* 126 A3
Nueva Esparta □, *Venezuela* 121 A5
Nueva Gerona, *Cuba* 116 B3
Nueva Imperial, *Chile* 128 A2
Nueva Palmira, *Uruguay* 126 C4
Nueva Rosita, *Mexico* 114 B4
Nueva San Salvador, *El Salv.* 116 D2
Nuéve de Julio, *Argentina* 126 D3
Nuevitas, *Cuba* 116 B4
Nuevo, G., *Argentina* 128 B4
Nuevo Guerrero, *Mexico* 115 B5
Nuevo Laredo, *Mexico* 115 B5
Nuevo León □, *Mexico* 114 C4
Nuevo Mundo, Cerro, *Bolivia* 124 E4
Nuevo Rocafuerte, *Ecuador* 120 D2
Nugget Pt., *N.Z.* 87 M2
Nugrus, Gebel, *Egypt* 76 C3
Nuhaka, *N.Z.* 87 H6
Nuits-St.-Georges, *France* 25 E11
Nukey Bluff, *Australia* 91 E2
Nukheila, *Sudan* 76 D2
Nuku'alofa, *Tonga* 87 E11
Nukus, *Uzbekistan* 44 E6
Nuland, *Neths.* 16 E6
Nulato, *U.S.A.* 96 B4
Nules, *Spain* 28 F4
Nullagine →, *Australia* 88 D3
Nullarbor, *Australia* 89 F5
Nullarbor Plain, *Australia* 89 F4
Numalla, L., *Australia* 91 D3
Numan, *Nigeria* 79 D7
Numansdorp, *Neths.* 16 E4
Numata, *Japan* 49 F9
Numatinna →, *Sudan* 77 F2
Numazu, *Japan* 49 G9
Numbulwar, *Australia* 90 A2
Numfoor, *Indonesia* 57 E8
Numurkah, *Australia* 91 F4
Nunaksaluk I., *Canada* 99 A7
Nuneaton, *U.K.* 13 E6
Nungo, *Mozam.* 83 E4
Nungwe, *Tanzania* 82 C3
Nunivak I., *U.S.A.* 96 B3
Nunkun, *India* 63 C7
Nunspeet, *Neths.* 16 D7
Nuoro, *Italy* 34 B2
Nuquí, *Colombia* 120 B2
Nūrābād, *Iran* 65 E8
Nure →, *Italy* 32 C6
Nuremburg = Nürnberg, *Germany* 19 F7
Nuri, *Mexico* 114 B3
Nurina, *Australia* 89 F4
Nuriootpa, *Australia* 91 E2
Nurlat, *Russia* 41 D17
Nürnberg, *Germany* 19 F7
Nurran, L. = Terewah, L., *Australia* 91 D4
Nurrari Lakes, *Australia* 89 E5
Nurri, *Italy* 34 C2
Nusa Barung, *Indonesia* 57 H15
Nusa Kambangan, *Indonesia* 57 G13
Nusa Tenggara Barat □, *Indonesia* 56 F5
Nusa Tenggara Timur □, *Indonesia* 57 F6
Nushki, *Pakistan* 62 E2
Nutak, *Canada* 97 C13
Nuth, *Neths.* 17 G7
Nutwood Downs, *Australia* 90 B1
Nuuk = Godthåb, *Greenland* 97 B14
Nuwakot, *Nepal* 63 E10
Nuweiba', *Egypt* 76 B3
Nuweveldberge, *S. Africa* 84 E3
Nuyts, C., *Australia* 89 F5
Nuyts Arch., *Australia* 91 E1
Nxau-Nxau, *Botswana* 84 B3
Nyaake, *Liberia* 78 E3
Nyack, *U.S.A.* 107 E11
Nyadal, *Sweden* 10 B11
Nyah West, *Australia* 91 F3
Nyahanga, *Tanzania* 82 C3
Nyahua, *Tanzania* 82 D3
Nyahururu, *Kenya* 82 B4
Nyainqentanglha Shan, *China* 54 C4
Nyakanazi, *Tanzania* 82 C3
Nyakrom, *Ghana* 79 D4
Nyâlâ, *Sudan* 77 E1
Nyamandhlovu, *Zimbabwe* 83 F2
Nyambiti, *Tanzania* 82 C3
Nyamwaga, *Tanzania* 82 C3
Nyandekwa, *Tanzania* 82 C3
Nyanding →, *Sudan* 77 F3
Nyangana, *Namibia* 84 B3
Nyanguge, *Tanzania* 82 C3
Nyankpala, *Ghana* 79 D4
Nyanza, *Burundi* 82 C2
Nyanza, *Rwanda* 82 C2
Nyanza □, *Kenya* 82 C3
Nyarling →, *Canada* 100 A6
Nyasa, L. = Malawi, L., *Africa* 83 E3
Nyazura, *Zimbabwe* 83 F3
Nyazwidzi →, *Zimbabwe* 83 F3
Nyborg, *Denmark* 11 J4
Nybro, *Sweden* 9 H13
Nyda, *Russia* 44 C8
Nyeri, *Kenya* 82 C4
Nyerol, *Sudan* 77 F3
Nyhem, *Sweden* 10 B9
Nyiel, *Sudan* 77 F3
Nyinahin, *Ghana* 78 D4
Nyirbátor, *Hungary* 21 H12
Nyíregyháza, *Hungary* 21 H11
Nykarleby, *Finland* 8 E17
Nykøbing, *Sjælland, Denmark* 11 J5
Nykøbing, *Storstrøm, Denmark* 11 K5
Nykøbing, *Viborg, Denmark* 11 H2
Nyköping, *Sweden* 11 F11
Nykvarn, *Sweden* 10 E11
Nyland, *Sweden* 10 A11
Nylstroom, *S. Africa* 85 C4
Nymagee, *Australia* 91 E4
Nymburk, *Czech.* 20 E5
Nynäshamn, *Sweden* 10 F11
Nyngan, *Australia* 91 E4
Nyon, *Switz.* 22 D2
Nyong →, *Cameroon* 79 E6
Nyons, *France* 27 D9
Nyord, *Denmark* 11 J6
Nyou, *Burkina Faso* 79 C4
Nysa, *Poland* 20 E7
Nysa →, *Europe* 18 C10
Nyssa, *U.S.A.* 110 E5
Nysted, *Denmark* 11 K5
Nyunzu, *Zaïre* 82 D2
Nyurba, *Russia* 45 C12
Nzega, *Tanzania* 82 C3
Nzega □, *Tanzania* 82 C3
N'Zérékoré, *Guinea* 78 D3
Nzeto, *Angola* 80 F2
Nzilo, Chutes de, *Zaïre* 83 E2
Nzubuka, *Tanzania* 82 C3

O

Ō-Shima, *Nagasaki, Japan* 49 G4
Ō-Shima, *Shizuoka, Japan* 49 G9
Oacoma, *U.S.A.* 108 D5
Oahe, L., *U.S.A.* 108 C4
Oahe Dam, *U.S.A.* 108 C4
Oahu, *U.S.A.* 102 H16
Oak Creek, *U.S.A.* 110 F10
Oak Harbor, *U.S.A.* 112 B4
Oak Hill, *U.S.A.* 104 G5
Oak Park, *U.S.A.* 104 E2
Oak Ridge, *U.S.A.* 105 G3
Oak View, *U.S.A.* 113 L7
Oakan-Dake, *Japan* 48 C12
Oakbank, *Australia* 91 E3
Oakdale, *Calif., U.S.A.* 111 H3
Oakdale, *La., U.S.A.* 109 K8
Oakengates, *U.K.* 12 E5
Oakes, *U.S.A.* 108 B5
Oakesdale, *U.S.A.* 110 C5
Oakey, *Australia* 91 D5
Oakham, *U.K.* 12 E7
Oakhurst, *U.S.A.* 112 H7
Oakland, *Calif., U.S.A.* 111 H2
Oakland, *Oreg., U.S.A.* 110 E2
Oakland City, *U.S.A.* 104 F2
Oakley, *Idaho, U.S.A.* 110 E7
Oakley, *Kans., U.S.A.* 108 F4
Oakover →, *Australia* 88 D3
Oakridge, *U.S.A.* 110 E2
Oakville, *U.S.A.* 112 D3
Oamaru, *N.Z.* 87 L3
Oasis, *Calif., U.S.A.* 113 M10
Oasis, *Nev., U.S.A.* 112 H9
Oates Land, *Antarctica* 5 C11
Oatman, *U.S.A.* 113 K12
Oaxaca, *Mexico* 115 D5
Oaxaca □, *Mexico* 115 D5
Ob →, *Russia* 44 C7
Oba, *Canada* 98 C3
Obala, *Cameroon* 79 E7
Obama, *Japan* 49 G7
Oban, *U.K.* 14 E3
Obbia, *Somali Rep.* 68 F4
Obdam, *Neths.* 16 C5
Obed, *Canada* 100 C5
Ober-Aagau, *Switz.* 22 B5
Obera, *Argentina* 127 B4
Oberalppass, *Switz.* 23 C7
Oberalpstock, *Switz.* 23 C7
Oberammergau, *Germany* 19 H7
Oberdrauburg, *Austria* 21 J2
Oberengadin, *Switz.* 23 C9
Oberentfelden, *Switz.* 22 B6
Oberhausen, *Germany* 18 D2
Oberkirch, *Germany* 19 G4
Oberland, *Switz.* 22 C5
Oberlin, *Kans., U.S.A.* 108 F4
Oberlin, *La., U.S.A.* 109 K8
Oberlin, *Ohio, U.S.A.* 106 E2
Obernai, *France* 25 D14
Oberndorf, *Germany* 19 G4
Oberon, *Australia* 91 E4
Oberpfälzer Wald, *Germany* 19 F8
Obersiggenthal, *Switz.* 23 B6
Oberstdorf, *Germany* 19 H6
Oberwil, *Switz.* 22 A5
Obi, Kepulauan, *Indonesia* 57 E7
Obi Is. = Obi, Kepulauan, *Indonesia* 57 E7
Obiaruku, *Nigeria* 79 D6
Óbidos, *Brazil* 121 D6
Óbidos, *Portugal* 31 F1
Obihiro, *Japan* 48 C11
Obilatu, *Indonesia* 57 E7
Obilnoye, *Russia* 43 C11
Obing, *Germany* 19 H8
Öbisfelde, *Germany* 18 C6
Objat, *France* 26 C5
Obluchye, *Russia* 45 E14
Obninsk, *Russia* 41 D10
Obo, *C.A.R.* 82 A2
Obo, *Ethiopia* 77 G4
Oboa, Mt., *Uganda* 82 B3
Obock, *Djibouti* 77 E5
Oborniki, *Poland* 20 C6
Oboyan, *Russia* 41 F10
Obozerskaya, *Russia* 44 C5
Obrovac, *Croatia* 33 D12
Obruk, *Turkey* 66 D5
Observatory Inlet, *Canada* 100 B3
Obshchi Syrt, *Kazakhstan* 6 E16

Obskaya Guba, *Russia* ... 44 C8
Obuasi, *Ghana* ... 79 D4
Obubra, *Nigeria* ... 79 D6
Obwalden □, *Switz.* ... 22 C6
Obzor, *Bulgaria* ... 38 G10
Ocala, *U.S.A.* ... 105 L4
Ocamo →, *Venezuela* ... 121 C4
Ocampo, *Mexico* ... 114 B3
Ocaña, *Colombia* ... 120 B3
Ocaña, *Spain* ... 28 F1
Oconomowoc, *U.S.A.* ... 108 D10
Ocate, *U.S.A.* ... 109 G2
Occidental, Cordillera, *Colombia* ... 120 C3
Occidental, Cordillera, *Peru* ... 124 C3
Ocean City, *N.J., U.S.A.* ... 104 F8
Ocean City, *Wash., U.S.A.* 112 C2
Ocean I. = Banaba, *Kiribati* ... 92 H8
Ocean Park, *U.S.A.* ... 112 D2
Oceano, *U.S.A.* ... 113 K6
Oceanport, *U.S.A.* ... 107 F10
Oceanside, *U.S.A.* ... 113 M9
Ochagavia, *Spain* ... 28 C3
Ochamchire, *Georgia* ... 43 E9
Ochamps, *Belgium* ... 17 J6
Ochil Hills, *U.K.* ... 14 E5
Ochre River, *Canada* ... 101 C9
Ochsenfurt, *Germany* ... 19 F6
Ochsenhausen, *Germany* . 19 G5
Ocilla, *U.S.A.* ... 105 K4
Ocmulgee →, *U.S.A.* ... 105 K4
Ocna Sibiului, *Romania* .. 38 D7
Ocoña, *Peru* ... 124 D3
Ocoña →, *Peru* ... 124 D3
Oconee →, *U.S.A.* ... 105 K4
Oconto, *U.S.A.* ... 104 C2
Oconto Falls, *U.S.A.* ... 104 C1
Ocosingo, *Mexico* ... 115 D6
Ocotal, *Nic.* ... 116 D2
Ocotlán, *Mexico* ... 114 C4
Ocquier, *Belgium* ... 17 H6
Ocreza →, *Portugal* ... 31 F3
Octave, *U.S.A.* ... 111 J7
Octeville, *France* ... 24 C5
Ocumare del Tuy, *Venezuela* ... 120 A4
Ocuri, *Bolivia* ... 125 D4
Oda, *Ghana* ... 79 D4
Ōda, *Japan* ... 49 G6
Oda, J., *Sudan* ... 76 C4
Ódáðahraun, *Iceland* ... 8 D5
Ödåkra, *Sweden* ... 11 H6
Odate, *Japan* ... 48 D10
Odawara, *Japan* ... 49 G9
Odda, *Norway* ... 9 F9
Odder, *Denmark* ... 11 J4
Oddur, *Somali Rep.* ... 68 G3
Ödeborg, *Sweden* ... 11 F5
Odei →, *Canada* ... 101 B9
Odemira, *Portugal* ... 31 H2
Ödemiş, *Turkey* ... 66 D3
Odendaalsrus, *S. Africa* .. 84 D4
Odense, *Denmark* ... 11 J4
Odenwald, *Germany* ... 19 F5
Oder →, *Germany* ... 18 B10
Oderzo, *Italy* ... 33 C9
Odesa = Odessa, *Ukraine* 42 C4
Odessa, *Canada* ... 107 B8
Odessa, *Ukraine* ... 42 C4
Odessa, *Tex., U.S.A.* ... 109 K3
Odessa, *Wash., U.S.A.* ... 110 C4
Odiakwe, *Botswana* ... 84 C4
Odiel →, *Spain* ... 31 H4
Odienné, *Ivory C.* ... 78 D3
Odintsovo, *Russia* ... 41 D10
Odiongan, *Phil.* ... 55 E4
Odobeşti, *Romania* ... 38 D10
O'Donnell, *U.S.A.* ... 109 J4
Odoorn, *Neths.* ... 16 C9
Odorheiu Secuiesc, *Romania* ... 38 C8
Odoyevo, *Russia* ... 41 E10
Odra →, *Poland* ... 20 B4
Odra →, *Spain* ... 30 C6
Odžaci, *Serbia* ... 21 K9
Odzi, *Zimbabwe* ... 85 B5
Oedelem, *Belgium* ... 17 F2
Oegstgeest, *Neths.* ... 16 D4
Oeiras, *Brazil* ... 122 C3
Oeiras, *Portugal* ... 31 G1
Oelrichs, *U.S.A.* ... 108 D3
Oelsnitz, *Germany* ... 18 E8
Oelwein, *U.S.A.* ... 108 D9
Oenpelli, *Australia* ... 88 B5
Of, *Turkey* ... 67 C9
Ofanto →, *Italy* ... 35 A9
Offa, *Nigeria* ... 79 D5
Offaly □, *Ireland* ... 15 C4
Offenbach, *Germany* ... 19 E4
Offenburg, *Germany* ... 19 G3
Offerdal, *Sweden* ... 10 A8
Offida, *Italy* ... 33 F10
Offranville, *France* ... 24 C8
Ofidhousa, *Greece* ... 39 N9
Ofotfjorden, *Norway* ... 8 B14
Ōfunato, *Japan* ... 48 E10
Oga, *Japan* ... 48 E9
Oga-Hantō, *Japan* ... 48 E9
Ogahalla, *Canada* ... 98 B2
Ōgaki, *Japan* ... 49 G8
Ogallala, *U.S.A.* ... 108 E4
Ogasawara Gunto, *Pac. Oc.* ... 92 E6
Ogbomosho, *Nigeria* ... 79 D5
Ogden, *Iowa, U.S.A.* ... 108 D8
Ogden, *Utah, U.S.A.* ... 110 F7
Ogdensburg, *U.S.A.* ... 107 B9
Ogeechee →, *U.S.A.* ... 105 K5
Ogilby, *U.S.A.* ... 113 N12
Oglio →, *Italy* ... 32 C7
Ogmore, *Australia* ... 90 C4
Ognon →, *France* ... 25 E12
Ogoja, *Nigeria* ... 79 D6
Ogoki →, *Canada* ... 98 B2
Ogoki L., *Canada* ... 98 B2
Ogoki Res., *Canada* ... 98 B2
Ogooué →, *Gabon* ... 80 E1
Ogosta →, *Bulgaria* ... 38 F6
Ogowe = Ogooué →, *Gabon* ... 80 E1
Ogr = Sharafa, *Sudan* ... 77 E2
Ogrein, *Sudan* ... 76 D3
Ogulin, *Croatia* ... 33 C12
Ogun □, *Nigeria* ... 79 D5
Oguta, *Nigeria* ... 79 D6
Ogwashi-Uku, *Nigeria* ... 79 D6
Ogwe, *Nigeria* ... 79 E6
Ohai, *N.Z.* ... 87 L2
Ohakune, *N.Z.* ... 87 H5
Ohanet, *Algeria* ... 75 C6
Ohata, *Japan* ... 48 D10
Ohau, L., *N.Z.* ... 87 L2
Ohey, *Belgium* ... 17 H6
Ohio □, *U.S.A.* ... 104 E3
Ohio →, *U.S.A.* ... 104 G1
Ohre →, *Czech.* ... 20 E4
Ohre →, *Germany* ... 18 C7
Ohrid, *Macedonia* ... 39 H3
Ohridsko, Jezero, *Macedonia* ... 39 H3
Ohrigstad, *S. Africa* ... 85 C5
Öhringen, *Germany* ... 19 F5
Oiapoque →, *Brazil* ... 121 C7
Oikou, *China* ... 51 E9
Oil City, *U.S.A.* ... 106 E5
Oildale, *U.S.A.* ... 113 K7
Oirschot, *Neths.* ... 17 E6
Oise □, *France* ... 25 C9
Oise →, *France* ... 25 D9
Oisterwijk, *Neths.* ... 17 E6
Ōita, *Japan* ... 49 H5
Ōita □, *Japan* ... 49 H5
Oiticica, *Brazil* ... 122 C3
Ojai, *U.S.A.* ... 113 L7
Ojinaga, *Mexico* ... 114 B4
Ojiya, *Japan* ... 49 F9
Ojos del Salado, Cerro, *Argentina* ... 126 B2
Oka →, *Russia* ... 41 C13
Okaba, *Indonesia* ... 57 F9
Okahandja, *Namibia* ... 84 C2
Okahukura, *N.Z.* ... 87 H5
Okanagan L., *Canada* ... 100 C5
Okandja, *Gabon* ... 80 E2
Okanogan, *U.S.A.* ... 110 B4
Okanogan →, *U.S.A.* ... 110 B4
Okaputa, *Namibia* ... 84 C2
Okara, *Pakistan* ... 62 D5
Okarito, *N.Z.* ... 87 K3
Okaukuejo, *Namibia* ... 84 B2
Okavango Swamps, *Botswana* ... 84 B3
Okaya, *Japan* ... 49 F9
Okayama, *Japan* ... 49 G6
Okayama □, *Japan* ... 49 G6
Okazaki, *Japan* ... 49 G8
Oke-Iho, *Nigeria* ... 79 D5
Okeechobee, *U.S.A.* ... 105 M5
Okeechobee, L., *U.S.A.* .. 105 M5
Okefenokee Swamp, *U.S.A.* ... 105 K4
Okehampton, *U.K.* ... 13 G3
Okene, *Nigeria* ... 79 D6
Oker →, *Germany* ... 18 C6
Okha, *Russia* ... 45 D15
Ókhi Óros, *Greece* ... 39 L7
Okhotsk, *Russia* ... 45 D15
Okhotsk, Sea of, *Asia* ... 45 D15
Okhotskiy Perevoz, *Russia* 45 C14
Okhotsko Kolymskoye, *Russia* ... 45 C16
Oki-Shotō, *Japan* ... 49 F6
Okiep, *S. Africa* ... 84 D2
Okigwi, *Nigeria* ... 79 D6
Okija, *Nigeria* ... 79 D6
Okinawa □, *Japan* ... 49 L3
Okinawa-Guntō, *Japan* ... 49 L3
Okinawa-Jima, *Japan* ... 49 L4
Okino-erabu-Shima, *Japan* 49 L4
Okitipupa, *Nigeria* ... 79 D5
Oklahoma □, *U.S.A.* ... 109 H6
Oklahoma City, *U.S.A.* ... 109 H6
Okmulgee, *U.S.A.* ... 109 H7
Oknitsa, *Ukraine* ... 42 B2
Okolo, *Uganda* ... 82 B3
Okolona, *U.S.A.* ... 109 H10
Okrika, *Nigeria* ... 79 E6
Oktabrsk, *Kazakhstan* ... 44 E6
Oktyabrsk, *Russia* ... 41 E16
Oktyabrskiy, *Belorussia* .. 40 E6
Oktyabrskoy Revolyutsii, Os., *Russia* ... 45 B10
Oktyabrskoye = Zhovtnevoye, *Ukraine* .. 42 C5
Oktyabrskoye, *Russia* ... 44 C7
Okulovka, *Russia* ... 40 B8
Okuru, *N.Z.* ... 87 K2
Okushiri-Tō, *Japan* ... 48 C9
Okuta, *Nigeria* ... 79 D5
Okwa →, *Botswana* ... 84 C3
Ola, *U.S.A.* ... 109 H8
Ólafsfjörður, *Iceland* ... 8 C4
Ólafsvík, *Iceland* ... 8 D2
Olancha, *U.S.A.* ... 113 J8
Olancha Pk., *U.S.A.* ... 113 J8
Olanchito, *Honduras* ... 116 C2
Öland, *Sweden* ... 9 H14
Olargues, *France* ... 26 E6
Olary, *Australia* ... 91 E3
Olascoaga, *Argentina* ... 126 D3
Olathe, *U.S.A.* ... 108 F7
Olavarría, *Argentina* ... 126 D3
Oława, *Poland* ... 20 E7
Ólbia, *Italy* ... 34 B2
Ólbia, G. di, *Italy* ... 34 B2
Old Bahama Chan. = Bahama, Canal Viejo de, *W. Indies* ... 116 B4
Old Baldy Pk. = San Antonio, Mt., *U.S.A.* .. 113 L9
Old Castile = Castilla y Leon □, *Spain* ... 30 D6
Old Castle, *Ireland* ... 15 C4
Old Cork, *Australia* ... 90 C3
Old Crow, *Canada* ... 96 B6
Old Dale, *U.S.A.* ... 113 L11
Old Dongola, *Sudan* ... 76 D3
Old Fletton, *U.K.* ... 13 E7
Old Forge, *N.Y., U.S.A.* ... 107 C10
Old Forge, *Pa., U.S.A.* ... 107 E9
Old Fort →, *Canada* ... 101 B6
Old Shinyanga, *Tanzania* . 82 C3
Old Speck Mt., *U.S.A.* ... 107 B14
Old Town, *U.S.A.* ... 99 D6
Old Wives L., *Canada* ... 101 C7
Oldbury, *U.K.* ... 13 F5
Oldeani, *Tanzania* ... 82 C4
Oldenburg, *Niedersachsen, Germany* ... 18 B4
Oldenburg, *Schleswig-Holstein, Germany* ... 18 A6
Oldenzaal, *Neths.* ... 16 D9
Oldham, *U.K.* ... 12 D5
Oldman →, *Canada* ... 100 D6
Olds, *Canada* ... 100 C6
Olean, *U.S.A.* ... 106 D6
Olėggio, *Italy* ... 32 C5
Oleiros, *Portugal* ... 30 F3
Olekma →, *Russia* ... 45 C13
Olekminsk, *Russia* ... 45 C13
Olema, *U.S.A.* ... 112 G4
Olen, *Belgium* ... 17 F5
Olenek, *Russia* ... 45 C12
Olenek →, *Russia* ... 45 B13
Olenino, *Russia* ... 40 C8
Oléron, I. d', *France* ... 26 C2
Oleśnica, *Poland* ... 20 D7
Olesno, *Poland* ... 20 E8
Olevsk, *Ukraine* ... 40 F5
Olga, *Russia* ... 45 E14
Olga, L., *Canada* ... 98 C4
Olga, Mt., *Australia* ... 89 E5
Ølgod, *Denmark* ... 11 J2
Olhão, *Portugal* ... 31 H3
Olib, *Croatia* ... 33 D11
Oliena, *Italy* ... 34 B2
Oliete, *Spain* ... 28 D4
Olifants →, *Africa* ... 85 C5
Olifantshoek, *S. Africa* ... 84 D3
Ólimbos, *Greece* ... 39 P10
Ólimbos, Óros, *Greece* ... 39 J5
Olímpia, *Brazil* ... 127 A6
Olinda, *Brazil* ... 122 C5
Olindiná, *Brazil* ... 122 D4
Olite, *Spain* ... 28 C3
Oliva, *Argentina* ... 126 C3
Oliva, *Spain* ... 29 G4
Oliva, Punta del, *Spain* ... 30 B5
Oliva de la Frontera, *Spain* 31 G4
Olivares, *Spain* ... 28 F2
Olivehurst, *U.S.A.* ... 112 F5
Oliveira, *Brazil* ... 123 F3
Oliveira de Azemeis, *Portugal* ... 30 E2
Oliveira dos Brejinhos, *Brazil* ... 123 D3
Olivenza, *Spain* ... 31 G3
Oliver, *Canada* ... 100 D5
Oliver L., *Canada* ... 101 B8
Olivone, *Switz.* ... 23 C7
Olkhovka, *Russia* ... 43 B11
Olkusz, *Poland* ... 20 E9
Ollagüe, *Chile* ... 126 A2
Olloy, *Belgium* ... 17 H5
Olmedo, *Spain* ... 30 D6
Olmos, *Peru* ... 124 B2
Olney, *Ill., U.S.A.* ... 104 F1
Olney, *Tex., U.S.A.* ... 109 J5
Oloma, *Cameroon* ... 79 E7
Olomane →, *Canada* ... 99 B7
Olomouc, *Czech.* ... 20 F7
Olongapo, *Phil.* ... 55 D4
Oloron, Gave d' →, *France* ... 26 E2
Oloron-Ste.-Marie, *France* 26 E3
Olot, *Spain* ... 28 C7
Olovo, *Bos.-H.* ... 21 L8
Olovyannaya, *Russia* ... 45 D12
Oloy →, *Russia* ... 45 C16
Olpe, *Germany* ... 18 D3
Olshanka, *Ukraine* ... 42 B4
Olshany, *Ukraine* ... 42 A6
Olst, *Neths.* ... 16 D8
Olsztyn, *Poland* ... 20 B10
Olt →, *Romania* ... 38 F7
Olten, *Switz.* ... 22 B5
Olteniţa, *Romania* ... 38 E9
Olton, *U.S.A.* ... 109 H3
Oltu, *Turkey* ... 67 C9
Olur, *Turkey* ... 67 C10
Olutanga, *Phil.* ... 55 H5
Olvega, *Spain* ... 28 D3
Olvera, *Spain* ... 31 J5
Olymbos, *Cyprus* ... 37 D12
Olympia, *Greece* ... 39 M4
Olympia, *U.S.A.* ... 112 D4
Olympic Mts., *U.S.A.* ... 112 C3
Olympic Nat. Park, *U.S.A.* 112 C3
Olympus, *Cyprus* ... 37 E11
Olympus, Mt. = Ólimbos, Óros, *Greece* ... 39 J5
Olympus, Mt., *U.S.A.* ... 112 C3
Olyphant, *U.S.A.* ... 107 E9
Om →, *Russia* ... 44 D8
Om Hajer, *Eritrea* ... 77 E4
Om Koi, *Thailand* ... 58 D2
Ōma, *Japan* ... 48 D10
Ōmachi, *Japan* ... 49 F8
Omae-Zaki, *Japan* ... 49 G9
Ōmagari, *Japan* ... 48 E10
Omagh, *U.K.* ... 15 B4
Omagh □, *U.K.* ... 15 B4
Omaha, *U.S.A.* ... 108 E7
Omak, *U.S.A.* ... 110 B4
Omalos, *Greece* ... 37 D5
Oman ■, *Asia* ... 68 C6
Oman, G. of, *Asia* ... 65 E8
Omaruru, *Namibia* ... 84 C2
Omaruru →, *Namibia* ... 84 C1
Omate, *Peru* ... 124 D3
Ombai, Selat, *Indonesia* .. 57 F6
Omboué, *Gabon* ... 80 E1
Ombrone →, *Italy* ... 32 F8
Omdurmân, *Sudan* ... 77 D3
Omegna, *Italy* ... 32 C5
Omeonga, *Zaïre* ... 82 C1
Ometepe, I. de, *Nic.* ... 116 D2
Ometepec, *Mexico* ... 115 D5
Ominato, *Japan* ... 48 D10
Omineca →, *Canada* ... 100 B4
Omiš, *Croatia* ... 33 E13
Omišalj, *Croatia* ... 33 C11
Omitara, *Namibia* ... 84 C2
Ōmiya, *Japan* ... 49 G9
Omme Å →, *Denmark* ... 11 J2
Ommen, *Neths.* ... 16 C8
Ömnögovĭ □, *Mongolia* .. 50 C3
Omo →, *Ethiopia* ... 77 F4
Omodhos, *Cyprus* ... 37 E11
Omolon →, *Russia* ... 45 C16
Omono-Gawa →, *Japan* . 48 E10
Omsk, *Russia* ... 44 D8
Omsukchan, *Russia* ... 45 C16
Ōmu, *Japan* ... 48 B11
Omul, Vf., *Romania* ... 38 D8
Ōmura, *Japan* ... 49 H4
Omuramba Omatako →, *Namibia* ... 81 H4
Omurtag, *Bulgaria* ... 38 F9
Ōmuta, *Japan* ... 49 H5
Omutninsk, *Russia* ... 41 B18
On, *Belgium* ... 17 H6
Oña, *Spain* ... 28 C1
Onaga, *U.S.A.* ... 108 F6
Onalaska, *U.S.A.* ... 108 D9
Onamia, *U.S.A.* ... 108 B8
Onancock, *U.S.A.* ... 104 G8
Onang, *Indonesia* ... 57 E5
Onaping L., *Canada* ... 98 C3
Oñate, *Spain* ... 28 B2
Onavas, *Mexico* ... 114 B3
Onawa, *U.S.A.* ... 108 D6
Onaway, *U.S.A.* ... 104 C3
Oncócua, *Angola* ... 84 B1
Onda, *Spain* ... 28 F4
Ondaejin, *N. Korea* ... 51 D15
Ondangua, *Namibia* ... 84 B2
Ondárroa, *Spain* ... 28 B2
Ondas →, *Brazil* ... 123 D3
Ondava →, *Slovak Rep.* . 20 G11
Onderdijk, *Neths.* ... 16 C6
Ondjiva, *Angola* ... 84 B2
Ondo, *Nigeria* ... 79 D5
Ondo □, *Nigeria* ... 79 D6
Öndörhaan, *Mongolia* ... 54 B6
Öndörshil, *Mongolia* ... 50 B5
Öndverðarnes, *Iceland* ... 8 D1
Onega, *Russia* ... 44 C4
Onega →, *Russia* ... 6 C13
Onega, G. of = Onezhskaya Guba, *Russia* ... 44 C4
Onega, L. = Onezhskoye Ozero, *Russia* ... 44 C4
Onehunga, *N.Z.* ... 87 G5
Oneida, *U.S.A.* ... 107 C9
Oneida L., *U.S.A.* ... 107 C9
O'Neill, *U.S.A.* ... 108 D5
Onekotan, Ostrov, *Russia* 45 E16
Onema, *Zaïre* ... 82 C1
Oneonta, *Ala., U.S.A.* ... 105 J2
Oneonta, *N.Y., U.S.A.* ... 107 D9
Onezhskaya Guba, *Russia* 44 C4
Onezhskoye Ozero, *Russia* 44 C4
Ongarue, *N.Z.* ... 87 H5
Ongerup, *Australia* ... 89 F2
Ongjin, *N. Korea* ... 51 F13
Ongkharak, *Thailand* ... 58 E3
Ongniud Qi, *China* ... 51 C10
Ongoka, *Zaïre* ... 82 C2
Ongole, *India* ... 60 M12
Ongon, *Mongolia* ... 50 B7
Onguren, *Russia* ... 45 D11
Onhaye, *Belgium* ... 17 H5
Oni, *Georgia* ... 43 E10
Onida, *U.S.A.* ... 108 C4
Onilahy →, *Madag.* ... 85 C7
Onitsha, *Nigeria* ... 79 D6
Onoda, *Japan* ... 49 G5
Onpyŏng-ni, *S. Korea* ... 51 H14
Ons, Is. d', *Spain* ... 30 C2
Onsala, *Sweden* ... 11 G6
Onslow, *Australia* ... 88 D2
Onslow B., *U.S.A.* ... 105 H7
Onstwedde, *Neths.* ... 16 B10
Ontake-San, *Japan* ... 49 G8
Ontaneda, *Spain* ... 30 B7
Ontario, *Calif., U.S.A.* ... 113 L9
Ontario, *Oreg., U.S.A.* ... 110 D5
Ontario □, *Canada* ... 98 B2
Ontario, L., *U.S.A.* ... 98 D4
Onteniente, *Spain* ... 29 G4
Ontonagon, *U.S.A.* ... 108 B10
Ontur, *Spain* ... 29 G3
Onyx, *U.S.A.* ... 113 K8
Oodnadatta, *Australia* ... 91 D2
Ooldea, *Australia* ... 89 F5
Ooltgensplaat, *Neths.* ... 17 E4
Oombulgurri, *Australia* ... 88 C4
Oona River, *Canada* ... 100 C2
Oordegem, *Belgium* ... 17 G3
Oorindi, *Australia* ... 90 C3
Oost-Vlaanderen □, *Belgium* ... 17 F3
Oost-Vlieland, *Neths.* ... 16 B6
Oostakker, *Belgium* ... 17 F3
Oostburg, *Neths.* ... 17 F3
Oostduinkerke, *Belgium* .. 17 F1
Oostelijk-Flevoland, *Neths.* 16 C7
Oostende, *Belgium* ... 17 F1
Oosterbeek, *Neths.* ... 16 E7
Oosterdijk, *Neths.* ... 16 C6
Oosterend, *Friesland, Neths.* ... 16 B6
Oosterend, *Noord-Holland, Neths.* ... 16 B5
Oosterhout, *Noord-Brabant, Neths.* . 17 E7
Oosterhout, *Noord-Brabant, Neths.* . 17 E5
Oosterschelde, *Neths.* ... 17 E4
Oosterwolde, *Neths.* ... 16 B8
Oosterzele, *Belgium* ... 17 G3
Oostkamp, *Belgium* ... 17 F2
Oostmalle, *Belgium* ... 17 F5
Oostrozebekke, *Belgium* ... 17 G2
Oostvleteven, *Belgium* ... 17 G1
Oostvoorne, *Neths.* ... 16 E4
Oostzaan, *Neths.* ... 16 D5
Ootacamund, *India* ... 60 P10
Ootmarsum, *Neths.* ... 16 D9
Ootsa L., *Canada* ... 100 C3
Opala, *Russia* ... 45 D16
Opala, *Zaïre* ... 82 C1
Opanake, *Sri Lanka* ... 60 R12
Opasatika, *Canada* ... 98 C3
Opasquia, *Canada* ... 101 C10
Opatija, *Croatia* ... 33 C11
Opava, *Czech.* ... 20 F7
Opeinde, *Neths.* ... 16 B8
Opelousas, *U.S.A.* ... 109 K8
Opémisca, L., *Canada* ... 98 C5
Opglabbeek, *Belgium* ... 17 F7
Opheim, *U.S.A.* ... 110 B10
Ophthalmia Ra., *Australia* 88 D2
Opi, *Nigeria* ... 79 D6
Opinaca →, *Canada* ... 98 B4
Opinaca L., *Canada* ... 98 B4
Opiskotish, L., *Canada* ... 99 B6
Oploo, *Neths.* ... 17 E7
Opmeer, *Neths.* ... 16 C5
Opobo, *Nigeria* ... 79 E6
Opochka, *Russia* ... 40 C6
Opoczno, *Poland* ... 20 D10
Opol, *Phil.* ... 55 G6
Opole, *Poland* ... 20 E7
Oporto = Porto, *Portugal* 30 D2
Opotiki, *N.Z.* ... 87 H6
Opp, *U.S.A.* ... 105 K2
Oppenheim, *Germany* ... 19 F4
Opperdoes, *Neths.* ... 16 C6
Oppido Mamertina, *Italy* . 35 D8
Oppland fylke □, *Norway* 10 C3
Oppstad, *Norway* ... 10 D5
Oprtalj, *Croatia* ... 33 C10
Opua, *N.Z.* ... 87 F5
Opunake, *N.Z.* ... 87 H4
Opuzen, *Croatia* ... 21 M7
Ora, *Cyprus* ... 37 E12
Ora, *Italy* ... 33 B8
Ora Banda, *Australia* ... 89 F3
Oracle, *U.S.A.* ... 111 K8
Oradea, *Romania* ... 38 B4
Öræfajökull, *Iceland* ... 8 D5
Orahovac, *Serbia* ... 21 N10
Orai, *India* ... 63 G8
Oraison, *France* ... 27 E9
Oral = Ural →, *Kazakhstan* ... 43 C14
Oral = Uralsk, *Kazakhstan* 44 D6
Oran, *Algeria* ... 75 A4
Oran, *Argentina* ... 126 A3

Orange = Oranje →, *S. Africa* 84 D2
Orange, *Australia* 91 E4
Orange, *France* 27 D8
Orange, *Calif., U.S.A.* 113 M9
Orange, *Mass., U.S.A.* 107 D12
Orange, *Tex., U.S.A.* 109 K8
Orange, *Va., U.S.A.* 104 F6
Orange, C., *Brazil* 121 C7
Orange Cove, *U.S.A.* 112 J7
Orange Free State □, *S. Africa* 84 D4
Orange Grove, *U.S.A.* 109 M6
Orange Walk, *Belize* 115 D7
Orangeburg, *U.S.A.* 105 J5
Orangeville, *Canada* 98 D3
Orani, *Phil.* 55 D4
Oranienburg, *Germany* 18 C9
Oranje →, *S. Africa* 84 D2
Oranje Vrystaat = Orange Free State □, *S. Africa* 84 D4
Oranjemund, *Namibia* 84 D2
Oranjerivier, *S. Africa* 84 D3
Oras, *Phil.* 55 E6
Orăştie, *Romania* 38 D6
Oraşul Stalin = Braşov, *Romania* 38 D8
Orava →, *Slovakia* 20 F9
Oravita, *Romania* 38 D4
Orb →, *France* 26 E7
Orba →, *Italy* 32 D5
Ørbæk, *Denmark* 11 J4
Orbe, *Switz.* 22 C3
Orbec, *France* 24 C7
Orbetello, *Italy* 33 F8
Órbigo →, *Spain* 30 C5
Orbost, *Australia* 91 F4
Orce, *Spain* 29 H2
Orce →, *Spain* 29 H2
Orchies, *France* 25 B10
Orchila, I., *Venezuela* 120 A4
Orco →, *Italy* 32 C4
Orcopampa, *Peru* 124 D3
Orcutt, *U.S.A.* 113 L6
Ord →, *Australia* 88 C4
Ord, Mt., *Australia* 88 C4
Ordenes, *Spain* 30 B2
Orderville, *U.S.A.* 111 H7
Ording, *Germany* 18 A4
Ordos = Mu Us Shamo, *Nei Mongol Zizhiqu, China* 50 E5
Ordos = Mu Us Shamo, *Nei Mongol Zizhiqu, China* 50 E5
Ordu, *Turkey* 67 C7
Ordu □, *Turkey* 67 C7
Orduña, *Álava, Spain* 28 C7
Orduña, *Granada, Spain* 29 H1
Ordway, *U.S.A.* 108 F3
Ordzhonikidze = Vladikavkaz, *Russia* 43 E11
Ordzhonikidze, *Ukraine* 42 C6
Ore, *Zaïre* 82 B2
Ore Mts. = Erzgebirge, *Germany* 18 E9
Orealla, *Guyana* 121 B6
Orebić, *Croatia* 21 M7
Örebro, *Sweden* 9 G13
Örebro län □, *Sweden* 9 G13
Oregon, *U.S.A.* 108 D10
Oregon □, *U.S.A.* 110 E3
Oregon City, *U.S.A.* 112 E4
Orekhov, *Ukraine* 42 C6
Orekhovo-Zuyevo, *Russia* 41 D11
Orel, *Russia* 41 E10
Orel →, *Ukraine* 42 B6
Orellana, Canal de, *Spain* 31 F5
Orellana, Pantano de, *Spain* 31 F5
Orellana la Vieja, *Spain* 31 F5
Orem, *U.S.A.* 110 F8
Ören, *Turkey* 66 E2
Orenburg, *Russia* 44 D6
Orense, *Spain* 30 C3
Orense □, *Spain* 30 C3
Orepuki, *N.Z.* 87 M1
Orestiás, *Greece* 39 H9
Øresund, *Europe* 11 J6
Orford Ness, *U.K.* 13 E9
Orgaña, *Spain* 28 C6
Organos, Pta. de los, *Canary Is.* 36 F2
Orgaz, *Spain* 31 F7
Orgeyev, *Moldavia* 42 C3
Orgon, *France* 27 E9
Orhaneli, *Turkey* 66 D3
Orhangazi, *Turkey* 66 C3
Orhon Gol →, *Mongolia* 54 A5
Ória, *Italy* 35 B10
Orient, *Australia* 91 D3
Oriental, Cordillera, *Bolivia* 125 D4
Oriental, Cordillera, *Colombia* 120 B3
Oriente, *Argentina* 126 D3
Origny-Ste.-Benoîte, *France* 25 C10
Orihuela, *Spain* 29 G4
Orihuela del Tremedal, *Spain* 28 E3
Oriku, *Albania* 39 J2
Orinduik, *Guyana* 121 C5
Orinoco →, *Venezuela* 121 B5
Orissa □, *India* 61 K14
Oristano, *Italy* 34 C1
Oristano, G. di, *Italy* 34 C1
Orituco →, *Venezuela* 120 B4
Orizaba, *Mexico* 115 D5
Orizona, *Brazil* 123 E2
Orjen, *Bos.-H.* 21 N8
Orjiva, *Spain* 29 J1
Orkanger, *Norway* 10 A3
Örkelljunga, *Sweden* 11 H7
Örkény, *Hungary* 21 H9
Orkla →, *Norway* 10 A3
Orkney, *S. Africa* 84 D4
Orkney □, *U.K.* 14 C6
Orkney Is., *U.K.* 14 C6
Orland, *U.S.A.* 112 F4
Orlando, *U.S.A.* 105 L5
Orlando, C. d', *Italy* 35 D7
Orléanais, *France* 25 E9
Orléans, *France* 25 E8
Orleans, *U.S.A.* 107 B12
Orléans, I. d', *Canada* 99 C5
Orlice →, *Czech.* 20 E6
Orlov, *Slovakia* 20 F10
Orlov Gay, *Russia* 41 F16
Ormara, *Pakistan* 60 G4
Ormea, *Italy* 32 D4
Ormília, *Greece* 39 J6
Ormoc, *Phil.* 55 F6
Ormond, *N.Z.* 87 H6
Ormond Beach, *U.S.A.* 105 L5
Ormož, *Slovenia* 33 B13
Ormstown, *Canada* 107 A11
Ornans, *France* 25 E13
Orne □, *France* 24 D7
Orne →, *France* 24 C6
Ørnhøj, *Denmark* 11 H2
Ornö, *Sweden* 10 E12
Örnsköldsvik, *Sweden* 10 A12
Oro, *N. Korea* 51 D14
Oro →, *Mexico* 114 B3
Oro Grande, *U.S.A.* 113 L9
Orobie, Alpi, *Italy* 32 B6
Orocué, *Colombia* 120 C3
Orodo, *Nigeria* 79 D6
Orogrande, *U.S.A.* 111 K10
Orol, *Spain* 30 B3
Oromocto, *Canada* 99 C6
Oron, *Nigeria* 79 E6
Oron, *Switz.* 22 C3
Orono, *Canada* 106 C6
Oropesa, *Spain* 30 F5
Oroquieta, *Phil.* 55 G5
Orós, *Brazil* 122 C4
Orosei, G. di, *Italy* 34 B2
Orosháza, *Hungary* 21 J10
Orotukan, *Russia* 45 C16
Oroville, *Calif., U.S.A.* 112 F5
Oroville, *Wash., U.S.A.* 110 B4
Oroville, L., *U.S.A.* 112 F5
Orroroo, *Australia* 91 E2
Orrville, *U.S.A.* 106 F3
Orsara di Púglia, *Italy* 35 A8
Orsha, *Belorussia* 40 D7
Orsières, *Switz.* 22 D4
Orsk, *Russia* 44 D6
Ørslev, *Denmark* 11 J5
Orsogna, *Italy* 33 F11
Orşova, *Romania* 38 E5
Ørsted, *Denmark* 11 H4
Orta, L. d', *Italy* 32 C5
Orta Nova, *Italy* 35 A8
Ortaca, *Turkey* 66 E3
Ortaköy, *Çorum, Turkey* 66 C6
Ortaköy, *Niğde, Turkey* 66 D6
Orte, *Italy* 33 F9
Ortegal, C., *Spain* 30 B3
Orteguaza →, *Colombia* 120 C2
Orthez, *France* 26 E3
Ortho, *Belgium* 17 H7
Ortigueira, *Spain* 30 B3
Orting, *U.S.A.* 112 C4
Ortles, *Italy* 32 B7
Ortón →, *Bolivia* 124 C4
Ortona, *Italy* 33 F11
Orūmīyeh, *Iran* 64 B5
Orūmīyeh, Daryācheh-ye, *Iran* 64 B5
Orune, *Italy* 34 B2
Oruro, *Bolivia* 124 D4
Oruro□, *Bolivia* 124 D4
Orust, *Sweden* 11 F5
Orūzgān □, *Afghan.* 60 C5
Orvault, *France* 24 E5
Orvieto, *Italy* 33 F9
Orwell, *U.S.A.* 106 E4
Orwell →, *U.K.* 13 E9
Oryakhovo, *Bulgaria* 38 F6
Orzinuovi, *Italy* 32 C6
Orzysz, *Poland* 20 B11
Osa, Pen. de, *Costa Rica* 116 E3
Osage, *Iowa, U.S.A.* 108 D8
Osage, *Wyo., U.S.A.* 108 D2
Osage →, *U.S.A.* 108 F9
Osage City, *U.S.A.* 108 F7
Ōsaka, *Japan* 49 G7
Osan, *S. Korea* 51 F14
Osawatomie, *U.S.A.* 108 F7
Osborne, *U.S.A.* 108 F5
Osceola, *Ark., U.S.A.* 109 H10
Osceola, *Iowa, U.S.A.* 108 E8
Oschatz, *Germany* 18 D9
Oschersleben, *Germany* 18 C7
Óschiri, *Italy* 34 B2
Oscoda, *U.S.A.* 106 B1
Ösel = Saaremaa, *Estonia* 40 B3
Osëry, *Russia* 41 D11
Osh, *Kirghizia* 44 E8
Oshawa, *Canada* 98 D4
Oshkosh, *Nebr., U.S.A.* 108 E3
Oshkosh, *Wis., U.S.A.* 108 C10
Oshmyany, *Belorussia* 40 D4
Oshnovīyeh, *Iran* 64 B5
Oshogbo, *Nigeria* 79 D5
Oshtorīnān, *Iran* 65 C6
Oshwe, *Zaïre* 80 E3
Osijek, *Croatia* 21 K8
Ósilo, *Italy* 34 B1
Osimo, *Italy* 33 E10
Osintorf, *Belorussia* 40 D7
Osipenko = Berdyansk, *Ukraine* 42 C7
Osipovichi, *Belorussia* 40 E6
Osizweni, *S. Africa* 85 D5
Oskaloosa, *U.S.A.* 108 E8
Oskarshamn, *Sweden* 9 H14
Oskélanéo, *Canada* 98 C4
Öskemen = Ust-Kamenogorsk, *Kazakhstan* 44 E9
Oskol →, *Ukraine* 41 G10
Oslo, *Norway* 10 E4
Oslob, *Phil.* 55 G5
Oslofjorden, *Norway* 10 E4
Osmanabad, *India* 60 K10
Osmancık, *Turkey* 42 F6
Osmaniye, *Turkey* 66 E7
Ösmo, *Sweden* 10 F11
Osnabrück, *Germany* 18 C4
Osor, *Italy* 33 D11
Osorio, *Brazil* 127 B5
Osorno, *Chile* 128 B2
Osorno, *Spain* 30 C6
Osorno □, *Chile* 128 B2
Osorno, Vol., *Chile* 128 B2
Osoyoos, *Canada* 100 D5
Ospika →, *Canada* 100 B4
Osprey Reef, *Australia* 90 A4
Oss, *Neths.* 16 E7
Ossa, Mt., *Australia* 90 G4
Óssa, Oros, *Greece* 39 K5
Ossa de Montiel, *Spain* 29 G2
Ossabaw I., *U.S.A.* 105 K5
Osse →, *France* 26 D4
Ossendrecht, *Neths.* 17 F4
Ossining, *U.S.A.* 107 E11
Ossipee, *U.S.A.* 107 C13
Ossokmanuan L., *Canada* 99 B7
Ossora, *Russia* 45 D17
Ostashkov, *Russia* 40 C8
Oste →, *Germany* 18 B5
Ostend = Oostende, *Belgium* 17 F1
Oster, *Ukraine* 40 F7
Osterburg, *Germany* 18 C7
Osterburken, *Germany* 19 F5
Österdalälven →, *Sweden* 9 F12
Östergötlands län □, *Sweden* 11 F9
Osterholz-Scharmbeck, *Germany* 18 B4
Østerild, *Denmark* 11 G2
Ostermundigen, *Switz.* 22 C4
Östersund, *Sweden* 10 A8
Østfold fylke □, *Norway* 10 E5
Ostfriesische Inseln, *Germany* 18 B3
Ostfriesland, *Germany* 18 B3
Óstia, Lido di, *Italy* 34 A5
Ostiglía, *Italy* 33 C8
Ostra, *Italy* 33 E10
Ostrava, *Czech.* 20 F8
Ostróda, *Poland* 20 B9
Ostrog, *Ukraine* 40 F5
Ostrogozhsk, *Russia* 41 F11
Ostrogróg Sźamotuły, *Poland* 20 C6
Ostrołęka, *Poland* 20 B11
Ostrov, *Bulgaria* 38 F7
Ostrov, *Romania* 38 E10
Ostrov, *Russia* 40 C6
Ostrów Mazowiecka, *Poland* 20 C11
Ostrów Wielkopolski, *Poland* 20 D7
Ostrowiec-Świętokrzyski, *Poland* 20 E11
Ostrzeszów, *Poland* 20 D7
Ostseebad-Kühlungsborn, *Germany* 18 A7
Osttirol □, *Austria* 19 J8
Ostuni, *Italy* 35 B10
Osum →, *Bulgaria* 38 F7
Osumi →, *Albania* 39 J3
Ōsumi-Kaikyō, *Japan* 49 J5
Ōsumi-Shotō, *Japan* 49 J5
Osun □, *Nigeria* 79 D5
Osuna, *Spain* 31 H5
Oswego, *U.S.A.* 107 C8
Oswestry, *U.K.* 12 E4
Oświecim, *Poland* 20 E9
Otago □, *N.Z.* 87 L2
Otago Harbour, *N.Z.* 87 L3
Ōtake, *Japan* 49 G6
Otaki, *N.Z.* 87 J5
Otaru, *Japan* 48 C10
Otaru-Wan = Ishikari-Wan, *Japan* 48 C10
Otava →, *Czech.* 20 F4
Otavalo, *Ecuador* 120 C2
Otavi, *Namibia* 84 B2
Otchinjau, *Angola* 84 B1
Otelec, *Romania* 38 D3
Otero de Rey, *Spain* 30 B3
Othello, *U.S.A.* 110 C4
Othonoí, *Greece* 39 K2
Óthris, Óros, *Greece* 39 K5
Otira Gorge, *N.Z.* 87 K3
Otis, *U.S.A.* 108 E3
Otjiwarongo, *Namibia* 84 C2
Otočac, *Croatia* 33 D12
Otoineppu, *Japan* 48 B11
Otorohanga, *N.Z.* 87 H5
Otoskwin →, *Canada* 98 B2
Otosquen, *Canada* 101 C8
Otranto, *Italy* 35 B11
Otranto, C. d', *Italy* 35 B11
Otranto, Str. of, *Italy* 35 B11
Otse, *S. Africa* 84 D4
Ōtsu, *Japan* 49 G7
Ōtsuki, *Japan* 49 G9
Otta, *Norway* 10 C3
Ottawa = Outaouais →, *Canada* 98 C5
Ottawa, *Canada* 98 C4
Ottawa, *Ill., U.S.A.* 108 E10
Ottawa, *Kans., U.S.A.* 108 F7
Ottawa Is., *Canada* 97 C11
Ottélé, *Cameroon* 79 E7
Otter L., *Canada* 101 B8
Otter Rapids, *Ont., Canada* 98 B3
Otter Rapids, *Sask., Canada* 101 B8
Otterndorf, *Germany* 18 B4
Otterup, *Denmark* 11 J4
Otterville, *Canada* 106 D4
Ottignies, *Belgium* 17 G5
Otto Beit Bridge, *Zimbabwe* 83 F2
Ottosdal, *S. Africa* 84 D4
Ottoshoop, *S. Africa* 84 D4
Ottsjön, *Sweden* 10 A7
Ottumwa, *U.S.A.* 108 E8
Otu, *Nigeria* 79 D5
Otukpa, *Nigeria* 79 D6
Oturkpo, *Nigeria* 79 D6
Otway, B., *Chile* 128 D2
Otway, C., *Australia* 91 F3
Otwock, *Poland* 20 C11
Ötz, *Austria* 19 H6
Ötz →, *Austria* 19 H6
Ötztaler Alpen, *Austria* 19 J7
Ou →, *Laos* 58 B4
Ou Neua, *Laos* 58 A3
Ou-Sammyaku, *Japan* 48 E10
Ouachita →, *U.S.A.* 109 K9
Ouachita, L., *U.S.A.* 109 H8
Ouachita Mts., *U.S.A.* 109 H7
Ouadâne, *Mauritania* 74 D2
Ouadda, *C.A.R.* 73 G9
Ouagadougou, *Burkina Faso* 79 C4
Ouahigouya, *Burkina Faso* 78 C4
Ouahila, *Algeria* 74 C3
Ouahran = Oran, *Algeria* 75 A4
Oualâta, *Mauritania* 78 B3
Ouallene, *Algeria* 75 D5
Ouanda Djallé, *C.A.R.* 73 G9
Ouango, *C.A.R.* 80 D4
Ouarâne, *Mauritania* 74 D2
Ouargla, *Algeria* 75 B6
Ouarkziz, Djebel, *Algeria* 74 C3
Ouarzazate, *Morocco* 74 B3
Ouatagouna, *Mali* 79 B5
Oubangi →, *Zaïre* 80 E3
Oubarakai, O. →, *Algeria* 75 C6
Ouche →, *France* 25 E12
Oud-Beijerland, *Neths.* 16 E4
Oud-Gastel, *Neths.* 17 E4
Oud Turnhout, *Belgium* 17 F6
Ouddorp, *Neths.* 16 E3
Oude-Pekela, *Neths.* 16 B10
Oude Rijn →, *Neths.* 16 D4
Oudega, *Neths.* 16 B8
Oudenaarde, *Belgium* 17 G3
Oudenbosch, *Neths.* 17 E5
Oudenburg, *Belgium* 17 F2
Ouderkerk, *Utrecht, Neths.* 16 D5
Ouderkerk, *Zuid-Holland, Neths.* 16 E5
Oudeschild, *Neths.* 16 B5
Oudewater, *Neths.* 16 D5
Oudkarspel, *Neths.* 16 C5
Oudon, *France* 24 E5
Oudtshoorn, *S. Africa* 84 E3
Oued Zem, *Morocco* 74 B3
Ouellé, *Ivory C.* 78 D4
Ouenza, *Algeria* 75 A6
Ouessa, *Burkina Faso* 78 C4
Ouessant, I. d', *France* 24 D1
Ouesso, *Congo* 80 D3
Ouest, Pte., *Canada* 99 C7
Ouezzane, *Morocco* 74 B3
Ouffet, *Belgium* 17 H6
Ouidah, *Benin* 79 D5
Ouistreham, *France* 24 C6
Oujda, *Morocco* 75 B4
Oujeft, *Mauritania* 74 D2
Ould Yenjé, *Mauritania* 78 B2
Ouled Djellal, *Algeria* 75 B6
Ouled Naïl, Mts. des, *Algeria* 75 B5
Oulmès, *Morocco* 74 B3
Oulu, *Finland* 8 D18
Oulu □ = Oulun lääni □, *Finland* 8 D19
Oulujärvi, *Finland* 8 D19
Oulujoki →, *Finland* 8 D18
Oulun lääni □, *Finland* 8 D19
Oulx, *Italy* 32 C3
Oum Chalouba, *Chad* 73 E9
Oum-el-Bouaghi, *Algeria* 75 A6
Oum el Ksi, *Algeria* 74 C3
Oum-er-Rbia, O. →, *Morocco* 74 B3
Oumè, *Ivory C.* 78 D3
Ounane, Dj., *Algeria* 75 C6
Ounguati, *Namibia* 84 C2
Ounianga-Kébir, *Chad* 73 E9
Ounianga Sérir, *Chad* 73 E9
Our →, *Lux.* 17 J8
Ouray, *U.S.A.* 111 G10
Ourcq →, *France* 25 C10
Oureg, Oued el →, *Algeria* 75 B5
Ourém, *Brazil* 122 B2
Ourense = Orense, *Spain* 30 C3
Ouricuri, *Brazil* 122 C3
Ourinhos, *Brazil* 127 A6
Ourique, *Portugal* 31 H2
Ouro Fino, *Brazil* 127 A6
Ouro Prêto, *Brazil* 123 F3
Ouro Sogui, *Senegal* 78 B2
Oursi, *Burkina Faso* 79 C4
Ourthe →, *Belgium* 17 H7
Ouse, *Australia* 90 G4
Ouse →, *E. Susx., U.K.* 13 G8
Ouse →, *N. Yorks., U.K.* 12 C8
Oust, *France* 26 F5
Oust →, *France* 24 E4
Outaouais →, *Canada* 98 C5
Outardes →, *Canada* 99 C6
Outat Oulad el Haj, *Morocco* 75 B4
Outer Hebrides, *U.K.* 14 D1
Outer I., *Canada* 99 B8
Outes, *Spain* 30 C2
Outjo, *Namibia* 84 C2
Outlook, *Canada* 101 C7
Outlook, *U.S.A.* 108 A2
Outreau, *France* 25 B8
Ouvèze →, *France* 27 E8
Ouyen, *Australia* 91 F3
Ouzouer-le-Marché, *France* 25 E8
Ovada, *Italy* 32 D5
Ovalau, *Fiji* 87 C8
Ovalle, *Chile* 126 C1
Ovar, *Portugal* 30 E2
Ovejas, *Colombia* 120 B2
Overdinkel, *Neths.* 16 D10
Overflakkee, *Neths.* 16 E4
Overijse, *Belgium* 17 G5
Overijssel □, *Neths.* 16 D9
Overijsselsch Kanaal →, *Neths.* 16 C8
Overpelt, *Belgium* 17 F6
Overton, *U.S.A.* 113 J12
Övertorneå, *Sweden* 8 C17
Ovid, *U.S.A.* 108 E3
Ovidiopol, *Ukraine* 42 C4
Oviedo, *Spain* 30 B5
Oviedo □, *Spain* 30 B5
Oviken, *Sweden* 10 A8
Oviksfjällen, *Sweden* 10 B7
Övör Hangay □, *Mongolia* 50 B2
Ovoro, *Nigeria* 79 D6
Ovruch, *Ukraine* 40 F6
Owaka, *N.Z.* 87 M2
Owase, *Japan* 49 G8
Owatonna, *U.S.A.* 108 C8
Owbeh, *Afghan.* 60 B3
Owego, *U.S.A.* 107 D8
Owen Falls, *Uganda* 82 B3
Owen Sound, *Canada* 98 D3
Owendo, *Gabon* 80 D1
Owens →, *U.S.A.* 112 J9
Owens L., *U.S.A.* 113 J9
Owensboro, *U.S.A.* 104 G2
Owensville, *U.S.A.* 108 F9
Owerri, *Nigeria* 79 D6
Owl →, *Canada* 101 B10
Owo, *Nigeria* 79 D6
Owosso, *U.S.A.* 104 D3
Owyhee, *U.S.A.* 110 F5
Owyhee →, *U.S.A.* 110 E5
Owyhee, L., *U.S.A.* 110 E5
Ox Mts., *Ireland* 15 B3
Oxapampa, *Peru* 124 C2
Oxelösund, *Sweden* 11 F11
Oxford, *N.Z.* 87 K4
Oxford, *U.K.* 13 F6
Oxford, *Miss., U.S.A.* 109 H10
Oxford, *N.C., U.S.A.* 105 G6
Oxford, *Ohio, U.S.A.* 104 F3
Oxford L., *Canada* 101 C9
Oxfordshire □, *U.K.* 13 F6
Oxley, *Australia* 91 E3
Oxnard, *U.S.A.* 113 L7
Oxus = Amudarya →, *Uzbekistan* 44 E6
Oya, *Malaysia* 56 D4
Oyama, *Japan* 49 F9
Oyapock →, *Fr. Guiana* 121 C7
Oyem, *Gabon* 80 D2
Oyen, *Canada* 101 C6
Øyeren, *Norway* 10 E5
Oykel →, *U.K.* 14 D4
Oymyakon, *Russia* 45 C15
Oyo, *Nigeria* 79 D5
Oyo □, *Nigeria* 79 D5
Oyón, *Peru* 124 C2
Oyonnax, *France* 27 B9
Oyster Bay, *U.S.A.* 107 F11

Ōyūbari, *Japan* 48 C11
Özalp, *Turkey* 67 D10
Ozamiz, *Phil.* 55 G5
Ozark, *Ala., U.S.A.* 105 K3
Ozark, *Ark., U.S.A.* 109 H8
Ozark, *Mo., U.S.A.* 109 G8
Ozark Plateau, *U.S.A.* 109 G9
Ozarks, L. of the, *U.S.A.* 108 F8
Ózd, *Hungary* 21 G10
Ozette L., *U.S.A.* 112 B2
Ozieri, *Italy* 34 B2
Ozona, *U.S.A.* 109 K4
Ozorków, *Poland* 20 D9
Ozuluama, *Mexico* 115 C5
Ozurgety, *Georgia* 43 F10

P

P.K. le Roux Dam, *S. Africa* 84 E3
Pa, *Burkina Faso* 78 C4
Pa-an, *Burma* 61 L20
Pa Mong Dam, *Thailand* 58 D4
Paal, *Belgium* 17 F6
Paamiut = Frederikshåb, *Greenland* 4 C5
Paar →, *Germany* 19 G6
Paarl, *S. Africa* 84 E2
Paatsi →, *Russia* 8 B20
Paauilo, *U.S.A.* 102 H17
Pab Hills, *Pakistan* 62 F2
Pabianice, *Poland* 20 D9
Pabna, *Bangla.* 61 G16
Pabo, *Uganda* 82 B3
Pacaás Novos, Serra dos, *Brazil* 125 C5
Pacaipampa, *Peru* 124 B2
Pacaja →, *Brazil* 122 B1
Pacajus, *Brazil* 122 B4
Pacaraima, Sierra, *Venezuela* 121 C5
Pacarán, *Peru* 124 C2
Pacaraos, *Peru* 124 C2
Pacasmayo, *Peru* 124 B2
Paceco, *Italy* 34 E5
Pachacamac, *Peru* 124 C2
Pachhar, *India* 62 G7
Pachino, *Italy* 35 F8
Pachitea →, *Peru* 124 B3
Pachiza, *Peru* 124 B2
Pacho, *Colombia* 120 B3
Pachpadra, *India* 60 G8
Pachuca, *Mexico* 115 C5
Pacific, *Canada* 100 C3
Pacific-Antarctic Ridge, *Pac. Oc.* 93 M16
Pacific Grove, *U.S.A.* 111 H3
Pacific Ocean, *Pac. Oc.* 93 G14
Pacifica, *U.S.A.* 112 H4
Pacitan, *Indonesia* 57 H14
Packwood, *U.S.A.* 112 D5
Pacuí →, *Brazil* 123 E2
Padaido, Kepulauan, *Indonesia* 57 E9
Padang, *Indonesia* 56 E2
Padangpanjang, *Indonesia* 56 E2
Padangsidempuan, *Indonesia* 56 D1
Padauari →, *Brazil* 121 D5
Padborg, *Denmark* 11 K3
Padcaya, *Bolivia* 125 E5
Paddockwood, *Canada* 101 C7
Paderborn, *Germany* 18 D4
Padilla, *Bolivia* 125 D5
Padloping Island, *Canada* 97 B13
Pádova, *Italy* 33 C8
Padra, *India* 62 H5
Padrauna, *India* 63 F10
Padre I., *U.S.A.* 109 M6
Padro, Mte., *France* 27 F12
Padrón, *Spain* 30 C2
Padstow, *U.K.* 13 G3
Padua = Pádova, *Italy* 33 C8
Paducah, *Ky., U.S.A.* 104 G1
Paducah, *Tex., U.S.A.* 109 H4
Padul, *Spain* 31 H7
Padula, *Italy* 35 B8
Paengnyong-do, *S. Korea* 51 F13
Paeroa, *N.Z.* 87 G5
Paesana, *Italy* 32 D4
Pafúri, *Mozam.* 85 C5
Pag, *Croatia* 33 D11
Paga, *Ghana* 79 C4
Pagadian, *Phil.* 55 H5
Pagai Selatan, P., *Indonesia* 56 E2
Pagai Utara, *Indonesia* 56 E2
Pagalu = Annobón, *Atl. Oc.* 71 G4
Pagastikós Kólpos, *Greece* 39 K6
Pagatan, *Indonesia* 56 E5
Page, *Ariz., U.S.A.* 111 H8
Page, *N. Dak., U.S.A.* 108 B6
Paglieta, *Italy* 33 F11
Pagny-sur-Moselle, *France* 25 D13
Pago Pago, *Amer. Samoa* 87 B13
Pagosa Springs, *U.S.A.* 111 H10
Pagwa River, *Canada* 98 B2
Pahala, *U.S.A.* 102 J17
Pahang →, *Malaysia* 59 L4
Pahiatua, *N.Z.* 87 J5
Pahokee, *U.S.A.* 105 M5
Pahrump, *U.S.A.* 113 J11
Pahute Mesa, *U.S.A.* 112 H10
Pai, *Thailand* 58 C2
Paia, *U.S.A.* 102 H16
Paicines, *U.S.A.* 112 J5
Paide, *Estonia* 40 B4
Paignton, *U.K.* 13 G4
Paiján, *Peru* 124 B2
Päijänne, *Finland* 9 F18
Paimbœuf, *France* 24 E4
Paimpol, *France* 24 D3
Painan, *Indonesia* 56 E2
Painesville, *U.S.A.* 106 E3
Paint Hills = Nouveau Comptoir, *Canada* 98 B4
Paint L., *Canada* 101 B9
Paint Rock, *U.S.A.* 109 K5
Painted Desert, *U.S.A.* 111 J8
Paintsville, *U.S.A.* 104 G4
País Vasco □, *Spain* 28 C2
Paisley, *Canada* 106 B3
Paisley, *U.K.* 14 F4
Paisley, *U.S.A.* 110 E3
Paita, *Peru* 124 B1
Paiva →, *Portugal* 30 D2
Paizhou, *China* 53 B9
Pajares, *Spain* 30 B5
Pajares, Puerto de, *Spain* 30 C5
Pak Lay, *Laos* 58 C3
Pak Phanang, *Thailand* 59 H3
Pak Sane, *Laos* 58 C4
Pak Song, *Laos* 58 E6
Pak Suong, *Laos* 58 C4
Pakaraima Mts., *Guyana* 121 B5
Pákhnes, *Greece* 37 D6
Pakistan ■, *Asia* 62 E3
Pakistan, East = Bangladesh ■, *Asia* 61 H17
Pakkading, *Laos* 58 C4
Pakokku, *Burma* 61 J19
Pakpattan, *Pakistan* 62 D5
Pakrac, *Croatia* 21 K7
Paks, *Hungary* 21 J8
Pakse, *Laos* 58 E5
Paktīā □, *Afghan.* 60 C6
Pakwach, *Uganda* 82 B3
Pala, *Chad* 73 G8
Pala, *U.S.A.* 113 M9
Pala, *Zaïre* 82 D2
Palabek, *Uganda* 82 B3
Palacios, *U.S.A.* 109 L6
Palafrugell, *Spain* 28 D8
Palagiano, *Italy* 35 B10
Palagonía, *Italy* 35 E7
Palagruža, *Croatia* 33 F13
Palaiókastron, *Greece* 37 D8
Palaiokhóra, *Greece* 37 D5
Palam, *India* 60 K10
Palamás, *Greece* 39 K5
Palamós, *Spain* 28 D8
Palampur, *India* 62 C7
Palana, *Australia* 90 F4
Palana, *Russia* 45 D16
Palanan, *Phil.* 55 C5
Palanan Pt., *Phil.* 55 C5
Palandri, *Pakistan* 63 C5
Palangkaraya, *Indonesia* 56 E4
Palani Hills, *India* 60 P10
Palanpur, *India* 62 G5
Palapye, *Botswana* 84 C4
Palas, *Pakistan* 63 B5
Palatka, *Russia* 45 C16
Palatka, *U.S.A.* 105 L5
Palau = Belau ■, *Pac. Oc.* 92 G5
Palawan, *Phil.* 55 G3
Palayankottai, *India* 60 Q10
Palazzo, Pte., *France* 27 F12
Palazzo San Gervásio, *Italy* 35 B8
Palazzolo Acreide, *Italy* 35 E7
Palca, *Chile* 124 D4
Paldiski, *Estonia* 40 B4
Paleleh, *Indonesia* 57 D6
Palembang, *Indonesia* 56 E2
Palena →, *Chile* 128 B2
Palena, L., *Chile* 128 B2
Palencia, *Spain* 30 C6
Palencia □, *Spain* 30 C6
Paleokastrítsa, *Greece* 37 A3
Paleometokho, *Cyprus* 37 D12
Palermo, *Colombia* 120 C2
Palermo, *Italy* 34 D6
Palermo, *U.S.A.* 110 G3
Palestine, *Asia* 69 D4
Palestine, *U.S.A.* 109 K7
Palestrina, *Italy* 34 A5
Paletwa, *Burma* 61 J18
Palghat, *India* 60 P10
Palgrave, Mt., *Australia* 88 D2
Pali, *India* 62 G5
Palinuro, C., *Italy* 35 B8
Palisade, *U.S.A.* 108 E4
Paliseul, *Belgium* 17 J6
Palitana, *India* 62 J4
Palizada, *Mexico* 115 D6
Palizzi, *Italy* 35 E8
Palk Bay, *Asia* 60 Q11
Palk Strait, *Asia* 60 Q11
Palkānah, *Iraq* 64 C5
Palla Road = Dinokwe, *Botswana* 84 C4
Pallanza = Verbánia, *Italy* 32 C5
Pallasovka, *Russia* 41 F15
Pallisa, *Uganda* 82 B3
Pallu, *India* 62 E6
Palm Beach, *U.S.A.* 105 M6
Palm Desert, *U.S.A.* 113 M10
Palm Is., *Australia* 90 B4
Palm Springs, *U.S.A.* 113 M10
Palma, *Mozam.* 83 E5
Palma →, *Brazil* 123 D2
Palma, B. de, *Spain* 36 B9
Palma de Mallorca, *Spain* 36 B9
Palma del Río, *Spain* 31 H5
Palma di Montechiaro, *Italy* 34 E6
Palma Soriano, *Cuba* 116 B4
Palmanova, *Italy* 33 C10
Palmares, *Brazil* 122 C4
Palmarito, *Venezuela* 120 B3
Palmarola, *Italy* 34 B5
Palmas, *Brazil* 127 B5
Palmas, C., *Liberia* 78 E3
Pálmas, G. di, *Italy* 34 C1
Palmas de Monte Alto, *Brazil* 123 D3
Palmdale, *U.S.A.* 113 L8
Palmeira, *Brazil* 123 G2
Palmeira dos Índios, *Brazil* 122 C4
Palmeirais, *Brazil* 122 C3
Palmeiras →, *Brazil* 123 D2
Palmeirinhas, Pta. das, *Angola* 80 F2
Palmela, *Portugal* 31 G2
Palmelo, *Brazil* 123 E2
Palmer, *U.S.A.* 96 B5
Palmer →, *Australia* 90 B3
Palmer Arch., *Antarctica* 5 C17
Palmer Lake, *U.S.A.* 108 F2
Palmer Land, *Antarctica* 5 D18
Palmerston, *Canada* 106 C4
Palmerston, *N.Z.* 87 L3
Palmerston North, *N.Z.* 87 J5
Palmerton, *U.S.A.* 107 F9
Palmetto, *U.S.A.* 105 M4
Palmi, *Italy* 35 D8
Palmira, *Argentina* 126 C2
Palmira, *Colombia* 120 C2
Palmyra = Tudmur, *Syria* 64 C3
Palmyra, *Mo., U.S.A.* 108 F9
Palmyra, *N.Y., U.S.A.* 106 C7
Palmyra Is., *Pac. Oc.* 93 G11
Palo Alto, *U.S.A.* 111 H2
Palo del Colle, *Italy* 35 A9
Palo Verde, *U.S.A.* 113 M12
Palombara Sabina, *Italy* 33 F9
Palompon, *Phil.* 55 F6
Palopo, *Indonesia* 57 E6
Palos, C. de, *Spain* 29 H4
Palos Verdes, *U.S.A.* 113 M8
Palos Verdes, Pt., *U.S.A.* 113 M8
Palouse, *U.S.A.* 110 C5
Palpa, *Peru* 124 C2
Palparara, *Australia* 90 C3
Pålsboda, *Sweden* 10 E9
Palu, *Indonesia* 57 E5
Paluan, *Phil.* 57 B6
Palwal, *India* 62 E7
Pama, *Burkina Faso* 79 C5
Pamanukan, *Indonesia* 57 G12
Pamekasan, *Indonesia* 57 G15
Pamiers, *France* 26 E5
Pamirs, *Tajikistan* 44 F8
Pamlico →, *U.S.A.* 105 H7
Pamlico Sd., *U.S.A.* 105 H8
Pampa, *U.S.A.* 109 H4
Pampa de Agma, *Argentina* 128 B3
Pampa de las Salinas, *Argentina* 126 C2
Pampa Grande, *Bolivia* 125 D5
Pampa Hermosa, *Peru* 124 B2
Pampanua, *Indonesia* 57 E6
Pamparato, *Italy* 32 D4
Pampas, *Argentina* 126 D3
Pampas, *Peru* 124 C3
Pampas →, *Peru* 124 C3
Pamphylia, *Turkey* 66 E4
Pamplona, *Colombia* 120 B3
Pamplona, *Spain* 28 C3
Pampoenpoort, *S. Africa* 84 E3
Pamukkale, *Turkey* 66 E3
Pan Xian, *China* 52 E5
Pana, *U.S.A.* 108 F10
Panabo, *Phil.* 55 H6
Panaca, *U.S.A.* 111 H6
Panagyurishte, *Bulgaria* 38 G7
Panaitan, *Indonesia* 57 G11
Panaji, *India* 60 M8
Panamá, *Panama* 116 E4
Panama ■, *Cent. Amer.* 116 E4
Panamá, G. de, *Panama* 116 E4
Panama Canal, *Panama* 116 E4
Panama City, *U.S.A.* 105 K3
Panamint Range, *U.S.A.* 113 J9
Panamint Springs, *U.S.A.* 113 J9
Panão, *Peru* 124 B2
Panaon I., *Phil.* 55 F6
Panare, *Thailand* 59 J3
Panarea, *Italy* 35 D8
Panaro →, *Italy* 32 D8
Panarukan, *Indonesia* 57 G15
Panay, *Phil.* 55 F5
Panay, G., *Phil.* 57 B6
Pancake Range, *U.S.A.* 111 G6
Pančevo, *Serbia, Yug.* 21 L10
Pancorbo, Paso, *Spain* 28 C1
Pandan, *Antique, Phil.* 55 F5
Pandan, *Catanduanes, Phil.* 55 D6
Pandegelang, *Indonesia* 57 G12
Pandharpur, *India* 60 L9
Pandilla, *Spain* 28 D1
Pando, *Uruguay* 127 C4
Pando □, *Bolivia* 124 C4
Pando, L. = Hope, L., *Australia* 91 D2
Pandokrátor, *Greece* 37 A3
Pandora, *Costa Rica* 116 E3
Panevėžys, *Lithuania* 40 D4
Panfilov, *Kazakhstan* 44 E8
Panfilovo, *Russia* 41 F13
Pang-Long, *Burma* 61 H21
Pang-Yang, *Burma* 61 H21
Panga, *Zaïre* 82 B2
Pangalanes, Canal des, *Madag.* 85 C8
Pangani, *Tanzania* 82 D4
Pangani □, *Tanzania* 82 D4
Pangani →, *Tanzania* 82 D4
Pangfou = Bengbu, *China* 51 H9
Pangil, *Zaïre* 82 C2
Pangkah, Tanjung, *Indonesia* 57 G15
Pangkajene, *Indonesia* 57 E5
Pangkalanbrandan, *Indonesia* 56 D1
Pangkalanbuun, *Indonesia* 56 E4
Pangkalansusu, *Indonesia* 56 D1
Pangkalpinang, *Indonesia* 56 E3
Pangkoh, *Indonesia* 56 E4
Pangnirtung, *Canada* 97 B13
Pangrango, *Indonesia* 57 G12
Panguipulli, *Chile* 128 A2
Panguitch, *U.S.A.* 111 H7
Pangutaran Group, *Phil.* 55 H4
Panhandle, *U.S.A.* 109 H4
Pani Mines, *India* 62 H5
Pania-Mutombo, *Zaïre* 82 D1
Panipat, *India* 62 E7
Panjal Range, *India* 62 C7
Panjgur, *Pakistan* 60 F4
Panjim = Panaji, *India* 60 M8
Panjinad Barrage, *Pakistan* 60 E7
Panjwai, *Afghan.* 62 D1
Pankshin, *Nigeria* 79 D6
Panmunjŏm, *N. Korea* 51 F14
Panna, *India* 63 G9
Panna Hills, *India* 63 G9
Pano Lefkara, *Cyprus* 37 E12
Pano Panayia, *Cyprus* 37 E11
Panorama, *Brazil* 127 A5
Pánormon, *Greece* 37 D6
Panshan, *China* 51 D12
Panshi, *China* 51 C14
Pantar, *Indonesia* 57 F6
Pante Macassar, *Indonesia* 57 F6
Pantelleria, *Italy* 34 F5
Pantón, *Spain* 30 C3
Pánuco, *Mexico* 115 C5
Panyam, *Nigeria* 79 D6
Panyu, *China* 53 F9
Pao →, *Anzoátegui, Venezuela* 121 B5
Pao →, *Apure, Venezuela* 120 B4
Páola, *Italy* 35 C9
Paola, *Malta* 37 D2
Paola, *U.S.A.* 108 F7
Paonia, *U.S.A.* 111 G10
Paoting = Baoding, *China* 50 E8
Paot'ou = Baotou, *China* 50 D6
Paoua, *C.A.R.* 73 G8
Pápa, *Hungary* 21 H7
Papagayo →, *Mexico* 115 D5
Papagayo, G. de, *Costa Rica* 116 D2
Papakura, *N.Z.* 87 G5
Papantla, *Mexico* 115 C5
Papar, *Malaysia* 56 C5
Pápas, Ákra, *Greece* 39 L4
Papenburg, *Germany* 18 B3
Paphlagonia, *Turkey* 66 C5
Paphos, *Cyprus* 37 E11
Papien Chiang = Da →, *Vietnam* 58 B5
Papigochic →, *Mexico* 114 B3
Paposo, *Chile* 126 B1
Papoutsa, *Cyprus* 37 E12
Papua New Guinea ■, *Oceania* 92 H6
Papuča, *Croatia* 33 D12
Papudo, *Chile* 126 C1
Papuk, *Croatia* 21 K7
Papun, *Burma* 61 K20
Papunya, *Australia* 88 D5
Pará = Belém, *Brazil* 122 B2
Pará □, *Brazil* 125 A7
Pará □, *Surinam* 121 B6
Parábita, *Italy* 35 B11
Paraburdoo, *Australia* 88 D2
Paracale, *Phil.* 55 D5
Paracas, Pen., *Peru* 124 C2
Paracatu, *Brazil* 123 E2
Paracatu →, *Brazil* 123 E2
Paracel Is. = Hsisha Chuntao, *Pac. Oc.* 56 A4
Parachilna, *Australia* 91 E2
Parachinar, *Pakistan* 62 C4
Paraćin, *Serbia, Yug.* 21 M11
Paracuru, *Brazil* 122 B4
Parada, Punta, *Peru* 124 D2
Paradas, *Spain* 31 H5
Paradela, *Spain* 30 C3
Paradhísi, *Greece* 37 C10
Paradip, *India* 61 J15
Paradise, *Calif., U.S.A.* 112 F5
Paradise, *Mont., U.S.A.* 110 C6
Paradise, *Nev., U.S.A.* 113 J11
Paradise →, *Canada* 99 B8
Paradise Valley, *U.S.A.* 110 F5
Parado, *Indonesia* 57 F5
Paragould, *U.S.A.* 109 G9
Paraguá →, *Bolivia* 125 C5
Paragua →, *Venezuela* 121 B5
Paraguaçu →, *Brazil* 123 D4
Paraguaçu Paulista, *Brazil* 127 A5
Paraguaipoa, *Venezuela* 120 A3
Paraguaná, Pen. de, *Venezuela* 120 A3
Paraguarí, *Paraguay* 126 B4
Paraguarí □, *Paraguay* 126 B4
Paraguay ■, *S. Amer.* 126 A4
Paraguay →, *Paraguay* 126 B4
Paraíba = João Pessoa, *Brazil* 122 C5
Paraíba □, *Brazil* 122 C4
Paraíba do Sul →, *Brazil* 123 F3
Parainen, *Finland* 9 F17
Paraiso, *Mexico* 115 D6
Parak, *Iran* 65 E7
Parakhino Paddubye, *Russia* 40 B8
Parakou, *Benin* 79 D5
Paralimni, *Cyprus* 37 D12
Paramaribo, *Surinam* 121 B6
Parambu, *Brazil* 122 C3
Paramillo, Nudo del, *Colombia* 120 B2
Paramirim, *Brazil* 123 D3
Paramirim →, *Brazil* 123 D3
Paramithiá, *Greece* 39 K3
Paramushir, Ostrov, *Russia* 45 D16
Paran →, *Israel* 69 E4
Paraná, *Argentina* 126 C3
Paranã, *Brazil* 123 D2
Paraná □, *Brazil* 127 A5
Paraná →, *Argentina* 126 C4
Paranaguá, *Brazil* 127 B6
Paranaíba →, *Brazil* 123 F1
Paranapanema →, *Brazil* 127 A5
Paranapiacaba, Serra do, *Brazil* 127 A6
Paranavaí, *Brazil* 127 A5
Parang, *Jolo, Phil.* 55 J4
Parang, *Mindanao, Phil.* 57 C6
Parangaba, *Brazil* 122 B4
Parapóla, *Greece* 39 N6
Paraspóri, Ákra, *Greece* 39 P10
Paratinga, *Brazil* 123 D3
Paratoo, *Australia* 91 E2
Parattah, *Australia* 90 G4
Paraúna, *Brazil* 123 E1
Paray-le-Monial, *France* 27 B8
Parbati →, *India* 62 G7
Parbhani, *India* 60 K10
Parchim, *Germany* 18 B7
Parczew, *Poland* 20 D12
Pardes Hanna, *Israel* 69 C3
Pardilla, *Spain* 30 D7
Pardo →, *Bahia, Brazil* 123 E4
Pardo →, *Mato Grosso, Brazil* 127 A5
Pardo →, *Minas Gerais, Brazil* 123 E3
Pardo →, *São Paulo, Brazil* 123 F2
Pardubice, *Czech.* 20 E5
Pare, *Indonesia* 57 G15
Pare □, *Tanzania* 82 C4
Pare Mts., *Tanzania* 82 C4
Parecis, Serra dos, *Brazil* 125 C6
Paredes de Nava, *Spain* 30 C6
Pareh, *Iran* 64 B5
Parelhas, *Brazil* 122 C4
Paren, *Russia* 45 C17
Parent, *Canada* 98 C5
Parent, L., *Canada* 98 C4
Parentis-en-Born, *France* 26 D2
Parepare, *Indonesia* 57 E5
Parfino, *Russia* 40 C7
Pargo, Pta. do, *Madeira* 36 D2
Paria, G. de, *Venezuela* 121 A5
Paria, Pen. de, *Venezuela* 121 A5
Pariaguán, *Venezuela* 121 B5
Pariaman, *Indonesia* 56 E2
Paricatuba, *Brazil* 121 D5
Paricutín, Cerro, *Mexico* 114 D4
Parigi, *Java, Indonesia* 57 G13
Parigi, *Sulawesi, Indonesia* 57 E6
Parika, *Guyana* 121 B6
Parima, Serra, *Brazil* 121 C5
Parinari, *Peru* 124 A3
Parîng, *Romania* 38 D6
Parintins, *Brazil* 121 D6
Pariparit Kyun, *Burma* 61 M18
Paris, *Canada* 98 D3
Paris, *France* 25 D9
Paris, *Idaho, U.S.A.* 110 E8
Paris, *Ky., U.S.A.* 104 F3
Paris, *Tenn., U.S.A.* 105 G1
Paris, *Tex., U.S.A.* 109 J7
Paris, Ville de □, *France* 25 D9
Parish, *U.S.A.* 107 C8
Pariti, *Indonesia* 57 F6
Park, *U.S.A.* 112 B4
Park City, *U.S.A.* 110 F8
Park Falls, *U.S.A.* 108 C9
Park Range, *U.S.A.* 110 G10
Park Rapids, *U.S.A.* 108 B7
Park River, *U.S.A.* 108 A6
Park Rynie, *S. Africa* 85 E5
Parkā Bandar, *Iran* 65 E8
Parker, *Ariz., U.S.A.* 113 L12
Parker, *S. Dak., U.S.A.* 108 D6
Parker Dam, *U.S.A.* 113 L12
Parkersburg, *U.S.A.* 104 F5

Parkerview, *Canada* 101 C8
Parkes, *Australia* 91 E4
Parkfield, *U.S.A.* 112 K6
Parkland, *U.S.A.* 112 C4
Parkside, *Canada* 101 C7
Parkston, *U.S.A.* 108 D5
Parksville, *Canada* 100 D4
Parma, *Italy* 32 D7
Parma, *Idaho, U.S.A.* 110 E5
Parma, *Ohio, U.S.A.* 106 E3
Parma →, *Italy* 32 D7
Parnaguá, *Brazil* 122 D3
Parnaíba, *Piauí, Brazil* 122 B3
Parnaíba, *São Paulo, Brazil* 125 D7
Parnaíba →, *Brazil* 122 B3
Parnamirim, *Brazil* 122 C4
Parnarama, *Brazil* 122 C3
Parnassós, *Greece* 39 L5
Párnis, *Greece* 39 L6
Párnon Óros, *Greece* 39 M5
Pärnu, *Estonia* 40 B4
Paroo →, *Australia* 91 E3
Páros, *Greece* 39 M8
Parowan, *U.S.A.* 111 H7
Parpaillon, *France* 27 D10
Parral, *Chile* 126 D1
Parramatta, *Australia* 91 E5
Parras, *Mexico* 114 B4
Parrett →, *U.K.* 13 F5
Parris I., *U.S.A.* 105 J5
Parrsboro, *Canada* 99 C7
Parry Is., *Canada* 4 B2
Parry Sound, *Canada* 98 C3
Parsberg, *Germany* 19 F7
Parshall, *U.S.A.* 108 B3
Parsnip →, *Canada* 100 B4
Parsons, *U.S.A.* 109 G7
Parsons Ra., *Australia* 90 A2
Partanna, *Italy* 34 E5
Parthenay, *France* 24 F6
Partinico, *Italy* 34 D6
Paru →, *Brazil* 121 D7
Parú →, *Venezuela* 120 C4
Paru de Oeste →, *Brazil* 121 C6
Parucito →, *Venezuela* 120 B4
Paruro, *Peru* 124 C3
Parvān □, *Afghan.* 60 B6
Parvatipuram, *India* 61 K13
Parys, *S. Africa* 84 D4
Pas-de-Calais □, *France* 25 B9
Pasadena, *Calif., U.S.A.* 113 L8
Pasadena, *Tex., U.S.A.* 109 L7
Pasaje, *Ecuador* 120 D2
Pasaje →, *Argentina* 126 B3
Pasay, *Phil.* 55 D4
Pascagoula, *U.S.A.* 109 K10
Pascagoula →, *U.S.A.* 109 K10
Paşcani, *Romania* 38 B9
Pasco, *U.S.A.* 110 C4
Pasco □, *Peru* 124 C2
Pasco, Cerro de, *Peru* 124 C2
Pascua, I. de, *Pac. Oc.* 93 K17
Pasewalk, *Germany* 18 B10
Pasfield L., *Canada* 101 B7
Pasha →, *Russia* 40 B8
Pashiwari, *Pakistan* 63 B6
Pashmakli = Smolyan, *Bulgaria* 39 H7
Pasinler, *Turkey* 67 D9
Pasirian, *Indonesia* 57 H15
Paskūh, *Iran* 65 E9
Pasley, C., *Australia* 89 F3
Pašman, *Croatia* 33 E12
Pasni, *Pakistan* 60 G3
Paso Cantinela, *Mexico* 113 N11
Paso de Indios, *Argentina* 128 B3
Paso de los Libres, *Argentina* 126 B4
Paso de los Toros, *Uruguay* 126 C4
Paso Flores, *Argentina* 128 B2
Paso Robles, *U.S.A.* 111 J3
Pasorapa, *Bolivia* 125 D5
Paspébiac, *Canada* 99 C6
Pasrur, *Pakistan* 62 C6
Passage West, *Ireland* 15 E3
Passaic, *U.S.A.* 107 F10
Passau, *Germany* 19 G9
Passendale, *Belgium* 17 G2
Passero, C., *Italy* 35 F8
Passo Fundo, *Brazil* 127 B5
Passos, *Brazil* 123 F2
Passow, *Germany* 18 B10
Passwang, *Switz.* 22 B5
Passy, *France* 27 C10
Pastaza □, *Ecuador* 120 D2
Pastaza →, *Peru* 120 D2
Pastęk, *Poland* 20 A9
Pasto, *Colombia* 120 C2
Pastos Bons, *Brazil* 122 C3
Pastrana, *Spain* 28 E2
Pasuruan, *Indonesia* 57 G15
Patagonia, *Argentina* 128 C2
Patagonia, *U.S.A.* 111 L8
Patambar, *Iran* 65 D9
Patan, *India* 60 H8
Patan, *Maharashtra, India* 62 H5
Patan, *Nepal* 61 F14
Patani, *Indonesia* 57 D7
Pataudi, *India* 62 E7
Patay, *France* 25 D8
Patchewollock, *Australia* 91 F3
Patchogue, *U.S.A.* 107 F11
Patea, *N.Z.* 87 H5
Pategi, *Nigeria* 79 D6
Patensie, *S. Africa* 84 E3
Paternò, *Italy* 35 E7
Pateros, *U.S.A.* 110 B4
Paterson, *U.S.A.* 107 F10
Paterson Ra., *Australia* 88 D3
Paterswolde, *Neths.* 16 B9
Pathankot, *India* 62 C6
Pathfinder Reservoir, *U.S.A.* 110 E10
Pathiu, *Thailand* 59 G2
Pathum Thani, *Thailand* 58 E3
Pati, *Indonesia* 57 G14
Patía, *Colombia* 120 C2
Patía →, *Colombia* 120 C2
Patiala, *India* 62 D7
Patine Kouka, *Senegal* 78 C2
Pativilca, *Peru* 124 C2
Patkai Bum, *India* 61 F19
Pátmos, *Greece* 39 M9
Patna, *India* 63 G11
Patnos, *Turkey* 67 D10
Patonga, *Uganda* 82 B3
Patos, *Brazil* 122 C4
Patos, L. dos, *Brazil* 127 C5
Patos de Minas, *Brazil* 123 E2
Patquía, *Argentina* 126 C2
Pátrai, *Greece* 39 L4
Pátraikós Kólpos, *Greece* 39 L4
Patricio Lynch, I., *Chile* 128 C1
Patrocínio, *Brazil* 123 E2
Patta, *Kenya* 82 C5
Pattada, *Italy* 34 B2
Pattani, *Thailand* 59 J3
Patten, *U.S.A.* 99 C6
Patterson, *Calif., U.S.A.* 111 H3
Patterson, *La., U.S.A.* 109 L9
Patterson, Mt., *U.S.A.* 112 G7
Patti, *India* 62 D6
Patti, *Italy* 35 D7
Pattoki, *Pakistan* 62 D5
Patton, *U.S.A.* 106 F6
Patu, *Brazil* 122 C4
Patuakhali, *Bangla.* 61 H17
Patuca →, *Honduras* 116 C3
Patuca, Punta, *Honduras* 116 C3
Pâturages, *Belgium* 17 H3
Pátzcuaro, *Mexico* 114 D4
Pau, *France* 26 E3
Pau, Gave de →, *France* 26 E2
Pau d' Arco, *Brazil* 122 C2
Pau dos Ferros, *Brazil* 122 C4
Paucartambo, *Peru* 124 C3
Pauillac, *France* 26 C3
Pauini, *Brazil* 124 B4
Pauini →, *Brazil* 121 D5
Pauk, *Burma* 61 J19
Paul I., *Canada* 99 A7
Paul Isnard, *Fr. Guiana* 121 C7
Paulhan, *France* 26 E7
Paulis = Isiro, *Zaïre* 82 B2
Paulista, *Brazil* 122 C5
Paulistana, *Brazil* 122 C3
Paullina, *U.S.A.* 108 D7
Paulo Afonso, *Brazil* 122 C4
Paulo de Faria, *Brazil* 123 F2
Paulpietersburg, *S. Africa* 85 D5
Pauls Valley, *U.S.A.* 109 H6
Pauma Valley, *U.S.A.* 113 M10
Pausa, *Peru* 124 D3
Pauto →, *Colombia* 120 B3
Pāveh, *Iran* 64 C5
Pavelets, *Russia* 41 E11
Pavia, *Italy* 32 C6
Pavlikeni, *Bulgaria* 38 F8
Pavlodar, *Kazakhstan* 44 D8
Pavlograd, *Ukraine* 42 B6
Pavlovo, *Russia* 41 D13
Pavlovo, *Russia* 45 C12
Pavlovsk, *Russia* 41 F12
Pavlovskaya, *Russia* 43 C8
Pavlovskiy-Posad, *Russia* 41 D11
Pavullo nel Frignano, *Italy* 32 D7
Pawhuska, *U.S.A.* 109 G6
Pawling, *U.S.A.* 107 E11
Pawnee, *U.S.A.* 109 G6
Pawnee City, *U.S.A.* 108 E6
Pawtucket, *U.S.A.* 107 E13
Paximádhia, *Greece* 37 D6
Paxoí, *Greece* 39 K3
Paxton, *Ill., U.S.A.* 104 E1
Paxton, *Nebr., U.S.A.* 108 E4
Payakumbuh, *Indonesia* 56 E2
Payerne, *Switz.* 22 C3
Payette, *U.S.A.* 110 D5
Paymogo, *Spain* 31 H3
Payne Bay = Bellin, *Canada* 97 B13
Payne L., *Canada* 97 C12
Paynes Find, *Australia* 89 E2
Paynesville, *Liberia* 78 D2
Paynesville, *U.S.A.* 108 C7
Paysandú, *Uruguay* 126 C4
Payson, *Ariz., U.S.A.* 111 J8
Payson, *Utah, U.S.A.* 110 F8
Paz →, *Guatemala* 116 D1
Paz, B. la, *Mexico* 114 C2
Pāzanān, *Iran* 65 D6
Pazar, *Turkey* 67 C9
Pazarcık, *Turkey* 66 E7
Pazardzhik, *Bulgaria* 38 G7
Pazin, *Croatia* 33 C10
Pazña, *Bolivia* 124 D4
Pčinja →, *Macedonia* 39 H4
Pe Ell, *U.S.A.* 112 D3
Peabody, *U.S.A.* 107 D14
Peace →, *Canada* 100 B6
Peace Point, *Canada* 100 B6
Peace River, *Canada* 100 B5
Peach Springs, *U.S.A.* 111 J7
Peak, The = Kinder Scout, *U.K.* 12 D6
Peak Downs, *Australia* 90 C4
Peak Downs Mine, *Australia* 90 C4
Peak Hill, *N.S.W., Australia* 91 E4
Peak Hill, *W. Austral., Australia* 89 E2
Peak Ra., *Australia* 90 C4
Peake, *Australia* 91 F2
Peake Cr. →, *Australia* 91 D2
Peale, Mt., *U.S.A.* 111 G9
Pearblossom, *U.S.A.* 113 L9
Pearl →, *U.S.A.* 109 K10
Pearl City, *U.S.A.* 102 H16
Pearsall, *U.S.A.* 109 L5
Pearse I., *Canada* 100 C2
Peary Land, *Greenland* 4 A6
Pease →, *U.S.A.* 109 H5
Pebane, *Mozam.* 83 F4
Pebas, *Peru* 120 D3
Pebble, I., *Falk. Is.* 128 D5
Pebble Beach, *U.S.A.* 112 J5
Peč, *Serbia, Yug.* 21 N10
Peçanha, *Brazil* 123 E3
Péccioli, *Italy* 32 E7
Pechea, *Romania* 38 D10
Pechenezhin, *Ukraine* 42 B1
Pechenga, *Russia* 44 C4
Pechiguera, Pta., *Canary Is.* 36 F6
Pechnezhskoye Vdkhr., *Ukraine* 42 A7
Pechora →, *Russia* 44 C6
Pechorskaya Guba, *Russia* 44 C6
Pecica, *Romania* 38 C4
Pečka, *Serbia, Yug.* 21 L9
Pécora, C., *Italy* 34 C1
Pečory, *Russia* 40 C5
Pecos, *U.S.A.* 109 K3
Pecos →, *U.S.A.* 109 L3
Pécs, *Hungary* 21 J8
Pedder, L., *Australia* 90 G4
Peddie, *S. Africa* 85 E4
Pédernales, *Dom. Rep.* 117 C5
Pedieos →, *Cyprus* 37 D12
Pedirka, *Australia* 91 D2
Pedra Azul, *Brazil* 123 E3
Pedra Grande, Recifes de, *Brazil* 123 E4
Pedras Negras, *Brazil* 125 C5
Pedreiras, *Brazil* 122 B3
Pedro Afonso, *Brazil* 122 C2
Pedro Cays, *Jamaica* 116 C4
Pedro Chico, *Colombia* 120 C3
Pedro de Valdivia, *Chile* 126 A2
Pedro Juan Caballero, *Paraguay* 127 A4
Pedro Muñoz, *Spain* 29 F2
Pedrógão Grande, *Portugal* 30 F2
Peebinga, *Australia* 91 E3
Peebles, *U.K.* 14 F5
Peekskill, *U.S.A.* 107 E11
Peel, *U.K.* 12 C3
Peel →, *Australia* 91 E5
Peel →, *Canada* 96 B6
Peene →, *Germany* 18 A9
Peera Peera Poolanna L., *Australia* 91 D2
Peers, *Canada* 100 C5
Pegasus Bay, *N.Z.* 87 K4
Pegnitz, *Germany* 19 F7
Pegnitz →, *Germany* 19 F6
Pego, *Spain* 29 G4
Pegu, *Burma* 61 L20
Pegu Yoma, *Burma* 61 K19
Pehuajó, *Argentina* 126 D3
Pei Xian, *China* 50 G9
Peine, *Chile* 126 A2
Peine, *Germany* 18 C6
Peip'ing = Beijing, *China* 50 E9
Peissenberg, *Germany* 19 H7
Peitz, *Germany* 18 D10
Peixe, *Brazil* 123 D2
Peixe →, *Brazil* 123 F1
Peixoto de Azeredo →, *Brazil* 125 C6
Peize, *Neths.* 16 B8
Pek →, *Serbia, Yug.* 21 L11
Pekalongan, *Indonesia* 57 G13
Pekan, *Malaysia* 59 L4
Pekanbaru, *Indonesia* 56 D2
Pekin, *U.S.A.* 108 E10
Peking = Beijing, *Beijing, China* 50 E9
Peking = Beijing, *Beijing, China* 50 E9
Pelabuhan Kelang, *Malaysia* 59 L3
Pelabuhan Ratu, Teluk, *Indonesia* 57 G12
Pelabuhanratu, *Indonesia* 57 G12
Pélagos, *Greece* 39 K7
Pelaihari, *Indonesia* 56 E4
Pelat, Mt., *France* 27 D10
Peleaga, *Romania* 38 D5
Pelechuco, *Bolivia* 124 C4
Pelée, Mt., *Martinique* 117 D7
Pelee, Pt., *Canada* 98 D3
Pelee I., *Canada* 98 D3
Pelejo, *Peru* 124 B2
Pelekech, *Kenya* 82 B4
Peleng, *Indonesia* 57 E6
Pelham, *U.S.A.* 105 K3
Pelhřimov, *Czech.* 20 F5
Pelican L., *Canada* 101 C8
Pelican Narrows, *Canada* 101 B8
Pelican Rapids, *Canada* 101 C8
Pelkosenniemi, *Finland* 8 C19
Pella, *S. Africa* 84 D2
Pella, *U.S.A.* 108 E8
Péllaro, *Italy* 35 D8
Pellworm, *Germany* 18 A4
Pelly →, *Canada* 96 B6
Pelly Bay, *Canada* 97 B11
Pelly L., *Canada* 96 B9
Peloponnese = Pelopónnisos □, *Greece* 39 M5
Pelopónnisos □, *Greece* 39 M5
Peloritani, Monti, *Italy* 35 D8
Peloro, C., *Italy* 35 D8
Pelorus Sd., *N.Z.* 87 J4
Pelotas, *Brazil* 127 C5
Pelvoux, Massif de, *France* 27 D10
Pemalang, *Indonesia* 57 G13
Pematangsiantar, *Indonesia* 56 D1
Pemba, *Mozam.* 83 E5
Pemba, *Zambia* 83 F2
Pemba Channel, *Tanzania* 82 D4
Pemba I., *Tanzania* 82 D4
Pemberton, *Australia* 89 F2
Pemberton, *Canada* 100 C4
Pembina, *U.S.A.* 101 D9
Pembina →, *U.S.A.* 101 D9
Pembine, *U.S.A.* 104 C2
Pembino, *U.S.A.* 108 A6
Pembroke, *Canada* 98 C4
Pembroke, *U.K.* 13 F3
Pembroke, *U.S.A.* 105 J5
Pen-y-Ghent, *U.K.* 12 C5
Peña, Sierra de la, *Spain* 28 C4
Peña de Francia, Sierra de, *Spain* 30 E4
Penafiel, *Portugal* 30 D2
Peñafiel, *Spain* 30 D6
Peñaflor, *Spain* 31 H5
Peñalara, Pico, *Spain* 30 E7
Penalva, *Brazil* 122 B2
Penamacôr, *Portugal* 30 E3
Penang = Pinang, *Malaysia* 59 K3
Penápolis, *Brazil* 127 A6
Peñaranda de Bracamonte, *Spain* 30 E5
Peñarroya-Pueblonuevo, *Spain* 31 G5
Peñas, C. de, *Spain* 30 B5
Penas, G. de, *Chile* 128 C2
Peñas, Pta., *Venezuela* 121 A5
Peñas de San Pedro, *Spain* 29 G2
Peñas del Chache, *Canary Is.* 36 E6
Peñausende, *Spain* 30 D5
Pench'i = Benxi, *China* 51 D12
Pend Oreille →, *U.S.A.* 110 B5
Pend Oreille L., *U.S.A.* 110 C5
Pendembu, *S. Leone* 78 D2
Pendências, *Brazil* 122 C4
Pender B., *Australia* 88 C3
Pendleton, *Calif., U.S.A.* 113 M9
Pendleton, *Oreg., U.S.A.* 110 D4
Penedo, *Brazil* 122 D4
Penetanguishene, *Canada* 98 D4
Peng Xian, *China* 52 B4
Pengalengan, *Indonesia* 57 G12
Penge, *Kasai Or., Zaïre* 82 D1
Penge, *Kivu, Zaïre* 82 C2
Penglai, *China* 51 F11
Pengshui, *China* 52 C7
Penguin, *Australia* 90 G4
Pengxi, *China* 52 B5
Pengze, *China* 53 C11
Penhalonga, *Zimbabwe* 83 F3
Peniche, *Portugal* 31 F1
Penicuik, *U.K.* 14 F5
Penida, *Indonesia* 56 F5
Peninsular Malaysia □, *Malaysia* 59 L4
Peñíscola, *Spain* 28 E5
Penitente, Serra dos, *Brazil* 122 C2
Penmarch, *France* 24 E2
Penmarch, Pte. de, *France* 24 E2
Penn Hills, *U.S.A.* 106 F5
Penn Yan, *U.S.A.* 106 D7
Pennabilli, *Italy* 33 E9
Pennant, *Canada* 101 C7
Penne, *Italy* 33 F10
Penner →, *India* 60 M12
Pennine, Alpi, *Alps* 32 B4
Pennines, *U.K.* 12 C5
Pennington, *U.S.A.* 112 F5
Pennino, Mte., *Italy* 33 E9
Pennsylvania □, *U.S.A.* 104 E6
Penny, *Canada* 100 C4
Peno, *Russia* 40 C8
Penola, *Australia* 91 F3
Penong, *Australia* 89 F5
Penonomé, *Panama* 116 E3
Penrith, *Australia* 91 E5
Penrith, *U.K.* 12 C5
Pensacola, *U.S.A.* 105 K2
Pensacola Mts., *Antarctica* 5 E1
Pense, *Canada* 101 C8
Penshurst, *Australia* 91 F3
Pentecoste, *Brazil* 122 B4
Penticton, *Canada* 100 D5
Pentland, *Australia* 90 C4
Pentland Firth, *U.K.* 14 C5
Pentland Hills, *U.K.* 14 F5
Penylan L., *Canada* 101 A7
Penza, *Russia* 41 E14
Penzance, *U.K.* 13 G2
Penzberg, *Germany* 19 H7
Penzhino, *Russia* 45 C17
Penzhinskaya Guba, *Russia* 45 C17
Penzlin, *Germany* 18 B9
Peoria, *Ariz., U.S.A.* 111 K7
Peoria, *Ill., U.S.A.* 108 E10
Pepingen, *Belgium* 17 G4
Pepinster, *Belgium* 17 G7
Pera Hd., *Australia* 90 A3
Perabumilih, *Indonesia* 56 E2
Perak →, *Malaysia* 59 K3
Perakhóra, *Greece* 39 L5
Perales de Alfambra, *Spain* 28 E3
Perales del Puerto, *Spain* 30 E4
Peralta, *Spain* 28 C3
Pérama, *Kérkira, Greece* 37 A3
Pérama, *Kríti, Greece* 37 D6
Percé, *Canada* 99 C7
Perche, *France* 24 D8
Perche, Collines du, *France* 24 D7
Percival Lakes, *Australia* 88 D4
Percy, *France* 24 D5
Percy Is., *Australia* 90 C5
Perdido →, *Argentina* 128 B3
Perdido, Mte., *Spain* 26 F4
Perdu, Mt. = Perdido, Mte., *Spain* 26 F4
Pereira, *Colombia* 120 C2
Pereira Barreto, *Brazil* 123 F1
Perekerten, *Australia* 91 E3
Perené →, *Peru* 124 C3
Perenjori, *Australia* 89 E2
Pereslavl-Zalesskiy, *Russia* 41 C11
Pereyaslav Khmelnitskiy, *Ukraine* 40 F7
Pérez, I., *Mexico* 115 C7
Pergamino, *Argentina* 126 C3
Pérgine Valsugano, *Italy* 33 B8
Pérgola, *Italy* 33 E9
Perham, *U.S.A.* 108 B7
Perhentian, Kepulauan, *Malaysia* 59 K4
Periam, *Romania* 38 C3
Péribonca →, *Canada* 99 C5
Péribonca, L., *Canada* 99 B5
Perico, *Argentina* 126 A2
Pericos, *Mexico* 114 B3
Périers, *France* 24 C5
Périgord, *France* 26 D4
Périgueux, *France* 26 C4
Perijá, Sierra de, *Colombia* 120 B3
Peristéra, *Greece* 39 K6
Peristerona →, *Cyprus* 37 D12
Perito Moreno, *Argentina* 128 C2
Peritoró, *Brazil* 122 B3
Perković, *Croatia* 33 E13
Perlas, Arch. de las, *Panama* 116 E4
Perlas, Punta de, *Nic.* 116 D3
Perleberg, *Germany* 18 B7
Perlevka, *Russia* 41 F11
Perm, *Russia* 44 D6
Pernambuco = Recife, *Brazil* 122 C5
Pernambuco □, *Brazil* 122 C4
Pernatty Lagoon, *Australia* 91 E2
Pernik, *Bulgaria* 38 G6
Peron, C., *Australia* 89 E1
Peron Is., *Australia* 88 B5
Peron Pen., *Australia* 89 E1
Péronne, *France* 25 C9
Péronnes, *Belgium* 17 H4
Perosa Argentina, *Italy* 32 D4
Perow, *Canada* 100 C3
Perpendicular Pt., *Australia* 91 E5
Perpignan, *France* 26 F6
Perris, *U.S.A.* 113 M9
Perros-Guirec, *France* 24 D3
Perry, *Fla., U.S.A.* 105 K4
Perry, *Ga., U.S.A.* 105 J4
Perry, *Iowa, U.S.A.* 108 E7
Perry, *Maine, U.S.A.* 105 C12
Perry, *Okla., U.S.A.* 109 G6
Perryton, *U.S.A.* 109 G4
Perryville, *U.S.A.* 109 G10
Perşembe, *Turkey* 67 C7
Perseverancia, *Bolivia* 125 C5
Persia = Iran ■, *Asia* 65 C7
Persian Gulf = Gulf, The, *Asia* 65 E6
Perstorp, *Sweden* 11 H7
Pertek, *Turkey* 67 D8
Perth, *Australia* 89 F2
Perth, *Canada* 98 D4
Perth, *U.K.* 14 E5
Perth Amboy, *U.S.A.* 107 F10
Pertuis, *France* 27 E9
Peru, *Ill., U.S.A.* 108 E10
Peru, *Ind., U.S.A.* 104 E2
Peru ■, *S. Amer.* 120 D2
Peru-Chile Trench, *Pac. Oc.* 93 K20
Perúgia, *Italy* 33 E9
Perušić, *Croatia* 33 D12
Péruwelz, *Belgium* 17 G3
Pervomaysk, *Russia* 41 D13
Pervomaysk, *Ukraine* 42 B4
Pervouralsk, *Russia* 44 D6
Perwez, *Belgium* 17 G5
Pes, Pta. del, *Spain* 36 C7
Pésaro, *Italy* 33 E9
Pescara, *Italy* 33 F11
Pescara →, *Italy* 33 F11
Peschanokopskoye, *Russia* 43 C9
Péscia, *Italy* 32 E7

Pescina, *Italy* 33 G10
Peseux, *Switz.* 22 C3
Peshawar, *Pakistan* 62 B4
Peshtigo, *U.S.A.* 104 C2
Peski, *Russia* 41 F13
Peskovka, *Russia* 41 B18
Pêso da Régua, *Portugal* 30 D3
Pesqueira, *Brazil* 122 C4
Pessac, *France* 26 D3
Pessoux, *Belgium* 17 H6
Pestovo, *Russia* 40 B9
Pestravka, *Russia* 41 E16
Petah Tiqwa, *Israel* 69 C3
Petaling Jaya, *Malaysia* 59 L3
Petaloudhes, *Greece* 37 C10
Petaluma, *U.S.A.* 112 G4
Petange, *Lux.* 17 J7
Petatlán, *Mexico* 114 D4
Petauke, *Zambia* 83 E3
Petawawa, *Canada* 98 C4
Petegem, *Belgium* 17 G3
Petén Itzá, L., *Guatemala* 116 C2
Peter I.s Øy, *Antarctica* 5 C16
Peter Pond L., *Canada* 101 B7
Peterbell, *Canada* 98 C3
Peterborough, *Australia* 91 E2
Peterborough, *Canada* 97 D12
Peterborough, *U.K.* 13 E7
Peterborough, *U.S.A.* 107 D13
Peterhead, *U.K.* 14 D7
Petermann Bjerg, *Greenland* 94 B17
Peter's Mine, *Guyana* 121 B6
Petersburg, *Alaska, U.S.A.* 100 B2
Petersburg, *Ind., U.S.A.* 104 F2
Petersburg, *Va., U.S.A.* 104 G7
Petersburg, *W. Va., U.S.A.* 104 F6
Petford, *Australia* 90 B3
Petília Policastro, *Italy* 35 C9
Petit Bois I., *U.S.A.* 105 K1
Petit-Cap, *Canada* 99 C7
Petit Goâve, *Haiti* 117 C5
Petit Lac Manicouagan, *Canada* 99 B6
Petit Saint Bernard, Col du, *Italy* 32 C3
Petitcodiac, *Canada* 99 C6
Petite Baleine →, *Canada* 98 A4
Petite Saguenay, *Canada* 99 C5
Petitsikapau, L., *Canada* 99 B6
Petlad, *India* 62 H5
Peto, *Mexico* 115 C7
Petone, *N.Z.* 87 J5
Petoskey, *U.S.A.* 104 C3
Petra, *Jordan* 69 E4
Petra, *Spain* 36 B10
Petra, Ostrova, *Russia* 4 B13
Petra Velikogo, Zaliv, *Russia* 48 C5
Petralia, *Italy* 35 E7
Petrel, *Spain* 29 G4
Petreto-Bicchisano, *France* 27 G12
Petrich, *Bulgaria* 39 H6
Petrijanec, *Croatia* 33 B13
Petrikov, *Belorussia* 40 E6
Petrinja, *Croatia* 33 C13
Petrograd = Sankt-Peterburg, *Russia* 40 B7
Petrolândia, *Brazil* 122 C4
Petrolia, *Canada* 98 D3
Petrolina, *Brazil* 122 C3
Petropavlovsk, *Kazakhstan* 44 D7
Petropavlovsk-Kamchatskiy, *Russia* 45 D16
Petropavlovskiy = Akhtubinsk, *Russia* 43 B12
Petrópolis, *Brazil* 123 F3
Petroşeni, *Romania* 38 D6
Petrova Gora, *Croatia* 33 C12
Petrovac, *Montenegro, Yug.* 21 N8
Petrovsk, *Russia* 41 E14
Petrovsk-Zabaykalskiy, *Russia* 45 D11
Petrovskoye = Svetlograd, *Russia* 43 D10
Petrozavodsk, *Russia* 44 C4
Petrus Steyn, *S. Africa* 85 D4
Petrusburg, *S. Africa* 84 D4
Petukhovka, *Belorussia* 40 E7
Peumo, *Chile* 126 C1
Peureulak, *Indonesia* 56 D1
Pevek, *Russia* 45 C18
Peveragno, *Italy* 32 D4
Peyrehorade, *France* 26 E2
Peyruis, *France* 27 D9
Pézenas, *France* 26 E7
Pfaffenhofen, *Germany* 19 G7
Pfäffikon, *Switz.* 23 B7
Pfarrkirchen, *Germany* 19 G8
Pfeffenhausen, *Germany* 19 G7
Pforzheim, *Germany* 19 G4
Pfullendorf, *Germany* 19 H5
Pfungstadt, *Germany* 19 F4
Phagwara, *India* 60 D9
Phaistós, *Greece* 37 D6
Phala, *Botswana* 84 C4
Phalera = Phulera, *India* 62 F6
Phalodi, *India* 62 F5
Phalsbourg, *France* 25 D14
Phan, *Thailand* 58 C2
Phan Rang, *Vietnam* 59 G7
Phan Ri = Hoa Da, *Vietnam* 59 G7
Phan Thiet, *Vietnam* 59 G7
Phanat Nikhom, *Thailand* 58 F3
Phangan, Ko, *Thailand* 59 H3
Phangnga, *Thailand* 59 H2
Phanh Bho Ho Chi Minh, *Vietnam* 59 G6
Phanom Sarakham, *Thailand* 58 F3
Pharenda, *India* 63 F10
Phatthalung, *Thailand* 59 J3
Phayao, *Thailand* 58 C2
Phelps, *N.Y., U.S.A.* 106 D7
Phelps, *Wis., U.S.A.* 108 B10
Phelps L., *Canada* 101 B8
Phenix City, *U.S.A.* 105 J3
Phet Buri, *Thailand* 58 F2
Phetchabun, *Thailand* 58 D3
Phetchabun, Thiu Khao, *Thailand* 58 E3
Phetchaburi = Phet Buri, *Thailand* 58 F2
Phi Phi, Ko, *Thailand* 59 J2
Phiafay, *Laos* 58 E6
Phibun Mangsahan, *Thailand* 58 E5
Phichai, *Thailand* 58 D3
Phichit, *Thailand* 58 D3
Philadelphia, *Miss., U.S.A.* 109 J10
Philadelphia, *N.Y., U.S.A.* 107 B9
Philadelphia, *Pa., U.S.A.* 107 F9
Philip, *U.S.A.* 108 C4
Philippeville, *Belgium* 17 H5
Philippi L., *Australia* 90 C2
Philippines ■, *Asia* 55 F5
Philippolis, *S. Africa* 84 E4
Philippopolis = Plovdiv, *Bulgaria* 38 G7
Philipsburg, *Mont., U.S.A.* 110 C7
Philipsburg, *Pa., U.S.A.* 106 F6
Philipstown, *S. Africa* 84 E3
Phillip I., *Australia* 91 F4
Phillips, *Tex., U.S.A.* 109 H4
Phillips, *Wis., U.S.A.* 108 C9
Phillipsburg, *Kans., U.S.A.* 108 F5
Phillipsburg, *N.J., U.S.A.* 107 F9
Phillott, *Australia* 91 D4
Philmont, *U.S.A.* 107 D11
Philomath, *U.S.A.* 110 D2
Phimai, *Thailand* 58 E4
Phitsanulok, *Thailand* 58 D3
Phnom Dangrek, *Thailand* 58 E5
Phnom Penh, *Cambodia* 59 G5
Phoenix, *Ariz., U.S.A.* 111 K7
Phoenix, *N.Y., U.S.A.* 107 C8
Phoenix Is., *Kiribati* 92 H10
Phoenixville, *U.S.A.* 107 F9
Phon, *Thailand* 58 E4
Phon Tiou, *Laos* 58 D5
Phong →, *Thailand* 58 D4
Phong Saly, *Laos* 58 B4
Phong Tho, *Vietnam* 58 A4
Phonhong, *Laos* 58 C4
Phonum, *Thailand* 59 H2
Phosphate Hill, *Australia* 90 C2
Photharam, *Thailand* 58 F2
Phra Chedi Sam Ong, *Thailand* 58 E2
Phra Nakhon Si Ayutthaya, *Thailand* 58 E3
Phra Thong, Ko, *Thailand* 59 H2
Phrae, *Thailand* 58 C3
Phrom Phiram, *Thailand* 58 D3
Phrygia, *Turkey* 66 D3
Phu Dien, *Vietnam* 58 C5
Phu Loi, *Laos* 58 B4
Phu Ly, *Vietnam* 58 B5
Phu Tho, *Vietnam* 58 B5
Phuc Yen, *Vietnam* 58 B5
Phuket, *Thailand* 59 J2
Phuket, Ko, *Thailand* 59 J2
Phulera, *India* 62 F6
Phumiphon, Khuan, *Thailand* 58 D2
Phun Phin, *Thailand* 59 H2
Piacá, *Brazil* 122 C2
Piacenza, *Italy* 32 C6
Piaçubaçu, *Brazil* 122 D4
Piádena, *Italy* 32 C7
Pialba, *Australia* 91 D5
Pian Cr. →, *Australia* 91 E4
Piana, *France* 27 F12
Pianella, *Italy* 33 F11
Pianoro, *Italy* 33 D8
Pianosa, *Puglia, Italy* 33 F12
Pianosa, *Toscana, Italy* 32 F7
Piapot, *Canada* 101 D7
Piare →, *Italy* 33 C9
Pias, *Portugal* 31 G3
Piaseczno, *Poland* 20 C11
Piatã, *Brazil* 123 D3
Piatra, *Romania* 38 F8
Piatra Neamţ, *Romania* 38 C9
Piauí □, *Brazil* 122 C3
Piaui →, *Brazil* 122 C3
Piave →, *Italy* 33 C9
Piazza Ármerina, *Italy* 35 E7
Pibor →, *Sudan* 77 F3
Pibor Post, *Sudan* 77 F3
Pica, *Chile* 124 E4
Picardie, *France* 25 C9
Picardie, Plaine de, *France* 25 C9
Picardy = Picardie, *France* 25 C9
Picayune, *U.S.A.* 109 K10
Picerno, *Italy* 35 B8
Pichilemu, *Chile* 126 C1
Pichincha, □, *Ecuador* 120 D2
Pickerel L., *Canada* 98 C1
Pickle Lake, *Canada* 98 B1
Pico Truncado, *Argentina* 128 C3
Picos, *Brazil* 122 C3
Picos Ancares, Sierra de, *Spain* 30 C4
Picota, *Peru* 124 B2
Picquigny, *France* 25 C9
Picton, *Australia* 91 E5
Picton, *Canada* 98 D4
Picton, *N.Z.* 87 J5
Picton, I., *Chile* 128 E3
Pictou, *Canada* 99 C7
Picture Butte, *Canada* 100 D6
Picuí, *Brazil* 122 C4
Picún Leufú, *Argentina* 128 A3
Pidurutalagala, *Sri Lanka* 60 R12
Piedecuesta, *Colombia* 120 B3
Piedicavallo, *Italy* 32 C4
Piedmont = Piemonte □, *Italy* 32 D4
Piedmont, *U.S.A.* 105 J3
Piedmont Plateau, *U.S.A.* 105 J5
Piedimonte d'Alife, *Italy* 35 A7
Piedra →, *Spain* 28 D3
Piedra del Anguila, *Argentina* 128 B2
Piedra Lais, *Venezuela* 120 C4
Piedrabuena, *Spain* 31 F6
Piedrahita, *Spain* 30 E5
Piedras, R. de las →, *Peru* 124 C4
Piedras Negras, *Mexico* 114 B4
Piemonte □, *Italy* 32 D4
Pierce, *U.S.A.* 110 C6
Piercefield, *U.S.A.* 107 B10
Pierre, *U.S.A.* 108 C4
Pierre Bénite, Barrage de la, *France* 27 C8
Pierre-de-Bresse, *France* 27 B9
Pierrefeu-du-Var, *France* 27 E10
Pierrefonds, *France* 25 C9
Pierrefontaine-les-Varans, *France* 25 E13
Pierrefort, *France* 26 D6
Pierrelatte, *France* 27 D8
Pieštany, *Slovakia* 20 G7
Piesting →, *Austria* 21 G6
Piet Retief, *S. Africa* 85 D5
Pietarsaari = Jakobstad, *Finland* 8 E17
Pietermaritzburg, *S. Africa* 85 D5
Pietersburg, *S. Africa* 85 C4
Pietraperzia, *Italy* 35 E7
Pietrasanta, *Italy* 32 E7
Pietrosu, *Romania* 38 B8
Pietrosul, *Romania* 38 B7
Pieve di Cadore, *Italy* 33 B9
Pieve di Teco, *Italy* 32 D4
Pievepélago, *Italy* 32 D7
Pigádhia, *Greece* 39 P10
Pigeon, *U.S.A.* 104 D4
Piggott, *U.S.A.* 109 G9
Pigna, *Italy* 32 E4
Pigüe, *Argentina* 126 D3
Pihani, *India* 63 F9
Pijnacker, *Neths.* 16 D4
Pikalevo, *Russia* 40 B9
Pikes Peak, *U.S.A.* 108 F2
Piketberg, *S. Africa* 84 E2
Pikeville, *U.S.A.* 104 G4
Pikou, *China* 51 E12
Pikwitonei, *Canada* 101 B9
Piła, *Poland* 20 B6
Pila, *Spain* 29 G3
Pilani, *India* 62 E6
Pilar, *Brazil* 122 C4
Pilar, *Paraguay* 126 B4
Pilas Group, *Phil.* 57 C6
Pilaya →, *Bolivia* 125 E5
Pilcomayo →, *Paraguay* 126 B4
Pilibhit, *India* 63 E8
Pilica →, *Poland* 20 D11
Pilkhawa, *India* 62 E7
Pillaro, *Ecuador* 120 D2
Pílos, *Greece* 39 N4
Pilot Mound, *Canada* 101 D9
Pilot Point, *U.S.A.* 109 J6
Pilot Rock, *U.S.A.* 110 D4
Pilsen = Plzeň, *Czech.* 20 F3
Pilštanj, *Slovenia* 33 B12
Pima, *U.S.A.* 111 K9
Pimba, *Australia* 91 E2
Pimenta Bueno, *Brazil* 125 C5
Pimentel, *Peru* 124 B2
Pina, *Spain* 28 D4
Pinamalayan, *Phil.* 55 E4
Pinang, *Malaysia* 59 K3
Pinar, C. del, *Spain* 36 B10
Pinar del Río, *Cuba* 116 B3
Pinarbaşi, *Turkey* 66 D7
Pinchang, *China* 52 B6
Pincher Creek, *Canada* 100 D6
Pinchi L., *Canada* 100 C4
Pinckneyville, *U.S.A.* 108 F10
Pîncota, *Romania* 38 C4
Pind Dadan Khan, *Pakistan* 62 C5
Pindar, *Australia* 89 E2
Pindaré →, *Brazil* 122 B3
Pindaré Mirim, *Brazil* 122 B2
Pindi Gheb, *Pakistan* 62 C5
Pindiga, *Nigeria* 79 D7
Pindobal, *Brazil* 122 B2
Pindos Óros, *Greece* 39 K4
Pindus Mts. = Pindos Óros, *Greece* 39 K4
Pine, *U.S.A.* 111 J8
Pine →, *Canada* 101 B7
Pine, C., *Canada* 99 C9
Pine Bluff, *U.S.A.* 109 H8
Pine City, *U.S.A.* 108 C8
Pine Falls, *Canada* 101 C9
Pine Flat L., *U.S.A.* 112 J7
Pine Pass, *Canada* 100 B4
Pine Point, *Canada* 100 A6
Pine Ridge, *U.S.A.* 108 D3
Pine River, *Canada* 101 C8
Pine River, *U.S.A.* 108 B7
Pine Valley, *U.S.A.* 113 N10
Pinecrest, *U.S.A.* 112 G6
Pinedale, *U.S.A.* 112 J7
Pinega →, *Russia* 44 C5
Pinehill, *Australia* 90 C4
Pinerolo, *Italy* 32 D4
Pineto, *Italy* 33 F11
Pinetop, *U.S.A.* 111 J9
Pinetown, *S. Africa* 85 D5
Pinetree, *U.S.A.* 110 E11
Pineville, *Ky., U.S.A.* 105 G4
Pineville, *La., U.S.A.* 109 K8
Piney, *France* 25 D11
Ping →, *Thailand* 58 E3
Pingaring, *Australia* 89 F2
Pingba, *China* 52 D6
Pingchuan, *China* 52 D3
Pingding, *China* 50 F7
Pingdingshan, *China* 50 H7
Pingdong, *Taiwan* 53 F13
Pingdu, *China* 51 F10
Pingelly, *Australia* 89 F2
Pingguo, *China* 52 F6
Pinghe, *China* 53 E11
Pinghu, *China* 53 B13
Pingjiang, *China* 53 C9
Pingle, *China* 53 E8
Pingli, *China* 52 A7
Pingliang, *China* 50 G4
Pinglu, *China* 50 E7
Pingluo, *China* 50 E4
Pingnan, *Fujian, China* 53 D12
Pingnan, *Guangxi Zhuangzu, China* 53 F8
Pingquan, *China* 51 D10
Pingrup, *Australia* 89 F2
Pingtan, *China* 53 E12
Pingtang, *China* 52 E6
Pingwu, *China* 50 H3
Pingxiang, *Guangxi Zhuangzu, China* 52 F6
Pingxiang, *Jiangxi, China* 53 D9
Pingyao, *China* 50 F7
Pingyi, *China* 51 G9
Pingyin, *China* 50 F9
Pingyuan, *Guangdong, China* 53 E10
Pingyuan, *Shandong, China* 50 F9
Pingyuanjie, *China* 52 F4
Pinhal, *Brazil* 127 A6
Pinheiro, *Brazil* 122 B2
Pinhel, *Portugal* 30 E3
Pinhuá →, *Brazil* 125 B4
Pini, *Indonesia* 56 D1
Piniós →, *Ilía, Greece* 39 M4
Piniós →, *Trikkala, Greece* 39 K5
Pinjarra, *Australia* 89 F2
Pink →, *Canada* 101 B8
Pinnacles, *Australia* 89 E3
Pinnacles, *U.S.A.* 112 J5
Pinnaroo, *Australia* 91 F3
Pinneberg, *Germany* 18 B5
Pino Hachado, Paso, *S. Amer.* 128 A2
Pinon Hills, *U.S.A.* 113 L9
Pinos, *Mexico* 114 C4
Pinos, Mt., *U.S.A.* 113 L7
Pinos Pt., *U.S.A.* 111 H3
Pinos Puente, *Spain* 31 H7
Pinotepa Nacional, *Mexico* 115 D5
Pinrang, *Indonesia* 57 E5
Pinsk, *Belorussia* 40 E5
Pintados, *Chile* 124 E4
Pintumba, *Australia* 89 F5
Pinyang, *China* 53 D13
Pinyug, *Russia* 44 C5
Pinzolo, *Italy* 32 B7
Pio XII, *Brazil* 122 B2
Pioche, *U.S.A.* 111 H6
Piombino, *Italy* 32 F7
Piombino, Canale di, *Italy* 32 F7
Pioner, Os., *Russia* 45 B10
Pionki, *Poland* 20 D11
Piorini →, *Brazil* 121 D5
Piorini, L., *Brazil* 121 D5
Piotrków Trybunalski, *Poland* 20 D9
Piove di Sacco, *Italy* 33 C9
Pīp, *Iran* 65 E9
Pipar, *India* 62 F5
Piparia, *India* 62 H8
Pipestone, *U.S.A.* 108 D6
Pipestone →, *Canada* 98 B2
Pipestone Cr. →, *Canada* 101 D8
Pipmuacan, Rés., *Canada* 99 C5
Pippingarra, *Australia* 88 D2
Pipriac, *France* 24 E5
Piqua, *U.S.A.* 104 E3
Piquet Carneiro, *Brazil* 122 C4
Piquiri →, *Brazil* 127 A5
Pīr Sohrāb, *Iran* 65 E9
Piracanjuba, *Brazil* 123 E2
Piracicaba, *Brazil* 127 A6
Piracuruca, *Brazil* 122 B3
Piræus = Piraiévs, *Greece* 39 M6
Piraiévs, *Greece* 39 M6
Piráino, *Italy* 35 D7
Pirajuí, *Brazil* 127 A6
Piran, *Slovenia* 33 C10
Pirané, *Argentina* 126 B4
Piranhas, *Brazil* 122 C4
Pirano = Piran, *Slovenia* 33 C10
Pirapemas, *Brazil* 122 B3
Pirapora, *Brazil* 123 E3
Piray →, *Bolivia* 125 D5
Pires do Rio, *Brazil* 123 E2
Pírgos, *Ilía, Greece* 39 M4
Pírgos, *Messinia, Greece* 39 N5
Pirgovo, *Bulgaria* 38 F8
Piriac-sur-Mer, *France* 24 E4
Piribebuy, *Paraguay* 126 B4
Pirin Planina, *Bulgaria* 39 H6
Pirineos, *Spain* 28 C6
Piripiri, *Brazil* 122 B3
Piritu, *Venezuela* 120 B4
Pirmasens, *Germany* 19 F3
Pirna, *Germany* 18 E9
Pirot, *Serbia, Yug.* 21 M12
Piru, *Indonesia* 57 E7
Piru, *U.S.A.* 113 L8
Piryatin, *Ukraine* 40 F8
Pisa, *Italy* 32 E7
Pisac, *Peru* 124 C3
Pisagua, *Chile* 124 D3
Pisarovina, *Croatia* 33 C12
Pisciotta, *Italy* 35 B8
Pisco, *Peru* 124 C2
Písek, *Czech.* 20 F4
Pishan, *China* 54 C2
Pishin Lora →, *Pakistan* 62 E1
Pisidia, *Turkey* 66 E4
Pising, *Indonesia* 57 F6
Pismo Beach, *U.S.A.* 113 K6
Pissos, *France* 26 D3
Pissouri, *Cyprus* 37 E11
Pisticci, *Italy* 35 B9
Pistóia, *Italy* 32 E7
Pistol B., *Canada* 101 A10
Pisuerga →, *Spain* 30 D6
Pisz, *Poland* 20 B11
Pitalito, *Colombia* 120 C2
Pitanga, *Brazil* 123 F1
Pitangui, *Brazil* 123 E3
Pitarpunga, L., *Australia* 91 E3
Pitcairn I., *Pac. Oc.* 93 K14
Pite älv →, *Sweden* 8 D16
Piteå, *Sweden* 8 D16
Piterka, *Russia* 41 F15
Piteşti, *Romania* 38 E7
Pithapuram, *India* 61 L13
Pithara, *Australia* 89 F2
Píthion, *Greece* 39 H9
Pithiviers, *France* 25 D9
Pitigliano, *Italy* 33 F8
Pitlochry, *U.K.* 14 E5
Pitrufquén, *Chile* 128 A2
Pitsilia □, *Cyprus* 37 E12
Pitt I., *Canada* 100 C3
Pittem, *Belgium* 17 F2
Pittsburg, *Kans., U.S.A.* 109 G7
Pittsburg, *Tex., U.S.A.* 109 J7
Pittsburgh, *U.S.A.* 106 F5
Pittsfield, *Ill., U.S.A.* 108 F9
Pittsfield, *Mass., U.S.A.* 107 D11
Pittsfield, *N.H., U.S.A.* 107 C13
Pittston, *U.S.A.* 107 E9
Pittsworth, *Australia* 91 D5
Pituri →, *Australia* 90 C2
Piuí, *Brazil* 123 F2
Pium, *Brazil* 122 D2
Piura, *Peru* 124 B1
Piura □, *Peru* 124 A2
Pivijay, *Colombia* 120 A3
Pixley, *U.S.A.* 112 K7
Piyai, *Greece* 39 K4
Pizarro, *Colombia* 120 C2
Pizol, *Switz.* 23 C8
Pizzo, *Italy* 35 D9
Placentia, *Canada* 99 C9
Placentia B., *Canada* 99 C9
Placer, *Phil.* 55 F5
Placerville, *U.S.A.* 112 G6
Placetas, *Cuba* 116 B4
Plaffeien, *Switz.* 22 C4
Plain Dealing, *U.S.A.* 109 J8
Plainfield, *U.S.A.* 107 F10
Plains, *Kans., U.S.A.* 109 G4
Plains, *Mont., U.S.A.* 110 C6
Plains, *Tex., U.S.A.* 109 J3
Plainview, *Nebr., U.S.A.* 108 D6
Plainview, *Tex., U.S.A.* 109 H4
Plainville, *U.S.A.* 108 F5
Plainwell, *U.S.A.* 104 D3
Plaisance, *France* 26 E4
Pláka, *Greece* 39 J8
Pláka, Ákra, *Greece* 37 D8
Plakhino, *Russia* 44 C9
Plana Cays, *Bahamas* 117 B5
Planada, *U.S.A.* 112 H6
Plancoët, *France* 24 D4
Plandište, *Serbia, Yug.* 21 K11
Planeta Rica, *Colombia* 120 B2
Planina, *Slovenia* 33 B12
Planina, *Slovenia* 33 C11
Plankinton, *U.S.A.* 108 D5
Plano, *U.S.A.* 109 J6
Plant City, *U.S.A.* 105 L4
Plaquemine, *U.S.A.* 109 K9
Plasencia, *Spain* 30 E4
Plaški, *Croatia* 33 C12
Plaster City, *U.S.A.* 113 N11
Plaster Rock, *Canada* 99 C6

Plastun, Russia 48 B8
Plata, Río de la, S. Amer. 126 C4
Platani →, Italy 34 E6
Plátanos, Greece 37 D5
Plateau □, Nigeria 79 D6
Plateau du Coteau du Missouri, U.S.A. 108 B4
Plato, Colombia 120 B3
Platta, Piz, Switz. 23 D9
Platte, U.S.A. 108 D5
Platte →, U.S.A. 108 F7
Platteville, U.S.A. 108 E2
Plattling, Germany 19 G8
Plattsburgh, U.S.A. 107 B11
Plattsmouth, U.S.A. 108 E7
Plau, Germany 18 B8
Plauen, Germany 18 E8
Plavinas, Latvia 40 C4
Plavnica, Montenegro, Yug. 21 N9
Plavsk, Russia 41 E10
Playa Blanca, Canary Is. 36 F6
Playa Blanca Sur, Canary Is. 36 F6
Playa de las Americas, Canary Is. 36 F3
Playa de Mogán, Canary Is. 36 G4
Playa del Inglés, Canary Is. 36 G4
Playa Esmerelda, Canary Is. 36 F5
Playgreen L., Canada 101 C9
Pleasant Bay, Canada 99 C7
Pleasant Hill, Calif., U.S.A. 112 H4
Pleasant Hill, Mo., U.S.A. 108 F7
Pleasanton, U.S.A. 109 L5
Pleasantville, U.S.A. 104 F8
Pléaux, France 26 C6
Pleiku, Vietnam 58 F7
Plélan-le-Grand, France 24 D4
Plémet-la-Pierre, France 24 D4
Pléneuf-Val-André, France 24 D4
Pleniţa, Romania 38 E6
Plenty →, Australia 90 C2
Plenty, B. of, N.Z. 87 G6
Plentywood, U.S.A. 108 A2
Plessisville, Canada 99 C5
Plestin-les-Grèves, France 24 D3
Pleszew, Poland 20 D7
Pleternica, Croatia 21 K7
Pletipi L., Canada 99 B5
Pleven, Bulgaria 38 F7
Plevlja, Montenegro, Yug. 21 M9
Płock, Poland 20 C9
Plöcken Passo, Italy 33 B9
Ploegsteert, Belgium 17 G1
Ploemeur, France 24 E3
Ploërmel, France 24 E4
Ploieşti, Romania 38 E9
Plombières-les-Bains, France 25 E13
Plomin, Croatia 33 C11
Plön, Germany 18 A6
Plöner See, Germany 18 A6
Plonge, Lac la, Canada 101 B7
Płońsk, Poland 20 C10
Płoty, Poland 20 B5
Plouaret, France 24 D3
Plouay, France 24 E3
Ploudalmézeau, France 24 D2
Plougasnou, France 24 D3
Plouha, France 24 D4
Plouhinec, France 24 E2
Plovdiv, Bulgaria 38 G7
Plum, U.S.A. 106 F5
Plum I., U.S.A. 107 E12
Plumas, U.S.A. 112 F7
Plummer, U.S.A. 110 C5
Plumtree, Zimbabwe 83 G2
Plunge, Lithuania 40 D2
Pluvigner, France 24 E3
Plymouth, U.K. 13 G3
Plymouth, Calif., U.S.A. 112 G6
Plymouth, Ind., U.S.A. 104 E2
Plymouth, Mass., U.S.A. 107 E14
Plymouth, N.C., U.S.A. 105 H7
Plymouth, N.H., U.S.A. 107 C13
Plymouth, Pa., U.S.A. 107 E9
Plymouth, Wis., U.S.A. 104 D2
Plynlimon = Pumlumon Fawr, U.K. 13 E4
Plyussa, Russia 40 B6
Plyussa →, Russia 40 B6
Plzeň, Czech. 20 F3
Pniewy, Poland 20 C6
Pô, Burkina Faso 79 C4
Po →, Italy 33 D9
Po, Foci del, Italy 33 D9
Po Hai = Bo Hai, China 51 E10
Pobé, Benin 79 D5
Pobeda, Russia 45 C15
Pobedino, Russia 45 E15
Pobedy Pik, Kirghizia 44 E8
Pobiedziska, Poland 20 C7
Pobla de Segur, Spain 28 C5
Pobladura de Valle, Spain 30 C5
Pocahontas, Ark., U.S.A. 109 G9
Pocahontas, Iowa, U.S.A. 108 D7
Pocatello, U.S.A. 110 E7
Pochep, Russia 40 E8
Pochinki, Russia 41 D14
Pochinok, Russia 40 D8
Pochutla, Mexico 115 D5
Poci, Venezuela 121 B5
Pocinhos, Brazil 122 C4
Pocito Casas, Mexico 114 B2
Poções, Brazil 123 D3
Pocomoke City, U.S.A. 104 F8
Poconé, Brazil 125 D6
Poços de Caldas, Brazil 127 A6
Poddebice, Poland 20 D8
Poděbrady, Czech. 20 E5
Podensac, France 26 D3
Podgorica, Montenegro, Yug. 21 N9
Podkamennaya Tunguska →, Russia 45 C10
Podlapac, Croatia 33 D12
Podolsk, Russia 41 D10
Podor, Senegal 78 B1
Podravska Slatina, Croatia 21 K7
Podujevo, Serbia, Yug. 21 N11
Poel, Germany 18 B7
Pofadder, S. Africa 84 D2
Pogamasing, Canada 98 C3
Poggiardo, Italy 35 B11
Poggibonsi, Italy 33 E8
Pogoanele, Romania 38 E9
Pogradeci, Albania 39 J3
Pogranitšnyi, Russia 48 B5
Poh, Indonesia 57 E6
Pohang, S. Korea 51 F15
Pohnpei, Pac. Oc. 92 G7
Pohorelá, Slovakia 20 G10
Pohorje, Slovenia 33 B12
Poiana Mare, Romania 38 F6
Poinsett, C., Antarctica 5 C8
Point Edward, Canada 98 D3
Point Pedro, Sri Lanka 60 Q12
Point Pleasant, N.J., U.S.A. 107 F10
Point Pleasant, W. Va., U.S.A. 104 F4
Pointe-à-la Hache, U.S.A. 109 L10
Pointe-à-Pitre, Guadeloupe 117 C7
Pointe Noire, Congo 80 E2
Poirino, Italy 32 D4
Poisonbush Ra., Australia 88 D3
Poissy, France 25 D9
Poitiers, France 24 F7
Poitou, France 26 B3
Poitou, Seuil du, France 26 B4
Poix de Picardie, France 25 C8
Poix-Terron, France 25 C11
Pojoaque Valley, U.S.A. 111 J11
Pokaran, India 60 F7
Pokataroo, Australia 91 D4
Poko, Sudan 77 F3
Poko, Zaïre 82 B2
Pokrov, Russia 41 D11
Pokrovsk, Russia 41 F15
Pokrovsk, Russia 45 C13
Pol, Spain 30 B3
Pola = Pula, Croatia 33 D10
Pola de Allande, Spain 30 B4
Pola de Lena, Spain 30 B5
Pola de Siero, Spain 30 B5
Pola de Somiedo, Spain 30 B4
Polacca, U.S.A. 111 J8
Polan, Iran 65 E9
Poland ■, Europe 20 C9
Polanów, Poland 20 A6
Polatsk = Polotsk, Belorussia 40 D6
Polcura, Chile 126 D1
Polden Hills, U.K. 13 F5
Polessk, Russia 40 D2
Polesye, Belorussia 40 E6
Polewali, Indonesia 57 E5
Polgar, Hungary 21 H11
Pŏlgyo-ri, S. Korea 51 G14
Poli, Cameroon 80 C2
Políaigos, Greece 39 N7
Policastro, G. di, Italy 35 C8
Police, Poland 20 B4
Polignano a Mare, Italy 35 B10
Poligny, France 25 F12
Políkhnitas, Greece 39 K9
Polillo Is., Phil. 55 D4
Polillo Strait, Phil. 55 D4
Polis, Cyprus 37 D11
Polístena, Italy 35 D9
Políyiros, Greece 39 J6
Polk, U.S.A. 106 E5
Polla, Italy 35 B8
Pollachi, India 60 P10
Pollensa, Spain 36 B10
Pollensa, B. de, Spain 36 B10
Póllica, Italy 35 B8
Pollino, Mte., Italy 35 C9
Pollock, U.S.A. 108 C4
Polna, Russia 40 B6
Polnovat, Russia 44 C7
Polo, U.S.A. 108 E10
Pologi, Ukraine 42 C7
Polonnoye, Ukraine 40 F5
Polotsk, Belorussia 40 D6
Polson, U.S.A. 110 C6
Poltava, Ukraine 42 B6
Polunochnoye, Russia 44 C7
Polynesia, Pac. Oc. 93 H11
Polynésie française □ = French Polynesia ■, Pac. Oc. 93 J13
Pomarance, Italy 32 E7
Pomarico, Italy 35 B9
Pomaro, Mexico 114 D4
Pombal, Brazil 122 C4
Pombal, Portugal 30 F2
Pómbia, Greece 37 D6
Pomeroy, Ohio, U.S.A. 104 F4
Pomeroy, Wash., U.S.A. 110 C5
Pomona, U.S.A. 113 L9
Pomorie, Bulgaria 38 G10
Pomos, Cyprus 37 D11
Pomos, C., Cyprus 37 D11
Pomoshnaya, Ukraine 42 B4
Pompano Beach, U.S.A. 105 M5
Pompei, Italy 35 B7
Pompey, France 25 D13
Pompeys Pillar, U.S.A. 110 D10
Ponape = Pohnpei, Pac. Oc. 92 G7
Ponask, L., Canada 98 B1
Ponass L., Canada 101 C8
Ponca, U.S.A. 108 D6
Ponca City, U.S.A. 109 G6
Ponce, Puerto Rico 117 C6
Ponchatoula, U.S.A. 109 K9
Poncheville, L., Canada 98 B4
Poncin, France 27 B9
Pond, U.S.A. 113 K7
Pond Inlet, Canada 97 A12
Pondicherry, India 60 P11
Pondrôme, Belgium 17 H6
Ponds, I. of, Canada 99 B8
Ponferrada, Spain 30 C4
Pongo, Wadi →, Sudan 77 F2
Poniatowa, Poland 20 D12
Ponikva, Slovenia 33 B12
Ponnani, India 60 P9
Ponnyadaung, Burma 61 J19
Ponoi →, Russia 44 C5
Ponoka, Canada 100 C6
Ponorogo, Indonesia 57 G14
Pons, France 26 C3
Pons, Spain 28 D6
Ponsul →, Portugal 31 F3
Pont-à-Celles, Belgium 17 G4
Pont-à-Mousson, France 25 D13
Pont-Audemer, France 24 C7
Pont-Aven, France 24 E3
Pont Canavese, Italy 32 C4
Pont-de-Roide, France 25 E13
Pont-de-Salars, France 26 D6
Pont-de-Vaux, France 25 F11
Pont-de-Veyle, France 27 B8
Pont-l'Abbé, France 24 E2
Pont-l'Évêque, France 24 C7
Pont-St.-Esprit, France 27 D8
Pont-sur-Yonne, France 25 D10
Ponta de Pedras, Brazil 122 B2
Ponta do Sol, Madeira 36 D2
Ponta Grossa, Brazil 127 B5
Ponta Pora, Brazil 127 A4
Pontacq, France 26 E3
Pontailler-sur-Saône, France 25 E12
Pontal →, Brazil 122 C3
Pontalina, Brazil 123 E2
Pontarlier, France 25 F13
Pontassieve, Italy 33 E8
Pontaubault, France 24 D5
Pontaumur, France 26 C6
Pontcharra, France 27 C10
Pontchartrain L., U.S.A. 109 K9
Pontchâteau, France 24 E4
Ponte Alta, Serra do, Brazil 123 E2
Ponte Alta do Norte, Brazil 122 D2
Ponte Branca, Brazil 125 D7
Ponte da Barca, Portugal 30 D2
Ponte de Sor, Portugal 31 F3
Ponte dell 'Olio, Italy 32 D6
Ponte di Legno, Italy 32 B7
Ponte do Lima, Portugal 30 D2
Ponte do Pungué, Mozam. 83 F3
Ponte-Leccia, France 27 F13
Ponte nell' Alpi, Italy 33 B9
Ponte Nova, Brazil 123 F3
Ponte San Martino, Italy 32 C4
Ponte San Pietro, Italy 32 C6
Pontebba, Italy 33 B10
Pontecorvo, Italy 34 A6
Pontedera, Italy 32 E7
Pontefract, U.K. 12 D6
Ponteix, Canada 101 D7
Pontelandolfo, Italy 35 A7
Pontevedra, Spain 30 C2
Pontevedra □, Spain 30 C2
Pontevedra, R. de →, Spain 30 C2
Pontevico, Italy 32 C7
Pontiac, Ill., U.S.A. 108 E10
Pontiac, Mich., U.S.A. 104 D4
Pontian Kecil, Malaysia 59 M4
Pontianak, Indonesia 56 E3
Pontic Mts. = Kuzey Anadolu Dağları, Turkey 66 C6
Pontine Is. = Ponziane, Isole, Italy 34 B5
Pontine Mts. = Kuzey Anadolu Dağları, Turkey 66 C6
Pontínia, Italy 34 A6
Pontivy, France 24 D4
Pontoise, France 25 C9
Ponton →, Canada 100 B5
Pontorson, France 24 D5
Pontrémoli, Italy 32 D6
Pontresina, Switz. 23 D9
Pontrieux, France 24 D3
Pontypool, Canada 106 B6
Pontypool, U.K. 13 F4
Pontypridd, U.K. 13 F4
Ponza, Italy 34 B5
Ponziane, Isole, Italy 34 B5
Poochera, Australia 91 E1
Poole, U.K. 13 G6
Pooley I., Canada 100 C3
Poona = Pune, India 60 K8
Pooncarie, Australia 91 E3
Poopelloe L., Australia 91 E3
Poopó, Bolivia 124 D4
Poopó, L. de, Bolivia 124 D4
Popanyinning, Australia 89 F2
Popayán, Colombia 120 C2
Poperinge, Belgium 17 G1
Popigay, Russia 45 B12
Popilta, L., Australia 91 E3
Popio L., Australia 91 E3
Poplar, U.S.A. 108 A2
Poplar →, Man., Canada 101 C9
Poplar →, N.W.T., Canada 100 A4
Poplar Bluff, U.S.A. 109 G9
Poplarville, U.S.A. 109 K10
Popocatepetl, Mexico 115 D5
Popokabaka, Zaïre 80 F3
Pópoli, Italy 33 F10
Popovača, Croatia 33 C13
Popovo, Bulgaria 38 F9
Poppel, Belgium 17 F6
Poprád, Slovakia 20 F10
Poprád →, Slovakia 20 F10
Porali →, Pakistan 62 G2
Porangaba, Brazil 124 B3
Porangatu, Brazil 123 D2
Porbandar, India 62 J3
Porce →, Colombia 120 B3
Porcher I., Canada 100 C2
Porco, Bolivia 125 D4
Porcos →, Brazil 123 D2
Porcuna, Spain 31 H6
Porcupine →, Canada 101 B8
Porcupine →, U.S.A. 96 B5
Pordenone, Italy 33 C9
Poreč, Croatia 33 C10
Porecatu, Brazil 123 F1
Poretskoye, Russia 41 D15
Pori, Finland 9 F16
Porjus, Sweden 8 C15
Porkhov, Russia 40 C6
Porkkala, Finland 9 G18
Porlamar, Venezuela 121 A5
Porlezza, Italy 32 B6
Porma →, Spain 30 C5
Pornic, France 24 E4
Poronaysk, Russia 45 E15
Póros, Greece 39 M6
Poroshiri-Dake, Japan 48 C11
Poroto Mts., Tanzania 83 D3
Porpoise B., Antarctica 5 C9
Porquerolles, I. de, France 27 F10
Porrentruy, Switz. 22 B4
Porreras, Spain 36 B10
Porretta, Passo di, Italy 32 D7
Porsangen, Norway 8 A18
Porsgrunn, Norway 10 E3
Port Adelaide, Australia 91 E2
Port Alberni, Canada 100 D4
Port Alfred, Canada 99 C5
Port Alfred, S. Africa 84 E4
Port Alice, Canada 100 C3
Port Allegany, U.S.A. 106 E6
Port Allen, U.S.A. 109 K9
Port Alma, Australia 90 C5
Port Angeles, U.S.A. 112 B3
Port Antonio, Jamaica 116 C4
Port Aransas, U.S.A. 109 M6
Port Arthur = Lüshun, China 51 E11
Port Arthur, Australia 90 G4
Port Arthur, U.S.A. 109 L8
Port au Port B., Canada 99 C8
Port-au-Prince, Haiti 117 C5
Port Augusta, Australia 91 E2
Port Augusta West, Australia 91 E2
Port Austin, U.S.A. 98 D3
Port Bell, Uganda 82 B3
Port Bergé Vaovao, Madag. 85 B8
Port Blandford, Canada 99 C9
Port Bou, Spain 28 C8
Port Bouët, Ivory C. 78 D4
Port Bradshaw, Australia 90 A2
Port Broughton, Australia 91 E2
Port Burwell, Canada 98 D3
Port Canning, India 63 H13
Port-Cartier, Canada 99 B6
Port Chalmers, N.Z. 87 L3
Port Chester, U.S.A. 107 F11
Port Clements, Canada 100 C2
Port Clinton, U.S.A. 104 E4
Port Colborne, Canada 98 D4
Port Coquitlam, Canada 100 D4
Port Credit, Canada 106 C5
Port Curtis, Australia 90 C5
Port Dalhousie, Canada 106 C5
Port Darwin, Australia 88 B5
Port Darwin, Falk. Is. 128 D5
Port Davey, Australia 90 G4
Port-de-Bouc, France 27 E8
Port-de-Paix, Haiti 117 C5
Port Dickson, Malaysia 59 L3
Port Douglas, Australia 90 B4
Port Dover, Canada 106 D4
Port Edward, Canada 100 C2
Port Elgin, Canada 98 D3
Port Elizabeth, S. Africa 84 E4
Port Ellen, U.K. 14 F2
Port-en-Bessin, France 24 C6
Port Erin, I. of Man 12 C3
Port Essington, Australia 88 B5
Port Etienne = Nouâdhibou, Mauritania 74 D1
Port Fairy, Australia 91 F3
Port Fouâd = Bûr Fuad, Egypt 76 H8
Port Gamble, U.S.A. 112 C4
Port-Gentil, Gabon 80 E1
Port Gibson, U.S.A. 109 K9
Port Glasgow, U.K. 14 F4
Port Harcourt, Nigeria 79 E6
Port Hardy, Canada 100 C3
Port Harrison = Inoucdjouac, Canada 97 C12
Port Hawkesbury, Canada 99 C7
Port Hedland, Australia 88 D2
Port Henry, U.S.A. 107 B11
Port Hood, Canada 99 C7
Port Hope, Canada 98 D4
Port Hueneme, U.S.A. 113 L7
Port Huron, U.S.A. 104 D4
Port Isabel, U.S.A. 109 M6
Port Jefferson, U.S.A. 107 F11
Port Jervis, U.S.A. 107 E10
Port-Joinville, France 24 F4
Port Katon, Russia 43 C8
Port Kelang = Pelabuhan Kelang, Malaysia 59 L3
Port Kembla, Australia 91 E5
Port Kenny, Australia 91 E1
Port-la-Nouvelle, France 26 E7
Port Laoise, Ireland 15 C4
Port Lavaca, U.S.A. 109 L6
Port-Leucate, France 26 F7
Port Lincoln, Australia 91 E2
Port Loko, S. Leone 78 D2
Port Louis, France 24 E3
Port Lyautey = Kenitra, Morocco 74 B3
Port MacDonnell, Australia 91 F3
Port Macquarie, Australia 91 E5
Port Maria, Jamaica 116 C4
Port Mellon, Canada 100 D4
Port-Menier, Canada 99 C7
Port Morant, Jamaica 116 C4
Port Moresby, Papua N. G. 92 H6
Port Mourant, Guyana 121 B6
Port Mouton, Canada 99 D7
Port Musgrave, Australia 90 A3
Port-Navalo, France 24 E4
Port Nelson, Canada 101 B10
Port Nolloth, S. Africa 84 D2
Port Nouveau-Québec, Canada 97 C13
Port O'Connor, U.S.A. 109 L6
Port of Spain, Trin. & Tob. 117 D7
Port Orchard, U.S.A. 112 C4
Port Orford, U.S.A. 110 E1
Port Pegasus, N.Z. 87 M1
Port Perry, Canada 98 D4
Port Phillip B., Australia 91 F3
Port Pirie, Australia 91 E2
Port Radium = Echo Bay, Canada 96 B8
Port Renfrew, Canada 100 D4
Port Roper, Australia 90 A2
Port Rowan, Canada 98 D3
Port Safaga = Bûr Safâga, Egypt 76 B3
Port Said = Bûr Sa'îd, Egypt 76 H8
Port St. Joe, U.S.A. 105 L3
Port St. Johns, S. Africa 85 E4
Port-St.-Louis-du-Rhône, France 27 E8
Port San Vicente, Phil. 55 B5
Port Sanilac, U.S.A. 98 D3
Port Saunders, Canada 99 B8
Port Severn, Canada 106 B5
Port Shepstone, S. Africa 85 E5
Port Simpson, Canada 100 C2
Port Stanley = Stanley, Falk. Is. 128 D5
Port Stanley, Canada 98 D3
Port Sudan = Bûr Sûdân, Sudan 76 D4
Port-sur-Saône, France 25 E13
Port Talbot, U.K. 13 F4
Port Taufiq = Bûr Taufiq, Egypt 76 J8
Port Townsend, U.S.A. 112 B4
Port-Vendres, France 26 F7
Port Wakefield, Australia 91 E2
Port Washington, U.S.A. 104 D2
Port Weld, Malaysia 59 K3
Portachuelo, Bolivia 125 D5
Portadown, U.K. 15 B5
Portage, U.S.A. 108 D10
Portage La Prairie, Canada 101 D9
Portageville, U.S.A. 109 G10
Portalegre, Portugal 31 F3
Portalegre □, Portugal 31 F3
Portales, U.S.A. 109 H3
Portarlington, Ireland 15 C4
Porteirinha, Brazil 123 E3
Portel, Brazil 122 B1
Portel, Portugal 31 G3
Porter L., N.W.T., Canada 101 A7
Porter L., Sask., Canada 101 B7
Porterville, S. Africa 84 E2
Porterville, U.S.A. 111 H4
Porthcawl, U.K. 13 F4
Porthill, U.S.A. 110 B5
Portile de Fier, Europe 38 E5
Portimão, Portugal 31 H2
Portland, N.S.W., Australia 91 E4
Portland, Vic., Australia 91 F3

Portland, *Canada* 107 B8
Portland, *Conn., U.S.A.* 107 E12
Portland, *Maine, U.S.A.* 99 D5
Portland, *Mich., U.S.A.* 104 D3
Portland, *Oreg., U.S.A.* 112 E4
Portland, I. of, *U.K.* 13 G5
Portland B., *Australia* 91 F3
Portland Bill, *U.K.* 13 G5
Portland Prom., *Canada* 97 C12
Portlands Roads, *Australia* 90 A3
Portneuf, *Canada* 99 C5
Pôrto, *Brazil* 122 B3
Porto, *France* 27 F12
Porto, *Portugal* 30 D2
Porto □, *Portugal* 30 D2
Porto, G. de, *France* 27 F12
Pôrto Acre, *Brazil* 124 B4
Pôrto Alegre, *Pará, Brazil* 121 D7
Pôrto Alegre, *Rio Grande do S., Brazil* 127 C5
Porto Amboim = Gunza, *Angola* 80 G2
Porto Argentera, *Italy* 32 D4
Porto Azzurro, *Italy* 32 F7
Porto Botte, *Italy* 34 C1
Pôrto Cajueiro, *Brazil* 125 C6
Porto Civitanova, *Italy* 33 E10
Porto Cristo, *Spain* 36 B10
Pôrto da Fôlha, *Brazil* 122 C4
Pôrto de Móz, *Brazil* 121 D7
Pôrto de Pedras, *Brazil* 122 C4
Pôrto des Meinacos, *Brazil* 125 C7
Porto Empédocle, *Italy* 34 E6
Pôrto Esperança, *Brazil* 125 D6
Pôrto Esperidão, *Brazil* 125 D6
Pôrto Franco, *Brazil* 122 C2
Porto Garibaldi, *Italy* 33 D9
Pôrto Grande, *Brazil* 121 C7
Pôrto Jofre, *Brazil* 125 D6
Pórto Lágo, *Greece* 39 J8
Porto Mendes, *Brazil* 127 A5
Porto Moniz, *Madeira* 36 D2
Pôrto Murtinho, *Brazil* 125 E6
Pôrto Nacional, *Brazil* 122 D2
Porto Novo, *Benin* 79 D5
Porto Petro, *Spain* 36 B10
Porto Recanati, *Italy* 33 E10
Porto San Giórgio, *Italy* 33 E10
Pôrto Santana, *Brazil* 121 D7
Porto Santo, *Madeira* 72 B1
Porto Santo Stefano, *Italy* 32 F8
Pôrto São José, *Brazil* 127 A5
Pôrto Seguro, *Brazil* 123 E4
Porto Tolle, *Italy* 33 D9
Porto Tórres, *Italy* 34 B1
Pôrto União, *Brazil* 127 B5
Pôrto Válter, *Brazil* 124 B3
Porto-Vecchio, *France* 27 G13
Pôrto Velho, *Brazil* 125 B5
Portobelo, *Panama* 116 E4
Portoferráio, *Italy* 32 F7
Portogruaro, *Italy* 33 C9
Portola, *U.S.A.* 112 F6
Portomaggiore, *Italy* 33 D8
Portoscuso, *Italy* 34 C1
Portovénere, *Italy* 32 D6
Portovíejo, *Ecuador* 120 D1
Portpatrick, *U.K.* 14 G3
Portree, *U.K.* 14 D2
Portrush, *U.K.* 15 A5
Portsall, *France* 24 D2
Portsmouth, *Domin.* 117 C7
Portsmouth, *U.K.* 13 G6
Portsmouth, *N.H., U.S.A.* 107 C14
Portsmouth, *Ohio, U.S.A.* 104 F4
Portsmouth, *R.I., U.S.A.* 107 E13
Portsmouth, *Va., U.S.A.* 104 G7
Portsoy, *U.K.* 14 D6
Porttipahta, *Finland* 8 B19
Portugal ■, *Europe* 30 F3
Portugalete, *Spain* 28 B1
Portuguesa □, *Venezuela* 120 B4
Portuguese-Guinea = Guinea-Bissau ■, *Africa* 78 C2
Portumna, *Ireland* 15 C3
Portville, *U.S.A.* 106 D6
Porvenir, *Bolivia* 124 C4
Porvenir, *Chile* 128 D2
Porvoo = Borgå, *Finland* 9 F18
Porzuna, *Spain* 31 F6
Posada →, *Italy* 34 B2
Posadas, *Argentina* 127 B4
Posadas, *Spain* 31 H5
Poschiavo, *Switz.* 23 D10
Posets, *Spain* 28 C5
Poshan = Boshan, *China* 51 F9
Posht-e-Badam, *Iran* 65 C7
Posídhion, Ákra, *Greece* 39 K6
Poso, *Indonesia* 57 E6
Posoegroenoe, *Surinam* 121 C6
Posong, *S. Korea* 51 G14
Posse, *Brazil* 123 D2
Possel, *C.A.R.* 80 C3
Possession I., *Antarctica* 5 D11
Pössneck, *Germany* 18 E7
Post, *U.S.A.* 109 J4
Post Falls, *U.S.A.* 110 C5
Postavy, *Belorussia* 40 D5
Poste Maurice Cortier, *Algeria* 75 D5
Postmasburg, *S. Africa* 84 D3
Postojna, *Slovenia* 33 C11
Poston, *U.S.A.* 113 M12
Potchefstroom, *S. Africa* 84 D4
Poté, *Brazil* 123 E3
Poteau, *U.S.A.* 109 H7
Poteet, *U.S.A.* 109 L5
Potelu, Lacul, *Romania* 38 F7
Potenza, *Italy* 35 B8
Potenza →, *Italy* 33 E10
Potenza Picena, *Italy* 33 E10
Poteriteri, L., *N.Z.* 87 M1
Potes, *Spain* 30 B6
Potgietersrus, *S. Africa* 85 C4
Poti, *Georgia* 43 E9
Potiraguá, *Brazil* 123 E4
Potiskum, *Nigeria* 79 C7
Potomac →, *U.S.A.* 104 F7
Potosí, *Bolivia* 125 D4
Potosí □, *Bolivia* 124 E4
Potosi Mt., *U.S.A.* 113 K11
Pototan, *Phil.* 55 F5
Potrerillos, *Chile* 126 B2
Potsdam, *Germany* 18 C9
Potsdam, *U.S.A.* 107 B10
Pottenstein, *Germany* 19 F7
Potter, *U.S.A.* 108 E3
Pottery Hill = Abû Ballas, *Egypt* 76 C2
Pottstown, *U.S.A.* 107 F9
Pottsville, *U.S.A.* 107 F8
Pottuvil, *Sri Lanka* 60 R12
Pouancé, *France* 24 E5
Pouce Coupé, *Canada* 100 B4
Poughkeepsie, *U.S.A.* 107 E11
Pouilly-sur-Loire, *France* 25 E9
Poulaphouca Res., *Ireland* 15 C5
Poulsbo, *U.S.A.* 112 C4
Pourri, Mt., *France* 27 C10
Pouso Alegre, *Mato Grosso, Brazil* 125 C6
Pouso Alegre, *Minas Gerais, Brazil* 127 A6
Pouzauges, *France* 24 F6
Povenets, *Russia* 44 C4
Poverty B., *N.Z.* 87 H7
Póvoa de Lanhosa, *Portugal* 30 D2
Póvoa de Varzim, *Portugal* 30 D2
Povorino, *Russia* 41 F13
Powassan, *Canada* 98 C4
Poway, *U.S.A.* 113 N9
Powder →, *U.S.A.* 108 B2
Powder River, *U.S.A.* 110 E10
Powell, *U.S.A.* 110 D9
Powell L., *U.S.A.* 111 H8
Powell River, *Canada* 100 D4
Powers, *Mich., U.S.A.* 104 C2
Powers, *Oreg., U.S.A.* 110 E1
Powers Lake, *U.S.A.* 108 A3
Powys □, *U.K.* 13 E4
Poxoreu, *Brazil* 125 D7
Poyang Hu, *China* 53 C11
Poyarkovo, *Russia* 45 E13
Poza de la Sal, *Spain* 28 C1
Poza Rica, *Mexico* 115 C5
Pozanti, *Turkey* 66 E6
Požarevac, *Serbia, Yug.* 21 L11
Pozi, *Taiwan* 53 F13
Poznań, *Poland* 20 C6
Pozo, *U.S.A.* 113 K6
Pozo Alcón, *Spain* 29 H2
Pozo Almonte, *Chile* 124 E4
Pozo Colorado, *Paraguay* 126 A4
Pozo del Dátil, *Mexico* 114 B2
Pozoblanco, *Spain* 31 G6
Pozuzo, *Peru* 124 C2
Pozzallo, *Italy* 35 F7
Pozzuoli, *Italy* 35 B7
Pra →, *Ghana* 79 D4
Prachin Buri, *Thailand* 58 E3
Prachuap Khiri Khan, *Thailand* 59 G2
Pradelles, *France* 26 D7
Pradera, *Colombia* 120 C2
Prades, *France* 26 F6
Prado, *Brazil* 123 E4
Prado del Rey, *Spain* 31 J5
Præstø, *Denmark* 11 J6
Pragersko, *Slovenia* 33 B12
Prague = Praha, *Czech.* 20 E4
Praha, *Czech.* 20 E4
Prahecq, *France* 26 B3
Prahova →, *Romania* 38 E8
Prahovo, *Serbia, Yug.* 21 L12
Praid, *Romania* 38 C8
Prainha, *Amazonas, Brazil* 125 B5
Prainha, *Pará, Brazil* 121 D7
Prairie, *Australia* 90 C3
Prairie →, *U.S.A.* 109 H5
Prairie City, *U.S.A.* 110 D4
Prairie du Chien, *U.S.A.* 108 D9
Prairies, *Canada* 96 C9
Pramánda, *Greece* 39 K4
Pran Buri, *Thailand* 58 F2
Prang, *Ghana* 79 D4
Prapat, *Indonesia* 56 D1
Prasonísi, Ákra, *Greece* 37 D9
Prata, *Brazil* 123 E2
Pratapgarh, *India* 62 G6
Prática di Mare, *Italy* 34 A5
Prätigau, *Switz.* 23 C9
Prato, *Italy* 32 E8
Prátola Peligna, *Italy* 33 F10
Pratovécchio, *Italy* 33 E8
Prats-de-Mollo-la-Preste, *France* 26 F6
Pratt, *U.S.A.* 109 G5
Pratteln, *Switz.* 22 A5
Prattville, *U.S.A.* 105 J2
Pravdinsk, *Russia* 41 C13
Pravia, *Spain* 30 B4
Praya, *Indonesia* 56 F5
Pré-en-Pail, *France* 24 D6
Pré St. Didier, *Italy* 32 C4
Precordillera, *Argentina* 126 C2
Predáppio, *Italy* 33 D8
Predazzo, *Italy* 33 B8
Predejane, *Serbia, Yug.* 21 N12
Preeceville, *Canada* 101 C8
Préfailles, *France* 24 E4
Pregonero, *Venezuela* 120 B3
Pregrada, *Croatia* 33 B12
Preko, *Croatia* 33 D12
Prelate, *Canada* 101 C7
Prelog, *Croatia* 33 B13
Premier, *Canada* 100 B3
Premont, *U.S.A.* 109 M5
Premuda, *Croatia* 33 D11
Prenjasi, *Albania* 39 H3
Prentice, *U.S.A.* 108 C9
Prenzlau, *Germany* 18 B9
Preobrazheniye, *Russia* 48 C6
Prepansko Jezero, *Macedonia* 39 J4
Preparis North Channel, *Ind. Oc.* 61 M18
Preparis South Channel, *Ind. Oc.* 61 M18
Přerov, *Czech.* 20 F7
Presanella, *Italy* 32 B7
Prescott, *Canada* 98 D4
Prescott, *Ariz., U.S.A.* 111 J7
Prescott, *Ark., U.S.A.* 109 J8
Preservation Inlet, *N.Z.* 87 M1
Preševo, *Serbia, Yug.* 21 N11
Presho, *U.S.A.* 108 D4
Presicce, *Italy* 35 C11
Presidencia de la Plaza, *Argentina* 126 B4
Presidencia Roque Saenz Peña, *Argentina* 126 B3
Presidente Epitácio, *Brazil* 123 F1
Presidente Hayes □, *Paraguay* 126 A4
Presidente Hermes, *Brazil* 125 C5
Presidente Prudente, *Brazil* 127 A5
Presidio, *Mexico* 114 B4
Presidio, *U.S.A.* 109 L2
Preslav, *Bulgaria* 38 F9
Prešov, *Slovakia* 20 F11
Prespa, L. = Prepansko Jezero, *Macedonia* 39 J4
Presque Isle, *U.S.A.* 99 C6
Prestbury, *U.K.* 13 F5
Prestea, *Ghana* 78 D4
Presteigne, *U.K.* 13 E5
Presto, *Bolivia* 125 D5
Preston, *Canada* 106 C4
Preston, *U.K.* 12 D5
Preston, *Idaho, U.S.A.* 110 E8
Preston, *Minn., U.S.A.* 108 D8
Preston, *Nev., U.S.A.* 110 G6
Preston, C., *Australia* 88 D2
Prestonpans, *U.K.* 14 F6
Prestwick, *U.K.* 14 F4
Prêto →, *Amazonas, Brazil* 121 D5
Prêto →, *Bahia, Brazil* 122 D3
Prêto do Igapó-Açu →, *Brazil* 121 D6
Pretoria, *S. Africa* 85 D4
Preuilly-sur-Claise, *France* 24 F7
Préveza, *Greece* 39 L3
Priazovskoye, *Ukraine* 42 C6
Pribilof Is., *Bering S.* 4 D17
Priboj, *Serbia, Yug.* 21 M9
Příbram, *Czech.* 20 F4
Price, *U.S.A.* 110 G8
Price I., *Canada* 100 C3
Prichalnaya, *Russia* 43 B11
Prichard, *U.S.A.* 105 K1
Priego, *Spain* 28 E2
Priego de Córdoba, *Spain* 31 H6
Priekule, *Latvia* 40 C2
Prien, *Germany* 19 H8
Prieska, *S. Africa* 84 D3
Priest →, *U.S.A.* 110 B5
Priest L., *U.S.A.* 110 B5
Priest Valley, *U.S.A.* 112 J6
Priestly, *Canada* 100 C3
Prievidza, *Slovakia* 20 G8
Prijedor, *Bos.-H.* 33 D13
Prikaspiyskaya Nizmennost, *Asia* 43 C13
Prilep, *Macedonia* 39 H4
Priluki, *Ukraine* 40 F8
Prime Seal I., *Australia* 90 G4
Primeira Cruz, *Brazil* 122 B3
Primorsko-Akhtarsk, *Russia* 42 C8
Primorskoye, *Ukraine* 42 C7
Primrose L., *Canada* 101 C7
Prince Albert, *Canada* 101 C7
Prince Albert, *S. Africa* 84 E3
Prince Albert Mts., *Antarctica* 5 D11
Prince Albert Nat. Park, *Canada* 101 C7
Prince Albert Pen., *Canada* 96 A8
Prince Albert Sd., *Canada* 96 A8
Prince Alfred, C., *Canada* 4 B1
Prince Charles I., *Canada* 97 B12
Prince Charles Mts., *Antarctica* 5 D6
Prince Edward I. □, *Canada* 99 C7
Prince Edward Is., *Ind. Oc.* 3 G11
Prince George, *Canada* 100 C4
Prince of Wales, C., *U.S.A.* 94 C3
Prince of Wales I., *Australia* 90 A3
Prince of Wales I., *Canada* 96 A10
Prince of Wales I., *U.S.A.* 100 B2
Prince Patrick I., *Canada* 4 B2
Prince Regent Inlet, *Canada* 4 B3
Prince Rupert, *Canada* 100 C2
Princenhage, *Neths.* 17 F5
Princesa Isabel, *Brazil* 122 C4
Princess Charlotte B., *Australia* 90 A3
Princess May Ras., *Australia* 88 C4
Princess Royal I., *Canada* 100 C3
Princeton, *Canada* 100 D4
Princeton, *Calif., U.S.A.* 112 F4
Princeton, *Ill., U.S.A.* 108 E10
Princeton, *Ind., U.S.A.* 104 F2
Princeton, *Ky., U.S.A.* 104 G2
Princeton, *Mo., U.S.A.* 108 E8
Princeton, *N.J., U.S.A.* 107 F10
Princeton, *W. Va., U.S.A.* 104 G5
Principe, I. de, *Atl. Oc.* 70 F4
Principe Chan., *Canada* 100 C2
Principe da Beira, *Brazil* 125 C5
Prineville, *U.S.A.* 110 D3
Prins Harald Kyst, *Antarctica* 5 D4
Prinsesse Astrid Kyst, *Antarctica* 5 D3
Prinsesse Ragnhild Kyst, *Antarctica* 5 D4
Prinzapolca, *Nic.* 116 D3
Prior, C., *Spain* 30 B2
Pripet = Pripyat →, *Europe* 40 F7
Pripet Marshes = Polesye, *Belorussia* 40 E6
Pripyat →, *Europe* 40 F7
Pripyat Marshes = Polesye, *Belorussia* 40 E6
Prislop, Pasul, *Romania* 38 B8
Pristen, *Russia* 41 F10
Priština, *Serbia, Yug.* 21 N11
Pritzwalk, *Germany* 18 B8
Privas, *France* 27 D8
Priverno, *Italy* 34 A6
Privolzhsk, *Russia* 41 C12
Privolzhskaya Vozvyshennost, *Russia* 41 F15
Privolzhskiy, *Russia* 41 F15
Privolzhye, *Russia* 41 E16
Priyutnoye, *Russia* 43 C10
Prizren, *Serbia, Yug.* 21 N10
Prizzi, *Italy* 34 E6
Prnjavor, *Bos.-H.* 21 L7
Probolinggo, *Indonesia* 57 G15
Procida, *Italy* 35 B7
Proddatur, *India* 60 M11
Prodhromos, *Cyprus* 37 E11
Proença-a-Nova, *Portugal* 31 F3
Prof. Van Blommestein Meer, *Surinam* 121 C6
Profítis Ilías, *Greece* 37 C9
Profondeville, *Belgium* 17 H5
Progreso, *Mexico* 115 C7
Prokhladnyy, *Russia* 43 E11
Prokletije, *Albania* 38 G2
Prokopyevsk, *Russia* 44 D9
Prokuplje, *Serbia, Yug.* 21 M11
Proletarskaya, *Russia* 43 C9
Prome = Pyè, *Burma* 61 K19
Prophet →, *Canada* 100 B4
Propriá, *Brazil* 122 D4
Propriano, *France* 27 G12
Proserpine, *Australia* 90 C4
Prosser, *U.S.A.* 110 C4
Prostějov, *Czech.* 20 F7
Proston, *Australia* 91 D5
Protection, *U.S.A.* 109 G5
Próti, *Greece* 39 M4
Provadiya, *Bulgaria* 38 F10
Proven, *Belgium* 17 G1
Provence, *France* 27 E9
Providence, *Ky., U.S.A.* 104 G2
Providence, *R.I., U.S.A.* 107 E13
Providence Bay, *Canada* 98 C3
Providence Mts., *U.S.A.* 111 J6
Providencia, *Ecuador* 120 D2
Providencia, I. de, *Colombia* 116 D3
Provideniya, *Russia* 45 C19
Provins, *France* 25 D10
Provo, *U.S.A.* 110 F8
Provost, *Canada* 101 C6
Prozor, *Bos.-H.* 21 M7
Prudentópolis, *Brazil* 123 G1
Prud'homme, *Canada* 101 C7
Prudnik, *Poland* 20 E7
Prüm, *Germany* 19 E2
Pruszcz Gdański, *Poland* 20 A8
Pruszków, *Poland* 20 C10
Prut →, *Romania* 38 D11
Pruzhany, *Belorussia* 40 E4
Prvič, *Croatia* 33 D11
Prydz B., *Antarctica* 5 C6
Pryluky = Priluki, *Ukraine* 40 F8
Pryor, *U.S.A.* 109 G7
Przasnysz, *Poland* 20 B10
Przedbórz, *Poland* 20 D9
Przemysl, *Poland* 20 F12
Przeworsk, *Poland* 20 E12
Przewóz, *Poland* 20 D4
Przhevalsk, *Kirghizia* 44 E8
Przysuchla, *Poland* 20 D10
Psakhná, *Greece* 39 L6
Psará, *Greece* 39 L8
Psel →, *Ukraine* 42 B5
Pserimos, *Greece* 39 N10
Psíra, *Greece* 37 D7
Pskov, *Russia* 40 C6
Psunj, *Croatia* 21 K7
Pszczyna, *Poland* 20 F8
Pteleón, *Greece* 39 K5
Ptich →, *Belorussia* 40 E6
Ptolemaís, *Greece* 39 J4
Ptuj, *Slovenia* 33 B12
Ptujska Gora, *Slovenia* 33 B12
Pu Xian, *China* 50 F6
Pua, *Thailand* 58 C3
Puán, *Argentina* 126 D3
Pu'an, *China* 52 E5
Puan, *S. Korea* 51 G14
Pubei, *China* 52 F7
Pucacuro →, *Peru* 120 D3
Pucallpa, *Peru* 124 B3
Pucará, *Bolivia* 125 D5
Pucará, *Peru* 124 D3
Pucarani, *Bolivia* 124 D4
Pucheng, *China* 53 D12
Pučišće, *Croatia* 33 E13
Pucka, Zatoka, *Poland* 20 A8
Puding, *China* 52 D5
Pudukkottai, *India* 60 P11
Puebla, *Mexico* 115 D5
Puebla □, *Mexico* 115 D5
Puebla de Alcocer, *Spain* 31 G5
Puebla de Don Fadrique, *Spain* 29 H2
Puebla de Don Rodrigo, *Spain* 31 F6
Puebla de Guzmán, *Spain* 31 H3
Puebla de Sanabria, *Spain* 30 C4
Puebla de Trives, *Spain* 30 C3
Puebla del Caramiñal, *Spain* 30 C2
Pueblo, *U.S.A.* 108 F2
Pueblo Hundido, *Chile* 126 B1
Pueblo Nuevo, *Venezuela* 120 B3
Puelches, *Argentina* 126 D2
Puelén, *Argentina* 126 D2
Puente Alto, *Chile* 126 C1
Puente del Arzobispo, *Spain* 30 F5
Puente-Genil, *Spain* 31 H6
Puente la Reina, *Spain* 28 C3
Puenteareas, *Spain* 30 C2
Puentedeume, *Spain* 30 B2
Puentes de Garcia Rodriguez, *Spain* 30 B3
Pu'er, *China* 52 F3
Puerco →, *U.S.A.* 111 J10
Puerto, *Canary Is.* 36 F2
Puerto Acosta, *Bolivia* 124 D4
Puerto Aisén, *Chile* 128 C2
Puerto Ángel, *Mexico* 115 D5
Puerto Arista, *Mexico* 115 D6
Puerto Armuelles, *Panama* 116 E3
Puerto Ayacucho, *Venezuela* 120 B4
Puerto Barrios, *Guatemala* 116 C2
Puerto Bermejo, *Argentina* 126 B4
Puerto Bermúdez, *Peru* 124 C3
Puerto Bolívar, *Ecuador* 120 D2
Puerto Cabello, *Venezuela* 120 A4
Puerto Cabezas, *Nic.* 116 D3
Puerto Cabo Gracias á Dios, *Nic.* 116 D3
Puerto Capaz = Jebba, *Morocco* 74 A4
Puerto Carreño, *Colombia* 120 B4
Puerto Castilla, *Honduras* 116 C2
Puerto Chicama, *Peru* 124 B2
Puerto Coig, *Argentina* 128 D3
Puerto Cortes, *Costa Rica* 116 E3
Puerto Cortés, *Honduras* 116 C2
Puerto Cumarebo, *Venezuela* 120 A4
Puerto de Alcudia, *Spain* 36 B10
Puerto de Andraitx, *Spain* 36 B9
Puerto de Cabrera, *Spain* 36 B9
Puerto de Gran Tarajal, *Canary Is.* 36 F5
Puerto de la Cruz, *Canary Is.* 36 F3
Puerto de Pozo Negro, *Canary Is.* 36 F6
Puerto de Santa María, *Spain* 31 J4
Puerto de Sóller, *Spain* 36 B9
Pto. del Carmen, *Canary Is.* 36 F6
Puerto del Rosario, *Canary Is.* 36 F6
Puerto Deseado, *Argentina* 128 C3
Puerto Guaraní, *Paraguay* 125 E6
Puerto Heath, *Bolivia* 124 C4
Puerto Huitoto, *Colombia* 120 C3
Puerto Inca, *Peru* 124 B3
Puerto Juárez, *Mexico* 115 C7
Puerto La Cruz, *Venezuela* 121 A5
Puerto Leguízamo, *Colombia* 120 D3
Puerto Limón, *Colombia* 120 C3
Puerto Lobos, *Argentina* 128 B3
Puerto López, *Colombia* 120 C3
Puerto Lumbreras, *Spain* 29 H3
Puerto Madryn, *Argentina* 128 B3
Puerto Maldonado, *Peru* 124 C4
Puerto Manotí, *Cuba* 116 B4

Puerto Mazarrón, Spain .. 29 H3
Puerto Mercedes, Colombia 120 C3
Puerto Miraña, Colombia . 120 D3
Puerto Montt, Chile 128 B2
Puerto Morelos, Mexico .. 115 C7
Puerto Nariño, Colombia . 120 C4
Puerto Natales, Chile 128 D2
Puerto Nuevo, Colombia . 120 B4
Puerto Nutrias, Venezuela 120 B4
Puerto Ordaz, Venezuela . 121 B5
Puerto Padre, Cuba 116 B4
Puerto Páez, Venezuela ... 120 B4
Puerto Peñasco, Mexico .. 114 A2
Puerto Pinasco, Paraguay . 126 A4
Puerto Pirámides, Argentina 128 B4
Puerto Plata, Dom. Rep. . 117 C5
Puerto Pollensa, Spain ... 36 B10
Puerto Portillo, Peru 124 B3
Puerto Princesa, Phil. 55 G3
Puerto Quellón, Chile 128 B2
Puerto Quepos, Costa Rica 116 E3
Puerto Real, Spain 31 J4
Puerto Rico, Bolivia 124 C4
Puerto Rico, Canary Is. .. 36 G4
Puerto Rico ■, W. Indies . 117 C6
Puerto Rico Trench, Atl. Oc. 117 C6
Puerto Saavedra, Chile ... 128 A2
Puerto Sastre, Paraguay .. 126 A4
Puerto Siles, Bolivia 125 C4
Puerto Suárez, Bolivia 125 D6
Puerto Tejada, Colombia . 120 C2
Puerto Umbría, Colombia 120 C2
Puerto Vallarta, Mexico .. 114 C3
Puerto Varas, Chile 128 B2
Puerto Villazón, Bolivia .. 125 C5
Puerto Wilches, Colombia 120 B3
Puertollano, Spain 31 G6
Puertomarin, Spain 30 C3
Puesto Cunambo, Peru ... 120 D2
Pueyrredón, L., Argentina 128 C2
Pugachev, Kazakhstan 41 F16
Puge, China 52 D4
Puge, Tanzania 82 C3
Puget Sound, U.S.A. 110 C2
Puget-Théniers, France ... 27 E10
Púglia □, Italy 35 B9
Pugŏdong, N. Korea 51 C16
Pugu, Tanzania 82 D4
Pūgūnzī, Iran 65 E8
Pui, Romania 38 D6
Puica, Peru 124 C3
Puig Mayor, Spain 36 B9
Puigcerdá, Spain 28 C6
Puigmal, Spain 28 C7
Puigpuñent, Spain 36 B9
Puisaye, Collines de la, France 25 E10
Puiseaux, France 25 D9
Pujilí, Ecuador 120 D2
Pujon-chosuji, N. Korea .. 51 D14
Puka, Albania 38 G2
Pukaki L., N.Z. 87 L3
Pukapuka, Cook Is. 93 J11
Pukatawagan, Canada 101 B8
Pukchin, N. Korea 51 D13
Pukchŏng, N. Korea 51 D15
Pukekohe, N.Z. 87 G5
Pukou, China 53 A12
Pula, Croatia 33 D10
Pula, Italy 34 D2
Pulacayo, Bolivia 124 E4
Pulaski, N.Y., U.S.A. 107 C8
Pulaski, Tenn., U.S.A. ... 105 H2
Pulaski, Va., U.S.A. 104 G5
Pulawy, Poland 20 D11
Pulga, U.S.A. 112 F5
Pulicat, L., India 60 N12
Pullman, U.S.A. 110 C5
Pulog, Phil. 55 C4
Pułtusk, Poland 20 C11
Pülümür, Turkey 67 D8
Pumlumon Fawr, U.K. 13 E4
Puna, Bolivia 125 D4
Puná, I., Ecuador 120 D1
Punakha, Bhutan 61 F16
Punasar, India 62 F5
Punata, Bolivia 125 D4
Punch, India 63 C6
Pune, India 60 K8
Pungsan, N. Korea 51 D15
Pungue, Ponte de, Mozam. 83 F3
Puning, China 53 F11
Punjab □, India 62 D6
Punjab □, Pakistan 62 E6
Puno, Peru 124 D3
Punta Alta, Argentina 128 A4
Punta Arenas, Chile 128 D2
Punta Cardón, Venezuela . 120 A3
Punta Coles, Peru 124 D3
Punta de Bombón, Peru .. 124 D3
Punta de Díaz, Chile 126 B1
Punta Delgado, Argentina 128 B4
Punta Gorda, Belize 115 D7
Punta Gorda, U.S.A. 105 M5
Punta Prieta, Mexico 114 B2
Punta Prima, Spain 36 B11
Puntabie, Australia 91 E1
Puntarenas, Costa Rica ... 116 E3
Punto Fijo, Venezuela 120 A3
Punxsatawney, U.S.A. 106 F5
Puqi, China 53 C9
Puquio, Peru 124 C3
Pur →, Russia 44 C8
Puracé, Vol., Colombia .. 120 C2
Puralia = Puruliya, India . 63 H12
Purbeck, Isle of, U.K. 13 G5
Purcell, U.S.A. 109 H6
Purchena Tetica, Spain ... 29 H2
Puri, India 61 K14
Purificación, Colombia ... 120 C3
Purmerend, Neths. 16 C5
Purnia, India 63 G12
Purukcahu, Indonesia 56 E4
Puruliya, India 63 H12
Purus →, Brazil 121 D5
Pŭrvomay, Bulgaria 38 G8
Purwakarta, Indonesia 57 G12
Purwodadi, Jawa, Indonesia 57 G14
Purwodadi, Jawa, Indonesia 57 G13
Purwokerto, Indonesia 57 G13
Purworejo, Indonesia 57 G14
Puryŏng, N. Korea 51 C15
Pusan, S. Korea 51 G15
Pushchino, Russia 45 D16
Pushkin, Russia 40 B7
Pushkino, Russia 41 F15
Pushkino, Russia 41 C10
Püspökladány, Hungary .. 21 H11
Pustoshka, Russia 40 C6
Putahow L., Canada 101 B8
Putao, Burma 61 F20
Putaruru, N.Z. 87 H5
Putbus, Germany 18 A9
Puthein Myit →, Burma . 61 M19
Putian, China 53 E12
Putignano, Italy 35 B10
Putina, Peru 124 C4
Puting, Tanjung, Indonesia 56 E4
Putlitz, Germany 18 B8
Putna →, Romania 38 D10
Putnam, U.S.A. 107 E13
Putorana, Gory, Russia ... 45 C10
Putre, Chile 124 D4
Puttalam, Sri Lanka 60 Q11
Putte, Neths. 17 F4
Putten, Neths. 16 D7
Puttgarden, Germany 18 A7
Putumayo →, S. Amer. .. 120 D4
Putuo, China 53 C14
Putussibau, Indonesia 56 D4
Puurs, Belgium 17 F4
Puy-de-Dôme, France 26 C6
Puy-de-Dôme □, France .. 26 C7
Puy-Guillaume, France ... 26 C7
Puy-l'Évêque, France 26 D5
Puyallup, U.S.A. 112 C4
Puyang, China 50 G8
Puyehue, Chile 128 B2
Puylaurens, France 26 E6
Puyo, Ecuador 120 D2
Pūzeh Rīg, Iran 65 E8
Pwani □, Tanzania 82 D4
Pweto, Zaïre 83 D2
Pwllheli, U.K. 12 E3
Pyana →, Russia 41 D15
Pyapon, Burma 61 L19
Pyasina →, Russia 45 B9
Pyatigorsk, Russia 43 D10
Pyatikhatki, Ukraine 42 B5
Pyè, Burma 61 K19
Pyinmana, Burma 61 K20
Pyla, C., Cyprus 37 E12
Pyŏktong, N. Korea 51 D13
Pyŏnggang, N. Korea 51 E14
Pyŏngtaek, S. Korea 51 F14
P'yŏngyang, N. Korea ... 51 E13
Pyote, U.S.A. 109 K3
Pyramid L., U.S.A. 110 G4
Pyramid Pk., U.S.A. 113 J10
Pyramids, Egypt 76 J7
Pyrénées, Europe 26 F4
Pyrénées-Atlantiques □, France 26 E3
Pyrénées-Orientales □, France 26 F6
Pyrzyce, Poland 20 B4
Pyshchug, Russia 41 B14
Pytalovo, Russia 40 C5
Pyttegga, Norway 10 B1
Pyu, Burma 61 K20

Q

Qaanaaq = Thule, Greenland 4 B4
Qachasnek, S. Africa 85 E4
Qādib, Yemen 68 E5
Qa'el Jafr, Jordan 69 E5
Qa'emābād, Iran 65 D9
Qā'emshahr, Iran 65 B7
Qagan Nur, China 50 C8
Qahar Youyi Zhongqi, China 50 D7
Qahremānshahr = Bākhtarān, Iran 64 C5
Qaidam Pendi, China 54 C4
Qajarīyeh, Iran 65 D6
Qala, Ras il, Malta 37 C1
Qala-i-Jadid, Afghan. 62 D2
Qala Yangi, Afghan. 62 B2
Qal'at al Akhḑar, Si. Arabia 64 E3
Qal'at Sukkar, Iraq 64 D5
Qal'eh Darreh, Iran 64 B5
Qal'eh Shaharak, Afghan. 60 B4
Qalyûb, Egypt 76 H7
Qamar, Ghubbat al, Yemen 68 D5
Qamdo, China 52 B1
Qamruddin Karez, Pakistan 62 D3
Qandahār, Afghan. 60 D4
Qandahār □, Afghan. 60 D4
Qapān, Iran 65 B7
Qaqortoq = Julianehåb, Greenland 4 C5
Qâra, Egypt 76 B2
Qara Qash →, India 63 B8
Qaraghandy = Karaganda, Kazakhstan 44 E8
Qārah, Si. Arabia 64 D4
Qardud, Sudan 77 E2
Qareh →, Iran 64 B5
Qareh Tekān, Iran 65 B6
Qarqan, China 54 C3
Qarqan He →, China 54 C3
Qarrasa, Sudan 77 E3
Qarshi = Karshi, Uzbekistan 44 F7
Qartabā, Lebanon 69 A4
Qaryat al Gharab, Iraq ... 64 D5
Qaryat al 'Ulyā, Si. Arabia 64 E5
Qasr 'Amra, Jordan 64 D3
Qaşr-e Qand, Iran 65 E9
Qasr Farâfra, Egypt 76 B2
Qatanā, Syria 69 B5
Qatar ■, Asia 65 E6
Qatlīsh, Iran 65 B8
Qattâra, Egypt 76 A2
Qattâra, Munkhafed el, Egypt 76 B2
Qattâra Depression = Qattâra, Munkhafed el, Egypt 76 B2
Qawām al Ḩamzah, Iraq .. 64 D5
Qāyen, Iran 65 C8
Qazaqstan = Kazakhstan ■, Asia 44 E7
Qazvin, Iran 65 B6
Qena, Egypt 76 B3
Qena, Wadi →, Egypt ... 76 B3
Qeqertarsuag = Disko, Greenland 4 C5
Qeqertarsuaq = Godhavn, Greenland 4 C5
Qeshlāq, Iran 64 C5
Qeshm, Iran 65 E8
Qezi'ot, Israel 69 E3
Qi Xian, China 50 G8
Qian Gorlos, China 51 B13
Qian Xian, China 50 G5
Qiancheng, China 52 D7
Qianjiang, Guangxi Zhuangzu, China 52 F7
Qianjiang, Hubei, China .. 53 B9
Qianjiang, Sichuan, China 52 C7
Qianshan, China 53 B11
Qianwei, China 52 C4
Qianxi, China 52 D6
Qianyang, Hunan, China . 53 D8
Qianyang, Shaanxi, China 50 G4
Qianyang, Zhejiang, China 53 B12
Qiaojia, China 52 D4
Qibā', Si. Arabia 64 E5
Qichun, China 53 B10
Qidong, Hunan, China ... 53 D9
Qidong, Jiangsu, China ... 53 B13
Qijiang, China 52 C6
Qila Safed, Pakistan 60 E2
Qila Saifullāh, Pakistan .. 62 D3
Qilian Shan, China 54 C4
Qimen, China 53 C11
Qin He →, China 50 G7
Qin Jiang →, China 53 D10
Qin Ling = Qinling Shandi, China 50 H5
Qin'an, China 50 G3
Qing Xian, China 50 E9
Qingcheng, China 51 F9
Qingdao, China 51 F11
Qingfeng, China 50 G8
Qinghai □, China 54 C4
Qinghai Hu, China 54 C5
Qinghecheng, China 51 D13
Qinghemen, China 51 D11
Qingjian, China 50 F6
Qingjiang, Jiangsu, China . 51 H10
Qingjiang, Jiangxi, China . 53 C10
Qingliu, China 53 D11
Qinglong, China 52 E5
Qingping, China 52 D6
Qingpu, China 53 B13
Qingshui, China 50 G4
Qingshuihe, China 50 E6
Qingtian, China 53 C13
Qingtongxia Shuiku, China 50 F3
Qingxi, China 52 D7
Qingxu, China 50 F7
Qingyang, Anhui, China .. 53 B11
Qingyang, Gansu, China .. 50 F4
Qingyi Jiang →, China ... 52 C4
Qingyuan, Guangdong, China 53 F9
Qingyuan, Liaoning, China 51 C13
Qingyuan, Zhejiang, China 53 D12
Qingyun, China 51 F9
Qingzhen, China 52 D6
Qinhuangdao, China 51 E10
Qinling Shandi, China ... 50 H5
Qinshui, China 50 G7
Qinyang, China 50 G7
Qinyuan, China 50 F7
Qinzhou, China 52 G7
Qionghai, China 58 C8
Qionglai, China 52 B4
Qionglai Shan, China 52 B4
Qiongshan, China 58 C8
Qiongzhou Haixia, China . 58 B8
Qiqihar, China 45 E13
Qiraîya, W. →, Egypt ... 69 E3
Qiryat Ata, Israel 69 C4
Qiryat Gat, Israel 69 D3
Qiryat Mal'akhi, Israel ... 69 D3
Qiryat Shemona, Israel ... 69 B4
Qiryat Yam, Israel 69 C4
Qishan, China 50 G4
Qishan, Taiwan 53 F13
Qitai, China 54 B3
Qiubei, China 52 E5
Qixia, China 51 F11
Qiyang, China 53 D8
Qojūr, Iran 64 B5
Qom, Iran 65 C6
Qomsheh, Iran 65 D6
Qostanay = Kustanay, Kazakhstan 44 D7
Qu Jiang →, China 52 B6
Qu Xian, Sichuan, China . 52 B6
Qu Xian, Zhejiang, China 53 C12
Quackenbrück, Germany . 18 C3
Quairading, Australia 89 F2
Quakertown, U.S.A. 107 F9
Qualeup, Australia 89 F2
Quambatook, Australia ... 91 F3
Quambone, Australia 91 E4
Quamby, Australia 90 C3
Quan Long, Vietnam 59 H5
Quanah, U.S.A. 109 H5
Quandialla, Australia 91 E4
Quang Ngai, Vietnam 58 E7
Quang Yen, Vietnam 58 B6
Quannan, China 53 E10
Quantock Hills, U.K. 13 F4
Quanzhou, Fujian, China . 53 E12
Quanzhou, Guangxi Zhuangzu, China 53 E8
Quaraí, Brazil 126 C4
Quarré-les-Tombes, France 25 E10
Quartu Sant' Elena, Italy . 34 C2
Quartzsite, U.S.A. 113 M12
Quatsino, Canada 100 C3
Quatsino Sd., Canada 100 C3
Qūchān, Iran 65 B8
Queanbeyan, Australia ... 91 F4
Québec, Canada 99 C5
Québec □, Canada 99 B6
Quedlinburg, Germany ... 18 D7
Queen Alexandra Ra., Antarctica 5 E11
Queen Charlotte, Canada . 100 C2
Queen Charlotte Bay, Falk. Is. 128 D4
Queen Charlotte Is., Canada 100 C2
Queen Charlotte Str., Canada 100 C3
Queen Elizabeth Is., Canada 94 B10
Queen Elizabeth Nat. Park, Uganda 82 C3
Queen Mary Land, Antarctica 5 D7
Queen Maud G., Canada . 96 B9
Queen Maud Land, Antarctica 5 D3
Queen Maud Mts., Antarctica 5 E13
Queens Chan., Australia .. 88 C4
Queenscliff, Australia 91 F3
Queensland □, Australia .. 90 C3
Queenstown, Australia ... 90 G4
Queenstown, N.Z. 87 L2
Queenstown, S. Africa ... 84 E4
Queets, U.S.A. 112 C2
Queguay Grande →, Uruguay 126 C4
Queimadas, Brazil 122 D4
Quela, Angola 80 F3
Quelimane, Mozam. 83 F4
Quelpart = Cheju Do, S. Korea 51 H14
Quemado, N. Mex., U.S.A. 111 J9
Quemado, Tex., U.S.A. .. 109 L4
Quemú-Quemú, Argentina 126 D3
Quequén, Argentina 126 D4
Querco, Peru 124 C3
Querétaro, Mexico 114 C4
Querétaro □, Mexico 114 C5
Querfurt, Germany 18 D7
Quesada, Spain 29 H1
Queshan, China 50 H8
Quesnel, Canada 100 C4
Quesnel →, Canada 100 C4
Quesnel L., Canada 100 C4
Questa, U.S.A. 111 H11
Questembert, France 24 E4
Quetena, Bolivia 124 E4
Quetico Prov. Park, Canada 98 C1
Quetrequile, Argentina ... 128 B3
Quetta, Pakistan 62 D2
Quevedo, Ecuador 120 D2
Quezaltenango, Guatemala 116 D1
Quezon City, Phil. 55 D4
Qufār, Si. Arabia 64 E4
Qui Nhon, Vietnam 58 F7
Quibaxe, Angola 80 F2
Quibdo, Colombia 120 B2
Quiberon, France 24 E3
Quíbor, Venezuela 120 B4
Quick, Canada 100 C3
Quickborn, Germany 18 B5
Quiet L., Canada 100 A2
Quiévrain, Belgium 17 H3
Quiindy, Paraguay 126 B4
Quila, Mexico 114 C3
Quilán, C., Chile 128 B2
Quilcene, U.S.A. 112 C4
Quilengues, Angola 81 G2
Quilimarí, Chile 126 C1
Quilino, Argentina 126 C3
Quillabamba, Peru 124 C3
Quillacollo, Bolivia 124 D4
Quillagua, Chile 126 A2
Quillaicillo, Chile 126 C1
Quillan, France 26 F6
Quillebeuf-sur-Seine, France 24 C7
Quillota, Chile 126 C1
Quilmes, Argentina 126 C4
Quilon, India 60 Q10
Quilpie, Australia 91 D3
Quilpué, Chile 126 C1
Quilua, Mozam. 83 F4
Quime, Bolivia 124 D4
Quimilí, Argentina 126 B3
Quimper, France 24 D2
Quimperlé, France 24 E3
Quinault →, U.S.A. 112 C2
Quincemil, Peru 124 C3
Quincy, Calif., U.S.A. ... 112 F6
Quincy, Fla., U.S.A. 105 K3
Quincy, Ill., U.S.A. 108 F9
Quincy, Mass., U.S.A. ... 107 D14
Quincy, Wash., U.S.A. ... 110 C4
Quines, Argentina 126 C2
Quinga, Mozam. 83 F5
Quingey, France 25 E12
Quintana de la Serena, Spain 31 G5
Quintana Roo □, Mexico . 115 D7
Quintanar de la Orden, Spain 28 F1
Quintanar de la Sierra, Spain 28 D2
Quintanar del Rey, Spain . 29 F3
Quintero, Chile 126 C1
Quintin, France 24 D4
Quinto, Spain 28 D4
Quinyambie, Australia ... 91 E3
Quípar →, Spain 29 G3
Quipungo, Angola 81 G2
Quirihue, Chile 126 D1
Quirindi, Australia 91 E5
Quiroga, Spain 30 C3
Quiruvilca, Peru 124 B2
Quissac, France 27 E8
Quissanga, Mozam. 83 E5
Quitilipi, Argentina 126 B3
Quitman, Ga., U.S.A. ... 105 K4
Quitman, Miss., U.S.A. .. 105 J1
Quitman, Tex., U.S.A. ... 109 J7
Quito, Ecuador 120 D2
Quixadá, Brazil 122 B4
Quixaxe, Mozam. 83 F5
Quixeramobim, Brazil ... 122 C4
Qujing, China 52 E4
Qul'ân, Jazâ'ir, Egypt ... 76 C4
Qumbu, S. Africa 85 E4
Quneitra, Syria 69 B4
Quoin I., Australia 88 B4
Quoin Pt., S. Africa 84 E2
Quondong, Australia 91 E3
Quorn, Australia 91 E2
Quqon = Kokand, Uzbekistan 44 E8
Qurein, Sudan 77 E3
Qurnat as Sawdā', Lebanon 69 A5
Qûs, Egypt 76 B3
Qusaybah, Iraq 64 C4
Quseir, Egypt 76 B3
Qūshchī, Iran 64 B5
Quthing, Lesotho 85 E4
Qūţīābād, Iran 65 C6
Quwo, China 50 G6
Quyang, China 50 E8
Quynh Nhai, Vietnam 58 B4
Quzi, China 50 F4
Qytet Stalin, Albania 39 J2
Qyzylorda = Kzyl-Orda, Kazakhstan 44 E7

R

Ra, Ko, Thailand 59 H2
Råå, Sweden 11 J6
Raahe, Finland 8 D18
Raalte, Neths. 16 D8
Raamsdonksveer, Neths. .. 17 E5
Raasay, U.K. 14 D2
Raasay, Sd. of, U.K. 14 D2
Rab, Croatia 33 D11
Raba, Indonesia 57 F5
Rába →, Hungary 21 H7
Rabaçal →, Portugal 30 D3
Rabah, Nigeria 79 C6
Rabai, Kenya 82 C4
Rabastens, France 26 E5
Rabastens-de-Bigorre, France 26 E4
Rabat, Malta 37 D1
Rabat, Morocco 74 B3

Rabaul, *Papua N. G.* 92 H7
Rabbit →, *Canada* 100 B3
Rabbit Lake, *Canada* 101 C7
Rabbitskin →, *Canada* 100 A4
Rabka, *Poland* 20 F9
Rābor, *Iran* 65 D8
Rácale, *Italy* 35 C11
Racalmuto, *Italy* 34 E6
Racconigi, *Italy* 32 D4
Race, C., *Canada* 99 C9
Rach Gia, *Vietnam* 59 G5
Raciąż, *Poland* 20 C10
Racibórz, *Poland* 20 E8
Racine, *U.S.A.* 104 D2
Rackerby, *U.S.A.* 112 F5
Radama, Nosy, *Madag.* 85 A8
Radama, Saikanosy, *Madag.* 85 A8
Rădăuţi, *Romania* 38 B8
Radbuza →, *Czech.* 20 F3
Radeburg, *Germany* 18 D9
Radeče, *Slovenia* 33 B12
Radekhov, *Ukraine* 40 F4
Radford, *U.S.A.* 104 G5
Radhanpur, *India* 62 H4
Radiska →, *Macedonia* 39 H3
Radisson, *Canada* 101 C7
Radium Hot Springs, *Canada* 100 C5
Radna, *Romania* 38 C4
Radnor Forest, *U.K.* 13 E4
Radolfzell, *Germany* 19 H4
Radom, *Poland* 20 D11
Radomir, *Bulgaria* 38 G6
Radomsko, *Poland* 20 D9
Radomyshl, *Ukraine* 40 F6
Radoviš, *Macedonia* 39 H5
Radovljica, *Slovenia* 33 B11
Radstock, *U.K.* 13 F5
Radstock, C., *Australia* 91 E1
Răducăneni, *Romania* 38 C10
Radviliškis, *Lithuania* 40 D3
Radville, *Canada* 101 D8
Rae, *Canada* 100 A5
Rae Bareli, *India* 63 F9
Rae Isthmus, *Canada* 97 B11
Raeren, *Belgium* 17 G8
Raeside, L., *Australia* 89 E3
Raetihi, *N.Z.* 87 H5
Rafaela, *Argentina* 126 C3
Rafah, *Egypt* 69 D3
Rafai, *C.A.R.* 82 B1
Raffadali, *Italy* 34 E6
Rafḥā, *Si. Arabia* 64 D4
Rafsanjān, *Iran* 65 D8
Raft Pt., *Australia* 88 C3
Ragag, *Sudan* 77 E1
Ragama, *Sri Lanka* 60 R11
Ragged, Mt., *Australia* 89 F3
Raglan, *Australia* 90 C5
Raglan, *N.Z.* 87 G5
Ragunda, *Sweden* 10 A10
Ragusa, *Italy* 35 F7
Raha, *Indonesia* 57 E6
Rahad, Nahr ed →, *Sudan* 77 E3
Rahad al Bardī, *Sudan* 73 F9
Rahaeng = Tak, *Thailand* 58 D2
Rahden, *Germany* 18 C4
Raheita, *Eritrea* 77 E5
Raḥīmah, *Si. Arabia* 65 E6
Rahimyar Khan, *Pakistan* 62 E4
Rāhjerd, *Iran* 65 C6
Raichur, *India* 60 L10
Raiganj, *India* 63 G13
Raigarh, *India* 61 J13
Raijua, *Indonesia* 57 F6
Railton, *Australia* 90 G4
Rainbow Lake, *Canada* 100 B5
Rainier, *U.S.A.* 112 D4
Rainier, Mt., *U.S.A.* 112 D5
Rainy L., *Canada* 101 D10
Rainy River, *Canada* 101 D10
Raipur, *India* 61 J12
Raj Nandgaon, *India* 61 J12
Raja, Ujung, *Indonesia* 56 D1
Raja Ampat, Kepulauan, *Indonesia* 57 E7
Rajahmundry, *India* 61 L12
Rajajooseppi, *Finland* 8 B20
Rajang →, *Malaysia* 56 D4
Rajapalaiyam, *India* 60 Q10
Rajasthan □, *India* 62 F5
Rajasthan Canal, *India* 62 E5
Rajauri, *India* 63 C6
Rajgarh, *Mad. P., India* 62 G7
Rajgarh, *Raj., India* 62 E6
Rajhenburg, *Slovenia* 33 B12
Rajkot, *India* 62 H4
Rajmahal Hills, *India* 63 G12
Rajpipla, *India* 60 J8
Rajpura, *India* 62 D7
Rajshahi, *Bangla.* 61 G16
Rajshahi □, *Bangla.* 63 G13
Rakaia, *N.Z.* 87 K4
Rakaia →, *N.Z.* 87 K4
Rakan, Ra's, *Qatar* 65 E6
Rakaposhi, *Pakistan* 63 A6
Rakata, Pulau, *Indonesia* 56 F3
Rakhni, *Pakistan* 62 D3
Rakitnoye, *Russia* 48 B7
Rakkestad, *Norway* 10 E5
Rakops, *Botswana* 84 C3
Rákospalota, *Hungary* 21 H9
Rakov, *Belorussia* 40 E5
Rakovica, *Croatia* 33 D12
Rakovník, *Czech.* 20 E3
Rakovski, *Bulgaria* 38 G7
Rakvere, *Estonia* 40 B5
Raleigh, *U.S.A.* 105 H6
Raleigh B., *U.S.A.* 105 H7
Ralja, *Serbia* 21 L10
Ralls, *U.S.A.* 109 J4
Ram →, *Canada* 100 A4
Rām Allāh, *Jordan* 69 D4
Ram Hd., *Australia* 91 F4
Rama, *Nic.* 116 D3
Ramacca, *Italy* 35 E7
Ramales de la Victoria, *Spain* 28 B1
Ramalho, Serra do, *Brazil* 123 D3
Raman, *Thailand* 59 J3
Ramanathapuram, *India* 60 Q11
Ramanetaka, B. de, *Madag.* 85 A8
Ramat Gan, *Israel* 69 C3
Ramatlhabama, *S. Africa* 84 D4
Ramban, *India* 63 C6
Rambervillers, *France* 25 D13
Rambipuji, *Indonesia* 57 H15
Rambouillet, *France* 25 D8
Ramea, *Canada* 99 C8
Ramechhap, *Nepal* 63 F12
Ramelau, *Indonesia* 57 F7
Ramenskoye, *Russia* 41 D11
Ramgarh, *Bihar, India* 63 H11
Ramgarh, *Raj., India* 62 F6
Ramgarh, *Raj., India* 62 F4
Rāmhormoz, *Iran* 65 D6
Ramīān, *Iran* 65 B7
Ramingining, *Australia* 90 A2
Ramla, *Israel* 69 D3
Ramlu, *Eritrea* 77 E5
Ramme, *Denmark* 11 H2
Ramnad = Ramanathapuram, *India* 60 Q11
Ramnagar, *India* 63 C6
Ramnäs, *Sweden* 10 E10
Ramon, *Russia* 41 F11
Ramona, *U.S.A.* 113 M10
Ramore, *Canada* 98 C3
Ramotswa, *Botswana* 84 C4
Rampur, *H.P., India* 62 D7
Rampur, *Mad. P., India* 62 H5
Rampur, *Ut. P., India* 63 E8
Rampur Hat, *India* 63 G12
Rampura, *India* 62 G6
Ramree I. = Ramree Kyun, *Burma* 61 K18
Ramree Kyun, *Burma* 61 K18
Rāmsar, *Iran* 65 B6
Ramsel, *Belgium* 17 F5
Ramsey, *Canada* 98 C3
Ramsey, *U.K.* 12 C3
Ramsgate, *U.K.* 13 F9
Ramsjö, *Sweden* 10 B9
Ramtek, *India* 60 J11
Ramvik, *Sweden* 10 B11
Ranaghat, *India* 63 H13
Ranahu, *Pakistan* 62 G3
Ranau, *Malaysia* 56 C5
Rancagua, *Chile* 126 C1
Rance, *Belgium* 17 H4
Rance →, *France* 24 D5
Rance, Barrage de la, *France* 24 D4
Rancharia, *Brazil* 123 F1
Rancheria →, *Canada* 100 A3
Ranchester, *U.S.A.* 110 D10
Ranchi, *India* 63 H11
Ranco, L., *Chile* 128 B2
Randan, *France* 26 B7
Randazzo, *Italy* 35 E7
Randers, *Denmark* 11 H4
Randers Fjord, *Denmark* 11 H4
Randfontein, *S. Africa* 85 D4
Randle, *U.S.A.* 112 D5
Randolph, *Mass., U.S.A.* 107 D13
Randolph, *N.Y., U.S.A.* 106 D6
Randolph, *Utah, U.S.A.* 110 F8
Randolph, *Vt., U.S.A.* 107 C12
Randsfjord, *Norway* 10 D4
Råne älv →, *Sweden* 8 D17
Rangae, *Thailand* 59 J3
Rangaunu B., *N.Z.* 87 F4
Rångedala, *Sweden* 11 G7
Rangeley, *U.S.A.* 107 B14
Rangely, *U.S.A.* 110 F9
Ranger, *U.S.A.* 109 J5
Rangia, *India* 61 F17
Rangiora, *N.Z.* 87 K4
Rangitaiki →, *N.Z.* 87 G6
Rangitata →, *N.Z.* 87 K3
Rangkasbitung, *Indonesia* 57 G12
Rangon →, *Burma* 61 L20
Rangoon, *Burma* 61 L20
Rangpur, *Bangla.* 61 G16
Rangsit, *Thailand* 58 F3
Ranibennur, *India* 60 M9
Raniganj, *India* 63 H12
Raniwara, *India* 60 G8
Rāniyah, *Iraq* 64 B5
Ranken →, *Australia* 90 C2
Rankin, *U.S.A.* 109 K4
Rankin Inlet, *Canada* 96 B10
Rankins Springs, *Australia* 91 E4
Rannoch, L., *U.K.* 14 E4
Rannoch Moor, *U.K.* 14 E4
Ranobe, Helodranon' i, *Madag.* 85 C7
Ranohira, *Madag.* 85 C8
Ranomafana, *Toamasina, Madag.* 85 B8
Ranomafana, *Toliara, Madag.* 85 C8
Ranong, *Thailand* 59 H2
Rānsa, *Iran* 65 C6
Ransiki, *Indonesia* 57 E8
Rantau, *Indonesia* 56 E5
Rantauprapat, *Indonesia* 56 D1
Rantekombola, *Indonesia* 57 E5
Rantoul, *U.S.A.* 104 E1
Ranum, *Denmark* 11 H3
Raon l'Étape, *France* 25 D13
Raoui, Erg er, *Algeria* 75 C4
Raoyang, *China* 50 E8
Rapa, *Pac. Oc.* 93 K13
Rapallo, *Italy* 32 D6
Rāpch, *Iran* 65 E8
Rapid →, *Canada* 100 B3
Rapid City, *U.S.A.* 108 D3
Rapid River, *U.S.A.* 104 C2
Rapides des Joachims, *Canada* 98 C4
Rapla, *Estonia* 40 B4
Rapperswil, *Switz.* 23 B7
Rapu Rapu I., *Phil.* 55 E6
Rarotonga, *Cook Is.* 93 K12
Ra's al' Ayn, *Syria* 64 B4
Ra's al Khaymah, *U.A.E.* 65 E8
Ra's al-Unuf, *Libya* 73 B8
Ra's an Naqb, *Jordan* 69 F4
Ras Bânâs, *Egypt* 76 C4
Ras Dashen, *Ethiopia* 77 E4
Ras el Ma, *Algeria* 75 B4
Ras Mallap, *Egypt* 76 J8
Râs Timirist, *Mauritania* 78 B1
Rasa, Punta, *Argentina* 128 B4
Rasca, Pta. de la, *Canary Is.* 36 G3
Raseiniai, *Lithuania* 40 D3
Rashad, *Sudan* 77 E3
Rashîd, *Egypt* 76 H7
Rashîd, Masabb, *Egypt* 76 H7
Rasht, *Iran* 65 B6
Rasi Salai, *Thailand* 58 E5
Raška, *Serbia* 21 M10
Rason L., *Australia* 89 E3
Raşova, *Romania* 38 E10
Rasra, *India* 63 G10
Rass el Oued, *Algeria* 75 A6
Rasskazovo, *Russia* 41 E12
Rastatt, *Germany* 19 G4
Rat Buri, *Thailand* 58 F2
Rat Islands, *U.S.A.* 96 C1
Rat River, *Canada* 100 A6
Ratangarh, *India* 62 E6
Raţāwī, *Iraq* 64 D5
Rath, *India* 63 G8
Rath Luirc, *Ireland* 15 D3
Rathdrum, *Ireland* 15 D5
Rathenow, *Germany* 18 C8
Rathkeale, *Ireland* 15 D3
Rathlin, *U.K.* 15 A5
Rathlin O'Birne I., *Ireland* 15 B3
Ratibor = Racibórz, *Poland* 20 E8
Ratlam, *India* 62 H6
Ratnagiri, *India* 60 L8
Raton, *U.S.A.* 109 G2
Rattaphum, *Thailand* 59 J3
Rattray Hd., *U.K.* 14 D7
Ratz, Mt., *Canada* 100 B2
Ratzeburg, *Germany* 18 B6
Raub, *Malaysia* 59 L3
Rauch, *Argentina* 126 D4
Raufarhöfn, *Iceland* 8 C6
Raufoss, *Norway* 10 D4
Raukumara Ra., *N.Z.* 87 H6
Raul Soares, *Brazil* 123 F3
Rauland, *Norway* 10 E2
Rauma, *Finland* 9 F16
Rauma →, *Norway* 10 B1
Raurkela, *India* 63 H11
Rausu-Dake, *Japan* 48 B12
Rava Russkaya, *Ukraine* 40 F3
Ravānsar, *Iran* 64 C5
Ravanusa, *Italy* 34 E6
Rāvar, *Iran* 65 D8
Ravels, *Belgium* 17 F6
Ravena, *U.S.A.* 107 D11
Ravenna, *Italy* 33 D9
Ravenna, *Nebr., U.S.A.* 108 E5
Ravenna, *Ohio, U.S.A.* 106 E3
Ravensburg, *Germany* 19 H5
Ravenshoe, *Australia* 90 B4
Ravenstein, *Neths.* 16 E7
Ravensthorpe, *Australia* 89 F3
Ravenswood, *Australia* 90 C4
Ravenswood, *U.S.A.* 104 F5
Ravi →, *Pakistan* 62 D4
Ravna Gora, *Croatia* 33 C11
Rawa Mazowiecka, *Poland* 20 D10
Rawalpindi, *Pakistan* 62 C5
Rawāndūz, *Iraq* 64 B5
Rawang, *Malaysia* 59 L3
Rawdon, *Canada* 98 C5
Rawene, *N.Z.* 87 F4
Rawicz, *Poland* 20 D6
Rawlinna, *Australia* 89 F4
Rawlins, *U.S.A.* 110 F10
Rawlinson Ra., *Australia* 89 D4
Rawson, *Argentina* 128 B3
Ray, *U.S.A.* 108 A3
Ray, C., *Canada* 99 C8
Rayadurg, *India* 60 M10
Rayagada, *India* 61 K13
Raychikhinsk, *Russia* 45 E13
Rāyen, *Iran* 65 D8
Raymond, *Canada* 100 D6
Raymond, *Calif., U.S.A.* 112 H7
Raymond, *Wash., U.S.A.* 112 D3
Raymondville, *U.S.A.* 109 M6
Raymore, *Canada* 101 C8
Rayne, *U.S.A.* 109 K8
Rayón, *Mexico* 114 B2
Rayong, *Thailand* 58 F3
Rayville, *U.S.A.* 109 J9
Raz, Pte. du, *France* 24 D2
Razan, *Iran* 65 C6
Ražana, *Serbia* 21 L9
Ražanj, *Serbia* 21 M11
Razdel'naya, *Ukraine* 42 C4
Razdolnoye, *Russia* 48 C5
Razdolnoye, *Ukraine* 42 D5
Razeh, *Iran* 65 C6
Razelm, Lacul, *Romania* 38 E12
Razgrad, *Bulgaria* 38 F9
Razmak, *Pakistan* 62 C3
Ré, I. de, *France* 26 B2
Reading, *U.K.* 13 F7
Reading, *U.S.A.* 107 F9
Real, Cordillera, *Bolivia* 124 D4
Realicó, *Argentina* 126 D3
Réalmont, *France* 26 E6
Reata, *Mexico* 114 B4
Rebais, *France* 25 D10
Rebecca, L., *Australia* 89 F3
Rebi, *Indonesia* 57 F8
Rebiana, *Libya* 73 D9
Rebun-Tō, *Japan* 48 B10
Recanati, *Italy* 33 E10
Recaş, *Romania* 38 D4
Recherche, Arch. of the, *Australia* 89 F3
Rechitsa, *Belorussia* 40 E7
Recht, *Belgium* 17 H8
Recife, *Brazil* 122 C5
Recklinghausen, *Germany* 17 E10
Reconquista, *Argentina* 126 B4
Recreio, *Brazil* 125 B6
Recreo, *Argentina* 126 B2
Recuay, *Peru* 124 B2
Red →, *La., U.S.A.* 109 K9
Red →, *N. Dak., U.S.A.* 108 A6
Red Bank, *U.S.A.* 107 F10
Red Bay, *Canada* 99 B8
Red Bluff, *U.S.A.* 110 F2
Red Bluff L., *U.S.A.* 109 K3
Red Cliffs, *Australia* 91 E3
Red Cloud, *U.S.A.* 108 E5
Red Deer, *Canada* 100 C6
Red Deer →, *Alta., Canada* 101 C6
Red Deer →, *Man., Canada* 101 C8
Red Deer L., *Canada* 101 C8
Red Indian L., *Canada* 99 C8
Red Lake, *Canada* 101 C10
Red Lake Falls, *U.S.A.* 108 B6
Red Lodge, *U.S.A.* 110 D9
Red Mountain, *U.S.A.* 113 K9
Red Oak, *U.S.A.* 108 E7
Red Rock, *Canada* 98 C2
Red Rock, L., *U.S.A.* 108 E8
Red Rocks Pt., *Australia* 89 F4
Red Sea, *Asia* 68 C2
Red Slate Mt., *U.S.A.* 112 H8
Red Sucker L., *Canada* 101 C10
Red Tower Pass = Turnu Rosu Pasul, *Romania* 38 D7
Red Wing, *U.S.A.* 108 C8
Rédange, *Lux.* 17 J7
Redbridge, *U.K.* 13 F8
Redcar, *U.K.* 12 C6
Redcliff, *Canada* 101 C6
Redcliffe, *Australia* 91 D5
Redcliffe, Mt., *Australia* 89 E3
Reddersburg, *S. Africa* 84 D4
Redding, *U.S.A.* 110 F2
Redditch, *U.K.* 13 E6
Redenção, *Brazil* 122 B4
Redfield, *U.S.A.* 108 C5
Redknife →, *Canada* 100 A5
Redlands, *U.S.A.* 113 M9
Redmond, *Australia* 89 F2
Redmond, *Oreg., U.S.A.* 110 D3
Redmond, *Wash., U.S.A.* 112 C4
Redon, *France* 24 E4
Redonda, *Antigua* 117 C7
Redondela, *Spain* 30 C2
Redondo, *Portugal* 31 G3
Redondo Beach, *U.S.A.* 113 M8
Redrock Pt., *Canada* 100 A5
Redruth, *U.K.* 13 G2
Redvers, *Canada* 101 D8
Redwater, *Canada* 100 C6
Redwood, *U.S.A.* 107 B9
Redwood City, *U.S.A.* 111 H2
Redwood Falls, *U.S.A.* 108 C7
Ree, L., *Ireland* 15 C4
Reed, L., *Canada* 101 C8
Reed City, *U.S.A.* 104 D3
Reeder, *U.S.A.* 108 B3
Reedley, *U.S.A.* 111 H4
Reedsburg, *U.S.A.* 108 D9
Reedsport, *U.S.A.* 110 E1
Reefton, *N.Z.* 87 K3
Refahiye, *Turkey* 67 D8
Refugio, *U.S.A.* 109 L6
Rega →, *Poland* 20 A5
Regalbuto, *Italy* 35 E7
Regen, *Germany* 19 G9
Regen →, *Germany* 19 F8
Regeneração, *Brazil* 122 C3
Regensburg, *Germany* 19 F8
Regensdorf, *Switz.* 23 B6
Réggio di Calábria, *Italy* 35 D8
Réggio nell' Emilia, *Italy* 32 D7
Regina, *Canada* 101 C8
Régina, *Fr. Guiana* 121 C7
Registro, *Brazil* 127 A6
Reguengos de Monsaraz, *Portugal* 31 G3
Rehar →, *India* 63 H10
Rehoboth, *Namibia* 84 C2
Rehovot, *Israel* 69 D3
Rei-Bouba, *Cameroon* 73 G7
Reichenbach, *Germany* 18 E8
Reichenbach, *Switz.* 22 C5
Reid, *Australia* 89 F4
Reid River, *Australia* 90 B4
Reiden, *Switz.* 22 B5
Reidsville, *U.S.A.* 105 G6
Reigate, *U.K.* 13 F7
Reillo, *Spain* 28 F3
Reims, *France* 25 C11
Reina Adelaida, Arch., *Chile* 128 D2
Reinach, *Aargau, Switz.* 22 B6
Reinach, *Basel, Switz.* 22 B5
Reinbeck, *U.S.A.* 108 D8
Reindeer →, *Canada* 101 B8
Reindeer I., *Canada* 101 C9
Reindeer L., *Canada* 101 B8
Reinga, C., *N.Z.* 87 F4
Reinosa, *Spain* 30 B6
Reinosa, Paso, *Spain* 30 C6
Reitdiep, *Neths.* 16 B8
Reitz, *S. Africa* 85 D4
Reivilo, *S. Africa* 84 D3
Rejmyre, *Sweden* 11 F9
Reka →, *Slovenia* 33 C11
Rekinniki, *Russia* 45 C17
Reliance, *Canada* 101 A7
Remad, Oued →, *Algeria* 75 B4
Rémalard, *France* 24 D7
Remarkable, Mt., *Australia* 91 E2
Rembang, *Indonesia* 57 G14
Remchi, *Algeria* 75 A4
Remedios, *Colombia* 120 B3
Remedios, *Panama* 116 E3
Remeshk, *Iran* 65 E8
Remich, *Lux.* 17 J8
Rémire, *Fr. Guiana* 121 C7
Remiremont, *France* 25 D13
Remo, *Ethiopia* 77 F5
Remontnoye, *Russia* 43 C10
Remoulins, *France* 27 E8
Remscheid, *Germany* 18 D3
Ren Xian, *China* 50 F8
Renascença, *Brazil* 120 D4
Rende, *Italy* 35 C9
Rendeux, *Belgium* 17 H7
Rendína, *Greece* 39 K4
Rendsburg, *Germany* 18 A5
Rene, *Russia* 45 C19
Renfrew, *Canada* 98 C4
Renfrew, *U.K.* 14 F4
Rengat, *Indonesia* 56 E2
Rengo, *Chile* 126 C1
Renhua, *China* 53 E9
Renhuai, *China* 52 D6
Reni, *Moldavia* 42 D3
Renk, *Sudan* 77 E3
Renkum, *Neths.* 16 E7
Renmark, *Australia* 91 E3
Rennell Sd., *Canada* 100 C2
Renner Springs T.O., *Australia* 90 B1
Rennes, *France* 24 D5
Rennes, Bassin de, *France* 24 E5
Reno, *U.S.A.* 112 F7
Reno →, *Italy* 33 D9
Renovo, *U.S.A.* 106 E7
Renqiu, *China* 50 E9
Rensselaer, *Ind., U.S.A.* 104 E2
Rensselaer, *N.Y., U.S.A.* 107 D11
Rentería, *Spain* 28 B3
Renton, *U.S.A.* 112 C4
Réo, *Burkina Faso* 78 C4
Reotipur, *India* 63 G10
Republic, *Mich., U.S.A.* 104 B2
Republic, *Wash., U.S.A.* 110 B4
Republican →, *U.S.A.* 108 F6
Republican City, *U.S.A.* 108 E5
Republiek, *Surinam* 121 B6
Repulse Bay, *Canada* 97 B11
Requena, *Peru* 124 B3
Requena, *Spain* 29 F3
Resadiye = Datça, *Turkey* 66 E2
Reşadiye, *Turkey* 66 C7
Resele, *Sweden* 10 A11
Reserve, *Canada* 101 C8
Reserve, *U.S.A.* 111 K9
Resht = Rasht, *Iran* 65 B6
Resistencia, *Argentina* 126 B4
Reşiţa, *Romania* 38 D4
Resolution I., *Canada* 97 B13
Resolution I., *N.Z.* 87 L1
Resplandes, *Brazil* 122 C2
Resplendor, *Brazil* 123 E3
Ressano Garcia, *Mozam.* 85 D5
Reston, *Canada* 101 D8
Retalhuleu, *Guatemala* 116 D1
Reteag, *Romania* 38 B7
Retenue, L. de, *Zaïre* 83 E2
Rethel, *France* 25 C11
Rethem, *Germany* 18 C5

Réthímnon, Greece 37 D6
Réthímnon □, Greece 37 D6
Retiche, Alpi, Switz. 23 D10
Retie, Belgium 17 F6
Retiers, France 24 E5
Retortillo, Spain 30 E4
Reuland, Belgium 17 H8
Réunion ■, Ind. Oc. 71 J9
Reus, Spain 28 D6
Reusel, Neths. 17 F6
Reuss →, Switz. 23 B6
Reutlingen, Germany 19 G5
Reutte, Austria 19 H6
Reuver, Neths. 17 F8
Reval = Tallinn, Estonia 40 B4
Revel, France 26 E6
Revelganj, India 63 G11
Revelstoke, Canada 100 C5
Reventazón, Peru 124 B1
Revigny-sur-Ornain, France 25 D11
Revilla Gigedo, Is., Pac. Oc. 93 F16
Revillagigedo I., U.S.A. 100 B2
Revin, France 25 C11
Revuè →, Mozam. 83 F3
Rewa, India 63 G9
Rewa →, Guyana 121 C6
Rewari, India 62 E7
Rexburg, U.S.A. 110 E8
Rey, Iran 65 C6
Rey, Rio del →, Nigeria 79 E6
Rey Malabo, Eq. Guin. 79 E6
Reyes, Bolivia 124 C4
Reyes, Pt., U.S.A. 112 H3
Reykjahlið, Iceland 8 D5
Reykjanes, Iceland 8 E2
Reykjavík, Iceland 8 D3
Reynolds, Canada 101 D9
Reynolds Ra., Australia 88 D5
Reynoldsville, U.S.A. 106 E6
Reynosa, Mexico 115 B5
Rēzekne, Latvia 40 C5
Rezvān, Iran 65 E8
Rharis, O. →, Algeria 75 C6
Rhayader, U.K. 13 E4
Rheden, Neths. 16 D8
Rhein, Canada 101 C8
Rhein →, Europe 16 E8
Rhein-Main-Donau-Kanal, Germany 19 F7
Rheinbach, Germany 18 E2
Rheine, Germany 18 C3
Rheineck, Switz. 23 B9
Rheinfelden, Switz. 22 A5
Rheinland-Pfalz □, Germany 19 E2
Rheinsberg, Germany 18 B8
Rheinwaldhorn, Switz. 23 D8
Rhenen, Neths. 16 E7
Rheriss, Oued →, Morocco 74 B4
Rheydt, Germany 18 D2
Rhin = Rhein →, Europe 16 E8
Rhinau, France 25 D14
Rhine = Rhein →, Europe 16 E8
Rhineland-Palatinate □ = Rheinland-Pfalz □, Germany 19 E2
Rhinelander, U.S.A. 108 C10
Rhino Camp, Uganda 82 B3
Rhir, Cap, Morocco 74 B3
Rhisnes, Belgium 17 G5
Rho, Italy 32 C6
Rhode Island □, U.S.A. 107 E13
Rhodes = Ródhos, Greece 37 C10
Rhodesia = Zimbabwe ■, Africa 83 F2
Rhodope Mts. = Rhodopi Planina, Bulgaria 39 H7
Rhodopi Planina, Bulgaria 39 H7
Rhön = Hohe Rhön, Germany 19 E5
Rhondda, U.K. 13 F4
Rhône □, France 27 C8
Rhône →, France 27 E8
Rhum, U.K. 14 E2
Rhyl, U.K. 12 D4
Rhymney, U.K. 13 F4
Ri-Aba, Eq. Guin. 79 E6
Riachão, Brazil 122 C2
Riacho de Santana, Brazil 123 D3
Rialma, Brazil 123 E2
Riaño, Spain 30 C5
Rians, France 27 E9
Riansares →, Spain 28 F1
Riasi, India 63 C6
Riau □, Indonesia 56 D2
Riau, Kepulauan, Indonesia 56 D2
Riau Arch. = Riau, Kepulauan, Indonesia 56 D2
Riaza, Spain 28 D1
Riaza →, Spain 28 D1
Riba de Saelices, Spain 28 E2
Ribadavia, Spain 30 C2
Ribadeo, Spain 30 B3
Ribadesella, Spain 30 B5
Ribamar, Brazil 122 B3
Ribas, Spain 28 C7
Ribas do Rio Pardo, Brazil 125 E7
Ribble →, U.K. 12 C5
Ribe, Denmark 11 J2
Ribeauvillé, France 25 D14
Ribécourt, France 25 C9
Ribeira, Spain 30 C2
Ribeira Brava, Madeira 36 D2
Ribeira do Pombal, Brazil 122 D4
Ribeirão Prêto, Brazil 127 A6
Ribeiro Gonçalves, Brazil 122 C2
Ribemont, France 25 C10
Ribera, Italy 34 E6
Ribérac, France 26 C4
Riberalta, Bolivia 125 C4
Ribnica, Slovenia 33 C11
Ribnitz-Damgarten, Germany 18 A8
Riccarton, N.Z. 87 K4
Riccia, Italy 35 A7
Riccione, Italy 33 D9
Rice, U.S.A. 113 L12
Rice L., Canada 106 B6
Rice Lake, U.S.A. 108 C9
Rich, Morocco 74 B4
Rich Hill, U.S.A. 109 F7
Richards Bay, S. Africa 85 D5
Richards L., Canada 101 B7
Richardson →, Canada 101 B6
Richardson Springs, U.S.A. 112 F5
Richardton, U.S.A. 108 B3
Riche, C., Australia 89 F2
Richelieu, France 24 E7
Richey, U.S.A. 108 B2
Richfield, Idaho, U.S.A. 110 E6
Richfield, Utah, U.S.A. 111 G8
Richford, U.S.A. 107 B12
Richibucto, Canada 99 C7
Richland, Ga., U.S.A. 105 J3
Richland, Oreg., U.S.A. 110 D5
Richland, Wash., U.S.A. 110 C4
Richland Center, U.S.A. 108 D9
Richlands, U.S.A. 104 G5
Richmond, N.S.W., Australia 91 E5
Richmond, Queens., Australia 90 C3
Richmond, N.Z. 87 J4
Richmond, S. Africa 85 D5
Richmond, U.K. 12 C6
Richmond, Calif., U.S.A. 112 H4
Richmond, Ind., U.S.A. 104 F3
Richmond, Ky., U.S.A. 104 G3
Richmond, Mich., U.S.A. 106 D2
Richmond, Mo., U.S.A. 108 F8
Richmond, Tex., U.S.A. 109 L7
Richmond, Utah, U.S.A. 110 F8
Richmond, Va., U.S.A. 104 G7
Richmond Ra., Australia 91 D5
Richmond-upon-Thames, U.K. 13 F7
Richterswil, Switz. 23 B7
Richton, U.S.A. 105 K1
Richwood, U.S.A. 104 F5
Ricla, Spain 28 D3
Ridder, Kazakhstan 44 D9
Ridderkerk, Neths. 16 E5
Riddes, Switz. 22 D4
Ridgecrest, U.S.A. 113 K9
Ridgedale, Canada 101 C8
Ridgefield, U.S.A. 112 E4
Ridgeland, U.S.A. 105 J5
Ridgelands, Australia 90 C5
Ridgetown, Canada 98 D3
Ridgewood, U.S.A. 107 F10
Ridgway, U.S.A. 106 E6
Riding Mountain Nat. Park, Canada 101 C8
Ridley, Mt., Australia 89 F3
Ried, Austria 21 G3
Riedlingen, Germany 19 G5
Riel, Neths. 17 E6
Rienza →, Italy 33 B8
Riesa, Germany 18 D9
Riesco, I., Chile 128 D2
Riesi, Italy 35 E7
Riet →, S. Africa 84 D3
Rieti, Italy 33 F9
Rieupeyroux, France 26 D6
Riez, France 27 E10
Riffe L., U.S.A. 112 D4
Rifle, U.S.A. 110 G10
Rifstangi, Iceland 8 C5
Rift Valley □, Kenya 82 B4
Rig Rig, Chad 73 F7
Riga, Latvia 40 C4
Riga, G. of = Rīgas Jūras Līcis, Latvia 40 C3
Rīgān, Iran 65 D8
Rīgas Jūras Līcis, Latvia 40 C3
Rigaud, Canada 107 A10
Rigby, U.S.A. 110 E8
Rīgestān □, Afghan. 60 D4
Riggins, U.S.A. 110 D5
Rignac, France 26 D6
Rigolet, Canada 99 B8
Riihimäki, Finland 9 F18
Riiser-Larsen-halvøya, Antarctica 5 C4
Rijau, Nigeria 79 C6
Rijeka, Croatia 33 C11
Rijen, Neths. 17 E5
Rijkevorsel, Belgium 17 F5
Rijn →, Neths. 16 D4
Rijnsburg, Neths. 16 D4
Rijssbergen, Neths. 17 E5
Rijssen, Neths. 16 D9
Rijswijk, Neths. 16 D4
Rike, Ethiopia 77 E4
Rikuzentakada, Japan 48 E10
Rila Planina, Bulgaria 38 G6
Riley, U.S.A. 110 E4
Rima →, Nigeria 79 C6
Rimah, Wadi ar →, Si. Arabia 64 E4
Rimavská Sobota, Slovakia 21 G10
Rimbey, Canada 100 C6
Rimbo, Sweden 10 E12
Rimi, Nigeria 79 C6
Rímini, Italy 33 D9
Rîmnicu Sărat, Romania 38 D10
Rîmnicu Vîlcea, Romania 38 D7
Rimouski, Canada 99 C6
Rimrock, U.S.A. 112 D5
Rinca, Indonesia 57 F5
Rincón de Romos, Mexico 114 C4
Rinconada, Argentina 126 A2
Ringarum, Sweden 11 F10
Ringe, Denmark 11 J4
Ringim, Nigeria 79 C6
Ringkøbing, Denmark 11 H2
Ringling, U.S.A. 110 C8
Ringsaker, Norway 10 D4
Ringsted, Denmark 11 J5
Ringvassøy, Norway 8 B15
Rinjani, Indonesia 56 F5
Rinteln, Germany 18 C5
Río, Punta del, Spain 29 J2
Rio Branco, Brazil 124 B4
Río Branco, Uruguay 127 C5
Rio Brilhante, Brazil 127 A5
Río Bueno, Chile 128 B2
Río Chico, Venezuela 120 A4
Rio Claro, Brazil 127 A6
Rio Claro, Trin. & Tob. 117 D7
Río Colorado, Argentina 128 A4
Río Cuarto, Argentina 126 C3
Rio das Pedras, Mozam. 85 C6
Rio de Contas, Brazil 123 D3
Rio de Janeiro, Brazil 123 F3
Rio de Janeiro □, Brazil 123 F3
Rio do Prado, Brazil 123 E3
Rio do Sul, Brazil 127 B6
Río Gallegos, Argentina 128 D3
Río Grande, Argentina 128 D3
Río Grande, Bolivia 124 E4
Rio Grande, Brazil 127 C5
Río Grande, Mexico 114 C4
Río Grande, Nic. 116 D3
Rio Grande →, U.S.A. 109 N6
Rio Grande City, U.S.A. 109 M5
Río Grande del Norte →, N. Amer. 103 E7
Rio Grande do Norte □, Brazil 122 C4
Rio Grande do Sul □, Brazil 127 C5
Río Hato, Panama 116 E3
Río Lagartos, Mexico 115 C7
Rio Largo, Brazil 122 C4
Rio Maior, Portugal 31 F2
Rio Marina, Italy 32 F7
Río Mayo, Argentina 128 C2
Río Mulatos, Bolivia 124 D4
Río Muni = Mbini □, Eq. Guin. 80 D2
Rio Negro, Brazil 127 B6
Río Negro, Chile 128 B2
Rio Negro, Pantanal do, Brazil 125 D6
Rio Pardo, Brazil 127 C5
Río Pico, Argentina 128 B2
Rio Real, Brazil 123 D4
Río Segundo, Argentina 126 C3
Río Tercero, Argentina 126 C3
Rio Tinto, Brazil 122 C4
Rio Tinto, Portugal 30 D2
Rio Verde, Brazil 123 E1
Río Verde, Mexico 115 C5
Rio Verde de Mato Grosso, Brazil 125 D7
Rio Vista, U.S.A. 112 G5
Ríobamba, Ecuador 120 D2
Ríohacha, Colombia 120 A3
Rioja, Peru 124 B2
Riom, France 26 C7
Riom-ès-Montagnes, France 26 C6
Rion-des-Landes, France 26 E3
Rionegro, Colombia 120 B2
Rionero in Vúlture, Italy 35 B8
Rioni →, Georgia 43 E9
Rios, Spain 30 D3
Riosucio, Caldas, Colombia 120 B2
Ríosucio, Choco, Colombia 120 B2
Riou L., Canada 101 B7
Rioz, France 25 E13
Riozinho →, Brazil 120 D4
Riparia, Dora →, Italy 32 C4
Ripatransone, Italy 33 F10
Ripley, Canada 106 B3
Ripley, Calif., U.S.A. 113 M12
Ripley, N.Y., U.S.A. 106 D5
Ripley, Tenn., U.S.A. 109 H10
Ripoll, Spain 28 C7
Ripon, U.K. 12 C6
Ripon, Calif., U.S.A. 112 H5
Ripon, Wis., U.S.A. 104 D1
Riposto, Italy 35 E8
Risalpur, Pakistan 62 B4
Risan, Montenegro, Yug. 21 N8
Risaralda □, Colombia 120 B2
Riscle, France 26 E3
Rishā', W. ar →, Si. Arabia 64 E5
Rishiri-Tō, Japan 48 B10
Rishon le Ziyyon, Israel 69 D3
Risle →, France 24 C7
Rison, U.S.A. 109 J8
Risør, Norway 11 F3
Rissani, Morocco 74 B4
Riti, Nigeria 79 D6
Rittman, U.S.A. 106 F3
Ritzville, U.S.A. 110 C4
Riva Bella, France 24 C6
Riva del Garda, Italy 32 C7
Rivadavia, Buenos Aires, Argentina 126 D3
Rivadavia, Mendoza, Argentina 126 C2
Rivadavia, Salta, Argentina 126 A3
Rivadavia, Chile 126 B1
Rivarolo Canavese, Italy 32 C4
Rivas, Nic. 116 D2
Rive-de-Gier, France 27 C8
River Cess, Liberia 78 D3
Rivera, Uruguay 127 C4
Riverdale, U.S.A. 112 J7
Riverhead, U.S.A. 107 F12
Riverhurst, Canada 101 C7
Riverina, Australia 89 E3
Rivers, Canada 101 C8
Rivers □, Nigeria 79 E6
Rivers, L. of the, Canada 101 D7
Rivers Inlet, Canada 100 C3
Riversdale, S. Africa 84 E3
Riverside, Calif., U.S.A. 113 M9
Riverside, Wyo., U.S.A. 110 F10
Riversleigh, Australia 90 B2
Riverton, Australia 91 E2
Riverton, Canada 101 C9
Riverton, N.Z. 87 M1
Riverton, U.S.A. 110 E9
Riverton Heights, U.S.A. 112 C4
Rives, France 27 C9
Rivesaltes, France 26 F6
Riviera, Europe 32 E5
Rivière-à-Pierre, Canada 99 C5
Rivière-au-Renard, Canada 99 C7
Rivière-du-Loup, Canada 99 C6
Rivière-Pentecôte, Canada 99 C6
Rivière-Pilote, Martinique 117 D7
Rivne = Rovno, Ukraine 40 F5
Rívoli, Italy 32 C4
Rivoli B., Australia 91 F3
Rixensart, Belgium 17 G5
Riyadh = Ar Riyāḍ, Si. Arabia 64 E5
Rize, Turkey 67 C9
Rize □, Turkey 67 C9
Rizhao, China 51 G10
Rizokarpaso, Cyprus 37 D13
Rizzuto, C., Italy 35 D10
Rjukan, Norway 10 E2
Roa, Norway 10 D4
Roa, Spain 30 D7
Road Town, Virgin Is. 117 C7
Roag, L., U.K. 14 C2
Roanne, France 27 B8
Roanoke, Ala., U.S.A. 105 J3
Roanoke, Va., U.S.A. 104 G6
Roanoke →, U.S.A. 105 H7
Roanoke I., U.S.A. 105 H8
Roanoke Rapids, U.S.A. 105 G7
Roatán, Honduras 116 C2
Robbins I., Australia 90 G4
Robe →, Australia 88 D2
Robe →, Ireland 15 C2
Röbel, Germany 18 B8
Robert Lee, U.S.A. 109 K4
Roberts, U.S.A. 110 E7
Robertsganj, India 63 G10
Robertson, S. Africa 84 E2
Robertson I., Antarctica 5 C18
Robertson Ra., Australia 88 D3
Robertsport, Liberia 78 D2
Robertstown, Australia 91 E2
Roberval, Canada 99 C5
Robeson Chan., Greenland 4 A4
Robinson →, Australia 90 B2
Robinson Ra., Australia 89 E2
Robinson River, Australia 90 B2
Robinvale, Australia 91 E3
Roblin, Canada 101 C8
Roboré, Bolivia 125 D6
Robson, Mt., Canada 100 C5
Robstown, U.S.A. 109 M6
Roca, C. da, Portugal 6 H4
Roca Partida, I., Mexico 114 D2
Rocas, I., Brazil 122 B5
Rocca d'Aspidé, Italy 35 B8
Rocca San Casciano, Italy 33 D8
Roccalbegna, Italy 33 F8
Roccastrada, Italy 33 F8
Roccella Iónica, Italy 35 D9
Rocha, Uruguay 127 C5
Rochdale, U.K. 12 D5
Rochechouart, France 26 C4
Rochedo, Brazil 125 D7
Rochefort, Belgium 17 H6
Rochefort, France 26 C3
Rochefort-en-Terre, France 24 E4
Rochelle, U.S.A. 108 E10
Rocher River, Canada 100 A6
Rocherath, Belgium 17 H8
Rocheservière, France 24 F5
Rochester, Canada 100 C6
Rochester, U.K. 13 F8
Rochester, Ind., U.S.A. 104 E2
Rochester, Minn., U.S.A. 108 C8
Rochester, N.H., U.S.A. 107 C14
Rochester, N.Y., U.S.A. 106 C7
Rociana, Spain 31 H4
Rociu, Romania 38 E8
Rock →, Canada 100 A3
Rock Hill, U.S.A. 105 H5
Rock Island, U.S.A. 108 E9
Rock Rapids, U.S.A. 108 D6
Rock River, U.S.A. 110 F11
Rock Sound, Bahamas 116 B4
Rock Springs, Mont., U.S.A. 110 C10
Rock Springs, Wyo., U.S.A. 110 F9
Rock Valley, U.S.A. 108 D6
Rockall, Atl. Oc. 6 D3
Rockanje, Neths. 16 E4
Rockdale, Tex., U.S.A. 109 K6
Rockdale, Wash., U.S.A. 112 C5
Rockefeller Plateau, Antarctica 5 E14
Rockford, U.S.A. 108 D10
Rockglen, Canada 101 D7
Rockhampton, Australia 90 C5
Rockhampton Downs, Australia 90 B2
Rockingham, Australia 89 F2
Rockingham B., Australia 90 B4
Rockingham Forest, U.K. 13 E7
Rocklake, U.S.A. 108 A5
Rockland, Canada 107 A9
Rockland, Idaho, U.S.A. 110 E7
Rockland, Maine, U.S.A. 99 D6
Rockland, Mich., U.S.A. 108 B10
Rocklin, U.S.A. 112 G5
Rockmart, U.S.A. 105 H3
Rockport, Mo., U.S.A. 108 E7
Rockport, Tex., U.S.A. 109 L6
Rocksprings, U.S.A. 109 K4
Rockville, Conn., U.S.A. 107 E12
Rockville, Md., U.S.A. 104 F7
Rockwall, U.S.A. 109 J6
Rockwell City, U.S.A. 108 D7
Rockwood, U.S.A. 105 H3
Rocky Ford, U.S.A. 108 F3
Rocky Gully, Australia 89 F2
Rocky Lane, Canada 100 B5
Rocky Mount, U.S.A. 105 H7
Rocky Mountain House, Canada 100 C6
Rocky Mts., N. Amer. 100 C4
Rockyford, Canada 100 C6
Rocroi, France 25 C11
Rod, Pakistan 60 E3
Rødberg, Norway 10 D2
Rødby, Denmark 11 K5
Rødbyhavn, Denmark 11 K5
Roddickton, Canada 99 B8
Rødding, Denmark 11 J3
Rødekro, Denmark 11 J3
Roden, Neths. 16 B8
Rødenes, Norway 10 E5
Rodenkirchen, Germany 18 B4
Roderick I., Canada 100 C3
Rodez, France 26 D6
Rodholívas, Greece 39 J6
Rodhopoú, Greece 37 D5
Ródhos, Greece 37 C10
Rodi Garganico, Italy 35 A8
Rodna, Romania 38 B7
Rodney, Canada 106 D3
Rodney, C., N.Z. 87 G5
Rodniki, Russia 41 C12
Rodriguez, Ind. Oc. 3 E13
Roe →, U.K. 15 A5
Roebling, U.S.A. 107 F10
Roebourne, Australia 88 D2
Roebuck B., Australia 88 C3
Roebuck Plains, Australia 88 C3
Roer →, Neths. 17 F7
Roermond, Neths. 17 F7
Roes Welcome Sd., Canada 97 B11
Roeselare, Belgium 17 G2
Rœulx, Belgium 17 G4
Rogachev, Belorussia 40 E7
Rogagua, L., Bolivia 124 C4
Rogaland fylke □, Norway 9 G9
Rogaška Slatina, Slovenia 33 B12
Rogatec, Slovenia 33 B12
Rogatin, Ukraine 40 G4
Rogdhia, Greece 37 D7
Rogers, U.S.A. 109 G7
Rogers City, U.S.A. 104 C4
Rogerson, U.S.A. 110 E6
Rogersville, U.S.A. 105 G4
Roggan River, Canada 98 B4
Roggel, Neths. 17 F7
Roggeveldberge, S. Africa 84 E3
Roggiano Gravina, Italy 35 C9
Rogliano, France 27 F13
Rogliano, Italy 35 C9
Rogoaguado, L., Bolivia 125 C4
Rogue →, U.S.A. 110 E1
Rohan, France 24 D4
Róhda, Greece 37 A3
Rohnert Park, U.S.A. 112 G4
Rohrbach-lès-Bitche, France 25 C14
Rohri, Pakistan 62 F3
Rohri Canal, Pakistan 62 F3
Rohtak, India 62 E7
Roi Et, Thailand 58 D4
Roisel, France 25 C10
Rojas, Argentina 126 C3
Rojo, C., Mexico 115 C5
Rokan →, Indonesia 56 D2
Rokeby, Australia 90 A3
Rokiškis, Lithuania 40 D4
Rokitno, Russia 40 F9
Rolândia, Brazil 127 A5
Rolde, Neths. 16 C9
Rolette, U.S.A. 108 A5
Rolla, Kans., U.S.A. 109 G4
Rolla, Mo., U.S.A. 109 G9

Rolla, *N. Dak., U.S.A.* 108 A5
Rollag, *Norway* 10 D3
Rolle, *Switz.* 22 D2
Rolleston, *Australia* 90 C4
Rollingstone, *Australia* 90 B4
Rom, *Sudan* 77 F3
Roma, *Australia* 91 D4
Roma, *Italy* 34 A5
Roma, *Sweden* 9 H15
Roman, *Romania* 38 C9
Roman, *Russia* 45 C12
Roman-Kosh, Gora, *Ukraine* 42 D6
Romanche →, *France* 27 C9
Romang, *Indonesia* 57 F7
Romãni, *Egypt* 69 E1
Romania ■, *Europe* 38 D8
Romano, Cayo, *Cuba* 116 B4
Romano di Lombardía, *Italy* 32 C6
Romanovka = Bessarabka, *Moldavia* 42 C3
Romans-sur-Isère, *France* 27 C9
Romanshorn, *Switz.* 23 A8
Romblon, *Phil.* 55 E5
Rombo □, *Tanzania* 82 C4
Rome = Roma, *Italy* 34 A5
Rome, *Ga., U.S.A.* 105 H3
Rome, *N.Y., U.S.A.* 107 C9
Romeleåsen, *Sweden* 11 J7
Romenay, *France* 27 B9
Romerike, *Norway* 10 D5
Romilly-sur-Seine, *France* 25 D10
Romîni, *Romania* 38 E7
Rommani, *Morocco* 74 B3
Romney, *U.S.A.* 104 F6
Romney Marsh, *U.K.* 13 F8
Romny, *Ukraine* 40 F8
Rømø, *Denmark* 11 J2
Romodan, *Ukraine* 40 G8
Romodanovo, *Russia* 41 D14
Romont, *Switz.* 22 C3
Romorantin-Lanthenay, *France* 25 E8
Romsdalen, *Norway* 10 B2
Ron, *Vietnam* 58 D6
Rona, *U.K.* 14 D3
Ronan, *U.S.A.* 110 C6
Roncador, Cayos, *Caribbean* 116 D3
Roncador, Serra do, *Brazil* 123 D1
Roncesvalles, Paso, *Spain* 28 B3
Ronceverte, *U.S.A.* 104 G5
Ronciglione, *Italy* 33 F9
Ronco →, *Italy* 33 D9
Ronda, *Spain* 31 J5
Ronda, Serranía de, *Spain* 31 J5
Rondane, *Norway* 10 C3
Rondón, *Colombia* 120 B3
Rondônia, *Brazil* 125 C5
Rondônia □, *Brazil* 125 C5
Rondonópolis, *Brazil* 125 D7
Rong Jiang →, *China* 52 E7
Rong Xian, *Guangxi Zhuangzu, China* 53 F8
Rong Xian, *Sichuan, China* 52 C5
Rong'an, *China* 52 E7
Rongchang, *China* 52 C5
Ronge, L. la, *Canada* 101 B7
Rongjiang, *China* 52 E7
Rongshui, *China* 52 E7
Ronne Ice Shelf, *Antarctica* 5 D18
Ronsard, C., *Australia* 89 D1
Ronse, *Belgium* 17 G3
Ronuro →, *Brazil* 125 C7
Roodepoort, *S. Africa* 85 D4
Roodeschool, *Neths.* 16 B9
Roof Butte, *U.S.A.* 111 H9
Roompot, *Neths.* 17 E3
Roorkee, *India* 62 E7
Roosendaal, *Neths.* 17 E4
Roosevelt, *Minn., U.S.A.* 108 A7
Roosevelt, *Utah, U.S.A.* 110 F8
Roosevelt →, *Brazil* 125 B5
Roosevelt, Mt., *Canada* 100 B3
Roosevelt I., *Antarctica* 5 D12
Roosevelt Res., *U.S.A.* 111 K8
Roper →, *Australia* 90 A2
Ropesville, *U.S.A.* 109 J3
Roque Pérez, *Argentina* 126 D4
Roquefort, *France* 26 D3
Roquemaure, *France* 27 D8
Roquetas, *Spain* 28 E5
Roquevaire, *France* 27 E9
Roraima □, *Brazil* 121 C5
Roraima, Mt., *Venezuela* 121 B5
Rorketon, *Canada* 101 C9
Røros, *Norway* 10 B5
Rorschach, *Switz.* 23 B8
Rosa, *Zambia* 83 D3
Rosa, C., *Algeria* 75 A6
Rosa, Monte, *Europe* 22 E5
Rosal, *Spain* 30 D2
Rosal de la Frontera, *Spain* 31 H3
Rosalia, *U.S.A.* 110 C5
Rosamond, *U.S.A.* 113 L8
Rosans, *France* 27 D9
Rosario, *Argentina* 126 C3
Rosário, *Brazil* 122 B3
Rosario, *Baja Calif. N., Mexico* 114 A1
Rosario, *Sinaloa, Mexico* 114 C3
Rosario, *Paraguay* 126 A4
Rosario, Villa del, *Venezuela* 120 A3
Rosario de la Frontera, *Argentina* 126 B3
Rosario de Lerma, *Argentina* 126 A2
Rosario del Tala, *Argentina* 126 C4
Rosário do Sul, *Brazil* 127 C5
Rosário Oeste, *Brazil* 125 C6
Rosarito, *U.S.A.* 113 N9
Rosarno, *Italy* 35 D8
Rosas, *Spain* 28 C8
Roscoe, *U.S.A.* 108 C5
Roscoff, *France* 24 D3
Roscommon, *Ireland* 15 C3
Roscommon, *U.S.A.* 104 C3
Roscommon □, *Ireland* 15 C3
Roscrea, *Ireland* 15 D4
Rose →, *Australia* 90 A2
Rose Blanche, *Canada* 99 C8
Rose Harbour, *Canada* 100 C2
Rose Pt., *Canada* 100 C2
Rose Valley, *Canada* 101 C8
Roseau, *Domin.* 117 C7
Roseau, *U.S.A.* 108 A7
Rosebery, *Australia* 90 G4
Rosebud, *U.S.A.* 109 K6
Roseburg, *U.S.A.* 110 E2
Rosedale, *Australia* 90 C5
Rosedale, *U.S.A.* 109 J9
Rosée, *Belgium* 17 H5
Roseland, *U.S.A.* 112 G4
Rosemary, *Canada* 100 C6
Rosenberg, *U.S.A.* 109 L7
Rosendaël, *France* 25 A9
Rosenheim, *Germany* 19 H8
Roseto degli Abruzzi, *Italy* 33 F11
Rosetown, *Canada* 101 C7
Rosetta = Rashîd, *Egypt* 76 H7
Roseville, *U.S.A.* 112 G5
Rosewood, *N. Terr., Australia* 88 C4
Rosewood, *Queens., Australia* 91 D5
Roshkhvār, *Iran* 65 C8
Rosières-en-Santerre, *France* 25 C9
Rosignano Marittimo, *Italy* 32 E7
Rosignol, *Guyana* 121 B6
Roşiori de Vede, *Romania* 38 E8
Rositsa, *Bulgaria* 38 F10
Rositsa →, *Bulgaria* 38 F8
Roskilde, *Denmark* 11 J6
Roskilde Amtskommune □, *Denmark* 11 J6
Roskilde Fjord, *Denmark* 11 J6
Roslavl, *Russia* 40 E8
Roslyn, *Australia* 91 E4
Rosmaninhal, *Portugal* 31 F3
Rosmead, *S. Africa* 84 E4
Røsnæs, *Denmark* 11 J4
Rosolini, *Italy* 35 F7
Rosporden, *France* 24 E3
Ross, *Australia* 90 G4
Ross, *N.Z.* 87 K3
Ross I., *Antarctica* 5 D11
Ross Ice Shelf, *Antarctica* 5 E12
Ross L., *U.S.A.* 110 B3
Ross-on-Wye, *U.K.* 13 F5
Ross Sea, *Antarctica* 5 D11
Rossa, *Switz.* 23 D8
Rossan Pt., *Ireland* 15 B3
Rossano Cálabro, *Italy* 35 C9
Rossburn, *Canada* 101 C8
Rosseau, *Canada* 106 A5
Rossignol, L., *Canada* 98 B5
Rossignol Res., *Canada* 99 D6
Rossland, *Canada* 100 D5
Rosslare, *Ireland* 15 D5
Rosslau, *Germany* 18 D8
Rosso, *Mauritania* 78 B1
Rossosh, *Russia* 43 A8
Rossport, *Canada* 98 C2
Rossum, *Neths.* 16 E6
Røssvatnet, *Norway* 8 D13
Rossville, *Australia* 90 B4
Rosthern, *Canada* 101 C7
Rostock, *Germany* 18 A8
Rostov, *Russia* 41 C11
Rostov, *Russia* 43 C8
Rostrenen, *France* 24 D3
Roswell, *U.S.A.* 109 J2
Rosyth, *U.K.* 14 E5
Rota, *Spain* 31 J4
Rotälven →, *Sweden* 10 C8
Rotan, *U.S.A.* 109 J4
Rotem, *Belgium* 17 F7
Rotenburg, *Germany* 18 B5
Roth, *Germany* 19 F7
Rothaargebirge, *Germany* 18 E4
Rothenburg, *Switz.* 23 B6
Rothenburg ob der Tauber, *Germany* 19 F6
Rother →, *U.K.* 13 G8
Rotherham, *U.K.* 12 D6
Rothes, *U.K.* 14 D5
Rothesay, *Canada* 99 C6
Rothesay, *U.K.* 14 F3
Rothrist, *Switz.* 22 B5
Roti, *Indonesia* 57 F6
Roto, *Australia* 91 E4
Rotondella, *Italy* 35 B9
Rotoroa, L., *N.Z.* 87 J4
Rotorua, *N.Z.* 87 H6
Rotorua, L., *N.Z.* 87 H6
Rotselaar, *Belgium* 17 G5
Rott →, *Germany* 19 G9
Rotten →, *Switz.* 22 D5
Rottenburg, *Germany* 19 G4
Rotterdam, *Neths.* 16 E5
Rottnest I., *Australia* 89 F2
Rottumeroog, *Neths.* 16 A9
Rottweil, *Germany* 19 G4
Rotuma, *Fiji* 92 J9
Roubaix, *France* 25 B10
Rouen, *France* 24 C8
Rouillac, *France* 26 C3
Rouleau, *Canada* 101 C8
Round Mt., *Australia* 91 E5
Round Mountain, *U.S.A.* 110 G5
Roundup, *U.S.A.* 110 C9
Roura, *Fr. Guiana* 121 C7
Rousay, *U.K.* 14 B5
Rouses Point, *U.S.A.* 107 B11
Roussillon, *Isère, France* 27 C8
Roussillon, *Pyrénées-Or., France* 26 F6
Rouveen, *Neths.* 16 C8
Rouxville, *S. Africa* 84 E4
Rouyn, *Canada* 98 C4
Rovaniemi, *Finland* 8 C18
Rovato, *Italy* 32 C7
Rovenki, *Ukraine* 43 B8
Rovereto, *Italy* 32 C8
Rovigo, *Italy* 33 C8
Rovinari, *Romania* 38 E6
Rovinj, *Croatia* 33 C10
Rovira, *Colombia* 120 C2
Rovno, *Ukraine* 40 F5
Rovnoye, *Russia* 41 F15
Rovuma →, *Tanzania* 83 E5
Row'ān, *Iran* 65 C6
Rowena, *Australia* 91 D4
Rowley Shoals, *Australia* 88 C2
Roxa, *Guinea-Biss.* 78 C1
Roxas, *Capiz, Phil.* 55 F5
Roxas, *Isabela, Phil.* 55 C4
Roxas, *Mindoro, Phil.* 55 E4
Roxboro, *U.S.A.* 105 G6
Roxborough Downs, *Australia* 90 C2
Roxburgh, *N.Z.* 87 L2
Roxen, *Sweden* 11 F9
Roy, *Mont., U.S.A.* 110 C9
Roy, *N. Mex., U.S.A.* 109 H2
Roy Hill, *Australia* 88 D2
Roya, Peña, *Spain* 28 E4
Royal Leamington Spa, *U.K.* 13 E6
Royan, *France* 26 C2
Roye, *France* 25 C9
Røyken, *Norway* 10 E4
Rožaj, *Montenegro, Yug.* 21 N10
Rozay-en-Brie, *France* 25 D9
Rozhishche, *Ukraine* 40 F4
Rŏžnava, *Slovakia* 20 G10
Rozoy-sur-Serre, *France* 25 C11
Rtishchevo, *Russia* 41 D13
Rúa, *Spain* 30 C3
Ruacaná, *Angola* 84 B1
Ruahine Ra., *N.Z.* 87 H6
Ruapehu, *N.Z.* 87 H5
Ruapuke I., *N.Z.* 87 M2
Ruâq, W. →, *Egypt* 69 F2
Rub' al Khali, *Si. Arabia* 68 D4
Rubeho Mts., *Tanzania* 82 D4
Rubezhnoye, *Ukraine* 42 B8
Rubh a' Mhail, *U.K.* 14 F2
Rubha Hunish, *U.K.* 14 D2
Rubiataba, *Brazil* 123 E2
Rubicon →, *U.S.A.* 112 G5
Rubicone →, *Italy* 33 D9
Rubinéia, *Brazil* 123 F1
Rubino, *Ivory C.* 78 D4
Rubio, *Venezuela* 120 B3
Rubizhne = Rubezhnoye, *Ukraine* 42 B8
Rubtsovsk, *Russia* 44 D9
Ruby L., *U.S.A.* 110 F6
Ruby Mts., *U.S.A.* 110 F6
Rucava, *Latvia* 40 C2
Rucheng, *China* 53 E9
Rud, *Norway* 10 D4
Rūd Sar, *Iran* 65 B6
Ruda Śląska, *Poland* 20 E8
Rudall, *Australia* 91 E2
Rudall →, *Australia* 88 D3
Ruden, *Germany* 18 A9
Rüdersdorf, *Germany* 18 C9
Rudewa, *Tanzania* 83 E3
Rudkøbing, *Denmark* 11 K4
Rudnik, *Serbia, Yug.* 21 L10
Rudnogorsk, *Russia* 45 D11
Rudnya, *Russia* 40 D7
Rudnyy, *Kazakhstan* 44 D7
Rudolf, Ostrov, *Russia* 44 A6
Rudolstadt, *Germany* 18 E7
Rudong, *China* 53 A13
Rudozem, *Bulgaria* 39 H7
Rudyard, *U.S.A.* 104 B3
Rue, *France* 25 B8
Ruelle, *France* 26 C4
Rufa'a, *Sudan* 77 E3
Ruffec, *France* 26 B4
Rufiji □, *Tanzania* 82 D4
Rufiji →, *Tanzania* 82 D4
Rufino, *Argentina* 126 C3
Rufisque, *Senegal* 78 C1
Rufunsa, *Zambia* 83 F2
Rugao, *China* 53 A13
Rugby, *U.K.* 13 E6
Rugby, *U.S.A.* 108 A5
Rügen, *Germany* 18 A9
Rugles, *France* 24 D7
Ruhengeri, *Rwanda* 82 C2
Ruhla, *Germany* 18 E6
Ruhland, *Germany* 18 D9
Ruhr →, *Germany* 18 D2
Ruhuhu →, *Tanzania* 83 E3
Rui Barbosa, *Brazil* 123 D3
Rui'an, *China* 53 D13
Ruichang, *China* 53 C10
Ruidosa, *U.S.A.* 109 L2
Ruidoso, *U.S.A.* 111 K11
Ruili, *China* 52 E1
Ruinen, *Neths.* 16 C8
Ruinerwold, *Neths.* 16 C8
Ruiten A Kanaal →, *Neths.* 16 C10
Ruivo, Pico, *Madeira* 36 D3
Rujm Tal'at al Jamā'ah, *Jordan* 69 E4
Ruk, *Pakistan* 62 F3
Rukwa □, *Tanzania* 82 D3
Rukwa L., *Tanzania* 82 D3
Rulhieres, C., *Australia* 88 B4
Rulles, *Belgium* 17 J7
Rum Cay, *Bahamas* 117 B5
Rum Jungle, *Australia* 88 B5
Ruma, *Serbia, Yug.* 21 K9
Rumāḥ, *Si. Arabia* 64 E5
Rumania = Romania ■, *Europe* 38 D8
Rumaylah, *Iraq* 64 D5
Rumbalara, *Australia* 90 D1
Rumbêk, *Sudan* 77 F2
Rumbeke, *Belgium* 17 G2
Rumelange, *Lux.* 17 K8
Rumford, *U.S.A.* 107 B14
Rumilly, *France* 27 C9
Rumoi, *Japan* 48 C10
Rumonge, *Burundi* 82 C2
Rumsey, *Canada* 100 C6
Rumula, *Australia* 90 B4
Rumuruti, *Kenya* 82 B4
Runan, *China* 50 H8
Runanga, *N.Z.* 87 K3
Runaway, C., *N.Z.* 87 G6
Runcorn, *U.K.* 12 D5
Rungwa, *Tanzania* 82 D3
Rungwa →, *Tanzania* 82 D3
Rungwe, *Tanzania* 83 D3
Rungwe □, *Tanzania* 83 D3
Runka, *Nigeria* 79 C6
Runton Ra., *Australia* 88 D3
Ruoqiang, *China* 54 C3
Rupa, *India* 61 F18
Rupar, *India* 62 D7
Rupat, *Indonesia* 56 D2
Rupert →, *Canada* 98 B4
Rupert House = Fort Rupert, *Canada* 98 B4
Rupununi →, *Guyana* 121 C6
Rur →, *Germany* 18 E2
Rurrenabaque, *Bolivia* 124 C4
Rus →, *Spain* 29 F2
Rusambo, *Zimbabwe* 83 F3
Rusape, *Zimbabwe* 83 F3
Ruschuk = Ruse, *Bulgaria* 38 F8
Ruse, *Bulgaria* 38 F8
Ruşeţu, *Romania* 38 E10
Rushan, *China* 51 F11
Rushden, *U.K.* 13 E7
Rushford, *U.S.A.* 108 D9
Rushville, *Ill., U.S.A.* 108 E9
Rushville, *Ind., U.S.A.* 104 F3
Rushville, *Nebr., U.S.A.* 108 D3
Rushworth, *Australia* 91 F4
Russas, *Brazil* 122 B4
Russell, *Canada* 101 C8
Russell, *U.S.A.* 108 F5
Russell L., *Man., Canada* 101 B8
Russell L., *N.W.T., Canada* 100 A5
Russellkonda, *India* 61 K14
Russellville, *Ala., U.S.A.* 105 H2
Russellville, *Ark., U.S.A.* 109 H8
Russellville, *Ky., U.S.A.* 105 G2
Russi, *Italy* 33 D9
Russia ■, *Eurasia* 45 C11
Russian →, *U.S.A.* 112 G3
Russkaya Polyana, *Kazakhstan* 44 D8
Russkoye Ustie, *Russia* 4 B15
Rustam, *Pakistan* 62 B5
Rustam Shahr, *Pakistan* 62 F2
Rustavi, *Georgia* 43 F11
Rustenburg, *S. Africa* 84 D4
Ruston, *U.S.A.* 109 J8
Ruswil, *Switz.* 22 B6
Rutana, *Burundi* 82 C2
Rute, *Spain* 31 H6
Ruteng, *Indonesia* 57 F6
Ruth, *Mich., U.S.A.* 106 C2
Ruth, *Nev., U.S.A.* 110 G6
Rutherford, *U.S.A.* 112 G4
Rutherglen, *U.K.* 14 F4
Rüti, *Switz.* 23 B7
Rutigliano, *Italy* 35 A10
Rutland Plains, *Australia* 90 B3
Rutledge →, *Canada* 101 A6
Rutledge L., *Canada* 101 A6
Rutshuru, *Zaïre* 82 C2
Ruurlo, *Neths.* 16 D8
Ruvo di Púglia, *Italy* 35 A9
Ruvu, *Tanzania* 82 D4
Ruvu →, *Tanzania* 82 D4
Ruvuma □, *Tanzania* 83 E4
Ruwais, *U.A.E.* 65 E7
Ruwenzori, *Africa* 82 B2
Ruyigi, *Burundi* 82 C3
Ruyuan, *China* 53 E9
Ruzayevka, *Russia* 41 D14
Ružomberok, *Slovakia* 20 F9
Rwanda ■, *Africa* 82 C3
Ry, *Denmark* 11 H3
Ryakhovo, *Bulgaria* 38 F9
Ryan, L., *U.K.* 14 G3
Ryazan, *Russia* 41 D11
Ryazhsk, *Russia* 41 E12
Rybache, *Kazakhstan* 44 E9
Rybinsk, *Russia* 41 B11
Rybinskoye Vdkhr., *Russia* 41 B11
Rybnik, *Poland* 20 E8
Rybnitsa, *Moldavia* 42 C3
Rybnoye, *Russia* 41 D11
Rychwał, *Poland* 20 C8
Ryde, *U.K.* 13 G6
Ryderwood, *U.S.A.* 112 D3
Rydöbruk, *Sweden* 11 H7
Rydułtowy, *Poland* 20 E8
Rye, *U.K.* 13 G8
Rye →, *U.K.* 12 C7
Rye Patch Reservoir, *U.S.A.* 110 F4
Ryegate, *U.S.A.* 110 C9
Rylsk, *Russia* 40 F9
Rylstone, *Australia* 91 E4
Ryōthu, *Japan* 48 E9
Rypin, *Poland* 20 B9
Ryūgasaki, *Japan* 49 G10
Ryūkyū Is. = Ryūkyū-rettō, *Japan* 49 M2
Ryūkyū-rettō, *Japan* 49 M2
Rzeszów, *Poland* 20 E11
Rzhev, *Russia* 40 C9

S

Sa, *Thailand* 58 C3
Sa Dec, *Vietnam* 59 G5
Sa'ādatābād, *Fārs, Iran* 65 D7
Sa'ādatābād, *Kermān, Iran* 65 D7
Saale →, *Germany* 18 D7
Saaler Bodden, *Germany* 18 A8
Saalfeld, *Germany* 18 E7
Saane →, *Switz.* 22 B4
Saar →, *Europe* 25 C13
Saarbrücken, *Germany* 19 F2
Saarburg, *Germany* 19 F2
Saaremaa, *Estonia* 40 B3
Saariselkä, *Finland* 8 B20
Saarland □, *Germany* 25 C13
Saarlouis, *Germany* 19 F2
Saas Fee, *Switz.* 22 D5
Sab 'Bi'ār, *Syria* 64 C3
Şaba, *W. Indies* 117 C7
Šabac, *Serbia, Yug.* 21 L9
Sabadell, *Spain* 28 D7
Sabah □, *Malaysia* 56 C5
Sabak Bernam, *Malaysia* 59 L3
Sábana de la Mar, *Dom. Rep.* 117 C6
Sábanalarga, *Colombia* 120 A3
Sabang, *Indonesia* 56 C1
Sabará, *Brazil* 123 E3
Sabarania, *Indonesia* 57 E9
Sabattis, *U.S.A.* 107 B10
Sabáudia, *Italy* 34 A6
Sabaya, *Bolivia* 124 D4
Sabhah, *Libya* 73 C7
Sabie, *S. Africa* 85 D5
Sabinal, *Mexico* 114 A3
Sabinal, *U.S.A.* 109 L5
Sabinal, Punta del, *Spain* 29 J2
Sabinas, *Mexico* 114 B4
Sabinas →, *Mexico* 114 B4
Sabinas Hidalgo, *Mexico* 114 B4
Sabine →, *U.S.A.* 109 L8
Sabine L., *U.S.A.* 109 L8
Sabine Pass, *U.S.A.* 109 L8
Sabinópolis, *Brazil* 123 E3
Sabinov, *Slovakia* 20 F11
Sabirabad, *Azerbaijan* 43 F13
Sabkhet el Bardawîl, *Egypt* 69 D2
Sablayan, *Phil.* 55 E4
Sable, C., *U.S.A.* 103 E10
Sable, C., *Canada* 99 D6
Sable I., *Canada* 99 D8
Sablé-sur-Sarthe, *France* 24 E6
Saboeiro, *Brazil* 122 C4
Sabolev, *Russia* 45 D16
Sabor →, *Portugal* 30 D3
Sabou, *Burkina Faso* 78 C4
Sabrātah, *Libya* 75 B7
Sabria, *Tunisia* 75 B6
Sabrina Coast, *Antarctica* 5 C9
Sabugal, *Portugal* 30 E3
Sabulubek, *Indonesia* 56 E1
Sabzevār, *Iran* 65 B8
Sabzvārān, *Iran* 65 D8
Sac City, *U.S.A.* 108 D7
Sacedón, *Spain* 28 E2
Sachigo →, *Canada* 98 A2
Sachigo, L., *Canada* 98 B1
Sachkhere, *Georgia* 43 E10
Sachseln, *Switz.* 23 C6
Sachsen □, *Germany* 18 E9
Sachsen-Anhalt □, *Germany* 18 D8
Sacile, *Italy* 33 C9
Sackets Harbor, *U.S.A.* 107 C8
Saco, *Maine, U.S.A.* 105 D10

Saco, *Mont., U.S.A.* 110 B10
Sacramento, *Brazil* 123 E2
Sacramento, *U.S.A.* 112 G5
Sacramento →, *U.S.A.* 112 G5
Sacramento Mts., *U.S.A.* 111 K11
Sacramento Valley, *U.S.A.* 112 G5
Sacratif, C., *Spain* 29 J1
Săcueni, *Romania* 38 B5
Sada, *Spain* 30 B2
Sádaba, *Spain* 28 C3
Sadani, *Tanzania* 82 D4
Sadao, *Thailand* 59 J3
Sadd el Aali, *Egypt* 76 C3
Saddle Mt., *U.S.A.* 112 E3
Sade, *Nigeria* 79 C7
Sadimi, *Zaïre* 83 D1
Sado, *Japan* 48 E9
Sado →, *Portugal* 31 G2
Sadon, *Burma* 61 G20
Sadon, *Russia* 43 E10
Sæby, *Denmark* 11 G4
Saegerstown, *U.S.A.* 106 E4
Saelices, *Spain* 28 F2
Safaga, *Egypt* 76 B3
Şafājah, *Si. Arabia* 64 E3
Säffle, *Sweden* 9 G12
Safford, *U.S.A.* 111 K9
Saffron Walden, *U.K.* 13 E8
Safi, *Morocco* 74 B3
Şafīābād, *Iran* 65 B8
Safīd Dasht, *Iran* 65 C6
Safīd Kūh, *Afghan.* 60 B3
Safonovo, *Russia* 40 D8
Safranbolu, *Turkey* 42 F5
Safwān, *Iraq* 64 D5
Sag Harbor, *U.S.A.* 107 F12
Saga, *Indonesia* 57 E8
Saga, *Japan* 49 H5
Saga □, *Japan* 49 H5
Sagae, *Japan* 48 E10
Sagala, *Mali* 78 C3
Sagar, *India* 60 M9
Sagara, L., *Tanzania* 82 D3
Sagay, *Phil.* 55 F5
Sagil, *Mongolia* 54 A4
Saginaw, *U.S.A.* 104 D4
Saginaw B., *U.S.A.* 104 D4
Sagīr, Zab as →, *Iraq* 64 C4
Sagleipie, *Liberia* 78 D3
Saglouc, *Canada* 97 B12
Sagŏ-ri, *S. Korea* 51 G14
Sagone, *France* 27 F12
Sagone, G. de, *France* 27 F12
Sagres, *Portugal* 31 J2
Sagua la Grande, *Cuba* 116 B3
Saguache, *U.S.A.* 111 G10
Saguenay →, *Canada* 99 C5
Sagunto, *Spain* 28 F4
Sahaba, *Sudan* 76 D3
Sahagún, *Colombia* 120 B2
Sahagún, *Spain* 30 C5
Saḩam al Jawlān, *Syria* 69 C4
Sahand, Kūh-e, *Iran* 64 B5
Sahara, *Africa* 70 D4
Saharan Atlas = Saharien, Atlas, *Algeria* 75 B5
Saharanpur, *India* 62 E7
Saharien, Atlas, *Algeria* 75 B5
Sahasinaka, *Madag.* 85 C8
Sahaswan, *India* 63 E8
Sahel, Canal du, *Mali* 78 C3
Sahibganj, *India* 63 G12
Sahiwal, *Pakistan* 62 D5
Şahneh, *Iran* 64 C5
Sahtaneh →, *Canada* 100 B4
Sahuaripa, *Mexico* 114 B3
Sahuarita, *U.S.A.* 111 L8
Sahuayo, *Mexico* 114 C4
Sahy, *Slovakia* 21 G8
Sai Buri, *Thailand* 59 J3
Sai-Cinza, *Brazil* 125 B6
Sa'id Bundas, *Sudan* 73 G9
Saïda, *Algeria* 75 B5
Saʿīdābād, *Kermān, Iran* 65 D7
Saʿīdābād, *Semnān, Iran* 65 B7
Saïdia, *Morocco* 75 A4
Sa'idiyeh, *Iran* 65 B6
Saidpur, *Bangla.* 61 G16
Saidu, *Pakistan* 63 B5
Saignelégier, *Switz.* 22 B3
Saignes, *France* 26 C6
Saigon = Phanh Bho Ho Chi Minh, *Vietnam* 59 G6
Saijō, *Japan* 49 H6
Saikhoa Ghat, *India* 61 F19
Saiki, *Japan* 49 H5
Saillans, *France* 27 D9
Sailolof, *Indonesia* 57 E8
Saimbeyli, *Turkey* 66 E7
Şa'in Dezh, *Iran* 64 B5
St. Abb's Head, *U.K.* 14 F6
St. Aegyd, *Austria* 21 H5
St.-Affrique, *France* 26 E6
St.-Agrève, *France* 27 C8
St.-Aignan, *France* 24 E8
St. Alban's, *Canada* 99 C8
St. Albans, *U.K.* 13 F7
St. Albans, *Vt., U.S.A.* 107 B11
St. Albans, *W. Va., U.S.A.* 104 F5
St. Alban's Head, *U.K.* 13 G5
St. Albert, *Canada* 100 C6
St.-Amand-en-Puisaye, *France* 25 E10
St.-Amand-les-Eaux, *France* 25 B10
St.-Amand-Mont-Rond, *France* 26 B6
St.-Amarin, *France* 25 E14
St.-Amour, *France* 27 B9
St.-André-de-Cubzac, *France* 26 D3
St.-André-de-l'Eure, *France* 24 D8
St.-André-les-Alpes, *France* 27 E10
St. Andrew's, *Canada* 99 C8
St. Andrews, *U.K.* 14 E6
St-Anicet, *Canada* 107 A10
St. Ann B., *Canada* 99 C7
St. Anne, *U.K.* 24 C4
St. Ann's Bay, *Jamaica* 116 C4
St. Anthony, *Canada* 99 B8
St. Anthony, *U.S.A.* 110 E8
St.-Antonin-Noble-Val, *France* 26 D5
St. Arnaud, *Australia* 91 F3
St. Arthur, *Canada* 99 C6
St. Asaph, *U.K.* 12 D4
St.-Astier, *France* 26 C4
St.-Aubin, *Switz.* 22 C3
St.-Aubin-du-Cormier, *France* 24 D5
St-Augustin-Saguenay, *Canada* 99 B8
St. Augustine, *U.S.A.* 105 L5
St. Austell, *U.K.* 13 G3
St.-Avold, *France* 25 C13
St.-Barthélemy, I., *W. Indies* 117 C7
St. Bee's Hd., *U.K.* 12 C4
St.-Benoît-du-Sault, *France* 26 B5
St.-Bernard, Col du Grand, *Europe* 22 E4
St.-Bernard, Col du Petit, *France* 27 C10
St.-Blaise, *Switz.* 22 B3
St. Boniface, *Canada* 101 D9
St.-Bonnet, *France* 27 D10
St.-Brévin-les-Pins, *France* 24 E4
St.-Brice-en-Coglès, *France* 24 D5
St. Bride's, *Canada* 99 C9
St. Brides B., *U.K.* 13 F2
St.-Brieuc, *France* 24 D4
St.-Calais, *France* 24 E7
St.-Cast-le-Guildo, *France* 24 D4
St. Catharines, *Canada* 98 D4
St. Catherines I., *U.S.A.* 105 K5
St. Catherine's Pt., *U.K.* 13 G6
St.-Céré, *France* 26 D5
St.-Cergue, *Switz.* 22 D2
St.-Cernin, *France* 26 C6
St.-Chamond, *France* 27 C8
St. Charles, *Ill., U.S.A.* 104 E1
St. Charles, *Mo., U.S.A.* 108 F9
St.-Chély-d'Apcher, *France* 26 D7
St.-Chinian, *France* 26 E6
St. Christopher = St. Kitts, *W. Indies* 117 C7
St. Christopher-Nevis ■, *W. Indies* 117 C7
St.-Ciers-sur-Gironde, *France* 26 C3
St. Clair, *Mich., U.S.A.* 106 D2
St. Clair, *Pa., U.S.A.* 107 F8
St. Clair, L., *Canada* 98 D3
St. Clairsville, *U.S.A.* 106 F4
St.-Claud, *France* 26 C4
St. Claude, *Canada* 101 D9
St.-Claude, *France* 27 B9
St. Cloud, *Fla., U.S.A.* 105 L5
St. Cloud, *Minn., U.S.A.* 108 C7
St-Coeur de Marie, *Canada* 99 C5
St. Cricq, C., *Australia* 89 E1
St. Croix, *Virgin Is.* 117 C7
St. Croix →, *U.S.A.* 108 C8
St. Croix Falls, *U.S.A.* 108 C8
St.-Cyr-sur-Mer, *France* 27 E9
St. David's, *Canada* 99 C8
St. David's, *U.K.* 13 F2
St. David's Head, *U.K.* 13 F2
St.-Denis, *France* 25 D9
St.-Denis-d'Orques, *France* 24 D6
St.-Dié, *France* 25 D13
St.-Dizier, *France* 25 D11
St.-Égrève, *France* 27 C9
St. Elias, Mt., *U.S.A.* 96 B5
St. Elias Mts., *Canada* 100 A1
St.-Élie, *Fr. Guiana* 121 C7
St.-Eloy-les-Mines, *France* 26 B6
St.-Émilion, *France* 26 D3
St.-Étienne, *France* 27 C8
St.-Étienne-de-Tinée, *France* 27 D10
St. Eugène, *Canada* 107 A10
St. Eustatius, *W. Indies* 117 C7
St-Félicien, *Canada* 98 C5
St.-Florent, *France* 27 F13
St.-Florent-sur-Cher, *France* 25 F9
St.-Florentin, *France* 25 D10
St.-Flour, *France* 26 C7
St.-Fons, *France* 27 C8
St. Francis, *U.S.A.* 108 F4
St. Francis →, *U.S.A.* 109 H9
St. Francis, C., *S. Africa* 84 E3
St. Francisville, *U.S.A.* 109 K9
St-François, L., *Canada* 107 A10
St.-Fulgent, *France* 24 F5
St-Gabriel-de-Brandon, *Canada* 98 C5
St. Gallen = Sankt Gallen, *Switz.* 23 B8
St.-Gaudens, *France* 26 E4
St.-Gengoux-le-National, *France* 27 B8
St.-Geniez-d'Olt, *France* 26 D6
St. George, *Australia* 91 D4
St. George, *Canada* 99 C6
St. George, *S.C., U.S.A.* 105 J5
St. George, *Utah, U.S.A.* 111 H7
St. George, C., *Canada* 99 C8
St. George, C., *U.S.A.* 105 L3
St. George Ra., *Australia* 88 C4
St-Georges, *Belgium* 17 G6
St. George's, *Canada* 99 C8
St-Georges, *Canada* 99 C5
St.-Georges, *Fr. Guiana* 121 C7
St. George's, *Grenada* 117 D7
St. George's B., *Canada* 99 C8
St. Georges Basin, *Australia* 88 C4
St. George's Channel, *U.K.* 15 E6
St.-Georges-de-Didonne, *France* 26 C3
St. Georges Hd., *Australia* 91 F5
St.-Gérard, *Belgium* 17 H5
St.-Germain-de-Calberte, *France* 26 D7
St.-Germain-des-Fossés, *France* 26 B7
St.-Germain-du-Plain, *France* 25 F11
St.-Germain-en-Laye, *France* 25 D9
St.-Germain-Laval, *France* 27 C8
St.-Germain-Lembron, *France* 26 C7
St.-Gervais-d'Auvergne, *France* 26 B6
St.-Gervais-les-Bains, *France* 27 C10
St.-Gildas, Pte. de, *France* 24 E4
St.-Gilles, *France* 27 E8
St.-Gilles-Croix-de-Vie, *France* 26 B2
St.-Gingolph, *Switz.* 22 D3
St.-Girons, *France* 26 F5
St. Gotthard P. = San Gottardo, Paso del, *Switz.* 23 C7
St.-Gualtier, *France* 24 F8
St.-Guénolé, *France* 24 E2
St. Helena, *U.S.A.* 110 G2
St. Helena ■, *Atl. Oc.* 2 E9
St. Helena, Mt., *U.S.A.* 112 G4
St. Helena B., *S. Africa* 84 E2
St. Helens, *Australia* 90 G4
St. Helens, *U.K.* 12 D5
St. Helens, *U.S.A.* 112 E4
St. Helens, Mt., *U.S.A.* 112 D4
St. Helier, *U.K.* 13 H5
St.-Hilaire-du-Harcouët, *France* 24 D5
St.-Hippolyte, *France* 25 E13
St.-Hippolyte-du-Fort, *France* 26 E7
St.-Honoré-les-Bains, *France* 25 F10
St-Hubert, *Belgium* 17 H6
St-Hyacinthe, *Canada* 98 C5
St. Ignace, *U.S.A.* 104 C3
St. Ignace I., *Canada* 98 C2
St. Ignatius, *U.S.A.* 110 C6
St-Imier, *Switz.* 22 B3
St. Ives, *Cambs., U.K.* 13 E7
St. Ives, *Corn., U.K.* 13 G2
St.-James, *France* 24 D5
St. James, *U.S.A.* 108 D7
St-Jean, *Canada* 98 C5
St-Jean →, *Canada* 99 B7
St-Jean, L., *Canada* 99 C5
St. Jean Baptiste, *Canada* 101 D9
St.-Jean-d'Angély, *France* 26 C3
St.-Jean-de-Bournay, *France* 27 C9
St.-Jean-de-Luz, *France* 26 E2
St.-Jean-de-Maurienne, *France* 27 C10
St.-Jean-de-Monts, *France* 24 F4
St.-Jean-du-Gard, *France* 26 D7
St.-Jean-en-Royans, *France* 27 C9
St-Jean-Port-Joli, *Canada* 99 C5
St-Jérôme, *Qué., Canada* 98 C5
St-Jérôme, *Qué., Canada* 99 C5
St. John, *Canada* 99 C6
St. John, *Kans., U.S.A.* 109 G5
St. John, *N. Dak., U.S.A.* 108 A5
St. John →, *U.S.A.* 99 C6
St. John, C., *Canada* 99 B8
St. John's, *Antigua* 117 C7
St. John's, *Canada* 99 C9
St. Johns, *Ariz., U.S.A.* 111 J9
St. Johns, *Mich., U.S.A.* 104 D3
St. Johns →, *U.S.A.* 105 K5
St. Johnsbury, *U.S.A.* 107 B12
St. Johnsville, *U.S.A.* 107 C10
St. Joseph, *La., U.S.A.* 109 K9
St. Joseph, *Mich., U.S.A.* 104 D2
St. Joseph, *Mo., U.S.A.* 108 F7
St. Joseph →, *U.S.A.* 104 D2
St. Joseph, I., *Canada* 98 C3
St. Joseph, L., *Canada* 98 B1
St-Jovite, *Canada* 98 C5
St.-Juéry, *France* 26 E6
St.-Julien-Chapteuil, *France* 27 C8
St.-Julien-du-Sault, *France* 25 D10
St.-Julien-en-Genevois, *France* 27 B10
St.-Junien, *France* 26 C4
St.-Just-en-Chaussée, *France* 25 C9
St.-Just-en-Chevalet, *France* 26 C7
St.-Justin, *France* 26 E3
St. Kilda, *N.Z.* 87 L3
St. Kitts, *W. Indies* 117 C7
St. Kitts-Nevis = St. Christopher-Nevis ■, *W. Indies* 117 C7
St. Laurent, *Canada* 101 C9
St.-Laurent, *Fr. Guiana* 121 B7
St.-Laurent-du-Pont, *France* 27 C9
St.-Laurent-en-Grandvaux, *France* 27 B9
St. Lawrence, *Australia* 90 C4
St. Lawrence, *Canada* 99 C8
St. Lawrence →, *Canada* 99 C6
St. Lawrence, Gulf of, *Canada* 99 C7
St. Lawrence I., *U.S.A.* 96 B3
St.-Léger, *Belgium* 17 J7
St. Leonard, *Canada* 99 C6
St.-Léonard-de-Noblat, *France* 26 C5
St. Lewis →, *Canada* 99 B8
St.-Lô, *France* 24 C5
St-Louis, *Senegal* 78 B1
St. Louis, *Mich., U.S.A.* 104 D3
St. Louis, *Mo., U.S.A.* 108 F9
St. Louis →, *U.S.A.* 108 B8
St.-Loup-sur-Semouse, *France* 25 E13
St. Lucia ■, *W. Indies* 117 D7
St. Lucia, L., *S. Africa* 85 D5
St. Lucia Channel, *W. Indies* 117 D7
St. Lunaire-Griquet, *Canada* 99 B8
St. Maarten, *W. Indies* 117 C7
St.-Maixent-l'École, *France* 26 B3
St.-Malo, *France* 24 D4
St.-Malo, G. de, *France* 24 D4
St.-Mandrier-sur-Mer, *France* 27 E9
St-Marc, *Haiti* 117 C5
St.-Marcellin, *France* 27 C9
St.-Marcouf, Is., *France* 24 C5
St. Maries, *U.S.A.* 110 C5
St-Martin, *W. Indies* 117 C7
St. Martin, L., *Canada* 101 C9
St.-Martin-de-Ré, *France* 26 B2
St.-Martin-Vésubie, *France* 27 D11
St. Martins, *Canada* 99 C6
St. Martinville, *U.S.A.* 109 K9
St.-Martory, *France* 26 E4
St. Mary Pk., *Australia* 91 E2
St. Marys, *Australia* 90 G4
St. Marys, *Canada* 106 C3
St. Mary's, *U.K.* 13 H1
St. Marys, *U.S.A.* 106 E6
St. Mary's, C., *Canada* 99 C9
St. Mary's B., *Canada* 99 C9
St. Marys Bay, *Canada* 99 D6
St.-Mathieu, Pte., *France* 24 D2
St. Matthews, I. = Zadetkyi Kyun, *Burma* 59 H2
St.-Maur-des-Fossés, *France* 25 D9
St. Maurice, *Switz.* 22 D4
St-Maurice →, *Canada* 98 C5
St.-Médard-de-Guizières, *France* 26 C3
St.-Méen-le-Grand, *France* 24 D4
St. Michael's Mount, *U.K.* 13 G2
St.-Michel-de-Maurienne, *France* 27 C10
St.-Mihiel, *France* 25 D12
St.-Nazaire, *France* 24 E4
St. Neots, *U.K.* 13 E7
St.-Nicolas-de-Port, *France* 25 D13
St. Niklass = Sint Niklaas, *Belgium* 17 F4
St. Niklaus, *Switz.* 22 D5
St.-Omer, *France* 25 B9
St-Pacome, *Canada* 99 C6
St.-Palais-sur-Mer, *France* 26 C2
St-Pamphile, *Canada* 99 C6
St.-Pardoux-la-Rivière, *France* 26 C4
St. Pascal, *Canada* 99 C6
St. Paul, *Canada* 100 C6
St. Paul, *Minn., U.S.A.* 108 C8
St. Paul, *Nebr., U.S.A.* 108 E5
St. Paul, I., *Ind. Oc.* 3 F13
St.-Paul-de-Fenouillet, *France* 26 F6
St. Paul I., *Canada* 99 C7
St.-Paul-lès-Dax, *France* 26 E2
St.-Péray, *France* 27 D8
St.-Père-en-Retz, *France* 24 E4
St. Peter, *U.S.A.* 108 C8
St. Peter Port, *Chan. Is.* 13 H5
St. Peters, *N.S., Canada* 99 C7
St. Peters, *P.E.I., Canada* 99 C7
St. Petersburg = Sankt-Peterburg, *Russia* 40 B7
St. Petersburg, *U.S.A.* 105 M4
St.-Philbert-de-Grand-Lieu, *France* 24 E5
St.-Pierre, *St- P. & M.* 99 C8
St-Pierre, L., *Canada* 98 C5
St.-Pierre-d'Oléron, *France* 26 C2
St.-Pierre-Église, *France* 24 C5
St.-Pierre-en-Port, *France* 24 C7
St.-Pierre et Miquelon □, *St- P. & M.* 99 C8
St.-Pierre-le-Moûtier, *France* 25 F10
St.-Pierre-sur-Dives, *France* 24 C6
St.-Pieters Leew, *Belgium* 17 G4
St.-Pol-de-Léon, *France* 24 D2
St.-Pol-sur-Mer, *France* 25 A9
St.-Pol-sur-Ternoise, *France* 25 B9
St.-Pons, *France* 26 E6
St.-Pourçain-sur-Sioule, *France* 26 B7
St.-Quay-Portrieux, *France* 24 D4
St.-Quentin, *France* 25 C10
St.-Rambert-d'Albon, *France* 27 C8
St.-Raphaël, *France* 27 E10
St. Regis, *U.S.A.* 110 C6
St.-Rémy-de-Provence, *France* 27 E8
St.-Renan, *France* 24 D2
St.-Saëns, *France* 24 C8
St.-Sauveur-en-Puisaye, *France* 25 E10
St.-Sauveur-le-Vicomte, *France* 24 C5
St.-Savin, *France* 26 B4
St.-Savinien, *France* 26 C3
St. Sebastien, Tanjon' i, *Madag.* 85 A8
St.-Seine-l'Abbaye, *France* 25 E11
St.-Sernin-sur-Rance, *France* 26 E6
St.-Servan-sur-Mer, *France* 24 D4
St.-Sever, *France* 26 E3
St.-Sever-Calvados, *France* 24 D5
St-Siméon, *Canada* 99 C6
St. Stephen, *Canada* 99 C6
St.-Sulpice, *France* 26 E5
St.-Sulpice-Laurière, *France* 26 B5
St.-Syprien, *France* 26 F7
St.-Thégonnec, *France* 24 D3
St. Thomas, *Canada* 98 D3
St. Thomas I., *Virgin Is.* 117 C7
St-Tite, *Canada* 98 C5
St.-Tropez, *France* 27 E10
St. Troud = Sint Truiden, *Belgium* 17 G6
St.-Vaast-la-Hougue, *France* 24 C5
St.-Valéry-en-Caux, *France* 24 C7
St.-Valéry-sur-Somme, *France* 25 B8
St.-Vallier, *France* 27 C8
St.-Vallier-de-Thiey, *France* 27 E10
St.-Varent, *France* 24 F6
St. Vincent, *W. Indies* 117 D7
St. Vincent, G., *Australia* 91 F2
St. Vincent & the Grenadines ■, *W. Indies* 117 D7
St.-Vincent-de-Tyrosse, *France* 26 E2
St. Vincent Passage, *W. Indies* 117 D7
St-Vith, *Belgium* 17 H8
St.-Yrieix-la-Perche, *France* 26 C5
Ste.-Adresse, *France* 24 C7
Ste-Agathe-des-Monts, *Canada* 98 C5
Ste-Anne de Beaupré, *Canada* 99 C5
Ste-Anne-des-Monts, *Canada* 99 C6
Ste-Croix, *Switz.* 22 C3
Ste.-Enimie, *France* 26 D7
Ste.-Foy-la-Grande, *France* 26 D4
Ste. Genevieve, *U.S.A.* 108 G9
Ste.-Hermine, *France* 26 B2
Ste.-Livrade-sur-Lot, *France* 26 D4
Ste-Marguerite →, *Canada* 99 B6
Ste.-Marie, *Martinique* 117 D7
Ste.-Marie-aux-Mines, *France* 25 D14
Ste-Marie de la Madeleine, *Canada* 99 C5
Ste.-Maure-de-Touraine, *France* 24 E7
Ste.-Maxime, *France* 27 E10
Ste.-Menehould, *France* 25 C11
Ste.-Mère-Église, *France* 24 C5
Ste.-Rose, *Guadeloupe* 117 C7
Ste. Rose du Lac, *Canada* 101 C9
Saintes, *France* 26 C3
Saintes, I. des, *Guadeloupe* 117 C7
Stes.-Maries-de-la-Mer, *France* 27 E8
Saintonge, *France* 26 C3
Saipan, *Pac. Oc.* 92 F6
Sairang, *India* 61 H18
Sairecábur, Cerro, *Bolivia* 126 A2
Saitama □, *Japan* 49 F9
Sajama, *Bolivia* 124 D4
Sajum, *India* 63 C8
Sak →, *S. Africa* 84 E3
Sakai, *Japan* 49 G7
Sakaide, *Japan* 49 G6
Sakaiminato, *Japan* 49 G6
Sakākah, *Si. Arabia* 64 D4
Sakakawea, L., *U.S.A.* 108 B3
Sakami, L., *Canada* 98 B4
Sâkâne, 'Erg i-n, *Mali* 74 D4
Sakania, *Zaïre* 83 E2
Sakarya = Adapazarı, *Turkey* 66 C4
Sakarya □, *Turkey* 66 C4
Sakarya →, *Turkey* 42 F4
Sakashima-Guntō, *Japan* 49 M2

Sakata, *Japan* 48 E9
Sakchu, *N. Korea* 51 D13
Sakeny →, *Madag.* 85 C8
Sakété, *Benin* 79 D5
Sakha = Yakut Republic □, *Russia* 45 C13
Sakhalin, *Russia* 45 D15
Sakhalinskiy Zaliv, *Russia* 45 D15
Šaki, *Ukraine* 42 D5
Šakiai, *Lithuania* 40 D3
Sakon Nakhon, *Thailand* 58 D5
Sakrand, *Pakistan* 62 F3
Sakrivier, *S. Africa* 84 E3
Sakskøbing, *Denmark* 11 K5
Sakuma, *Japan* 49 G8
Sakurai, *Japan* 49 G7
Sal →, *Russia* 43 C9
Sala, *Sweden* 9 G14
Sala Consilina, *Italy* 35 B8
Sala-y-Gómez, *Pac. Oc.* 93 K17
Salaberry-de-Valleyfield, *Canada* 98 C5
Saladas, *Argentina* 126 B4
Saladillo, *Argentina* 126 D4
Salado →, *Buenos Aires, Argentina* 126 D4
Salado →, *La Pampa, Argentina* 128 A3
Salado →, *Río Negro, Argentina* 128 B3
Salado →, *Santa Fe, Argentina* 126 C3
Salado →, *Mexico* 114 B5
Salaga, *Ghana* 79 D4
Sālah, *Syria* 69 C5
Sálakhos, *Greece* 37 C9
Salala, *Liberia* 78 D2
Salala, *Sudan* 76 C4
Salālah, *Oman* 68 D5
Salamanca, *Chile* 126 C1
Salamanca, *Spain* 30 E5
Salamanca, *U.S.A.* 106 D6
Salamanca □, *Spain* 30 E5
Salāmatābād, *Iran* 64 C5
Salamina, *Colombia* 120 B2
Salamis, *Cyprus* 37 D12
Salamis, *Greece* 39 M6
Salar de Atacama, *Chile* 126 A2
Salar de Uyuni, *Bolivia* 124 E4
Sălard, *Romania* 38 B5
Salas, *Spain* 30 B4
Salas de los Infantes, *Spain* 28 C1
Salatiga, *Indonesia* 57 G14
Salaverry, *Peru* 124 B2
Salawati, *Indonesia* 57 E8
Salayar, *Indonesia* 57 F6
Salazar →, *Spain* 28 C3
Salbris, *France* 25 E9
Salcombe, *U.K.* 13 G4
Salda Gölü, *Turkey* 66 E3
Saldaña, *Spain* 30 C6
Saldanha, *S. Africa* 84 E2
Saldanha B., *S. Africa* 84 E2
Saldus, *Latvia* 40 C3
Sale, *Australia* 91 F4
Salé, *Morocco* 74 B3
Sale, *U.K.* 12 D5
Salekhard, *Russia* 44 C7
Salem, *India* 60 P11
Salem, *Ind., U.S.A.* 104 F2
Salem, *Mass., U.S.A.* 107 D14
Salem, *Mo., U.S.A.* 109 G9
Salem, *N.J., U.S.A.* 104 F8
Salem, *Ohio, U.S.A.* 106 F4
Salem, *Oreg., U.S.A.* 110 D2
Salem, *S. Dak., U.S.A.* 108 D6
Salem, *Va., U.S.A.* 104 G5
Salemi, *Italy* 34 E5
Salernes, *France* 27 E10
Salerno, *Italy* 35 B7
Salerno, G. di, *Italy* 35 B7
Salford, *U.K.* 12 D5
Salgir →, *Ukraine* 42 D6
Salgótarján, *Hungary* 21 G9
Salgueiro, *Brazil* 122 C4
Salida, *U.S.A.* 102 C5
Salies-de-Béarn, *France* 26 E3
Salihli, *Turkey* 66 D3
Salima, *Malawi* 81 G6
Salina, *Italy* 35 D7
Salina, *U.S.A.* 108 F6
Salina Cruz, *Mexico* 115 D5
Salinas, *Brazil* 123 E3
Salinas, *Chile* 126 A2
Salinas, *Ecuador* 120 D1
Salinas, *U.S.A.* 111 H3
Salinas →, *Guatemala* 115 D6
Salinas →, *U.S.A.* 111 H3
Salinas, B. de, *Nic.* 116 D2
Salinas, C. de, *Spain* 36 B10
Salinas, Pampa de las, *Argentina* 126 C2
Salinas Ambargasta, *Argentina* 126 B3
Salinas de Hidalgo, *Mexico* 114 C4
Salinas Grandes, *Argentina* 126 B2
Saline →, *Ark., U.S.A.* 109 J8
Saline →, *Kans., U.S.A.* 108 F6
Salines, *Spain* 36 B10
Salinópolis, *Brazil* 122 B2
Salins-les-Bains, *France* 25 F12
Salir, *Portugal* 31 H2
Salisbury = Harare, *Zimbabwe* 83 F3
Salisbury, *Australia* 91 E2
Salisbury, *U.K.* 13 F6
Salisbury, *Md., U.S.A.* 104 F8
Salisbury, *N.C., U.S.A.* 105 H5
Salisbury Plain, *U.K.* 13 F6
Sălişte, *Romania* 38 D6
Salitre →, *Brazil* 122 C3
Salka, *Nigeria* 79 C5
Salkhad, *Jordan* 69 C5
Sallent, *Spain* 28 D6
Salles-Curan, *France* 26 D6
Salling, *Denmark* 11 H2
Sallisaw, *U.S.A.* 109 H7
Sallom Junction, *Sudan* 76 D4
Salmās, *Iran* 64 B5
Salmerón, *Spain* 28 E2
Salmo, *Canada* 100 D5
Salmon, *U.S.A.* 110 D7
Salmon →, *Canada* 100 C4
Salmon →, *U.S.A.* 110 D5
Salmon Arm, *Canada* 100 C5
Salmon Falls, *U.S.A.* 110 E6
Salmon Gums, *Australia* 89 F3
Salmon Res., *Canada* 99 C8
Salmon River Mts., *U.S.A.* 110 D6
Salo, *Finland* 9 F17
Salò, *Italy* 32 C7
Salobreña, *Spain* 31 J7
Salome, *U.S.A.* 113 M13
Salon-de-Provence, *France* 27 E9
Salonica = Thessaloníki, *Greece* 39 J5
Salonta, *Romania* 38 C4
Salor →, *Spain* 31 F3
Salou, C., *Spain* 28 D6
Salsacate, *Argentina* 126 C2
Salses, *France* 26 F6
Salsk, *Russia* 43 C9
Salso →, *Italy* 34 E6
Salsomaggiore, *Italy* 32 D6
Salt →, *Canada* 100 B6
Salt →, *U.S.A.* 111 K7
Salt Creek, *Australia* 91 F2
Salt Fork Arkansas →, *U.S.A.* 109 G6
Salt Lake City, *U.S.A.* 110 F8
Salt Range, *Pakistan* 62 C5
Salta, *Argentina* 126 A2
Salta □, *Argentina* 126 A2
Saltcoats, *U.K.* 14 F4
Saltee Is., *Ireland* 15 D5
Saltfjorden, *Norway* 8 C13
Saltholm, *Denmark* 11 J6
Salthólmavík, *Iceland* 8 D3
Saltillo, *Mexico* 114 B4
Salto, *Argentina* 126 C3
Salto, *Uruguay* 126 C4
Salto da Divisa, *Brazil* 123 E4
Salton City, *U.S.A.* 113 M11
Salton Sea, *U.S.A.* 113 M11
Saltpond, *Ghana* 79 D4
Saltsjöbaden, *Sweden* 10 E12
Saltville, *U.S.A.* 104 G5
Saluda →, *U.S.A.* 105 H5
Salûm, *Egypt* 76 A2
Salûm, Khâlig el, *Egypt* 76 A2
Salur, *India* 61 K13
Salut, Is. du, *Fr. Guiana* 121 B7
Saluzzo, *Italy* 32 D4
Salvación, B., *Chile* 128 D1
Salvador, *Brazil* 123 D4
Salvador, *Canada* 101 C7
Salvador, L., *U.S.A.* 109 L9
Salvaterra, *Brazil* 122 B2
Salvaterra de Magos, *Portugal* 31 F2
Sálvora, I., *Spain* 30 C2
Salween →, *Burma* 61 L20
Salyany, *Azerbaijan* 67 D13
Salyersville, *U.S.A.* 104 G4
Salza →, *Austria* 21 H4
Salzach →, *Austria* 21 G2
Salzburg, *Austria* 21 H3
Salzgitter, *Germany* 18 C6
Salzwedel, *Germany* 18 C7
Sam Neua, *Laos* 58 B5
Sam Ngao, *Thailand* 58 D2
Sam Rayburn Reservoir, *U.S.A.* 109 K7
Sam Son, *Vietnam* 58 C5
Sam Teu, *Laos* 58 C5
Sama, *Russia* 44 C7
Sama de Langreo, *Spain* 30 B5
Samagaltai, *Russia* 45 D10
Samaipata, *Bolivia* 125 D5
Samales Group, *Phil.* 55 J4
Samâlût, *Egypt* 76 J7
Samana, *India* 62 D7
Samana Cay, *Bahamas* 117 B5
Samandağı, *Turkey* 66 E6
Samanga, *Tanzania* 83 D4
Samangwa, *Zaïre* 82 C1
Samani, *Japan* 48 C11
Samar, *Phil.* 55 F6
Samara, *Russia* 41 E17
Samaria = Shōmrōn, *Jordan* 69 C4
Samariá, *Greece* 37 D5
Samarinda, *Indonesia* 56 E5
Samarkand, *Uzbekistan* 44 F7
Samarqand = Samarkand, *Uzbekistan* 44 F7
Sāmarrā, *Iraq* 64 C4
Samastipur, *India* 63 G11
Samatan, *France* 26 E4
Samaúma, *Brazil* 125 B5
Samba, *India* 63 C6
Samba, *Zaïre* 82 C2
Sambaíba, *Brazil* 122 C2
Sambalpur, *India* 61 J14
Sambar, Tanjung, *Indonesia* 56 E4
Sambas, *Indonesia* 56 D3
Sambava, *Madag.* 85 A9
Sambawizi, *Zimbabwe* 83 F2
Sambhal, *India* 63 E8
Sambhar, *India* 62 F6
Sambiase, *Italy* 35 D9
Sambonifacio, *Italy* 32 C8
Sambor, *Cambodia* 58 F6
Sambor, *Ukraine* 40 G3
Sambre →, *Europe* 17 H5
Sambuca di Sicilia, *Italy* 34 E6
Samburu □, *Kenya* 82 B4
Samchŏk, *S. Korea* 51 F15
Samchonpo, *S. Korea* 51 G15
Same, *Tanzania* 82 C4
Samedan, *Switz.* 23 C9
Samer, *France* 25 B8
Samfya, *Zambia* 83 E2
Sámi, *Greece* 39 L3
Samnah, *Si. Arabia* 64 E3
Samnaun, *Switz.* 23 C10
Samo Alto, *Chile* 126 C1
Samobor, *Croatia* 33 C12
Samoëns, *France* 27 B10
Samokov, *Bulgaria* 38 G6
Samoorombón, B., *Argentina* 126 D4
Samorogouan, *Burkina Faso* 78 C4
Sámos, *Greece* 39 M9
Samoš, *Serbia, Yug.* 21 K10
Samos, *Spain* 30 C3
Samothráki, *Évros, Greece* 39 J8
Samothráki, *Kérkira, Greece* 37 A3
Samoylovka, *Russia* 41 F13
Sampa, *Ghana* 78 D4
Sampacho, *Argentina* 126 C3
Sampang, *Indonesia* 57 G15
Samper de Calanda, *Spain* 28 D4
Sampit, *Indonesia* 56 E4
Sampit, Teluk, *Indonesia* 56 E4
Samrée, *Belgium* 17 H7
Samrong, *Cambodia* 58 E4
Samrong, *Thailand* 58 E3
Samsø, *Denmark* 11 J4
Samsø Bælt, *Denmark* 11 J4
Samsun, *Turkey* 66 C7
Samtredia, *Georgia* 43 E10
Samui, Ko, *Thailand* 59 H3
Samun □, *Turkey* 66 C7
Samur →, *Azerbaijan* 43 F13
Samusole, *Zaïre* 83 E1
Samut Prakan, *Thailand* 58 F3
Samut Sakhon, *Thailand* 58 F3
Samut Songkhram →, *Thailand* 58 F3
Samwari, *Pakistan* 62 E2
San, *Mali* 78 C4
San →, *Cambodia* 58 F5
San →, *Poland* 20 E11
San Adrián, C. de, *Spain* 30 B2
San Agustín, *Colombia* 120 C2
San Agustin, C., *Phil.* 55 H7
San Agustín de Valle Fértil, *Argentina* 126 C2
San Ambrosio, *Pac. Oc.* 93 K20
San Andreas, *U.S.A.* 112 G6
San Andrés, I. de, *Caribbean* 116 D3
San Andres Mts., *U.S.A.* 111 K10
San Andrés Tuxtla, *Mexico* 115 D5
San Angelo, *U.S.A.* 109 K4
San Anselmo, *U.S.A.* 112 H4
San Antonio, *Belize* 115 D7
San Antonio, *Chile* 126 C1
San Antonio, *Phil.* 55 D4
San Antonio, *N. Mex., U.S.A.* 111 K10
San Antonio, *Tex., U.S.A.* 109 L5
San Antonio, *Venezuela* 120 C4
San Antonio →, *U.S.A.* 109 L6
San Antonio, C., *Argentina* 126 D4
San Antonio, C., *Cuba* 116 B3
San Antonio, C. de, *Spain* 29 G5
San Antonio, Mt., *U.S.A.* 113 L9
San Antonio Abad, *Spain* 36 C7
San Antonio de los Baños, *Cuba* 116 B3
San Antonio de los Cobres, *Argentina* 126 A2
San Antonio Oeste, *Argentina* 128 B4
San Arcángelo, *Italy* 35 B9
San Ardo, *U.S.A.* 112 J6
San Augustín, *Canary Is.* 36 G4
San Augustine, *U.S.A.* 109 K7
San Bartolomé, *Canary Is.* 36 F6
San Bartolomé de Tirajana, *Canary Is.* 36 G4
San Bartolomeo in Galdo, *Italy* 35 A8
San Benedetto, *Italy* 32 C7
San Benedetto del Tronto, *Italy* 33 F10
San Benedicto, I., *Mexico* 114 D2
San Benito, *U.S.A.* 109 M6
San Benito →, *U.S.A.* 112 J5
San Benito Mt., *U.S.A.* 112 J6
San Bernardino, *U.S.A.* 113 L9
San Bernardino, Paso del, *Switz.* 23 D8
San Bernardino Mts., *U.S.A.* 113 L10
San Bernardino Str., *Phil.* 55 E6
San Bernardo, *Chile* 126 C1
San Bernardo, I. de, *Colombia* 120 B2
San Blas, *Mexico* 114 B3
San Blas, Arch. de, *Panama* 116 E4
San Blas, C., *U.S.A.* 105 L3
San Borja, *Bolivia* 124 C4
San Buenaventura, *Bolivia* 124 C4
San Buenaventura, *Mexico* 114 B4
San Carlos = Butuku-Luba, *Eq. Guin.* 79 E6
San Carlos, *Argentina* 126 C2
San Carlos, *Bolivia* 125 D5
San Carlos, *Chile* 126 D1
San Carlos, *Mexico* 114 B4
San Carlos, *Nic.* 116 D3
San Carlos, *Negros, Phil.* 55 F5
San Carlos, *Pangasinan, Phil.* 55 D4
San Carlos, *Spain* 36 B8
San Carlos, *Uruguay* 127 C5
San Carlos, *U.S.A.* 111 K8
San Carlos, *Amazonas, Venezuela* 120 C4
San Carlos, *Cojedes, Venezuela* 120 B4
San Carlos de Bariloche, *Argentina* 128 B2
San Carlos de la Rápita, *Spain* 28 E5
San Carlos del Zulia, *Venezuela* 120 B3
San Carlos L., *U.S.A.* 111 K8
San Cataldo, *Italy* 34 E6
San Celoni, *Spain* 28 D7
San Clemente, *Chile* 126 D1
San Clemente, *Spain* 29 F2
San Clemente, *U.S.A.* 113 M9
San Clemente I., *U.S.A.* 113 N8
San Constanzo, *Italy* 33 E10
San Cristóbal, *Argentina* 126 C3
San Cristóbal, *Colombia* 120 D3
San Cristóbal, *Dom. Rep.* 117 C5
San Cristóbal, *Mexico* 115 D6
San Cristóbal, *Spain* 36 B11
San Cristóbal, *Venezuela* 120 B3
San Damiano d'Asti, *Italy* 32 D5
San Daniele del Friuli, *Italy* 33 B10
San Demétrio Corone, *Italy* 35 C9
San Diego, *Calif., U.S.A.* 113 N9
San Diego, *Tex., U.S.A.* 109 M5
San Diego, C., *Argentina* 128 D3
San Diego de la Unión, *Mexico* 114 C4
San Dimitri, Ras, *Malta* 37 C1
San Donà di Piave, *Italy* 33 C9
San Elpídio a Mare, *Italy* 33 E10
San Estanislao, *Paraguay* 126 A4
San Esteban de Gormaz, *Spain* 28 D1
San Felice sul Panaro, *Italy* 32 D8
San Felipe, *Chile* 126 C1
San Felipe, *Colombia* 120 C4
San Felipe, *Mexico* 114 A2
San Felipe, *Venezuela* 120 A4
San Felipe →, *U.S.A.* 113 M11
San Felíu de Guíxols, *Spain* 28 D8
San Felíu de Llobregat, *Spain* 28 D7
San Félix, *Pac. Oc.* 93 K20
San Fernando, *Chile* 126 C1
San Fernando, *Mexico* 114 B1
San Fernando, *La Union, Phil.* 55 C4
San Fernando, *Pampanga, Phil.* 55 D4
San Fernando, *Baleares, Spain* 36 C7
San Fernando, *Cádiz, Spain* 31 J4
San Fernando, *Trin. & Tob.* 117 D7
San Fernando, *U.S.A.* 113 L8
San Fernando →, *Mexico* 114 C5
San Fernando de Apure, *Venezuela* 120 B4
San Fernando de Atabapo, *Venezuela* 120 C4
San Fernando di Púglia, *Italy* 35 A9
San Francisco, *Argentina* 126 C3
San Francisco, *Bolivia* 125 D4
San Francisco, *U.S.A.* 111 H2
San Francisco →, *U.S.A.* 111 K9
San Francisco, Paso de, *S. Amer.* 126 B2
San Francisco de Macorîs, *Dom. Rep.* 117 C5
San Francisco del Monte de Oro, *Argentina* 126 C2
San Francisco del Oro, *Mexico* 114 B3
San Francisco Javier, *Spain* 36 C7
San Francisco Solano, Pta., *Colombia* 120 B2
San Fratello, *Italy* 35 D7
San Gabriel, *Ecuador* 120 C2
San Gavino Monreale, *Italy* 34 C1
San Gil, *Colombia* 120 B3
San Gimignano, *Italy* 32 E8
San Giórgio di Nogaro, *Italy* 33 C10
San Giórgio Iónico, *Italy* 35 B10
San Giovanni Bianco, *Italy* 32 C6
San Giovanni in Fiore, *Italy* 35 C9
San Giovanni in Persiceto, *Italy* 33 D8
San Giovanni Rotondo, *Italy* 35 A8
San Giovanni Valdarno, *Italy* 33 E8
San Giuliano Terme, *Italy* 32 E7
San Gorgonio Mt., *U.S.A.* 113 L10
San Gottardo, Paso del, *Switz.* 23 C7
San Gregorio, *Uruguay* 127 C4
San Gregorio, *U.S.A.* 112 H4
San Guiseppe Iato, *Italy* 34 E6
San Ignacio, *Belize* 115 D7
San Ignacio, *Bolivia* 125 D5
San Ignacio, *Mexico* 114 B2
San Ignacio, *Paraguay* 126 B4
San Ignacio, L., *Mexico* 114 B2
San Ildefonso, C., *Phil.* 55 C5
San Isidro, *Argentina* 126 C4
San Jacinto, *Colombia* 120 B2
San Jacinto, *U.S.A.* 113 M10
San Jaime, *Spain* 36 B11
San Javier, *Misiones, Argentina* 127 B4
San Javier, *Santa Fe, Argentina* 126 C4
San Javier, *Beni, Bolivia* 125 C5
San Javier, *Santa Cruz, Bolivia* 125 D5
San Javier, *Chile* 126 D1
San Javier, *Spain* 29 H4
San Jerónimo, Sa. de, *Colombia* 120 B2
San Jeronimo Taviche, *Mexico* 115 D5
San Joaquín, *Bolivia* 125 C5
San Joaquin, *U.S.A.* 112 J6
San Joaquín, *Venezuela* 120 A4
San Joaquín →, *Bolivia* 125 C5
San Joaquin →, *U.S.A.* 111 G3
San Joaquin Valley, *U.S.A.* 112 J6
San Jordi, *Spain* 36 B9
San Jorge, *Argentina* 126 C3
San Jorge, *Spain* 36 C7
San Jorge, B. de, *Mexico* 114 A2
San Jorge, G., *Argentina* 128 C3
San Jorge, G. de, *Spain* 28 E4
San José, *Bolivia* 125 D5
San José, *Costa Rica* 116 E3
San José, *Guatemala* 116 D1
San José, *Mexico* 114 C2
San Jose, *Phil.* 55 D4
San José, *Spain* 36 C7
San Jose, *U.S.A.* 111 H3
San Jose →, *U.S.A.* 111 J10
San Jose de Buenovista, *Phil.* 55 E4
San José de Feliciano, *Argentina* 126 C4
San José de Jáchal, *Argentina* 126 C2
San José de Mayo, *Uruguay* 126 C4
San José de Ocune, *Colombia* 120 C3
San José de Uchapiamonas, *Bolivia* 124 C4
San José del Cabo, *Mexico* 114 C3
San José del Guaviare, *Colombia* 120 C3
San José do Anauá, *Brazil* 121 C5
San Juan, *Argentina* 126 C2
San Juan, *Colombia* 120 B2
San Juan, *Mexico* 114 C4
San Juan, *Ica, Peru* 124 D2
San Juan, *Puno, Peru* 124 C4
San Juan, *Phil.* 55 G7
San Juan, *Puerto Rico* 117 C6
San Juan □, *Argentina* 126 C2
San Juan →, *Argentina* 126 C2
San Juan →, *Bolivia* 125 E4
San Juan →, *Colombia* 120 C2
San Juan →, *Nic.* 116 D3
San Juan →, *U.S.A.* 111 H8
San Juan →, *Venezuela* 121 A5
San Juan, C., *Eq. Guin.* 80 D1
San Juan Bautista, *Paraguay* 126 B4
San Juan Bautista, *Spain* 36 B8
San Juan Bautista, *U.S.A.* 111 H3
San Juan Bautista Valle Nacional, *Mexico* 115 D5
San Juan Capistrano, *U.S.A.* 113 M9
San Juan Cr. →, *U.S.A.* 112 J5
San Juan de Guadalupe, *Mexico* 114 C4
San Juan de los Morros, *Venezuela* 120 B4
San Juan del César, *Colombia* 120 A3
San Juan del Norte, *Nic.* 116 D3
San Juan del Norte, B. de, *Nic.* 116 D3
San Juan del Puerto, *Spain* 31 H4
San Juan del Río, *Mexico* 115 C5
San Juan del Sur, *Nic.* 116 D2
San Juan I., *U.S.A.* 112 B3
San Juan Mts., *U.S.A.* 111 H10
San Julián, *Argentina* 128 C3
San Just, Sierra de, *Spain* 28 E4
San Justo, *Argentina* 126 C3
San Kamphaeng, *Thailand* 58 C2
San Lázaro, C., *Mexico* 114 C2

San Lázaro, Sa., *Mexico* 114 C3
San Leandro, *U.S.A.* 111 H2
San Leonardo, *Spain* 28 D1
San Lorenzo, *Argentina* 126 C3
San Lorenzo, *Beni, Bolivia* 125 D4
San Lorenzo, *Tarija, Bolivia* 125 E5
San Lorenzo, *Ecuador* 120 C2
San Lorenzo, *Paraguay* 126 B4
San Lorenzo, *Spain* 36 B10
San Lorenzo, *Venezuela* 120 B3
San Lorenzo →, *Mexico* 114 C3
San Lorenzo, I., *Mexico* 114 B2
San Lorenzo, I., *Peru* 124 C2
San Lorenzo, Mt., *Argentina* 128 C2
San Lorenzo de la Parrilla, *Spain* 28 F2
San Lorenzo de Morunys, *Spain* 28 C6
San Lucas, *Bolivia* 125 E4
San Lucas, *Baja Calif. S., Mexico* 114 C3
San Lucas, *Baja Calif. S., Mexico* 114 B2
San Lucas, *U.S.A.* 112 J5
San Lucas, C., *Mexico* 114 C3
San Lúcido, *Italy* 35 C9
San Luis, *Argentina* 126 C2
San Luis, *Cuba* 116 B3
San Luis, *Guatemala* 116 C2
San Luis, *U.S.A.* 111 H11
San Luis □, *Argentina* 126 C2
San Luis, I., *Mexico* 114 B2
San Luis, L. de, *Bolivia* 125 C5
San Luis, Sierra de, *Argentina* 126 C2
San Luis de la Paz, *Mexico* 114 C4
San Luis Obispo, *U.S.A.* 113 K6
San Luis Potosí, *Mexico* 114 C4
San Luis Potosí □, *Mexico* 114 C4
San Luis Reservoir, *U.S.A.* 112 H5
San Luis Río Colorado, *Mexico* 114 A2
San Marco Argentano, *Italy* 35 C9
San Marco dei Cavoti, *Italy* 35 A7
San Marco in Lámis, *Italy* 35 A8
San Marcos, *Colombia* 120 B2
San Marcos, *Guatemala* 116 D1
San Marcos, *Mexico* 114 B2
San Marcos, *U.S.A.* 109 L6
San Marino ■, *Europe* 33 E9
San Martín, *Argentina* 126 C2
San Martín, *Colombia* 120 C3
San Martin →, *Bolivia* 125 C5
San Martín, L., *Argentina* 128 C2
San Martin de los Andes, *Argentina* 128 B2
San Martín de Valdeiglesias, *Spain* 30 E6
San Martino de Calvi, *Italy* 32 C6
San Mateo, *Phil.* 55 C4
San Mateo, *Baleares, Spain* 36 B7
San Mateo, *Valencia, Spain* 28 E5
San Mateo, *U.S.A.* 111 H2
San Matías, *Bolivia* 125 D6
San Matías, G., *Argentina* 128 B4
San Miguel, *El Salv.* 116 D2
San Miguel, *Panama* 116 E4
San Miguel, *Spain* 36 B7
San Miguel, *U.S.A.* 111 J3
San Miguel, *Venezuela* 120 B4
San Miguel →, *Bolivia* 125 C5
San Miguel →, *S. Amer.* 120 C2
San Miguel de Huachi, *Bolivia* 124 D4
San Miguel de Salinas, *Spain* 29 H4
San Miguel de Tucumán, *Argentina* 126 B2
San Miguel del Monte, *Argentina* 126 D4
San Miguel I., *U.S.A.* 113 L6
San Miniato, *Italy* 32 E7
San Narciso, *Phil.* 55 D4
San Nicolás, *Canary Is.* 36 G4
San Nicolas, *Phil.* 55 B4
San Nicolás de los Arroyas, *Argentina* 126 C3
San Nicolas I., *U.S.A.* 113 M7
San Onofre, *Colombia* 120 B2
San Onofre, *U.S.A.* 113 M9
San Pablo, *Bolivia* 126 A2
San Pablo, *Phil.* 55 D4
San Paolo di Civitate, *Italy* 35 A8
San Pedro, *Buenos Aires, Argentina* 127 B5
San Pedro, *Jujuy, Argentina* 126 A3
San Pedro, *Colombia* 120 C3
San-Pédro, *Ivory C.* 78 E3
San Pedro, *Mexico* 114 C2
San Pedro, *Peru* 124 C3
San Pedro □, *Paraguay* 126 A4
San Pedro →, *Chihuahua, Mexico* 114 B3
San Pedro →, *Michoacan, Mexico* 114 D4
San Pedro →, *Nayarit, Mexico* 114 C3
San Pedro →, *U.S.A.* 111 K8
San Pedro, Pta., *Chile* 126 B1
San Pedro, Sierra de, *Spain* 31 F4
San Pedro Channel, *U.S.A.* 113 M8
San Pedro de Arimena, *Colombia* 120 C3
San Pedro de Atacama, *Chile* 126 A2
San Pedro de Jujuy, *Argentina* 126 A3
San Pedro de las Colonias, *Mexico* 114 B4
San Pedro de Lloc, *Peru* 124 B2
San Pedro de Macorís, *Dom. Rep.* 117 C6
San Pedro del Norte, *Nic.* 116 D3
San Pedro del Paraná, *Paraguay* 126 B4
San Pedro del Pinatar, *Spain* 29 H4
San Pedro Mártir, Sierra, *Mexico* 114 A1
San Pedro Mixtepec, *Mexico* 115 D5
San Pedro Ocampo = Melchor Ocampo, *Mexico* 114 C4
San Pedro Sula, *Honduras* 116 C2
San Pietro, I., *Italy* 34 C1
San Pietro Vernótico, *Italy* 35 B11
San Quintín, *Mexico* 114 A1
San Rafael, *Argentina* 126 C2
San Rafael, *Calif., U.S.A.* 112 H4
San Rafael, *N. Mex., U.S.A.* 111 J10
San Rafael, *Venezuela* 120 A3
San Rafael Mt., *U.S.A.* 113 L7
San Rafael Mts., *U.S.A.* 113 L7
San Ramón, *Bolivia* 125 C5
San Ramón, *Peru* 124 C2
San Ramón de la Nueva Orán, *Argentina* 126 A3
San Remo, *Italy* 32 E4
San Román, C., *Venezuela* 120 A3
San Roque, *Argentina* 126 B4
San Roque, *Spain* 31 J5
San Rosendo, *Chile* 126 D1
San Saba, *U.S.A.* 109 K5
San Salvador, *Bahamas* 117 B5
San Salvador, *El Salv.* 116 D2
San Salvador, *Spain* 36 B10
San Salvador de Jujuy, *Argentina* 126 A3
San Salvador I., *Bahamas* 117 B5
San Sebastián, *Argentina* 128 D3
San Sebastián, *Spain* 28 B3
San Sebastián, *Venezuela* 120 B4
San Sebastian de la Gomera, *Canary Is.* 36 F2
San Serra, *Spain* 36 B10
San Serverino Marche, *Italy* 33 E10
San Simeon, *U.S.A.* 112 K5
San Simon, *U.S.A.* 111 K9
San Stéfano di Cadore, *Italy* 33 B9
San Telmo, *Mexico* 114 A1
San Telmo, *Spain* 36 B9
San Tiburcio, *Mexico* 114 C4
San Valentin, Mte., *Chile* 128 C2
San Vicente de Alcántara, *Spain* 31 F3
San Vicente de la Barquera, *Spain* 30 B6
San Vicente del Caguán, *Colombia* 120 C3
San Vincenzo, *Italy* 32 E7
San Vito, *Italy* 34 C2
San Vito, C., *Italy* 34 D5
San Vito al Tagliamento, *Italy* 33 C9
San Vito Chietino, *Italy* 33 F11
San Vito dei Normanni, *Italy* 35 B10
San Yanaro, *Colombia* 120 C4
San Ygnacio, *U.S.A.* 109 M5
Saña, *Peru* 124 B2
Sana', *Yemen* 68 D3
Sana →, *Bos.-H.* 33 C13
Sanaba, *Burkina Faso* 78 C4
Şanāfīr, *Si. Arabia* 76 B3
Sanaga →, *Cameroon* 79 E6
Sanaloa, Presa, *Mexico* 114 C3
Sanana, *Indonesia* 57 E7
Sanand, *India* 62 H5
Sanandaj, *Iran* 64 C5
Sanandita, *Bolivia* 126 A3
Sanary-sur-Mer, *France* 27 E9
Sanawad, *India* 62 H7
Sancellas, *Spain* 36 B9
Sancergues, *France* 25 E9
Sancerre, *France* 25 E9
Sancerrois, Collines du, *France* 25 E9
Sancha He →, *China* 52 D6
Sanchahe, *China* 51 B14
Sánchez, *Dom. Rep.* 117 C6
Sanchor, *India* 62 G4
Sanco Pt., *Phil.* 57 C7
Sancoins, *France* 25 F9
Sancti-Spíritus, *Cuba* 116 B4
Sancy, Puy de, *France* 26 C6
Sand →, *S. Africa* 85 C5
Sand Springs, *U.S.A.* 109 G6
Sanda, *Japan* 49 G7
Sandakan, *Malaysia* 56 C5
Sandan = Sambor, *Cambodia* 58 F6
Sandanski, *Bulgaria* 39 H6
Sandaré, *Mali* 78 C2
Sanday, *U.K.* 14 B6
Sandefjord, *Norway* 10 E4
Sanders, *U.S.A.* 111 J9
Sanderson, *U.S.A.* 109 K3
Sandfly L., *Canada* 101 B7
Sandgate, *Australia* 91 D5
Sandía, *Peru* 124 C4
Sandıklı, *Turkey* 66 D4
Sandnes, *Norway* 9 G8
Sandness, *U.K.* 14 A7
Sandoa, *Zaïre* 80 F4
Sandona, *Colombia* 120 C2
Sandover →, *Australia* 90 C2
Sandoway, *Burma* 61 K19
Sandpoint, *U.S.A.* 110 B5
Sandringham, *U.K.* 12 E8
Sandslån, *Sweden* 10 A11
Sandspit, *Canada* 100 C2
Sandstone, *Australia* 89 E2
Sandu, *China* 52 E6
Sandusky, *Mich., U.S.A.* 98 D3
Sandusky, *Ohio, U.S.A.* 106 E2
Sandvig, *Sweden* 11 J8
Sandviken, *Sweden* 9 F14
Sandwich, C., *Australia* 90 B4
Sandwich B., *Canada* 99 B8
Sandwich B., *Namibia* 84 C1
Sandwip Chan., *Bangla.* 61 H17
Sandy, *Nev., U.S.A.* 113 K11
Sandy, *Oreg., U.S.A.* 112 E4
Sandy Bight, *Australia* 89 F3
Sandy C., *Queens., Australia* 90 C5
Sandy C., *Tas., Australia* 90 G3
Sandy Cay, *Bahamas* 117 B4
Sandy Cr. →, *U.S.A.* 110 F9
Sandy L., *Canada* 98 B1
Sandy Lake, *Canada* 98 B1
Sandy Narrows, *Canada* 101 B8
Sanford, *Fla., U.S.A.* 105 L5
Sanford, *Maine, U.S.A.* 107 C14
Sanford, *N.C., U.S.A.* 105 H6
Sanford →, *Australia* 89 E2
Sanford, Mt., *U.S.A.* 96 B5
Sang-i-Masha, *Afghan.* 62 C2
Sanga, *Mozam.* 83 E4
Sanga →, *Congo* 80 E3
Sanga-Tolon, *Russia* 45 C15
Sangamner, *India* 60 K9
Sangar, *Afghan.* 62 C1
Sangar, *Russia* 45 C13
Sangar Sarai, *Afghan.* 62 B4
Sangasangadalam, *Indonesia* 56 E5
Sangay, *Ecuador* 120 D2
Sange, *Zaïre* 82 D2
Sangeang, *Indonesia* 57 F5
Sanger, *U.S.A.* 111 H4
Sangerhausen, *Germany* 18 D7
Sanggan He →, *China* 50 E9
Sanggau, *Indonesia* 56 D4
Sangihe, Kepulauan, *Indonesia* 57 D7
Sangihe, P., *Indonesia* 57 D7
Sangju, *S. Korea* 51 F15
Sangkapura, *Indonesia* 56 F4
Sangkhla, *Thailand* 58 E2
Sangli, *India* 60 L9
Sangmélina, *Cameroon* 79 E7
Sangonera →, *Spain* 29 H3
Sangre de Cristo Mts., *U.S.A.* 109 G2
Sangro →, *Italy* 33 F11
Sangudo, *Canada* 100 C6
Sangue →, *Brazil* 125 C6
Sangüesa, *Spain* 28 C3
Sanguinaires, Is., *France* 27 G12
Sangzhi, *China* 53 C8
Sanhala, *Ivory C.* 78 C3
Sāniyah, *Iraq* 64 C4
Sanje, *Uganda* 82 C3
Sanjiang, *China* 52 E7
Sanjo, *Japan* 48 F9
Sankt Antönien, *Switz.* 23 C9
Sankt Blasien, *Germany* 19 H4
Sankt Gallen, *Switz.* 23 B8
Sankt Gallen □, *Switz.* 23 B8
Sankt Goar, *Germany* 19 E3
Sankt Ingbert, *Germany* 19 F3
Sankt Margrethen, *Switz.* 23 B9
Sankt Moritz, *Switz.* 23 D9
Sankt-Peterburg, *Russia* 40 B7
Sankt Pölten, *Austria* 21 G5
Sankt Valentin, *Austria* 21 G4
Sankt Veit, *Austria* 21 J4
Sankt Wendel, *Germany* 19 F3
Sankuru →, *Zaïre* 80 E4
Sanlúcar de Barrameda, *Spain* 31 J4
Sanlúcar la Mayor, *Spain* 31 H4
Sanluri, *Italy* 34 C1
Sanmenxia, *China* 50 G6
Sanming, *China* 53 D11
Sannaspos, *S. Africa* 84 D4
Sannicandro Gargánico, *Italy* 35 A8
Sannidal, *Norway* 10 F3
Sannieshof, *S. Africa* 84 D4
Sannīn, J., *Lebanon* 69 B4
Sanok, *Poland* 20 F12
Sanquhar, *U.K.* 14 F5
Sansanding Dam, *Mali* 78 C3
Sansepolcro, *Italy* 33 E9
Sansha, *China* 53 D13
Sanshui, *China* 53 F9
Sanski Most, *Bos.-H.* 33 D13
Sansui, *China* 52 D7
Santa, *Peru* 124 B2
Sant' Ágata de Goti, *Italy* 35 A7
Sant' Ágata di Militello, *Italy* 35 D7
Santa Ana, *Beni, Bolivia* 125 C4
Santa Ana, *Santa Cruz, Bolivia* 125 D6
Santa Ana, *Santa Cruz, Bolivia* 125 D5
Santa Ana, *Ecuador* 120 D1
Santa Ana, *El Salv.* 116 D2
Santa Ana, *Mexico* 114 A2
Santa Ana, *U.S.A.* 113 M9
Santa Ana →, *Venezuela* 120 B3
Sant' Ángelo Lodigiano, *Italy* 32 C6
Sant' Antíoco, *Italy* 34 C1
Sant' Arcángelo di Romagna, *Italy* 33 D9
Santa Bárbara, *Colombia* 120 B2
Santa Bárbara, *Honduras* 116 D2
Santa Bárbara, *Mexico* 114 B3
Santa Bárbara, *Spain* 28 E5
Santa Barbara, *U.S.A.* 113 L7
Santa Bárbara, *Venezuela* 120 B3
Santa Bárbara, Mt., *Spain* 29 H2
Santa Barbara Channel, *U.S.A.* 113 L7
Santa Barbara I., *U.S.A.* 113 M7
Santa Catalina, *Colombia* 120 A2
Santa Catalina, *Mexico* 114 B2
Santa Catalina, Gulf of, *U.S.A.* 113 N9
Santa Catalina I., *U.S.A.* 113 M8
Santa Catarina □, *Brazil* 127 B6
Santa Catarina, I. de, *Brazil* 127 B6
Santa Caterina Villarmosa, *Italy* 35 E7
Santa Cecília, *Brazil* 127 B5
Santa Clara, *Cuba* 116 B4
Santa Clara, *Calif., U.S.A.* 111 H3
Santa Clara, *Utah, U.S.A.* 111 H7
Santa Clara de Olimar, *Uruguay* 127 C5
Santa Clotilde, *Peru* 120 D3
Santa Coloma de Farners, *Spain* 28 D7
Santa Coloma de Gramanet, *Spain* 28 D7
Santa Comba, *Spain* 30 B2
Santa Croce Camerina, *Italy* 35 F7
Santa Croce di Magliano, *Italy* 35 A7
Santa Cruz, *Argentina* 128 D3
Santa Cruz, *Bolivia* 125 D5
Santa Cruz, *Brazil* 122 C4
Santa Cruz, *Chile* 126 C1
Santa Cruz, *Costa Rica* 116 D2
Santa Cruz, *Madeira* 36 D3
Santa Cruz, *Peru* 124 B2
Santa Cruz, *Phil.* 55 D4
Santa Cruz, *U.S.A.* 111 H2
Santa Cruz, *Venezuela* 121 B5
Santa Cruz □, *Argentina* 128 C3
Santa Cruz □, *Bolivia* 125 D5
Santa Cruz →, *Argentina* 128 D3
Santa Cruz Cabrália, *Brazil* 123 E4
Santa Cruz de la Palma, *Canary Is.* 36 F2
Santa Cruz de Mudela, *Spain* 29 G1
Santa Cruz de Tenerife, *Canary Is.* 36 F3
Santa Cruz del Norte, *Cuba* 116 B3
Santa Cruz del Retamar, *Spain* 30 E6
Santa Cruz del Sur, *Cuba* 116 B4
Santa Cruz do Rio Pardo, *Brazil* 127 A6
Santa Cruz do Sul, *Brazil* 127 B5
Santa Cruz I., *Solomon Is.* 92 J8
Santa Cruz I., *U.S.A.* 113 M7
Santa Domingo, Cay, *Bahamas* 116 B4
Santa Elena, *Argentina* 126 C4
Santa Elena, *Ecuador* 120 D1
Santa Elena, C., *Costa Rica* 116 D2
Sant' Eufémia, G. di, *Italy* 35 D9
Santa Eugenia, Pta., *Mexico* 114 B1
Santa Eulalia, *Spain* 36 C8
Santa Fe, *Argentina* 126 C3
Santa Fe, *Spain* 31 H7
Santa Fe, *U.S.A.* 111 J11
Santa Fé □, *Argentina* 126 C3
Santa Filomena, *Brazil* 122 C2
Santa Galdana, *Spain* 36 B10
Santa Gertrudis, *Spain* 36 B7
Santa Helena, *Brazil* 122 B2
Santa Helena de Goiás, *Brazil* 123 E1
Santa Inês, *Brazil* 123 D4
Santa Inés, *Baleares, Spain* 36 B7
Santa Inés, *Extremadura, Spain* 31 G5
Santa Inés, I., *Chile* 128 D2
Santa Isabel = Rey Malabo, *Eq. Guin.* 79 E6
Santa Isabel, *Argentina* 126 D2
Santa Isabel, *Brazil* 123 D1
Santa Isabel, Pico, *Eq. Guin.* 79 E6
Santa Isabel do Araguaia, *Brazil* 122 C2
Santa Isabel do Morro, *Brazil* 123 D1
Santa Lucía, *Corrientes, Argentina* 126 B4
Santa Lucía, *San Juan, Argentina* 126 C2
Santa Lucía, *Spain* 29 H4
Santa Lucia, *Uruguay* 126 C4
Santa Lucia Range, *U.S.A.* 111 J3
Santa Magdalena, I., *Mexico* 114 C2
Santa Margarita, *Argentina* 126 D3
Santa Margarita, *Mexico* 114 C2
Santa Margarita, *Spain* 36 B10
Santa Margarita, *U.S.A.* 112 K6
Santa Margarita →, *U.S.A.* 113 M9
Santa Margherita, *Italy* 32 D6
Santa María, *Argentina* 126 B2
Santa Maria, *Brazil* 127 B5
Santa Maria, *Phil.* 55 C4
Santa Maria, *Spain* 36 B9
Santa Maria, *Switz.* 23 C10
Santa Maria, *U.S.A.* 113 L6
Santa María →, *Mexico* 114 A3
Santa María, B. de, *Mexico* 114 B3
Santa Maria, C. de, *Portugal* 31 J3
Santa Maria Capua Vetere, *Italy* 35 A7
Santa Maria da Vitória, *Brazil* 123 D3
Santa María de Ipire, *Venezuela* 121 B4
Santa Maria di Leuca, C., *Italy* 35 C11
Santa Maria do Suaçuí, *Brazil* 123 E3
Santa Maria dos Marmelos, *Brazil* 125 B5
Santa María la Real de Nieva, *Spain* 30 D6
Santa Marta, *Colombia* 120 A3
Santa Marta, *Spain* 31 G4
Santa Marta, Ría de, *Spain* 30 B3
Santa Marta, Sierra Nevada de, *Colombia* 120 A3
Santa Marta Grande, C., *Brazil* 127 B6
Santa Maura = Levkás, *Greece* 39 L3
Santa Monica, *U.S.A.* 113 M8
Santa Olalla, *Huelva, Spain* 31 H4
Santa Olalla, *Toledo, Spain* 30 E6
Sant' Onofrio, *Italy* 35 D9
Santa Pola, *Spain* 29 G4
Santa Ponsa, *Spain* 36 B9
Santa Quitéria, *Brazil* 122 B3
Santa Rita, *U.S.A.* 111 K10
Santa Rita, *Guarico, Venezuela* 120 B4
Santa Rita, *Zulia, Venezuela* 120 A3
Santa Rita do Araquaia, *Brazil* 125 D7
Santa Rosa, *La Pampa, Argentina* 126 D3
Santa Rosa, *San Luis, Argentina* 126 C2
Santa Rosa, *Bolivia* 124 C4
Santa Rosa, *Brazil* 127 B5
Santa Rosa, *Colombia* 120 C4
Santa Rosa, *Ecuador* 120 D2
Santa Rosa, *Peru* 124 C3
Santa Rosa, *Calif., U.S.A.* 112 G4
Santa Rosa, *N. Mex., U.S.A.* 109 H2
Santa Rosa, *Venezuela* 120 C4
Santa Rosa de Cabal, *Colombia* 120 C2
Santa Rosa de Copán, *Honduras* 116 D2
Santa Rosa de Osos, *Colombia* 120 B2
Santa Rosa de Río Primero, *Argentina* 126 C3
Santa Rosa de Viterbo, *Colombia* 120 B3
Santa Rosa del Palmar, *Bolivia* 125 D5
Santa Rosa I., *Calif., U.S.A.* 113 M6
Santa Rosa I., *Fla., U.S.A.* 105 K2
Santa Rosa Range, *U.S.A.* 110 F5
Santa Rosalía, *Mexico* 114 B2
Santa Sofia, *Italy* 33 E8
Santa Sylvina, *Argentina* 126 B3
Santa Tecla = Nueva San Salvador, *El Salv.* 116 D2
Santa Teresa, *Argentina* 126 C3
Santa Teresa, *Brazil* 123 E3
Santa Teresa, *Mexico* 115 B5
Santa Teresa, *Venezuela* 121 C5
Santa Teresa di Riva, *Italy* 35 E8
Santa Teresa Gallura, *Italy* 34 A2
Santa Vitória, *Brazil* 123 E1
Santa Vitória do Palmar, *Brazil* 127 C5
Santa Ynez →, *U.S.A.* 113 L6
Santa Ynez Mts., *U.S.A.* 113 L6
Santa Ysabel, *U.S.A.* 113 M10
Santadi, *Italy* 34 C1
Santai, *China* 52 B5
Santaluz, *Brazil* 122 D4
Santana, *Brazil* 123 D3
Santana, *Madeira* 36 D3
Santana, Coxilha de, *Brazil* 127 C4
Santana do Ipanema, *Brazil* 122 C4

Santana do Livramento, *Brazil* 127 C4
Santanayi, *Spain* 36 B10
Santander, *Colombia* 120 C2
Santander, *Spain* 30 B7
Santander Jiménez, *Mexico* 115 C5
Santaquin, *U.S.A.* 110 G8
Santarém, *Brazil* 121 D7
Santarém, *Portugal* 31 F2
Santarém □, *Portugal* 31 F2
Santaren Channel, *W. Indies* 116 B4
Santee, *U.S.A.* 113 N10
Santéramo in Colle, *Italy* 35 B9
Santerno →, *Italy* 33 D8
Santhia, *Italy* 32 C5
Santiago, *Bolivia* 125 D6
Santiago, *Brazil* 127 B5
Santiago, *Chile* 126 C1
Santiago, *Panama* 116 E3
Santiago, *Peru* 124 C2
Santiago, *Phil.* 55 C4
Santiago □, *Chile* 126 C1
Santiago →, *Peru* 120 D2
Santiago, C., *Chile* 128 D1
Santiago, Punta de, *Eq. Guin.* 79 E6
Santiago, Serranía de, *Bolivia* 125 D6
Santiago de Chuco, *Peru* 124 B2
Santiago de Compostela, *Spain* 30 C2
Santiago de Cuba, *Cuba* 116 C4
Santiago de los Cabelleros, *Dom. Rep.* 117 C5
Santiago del Estero, *Argentina* 126 B3
Santiago del Estero □, *Argentina* 126 B3
Santiago del Teide, *Canary Is.* 36 F3
Santiago do Cacém, *Portugal* 31 G2
Santiago Ixcuintla, *Mexico* 114 C3
Santiago Papasquiaro, *Mexico* 114 B3
Santiaguillo, L. de, *Mexico* 114 C4
Santillana del Mar, *Spain* 30 B6
Säntis, *Switz.* 23 B8
Santisteban del Puerto, *Spain* 29 G1
Santo →, *Peru* 124 B2
Santo Amaro, *Brazil* 123 D4
Santo Anastácio, *Brazil* 127 A5
Santo André, *Brazil* 127 A6
Santo Ângelo, *Brazil* 127 B5
Santo Antonio, *Brazil* 125 D6
Santo Antônio de Jesus, *Brazil* 123 D4
Santo Antônio do Içá, *Brazil* 120 D4
Santo Antônio do Leverger, *Brazil* 125 D6
Santo Corazón, *Bolivia* 125 D6
Santo Domingo, *Dom. Rep.* 117 C6
Santo Domingo, *Baja Calif. N., Mexico* 114 A1
Santo Domingo, *Baja Calif. S., Mexico* 114 B2
Santo Domingo, *Nic.* 116 D3
Santo Domingo de la Calzada, *Spain* 28 C2
Santo Domingo de los Colorados, *Ecuador* 120 D2
Santo Stéfano di Camastro, *Italy* 35 D7
Santo Stino di Livenza, *Italy* 33 C9
Santo Tirso, *Portugal* 30 D2
Santo Tomás, *Mexico* 114 A1
Santo Tomás, *Peru* 124 C3
Santo Tomé, *Argentina* 127 B4
Santo Tomé de Guayana = Ciudad Guayana, *Venezuela* 121 B5
Santoña, *Spain* 30 B7
Santos, *Brazil* 127 A6
Santos, Sierra de los, *Spain* 31 G5
Santos Dumont, *Brazil* 123 F3
Santpoort, *Neths.* 16 D5
Sanvignes-les-Mines, *France* 25 F11
Sanyuan, *China* 50 G5
Sanza Pombo, *Angola* 80 F3
São Anastácio, *Brazil* 127 A5
São Bartolomeu de Messines, *Portugal* 31 H2
São Benedito, *Brazil* 122 B3
São Bento, *Brazil* 122 B3
São Bento do Norte, *Brazil* 122 C4
São Bernado de Campo, *Brazil* 123 F2
São Borja, *Brazil* 127 B4
São Bras d'Alportel, *Portugal* 31 H3
São Caitano, *Brazil* 122 C4
São Carlos, *Brazil* 127 A6
São Cristóvão, *Brazil* 122 D4
São Domingos, *Brazil* 123 D2
São Domingos do Maranhão, *Brazil* 122 C3
São Félix, *Brazil* 123 D1
São Francisco, *Brazil* 123 E3
São Francisco →, *Brazil* 122 D4
São Francisco do Maranhão, *Brazil* 122 C3
São Francisco do Sul, *Brazil* 127 B6
São Gabriel, *Brazil* 127 C5
São Gabriel da Palha, *Brazil* 123 E3
São Gonçalo, *Brazil* 123 F3
São Gotardo, *Brazil* 123 E2
Sao Hill, *Tanzania* 83 D4
São João da Boa Vista, *Brazil* 127 A6
São João da Pesqueira, *Portugal* 30 D3
São João da Ponte, *Brazil* 123 E3
São João del Rei, *Brazil* 123 F3
São João do Araguaia, *Brazil* 122 C2
São João do Paraíso, *Brazil* 123 E3
São João do Piauí, *Brazil* 122 C3
São João dos Patos, *Brazil* 122 C3
São Joaquim da Barra, *Brazil* 123 F2
São Jorge, Pta. de, *Madeira* 36 D3
São José, B. de, *Brazil* 122 B3
São José da Laje, *Brazil* 122 C4
São José de Mipibu, *Brazil* 122 C4
São José do Peixe, *Brazil* 122 C3
São José do Rio Prêto, *Brazil* 127 A6
São José dos Campos, *Brazil* 127 A6
São Leopoldo, *Brazil* 127 B5
São Lourenço, *Brazil* 123 F2
São Lourenço →, *Brazil* 125 D6
São Lourenço, Pantanal do, *Brazil* 125 D6
São Lourenço, Pta. de, *Madeira* 36 D3
São Luís, *Brazil* 122 B3
São Luís do Curu, *Brazil* 122 B4
São Luís Gonzaga, *Brazil* 127 B5
São Marcos →, *Brazil* 123 E2
São Marcos, B. de, *Brazil* 122 B3
São Martinho, *Portugal* 30 E2
São Mateus, *Brazil* 123 E4
São Mateus →, *Brazil* 123 E4
São Miguel do Araguaia, *Brazil* 123 D1
São Miguel dos Campos, *Brazil* 122 C4
São Nicolau →, *Brazil* 122 C3
São Paulo, *Brazil* 127 A6
São Paulo □, *Brazil* 127 A6
São Paulo, I., *Atl. Oc.* 2 D8
São Paulo de Olivença, *Brazil* 120 D4
São Pedro do Sul, *Portugal* 30 E2
São Rafael, *Brazil* 122 C4
São Raimundo das Mangabeiras, *Brazil* 122 C2
São Raimundo Nonato, *Brazil* 122 C3
São Romão, *Brazil* 123 E2
São Roque, *Madeira* 36 D3
São Roque, C. de, *Brazil* 122 C4
São Sebastião, I. de, *Brazil* 127 A6
São Sebastião do Paraíso, *Brazil* 127 A6
São Simão, *Brazil* 123 E1
São Teotónio, *Portugal* 31 H2
São Tomé, *Atl. Oc.* 70 F4
São Tomé, *Brazil* 122 C4
São Tomé, C. de, *Brazil* 123 F3
São Tomé & Principe ■, *Africa* 71 F4
São Vicente, *Brazil* 127 A6
São Vicente, *Madeira* 36 D2
São Vicente, C. de, *Portugal* 31 H2
Saona, I., *Dom. Rep.* 117 C6
Saône →, *France* 27 C8
Saône-et-Loire □, *France* 25 F11
Saonek, *Indonesia* 57 E8
Saoura, O. →, *Algeria* 75 C4
Sapanca, *Turkey* 66 C4
Sapão →, *Brazil* 122 D2
Saparua, *Indonesia* 57 E7
Sapé, *Brazil* 122 C4
Sapele, *Nigeria* 79 D6
Sapelo I., *U.S.A.* 105 K5
Sapiéntza, *Greece* 39 N4
Sapone, *Burkina Faso* 79 C4
Saposoa, *Peru* 124 B2
Sapozhok, *Russia* 41 E12
Sappemeer, *Neths.* 16 B9
Sappho, *U.S.A.* 112 B2
Sapporo, *Japan* 48 C10
Sapri, *Italy* 35 B8
Sapudi, *Indonesia* 57 G16
Sapulpa, *U.S.A.* 109 G7
Saqqez, *Iran* 64 B5
Sar Dasht, *Iran* 65 C6
Sar Gachīneh, *Iran* 65 D6
Sar Planina, *Macedonia* 38 G4
Sara, *Burkina Faso* 78 C4
Sara, *Phil.* 55 F5
Sara Buri, *Thailand* 58 E3
Sarāb, *Iran* 64 B5
Sarabadi, *Iraq* 64 C5
Sarada →, *India* 61 F12
Saragossa = Zaragoza, *Spain* 28 D4
Saraguro, *Ecuador* 120 D2
Sarajevo, *Bos.-H.* 21 M8
Saramacca □, *Surinam* 121 C6
Saramacca →, *Surinam* 121 B6
Saran, G., *Indonesia* 56 E4
Saranac Lake, *U.S.A.* 107 B10
Saranda, *Tanzania* 82 D3
Sarandí del Yi, *Uruguay* 127 C4
Sarandí Grande, *Uruguay* 126 C4
Sarangani B., *Phil.* 55 J6
Sarangani Is., *Phil.* 55 J6
Sarangarh, *India* 61 J13
Saransk, *Russia* 41 D14
Sarapul, *Russia* 44 D6
Sarasota, *U.S.A.* 105 M4
Saratoga, *Calif., U.S.A.* 112 H4
Saratoga, *Wyo., U.S.A.* 110 F10
Saratoga Springs, *U.S.A.* 107 C11
Saratov, *Russia* 41 F15
Saravane, *Laos* 58 E6
Sarawak □, *Malaysia* 56 D4
Saray, *Turkey* 67 D11
Saraya, *Senegal* 78 C2
Sarayköy, *Turkey* 66 E3
Sarayönü, *Turkey* 66 D5
Sarbāz, *Iran* 65 E9
Sarbīsheh, *Iran* 65 C8
Sarca →, *Italy* 32 C7
Sarda → = Sarada →, *India* 61 F12
Sardalas, *Libya* 75 C7
Sardarshahr, *India* 62 E6
Sardegna, *Italy* 34 B2
Sardhana, *India* 62 E7
Sardina, Pta., *Canary Is.* 36 F4
Sardinata, *Colombia* 120 B3
Sardinia = Sardegna, *Italy* 34 B2
Sardis, *Turkey* 66 D3
Sārdūīyeh = Dar Mazār, *Iran* 65 D8
Saréyamou, *Mali* 78 B4
Sargent, *U.S.A.* 108 E5
Sargodha, *Pakistan* 62 C5
Sarh, *Chad* 73 G8
Sarhro, Djebel, *Morocco* 74 B3
Sārī, *Iran* 65 B7
Sária, *Greece* 39 P10
Sarıgöl, *Turkey* 66 D3
Sarikamiş, *Turkey* 67 C10
Sarıkaya, *Turkey* 66 D6
Sarikei, *Malaysia* 56 D4
Sarina, *Australia* 90 C4
Sariñena, *Spain* 28 D4
Sarita, *U.S.A.* 109 M6
Sariwŏn, *N. Korea* 51 E13
Sark, *Chan. Is.* 13 H5
Sarkad, *Hungary* 21 J11
Şarkışla, *Turkey* 66 D7
Şarköy, *Turkey* 66 C2
Sarlat-la-Canéda, *France* 26 D5
Sarles, *U.S.A.* 108 A5
Sărmaşu, *Romania* 38 C7
Sarmi, *Indonesia* 57 E9
Sarmiento, *Argentina* 128 C3
Särna, *Sweden* 10 C7
Sarnano, *Italy* 33 E10
Sarnen, *Switz.* 22 C6
Sarnia, *Canada* 98 D3
Sarno, *Italy* 35 B7
Sarny, *Ukraine* 40 F5
Särö, *Sweden* 11 G5
Sarolangun, *Indonesia* 56 E2
Saronikós Kólpos, *Greece* 39 M6
Saronno, *Italy* 32 C6
Saros Körfezi, *Turkey* 66 C2
Sárospatak, *Hungary* 21 G11
Sarova, *Russia* 41 D13
Sarpsborg, *Norway* 10 E5
Sarracín, *Spain* 28 C1
Sarralbe, *France* 25 D14
Sarre = Saar →, *Europe* 25 C13
Sarre-Union, *France* 25 D14
Sarrebourg, *France* 25 D14
Sarreguemines, *France* 25 C14
Sarriá, *Spain* 30 C3
Sarrión, *Spain* 28 E4
Sarro, *Mali* 78 C3
Sarstedt, *Germany* 18 C5
Sartène, *France* 27 G12
Sarthe □, *France* 24 E7
Sarthe →, *France* 24 E6
Sartilly, *France* 24 D5
Sartynya, *Russia* 44 C7
Sárvár, *Hungary* 21 H6
Sarvestān, *Iran* 65 D7
Särvfjället, *Sweden* 10 B7
Sárviz →, *Hungary* 21 J8
Sary-Tash, *Kirghizia* 44 F8
Sarych, Mys, *Ukraine* 42 D5
Saryshagan, *Kazakhstan* 44 E8
Sarzana, *Italy* 32 D6
Sarzeau, *France* 24 E4
Sas van Gent, *Neths.* 17 F3
Sasabeneh, *Ethiopia* 68 F3
Sasaram, *India* 63 G11
Sasebo, *Japan* 49 H4
Saser, *India* 63 B7
Saskatchewan □, *Canada* 101 C7
Saskatchewan →, *Canada* 101 C8
Saskatoon, *Canada* 101 C7
Saskylakh, *Russia* 45 B12
Sasnovka, *Russia* 41 C17
Sasolburg, *S. Africa* 85 D4
Sasovo, *Russia* 41 D12
Sassandra, *Ivory C.* 78 E3
Sassandra →, *Ivory C.* 78 E3
Sássari, *Italy* 34 B1
Sassenheim, *Neths.* 16 D5
Sassnitz, *Germany* 18 A9
Sasso Marconi, *Italy* 33 D8
Sassocorvaro, *Italy* 33 E9
Sassoferrato, *Italy* 33 E9
Sassuolo, *Italy* 32 D7
Sástago, *Spain* 28 D4
Sastown, *Liberia* 78 E3
Sasumua Dam, *Kenya* 82 C4
Sata-Misaki, *Japan* 49 J5
Satadougou, *Mali* 78 C2
Satanta, *U.S.A.* 109 G4
Satara, *India* 60 L8
Satilla →, *U.S.A.* 105 K5
Satipo, *Peru* 124 C3
Satmala Hills, *India* 60 J9
Şatna, *India* 63 G9
Šator, *Bos.-H.* 33 D13
Sátoraljaújhely, *Hungary* 21 G11
Satpura Ra., *India* 62 J7
Satrup, *Germany* 18 A5
Satsuna-Shotō, *Japan* 49 K5
Sattahip, *Thailand* 58 F3
Satu Mare, *Romania* 38 B5
Satui, *Indonesia* 56 E5
Satun, *Thailand* 59 J3
Saturnina →, *Brazil* 125 C6
Sauce, *Argentina* 126 C4
Sauceda, *Mexico* 114 B4
Saucillo, *Mexico* 114 B3
Sauda, *Norway* 9 G9
Saúde, *Brazil* 122 D3
Sauðarkrókur, *Iceland* 8 D4
Saudi Arabia ■, *Asia* 68 B3
Sauer →, *Germany* 17 J9
Saugeen →, *Canada* 106 B3
Saugerties, *U.S.A.* 107 D11
Saugues, *France* 26 D7
Sauherad, *Norway* 10 E3
Saujon, *France* 26 C3
Sauk Centre, *U.S.A.* 108 C7
Sauk Rapids, *U.S.A.* 108 C7
Saül, *Fr. Guiana* 121 C7
Saulgau, *Germany* 19 G5
Saulieu, *France* 25 E11
Sault, *France* 27 D9
Sault Ste. Marie, *Canada* 98 C3
Sault Ste. Marie, *U.S.A.* 104 B3
Saumlaki, *Indonesia* 57 F8
Saumur, *France* 24 E6
Saunders C., *N.Z.* 87 L3
Saunders I., *Antarctica* 5 B1
Saunders Point, *Australia* 89 E4
Saurbær, *Borgarfjarðarsýsla, Iceland* 8 D3
Saurbær, *Eyjafjarðarsýsla, Iceland* 8 D4
Sauri, *Nigeria* 79 C6
Saurimo, *Angola* 80 F4
Sausalito, *U.S.A.* 112 H4
Sautatá, *Colombia* 120 B2
Sauveterre-de-Béarn, *France* 26 E3
Sauzé-Vaussais, *France* 26 B4
Savá, *Honduras* 116 C2
Sava →, *Serbia, Yug.* 21 L10
Savage, *U.S.A.* 108 B2
Savage I. = Niue, *Cook Is.* 93 J11
Savai'i, *W. Samoa* 87 A12
Savalou, *Benin* 79 D5
Savane, *Mozam.* 83 F4
Savanna, *U.S.A.* 108 D9
Savanna la Mar, *Jamaica* 116 C4
Savannah, *Ga., U.S.A.* 105 J5
Savannah, *Mo., U.S.A.* 108 F7
Savannah, *Tenn., U.S.A.* 105 H1
Savannah →, *U.S.A.* 105 J5
Savannakhet, *Laos* 58 D5
Savant L., *Canada* 98 B1
Savant Lake, *Canada* 98 B1
Savanur, *India* 60 M9
Savé, *Benin* 79 D5
Save →, *France* 26 E5
Save →, *Mozam.* 85 C5
Sāveh, *Iran* 65 C6
Savelugu, *Ghana* 79 D4
Savenay, *France* 24 E5
Saverdun, *France* 26 E5
Saverne, *France* 25 D14
Savièse, *Switz.* 22 D4
Savigliano, *Italy* 32 D4
Savigny-sur-Braye, *France* 24 E7
Saviñao, *Spain* 30 C3
Savio →, *Italy* 33 D9
Savognin, *Switz.* 23 C9
Savoie □, *France* 27 C10
Savona, *Italy* 32 D5
Sawahlunto, *Indonesia* 56 E2
Sawai, *Indonesia* 57 E7
Sawai Madhopur, *India* 62 F7
Sawang Daen Din, *Thailand* 58 D4
Sawankhalok, *Thailand* 58 D2
Sawara, *Japan* 49 G10
Sawatch Mts., *U.S.A.* 111 G10
Sawel, *U.K.* 15 B4
Sawi, *Thailand* 59 G2
Sawmills, *Zimbabwe* 83 F2
Sawu, *Indonesia* 57 F6
Sawu Sea, *Indonesia* 57 F6
Saxby →, *Australia* 90 B3
Saxon, *Switz.* 22 D4
Saxony, Lower = Niedersachsen □, *Germany* 18 C5
Saxton, *U.S.A.* 106 F6
Say, *Niger* 79 C5
Saya, *Nigeria* 79 D5
Sayabec, *Canada* 99 C6
Sayaboury, *Laos* 58 C3
Sayán, *Peru* 124 C2
Sayan, Vostochnyy, *Russia* 45 D10
Sayan, Zapadnyy, *Russia* 45 D10
Sayasan, *Russia* 43 E12
Saydā, *Lebanon* 69 B4
Sayhan-Ovoo, *Mongolia* 50 B2
Sayhandulaan, *Mongolia* 50 B5
Sayḩut, *Yemen* 68 D5
Saynshand, *Mongolia* 50 B6
Sayre, *Okla., U.S.A.* 109 H5
Sayre, *Pa., U.S.A.* 107 E8
Sayula, *Mexico* 114 D4
Sazin, *Pakistan* 63 B5
Sazlika →, *Bulgaria* 39 H8
Sbeïtla, *Tunisia* 75 A6
Scaër, *France* 24 D3
Scafell Pikes, *U.K.* 12 C4
Scalea, *Italy* 35 C8
Scalpay, *U.K.* 14 D2
Scandia, *Canada* 100 C6
Scandiano, *Italy* 32 D7
Scandinavia, *Europe* 8 E12
Scansano, *Italy* 33 F8
Scapa Flow, *U.K.* 14 C5
Scappoose, *U.S.A.* 112 E4
Scarborough, *Trin. & Tob.* 117 D7
Scarborough, *U.K.* 12 C7
Scebeli, Wabi →, *Somali Rep.* 68 G3
Šćedro, *Croatia* 33 E13
Scenic, *U.S.A.* 108 D3
Schaal See, *Germany* 18 B6
Schaan, *Liech.* 23 B9
Schaesberg, *Neths.* 17 G8
Schaffen, *Belgium* 17 G6
Schaffhausen, *Switz.* 23 A7
Schaffhausen □, *Switz.* 23 A7
Schagen, *Neths.* 16 C5
Schaijk, *Neths.* 16 E7
Schalkhaar, *Neths.* 16 D8
Schalkwijk, *Neths.* 16 E6
Schangnau, *Switz.* 22 C5
Schänis, *Switz.* 23 B8
Schärding, *Austria* 20 G3
Scharhörn, *Germany* 18 B4
Scharnitz, *Austria* 19 H7
Scheessel, *Germany* 18 B5
Schefferville, *Canada* 99 B6
Schelde →, *Belgium* 17 F4
Schell Creek Ra., *U.S.A.* 110 G6
Schenectady, *U.S.A.* 107 D11
Scherfede, *Germany* 18 D5
Scherpenheuvel, *Belgium* 17 G5
Scherpenisse, *Neths.* 17 E4
Scherpenzeel, *Neths.* 16 D7
Schesaplana, *Switz.* 23 B9
Schesslitz, *Germany* 19 F7
Scheveningen, *Neths.* 16 D4
Schiedam, *Neths.* 16 E4
Schiermonnikoog, *Neths.* 16 B8
Schiers, *Switz.* 23 C9
Schifferstadt, *Germany* 19 F4
Schifflange, *Lux.* 17 K8
Schijndel, *Neths.* 17 E6
Schiltigheim, *France* 25 D14
Schio, *Italy* 33 C8
Schipbeek, *Neths.* 16 D8
Schipluiden, *Neths.* 16 E4
Schirmeck, *France* 25 D14
Schlei →, *Germany* 18 A5
Schleiden, *Germany* 18 E2
Schleiz, *Germany* 18 E7
Schleswig, *Germany* 18 A5
Schleswig-Holstein □, *Germany* 18 A5
Schlieren, *Switz.* 23 B6
Schlüchtern, *Germany* 19 E5
Schmalkalden, *Germany* 18 E6
Schmölln, *Brandenburg, Germany* 18 B10
Schmölln, *Thüringen, Germany* 18 E8
Schneeberg, *Austria* 21 H5
Schneeberg, *Germany* 18 E8
Schoenberg, *Belgium* 17 H8
Schofield, *U.S.A.* 108 C10
Scholls, *U.S.A.* 112 E4
Schönberg, *Mecklenburg-Vorpommern, Germany* 18 B6
Schönberg, *Schleswig-Holstein, Germany* 18 A6
Schönebeck, *Germany* 18 C7
Schönenwerd, *Switz.* 22 B5
Schongau, *Germany* 19 H6
Schöningen, *Germany* 18 C6
Schoondijke, *Neths.* 17 F3
Schoonebeek, *Neths.* 16 C9
Schoonhoven, *Neths.* 16 E5
Schoorl, *Neths.* 16 C5
Schortens, *Germany* 18 B3
Schoten, *Belgium* 17 F5
Schouten I., *Australia* 90 G4
Schouten Is. = Supriori, Kepulauan, *Indonesia* 57 E9
Schouwen, *Neths.* 17 E3
Schramberg, *Germany* 19 G4
Schrankogl, *Austria* 19 H7
Schreckhorn, *Switz.* 22 C6
Schreiber, *Canada* 98 C2
Schrobenhausen, *Germany* 19 G7
Schruns, *Austria* 19 H5
Schuler, *Canada* 101 C6

Schuls, *Switz.* 23 C10
Schumacher, *Canada* 98 C3
Schüpfen, *Switz.* 22 B4
Schüpfheim, *Switz.* 22 C6
Schurz, *U.S.A.* 110 G4
Schuyler, *U.S.A.* 108 E6
Schuylkill Haven, *U.S.A.* 107 F8
Schwabach, *Germany* 19 F7
Schwäbisch Gmünd, *Germany* 19 G5
Schwäbisch Hall, *Germany* 19 F5
Schwäbische Alb, *Germany* 19 G5
Schwabmünchen, *Germany* 19 G6
Schwanden, *Switz.* 23 C8
Schwandorf, *Germany* 19 F8
Schwaner, Pegunungan, *Indonesia* 56 E4
Schwarmstedt, *Germany* 18 C5
Schwärze, *Germany* 18 C9
Schwarze Elster →, *Germany* 18 D8
Schwarzenberg, *Germany* 18 E8
Schwarzenburg, *Switz.* 22 C4
Schwarzwald, *Germany* 19 H4
Schwaz, *Austria* 19 H7
Schwedt, *Germany* 18 B10
Schweinfurt, *Germany* 19 E6
Schweizer Mittelland, *Switz.* 22 C4
Schweizer-Reneke, *S. Africa* 84 D4
Schwenningen, *Germany* 19 G4
Schwerin, *Germany* 18 B7
Schweriner See, *Germany* 18 B7
Schwetzingen, *Germany* 19 F4
Schwyz, *Switz.* 23 B7
Schwyz □, *Switz.* 23 B7
Sciacca, *Italy* 34 E6
Scicli, *Italy* 35 F7
Scilla, *Italy* 35 D8
Scilly, Isles of, *U.K.* 13 H1
Ścinawa, *Poland* 20 D6
Scioto →, *U.S.A.* 104 F4
Scobey, *U.S.A.* 108 A2
Scone, *Australia* 91 E5
Scordia, *Italy* 35 E7
Scoresbysund, *Greenland* 4 B6
Scorno, Punta dello, *Italy* 34 A1
Scotia, *Calif., U.S.A.* 110 F1
Scotia, *N.Y., U.S.A.* 107 D11
Scotia Sea, *Antarctica* 5 B18
Scotland, *U.S.A.* 108 D6
Scotland □, *U.K.* 14 E5
Scotland Neck, *U.S.A.* 105 G7
Scott, C., *Australia* 88 B4
Scott City, *U.S.A.* 108 F4
Scott Glacier, *Antarctica* 5 C8
Scott I., *Antarctica* 5 C11
Scott Inlet, *Canada* 97 A12
Scott Is., *Canada* 100 C3
Scott L., *Canada* 101 B7
Scott Reef, *Australia* 88 B3
Scottburgh, *S. Africa* 85 E5
Scottdale, *U.S.A.* 106 F5
Scottsbluff, *U.S.A.* 108 E3
Scottsboro, *U.S.A.* 105 H2
Scottsburg, *U.S.A.* 104 F3
Scottsdale, *Australia* 90 G4
Scottsville, *Ky., U.S.A.* 105 G2
Scottsville, *N.Y., U.S.A.* 106 C7
Scottville, *U.S.A.* 104 D2
Scranton, *U.S.A.* 107 E9
Scugog, L., *Canada* 106 B6
Scunthorpe, *U.K.* 12 D7
Scuol, *Switz.* 23 C10
Scusciuban, *Somali Rep.* 68 E5
Scutari = Üsküdar, *Turkey* 39 H11
Seabra, *Brazil* 123 D3
Seabrook, L., *Australia* 89 F2
Seaford, *U.S.A.* 104 F8
Seaforth, *Canada* 98 D3
Seagraves, *U.S.A.* 109 J3
Seal →, *Canada* 101 B10
Seal Cove, *Canada* 99 C8
Seal L., *Canada* 99 B7
Sealy, *U.S.A.* 109 L6
Searchlight, *U.S.A.* 113 K12
Searcy, *U.S.A.* 109 H9
Searles L., *U.S.A.* 113 K9
Seaside, *Calif., U.S.A.* 112 J5
Seaside, *Oreg., U.S.A.* 112 E3
Seaspray, *Australia* 91 F4
Seattle, *U.S.A.* 112 C4
Seaview Ra., *Australia* 90 B4
Sebastián Vizcaíno, B., *Mexico* 114 B2
Sebastopol = Sevastopol, *Ukraine* 42 D5
Sebastopol, *U.S.A.* 112 G4
Sebderat, *Eritrea* 77 D4
Sebdou, *Algeria* 75 B4
Seben, *Turkey* 66 C4
Sebewaing, *U.S.A.* 104 D4
Sebezh, *Russia* 40 C6
Sebha = Sabhah, *Libya* 73 C7
Sébi, *Mali* 78 B4
Şebinkarahisar, *Turkey* 42 F8
Sebiş, *Romania* 38 C5
Sebkhet Te-n-Dghâmcha, *Mauritania* 78 B1
Sebkra Azzel Mati, *Algeria* 75 C5
Sebkra Mekerghene, *Algeria* 75 C5
Sebnitz, *Germany* 18 E10
Sebou, Oued →, *Morocco* 74 B3
Sebring, *Fla., U.S.A.* 105 M5
Sebring, *Ohio, U.S.A.* 106 F3
Sebringville, *Canada* 106 C3
Sebta = Ceuta, *Morocco* 74 A3
Sebuku, *Indonesia* 56 E5
Sebuku, Teluk, *Malaysia* 56 D5
Secchia →, *Italy* 32 C8
Sechelt, *Canada* 100 D4
Sechura, *Peru* 124 B1
Sechura, Desierto de, *Peru* 124 B1
Seclin, *France* 25 B10
Secondigny, *France* 24 F6
Secretary I., *N.Z.* 87 L1
Secunderabad, *India* 60 L11
Sécure →, *Bolivia* 125 D5
Sedalia, *U.S.A.* 108 F8
Sedan, *Australia* 91 E2
Sedan, *France* 25 C11
Sedan, *U.S.A.* 109 G6
Sedano, *Spain* 28 C1
Seddon, *N.Z.* 87 J5
Seddonville, *N.Z.* 87 J4
Sedeh, *Fārs, Iran* 65 D7
Sedeh, *Khorāsān, Iran* 65 C8
Sederot, *Israel* 69 D3
Sedgewick, *Canada* 100 C6
Sedhiou, *Senegal* 78 C1
Sedičany, *Czech.* 20 F4
Sedico, *Italy* 33 B9
Sedley, *Canada* 101 C8
Sedova, Pik, *Russia* 44 B6
Sedrata, *Algeria* 75 A6
Sedro-Woolley, *U.S.A.* 112 B4
Sedrun, *Switz.* 23 C7
Šeduva, *Lithuania* 40 D3
Seebad Ahlbeck, *Germany* 18 B10
Seehausen, *Germany* 18 C7
Seeheim, *Namibia* 84 D2
Seekoei →, *S. Africa* 84 E4
Seelaw, *Germany* 18 C10
Sées, *France* 24 D7
Seesen, *Germany* 18 D6
Sefadu, *S. Leone* 78 D2
Seferihisar, *Turkey* 66 D2
Séfeto, *Mali* 78 C3
Sefrou, *Morocco* 74 B4
Sefwi Bekwai, *Ghana* 78 D4
Segamat, *Malaysia* 59 L4
Segarcea, *Romania* 38 E6
Segbwema, *S. Leone* 78 D2
Seget, *Indonesia* 57 E8
Seggueur, O. →, *Algeria* 75 B5
Segonzac, *France* 26 C3
Segorbe, *Spain* 28 F4
Ségou, *Mali* 78 C3
Segovia = Coco →, *Cent. Amer.* 116 D3
Segovia, *Colombia* 120 B3
Segovia, *Spain* 30 E6
Segovia □, *Spain* 30 E6
Segré, *France* 24 E6
Segre →, *Spain* 28 D5
Séguéla, *Ivory C.* 78 D3
Seguin, *U.S.A.* 109 L6
Segundo →, *Argentina* 126 C3
Segura →, *Spain* 29 G4
Segura, Sierra de, *Spain* 29 G2
Seh Qal'eh, *Iran* 65 C8
Sehitwa, *Botswana* 84 C3
Sehore, *India* 62 H7
Sehwan, *Pakistan* 62 F2
Şeica Mare, *Romania* 38 C7
Seiland, *Norway* 8 A17
Seiling, *U.S.A.* 109 G5
Seille →, *France* 27 B8
Seilles, *Belgium* 17 G6
Sein, I. de, *France* 24 D2
Seinäjoki →, *Finland* 8 E17
Seine →, *France* 24 C7
Seine, B. de la, *France* 24 C6
Seine-et-Marne □, *France* 25 D9
Seine-Maritime □, *France* 24 C7
Seine-St.-Denis □, *France* 25 D9
Seistan, *Iran* 65 D9
Sejerø, *Denmark* 11 J5
Sejerø Bugt, *Denmark* 11 J5
Seka, *Ethiopia* 77 F4
Sekayu, *Indonesia* 56 E2
Seke, *Tanzania* 82 C3
Sekenke, *Tanzania* 82 C3
Sekken Veøy, *Norway* 10 B1
Sekondi-Takoradi, *Ghana* 78 E4
Sekuma, *Botswana* 84 C3
Selah, *U.S.A.* 110 C3
Selama, *Malaysia* 59 K3
Selárgius, *Italy* 34 C2
Selaru, *Indonesia* 57 F8
Selb, *Germany* 19 E8
Selby, *U.K.* 12 D6
Selby, *U.S.A.* 108 C4
Selca, *Croatia* 33 E13
Selçuk, *Turkey* 66 E2
Selden, *U.S.A.* 108 F4
Sele →, *Italy* 35 B7
Selemdzha →, *Russia* 45 D13
Selenga = Selenge Mörön →, *Asia* 54 A5
Selenge Mörön →, *Asia* 54 A5
Selenica, *Albania* 39 J2
Selenter See, *Germany* 18 A6
Sélestat, *France* 25 D14
Seletan, Tg., *Indonesia* 56 E4
Seletin, *Romania* 38 B8
Selfridge, *U.S.A.* 108 B4
Sélibabi, *Mauritania* 78 B2
Seliger, Oz., *Russia* 40 C8
Seligman, *U.S.A.* 111 J7
Şelim, *Turkey* 43 F10
Selîma, El Wâhât el, *Sudan* 76 C2
Selinda Spillway, *Botswana* 84 B3
Selinoús, *Greece* 39 M4
Selizharovo, *Russia* 40 C8
Seljord, *Norway* 10 E2
Selkirk, *Canada* 101 C9
Selkirk, *U.K.* 14 F6
Selkirk I., *Canada* 101 C9
Selkirk Mts., *Canada* 100 C5
Selles-sur-Cher, *France* 25 E8
Selliá, *Greece* 37 D6
Sellières, *France* 25 F12
Sells, *U.S.A.* 111 L8
Sellye, *Hungary* 21 K7
Selma, *Ala., U.S.A.* 105 J2
Selma, *Calif., U.S.A.* 111 H4
Selma, *N.C., U.S.A.* 105 H6
Selmer, *U.S.A.* 105 H1
Selongey, *France* 25 E12
Selowandoma Falls, *Zimbabwe* 83 G3
Selpele, *Indonesia* 57 E8
Selsey Bill, *U.K.* 13 G7
Seltz, *France* 25 D15
Selu, *Indonesia* 57 F8
Sélune →, *France* 24 D5
Selva, *Argentina* 126 B3
Selva, *Italy* 33 B8
Selva, *Spain* 28 D6
Selvas, *Brazil* 124 B4
Selwyn, *Australia* 90 C3
Selwyn L., *Canada* 101 A8
Selwyn Ra., *Australia* 90 C3
Seman →, *Albania* 39 J2
Semara, *W. Sahara* 74 C2
Semarang, *Indonesia* 57 G14
Semau, *Indonesia* 57 F6
Sembabule, *Uganda* 82 C3
Sémé, *Senegal* 78 B2
Semeih, *Sudan* 77 E3
Semenov, *Russia* 41 C14
Semenovka, *Ukraine* 40 E8
Semenovka, *Ukraine* 42 B5
Semeru, *Indonesia* 57 H15
Semey = Semipalatinsk, *Kazakhstan* 44 D9
Semiluki, *Russia* 41 F11
Seminoe Reservoir, *U.S.A.* 110 E10
Seminole, *Okla., U.S.A.* 109 H6
Seminole, *Tex., U.S.A.* 109 J3
Semiozernoye, *Kazakhstan* 44 D7
Semipalatinsk, *Kazakhstan* 44 D9
Semirara Is., *Phil.* 55 F4
Semisopochnoi I., *U.S.A.* 96 C2
Semitau, *Indonesia* 56 D4
Semiyarskoye, *Kazakhstan* 44 D8
Semmering Pass, *Austria* 21 H5
Semnān, *Iran* 65 C7
Semnān □, *Iran* 65 C7
Semois →, *Europe* 17 J5
Semporna, *Malaysia* 57 D5
Semuda, *Indonesia* 56 E4
Semur-en-Auxois, *France* 25 E11
Sena, *Bolivia* 124 C4
Senā, *Iran* 65 D6
Sena, *Mozam.* 83 F3
Sena →, *Bolivia* 124 C4
Sena Madureira, *Brazil* 124 B4
Senador Pompeu, *Brazil* 122 C4
Senaja, *Malaysia* 56 C5
Senaki, *Georgia* 43 E10
Senanga, *Zambia* 84 B3
Senatobia, *U.S.A.* 109 H10
Sendafa, *Ethiopia* 77 F4
Sendai, *Kagoshima, Japan* 49 J5
Sendai, *Miyagi, Japan* 48 E10
Sendai-Wan, *Japan* 48 E10
Sendenhorst, *Germany* 18 D3
Seneca, *Oreg., U.S.A.* 110 D4
Seneca, *S.C., U.S.A.* 105 H4
Seneca Falls, *U.S.A.* 107 D8
Seneca L., *U.S.A.* 106 D8
Seneffe, *Belgium* 17 G4
Senegal ■, *W. Afr.* 78 C2
Senegal →, *W. Afr.* 78 B1
Senegambia, *Africa* 70 E2
Senekal, *S. Africa* 85 D4
Senftenberg, *Germany* 18 D10
Senga Hill, *Zambia* 83 D3
Senge Khambab = Indus →, *Pakistan* 62 G2
Sengerema □, *Tanzania* 82 C3
Sengiley, *Russia* 41 E16
Sengkang, *Indonesia* 57 E6
Sengua →, *Zimbabwe* 83 F2
Senguerr →, *Argentina* 128 C3
Senhor-do-Bonfim, *Brazil* 122 D3
Senica, *Slovak Rep.* 20 G7
Senigállia, *Italy* 33 E10
Senio →, *Italy* 33 D9
Senirkent, *Turkey* 66 D4
Senise, *Italy* 35 B9
Senj, *Croatia* 33 D11
Senja, *Norway* 8 B14
Senlis, *France* 25 C9
Senmonorom, *Cambodia* 58 F6
Sennâr, *Sudan* 77 E3
Senne →, *Belgium* 17 G4
Senneterre, *Canada* 98 C4
Senniquelle, *Liberia* 78 D3
Senno, *Belorussia* 40 D6
Sennori, *Italy* 34 B1
Seno, *Laos* 58 D5
Senonches, *France* 24 D8
Senorbì, *Italy* 34 C2
Senožeče, *Slovenia* 33 C11
Sens, *France* 25 D10
Senta, *Serbia* 21 K10
Sentery, *Zaïre* 82 D2
Sentinel, *U.S.A.* 111 K7
Sentolo, *Indonesia* 57 G14
Senya Beraku, *Ghana* 79 D4
Seo de Urgel, *Spain* 28 C6
Seohara, *India* 63 E8
Seoni, *India* 63 H8
Seoul = Sŏul, *S. Korea* 51 F14
Separation Point, *Canada* 99 B8
Sepīdān, *Iran* 65 D7
Sepo-ri, *N. Korea* 51 E14
Sepone, *Laos* 58 D6
Sept-Îles, *Canada* 99 B6
Septemvri, *Bulgaria* 38 G7
Sepúlveda, *Spain* 30 D7
Sequeros, *Spain* 30 E4
Sequim, *U.S.A.* 112 B3
Sequoia National Park, *U.S.A.* 111 H4
Serafimovich, *Russia* 43 B10
Seraing, *Belgium* 17 G7
Seraja, *Indonesia* 59 L7
Serakhis →, *Cyprus* 37 D11
Seram, *Indonesia* 57 E7
Seram Laut, Kepulauan, *Indonesia* 57 E8
Seram Sea, *Indonesia* 57 E7
Serang, *Indonesia* 57 G12
Serasan, *Indonesia* 59 L7
Seravezza, *Italy* 32 E7
Serbia □, *Yugoslavia* 21 M11
Serdo, *Ethiopia* 77 E5
Serdobsk, *Russia* 41 E14
Serëdka, *Russia* 40 B6
Şereflikoçhisar, *Turkey* 66 D5
Seregno, *Italy* 32 C6
Seremban, *Malaysia* 59 L3
Serengeti □, *Tanzania* 82 C3
Serengeti Plain, *Tanzania* 82 C3
Serenje, *Zambia* 83 E3
Sereth = Siret →, *Romania* 38 D11
Sergach, *Russia* 41 D14
Serge →, *Spain* 28 D5
Sergino, *Russia* 44 C7
Sergipe □, *Brazil* 122 D4
Sergiyev Posad, *Russia* 41 C11
Seria, *Brunei* 56 D4
Serian, *Malaysia* 56 D4
Seriate, *Italy* 32 C6
Seribu, Kepulauan, *Indonesia* 56 F3
Sérifontaine, *France* 25 C8
Sérifos, *Greece* 39 M7
Sérignan, *France* 26 E7
Serik, *Turkey* 66 E4
Seringapatam Reef, *Australia* 88 B3
Sermaize-les-Bains, *France* 25 D11
Sermata, *Indonesia* 57 F7
Sérmide, *Italy* 33 C8
Sernovodsk, *Russia* 41 E17
Serny Zavod, *Turkmenistan* 44 F6
Serón, *Spain* 29 H2
Serós, *Spain* 28 D5
Serov, *Russia* 44 D7
Serowe, *Botswana* 84 C4
Serpa, *Portugal* 31 H3
Serpeddi, Punta, *Italy* 34 C2
Serpentara, *Italy* 34 C2
Serpentine, *Australia* 89 F2
Serpentine Lakes, *Australia* 89 E4
Serpis →, *Spain* 29 G4
Serpukhov, *Russia* 41 D10
Serra do Navio, *Brazil* 121 C7
Serra San Bruno, *Italy* 35 D9
Serra Talhada, *Brazil* 122 C4
Serracapriola, *Italy* 35 A8
Serradilla, *Spain* 30 F4
Sérrai, *Greece* 39 H6
Serramanna, *Italy* 34 C1
Serrat, C., *Tunisia* 75 A6
Serre-Ponçon, L. de, *France* 27 D10
Serres, *France* 27 D9
Serrezuela, *Argentina* 126 C2
Serrinha, *Brazil* 123 D4
Serrita, *Brazil* 122 C4
Sersale, *Italy* 35 C9
Sertã, *Portugal* 30 F2
Sertânia, *Brazil* 122 C4
Sertanópolis, *Brazil* 127 A5
Sêrtar, *China* 52 A3
Sertig, *Switz.* 23 C9
Serua, *Indonesia* 57 F8
Serui, *Indonesia* 57 E9
Serule, *Botswana* 84 C4
Sérvia, *Greece* 39 J4
Sese Is., *Uganda* 82 C3
Sesepe, *Indonesia* 57 E7
Sesfontein, *Namibia* 84 B1
Sesheke, *Zambia* 84 B3
Sesia →, *Italy* 32 C5
Sesimbra, *Portugal* 31 G1
Sessa Aurunca, *Italy* 34 A6
S'estañol, *Spain* 36 B9
Sesto San Giovanni, *Italy* 32 C6
Sestri Levante, *Italy* 32 D6
Sestrières, *Italy* 32 D3
Sestrunj, *Croatia* 33 D12
Sestu, *Italy* 34 C2
Sesvenna, *Switz.* 23 C10
Setana, *Japan* 48 C9
Sète, *France* 26 E7
Sete Lagôas, *Brazil* 123 E3
Sétif, *Algeria* 75 A6
Seto, *Japan* 49 G8
Setonaikai, *Japan* 49 G6
Settat, *Morocco* 74 B3
Setté-Cama, *Gabon* 80 E1
Séttimo Tor, *Italy* 32 C4
Setting L., *Canada* 101 B9
Settle, *U.K.* 12 C5
Settlement Pt., *Bahamas* 105 M6
Setto Calende, *Italy* 32 C5
Setúbal, *Portugal* 31 G2
Setúbal □, *Portugal* 31 G2
Setúbal, B. de, *Portugal* 31 G2
Seugne →, *France* 26 C3
Seulimeum, *Indonesia* 56 C1
Seuzach, *Switz.* 23 A7
Sevan, *Armenia* 43 F11
Sevan, Ozero, *Armenia* 43 F11
Sevastopol, *Ukraine* 42 D5
Sevelen, *Switz.* 23 B8
Seven Emu, *Australia* 90 B2
Seven Sisters, *Canada* 100 C3
Sevenum, *Neths.* 17 F8
Sever →, *Spain* 31 F3
Sévérac-le-Château, *France* 26 D7
Severn →, *Canada* 98 A2
Severn →, *U.K.* 13 F5
Severn L., *Canada* 98 B1
Severnaya Zemlya, *Russia* 45 B10
Severo-Kurilsk, *Russia* 45 D16
Severo-Yeniseyskiy, *Russia* 45 C10
Severodonetsk, *Ukraine* 43 B8
Severodvinsk, *Russia* 44 C4
Sevier, *U.S.A.* 111 G7
Sevier →, *U.S.A.* 111 G7
Sevier L., *U.S.A.* 110 G7
Sevilla, *Colombia* 120 C2
Sevilla, *Spain* 31 H5
Sevilla □, *Spain* 31 H5
Seville = Sevilla, *Spain* 31 H5
Sevnica, *Slovenia* 33 B12
Sèvre-Nantaise →, *France* 24 E5
Sèvre-Niortaise →, *France* 26 B3
Sevsk, *Russia* 40 E9
Seward, *Alaska, U.S.A.* 96 B5
Seward, *Nebr., U.S.A.* 108 E6
Seward Pen., *U.S.A.* 96 B3
Sewell, *Chile* 126 C1
Sewer, *Indonesia* 57 F8
Sewickley, *U.S.A.* 106 F4
Sexbierum, *Neths.* 16 B6
Sexsmith, *Canada* 100 B5
Seychelles ■, *Ind. Oc.* 47 K9
Seyðisfjörður, *Iceland* 8 D7
Seydvān, *Iran* 64 B5
Seyfe Gölü, *Turkey* 66 D6
Seyhan Barajı, *Turkey* 66 E6
Seyitgazi, *Turkey* 66 D4
Seym →, *Ukraine* 40 F8
Seymchan, *Russia* 45 C16
Seymour, *Australia* 91 F4
Seymour, *S. Africa* 85 E4
Seymour, *Conn., U.S.A.* 107 E11
Seymour, *Ind., U.S.A.* 104 F3
Seymour, *Tex., U.S.A.* 109 J5
Seymour, *Wis., U.S.A.* 104 C1
Seyne, *France* 27 D10
Seyssel, *France* 27 C9
Sežana, *Slovenia* 33 C10
Sézanne, *France* 25 D10
Sezze, *Italy* 34 A6
Sfax, *Tunisia* 75 B7
Sfintu Gheorghe, *Romania* 38 D8
Sfintu Gheorghe, Braţul →, *Romania* 38 E12
Sha Xi →, *China* 53 D12
Sha Xian, *China* 53 D11
Shaanxi □, *China* 50 G5
Shaba □, *Zaïre* 82 D2
Shabunda, *Zaïre* 82 C2
Shache, *China* 54 C2
Shackleton Ice Shelf, *Antarctica* 5 C8
Shackleton Inlet, *Antarctica* 5 E11
Shādegān, *Iran* 65 D6
Shadi, *China* 53 D10
Shadi, *India* 63 C7
Shadrinsk, *Russia* 44 D7
Shaffa, *Nigeria* 79 C7
Shafter, *Calif., U.S.A.* 113 K7
Shafter, *Tex., U.S.A.* 109 L2
Shaftesbury, *U.K.* 13 F5
Shagamu, *Nigeria* 79 D5
Shagram, *Pakistan* 63 A5
Shah Bunder, *Pakistan* 62 G2
Shahabad, *Punjab, India* 62 D7
Shahabad, *Raj., India* 62 G7
Shahabad, *Ut. P., India* 63 F8
Shahadpur, *Pakistan* 62 G3
Shahba, *Syria* 69 C5
Shahdād, *Iran* 65 D8
Shahdadkot, *Pakistan* 62 F2
Shahe, *China* 50 F8
Shahganj, *India* 63 F10
Shahgarh, *India* 60 F6
Shaḥḥāt, *Libya* 73 B9
Shahjahanpur, *India* 63 F8
Shahpur, *India* 62 H7
Shahpur, *Pakistan* 62 E3
Shahpura, *India* 63 H9
Shahr Kord, *Iran* 65 C6
Shāhrakht, *Iran* 65 C9
Shahrig, *Pakistan* 62 D2
Shahukou, *China* 50 D7

Shaikhabad, *Afghan.* 62 B3
Shajapur, *India* 62 H7
Shakargarh, *Pakistan* 62 C6
Shakawe, *Botswana* 84 B3
Shaker Heights, *U.S.A.* 106 E3
Shakhty, *Russia* 43 C9
Shakhunya, *Russia* 41 C15
Shaki, *Nigeria* 79 D5
Shakopee, *U.S.A.* 108 C8
Shala, L., *Ethiopia* 77 F4
Shallow Lake, *Canada* 106 B3
Shaluli Shan, *China* 52 B2
Shām, *Iran* 65 E8
Shamâl Dârfûr □, *Sudan* 77 D2
Shamâl Kordofân □, *Sudan* 77 D2
Shamattawa, *Canada* 101 B10
Shamattawa →, *Canada* 98 A2
Shambe, *Sudan* 77 F3
Shambu, *Ethiopia* 77 F4
Shamīl, *Iran* 65 E8
Shamkhor, *Azerbaijan* 43 F12
Shāmkūh, *Iran* 65 C8
Shamli, *India* 62 E7
Shamo = Gobi, *Asia* 50 C5
Shamo, L., *Ethiopia* 77 F4
Shamokin, *U.S.A.* 107 F8
Shamrock, *U.S.A.* 109 H4
Shamva, *Zimbabwe* 83 F3
Shan □, *Burma* 61 J21
Shan Xian, *China* 50 G9
Shanan →, *Ethiopia* 77 F5
Shanchengzhen, *China* 51 C13
Shāndak, *Iran* 65 D9
Shandon, *U.S.A.* 112 K6
Shandong □, *China* 51 F10
Shandong Bandao, *China* 51 F11
Shang Xian, *China* 50 H5
Shangalowe, *Zaïre* 83 E2
Shangani →, *Zimbabwe* 83 F2
Shangbancheng, *China* 51 D10
Shangcai, *China* 53 A10
Shangcheng, *China* 53 B10
Shangchuan Dao, *China* 53 G9
Shangdu, *China* 50 D7
Shanggao, *China* 53 C10
Shanghai, *China* 53 B13
Shanghang, *China* 53 E11
Shanghe, *China* 51 F9
Shangjin, *China* 53 A8
Shanglin, *China* 52 F7
Shangnan, *China* 50 H6
Shangqiu, *China* 50 G8
Shangrao, *China* 53 C11
Shangshui, *China* 50 H8
Shangsi, *China* 52 F6
Shangyou, *China* 53 E10
Shangzhi, *China* 51 B14
Shanhetun, *China* 51 B14
Shani, *Nigeria* 79 C7
Shaniko, *U.S.A.* 110 D3
Shannon, *Greenland* 4 B7
Shannon, *N.Z.* 87 J5
Shannon →, *Ireland* 15 D2
Shansi = Shanxi □, *China* 50 F7
Shantar, Ostrov Bolshoy, *Russia* 45 D14
Shantipur, *India* 63 H13
Shantou, *China* 53 F11
Shantung = Shandong □, *China* 51 F10
Shanxi □, *China* 50 F7
Shanyang, *China* 50 H5
Shanyin, *China* 50 E7
Shaoguan, *China* 53 E9
Shaowu, *China* 53 D11
Shaoxing, *China* 53 C13
Shaoyang, *Hunan, China* 53 D8
Shaoyang, *Hunan, China* 53 D8
Shapinsay, *U.K.* 14 B6
Shaqra', *Si. Arabia* 64 E5
Shaqrā', *Yemen* 68 E4
Sharafa, *Sudan* 77 E2
Sharbot Lake, *Canada* 107 B8
Shari, *Japan* 48 C12
Sharjah = Ash Shāriqah, *U.A.E.* 65 E7
Shark B., *Australia* 89 E1
Sharm el Sheikh, *Egypt* 76 B3
Sharon, *Mass., U.S.A.* 107 D13
Sharon, *Pa., U.S.A.* 106 E4
Sharon Springs, *U.S.A.* 108 F4
Sharp Pt., *Australia* 90 A3
Sharpe L., *Canada* 101 C10
Sharpsville, *U.S.A.* 106 E4
Sharq el Istiwa'iya □, *Sudan* 77 F3
Sharya, *Russia* 41 B14
Shasha, *Ethiopia* 77 F4
Shashemene, *Ethiopia* 77 F4
Shashi, *Botswana* 85 C4
Shashi, *China* 53 B9
Shashi →, *Africa* 83 G2
Shasta, Mt., *U.S.A.* 110 F2
Shasta L., *U.S.A.* 110 F2
Shatsk, *Russia* 41 D12
Shatt al'Arab →, *Iraq* 65 D6
Shattuck, *U.S.A.* 109 G5
Shatura, *Russia* 41 D11
Shaumyani, *Georgia* 43 F11
Shaunavon, *Canada* 101 D7
Shaver L., *U.S.A.* 112 H7
Shaw →, *Australia* 88 D2
Shaw I., *Australia* 90 C4
Shawan, *China* 54 B3
Shawanaga, *Canada* 106 A4
Shawano, *U.S.A.* 104 C1
Shawinigan, *Canada* 98 C5
Shawnee, *U.S.A.* 109 H6
Shaybārā, *Si. Arabia* 64 E3
Shayib el Banat, Gebel, *Egypt* 76 B3
Shaykh Sa'īd, *Iraq* 64 C5
Shchekino, *Russia* 41 D10
Shcherbakov = Rybinsk, *Russia* 41 B11
Shchigri, *Russia* 41 F10
Shchors, *Ukraine* 40 F7
Shchuchiosk, *Kazakhstan* 44 D8
She Xian, *Anhui, China* 53 C12
She Xian, *Hebei, China* 50 F7
Shea, *Guyana* 121 C6
Shebekino, *Russia* 41 F10
Shebele = Scebeli, Wabi →, *Somali Rep.* 68 G3
Sheboygan, *U.S.A.* 104 D2
Shediac, *Canada* 99 C7
Sheelin, L., *Ireland* 15 C4
Sheep Haven, *Ireland* 15 A4
Sheerness, *U.K.* 13 F8
Sheet Harbour, *Canada* 99 D7
Sheffield, *U.K.* 12 D6
Sheffield, *Ala., U.S.A.* 105 H2
Sheffield, *Mass., U.S.A.* 107 D11
Sheffield, *Pa., U.S.A.* 106 E5
Sheffield, *Tex., U.S.A.* 109 K4
Sheho, *Canada* 101 C8
Shehojele, *Ethiopia* 77 E4
Shehong, *China* 52 B5
Shehuen →, *Argentina* 128 C3
Sheikhpura, *India* 63 G11
Shek Hasan, *Ethiopia* 77 E4
Shekhupura, *Pakistan* 62 D5
Sheki, *Azerbaijan* 43 F12
Sheksna →, *Russia* 41 B11
Shelburne, *N.S., Canada* 99 D6
Shelburne, *Ont., Canada* 98 D3
Shelburne, *U.S.A.* 107 B11
Shelburne B., *Australia* 90 A3
Shelburne Falls, *U.S.A.* 107 D12
Shelby, *Mich., U.S.A.* 104 D2
Shelby, *Mont., U.S.A.* 110 B8
Shelby, *N.C., U.S.A.* 105 H5
Shelby, *Ohio, U.S.A.* 106 F2
Shelbyville, *Ill., U.S.A.* 108 F10
Shelbyville, *Ind., U.S.A.* 104 F3
Shelbyville, *Tenn., U.S.A.* 105 H2
Sheldon, *U.S.A.* 108 D7
Sheldrake, *Canada* 99 B7
Shelikhova, Zaliv, *Russia* 45 D16
Shell Lake, *Canada* 101 C7
Shell Lakes, *Australia* 89 E4
Shellbrook, *Canada* 101 C7
Shellharbour, *Australia* 91 E5
Shelling Rocks, *Ireland* 15 E1
Shelon →, *Russia* 40 B7
Shelton, *Conn., U.S.A.* 107 E11
Shelton, *Wash., U.S.A.* 112 C3
Shemakha, *Azerbaijan* 43 F13
Shen Xian, *China* 50 F8
Shenandoah, *Iowa, U.S.A.* 108 E7
Shenandoah, *Pa., U.S.A.* 107 F8
Shenandoah, *Va., U.S.A.* 104 F6
Shenandoah →, *U.S.A.* 104 F7
Shenchi, *China* 50 E7
Shendam, *Nigeria* 79 D6
Shendî, *Sudan* 77 D3
Sheng Xian, *China* 53 C13
Shengfang, *China* 50 E9
Shëngjergji, *Albania* 39 H3
Shëngjini, *Albania* 39 H2
Shenjingzi, *China* 51 B13
Shenmu, *China* 50 E6
Shennongjia, *China* 53 B8
Shenqiu, *China* 50 H8
Shenqiucheng, *China* 50 H8
Shensi = Shaanxi □, *China* 50 G5
Shenyang, *China* 51 D12
Shepetovka, *Ukraine* 40 F5
Shepopur Kalan, *India* 60 G10
Shepparton, *Australia* 91 F4
Sheqi, *China* 50 H7
Sher Qila, *Pakistan* 63 A6
Sherborne, *U.K.* 13 G5
Sherbro I., *S. Leone* 78 D2
Sherbrooke, *Canada* 99 C5
Shereik, *Sudan* 76 D3
Sheridan, *Ark., U.S.A.* 109 H8
Sheridan, *Wyo., U.S.A.* 110 D10
Sherkot, *India* 63 E8
Sherman, *U.S.A.* 109 J6
Sherridon, *Canada* 101 B8
Sherwood, *N. Dak., U.S.A.* 108 A4
Sherwood, *Tex., U.S.A.* 109 K4
Sherwood Forest, *U.K.* 12 D6
Sheslay, *Canada* 100 B2
Sheslay →, *Canada* 100 B2
Shethanei L., *Canada* 101 B9
Shetland □, *U.K.* 14 A7
Shetland Is., *U.K.* 14 A7
Shewa □, *Ethiopia* 77 F4
Shewa Gimira, *Ethiopia* 77 F4
Sheyenne, *U.S.A.* 108 B5
Sheyenne →, *U.S.A.* 108 B6
Shibām, *Yemen* 68 D4
Shibata, *Japan* 48 F9
Shibecha, *Japan* 48 C12
Shibetsu, *Japan* 48 B11
Shibîn el Kôm, *Egypt* 76 H7
Shibîn el Qanâtir, *Egypt* 76 H7
Shibing, *China* 52 D7
Shibogama L., *Canada* 98 B2
Shibushi, *Japan* 49 J5
Shicheng, *China* 53 D11
Shickshock Mts. = Chic-Chocs, Mts., *Canada* 99 C6
Shidao, *China* 51 F12
Shidian, *China* 52 E2
Shido, *Japan* 49 G7
Shiel, L., *U.K.* 14 E3
Shield, C., *Australia* 90 A2
Shiga □, *Japan* 49 G8
Shigaib, *Sudan* 73 E9
Shigu, *China* 52 D2
Shiguaigou, *China* 50 D6
Shihchiachuangi = Shijiazhuang, *China* 50 E8
Shijiazhuang, *China* 50 E8
Shijiu Hu, *China* 53 B12
Shikarpur, *India* 62 E8
Shikarpur, *Pakistan* 62 F3
Shikoku □, *Japan* 49 H6
Shikoku-Sanchi, *Japan* 49 H6
Shilabo, *Ethiopia* 68 F3
Shiliguri, *India* 61 F16
Shilka, *Russia* 45 D12
Shilka →, *Russia* 45 D13
Shillelagh, *Ireland* 15 D5
Shillong, *India* 61 G17
Shilo, *Jordan* 69 C4
Shilong, *China* 53 F9
Shilou, *China* 50 F6
Shilovo, *Russia* 41 D12
Shimabara, *Japan* 49 H5
Shimada, *Japan* 49 G9
Shimane □, *Japan* 49 G6
Shimanovsk, *Russia* 45 D13
Shimen, *China* 53 C8
Shimenjie, *China* 53 C11
Shimian, *China* 52 C4
Shimizu, *Japan* 49 G9
Shimodate, *Japan* 49 F9
Shimoga, *India* 60 N9
Shimoni, *Kenya* 82 C4
Shimonoseki, *Japan* 49 H5
Shimpuru Rapids, *Angola* 84 B2
Shimsk, *Russia* 40 B7
Shin, L., *U.K.* 14 C4
Shin-Tone →, *Japan* 49 G10
Shinan, *China* 52 F7
Shinano →, *Japan* 49 F9
Shīndand, *Afghan.* 60 C3
Shingleton, *U.S.A.* 98 C2
Shingū, *Japan* 49 H7
Shinjō, *Japan* 48 E10
Shinkafe, *Nigeria* 79 C6
Shinshār, *Syria* 69 A5
Shinyanga, *Tanzania* 82 C3
Shinyanga □, *Tanzania* 82 C3
Shiogama, *Japan* 48 E10
Shiojiri, *Japan* 49 F8
Ship I., *U.S.A.* 109 K10
Shipehenski Prokhod, *Bulgaria* 38 G8
Shiping, *China* 52 F4
Shipki La, *India* 60 D11
Shippegan, *Canada* 99 C7
Shippensburg, *U.S.A.* 106 F7
Shiprock, *U.S.A.* 111 H9
Shiqian, *China* 52 D7
Shiqma, N. →, *Israel* 69 D3
Shiquan, *China* 50 H5
Shīr Kūh, *Iran* 65 D7
Shiragami-Misaki, *Japan* 48 D10
Shirakawa, *Fukushima, Japan* 49 F10
Shirakawa, *Gifu, Japan* 49 F8
Shirane-San, *Gumma, Japan* 49 F9
Shirane-San, *Yamanashi, Japan* 49 G9
Shiraoi, *Japan* 48 C10
Shīrāz, *Iran* 65 D7
Shirbin, *Egypt* 76 H7
Shire →, *Africa* 83 F4
Shiretoko-Misaki, *Japan* 48 B12
Shirinab →, *Pakistan* 62 D2
Shiringushi, *Russia* 41 E13
Shiriya-Zaki, *Japan* 48 D10
Shiroishi, *Japan* 48 E10
Shīrvān, *Iran* 65 B8
Shirwa, L. = Chilwa, L., *Malawi* 83 F4
Shishou, *China* 53 C9
Shitai, *China* 53 B11
Shivpuri, *India* 62 G7
Shixian, *China* 51 C15
Shixing, *China* 53 E10
Shiyan, *China* 53 A8
Shiyata, *Egypt* 76 B2
Shizhu, *China* 52 C7
Shizong, *China* 52 E5
Shizuishan, *China* 50 E4
Shizuoka, *Japan* 49 G9
Shizuoka □, *Japan* 49 G9
Shklov, *Belorussia* 40 D7
Shkoder = Shkodra, *Albania* 38 G2
Shkodra, *Albania* 38 G2
Shkumbini →, *Albania* 39 H2
Shmidta, O., *Russia* 45 A10
Shō-Gawa →, *Japan* 49 F8
Shoal Lake, *Canada* 101 C8
Shōdo-Shima, *Japan* 49 G7
Shoeburyness, *U.K.* 13 F8
Sholapur = Solapur, *India* 60 L9
Shologontsy, *Russia* 45 C12
Shōmrōn, *Jordan* 69 C4
Shoshone, *Calif., U.S.A.* 113 K10
Shoshone, *Idaho, U.S.A.* 110 E6
Shoshone L., *U.S.A.* 110 D8
Shoshone Mts., *U.S.A.* 110 G5
Shoshong, *Botswana* 84 C4
Shoshoni, *U.S.A.* 110 E9
Shostka, *Ukraine* 40 F8
Shou Xian, *China* 53 A11
Shouchang, *China* 53 C12
Shouguang, *China* 51 F10
Shouning, *China* 53 D12
Shouyang, *China* 50 F7
Show Low, *U.S.A.* 111 J9
Shpola, *Ukraine* 42 B4
Shreveport, *U.S.A.* 109 J8
Shrewsbury, *U.K.* 12 E5
Shrirampur, *India* 63 H13
Shropshire □, *U.K.* 13 E5
Shuangbai, *China* 52 E3
Shuangcheng, *China* 51 B14
Shuangfeng, *China* 53 D9
Shuanggou, *China* 51 G9
Shuangjiang, *China* 52 F2
Shuangliao, *China* 51 C12
Shuangshanzi, *China* 51 D10
Shuangyang, *China* 51 C13
Shuangyashan, *China* 54 B8
Shucheng, *China* 53 B11
Shuguri Falls, *Tanzania* 83 D4
Shuicheng, *China* 52 D5
Shuiji, *China* 53 D12
Shuiye, *China* 50 F8
Shujalpur, *India* 62 H7
Shukpa Kunzang, *India* 63 B8
Shulan, *China* 51 B14
Shule, *China* 54 C2
Shumagin Is., *U.S.A.* 96 C4
Shumerlya, *Russia* 41 D15
Shumikha, *Russia* 44 D7
Shunchang, *China* 53 D11
Shunde, *China* 53 F9
Shungay, *Kazakhstan* 43 B12
Shungnak, *U.S.A.* 96 B4
Shuo Xian, *China* 50 E7
Shūr →, *Iran* 65 D7
Shūr Āb, *Iran* 65 C6
Shūr Gaz, *Iran* 65 D8
Shūrāb, *Iran* 65 C8
Shūrjestān, *Iran* 65 D7
Shurma, *Russia* 41 C17
Shurugwi, *Zimbabwe* 83 F3
Shūsf, *Iran* 65 D9
Shūshtar, *Iran* 65 D6
Shuswap L., *Canada* 100 C5
Shuya, *Russia* 41 C12
Shuyang, *China* 51 G10
Shūzū, *Iran* 65 D7
Shwebo, *Burma* 61 H19
Shwegu, *Burma* 61 G20
Shweli →, *Burma* 61 H20
Shymkent = Chimkent, *Kazakhstan* 44 E7
Shyok, *India* 63 B8
Shyok →, *Pakistan* 63 B6
Si Chon, *Thailand* 59 H2
Si Kiang = Xi Jiang →, *China* 53 F9
Si-ngan = Xi'an, *China* 50 G5
Si Prachan, *Thailand* 58 E3
Si Racha, *Thailand* 58 F3
Si Xian, *China* 51 H9
Siahan Range, *Pakistan* 60 F4
Siaksrindrapura, *Indonesia* 56 D2
Sialkot, *Pakistan* 62 C6
Siam = Thailand ■, *Asia* 58 E4
Siantan, P., *Indonesia* 59 L6
Siàpo →, *Venezuela* 120 C4
Sīāreh, *Iran* 65 D9
Siargao, *Phil.* 55 G7
Siari, *Pakistan* 63 B7
Siasi, *Phil.* 57 C6
Siasi I., *Phil.* 55 J4
Siátista, *Greece* 39 J4
Šiau, *Indonesia* 57 D7
Šiauliai, *Lithuania* 40 D3
Siaya □, *Kenya* 82 B3
Siazan, *Azerbaijan* 43 F13
Sibâi, Gebel el, *Egypt* 76 B3
Sibari, *Italy* 35 C9
Sibasa, *S. Africa* 85 C5
Šibayi, L., *S. Africa* 85 D5
Šibenik, *Croatia* 33 E12
Siberia, *Russia* 4 D13
Siberut, *Indonesia* 56 E1
Sibi, *Pakistan* 62 E2
Sibil, *Indonesia* 57 E10
Sibiti, *Congo* 80 E2
Sibiu, *Romania* 38 D7
Sibley, *Iowa, U.S.A.* 108 D7
Sibley, *La., U.S.A.* 109 J8
Sibolga, *Indonesia* 56 D1
Sibret, *Belgium* 17 J7
Sibsagar, *India* 61 F19
Sibu, *Malaysia* 56 D4
Sibuco, *Phil.* 55 H5
Sibuguey B., *Phil.* 55 H5
Sibutu, *Phil.* 57 D5
Sibutu Group, *Phil.* 55 J3
Sibutu Passage, *E. Indies* 57 D5
Sibuyan, *Phil.* 55 E5
Sibuyan Sea, *Phil.* 55 E5
Sicamous, *Canada* 100 C5
Sichuan □, *China* 52 B5
Sicilia, *Italy* 35 E7
Sicilia □, *Italy* 35 E7
Sicilia, Canale di, *Italy* 34 E5
Sicilian Channel = Sicilia, Canale di, *Italy* 34 E5
Sicily = Sicilia, *Italy* 35 E7
Sicuani, *Peru* 124 C3
Siculiana, *Italy* 34 E6
Sidamo □, *Ethiopia* 77 G4
Sidaouet, *Niger* 79 B6
Sidári, *Greece* 37 A3
Siddeburen, *Neths.* 16 B9
Siddhapur, *India* 62 H5
Siddipet, *India* 60 K11
Side, *Turkey* 66 E4
Sidéradougou, *Burkina Faso* 78 C4
Siderno Marina, *Italy* 35 D9
Sídheros, Ákra, *Greece* 37 D8
Sidhirókastron, *Greece* 39 H6
Sîdi Abd el Rahmân, *Egypt* 76 H6
Sîdi Barrâni, *Egypt* 76 A2
Sidi-bel-Abbès, *Algeria* 75 A4
Sidi Bennour, *Morocco* 74 B3
Sidi Haneish, *Egypt* 76 A2
Sidi Kacem, *Morocco* 74 B3
Sidi Omar, *Egypt* 76 A1
Sidi Slimane, *Morocco* 74 B3
Sidi Smaïl, *Morocco* 74 B3
Sidlaw Hills, *U.K.* 14 E5
Sidley, Mt., *Antarctica* 5 D14
Sidmouth, *U.K.* 13 G4
Sidmouth, C., *Australia* 90 A3
Sidney, *Canada* 100 D4
Sidney, *Mont., U.S.A.* 108 B2
Sidney, *N.Y., U.S.A.* 107 D9
Sidney, *Nebr., U.S.A.* 108 E3
Sidney, *Ohio, U.S.A.* 104 E3
Sidoarjo, *Indonesia* 57 G15
Sidon = Saydā, *Lebanon* 69 B4
Sidra, G. of = Surt, Khalīj, *Libya* 73 B8
Siedlce, *Poland* 20 C12
Sieg →, *Germany* 18 E3
Siegburg, *Germany* 18 E3
Siegen, *Germany* 18 E4
Siem Pang, *Cambodia* 58 E6
Siem Reap, *Cambodia* 58 F4
Siena, *Italy* 33 E8
Sieradź, *Poland* 20 D8
Sierck-les-Bains, *France* 25 C13
Sierpc, *Poland* 20 C9
Sierpe, Bocas de la, *Venezuela* 121 B5
Sierra Blanca, *U.S.A.* 111 L11
Sierra Blanca Peak, *U.S.A.* 111 K11
Sierra City, *U.S.A.* 112 F6
Sierra Colorada, *Argentina* 128 B3
Sierra de Yeguas, *Spain* 31 H6
Sierra Gorda, *Chile* 126 A2
Sierra Grande, *Argentina* 128 B3
Sierra Leone ■, *W. Afr.* 78 D2
Sierra Madre, *Mexico* 115 D6
Sierra Mojada, *Mexico* 114 B4
Sierraville, *U.S.A.* 112 F6
Sierre, *Switz.* 22 D5
Sif Fatima, *Algeria* 75 B6
Sífnos, *Greece* 39 N7
Sifton, *Canada* 101 C8
Sifton Pass, *Canada* 100 B3
Sig, *Algeria* 75 A4
Sigdal, *Norway* 10 D3
Sigean, *France* 26 E6
Sighetu-Marmatiei, *Romania* 38 B6
Sighişoara, *Romania* 38 C7
Sigli, *Indonesia* 56 C1
Siglufjörður, *Iceland* 8 C4
Sigmaringen, *Germany* 19 G5
Signakhi, *Georgia* 43 F11
Signal, *U.S.A.* 113 L13
Signal Pk., *U.S.A.* 113 M12
Signau, *Switz.* 22 C5
Signy-l'Abbaye, *France* 25 C11
Sigsig, *Ecuador* 120 D2
Sigtuna, *Sweden* 10 E11
Sigüenza, *Spain* 28 D2
Siguiri, *Guinea* 78 C3
Sigulda, *Latvia* 40 C4
Sigurd, *U.S.A.* 111 G8
Sihanoukville = Kompong Som, *Cambodia* 59 G4
Sihaus, *Peru* 124 B2
Sihui, *China* 53 F9
Siirt, *Turkey* 67 E9
Siirt □, *Turkey* 67 E9
Sijarira Ra., *Zimbabwe* 83 F2
Sikao, *Thailand* 59 J2
Sikar, *India* 62 F6
Sikasso, *Mali* 78 C3
Sikeston, *U.S.A.* 109 G10
Sikhote Alin, Khrebet, *Russia* 45 E14
Sikhote Alin Ra. = Sikhote Alin, Khrebet, *Russia* 45 E14
Sikiá., *Greece* 39 J6
Síkinos, *Greece* 39 N8
Sikkani Chief →, *Canada* 100 B4
Sikkim □, *India* 61 F16
Sikotu-Ko, *Japan* 48 C10
Sil →, *Spain* 30 C3
Silacayoapan, *Mexico* 115 D5
Silandro, *Italy* 32 B7
Silay, *Phil.* 55 F5
Silba, *Croatia* 33 D11
Silchar, *India* 61 G18
Silcox, *Canada* 101 B10
Şile, *Turkey* 66 C3
Silenrieux, *Belgium* 17 H4

Siler City, *U.S.A.* 105 H6
Silesia = Śląsk, *Poland* 20 E6
Silet, *Algeria* 75 D5
Silgarhi Doti, *Nepal* 63 E9
Silghat, *India* 61 F18
Silifke, *Turkey* 66 E5
Siliguri = Shiliguri, *India* 61 F16
Siling Co, *China* 54 C3
Silíqua, *Italy* 34 C1
Silistra, *Bulgaria* 38 E10
Silivri, *Turkey* 66 C3
Siljan, *Sweden* 9 F13
Silkeborg, *Denmark* 11 H3
Sillajhuay, Cordillera, *Chile* 124 D4
Sillé-le-Guillaume, *France* 24 D6
Sillustani, *Peru* 124 D3
Siloam Springs, *U.S.A.* 109 G7
Silopi, *Turkey* 67 E10
Silsbee, *U.S.A.* 109 K7
Šilute, *Lithuania* 40 D2
Silva Porto = Kuito, *Angola* 81 G3
Silvan, *Turkey* 67 D9
Silvaplana, *Switz.* 23 D9
Silver City, *N. Mex., U.S.A.* 111 K9
Silver City, *Nev., U.S.A.* 110 G4
Silver Cr. →, *U.S.A.* 110 E4
Silver Creek, *U.S.A.* 106 D5
Silver L., *Calif., U.S.A.* 112 G6
Silver L., *Calif., U.S.A.* 113 K10
Silver Lake, *U.S.A.* 110 E3
Silver Streams, *S. Africa* 84 D3
Silverton, *Colo., U.S.A.* 111 H10
Silverton, *Tex., U.S.A.* 109 H4
Silves, *Portugal* 31 H2
Silvi, *Italy* 33 F11
Silvia, *Colombia* 120 C2
Silvies →, *U.S.A.* 110 E4
Silvolde, *Neths.* 16 E8
Silvretta-Gruppe, *Switz.* 23 C10
Silwa Bahari, *Egypt* 76 C3
Silz, *Austria* 19 H6
Sim, C., *Morocco* 74 B3
Simanggang, *Malaysia* 56 D4
Simao, *China* 52 F3
Simão Dias, *Brazil* 122 D4
Simard, L., *Canada* 98 C4
Simav, *Turkey* 66 D3
Simba, *Tanzania* 82 C4
Simbach, *Germany* 19 G9
Simbirsk, *Russia* 41 D16
Simbo, *Tanzania* 82 C2
Simcoe, *Canada* 98 D3
Simcoe, L., *Canada* 98 D4
Simenga, *Russia* 45 C11
Simeto →, *Italy* 35 E8
Simeulue, *Indonesia* 56 D1
Simferopol, *Ukraine* 42 D6
Sími, *Greece* 39 N10
Simi Valley, *U.S.A.* 113 L8
Simikot, *Nepal* 63 E9
Simití, *Colombia* 120 B3
Simla, *India* 62 D7
Şimleu-Silvaniei, *Romania* 38 B5
Simme →, *Switz.* 22 C4
Simmern, *Germany* 19 F3
Simmie, *Canada* 101 D7
Simmler, *U.S.A.* 113 K7
Simões, *Brazil* 122 C3
Simojärvi, *Finland* 8 C19
Simojoki →, *Finland* 8 D18
Simojovel, *Mexico* 115 D6
Simonette →, *Canada* 100 B5
Simonstown, *S. Africa* 84 E2
Simplício Mendes, *Brazil* 122 C3
Simplon, *Switz.* 22 D6
Simplon Pass = Simplonpass, *Switz.* 22 D6
Simplon Tunnel, *Switz.* 22 D6
Simplonpass, *Switz.* 22 D6
Simpson Desert, *Australia* 90 D2
Simpungdong, *N. Korea* 51 D15
Simunjan, *Malaysia* 56 D4
Simushir, Ostrov, *Russia* 45 E16
Sinabang, *Indonesia* 56 D1
Sinadogo, *Somali Rep.* 68 F4
Sinai = Es Sînâ', *Egypt* 76 J8
Sinai, Mt. = Mûsa, G., *Egypt* 76 J8
Sinai Peninsula, *Egypt* 69 F2
Sinaia, *Romania* 38 D8
Sinaloa □, *Mexico* 114 C3
Sinaloa de Levya, *Mexico* 114 B3
Sinalunga, *Italy* 33 E8
Sinan, *China* 52 D7
Sinarádhes, *Greece* 37 A3
Sīnāwan, *Libya* 75 B7
Sincé, *Colombia* 120 B2
Sincelejo, *Colombia* 120 B2
Sinchang, *N. Korea* 51 D15
Sinchang-ni, *N. Korea* 51 E14
Sinclair, *U.S.A.* 110 F10
Sinclair Mills, *Canada* 100 C4
Sincorá, Serra do, *Brazil* 123 D3
Sind, *Pakistan* 62 G3
Sind □, *Pakistan* 62 F3
Sind →, *India* 63 B6
Sind Sagar Doab, *Pakistan* 62 D4
Sindal, *Denmark* 11 G4
Sindangan, *Phil.* 55 G5
Sindangbarang, *Indonesia* 57 G12
Sinde, *Zambia* 83 F2
Sinegorski, *Russia* 43 C9
Sinelnikovo, *Ukraine* 42 B6
Sines, *Portugal* 31 H2
Sines, C. de, *Portugal* 31 H2
Sineu, *Spain* 36 B10
Sinfra, *Ivory C.* 78 D3
Sing Buri, *Thailand* 58 E3
Singa, *Sudan* 77 E3
Singapore ■, *Asia* 59 M4
Singapore, Straits of, *Asia* 59 M5
Singaraja, *Indonesia* 56 F5
Singen, *Germany* 19 H4
Singida, *Tanzania* 82 C3
Singida □, *Tanzania* 82 D3
Singitikós Kólpos, *Greece* 39 J6
Singkaling Hkamti, *Burma* 61 G19
Singkawang, *Indonesia* 56 D3
Singleton, *Australia* 91 E5
Singleton, Mt., *N. Terr., Australia* 88 D5
Singleton, Mt., *W. Austral., Australia* 89 E2
Singoli, *India* 62 G6
Singora = Songkhla, *Thailand* 59 J3
Singosan, *N. Korea* 51 E14
Sinhung, *N. Korea* 51 D14
Sînî □, *Egypt* 69 F2
Siniscóla, *Italy* 34 B2
Sinj, *Croatia* 33 E13
Sinjai, *Indonesia* 57 F6
Sinjār, *Iraq* 64 B4
Sinkat, *Sudan* 76 D4
Sinkiang Uighur = Xinjiang Uygur Zizhiqu □, *China* 54 B3
Sinmak, *N. Korea* 51 E14
Sinnai, *Italy* 34 C2
Sinni →, *Italy* 35 B9
Sinnuris, *Egypt* 76 J7
Sinoe, L., *Romania* 38 E11
Sinop, *Turkey* 42 E6
Sinop □, *Turkey* 66 C6
Sinpo, *N. Korea* 51 E15
Sins, *Switz.* 23 B6
Sinskoye, *Russia* 45 C13
Sint-Amandsberg, *Belgium* 17 F3
Sint Annaland, *Neths.* 17 E4
Sint Annaparoch, *Neths.* 16 B7
Sint-Denijs, *Belgium* 17 G2
Sint Eustatius, I., *Neth. Ant.* 117 C7
Sint-Genesius-Rode, *Belgium* 17 G4
Sint-Gillis-Waas, *Belgium* 17 F4
Sint-Huibrechts-Lille, *Belgium* 17 F6
Sint-Katelinje-Waver, *Belgium* 17 F5
Sint-Kruis, *Belgium* 17 F2
Sint-Laureins, *Belgium* 17 F3
Sint Maarten, I., *W. Indies* 117 C7
Sint-Michiels, *Belgium* 17 F2
Sint Nicolaasga, *Neths.* 16 C7
Sint Niklaas, *Belgium* 17 F4
Sint Oedenrode, *Neths.* 17 E6
Sint Pancras, *Neths.* 16 C5
Sint Philipsland, *Neths.* 17 E4
Sint Truiden, *Belgium* 17 G6
Sint Willebrord, *Neths.* 17 E5
Sîntana, *Romania* 38 C4
Sintang, *Indonesia* 56 D4
Sintjohannesga, *Neths.* 16 C7
Sinton, *U.S.A.* 109 L6
Sintra, *Portugal* 31 G1
Sinŭiju, *N. Korea* 51 D13
Sinyukha →, *Ukraine* 42 B4
Siocon, *Phil.* 55 H5
Siófok, *Hungary* 21 J8
Sioma, *Zambia* 84 B3
Sion, *Switz.* 22 D4
Sioux City, *U.S.A.* 108 D6
Sioux Falls, *U.S.A.* 108 D6
Sioux Lookout, *Canada* 98 B1
Sip Song Chau Thai, *Vietnam* 58 B4
Sipalay, *Phil.* 55 G5
Siping, *China* 51 C13
Sipiwesk L., *Canada* 101 B9
Sipora, *Indonesia* 56 E1
Siquia →, *Nic.* 116 D3
Siquijor, *Phil.* 55 G5
Siquirres, *Costa Rica* 116 D3
Siquisique, *Venezuela* 120 A4
Sir Edward Pellew Group, *Australia* 90 B2
Sir Graham Moore Is., *Australia* 88 B4
Siracusa, *Italy* 35 E8
Sirajganj, *Bangla.* 63 G13
Sirakoro, *Mali* 78 C3
Şiran, *Turkey* 67 C8
Sirasso, *Ivory C.* 78 D3
Sīrdān, *Iran* 65 B6
Sirer, *Spain* 36 C7
Siret, *Romania* 38 B9
Siret →, *Romania* 38 D11
Şiria, *Romania* 38 C4
Sirino, Monte, *Italy* 35 B8
Sírna, *Greece* 39 N9
Sirnach, *Switz.* 23 B7
Şirnak, *Turkey* 67 E10
Sirohi, *India* 62 G5
Sironj, *India* 62 G7
Síros, *Greece* 39 M7
Sirretta Pk., *U.S.A.* 113 K8
Sirsa, *India* 62 E6
Siruela, *Spain* 31 G5
Sisak, *Croatia* 33 C13
Sisaket, *Thailand* 58 E5
Sisante, *Spain* 29 F2
Sisargas, Is., *Spain* 30 B2
Sishen, *S. Africa* 84 D3
Sishui, *Henan, China* 50 G7
Sishui, *Shandong, China* 51 G9
Sisipuk L., *Canada* 101 B8
Sisophon, *Cambodia* 58 F4
Sissach, *Switz.* 22 B5
Sisseton, *U.S.A.* 108 C6
Sissonne, *France* 25 C10
Sīstān va Balūchestān □, *Iran* 65 E9
Sisteron, *France* 27 D9
Sisters, *U.S.A.* 110 D3
Sitamarhi, *India* 63 F11
Sitapur, *India* 63 F9
Siteki, *Swaziland* 85 D5
Sitges, *Spain* 28 D6
Sitía, *Greece* 37 D8
Sítio da Abadia, *Brazil* 123 D2
Sitka, *U.S.A.* 96 C6
Sitoti, *Botswana* 84 C3
Sitra, *Egypt* 76 B2
Sittang Myit →, *Burma* 61 L20
Sittard, *Neths.* 17 G7
Sittensen, *Germany* 18 B5
Sittona, *Eritrea* 77 E4
Sittwe, *Burma* 61 J18
Siuna, *Nic.* 116 D3
Siuri, *India* 63 H12
Sivana, *India* 62 E8
Sīvand, *Iran* 65 D7
Sivas, *Turkey* 66 D7
Sivas □, *Turkey* 66 D7
Siverek, *Turkey* 67 E8
Sivrihisar, *Turkey* 66 D4
Sivry, *Belgium* 17 H4
Sîwa, *Egypt* 76 B2
Sîwa, El Wâhât es, *Egypt* 76 B2
Siwalik Range, *Nepal* 63 F10
Siwan, *India* 63 F11
Siyâl, Jazâ'ir, *Egypt* 76 C4
Sizewell, *U.K.* 13 E9
Siziwang Qi, *China* 50 D6
Sjælland, *Denmark* 11 J5
Sjællands Odde, *Denmark* 11 J5
Själevad, *Sweden* 10 A12
Sjenica, *Serbia* 21 M10
Sjoa, *Norway* 10 C3
Sjöbo, *Sweden* 11 J7
Sjösa, *Sweden* 11 F11
Sjumen = Šumen, *Bulgaria* 38 F9
Skadovsk, *Ukraine* 42 C5
Skagafjörður, *Iceland* 8 D4
Skagastølstindane, *Norway* 9 F9
Skagen, *Denmark* 11 G4
Skagerrak, *Denmark* 11 G3
Skagit →, *U.S.A.* 112 B4
Skagway, *U.S.A.* 100 B1
Skaidi, *Norway* 8 A18
Skala Podolskaya, *Ukraine* 42 B2
Skalat, *Ukraine* 40 G4
Skalni Dol = Kamenyak, *Bulgaria* 38 F9
Skals, *Denmark* 11 H3
Skanderborg, *Denmark* 11 H3
Skanör, *Sweden* 11 J6
Skara, *Sweden* 9 G12
Skaraborgs län □, *Sweden* 9 G12
Skardu, *Pakistan* 63 B6
Skarrild, *Denmark* 11 J2
Skarzysko Kamienna, *Poland* 20 D10
Skebokvarn, *Sweden* 10 E10
Skeena →, *Canada* 100 C2
Skeena Mts., *Canada* 100 B3
Skegness, *U.K.* 12 D8
Skeldon, *Guyana* 121 B6
Skellefte älv →, *Sweden* 8 D16
Skellefteå, *Sweden* 8 D16
Skelleftehamn, *Sweden* 8 D16
Skender Vakuf, *Bos.-H.* 21 L7
Skene, *Sweden* 11 G6
Skerries, The, *U.K.* 12 D3
Skhoinoúsa, *Greece* 39 N8
Ski, *Norway* 10 E4
Skíathos, *Greece* 39 K6
Skibbereen, *Ireland* 15 E2
Skiddaw, *U.K.* 12 C4
Skien, *Norway* 10 E3
Skierniewice, *Poland* 20 D10
Skikda, *Algeria* 75 A6
Skilloura, *Cyprus* 37 D12
Skinári, Ákra, *Greece* 39 M3
Skipton, *Australia* 91 F3
Skipton, *U.K.* 12 D5
Skirmish Pt., *Australia* 90 A1
Skíros, *Greece* 39 L7
Skivarp, *Sweden* 11 J7
Skive, *Denmark* 11 H3
Skjálfandafljót →, *Iceland* 8 D5
Skjálfandi, *Iceland* 8 C5
Skjeberg, *Norway* 10 E5
Skjern, *Denmark* 11 J2
Škofja Loka, *Slovenia* 33 B11
Skoghall, *Sweden* 9 G12
Skole, *Ukraine* 40 G3
Skópelos, *Greece* 39 K6
Skopí, *Greece* 37 D8
Skopin, *Russia* 41 E11
Skopje, *Macedonia* 39 G4
Skórcz, *Poland* 20 B8
Skövde, *Sweden* 9 G12
Skovorodino, *Russia* 45 D13
Skowhegan, *U.S.A.* 99 D6
Skownan, *Canada* 101 C9
Skradin, *Croatia* 33 E12
Skreanäs, *Sweden* 11 H6
Skudeneshavn, *Norway* 9 G8
Skull, *Ireland* 15 E2
Skultorp, *Sweden* 11 F7
Skunk →, *U.S.A.* 108 E9
Skuodas, *Lithuania* 40 C2
Skurup, *Sweden* 11 J7
Skutskär, *Sweden* 10 D11
Skvira, *Ukraine* 42 B3
Skwierzyna, *Poland* 20 C5
Skye, *U.K.* 14 D2
Skykomish, *U.S.A.* 110 C3
Skyros = Skíros, *Greece* 39 L7
Slagelse, *Denmark* 11 J5
Slagharen, *Neths.* 16 C9
Slamet, *Indonesia* 56 F3
Slaney →, *Ireland* 15 D5
Slangerup, *Denmark* 11 J6
Slano, *Croatia* 21 N7
Slantsy, *Russia* 40 B6
Śląsk, *Poland* 20 E6
Slate Is., *Canada* 98 C2
Slatina, *Romania* 38 E7
Slaton, *U.S.A.* 109 J4
Slave →, *Canada* 100 A6
Slave Coast, *W. Afr.* 70 F4
Slave Lake, *Canada* 100 B6
Slave Pt., *Canada* 100 A5
Slavgorod, *Russia* 44 D8
Slavnoye, *Belorussia* 40 D6
Slavonska Požega, *Croatia* 21 K7
Slavonski Brod, *Croatia* 21 K8
Slavuta, *Ukraine* 40 F5
Slavyanka, *Russia* 48 C5
Slavyansk, *Ukraine* 42 B7
Slavyansk-na-Kubani, *Russia* 42 D8
Sławno, *Poland* 20 A6
Sławoborze, *Poland* 20 B5
Sleaford, *U.K.* 12 E7
Sleaford B., *Australia* 91 E2
Sleat, Sd. of, *U.K.* 14 D3
Sleeper Is., *Canada* 97 C11
Sleepy Eye, *U.S.A.* 108 C7
Sleidinge, *Belgium* 17 F3
Sleman, *Indonesia* 57 G14
Slemon L., *Canada* 100 A5
Slidell, *U.S.A.* 109 K10
Sliedrecht, *Neths.* 16 E5
Sliema, *Malta* 37 D2
Slieve Aughty, *Ireland* 15 C3
Slieve Bloom, *Ireland* 15 C4
Slieve Donard, *U.K.* 15 B6
Slieve Gullion, *U.K.* 15 B5
Slieve Mish, *Ireland* 15 D2
Slievenamon, *Ireland* 15 D4
Sligo, *Ireland* 15 B3
Sligo □, *Ireland* 15 B3
Sligo B., *Ireland* 15 B3
Slijpe, *Belgium* 17 F1
Slikkerveer, *Neths.* 16 E5
Slite, *Sweden* 9 H15
Sliven, *Bulgaria* 38 G9
Slivnitsa, *Bulgaria* 38 G6
Sljeme, *Croatia* 33 C12
Sloan, *U.S.A.* 113 K11
Sloansville, *U.S.A.* 107 D10
Slobodskoy, *Russia* 41 B17
Slobozia, *Romania* 38 E10
Slocan, *Canada* 100 D5
Slochteren, *Neths.* 16 B9
Slöinge, *Sweden* 11 H6
Slonim, *Belorussia* 40 E4
Slotermeer, *Neths.* 16 C7
Slough, *U.K.* 13 F7
Sloughhouse, *U.S.A.* 112 G5
Slovak Rep. ■, *Europe* 20 G9
Slovakia = Slovak Rep. ■, *Europe* 20 G9
Slovakian Ore Mts. = Slovenské Rudohorie, *Slovak Rep.* 20 G9
Slovenia ■, *Europe* 33 C11
Slovenija = Slovenia ■, *Europe* 33 C11
Slovenj Gradec, *Slovenia* 33 B12
Slovenska Bistrica, *Slovenia* 33 B12
Slovenská Republika = Slovak Rep. ■, *Europe* 20 G9
Slovenské Rudohorie, *Slovak Rep.* 20 G9
Slovyansk = Slavyansk, *Ukraine* 42 B7
Słubice, *Poland* 20 C4
Sluch →, *Ukraine* 40 F5
Sluis, *Neths.* 17 F2
Slunj, *Croatia* 33 C12
Słupca, *Poland* 20 C7
Słupsk, *Poland* 20 A7
Slurry, *S. Africa* 84 D4
Slutsk, *Belorussia* 40 E5
Slyne Hd., *Ireland* 15 C1
Slyudyanka, *Russia* 45 D11
Smålandsfarvandet, *Denmark* 11 J5
Smålandsstenar, *Sweden* 11 G7
Smalltree L., *Canada* 101 A7
Smara, *Morocco* 72 B3
Smarje, *Slovenia* 33 B12
Smartt Syndicate Dam, *S. Africa* 84 E3
Smartville, *U.S.A.* 112 F5
Smeaton, *Canada* 101 C8
Smederevo, *Serbia* 21 L10
Smederevska Palanka, *Serbia* 21 L10
Smela, *Ukraine* 42 B4
Smethport, *U.S.A.* 106 E6
Smidovich, *Russia* 45 E14
Smilde, *Neths.* 16 C8
Smiley, *Canada* 101 C7
Smith, *Canada* 100 B6
Smith →, *Canada* 100 B3
Smith Arm, *Canada* 96 B7
Smith Center, *U.S.A.* 108 F5
Smith Sund, *Greenland* 4 B4
Smithburne →, *Australia* 90 B3
Smithers, *Canada* 100 C3
Smithfield, *S. Africa* 85 E4
Smithfield, *N.C., U.S.A.* 105 H6
Smithfield, *Utah, U.S.A.* 110 F8
Smiths Falls, *Canada* 98 D4
Smithton, *Australia* 90 G4
Smithtown, *Australia* 91 E5
Smithville, *Canada* 106 C5
Smithville, *U.S.A.* 109 K6
Smoky →, *Canada* 100 B5
Smoky Bay, *Australia* 91 E1
Smoky Falls, *Canada* 98 B3
Smoky Hill →, *U.S.A.* 108 F6
Smoky Lake, *Canada* 100 C6
Smøla, *Norway* 10 A2
Smolensk, *Russia* 40 D8
Smolikas, Óros, *Greece* 39 J3
Smolník, *Slovak Rep.* 20 G10
Smolyan, *Bulgaria* 39 H7
Smooth Rock Falls, *Canada* 98 C3
Smoothstone L., *Canada* 101 C7
Smorgon, *Belorussia* 40 D5
Smyadovo, *Bulgaria* 38 F10
Smyrna = İzmir, *Turkey* 66 D2
Snaefell, *U.K.* 12 C3
Snæfellsjökull, *Iceland* 8 D2
Snake →, *U.S.A.* 110 C4
Snake I., *Australia* 91 F4
Snake L., *Canada* 101 B7
Snake Range, *U.S.A.* 110 G6
Snake River Plain, *U.S.A.* 110 E7
Snarum, *Norway* 10 D3
Snedsted, *Denmark* 11 H2
Sneek, *Neths.* 16 B7
Sneeker-meer, *Neths.* 16 B7
Sneeuberge, *S. Africa* 84 E3
Snejbjerg, *Denmark* 11 H2
Snelling, *U.S.A.* 112 H6
Snezhnoye, *Ukraine* 43 C8
Snežnik, *Slovenia* 33 C11
Snigirevka, *Ukraine* 42 C5
Snizort, L., *U.K.* 14 D2
Snøhetta, *Norway* 10 B3
Snohomish, *U.S.A.* 112 C4
Snoul, *Cambodia* 59 F6
Snow Hill, *U.S.A.* 104 F8
Snow Lake, *Canada* 101 C8
Snow Mt., *U.S.A.* 112 F4
Snowbird L., *Canada* 101 A8
Snowdon, *U.K.* 12 D3
Snowdrift, *Canada* 101 A6
Snowdrift →, *Canada* 101 A6
Snowflake, *U.S.A.* 111 J8
Snowshoe Pk., *U.S.A.* 110 B6
Snowtown, *Australia* 91 E2
Snowville, *U.S.A.* 110 F7
Snowy →, *Australia* 91 F4
Snowy Mts., *Australia* 91 F4
Snug Corner, *Bahamas* 117 B5
Snyatyn, *Ukraine* 42 B1
Snyder, *Okla., U.S.A.* 109 H5
Snyder, *Tex., U.S.A.* 109 J4
Soacha, *Colombia* 120 C3
Soahanina, *Madag.* 85 B7
Soalala, *Madag.* 85 B8
Soan →, *Pakistan* 62 C4
Soanierana-Ivongo, *Madag.* 85 B8
Soap Lake, *U.S.A.* 110 C4
Sobat, Nahr →, *Sudan* 77 F3
Sobhapur, *India* 62 H8
Sobinka, *Russia* 41 D12
Sobótka, *Poland* 20 E6
Sobrado, *Spain* 30 B2
Sobral, *Brazil* 122 B3
Sobreira Formosa, *Portugal* 31 F3
Soc Giang, *Vietnam* 58 A6
Soc Trang, *Vietnam* 59 H5
Soča →, *Europe* 33 B10
Sochaczew, *Poland* 20 C10
Soch'e = Shache, *China* 54 C2
Sochi, *Russia* 43 E8
Société, Is. de la, *Pac. Oc.* 93 J12
Society Is. = Société, Is. de la, *Pac. Oc.* 93 J12
Socompa, Portezuelo de, *Chile* 126 A2
Socorro, *Colombia* 120 B3
Socorro, *U.S.A.* 111 J10
Socorro, I., *Mexico* 114 D2
Socotra, *Ind. Oc.* 68 E5
Socuéllmos, *Spain* 29 F2
Soda L., *U.S.A.* 111 J5
Soda Plains, *India* 63 B8
Soda Springs, *U.S.A.* 110 E8
Söderhamn, *Sweden* 9 F14
Söderköping, *Sweden* 9 G14
Södermanlands län □, *Sweden* 10 E10
Södertälje, *Sweden* 10 E11
Sodiri, *Sudan* 77 E2
Sodo, *Ethiopia* 77 F4
Sodražica, *Slovenia* 33 C11
Sodus, *U.S.A.* 106 C7

Soekmekaar, *S. Africa* 85 C4
Soest, *Germany* 18 D4
Soest, *Neths.* 16 D6
Soestdijk, *Neths.* 16 D6
Sofádhes, *Greece* 39 K5
Sofara, *Mali* 78 C4
Sofia = Sofiya, *Bulgaria* 38 G6
Sofia →, *Madag.* 85 B8
Sofievka, *Ukraine* 42 B5
Sofiiski, *Russia* 45 D14
Sofikón, *Greece* 39 M6
Sofiya, *Bulgaria* 38 G6
Sōfu-Gan, *Japan* 49 K10
Sogakofe, *Ghana* 79 D5
Sogamoso, *Colombia* 120 B3
Sogār, *Iran* 65 E8
Sögel, *Germany* 18 C3
Sogn og Fjordane fylke □, *Norway* 9 F9
Sogndalsfjøra, *Norway* 9 F9
Sognefjorden, *Norway* 9 F8
Söğüt, *Turkey* 66 C4
Söğüt Gölü, *Turkey* 66 E3
Sŏgwi-po, *S. Korea* 51 H14
Soh, *Iran* 65 C6
Sohâg, *Egypt* 76 B3
Sŏhori, *N. Korea* 51 D15
Soignies, *Belgium* 17 G4
Soira, *Eritrea* 77 E4
Soissons, *France* 25 C10
Sōja, *Japan* 49 G6
Sojat, *India* 62 G5
Sok →, *Russia* 41 E17
Sokal, *Ukraine* 40 F4
Söke, *Turkey* 66 E2
Sokelo, *Zaïre* 83 D1
Sokhumi = Sukhumi, *Georgia* 43 E9
Sokki, Oued In →, *Algeria* 75 C5
Sokna, *Norway* 10 D3
Soknedal, *Norway* 10 B4
Soko Banja, *Serbia* 21 M11
Sokodé, *Togo* 79 D5
Sokol, *Russia* 41 B12
Sokółka, *Poland* 20 B13
Sokolo, *Mali* 78 C3
Sokołów Małpolski, *Poland* 20 E12
Sokołów Podlaski, *Poland* 20 C12
Sokoto, *Nigeria* 79 C6
Sokoto □, *Nigeria* 79 C6
Sokoto →, *Nigeria* 79 C5
Sol Iletsk, *Russia* 44 D6
Solai, *Kenya* 82 B4
Solano, *Phil.* 55 C4
Solapur, *India* 60 L9
Solares, *Spain* 30 B7
Soléa □, *Cyprus* 37 D12
Solec Kujawski, *Poland* 20 B8
Soledad, *Colombia* 120 A3
Soledad, *U.S.A.* 111 H3
Soledad, *Venezuela* 121 B5
Solent, The, *U.K.* 13 G6
Solenzara, *France* 27 G13
Solesmes, *France* 25 B10
Solfonn, *Norway* 9 F9
Solhan, *Turkey* 67 D9
Soligalich, *Russia* 41 B13
Soligorsk, *Belorussia* 40 E5
Solikamsk, *Russia* 44 D6
Solila, *Madag.* 85 C8
Solimões = Amazonas →, *S. Amer.* 121 D7
Solingen, *Germany* 17 F10
Sollebrunn, *Sweden* 11 F6
Sollefteå, *Sweden* 10 A11
Sollentuna, *Sweden* 10 E11
Sóller, *Spain* 36 B9
Solling, *Germany* 18 D5
Solna, *Sweden* 10 E12
Solnechnogorsk, *Russia* 41 C10
Sologne, *France* 25 E8
Solok, *Indonesia* 56 E2
Sololá, *Guatemala* 116 D1
Solomon, N. Fork →, *U.S.A.* 108 F5
Solomon, S. Fork →, *U.S.A.* 108 F5
Solomon Is. ■, *Pac. Oc.* 92 H7
Solon, *China* 54 B7
Solon Springs, *U.S.A.* 108 B9
Solonópole, *Brazil* 122 C4
Solor, *Indonesia* 57 F6
Solotcha, *Russia* 41 D11
Solothurn, *Switz.* 22 B5
Solothurn □, *Switz.* 22 B5
Solsona, *Spain* 28 D6
Solta, *Croatia* 33 E13
Solṭānābād, *Khorāsān, Iran* 65 C8
Solṭānābād, *Khorāsān, Iran* 65 B8
Solṭānābād, *Markazī, Iran* 65 C6
Soltau, *Germany* 18 C5
Soltsy, *Russia* 40 B7
Solunska Glava, *Macedonia* 39 H4
Solvang, *U.S.A.* 113 L6
Solvay, *U.S.A.* 107 C8
Solway Firth, *U.K.* 12 C4
Solwezi, *Zambia* 83 E2
Sōma, *Japan* 48 F10
Soma, *Turkey* 66 D2
Somali Rep. ■, *Africa* 68 F4
Somalia ■ = Somali Rep. ■, *Africa* 68 F4
Sombernon, *France* 25 E11
Sombor, *Serbia* 21 K9
Sombra, *Canada* 106 D2
Sombrerete, *Mexico* 114 C4
Sombrero, *Anguilla* 117 C7
Somers, *U.S.A.* 110 B6
Somerset, *Canada* 101 D9
Somerset, *Colo., U.S.A.* 111 G10
Somerset, *Ky., U.S.A.* 104 G3
Somerset, *Mass., U.S.A.* 107 E13
Somerset, *Pa., U.S.A.* 106 F5
Somerset □, *U.K.* 13 F5
Somerset East, *S. Africa* 84 E4
Somerset I., *Canada* 96 A10
Somerset West, *S. Africa* 84 E2
Somerton, *U.S.A.* 111 K6
Somerville, *U.S.A.* 107 F10
Someş →, *Romania* 38 B5
Someşul Mare →, *Romania* 38 B7
Somma Lombardo, *Italy* 32 C5
Somma Vesuviana, *Italy* 35 B7
Sommariva, *Australia* 91 D4
Sommatino, *Italy* 34 E6
Somme □, *France* 25 C9
Somme →, *France* 25 B8
Somme, B. de la, *France* 24 B8
Sommelsdijk, *Neths.* 16 E4
Sommepy-Tahure, *France* 25 C11
Sömmerda, *Germany* 18 D7
Sommesous, *France* 25 D11
Sommières, *France* 27 E8
Somoto, *Nic.* 116 D2
Sompolno, *Poland* 20 C8
Somport, Paso, *Spain* 28 C4
Somport, Puerto de, *Spain* 28 C4
Somuncurá, Meseta de, *Argentina* 128 B3
Son, *Neths.* 17 E6
Son, *Norway* 10 E4
Son, *Spain* 30 C2
Son Ha, *Vietnam* 58 E7
Son Hoa, *Vietnam* 58 F7
Son La, *Vietnam* 58 B4
Son Tay, *Vietnam* 58 B5
Soná, *Panama* 116 E3
Sonamarg, *India* 63 B6
Sonamukhi, *India* 63 H12
Sŏnchŏn, *N. Korea* 51 E13
Soncino, *Italy* 32 C6
Sondags →, *S. Africa* 84 E4
Sóndalo, *Italy* 32 B7
Sondar, *India* 63 C6
Sønder Omme, *Denmark* 11 J2
Sønder Tornby, *Denmark* 11 G3
Sønderborg, *Denmark* 11 K3
Sønderjyllands Amtskommune □, *Denmark* 11 J3
Sondershausen, *Germany* 18 D6
Søndre Strømfjord, *Greenland* 97 B14
Sóndrio, *Italy* 32 B6
Sone, *Mozam.* 83 F3
Sonepur, *India* 61 J13
Song, *Thailand* 58 C3
Song Cau, *Vietnam* 58 F7
Song Xian, *China* 50 G7
Songchŏn, *N. Korea* 51 E14
Songea, *Tanzania* 83 E4
Songea □, *Tanzania* 83 E4
Songeons, *France* 25 C8
Songhua Hu, *China* 51 C14
Songhua Jiang →, *China* 54 B8
Songjiang, *China* 53 B13
Songjin, *N. Korea* 51 D15
Songjŏng-ni, *S. Korea* 51 G14
Songkan, *China* 52 C6
Songkhla, *Thailand* 59 J3
Songming, *China* 52 E4
Songnim, *N. Korea* 51 E13
Songpan, *China* 52 A4
Songtao, *China* 52 C7
Songwe, *Zaïre* 82 C2
Songwe →, *Africa* 83 D3
Songxi, *China* 53 D12
Songzi, *China* 53 B8
Sonid Youqi, *China* 50 C7
Sonipat, *India* 62 E7
Sonkovo, *Russia* 41 C10
Sonmiani, *Pakistan* 62 G2
Sonnino, *Italy* 34 A6
Sono →, *Goiás, Brazil* 122 C2
Sono →, *Minas Gerais, Brazil* 123 E2
Sonogno, *Switz.* 23 D7
Sonora, *Calif., U.S.A.* 111 H3
Sonora, *Tex., U.S.A.* 109 K4
Sonora □, *Mexico* 114 B2
Sonora →, *Mexico* 114 B2
Sonora Desert, *U.S.A.* 113 M12
Sonoyta, *Mexico* 114 A2
Sŏnsan, *S. Korea* 51 F15
Sonsonate, *El Salv.* 116 D2
Sonthofen, *Germany* 19 H6
Soochow = Suzhou, *China* 53 B13
Sop Hao, *Laos* 58 B5
Sop Prap, *Thailand* 58 D2
Sopachuy, *Bolivia* 125 D5
Sopi, *Indonesia* 57 D7
Sopo, Nahr →, *Sudan* 77 F2
Sopot, *Poland* 20 A8
Sopotnica, *Macedonia* 39 H4
Sopron, *Hungary* 21 H6
Sop's Arm, *Canada* 99 C8
Sopur, *India* 63 B6
Sør-Rondane, *Antarctica* 5 D4
Sør-Trøndelag fylke □, *Norway* 10 B3
Sora, *Italy* 34 A6
Sorah, *Pakistan* 62 F3
Söråker, *Sweden* 10 B11
Sorano, *Italy* 33 F8
Sorata, *Bolivia* 124 D4
Sorbas, *Spain* 29 H2
Sorel, *Canada* 98 C5
Sörenberg, *Switz.* 22 C6
Soreq, N. →, *Israel* 69 D3
Soresina, *Italy* 32 C6
Sorgono, *Italy* 34 B2
Sorgues, *France* 27 D8
Sorgun, *Turkey* 66 D6
Soria, *Spain* 28 D2
Soria □, *Spain* 28 D2
Soriano, *Uruguay* 126 C4
Soriano nel Cimino, *Italy* 33 F9
Sorkh, Kuh-e, *Iran* 65 C8
Sorø, *Denmark* 11 J5
Soro, *Guinea* 78 C3
Sorocaba, *Brazil* 127 A6
Soroki, *Moldavia* 42 B3
Soron, *India* 63 F8
Sorong, *Indonesia* 57 E8
Soroní, *Greece* 37 C10
Soroti, *Uganda* 82 B3
Sørøya, *Norway* 8 A17
Sørøysundet, *Norway* 8 A17
Sorraia →, *Portugal* 31 G2
Sorrento, *Australia* 91 F3
Sorrento, *Italy* 35 B7
Sorsele, *Sweden* 8 D14
Sorso, *Italy* 34 B1
Sorsogon, *Phil.* 55 E6
Sortino, *Italy* 35 E8
Sorvizhi, *Russia* 41 C16
Sos, *Spain* 28 C3
Sŏsan, *S. Korea* 51 F14
Soscumica, L., *Canada* 98 B4
Sosna →, *Russia* 41 E11
Sosnovka, *Russia* 41 E12
Sosnovka, *Russia* 45 D11
Sosnowiec, *Poland* 20 E9
Sospel, *France* 27 E11
Sostanj, *Slovenia* 33 B12
Sŏsura, *N. Korea* 51 C16
Soto la Marina →, *Mexico* 115 C5
Soto y Amío, *Spain* 30 C5
Sotteville-lès-Rouen, *France* 24 C8
Sotuta, *Mexico* 115 C7
Souanké, *Congo* 80 D2
Soúdha, *Greece* 37 D6
Soúdhas, Kólpos, *Greece* 37 D6
Sougne-Remouchamps, *Belgium* 17 H7
Souillac, *France* 26 D5
Souk-Ahras, *Algeria* 75 A6
Souk el Arba du Rharb, *Morocco* 74 B3
Soukhouma, *Laos* 58 E5
Sŏul, *S. Korea* 51 F14
Soulac-sur-Mer, *France* 26 C2
Soultz-sous-Forêts, *France* 25 D14
Soumagne, *Belgium* 17 G7
Sound, The = Øresund, *Europe* 11 J6
Sound, The, *U.K.* 13 G3
Soúnion, Ákra, *Greece* 39 M7
Sour el Ghozlane, *Algeria* 75 A5
Sources, Mt. aux, *Lesotho* 85 D4
Sourdeval, *France* 24 D6
Soure, *Brazil* 122 B2
Soure, *Portugal* 30 E2
Souris, *Man., Canada* 101 D8
Souris, *P.E.I., Canada* 99 C7
Souris →, *Canada* 108 A5
Sousa, *Brazil* 122 C4
Sousel, *Brazil* 122 B1
Sousel, *Portugal* 31 G3
Souss, O. →, *Morocco* 74 B3
Sousse, *Tunisia* 75 A7
Soustons, *France* 26 E2
South Africa ■, *Africa* 84 E3
South Aulatsivik I., *Canada* 99 A7
South Australia □, *Australia* 91 E2
South Baldy, *U.S.A.* 111 J10
South Bend, *Ind., U.S.A.* 104 E2
South Bend, *Wash., U.S.A.* 112 D3
South Boston, *U.S.A.* 105 G6
South Branch, *Canada* 99 C8
South Brook, *Canada* 99 C8
South Buganda □, *Uganda* 82 C3
South Carolina □, *U.S.A.* 105 J5
South Charleston, *U.S.A.* 104 F5
South China Sea, *Asia* 56 C4
South Dakota □, *U.S.A.* 108 C5
South Downs, *U.K.* 13 G7
South East C., *Australia* 90 G4
South East Is., *Australia* 89 F3
South Esk →, *U.K.* 14 E5
South Foreland, *U.K.* 13 F9
South Fork →, *U.S.A.* 110 C7
South Fork, American →, *U.S.A.* 112 G5
South Fork, Feather →, *U.S.A.* 112 F5
South Georgia, *Antarctica* 5 B1
South Glamorgan □, *U.K.* 13 F4
South Haven, *U.S.A.* 104 D2
South Henik, L., *Canada* 101 A9
South Honshu Ridge, *Pac. Oc.* 92 E6
South Horr, *Kenya* 82 B4
South I., *Kenya* 82 B4
South I., *N.Z.* 87 L3
South Invercargill, *N.Z.* 87 M2
South Knife →, *Canada* 101 B10
South Korea ■, *Asia* 51 F15
South Lake Tahoe, *U.S.A.* 112 G6
South Loup →, *U.S.A.* 108 E5
South Magnetic Pole, *Antarctica* 5 C9
South Milwaukee, *U.S.A.* 104 D2
South Molton, *U.K.* 13 F4
South Nahanni →, *Canada* 100 A4
South Natuna Is. = Natuna Selatan, Kepulauan, *Indonesia* 59 L7
South Negril Pt., *Jamaica* 116 C4
South Orkney Is., *Antarctica* 5 C18
South Pagai, I. = Pagai Selatan, P., *Indonesia* 56 E2
South Pass, *U.S.A.* 110 E9
South Pittsburg, *U.S.A.* 105 H3
South Platte →, *U.S.A.* 108 E4
South Pole, *Antarctica* 5 E
South Porcupine, *Canada* 98 C3
South River, *Canada* 98 C4
South River, *U.S.A.* 107 F10
South Ronaldsay, *U.K.* 14 C6
South Sandwich Is., *Antarctica* 5 B1
South Saskatchewan →, *Canada* 101 C7
South Seal →, *Canada* 101 B9
South Shetland Is., *Antarctica* 5 C18
South Shields, *U.K.* 12 C6
South Sioux City, *U.S.A.* 108 D6
South Taranaki Bight, *N.Z.* 87 H5
South Thompson →, *Canada* 100 C4
South Twin I., *Canada* 98 B4
South Tyne →, *U.K.* 12 C5
South Uist, *U.K.* 14 D1
South West Africa = Namibia ■, *Africa* 84 C2
South West C., *Australia* 90 G4
South Yorkshire □, *U.K.* 12 D6
Southampton, *Canada* 98 D3
Southampton, *U.K.* 13 G6
Southampton, *U.S.A.* 107 F12
Southampton I., *Canada* 97 B11
Southbridge, *N.Z.* 87 K4
Southbridge, *U.S.A.* 107 D12
Southend, *Canada* 101 B8
Southend-on-Sea, *U.K.* 13 F8
Southern □, *Malawi* 83 F4
Southern □, *S. Leone* 78 D2
Southern □, *Zambia* 83 F2
Southern Alps, *N.Z.* 87 K3
Southern Cross, *Australia* 89 F2
Southern Hills, *Australia* 89 F3
Southern Indian L., *Canada* 101 B9
Southern Ocean, *Antarctica* 5 C6
Southern Pines, *U.S.A.* 105 H6
Southern Uplands, *U.K.* 14 F5
Southington, *U.S.A.* 107 E12
Southold, *U.S.A.* 107 E12
Southport, *Australia* 91 D5
Southport, *U.K.* 12 D4
Southport, *U.S.A.* 105 J6
Southwest C., *N.Z.* 87 M1
Southwold, *U.K.* 13 E9
Soutpansberg, *S. Africa* 85 C4
Souvigny, *France* 26 B7
Sovetsk, *Russia* 40 D2
Sovetsk, *Russia* 41 C16
Sovetskaya Gavan, *Russia* 45 E15
Sovicille, *Italy* 33 E8
Soviet Union = Commonwealth of Independent States ■, *Eurasia* 45 D11
Sovra, *Croatia* 21 N7
Soweto, *S. Africa* 85 D4
Sōya-Kaikyō = La Perouse Str., *Asia* 48 B11
Sōya-Misaki, *Japan* 48 B10
Soyo, *Angola* 80 F2
Sozh →, *Belorussia* 40 F7
Sozopol, *Bulgaria* 38 G10
Spa, *Belgium* 17 H7
Spain ■, *Europe* 7 H5
Spakenburg, *Neths.* 16 D6
Spalding, *Australia* 91 E2
Spalding, *U.K.* 12 E7
Spalding, *U.S.A.* 108 E5
Spangler, *U.S.A.* 106 F6
Spaniard's Bay, *Canada* 99 C9
Spanish, *Canada* 98 C3
Spanish Fork, *U.S.A.* 110 F8
Spanish Town, *Jamaica* 116 C4
Sparks, *U.S.A.* 112 F7
Sparta = Spárti, *Greece* 39 M5
Sparta, *Ga., U.S.A.* 105 J4
Sparta, *Wis., U.S.A.* 108 D9
Spartanburg, *U.S.A.* 105 H4
Spartansburg, *U.S.A.* 106 E5
Spartel, C., *Morocco* 74 A3
Spárti, *Greece* 39 M5
Spartivento, C., *Calabria, Italy* 35 E9
Spartivento, C., *Sard., Italy* 34 D1
Spas-Demensk, *Russia* 40 D8
Spas-Klepiki, *Russia* 41 D12
Spassk-Dalniy, *Russia* 45 E14
Spassk-Ryazanskiy, *Russia* 41 D12
Spátha, Ákra, *Greece* 37 D5
Spatsizi →, *Canada* 100 B3
Spearfish, *U.S.A.* 108 C3
Spearman, *U.S.A.* 109 G4
Speer, *Switz.* 23 B8
Speers, *Canada* 101 C7
Speightstown, *Barbados* 117 D8
Speke Gulf, *Tanzania* 82 C3
Spekholzerheide, *Neths.* 17 G8
Spence Bay, *Canada* 96 B10
Spencer, *Idaho, U.S.A.* 110 D7
Spencer, *Iowa, U.S.A.* 108 D7
Spencer, *N.Y., U.S.A.* 107 D8
Spencer, *Nebr., U.S.A.* 108 D5
Spencer, *W. Va., U.S.A.* 104 F5
Spencer, C., *Australia* 91 F2
Spencer B., *Namibia* 84 D1
Spencer G., *Australia* 91 E2
Spencerville, *Canada* 107 B9
Spences Bridge, *Canada* 100 C4
Spenser Mts., *N.Z.* 87 K4
Sperkhiós →, *Greece* 39 L5
Sperrin Mts., *U.K.* 15 B5
Spessart, *Germany* 19 E5
Spétsai, *Greece* 39 M6
Spey →, *U.K.* 14 D5
Speyer, *Germany* 19 F4
Speyer →, *Germany* 19 F4
Spezzano Albanese, *Italy* 35 C9
Spiekeroog, *Germany* 18 B3
Spielfeld, *Austria* 33 B12
Spiez, *Switz.* 22 C5
Spijk, *Neths.* 16 B9
Spijkenisse, *Neths.* 16 E4
Spíli, *Greece* 37 D6
Spilimbergo, *Italy* 33 B9
Spin Baldak = Qala-i-Jadid, *Afghan.* 62 D2
Spinalónga, *Greece* 37 D7
Spinazzola, *Italy* 35 B9
Spirit Lake, *Idaho, U.S.A.* 110 C5
Spirit Lake, *Wash., U.S.A.* 112 D4
Spirit River, *Canada* 100 B5
Spiritwood, *Canada* 101 C7
Spišská Nová Ves, *Slovak Rep.* 20 G10
Spithead, *U.K.* 13 G6
Spittal, *Austria* 21 J3
Spitzbergen = Svalbard, *Arctic* 4 B8
Split, *Croatia* 33 E13
Split L., *Canada* 101 B9
Splitski Kanal, *Croatia* 33 E13
Splügen, *Switz.* 23 C8
Splügenpass, *Switz.* 23 C8
Spofford, *U.S.A.* 109 L4
Spokane, *U.S.A.* 110 C5
Spoleto, *Italy* 33 F9
Spooner, *U.S.A.* 108 C9
Sporyy Navolok, Mys, *Russia* 44 B7
Spragge, *Canada* 98 C3
Sprague, *U.S.A.* 110 C5
Sprague River, *U.S.A.* 110 E3
Spratly I., *S. China Sea* 56 C4
Spray, *U.S.A.* 110 D4
Spree →, *Germany* 18 C9
Spremberg, *Germany* 18 D10
Sprimont, *Belgium* 17 G7
Spring City, *U.S.A.* 110 G8
Spring Garden, *U.S.A.* 112 F6
Spring Mts., *U.S.A.* 111 H6
Spring Valley, *Calif., U.S.A.* 113 N10
Spring Valley, *Minn., U.S.A.* 108 D8
Springbok, *S. Africa* 84 D2
Springdale, *Canada* 99 C8
Springdale, *Ark., U.S.A.* 109 G7
Springdale, *Wash., U.S.A.* 110 B5
Springe, *Germany* 18 C5
Springer, *U.S.A.* 109 G2
Springerville, *U.S.A.* 111 J9
Springfield, *Canada* 106 D4
Springfield, *N.Z.* 87 K3
Springfield, *Colo., U.S.A.* 109 G3
Springfield, *Ill., U.S.A.* 108 F10
Springfield, *Mass., U.S.A.* 107 D12
Springfield, *Mo., U.S.A.* 109 G8
Springfield, *Ohio, U.S.A.* 104 F4
Springfield, *Oreg., U.S.A.* 110 D2
Springfield, *Tenn., U.S.A.* 105 G2
Springfield, *Vt., U.S.A.* 107 C12
Springfontein, *S. Africa* 84 E4
Springhill, *Canada* 99 C7
Springhouse, *Canada* 100 C4
Springhurst, *Australia* 91 F4
Springs, *S. Africa* 85 D4
Springsure, *Australia* 90 C4
Springvale, *Queens., Australia* 90 C3
Springvale, *W. Austral., Australia* 88 C4
Springvale, *U.S.A.* 107 C14
Springville, *Calif., U.S.A.* 112 J8
Springville, *N.Y., U.S.A.* 106 D6
Springville, *Utah, U.S.A.* 110 F8
Springwater, *Canada* 101 C7
Spruce-Creek, *U.S.A.* 106 F6
Spur, *U.S.A.* 109 J4
Spurn Hd., *U.K.* 12 D8
Spuž, *Montenegro* 21 N9
Spuzzum, *Canada* 100 D4
Squam L., *U.S.A.* 107 C13
Squamish, *Canada* 100 D4
Square Islands, *Canada* 99 B8
Squillace, G. di, *Italy* 35 D9

Squinzano, *Italy* 35 B11
Squires, Mt., *Australia* 89 E4
Sragen, *Indonesia* 57 G14
Srbac, *Bos.-H* 21 K7
Srbija = Serbia □, *Yugoslavia* 21 M11
Srbobran, *Serbia, Yug.* 21 K9
Sre Khtum, *Cambodia* 59 F6
Sre Umbell, *Cambodia* 59 G4
Srebrnica, *Bos.-H.* 21 L9
Sredinny Ra. = Sredinnyy Khrebet, *Russia* 45 D16
Sredinnyy Khrebet, *Russia* 45 D16
Središče, *Slovenia* 33 B13
Sredna Gora, *Bulgaria* 38 G7
Sredne Tambovskoye, *Russia* 45 D14
Srednekolymsk, *Russia* 45 C16
Srednevilyuysk, *Russia* 45 C13
Śrem, *Poland* 20 C7
Sremska Mitrovica, *Serbia, Yug.* 21 L9
Srepok →, *Cambodia* 58 F6
Sretensk, *Russia* 45 D12
Sri Lanka ■, *Asia* 60 R12
Srikakulam, *India* 61 K13
Srinagar, *India* 63 B6
Środa Wielkopolski, *Poland* 20 C7
Srpska Itabej, *Serbia, Yug.* 21 K10
Staaten →, *Australia* 90 B3
Staberhuk, *Germany* 18 A7
Stabroek, *Belgium* 17 F4
Stad Delden, *Neths.* 16 D9
Stade, *Germany* 18 B5
Staden, *Belgium* 17 G2
Staðarhólskirkja, *Iceland* 8 D3
Städjan, *Sweden* 10 C6
Stadlandet, *Norway* 8 E8
Stadskanaal, *Neths.* 16 B9
Stadthagen, *Germany* 18 C5
Stadtlohn, *Germany* 18 D2
Stadtroda, *Germany* 18 E7
Stäfa, *Switz.* 23 B7
Stafafell, *Iceland* 8 D6
Staffa, *U.K.* 14 E2
Stafford, *U.K.* 12 E5
Stafford, *U.S.A.* 109 G5
Stafford Springs, *U.S.A.* 107 E12
Staffordshire □, *U.K.* 12 E5
Stagnone, *Italy* 34 E5
Staines, *U.K.* 13 F7
Stakhanov = Kadiyevka, *Ukraine* 43 B8
Stalden, *Switz.* 22 D5
Stalingrad = Volgograd, *Russia* 43 B11
Staliniri = Tskhinvali, *Georgia* 43 E11
Stalino = Donetsk, *Ukraine* 42 C7
Stalinogorsk = Novomoskovsk, *Russia* 41 D11
Stalis, *Greece* 37 D7
Stalowa Wola, *Poland* 20 E12
Stalybridge, *U.K.* 12 D5
Stamford, *Australia* 90 C3
Stamford, *U.K.* 13 E7
Stamford, *Conn., U.S.A.* 107 E11
Stamford, *Tex., U.S.A.* 109 J5
Stamps, *U.S.A.* 109 J8
Stanberry, *U.S.A.* 108 E7
Stančevo = Kalipetrovo, *Bulgaria* 38 E10
Standerton, *S. Africa* 85 D4
Standish, *U.S.A.* 104 D4
Stanford, *U.S.A.* 110 C8
Stange, *Norway* 10 D5
Stanger, *S. Africa* 85 D5
Stanislaus →, *U.S.A.* 112 H5
Stanislav = Ivano-Frankovsk, *Ukraine* 40 G4
Stanke Dimitrov, *Bulgaria* 38 G6
Stanley, *Australia* 90 G4
Stanley, *N.B., Canada* 99 C6
Stanley, *Sask., Canada* 101 B8
Stanley, *Falk. Is.* 128 D5
Stanley, *Idaho, U.S.A.* 110 D6
Stanley, *N. Dak., U.S.A.* 108 A3
Stanley, *N.Y., U.S.A.* 106 D7
Stanley, *Wis., U.S.A.* 108 C9
Stanovoy Khrebet, *Russia* 45 D13
Stanovoy Ra. = Stanovoy Khrebet, *Russia* 45 D13
Stans, *Switz.* 23 C6
Stansmore Ra., *Australia* 88 D4
Stanthorpe, *Australia* 91 D5
Stanton, *U.S.A.* 109 J4
Stanwood, *U.S.A.* 112 B4
Staphorst, *Neths.* 16 C8
Staples, *U.S.A.* 108 B7
Stapleton, *U.S.A.* 108 E4
Star City, *Canada* 101 C8
Stara-minskaya, *Russia* 43 C8
Stara Moravica, *Serbia, Yug.* 21 K9
Stara Planina, *Bulgaria* 38 F6
Stara Zagora, *Bulgaria* 38 G8
Starachowice, *Poland* 20 D11
Starashcherbinovskaya, *Russia* 43 C8
Staraya Russa, *Russia* 40 C7
Starbuck I., *Kiribati* 93 H12
Stargard Szczeciński, *Poland* 20 B5
Stari Trg, *Slovenia* 33 C12
Staritsa, *Russia* 40 C9
Stärke, *U.S.A.* 105 K4
Starkville, *Colo., U.S.A.* 109 G2
Starkville, *Miss., U.S.A.* 105 J1
Starnberg, *Germany* 19 G7
Starnberger See, *Germany* 19 H7
Starobelsk, *Ukraine* 43 B8
Starodub, *Russia* 40 E8
Starogard, *Poland* 20 B8
Starokonstantinov, *Ukraine* 42 B2
Start Pt., *U.K.* 13 G4
Staryy Biryuzyak, *Russia* 43 D12
Staryy Chartoriysk, *Ukraine* 40 F4
Staryy Kheydzhan, *Russia* 45 C15
Staryy Krym, *Ukraine* 42 D6
Staryy Oskol, *Russia* 41 F10
Stassfurt, *Germany* 18 D7
State College, *U.S.A.* 106 F7
Stateline, *U.S.A.* 112 G7
Staten, I. = Estados, I. de Los, *Argentina* 128 D4
Staten I., *U.S.A.* 107 F10
Statesboro, *U.S.A.* 105 J5
Statesville, *U.S.A.* 105 H5
Stauffer, *U.S.A.* 113 L7
Staunton, *Ill., U.S.A.* 108 F10
Staunton, *Va., U.S.A.* 104 F6
Stavanger, *Norway* 9 G8
Staveley, *N.Z.* 87 K3
Stavelot, *Belgium* 17 H7
Stavenhagen, *Germany* 18 B8
Stavenisse, *Neths.* 17 E4
Staveren, *Neths.* 16 C6
Stavern, *Norway* 10 F4
Stavre, *Sweden* 10 B9
Stavropol, *Russia* 43 D10
Stavros, *Cyprus* 37 D11
Stavrós, *Greece* 37 D6
Stavros, Ákra, *Greece* 37 D6
Stavroúpolis, *Greece* 39 H7
Stawell, *Australia* 91 F3
Stawell →, *Australia* 90 C3
Stawiszyn, *Poland* 20 D8
Stayner, *Canada* 106 B4
Steamboat Springs, *U.S.A.* 110 F10
Steckborn, *Switz.* 23 A7
Steele, *U.S.A.* 108 B5
Steelton, *U.S.A.* 106 F8
Steelville, *U.S.A.* 109 G9
Steen River, *Canada* 100 B5
Steenbergen, *Neths.* 17 E4
Steenkool = Bintuni, *Indonesia* 57 E8
Steenvoorde, *France* 25 B9
Steenwijk, *Neths.* 16 C8
Steep Pt., *Australia* 89 E1
Steep Rock, *Canada* 101 C9
Ştefăneşti, *Romania* 38 B10
Stefanie L. = Chew Bahir, *Ethiopia* 77 G4
Stefansson Bay, *Antarctica* 5 C5
Steffisburg, *Switz.* 22 C5
Stege, *Denmark* 11 K6
Steiermark □, *Austria* 21 H5
Steigerwald, *Germany* 19 F6
Steilacoom, *U.S.A.* 112 C4
Stein, *Neths.* 17 G7
Steinbach, *Canada* 101 D9
Steinfort, *Lux.* 17 J7
Steinfurt, *Germany* 18 C3
Steinheim, *Germany* 18 D5
Steinhuder Meer, *Germany* 18 C5
Steinkjer, *Norway* 8 E11
Steinkopf, *S. Africa* 84 D2
Stekene, *Belgium* 17 F4
Stellarton, *Canada* 99 C7
Stellenbosch, *S. Africa* 84 E2
Stellendam, *Neths.* 16 E4
Stelvio, Paso dello, *Italy* 23 C10
Stemshaug, *Norway* 10 A2
Stendal, *Germany* 18 C7
Stene, *Belgium* 17 F1
Stensele, *Sweden* 8 D14
Stenstorp, *Sweden* 11 F7
Stepanakert = Khankendy, *Azerbaijan* 67 D12
Stephen, *U.S.A.* 108 A6
Stephens Creek, *Australia* 91 E3
Stephens I., *Canada* 100 C2
Stephenville, *Canada* 99 C8
Stephenville, *U.S.A.* 109 J5
Stepnica, *Poland* 20 B4
Stepnoi = Elista, *Russia* 43 C11
Stepnyak, *Kazakhstan* 44 D8
Steppe, *Asia* 46 E9
Sterkstroom, *S. Africa* 84 E4
Sterling, *Colo., U.S.A.* 108 E3
Sterling, *Ill., U.S.A.* 108 E10
Sterling, *Kans., U.S.A.* 108 F5
Sterling City, *U.S.A.* 109 K4
Sterling Run, *U.S.A.* 106 E6
Sterlitamak, *Russia* 44 D6
Sternberg, *Germany* 18 B7
Šternberk, *Czech.* 20 F7
Stérnes, *Greece* 37 D6
Stettin = Szczecin, *Poland* 20 B4
Stettiner Haff, *Germany* 18 B10
Stettler, *Canada* 100 C6
Steubenville, *U.S.A.* 106 F4
Stevens Point, *U.S.A.* 108 C10
Stevenson, *U.S.A.* 112 E5
Stevenson L., *Canada* 101 C9
Stevns Klint, *Denmark* 11 J6
Stewart, *B.C., Canada* 100 B3
Stewart, *N.W.T., Canada* 96 B6
Stewart, *U.S.A.* 112 F7
Stewart, C., *Australia* 90 A1
Stewart, I., *Chile* 128 D2
Stewart I., *N.Z.* 87 M1
Stewarts Point, *U.S.A.* 112 G3
Stewiacke, *Canada* 99 C7
Steynsburg, *S. Africa* 84 E4
Steyr, *Austria* 21 G4
Steytlerville, *S. Africa* 84 E3
Stia, *Italy* 33 E8
Stiens, *Neths.* 16 B7
Stigler, *U.S.A.* 109 H7
Stigliano, *Italy* 35 B9
Stigsnæs, *Denmark* 11 J5
Stigtomta, *Sweden* 11 F10
Stikine →, *Canada* 100 B2
Stilfontein, *S. Africa* 84 D4
Stilís, *Greece* 39 L5
Stillwater, *N.Z.* 87 K3
Stillwater, *Minn., U.S.A.* 108 C8
Stillwater, *N.Y., U.S.A.* 107 D11
Stillwater, *Okla., U.S.A.* 109 G6
Stillwater Range, *U.S.A.* 110 G4
Stilwell, *U.S.A.* 109 H7
Štip, *Macedonia* 39 H5
Stíra, *Greece* 39 L7
Stirling, *Australia* 90 B3
Stirling, *Canada* 100 D6
Stirling, *U.K.* 14 E5
Stirling Ra., *Australia* 89 F2
Stittsville, *Canada* 107 A9
Stockach, *Germany* 19 H5
Stockerau, *Austria* 21 G6
Stockett, *U.S.A.* 110 C8
Stockholm, *Sweden* 10 E12
Stockholms län □, *Sweden* 10 E12
Stockhorn, *Switz.* 22 C5
Stockport, *U.K.* 12 D5
Stockton, *Calif., U.S.A.* 111 H3
Stockton, *Kans., U.S.A.* 108 F5
Stockton, *Mo., U.S.A.* 109 G8
Stockton-on-Tees, *U.K.* 12 C6
Stockvik, *Sweden* 10 B11
Stöde, *Sweden* 10 B10
Stogovo, *Macedonia* 39 H3
Stoke on Trent, *U.K.* 12 D5
Stokes Bay, *Canada* 98 C3
Stokes Pt., *Australia* 90 G3
Stokes Ra., *Australia* 88 C5
Stokkseyri, *Iceland* 8 E3
Stokksnes, *Iceland* 8 D6
Stolac, *Bos.-H.* 21 M7
Stolberg, *Germany* 18 E2
Stolbovaya, *Russia* 41 D10
Stolbovaya, *Russia* 45 C16
Stolbovoy, Ostrov, *Russia* 45 D17
Stolbtsy, *Belorussia* 40 E5
Stolin, *Belorussia* 40 F5
Stolwijk, *Neths.* 16 E5
Stomíon, *Greece* 37 D5
Ston, *Croatia* 21 N7
Stonehaven, *U.K.* 14 E6
Stonehenge, *Australia* 90 C3
Stonewall, *Canada* 101 C9
Stony L., *Man., Canada* 101 B9
Stony L., *Ont., Canada* 106 B6
Stony Rapids, *Canada* 101 B7
Stony Tunguska = Podkamennaya Tunguska →, *Russia* 45 C10
Stonyford, *U.S.A.* 112 F4
Stopnica, *Poland* 20 E10
Stora Lulevatten, *Sweden* 8 C15
Stora Sjöfallet, *Sweden* 8 C15
Storavan, *Sweden* 8 D15
Store Bælt, *Denmark* 11 J5
Store Creek, *Australia* 91 E4
Store Heddinge, *Denmark* 11 J6
Støren, *Norway* 10 A4
Storlulea = Stora Lulevatten, *Sweden* 8 C15
Storm B., *Australia* 90 G4
Storm Lake, *U.S.A.* 108 D7
Stormberge, *S. Africa* 84 E4
Stormsrivier, *S. Africa* 84 E3
Stornoway, *U.K.* 14 C2
Storozhinets, *Ukraine* 42 B1
Storsjö, *Sweden* 10 B7
Storsjøen, *Hedmark, Norway* 10 D5
Storsjøen, *Hedmark, Norway* 10 C5
Storsjön, *Sweden* 10 B7
Storstrøms Amt. □, *Denmark* 11 K5
Storuman, *Sweden* 8 D14
Stoughton, *Canada* 101 D8
Stour →, *Dorset, U.K.* 13 G5
Stour →, *Here. & Worcs., U.K.* 13 E5
Stour →, *Kent, U.K.* 13 F9
Stour →, *Suffolk, U.K.* 13 F9
Stourbridge, *U.K.* 13 E5
Stout, L., *Canada* 101 C10
Stove Pipe Wells Village, *U.S.A.* 113 J9
Stowmarket, *U.K.* 13 E9
Strabane, *U.K.* 15 B4
Strabane □, *U.K.* 15 B4
Stracin, *Macedonia* 38 G5
Stradella, *Italy* 32 C6
Strahan, *Australia* 90 G4
Strakonice, *Czech.* 20 F3
Straldzha, *Bulgaria* 38 G9
Stralsund, *Germany* 18 A9
Strand, *S. Africa* 84 E2
Strangford L., *U.K.* 15 B6
Strängnäs, *Sweden* 10 E11
Strangsville, *U.S.A.* 106 E3
Stranraer, *U.K.* 14 G3
Strasbourg, *Canada* 101 C8
Strasbourg, *France* 25 D14
Strasburg, *Germany* 18 B9
Strasburg, *U.S.A.* 108 B4
Strassen, *Lux.* 17 J8
Stratford, *Canada* 98 D3
Stratford, *N.Z.* 87 H5
Stratford, *Calif., U.S.A.* 111 H4
Stratford, *Conn., U.S.A.* 107 E11
Stratford, *Tex., U.S.A.* 109 G3
Stratford-upon-Avon, *U.K.* 13 E6
Strath Spey, *U.K.* 14 D5
Strathalbyn, *Australia* 91 F2
Strathclyde □, *U.K.* 14 F4
Strathcona Prov. Park, *Canada* 100 D3
Strathmore, *Australia* 90 B3
Strathmore, *Canada* 100 C6
Strathmore, *U.K.* 14 E5
Strathmore, *U.S.A.* 112 J7
Strathnaver, *Canada* 100 C4
Strathpeffer, *U.K.* 14 D4
Strathroy, *Canada* 98 D3
Strathy Pt., *U.K.* 14 C4
Stratton, *U.S.A.* 108 F3
Straubing, *Germany* 19 G8
Straumnes, *Iceland* 8 C2
Strausberg, *Germany* 18 C9
Strawberry Reservoir, *U.S.A.* 110 F8
Strawn, *U.S.A.* 109 J5
Strážnice, *Czech.* 20 G7
Streaky B., *Australia* 91 E1
Streaky Bay, *Australia* 91 E1
Streator, *U.S.A.* 108 E10
Streé, *Belgium* 17 H4
Streeter, *U.S.A.* 108 B5
Streetsville, *Canada* 106 C5
Strehaia, *Romania* 38 E6
Strelcha, *Bulgaria* 38 G7
Strelka, *Russia* 45 D10
Streng →, *Cambodia* 58 F4
Strésa, *Italy* 32 C5
Strezhevoy, *Russia* 44 C8
Stříbro, *Czech.* 20 F3
Strijen, *Neths.* 16 E5
Strimón →, *Greece* 39 J6
Strimonikós Kólpos, *Greece* 39 J6
Stroeder, *Argentina* 128 B4
Strofádhes, *Greece* 39 M4
Strömbacka, *Sweden* 10 C10
Strómboli, *Italy* 35 D8
Stromeferry, *U.K.* 14 D3
Stromness, *U.K.* 14 C5
Ströms vattudal, *Sweden* 8 D13
Strömstad, *Sweden* 9 G11
Strömsund, *Sweden* 8 E13
Stróngoli, *Italy* 35 C10
Stronsay, *U.K.* 14 B6
Stronsburg, *U.S.A.* 108 E6
Stroud, *U.K.* 13 F5
Stroud Road, *Australia* 91 E5
Stroudsburg, *U.S.A.* 107 F9
Stroumbi, *Cyprus* 37 E11
Struer, *Denmark* 11 H2
Struga, *Macedonia* 39 H3
Strugi Krasnyye, *Russia* 40 B6
Strumica, *Macedonia* 39 H5
Strumica →, *Europe* 39 H6
Struthers, *Canada* 98 C2
Struthers, *U.S.A.* 106 E4
Stryi, *Ukraine* 40 G3
Stryker, *U.S.A.* 110 B6
Strzegom, *Poland* 20 E6
Strzelce Krajeńskie, *Poland* 20 C5
Strzelecki Cr. →, *Australia* 91 D2
Strzelin, *Poland* 20 E7
Strzelno, *Poland* 20 C8
Strzyżów, *Poland* 20 F11
Stuart, *Fla., U.S.A.* 105 M5
Stuart, *Nebr., U.S.A.* 108 D5
Stuart →, *Canada* 100 C4
Stuart Bluff Ra., *Australia* 88 D5
Stuart L., *Canada* 100 C4
Stuart Ra., *Australia* 91 D1
Stubbekøbing, *Denmark* 11 K6
Stugun, *Sweden* 10 A9
Stull, L., *Canada* 98 B1
Stung Treng, *Cambodia* 58 F5
Stupart →, *Canada* 101 B10
Stupino, *Russia* 41 D11
Sturgeon B., *Canada* 101 C9
Sturgeon Bay, *U.S.A.* 104 C2
Sturgeon Falls, *Canada* 98 C4
Sturgeon L., *Alta., Canada* 100 B5
Sturgeon L., *Ont., Canada* 106 B6
Sturgeon L., *Ont., Canada* 98 B1
Sturgis, *Mich., U.S.A.* 104 E3
Sturgis, *S. Dak., U.S.A.* 108 C3
Sturt Cr. →, *Australia* 88 C4
Sturt Creek, *Australia* 88 C4
Stutterheim, *S. Africa* 84 E4
Stuttgart, *Germany* 19 G5
Stuttgart, *U.S.A.* 109 H9
Stuyvesant, *U.S.A.* 107 D11
Stykkishólmur, *Iceland* 8 D2
Styr →, *Belorussia* 40 E5
Styria = Steiermark □, *Austria* 21 H5
Su Xian, *China* 50 H9
Suakin, *Sudan* 76 D4
Suan, *N. Korea* 51 E14
Suapure →, *Venezuela* 120 B4
Suaqui, *Mexico* 114 B3
Suatá →, *Venezuela* 121 B4
Subang, *Indonesia* 57 G12
Subansiri →, *India* 61 F18
Subayhah, *Si. Arabia* 64 D3
Subi, *Indonesia* 59 L7
Subiaco, *Italy* 33 G10
Subotica, *Serbia, Yug.* 21 J9
Success, *Canada* 101 C7
Suceava, *Romania* 38 B9
Suceava →, *Romania* 38 B9
Sucha-Beskidzka, *Poland* 20 F9
Suchan, *Poland* 20 B5
Suchan, *Russia* 48 C6
Suchitoto, *El Salv.* 116 D2
Suchou = Suzhou, *China* 53 B13
Süchow = Xuzhou, *China* 51 G9
Suchowola, *Poland* 20 B13
Sucio →, *Colombia* 120 B2
Suck →, *Ireland* 15 C3
Sucre, *Bolivia* 125 D4
Sucre, *Colombia* 120 B3
Sucre □, *Colombia* 120 B2
Sucre □, *Venezuela* 121 A5
Sucuaro, *Colombia* 120 C4
Sućuraj, *Croatia* 33 E14
Sucuriju, *Brazil* 122 A2
Sucuriú →, *Brazil* 125 E7
Sud, Pte., *Canada* 99 C7
Sud-Ouest, Pte. du, *Canada* 99 C7
Suda →, *Russia* 41 B10
Sudak, *Ukraine* 42 D6
Sudan, *U.S.A.* 109 H3
Sudan ■, *Africa* 77 E3
Suday, *Russia* 41 B13
Sudbury, *Canada* 98 C3
Sudbury, *U.K.* 13 E8
Sûdd, *Sudan* 77 F2
Suddie, *Guyana* 121 B6
Süderbrarup, *Germany* 18 A5
Süderlügum, *Germany* 18 A4
Süderoog-Sand, *Germany* 18 A4
Sudeten Mts. = Sudety, *Europe* 20 E6
Sudety, *Europe* 20 E6
Sudi, *Tanzania* 83 E4
Sudirman, Pegunungan, *Indonesia* 57 E9
Sudogda, *Russia* 41 D12
Sudr, *Egypt* 76 J8
Sudzha, *Russia* 40 F9
Sueca, *Spain* 29 F4
Suedala, *Sweden* 11 J7
Suez = El Suweis, *Egypt* 76 J8
Suez, G. of = Suweis, Khalîg el, *Egypt* 76 J8
Suez Canal = Suweis, Qanâl es, *Egypt* 76 H8
Suffield, *Canada* 101 C6
Suffolk, *U.S.A.* 104 G7
Suffolk □, *U.K.* 13 E9
Sugar City, *U.S.A.* 108 F3
Suğla Gölü, *Turkey* 66 E5
Sugluk = Saglouc, *Canada* 97 B12
Sugny, *Belgium* 17 J5
Suhaia, L., *Romania* 38 F8
Suhār, *Oman* 65 E8
Suhbaatar, *Mongolia* 54 A5
Sühbaatar □, *Mongolia* 50 B8
Suhl, *Germany* 18 E6
Suhr, *Switz.* 22 B6
Şuhut, *Turkey* 66 D4
Sui Xian, *Henan, China* 50 G8
Sui Xian, *Henan, China* 53 B9
Suiá Missu →, *Brazil* 125 C7
Suichang, *China* 53 C12
Suichuan, *China* 53 D10
Suide, *China* 50 F6
Suifenhe, *China* 51 B16
Suihua, *China* 54 B7
Suijiang, *China* 52 C4
Suining, *Hunan, China* 53 D8
Suining, *Jiangsu, China* 51 H9
Suining, *Sichuan, China* 52 B5
Suiping, *China* 50 H7
Suippes, *France* 25 C11
Suir →, *Ireland* 15 D4
Suixi, *China* 53 G8
Suiyang, *Guizhou, China* 52 D6
Suiyang, *Heilongjiang, China* 51 B16
Suizhong, *China* 51 D11
Sujangarh, *India* 62 F6
Sukabumi, *Indonesia* 57 G12
Sukadana, *Kalimantan, Indonesia* 56 E3
Sukadana, *Sumatera, Indonesia* 56 F3
Sukagawa, *Japan* 49 F10
Sukaraja, *Indonesia* 56 E4
Sukarnapura = Jayapura, *Indonesia* 57 E10
Sukchŏn, *N. Korea* 51 E13
Sukhinichi, *Russia* 40 D9
Sukhona →, *Russia* 44 D4
Sukhothai, *Thailand* 58 D2
Sukhumi, *Georgia* 43 E9
Sukkur, *Pakistan* 62 F3
Sukkur Barrage, *Pakistan* 62 F3
Sukumo, *Japan* 49 H6
Sukunka →, *Canada* 100 B4
Sul, Canal do, *Brazil* 122 B2
Sula →, *Ukraine* 40 G8
Sula, Kepulauan, *Indonesia* 57 E7
Sulaco →, *Honduras* 116 C2
Sulaiman Range, *Pakistan* 62 D3
Sulak →, *Russia* 43 E12
Sūlār, *Iran* 65 D6

Sulawesi □, *Indonesia* 57 E6
Sulawesi Sea, *Indonesia* 57 D6
Sulechów, *Poland* 20 C5
Sulejów, *Poland* 20 D9
Sulgen, *Switz.* 23 A8
Sulima, *S. Leone* 78 D2
Sulina, *Romania* 38 D12
Sulina, Braţul →, *Romania* 38 D12
Sulingen, *Germany* 18 C4
Sulitälma, *Sweden* 8 C14
Sulitjelma, *Norway* 8 C14
Sullana, *Peru* 124 A1
Sullivan, *Ill., U.S.A.* 108 F10
Sullivan, *Ind., U.S.A.* 104 F2
Sullivan, *Mo., U.S.A.* 108 F9
Sullivan Bay, *Canada* 100 C3
Sully-sur-Loire, *France* 25 E9
Sulmona, *Italy* 33 F10
Sulphur, *La., U.S.A.* 109 K8
Sulphur, *Okla., U.S.A.* 109 H6
Sulphur Pt., *Canada* 100 A6
Sulphur Springs, *U.S.A.* 109 J7
Sulphur Springs Draw →, *U.S.A.* 109 J4
Sultan, *Canada* 98 C3
Sultan, *U.S.A.* 112 C5
Sultanpur, *India* 63 F10
Sulu Arch., *Phil.* 55 J4
Sulu Sea, *E. Indies* 55 G4
Sülüklü, *Turkey* 66 D5
Sululta, *Ethiopia* 77 F4
Suluova, *Turkey* 66 C6
Suluq, *Libya* 73 B9
Sulzbach, *Germany* 19 F3
Sulzbach-Rosenberg, *Germany* 19 F7
Sulzberger Ice Shelf, *Antarctica* 5 D10
Sumalata, *Indonesia* 57 D6
Sumampa, *Argentina* 126 B3
Sumatera □, *Indonesia* 56 D2
Sumatra = Sumatera □, *Indonesia* 56 D2
Sumatra, *U.S.A.* 110 C10
Sumba, *Indonesia* 57 F5
Sumba, Selat, *Indonesia* 57 F5
Sumbawa, *Indonesia* 56 F5
Sumbawa Besar, *Indonesia* 56 F5
Sumbawanga □, *Tanzania* 82 D3
Sumbe, *Angola* 80 G2
Sumburgh Hd., *U.K.* 14 B7
Sumdo, *India* 63 B8
Sumé, *Brazil* 122 C4
Sumedang, *Indonesia* 57 G12
Šumen, *Bulgaria* 38 F9
Sumenep, *Indonesia* 57 G15
Sumgait, *Azerbaijan* 43 F13
Sumiswald, *Switz.* 22 B5
Summer L., *U.S.A.* 110 E3
Summerland, *Canada* 100 D5
Summerside, *Canada* 99 C7
Summerville, *Ga., U.S.A.* 105 H3
Summerville, *S.C., U.S.A.* 105 J5
Summit Lake, *Canada* 100 C4
Summit Peak, *U.S.A.* 111 H10
Sumner, *Iowa, U.S.A.* 108 D8
Sumner, *Wash., U.S.A.* 112 C4
Sumoto, *Japan* 49 G7
Sumqayit = Sumgait, *Azerbaijan* 43 F13
Sumter, *U.S.A.* 105 J5
Sumy, *Ukraine* 40 F9
Sun City, *Ariz., U.S.A.* 111 K7
Sun City, *Calif., U.S.A.* 113 M9
Sunagawa, *Japan* 48 C10
Sunan, *N. Korea* 51 E13
Sunart, L., *U.K.* 14 E3
Sunburst, *U.S.A.* 110 B8
Sunbury, *Australia* 91 F3
Sunbury, *U.S.A.* 107 F8
Sunchales, *Argentina* 126 C3
Suncho Corral, *Argentina* 126 B3
Sunchon, *S. Korea* 51 G14
Suncook, *U.S.A.* 107 C13
Sunda, Selat, *Indonesia* 56 F3
Sunda Is., *Indonesia* 46 K14
Sunda Str. = Sunda, Selat, *Indonesia* 56 F3
Sundance, *U.S.A.* 108 C2
Sundarbans, The, *Asia* 61 J16
Sundargarh, *India* 61 H14
Sundays = Sondags →, *S. Africa* 84 E4
Sundbyberg, *Sweden* 10 E11
Sunderland, *Canada* 106 B5
Sunderland, *U.K.* 12 C6
Sundre, *Canada* 100 C6
Sundridge, *Canada* 98 C4
Sunds, *Denmark* 11 H3
Sundsjö, *Sweden* 10 B9
Sundsvall, *Sweden* 10 B11
Sung Hei, *Vietnam* 59 G6
Sungai Kolok, *Thailand* 59 J3
Sungai Lembing, *Malaysia* 59 L4
Sungai Patani, *Malaysia* 59 K3
Sungaigerong, *Indonesia* 56 E2
Sungailiat, *Indonesia* 56 E3
Sungaipakning, *Indonesia* 56 D2
Sungaipenuh, *Indonesia* 56 E2
Sungaitiram, *Indonesia* 56 E5
Sungari = Songhua Jiang →, *China* 54 B8
Sungguminasa, *Indonesia* 57 F5
Sunghua Chiang = Songhua Jiang →, *China* 54 B8
Sungikai, *Sudan* 77 E2
Sungurlu, *Turkey* 42 F6
Sunja, *Croatia* 33 C13
Sunnyside, *Utah, U.S.A.* 110 G8
Sunnyside, *Wash., U.S.A.* 110 C3
Sunnyvale, *U.S.A.* 111 H2
Sunray, *U.S.A.* 109 G4
Suntar, *Russia* 45 C12
Sunyani, *Ghana* 78 D4
Supai, *U.S.A.* 111 H7
Supamo →, *Venezuela* 121 B5
Supaul, *India* 63 F12
Supe, *Peru* 124 C2
Superior, *Ariz., U.S.A.* 111 K8
Superior, *Mont., U.S.A.* 110 C6
Superior, *Nebr., U.S.A.* 108 E5
Superior, *Wis., U.S.A.* 108 B8
Superior, L., *U.S.A.* 98 C2
Supetar, *Croatia* 33 E13
Suphan Buri, *Thailand* 58 E3
Suphan Dağı, *Turkey* 67 D10
Supriori, Kepulauan, *Indonesia* 57 E9
Supung Sk., *China* 51 D13
Sūq Suwayq, *Si. Arabia* 64 E3
Suqian, *China* 51 H10
Sūr, *Lebanon* 69 B4
Sur, Pt., *U.S.A.* 111 H3
Sura →, *Russia* 41 C15
Surab, *Pakistan* 62 E2
Surabaja = Surabaya, *Indonesia* 57 G15
Surabaya, *Indonesia* 57 G15
Suraia, *Romania* 38 D10
Surakarta, *Indonesia* 57 G14
Surakhany, *Azerbaijan* 43 F14
Surat, *Australia* 91 D4
Surat, *India* 60 J8
Surat Thani, *Thailand* 59 H2
Suratgarh, *India* 62 E5
Surazh, *Belorussia* 40 D7
Surazh, *Russia* 40 E8
Surduc Pasul, *Romania* 38 D6
Surdulica, *Serbia, Yug.* 21 N12
Sûre = Sauer →, *Germany* 17 J9
Surendranagar, *India* 62 H4
Surf, *U.S.A.* 113 L6
Surgères, *France* 26 B3
Surgut, *Russia* 44 C8
Surhuisterveen, *Neths.* 16 B8
Suriapet, *India* 60 L11
Surigao, *Phil.* 55 G6
Surigao Strait, *Phil.* 55 F6
Surin, *Thailand* 58 E4
Surin Nua, Ko, *Thailand* 59 H1
Surinam ■, *S. Amer.* 121 C6
Suriname □, *Surinam* 121 B6
Suriname ■ = Surinam ■, *S. Amer.* 121 C6
Suriname →, *Surinam* 121 B6
Sūrmaq, *Iran* 65 D7
Sürmene, *Turkey* 43 F9
Surovikino, *Russia* 43 B10
Surprise L., *Canada* 100 B2
Surrey □, *U.K.* 13 F7
Sursee, *Switz.* 22 B6
Sursk, *Russia* 41 E14
Surt, *Libya* 73 B8
Surt, Khalīj, *Libya* 73 B8
Surtsey, *Iceland* 8 E3
Surubim, *Brazil* 122 C4
Sürüç, *Turkey* 67 E8
Suruga-Wan, *Japan* 49 G9
Surumu →, *Brazil* 121 C5
Susa, *Italy* 32 C4
Suså →, *Denmark* 11 J5
Sušac, *Croatia* 33 F13
Susak, *Croatia* 33 D11
Susaki, *Japan* 49 H6
Süsangerd, *Iran* 65 D6
Susanino, *Russia* 45 D15
Susanville, *U.S.A.* 110 F3
Susch, *Switz.* 23 C10
Suşehri, *Turkey* 67 C8
Susong, *China* 53 B11
Susquehanna →, *U.S.A.* 107 G8
Susquehanna Depot, *U.S.A.* 107 E9
Susques, *Argentina* 126 A2
Sussex, *Canada* 99 C6
Sussex, *U.S.A.* 107 E10
Sussex, E. □, *U.K.* 13 G8
Sussex, W. □, *U.K.* 13 G7
Susteren, *Neths.* 17 F7
Sustut →, *Canada* 100 B3
Susuman, *Russia* 45 C15
Susunu, *Indonesia* 57 E8
Susurluk, *Turkey* 66 D3
Susuz, *Turkey* 67 C10
Sütçüler, *Turkey* 66 E4
Sutherland, *S. Africa* 84 E3
Sutherland, *U.S.A.* 108 E4
Sutherland Falls, *N.Z.* 87 L1
Sutherlin, *U.S.A.* 110 E2
Sutivan, *Croatia* 33 E13
Sutlej →, *Pakistan* 62 E4
Sutter, *U.S.A.* 112 F5
Sutter Creek, *U.S.A.* 112 G6
Sutton, *Canada* 107 A12
Sutton, *U.S.A.* 108 E6
Sutton →, *Canada* 98 A3
Sutton in Ashfield, *U.K.* 12 D6
Suttor →, *Australia* 90 C4
Suttsu, *Japan* 48 C10
Suva, *Fiji* 87 D8
Suva Reka, *Serbia, Yug.* 21 N10
Suvo Rudište, *Serbia, Yug.* 21 M10
Suvorov, *Russia* 41 D10
Suvorov Is. = Suwarrow Is., *Cook Is.* 93 J11
Suwałki, *Poland* 20 A12
Suwannaphum, *Thailand* 58 E4
Suwannee →, *U.S.A.* 105 L4
Suwanose-Jima, *Japan* 49 K4
Suwarrow Is., *Cook Is.* 93 J11
Suwayq aş Şuqban, *Iraq* 64 D5
Suweis, Khalîg el, *Egypt* 76 J8
Suweis, Qanâl es, *Egypt* 76 H8
Suwŏn, *S. Korea* 51 F14
Suzdal, *Russia* 41 C12
Suzhou, *China* 53 B13
Suzu, *Japan* 49 F8
Suzu-Misaki, *Japan* 49 F8
Suzuka, *Japan* 49 G8
Suzzara, *Italy* 32 C7
Svalbard, *Arctic* 4 B8
Svalbarð, *Iceland* 8 C6
Svalöv, *Sweden* 11 J7
Svanvik, *Norway* 8 B21
Svappavaara, *Sweden* 8 C16
Svarstad, *Norway* 10 E3
Svartisen, *Norway* 8 C12
Svartvik, *Sweden* 10 B11
Svatovo, *Ukraine* 42 B8
Svay Chek, *Cambodia* 58 F4
Svay Rieng, *Cambodia* 59 G5
Svealand □, *Sweden* 9 G13
Sveg, *Sweden* 9 E13
Svendborg, *Denmark* 11 J4
Svene, *Norway* 10 E3
Svenljunga, *Sweden* 11 G7
Svenstrup, *Denmark* 11 H3
Sverdlovsk = Yekaterinburg, *Russia* 44 D7
Sverdlovsk, *Ukraine* 43 B8
Sverdrup Is., *Canada* 4 B3
Svetac, *Croatia* 33 E12
Sveti Ivan Zelina, *Croatia* 33 C13
Sveti Jurij, *Slovenia* 33 B12
Sveti Lenart, *Slovenia* 33 B12
Sveti Nikole, *Macedonia* 39 H4
Sveti Trojica, *Slovenia* 33 B12
Svetlaya, *Russia* 48 A9
Svetlogorsk, *Belorussia* 40 E6
Svetlograd, *Russia* 43 D10
Svetlovodsk, *Ukraine* 40 G8
Svetozarevo, *Serbia, Yug.* 21 L11
Svidník, *Slovakia* 20 F11
Svilaja Planina, *Croatia* 33 E13
Svilengrad, *Bulgaria* 39 H9
Svir →, *Russia* 6 C12
Svishtov, *Bulgaria* 38 F8
Svisloch, *Belorussia* 40 E4
Svitava →, *Czech.* 20 F6
Svitavy, *Czech.* 20 F6
Svobodnyy, *Russia* 45 D13
Svolvær, *Norway* 8 B13
Svratka →, *Czech.* 20 F6
Svrljig, *Serbia, Yug.* 21 M12
Swabian Alps = Schwäbische Alb, *Germany* 19 G5
Swainsboro, *U.S.A.* 105 J4
Swakopmund, *Namibia* 84 C1
Swale →, *U.K.* 12 C6
Swalmen, *Neths.* 17 F8
Swan Hill, *Australia* 91 F3
Swan Hills, *Canada* 100 C5
Swan Is., *W. Indies* 116 C3
Swan L., *Canada* 101 C8
Swan River, *Canada* 101 C8
Swanage, *U.K.* 13 G6
Swansea, *Australia* 91 E5
Swansea, *U.K.* 13 F4
Swar →, *Pakistan* 63 B5
Swartberge, *S. Africa* 84 E3
Swartmodder, *S. Africa* 84 D3
Swartruggens, *S. Africa* 84 D4
Swarzędz, *Poland* 20 C7
Swastika, *Canada* 98 C3
Swatow = Shantou, *China* 53 F11
Swaziland ■, *Africa* 85 D5
Sweden ■, *Europe* 9 H13
Swedru, *Ghana* 79 D4
Sweet Home, *U.S.A.* 110 D2
Sweetwater, *Nev., U.S.A.* 112 G7
Sweetwater, *Tex., U.S.A.* 109 J4
Sweetwater →, *U.S.A.* 110 E10
Swellendam, *S. Africa* 84 E3
Świdnica, *Poland* 20 E6
Świdnik, *Poland* 20 D12
Świdwin, *Poland* 20 B5
Świebodzin, *Poland* 20 C5
Świecie, *Poland* 20 B8
Świętokrzyskie, Góry, *Poland* 20 E10
Swift Current, *Canada* 101 C7
Swiftcurrent →, *Canada* 101 C7
Swilly, L., *Ireland* 15 A4
Swindle, I., *Canada* 100 C3
Swindon, *U.K.* 13 F6
Swinemünde = Świnoujście, *Poland* 20 B4
Świnoujście, *Poland* 20 B4
Switzerland ■, *Europe* 22 D6
Swords, *Ireland* 15 C5
Syasstroy, *Russia* 40 A8
Sychevka, *Russia* 40 D9
Sydney, *Australia* 91 E5
Sydney, *Canada* 99 C7
Sydney Mines, *Canada* 99 C7
Sydprøven, *Greenland* 4 C5
Sydra G. of = Surt, Khalīj, *Libya* 73 B8
Syke, *Germany* 18 C4
Syktyvkar, *Russia* 44 C6
Sylacauga, *U.S.A.* 105 J2
Sylarna, *Sweden* 8 E12
Sylhet, *Bangla.* 61 G17
Sylt, *Germany* 18 A4
Sylvan Lake, *Canada* 100 C6
Sylvania, *U.S.A.* 105 J5
Sylvester, *U.S.A.* 105 K4
Sym, *Russia* 44 C9
Symón, *Mexico* 114 C4
Synnott Ra., *Australia* 88 C4
Syracuse, *Kans., U.S.A.* 109 F4
Syracuse, *N.Y., U.S.A.* 107 C8
Syrdarya →, *Kazakhstan* 44 E7
Syria ■, *Asia* 64 C3
Syul'dzhyukyor, *Russia* 45 C12
Syzran, *Russia* 41 E16
Szaraz →, *Hungary* 21 J10
Szarvas, *Hungary* 21 J10
Szczebrzeszyn, *Poland* 20 E12
Szczecin, *Poland* 20 B4
Szczecinek, *Poland* 20 B6
Szczekocimy, *Poland* 20 E9
Szczytno, *Poland* 20 B11
Szechwan = Sichuan □, *China* 52 B5
Szeged, *Hungary* 21 J10
Szeghalom, *Hungary* 21 H11
Székesfehérvár, *Hungary* 21 H8
Szekszárd, *Hungary* 21 J8
Szendrö, *Hungary* 21 G10
Szentendre, *Hungary* 21 H9
Szentes, *Hungary* 21 J10
Szentgotthárd, *Hungary* 21 J6
Szentlörinc, *Hungary* 21 J8
Szigetvár, *Hungary* 21 J7
Szolnok, *Hungary* 21 H10
Szombathely, *Hungary* 21 H6
Szprotawa, *Poland* 20 D5
Szydłowiec, *Poland* 20 D10
Szypliszki, *Poland* 20 A13

T

't Harde, *Neths.* 16 D7
't Zandt, *Neths.* 16 B9
Ta Khli Khok, *Thailand* 58 E3
Ta Lai, *Vietnam* 59 G6
Tabacal, *Argentina* 126 A3
Tabaco, *Phil.* 55 E5
Tabagné, *Ivory C.* 78 D4
Ţābah, *Si. Arabia* 64 E4
Tabajara, *Brazil* 125 B5
Tabalos, *Peru* 124 B2
Tabarca, I. de, *Spain* 29 G4
Tabarka, *Tunisia* 75 A6
Ţabas, *Khorāsān, Iran* 65 C9
Ţabas, *Khorāsān, Iran* 65 C8
Tabasará, Serranía de, *Panama* 116 E3
Tabasco □, *Mexico* 115 D6
Tabatinga, Serra da, *Brazil* 122 D3
Tabāzīn, *Iran* 65 D8
Tabelbala, Kahal de, *Algeria* 75 C4
Taber, *Canada* 100 D6
Tabernas, *Spain* 29 H2
Tabernes de Valldigna, *Spain* 29 F4
Tabira, *Brazil* 122 C4
Tablas, *Phil.* 55 E5
Tablas Strait, *Phil.* 55 E4
Table B. = Tafelbaai, *S. Africa* 84 E2
Table B., *Canada* 99 B8
Table Mt., *S. Africa* 84 E2
Tableland, *Australia* 88 C4
Tabletop, Mt., *Australia* 90 C4
Tábor, *Czech.* 20 F4
Tabora, *Tanzania* 82 D3
Tabora □, *Tanzania* 82 D3
Tabou, *Ivory C.* 78 E3
Tabrīz, *Iran* 64 B5
Tabuaeran, *Pac. Oc.* 93 G12
Tabuelan, *Phil.* 55 F5
Tabuenca, *Spain* 28 D3
Tabūk, *Si. Arabia* 64 D3
Tacámbaro de Codallos, *Mexico* 114 D4
Tacheng, *China* 54 B3
Tach'ing Shan = Daqing Shan, *China* 50 D6
Táchira □, *Venezuela* 120 B3
Tácina →, *Italy* 35 D9
Tacloban, *Phil.* 55 F6
Tacna, *Peru* 124 D3
Tacna □, *Peru* 124 D3
Tacoma, *U.S.A.* 112 C4
Tacuarembó, *Uruguay* 127 C4
Tacutu →, *Brazil* 121 C5
Tademaït, Plateau du, *Algeria* 75 C5
Tadent, O. →, *Algeria* 75 D6
Tadjerdjeri, O. →, *Algeria* 75 C6
Tadjerouna, *Algeria* 75 B5
Tadjettaret, O. →, *Algeria* 75 D6
Tadjmout, *Oasis, Algeria* 75 B5
Tadjmout, *Saoura, Algeria* 75 C5
Tadjoura, *Djibouti* 68 E3
Tadjoura, Golfe de, *Djibouti* 77 E5
Tadmor, *N.Z.* 87 J4
Tadoule, L., *Canada* 101 B9
Tadoussac, *Canada* 99 C6
Tadzhikistan = Tajikistan ■, *Asia* 44 F8
Taechŏn-ni, *S. Korea* 51 F14
Taegu, *S. Korea* 51 G15
Taegwan, *N. Korea* 51 D13
Taejŏn, *S. Korea* 51 F14
Tafalla, *Spain* 28 C3
Tafar, *Sudan* 77 F2
Tafassasset, O. →, *Algeria* 75 D6
Tafelbaai, *S. Africa* 84 E2
Tafelney, C., *Morocco* 74 B3
Tafermaar, *Indonesia* 57 F8
Taffermit, *Morocco* 74 C3
Tafí Viejo, *Argentina* 126 B2
Tafīhān, *Iran* 65 D7
Tafiré, *Ivory C.* 78 D3
Tafnidilt, *Morocco* 74 C2
Tafraoute, *Morocco* 74 C3
Taft, *Iran* 65 D7
Taft, *Phil.* 55 F6
Taft, *Calif., U.S.A.* 113 K7
Taft, *Tex., U.S.A.* 109 M6
Taga Dzong, *Bhutan* 61 F16
Taganrog, *Russia* 43 C8
Taganrogskiy Zaliv, *Russia* 42 C8
Tagânt, *Mauritania* 78 B2
Tagatay, *Phil.* 55 D4
Tagbilaran, *Phil.* 55 G5
Tággia, *Italy* 32 E4
Taghzout, *Morocco* 74 B4
Tagish, *Canada* 100 A2
Tagish L., *Canada* 100 A2
Tagliacozzo, *Italy* 33 F10
Tagliamento →, *Italy* 33 C10
Táglio di Po, *Italy* 33 D9
Tagna, *Colombia* 120 D3
Tago, *Phil.* 55 G7
Tagomago, I. de, *Spain* 36 B8
Taguatinga, *Brazil* 123 D3
Tagudin, *Phil.* 55 C4
Tagum, *Phil.* 55 H6
Tagus = Tejo →, *Europe* 31 G1
Tahakopa, *N.Z.* 87 M2
Tahala, *Morocco* 74 B4
Tahan, Gunong, *Malaysia* 59 K4
Tahat, *Algeria* 75 D6
Tāherī, *Iran* 65 E7
Tahiti, *Pac. Oc.* 93 J13
Tahoe, L., *U.S.A.* 112 G6
Tahoe City, *U.S.A.* 112 F6
Taholah, *U.S.A.* 112 C2
Tahoua, *Niger* 79 C6
Tahta, *Egypt* 76 B3
Tahtali Dağları, *Turkey* 66 D6
Tahuamanu →, *Bolivia* 124 C4
Tahulandang, *Indonesia* 57 D7
Tahuna, *Indonesia* 57 D7
Taï, *Ivory C.* 78 D3
Tai Hu, *China* 54 C7
Tai Shan, *China* 51 F9
Tai Xian, *China* 53 A13
Tai'an, *China* 51 F9
Taibei, *Taiwan* 53 E13
Taibique, *Canary Is.* 36 G2
Taibus Qi, *China* 50 D8
T'aichung = Taizhong, *Taiwan* 53 E13
Taidong, *Taiwan* 53 F13
Taieri →, *N.Z.* 87 M3
Taigu, *China* 50 F7
Taihang Shan, *China* 50 G7
Taihape, *N.Z.* 87 H5
Taihe, *Anhui, China* 50 H8
Taihe, *Jiangxi, China* 53 D10
Taihu, *China* 53 B11
Taijiang, *China* 52 D7
Taikang, *China* 50 G8
Tailem Bend, *Australia* 91 F2
Tailfingen, *Germany* 19 G5
Taimyr Peninsula = Taymyr, Poluostrov, *Russia* 45 B11
Tain, *U.K.* 14 D4
Tainan, *Taiwan* 53 F13
Taínaron, Ákra, *Greece* 39 N5
Taining, *China* 53 D11
Taintignies, *Belgium* 17 G2
Taiobeiras, *Brazil* 123 E3
T'aipei = Taibei, *Taiwan* 53 E13
Taiping, *China* 53 B12
Taiping, *Malaysia* 59 K3
Taipingzhen, *China* 50 H6
Taipu, *Brazil* 122 C4
Taishan, *China* 53 F9
Taishun, *China* 53 D12
Taita □, *Kenya* 82 C4
Taita Hills, *Kenya* 82 C4
Taitao, C., *Chile* 128 C1
Taitao, Pen. de, *Chile* 128 C2
Taivalkoski, *Finland* 8 D20
Taiwan ■, *Asia* 53 F13
Taiwan Shan, *Taiwan* 53 F13
Taixing, *China* 53 A13
Taïyetos Óros, *Greece* 39 N5
Taiyiba, *Israel* 69 C4
Taiyuan, *China* 50 F7
Taizhong, *Taiwan* 53 E13
Taizhou, *China* 53 A12
Taizhou Liedao, *China* 53 C13
Ta'izz, *Yemen* 68 E3
Tājābād, *Iran* 65 D7

Tajapuru, Furo do, *Brazil* 122 B1
Tajikistan ■, *Asia* 44 F8
Tajima, *Japan* 49 F9
Tajo = Tejo →, *Europe* 31 G1
Tajrīsh, *Iran* 65 C6
Tājūrā, *Libya* 73 B7
Tak, *Thailand* 58 D2
Takāb, *Iran* 64 B5
Takachiho, *Japan* 49 H5
Takada, *Japan* 49 F9
Takahagi, *Japan* 49 F10
Takaka, *N.Z.* 87 J4
Takamatsu, *Japan* 49 G7
Takaoka, *Japan* 49 F8
Takapuna, *N.Z.* 87 G5
Takasaki, *Japan* 49 F9
Takatsuki, *Japan* 49 G7
Takaungu, *Kenya* 82 C4
Takayama, *Japan* 49 F8
Take-Shima, *Japan* 49 J5
Takefu, *Japan* 49 G8
Takengon, *Indonesia* 56 D1
Takeo, *Cambodia* 59 G5
Takeo, *Japan* 49 H5
Tåkern, *Sweden* 11 F8
Tākestān, *Iran* 65 C6
Taketa, *Japan* 49 H5
Takh, *India* 63 C7
Takhman, *Cambodia* 59 G5
Takikawa, *Japan* 48 C10
Takla L., *Canada* 100 B3
Takla Landing, *Canada* 100 B3
Takla Makan = Taklamakan Shamo, *China* 54 C3
Taklamakan Shamo, *China* 54 C3
Taku →, *Canada* 100 B2
Takum, *Nigeria* 79 D6
Takutu →, *Guyana* 121 C5
Tal Halāl, *Iran* 65 D7
Tala, *Uruguay* 127 C4
Talacogan, *Phil.* 55 G6
Talagante, *Chile* 126 C1
Talaïnt, *Morocco* 74 C3
Talak, *Niger* 79 B6
Talamanca, Cordillera de, *Cent. Amer.* 116 E3
Talara, *Peru* 124 A1
Talas, *Kirghizia* 44 E8
Talas, *Turkey* 66 D6
Talâta, *Egypt* 69 E1
Talata Mafara, *Nigeria* 79 C6
Talaud, Kepulauan, *Indonesia* 57 D7
Talaud Is. = Talaud, Kepulauan, *Indonesia* 57 D7
Talavera de la Reina, *Spain* 30 F6
Talawana, *Australia* 88 D3
Talayan, *Phil.* 55 H6
Talbert, Sillon de, *France* 24 D3
Talbot, C., *Australia* 88 B4
Talbragar →, *Australia* 91 E4
Talca, *Chile* 126 D1
Talca □, *Chile* 126 D1
Talcahuano, *Chile* 126 D1
Talcher, *India* 61 J14
Talcho, *Niger* 79 C5
Taldy Kurgan, *Kazakhstan* 44 E8
Taldyqorghan = Taldy Kurgan, *Kazakhstan* 44 E8
Talesh, *Iran* 65 B6
Ţalesh, Kūhhā-ye, *Iran* 65 B6
Talguharai, *Sudan* 76 D4
Tali Post, *Sudan* 77 F3
Taliabu, *Indonesia* 57 E6
Talibon, *Phil.* 57 B6
Talibong, Ko, *Thailand* 59 J2
Talihina, *U.S.A.* 109 H7
Talisayan, *Phil.* 55 G6
Taliwang, *Indonesia* 56 F5
Tall 'Asūr, *Jordan* 69 D4
Tall Kalakh, *Syria* 69 A5
Talla, *Egypt* 76 J7
Talladega, *U.S.A.* 105 J2
Tallahassee, *U.S.A.* 105 K3
Tallangatta, *Australia* 91 F4
Tallarook, *Australia* 91 F4
Tallering Pk., *Australia* 89 E2
Tallinn, *Estonia* 40 B4
Tallulah, *U.S.A.* 109 J9
Talmest, *Morocco* 74 B3
Talmont, *France* 26 B2
Talnoye, *Ukraine* 42 B4
Talodi, *Sudan* 77 E3
Talovaya, *Russia* 41 F12
Talpa de Allende, *Mexico* 114 C4
Talsi, *Latvia* 40 C3
Talsinnt, *Morocco* 75 B4
Taltal, *Chile* 126 B1
Taltson →, *Canada* 100 A6
Talwood, *Australia* 91 D4
Talyawalka Cr. →, *Australia* 91 E3
Tam Chau, *Vietnam* 59 G5
Tam Ky, *Vietnam* 58 E7
Tam Quan, *Vietnam* 58 E7
Tama, *U.S.A.* 108 E8
Tamala, *Australia* 89 E1
Tamalameque, *Colombia* 120 B3
Tamale, *Ghana* 79 D4
Taman, *Russia* 42 D7
Tamanar, *Morocco* 74 B3
Tamano, *Japan* 49 G6
Tamanrasset, *Algeria* 75 D6
Tamanrasset, O. →, *Algeria* 75 D5
Tamaqua, *U.S.A.* 107 F9
Tamar →, *U.K.* 13 G3
Támara, *Colombia* 120 B3
Tamarang, *Australia* 91 E5
Tamarinda, *Spain* 36 B10
Tamarite de Litera, *Spain* 28 D5
Tamashima, *Japan* 49 G6
Tamaské, *Niger* 79 C6
Tamaulipas □, *Mexico* 115 C5
Tamaulipas, Sierra de, *Mexico* 115 C5
Tamazula, *Mexico* 114 C3
Tamazunchale, *Mexico* 115 C5
Tamba-Dabatou, *Guinea* 78 C2
Tambacounda, *Senegal* 78 C2
Tambelan, Kepulauan, *Indonesia* 56 D3
Tambellup, *Australia* 89 F2
Tambo, *Australia* 90 C4
Tambo, *Peru* 124 C3
Tambo →, *Peru* 124 C3
Tambo de Mora, *Peru* 124 C2
Tambobamba, *Peru* 124 C3
Tambohorano, *Madag.* 85 B7
Tambopata →, *Peru* 124 C4
Tambora, *Indonesia* 56 F5
Tambov, *Russia* 41 E12
Tambre →, *Spain* 30 C2
Tambuku, *Indonesia* 57 G15
Tamburâ, *Sudan* 77 F2
Tâmchekket, *Mauritania* 78 B2
Tame, *Colombia* 120 B3
Tamega →, *Portugal* 30 D2
Tamelelt, *Morocco* 74 B3
Tamenglong, *India* 61 G18
Tamerza, *Tunisia* 75 B6
Tamgak, Mts., *Niger* 72 E6
Tamiahua, L. de, *Mexico* 115 C5
Tamil Nadu □, *India* 60 P10
Tamines, *Belgium* 17 H5
Tamis →, *Serbia, Yug.* 38 E3
Tamluk, *India* 63 H12
Tammerfors = Tampere, *Finland* 9 F17
Tammisaari, *Finland* 9 F17
Tamo Abu, Pegunungan, *Malaysia* 56 D5
Tampa, *U.S.A.* 105 M4
Tampa B., *U.S.A.* 105 M4
Tampere, *Finland* 9 F17
Tampico, *Mexico* 115 C5
Tampin, *Malaysia* 59 L4
Tamri, *Morocco* 74 B3
Tamrida = Qādib, *Yemen* 68 E5
Tamsagbulag, *Mongolia* 54 B6
Tamsalu, *Estonia* 40 B5
Tamu, *Burma* 61 G19
Tamuja →, *Spain* 31 F4
Tamworth, *Australia* 91 E5
Tamworth, *U.K.* 13 E6
Tamyang, *S. Korea* 51 G14
Tan An, *Vietnam* 59 G6
Tan-tan, *Morocco* 74 C2
Tana, *Norway* 8 A20
Tana →, *Kenya* 82 C5
Tana →, *Norway* 8 A20
Tana, L., *Ethiopia* 77 E4
Tana River, *Kenya* 82 C4
Tanabe, *Japan* 49 H7
Tanabi, *Brazil* 123 F2
Tanafjorden, *Norway* 8 A20
Tanaga, Pta., *Canary Is.* 36 G1
Tanagro →, *Italy* 35 B8
Tanahbala, *Indonesia* 56 E1
Tanahgrogot, *Indonesia* 56 E5
Tanahjampea, *Indonesia* 57 F6
Tanahmasa, *Indonesia* 56 E1
Tanahmerah, *Indonesia* 57 F10
Tanakura, *Japan* 49 F10
Tanami, *Australia* 88 C4
Tanami Desert, *Australia* 88 C5
Tanana, *U.S.A.* 96 B4
Tanana →, *U.S.A.* 96 B4
Tananarive = Antananarivo, *Madag.* 85 B8
Tanannt, *Morocco* 74 B3
Tánaro →, *Italy* 32 C5
Tanaunella, *Italy* 34 B2
Tanbar, *Australia* 90 D3
Tancarville, *France* 24 C7
Tancheng, *China* 51 G10
Tanchŏn, *N. Korea* 51 D15
Tanda, *Ut. P., India* 63 F10
Tanda, *Ut. P., India* 63 E8
Tanda, *Ivory C.* 78 D4
Tandag, *Phil.* 55 G7
Tandaia, *Tanzania* 83 D3
Tăndărei, *Romania* 38 E10
Tandaué, *Angola* 84 B2
Tandil, *Argentina* 126 D4
Tandil, Sa. del, *Argentina* 126 D4
Tandlianwala, *Pakistan* 62 D5
Tando Adam, *Pakistan* 62 G3
Tandou L., *Australia* 91 E3
Tandsbyn, *Sweden* 10 A8
Tane-ga-Shima, *Japan* 49 J5
Taneatua, *N.Z.* 87 H6
Tanen Tong Dan, *Burma* 58 D2
Tanezrouft, *Algeria* 75 D5
Tang, Koh, *Cambodia* 59 G4
Tang Krasang, *Cambodia* 58 F5
Tanga, *Tanzania* 82 D4
Tanga □, *Tanzania* 82 D4
Tanganyika, L., *Africa* 82 D2
Tanger, *Morocco* 74 A3
Tangerang, *Indonesia* 57 G12
Tangerhütte, *Germany* 18 C7
Tangermünde, *Germany* 18 C7
Tanggu, *China* 51 E9
Tanggula Shan, *China* 54 C4
Tanghe, *China* 50 H7
Tangier = Tanger, *Morocco* 74 A3
Tangorin P.O., *Australia* 90 C3
Tangshan, *China* 51 E10
Tangtou, *China* 51 G10
Tanguiéta, *Benin* 79 C5
Tangxi, *China* 53 C12
Tangyan He →, *China* 52 C7
Tanimbar, Kepulauan, *Indonesia* 57 F8
Tanimbar Is. = Tanimbar, Kepulauan, *Indonesia* 57 F8
Taninges, *France* 27 B10
Tanjay, *Phil.* 55 G5
Tanjong Malim, *Malaysia* 59 L3
Tanjore = Thanjavur, *India* 60 P11
Tanjung, *Indonesia* 56 E5
Tanjungbalai, *Indonesia* 56 D1
Tanjungbatu, *Indonesia* 56 D5
Tanjungkarang Telukbetung, *Indonesia* 56 F3
Tanjungpandan, *Indonesia* 56 E3
Tanjungpinang, *Indonesia* 56 D2
Tanjungpriok, *Indonesia* 57 G12
Tanjungredeb, *Indonesia* 56 D5
Tanjungselor, *Indonesia* 56 D5
Tank, *Pakistan* 62 C4
Tänndalen, *Sweden* 10 B6
Tannis Bugt, *Denmark* 11 G4
Tannu-Ola, *Russia* 45 D10
Tano →, *Ghana* 78 D4
Tanon Str., *Phil.* 55 F5
Tanout, *Niger* 79 C6
Tanquinho, *Brazil* 123 D4
Tanta, *Egypt* 76 H7
Tantoyuca, *Mexico* 115 C5
Tantung = Dandong, *China* 51 D13
Tanumshede, *Sweden* 11 F5
Tanunda, *Australia* 91 E2
Tanus, *France* 26 D6
Tanyeri, *Turkey* 67 D8
Tanzania ■, *Africa* 82 D3
Tanzilla →, *Canada* 100 B2
Tao Ko, *Thailand* 59 G2
Tao'an, *China* 51 B12
Tao'er He →, *China* 51 B13
Taohua Dao, *China* 53 C14
Taolanaro, *Madag.* 85 D8
Taole, *China* 50 E4
Taormina, *Italy* 35 E8
Taos, *U.S.A.* 111 H11
Taoudenni, *Mali* 74 D4
Taoudrart, Adrar, *Algeria* 75 D5
Taounate, *Morocco* 74 B4
Taourirt, *Algeria* 75 C5
Taourirt, *Morocco* 75 B4
Taouz, *Morocco* 74 B4
Taoyuan, *China* 53 C8
Taoyuan, *Taiwan* 53 E13
Tapa, *Estonia* 40 B4
Tapa Shan = Daba Shan, *China* 52 B7
Tapachula, *Mexico* 115 E6
Tapah, *Malaysia* 59 K3
Tapajós →, *Brazil* 121 D7
Tapaktuan, *Indonesia* 56 D1
Tapanahoni →, *Surinam* 121 C7
Tapanui, *N.Z.* 87 L2
Tapauá, *Brazil* 125 B5
Tapauá →, *Brazil* 125 B5
Tapeta, *Liberia* 78 D3
Taphan Hin, *Thailand* 58 D3
Tapi →, *India* 60 J8
Tapia, *Spain* 30 B4
Tápiószele, *Hungary* 21 H9
Tapiraí, *Brazil* 123 E2
Tapirapé →, *Brazil* 122 D1
Tapirapecó, Serra, *Venezuela* 121 C5
Tapirapuã, *Brazil* 125 C6
Tapoeripa, *Surinam* 121 B6
Tapolca, *Hungary* 21 J7
Tappahannock, *U.S.A.* 104 G7
Tapuaenuku, Mt., *N.Z.* 87 J4
Tapul Group, *Phil.* 55 J4
Tapurucuará, *Brazil* 121 D4
Taqīābād, *Iran* 65 C8
Ţaqţaq, *Iraq* 64 C5
Taquara, *Brazil* 127 B5
Taquari →, *Brazil* 125 D6
Taquaritinga, *Brazil* 123 F2
Tara, *Australia* 91 D5
Tara, *Canada* 106 B3
Tara, *Russia* 44 D8
Tara, *Zambia* 83 F2
Tara →, *Russia* 44 D8
Taraba □, *Nigeria* 79 D7
Tarabagatay, Khrebet, *Kazakhstan* 44 E9
Tarabuco, *Bolivia* 125 D5
Tarābulus, *Lebanon* 69 A4
Tarābulus, *Libya* 75 B7
Tarahouahout, *Algeria* 75 D6
Tarajalejo, *Canary Is.* 36 F5
Tarakan, *Indonesia* 56 D5
Tarakit, Mt., *Kenya* 82 B4
Taralga, *Australia* 91 E4
Tarama-Jima, *Japan* 49 M2
Taranagar, *India* 62 E6
Taranaki □, *N.Z.* 87 H5
Tarancón, *Spain* 28 E1
Taranga, *India* 62 H5
Taranga Hill, *India* 62 H5
Táranto, *Italy* 35 B10
Táranto, G. di, *Italy* 35 B10
Tarapacá, *Colombia* 120 D4
Tarapacá □, *Chile* 126 A2
Tarapoto, *Peru* 124 B2
Taraquá, *Brazil* 120 C4
Tarare, *France* 27 C8
Tararua Ra., *N.Z.* 87 J5
Tarascon, *France* 27 E8
Tarascon-sur-Ariège, *France* 26 F5
Tarashcha, *Ukraine* 42 B4
Tarata, *Peru* 124 D3
Tarauacá, *Brazil* 124 B3
Tarauacá →, *Brazil* 124 B4
Taravo →, *France* 27 G12
Tarawera, *N.Z.* 87 H6
Tarawera L., *N.Z.* 87 H6
Tarazona, *Spain* 28 D3
Tarazona de la Mancha, *Spain* 29 F3
Tarbat Ness, *U.K.* 14 D5
Tarbela Dam, *Pakistan* 62 B5
Tarbert, *Strath., U.K.* 14 F3
Tarbert, *W. Isles, U.K.* 14 D2
Tarbes, *France* 26 E4
Tarboro, *U.S.A.* 105 H7
Tarbrax, *Australia* 90 C3
Tarcento, *Italy* 33 B10
Tarcoola, *Australia* 91 E1
Tarcoon, *Australia* 91 E4
Tardets-Sorholus, *France* 26 E3
Tardoire →, *France* 26 C4
Taree, *Australia* 91 E5
Tarentaise, *France* 27 C10
Tarf, Ras, *Morocco* 74 A3
Tarfa, Wadi el →, *Egypt* 76 J7
Tarfaya, *Morocco* 74 C2
Targon, *France* 26 D3
Targuist, *Morocco* 74 B4
Tarhbalt, *Morocco* 74 B3
Tarhit, *Algeria* 75 B4
Táriba, *Venezuela* 120 B3
Tarifa, *Spain* 31 J5
Tarija, *Bolivia* 126 A3
Tarija □, *Bolivia* 126 A3
Tariku →, *Indonesia* 57 E9
Tarim Basin = Tarim Pendi, *China* 54 C3
Tarim He →, *China* 54 C3
Tarim Pendi, *China* 54 C3
Tarime □, *Tanzania* 82 C3
Taritatu →, *Indonesia* 57 E9
Tarka →, *S. Africa* 84 E4
Tarkastad, *S. Africa* 84 E4
Tarkhankut, Mys, *Ukraine* 42 D5
Tarko Sale, *Russia* 44 C8
Tarkwa, *Ghana* 78 D4
Tarlac, *Phil.* 55 D4
Tarlton Downs, *Australia* 90 C2
Tarm, *Denmark* 11 J2
Tarma, *Peru* 124 C2
Tarn □, *France* 26 E6
Tarn →, *France* 26 D5
Tarn-et-Garonne □, *France* 26 D5
Tarna →, *Hungary* 21 H9
Tårnby, *Denmark* 11 J6
Tarnobrzeg, *Poland* 20 E11
Tarnów, *Poland* 20 F11
Táro →, *Italy* 32 D7
Taroom, *Australia* 91 D4
Taroudannt, *Morocco* 74 B3
Tarp, *Germany* 18 A5
Tarpon Springs, *U.S.A.* 105 L4
Tarquínia, *Italy* 33 F8
Tarragona, *Spain* 28 D6
Tarragona □, *Spain* 28 D6
Tarrasa, *Spain* 28 D7
Tárrega, *Spain* 28 D6
Tarrytown, *U.S.A.* 107 E11
Tarshiha = Me'ona, *Israel* 69 B4
Tarso Emissi, *Chad* 73 D8
Tarsus, *Turkey* 66 E6
Tartagal, *Argentina* 126 A3
Tartas, *France* 26 E3
Tartu, *Estonia* 40 B5
Ţarţūs, *Syria* 64 C2
Tarumirim, *Brazil* 123 E3
Tarumizu, *Japan* 49 J5
Tarussa, *Russia* 41 D10
Tarutao, Ko, *Thailand* 59 J2
Tarutung, *Indonesia* 56 D1
Tarvisio, *Italy* 33 B10
Tarz Ulli, *Libya* 75 C7
Tasāwah, *Libya* 73 C7
Taschereau, *Canada* 98 C4
Taseko →, *Canada* 100 C4
Tash-Kumyr, *Kirghizia* 44 E8
Tashauz, *Turkmenistan* 44 E6
Tashi Chho Dzong = Thimphu, *Bhutan* 61 F16
Tashkent, *Uzbekistan* 44 E7
Tashtagol, *Russia* 44 D9
Tasikmalaya, *Indonesia* 57 G13
Tåsjön, *Sweden* 8 D13
Taskan, *Russia* 45 C16
Taşköprü, *Turkey* 42 F6
Tasman B., *N.Z.* 87 J4
Tasman Mts., *N.Z.* 87 J4
Tasman Pen., *Australia* 90 G4
Tasman Sea, *Pac. Oc.* 92 L8
Tasmania □, *Australia* 90 G4
Tăşnad, *Romania* 38 B5
Tassil Tin-Rerhoh, *Algeria* 75 D5
Tassili n-Ajjer, *Algeria* 75 C6
Tassili-Oua-n-Ahaggar, *Algeria* 75 D6
Tasu Sd., *Canada* 100 C2
Tata, *Morocco* 74 C3
Tatabánya, *Hungary* 21 H8
Tatahouine, *Tunisia* 75 B7
Tatar Republic □, *Russia* 44 D6
Tatarbunary, *Ukraine* 42 D3
Tatarsk, *Russia* 44 D8
Tateyama, *Japan* 49 G9
Tathlina L., *Canada* 100 A5
Tathra, *Australia* 91 F4
Tatinnai L., *Canada* 101 A9
Tatnam, C., *Canada* 101 B10
Tatra = Tatry, *Slovakia* 20 F9
Tatry, *Slovakia* 20 F9
Tatsuno, *Japan* 49 G7
Tatta, *Pakistan* 62 G2
Tatuī, *Brazil* 127 A6
Tatum, *U.S.A.* 109 J3
Tat'ung = Datong, *China* 50 D7
Tatvan, *Turkey* 67 D10
Tauá, *Brazil* 122 C3
Taubaté, *Brazil* 127 A6
Tauberbischofsheim, *Germany* 19 F5
Taucha, *Germany* 18 D8
Taufikia, *Sudan* 77 F3
Taumarunui, *N.Z.* 87 H5
Taumaturgo, *Brazil* 124 B3
Taung, *S. Africa* 84 D3
Taungdwingyi, *Burma* 61 J19
Taunggyi, *Burma* 61 J20
Taungup, *Burma* 61 K19
Taungup Pass, *Burma* 61 K19
Taungup Taunggya, *Burma* 61 K18
Taunsa Barrage, *Pakistan* 62 D4
Taunton, *U.K.* 13 F4
Taunton, *U.S.A.* 107 E13
Taunus, *Germany* 19 E4
Taupo, *N.Z.* 87 H6
Taupo, L., *N.Z.* 87 H5
Taurage, *Lithuania* 40 D3
Tauranga, *N.Z.* 87 G6
Tauranga Harb., *N.Z.* 87 G6
Taurianova, *Italy* 35 D9
Taurus Mts. = Toros Dağları, *Turkey* 66 E5
Tauste, *Spain* 28 D3
Tauz, *Azerbaijan* 43 F11
Tavannes, *Switz.* 22 B4
Tavda, *Russia* 44 D7
Tavda →, *Russia* 44 D7
Taverny, *France* 25 C9
Taveta, *Tanzania* 82 C4
Taveuni, *Fiji* 87 C9
Tavignano →, *France* 27 F13
Tavira, *Portugal* 31 H3
Tavistock, *Canada* 106 C4
Tavistock, *U.K.* 13 G3
Tavolara, *Italy* 34 B2
Távora →, *Portugal* 30 D3
Tavoy, *Burma* 58 E2
Tavşanlı, *Turkey* 66 D3
Taw →, *U.K.* 13 F3
Tawas City, *U.S.A.* 104 C4
Tawau, *Malaysia* 56 D5
Tawitawi, *Phil.* 55 J4
Taxila, *Pakistan* 62 C5
Tay →, *U.K.* 14 E5
Tay, Firth of, *U.K.* 14 E5
Tay, L., *Australia* 89 F3
Tay, L., *U.K.* 14 E4
Tay Ninh, *Vietnam* 59 G6
Tayabamba, *Peru* 124 B2
Tayabas Bay, *Phil.* 55 E4
Taylakovy, *Russia* 44 D8
Taylor, *Canada* 100 B4
Taylor, *Nebr., U.S.A.* 108 E5
Taylor, *Pa., U.S.A.* 107 E9
Taylor, *Tex., U.S.A.* 109 K6
Taylor, Mt., *U.S.A.* 111 J10
Taylorville, *U.S.A.* 108 F10
Taymā, *Si. Arabia* 64 E3
Taymyr, Oz., *Russia* 45 B11
Taymyr, Poluostrov, *Russia* 45 B11
Tayport, *U.K.* 14 E6
Tayshet, *Russia* 45 D10
Tayside □, *U.K.* 14 E5
Taytay, *Phil.* 55 F3
Taz →, *Russia* 44 C8
Taza, *Morocco* 74 B4
Tāzah Khurmātū, *Iraq* 64 C5
Tazawa-Ko, *Japan* 48 E10
Tazenakht, *Morocco* 74 B3
Tazin L., *Canada* 101 B7
Tazoult, *Algeria* 75 A6
Tazovskiy, *Russia* 44 C8
Tbilisi, *Georgia* 43 F11
Tchad = Chad ■, *Africa* 73 E8
Tchad, L., *Chad* 73 F7
Tchaourou, *Benin* 79 D5
Tch'eng-tou = Chengdu, *China* 52 B5
Tchentlo L., *Canada* 100 B4
Tchibanga, *Gabon* 80 E2
Tchien, *Liberia* 78 D3
Tchin Tabaraden, *Niger* 79 B6
Tch'ong-k'ing = Chongqing, *China* 52 C6
Tczew, *Poland* 20 A8
Te Anau, L., *N.Z.* 87 L1
Te Aroha, *N.Z.* 87 G5
Te Awamutu, *N.Z.* 87 H5
Te Kuiti, *N.Z.* 87 H5

Te Puke, *N.Z.* 87 G6
Te Waewae B., *N.Z.* 87 M1
Tea →, *Brazil* 120 D4
Tea Tree, *Australia* 90 C1
Teague, *U.S.A.* 109 K6
Teano, *Italy* 35 A7
Teapa, *Mexico* 115 D6
Teba, *Spain* 31 J6
Tebakang, *Malaysia* 56 D4
Teberda, *Russia* 43 E9
Tébessa, *Algeria* 75 A6
Tebicuary →, *Paraguay* 126 B4
Tebingtinggi, *Indonesia* 56 D1
Tébourba, *Tunisia* 75 A6
Téboursouk, *Tunisia* 75 A6
Tebulos, *Russia* 43 E11
Tecate, *Mexico* 113 N10
Tecer Dağı, *Turkey* 66 D7
Tech →, *France* 26 F7
Techiman, *Ghana* 78 D4
Tecka, *Argentina* 128 B2
Tecomán, *Mexico* 114 D4
Tecopa, *U.S.A.* 113 K10
Tecoripa, *Mexico* 114 B3
Tecuala, *Mexico* 114 C3
Tecuci, *Romania* 38 D10
Tecumseh, *U.S.A.* 104 D4
Tedzhen, *Turkmenistan* 44 F7
Tees →, *U.K.* 12 C6
Teesside, *U.K.* 12 C6
Teeswater, *Canada* 106 C3
Tefé, *Brazil* 121 D5
Tefé →, *Brazil* 121 D5
Tefenni, *Turkey* 66 E3
Tegal, *Indonesia* 57 G13
Tegelen, *Neths.* 17 F8
Tegernsee, *Germany* 19 H7
Teggiano, *Italy* 35 B8
Teghra, *India* 63 G11
Tegid, L. = Bala, L., *U.K.* 12 E4
Tegina, *Nigeria* 79 C6
Tegucigalpa, *Honduras* 116 D2
Tehachapi, *U.S.A.* 113 K8
Tehachapi Mts., *U.S.A.* 113 L8
Tehamiyam, *Sudan* 76 D4
Tehilla, *Sudan* 76 D4
Téhini, *Ivory C.* 78 D4
Tehrān, *Iran* 65 C6
Tehuacán, *Mexico* 115 D5
Tehuantepec, *Mexico* 115 D5
Tehuantepec, G. de, *Mexico* 115 D5
Tehuantepec, Istmo de, *Mexico* 115 D6
Teide, *Canary Is.* 36 F3
Teifi →, *U.K.* 13 E3
Teign →, *U.K.* 13 G4
Teignmouth, *U.K.* 13 G4
Teixeira, *Brazil* 122 C4
Teixeira Pinto, *Guinea-Biss.* 78 C1
Tejo →, *Europe* 31 G1
Tejon Pass, *U.S.A.* 113 L8
Tekamah, *U.S.A.* 108 E6
Tekapo, L., *N.Z.* 87 K3
Tekax, *Mexico* 115 C7
Tekeli, *Kazakhstan* 44 E8
Tekeze →, *Ethiopia* 77 E4
Tekija, *Serbia* 21 L12
Tekirdağ, *Turkey* 66 C2
Tekirdağ □, *Turkey* 66 C2
Tekkali, *India* 61 K14
Tekke, *Turkey* 66 C7
Tekman, *Turkey* 67 D9
Tekoa, *U.S.A.* 110 C5
Tekouiât, O. →, *Algeria* 75 D5
Tel Aviv-Yafo, *Israel* 69 C3
Tel Lakhish, *Israel* 69 D3
Tel Megiddo, *Israel* 69 C4
Tela, *Honduras* 116 C2
Télagh, *Algeria* 75 B4
Telanaipura = Jambi, *Indonesia* 56 E2
Telavi, *Georgia* 43 F11
Telde, *Canary Is.* 36 G4
Telegraph Creek, *Canada* 100 B2
Telekhany, *Belorussia* 40 E4
Telemark fylke □, *Norway* 10 E2
Telén, *Argentina* 126 D2
Teleng, *Iran* 65 E9
Teleño, *Spain* 30 C4
Teleorman →, *Romania* 38 E8
Teles Pires →, *Brazil* 125 B6
Telescope Pk., *U.S.A.* 113 J9
Teletaye, *Mali* 79 B5
Telford, *U.K.* 12 E5
Telfs, *Austria* 19 H7
Télimélé, *Guinea* 78 C2
Telkwa, *Canada* 100 C3
Tell City, *U.S.A.* 104 G2
Tellicherry, *India* 60 P9
Tellin, *Belgium* 17 H6
Telluride, *U.S.A.* 111 H10
Teloloapán, *Mexico* 115 D5
Telpos Iz, *Russia* 6 C17
Telsen, *Argentina* 128 B3
Telšiai, *Lithuania* 40 D3
Teltow, *Germany* 18 C9
Teluk Anson, *Malaysia* 59 K3
Teluk Betung = Tanjungkarang Telukbetung, *Indonesia* 56 F3
Teluk Intan = Teluk Anson, *Malaysia* 59 K3
Telukbutun, *Indonesia* 59 K7
Telukdalem, *Indonesia* 56 D1
Tema, *Ghana* 79 D5
Temanggung, *Indonesia* 57 G14
Temapache, *Mexico* 115 C5
Temax, *Mexico* 115 C7
Temba, *S. Africa* 85 D4
Tembe, *Zaïre* 82 C2
Temblador, *Venezuela* 121 B5
Tembleque, *Spain* 28 F1
Temblor Range, *U.S.A.* 113 K7
Teme →, *U.K.* 13 E5
Temecula, *U.S.A.* 113 M9
Temerloh, *Malaysia* 59 L4
Temir, *Kazakhstan* 44 E6
Temirtau, *Kazakhstan* 44 D8
Temirtau, *Russia* 44 D9
Témiscaming, *Canada* 98 C4
Temma, *Australia* 90 G3
Temnikov, *Russia* 41 D13
Temo →, *Italy* 34 B1
Temora, *Australia* 91 E4
Temosachic, *Mexico* 114 B3
Tempe, *U.S.A.* 111 K8
Tempe Downs, *Australia* 88 D5
Témpio Pausania, *Italy* 34 B2
Tempiute, *U.S.A.* 112 H11
Temple, *U.S.A.* 109 K6
Temple B., *Australia* 90 A3
Templemore, *Ireland* 15 D4
Templeton, *U.S.A.* 112 K6
Templeton →, *Australia* 90 C2
Templeuve, *Belgium* 17 G2
Templin, *Germany* 18 B9
Tempoal, *Mexico* 115 C5
Temryuk, *Russia* 42 D7
Temse, *Belgium* 17 F4
Temska →, *Serbia* 21 M12
Temuco, *Chile* 128 A2
Temuka, *N.Z.* 87 L3
Ten Boer, *Neths.* 16 B9
Tena, *Ecuador* 120 D2
Tenabo, *Mexico* 115 C6
Tenaha, *U.S.A.* 109 K7
Tenali, *India* 60 L12
Tenancingo, *Mexico* 115 D5
Tenango, *Mexico* 115 D5
Tenasserim, *Burma* 59 F2
Tenasserim □, *Burma* 58 F2
Tenay, *France* 27 C9
Tenby, *U.K.* 13 F3
Tenda, Col di, *France* 27 D11
Tendaho, *Ethiopia* 68 E3
Tende, *France* 27 D11
Tendelti, *Sudan* 77 E3
Tendjedi, Adrar, *Algeria* 75 D6
Tendrara, *Morocco* 75 B4
Tendre, Mt., *Switz.* 22 C2
Teneida, *Egypt* 76 B2
Tenente Marques →, *Brazil* 125 C6
Ténéré, *Niger* 79 B7
Tenerife, *Canary Is.* 36 F3
Tenerife, Pico, *Canary Is.* 36 G1
Ténès, *Algeria* 75 A5
Teng Xian, *Guangxi Zhuangzu, China* 53 F8
Teng Xian, *Shandong, China* 51 G9
Tengah □, *Indonesia* 57 E6
Tengah Kepulauan, *Indonesia* 56 F5
Tengchong, *China* 52 E2
Tengchowfu = Penglai, *China* 51 F11
Tenggara □, *Indonesia* 57 E6
Tenggarong, *Indonesia* 56 E5
Tenggol, P., *Malaysia* 59 K4
Tengiz, Ozero, *Kazakhstan* 44 D7
Tenigerbad, *Switz.* 23 C7
Tenino, *U.S.A.* 112 D4
Tenkasi, *India* 60 Q10
Tenke, *Shaba, Zaïre* 83 E2
Tenke, *Shaba, Zaïre* 83 E2
Tenkodogo, *Burkina Faso* 79 C4
Tenna →, *Italy* 33 E10
Tennant Creek, *Australia* 90 B1
Tennessee □, *U.S.A.* 105 H2
Tennessee →, *U.S.A.* 104 G1
Tenneville, *Belgium* 17 H7
Tennille, *U.S.A.* 105 J4
Tennsift, Oued →, *Morocco* 74 B3
Teno, Pta. de, *Canary Is.* 36 F3
Tenom, *Malaysia* 56 C5
Tenosique, *Mexico* 115 D6
Tenryū-Gawa →, *Japan* 49 G8
Tent L., *Canada* 101 A7
Tenterfield, *Australia* 91 D5
Teófilo Otoni, *Brazil* 123 E3
Teotihuacán, *Mexico* 115 D5
Tepa, *Indonesia* 57 F7
Tepalcatepec →, *Mexico* 114 D4
Tepehuanes, *Mexico* 114 B3
Tepequem, Serra, *Brazil* 121 C5
Tepetongo, *Mexico* 114 C4
Tepic, *Mexico* 114 C4
Tepoca, C., *Mexico* 114 A2
Tequila, *Mexico* 114 C4
Ter →, *Spain* 28 C8
Ter Apel, *Neths.* 16 C10
Téra, *Niger* 79 C5
Tera →, *Spain* 30 D5
Teraina, *Kiribati* 93 G11
Téramo, *Italy* 33 F10
Terang, *Australia* 91 F3
Terborg, *Neths.* 16 E8
Tercan, *Turkey* 67 D9
Tercero →, *Argentina* 126 C3
Terebovlya, *Ukraine* 40 G4
Terek →, *Russia* 43 E12
Terenos, *Brazil* 125 E7
Tereshka →, *Russia* 41 F15
Teresina, *Brazil* 122 C3
Teresinha, *Brazil* 121 C7
Terewah, L., *Australia* 91 D4
Terges →, *Portugal* 31 H3
Tergnier, *France* 25 C10
Terhazza, *Mali* 74 D3
Terheijden, *Neths.* 17 E5
Teridgerie Cr. →, *Australia* 91 E4
Terlizzi, *Italy* 35 A9
Terme, *Turkey* 42 F7
Termez, *Uzbekistan* 44 F7
Términi Imerese, *Italy* 34 E6
Términos, L. de, *Mexico* 115 D6
Térmoli, *Italy* 33 F12
Ternate, *Indonesia* 57 D7
Terneuzen, *Neths.* 17 F3
Terney, *Russia* 45 E14
Terni, *Italy* 33 F9
Ternitz, *Austria* 21 H6
Ternopol, *Ukraine* 42 B1
Terowie, *N.S.W., Australia* 91 E4
Terowie, *S. Austral., Australia* 91 E2
Terra Bella, *U.S.A.* 113 K7
Terrace, *Canada* 100 C3
Terrace Bay, *Canada* 98 C2
Terracina, *Italy* 34 A6
Terralba, *Italy* 34 C1
Terranova = Ólbia, *Italy* 34 B2
Terranuova Bracciolini, *Italy* 33 E8
Terrasini Favarotta, *Italy* 34 D6
Terrassa = Tarrasa, *Spain* 28 D7
Terrasson-la-Villedieu, *France* 26 C5
Terre Haute, *U.S.A.* 104 F2
Terrebonne B., *U.S.A.* 109 L9
Terrecht, *Mali* 75 D4
Terrell, *U.S.A.* 109 J6
Terrenceville, *Canada* 99 C9
Terrick Terrick, *Australia* 90 C4
Terry, *U.S.A.* 108 B2
Terschelling, *Neths.* 16 B6
Terter →, *Azerbaijan* 43 F12
Teruel, *Spain* 28 E3
Teruel □, *Spain* 28 E4
Tervel, *Bulgaria* 38 F10
Tervola, *Finland* 8 C18
Teryaweyna L., *Australia* 91 E3
Tešanj, *Bos.-H.* 21 L7
Teseney, *Eritrea* 77 D4
Tesha →, *Russia* 41 D13
Teshio, *Japan* 48 B10
Teshio-Gawa →, *Japan* 48 B10
Tesiyn Gol →, *Mongolia* 54 A4
Teslin, *Canada* 100 A2
Teslin →, *Canada* 100 A2
Teslin L., *Canada* 100 A2
Tesouro, *Brazil* 125 D7
Tessalit, *Mali* 79 A5
Tessaoua, *Niger* 79 C6
Tessenderlo, *Belgium* 17 F6
Tessin, *Germany* 18 A8
Tessit, *Mali* 79 B5
Test →, *U.K.* 13 F6
Testa del Gargano, *Italy* 35 A9
Têt →, *France* 26 F7
Tetachuck L., *Canada* 100 C3
Tetas, Pta., *Chile* 126 A1
Tete, *Mozam.* 83 F3
Tete □, *Mozam.* 83 F3
Teterev →, *Ukraine* 40 F7
Teteringen, *Neths.* 17 E5
Teterow, *Germany* 18 B8
Teteven, *Bulgaria* 38 G7
Tethul →, *Canada* 100 A6
Tetiyev, *Ukraine* 42 B3
Teton →, *U.S.A.* 110 C8
Tétouan, *Morocco* 74 A3
Tetovo, *Macedonia* 38 G4
Tetuán = Tétouan, *Morocco* 74 A3
Tetyukhe Pristan, *Russia* 48 B7
Tetyushi, *Russia* 41 D16
Teuco →, *Argentina* 126 B3
Teufen, *Switz.* 23 B8
Teulada, *Italy* 34 D1
Teulon, *Canada* 101 C9
Teun, *Indonesia* 57 F7
Teutoburger Wald, *Germany* 18 C4
Tevere →, *Italy* 33 G9
Teverya, *Israel* 69 C4
Teviot →, *U.K.* 14 F6
Tewantin, *Australia* 91 D5
Tewkesbury, *U.K.* 13 F5
Texada I., *Canada* 100 D4
Texarkana, *Ark., U.S.A.* 109 J8
Texarkana, *Tex., U.S.A.* 109 J7
Texas, *Australia* 91 D5
Texas □, *U.S.A.* 109 K5
Texas City, *U.S.A.* 109 L7
Texel, *Neths.* 16 B5
Texhoma, *U.S.A.* 109 G4
Texline, *U.S.A.* 109 G3
Texoma, L., *U.S.A.* 109 J6
Teykovo, *Russia* 41 C12
Teza →, *Russia* 41 C12
Tezin, *Afghan.* 62 B3
Teziutlán, *Mexico* 115 D5
Tezpur, *India* 61 F18
Tezzeron L., *Canada* 100 C4
Tha-anne →, *Canada* 101 A10
Tha Deua, *Laos* 58 D4
Tha Deua, *Laos* 58 C3
Tha Pla, *Thailand* 58 D3
Tha Rua, *Thailand* 58 E3
Tha Sala, *Thailand* 59 H2
Tha Song Yang, *Thailand* 58 D1
Thaba Nchu, *S. Africa* 84 D4
Thaba Putsoa, *Lesotho* 85 D4
Thabana Ntlenyana, *Lesotho* 85 D4
Thabazimbi, *S. Africa* 85 C4
Thai Binh, *Vietnam* 58 B6
Thai Hoa, *Vietnam* 58 C5
Thai Muang, *Thailand* 59 H2
Thai Nguyen, *Vietnam* 58 B5
Thailand ■, *Asia* 58 E4
Thailand, G. of, *Asia* 59 G3
Thakhek, *Laos* 58 D5
Thal, *Pakistan* 62 C4
Thal Desert, *Pakistan* 62 D4
Thala, *Tunisia* 75 A6
Thala La, *Burma* 61 E20
Thalabarivat, *Cambodia* 58 F5
Thalkirch, *Switz.* 23 C8
Thallon, *Australia* 91 D4
Thalwil, *Switz.* 23 B7
Thame →, *U.K.* 13 F6
Thames, *N.Z.* 87 G5
Thames →, *Canada* 98 D3
Thames →, *U.K.* 13 F8
Thames →, *U.S.A.* 107 E12
Thamesford, *Canada* 106 C3
Thamesville, *Canada* 106 D3
Than Uyen, *Vietnam* 58 B4
Thane, *India* 60 K8
Thanesar, *India* 62 D7
Thanet, I. of, *U.K.* 13 F9
Thangoo, *Australia* 88 C3
Thangool, *Australia* 90 C5
Thanh Hoa, *Vietnam* 58 C5
Thanh Hung, *Vietnam* 59 H5
Thanh Pho Ho Chi Minh = Phanh Bho Ho Chi Minh, *Vietnam* 59 G6
Thanh Thuy, *Vietnam* 58 A5
Thanjavur, *India* 60 P11
Thann, *France* 25 E14
Thaon-les-Vosges, *France* 25 D13
Thap Sakae, *Thailand* 59 G2
Thap Than, *Thailand* 58 E2
Thar Desert, *India* 62 F4
Tharad, *India* 62 G4
Thargomindah, *Australia* 91 D3
Tharrawaddy, *Burma* 61 L19
Tharthar, W. →, *Iraq* 64 C4
Thásos, *Greece* 39 J7
That Khe, *Vietnam* 58 A6
Thatcher, *Ariz., U.S.A.* 111 K9
Thatcher, *Colo., U.S.A.* 109 G2
Thaton, *Burma* 61 L20
Thau, Bassin de, *France* 26 E7
Thaungdut, *Burma* 61 G19
Thayer, *U.S.A.* 109 G9
Thayetmyo, *Burma* 61 K19
Thayngen, *Switz.* 23 A7
Thazi, *Burma* 61 J20
The Alberga →, *Australia* 91 D2
The Bight, *Bahamas* 117 B4
The Coorong, *Australia* 91 F2
The Dalles, *U.S.A.* 110 D3
The English Company's Is., *Australia* 90 A2
The Frome →, *Australia* 91 D2
The Grampians, *Australia* 91 F3
The Great Divide = Great Dividing Ra., *Australia* 90 C4
The Hague = 's-Gravenhage, *Neths.* 16 D4
The Hamilton →, *Australia* 91 D2
The Macumba →, *Australia* 91 D2
The Neales →, *Australia* 91 D2
The Officer →, *Australia* 89 E5
The Pas, *Canada* 101 C8
The Range, *Zimbabwe* 83 F3
The Rock, *Australia* 91 F4
The Salt L., *Australia* 91 E3
The Stevenson →, *Australia* 91 D2
The Warburton →, *Australia* 91 D2
Thebes = Thívai, *Greece* 39 L6
Thebes, *Egypt* 76 B3
Thedford, *Canada* 106 C3
Thedford, *U.S.A.* 108 E4
Theebine, *Australia* 91 D5
Thekulthili L., *Canada* 101 A7
Thelon →, *Canada* 101 A8
Thénezay, *France* 24 F6
Thenia, *Algeria* 75 A5
Thenon, *France* 26 C5
Theodore, *Australia* 90 C5
Thepha, *Thailand* 59 J3
Thérain →, *France* 25 C9
Theresa, *U.S.A.* 107 B9
Thermaïkos Kólpos, *Greece* 39 J5
Thermopolis, *U.S.A.* 110 E9
Thermopylae P., *Greece* 39 L5
Thessalía □, *Greece* 39 L4
Thessalon, *Canada* 98 C3
Thessaloníki, *Greece* 39 J5
Thessaloniki, Gulf of = Thermaïkos Kólpos, *Greece* 39 J5
Thessaly = Thessalía □, *Greece* 39 L4
Thetford, *U.K.* 13 E8
Thetford Mines, *Canada* 99 C5
Theun →, *Laos* 58 C5
Theunissen, *S. Africa* 84 D4
Theux, *Belgium* 17 G7
Thevenard, *Australia* 91 E1
Thiámis →, *Greece* 39 K3
Thiberville, *France* 24 C7
Thibodaux, *U.S.A.* 109 L9
Thicket Portage, *Canada* 101 B9
Thief River Falls, *U.S.A.* 108 A6
Thiel Mts., *Antarctica* 5 E16
Thiene, *Italy* 33 C8
Thiérache, *France* 25 C10
Thiers, *France* 26 C7
Thies, *Senegal* 78 C1
Thiet, *Sudan* 77 F2
Thika, *Kenya* 82 C4
Thikombia, *Fiji* 87 B9
Thille-Boubacar, *Senegal* 78 B1
Thimphu, *Bhutan* 61 F16
þingvallavatn, *Iceland* 8 D3
Thionville, *France* 25 C13
Thíra, *Greece* 39 N8
Thirasía, *Greece* 39 N8
Thirsk, *U.K.* 12 C6
Thisted, *Denmark* 9 H10
Thistle I., *Australia* 91 F2
Thívai, *Greece* 39 L6
Thiviers, *France* 26 C4
Thizy, *France* 27 B8
þjórsá →, *Iceland* 8 E3
Thlewiaza →, *Man., Canada* 101 B8
Thlewiaza →, *N.W.T., Canada* 101 A10
Thmar Puok, *Cambodia* 58 F4
Tho Vinh, *Vietnam* 58 C5
Thoa →, *Canada* 101 A7
Thoen, *Thailand* 58 D2
Thoeng, *Thailand* 58 C3
Thoissey, *France* 27 B8
Tholdi, *Pakistan* 63 B7
Tholen, *Neths.* 17 E4
Thomas, *Okla., U.S.A.* 109 H5
Thomas, *W. Va., U.S.A.* 104 F6
Thomas, L., *Australia* 91 D2
Thomaston, *U.S.A.* 105 J3
Thomasville, *Ala., U.S.A.* 105 K2
Thomasville, *Ga., U.S.A.* 105 K3
Thomasville, *N.C., U.S.A.* 105 H5
Thommen, *Belgium* 17 H8
Thompson, *Canada* 101 B9
Thompson, *U.S.A.* 111 G9
Thompson →, *Canada* 100 C4
Thompson →, *U.S.A.* 108 F8
Thompson Falls, *U.S.A.* 110 C6
Thompson Landing, *Canada* 101 A6
Thompson Pk., *U.S.A.* 110 F2
Thomson's Falls = Nyahururu, *Kenya* 82 B4
Thon Buri, *Thailand* 59 F3
Thônes, *France* 27 C10
Thonon-les-Bains, *France* 27 B10
Thorez, *Ukraine* 43 B8
þórisvatn, *Iceland* 8 D4
þorlákshöfn, *Iceland* 8 E3
Thornaby on Tees, *U.K.* 12 C6
Thornbury, *Canada* 106 B4
Thorold, *Canada* 106 C5
þórshöfn, *Iceland* 8 C6
Thouarcé, *France* 24 E6
Thouars, *France* 24 F6
Thouin, C., *Australia* 88 D2
Thousand Oaks, *U.S.A.* 113 L8
Thrace, *Turkey* 66 C2
Thrakikón Pélagos, *Greece* 39 J8
Three Forks, *U.S.A.* 110 D8
Three Hills, *Canada* 100 C6
Three Hummock I., *Australia* 90 G3
Three Lakes, *U.S.A.* 108 C10
Three Points, C., *Ghana* 78 E4
Three Rivers, *Australia* 89 E2
Three Rivers, *Calif., U.S.A.* 112 J8
Three Rivers, *Tex., U.S.A.* 109 L5
Three Sisters, *U.S.A.* 110 D3
Throssell, L., *Australia* 89 E3
Throssell Ra., *Australia* 88 D3
Thuan Hoa, *Vietnam* 59 H5
Thubun Lakes, *Canada* 101 A6
Thueyts, *France* 27 D8
Thuillies, *Belgium* 17 H4
Thuin, *Belgium* 17 H4
Thuir, *France* 26 F6
Thule, *Greenland* 4 B4
Thun, *Switz.* 22 C5
Thundelarra, *Australia* 89 E2
Thunder B., *U.S.A.* 106 B1
Thunder Bay, *Canada* 98 C2
Thunersee, *Switz.* 22 C5
Thung Song, *Thailand* 59 H2
Thunkar, *Bhutan* 61 F17
Thuong Tra, *Vietnam* 58 D6
Thur →, *Switz.* 23 A8
Thurgau □, *Switz.* 23 A8
Thüringen □, *Germany* 18 E7
Thüringer Wald, *Germany* 18 E7
Thurles, *Ireland* 15 D4

Thurloo Downs, *Australia* **91 D3**
Thurn P., *Austria* **19 H8**
Thursday I., *Australia* **90 A3**
Thurso, *Canada* **98 C4**
Thurso, *U.K.* **14 C5**
Thurston I., *Antarctica* **5 D16**
Thury-Harcourt, *France* **24 D6**
Thusis, *Switz.* **23 C8**
Thutade L., *Canada* **100 B3**
Thyborøn, *Denmark* **11 H2**
Thylungra, *Australia* **91 D3**
Thyolo, *Malawi* **83 F4**
Thysville = Mbanza Ngungu, *Zaïre* **80 F2**
Ti-n-Barraouene, O. →, *Africa* **79 B5**
Ti-n-Medjerdam, O. →, *Algeria* **75 C5**
Ti-n-Tarabine, O. →, *Algeria* **75 D6**
Ti-n-Zaouatene, *Algeria* **75 E5**
Tia, *Australia* **91 E5**
Tiahuanacu, *Bolivia* **124 D4**
Tian Shan, *China* **54 B3**
Tianchang, *China* **53 A12**
Tiandong, *China* **52 F6**
Tian'e, *China* **52 E6**
Tianguá, *Brazil* **122 B3**
Tianhe, *China* **52 E7**
Tianjin, *China* **51 E9**
Tiankoura, *Burkina Faso* **78 C4**
Tianlin, *China* **52 E6**
Tianmen, *China* **53 B9**
Tianquan, *China* **52 B4**
Tianshui, *China* **50 G3**
Tiantai, *China* **53 C13**
Tianyang, *China* **52 F6**
Tianzhen, *China* **50 D8**
Tianzhu, *China* **52 D7**
Tianzhuangtai, *China* **51 D12**
Tiaret, *Algeria* **75 A5**
Tiassalé, *Ivory C.* **78 D4**
Tibagi, *Brazil* **127 A5**
Tibagi →, *Brazil* **127 A5**
Tibati, *Cameroon* **79 D7**
Tiber = Tevere →, *Italy* **33 G9**
Tiber Reservoir, *U.S.A.* **110 B8**
Tiberias = Teverya, *Israel* **69 C4**
Tiberias, L. = Yam Kinneret, *Israel* **69 C4**
Tibesti, *Chad* **73 D8**
Tibet = Xizang □, *China* **54 C3**
Tibiao, *Phil.* **55 F5**
Tibiri, *Niger* **79 C6**
Ţibleş, *Romania* **38 B7**
Tibnī, *Syria* **64 C3**
Tibooburra, *Australia* **91 D3**
Tibro, *Sweden* **11 F8**
Tibugá, G. de, *Colombia* **120 B2**
Tiburón, *Mexico* **114 B2**
Ticao I., *Phil.* **55 E5**
Tîchît, *Mauritania* **78 B3**
Tichla, *Mauritania* **74 D2**
Ticho, *Ethiopia* **77 F4**
Ticino □, *Switz.* **23 D7**
Ticino →, *Italy* **32 C6**
Ticonderoga, *U.S.A.* **107 C11**
Ticul, *Mexico* **115 C7**
Tidaholm, *Sweden* **11 F7**
Tiddim, *Burma* **61 H18**
Tideridjaouine, Adrar, *Algeria* **75 D5**
Tidikelt, *Algeria* **75 C5**
Tidjikja, *Mauritania* **78 B2**
Tidore, *Indonesia* **57 D7**
Tiébissou, *Ivory C.* **78 D3**
Tiefencastel, *Switz.* **23 C9**
Tiel, *Neths.* **16 E6**
Tiel, *Senegal* **78 C1**
Tieling, *China* **51 C12**
Tielt, *Belgium* **17 F2**
Tien Shan, *Asia* **46 E11**
Tien-tsin = Tianjin, *China* **51 E9**
Tien Yen, *Vietnam* **58 B6**
T'ienching = Tianjin, *China* **51 E9**
Tienen, *Belgium* **17 G5**
Tiénigbé, *Ivory C.* **78 D3**
Tientsin = Tianjin, *China* **51 E9**
Tierra Amarilla, *Chile* **126 B1**
Tierra Amarilla, *U.S.A.* **111 H10**
Tierra Colorada, *Mexico* **115 D5**
Tierra de Barros, *Spain* **31 G4**
Tierra de Campos, *Spain* **30 C6**
Tierra del Fuego □, *Argentina* **128 D3**
Tierra del Fuego, I. Gr. de, *Argentina* **128 D3**
Tierralta, *Colombia* **120 B2**
Tiétar →, *Spain* **30 F4**
Tieté →, *Brazil* **127 A5**
Tieyon, *Australia* **91 D1**
Tifarati, *W. Sahara* **74 C2**
Tiffin, *U.S.A.* **104 E4**
Tiflèt, *Morocco* **74 B3**
Tiflis = Tbilisi, *Georgia* **43 F11**
Tifton, *U.S.A.* **105 K4**
Tifu, *Indonesia* **57 E7**
Tigil, *Russia* **45 D16**
Tignish, *Canada* **99 C7**
Tigray □, *Ethiopia* **77 E4**
Tigre →, *Peru* **120 D3**
Tigre →, *Venezuela* **121 B5**
Tigris = Dijlah, Nahr →, *Asia* **64 D5**
Tiguentourine, *Algeria* **75 C6**
Tigyaing, *Burma* **61 H20**
Tigzerte, O. →, *Morocco* **74 C3**
Tîh, Gebel el, *Egypt* **76 J8**
Tihodaine, Dunes de, *Algeria* **75 C6**
Tijesno, *Croatia* **33 E12**
Tījī, *Libya* **75 B7**
Tijuana, *Mexico* **113 N9**
Tikal, *Guatemala* **116 C2**
Tikamgarh, *India* **63 G8**
Tikhoretsk, *Russia* **43 D9**
Tikhvin, *Russia* **40 B8**
Tikkadouine, Adrar, *Algeria* **75 D5**
Tiko, *Cameroon* **79 E6**
Tikrīt, *Iraq* **64 C4**
Tiksi, *Russia* **45 B13**
Tilamuta, *Indonesia* **57 D6**
Tilburg, *Neths.* **17 E6**
Tilbury, *Canada* **98 D3**
Tilbury, *U.K.* **13 F8**
Tilcara, *Argentina* **126 A2**
Tilden, *Nebr., U.S.A.* **108 D6**
Tilden, *Tex., U.S.A.* **109 L5**
Tilemses, *Niger* **79 B5**
Tilemsi, Vallée du, *Mali* **79 B5**
Tilhar, *India* **63 F8**
Tilia, O. →, *Algeria* **75 C5**
Tilichiki, *Russia* **45 C17**
Tiligul →, *Ukraine* **42 C4**
Tililane, *Algeria* **75 C4**
Tílissos, *Greece* **37 D7**
Till →, *U.K.* **12 B5**
Tillabéri, *Niger* **79 C5**
Tillamook, *U.S.A.* **110 D2**
Tillberga, *Sweden* **10 E10**
Tillia, *Niger* **79 B5**
Tillsonburg, *Canada* **98 D3**
Tillyeria □, *Cyprus* **37 D11**
Tílos, *Greece* **39 N10**
Tilpa, *Australia* **91 E3**
Tilrhemt, *Algeria* **75 B5**
Tilsit = Sovetsk, *Russia* **40 D2**
Tilt →, *U.K.* **14 E5**
Tilton, *U.S.A.* **107 C13**
Timagami L., *Canada* **98 C3**
Timaru, *N.Z.* **87 L3**
Timashevsk, *Russia* **43 D8**
Timau, *Italy* **33 B10**
Timau, *Kenya* **82 B4**
Timbákion, *Greece* **37 D6**
Timbaúba, *Brazil* **122 C4**
Timbedgha, *Mauritania* **78 B3**
Timber Lake, *U.S.A.* **108 C4**
Timber Mt., *U.S.A.* **112 H10**
Timbío, *Colombia* **120 C2**
Timbiqui, *Colombia* **120 C2**
Timboon, *Australia* **91 F3**
Timbuktu = Tombouctou, *Mali* **78 B4**
Timellouline, *Algeria* **75 C6**
Timétrine Montagnes, *Mali* **79 B4**
Timfristós, Óros, *Greece* **39 L4**
Timhadit, *Morocco* **74 B3**
Timi, *Cyprus* **37 E11**
Timia, *Niger* **79 B6**
Timimoun, *Algeria* **75 C5**
Timiş = Tamis →, *Serbia* **38 E3**
Timişoara, *Romania* **38 D4**
Timmins, *Canada* **98 C3**
Timok →, *Serbia* **21 L12**
Timon, *Brazil* **122 C3**
Timor, *Indonesia* **57 F7**
Timor □, *Indonesia* **57 F7**
Timor Sea, *Ind. Oc.* **88 B4**
Tin Alkoum, *Algeria* **75 D7**
Tin Gornai, *Mali* **79 B4**
Tin Mt., *U.S.A.* **112 J9**
Tîna, Khalîg el, *Egypt* **76 H8**
Tinaca Pt., *Phil.* **55 J6**
Tinaco, *Venezuela* **120 B4**
Tinafak, O. →, *Algeria* **75 C6**
Tinajo, *Canary Is.* **36 E6**
Tinaquillo, *Venezuela* **120 B4**
Tinca, *Romania* **38 C4**
Tinchebray, *France* **24 D6**
Tindouf, *Algeria* **74 C3**
Tinée →, *France* **27 E11**
Tineo, *Spain* **30 B4**
Tinerhir, *Morocco* **74 B3**
Tinfouchi, *Algeria* **74 C3**
Ting Jiang →, *China* **53 E11**
Tinggi, Pulau, *Malaysia* **59 L5**
Tinglev, *Denmark* **11 K3**
Tingo Maria, *Peru* **124 B2**
Tinh Bien, *Vietnam* **59 G5**
Tinharé, I. de, *Brazil* **123 D4**
Tinjoub, *Algeria* **72 C3**
Tinkurrin, *Australia* **89 F2**
Tinnevelly = Tirunelveli, *India* **60 Q10**
Tinnoset, *Norway* **10 E3**
Tinnsjø, *Norway* **10 E2**
Tinogasta, *Argentina* **126 B2**
Tínos, *Greece* **39 M8**
Tiñoso, C., *Spain* **29 H3**
Tinta, *Peru* **124 C3**
Tintigny, *Belgium* **17 J7**
Tintina, *Argentina* **126 B3**
Tintinara, *Australia* **91 F3**
Tinto →, *Spain* **31 H4**
Tioga, *U.S.A.* **106 E7**
Tioman, Pulau, *Malaysia* **59 L5**
Tione di Trento, *Italy* **32 B7**
Tionesta, *U.S.A.* **106 E5**
Tior, *Sudan* **77 F3**
Tioulilin, *Algeria* **75 C4**
Tipongpani, *India* **61 F19**
Tipperary, *Ireland* **15 D3**
Tipperary □, *Ireland* **15 D4**
Tipton, *U.K.* **13 E5**
Tipton, *Calif., U.S.A.* **111 H4**
Tipton, *Ind., U.S.A.* **104 E2**
Tipton, *Iowa, U.S.A.* **108 E9**
Tipton Mt., *U.S.A.* **113 K12**
Tiptonville, *U.S.A.* **109 G10**
Tiquié →, *Brazil* **120 C4**
Tiracambu, Serra do, *Brazil* **122 B2**
Tīrān, *Iran* **65 C6**
Tīrân, *Si. Arabia* **76 B3**
Tirana, *Albania* **39 H2**
Tiranë = Tirana, *Albania* **39 H2**
Tirano, *Italy* **32 B7**
Tiraspol, *Moldavia* **42 C3**
Tirat Karmel, *Israel* **69 C3**
Tiratimine, *Algeria* **75 C5**
Tirdout, *Mali* **79 B4**
Tire, *Turkey* **66 D2**
Tirebolu, *Turkey* **67 C8**
Tiree, *U.K.* **14 E2**
Tîrgovişte, *Romania* **38 E8**
Tîrgu Frumos, *Romania* **38 B10**
Tîrgu-Jiu, *Romania* **38 D6**
Tîrgu Mureş, *Romania* **38 C7**
Tîrgu Neamţ, *Romania* **38 B9**
Tîrgu Ocna, *Romania* **38 C9**
Tîrgu Secuiesc, *Romania* **38 D9**
Tirich Mir, *Pakistan* **60 A7**
Tiriola, *Italy* **35 D9**
Tiririca, Serra da, *Brazil* **123 E2**
Tiris, *W. Sahara* **74 D2**
Tîrnava Mare →, *Romania* **38 C7**
Tîrnava Mică →, *Romania* **38 C7**
Tîrnăveni, *Romania* **38 C7**
Tírnavos, *Greece* **39 K5**
Tirodi, *India* **60 J11**
Tiros, *Brazil* **123 E2**
Tirschenreuth, *Germany* **19 F8**
Tirso →, *Italy* **34 C1**
Tirso, L. del, *Italy* **34 B1**
Tiruchchirappalli, *India* **60 P11**
Tirunelveli, *India* **60 Q10**
Tirupati, *India* **60 N11**
Tiruppur, *India* **60 P10**
Tiruvannamalai, *India* **60 N11**
Tisa →, *Hungary* **21 J10**
Tisa →, *Serbia* **21 K10**
Tisdale, *Canada* **101 C8**
Tishomingo, *U.S.A.* **109 H6**
Tisnaren, *Sweden* **10 F9**
Tisovec, *Slovak Rep.* **20 G9**
Tissemsilt, *Algeria* **75 A5**
Tissint, *Morocco* **74 C3**
Tissø, *Denmark* **11 J5**
Tisza = Tisa →, *Hungary* **21 J10**
Tiszafüred, *Hungary* **21 H10**
Tiszavasvári, *Hungary* **21 H11**
Tit, *Ahaggar, Algeria* **75 D6**
Tit, *Tademait, Algeria* **75 C5**
Tit-Ary, *Russia* **45 B13**
Titaguas, *Spain* **28 F3**
Titel, *Serbia* **21 K10**
Tithwal, *Pakistan* **63 B5**
Titicaca, L., *S. Amer.* **124 D4**
Titiwa, *Nigeria* **79 C7**
Titlis, *Switz.* **23 C6**
Titograd = Podgorica, *Montenegro* **21 N9**
Titov Veles, *Macedonia* **39 H4**
Titova Korenica, *Croatia* **33 D12**
Titovo Užice, *Serbia* **21 M9**
Titule, *Zaïre* **82 B2**
Titumate, *Colombia* **120 B2**
Titusville, *Fla., U.S.A.* **105 L5**
Titusville, *Pa., U.S.A.* **106 E5**
Tivaouane, *Senegal* **78 C1**
Tiveden, *Sweden* **11 F8**
Tiverton, *U.K.* **13 G4**
Tívoli, *Italy* **33 G9**
Tiyo, *Eritrea* **77 E5**
Tizga, *Morocco* **74 B3**
Ti'zi N'Isli, *Morocco* **74 B3**
Tizi-Ouzou, *Algeria* **75 A5**
Tizimín, *Mexico* **115 C7**
Tiznados →, *Venezuela* **120 B4**
Tiznit, *Morocco* **74 C3**
Tjeggelvas, *Sweden* **8 C14**
Tjeukemeer, *Neths.* **16 C7**
Tjirebon = Cirebon, *Indonesia* **57 G13**
Tjøme, *Norway* **10 E4**
Tjonger Kanaal, *Neths.* **16 C7**
Tjörn, *Sweden* **11 G5**
Tkibuli, *Georgia* **43 E10**
Tkvarcheli, *Georgia* **43 E9**
Tlacotalpan, *Mexico* **115 D5**
Tlahualilo, *Mexico* **114 B4**
Tlaquepaque, *Mexico* **114 C4**
Tlaxcala, *Mexico* **115 D5**
Tlaxcala □, *Mexico* **115 D5**
Tlaxiaco, *Mexico* **115 D5**
Tlell, *Canada* **100 C2**
Tlemcen, *Algeria* **75 B4**
Tleta Sidi Bouguedra, *Morocco* **74 B3**
Tlumach, *Ukraine* **42 B1**
Tlyarata, *Russia* **43 E12**
Tmassah, *Libya* **73 C8**
Tnine d'Anglou, *Morocco* **74 C3**
To Bong, *Vietnam* **58 F7**
Toad →, *Canada* **100 B4**
Toamasina, *Madag.* **85 B8**
Toamasina □, *Madag.* **85 B8**
Toay, *Argentina* **126 D3**
Toba, *Japan* **49 G8**
Toba Kakar, *Pakistan* **62 D3**
Toba Tek Singh, *Pakistan* **62 D5**
Tobago, *W. Indies* **117 D7**
Tobarra, *Spain* **29 G3**
Tobelo, *Indonesia* **57 D7**
Tobermorey, *Australia* **90 C2**
Tobermory, *Canada* **98 C3**
Tobermory, *U.K.* **14 E2**
Tobin, *U.S.A.* **112 F5**
Tobin, L., *Australia* **88 D4**
Tobin L., *Canada* **101 C8**
Toboali, *Indonesia* **56 E3**
Tobol, *Kazakhstan* **44 D7**
Tobol →, *Russia* **44 D7**
Toboli, *Indonesia* **57 E6**
Tobolsk, *Russia* **44 D7**
Tobruk = Tubruq, *Libya* **73 B9**
Tobyhanna, *U.S.A.* **107 E9**
Tocache Nuevo, *Peru* **124 B2**
Tocantínia, *Brazil* **122 C2**
Tocantinópolis, *Brazil* **122 C2**
Tocantins →, *Brazil* **122 B2**
Toccoa, *U.S.A.* **105 H4**
Toce →, *Italy* **32 C5**
Tochigi, *Japan* **49 F9**
Tochigi □, *Japan* **49 F9**
Tocina, *Spain* **31 H5**
Tocopilla, *Chile* **126 A1**
Tocumwal, *Australia* **91 F4**
Tocuyo →, *Venezuela* **120 A4**
Tocuyo de la Costa, *Venezuela* **120 A4**
Todd →, *Australia* **90 C2**
Todeli, *Indonesia* **57 E6**
Todenyang, *Kenya* **82 B4**
Todi, *Italy* **33 F9**
Tödi, *Switz.* **23 C7**
Todos os Santos, B. de, *Brazil* **123 D4**
Todos Santos, *Mexico* **114 C2**
Todtnau, *Germany* **19 H3**
Toecé, *Burkina Faso* **79 C4**
Tofield, *Canada* **100 C6**
Tofino, *Canada* **100 D3**
Töfsingdalens nationalpark, *Sweden* **10 B6**
Toftlund, *Denmark* **11 J3**
Tofua, *Tonga* **87 D11**
Tōgane, *Japan* **49 G10**
Togba, *Mauritania* **78 B2**
Toggenburg, *Switz.* **23 B8**
Togian, Kepulauan, *Indonesia* **57 E6**
Togliatti, *Russia* **41 E16**
Togo ■, *W. Afr.* **79 D5**
Togtoh, *China* **50 D6**
Tohma →, *Turkey* **67 D8**
Tōhoku □, *Japan* **48 E10**
Toinya, *Sudan* **77 F2**
Tojikiston = Tajikistan ■, *Asia* **44 F8**
Tojo, *Indonesia* **57 E6**
Tōjō, *Japan* **49 G6**
Toka, *Guyana* **121 C6**
Tokachi-Dake, *Japan* **48 C11**
Tokachi-Gawa →, *Japan* **48 C11**
Tokaj, *Hungary* **21 G11**
Tokala, *Indonesia* **57 E6**
Tōkamachi, *Japan* **49 F9**
Tokanui, *N.Z.* **87 M2**
Tokar, *Sudan* **76 D4**
Tokara-Rettō, *Japan* **49 K4**
Tokarahi, *N.Z.* **87 L3**
Tokashiki-Shima, *Japan* **49 L3**
Tokat, *Turkey* **66 C7**
Tokat □, *Turkey* **66 C7**
Tŏkchŏn, *N. Korea* **51 E14**
Tokeland, *U.S.A.* **112 D3**
Tokelau Is., *Pac. Oc.* **92 H10**
Tokmak, *Kirghizia* **44 E8**
Toko Ra., *Australia* **90 C2**
Tokoro-Gawa →, *Japan* **48 B12**
Tokuno-Shima, *Japan* **49 L4**
Tokushima, *Japan* **49 G7**
Tokushima □, *Japan* **49 H7**
Tokuyama, *Japan* **49 G5**
Tōkyō, *Japan* **49 G9**
Tolaga Bay, *N.Z.* **87 H7**
Tolbukhin, *Bulgaria* **38 F10**
Toledo, *Spain* **30 F6**
Toledo, *Ohio, U.S.A.* **104 E4**
Toledo, *Oreg., U.S.A.* **110 D2**
Toledo, *Wash., U.S.A.* **110 C2**
Toledo, Montes de, *Spain* **31 F6**
Tolentino, *Italy* **33 E10**
Tolga, *Algeria* **75 B6**
Tolga, *Norway* **10 B5**
Toliara, *Madag.* **85 C7**
Toliara □, *Madag.* **85 C8**
Tolima, *Colombia* **120 C2**
Tolima □, *Colombia* **120 C2**
Tolitoli, *Indonesia* **57 D6**
Tolkamer, *Neths.* **16 E8**
Tolleson, *U.S.A.* **111 K7**
Tollhouse, *U.S.A.* **112 H7**
Tolmachevo, *Russia* **40 B6**
Tolmezzo, *Italy* **33 B10**
Tolmin, *Slovenia* **33 B10**
Tolo, *Zaïre* **80 E3**
Tolo, Teluk, *Indonesia* **57 E6**
Tolochin, *Belorussia* **40 D6**
Tolosa, *Spain* **28 B2**
Tolox, *Spain* **31 J6**
Toltén, *Chile* **128 A2**
Toluca, *Mexico* **115 D5**
Tom Burke, *S. Africa* **85 C4**
Tom Price, *Australia* **88 D2**
Tomah, *U.S.A.* **108 D9**
Tomahawk, *U.S.A.* **108 C10**
Tomakomai, *Japan* **48 C10**
Tomales, *U.S.A.* **112 G4**
Tomales B., *U.S.A.* **112 G3**
Tomar, *Portugal* **31 F2**
Tomarza, *Turkey* **66 D6**
Tomás Barrón, *Bolivia* **124 D4**
Tomaszów Mazowiecki, *Poland* **20 D9**
Tomatlán, *Mexico* **114 D3**
Tombador, Serra do, *Brazil* **125 C6**
Tombé, *Sudan* **77 F3**
Tombigbee →, *U.S.A.* **105 K2**
Tombouctou, *Mali* **78 B4**
Tombstone, *U.S.A.* **111 L8**
Tombua, *Angola* **84 B1**
Tomé, *Chile* **126 D1**
Tomé-Açu, *Brazil* **122 B2**
Tomelilla, *Sweden* **11 J7**
Tomelloso, *Spain* **29 F1**
Tomingley, *Australia* **91 E4**
Tomini, *Indonesia* **57 D6**
Tomini, Teluk, *Indonesia* **57 E6**
Tominian, *Mali* **78 C4**
Tomiño, *Spain* **30 D2**
Tomkinson Ras., *Australia* **89 E4**
Tommot, *Russia* **45 D13**
Tomnavoulin, *U.K.* **14 D5**
Tomnop Ta Suos, *Cambodia* **59 G5**
Tomo, *Colombia* **120 C4**
Tomo →, *Colombia* **120 B4**
Toms Place, *U.S.A.* **112 H8**
Toms River, *U.S.A.* **107 G10**
Tomsk, *Russia* **44 D9**
Tonalá, *Mexico* **115 D6**
Tonale, Passo del, *Italy* **32 B7**
Tonalea, *U.S.A.* **111 H8**
Tonantins, *Brazil* **120 D4**
Tonasket, *U.S.A.* **110 B4**
Tonate, *Fr. Guiana* **121 C7**
Tonawanda, *U.S.A.* **106 D6**
Tonbridge, *U.K.* **13 F8**
Tondano, *Indonesia* **57 D6**
Tondela, *Portugal* **30 E2**
Tønder, *Denmark* **11 K2**
Tondi Kiwindi, *Niger* **79 C5**
Tondibi, *Mali* **79 B4**
Tonekābon, *Iran* **65 B6**
Tong Xian, *China* **50 E9**
Tonga ■, *Pac. Oc.* **87 D11**
Tonga Trench, *Pac. Oc.* **92 J10**
Tongaat, *S. Africa* **85 D5**
Tong'an, *China* **53 E12**
Tongareva, *Cook Is.* **93 H12**
Tongatapu, *Tonga* **87 E11**
Tongbai, *China* **53 A9**
Tongcheng, *Anhui, China* **53 B11**
Tongcheng, *Hubei, China* **53 C9**
Tongchŏn-ni, *N. Korea* **51 E14**
Tongchuan, *China* **50 G5**
Tongdao, *China* **52 D7**
Tongeren, *Belgium* **17 G6**
Tonggu, *China* **53 C10**
Tongguan, *China* **50 G6**
Tonghai, *China* **52 E4**
Tonghua, *China* **51 D13**
Tongjiang, *Heilongjiang, China* **54 B8**
Tongjiang, *Sichuan, China* **52 B6**
Tongjosŏn Man, *N. Korea* **51 E14**
Tongking, G. of = Tonkin, G. of, *Asia* **58 B7**
Tongliang, *China* **52 C6**
Tongliao, *China* **51 C12**
Tongling, *China* **53 B11**
Tonglu, *China* **53 C12**
Tongnae, *S. Korea* **51 G15**
Tongnan, *China* **52 B5**
Tongobory, *Madag.* **85 C7**
Tongoy, *Chile* **126 C1**
Tongren, *China* **52 D7**
Tongres = Tongeren, *Belgium* **17 G6**
Tongsa Dzong, *Bhutan* **61 F17**
Tongue, *U.K.* **14 C4**
Tongue →, *U.S.A.* **108 B2**
Tongwei, *China* **50 G3**
Tongxin, *China* **50 F3**
Tongyang, *N. Korea* **51 E14**
Tongyu, *China* **51 B12**
Tongzi, *China* **52 C6**
Tonj, *Sudan* **77 F2**
Tonk, *India* **62 F6**
Tonkawa, *U.S.A.* **109 G6**
Tonkin = Bac Phan, *Vietnam* **58 B5**
Tonkin, G. of, *Asia* **58 B7**
Tonlé Sap, *Cambodia* **58 F4**
Tonnay-Charente, *France* **26 C3**
Tonneins, *France* **26 D4**
Tonnerre, *France* **25 E10**
Tönning, *Germany* **18 A4**
Tono, *Japan* **48 E10**
Tonopah, *U.S.A.* **111 G5**
Tonosí, *Panama* **116 E3**
Tønsberg, *Norway* **10 E4**
Tooele, *U.S.A.* **110 F7**
Toompine, *Australia* **91 D3**
Toonpan, *Australia* **90 B4**

Toora, *Australia* 91 F4
Toora-Khem, *Russia* 45 D10
Toowoomba, *Australia* 91 D5
Topalu, *Romania* 38 E11
Topaz, *U.S.A.* 112 G7
Topeka, *U.S.A.* 108 F7
Topki, *Russia* 44 D9
Topl'a →, *Slovakia* 20 G11
Topley, *Canada* 100 C3
Toplica →, *Serbia, Yug.* 21 M11
Toplița, *Romania* 38 C8
Topocalma, Pta., *Chile* 126 C1
Topock, *U.S.A.* 113 L12
Topola, *Serbia, Yug.* 21 L10
Topoľčany, *Slovakia* 20 G8
Topoli, *Kazakhstan* 43 C14
Topolnitsa →, *Bulgaria* 38 G7
Topolobampo, *Mexico* 114 B3
Topolovgrad, *Bulgaria* 38 G9
Toppenish, *U.S.A.* 110 C3
Topusko, *Croatia* 33 C12
Toquepala, *Peru* 124 D3
Torá, *Spain* 28 D6
Tora Kit, *Sudan* 77 E3
Toraka Vestale, *Madag.* 85 B7
Torata, *Peru* 124 D3
Torbalı, *Turkey* 66 D2
Torbay, *Canada* 99 C9
Torbay, *U.K.* 13 G4
Tørdal, *Norway* 10 E2
Tordesillas, *Spain* 30 D6
Tordoya, *Spain* 30 B2
Töreboda, *Sweden* 11 F8
Torfajökull, *Iceland* 8 E4
Torgau, *Germany* 18 D8
Torgelow, *Germany* 18 B9
Torhout, *Belgium* 17 F2
Tori, *Ethiopia* 77 F3
Tori-Shima, *Japan* 49 J10
Torigni-sur-Vire, *France* 24 C6
Torija, *Spain* 28 E1
Torin, *Mexico* 114 B2
Toriñana, C., *Spain* 30 B1
Torino, *Italy* 32 C4
Torit, *Sudan* 77 G3
Torkovichi, *Russia* 40 B7
Tormes →, *Spain* 30 D4
Tornado Mt., *Canada* 100 D6
Torne älv →, *Sweden* 8 D18
Torneå = Tornio, *Finland* 8 D18
Torneträsk, *Sweden* 8 B15
Tornio, *Finland* 8 D18
Tornionjoki →, *Finland* 8 D18
Tornquist, *Argentina* 126 D3
Toro, *Baleares, Spain* 36 B11
Toro, *Zamora, Spain* 30 D5
Torö, *Sweden* 11 F11
Toro, Cerro del, *Chile* 126 B2
Toro Pk., *U.S.A.* 113 M10
Törökszentmiklós, *Hungary* 21 H10
Toroníos Kólpos, *Greece* 39 J6
Toronto, *Australia* 91 E5
Toronto, *Canada* 98 D4
Toronto, *U.S.A.* 106 F4
Toropets, *Russia* 40 C7
Tororo, *Uganda* 82 B3
Toros Dağları, *Turkey* 66 E5
Torotoro, *Bolivia* 125 D4
Torpshammar, *Sweden* 10 B10
Torquay, *Canada* 101 D8
Torquay, *U.K.* 13 G4
Torquemada, *Spain* 30 C6
Torralba de Calatrava, *Spain* 31 F7
Torrance, *U.S.A.* 113 M8
Torrão, *Portugal* 31 G2
Torre Annunziata, *Italy* 35 B7
Tôrre de Moncorvo, *Portugal* 30 D3
Torre del Greco, *Italy* 35 B7
Torre del Mar, *Spain* 31 J6
Torre-Pacheco, *Spain* 29 H4
Torre Pellice, *Italy* 32 D4
Torreblanca, *Spain* 28 E5
Torrecampo, *Spain* 31 G6
Torrecilla en Cameros, *Spain* 28 C2
Torredembarra, *Spain* 28 D6
Torredonjimeno, *Spain* 31 H7
Torrejoncillo, *Spain* 30 F4
Torrelaguna, *Spain* 28 E1
Torrelavega, *Spain* 30 B6
Torremaggiore, *Italy* 35 A8
Torremolinos, *Spain* 31 J6
Torrens, L., *Australia* 91 E2
Torrens Cr. →, *Australia* 90 C4
Torrens Creek, *Australia* 90 C4
Torrente, *Spain* 29 F4
Torrenueva, *Spain* 29 G1
Torreón, *Mexico* 114 B4
Torreperogil, *Spain* 29 G1
Torres, *Mexico* 114 B2
Torres Novas, *Portugal* 31 F2
Torres Strait, *Australia* 92 H6
Torres Vedras, *Portugal* 31 F1
Torrevieja, *Spain* 29 H4
Torrey, *U.S.A.* 111 G8
Torridge →, *U.K.* 13 G3
Torridon, L., *U.K.* 14 D3
Torrijos, *Spain* 30 F6
Torrington, *Conn., U.S.A.* 107 E11
Torrington, *Wyo., U.S.A.* 108 D2
Torroella de Montgri, *Spain* 28 C8
Torrox, *Spain* 31 J7
Torsö, *Sweden* 11 F7
Tortola, *Virgin Is.* 117 C7
Tórtoles de Esgueva, *Spain* 30 D6
Tortona, *Italy* 32 D5
Tortoreto, *Italy* 33 F10
Tortorici, *Italy* 35 D7
Tortosa, *Spain* 28 E5
Tortosa, C., *Spain* 28 E5
Tortosendo, *Portugal* 30 E3
Tortue, I. de la, *Haiti* 117 B5
Tortum, *Turkey* 67 C9
Ţorūd, *Iran* 65 C7
Torul, *Turkey* 67 C8
Toruń, *Poland* 20 B8
Torup, *Denmark* 11 G3
Torup, *Sweden* 11 H7
Tory I., *Ireland* 15 A3
Torysa →, *Slovakia* 20 G11
Torzhok, *Russia* 40 C9
Tosa, *Japan* 49 H6
Tosa-Shimizu, *Japan* 49 H6
Tosa-Wan, *Japan* 49 H6
Toscana, *Italy* 32 E8
Toscano, Arcipelago, *Italy* 32 F7
Toshkent = Tashkent, *Uzbekistan* 44 E7
Tosno, *Russia* 40 B7
Tossa, *Spain* 28 D7
Tostado, *Argentina* 126 B3
Tostedt, *Germany* 18 B5
Tostón, Pta. de, *Canary Is.* 36 F5
Tosu, *Japan* 49 H5
Tosya, *Turkey* 66 C6
Totana, *Spain* 29 H3
Toten, *Norway* 10 D4
Toteng, *Botswana* 84 C3
Tôtes, *France* 24 C8
Tótkomlós, *Hungary* 21 J10
Totma, *Russia* 41 B13
Totnes, *U.K.* 13 G4
Totness, *Surinam* 121 B6
Totonicapán, *Guatemala* 116 D1
Totora, *Bolivia* 125 D4
Totten Glacier, *Antarctica* 5 C8
Tottenham, *Australia* 91 E4
Tottenham, *Canada* 106 B5
Tottori, *Japan* 49 G7
Tottori □, *Japan* 49 G7
Touat, *Algeria* 75 C5
Touba, *Ivory C.* 78 D3
Toubkal, Djebel, *Morocco* 74 B3
Toucy, *France* 25 E10
Tougan, *Burkina Faso* 78 C4
Touggourt, *Algeria* 75 B6
Tougué, *Guinea* 78 C2
Toukmatine, *Algeria* 75 D6
Toul, *France* 25 D12
Toulepleu, *Ivory C.* 78 D3
Toulon, *France* 27 E9
Toulouse, *France* 26 E5
Toummo, *Niger* 73 D7
Toumodi, *Ivory C.* 78 D3
Tounassine, Hamada, *Algeria* 74 C3
Toungoo, *Burma* 61 K20
Touques →, *France* 24 C7
Touraine, *France* 24 E7
Tourane = Da Nang, *Vietnam* 58 D7
Tourcoing, *France* 25 B10
Tourine, *Mauritania* 74 D2
Tournai, *Belgium* 17 G2
Tournan-en-Brie, *France* 25 D9
Tournay, *France* 26 E4
Tournon, *France* 27 C8
Tournon-St.-Martin, *France* 24 F7
Tournus, *France* 27 B8
Touros, *Brazil* 122 C4
Tours, *France* 24 E7
Touwsrivier, *S. Africa* 84 E3
Tovar, *Venezuela* 120 B3
Tovarkovskiy, *Russia* 41 E11
Tovdal, *Norway* 11 F2
Tovdalselva →, *Norway* 11 F2
Towada, *Japan* 48 D10
Towada-Ko, *Japan* 48 D10
Towamba, *Australia* 91 F4
Towanda, *U.S.A.* 107 E8
Towang, *India* 61 F17
Tower, *U.S.A.* 108 B8
Towerhill Cr. →, *Australia* 90 C3
Towner, *U.S.A.* 108 A4
Townsend, *U.S.A.* 110 C8
Townshend I., *Australia* 90 C5
Townsville, *Australia* 90 B4
Towson, *U.S.A.* 104 F7
Toya-Ko, *Japan* 48 C10
Toyah, *U.S.A.* 109 K3
Toyahvale, *U.S.A.* 109 K3
Toyama, *Japan* 49 F8
Toyama □, *Japan* 49 F8
Toyama-Wan, *Japan* 49 F8
Toyohashi, *Japan* 49 G8
Toyokawa, *Japan* 49 G8
Toyonaka, *Japan* 49 G7
Toyooka, *Japan* 49 G7
Toyota, *Japan* 49 G8
Tozeur, *Tunisia* 75 B6
Tra On, *Vietnam* 59 H5
Trabancos →, *Spain* 30 D5
Traben Trarbach, *Germany* 19 F3
Trabzon, *Turkey* 42 F8
Trabzon □, *Turkey* 67 C8
Tracadie, *Canada* 99 C7
Tracy, *Calif., U.S.A.* 111 H3
Tracy, *Minn., U.S.A.* 108 C7
Tradate, *Italy* 32 C5
Tradovoye, *Russia* 48 C6
Trafalgar, C., *Spain* 31 J4
Traiguén, *Chile* 128 A2
Trail, *Canada* 100 D5
Trainor L., *Canada* 100 A4
Traíra →, *Brazil* 120 D4
Trákhonas, *Cyprus* 37 D12
Tralee, *Ireland* 15 D2
Tralee B., *Ireland* 15 D2
Tramelan, *Switz.* 22 B4
Tramore, *Ireland* 15 D4
Tran Ninh, Cao Nguyen, *Laos* 58 C4
Tranås, *Sweden* 9 G13
Trancas, *Argentina* 126 B2
Trancoso, *Portugal* 30 E3
Tranebjerg, *Denmark* 11 J4
Tranemo, *Sweden* 11 G7
Trang, *Thailand* 59 J2
Trangahy, *Madag.* 85 B7
Trangan, *Indonesia* 57 F8
Trangie, *Australia* 91 E4
Trångsviken, *Sweden* 10 A8
Trani, *Italy* 35 A9
Tranoroa, *Madag.* 85 C8
Tranqueras, *Uruguay* 127 C4
Trans Nzoia □, *Kenya* 82 B3
Transantarctic Mts., *Antarctica* 5 E12
Transcaucasia = Zakavkazye, *Asia* 43 F11
Transcona, *Canada* 101 D9
Transilvania, *Romania* 38 D8
Transkei □, *S. Africa* 85 E4
Transvaal □, *S. Africa* 84 D4
Transylvania = Transilvania, *Romania* 38 D8
Transylvanian Alps, *Romania* 6 F10
Trápani, *Italy* 34 D5
Trapper Pk., *U.S.A.* 110 D6
Traralgon, *Australia* 91 F4
Trarza, *Mauritania* 78 B2
Trasacco, *Italy* 33 G10
Trăscău, Munţii, *Romania* 38 C6
Trasimeno, L., *Italy* 33 E9
Trat, *Thailand* 59 F4
Traun, *Austria* 21 G4
Traunstein, *Germany* 19 H8
Tråvad, *Sweden* 11 F7
Traveller's L., *Australia* 91 E3
Travemünde, *Germany* 18 B6
Travers, Mt., *N.Z.* 87 K4
Traverse City, *U.S.A.* 104 C3
Travnik, *Bos.-H.* 21 L7
Trayning, *Australia* 89 F2
Trazo, *Spain* 30 B2
Trbovlje, *Slovenia* 33 B12
Trébbia →, *Italy* 32 C6
Trebel →, *Germany* 18 B9
Trebinje, *Bos.-H., Yug.* 21 N8
Trebisacce, *Italy* 35 C9
Trebišnica →, *Bos.-H.* 21 N8
Trebišov, *Slovakia* 20 G11
Trebižat →, *Bos.-H.* 21 M7
Trebnje, *Slovenia* 33 C12
Třeboň, *Czech.* 20 G4
Trebujena, *Spain* 31 J4
Trecate, *Italy* 32 C5
Trece Martires, *Phil.* 55 D4
Tredegar, *U.K.* 13 F4
Tregaron, *U.K.* 13 E4
Trégastel-Plage, *France* 24 D3
Tregnago, *Italy* 33 C8
Tregrosse Is., *Australia* 90 B5
Tréguier, *France* 24 D3
Trégunc, *France* 24 E3
Treherne, *Canada* 101 D9
Tréia, *Italy* 33 E10
Treignac, *France* 26 C5
Treinta y Tres, *Uruguay* 127 C5
Treis, *Germany* 19 E3
Trekveld, *S. Africa* 84 E2
Trelde Næs, *Denmark* 11 J3
Trelew, *Argentina* 128 B3
Trélissac, *France* 26 C4
Trelleborg, *Sweden* 11 J7
Trélon, *France* 25 B11
Tremiti, *Italy* 33 F12
Tremonton, *U.S.A.* 110 F7
Tremp, *Spain* 28 C5
Trenche →, *Canada* 98 C5
Trenčín, *Slovakia* 20 G8
Trenggalek, *Indonesia* 57 H14
Trenque Lauquen, *Argentina* 126 D3
Trent →, *U.K.* 12 D7
Trentino-Alto Adige □, *Italy* 32 B8
Trento, *Italy* 32 B8
Trenton, *Canada* 98 D4
Trenton, *Mo., U.S.A.* 108 E8
Trenton, *N.J., U.S.A.* 107 F10
Trenton, *Nebr., U.S.A.* 108 E4
Trenton, *Tenn., U.S.A.* 109 H10
Trepassey, *Canada* 99 C9
Trepuzzi, *Italy* 35 B11
Tres Arroyos, *Argentina* 126 D3
Três Corações, *Brazil* 123 F2
Três Lagoas, *Brazil* 123 F1
Tres Lagos →, *Argentina* 128 C2
Tres Marías, *Mexico* 114 C3
Três Marias, Represa, *Brazil* 123 E2
Tres Montes, C., *Chile* 128 C1
Tres Pinos, *U.S.A.* 112 J5
Três Pontas, *Brazil* 123 F2
Tres Puentes, *Chile* 126 B1
Tres Puntas, C., *Argentina* 128 C3
Três Rios, *Brazil* 123 F3
Tres Valles, *Mexico* 115 D5
Treska →, *Macedonia* 39 H4
Trespaderne, *Spain* 28 C1
Trets, *France* 27 E9
Treuchtlingen, *Germany* 19 G6
Treuenbrietzen, *Germany* 18 C8
Treungen, *Norway* 9 G10
Trevíglio, *Italy* 32 C6
Trevínca, Peña, *Spain* 30 C4
Treviso, *Italy* 33 C9
Trévoux, *France* 27 C8
Treysa, *Germany* 18 E5
Trgovište, *Serbia, Yug.* 21 N12
Triabunna, *Australia* 90 G4
Triánda, *Greece* 37 C10
Triang, *Malaysia* 59 L4
Triaucourt-en-Argonne, *France* 25 D12
Tribsees, *Germany* 18 A8
Tribulation, C., *Australia* 90 B4
Tribune, *U.S.A.* 108 F4
Tricárico, *Italy* 35 B9
Tricase, *Italy* 35 C11
Trichinopoly = Tiruchchirappalli, *India* 60 P11
Trichur, *India* 60 P10
Trida, *Australia* 91 E4
Trier, *Germany* 19 F2
Trieste, *Italy* 33 C10
Trieste, G. di, *Italy* 33 C10
Trieux →, *France* 24 D3
Triggiano, *Italy* 35 A9
Triglav, *Slovenia* 33 B10
Trigno →, *Italy* 33 F11
Trigueros, *Spain* 31 H4
Trikhonis, Límni, *Greece* 39 L4
Tríkkala, *Greece* 39 K4
Trikomo, *Cyprus* 37 D12
Trikora, Puncak, *Indonesia* 57 E9
Trilj, *Croatia* 33 E13
Trillo, *Spain* 28 E2
Trim, *Ireland* 15 C5
Trincomalee, *Sri Lanka* 60 Q12
Trindade, *Brazil* 123 E2
Trindade, I., *Atl. Oc.* 2 F8
Trinidad, *Bolivia* 125 C5
Trinidad, *Colombia* 120 B3
Trinidad, *Cuba* 116 B3
Trinidad, *Uruguay* 126 C4
Trinidad, *U.S.A.* 109 G2
Trinidad, *W. Indies* 117 D7
Trinidad →, *Mexico* 115 D5
Trinidad, G., *Chile* 128 C1
Trinidad, I., *Argentina* 128 A4
Trinidad & Tobago ■, *W. Indies* 117 D7
Trinitápoli, *Italy* 35 A9
Trinity, *Canada* 99 C9
Trinity, *U.S.A.* 109 K7
Trinity →, *Calif., U.S.A.* 110 F2
Trinity →, *Tex., U.S.A.* 109 L7
Trinity B., *Canada* 99 C9
Trinity Range, *U.S.A.* 110 F4
Trinkitat, *Sudan* 76 D4
Trino, *Italy* 32 C5
Trion, *U.S.A.* 105 H3
Trionto, C., *Italy* 35 C9
Triora, *Italy* 32 E4
Tripoli = Tarābulus, *Lebanon* 69 A4
Tripoli = Tarābulus, *Libya* 75 B7
Tripp, *U.S.A.* 108 D6
Tripura □, *India* 61 H17
Tripylos, *Cyprus* 37 E11
Trischen, *Germany* 18 A4
Tristan da Cunha, *Atl. Oc.* 2 F9
Trivandrum, *India* 60 Q10
Trivento, *Italy* 35 A7
Trnava, *Slovakia* 21 G7
Trochu, *Canada* 100 C6
Trodely I., *Canada* 98 B4
Trogir, *Croatia* 33 E13
Troglav, *Croatia* 33 E13
Trøgstad, *Norway* 10 E5
Tróia, *Italy* 35 A8
Troilus, L., *Canada* 98 B5
Troina, *Italy* 35 E7
Trois Fourches, Cap des, *Morocco* 75 A4
Trois-Pistoles, *Canada* 99 C6
Trois-Rivières, *Canada* 98 C5
Troisvierges, *Belgium* 17 H8
Troitsk, *Russia* 44 D7
Troitsko Pechorsk, *Russia* 44 C6
Trölladyngja, *Iceland* 8 D5
Trollhättan, *Sweden* 11 F6
Trollheimen, *Norway* 10 B3
Trombetas →, *Brazil* 121 D6
Troms fylke □, *Norway* 8 B15
Tromsø, *Norway* 8 B15
Trona, *U.S.A.* 113 K9
Tronador, *Argentina* 128 B2
Trondheim, *Norway* 10 A4
Trondheimsfjorden, *Norway* 8 E11
Trönninge, *Sweden* 11 H6
Trönö, *Sweden* 10 C10
Tronto →, *Italy* 33 F10
Troodos, *Cyprus* 37 E11
Troon, *U.K.* 14 F4
Tropea, *Italy* 35 D8
Tropic, *U.S.A.* 111 H7
Tropoja, *Albania* 38 G3
Trossachs, The, *U.K.* 14 E4
Trostan, *U.K.* 15 A5
Trostberg, *Germany* 19 G8
Trostyanets, *Ukraine* 40 F9
Trotternish, *U.K.* 14 D2
Troup, *U.S.A.* 109 J7
Trout →, *Canada* 100 A5
Trout L., *N.W.T., Canada* 100 A4
Trout L., *Ont., Canada* 101 C10
Trout Lake, *Mich., U.S.A.* 98 C2
Trout Lake, *Wash., U.S.A.* 112 E5
Trout River, *Canada* 99 C8
Trouville-sur-Mer, *France* 24 C7
Trowbridge, *U.K.* 13 F5
Troy, *Turkey* 66 D2
Troy, *Ala., U.S.A.* 105 K3
Troy, *Idaho, U.S.A.* 110 C5
Troy, *Kans., U.S.A.* 108 F7
Troy, *Mo., U.S.A.* 108 F9
Troy, *Mont., U.S.A.* 110 B6
Troy, *N.Y., U.S.A.* 107 D11
Troy, *Ohio, U.S.A.* 104 E3
Troyan, *Bulgaria* 38 G7
Troyes, *France* 25 D11
Trpanj, *Croatia* 21 M7
Trstena, *Slovakia* 20 F9
Trstenik, *Serbia, Yug.* 21 M10
Trubchevsk, *Russia* 40 E8
Trucial States = United Arab Emirates ■, *Asia* 65 F7
Truckee, *U.S.A.* 112 F6
Trujillo, *Colombia* 120 C2
Trujillo, *Honduras* 116 C2
Trujillo, *Peru* 124 B2
Trujillo, *Spain* 31 F5
Trujillo, *U.S.A.* 109 H2
Trujillo, *Venezuela* 120 B3
Trujillo □, *Venezuela* 120 B3
Truk, *Pac. Oc.* 92 G7
Trumann, *U.S.A.* 109 H9
Trumbull, Mt., *U.S.A.* 111 H7
Trun, *France* 24 D7
Trun, *Switz.* 23 C7
Trundle, *Australia* 91 E4
Trung-Phan, *Vietnam* 58 E7
Truro, *Canada* 99 C7
Truro, *U.K.* 13 G2
Truslove, *Australia* 89 F3
Trustrup, *Denmark* 11 H4
Truth or Consequences, *U.S.A.* 111 K10
Trutnov, *Czech.* 20 E5
Truyère →, *France* 26 D6
Tryavna, *Bulgaria* 38 G8
Tryon, *U.S.A.* 105 H4
Tryonville, *U.S.A.* 106 E5
Trzcianka, *Poland* 20 B6
Trzebiatów, *Poland* 20 A5
Trzebiez, *Poland* 20 B4
Trzebinia-Siersza, *Poland* 20 E9
Trzebnica, *Poland* 20 D7
Tržič, *Slovenia* 33 B11
Tsageri, *Georgia* 43 E10
Tsaratanana, *Madag.* 85 B8
Tsaratanana, Mt. de, *Madag.* 85 A8
Tsarevo = Michurin, *Bulgaria* 38 G10
Tsarichanka, *Ukraine* 42 B6
Tsau, *Botswana* 84 C3
Tsebrikovo, *Ukraine* 42 C4
Tselinograd, *Kazakhstan* 44 D8
Tsetserleg, *Mongolia* 54 B5
Tshabong, *Botswana* 84 D3
Tshane, *Botswana* 84 C3
Tshela, *Zaïre* 80 E2
Tshesebe, *Botswana* 85 C4
Tshibeke, *Zaïre* 82 C2
Tshibinda, *Zaïre* 82 C2
Tshikapa, *Zaïre* 80 F4
Tshilenge, *Zaïre* 82 D1
Tshinsenda, *Zaïre* 83 E2
Tshofa, *Zaïre* 82 D2
Tshwane, *Botswana* 84 C3
Tsigara, *Botswana* 84 C4
Tsihombe, *Madag.* 85 D8
Tsimlyansk, *Russia* 43 C10
Tsimlyansk Res. = Tsimlyanskoye Vdkhr., *Russia* 43 B10
Tsimlyanskoye Vdkhr., *Russia* 43 B10
Tsinan = Jinan, *China* 50 F9
Tsineng, *S. Africa* 84 D3
Tsinghai = Qinghai □, *China* 54 C4
Tsingtao = Qingdao, *China* 51 F11
Tsinjomitondraka, *Madag.* 85 B8
Tsiroanomandidy, *Madag.* 85 B8
Tsivilsk, *Russia* 41 D15
Tsivory, *Madag.* 85 C8
Tskhinvali, *Georgia* 43 E11
Tsna →, *Russia* 41 D12
Tso Moriri, L., *India* 63 C8
Tsodilo Hill, *Botswana* 84 B3
Tsogttsetsiy, *Mongolia* 50 C3
Tsolo, *S. Africa* 85 E4
Tsomo, *S. Africa* 85 E4
Tsu, *Japan* 49 G8
Tsu L., *Canada* 100 A6
Tsuchiura, *Japan* 49 F10
Tsugaru-Kaikyō, *Japan* 48 D10
Tsumeb, *Namibia* 84 B2
Tsumis, *Namibia* 84 C2

Tsuruga, *Japan* 49 G8
Tsurugi-San, *Japan* 49 H7
Tsuruoka, *Japan* 48 E9
Tsushima, *Gifu, Japan* 49 G8
Tsushima, *Nagasaki, Japan* 49 G4
Tsvetkovo, *Ukraine* 42 B4
Tua →, *Portugal* 30 D3
Tual, *Indonesia* 57 F8
Tuam, *Ireland* 15 C3
Tuamotu Arch. = Tuamotu Is., *Pac. Oc.* 93 J13
Tuamotu Is., *Pac. Oc.* 93 J13
Tuamotu Ridge, *Pac. Oc.* 93 K14
Tuanfeng, *China* 53 B10
Tuanxi, *China* 52 D6
Tuao, *Phil.* 55 C4
Tuapse, *Russia* 43 D8
Tuatapere, *N.Z.* 87 M1
Tuba City, *U.S.A.* 111 H8
Tuban, *Indonesia* 57 G15
Tubarão, *Brazil* 127 B6
Tūbās, *Jordan* 69 C4
Tubau, *Malaysia* 56 D4
Tubbergen, *Neths.* 16 D9
Tübingen, *Germany* 19 G5
Tubize, *Belgium* 17 G4
Tubruq, *Libya* 73 B9
Tubuai Is., *Pac. Oc.* 93 K12
Tuc Trung, *Vietnam* 59 G6
Tucacas, *Venezuela* 120 A4
Tucano, *Brazil* 122 D4
Tuchang, *Taiwan* 53 E13
Tuchodi →, *Canada* 100 B4
Tuchola, *Poland* 20 B7
Tucson, *U.S.A.* 111 K8
Tucumán □, *Argentina* 126 B2
Tucumcari, *U.S.A.* 109 H3
Tucunaré, *Brazil* 125 B6
Tucupido, *Venezuela* 120 B4
Tucupita, *Venezuela* 121 B5
Tucuruí, *Brazil* 122 B2
Tudela, *Spain* 28 C3
Tudela de Duero, *Spain* 30 D6
Tudmur, *Syria* 64 C3
Tudor, L., *Canada* 99 A6
Tudora, *Romania* 38 B9
Tuella →, *Portugal* 30 D3
Tuen, *Australia* 91 D4
Tueré →, *Brazil* 122 B1
Tugela →, *S. Africa* 85 D5
Tuguegarao, *Phil.* 55 C4
Tugur, *Russia* 45 D14
Tuineje, *Canary Is.* 36 F5
Tukangbesi, Kepulauan, *Indonesia* 57 F6
Tukarak I., *Canada* 98 A4
Tukayyid, *Iraq* 64 D5
Tûkh, *Egypt* 76 H7
Tukobo, *Ghana* 78 D4
Tūkrah, *Libya* 73 B9
Tuktoyaktuk, *Canada* 96 B6
Tukums, *Latvia* 40 C3
Tukuyu, *Tanzania* 83 D3
Tula, *Hidalgo, Mexico* 115 C5
Tula, *Tamaulipas, Mexico* 115 C5
Tula, *Nigeria* 79 D7
Tula, *Russia* 41 D10
Tulancingo, *Mexico* 115 C5
Tulare, *U.S.A.* 111 H4
Tulare Lake Bed, *U.S.A.* 111 J4
Tularosa, *U.S.A.* 111 K10
Tulbagh, *S. Africa* 84 E2
Tulcán, *Ecuador* 120 C2
Tulcea, *Romania* 38 D11
Tulchin, *Ukraine* 42 B3
Tūleh, *Iran* 65 C7
Tulemalu L., *Canada* 101 A9
Tuli, *Indonesia* 57 E6
Tuli, *Zimbabwe* 83 G2
Tulia, *U.S.A.* 109 H4
Ţūlkarm, *Jordan* 69 C4
Tullahoma, *U.S.A.* 105 H2
Tullamore, *Australia* 91 E4
Tullamore, *Ireland* 15 C4
Tulle, *France* 26 C5
Tullibigeal, *Australia* 91 E4
Tullins, *France* 27 C9
Tulln, *Austria* 21 G6
Tullow, *Ireland* 15 D4
Tullus, *Sudan* 77 E1
Tully, *Australia* 90 B4
Ţulmaythah, *Libya* 73 B9
Tulmur, *Australia* 90 C3
Tulnici, *Romania* 38 D9
Tulovo, *Bulgaria* 38 G8
Tulsa, *U.S.A.* 109 G7
Tulsequah, *Canada* 100 B2
Tulu Milki, *Ethiopia* 77 F4
Tulu Welel, *Ethiopia* 77 F3
Tulua, *Colombia* 120 C2
Tulun, *Russia* 45 D11
Tulungagung, *Indonesia* 56 F4
Tum, *Indonesia* 57 E8
Tuma, *Russia* 41 D12
Tuma →, *Nic.* 116 D3
Tumaco, *Colombia* 120 C2
Tumaco, Ensenada, *Colombia* 120 C2
Tumatumari, *Guyana* 121 B6
Tumba, *Sweden* 10 E11
Tumba, L., *Zaïre* 80 E3
Tumbarumba, *Australia* 91 F4
Tumbaya, *Argentina* 126 A2
Túmbes, *Peru* 124 A1
Tumbes □, *Peru* 124 A1
Tumbwe, *Zaïre* 83 E2
Tumby Bay, *Australia* 91 E2
Tumd Youqi, *China* 50 D6
Tumen, *China* 51 C15
Tumen Jiang →, *China* 51 C16
Tumeremo, *Venezuela* 121 B5
Tumiritinga, *Brazil* 123 E3
Tumkur, *India* 60 N10
Tummel, L., *U.K.* 14 E5
Tump, *Pakistan* 60 F3
Tumpat, *Malaysia* 59 J4
Tumu, *Ghana* 78 C4
Tumucumaque, Serra, *Brazil* 121 C7
Tumupasa, *Bolivia* 124 C4
Tumut, *Australia* 91 F4
Tumwater, *U.S.A.* 110 C2
Tunas de Zaza, *Cuba* 116 B4
Tunbridge Wells, *U.K.* 13 F8
Tunceli, *Turkey* 67 D8
Tunceli □, *Turkey* 67 D8
Tuncurry, *Australia* 91 E5
Tunduru, *Tanzania* 83 E4
Tunduru □, *Tanzania* 83 E4
Tundzha →, *Bulgaria* 39 H9
Tunga Pass, *India* 61 E19
Tungabhadra →, *India* 60 M11
Tungaru, *Sudan* 77 E3
Tungla, *Nic.* 116 D3
Tungnafellsjökull, *Iceland* 8 D5
Tungsten, *Canada* 100 A3
Tungurahua □, *Ecuador* 120 D2
Tunguska, Nizhnyaya →, *Russia* 45 C9
Tunia, *Colombia* 120 C2
Tunica, *U.S.A.* 109 H9
Tunis, *Tunisia* 75 A7
Tunis, Golfe de, *Tunisia* 75 A7
Tunisia ■, *Africa* 75 B6
Tunja, *Colombia* 120 B3
Tunkhannock, *U.S.A.* 107 E9
Tunliu, *China* 50 F7
Tunnsjøen, *Norway* 8 D12
Tunungayualok I., *Canada* 99 A7
Tunuyán, *Argentina* 126 C2
Tunuyán →, *Argentina* 126 C2
Tunxi, *China* 53 C12
Tuo Jiang →, *China* 52 C5
Tuolumne, *U.S.A.* 111 H3
Tuolumne →, *U.S.A.* 112 H5
Tuoy-Khaya, *Russia* 45 C12
Tūp Āghāj, *Iran* 64 B5
Tupã, *Brazil* 127 A5
Tupaciguara, *Brazil* 123 E2
Tupelo, *U.S.A.* 105 H1
Tupik, *Russia* 40 D8
Tupik, *Russia* 45 D12
Tupinambaranas, *Brazil* 121 D6
Tupirama, *Brazil* 122 C2
Tupiratins, *Brazil* 122 C2
Tupiza, *Bolivia* 126 A2
Tupman, *U.S.A.* 113 K7
Tupper, *Canada* 100 B4
Tupper Lake, *U.S.A.* 107 B10
Tupungato, Cerro, *S. Amer.* 126 C2
Tuquan, *China* 51 B11
Túquerres, *Colombia* 120 C2
Tura, *Russia* 45 C11
Turabah, *Si. Arabia* 64 D4
Turagua, Serranía, *Venezuela* 121 B5
Tūrān, *Iran* 65 C8
Turan, *Russia* 45 D10
Turayf, *Si. Arabia* 64 D3
Turbenthal, *Switz.* 23 B7
Turégano, *Spain* 30 D6
Turek, *Poland* 20 C8
Turen, *Venezuela* 120 B4
Turfan = Turpan, *China* 54 B3
Turfan Depression = Turpan Hami, *China* 54 B3
Tŭrgovishte, *Bulgaria* 38 F9
Turgutlu, *Turkey* 66 D2
Turhal, *Turkey* 42 F7
Turia →, *Spain* 29 F4
Turiaçu, *Brazil* 122 B2
Turiaçu →, *Brazil* 122 B2
Turin = Torino, *Italy* 32 C4
Turin, *Canada* 100 D6
Turka, *Ukraine* 40 G3
Turkana □, *Kenya* 82 B4
Turkana, L., *Africa* 82 B4
Turkestan, *Kazakhstan* 44 E7
Túrkeve, *Hungary* 21 H10
Turkey ■, *Eurasia* 66 D7
Turkey Creek, *Australia* 88 C4
Turki, *Russia* 41 F13
Turkmenistan ■, *Asia* 44 F6
Türkoğlu, *Turkey* 66 E7
Turks & Caicos Is. ■, *W. Indies* 117 B5
Turks Island Passage, *W. Indies* 117 B5
Turku, *Finland* 9 F17
Turkwe →, *Kenya* 82 B4
Turlock, *U.S.A.* 111 H3
Turnagain →, *Canada* 100 B3
Turnagain, C., *N.Z.* 87 J6
Turneffe Is., *Belize* 115 D7
Turner, *Australia* 88 C4
Turner, *U.S.A.* 110 B9
Turner Pt., *Australia* 90 A1
Turner Valley, *Canada* 100 C6
Turners Falls, *U.S.A.* 107 D12
Turnhout, *Belgium* 17 F5
Turnor L., *Canada* 101 B7
Tŭrnovo, *Bulgaria* 38 F8
Turnu Măgurele, *Romania* 38 F7
Turnu Rosu Pasul, *Romania* 38 D7
Turon, *U.S.A.* 109 G5
Turpan, *China* 54 B3
Turpan Hami, *China* 54 B3
Turriff, *U.K.* 14 D6
Tursāq, *Iraq* 64 C5
Tursha, *Russia* 41 C15
Tursi, *Italy* 35 B9
Turtle Head I., *Australia* 90 A3
Turtle L., *Canada* 101 C7
Turtle Lake, *N. Dak., U.S.A.* 108 B4
Turtle Lake, *Wis., U.S.A.* 108 C8
Turtleford, *Canada* 101 C7
Turukhansk, *Russia* 45 C9
Turun ja Porin lääni □, *Finland* 9 F17
Turzovka, *Slovakia* 20 F8
Tuscaloosa, *U.S.A.* 105 J2
Tuscánia, *Italy* 33 F8
Tuscany = Toscana, *Italy* 32 E8
Tuscola, *Ill., U.S.A.* 104 F1
Tuscola, *Tex., U.S.A.* 109 J5
Tuscumbia, *U.S.A.* 105 H2
Tuskar Rock, *Ireland* 15 D5
Tuskegee, *U.S.A.* 105 J3
Tustna, *Norway* 10 A2
Tutak, *Turkey* 67 D10
Tutayev, *Russia* 41 C11
Tuticorin, *India* 60 Q11
Tutin, *Serbia, Yug.* 21 N10
Tutóia, *Brazil* 122 B3
Tutong, *Brunei* 56 D4
Tutova →, *Romania* 38 C10
Tutrakan, *Bulgaria* 38 E9
Tutshi L., *Canada* 100 B2
Tuttle, *U.S.A.* 108 B5
Tuttlingen, *Germany* 19 H4
Tutuala, *Indonesia* 57 F7
Tutuila, *Amer. Samoa* 87 B13
Tututepec, *Mexico* 115 D5
Tuva Republic □, *Russia* 45 D10
Tuvalu ■, *Pac. Oc.* 92 H9
Tuxpan, *Mexico* 115 C5
Tuxtla Gutiérrez, *Mexico* 115 D6
Tuy, *Spain* 30 C2
Tuy An, *Vietnam* 58 F7
Tuy Duc, *Vietnam* 59 F6
Tuy Hoa, *Vietnam* 58 F7
Tuy Phong, *Vietnam* 59 G7
Tuya L., *Canada* 100 B2
Tuyen Hoa, *Vietnam* 58 D6
Tuyen Quang, *Vietnam* 58 B5
Tūysarkān, *Iran* 65 C6
Tuz Gölü, *Turkey* 66 D5
Ţūz Khurmātū, *Iraq* 64 C5
Tuzla, *Bos.-H.* 21 L8
Tuzla Gölü, *Turkey* 66 D6
Tuzlov →, *Russia* 43 C8
Tvååker, *Sweden* 11 G6
Tvedestrand, *Norway* 11 F2
Tver, *Russia* 41 C9
Tvŭrditsa, *Bulgaria* 38 G8
Twain, *U.S.A.* 112 E5
Twain Harte, *U.S.A.* 112 G6
Tweed, *Canada* 106 B7
Tweed →, *U.K.* 14 F7
Tweed Heads, *Australia* 91 D5
Tweedsmuir Prov. Park, *Canada* 100 C3
Twello, *Neths.* 16 D8
Twentynine Palms, *U.S.A.* 113 L10
Twillingate, *Canada* 99 C9
Twin Bridges, *U.S.A.* 110 D7
Twin Falls, *U.S.A.* 110 E6
Twin Valley, *U.S.A.* 108 B6
Twisp, *U.S.A.* 110 B3
Twistringen, *Germany* 18 C4
Two Harbors, *U.S.A.* 108 B9
Two Hills, *Canada* 100 C6
Two Rivers, *U.S.A.* 104 C2
Twofold B., *Australia* 91 F4
Tychy, *Poland* 20 E8
Tykocin, *Poland* 20 B12
Tyldal, *Norway* 10 B4
Tyler, *U.S.A.* 103 D7
Tyler, *Minn., U.S.A.* 108 C6
Tyler, *Tex., U.S.A.* 109 J7
Týn nad Vltavou, *Czech.* 20 F4
Tynda, *Russia* 45 D13
Tyne →, *U.K.* 12 C6
Tyne & Wear □, *U.K.* 12 C6
Tynemouth, *U.K.* 12 B6
Tynset, *Norway* 10 B4
Tyre = Sūr, *Lebanon* 69 B4
Tyrifjorden, *Norway* 10 D4
Tyringe, *Sweden* 11 H7
Tyristrand, *Norway* 10 D4
Tyrnyauz, *Russia* 43 E10
Tyrone, *U.S.A.* 106 F6
Tyrrell →, *Australia* 91 F3
Tyrrell, L., *Australia* 91 F3
Tyrrell Arm, *Canada* 101 A9
Tyrrell L., *Canada* 101 A7
Tyrrhenian Sea, *Europe* 34 B5
Tysfjorden, *Norway* 8 B14
Tystberga, *Sweden* 11 F11
Tyub Karagan, Mys, *Kazakhstan* 43 D14
Tyuleniy, *Russia* 43 D12
Tyumen, *Russia* 44 D7
Tywi →, *U.K.* 13 F3
Tywyn, *U.K.* 13 E3
Tzaneen, *S. Africa* 85 C5
Tzermiádhes, *Greece* 37 D7
Tzermiádhes Neápolis, *Greece* 39 P8
Tzoumérka, Óros, *Greece* 39 K4
Tzukong = Zigong, *China* 52 C5
Tzummarum, *Neths.* 16 B7

U

U Taphao, *Thailand* 58 F3
U.S.A. = United States of America ■, *N. Amer.* 102 C7
Uachadi, Sierra, *Venezuela* 121 C4
Uainambi, *Colombia* 120 C4
Uanda, *Australia* 90 C3
Uarsciek, *Somali Rep.* 68 G4
Uasin □, *Kenya* 82 B4
Uato-Udo, *Indonesia* 57 F7
Uatumã →, *Brazil* 121 D6
Uauá, *Brazil* 122 C4
Uaupés, *Brazil* 120 D4
Uaupés →, *Brazil* 120 C4
Uaxactún, *Guatemala* 116 C2
Ubá, *Brazil* 123 F3
Ubaitaba, *Brazil* 123 D4
Ubangi = Oubangi →, *Zaïre* 80 E3
Ubaté, *Colombia* 120 B3
Ubauro, *Pakistan* 62 E3
Ubaye →, *France* 27 D10
Ube, *Japan* 49 H5
Ubeda, *Spain* 29 G1
Uberaba, *Brazil* 123 E2
Uberaba, L., *Brazil* 125 D6
Uberlândia, *Brazil* 123 E2
Überlingen, *Germany* 19 H5
Ubiaja, *Nigeria* 79 D6
Ubolratna Res., *Thailand* 58 D4
Ubombo, *S. Africa* 85 D5
Ubon Ratchathani, *Thailand* 58 E5
Ubondo, *Zaïre* 82 C2
Ubort →, *Belorussia* 40 E6
Ubrique, *Spain* 31 J5
Ubundu, *Zaïre* 82 C2
Ucayali →, *Peru* 124 A3
Uccle, *Belgium* 17 G4
Uchi Lake, *Canada* 101 C10
Uchiura-Wan, *Japan* 48 C10
Uchiza, *Peru* 124 B2
Uchte, *Germany* 18 C4
Uchur →, *Russia* 45 D14
Ucluelet, *Canada* 100 D3
Ucuriş, *Romania* 38 C4
Uda →, *Russia* 45 D14
Udaipur, *India* 62 G5
Udaipur Garhi, *Nepal* 63 F12
Udbina, *Croatia* 33 D12
Uddel, *Neths.* 16 D7
Uddevalla, *Sweden* 11 F5
Uddjaur, *Sweden* 8 D16
Uden, *Neths.* 17 E7
Udgir, *India* 60 K10
Udhampur, *India* 63 C6
Udi, *Nigeria* 79 D6
Údine, *Italy* 33 B10
Udmurt Republic □, *Russia* 44 D6
Udon Thani, *Thailand* 58 D4
Udupi, *India* 60 N9
Udvoy Balkan, *Bulgaria* 38 G9
Udzungwa Range, *Tanzania* 83 D4
Ueckermünde, *Germany* 18 B10
Ueda, *Japan* 49 F9
Uedineniya, Os., *Russia* 4 B12
Uele →, *Zaïre* 80 D4
Uelen, *Russia* 45 C19
Uelzen, *Germany* 18 C6
Uetendorf, *Switz.* 22 C5
Ufa, *Russia* 44 D6
Uffenheim, *Germany* 19 F6
Ugab →, *Namibia* 84 C1
Ugalla →, *Tanzania* 82 D3
Uganda ■, *Africa* 82 B3
Ugchelen, *Neths.* 16 D7
Ugento, *Italy* 35 C11
Ugep, *Nigeria* 79 D6
Ugie, *S. Africa* 85 E4
Ugijar, *Spain* 29 J1
Ugine, *France* 27 C10
Uglegorsk, *Russia* 45 E15
Uglich, *Russia* 41 C11
Ugljane, *Croatia* 33 E13
Ugolyak, *Russia* 45 C13
Ugra →, *Russia* 41 D10
Ugûn Mûsa, *Egypt* 69 F1
Ugŭrchin, *Bulgaria* 38 F7
Uh →, *Slovakia* 21 G11
Uherske Hradiště, *Czech.* 20 F7
Uhrichsville, *U.S.A.* 106 F3
Uíge, *Angola* 80 F2
Uijŏngbu, *S. Korea* 51 F14
Ŭiju, *N. Korea* 51 D13
Uinta Mts., *U.S.A.* 110 F8
Uitenhage, *S. Africa* 84 E4
Uitgeest, *Neths.* 16 C5
Uithoorn, *Neths.* 16 D5
Uithuizen, *Neths.* 16 B9
Uitkerke, *Belgium* 17 F2
Újfehértó, *Hungary* 21 H11
Ujhani, *India* 63 F8
Uji-guntō, *Japan* 49 J4
Ujjain, *India* 62 H6
Újpest, *Hungary* 21 H9
Újszász, *Hungary* 21 H10
Ujung Pandang, *Indonesia* 57 F5
Uka, *Russia* 45 D17
Ukara I., *Tanzania* 82 C3
Uke-Shima, *Japan* 49 K4
Ukerewe □, *Tanzania* 82 C3
Ukerewe I., *Tanzania* 82 C3
Ukholovo, *Russia* 41 E12
Ukhrul, *India* 61 G19
Ukhta, *Russia* 44 C6
Ukiah, *U.S.A.* 112 F3
Ukki Fort, *India* 63 C7
Ukmerge, *Lithuania* 40 D4
Ukraine ■, *Europe* 42 B4
Ukwi, *Botswana* 84 C3
Ulaanbaatar, *Mongolia* 45 E11
Ulaangom, *Mongolia* 54 A4
Ulamba, *Zaïre* 83 D1
Ulan Bator = Ulaanbaatar, *Mongolia* 45 E11
Ulan Ude, *Russia* 45 D11
Ulanga □, *Tanzania* 83 D4
Ulanów, *Poland* 20 E12
Ulaş, *Turkey* 66 D7
Ulaya, *Morogoro, Tanzania* 82 D4
Ulaya, *Tabora, Tanzania* 82 C3
Ulcinj, *Montenegro, Yug.* 39 H2
Ulco, *S. Africa* 84 D3
Ulfborg, *Denmark* 11 H2
Ulft, *Neths.* 16 E8
Ulhasnagar, *India* 60 K8
Uljma, *Serbia, Yug.* 21 K11
Ulla →, *Spain* 30 C2
Ulladulla, *Australia* 91 F5
Ullånger, *Sweden* 10 B12
Ullapool, *U.K.* 14 D3
Ullared, *Sweden* 11 G6
Ulldecona, *Spain* 28 E5
Ullswater, *U.K.* 12 C5
Ullung-do, *S. Korea* 51 F16
Ulm, *Germany* 19 G5
Ulmarra, *Australia* 91 D5
Ulmeni, *Romania* 38 D9
Ulonguè, *Mozam.* 83 E3
Ulricehamn, *Sweden* 9 H12
Ulrum, *Neths.* 16 B8
Ulsan, *S. Korea* 51 G15
Ulsberg, *Norway* 10 B3
Ulster □, *U.K.* 15 B5
Ulubaria, *India* 63 H13
Ulubat Gölü, *Turkey* 66 C3
Ulubey, *Turkey* 66 D3
Uluborlu, *Turkey* 66 D4
Uludağ, *Turkey* 66 C3
Uludere, *Turkey* 67 E10
Uluguru Mts., *Tanzania* 82 D4
Ulukışla, *Turkey* 66 E6
Ulungur He →, *China* 54 B3
Ulutau, *Kazakhstan* 44 E7
Ulvenhout, *Neths.* 17 E5
Ulverston, *U.K.* 12 C4
Ulverstone, *Australia* 90 G4
Ulya, *Russia* 45 D15
Ulyanovsk = Simbirsk, *Russia* 41 D16
Ulyasutay, *Mongolia* 54 B4
Ulysses, *U.S.A.* 109 G4
Umag, *Croatia* 33 C10
Umala, *Bolivia* 124 D4
Uman, *Ukraine* 42 B4
Umaria, *India* 61 H12
Umarkot, *Pakistan* 60 G6
Umatilla, *U.S.A.* 110 D4
Umba, *Russia* 44 C4
Umbertide, *Italy* 33 E9
Umbrella Mts., *N.Z.* 87 L2
Umbria □, *Italy* 33 F9
Ume älv →, *Sweden* 8 E16
Umeå, *Sweden* 8 E16
Umera, *Indonesia* 57 E7
Umfuli →, *Zimbabwe* 83 F2
Umgusa, *Zimbabwe* 83 F2
Umka, *Serbia, Yug.* 21 L10
Umkomaas, *S. Africa* 85 E5
Umm ad Daraj, J., *Jordan* 69 C4
Umm al Qaywayn, *U.A.E.* 65 E7
Umm al Qittayn, *Jordan* 69 C5
Umm Arda, *Sudan* 77 D3
Umm Bāb, *Qatar* 65 E6
Umm Bel, *Sudan* 77 E2
Umm Dubban, *Sudan* 77 D3
Umm el Fahm, *Israel* 69 C4
Umm Koweika, *Sudan* 77 E3
Umm Lajj, *Si. Arabia* 64 E3
Umm Merwa, *Sudan* 76 D3
Umm Ruwaba, *Sudan* 77 E3
Umm Sidr, *Sudan* 77 E2
Ummanz, *Germany* 18 A9
Umnak I., *U.S.A.* 96 C3
Umniati →, *Zimbabwe* 83 F2
Umpqua →, *U.S.A.* 110 E1
Umreth, *India* 62 H5
Umtata, *S. Africa* 85 E4
Umuahia, *Nigeria* 79 D6
Umuarama, *Brazil* 127 A5
Umvukwe Ra., *Zimbabwe* 83 F3
Umzimvubu = Port St. Johns, *S. Africa* 85 E4
Umzingwane →, *Zimbabwe* 83 G2
Umzinto, *S. Africa* 85 E5
Una, *India* 62 J4
Una →, *Bos.-H.* 33 C13
Unac →, *Bos.-H.* 33 D13

Unadilla, *U.S.A.* 107 D9
Unalaska, *U.S.A.* 96 C3
Uncastillo, *Spain* 28 C3
Uncía, *Bolivia* 124 D4
Uncompahgre Peak, *U.S.A.* 111 G10
Unden, *Sweden* 11 F8
Underberg, *S. Africa* 85 D4
Underbool, *Australia* 91 F3
Undersaker, *Sweden* 10 A7
Undersvik, *Sweden* 10 C10
Unecha, *Russia* 40 E8
Uneiuxi →, *Brazil* 120 D4
Ungarie, *Australia* 91 E4
Ungarra, *Australia* 91 E2
Ungava B., *Canada* 97 C13
Ungava Pen., *Canada* 97 C12
Ungeny, *Moldavia* 42 C2
Unggi, *N. Korea* 51 C16
Ungwatiri, *Sudan* 77 D4
Uni, *Russia* 41 C17
União da Vitória, *Brazil* 127 B5
União dos Palmares, *Brazil* 122 C4
Unije, *Croatia* 33 D11
Unimak I., *U.S.A.* 96 C3
Unini →, *Brazil* 121 D5
Union, *Miss., U.S.A.* 109 J10
Union, *Mo., U.S.A.* 108 F9
Union, *S.C., U.S.A.* 105 H5
Union, Mt., *U.S.A.* 111 J7
Union City, *Calif., U.S.A.* 112 H4
Union City, *N.J., U.S.A.* 107 F10
Union City, *Pa., U.S.A.* 106 E5
Union City, *Tenn., U.S.A.* 109 G10
Union Gap, *U.S.A.* 110 C3
Union of Soviet Socialist Republics = Commonwealth of Independent States ■, *Eurasia* 45 D11
Union Springs, *U.S.A.* 105 J3
Uniondale, *S. Africa* 84 E3
Uniontown, *U.S.A.* 104 F6
Unionville, *U.S.A.* 108 E8
United Arab Emirates ■, *Asia* 65 F7
United Kingdom ■, *Europe* 7 E5
United States of America ■, *N. Amer.* 102 C7
Unity, *Canada* 101 C7
Universales, Mtes., *Spain* 28 E3
Unjha, *India* 62 H5
Unnao, *India* 63 F9
Uno, Ilha, *Guinea-Biss.* 78 C1
Unst, *U.K.* 14 A8
Unstrut →, *Germany* 18 D7
Unter-engadin, *Switz.* 23 C10
Unterägeri, *Switz.* 23 B7
Unterkulm, *Switz.* 22 B6
Unterseen, *Switz.* 22 C5
Unterwaldner Alpen, *Switz.* 23 C6
Unuk →, *Canada* 100 B2
Ünye, *Turkey* 42 F7
Unzha, *Russia* 41 B14
Unzha →, *Russia* 41 C13
Uors, *Switz.* 23 C8
Uozu, *Japan* 49 F8
Upa →, *Czech.* 20 E6
Upata, *Venezuela* 121 B5
Upemba, L., *Zaïre* 83 D2
Upernavik, *Greenland* 4 B5
Upington, *S. Africa* 84 D3
Upleta, *India* 62 J4
Upolu, *W. Samoa* 87 A13
Upper Alkali Lake, *U.S.A.* 110 F3
Upper Arrow L., *Canada* 100 C5
Upper Foster L., *Canada* 101 B7
Upper Hutt, *N.Z.* 87 J5
Upper Klamath L., *U.S.A.* 110 E3
Upper Lake, *U.S.A.* 112 F4
Upper Musquodoboit, *Canada* 99 C7
Upper Red L., *U.S.A.* 108 A7
Upper Sandusky, *U.S.A.* 104 E4
Upper Volta = Burkina Faso ■, *Africa* 78 C4
Upphärad, *Sweden* 11 F6
Uppsala, *Sweden* 10 E11
Uppsala län □, *Sweden* 9 G14
Upshi, *India* 63 C7
Upstart, C., *Australia* 90 B4
Upton, *U.S.A.* 108 C2
Ur, *Iraq* 64 D5
Urabá, G. de, *Colombia* 120 B2
Uracara, *Brazil* 121 D6
Urad Qianqi, *China* 50 D5
Urakawa, *Japan* 48 C11
Ural, *Australia* 91 E4
Ural →, *Kazakhstan* 43 C14
Ural Mts. = Uralskie Gory, *Russia* 44 D6
Uralla, *Australia* 91 E5
Uralsk, *Kazakhstan* 44 D6
Uralskie Gory, *Russia* 44 D6
Urambo, *Tanzania* 82 D3
Urambo □, *Tanzania* 82 D3
Urandangi, *Australia* 90 C2
Uranium City, *Canada* 101 B7
Uranquinty, *Australia* 91 F4
Uraricaá →, *Brazil* 121 C5
Uraricuera →, *Brazil* 121 C5
Urawa, *Japan* 49 G9
Uray, *Russia* 44 C7
'Uray'irah, *Si. Arabia* 65 E6
Urbana, *Ill., U.S.A.* 104 E1
Urbana, *Ohio, U.S.A.* 104 E4
Urbánia, *Italy* 33 E9
Urbano Santos, *Brazil* 122 B3
Urbel →, *Spain* 28 C1
Urbino, *Italy* 33 E9
Urbión, Picos de, *Spain* 28 C2
Urcos, *Peru* 124 C3
Urda, *Kazakhstan* 43 B12
Urda, *Spain* 31 F7
Urdinarrain, *Argentina* 126 C4
Urdos, *France* 26 F3
Urdzhar, *Kazakhstan* 44 E9
Ure →, *U.K.* 12 C6
Uren, *Russia* 41 C14
Ures, *Mexico* 114 B2
Urfa, *Turkey* 67 E8
Urfa □, *Turkey* 67 E8
Urfahr, *Austria* 21 G4
Urganch = Urgench, *Uzbekistan* 44 E7
Urgench, *Uzbekistan* 44 E7
Uri, *India* 63 B6
Uri □, *Switz.* 23 C7
Uribante →, *Venezuela* 120 B3
Uribe, *Colombia* 120 C3
Uribia, *Colombia* 120 A3
Uriondo, *Bolivia* 126 A3
Urique, *Mexico* 114 B3
Urique →, *Mexico* 114 B3
Urirotstock, *Switz.* 23 C7
Urk, *Neths.* 16 C7
Urla, *Turkey* 66 D2
Urlati, *Romania* 38 E9
Urmia = Orūmīyeh, *Iran* 64 B5
Urmia, L. = Orūmīyeh, Daryācheh-ye, *Iran* 64 B5
Urner Alpen, *Switz.* 23 C7
Uroševac, *Serbia, Yug.* 21 N11
Urrao, *Colombia* 120 B2
Ursus, *Poland* 20 C10
Uruaçu, *Brazil* 123 D2
Uruana, *Brazil* 123 E2
Uruapan, *Mexico* 114 D4
Uruará →, *Brazil* 121 D7
Urubamba, *Peru* 124 C3
Urubamba →, *Peru* 124 C3
Urubaxi →, *Brazil* 121 D5
Urubu →, *Brazil* 121 D6
Uruçara, *Brazil* 121 D6
Uruçuí, *Brazil* 122 C3
Uruçuí, Serra do, *Brazil* 122 C3
Uruçuí Prêto →, *Brazil* 122 C3
Urucuia →, *Brazil* 123 E2
Urucurituba, *Brazil* 121 D6
Uruguai →, *Brazil* 127 B5
Uruguaiana, *Brazil* 126 B4
Uruguay ■, *S. Amer.* 126 C4
Uruguay →, *S. Amer.* 126 C4
Urumchi = Ürümqi, *China* 44 E9
Ürümqi, *China* 44 E9
Urup →, *Russia* 43 D9
Urup, Os., *Russia* 45 E16
Urutaí, *Brazil* 123 E2
Uryung-Khaya, *Russia* 45 B12
Uryupinsk, *Russia* 41 F12
Urzhum, *Russia* 41 C16
Urziceni, *Romania* 38 E9
Uşak, *Turkey* 66 D3
Uşak □, *Turkey* 66 D3
Usakos, *Namibia* 84 C2
Usborne, Mt., *Falk. Is.* 128 D5
Ušće, *Serbia, Yug.* 21 M10
Usedom, *Germany* 18 B9
'Usfān, *Si. Arabia* 76 C4
Ush-Tobe, *Kazakhstan* 44 E8
Ushakova, Os., *Russia* 4 A12
Ushant = Ouessant, I. d', *France* 24 D1
Ushashi, *Tanzania* 82 C3
Ushat, *Sudan* 77 F2
Ushibuka, *Japan* 49 H5
Ushuaia, *Argentina* 128 D3
Ushumun, *Russia* 45 D13
Usk →, *U.K.* 13 F5
Üsküdar, *Turkey* 39 H11
Uslar, *Germany* 18 D5
Usman, *Russia* 41 E11
Usoke, *Tanzania* 82 D3
Usolye Sibirskoye, *Russia* 45 D11
Usoro, *Nigeria* 79 D6
Uspallata, P. de, *Argentina* 126 C2
Uspenskiy, *Kazakhstan* 44 E8
Usquert, *Neths.* 16 B9
Ussel, *France* 26 C6
Ussuri →, *Asia* 48 A7
Ussuriysk, *Russia* 45 E14
Ussurka, *Russia* 48 B6
Ust-Aldan = Batamay, *Russia* 45 C13
Ust Amginskoye = Khandyga, *Russia* 45 C14
Ust-Bolsheretsk, *Russia* 45 D16
Ust Buzulukskaya, *Russia* 41 F13
Ust Chaun, *Russia* 45 C18
Ust-Donetskiy, *Russia* 43 C9
Ust'-Ilga, *Russia* 45 D11
Ust Ilimpeya = Yukti, *Russia* 45 C11
Ust-Ilimsk, *Russia* 45 D11
Ust Ishim, *Russia* 44 D8
Ust-Kamchatsk, *Russia* 45 D17
Ust-Kamenogorsk, *Kazakhstan* 44 E9
Ust-Karenga, *Russia* 45 D12
Ust Khayryuzova, *Russia* 45 D16
Ust-Kut, *Russia* 45 D11
Ust Kuyga, *Russia* 45 B14
Ust-Labinsk, *Russia* 43 D8
Ust Luga, *Russia* 40 B6
Ust Maya, *Russia* 45 C14
Ust-Mil, *Russia* 45 D14
Ust-Nera, *Russia* 45 C15
Ust-Nyukzha, *Russia* 45 D13
Ust Olenek, *Russia* 45 B12
Ust-Omchug, *Russia* 45 C15
Ust Port, *Russia* 44 C9
Ust Tsilma, *Russia* 44 C6
Ust-Tungir, *Russia* 45 D13
Ust Urt = Ustyurt, Plato, *Kazakhstan* 44 E6
Ust Vorkuta, *Russia* 44 C7
Ustaoset, *Norway* 10 D2
Ustaritz, *France* 26 E2
Uste, *Russia* 41 B11
Uster, *Switz.* 23 B7
Ústí nad Labem, *Czech.* 20 E4
Ústí nad Orlicí, *Czech.* 20 F6
Ustica, *Italy* 34 D6
Ustinov = Izhevsk, *Russia* 44 D6
Ustka, *Poland* 20 A6
Ustrzyki Dolne, *Poland* 20 F12
Ustye, *Russia* 45 D10
Ustyurt, Plato, *Kazakhstan* 44 E6
Ustyuzhna, *Russia* 41 B10
Usu, *China* 54 B3
Usuki, *Japan* 49 H5
Usulután, *El Salv.* 116 D2
Usumacinta →, *Mexico* 115 D6
Usumbura = Bujumbura, *Burundi* 82 C2
Usure, *Tanzania* 82 C3
Uta, *Indonesia* 57 E9
Utah □, *U.S.A.* 110 G8
Utah, L., *U.S.A.* 110 F8
Ute Creek →, *U.S.A.* 109 H3
Utena, *Lithuania* 40 D4
Ütersen, *Germany* 18 B5
Utete, *Tanzania* 82 D4
Uthai Thani, *Thailand* 58 E3
Uthal, *Pakistan* 62 G2
Utiariti, *Brazil* 125 C6
Utica, *N.Y., U.S.A.* 107 C9
Utica, *Ohio, U.S.A.* 106 F2
Utiel, *Spain* 28 F3
Utik L., *Canada* 101 B9
Utikuma L., *Canada* 100 B5
Utinga, *Brazil* 123 D3
Utrecht, *Neths.* 16 D6
Utrecht, *S. Africa* 85 D5
Utrecht □, *Neths.* 16 D6
Utrera, *Spain* 31 H5
Utsjoki, *Finland* 8 B19
Utsunomiya, *Japan* 49 F9
Uttar Pradesh □, *India* 63 F9
Uttaradit, *Thailand* 58 D3
Uttoxeter, *U.K.* 12 E6
Ütze, *Germany* 18 C6
Uudenmaan lääni □, *Finland* 9 F18
Uusikaarlepyy, *Finland* 8 E17
Uusikaupunki, *Finland* 9 F16
Uva, *Russia* 41 C18
Uvá →, *Colombia* 120 C3
Uvalde, *U.S.A.* 109 L5
Uvarovo, *Russia* 41 F13
Uvat, *Russia* 44 D7
Uvinza, *Tanzania* 82 D3
Uvira, *Zaïre* 82 C2
Uvs Nuur, *Mongolia* 54 A4
Uwajima, *Japan* 49 H6
Uweinat, Jebel, *Sudan* 76 C1
Uxbridge, *Canada* 106 B5
Uxin Qi, *China* 50 E5
Uxmal, *Mexico* 115 C7
Uyandi, *Russia* 45 C15
Uyo, *Nigeria* 79 D6
Uyuni, *Bolivia* 124 E4
Uzbekistan ■, *Asia* 44 E7
Uzen, Bol. →, *Kazakhstan* 41 G16
Uzen, Mal. →, *Kazakhstan* 41 G16
Uzerche, *France* 26 C5
Uzès, *France* 27 D8
Uzh →, *Ukraine* 40 F7
Uzhgorod, *Ukraine* 40 G3
Uzlovaya, *Russia* 41 E11
Uzunköprü, *Turkey* 39 H9
Uzwil, *Switz.* 23 B8

V

Vaal →, *S. Africa* 84 D3
Vaal Dam, *S. Africa* 85 D4
Vaals, *Neths.* 17 G8
Vaalwater, *S. Africa* 85 C4
Vaasa, *Finland* 8 E16
Vaasan lääni □, *Finland* 8 E17
Vaassen, *Neths.* 16 D7
Vabre, *France* 26 E6
Vác, *Hungary* 21 H9
Vacaria, *Brazil* 127 B5
Vacaville, *U.S.A.* 112 G5
Vaccarès, Étang de, *France* 27 E8
Vach →, *Russia* 44 C8
Vache, I.-à-, *Haiti* 117 C5
Vadnagar, *India* 62 H5
Vado Lígure, *Italy* 32 D5
Vadodara, *India* 62 H5
Vadsø, *Norway* 8 A20
Vadstena, *Sweden* 11 F8
Vaduz, *Liech.* 23 B9
Værøy, *Norway* 8 C12
Vagnhärad, *Sweden* 10 F11
Vagos, *Portugal* 30 E2
Váh →, *Slovakia* 21 H8
Vahsel B., *Antarctica* 5 D1
Vái, *Greece* 37 D8
Vaigach, *Russia* 44 B6
Vaiges, *France* 24 D6
Vaihingen, *Germany* 19 G4
Vailly-sur-Aisne, *France* 25 C10
Vaison-la-Romaine, *France* 27 D9
Vakfikebir, *Turkey* 67 C8
Val-de-Marne □, *France* 25 D9
Val-d'Oise □, *France* 25 C9
Val d'Or, *Canada* 98 C4
Val Marie, *Canada* 101 D7
Valadares, *Portugal* 30 D2
Valahia, *Romania* 38 E8
Valais □, *Switz.* 22 D5
Valais, Alpes du, *Switz.* 22 D5
Valandovo, *Macedonia* 39 H5
Valcheta, *Argentina* 128 B3
Valdagno, *Italy* 33 C8
Valday, *Russia* 40 C8
Valdayskaya Vozvyshennost, *Russia* 40 C8
Valdeazogues →, *Spain* 31 G6
Valdemarsvik, *Sweden* 11 F10
Valdepeñas, *Ciudad Real, Spain* 31 G7
Valdepeñas, *Jaén, Spain* 31 H7
Valderaduey →, *Spain* 30 D5
Valderrobres, *Spain* 28 E5
Valdés, Pen., *Argentina* 128 B4
Valdez, *Ecuador* 120 C2
Valdez, *U.S.A.* 96 B5
Valdivia, *Chile* 128 A2
Valdivia, *Colombia* 120 B2
Valdivia □, *Chile* 128 B2
Valdobbiádene, *Italy* 33 C9
Valdosta, *U.S.A.* 105 K4
Valdoviño, *Spain* 30 B2
Valdres, *Norway* 10 D3
Vale, *Georgia* 43 F10
Vale, *U.S.A.* 110 E5
Valea lui Mihai, *Romania* 38 B5
Valença, *Brazil* 123 D4
Valença, *Portugal* 30 C2
Valença do Piauí, *Brazil* 122 C3
Valençay, *France* 25 E8
Valence, *Drôme, France* 27 D8
Valence, *Tarn-et-Garonne, France* 26 D4
Valencia, *Spain* 29 F4
Valencia, *Venezuela* 120 A4
Valencia □, *Spain* 29 F4
Valencia, Albufera de, *Spain* 29 F4
Valencia, G. de, *Spain* 29 F5
Valencia de Alcántara, *Spain* 31 F3
Valencia de Don Juan, *Spain* 30 C5
Valencia del Ventoso, *Spain* 31 G4
Valenciennes, *France* 25 B10
Valensole, *France* 27 E9
Valentia Harbour, *Ireland* 15 E1
Valentia I., *Ireland* 15 E1
Valentim, Sa. do, *Brazil* 122 C3
Valentin, *Russia* 48 C7
Valentine, *Nebr., U.S.A.* 108 D4
Valentine, *Tex., U.S.A.* 109 K2
Valenza, *Italy* 32 C5
Valera, *Venezuela* 120 B3
Valguarnera Caropepe, *Italy* 35 E7
Valier, *U.S.A.* 110 B7
Valinco, G. de, *France* 27 G12
Valjevo, *Serbia, Yug.* 21 L9
Valka, *Estonia* 40 C5
Valkeakoski, *Finland* 9 F18
Valkenburg, *Neths.* 17 G7
Valkenswaard, *Neths.* 17 F6
Vall de Uxó, *Spain* 28 F4
Valla, *Sweden* 10 E10
Valladolid, *Mexico* 115 C7
Valladolid, *Spain* 30 D6
Valladolid □, *Spain* 30 D6
Vallata, *Italy* 35 A8
Valldemosa, *Spain* 36 B9
Valle d'Aosta □, *Italy* 32 C4
Valle de Arán, *Spain* 28 C5
Valle de Cabuérniga, *Spain* 30 B6
Valle de la Pascua, *Venezuela* 120 B4
Valle de las Palmas, *Mexico* 113 N10
Valle de Santiago, *Mexico* 114 C4
Valle de Suchil, *Mexico* 114 C4
Valle de Zaragoza, *Mexico* 114 B3
Valle del Cauca □, *Colombia* 120 C2
Valle Fértil, Sierra del, *Argentina* 126 C2
Valle Hermoso, *Mexico* 115 B5
Vallecas, *Spain* 30 E7
Valledupar, *Colombia* 120 A3
Vallehermoso, *Canary Is.* 36 F2
Vallejo, *U.S.A.* 112 G4
Vallenar, *Chile* 126 B1
Valleraugue, *France* 26 D7
Vallet, *France* 24 E5
Valletta, *Malta* 37 D2
Valley Center, *U.S.A.* 113 M9
Valley City, *U.S.A.* 108 B6
Valley Falls, *U.S.A.* 110 E3
Valley Springs, *U.S.A.* 112 G6
Valley Wells, *U.S.A.* 113 K11
Valleyview, *Canada* 100 B5
Valli di Comácchio, *Italy* 33 D9
Vallimanca, Arroyo, *Argentina* 126 D4
Vallo della Lucánia, *Italy* 35 B8
Vallon-Pont-d'Arc, *France* 27 D8
Vallorbe, *Switz.* 22 C2
Valls, *Spain* 28 D6
Vallsta, *Sweden* 10 C10
Valmaseda, *Spain* 28 B1
Valmiera, *Latvia* 40 C4
Valmont, *France* 24 C7
Valmontone, *Italy* 34 A5
Valmy, *France* 25 C11
Valnera, Mte., *Spain* 28 B1
Valognes, *France* 24 C5
Valona = Vlóra, *Albania* 39 J2
Valongo, *Portugal* 30 D2
Valpaços, *Portugal* 30 D3
Valparaíso, *Chile* 126 C1
Valparaíso, *Mexico* 114 C4
Valparaiso, *U.S.A.* 104 E2
Valparaíso □, *Chile* 126 C1
Valpovo, *Croatia* 21 K8
Valréas, *France* 27 D8
Vals, *Switz.* 23 C8
Vals →, *S. Africa* 84 D4
Vals, Tanjung, *Indonesia* 57 F9
Vals-les-Bains, *France* 27 D8
Valsad, *India* 60 J8
Valskog, *Sweden* 10 E9
Válta, *Greece* 39 J6
Valtellina, *Italy* 32 B6
Valuyki, *Russia* 41 F11
Valverde, *Canary Is.* 36 G2
Valverde del Camino, *Spain* 31 H4
Valverde del Fresno, *Spain* 30 E4
Vama, *Romania* 38 B8
Vámos, *Greece* 37 D6
Van, *Turkey* 67 D10
Van □, *Turkey* 67 D10
Van, L. = Van Gölü, *Turkey* 67 D10
Van Alstyne, *U.S.A.* 109 J6
Van Bruyssel, *Canada* 99 C5
Van Buren, *Canada* 99 C6
Van Buren, *Ark., U.S.A.* 109 H7
Van Buren, *Maine, U.S.A.* 105 B11
Van Buren, *Mo., U.S.A.* 109 G9
Van Canh, *Vietnam* 58 F7
Van Diemen, C., *N. Terr., Australia* 88 B5
Van Diemen, C., *Queens., Australia* 90 B2
Van Diemen G., *Australia* 88 B5
Van Gölü, *Turkey* 67 D10
Van Horn, *U.S.A.* 109 K2
Van Ninh, *Vietnam* 58 F7
Van Reenen P., *S. Africa* 85 D4
Van Rees, Pegunungan, *Indonesia* 57 E9
Van Tassell, *U.S.A.* 108 D2
Van Wert, *U.S.A.* 104 E3
Van Yen, *Vietnam* 58 B5
Vanavara, *Russia* 45 C11
Vancouver, *Canada* 100 D4
Vancouver, *U.S.A.* 112 E4
Vancouver, C., *Australia* 89 G2
Vancouver I., *Canada* 100 D3
Vandalia, *Ill., U.S.A.* 108 F10
Vandalia, *Mo., U.S.A.* 108 F9
Vandenburg, *U.S.A.* 113 L6
Vanderbijlpark, *S. Africa* 85 D4
Vandergrift, *U.S.A.* 106 F5
Vanderhoof, *Canada* 100 C4
Vanderlin I., *Australia* 90 B2
Vandyke, *Australia* 90 C4
Vänern, *Sweden* 11 F7
Vänersborg, *Sweden* 11 F6
Vang Vieng, *Laos* 58 C4
Vanga, *Kenya* 82 C4
Vangaindrano, *Madag.* 85 C8
Vanguard, *Canada* 101 D7
Vanier, *Canada* 98 C4
Vankarem, *Russia* 45 C18
Vankleek Hill, *Canada* 98 C5
Vanna, *Norway* 8 A15
Vännäs, *Sweden* 8 E15
Vannes, *France* 24 E4
Vanoise, Massif de la, *France* 27 C10
Vanrhynsdorp, *S. Africa* 84 E2
Vanrook, *Australia* 90 B3
Vansbro, *Sweden* 9 F13
Vansittart B., *Australia* 88 B4
Vanthli, *India* 62 J4
Vanua Levu, *Fiji* 87 C8
Vanua Mbalavu, *Fiji* 87 C9
Vanuatu ■, *Pac. Oc.* 92 J8
Vanwyksvlei, *S. Africa* 84 E3
Vanzylsrus, *S. Africa* 84 D3
Vapnyarka, *Ukraine* 42 B3
Var □, *France* 27 E10
Var →, *France* 27 E11
Vara, *Sweden* 11 F6
Varades, *France* 24 E5
Varaita →, *Italy* 32 D4
Varallo, *Italy* 32 C5

Varanasi, *India* 63 G10
Varangerfjorden, *Norway* 8 A20
Varaždin, *Croatia* 33 B13
Varazze, *Italy* 32 D5
Varberg, *Sweden* 11 G6
Vardar = Axiós →, *Greece* 39 J5
Varde, *Denmark* 11 J2
Varde Å →, *Denmark* 11 J2
Varel, *Germany* 18 B4
Varella, Mui, *Vietnam* 58 F7
Varena, *Lithuania* 40 D4
Varennes-sur-Allier, *France* 26 B7
Vareš, *Bos.-H.* 21 L8
Varese, *Italy* 32 C5
Varese Lígure, *Italy* 32 D6
Vårgårda, *Sweden* 11 F6
Vargem Bonita, *Brazil* 123 F2
Vargem Grande, *Brazil* 122 B3
Varginha, *Brazil* 127 A6
Vargön, *Sweden* 11 F6
Variadero, *U.S.A.* 109 H2
Varillas, *Chile* 126 A1
Väring, *Sweden* 11 F8
Värmlands län □, *Sweden* 9 G12
Varna, *Bulgaria* 38 F10
Värnamo, *Sweden* 9 H13
Värö, *Sweden* 11 G6
Vars, *Canada* 107 A9
Varsseveld, *Neths.* 16 E8
Varto, *Turkey* 67 D9
Varvarin, *Serbia, Yug.* 21 M11
Varzaneh, *Iran* 65 C7
Várzea Alegre, *Brazil* 122 C4
Várzea da Palma, *Brazil* 123 E3
Várzea Grande, *Brazil* 125 D6
Varzi, *Italy* 32 D6
Varzo, *Italy* 32 B5
Varzy, *France* 25 E10
Vasa, *Finland* 8 E16
Vasa Barris →, *Brazil* 122 D4
Vascão →, *Portugal* 31 H3
Vaşcău, *Romania* 38 C5
Vascongadas = País Vasco □, *Spain* 28 C2
Vasht = Khāsh, *Iran* 60 E2
Vasilevichi, *Belorussia* 40 E6
Vasilikón, *Greece* 39 L6
Vasilkov, *Ukraine* 40 F7
Vaslui, *Romania* 38 C10
Vassar, *Canada* 101 D9
Vassar, *U.S.A.* 104 D4
Västerås, *Sweden* 10 E10
Västerbottens län □, *Sweden* 8 D14
Västernorrlands län □, *Sweden* 10 A11
Västervik, *Sweden* 9 H14
Västmanlands län □, *Sweden* 9 G14
Vasto, *Italy* 33 F11
Vasvár, *Hungary* 21 H6
Vatan, *France* 25 E8
Vathí, *Greece* 39 M10
Váthia, *Greece* 39 N5
Vatican City ■, *Europe* 33 G9
Vaticano, C., *Italy* 35 D8
Vatili, *Cyprus* 37 D12
Vatnajökull, *Iceland* 8 D5
Vatnås, *Norway* 10 E3
Vatneyri, *Iceland* 8 D2
Vatoa, *Fiji* 87 D9
Vatólakkos, *Greece* 37 D5
Vatoloha, *Madag.* 85 B8
Vatomandry, *Madag.* 85 B8
Vatra-Dornei, *Romania* 38 B8
Vättern, *Sweden* 11 F8
Vättis, *Switz.* 23 C8
Vaucluse □, *France* 27 E9
Vaucouleurs, *France* 25 D12
Vaud □, *Switz.* 22 C2
Vaughn, *Mont., U.S.A.* 110 C8
Vaughn, *N. Mex., U.S.A.* 111 J11
Vaulruz, *Switz.* 22 C3
Vaupés = Uaupés →, *Brazil* 120 C4
Vaupes □, *Colombia* 120 C3
Vauvert, *France* 27 E8
Vauxhall, *Canada* 100 C6
Vava'u, *Tonga* 87 D11
Vavoua, *Ivory C.* 78 D3
Vaxholm, *Sweden* 10 E12
Växjö, *Sweden* 9 H13
Vaygach, Ostrov, *Russia* 44 C6
Váyia, Ákra, *Greece* 37 C10
Veadeiros, *Brazil* 123 D2
Vechta, *Germany* 18 C4
Vechte →, *Neths.* 16 C8
Vecsés, *Hungary* 21 H9
Veddige, *Sweden* 11 G6
Vedea →, *Romania* 38 F8
Vedia, *Argentina* 126 C3
Vedra, I. del, *Spain* 36 C7
Vedrin, *Belgium* 17 G5
Veendam, *Neths.* 16 B9
Veenendaal, *Neths.* 16 D7
Veerle, *Belgium* 17 F5
Vefsna →, *Norway* 8 D12
Vega, *Norway* 8 D11
Vega, *U.S.A.* 109 H3
Vegadeo, *Spain* 30 B3
Vegafjorden, *Norway* 8 D12
Veghel, *Neths.* 17 E7
Vegorritis, Límni, *Greece* 39 J4
Vegreville, *Canada* 100 C6
Vegusdal, *Norway* 11 F2
Veii, *Italy* 33 F9
Vejen, *Denmark* 11 J3
Vejer de la Frontera, *Spain* 31 J5
Vejle, *Denmark* 11 J3
Vejle Fjord, *Denmark* 11 J3
Vela Luka, *Croatia* 33 F13
Velas, C., *Costa Rica* 116 D2
Velasco, Sierra de, *Argentina* 126 B2
Velay, Mts. du, *France* 26 D7
Velddrif, *S. Africa* 84 E2
Veldegem, *Belgium* 17 F2
Velden, *Neths.* 17 F8
Veldhoven, *Neths.* 17 F6
Velebit Planina, *Croatia* 33 D12
Velebitski Kanal, *Croatia* 33 D11
Veleka →, *Bulgaria* 38 G10
Velenje, *Slovenia* 33 B12
Velestínon, *Greece* 39 K5
Vélez, *Colombia* 120 B3
Vélez Blanco, *Spain* 29 H2
Vélez Málaga, *Spain* 31 J6
Vélez Rubio, *Spain* 29 H2
Velhas →, *Brazil* 123 E3
Velika, *Croatia* 21 K7
Velika Gorica, *Croatia* 33 C13
Velika Kapela, *Croatia* 33 C12
Velika Kladuša, *Bos.-H.* 33 C12
Velika Morava →, *Serbia, Yug.* 21 L11
Velikaya →, *Russia* 40 C6
Velikaya Kema, *Russia* 48 B8
Velikaya Lepetikha, *Ukraine* 42 C5
Velike Lašče, *Slovenia* 33 C11
Velikiye Luki, *Russia* 40 C7
Velikonda Range, *India* 60 M11
Velikoye, Oz., *Russia* 41 D12
Velingrad, *Bulgaria* 39 G6
Velino, Mte., *Italy* 33 F10
Velizh, *Russia* 40 D7
Velke Meziřici, *Czech.* 20 F6
Velletri, *Italy* 34 A5
Vellinge, *Sweden* 11 J7
Vellore, *India* 60 N11
Velp, *Neths.* 16 D7
Velsen-Noord, *Neths.* 16 D5
Velten, *Germany* 18 C9
Veluwe Meer, *Neths.* 16 D7
Velva, *U.S.A.* 108 A4
Veme, *Norway* 10 D4
Ven, *Sweden* 11 J6
Venaco, *France* 27 F13
Venado Tuerto, *Argentina* 126 C3
Venafro, *Italy* 35 A7
Venarey-les-Laumes, *France* 25 E11
Venaria, *Italy* 32 C4
Venčane, *Serbia, Yug.* 21 L10
Vence, *France* 27 E11
Venda □, *S. Africa* 85 C5
Vendas Novas, *Portugal* 31 G2
Vendée □, *France* 24 F5
Vendée →, *France* 24 F5
Vendéen, Bocage, *France* 26 B2
Vendeuvre-sur-Barse, *France* 25 D11
Vendôme, *France* 24 E8
Vendrell, *Spain* 28 D6
Vendsyssel, *Denmark* 11 G4
Véneta, L., *Italy* 33 C9
Véneto □, *Italy* 33 C8
Venev, *Russia* 41 D11
Venézia, *Italy* 33 C9
Venézia, G. di, *Italy* 33 C10
Venezuela ■, *S. Amer.* 120 B4
Venezuela, G. de, *Venezuela* 120 A3
Vengurla, *India* 60 M8
Venice = Venézia, *Italy* 33 C9
Venkatapuram, *India* 61 K12
Venlo, *Neths.* 17 F8
Venraij, *Neths.* 17 E7
Venta de Cardeña, *Spain* 31 G6
Venta de San Rafael, *Spain* 30 E6
Ventana, Punta de la, *Mexico* 114 C3
Ventana, Sa. de la, *Argentina* 126 D3
Ventersburg, *S. Africa* 84 D4
Venterstad, *S. Africa* 84 E4
Ventimíglia, *Italy* 32 E4
Ventnor, *U.K.* 13 G6
Ventotene, *Italy* 34 B6
Ventoux, Mt., *France* 27 D9
Ventspils, *Latvia* 9 H16
Ventuarí →, *Venezuela* 120 C4
Ventucopa, *U.S.A.* 113 L7
Ventura, *U.S.A.* 113 L7
Venus B., *Australia* 91 F4
Vera, *Argentina* 126 B3
Vera, *Spain* 29 H3
Veracruz, *Mexico* 115 D5
Veracruz □, *Mexico* 115 D5
Veraval, *India* 62 J4
Verbánia, *Italy* 32 C5
Verbicaro, *Italy* 35 C8
Verbier, *Switz.* 22 D4
Vercelli, *Italy* 32 C5
Verchovchevo, *Ukraine* 42 B6
Verdalsøra, *Norway* 8 E11
Verde →, *Argentina* 128 B3
Verde →, *Goiás, Brazil* 123 E1
Verde →, *Goiás, Brazil* 123 E1
Verde →, *Mato Grosso, Brazil* 125 E7
Verde →, *Mato Grosso, Brazil* 125 C6
Verde →, *Chihuahua, Mexico* 114 B3
Verde →, *Oaxaca, Mexico* 115 D5
Verde →, *Veracruz, Mexico* 114 C4
Verde →, *Paraguay* 126 A4
Verde, Cay, *Bahamas* 116 B4
Verde Grande →, *Brazil* 123 E3
Verde Island Pass, *Phil.* 55 E4
Verde Pequeno →, *Brazil* 123 D3
Verden, *Germany* 18 C5
Verdi, *U.S.A.* 112 F7
Verdigre, *U.S.A.* 108 D5
Verdon →, *France* 27 E9
Verdun, *France* 25 C12
Verdun-sur-le-Doubs, *France* 25 F12
Vereeniging, *S. Africa* 85 D4
Vérendrye, Parc Prov. de la, *Canada* 98 C4
Verga, C., *Guinea* 78 C2
Vergato, *Italy* 32 D8
Vergemont, *Australia* 90 C3
Vergemont Cr. →, *Australia* 90 C3
Vergennes, *U.S.A.* 107 B11
Vergt, *France* 26 C4
Verín, *Spain* 30 D3
Veriña, *Spain* 30 B5
Verkhnedvinsk, *Belorussia* 40 D5
Verkhnevilyuysk, *Russia* 45 C13
Verkhneye Kalinino, *Russia* 45 D11
Verkhniy Baskunchak, *Russia* 43 B12
Verkhovye, *Russia* 41 E10
Verkhoyansk, *Russia* 45 C14
Verkhoyansk Ra. = Verkhoyanskiy Khrebet, *Russia* 45 C13
Verkhoyanskiy Khrebet, *Russia* 45 C13
Verlo, *Canada* 101 C7
Verma, *Norway* 10 B2
Vermenton, *France* 25 E10
Vermilion, *Canada* 101 C6
Vermilion →, *Alta., Canada* 101 C6
Vermilion →, *Qué., Canada* 98 C5
Vermilion, B., *U.S.A.* 109 L9
Vermilion Bay, *Canada* 101 D10
Vermilion Chutes, *Canada* 100 B6
Vermilion L., *U.S.A.* 108 B8
Vermillion, *U.S.A.* 108 D6
Vermont □, *U.S.A.* 107 C12
Vernal, *U.S.A.* 110 F9
Vernalis, *U.S.A.* 112 H5
Vernayaz, *Switz.* 22 D4
Verner, *Canada* 98 C3
Verneuil-sur-Avre, *France* 24 D7
Verneukpan, *S. Africa* 84 D3
Vernier, *Switz.* 22 D2
Vernon, *Canada* 100 C5
Vernon, *France* 24 C8
Vernon, *U.S.A.* 109 H5
Vernonia, *U.S.A.* 112 E3
Vero Beach, *U.S.A.* 105 M5
Véroia, *Greece* 39 J5
Verolanuova, *Italy* 32 C7
Véroli, *Italy* 34 A6
Verona, *Italy* 32 C8
Veropol, *Russia* 45 C17
Versailles, *France* 25 D9
Versalles, *Bolivia* 125 C5
Versoix, *Switz.* 22 D2
Vert, C., *Senegal* 78 C1
Vertou, *France* 24 E5
Vertus, *France* 25 D11
Verulam, *S. Africa* 85 D5
Verviers, *Belgium* 17 G7
Vervins, *France* 25 C10
Verzej, *Slovenia* 33 B13
Vescavoto, *France* 27 F13
Vesdre →, *Belgium* 17 G7
Veselí nad Lužnicí, *Czech.* 20 F4
Veselovskoye Vdkhr., *Russia* 43 C9
Veshenskaya, *Russia* 43 B9
Vesle →, *France* 25 C10
Vesoul, *France* 25 E13
Vessigebro, *Sweden* 11 H6
Vest-Agder fylke □, *Norway* 9 G9
Vesterålen, *Norway* 8 B13
Vestersche Veld, *Neths.* 16 C8
Vestfjorden, *Norway* 8 C13
Vestfold fylke □, *Norway* 9 G11
Vestmannaeyjar, *Iceland* 8 E3
Vestmarka, *Norway* 10 E5
Vestone, *Italy* 32 C7
Vestsjællands Amtskommune □, *Denmark* 11 J5
Vestspitsbergen, *Svalbard* 4 B8
Vestvågøy, *Norway* 8 B12
Vesuvio, *Italy* 35 B7
Vesuvius, Mt. = Vesuvio, *Italy* 35 B7
Vesyegonsk, *Russia* 41 B10
Veszprém, *Hungary* 21 H7
Vésztő, *Hungary* 21 J11
Vetlanda, *Sweden* 9 H13
Vetluga, *Russia* 41 C14
Vetlugu →, *Russia* 41 C15
Vetluzhskiy, *Russia* 41 C14
Vetovo, *Bulgaria* 38 F9
Vetralla, *Italy* 33 F9
Vettore, Monte, *Italy* 33 F10
Veurne, *Belgium* 17 F1
Vevey, *Switz.* 22 D3
Veynes, *France* 27 D9
Veys, *Iran* 65 D6
Vézelise, *France* 25 D13
Vézère →, *France* 26 D4
Vezirköprü, *Turkey* 66 C6
Vi Thanh, *Vietnam* 59 H5
Viacha, *Bolivia* 124 D4
Viadana, *Italy* 32 D7
Viamão, *Brazil* 127 C5
Viana, *Brazil* 122 B3
Viana, *Spain* 28 C2
Viana del Bollo, *Spain* 30 C3
Viana do Alentejo, *Portugal* 31 G3
Viana do Castelo, *Portugal* 30 D2
Vianden, *Belgium* 17 J8
Vianen, *Neths.* 16 E6
Vianna do Castelo □, *Portugal* 30 D2
Vianópolis, *Brazil* 123 E2
Viar →, *Spain* 31 H5
Viaréggio, *Italy* 32 E7
Viaur →, *France* 26 D5
Vibank, *Canada* 101 C8
Vibo Valéntia, *Italy* 35 D9
Viborg, *Denmark* 11 H3
Vibraye, *France* 24 D7
Vic-en-Bigorre, *France* 26 E4
Vic-Fézensac, *France* 26 E4
Vic-sur-Cère, *France* 26 D6
Vicenza, *Italy* 33 C8
Vich, *Spain* 28 D7
Vichada □, *Colombia* 120 C4
Vichada →, *Colombia* 120 C4
Vichuga, *Russia* 41 C12
Vichy, *France* 26 B7
Vicksburg, *Ariz., U.S.A.* 113 M13
Vicksburg, *Mich., U.S.A.* 104 D3
Vicksburg, *Miss., U.S.A.* 109 J9
Vico, L. di, *Italy* 33 F9
Vico del Gargaro, *Italy* 35 A8
Viçosa, *Brazil* 122 C4
Viçosa do Ceará, *Brazil* 122 B3
Vicosoprano, *Switz.* 23 D9
Victor, *India* 62 J4
Victor, *Colo., U.S.A.* 108 F2
Victor, *N.Y., U.S.A.* 106 D7
Victor Harbor, *Australia* 91 F2
Victoria, *Argentina* 126 C3
Victoria, *Canada* 100 D4
Victoria, *Chile* 128 A2
Victoria, *Guinea* 78 C2
Victoria, *Malaysia* 56 C5
Victoria, *Malta* 37 C1
Victoria, *Phil.* 55 D4
Victoria, *Kans., U.S.A.* 108 F5
Victoria, *Tex., U.S.A.* 109 L6
Victoria □, *Australia* 91 F3
Victoria →, *Australia* 88 C4
Victoria, Grand L., *Canada* 98 C4
Victoria, L., *Africa* 82 C3
Victoria, L., *Australia* 91 E3
Victoria Beach, *Canada* 101 C9
Victoria de Durango, *Mexico* 114 C4
Victoria de las Tunas, *Cuba* 116 B4
Victoria Falls, *Zimbabwe* 83 F2
Victoria Harbour, *Canada* 98 D4
Victoria I., *Canada* 96 A8
Victoria Ld., *Antarctica* 5 D11
Victoria Nile →, *Uganda* 82 B3
Victoria Res., *Canada* 99 C8
Victoria River Downs, *Australia* 88 C5
Victoria Taungdeik, *Burma* 61 J18
Victoria West, *S. Africa* 84 E3
Victorias, *Phil.* 55 F5
Victoriaville, *Canada* 99 C5
Victorica, *Argentina* 126 D2
Victorville, *U.S.A.* 113 L9
Vicuña, *Chile* 126 C1
Vicuña Mackenna, *Argentina* 126 C3
Vidal, *U.S.A.* 113 L12
Vidal Junction, *U.S.A.* 113 L12
Vidalia, *U.S.A.* 105 J4
Vidauban, *France* 27 E10
Vídho, *Greece* 37 A3
Vidigueira, *Portugal* 31 G3
Vidin, *Bulgaria* 38 F5
Vidio, C., *Spain* 30 B4
Vidisha, *India* 62 H7
Vidzy, *Belorussia* 40 D5
Viechtach, *Germany* 19 F8
Viedma, *Argentina* 128 B4
Viedma, L., *Argentina* 128 C2
Vieira, *Portugal* 30 D2
Viella, *Spain* 28 C5
Vielsalm, *Belgium* 17 H7
Vienenburg, *Germany* 18 D6
Vieng Pou Kha, *Laos* 58 B3
Vienna = Wien, *Austria* 21 G6
Vienna, *U.S.A.* 109 G10
Vienne, *France* 27 C8
Vienne □, *France* 26 B4
Vienne →, *France* 24 E7
Vientiane, *Laos* 58 D4
Vientos, Paso de los, *Caribbean* 117 C5
Vierlingsbeek, *Neths.* 17 E8
Viersen, *Germany* 18 D2
Vierwaldstättersee, *Switz.* 23 C7
Vierzon, *France* 25 E9
Vieste, *Italy* 35 A9
Vietnam ■, *Asia* 58 C5
Vieux-Boucau-les-Bains, *France* 26 E2
Vif, *France* 27 C9
Vigan, *Phil.* 55 C4
Vigévano, *Italy* 32 C5
Vigia, *Brazil* 122 B2
Vigía Chico, *Mexico* 115 D7
Víglas, Ákra, *Greece* 37 D9
Vignemale, Pic du, *France* 26 F3
Vigneulles-lès-Hattonchâtel, *France* 25 D12
Vignola, *Italy* 32 D8
Vigo, *Spain* 30 C2
Vigo, Ría de, *Spain* 30 C2
Vihiers, *France* 24 E6
Vijayawada, *India* 61 L12
Vijfhuizen, *Neths.* 16 D5
Viken, *Sweden* 11 F8
Viking, *Canada* 100 C6
Vikna, *Norway* 8 D11
Viksjö, *Sweden* 10 B11
Vikulovo, *Russia* 44 D8
Vila da Maganja, *Mozam.* 83 F4
Vila de João Belo = Xai-Xai, *Mozam.* 85 D5
Vila de Rei, *Portugal* 31 F2
Vila do Bispo, *Portugal* 31 H2
Vila do Chibuto, *Mozam.* 85 C5
Vila do Conde, *Portugal* 30 D2
Vila Franca de Xira, *Portugal* 31 G2
Vila Gamito, *Mozam.* 83 E3
Vila Gomes da Costa, *Mozam.* 85 C5
Vila Machado, *Mozam.* 83 F3
Vila Mouzinho, *Mozam.* 83 E3
Vila Nova de Foscôa, *Portugal* 30 D3
Vila Nova de Ourém, *Portugal* 31 F2
Vila Novo de Gaia, *Portugal* 30 D2
Vila Pouca de Aguiar, *Portugal* 30 D3
Vila Real, *Portugal* 30 D3
Vila Real de Santo António, *Portugal* 31 H3
Vila Vasco da Gama, *Mozam.* 83 E3
Vila Velha, *Amapá, Brazil* 121 C7
Vila Velha, *Espirito Santo, Brazil* 123 F3
Vila Viçosa, *Portugal* 31 G3
Vilaboa, *Spain* 30 C2
Vilaine →, *France* 24 E4
Vilanandro, Tanjona, *Madag.* 85 B7
Vilanculos, *Mozam.* 85 C6
Vilar Formosa, *Portugal* 30 E4
Vilareal □, *Portugal* 30 D3
Vilaseca-Salou, *Spain* 28 D6
Vilcabamba, Cordillera, *Peru* 124 C3
Vilcanchos, *Peru* 124 C3
Vileyka, *Belorussia* 40 D5
Vilhelmina, *Sweden* 8 D14
Vilhena, *Brazil* 125 C5
Viliga, *Russia* 45 C16
Viliya →, *Lithuania* 40 D3
Viljandi, *Estonia* 40 B4
Vilkovo, *Ukraine* 42 D3
Villa Abecia, *Bolivia* 126 A2
Villa Ahumada, *Mexico* 114 A3
Villa Ana, *Argentina* 126 B4
Villa Ángela, *Argentina* 126 B3
Villa Bella, *Bolivia* 125 C4
Villa Bens = Tarfaya, *Morocco* 74 C2
Villa Cañás, *Argentina* 126 C3
Villa Carlos, *Spain* 36 B11
Villa Cisneros = Dakhla, *W. Sahara* 74 D1
Villa Colón, *Argentina* 126 C2
Villa Constitución, *Argentina* 126 C3
Villa de Cura, *Venezuela* 120 A4
Villa de María, *Argentina* 126 B3
Villa del Rosario, *Venezuela* 120 A3
Villa Dolores, *Argentina* 126 C2
Villa Frontera, *Mexico* 114 B4
Villa Guillermina, *Argentina* 126 B4
Villa Hayes, *Paraguay* 126 B4
Villa Iris, *Argentina* 126 D3
Villa Juárez, *Mexico* 114 B4
Villa María, *Argentina* 126 C3
Villa Mazán, *Argentina* 126 B2
Villa Minozzo, *Italy* 32 D7
Villa Montes, *Bolivia* 126 A3
Villa Ocampo, *Argentina* 126 B4
Villa Ocampo, *Mexico* 114 B3
Villa Ojo de Agua, *Argentina* 126 B3
Villa San Giovanni, *Italy* 35 D8
Villa San José, *Argentina* 126 C4

HW0075 4891

PENGUIN BOOKS

KICKED, BITTEN, AND SCRATCHED

Amy Sutherland is the author of *Cookoff: Recipe Fever in America*, which was selected by Barnes and Noble for its Discover Great New Writers program and was included in Amazon.com's list of the best fifty books of the year. Her articles have appeared in the *Los Angeles Times*, *The Boston Globe*, and *Cooking Light*, among other publications. Her article "What Shamu Taught Me About a Happy Marriage" was the *New York Times*'s most e-mailed article of 2006. She was a features writer for daily newspapers in Maine and Vermont for twelve years. The author lives in Boston, Massachusetts, and Portland, Maine, with her husband, Scott, and their two dogs, Dixie and Penny.

Kicked, Bitten, and Scratched

Life and Lessons at the World's Premier School for Exotic Animal Trainers

Amy Sutherland

Penguin Books

For Ann Early, my Aunt Pretty,
who held my young fingers
to the earth's quick pulse

PENGUIN BOOKS
Published by the Penguin Group
Penguin Group (USA) Inc., 375 Hudson Street, New York, New York 10014, U.S.A.
Penguin Group (Canada), 90 Eglinton Avenue East, Suite 700, Toronto,
Ontario, Canada M4P 2Y3 (a division of Pearson Penguin Canada Inc.)
Penguin Books Ltd, 80 Strand, London WC2R 0RL, England
Penguin Ireland, 25 St Stephen's Green, Dublin 2, Ireland (a division of Penguin Books Ltd)
Penguin Group (Australia), 250 Camberwell Road, Camberwell,
Victoria 3124, Australia (a division of Pearson Australia Group Pty Ltd)
Penguin Books India Pvt Ltd, 11 Community Centre,
Panchsheel Park, New Delhi – 110 017, India
Penguin Group (NZ), 67 Apollo Drive, Rosedale, North Shore 0745,
Auckland, New Zealand (a division of Pearson New Zealand Ltd)
Penguin Books (South Africa) (Pty) Ltd, 24 Sturdee Avenue,
Rosebank, Johannesburg 2196, South Africa

Penguin Books Ltd, Registered Offices:
80 Strand, London WC2R 0RL, England

First published in the United States of America by Viking Penguin,
a member of Penguin Group (USA) Inc. 2006 Published in Penguin Books 2007

10 9 8 7 6 5 4 3 2 1

Copyright © Amy Sutherland, 2006
All rights reserved

Photograph on the title page of a kinkajou © Anup Shah/Photodisc Green/Getty Images

THE LIBRARY OF CONGRESS HAS CATALOGED THE HARDCOVER EDITION AS FOLLOWS:
Sutherland, Amy.
Kicked, bitten, and scratched : life and lessons at the world's premier
school for exotic animal trainers / Amy Sutherland.
p. cm.
ISBN 0-670-03768-0 (hc.)
ISBN 978-0-14-311194-8 (pbk.)
1. Moorpark College. Exotic Animal Training and Management Program
2. Animal trainers—Vocational guidance—California. 3. Exotic animals—California.
I. Title.
SF83.C23M667 2006
636.088'8023—dc22 2005057474

Printed in the United States of America
Designed by Nancy Resnick

Except in the United States of America, this book is sold subject to the condition
that it shall not, by way of trade or otherwise, be lent, resold, hired out, or otherwise
circulated without the publisher's prior consent in any form of binding or cover other
than that in which it is published and without a similar condition including
this condition being imposed on the subsequent purchaser.

The scanning, uploading and distribution of this book via the Internet or via any other means
without the permission of the publisher is illegal and punishable by law. Please purchase only
authorized electronic editions, and do not participate in or encourage electronic piracy
of copyrighted materials. Your support of the author's rights is appreciated.

Contents

Preface vii

Introduction xi

Orientation 1

Behaviors 24

September 35

Nutrition 47

Animal People 55

October 62

Briz 87

The Fire 101

Elephants 116

November 133

Baboon Here! 144

December 152

Dr. Peddie 168

Walking Big Cats 178

Falling in Love 192
Birdman Bites 208
Dolphin Dreams 215
February 226
March 243
Baltimore 261
Spring 274
Graduation 287
The Zoo Is Theirs 299
August 312

Acknowledgments 319

Preface

While working on this book, spending hours watching animal trainers accomplish the seemingly impossible, teaching a hyena to fetch and a baboon to ride a skateboard, I got to thinking of a certain species—the American husband. Maybe, I thought, the techniques used to teach elephants to paint and dolphins to flip, might work with this animal, in particular with the subspecies known as Scott Sutherland.

At home, I went to work. I adopted the trainer's motto "the animal is never wrong." I analyzed my husband's behavior like a trainer does a badger's or a tiger's. I used techniques with scientific names. I did this half as a goof—nothing I tried before was this much fun—but in short order I got results.

On June 25, 2006, I announced via a column in *The New York Times,* how I had improved my marriage using the principles of progressive exotic animal training. By noon or sooner, my column, entitled, "What Shamu Taught Me about a Happy Marriage," became the most e-mailed story off the *Times* Web site. There it remained for the next thirty days, much to my shock.

My phone began to ring. I was interviewed by reporters in Australia, Colombia, Brazil, France, Belgium, Turkey, and Germany. My column was blogged. I was called a devil shrew on a right-wing Web site, which I consider a kind of honor. I was interviewed on NPR, MSNBC, and the *Today Show*. My inbox filled up with fan mail. A few psychiatrists wrote to congratulate me. An acquaintance was given a copy of my column by her marriage therapist. My musings inspired a *Sylvia* cartoon.

Before long, I had a new book contract followed by a movie deal. Now exotic animal training had not only improved my marriage but changed my life.

I was asked over and over why I thought my column had hit such a chord. The short answer is, I really don't know. The long answer is I think people are hungry for a fresh way to negotiate the small, daily annoyances that can poison a marriage. You don't want to go to a counselor for every little thing, but all those little things in sum can finally land you there. Being social animals, we instinctively want to get along, especially with our spouses. But as another sock hits the floor or toilet seat is left up, the fur flies.

Second, I think many people, like myself, welcome proof that, indeed, we humans are squarely in the animal kingdom. There's something comforting to knowing that the same approach that can be used to teach a hermit crab to ring a bell for its dinner or a killer whale to breach on command can be used to teach us highest of primates to take the trash out. We may have the biggest, wrinkliest brains, but that does not make us immune to basic behavioral principles that apply to all organisms. We are truly not alone on this planet.

Nearly four years ago, I walked into an unusual zoo in southern California never, ever expecting that I was embarking on a path that would lead far beyond the compound's high fence, both figuratively and literally.

Trainers teach what they call an "A to B," meaning getting an animal to go from here to there. Writing and reporting has trained me to go from A to wherever. B is always out there, somewhere, but it's never where or what I expected. Thank god.

Introduction

I have always considered myself an animal person, meaning I not only felt at ease with most things furred, feathered, scaled, even fanged, but moreover, I found them an endlessly compelling and integral part of the world. A life without this passion has always struck me as a lesser one, and I admit to being a hard judge of people who do not share my love for the animal kingdom. At worst, I consider them suspicious; at best, deeply flawed. Perhaps my love of animals, which I admit I consider a superior trait, is simply a by-product of my upbringing. Despite its standard white suburban backdrop, my childhood managed to stray from the stereotype, thanks to a fun-loving mother and the unruly woods that breached our trim backyard.

I grew up with the requisite cats and dogs, mostly strays. There was Curly, a handsome mutt with a wavy coat worthy of a Breck Girl. There was Tang, a low-to-the-ground terrier mix, who always ran in a diagonal line and whose sizable balls, which nearly dragged between his short legs, could not go unnoticed even by the most modest of dog lovers. We also had three ducks one summer that chased us while we played Wiffle ball and overfertilized our and our neighbors' yards with their voluminous and slippery green dung. We temporarily housed turtles that lumbered along the road after rainstorms. One had three legs and dragged a corner of its shell in a way that broke our hearts. We kept it longer than the requisite week and fed it full of iceberg lettuce. One Easter we got a black-and-white bunny that hopped around the house, despite our cat and dog, depositing neat piles of raisin-sized poops my mom vacuumed up. When the bunny became a good-sized rabbit and the poops grew plumper, we put it outside, assuming it would prefer to live in the great outdoors with other rabbits. Instead, the bunny stayed close to home, hopping among the shrubs in our front yard. Most nights, the rabbit would wait in the garage for my father to come home from work and scratch its long ears. When I was in high school we got a dove, Eleanor, who spent her days cooing to her image in a mirror, laying eggs in our hanging plants, and trying to land on our heads. There were also guppies and hamsters along the way, though we were put off by their maternal cannibalism. The sound of a mother hamster munching her baby with lip-smacking relish still rings in my ears.

Beyond our household and its menagerie, we found the animal kingdom thriving in our suburban neighborhood. Just a few houses down, an older girl I much admired kept pet chickens that ran loose, lending an incongruous country touch to the new suburb. A couple of streets over, a raucous family of nine kept baby raccoons. My sister, our friend Bunny, and I spent whole afternoons wading ankle-deep in a wide creek, turning rocks over, looking for crayfish. The few we managed to get our small hands on—they were fast—we'd collect in a pail, only to empty it back into the creek's shallow, clear waters before heading home for cream-cheese-and-jelly sandwiches. At night, we tossed pebbles into the dark sky, provoking bats to dive-bomb us as we threw ourselves flat on the grass. We hiked through local farm fields filled with cows without a second thought, until one chased us down a hill. We only escaped being stampeded by throwing ourselves over a fence; then we lay there windless and laughing. The marauding cow stood stolidly by on the other side of the fence staring at us, as if to make its point.

When I left home and took up apartment life, my love of animals was mostly expressed vicariously. None of the landlords allowed dogs. I am allergic to cats. I would never, ever get another hamster. Besides, my life was too peripatetic for pets. Urban animals were a touch too urban, such as the obese raccoon that each night climbed a fire escape on my building, begging for food from window to window. Squirrels ate a hole in the kitchen screen of one apartment and regularly slipped in while I was out, raiding my trash can or pilfering a muffin I'd left on the counter and then, for some reason, retiring to my bathtub for their feast.

I was left to satisfy myself by petting any dog that came within arm's length and watching all things nature on television. I dreamed of buying a house, not to have the house so much as to get a dog, to have a small yard where I could hang a bird feeder, and maybe even to find a snake or two in the grass. Finally, in the spring of 1999, having acquired a house and a bit of stability, my husband and I drove two hours down the coast of Maine to New Hampshire to the home of a haughty breeder of Australian shepherds. We were there to collect an eight-week-old female red tricolor. As we expected, we fell hard. After being sized up by the taciturn breeder and deemed worthy—just barely—of an Aussie, she lent us a puppy crate, and we loaded our furry charge into the backseat. On the drive home, the pup whimpered in her crate on the backseat as we debated names and unwittingly drove through the night to a new and much richer life.

I had grown up in the era when everybody let their suburban pooches run. I had neither trained a dog nor known a trained dog. Dixie, as we named her, required training. She's a herding dog, and herding dogs need direction, as trainers say euphemistically. So Dixie and I went off to puppy school and then to general obedience and agility classes, all taught by an enlightened trainer I happened upon. To my surprise, I did most of the learning and struggled to keep up with Dixie, a far quicker study. The classes, what with the barking and trying to hold the leash, clicker, and treats in one hand, could be unbelievably aggravating. I felt like a miserable failure most of the time. I stuck with it, because it soon became clear that training opened a two-way line of communication between me and Dixie. More than that, it gave me a way to communicate with another species—an unexpected thrill. I felt an underused lobe in my brain rev up each time I worked with Dixie. It was a blissfully nonverbal lobe that read body language, one that considered the world from another species' point of view. Briefly, I was liberated from my overwhelming humanness. I was hooked.

Eventually, I found myself on the Paris set of *102 Dalmatians* on an assignment for *Disney* magazine. There was a small army of trainers with their menagerie of animals, mostly dogs (a borzoi, two French poodles, a bulldog, a border terrier, and, of course, dalmatians), and a few parrots. I hung out with the trainers from Birds & Animals Unlimited day after day, watching how they calmly got their dogs to run through moving traffic or how they hid behind trees or mailboxes to give their canine actors hand commands during takes. If I wasn't with them, I was chewing the fat with the American Humane Association rep on the set, who was a horse trainer also. I basically talked animals all day. I talked about how to knit a sweater for a dachshund, why a French trainer's authoritarian style wasn't working with his two poodles, and how to tell when a dog was stressed. On the film set, I was surrounded by the nerve-wracking, nitty-gritty construction of fiction, but I had taken refuge in a real world as magical as make-believe, a world in which people knew essentially how to talk to animals. In my notes was the name of the school nearly all the trainers had attended: a small community college in Southern California called the Exotic Animal Training and Management Program at Moorpark College. That such a place, a college that taught people to train everything from rabbits to tigers, existed struck me as incredible. When I got home I wrote MOORPARK on a piece of lined paper. Inspired, I taught Dixie to bring in the newspaper.

Our passions often lead us down paths that we don't even realize we are on until we arrive at an unexpected but welcome destination. In July 2003, I found myself standing atop an arid hill on the outside of a high chain-link fence with a gregarious vet by my side. A sign read America's Teaching Zoo. That turned out to be a humble claim for what lay beyond the gate, as my guide, the vet, would show me. Within was a secret garden full of small mysteries, deep passions, unexpected heartbreak, rare beauty, and high comedy. For a year I lived within what seemed at times to be a childhood storybook come to life. I went on emu walks, smiled at a baboon who smiled back, got a kiss from a sea lion, played with a baby orangutan, and touched my first snake—a king snake. I watched as students taught a hyena to spin, a camel to play basketball, and a baboon to get in a crate and close the door behind itself. I spent long days among fellow animal lovers to whom I never had to explain why I so adored the pygmy goat or why I never tired of going for walks with the cougar brothers. In a way, I suppose, I was reliving those aimless days of my youth that were filled with crayfish, bats, frogs, dogs, and chickens. Only now they were full of badgers, servals, miniature horses, and capuchin monkeys.

I had come cross-country for a good subject. What I didn't expect was that my time at the teaching zoo would change me, corny as that sounds, and for the better, as I suspect it does anyone who spends much time there. For who can spend any time within a magical kingdom, even a flawed one, and not return to the black-and-white world changed, if only by knowing that the seemingly impossible does exist?

Orientation

On an August day, under a sharp blue California sky with a view of the umber Santa Susana Mountains behind him so beautiful it can make you forget the pounding 100° heat, Dr. Jim Peddie stands in the shade and speaks of death. As a veterinarian who has euthanized hundreds of people's beloved pets during his long career, he knows death too well but he has never grown comfortable with that moment when life slips away at his say. "Everyone thinks death should be peaceful, but it seldom is," he says, his hands in his jeans pockets, his face pinched, and his voice raw.

Before him are fifty-one faces scattered over metal risers in a small outdoor theater. The smooth, tan faces belong to the incoming class of students or—as they will be referred to for the next twelve months—the *first years* in the Exotic Animal Training and Management Program at Moorpark College (EATM). This new crop of aspiring exotic animal trainers are nearly all women, forty-seven out of fifty-one. Most are in their early to mid-twenties, many of them tall. They are dressed for the heat in shorts, visors, and tank tops.

Tattoos scroll across their shoulders or lower backs. They look eager, optimistic. This is their first step toward a bright, sunny future. Death—that dark, distant star—is the last thing on their minds.

Still, Dr. Peddie's gravity is not lost on them. Nobody smiles. Their sunglassed eyes all rest quietly and attentively on the broad-shouldered, fatherly vet. The change in tone is oddly striking in what has been up to now an overwhelming, yet giddy, few days of meet and greets. On their orientation week schedules, this one-hour slot is listed blandly as Processing Food Animals. Most of the new first years know what is coming and have steeled themselves, though there's a rumor they may be spared this gruesome initiation rite that requires animal lovers to prove their love by killing a bird with their bare hands. It's an early litmus test of whether the first years are tough enough for the program, because the school is not, as Dr. Peddie says, for people who think animals are cute.

Birds of prey and reptiles require freshly killed prey, Dr. Peddie explains. In captivity, some can be trained to eat dead animals, but others must have their caretakers hunt for them. Consequently, the school teaches students how to humanely kill pigeons and rats. Every student must break a pigeon's neck with her hands, what they call pulling a pigeon, or gas a rat before she can graduate. There is no way around it, the vet explains. Crying vegetarian won't get you out of it, nor will your religious beliefs. "I feel it is important you do it so you know you can do it," he says. "We've had [graduates] lose jobs because of this. You people are animal people, and this is part of animal care. We do this right up front and early."

He describes how the birds' wings flutter, the small black eyes blink, and the head pops off in your palm. As you pull, you may feel the spinal column stretch like a piece of elastic. Despite the medieval style of execution, this is the quickest way to render the birds unconscious, he says, and is thus the most humane. "People deal with this differently," he explains. "Some people will break down crying, some will burst out laughing like they are giddy. Either one is the same thing, a release, so don't be critical of how someone reacts. They're not laughing because they are ecstatic. They are ecstatically uncomfortable."

Usually at this point, a current student gently takes a bird, wings flapping, with one hand and leans over a trash can. With her other hand, she quickly jerks its nut-shaped head, cracking its small vertebrae and tearing the neck; she drops the head, which lands with a small thump on the bottom of the can. Then Dr. Peddie asks for a half dozen volunteers to step forward for this odd baptism. Today, this is not to be. After all this buildup, it turns out the rumor is true. Fortunately or unfortunately (depending on whether you'd just as soon get it over with or prefer to procrastinate pulling a pigeon until the very last day of school), there are no birds to kill. To head off the spread of Newcastle disease, a contagious and deadly virus, a statewide quarantine has stopped all sales of birds, Dr. Peddie explains. He hopes to have some pigeons soon, he says. He apologizes.

Death, however, will not be denied on this sunny day. Instead, a half dozen unlucky rats will be smothered with CO_2. Before a collective sigh of relief can be exhaled, a trio of women in their twenties wheels in a shoulder-high metal tank of the gas, precariously strapped to a handcart by a bungee cord, and totes in a plastic bin of rats. These women are *second years,* meaning they are in the second year of the program. Moreover, they are the Rat Room managers. They oversee a small colony of rats in a room the size of a large walk-in closet. The rats are raised to feed the zoo's reptiles and birds of prey. A Rat Room manager with schoolmarm glasses and visor pulled low cinches a spotted rodent around the shoulders with her thumb and index finger and hoists it up for all to see. Except for its busy nose, the bright-eyed rat goes slack, its pink tail hanging straight. "Be careful, because they will, I repeat *will,* bite you," she says.

Everything is ready to go. All that is needed is a plastic bin, a small plastic garbage bag, the CO_2, and, of course, the rats. The managers are at pains to explain themselves and keep repeating that they do not relish their task. “Then we feed the golden eagle and see the enjoyment he gets out of the food. It’s the circle of life,” one manager, unsmiling and squinting in the sun, explains. “If you are upset by it, if you want to cry, go for it,” she says. “If it’s upsetting to you, let your emotions out.”

A Rat Room manager quickly, unceremoniously loads six rats, noses twitching, little ears upright, into a plastic bin covered by a small green garbage bag. There’s hardly enough time to spit out a good-bye. Another manager closes the bag around the carbon dioxide tube. The other holds her hands down on the rats, because they sometimes push their way out. The third manager opens the gas valve. In the bleachers, no one says a word. The two minutes tick away slowly as everyone stares at the plastic bag. There are no noticeable rustlings in the bin. No squeaks for help. The gas is turned off. The now limp rats are removed one by one. The managers lightly tap the eyes with their index fingers to make sure the rats are stone dead. There is no blood, no smell.

While men are embarrassed to cry, women can be embarrassed not to, but there is nary a sniffle. Instead of a wet-hanky fest, there is a solemn hush. This is broken as the new first years raise their hands and ask practical questions like how often do they gas rats and for how long exactly. The bin of gassed rats is whisked away to a freezer. The canister of CO_2 is wheeled offstage. That’s enough of death for one day.

A sheep zips across the back of the outdoor stage. A pig, his hide a sooty black, ambles out and pokes at a ratty red carpet with his nose until the length of it unfurls and two chunks of apple pop out. Having devoured them, he lazily saunters offstage, his scrawny tail giving a little twitch as he exits. “We’re going to need to cut his tusks again,” Dr. Peddie sighs, sitting in the bleachers next to me. The first years will find that the sudden shift in mood is emblematic of life at EATM, where emotions run high and the unexpected is around every corner.

Orientation is packed with traditions, one of which is the off-color show the second years present. It's a chance for them to strut their training stuff and cut loose after a long, grinding summer of running the teaching zoo by themselves. What follows is a ribald beauty pageant of beasts that breaks all the rules of a proper animal education presentation. They even have the animals do *tricks,* a forbidden word among enlightened trainers, who prefer *behaviors* instead. In one hand, the MC carries two dead squirrels frozen in an amorous embrace. He occasionally holds them to his sweaty brow. When a student rides Kaleb, the caramel-colored camel, onstage, the MC says, "Here's a big hairy beast onstage with a camel underneath." He warns that Kaleb could "freak out at any minute" and notes that a camel has thick knee pads and prehensile lips. "When would that come in handy?"

Another student totes Happy, the American alligator, onstage like a big log. The MC rattles off some alligator stats—they are exothermic, only grow as big as their enclosure, and have extra eyelids—then encourages his audience to take the Velcro strap off his snout. "Really, it's like opening a present." He adds, "Their skin makes excellent shoes and purses." He pauses. "Would you ever say that in a regular show?" None of the first years answers. Just laughter. "First years, what have you learned in your first three days? Wake up!" he taunts.

Half the show's humor comes at the student handlers' expense. A good number of the animals don't do as told. A little big-eared fox suddenly bounds off a student's shoulder as she exits the stage; despite her trainer's protests, C.J., the coyote, takes a long drink of water from a shallow moat that rings the stage; Julietta, the emu, won't take her exit; Banjo, the macaw, won't get on his roller skates.

Finally, the stage is hosed down, techno music is cranked up, and the star arrives. Schmoo, the twenty-four-year-old sea lion, head up and barking joyfully, bounds onstage like a rock star with her band—in this case, her four student trainers. Schmoo isn't just the star of the show but of the whole program, with her 170-plus commands and her long list of movie and commercial credits.

Schmoo zips back and forth between the student trainers as they put her through her paces, tossing her chunks of slippery squid. She quickly rolls over and coats herself with specks of dirt, barks jubilantly, raises a flipper to her brow in a quick salute, and sticks her tongue out like a third grader. When a trainer points her finger and says, "Bang!" Schmoo collapses in an overly dramatic heap worthy of a silent screen diva. When a trainer says, "Shark!" she tosses a flipper up to imitate the killer. She tips far forward on her breast and pitches her tail happily into the air. Then Schmoo does the reverse, rising up on her tail, throwing her flippers out, and pointing her nose heavenward like an angel.

The first-year students are rapt. They lean forward and smile broadly. This is why they are here, why they'll endure a brutal schedule, give up their social life, and take on huge student loans. A year from now it could be they who are having a high time tossing squid to this incredible creature and singing out "Shark!" This is proof, however fleeting, that their farfetched dreams of working with animals can come true. What they don't know is that, backstage, Gabby, the Catalina macaw, has bitten one of the second years badly enough that she has been rushed to the campus Health Center. Dreams always come with a price, whether it's money, time, or blood.

It is now the third day of what is likely to be the hardest twenty-one months of any first year's life. This orientation week—a busy string of potlucks, ice breakers, and gag gifts—is a deceptive introduction to life at the school. However, the week is peppered with advice and announcements that foreshadow what's ahead. Starting next week, the first years won't have an official vacation until next summer. They will work most, if not all, holidays and most weekends. Four days a week they are due here by 6:30 A.M. and won't leave until 5 P.M. During these long days, they will care for the teaching zoo of some 150 to 200 animals, doing everything from hosing out the cages to answering the phones. When not cleaning, feeding, or even weeding, they will attend classes—one of the few times they get to sit down during the day, which often induces deep naps complete with drooling and snoring. In the evening, drowsy from the day, they will study animal anatomy tomes and memorize agonizingly long lists of Latin species names. As an alum puts it, the school "pretty much owns you."

Students will follow a list of rules worthy of the Marines. Their uniforms must be kept clean; shorts cannot be too short; earrings cannot be too long; bra straps cannot show; sleeves must not be rolled. They cannot use their cell phones at the zoo. They cannot smoke. They cannot run or laugh near the primates' cages. Most important, they cannot be late for the morning cleaning. If these rules are repeatedly broached or if a grade slips below a C in any class, they will be kicked out. Four students among the class of 2004 got the boot last year.

They could be chomped, mauled, or even killed by an animal. Even the smallest nick could produce a surly infection. They might catch a zoonotic disease—anything from parrot fever to bubonic plague. "Wash your hands," a staffer reminds them. "The last thing we want is any of our students coming down with worms." Dr. Peddie warns that their romances, especially new ones, may not survive. They will not have a social life beyond the zoo. Tell your family you'll hardly see them, Dr. Peddie instructs. Working part-time is strongly discouraged. Money will be tight. As the letter to prospective students ominously warns, "You will not have much time for yourself, so make sure areas of your life are in order."

They will live and die by their planners, in which they will chart out their days in fifteen-minute increments and write endless to-do lists. They will get what they call EATM hands: hands that are cracked, cracks that are filled with dirt, dirt that can't be washed out, no matter how hard they scrub. They will keep an extra set of clothes or two in the car because, as a staffer tells them, "If the tiger sprays you, you don't want to go around smelling like urine all day."

The students will suck it up and count their blessings because they have gotten into the premier program in the country, if not the world. This is the Harvard for exotic animal trainers. It's also the only academic program for trainers. Santa Fe Community College in Gainesville, Florida, has a zoo as well, but its program is primarily for zookeepers. If you want to be a trainer, Moorpark is the school for you. The general public may never have heard of it, but anyone in the animal industry has. Graduates work in zoos across the country, in Hollywood, the U.S. Navy, Ringling Bros., Guide Dogs for the Blind, and SeaWorld. They work in sanctuaries, aquariums, animal parks, and research facilities. Most of the trainers at Universal Studios' animal show are Moorparkers, as they are known. A few years back, the San Diego Zoo and Wild Animal Park, one of the country's top zoos, filled seven openings with recent grads of the program. Julie Scardina, the animal ambassador for SeaWorld and one of the country's most visible trainers with regular stints on *The Tonight Show* with Jay Leno, is a Moorparker.

EATM perches on a ridge overlooking the college's ultragreen football field and driving range on one side, the orderly houses of the commuter burg on the other side. To the east is a range of arid, muscle-bound mountains. To the west, the four lanes of a highway bend through a treeless landscape. The highway occasionally backs up, reminding you that Los Angeles is only fifty miles to the southwest.

EATM's entrance is tucked into an out-of-the-way corner of the community college, at the far end of its moatlike parking lot. The sign out front reads America's Teaching Zoo, but no one calls it that except when they answer the telephone. Students and staff refer to the program as EATM (pronounced "EE-tem") or just Moorpark. Looking through the high chain-link front gate, all you can see is a small outdoor theater, an unassuming huddle of buildings, some olive trees, and a single-lane blacktop road running away from you. There is not an animal in sight, though you might hear a doleful wolf howl or a cranky cockatoo shriek. Those are the only clues to the reason why this gate must always be kept closed.

Just inside the gate down a grassy slope on the left is a small aviary. Nearby, Clarence, the septuagenarian Galapagos tortoise, with his impossibly long neck stretched full-out, is likely to slowly turn his rocklike head, as if it moved on hydraulics, to look at you. On the right is an outdoor theater with a bare earth stage and metal bleachers. A short walk farther, there are a few low, unassuming buildings. This is the hub of the zoo, where the front office and the two classrooms, Zoo 1 and Zoo 2, are located.

The zoo stretches the length of the ridge, which makes for stunning views of the surrounding mountains and foothills and near constant, welcome breezes. An oblong-shaped road circles the teaching zoo's animals. Down the western side, the road is made of blacktop, lined with benches, and shaded by willowy pepper trees. This is the front road, where the public is allowed to wander on Saturdays and Sundays. The road turns to gravel along the zoo's eastern flank. This is the back road. The entrances to the animal cages can be found here. Consequently, this is the road favored by students, and you hear them crunching down it all day long.

Although EATM opens the gate to the public on the weekends and for field trip after field trip of kids lugging backpacks, it is first and foremost a school, which means it looks different from most zoos. In an age of lush zoos with enclosures that resemble African grasslands or polar ice floes, EATM has a bare-bones, old-fashioned look. Though the grounds are well landscaped with bird-of-paradise, cactus, roses, trumpet vines, mulberry trees, and oleander bushes, the animals are in cages, and there are no efforts to conceal that. The Bengal tiger, Taj, glares at you from behind bars. There are no chapter-long labels explaining mating and eating habits or lecturing the public on endangered species or rain forest decimation. At most, there's the species name, and often not even that.

The cages may look as if someone just emptied their office trash can in them. Student keepers are forever stocking the enclosures with all sorts of things to keep the animals busy and stimulated. This is called behavioral enrichment or B.E. In the parrot cages, there are hefty Los Angeles Yellow Pages with sunflower seeds tucked inside and rolls of unraveled toilet paper. Leafy branches are stuck through the primate cages for the animals to pluck, and big blocks of frozen Tang are left on the floor for them to lick. There are bowling balls for the cougars. Goblin, a baboon, cuddles a menagerie of stuffed animals.

You'll see other things you'd never see in a regular zoo. You might spot a student with a French manicure reaching her fingers through the bars and digging her shiny nails into the head of a hyena that's gone limp from the joy of a good scratch. You might see a gibbon, its long slender arms stretched through the cage, meticulously picking bits of dried skin off a student's arms. You might see Legend, the wolf, out for a stroll on her leash or Harrison, the Harris hawk, winging back and forth between two trainers. The teaching zoo is a lab where students can lay their hands on many different types of feathers, scales, and fur, and that is what makes the program so unusual.

So far during orientation week, the students have gotten to touch only two animals: the easygoing Chilean rose-haired tarantula, Rochelle, or any of the three-inch-long Madagascar hissing cockroaches. More people want to hold the tarantula that bites than the cockroaches that don't. These are two of the very few animals the first years will be able to touch until well into next semester. In fact, they are not even allowed to speak to most of the zoo's residents. If Taj chuffs at them, they may chuff back, but only one breathy greeting. They can talk to and handle the rats, the bunnies, the sugar gliders, the chinchillas, the opossums, all the reptiles, and Nova, the great horned owl. That's it for now. Sometime next winter they can say hello to Zulu, the mandrill, and Benny, the ancient capuchin. Until then lips must remain zipped. Students may not even linger in front of a cage long enough for an animal to notice them or, in some cases, make eye contact. The first years are like the cleaning staff of a high-end hotel, busy but invisible, and any interaction with the well-turned-out guests is absolutely forbidden. They clean the animals' poop out of their cages, but they mustn't utter a word. If a parrot says "Hi," the first years must turn a deaf ear, no matter how rude they feel.

There are a number of practical reasons for this legendary rule. The animals are generally unnerved by the arrival of new students each August. For example, Rosie, a baboon, is likely to scream and shake her cage like a berserk mental patient, the first years are told, until she gets used to them. Too much attention from these new faces may not only upset the animals but also distract them from their training regimen and cause them to lose their learned commands. They may confuse "Circle!" with "Speak!" or start waving when they should sit. The rule is especially important for the primates, who, as social creatures go, can be mighty prickly. For them, eye contact can translate as aggression. Look at a primate too long and he'll think you want a piece of him. The pissed-off monkey may then vent his rage on his unwitting trainer. Moreover, the rule is a test that the first years will do as they are told and that they will exercise great discipline in the face of great temptation. Everyone is rightly anxious about this rule. For these students, talking to an animal is a reflex as natural as breathing. The first years worry that without thinking they'll utter a "Hi, cutie!" or a "Hi, sweetie!" and the next thing they know, they'll have their walking papers.

"Don't talk to anything," Chris Jenkins, a second year, tells two first years, while they are standing in front of George, the fennec fox. George looks like a fairy-tale character curled in an afghan, softly whimpering for attention. George not only provokes an overwhelming urge to say hello but also to cradle him in your arms like a baby and sing a lullaby. "It's very unnatural to not say 'Hi' to animals, but everyone is listening," he continues. "There are severe consequences. It affects your grades, your animal assignments, it could even get you kicked out. Every year there's a couple who do it."

It is now Thursday, the fourth day of orientation week, and Jenkins, one of the best liked and most respected students in his class, is giving two first years another tour of the teaching zoo. This one is a behind-the-scenes look. The two first years, Susan Patch and Linda Castaneda, have had their pens and notebooks out all along the way. Jenkins starts at the aviary at the front of the zoo, where he tells them the turacos "like to buzz heads." The noisy guy is the plover, and the pheasant doesn't have a name—"just pheasant." Jenkins points out that Clarence, next door, is the only animal first years are allowed to hose off.

Jenkins leads them across the front road and behind the outdoor theater, where Happy, the alligator submerged out of sight in his pool, and two tortoises live. Here, Little Joe, much the smaller of the two, mounts Tremor and thrusts away, his hooked mouth opening and closing. Both Castaneda and Patch briefly quit taking notes. "It's like turtle porn," Jenkins says before turning to go backstage of the school's outdoor theater where he slides open the lid to a box, and several sets of eyes blink in the light. He's awakened the sugar gliders. Next, Jenkins points out the rabbits in their cages. If it's over 100°, put a water bottle in with them, he says. They stroll past the front office and through the squawky ruckus of Parrot Garden, where, Jenkins warns, you can accidentally get locked in the cages. As the threesome pauses by the emu's enclosure, Jenkins explains that when they clean her cage one student goes in and holds the emu down. Both Castaneda and Patch quietly contemplate this, while looking at the towering bird with her monster-sized feet. "It sounds worse than it is," Jenkins says.

Now they are in what's called the Show area near George. It's so hot that nearby Buttercup, the only trained badger in the country, Jenkins tells them, lies flat on her back, paws in the air. "She looks like roadkill right now," he says. "She's dug a hole nine feet deep." A trainer in the cage with Hudson keeps chanting, "Good beaver." They step up to the pen where Hamilton, the Yucatan mini-pig, lives and look down on his tattered black ears. He's not so mini, weighing in at 180 pounds. There's a rock in his pool, Jenkins says, because he likes to push it over. Castaneda and Patch scribble down the detail.

Next door, they duck into Carnivores, the area that everyone calls Big Carns, where three cougars, a Bengal tiger, an African lioness, a coyote, a wolf, a hyena, and two servals sleep most of the day away. The servals both bare their fangs and hiss. "Watch your fingers with them. They'll get you," Jenkins says. "The locks with red paint mean only staff can open those cages." They continue down the back road, and then through another gate, where the smell of a farm, that earthy mix of poop and hay, and sea lion barks fill the air. This area is called Hoofstock, which the sheep, deer, a miniature horse, the pigs, camels, and Schmoo call home. Jenkins demonstrates how the two camels can lean way out of their enclosures and trap you in the far end of Hoofstock. "These guys you need to watch out for."

Jenkins looks at his watch. He is due to walk Olive, the baboon, so he rushes through the rest, quickly ducking into the Reptile Room, a converted railroad car that smells like overripe fruit. He tells them to make sure the tarantula has water in her bowl, that none of the reptiles are venomous, and don't let Morty, the Burmese python, get too hungry. If so, he'll think his student handlers are dinner and squeeze them too hard. They sprint through Nutrition, a building devoted to making the animals' meals. He shows them the terrarium, where the mealworms are grown for the reptiles' dinners. They speed walk around Primate Gardens while the capuchins squabble and chatter. "These guys are hair grabbers and pullers," Jenkins says. He stops at the back of Primate Gardens and points to one last gate, this one between the lemurs' and the binturongs' cages. That gate leads to Quarantine, where a mishmash of animals—a raven, a snapping turtle, an arctic fox, a dog, among others—live. Then Jenkins is off, as Castaneda and Patch still write, hoping against hope to commit at least a small chunk of this avalanche of information to memory.

Patch is a lean, poker-faced beauty. She has a matter-of-fact manner and an athlete's grace. Blue rhinestone studs run up both her earlobes. Castaneda is nearly six feet tall and striking. Like many tall women, she slouches slightly. She has very pale, lightly freckled skin, black hair, and cultivates a kind of hip, bookish look. She wears a CamelbaK, the mouthpiece of which is draped over her shoulder and leaking water down her T-shirt. Both women are fairly typical of EATM students these days. They are in their twenties, they already have bachelor's degrees, and they are using this two-year associate's program as a kind of graduate program.

Patch, twenty-two, grew up in San Diego, where she regularly visited the city's world-class zoo and early on set her sights on working there. Her young life has been one calculated move after another to that end. Despite low pay, zookeepers' jobs are highly competitive, especially at a zoo with the reputation of San Diego's.

Patch began building her resume at the University of California, Davis, where she studied animal science, cared for the school's barnyard of animals, and trained a cow to be led on a halter. To beef up her animal experience, Patch volunteered at the San Diego Zoo, giving health exams to boas and iguanas at the reptile center. She worked part-time for her mother, a research scientist, plucking ovaries out of mice lying prone under a microscope.

By comparison, Castaneda, twenty-seven, discovered her affinity for animals relatively late. She grew up in Lynwood, where the wildlife was limited to rats and pigeons. She didn't see a squirrel or a woodpecker, she says, until she went to Lewis and Clark College in Portland, Oregon, on a scholarship. She started out premed, "so my parents could say they have a doctor in the family," but decided that animals needed more help.

After college, Castaneda moved back to Los Angeles with a degree in biology and taught science to grade schoolers and high school freshmen on her home turf, the inner city. She signed on for a summer gig as a research assistant helping a professor in Cameroon study the habits of hornbills and primates in the rain forest. She had to walk the eighteen miles into the jungle camp and ran out of water with four miles to go. The days in the rain forest were long, the nights uncomfortable and buggy, but the trip convinced Castaneda that her future truly belonged with animals. When she got home she applied to EATM.

Castaneda essentially moves through the world incognito. She's a Mexican American who grew up in the inner city, but people assume she's middle class and white. This leads to some awkward situations. People make racist remarks to her—outright ones or backhanded ones like "You could totally pass for being white." Even other Hispanics think she's white and doesn't speak Spanish. Her father is a retired machine operator who never really learned to speak English. Her mother, on the other hand, not only learned to speak English, but earned a high school degree, then a bachelor's, and finally a master's in linguistics. Nearly all the girls Castaneda went to school with, she says, got pregnant. Castaneda's family and work ethic made her different. "When my mother was my age she had three children and didn't speak English," she says. "I have no children, no house payment. I have no excuse for failure." So, like many second generation immigrants, Castaneda is under some pressure to succeed, even if it's self-imposed.

Both Patch and Castaneda are smart, confident young women. Neither worries that she will wash out of EATM. Both are aiming for straight A's. Patch thinks her UC Davis degree will stand her in good stead at EATM. Castaneda knows she can work harder than most anyone. Besides, after her trip to Cameroon and teaching, Castaneda feels especially unflappable. "What can EATM do to me that a fifth grade punk already hasn't done?"

Tonight yet another social function is on the schedule, the last one of the busy week—a bonfire. As tradition has it, the second years are the hosts, so they pack up a load of firewood, boxes of graham crackers, cans of chocolate icing, and marshmallows and head west to the broad beaches of Oxnard, where the temperature is a good thirty degrees cooler—a welcome change from the day's heat. After a good-sized fire is stoked, the students settle down in a kind of circle, second years on one side, first years on the other. I settle on a neutral spot in the circle where I have first years to one side, second years to the other. The conversation is, naturally, about animals. A second year tells me that she dreamed of being a dolphin trainer when she grew up in landlocked Wyoming. Another says that when her parents offered her the choice between the traditional Mexican coming out party or a horse for her fifteenth birthday, she chose a horse. A first year from Georgia tells me about volunteering at a shelter for fawns.

A woman had cleared all the furniture out of her house and filled it with cribs for orphaned fawns. When they jumped out, the first year would put them back in their cribs. "I totally love deer," she gushes.

If the first years feel a little as if they have intruded on someone else's party, they are not to blame. Many of the second years talk among themselves and ignore the first years. They crack inside jokes and sit close to each other. By comparison, the first years sit stiff and quiet. They don't know the second years or each other. They look over the flames at their very confident, very comfortable upperclassmen. As they've already been told on several occasions by staffers, this class of second years is exceptional and may be the best class ever.

It could be the second years are feeling too giddy just now to be good hosts. For them, the worst of the program is nearly behind them and they are about to come into the full wealth of being second years: field trips, later mornings, much more time with their animals. Essentially, they will be promoted to middle management. They will oversee all the scrubbing and make sure the first years follow the rules. This is why many of the EATM grads do not have fond memories of their second years. They are their bosses. This class of second years has sworn among themselves that they will be nice to their first years, mentors rather than shrews. But I've been told every class of second years makes this solemn pledge to themselves. All these students are here to learn animal behavior, but it's human behavior, often their own, that is most likely to trip them up.

As the evening deepens and the surf grows louder, the students go around the circle giving their names and ages. Then a game of telephone is begun, quickly becomes off-color, and then peters out. Marshmallows are spiked on foraged sticks and dunked into the fire, where they flame like mini-meteors, shooting sparks of burnt sugar into the black night. The flames reflect in young eyes that are eagerly, nervously turned toward the future. As the fire's crackling punctuates the lulling song of the surf, some of the first years wonder if they will shine; others, if they will make it. All of them consider the possibility that in the next year, month, or even week, they may be kicked, bitten, or scratched.

By Friday morning, the first years have dropped several hundred dollars at the bookstore on weighty textbooks on animal anatomy and an array of sweatshirts, tank tops, and polo shirts with the EATM logo. Now it's work day, the last day of orientation week and the traditional scrubbing of the teaching zoo from one end to the other. Both classes of students, numbering ninety-seven strong, will march through the compound with mops and buckets in hand. As the thermometer again hovers around 100°, students take brooms and knock cobwebs off evergreen bushes. They sponge the black mildew off the walls in the Reptile Room and pull a small tree out of Happy's sun-baked enclosure. All twenty-six bins of rodents are placed on desks in Zoo 1 so the Rat Room can be hosed. Legend, the wolf, stands and watches as three blond students wrestle a huge stainless steel sink down the front road.

I find Terri Fidone, a first year with dark eyes and a long black ponytail, at the back of the zoo, shovel in hand, contemplating an unenviable task. She has been assigned to scrub out the Dumpsters. The problem is they are full, and the truck that could empty them is off on an errand. If the truck doesn't show up soon, Fidone will have to climb into the Dumpster and shovel out the trash. "If I have to, I will, but I will be really bummed out," she says in her low voice. Until recently, Fidone was working on her bachelor's in biology while serving cocktails at the world's biggest casino, the mammoth MGM Mirage in Vegas. She started waiting tables when she was seventeen, then graduated to cocktail waitress. The tips were on average $100 to $200 a night—more if she worked the baccarat room, less if she worked the nickel slots. Once, a high roller at the roulette table threw her a $1,000 chip. When she dropped an organic chemistry class at the University of Nevada in Las Vegas because she was failing, she made a pact with herself to use the time she would have been in that class productively. She noticed a billboard for Keepers of the Wild, a sanctuary for exotic animals about an hour's drive southwest from Vegas across the Arizona state line, and signed up to volunteer there. While cleaning out the big cats' cages, she discovered that she "could shovel crap for eight hours and I'd rather be there than go to work and earn money."

After nearly ten years, she quit her job at the MGM in July to attend EATM. Now she's contemplating life as an EATM student, which means no more $100 sushi splurges or buying brand-name groceries. It will be generics for the next two years. "I have to get used to going to the bank to get money," she says. "Before, I always had cash on hand." A voice on the intercom asks if anyone knows where a pickax is. The truck arrives and Fidone is spared. She goes looking for sponges and a bucket.

The cleaning frenzy continues around me. Oddly enough, there's a lot of fussing over insects. The Reptile Room managers call out, "Ooh, spiders!" as they wipe down the walls. A threesome in the iguana enclosure hops and chants, "Yuck! Yuck!" as an ant colony they've disrupted streams up their bare legs. By the front office, Castaneda, still wearing her CamelbaK, points out a tarantula wasp to me, the big furry spider's only predator. It's about as big as a praying mantis and has a shiny black body and alarmingly orange wings. As Castaneda calmly explains to me how the wasp can paralyze a tarantula, the thing flaps its menacing wings, lifts off from the lawn like a helicopter, turns in our direction, and buzzes past us. Castaneda holds her ground and says calmly, "There it goes." Other students nearby—women who aspire to pet tigers and handle boas—shriek, duck, and run for it. Someone yells, "What the hell is that?" Turns out animal people are not necessarily bug people.

As the sun grows stronger, people zigzag like drunks as they walk from patch of shade to patch of shade, toting buckets and mops. They stand in the parrot misters. They squirt each other with hoses. Anita Wischhusen has sweated through her baggy tank top, a large wet stain spreading across her back, another pooling between her breasts. Despite the heat and hard work, she wisecracks loudly and cackles huskily at her own jokes. At forty-five, she is the second oldest student in the class of 2005.

Wischhusen is naturally loud but thoughtful. She has a gray, fuzzy mullet haircut and a dirty-brown tan. Her car is covered with pro-animal bumper stickers, even one that proclaims her membership in People for the Ethical Treatment of Animals (PETA), which is a kind of dirty word around EATM, but Wischhusen is not one to fit in. She grew up wanting to be a vet but didn't have the heart to euthanize animals. Her parents pushed her toward a secure career, so she went into computers. Her career may have been secure, but her lifestyle was not. When she wasn't at the keyboard, she was partying as hard as a Hell's Angel. At forty, after another night of drugging and drinking, she nodded off at the wheel, plowed into a highway median, broke her jaw, and landed in a court-ordered thirty-day rehab program. "The program told me to stop drinking, but did not tell me why I drank," she says.

When her brother came out, it occurred to Wischhusen for the first time that perhaps she was gay too. She'd always dated men and had sex "and all that, but it didn't do much for me." Maybe, she wondered, that was why she drained whole bottles of amber tequila at a sitting. In short order, she was not only sober but also had a serious girlfriend, a traffic cop with a daughter. At last, her personal life was in order. Then California's robust tech economy wilted, and Wischhusen was laid off from three jobs in a row.

After the final pink slip, Wischhusen thought back to her younger self, the one who dreamed of working with animals. She decided to go to EATM. That she is here is a small miracle. It took a couple of applications to get in. In the meantime, her father died of melanoma, the treatment for which used up the money her parents said she could have for EATM. Her girlfriend's daughter suffered a brain aneurysm. Wischhusen, who was teaching the girl to speak again, worried that she now had neither the money nor the time for EATM. Her girlfriend pushed her to go. Wischhusen sits for a moment in the shade, dabs at her wet shirt with a towel, and says happily, "I have no life now."

The first year students aren't the only new faces at the zoo this week. Amber Cavett, an outgoing, athletic-looking second year, leads me to the far end of the zoo through the gate at the back of Primate Gardens and into Quarantine. Here, we find Samburu. Samburu is a caracal, a small, fawn-colored African cat with tassels of black fur that droop decoratively from the tip of each ear. An EATM faculty member drove him from Northern California through the cool night and deposited him here this morning. The eleven-year-old cat is in the cage next to Tango, an arctic fox. While Tango pants loudly, the caracal lounges on a bed of hay in a box mounted about five feet up one wall of his cage. Word is that he's ornery, even nasty, but he seems quite demure just now. This is Cavett's first look at her new charge. She will train him for a grade this semester. She's fascinated but apprehensive because of his bad reputation. She's hoping to teach him to go into a crate on command—nothing too fancy. "They have round eyes rather than slitted like other cats because they hunt birds," Cavett says, looking at him. "They aren't nocturnal. They are crepuscular." You wouldn't know it by her upbeat nature, but Cavett has had one tough summer. Chance, the huge binturong (a native of Southeast

Asia that resembles a kind of raccoon on steroids with a huge prehensile tail to boot), bit her finger while she was showing off some training for her mother. He sank his teeth into her middle finger down to the bone. She couldn't bend it for two weeks. In June, she became the emu's lead keeper. Every day since, Julietta has tried to attack Cavett. When the 200-pound bird feels peevish, which is all summer, she rises up, stretches out her strange, turquoise neck, and then whacks at the nearest human with her beak. As if that wasn't bad enough, Julietta will kick with her three-toed feet. Whenever Julietta came after Cavett, she jumped back, even yelped. Cavett was told she had to get over her fears or she couldn't be Julietta's lead keeper. So Cavett drew on her experience as a scholarship runner at a community college in Oregon, where she put on a brave face for races even when she was terrified of losing. Cavett suppressed the urge to run for her life when Julietta attacked, stepped near the emu, and grabbed her blue, hairy neck. "If you stand really close to her, she can't kick you," she says.

We head to Nutrition to fetch Samburu his first meal at EATM. There we find various second years busily making dinner for their charges. They pluck whole rabbits from the walk-in freezer. They scoop crickets out of a terrarium. They unscrew jars of bright orange and green baby food. Cavett takes a cleaver and whacks off the head and feet of a frozen yellow chick. She pulls the stringy fat from three chicken necks, then chops them into bite-size chunks. She measures out 40 grams of canned horsemeat. Back in Quarantine, Cavett steps between Tango's and Samburu's cages. She will feed him by hand to develop a bond with him. She squats and tentatively holds out a piece of chicken neck in her fingertips, reaching through the bars at shoulder height. With a loud hiss, Samburu explodes out of his raised box, bounds to the bars, bares his teeth, and snatches the chicken neck from Cavett. "Okay, I'm a little scared," she says, holding her ground but turning her face away from him.

Samburu zips back into his box, jumps the five feet down to the floor of his cage, and bounces back up, hissing and growling loudly. Cavett holds another piece of meat through the bars. The cat leaps back down, grabs the meat with his teeth, inhales it, runs in a quick circle, and then suddenly, surprisingly, lies down on his stomach. He places his front paws neatly under him and gobbles up everything Cavett holds out to him. He gets up every once in a while and runs around the cage, only to settle right back down for more chow. "See that circle behavior?" Cavett asks. "I could put that on cue." Behind Cavett, Tango, perhaps inspired by Samburu's ruckus, gives himself a nice scratch. He runs back and forth along a series of wooden scrub brushes wired to his cage. The yellow bristles pull loose strands of his plush white fur. Tango pants happily. Samburu keeps hissing, but now it's a light, steady, contented-sounding drone. Cavett smiles. The summer is nearly over. The first feeding couldn't be going any better. This cranky, crepuscular cat with the fancy ears might just change her luck.

Behaviors

Animal training has been around since the first caveman threw a chunk of grilled mastodon to a hungry wolf lurking at the shadowy edge of the campfire light. Since then, we have taught dogs to herd, falcons to hunt on command, elephants to log, cheetahs to walk on leashes, lions to pull chariots, chimps to roller skate, and parrots to sing "Yankee Doodle Dandy." During nearly all that long history, no one truly understood training. Whether a trainer used brute force or kindness, nobody knew exactly why a technique worked or didn't. Animal training was like alchemy. That was until Ivan Petrovich Pavlov of the drooling dog and B. F. Skinner of the Ping-Pong-playing pigeons came along; they found the science behind the magic.

While researching digestion, Pavlov noticed that his research dogs drooled at the sight of white lab coats. That got the Russian physiologist thinking about involuntary reflexes. Could they be induced? he wondered. To answer that question, he placed a harnessed dog in a soundproof room. Each time a bell sounded, a puff of food powder was blown in its mouth. The dog would salivate.

Eventually, the pooch's brain linked the sound of the bell with a lip-smacking whiff of the powder. Then, all it took was one ding to make the dog slobber.

On the surface this seems a useless bit of information, but Pavlov's discovery had profound meaning for the fledgling field of behaviorism. He proved a reflex could be provoked through association. He dubbed this learning to connect one thing with another a conditioned response or reflex. It goes on all around us; for instance, a patient winces at the sight of a syringe or a kitty prances to the kitchen at the sound of a can opener. The behavioral equation is simple: A = B.

Pavlov's theory opened the door to a room that Skinner furnished. In his 1938 book, *The Behavior of Organisms,* Skinner introduced his new theory, *operant conditioning*. Through countless experiments with pigeons at Harvard University, Skinner demonstrated that behavior is shaped by its consequences. If a pigeon was rewarded for something it did, the bird would repeat that behavior. If the cooing bird gets a bit of grain for pecking a piano key, you can bet the bird will peck that key again and again and again. As long as the grain is forthcoming, the winged virtuoso will play on. What animal trainers had long assumed, Skinner demonstrated was a scientific truth.

Skinner's research also proved that rewards worked better than punishment. Not that punishment didn't change behavior; it did but not always as desired. A pigeon, or a person for that matter, is likely to look for ways to simply avoid the punishment. For example, police punish drivers who go above the speed limit. That discourages a number of lead foots, but a good number continue speeding with an eye out for police cars. Skinner found that rewards got the job done more effectively. For a species wedded to punishment, this was, and still is, revolutionary.

Skinner elaborated on the principles of operant conditioning in detail and came up with a whole vocabulary as well as equations and graphs with elegant curves. Along the way, he taught pigeons to play "Take Me Out to the Ball Game" and to walk in figure eights. He even taught the birds how to guide a missile by pecking at a target. He hoped his findings would make for a kinder world for his own species. Though that goal eluded Skinner, he changed animal training for good and for the better. He proved scientifically that a chunk of meat could generally accomplish more than the crack of a whip. Operant conditioning also gave animal training a level of seriousness, a scientific heft, it had never had. He took animal training out of the realm of the carny, the outsider, and plopped it down in the lab, where it might finally get some respect.

The wild animal tamers of yesteryear, a chair in one hand and a whip in the other, are now just images in old circus posters. Today we have exotic animal trainers. No enlightened trainer worth his clicker speaks of *tricks,* a word that conjures up the politically incorrect big top and the darker aspects of animal training. Animals are taught *behaviors*. They aren't kept in cages but *enclosures*. Times have changed and this linguistic shift reflects that.

Over the past two decades or so, the number of trainers using the principles of operant conditioning and positive reinforcement has grown steadily. Julie Scardina of SeaWorld says it's still not the dominant technique, but it is more and more broadly used. Clicker training, which is based on operant conditioning, has taken the dog world by storm and is on the rise among horse and bird trainers. Ken Ramirez, who oversees the training staff of the Shedd Aquarium, says, "When I look at where training was when I started in 1976, and where it is today, it's quite an evolution." Moreover, the whole idea of how to use training has changed. Training is no longer limited to the circus or the movie set. It is used in wildlife sanctuaries, zoos, animal shelters, research facilities, and educational programs. In his weighty manual, *Animal Training: Successful Animal Management Through Positive Reinforcement,* Ramirez writes that training today is "the cornerstone of a good animal care program." Scardina says that through training "you can make an animal's life safer, more positive and more interesting."

Training is now used to teach animals to cooperate with medical procedures, such as blood draws and ultrasounds—procedures for which they once would have been sedated. They are trained for general care; for instance, an elephant is taught to hold its foot up for a needed filing and dolphins are taught to give blowhole samples. Training is used for mental stimulation and exercise. Captive animals are trained to walk on leashes so they can stretch their legs and get a change of scenery. Gary and Kari Johnson start every morning at their private elephant compound in Southern California by leading their herd of pachyderms, each trunk holding the tail of the animal in front of it, on a bracing walk. Animals are trained so they can travel or go in front of crowds without undue stress. David Jackson of Zoo To You, a well-known educational outreach program in California, is often asked what drug he gives Jasmine, his Bengal tiger, that she'll lie still at his feet during his presentations. "People don't realize that she's been trained to do that," he says. "She's so calm and comfortable, nobody has a clue."

Enlightened trainers learn the animal's natural history to better understand the species. It makes a difference that a lion is a social animal and a tiger is not, that a horse is a prey animal and a wolf is not. Trainers study up on a species' natural behaviors so they know what will come easily to an animal and what won't. For example, baboons jump in the wild as a way to make themselves look bigger. In the open ocean, wild dolphins arc high out of the water just as they are trained to do in shows. Trainers learn an animal's physiology so they know what it can and can't do. Elephants cannot jump, though they can stand on their back feet.

As Ramirez writes, a contemporary trainer is "a keeper, a biologist, a mammalogist, an ethologist and much more."

Added to that is the fact that training is no longer thought of as a means to dominate an animal but rather as a means to communicate. Through operant conditioning a common language can be found, a mostly nonverbal one. As Karen Pryor says, this is a two-way system: "It is really an eerie thrill when the animal turns the training system around and uses it to communicate with you." Al Kordowski, an EATM grad and longtime marine mammal trainer with SeaWorld, explains it this way: "Imagine your best friend couldn't talk but you find a way to communicate and both achieve something together. That to me is it," he says. "We have a hard enough time communicating with each other. You've achieved something most people can't achieve in their day-to-day life, and you've done it with a wild animal."

EATM is credited with producing many of the foot soldiers in this training revolution. The program has graduated legions of trainers versed in operant conditioning and progressive animal care. These grads have infiltrated the animal industry from top to bottom, changing it as they went. Netta Banks, an EATM grad who works for the American Humane Association, monitoring animals on film and television sets, says, "Ninety-seven percent of young trainers are from the Moorpark program. They have raised the bar for zookeepers, for animal trainers and wildlife educators." The program's grads used to go primarily to marine parks, studio companies, and the circus. Now, more and more EATM grads land jobs at zoos and aquariums, thus spreading their training knowledge into those arenas. The school has also taken a formerly secretive skill and made it an academic curriculum at a public college open to all. In the past, aspiring trainers broke into the profession by cleaning cages at the circus or for a movie trainer until luck gave them a chance. There was no direct career path. Once EATM opened its doors, that changed.

* * *

Gary Wilson has taught the behavior and training classes at the school since 1985. Though he's nearly fifty, Wilson is still handsome in a boyish, clean-cut way. He runs regularly. He has a low-key but friendly, talkative manner. He seems more the thinker in a world of doers—someone as drawn to abstract ideas as he is to animals, who's as happy to discuss evolutionary biology as how to get Nick, the miniature horse, to blow a party horn. He teaches Sunday school at the Methodist church that his wife and two children attend. He's prone to giggling and has a wry sense of humor that can be lost on his students. He often wears a belt buckle with a lion's head emblazoned on it.

Wilson is an alum of the program, as is his wife, Cindy, who also teaches at EATM. He graduated in 1977 with Scardina. Both applied for a killer whale training job at SeaWorld. Scardina got the job and became the second female trainer at the park. Wilson got a job at Six Flags Magic Mountain, an amusement park, where he walked a lion on a leash. The lion, which had been in Tarzan movies, was missing the tuft of fur at the end of his tail. Wilson would lead him through a petting zoo, then clip him on to a front porch, where he slept the day away. People could pay $5 to have their picture taken with him. "People would hand you their baby to set by the lion, and you'd ask if they wanted to get in the picture and they didn't want to get near the lion," Wilson says.

Wilson then worked for two years with the Navy training dolphins. One of his cetacean protégés, K-Dog, was deployed in Iraq in 2003. He didn't find the Navy or training dolphins intellectually stimulating enough and went back to school. Eventually, he earned a master's in biological sciences from the University of California, Santa Barbara, in 1985. He started teaching at EATM while he was still working on his bachelor's, then joined the faculty full time after earning his master's. "My interest in training animals was an interest in helping animals," he says. "I saw this job as a chance to have a greater impact."

Like most marine mammal trainers, Wilson strongly emphasizes using positive reinforcement. He's an optimist whose leitmotif is "Try it." As one student tells me, "What's so awesome about him is that he thinks anything is possible." He's famous among his students for thinking up pie-in-the-sky behaviors for them to train. It's rumored that he once suggested that a student teach one of the school's capuchins to ride in a small basket hung from a helium balloon. When I ask Wilson if he did, he says he doesn't recall that, but it sounds like a fun idea. A few of the other trainers on the EATM staff think he may be overly optimistic and not cautious enough with the animals. He has, in fact, been attacked a couple of times. In one class graduation program he was described as the "animal chew toy."

Wilson first broaches operant conditioning in Animal Behavior, which the students take during either of their first two semesters. Wilson says the principles of operant conditioning aren't that hard to learn, but applying them is a different matter. That's why in the lab that accompanies the class, students train rats to run a maze. They learn to use a clicker, a small novelty store noisemaker, to tell an animal when it does the correct behavior, as a dolphin trainer uses a whistle. Wilson also lectures on the honeybee's waggle dance, the songbird's sub song, and the eel's long migration across the Atlantic Ocean. He speaks of filial imprinting, altruism, and the pecking order in chickens. He depicts the endless, intricate behaviors that, like the inner workings of a clock, make the animal kingdom tick.

In the summer, Wilson teaches a class in training using Pryor's *Don't Shoot the Dog!* and Ramirez's book. For that class's lab, students train two of the zoo residents for a grade. As with the rats, they nearly all work with treats, rewarding the animals when they do something right. Students meet one-on-one with Wilson on a regular basis to discuss their progress or any problems they are having. In the following two semesters, when they are second years, the students work with different animals. By graduation, the students have trained a hoofstock, a primate, a carnivore, and a bird as well as cared for a dozen or more animals.

Wilson finds that some people are natural trainers. They have an eye for body language. They are patient and calm. Trainers often refer to this as "animal sense." Plenty of trainers think that you have to be born with it and that, like common sense, it cannot be taught. Dr. Peddie is in this camp. Wilson disagrees. He finds some students are not natural trainers, but learn the skill from coursework and practice. Sometimes this latter group can outshine the natural trainers, who just try to get by on their instincts. The students who polish their inborn talent with what they learn in the classroom make the best trainers, he says. Then there are some students who just never get it, no matter how passionate they are about animals or how hard they study. "When it doesn't come together for some, I joke about dental hygiene school," he says.

Training is generally harder than most people assume, especially people who consider themselves good with animals. As one trainer put it, "It tweaks your head psychologically." It's like a Zen Buddhist lesson in self-control. You must be an intense observer, yet always think ahead, anticipate the animal's response, what one trainer refers to as "proactive second guessing." You have to think on your feet while always remaining calm. You must be confident yet cautious. If you make a mistake, you could teach the wrong behavior or even get hurt. If you get it right, as Kordowski says, "It's an adrenaline rush."

For the fall semester, Wilson has the students train husbandry behaviors, meaning anything that would help with the animal's care. One student has decided to teach Zulu, the mandrill, to offer his arm for an injection. Another has been assigned to teach Gee Whiz, the llama who doesn't like to be touched, to stand still and be brushed. One has set her sights on lifting Spitz, a serval, in her arms. Mary VanHollebeke has chosen, to Wilson's thinking, one of the hardest training assignments: to get near Starsky, the teaching zoo's Patagonian cavy. That may sound like a small order compared to teaching a baboon to be jabbed willingly with a hypodermic needle, but there are few animals at the zoo as skittish as the cavy.

The cavy spends his days on alert, twitching his nose ever so slightly with his ears pricked. Everything scares him. On the arid grasslands of southern Argentina he could flee a predator, sprinting up to fifty miles per hour, but in a cage—even a roomy one—there is nowhere to run. The large South American rodent looks like a rabbit crossed with a small deer. He has bunnylike eyes and large, upright ears. His slender legs are long and the toes on his feet resemble hooves. He has a fawn-colored coat with white along his belly and between his back legs; his rump is edged with a slight skirt of fur. Starsky arrived this past spring with another cavy that soon became sick and died. That left Starsky, an animal that usually lives in pairs or threesomes in the wild, alone—that is, except for VanHollebeke.

Starsky is new to the training game, as they say at EATM. VanHollebeke is the first student to work with him, and that alone should make her task slow going. Animals eventually understand training in concept and that if they do as asked, a reward is in the offing. An animal brand new to training, such as Starsky, is typically confused by the whole process.

VanHollebeke began this past summer, sitting very quietly by a tree about ten feet away from his cage, letting the cavy get used to her. In training talk, this is what they call desensitizing. She held perfectly still, which doesn't come naturally to VanHollebeke, who charges through the day until she collapses into bed at night. If VanHollebeke moved, even to push a loose hair away from her face, the big-eyed rodent would dash to the far end of his cage. If he got really scared, he'd jump madly against his cage, even scrape himself. And so VanHollebeke took her sweet time.

Once the cavy got used to VanHollebeke in one spot, she'd move a step closer to his cage. If the cavy was unbothered, she would reward him by taking a step back. Slowly, VanHollebeke worked her way toward the cavy, inching closer and closer. When she got within a few feet of his cage, she taped a spoon to a long stick. If VanHollebeke stepped closer and Starsky held his ground, she would slip the spoon on a stick through the bars and deposit a snack of alfalfa pellets on the ground.

By the end of the summer, the second year was finally able to slip inside the cavy's cage and sit on the concrete ledge near the door without scaring Starsky too badly, though he kept his distance. Now, as often as she can, VanHollebeke sits in his cage. Perched on the ledge, quiet and still, VanHollebeke says she does a lot of thinking. Meanwhile, the cavy hides behind a bush at the far end of his cage and occasionally peeks out with one large, unblinking eye.

VanHollebeke is a tall, dynamic beauty with an oval face and straight dark hair that reaches far down her back. She is an unlikely candidate for a training task worthy of a monk. She likes things to be perfect and to go as planned, and when they don't, she has a short temper and a sharp tongue. She's much more calm with animals, she says, and is drawn to the distressed, difficult ones. VanHollebeke, like many EATM students, originally thought she'd be a vet. She was putting herself through college in Michigan, going part time and taking pre-vet courses. One night her mother couldn't sleep, turned on the television, and saw a program about EATM. Though it was 4:30 A.M., she woke her daughter.

A year into the program, VanHollebeke has found that training is not for her. She does not, she admits, have the patience for it, especially all the repetition. She likes caring for the animals, especially making their lives more interesting with behavioral enrichment. She brings Starsky corn on the cob and browse. She stacks up his hay in a pile so he can busy himself stamping it back out.

VanHollebeke also likes a challenge, even one within herself. What better way could there be to learn patience than by ever so slowly convincing a South American rodent to trust her? Seated in the shade of Starsky's cage as he tucks his small, fleet figure behind the bush, VanHollebeke seeks a serenity that has eluded her. She also dreams the impossible—of touching this Patagonian cavy before she graduates next May.

September

For the two weeks following orientation the new students take notes until their fingers cramp. It's the worst injury they risk just now. Each morning, they follow Brenda Woodhouse around for a crash course in running the teaching zoo. Woodhouse, who's trained dolphins at Chicago's Brookfield Zoo and worked at the bird show at the Los Angeles Zoo, has a job similar to a drill sergeant. She must get her new recruits up to speed fast. She has to instill in them a long list of the dos and don'ts of zookeeping at EATM. She has to teach them how a zoo is in the details, that the smallest oversight—one forgotten parrot feeding, one tool absentmindedly left near a primate's cage—can have huge, even tragic, consequences.

A new keeper hired at a typical zoo would have to learn how to run only a portion of it. At EATM the first years have to learn an entire zoo as fast as they can. When cleaning the chinchilla's cage, they should let him take a dust bath for a minute or two. Zulu, the mandrill, gets a cup of juice in a *paper* cup. Three times a week the algae on Sally, the snapping turtle's shell should be gently scrubbed off.

The first years learn the three *Ls*: life, liquid, locks. A keeper should always check to make sure an animal is alive in its cage, that it has water, and that the cage is locked. Woodhouse shows them where the red emergency phones are. They learn why they must always wear a whistle. If an animal gets loose, you blow your lungs out. If you hear a whistle, duck into a classroom, a storage shed, or even an animal cage. Woodhouse tells them if a primate grabs them through a cage, not to scream or yank, which is fun for the monkey. If a big cat attacks you, roll into a ball. If a camel knocks you down, roll away from it. If there's an earthquake, all the students who can should report to the teaching zoo. If there's a fire, there's no emergency plan for that just yet. It's coming soon, Woodhouse says.

Woodhouse shows them how to put on the miniature horse's halter, which is simple enough, how to walk the emu, which can require some running backward, and how to tie a falconry knot with one hand. They learn how to pick up the big snakes so their body weight is properly supported. If they grab just the head and the tail, they are told, the snake's spine may snap. It's a lot to take in all at once. Woodhouse knows it. She teaches with a big smile, lots of encouragement, and a voice that naturally booms. She's got a maternal touch, but no one doubts she means business, especially after she begins marking students tardy. The first years are due at 6:30 A.M. sharp. It's an adjustment. They speed through the early morning fog, blitz into the parking lot, barely turn off the ignition before they have a foot out the car door, then sprint for the front gate, where they fumble with the latch, losing precious seconds. When the classroom clock's hands reach 6:30 A.M. exactly, Woodhouse starts reading down the roll.

On the first Wednesday, Larissa Comb, a Colgate University graduate and a former Wall Street stockbroker, pulls into the parking lot with only minutes to spare. She's about to dash for the front gate when she notices a second year taking her time. Comb must have more time than she thinks. She slows her pace. What she doesn't know is that Woodhouse reads the names alphabetically. Comb also doesn't know that the second year strolling through the parking lot's last name begins with *Z*.

When Comb slips into the classroom, Woodhouse has just read through the Cs. Comb grabs a seat and doesn't say anything until Woodhouse has read the entire roll. Though she was only thirty seconds late, Comb is docked for the amount of time lost until she announced her presence—three minutes. She should have yelled "Here!" as soon as she stepped in the door. The longer the tardiness, the more docked points. Comb just lost two. That's a pittance, really. What worries Comb is that just ten days into the program she can already kiss her sterling record good-bye. Her heart sinks. This is why: In the winter the first years will ask for the animals they would like to work with come summer. The staff considers the requests based on the students' grades and attendance. Straight-A students with perfect attendance get first dibs. The students with less stellar records get the leftovers. Comb just slid down a rung.

When not following Woodhouse around the zoo, the first years hole up in the air-conditioned chill of Zoo 2, the larger of the program's two classrooms. In Anatomy and Physiology (A&P), Dr. Peddie, like an old fire-and-brimstone preacher, strikes the fear of zoonotic diseases into the first years' hearts. With relish the vet regales the first years with the symptoms of rabies, bubonic plague, and his personal favorite, Valley Fever. "I tell them you can end up wearing diapers," he chortles to me. "That is always an attention grabber." His point is simple—wash your hands, wash your hands, wash your hands.

The average first year takes seven classes. In Animal Diversity they begin to work their way through the animal kingdom slide by slide, starting with sponges (phylum Porifera), jotting down the family, genus, and common name of each species as they go. In Animal Behavior they dive into the theoretical underpinnings of operant conditioning and how to care for a rat. Gary Wilson teaches both classes. He is a notoriously tough test giver, who will mark off an answer if it isn't worded exactly so. Second years have warned the first years not to take more than one "Gary class" per semester. In addition to the class on zookeeping, Woodhouse runs a class on conservation and another on wildlife education.

Classes have started for the second years as well, though not nearly as many. In Dr. Peddie's vet procedure class they study skin, from calluses to carcinomas. In Wilson's training class they discuss how, through bad timing, you can accidentally teach an animal an unintended or unwanted behavior, what is called superstitious behavior. The second years still spend most of their time running the teaching zoo as they did this summer.

From August to early May, both classes, 100 or so strong, work at the zoo, but once the second years graduate, half as many students are left for the same job. This summer, as with most summers here, the mercury regularly shot over 100°. A few students fainted from dehydration. They stood in the walk-in freezer in Nutrition to cool down. Under the sun, the animals' poop bloomed to a pungent ripeness, especially in Hoofstock, where the camels and sheep scatter droplets all day long. When they weren't cleaning, feeding, or training, the students were putting on education shows for zoo visitors.

The summer has exhausted them. The second years try not to lick their collective chops or count the hours until the first years take over the lion's share of hosing, raking, poop scraping, and chopping up dead chicks. However, this also means sharing what has gotten to feel like their zoo. The latter may prove harder than the former.

* * *

On the last day of August, a Sunday, the baton is finally passed. The first years fan out across the zoo and go to work. Linda Castaneda spends her first week cleaning in Hoofstock. When Castaneda goes in with the sheep, they give her a once-over, bumping her with their soft black noses, inquisitively baaing at her. She refrains from baaing back. She starts to smell like "butt." There's a mystery brown spot on her shirt. When her boyfriend does their laundry, an animal turd rolls out of the cuff of her pants.

Being brand new to zookeeping, the first years immediately begin to make mistakes. Castaneda leaves the wheelbarrow too close to a camel's enclosure. One first year forgets she shouldn't let the guenons get overhead while she's cleaning their cage. Ramon, the male, pees on her head. While scrubbing the Reptile Room, a first year plops Dot, the yellow leopard gecko, on her shoulder, thinking she'll stick there. She doesn't. The gecko tumbles to the floor. Dot survives that free fall only to have another first year on the very next day plop her on her shoulder; again Dot tumbles tail over snout. The first years, humiliated, learn their lesson: not all geckos stick.

Michlyn Hines, who's in charge of running the teaching zoo, comes across a first year who has hung a lock on a cage where Samantha, the gibbon, can reach it. Hines no sooner finishes telling the girl about the lock than the first year begins sweeping about a foot from Samantha's cage, where the gibbon, a notorious arm grabber and hair yanker, could easily reach her. Already there's animal interaction—too much of it. A first year is repeatedly caught chatting to the lemurs. One first year insists on leaning her face in close to the mandrill's cage, a no-no. First years greet Abbey, the dog, when she's out for her morning stroll. They are all told to zip it. It's largely up to the second years to enforce the rules and that power can't help going to some people's heads. Some, even though they said they wouldn't, get a little bossy and a little superior. They scold when cages aren't clean enough, when logs aren't filled out correctly, or when the tortoises' overhead light isn't turned on. They make the first years raise their arms to see if their shirts stay tucked in, per the dress code. They report the first years' mistakes to the staff.

This makes the first years alternately skittish and resentful. The first years complain that second years talk to them as if they are stupid. A good number of the students have worked with animals before and don't appreciate being treated as if they know nothing. One chafes when a second year tells her how to roll up a hose. Anita Wischhusen, forty-something, with a full résumé of professional jobs, is written up by a second year half her age and half her size for not "taking direction." Wischhusen shoots her dirty looks whenever she can and bad-mouths her. First years can't help noticing the second years breaking a rule or two, answering their cell phones on the back road, or going into animal cages without the required second person to back them up.

At student council meetings, Becki Brunelli, a second year, tries to keep the peace. She reminds her classmates to be understanding with the first years. At thirty-three, she's one of the oldest in her class. She has an easygoing manner, but nothing gets past her. She's tall, has a head of long, kinky brown hair and a lilting voice. She loves rats and has one tattooed on her ankle. She is a strict vegetarian. She is one of Dr. Peddie's favorites. He's cooking up a way to hire her at EATM after she graduates this spring. That would suit Brunelli just fine.

Maybe because she's so capable and because she could do most anything she set her mind on, Brunelli has had trouble settling on a career. She was an elementary school teacher. Then she went back to school to study anthropology. Brunelli did that for two years and then switched to computer science. She got a job as a Web designer for Warner Brothers. She made a sizable paycheck there but found that so many long days in front of the computer wore her down. She got out of shape. Her natural ebullience waned.

On a whim, Brunelli went on a trip to the rain forest. Not long after touching down in Iquitos, Peru, she felt younger and healthier as she soaked up the oxygen-laden, moist air. Each night she fell into a sleep so deep that the din of the nighttime rain forest never disturbed her. She realized she had to escape the cage she had made for herself, her fluorescent-lit cubicle, and make a different life. When she returned to Los Angeles, she resolved to change careers again. This time it would be animal trainer.

At EATM, she's gotten nearly straight A's, except for one B in behavior lab class, where her rat would not run its maze. She's a class leader. She's as happy as anyone who's happened upon their calling. However, a few things do nag.

As Dr. Peddie warns all students, EATM often trumps love. Over the years, the program's demands have caused its share of breakups and divorces. When students' grades slip, one of the first questions Dr. Peddie asks is "Do you have a boyfriend?" If the answer is yes, "Are you having trouble with him?" Though Brunelli's grades don't show it, she is. For the first year of the program she lived with her boyfriend, an actor, but they saw so little of each other, she decided this summer to move closer to the school and do away with her hour-long commute. They haven't broken up. In fact, Brunelli, always the optimist, hopes the change will improve their relationship.

Brunelli's other distraction is the number of credit card bills that land in her mailbox each month. She came to EATM with a goodly amount of debt, chiefly student loans. Then it took her some time to adjust from a $70,000 salary to the near zero income of a student, and her bills have only gotten bigger. This debt weighs on her, especially when she thinks of her newly chosen profession. Entry-level pay is low for many animal jobs, about $8 an hour. Having found her calling, Brunelli wonders if she can afford it.

For now, she throws herself into life at the school. She is on three committees, including the student council, does all the zoo's scheduling, and cooks up schemes to raise money for the school. This semester she's assigned to Rowdy, the skunk; Nuez, the agouti; Malaika, the African gray parrot; and Goblin, the thirty-year-old hamadryas baboon. Goblin is her favorite, though Brunelli hates to say so. The baboon has a sweet disposition and spends most of her day grooming her stuffed animals. She loves yogurt so much she will throw it up into her mouth for a second, third, and fourth taste. Brunelli often sets up a chair next to Goblin's cage so the baboon can trace every follicle, mole, and bump on her forearm. It's so relaxing that the baboon goes into a meditative trance and Brunelli falls asleep. Brunelli is training Goblin to let her insert an ear thermometer. She's already taught the baboon to hold her ear near her cage bars. Now, once a day or so, Brunelli crouches down and pokes her finger into the baboon's ear, getting her used to that first.

After a long day at the teaching zoo, Brunelli often goes home at night to find Harry, an orangutan, sitting in her living room. Her roommate works at the Universal Studios animal show and brings the primate home for sleepovers. "I never get tired of animals," she says. "No matter what's going on in the rest of my life, I can go hang out with animals. It's always therapeutic." In other words, it's hard to worry about your love life crumbling or impossibly high debts when you are watching TV with an orangutan.

The teaching zoo's inhabitants are the constant at EATM. They come and go, but many of the inhabitants have called the teaching zoo home for most of their lives. Laramie, the one-winged golden eagle, arrived in 1977. Koko, the forty-one-year-old capuchin, moved in in 1975. Precious, the anaconda, has lived here for almost thirty years. It's the students that change regularly, and this is not lost on the animals. Even though the temperatures are still hot enough to nap most of the day, the teaching zoo's residents notice the new, inexperienced keepers. Taj, the Bengal tiger, eyes flashing green, back slung low, stalks the first years as they clean by her cage. In Primate Gardens, Samantha lets loose with her warning call, a slow building whoop. Rosie, the olive baboon, screams at any new student who dares to walk near her cage.

Most of the teaching zoo's animals are donated. Some are gifts or loans from movie trainers, such as Abbey and the camels, Kaleb and Sirocco. Some come from private owners who found that a Bengal tiger or a serval do not make a good pet. Some are abandoned or rescued animals that need a home, such as Buttercup, the badger who was found at a Moorpark gas station when she was a baby. She had a puncture wound. There are as many hard-luck stories as you'd find in a Dickensian orphanage: Happy, the alligator, is about half the size he should be, because a man raised him in a bathtub and fed him fast-food hamburgers; Olive, the olive baboon, was illegally captured and confiscated while still a baby; Tyson, the military macaw, has breathing problems from being stuffed within a car door to be smuggled into the United States.

On the flip side, some of the EATM animals have impressive resumes. Puppy, the turkey vulture, was in *Airplane,* sitting on Peter Graves's shoulder as the plane dived. Schmoo was in *The Golden Seal* when she was only six months old. For years, Schmoo was the only trained sea lion in the business. She appeared in the TV series *Dharma and Greg* and did commercials for Frigidaire, DuPont, and Saran Wrap. Sirocco, the white camel, appeared in the movie *The Mummy*.

As in most zoos, many of the animals at EATM are in their golden years. This keeps Dr. Peddie as busy as a doctor in a rest home. Louie, the ancient prairie dog, has lost the use of his back legs and pulls himself around. Koko shakes from old age. Schmoo is nearly blind from cataracts. Her hearing is going. She is epileptic, for which she takes phenobarbital. She also has ulcers. She takes Zantac for that. In all, she gets twelve pills and vitamins every day, all of which are stuffed into the fish she eats.

Dr. Peddie's job is made easier and harder by the students, who are quick to tug on the vet's sleeve. "If an animal hiccups twice in the wrong way I'm alerted," he says. He has to filter out what are honest concerns and what are overreactions. Like new parents, the students have a tendency to worry. "We have all the rejects, the ancient ones, and the students keep falling in love with them," he says. As usual, several of the zoo's inhabitants demand Dr. Peddie's attention. The rabbits have walking dandruff. Their bedraggled coats are filled with Cheyletiella mites. Samuel, the corn snake, has five eggs stuck in her uterus. When you turn her upside down, you can see the lumps. The first surprise was that Samuel, who everyone assumed was male and thus the name, laid a clutch of a dozen or so eggs last spring. The Reptile Room managers suspected she had more in her, but the snake ate and defecated through the summer, so they didn't say anything to the vet. Recently, Samuel became irritable, so the managers spoke up. Dr. Peddie gives the corn snake a medication to make her pass the eggs, but none of them budges. Then the vet tries to draw them out with a syringe, but the eggs are, as he says, "too cheesy." There is one last option: squeezing them out with his two big hands. Dr. Peddie puts that task on his long to-do list.

Most worrisome is Zeus's case. Zeus is a female green iguana, who, like Samuel, was believed to be male until she started laying eggs. No one knows her age but the assumption is that the iguana's old. Certainly Zeus moves likes she is, mostly dragging herself around by her front legs, her back legs limp behind her. The reason becomes obvious when Dr. Peddie holds up a set of X-rays in class. The vertebrae in her lower back have fused together, possibly from a bad break. Dr. Peddie shows the students the X-ray, not just to teach them but also to prepare them for what comes next—putting her down. The vet is in no rush. When it comes to euthanizing an animal, Dr. Peddie believes in the art of diplomacy and consensus building. He will hold off putting an animal down, if it's not in too much pain, until the majority of students are ready. Sometimes the staff, even students, think he's too slow to pull the trigger.

By the last week of the month, the first years sag under the weight of classes and morning cleanings. Dr. Peddie confides to me that he's a little worried, that this new class is "fragile." The first years are on average younger than the second years. They appear to have more personal problems. The second years complain that they aren't at the teaching zoo enough. Woodhouse thinks they are doing okay, but admits the first years are not jelling as a class. They are getting a rep, like every class of students that has passed through EATM, but it is not a good one. This pains the overachievers, like Castaneda. But who could possibly measure up to the second years? The staff adores them. For the lowly first years, resentment builds. While the first years slave away like Cinderellas, the second years have all the fun. They dissect rats; they cavort with the animals; they run out for big bags of fast food; they go to scuba class. It also doesn't help that the second years don't invite the first years to their parties and that they sometimes don't even acknowledge them when they walk into a room.

The first years, Castaneda tells me, "feel like they are drowning." Many first years are surprised by the program's academic rigors. For Wilson's Diversity test, the students need to memorize forty-four slides with each animal's family, genus, species, order, and common names in that exact order. Everyone carries flashcards all the time, glancing through them as they rush down the zoo's front road. A detailed drawing of the entire zoo is due in Woodhouse's class. A test in Dr. Peddie's Anatomy is in the offing.

Students who'd given up their ambitions to be vets because they didn't fare well in science classes find themselves again struggling with science classes. Even a student like Comb, who got good grades at Colgate without killing herself, says, "This is the first thing I've had to work hard at. It's a different kind of difficult. In college I used to take a break and play my violin. Here I'm too tired. Every piece of you is exhausted."

One first year teeters on the edge, having come late to the morning cleaning several times. The first years look to their left and right and wonder who won't make it through the first semester. Add to that, the Newcastle quarantine has ended, and that means there are pigeons to be had. Any day now, the first years will be expected to break some bird's neck with their bare hands.

Nutrition

Humans have a deep urge to feed animals. Note the bird feeders that dot our yards and the piles of oily french fries left for noisy gulls. We leave out food for foxes, deer, opossums, rabbits, and squirrels. Though it's illegal, more and more people feed wild dolphins in Florida, Texas, and the Carolinas. Some people even pay for the chance to serve sharks dinner. National parks warn visitors not to give leftovers to bears, mule deer, moose, coyotes, prairie dogs, marmots, and so on. This human drive is not limited to our borders. Down under, the Tasmanian Wildlife Service warns visitors not to feed wallabies, currawongs, and Tasmanian devils. At zoos, people are forever chucking candy in with monkeys or tossing marshmallows over the fence to polar bears, despite signs asking them not to. Eric Baratay and Elisabeth Hardouin-Fugier write in *Zoo: A History of Zoological Gardens in the West* that on a day in 1957, visitors to Antwerp's zoo fed an elephant 1,706 peanuts, 1,089 pieces of bread, 1,330 sweets, 811 biscuits, 198 orange segments, 17 apples, 7 ice creams, and 1 hamburger.

Why all the feeding? Food is a common currency. Every living creature needs it, craves it. A handout is the surest means to some kind of interaction with a wild animal. Moreover, food is love for humans. For us, offering a morsel is an engraved invitation to cross-species friendship, though an animal sees the exchange in a much more utilitarian way. This need to feed is deeply satisfied at EATM, where the students are supposed to feed the animals.

All the food prep goes on in Nutrition, a building that seems to constantly echo with the thwack of a dull knife and the kerplunk of monkey chow dropping into stainless steel bowls. As a radio blares, EATM students hurriedly pulverize melon, scramble eggs, and rend heads of romaine. The room is shiny with stainless steel counters. There are shelves packed with jars of brightly colored baby food, plastic bins of freckled bananas, box after box of oatmeal. Nutrition is perfumed with the thick aroma of slightly overripe fruit. Much of the produce is donated by area grocery stores, and so the lettuce may be slightly wilted, the grapes a bit shriveled, the yellow squash dimpled with rot.

Though the room is filled with food, you can quickly lose your appetite here. In the large walk-in freezer there are frosty, headless pigeon bodies, plastic cups of pink baby rats, and buckets of thick, soupy blood left over from thawing horsemeat for the big cats. The students whack slippery chicken necks into chunks. They collect mealworms and crickets. They squeeze the remaining yolk out of the pearly baby chicks with their fingers.

Prep work here can be straightforward or a creative outlet for the students. Food provides the building blocks for a lot of behavioral enrichment. Students artistically lay lettuce leaves and strawberries on a tray for the tortoises, which prefer brightly colored produce. Students stuff meat inside coconut shells for Savuti, the hyena. They freeze blocks of blood for the big cats to lick with their rasplike tongues. Even a slight change in preparation makes for B.E., so the students cook rice in coconut milk or dice vegetables extra small. They offer whole pieces of fruit or a snail still in its shell. All these culinary variations break the routine for the students as well. Behavioral enrichment is a two-way street.

For most animals, the students need only to prepare the correct amount of food, deliver it to the cage, and keep the records up to date. For a few others, feeding is a little more involved. When serving the snakes their very occasional rat, the students have to remember not to handle a prey animal beforehand. Snakes hunt with the nose, and if your hand smells like a rabbit, they may bite that. If you are assigned to Schmoo, you will be forever thawing, rinsing, and sorting fish, not to mention removing small squid from the pen. If you are assigned to either of the two eagles, you'll be setting traps for squirrels and rabbits around the teaching zoo and then gassing them to feed to Laramie or Ghost. Then there is Nick, the not-so-miniature horse.

Nick is, as an EATM staffer puts it, "oinky fat." A year and a half ago he weighed 285 pounds, according to zoo records. Over a six-month stretch the mini-horse's weight soared to 337 pounds. Now he hovers around the 300 mark. That's still too hefty. His student trainers could cut back his food, but that's not the problem. The problem is that Nick's a thief and, worse, he's stealing from his best friend.

At the teaching zoo, Nick is a popular animal with the students and the public. He knows about sixteen behaviors, including sticking his tongue out and turning in a circle. He is good-looking, with a caramel-colored coat and a long blond mane that hangs dashingly across his forehead. Nick came to the teaching zoo in 1997. He arrived with the llama, Gee Whiz, or Whiz, as a lot of the students call him. The hooved twosome were rejects from a petting zoo of sorts. Neither liked strangers touching him. Whiz has quite an underbite. He has large eyes, and his coat resembles a big, rumpled sweater. Regardless, Whiz has a regal bearing. He stands much taller than Nick, though the horse is wider.

Hoofstock generally do better with company, so the twosome live in the same corral near the camels, the little pigs, and the mule deer. Nick and Whiz are boon companions. They often stand side by side. Nick, however, is not the best corral mate. He steals Whiz's food. The llama has bad teeth. Trainers must moisten his pellets. Still, Whiz eats slowly, chewing in exaggerated, clockwise rotations while he stares ahead. Before Whiz can finish his dinner, Nick polishes off his own meal of oat hay and then sticks his handsome muzzle in the llama's bin for second helpings.

The second years assigned to work with Nick this fall semester are determined to slim the tubby horse. They have started him on a new exercise regimen. In addition to his daily walks around the compound, they now take him into the teaching zoo's smaller amphitheater, remove his bridle, and let the boy run. Like a rodeo horse, Nick tears around in mad circles and figure eights, kicking up a spray of dust and wood chips with his back legs as he goes. The commotion usually makes C.J., the coyote, yip and Legend, the wolf, howl in their nearby cages.

One of the student trainers, Jena Anderson, a tall young woman from Minnesota with big blue eyes and a deep, melodic voice, has begun retraining the horse to pull a one-person cart for a grade this semester. She's started by reteaching Nick to run wide circles while on a lead, what is called lunging. She finds Nick is out of shape. When she directs him to keep running, Nick looks at her as if to say, "You gotta be kidding me." "He's a moocher and a slacker," Anderson says.

Anderson is low-key but determined and accomplished. She has a degree in fine arts from St. Olaf College, taught art history, directed a church choir, and was a director of a vet clinic. When she called the Minnesota Zoo asking about careers working with animals, they told her about EATM. She spent a year working at a religious camp in California to get residency so that EATM would fit her budget. She describes herself as a recovering Catholic and "practicing Christian. . . . I don't go around saying praise Jesus," she says. While she was working at the camp, nine ministers took her out for a drink and tried to convince Anderson that she should go to divinity school. "That's not what God is telling me to do," she says.

If you had to bet on her or Nick winning this battle of the bulge, you'd put a big pile of money down on Anderson. She's not only exercising him more but also doing her best to outsmart the ravenous horse. She has moved Whiz's food trough out of Nick's reach, tying it high on a bar in the corral. That seems to be working, but there are reports that Nick has taken to ramming Whiz in the neck while he is chewing, making the llama drop his half-chewed meal on the ground.

Amy Mohelnitzky has the opposite problem. The second year puzzles over how to get a certain animal to eat her breakfast and, like a worried mother, tries her wiles in the kitchen, cajoles, and generally frets. The object of her concern lives at the back of the teaching zoo, where unexpected barks can surprise a visitor. This is where Abbey, the teaching zoo's briard mix, lives.

Abbey is one of the few animals at the zoo who could give Schmoo a run for her money in the training department. She's on loan to the teaching zoo from a studio trainer and has a long list of commercial credits, including advertisements for PetSmart. Abbey is also what Dr. Peddie calls a "difficult keep," which makes her a good addition to a teaching zoo. Her long, glamorous coat, which is a smoky black down the back and cream-colored around the face, ruff, and down the legs, requires constant attention to keep it untangled and flowing. A few days without grooming and Abbey begins to look like a Rastafarian who fell in a mud puddle.

Like many a starlet, the pooch has a finicky appetite and always prefers attention to a treat. Consequently, her svelte figure often becomes a little too svelte. When you weave your fingers through her coat, you easily feel her ribs and her narrow waist. Though she'll usually eat in the evening, most mornings Abbey turns her soft black nose up at breakfast. When the briard mix doesn't eat, she always throws up a puddle of watery, yellow bile. Then the pup doesn't feel up to training. This has been her story since coming to the teaching zoo two years ago.

Abbey, a dog living at a zoo, can't help looking out of place amid the big cats, iguanas, baboons, and macaws. She lives at the far end of the zoo because her excited woofs scare the other animals, especially the three spider monkeys that madly whirl around their cage and puff their chests out as Abbey trots by. As part of the first years' long list of zookeeping duties, Abbey is walked on her leash each morning. Her coat flowing, her pink tongue poking out, Abbey sashays past the screaming capuchins, the big-eyed camels, and the snoozing mountain lions, barking and barking as she prances along. The only animal she notices is Legend. Any student walking Abbey down the front road knows she has to tighten her grip on the leash and flex her biceps as they near Legend, because the two canids carry on like mortal enemies. Legend lunges at her cage and growls a low, toothy threat while Abbey pulls her leash taut, straining with all her might to get at Legend.

A dog at a zoo—even a studio dog with a long list of commercial credits—is a bit of a second-class citizen. Everyone loves her, but she is not an exotic, and that is what the students came to train. Many have already had dogs, and there is a feeling that training one when you could be training a Bengal tiger is a missed opportunity. Never mind that there are far more jobs training dogs, whether for the movies, for sniffing work, or for therapy, than there are jobs training exotics. Also, dogs, compared to the rest of the teaching zoo's inhabitants, are not dangerous. This was not lost on Mohelnitzky. While some of the EATM students get a buzz off working with dangerous animals, Mohelnitzky does not. She admits to being afraid of some of the animals, though she's as brave as any of the students. On stage one time, Kaleb, the dromedary, kicked his legs out in a mad, threatening jig, thrashing his head to and fro, and tossed Mohelnitzky around like a rag doll while she clung to his reins. She fell on her knee so hard that she couldn't walk for two days. Abbey not only offers a break from steeling her nerves but also the dog actually craves her attention. "Most animals are like give me my food and leave me alone," Mohelnitzky says. "Coming out of the cage is the happiest thing for Abbey." Besides, Mohelnitzky is head over heels in love with Abbey, and that love salves a wound.

Mohelnitzky is pretty, like many of the EATM students, though she's of average height; most of the EATM girls are tall. Mohelnitzky always looks put together. She wears makeup. She complains she's in the worst shape ever but doesn't look it. She's from Wisconsin. When she was nineteen, Mohelnitzky moved with her then boyfriend now husband to California. He's an actor who dreams of having his own talk show. Mohelnitzky came to the West without a dream per se. She had always loved animals but never thought there was any kind of career working with them. She studied nutrition for one year in college and got a job as a personal trainer in Santa Monica. She found out about EATM during a visit to the San Diego Wild Animal Park, quit her job, and began waiting tables and working in a vet's office so that she could take the prerequisites for the program.

During her first year at EATM, Mohelnitzky came home one night to see a blood stain on her front doormat. A workman at their apartment complex had let himself in to do some work. If they had known he was coming, they would have shut Barney, their little beagle mix, in the bedroom. They didn't. When the workman opened their front door, he let Barney out. The pooch ran into traffic and was killed. The couple was heartbroken. They moved.

Once again Mohelnitzky spends her days thinking about a dog. Abbey's previous student trainers didn't get her out of her cage much. She thinks that might be part of her stomach problems, that Abbey doesn't get enough exercise. She springs Abbey from the cage whenever she can and takes her to every class with her. When it's too hot or rainy, Mohelnitzky puts Abbey in the front office, even though some staff members grumble. She's started feeding her twice a day, rather than just in the evening, which had been the practice. Mohelnitzky wonders if she has an ulcer. These late summer mornings, she mixes cooked vegetables and a can of wet dog food into her kibble, garnishes it with a sprinkle of acidophilus powder, and heads to Abbey's cage to tempt this picky pooch's appetite. "If she were a tiger, I think more would be done for her," Mohelnitzky says, "but she's just the dog."

Animal People

Among the ninety-seven students currently enrolled at EATM there is a house husband, an eighteen-year-old vegan from Colorado, a plumber who used to earn $50 an hour, and a young New Yorker whose ultimate goal is to get a Ph.D. in evolutionary psychology. Most of the students are from California, but some hail from West Virginia, Iowa, North Carolina, Michigan, Washington, and even Peru and Argentina. A goodly number have bachelor's degrees. A few are in their forties and a handful are in their thirties. They are changing careers, getting that college degree that may have eluded them years back, working a midlife crisis out of their system, or all of the above. The bulk of the students are in their early to mid-twenties. A couple are fresh out of high school. Many of the EATM students are paying their own way, moonlighting as vet techs or manning registers in video stores, racking up credit card debt, and taking out personal loans.

Despite the differences in ages and backgrounds, the EATM students talk of feeling deeply at home, of finally being in their tribe. They are. They are all animal people. This may make the school a headier experience than it already is. Many of these students have always felt out of step with the world. Here, they can talk about animals all day and no one will give them a sideways glance. Being among their own has its downside, though: animal people typically aren't at their best with people, even other animal people.

The term *animal people* gets tossed around a lot at EATM and among professional trainers, but when you start asking what it means exactly, not everyone is sure. What becomes clear, though, is that the term is a double-edged sword—a badge of honor on the one hand, shorthand for misfit on the other. Gary Johnson sums it up when he tells me that an animal person is "someone who will work long and hard. It's whatever it takes to get the job done. Animals don't care about workers' comp or coffee breaks." Then he adds, "People who hang around animals tend to be on the strange side."

The simple definition of this term is that animal people are passionate about animals. Animals are not on the outskirts of life but at its very core. Typically, they have felt this way their entire life. One EATM student told me that when she was a kid and played house with her friends, she always volunteered to be the dog. Another got the idea to be a dolphin trainer when she was five, though her family had no pets other than a guinea pig and she grew up in a small town in Wyoming far from the ocean or a zoo. Others told stories of feeding the family pets and of nursing ailing bunnies.

Most children are strongly drawn to animals, but for some that feeling does not wane as they grow up but rather it intensifies. Any child watching a trainer in a shiny wet suit ride atop a killer whale might think, I'd like to do that, but an animal person holds tight to that dream. It's reflected in how students apply over and over to EATM (one as many as five times) or attempt to return after being kicked out. A number of professional trainers told me that that their job was not a career but an identity. "This isn't what I do," says Kris Romero, an EATM grad and staff member. "This is what I am."

Now it's a fine line between loving animals deeply and preferring their company to your own species. It's a line some animal people drift across, and this is where the misfit connotation comes from. Dr. Peddie puts it diplomatically, saying some animal people don't communicate well with people and so take refuge in the animal kingdom, telling their deepest secrets to their hamster or plastering their bedrooms with posters of horses and lions. Mark Forbes, an EATM alum who is second in charge at the studio company Birds & Animals Unlimited, puts it less diplomatically: "There are so many animal people that are horrid at dealing with people."

I found most animal people to be energetic, strong-willed extroverts, though I did run across some walking stereotypes. I found a surprising machismo for a profession that is dominated by women. Trainers rarely fail to mention how hard their job is, whether the physical work or the long hours. I heard the buzzword 24/7 over and over. "They take pride in how difficult it is," Dr. Peddie says. Trainers spoke of their profession as a calling on a par with joining a convent or monastery. Michlyn Hines, who worked at the Los Angeles Zoo for seventeen years before joining the staff at EATM, says in the eighties few women zookeepers had children; the job was considered too consuming to accommodate motherhood. I also found animal people generally opinionated and competitive. They can be quick to criticize one another for everything, from how someone keeps her compound to her training techniques. Karen Rosa, head of the American Humane Association's Film & TV Unit, hears studio trainers tear each other down on a regular basis.

As Brenda Woodhouse points out, animal training builds ego, and that ego gets the better of some trainers. Though they might be only a few months into the program, even EATM students don't shy away from offering scathing opinions of professional trainers, not to mention of each other. If I mention one to another, I often get the lowdown on the other student's failings: one has to have everything her way; another is a know-it-all; X is retarded; Y is a bitch; Z doesn't have a lick of animal sense. The second years get along famously and generally don't trash each other, with a few exceptions such as the classmate who has gotten a reputation as a pathological liar. When it comes to the first years, though, many of the second years let it rip: the first years this; the first years that. The first years often turn on themselves, grousing about their student council and gnashing their teeth over every misstep their classmates take. "There's more stupid people here than I thought existed," says Wischhusen of her class.

Like new mothers, EATM students are forever gauging who is the most devoted. There's nothing like nurturing to bring out women's competitive streak. Everyone notices when someone takes time off from the teaching zoo. "If she doesn't have to be at the zoo, then she's not here," is a recurrent criticism. If you are not there every day all day, you are considered a fair-weather animal person. Terri Fidone spends time with her new boyfriend on the weekend. Students notice. Wischhusen stays home with her girlfriend when she can. Students notice. There is tsk-tsking over a first year who sits in her car in the teaching zoo parking lot listening to the radio one afternoon.

That EATM students can be so fractious is ironic, because training and operant conditioning work on humans too. An EATM staffer tells me, "It helps you understand why people do the things they do. They are learning such good people skills. I'm sure they thought [the program] was all about animals." That lesson is, obviously, often lost on the students.

Does the school have a testy tone because there are so many animal people at EATM or because there are so many women?

A preponderance of X chromosomes usually makes for what one EATM staffer calls the drama du jour. There are cliques, plenty of hurt feelings, a steady stream of gossip, and roommate problems. The college's psychologist, Laura Forsythe, says at one time she was seeing three women, separately, from the same house. Forsythe says the psychologist before her said to expect a lot of EATM students. He was right. She finds the same problems—depression, eating disorders, even suicidal tendencies—that she finds in the overall student body but with more frequency among the EATM students. "People talk about it being a hothouse," she says. She hears similar complaints from students in the nursing program, which is also dominated by women. EATM students, Forsythe says, may suffer more because they are so isolated. The program is so consuming they have little time for a social life, let alone eating well. If only the vending machine had less candy and more high-protein snacks, Forsythe despairs.

For some of the students, though, the experience is a revelation. A number told me that they had always had trouble getting along with women until EATM. Here they find the best friends they've ever had. You can tell who's close to whom by where they sit in Zoo 2 during class. The buddies clump together in twosomes or groups of three and four. Loners, such as Wischhusen and Fidone, tend to sit in the very front row or toward the back.

That there are so many women at EATM comes as a surprise to many. The image most people have of animal trainers is men in fancy getups with big cats like Siegfried & Roy or the late Gunther Gebel-Williams of Ringling Bros. and Barnum & Bailey Circus. Also, women are not generally drawn to dangerous work, which animal training is, but then most dangerous work—mining, commercial fishing, truck driving—does not include caretaking.

Women have dominated the student body at EATM since the program opened its doors in 1974. There has been only one class with a nearly even gender split. In the school's early years, the female student body was a bellwether of change. By the eighties, more and more women became zookeepers, historically a man's job. They now represent 75 percent of keepers nationwide, according to a 2000 survey by the American Association of Zoo Keepers. In 1977, Julie Scardina was the second female trainer hired by SeaWorld. Now women count for more than half of the company's trainers.

The number of men has declined as the education requirements for keeping and training jobs has increased but the pay hasn't. Not so long ago, a zookeeper didn't even need a high school diploma, just the muscle to hoist a fifty-pound bag of feed. Now a college degree is expected for jobs that pay not much more than the minimum wage and still require scooping poop. This may have deterred men but not women, who are generally more willing to accept lower wages in exchange for following their dreams.

The preponderance of women at EATM makes for a strange hybrid—a boot camp crossed with a sorority. There are all the rules, the physical demands, the early morning reveille, the uniforms, and the class hierarchy of a military school. According to Dr. Peddie, the school is designed, like the Marines, to break the students down in the first semester, then build them back up again. However, a female faculty member burst out laughing when I told her he said this. Dr. Peddie may exaggerate, but the program is an ordeal physically and mentally. Mixed into the rigorous regimen are all kinds of girly rituals of parties, gift giving, and skits. "You're working with animal poop, getting sweaty, getting huge muscles, you have to do something that is girly," says first year Larissa Comb. Like Catholic school girls, the EATM students gussy up their uniforms with accessories. They strap on shimmering belts, pull on socks with paw prints, and clip on silver earrings in the shape of arcing dolphins. Fidone sports diamond earrings her new boyfriend gave her. Susan Patch has a small clock in the shape of a ladybug hanging from a belt loop. A first year wears striking woven belts she brought with her from Argentina. Some do go into deep schlump mode, hiding under caftan-sized jackets and pulling visors low over unwashed hair, but plenty of the students brush on mascara and even nail polish. They dab on lip gloss before taking the serval for a walk. They change their hairstyle or color as often as runway models. In these details they retain their femaleness, not to mention their individuality, as EATM grinds them down and builds them back up to the gold standard of animal people.

The irony is that before too long animal people may be on the endangered species list themselves. Working with animals is less and less a safe haven for misanthropes and introverts. Movie trainers have to work with a long list of people on the set. Most killer whale and dolphin trainers are performers. Even zookeepers are expected to set down their rakes and talk to the public more and more. A growing number of animal interaction programs, such as Discovery Cove in Florida, require trainers to work closely with the public. That is why at EATM students have to learn to speak in public and work as a team. At the school, they also learn how to behave within an overwhelmingly social hive. If EATM truly succeeds, by the time they graduate, these animal people will be people people.

October

On the first Saturday of the month, the EATM students leave their uniforms at home, slip into their civvies, and gather for a party in the San Fernando Valley at Trevor Jahangard's house. Jahangard is one of the two male second years and at twenty is one of the youngest students in his class. Some of the second years refer to him as "our baby" and tease him like a younger brother. He lives with his family, who regularly host huge get-togethers of their Jewish, Iranian, Mexican, and African American relatives. So a dinner party for some eighty EATM students and staff isn't that big a stretch. Long tables line the backyard. There's a ping-pong table in one of two living rooms and a pool table in the other. His mother has laid out a prodigious buffet of Persian food. There are platters of beef stew with lentils, cucumbers doused with yogurt, a chicken salad dotted with peas, and planks of pita. Pomegranate seeds shimmer like so many rubies in a large bowl.

What with lip gloss applied and hair curled, some of the students are almost unrecognizable from their EATM selves. Silver belly button rings twinkle and inky tattoos peek out from under low cut T-shirts. Some have brought boyfriends, so there are far more males in the mix, which seems to make for a mellower mood. Most of the students slouch on couches and watch various games unfold. Dr. Peddie picks up a pool stick. A number of students gather to heckle him. Linda Castaneda, I, and some first years hover near the buffet table. We snack on wedges of pita and talk of Siegfried & Roy. Just last night, Montecore, a seven-year-old white tiger, bit Roy Horn on the neck during a performance and dragged him offstage as if he were a felled deer. Horn's in critical condition. We debate the story the Siegfried & Roy camp has floated, that the tiger was somehow helping Horn. These novice trainers don't buy it. "He went right for his jugular. That means he thought of him as prey," Castaneda says.

Horn's attack is a visceral reminder to these young women that they have embarked on a dangerous profession. Even the most skilled trainers are at risk. VanHollebeke's mother has already called to tell her she can't work with big cats. Before she entered the program, Susan Patch's father made her promise that she'd never work with elephants. But you don't have to work with a powerful predator or gargantuan herbivore to put yourself in harm's way. As they say over and over at EATM, anything with a mouth bites.

Though the first years long for animal interaction, they mean the friendly kind, but you can't have that without tempting the toothy, snarly kind. There are hundreds of ways to get hurt at the teaching zoo. Brenda Woodhouse teaches the first years the finer points of keeping safe here and in their future jobs. She instructs the first years to locate an animal in its cage before going in, have escape routes in mind, and be ready to fight the animal if it comes to that. They should know the animal's behavior, Woodhouse says, so they can decipher its body language. An animal doing something out of the normal—say, roaming its cage when it normally sleeps—can be a bad sign. Watch out for a primate shaking its cage or bouncing up and down rigidly. Keep an eye on a parrot's beak and don't let the birds get above you. An angry tiger's eyes will flash green. A mountain lion is more aggressive than people assume. Always, always back out of a cage. Woodhouse can give pointer after pointer, but ultimately it's up to these students to find the midpoint between too much fear and not enough. Caution requires a careful balancing act that will come naturally to some and elude others, no matter how hard they try. The animals will notice if they are scared or careless. Some species will be forgiving; others will not.

Though the teaching zoo is run largely by people brand new to working with exotic animals, most injuries are inflicted by tools. There have been a few close calls. A student was bitten badly on the arms by a baboon. Another was mauled by a tapir. One student was attacked by a lion. This was in the 1980s when the teaching zoo was in cramped quarters down by the football field. As Gary Wilson tells it, the student was feeding animals in a row of cages, working her way toward the lions. The lions were in a large arena at the time. A tunnel led from their arena to their cages. It was blocked with a plywood board. In a fit of excitement, Hatari, the male lion, banged on the board so hard he broke the chain that connected the tunnel to the arena. The lion charged through the resulting narrow breach. The student with the food had her back to the big cat and never saw or heard him coming. The lion grabbed her from behind, sinking his canines into her neck and shoulder. A male student struck Hatari with a rake, breaking it over the cat's back, according to one alum. The lion let go and hightailed it to a corner of the compound. He hid behind a barn. Jamie LoVullo, who was then a student at the school, says, "It was the first time you learned that an animal you loved could kill you."

The injured student survived, but the bite caused nerve damage to her face. Whether EATM would survive wasn't certain at first. The student sued the school and the EATM staff, including the then director, Bill Brisby. They settled out of court. Wilson heard the student used the settlement to start a dolphin swim program in the Bahamas. EATM continued. Hatari was not put down.

All the students know the story of the lion bite, but over the years it has been turned around some, as many EATM tales are. There are rumors that she hadn't told the school that she was hard of hearing and a hemophiliac. Wilson says he doubts she was a bleeder; she resisted going to the emergency room after the attack, he says—not typical hemophiliac behavior. She was somewhat deaf, Wilson says, but as he remembers, it didn't make a difference. The students who saw the lion escape never had a chance to warn her.

Wilson himself has been attacked twice at the school. In 2000, Kissu, the declawed mountain lion, turned on him while he was in a caged area with the cat. It was orientation week. A film crew from *Animal Planet* was at the teaching zoo. Wilson was leading the cougar through a caged corridor to a play area. The cat dawdled. Wilson called, "Kitty, kitty!" Kissu turned and looked at him. His pupils had become huge, black discs. Wilson knew he was in trouble. He didn't have a bobstick, which was a mistake. Kissu lunged at Wilson and bit down on his elbow. He had on a sweatshirt and a jacket, so the mountain lion's teeth did not puncture him. Wilson knocked the cat off and grabbed him by the scruff. He tried to push Kissu into his cage, but the cougar charged back out and sank his canines into Wilson's rump. Wilson grabbed the cougar by the back of the neck again, and this time shoved him into his cage. *Animal Planet* caught the white-faced Wilson fresh from the attack as he told Dr. Peddie what had just happened. "What saved me was that he didn't have claws," Wilson says. A Dutch student raced Wilson in his BMW to the emergency room. "That was probably the scariest part of the whole thing."

Afterward, Wilson wondered what had triggered Kissu's attack. He had taken care of the cat in his home when Kissu was a cub and had spent hours sitting in his cage. He called Sled Reynolds, a professional trainer who lends the teaching zoo its camels. Wilson asked Reynolds why he thought Kissu had attacked him. He doesn't need an excuse, Reynolds told Wilson. "I tend to be more analytical than that, but he's probably right. Even though an animal is an animal you have worked with a long time, they can still turn on you."

Wilson still dreams of Kissu charging at him, his canines bared, his pupils like big black holes. It's not his only recurring nightmare. He also dreams of the time when Lulu, a camel, nearly killed him. That was more harrowing, he says, because there was nothing he could do. In the spring of 2002, Lulu delivered Kaleb at the teaching zoo. Wilson had stopped by the school with his wife, Cindy, and their two children to visit the baby camel. Some students and staff milled around. Before leaving, Wilson tried to milk Lulu. The camel, who Brenda Woodhouse says was grinding her teeth and seemed agitated, was in no mood to have her teats pulled. As Wilson leaned under her, Lulu kicked him with her front legs, knocking him to the ground. Then she sat down on him, pressing him into the hard-packed earth with her belly. Wilson heard his ribs crack. His arm was twisted. Woodhouse says all you could see of Wilson were his legs sticking out from under Lulu. "I was just pinned," Wilson says. "I thought this is a really shitty way to die. In the dirt, under a camel's belly. I can't breathe. I'll pass out."

People screamed and pushed. The camel wouldn't budge until a student stabbed her in the side with a Leatherman. Wilson escaped. His arm was hurt and some ribs were broken. The more serious damage may have been to his psyche. In recent years, Wilson has started to have panic attacks. He thinks it's due to years of sixty-to-eighty-hour-long weeks he pulled over the years, but the camel attack, not to mention the cougar attack, couldn't have helped. Still, having a camel try to kill you has its benefits. Always the optimist, Wilson says, "I feel fortunate I came close to death. I appreciate life more."

In actuality, it's the animals you least suspect that inflict the most wounds at the teaching zoo. This past summer, Sequoia, the demure-looking mule deer, beat up a second year who was training her. The student was in the deer's pen when Sequoia rose up on her back legs and clocked the second year with her front hooves. The blow cracked open the student's head and left dark bruises all over her chest and legs. Maybe the deer went ballistic because the second year had been in Big Carns and smelled like the cats. Maybe it was a jealous rage. The student was dating Sequoia's favorite human, the gardener at the zoo, who lovingly brings the deer browse and sits by her cage. "Deer aren't very nice," she tells me. "They can be very aggressive. Nobody told me that until I got on her."

Back in May, Birdman, the kinkajou, nailed Mary VanHollebeke. Kinkajous resemble fairy-tale animals, with big, luminous eyes, pertly pointed noses, and long curlicue tails. They are nocturnal, so when VanHollebeke stepped into Birdman's cage to leave his food, usually he snoozed away in his dark den box. That day she leaned over to set his bowl of food on the ground and stood up to find, to her surprise, the kinkajou out on his shelf. He bit her right hand and then her left, sinking his teeth deep into her flesh. He held on. VanHollebeke tucked Birdman between her legs and squeezed, so the kinkajou couldn't thrash. Another student tried to scare, poke, and pry Birdman off. He wouldn't budge. VanHollebeke could hear him slurping her blood. After a few minutes, Birdman finally let go. He'd bitten all the way through her hand. "There was a lot of blood," she told me. "It was all over." An infection took root in one hand. VanHollebeke had to go on an antibiotic drip every four hours. She wore bandages on both hands for two weeks. She needed two months of physical therapy to repair the muscle and nerve damage to her left hand. VanHollebeke ends her story by saying, "He's got the sweetest face in the world."

The most recent emergency room visit was the work of Gabby, the parrot. The macaws, with their sharp hooked beaks strong enough to break a finger, inflict many of the wounds at the teaching zoo. Students work with them at close range, and the parrots can be quite peevish. Gabby is the same parrot who punctured a student trainer's hand during orientation week. Two weeks ago, the parrot bit again, this time on the student's lip. The second year had leaned close to the bird for a kiss. Instead, she felt a sharp pinch, the warm ooze of blood, and a flap of her lip roll into her mouth. Her mother paid for a plastic surgeon to stitch her lower lip back together.

Students who have been munched wear their scars like purple hearts. They describe them with a mix of world-weariness and self-mockery. There is some relief in being hurt, in knowing exactly what it's like to be chomped or rammed, in knowing you survived, and in knowing that you are not infallible. An animal bite takes a bit of the ego out of these young trainers, which can be a good thing. It's the students who get bitten repeatedly that the staff worries about. They have their eye on one first year who has already been bitten a couple of times, including a chomp from a lemur.

The unscathed—nearly all the first years, including Castaneda, and some of the second years, including Brunelli—may dread the unknown. However, having skin that has never been breached by fangs or beak and never been bruised by horn or hoof may make you feel superior. Even the levelheaded Brunelli can't help feeling a tad proud of her no-bite status. To her, it's proof that she may be a natural with animals. This confidence is unlikely to survive EATM. Few students graduate without a nip, if not a puncture wound or two.

As for Horn, the general consensus near the buffet table is that the showman had been playing with fire for years by bunking with tigers, romping with tigers, and snuggling with tigers. They are, after all, tigers. Up until now, despite his talents, Horn had been lucky. And whatever happened on stage, Horn was very unlucky to have fallen down in front of his tiger. These trainers in training know enough to realize you never want to resemble prey to a large, toothy, muscular predator.

The conversation runs out of steam, so we head outside into the dark to see the mews Jahangard has built in a corner of his family's backyard. In addition to going to EATM, Jahangard is apprenticing to be a falconer, a consuming process on its own. The party is still going strong, though some of the revelers have to get up at 6 A.M. or so. On the back porch, a first year tells Dr. Peddie a fart story. He guffaws. Then he regales us with one of his classics, the one about Boobs Mackenzie. Not long after she'd had a botched breast reduction, Boobs brought in her dog. She said, "Dr. Peddie, would you look at this?" He thought she meant something about the dog. She lifted up her blouse. As he tells it, "She had her nipples pointing south, right at the floor." He laughs at his own story. As the clock nears 11 P.M., people start to say their goodbyes and drift toward their cars, as the prospect of hosing poop on too little sleep, and possibly with a hangover, begins to weigh on their young minds.

At 8 A.M. the next morning, a deep fog cloaks the zoo, softening the hard edges of the chain-link front gate. As I walk through the gauzy mist, a bespectacled female figure near the front office calls out to me, "You've come at a great time. We've got eighty pigeons."

That is eighty decrepit homing pigeons to be pulled. Eighty pigeons is an unprecedented number of birds; usually, the school gets a dozen or so at a time. The birds always arrive unannounced, but once here, they are quickly dispensed with. The owner of the pigeons, a guy who has been bringing them here since EATM started, lifts them out one by one and hands them to a second year who goes by the name of CVP. She's well liked by both classes. She has a round face and a very feminine voice that nearly trills. As the owner hands her the pigeons, he points out especially old ones for me to see, such as one with a very craggy waddle. I don't really want to see the birds, so I keep my eyes on my notebook. The pigeons coo and coo. CVP matter-of-factly loads them into two crates, then totes them down the front road to the hay barn, which is next to the Rat Room and across from Zulu's cage in Primate Gardens.

Word spreads quickly, and before long a small circle of apprehensive, quiet women in sweatshirts has formed by the barn. These nurturers have come to be executioners. CVP has set the two crates of softly cooing pigeons next to two large garbage cans. Just behind her in the barn, another second year has set up a butcher station. The gray light glints off the large cleaver with which she'll chop off the wings and feet.

"We're here for you," CVP says to the small circle. "If you want to cry, cry on our shoulders. Some people cry. Some people laugh. Try to respect how people react."

The small circle freezes in place. Some put their fingers in their mouths. CVP plucks a bird out of a crate and calms its fluttering wings. She wraps her left hand around its body. "It's dislocation. You'll pick up the bird and pull its head right off." With her right hand, she hooks her index and middle finger around the bird's head, so the knuckles of each hand are touching. "My hands are tiny," she says to herself. "Don't let them get loose. They're homing pigeons. They'll fly home."

She leans over and into the garbage can, pressing the bird against the side. "Blood will squirt out. Don't look down at the bottom of the bucket. They might blink. [The body] will twitch for about a minute and a half, so press it against the side of the can." And then unexpectedly, without missing a beat, she jerks her right arm and off pops the pigeon's head. We don't see it, but hear it thud on the bottom of the garbage can. "The quicker you do it, the better. The longer you take, the worse it gets," she says. "He's still twitching."

The small group frowns and shifts from foot to foot. There are a few doleful uh-uhs. Everyone is clearly uncomfortable, but there's not one tear or giggle. The first two volunteers step forward. One says,."I think I might laugh." They both lean over the can, birds in hand, follow CVP's orders, and quickly pull the heads off. They turn their heads so they can't see the bottom of the bucket. The one who thought she'd laugh smiles uncontrollably and titters slightly as they stand there forever, waiting for the bird's nervous system to still. When they hand the pigeon bodies over to be chopped, their hands are slick with blood. "Oh my god," someone in the circle says. Another two volunteers step up, including the bright-eyed first year from Georgia who took care of baby deer. "Give me an ugly one," she says.

As the cleaver chops away in the background, the two first years dutifully take the birds in hand, lean over the can, and pull. Then the Georgian lets loose with a kind of play by play. "Mine moves too much; uh, mine moves too much. He's trying to walk." She half smiles, half grimaces as she holds the jerky body against the can. "There's like juice all over my hand. It just shot up my pants." Waiting students stare at their feet and rub their hands on their pants.

Some more first years, including Castaneda, arrive just as this twosome hand over their pigeons and march off with their bloodied hands held in front of them like zombies. The cleaver thwack-thwacks in the barn. "Is that blood?" one of the students who just walked up asks. "I'm going to faint." Castaneda jumps in. "Can I get an ugly one?" she asks. Maybe because she missed

CVP's matter-of-fact introduction, Castaneda is the first student to look clearly upset as she takes a pigeon in her hand and assumes the execution position at the garbage can. So does her partner. CVP coaches them. When Castaneda pulls, the head doesn't come off; she has to jerk a second time. "Oh god," she moans. Her partner begins to cry. Castaneda wells up. They hand over their birds and wipe their eyes on their upper arms as blood drips off their fingers.

Just then, a slight, older student with bleached blond hair walks up. This is Chandra Cohn. She is already crying—tears running down her cheeks, eyes red, sniffling, the works. The mood quickly tumbles downhill. What was grim but businesslike suddenly becomes the scene of a tragic accident or massacre. Thwack! Thwack! the cleaver pounds. One pigeon sits in a crate by itself. It's so pretty no one will pull it.

"This is the hardest thing you'll ever have to do here," CVP says, trying to restore calm. She says this with the slick red hands of an ax murderer. When she hasn't been showing first years the drill, she's been pulling pigeons like a machine. There are just so many birds to kill, far more than the first years can handle. A couple of other second years have arrived to help and quickly begin popping heads off. "Whoa, got a squirter," one says. "Dude, this one is blinking."

The group of onlookers grows as a few staff members and second years arrive to watch. They mean well, but the onlookers add to the ghoulish spectacle. The student from Argentina with the stylish belts and earrings that dangle more than they should pulls halfheartedly with lips trembling, wailing, "I can't do it." A student standing back from the group near Primate Gardens lets out a deep sob and walks off. Another student pops a head off, then drops the bird's body, which thrashes in the can, its wings rustling the plastic garbage bag. She has to reach in and grab it. She opens her mouth so wide in disgust you can see her silver tongue stud. The pigeons in the crates grow quiet and still.

"Whoa, got a live one," calls the second year, chopping away as a headless body flaps across her cutting board. Somehow Cohn summons the nerve to step up to the garbage can, but when she pulls her pigeon she sobs uncontrollably and shakes. Next to her, CVP pops another head off. A very small first year with an upturned nose and a pretty, starlet way about her strolls up with her pants tucked into her wellies. She smiles and says, "I want to do it before I get sick and pass out."

"We know first aid," CVP says.

"I have a problem with anxiety," the first year says, smiling, and paces in a circle, while CVP collects a bird for her.

"You're going to realize you're going to do things you never thought you could," another second year volunteers.

The first year jumps from foot to foot. Finally, bird in hand, the demure student leans over the can—the smile, a bit sad now, still on her face. She turns her head, jerks her arm, and, poised, pulls the bird's head off.

Some of the students who went first have drifted back, their hands now clean. They've come for their pigeon bands. It's an EATM tradition to keep a shiny leg band from a pigeon you've pulled. Typically, people add them to their key chains. They are half badges of honor, half mementos of the sacrificed birds. The bands are also, well, pretty. "Can I have a blue band?" a student with eyes still red from crying asks. Even Cohn, who took it worse than anyone, returns for a band, though she's still sniffling. "The pigeon was the same color as my bird," she whimpers as she holds her hand out for the band.

The morning wears on and the hysteria passes. Eyes are dried. Notes are compared. Pigeon bands are wedged onto key chains. Castaneda tries not to think about the way she could feel the bird's vertebrae pull apart and how its warm body trembled in her palm. As I walk up the front road, I run into Anita Wischhusen. I ask why she didn't pull a pigeon. Because, she informs me, she has no intention of doing so—period. She's hoping for another outbreak of Newcastle disease. If not that, she'll find a loophole in the school's rules. Before I get to ask her why, we reach the front office and are within earshot of a staff member. Wischhusen goes quiet and walks away from me. She returns and hands me a note that reads, "I can't talk about the pigeons in front of Holly. I don't want her to know."

The pigeon bodies are stashed in the freezer for the next twenty-four hours to kill any parasites. The feet are thrown away. The wings are for the taking. They make good behavioral enrichment for the big cats, monkeys, and raccoons. In Nutrition, Amber Cavett collects a couple of pigeon wings, pokes holes in them with a knife, and threads strings through the holes. I follow her down to Samburu's cage. He hisses at us as we walk up to him. She's been training him to take food more calmly but making only marginal progress. While the caracal is closed off to one side of his cage, Cavett slips into the empty half and ties the wings to the top of the enclosure so they dangle like a mobile.

She steps out and lifts a gate. Samburu rockets into the other half of his cage. The raccoon next door has scaled the side of his enclosure to see what all the fuss is. Samburu turns his face up to the wings, sniffs, then shoots straight up about four feet, front legs extended, and bats the wings with both paws. They sway like piñatas. A few more lightning-quick jumps and bats, and he's got the wings down and one in his mouth. The caracal lies belly down on the floor as he devours the wing. The feathers fan absurdly out of his mouth, the bones cracking loudly between his teeth as the cycle of life spins on.

The next morning, as I walk in from the parking lot just shy of

7 A.M., the dark silhouette of a student shoots past me in the gloom. Her name is near the top of the alphabet on the roll call. The teaching zoo's lights color the morning mist lavender. Just down the front road, the heat lamps glow a hazy orange in Parrot Gardens. The birds squawk lazily. A low mooing emanates from deep within the zoo. Clarence slowly lifts his anvil-shaped head and looks my way. At the morning meeting inside Zoo 1, CVP stands and congratulates yesterday's pigeon pullers. "We're very proud of you," she says. There's talk of which vents should be open or closed in Primate Gardens, warnings to keep extension cords out of animals' reach, and an announcement that the garbage disposal in Nutrition is clogged. The meeting over, the students sleepily zip their hoodies, hunch their shoulders against a damp chill, and head into the early morning gloom.

I walk with Castaneda down the gravel back road to Big Carns. She's still upset that pulling a pigeon upset her. Castaneda is five foot eleven inches. She's been patronizingly called "a big girl." She used to be even bigger and keeps a photo of herself seventy-five pounds heavier taped inside her planner. Whatever her weight, she's never felt or acted girly. In her family "whatever happens, I'm the one who has to be okay with it. I even cleaned out my sister's litter box when it was like sludge," she tells me. Standing by the cougar boys, Sage and Spirit, who bound about boxing with each other, she pauses and then says, "Just think about it. How can you murder something with your own hands?" She shakes her head.

"We don't seem to have any poop today," VanHollebeke calls. She's in charge of the cleaning crew of first years in Big Carns this morning. A day without poop here is a holiday. Most everyone agrees that the big cats produce some of the nastiest-smelling guano. As students gingerly pick up log after log with tongs, they often have to pause and turn their heads. The stink is solid and it gathers at the back of your mouth. One first year even pulls his T-shirt up over his nose to fend off the stench.

The cages in this area form a large letter C. This is what Taj, Kissu, Sage and Sprit, Kiara, Savuti, and Legend call home. C.J. also lives here, as do two servals. In the middle is the arena, a roomy enclosure with logs, a den box, and platforms. Several of the animals take turns spending a day per week in the arena. It gives them a change of scenery, room to stretch, and a bed of grass to lounge on.

Cleaning in Big Carns is like working in a federal prison. Doors have to be carefully locked, then unlocked, then locked again. Nearly every morning an animal is moved or "switched," as they say, into the arena. This involves a sequence of opening and closing doors that looks simple enough, but if one little mistake is made, an animal or human could end up hurt or dead. That is why a staff member is always present. Today, Legend comes out and Kissu goes in. This requires Legend to pass Kiara's cage, where the wolf and the lioness will go at it through the chain-link. Though they have been neighbors for five years or so, given the chance to quarrel violently, they will, so Kiara has to be closed into her bedroom. That takes some chicken necks and some pleading, but eventually the lioness sashays to her den box.

The wolf returns to her cage, and a small army of students swarm into the empty arena to spruce it up for Kissu. Students carry in a basket filled with cheap colognes, spices, talcum powder, spray deodorant, mouthwash, and lotion. Like the pigeon wings, these scents are behavioral enrichment for the big cats—something to mix up their day and a chance to use their natural instincts. The students dab perfume here and sprinkle onion powder there. One of the spices makes Kissu so ecstatic she drools and rolls on her back, but no one is sure whether it's the roast beef seasoning or the poultry seasoning or maybe the steak seasoning, so they scatter them all. Students exit, locks are unlocked, doors opened and closed. Kissu bolts into the arena, lips parted, eyes bright, darting from log to stump to rock, breathing deeply.

Taj, the nine-year-old Bengal tiger, has a cage twice as big as the others with a view of the back road. Here, she can slink along an end of her cage, stalking students and other animals on leashed walks as they go by. She also has a pool, in which she lounges with her tail draped over the side. Anita Wischhusen gingerly pokes a piece of chicken neck through the bars to lure the tiger to one side of her cage so they can clean the other half. "Don't put your fingers through," Brenda Woodhouse warns. With a low rumble, Taj steps her way and snatches the neck with her large teeth from Wischhusen's grasp. The student shudders, squeezes her eyes closed, and giggles as if she's just been tickled. As Wischhusen steps back from the cage, she says to me, "It's hard not to talk to Taj. I just found out that you can chuff at her."

"Only if she chuffs at you first," Castaneda says, standing nearby.

"Has she chuffed at you?" Wischhusen asks.

"No," Castaneda answers.

"Well, you got Schmoo for Davis week," Wischhusen retorts.

This is a very sore point for Wischhusen just now; it's becoming the same for Castaneda. While the second years take an upcoming, weeklong field trip, the first years have been assigned to take care of various animals. The competition was intense, as usual, for Schmoo. Only the star students get the star animal.

Schmoo is the only marine mammal at EATM. She is also the most time-consuming animal at the teaching zoo. Her student trainers spend hours thawing her mackerel and squid. She is in most of the zoo's educational shows. Her long list of commands must be regularly rehearsed so she doesn't forget them. Her student trainers are forever cleaning or fixing her pool, which was meant for a backyard, not for a sea lion. Consequently, staff assigns Schmoo only to students with straight A's and perfect attendance, even if they are only temporary caretakers. That is because the sea lion takes so much work that students' grades often suffer; the students have to be in a position to let their grades slip without risk of flunking out.

About a dozen first years asked to be assigned to Schmoo for the week. Only four were chosen. Wischhusen, who does not have straight A's, was not one of them, and she's pissed. She suspects it's because she is in her forties. However, she did get Kiara, which is far from a booby prize. Castaneda, who has straight A's and nary a blemish on her attendance record, got Schmoo. This is one of the main reasons she has worked so hard: to win these kinds of plum assignments. But what she didn't expect were the resentful comments. Wischhusen's isn't the first, and Castaneda is getting tired of it.

"Well, you got Kiara," Castaneda counters as Wischhusen in her pink wellies walks off.

Gary Wilson stands by the front office watching a second year with almond-shaped eyes and hair down to her waist give Cyrano, a blue and gold macaw with a slightly crooked mouth, a pedicure. She saws away with an emery board on his front nails. Cyrano keeps trying to pinch her hand with his black beak. Wilson watches briefly, pokes around at his palm-sized computer, and then announces her grade: "I'll give you an 85." He and the student walk to the other end of the zoo, where she collects Bubbles, a young opossum with beady, glassine eyes and little, fluttering black ears. The second year hooks a leash on the opossum, and Bubbles trots alongside her like a puppy out for a walk. "She's doing fewer open-mouthed threats," the second year tells Wilson. He gives her a 95.

Time always flies at EATM. It is already midterm week for the second years. They have to demonstrate how well they have trained their animals so far this semester. The way it works is that

Wilson, his PDA in one hand, a small video camera in the other, roams the zoo, meeting students at various cages at appointed times. He nearly always runs late, so the students often wait nervously by their animals, warming them up or gauging their frame of mind. Wilson, considered a tough grader in his academic courses, is a softer touch in his training lab. He often gives the students the benefit of the doubt: animals have moods; they don't feel well sometimes; they get distracted by scents, sounds, and sights; they can be scared by the wind or a maintenance truck driving by. Still, students are embarrassed and frustrated when after weeks of training their animals appear to have amnesia or, worse, nip them during a midterm or final.

Wilson also considers the animal itself, how experienced it is. He expects the students to teach more ambitious behaviors to veterans of training such as Abbey or Nick. For her midterm, Amy Mohelnitzky trimmed Abbey's toenails, though the pooch will only let the second year do it when she's lying on her side. Wilson gives her a 100. Anderson demonstrates the progress she's making in teaching Nick to pull a cart. So far, Anderson's gotten the chubby horse to wear blinders and a halter. She attached two bamboo poles to his halter and trained him to pull those. Nick complies but he's tense. Anderson gets a 90.

For nervous prey animals like Starsky, Wilson has far lower expectations. During her midterm, VanHollebeke sits on the concrete ledge and holds out the elongated spoon filled with alfalfa pellets to the wary cavy hiding at the back of his cage. She gets a B. Wilson also considers the species. In terms of brain power, Wilson says the reptiles are the hardest to train. Marlowe Robertson, a second year with a fondness for reptiles, is the first to have made any headway with Happy, the alligator, having trained him to follow a target pole. On the flip side, primates have so much brain power, Wilson says, "They have all day to think about how to do the least amount of work for a treat."

At the far end of the zoo, Wilson finds Becki Brunelli waiting by Goblin. Brunelli has graduated from sticking her finger in Goblin's ear to prodding it with a spoon. She squats down by Goblin's cage and calls the baboon over. Goblin lopes over and on Brunelli's command presses her nose against her cage.

"Ear," Brunelli says.

Goblin turns her head sideways, bringing her ear closer to the cage. Brunelli slides the shiny handle through the bars and toward Goblin's ear. She misses her target slightly. Goblin's eyes widen and she jumps as if she's been goosed. "Sorry," Brunelli says to Goblin and then puts the spoon handle in the baboon's ear. Wilson gives her a 95, docking Brunelli five points for her poor aim.

Next, Wilson meets up with a petite, freckled second year by Friday the raccoon's cage. The second year steps inside the cage with a scale. As soon as she sets it down, Friday tries to jump on. "Station! station!" she repeats, but the raccoon wants on that scale. The second year has to block Friday with her arms while she readies the scale. She and Wilson crack up. Despite the raccoon's enthusiasm, she gets a 90: "His stationing needs to be more solid," Wilson says.

Wilson ends the morning at the hornbills' pen with the second year he considers to be one of the best trainers in her class, April Matott, a small, understated blonde from Albany, New York. Matott asks Wilhelmina, a thirty-year-old Abyssinian ground hornbill with a crippled wing, to step up on a perch. The ancient, unsteady bird complies. This is a major accomplishment because early in her training Wilhelmina fell and accidentally spiked herself on a shoot of bamboo. Matott gets a 100.

"There's only a few students who are training the animal and not vice versa," Wilson tells me.

* * *

There are many unexpected lessons at the teaching zoo. Students learn that the camel's breath smells like rotting, fermenting broth, that the owl's poop is stinky and sticky, that tortoises pass loud, stinky bursts of methane. "I've learned that everything farts," a first year from New York City tells me. EATM desensitizes these students to things that would make most people vomit. A squirrel monkey pooped on a student's head. "It was like apple sauce," she says. A first year tipped over a bucket of blood in Nutrition. It dumped into her boot. While another was organizing the walk-in freezer, a shelf full of frozen pigeon parts showered down on her. A frozen, headless pigeon body hit her in the mouth. Feathers stuck to her lips.

During the morning cleaning, a small contingent tiptoes into Zulu's cage, gingerly stepping over creamy pools of his ejaculate. A first year accidentally dipped her hand in one. In the Rat Room, students scan the bins looking for half-cannibalized rats to pluck out. While hosing poop out of cages, many a student has shot a stream hard at a log, only to have the water splash up into their mouths. And then there's Dr. Peddie.

No one can quite prepare you for the vet's ability to make your stomach turn. He lulls you with scientific terms, then bam! He hits you in the gut with a vivid description of an abscess. By their very nature his vet classes cover nauseating material, but he just seems to relish it.

Take this morning's lecture, for example. It starts out innocently enough as he describes neutrophils, lymphocytes, eosinophils, basophils, and monocytes to a class of second years. A few struggle to stay awake to note down what the various white blood cells do, their ponytails swaying as their heads droop. "It's hard to make blood interesting," the vet confesses, his brow knitting.

He cuts to a favorite topic, not exactly a crowd-pleaser, but one that is sure to wake a few sleepy heads—pus. He recounts the story of his best friend, who just had surgery; the incision became infected. Pus was just pouring out of it, he exclaims. "I don't like your stories," a student in back says. He flashes slides of sick animals: a puppy with lockjaw, a lamb that has to be put down. "Not all pus is liquid. This pus is like cheese," he says.

"Yuck," someone says, which prompts a chorus of shushes. An image of two large worms flashes. Someone moans, "Oh man."

Last but not least is the image of a goat with something indistinguishable but hugely swollen hanging off its behind. "You're looking at the south end," Dr. Peddie chortles, pointing at the slide. "That is his scrotum. It's as big as a melon. *This* is full of pus."

The next morning finds the vet far less jovial. Dr. Peddie has ruled today, the second Tuesday in October, Zeus's last. Dr. Peddie will put down the ailing iguana some time this morning, after the students are done cleaning the zoo and before class.

Down in the claustrophobic Reptile Room, where the snakes and lizards are stacked in cages one atop the other, the morning's cleaning is just wrapping up. "Everybody pooped today," Jena Anderson tells me proudly. "Everybody had stinky poop." Now they've moved on to feeding. Anderson attends her "barbecue." She's arranged pinkies and fuzzies, dead baby rats with black eyes bulging through their paper-thin eyelids, on a space heater like so many hot dogs. While the pinkies and fuzzies heat, Anderson heads over to Nutrition to make the turtles' breakfast. She loads produce onto a tray and then adds two roses dusted with cookie crumbs. "Presentation is everything," she says. "Bon appétit."

In addition to training Nick, Anderson is a Reptile Room manager. She and five other classmates oversee the general care of the teaching zoo's scaled collection. This includes several very large snakes: Precious, the yellow anaconda; Morty, the Burmese python;

and Ceylon, the Indian python. There are smaller snakes, such as Mupu II, the California Mountain king snake, and Kia and Kio, the sand boas. They recently produced a pile of wriggling baby sand boas. Conan, the popular Chinese water dragon, lives here, lounging in a pool shaped like a volcano. So does Howie, the blue-tongued skink owned by a movie trainer, who retrieves the lizard for a job occasionally, and Dot, the African gecko that doesn't stick.

In each class, there are typically only a handful of students interested in the reptiles. Usually, there are also a handful who'd rather go through life never having touched a snake. They'll have to get over that. Currently, only Happy, the alligator, is trained, but a good number of the reptiles are used in the teaching zoo's shows. A favorite stunt for private birthday shows is to get a group of volunteers from the audience, have the kids line up, close their eyes, and hold their arms out. Then the EATM students lug out Ceylon and drape her over the kids' outstretched arms. And when you clean the Reptile Room, there's a good chance you'll have to touch a snake or two. The large snakes like Precious are carried outside and allowed to slither around on the pavement for a stretch.

This morning in the Reptile Room, all the animals have been fed except for Zeus. No last meal. No last cleaning either. She sits near the back of her cage oblivious to her fate. Marlowe Robertson arrives looking forlorn. She is Happy's trainer and, like Anderson, a Reptile Room manager. She has on a big leather glove. She slides open the glass door to Zeus's cage and reaches in. Two more Reptile Room managers appear. They collect Blaze, the corn snake, and load him into a carrier. The snake has been very sluggish and may need to be euthanized as well. We start up the gravel back road, a large lizard's life weighing on our minds. Robertson carries Zeus on her upturned palm. The iguana remains still, her rounded nose forward. Robertson's eyes are wide and moist. No one talks, except that when we pass Wendell, the pygmy goat, standing atop his box, Robertson sings out in a wobbly goat voice, "Hello, Wendell." He flicks his black tassel of a tail. On we walk. The lethargic corn snake nearly wiggles out of its carrier in a burst of unexpected energy. By Parrot Gardens, a dark-eyed second year hurries up to us. "Can we say good-bye?" She strokes Zeus's head and stares into the lizard's unblinking eyes.

Dr. Peddie leans out of Zoo 1, tight-lipped, grim-looking, with rubber gloves on, and a syringe in one hand. He waves us in and quickly gets down to business. While Robertson holds her, Dr. Peddie injects a dose of pentobarbital sodium into Zeus's ribs. Suddenly, she is animated and trying to squirm out of Robertson's hold. This is typical of animals about to be put down, Dr. Peddie says. He has Robertson hold Zeus's belly down on the table in Zoo 1 so that the lizard's tail drapes over the side. Dr. Peddie gets down on one knee and injects another dose of the barbiturate into the base of the iguana, just under her tail. He gets lucky and hits a major vein.

"Reptiles have low blood pressure," he says. "This is going to take awhile." Robertson holds the lizard against her chest. Zeus grows stiller, but waves her head around occasionally. "Be careful because she can still bite you," Dr. Peddie warns. As death slowly comes for the lizard, the vet examines the corn snake, which seems to have miraculously recovered. Dr. Peddie sets the snake on the table, then rolls it over. The corn snake quickly rights about half of itself: not bad. Dr. Peddie gives the corn snake a reprieve. Meanwhile, the tip of Zeus's pink tongue lolls a bit. Then her eyes slide closed, but her sides still push in and out. Her plump tongue protrudes more and more.

Her whole tongue sticks out. Her stillness is indisputable. Robertson smothers a sob. Tears run down her cheeks. Dr. Peddie holds up a plastic garbage bag, and Robertson gently lowers the iguana inside. She wraps both her arms around the bag and clutches Zeus in a way she never could while the lizard lived. Holding the dead iguana close, Robertson walks out of the classroom into the constant California sunshine.

Later, after the bunnies have been bathed, after a student has nearly been knocked down by Sequoia while leashing the mule deer for her midterm (Wilson gave her an 80), after Rosie, the baboon, and Abbey have almost run into each other while out on walks, and after Dr. Peddie has lectured the first years on what he calls the wow of the heart, all the second years gather for one last look at Zeus in Zoo 1.

Her still body slides out of the green plastic bag onto the very same table where the iguana got her lethal injections. The students gather around. A single fly buzzes the room. The iguana's pink tongue flaps sloppily. The vet points out the papery layers of loose skin on Zeus. She'd begun to molt, he says. Her front legs are robust, but her back legs are withered and flaccid. Robertson stands next to Dr. Peddie. She looks on, interested but sad, as the vet turns the iguana on her back. He cuts a neat straight line right up Zeus's belly, exposing her glistening pink insides. There are yellow-orange globs of fat tucked around her three-chambered heart. Dr. Peddie runs his fingers along her intestine. "This is called slipping the guts," he says. "I feel something like tapioca pearls."

"Eew," someone moans.

"See, there is one hole for everything, pooping and giving birth," he adds. The only abnormality he finds is a small yellow cyst on the liver. He pinches the cyst and a discharge comes out. "It's cheesy," he says. Then he pokes Zeus's small heart with his scissors. The meaty pump seizes. That sets off a wail of disgust followed by hearty chuckles. Some students shake their hands, squirm, or roll their eyes.

"Do it again, Dr. Freakenstein," someone calls.

A mischievous grin on his face, Dr. Peddie pokes Zeus's heart again. It lurches, prompting more cries and laughs. Robertson, stone-faced, strokes the dead lizard's foot with her index finger and says a silent good-bye.

Briz

Bill Brisby appears to have had some kind of midlife crisis—a rather spectacular one. Like a solar flare, its effects spread far and wide and can still be felt. In the 1960s, he was an award-winning high school science teacher. He had a crew cut, geeky, thick-framed glasses, and was even a bit pudgy, according to his longtime friend and colleague Lynn Doria. He lived with his wife, Beverly, and three children. By the end of the 1970s he had morphed into an exotic animal trainer and started a one-of-a-kind school. He let his close-cropped hair grow beyond his ears and sprouted a shaggy, graying beard. He dressed in khaki, adopting that African big hunter look that so many trainers and zookeepers favor. He divorced his wife of twenty-six years and married one of his students thirty years his junior. "Everything about him changed," says Doria. "He went from one extreme to the other. He never found the middle."

Briz, as everyone still calls him, was the kind of man who is easily mythologized even while still alive. He had the bravado of a man who could wrestle with a lion—and did. He was a charismatic, inspiring teacher, the kind that could beat you down and build you up at the same time. Former students still recite Brizisms such as: "When you know everything, you know nothing," "It's okay not to know something, but go find it out," or my personal favorite: "You can train a chicken and do a great act in Vegas."

He had the sharp eye of an entrepreneur, spotting an opportunity from a far distance. He was audacious enough to teach himself how to train dangerous animals. He was a glass-half-full type who believed in the power of hard work and pushing yourself to the limit. He didn't need much sleep. His second and much younger wife had trouble keeping up with him. He had big hands and a big voice. He was a ruggedly handsome alpha male who did things his way, no matter who it pissed off. Women—particularly young women—were drawn to him.

Most everyone says that you either loved or hated Briz, which may be more myth than truth. I eventually realized this was a polite way of saying he could be a first-class asshole. I did come across a few alums who hated him, but even they had a deep, if grudging, respect for the man who made such a wild dream come true. "Some people thought he was arrogant," says Jamie LoVullo (EATM '83). "I thought he was incredible. Of course, he wasn't perfect."

There's not too much in Briz's early life that points to his later transformation. According to a lengthy obituary, Briz was born in 1924 and grew up in LA's Compton long before it became known for gang warfare and inner-city strife. His family had animals—nothing exotic, but plenty of cats, dogs, chickens, goats, and rabbits. Though he taught science most of his career, his B.S. was in physical education from Colorado A&M, according to college records. He embarked on what would appear to be a fairly ordinary life and career, coaching football and teaching at Fillmore High School, where he remained from 1950 to 1969. However, Briz wasn't ordinary. At home, his family had foxes, raccoons, a South

American tree otter, ducks, a ring-tailed cat, and rabbits. He became head of the science department. He won awards. He set up an outdoor classroom on Rincon Island, a man-made island off the coast near Santa Barbara. He convinced Edward Teller, the father of the H-bomb, and Charles Richter, who invented the earthquake scale, to speak to his science club. He invited exotic animal trainers Hubert Wells and Wally Ross to visit his classroom.

There are various myths about Briz. One is that in the 1960s he trained dolphins in the Navy's program at Point Mugu in Malibu. His obituary says he was the curator of the center's aquarium; however, Dr. Sam Ridgeway, who began the Navy's marine mammal program, says Briz never worked there. Ridgeway recalls Briz's coming to the lagoon for water samples, but that's it. Everyone assumes that Briz had a degree in science, but he followed his physical education degree with a master's in secondary administration, receiving that degree in 1969 from the University of Southern California. That same year he joined the faculty at the newly minted Moorpark College. Built on 134 acres of old ranch land in what was then primarily a farming town, the school opened in 1967 and its student body quickly swelled.

In 1971, Briz taught a course in wild animal training and management. He lectured on training and behavior one day a week and on another took the class to different facilities, such as the former MarineLand USA. A number of his students were offered jobs. That got him thinking. According to Doria, he and Wally Ross and Martine Colette, who now runs a sanctuary called the Wildlife WayStation, discussed setting up a school for trainers. When that didn't pan out, Briz proposed the idea to Moorpark. He suggested a new major, one that would prepare students for jobs in animal parks, zoos, aquariums, and even circuses. These were vocations no community college had prepared students for in the past. A new institution is usually a fairly open-minded one, and Briz was persuasive. Moorpark bit. "He hit the time when the emphasis was on adult ed," says Dr. Peddie. "EATM came into that. Moorpark started a program in aviation at the same time. A lot of these programs fell by the wayside, but EATM didn't."

It was 1974 before Briz had enough courses to constitute a major. Doria, who had a house full of mangy kittens, opossums nicked by lawn mowers, and birds with faulty wings, became the program's first graduate, Briz's girlfriend, and his accomplice. He called her Little Red. A small woman with prominent cheekbones and a mane of red hair, Doria had moved from her hometown of Chicago to Los Angeles to be an actor. As soon as she graduated, Doria joined the EATM staff. She retired in 2000.

The twosome began rounding up animals for the teaching zoo, starting with Kiska. They drove down to Van Nuys to pick up the eight-month-old wolf that they'd been told was tame. He was not; he had been raised with a dog that he romped with but was not used to people. They had to push the wolf into the back of Briz's truck, which was covered by a camper shell. The wolf hid for two days on the top shelf of the camper. Doria and Briz took turns sitting in the camper with him, trying to accustom the young wolf to their presence. "I wondered if this was a good idea," Doria says. "I would never do that again. I didn't know any better." At the time, Doria assumed Briz had worked with a wolf before. Years later, she says, "He told me he was faking it."

When the wolf finally emerged from the camper, they leashed him to a post during the day and housed him in a cage in a maintenance building at night. They named him Kiska. The first official class of students did their night watch with Kiska, then the teaching zoo's only animal. Before long the compound began to bulge. It was the loosey-goosey seventies in southern California, when you could buy a baby elephant from the local tire store. People dropped off unwanted, unusual pets. Briz, Dr. Peddie says, could never say no. The students built the pens and cages to keep up with the new arrivals. The original compound was small, about three-quarters of an acre, and dense. You could see from one end to the other. It sat at the far end of the football field on low ground that regularly flooded during heavy rains. Students would get in trouble for riding the camel on the well-groomed turf.

Briz and Doria drove to Long Beach to collect two neurotic pet capuchins, one of which, Koko, still lives at the teaching zoo. They put them in a cage atop the station wagon and zoomed back up the highway. Briz got word that a safari park in Irvine had a lion cub they didn't want—a male with a chunk bitten out of his ear. Briz, Doria, and some students loaded the cub, which turned out to be a female the size of a Great Dane, into the back of a station wagon. They named her Carol. Briz and Doria had often snuck animals into the zoo, unbeknownst to the college honchos. There was no hiding the lion. Administrators asked Briz how he would pay for the upkeep of the king of the jungle and the rest of his expanding zoo. With educational shows, Briz answered. EATM itself would pay for most of the teaching zoo's upkeep, as it still does. That appeased the administrators. Briz, untethered from the college's purse strings, had even more freedom to run his kingdom as he saw fit.

It was *his* kingdom: Briz picked the animals and picked the students. He ran the program like a military school—an odd choice for a man who told Doria he had washed out of the service after an emotional breakdown. At EATM, he was the brass and nothing made the point clearer than the pipes. They were neatly stacked at one end of the zoo. They were sewer-sized, maybe twenty feet long. They were rusting metal. It took five or six people to lift just one. During orientation week, Briz would order the new first years to move the piles of pipes to the other end of the zoo. If they dared to ask why, the answer was a gruff "Because I say so." It was hot. They got blisters. The blisters broke on the pipes. Briz yelled at them, calling them "stupid broads." After the pipes were neatly stacked in their new location, they would sit there rusting until the following fall when the next new class arrived. Then the new students would lug the pipes back to the other end of the compound, and so it went year after year.

"He was a total dictator, also to his staff," says Dr. Peddie. "I was one of the few people he did not lock horns with. Not that the students didn't love him. They feared him."

"If he told you to jump off a cliff, you might have," says Dorothy Belanger, a senior keeper at the Los Angeles Zoo, who graduated from the program and now works there part time.

If you wanted democracy you came to the wrong place. Briz didn't suffer anyone questioning his authority, which rankled some students. One alum told me he was more a bully than a leader, one who favored pretty girls and loaded his tests with trick questions. If he didn't like you, he'd make it clear. His big, booming voice could be heard the length of the compound. He believed in the crucible approach. When Susan Cox was a student in 1985, she asked Briz if she could quit working with the parrots because they wouldn't stop biting her, tearing her hands to shreds. No was the answer. When Diane Cahill, Briz's second wife, was a student, she hid her snake phobia from him, knowing if he found out, he'd assign her to one.

Students were required to be at the school at 6 A.M. every day of the week from September until June. Every third or fourth night they had to stay over, sleeping on hay in a barn or in with the reptiles, which occasionally got out. "We worked, worked, worked," LoVullo says. Kris Romero, who graduated in '88 and teaches part time at the school, remembers being so exhausted that she hallucinated seeing ants all over a countertop. If you got three tardies, you were out. Briz counted tardies as being late for or missing one class. If you missed a morning with three classes, bingo! You hit your limit; off you went. There was no grievance procedure. One alum told me of students setting up other students for a third tardy so that they would be expelled. "I saw some good animal people get kicked out," says Cox.

Briz's point was that the animals come first. He knew he couldn't make his students animal experts, but he could instill in them an exceptional work ethic for a field that requires utter devotion and long hours. "He wanted you to be married, like a nun would be married to Jesus," Doria says. Gary Wilson says students obliged because it created an esprit de corps. "Why do people become a Navy Seal and go through that hell?" he asks. "It's because it's an elite. It's an accomplishment."

Typically in these years, only half a class made it to graduation, what with students getting kicked out and dropping out. When Wilson went, his class started with thirty; fifteen made it across the finish line. When Brenda Woodhouse (EATM '80) graduated, only sixteen out of her class of forty were on hand. Many of the casualties were men. The college pressed Briz to accept more male students because there were so few and those few were often thrown out. "He was at odds with men," says Alan Kordowski (EATM '76), curator of mammal training at SeaWorld in Orlando. "So we didn't get along."

If Briz had trouble with men, he'd created the perfect world for himself. From the get-go, EATM attracted female students. Long hours of endless cleaning never discourages women the way it does men. It was a gender imbalance that proved a great temptation. "It was Candyland," says Doria. After his divorce, Briz became engaged to Doria, who was fifteen years his junior. Then he broke it off to marry Cahill, who was thirty years his junior. Dr. Peddie says Briz was a sexual athlete. "His students would give him anything. I think many of his students did."

The largely female student body combined with Briz's military style of running the school made for an odd mix that continues today. As many sports coaches know, most young men need to be knocked down a peg or two, but most young women need the reverse. Females do not generally respond well to being beaten down, criticized, and subjected to ironclad rules. Kordowski says

Briz did it to toughen them up. "Back then women were in the industry, but all the bosses were men."

Cox says Briz told them they could expect to have to sleep with their bosses. He would say things like "Come here, little girl." "He was harsh. He was brutal. He was sarcastic," she says. She's grateful for it. She went to EATM when she was thirty-six, married, and had two kids. She had grown up a latchkey kid in a family that taught her to think small. She married young and let her husband run her life. Without Briz and EATM, she says, "I would not be who I am today. I'd still be afraid to drive on freeways, afraid to go places by myself. I wouldn't have done any of the things I've done."

LoVullo, who is a rep on movie sets for the American Humane Association, was, as she admits, "a really horrible teenager." She snuck boyfriends into her house. She ran away. She wanted to drop out of school. Then she heard of EATM. A competitive horseback rider, LoVullo could envision a future working with animals and had a reason to stick out high school. Animals and EATM got her on the right track, and she mostly credits Briz's tough love. "I'll never say a bad word about him." After graduation, LoVullo kept in touch with Briz. She found that once she was no longer an EATM student, Briz was a bit of a teddy bear. "He played the part of a hard-ass," she says. "That's not really who he was. That is what he did to make better students."

For many of the alums from the Briz era, these were the glory days of EATM, a golden, not-so-distant past when the school ran as it should. The students would trek up to nearby Carlisle Canyon to take training classes with Cheryl Shawver of Animal Actors of Hollywood. The company's owner, Hubert Wells, the legendary movie trainer with a suave Hungarian accent, kept some of his animals at the teaching zoo, including the very first Schmoo.

Though Wells didn't teach, he'd give a talk here and there. While a student, Cahill helped Wells raise a pack of wolves for the film *Never Cry Wolf*. LoVullo remembers Wells arriving and opening the back of his truck to let three lions out. They trotted alongside him off leash. "He was a god to us," she says. Wally Ross, the circus man and movie trainer, was about as well. When EATM briefly took in a young elephant that a local group of Hare Krishna couldn't handle, Ross supervised its student handlers. Frank Inn lumbered through the gate, then an old and very fat man, and put Benji through his paces to wow the students. He even gave Briz a look-alike pooch.

It was not such a shining era, though, for many of the college's administrators. A stickler for his own rules, Briz repeatedly flouted the college's. Briz pretty much ran EATM as he pleased. He was bounced from exasperated dean to exasperated dean. "I don't know if rules applied in his mind," says Brenda Woodhouse. "He had majorly pissed off the administration. No one wanted to deal with him."

When Briz retired in 1985 at sixty, the college named Wilson, then a part-time instructor, the new EATM director. Briz chose him as his successor. Doria had hoped to take over but she didn't have a graduate degree. Wilson did. It was an opportunity of a lifetime but an impossible task. Briz's shadow loomed large. It didn't help that Briz stayed around another year to teach one last class as Wilson tried to take charge. Briz was larger than life; Wilson was—is—not. Where Briz boomed, Wilson talked. Like an old-time preacher, Briz had struck the students with a mix of fear and awe. Wilson was young and approachable, a scientist at heart. Where Briz was obviously passionate and outspoken, Wilson is understated, and his ever-present smile is hard to read at times.

Wilson set about making amends with college administrators and making the program less of an outcast. He beefed it up academically and he codified the rules Briz had carried in his head, putting them to paper in a handbook. Alums and staff began to worry that EATM was losing its edge, that it wouldn't survive without Briz. Briz voiced his displeasure with Wilson's changes to the students, undercutting the new director's authority. "There was pressure from the college to make the students come first, the animals come second," Doria says. "[Gary] was more for the students. He was gentler. He was trying to be the softer side of EATM." But then anyone would look like a softy compared to Briz.

Nearly two decades since Briz retired, the hand-wringing over EATM continues. Alums still complain that the program is no longer tough enough, even those students who studied there when Wilson, the alleged softy, was director from 1985 to 2001. They say the school is no longer the gold standard, that the graduates are arrogant, demanding, and even whiny. "They are stripping away everything which made it special," says Netta Banks, a rep for the American Humane Association's Film & TV Unit.

The complaints have become even louder since Dr. Peddie took charge in 2001, though the alums don't blame the vet but rather the college administration. Brenda Shubert, who became EATM's dean in 1999, has brought the program into the fold, making it less a private school within a public college. In so doing, she changed EATM requirements that essentially weren't legal at a community college in California, a necessity in an age when people are not shy about going to court. For example, students are no longer required to be at the zoo seven days a week, though many still come that often. The old rule made the students spend hours at the zoo for which they received no course credits. This was not kosher. Now they are broken into two groups: one cleans Sunday through Wednesday; the other cleans Wednesday through Saturday. The cleaning is now part of a course called Zoo Skills, for which they get three credits.

The alums don't like this, but what really bothers them is that night watches are no more. Previously, students had stayed overnight on the compound with no faculty supervision. The college ruled that practice a liability bomb ready to go off. Night watch, says EATM staffer Mara Rodriguez, was "what made it real. That you were going to become a wild animal trainer." People speak of it reverently, as some kind of baptism. There was even an EATM superstition that the animals spoke at midnight on Christmas Eve. Mark Forbes of the studio training company Birds & Animals Unlimited is one of the few EATM alums I spoke to who downplayed night watch. "We'd go around and wake animals up," he says. "What are you going to do if an animal is in trouble? It was just to make it hard. It wasn't necessarily good for the animals, nor did it make you a better trainer."

What Forbes doesn't like is the lottery. In the past, the application process to EATM was long and involved, similar to a graduate program. You needed three letters of recommendation and you had to have work experience with exotic animals already. Of the 400 or so who applied, 100 or more were interviewed by the staff, who then chose the incoming class of about 50. Moorpark College is required by law to accept any student with a high school degree or equivalent. That EATM was picking and choosing its students was illegal for all those years. Beginning with the class of 2003, students are selected by lottery. They must have completed five prerequisites, such as freshman English and introductory biology, and they must attend a meeting for prospective students at the teaching zoo in April or May. This policy has greatly reduced the pool of applicants to about 100. Now, your chance of getting into the program, according to EATM's Web site, is about 1 in 2. Incoming students, however, can no longer claim a certain cachet. Getting into EATM is no longer proof that you are exceptional, just that you are lucky. So far, lady luck, the staff says, appears to be on their side. Dr. Peddie says the students selected by lottery are just as good. His beloved second years—one of the best classes ever—were chosen by chance. This does not allay worries, though. "At Moorpark they used to be able to guarantee they'd gotten the best," says Gary Priest, the curator of behavior at the San Diego Zoo and Wild Animal Park. "Now they can't."

What if you take a glass-half-full approach to EATM? The physical demands may have waned, but the academic demands have waxed dramatically. Now that the students are not so physically exhausted, they can study more. There are eight 4.0s currently. The attrition rate has dropped significantly, from 50 percent to 10 percent or less. Students also get more experience with the animals. Under Briz they generally worked with one animal per semester. Now they care for a minimum of four animals and train two.

The animals have it better. The compound, which was moved to the top of the ridge in 1990, is a big improvement over the cramped quarters of the original. In 2002, a staff position was created specifically to manage the teaching zoo. Michlyn Hines (EATM '84) was hired away from the Los Angeles Zoo, where she had worked for seventeen years. Since joining the staff, she has set about making the teaching zoo more professional, including plans to apply for accreditation with the American Zoo and Aquarium Association (AZA). Accreditation will raise the teaching zoo's status and make it possible for other zoos to lend animals to EATM. Plans are in the works for EATM to get a brand-new building; the college has approved $7.9 million for a new two-story building that will include classrooms, a dining room, a box office, and even a gift shop. If all goes according to plan, construction will begin in 2006.

So why don't alums notice these changes? Rodriguez says that the more the school changes "the less they can relate to it. There's a fear in that. They don't know how it works anymore." Mark Forbes says alums romanticize how hard the program was. "That way we can feel what we did had meaning. There wasn't a point to working that hard. Zookeepers don't work that hard." I also began to wonder if it isn't just human nature, that urge to lord it over younger generations because you had it tough. Or maybe it's animal people just being animal people. The truth is that the way Briz ran the program would be impossible today. It should have been impossible then—a teacher at a public school tossing students out at whim, making them work slave hours, sleeping with the students, and calling them "broads." These excesses have long since been huge no-no's on college campuses. Briz is lucky he got out when he did, before some student thought to take him to court.

It's also lucky Briz came along when he did, at a time when John Wayne types could still get things done in their big personality way without setting off an avalanche of grievances and court cases. In this sensitive, liability-obsessed age, it's hard to imagine anyone creating anything as outrageous as EATM or a renegade on the scale of Briz wrestling with lions in the hallowed halls of academia. For better or worse, the Brizes of the world are an endangered species.

After he retired, Briz moved with Cahill and their daughter to Camp Nelson in the Sequoia National Forest. There he morphed a third time, this time into the Owl Man. As a science teacher at the Clemmie Gill School of Science and Conservation, Briz donned a suit of buckskin and lectured to fifth graders while holding a horned owl on one arm. He'd become a kind of aging man of the mountains, a thinking man's Paul Bunyan. He was still a rule breaker. He took Sammy, his Lhasa apso with a horrible underbite, with him to work, though it wasn't allowed. He'd put the little dog out on his nature trail and use him as an example of a vertebrate.

He and Cahill divorced in 1988. By 1991, Parkinson's disease and prostate cancer had made Briz retire for good. Eventually, his son moved him to a retirement home, where, according to his obituary, he watched football and read Louis L'Amour westerns. On his front door he hung a photo of himself with his favorite lion, Chad. When Doria visited him, they'd talk about EATM. He told her he'd rather see it closed than come to what it had. An EATM alum, Gary Mui, interviewed him there for a film he was making about the school. Cox went with Mui. Briz was feeble, she says, though he still had "that twinkle." In the film, Briz's voice is weak. He looks at the camera through big glasses and describes in a low mumble how he used to irk his family during hikes by never letting them sit down when they were tired, making them push on just a bit and then a bit more. "You can always go a little farther," he murmurs. "You can get a lot of things done you didn't think you could."

On New Year's Eve 2000, Doria called him on the phone. They chatted briefly. He said he was tired. Briz died the next morning. He was seventy-six. He couldn't go any further.

The Fire

The third week of October the first years get the zoo to themselves at last. The second years pile into three vans and head north for the traditional whirlwind field trip referred to as Davis week. Like new mothers hiring babysitters, they leave long lists of dos and don'ts for the first yeas. They drive off fretting that their animals will not survive without them. These worries, however, recede as the second years ask for behaviors from an elephant at Six Flags Marine World in Vallejo, play with the puppies at Guide Dogs for the Blind in San Rafael, and feed giraffes at Safari West in Santa Rosa.

Back at the zoo, the first years get at least a little of what they have longed for—animal interaction. They chat with Louie, the geriatric prairie dog. They tender chicken necks through the bars to cougars. However, it is not the lovefest they dream of. The first years can only interact with the animals they have been assigned to, and the second years have set strict limits on that. Mostly, first years are allowed only to say "Hi" and "Bye" to their charges—no baby talk, no gossiping, no existential conversations. The first years assigned to Rosie, the baboon, are allowed two additional words: "Good girl." The ones working with Rio can ask the blue and gold macaw for behaviors inside her cage but cannot pick her up. Wischhusen gets more interaction than most. When she tells Kiara to go into her den box, the lion thunders right in her face. "The power of her roar exhilarated me," she says.

The first years assigned to Schmoo are forbidden to chat up the sea lion and must keep to perfunctory greetings. Nor may they ask her for behaviors—nary a wave. This seems to put Schmoo in a mood. The sea lion is typically as busy as a socialite. With her second year trainers gone, the sea lion's schedule of shows and training sessions comes to a standstill. She sinks into a funk deeper than her pool and refuses to eat.

At 7 A.M., 9 A.M., 12 noon, and 4 P.M., one of the four temporary Schmoo girls appears at the sea lion's cage with a plastic container of smelt, mackerel, and squid carefully prepared for her highness. They usually leave with what they came with—a full container. Each time Linda Castaneda steps close to the fence, Schmoo jumps out of her pool and waddles over to see who's there. "Hi, Schmoooooo," Castaneda coos. Nearly blind and somewhat deaf, Schmoo takes a beat or two, nose upraised, whiskers twittering, head cocked, and then she realizes the silhouette is not one of her usual trainers. As Castaneda dangles a mackerel by its tail before her, Schmoo turns up her nose and closes her mouth tight. We are a species that takes things personally, especially a refused morsel. Snubbed, the star student sighs, frowns, and turns away from the star animal. For Castaneda what was an honor quickly becomes a royal pain in the neck. She's taken to calling Schmoo a "punk" or a "brat." She does not savor the prospect of telling the second years that they couldn't get Schmoo to eat.

To Schmoo, Castaneda and the three other first years must seem very dull. They want to give her fish for free—no barks, no spins—but Schmoo is used to working for her food. Handouts just won't do for this prima donna. The hunger strike is doubly worrisome: no fish means no meds for the aging sea lion. Schmoo has done this in the past when previous second-year trainers have left her in the care of first years. Because this is a teaching zoo, the staff wants the first years to figure Schmoo out and to tempt her appetite. The learning experience, though, cannot go on indefinitely or the cost of the lesson could be one dead epileptic sea lion.

During Davis week temperatures top 100° every day, though it's late October. The air in Hoofstock grows thick as the plentiful camel and sheep poop bakes in the sun. The doors are swung open on the Reptile Room. The big cats snooze the day away, rousing to swat at the flies that buzz their ears. The Santa Ana winds gust southwest, rasping the already withered landscape; there's been no meaningful rain since June. All the foothills surrounding the zoo have faded to dun brown under a garishly blue sky. Brush fires have broken out across Southern California, including a sizable one in Burbank, where the palm trees are reported to be burning "like tiki torches."

The crisped terrain around Moorpark may look like it could self-combust, but wildfires in Burbank seem a distant threat. Each fire season there's some smoke on the horizon here, even flames, but nothing very serious. It's earthquakes that people worry about around here.

As the week wears on, three things remain constant: Schmoo won't eat, the Santa Anas won't let up, and the mercury won't dip. The staff steps in with Schmoo and takes over feeding the sea lion. They can ask her for behaviors in exchange for food. Schmoo quickly gets her appetite back. The temporary Schmoo girls breathe a sigh of relief but feel defeated, especially Castaneda.

The class suffers its first casualty, a first year who has been repeatedly late for the morning cleaning. She came at noon one day and forgot to feed the sheep once. Some first years think she got what she deserved, but others come to her defense. With the second years gone, no bosses and no snitches, a bit of anarchy breaks out amid the first years. They yak away with their animals. One first year ignores her second year's diet orders for Clarence and starts stuffing the Galapagos tortoise with produce. The heat and the responsibility begin to fray people's nerves.

Weather forecasters promise cooler temps are on the way, but the thermometer registers 106° on Wednesday. On Thursday wild fires spark north of Moorpark in Piru, still well away from the teaching zoo on the far side of a river and a mountain range. Then on Friday a new line of fires ignites to the northeast in Val Verde near Santa Clarita. These blazes, too, are miles off on the other side of mountains, so no one worries at the zoo. However, the staff and first years can't help noticing that gray smoke like a low, dirty cloud peeks over the mountains' jagged ridge. What they don't know is that this plume is so big it's visible from space.

On Saturday the Santa Anas drive the faraway blaze and its murk west. In Moorpark the smoke thickens to a gauzy blanket. Like a smoldering coal, the sun glows red through the haze. The smell of a bonfire spices the air. In Big Carns, the cats pace peevishly and lift their noses into the sooty air. During morning cleaning in the Reptile Room the animals are antsy, odd: when Ceylon is set out on the blacktop to stretch, the Indian python tries to slither away; Precious, the yellow anaconda, does the same; Morty, the Burmese python with fangs bared, strikes at the plastic door to his cage. The zoo is open to the public on Saturday, but families arrive only to cut their visits short. The air is thick, and the temperature is well over 100° again. Residents near the college hose down their roofs and yards just in case. As the smog waxes and wanes, the first years start asking, "What if?"

Mara Rodriguez, the only staff person at the teaching zoo, tells them not to worry about a fire. She's seen smoke like this before. Rodriguez is in her mid-thirties. Though she doesn't, she looks like she spends a lot of time at the beach. Her shoulder length hair is streaked blond, and she has a tan. Hanging next to a couple of to-go menus on her office door is a quotation from Maya Angelou: "If you don't like something, change it. If you can't change it, change your attitude. No matter what, don't complain."

Rodriguez is an anomaly among animal people because she isn't one: "I'm passionate, but not like the rest of them, all these people goo-goo over animals. I've never been like that." Growing up, she didn't go to horse camp. She didn't lacquer her bedroom walls with tiger posters. She didn't even feed the family dog. "I'm a people person," she says. "I didn't grow up singing to my chickens. I was a city girl who went to the mall." She was, however, taken to SeaWorld as a kid, and that's what got her thinking about EATM. She was accepted in 1988. "When I got here I finally found something I was good at," she says. "It came easier to me than anything had."

After graduation, she got a job at Animal Actors of Hollywood. Rodriguez worked long hours on the set but made good money. She even ended up on camera. For *House Arrest* she clung to an air conditioner as rats ran down her arms and back. On *Full House* she doubled for a cast member, letting a dog lick chicken baby food off her face. "I've done everything. I'm the luckiest person in the world," she says.

At EATM Rodriguez weighed 190 pounds but as a movie trainer she slimmed down, thanks to a penchant for laxatives and puking. Eventually, she got over her eating disorder, but it took years. Now she keeps a keen eye on the EATM students, watching for telltale signs, such as girls who touch their bodies a lot or go from a size 8 to a 2. She has her eye on two blond second years who are just too thin.

Rodriguez thinks of herself as a role model for the students. She can show them that a regular person, even a girly girl, can work in this macho field. Even though she regularly walks the cougar brothers on chains around the zoo, Rodriguez keeps her nails long and impeccably manicured. Her lips are always shiny with lip gloss. “I don’t want to become the stereotype, someone who is always dirty, lives in a trailer, and wears baggy clothes,” she says. “Some of these girls try to be very masculine. I don’t mind asking a guy to move something for me.” She’s also a single mom in a field where plenty of women still don’t have children, especially studio trainers. Her son, Noah, is five. She’d rather be with him than do anything else. “Animals are important, but not the most important.”

Around 3 P.M., about the time the flames in Val Verde leapfrog highway 126 and hop west toward Moorpark, white ash as thick as snow begins falling at the zoo. Sitting by Clarence’s enclosure, Anita Wischhusen listens to cinders like snowflakes softly pelt the tree leaves. With the second years due back late tonight, today is the last day the first years have the teaching zoo to themselves. Many of them bring their parents up to meet the animals they have briefly cared for. Wischhusen’s girlfriend takes a picture of her feeding Kiara.

Around 4 P.M., as usual, the students start closing the zoo for the night. Castaneda gets in her car and heads for home in the San Fernando valley. Wischhusen and her girlfriend sit on the back of her pickup truck in the parking lot watching the smoke, now as dark as a thunderhead, roil to the east. Though the sun dips near the horizon, it is still 100°. Sara Stresky, a student with pale skin and a broad forehead from West Virginia, feeds Chui, the white-nosed coati, and Buttercup, the badger. She takes one last walk around the zoo to snap photos of the smoke and then leaves. Stresky doesn't get far down the road when she sees flames cresting the hills very near the college. She calls Rodriguez on her cell phone and turns her car around.

Rodriguez, who not only hoped for the best all day but also expected it, walks out the front gate to see for herself. The sky is a sooty black, and a huddle of police cars and fire trucks are in the college's parking lot. She calls for students to start putting together crates, just in case. Then, before she steps back into the teaching zoo, a friend drives up. Get out, her friend tells her; the fires are closer than you think. The police turn on their sirens and over loudspeakers order people to evacuate.

Behind Rodriguez, 150 or so animals sit in their cages. There aren't enough crates or people to move them. The ten or so first years still at the zoo have never handled most of the animals. The second years have all the school's vans. There is no emergency plan for a fire. It's up to Rodriguez to come up with one this second. As the sky flashes orange through swirling smoke, Rodriguez turns on her heel and attempts the impossible.

One student is sent to the phone to call for help and reaches several staff members, who set off in their cars toward the zoo. Castaneda, reached by cell phone in her car, turns around. Flames now crackle along the highway. She bursts into tears. At the school, Wischhusen runs for wet towels and face masks. A few students construct crates in front of Zoo 1. The rest dash to Parrot Gardens to pack up the birds first because the smoke will smother their delicate lungs. Stresky charges into Banjo's cage. The macaw chomps her arms and hands over and over each time she reaches for him. Chieftain nails another first year in the stomach as she tries to grab him. Cookie, a loquacious African gray, goes into a crate—no problem. In the mayhem, Bwana, a turaco, flies off. Somehow, all the macaws are crated.

Stresky grabs a falconer's glove and runs to the Mews to get Laramie, the golden eagle. He reaches with one taloned foot toward her gloved hand but won't step up with the other. Without a hood on he won't climb on her glove, but Stresky doesn't know that. Finally, the eagle jumps to the floor, and Stresky herds him into a crate. She chases a raccoon endlessly around its cage trying to get the critter crated, gives up, and runs to the bobcat's cage to help another student. The cat hisses and bats at them. They back off, crate the serval next door, and return to the bobcat. This time he complies. Then Stresky hears Abbey's emphatic barks. I can't believe no one got her, she thinks, as she runs to the far end of the teaching zoo. She opens the cage door, and the briard mix bounds out and follows Stresky up the front road as if this were a great game. Stresky opens a truck door, and Abbey jumps happily onto the seat next to the crated bobcat.

Hudson, the beaver, is snatched from his pool. Helicopters flutter overhead. Adrenaline crests. Someone yells to keep calm. Students' tears pool atop their face masks. A first year assigned to Rosie, the baboon, for the week summons his courage and steps into her cage. He asks her to leash on. The baboon coolly does as told, even pausing at the door to her cage, as she's been trained to do. Nearby, a first year does something VanHollebeke has spent months hoping to do: she touches the cavy. She dives at Starsky, grabs him by the back legs, and tosses him into a crate.

Rodriguez, having rounded up and crated three squirrel monkeys, realizes that the biggest danger now is the pandemonium. She orders hysterical students to leave and keeps her own fears that the flames have them trapped to herself. While the first years worry about the animals' fate, Rodriguez worries about her own life and her five-year-old son and thinks, I don't want to die for the animals.

Michlyn Hines and her husband speed along back roads as

trees kindle like firewood and flickering embers drift by. They keep running into road blocks where they backtrack or beg to be let through. Her cell phone rings, and a first year says through hysterical tears, "We're evacuating the zoo. We don't have all the animals." The line goes dead.

Somehow, staff members Kris Romero and Holly Tumas make it to the teaching zoo, but with only moments to spare. Both women head for their favorite animal. Tumas scoops up a baby gibbon from Primate Gardens. Romero runs for her beloved turkey vulture, Puppy. When she was a student, she napped in the grass with the bird at her side. She let him pluck food from her teeth with his beak. As Romero drags a huge crate into his mews, Puppy flies out the door and up onto a fence post. Romero knows he can't out-fly the fire. She climbs the post and reaches for the vulture. He bites her outstretched arms over and over until she finally gets ahold of him.

A first year, noticing Olive still in her cage, opens the door. The baboon sits by the doorway as she is supposed to, but when the first year tries to leash her, the baboon threatens her. The student starts up the back road with Olive following. She leads the baboon into Zoo 1, closes the door, and gets Rodriguez. When Rodriguez sees Olive sitting on a desk, she is shocked that the baboon is not leashed. Now there are two problems: the fire and a loose baboon. Rodriguez can't leave her in Zoo 1. What if someone comes and opens the door not knowing there is a baboon inside? Rodriguez grabs a bunch of grapes off a desk to lure Olive into a crate set in the classroom doorway. The baboon screams at her and jumps over the crate and outside. Olive lopes toward Parrot Gardens while visions of the baboon running off into the surrounding neighborhood flash through Rodriguez's mind. Just then, Olive turns back and ambles into the crate.

Another student walks Nick to the front of the zoo, but the miniature horse is not small enough to fit in anybody's car.

Rodriguez leads Nick back to Parrot Gardens and puts the horse in a cage there. She finds Julietta, the emu she hand raised, loose. Though she's terrified of dying herself, Rodriguez can't leave the big dumb bird like this. She shepherds the emu into another parrot cage.

Over the loudspeaker the police announce, "If you do not go now we are not responsible for your lives." Students dump the contents of their cars onto the parking lot to make room for the animals. Wischhusen packs her truck with squirrel monkeys and birds. Castaneda tosses everything out of her car except her Diversity notes—there is a test next week—and loads four parrots, one squirrel monkey, and George, the fennec fox. Students sprint through the zoo turning on faucets and sprinklers, looking into the faces of Zulu, the mandrill baboon, Taj, the Bengal tiger, Savuti, the hyena, Kaleb, the camel, even Schmoo to say a quiet "I'm sorry. Good-bye." They open the door to the aviary so the plover, pheasant, wood duck, and turaco can fly away. Then they drive off into the smoke, darkness, and flames.

By now the blaze burns to three sides of the college. Since 3 P.M. when Wischhusen sat listening to the ash fall, the fire, like a fast approaching army, has marched ten miles west and encircled Moorpark. It burns wherever they look. The caravan stops briefly at a nearby burrito shop, but the flames are still too close, so they push on to the vast Target parking lot near the highway, hoping the sea of blacktop will protect them. They set up camp away from curious onlookers and between the back of the store and a large retaining wall. Students stampede into Target and take towels, bottled water, and anything that will make the fifty or so animals more comfortable. Crates are rearranged so that the birds are moved into cars that have air conditioning. Some students leave to rescue their pets at home. The rest wait, cry, and wonder if the teaching zoo is burning.

Hines and her husband finally arrive at the teaching zoo's front gate. She calls down to Target to tell them it is unscathed. Tumas and Rodriguez return. Other alumni and staff arrive. In about forty minutes another thirty or so animals are hurriedly crated, including the wolf, and evacuated. Dr. Peddie, who, like Hines, navigated a maze of back roads and police blockades, catches up with the makeshift zoo at Target. Everyone settles in, prepared to spend the night. They set up a first aid station and begin rounds, checking the animals in their crates. They keep a wary eye on the flames that color the night an ominous orange.

After a harrowing ride, the vans of second years stream into the Target parking lot at about 8:30. They bound out and frantically look for their animals. There is plenty of hugging and crying, but some second years shoo the first years away from the crates, while others don't think to ask the first years if they are okay. One second year announces that they may no longer talk to the animals.

The hill behind Target sparks. The EATM staff decides to return to the teaching zoo, where there is food and water for the animals and no curious public. The caravan winds its way back through the thick dark. Back at the zoo, the animals that have been crated are moved into the school's vans with the air conditioning running. The vans are parked in a single line pointing toward the front gate, ready to stream out at a moment's notice.

As the fire devours the sage brush, cactus, and paltry trees on the hills around the teaching zoo, any remaining animal that can be crated is. Samburu, the ornery caracal, is lassoed with a catch pole. The snakes and lizards are put in anything that can hold them, whether it be a trash can or a Tupperware container. Trailers are put on standby in Hoofstock for the animals there.

Brunelli finds Goblin on a high shelf in her cage, a blanket pulled over her head. The baboon must be sedated so she can be crated. Brunelli and another student tell Goblin to go to her bedroom, the alcove off her cage, where Dr. Peddie can more easily dart her. Brunelli tempts her with a watermelon chunk. Nothing doing. Brunelli puts stuffed animals in the bedroom. Goblin refuses. The baboon screams. She defecates all over her cage. Time is running out. Dr. Peddie takes aim at a moving target, the frantic baboon. Goblin soon swoons. Amid the mayhem, the crackling, and the smoke, Brunelli gently lifts Goblin and is struck by how light the baboon is while lowering her into a crate.

Dr. Peddie does not have enough anesthesia to knock down all the truly dangerous animals and, in general, he'd rather not. Anesthetizing an animal is a very risky business, especially when you don't know the animal's weight. If you guess just slightly wrong, you could have a dead lion on your hands. The big cats and Savuti are put in their concrete den boxes, which are then covered with wet blankets. Anything flammable is removed from their cages. If they have to evacuate again, the big carnivores as well as Zulu the mandrill will remain behind once more.

The students settle in for a night watch. The second years, back in charge, send the first years home. At about 2 A.M., the flames reach to the stars, and the sky pulsates and roars. The fire slides down the hill immediately west of the college like a lava flow. If the winds shift, the blaze may lunge at the school. The staff and students, people who spend their days gauging a lion's mood or anticipating a capuchin's next move, watch helplessly as this hungry beast rages through the night before their eyes. Operant conditioning holds no sway with this creature.

* * *

The wind does not shift. The blaze recedes. Sunday morning breaks. The fire burned in a horseshoe shape, passing Moorpark on either side. The zoo, the college, the surrounding neighborhoods are an oasis of green in a world of black. The only signs of life are a few old oak trees that somehow weathered the conflagration. Their time may still come. Brush fires spark here and there, their flames writhing in the hot wind. Throughout the day, everyone remains at the ready to evacuate. Crated animals are checked every half hour. They grow agitated in the closed, increasingly dirty quarters that are filling up with urine and feces. Buttercup, the badger, tries to dig her way out of her crate. Rowdy, the baby skunk, hides in a corner of his. The spider monkeys chatter nervously. A couple of students trail Bwana as he flaps around the teaching zoo, trying to recapture the turaco. Everyone's eyes smart and lungs strain from the smoke and ash. Everyone is exhausted. Some are punch-drunk. Dr. Peddie, who spent the night as well, tries to send some of them home to sleep, but no one will leave. Who can nap when the world may still go up in flames?

All the zoo's birds, reptiles, and some of the small mammals have been moved to another facility where they can breathe more easily. To the east, the fire licks at the Ronald Reagan Presidential Library. The highway that runs in front of the school remains closed. In the mid-afternoon, the ground shimmies underfoot. Wischhusen, taking a break in an air-conditioned classroom, looks up and says, "I think that was an earthquake." She's right.

During rounds, students notice that Tango, the cheery arctic fox, is breathing hard. However, he always pants; with his furred foot pads and dense coat, he's made for life on the permafrost, not in this parched landscape. He's also lethargic. Dr. Peddie is fetched. The fox is moved to an air-conditioned classroom. His body temperature is 108°. Tango must be chilled. The fox is attached to an IV, injected with steroids, and given a cool-water enema. His furry paws are dipped in ice water. His body temp dips to 101°. For a few hours the fox is stabilized and everyone breathes a sigh of relief. Suddenly, Tango pants his last pant. The teaching zoo has lost its first animal to the fire.

By Sunday night the fire recedes, so the animals are returned to their cages. Still, students and some staff stay overnight again just in case a passing ember should alight. Smoke still shrouds the zoo. Flickers spark on the horizon here and there. Over the next few days, the fires smolder, then die. The sky showers ash. It catches in everyone's hair. Students scrub the teaching zoo from top to bottom. Bwana, the turaco, flies around the zoo until he can't resist a handful of grapes held aloft. He returns to his cage. Kermit, a noble macaw, is found dead on the bottom of his cage, making him the second casualty. All the birds set loose from the aviary return, except for the pheasant.

It could have been so much worse. Most of the animals willingly were crated. Relatively few animals were hurt. Olive could have escaped but she didn't. Ignorance was bliss for the first years, who didn't fully realize the risks they took to crate certain of the various animals. If they had, they might not have evacuated as many. Everyone walks around with a renewed sense of life, that surge of optimism that follows a missed bullet. From the zoo, they look around at the scorched hills and feel incredibly lucky and profoundly aware of the rush of time. Life—these young students think for the first time—is short.

Maybe because of heightened emotions, after a few harmonious days the good feelings begin to evaporate. The second years, worried that all their training was undone by the evacuation, want to return to normal. That means no animal interaction for the first years. The first years, having risked their lives for some of the animals, can't let go. Haven't they earned the right to talk to the animals? Aren't they heroes? The second years think they are being dramatic.

After a couple of weeks of sniping, Dr. Peddie asks the college's psychologist to come up. Everyone gathers in Zoo 2. Even some staff members cry as they relive the fire. The psychologist explains post-traumatic stress syndrome. A second year accuses the first years of not respecting her class. A first year recounts how she feared for her life during the first evacuation. Someone says she would "die for her animals." Others raise their eyebrows and think to themselves, I would not. When it's over, some students feel better, some don't. Like a bad burn, hurt feelings can be a long time healing.

Elephants

Over the past three days April Matott has scooped elephant poop from dawn until dusk. The seven Asian elephants at Have Trunk Will Travel, a noted private facility, produce as much as fifteen wheelbarrow loads a day. It all must be cleared away with an elephant-sized pooper-scooper—a shovel. This is a novel experience for the second year. At EATM she became familiar with all kinds of dung, from the big snakes' squishy bowel movements, striated with undigested white rat fur, to the llama's beanlike droppings that bounce as they hit the ground. Elephant poop, however, has remained an unknown until now.

This is what the twenty-one-year-old has learned so far: pachyderms defecate nearly as often as sheep, but in lumps the size of melons or even loaves of bread. As guano goes, it's hardly smelly. The weedy potpourri of hay and grass smells something like chamomile tea spiked with nostril-dilating eucalyptus. What the dung lacks in stench it makes up for in heft. When the diminutive Matott lifts her shovel and stands at the ready behind a set of great gray haunches with a raised tail, she must flex her arms, because the soon-to-emerge dung will land with forceful kerplunks. If she doesn't hold on tight, the plummeting, steamy elephant missiles could knock the shovel right out of her hands.

This has not been the EATM student's only lesson during her brief internship here at the elephant ranch. In short order, she's learned that life with elephants is consuming, if not dangerous, increasingly controversial, and possibly heartbreaking. As EATM drums into the students nonstop, working with animals is a lifestyle, not a job. But to be an elephant trainer demands an unwavering devotion. The reward is a profound bond with the world's largest land mammal. The ranks of humans that can claim this privilege are small and growing smaller.

It is the second week of November, what they call project week around EATM, when the second years go on one-week internships. It is a chance, however brief, to leave the dreamlike but hermetic confines of EATM for a taste of life amid professional trainers and zookeepers. Once again, the second years leave the animals in the hands of first years who aren't too sorry to see them go. Relations have improved, but the tension between the two classes, like the smell of smoke that lingers around the teaching zoo, has yet to blow over.

Most of the second years haven't gone far for the week because California is rife with zoos, animal parks, aquariums, and studio companies. Becki Brunelli and Trevor Jahangard headed north to work with baboon trainer Kevin Keith in Vallejo. Mary VanHollebeke decamped for the Folsom City Zoo. Amy Mohelnitzky hooked up with a studio company in the Los Angeles area. Twenty-one-year-old Matott climbed into her '94 Plymouth, a high school graduation gift, and drove two hours southeast and checked into a cheap motel in Lake Elsinore, the town closest to Have Trunk.

Animal people typically break into groups roughly by species: marine mammals, big cats, primates, dogs, birds, or elephants. The last group is perhaps smallest, possibly because they have the fewest opportunities. Members of the American Zoo and Aquarium Association house some 305 elephants (160 Asian and 145 African). Private facilities such as Have Trunk care for another 200 to 300. They are tended by some 600 elephant trainers, according to a 1997 report by the U.S. Department of Labor.

Elephant trainers have one of the longest apprenticeships of any trainers, spending years learning how to control an animal twenty-five to fifty times their size. In addition to patience, they need guts. A slightly pissed off elephant can kill a keeper with a mere push or a kick. It's a perilous job, because elephant keepers and trainers traditionally have worked hands-on with the animals. At a zoo, you won't find keepers going in with the rhinos or the gorillas, but you may find them in with the elephants.

That age-old system, though, has begun to fade as more and more American zoos switch to what is called protected contact, which requires keepers to work with the elephants through the cage bars. With that change, the hands-on approach is not being passed along to a younger generation. Gary and Kari Johnson, owners of Have Trunk, worry that their way of working will soon be a lost art.

In fact, the whole profession may soon be on the endangered list. With the 1973 ban on importing Asian elephants plus the limited success of breeding in captivity, the number of elephants in North America is bound to dwindle. Elephants have also become the poster animal for People for the Ethical Treatment of Animals and its ilk. Circuses and zoos are pressured to retire their elephants to sanctuaries. Elephant trainers, good and bad alike, are smeared by animal rights protesters. Anyone with ideas about becoming an elephant trainer can't help but think twice. The road is long, uphill, and may lead nowhere.

The Johnsons at Have Trunk Will Travel take one EATM student for one week each year. This is one of the few shots an EATM student has at getting any elephant experience. The teaching zoo does not have a pachyderm for several reasons. Elephants are slow to make bonds and the teaching zoo's rotating student trainers would make these huge, hierarchical mammals hard to control and dangerous. Elephants are also expensive to keep, given that a typical one chews through about 200 pounds of hay a day.

Moreover, there aren't typically enough students interested in working with elephants to justify the cost, usually only one or two students per class, according to Dr. Peddie. Among the second years, they are Becki Brunelli and a young woman from Baltimore. Matott isn't one, so Dr. Peddie was surprised when she asked him to recommend her to Have Trunk.

Matott is a generalist. She hasn't cast her lot with one species. After EATM, she might like to work for an educational outreach facility, but she has an open mind about her future. All Matott knows is that she'd like to move back near her family in Albany, New York. Matott is small, her manner understated, so much so she can be easy to miss, especially among so many strong personalities. Her voice has a slight squeak to it. Her jackets and sweatshirts are always about two sizes too big and her straight dark-blond hair often a tad disheveled. She has a nose ring. She's paying her own way through school, working as a vet tech at an animal emergency clinic. She adopted a badly burned stray kitten that showed up at the clinic after the recent fire. The kitten joins Matott's other cat, as well as two rats and two hedgehogs.

In addition to training Wilhelmina, the hornbill, to step up onto a perch, Matott trained the teaching zoo's two guenons to get inside a crate. She also works with Abbey; Julietta, the emu; Sly, an opossum; one of the pigs; and Ghost, the clumsy bald eagle. Despite Matott's small size, whenever Ghost bates, lunging off her hand while wildly flapping his wings, she calmly swings the eagle in a neat circle back onto her gloved hand. Once the eagle gave her breast a good pinch with his hooked beak. Matott didn't flinch, just pursed her lips and blew a piece of hair that had fallen across her eyes out of the way.

Dr. Peddie is careful about who he sends to Have Trunk. First, the Johnsons are his close friends. Second, the Johnsons suffer no slouches, and by slouches they mean anyone who can't shovel elephant poop twelve hours a day. They are considered some of the top, if not *the* top, trainers in the country, Dr. Peddie says, and they run a facility that is tidier than a ritzy resort. Also, he wants to send someone humble enough to realize they aren't going to learn anything about training elephants. How could they in just a week? What they'll learn is how to sweep the barn, rake the crushed-granite yard, brush an elephant, and, of course, shovel poop. "It sounds like it's nothing but there's a lot to it," says Kari Johnson.

Have Trunk Will Travel is a ten-acre ranch tucked into the rolling hills of Perris, an impoverished rural community south of LA. You might never know the ranch was there, the way it's hidden behind a hill. As I pull up to the gate, I wonder if I'm lost even though I've followed Kari's directions, turning at a trailer with two satellite dishes aimed at the expansive blue sky. There is no sign of the small elephant herd. No trumpet calls, no flapping ears anywhere in sight. Through the entry gate, I can see the drive is lined with perfectly spaced palms and cypress trees cut into elongated barrel shapes. The gate rolls back. I slowly drive past a yard full of ponies. A large house to my left perches over grassy fields. Everything is spic and span and so still it seems deserted. Then I notice some movement. Two trunks wag in tandem. A pair of elephants stand side by side on a hillside. As I follow the drive it descends to a large lot that circles a barn, and I spot more trunks and flapping ears. Kari meets me at my car. She has a head of red hair. She comes across as ladylike yet earthy and strong. Like most animal trainers I meet, she has a physical assuredness about her. Her figure has spread some in middle age, but, as she says, she's "fat but fit."

The elephants have recently finished their morning regimen: a brisk, single file walk around the property, a snack of grass in a neighbor's field, a bath, and a training session. Kari points out who is who in the herd. That's Tess and Becky, the two best friends standing close together on the hillside. Tusko, their bull, is in an enclosure on one side of the barn. The four other females—Tai, Kitty, Dixie, and Rosie—keep him company this morning. No day is the same at Have Trunk Will Travel. The Johnsons are always changing the elephants' routine, putting them in different enclosures, and training them different behaviors to keep them from getting in a rut.

Kari leads me up to the office on the top floor of the barn with its black leather furniture, elephant knickknacks, and views of the compound. Out one window, I see Matott push a wheelbarrow of dung the color of golden fall leaves. Photos of the elephants at work cover the white office walls. In one, Tai holds Goldie Hawn aloft with her trunk. In another, Daryl Hannah lounges along Dixie's spine. An elephant balances on huge fake roller skates in an ad for Korean Airlines. "That was shot in the barn here," Kari says.

Kari goes off to collect Gary. Meanwhile, I chat with Joanne Smith, an EATM grad who has worked here for nine years—longer than anyone. Smith has on a full face of makeup and a baseball cap that reads I'm Having a Bad Hair Day. Smith was always nuts for elephants as far back as she can remember. EATM didn't really prepare her for her heart's desire, but, as she says, "You can't learn anything about training elephants from a book." When Smith graduated in 1989, she took a job with the elephants at the Racine Zoo in Wisconsin. "My mom was afraid, because you don't make much money in this business," she says. When the elephants were moved to warmer climes in Texas, Smith nearly followed but instead signed on with the Johnsons, because their "elephants can go everywhere. Most zoos' [elephants] don't do the amount of stuff they do." The herd travels around the country in a small fleet of semis. They play soccer and baseball with their trainers. They even paint. Smith prefers Dixie's nice long strokes to Kitty's slapdash style. The only trick, she says, is teaching them to keep dunking their brushes in the water jar.

"I just ended up doing exactly what I wanted," she says, and smiles. Not that it's been easy. Despite her long employ with the Johnsons, she still considers herself a trainer in training. Gary is also known for his exacting standards. Many other apprentice trainers have come and gone while Smith has been with the Johnsons. Her marriage caved under the long hours and demands. Ultimately, her husband didn't like the fact that the elephants came first. They have to, she says. Now she lives on the grounds, works every other weekend, every other night, and rarely socializes.

Smith runs off to the dentist. Out the window, I see Matott cross the lot with a rake in hand. Kari comes up the steps with Gary behind her. He has the bulky forearms of an old-time iron man. His thick hair sprouts in a widow's peak over his low broad forehead. His voice is deep and he speaks slowly. Gary got his first elephant in 1970 when he was sixteen. Back then, all you needed in order to get an elephant was the money. Gary didn't even have that. He traded a llama and two pygmy goats for his first elephant, Sammy, a male that was part of a small petting zoo at an Italian restaurant. Gary had a good idea what he was getting into. He'd worked at a petting zoo, sweeping poop at first but eventually graduating to running the elephant ride. When he was fourteen, he'd lied about his age and spent a summer with Ringling Bros. working with an elephant. Eventually he was kicked out of school for playing hooky so he could spend an afternoon watching elephants at a shopping center. Still, he admits that buying his own was "a weirdo thing to do."

Gary kept Sammy on his parents' twenty-acre ranch in Anaheim. He housed him in his family's oversized garage and trained him mostly by trial and error. Then the elephant reached sexual maturity and got too aggressive. Gary sent Sammy to a park in Mexico. In 1978, he got Tai, the herd's thirty-five-year-old matriarch and star performer. As Kari likes to say, "Gary got Tai before I got Gary." After all these years, elephants still have their hold on him. He'll forget to come in for meals, Kari says. "He's hard to manage. You can't make him not do it."

Kari fell into elephant training. It was the family business. Her stepfather was Robert "Smokey" Jones, a world famous elephant trainer. He trained circus and zoo elephants around the country. With his partner, he trained an elephant to water ski. Traditionally, elephants have been trained through dominance and often heavy use of the bull hook. Jones used a more enlightened approach that relied on cooperation and consistency. He studied the elephants and got to know their habits, the way their minds worked, just as Gary and Kari have.

Kari wasn't all that interested in elephant training but she began working with them when she was thirteen or fourteen. She was fifteen when Gary began hanging around her stepdad. She thought he was a hick. Ten or so years later, Kari finally noticed how cute he was. By then, Gary had three elephants. Unlike most women, Kari didn't mind the package deal. The couple was so busy living and breathing elephants they never really dated. "We meant to," Kari says. "We just moved in together." While they were at a convention in Las Vegas, Gary asked Kari, "Do you want to go ahead and get married?" They squeezed the nuptials into a busy day, went back to their room, and toasted each other with Diet Coke poured into two cups from the hotel bathroom. Elephants encircle their wedding bands.

Keeping your own elephant is expensive. You need not only mountains of hay but also a place big enough to keep the animal. However, an elephant doesn't really leave time for having a job. You need to pay for the elephant with the elephant. So an elephant naturally becomes your job and your life, as it has with the Johnsons.

Movie work pays the best. Gary and Tai have made a long list of films, including *George of the Jungle* and *The Jungle Book*. Film jobs, unfortunately, are sporadic. So the couple take their elephants to fairs, zoos, and even pumpkin patches, where people clamber on without realizing they are on the back of a Hollywood star. Lately, they've been hiring out Tai for traditional Indian weddings, in which the groom, dressed in white from head to toe, sits in a special saddle and rides the animal to the ceremony.

The Johnsons are obviously happy with their unusual life. There are just two clouds on their otherwise clear horizon. The first is obvious: the animal rights movement. They picket the elephant rides the Johnsons offer at the Santa Ana Zoo. They have tried to ban exotics in communities around California, including the Johnsons' own Riverside County. If the elephants can't work, the Johnsons would not be able to afford to keep them. It hasn't come to that, but they worry. All the fighting and the constant testifying take them away from their work. When the Riverside ban was proposed, the Johnsons had to let their business go to fight the ordinance. Kari has testified at city councils, legislative committees, and even before the U.S. Congress. The Johnsons can't help feeling defensive, so much so that when I ask them if they rescued their elephants, Kari bristles and says, "We got them as they became available." She admits that they have paid more than they should have for some of their elephants "to get them out of a situation," but she won't use the word *rescue*. It's "too self important," she says. She won't use the enemy's vocabulary.

If Kari seems bitter, it's worth noting that the animal rights people kicked her when she was down, which brings us to the other dark cloud. This one, which has hung so low over the ranch for nearly five years, may soon lift.

I follow Kari outside for a tour of the compound. We start with Tusko, the 12,000-pound bull with a billboard-sized forehead. He is twice the size of any of the females. His dun-colored skin has an apricot sheen from all the dust he's sprayed on himself. He is the only elephant they cannot go in the enclosure with. Male elephants are much more dangerous because they are so big and aggressive, especially when they go into musth.

Tusko is part of the Johnsons' plan for the future—not just their own future but the future of Asian elephants. The Johnsons' income not only keeps the elephants in hay, the ranch in decomposed granite, and the Johnsons in their house but also funds the couple's breeding program. They are part of a countrywide effort to breed Asian elephants in captivity. As wild Asian elephant populations dwindle, people like the Johnsons believe that breeding captive animals will save the species. They are members of the AZA's Species Survival Plan Program. They are also one of the few private facilities that is AZA-accredited.

To this end, Tusko, the behemoth, was added to their herd. However, their jumbo-sized lothario was a disappointment at first. He didn't seem to know where to put his huge winky-tink, as Kari calls it, so they sent him off to a breeding facility for some much needed practice. After about a year, Tusko knocked up a female there. The Johnsons sent for their stud.

Kari walks me down a line of shiny gray trucks, including two semis neatly parked at the far end of the compound. They were especially designed by Gary for transporting the girls. They have air conditioning. One has a screen so the elephants can see out, but people can't see in. There are other clever inventions at the ranch, such as a Dumpster set in the ground and landscaped right up to the edges. You can't see it's full of poop until you're standing nearly on top of it.

As we round one end of the barn, we see the end of a trunk snaking over a fence delicately reaching for a flowering bush. "I see you miss Dixie," Kari calls. Dixie is the oldest at nearly forty, but she's not nearly as big as Tai, who has about a thousand pounds on her. Dixie is a talker. She even moos like a cow. Dixie, Kitty, Tai, and Rosie have moved over to the enclosure next door to Tusko. Here, they coat themselves with dust, elephant sunblock basically. They snack on the branches of the eucalyptus, cottonwood, and pine willow trees. They play, running and throwing sticks at each other, and they nap. As Tai settles down for a late-morning snooze, going down on one knee, then rolling slowly onto her side, the other three elephants gather round like ladies in waiting.

In the hillside enclosure, Tess and Becky continue to move in tandem like Siamese twins. These best friends may have a secret in common: both mated with Tusko this fall. Both might be pregnant. It's about ten weeks before you can know for sure. Tusko will soon get a third time at bat. Rosie is due to cycle soon. If all goes well, there may be three babies on the way. These wouldn't be the first babies, and this is what makes Kari's eyes go bright with that sharp brightness that precedes tears, though she can now talk about Amos and Annie without crying.

Five years ago, two baby elephants frolicked on this ranch—two wonderful, goofy baby elephants. Tess gave birth to 300-pound Annie with Dr. Peddie's help on July 30, 1998. She arrived feet first and got up right away. Annie looked like her mom. Her ears came to a pretty point and her smooth skin was dark. A month later, Becky had Amos after a long delivery. He was very hairy like his mom. Amos didn't have Annie's pizzazz but was lovable all the same. Everyone fell hard for these two babies, who splashed in their Barbie swimming pool and chased each other all day long. Like a proud mom, Kari took their photos to the bank and the tellers passed them around. Joanne Smith secretly taught Amos to paint and gave the Johnsons his masterpiece for a Christmas present. The Johnsons had a TV monitor in their room so they could keep an eye on the babies at night. They would stay up late watching the twosome wrestle and play. Gary called it E-TV.

On an early spring morning in 1999, Annie suddenly became ill. Dr. Peddie was out of town, but two top elephant vets happened to be in the area. They were called to the ranch. Annie's lungs were filling with fluid. The eight-month-old elephant was given intravenous antibiotics but she got sicker and sicker. At the end of the day, as Kari conferred with Dr. Peddie on the phone, Annie's heart stopped.

Kari grieved like a bereaved mother, long and hard. She wished she could be like Tess, who trumpeted and paced inconsolably for days and then got over it. An animal rights activist accused the Johnsons of having separated Annie from her mother and thus prompting her death. In fact, mother and daughter had never been apart. The autopsy showed nothing conclusive. All the Johnsons knew was that they had two baby elephants and then they had one.

Then they had none.

That summer, Amos succumbed to a twisted intestine on Gary's birthday, August 8. Joanne Smith says it was the worst thing she ever went through. Dr. Peddie says he's tried to block the deaths out of his memory. "Those babies were the best thing that ever happened to us," Kari says. "Losing them was the worst thing that ever happened."

* * *

Matott has been cleaning alongside David Smith, the Johnsons' newest employee, since 6:30 A.M. If either is tired, it doesn't show. Smith, who is not related to Joanne Smith, graduated from EATM just last spring. He has a lithe build, a thin face with a small chin, and close-cropped hair. He is friendly but serious, weighing his words as he speaks. He lives in a trailer on the property and gets to see his girlfriend only once a week on his day off. He works twelve-hour days at a minimum and doesn't make much money. He has a master's degree.

Smith was an environmental technician in the Los Angeles area for ten years. He began to wonder if he was making a difference, if the long days were worth it. His volunteer work at an animal refuge made him decide to go to EATM at thirty-four. Smith did a one-week internship with Have Trunk last fall. He didn't have his heart set on working with elephants, but the Johnsons' conservation work appealed to the environmentalist in him. The Johnsons hired him when he graduated. His primary duty now is to clean the ranch, but eventually the Johnsons hope to make a free-contact elephant trainer out of him and thus pass on their method to a younger generation. "It is kind of amazing, what an opportunity it is," Dave says. "There's nothing like this situation in the country."

This apprenticeship is slow going; it not only takes time to bond with an elephant (as much as two years) but also to master the fine nuances of the profession. Over the years, the Johnsons have started to teach a half dozen or so would-be trainers, only to have them give up midstream. By taking Smith on, they are gambling a good chunk of time. It will be a couple of years before they'll know whether Smith can develop the instinct to be two to three steps ahead of an elephant. If he doesn't, "he'll still be a good guy," Kari says. "He just won't be a great elephant guy." When I ask Smith how he feels about the long road ahead, he says, "Best not to entertain those thoughts."

He took some baby steps this summer, and picked up pointers, such as elephants respond best to quiet, calm commands. He got acquainted with the herd and they with him. Mostly, though, he helped getting the elephants back and forth from various fairs and festivals. Since September, he's been working on training each day with Becky or Rosie. He finds there's such a big gap in knowledge between him and the other trainers, they can't always explain to him what he's doing wrong. He gets discouraged. "Handling elephants is supremely more difficult than it looks," he says.

Not long after lunch, he and Matott briefly set aside their shovels and wheelbarrows. Becky, Smith's practice elephant, is collected from the hillside enclosure. She is sociable and a good sport. She's young at only twenty-five. She will still add another thousand pounds over the next ten years. She's the hairiest of the herd, with a fuzzy halo of wiry black hair on her brow and shoulders. She has ugly rough calluses on her temples that resemble patches of gravel, but as Kari says, "She's so cute it doesn't matter." At this point, Becky knows far more about elephant training than Dave does.

Kari has Dave start by walking Becky in a circle. They stroll around quickly, Becky keeping abreast of Dave's shoulder. He carries a bull hook in his hand, but like the Johnsons, rarely uses it and then only as a guide. The Johnsons, like Kari's stepdad, rely on rewards and consistency to train their elephants. They don't call it operant conditioning, but that is essentially what they are using. Kari, Matott, and I stand in the middle of the circle, turning and craning our necks as Smith and Becky circle us. The point is to keep Becky by his side, not to let her lag behind or surge ahead. This is what Dave has to learn first—how to lead Becky. "If you can't do that, you can't do anything," Kari says.

Kari tells Dave to stop and have Becky swing around. "Get in line," he commands quietly. Becky stops and turns to face him.

"Steady," he says. Becky's body should be at a neat ninety-degree angle to Dave. If she's not, that's her way of testing the novice trainer. The bulk of an elephant is hard to size up. Not hearing any encouragement from Kari, Dave turns to look at her. "Where's the front?" Kari asks. Dave looks as if he isn't quite sure. He good-naturedly walks around Becky and keeps asking her to move a bit here, a bit there. It's like trying to get an SUV perfectly straight in a parking space. Becky moves a bit forward, and her rear end goes out of whack. "She's past center," Kari says. "Do you see the front?"

If Kari has a note of impatience in her voice, Smith seems unfazed. He finally gets Becky into a correct position and then says, "Trunk." Becky raises her trunk high. "Foot," Smith says and Becky, as crows squawk nearby, daintily lifts one rounded front foot so that you can see its sole is pink. Then he walks a circle around her. "Can you tell April why you are doing that?" Kari asks.

"I don't want her to think that she can move when I move," he says.

Off they go again, man and elephant padding around and around in the afternoon sun. Dave stops Becky whenever Kari tells him to and goes through the same drill over and over. "Get in line," he says, and Becky swings her bulk around. "Steady," he says, then straightens her out. Dave has her raise her trunk and then a foot, and they return to their hypnotizing circles. After several attempts, Smith nails it on his first try: Becky stops on a dime and swings into place with the precision of a Marine.

"She's very straight. Good," Kari says.

After a few more spins around, Kari stops them so Becky can go to the bathroom. Matott dashes behind Becky with a shovel while Kari commands, "Go potty." Becky rumbles, squeaks like air being let out of a balloon, and then roars. One loaf pops out and hits April's waiting shovel. The afternoon wanes and there is yet more cleaning, more poop to be tidied up. That's enough practice for one day. Dave strides through the gate into the hillside enclosure with Becky right by his side. "Now, Dave, you know better than that," Kari scolds. An elephant as placid as Becky could inadvertently smash him against the gate. Kari's reprimand breaks the quiet magic of the past half hour. It is a reminder that just one little mistake could have dire consequences. This is one of the tricks of elephant training—never forgetting for one second that these intelligent, personable beasts could hurt or even kill you.

Dave and Matott rush over to feed the ponies, Gary's "hobby," then back to ready the elephants for the night. In the fading light, they scoop Tusko's enclosure while the bull devours hay and loudly slurps water. The female elephants dip down on one knee and roll on their sides for a brushing. Then they rise and clasp one another's tails with their trunks and step lightly out of their enclosure. They stop and swing to face Kari, who commands, "Get busy." Kari walks between the elephants, chirping, and tickles their bellies with her fingers. "Oooo, ooo," she coos. There is much rumbling and straining. Matott is back in position behind the elephants, trying to gauge who's about to let loose. As she gives up on one raised tail to step to another, a steamy lump tumbles out. She swings her shovel back but it's too late. "I missed it," she wails.

"Tails," Kari says. The four females take one another's tails again and walk single file through the deepening night and into the barn. Soon the roomy barn fills up with their swaying bulk. Most of the night, Kari says, they will eat. They won't sleep until near dawn. The girls line up in specific order, so best friends are next to each other. From left to right, it goes Becky, Tess, then the mischievous Kitty, the matriarch Tai, chatty Dixie, and little Rosie. One foot in front and one foot in back is chained to keep them in this order. This makes for a peaceful night and keeps them from eating each other's food—well, almost.

The noshing has already begun. Becky eats from her pile of hay and helps herself to Tess and Kitty's on either side. Rosie pushes her pile out of reach of the herd. Tai doesn't seem to care who snacks from her stack of hay. Though they all defecated outside, they are already at it again in the barn. Matott and Smith push a wheelbarrow down the line of large bottoms. Then, though their long day is officially done, the two humans slouch on hay bales and watch the elephants dine. Elephants may move with an uncanny silence given their size but they are noisy eaters. They smack their great lips and grind their teeth. They breathe heavily. They play with their hay using their trunks. They chew and chew in great circular motions. It is mesmerizing. Eventually, Matott and Smith rouse themselves and reluctantly leave. Matott has a test to study for. Both have another early morning ahead.

On the last day of her week, Matott is rewarded. The Johnsons give her a T-shirt that Rosie and Tess painted. She climbs atop Tai for a ride. Matott lies on the ground as the elephant leans over, gently takes the young woman's leg in her mouth, and then lifts her. Though Tai's teeth pinch a little, Matott smiles for the camera.

It's been a good week, Matott thinks. She's learned a lot, including that elephant training is not for her, at least not right now. She noticed that everyone who works for Have Trunk Will Travel lives there and that they rarely leave the compound without the elephants. She wants to work with a range of animals. She also wants time for her own animals, for friends, and for other experiences. She's not quite ready to devote herself to one all-consuming species, even if it's the beautiful, mighty, and intelligent elephant. She's young. Matott's not ready to give her life away, at least not yet.

November

Back at EATM, Austin and Alamo, the once adorable prairie dogs that arrived earlier this fall, have gone into rut. They now prefer biting to cuddling. Austin nailed Castaneda, nicking her on the leg, then digging his little incisors into her thumb. It was her first bite. "It seems silly to be bitten by a herbivore," she tells me.

Leftover Halloween pumpkins are stacked outside of Nutrition. The big cats will get to swat them around like gazelle heads. The November chill has chased the flies out of Hoofstock. Tremor and Little Joe, the tortoises, have been moved into a tub in the Reptile Room. Legend's fur thickens. So does Nick's. The miniature horse remains plenty plump no matter what Jena Anderson does. She tried putting the llama's food on an upturned garbage can lid outside the corral beyond Nick's reach. The lid, though, fills with water when it rains. She'll have to think of something else.

With the second years gone on projects, the first years work at triple time. Terri Fidone, the former Vegas cocktail waitress, babysits

Abbey while Mohelnitzky is away. It's like caring for a heartsick lover. Abbey shreds her blankets. She throws up more than usual. She refuses breakfast though Fidone douses her food with scrambled eggs and barbecue sauce, as Mohelnitzky instructed. At least the pooch has moved to better quarters, the arctic fox's old digs at the front of Quarantine. Now Abbey can see the goings on in Primate Gardens, such as the binturong, Chance, being fed or students training the lemurs, Obi-wan and Jenga.

Without the second years the zoo feels slightly deserted. On a Wednesday afternoon, I find only a few students trundling about in their wellies, eyes glued to flash cards in their hands. Looking south over the green athletic fields, the banks of the foothills are an ugly black in every direction. The faintest scent of wood smoke wafts over the teaching zoo. In Primate Gardens, Zulu chomps a head of romaine lettuce while watching TV. Someone has plugged the small black-and-white set into a heavy orange extension cord and set it on a chair outside his cage. The sound is turned off. The baboon sits on his puffed pink bottom, motionless except for absentmindedly scratching himself here and there, while he watches a car commercial.

I run into Castaneda, who's on her way to feed the cougar brothers a slippery mix of chicken necks and ground mystery meat shaped into balls. As we walk up the back road, we look north toward the tarnished landscape beyond the zoo's lush green. "How do you like the Happy Face?" Linda asks me, pointing out the maniacally smiling cartoon someone has etched into a charred hillside. The flames have long since receded, but the fire burns on. Mary VanHollebeke has had to start over from the beginning with Starsky's training. Ash still accumulates in the animals' cages. Mara Rodriguez's car only recently ceased smelling of smoke. Work has begun on an emergency plan for a fire. Goblin, the baboon, is being crate trained.

Inside Big Carns, Castaneda and another first year go to opposite sides of the cage and each calls over one of the cougar brothers. Castaneda gets Sage to climb onto a high shelf in his cage and then starts pushing meatballs through the bars into the cat's waiting mouth with the palms of her hands. Castaneda gingerly offers a chicken neck through the bars so he has to tip his head up to munch it. He crunches the bones loudly. When you hear that, Castaneda says, you can't help wondering if they snagged your finger. Cage bars are no guarantee against getting hurt. Samburu recently hooked a second year's finger, splitting it right up the meaty tip, while she was feeding him through the bars.

"I love you all," Castaneda says to her fingers. "If I lose one, I'll miss you. Nothing personal." The cougars purr and make happy kitty sounds. Castaneda chatters in response. "Isn't that yummy?" Savuti, the hyena, stands at attention one cage over, watching the feast. Susan Patch pauses along the front road to watch.

"Why do you hold the food high up like that?" Patch asks Castaneda.

"Holly said to, because if he eats too fast he'll throw up."

Patch looks dubious. She often does. Patch's gotten a bit of a reputation as a know-it-all, but she *does* have a degree in animal science. Patch's skin, like a lot of EATM students, has broken out. Unlike a lot of EATM students, she has lost weight. A former competitive rower, Patch thinks it's because she's losing muscle mass. She'd be the only one. Biceps and abs are generally on the increase. So are bellies and bottoms. Midriffs lap over khakis. Upper arms swell and jiggle. It seems impossible that you could gain weight here, but then you see the grab bags of candy passed around classrooms, the cartons of steamy fast food imported by the hour, and the boxes of slicked doughnuts at every kind of meeting.

The strain of this first semester takes its toll. EATM exacerbates any problems or flaws the students have. Larissa Comb is heartbroken over a relationship that ended. At EATM, where there's no time to date, her loneliness deepens. Another first year counts her pennies and pays for her groceries with food stamps. This is Chandra Cohn, the lean, long-faced first year who bawled loudly over pulling her pigeon. Just before orientation her husband asked her for a separation. Now she's scrambling to pay the rent on the room that she, her daughter, a ferret, two rats, and two hermit crabs share in a houseful of students. Castaneda's rheumatoid arthritis has flared, not to mention her allergies. When she worked in the Rat Room, her eyes became swollen even though she wore a face mask. She got a sinus infection. Her perfectionist ways also get the better of her. She copies her classroom notes, writing them out in her neat print so they are "pretty." EATM doesn't leave time for getting things just right, but Castaneda can't stop herself.

One of the rules of training is to not let your animal get too frustrated, but EATM does not always practice with its own students what it preaches. First years agree they would do better if they could just talk to the animals, touch them. They are, after all, animal people. Still, nobody drops out as students did in the past.

Sage passes on the last chicken neck Castaneda offers. "That's funny," she says. Castaneda holds her hand up against the cougar's cage. As Sage licks the meaty gunk off her palm we hear someone call, "I love you Schmoo." Schmoo—not one of Castaneda's favorite animals these days! While the cougar happily takes nearly every morsel Castaneda tenders, the sea lion will not. With the second years gone, Schmoo has resumed her hunger strike. I follow Castaneda out of Big Carns and down the back road toward Schmoo. As we walk, we can hear the sea lion's low, guttural rumble, almost like an old man clearing his throat. As a tall, redheaded first year passes us, she blurts out proudly, "My monkey caught a bird."

We meet up with the other temporary Schmoo girls and Gary Wilson, who's come to see if he can tempt the sea lion to eat. Schmoo's pool gurgles. Sirocco and Kaleb, the camels, turn their large snouts our way. Wilson has an idea: forget putting the pills in the fish. Wilson calls Schmoo over and opens the gate. She waddles out, her dark eyes shining, her extra-long whiskers glistening in the sun. Wilson rattles off commands, to which Schmoo energetically responds, throwing her tail up, waving a flipper, and rolling over on the hard-packed earth. "Open!" Wilson says. The sea lion opens her mouth, exposing two banks of black teeth and a bubblegum-pink tongue. One of the temporary Schmoo girls, a blonde with a high voice, quickly tosses a handful of pills in. Mission accomplished.

Wilson keeps working Schmoo, commanding her to turn left, to circle, wiggle her whiskers, and roll over. He rewards her with fish and squid, which she gobbles down. By now, her dark stomach is pebbled with light specks of dirt. "Touch!" Wilson says and rubs her belly. Schmoo opens her mouth as if it tickles, then downs a glob of squid Wilson tosses her. The temporary Schmoo girls stand in the shade watching, not smiling.

"She wouldn't even take fish from us," Castaneda harrumphs.

"She's acted like she hated us," the blonde says.

"She snubs us," Castaneda says.

"I swear she rolls her eyes at us," the blonde counters.

"Look how happy she is with him," Castaneda says.

Suddenly Schmoo lunges at Wilson with her teeth bared. He jumps back. The Schmoo girls tense. "Relax," he says. The sea lion closes her mouth and loosens her posture. The temporary Schmoo girls, though, remain rigid.

Brenda Woodhouse is not a morning person by nature. Nevertheless, five days a week she rises at 4:30 A.M., when night still has its black hold on the sky, and drives fifty-two miles from her home in Acton to EATM. She's due at the school before 6:30 A.M., when she starts calling the roll in her clear, strong voice and marking down who's late. She says she never gets enough sleep, but it doesn't show. At this early hour, when the students hunch over their desks and recede into their sweatshirts, Woodhouse, who naturally walks fast, talks fast, and thinks fast, is on full alert.

This morning, like all mornings, she's here, there, and everywhere at the zoo, supervising inexperienced students as best she can, answering questions as she goes. I have to trot to keep up with her as she strides down the back road. As she rounds Nutrition, a first year dashes over to her, something grasped in her hand. She opens her fingers. It's a baby rat, a pinkie, with its shoulder bone sticking out. "We're out of gas," the student says. Woodhouse suggests crushing it quickly with a rock.

Woodhouse is heavy set and strong. Her blond hair falls to her shoulders. She has wide-set eyes and a rounded nose. She moves her hands a lot when she talks. She's magnetic. Growing up, she was the link between her deaf parents and the world of sound. Her parents signed at home but only lip-read in public; signing had a stigma then. Both could speak, Woodhouse says, in uninflected monotones. Still, they leaned on their only child. It may have been too much responsibility for a child, but Woodhouse's unusual upbringing prepared her for communicating in a nonverbal world. "I grew up reading body language," she says.

She thought she'd work with deaf people and studied psychology in college. Then she found out about EATM and changed course. She would be a different kind of interpreter, a link between the animal world and our own. It was the Briz years. Woodhouse didn't think she'd made much of an impression on him because he always called her Louise. She left the program two months early without graduating to take her dream job, working with marine mammals at Chicago's Brookfield Zoo. She loved it there among the zoo's five dolphins, three California sea lions, one walrus, and one harbor seal. It was a union job that paid well. She had not worked with EATM's sole marine mammal, Schmoo 1, a more affable sea lion than the current Schmoo, but Woodhouse learned on the job. There were only two things she didn't like: jumping in and out of the chilly dolphin pools in the winter and handling endless buckets of fish. A visitor once asked her how she got dates, smelling like fish. In fact, she was married to her high school sweetheart. She left her job after she had the first of her two kids.

Her family moved back west. Her husband is a high school guidance counselor. Woodhouse took a part-time job with the bird show at the Los Angeles Zoo. She also trained the drills, large, tailess monkeys related to mandrills, for artificial insemination. Then in 1994, she joined the EATM faculty. She's an upbeat, gregarious teacher. Animals still have a hold on her, especially anything with hooves, but now her focus is on her own species.

Just a few steps farther past Nutrition, another student approaches Woodhouse. "Can Zulu have this?" she says, holding out a toy green frog with stuffing coming out. "No," Woodhouse says. The student disappears into the barn and returns with a stuffed, floppy-eared, purple bunny with its button eyes removed. "Yes," Woodhouse rules.

We all walk over to his cage. Zulu grabs a rubber wellie and slowly climbs onto one of his shelves. With his elaborate coloring, Zulu is at times regal, at times clownish. A stripe of cherry red runs down the middle of his face over his nose and upper lip. To either side of the stripe, his cheeks are a faded blue. His beard is a lemony blond, his chest hair a creamy white, and his balls an impossible violet.

His pace is unhurried. He's rather aloof compared to the busy, chattering spider monkeys next door. He spends much of his day quietly watching the students scurry about. However, should you approach his cage, his lips will spread in that exaggerated clownish grin with the yellow canines overlapping his bottom lip. It's quite a sight. The rule with primates is that a smile suggests fear.

With Zulu, though, a smile is what it looks like, a howdy-do. He is nearly ten. He's been living at the teaching zoo for five years. He is owned by a professional trainer, Monty Cox, and his wife, Anna, who bought him when he was seven weeks old. Anna raised him at home, even teaching him to sit at her breakfast bar and eat with a spoon. By the time his canines came in, Zulu was far less cute and far more dangerous. Also, the Coxes did not have a permit to keep him in their home. EATM took the mandrill in.

At the zoo, Zulu whiles away his day with his collection of all things rubber: boots, balls, even a basketball. He loves bubble gum. The colors on his face light up when he's handed a new rubber toy. He'll drool. He often masturbates, tucking a wellie between his legs, rubbing it just so. This embarrasses, if not revolts, some of the students. They stop by his cage to say hello, only to notice the jerking of his hips; and with a surprised "Oh!" they turn on their heels. Woodhouse says all the male primates at the teaching zoo masturbate a good deal, but she's never seen one use a tool before.

Sunni Robertson, a cheerful first year with olive skin, is taking care of his highness this week. Robertson is trying him on for size. She might ask to be his trainer next year. He is quite an undertaking, as his current second year trainers will tell you. First, there is the pinching. Zulu can reach his hairy arm through his cage. His student trainers often sit within reach of the mandrill to groom him or just to keep him company. Should they annoy him, say by moving too quickly while grooming, Zulu will reach through the cage bars and squeeze their arms, pressing his black nails into their skin with relish. Moreover, if a student trainer ticks him off in general, maybe by talking to a friend near his cage when he wants her full attention, she is instructed to hold her arms up to the cage and let him pinch them, which he does. Otherwise, the thinking goes, he will stay mad. Having vented his rage, Zulu gets over it. The student trainer, having been grabbed, gets a bruise. He's like an abusive boyfriend. My guess is that no man would agree to this, but all Zulu's female trainers submit to his punishing grip.

Zulu offers the most painful lesson in how a trainer must consider an animal's natural history. In the wild, as Cindy Wilson explains it, Zulu would live with a harem of female mandrills. They would be with him all the time. Here at EATM, the student trainers substitute for his harem, but they disappear for long stretches every night, so Zulu, like an insecure king, has to keep reasserting his male dominance over his female subjects.

Certainly his headaches don't improve his mood. Whenever he gets a bad one, Zulu pulls on an ear. Bright lights will bother his eyes. He can even seem temporarily blind. No one knows exactly what to do for him. He's never had an MRI, Dr. Peddie says, because Anna is afraid to have him anesthetized. Zulu is a package deal. Anna visits him regularly and still has a fair amount to say about his care. Many students don't want to deal with someone who is not on the school's staff. Also, many of the students don't approve of Anna because she feeds Zulu burritos, pumpkin pies, and other junk food fit for a teenager. The mandrill has quite a beer gut, and the students blame Anna for it though she comes only every couple of weeks or so.

That's a lot to consider, but this week has gone well so far, Robertson says. Zulu hasn't scared her off, but she's not sure she's up to the pinching. While we stand by his cage talking, the king sits above us on a shelf in his cage, holding his scepter in one hand—a wellie.

At 8:30 A.M., the appointed time for Schmoo's morning feeding, the temporary Schmoo girl with blond hair and a high voice arrives at the sea lion's cage with a slick pile of freshly thawed fish and squid and a handful of pills. When she calls Schmoo over, she immediately obliges. "Open!" the student chirps and to our mutual shock, Schmoo does. The first year fumbles the pills and before she can toss them into Schmoo's mouth, the sea lion closes her trap. The first year groans. "Open! Open! Open!" she chirps, but nothing doing. Schmoo turns, waddles back to her pool, dives in one side and out another, slides into her favorite corner, and lifts her whiskered nose to the sun.

"Schmoo, you big brat," the first year says. "You don't want to listen to me. You're being silly." She calls Schmoo over again. The sea lion indulges her and scoots back over. "Open!" she tries again. A moment or two passes. We stare at her. Will she, won't she? The sea lion opens wide. The first year tosses in pill after pill, jumps, and pumps her fists in the air.

"I love you Schmoo," she squeals.

Schmoo isn't quite done being finicky, however. She won't eat any fish or squid. That the diva deigned to take the pills is more than enough. In fact, the student reports, it feels like Christmas.

Later, when I report to Castaneda that Schmoo finally took her pills, she looks equally relieved and irked. She would have liked to be the one who got the sea lion to take her meds. She has straight A's and a bachelor's from a respected college. She managed teenage punks in an inner-city school. She lived in an African jungle for weeks. Still, an elderly, nearly blind sea lion has gotten the better of this perfectionist.

The next day, a Saturday, the cleaning starts at a leisurely 8 A.M. There are no classes and the teaching zoo doesn't open to the public until 11 A.M., so the pace slows just a hair. In Hoofstock, two easygoing EATM students fill a wheelbarrow with poop from the sheep, the pigs, the deer, and the camels. Another first year stops by to pluck a log or two from the wheelbarrow for Savuti the hyena; he likes to roll in it. Sirocco and Kaleb watch the cleaning proceed with their heavily lashed eyes. Schmoo sits in her corner, nose turned skyward.

Now that the flies have waned, this is one of my favorite spots in the zoo. With pens rather than cages, it's airy and sunny. The sounds are soothing, from the sheep's rhythmic baaing to the water lapping in Schmoo's pool. The animals are mostly familiar, knowable. Though you have to be careful that you don't get too relaxed. As I'm talking to Adam Hyde, a towering, soft-fleshed eighteen-year-old who wears clothes two sizes too big, Sirocco, the white camel (the one with a bad reputation), leans over and presses his nose against Adam's arm. Hyde jumps and nearly trips over a salt lick. The other first year and I freeze. "That was enough to scare the hell out of me," Hyde says. He turns to Sirocco. "Putz," he says, recovering his teenage swagger. We laugh.

Castaneda, with her sure stride, comes through the gate, clutching Schmoo's plastic pill holder. From across Hoofstock, I watch as she calls Schmoo over. The sea lion, who always moves faster than you expect, zips right over. "Open!" Castaneda commands. Schmoo obliges. Castaneda tosses the pills in matter-of-factly. No fist pumping, no jumping up and down or squealing.

"It's nice not to be responsible for killing the sea lion," Castaneda says and turns on her heel and walks off. It's too little too late. This star student will pass on the star animal. She will not ask for Schmoo.

Baboon Here!

One December morning I arrive at the teaching zoo to find Rosie, the olive baboon, and Trevor Jahangard sitting side by side in the shade. They have settled on a bench not far from the front gate overlooking the Aviary and Clarence. Below, a bunny hops through the huge tortoise's lettuce-strewn enclosure. Clarence doesn't notice. He's trained his beady black eyes on the unlikely pair—the man and the baboon.

Rosie and Trevor resemble two old friends quietly enjoying each other's company on a sunny morning. It is brisk, but Jahangard has on a muscle shirt and shorts, which he seems to favor no matter the temperature. He clutches one end of Rosie's leash, which hooks to a belt low on the monkey's hips. Her legs stick out straight from the bench. Her expression is serene, though her copper-colored eyes look a tad serious. One black hand is tucked under a leg. Chris Jenkins leans on a wooden cane nearby. When I approach the threesome, he calls, "Baboon here!" I stop to chat, though I know I'm intruding on a male enclave of a sort.

That there are so many female students at EATM is generally a blessing for the few males in the program but a bit of a mixed one. Alum Mark Forbes says he loved being with so many girls and dated three of them. Once when Adam Hyde complained he needed a break from the "estrogen fest," a female student shot back: "Pu-leeze, you love it. You've never been around so many gorgeous women in your life." If the men are single, the school is a testosterone-laden male's dream come true. Numbers and time are on their side. There are currently 6 male students and 89 females, roughly a 1 to 14 ratio. EATM leaves the women little time to hunt for men elsewhere. As Rodriguez tells me, even the biggest dorks get laid at EATM. Of the six males in the two classes, the oldest is married, and Jenkins lives with his longtime, non-EATM girlfriend. That improves the ratio to 1 to 22. Jahangard kind of dates one of his fellow second years, a sharp, striking woman nearly ten years his senior. One of the first-year males is in an on-again, off-again romance with a classmate. Take them out of the running, and now the ratio is 1 to 44. Though Adam Hyde is just eighteen, chunky, and still has a high school smart-alecky bravado that doesn't play well with women over sixteen, the odds are on his side.

On the downside, the preponderance of women makes for all the presents and hugging. Even alpha females, who brave cougars and regularly hoist fifty-pound bags of feed, can get to squealing and trilling, not to mention gossiping. Jahangard tells me the women are more quarrelsome, that they have to talk about everything, and he doesn't need to. "I'm like, 'It's okay. It doesn't matter,' " he says.

When Jahangard and Jenkins crave some quiet male bonding, they can briefly leave the girliness behind and get Rosie out. Rosie is twenty. She came to EATM at four months. Her deep olive green coat is speckled with white. She weighs maybe thirty pounds. This is the first of Rosie's two daily walks. Jenkins, as backup, comes along each time. The threesome's walk can be an efficient twenty-minute turn around the compound or a lounge in the sun on the bleachers in Wildlife Theater. During these sessions, Rosie often grooms Jahangard, meticulously scanning his legs and arms with her black fingers, as the two men shoot the bull. "It's really comforting except when she pulls hairs out," Jahangard says.

What makes Rosie a males-only club is that only men can be assigned to her as trainers or backups. The thinking behind this has to do with how a female baboon would live in the wild. There, she would readily submit to male baboons, who are twice as big as females. The boys also have much bigger canines, some as big as a leopard's, and they will sink those into any uppity girl baboon. In the wild, male baboons are vagabonds. They leave their birth group when they reach sexual maturity and join up with another troupe, only to strike out again eventually. The females are stay-at-home types, remaining in their birth troupe their entire life. Girl baboons inherit their rank from their mother, so they don't scrap as often or as intensely as males do. However, they will readily battle any female from outside their troupe.

Instinctively, Rosie is inclined to challenge new female trainers, whom she's likely to view as coming from outside her troupe. She does this either by ignoring them or—worse—attacking them. Though she's had her canines pulled, Rosie's still got a mouthful of teeth, not to mention freakish strength. When Gary Wilson took over the school in 1985, Rosie still had female trainers. She got feisty toward one and eventually sank her teeth into the student's hands. Wilson says the student looked as if she had slit her wrists. After that, Wilson decided it would be only male trainers for Rosie. With men, Rosie is all lady, as in the throwback, kid-gloved kind. She doesn't mind that her male trainers come and go. She accepts each one of them as the boss, even a twenty-year-old like Jahangard.

Olive, the teaching zoo's other olive baboon, is a slightly different story. While Olive also requires a male trainer, she can have female backups. The thinking is that Olive is not as confident as Rosie and therefore would not be as likely to threaten a female backup. Rosie was born in captivity and handled by humans from an early age. Olive was captured from the wild and had a youth like a Charles Dickens character. She was caught illegally along with her mother in Africa. Olive was confiscated. The good intentions went awry as the baby baboon was separated from her mother and then housed alone during her impressionable youth. Consequently, Olive, now sixteen, can be very neurotic, shaking her den box, banging her head against it, self-mutilating, and pulling out fur. Her cage is littered with toys, mirrors, pieces of fabric—anything to keep her occupied. Still, the school doesn't risk giving her a female trainer. On the rare occasion that her female backups have asked her anything, Olive has ignored them. She really has eyes only for Jenkins. "Primates in general are incredibly chauvinistic," says Kevin Keith, an EATM grad and one of the few professional baboon trainers in the country.

Keith says it's not out of the question for a woman to train baboons. He knows of a female trainer who even works with male baboons. She is experienced, has an established relationship with the baboons, and is tough, he says. A female trainer can even have some advantages. "She can flirt with them," he says. At EATM, Goblin, the hamadryas baboon, has all female trainers, but that's because students work with her through the cage. She does not come out for walks like Rosie and Olive.

Pairing male trainers with Rosie and Olive is one of the many examples of how EATM students are taught to consider an animal's instincts and behavior. Students always hold macaws so they are above the birds, because in the parrot world whoever is higher is dominant. When students walk Julietta, the emu, three or so students trot alongside her. An emu is a herd animal and will stay with a group. Should Rosie or Olive ever challenge Jenkins or Jahangard, they are taught to grab the monkeys, push them to the ground, and hold them there—essentially what a dominant male baboon would do. Neither has had to do that so far. Keith takes it one step further at his facility. On the rare occasion that one of his baboons seriously challenges him, Keith will hold his baboon down and bite it on the back of the neck just enough to remind it he's in charge, as baboons do to each other. "I had to learn to hold my cheeks back when I bit. I bit my own cheeks." He rarely does it, but when he does, the bite works, he says. "You have to have that dominance or you are done."

Rosie and Olive aren't the only animals at the teaching zoo to whom gender matters. Neither C.J., the coyote, nor Legend, the wolf, cares for men. C.J. dislikes them intensely. She so dislikes Hyde, the towering teenager, that whenever he is anywhere near her cage, she barks and barks and barks. Julietta is with C.J., and decidedly doesn't like men. Once, as a group of students were getting her out for a walk, the emu swung her fuzzy blue head at Jenkins as if it were a club. As everyone collectively gasped, Jenkins coolly stepped close and grabbed the bird's long neck, which immediately calmed her down, and then said matter-of-factly, "She hates me." On the flip side, Ozz, the Geoffrey tamarin, prefers men.

Because there are always so few male students at EATM, chances are good that if you are a man you will be assigned to a baboon. You won't even have to score top grades or perfect attendance to get these high-status animals, unlike students who vie for Schmoo. However, Jenkins and Jahangard happen to be A students. Jenkins has clean-cut good looks (a style he undermines occasionally by shaving his head), bright eyes, and a high-pitched honk of a laugh. Jahangard has a long jutting jaw, dark curly hair, and rounded ears that stick out a bit. He's got the lean, muscular physique of a wrestler. He's easygoing, but his female classmates say he's got some ego.

Jahangard knew he wanted a baboon from the get-go, but there were originally five guys in his class. He had a little competition at least. Then two guys dropped out before school and a third not long after classes started. Jahangard was assured a baboon. Luckily, Jahangard and Jenkins did not have their hearts set on the same one. Jenkins, who has a psychology degree from UC Davis, was drawn to Olive's troubled personality. Jahangard just wanted to train behaviors, not psychoanalyze neuroses. Rosie was the one for him. She knows between seventy and eighty commands, and her standing flip will make you dizzy.

The fact that college students learn to work hands-on with the baboons here is a unique opportunity. There are few places to learn on the job, because only a small number of zoos or facilities bring their baboons out. Keith got his first baboon experience at EATM working with Balentino, a male who used to live at the teaching zoo. Keith was petrified of him. "It's like a race car driver. You might be fearful to get in the car but you're so fascinated by it." When Keith went in his cage, he'd square his shoulders and make his six-foot-five-inch frame look even bigger. Balentino would scream at him. Keith thought it was aggression. In fact, Keith was scaring the bejesus out of the baboon. He had to relax his posture.

After EATM, he worked at the animal show at Universal Studios and then at Six Flags Marine World in Vallejo, where he trained chimps. He gravitated back to the underappreciated baboons, eventually creating his own facility where he keeps four baboons and a mandrill, which he walks on a leash. Keith is one of a handful of baboon trainers nationwide. No one wants to work with the baboons much, he says. "They have red butts. They are aggressive." He not only likes the big monkeys, but sees his baboon facility as a wise business move. As pressure grows from animal rights organizations to not use chimps in entertainment, Keith expects demand for trained baboons to grow. They are quick thinkers, Keith says, and can work their whole life, unlike chimpanzees, which have to be retired when they become sexually mature at around ten. "[Baboons] are more socially intelligent," he says. "They always want to be in a group. They are like dogs. As long as you treat them in a positive manner, they love to be trained."

All the baboon walking makes for a busy day, especially for Jenkins. He gets Olive out at least once, usually twice, for walks. He is a backup for each of Rosie's two walks with Jahangard. Also, he has to follow along when Jahangard gets Rosie out for education shows in Wildlife Theatre. As the backup, Jenkins mostly runs interference, keeping onlookers from getting too close. He carries a cane, which is used primarily as a visual barricade to overeager humans, typically children, who often mistake Olive or Rosie for dogs. The backup is also there to keep passersby away from the trainer. The rule is nobody touches either trainer when they have Rosie or Olive out; you shouldn't even raise your voice to them. Either baboon might see that as a threat to their main man.

Olive's and Rosie's walks are not so much constitutionals as a change of pace in their captive lives. The promenades also keep them comfortable with being outside their cages. When Olive strolls with Jenkins, she is very alert, looking everywhere, examining the ground for food, keeping a constant eye on Jenkins. She pauses to smell bushes or to tuck a piece of bamboo in her cheek pocket. Rosie, on the other hand, is businesslike, almost blasé.

Both men keep one eye on their baboon and one eye on the world around them, scanning the horizon for anything that might upset their monkeys. For example, Rosie hates things that flap in the wind. Should something unsettle her, Jahangard will give her commands, such as asking her to take his hand, in order to calm her and get her focused on him. He does the same if Rosie shows any flicker of aggression—say if she eye-flashes a female student. This morning she is lovey-dovey. Jahangard asks for a kiss, and Rosie complies with a soft peck on his cheek. She drops from the bench and hunches on the ground by Jahangard's feet where she begins methodically sorting through the dark hair on his legs.

Rosie knows so many commands that it is hard to come up with new ones to teach her. For the winter semester, Jahangard will train her to voluntarily take an injection. He had thought of pricking her in her pink pillowy bottom, but the sciatic nerve is there. That means he'll have to prick her in the thigh. To do that, he'll have to face her, which makes him a little nervous. "All she has to do is bite me in the face." Rosie has rejoined Jahangard on the bench. He gooses her thigh to show how he's starting the injection training. Rosie starts a little and pops her bright eyes. This summer he trained her to let him reach in her cheek pouch. He demonstrates that too, poking his index finger in her mouth and prodding about while the monkey stares off in the distance.

Jahangard also trained her to climb atop the school van and leap into his arms like a damsel in distress. He gets up to show me. Rosie bounds on the hood. Jahangard thrusts one of his legs out. He opens his arms to the waiting baboon. She jumps easily into his waiting embrace, her black hands outstretched, her tail flying up behind her. Her feet land on his thigh. Her arms snug the young man around his neck. For a moment, human and baboon clasp like lovers.

Nearby, the jingle of female voices rises as EATM students file into Zoo 1. The day charges ahead. The men turn to walk Rosie back to her cage, the baboon following along on all fours. As the threesome ambles down the front road, Jenkins calls in his clear voice, "Baboon here!"

December

Despite the constant rush of life—the feeding, the cleaning, the gossiping, the studying—death is always in the wings at EATM. The students must learn to say good-bye for good. In early December, Mama Dolly, the doddering, ancient matriarch of the sheep, quits eating. Dr. Peddie holds a stethoscope to her stomach and listens for a sound like fingers rubbing against a wall. It's not there. That means the fourth chamber of her stomach has quit working. She is slowly starving to death. The vet rules that her time has come.

She's already lasted longer than anyone had expected. When the school bought six black-faced Suffolk lambs, the breeder threw in Mama. She could no longer breed but the ancient sheep could still be a leader. All grown up, the small flock of sheep still bleat hopelessly whenever Mama leaves the pen for a show or a training session.

The dowager arrived with an aging digestive tract. The stomachs of hoofstock churn and churn as they brew hay into a nutritional soup. Their guts eventually wear out from all that churning and brewing. As Mama's tummy failed, she has filled with gas, so much so the sheep has become noticeably lopsided. If you push her bulging side, Mama burps.

One early morning, Dr. Peddie again becomes a reluctant angel of death. CVP, Mama's student trainer and the crack pigeon puller, begs off death for once. Kristin Gieseker-Hopkins, an exuberant blond Texan who goes by the name of Kage, volunteers to take her place. She is the trainer of Sadie, the biggest of the small flock and the one that picks on the other sheep. Mama usually won't let anyone other than CVP halter her, but Kage thinks she has a shot; Mama knows her.

Turns out that Mama can hardly move. Kage and another second year have to lift Mama and half carry her out of the pen. Dr. Peddie warns them: when hoofstock are put down, there's nothing peaceful about it. They are given the initial sedative standing up. The animals sometimes go rigid, as if they've been shocked, and then collapse dramatically. Last year, when Dr. Peddie put down Bob, the hugely popular water buffalo, his great bulk not only hit the deck like a boulder, but he bellowed and cried.

Standing near Schmoo's enclosure, Dr. Peddie injects Mama with an overdose of a sedative. The queen sheep does not make much noise though she goes down hard. Her head lands in Kage's lap. She gurgles. That's unnerving, but what really starts to bother Kage is that the four sheep, including her Sadie, quietly watch the proceedings like witnesses at an execution. They never turn their coal black faces away. Their eyes, with those horizontal slashes of pupil, stare. Kage looks down and notices that Mama has dribbled a yellowish-green stain on her gym shoe.

It's Christmastime. This week, the students are playing Secret Santa, leaving little surprise gift bags on one another's desks. They have their pictures taken with Clarence, the Galapagos tortoise, whose shell is festooned with big red bows. Mostly, though, they fret. The holidays are lost to the nail biting of finals. In fact, the school's official holiday party is scheduled for mid-January, when the students can actually enjoy it.

For the Diversity final first years have to memorize over two hundred animals from sponges to storks. One morning, I find the metal picnic tables near the front gate full of first years flipping through handfuls of cards, their eyes scanning back and forth. There's much nervous tittering until a tall redhead snaps, "Everyone shut up!" One student, teetering on the edge of flunking Diversity, has broken out in hives. Linda Castaneda has bloodshot eyes. Sara Stresky, who rescued animals during the fire, has a migraine. Diversity is not her problem; she already dropped that class because she was failing. Her problem is Dr. Peddie's Anatomy and Physiology class. She needs a high score on the final to pass the class. For the test, she tells me, she'll have to take her meds for an attention deficit disorder.

The second years, as usual, don't seem nearly as anxious, though they have tests too. Most of the animals oblige and Training finals go swimmingly. Goblin, the baboon, presses the side of her head against her cage while Brunelli slides a thermometer into the baboon's ear. Brunelli's aim is solid this time. The only hitch is the thermometer doesn't seem to work. Amber Cavett was overambitious when she dreamed of training Samburu, the cranky caracal, to walk on a leash, but she shows Wilson she has taught the cat to present his front paws for a nail clipping. April Matott instructs Hamilton, the Yucatán miniature pig, to stay put while she measures his not-so-miniature hooked tusks. They all get A's.

Jena Anderson, Nick's trainer, only hooked the mini-horse up to the cart last week, but he gamely pulls it for her final. Though millions of horses have been taught to tow countless carts, it's still an amazing accomplishment. Anderson has convincd a prey animal to pull something it can't see. Anderson scores an A. If she was graded on his weight reduction, the score might be lower. Despite her best efforts, Nick is still a fatty. After Nick and Whiz recently moved to a new corral, Anderson tried again to tie the llama's food basket out of the horse's reach. Before long, Nick managed to knock Whiz's food out of the basket with his muzzle. Anderson gives up. The horse wins the battle of the bulge.

Likewise, after a semester-long effort, Mohelnitzky has not gotten to the bottom of Abbey's stomach troubles. Neither acidophilus nor Zantac makes a lick of difference; the pooch still pukes bile most mornings. Mohelnitzky did train the dog to zip over an A-frame, but Abbey doesn't do as well weaving through a series of poles stuck in the ground, so Mohelnitzky gets a B for her final.

A few animals do not cooperate, reminding these students of their fundamental wildness. On this sunny morning, Kage rouses Todd, the albino red fox, from a nap for her final. Big mistake: Todd, her beloved canine, does not like to be woken from a snooze. At first, he won't get off the shelf at the back of his cage. "That's unusual," Kage says. Still, her final gets off to a good start. He gets on a scale as told, and weighs in at 18.2 pounds. Todd wags his fluffy tail at Wilson, who stands outside the cage, and lets Kage stick her finger covered with toothpaste in his mouth. It's when she gets out nail clippers that everything slides south in a hurry.

When she tries to clip his toenails, Todd bares his teeth at her, even snaps close to her cheeks. "Cut it out," Kage barks and stands her ground. "What is your issue?" A professional trainer might step back, but Kage's grade is on the line. Wilson is watching. She runs the fox through a series of commands. Todd settles down. The fox lets her take a back foot while he stares kind of haplessly at Wilson. "It's so hard to be a fox named Todd," Kage says. Her gamble pays off. Wilson gives her a 100.

A little later, VanHollebeke steps into Starsky's cage and plops down on the berm of concrete. The cavy darts to a far corner of his cage, his little white skirt quivering. Starsky ducks behind a plastic igloo-shaped doghouse covered with pine boughs. VanHollebeke's oversized jacket rustles as she stretches out her arm. She holds her long stick with a spoon taped onto the end. In the spoon is a small pile of alfalfa pellets.

"Come here, handsome," VanHollebeke calls. "It's okay."

She lets out a big sigh. Since the fire, she's regained Starsky's trust, inching her way back into his cage, but you can't tell that just now. The cavy takes a baby step out from behind the igloo, one wide eye trained on us. His little body is rigid like a sculpture. We wait. He waits. VanHollebeke holds the spoon. The humans and the cavy all stand stock still. Around us life pulses. Buttercup, the badger, burrows through a mound of shredded paper with her flipperlike paws. Rosie, the baboon, lounges on her back atop her den box. Hudson, the beaver, strips bark off a bough with his orange teeth. Starsky looks as if a taxidermist got ahold of him, except for the faintest twittering of his whiskers.

"It's so very scary," VanHollebeke says. "I know, bubba." She shakes her head and sighs again. "He did it this morning." The standoff continues. To the cavy's thinking, it's a matter of life and death; for VanHollebeke, only a grade is at stake.

"I'm ready to quit when you are," she snaps. VanHollebeke stands up and steps forward to rake up the pellets she accidentally spilled from the spoon. In one quick hop, Starsky is back behind the igloo. Van Hollebeke seems on the verge of losing her famous temper, and if she wasn't in the cage with the scaredy-cat cavy, she might.

"Ninety-five," Wilson says. "I'll give you the benefit of the doubt."

"I'm determined to touch him before I leave this place," VanHollebeke says and purses her lips. Starsky pokes his head out from behind the igloo again, sees VanHollebeke's figure looming, and vanishes.

* * *

That afternoon in Zoo 2, the first years sit in the dark with pens in hand. They take a collective deep breath as image after image flashes by. They chew their lips, tap their pens against their forehead, squirm in their seats. An hour and a half later, they stumble out into the sunshine, squinting. Now, they all breathe a sigh of relief. "I'm going to have a slide-burning party," a first year announces.

The second-guessing begins. "What was the blue bird with the funny head?" one first year asks, holding her hands atop her head and waggling her fingers to demonstrate its crown of feathers. "What kind of rhino was that," Castaneda asks, "a black rhino or an Indian rhino?" "Black," say a few. "Indian," counter others. "It could have been worse," Castaneda says, her eyes pinched from too little sleep. "He could have given us all four rhinos. He only gave us one."

Castaneda guesses that she missed eight questions, if she counts the rhino. That gives her a B, but good enough to keep her A in the class, which preserves her perfect record. If only her classmates could be as diligent! She turns to show me the first years' most recent gaffe. My eyes scan the back of her sweatshirt. Each class creates a design for its sweatshirt. The first years went a little philosophical, using a quote from Gandhi, but they misspelled his name; the *h* is missing. Castaneda, the driven daughter of immigrants, frowns over her shoulder at me.

I follow Susan Patch back inside Zoo 2. She's going to give Missy, her rat, the last practice run on her Wild West–themed maze. The test is tomorrow. Missy has a black head with dark pink ears and a stripe down the back of her shiny coat. Patch plops Missy on her shoulder. She hasn't just trained her rat to run a maze. She's created a piece of theater. The maze is a mini multilevel stage set. The top level has a painted backdrop of snowcapped mountains; the next level resembles the Grand Canyon; the level below that has a diorama of cactuses. On the bottom is a little saloon, complete with swinging doors, Patch created with popsicle sticks.

She made up a story for the maze—a kind of classic Western, but starring a girl rat. As Patch tells it, Missy has to brave a mine shaft (a toilet paper tube), cross a precarious rope bridge over a gorge, climb down a ladder to the desert below, where she must wind her way through cactuses (weave poles) and forge the River Plastico (a plastic container of water). When Missy gets to town, night has fallen. "What would any rat do?" Patch asks. "Go to the local bar." Missy pushes open swinging doors, tosses back a shot at the bar, and plays poker. Patch trained Missy to press her nose to her thumb, which Patch always sets atop the Queen of Hearts. Because she's a wily rodent, Patch explains, Missy cheats at cards, and thus "makes a hasty exit." The rat opens a little window and dives through it.

Patch has trained Missy on the maze twice a day, every day for three weeks, rewarding her with dried banana chips and sunflower seeds split in half. Like a coach, Patch warms Missy up with a massage and then plenty of chatter. As the rat noses around Patch's shoulders, ducking under her ponytail, and climbing in and out of her hood, the first year prattles on. "Are you ready? Are you ready?" Then she sets her hand on the top of the maze and trills, "Go, Missy!" Missy gamely trots the length of her arm and begins her journey through the Wild West. She takes her time going over the gorge. "Come on, you slug," Patch says. Missy stops amid the cactus weave poles to bathe herself, rubbing her little lavender-pink paws over her face. "No baths," Patch says. "Gary says they bathe when they are nervous." When Missy gets to the Rio Plastico, she takes a sip before ambling over the little bridge. She jumps down to the saloon and stalls by the swinging doors, then ignores the handful of playing cards Patch holds up to her. Patch grabs Missy and deposits the rat back on her shoulder.

"Are you ready? Are you ready? We'll be faster tomorrow. You betcha."

By the third run Missy begins to pick up a head of steam, and on the fourth go she smokes the maze, zipping over the rope bridge and dashing through the weave poles, her little head bobbing left, right, left, right. She bounds over the Rio Plastico, throws open the saloon's swinging doors with her little pink paws, dips her nose into the thimble Patch is using for a shot glass, picks the high card, and bolts out the window.

Patch, wanting to end the practice on a high note, calls it a day. Back in her cage, Missy thirstily takes a pull on her water bottle, her pink nose twitching all the while. "If anything happens to her overnight," Patch says, looking at Missy, "I'm screwed."

The next morning, I drive to EATM along an empty highway under a full moon. The road curves gently like a wide river through the burned, bald hillsides. They are black no more. The scorched landscape, at least at this early hour, glitters like a forgotten family heirloom. Time and winter's cool moistness have burnished the landscape bronze. Under the thin dawn light, the charred, bent-over cactuses resemble gilded filigree. Swaths of fire retardant are the milky green of oxidizing copper.

EATM students zoom into the parking lot, grab their backpacks, and rush for the gate. The vegan from Colorado runs past me as I open the tall chain-link gate. She mutters hello as she goes by. She's trailing the main pack of students by about thirty seconds—thirty seconds that could make her tardy; thirty seconds that could keep her from training the animal she's set her heart on. The minutes, the seconds, pass with such consequence at this early hour.

Every Wednesday morning all the students and most of the staff meet. It's the one chance each week to pass on zoo news to pretty much everyone at once. So, as soon as the hoses are coiled and rakes set aside, all the students file into Zoo 2. The second years sit close together, massage each other, and pass boxes of slick doughnuts among themselves. The first years seem by comparison sunken-eyed and harried. A number of them have their rats in tow, enclosed in little cages they clutch like pocketbooks. The maze test is this afternoon. Michlyn Hines announces that the zoo's truck is out of oil. The mother of one of the second years is dying of cancer, and Hines needs student volunteers to cover the absent student's cleaning shifts. A young water buffalo is moving in next week. It's coming with a zebu. Taj, the Bengal tiger, has runny poop. Wendell, the pygmy goat, has blood in his urine.

As usual, Brunelli has one, two, or three announcements between student council, the yearbook, and her fund-raising schemes. Kage, nicknamed The Dish Nazi, stands up and complains that people are *still* leaving their dirty bowls in Nutrition. Chris Jenkins rises to say a broken bulb was found in the enclosure with Sally, the snapping turtle; the zoo is almost out of crickets; and don't touch the baby sand boas. They'll be for sale soon.

The day unspools like any other day at the teaching zoo, except that it isn't for about a dozen first years. Today is a pivotal day for them—their first chance to demonstrate their training chops for a grade. The test is also their first taste of what it's like to have their fate hang on an animal, in this case a rat. Come mid-afternoon, Zoo 2 buzzes with cheerleading. With just a few minutes left before the rat maze test, first years coach their rodents through practice runs. "Jump it!" "Cross it!" "Rope!" Kristy Marson, one of the most enthusiastic students in her class, is the loudest. Her black ponytail bobs furiously as her rat bounds into a makeshift mini-tram and rides it to a lower level in the maze. Only Marissa Williams is quiet. Williams has big pretty eyes and a dancer's figure and grace. She watches dejectedly as her rat dangles from a rope ladder. It won't climb. Her first two rats became sick, sneezing so hard they got bloody noses. She got a third rat, but it became ill, too. Dr. Peddie prescribed antibiotics, and the rats recovered but not soon enough. Williams only started training one last night.

At the top of her maze is a little TV set. The rat is supposed to put his head in it, so that his little furry face fills the picture tube. He pokes his pointed pink nose in, twitters his whiskers, and then starts to rub his paws over his face. He's taking a bath. Williams sighs. Wilson teaches that if an animal gets a behavior wrong, it's the trainer's fault, not the animal's. Williams's expression says she's having a hard time not blaming her rat, or at least her luck.

The rules for the rat maze test are simple, as Wilson explains: Each student has three minutes. If the rat runs the maze more than once, Wilson will grade the best run. He will deduct for touching the rat or feeding it while in the maze. It doesn't matter if you use verbal cues or not. They will go in alphabetical order, but you can volunteer to go earlier, which is what Patch does. She will be tenth.

The first rat runs a bare-bones maze of foam board with no problem and pops merrily out a window at the end. The second rat, a plump one, stalls in the middle of his run. The third student pulls a rat from her hoodie, and it blasts through an elaborate model prison, climbing a mini razor-wire fence and jumping into the back of a getaway truck with the word FREE written on the side. Everyone claps. The next rat—a rosy, hairless number—runs around like a windup toy, here, there, everywhere but into his maze. As her grade plummets, the student can't help laughing. Wilson cracks up too.

Then Marson gets up. "Sorry, I have to be loud for my rat," she says. As Marson bounces and chants, her rat races through the maze, even swimming across a little pool, her pink paws doing a kind of breast stroke. After her rat blasts through a sixth time with the three-minute clock yet to run out, Wilson says, "You can stop now. Your grade can't get any better."

"My rat just peed all over me," another student announces, and leaves the classroom. A few more students get up, including one of the few guys in the class. With a knit cap pulled down over his eyebrows, he stands still and silently watches as his rat bobs through a clear plastic maze. Finally, Patch is up. She steps to the front of the room.

"Sorry, I talk to my rat," she says.

"Susan, you have whole conversations with your rat," Wilson responds.

As Patch places her maze on the table, the mountain backdrop at the top comes loose. Marson volunteers to hold it in place. Missy scampers back and forth along Patch's shoulders and under her ponytail. "It's going to be good. I'm going to get you. I think you can do it, baby girl. Okeydokey, okeydokey," Patch chatters, then sets her hand on the right side of the maze. Missy scampers down, but freezes when she sees Marson, her face looming over the toilet paper roll mine shaft. Marson ducks out of sight, but Missy is spooked.

Patch starts over. This time Missy ignores Marson and trots through the mine shaft but halfheartedly. The rat takes her time on the rope bridge, meanders through the cactus weave poles, pads around the bridge, freezes outside the swinging doors to the saloon, and rubs her little paws worriedly over her face. Missy's clearly not feeling very cowgirl. "I'm going to beg," Patch says. "Don't do this to me. Don't take a bath. We don't have time for this. I'm going to poke you." Patch picks her up for a second run, but Wilson calls time. Patch plops Missy back on her shoulder. "That was not real fast, not real slick, not fast or slick, but it was all right," Patch says.

After Patch, a student gets up with a fancy maze in the shape of a two-masted schooner. The rat's performance is less impressive; it won't even ring the bell. The next student pleads with her rodent, "Don't you dare do this to me." Another says, "Come on, momma wants to pass this class." The last student to go is Williams. Her rat manages a bit of the maze, even scoots up some of the rope, but then, as usual, bathes by the little TV set. Williams frowns and sighs. "I'm not one to beg rats," she says. She waits out the clock basically. When Wilson calls time she dejectedly picks up her rat and walks away, leaving her maze behind.

"Kristy, you won," someone calls.

"I didn't win," she says. "There's nothing to win."

"You ruined the curve," Wilson says.

It's always something with Schmoo. Her pool needs fixing or she's not eating. Over the past five days, she's gotten toothy, even bitey. On Saturday, Schmoo totally ignored one of her student trainers during a show. A staff member had to step in. Two days ago she clamped on to one of her student trainers' thighs. "I was stunned stupid that I was that stupid," she tells me. "You're always expecting the unexpected to happen, but when it does you're shocked." The bruise on her leg looks like she ran into a coffee table. This morning Schmoo, her black teeth bared, charged another student trainer twice and chased her a good twenty feet. This student now keeps six feet between her and the sea lion.

In addition to the aggression, Schmoo has also stopped eating in the morning. Yesterday she turned her nose up at all fish until 3:30 P.M. Now Wilson slumps in a collapsible chair in the shade near her cage. His brim is pulled low. He was up until 2 A.M. writing the Diversity final. The Schmoo girls, the sea lion's four second-year trainers, stand nearby. All four have various shades of blond hair. The object of their consternation sits in her corner, her long whiskers glowing in the late afternoon sun.

Five human brains join forces to decipher one sea lion brain. This is the crux of training, trying to think like an animal, which turns out to be not so easy for humans. Maybe it's her pool. It's dirty enough to make even the most levelheaded sea lion peevish. The swirling water is a murky brown, and when Schmoo hops out of it, the smell of sewage follows her. The filter, which was meant for a swimming pool, just isn't up to all the poop and sand, but the school can't afford another.

Wilson suggests using rewards other than food, such as pieces of ice or spray from a mister bottle—in behaviorspeak "a secondary reinforcer." He explains that most places work with big, 500-pound male sea lions that are very confident and very food-driven, so they are not as complicated as the comparatively petite Schmoo. Wilson and the second years chew on this for a while, but no conclusions are reached. He leaves, and the trainers get the recalcitrant sea lion out of her roomy enclosure. She happily waddles out and starts working with one of the second years, the one she bared her teeth at this morning. Schmoo salutes, sticks her tongue out, and flips her tail up. Then the trainer turns to me and asks, "Ever been kissed by a sea lion?"

"No," I answer, and before I know it, the trainer points Schmoo in my direction and commands "Kiss!" She's scooting my way, her near-blind eyes fixed on me. The conversation I've just heard about her charging and biting races through my head. I close my eyes extra tight and purse my lips so they are as far away from my face as possible. Our kiss is more Eskimo than anything. We bump noses clumsily. I feel her coarse whiskers against my cheeks. She exhales and her sea lion breath rushes up my nose. I hear a light grunt, and she's gone. My face is intact, though I can't help checking my nose with one hand. It's moist on the end. I smile long and hard and, for some reason, blink back tears.

The training session continues with each of the four second years taking turns. One second year kicks a soccer ball at Schmoo, and the sea lion bounces it back with her nose. The student gets a cart out. Schmoo hops aboard and waves one flipper as the second year pulls it around the middle of Hoofstock. Both camels watch the sea lion wheel by like a beauty queen in a parade. All seems normal. The last trainer, an especially cool-headed second year, orders the sea lion into the large box to one side of her enclosure. Schmoo complies. The student steps into Schmoo's enclosure to reward the sea lion with fish. Then, as the student turns to leave, Schmoo waddles after her. The second year orders her back. Schmoo, all black teeth, charges. The rest of us gasp.

The student backs up out of the cage a good ten feet before Schmoo stops. "Relax!" she commands, and Schmoo does. As the second year walks the sea lion back to her box, Schmoo flashes those black teeth again right by the student's waist. The second year dodges Schmoo, keeps her composure, and orders Schmoo back into her box. The sea lion obliges as if nothing has happened. The student closes the gate. The four Schmoo girls shake their heads, then walk to Nutrition to rinse the fish goo off their hands. I nervously touch the end of my nose, still damp from my sea lion kiss.

Before finals week is out, Brunelli breaks up with her actor boyfriend. She doesn't blame EATM but guesses the program hastened along the inevitable. She's relieved and even has someone in mind to date, a teller at her bank. Still, the day of the breakup, she asks another student to feed Rowdy, the skunk, and goes home upset. Sequoia, the deer, drags a second year, a young woman from Salt Lake City with a dry sense of humor, down the back road. The deer snaps the chain taut and the second year is briefly airborne. The student comes down hard, rips a wad of flesh off her elbow, and lets go. Sequoia's tail flashes as the deer bolts away. "Deer loose!" someone yells. Sequoia comes to an abrupt stop by the door to Hoofstock, where the school's gardener, the deer's favorite human, catches her.

Second years begin what they call turnovers, essentially the process of one student trainer passing their animal to the next student trainer. They demonstrate commands, detail likes and dislikes, show them how to make the animals' dinners. One afternoon, April Matott watches while another second year puts Savuti the hyena through his paces. To the command "Look cute!" he puts his front paws up on a den box and looks back over his shoulder. "You have to tell him he looks cute," the Savuti trainer tells Matott. You can train him to obey commands in one session, she says. The trick, she tells Matott, is your timing must always be precise.

There's a potluck lunch, during which the Secret Santas are revealed and more presents are exchanged. The strain of the week shows. Despite the thumping bass of a boom box, Chris Jenkins falls asleep at the back of the classroom with Abbey's leash in his hand. The dog naps at his feet. Castaneda's eyes are still bloodshot. Sara Stresky tells me she thinks she might have flunked Dr. Peddie's test. The morning cleaning ran over that day, and she arrived a half hour late for the test. She forgot to take her meds for her learning disorder. Will she be the next in her class to go?

Kage's week, which started with holding Mama Dolly while she was put down, never improved. After Todd, the fox, tried to bite her during her final, Benny, her capuchin monkey, nipped her. So did Alamo, the prairie dog. Finally, when she went to get Sadie out for a show, the sheep ran from Kage as if she were afraid for her life. Sadie won't even take food from Kage, which is unheard of with ever-hungry sheep. Wilson teaches that animals associate events that happen simultaneously or close together. If a dog is going through a doorway when a car backfires outside, the dog is likely to be afraid of doorways from then on. What went through Sadie's mind when she watched as Mama Dolly collapsed in Kage's arms? The sheep balks as Kage tries to lead her up the back road. Sadie digs in hoof after hoof.

Dr. Peddie

There are some things you should know about Dr. Jim Peddie. He is deaf in his left ear. He is a good storyteller, so much so that when he tells you the same story a second and even a third time, you don't mind. Nothing grosses him out. He can eat with gusto while discussing the components of tears: oil, water, and snot. He's all boy. He fishes. He loves cars, planes—basically, anything that moves.

Dr. Peddie has a beautiful, smart wife. He made a bundle. He was a vet to the stars. He's delivered baby elephants, removed a garden hose from a hyena's stomach, and brought black leopards back from the brink of death. He flew to Africa and helped paint a lion white. He stood in the wings of the Academy Awards, a blow dart pipe aimed at Bart the Bear, in case the 1,500-pound Kodiak onstage attacked Mike Myers.

He's lived an incredible life. Not a fairy-tale life—there have been some bumps along the way—but a big, rich, exciting life. He still can't believe it, and his voice can fill with wonder, as if he's no idea how it happened, his life. But he knows. True, this country boy from Pennsylvania is talented and personable, but plenty of people are. Dr. Peddie's put in long days for years and years. He's always kept farmers' hours—rising in the dark, often toiling well into the evening. He hasn't slept more than six hours in years. "I've worked ever since I can remember," he says.

Now, he says, he's tired—tired of paperwork, committee meetings, putting animals to sleep, and arguing. He looks fit, but decades of overwork have left him with a list of health problems longer than Schmoo's. He's got spastic colon, vertigo, migraine headaches, and carpal tunnel syndrome. Every day his thyroid destroys a little bit more of itself. It's time to slow down, he says. He wants to tinker with his collection of small antique engines, buy a boat, and travel with his wife. Still, I'm not entirely convinced. It's hard to believe that a man who idles at such a high rpm can slow his pace, even if he wants to.

We are sitting in a dimly lit Chinese restaurant in a low-slung shopping mall off the 101 in Oxnard. There's a soothing hush to the restaurant. Before us is an overwhelming spread: a stack of moo shu pancakes, a slick stir-fry, and a bowl of white rice. Dr. Peddie digs in. It's not long past 6 P.M. Dr. Peddie eats like a farmhand—voraciously and on the early side. Once when I ferried a box of barbecue takeout to his beach house in Ventura, I arrived at 6:45 P.M. to find him pacing his driveway like a ravenous big cat.

Dr. Peddie looks like a guy who would list splitting wood as one of his hobbies. He is tall, big in the shoulders, and a little broad of girth. He has a wide-open face that is easy to read. He purses his lips, scrunches his nose, even rolls his eyes. He sports oversized wire-rimmed glasses and favors baseball caps, but takes them off inside, as he has for dinner. He is one of the best dinner partners you can have. Not only does he have good stories to tell, though you might not want to hear the one about the constipated elephant while you're eating, but also he's interested in most everything, solicitous, says what's on his mind, and laughs heartily at your jokes. His only fault as a conversationalist is that he's prone to exaggerate. Someone he likes is the gold standard; someone he doesn't is the biggest asshole who ever lived. One of his oldest friends jokes that Dr. Peddie inflates all the numbers in his stories by at least 30 percent. His wife used to correct him as he embellished his tales but gave up.

This is his perhaps-somewhat-embellished story. Dr. Peddie set his sights on becoming a dairy vet early on. It was a logical choice for an ambitious boy in Williamsport, Pennsylvania. The town, a county seat, straddles the west branch of the Susquehanna River as it slips through the foothills of the Allegheny Mountains. Other than the surrounding terrain of deep woods, old mountains, and plentiful rivers, Williamsport didn't have a lot going for it then. The former lumber town was a town of small dreams, the vet says. Unemployment was high. Most jobs there were blue collar. Even though his family was middle class—his father was an airplane mechanic, his mother a teacher—Dr. Peddie grew up feeling that the wolf was at the door. That gnawing sense of impending destitution, combined with his mother's forever telling him to get busy, even if he was reading a book, made for a boy who became a driven, restless man.

"All of the years I've known him, he's either going ninety miles per hour or he's asleep," says his wife, Linda.

He was the first member of his family to go to a four-year college. He attended Cornell University for seven years: three years pre-vet, four years in vet school. His only sibling, a younger brother, followed the same path. Dr. Peddie's central accomplishment at Cornell, which he still boasts about regularly, was snagging the only female student in the vet class of '65, the then Linda Reeve. Linda hailed from a farm town on the far end of Long Island. At first, she didn't know what to make of the unsophisticated young man from Pennsylvania. He could be so candid it hurt, Linda says. She did notice his hands. During dissections, he moved them with such sureness and ease. On their first date, they stopped for gas, and he swapped fishing stories with the attendant. She liked the way that he could "scratch and spit with the best of them."

Dr. Peddie saw himself as the future James Herriot of central Pennsylvania, but Linda changed this. As he puts it, she told him "there ain't no way in hell that I'm going to work on cows." Each had spent a glorious summer in California. In 1965, they married during spring break, graduated, packed their car, and turned it west. They had hardly settled in when Dr. Peddie was drafted. He spent his two-year tour of duty not in the jungles of Vietnam but in the walk-in freezers of Fort Lee, Virginia. He oversaw the base's food safety. Though he stayed stateside, Dr. Peddie still got hurt. He pulled up along a tank on a firing range just as it ka-boomed. His left ear instantly began ringing and has never stopped.

Discharged, he and Linda returned again to California with the first of their two daughters in tow. They both joined the staff at Conejo Valley Veterinary Clinic in Thousand Oaks. Bob Miller, now a famous equine specialist, had started the practice in his garage, using an ironing board for an operating table, Linda says. By 1968, when the Peddies came on board, the practice called a building on Thousand Oaks's main street home. Though Thousands Oaks has since morphed into a hopping commuter burg with SUVs barreling from shopping plaza to shopping plaza, in the late sixties it was still an outpost, one where you might see a lion chained along the main drag or maybe even an elephant out for a stroll.

Just down the street from the clinic was Jungleland. The wild animal park was started in 1927 by the animal importer Louis Goebels. In its heyday, Jungleland drew crowds from LA to see its performing lions, tigers, elephants, and chimps. Circuses wintered on the park's grounds. Lions' roars and peacocks' screeches roused locals from their dreams. Schoolchildren were kept home for the day when six mountain lions escaped from the park. By the 1960s, the park's glory days were behind it, but it was still open to the public and the animals continued to work in movies and television. The trainers Hubert Wells and Wally Ross worked there as well as old-timers like Mabel Stark, the heavily scarred tiger trainer who had been a Ringling Bros. star long before.

Conejo Valley Vet cared for the animals, though none of the vets was trained for exotics. Vet schools then rarely broached the subject of exotic animal medicine. Dr. Murray Fowler at the University of California, Davis, offered the first course ever in exotic animal medicine in 1967. Until then, how to sew up a torn elephant trunk or treat a constipated cougar was acquired on the job and passed down by word of mouth.

Before Jungleland, the most unusual animal the Peddies had worked on was a wild boar in vet school. "We had zippo for confidence," Linda says. "Miller's approach was, well, 'What kind of animal is it like?' He thought if we don't try to help them, who will?" Dr. Peddie answered an emergency call from Jungleland about a sick black leopard. He found not a sick cat but a nearly dead cat. Her uterus had ruptured, dumping her three unborn cubs into her abdominal cavity. He operated on her at the clinic, saving her and the cubs. "I was wetting my pants," he says. "Nobody ever said anything about leopards in vet school, but, hell, I did this."

Dr. Peddie loved the adrenaline rush of working with exotics, the thinking on his feet, the pioneering aspect of it. Working on exotics was a tricky business then. There were few sedatives to choose from. Owners rarely knew the weight of their animals. If you gave an animal too much anesthetic, you could kill it; too little, the animal could kill you. Dr. Peddie once had a tiger sit up on the operating table. "I was always pooping in my pants when I worked on these animals."

His confidence grew quickly. He anesthetized Jungleland's mandrill, which he was treating for lymphatic leukemia. After the treatment was completed, he and Miller loaded the doped mandrill into a pickup truck. Dr. Peddie sat the mandrill on his lap, propping the animal up in the passenger window so passing cars would see his exotically colored face. They drove to his house, leaned the mandrill up against the door, rang the doorbell, and hid out of sight. When Linda answered, she took one look and said, "Whose idea of a joke is this?" It wasn't the effect the vets were after. They took the mandrill over to his neighbors'. That woman opened her door and screamed. Satisfied, the vets returned to driving the mandrill around town.

By the 1960s the animals at Jungleland did not always get the best food, if they even got enough. Consequently, the Conejo vets saw cases they had only read about in textbooks. The Asiatic deer got oleander poisoning from chewing cuttings near their cage. All the tigers fell into Rip Van Winkle–like slumbers. The cats had dined on a horse, including its liver, that had been euthanized with barbiturates. Four of the tigers died. The survivors snoozed for as long as four days.

In 1969, Jungleland finally closed. One of its lions took a bite out of Jayne Mansfield's son while the movie star was posing for publicity shots. She sued for big bucks. The park's 1,800 animals were auctioned off. Still, there were plenty of exotic animals in the area. There were movie trainers and circuses scattered around. Hubert Wells had started his own company, Animal Actors of Hollywood. "I came to realize that a lot of these people were very decent people," Dr. Peddie says. "They were tremendously devoted to their animals. You always hear about these people beating the animals. It was 180 degrees from that."

Not long after he started EATM, Bill Brisby had asked Dr. Peddie to teach a class. Dr. Peddie thought the program sounded flaky and begged off. By 1977 he had changed his mind and began teaching there one night a week, lecturing on parrot nutrition or how to diagnose pinkeye, from 6 to 10 P.M. each Monday. His exhaustive essay tests quickly became notorious. His focus remained the practice, and he became a partner as well as business manager. He cranked out eight surgeries a day. Those hands that Linda Reeve fell for could work magic inside and out. Not only could he patch the animals back together, but they hardly had scars. Vet work is hard, physical work, especially surgery. What with the surgeries, working weekends, and never sleeping enough, Dr. Peddie wore out. His hands ached and tingled from carpal tunnel syndrome. He cashed in his share of the practice and signed on to teach full time and be the staff vet at EATM. He was forty-nine. The plan was to slow down and take vacations and holidays. He tried to but couldn't.

Gary Gero, a top Hollywood trainer who runs the show at Universal Studios, asked the vet to visit his facility once a month and give the animals general vet care. It was such good money, Dr. Peddie could not say no. In short order, word spread about Dr. Peddie among studio trainers, and the Peddies found themselves with a new business—a vet practice for movie and TV animals. They called it Drs. Peddie. Life sped up to double time, then triple time. They both worked seven days a week. Dr. Peddie taught his classes, cared for the teaching zoo, then drove off to tend Moose, the Jack Russell terrier on *Frasier,* or zipped over to Universal Studios to check on an orangutan.

This was as glamorous as vet work could get. Trainers solicited his opinion. He hung out on movie sets. He jetted to Australia to be on the set of *Babe 2*. He zigzagged around Southeast Asia with a trainer looking for an orangutan to use in the movie. "It was really stimulating," Jim said. "It's the people. They made my mind work. I'm a different person with them. My thought process kicks up a notch."

It was not so stimulating for his wife. Linda was stuck at home. She was mission control, piloting the business and the substantial paperwork. Every time an animal went on a foreign set, document upon document was needed. "If I went grocery shopping, when I got back there'd be twelve to fourteen messages on the machine," she says. "I gave up reading. I had no life outside of the practice. He was running around the countryside while I was at home doing the books."

In 1999 all of Linda's joints ballooned and throbbed. A year later Dr. Peddie's joints blew up too. He also developed vertigo that brought on spells of spinning that were so bad he threw up for hours. Though he'd had surgery, his carpal tunnel syndrome flared. His hands would fall asleep and he couldn't hold a syringe. Still, the vet couldn't stop, not even slow down. In 2001, between jobs, he zoomed off for his annual all-guys luxe fishing trip in Alaska. He came home to find that Drs. Peddie was no more.

"I shut down the business because I'd had it," Linda says. "I knew he was compromised as he was. It was ridiculous to go off on a fishing trip. He couldn't even tie a tie. I told him when he left, 'I'm shutting this down.' He loved to be a vet to the stars. It was a larger-than-life kind of thing. . . . I said, 'Jim, the animals you're dealing with know you're compromised. They know it inherently.' " Dr. Peddie was furious. "It was my identity," he says.

No matter how down to earth or confident Dr. Peddie is, he cares about status. He'll admit it. He was a big somebody and now, thanks to Linda, he wasn't. Luckily, he still had EATM. That same year, Dr. Peddie, somewhat to his surprise, ascended to the position of department chair of EATM. The program had a new dean, Brenda Shubert. She made big changes, which resulted in Gary Wilson's stepping down as EATM director. Shubert asked Dr. Peddie to take over. If he didn't, the college was going to bring in someone from outside of the program. Dr. Peddie did so reluctantly, he says, which caused a falling out between the vet and Wilson. They have been at loggerheads ever since. You will rarely even find them at the same social event. Few, if any, of the students know about this rift, because the tensions play out in staff meetings behind closed doors. The all-female staff, though, is keenly aware of the bad relations. You could write it off as a struggle between two alpha males, which is likely part of it, but both men have very different styles and very different personalities. Wilson is a thinker, a dreamer; the vet is a doer, Mr. Practical. Whatever the cause, the two men just do not agree, and Dr. Peddie is tired of arguing.

As head of the program, Dr. Peddie's been approachable, not a mythic character like Briz. He might be gruff with students on occasion, when he wearies of their various false alarms about the animals. For a man's man, he's at home with women, which is a good thing at EATM. He can be a bit fatherly, maybe because he has two daughters. He tells me students often ask him for medical advice, confiding in him that they have a rash or that it burns when they pee. "I draw the line at, 'Will you feel this lump?'"

Dr. Peddie, like most men, also enjoys the company of attractive young women. During my first visit to the school, I scanned the photos of second years posted in the student lounge and asked the vet, What was with all the babes? He acted surprised, looked closer at the photos, as if he'd never noticed. He'd noticed.

The vet still feels bad about Mama Dolly, he says, as we make a dent in the moo shu chicken and stir-fry. "It's a sense of failure," he says. A couple of other animals at the teaching zoo hover at death's door. George has some mysterious ailment that makes the little fox as dizzy as a drunk. Louie, the ancient prairie dog, who's paralyzed from the waist down, steadily declines. Schmoo always worries him. She seems fit, but given her epilepsy and age, she's fragile. "I hope I get out of here before she crashes," he says.

Dr. Peddie will retire this coming May. He will have taught twenty-six years. He tried to make his exit last year, but the college president talked him out of retiring. His wife was disappointed.

Just one more year, he promised her. Just one more year, he told the president. He's keeping his bargain, though the first years hope to change his mind. He's ordered a boat to be built up in Paso Robles. He and Linda plan to go to New Zealand. He's anointed his successor: Brenda Woodhouse. Next fall, she'll become EATM's first female director.

What will Dr. Peddie's leaving mean for EATM? The vet has taught at the school longer than anyone. Unlike the time when Briz retired, nowadays no one is worried about the fate of the school, though some staff members wonder how it will fare without the vet's business sense and his good relations with the dean. What will it mean for the vet? "It's scary, this idea of shutting it down," he says. Still, you can already sense a bit of detachment in Dr. Peddie and that his future lies elsewhere, outside of the teaching zoo's front gate. He hasn't even gotten to know many of the first years' names. Come next summer, there will be no more grading tests, no more college meetings, no more paperwork, no more putting animals down—just fishing, trips with his wife, tinkering with his boat, and more fishing. His only worry is, can he be a nobody?

Walking Big Cats

The few weeks between the end of the first semester and the start of the second is a long vacation for most Moorpark College students but not for the EATM students. While the holiday break shutters the campus, the teaching zoo hops. There aren't any classes, but students must still tend to their charges, and not even Christmas liberates them from scooping poop. The only student to get a vacation is the one EATM student who is an EATM student no more. As she feared, Sara Stresky did not pass Dr. Peddie's test. He takes her in his office to tell her that she is out. Dr. Peddie always has a box of tissues ready for these meetings. Stresky digs into the box, wipes away tears. She can no longer venture past the front office during the week. She can't pull on her EATM coat, sweatshirt, or T-shirt. She must wait for the weekend like the rest of the general public to stroll down the front road. There is one advantage to her new low status: on Saturday and Sunday, Stresky, like any visitor, can chatter away with the teaching zoo's residents to her heart's content.

Stresky is the semester's third casualty. A seond year, the reputed pathological liar, finally got the boot in December, after repeatedly reporting late. In the past EATM students mostly washed out or quit because of the physical demands. Now, the academic demands are more often the culprit. Dr. Peddie says students focus on their zoo duties at the expense of studying. That may be so, but perhaps the students are only doing as told. The staff constantly chants the mantra, "The animals come first."

During the holiday break, the long-awaited water buffalo, Walter, arrives with his bosom companion, not a zebu, but a Scottish highland cow named Dunny. The twosome move into a pen in Hoofstock along the front road. They stand side by side, roughhouse occasionally, and look exceptionally cute for bovines. Somehow, like two mischievous boys, they manage to turn a water faucet on and flood Hoofstock twice. Walter's young horns sprout from his rounded forehead. They are only half as long as his ears. Dunny's enormous bulk is covered with a dense, caramel-colored coat worthy of a woolly mammoth. Kaleb, the camel, leans his long neck over the corral fence and sucks on Dunny's coat. The Scottish cow just stands there.

For two weeks George the ailing Fennec Fox pads in dizzy circles, his head cocked as if listening for a faraway rustling with his two large ears. All his tests come back normal, neither a blood cell out of place nor a worrisome shadow on his wee brain. After his student trainers find him trembling uncontrollaby one early January morning, Dr. Peddie euthanizes the small fox and then sends his little body off for an autopsy, in case he had something contagious such as meningitis. Meanwhile, one of the teaching zoo's pigeons, a white one, is found dead. Somehow, amid the small flock, it starved. Some students cast an accusing eye at the pigeon's second-year keepers. This is the place to make mistakes, Dr. Peddie says. That is why it's called a teaching zoo.

Becki Brunelli recovered quickly from her breakup. She's had several dates, including the bank teller and a contestant on the television reality show *The Bachelor*. However, there is a new male in her life who causes her endless pain—Cain, the chattering lory. Brunelli is assigned to the small nectar feeder for next semester. To that end, she's begun handling Cain so they can get used to each other, but every time Brunelli takes the little, loquacious lory out of his cage, he pierces her with his needlelike beak over and over. Her hands and forearms are polka-dotted with bruises and punctures. It's a comeuppance for the heretofore unbitten Brunelli. This little red bird with green wings has made a confident, smart, beautiful, energetic woman second-guess herself. "For me, most of my animals have taken to me pretty well," she tells me. "Your ego wants to say, animals like me. Then you have an animal who doesn't take to you. And you realize it's not about you."

This three-week stretch is another chance for second years to head off on projects. Most stay close to the zoo and save their money (they often have to pay transportation, and room and board for the projects). Trevor Jahangard and then Chris Jenkins head off to a Hawaiian resort to work for a dolphin interaction program. Another student boards a plane to Bermuda to work with cetaceans there. Carissa Arellanes packs for far less tropical climes. She stuffs her suitcase with winter clothing and flies east to spend a week at the Cincinnati Zoo's Cat Ambassador Program.

On a Friday morning in early January, we set out across the broad parking lot at the Cincinnati Zoo—two trainers, Arellanes, I, and one serval on a leash. Mara, the serval, is so excited that the black line of fur down her back bristles. She bounces about the feet of her handler, Jennifer Good. The cat has tripped Good in the past with all her happy bounding. Mara flashes her tail back and forth. With the delicate steps of a ballet dancer in toe shoes, the serval's feet hardly touch the snow-dusted blacktop. Still, Mara leaves tiny little black paw prints on the field of white.

As we walk, the serval darts right, unreeling the black cord of her retractable leash. The cat lowers her nose to the snow, inhales deeply, then raises her small head topped with impossibly big, perked-up ears for a look around. Suddenly Mara throws her spindly front legs out and rushes back to Good in a couple of giddy strides. Good catches the serval between her legs and gives her narrow chest a rub. The cat's off again, this time to the left. She rubs up against Arellanes's legs, arching her back like a house cat. Mara's enthusiasm is infectious. None of us can help smiling, though the air is sharp with cold and a gray sky heavy with winter looms overhead. We sniffle, stuff our throbbing hands in our pockets, and walk into the frigid day behind this joyful African cat.

Mara resides in a small compound on a rise behind some trees to one side of the Cincinnati Zoo's parking lot. Here live two ocelots; a lynx; a young fishing cat; two cougars; four house cats; a male and female cheetah; and, surprisingly, one very large dog, an Anatolian shepherd. They are the zoo's Cat Ambassadors. These felines are trotted on leash into classrooms, where they strut their stuff. The ocelot scales an upright pole, then climbs back down head first. The serval, with its spindly front legs outstretched, hops high into the air. The cheetahs, well, just sit and be cheetahs, which seems to be more than enough to enthrall an audience.

The Cat Ambassador Program is emblematic of a seismic shift in thinking at zoos, the idea that captive animals can help save those in the wild. Many zoos these days have restyled themselves as conservation organizations. They invest in breeding programs to save endangered species, such as the Asian elephant, if only in captivity. They pair with conservation groups working in the wild. The Cincinnati Zoo has about thirty such affiliations, including the Cheetah Conservation Fund, Brazilian Ocelot Conservation Project, and the Fishing Cat Conservation Project. Moreover, zoos with their animals can give a faraway crisis some immediacy. If you see a mandrill in all his multicolored glory in a zoo, the thinking goes, you will be more sympathetic to its plight on the other side of the globe. You may even write a check. Thus the wordy panels hung by many a zoo cage detailing habitat destruction and the like, which can make a visit to the zoo a depressing meditation on human folly. The zoo's Cat Ambassador Program takes this approach one step further, by taking the animal out of the cage, out of the zoo, and into the everyday world. A cheetah sitting languidly on a desk leaves a much bigger impression than that same cheetah in a cage. "It's what we call the wow factor," Good says.

This program and others like it are made possible by trainers. Your average zookeeper does not know how to walk a wildcat on a leash. If you're going to bring exotic animals into classrooms, you better have someone who knows something about training on your zoo staff, and this is where EATM comes in. Three out of the four staffers for the Cat Ambassador Program are EATM graduates, including Good, who leads Mara back to her cage and collects Sihel, the ocelot. Sihel's cry is a fierce "REE-ow." She has chewed all of her toys. The ocelot is given a hunk of bone to gnaw on every night so she'll leave her own tail alone. Despite her wild ways, she is the first ocelot born from a frozen embryo; *sihel* is Mayan for "born again."

Compared to the prancing Mara, Sihel slinks out onto the blacktop, back hung low, eyes bright. She prowls the sides of the parking lot, where the snow cover is thicker. Good punts a chunk of snow her way. Sihel pounces on it. Another trainer heaves a snowball ahead of the cat. Sihel pees on it, then eyes a large, spiny stick. Good pauses so the ocelot can hoist it in her mouth. Sihel carries her head high, stretching her neck so she can drag the stick along. Before going back inside the compound, Good orders the ocelot to drop the stick for a treat. Sihel obliges, but a low grumble emanates from her chest.

Good leashes up Minnow, the program's new fishing cat, a young one that's not much bigger than a house cat. She has a pink nose and webbed paws for scooping prey out of the streams of Southeast Asia and India. Her gray coat is flecked with dark spots. We've just started down the sidewalk toward the parking lot when a long-limbed woman lopes up, takes a look at Minnow, and chortles, "That's not a cat. What is that?"

This is Cathryn Hilker. Hilker started what became the Cat Ambassador Program in 1981, when she began taking a cheetah into classrooms. Exotic cat trainers have a reputation for big, extroverted personalities, and Hilker fits the bill. In her seventies, she frosts her graying hair with blond. She wears big glasses that slightly distort her eyes. Her low, melodious voice naturally projects. There's something Lucille Ball about her, from her leggy tallness to her quick sense of humor. She relishes absurdity and tells stories that are funny at her own expense. When I ask how long she's worked at the zoo, she answers, "The only person who'd been here longer than I have is the hippopotamus, and he died." Hilker makes animal rights people froth, as you would expect, but she's rattled some zoo supporters as well. She once ran a cheetah on a race track. "Everyone was mad at me," Hilker says. "I thought it was so much fun. People are so uptight."

Hilker grew up on a farm in Mason, Ohio, a rural county to the north of Cincinnati, where she became an avid horsewoman; she showed; she foxhunted. She taught English at a private school, married at thirty-eight, and had one son. Then she adopted a ten-week-old cheetah. "Before cats, all horses and self-indulgence," she says. "After cats, my entire life is devoted to serving the cheetah."

Hilker's cause is the fastest land animal. A cheetah can hit sixty to seventy miles per hour in a few seconds, an acceleration any automaker would envy. Everything about the cheetah is designed for speed, from its oversized liver to its small head that offers little wind resistance. It's the only cat that doesn't have a collarbone.

Without it, the cheetah can stretch its front legs straight out for a stride that measures twenty-six feet long. The cheetah's flat tail acts like a rudder. The cat's pads are tough like tire treads.

The cat's speed, good looks, and relative docility have made it a favorite with man since antiquity. As early as 3000 BC, the Sumerians leashed cheetahs and hunted with them. Called coursing, hunting with cheetahs became an enduring sport from Europe to China. The cheetah wore a hood, as a falcon would, and once it was removed, the cat sprinted for the prey. Akbar the Great, an Indian mogul of the sixteenth century, reportedly had over 9,000 coursing cheetahs. The demand for hunting cheetahs drained wild populations, and by the early 1900s, India had to import cheetahs from Africa for hunting. Still, at the turn of the century an estimated 100,000 cheetahs roamed Asia and Africa. Now those numbers have dwindled to an estimated 12,500 cats, nearly all of which are in Africa.

The deck is hugely stacked against the cheetah, from the fur trade to habitat loss. African farmers consider them pests and regularly shoot them the way American ranchers once did the wolf. Added to that is the fact that today's wild cheetah population is deeply inbred, thanks to the Ice Age. That chilly stretch of time so reduced the number of cats that their gene pool today is a teeny one. Consequently, they are prone to disease and reproduce poorly. According to the Cheetah Conservation Fund, only one in ten cubs born in the wild makes it to adulthood. Though zoos have had luck breeding many species, the cheetah is not one of them. That this specialized marvel is still with us on planet Earth is no small miracle.

However, this is not what Hilker was thinking about when she first proposed to the director of the Cincinnati Zoo getting an animal or two out of their cages. As she remembers, "He said, 'That's the dumbest idea I ever heard.' " In the seventies, her idea was revolutionary. Most zoos then were museums, where animals were displayed like living sculptures. Hilker got the okay to get a horned owl out of its cage. She wasn't to do anything but hold the bird and talk about it. Whenever she did, visitors surged around her. "When you get out behind the bars and out behind the moat, you give the animal an immediacy," Hilker says.

Hilker asked a friend, Jack Maier, then president of Frisch's Big Boy restaurants, to donate $5,000 to start a program of taking a few animals—a snake, the horned owl, an opossum—to schools in what became the zoo's outreach program. Then she got Maier to fund Frisch's Discovery Center, where the public could see some animals up close, even touch some. She asked the zoo director if one of the lion cubs that was rejected by its mother could move to the center. He said, "Yes, but don't take it off the grounds." Hilker took the lion cub home at night and brought it to the zoo each day. People lined up ten-deep to see him.

She was on a roll. She asked for her very favorite animal, a cheetah. "To my utter astonishment, I was told I could go to Columbus and get one." The Columbus Zoo loaned the Cincinnati Zoo one of two cubs. The cheetah was about the size of a house cat and still had her mantel, the long, fawn-colored fuzz that grows along a cheetah cub's back. Her name was *Maliki,* Swahili for "Angel." "I had no idea what it was like to have a wild animal give you its heart," she says. "Everything about it cut me like a knife."

For the first year, Angel slept with Hilker and her husband. She played with the couple's harlequin Great Dane, Dominic. By the time she was a year and a half, Angel was a fully grown, eighty-pound cheetah and stood twenty-eight inches. She measured five and a half feet from her nose to the tip of her tail. While still a cub, Hilker began taking the cat to schools. The cheetah was called the zoo's Wildlife Ambassador of Goodwill. Angel sat and Hilker talked. She talked about cheetahs, about wild animals, why they are important, about the "web of life."

Zoo honchos were worried they would be criticized for having a cheetah on a leash, Hilker says, but the public and the media were fascinated. "Money started to come in." The twosome became national—even international—celebrities of a sort. They made the rounds of national talk shows. Angel licked David Letterman and jumped on the couch with Regis and Kathie Lee. They met Prince Charles in Palm Springs.

Zookeepers in Cincinnati begrudged her her success, Hilker says. Angel, they sniffed, was not a *true* wildcat; she'd been tainted by training. Training was a bad word at zoos. The T word has circus connotations and bespeaks tricks, even costumes. Zoos considered themselves serious educational institutions and anything that verged on entertainment was suspect. A cheetah on a leash sounded like too much fun. "It was totally disapproved of," Hilker says. Still, she says, "Some of the zookeepers who were the most vocal critics would call and say, 'Hi, my parents are in town. Could they come see Angel?' That was very rewarding."

Angel was so in demand, the Cincinnati Zoo enlisted more cats. Carrie, a mountain lion Hilker raised on her farm, "a teeny, runty cat," she says, was drafted into service. Then the serval Mara and a snow leopard moved in. The Cat Ambassadors became one of the zoo's most visible programs and a national model. "Now everyone wants to mimic the program," Hilker says. "There have been some horrific ones because they don't want to invest in the training. Cheetahs are not pussycats. When they get angry they strike."

You just don't hook up an exotic cat and go for a stroll as you would a dog, though trainers who know how to walk a tiger or cougar make it look that easy. Mara Rodriguez does. At EATM, Rodriguez walks at least one of the two cougar brothers, Sage and Spirit, nearly every day she's there, chaining a cat and hooking her fingers with her long manicured nails through the links for a better grip.

"I seem calm and mellow [when I walk them], but if people could only see inside my head with everything going on and all the gray hairs under my dye job," she says.

Rodriguez has been walking big cats for twelve years. When Rodriguez was a student at EATM, none of the cats came out on a leash, so she learned on the job at Animal Actors of Hollywood. Rodriguez started with cubs, which weren't as scary, and worked her way up to tigers. Along the way, she built up the needed confidence. "Working with cats, you don't even get okay until about two years," she says. "You have to walk without fear. . . . Once you look comfortable to other people you're getting somewhere."

When Hilker decided to leash up big cats, she knew she needed help. She had trained dogs and horses but never a wild animal. She hired two trainers to coach her: first, a woman who had leash-trained a cheetah at Six Flags Marine World; second, a sarcastic EATM grad, who spent three summers teaching Hilker. "She was merciless all day, every day," Hilker says. "I'd go home and cry on the way home. I paid her my money. Me. My money. And she was merciless."

To walk a big cat is to learn how to bluff. You want them to think that you are in charge, though the cats are stronger, faster, and have sharper teeth. The bluff comes from being confident and consistent. Hilker learned to not let the cat ever get away with anything, and to always know in advance what she wanted the animal to do and where she wanted to lead it. She learned how to get a lounging cat up for a walk. She learned that different cats require different approaches. Hilker needed to be forceful with Carrie, the cougar, who preferred sitting to walking and was bullheaded compared to the cooperative Angel. Cougars don't take offense at being corrected, but if you discipline a cheetah, Hilker says, "they are in an instant snit. They will close their eyes and go rigid. . . . They are Miss Priss with high heels and a tutu on."

Angel was a perfect starter cat for Hilker. She was forgiving of the trainer's early blunders. In eleven years, Angel struck Hilker only once. During a presentation, a kid crawled under the table Angel was sitting on and pulled the cheetah's tail. Spooked, Angel swatted Hilker and her dewclaw caught the trainer's arm. The cheetah watched in fascination as blood ran down Hilker's arm.

Angel died in 1992. In her memory Hilker created the Angel Fund. Donations to the fund support the Cheetah Conservation Fund, which works to save the cat in Namibia. Namibia has the largest population of wild cheetahs, but their numbers are dropping. Using an innovative approach, the program gives farmers Anatolian shepherds, an ancient Turkish breed, to protect their livestock. With the dogs protecting their livestock, the farmers don't feel compelled to kill cheetahs.

This explains why there is a dog in the Cat Ambassador Program. Alexa joined the program as a puppy so that people could see the breed that was helping save the cheetah. While in Namibia the shepherd and the cheetah are not on friendly terms, here in Cincinnati they are boon companions. Sara, one of the program's two current cheetahs, and Alexa got to know each other out at Hilker's farm. At first there was plenty of fighting, but now the twosome are very simpatico. At the zoo, they are roommates. They still play, but Sara tires of it first, whereas Alexa could wrestle all day. They are only separated at feeding time. Dinner can bring back the old growling.

Though Hilker is quite underdressed for the winter day in a sweater and silk scarf, she wants to show me how you walk a cougar. It's near closing time, 5 P.M., and the pale winter light has just begun to fade. Hilker grabs a heavy chain and heads into one of the cougars' outdoor enclosures. From where I'm standing,

I can't see her but I can hear her. "There you are, you big ugly cougar," she says. "Why are you sitting there looking at me like you might attack me? Get over here, you mean thing." She emerges with the fawn-colored cougar, holding the chain in her gloveless hand. Arellanes and Good join us. The cold clamps on us like a vise as we trod across the parking lot for the last cat walk of the day.

The cougar is matter-of-fact. She neither bounds like the serval nor hunts like the ocelot. "She just trundles along," Hilker says, kicking some snow the cat's way. Hilker hears a car and stops. Cars can rattle the cat. When the engine's purr fades into the distance, we turn to go. The cougar remains seated. This is what Hilker wanted to show me. She applies steady pressure on the chain, and before long the cougar obliges. A cheetah treated this way would pitch a tantrum, Hilker says.

"Let's leave cougar prints," she says. "I love leaving cougar prints."

Just outside the parking lot's fence, brick houses line the street. The low winter sun glints pink in their windows. We cross the snow-glazed lot, a trail of paw prints behind us. We arrive at two picnic tables. Hilker orders the cougar up on one, then tells her to leap to the other, which the cat does in a flash. When Hilker asks the cougar to sit, the cat doesn't budge. Good tells Hilker she's using the wrong hand signal. "Oh," Hilker says; she points her index finger at the sky, and the cougar complies. Arellanes and I pose for photos. We pull off our gloves and dig our fingers into the cougar's rough, dense fur, like a coarse rug. We smile for the camera. The cougar purrs.

Trainers have a great and unusual gift to share, to make the impossible possible, and most are generous with it. Hilker is no different. After the cougar is put away and the staff has left, she turns to me and asks, "Want to pet a cheetah?" Before I know it, we are standing outside Sara's small indoor cage as Hilker looks me over for anything that might catch the cat's eye. She has me put down my bag and take off my gloves. She wonders out loud about my coat with its loose, nubby weave, but rules that I can keep it on. A small distant voice in my head sounds an alarm, but when Hilker opens the cage door I follow her in.

Sara lounges on her raised, rectangular bed filled with hay. Hilker sinks down next to her and sighs happily. This is the first she's seen the cheetah since a recent trip. "I couldn't wait to get back and thump my cats," she says. Hilker drapes her right arm over Sara and scratches her neck with her left hand.

I do not exude confidence, and I know it. I'm less scared than awkward. I feel like I should curtsy or bow. Hilker motions me to sit down on a second bed, close to Sara's, and to pet her on her shoulder. I reach out and gently touch her. The cheetah doesn't even turn her head. Her shoulder is bony. Her fur is like chenille. I'm dumbstruck by the sight of my own hand against cheetah spots.

I tentatively stroke Sara with my fingertips as Hilker chatters casually about her vacation. I can hardly respond at first. A satisfied purr sounds deep inside the cheetah. The cat turns to look at me once or twice but mostly can't be bothered. Before long, I find myself ruffling her fur with my fingers as if she's a dog, and talking away to Hilker. Suddenly, two women chatting in a cage with a cheetah between them seems the most natural thing in the world, and that's the marvel of it.

That evening, Hilker leans against a table with Sara posed on one side and Alexa the shepherd on the other side. About a dozen people have turned out on this frigid night ostensibly to hear Hilker speak, but really to be in the same room with a cheetah. The small group smile daftly and sit up straight in their seats. "All my friends were jealous when I told them what we were doing to-night," a woman gushes to Hilker. Hilker leans against a table, her long legs crossed at the ankles before her. "You're a good kitty," Hilker says. For the umpteenth time in the past twenty-five years, Hilker tells of her true love, this cat with the flexible spine and aerodynamic tail. She points out Sara's dewclaw and the black teardrops under her eyes. The cat and dog hold their heads high and stare straight ahead while two Cat Ambassador staffers clutch their leashes. As if bored, Sara raises a paw and licks it gently. "Are you primping?" Hilker turns and asks. The cheetah shifts, as if to get down, and a trainer stops her.

On the other side, eager-eyed Alexa pants. When she's asked to speak on command, Alexa woofs enthusiastically. When the trainer leads the dog through the small audience, Alexa slaps the air with her tail and solicits pats with her bright eyes and soft, moist nose. In Namibia, one of these dogs killed two male baboons, Hilker says.

Then it's Sara's turn to step down. The cat refuses. She's peeved about being stopped earlier. It is, as Hilker says, "so cheetah." After much coaxing, the cheetah hops down as if it were her idea to begin with and saunters back and forth through the audience, her shoulder blades shifting dramatically from side to side. She slinks like a runway model. People lean forward in their seats, crane their heads for a better look, and sigh. A man at the end of a row bends at the waist so that his face is even with Sara's as the cheetah slides by. The wow factor is clearly at work. Hilker smiles yet again at this simple magic. "Isn't it charming to have a cheetah walk right by your face," she says. "Aren't we silly?"

Falling in Love

Love is in the air at the teaching zoo these days. The first years ponder their affections for various animals, divining crushes from true devotion, considering compatibility versus sheer magnetism. One enthusiastically proclaims her love for the turkey vulture to me. Another confides he's got a thing for the binturong. A first year from Virginia has given her heart to a nippy macaw. All this lovesickness has a reason. The first years must turn in their animal requests in less than a week, by January 21. These will be the animals they will work with come summer semester, when the second years have graduated and gone. Summer is still four months away, but it's the first light on the dark horizon, the first promise of meaningful animal contact to come.

The first years must pick animals in four categories: primates, carnivores, birds, and hoofstock. In each category they can list their choices in descending order, from most desired to least. It's something like making a Christmas list. And who gets what will have something to do with who's been naughty or nice. These assignments are the big payoff for the months of hard work.

In the Briz years, he pretty much chose who got assigned to what animal. Now there is a system with a scientific bent. The staff ranks the students according to grades, attendance, and how much time they have weeded or painted around the teaching zoo, what they call volunteer hours. The students with all the possible points, such as Linda Castaneda, Susan Patch, and Terri Fidone, land at the top of the list. The animals in demand, such as Schmoo and Taj, go to these students. Then the staff starts working down the names. The lower your grades, the spottier your attendance, the farther down your name falls. If you are near the bottom, well, you'll get the animals that are left, the ones no one wanted.

This system is the reason why that one morning Larissa Comb rolled in thirty seconds late haunts the former stockbroker. She has straight A's, worked all her volunteer hours, and was only late that once. But that one blunder sent her name trailing down the list. Still, Comb takes her chances and asks for Schmoo, though she doesn't have all her points and knows about a dozen students would like the sea lion.

Tony Capovilla does not have straight A's but he can pretty much expect to get the only animal he wants: Rosie. The former plumber came to EATM just to work with her, which was a bit of a risk. There are four men among the first years. As it turned out, though, one, a former Federal Express driver and father of two, does not want to work the baboons. He thinks they are scary, not to mention time consuming. He'd rather put the hours into Max, the neurotic military macaw he's fallen for. So that nearly guarantees Capovilla Rosie.

These requests are especially freighted, because this is when the first years choose what they call their year-longs, which is what Rosie is. Most of the animals at the teaching zoo get a new set of trainers every semester, but some the students work with for twelve months. This includes all the primates and Schmoo. A year is quite a long engagement, so the students gnash their teeth, scheme, and strategize.

Anita Wischhusen tells me disgustedly that some first years keep their animal requests to themselves. "They say, 'I'm not going to tell you because you'll ask for them.' That so doesn't make sense." Wischhusen does not have the grades for Schmoo, so she won't ask for her. She doesn't quite for Taj, but she's requested the tigress anyway. In the bird category she's asking for a "turaco, turaco, and turaco. I don't want a bird who will bite. I'm not a bird person." She's leaning toward Zulu for her primate.

Patch is one of those first years keeping her choices to herself. She's trying to avoid the competition, jealousy, and resentment that swirls around animal assignments, but, as Wischhusen makes clear, that's nearly impossible. Patch's first picks are Goblin, the hamadryas baboon; Laramie, the eagle; Sage and Spirit, the cougar brothers; and Lulu, the recently arrived pregnant camel. Like Wischhusen, Castaneda does not want a parrot. Like Patch, she wants the cougar brothers. She'll also ask for Scooter, the capuchin, and the two-for-one deal, Walter and Dunny. She figures the young water buffalo and the Scottish cow will be a good way to build her confidence for a camel later.

First years also consider who will be their co-trainers. As many as four students are assigned to each animal. So if you hear a fellow student—a known slacker or malcontent—is asking for the same animal as you, you might think again. There are a first year or two who fall into this category. One in particular has a reputation for worming out of work. Bets are on her, a young student with unkempt long hair and moist eyes, being the next to wash out.

As with all things at EATM, the animal requests provoke much discussion and anxiety. Things here so naturally rise to a fevered pitch, if only because everyone is so exhausted. The first years fret like brides waiting for word of their arranged marriages.

In their more levelheaded moments, the first years say they will love whatever animal they get. Time after time that has proved true, says Dr. Peddie.

For nearly every animal, there is some wide-eyed, love-struck student. "I never thought I'd fall in love with this cavy," Mary Van-Hollebeke says. Her affections crept up on her even though, as she says, the cavy "doesn't give much back." When she thinks of her spring graduation, she says, "He's the animal I'll miss the most." Kage adores Benny, the ancient capuchin, even though he's bit her, masturbates regularly, and resembles a character from a Stephen King novel with his hairless, curled tail. Two second years are devoted to Louie, the paraplegic prairie dog that rarely emerges from his den box. Even the teaching zoo's gardener fell hard.

The tall, muscular fellow with a constant tan and ready smile dotes on Sequoia, the mule deer. One day as he was nervously trimming the acacia bush by Sequoia's cage, the deer trotted over. She poked her soft muzzle through the fence and licked his arms. At first, he worried that Sequoia might bite him, but before long he was smitten. Now he brings the deer bundles of browse to chew. When the east winds gust, it rattles Sequoia, so he sits outside her cage to calm her. Last year, when Sequoia pummeled a second year, the gardener found himself terribly torn. He was dating the student. "I thought, poor Stephanie. Then I'd think, poor Sequoia." Eyewitnesses claim he yelled, "Don't hurt her," meaning Sequoia.

Becki Brunelli has developed a big soft spot for Nuez, the Central American agouti. "I like rats so much and he's a big rat," she says. "He's kind of an underdog and I always like underdogs." He's the size of a house cat and has a shiny cinnamon-colored coat stippled with black. His head is shaped like a squirrel's but with a longer muzzle. At first glance he looks tailless but between his rounded haunches is a tiny bald nub, just enough to remind you he's a rodent.

Brunelli is one of the few, if not the only, students who will pick up Nuez and cuddle. That's because Nuez is known as the rodent squirt gun. Male agoutis spray female agoutis with urine as a come-on of sorts. Nuez tries the same technique on the students. Just inside the cage door Brunelli keeps a plastic cafeteria tray to shield herself from Nuez's love sprays.

Many of the EATM students dislike rats to begin with, especially one that squirts. A number of the students assume it's ejaculate that Nuez jets at them. One calls it his "special sauce." Brunelli always corrects them. It's urine, she reassures them. Brunelli has lobbied hard for Nuez, urging first years to request him as an animal assignment. "Whenever anyone says anything bad about him, I always say, 'But he's so cute.' "

To prove her point to me, we head down to Nuez's cage behind Nutrition. Brunelli swings open the door, and Nuez rises up on his back legs. "Don't you spray me," Brunelli says. She emerges cuddling the agouti like a baby, his soft nose tucked into her neck. He rubs his face along her throat, and gives her a peck on the cheek. He's so happy he squeaks. Two first years wander over, curious.

"Is he a rodent?" one asks.

"Does he bite?" queries the other.

Just nibbles, Brunelli explains, love nibbles. She launches into her pitch about how affectionate Nuez is while the rodent snuggles close. First years often look on with obvious envy as second years embrace their animals, but not now. The two first years look dubious, even a bit revolted. "He's trying to seduce you," one says to Brunelli.

"They mate for life," Brunelli says, which I don't think is much of a selling point—at least not for these two.

Brunelli isn't the only second year actively lobbying first years, urging them to ask for their animals. Kage has recruited a first year for Todd, the fox, and has groomed another for Benny. VanHollebeke pleads with first years on her cavy's behalf. Oddly enough, Amy Mohelnitzky finds herself lobbying for Abbey. She loves the dog so much that's she asked to train her again this semester, but none of the first years are interested in the canine star. To them, she's just a dog—moreover, a high maintenance one that needs bathing and brushing and fussing over her food. Why would they work with a dog that has a bad stomach when they could train a perfectly healthy lioness?

It doesn't help that Abbey has been more miserable of late. Mohelnitzky picks a staffer's brain on what might calm the poor dog's stomach. Nothing has worked so far. As they talk, the staffer mentions that Abbey would do better in a home. Mohelnitzky raises her eyebrows. "Would you want her?" the staffer asks. Not long after, Mohelnitzky asks her apartment manager if she could have a dog. He says no.

It's the first week of second semester. A few of the big carns, such as Legend, have leftover Christmas trees in their cages. They can pounce on them as if they were big prey. The lemon trees hang heavy with fruit by the pen of Clarence, the Galapagos tortoise. The mornings dip below freezing, and the sun is slow to emerge over the mountaintops to the east. The students don headlamps like coal miners, aiming the beams through the dark at cage floors, scanning for wayward turds.

The first years gird themselves for what they are warned will be an even tougher semester. How can that be? they wonder. This is how: in addition to classes, the first years will be the worker bees for the Spring Spectacular, the school's annual fund-raiser. That means cleaning the zoo, studying for class, building sets and props, and tons more schlepping in general. A student from Argentina gets to shaking just thinking of the semester ahead. Susan Patch, as usual, remains unflappable. She's signed up for kick boxing this semester.

The first years' reputation sinks a little lower. A classmate went in with the capuchin troupe by herself to clean, which is against the rules. She thought she had closed the chattering monkeys off to one side of their baleen cage, but the alpha capuchin slipped through to her side. She fled, leaving tools behind. Another first year opened a door in Big Carns too soon while moving an animal into the arena. Castaneda and the other go-getters among the class resent being lumped in with the screwups. How will they ever measure up to the second years at this rate?

For their last semester at EATM, the second years have relatively few courses remaining. The focus of all their energies will be Spring Spec, specifically "Welcome to the Jungle," a kind of hallucinatory, wordy tale of a circus train crashing on an island. The show has a big cast and includes many cameo appeareances by teaching zoo animals. By March, the second years must learn their lines and teach the animal actors their parts.

Before any training can start, though, the turnovers have to be complete. This process always riles up some of the animals. Samburu the caracal has gotten so aggressive during feedings, knocking his face into the bars, that he's skinned his nose. Salsa, a Catalina macaw, has gotten nippy. Cain, the chattering lory, wouldn't quit biting Brunelli, so she quit handling the bird. Instead, she sits outside the cage, hoping to make friends from a distance.

Depending on the animals, turnover can take hours, days, or even months. The process for Birdman, the kinkajou, is simple. Birdman's current trainer demonstrates how to crate the critter, and Jahangard's set to go. While Jahangard is in the cage, though, something funny happens. The kinkajou opens his mouth wide as if to bite the student. His current trainer, who nuzzles the kinkajou with her face, has never seen Birdman do that. On the other end of the spectrum, the turnover for the cougar boys can last the whole semester. If all goes according to plan, by that time each of the students will have walked a cougar on a chain around the teaching zoo.

Mara Rodriguez runs the changeover. In fact, the students never work with the cougar brothers without Rodriguez present. This afternoon, she steps into the arena in the center of Big Carns with Sage and Spirit. As usual, Rodriguez is put together with her well-fitting clothes, mirrored wraparound sunglasses, and long nails painted a bruised maroon. In a corner of the arena, two second years keep Spirit busy so Rodriguez can work with Sage, the mellower of the two cats, on the opposite side.

Rodriguez starts each turnover by acquainting the students with the cougars and vice versa. This is a case where desensitization works both ways. However, the brothers have a head start. Sage and Spirit are far more used to humans than these three young women are accustomed to standing next to a mountain lion. To work with the cougars, the students have to learn a delicate balancing act: how to be relaxed yet attentive, confident yet cautious. They have to find that spot where opposite impulses harmonize. If they don't, they risk getting hurt or worse.

In the afternoon sun, three second years lean against the high chain-link fence, staring, as if hypnotized by Sage. The cougar, his eyes closed, lounges on the ground by Rodriguez's feet. Rodriguez calls in one of the second years, a pear-shaped young woman with straight hair down her back. She steps through the gate looking less frightened than awkward. Rodriguez tells her to tuck in the dangling strings of her sweatshirt hood and then motions her over to Sage. "You can pet him," Rodriguez says. "You can lean down to do so but don't ever reach down and tie your shoe or massage your ankle."

The student squats and tentatively strokes the cat. Sage licks a round paw and scratches his head. He never looks at the second year. Off in the corner, the students playing with Spirit laugh and gossip.

"I'm going to have you walk from here to here, and don't look weird," Rodriguez tells the student. "I don't want you looking around, running into things. He'll notice that. Be confident." The second year walks a few steps one direction and then back as we all watch. She looks self-conscious. The humans watch her. The cat does not.

That student comes out and the next goes in—Jena Anderson, the second year who taught Nick to pull the cart. Rodriguez has her tuck in her sweatshirt strings also. Anderson, who typically is poised, now looks just the slightest bit bug-eyed. Spirit wanders over from the far corner. Anderson turns, sees Spirit, and freezes. The second years in the corner of the arena call the stray cougar back. "You just get the hell out of the way if [the cougars] look like they will chase each other," Rodriguez says.

Sage remains detached. He pulls himself up and saunters in Anderson's direction. Again, Anderson freezes. "If they don't pay attention to you, it's no big deal," Rodriguez says, walking alongside the cat. Then, as Rodriguez steps over a log lying on the ground, she catches her pants leg on a branch. She almost trips—exactly what you don't want to do. Rodriguez catches herself, stumbling ever so slightly.

Anderson switches off with the third student, who stands around the drowsy cat. She walks from here to there, as Rodriguez tells her, tries not to act weird, and tries not to act like she's in a cage with a dangerous animal. The indifferent cat stretches out on the ground, lazily squinting. "It seems boring, but I hope you guys appreciate that there are people in the cage," Rodriguez says. "You want [the cougars] to not care."

* * *

Come second semester, first years can sign up for the first of three classes on primates taught by Cindy Wilson, Gary's wife. The couple began dating in high school and went to EATM together. She works part time at the zoo. In addition to the primate classes, Cindy oversees the behavioral enrichment program. She is prone to small, wry, almost inscrutable smiles and is typically soft-spoken, that is, until she uses her primate voice. Then she booms, so most any primate, including a human, will stop in its tracks. She's a motherly figure to many of the students, a role she enjoys. A past class nicknamed her Momma Cindy. She's been known to hand out Twinkies to students who answer questions correctly in class.

Cindy Wilson learned about primates from working with them firsthand. When Gary was the director, she stopped by the college to pick up his paycheck and came home with a six-day-old rhesus macaque. "At first I was overwhelmed," she tells me. "Within twenty-four hours we had bonded. I said, 'He can stay.' " His last feeding was at midnight. By four months, he could scale the refrigerator. Gary built a jungle gym of PVC pipes in their living room. Cindy had found her niche. "With primates I'll never know all I need to know," she says. "It's a very dynamic relationship."

She's using today's class as an introduction to some of the primates, knowing the first years have to finalize their animal requests. So we walk down the front road en masse to Zulu's cage, where several of his second year trainers stand waiting. Zulu sits on his shelf behind them, nonchalantly chewing gum. Kristina Nelson, the coolheaded Iowan whom Schmoo charged last month, starts. "A lot of people pass on asking for him because you have to deal with his owner," she says. "Everyone who comes with Zulu is very nice." That pretty much concludes the sales job. What follows sounds like a support group for abused wives, all married to the same polygamist husband.

"He's spoiled rotten," Nelson continues. "He's the biggest spoiled baby. He's left bruises on us."

"It's hard because he threatens the whole time," chimes in another trainer, a reedy brunette. "He grabbed me a lot. I quit grooming with him in the summer." While she talks, Mary Van-Hollebeke blows slowly into Zulu's mouth to keep his highness happy.

"The first time he grabbed me, my legs shook," Nelson says. "You have to pet him, not groom him. You have to go the right direction on his fur." If you don't, he'll grab you, she adds.

Someone nearby mutters, "I don't think so." Everyone squints into the sun and looks dubious. Cindy explains about the harem Zulu would have in the wild and how he has to assert his authority over his female trainer. The first years look at her, nodding blankly.

"He scared me more than anything," says the brunette. "I have scars on my hands from his nails."

"Even feeding at first was terrifying," says Nelson. He's left bruises in the shape of handprints on their arms. You have to let him squeeze your arm, she insists, or he'll stay mad. Maybe sensing that she's overdone it, Nelson adds, "When you go away and come back, he's so ecstatic to see you."

Zulu, one arm draped over a knee, looks as if he's calmly listening, carefully considering all that's being said. VanHollebeke softly strokes the side of his big head, which he leans up against the bars. As the group shifts around the corner to Goblin's cage, there are some shared glances, some mutterings about not wanting to be grabbed. Sunni Robertson, who took care of Zulu in the fall, has decided the mandrill is not for her. Wischhusen, who's afraid of the macaws, is unintimidated. She will ask for the mandrill, her "monkey in drag."

A second year with big brown eyes leans her back against Goblin's cage. The baboon carefully works her black fingers along the second year's hairline, careful to leave the student's barrette in place. Cindy explains that the second year grooms with Goblin so the baboon will feel comfortable with the group of students gathered round. It's a show of solidarity, the second year's way of saying to the baboon, "I'm on your side." Goblin loudly smacks her lips together, a sign of contentment and friendship. The only downside to Goblin, the brown-eyed second year says, is that her turnover will be very slow, but otherwise she is a honey. The first years smile. Some even sigh enviously. This is more like it. Who would volunteer to be grabbed when they could be groomed? The first years are, after all, only human.

The next day, Saturday, a few second years dawdle in the chill morning air by the wolf's cage. Legend bounds about excitedly, her white tail flashing, her lips parted. Even C.J., the coyote, is wound up in the cage next door. The coyote bites at her hind leg, turning tight circles as she does. Holly Tumas strides up and pulls out a heavy key chain. Tumas, who has taught at the school since 1999, has her baseball cap pulled low over her long, straight, dark brown hair. Former male students nicknamed her "Hottie." She laughs a great joyful laugh. Though she is a stickler for the teaching zoo's rules, she is approachable and friendly. She is Legend's alpha female.

To be Legend's alpha takes more subtlety than you'd assume. You can't throw your weight aound; you'll scare the wolf. Scared, Legend becomes aggressive. With her upright posture and solid voice, Tumas broadcasts that she is top rank. Her long friendship with the wolf helps. Tumas has known Legend for six years, since she graduated in 1997. She got a job with the animal show at Magic Mountain, a theme park in Valencia, where she trained and walked Legend, or Ledgy, as she is called at EATM. When the park sold off its animals, Tumas and then, later, Legend joined

EATM. If the wolf ever second-guesses Tumas's dominance, she takes over a few of Legend's feedings in order to reestablish that she is top wolf in this small pack.

Female students typically need speech lessons to work with Legend. As one second year says, she's working on her "Legend voice." The natural female speaking pattern—that musical jingle—does not lend itself to training a wolf. The students can't use the high, chirpy singsongs they so often do with the other animals. They can't slide up a note at the end of a command, making it sound like a question. They have to make their voices lower and firmer. Men, however, must do the reverse. Men, especially the more testosterone-laden, make Legend nervous. Even those with a soft touch, such as Chris Jenkins, can unnerve the female wolf. Consequently, male students learn to tone down their masculinity.

Legend calls a corner cage along the front road home. Her archenemy, Kiara, the lioness, is her neighbor on one side; her best buddy, C.J., the coyote, is on the other. The wolf's coat is the color of oatmeal, except for the darker patches that outline the bridge of her nose, the points of her ears, and the curve of her haunches. She has amber eyes and a jet black nose. Tumas says she is an extra-social wolf, a trait that has deepened as Legend has aged. Now ten, she craves the student's company. "She's such a good wolf," Tumas says. "It's common for people not to think of her as a full wolf. It's so wrong. Her aggression can come lightning fast. I've seen it." Legend also has a thing for Michael Jackson's "Man in the Mirror." Whenever she hears the pop ballad, she howls.

Somehow Legend always knows when she's going for a walk. That is why she and C.J. are excited. Though the coyote is not coming out, the two canines consider themselves members of the same pack, so what happens to one has an effect on the other. That Legend is a pack animal makes her training altogether different from the cougars'. The cats are solitary creatures and don't require social attachments. Legend, however, yearns to be in a group. To train and walk the wolf, the students must become her pack members. This is a process dictated by the wolf. Some students Legend welcomes into the pack faster than others. She readily accepted one of the second years because the student trains C.J. If the coyote counts her as a pack member, the wolf automatically does too.

The key to gaining entrance to Legend's pack, Tumas says, is to take it slow. "If [the students] push too hard, it sets them back." As a first step, you sit near the wolf's cage. Eventually, you talk to Legend and feed her. Then you wait for Legend to sniff your hands or offer her furry flank along the enclosure—what's called presenting. Once you have that stamp of approval, you step into the wolf's cage with Tumas. There, you stand and wait for Legend's next signal. This may take several sessions. Once Legend rubs her legs against you or smells your hand, you are an official pack member. Only then can you learn to walk the wolf.

Taking Legend out of her cage is something like the changing of the guard. It's a highly regimented system during which Tumas announces every move, such as the lock being unlocked, and the cage door being opened. Tumas steps through the door first, closing it behind her. Then a student does the same. When they are in the cage, they never, ever turn their backs on Legend. Meanwhile, as Tumas commands, Legend sits on a tree stump in the middle of the cage. Today, Legend is so excited, like a dog anticipating a trip to the park, that she skips off her stump and prances over to Tumas. "On your mark," Tumas orders in her wolf voice. Legend does as told by her alpha.

A slouchy second year, who has recently become a pack member, squeezes in behind Tumas. Today, she will learn the first step of walking the wolf, catching her up. The two women move to either side of the wolf. The student holds out a looped rope. On her command, Legend leaps forward off the stump as the student kind of lassos her. Her aim is slightly off, but the wolf's head goes through the loop, if just barely. While the student holds the rope, Tumas leans over Legend and hooks on a heavy chain.

Legend passes through a series of doors, and the band parades up the back road. Tumas grips the chain today, but eventually all the students will take it. For now, they take up assigned positions, like sentries, around the wolf. Everyone hustles to keep up. The cougars poke along on their walks, meander from here to there. Legend is all business. After stopping to pee on a eucalyptus bush, Legend strides along in a straight line, hardly breaking her pace to inhale a smell here and there. Her head held low, she pants lightly. The chain jingles. Legend pauses briefly to press her nose to a building. "Stopping!" a student out front calls. Then we're off again.

Tumas keeps an eye peeled for squirrels and rabbits, even a dog being walked outside the zoo's fence—anything that might catch Legend's predator eye. If the wolf was to sprint, Tumas would dig her heels in, cling to the chain, and lean back like a water skier. Tumas has never had to do that, though she flexed her biceps hard once when Legend lunged at an empty animal crate.

We turn into Wildlife Theater, which is empty just now, though visitors have begun to trickle in to the teaching zoo. Tumas orders Legend onto a tree stump in the middle of the earthen stage surrounded by empty metal bleachers. The wolf neatly steps up and balances gracefully atop the log. A little boy wanders around the bleachers and stops dumbstruck. "Is that a wolf?" he asks.

Legend's eyes remain on Tumas. "Good stay," she says. Tumas and the students raise their chins and begin to howl. Legend looks from person to person, cocking her head curiously, and flutters her tail. The humans persist. Legend seems nearly to shrug her shoulders, then raises her black nose and pushes her ears back.

She joins in with a rich howl heavy with beauty and longing. Legend's call resonates in your chest, fills you up. Tumas and the students hardly touch the real thing. They let Legend take the lead, and the small choir raise their voices to the heavens above like countless packs before them.

Birdman Bites

During a morning cleaning in January, Trevor Jahangard strides the length of the zoo and pushes the chain-link gate to Quarantine open. This is where Birdman, the kinkajou, lives. Jahangard's low-key manner belies how much he accomplishes every day. In addition to EATM, he's apprenticing to be a falconer and taking night classes in calculus and chemistry this semester. Like many EATM students, Jahangard discovered his love for animals early on, but in an atypical way. When Jahangard was six his family went to visit his father's relatives in Iran. At nearly every house they visited, the host would ritualistically kill a sheep, slit its throat, say a prayer in Farsi, and then butcher it in the backyard. "I was fascinated. I told my mother I wanted to be a butcher. I told her I wanted to cut up animals. She said, 'Why not become a vet?' "

Neither of his parents cared much for animals. His mother is allergic to rabbits, cats, and dogs. His father and his side of the family revile snakes and aren't in the custom of keeping pets. Still, Jahangard's parents let him fill terrariums with snakes, salamanders, and frogs. At nine, Jahangard bred and sold lovebirds. He bred cockatoos as well. He attended a magnet school at the Los Angeles Zoo and from there came directly to EATM. He wants to train primates.

Jahangard asked for the kinkajou this semester because he wanted an animal that wouldn't take too much of his time. He's busy enough training Rosie and working on Spring Spec. Still, like most EATM students, he has big ideas about what he can accomplish in a few months' training. He plans to train the kinkajou to come out of his cage on a leash. This will be for a grade. The fact that the kinkajou locked on to VanHollebeke's hand last May does not worry him. He's trained Kaleb, Rosie, and the cougar brothers. A small member of the raccoon family weighing only five or so pounds shouldn't be a problem.

Kinkajous are enchanting, otherworldly-looking animals, with their wide shiny eyes, little pink snout and ears, long prehensile tail, and narrow, serpentine tongue. The underside of their paws, crossed by lifelines, looks shockingly human. Their feet rotate 180 degrees. Their teeth are as sharp as a predator's though they prefer fruit, insects, and an occasional long drink of nectar. Their coats are waterproof like a beaver's or otter's.

They snooze away the day high above the ground in the rain forest canopy of Central and South America. They are often called honey bears and kept as pets. The word around EATM is that Birdman formerly belonged to the actress Kirstie Alley. Now the kinkajou bunks in a cage next to Wakwa, a raven. Here he sleeps curled up in a blanket in his den box. He does not rouse easily. Students can spend as much as a half hour waking the kinkajou for a training session.

Jahangard's been told Birdman has diarrhea. A first year who may ask for the kinkajou for this summer (the Georgian who cared for a houseful of baby deer) tags along with Jahangard. Birdman does have the runs. The kinkajou has also pulled his blankets out of his den box and, uncharacteristically, he is on the cage floor. Jahangard goes in to put the blankets back, but he's hardly stepped inside when Birdman springs at him and latches on to his knee. Jahangard quickly knocks the animal off and sets Birdman down on the cage floor. Before Jahangard can leave, Birdman bites down hard on the knuckle of his right index finger. The kinkajou curls its legs and tail around Jahangard's arm as if it were a tree branch.

Jahangard has no intention of letting Birdman clamp on to him for five minutes the way he did to VanHollebeke. Jahangard grabs the kinkajou's small head and tries to pry him off. Birdman bites down harder, sinking his canines deeper into Jahangard's knuckle and palm. Get the hose, he tells the Georgian. She grabs the hose but when she turns it on, it runs dry. There's a kink. She runs back to unravel it. Meanwhile rivulets of Jahangard's blood stream down his arm and drip on the cage floor as the kinkajou bears down. The hose gushes. The Georgian aims it at Birdman's eyes and mouth, blasting the honey bear. Birdman does not budge.

They give up on the hose. Jahangard squeezes the back of Birdman's head with all his might. Finally, the kinkajou's jaws ease. Jahangard throws Birdman down hard to stun him, then turns for the door. Birdman stays put on the ground. As he exits the cage, Jahangard worries that maybe he's hurt Birdman. He makes a beeline for Nutrition, dripping blood through Primate Gardens as he goes. He scrubs the puncture wounds with Betadine. Then he hurries through the zoo, out the front gate, and across the vast parking lot to the Health Center.

There, a nurse eyes the wound and orders Jahangard to soak it in Betadine for twenty minutes. She writes him a prescription for antibiotics and sends him for an X-ray. His knuckle has been punctured and crushed. Luckily, no stray bone fragments are found knocking about. All Jahangard has to worry about is an infection.

That is a big worry. The bacteria that thrive in the kinkajou's mouth now call Jahangard's knuckle home. A bite from a kinkajou isn't likely to kill you, but an infection very well might.

The nurses at Moorpark College see cases that few, if any, other college health centers do. They treat what have become run-of-the-mill ailments on college campuses—the eating disorders, depressions, and STDs—plus camel bites to the breast and puncture wounds from parrots. They see fungal infections and bug bites that would be more at home in a tropical country. The EATM students keep them on their nursing toes. "I love it. It's so out of the normal that it's fun," says Sharon Manakas, the center's coordinator.

The students are frequent visitors with normal and abnormal problems. As I sat in the lobby waiting to meet with Manakas one afternoon, in the course of about thirty minutes four EATM students came by. One first year stopped in because she thought she'd broken a finger. When she couldn't see a nurse right away, she decided to soldier on with her lame finger.

In recent years, Manakas has gotten the Health Center more involved in EATM. They have a letter ready to go with any EATM student headed to the emergency room, explaining that animal bites should not always be sutured. The nurses give the first years checkups and have them fill out a long questionnaire. Depending on what they find, the nursing staff keeps an eye on some of them. They will pull students in for meetings if they are repeatedly bitten. Manakas rightly worries that there are many wounds she never sees, because the students don't report bites because they don't want unsafe credits. Even small rat bites are prone to bad infections. A nick on Linda Castaneda's hand from a prairie dog got infected and took a month to heal.

It's not just the bites that worry Manakas but the way the program physically and mentally grinds people down. She wishes the students took better care of themselves, but the program teaches them that the animals always come first. Manakas sees herself as a counterbalance to this emphasis. Don't get her wrong—Manakas loves animals. Over her desk, she even has a black-and-white photo of Bob, the zoo's beloved, deceased water buffalo, with a tire hanging from one horn. She just doesn't like animals more than people.

Sometimes this has put her at odds with the EATM staff. After a macaque nearly ripped the eyelid off a male student, Manakas pressed for the monkeys to be removed. The injury was bad enough, but more worrisome was that macaques are possible herpes B carriers. There is no reliable test for herpes B, and the macaques can shed it without any apparent symptoms. The chance of catching herpes B from a monkey is slim, according to a National Institutes of Health report, but if you do, write your will. The injured student had to be repeatedly tested, which put the nursing staff at risk of contracting the virus as well, Manakas says. The surgical team that mended his eye was also in danger of infection. Manakas thought it too great a risk for a public teaching facility. The Wilsons, who had hand-raised the macaques, fought to keep them but lost the battle. The monkeys moved out.

Animal bites are a constant danger at the teaching zoo, but the real threats are the infections that can bloom so easily. Bacteria are far wilier than the wildest animal. In fact, the students needn't be bitten to get an infection. One student contracted a blazing infection from cleaning the turtle pool with a scratch on her hand. The teaching zoo is rife with bacteria, no matter how the students clean and clean. That is why Dr. Peddie harps on hand washing. There's a picture of the vet looking unusually stern over the sink in Nutrition with a caption inked in: Dr. Peddie says, Wash your hands. Most students comply, which makes for endless cases of eczema. Then infections take root in the cracks in their hands.

The day after the bite, Jahangard's hand puffs and reddens. Despite all the Betadine and the antibiotics, his knuckle is infected. This is especially bad news because an infection in a joint can wreak havoc, causing nerve damage or morphing into a bone infection. Jahangard goes to the emergency room, where he is hooked up to an intravenous drip of antibiotics. The next day his knuckle blooms bigger, redder, and angrier. Back he goes to the ER, where they switch the IV drip to a stronger antibiotic, Vancomycin. Jahangard returns a third day for another bag. The swelling stalls. He returns Sunday for one last bag. He's sent home with two different oral antibiotics. There is no nerve damage. Though it will be tender for weeks, Jahangard should have full movement of his index finger.

The student abandons his plan to train Birdman to walk on a leash. Now his goal will be "to not get chewed." The Georgian has decided not to ask for Birdman. That's no surprise, but her logic is. "He had to hurt the kinkajou to get him off of him," she tells me. "If that was me, I'd let him chew my arm off. I'm not at that point where I could hurt an animal to save myself. So I thought I shouldn't ask for him."

Dr. Peddie worries the Health Center did too little for Jahangard. He thinks they should have gone in with bigger antibiotic guns from the start. He invites the nurses up for a tour of the zoo, during which the vet describes the various bites its residents can inflict, the size of their teeth, and the bacteria that live in their mouths. In the Reptile Room, he tells them that any snake bite should be x-rayed. The reptiles' teeth break easily and can be left behind in a wound, where they will fester. Near Schmoo's cage he describes fish-handlers' disease and how the small scrapes and cuts the students get on their hands while rinsing the mackerel can get infected. As they tour the Mews, the vet explains how the eagles can lock their talons, which can cause a crushing injury. In Parrot Garden, he mentions that a macaw can break a broomstick with its beak. The Health Center nurses eat it up. This is why they love EATM.

Dolphin Dreams

Today is a big day for the aspiring dolphin trainers among the second years. They will make a pilgrimage to Mecca, aka SeaWorld. There, childhood dreams of passing the day in a snug wet suit with a smiley cetacean are a reality for a chosen few. Moreover, if you want to be a dolphin trainer, this is where most of the jobs are; with three SeaWorlds and various amusement parks, Anheuser-Busch employs more marine mammal trainers than anyone. That explains why one second year, who's wanted to be a dolphin trainer since she was five, rises early to carefully curl her long blond locks. She wants to look her best, just in case. Who knows, maybe some SeaWorld honcho will discover her.

This weeklong field trip in mid-February started at Have Trunk Will Travel, where Dave Smith showed off his newly acquired elephant training chops, then proceeded to the San Diego Zoo, where the second years each patted a cheetah on the head. This morning, the group slips through a security gate at SeaWorld to meet up with a mustachioed, seasoned trainer. As expected, he goes on and on about how hard the job is. He's preaching to the converted. What the second years want is the inside track, how to get the impossible—a job.

He became a dolphin trainer in 1976, back when people just happened into the profession. Times have changed. Basically, no one can just fall into the job now. He tells them to get scuba- and CPR-certified, to join the International Marine Animal Trainers Association (IMATA), and to get a college degree. In interviews, he tells them, don't say you want to only work with dolphins. You may have to work with sea otters, even walruses, to get your foot in the door. Don't mention any spiritual connections you might have with cetaceans. "If someone says in an interview, 'I was a dolphin in a previous life,' uh, they're out of here," he says. Give yourself any edge you can, because, "everyone wants to be a dolphin trainer. They'll kill you for it."

The second years follow him past what looks like a big water purifying plant, with huge, bulbous tanks that hum loudly, and through a doorway to the edge of a perfectly turquoise pool, as shiny as a jewel. Nanook, a white beluga whale, bobs in the middle. A bright red ball shimmies across the water. The scene looks like an abstract painting, the colors are so strong and pure and the shapes of the pool and the whale so simple and clean. To one side of the pool, two smaller, grayish females patiently rest their rounded chins in the hands of a trainer. Nanook likes to boss them around and lets loose with a sharp shriek like a seagull's at the girls. "We have to ignore that," the trainer says.

Belugas may be more striking than dolphins but they are not as acrobatic. They can neither jump nor spin. The trainer commands Nanook to get on a poolside scale. The whale gives it a halfhearted try, barely getting his rounded chin on the scale before sliding back into the pool. Then he hoists his great alabaster hulk on the scale. He jauntily tosses his tail up as the numbers tick higher and higher. The beluga weighs 2,000 pounds. Thus establishing his grandeur,

Nanook sinks quietly back into the pool, becoming a ghostly white shadow just beneath the broken blue surface.

Every class at EATM has at least a few wannabe dolphin trainers. This may seem odd, given the fact that the teaching zoo does not have a dolphin. In fact, the only marine mammal is the temperamental Schmoo. Gary Wilson has long dreamed of erecting a small marine mammal facility at the school, but EATM can hardly afford Schmoo's freezer full of mackerel and squid. No tanks are in the offing. The lack of marine mammals, though, does not deter students. EATM teaches you the principles of operant conditioning, the common language of dolphin trainers. Lots of alumni have landed jobs at SeaWorld parks, aquarium shows, and the Navy's International Marine Mammal Project in San Diego. When Brenda Woodhouse attended the school, she was not assigned to the zoo's sea lion. Still, she got a job as a dolphin trainer. The same is true for Wilson, who worked for the Navy. Of the ten or so second years who want to train marine mammals, only two are assigned to Schmoo. The rest make do training flipperless animals.

An EATM degree gives them an edge, but it is no guarantee of a wet suit. As the SeaWorld trainer says, competition is brutal. You might have an easier time becoming a Hollywood star. There are far more dolphin trainers than there are jobs. The International Marine Animal Trainers Association has 1,200 members spread over thirty-five countries, and not all of them work with dolphins. The field has grown some, thanks to interaction programs, but the profession remains tiny. Tom La Puzza, spokesman for the U.S. Navy's International Marine Mammal Project, regularly gets calls from parents of children who have decided on dolphin training as their future career. "They'll say, 'I know it's a hard field to get into,' " he says. "They have no idea."

Why is this? Simply put, because humans are gaga over dolphins. New Age types see an enlightened old soul in the dolphin's smiley gape. Parents plunge autistic, deaf, and terminally ill children in with dolphins, as if the animals had healing powers. Tourists pay big bucks at interaction programs from Tahiti to Mexico to frolic with the cetaceans. At SeaWorld, an average of 100 people a day in the summer plunk down $150 each to get in a pool with the park's dolphins. Often there are tears. An entertainment lawyer, a big guy over six feet tall, bawled his eyes out in the dolphin pool recently. "It's emotional because they've always had this fantasy and suddenly they are living it, and they are overwhelmed," says SeaWorld trainer Suzanne Morgan.

Visitors at the park regularly hold their babies out over the dolphin pool, not to mention the killer whale pool. A family once begged Morgan to let their child who was dying of cancer pet a dolphin before he left this world. Morgan caved and arranged for the family to have some private face time with the dolphins. When the family showed, the dying child was a bubbly, rosy-cheeked baby, and it was the adults who seemed keenest to pet a dolphin. It wasn't the first time Morgan had been sold a line.

No wonder we are so infatuated. Most people have been introduced to dolphins via the stage and screen, which have hyped the animals' charms. Americans of a certain age can still hum the theme song from *Flipper* or mimic the daft lines chirped by the cetaceans in *The Day of the Dolphin*. If you visited SeaWorld as a kid, chances are you left with high-flying dreams of swimming with dolphins or riding a killer whale. Erin Ford, an EATM student from Baltimore, says that "when I saw the trainer come shooting out of the water on the whale's rostrum, I knew that had to be me one day." She was eleven.

As animals in captivity go, dolphins are not such a troubling sight. Instead of a motionless zoo animal behind bars, dolphins frolic in sparkling blue water. We look at the zoo animal and think prison. We look at the dolphins and think swimming pool. Even their trained stunts look more like sports than circus tricks. They are exotic, almost otherworldly, yet familiar. Dolphins live in groups, like us, and with that ever-present smile, they look happy and friendly. They have an athletic grace we find irresistible, not to mention big brains that always wow us humans. "People assume that they are smarter than we are," says Al Kordowski, a longtime trainer at SeaWorld in Orlando.

Dolphin trainers acquire a good deal of their mystique by association. The trainers appear to hold godlike powers when, with a simple flick of the wrist, they command this sleek creature to flip higher than an Olympic gymnast. People will look at a tiger trainer and think that guy has balls. They look at a dolphin trainer and think that guy has brains. "You put on a wet suit and it's like you are a superhero," says Dave McCain, a trainer at SeaWorld in San Diego.

Like their charges, dolphin trainers have traditionally been fit and good-looking. They resemble young college coeds working part time on summer break. They have the bronze skin and bleached hair of surfers and lifeguards. Though many dolphin trainers are essentially entertainers, they have the aura of science about them, unlike circus or movie trainers. Dolphin trainers have their own jargon, bandying about terms like *delta, conditioned stimuli,* and *variable reinforcement*. They are an elite: "There are lots of doctors, accountants, and lawyers," Morgan says. "We're a small, tiny club."

Dolphin training, however, is not the perfect job. For one thing, dolphins bite. They can also ram with their rostrums hard enough to break ribs. Peeved, they can push a trainer out of the water or pin him to the bottom of the tank. In *Lads Before the Wind,* Karen Pryor writes of dolphins' whacking trainers on the head with their tail flukes, blasting them with sonar "you could feel in your bones," and swimming headlong at trainers, only to stop just shy of ramming them.

Dolphin training is just plain hard work. "It's lugging buckets. It's squirting poop," says Morgan. You have to be a crack swimmer. To get a job at SeaWorld, you must swim 220 feet, half of it underwater, and dive 24 feet to retrieve a small weight. Rain or shine, dolphin trainers are outside. All day long, they jump in and out of 52° saltwater pools. The numbing water makes their ear canals swell. Their knees, shoulders, necks, and backs ache. They are prone to sinus infections. Kordowski says trainers swap tricks on how to blow the water out of their sinus cavities.

Dolphin training is especially unglamorous at the start, painfully so if you are a college graduate. Dolphin trainers begin their careers in the fish room, rinsing and weighing bucket after bucket of slimy mackerel, squid, and the like. They work weekends and holidays. They earn a pittance. Even after having paid their dues, they will never get rich. Kordowski says a marine mammal trainer is lucky to make between $25,000 and $30,000. "You can't be head of household and have this job," Morgan says. The guys who stay in the profession, she says, are largely unmarried or gay. Then why do dolphin trainers persist in such trying, underpaid jobs? The answer is obvious. "There are so many cute faces," Morgan says. "It's so self-perpetuating. It just never gets old. . . . It all comes down to that you can get in a pool with a dolphin."

Dolphin training is a relatively recent phenomenon. The first dolphin show in this country was held in 1938 at Marineland in St. Augustine, Florida. It wasn't until the late fifties and early sixties that dolphin training picked up a head of steam, inspired in part by a growing scientific interest. Though Aristotle observed that dolphins gave live birth and suckled their young, little was known about the animals well into the twentieth century. As Dr. Sam Ridgeway writes in *The Dolphin Doctor,* between 1963 and 1973, during which the Apollo program landed a man on the moon, three species of dolphins were studied for the first time.

At Marineland of the Pacific, the world's biggest oceanarium when it opened in 1954 near Los Angeles, zoologist Ken Norris pioneered the study of echolocation with the park's dolphins. In 1962, the U.S. Navy studied the dolphins' knack for diving to great depths without consequence. At the base on Point Mugu in Ventura County, Dr. Ridgeway recruited Wally Ross, the circus trainer who had worked at Jungleland and taught some at EATM, to train Tuffy, a recalcitrant bottlenose with a crescent-shaped scar down its side. Tuffy became the first trained dolphin to work in the open ocean. He dove over 200 feet ferrying tools to SeaLab.

A couple thousand miles out in the Pacific, Pryor cracked a weighty tome on operant conditioning at Sea Life Park in Hawaii. Her husband had started the park in 1963 as a hybrid, an oceanarium that would support a research facility. He drafted her to train the wild-caught dolphins. She had limited experience, training Welsh ponies and her pet dogs, but found Skinner's principles worked beautifully. In *Lads Before the Wind* she writes, "I could see that, given this handful of facts, this elegant system called 'operant conditioning,' one could train any animal to do anything it was physically capable of doing."

To research captive dolphins, they had to be trained to at least a certain extent. If you wanted to test a dolphin's echolocations, you had to teach the animal to wear eye cups. Training dolphins required an entirely different approach from any other animal. If you did something a dolphin didn't like, it could just swim away. Reins, bits, cattle prods, elephant hooks, and the like were out of the question. There's no dominating an animal you can't get your hands on easily and that can just disappear under water. Dolphins could not be forced to work; they had to be enticed.

Early dolphin trainers went to work with whistles, buckets of fish, and operant conditioning manuals. They came up with other rewards—ice, squirts with a hose, a look in a mirror—so a dolphin full of fish would keep working. Using science, they made training fun for an animal.

Though Skinner's principles were used by other types of animal trainers, even if they didn't call it that, marine mammal trainers were the first to wholly embrace the science. They worked out a vocabulary. They standardized their hand cues. Dolphin trainers began getting degrees in psychology and behavior science. They began using training in a holistic way to teach animals to travel and to accept medical treatments. They explained what they were doing in scientific terms, which still isn't the case with many animal trainers. While movie trainers used *affection training* or circus trainers used *gentling*, dolphin trainers used operant conditioning. Unlike many animal trainers, who tend to be competitive and secretive, marine mammal trainers pulled together as a profession. IMATA was founded in 1972.

All this put marine mammal trainers at the forefront of modern training, where they remain. Three of the most influential trainers, Karen Pryor, Gary Priest of the San Diego Zoo, and Ken Ramirez at the Shedd, are all marine mammal trainers. For the past thirty years, marine mammal trainers have beaten the drum for operant conditioning and, moreover, positive reinforcement. At the Shedd, the trainers don't even have a means to tell their animals no. "Once you have the ability to say no," Ramirez says, "you overuse it." Ramirez and his ilk have demonstrated that you needn't punish or coerce your animals to train them. That has been an eye-opener, especially to dog trainers, who traditionally relied on coercion and dominance. This sunny approach is not only better for the animals, but has made training a lot more palatable to institutions such as zoos and sanctuaries.

Marine mammal trainers, especially dolphin trainers, are often considered prima donnas, especially because of their hard-to-follow lingo. One EATM student told me she thought dolphin trainers were snooty. That's the price you pay for being leaders in your field: resentment. For how much longer will the marine mammal trainers lead the pack? The zoo world is certainly fast on their heels, though they have a ways to go. Certainly bird and dog trainers could give them a strong run for their money any day now. When that day comes—when the marine mammal trainers lose their lead—it will be good news for captive animals.

Throughout the morning, the second years wander the park. They hold their hair back with one hand and poke their free arm elbow deep into the bat ray pool to stroke the strange creatures' smooth, hard backs. They watch as penguins frolic under the chilly spray of a snow gun. They stroke the rubbery rostrums of dolphins. Many of the students have been here before, some repeatedly, and have grown a touch jaded. When I mention that the killer whales and trainers are having a play session, one says, "Been there, done that," and heads into the gift shop. Meanwhile, the second year with the curled hair slips off to a quiet spot to call and confirm the date for her swim test at SeaWorld Miami.

Everyone gathers for lunch, where a number of students order a child's meal, because it comes in a plastic holder shaped like a dolphin. I can't help watching one student, a pretty, but very slim one, feast on only the mountain of french fries from her kiddy lunch. She douses them with ranch dressing. Afterward, everyone plops down on a soft stretch of lawn to watch the SeaWorld bird trainers. They bring out Ruby, a fluorescent red ibis, and instruct her to land on a few heads. Ruby slips and slides in Brunelli's curly locks until she lands on her sunglasses and perches there. A black vulture chases the trainers around like a puppy with a funny, waddling run.

We head over to The Shamu Adventure stadium, where three female trainers ride killer whales like surfboards, balancing on their black noses, arms spread to steady themselves. Standing atop the whales' noses, they explode from the pool like human cannonballs. As woman and whale reach the apex of their jump, both arch and dive neatly back into the choppy turquoise waters. Several whales rise up in unison, flippers akimbo, their white bellies shimmering in the afternoon sun. The spectacle is like something Louis XIV would have thought up to wow his jaded court. The bleachers are not filled with aristocrats in feathers and velvet but with tons of shrieking kids in shorts, begging to be splashed by these orcas. The whales are only too happy to oblige. Waves wash over children as they rush toward the pool. Amid the splashing, the Shamus' acrobatics, and the general controlled mayhem of the scene, a second year next to me—an aspiring tiger trainer—wells up. "It's so emotional," she says.

The day ends at Dolphin Stadium, which has a kind of Spanish-mission-meets-rocky-lagoon look to it, with a lighthouse mixed in. There are four dolphins (Duncan, Dolly, Sidney, and Buster) and two pilot whales (Shadow and Bubbles). Bubbles is forty-five. Her age doesn't show. During the customary splashing, she smashes the surface with her dorsal fin, producing frothy waves that chase parents from the front rows. Duncan soars in a tidy arc over a rope twenty-seven feet above the pool. The dolphins are so much smaller and fleeter than the killer whales, but their performance is more poetic, even in its sillier moments. They ferry trainers around the pool. They leap in pairs. They flip and spin with impossible ease. They are the ultimate synchronized swimmers.

After all the families empty out, the second years stay behind, and the dolphin trainers come out in their dripping wet suits. Small puddles collect at their feet. Though the trainers are experienced public speakers, they stand so the EATM students must look into the sun. Everyone has their hands to their brows to shade their eyes. The real distraction, though, is in the pool. As a senior trainer, a super-composed blonde in her thirties, talks about *bridging* and *secondary reinforcements,* the dolphins sail past in the pool, going round and round like an underwater merry-go-round. One animal, a stripe of white down its side, dreamily swims by upside down, its eyes squeezed closed. A pilot whale cruises by over and over with the same little dolphin tucked by his side. One dolphin finally pokes his head out, leans his chin on the pool's glass wall, and stares at the group. No one can resist returning the look. Who can pay attention to anything when a dolphin is eyeballing you?

February

Salsa, the Catalina macaw, won't fly across the stage. Hudson, the beaver, misses his cue. Curly, one of the three mini potbellied pigs, trots on and offstage a couple of times before his trainer scoops up his little black body. Sadie, the sheep, baas loudly backstage. Only Abbey seems to have her part down, lounging on stage, pink tongue unfurled in a quiet pant.

The two casts of "Welcome to the Jungle," the centerpiece of Spring Spec, have been rehearsing for a month. Every morning, one of the two casts takes over Wildlife Theater, and for a good three hours these aspiring animal trainers channel all their overachiever energy into putting on a show. There's something very summer camp about the whole endeavor, yet a lot rides on the production. Spring Spec raises a goodly chunk of money for EATM over its three weekends. Last year, the event snagged nearly $40,000.

Brenda Woodhouse and Jena Anderson, the director of this cast, sit in the bleachers with notebooks in their laps. Anderson has a degree in fine arts and has directed a church choir, so she knows her way around the stage. She's one of the few in her class who does. Most of the students are new as it is to public speaking and now here they are acting.

This Monday morning's run-through is the first time the animals have joined the second years on stage. There has been confusion enough just among the humans, many of whom still don't know their lines or blocking, but add in the animals, and pandemonium rages. Students forget to get their animals, and most animals don't know their trained behaviors. When Rio, the blue and gold macaw, is supposed to appear, someone says, "Rio's in the show?" While many of the animals won't even come out onstage, the pigs can't get enough of the limelight, especially Hamilton, the not-so-miniature Yucatan pig, who lumbers on at every chance he can get.

"Is the rabbit coming?" someone yells.

As with all things EATM, the script is ambitious, which explains why the second years still struggle with their lines. Surprisingly, the text calls for far less from the animals. They are bit players mostly, making cameo appearances as they run or flap across the stage. In the school's old days, the animals were the stars of Spring Spec's precursor, Family Circus. Back then students dressed up in glittery circus costumes and ran ponies with headdresses in hypnotic circles. When circuses became politically incorrect, the school switched to the more neutral edutainment approach. For this show few are being trained to do anything flashy. Students are teaching two parrots to wing into the bleachers and collect a dollar bill from an audience member. Progress has been slow on that stunt. Student trainers spend most of their time just desensitizing the animals to all the distractions onstage.

That is obviously easier said than done. Up until now, the second years have worked their animals in the relative peace and quiet of the teaching zoo grounds. The animals used in the educational shows typically take the stage one at a time. Here, they must follow commands in a vortex of distractions: actors in costume running by, audience members laughing loudly, and other animals onstage. This explains why during rehearsal so many of the animals freeze, as Mazoe, the serval, does. The big-eared cat turns her eyes slowly around the stage and then to the few of us in the bleachers. Paco, a white-nosed coati, is more at ease, walking neatly on his leash. Then Precious, the boa constrictor, squeezes a second year's arm so hard she forgets her line. "I'm getting constricted here," she says.

As Becki Brunelli stands stage right with Malaika, the nervous Nellie parrot, perched on her raised hand, a piece of scenery behind them tilts dangerously forward. "Watch out!" a universal cry breaks out just as the fake wall tumbles, and Brunelli barely steps out of harm's way. She turns to take the bird offstage, but Woodhouse stops her. "Keep it positive for Malaika," she calls.

Nick, the miniature horse, charges onstage at a full gallop, his hooves kicking up dust, his mane flowing. "Whoa!" Woodhouse yells from the bleachers. Nick composes himself and turns a pretty circle and then bows. Hamilton struts back onstage with his trainer in pursuit. When Salsa refuses to spread her wings a second time, her trainer says, "Salsa, fly, damn it!" Olive ambles out on a leash, a banana peel in one hand, looking a bit uneasy. "Come on, sweetie," her trainer Chris Jenkins coos. The run-through of the hour-long show has taken two hours.

"How's it look, Jena?" someone asks Anderson in the stands.

"We'll see," the director answers.

It's mid-February. Though the calendar technically declares the season winter, there are early signs of spring. Legend's meals have shrunk; she doesn't need as much to eat as temperatures rise. The sun crests the mountains to the east earlier and earlier. The students can leave their headlamps in their lockers during the morning cleaning.

The teaching zoo's various newcomers have settled in. Lulu's sides bulge obviously now. The pregnant camel is docile and lovely and everything her son Kaleb and certainly Sirocco aren't. Nick *looks* as if he were pregnant. Despite the efforts of a new set of student trainers, the horse has gained weight, ballooning to 310 pounds. Walter, the kid water buffalo, has become a teaching zoo favorite. He so loves being brushed that he sinks onto his side with bliss. If you rub your hand over his hide, your fingers smell like goat cheese afterward.

Mohelnitzky continues to tinker with Abbey's diet, adding more and more wet food, heaps of ramen noodles, and cans of chicken broth until the dog's meals are a soupy heap. The student adds Mylanta to her evening meal and crosses her fingers. Mary VanHollebeke is not training Starsky for a grade this semester, but she hasn't given up on touching the cavy. She still spends hours each week convincing the big-eyed critter to come close. It's beginning to pay off. He'll pretty reliably eat from the spoon taped to a stick if VanHollebeke holds it very still as she sits in his cage. The student shortens the handle ever so little, so that without realizing it, Starsky is inching toward VanHollebeke as he nibbles on pellets.

Schmoo is less aggressive these days, but still flashes her black teeth on occasion, keeping everyone on their toes. Cain quit puncturing Brunelli recently, but then started sinking his beak into another second year. Samburu, the caracal, hooked a second year's middle finger. She was teaching him a touch behavior, meaning she touches him and not the other way around, as it turned out.

Jahangard spends most of his day with Rosie, the baboon, leaving little time for Birdman, the pit bull kinkajou. That's fine with Jahangard. "Not that I don't like the kinkajou, but I don't like the kinkajou," he says. Still he has to train him for a grade, pulling Birdman from his den box, which seems like a small order until you look at Jahangard's hand. His knuckle is still puffed and sensitive.

Another group of first years begin training rats, toting the rodents to Zoo 2 so they will get used to the classroom. While Wilson lectures, the rats suck noisily from their water bottles and rustle in beds of shredded newspaper. They squat and pee on the tables. Students quickly dab up the small amber pools, as nearby someone eats an overstuffed pita sandwich or a tub of yogurt. A rat occasionally tumbles to the floor or a fight breaks out. After one scuffle, Dr. Peddie patched a wounded rat together with Super Glue.

Linda Castaneda got two hairless rats, hoping their baldness would not trip her asthma. They have. She's so allergic to them she can't sleep at night. She sits up coughing and wheezing. Because they are hairless, the rats can't sleep outside. They'd get too cold. "I almost got in my car at 2 A.M. the other night so I could sleep," she tells me, her voice decreasing to a whisper by the end of the sentence as she runs out of breath. She's returning the pink critters. After she does that, she's going to the Health Center for some antidepressants, she says. Her urge to do things just so combined with EATM's endless demands have stretched her to cracking. She's hoping some pills will purge her of perfectionism. "I'd like to see what life is like without all the noise in my head."

Most of the first years are keyed up over animal assignments, which will be announced in a couple of days. The first year from Argentina has broken out in hives. While emceeing a show for a class of grade schoolers, another first year suddenly walks offstage and throws up from nerves. An older student wakes in the middle of the night from a vivid dream in which she got the serval. Only Chandra Cohn's mind seems elsewhere. The financially beleaguered mom doesn't fret because she doubts she'll get any of the animals she asked for. She didn't have the grades, especially not for Ebony, the raven, whom she longs for. Besides, she's got bigger worries. She always does.

Cohn, the lean, long-faced first year who bawled loudly over pulling her pigeon, counts her pennies each month. She's paying for her groceries with food stamps. She often forgoes lunch, seeming to survive off soda and cigarettes. This isn't the way EATM was supposed to go. After she graduated from high school, she landed a job with movie trainer Bob Dunn. She got pregnant and that changed her plans. She married, had a second child, and worked as a secretary. Over the years, Cohn applied to EATM five times and got in once. Her husband wouldn't let her go, she says. This time he encouraged her. Then last summer, not long before school started, he told her he wanted to separate.

She rented a room in a house where nine or so other students live. Then the younger of her two daughters moved in with her. Her landlord raised the rent. Most nights—after she's helped her daughter with her homework, done her own, and cared for her ferret, two rats, and two hermit crabs—she gets to bed about 2 A.M., which explains why her eyes are always lined with red. Now her ex has sued her for child support.

The funny thing about Cohn is that you'd expect EATM would push her over the brink. It has the opposite effect on her. While the other first years grouse about the program, the animals get Cohn through the day. Here, she can find some peace of mind from the unpredictableness of life beyond the front gate. "I hear the parrots and primates when I come in and it just makes me happy," she says to me while watching Savuti, the hyena, lounge in his cage.

Cohn's observing him for Wilson's Behavior class. She's set her cell phone to ring every thirty seconds. When it chimes, she notes what the hyena is doing, which looks to me like sleeping. "No," she says, her voice lifting, her face brightening. She's discovered there's a difference between when he's resting and when he's sleeping. "Resting, he occasionally lifts his head or moves; sleeping, he's out cold."

Savuti is one of the zoo's biggest surprises. He's enthusiastic, generous, creative, funny, and—something I never thought I'd say about a spotted hyena—lovable. Not only is he one of the best trained animals on the compound, he is the most eager. He gets overexcited with his trainers, trying to anticipate the next command, offering three behaviors when one will do.

There are a few tricks to training Savuti. You work with him through the cage. Second, you must never forget that he is a hyena. That means always watching where your fingers are. Let's put it this way: Savuti cannot have bowling balls with finger holes, because he can break them apart with his jaw. Next, you have to learn the long list of his commands. If the animals don't keep doing their commands, they forget them. That's why animals at the teaching zoo are forever "losing behaviors," as the staff says.

This semester, April Matott and Carrie Hakanson are assigned to Savutes, as the students often call him. Matott is training him to press his left side against the cage bars. Hakanson, whom I find by Savuti's cage later in the day, is twenty-nine and a self-described tomboy who worked with howler monkeys in Costa Rica. She is teaching the hyena to spin but not for a grade. This is the kind of thing EATM students do just for fun—teach a hyena to pirouette. Another student has taught Kaleb, the camel, to dunk a basketball this semester.

"Maybe not a three-sixty," Hakanson says, looking at Savuti, who stares back, his head cocked, "but something dramatic."

Hakanson has worked with two of his existing commands, jump and circle, saying them in quick succession so he is in constant motion. The hyena stands close to the bars, waiting, his big eyes glued to Hakanson. She warms him up with a jump, a sit, and a fetch. She asks him to hold still while she pinches his shoulder through the cage. This is for an injection behavior. "Walk it!" she says. Savuti throws his front paws up on the bars and walks sideways on his hind legs down the cage. Then the second year says

"Spin!" He turns a bit to the left and looks at her with a question in his eye, as if to ask, "Is that it?" She says, "Spin!" This time he tosses himself up in the air like a clumsy dancer and comes down hard with his chin on a log. Unfazed, the hyena rushes back to the bars for a chicken neck, which Hakanson gingerly proffers through the bars.

Late afternoon at the teaching zoo is magical. This is when students tend to get the animals out for a stroll. Calls of "Pig here!" or "Coyote here!" echo across the compound. The students sprint alongside the crazy emu, Julietta. They plead with Spitz, the serval, who lies down every few steps, to please get up. They unreel Scooter's leash so the capuchin monkey can scale her favorite tree, the mulberry near Clarence's enclosure. Walter and Dunny's trainers pull on their leather gloves and promenade with the bulky twosome. If they get too far apart, Dunny stops and Walter cries. The students have to get staff approval for who is out when, because you don't want, say, Legend, a wolf, and Sequoia, a mule deer, running into each other.

This afternoon, Mara Rodriguez steers Spirit, the cougar, down the back road. Spirit is the larger of the two cougar brothers and his fawn-colored coat darkens around his mouth. Though they are well into the semseter, the students aren't ready to take the leash yet. Three of them shadow Rogriguez and the cat.

Spirit stops to smell where Walter peed. He jumps a bit for no apparent reason. Spirit hasn't been on a walk recently. He seems a hair skittish. "If that cat drags me, jump on my chain," Rodriguez says. The students nod. Spirit did drag her once. Rodriguez had noticed just the slightest change in the cougar's gait. Ten steps later, Spirit bolted. Rodriguez threw herself flat out on the ground, spreading her feet, making herself as hard to drag as possible. Still, Spirit pulled her down the back road, scraping the skin off her arms, ripping her shirt and pants. "I'm lucky," she says. "This is such a dangerous field. What has happened to me isn't major, but the major stuff could kill you."

As the posse rounds Nutrition, they come upon a maintenance guy changing a tire on a Bobcat. This clearly unsettles Spirit, who doesn't like cars. They retreat up the back road. Spirit digs in his paws by Sequoia's cage. Rodriguez stops, and the cougar nuzzles her leg. "Are you having a bad day?" she asks. When she turns to go, he freezes, then moves to go in the other direction. Rodriguez bends down on one knee and pulls the chain in link by link so it is nearly taut. "I'll get him to come to me," she says. Once he does, she stands and walks the way Spirit wanted to go. You always want a cat to think his idea was, in fact, your idea.

Eventually, we turn into the section between Hoofstock and Big Carns, where there is a small outdoor theater, and close the gate behind us. Rodriguez orders the cougar up on a stump, and he sits neatly atop the log, his tail draping down the side. She leads the cougar over to where the ground is cushioned with reddish cedar chips. Here, Spirit stretches out on the rich-smelling mattress of mulch. Jena Anderson steps behind the cat, leans down, and starts massaging his shoulders. "Go Jena," another student says, then points out that Anderson's ties from her hoodie are loose.

"You have to know what you are dangling," Rodriguez says.

Rodgriguez hands the leash to Anderson, who clutches it while the other two students take turns stroking the lounging cat. This is another step along the way to learning to walk the cougar. Next door, Legend howls long and hard as C.J., the coyote, leaves her cage for a walk. A low bark rumbles from Schmoo's direction. The scene is deceptively peaceful, five women gathered around a sleepy cougar in the late afternoon sun. Rodriguez knows better, that the calm could break suddenly. She gazes down at the cougar sprawled near her feet and says, "Sometimes I wonder if I'm the biggest idiot but I just think I have something to share that is so neat."

The day finally arrives. On a drizzly morning, the students file into Zoo 2 for the Wednesday meeting. The first years are like kids on Christmas morning, giggling, sitting on the edge of their seats. Announcements, such as "Do not take your rats to the school cafeteria," are kept to a minimum, then the second years are chased from the room. This is, finally, the first years' moment.

Woodhouse hands a folded sheet of paper to every first year, but tells them not to open them just yet. She ran out of herbivores this year and there were more requests for Wendell, the goat, than ever before, she says. The first years nervously fiddle with the pieces of paper. "I'll just keep talking," she says with a laugh. "Anyway, I hope you appreciate every animal you get."

The fluttering of paper fills the room, followed by a few seconds of quiet as eyes scan the long, dense list and then cheering breaks out. First years jump out of their seats and hug each other, yelling, "I got Puppy!" or "I got Cowboy!" Two first years assigned to Laramie, the one-winged eagle, jump into each other's arms. "I'm going to pee in my pants," another first year calls out. Wischhusen dials her girlfriend on her cell. "I got Taj and Zulu," she says.

The Argentinean who broke out in hives stands stunned: she got the animals she asked for, including Savuti, despite her less than perfect grades. Cohn did not get her favorite, Ebony, the raven, but she did get C.J. Patch, Fidone, and Castaneda all got their requests. Castaneda has been assigned to her beloved cougar brothers and the bovine duo, Walter and Dunny. "I got all my first choices," Castaneda says. "It pays to work hard."

Does it? Before the first years leave the room, there's muttering about a student who's been assigned to Schmoo. She dropped Diversity last semester to keep a 4.0. She is also assigned to the zoo's young gibbon. The consensus is quick and sure. She doesn't deserve them.

Larissa Comb sits amid the cheering and carrying on and sinks. Around her are students with lower grades rejoicing, trilling. The straight-A student, a generally all-around accomplished person, got only one of her first picks, a pig. She did not get Schmoo or Goblin, the baboon, or Rio, the macaw. Not that she doesn't like her animals, but she can't help feeling all her hard work has gone unrewarded. She knows why: that one morning she was thirty seconds late last fall.

Combs isn't the only deflated person in the room. The second years rushed into Zoo 2 to congratulate the first years. Mohelnitzky can't find anyone to hug. No first year has been assigned to Abbey. That means nobody asked to work with the dog.

Outside a light sprinkle falls. The morning's rehearsal is canceled. The primates hate rain. The humidity bothers Baxter's arthritis. The second years wander off into the gray, wet morning. The trilling quiets as most of the first years settle in for Dr. Peddie's Animal Nutrition class. He's in classic form. Today's lecture on the minerals animals need in their diet begins with the vet describing his grandmother's goiter, holding his hands up to show just how big it was. "It weighed four to five pounds," he exults.

"Ugh," someone moans in the back of the class.

Over the next hour and a half, he describes a sphincter as "like a drawstring purse," draws a strange-looking cow, which prompts a student to ask, "Dr. Peddie, is that *T. rex*?" He tells them a ruminant's stomach is about the size of a fifty-five-gallon drum and it's full "of a sludge of dead bodies," like a "thick soup." He recounts how he tried to pull a loose tooth from an elephant with the help of a screwdriver and a flashlight. He couldn't pry it free. If you don't pull the tooth, when it falls out, the elephant swallows it.

Quite some time later, after a long journey through the pachyderm's organlike digestive tract, he explains, it appears in the animal's hefty stool. The elephant trainers, he says, gave him the tooth for Christmas.

"Which end did it come out of?" someone yells. His hearing aid must be turned low, because the vet returns to his *T. rex* cow on the board and scrawls some curlicue innards.

By the time class ends, a list of what they call the extra animals, the animals that no one requested and that still need student trainers assigned to them, has been posted outside of the main office. The first years gather round. There are all the usual suspects: the emu, the alligator, the kinkajou, and Starsky, the cavy. There, second from the top, is Abbey. Seeing her name, a tall student next to me says, "I didn't come all the way from Colorado to train a dog."

What these students do every day is controversial. Same with the staff. That EATM even exists is controversial to some extent. That is now true of any animal park, circus, zoo, or aquarium. Though their dreams of working with animals may have been born in the innocence of childhood, animal trainers now find themselves on the front lines of a fight they didn't pick. No matter how good their intentions, they are the declared enemy of the animal rights movement.

That hasn't always been the case. When Gary Johnson bought his first elephant in 1970, he never imagined that one day protesters would heckle his elephant rides at the Santa Ana Zoo. It never occurred to his wife, Kari, that as part of being an elephant trainer she would testify to a congressional committee.

The animal rights movement has been on the offensive for quite a stretch. In response, zoos, animal parks, and trainers have often offered a muddled, halfhearted defense. If the tables are to turn, animal trainers and keepers need to bone up on the legislative system and hone their PR skills. At the very least, they need to think out their position, to have a well-reasoned rationale for why they do what they do. It's not only the animal rights movement they will have to answer to but also any Joe Public that asks them why a big cat sleeps so much in its cage. You don't have to be a PETA member to feel uncomfortable about animals in captivity. Michlyn Hines says she meets people all the time who hate zoos. Becki Brunelli recently had a first date with a man who told her the teaching zoo's animals should be set loose, that they'd be better off squashed on the LA freeways. "I don't think we'll go out again," she says.

There isn't much time in the day at the teaching zoo for philosophy or philosophizing. That is where Animal Ethics comes in. The class is taught on Wednesday evening from 6 to 9 P.M. during the second semester by Leland Shapiro, a professor of animal science at nearby Pierce College who moonlights at EATM. He's completed two postdoctoral studies in bioethics. When he started teaching the course in the late nineties, he found no other like it. He wrote his own textbook.

In Shapiro's class, the EATM students hear names like René Descartes, John Stuart Mill, Chief Seattle, and Gandhi ("To believe something and not live it is dishonest"). They learn how various religions regard animals—that Judaism forbids castration of animals, and Islam teaches that animals should not be used in entertainment. They learn the difference between Malthusianism and dominionism, between animal rights and animal welfare, and between vegetarian and vegan.

Much of Shapiro's class is devoted to the gray area in a debate that's often been cast as black and white. He tells them that Adolf Hitler was a vegetarian. The Dalai Lama eats meat, per his doctor's orders. He points out that there is a cure for the formerly fatal parvovirus, thanks to medical research done on dogs that were given parvo. Medical research on animals produced vaccines for tetanus, polio, diphtheria, smallpox, and whooping cough. Do the ends justify the means? What moral obligation do we have to animals? To ourselves? These are questions that would make the students squirm in their seats if they weren't so tired.

Tonight he mentions the dilemma of Premarin, an estrogen drug used by millions of postmenopausal women made from pregnant mare urine. The horses are kept in a barn stall for six months a year. Even if they weren't pregnant, Shapiro points out, they'd be kept in the barn through the frigid North Dakota winter. Most Premarin is produced by mares on small family farms, he says. Estrogen can be made synthetically, but it's not quite the same as the estrogen produced by the mares. Are the farmers right or wrong to use the mares so? His point is to get the students thinking, rather than accepting popular ideas without examining them.

The EATM students are of various mind-sets, though it's safe to say that everyone agrees captive animals should be well cared for. Brunelli is a strict vegetarian but would like to be a movie trainer. Another student believes animals should be used only for education, meaning zoos are okay but animal parks like SeaWorld are not. Many of the students object to circuses. Not Linda Castaneda. Anita Wischhusen's worked at a dog pound where she had to put the animals to sleep. Among the many stickers on her car, there is one for PETA.

PETA, the biggest and best known animal rights organization, is a four-letter word at EATM. The animal rights movement, with its misinformation and its clandestine techniques, has put anyone who works with animals on guard, including EATM, and made for a bunker mentality. The school is very wary of anyone expressing animal rights sentiments—so wary, in fact, that when, as an April Fools' prank, a group of EATM students posed as animal rights protesters outside the front gate a few years back, they were all summarily expelled by Wilson. Dr. Peddie says if he suspects a prospective student is an animal rights plant, he removes their name from the lottery. The barbed wire perimeter fence around the teaching zoo is not just to keep animals in but also, as at the Johnsons' ranch, possible intruders out, especially animal rights believers with ideas of opening the cage doors.

Not long into this project I found out just how wary the school is. When a young alumna I interviewed misconstrued my questions, she called EATM. She didn't complain about my line of questions but rather suspected I was an animal rights spy, an accusation some staff members took seriously.

Turns out it's not that easy to prove that you are not an animal rights spy. If you were, wouldn't you cover your tracks? I found myself, a horse racing fan, a zoo supporter, and a devoted carnivore, making a long list of character references, from my book editor to an old boss, who could verify that I am a journalist, not a PETA informer. It was a good lesson that brought home to me just how nervous people in the animal industry are, and understandably so.

Suzanne Morgan, the longtime trainer at SeaWorld, told me of a day at the company's Ohio park when the employees were alerted to be on the watch for animal rights protesters. The company had gotten word that something was afoot. What, exactly, nobody knew. Would they try to release the animals? Would they vandalize the park? Hurt the workers? The employees, easy to spot in their uniforms among the milling visitors, felt like sitting ducks, Morgan says.

The movie trainer Hubert Wells has gotten death threats repeatedly. One caller threatened to kill him over his work in *Out of Africa*. In the movie, Karen Blixen and Denys Finch Hatton, played by Meryl Streep and Robert Redford, shoot two charging lions. Wells dug a hole and filled it with padding. The charging lions dropped out of sight into the hole, making it look as if they had dropped dead. His only crime may have been in making it look too convincing. "I know you killed those lions," the caller would growl.

As part of the animal show at Universal Studios, a marshal eagle flies in front of a wind machine. During one performance that Mark Forbes emceed, as the bird flapped, "a lady stood up and yelled, 'This is disgusting,' and started running up and down the stands screaming. Security escorted her out." Forbes tried to recover the show by cracking, "Sorry, folks, I told Mom to stay home today." Nobody laughed.

On the flip side, some trainers told me, Morgan included, that the animal rights movement, despite its heavy-handed tactics and misinformation, has kept the animal industry on its toes in a good way. Karen Rosa, director of the American Humane Association's Film & TV Unit, says PETA and the like have worked in their favor. Movie companies and trainers have become more willing to work with her watchdog group. The association's stamp of approval on a movie gives producers some ammo against any criticism from animal rights groups.

Animal ethics is a heavy, even discouraging subject, but Shapiro does what he can to keep it light. Tonight's class includes two student skits. For the first, two second year students stoop behind a table at the front of the room and perform a hand puppet show on the pros and cons of chicken farming, complete with a catchy song, the chorus of which, "More meat, more money," they sing in high, chirpy voices. The whole room cracks up. "Humor can relax people, not to change their minds, but to see the other's point of view," Shapiro says.

Tonight's class ends a little early. The students close their notebooks and stuff them in their backpacks. They trudge into the dark, take a last look back at the peaceful zoo behind them, then slip through the front gate to the parking lot. The animals, the source of so much philosophical debate, so much consternation, snooze in their cages.

* * *

By the end of the week, a list of who has been assigned to the extra animals is posted by the front office. When Mohelnitzky sees who's been assigned to Abbey, she's crestfallen. She approves of one of the first years, but the other two worry her. She overheard them complaining about Abbey, and one of the two is the first year everyone expects to flunk out or be kicked out. Mohelnitzky goes home depressed. She even cries. She asks her apartment manager again if she can have a dog. He suggests she write a letter to the building's owner. With pen in hand, Mohelnitzky carefully words her request, hoping against hope to bring a zoo dog home.

March

Even though they are close, human and hyena, only inches apart, there are bars between them. April Matott, the second year who went to Have Trunk Will Travel back in the fall, kneels just outside Savuti's cage. The bright-eyed hyena sidles up to the bars. It's the first day of March, a Monday. Matott is running on a few hours of sleep. Though Dr. Peddie does all he can to discourage the students from working part-time jobs, some just have to, and Matott is one of those. She didn't get home from her job at the emergency vet clinic until 2 or 3 A.M., then arrived at the teaching zoo by 6:30 A.M.

She's showing a first year, the Argentinean prone to hives, how a command works. Matott's taught Savuti to let her scratch his left side. She balls her left hand and holds it against the cage. She orders Savuti to press his nose to her fist while she digs into his oily coat with the fingers on her right hand. Matott doesn't use a clicker because Savuti's grown snappish recently, lunging at the bars for his rewards of chicken necks. Matott thinks the clicker aggravates this aggression, so instead she just says, "Good."

Holding her left fist against the cage bars, Matott calls, "Target!" She raises her voice to be heard over the nearby racket of men repairing a drain. The machine they are using backfires with a loud crack. In a flash, Savuti turns his head and bites down on the fingertips of Matott's right hand. "He's got my hand," Matott says.

Savuti pulls, looks confused. Matott is confused, too. She thought her fingers were safely on her side of the bars. Let go, she thinks. She pulls back. The hyena hangs on. She calmly tells the first year to get the hose. The Argentinean dashes for it, but the hose is missing. The construction crew has it.

The delicate tug-of-war between human and hyena continues. Matott hears the snap of a bone break. There goes a finger, she thinks. Then, magically, Savuti unclenches his jaw. Matott's hand is hers again.

The students leave the bewildered hyena. Matott asks the Argentinean to look at her hand to see if all her fingers are there. The Argentinean has a blood phobia. Even the words *vein* or *heart* have made her woozy in the past. She braces herself and looks at the small hand before her. She counts five fingers. The middle one looks as if it's been smashed in a car door. To her relief, the Argentinean does not faint. To her relief, Matott has all her digits.

At the Health Center, a nurse examines Matott's hand and sends her to the emergency room for an X-ray. Matott's middle finger is broken. There's a good-sized hole in the top of her nail where Savuti's tooth punctured it. The nail is not likely to grow back. Matott's referred to a hand specialist.

At EATM they like to say that anything with a mouth bites. That's usually easy to remember around the big carns with their huge, shiny canines. That's harder to keep in mind with the cuter, cuddlier animals, and so the students seem to be forever getting nibbled by the prairie dogs or the baby skunks, one of which has been nicknamed Boob Biter. The funny thing about Savuti is, as dangerous carnivores go, he's cute, really cute. Dr. Peddie says that's why Savuti chomps a student every few years. The hyena got one student twice, the vet says. They let their guard down. Matott says that wasn't the case for her. She thinks Savuti mistook the backfire for a clicker and her pink finger for a chicken neck.

So the new month starts with a bite, a bad one, but it could have been so much worse. Matott is lucky not only to have all her fingers, but that Savuti bit her right hand. Matott needs her left hand to man Laramie, the one-winged eagle, in the Spring Spec show.

Preparations for Spring Spec have built to a fevered pitch. Though classes continue and job searches have begun, all anyone thinks or talks about at the school is Spring Spec, essentially a party that lasts for three weekends. The zoo is scrubbed, weeded, and raked. A team of students with paint brushes dab a dense jungle scene on the backdrop of Wildlife Theater. Costumes are stitched, flowers planted. Emu eggs are carefully emptied so they can be sold. Buttercup's paws are dunked in pink and black paint, so the badger can trot across pieces of paper and make paintings to sell.

There are a few snafus. Spring Spec T-shirts are printed, but the first years, being first years, got them wrong. The second years nail down their lines and polish their animals' training. Though the first years seem to do most of the heavy lifting for the event, overseeing countless details, crewing for the show, and organizing tours, the second years, as tradition would have it, consider it their Spring Spec. And being EATM students, they think of it competitively. They want to raise more money than the class before them, their second years.

The day of the press preview arrives. When the morning breaks and the cast convenes, they discover a costume is missing. Someone took it home to wash because Hudson, the beaver, peed on the costume. Beaver pee or not, the show must go on. Julietta opens the show, high-stepping around the stage, her bluish head slightly bobbing. A small flock of homing pigeons wing overhead, a gray flurry, to the top of the bleachers where a box awaits them—no problem. Baxter gamely, if slowly, carries tools on stage. Rosie throws kisses to the audience and leaps into Trevor's arms.

There are a few animal gaffes, but that's to be expected. When the sheep canter out, one starts chewing on a vine at the back of the stage and doesn't exit on cue. Mary VanHollebeke reaches out from the wings and grabs her halter. The jungle backdrop, which the students added details to just last night, confuses some of the animals. The rats try to climb the freshly painted branches. Puppy, the turkey vulture, his black wings thrown wide, glides past his stump and lands on a video camera. The trainers forgot to bait the stump.

Whatever missteps there are, Schmoo more than makes up for. The sea lion is on. For the finale she balances a ball on her nose, waves a flipper, and smacks a trainer on the bottom. She's a whirling dervish. Everyone cheers and claps. By the time Schmoo's finished, she's speckled in golden bits of earth and glittering like a star.

The following day, the teaching zoo throws its doors open for the first official day of Spring Spec 2004. An army of families in gym shoes pushing strollers marches through. Though "Welcome to the Jungle" has been the focus of attention, there is plenty else to do and the crowd fans out across the compound. There is face painting and a coconut toss. You can take a behind-the-scenes tour of the zoo, which includes a visit to Nutrition, where you can sample monkey chow or bird senet and stroll up the regularly off-limits back road. Tour takers are treated to insider information, such as why Taj, the tiger, is tucked in her den box today; she's afraid of strollers.

The second years trot out various zoo residents. Legend steps up on a tree stump. A student trainer hits the play button on a boom box, and the opening strains of Michael Jackson's "Man in the Mirror" tinkle. Legend's eyes widen. The wolf raises her nose to the sky and howls along to the pop ballad.

At the far end of the zoo, down a hill from Primate Gardens, there's Creature Feature. This is where a long list of professional trainers show off their chops. Nearby, two young women construct a combo information booth–playpen. Inside, a young orangutan named Pebbles in a disposable diaper gambols, tossing toys about, draping her long arms around her trainer's neck, and occasionally trying to scale the fence. She's henna red and restless as a toddler. Pebbles is a huge distraction to the EATM students, especially the interaction-starved first years, some of whom cluster around cooing at her when they should be off giving a tour.

"She's a princess," one of her trainers tells me. "She knows she's pretty."

The two women, who work for the movie trainer Bob Dunn, have brought Pebbles along to raise money for a retirement home for primates in the entertainment industry. A $5 contribution will buy you entry into Pebbles's pen. I hand over a donation and step through the fence. Pebbles is far less interested in me than I am in her. So the trainers give me an orange drink and that catches Pebbles's eye. After I tip the drink so she can take a swallow, the toddler orangutan lets me scratch her back. Her hair is coarse and her back flat and solid as a board. An EATM student walks up to the booth and demands, "How come you get to do that?"

Two little girls rush the fence. Pebbles slips out from under my fingers and over to the girls. She's clearly more interested in primates her age. The younger girl, maybe two or three, is Pebbles's height and the two look each other in the eye. Their parents quickly hand over $5, get out their camera, and the twosome steps into Pebbles's playpen. The girls are less interested in Pebbles than in her toy box, which they immediately inspect. Pebbles holds up toys for them to see. The girls poke around, reach in, and grab a thing or two, oblivious to the orangutan standing right next to them. "When will you ever get to play with an orangutan again?" the mother pleads. This once-in-a-lifetime moment is lost on the youngsters, whose open minds have yet to draw a clear line between humans and animals.

The EATM students dash back and forth across the zoo, from cages to tours to the stage. They aren't allowed to eat in public, so some scarf down snow cones as they stride behind the front office. When they get a few minutes to actually sit down, they duck into Zoo 2 and devour whole sandwiches with the speed of a big cat.

There are four performances of "Welcome to the Jungle," two by each cast. The show has a circus, a train wreck, a mime, a villain, a scene from *Gilligan's Island,* a central mystery, and a referee. It's Oscar Wilde meets Steve Martin. It's very inventive and the cast carries it off gamely, but the intricate wordplay and dense plot make for a long show by family entertainment standards. The metal bleachers creak and groan with restlessness. Wriggly preschoolers are lugged out mid-show.

By late afternoon, everyone is beat and, understandably, tempers begin to flare. Susan Patch notices that Adam Hyde is backing up Trevor Jahangard with Rosie, the baboon, when he should be cleaning. Up until now, Patch has made a point of keeping an even keel, of not taking things personally, but something about this makes her snap. She doesn't yell but, as she puts it later, suggests "not very politely" that Hyde should help out. Hyde, with Rosie nearby, does as he's been taught. He checks his temper. Jahangard tells Patch, "Not now." They are both thinking of Rosie, who doesn't bat an eye but is sure to have noticed that a female, moreover an outsider, has challenged her man. In a moment of being too human, Patch has just committed a social offense in the baboon's world.

It's not long before Patch realizes her error. A second year who saw the scene confronts her. Patch feels her up-to-now clean record, her straight A's, and her perfect attendance slip through her hands. It hits the model student hard. Uncharacteristically, she feels like crying, so the moment Patch is done for the day, she runs for the parking lot. Then she hears Holly Tumas call her name across the stretch of tar. Patch turns, apologizes, and bursts into tears as the other students file by to their cars. Hyde goes home and calls all his friends to discuss human behavior, what he calls Bitchfest 2004.

A carpet of green has unrolled over the hills around the teaching zoo. Sunny yellow wild mustard crowds the valleys. The reminders of last fall's blaze, the skeletons of charred trees with their branches raised skyward and the wiry black balls of crisped sagebrush, still dot the landscape but they look less ominous, more incongruous. The spring sun is hot enough that Wendell, the goat, and Baxter, the pig, nap in the afternoon rays. The reptiles take turns basking in the sun in an outside cage by Nutrition.

Second years fill in Buttercup's hole. Before they dump in the two wheelbarrows of dirt, one student sticks her head down the badger's lair, but can't see the bottom. While out on a walk, Mara Rodriguez chucks Spirit quickly under the chin to remind him who's in charge. He's been ignoring commands. As she says, "If you have a cat on the end of a chain who doesn't listen to you, you're in trouble."

Fewer and fewer first years retain their flawless records. Patch was given a learning contract, essentially a warning, for snapping at Hyde in front of Rosie. Like Patch, Castaneda has fallen from grace. On a recent morning, she drove through a deep fog up the 101, arriving at her usual 5:30 A.M. Then she fell asleep in her car.

She snoozed as other students pulled into the lot and headed into the teaching zoo. No one stopped to rouse her. Her cell phone rang at 6:01 A.M. A fellow first year was calling her from Zoo 1. They had just read her name off the roll.

Chris Jenkins, who trains Olive, announces at a weekly meeting that he's gotten engaged. Everyone cries and cheers. So far, Dr. Peddie's dire predictions of relationship mayhem have not proved true. No marriages have crashed. Serious relationships have held steady. Romances have even bloomed. Terri Fidone often sparkles with pieces of diamond jewelry her boyfriend gives her. He regularly sends text messages that he loves her. The trick to keeping love alive at EATM, Castaneda's live-in boyfriend tells me, is that you accept the teaching zoo as the be-all and end-all for twenty-two months. "I hear everything three times," he says. "When I get home, over dinner, and before we go to bed." Oh, and a fourth: "When she calls her mother or her sister." He's taken over the grocery shopping and laundry. He's learned how to get monkey pee out of her shirts.

Dr. Peddie has gotten a huge shiny new red truck. He needed it, he says, to trailer his new boat that he's docked in Santa Barbara. However, I suspect that the vet, being a man's man, just wanted a big truck. He asks most everybody who walks within five feet of him, "Have you seen my truck?"

He's happy to talk about his retirement gear, but the actual leaving makes his voice tight. Not that he's changed his mind, however much the first years plead. It's just that he can't help feeling a bit anxious. His elderly mother telephones in a worried voice and asks how he can afford this. He can easily, but her question eats at him. His father worked well into his eighties. By his parents' standards, "he's quitting." Then there's the retirement party. Mara Rodriguez has invited four hundred people to a picnic next month. When that subject comes up, his eyes shift from side to side and he draws his lips in. "I don't like being the center of attention," he says. I can't help taking pity on him and ask him something about his truck. His face loosens. He smiles.

The Monday morning after Spring Spec, when a pale fog swaths the teaching zoo, Dr. Peddie pilots his other truck, the old green one with all his vet equipment in the back, to Primate Gardens. The primates are due for their annual TB tests. It's stressful for the vet, for the primates, and for Gary Wilson, who has to catch some of them. "I think I'm slowing down," Wilson says.

This testing will be slightly easier because Goblin was crate-trained last fall after the fire. Last year the baboon had to be darted, but this time on a student's command she goes in her crate and pulls the door closed behind her. Her four student trainers, includng Brunelli, then make themselves scarce, so the baboon won't associate them with what's to come. They don't want to lose Goblin's trust.

Samantha, the gibbon, lets loose with one of her alarm calls—a long whoop—as Gary and Cindy Wilson enter Goblin's cage. They pick up the crate and tip it, so Dr. Peddie can inject the baboon with a sedative. He warns the Wilsons, "She's strong enough to break out of there." She doesn't. They set the crate down and wait for the drug to take effect.

Benji, the vervet monkey, is another story. He's new to the zoo and this will be the first time Wilson will net him. The arboreal monkey has turquoise balls and big fangs. When a second year trainer opens the door to his round enclosure, to her surprise, the latch drops off in her hand. With his agile black fingers, Benji had worked off a nut.

She and another second year shoo Benji into his bedroom, the small room at the back of his cage, where Gary Wilson awaits him. From outside, all you can see are Wilson's bare legs, to which a student wonders out loud, "Why does he have shorts on?" Then

Benji screams and lunges, and there's a flash of fangs and Wilson's legs jumping. The small group outside of the cage tense, gasp, and lean forward. Somehow, the horrible-sounding scene ends up with Benji in Wilson's net. "You should have worn pants," someone says to Wilson. "I should have worn a cup," he responds.

Dr. Peddie pricks Benji through the net. By now, Goblin is so drowsy her second year trainers, including Brunelli, have lifted her out of her crate and set her on a table where the vet can examine her. The baboon leans against Brunelli as the vet pricks her for a tuberculosis test, then checks her teeth, and listens to her heart beat. These annual tests teach the students about what's involved in the animals' general care and how they can help as trainers, such as getting Goblin to hop inside her crate. But the loving often supersedes the learning. Brunelli and Goblin's three other second-year trainers gather round the baboon and do what they normally can't—stroke her and snuggle her. They remark on how soft her skin is. They run their fingertips along her arms, touch her nose, and massage the soles of her feet. Brunelli wraps her arms around the sagging baboon and smiles for the camera. First years stand to the side, enviously watching the love fest. Goblin's tongue hangs out a bit. The baboon lets out a soft sigh.

With the first weekend of Spring Spec behind them, the second years turn their attention back to turnovers. They have to hand over their animals to the first years before they graduate in early May. That seems like plenty of time but it isn't, because turnovers in the spring are long and protracted. The first years, what with classes and the all-consuming Spring Spec, have gotten behind on the many steps of turnovers. The second years press them to pick up the pace. A flurry of notes are posted by the front office, listing turnover appointments by various cages. Mary VanHollebeke yells at Castaneda and the other first-year trainers on Walter and

Dunny. When a first year steps out of class, a second year chides him for missing a feeding with the macaw, Max. "I was in class," he pleads. "Until you've observed a feeding, you can't talk to him," she says. "Then you can give him a nut and say 'Hi.' "

"The second years are giving us a ration of shit," says Chandra Cohn. She's behind on all her turnovers, the furthest being on Samantha, the gibbon. The second year on Boots, the opossum, though, has been giving her the hardest time. "I don't want to even talk about the opossum," Cohn says.

A first year on Puppy, the turkey vulture, has worked up to step 4 in the bird's turnover, learning how to wrap your upper arms with Ace bandages. That done, she proceeds to step 5, pulls on thick leather gloves, and picks up the vulture. With his serrated beak, Puppy grabs and twists her arms—thus the Ace bandages, despite which the bird still leaves bruises. He pulls back her heavy leather gloves and bites her bare forearm. Likewise, Laramie, the one-winged eagle, jabs at his keepers' eyes with his hooked beak. Consequently, they all wear sunglasses. Still, the eagle leaves his mark on these trainers; their foreheads are dotted with small scabs. Susan Patch, who's assigned to the eagle for summer semester, has learned how to gas rats and trap bunnies. That step in the turnover complete, she can now say "Hi" to Laramie. At home, she strengthens her left arm so that she can hoist the eagle. She clutches an eight-pound weight in her left hand while extending her arm. Her muscles strain and quiver. Laramie weighs eleven pounds.

Anita Wischhusen whiles away hours by Zulu's cage, getting to know his honor. She does not groom with him, so the mandrill hasn't had a chance to pinch her yet, but she's worried about when the time will come. "My reaction when something hurts is to pull back," she says, which will make him squeeze harder.

Though Tony Capovilla and Adam Hyde were both assigned to Rosie, the turnover has focused on Hyde. Rosie is already plenty comfortable with Capovilla. She even barks hello to him. Hyde she doesn't know so well. Hyde wants to be a tiger trainer. His looming height will work to his advantage with big cats but not so much so with Rosie. He could easily intimidate the female baboon, though he never has that effect on his fellow students. The lumbering eighteen-year-old learns to look smaller and less threatening. Jahangard tells Hyde never to look at Rosie directly but always from the side. When he walks with the baboon, Hyde slouches. He keeps his voice low and calm—none of his usual cracks or cutting up. So far, the baboon flinched only once, when Hyde offered her a treat.

No matter the primate, Cindy Wilson counsels the students to make their acquaintance slowly. Primates, except for us, are not ones to make friends quickly. If the students push too hard, the primates might push back, only with bared teeth. "Nobody at this point should be getting bitten," she tells them in class. "If you are seeing aggression, you need to change what you are doing. You should be building a bond now." That's why all the primates have lengthy, complicated turnovers. Olive's takes the longest, sixteen weeks. Even the turnover for Scooter, the outgoing capuchin monkey, can take months in some cases.

Hierarchy is a big deal to Scooter, as it is to all primates. Carrie Hakanson is the most dominant of the monkey's second-year trainers, so much so that she can freak out the capuchin just by asking for behaviors. If Scooter is on a tree branch above Hakanson and the second year looks up at her, the monkey will crouch down, a submissive posture. The way Scooter's turnover works is that the four first years go one at a time, from the least dominant personality to the most. Hakanson picked the order and, to my surprise and hers, Castaneda is the first to go, meaning she's the least assertive of the four. This is the first time in her five-foot-eleven-inch life she's been described as such. Number two is a similarly tall woman who wears size 12 shoes. Number three is a former 911 dispatcher with a low, gravelly voice. Terri Fidone is number four.

Hakanson collects the monkey from her cage, takes her hand, and lifts Scooter onto her shoulder. The group ambles up the front road and settles on the curb near one of Scooter's favorite trees, a mulberry near Clarence's enclosure. Hakanson directs Castaneda to sit close to her. The rest of us sit off to the side, per her instructions. On her long lead, Scooter effortlessly scales the mulberry. Hakanson points out a lizard on the tree to the monkey. Scooter doesn't seem to see it, then suddenly her little hands flash, and the lizard tail is sticking out of her mouth as she crunches. Everyone wails. Hakanson calls "Fix it!" and the capuchin rappels down the tree, pulling her lead in as she goes, working black hand over black hand, unraveling its various tangles as she descends. Then she bounds on number two's and number three's knees. Hakanson calls her off, because she doesn't want Scooter to get too friendly with them yet. When Scooter lands on my knees, Hakanson leaves her there. I'm inconsequential, kind of an interesting piece of scenery in the scheme of things, which I find slightly insulting.

Scooter eyes me briefly, scrunches her brow. I hold still and avert my eyes. Then she grooms herself, including a couple of grabs at her crotch, as she balances delicately on my bent knee. As I watch Scooter out of the corner of my eye, I accept my low status in this troupe. Sitting next to me, numbers two and three in the hierarchy still grapple with their respective spots in the lineup. Neither is happy.

"I thought I was pretty opinionated," grouses number two, thinking she should be higher.

"There's no way I'm more dominant than you," says number three, thinking she should be lower. Hierarchy is a big deal for primates, and that includes us.

* * *

There's not much to Abbey's turnover, other than learning to feed her, which is no simple matter. Mohelnitzky tried dosing the dog with Mylanta at night, but that didn't seem to solve her stomach problems either. Undeterred, Mohelnitzky now pours the milky potion down Abbey's throat in the morning. She has trained Abbey to run over an A-frame and through a tunnel for the preshow of "Welcome to the Jungle," but if her stomach bothers her, the pooch won't perform.

In Nutrition, Mohelnitzky shows the students assigned to Abbey how to make the finicky dog's breakfast. In the walk-in freezer, Mohelnitzky pulls down Abbey's tray from a high shelf to show the first years. There is a container of scrambled eggs, pureed chicken noodle soup, and a sticky bottle of barbecue sauce. As Mohelnitzky ladles a gooey mess of soup, eggs, and ramen noodles dotted with kibble into a bowl, she explains that she feeds Abbey 200 grams in the morning and 450 grams in the evening. "Give her whatever is working at the time, and currently it's ramen noodles," she says. "You don't have to worry about this dog getting fat. She is very pampered and very spoiled, so you guys need to keep it up."

What Mohelnitzky doesn't tell them is that she is probably wasting their time. Her landlord said she can have a dog, that he'll make this one exception. That done, she asked the studio training company that owns Abbey if the dog can live with her. They also said yes. There is one last step. She has to submit the request in writing to the EATM staff. Again, Mohelnitzy picks up her pen for Abbey.

Thursday morning, Brenda Woodhouse tries to read the roll as if nothing has happened. She sends the students out on the compound as if it were any other day. She and Rodriguez have agreed not to say anything just yet, but they don't know how long they can keep their emotions in check.

When the zoo has been scrubbed from back to front, the sheep pellets in Hoofstock raked up, and the parrots fed, the students file back into Zoo 1, as they do every morning, to check in, to report anything amiss, to pause briefly before rushing headlong into another busy day. They sink into their chairs. After they are seated, four second years arrive and walk to the front of the classroom. Their faces are tight, splotchy, as if they have been crying.

The EATM staff forever reminds the students to expect the unexpected. An animal can lunge at you out of the blue, bite you in a flash, and escape through a door that is hardly cracked. The animals are wild, no matter how long they are in cages, no matter how close you bond to them. Nature has designed them to be unpredictable. And so is life, but who thinks of that when each day a camel might try to knock you down or a hyena might take off a finger? When these are your worries, the everyday concerns of the world beyond the front gate so easily recede into the far, inconsequential distance. But the front gate only keeps the animals in. It does not keep life, with all its vagaries and fundamental wildness, out.

A second year has died. The words stop time in the room, as the students quickly weigh them. Then their heaviness settles, their razor sharpness cuts. The students gasp and let out small cries. Their mouths slacken. They press their palms to their cheeks as if to scream. Megan Thomas, the second year who ate french fries with a pool of ranch dressing at SeaWorld, who trained Hudson, the beaver, to stand up in his stream, who always smiled and never complained, who just turned twenty-five on Sunday, died in her sleep last night. Her boyfriend couldn't wake her. Her roommates, the young women telling them this unbelievable news, tried to rouse her and couldn't. They gave her CPR. They called 911. Nothing changed the fact that this beautiful, talented girl, who dreamed of training tigers in Las Vegas, was dead.

Everyone sobs, hugs, and staggers out of the room drunk with grief and shock and the absurdity of it all. Not a bite, not a scratch, not a kick. Like Sleeping Beauty, she slipped away from them unscathed in the comfort of her own bed.

"Did she have a heart condition?" students ask. Nobody knows. What could snatch a young woman's life in the middle of the night? There is no ready answer. Rodriguez can't help wondering about her weight, how thin Megan was. Michlyn Hines was worried enough about Megan and a few other students that she had called the Health Center recently. The director was on vacation; she just returned today.

Classes are canceled. So are rehearsals and any kind of appointment. A place so full of bustling activity grinds to an unnerving halt. No one knows what to do with themselves, except for Anita Wischhusen, who gets busy in the front office with some computer work and, perhaps because she's old enough to be world-weary, takes a philosophical approach. "It's the cycle of life," she says grimly.

Many of the second years leave for the house Megan shared with three other EATM students and her longtime boyfriend, where her parents are already busy planning her funeral. The remaining students move in slow motion. Some sit and rest their heads in their hands. In the front office, Kage, the vivacious Texan, lays her head in Brunelli's lap and the two women sob. Others wander off down the front road. Trevor Jahangard and Adam Hyde go to get Rosie out for a stroll. Mary VanHollebeke walks back to Zulu's cage, and the kingly mandrill leans his shoulder against the bars for her to groom, something he hasn't done in a long time. Brunelli settles down next to Goblin's cage.

The students are taught that if they are upset or mad, they should not work with the animals, especially the primates. They will be too distracted to notice the small, telling details of an animal's behavior. Still, the staff doesn't stop any of the students. Suddenly, the certainty of the animals—that they must be fed, walked, and cared for, no matter what—is a deep comfort amid unfathomable uncertainties. The day's lesson has been their hardest at EATM yet: that life, like a wild animal, can never be tamed.

Life can't pause for long at the teaching zoo. There's talk of canceling Spring Spec, but that's impossible. Tomorrow the crowds will return for the second weekend of the zoo-wide extravaganza. Both casts of "Welcome to the Jungle" need to rehearse the freshly cut scripts. One cast, the one that had Megan in it, has to figure out how to get along without her. The rehearsal starts and stops as hollow-eyed second years stumble around the stage and, here and there, break down in tears. The show is supposed to be funny, and funny just doesn't feel right, right now. Funny also doesn't work with actors crying onstage.

Meanwhile, a mob of prospective students and their parents and boyfriends arrives. Anyone who has applied to the program must attend one of these daylong programs. To some degree, these meetings are meant to haze prospective students, to scare off the ones who think animals are cute or have dreams of playing with Bambi. Dr. Peddie does the best he can. He tells them about the lion attack, he warns them that the program will destroy relationships, that parents should not expect to see their sons and daughters for the duration. If you have medical problems, you ought to think twice, he says.

Though Dr. Peddie gives it his all, he can't hold a candle to Tony Capovilla. He's volunteered to give a small group of prospective students and their families a tour of the teaching zoo. Each time I visit the zoo, I'm somewhat surprised to find Capovilla still here. No one has quit the program this year, but if anyone does, my bet would be on Capovilla. Though he has hung in and worked hard, he always seems on the edge of leaving EATM and returning to his $50-an-hour plumber's life. He'll say as much, never hiding his frustration with the program.

Capovilla has a high, rounded forehead, which is often sunburned, a strong chin, and an expressive face. He speaks with a tight-jawed drawl and is in his early thirties. His mother offered to pay his way to EATM. Capovilla thought going to the program would be kind of a vacation from earning a living. He couldn't have been more wrong.

Capovilla's tour makes for a rather discouraging but honest introduction, a counterbalance to the breathless enthusiasm of some of his classmates. The prospective students with their sunny expressions clearly don't quite know how to take some of the things he says in his growly twang, such as "You're worse than a slave, because you pay to do this work" or "You have an easy life now. Enjoy it. I wish I did." At the Rat Room, he encourages them to lean in and "just take a little smell." He tells them, "You'll get used to seeing frozen pigeon heads." Still, try as he may, not even Capovilla can burst their bubble. Now that they have walked through the front gate and seen their dreams in the flesh, few will be turned away.

On Saturday, after the crowds leave, the pots of face paint are capped, the costumes are stashed, and the spilled snow cones are hosed off the front road, everyone gathers in Wildlife Theater for a memorial service. One by one, the animals Megan cared for and trained are brought out onstage. For the first time ever, Clarence, lured by chunks of watermelon, lumbers from his enclosure all the way to the theater. It takes the tortoise an hour. Brunelli brings out Malaika and demonstrates what Megan taught the parrot—a wolf whistle. VanHollebeke fights back tears and lugs out a rabbit. Another student, looking down at her feet, ferries out Nova, the horned owl. Megan used to hoot at him, she says. Hudson is plopped in the pool. The parade continues as dusk turns to night. The humans in the bleachers quietly watch the animals as the dark washes over them.

Baltimore

On the first Monday of April a cold wind grazes Baltimore's waterfront, winter's frosty good-bye kiss on spring's young cheek. The tentative daffodils shiver. The chill air ruffles the green grass and teases the harbor into frosty waves. Though the sun shines, it's a good day to hole up, and that's what a couple hundred zookeepers and animal trainers do in a hotel along the harbor. In a spacious, windowless conference room, they pull up chairs at long tables covered with white tablecloths and pour themselves tall glasses of chilled water. They uncap pens and flip crisp pages of fresh notebooks, ready for reports from the front lines of a revolution that promises an even sunnier future than the budding bulbs outside.

This is the fourth annual meeting of the Animal Behavioral Management Alliance (ABMA). ABMA focuses solely on training. As such, the organization is a rare thing, what animal people call pan-species. At this conference, parrot trainers are elbow to elbow with aquarists and tiger keepers. ABMA's singular focus on training seems straightforward enough, but the truth is the organization sees training as just a tool to reach its broader goal—changing the captive animal world for the better. If ABMA has its way, zoo animals won't have to be sedated for routine medical procedures. They won't be hosed to get them to move from their cage to their zoo exhibit. Big cats won't pace their days away. Monkeys won't neurotically pull their fur out.

Though ABMA's vision may sound utopian, it does not call for blind faith; it is based on the sound science of operant conditioning. As one member puts it, B. F. Skinner "is the father of our industry." ABMA knows seeing is believing, and over the next five days this conference is designed to offer example after example of how Skinner's principles can improve not only the lives of captive animals but the keepers' as well. This week's schedule includes talks on training a black mamba snake to press its nose to a target pole, a gator to rocket out of a murky pond on command, and a dart frog to jump on a mini-scale to be weighed. This morning's lineup alone will cover training African wild dogs, nutria, and fish crows.

ABMA was started in 2000, primarily by marine mammal trainers who sensed a growing hunger among zookeepers and other animal professionals for their techniques. Since then, membership has nearly doubled to about 350. That ABMA exists is proof of the seismic shift in thinking at zoos. Not long ago, training was taboo. An EATM alum told me that when she graduated in 1990, if you wanted to work at a zoo you had to keep your training prowess a secret. It would be a huge black mark. At worst, trainers were equated with circus folk. At best, they were considered prima donnas.

The tables have begun to turn over the past ten years, as zoos have realized the practical benefits of training. Dorothy Belanger, an EATM grad and part-time staffer, offers a case in point. When Belanger was assigned to the Sumatran tigers in 1996, she leapfrogged over more senior keepers, which caused some grumbling. Why was she promoted out of line? Because, Belanger says, she had trained a diabetic gibbon to voluntarily offer its arm for insulin shots.

To some degree, this year's ABMA conference will preach to the converted. Many of the keepers and trainers here know at least a bit of operant conditioning. This conference, though, is sure to rev them up and send them home like so many ardent missionaries, which is good. There are still old-school zoo directors and senior zookeepers to sway whom one attendee refers to as "dead weight." The older keepers can be entrenched, says Gary Priest. "It's not what they signed up for."

Zookeepers predominate here, but there are some dog trainers, an ethologist from Sweden, and even a gymnastics coach, for some reason. Most are young, as are the foot soldiers of any revolution. Most are women, reflecting the gender imbalance of the field. Most are in sweatshirts or polo shirts in solid colors with zoo emblems emblazoned on them. They make their fashion statements with their accessories: socks with tiger stripes, sterling silver animals dangling from their ears, canvas bags covered with paw prints.

A clutch of EATM students, all second years, take up one long table near the front. They are here with Cindy and Gary Wilson. He is one of ABMA's founding directors. Most of the group, eleven of them, bunk down each night at a student's sister's house south of Baltimore. They sleep on couches and the floor, which explains how tired they all look. They drive an hour here each morning in two SUVs they've rented with pooled funds.

Though it's early April, the second years are already done with classes for the semester. Their last month of school is devoted to special projects and job searches. This conference counts as a special project. Three of the students will give a presentation later this week on B.E. at the teaching zoo. Tomorrow, Sarah Harrison and Priscilla Carbajal will speak on the evacuation during the fire. This would have been an emotional presentation in any case, but now it's more so. Their close friend Megan Thomas was to give the lecture with them. The smiley young woman who was to speak about the fire that nearly destroyed the zoo has died somehow. That they are here without Megan is a constant reminder not just of her death but of death itself, so amid all the conference's chatter and buoyancy, the EATM students wander sadly. They should make connections and hand out resumes to training bigwigs. Instead, they cling to each other, as people with heavy hearts do, moving through the cheery crowd like a family in mourning.

Karen Pryor, author, pioneering dolphin trainer, scientist, is also here, if only fleetingly this morning, to give the keynote address. Pryor, in her early seventies, has auburn hair cut in a no-nonsense pageboy. She's of average height, has long, lean arms and a low, melodic voice. She has a good sense of humor and an especially sunny smile. Pryor is a natural storyteller and has a down-to-earth way of talking about training.

She is a star in this crowd—a woman who was training dolphins well before many people in the room were born, who wrote a definitive and easily digestible book on operant conditioning, and who saw the broad implications of Skinner's findings for captive animals long before anyone else did. Her central point is this—hang in there. "One way to change your world is to outlive your critics," she says. If you find your zoo administration pooh-poohs training just persist, she advises. Pryor has, and look at her. She's gone from outcast to luminary. "Open hostility," she tells them, "is one of the best signs that you are making progress."

Pryor comes from a long line of ministers on one side and a secular radical or two on the other. She has three children and seven grandchildren. She's been married and divorced twice. Her first husband, who founded Sea Life Park, fired her from her dolphin training post, essentially for insubordination. She was married a second time, to Jon Lindbergh, son of Charles Lindbergh. She lived with him in the mountains outside Seattle for fifteen years, where she caught up on her scientific writing. Now she lives by herself in the Boston area with her two dogs, a border terrier named Twitchett and a German harlequin poodle named Misha. They are clicker trained.

Pryor considers herself a scientist foremost and has been a link between the animal training world and the behaviorists, some of whom have been appalled at how Skinner's ideas have been usurped to teach dolphins to flip. Pryor is well versed in the abstract notions of her field but isn't above teaching a damselfish to swim through a hoop or a hermit crab to yank on a string for its dinner. She is also an optimist, the way anyone who has sparked two revolutions in her lifetime would be. Before she hung a dolphin whistle around her neck, Pryor changed the way people thought about breast feeding with her book *Nursing Your Baby*. Then Pryor fell into dolphin training and became a pioneer in that field.

Pryor hung up her dolphin whistle in 1974 and wrote *Lads Before the Wind* about her adventures teaching the cetaceans. When she moved to New York City with her teeange daughter to be a freelance writer, Pryor assumed her life as an animal trainer was over. Not long after her migration east, however, she was enlisted by Smithsonian's National Zoo to solve some behavior problems, such as why the polar bears banged on their cage doors all day. Pryor taught the keepers what she had learned with dolphins. In turn, she learned that operant conditioning knew no bounds specieswise. Like other early dolphin trainers, Pryor had assumed Skinner's principles truly worked only with marine mammals. She'd just proven herself wrong.

For Pryor, it was a eureka experience plain and simple. Not so for the zoo world. They criticized Pryor for teaching animals "nonnaturalistic" behaviors or harrumphed that she made them into robots. "It's not fun to be ahead of your time," she says. "Everyone in the field thinks you're nuts."

When a tennis coach asked Pryor at a dinner party to recommend a book on how to use operant conditioning on the court, a light went off in the author's head. She wrote *Don't Shoot the Dog!* to explain operant conditioning in the most conversational tone possible, in hopes people from all walks of life would use Skinnerian principles. Pryor wrote the book primarily, she says, "to get people to stop yelling at their kids." The 1984 book did not reach the broad public Pryor had hoped for, but, to her surprise, dog trainers embraced it enthusiastically. The book inspired the clicker-training movement that has taken dog obedience classes by storm. Meanwhile, her book slowly became the basic primer for trainers of all ilks.

Pryor could rest on her laurels but she doesn't. "Is there a point where you can stop pushing?" she asks. "I don't know." She's curious to see what's ahead and just how far operant conditioning can go. In her talk this morning, she mentions in passing that gymnastics coaches have begun to use a form of clicker training with their athletes. They call this training "tagging"; the clickers, "taggers." It is somewhat lost on this crowd, but Pryor has said something rather startling. The dolphin trainer has now set her sights on another species—humans—to see how operant conditioning can better life for them.

The afternoon includes a talk by trainers at SeaWorld in San Diego on how they recruit young visitors to smear peanut butter on the polar bears' boomer ball or let them shoot wads of cream cheese into their enclosure. It makes the kids and the bears happy. Trainers from the San Diego Zoo and Wild Animal Park show a video of their cheetah streaking after a lure. They learned to do so from none other than Cathryn Hilker at the Cincinnati Zoo. A trainer at a dolphin interaction program in Hawaii describes how guests merrily clean the dolphins' long row of teeth with a Waterpik, feel for their dorsal vein, and place eyecups on them. After dinner, the long day ends with a workshop on aggression led by two trainers who started their careers with killer whales, Gary Priest and Thad Lacinak, who as corporate curator of training for SeaWorld's various parks oversees more than three hundred trainers.

The two men go at the subject alternately like stand-up comics or preachers. Priest teases Lacinak about his pet Chihuahua, Peanut. "I think you need your estrogen levels checked," he needles. "I'm not the one who was a hairdresser," Lacinak shoots back, referring to Priest's previous career. Then they show frightening footage of an elephant tossing a keeper across an enclosure. They recount hellfire-and-brimstone stories of trainers getting hurt or, worse, killed. Their message is simple: do not punish your animals. Aggression provokes aggression, setting off a troubling cycle. Every time your animal bites or lunges at you, it makes it more likely it'll do it again. "It's fun for animals to aggress," Lacinak says. "When you win the fight, it feels good."

This is the marine mammal trainers' bailiwick. In the early days of the field, trainers quickly realized aversive techniques just plain didn't work. A lot of early killer whale trainers were hurt, Lacinak says, until they learned never, ever to correct the orcas. Marine mammal trainers figure if they can use only positive reinforcement, every trainer ought to be able to do the same. Not only is it a more moral way to work, it's more effective and safer, they say, and so Lacinak and Priest hammer away. Don't withhold food, they counsel. A hungry animal gets aggressive fast. Don't hose animals. They only become desensitized to it and begin to think of you as annoying or threatening. Don't use a shield with sea lions. "All it does is piss them off," Lacinak says. "Every time you use an aversive you are hurting your relationship with that animal."

This is an ongoing debate in the training world, because there are shades of punishment and what constitutes an aversive technique. Using a bit and reins on a horse is aversive. So is a whip. While many trainers would consider whipping a horse cruel, not to mention pointless, few would dispense with a bit and reins. What exactly is negative can be very subjective. It's safe to say most people here prefer positive training techniques, or they wouldn't bother with operant conditioning to begin with. Some trainers, though, think using only positive reinforcement is impractical if not impossible, especially when working with big, dangerous animals, to which hierarchy matters. How do you convince a pushy camel you're the boss when he digs in his two-toed feet or bites you in the ribs? At the teaching zoo, if Kaleb, the camel, won't lie down, the students pull down hard on his lead or pop him on the nose with a fist to remind him they are in charge. Lacinak and Priest would not approve, and therein lies the basic philosophical rub.

"Get your animals to like you," Priest says. "Don't punish them." Priest knows he has some convincing to do. Keepers and trainers are humans, and humans are primates, and primates are naturally inclined to dominate and to punish when a little encouragement would do. "Changing the behavior of the animals isn't as easy as changing the behavior of the keepers," he tells the audience. Priest should know.

Like Pryor, Priest is a star in this circle. He's a handsome man with a thick, graying beard. He wears Hawaiian-style shirts with loud prints. Though he's deeply religious, he's got an off-color sense of humor. He's come a long way from his early cowboy days of killer whale training. Like so many of those early trainers, Priest ended up in a tank with an orca by chance. While going to college, Priest worked as a grocery checker, a job he loathed. A woman who worked in the human resources department at SeaWorld came through his aisle. Priest, who is extremely personable, struck up a conversation. Luckily, she had a big order, and by the time he'd rung up her groceries, she told him the park was hiring. He'd never been to SeaWorld, but a job there sounded like more fun than ringing a cash register.

He worked the 4 A.M. shift in the fish house. It was 1970. Killer whales had only been in captivity for five years. Trainers were figuring it out as they went. One morning, not long into his employ, Priest's boss called him over. The killer whale trainer was walking funny, gingerly. He told Priest that he'd be riding the killer whale today. "I was so stunned I never had to worry about stage fright, because I was so afraid of being peeled out of my wet suit like a banana and eaten," he says. "My big break was because of his hemorrhoids."

Priest quit school and became a full-time killer whale trainer. He loved the work, but another SeaWorld boss frustrated him, so he left the park in 1975. Priest went to barber school and cut hair for about five years. He returned to animal training in 1983, when the world-renowned San Diego Zoo hired him as a one-person training department.

In his early days at the zoo some keepers, Priest says, "got their noses bent out of shape" over taking suggestions from a killer whale trainer. Then along came Loon, the diabetic drill. Back then, the only way to get a blood test from a monkey was to sedate him. There was no way Loon could survive having that done repeatedly each day to monitor his glucose level. Normally, the zoo would have had two choices: change his diet and hope against hope or euthanize him.

Marine mammal trainers had long taught husbandry procedures like blood draws. Priest thought, why not try it with a drill? He pulled on tufts of fur on Loon's arm while grooming him. He got the drill to stick his arm through a plastic tube and keep it there. Eventually, Loon would offer his arm through the cage for thrice-daily blood tests. This was revolutionary in the zoo world, which hadn't really considered the medical benefits of training. Priest became a celebrity and, more important, a catalyst for change.

The trainer didn't get to enjoy the limelight for long. In 1991, one of the elephant trainers was killed at the zoo's sister organization, the San Diego Wild Animal Park. Priest was recruited to change how the keepers worked with the elephants to make it safer. People are forever saying the U.S. Department of Labor considers the job of elephant keeper one of the most dangerous in the country, more dangerous than mining or police work. That depends somewhat on how you spin the statistics, and sensationalizes something that doesn't really need sensationalizing. The point is that working with elephants is very, very risky. As Priest puts it, "Elephants don't leave bruises. They leave stains."

For well over four millennia, elephant trainers have taken that chance. Traditionally, the animals are worked in "free contact," meaning human and elephant side by side, no barrier. This is how Gary and Kari Johnson at Have Trunk Will Travel work their female elephants. This system is based on dominance and use of the elephant hook. The Johnsons use the hook as a guide and as an extension of the arm, in the way that many big cat trainers use a whip. However, some old-school trainers assert themselves with heavy use of the elephant hook, especially in Asia. To Priest "it's a system based on negatives."

This age-old system also relies on a long, steady bond between human and animal as well as a trainer with years of experience. As the circus trainers who once took up the steadier life of zoo jobs have disappeared and the older generation of elephant keepers retire, the pool of experienced trainers has shrunk. The younger zookeepers taking their jobs don't have nearly as much experience. Zoos can't always afford the three to five years to train these novice keepers, so many go into the elephant yard without being well prepared. When a keeper is hurt or, worse, killed, it is usually a young one, Priest says.

At the Wild Animal Park, Priest advocated that the elephants be worked in "protected contact," meaning through cage bars, and solely with positive reinforcement. Priest says the elephants learned quickly; the keepers, not so fast. At first they ignored him. Then they argued with him. They vandalized his car. In operant-conditioning talk, they gave Priest lots of aversive stimuli—bucketfuls. "It's mighty reinforcing to go in with elephants and be treated like an elephant," Priest says. "It's so cool. I never appreciated the bond between keepers and elephants. Now, they are no longer part of the herd."

Priest persisted and his system prevailed. Ultimately, all the zoo's elephant trainers who had worked in free contact either quit or were transferred, Priest says. The elephants could make the change, but the humans couldn't. More than ten years later, more and more zoos have switched to protected contact, a trend that is still controversial among elephant keepers and trainers. To this day, Priest says, he remains a pariah among free-contact elephant trainers. Regardless, his career has flourished. Now, as curator of applied behavior, he oversees fifty people at the San Diego Zoo and Wild Animal Park. He consults at zoos around the country and the world.

His work is now largely with people, and he misses the "aha experience" that comes with animal training. What's more important, he says, is that he pass the training baton to the next generation. The revolution is young, and there are still battles to be fought, but Priest compares everything to his wrangle with the elephant keepers. Nothing much seems like that big a fight, after that.

The next morning, a Tuesday, the weather shifts dramatically. The chill wind abates and warmer temperatures soften the air. Anyone who threw on a winter coat to walk to the National Aquarium finds herself shedding it. The day starts with a lean breakfast of limp pastries and so-so coffee, but everything is uphill from there. There's the brand new dolphin show in a sunny theater. It's classic edutainment, with a loud, rocking sound track and two large video screens that flash close-ups of the dolphins. Conference attendees wander the aquarium's dark halls, watching spectral rays glide, hammerhead sharks cruise, and puffer fish bulge. In one darkened tank, a giant Pacific octopus curls a tentacle around a jar. When they reach the fifth floor, conference-goers squint into the light of an early spring day. Their cheeks suddenly feel dewy. They've stepped into the aquarium's man-made rain forest, complete with the loud, raspy bird calls of fidgety blue-gray tanagers and golden tamarins romping in the tree canopy overhead. The monkeys, an aquarium trainer proudly tells me, pee on command.

Back at the hotel, everyone settles in for another afternoon of startling presentations. Priest introduces two trainers from The Living Seas, a 6.2-million-gallon aquarium at Walt Disney World's Epcot, by saying they've used operant conditioning on "an animal no one even dreamed of training just a few years ago." He's referring to the aquarium's two spotted eagle rays, Dottie and Lance, who each have a five-foot wingspan. The two rays had become nuisances. Dottie and Lance accosted divers who got in the tank to feed the fish, pinched them with their hard pallets and pulled their regulators out of their mouths. The two rays even ganged up on guest divers in the tank.

This couldn't go on. The aquarists had nothing to lose. They tried something unheard of—training rays. It was slow going, eighty sessions over four months. By the end, the rays were trained to swim to a PVC elbow filled with clams. A diver would hold the PVC feeder away from his body. No more pinching, no more grabbing their regulators. Now, if a ray swims toward an empty-handed diver, he just points to the diver with the feeder. The ray will turn its wide wings and sail in that direction.

In following talks, there are mentions of sharks trained to go to a station to be fed, a parrot taught to stick his head in a nebulizer, and elephants who will stand still for artificial insemination. Then it's time for the two EATM students to talk about the fire. Gary Wilson introduces them. While he stands at the podium, behind him Harrison blinks back tears, and Carbajal fans her face with her hand. Their fellow students sit up straight and smile to buoy their friends. The charged emotions are out of place in what has been up until now a day of wonders, and the audience seems confused. Wilson explains that one of the students who was to give this talk has just died, and a hushed understanding falls over the room.

Harrison and Carbajal gather themselves and in steady voices recount the few days last fall when the zoo stood in peril. Maybe they are distracted from their grief by the memory of another trauma, the fire, only five months ago. They flash pictures of moon-high flames. They describe the initial evacuation, the long night spent ready to decamp a second time, and the changes that have been made since. A fire emergency plan has been written. Animals have been crate-trained. Their composure does not crack until the very end when a photo of Megan Thomas, smiling her huge, bright smile, flashes before the room.

To the attendees, this is a beautiful young girl snatched too soon. To the EATM students, this is their dearest friend, a peer who inexplicably died, the bad ending of what had been their fairy tale at the teaching zoo. They have learned that the power of operant conditioning is not limitless. No training technique can lessen their pain.

Spring

The morning of Dr. Peddie's retirement party, the vet sits down at his computer in the couple's downstairs office to write a speech. He has a bug and doesn't feel well, but what worries him more are all the people who will gather today because of him. Mara Rodriguez told him three hundred have RSVPed for the picnic. He's shocked. It's embarrassing, being the center of attention, and unnerving that his career at EATM, his career in general, is truly ending. He's retiring. He has the new boat to prove it. Who will he be? he asks himself again, the same question that has echoed in his mind for weeks. He chases away those thoughts and concentrates on the black screen before him. Unshaved, in jeans and a sweatshirt, he sits here, a guy's guy, and looking like it just now, and thinks about the women who have shaped his life, who helped him get from here to there. They've made all the difference.

"Do you know what time it is?" one of these women, his wife, Linda, calls down the stairs to his office.

Over at the Underwood Family Farm in Moorpark, Rodriguez

and a handful of EATM students, the ones who volunteer for everything, such as Becki Brunelli, make final preparations for the outdoor fete. They dump sacks of pretzels into bowls. They arrange centerpieces of goldfish bowls and shells on small squares of netting. They toss up a table near the farm entrance and pen name tags. They erect poster boards plastered with photos of Dr. Peddie atop a tricycle, reaching up a cow's rectum at vet school, and reeling out yet another fishing line. Blue tablecloths fly from their hands. The wind has risen. The clouds gather and darken overhead.

As they work, there's talk, as always, of the teaching zoo and of their animals. A first year explains her black eye. A small South American monkey the size of a squirrel pounced on the back of her head. Then it "bitch-slapped me." Linda Castaneda recounts how Dunny, the Scottish cow, recently pinned her against a fence near Schmoo's enclosure. The next time Castaneda walked him, she was so scared her legs shook. Dunny's best friend, the once adorable Walter, the water buffalo, horned her onstage with his ever-growing rack. Castaneda asked for the cow and water buffalo pair to build her confidence for a camel later, but she's thinking she got the order in reverse.

The party is a family affair. There's a petting zoo and hayrides. The farm, on a flat stretch of fertile earth between some mounded hills, is owned by Craig Underwood, the vet's best and oldest friend. It's a pivotal place for Dr. Peddie. This is the farm where the vet spent a bucolic summer during college, when he made a lifelong friend and fell in love with the arid, open landscape that would become his home. He can stand here today and see how right the promise of that summer was. That is, if he finishes his speech and hightails it over there.

About 3 P.M., cars pull into the parking lot. The cars disgorge vet techs, movie animal trainers, and zookeepers. Former students have flown in from all over the country. Students plaster name tags on guests as they file in. Everyone tips back a large plastic cup of beer and catches up. The sky breaks, and the sun bobs out behind blue-lined clouds. In short order, the parking lot fills.

Dr. Peddie arrives seeming a little keyed up, apologizing for being late, though he's not. Linda smiles and looks stunning in a red leather coat. Before the vet grows more nervous, he's swept into a crowd of old friends and acquaintances. "Oh, my god" becomes his constant refrain as he whirls away. As I pass the vet later, I hear him say to a woman, "Sounds like persistent sinusitis to me."

The gathering is a bit of a who's who in the training world. Cheryl Shawver, owner of Animal Actors of Hollywood, is here all in black. So is Hubert Wells. The dapper Hungarian, still handsome in his seventies, has been friends with the vet since the last years of Jungleland. Dr. Peddie calls "Hubie" his idol because the trainer has had such beautiful girlfriends, including one now who is half his age. Wells could pass as a movie star and speaks in declarative sentences like "A Jack Russell is the only kind of dog to have." He has a scar from every big cat except a leopard: "They've all put a hole in my butt." Wells's approach to training is matter-of-fact, almost to the point of being profound. "You have to explain to the animal what you want," he says. "If something doesn't work, try to think of something else."

The younger generation of movie trainers, such as Mark Forbes, toss back beers here, too, and they offer a study in contrasts, demonstrating that a renegade job has become more of a career. They are Dr. Peddie's former students. They have EATM degrees, unlike the self-taught older generation. They also don't have the big personalities. Forbes, who has worked on a long list of movies from *Homeward Bound II* to *Hidalgo*, is more likely to demystify the profession, saying things like "It's not rocket science." With his thick reddish hair and lean frame, he comes across as the guy next door. "In the past, [studio trainers] were larger-than-life characters," Forbes says. "It does something for them to be this character. It never worked for me. It never gets a better shot or gets animals to work better." Many of the older trainers trained big cats and bears—dangerous animals that naturally made them look macho. Forbes is happy with dogs. "[Big] cat trainers say, 'How can you go on the set [with a dog]? People don't respect you.' "

About the time the second hayride rolls out, the sky dims to gray again and the wind picks up a notch. As people settle in with plates of barbecue, napkins take flight like so many white birds. The board of Dr. Peddie photos blows over. The mercury sinks steadily. You can tell who got here when by what kind of coat they wear. Early comers shiver in cotton sweaters and Windbreakers, while the latecomers look comfortable in down jackets. Everyone gobbles, while clinging to a paper plate of chicken and glancing overhead. Sure enough, an icy, hard rain pours.

Everyone crams in with the caterers under a small pavilion. Rodriguez, who spent months planning this party, climbs atop a table and says, "This really isn't what I had in mind." Speakers are pulled up from the crowd onto the table. Lynn Doria cracks about how much hair the vet has lost. Shawver tells the crowd about the time when an elephant got a rock stuck in its trunk and the vet told her, "Let's wait and see if it's there tomorrow."

A fellow vet tells how Dr. Peddie confided in her that he comes up with his speeches while sitting on the john. Craig Underwood drawls, "I think Jim has been retiring for about twenty years." He tells them how Dr. Peddie exaggerates, even about how many pork chops he ate, and how the vet's penchant for the earthy and grotesque changed his family's table conversation so many years ago. "I'm grateful for the summer of 1963," he says, and the two men tear up. "Now I think he should run for political office," to which everyone cheers.

Then it's the vet's turn. Holding his freshly written speech atop the table, he tells the moist, tight crowd about the women in his life, starting with his ninety-one-year-old mother, who told him this morning on the phone "to stand up straight and talk up" when he gave his speech. He thanks Craig Underwood's mother for hosting him that fateful summer. He thanks Shawver for believing in him. He thanks the female vet techs who always reminded him that the animals were flesh and blood, not anatomical specimens. Even the young females at EATM get a nod for hanging on his every word. "It was like I died and went to heaven," he says. Last, he comes to his "queen," Linda, who kept him from becoming "a cantankerous old vet, treating old dairy cows," and the only important woman in his life, he says, "that I've slept with."

Then the rain stops, and the crowd fans out a bit. A rainbow stripes the sky. Dr. Peddie exhales and says, "I've had nightmares about today, but I've thoroughly enjoyed myself."

Up at the zoo, a new bench with a lion's head at one end and its rump at the other has been placed along the front road overlooking the aviary. Megan Thomas's parents paid for it in memory of their daughter. There is no official word on what caused Megan's death, only rumors of diet pills and the like. Students are left to sit on the bench and ponder the mystery.

One parrot bit off another's toe, a sickly prairie dog had to be euthanized, and Todd, the fox, moved in next to Starsky, the cavy. This relocation has unforeseen consequences. The extroverted fox brings the wallflower cavy out of his shell in a way Mary VanHollebeke has been unable to. His new neighbor emboldens Starsky. Now, when VanHollebeke steps into Starksy's cage, she finds the creature less jittery, even confident.

Over the past few months, the second year has methodically backed up the spoon until it is nearly in her hand. One spring afternoon, as the fox frolics next door, VanHollebeke slips the spoon into her palm and freezes. The cavy leans over and nibbles a pellet or two. She can feel his warm breath on her hand. This isn't officially touching him, but it's damn close. Adrenaline pumps into her veins, but she remains stock-still. One celebratory yelp and her months of painstaking work will be undone. Nearly a year since she first began standing outside the cavy's cage, VanHollebeke watches silently as the teaching zoo's most skittish animal eats from her hand.

With many turnovers finished or almost done, there are no more complaints about a lack of animal interaction among the first years. The cross-species contact soothes like a salve. I find Chandra Cohn, who usually is bug-eyed and straight-mouthed with exhaustion, now wearing a beatific smile on her face. "I just groomed with Samantha for the first time," she tells me one April morning. That the gibbon in Primate Gardens ran her fingers over Cohn's thin arms, inspecting her scabs and moles, means the primate has accepted the harried human into her troop. Under the monkey's searching fingertips, Cohn finds her worries recede.

Animal interaction does not do the trick for Terri Fidone. Oddly enough, Fidone, who has weathered the program better than most, finally begins to sag. Though she's kept to herself, spending her free time with her boyfriend, not joining any of the cliques or listening to the gossip, the competition finally wears her down. "Everybody is so concerned about what everybody else is doing. . . . I feel the vibes. People want to know my business," the former cocktail waitress says. When her aunt died recently out of the blue, she was too upset to go for a cougar walk. Another first year remarked on her absence, which irked her. She misses her family in Las Vegas, even her parents' two teacup poodles. For the first time, she thinks of quitting. She doesn't.

Of her four turnovers, Fidone is furthest along with Kaleb, the dromedary camel. Kaleb is personable and will step close to anyone near his corral, as he lazily blinks his heavily lashed eyes. Like all camels', his breath stinks. Students often feed him whole lemons off the trees near the front office to improve his bad breath. Kaleb and his mother, Lulu, are the biggest animals at the teaching zoo. Kaleb weighs more than one thousand pounds. They are also some of the smartest residents, more so than their stolid countenance may let on. Cindy Wilson says camels are like primates, only they can kill you much faster.

Kaleb is well behaved generally, but also sneaky. He plans his "naughty moves," as a second year puts it, where he'll push a student toward a tree or wall. The student trainers change the route of his walks so he can't think ahead. The boy also bloops. This is an EATM word for the camels' kicking their legs wildly and thrashing about. The camels do it when they are scared or agitated.

Over the past year, a number of the student trainers have been hurt while Kaleb blooped. He hit one in the jaw, knocked the wind out of another, and split open the head of a third. Students must learn to anticipate a bloop by learning the signs: he raises his tail, puts his ears back, raises his head, and tenses his body. He also tends to bloop right before meal time, in Primate Gardens and along the mulch path near Clarence's enclosure. Whether it's the bumpy texture of the mulch under his padded feet or the strange sight of the humongous turtle, Kaleb nearly always goes bananas there.

This is where the second years show Fidone what a bloop looks like and how to handle the melee. As Kaleb begins to shuffle in a lively manner over the mulch, one second year pulls down hard on his lead. That cinches the stud chain over Kaleb's nose and lowers his head so she can better control him. The second years also bring Kaleb here to bloop just for the heck of it, to work it out of his system. They call it his happy dance. However, some trainers would consider this rehearsed aggression, meaning that the more Kaleb gets to bloop, the more he will bloop. It's fun for the camel. The thing is, in a weird way, it's also fun for the students. It's inordinately satisfying to overcome your fears and get a one-thousand-pound-plus animal to calm down. That's why Fidone asked for him.

Lulu, on the other hand, is as ladylike as camels come. Susan

Patch has not had to learn about bloops. Lulu hasn't done that once since arriving at the teaching zoo this past winter. Rather, Patch and another first year, Crystal Oswald, a tall, striking redhead with an oval face and long stride, prepare for motherhood. Lulu is obviously pregnant now. She's lopsided even. Her sides bulge so much that a student walking by her says, "I get cramps just looking at her."

The camel weighs nearly 1,500 pounds, 70 of which she gained in three weeks. Patch and Oswald think Lulu could be a momma any day now. They handle Lulu's teats, trying to desensitize the camel to being touched there. Lulu is fidgety, uncomfortable, like any expectant mother. When Patch and Oswald ready the camel for an education show one April morning, Lulu refuses to be brushed, shifting her wide sides away. "She's being a bitch," Patch says, walking after the camel with a brush. Not even white wedges of apple persuade her to hold still for a grooming. The camel takes them in her mouth only to let the chunks fall to the ground.

Later that same day in Anatomy and Physiology class, Dr. Peddie says that when hoofstock give birth, the labor is violent and fast. The young are born feet first and ready to run with their moms. As the female nears delivery, her vulva streams clear mucus and she stops eating. "Lulu won't take treats," Oswald calls from the back of the classroom. Dr. Peddie pulls a lavender bandana out of his pocket and blows his nose hard on it.

"Tell your vasectomy story," someone in the front row pipes up.

"Oh god," he says, shifting from foot to foot in a kind of "If I must" jig and then, maybe sensing that his days of having a rapt audience of young women for his off-color stories are numbered, launches into the tale. And so the EATM class of 2005 becomes the very last to learn that Dr. Peddie's Novocain block didn't work, that, wearing nothing but socks and lying spread-eagle in the stirrups, he realized he knew the attending nurse, and that the doctor accidentally shocked the vet, which made his legs shoot straight out. "I kicked his glasses off," Dr. Peddie says, smiling.

The second years do not graduate until the first Saturday of May, a few weeks off, but there's little for them to do at the teaching zoo in these final weeks. Their classes are done. Many have already turned over their animals to the first years. Mostly, they roam the grounds with their pals, dash off for bags of steamy fast food, and get animals out.

Still, until graduation, they are technically in charge. They remind the first years in so many ways, small and otherwise. They didn't let the first years make comments on a video tribute to the vet that played at his picnic. They have not invited the first years to the Dr. Peddie roast next month. They grouse about how inept the first years are and make dire predictions. "People will be going to the hospital," a second year ominously tells me.

There is some cause for concern. A first year got out the bobcat without staff permission. Another let Dunny, the Scottish cow, out by accident. Are the first years that bad? I ask the staff. No, they say. This is how it goes each year, they tell me. The second years believe only they can run the teaching zoo and that mayhem will break out as soon as they leave. The first years cannot shine, Rodriguez says, until the second years leave.

For now, the first years, like downtrodden younger siblings, are alternately resentful and intimidated. They are also more harried than ever. They effectively run the zoo, though the staff has yet to give them cage keys. They have to ask the second years to open the doors for them, which is a pain. The first years still have classes. They study the structure of the eye and watch slides of ungulates. They listen to Wilson lecture on dominance. He says some people think that hierarchy is maintained by subordinate animals, and not vice versa. As a graduate student, Wilson studied white-crowned sparrows. The brighter the sparrow's crown, the higher it is in the flock hierarchy. He painted one sparrow's crown brighter. As he guessed, the other birds began to treat the one with Wilson's highlights as boss. This lesson is very apropos just now. The first years still kowtow to the second years, though they are essentially painted sparrows. The paint will soon wear off.

That the first years' time is coming becomes obvious at a weekly meeting. The first years drag themselves into Zoo 2 and settle heavily in their chairs. Hollow-eyed, they wearily rest their heads in their hands. Sitting on tables at the back of the room, the second years pass glazed doughnuts, laugh as if at a reunion, and swing their legs. Woodhouse announces that she has cage keys for the first years. They sit up in their seats and cheer. The second years in back quit jauntily swinging their legs. They slouch and look deflated. The zoo will go on without them.

A week after Dr. Peddie's party, not long before the teaching zoo closes for the day, a Saturday, Crystal Oswald strides down the back road with her red ponytail swinging and her hands full of dishes. She looks over into Hoofstock. Lulu lies on her side. Water jets out of the camel's behind. The baby is coming. Now. Oswald calls up to the front office. "Lulu's water broke," she says into the phone. Give her a bucket of water, the staff member replies. "No, the other water," Oswald says.

In short order, a slender white camel dives front hooves first from Lulu's womb and lands in a kind of tumbled, leggy heap on the bare ground. He's white and fuzzy like a lamb. His fur is darker around his eyes and at the very slight curve that is his immature hump. He doesn't stand up to feed, though Lulu pokes his behind with her nose. This worries everyone. Lulu's last baby did the same thing.

Patch, who was touring the Reagan Library with her parents

when the baby was born, arrives and prepares to spend the night at the teaching zoo with Oswald. The baby does not have an official name, but everyone starts calling him Charlie, naming him after a retired engineer who haunts the teaching zoo each weekend. Charlie hiccups and shivers, signs of possible electrolyte imbalance or an infection.

Dr. Peddie is out of town, so another vet checks the leggy baby twice during the night. He says to bottle-feed Charlie. Someone is sent to buy goat's milk at Ralph's. A calf's nipple is found for the bottle. Every two hours they lift him up and hold the bottle to his young lips. The last time Lulu had a baby, she crushed Wilson, so the camel is tied to a corral bar while they feed Charlie. This maddens the new momma. Lulu moans and groans and swings her wide hips around.

By 10 A.M. the next morning, Sunday, Charlie stands up, though he is as wobbly as a drunk. Before long, he makes a sucking face, as if he might know what he's doing. Students and staff try holding the clumsy baby camel up to Lulu's udder, but because she's tied up, she won't hold still. Patch and Oswald suggest leaving her untied, but staff won't risk it, not after what happened to Wilson last time.

By Monday morning, the temperatures rise uncharacteristically for April, zooming toward 100°. If you lean against Lulu's corral, the bars lightly singe your bare hands or arms. Quite a crowd gathers in Hoofstock. Students and staff hover along the corral's edge, eyes trained on a strange, awkward dance before them. Michlyn Hines, looking pale and resolute, holds the baby camel on his feet with Fidone's help. Oswald clutches Lulu's lead, trying to still the restless momma camel. Hines, with one arm hooked under Charlie's small belly, reaches out with the other and grasps a nipple that dangles from Lulu's swollen udder, pulling it toward the baby's face, as if to say "here." This is risky work, but Hines worries that Charlie has yet to get a long drink of Lulu's colostrum. Despite the students' efforts, the camel still doesn't like having her udder touched. Who can blame her, really? Lulu moans deeply, like the sound of a ship creaking at sea, and pulls away. The baby blinks his black eyes. He totters in Hines's and Fidone's arms, as they steer him unsteadily toward his mother.

This quiet, so-far-unproductive waltz seems to go on indefinitely, then a statuesque blonde steps into the corral. She's an EATM grad, a trainer from the studio company that owns Lulu. She takes Lulu's halter from Oswald, who looks miffed. In short order, the calm breaks and there's yelling and dust flying. The blonde pops Lulu repeatedly on the nose and legs with the lead as the camel pulls back and digs her padded feet in. When Lulu resists, the blonde commands her to walk in circles. Lulu groans. The trainer wants Lulu to hold still so she can be milked. Every time a vet who has stepped into the corral gets close, Lulu jerks away. Whenever Lulu does this, the trainer pops her and they tussle. There's more dust and yelling. It's quite a scene, especially at EATM, where the animals are rarely handled this roughly. It also looks worse than it is, if only because so much dust whirls around.

"Oh, the children," someone says. A school group is coming down the front road.

Eventually, the blond trainer wins the day, and Lulu settles down, does as she's told, and holds still for the vet to pull her teats, but he doesn't manage to get much milk out. "You can't hurt her," the trainer says to Oswald, standing by the corral. "You can't let her get away with anything." Oswald, lips tight, doesn't say anything.

Rodriguez steps into the corral to give Charlie a bottle of goat's milk. The crowd disbands, and mother and child are left in peace briefly. Later, when I ask Wilson what he thought of the trainer's handling of Lulu, he says it doesn't bother him. He would always rather use positive training methods, but they take longer and time was of the essence. Lulu had to be milked.

In the afternoon, after a second year suggests that Lulu's lead be held loosely so she can touch Charlie as he nurses (the same idea Patch and Oswald mentioned Saturday night), the staff gives it a try. That done, Lulu, her nose nuzzling her boy on the rump, stands still for Charlie to nurse. Though Charlie now suckles on his own, there are two more night watches. Patch and Oswald stay for parts of both.

Motherhood takes its toll—not so much on Lulu as on Hines, Patch, and Oswald. Hines becomes so exhausted she can hardly string a sentence together. When she proposes to Dr. Peddie that they insert a stomach tube in little Charlie, the vet asks her when was the last time she ate or slept? He buys her lunch and convinces her the baby is fine: "He needs to bond with his mother."

So far, tending a newborn camel has turned out to be far more work than Patch or Oswald expected. They hadn't counted on staying up four nights in a row right before finals. When Patch sits down on Wednesday morning to take Dr. Peddie's Animal Nutrition test, she falls dead asleep atop her essay booklet. Oswald finds she can't spell anything or write in a straight line. When Patch rouses herself, she reads over her test and realizes she's penned some crazy answers as she fell into her doze. She'd written that you defrost fish by sitting it in a warm bath for five minutes, when she knows that you thaw it overnight in the fridge. The baby camel nearly cost her a grade.

Meanwhile, down in Hoofstock, a baby camel latches on to his mother's nipple whenever she nuzzles his behind with her soft nose. The pulse of the zoo quickens, and the cycle of life spins on, immune to exams, job searches, exhaustion, and the other makings of human drama.

Graduation

Most of the second years are far too young to remember the sexual revolution. To them it sounds like a quaint, distant historical period. Still, there's much tittering as we stand before an epicenter of that more-shattering time. For their very last field trip, the second years find themselves before a Tudor-style house with sprawling grounds in Beverly Hills—the Playboy Mansion. They've come to see the animals, and not the party kind. Hefner has what so many animal people dream of—his very own zoo.

He bought the mansion in 1971, the year *Playboy*'s monthly circulation peaked at seven million, his clubs numbered twenty-three, and his two-eared emblem radiated sexy good taste worldwide. In the early seventies, Hefner was at the tip-top of his zenith. Like so many fat cats before him with cash to burn and status to flaunt, Hef built a zoo.

As long as there has been privilege and wealth, there have been private zoos. The Chinese emperor Wen Wang created a zoo he called the Garden of Intelligence just before 1000 BC. About the same time, the biblical King Solomon started the tradition in Israel. Assyrian and Babylonian kings followed suit. The Roman upper class kept stags and wild boar on the grounds of their villas for hunting as well as for display. Menageries declined after the collapse of the Roman empire, but collections were maintained by European heavyweights, such as Charlemagne in the eighth century and Henry I of England in the twelfth. From the fourteenth to eighteenth centuries, any European royal or aristocrat worth his title had his own zoo. Some of these early menageries evolved into the West's first public zoos in the nineteenth century. Since then, private zoos have been a waning tradition but, as Hefner's proves, not a dead one.

Unlike many other collections through the ages, Hefner's is low on powerhouse species. There are no big cats and no bears. Rather, Hefner seems to prefer beauty to power, and so there are lots and lots of birds: dazzling rare pheasants, leggy African crowned cranes, and rounded trumpeters. Though Hefner's zoo of some 100 animals is private, it has some of the serious aspirations of a public one. That's where our tour guide, John Heston, comes in. He's run the zoo for nearly thirty years.

Heston is a down-to-earth high school science teacher who describes himself as "a farm kid from Oklahoma." He has a bit of a drawl from the open country of his youth. He seems slightly out of place amid the splendor of the mansion. Like so many people the second years have met on field trips, Heston did not follow any career path, so he can't offer a lot of pointers for their job searches. He did not attend EATM, though he has two keepers on his small staff who did. Heston fell into the job in 1975 while he was working on his bachelor's in biology. At that point, the collection was not very healthy. The first order of business was to identify all the animals. That done, Heston studied up on how best to care for them. Before long, animals in the collection not only began to live longer but began to breed. Heston moved on to things like behavioral enrichment, training, and conservation.

Hefner, he tells us, bought the house because Barbie Benton wanted a tennis court, and it had one. "She was a nice lady," he says. The zoo was added early on, and some of the birds have been here from the get-go. Heston leads us around the corner of the house, where the lawn falls away in an undulating sweep like a gentle waterfall. Peacocks, their long tails dragging on the turf like the trains of evening gowns, cock their shiny blue heads to look at us. We round another corner and find geese, cranes, flamingos, and ibis leisurely poking through the backyard with their beaks. Hef, Heston tells us, believes in minimum confinement, so many of the birds wander the estate all day.

The second years quickly duck into the steamy and infamous grotto off Hefner's bright blue pool, then follow Heston single file across the plush turf. This prompts the geese to flap off. A trumpeter named Truman falls into line with us. For the rest of the walk, there is a chorus of "Watch out for Truman!" and "Don't step on Truman!" as the fearless bird steps on our heels. The group advances along a stone path over a stream thick with tubby koi. A net draped over the flowing water prevents the birds from eating the fish for dinner. Heston tugs back a heavy soundproofing curtain, and macaw shrieks pierce the air.

The path weaves between roomy cages of spider monkeys, yellow squirrel monkeys, and tamarins. The cages are shaded by trees, and the small zoo has a tropical rain forest feel to it. Heston has a waiver so the zoo can keep different species in the same cages. For example, there are bunnies in with some crested cranes. "It makes their life more interesting," Heston says.

He steps in with a pair of squirrel monkeys. The two climb aboard his shoulders and drape their long arms around him. They came from a Dumpster in Newbury Park, he says. "They are a lot like people but they are incredibly honest." He lifts them from his shoulders to go, and they hover by the door as he steps out backward. "It took six months of training to get them to let me leave."

As we near a cage full of exotically colored pheasants, a crested crane steps in our path, blocking the way, and looking surprisingly menacing for something with such spindly legs. "That's Spot," Heston says, and shoos him off. The bird was raised by hand and ate dog food, he explains. "That's why Hefner called him Spot." We duck into a series of stone buildings. Inside it's moist and close. This is where the hornbills Heston breeds live.

Since the late '70s, Heston has bred a long list of endangered hornbills, starting with Jackson's hornbills. Since then he's raised Taricitic hornbills, Oriental pied hornbills, and black Malaysian hornbills, to name just a few. He is currently working on the large bar-pouched wreathed hornbills. The species, he says, "has one foot on a banana peel." If it weren't for a project like this, he probably wouldn't have stuck at the zoo for all these years. This gives the extravagance a purpose and some intellectual import. Otherwise, the zoo would exist only for one man's pleasure.

There are reminders everywhere of that man's pleasures. Heston takes us over to the gaming room, where a few of the students tackle the roomful of video games. Second years pile into a mirror-lined, pillow-strewn den and smile for the camera. The tour ends back at the shimmering pool where coffee and pastries await. "Fruit salad," someone calls, and the young women with plates in hand surge around a voluminous bowl of cantaloupe, honeydew, and berries. As the EATM students merrily fork chunks of melon, a goose pads across the lawn. A crested crane turns his fancy head to the sky. A flamingo balances on one leg.

The unseasonably hot temperatures persist into May, with the mercury cresting at 90° at midday in Moorpark. The early heat singes the green hills. As they wither to brown, the blackened scars of last fall's fire recede into the dun-colored landscape. At the teaching zoo, Aladdin, the chinchilla, has been moved into the air-conditioned cool of the supply closet off Zoo 1. The sheep and Gee Whiz, the llama, have been sheared. The llama vaguely resembles a Q-tip with his tufted tail and shaggy head.

On the first Monday in May, another round of primates, including Scooter, are given TB tests. I find Linda Castaneda seated in the air-conditioned comfort of Zoo 1 with Scooter mewing in a crate before her. "Take a nap!" Castaneda coos in her Scooter voice, which is high and uncharacteristically girly for her. Castaneda fills out feeding logs while waiting for the monkey to rouse from the anesthetic. She has hives on the base of her neck from letting her rat run around her shoulders. She's been at the zoo every day, she tells me, since January 31. Castaneda has switched from Zoloft, which made her crabby, to Wellbutrin, still hoping to tame her perfectionist ways.

The baby camel has been named Sahara officially, though Susan Patch still often calls him Charlie. In Hoofstock, I find Patch and two other students scrubbing the young camel. One works her fingers through the caked poop in his tail. Lulu stands nearby, her eyes trained on her goofy boy. Her coat has fallen out in big, mangy-looking chunks since delivering her baby. In a corral one over, the freshly sheared sheep look up. Dunny and Walter butt heads lightly. Schmoo suns herself in her corner.

Though the students squirt Sahara, he totters over for more of the same. This is good. The plan is to get Sahara used to handling so that, unlike his mother, he won't mind the touch of human hands. Adam Hyde swings open the gate to Hoofstock. He's been recruited to scoop Sahara up so he can be weighed, though he didn't expect to hoist a wet camel. Hyde cups the animal's neck with one arm and his belly with the other and steps on a scale. Together, camel and first year weigh 358½ pounds. Hyde sets the camel down and steps back on the scale. He weighs 252. "I've lost weight," he exclaims. Sahara has gained nearly twenty pounds in the ten days since he was born. The baby camel now weighs 106½.

The new crop of Schmoo girls file into Hoofstock. They are still learning the sea lion's commands—they write them on their arms—and her fickle ways. They've already begun to sing their commands in clear, high voices just like the second years. Today, they saw her wander for the first time, while she was doing an education show this morning with the second years. *Wandering* is teaching zoo talk for when the temperamental sea lion zones out and ignores commands. Nobody knows why she wanders. Maybe the unseasonable heat puts her in a mood. Maybe a small seizure rattles her. Maybe she is just being Schmoo.

Two of the second year Schmoo girls arrive. "Has anyone showed you sneaky-walk?" one asks. The second years open Schmoo's enclosure, and the shiny dowager scoots out. Sneaky-walk is like something out of a Marx Brothers film, basically a goofy, shadow walk. Schmoo follows the trainer, and each time the trainer stops and looks over her shoulder, the sea lion does the same. Schmoo is not the least bit wandery now, and turns her black head just at the right moment. Her timing is right on, despite her bad hearing and cataracts. The new Schmoo girls try to concentrate, to soak up the finer points of sneaky-walk, but they can't help laughing.

For the first years, this is the last week of classes before finals. One is on academic probation and may soon be saying adieu. In Dr. Peddie's A&P, they take notes on white muscle disease, which leaves the tissue looking like "acid poured on a steak," the vet says, ruining yet another food for his students. In Diversity, they are close to the end of a very long list of species, nearing the scavengers and what is listed on the outline as "most abundant large decomposers," seven vultures and one stork. In Behavior, Wilson hits a philosophical note: "Thinking freedom is a good thing is a very anthropomorphic view," he says.

In addition to the rat maze exam this week, there is the knot test. In between classes, first years sit cross-legged on the small lawn in front of Zoo 1 tying and untying, practicing the thirty some knots Wilson taught them. The teacher prowls the zoo looking for students to test. They duck into supply sheds to hide from him. When Wilson catches up with Chandra Cohn, she shows him the two or three she knows. She has bigger tangles on her mind, such as how she will pay the rent this month. Her student loan has gone AWOL.

This is the last week, period, for the second years. Next week they'll be like any visitors to the zoo, restricted to the front road, unable to open a cage, and forbidden, like a first year, from animal interaction. "Graduation is going to be hard," Mohelnitzky says. "I don't want it to end. I don't want to say good-bye." Another second year tells me that graduating is like getting out of prison: "You think you can't wait to get out but then you don't know what to do." Another tells me after twenty-two months in her uniform, "I've forgotten how to put outfits together."

It's a week of last this and last that. Every time I walk past Buttercup's cage, one of her second-year trainers presses the badger's square, flat body to her chest. Second years throw a leg over Kaleb for one last camel ride. They pull up chairs to primate cages for extra grooming sessions.

Rosie, the baboon, knows the drill, that Jahangard will soon leave her. In her way, the baboon says good-bye first; she quits obeying his commands. When he tells her to get in her crate, Rosie doesn't. A dominant male baboon would let Rosie have it for this infraction—push her or bite her. Jahangard takes the middle road. He has Adam Hyde and Tony Capovilla stand behind him and the three men stare at the uppity female baboon together.

Mary VanHollebeke accepts defeat with Starsky, the cavy, though she came mighty close. She'll graduate without touching the cavy as she had dreamed. After eating out of her hand a few times last month, Starsky never came as close to VanHollebeke again. "I thought I'd make more progress," she sighs by his cage. "I'd planned for him to be out by now." Her efforts have not been for naught. Starsky is less scared of humans, especially a certain human with long dark brown hair. Moreover, VanHollebeke leaves EATM with a newfound patience. As the human accustomed the cavy to her looming presence, the small South American rodent desensitized VanHollebeke to the fast ticking of the clock inside her head.

Amy Mohelnitzky is the only one that doesn't have to say good-bye to her favorite animal. The staff approved Mohelnitzky's request. Abbey will go home with her. The pooch will still belong to the studio company, but she'll live with Mohelnitzky and her husband. Earlier this week, some of the second years threw her a shower. They gave her dog toys, a blanket, poop pickup bags, and food bowls on a raised stand so the briard mix doesn't have to strain her neck when she eats. Mohelnitzky still doesn't know for sure when Abbey can move out of the zoo. Abbey has to stay until the teaching zoo gets another dog.

The second years dread saying good-bye to each other as well. Next week they will scatter. The one who curled her hair for her SeaWorld visit has gotten a dream job at Discovery Cove in Florida. CVP, pigeon puller extraordinaire, will move up to Vallejo to work with sea lions for the summer. Two second years are off to the Point Defiance Zoo in Tacoma, Washington. Another is moving to Portland, Oregon, where she hopes to land a job with Guide Dogs for the Blind. April Matott will drive her ancient Plymouth back to her hometown of Albany, New York, and look for work there.

Not everyone will depart for farther points. Mohelnitzky will teach puppy training classes at night and work as a receptionist for a vet during the day. Chris Jenkins, Olive's trainer, landed a job with an education outreach program in Pasadena. Two other students found work at Animal Actors of Hollywood in Thousand Oaks. VanHollebeke will work at the teaching zoo's summer camp. And Becki Brunelli, to my surprise, has taken a part-time job with an area studio company. Brunelli kept hoping that some kind of job would open at EATM or even at Moorpark College, but one never did. As graduation neared, she saw the job with the movie trainer and thought, why not? Dr. Peddie gave her a rave review.

The thing is, film work probably pays less, at least starting out, than most any other animal work. New movie trainers typically work as cleaners, as Brunelli will. She's being paid $700 a month to clean and care for 35 dogs, 20 cats, a couple of raccoons, and sundry other animals. If Brunelli goes on a set, her hourly wage jumps from $8 an hour to $32, but for as long as she's on the shoot only. The trick is to get on a set. New movie trainers often train an animal new to a facility, in hopes it will be needed for a shoot. The more in demand the animal becomes, the more money that trainer makes. That could take some time and is a bit of a gamble. In the short run, Brunelli will supplement her meager wages with computer work. With her student loans and credit card debt, she'll have to.

The final week is riddled with parties and rituals, like a summer camp winding up for the season. This morning, Thursday, is the willing ceremony, a kind of changing of the guard meets baby shower. It marks the official turning over of the animals from the second years to the first years. As usual, there are presents involved. Everyone convenes in Wildlife Theater, the first years on one side, the second years on the other. VanHollebeke and Brunelli call out various areas, starting with Big Carns. Then students stomp down the creaky bleachers to the stage en masse. Squealing and hugging rule as the second years give halters, chunks of salmon, brushes, marshmallows, handmade key chains, and bags of Goldfish to the first years. Then the first years hand over presents to their second-year buddies. For the moment at least, any bad feelings between the classes evaporate as the air fills with the sound of gift paper ripping and animal print socks and the like being unwrapped.

There's another party Thursday night, and then Friday families alight at various nearby airports. The second years tour them through the zoo and demonstrate the magic they have learned with various animals. The day's mood is merry like a holiday's, between the second years' excitement and first years' seeing the end in sight. That is, until the king tumbles.

Not long past noon, Zulu falls off a platform in his enclosure. A student hears him land with a thump and arrives to find the mandrill on the ground having a seizure. Word spreads quickly, and in short order a number of his trainers rush to his side with worried expressions on their faces. The mandrill sits cross-legged on the ground, something no one has seen him do before. He furrows his brow. The blue in his face pales to the color of threadbare denim. He doesn't smile his big, fanged, clown smile. VanHollebeke and Kristina Nelson, the coolheaded Iowan, stroke his hands and look deep into his mournful eyes.

"Was he fed anything different?" Nelson asks two first years standing nearby. No, they say, nothing was different.

Zulu's owner has been called; his medical care is up to her. The sudents have some theories, that this has to do with his migraines, and that he ought to have an MRI. They hold his hands through the cage and comfort the fallen king. Even in his reduced state, Zulu appears to enjoy all the female attention. He scratches himself and even picks at some dried poop on his butt—small, welcome signs of his regular self. His timing is horrible. It was going to be hard enough for his second-year trainers to leave him, but now, like this, how can they?

"I'm staying here," Nelson says, clutching the hand of the ailing mandrill.

The crush of time is slowed by nonstop graduation festivities, which I'm beginning to think is the point. Friday night there's the Dr. Peddie roast up at the zoo. As people filter in, they deposit flowers on Megan's bench, tie balloons to it, and then join an endless line for burgers. The vet looks chipper, though he reports recurring dreams of traveling and not being able to reach his wife on the phone, from which he wakes up in a cold sweat.

The roast, as all things EATM, is a long and ambitious affair. It begins in Zoo 2 with a slide show. There are photos of Dr. Peddie asleep in his underwear and with his arm up various animals' behinds. Back outside, as the light fades, Castaneda presents him with a nautical compass from the first years. There are funny, touching tributes from the second years, too, though one mentions that Dr. Peddie always teased her about her past visits to bondage clubs and another, the zoo's gardener—the one who loves Sequoia, the deer—tells the bleacher full of parents, younger siblings, and grandparents about how the vet warned him that "he'd screw himself to death." Brunelli, the emcee, looks mortified. "All I can say is, I'm sorry," she says, before asking Dr. Peddie to say a few words. Then the vet relates his story about how, as a joke, he told the dean of the college that he accepts only students with a C-cup or bigger to EATM.

As the evening winds to an end and families and students filter out, a small group remains behind to spend the night with Zulu. For their very last twenty-four hours, a few second years get to do night watch. It turns out to be uneventful. The mandrill sleeps the night away on his platform, rising at daybreak. He tugs on his left ear and scratches his lower back. At about 6:45 A.M. he has a cup of warm broth and throws it up. Close to 8 A.M. he pulls his penis, ejaculates, and eats his sperm. Zulu is clearly feeling more himself.

Not long after Zulu improves, the second years with their families in tow return for another tradition, Family Circus. For two and a half hours, the students trot out their various animals. Schmoo, as always, closes the show, entering stage right with a ball balanced on her upraised nose. Not long into her act, though, the sea lion ignores a trainer when she asks for a kiss. Schmoo is wandering. The trainers cut her act short and, without seeming obvious, usher the star offstage.

The afternoon is one long drawn-out good-bye. It's hard not to feel bad for the second years. The Schmoo girls burst into tears after their last training session. One student walks around the teaching zoo crying her eyes out. Brunelli settles into a chair by Goblin's cage and lets the olive baboon gently groom her hand.

As the sun slowly dips and the heat of the day lifts, the second years gather backstage in Wildlife Theater to line up for the graduation ceremony. "We'll have to ask the first years to open the front gate for us," one grumbles in line. They march out. There are floating candles in the shallow moat around the dirt stage. The bleachers are packed with video camera–toting relatives. The mountaintops that burst into flame last fall glow pink in the early dusk. There's applause and inspiring speeches from staff members and classmates. Jenkins tells the crowd that this is a wonderful place but not an easy place to be. Gary Wilson hands out their certificates one by one. Then the students intone the EATM pledge ending, "I accept the challenges which lie ahead of me. I will represent with pride, dignity, and honor the Exotic Animal Training and Management Program of Moorpark College."

Finally, the moment has arrived. The new graduates embrace their families and friends and hug staff members one last time. If they tarry, no one rushes them. Slowly, they trickle out into the wide world, glancing back as the front gate closes behind them.

The Zoo Is Theirs

The first years' tenure at the teaching zoo begins, as you might expect, dramatically. When finals are posted, the first year who is on probation passes, at which her classmates cheer, but two others flunk out. That brings the casualties for the class to four. One student is not a surprise: she's the one everyone expected to get kicked out, the slacker who made Mohelnitzky decide to adopt Abbey. She missed a C by 10 points in Anatomy and Physiology. She's shown the front gate.

The other first year is a surprise. It's Tony Capovilla, one of Rosie's new trainers. A few months ago that might have been a relief to the former plumber, but not now. Though he's grumbled about the program in the past, he has come around and accepted how consuming it is. Capovilla is stunned. He thought he had a B going into his Diversity final but, given that test score, Capovilla missed a C by a fraction of a point. Dr. Peddie, as one of his final duties before retiring, tells Capovilla he's out, that it's the student's decision when he's done, now or at the end of the week. Now, Capovilla says, and shows himself the front gate. He could reenter the program a year from now but he would join a class with six other men, which means he could not count on training Rosie, the baboon—the reason he came to EATM in the first place.

This means that Rosie now has one trainer, Adam Hyde, and Hyde does not have a backup. The only way Rosie can come out for a walk right now is if Cindy Wilson comes along. When she does, Hyde feels self-conscious, he the primate novice, she the expert. Rosie seems to notice his discomfort and challenges Hyde. When he gives her a command, the baboon looks at Wilson. It's the baboon's way of asking, Who is in charge here?

Within a week, the slacker is back. Dr. Peddie, in what he says is an effort to "be an all-around-bitchin-good guy," cut her a deal, what he thought was a secret deal. Within about twelve hours it wasn't. Nothing ever is at EATM. Going over her final, the vet finds an answer that he could give her 10 more points on. The correct information is there, though not in the proper order. This girl pulls on his heart strings. Her personal life is a mess, he says. The vet will pass her, he tells her, but she must read *Ten Stupid Things Women Do to Mess Up Their Lives* by Laura C. Schlessinger and write a book report. He realizes it was a weak moment. "She is not someone to go to the mat for," he tells me on the phone.

Brenda Woodhouse, newly in charge, hears of Dr. Peddie's "secret" deal from Capovilla, who arrives in her office with all his quizzes from Diversity under his arm. "I'm shocked Dr. Peddie thought anything would stay a secret here," she says. Capovilla meets with Wilson, too, and the two of them go over the tests and find a score that was entered incorrectly, a 26 that should have been a 27. That gives Capovilla the sliver of a point he needs to pass Diversity. In like manner, he rejoins the program. The first years are glad to have him back, but some can't help wondering if he, too, was given a deal, if only for Rosie's sake.

That's just the start of what sounds like a rocky first few weeks. Ebony, the raven, bolts, flying through the legs of the student blocking the cage door. Paco, the white-nosed coati, likewise escapes, and is found trundling around Maintenance. While onstage, Friday, a raccoon, scampers into the bleachers. The students catch up with him on the aviary lawn. Zeta, a turaco, flies off and flaps around the zoo for twenty-four hours before she is lured back to her cage. One student gets docked unsafe credits for forcing Julietta, the emu, on the scale along the back road. Then the same student is bitten on the finger by one of the lemurs. Next she lets Zeta out by accident, which she blames on her bandaged finger.

"It's just frustrating if you are killing yourself for this," Castaneda says. "We'll be judged on their slacker asses." Castaneda has given up on medicating her perfectionism; Wellbutrin gave her a "gnarly" rash and nightmares. She's thinking now, though, given how much all the recent screwups bother her, that maybe the drug worked. When she posts a note about Dunny throwing up by Zoo 1, she tears it a bit. She pauses and considers taking the note down and redoing it. She doesn't have the time, so resists the urge. EATM, with its impossible to-do list, may accomplish what the antidepressants didn't—train her to be less than perfect.

Michlyn Hines struggles to make the teaching zoo run like a professional zoo. She threatens to lower grades if students don't catch up with the zoo's paperwork, reminds them to keep the front gate closed, and referees disputes. Most of the first years get along fine, but the few who don't do so dramatically. "There were no personality conflicts in the class before," Hines says. "Now I have two trainers on a bird who won't talk to each other." She's referring to Anita Wischhusen and a young woman assigned to Zeta, the turaco. Two of the Schmoo girls don't get along either. Then not long after he returns, Capovilla gets into a shoving match with an older male student.

Capovilla had gotten Rosie out of her cage and then called up to the office to see if he could walk her. Technically, Capovilla should have asked before getting the baboon out. The older student, a broad-shouldered man with a soft voice, said so to Capovilla. Moreover, he said it in front of Rosie. Capovilla kept his temper but after he put the baboon away, he saw the older student stepping out of Zoo 1 and he let his rage rip. "He threatened my life," Capovilla says.

The kinkajou, now nicknamed Cujo, sinks his teeth into the third hand in just over a year. Kristy Marson—a star in her class, a Schmoo girl, a student seemingly born to train—ends up with the kinkajou attached to her hand like Jahangard and VanHollebeke before her. The staff rules that students will no longer go in with Birdman. They will train him from outside his cage, just as they do the tiger, lion, and hyena.

Then Ronald Reagan has to go and die. All the mourners pull their cars into Moorpark College's lot and from there are ferried over to the Ronald Reagan Presidential Library, where the former president lies in state. This means there's essentially no place for the EATM students to park. For two days a skeletal crew of students tends the teaching zoo. Now that the zoo is theirs, the first years wonder if they will ever get in the groove.

By late June, I find that they have. The first years have new confidence, as the staff predicted they would. No longer intimidated by their second years, their brows unknit, and joints loosen. Smiles are common. There's a new ease in their step. They have taken charge. Holly Tumas says the class is doing well, "more than second years expected, more than first years expected."

Though they've been training their animals for less than a month, the first years are making quick progress. Sahara, the baby camel, lets Susan Patch and Crystal Oswald put their fingers in his soft mouth. A first year has taught Schmoo to keep two feet of stomach tubing down her throat. All the new cougar trainers have taken the chain while on a walk. A first year, one who aspires to get a Ph.D., has taught Cookie, the loquacious gray parrot, to whistle part of *The Andy Griffith Show*'s theme song.

Marissa Williams, a pretty young horsewoman from North Carolina, has taken over Nick's training, which includes his weight problem. She has yet to take some pounds off the maxi-mini horse, but Nick is fitter. Nick still pesters Gee Whiz until the llama spits food at him, which the horse then gobbles up. Williams figures that's a lost cause and just keeps the horse moving. She's organized teams of walkers to get him out for romps twice a week. She runs him in wide circles on the aviary lawn. She hooks him up to the cart and trots him around the zoo.

Zulu has improved. He flashes me his signature fanged smile while he relishes a wad of gum with big, exaggerated, lip-smacking chews. He hasn't had any more seizures. In the dry summer heat, his butt pad has dried out and cracked, getting blood all over his cage, but, nevertheless, he seems his old regal self. He's groomed with all four of his new trainers—a sign he has accepted them, though he often grabs Wischhusen during these sessions. The first time he grabbed her he pinched her until she got a bruise. Then he dug his fingernails into the bruise until he drew blood. "He's cruel," she says. "He's a little shit."

The mandrill and Wischhusen are in a bit of a power struggle, which comes as no surprise. Wischhusen goes her own way. She's made it this far without pulling a pigeon, mostly because she just doesn't want to. Now she's going against everybody's advice with Zulu. When Wischhusen irks the mandrill, she does not offer her arm to Zulu for a punishing squeeze. She has trouble, not surprisingly, being subordinate. It is not in her nature, which is probably why she is so drawn to Taj. Training a tiger is all about being dominant, which Wischhusen has no problem with, given her broad shoulders and football coach's voice. With Zulu it's the reverse, and Wischhusen cannot bring herself to curtsy to the king. She will not submit by letting him vent his rage on her arm. Wischhusen thinks her approach is worth a try. "They said he wouldn't eat cooked yams and he does," she says.

The irony is that Zulu consequently grabs Wischhusen more than any of the four trainers. Often when she sits close to his cage or grooms with him, Zulu snatches her arms with his black hands and clenches with all his mandrill might. Sometimes it scares Wischhusen so badly it makes her legs shake.

There's plenty of news of the recently graduated second years. A couple have moved to Hawaii and another to Mexico in pursuit of dolphin training jobs. One recent graduate has left movie training for educational outreach work. Another had a change of heart before she even started with a studio trainer, did a brief turn teaching at a dog training school, quit that job, and has started her own dog training business.

Becki Brunelli fills me in over a dinner of Mexican food in a roadside restaurant in Moorpark. She orders chicken fajitas without the chicken. We eat on the early side, as the sunshine just barely slants, because Brunelli's due again on a movie set tomorrow morning at 4:30 A.M. She was there today. The domestic cat she was working with got loose and ran around the set, which got Brunelli in hot water with her new boss. She shrugs her shoulders. Ever the optimist, she says it was a learning experience.

Brunelli herself has adjusted fine to life after EATM. She's as bright-eyed and energetic as always. She's single again, she says with a smile. "Right now, I can't see myself with anyone. I'm not lonely. What I want now is adventure." Her days, though, are spent mostly raking up dog poop and scraping dried pigeon droppings off the bottom of their cages. She has splinters in her fingers. "It just sucks. It's like being a first year again," she says. She worries that her coworker is a teenager with a high school diploma. Brunelli, thirty-four, has two college degrees, not to mention graduate work, under her belt.

As we sip frosty margaritas and a motorcycle blares into the parking lot outside, Brunelli says she and her fellow graduates are working in facilities that are not as well kept as the teaching zoo. At the trainer's facility, Brunelli says, water bowls are filled only if they are empty. At EATM the water was changed every day regardless, she says. I detect a touch of what Dr. Peddie calls the EATM curse. Graduates have gotten a reputation for being know-it-alls and telling employers how to keep their facilities or train their animals. Dr. Peddie warns new graduates to keep their lips locked, but that's not always easy for animal people when it comes to animals.

In Wilson's training class, the first years get down to the nitty-gritty of using operant conditioning. It's one thing to understand the principles, another to put them to work. Wilson says students having trained a rat think they know it all. Obviously, they don't.

One of the biggest hurdles for a novice trainer to get over is being human. Despite our big brains, we have trouble looking at the world through another species' eyes. We're so busy thinking, we have trouble paying attention to what we are doing. We fidget, so our body language is a mishmash of signals that could confuse the most intelligent species. We are naturally bossy and expect human traits like obedience and loyalty from the animal kingdom. We take things personally.

Wilson devotes a chunk of a class to anthropomorphism. The English language lends itself to such, but Wilson warns, "The danger is, if we are being really anthropomorphic, it could lead to bad decisions." He cautions the students against saying things like "The animal is glad to see me" or "The animal loves me but hates my co-trainer." Animals are not emotional. Humans are.

"We want you to care about all the animals, even the rats in the breeding colony, but you can't let animals get away with things because you want to be a friend rather than a trainer.

"You have to be consistent," he says. "You can't be a buddy."

That isn't a hard lesson for Castaneda just now with Walter, the once-adorable water buffalo. No one feels much like petting him these days, though he's still technically a baby. He waves those ever-growing horns around. He digs in his hooves on walks. He tried to ram a sheep backstage. It took five people to stop him, including the sizable Hyde. Castaneda and his other student trainers think the problem is the rather large pair of testicles hanging low between Walter's haunches. Castaneda and his other student trainers want the punk water buffalo "chopped," meaning castrated.

Castaneda assumed that of the animals she was assigned to, the cougars were the most dangerous. Now she thinks it's Walter. She's still shook up over a walk last week. Wilson suggested separating Walter and Dunny, the constant companions, during the stroll. Dunny was led ahead and into the hay barn where Walter couldn't see him. The water buffalo panicked and charged after his furry, bovine friend, pulling a frightened Castaneda along with him. If he were a large cat, she could throw herself down. If he were a camel, she could pull his head down. With a water buffalo, all she could do was run alongside as Walter frantically looked for his pal. The experience taught Castaneda that she needed a pair of steel-toed boots.

Ever since Walter took off, his trainers are uneasy about getting the duo out. A minimum of three trainers is needed to walk "the cows," but these days it's hard to find three willing students. Though she's scared as well, Castaneda worries the twosome isn't getting any exercise. Today, she and three students gather at Dunny and Walter's corral because Woodhouse is going to come along on the walk and offer pointers, which makes everyone feel more confident.

The two bovines smell of citronella. Ash-colored stripes have emerged on Walter's chest and legs. Dunny has put on weight. A student to either side of him, the Scottish cow lumbers out, his big woolly coat a beautiful caramel color in the sun. No problem.

Then Castaneda in her leather gloves and big boots leashes Walter up in the corral and turns him toward the gate. He immediately plants his heels and wags his head with those now enormous horns. Castaneda hangs on for her life, flexing her arms, gritting her teeth, but she's really no match.

"I wouldn't put up with that," Woodhouse says. "Put on a second lead."

A first year with blue eyes and chestnut hair to her shoulders attaches a second lead on the other side. Woodhouse shows the students how to turn the water buffalo. One student holds still, the pivot point, and the other walks him around. It's a simple but effective system that gives the two young women some control.

Walter's slightly better behaved coming out of the corral but then heads for a tuft of grass near Lulu's enclosure, and another wrestling match ensues. The two students dig in their heels and pull back on his head. Somehow they get him across Hoofstock and out the gate, though Woodhouse tells them they should always go ahead of the water buffalo, "so he doesn't pin you."

We start up the back road. Two enormous bovines and six women. We are briefly a picture of pastoral calm, that is, until Walter swings his great horned head toward another patch of grass, and another battle royal begins, with Castaneda and the brown-haired first year pulling back and Walter pushing forward. "Do you ever whack him?" Woodhouse asks.

"Gary discourages us from slapping him," Castaneda says. Woodhouse smiles.

We continue up the back road, amble past Zoo 1 and the office, heading toward the front gate. When we arrive near Megan's bench, about the time Clarence cranes his head our way, Walter steps off the blacktop onto the grass, dragging the students with him. "I'd take him out of there because he's just reinforcing himself for being a pain in the ass," Woodhouse says.

The two women tussle with the adolescent buffalo, try pivoting him, but get nowhere. Then in a flash, Woodhouse like a superhero whacks Walter on the neck with the palm of her hand, grabs his lead, and single-handedly pulls him back on the blacktop. It's a sight to behold. We all look at Woodhouse with silent awe. Walter seems just as surprised as the rest of us.

For the rest of the walk Walter just trots along like his old baby self. We take a spin down the front road and then double back. Gee Whiz turns his head to watch us pass. Harrison, the Harris hawk, squawks at us. Dunny stops to take a long voluminous pee. Castaneda blocks Walter's view. "He likes to drink Dunny's pee," she explains. When they stop by the scales, Dunny weighs in at 1,022 pounds, nearly 50 pounds heavier than he was a month ago. At 800 pounds, Walter has gained 80, but he is still growing. Once the two bovine buddies are put back in their corral, they playfully start butting heads. "You're a brat," Castaneda says to Walter.

Woodhouse says the crack she gave the water buffalo was like a flyswatter's to him. It was meant to get his attention, she says, which it did clearly. The trick is to use it judiciously, she tells them. If you don't, it will lose its meaning.

Like Castaneda, Terri Fidone learns an animal needn't have claws or fangs to be dangerous. She, too, assumed the cougar brothers were the most worrisome animals she'd be working with. In fact, it's a domestic animal, Kaleb. "Odds of [the cougars] attacking are very low," she says. "With a camel, every day it could happen."

Kaleb bloops and bloops and bloops. One time by the aviary lawn, Fidone could not get the camel to stop. Though she pulled hard on Kaleb's lead, she could not get the camel's head down. Kaleb kicked her in the back, knocking Fidone forward onto her knees. When she fell, she lost hold of the lead. He could have stomped her. Instead, he quit blooping and stood still by her side. As Fidone walked him back to Hoofstock she realized she couldn't hear. All the adrenaline coursing through her veins had temporarily turned off her hearing. Her nerves were shaken. Worse, her pride was hurt.

Fidone's not sure why Kaleb's become so incorrigible. She wonders if the second years had him bloop too much. He tends to bloop when she has the lead. Could that be because she's training him for a grade? Wilson, inspired by the recent ABMA conference, has instructed the first years to use more positive reinforcement with Kaleb. They give him wedges of sweet potato for walking well and staying calm, though the treats seem to have the opposite effect on him. He's pushy. Could it be this change in approach? Or is the four-year-old reaching sexual maturity? Only Kaleb knows.

Fidone is no chicken. She's skydived. She rides motorcycles. She's served drinks in the world's biggest casino. She's tough and likes a challenge, even one with a big, fatty hump. Still, there are some days she can't bring herself to get the camel out for a walk. "It's so trying with him at times. You think, am I going to live today?"

There's a new resident at the zoo. You can see him if you stand at the back of Primate Gardens and look between the lemurs' and the binturong's cages into Quarantine. Chances are, he'll look right back at you with such eager, glad eyes it can break your heart. The teaching zoo has a new dog.

Kasey came from a pound in Las Vegas with a case of kennel cough. His age is guessed at one and a half. He's a mutt but looks like he has a lot of Australian shepherd in him. He certainly has the breed's bright, attentive eyes and fluffy coat. He's moved into Abbey's old digs next to Samburu, the ornery caracal.

A zoo is a lot for a young dog to get used to. When Kasey first arrived he barked his head off in his new, exotic home. Now the pooch is relatively quiet. The primates aren't bothered by him, nor is Legend. Consequently, Kasey's easier to walk than Abbey was. He eats only dry kibble, which he gobbles right up. Yet Kasey is no star like his predecessor. The pup knows only one command—Sit! He has no manners. He pulls on his leash and jumps on people excitedly. He's pent up with young energy and easily becomes overexcited. Consequently, two of his student trainers lead him to the front of the line for a campus walk one afternoon. That way, Kasey won't be distracted by the assortment of animals trailing behind him.

This campus walk heads out the back gate and along a dirt road that curves down a hill to the playing fields below the zoo. Larissa Comb holds Nick's halter. Three students, their arms held high and crooked, carry macaws on their hands. Rosie ambles along on her leash next to Capovilla and Hyde. Holly Tumas carries a young gibbon in her arms.

As the group turns to walk out on the baseball field, Kasey starts barking, and his trainers stop to calm him. "That dog is crazy," someone holding a macaw says. The students with their various animals pause briefly and then push on. At first Kasey doesn't seem too rattled by the procession passing him, but then Rosie jumps up on some jungle gym bars. That does it. The dog lunges on his lead and woofs his lungs out at the baboon. Both trainers grab hold of his leash and flex their arms. Even after the campus walk has moved off across the lush, grassy field, Kasey still goes bonkers. His student trainers stand by his side and watch the group walk away. "They won't wait for us when he is having trouble," one says. "If it was another animal, they would wait," the other says. Kasey bugs his eyes at the receding baboon.

The group settles on a cushy carpet of lime green grass that sparkles in the afternoon sun. The athletic field is a brilliant oasis amid the browned foothills. It's not too hot and a soft breeze blows. The occasional pop of a bat hitting a ball sounds. A team practices nearby. Tumas sets the gibbon down, and the monkey joyfully stretches out on her belly on the turf. Rosie carefully picks through the blades and, having found one that is to her liking, plucks it and pops it in her mouth. Two young boys on bikes ride past, never seeming to notice the baboon sitting on the lawn. Comb runs with Nick at her side across the field and then back. Susan Patch does a cartwheel.

Now that the teaching zoo is theirs, the summer promises to be long and busy. For a moment, though, they pause and relish the fullness of a beautiful day, from the sun burnishing their faces to the lemon-scented grass as fresh and inviting as a newly made bed. Before too long the group pulls itself to its feet and, holding leashes and reins, drifts across the carpet of green, meanders up the scrubby hill, and vanishes like a dream.

August

As the summer progresses, the second years' warning proves true: this is the most demanding semester yet. There are only half as many people to clean the teaching zoo. There are still classes to study for, presentations to give, and now animals to train. They are even required to spend a few days volunteering at area zoos. Yet it's so satisfying to work with the animals, to lay their hands on them, talk to them, and teach them, that the first years find they can soldier on through the long days under the inland California sun. The rush of time at the teaching zoo, the endless highs and lows, and the days packed with the unusual and wondrous pull them through their weariest moments.

In July alone, Walter, the water buffalo, is castrated, another first year flunks out, and the capuchins break out of their double-baleen cage. One hot morning, Susan Patch notices something skitter through Primate Gardens, a rabbit, she thinks. Then she realizes it's a monkey. Patch sprints up the front road, throws open the door to Zoo 2, and, out of breath, wheezes to the crowd, "Capuchins out!"

The clever troupe had worked off a bolt or two on their cage. The students get a hasty, hands-on lesson in what to do when an animal escapes. One, Flash, is quickly recaptured, but Elvis, the alpha male, laps the campus. The student from Georgia who took care of fawns climbs atop a batting cage, pulls on leather monkey gloves, sits cross-legged, and waits. Elvis runs across her lap a few times, stopping once to lean his flat nose close to hers. As he scampers over her legs one more time, she grabs him.

Elvis bites down hard on her hand. She holds on to the monkey's waist. He is returned to his cage. The first year pulls off her glove and finds to her amazement the bite did not break her skin. Later, when another monkey pees on her hand, it swells and turns red. An invisible wound has somehow become infected.

The students practice what they learn in Wilson's training class on the zoo to good effect. Castaneda teaches Scooter, a capuchin, to climb into a bucket and the now much more mellow Walter to stand on a mark. Adam Hyde teaches Rosie to ride a skate board and to let him brush her teeth. Anita Wischhusen trains Taj to sit on a fake scale that she slides under the tiger's cage but makes little progress with her novel approach to Zulu. The mandrill regularly grabs her, putting Wischhusen in her place. In fact, she's the most subordinate among the four student trainers. Kristy Marson, working outside his cage, teaches Birdman, the kinkajou, to go into a crate on command.

Marissa Williams teaches Nick to step as prettily as the Lipizzaner Stallions and, moreover, manages to thin the horse. At last Nick drops below 300, to 290 pounds. His middle no longer bulges. He no longer huffs and puffs when he pulls the cart.

Patch trains Sahara, the baby camel, to be haltered and led. That done, Sahara goes for his first trailer ride, to Burbank to *The Tonight Show* with Jay Leno. His mom, Lulu, comes along for the ride. During the rehearsal, Harry, as he is nicknamed, nervously pees a bit on the rubber mats under him, but settles down nicely. However, when the full band begins to play, the poor baby camel screams and security men come running. Patch holds her hand over his soft mouth but to little avail. Then, after the lantern-jawed comedian dawdles with a caracal, time runs out for Harry.

Chandra Cohn, no longer able to afford her rent, moves home with her mother in Resada. As the summer passes, her much-needed student loan never materializes. Cohn takes her mind off her troubles by teaching Wilhelmina, the hornbill, to get in a crate. Cohn, who was once very disappointed that she didn't get Ebony, the raven, falls in love with the awkward bird with the bald wing.

Terri Fidone trains Kaleb to go to a mark and cush, but he is no better behaved on walks. On a Saturday in August, as Fidone walks Kaleb into Hoofstock, the camel pitches yet another fit. Fidone trips over the railroad ties along a flower bed by Schmoo's enclosure. She falls hard and cracks her head against a fence pole. The camel could easily stomp her, so Fidone bounces up as fast as she can, her crop still in her hand. Afterward, Fidone is covered with sweat. She shakes. A knot swells on her head. She sends a classmate up to Wildlife Theatre to say she can't do the rest of the show. "Still, it's been a great experience," she says of Kaleb. "I don't want to give him up. It's such an adrenaline rush."

The new vet, Cynthia Stringfield, arrives. She gives the collection a once-over. A macaw has a sour crop, a gibbon has a wound that won't heal, and Mazoe, a serval, has blood in her urine, but the collection is in good shape. Stringfield is a slim, long-limbed woman with a square jaw. At the Los Angeles Zoo, she was one of two or three vets that cared for twelve to eighteen hundred animals. She expects EATM's collection to be much more manageable. What's new to her is teaching and students—EATM students to be exact. They may prove, as Dr. Peddie has warned her, to be the most demanding species at the teaching zoo.

Beyond the zoo's fence, Dr. Peddie finds to his surprise that he takes to retirement quickly. There's no more wondering out loud about his identity. The vet finds he'd rather tinker with his boat than contemplate existential questions. He pops up to EATM off and on. In early August, he's due back on campus to receive the college's most prestigious teaching award, the Distinguished Faculty Chair. "You know, they give you an actual chair," he tells me, "a rocking chair."

Reports of the second years continue to filter in. One has gotten a job training dolphins at Sea Life Park in Hawaii. Another has gotten a boob job. Trevor Jahangard has had his tonsils out and shaved his head. After finishing up the summer camp at EATM, Mary VanHollebeke moves to Las Vegas and waits tables so she can begin paying off her student loans. After six weeks on the job, Becki Brunelli quits. The owner accused her of trying to meet movie stars. The two did not jibe, Brunelli says. She leaves LA, as well, and returns to her hometown in Northern California to be near her family. She's fallen in love and moves in with an old boyfriend. She gets a job designing Web pages. Like VanHollebeke, Brunelli puts off her dream of working with animals while she pays off her credit cards.

In a dog park along the poky Los Angeles River in Encino, Amy Mohelnitzky leans over to unhook a leash. That done, Abbey gallops across a flat expanse of grass. Her long coat blows back. Abbey stops to nose a dachshund, then she's off again. Her paws hardly seem to hit the ground as she falls in beside a mutt chasing a ball.

Abbey has taken to the life of a house dog. The pooch sleeps on a bed Mohelnitzky's mother sewed for her and sent from Wisconsin. She doesn't bark nearly as much anymore—really only here at the dog park—but who can blame her? When Mohelnitzky first brought Abbey home, she continued to feed the mutt a sloppy pile of noodles, cottage cheese, chicken broth, and rice. That wasn't working, so she tried just plain kibble with hot water. Now the dog rarely pukes. She eats nearly every meal. If Abbey hesitates to eat breakfast, Mohelnitzky calls one of her two cats over to the bowl, and that revives the dog's appetite. Like Abbey, Mohelnitzky has adjusted well to life after EATM. She works in a vet's office during the day and teaches puppy training a couple of nights a week. "It's nice to have a normal life," she says as we watch Abbey sprint, a flash of white across a seemingly endless stretch of green.

In the second week of August at about the time the pomegranates ripen on the tree near the front office, the front gate swings open and a new crop of students pours into the teaching zoo. With their arrival, the first years now officially become second years. As deeply tanned as field workers, they look around and find only three missing from their ranks. The rest have made it, even the slacker, though some have scars to show for their time here. Having survived the crucible of the last twelve months, they breathe a sigh of relief as they contemplate the riches just ahead: later mornings, field trips, and projects.

On the first day of orientation week, the new students kerthunk up the metal bleachers of Wildlife Theatre and take seats. Wilson talks to them of death. Susan Patch demonstrates how to gas a rat, and how to flick their little eyes to make sure they are dead. Another newly minted second year shows how to pull a pigeon, talking as she takes a bird in hand, leans over a trash can, and neatly twists its head off. The bleachers remain quiet, but when volunteers are requested, a good dozen hands shoot up, more than they have birds for. One newbie asks, if you don't get the head off, do you still get credit? Wilson says yes.

Just as their own second years did, the new second years agree to be kinder to their first years: they will invite them to their parties, share their doughnuts, and learn their names. They will make them feel welcome. History, however, and human behavior are against them. Few classes have jibed but it's worth a try. Maybe this underdog of a class can do it. Certainly, they've come further than the staff or they themselves expected.

The new second years look into the bleachers at the eager, fresh faces and see themselves a year ago—green, unsure, perhaps even scared. Can it be that just last August they sat there watching as Schmoo, glistening in the sun, jubilantly frolicked onstage with her trainers? They've given themselves over body and soul to the cloistered life of the teaching zoo. They've said good-bye to nearly a dozen animals. They've lived through a fire and a death. They've withstood punishing exams, gossip, and bites. They've killed a bird with their bare hands. They've learned how to walk a cougar, groom a baboon, cuddle a badger, hold a boa constrictor, and train a temperamental sea lion. Having done all that, anything seems possible.

Acknowledgments

How do you thank someone for leading the way to the most fascinating experience of your life? It was a lucky day the day I met Dr. Jim Peddie. A long list of people helped me with this project, but Dr. Peddie was the first, the one who made it all possible. This fireball of a vet was my trusty, personable guide throughout, even coming to my rescue on one occasion. He may have ruined dairy foods for me by referring to pus as "cheesy," but it was a small price to pay for his invaluable help, not to mention his company.

Likewise, I owe the outstanding staff at EATM an enormous debt: Gary and Cindy Wilson, Brenda Woodhouse, Michlyn Hines, Chuck Brinkman, Mara Rodriguez, Holly Tumas, Dorothy Belanger, Leland Shapiro, and Kris Romero. It's not easy to have a reporter knocking around asking you question after question while you leash a cougar or demonstrate how to net a monkey, but they did so with grace and good humor. They gave me open access to the school, which was key to this book. For that, I also thank the program's dean, Brenda Shubert, and Moorpark College president Eva Conrad. Former EATM staff Lynn Doria, Susan Cox, and Diane Cahill generously showed me the long view of the school. And if it weren't for Bill Brisby, EATM's founder, there would be no school for me to have written about. His big, crazy dream has made the smaller dreams of countless others come true, mine included.

Most of my time on this project was spent on the compound with the students and the animals. In fact, I often found myself hanging out at the teaching zoo long after I should have gone home. I am especially grateful to Becki Brunelli, Linda Castaneda, Susan Patch, and Trevor Jahangard, who were extraordinarily generous with their time and thoughts. I miss our cageside chats. Students Anita Wischhusen, Terri Fidone, Adam Hyde, Amber Cavett, Jenn Donovan, Carrie Hakanson, Amy Mohelnitzky, Mary VanHollebeke, Jena Anderson, Crystal Pieroni, and Chris Jenkins all lent a helping hand as well. I could go on. In short, I am forever indebted to the EATM classes of 2003 and 2004, by whose aplomb I will forever be awed.

A long list of professional animal trainers took time from their busy lives to talk to me, even let me pet an animal or two: Julie Scardina, Suzanne Morgan, and Al Kordowski at SeaWorld; Mark Forbes and Gary Mui at Birds and Animals Unlimited; Dave and Anita Jackson at Zoo to You: John Heston at the Playboy Mansion Zoo; Cathryn Hilker and Jennifer Good at the Cincinnati Zoo; Gary and Kari Johnson and their staff at Have Trunk Will Travel; Ken Ramirez at the Shedd Aquarium; Gary Priest at the San Diego Zoo and Wild Animal Park; and training revolutionary and author Karen Pryor.

As this project proved as wily as the wildest beast, my agent Jane Chelius kept me sane with her encouragement and excellent counsel. My editor, the estimable Ray Roberts, kept me on course with a potent mix of chiding and cheerleading. I suspect he was a lion tamer in a previous life. I'm also grateful to all the staff at Viking who helped make this book a reality.

I owe a debt of gratitude to one of my oldest and best friends, the talented, beautiful Lisa Stiepock, who by giving me a magazine assignment set me on the path to this book. As always, friends and family (thanks, Ma!) shored me up when the going got tough. None, however, did so as much as my soul mate, Scott Sutherland. There should be a section in heaven reserved for the spouses of authors, and if there is any justice, it will have unlimited supplies of bike magazines for my sweet, smart, handsome husband.

Lastly, how do you thank animals, the guiding spirits of this book? I owed them before I even set out on this adventure. All I can offer by way of gratitude is what any of us can, to always keep their best interests at heart. For without animals, there would be little, if any, magic in the world.

MW00758354

CAT *in the* DARK

Books by Shirley Rousseau Murphy

Cat on the Edge
Cat Under Fire
Cat Raise the Dead
Cat in the Dark

Published by HarperPrism

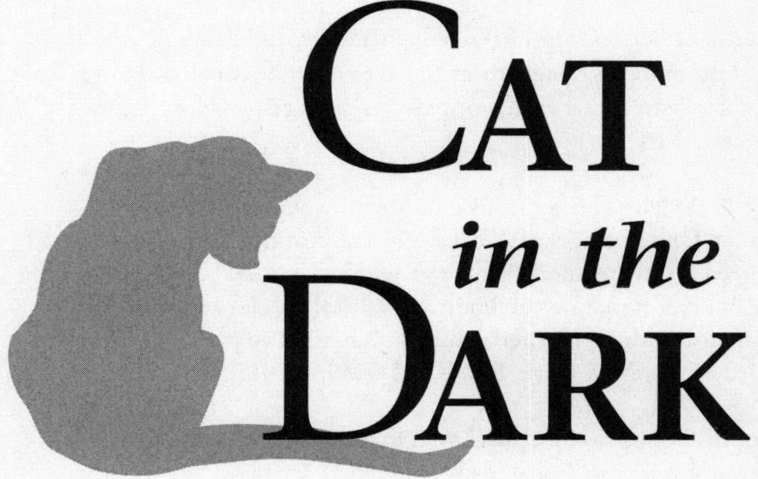

Cat in the Dark

Shirley Rousseau Murphy

HarperPrism

HarperPrism
A Division of HarperCollins*Publishers*
10 East 53rd Street, New York, NY 10022-5299

This is a work of fiction. The characters, incidents, and dialogues are products of the author's imagination and are not to be construed as real. Any resemblance to actual events or persons, living or dead, is entirely coincidental.

Copyright © 1999 by Shirley Rousseau Murphy. All rights reserved. Printed in the United States of America. No part of this book may be used or reproduced in any manner whatsoever without written permission except in the case of brief quotations embodied in critical articles and reviews. For information address HarperCollins Publishers Inc., 10 East 53rd Street, New York, NY 10022-5299.

HarperCollins books may be purchased for educational, business, or sales promotional use. For information please write: Special Markets Department, HarperCollins Publishers Inc., 10 East 53rd Street, New York, NY 10022-5299

FIRST EDITION

Library of Congress Cataloging-in-Publication Data

Murphy, Shirley Rousseau.
Cat in the dark / Shirley Rousseau Murphy. — 1st U.S. ed.
p. cm.
ISBN 0-06-105096-2
1. Cats—Fiction. I. Title.
PS3563.U7619C35 1999
813' .54—dc21 98-39206

Visit HarperPrism on the World Wide Web at
http://www.harperprism.com

99 00 01 02 ❖/RRD 10 9 8 7 6 5 4 3 2 1

For those who wonder about their cats.
And for the cats who don't need to wonder, for the cats who know.

And, of course, for Joe Cat.
And this time, too, for Lucy and skybound E.L.T.

And always for Pat for his laughter in the right places
and his support and advice.

1

THE CAT crouched in darkness beneath the library desk, her tabby stripes mingled with the shadows, her green eyes flashing light, her tail switching impatiently as she watched the last patrons linger around the circulation counter. Did humans *have* to dawdle, wasting their time and hers? What *was* it about closing hour that made people so incredibly slow?

Above her the library windows were black, and out in the night the oaks' ancient branches twisted against the glass, the moon's rising light reflecting along their limbs and picking out the rooftops beyond. The time was nine-fifteen. Time to turn out the lights. Time to leave these hallowed rooms to her. Would people never leave? She was so irritated she almost shouted at them to get lost, that this was her turf now.

Beyond the table and chair legs, out past the open door, the library's front garden glowed waxen in the moonlight, the spider lilies as ghostly pale as the white reaching fingers of a dead man. Three women moved out into the garden along the stone path, beneath the oak trees' dark shelter, heading toward the street; behind them, Mavity Flowers hurried out toting her heavy book bag, her white maid's uniform as bright as moonstruck snow, her gray, wiry hair ruffled by the sea wind. Her white polyester skirt was deeply wrinkled in the rear from sitting for nearly an hour delving through the romance novels, choosing half a dozen unlikely dreams in which to lose herself. Dulcie imagined Mavity hastening home to her tiny cottage, making herself a cup of tea, getting comfy, maybe slipping into her bathrobe and putting her feet up for an evening's read—for a few hours' escape and pleasure after scrubbing and vacuuming all day in other people's houses.

Mavity was a dear friend of Dulcie's housemate; she and Wilma had known each other since elementary school, more than fifty years. Wilma was the tall one, strong and self-sufficient, while Mavity was such a small person, so wrinkled and frail-looking that people treated her as if she should be watched over—even if she did work as hard as a woman half her age. Mavity wasn't a cat lover, but she and Dulcie were friends. She always stroked Dulcie and talked to her when she stopped by Wilma's; Mavity told Dulcie she was beautiful, that her chocolate-dark stripes were as lovely as mink, that Dulcie was a very special cat.

But the little lady had no idea how special. The truth would have terrified her. The notion that Dulcie had read (and found tedious) most of the stories that she, herself, was toting home tonight, would have shaken Mavity Flowers right down to her scruffy white oxfords.

Through the open front door, Dulcie watched Mavity hurry to the corner and turn beneath the yellow glow of the streetlamp to disappear down the dark side street into a tunnel of blackness beneath a double row of densely massed eucalyptus trees. But within the library, seven patrons still lingered.

And from the media room at the back, four more dawdlers appeared, their feet scuffing along inches from Dulcie's nose—silk-clad ankles in stilted high heels, a boy's bony bare feet in leather sandals, a child's little white shoes and lace-ruffled white socks following Mama's worn loafers. And all of them as slow as cockroaches in molasses, stopping to examine the shelved books and flip through the racked magazines. Dulcie, hunching against the carpet, sighed and closed her eyes. Dawdling was a *cat's* prerogative, humans didn't have the talent. Only a cat could perform that slow, malingering dance, the *half-in-half-out-the-door* routine, with the required insolence and grace.

She was not often so rude in her assessment of human frailties. During the daytime hours, she was a model of feline amenity, endlessly obliging to the library patrons, purring for them and smiling when the old folks and children petted and fussed over her, and she truly loved them. Being official library cat was deeply rewarding. And at home with Wilma she considered herself beautifully laid-back; she and Wilma had a lovely life together. But when night fell, when the dark winds shook the oaks and pines and rattled the eucalyptus leaves, her patina of civilization gave way and the ancient wildness rose in her, primitive passions took her—and a powerful and insatiable curiosity drove her. Now, eager to get on with her own agenda, she was stifled not only by lingering humans but was put off far more by the too-watchful gaze of the head librarian.

Jingling her keys, Freda Brackett paced before the circulation desk as sour-faced as a bad-tempered possum and as impatient for people to leave as was Dulcie herself—though for far different reasons. Freda couldn't wait to be free of the books and their related routines for a few hours, while Dulcie couldn't wait to get at the thousands of volumes, as eager as a child waiting to be alone in the candy store.

Freda had held the position of head librarian for two months. During that time, she had wasted not an ounce of love on the library and its contents, on the patrons, or on anyone or anything connected with the job. But what could you expect of a political appointee?

The favorite niece of a city council member, Freda had been selected over several more desirable applicants among the library's own staff. Having come to Molena Point from a large and businesslike city library, she ran this small, cozy establishment in the same way. Her only objective was to streamline operations until the Molena Point Library functioned as coldly and impersonally as the institution she had abandoned. In just two months the woman's rigid rules had eaten away at the warm, small-village atmosphere like a rat demolishing last night's cake.

She discouraged the villagers from using the library as a meeting place, and she tried to deter any friendliness among the staff. Certainly she disapproved of librarians being friends with the patrons—an impossibility in a small town. Her rules prevented staff from performing special favors for any patron and she even disapproved of helping with book selection and research, the two main reasons for library service.

And as for Dulcie, an official library cat was an abomination. A cat on the premises was as inappropriate and unsanitary as a dog turd on Freda's supper plate.

But a political appointee didn't have to care about the job, they were in it only for the money or prestige. If they loved their work they would have excelled at it and thus been hired on their own merits. Political appointees were, in Dulcie's opinion, always bad news. Just last summer a police detective who was handed his job by the mayor created near disaster in the village when he botched a murder investigation.

Dulcie smiled, licking her whiskers.

Detective Marritt hadn't lasted long, thanks to some quick paw-work. She and Joe Grey, moving fast, had uncovered evidence so incriminating that the real killer had been indicted, and Detective Marritt had been fired—out on the street. A little feline intervention had made him look like mouse dirt.

She wished they could do the same number on Freda.

Behind the circulation desk, Dulcie's housemate, Wilma Getz, moved back and forth arranging books on the reserve shelf, her long, silver hair bound back with a turquoise clip, her white turtleneck sweater and black blazer setting off to advantage her slim, faded jeans. The two women were about the same age, but Wilma had remained lithe and fresh, while Freda looked dried-up and sharp-angled and sour—and her clothes always smelled of mothballs. Dulcie, watching the two women, did not expect what was coming.

"Get your cat, Wilma. You are to take it home with you tonight."

"She's all right inside—she'll go out later through her cat door."

"You will take it home with you. I don't want it here at night. There's too much possibility of damage. Animals have no place in a library. You are fortunate that, so far, I have allowed it to remain during the day."

Wilma laid aside the books she was arranging and fixed Freda with a level look. "Dulcie is not a destructive cat. Her manners, as you should have observed, are impeccable."

"No cat can be trusted. You have no way to know what it might do. You will take it home with you."

Dulcie, peering from the shadows, dug her claws hard into the carpet—she'd like to tear it to shreds. Or tear Freda to shreds, flay her like a cornered rat. She imagined Freda as a hunting trophy, the woman's head mounted over the circulation desk like the deer head over Morrie's Bar.

Wilma picked up her purse. "Dulcie has a right to be here. She *is* the library cat. She was appointed by the mayor and she is of great value to us. Have you forgotten that her presence has doubled the children's book circulation?"

"That is such a ridiculous notion. The library is a center for sophisticated research tools, Ms. Getz. It is not a petting zoo."

"This is a small village library, Freda. It is geared to patrons who want to spend a few pleasant hours."

"Even if that were its purpose, what does that have to do with a *cat?*"

"Our patrons like having a little cat to pet and to talk to." Wilma gave Freda a gentle smile. "You've seen the statistics. Duclie has brought in patrons who never came to the library before, and who are now regulars."

"Ms. Getz, the city hired me to run a library, not an animal shelter. There is absolutely no precedent for . . ."

"You know quite well there is precedent. Do you think the libraries that keep a cat are run by idiots? There are library cats all across the country, and every one of them is credited with large increases in circulation. Do you think the librarians in El Centro and Hayward and Hood River, in Niagara Falls, Fort Worth, and in a dozen other states would bother to keep a library cat if the cat did not perform a valuable service?"

"Very likely those libraries have a mouse problem and were forced to keep a cat. You are truly paranoid about this foolishness. I would hope your reference work is of a more scholarly . . ."

Wilma folded her hands loosely in front of her, a gesture Dulcie knew well when Wilma longed to punch someone. "Why don't *you* do *your* research, Freda? Library cats date at least as far back as the eighteen-hundreds, not only here but in England and Italy. There have been nonfiction books published on the library cat, a videotape is now being produced, and at least one thesis has been written on the subject—to say nothing of the Library Cat Society, which is a *national* organization of librarians and library cat supporters."

Beneath the reference desk, Dulcie smiled. Wilma hadn't spent thirty years putting down pushy federal parolees for nothing.

"Since Dulcie came," Wilma reminded Freda, "our children's reading program has grown so popular we've had to start three new groups—because of Dulcie. She draws out the shy children, and when new children come in to pet her, very often they discover a brand-new love for books. And they adore having her with them during story hour, snuggling among the cushions."

Dulcie wanted to cheer, to do a little cat-dance to thank Wilma—but as Freda turned away, the expression on the woman's face made Dulcie back deeper under the desk, an icy shiver passing over her.

If she had been an ordinary cat, Wilma would take her away for her own safety, because who knew what Freda might do? How could an ordinary cat fathom the lengths Freda Brackett might go to, to get rid of her?

But Dulcie was not ordinary. She was quite aware of the woman's malice and, despite Wilma's worries, she knew how to keep out of Freda's way.

Freda, turning her back on Wilma, motioned her assistant to put out the lights. Bernine Sage hurried out from the book stacks, heading for the electrical switches behind the circulation desk, her smoothly coiled red hair gleaming in the overhead light, her slim black suit describing exactly Bernine's businesslike attitude. She was not a librarian but a computer expert and a bookkeeper—a perfect choice as Freda's assistant, to bring the backward village institution into the twenty-first century. Bernine, during the exchange between Freda and Wilma, had stood in the shadows as alert as an armed guard ready to support her superior.

Bernine and Wilma had known each other for many years; Bernine was, as far as she could be, Wilma's friend. But friendship ended where her bread was buttered.

Dulcie's own relationship with Bernine was one of a fear far more complicated than her wariness of Freda Brackett. Bernine Sage had acquired her dislike of cats in an unusual way, and she knew too much about certain kinds of cats. If she got started on Celtic history and the ancient, speaking cats, and began spilling her theories to Freda and quoting mythology, she could set Ms. Brackett off in a frightening new direction. A real witch-hunt—cat hunt—focused on her; though she was neither witch nor witch's cat, Dulcie thought demurely.

But what she *was* could be no less terrifying to an unsympathetic and unimaginative human.

Now, as Bernine threw the switches for the overhead lights, the library rooms dimmed to a soft glow where a few desk lamps still burned, and the last patrons headed out. But Wilma glanced across the room to Dulcie, her message as clear as if she had spoken: She would not take Dulcie home—she would not give in to Freda. But her look implored Dulcie to go on out and let the woman cool down. Her gaze said clearly that she wouldn't sleep unless she knew Dulcie was safe.

Within the shadows, Dulcie blinked her eyes slowly, trying to look compliant, trying to ease her friend.

But she had no intention of leaving. Crouched on the carpet, her tail switching, she waited impatiently as Freda and Bernine, and then Wilma, moved toward the door. Bernine paused to throw the last switch, and the desk lamps went dark, casting the room into blackness. For an instant Dulcie was blind, but before the dead bolt slid home her night vision kicked in and the darkness turned transparent, the tables and chairs reemerged, and across the book-lined walls, the blowing shadows of the oaks swam and shivered.

Alone. At last she was alone.

Trotting out from beneath the desk, she leaped to its top and spun, chasing her tail, then flew to the floor again and hit the carpet running, racing through the reading rooms under tables and desks, tearing through moonlight and shadow. Around her, the darkened rooms seemed larger, as if the daytime walls had melted away into wind-tossed space. Leaping to a bookshelf, she pawed down a claw-marked volume. With a soft thud it hit the carpet.

Carrying it in her teeth, she sprang to a table where the moon's light shone brightest. Pawing the book open, she soon was wandering Africa, prowling the open grasslands, her nostrils filled with the sharp scent of wildebeest and antelope, and around her the African night reeled away to mountains so tall they vanished among the stars. Feasting on gazelle, she raced across grassy plains so vast that if Molena Point were set down there, it would seem only a child's toy village. Roaring and chuffing, she was a leopard padding among clay huts terrifying sleeping humans, leaving gigantic pawprints in the dust for unlucky hunters to follow. And when at last she was overwhelmed by Africa's immense spaces, she turned to the close, confining alleys of tenth-century England, to tales of narrow medieval streets.

But too soon those tales turned dark. Hecate wooed her. Evil beckoned to her. She blundered into stories of witches in cat-form and of cat familiars. Medieval humans stalked her, folk terrified by the sight of a cat and wanting only to kill it. Trapped by that era of cruelty, she was sucked down into darkness, unable to shake the bloody and horror-ridden images. These stories were nothing like the gentler, Celtic dramas that she liked to browse through when ancient peoples, taking cat-form, wandered down to a netherworld beneath the soft green hills, when the magical race that was kin to both man and cat could take the shape of either. When that ancient tribe of speaking cats to which she and Joe belonged—and of which they might be nearly the last survivors—had been understood and loved by the Celts. Unable to rid herself of the darker visions, she backed away from the open book, slashing at the offending volume, almost bereft of her reason.

Then she whirled away to crouch at the edge of the table, shocked at her own loss of control.

What am I doing? There is nothing here, only stories. Words on a page, nothing more. That evil time is gone, ages gone. Why am I crouching here trembling like a terrified hunk of cat fur? What set me off like that, to nearly lose myself? Shivering, she felt almost as if someone had fixed dark thoughts on her. Lashing her tail, disgusted by her pointless fear, by her sudden failure of spirit, she leaped to the floor and fled through Wilma's office and out her cat door into the night, into the soft and welcoming night, into Molena Point's safe and moonlit night.

2

IN THE BEDROOM of the white Cape Cod cottage, moonlight shone through the open windows and a fitful breeze fingered across the bed, teasing the ears of the tomcat who slept curled in the blankets, his muscular body gleaming as sleek as gray velvet. Beside him on the double bed, his human housemate snored softly, clutching the pillow for warmth, unaware that Joe Grey had clawed away the covers into a comfortable and exclusive nest. Clyde, naked and chilled, was too deep in sleep to wake and retrieve the blankets, but Joe Grey stirred as the breeze quickened, his white paws flexed and his nose lifted, catching an elusive scent.

He woke fully, staring toward the open window, drawing his lips back in a grimace at the stink he detected on the cool night air.

Tomcat.

The smell that came to him on the ocean breeze was the rank odor of an unknown tom—a stranger in the village.

Joe might not encounter a village tom for months, but he knew each one, knew what routes he favored and which pals he hung out with, by the scent marks left on storefronts and tree trunks, aromas as individual as hand-lettered placards stating name and residence. He knew the smell of every cat in Molena Point, but this one was exotic and foreign.

Joe tolerated the regular village toms, because how could he not? Without some degree of civility, life would degenerate into a succession of endless and meaningless battles. One restrained oneself until the prize was greatest, until a queen in heat ruled the night—then it was war, bloody and decisive.

But no amount of civilized restraint among the village toms left room for strangers on their turf.

This could be a stray from the wharf who had decided to prowl among the shops, or maybe some tourist's cat; whatever the case, he didn't like the intruder's belligerent, testosterone-heavy message. The beast's odor reeked of insolence and of a bold and dark malaise—a hotly aggressive, sour aroma. The cat smelled like trouble.

In the moon's glow, the cottage bedroom was lent a charm not apparent in the daytime. A plain room, it was suited to a simple bachelor's spartan tastes, comfortable but shabby, the pine dresser and pine nightstand sturdily made and ugly, the ladder-back chair old and scarred. But now, in the moonlight, the unadorned white walls were enlivened by the shifting shadows of the oak trees that spread just outside the window, their knotted patterns softening the room's stark lines and offering a sense of mystery and depth. And beside the bed, a thick, ruby-toned Persian rug added a single touch of luxury, gleaming like jewels in the moonlight—a tender and extravagant gift from one of Clyde's former lovers.

Pawing free of the confining bedcovers, Joe Grey walked heavily across the bed and across Clyde's stomach and dropped down to the thick, soft rug. Clyde, grunting, raised up and glared at him.

"Why the hell do you do that? You're heavy as a damned moose!"

Joe smiled and dug his claws into the rug's silky pile.

Clyde's black hair was wild from sleep, his cheeks dark with a day's growth of stubble. A line of black grease streaked his forehead, residue from the innards of some ailing Rolls Royce or Mercedes.

"You have the whole damned bed to walk on. Can't you show a little consideration? I don't walk on your stomach."

Joe dug his claws deeper into the Persian weave, his yellow eyes sly with amusement. "You work out, you're always bragging about your great stomach muscles—you shouldn't even feel my featherweight. Anyway, you were snoring so loud, so deep under, that a Great Dane on your stomach shouldn't have waked you."

"Get the hell out of here. Go on out and hunt, let me get some sleep. Go roll in warm blood or whatever you do at night."

"For your information, I'm going straight to the library. What more sedate and respectable destination could one possibly . . ."

"Can it, Joe. Of course you're going to the library—but only to get Dulcie. Then off to murder some helpless animal, attack some innocent little mouse or cute, cuddly rabbit. Look at you—that killer expression plastered all over your furry face."

"Rabbits are not cuddly. A rabbit can be as vicious as a bullterrier—their claws are incredibly sharp. And what gives you the slightest clue to Dulcie's and my plans for the evening? You're suddenly an authority on the behavior of *felis domesticus?*"

Clyde doubled the pillow behind his head. "I don't have to be an authority to smell the blood on your breath when you come stomping in at dawn."

"I don't come in here at dawn. I go directly to the kitchen, minding my own business."

"And trailing muddy pawprints all over the kitchen table. Can't you wash like a normal cat? You get so much mud on the morning paper, who can read it?"

"I have no trouble reading it. Though why anyone would waste more than five minutes on that rag is hard to understand."

Clyde picked up the clock, which he kept facedown on the night table. The luminous dial said twelve thirty-three. "It's late, Joe. Get on out of here. Save your sarcasm for Dulcie. Some of us have to get up in the morning, go to work to support the indigent members of the household."

"I can support myself very nicely, thank you. I let you think otherwise simply to make you feel needed, to let you think you perform some useful function in the world."

Padding across the oak floor, Joe pawed open the bedroom door. "So go to sleep. Sleep your life away." Giving Clyde a last, narrow glare, he left the room. Behind him, he heard Clyde groan and pound his pillow and roll over.

Trotting down the hall and through the living room, brushing past his own tattered, hair-matted easy chair, he slipped out through his cat door. He supposed he should feel sorry for Clyde. How could a mere human, with inferior human senses, appreciate the glory of the moonlit night that surrounded him as he headed across the village?

To his right, above the village roofs, the Molena Point hills rose round and silvered like the pale, humped backs of grazing beasts. All around him, the shop windows gleamed with lunar light, and as he crossed Ocean Avenue with its eucalyptus-shaded median, the trees' narrow leaves, long and polished, reflected the moon's glow like silver fish hung from the branches—thousands, millions of bright fish. No human, with inferior human eyesight, could appreciate such a night. No human, with dull human hearing and minimal sense of smell, could enjoy any of the glories of the natural world as vividly as did a cat. Clyde, poor pitiful biped, didn't have a clue.

Trotting up the moon-whitened sidewalk, he caught again the scent of the vagrant tom and followed it on the shifting wind, watching for any stealthy movement in the tangled shadows. But then, hurrying past the softly lit shops and galleries, he lost that sour odor; now, passing a block of real estate offices and little cafes, sniffing at the doors and at the oversized flower pots that stood along the curb, he smelled only dog urine and the markings of the cats he knew. The tom had, somewhere behind him, taken a different route.

Approaching Dulcie's cat door, which had been cut at the back of the library into Wilma's office, he startled at a sound within—and the door flap exploded out and Dulcie shot through nearly on top of him, her green eyes wildly blazing.

She froze, staring at him. She said no word. She lashed her tail and spun away again, racing for the nearest tree and up it, swarming up to the roofs.

Puzzled and concerned, he followed her.

Was she simply moon-maddened, wild with the pull of the full moon? Or had something frightened her in the library's dark rooms?

With Dulcie, who knew? His lady's moods could explode as crazily as moths flung in a windstorm.

At least he hadn't scented the strange tom around her door, he thought with relief as he gained the moonlit peaks.

Already she had disappeared. But her scent was there, warm and sweet, leading away into dense blackness between a tangle of vent pipes that rose from a roof as silvered and flat as a frozen pond. Slipping between the slashing shadows, he galloped past a dozen east-facing windows that reflected a dozen pale moons. Rearing up to look across the roofs for her, peering beneath overhangs and around dormers, he softly called to her. He spoke her name half a dozen times before he grew uneasy, began to worry that the tom had found her first.

Most toms wouldn't harm a female, but there was always the nasty-tempered beast who liked to hurt a lady more than he liked to love her, the unusual, twisted male who fed on fear and pain—beasts little different from a similarly warped human. Except there were far fewer such cats than men.

Not that Dulcie couldn't take care of herself. There wasn't a dog in Molena Point who would tangle with his lady. But despite Dulcie's temper and her swift claws, Joe searched with growing concern, hurrying along the peaks and watching the shadows and calling. Beneath the moon's shifting light he could see nothing alive but the darting bats that skimmed the rooftops sucking up bugs and squeaking their shrill radar cries.

Suddenly the tom's scent hit him strong, clinging to the wall of a little, one-room penthouse.

Sniffing at the window, Joe could smell where the cat had

rubbed his cheek along the glass, arrogantly marking this territory as if it were his own.

Peering in through the dusty pane, he studied the old desk stacked with papers and catalogs and the shelves behind, crammed with books and ledgers. What had the tom seen in there of interest?

Beyond the desk a spiral staircase led down to the bookstore below. Maybe this cat, like Dulcie and like Joe himself, found a bookstore inviting; certainly bookstores had a warm coziness, and they always smelled safe.

Maybe the cat had taken up residence there; maybe the two young women who kept the shop had adopted him, picked him up on the highway or at the animal pound. How would they know that Molena Point already had enough tomcats? And why would they care? Why would a human care about the delicate balance of territory necessary to the village males?

A nudge against his flank spun him around crouched to attack.

Dulcie bounced aside laughing, her green eyes flashing. Cuffing his face, she raced to the edge of the roof and dropped off, plummeting down into the concrete canyon—he heard her claws catch on an awning.

Crouching on the rain gutter, he looked down where she clung in the swaying canvas, her eyes blazing. Lashing her tail, she leaped up past him to the roof again and sped away. He burst after her and they fled along the rooftops laughing with human voices.

"You can't escape . . ."

"No scruffy tom can catch me . . ."

"No hoyden queen can outrun *this* tomcat, baby."

"Try me." She laughed, scorching away into the dark and twisted shadows. And who was to hear them? Below, the village slept. No one would hear them laughing and talking—no one, seeing them racing across the rooftops, would connect two cats with human voices. Wildly they fled across the peaks, leaping from shingled hip to dormer and up the winding stairs of the courthouse tower, swiftly up to its high, open lookout.

On the small circular terrace beneath the tower's conical roof they trotted along the top of the brick rail, looking down at the world spread all below them, at a vast mosaic stained to silver and black. Nothing moved there, only the cloud shadows slipping across and the little bats jittering and darting on the fitful wind.

But then as they padded along the rail, stepping around the outside of the tower's four pillars on a narrow row of bricks, something stirred below them.

In the sea of darkness an inky patch shifted suddenly and slunk out of the shadows.

He stood staring up at them, black and bold among the rooftops. A huge beast. Black as sin. The biggest tomcat Joe had ever seen—broad of shoulder, wide of head, solid as a panther. He moved with the grace of a panther, swaggering across the roof directly below them, belligerent and predaceous and staring up narrow-eyed, intently watching them, his slitted, amber eyes flashing fire—and his gaze was fully on Dulcie, keen with speculation.

3

ON THE ROOFS below Joe and Dulcie the tomcat sauntered along a sharp peak, swaying his broad shoulders with authority and staring coldly up at them where they crouched high on the rail of the tower. Though he dismissed Joe, hardly noticing him, his gaze lingered keenly on Dulcie, making her shiver. Then he smiled and, turning away again, began to stalk between the chimneys, his gaze fixed on a skylight's clear dome; crouched over the moonstruck bubble, he peered down intently through the curving glass.

From their high vantage, Dulcie watched him with interest. "Blue Moss Cafe," she said softly. "What's he looking at? What's so fascinating? They're closed for the night." There would not be so much as a bread crust remaining on the small round tables, not a crumb visible in the stainless steel kitchen; she and Joe had often looked in, sniffing the good smell of beef stew, watching the happy diners. The cat seemed to study every detail of the dim, closed restaurant, remaining so for some moments before he moved on again to peer into an attic and then into a darkened penthouse. There were apartments above some of the shops, and where a room was lighted, he kept his distance, circling around to avoid any wash of light spilling upon him. Approaching an angled, tilting skylight, he hunkered over the dark, dusty panes—and froze.

Whatever he saw below him down in the dusty-dim environs of Medder's Antiques had jerked him to full alert. Lashing his tail, he clawed at the glass, every line of his muscled body focused and intent, fixated on the little crowded antique store and its ancient, dusty furniture, perhaps studying some odd accouterment of human culture—maybe an antique rattrap or silk umbrella or silver snuffbox. A faint glow seeped up from a nightlight somewhere within, dully igniting the skylight's grimy panes and silhouetting the black cat's broad head and thick shoulders. Clawing at the metal frame, digging and pulling, he soon forced the skylight open.

Heaving his shoulder into the crack, he pushed the glass up, rolled underneath, and dropped out of sight as the glass thumped closed behind him; the leap would be ten or twelve feet down among dust-scented Victorian chairs and cluttered china cabinets.

"Come on!" Dulcie hissed. Leaping from the rail, she fled down the tower's dark, winding stairs. Joe raced close, pressing against her, gripped by a nameless fear for her; he didn't like to think what kind of cat this was, breaking and entering like a human thief.

Side by side they crouched over the skylight looking down where the cat had vanished among the jumbled furniture. Nothing moved. The reflections across a row of glass-faced china cabinets were as still as if time itself had stopped, the images of carved fretwork and tattered silk shawls lifeless and eternal, a dead montage. A heap of musical instruments, violins and trumpets and guitars, lay tumbled into the arms of a Victorian setee. An ancient bicycle wore a display of feathered hats suspended from its seat and handlebars. The cats heard no sound from the shop, only the hush of breeze around them tickling across the rooftops punctuated by the high-frequency calls of the little bats.

Clink. A metallic clunk jarred the night. Then a familiar scraping sound as the front door opened. The tinkle of its bell stifled quickly, as if someone had grabbed the clapper.

Two men spoke, their voices muted. The cats heard the scuff of shoes crossing the shop but could see no one. Soon they heard wooden drawers sliding out, then the ring of the shop's old-fashioned cash register as its drawer sprang open—sounds they knew well from visiting widow Medder. Joe found himself listening for a police car down on the street, hoping that a silent alarm might have gone off, alerting a patrol unit.

But would Mrs. Medder have an alarm, when she didn't even have a computer or a fax machine?

Celia Medder had opened the shop a year ago, after losing her husband and young child in a boating accident down near Santa Barbara; she had moved to Molena Point wanting to escape her painful memories, had started the little shop with her own antique furniture from the large home she no longer wanted, slowly buying more, driving once a month up into the gold-rush towns north of Sacramento looking for bargains. It had not been easy to make a go of her new business. The cats were fond of her; she always welcomed them, never chased them off the sofas or Victorian chairs. She would brush up the satin when they jumped down, but she never spoke to them harshly.

The night was so still that they needn't look over to know the street was empty. No soft radio from a police unit, no whisper of tires, no footsteps.

"Why would a burglar break into a used furniture shop?" Dulcie whispered. "Why not a bank or jewelry store? And where did that cat come from?" She cut him a sideways look. "A trained cat? Trained to open skylights? I don't think so."

Below them the reflections jumped suddenly across the china cabinets. A dozen images flared and swam as a man slipped between the crowded furniture, edging between chairs and couches. A thin, small man—hunched shoulders, a slouch hat, a wrinkled leather flight jacket. The black cat joined him, circling around his ankles, rubbing and preening. Suddenly all the history of their ancient race tumbled through Dulcie's head—Celtic kings, underground worlds, sleek shape-shifting princesses—all the old tales that the rest of the world thought of as fairy tales and that she knew were not. And the idea that this black burglar might be like themselves both excited and frightened her.

Man and cat moved through the room, out of sight. Dulcie and Joe heard cupboard doors sliding, then the clink of metal on metal, then the buzz of an electric tool.

"Drill," Joe said. "Sounds like they've found the safe."

"They must have had it spotted. It wasn't that easy to find, hidden in the back of that old cupboard."

Joe clawed at the skylight, digging at its frame to force the glass open, but before he could slide in, Dulcie bit the scruff of his neck, jerking him away. The skylight dropped with a thud.

He spun around, hissing at her. "Thank you very much. Now they know we're here. Just leave me alone, Dulcie."

"I won't. You'd be trapped down there. They could kill you before you got out. You think *that* will help Mrs. Medder? You think getting dead will catch a thief? And they didn't hear a thing. How could they, with the noise that drill's making?"

But the drilling stopped. In the silence they heard a series of thuds and bumps. Dulcie crept closer, listening. "What did they do, drill the lock off?"

"I'm guessing they drilled a small hole—enough to stick a periscope inside."

She gave him a narrow, amused glance.

"Not kidding. Miniature periscope, with a light on it."

"Sure."

He sighed impatiently. "A safe's lock is made of flat plates. Okay? Each one turns when you spin the dial. When you get them lined up, the lock opens."

"So?"

"So, if you can see them from the inside, you can line them up. The burglar drills a hole, puts the little periscope in—Captain Harper has one. It's about as big as a pencil but with a flexible neck. You stick it into the safe and watch the plates while you turn the dial."

Her green eyes widened. "You're serious."

"Harper showed Clyde. He took it from the evidence room after it wasn't needed anymore."

"No wonder you hang around home when the law comes over to play poker. It's wonderful, the things you learn from Max Harper."

"You needn't be sarcastic."

"I'm not being . . ." She stopped to listen. They heard the front door open and close and footsteps going away. Leaping to the roof's edge, they crouched with their paws in the gutter, peering down.

Below them, the sidewalk was empty. No sign of man nor cat. But footsteps whispered away, around the corner. Joe crouched to drop down to the awning. "We need a phone—need to call Harper. Maybe a squad car can pick them up before they get away."

"Not this time," she said softly.

He turned to stare at her, his yellow eyes wide. "What's with you?"

"You want Harper to know that one of the burglars is a cat?"

"I don't intend to tell him about the cat."

"So you don't say a word about the cat. Harper picks up the burglar. You know how tough he can be. There's no sign of forced entry, and Harper keeps at the guy about how he got in, until he caves. Tells Harper that a cat let him in, that he uses a trained cat."

"Come on, Dulcie. The cat is his secret weapon. He'll protect that beast like Fort Knox."

She gave him a long look. "There'll be cat hairs all over the store, on the guy's clothes, and around the skylight. Even if the guy keeps his secret, Harper will be suspicious. You know how thorough he is—and how paranoid about cats. You know how nervous he gets when there's a cat anywhere near a case."

Over the past year, Joe and Dulcie's telephone tips to Max Harper, in the guise of interested citizens, had led to key arrests in three Molena Point murders, resulting in six convictions. But each time, the cats themselves had been seen in embarrassing situations. This, and the fact that some of their tips had involved evidence that couldn't possibly have been discovered by a human informant, tended to make Max Harper nervous. He had, in short, some well-founded suspicions involving the feline persuasion.

"We don't need to add to his unease," Dulcie said. She looked deeply at Joe. "Let's leave this one alone. I have a bad feeling about this."

"Dulcie, sometimes you . . ."

Below them a shadow moved in the blackness at the edge of the awning. And the blackness exploded up at them—the black cat hit the roof inches from Joe, his fangs white in the moonlight, his claws gleaming sharp as knives, going straight for Joe's throat.

Dulcie charged between them.

The black tom froze, staring at her.

Joe and Dulcie faced the black cat, rigid with challenge.

Not a sound, not a twitch.

Then the tom relaxed, leering at Dulcie, his tail lashing provocatively, his neck bowed like the neck of a bull; when he smiled, his eyes burned keener than the fires of hell.

"I am Azrael."

Joe circled him, rumbling and snarling.

"Azrael," Dulcie said, moving between Joe and the black tom. "Azrael means Death Angel." She watched the cat intently.

The presence of another like themselves should be a cause for joy. Where had he come from? Why was he here in their village? As Joe moved again to attack, she cut him a look of warning. What good were teeth and claws, if they found out nothing about this cat?

"Azrael," she mewed softly, recalling the dark mythology. "Azrael of the million dark veils. Azrael who can spin the world on one claw.

"Azrael whose golden throne gleams in the sixth Heaven," she purred, glaring at Joe to be still. "Azrael of the four black wings and the four faces, and a thousand watchful eyes."

The tom smiled and preened at her but glanced narrowly at Joe.

"Azrael who stole from that store," Dulcie said, trying to sound amused. "Azrael who helped that man steal."

The black tom laughed. "And what do you think we stole? That junk furniture? Did you see him carrying away old chairs and hat racks?"

"You took her money."

"If we did, little queen, that's none of your affair." His purr was a ragged rumble; he towered over her, slow and insinuating; his amber eyes caressed her, devoured her—but when he reached out his nose to sniff her tail, she whirled, screaming feline curses, and Joe exploded, biting and slashing him, sinking his claws into the tom's back and neck. The two toms spun in a clawing, yowling whirlwind across the roofs, raking fur and swearing until Dulcie again thrust herself between them, fighting them both.

They spun apart and backed off, circling and snarling, crouching to leap again for the tender parts.

Joe attacked first—blood spattered Dulcie's face. But the tom sent him flying against a chimney. Joe shook his head and bolted into Azrael, cursing a string of human insults until Dulcie again drove them apart, battling like a wildcat; neither tom would hurt a queen.

"You want to bring the cops?" she hissed at them. "There are apartments above these shops. You make enough noise, someone will call the station."

The black tom smiled and turned away. He began to wash, as casual and easy as if there had never been a battle. But soon he paused, and drew himself up tall and erect like an Egyptian statue carved from ebony. "You two little cats," he said, looking them over as if they amused him. "You two little cats—I see death around you."

He studied them haughtily. "Do you not sense death?" He licked his paw. "There will be death in this village. Human death. I sense death—three human corpses. Death before the moon is again full.

"I see you two little cats standing over the bodies. I see your foolish pain—because humans are dead." He laughed coldly. "Humans. How very silly. Why would you care that a human dies? The world is overrun with humans."

"What do . . ." Dulcie began.

But a whistle from the street jerked the tomcat up, a call as soft as the cry of a night bird. He turned, leaped down into the awning, and was gone. They heard a muffled *oof* of breath as he hit the street. Heard his human partner speak to him, then footsteps.

Looking over the roof's edge, they watched the two drift away, up the street into darkness. Joe crouched to follow, but Dulcie pressed against him, urging him away from the edge.

"Don't," she said. "Please don't—he frightens me." She was demure and quiet. If she had ranted and snarled at him, he would have been off at once, after the pair.

"He scares me," she repeated, sitting down on the shingles. Joe looked back at her crossly, knowing he'd be sorry he hadn't followed. But he was puzzled, too. Dulcie was seldom afraid. Not this shivering, shrinking, huge-eyed kind of fear.

"Please," she said, "leave him alone. He might be like us. There might be a wonderful mystery about him. But he terrifies me."

Later, in the small hours when Joe and Dulcie had parted, as she snuggled down in the quilt beside Wilma, she dreamed of Azrael, and in sleep she shivered. Caught by the tom's amber eyes, she followed him along medieval lanes, was both frightened of him and fascinated. Winding across ancient rooftops they slipped among gargoyles and mythic creatures twisted and grotesque, beasts that mirrored the black tom's dark nature. Azrael before her, drawing her on, charming her, leading her in dream until she began to lose all judgment.

She'd always had vivid dreams. Sometimes, prophetic dreams. But this drama woke her, clawing the blankets, hissing with fear and unwanted emotions. Her thrashing woke Wilma, who sat up in bed and gathered Dulcie close, her long gray hair falling around them, her flannel nightgown warm against Dulcie. "Nightmare? A bad nightmare?"

Dulcie said nothing. She lay shivering against Wilma, trying to purr, feeling very ashamed of the way the black tom had made her feel.

She was Joe Grey's lady; her preoccupation with the stranger, even in dream, deeply upset her.

Wilma didn't press her for answers. She stroked Dulcie until she slept again, and this time as Dulcie dropped into the deep well of sleep she held her thoughts on Joe Grey and on home and on Wilma, pressing into her mind everyone dear to her, shutting out dark Azrael.

It was not until the next morning that Joe, brushing past Clyde's bare feet, leaping to the kitchen table and pawing open the morning *Gazette*, learned more about the burglary at Medder's Antiques. He read the article as Clyde stood at the stove frying eggs. Two over-easy for Clyde, one sunny-side up for Joe. Around Clyde's feet the three household cats and the elderly black Labrador crouched on the kitchen floor eating kibble, each at his or her own bowl. Only Joe was served breakfast on the table, and he certainly wasn't having kibble.

Clyde said kibble was good for his teeth, but so were whole wheat kitty treats laced with fish oil and added vitamins from Molena Point's Pet Gourmet. Choosing between P.G.'s delightful confections and store-bought kibble was no contest. Two of P.G.'s fish-shaped delicacies, at this moment, lay on his breakfast plate, which Clyde had placed just beside the newspaper. Clyde had arranged four sardines as well, and a thin slice of Brie, a nicely planned repast awaiting only the fried egg.

It had taken a bit of doing to get Clyde trained, but the effort had been worth it.

Standing on the morning paper sniffing the delicate aroma of good, imported sardines, he read the *Gazette*'s account of the burglary. The police did not know how the burglar had gotten into the store. There had been no sign of forced entry. No item of merchandise seemed to be missing. Fifteen hundred dollars had been taken, three hundred from the cash register, the balance from the locked safe. The safe had been drilled, a very professional job. Joe didn't know he was growling until Clyde turned from the stove.

"What? What are you reading?" Clyde brought the skillet to the table, dished up the eggs, then picked Joe up as if he were a bag of flour so he could see the paper.

Joe dangled impatiently as Clyde read.

Clyde set Joe down again, making no comment, and turned away, his face closed and remote.

They had been through this too many times. Clyde didn't like him messing around with burglaries and murders and police business. And Joe was going to do as he pleased. There was no way Clyde could stop him short of locking him in a cage. And Clyde Damen, even at his worst, would never consider such a deed—never be fool enough to attempt it.

Clyde sat down at the table and dumped pepper on his eggs. "So this is why you've been scowling and snarling all morning, this burglary."

"I haven't been scowling and snarling." Joe slurped up a sardine, dipping it in egg yolk. "Why would I bother with a simple break-and-enter? Max Harper can handle that stuff."

"Oh? Those small crimes are beneath you? So, then, what's with the worried scowl?"

Joe looked at him blankly and nipped off a bite of Brie.

Clyde reached across the table and nudged him. "What's going on? What's with you?"

"Nothing," Joe said coldly. "Is there some law that I have to tell you all my business?"

Clyde raised an eyebrow.

"So there's a new cat in the village. It's nothing to worry you, nothing for you to fret over."

Clyde was silent a moment, watching him. "I take it this is a tomcat. What did he do, come onto Dulcie?"

Joe glared.

Clyde grinned. "What else would make you so surly?" He mopped up egg with his toast. "I imagine you can handle the beast. I don't suppose this cat has anything to do with last night's burglary?"

Joe widened his eyes and laughed. "In what way? What would a cat have to do with a burglary? It's too early in the morning for dumb questions."

Clyde looked at him deeply, then rose and fetched the coffeepot, poured a fresh cup.

"You get the Sheetrock all torn out?"

"We did, and hauled it to the dump. No more Sheetrock dust, you and Dulcie can hunt mice to your little hearts' content without sneezing—until we start hanging new Sheetrock, of course."

The five-apartment unit that Clyde had bought was a venture Joe considered incredibly foolhardy. No way Clyde Damen was going to turn that neglected dump into a sound rental investment. The fact that Clyde was working on the project himself turned Joe weak with amusement.

The only sensible thing Clyde had done on the venture was to hire his girlfriend, Charlie Getz, who operated Charlie's Fix-It, Clean-It. Charlie's business was relatively new. She had only a small crew—just two women—but she did good work. Her cleaning lady was sixty-year-old Mavity Flowers, who was a tiny, skinny creature but a surprisingly hard worker. The other employee, Pearl Ann Jamison, was a real find. Pearl Ann not only cleaned for Charlie, she was handy at light carpentry and could turn out professional Sheetrock work, from installation of the heavy wallboard to mudding and taping. The rest of the work on the building, the wiring and plumbing, Charlie and Clyde were farming out to subcontractors.

Joe finished his breakfast, nosed his plate out of the way, and began to wash, thinking about the burglary. He supposed the antique shop had been the first, as he'd seen nothing in the papers about any other similar thefts. He didn't let himself dwell on the nature of the black tom or where he came from but kept his mind on the immediate problem, wondering what other small village businesses the man and cat planned to hit.

But maybe this had been a one-time deal. Maybe the pair was just passing through, heading up the coast—maybe they'd simply needed some walking-around money. Maybe they were already gone, had hauled out of Molena Point for parts unknown.

Sure. The village should be so lucky.

No, this burglary hadn't been impromptu. The planning was too precise, the team's moves too deliberate and assured, as if they had done their research. As if they knew very well that the quiet village was a sitting duck, and they knew just how to pluck it.

He hated to think that that cat might have been prowling the shops for days—maybe weeks—and he and Dulcie hadn't known about it, hadn't scented the beast or seen him. He imagined the cat and the old man idling in Mrs. Medder's antique shop getting friendly with her, the old man making small talk as he cased the place looking for a safe or a burglar alarm, the black tom wandering innocently rubbing around the old woman's ankles, purring and perhaps accepting little tidbits of her lunch while he, too, checked the layout, leaped up to stare into the drawer of the open cash register, and searched the shadows for an alarm system.

He didn't like that scenario. It was bad enough for a human to steal from the village shops. A cat had no business doing this stuff.

Leaping from the table to the sink, pacing restlessly across the counter and glaring out the window, Joe wished he'd followed those two last night. He wouldn't make that mistake again. Dulcie could find excuses to avoid confronting the black tomcat if she chose, but he was going to nail that little team. Licking egg from his whiskers as he watched the rising sun lift above the Molena Point hills, Joe Grey's lust for justice flamed at least as bright as that solar orb—burned with a commitment as powerful and predatory as any human cop.

4

CHARLIE GETZ had no reason to suspect, when she woke early Saturday morning, that she was about to be evicted from her cozy new apartment, that by the time most of the village sat down to breakfast she'd be shoving cardboard boxes and canvas duffles into her decrepit Chevy van, dumping all her worldly possessions back into her aunt's garage—from which she had so recently removed them. Thrown out, given the boot, on the most special day of her life, on a day that she had wanted to be perfect.

She'd already spent three months sponging off Aunt Wilma, had moved in with Wilma jobless and nearly broke and with no prospects, had lived rent-free in Wilma's guest room after abandoning her failed career.

During that time she'd launched her new venture, put what little cash she had into running ads, buying the old van and used cleaning and carpentry equipment, hiring the best help she could find on short notice. She was twenty-eight years old. Starting Charlie's Fix-It, Clean-It and renting her own apartment, taking responsibility for her own life after wasting six years in San Francisco had been one big strike for independence. A huge step toward joining—belatedly—the adult world.

Now here she was back to square one, homeless again.

She had loved being with Wilma, loved coming home to a cozy house, to a blazing fire and a nice hot meal, loved being pampered, but she valued, more, being her own provider.

Now, waking at dawn before she had any notion that an eviction notice was tucked beside her front door, she snuggled down into the covers, looking around her little studio with deep satisfaction. The one room pleased her immensely, though the furnishings weren't much, just her easel, her single cot, her secondhand breakfast table, and two mismatched wooden chairs. Open cardboard boxes stacked on their sides like shelves held her neatly folded clothes. But through her open windows a cool breeze blew in, smelling pleasantly of the sea, and above the village rooftops the sunrise, this morning, was a wonder of watercolor tints, from pink to pale orange streaked among islands of dark clouds.

The coastal foothills would be brightening now as the sun rose behind them, casting its light down on the small village, onto the narrow, wandering lanes and dark, leathery oak trees and the maze of slanted, angled rooftops, and reflecting from the windows of the little restaurants and shops—the morning sun sending its light into the windows of the Aronson Gallery onto her own drawings, picking out her work with fingers of light.

What a strange sensation, to think that she belonged to a gallery, that her work was to be part of a real exhibit. She still couldn't believe her luck, not only to be included with six well-known artists but to see her drawings occupying more than half the gallery's front window—a real vote of confidence for a newcomer. The exhibit had been a bonus out of nowhere, unforeseen and amazing.

Four years of art school and two years trying to find her way as a commercial artist, a dozen trial-and-error, entry-level advertising jobs that she knew weren't right for her, nor she for them, had led at last to the realization that she would never make a living in the art world. Her failure had left her feeling totally defeated—a misfit not only in her chosen field but in life. Only now, after she had abandoned all idea of supporting herself in the arts, had anyone been interested in her drawings.

Reaching to her nightstand, she switched on the travel-size coffeepot that she had prepared the night before, wondering if her flowered India skirt and sandals and the low-necked blue T-shirt *were* the right clothes for the opening or if she'd better try the black dress again, with the silver necklace her aunt had loaned her. She imagined the gallery as it would be tonight, lighted and festive, thinking about the crowd of strangers, hoping she could remember people's names.

As the scent of coffee filled the room she sat up, pushing her pillow behind her, and poured a steaming mug, blowing on the brew to cool it. Coffee in bed was pure luxury, a little moment to spoil herself before she started the day, pulled on her jeans and boots and a work shirt, and hurried out to be on the job by eight, installing Sheetrock and trying to figure out how to do things she'd never done before. She would not, once she got moving, stop again until dark overtook her, except for a hasty sandwich with her girls, maybe with Clyde, and with whatever subcontractor might be working.

Leaning back into the pillows, she planned her day and the week ahead, laying out the work for the plumber, the sprinkler man, and the electrician, and watching, through her open windows, the sky brighten to flame, the sunrise staining the room, and laying a wash of pink over her framed drawings. Her studies of the two cats looked back at her, so alert and expectant that she had to smile. Dulcie had such a wicked little grin, such a slant-eyed, knowing look, as if she kept some wonderful secret.

The portraits of Joe Grey were more reserved. Tomcat dignity, she thought, amused. Drawing Joe was like drawing draped satin or polished pewter—the tomcat was so sleek and beautifully muscled, his charcoal-gray coat gleaming like velvet.

But his gaze was imperious. So deeply appraising that sometimes he made her uncomfortable. Sometimes she could swear that she saw, in Joe Grey's eyes, a judgment far too perceptive, a watchfulness too aware and intense for any cat.

Charlie didn't understand what it was about those two; both cats had a presence that set them apart from other felines.

Maybe she just knew them better. Maybe all cats had that quality of awareness, when you knew them. Her thoughts fled to last night when she had stood alone in the moonlit village looking up at the black rooftops, stood touched by that vast, wheeling space, and had glimpsed two cats leaping between the rooftops across the pale, night sky, and she felt again a wonderful delight in their freedom.

She had gone out to dinner alone, hadn't felt like a can of soup or peanut butter and crackers, which was all her bare cupboard had offered. And she didn't feel like calling Clyde. Their dating was casual; he probably would have been happy to run out for a quick hamburger, but she'd wanted to be by herself. Besides, she'd been with him half the day, working on the house. She'd been tired and irritable from dealing with a hired carpenter, had wanted to walk the village alone, watch the evening draw down, have a quiet dinner and then home to bed. When she had taken on the job of refurbishing Clyde's newly purchased relic of an apartment house, she had bitten off almost more than she could chew. She'd had no intention, when she started Charlie's Fix-It, Clean-It, of becoming a remodeling service. The business was meant to be just what it said: minor household repairs and painting—replacing a few shingles, spiffing up the yard, window washing, gutter cleaning, a good scrub down, total maintenance for the village homes and cottages. Not tearing out and replacing walls, supervising workmen, replacing ancient plumbing. She had no contractor's license, but Clyde was, for all practical purposes, his own contractor. All they had to do was satisfy the various building inspectors.

She'd gotten home from work as the summer twilight faded into a clear, chill night, had peeled off her sweaty jeans and shirt, showered, put on clean denims and a warm sweater. Leaving her apartment, she had walked through the village down to the shore ten blocks south, moving quickly between wandering tourists. This was the beginning of the Fourth of July weekend, and along the narrow streets, NO VACANCY signs glowed discreetly among climbing nasturtiums and bougainvillea.

She had chosen a circuitous route, cutting across Ocean to the south side of the village, slowing to look in the windows of the Latin American Boutique, enjoying the brightly painted carvings and red-toned weavings, admiring and coveting the beautiful crafts and trying not to make nose prints on the glass.

She had met the shop's owner, Sue Marble, a white-haired woman of maybe fifty who, people said, kept the store primarily so she could claim a tax write-off on her frequent Latin American trips. Not a bad deal, more power to her.

But as she had moved along beside the window, a Peruvian death mask gleamed through her own reflection, an ugly face superimposed over her face, framed by her wild red hair. The image had amused her—then frightened her. Swiftly she had turned away, hurried away toward the shore.

She hit the beach at Tenth Avenue, and had walked south a mile on the hard sand, then turned back up Ocean to The Bakery, thinking that a glass of Chablis would be nice, and perhaps crab Newburg. She thought sometimes that she led herself through life only with these little treats, like beguiling a mule with a carrot.

But why not treat herself? Tuck some bits of fun in with the hard work? Hanging Sheetrock all day was no picnic—and the heavy work had left her ravenous.

The Bakery, a rambling structure of weathered shingles, had been a summer-vacation house in the early 1900s. A deep porch ran along the front, facing a little seaside park of sand dunes and low, twisted oak trees spreading like dark, giant hands over the curves of sand and sweeps of dark ice plant. She'd been disappointed that all the terrace tables were taken, but then had spied a small corner table and soon was settled facing the darkening dunes, ordering wine and the Newburg, quietly celebrating the first gallery exhibit of her drawings.

After her father died, it was her mother's subtle control that had eased her in the direction of art school, to develop the talent her mother thought was her strongest. Her mother would not consider that her skills at repair work and at organizing the work of others had any value. Sipping her wine, Charlie thought about her mother with regret and disappointment. Her mother had died a year before she finished art school.

Beyond The Bakery veranda, the breaking waves were tipped with phosphorescence, and above them the night sky flowed like surging water, its light seeming also to ebb and change. She'd been so physically tired from the day's work that the Chablis had given her a nice buzz, and the conversations around her were subdued, a relaxed ambience of soft voices against the hushing surf. When her Newburg arrived she'd made herself eat slowly, not wolf the good dish but savor each bite—had to remind herself this wasn't noon on the job, eating a sandwich with the work crew and with Mavity and Pearl Ann and Clyde, all of them starved. Had to remind herself this was not supper with Clyde. Eating with Clyde was much like eating with the carpenters; she was inclined to follow his lead, devour her meal as if it would remain on the table only briefly and must be consumed before it got away.

But Clyde was good company. And he was honest, quick to see the truth of a situation. If he was lacking in some social graces, who cared? There was nothing put-on or fake about him.

That first morning, when they went up to look at the five-apartment building after he signed the escrow papers, he'd been so excited. Leading her in through the weedy patio and through those moldering rooms, he'd been deep in the grip of euphoria, imagining what the place would look like when they'd refurbished it—imagining he could do most of the work himself, just a little help from her. *Just a little paint, Charlie. A bit of patching.* They'd agreed to exchange labor. She'd help with the house, presenting him with bills that he'd honor by working on her declining Chevy van.

Of course there was more needed than patching, but the five apartments had nice large rooms and high ceilings, and Clyde had envisioned the final result just as clearly as he saw the possibilities in restoring an old, vintage car.

The difference was, he knew what it took to restore a car. Beneath his skilled hands the Mercedeses and BMWs and Bentleys of Molena Point purred and gleamed, as cared for as fine jewelry. But Clyde was no carpenter. To Clyde Damen, carpentry was a foreign language.

In order to pay cash for the building, he had sold his five beautifully restored antique cars, including the classic red Packard touring car that he so loved. The sales nearly broke his heart, he had done every speck of work on those cars himself in his spare time. But he was too tight to pay interest on a mortgage, and she didn't blame him.

As the dining terrace began to empty, she had dawdled over her dinner enjoying her own company, quietly watching the surf's endless rolling, feeling its power—spawned by the interplay of wind, the moon's pull, and the centrifugal whirling of the earth. The sea's unending motion seemed to repeat the eternal power of the universe—its vast and unceasing life.

She relished her idle thoughts, her idle moments, the little pauses in which to let her mind roam.

After the Newburg she had treated herself to a flan and coffee, and it was past midnight when she paid her bill, left the veranda, and headed home through the softly lighted village. The streets were nearly empty. She imagined the tourists all tucked up in their motel rooms, with maybe a fire burning on the hearth, perhaps wrapped in their warm robes nursing a nightcap of brandy.

Walking home, she had paused to look in the window of a sporting goods shop at a beautiful leather coat that she would never buy; she'd rather have a new cement mixer. It was then, turning away, that her glance was drawn to the rooftops by swift movement: Two dark shadows had sailed between the peaks. She had caught only a glimpse. Owls? A pair of large night birds?

But they were gone, the sky was empty.

No, there they were. Two silhouettes, not flying but racing along a peaked ridge, leaping from roof to roof then dropping out of sight.

Cats! They were cats; she had seen a lashing tail against the clouds and sharply peaked ears. Two cats, playing across the rooftops.

And she had to laugh. There was no mistaking Joe Grey's tail-less posterior, and his white paws and white nose. She had stood very still, setting carefully into memory the cats' swift flight against the pale clouds. They appeared again, and as they fled up another peak and leaped between dark ridges, scorching in and out among the tilting roofs, she had itched for a piece of charcoal, a bit of paper.

As she stood watching them, she heard a young couple laughing somewhere ahead, the woman's voice soft. Glancing to the street she didn't see the man and woman, but their conversation was playful, challenging and happy; she couldn't make out their words. Then silence, as if they had turned up a side street.

And the cats were gone. She had stood alone on the sidewalk, her painter's mind teeming with the two racing felines, with the joy of their carefree flight.

But now, lying in bed, seeing the leaping cats among the darkly angled rooftops, she felt a sudden chill.

Puzzled, sliding out of bed, she refilled her coffee cup and stood before the easel looking at the quick sketch she had done, from memory, before she went to sleep, the swift lines of charcoal on newsprint, her hasty strokes blocking in jutting roof lines against the sky, and the lithe, swift cats leaping across—and a sense of threat was there, that she had not meant to lend to the scene. Studying the drawing, she shivered.

Last night she had been so charmed by the cats' grace and freedom, by their wild joy; she had felt only pleasure in the hasty drawing—but she saw now that the drawing did not reflect joy. Its spirit was dark, pensive. Somehow she had infused the composition with foreboding. Its shadowed angles implied a dark threat.

Threat *to* the cats? Or threat *because* of the cats?

Perplexed, she turned away. Carrying her coffee, she headed for the shower.

The bathroom was tiny. Setting her coffee cup on the edge of the sink basin, she slid under the hot, steaming water of the shower, her mind fully on the sketch.

What had guided her hand last night? Those two little cats were dear to her; she had gotten to know Dulcie well while she was staying with Wilma. And if not for her drawings of Joe and Dulcie, sketching them for her own pleasure, her work would not have been seen by Sicily Aronson. She would never have been invited to join Sicily's prestigious group. Without Joe and Dulcie, there would be no exhibit for her tonight at Sicily's fine gallery.

Letting the hot water pound on her back, reaching out for a sip of coffee, she told herself she had better get her mind on the day's work. She had building materials to order and three subcontractors to juggle so they didn't get in each other's way. Coming out of the shower to dress and make a peanut-butter sandwich, checking over her work list, she forgot the dark drawing.

But then as she opened the front door, carrying her denim work jacket and the paper bag with her lunch, a folded sheet of paper fluttered down against her boot, as if it had been stuffed between the door and the molding. Snatching it up before it blew away, unfolding it, she read the neatly typed message.

> Charlie:
>
> You'd be a good tenant, if you didn't clutter up the yard. You've had a week, and two previous warnings, to get your stuff out of the backyard. The other tenants are complaining. They want to lie in the sun back there, not fall over wheelbarrows and shovels. I have no choice. You are in violation of your rental contract. This is a formal notice to vacate the apartment and all premises by tonight. Any item you leave behind, inside the apartment or in the yard—cement mixer, buckets, the entire clutter—will be mine to keep and dispose of.

She set her lunch bag on the porch, dropped her jacket on top, and read the note again. Looking down toward her landlord's apartment, just below hers, she wanted to snatch up that neat little man and smear him all over his neat little yard.

Swinging back inside, she grabbed her stacked cardboard boxes and began shoving dishes and pots and pans in on top of her folded clothes. Jerking her few hanging garments from the closet, she rolled them into a bundle, snatched her framed drawings off the wall, and carried the first load down to her van. Halfway through her packing, she grabbed up the phone and called Clyde, told him she'd be a bit late. Didn't tell him why. And within an hour she was out of there, chalking up another defeat.

5

THE BRIGHTLY lighted gallery, from the aspect of the two cats, was an obstacle course of human legs and feet. They had to move lively toward the back to avoid being stepped on by spike heels, wedge sandals, and hard, polished oxfords that looked as lethal as sledgehammers. Slinking between silken ankles and well-creased trouser cuffs, they slipped beneath Sicily Aronson's desk into shadow where they could watch, untrampled, the champagne-fueled festivities.

In Joe's opinion, the way to attend an art exhibit was from, say, a rooftop several blocks removed. But Dulcie had to be in the middle, listening to the tangle of conversations, sniffing expensive French perfumes and admiring dangling jewelry and elegant hair arrangements. "No one will notice us—they're all talking at once, trying to impress each other."

"Right. Of course Sicily won't notice us. So why is she swooping in this direction like a hungry barn owl?" The gallery owner was pushing through the crowd with her usual exuberance. "On stage," Joe muttered. "Always on stage." She was dressed in silver lamé evening pajamas that flapped around her ankles, a flowing silver scarf that swung around her thin thighs, and an amazing array of clinking jewelry. Kneeling and laughing, she peered under the desk at them, then scooped Dulcie into her arms. Pulling Joe out, too, she cuddled them like two teddy bears; Joe had to grit his teeth to keep from clawing her, and of course Dulcie gave him that *don't-you-dare* scowl.

"You two look beautiful, so sleek and brushed," Sicily cooed, snuggling them against her silver bosom. "This is lovely to have you here—after all, you are the main models, you dear cats. Did Wilma bring you? Where is Wilma?"

Joe wanted to throw up. Dulcie purred extravagantly—she was such a sucker for this stuff. Whenever she visited Sicily, wandering into the gallery, Sicily had a treat for her, a little snack put aside from Molena Point's Pet Gourmet. And Sicily kept a soft sweater for Dulcie to nap on; she had figured out quickly that to Dulcie, pretty garments, silk and velvet and cashmere, were the pièce de résistance. Only once, when Dulcie trotted out of the shop dragging a handwoven vicuña scarf, did Sicily fling a cross word at her and run out to retrieve the treasure. Now, fawning and petting them and effectively blocking their escape, she reached behind the desk to fetch a blue velvet cushion and laid it on the blotter. "You two stay right here—just curl up and look pretty—and I'll fix a plate for you." Leaning down, she stared into Joe's eyes, stroking him and scratching behind his ears. "Caviar, Joe Grey? Smoked turkey?"

Joe felt himself weakening.

But as Sicily left them, a big woman in a plum-colored dress descended, pushing her way out of the crowd. "Oh, the two little models. Oh, look how sweet."

Joe growled and raised his paw. Dulcie nudged him.

"Isn't that cute. Look at him put up his paw to shake hands. Just like a little dog."

The lady's male companion had sensibly stepped back from Joe. But the woman reached for him. "Oh, they look *just* like their portraits. Such dear little cats. Come and pet them, Howard. Look how sweet, the way they're posing here on the desk, so obedient."

She patted Joe on the head like a dog, a gesture guaranteed, under most circumstances, to elicit a bloody stump. He held his temper with heroic effort, but he calmed as she chose a slice of ham from her plate and gave them each a share.

He was beginning to feel more charitable when a woman in a white dress joined them. "Oh, the darling kitties, the kitties in the drawings." And an elderly couple headed their way, practically cooing. A regular crowd was gathering. Joe eyed them sourly. Even the good party food wasn't enough to put up with this. As other guests circled the desk reaching to pet them, Joe lost it. Lashing out at the nearest hand, he leaped past it, hit the floor running, sped out the door and across the street and up a bougainvillea vine. Didn't stop until he was on the roof of Mara's Leather Shop, pacing among the vents.

Dulcie didn't follow him. Probably she'd stay in there all night, lapping up the attention.

Stretching out beside a warm chimney, he dozed intermittently and irritably. His view from the roof was directly in through the gallery's wide windows and open front door, where the crowd had gathered around a white-clothed table as a tuxedoed waiter served champagne. It was more than an hour before Dulcie came trotting out between a tangle of elegantly clad ankles, scanned the rooftops, and saw him looking over. Lifting her tail like a happy flag, she crossed the street and swarmed up the vine to join him.

"You didn't have to be so surly. You knew we'd be petted. Cats in a public place always get petted."

"*Petted?* Mauled is the word. You said no one would notice us."

She settled down beside him, her belly against the warm shingles. "You missed some good party food."

"I'll have my share in the alley."

"Suit yourself. I had duck liver canapés from the hand of my favorite movie star." She sighed deeply. "He might be sixty-some, but he's some macho hombre."

"Big deal. So some Hollywood biggie feeds you duck liver like a zoo animal."

"Not at all. He was very polite and cordial. And he's not from Hollywood; you know very well that he lives in Molena Point. What a nice man. He treated *me* like a celebrity—he told me I have beautiful eyes." And she gave him a clear green glance, bright and provocative.

Joe turned away crossly. "So where are Charlie and Clyde? Fashionably late is one thing. Charlie's going to miss her own party."

"They'll show. Clyde told Wilma he'd keep Charlie away until there was a real mob, until she could make a big entrance."

"This *is* a mob. And Charlie isn't the kind for a big entrance."

"She will be, tonight."

Joe snorted.

"It's her party. Why not a grand entrance?"

"Females. Everything for show."

"I've seen you make a big entrance—stroll into the living room when Clyde has company. Wait until conversation's in full swing, then swagger in so everyone stops talking. Starts calling to you, *kitty kitty kitty*, and making little lovey noises."

"That is a totally different matter. That is done for a specific purpose."

Dulcie cut her eyes at him, and smiled.

The game was to get the crowd's attention and then, when they were all calling and making a fuss, to pick out the person who remained withdrawn and quiet. Who did *not* want to pet the kitty.

Immediately one made a beeline for the cat hater. A jump into their lap, a persistent rubbing and kneading and waving your tail in their face, and the result was most rewarding. If your victim had a really severe case of ailurophobia, the effect was spectacular.

When the routine worked really well, when you had picked the right mark, your victim would turn as white as skimmed milk. If you could drool and rub your face against theirs, that was even better. There was nothing half as satisfying as a nice evening of ailurophobe harassment. Such little moments were to be treasured—such fleeting pleasures in life made up for all the millions of human rebuffs, for centuries of shabby human slights and maltreatment.

"Here they come," Dulcie said, pressing forward over the roof gutter, her ears pricked, the tip of her tail twitching with excitement.

Clyde pulled up directly in front of the gallery, his yellow '29 Chevy convertible commanding immediate attention. This was the car's maiden appearance. The top was down, and the machine was dazzling. He had completely overhauled the vintage model, had given it mirror-bright metal detailing, pearly, canary-toned paint, pale yellow leather upholstery, and of course the engine purred like a world-champion Siamese. The car's creamy tones set off Charlie's flaming hair to perfection.

Her red, curling mane hung loose across her shoulders over a dark tank top, and as Clyde handed her out, her flowered India skirt swirled around her ankles in shades of red, pink, and orange. The cats had never seen Charlie in high-heeled sandals, had never seen her in a skirt.

"Wow," Joe said, hanging over the roof, ogling.

"Oh, my," Dulcie said. "She's beautiful."

Tonight they saw none of Charlie's usual shyness. She looked totally wired, her cheeks flaming as she took Clyde's hand and stepped to the curb.

Clyde's chivalry prompted them to stare, too, as he gave Charlie his arm and escorted her into the gallery. Clyde himself looked elegant, scrubbed and shaven and sharply turned out in a black sport coat over a white turtleneck and a good-looking pair of jeans. For Clyde, this was formal attire.

"There's the mayor," Dulcie said, "and his wife. And look—the president of the art association."

Joe didn't know the president of the art association from a rat's posterior. Nor did he care. But he cared about Clyde and Charlie. He watched with almost parental pride as they pushed into the gallery and were mobbed with greetings and well-wishers. Crouched on the edge of the roof, the two cats totally enjoyed Charlie's happy moment. They remained watching as the party spilled out onto the sidewalk among a din of conversation and laughter, and the scents of perfumes and champagne and caviar caressed them on the night breeze.

But later when two waiters headed away toward Jolly's Deli carrying a stack of nearly empty trays that they had replaced with fresh servings, the cats left the roof, padding along behind them, their attention on those delectable scraps.

Jolly's Deli catered most of the local affairs, the gallery openings and weddings and the nicest parties. And whatever delicacies were left over, George Jolly set out on paper plates in the alley for the enjoyment of the village cats.

Of course the old man put out deli scraps several times every day, but party fare was the best. An astute cat, if he checked the *Gazette*'s social page or simply used his nose, could dine as elegantly, in Jolly's alley, as Molena Point's rich and famous.

And the alley provided more than a free handout. Through frequent use, it had become the city version of a feline hunting path, a communal by-way shared by all the local cats.

Some people view cats as reclusive loners, but that is not the case. Any cat could tell you that a feline is simply more discerning than a dog, that cats take a subtler view of social interaction.

When several cats happened into the alley at one time, they did not circle each other snarling like ill-mannered hounds—unless, of course, they were toms on the make. But in a simple social situation, each cat sat down to quietly study his or her peers, communicating in a civilized manner by flick of ear, by narrowing of eyes, by twitching tail, following a perceptive protocol as to who should proceed first, who merited the warmest patch of sunshine or the preferred bench on which to nap.

The village cats had established in Jolly's alley, as well, a center for feline messages, a handy post office where, through scents left on flowerpot and doorway, one could learn which cats were with kitten or had had their kittens, which ladies were feeling amorous, or if there was a new cat in the village.

Only in the hierarchy of the supper plate did the biggest and strongest prevail—but George Jolly did not tolerate fights.

Such social commerce pleased Joe and Dulcie despite the void that separated them from normal cats. After all, every cat was unique. The lack of human language didn't make the other cats imperceptive or unwise; each could enjoy the world in his own way. And, Joe thought, how many cats would *want* to read the newspaper or use the phone?

But tonight they had the alley to themselves, the little brick-paved retreat was their own small corner of civilized ambiance, softly lit by the wrought-iron lamps at either end of the lane, perfumed by the jasmine vine that concealed Jolly's garbage cans.

The two waiters had disappeared inside, but George Jolly must have been watching for visitors, because as the cats flopped down to roll on the warm bricks, the back door opened and the old man was there, his white apron extending wide over his ample stomach as he knelt to place a paper plate before them, a little snack of smoked salmon and chopped egg and Beluga caviar.

They approached the offering purring, Dulcie waving her tail, and George Jolly stood smiling and nodding. Jolly loved providing these little repasts—he took a deep delight in the cats' pleasure.

Kneeling for a moment to stroke them, he soon rose again and turned away to his kitchen like any good chef, allowing his guests privacy in which to enjoy their meal. They were crouched over the plate nibbling at the caviar when, above them, a dark shadow leaped across the sky from roof to roof, and the black tom paced the shingles looking down at them—observing the loaded deli plate.

Dropping to an awning and then to the bricks, he swaggered toward them snarling a challenge deep in his throat, a growl of greed and dominance.

Dulcie screamed at him and crouched to slash; Joe flew at him, raking. At the same moment, the back door flew open and George Jolly ran out swinging a saucepan.

"No fighting! You cats don't fight here! You cats behave in my alley!"

Joe and Dulcie backed away glancing at each other, but Azrael stood his ground, snarling and spitting at Jolly.

"Stop that, you black beast. Don't you challenge me!" Jolly hefted the pan. "You eat nice or I don't feed you. I take the plate away." He looked hard at the three of them. "I don't put out my best imported for you to act like street rabble—you are Molena Point cats, not alley bums.

"Except you," Jolly said, glaring at Azrael. "I don't know you, you black monster. Well, wherever you come from, you snarl again, you get a smack in the muzzle."

George Jolly could never have guessed the true effect of his words. He had no idea that the three cats understood him, he knew only that his tone would frighten and perhaps shame them. He glared hard at Azrael—Azrael blazed back at him, his amber eyes sparking rage, and he began to stalk the old man, crouching as if he would spring straight into Jolly's face.

"Don't you threaten me," Jolly snapped, swinging the saucepan. "You learn some manners or you'll be snarling at the dogcatcher." He stood glaring until Azrael backed away switching his tail, his head high, and turned and swaggered off up the alley—until the formidable Death Angel vanished into the night.

Joe and Dulcie did not see Azrael again until some hours later as they prowled the rooftops. Pale clouds had gathered across the moon, and there was no sound; the bats had gone to roost or perch or whatever bats did hanging upside down in their pokey little niches beneath the eaves. Who knew why bats would hunt one night and not the next? Presumably, Joe thought, it had to do with how bright the sky—yet why would bats care, when they hunted by radar? On the roofs around them, the shadows were marbled by moonlight. Above them they heard a barn owl call, sending shivers. Even Joe Grey respected the claws and beak of the barn owl.

When the clouds parted and the full moon brightened the rooftops, across the moon's face the owl came winging. He swooped low and silent. The cats crouched to run. Screaming a booming cry, he dove, heading for the shadows beyond them.

They heard the boom of his wings beating against the roof, and heard screaming—the owl's scream and a cat's scream, then the frantic flurrying of feathers, the thud of bodies . . .

The owl exploded into the sky and was gone.

And in the moon's gleam the black cat sauntered out swaggering and spitting feathers.

Unaware of them, he slipped along seeming none the worse for his encounter. Pausing as before at each window and skylight, looking in, he lingered at a thin dormer window. He reared suddenly, clawing at the frame.

A wrenching creak slashed the night as the casement banged open.

Below on the street the cats heard footsteps, and when they fled over the roofs to look, they saw Azrael's human partner pacing, peering impatiently in through a glass door below a liquor store sign, his gray hair tangled around the collar of his wrinkled leather jacket, his boots, when he fidgeted, chuffing softly on the concrete.

The instant the door opened from inside, the old man slipped in. The cats, dropping down onto the hanging sign then to the sidewalk, crouched beneath a car where they could see through the plate glass.

Within, a faint, swinging light shone as the old man shielded his flashlight behind his hand, directing its beam along rows of bottles where Azrael paced, his tail lashing against the rich labels.

At the cash register, the old man bent over the lock and inserted a metal pick, his thin face lined and intent.

Within minutes he had the drawer open and was snatching out stacks of bills. Cleaning out the shallow tray, he lifted it, spilling loose change onto the floor as he grabbed at the larger bills that lay beneath; the night was so still they heard every coin drop.

"Why do shopkeepers do that?" Dulcie whispered. "Why do they leave money in the register?"

"Because the village has never had that much trouble. Don't you wonder if this old boy knew that—if he knew what an easy mark Molena Point is? Yet he has to be a stranger—I'd remember that old man."

They watched him stuff wads of bills into his pockets while, behind him, Azrael wound back and forth along the liquor shelf smiling and rubbing against the bottles.

"Cut the purring!" the old man snapped. "You sound like a spavined outboard. And don't leave cat hair stuck to everything."

"I never leave cat hair. Have you ever seen me shed?"

"Of course you shed. Everything I own is covered with black fur."

Azrael leaned from the shelf, peering over his partner's shoulder. "Get those tens—they can't trace tens so easy."

"Who's going to trace anything? No one marks their money in this burg. You're talking like some big-assed bank artist."

"How do you know they don't?"

"Don't be so paranoid."

"It's you that's paranoid—getting jumpy because I purr and grousing about cat hair."

The old man smoothed his thin gloves where they had wrinkled over his fingers and closed the register, and the two slipped out the front door.

"Don't forget to lock it," the cat hissed.

"Don't be so damn bossy."

"Don't get smart with me, old man. You'll be running this party alone."

The man and cat stiffened as, half a block away, a prowling police car turned into the street. As it shone its light along the storefronts in routine inspection, the two burglars slid through the shadows into the alley, were gone as completely as if they had never been there.

The patrol car didn't slow. The moment it had passed, the two appeared again, heading up Ocean. As they moved away, Joe and Dulcie followed, slipping along beneath the parked cars. Joe was determined to stay with them tonight, to see where they went to ground. Dulcie didn't like this, but she was unwilling to stay behind.

The two burglars proceeded up Ocean for four blocks, then turned down toward the Fish Shack. The old man paused before entering. "You want the cod or the shrimp?"

"The shrimp—what these stateside yokels pass off as shrimp. Poor substitute for what we get at home."

"You're not at home, so stop bitching." The little man disappeared inside. The cat turned away to the curb where he sniffed at the messages left by passing four-legged citizens. If he scented Joe and Dulcie over the smell of other cats and dogs and fish and axle grease, he gave no indication. His partner returned dangling a white paper bag liberally splotched with grease.

"No shrimp. You'll have to eat fish and chips."

"Couldn't you have gotten crab?"

"Didn't think to ask. Let's get on, before the law comes back." And off they went, man and cat walking side by side bickering companionably, two swaggering lowlifes with the cocky walk of drunks leaving a cheap bar.

6

BEYOND WILMA'S open shutters, the neighborhood was drowned by fog, the cottages and trees hidden in the thick mist, the gnarled branches of the oak tree that ruled her front garden faded as white as if the tree had vanished and only its ghost remained. Standing at the window sipping her morning coffee, she thought that it was the coastal fog, as much as Molena Point's balmy days, that had drawn her back to her childhood village to spend her retirement years. She had always loved the fog, loved its mystery—had wandered the foggy neighborhoods as a little girl pretending she had slipped into a secret and magical world.

At dawn this morning, she had taken a long walk along the shore listening to the breakers muffled and hidden within the white vail, then home again to a hot cup of coffee and to prepare breakfast for her company.

Behind her, the Sunday paper lay scattered comfortably across her Kirman rug, and beside the fire, Clyde sprawled on the velvet loveseat reading the sports page. On the other side of the hearth, lounging in the flowered chaise, Bernine Sage pored over the financial section. Neither had spoken in some time. Clyde's preoccupation was normal; Bernine's silence came across as self-centered and cold.

She would not ordinarily have invited Bernine to breakfast or for any meal, but this morning she'd had no choice. Bernine had been at her door late last night when she arrived home from the opening. Having fought with her current lover, needing a place to stay, she seemed to think that it was Wilma's responsibility to offer her a bed; she hadn't asked if Wilma *had* company or if her presence would be inconvenient. "Why I ever moved in with that idiot—what a selfish clod. And not a motel room left. I've called and called. Damn the holidays."

After getting Bernine settled, Wilma had left a note on the kitchen table hoping Charlie would see it.

Bernine is in the guest room with you, I'm sorry. She had a fight with her live-in.

Charlie had seen the note, all right. When Wilma came out at five this morning, the scrap of paper was in the trash, wadded into a tight ball.

Bernine had dressed for brunch this morning not in jeans like everyone else, but in a pink velvet leisure suit, gold belt, gold lizard sandals, and gold earrings, and had wound her coppery hair into a flawless French twist decorated with gold chains—just a bit much in this house, in this company, Wilma thought, hiding a smile. Her own concession to company for breakfast had been to put on a fresh white sweatshirt over her jeans. And Clyde, of course, was nattily attired in ancient, frayed cut-offs, a faded purple polo shirt with a large ragged hole in the pocket, and grease-stained sandals.

Bernine had greeted him, when he and Joe arrived, with a raised eyebrow and a shake of her elegant head. "You brought your *cat?* You brought your cat to breakfast? You actually walked over here, through the village, with a cat tagging along?"

Clyde had stared at her.

"Well," she said, "it's foggy. Maybe no one saw you."

"What difference if someone saw us? We—I do this all the time, take the cat for a walk."

"I'm surprised that a cat would follow you. What do you do, carry little treats to urge it along? Don't people laugh—a grown man walking a cat?"

"Why should anyone laugh? Why should I *care?* Everyone knows Joe. Most people speak to him. And the tourists love it; they all want to pet him." Clyde smiled. "Some rather interesting tourists, as a matter of fact." And he turned away, snatching up the Sunday paper, looking for the sports page.

Now the cat in question lay patiently awaiting the breakfast casserole. Stretched across the couch beside Dulcie, the two of them occupied as much of the blue velvet expanse as they could manage, comfortably watching the fire and dozing. Their occasional glances up at Wilma communicated clearly their pleasure in this lazy Sunday morning before the blazing fire, with their friends around them—and with the front page of the Molena Point *Gazette* lying on the floor where she had casually dropped it so that they could read the lead article. As they read, their little cat faces keen with interest, she had busied herself at the coffee table rearranging the magazines, effectively blocking Bernine's view. But then the cats, finishing the half-page account of the liquor store burglary, had put on dull, sleepy faces again, diligently practicing their best fuzzy-minded expressions.

The two cats looked beautiful this morning, Wilma thought, sleek and healthy, their coats set off by the blue velvet cushions, Dulcie's curving, chocolate stripes as dark as mink, her pale, peach tinted ears and paws freshly washed. And Joe always looked as if he had groomed himself for a formal event, his charcoal-gray coat shining, his white paws, white chest, and white nose as pristine as new snow.

Wilma didn't speak to them in front of Bernine, even to prattle baby talk as one would to ordinary pets; their responsive glances were sometimes more intelligent than they intended, and

Bernine was far too watchful. The history that Bernine had picked up from a previous boyfriend, the Welsh mythology of unnatural and remarkable cats that had peopled the ancient world, was better not stirred even in the smallest way. Better not to set Bernine off with the faintest hint of immediate feline strangeness.

In fact, having Bernine in the house with Dulcie was not at all comfortable. She just hoped Bernine would find a place soon. And certainly Bernine's intrusion into the guest room was not a happy situation for Charlie who, half an hour ago, had disappeared in the direction of the garage, silent and uncommunicative. Wilma knew she would be out there sulking as she unloaded her possessions from the van. Already cross at the eviction from her apartment—though she hadn't let her anger spoil last night's gallery opening—her sullenness was multiplied by Bernine's unexpected presence. Bernine was not Charlie's favorite person.

Earlier this morning when the two young women had coffee in the kitchen, Charlie had made no effort to be civil, had hardly spoken to Bernine. Wilma hoped that when Mavity arrived, her old friend would ease the atmosphere, that her earthy temperament would soften their various moods. Mavity might be ascerbic, without subtlety or guile, but her very honesty made her comfortable to be near.

As she picked up the coffeepot from the desk and moved across the room to fill Clyde's cup, she watched the cats sniffing the good smells from the kitchen and licking their whiskers. She could just imagine Bernine's sarcasm when the cats were fed from the same menu as the guests.

Clyde lowered the sports page and held out his cup. "Charlie going to stay out in the garage all morning? What's she doing?"

"Unloading her tools and equipment—she'll be in shortly. You could go out and help her."

Clyde sipped his coffee, shook his head, and dug out the editorial section, burying himself again. Bernine watched him, amused. Very likely, Wilma thought, Bernine understood Charlie's temper—and the reason for it—far better than did Clyde.

* * *

Dulcie watched Clyde, too, and she wanted to whop him, wished she could chase him out to the garage with Charlie. Didn't he know Charlie was jealous? That she was out there sulking not over the eviction, or simply over Bernine's presence, but over Bernine's proximity to Clyde himself? Males could be so dense.

But you didn't need female perception, or feline perception, to see that Bernine's sophistication and elegant clothes and carefully groomed good looks, coupled with her superior and amused attitude, made big-boned Charlie Getz feel totally inadequate. You didn't need female-cat intelligence to see that Charlie didn't want Bernine anywhere near Clyde Damen.

Scowling at Clyde, she realized that Bernine was watching her, and she turned away, closing her eyes and tucking her nose beneath her paw, praying for patience. *Must* the woman stare? It was hard enough to avoid Bernine at the library, without being shut in, at home, with that cat hater.

Why were anti-cat people so one-sided? So rigid? So coldly judgmental?

And how strange that the very things Bernine claimed to value in her own life, her independence and self-sufficiency, she couldn't abide in a sweet little cat.

Beside her on the couch, Joe was avoiding Bernine's gaze by restlessly washing, his yellow eyes angrily slitted, his ears flat to his head. He'd been cross and edgy anyway, since last night when they followed the old man and Azrael and lost them. And then the front page of the *Gazette* this morning hadn't helped, had turned him as bad-tempered as a cornered possum.

The Molena Point *Gazette* didn't concern itself with news beyond the village. Problems in the world at large could be reported by the *San Francisco Chronicle* or the *Examiner*. The *Gazette* was interested only in local matters, and last night's break-in occupied half the front page, above the fold.

SECOND BURGLARY HITS VILLAGE

A break-in last night at Jewel's Liquors netted the burglars over two thousand dollars from a locked cash register. This is the second such burglary in a week. Police have, at this time, no clue to the identity of the robber.

Police Captain Max Harper told reporters that though the department performed a thorough investigation, they found no mark of forced entry on the doors or on the window casings and no fingerprints. The crime was discovered by the store's owner, Leo Jewel, when he went in early this morning to restock the shelves and prepare a bank deposit. When Jewel opened the register he found only loose change, and loose change had been spilled on the floor.

Captain Harper said the burglar's mode of operation matched that of the Medder's Antiques burglary earlier this week. "It is possible," Harper said, "that the burglar obtained duplicate keys to both stores, and that he picked the cash register's lock."

Leo Jewel told reporters he was certain he had locked both the front and the alley doors. He said that no one else had a key to the store. He had closed up at ten as usual. Captain Harper encourages all store owners to check their door and window locks, to bank their deposits before they close for the night, and to consider installing an alarm system. Harper assured reporters that street patrols had been increased, and that any information supplied by a witness will be held in confidence, that no witness would be identified to the public.

Dulcie wondered if the police had collected any black cat hairs. She wondered what good the stolen money was, to Azrael. *So the old man buys him a few cans of tuna. So big deal.* But she didn't imagine for a minute that any monetary gain drove Azrael. The black tom, in her opinion, was twisted with power-hunger, took a keen and sadistic pleasure in seeing a human's hard-won earnings stolen—was the kind of creature who got his kicks by making others miserable. For surely a chill meanness emanated from the cat who liked to call himself the Death Angel; he reeked of rank cruelty as distinctive as his tomcat smell.

When the doorbell blared, she jumped nearly out of her skin. As Wilma opened the door, Mavity Flowers emerged from the mist, her kinky gray hair covered by a shabby wool scarf beaded with fog. Beneath her old, damp coat, her attire this morning was the same that she wore for work, an ancient rayon pants uniform, which, Dulcie would guess, she had purchased at the Salvage Shop and which had, before Mavity ever saw it, already endured a lifetime of laundering and bleaching. Mavity varied her three pants uniforms with four uniform dresses, all old and tired but serviceable. She hugged Wilma, her voice typically scratchy.

"Smells like heaven in here. Am I late? What are you cooking?" She pulled off the ragged scarf, shook herself as if to shake away remnants of the fog. "Morning, Clyde. Bernine.

"Had to clear the mops and brooms out of my Bug. Dora and Ralph's plane gets in at eleven. My niece," she told Bernine, "from Georgia. They bring everything but the roof of the house. My poor little car will be loaded. I only hope we make it home, all that luggage and those two big people. I should've rented a trailer."

Dulcie imagined Mavity hauling her portly niece and nephew-in-law in a trailer like steers in a cattle truck, rattling down the freeway. Bernine looked at Mavity and didn't answer. Mavity's minimal attention to social skills and her rigid honesty were not high on Bernine's list. Yet it was those very qualities that had deeply endeared her to Wilma. Mavity's raspy voice echoed precisely her strained temper this morning; she had been volatile ever since her brother arrived two weeks ago.

Greeley Urzey visited his sister every few years, and he liked to have his daughter and her husband fly out from the east to be with him; but it took Mavity only a few days with a houseful of company before she grew short-tempered.

"That house isn't hardly big enough for Greeley and me, and with Dora and Ralph we'll be like sardines. They always have the bedroom, neither one can abide the couch, and they bring enough stuff for a year, suitcases all over. Greeley and me in the sitting room, him on the couch, me on that rickety cot, and Greeley snoring to shake the whole house."

Dulcie and Joe glanced at each other, suppressing a laugh.

"It *is* a small house," Wilma said kindly, sitting down on the couch beside Dulcie and patting a space for Mavity.

Mavity sat stroking Dulcie, then reached to pet Joe. "You're a nice cat, Joe Grey. I wish all tomcats were as clean and polite."

She looked at Wilma, shaking her head. "Can you believe that Greeley brought a *cat* with him! A great big, ugly cat. Carried it right on the plane with him. He found it on the streets of Panama; it probably has every disease. My whole house smells of tomcat. I can't believe Greeley would do such a thing—a cat, all that way from Panama. Took it on board, in a cage. Three thousand miles. I didn't think even Greeley could be so stupid.

"He could have left it home, could have paid some neighbor to feed it. They have maids down there—everyone has a maid, even Greeley, to clean up and take care of things. The maid could have fed an animal. Greeley never did have any sense. Who in their right mind would travel all that way carting a stray cat? It's sure to get lost up here, wander off, and then Greeley will have a fit."

Bernine had put aside the financial page. "Can't you board it somewhere?" she asked coldly. "Surely there are kennels for cats."

"First thing I told Greeley, but he wouldn't hear of it."

Bernine shrugged and returned to the newspaper. Dulcie, fascinated, sniffed at Mavity's uniform searching for the cat's scent.

But she could smell only the nose-itching jolt of Mavity's gardenia-scented bath powder. Leaping to the floor, she sniffed of Mavity's shoes.

No hint of cat there. Mavity's white leather oxfords smelled of shoe polish and of a marigold Mavity must have stepped on coming up the walk; the flower's golden color was streaked up the white leather. Frustrated with her inability to scent the strange tomcat, she curled up again on the couch, quietly regarding Mavity.

"I told Greeley that cat could do its business outdoors. Why ever not, when I live right there on the edge of a whole marsh full of sand? But no, even if the cat goes outside, it still has to have a fresh sandbox, right there in the kitchen. Talk about spoiled—talk about stink.

"I told Greeley it's his job to change the sand, go down to the marsh and get fresh sand, but I have to keep telling and telling him. And to top it off, the cat has sprayed all over my furniture—the whole house reeks of it. Oh, my, what a mess. I'll never get it clean. Why do tomcats do that?"

Dulcie almost choked with suppressed laughter. She daren't look at Joe for fear she'd lose control.

"Well, in spite of that beast, it's good to have Greeley. It's been four years since he was here. After all, Greeley and Dora and Ralph—they're all the family I have."

Mavity grinned. "I guess my little car will hold the two of them and the luggage; it always has before." She glanced at Bernine and reached to stroke Dulcie. "It's not every day your only family comes for a visit."

Swallowing back her amusement, Dulcie rolled over, her paws waving in the air. Mavity was so dear—she could complain one minute, then turn around and do something thoughtful. She had cooked all week, making cakes and casseroles for Greeley and his daughter and son-in-law so they would enjoy their stay.

Dulcie didn't realize she was smiling until Wilma scowled a sharp warning and rose hastily, pulling Mavity up.

"The frittata's done," Wilma said. "It will burn. Let's take up breakfast." She headed for the kitchen, urging Mavity along, shooting Dulcie such a stern look of warning that Dulcie flipped over, flew off the couch, bolted through the house to the bedroom and under Wilma's bed.

Crouched in the dark she swallowed back a mewing laugh—at Mavity, and at Wilma's look of anger because she'd been smiling—trying not to laugh out loud. It was terrible to have to stifle her amusement. Didn't Wilma understand how hard that was? Sometimes, Dulcie thought, she might as well plaster a Band-Aid over her whiskers.

Lying on her back on the thick bedroom rug, staring up at the underside of the box springs, she considered Greeley and his tomcat.

Were these two the burglars?

But that was not possible. It would never happen, the solution to a crime fall into their furry laps as easy as mice dumped from a cage.

Last night she and Joe had followed the old man and Azrael clear across the village before they lost them. Keeping to the darkest shadows, they had tailed them to the busy edge of Highway One, had drawn back warily from the cars whizzing by—had watched the cat leap to the old man's shoulder and the man run across between the fast vehicles where no sensible animal would venture.

Pausing on the curb, their noses practically in the line of fast cars and breathing enough carbon monoxide to put down an ox, they had argued hotly about whether to follow the two across that death trap—argued while Azrael and the old man hurried away down the block.

"You can go out there and get squashed if you want," she'd told him, "but I'm not. It's dark as pitch, those drivers can't see you, and no stupid burglar is worth being squashed into sandwich meat."

And for once she had been able to bully Joe—or for once he had shown some common sense.

But then, watching the pair hurry two blocks south and double back and cross the highway again, toward the village, their tempers blazed.

"They duped us!" Joe hissed. "Led us like two stupid kittens following a string—hoping we'd be smashed on the highway." And he crouched to race after them.

But she wasn't having any more. "We could tail them all night. As long as they know we're following, they're not about to go home."

"They have to go home sometime—have to sleep sometime."

"They'll sleep on a bench. Just see if they don't."

But Joe had shadowed them for over an hour, and she tagged

along—until Joe realized that Azrael knew they were still following, knew exactly where they were on the black street, that the cat had senses like a laser.

But now—what if Mavity's brother and his cat were the burglars?

Certainly everything fit. Greeley had been here for two weeks. Both burglaries had occurred within that time. The old man looked the right age to be Mavity's brother, and, more to the point, he was small like Mavity, with the same wiry frame.

There was, Dulcie thought, a family resemblance, the deeply cleft upper lip, the same kind of dry wrinkles, the same coloring. Though Mavity's hair was gray, and the burglar's was ordinary brown, with gray coming in around his ears.

If the burglar *was* Greeley, then, as sure as mice had tails, he had stashed the money somewhere in Mavity's cottage. Where else would he hide it? He didn't live in Molena Point; it wasn't as if he had access to unlimited hiding places. Greeley was practically a stranger in the village.

As she flipped over, clawing with excitement into the carpet, wondering when would be the best time to slip into Mavity's cottage and search for the stolen cash, beside her the bedspread moved and Joe peered under, his yellow eyes dark and his expression smug.

"So," he whispered. "This one dropped right into our paws. Did you smell Azrael on her?"

"No, I didn't. We can't be sure . . ."

"Of course we're sure. There's no such thing as coincidence." He looked at her intently. "New man in town, brings his cat all the way from Panama. Why would he bring a cat all that way, unless he had some use for it? And that old burglar," Joe said, "even looks like Mavity."

Twitching a whisker, he rolled over, grinning, as pleased as any human cop who'd run the prints and come up with a positive ID.

7

CHARLIE HAULED the last duffle from her van and dumped it in Wilma's garage, enjoying the chill fog that pressed around the open garage and lay dense across the garden—but not enjoying, so much, shifting all her gear once again.

As a child she had loved to play "movers," filling cardboard-box "moving vans" with toys and sliding them along a route carefully planned to bring all her family and friends together into a tight little compound. At six years old, moving had satisfied a yearning need in her. At twenty-eight, hauling her worldly goods around in pasteboard boxes was right up there with having a double bypass.

Stacking her cartons of jumbled kitchen utensils and clothes against the wall beside Wilma's car, she sniffed the aroma from the kitchen, the delicious scent of ham and onions and cheese. But, hungry as she was, she didn't relish having to sit at the table with Bernine.

She considered making an excuse and skipping breakfast, but that would hurt Wilma. It wasn't Wilma's fault that Bernine had moved in uninvited; she could hardly have let the woman sleep on the street—though the image *did* appeal. And not only had

Bernine taken over the guest room, she was sitting in there with Clyde right now, all cozy beside the fire, and Clyde hadn't made the slightest effort to come out and keep *her* company.

Coming home last night from the opening, she'd been on such a high, had returned Clyde's kisses with more than her usual ardor; they'd had such a good time. And now, this morning, he seemed totally distant.

Slamming the last box into place, she wheeled her cement mixer out of the van and rolled it around behind the garage, parking it next to her two wheelbarrows, throwing a tarp over the equipment to keep out some of the damp. Wilma's backyard was as narrow as an alley, stopping abruptly at the steep, overgrown hillside. The front yard was where Wilma's flowers bloomed in rich tangles of color between the stone walks. Wilma, having no use for a lawn, had built an English garden, had worked the soil beds with peat and manure until they were as rich as potting mixture, creating an environ where, even beneath the oak tree, her blooms thrived.

Closing the van's side door, Charlie stood a moment gearing herself to go back inside. Last night when Clyde gave her a last lingering kiss and drove off in the yellow roadster, waving, she had headed for bed wanting to stretch out and relive every lovely moment of the evening, from the festive arrival Clyde had planned for her, and all the compliments about her work, to Clyde's very welcome warmth. But then, coming into the guest room, there was Bernine in *her* bed, on the side of the room she thought of as absolutely her own, and Bernine's clothes scattered all over as if she'd moved in forever. Bernine had been sound asleep, her creamy complexion glowing, her red hair spread across the pillow as if she was about to have her picture taken for some girlie magazine or maybe welcome a midnight lover.

A silk skirt lay across the chair, a pink cashmere sweater was tossed on the dresser, and Bernine's handmade Italian boots were thrown on the other bed beside a suede coat that must have cost more than six cement mixers. Surveying the takeover, feeling as if she'd been twice evicted, she'd gone back into the kitchen to cool down, to make herself a cup of cocoa. It was then that she found the note, folded on the table and weighted down with the salt shaker.

She'd read it, said a few rude words, wadded it up, and thrown it in the trash. Had stood at the stove stirring hot milk, thinking she would sleep in the van.

But of course she hadn't. She'd gone to bed at last, dumping Bernine's boots and coat on the floor, creeping into the other bed deeply angry and knowing she was being childish.

This morning, coming down the hall from the shower, she'd avoided looking at Bernine sleeping so prettily—and had avoided looking in the mirror at her own unruly hair and her thousand freckles, had pulled on her jeans and her faded sweatshirt, her scuffed boots, tied back her wild mane with a shoestring, and slipped out of the room only to catch a glimpse of Bernine's slitted eyes, watching her, before she turned over, pulling the covers up.

Then in the kitchen she'd hardly poured her coffee before Bernine came drifting in, yawning, tying a silk wrapper around her slim figure. And now the woman was in there with Clyde, all dressed up and smelling like the perfume counter at Saks. She hoped Bernine's soured love life, or whatever had left her temporarily homeless, had been suitably painful.

An old boyfriend once told her that her temper came from insecurity, that her anger flared when she felt she was not in control of a situation, that if she would just take positive action, put herself in control, she wouldn't get so raging mad.

Maybe he was right. She was considering what positive action she would like to take against Bernine when Mavity's VW Bug pulled to the curb, its rusted body settling with little ticks and grunts like some ancient, tired cart horse.

Watching Mavity slide out, small and quick, and hurry to the front door, Charlie began to feel easier. Mavity always had that effect. And at last she went on in, across the roofed back porch to the kitchen.

Wilma's kitchen was cozy and welcoming with its blue-and-white wallpaper, its patterned blue counter tile and deep blue linoleum. The big round table was set with flowered placemats, Wilma's white ironware, and a bunch of daisies from the garden. Charlie poured herself a cup of coffee as Wilma and Mavity came in, Mavity's short gray hair kinky from the fog, her worn white uniform freshly washed and pressed.

As Wilma took a casserole from the oven and put a loaf of sliced bread in the microwave, Charlie mixed the frozen orange juice, and Mavity got out the butter and jam. Clyde schlepped into the kitchen hitching up his cut-offs, looking endearingly seedy. His disheveled appearance cheered Charlie greatly—why would Bernine be interested in a guy who looked like he'd slept in some alley?

On the table, the frittata casserole glistened with melted cheese; the Sicilian bread came out of the oven steaming hot. The bowl of fresh oranges and kiwi, mango and papaya was aromatic and inviting. As they took their places, the two cats trooped in, licking their whiskers, and sat down intently watching the table. Charlie wished she could read their minds; though at the moment there was no need, their thoughts were obvious—two little freeloaders, waiting for their share.

When they were seated, Wilma bowed her head, preparing to say grace. Charlie liked that in her aunt. Wilma might be modern in most ways, but true to family tradition she liked a little prayer on Sunday morning, and that was, to Charlie, a comfortable way to start the week.

But the prospect of a morning prayer seemed to make Bernine uneasy; she glanced away looking embarrassed. As if the baring of any true reverence or depth of feeling was not, to Bernine, socially acceptable—or, Charlie thought, was beyond what Bernine understood.

"Thank you for this abundance," Wilma said. "Bless the earth we live upon, bless all the animals, and bless us, each one, in our separate and creative endeavors."

"And," Clyde added, "bless the little cats."

Amused, Charlie glanced down at the cats. She could swear that Dulcie was smiling, the corners of the little tabby's mouth turned up, and that Joe Grey had narrowed his yellow eyes with pleasure. Maybe they were reacting to the gentle tone of Clyde's and Wilma's voices, combined with the good smell of breakfast. Now the cats' gazes turned hungrily again to the table as Wilma cut the frittata into pie-shaped wedges and served the plates. Five plates, and a plate for Joe and Dulcie, which she set on the floor beside her chair, evoking an expression of shock and pain from Bernine.

Wilma passed Clyde's plate last. "How's work going on the apartments?"

"A few complications—it'll be a while before we're ready for you to landscape the patio. But between Charlie's expertise and my bumbling we'll get it done."

"Thank goodness for Mavity," Charlie said, patting Mavity's hand. "We couldn't do without you."

"Couldn't do without Pearl Ann," Mavity said. "I'm the scrub team," she explained to Bernine. "But Pearl Ann does other stuff. I don't know nothing about taping Sheetrock. Pearl Ann's a regular whiz—she can tape Sheetrock, grout tile, she can do anything. She says her daddy was a building contractor and she grew up on the job sites."

Clyde passed Mavity the butter. "Pearl Ann would be just about perfect, if she'd improve her attitude."

"I invited her to breakfast," Wilma said, "but she planned to hike down the coast this morning." Pearl Ann Jamison, tall and plain and quiet, was fond of solitary pursuits, seemed to prefer her own dour company to the presence of others. But, as Mavity said, she was a good worker.

Mavity glanced at her watch. "I don't want to be late, leave Dora and Ralph sitting in the airport."

"They don't get in until eleven," Wilma said, and she dished up another helping of frittata for Mavity. "Maybe they won't stay too long," she added sympathetically.

"One of those night flights," Mavity told Bernine. "Catching the shuttle up from L.A. They bring enough luggage for a year."

"Yes, you said that," Bernine told her dryly.

"And with my brother here, too, my little place is straining at the seams. Maybe one of these days I can afford a bigger house," Mavity rambled amiably. "Two guest rooms would be nice. I plan to start looking when my investments have grown a bit more. That Winthrop Jergen, he's a regular genius, the way he's earned money for me."

Bernine gave Mavity her full attention. "You have someone helping you with your—savings?"

"Winthrop Jergen," Mavity said. "My investment counselor. Doesn't that sound grand? He lives right there in Clyde's upstairs apartment, was living there when Clyde bought the place."

"Oh," Bernine said. "I see." As if Mavity had told her that Jergen meted out his financial advice from the local phone booth.

"He has clients all over the village," Mavity said. "Some of Clyde's wealthiest customers come to Mr. Jergen. They pull up out in front there in their Lincolns and BMWs."

Bernine raised an eyebrow.

"He moved here from Seattle," Mavity continued. "He's partly retired. Said his doctor wanted him to work at a slower pace, that his Seattle job was too frantic, hard on his blood pressure."

She gave an embarrassed laugh. "He talks to me sometimes, when I'm cleaning. He's very young—but so dedicated. That conscientious kind, you know. They're hard on themselves."

"And he does your—investments," Bernine said with a little twisted smile.

"Oh, yes, the bit of savings we had before my husband died, and part of my salary, too." Mavity launched into a lengthy description of the wonders that Winthrop Jergen had accomplished for her, the stocks he had bought and sold. "My account has almost tripled. I never thought I'd be an investor." She described Jergen's financial techniques as if she had memorized, word for word, the information Jergen had given her, passing this on with only partial comprehension.

Bernine had laid down her fork, listening to Mavity. "He must be quite a manager. You say he's young?"

"Oh, yes. Maybe forty. A good-looking man. Prematurely silver hair, all blow-dried like some TV news anchor. Expensive suits. White shirt and tie every day, even if he does work at home. And that office of his, there in the big living room, it's real fancy. Solid cherry desk, fancy computer and all."

Bernine rewarded Mavity with a truly bright smile. "Your Mr. Jergen sounds most impressive."

Dulcie, watching Bernine, envisioned a fox at the hen coop.

"But I do worry about him." Mavity leaned toward Clyde, her elbows comfortably on the table. "You know that man that watches your apartment building? The one who's there sometimes in the evening, standing across the street so quiet?"

"What about him?"

"I think sometimes that Mr. Jergen, with all the money he must have—I wonder if that man . . ."

"Wonder what?" Clyde said impatiently.

Mavity looked uncertain. "Would Mr. Jergen be so rich that man would rob him?"

Clyde, trying to hide a frown of annoyance, patted Mavity's hand. "He's just watching—you know how guys like to stand around watching builders. Have you ever seen a house under construction without a bunch of rubberneckers?"

"I suppose," Mavity said, unconvinced. "But Mr. Jergen is such a nice man, and—I guess sort of innocent."

Bernine's eyes widened subtly. She folded her napkin, smiling at Clyde. "This Mr. Jergen sounds like a very exceptional person. Do you take care of his car?"

Clyde stared at her.

Dulcie and Joe glanced at one another.

"Of course Clyde takes care of his car," Mavity said. "Mr. Jergen has a lovely black Mercedes, a fancy little sports model, brand-new. White leather seats. A CD player and a phone, of course."

The little woman smiled. "He deserves to have nice things, the way he helps others. I expect Mr. Jergen has changed a lot of lives. Why, he even signed a petition to help Dulcie—the library cat petition, you know. I carry one everywhere."

Wilma rose to fetch the coffeepot, wondering if Mavity had forgotten that Bernine sided totally with Freda Brackett in the matter of Dulcie's fate.

This was the second time in a year that petitions had been circulated to keep Dulcie as official library cat, and the first round had been only a small effort compared to the present campaign. At that time, the one cat-hating librarian had quit her job in a temper saying that cats made her sneeze (no one had ever heard her sneeze). The furor had been short-lived and was all but forgotten. But now, because of the hardhanded ranting of Freda Brackett, all the librarians, except Bernine, and many of the patrons had been walking the village from door to door getting signatures in support of Dulcie. Even Wilma's young friend, twelve-year-old Dillon Thurwell, had collected nearly a hundred signatures.

Mavity busied herself picking up her dishes, and she soon left for the airport, her decrepit VW ratting away through the thinning fog. Strange, Dulcie thought, that at breakfast no one had mentioned the two burglaries. Usually such an incident in the village was a prime topic of conversation.

She guessed Bernine had been too interested in Winthrop Jergen to think about burglaries, and certainly Clyde wouldn't mention them in front of her and Joe; Clyde hated when they got interested in a local crime. He said their meddling complicated his life to distraction, that they were making an old man of him—but Clyde knew he couldn't change them. Anyway, their interests gave him something to grouse about. As she and Joe slipped out into the fog through her cat door and headed up the hills, their thoughts were entirely on the burglaries and on Mavity's brother, Greeley, and his traveling tomcat.

"If Greeley is the burglar," she said, "we need some hard evidence for Captain Harper."

He looked at her quizzically. "Why the change of mind? You were all for keeping this from Harper."

"I've been thinking—if Harper doesn't find the burglar and make an arrest, he'll set up a stakeout. And what if they see Azrael break into a shop? That would really tear it. What if the *Gazette* got hold of that?"

"Harper isn't going to tell the press that kind of thing."

"But one of his men might. Maybe the uniforms on stakeout would tell someone. What if Lieutenant Brennan or Officer Wendell sees Azrael open a skylight and slip in, and then there's a burglary and they start blabbing around the department?"

Joe sighed. "You're not happy if we finger the old man, and you're not happy if we don't. I swear, Dulcie, you can worry a problem right down to a grease spot. What is it with females? Why do you make things so damned complicated?"

"We don't make things complicated. We simply attend to details. Females are thorough—we want to see the whole picture."

Joe said nothing. There were times when it was better to keep his mouth shut. Trotting across the grassy park above the Highway One tunnel, they headed up a winding residential street, toward the wild hills beyond.

"And," she said, "if Brennan and Wendell did see Azrael break in, they'd start putting things together—remembering the times *we've* been under their feet at a crime scene."

"Dulcie, who would believe that stuff? If a cop talked like that, they'd laugh him out of the department. No one would believe . . ."

"People *would* believe it," she said impatiently. "The story's so bizarre, the press would love it. The papers would have a field day. Every tabloid would run it, front page. And every nut in the country would believe it. People would flock to Molena Point wanting to see the trained burglar-cat. Or, heaven forbid, the talking cat. If *that* got in the news . . ."

"Dulcie, you're letting your imagination go crazy."

But he knew she was right. He cut a look at her, kneading his claws in the warm earth. "If we can find the stolen money and get it to Harper, and if the guy's prints are on it, Harper will make the arrest without a stakeout. And the cops will never know about Azrael."

"If there *are* any prints on the money, with those gloves the old man was wearing."

"Likely he'd count the money after he stole it," Joe said. "Why would he wear gloves then? Harper gets the prints, arrests the old man, and you can bet your whiskers that tomcat won't hang around. He'd be long gone. And good riddance."

"Except," she said, "that old man might *tell* the cops about Azrael, just to take the heat off himself. Figure he could make himself famous and create enough interest, enough sympathy for the talking cat, enough public outcry, that he'd be acquitted."

"That's really way out."

"Is it? Look at the court trials just this year, where public opinion has swayed the verdict."

He looked at her intently. She was right. "Talking cat confesses to robberies. Verbose kitty discovered in California village."

She twitched her whiskers with amusement. "Tomcat perjures himself on witness stand."

"Speaking cat insults presiding judge, is cited for contempt."

Dulcie smiled. "County attorney goes for feline conviction. Judge rules that jury must include proper quota of cat lovers."

"Or cats," he said. "Tomcats sit on jury . . ."

"Cat excused because she's nursing kittens . . ." She rolled over, convulsed with feline glee.

"But," she said at last, "what about the murders? We don't . . ."

"What murders?"

"The three deaths. Azrael said he saw death—three murders."

"You don't believe that stuff. Come on, Dulcie, that's tomcat grandstanding. *There will be murder in this village . . .*" Joe mimicked. "*I smell death, death before the moon is full . . .*" He yowled with amusement. "*I see you two little cats standing over the bodies . . .* Oh, boy, talk about chutzpah."

"But . . ."

"So who is going to be murdered over a couple of little, two-bit burglaries? Come on, Dulcie. He was giving you a line. That tomcat's nothing but a con artist, an overblown bag of hot air."

But Dulcie lashed her tail and laid back her ears. "There *could* be truth in what Azrael said." With all his talk of voodoo and dark magic, *was* the foreign tomcat able to see into the future?

Certainly there was a sense of otherness about Azrael—a dark aura seemed to cling around him like a grim shadow. And certainly when she read about cats like themselves, a thread of dark prophetic talents wound through the ancient myths.

Who knew, she thought, shivering, what terrifying skills the black tom might have learned in those far and exotic lands?

8

DORA AND RALPH Sleuder's shuttle from L.A. was due to land at 11:03, and as Mavity headed up the freeway for Peninsula Airport, her VW chugging along with the scattered Sunday traffic, the fog was lifting; the day was going to be pretty, clear and bright.

Wilma's elegant breakfast had been a lovely way to end the week; though the pleasant company made her realize how much time she spent alone. It would be nice to have Dora and Ralph with her, despite her crowded little house. She did miss her family.

She really ought to entertain them better, ought to get Wilma's recipe for that elegant casserole. All she ever made for breakfast was eggs and bacon or cereal. Well, of course she'd be making grits. Dora couldn't face a morning without grits—she always brought instant grits with her from Georgia. The first time Mavity heard of instant grits, which were more common in the south than instant oatmeal, she'd doubled over laughing. But after all, it was a southern staple. And Dora worked hard at home. On the farm, breakfast was a mainstay. Dora grew up in a household where her mother rose every morning at four to fix grits and eggs and salty country ham and homemade biscuits from scratch, a real farm breakfast. Biscuits and redeye gravy became Greeley's favorite after he married a southern girl at eighteen and moved south to her father's farm.

Greeley and his wife had had only the one child, only Dora, and for thirty years he had lived that life, so different from how he grew up here in California. Imagine, getting out to the fields every morning before daylight. You'd think Dora would want to get off the farm, but no, she and Ralph still planted and harvested and hauled produce to market, though they had some help now. And now they had that junk car business, too. Ralph called it a "recycled parts exchange."

For herself, she'd rather clean other people's houses than do that backbreaking field labor. After a day's work, her time was her own. No sick cows to tend, no broken water lines or dried up crops to worry over. She could come home, make a nice cup of tea, put up her feet, and forget the world around her.

And maybe Greeley hadn't liked it all that well, either, because the minute Dora's mother died—Dora was already married—Greeley hit out for Panama, and the next thing she knew, he'd learned to be a deep-sea diver. That had shocked everyone. Who knew that all those years, Greeley Urzey had such a strange, unnatural longing?

Well, he was happy living down there in Central America, doing his underwater repairs for the Panama Canal people, and Dora and Ralph were happy with their farm and their junk business. *And I'm happy*, Mavity thought, *except I wish Lou was still here, that he wasn't taken away from me so soon.* She shoved aside the word *lonely*, pushed it down deep where it wouldn't nudge at her. She knew she'd soon be grousing because of too much family, longing for some loneliness—well, for some privacy.

Never happy. That's the trouble with me. Maybe that's the trouble with everyone, always something that doesn't suit. I wonder what it'll be like in the next world—I wonder if you really are happy forever?

She had given herself plenty of time heading for the airport, and in the brightening morning she took pleasure in the Molena Point hills that flanked the little freeway, the dense pine and cypress woods rising dark against the blue sky, and the small valleys still thick with mist. Ahead, down the hills, the fog was breaking apart over the wide scar of the airport that slashed between the houses and woods. Greeley had wanted to come along, and she could have swung by the house to get him if she'd had room, but he ought to have known the Bug wouldn't handle another passenger plus a mountain of baggage. Even though Dora and Ralph traveled with all those suitcases, she'd never seen either of them wearing anything but jeans and T-shirts or sweatshirts printed in Day-Glo with some crazy message. Besides, they were not small people. Each time she saw her niece and Ralph, their girth had spread a little, expanding like warm bread dough.

But they were a sweet couple, and she'd get them tucked into the car one way or another. Maybe by their next visit she would have a bigger house, three nice bedrooms, one on the main level for herself, two upstairs for company. Not too big, though. Too much to clean. Maybe a place up in the hills. She wondered why Wilma didn't open an account with Mr. Jergen and increase her own pension. Sometimes she didn't understand Wilma; sometimes she thought Wilma's career as a parole officer had left her with no trust at all. Wilma relied on her close friends, but she didn't have much faith in other folks.

Turning off the freeway into the small airport, she drove slowly past the glass doors of the little terminal but didn't park in front. You could never depend on that fifteen-minute parking. They'd give you a ticket one second after your time was up—as if the meter maid was lurking just around the corner, hungry to make her quota. Continuing on down the hill, she pulled into a short-term space, locked the car, and headed double-time back up the steep incline.

Pushing open the glass door, her frizzy gray hair was reflected, and her thin old body, straight as a stick in her white uniform. She might look frowsy, but she was in better shape than most women half her age. She wasn't even breathing hard after the steep climb—and she didn't have to pay some expensive gym to keep fit.

She *got* paid for doing her workouts scrubbing and polishing and sweeping, right on the job.

Greeley was the same as her, as lean as a hard-running hound. Dora, being Greeley's daughter, ought to be the same, but she took after her mother. Ample, Greeley said.

Still, Dora didn't have Greeley's quick temper, and that was a blessing.

Peninsula Airport was so small that most of its flights were commuter planes. The runways would take a 737 if some airline ever decided to put on a straight run, but no one had. Crossing the lobby toward the three gates, she saw that all three of the little glassed-in waiting areas were empty. To her left at the Delta desk a lone clerk stood staring into space as if sleeping on his feet.

In the larger general waiting room to her right, only three travelers occupied the long lines of worn chairs. Two men sat slumped and dozing, as if they might have traveled all night or maybe waited there all night huddled down into the cracked leather. She couldn't see much of the man behind the pillar, just his legs. She had the impression of limpness; maybe he was asleep, too.

She thought she'd like a cup of coffee but, checking her watch by the airport clock, there really wasn't that much time. Anyway the airport coffee was expensive and not worth hiking upstairs, throwing away a buck and a half. Wilma's coffee was better. And where would she put another cup? She was so full of breakfast her ears bulged.

Choosing a seat in the middle of a row of attached chairs, she settled down where she would be able to see the incoming plane but away from the overflowing ashtrays and their stink of stale cigarettes. After one week with Greeley smoking in the house, she longed never to see another cigarette; her little cottage smelled not only of cat, but like a cheap bar as well.

She could have put up one of those THANK YOU FOR NOT SMOKING signs in the living room. Not that Greeley would pay any attention. He'd pitch a fit if she tried to make him go outdoors to smoke.

Between the stink of cigarettes and the stink of that cat, she'd have to burn her home to the ground to get the smell out.

Mavity's cottage, anywhere else but Molena Point, would be called a shack. It was a low-roofed, California-style clapboard, one step up from a single-wide trailer. But in the upbeat seaside village, it had value. Well, she thought, the land had value. Located right on the bay, it was real waterfront property, even if the bay, at that point, was muddy and smelly.

One would think, from looking at the Molena Point map, that her house faced a wide bathing beach. In fact, her little bit of land occupied a strip of marsh between the bay and the river—oh, it had patches of beach sand, but with heavy sea grass growing through. And the marsh was sometimes in flood. All the foundations along the shore were real high, and in bad weather one wanted to have buckets handy. The lower part of her house was stained dark with blackish slime that, as many times as she hosed and scrubbed it, just kept getting darker.

She hadn't thought much about her property value until Winthrop Jergen pointed out just how dear that land might be and had explained to her how much she could borrow on it, if she chose to invest more heavily. But she hesitated at the thought of a mortgage. She would hate to have something happen, though of course nothing would happen.

She did love the view from her porch; she loved the marsh and the sea birds, the gulls and the pelicans and terns. The land just above her place, up the hill where the old Spanish mission rose against the sky, was pricey property. There were fine, expensive homes up there bordering the valley road; and the old mission was there. She loved to hear its bells ringing for mass on Sunday morning.

Dora said the bells brought her right up out of a sound sleep. But what was wrong with that? Being southern, they got up for church, anyway. They always trotted off to mass, even if they weren't Catholic. Ralph said it was good for the soul to worship with a little variety.

The airport loudspeaker crackled, announcing the incoming commuter flight from L.A., and she rose and moved into waiting area number three and stood at the window. The runway was still empty, the sky empty.

It had been a long time since she'd seen Dora and Ralph, though they had talked on the phone quite a lot recently. Now that Greeley was considering moving back to California, she thought the Sleuders might decide to come out to the coast, too, maybe settle down inland where property was cheaper. Since they had that terrible financial loss last year, she supposed they didn't have a lot of money. Well, the only reason *she* could afford to be here was because she and Lou had bought their little place nearly forty years ago when prices along the marsh were nothing. And both of them always worked, too. Their cottage had been only a couple thousand dollars, back then, and was called a fishing shack.

She'd buried Lou in the Molena Point Cemetery thirteen years ago last April, and she had to admit, if only to herself, she *was* lonely—lonely and sometimes afraid.

Well, maybe she wasn't the only one who was lonely. Before Ralph made their plane reservations, Dora had called her four times in one week, long chatty calls, as if she, too, needed family. Then Dora surprised her by deciding to head out her way, when they didn't even know if Greeley was coming. Usually it was Greeley who set the dates, far in advance, when he could get off work.

The small, twin-engine commuter flashed across the sky. Mavity pressed against the glass watching as it came taxiing back, its turbo engines throbbing, and slowed and turned and pulled up before the building. She watched two men push the rolling metal stair up to its door, watched the baggage cart run out to the plane, and stood looking for Dora and Ralph. There was no first class on the commuter, so they might even be first in line.

Waiting for her family, she did not see the thin-faced man behind the pillar shift in his chair for a better view of the plane—a pale, waxen-faced man with light brown hair hanging down his back in a ponytail, pale brown eyes. His brown cords and brown polo shirt were deeply wrinkled, his imitation leather loafers pulled on over bare feet.

Half hidden behind the post, Troy Hoke had observed Mavity since she arrived, and now, watching the disembarking passengers, he smiled as Dora and Ralph Sleuder came ponderously down the metal steps and headed across the tarmac toward the building. Dora's T-shirt said GEORGIA PEACH, stenciled over the picture of a huge pink peach, and Ralph's shirt told the world that he was a GEORGIA BULLDOGS fan. As they came into the glass-walled waiting room, Hoke lifted his newspaper again. The two big people surged inside, laughing and engulfing Mavity in hugs. He kept the newspaper raised as the three stepped to the moving baggage belt and stood talking, waiting for the luggage. He had parked at the far end of the long-term section and, coming up into the terminal forty-five minutes before Mavity arrived, he had loitered in the gift shop reading magazines until he saw Mavity's old VW Bug pull by the glass doors heading for the parking lot. Had watched her come quickly up the hill again, in that familiar, impatient jerking way she had, and swing in through the glass doors to check the flight postings.

The luggage was being unloaded, the two baggage handlers throwing it off the cart onto the belt. It took a while for the Sleuders to retrieve their suitcases, slowly building a tilting mountain of baggage. He watched the two hefty folk and Mavity slide and drag suitcases across the lobby to the main door, where Dora and Ralph waited beside their belongings while Mavity went to get her car, pulling into the loading zone. He was amused at their efforts to stow all the bags into the interior of the VW and in the hood. They rearranged the load three times before they could close the doors. Dora sat in the front seat balancing a big duffle on her lap. Ralph, in the back, was buried under three suitcases. Not until he saw the VW drive off and turn toward the freeway did the thin-faced man leave the terminal, taking his time as he walked to his car and then headed for Molena Point.

*   *   *

Mavity's little car was so loaded she thought its springs would flatten right down to the ground. Leaving the terminal, she was certain the tailpipe would drag along the concrete. Before she left home she'd removed all her cleaning stuff—brooms, mops, her two vacuum cleaners, the canister model and the old Hoover upright, and her scrub buckets and plastic carrier fitted out with bottles of cleaning solutions and window scrapers and rags—had left it all in the carport hoping Greeley's cat wouldn't pee on everything. Now, beside her, Dora sat pinned down by the big duffle bag and by her bed pillow, which she always carried when she traveled because without it she couldn't sleep. Dora's arm pooched over the gearshift, and her thigh squished against it so hard that they might have to drive the freeway in low gear.

"Where's Greeley?" Ralph asked, looking around the VW as if he expected his father-in-law to materialize from beneath a suitcase.

"He's really anxious to see you," Mavity said. "Too bad there wasn't room in the car."

"How long is it to the house?" Dora said nervously. "I should have stopped in the ladies' room."

"Ten minutes," Mavity lied, cutting the time in half. "You remember. Only a little while. You can hold it."

"Is there a Burger King near? We could stop there for the restroom. Or a McDonald's?"

Patiently Mavity swung down an off-ramp to McDonald's and watched Dora make a trip inside. When Dora wedged herself back into the car she was toting a white paper bag emblazoned with the golden arches and smelling of hamburger and onions. She handed Ralph a double burger, its wrapping damp with mustard, and shoved a giant paper cup between her knees.

Mavity, pulling onto the freeway again, was glad the Sunday traffic wasn't heavy. Already she was beginning to feel like a sardine packed too tight. She tried to keep her mind on the cool, piney sea wind blowing in through her open window. Ahead, as she turned toward Molena Point, the wide expanse of sea with the sun on it eased the tight feeling across her shoulders. But when they turned off the highway into the village, Dora said, "I'd love to see where you work, where they're doing that remodeling. Could we stop by there?" Dora loved anything to do with houses.

"We can come back," Mavity told her. "After we unload. Or this evening after supper we can take a run up, the four of us." If she didn't get out of the crammed car soon she was going to have one of those shaky attacks that left her feeling weak.

But Dora's face crumpled with disappointment.

"Or what about tomorrow morning?" Mavity said quickly. "You and Ralph and Greeley can drop me off for work, take your time looking at the building—though it's just a mess of lumber and Sheetrock—then you can have the car for the day, go out for a nice lunch, and pick me up at five. How would that suit you?" She seldom offered her car when they were visiting, because she needed it for work, and she knew Dora wouldn't refuse.

Dora nodded, despite the disappointment that pulled down her soft jowels. Mavity only hoped she could show them through the apartments quickly tomorrow, without getting in everyone's way. Dora seemed totally set on seeing the project, and when Dora got her mind on something, it was hard to distract her.

They found Greeley at home in the kitchen frying chicken. He made drinks for Dora and Ralph, and they sat in lawn chairs out on the grass, looking at the bay, talking and catching up, until Dora and Ralph got hungry.

Dora didn't mention the apartment building again during dinner, but Monday morning she and Ralph were up early getting themselves ready, getting in Mavity's way as she tried to wash and dress.

And up at the apartments, they insisted on poking through every room, bothering the two carpenters and chattering to Pearl Ann and Charlie, who were busy hanging Sheetrock, slowing everyone's work until Pearl Ann opened a can of paint thinner and accidentally spilled some on Dora, and that sent Dora off with Ralph in the VW to change her clothes.

She thought it strange that Dora had seemed to avoid the patio, keeping to its roofed walkway or inside the apartments, but glancing out often—almost as if she didn't want to be seen, though there was no one living in the apartments, only Mr. Jergen, and his office lights weren't burning; the upstairs windows were dark as if he had gone out. Maybe Dora, looking out at the flower beds, had developed an interest in landscaping. Heaven knew, the patio could use some nice plants and bushes; it must look to Dora like last year's dried-up farm stubble.

Well, despite Dora's peculiarities, it was good that she had gotten her mind off her troubles; this was not an easy time for the Sleuders. Mavity guessed she ought to be a bit more tolerant of Dora's irritating manner.

9

AT THREE O'CLOCK on Tuesday morning across the moonlit village nothing stirred, no hush of tires on the damp streets, no rumble of car engines beneath the cloud-veiled moon; the tangle of cottages and shops and sheltering trees was so still the village might have been cast beneath some hoary wizard's hundred-year enchantment. The white walls of Clyde Damen's cottage and its ragged lawn were patterned with the ancient scriptures of tree shadow as still as if frozen in time. But suddenly a shadow broke away, racing across the mottled lawn and up the steps and in through the cat door, his white paws flashing.

Tracking mud across the carpet, Joe Grey trotted through the sleeping house accompanied by comforting and familiar sounds; the creak in the floor as he crossed the hall, Clyde's irregular snoring from the bedroom, and beyond the kitchen door, old Rube gently snuffling his own doggy snores. Joe pictured the Labrador sprawled on the bottom bunk in the laundry, among the tangle of cats, all sleeping deeply. The four household animals had slept thus ever since Barney died, dog and cats crowding together to ease their loneliness for the elderly golden retriever.

Joe missed Barney, too. The old golden had been a clown,

always into something, dragging Clyde's Levis and gym equipment all over the house, huffing and growling in the kitchen as he goaded the white cat to knock a pack of cookies off the top of the refrigerator.

Moving swiftly down the hall, Joe's nostrils were filled with the stench of human sleep laced with beer and garlic. Loping across the bedroom's antique rug, he sprang onto the blankets inscribing muddy pawprints, avoiding Clyde's stomach by leaping over his housemate. Kneading the empty pillow, he stretched out across it and began to wash.

Around him, the room was a montage of twisted tree shadows, as dense as if he resided in a jungle—though the thought of jungle irritated him, reminded him of the invading tom. As he washed, Clyde stirred and moaned—and woke, leaning up to stare.

"What the hell are you doing? You're shaking the whole damned bed."

"How could I shake the bed? I was simply washing my face. You're so sensitive."

Clyde snatched up the digital clock. "It's three A.M. I was sound asleep."

"You wouldn't want me to go to sleep unbathed."

"I don't care if you never take a bath—if you call that disgusting licking *bathing*." Clyde flipped on the bedside lamp, scowling at him.

"My God. I might as well have a platoon of muddy marines marching across the sheets. Can't you wash outside? When I go to bed, I don't drag half the garden in. And I don't do all that stomping and wiggling."

"*You* have hot and cold running water and a stack of nice thick bath towels. All I have is my poor little cat tongue."

Clyde sighed. "I presume the hunting was successful, by the amount of blood on your face. And by the fact that you are not out in the kitchen banging around clawing open the kibble box, ripping through the entire supply of cat goodies."

"When have I ever done that after a night's hunt? Of course

the hunting was successful. Was, in fact, very fine. The full moon, even with clouds streaked across it, makes the rabbits wild.

"It's the lunar pull," Joe told Clyde, giving him a narrow leer. "Oh, the rabbits danced tonight. Spun and danced across the hills as if there wasn't a cat within miles. Lovely rabbits. Such tender little rabbits."

"Please. Spare me your feline sadism."

"What we do is certainly not sadism. We are part of a complicated and essential balance of nature—a part, if you will, of the God-given food chain. An essential link in the necessary . . ."

Clyde snatched up his pillow and whacked Joe. *"Stop talking. Stop washing. Stop shaking the bed. Shut up and lie still and get the hell to sleep."*

Joe crawled out from under the pillow, his ears back, his head ducked low, and his bared teeth gleaming sharp as knives.

Clyde drew back, staring at him. "What? What's the matter? I hardly tapped you."

"You didn't *tap* me. You *whacked* me. In all our years together, you've never hit me. What's with you? How come you're so irritable?"

"*I'm* irritable? You're the bad-tempered one—I thought you were going to take my arm off." Clyde peered closer, looking him over. "You and Dulcie have a fight?"

"You're so witty. No we didn't have a fight. I simply don't like being hit. Fun is one thing, but that was real anger. And why would Dulcie and I fight? For your information, I left Dulcie on Ocean Avenue staring in the window of that new Latin American shop, drooling over all that handmade stuff they sell. And why are *you* so edgy? You and Charlie have a fight?"

"Of course not. She . . ." Clyde paused, frowning. "Well she was a bit cool."

"And you're taking it out on me. Venting your bad mood on a defenseless little cat. What did you fight about?"

"Nothing. She was just cool. She's been cool ever since Sunday morning. Who knows what's with women?"

"Bernine," Joe said and resumed washing his paws.

"Bernine *what?*"

Joe shrugged.

"You mean she's in a bad temper because Bernine's staying with Wilma? But why get angry at me?"

"You figure it out. I'm not going to draw pictures for you. I don't suppose you would want to get up and pour me a bowl of milk. I'm incredibly thirsty."

"You're not saying—Charlie's not *jealous.* Jealous of Bernine Sage?"

"Milk is good for the stomach after a full meal of raw game. A nice chilled drink of milk would ease my mood, and would wash down that cottontail with just the right dietetic balance."

"Why the hell would she be jealous of Bernine? Bernine Sage is nothing—a bimbo, a gold digger. Doesn't Charlie . . . ? Bernine doesn't care about anything but Bernine. What's to be jealous of?"

"If you would keep a bowl of milk in the refrigerator where I can reach it, I wouldn't have to ask. It's demeaning to have to beg. I have no trouble opening the refrigerator, but without fingers and a thumb I really can't manage the milk bottle."

"Please, spare me the details."

"And have a glass yourself—it will help you sleep."

"I was asleep, until you decided to take a bath. And now you want me to get up out of a nice warm bed and freeze my feet on the linoleum, to . . ."

"Slippers. Put on your slippers. Put on a robe—unless you really enjoy schlepping around the kitchen naked, with the shades up, giving the neighbors a thrill."

"I am not naked. I have on shorts. I am not going to get out of bed. I am not going to go out to the kitchen and wake up the other animals, to pour you a bowl of milk. I can't even describe the rudeness of such a request—all so you can wash down your bloody kill. That is as barbaric as some African headhunter drinking blood and milk. The Watusi or something."

"Masai. They are not headhunters. The Masai are a wise and

ancient people. They drink milk mixed with the blood of their cattle to give them strength. It is an important Masai ritual, a meaningful and religious experience. *They* know that milk is nourishing to the soul as well as to the body of a tired hunter. And if you want to talk disgusting, what about those Sugar Puffs or Honey Pops or whatever you eat for breakfast with all that pyridoxine hydrochloride and palmitate, to name just a few foreign substances. You think that's not putting strange things in your stomach?" Joe kneaded the pillow; its springy softness gave him the same sense of security he had known in kittenhood kneading at his mother's warm belly. "There's a fresh half-gallon of milk in the refrigerator, whole milk."

Clyde sighed, rose, and began to search for his slippers. Joe watched him for a moment then galloped along past him to the kitchen.

And as Joe drank milk out of his favorite bowl, which Clyde had placed on the breakfast table, and below him on the floor the other animals slurped up their own hastily supplied treats, Clyde sat at the table drinking cold coffee left over from the morning before.

"I hope you killed that rabbit quickly and didn't tease it. I don't like to think of you and Dulcie tormenting . . ." Clyde shook his head. "For two intelligent beings, you really ought to show more restraint. What good is it to be sentient, to be master of a culturally advanced language, and, supposedly, of advanced thought patterns, and still act like barbarians?"

"The rabbit died quickly. Dulcie broke its neck. Does that make you happy? It was a big buck—a huge buck, maybe the granddaddy of rabbits. It clawed her in the belly, too. For your information, a rabbit can be as vicious as a Doberman when you . . ."

"Wouldn't you be vicious if someone was trying to flay you for supper?"

"We're cats. We're hunters. God put rabbits on the earth for cats to hunt—it's what we do. You want we should go on food stamps?"

Finished with his milk, he dropped to the cold linoleum,

Clyde turned off the light, and they trucked back to bed again. But, getting settled, clawing his side of the blanket into a satisfactory nest, Joe began to worry about Dulcie.

When he had left her in the village, not an hour before, he thought he glimpsed a shadow moving across the rooftops. Probably a raccoon or possum had climbed to the rooftops to scavenge bird's nests. And even if it had been Azrael, Dulcie would be in control; she was quite capable of bloodying Azrael if he got fresh.

Or, he hoped she was.

The moon's light cast the sidewalk and shops into a labyrinth of confusing shadows, but the street seemed empty, and Dulcie heard no sound, nor had noticed anything moving except, high above her, the little bats darting and squeaking. Her attention was centered on the shop window against which she stood, her paws pressed to the glass, the bright colors of weavings and carvings and clay figures softly illuminated into a rainbow of brilliance. Oh, the bright art drew her. Pushing her nose against the pane, she sniffed the exotic scents that seeped through, aromas no human would detect; the faint drift of sour foreign dyes, of rare woods and leathers, the heavy stink of sheep fat from the handmade wool rugs and blankets. Studying the bold Colombian and Peruvian patterns, she thought that their strange-looking horses and deer and cats were closer akin to mythological animals than to real beasts.

Closer akin to me, she thought.

The notion startled her, shocked her, made her shiver.

The idea must have been playing on her mind without realizing, from the myths she had read—the notion that she was strange and out of sync with the world.

It isn't so. I am real flesh and blood, not some weird mythical beast. I am only different.

Just a little bit different.

And stubbornly she returned her attention to the bright and foreign wares.

She had, coming down the street, paused at each shop to stand on her hind paws and stare in, admiring handprinted silk blouses and cashmere sweaters and handmade silver jewelry, her hunger for those lovely embellishments making her purr and purr with longing.

Now, dropping to all fours, she slipped into the garden that ran beside the shop and trotted along to the back, staring up at the transom above the back door.

She did not intend to steal—as she had, in the past, stolen silky garments from her neighbors. She meant only to get nearer the lovely wares, to sniff and feel and enjoy.

Swarming up a purple-blooming bougainvillea vine that climbed the shop wall, forcing up between its tangle of rough, woody limbs, she clung above the back door, clawing at the narrow transom until the hinged window dropped inward. It stopped halfway, held by a chain.

Crawling through on the slanted glass, she jumped down to a stack of packing crates, then to the floor.

She was in the shop's storeroom. It smelled of packing straw and the sour scent of the raw mahogany crates that had been shipped from South America.

Trotting into the big showroom, she was surrounded by primitive weavings and carvings and paintings, was immersed in a gallery of the exotic, every tabletop and display case filled with unusual treasures. Leaping to a counter, she nosed at straw figures and clay beasts, at painted wooden animals and medieval-looking iron wall hangings and applique pictures made from tiny bits of cloth. Lying down on a stack of wool sweaters as soft as the down of a baby bird, she rolled luxuriously, purring and humming a happy, half-cat, half-human song of delight.

It had been a long time since she'd coveted anything so fiercely as these lovely creations.

Choosing the softest sweater, a medley of rust and cream and black that complemented her own tabby coat, she forgot her good intentions. Dragging it between her front paws—like a leopard dragging an antelope—she headed across the floor to the storeroom. There she gazed up toward the high window, her head swimming with the heady pleasure of taking, all for herself, something so beautiful. She was crouched to leap when a sharp thud made her spin around, bristling.

She could smell him before she saw him. In the inky gloom, he was a whisper of black on black, his amber eyes gleaming, watching her. Sauntering out of the darkness, he smiled with smug superiority. "What have you stolen, my dear?"

She crouched, glaring.

"My, my. Would you report me and Greeley to the police, when you're nothing but a thief yourself? Tell me, Dulcie, where are you taking that lovely vicuña sweater?"

"I'm taking it to nap on it," she lied, "in the storeroom, away from the display lights. Is there a law against that?"

The tomcat sat down, cutting her a wicked smile. "You don't steal, my dear? You have never stolen from, say, your neighbors? Never slipped into their houses and carried away silk underwear, never stolen a black silk stocking or a lace teddy?"

Her heart pounded; if she had been human, her face would have flamed red.

"My dear Dulcie, I know all about your little escapades. About the box that your Wilma Getz keeps on her back porch so the neighbors can retrieve their stolen clothes, about Mr. Warren's chamois gloves that were a present from his wife, about Wilma's own expensive watch that was 'lost' under the bathtub for nearly a year."

She watched him narrowly. Where had he heard such things? All her neighbors knew, but . . . *Mavity.* It had to be Mavity—she could have heard it anywhere. She'd probably told that cute little story to Greeley, having no idea she would hurt Dulcie.

"Mavity thinks you're charming," Azrael told her, "dragging home the neighbor's underwear."

The tomcat twitched his whiskers. "And Greeley, of course, was most fascinated by your display of, shall we say, perspicacity and guile."

He looked up to the shelves above them, drawing her gaze to a row of ugly black carvings. "Those figures up there, my dear, those ugly little feathered men—you *do* know that those are voodoo dolls?"

"So?"

"That dark voodoo magic is of great importance." His smile was oily.

"It is that kind of darkness in you, Dulcie, that entices you to steal. Oh, yes, my dear, we are alike in that.

"You know the tales of the black cat," he said softly, "of the witch's familiar. Those are the tales of the dark within us—that is the darkness that invites the joy of thieving, my dear. That is the darkness speaking within your nature."

She had backed away from him, her paw raised to slash him, but his golden eyes held her, his pupils huge and black, his purring voice drawing her, enticing her.

"You and I, Dulcie, we belong to the dark. Such magic and passion are rare, are to be treasured.

"Oh, yes, the dark ways call to you, sweet tabby. The dark, voodoo ways." He narrowed his eyes, his purr rumbling. "Voodoo magic. Black magic. Shall I say the spells for you, the dark spells? The magic so dear to your jungle brothers? Come, my Dulcie . . ." and he slid close against her, making her tremble.

She spun away from him hissing and crouched to leap to the transom, but he blocked her way. She fled into the showroom. He followed.

"In the jungle, my dear, the voodoo witches make dark enchantments, such exotic and exciting spells—spells to sicken and waste your enemies—and love spells, my dear . . ."

She leaped away but he was there pressing against her. When she lashed out at him, his topaz eyes burned with amusement and his black tail described a measured dance.

"My dark powers fascinate you, sweet Dulcie. My cunning is human cunning, but beneath my black fur, my skin is marked by the spots of the jungle cat.

"I have teased jungle dragons as big as two men and have come away unscathed. I have hunted among constrictors twenty feet long, have dodged snakes so huge they could swallow a dozen cats." And the tomcat's words and his steamy gaze filled her with visions she didn't want.

"I have hunted in the mangrove trees, dodging hairy beasts with the faces of ghosts, creatures that hang upside down among the branches, their curving claws reaching as sharp as butcher knives, their coats swarming with vermin." The black tom purred deep in his throat. "I have witnessed human voodoo rites where an image of Christ is painted with goat's blood and common cats are skinned alive, their innards . . ."

"Stop it!" She twisted away, leaping to the top of a cabinet—but again he was beside her, his eyes wild, her distress exciting him. "Come run with me, Dulcie of the laughing eyes. Come with me down the shore under the full moon. Come where the marsh birds nest, where we can suck bird's eggs and eat the soft, sweet baby birds, where we can haze the bedraggled stray cats that cower beneath the docks, the starving common cats that crouch mute beneath the pier. Come, sweet Dulcie . . ."

His words, frightening and cruel, stirred a wildness in her, and the tom pressed her down, began to lick her ear. "Come with me, sweet Dulcie, before the moon is gone. Come now while the night is on us." His voice was soft, beguiling, dizzying her.

She raked him hard across the nose and leaped away, knocking sweaters to the floor, tipping a tall wooden man that fell with a crash behind her as she fled through the storeroom and up the pile of crates and out the transom.

Dropping down the vine to the mist-damp sidewalk, she fled up the side lane and across Eighth, across Seventh and then Ocean past the darkened, empty shops, never looking back, her heart pounding so hard she couldn't have heard a dozen beasts chasing her, certainly couldn't have heard the soft padding of Azrael's swift pursuit.

But when, stopping in the shadow of a car, she crouched to look behind her, the sidewalk and street were empty. Above her, along the rooftops, nothing moved.

What had happened to her back there? Despite her anger, she had been nearly lost in a cocoon of dark desire.

Pheromones, she told herself. *Nothing but a chemical reaction. His sooty ways have nothing to do with real life.*

Shaken with repugnance at herself, she spun away again racing for home, speeding past the closed shops and at last hitting her own street, storming across Wilma's garden, trampling the flowers, up the back steps and in through her cat door, terrified of the dark stranger and terrified of herself.

Crouching on the linoleum, she watched her door swinging back and forth, unable to shake the notion that he would come charging through.

But after a long time when the plastic door grew still and remained pale, without any looming shadow, she tried to calm herself, washing and smoothing her ruffled fur and licking at her sweating paws.

She felt bruised with shame. She had for one long moment abandoned Joe Grey—for one moment abandoned the bright clarity of life and slipped toward something dark, something rancid with evil.

Azrael's twisted ways were not her ways.

She was not an ignorant, simple beast to whom a dalliance with Azrael would be of no importance. She was sentient; she and Joe Grey bore within themselves a rare and wonderful gift. With human intelligence came judgment. And with judgment came commitment, an eternal and steely obligation and joy from which one did not turn away.

In her gullible and foolish desire, she had nearly breeched that commitment.

There would never be another like Joe Grey, another who

touched her with Joe's sweet magic. She and Joe belonged to each other; their souls were forever linked. How could she have warmed, for the merest instant, to Azrael's evil charms?

Pheromones, she told herself, and defiantly she stared at her cat door ready to destroy any intruder.

10

LATER THAT MORNING, in the patio of the Spanish-style structure, where piles of new lumber lay across the dry, neglected flower beds, from within a downstairs apartment came the sudden ragged whine of a skill-saw, jarring the two cats as they padded in through the arch past a stack of two-by-fours. The air was heavy with the scent of raw wood, sweet and sharp.

Joe couldn't count how many mice he and Dulcie had killed in the tall grass that surrounded this building, before Clyde bought the place. Situated high above the village, the two-story derelict stood alone on the crest of the hill facing a dead-end street. The day Clyde decided to buy it was the first time Joe had gained access or wanted to enter the musty rooms. Even the exterior smelled moldy; the place was a dump, the walls stained and badly in need of paint, the roof tiles faded and mossy, the roof gutter hanging loose.

That day, trotting close to Clyde entering the front apartment beneath festoons of cobwebs as thick as theater curtains, he was put in mind of a Charles Addams creepy cartoon; beneath the cobwebs and peeling wallpaper hung old-fashioned, imitation gas lights; under Joe's paws, the ancient floors were deeply scarred as if generations of gigantic rats had dug and gnawed at the wood.

"You're going to buy this heap?"

"Made an offer today," Clyde had said proudly.

"I hope it was a low offer. What are they asking for this monstrosity?"

"Seven hundred."

"Seven hundred dollars? Well . . ."

"Seven hundred thousand."

"Seven hundred *thousand?*" He had stared at Clyde, unbelieving.

Over the sour smell of accumulated dirt he could smell dead spiders, dead lizards, and generations of decomposing mouse turds. "And who is going to clean and restore this nightmare?"

"I am, of course. Why else would I . . ."

"You? *You* are going to repair this place? Clyde Damen who can't even change a lightbulb without a major theatrical production? *You're* going to do the work here? *This* is your sound financial investment, and you're going to protect that investment by working on it yourself?"

"May I point out that one apartment *has* been refurbished, that it looks great and is rented for a nice fifteen hundred a month? That most of what you're seeing is simply dirt, Joe. The place will be totally different when it's cleaned and painted. You take five apartments at fifteen hundred each . . ."

"Less taxes. Less insurance—fire insurance, liability insurance, earthquake insurance—less yard maintenance, utility bills, general upkeep . . ."

"After expenses," Clyde had said patiently, "I figure ten, maybe twelve percent profit. Plus a nice depreciation write-off, to say nothing of eventual appreciation, a solid capital gain somewhere down the line."

"*Capital gain? Appreciation?*" Joe had sneezed with disgust, imagining within these walls vast colonies of termites—overlooked by the building inspectors—chewing away on the studs and beams, weakening the interior structure until one day, without warning, the walls would come crashing down. He had envisioned, as well, flooded bathrooms when the decrepit plumbing gave way and faulty wiring, which at the first opportunity would short out, emit rivers of sparks, and ignite the entire building.

Which, he thought, might be the best solution.

"It *is* insured?"

"Of course it's insured."

"I can't believe you made an offer on this. I can't believe you sold those five antique cars—those cars that were worth a fortune and that you loved like your own children, those cars you spent half your life restoring—sold them to buy *this*. Ten years from now when you're old and feeble and still working on this monstrosity and are so in debt you'll never . . ."

"In ten years I will not be old and feeble. I am in the prime of my life. And what the hell do you know about houses? What does a cat know about the value of real estate?" Clyde had turned away really angry, hadn't spoken to him for the rest of the day—just because he'd pointed out a few obvious truths.

And, what was worse, Dulcie had sided with Clyde. One look at the inside of the place and she was thrilled. "Don't be such a grouch, Joe. It's lovely. It has loads of charm. Big rooms, nice high ceilings. All it needs is . . ."

"The wrecking ball," Joe had snapped. "Can you imagine *Clyde* fixing it up? Clyde, who had to beg Charlie to repair our leaky roof?"

"Maybe he'll surprise you. I think the house will be good for him." And she had strolled away waving her tail, padding through the dust and assessing the cavernous and musty spaces like some high-powered interior designer. Staring above her at the tall windows, trotting across the splintery floors through rooms so hollow that her smallest mew echoed, Dulcie could see only fresh paint, clean window glass, deep windowseats with puffy cushions, soft carpets to roll on. "With Charlie's help," she had said, "he'll make it look wonderful."

"They're both crazy, repairing old junkers—Clyde fixing up this place, Charlie trying to save that heap of a VW. So he rebuilds the engine for her, does the body work, takes out the dings and rust holes, gives it new paint . . ."

"And fits out the interior," Dulcie said, "with racks and cupboards for her cleaning and repair equipment—for vacuum cleaners, ladders, paint, mops, cleaning chemicals. It'll be nice, too, Joe. You'll see."

Charlie had made it clear that her work on the apartments would be part-time, that her other customers came first. Her new business was less than a year old; she couldn't afford to treat her customers badly or to turn customers away. She was lucky to have Pearl Ann on the job. Pearl Ann Jamison, besides having useful carpentry skills, was steadier, Charlie said, than most of the men she'd hired. Except for her solitary hikes up and down the coast, Pearl Ann seemed to want no other life but hard work. Pearl Ann's only faults were a sour disposition and a dislike of cleaning any house or apartment while the occupant was at home. She said that the resident, watching over her shoulder, flustered her, made her feel self-conscious.

Now, the cats sat down in a weed-filled flower bed, listening for any mole that might be working beneath the earth. The patio was sunny and warm. The building that surrounded them on three sides contained five apartments, three up and two down, allowing space on the main level for a bank of five garages that were entered from a driveway along the far side of the building. Winthrop Jergen's apartment was directly above the garages. Strange, Joe thought, that well-groomed, obviously well-to-do and discerning Winthrop Jergen, with his elegant suits, nice furniture, and expensive Mercedes would want to live in such a shabby place, to say nothing of putting up with the annoyance of a renovation project, with the grating whine of skill-saws and endless hammering, as he tried to concentrate on financial matters in his home office. But despite the noise, Jergen seemed content. Joe had heard him tell his clients that he liked the privacy and that he was totally enamored of the magnificent view. From Jergen's office window he had a wide vista down the Molena Point hills to the village rooftops and the sea beyond; he said the offbeat location suited him exactly.

And Clyde was happy to have the rent, to help pay for materials while he was restoring the other four units.

Dulcie and Joe watched, through the open door of the back apartment, Charlie set up a stepladder and begin to patch the living-room ceiling; the patching compound smelled like peppermint toothpaste. Above them, through an upstairs window, they could hear the sliding *scuff, scuff* of a trowel and could see Pearl Ann mudding Sheetrock. All the windows stood open except those to Jergen's rooms; Winthrop Jergen kept his office windows tightly closed to prevent damage to his computer.

As the cats sunned in the patio, Mavity Flowers came out of the back apartment and headed upstairs, hauling her mop and bucket, her vacuum cleaner, and cleaning caddy. The cats, hoping she might stir up a last, lingering mouse, followed her as far as the stairwell, where they slipped beneath the steps.

The dusty space under the stairs still smelled of mouse, though they had wiped out most of the colony—mice as easy to catch as snatching goldfish from a glass bowl, the indolent creatures having lived too long in the vacant rooms. Winthrop Jergen's only complaint when Clyde took over as landlord was the persistence of the apartment's small rodents. A week after Joe and Dulcie got to work, Jergen's complaints ceased. He had no idea that the cats hunted in his rooms; the notion would have given him fits. The man was incredibly picky—didn't want ocean air or dust to touch his computer, so probably cat hair would be the kiss of death.

But the mice were gone, and it was while hunting the rodent colony that they had found the hidden entrance into Jergen's rooms.

To the left of the stairs was a two-foot-wide dead space between the walls, running floor to ceiling. It could be entered from a hole beneath the third step, where the cats now crouched. Very likely Clyde would soon discover the space, which ran along beside the garages, and turn it into a storage closet or something equally useful and dull. Meantime, the vertical tunnel led directly up to Winthrop Jergen's kitchen. There, a hinged flap opened beneath the sink, apparently some kind of clean-out access for the plumbing, so a workman could reach through to the pipes—an access plenty large enough to admit a mouse, a rat, or an interested cat into Jergen's rooms.

Now, scrambling up inside the wall from fire block to fire block, they crouched beneath Jergen's kitchen sink listening to Mavity's vacuum cleaner thundering back and forth across the living-room rug; the machine emitted a faint scent of fresh lavender, which Mavity liked to add to the empty bag. They could not, this morning, detect any scent of new mice that might have entered the premises, but all visits to Jergen's rooms were of interest, particularly to Dulcie with her curiosity about computers—she was familiar with the library functions but spreadsheets were a whole new game.

Waiting until Mavity headed for the bedroom, they crossed the kitchen and sat down in the doorway, ready to vanish if the financier turned around. He sat with his back to them, totally occupied with the numbers on the screen.

Jergen's office took up one end of the spacious living room. His handsome cherry-wood desk stood against the front windows, looking down the Molena Point hills—though all the cats could see from floor level was the blue sky and a few clouds, whose dark undersides hinted of rain.

The light of Jergen's computer cast a faint blue gleam across his well-styled silver hair. His busy fingers produced a soft, constant clicking on the keys. His pale gray suit was smoothly tailored. His shoes, in the cats' direct line of sight, were of soft, gleaming black leather. Everything about Winthrop Jergen presented an aura of expensive good taste.

To Jergen's right stood two cherry file cabinets, then a row of tall bookshelves filled with professional-looking volumes. The thick Kirman rug was oversized, fitting nearly to the pale walls, its colors of ivory and salmon forming a soft background to the creamy leather couch and the rose silk easy chairs. The six etchings on the left wall were delicately detailed studies of far and exotic cities, each with unusual rooftops: conical roofs, fluted roofs, straw ones topping stone huts, and a vista with sharply peaked domes. Each city flanked a seaport, as if perhaps the etchings embodied Jergen's dreams of far and extensive travel. The vacuuming ceased, and the cats backed into shadow. As Mavity returned with a lemon-scented cloth and began to dust the end tables, Jergen stopped typing.

"Mavity, would you hand me that file? There on the credenza?"

She picked up a file from the cherry credenza, brought it across to him, her work-worn hands dry and wrinkled compared to Jergen's smooth hands and neatly manicured nails.

"And that book—the black account book."

Obediently she brought the book to him, complying as a kindergartner might obey a revered teacher.

"Thank you, Mavity. Your Coca-Cola stock is doing very well; you should expect a nice dividend soon. And though I can't be certain, it appears the Home Depot stock should split this month, and that will give you a really handsome bonus."

Mavity beamed. "I don't know no way to thank you, Mr. Jergen, for all you're doing for me."

"But, Mavity, your good fortune is in my interest, too. After all, I enjoy a nice percent of your earnings."

"Oh, and you deserve it," she said hastily. "You earn every penny and more."

Jergen smiled. "It's a fair exchange. I expect your niece and her husband have arrived by now, for their visit? Didn't you tell me they were coming this week?"

"Oh, yes, all tucked up in my little place, and enjoying the beach." Mavity began to wind her vacuum cleaner cord, turning away to straighten it.

Jergen smiled briefly and returned to his computer; he began to work again, deep into columns of numbers. Dulcie's eyes widened at the large amounts of money flashing on the screen and at the names of the impressive financial institutions—firms mentioned with serious respect in the library's reference department. But soon both cats grew impatient with a world so far removed, that they could not smell or taste or deal with directly, and they slipped away, leaping down within the dark wall, crouching at the bottom.

In the musty shadows of the narrow, hidden space, Dulcie's eyes were as black as midnight. "Mavity trusts Jergen totally. She thinks he hung the moon. Why does he make me uneasy?"

Joe looked at her and shrugged. "Don't start, Dulcie. There's nothing wrong with Jergen. You're just bored—looking for trouble."

She hissed at him but said nothing as they padded out beneath the stairs into the sunny patio. And they both forgot Winthrop Jergen when a pale blue BMW pulled up in front.

Bernine Sage swung out and came into the patio, her high heels clicking sharply across the worn bricks. Pausing, she glanced through the open doors of the two first-floor apartments.

In the back apartment Charlie had stopped work. She stood quietly on her ladder watching Bernine, but she did not call out to her. Not until Bernine headed purposefully in her direction did Charlie come down the ladder. "Looking for Clyde?" Her tone was not cordial.

"I have an appointment with Winthrop Jergen," Bernine said cooly. "Is it upstairs? How do I . . . ?"

Charlie pointed toward the stairwell. Bernine said nothing more but headed across the patio.

Behind her, relief softened Charlie's face. And from an upper-floor window, Pearl Ann stood at the glass watching the little scene with a dry, amused smile.

The cats listened to the clink of Bernine's heels on the stairs, then her soft knock.

"She doesn't waste any time, does she?" Dulcie said with a cutting little mew.

Joe shrugged. "She'll start off talking investments, then come onto him. The woman's a leech." He curled up in the sunny weeds, yawning.

Dulcie curled up beside him, watching and listening. And it wasn't half an hour later that they heard the upstairs door open and heard Bernine say softly, "Twelve-thirty, then. See you tomorrow." And she clicked down the steps and left the patio with a smug, self-satisfied expression. Her fast work, even for Bernine, piqued Dulcie's interest like the sound of mice scratching at a baseboard.

She watched Bernine drive away, then looked up at Jergen's apartment. "Does he realize she's a little gold digger? He seems smarter than that."

"Maybe *he's* playing at some game—maybe he sees right through her."

Dulcie smiled. "I want to see this. I want to see how he looks when he leaves to pick her up, what he's wearing . . ."

"That's incredibly nosy. What difference . . ."

"What he's wearing," she said with patient female logic, "will indicate what he has in mind—what he thinks of Bernine."

And Dulcie's curiosity drew them back the next day to the patio, where they lay napping in the sun as Winthrop Jergen left his apartment. The sight of him made Dulcie laugh.

"Just as I thought. Trying to look like a twenty-year-old."

He was dressed in a black turtleneck sweater that set off his sleek silver hair, tight black slacks, a tan suede sport coat, and suede boots. "Right," Dulcie said, smirking. "Bernine made a big impression. Don't be surprised if she takes him for a nice sum—she has a way with her lovers."

But Joe was watching Pearl Ann gathering up her cleaning equipment as Jergen's Mercedes pulled away. Joe rose as she headed for the stairs.

"This isn't Jergen's regular cleaning day," he said, as Pearl Ann slipped quickly inside. "Come on."

In another minute they were crouched beneath Jergen's sink, waiting for the customary cleaning sounds, for Pearl Ann's vacuum to start. They heard only silence, then the jingle of keys and a file drawer sliding open.

Slipping to the kitchen door, they watched Pearl Ann sitting at Winthrop Jergen's desk examining the hanging files in an open drawer. Her keys dangled on their familiar gold chain from the drawer's lock.

Searching through the files, she removed one occasionally and laid it on the desk, paging through. Then she turned on Jergen's computer. She seemed quite at home with the machine, scrolling through vast columns of numbers. But every few minutes she rose to lean over the desk, looking down at the street below, her jumpsuit tight across her slim rear. The scent of her jasmine cologne was so sharp that Dulcie had to press her nose against her paw to keep from sneezing. After a long perusal of both hard copy and computer files, she removed a floppy disk from her pocket and slipped it into the machine.

"Copies," Dulcie breathed against Joe's ear. "She's making copies. She's using a code. How does she know his code?" At night in the library, after some instruction from Wilma, she found the computer a challenge, though she still preferred the feel of book pages beneath her paws. She knew about codes, Wilma had shown her that; Wilma kept a few things on her computer she didn't want the whole library to know.

When Pearl Ann seemed finished with the financial sheets, she pulled up a file of Jergen's business letters, quickly read through them and copied them, then dropped the disk in her pocket and turned off the machine. As she turned to put away the files, a whiff of her perfume engulfed the cats, and without warning, Dulcie sneezed.

Pearl Ann whirled and saw them.

"Cats! My God! Get out of here! What are you doing in here! He'll have a fit. How did you get in here!"

Crouching, they backed away. Neither Joe nor Dulcie cared to run beneath the sink and reveal their secret entrance. And the front door was securely closed.

"Scat! Go on, get out!" She snatched up her mop, shaking it at them.

They didn't move.

"You nervy little beasts! Go *on*, get out of here!" Her voice was hoarse with impatience.

They turned toward the front door, hoping she'd open it, but they weren't fast enough. She shouted again and lunged at them, exhibiting a temper they hadn't guessed at.

They'd never gotten friendly with Pearl Ann, nor she with them. She did her work, and they went about their business, all perfectly civil. But now that they were in her way, they saw a more violent side to Pearl Ann Jamison. Swinging her mop, she advanced on Dulcie, trapping her against the file cabinet. "You nasty little beast."

Dulcie fought the mop, enraging Pearl Ann, who swooped and grabbed her, snatched her up, avoiding her claws, and shook her hard.

Joe leaped at Pearl Ann, clawing her leg to make her drop Dulcie. Gasping, she hit him and swung Dulcie up. "*Damn* cats! Damn!" she croaked. Jerking the door open, she pitched Dulcie down the stairwell.

Joe barely skinned through as she slammed the door; below him Dulcie fell, unable to find her footing. He flew down the stairs, ramming against her, pushing her into the baseboard to stop her headlong tumble. Pressing against her, he could feel her heart pounding.

"You okay?" he asked, as they crouched shivering on the steps.

"I think so. I couldn't get my paws under me."

"What was she so angry about? What's with her?" He licked her face, trying to calm her. "Do you hurt anywhere?"

"I'm all right. I guess she doesn't like cats. I never saw that side of her before." Her voice was shaky. She licked hard at her left shoulder.

"Whatever she was doing in there, she was nervous as a rat in a cement mixer. Come on, let's get out of here."

They beat it out through the patio, didn't stop until they were across the street on their own turf, hidden in the tall grass.

"So what *was* she doing?" Joe said, nosing at Dulcie's hurt shoulder. "Is she trying to rip him off? First Bernine came onto him, and now Pearl Ann's nosing around." He looked intently at Dulcie. "What, exactly, was she doing at the computer?"

"I couldn't make much of it, all those numbers make my head reel. You'd have to have an accounting degree."

"Maybe she's running a scam. Hire onto a job, look for something to steal. But what would she . . . ?"

"Could she be the law?" Dulcie wondered. "Or a private detective? Maybe checking on Jergen?"

"Checking on him for what?"

"I don't know. Or maybe investigating one of his clients?"

Joe frowned, the white mark down his nose squeezing into a scowl. "Anything's possible."

"Whatever she was doing, and in spite of getting sworn at and tossed downstairs, I'm as much on her side as Jergen's. Sometimes that man makes me twitch. Always so smooth and restrained—and always *so* well-groomed."

Joe grinned. "Not like Clyde—earthy and honest." But then he sat lost in thought.

"Did Bernine get Jergen away so Pearl Ann could snoop?" Dulcie asked.

Joe looked at her and said nothing. Was there a crime here, or were they painting more into this than was there?

She said, "Pearl Ann was snooping for some reason. And Bernine—even for Bernine—really did come onto him pretty fast."

The cats looked intently at each other, the two incidents, together, as compelling to them as a wounded bird fluttering before their noses.

11

WALKING ALONG Dolores Street carrying a bowl of potato salad and a six-pack of beer, Charlie glanced up as Wilma nudged her, nodding ahead to where a black Mercedes convertible had slowed to turn the corner. From the driver's seat, Winthrop Jergen raised his hand in greeting. Sitting close beside him, Bernine gave them a tight little smile, cold and patronizing. The tall redhead was elegantly dressed in a sleek black, bare-shouldered frock, her russet hair coiled high and caught with a band of black.

"She doesn't waste any time," Charlie said. "Lunch yesterday and now dinner. Wonder where they're going."

"Somewhere expensive, if I know Bernine." Wilma shifted the bag of French bread to her other hand and reached up to steady Dulcie, who was riding on her shoulder. "Mavity's remarks on Sunday, about Jergen's financial acumen, were like gunfire to the troops."

"It's amazing she didn't already know him, considering he's a well-to-do bachelor."

"A rare oversight. I've known Bernine half my life, and she seldom misses such a plum." Glancing around at Dulcie, Wilma winked. Dulcie narrowed her eyes in answer. But as the convertible turned the corner and disappeared, she turned her attention to the shop windows, dismissing Bernine's little games, enjoying the elevated view from Wilma's shoulder. Her high perch was a liberating change from being level with the bottoms of doorways—from breathing the smell of hot rubber tires and dog pee and having to stand on her hind paws to see a store display. One had, at twelve inches from the sidewalk, a somewhat limited perspective.

Charlie, pausing at a dress shop, stared covetously in at a creamy velvet cocktail suit, where the sleek, dark-haired mannequin posed against a background of city lights. "Wish I could wear that stuff—and could look like that."

"Of course you can wear it, and of course you can look like that, or better. That ivory velvet would be smashing with your red hair."

"Right. And where would I wear it? For four hundred dollars, I'd rather have a Bosch drill, some new sawhorses, and a heavier sander." Charlie laughed and moved on, looking around her with pleasure at the small village. Over the rooftops, the eastern hills were burnished by early-evening light, the windows of the scattered hillside houses reflecting gold and catching images of the sinking sun. Close around them along the narrow streets, the sprawling oaks, the tubs of flowers, the little benches, and the used-brick facades and jutting bay windows caught the light, so brilliant with color and yet so cozy that she felt her heart skip.

"This village—how lucky we are. The first time I ever saw it, I knew that I'd come home."

Wilma nodded. "Some people are born for fast highways, for tall buildings, but you and I, we're happier with the small places, the people-friendly places, with the little, interesting details—and with having everything we need right within walking distance.

"I like sensing the land under me, too. The way the old cypress trees cling to the great rims of rock and the rock ridges drop away into the sea like the spine of some ancient, half-emerged animal.

In the city," Wilma said, "I can't sense the earth. I couldn't wait, when I retired, to move back home.

"I like knowing that these old trees were here before there was a village, when this coastal land was all wild—range cattle and grizzly bear country." Wilma put her hand on Dulcie as they crossed the southbound lane of Ocean, toward the wide, grassy stretch of the tree-shaded median.

"I bet you had enough of big city crime, too."

Wilma nodded. "In Molena Point, I don't have to watch my backside."

Charlie laughed. "People-friendly," she agreed.

And cat-friendly, Dulcie thought. Compared to San Francisco's mean alleys, which Joe had described in frightening detail—the bad-tempered, roving dogs, the speeding cars, the drunks reaching out from doorways to snatch a little cat and hurt it—compared to these, Molena Point really *was* cat heaven, just as Clyde told Joe.

Clyde said Joe was lucky to have landed here. And despite Joe's smart-mouthed replies, Joe Grey knew he was lucky—he just would never admit it.

Beyond Ocean, as they approached Clyde's white Cape Cod cottage, Dulcie could smell the smokey-meaty scent from Clyde's barbeque and could hear Clyde's CD playing a soft jazz trumpet. Pete Fountain, she thought, purring as she leaped down from Wilma's shoulder and in through Joe's cat door.

In Clyde's weedy backyard, a thick London broil sizzled on the grill. Clyde and Max Harper sat comfortably in folding chairs sipping beer. Harper, lean and leathery, looked even thinner out of uniform, dressed in soft jeans and Western shirt. Above the two men, in the maple tree, Joe Grey sprawled along a branch, watching sleepy-eyed as Dulcie threaded out the back door between Wilma's and Charlie's ankles. The little tabby headed across the yard, slowed by the inspection of the household cats sniffing and rubbing against her and by Rube's wet licks across her face. The old Labrador loved

Dulcie, and she was always patient with him; she never scratched him for his blundering clumsiness and sloppy greetings. Trotting quickly across the grass, escaping the menagerie, she swarmed up the tree to settle on the branch beside Joe, her weight dropping them a bit lower among the leaf cover.

Below them the picnic table was set for four and loaded with jars of condiments, paper napkins, plastic plates, bowls of chips and dip, and now Wilma's covered bowl of potato salad. Wilma laid the foil-wrapped garlic bread at the back of the grill and put her beer in the Styrofoam cooler, tossing one to Charlie and opening one for herself. As she sat down, Clyde handed her a sheaf of papers.

Looking them over, she smiled. "What did you do, Max, threaten your men with desk duty if they didn't sign a petition? Looks like you got signatures from the jail regulars, too."

"Of course," Harper said. "Drug dealers, pimps, they're all there."

She looked up at Clyde. "Two of these petitions are yours. You've been intimidating your automotive customers."

Clyde tossed a roll of paper towels on the table. "They don't sign the petition, they don't get their car—though most of them were pleased to sign it." He tipped up his beer, took a long swallow. "All this damn fuss. If the village wants a library cat, what's the harm? This Brackett woman is a piece of work."

"Next thing," Harper said, "she'll be complaining because my men circulated petitions on their own time."

"She'll try to get an ordinance against that, too," Charlie said.

"She'd have a hard time," Harper said. "Those petitions aren't for financial or political gain, they're for a cat. A poor, simple cat."

Dulcie cut her eyes at Joe. *A poor, simple cat?* But she had to smile. For someone so wary of certain felines, Max Harper had responded to the library cat battle like a real gentleman—though if he knew the petitions were to help one of his telephone informants, he might go into shock.

Clyde adjusted the height of the grill to keep the meat from burning. The aroma of the London broil made the cats lick their whiskers.

Harper looked at Charlie. "So your landlord tossed you out."

"I'm back freeloading on Wilma."

"And you've joined Sicily Aronson's group," he said. "I stopped in the gallery to have a look." He nodded his approval. "Your animals are very fine." Charlie's cheeks reddened. Harper glanced up at Dulcie and Joe as if inspecting them for a likeness. "You make those cats look . . ."

He paused, frowning, seemed to revise what he'd started to say. "It's fine work, Charlie. And the Aronson is a good gallery—Sicily's people sell very well. I think your work will be very much in demand."

Charlie smiled. "That would be nice—it would be great to fatten up my bank account, stop feeling shaky about money."

"It'll come," Harper said. "And Charlie's Fix-It, Clean-It appears to be doing well—except," he said, glancing at Clyde, "you need to be careful about questionable clients."

"If you hit it big," Clyde said, "if you sell a lot of drawings, you could put some money with Jergen, go for the high earnings. A bank doesn't pay much interest."

"I don't like the uncertainty," Charlie told him. "Call me chicken, but I'd rather depend on a small and steady interest."

Clyde tested the meat, slicing into one end, a tiny cut that ran bloody. In the tree above, the cats watched, mesmerized.

Harper passed Charlie a beer. "Have you found a new apartment?"

"Haven't had time to look. Or maybe I haven't had the incentive," Charlie said. "I get pretty comfortable with Wilma."

"There are a couple of cottages empty down near Mavity's place. We cleared one last week—busted the tenant for grass."

"Just what I want. Handy to my friendly neighborhood drug dealer."

"In fact, it's pretty clean down there. We manage to keep them at bay."

Molena Point depended for much of its income on tourism, and Harper did his best to keep the village straight, to stay on top of any drug activity. But even Molena Point had occasional problems. Several months ago, Joe remembered, there'd been an influx of PCP and crack. Harper had made three cases and got three convictions. In this town, the dealers went to jail. Harper had said that some of the drugs coming into the village were designer stuff, experimental pills.

Clyde said, "I could turn one of the new apartments into two studios. You could rent one of those."

"Your permit doesn't allow for more than five residences," Charlie said.

"Or you could move in here, with me."

Charlie blushed. "If I move in with you, Clyde Damen, I'll sleep in the laundry with the cats and Rube."

At the sound of his name, Rube lifted his head, staring bleerily at Charlie. The old dog's cataracts made his eyes dull and milky. His black muzzle was salted with white hairs. When Charlie reached to pet him, Rube leaned his head against her leg. The three household cats wound around Clyde's ankles as he removed the steak from the grill. But when the foursome was seated, it was Charlie who took up a knife and cut off bits of her steak for the animals.

The CDs played softly a string of Preservation Hall jazz numbers, the beer was ice cold, the steak pink and tender, the conversation comfortable, and as evening drew down, the fog gathered, fuzzing the outdoor lights and enclosing the backyard until it seemed untouched by the outside world. It was not until the four had finished dinner, the animals had had their fill, and Charlie was pouring coffee, that Harper mentioned the burglaries.

There had been a third break-in, at Waverly's Leather Goods. "They got over four thousand in small bills. Didn't take anything else, just the cash." Waverly's was the most exclusive leather shop in the village. "We have one partial print—we're hoping it's his. The guy's real careful.

"The print doesn't match any of the employees, but it will take a few days to get a make. He may have taken off his gloves for a minute while he was working on the safe."

"Are you still going on the theory the burglar's getting hold of the store keys?" Wilma asked.

Harper shrugged. "We're checking the locksmiths. Or he could simply be skilled with locks." He started to say something more, then hesitated, seemed to change his mind.

In the tree above him, the cats stared up at the sky, following the antics of the diving bats that wheeled among the treetops, but taking in Harper's every word.

Wilma, glancing up at them, exchanged a look with Clyde and turned away torn between a scowl and a laugh. The cats aggravated them both—but they were so wonderful and amazing that Wilma wished, sometimes, that she could follow them unseen and miss nothing.

It was not until the company had left, around midnight, that Clyde vented his own reaction. As Joe settled down, pawing at the bed covers, Clyde pulled off his shirt and emptied his pockets onto the dresser. "So what gives?"

"What gives about what?"

"You're very closemouthed about these burglaries." He turned to look at Joe. "Why the silence? There is no crime in Molena that you and Dulcie don't get involved with."

Joe looked up at him dully.

"Come on, Joe."

Joe yawned.

"*What?* Suddenly I'm the enemy? You think I can't be trusted?"

"We're not interested in these petty thefts."

"Of course you're interested. And isn't it nice, once in a while, to share your thoughts, to have some human feedback?"

"We're not investigating anything. Three amateurish little burglaries—Harper can handle that stuff."

"You have, in the past, not only confided in me, but picked up some rather useful information, thanks to yours truly."

Joe only looked at him.

"Clues you would surely have missed if Max and I didn't play poker, if you didn't scrounge around on the poker table, eavesdropping. But now you're too good to talk to me?"

Joe yawned again. "I am eternally grateful for your help on previous occasions. But at the moment I am not in need of information. We're not interested." Turning over on the pillow, with his back to Clyde, he began to work on his claws, pulling off the old sheaths.

He and Dulcie already knew who the perp was. As soon as they checked out Mavity's brother, Greeley, and found where he'd stashed the money, they'd tip Harper. And that would wrap it up. If the prints on the stolen bills matched the print from the leather shop, Harper would have Greeley cold.

Biting at his claws to release the sharp new lances and listening to Clyde noisily brushing his teeth in the bathroom, he quickly laid his plan.

Dulcie wasn't going to like the drill.

But she'd asked for it. If she wanted to play cute with the black tomcat, wanted to cut her eyes at Azrael, then she could make herself useful.

12

MAVITY FLOWERS'S cottage stood on pilings across a narrow road from the bay and marsh, crowded among similar dwellings, their walls cardboard-thin, their roofs flat and low, their stilted supports stained with mud from years of soaking during the highest tides. Mavity's VW Bug was parked on the cracked cement drive that skirted close to the house. Beyond the car, at the back, the open carport was crowded with pasteboard boxes, an old table, a wooden sawhorse, two worn tires, and a broken grocery cart. Joe, approaching the yard from across the road through the tall marsh grass, skirted pools of black mud that smelled fishy and sour; then as he crossed the narrow road, Azrael's scent came strong to him, clinging to the scruffy lawn.

Following the tomcat's aroma up onto Mavity's porch, he sniffed at the house wall, below an open window. Above him, the window screen had been removed and the window propped open, and black cat hairs clung to the sill. Mavity might complain about the tomcat, but she treated him cordially enough. From within the cottage, the smell of fried eggs and coffee wrapped around Joe, and he could hear silverware clatter against a plate.

"Eat up, Greeley, or I'll be late."

"Eating as fast as I can," a man replied. "You hadn't ought to rush a man in the morning."

"If you're coming with me, you'll get a move on."

Below the window, Joe Grey smiled. He'd hit pay dirt. That raspy, hoarse croak was unmistakable; he could hear again the wizened old man arguing with Azrael over their takeout fish and chips. Greeley was their man. No doubt about it. Mavity's own brother was their light-fingered, cat-consorting thief.

Luck, Joe thought. *Or the great cat god's smiling*. And, sitting down beneath the window, he prepared to wait.

Once Mavity left for work, taking Greeley with her, he'd have only Dora and Ralph to worry about—if, indeed, they were out of bed yet. Mavity said the portly couple liked to sleep late, and if the great cat god hung around, he might not even have to dodge the Sleuders; maybe they'd sleep through his search.

As for Azrael, at the moment that tomcat was otherwise occupied.

But to make sure, Joe dropped from the porch to the yard and prowled among the pilings, sniffing for Dulcie's scent.

Yes, he found where she had marked a path, her provocative female aroma leading away toward the village, a trail that no tomcat would ignore. He imagined her, even now, trotting across the rooftops close beside Azrael, her tail waving, her green eyes cutting shyly at the tom, distracting him just as they'd planned.

He sat down beside a blackened piling, trying to calm his frayed nerves, wondering if this idea had been so smart.

But Dulcie wouldn't betray him. And as far as her safety, his lady could whip a room full of German shepherds with one paw tied behind. He imagined her dodging Azrael's unwanted advances, subtly leading him on a wild chase far from Mavity's cottage, handling the situation with such guile that she would not need to smack the foreign beast.

"Get your jacket, Greeley, or I'll be late." Inside, a chair scraped and dishes were being stacked, then water ran in the sink. He caught the sharp smell of dish soap, imagined Mavity standing just a few feet from him washing up the breakfast plates. Then the water was turned off. Soon the door opened, and from beneath the deck he watched their hurrying feet descend the steps, Mavity's white jogging shoes and Greeley's dark loafers.

He got a look at him as they headed for her VW. This was their man, all right.

Greeley wasn't much taller than Mavity. He wore the wrinkled leather jacket with the cuffs turned up and the collar pushing at his shaggy gray hair. Joe could see him again rifling Mrs. Medder's cash register.

The car doors slammed and Mavity backed out, turning up Shoreline toward the village. Joe did not enter the house at once but listened for Dora and Ralph. When, after some minutes, he had heard nothing but the sea wind hushing through the marsh grass behind him, he leaped to the sill and slipped in through the open window.

Pausing above the sink, his nose was filled with the smell of greasy eggs and soapsuds. The kitchen was open to the small living room, with barely space between for the tiny breakfast table pushed against the back of the couch. A faded, overstuffed chair faced the couch, along with a small desk and a narrow cot covered with a plaid blanket. A TV jammed between the desk and a bookcase completed the decor. The ceiling was low, the walls pale tan. To his right, from the darkened bedroom, he heard slow, even breathing.

There was only the one bedroom, and through the open door he studied the piled suitcases, the closed blinds, the two big mounds sprawled beneath the blankets. When neither Dora nor Ralph stirred, he padded along the kitchen counter and across the breakfast table to the back of the couch.

At one end of the couch was a stack of folded sheets and blankets and a bed pillow. Dropping down to the rug, he inspected first beneath the furniture and found, under the cot, a battered leather suitcase.

The clasp was devilishly hard to open. Digging at it with stubborn claws, at last he sprang it.

He found within only socks, underwear, a shaving kit, and a pair of wrinkled pajamas. The shaving kit, which was unzipped, had an inner pocket. Pawing this open, thinking Greeley might have stashed some of the money there, he narrowly missed cutting his pad on Greeley's used razor blades. Why would anyone save old razor blades?

Nosing into the suitcase under the false bottom, which was meant to keep the bag rigid, he found nothing but a small notebook containing some foreign addresses and Greeley's plane ticket. Sliding the ticket from its envelope, he saw that Greeley had not yet made his return reservation. Pushing everything back in order, he turned away. Listening to the lonely wind buffet the cottage, he headed for the bedroom.

Long before Joe entered Mavity's cottage, across the village on the dark rooftops where the sea wind scudded and danced, Dulcie slunk along a roof's edge watching the street below. Around her, the dark trees hushed and rattled, and the moon's fitful light jumped and fled; above her, telephone lines swung in an erratic dance, and in an open dormer window white curtains whipped like frantic ghosts. By the strike of the courthouse clock she had been on the rooftops since three, and it was now nearly six. She had not seen Azrael. She was beginning to worry that he had not left Mavity's cottage or had returned to it, surprising Joe in his search.

Had she not marked her trail clearly enough, on her way from the marsh? Or had she marked it too clearly? Rubbing her whiskers on every surface and leaving little damp messages, had she made Azrael suspicious? She prayed that he hadn't guessed their plan, that he was lying in wait for Joe. She longed to turn back to Mavity's, but she might only lead him there. She could do nothing but keep on searching, casually marking her trail across the rooftops.

Then suddenly, in the shadows of the alley, was that the tomcat? Quickly she dropped down to an oak branch and crossed the six-foot chasm to the roof of the Swiss Cafe.

Stretching out along the rain gutter, she watched the dark montage of shadows that she thought had moved.

Now all was still. No sign of Azrael.

At last she slipped to the corner where she could see the street. She waited there, watching, until the glow of the street lamps began to fade and the sky grew to the color of pewter beneath dark, scudding clouds. The courthouse clock struck six-thirty. Maybe the tomcat *had* returned to Mavity's and at this moment he and Joe were locked in terrible battle.

A lone car hushed along Ocean as an early riser headed for work. A shopkeeper set a box of trash at the curb then began to water his curbside garden of ferns and geraniums. Dulcie was about to turn away, to seek Azrael along other streets when from beneath a parked truck the black tom swaggered out, nose to the gusting wind. Pausing just below her, he licked his paw and washed his whiskers. He seemed restless, kept glancing away in the direction of the marsh. Was he aware of her? Did some sixth sense nudge him? When he started away, Dulcie followed quickly along the roof's edge.

But then he paused at the Red Skillet Cafe, stood peering into the patio, sniffing deeply the scents from last night's grilled salmon and halibut. As Dulcie hunched on the rooftop, he padded through the wrought-iron gate to wind among the tables. Immediately a mockingbird, snatching up crumbs, attacked him—and exploded in a storm of feathers, with a naked backside. The black tom smiled, licked his whiskers, and prowled among the tables, gulping bits of charred fish like some half-starved stray—but still he seemed edgy and unsettled, glancing away again and again in the direction of Mavity's cottage.

Quickly Dulcie, her heart pounding half with fear, half with excitement, dropped to the pavement and hurried after him.

Beyond the iron gate, Azrael was turned away. But his ears flicked. His tail lashed. His body stiffened as he sensed a presence behind him. As she slipped in through the bars, he whirled to face her.

She paused, her paw softly lifted.

His gaze narrowed to a sly caress.

They stared at each other in silence. Azrael flattened his whiskers, offered subtle body talk meant to set the stage for mating.

Dulcie gave him a slow smile. This wasn't going to be easy, to delay him yet avoid the snuggling games. She felt like a lady cop playing street hustler.

"Where is your friend, my dear? Your little gray friend? Does he know you're out alone?"

She wound among the chair legs, her tail high, her stroll sultry, her heart pounding so hard she could hear it. Azrael trotted close to her, his amber eyes deep and golden; when he bowed his neck, towering over her, she felt small suddenly, and frail.

Dora and Ralph Sleuder slept deeply, their even breathing unchanged as Joe prowled the dim bedroom. Pawing through a suitcase that lay open on the floor, he dug into its pockets and searched under the clothes, taking considerable trouble to push everything back in the same jumble as he'd found it.

He was nosing into a big duffle bag when the bedsprings creaked and Ralph stirred and sneezed. Fleeing to the kitchen, Joe leaped on the table and shot to the top of the refrigerator. Crouching behind a metal canister and a bag of potato chips, he watched Ralph swing to the floor and pad away toward the bathroom, nattily attired in striped green boxer shorts that dropped beneath his bare belly.

Making himself comfortable behind the chips, he was careful not to brush its crinkly cellophane or against the package of cookies. Amazing what a person could cram atop a refrigerator. Clyde favored beer, and an assortment of cat and dog kibble—all the essentials readily at hand.

The bedsprings squeaked again, and Dora rose, her ample curves voluminous in a pink-and-green flowered nightie. Not bothering to wash or comb her hair, she padded into the kitchen, looked out the window, and glanced into the living room.

Returning to the bedroom, she began to open the drawers in the tall dresser, carefully examining the contents of each, her movements quick and watchful.

From the bathroom, the toilet flushed, and Ralph returned to start on the other dresser, pawing through Mavity's personal belongings.

"Nothing," Dora said at last, closing the bottom drawer. "She must have a lot of time on her hands, to keep her drawers so neated up."

Ralph slammed a drawer closed. "Maybe in the living room."

"Start on the desk. I'll look in the bookcase. Daddy'll have dropped her at work by now, so she won't come charging back forgetting her lunch or whatever. That gave me the cold sweats yesterday when she did that."

"What about your daddy? How soon will he be back?"

"Depends. If he decided to drive over to Monterey—haircuts are cheaper over there—he'll be a while."

Watching Dora go through the bookcase, pulling romance novels from the shelves to look behind then shoving them back, watching Ralph finger through the contents of Mavity's desk, Joe grew so interested that he backed into the cookies. The brittle crunch brought both Dora and Ralph swinging around to stare toward the kitchen. He remained frozen behind the canister, as still as one of those plaster amusement park cats—a gray plaster cat with white markings.

"Heat," Ralph said, seeing no one in the kitchen. "Thought it was that stinking Azrael coming through the window, but it was just heat—them chip bags pop in the heat. Makes 'em rancid, too."

Joe watched, puzzled, as the two pudgy people resumed their investigation. If they were looking for Greeley's stolen money, why had they searched Mavity's bedroom? Why not go directly to Greeley's suitcase, as he himself had done?

But maybe they'd already searched there. Or did they think

that Mavity had hidden the money? Did they think she was Greeley's accomplice?

Not Mavity. He couldn't think that.

The smell of chips was so strong he could taste them. What did they put in that stuff? Looking out, he watched Ralph remove papers from the desk drawers and shuffle through them, scanning Mavity's letters and bills, and he grew certain Ralph wasn't looking for the money. But what, then?

The desk had seven drawers. Digging into the bottom drawer, Ralph raised up, fanning a stack of white paper. "*Got it! I got it!*"

Dora hurried in, her short, flowered nightie flapping around her meaty white legs, and snatched the papers from him. Leaning against the desk, she rifled through—then waved the papers and laughed, hugged Ralph and did a little dance around him, wriggling provocatively.

"Take a good look," she said, handing them back, "while I get set up." And she vanished into the bedroom. Joe heard a click, as if a suitcase had opened. She returned carrying a small copier machine. Glancing out the window toward the drive, she set it on the kitchen table and began to search for an outlet.

"Hurry up. Unplug the toaster. A haircut doesn't take forever. Your dad . . ."

"I am hurrying. Give me the statements." Jerking out the toaster cord, she jammed in the plug, flipped the switch, and stood shuffling through the sheaf of papers until a green light came on.

Slipping to the edge of the refrigerator, Joe could just see a letterhead above Mavity's name and address. WINTHROP JERGEN, FINANCIAL ADVISOR.

Dora made two copies of each page and separated them into two piles. When she was halfway through, Ralph stopped her. "You better call him. I'll finish."

"You call him."

"No. You're the one started this. You do it."

Sighing, she fished a slip of paper from her pocket, picked up the phone from the desk and carried it to the coffee table dragging the cord, sat down on the couch where she could be comfortable. "I hope he's there."

"He said he'd wait for the call."

"Why is it so hard to get him on the phone?"

"Just call, Dora. Before your daddy gets back."

While Ralph ran copies, she punched in seven clicks. No area code, so it was a local call. Waiting for her party to pick up, she glanced directly toward the refrigerator. Joe held his breath, didn't twitch a whisker.

Abruptly she returned her attention to the phone. She didn't say hello, she offered no cordial introduction, just started talking.

"We have them."

A pause.

"I can't. Dad has the car. He took Mavity to work. He's getting a haircut—I told you he'd get one today. He'll be back any minute."

Silence.

"All right. But hurry."

She hung up. "He's on his way." She headed for the bedroom and in a few minutes returned dressed in tight jeans and a T-shirt that told the world she liked hot cars and champagne, carrying a large leather briefcase. Ralph finished up the copies, straightened the two stacks, and put the originals back in the bottom desk drawer. Dora carried one stack into the bedroom, then unplugged the copier and slipped it into the briefcase, tucking the other set of pages on top.

When Ralph padded into the kitchen to make coffee, Joe froze again. The couple sat at the table, not five feet from him, sipping coffee and waiting.

"Where can he be?" Dora grumbled. "What's taking so long?"

After twenty minutes by the kitchen clock, she fetched a plate of cake from the cupboard and cut two thick slices.

Ten minutes more, and another ten. They had poured the last of the coffee and Joe felt ready to pitch a fit—it was an interminable wait for both the Sleuders and their silent audience. At last a car came down the street.

"That has to be him. Where has he been?" Dora patted her hair and straightened her shirt. "What in the world took him so long?"

But the car went on by. Joe heard it stop a block away, heard the car door slam. In a minute, footsteps came up the street, turning to the house.

"That's him," Ralph said. A shadow loomed beyond the louvered glass: a thin man. Dora pulled the door open.

"Had car trouble," the man said, stepping inside. "Left it up the block. It's running rough as a paint shaker."

Joe, watching him, was rigid with amazement.

He was of medium height and slight of build, his light brown hair tied in a ponytail that flopped over the hood of his blue windbreaker.

This was the man who lingered around the apartments. The silent watcher. Joe caught a whiff of motor grease as he moved past Dora to the table.

"Let's have a look."

Dora opened the briefcase and handed him the copies.

"Shuffle them out, Dora. My hands are greasy from the car."

She spread the statements across the kitchen table; he stood scanning them as she sorted through, then looked up at her, smiling.

"This is what we want. Exactly. You've done a good job here." He winked at her. "You two are quite something."

The man watched as Dora put the papers in a neat pile again and slid them back into the briefcase on top the copier, carefully closing the lid.

Removing a white handkerchief from his pocket, he wrapped it around the handle. "No need to get grease on the leather. I'm just filthy." He smiled again, holding the briefcase away from his pantleg, and moved toward the door. "Wish me luck, folks, that I can nurse the old car into the village."

"I could phone for a tow truck," Dora offered.

"I'll take it slow. I think it's the carburetor, but I should be able to make it to the garage all right." He stared down at his dirty hands, let Dora open the door for him.

The man's name was never spoken. When he had gone, Joe endured what seemed eternal confinement between the chips and cookies while Dora fixed breakfast and the two folks ate a never-ending meal of fried sausage, fried eggs, instant grits, toast, and coffee. At first the smells made him hungry, but after prolonged exposure, he wanted to throw up. He woke from a fitful doze as Dora began to do the dishes, running hot water into the sink, plunging her hands into the suds.

When she had put the dishes in the drain, she hurried to the bedroom and returned wearing a yellow-and-purple mumu and flipflops and carrying a blanket and a beach umbrella. Ralph padded out dressed in skin-tight black exercise shorts and a red tank top straining across his considerable girth. Joe watched them toddle down the steps and plow through the muddy, sandy marsh to a streak of sand at the edge of the water, watched them spread their towels on the fish-scented shore. As Ralph put up the beach umbrella, Joe leaped down from the refrigerator and resumed his own search, swiftly prowling, poking with a nervous paw.

He found no other suitcase smelling of Greeley. He dug into the bags belonging to Dora and Ralph, then looked for the money beneath the beds and up under the bedsprings and under the couch cushions, all the while listening for footsteps on the porch or the sound of a car—or the soft thump of paws hitting the windowsill.

He tossed the bathroom, too, then pawed open the kitchen cabinets. He fought open the refrigerator but found no wrapped package that might contain money. Standing on the kitchen counter, he was just able to open the freezer, a favored place for householders to hide their valuables according to Max Harper. Leaning into the cold, he sniffed several paper-wrapped packages, but the smell of each matched its handwritten label: pork chops, shrimp, green beans. He nearly froze his ears off. Being practically inside the freezer, trying to listen for intruders, feeling as nervous as a mouse in a tin bucket, he backed out gratefully into the warm kitchen.

When he could think of nowhere else to look—couldn't figure a way to take the top off the toilet tank or remove the light fixtures—he gave up, sprang out the open window, and trotted up the hill behind the cottage. Fleeing the scene through the woods, he hit the wide gardens above, galloping between those substantial homes wondering where Greeley had hidden the money and what Dora and Ralph were up to. Telling himself that Dora Sleuder wouldn't rip off her own aunt Mavity.

13

WINTHROP JERGEN liked to tell his clients that he was a sentimental nonconformist, that he would endure almost any inconvenience so he could enjoy the magnificent view from his out-of-the-way office-apartment.

In fact, the view meant nothing. That wondrous vista down the Molena Point hills wasn't even visible when he sat at his desk, only the tops of a few ragged trees and empty sky. He had to stand up or move to the couch before the glare of sun-glazed rooftops stabbed at his vision. And this morning the so-called view was a mass of wind-churned trees and ugly whitecaps. That was the trouble with being close to the water, these violent winds whipping inland. Now, standing at his desk looking down to the dead-end street below, observing the weeds and the three battered service trucks parked behind Charlie Getz's rusting van, he wondered why he tolerated this disreputable display.

According to the provisions of his lease, he could have refused to let Damen undertake the remodeling, but he thought it better to endure a few months' annoyance in order to acquire a more respectable environ. And it was always possible that Damen would overextend himself, sink more money into the project than he could manage, and would be in need of cash, perhaps a personal loan.

Glancing at his watch, he left his desk and in the bathroom removed his sport coat, tucked a clean bath towel over his white shirt and tie, ran hot water into a washcloth and steamed his face, bringing up a ruddy color and relaxing the tightness that prevailed after he'd been at work for several hours. He brushed his teeth, used the blow-dryer to touch up his hair, removed the towel, and washed his hands. He was to pick up Bernine at twelve-thirty. He'd had trouble getting a reservation on a Saturday, but Bernine had raved about the Windborne. The restaurant was indeed charming, a rustic, secluded aerie clinging to the seacliffs south of the village. Bernine said she liked the ambiance. The moneyed ambiance, he thought, amused. As long as Bernine wasn't buying. If he kept this up, lunch or dinner every day, she could prove to be expensive.

He wasn't sure whether Bernine Sage would become a client or a lover, or both. It didn't matter. One way or another, she would be useful. She was blatantly obvious in coming onto him, but she was a good-looker, kept herself groomed and dressed in a style that commanded attention. A nice showpiece. And she seemed to know her way around, knew a lot of worthwhile, influential people.

As long as they understood each other, the relationship could be mutually entertaining. With Bernine on his arm he got plenty of appraising looks. She attracted interest, and interest, in a certain strata, meant money.

Straightening his tie and slipping back into his sport coat, he returned to the computer screen to finish up a last group of entries. He checked his figures, then closed and secured the file with a code and punched in the screen saver, a slowly wheeling montage of various foreign currencies. Putting his backup disks safely in the file cabinet, he locked it and locked the desk, left no disk or hard copy accessible. And without the code, no one could access his hard drive.

Surely no one around here had reason to snoop, or very likely had the knowledge to override his code. But he made it a point to follow set routines. He was successful in large part because he did not deviate from carefully chosen and rigorously observed procedures.

Two incidents of the morning did bother him, however. Small mistakes he must have made, though he abhorred carelessness.

He had found a number error in the Benson file. And he had found, in a hard copy file for the Dawson account, two spreadsheets out of order. Such small inefficiencies could lead to far more serious errors. He did not allow such carelessness in others, and he certainly couldn't sanction it in himself.

Locking the apartment, heading down the stairs jingling his keys, he paused at the bottom of the steps glancing to his right into the weedy patio at the stacks of lumber, the sawhorses, and crated plumbing fixtures. He hoped this project wouldn't last forever. Turning left from the stairwell, he stepped out onto the driveway and to the bank of garages. Activating his pocket remote, he opened his single garage door, backed the Mercedes out, and headed down the hills.

Molena Point's shops and cottages were appallingly picturesque. In his opinion, a regular Disney World, though he would not say that to anyone. As for the crowds of tourists, those people might as well be in Fantasyland, they were so busy spending money on foolish whims. No thought to solid investment. No, the tourists weren't for him. It was Molena Point's established residents who made up the predictable cadre of his clients.

Parking in the short-term green zone in front of the Molena Point Library, he had intended to wait for Bernine in the car, but on impulse he swung out and moved through the deep garden, along the stone walk, and in through the dark, heavily carved doors of the sprawling Mediterranean building.

The central reading room was brightly lighted, its white walls and spaciousness offsetting the dark tables and bookcases. Through an office door he could see Bernine, dressed in a short pink suit, standing near a desk beside the head librarian—Freda something—a frowsy scarecrow of a woman who seemed to be scolding a third party standing nearly out of sight beyond the door. Interested, he wandered in that direction, pausing beside the book stacks.

He could see a bit of the third woman, with her back to him. Red sweatshirt, long gray hair caught back with a silver clip, faded jeans. That would be the Getz woman, the person Bernine was staying with.

Plucking a book from the shelf, something about Scottish bed-and-breakfasts, he stood slowly turning the pages, listening for any stray information that might be useful.

They were arguing about a cat. *A cat*—that cat that had caused all the fuss in the newspaper, the animal they called the library cat. Freda was giving the tall, gray-haired woman a real dressing-down. And she had considerable skill at it, too; she handled her authority with style, splendidly high-handed and thorough.

And certainly Bernine, standing at full attention, was being very politic; her few comments, when Freda spoke to her, were as smooth as butter. How insane, all this fuss over some cat. You couldn't walk the street without someone wanting you to sign a petition.

He turned away as this Wilma person came out. She was actually carrying the cat, holding the animal across her shoulder like a baby. She crossed the reading room rigid with anger and disappeared through an office door.

From behind the closed door he heard her talking to someone, softly arguing. Curious, he moved closer. The other voice was so soft he could not make out the words, but both women were angry. He had a strong desire to see the other speaker, such a sudden, intense curiosity that he was tempted to push open the door.

Shutting the door behind her, Wilma set Dulcie on the desk. "That woman! How did we ever get saddled with her?"

"I'd like to slash her," Dulcie hissed, her green eyes blazing. "Eviscerate her like a dead toad."

Glancing at the door, Wilma lowered her voice. "She frightens me. We don't know what she might do." She reached to stroke

Dulcie. "Won't you agree to leave the library for a while?"

Dulcie's eyes widened.

"She could be capable of anything. I don't want you hurt."

Dulcie glared, her ears flat. "I can take care of myself."

"I know that. I know you can be all teeth and claws. But Freda is bigger, and she has the advantage of any number of large, heavy weapons. She could block your cat door and corner you, trap you in one of the offices. She might even turn on the gas. This petition movement has her in a rage. She's livid that the town and her own staff are trying to override her."

"You think she'd turn on the gas and risk blowing the place up? Don't be silly. And so she blocks my cat door. You know I can open any door in this library—the back door, the front door, the door to the side street. I can turn the knobs and, with a little time, I can turn every one of these dead bolts."

Wilma stroked her diffidently. "I know how skilled you are. And I know your hearing and eyesight are far superior, that there's no way she could slip up on you. But you refuse to admit that, simply because of size, a human might have some advantage. She's cruel, Dulcie. And she's angry!"

Dulcie turned away and began to wash, every lick across her tabby fur telegraphing her disdain.

Wilma walked around the desk and sat down facing her. "Please, won't you stay in my office during the day? Near your cat door? And stay away at night until the petitions go to the city council?"

Dulcie leaped off the desk, lashing her tail, and without another word pushed out her cat door. She'd had a difficult morning already, before Freda started in, and now Wilma. Tired and cross beyond toleration from leading Azrael around the village while trying to avoid his intimacies, she had come into the library needing a long nap, and there was Freda making another fuss. And now Wilma roiling at her. She felt as irritable as a bee trapped against the window; she wanted only to be left alone.

Azrael had pretended to enjoy her company as she gave him the grand tour, showed him the best places to hunt wharf rats, demurely led him along the shore and into the warehouses; as she showed him the meanest dogs to avoid and where the best restaurant garbage was judiciously hidden out of sight of wandering tourists—not that any village cat frequented such places. Why should they, when they could enjoy George Jolly's offerings? But the entire morning she didn't dare let her guard down. He had only one thing on his mind—he *would* keep nuzzling her. She had swayed on a tightrope between seeking to distract Azrael while Joe searched Mavity's cottage—and fighting her own distressing fascination. She didn't want to find Azrael charming; she didn't want to be drawn to him.

Well he *was* a good storyteller. Lying in the sun on Molena Point's fishy-smelling pier, he had told her wonderful tales of the jungle, had shown her the jungle's mysterious, leafy world awash in emerald light, the rain approaching like a silver curtain to drench the giant leaves and vines then move on again, a silver waterfall receding, glinting with the sun's fire.

He had shown her the steaming city sidewalks crowded with dirty children begging for food and stealing anything their fingers touched, had shown her black buzzards bigger than any street cat hunched above her on the rooftops, diving heavily to snatch garbage from the sidewalks; had shown her tangles of fishing boats tied to the wharves, then buckets of silver cod dumped flopping on the pier. His stories were so vivid that she could smell the stench of the open market where fly-covered sides of beef hung rotting in the tropical sun—and the tomcat's soft-spoken Spanish phrases enticed her, caressed her, though she did not understand their meaning.

She had ignored the darkness surrounding Azrael, the cloying heaviness beneath his sweet Spanish phrases—until he repeated his ugly predictions of murder.

"The people in this village, that woman Bernine Sage, and this investment person, and your Wilma Getz and her niece and that auto mechanic, all of them are drawing close to death. As unable to pull away as leaves blown to the edge of a dark pool." And Azrael had smiled as if greatly enjoying the prospect of human death. Rising, he had peered down into the shadowed world of mud and pilings below them, where Molena Point's small colony of stray cats eked out a meager living.

Suddenly, lashing his tail, he had leaped off the pier and shouldered into the shadows below, snarling and belligerent, routing the cowering strays, tormenting and bullying those thin cats, had sent them slinking away into dark niches to crouch terrified between the damp boulders.

Shocked, she had stormed after him and driven him back with steely claws. To hell with guile and sweet smiles.

But at her attack, his amber eyes had widened with amazement. "What's the matter? They're only common cats. They're not like us. Come on, Dulcie, have a little fun—they're only stupid beasts."

"You think they're stupid because they can't speak? You think they're without feelings? Without their own sensibilities and their own unique ways?"

He had only looked at her.

"Common cats have knowledge," she had said softly. She was hot with anger, but she daren't enrage him—not until Joe had finished with Mavity's cottage. "Can't you see," she had mewed gently, "that they have feelings, too?" All the while, she wanted to tear the stuffings out of him, he was *so* arrogant—this cat couldn't see a whisker-length beyond his ego-driven nose.

Disdainfully he had flicked his tail at her silly notions and stalked away. And she, chagrined, had swallowed her pride and galloped after him, sidling against his shoulder.

He'd glanced down at her, leering smugly again, turning on the charm, rubbing his whiskers against hers. She had held her tongue with great effort and spun away from the wharf, laughing softly and leading him a wild chase through the village. The cat was so incredibly boorish. Who needed a tom that viewed other cats so brutally, who viewed a female not as an interesting companion or hunting partner, but as a faceless object meant only to mount, only for male gratification?

And when at long last she heard the tower clock strike ten, and knew that Joe would have left Mavity's, she gave Azrael the slip. Making a tangled way among and through the shops, through enough varied scents—spices, perfumes, shoe polish—to hide her trail, she had slipped into the library guessing that, even if Azrael tracked her, he wouldn't follow her into that sanctuary of strict rules where he'd likely be thrown out on his lashing black tail.

Alone at last, she'd had a little wash and settled into the shelves of medieval history for a quiet nap. But it wasn't two hours later that she woke to Wilma and Freda arguing.

Alarmed, she had leaped down and trotted into Freda's office to rub against Wilma's ankles—whether out of support for Wilma or out of curiosity, she wasn't sure. And Wilma had picked her up and cuddled her, as together they took the blast of Freda Brackett's temper.

Jergen watched his lunch date emerge from the head librarian's office looking like a million dollars in the pale pink suit, its tight skirt at midthigh, the low-cut jacket setting off a touch of cleavage and Bernine's golden tan. Her red hair, piled high and curly, was woven with a flowered silk scarf in shades of red and pink. The minute she saw him, she turned on the dazzle, gave him a bright and knowing smile.

"Ready for champagne?" he said, offering his arm. "Our reservations are for one." Escorting her out, their passage was followed by the envious stares of several women behind the checkout counter. They made, Jergen was fully aware, an unusually handsome couple, well turned-out and enviable.

Crossing the garden, he stopped to pick a red carnation for Bernine. He was handing her into the car when, glancing across the street, he saw a portly couple entering an antique shop. He forgot Bernine and froze, stood staring—felt as if his blood had drained away.

But, no. Surely he was mistaken. That could not have been the Sleuders. Not Dora and Ralph Sleuder.

How would those two get here to Molena Point, and why would they come here? No, he had only imagined the resemblance. Taking himself in hand, he settled Bernine within the Mercedes, went around and slipped behind the wheel. The Sleuders wouldn't be here, three thousand miles from Georgia. If those two hicks took a vacation anywhere, it would be to Disney World or to Macon, Georgia, to look at the restored southern mansions.

But, pulling out into the slow traffic, he continued to watch the antique shop. Now he could only catch a glimpse of the couple. Behind him, the traffic began to honk. Damn tourists. Moving on to the corner, he made a U-turn and came back on the other side, driving slowly. He was glad he had put the top up, so he was less visible. Passing the shop, he caught a clear look at the woman.

My God. It *was* Dora Sleuder. Or her exact double. And then Ralph moved into view—the heavy chin, the receeding hairline and protruding belly.

This could not be happening.

What earthly event could have brought those people here? Brought those two bucolic hicks across the country? *No one* knew *he* was here. He had taken every precaution to cover his trail. He drove on by, trying to pull himself together, very aware of Bernine watching him, every line of her body rigid with curiosity.

Someone once said that wherever you traveled, even halfway around the world, in any group of a hundred people you had a 50 percent chance of meeting someone you knew, simply by coincidence, by the law of averages.

Surely this was coincidence. What else could it be?

But the worst scenario was that the Sleuders *had* come here to find him.

So? What could they do if they did find him?

Circling the block, he tried to puzzle out who could have sent them to Molena Point. Who, among his acquaintances, might be linked to them?

So far as he knew, only one of his clients had any ties to the east coast, and that was Mavity Flowers, whose niece came from one of the southern states. Mavity hadn't mentioned the niece's name and he hadn't any reason to ask.

What a nasty coincidence if Dora turned out to be Mavity's niece.

But no, that was too far-fetched. That sort of concurrence didn't happen, would be quite impossible.

However, the fact remained that those two dull people were here. He had to wonder if, despite their simple rural set of mind, they had somehow tracked him.

Whatever the scenario—happenstance or deliberate snooping—the reality was that if he remained in this small, close town where everyone knew everyone's business, the Sleuders would find him.

He began to sweat, considering what action to take.

Beside him, Bernine was growing restless. Smiling, he laid his hand over hers. "The couch in that antique shop, that dark wicker couch. It's exactly what I've been looking for. I want to go back after lunch. If it's as nice as it looks, it will fit my apartment perfectly—just the contrast I want to the modern leather."

Bernine looked skeptical.

"Imagine it done up in some kind of silk, perhaps a Chinese print. You know about that kind of thing; you have wonderful taste. Would you have time, after lunch, to take a look?"

He could see she wasn't buying it but that she appreciated the lie.

"I'd love to. Maybe we can find the right fabric in one of the local shops."

He liked the speculative way she watched him, trying to read his real purpose, almost licking her lips over the intrigue. Strangely, her interest calmed him. Perhaps, he thought, Bernine could be useful, if he needed help with the Sleuders.

But as the Mercedes turned off Ocean, picking up speed heading down the coast, neither Jergen or Bernine had seen a woman watching them from an upstairs window as they slowly circled the block.

14

FROM THE FRESHLY washed windows of her new apartment, Charlie, taking a break from cleaning, watched Bernine Sage and Winthrop Jergen leave the library across Ocean looking very handsome, Bernine in a short-skirted pink suit, Jergen wearing a tweed sport coat and pale slacks. The couple, in less than a week, had become an item. And that was all right with her.

She had come to the window for the hundredth time, she thought, amused at herself, to admire her brand-new view of the village rooftops and of Ocean's tree-shaded median and the library's bright gardens. Now, watching Jergen lean to open the passenger door for Bernine, she saw him suddenly go rigid, straightening up and seeming to forget Bernine as he stared across the median at something on the street below her.

Craning to look down, she could see nothing unusual, just window-shoppers, two shopkeepers hurrying by, probably on their way to lunch, and a meter maid marking tires. Directly below her, lying on a bench in the sun, a huge black cat was stretched out, ignoring the people who surged around him, in a most uncatlike manner. Most cats didn't want to sleep anywhere near strangers, but this one seemed to think he owned the sidewalk. Winthrop

Jergen was still staring but then he seemed to shake himself. He turned, handing Bernine into the car.

Pulling away from the curb, he crept along slowly, still looking, until irate drivers behind him began to honk. He speeded up only a little, and when he reached the corner where Ocean Avenue stopped at the beach, he made a U-turn and came back up the northbound lane, pausing just below her window and tying up traffic again before the bleating horns drove him on. The cat, on its bench, stared irritably at the noise. Charlie left the window to resume her cleaning, to finish scrubbing the kitchen alcove. A new home was never hers until she had dug out the crevice dirt and scoured and burnished every surface.

She finished cleaning just after one and headed for Wilma's to pick up her clothes and tools and meager furniture, thankful that Bernine wouldn't be there watching her pack, making sarcastic comments. She'd had enough of that this morning. When Clyde picked her up for an early trip to the plumbing supply houses, he had come in for coffee and of course Bernine was up, looking fetching in a tangerine silk dressing gown.

"A breakfast date," Bernine had purred smugly. "Now, isn't that romantic." She had looked them over as if she'd discovered two children playing doctor in the closet. "And where are you two off to, so early?"

"Plumbing supply," Clyde had said gruffly, gulping his coffee. "Come on, Charlie, they open in thirty minutes." Turning his back on Bernine, he had gone on out to the truck. Charlie had followed him, smiling.

They had had a lovely morning prowling through plumbing showrooms looking at showers, basins, at elegant brass faucets and towel racks. Not everyone's idea of fun, but the excursion had suited them both. She had been back in Molena Point in time to pick up the key from her new landlord and get her studio ready to move into.

Now, parking in Wilma's drive, she let herself into the kitchen, went down the hall to the guest room and began to fold her clothes into a duffle bag. As she was hiking her stuff out to the van, Wilma pulled up the drive beside her.

"Short day," Wilma said, at her questioning look. "I took off at noon." She looked angry, as if she'd not had a pleasant morning. Little tabby Dulcie sat hunched on the seat beside her, sulkily washing her paws. Wilma looked at Charlie's tools and bags piled on the drive, looked at Charlie, and her disappointment was clear.

"I found an apartment," Charlie said softly.

"Is it nice?" Wilma smiled, doing her best to be pleased. "Where is it?"

"Just across from the library—I can run in anytime, and you can run over for lunch or for dinner." Charlie reached to touch her aunt's shoulder. "I love being with you. How could I not, the way you spoil me? It's just—I feel a burden, coming back again after being here so long."

Wilma grinned. "It's just that you like your privacy—and detest being stuck with Bernine."

Charlie shrugged. "That, too. But . . ."

"Ever since you were a little girl," Wilma said, "you've valued your own space. I'm going to make a chicken sandwich. You have time for lunch?"

"Sure, I do."

Charlie finished loading up and went into the kitchen where Wilma was slicing white meat off a roast chicken. She sat down, stroking Dulcie who lay curled up on a kitchen chair. Wilma said, "I hadn't much choice, about Bernine."

"I know that. You have enough problem with her at the library. No need to antagonize her any more—until the petitions are in. She's a troublemaker." She got up to pour herself a glass of milk. "But maybe she'll be in a nicer mood for a while, now that she's dating Winthrop Jergen. I saw them coming out of the library at noon, like they were having lunch."

"Who knows how that will turn out?" Wilma said. She set the sandwiches on the table. "Tell me about your apartment."

"It's one big room—fresh white paint, a wonderful view of the village, and there's a garage off the alley, for storage. The stairs go down to a little foyer between the antique shop and the camera store; you can go from there to the street or back to the alley. There's a deli down at the corner, but not as good as Jolly's, and . . . But you know every shop on that street."

Wilma nodded. "You'll enjoy living there."

"You and Dulcie are invited to dinner as soon as I get settled." She finished her sandwich quickly, petted Dulcie again, and headed back to her new apartment to unload her boxes and tools. Seemed like she'd spent half her life lately carting her stuff around. After hiking her duffles and folding bed up the stairs, she put fresh sheets on the bed, slapped new shelf paper in the cupboards, and unpacked her few kitchen supplies. By three o'clock she had stored her tools in the garage and was headed back for the job to check on the plumber, see if he'd finished roughing in the changes to the ground-floor bathrooms.

Parking before the building, coming in through the patio, she glanced up at Winthrop Jergen's windows and was surprised that they were open—this wasn't his regular cleaning day, and he never opened the windows, only the girls did. Then she saw Pearl Ann through the bathroom window, working at something, and remembered that he'd wanted some repairs done. She hoped Pearl Ann would close up when she left or they'd all hear about it. Heading across the patio into the back apartment, she saw that Pearl Ann had finished mudding the Sheetrock in those rooms, and had cleaned her tools and left them dry and shining on the work table, had left the container of mud well sealed. Pearl Ann was always careful with her equipment.

Many women didn't like to mess with Sheetrock, partly because the drywall panels were hellishly heavy for a woman to handle. But Pearl Ann was good at the work, and she used a specially made wedge to lift the panels without straining so she could nail them in place. And her taping and mudding was as good as any full-time professional. She used the big float, giving it long, bold sweeps; she said she had learned from her dad.

Charlie was in the kitchen of the back apartment, which they used as an office and storeroom, when she saw the two cats come trotting into the patio from the hills below. It always amazed her how far and how quickly cats could travel. Less than two hours ago, she'd been feeding Dulcie bits of her chicken sandwich in Wilma's sunny kitchen.

But these two roamed all over the hills; according to Clyde and Wilma, they were excellent hunters. She could imagine Joe Grey killing most anything, but it was hard to think of soft little Dulcie with blood and gore on her claws. Now, watching Dulcie roll on the sun-warmed bricks, she could almost feel in her own body the cat's deep relaxion and well-being.

But soon Dulcie rose again, looking around eagerly—as if all set to rout a colony of mice. She looked secretive, too. As if, Charlie thought, she was about to embark on some urgent clandestine mission.

I have too much imagination.

Maybe I never grew up—still carting around my childhood fancies.

But the two cats did bother her. So often they appeared bound somewhere with intense purpose—bound on a specific errand, not just wandering. Cats not aware only of the moment but focused on some future and urgent matter.

These, Charlie Getz, are not sensible thoughts you're having. You ought to be making a building supply list.

Yet even as she watched, the cats rose and trotted purposefully away across the patio in a most responsible and businesslike manner.

Maybe they knew it was nearly quitting time. Maybe they were waiting for Clyde; he usually showed up about now. A dog would go to the door at the time his master was due home, so why not a cat? A dog would show up at the bus stop to escort his kid home from school. Certainly cats were at least as smart as dogs—she'd read some startling things about the abilities of cats. She watched the cats cross the patio, looking up at Winthrop Jergen's windows as if watching the flashes of Pearl Ann's polishing cloth. Sweeping across the glass, it must look, to them, like some trapped and frantic bird.

But suddenly they glanced back and saw her looking out. They turned away abruptly to sniff at the edge of a flower bed. Turned away so deliberately that she felt as if she'd been snubbed. Had been summarily dismissed.

Amused by her own imaginings, she opened the kitchen door and told the cats, "Clyde's not here yet."

They looked around at her, their eyes wide and startled.

"He's bringing some kitchen cabinets. If you're looking for a ride home, just wait around, guys."

The cats gave her a piercing look then closed their eyes, in unison, and turned away—as if the sound of her voice annoyed them. And when, half an hour later, Clyde arrived with the cabinets, Joe and Dulcie had disappeared.

"They'll come home when they're ready," he said.

"Don't you worry about them? Don't you wonder where they go?"

"Sure I worry. They're cats. People worry about their cats. Every time some village cat doesn't show up for supper, you can hear his owner shouting all over Molena Point."

He looked at her helplessly. "So what am I supposed to do? Follow Joe around? I can't lock him in the house, Charlie. Do that, and I might as well put him in a cage."

He seemed very intense about this. Well, she thought, Clyde loved his cat.

They unloaded the kitchen cabinets and set them in the front apartment; this was the only apartment to get new cupboards, thanks to the last tenant who had painted the old ones bright red. The new units were pale oak and prefinished. When Clyde was ready to head home, the cats were nowhere to be found, though he shouted for Joe several times. If the tomcat was around, he would usually come trotting to Clyde's summons, as responsive as any dog. Clyde called him again, waited, then swung into his truck.

She stared at him.

"They'll come home when they feel like it." He searched her

face for understanding. "I can't keep him confined, treat him like an overcontrolled lap dog. What good would Joe's life be, if I told him what to do all the time?"

She watched him turn the truck around at the dead end and pull away toward the village, his words resonating strangely. *What good would Joe's life be, if I told him what to do all the time?*

A puzzling turn of phrase. For some reason, the question, thus stated, left her filled with both unease and excitement.

Tossing some tools in through the side door of the van, she went back inside to get a ladder. Slipping it in on top of the tools, she pulled the door closed. She wanted to hang some drawings tonight and put up bookshelves. As she locked up the building, she called the cats, checking each apartment so not to shut them in.

She didn't find them. No sign of the little beasts. She didn't know why she worried about them. As Clyde said, they were off hunting somewhere.

But when she slid into her van, there they were on the front passenger seat, sitting side by side, watching her as expectantly as a taxi fare waiting for the driver, urging him to get a move on.

15

JOLLY'S ALLEY was no longer a pretty retreat for either tourist or village cat. Beneath the darkening sky where the first stars shone, the cozy brick lane with its little shops looked like a garbage dump. The light of its two wrought-iron lamps shone down upon a mess of greasy paper wrappers, broken eggshells, sandwich crusts, and chewed chicken bones. Wadded paper napkins and broken Styrofoam cups spilled from the two overturned refuse cans, and the smears of cold spaghetti and slaw and potato salad were stuck liberally with tufts of torn-out cat fur—a dozen colors of fur, telling the tale of a huge battle.

Joe and Dulcie, pausing at the alley's entrance, surveyed the mess with amazement, then outrage. Dulcie's ears went back and her tail lashed. Joe crouched as if to spring on whatever feline culprit remained.

But no culprit was visible, the battling cats had fled. Only the tufts of fur told the story, and their pawprints deep in the potato salad—and the stink of fear that lingered, as sharp as the smell of gunpowder after a frontline skirmish.

And, stronger even than the fear-stink, was the odor of the perpetrator—the belligerent reek of the black tomcat.

Sniffing Azrael's scent, Joe and Dulcie padded across the greasy bricks, peering into the shadows beneath the jasmine vine, searching for him.

Suddenly above them a shadow exploded between the rooftops and dropped down within the jasmine vine, dark and swift.

The black tom sauntered out of the foliage, his bullish shoulders swaggering, his amber eyes burning. Looking around at the devastation, he smiled and licked his whiskers.

Joe's growl was deep. "I suppose you waited until all the cats congregated for an evening's snack, then attacked them. Did you trap the smallest ones behind the garbage cans, so you could bloody them?"

Azrael widened his amber eyes. "And what business is it of yours, little cat? What are you, keeper of the village kitties?" Crouching, he circled Joe, his teeth bared, his eyes blazing.

Joe leaped, biting into Azrael's shoulder, raking his hind claws hard down Azrael's belly. Azrael clawed him in the neck. They spun, a tangle of slashing and screaming, then Azrael had Joe by the throat, forcing him down. Joe twisted free and bit him in the flank as Dulcie lunged into the fray. Together they pinned the tomcat. Under their violent double assault, he went limp. When they drew back, he fled to a safer position.

Now suddenly he was all smiles, waving his tail, curving and winding around a lamppost, the change swift and decisive. Chirruping and purring, he fixed his gaze on Dulcie.

"If I had guessed, my dear, that you would be here this evening, we could have feasted together—after I routed that rabble, of course. Or perhaps," he said softly, "you would have enjoyed that little skirmish—a little playful challenge to get your blood up. Hold!" he said as Joe moved to attack. "I have news. Information that will interest you."

But Joe leaped tearing at Azrael's ear and shoulder, and again the two were a screaming whirlwind—until the deli door crashed open and George Jolly ran out swinging a bucket. A cascade of dishwater hit them. Azrael bolted under a bench. Joe backed away, shocked, licking greasy dishwater from his whiskers.

"Look at this mess! At the mess you cats made." Jolly fixed his gaze on Joe. "What kind of behavior is this? I go away for half an hour and you trash my alley! And on a Sunday, too—with the village full of visitors. You! I'd thought better of you, gray tomcat. Why would you do this?"

He looked hard at Dulcie. "Tomcats! Stupid fighting tomcats. All this over a lady? *Shame. For shame.*" He shook his head sadly. "I feed you no more, you tomcats. I feed no one. You disappoint me. You're nothing but common street rowdies!"

Turning his back, he went inside. But he was out again at once, carrying a broom and dustpan. Irritably he righted the garbage cans and began to sweep, filling the dustpan over and over, dumping garbage back into the metal barrels. Azrael had disappeared, and as Jolly unwound a hose, Joe and Dulcie fled to the end of the alley.

Bouncing a hard spray across the bricks, Jolly washed up every smear, hosing the last crumbs into the drainage grid. Giving Joe a disgusted look, he disappeared inside. As he shut the door, Azrael dropped down from the roof. Ignoring Joe, he sidled up to Dulcie, looking incredibly smug.

"Such a charming companion you were the other morning, my dear Dulcie—diverting me so cleverly, while your crude friend, here, tossed Mavity's cottage."

He eyed Joe narrowly. "What were you looking for, gray cat, prowling Mavity's home while Dulcie performed her little ruse?"

Joe washed his paws, sleeking the white fur, and spread his claws to lick them dry.

"If you so enjoy snooping," Azrael told him, "if you *like* poking into human business—which I find incredibly boring—you might be interested in last night's telephone conversation. Though I would prefer to share my information privately, with the lady," Azrael said, purring.

Dulcie looked at him coldly. "Share it with both of us. One

does not hunt another's turf without shedding blood. What was this conversation? Why would we be interested?"

"An invitation to dinner," Azrael told her. "Someone in the village has invited Dora and Ralph out to dinner—without Mavity or Greeley."

"Humans go out to dinner frequently," Dulcie said, yawning.

"They are keeping this dinner a secret. They've told no one. The reservation is at a very fancy restaurant, much too elegant for those two Georgia hicks."

Dulcie yawned in his face. "Who made such an invitation?"

"They got a phone call, so I only heard one side. Heard Dora say *Winthrop*. Couldn't tell if she was talking *to* Winthrop Jergen or about him. You know Jergen—Mavity's financial guru."

"We know him," Joe said, turning from Azrael to wash his hind paw.

Azrael sat tall, puffing himself up, lashing his thick black tail. "Why would a big-time financial advisor take those two rednecks to dinner? And why wouldn't they tell Mavity and Greeley? Not a word," Azrael said, narrowing his amber eyes.

"Maybe the Sleuders want to invest," Dulcie suggested. "Surely Mavity bragged about Jergen—about how much money he's earned for her."

"Then why not invite her along? But what a laugh—*she* hasn't any business investing, she's nothing but a scrub woman. A bad-tempered, mean-spirited scrub woman, the way she treats visitors."

Dulcie looked hard at him. "The way she treats dirty-mannered tomcats? At least her money is her own. She didn't steal it, like her brother."

"If she'd learned from Greeley she wouldn't be mopping floors—not that I care what happens to that one."

"Where is this dinner?" Dulcie said. "What restaurant?"

"Pander's. Real fancy, people all dressed up, BMWs and stretch limos, street lined with Lincolns and New Yorkers. You should have seen Dora swoon. The minute she hung up the phone she rushed into the bedroom, fussing about dresses, pulling clothes out of her suitcase, holding them up and looking in the mirror."

Azrael smiled. "But when Mavity got home, Dora was suddenly real busy doing up the dishes, cleaning up the kitchen. No hint of the big invitation."

"Why didn't *you* tell Greeley?" Dulcie asked.

"Waiting to see what happens," Azrael said cooly. "To see where this little adventure leads." He licked his paw, smug and self-assured. "Sometimes it pays to hold back a little something from Greeley."

He rose, lashing his tail. "Greeley's blind when it comes to Dora. He'd never believe that Dora lied to him. When it comes to Dora, he wouldn't believe even me." And for a moment, the black tom looked almost pitiful.

"Greeley didn't believe that Dora nearly killed me with that damned frying pan," he hissed. "The minute he leaves the house she starts throwing stuff—but he says I'm lying."

"When is this fancy dinner?" Joe said. "And why are you telling us?"

Azrael's face became a sleek black mask. "I told you—that night on the rooftops, I told you. I sense death." He looked at Joe almost helplessly. "This dinner . . . Visions of death. I do not want it to touch Greeley."

The black tom shook himself. "If I spy on Dora and Ralph, if they see me prowling the restaurant, Dora'll pitch a fit, have the whole place down on me." He looked at Joe a long time. "She'd pay no attention to you—you'd be just a neighborhood cat lurking. You can slip under the tables. Try the terrace first. She seemed impressed that they might sit on the upstairs terrace, with a view down on the village." Azrael gave a toothy laugh. "What's the big deal about rooftops?" He fixed Joe with another level look. "You can find out what Dora and Ralph are up to—find out if it will harm Greeley."

"Why would his own daughter do something to hurt him?" Dulcie asked.

"Maybe she wouldn't mean to harm him. Maybe she wouldn't understand the implications."

"You're making too much . . ." Joe began.

"I sense death around Greeley," the cat yowled. "I see death."

"Even if you do, why should we get involved?" Joe asked coldly. "What's in it for us?"

The black tom gave Joe a deep and knowing look. "You will do it. You dance to curiosity as some cats dance to catnip. You two are riven with inquisitiveness.

"And with righteousness," Azrael continued smugly. "If you think the law will be broken, that there's a crime, that a human will be harmed, you little cats will do it."

Joe crouched to rake him again, but the tom ignored him, twitching a long black whisker.

"You nosed into every possession Dora and Ralph have. You left your scent on every smallest bit of clothing. If you thirst for knowledge and justice, if you stalk after lawbreakers, how could you *not* run surveillance—as your Captain Harper would say—on this intriguing little meeting?"

They watched him intently, Joe angrily, Dulcie with increasing interest.

"Tonight," Azrael said softly, narrowing his flame-golden eyes. "Seven-thirty. They're to take a cab." And he slipped away, vanishing among the shadows.

Dulcie looked after him with speculation.

Joe said, "What's he trying to pull? There's no crime, nothing has happened. What a lot of . . ."

She kept looking where Azrael had vanished, and an eager, hotly curious expression gleamed like fire in her wide green eyes.

"He's setting us up, Dulcie."

"Why would he set us up? I don't think so. Did you see his eyes when he talked about Greeley? That was—that was a plea for help."

"Come on, Dulcie. A plea for help from the likes of him? That cat cares about no one."

"He cares about Greeley." She gave Joe a deep green look. "He loves Greeley. I'm going over there to Pander's."

"Come on, Dulcie. You let him sucker you right in."

"Into *what?* What could he do? What harm can come of it?"

"Dulcie . . ."

"Do as you please," she hissed. "I want to know what this is about." And she trotted away, switching her tail, heading for Pander's.

Joe galloped after her, leaned down and licked her ear. "Totally stubborn," he said, laughing.

She paused, widened her eyes at him, purring.

"Hardheaded." He licked her whiskers. "And totally fascinating."

She gave him a green-eyed dazzle and a whisker kiss.

"So what the hell?" Joe purred. "So we slip into Pander's, maybe cadge a scrap of fillet. So what could happen?"

16

CROUCHING close together beneath a red convertible, the cats licked their whiskers at the delicious smells from Pander's, the aroma of roast lamb and wine-basted venison and, Dulcie thought, scallops simmered in a light sherry. But the elegant scents were the only hints of Pander's delights, for the building itself was not inviting. From the street it looked as stark as a slum-district police precinct.

The brick face of the plain, two-story structure rose directly from the sidewalk with no architectural grace, not even a window through which to glimpse the restaurant's elegantly clad diners. The closed door was painfully austere, with no potted tree or flower or vine beside it, in the usual Molena Point style, to break the severity. Only the expensive cars parked at the curb and the delicious aromas wafting out hinted at the pleasures of Pander's as the cats waited for Dora and Ralph Sleuder to appear.

Despite the gourmet allure, Joe would just as soon be home catching a nap as spying in that rarified environ, dodging the sharp eyes and hard shoes of unsympathetic waiters.

"What if we can't get in?" Dulcie said softly, studying the blank, closed facade.

"Should have phoned for a reservation. We'd like two cushions laid on a corner table, my good man. We'll have the venison—you can dispense with the silverware."

She just looked at him.

"We'll go over the roof," he said more gently. "Drop down onto the terrace." The second-floor dining terrace, at the back, boasted no outer access, only the stairs from within the main dining room.

"But, Joe, the minute we look over the edge of the roof and the terrace lights hit us, we're like ducks in a shooting gallery."

"Who's going to look up at the roof? They'll all be busy with their menus and drinks and impressing each other." He looked hard at her. "I still say it's a setup. I don't trust anything that lying alley cat tells us."

"He looked really worried. I think he truly wanted our help. Maybe his prediction of murder isn't all imagination, maybe Greeley is in danger, and we can find out why."

Joe shrugged. "Maybe Jergen found out that Greeley's stealing. Maybe he's going to hit Dora for blackmail—she forks over or he turns in her father."

"That sounds flimsy. How would he even know Greeley? For that matter, how does he know Dora and Ralph?" Her green eyes narrowed. "Why this dinner so soon after Dora and Ralph copied Mavity's financial statements?"

"As to that, what about Pearl Ann snooping into Jergen's computer? Is there some connection? And," he said, "need I point out again that there's been no crime committed? That this is all simply conjecture?"

She gave him that don't-be-stupid look, her eyes round and dark. "When people start prying into other people's business, copying their personal papers, accessing their computer files, either a crime's been committed or one's about to be. *Someone's* up to no good. We just don't know who." And she settled closer to Joe beneath the convertible to await Jergen's little dinner party.

The Sleuders had not yet made an appearance when Pander's

door opened, a middle-aged couple came out, and the cats glimpsed, within, a tuxedoed maître d' of such rigid stance that one had to assume, should he discover a trespassing cat, he would snatch it up by its tail and call the dog-catcher. They had been waiting for some time when they realized they were not the only observers lingering near Pander's closed door.

Across the street a man stood in the shadowed recess between two buildings, a thin, stooped man, pale and very still, watching Pander's: the Sleuders' mysterious friend and courier. The man who loitered, in the evenings, outside Clyde's apartment building.

"He gives me the shivers," Dulcie whispered. The cats watched him for a moment then slipped away beneath the line of cars and around the corner to the back alley.

They hoped to find the kitchen door propped open, a common practice among Molena Point restaurants during the summer to release the accumulated heat of the day and to let out the warm breath of the cookstove.

But the rear door was securely shut, the entire building sealed tighter than Max Harper's jail.

"Spotlights or not," Joe said, "let's hit the roof." And he took off for the end of the building, swarming up a bougainvillea vine through clusters of brick red flowers. With Dulcie close behind him, they padded across Pander's low, tarred roof toward the blinding light that flowed up from the terrace. Soft voices rose, too, and laughter, accompanied by the tinkling of crystal.

Crouching at the edge, their paws in the roof gutter and their eyes slitted against the glare, they peered down onto two rows of snowy-clothed tables and the heads of sleekly coiffed women in low-cut gowns and neatly tailored gentlemen; the tables were set with fine china and heavy silver, and the enticing aromas engulfed the cats in a cloud of gourmet nirvana. Only with effort did they resist the urge to drop onto the nearest table and grab a few bites, then run like hell.

But they hadn't come here to play, to create chaos in Pander's elegant retreat, as amusing as that might be.

Along the terrace wall, dark-leafed, potted trees stood judiciously placed to offer the diners a hint of privacy between their tables. The cats did not see Dora and Ralph. But a serving cart stood directly below them, and in a flash of tabby and gray they dropped down onto it then onto the terrace, slipping beneath the cart, finding their privacy in the shadows between its wheels.

From this shelter, their view down the veranda was a forest of table and chair legs, slim ankles, pant cuffs, and gleaming oxfords. A waiter passed, inches from their noses, his hard black shoes creaking on the tiles. To their right, a pair of glass doors opened to the interior dining room. They knew from their housemates' descriptions that Pander's had four dining rooms, all richly appointed with fine antique furniture and crystal chandeliers, and the tables set with porcelain and sterling and rock crystal. Both Wilma and Clyde favored Pander's for special occasions, for a birthday or for the anniversary of Wilma's retirement. The staff was quiet and well-trained, none of the *my-name-is-George-and-I'll-be-your-waiter* routine, and none of the overbearing showmanship of some expensive but tasteless restaurants that catered to the nouveau riche, waiters with bold opinions and flashy smiles. Pander's existed for the comfort and pleasure of its guests, not to put on a floor show.

When Wilma did dine at Pander's, she would bring home to Dulcie some small and delectable morsel saved from her plate, wrapped by her waiter in gold foil and tucked into a little gold carton printed with Panders' logo. Once she had brought a small portion of beef Wellington, another time a little serving of pheasant stuffed with quail. She had served these to Dulcie on the good china, too, making of the occasion a delightful party. Pander's was one of the human institutions about which Dulcie liked to weave daydreams, harmless little fantasies in which she was a human person dressed in silk and diamonds and perhaps a faux-leopard scarf, little imaginary dramas that delighted her and hurt no one.

But now she began to worry. "What if they didn't get a terrace table? If they're not here when the courthouse clock chimes eight, we'll have to try the dining rooms, slip along under the dessert cart when they wheel it in that direction."

"I'm not going through that routine again. Creeping around on our bellies between squeaking wheels. I had enough of that in the nursing home."

"At least you didn't have to worry about your tail getting under the wheels." She cut him an amused glance. "A docked tail does have its upside.

"And," she said, "your short tail makes you look incredibly handsome—even more macho. The drunk who stepped on your tail and broke it—he didn't know he was doing you such a big favor."

The terrace was filling up, several parties had entered; only two tables remained empty, and no sign of the Sleuders. The cats were crouched to make a dash for the inner door when they saw Dora and Ralph coming through.

"There they . . ." She stopped, staring.

Joe did a double take.

The Sleuders' host was not Winthrop Jergen.

Dora and Ralph's dinner companion, gently ushering them in behind the maître d', was Bernine Sage, her red hair wound high with bands of gold, her orange-and-pink flowered suit summery and cool—making Dora and Ralph look so shabby that Dulcie felt embarrassed for them.

Dora had chosen a black dress, possibly to make herself appear thinner, but the black was rusty and faded, as if she had owned the dress for a very long time, and her black stockings were of the extra-support, elasticized variety. Ralph was dressed in a gray pinstripe suit with amazingly wide lapels, a shirt that should have been put through a tub of bleach, and a broad necktie with black-and-white dominoes printed across it. His socks were pale blue.

As the three were seated, the cats flashed across open space and beneath the table nearest to their cart. Slipping behind a potted tree to the next table, winding between silk-clad ankles and satin pumps and polished Balley loafers, they were careful to avoid physical contact with the clientele, not to brush against someone's ankle and elicit startled screams and have waiters on them as thick as summer fleas.

Moving warily, their progress alternating between swift blurs and slinky paw-work, they gained the end of the terrace and slipped under the Sleuders' table, crouching beside Bernine's pink high heels and nude stockings, Dulcie tucking her tail under so not to tickle those slim ankles.

Dora's black shoes were a size too small. Her skin pooched over and her thick stockings wrinkled. Ralph was wearing, over his baby blue socks, black penny loafers with dimes in the slots. The threesome was seated so that the Sleuders could enjoy the view out over the village rooftops. Bernine's vantage commanded the terrace tables and their occupants; she could watch the room while seeming to give the preferred seating to her guests. Their conversation was hesitant, almost shy. Above the cats, a menu rattled. Dora shifted in her chair, rearranging her feet so Joe had to back away. She asked Bernine about Molena Point's weather in the winter, and Ralph inquired about the offshore fishing. The cats were starting to doze when a waiter came to take the drink orders. Dora ordered something called a white moose, Ralph liked his Jack Daniel's straight with no chaser, and Bernine favored a Perrier.

When the waiter had gone, Bernine said, "How is Mavity feeling—is she all right? She's working so hard. I worry about her. House cleaning is terribly heavy work for a woman of her years."

Dora's voice bristled. "Mavity has always worked hard."

"I know Charlie is shorthanded," Bernine confided, "but Mavity isn't so young anymore."

"Hard work is the way she and Daddy grew up; they thrive on it. Both of them worked in the family grocery since they were in grammar school. It was right there on Valley Road when this part of Molena Point was mostly little farms," Dora told her. "Mavity and Daddy wouldn't know what to do without hard work. Daddy was the same on the farm, always working."

"Well, I suppose she does want the work just now, since she's investing every penny. She's so excited about increasing her savings."

There was a pause as their drinks arrived, the waiter's hard black shoes moving around the table, the sound of ice tinkling, the sharp scent of alcohol tickling the cats' noses. "But I do wonder," Bernine said, "about these investments of hers. Mavity is thrilled with the money, but this Winthrop Jergen . . ." Another long pause. Dora began to wiggle her left toe. Ralph's feet became very still. Bernine said tentatively, "I wonder sometimes if Mr. Jergen is—quite to be trusted."

No one responded. Under the table, Ralph tapped his foot softly. Dora shifted position, pressed one foot tightly against the other.

Bernine said, "The kind of money Mavity's making seems—well, nearly too good to be true.

"Though I don't see how Mr. Jergen could cheat her," she hastened. "After all, she must get a regular monthly statement. And she told me herself, she drew two hundred dollars from her profits just last week to do a few things to the house, buy some new dishes."

Dora made a strange little sound. "Oh, the dishes are lovely. Real Franciscan pottery, just like Mama had. Well, she didn't have to do that, just because we were coming. Didn't have to do anything for us."

"She wanted to," Bernine said. "And I guess she can afford it, all right. I'd love to invest with Mr. Jergen, but I—I don't know. Investments make me so nervous."

"Investing with that Je . . ." Ralph began. Under the table, Dora kicked him.

"Still," Bernine went on smoothly, "if Mavity can make that kind of money . . . Well, maybe I *would* like to try."

Ralph cleared his throat. "I—I wouldn't do that." Dora kicked him again, barely missing Joe, and the cats backed away against the terrace wall. There was another pause, as if Bernine might have looked at Ralph with surprise.

"Do—do you have any—special reluctance?" she asked. "I know so very little about investments."

Dulcie cut her eyes at Joe, amused. This was hugely entertaining. Whatever Bernine was playing at, she must seem, to Dora and Ralph, the height of sophistication—it must be a heady experience for Ralph to find Bernine Sage asking his advice.

Ralph leaned closer to Bernine's chair. "I would be careful about investing with Jergen." And Dora's heel pressed hard against his ankle.

"Oh?" Bernine said softly. "You're not telling me there's something wrong?"

The waiter approached and they heard the tinkle of fresh drinks. There was a long interval concerned with ordering, with crab mornay, with a salad of baby lettuces, cuts of rare fillet, and a broiled lobster—a discussion that left the cats sniffing around under the table for any leftovers from previous diners.

"I can't believe . . ." Bernine began when the waiter had gone, "I can't dream that Mavity's Mr. Jergen . . . Are you saying that Mr. Jergen . . . ?" She paused delicately, her hand beneath the table seeming to accidentally brush Ralph's hand. The cats watched, fascinated, as Ralph tentatively stroked Bernine's fingers. Dulcie could picture Bernine giving him a steamy gaze from beneath her mascara-heavy lashes.

Ralph cleared his throat and shifted his hand guiltily as if he thought Dora might have noticed his preoccupation. "I would not invest with Mr. Jergen," he said bluntly.

"Ralph . . ." Dora said.

"We—Dora and I—we are very worried about Mavity."

"But she's made such wonderful money," Bernine said. "She told me her profits have been . . ."

Dora sighed, pressing one toe against the other as if to relieve her tension. "I don't think we should be talking about this, Ralph. After all, we . . ."

"Dora, be reasonable. Do you want this poor girl to . . . Do you want the same thing to happen to Bernine?"

Bernine leaned forward, tucking her sandaled toe behind her ankle in a little spurt of elation. As if she had whispered to herself, *Bingo! Gotcha.*

"All right," Dora said reluctantly. "If you want to do this, Ralph, all right. But we have been far too trusting in the past, and I . . ."

"Dora, this is different. Can't you see this is different?"

Dora sighed.

Ralph leaned close to Bernine, clutching her hand earnestly beneath the table, as if in a spasm of heart-to-heart communication. "Winthrop Jergen—it's hard to tell you this, my dear. But Winthrop Jergen is a—professional confidence artist."

Bernine caught her breath.

"We have the proof," Ralph said. "All the court proceedings are available, back in Georgia."

"You mean he's—been to jail?"

"Jergen wasn't convicted," Ralph told her, "but he's guilty as sin."

"We only hope," Dora said, "that we can convince Mavity of this. That she will accept the truth. We haven't told her yet. We wanted . . ."

This time it was Ralph's turn to kick, his black loafer thumping Dora's ankle.

"We only hope that she can pull out of this in time," Ralph said. "Before Jergen gets away with her money. She doesn't . . ."

The waiter returned with their salads. In the island of silence as he served, the cats curled down more comfortably against the wall. When he had gone Ralph leaned, again, toward Bernine.

"Winthrop Jergen, my dear, robbed us of nearly all our life savings."

"Oh. Oh, don't tell me that. Oh, how terrible for you. I can't believe this." Bernine's toe wiggled with excitement.

"We've gotten none of our money back," Ralph told her. "All gone. Police couldn't find a trace, not a bank account, nothing."

Dora uncrossed her ankles, setting her feet solidly. "Jergen arranged his little scheme so his partner went to prison. Jergen got off free—went totally free."

"But where did this all happen? And when?" Bernine asked, puzzled.

"In Georgia, and not many months ago," Dora told her. "Not long before Christmas—it was a terrible Christmas for us. Terrible."

"But what brought him here? How did you know he was here? Did Mavity . . . ?"

"Mavity told us about her wonderful investments," Ralph said. "She hoped we might be able to make back some of our losses."

"And," Dora said, "when she described Jergen, we began to suspect that this might be Warren Cumming—that's his real name."

"Seemed impossible it could be the same man," Ralph said. "But when we checked Cumming's phone in Georgia, it had been disconnected. And when we went to his office, it was empty; he'd moved out. Mavity's description of Jergen sounded so much like Cumming that we decided to find out. So when we told . . ."

Dora kicked again. Poor Ralph was going to have a black-and-blue ankle.

"When we told our Georgia friends we were coming out here," Ralph mumbled, "they wished us luck. You have to understand how angry we were, that Jergen got off free."

"Scot-free," Dora said. "Looks like he came right on out here, took a new name, started right up again, cheating people—cheating my own aunt."

"But . . ." Bernine began.

"I suppose he got a new driver's license," Dora said. "Got all those fake cards like you read about, social security, who knows what else?"

Ralph shifted his feet. "All we can do, now, is try to convince poor Mavity of the truth. She thinks that man hung the moon. But with some proof . . ."

"Now," Dora said loudly, pressing her knee against his, "now all we can do is help Mavity cope with this. That's all we can ever do."

As their entrées were served, the conversation deteriorated to a replay of everyone's concerns for Mavity, punctuated by the sounds of cutlery on china and occasional smacking from Ralph. The cats had nearly dozed off again when the main course was concluded and their waiter took the plates and brought coffee and the dessert cart. Bernine declined dessert. Dora chose a pecan and caramel torte with whipped cream. Ralph selected a double cream puff with chocolate sauce. Dulcie was partial to the small custard tart on the bottom shelf. Lifting it gently from its pleated white doily, she and Joe indulged. Above them, the conversation turned to Molena Point's tourist attractions, then back to Mavity, to how shocked Bernine was and how worried they all were for Mavity's well-being. When again the dessert cart passed their table, the cats went away beneath it, licking cream from their whiskers.

As the waiter parked the cart at the end of the terrace and turned away, the cats sprang to its top shelf skillfully missing cakes and pies and tortes. Leaping to the roof, they dislodged one small piece of cherry pie, sent it skidding across the terrace. They heard it hit and didn't look back, sped racing across the roof and didn't stop until they reached the end of the block.

Pausing beside a warm heat vent, they had a leisurely and calming wash to settle their nerves. "What's that hussy up to?" Joe said, licking his paws.

"Don't forget, she worked for years as a secretary for the San Francisco probation office. That's where Wilma first knew her."

"So?"

"She must know a lot of probation officers and law enforcement people. And those guys, when they retire, sometimes start private investigative services. Wilma knows several P.O.s who . . ."

"You think she's *investigating* Dora and Ralph? Or investigating Jergen? Come on, Dulcie. Can you picture Bernine doing anything to help the law?"

"She would for money—she'd do anything for money."

"And what about the watcher?" He peered over the roof to see if the man was still there, but he had gone—or had moved to a new vantage. "He appears to have masterminded the copying of Mavity's financial statements," Joe said. "*He* could be some kind of cop—that's more believable than Bernine helping the law."

He began to pace the roof, across the warm, tarry surface. "And what about Pearl Ann, snooping on Jergen?" He looked at Dulcie intently. "Who's the cop, here? And who's the rip-off artist?"

As they discussed the puzzle, thirty feet below them the sidewalk was busy with tourists, the after-dinner crowd heading home, lingering at the shop windows, and late diners coming from art exhibits or leaving the local theater, heading for various village restaurants. They saw, scattered among the crowd, two women and an elderly man carrying library cat petitions, stopping each tourist to show newspaper clippings with Dulcie's picture.

"Who's checking those signatures," Joe said, amused. "These people aren't village residents."

"They use the library, though," she said defensively. "Lots of visitors do. Wilma makes out temporary cards all the time."

Directly below them a couple in jeans stood arguing about whether to drive on to San Francisco or stay in Molena Point, and up at the corner three college-age girls flirted with their male escort, each angling prettily for his attention. Ordinarily the cats enjoyed watching tourists, they liked hanging over the roof making fun of people, but tonight their attention returned quickly to Bernine and the Sleuders, worrying at the tangle as intently as they would worry at an illusive mouse.

But, as it turned out, they had little time to circle the quarry before Azrael's prediction came true. Before there was, indeed, a murder. An event that sucked in Joe and Dulcie like flies into a spider web.

17

I SEE DEATH *around you . . . death before the moon is full,* Azrael had told them—almost as if the black tom could himself bring death with his dark magic, as if this beast were indeed the Death Angel. Whatever the truth, two days after Azrael beguiled Joe and Dulcie into spying at Pander's restaurant, death reached out just as he predicted.

It was barely eight A.M., Tuesday morning, as they entered the empty library, slipping in through Dulcie's cat door, their bellies full of fat mice, meaning to curl up on the children's window seat for a little nap before opening time. The cushioned retreat, where the children listened to stories, was at this hour Dulcie's private domain.

According to Freda Brackett, Dulcie had turned the long window seat and the inviting tangle of brightly flowered pillows into a nest of cat hair, fleas, and ringworm, but the children thought differently. They loved finding Dulcie among the cushions to snuggle as they listened to the librarian's stories; they all fought to hold her and sit close to her.

But now this early morning there were as yet no children and the wide bay window was theirs, the only sounds the occasional *whish* of passing cars away across the garden and the distant purling of the sea; crossing the reading room, the cats could feel, through the floor and carpet, the sea's constant muffled heartbeat.

Dulcie thought it so odd that Wilma couldn't feel the surf beating unless she was right there at the shore. How sad, what humans missed. Nor had Wilma, just last week, felt the preearthquake tremors that sent Dulcie under the bed at two in the morning, yowling until Wilma took shelter in the closet, the two of them waiting for the earthquake to hit, for heavy objects to start falling.

The ensuing quake had been nothing, amusingly small, no more damage done than a few drinking glasses broken and a crack in the bathroom wall—by California standards, hardly worth getting out of bed for—though Dulcie had not been able to determine its severity by its preshock tremors.

Now, leaping to the window seat, kneading the pillows, the cats yawned and stretched, ready for a nap—and stopped.

They went rigid, hissing, backing away from the glass.

A smell assailed them, unnatural and alarming.

Not the sweet aroma of little children and candy wrappers and the librarians' subtle perfume.

A stink of death seeped in around the glass—nor was it the scent of a dead animal, not the smell of freshly killed rabbit or squirrel. No. The smell they tasted, flehming and growling, was the stink of human death.

Crouched and tense, they approached the glass, stood pressed against the window looking down into the depths of the tangled garden.

Beyond the window, the building's two wings jutted out to form a partially walled disarray of blooms that reached up thick as a jungle beneath the children's window. Spider lilies, tapping at the glass, were tall and thick, their delicate blossoms curled like reaching hands. Beyond the lilies, flowering bushes glowed, and tangles of blue iris. On the east wall, a mass of climbing yellow nasturtiums shone yellow as sunshine, and above the jungle of blooms the oak trees twisted their sturdy, dark limbs and jade foliage against the morning sky.

Beyond the garden stood Ocean Avenue's double row of eucalyptus trees and then, across the divided street, the crowded, two-story shops. But it was the flower bed beneath the bay window and what lay crushing the blooms, that held the cats' attention, that made every hair rise, that drew Joe's lips back in a keening snarl and made Dulcie catch her breath with a shocked mewl.

Below the jutting window a man knelt. As the cats watched, he reached to touch the two bodies that lay sprawled together unmoving, their fleshy, blue-veined, half-naked limbs shockingly white.

Greeley Urzey knelt stroking Dora's limp hand, reaching to touch her bare, white leg, her naked limbs heavy and comatose. Both Ralph's and Dora's clothes were half-torn off—not as if they had been attacked, rather as if they had flung off their garments in a wild and frenzied dance, an insane gavotte. And across the garden, an erratic path twisted, raw with crushed foliage and flowers, a maddened trail plunging in from Ocean Avenue.

One of Ralph's penny loafers lay yards away from him among a bed of daisies, its dime gleaming in the morning light. The cats could see, across the street, what might be a sweater dropped on the curb.

They drew back as Greeley clasped together his shaking hands and rose, his whole being seeming to tremble, the expression on his face frightened and confused.

He stood staring uncertainly around the garden, then wandered away up the path, his gait slow and hesitant. As he stumbled along Ocean, the black cat dropped down out of an oak tree and fell into step beside him.

At the same instant, Joe and Dulcie leaped from the window seat and scorched across the library and out Dulcie's cat door. They reached the front garden just as Greeley and Azrael turned the corner, disappearing into a tunnel of dark, low-growing cypress trees.

The two cats grimaced at the death smell, softened by the scent of crushed lilies. Joe placed an exploring paw on Ralph's arm.

Dulcie nosed at Dora's hand—and drew back from the icy flesh. She looked at Joe, stricken.

"Greeley didn't do this. Greeley didn't do this terrible thing, not to his own daughter."

"Maybe he just found them. They've been dead for hours, Dulcie. If he killed them, why would he come back?"

"But if he just found them, why wouldn't he head for the police station? He went in the opposite direction."

"Maybe he was too upset. Maybe he'll call the cops from somewhere. Maybe go home to Mavity, call from there."

"Oh, Joe, these poor, silly people. What did they do, that they would die in such—distress?" She pressed close to him, thinking of the stolen computer printouts, then of Ralph and Dora's feet beneath the table at Pander's, Ralph's penny loafers beside Bernine's silk-clad ankles, thinking of Dora kicking Ralph when his remarks didn't suit her.

"Whatever they did, they were just simple folk. Who would kill them?" She stared at the tangle of pale, twisted limbs, shocked by their raw whiteness. The Sleuders were such very bulgy people, their limbs lumpy and misshapen. It must be terrible not to have a nice coat of sleek, concealing fur to cover your fat places and your rawness. She watched Joe sniff at Ralph's nose and mouth—he made a flehming face, raising his lip and flattening his ears.

He smelled Dora's face, too, scowling. "Drugs? Were they into drugs?"

"Don't be silly. Dora and Ralph Sleuder?"

"What else would smell so foreign?"

She sniffed at the dead couple's faces and backed away sneezing at the strange, pungent odor. "We'd better call the dispatcher."

As they started toward her cat door, he stopped suddenly, pressing her back. "Dulcie, wait."

She paused, one paw lifted. "What? It's nearly opening time; the staff will be coming to work. What's the matter?"

"Isn't children's story hour this morning?"

"Oh! Oh, my! Come on!" She dodged past him. "They'll be crowding in any minute, running to the window." And she took off round the side of the building.

Twice a week story hour began at eight-fifteen. The kids came flocking in, breaking away from their parents, laughing and pummeling each other and heading straight for the window seat, leaping into the cushions in a frenzy of enthusiasm, pressing their noses to the glass to look out. Children were always drawn to windows—as surely as kittens were drawn to dangling string. Entering any room, children flocked to the glass as if, like Alice, they expected to find beyond the pane any number of exotic new worlds.

This morning, beyond this glass, they'd find an exotic world, all right—a scene never meant for a child's viewing. But now, as she leaped for her cat door to call the precinct, Joe barged into her again, blocking her way.

"What?" she hissed, shouldering him aside.

"Listen, Dulcie. What would happen if we don't call the cops?"

She stared at him, shocked. "The children would be . . . We can't let them see those bodies. They'd . . ."

"They'd start screaming," Joe suggested. "Screaming, giggling, making jokes to hide their fear and confusion. Their parents . . ." He licked a whisker and smiled wickedly. "Their parents would see the dead bodies and pitch a fit—that the library would let the children see this."

He began to purr. "Those parents would put Freda right on the hot seat."

She looked at him, her eyes widening. She didn't breathe. What he was suggesting was terrible.

"How embarrassing for Freda," Joe said softly.

"No!" she said, shouldering past him. "I won't do that. It would be dreadful for the children."

"Those kids are tougher than you think. All they'll need is

plenty of hugging and a chance to talk it out with their mom or dad—any good parent could put a positive spin on the experience. Turn a shocking situation into something positive—as long as the kids are hugged and loved."

"No!" she said, pressing past him.

But again he blocked her, licking his whiskers. "It would be the parents who are stressed. And they'd dump it all on Freda—complaints to the mayor, to the city council, letters to the editor, follow-up editorials. Enough fuss," Joe said, his yellow eyes burning, "to get Freda fired."

There was a long silence. Joe's eyes gleamed with the devil's own light.

"No, Joe. We can't! Not frighten the children like that—not to spite Freda, not to spite anyone." Hotly she slashed at him and bolted through her cat door into Wilma's office where she could call the station.

But she was too late.

As she leaped for Wilma's office she heard two librarians talking, heard Freda call out as she came in through the back door, and the next moment she heard children running up the walk past the hidden, flower-shrouded bodies, heard them racing across the reading room straight for their window seat.

18

THE LIBRARY and garden were crawling with cops. From the roof, Joe Grey watched three medics kneel among the lilies beside the bodies of Dora and Ralph Sleuder. Unable to observe all the action from inside, he had streaked up the back of the building to the roof, leaving Dulcie inside on the book stacks doing interior surveillance. The police action upon entering the garden had been swift and precise as each man swung to his appointed job.

But now the medics, unable to help the deceased, rose again and moved away, nodding to the police photographer. He, pushing back his shoulder-length black hair, knelt among the flowers to shoot close-ups first of the victims' faces, then of their raw white limbs, recording from every possible camera position; loading new film, at last he turned from the bodies to photograph the surround, the window above the corpses, the white stucco wall, and the garden itself, calling an assistant to part the lilies so he could shoot the earth beneath. Across the garden, Freda Brackett's angry accusations rose sharply.

She stood before the library's open front door, toe to toe with Max Harper, her words burning like flames. Harper listened to her harangue without speaking, his thin face frozen into complicated lines of distaste that made Joe laugh. Didn't Freda see the deep anger in the police captain's eyes—and the spark of cold amusement?

"What kind of police force *is* this, Captain Harper, to let such a shocking crime occur practically inside the library! This is beyond excuse. You have no idea the damage this will cause the children. What kind of police would subject children to this nightmare? Any well-run police force would have prevented this shocking event. You . . ."

Joe ceased to listen to her—as he suspected Harper had, too. The aftermath of the Sleuders' deaths was turning out pretty much as he'd thought—and as Dulcie had feared. The children, on arriving for story hour and discovering the bodies, had crowded against the window, pushing each other out of the way, shocked at first, then quickly out of control. Staring down through the glass, smearing it with their noses and with sticky fingers, they screamed then laughed, working themselves into a furor of shrill giggles that did not abate until their parents dragged them away. Not even the ululation of sirens careening through the village had quieted them, nor had the arrival of the ambulance and four police cars skidding to the curb; they only shouted louder, fought harder to see every detail.

Out beyond the garden, two officers were clearing the street and putting up cordons at the ends of the block. At both corners, pedestrians had gathered, idle onlookers drawn to tragedy, some out of empathy but most with prurient curiosity. Of all those who crowded to look, Joe was the only observer enjoying a rooftop vantage. Lying with his chin propped on his paws and his paws resting on the roof gutter, his alert gray ears caught every whisper.

He watched the evidence officer lift lint and debris from the bodies and the surround and mark the evidence bags as to content and location. Watched him go over the victims' clothes with the department's tiny vacuum cleaner and wondered if any lint had fallen from Greeley's clothes when he knelt over Dora—or, for that matter, if the lab would find black cat hairs—or traces of their own fur where he and Dulcie had sniffed at the victims' faces.

Well, so Harper found cat hairs. So what was he going to do? There'd been cat hairs at other murder scenes. He watched the fingerprint specialist dust the deceased's clothing and skin and the window and the slick green lily leaves, carefully lifting prints. Watched the forensic pathologist arrive—a white-haired man stepping out of an ancient gray Cadillac—to examine the bodies, place bags over the victim's hands, and wrap Dora and Ralph for transport to the morgue. As the courthouse clock chimed ten-thirty, the forensics team moved inside the library, and so did Joe Grey, heading for the book stack where Dulcie sat twitching her tail, highly amused as she listened to a little group of irate mothers.

Lieutenant Brennan, heavy in his tight uniform, stood talking with the five women and their excited preschoolers, the little ones wiggling and shouting. Three-year-old James Truesdel wanted to know why those people were asleep in the garden, and Nancy Phillips, with five-year-old superiority, told him they were not asleep, they were dead. *She* wanted to know: "How did they get dead, with their clothes off?" And five-year-old Albert Leddy, trying to drag his mother back toward the window seat from which he had been extricated, pitched such a tantrum, kicking his mother in the shins, that if he'd been a kitten Dulcie would have whacked him hard and nipped his nervy little ears.

But she had to smile, too, because from the temper of the parents, the pro-library cat group had snatched the day just as Joe had predicted, had grabbed opportunity by the tail. As Freda Brackett left Captain Harper and came back inside, nine parents converged on her, and James Truesdel's mother began to question her in a manner that indicated there would soon be a hotly phrased letter in the *Gazette*.

Behind Freda, Bernine Sage manned the three constantly ringing phone lines—word traveled fast in the village—giving dry, uninformative answers. It was hard to tell whether Bernine was an island of efficiency or of total indifference. Dulcie glanced up to the door as a young man bolted in, having talked his way past the police guard.

Danny McCoy was disheveled and breathing hard, his red hair tousled; having obviously rushed over from the *Gazette* offices, he exchanged a look of complicity with Mrs. Leddy.

Danny, too, was a mover and shaker on Dulcie's behalf. He had done several columns supporting the library cat and had made a big deal that library cats were a growing trend across the country. He had done a really nice article on the Library Cat Society, interviewing its president and several of its members and quoting from the society's quarterly newsletters about the popularity of individual library cats in Minden, Nevada, Eastham, Massachusetts, and, closer to home, El Centro. Now, deftly trapping Freda between the checkout desk and a book cart, he began with the standard questions: Who had found the bodies? What time where they discovered? Then he moved on to the question of why the children had been allowed to see the murder victims, why they had not been supervised, to avoid such ugly experience.

"We didn't know the bodies were *there*," Freda snapped. "One does not come to work expecting to find dead bodies outside the children's room. The police are supposed to patrol that street. Why didn't *they* see the bodies? This Captain Harper was extremely lax to allow such an occurrence. This is not New York City. This is a small, quiet town. What else do the police have to do, but keep the streets and public buildings safe?"

"But, Ms. Brackett, why were the children allowed to view the corpses?"

"I told you. We didn't know they were there! Can't you understand me? It was the *children* who discovered the tragedy. *We* don't go into the children's room first thing in the morning. We are far too busy preparing to open the library, preparing the checkout machine, clearing the bookdrop, starting up the computers . . ."

"No one looked out the window before the children arrived?"

"Of course not. Why would we? Don't you listen? We had no reason to look out. The children's librarian was at her desk getting ready for story hour. This work takes a good deal of preliminary attention. My staff does not have time to dawdle, gawking out windows, Mr. McCoy."

"So you let the children run in there, without any supervision, and view a shocking and frightening death scene."

Dulcie smiled with appreciation. Danny was being totally unfair. Taunting Freda and shaping his own biased agenda. The article he was preparing to write would be scathing—he was going to cream Freda.

Purring and rolling over, she watched Joe slip in the front door and across the reading room behind the feet of several officers. He made one leap to a reading table, another to the top of the book stack, landed beside her with a soft thud, purring.

"Where's Mavity?" she whispered. "Did someone go to find her, to tell her about Dora and Ralph? Did they go to look for Greeley?"

"Harper sent an officer to find Mavity. I don't know about Greeley." And he settled down to watch Danny torment Freda, the young reporter playing her as skillfully as any cat baiting an angry rat.

"Exactly what degree of damage, Ms. Brackett, might this event have done to the children? Is it possible, would you say, that some of the children will need psychiatric help? Perhaps trauma counseling? Is the library insured for that kind of . . ."

"The city sees to our insurance, Mr. McCoy. I don't have time for this foolishness. If the children glimpsed a murder scene, that is no different from what they see on television."

Mrs. Truesdel moved closer to join them. "That is not what you told Captain Harper, Ms. Brackett. You said the children would probably need therapy. And as far as television," Mrs. Truesdel said, "I don't let my five-year-old watch violent TV. Nor do my friends. We *try* to protect our small children from undue violence. Certainly we don't expect them to witness two shocking deaths during story hour."

"This experience," Danny said, "will give them far worse nightmares then any TV show." He moved closer to Freda. "Certainly this ugly look at death has been far more harmful to the children than, say, finding a little cat in the library."

"Dead bodies, Mr. McCoy, seen through a window, cannot bite the children or communicate to them some life-threatening disease."

"I don't follow you. The library cat is healthy. What disease do you think she . . ."

"Rabies, Mr. McCoy. Lyme disease. Cat scratch fever—all of which can kill, if not treated. In the past year, in this county alone, there have been fifteen cases of rabies. And the statistics on Lyme disease . . ."

"But Dulcie has had her rabies shots. She has excellent veterinary care—she's not a diseased stray off the streets. And to my knowledge there have been no cases of Lyme disease in this coastal area."

"A cat's bite or scratch," Freda snapped, "is notoriously filthy."

"Has she ever bitten or scratched a child?"

"There is always the chance she will. Cats are half-wild creatures; they are never really domesticated."

Atop the book stack, Dulcie's eyes blazed. If ever she did yearn to bite and scratch, this was the moment. If ever she abandoned her domesticated ways, now was the time.

Beside her, Joe was nearly choking with laughter, his ears and whiskers twitching, his mouth open in a wide grin.

Soon Danny, having taken enough quotes from Freda for a scathing article, smiled sweetly at her, turned away, and approached three other mothers and their children. He was deep into conversation with them, writing down their comments, when another squad car pulled to the curb and an officer hurried up the path looking for Captain Harper, who stood just inside the door talking to the photographer.

"We didn't find Mavity Flowers," he told Harper. "She wasn't at home or at work up at Damen's apartments. And we haven't found Greeley Urzey."

Joe and Dulcie looked at each other. Dulcie whispered, "Has Greeley skipped? *Did* he do it?"

"No way, Dulcie. He . . ." Joe paused, scowling. "Here comes Clyde. He doesn't look too happy."

Hurrying up the walk, stepping over the yellow ribbon barrier and past the police guard, Clyde, like Danny, was disheveled and red-faced. Rushing in, nodding to Harper, he spotted Joe atop the book stack.

Sprinting across the room, he snatched Joe by the scruff of the neck and swung him down onto his shoulder, giving Joe a glare that would turn a Doberman to stone.

"Claws in," he hissed. "Put your claws *in*. And stay right there. Not a move. Not a snarl out of you."

Joe was shocked and hurt. What had he done? And he could say nothing. In public, he had no chance to defend himself.

Clyde looked up at Dulcie more gently. "Would you two like some breakfast?" He reached up for her. She gave him an innocent green gaze and slipped down willingly into his arms, soft and innocent, her claws hidden, her little cat smile so beatific Joe thought he'd throw up; he turned away from her, disgusted.

"It's time you two were out of here," Clyde said softly, meaning: *Stay away from this! Leave it alone! Forget it.* Carrying them out, Joe on his shoulder and Dulcie in his arms, he hurried around the block to his car and plunked them down in the ragged front seat. He was driving his latest acquisition, a battered '32 Ford that sounded like a spavined lawnmower. Starting the engine with a deafening clatter, he headed for Wilma's house.

When Clyde had sold his antique red Packard touring car to help pay for the apartment building, he'd started driving an old Mercedes he'd fixed up. The car was all right except for its color. Joe had refused to ride in the baby pink Mercedes. Clyde himself had taken all the ribbing he could stand, then sold the Mercedes and finished up the last details on the yellow '29 Chevy convertible in which he had escorted Charlie to the gallery opening. But then he'd picked up this Ford; he always had to have some old clunker to refurbish. Eventually he would turn it into a beauty, but meantime a ride in the heap was like being transported in a bucket of rattling tin cans. Driving to Wilma's, Clyde didn't speak to them. They crouched together hunched and cross as he parked at Wilma's curb.

She was on her hands and knees in the garden, transplanting gazanias, thinning out the low yellow flowers. As Clyde killed the rattling engine, the cats leaped out.

Wilma sat back on her heels, looking them over, her eyes widening with suspicion. "What?" she said. "What have they done now?"

Dulcie stared at her, hurt.

Joe didn't wait to hear Clyde's biased accusations. He shot past Wilma through the garden and around the house and up the hill at the back. To hell with humans.

Soon Dulcie came trotting along, looking chastened, and they took off up the hills to hunt—to let the atmosphere cool down.

19

CHARLIE WAS on a ladder painting the downstairs front bedroom when she saw Max Harper's police unit pull up out in front. As he came across the patio, something about his drawn look and the resigned set of his shoulders brought her down the ladder. Wiping her hands, she stepped to the open door.

Lieutenant Brennan had been up earlier looking for Mavity, but he wouldn't tell her why. She'd told him to try Mavity's cottage, that very likely Mavity had slept in, that she did that sometimes, that when she woke up she'd phone the apartments frantic and apologetic. But now, watching Harper, a chill held Charlie. His solemn expression made her stomach lurch.

She hadn't gotten to work herself until ten, had made a run around the coast to Hudson's Building Supply to pick up an order of some special tile and paint, some varnish, five gallons of mud, and some finishing nails. She'd had a cup of coffee with the owner, John Hudson, had helped him load her order then headed back. When she got to work, Mavity's VW wasn't parked in front, nor had Pearl Ann seen her.

Harper stopped in the open doorway.

"Clyde's not here," she said, motioning him on in, searching the captain's solemn brown eyes.

"Clyde's at the library," he said. "Or he was. He left just before I did. I'm looking for Mavity."

"Didn't Brennan find her? He was here."

Harper turned from her, wandered the big room, studying the sanded Sheetrock and the half-painted ceiling. The units were being done so piecemeal that sometimes it even confused her, one room finished and painted while the next room was hardly started; but with their crew, it seemed to be working. Max turned to look at her, his back to the windows.

"What is it?" she said softly.

"Mavity's niece and her husband. They were found dead this morning."

"Dora and Ralph?" She stood a moment trying to take that in. Dora and Ralph Sleuder? "Was—was there an accident? A car accident?"

"We found them in the garden outside the library."

"The library garden? I don't understand. How could . . . Why would . . . ?"

"The call came in around eight forty-five this morning."

She tried to collect herself. "What happened? An accident in the garden? But I didn't see anything—well, but I left around seven." She knew she wasn't making sense.

"You were in the garden?"

"No. Across the street."

"Oh, yes, you moved into that apartment above Joan's Antiques."

She nodded. "I drank my coffee looking out."

"And you saw nothing unusual?"

"The garden was—I saw no one there. I thought I saw something move inside the window, but it was just those pillows against the glass. Dora and Ralph can't be dead."

"You thought you saw something moving?"

"I think it was just the pillows—or it could have been the cat, she sleeps in the window sometimes."

"And you didn't see anyone in the garden? Or on the street?"

"I didn't notice anyone. But I was only at the window long enough to drink my coffee."

"And you saw nothing different about the garden?"

"No." She thought a minute. "Yes. There was some kind of shadow in the lilies. As if something had crushed them. They're so thick and tall, it's hard to be sure. But there seemed to be a dark place, as if maybe a dog had slept there and broken the flowers."

Harper was quiet, watching her. "Did you know the Sleuders well?"

"No. I met them the day after they arrived, they came up to see the apartments—rubbernecking, I guess. Mavity didn't seem too happy about it."

"Have you any idea if they were into drugs—anything Mavity might have said?"

Charlie stared at him. "Drugs? Those two country people? My God, I wouldn't think so. Are you saying—what? They died of an overdose?"

"We don't know yet. Lab's working on it."

"Could they have taken—could it be some medication? I can't imagine drugs. Oh, poor Mavity. Have you told her? No, you came to find her. Have you been to the house?"

"I sent Brennan earlier. No one was home."

She snatched up her purse and keys. "We have to find her. She could be . . ." She looked at him imploringly. "I want to find Mavity."

In the squad car, as Max spun a U-turn and headed down the hill, he described for her the murder scene outside the children's room. It sickened her to think of Dora and Ralph lying there in the garden dead, half-naked as if they might have been on some wild and terrifying high.

"PCP could do that," Harper said. "Or crack, or one of the designer drugs." His words made her see Mavity lying dead, too; she couldn't shake her concern.

They found Mavity's VW parked in front of her cottage. Mavity was inside, perfectly safe, just finishing breakfast. Charlie grabbed her and hugged her. The little woman stepped back from Charlie, puzzled.

"I just called the apartments," she told Charlie. "I know I'm late. I'm sorry, I meant to call earlier but . . . I went for a walk down the marsh," she said lamely. "The time got away from me." She frowned at Charlie and at Harper. "What? What is it?"

Harper glanced toward the sitting room. Mavity motioned them in, past the kitchen. He sat on the couch taking Mavity's hand and easing her down beside him. Her short white hair was rumpled from the sea wind. Her face had gone deadly solemn.

"Mavity, did Dora and Ralph come home last night?"

"No. That's why I went to the beach. I was looking for them."

She twisted the hem of her white uniform jacket and folded it into a knot. "I thought maybe they got up early, didn't eat breakfast, or went out to eat, and that they were sitting out on the beach. But I . . ." She looked at him intently. "They've never stayed away overnight. And Greeley's gone, too. But Greeley does that. Out at all hours, that's no surprise."

"Were Dora and Ralph home for dinner last night?"

She smoothed her jacket hem and clasped her hands together. "No. Two nights running, they've gone out alone in the evening. Didn't tell me where, didn't tell Greeley."

"Sunday night was the first time?"

"Sunday, yes. They left before I got home from work, and they came home around nine-thirty. They were all dressed up. They went right to bed, wouldn't say where they'd been. What is this about? Where are they?"

Charlie sat down beside her, glancing across her to Max.

"Mavity," Max said gently, "there's been an accident."

She watched him, said nothing.

"Dora and Ralph were found this morning. They were found together. They're dead, Mavity. I'm so sorry."

"They can't be dead. I saw them just last night, all dressed up. They were fine last night." She reached for Charlie's hand. "There must be some mistake. I saw them just last night."

Charlie took both Mavity's hands in hers, held them tightly.

Mavity looked at them nakedly. "A car accident? Was it the taxi? Was there an accident with the taxi?"

"No," Harper said. "Where did they go to dinner? Why didn't you and Greeley go?"

"We weren't asked—neither time. They wouldn't say where they were going." She was squeezing Charlie's hand so hard that Charlie's fingers popped. "*Was there an accident?*"

Charlie glanced helplessly at Harper.

Max said, "No. It was not a car accident. You're sure they didn't come home last night?"

"I don't think so. But Dora always makes the bed, so they might have been here. But Greeley—Greeley wasn't home. He does that. Goes walking at night. Walking all night with that cat. Says it calms his nerves."

"When you got up this morning," Harper said, "no one was here? No beds had been slept in?"

"The beds were made up. No one was here, no dirty dishes in the sink. Neat as a pin." She began to shiver.

Charlie lifted a folded blanket from the end of the couch and wrapped it around the little woman.

"Were they upset about anything?" Harper asked her.

Mavity just looked at him.

Charlie squeezed her shoulder. "Mavity?"

"Nothing really. Just—Greeley and Dora had a fight. Greeley left angry, really mad—but Greeley has a short temper. He doesn't stay mad. He gets right over it."

"What was the fight about?" Harper said patiently.

She shook her head. "No one would say. Wouldn't tell me. That really hurt. All the secrecy. Secrets about where they were going. Secrets about why they fought.

"I can't imagine what they couldn't tell me. I would have driven them if they'd wanted. But no, they didn't want me to bother; they had to have a cab. Was it the cab?" she repeated. "Did it have a wreck?"

"No," Charlie said, "they weren't in a wreck. They may have gotten sick suddenly."

"Sick?" She looked at them, puzzled. "Sick from the food? From their dinner?"

"We're not sure what happened," Harper said. "There will be an autopsy. Were—were they into drugs, do you know?"

"*Drugs?*" Her eyes blazed with shock. "*Dora and Ralph? Of course not.* I can't imagine such a thing." She hugged herself, seemed unable to get warm despite the blanket. "How can I tell this to Greeley? *Drugs?* Oh, you're mistaken."

"The autopsy will tell us," Harper said.

"I don't know how to tell Greeley that Dora . . . She's his only child. She—he didn't see her often, but she's—she was all he had." Mavity shook her head. "Greeley will think it's his fault."

"Why?" Harper said.

"Because they fought, because he left the house angry."

"And you have no idea what they fought about?"

"It was going on when I got home. I guess they didn't hear the car. Greeley was shouting at Dora, that she was making trouble for nothing, that they had no right—then they heard me on the porch and that was the end of it, when I came in. Greeley stomped out with that cat following him, and then Dora and Ralph left all dressed up again, wouldn't say anything more."

Charlie rose, stepped into the kitchen, rinsed out the coffeepot, and refilled it. Mavity said, "It was only a family tiff. Maybe Dora and Ralph, going out alone, made Greeley mad. Who would they go with? They don't know anyone in Molena Point."

"And Greeley was out all night," Harper said.

"I would have heard him come in. He sleeps on the couch right here, and me on the cot. And he always leaves his bed unmade, leaves a mess for me to straighten, sheets half on the floor."

"Are his clothes still here? His luggage?"

"He only has the one bag." She rose and peered in between the recliner chair and the television. "It's here." She picked up the bag, looked in. "Full of clothes." She went to check the bathroom.

"Shaving kit's there on the sink."

Harper said, "Does he always travel so light?"

She nodded. "He never packs much in the way of clothes, says he can buy what he needs. He would have checked the one bag, though, because he carried that cat on board. Right in the cabin, in its cage—one of those carrier things." She opened the washing machine, which stood in a corner of the kitchen, and peered in.

"Left a shirt to be washed, some socks, and a pair of shorts." She looked across at Harper. "Greeley wouldn't go away for good—back to Panama—and not tell me." She pressed her fist to her lips. "Captain Harper, where is Greeley? Greeley has to be all right—Greeley's all I have now."

"We don't know where he is," Harper said. "I'm sure he'll turn up. My officers are looking for him."

They drank their coffee in silence. Max did not light a cigarette but Charlie could tell he wanted one. He asked Mavity if he could search Dora and Ralph's belongings.

"Yes. But what for? Well, it don't matter. They can't complain now," she said, her voice shaking.

"Maybe I'll find something to tell us where they went last night, maybe some scrap of paper with an address, something to help us understand what happened."

"Their bags are in the bedroom—their clothes are in the closet and scattered all over."

Harper rose. "I'd like both of you to come in while I search."

They made a little procession, carrying their coffee cups into the small bedroom. Harper's lean figure moved neatly among the clutter. Charlie stood in the bedroom doorway sipping her coffee, watching Max search for drugs as well as for evidence of the Sleuders' dinner destination. She didn't like having to witness this. The necessity for a search, coupled with Mavity's own distress, made her feel frightened and sick.

She watched him examine each item of clothing, going through pockets, sorting carefully through the contents of each of the Sleuders' five bags and examining the bags themselves, the pockets and the lining. It was in the last bag, a big duffle, that he withdrew a thick packet of legal-size papers divided into two stacks, each held by a metal clip.

"Mavity, I'd like to keep these as evidence. I'll give you a receipt for them."

"Sure you can keep them. What are they?"

Harper looked at her, surprised. "Didn't you know that Dora had your financial statements?" He handed one of the packets to her.

She stared at the papers, at her name and address beneath Winthrop Jergen's letterhead. "These are *my* statements, from Mr. Jergen." She looked at Harper, puzzled. "Dora took my statements? Why would she do that? These are none of her business. Dora wouldn't . . ."

She hurried to the front room. They watched her open the bottom desk drawer, removing a similar stack of legal-size papers.

"But my statements are here."

She looked hard at Harper. Carefully she examined the two stacks.

"She copied them. See where I made some little notes? On the copies, you can barely see the pencil marks."

She sat down on the couch, looking very small. "Why would Dora do that? What could she want with my statements?"

Harper handed her the other set of legal-size papers that he had taken from the Sleuders' duffle bag. These statements had a different letterhead, under the name Cumming, and were dated the previous year, detailing the Sleuders' own stock earnings.

She looked at them, looked up at him. "I don't understand. Dora and Ralph had some investment problems last year, about the time these are dated."

"What kind of problems?"

"They were cheated of a lot of money. The men were caught, and one of them went to prison."

"Is that the name of the firm that cheated them?"

"It could be. Yes, I think it is."

"You said only one of the members was convicted?"

"Yes. Dora was very upset because the other man, Warren Cumming, went free."

"Did Greeley know about the swindle?"

"Oh, yes. He wrote me all about it—he was furious. And of course Dora called me several times. She'd get so angry, with the trial and all." She looked again at the Sleuders' statements.

"Look here, at Dora's little squiggly marks beside some of these stocks. I have some of the same stock. Coca-Cola, Home Depot. Maybe," she said, "maybe Dora was comparing how much she and Ralph made on that stock—before they were swindled—with how much I've made. It doesn't really make sense, but Dora's—was funny that way. And she was so bitter about their loss. Well, anyone would be bitter!"

Harper put his arm around her. "Later today, when you feel up to it, would you come down to the station and give me a formal statement?"

"Yes, if I have to." She was very pale. "I'll look for Greeley first, and then I'll come. I—I'll need to make arrangements—funeral arrangements."

"Not yet," Harper said. "I'll let you know when you can do that. You don't have any idea where Greeley might have gone? Where he might have stayed last night?"

"No. He's a night owl. But he can't go very far without a car—he's too cheap to take a cab."

She moved away from Harper, looking up at him. "Thank you, Captain Harper. Soon as I get myself together I'll drive around the village, see if I can find him. I don't know how I'm going to tell him about Dora."

Charlie stayed with Mavity for a while after Harper left, making her a cup of tea and fetching her an aspirin from the medicine cabinet. When Mavity felt better, she drove Charlie up to work, then went to look for Greeley.

Charlie, getting back to work, kept puzzling over Dora and

Ralph. They had seemed such simple folk, plain and uncomplicated, not the kind to deceive Mavity, and surely not the kind to be into drugs. That strange twist, if it was true, put a whole new light on Dora and Ralph Sleuder.

Pulling on her painting shirt and climbing back on the ladder, she was unable to stop worrying over the Sleuders, unable to stop wondering what Harper would uncover when he looked into their background—wondering how much Mavity might not have known about her dead niece.

20

YOU'D THINK he'd have the courtesy to call me," Mavity complained, "but not Greeley. Always been that way. Walk out, gone a couple of days, and then home again and never a word." She'd pulled herself from the shocked, quiet state she'd been in that morning and was herself again, cross and abrasive, and Charlie was glad to hear the little woman grousing. They were in the back apartment, in the kitchen-office. It was three-thirty in the afternoon and Mavity, after searching futilely for Greeley, had just gotten to work.

"Ever since we were in high school, he's gone off like that. Drove Mama crazy. She called the police once, reported him missing, and when Greeley found out, he pitched a fit. Left home for three weeks, no one knew where." Mavity shook her head. "Mama never did that again—she just let him ramble." The little woman was wound tight, her voice brittle with worry. She had shown up dragging her cleaning things. "I need to do something. I can't bear to stay home by myself. I left him a note, to call me up here."

"If you feel like it, you can go up and help Pearl Ann. Mr. Jergen wanted some extras, and it had to be today. Some repairs—he wants the work done while he's out. Pearl Ann has a dental appointment so she can't stay too long, then she's catching the Greyhound to San Francisco."

"San Francisco? Pearl Ann never goes anywhere. I've never known her to do anything but tramp the cliffs. Hiking, she calls it. Why in the world is she going to San Francisco?"

Charlie laughed. "This will be her first trip to the city, and she seems thrilled. It'll be good for her. She wants to see the Golden Gate, Coit Tower, all the tourist stuff. I've never seen her so talkative. She even showed me the silk pants and blazer she bought for the trip.

"She'll have time to do Jergen's extras, if you help her. He wants the refrigerator cleaned, said the ice tasted bad. Pearl Ann missed it last week. And he wanted some repairs in the bathroom, said a towel rack had pulled out of the wall and the shower is leaking. It needs caulking—these old tile showers. I told him Pearl Ann had to leave early to catch her bus, but what does he care? You sure you feel up to working?"

"I'll feel better keeping busy. There's nothing I can do about Greeley, only wait. The police are looking for him," Mavity said darkly. Finishing her coffee, she headed toward the stairs carrying her cleaning equipment, and Charlie left to take care of the Blackburn house, do the weekly cleaning and half a dozen small repairs. This was her regular work, the kind of miscellaneous little jobs for which she had started Charlie's Fix-It, Clean-It and for which she was building a good reputation in Molena Point. What her customers valued most was being able to make one phone call, have the house cleaned and the yard work and repairs tended to all at once. One call, one stop. Her customers didn't know that every repair was a challenge, that she carried an entire library of helpful volumes in the van, detailed instructions to refer to if she ran into trouble. Only three times, so far, had she been forced to call in a subcontractor.

She was urging the old Chevy up the hill when she saw two cats racing through the tall grass and recognized Joe Grey's tailless gallop and his flashy white markings. Beside him, Dulcie blended into the grassy shadows like a dark little tiger. It still amazed her that they traveled so far. The freedom of their racing flight made her itch for paper and charcoal, and when they vanished into a tangle of Scotch broom, she slowed the van, watching for them to reappear.

They came out of the bushes suddenly and sat down near the street, regarding her van as she moved slowly by. They looked almost as if they *knew* the vehicle, as if they were quite aware that she was at the wheel and wondered what she was gawking at.

She stopped the van and let it idle, to see what they would do.

They glanced at each other, a strange little look between them, then they rose again and trotted away. Turning their backs, they disappeared into the meadow grass as if dismissing her.

Driving on, she couldn't rid herself of the notion that Joe and Dulcie had cut her dead. Had not wanted her snooping, had all but told her to mind her own business. Even after she began the Blackburns' repairs she kept seeing the two cats turning to look at her, seeing their impatient, irritated expressions.

The Blackburn house was a small, handsome Tudor with gray stone walls, brick detailing, and a shake roof. Letting herself in, she did a light weekly cleaning, fixed the sticking latch on the back gate, and put new washers in a dripping faucet. Mrs. Blackburn had left her check on the hall table with a plate of chocolate chip cookies and a note.

Charlie, Becky made a ton of these for school, and I snagged a few. There's milk in the refrigerator.

She sat at the Blackburns' kitchen table enjoying the cookies and milk, then put her plate and glass in the dishwasher and headed back for the apartments.

She arrived just after six. Mavity had left, her VW Bug was gone. She checked the work Pearl Ann had finished, her patches on the back wall of the building so cleverly stippled that, once the wall was painted, no one would ever guess there had been need for repairs. As she headed out again through the patio, she heard a little clicking noise.

Glancing above her, she saw that Winthrop Jergen's windows were open, the louvered metal shade blowing gently against the molding.

She wondered if Pearl Ann had missed her appointment and was still there, because Jergen never opened the windows. Strange that both Pearl Ann and Mavity would forget to shut them, considering the angry exchanges they'd had with Jergen. Though she could hardly blame Mavity for forgetting, with the events of the morning.

Heading up the stairs, she knocked twice and when Jergen didn't answer she let herself in. He didn't much like her having a key, but as long as she contracted to clean for him, both she and Mavity had keys. She thought, when she pushed the door open, that he must be there after all, and she called out to him, because beyond the entry she could see the glow of his computer screen.

He didn't answer. But she could see a spreadsheet on the screen, long columns of numbers. Her attention focused on the room itself, on the overturned lamp hanging off the desk by its cord, on the toppled swivel chair lying amidst scattered in-boxes and file folders. On Winthrop Jergen lying beside the chair, his blood staining the papers and seeping into the Kirman rug.

Charlie remained absolutely still. Looking. Trying to take in what she was seeing.

He lay twisted on his side, his white shirt and pale blue suit blood-soaked. His throat was ripped open in a wide wound like a ragged hank of bleeding meat.

A cleaning cloth lay beside him in a pool of blood, the kind of plaid mesh cloth that she bought in quantity. Though he couldn't possibly be alive, she knelt and touched his wrist. There was, of course, no pulse. No one could live with that terrible wound, with their throat ripped away. She felt nauseated, could feel the cookies and milk want to come up.

Stepping carefully around Jergen's body, trying not to be sick, trying to stay out of the blood, she moved to the desk, fished an identical cleaning cloth from her pocket, and used it to pick up the phone.

But then she quietly laid it down again and grabbed up a heavy postal scale and turned to face the room, appalled at her own stupidity. If the killer was still in the apartment, she had to get out.

What was she was going to do, fend him off with a postal scale?

But she had no other weapon.

Warily she moved into the bedroom, checking the closet, then the bath. Finding those spaces empty, she approached the kitchen, knowing she should run, get out—knowing this was crazy, that this could not be happening. It was bright afternoon in a village as respectable and civilized as a cup of afternoon tea. Through Jergen's front windows, the low sun gleamed gently, sending sparkles across the calm sea and across the village rooftops; this was Molena Point, tame and quiet, not New York or L.A. with their news of bloody daytime murders.

Finding the kitchen empty, she returned to Jergen's desk, and using the cleaning rag to pick up the phone, she called 911.

But even as she dialed, she wondered if she'd locked the front door behind her. And, waiting for the dispatcher, she laid down the receiver and fled to the door and locked it.

She returned to the desk to hear the dispatcher shouting, "Hello? Hello?"

Standing over Jergen's body, holding the phone in the dustrag, she began to shiver. The metallic smell of blood and the smell of other bodily releases sickened her. She gave the address and stood staring down at Jergen's bloody face and bloody, torn throat, unable to hang up or to look away.

The only dead people she had encountered in her twenty-eight years were those from whom all signs of violence or distress had been gently wiped away, bodies thoughtfully groomed and arranged in the clean satin lining of expensive caskets—an elderly neighbor when she was twelve, her mother's cousin Marie two years later. Her father, when she was eighteen, and her mother when she was in art school. All the deceased were dressed in their Sunday best, their hands calmly folded over their demure chests, her mother's gold wedding band gleaming on her pale finger.

In the room's silence, the faint hum of the computer was like a thin voice whispering to her. Moving past the end of the desk and the two low file cabinets, she saw, for the first time, what appeared to be the murder weapon; though for a long moment she looked at it uncomprehending.

On the rug beside the file cabinets lay the metal divider from an ice cube tray. Blood covered its protruding aluminum handle and had run down into the little squares turning them as red as if someone had ejected a double line of red ice cubes—blood ice cubes. There should be a little wooden stick in each like the frozen orange-juice suckers that mothers made to keep their kids from eating junk.

Sirens screamed, coming up the hill. She backed away from the bloody kitchen utensil and moved unsteadily to the wide window beyond the couch. Standing at the glass, she watched the emergency vehicle careen into the lane, followed by two squad cars, watched two medics jump out loaded with an oxygen tank and black bags—as if her report of death had been faulty, as if the caller might have misjudged the condition of the victim. As if Winthrop Jergen still had a chance at life. Behind the medics, Max Harper swung out of his police unit, and two more uniformed officers from the other squad car double-timed through the patio as she hurried to unlock the door.

21

HIGH UP THE HILLS, a narrow hunting trail led beneath a tangle of toyon bushes, a track no wider than a cat's shoulders, and along the path in a spill of sunshine, Joe and Dulcie crouched feasting on a fat mouse, the last of five sweet morsels they had caught within the hour skittering among the roots and leaves. Above the cats, the toyon's hollylike berries were hard and green, having just emerged from their summer blossoms; the afternoon was warm and still, the only sound was the twittering of some sparrows pottering among the upper leaves.

Suddenly sirens screamed, blasting up from the village.

Rearing tall so they could see down the hills, the cats watched an ambulance careen up the winding streets followed by two police units, and skid into the dead-end street below Clyde's apartments—and they took off down the hills, Joe with visions of Clyde falling off the roof, Dulcie's sudden fear involving the power saws. Bolting down the slopes, charging through bushes and tall grass and across the last street, they scorched past the hot rubber stink of the ambulance and squad cars and into the patio.

Men's voices from above them, from Winthrop Jergen's open windows. The police radio. Max Harper's quick commands—and the faint but unmistakable smell of human blood. Racing under the stairs and up the inner wall, they slipped beneath Jergen's sink and pushed the cabinet door open.

The smell of blood, of death.

Slinking across the linoleum, they crouched at the edge of the living room. The instant the uniforms' backs were turned, they bolted under the cherry credenza, peering out at Winthrop Jergen's sprawled body. The smell of his shaving lotion mixed strangely with the stench of death.

The lamps were all lit, every light burning except the lamp that hung over the edge of the desk. The toppled swivel chair and scattered papers and files were all soaked with Jergen's blood. As the medics rose and moved away, the cats got a good look at Jergen, his throat ripped as brutally as if a leopard or tiger had been at him—but this was not a hunting kill, this was the result of human malice.

As the photographer got to work, the flashing strobe lights nearly blinded the cats, forcing them to squeeze their eyes shut. The after-flashes, the blazing white reverse-images of Jergen's body, were as eerie as if his light-propelled spirit kept flashing back, trying to rejoin his corpse.

Beyond the windows, clouds had begun to gather, dimming the late afternoon. The tangle of officers' feet moving carefully across the Kirman rug, skirting around the body, Charlie sitting quietly on the couch out of the way, and the familiar forensics routines filled the cats' vision and minds as the photographer shot his last roll and Officer Kathleen Ray began to collect evidence, her dark hair swinging around her shoulders. The first item she bagged, lifting it carefully from the floor beyond the file cabinets, held the cats' complete attention.

A device from the freezer, the thing that held the ice cubes, but covered with blood, dripping blood, its handle sticking up like a bloody knife, making them see too vividly a human hand jabbing and jabbing that blunt instrument into Jergen's soft flesh.

The cats' own bloodthirst was normal; it was the way God had made them. They were hunters, they killed for food and to train their young—well maybe sometimes for sport. But this violent act by some unknown human had nothing to do with hunting—for a human to brutally maim one of their own kind out of rage or sadism or greed was, to Joe and Dulcie, a shocking degradation of the human condition. To imagine that vicious abandon in a human deeply distressed Dulcie; she did not like thinking about humans in that way.

Pushing closer to Joe, she watched Officer Ray's familiar procedures, the tweezers, the tedious routine of picking up each fleck of evidence, the bagging and labeling, and slowly the thoroughness of her actions began to ease Dulcie. She imagined the intricacies of the laboratory studies that would follow, the carefully established methods, and a sense of rightness filled her.

Then the fingerprinting began, the black powder, the lifting tape, the fingerprint cards, all carefully thought out and calming, techniques that were the result of a wonderful human intelligence.

Humans might be sense-challenged, without a cat's balance and keen hearing and superior sense of touch, to say nothing of the cat's night vision, but the human's inventiveness and mental skills made up for those failures—people might be capable of brutality, in a shocking short circuit of the human spirit, but the best of mankind were still wonderful to observe.

And, she thought, *what are we—what are Joe and I, that we can understand the achievements of humankind?*

By the time the forensics team had finished, night had closed around the apartment, the black windows reflecting the blaze of lights within, turning the room stark and grim. The coroner arrived, completed his examination and bagged the body, and slid it onto a stretcher. As the paramedics carried it out, Officer Ray collected the last bits of evidence from where the corpse had lain. No one had touched the computer, except to lift fingerprints from the keyboard and monitor. The screen still glowed pale green, etching into the delicate glass the image of a financial spreadsheet.

Max Harper had sent Officer Wendell over to Mavity's cottage to take her down to the station, and patrol units were looking for Pearl Ann. Harper sat with Charlie on the couch, questioning her. "Did you *see* Mavity and Pearl Ann come up here to clean?"

"Pearl Ann was up here. I could see her through Jergen's bathroom window, probably repairing the towel rack. Mavity was headed for the stairs when I left, carrying her cleaning things. But, no, I didn't see Mavity enter the apartment."

"What time was that?"

"Around three-fifteen, I think. I got to the Blackburns' about three-thirty. I usually take Mavity with me; she cleans while I do the repairs. But today—Jergen had asked for some extras, so I sent her up to help Pearl Ann."

"What sort of extras?"

"Clean the refrigerator, fix the towel rack that had pulled out of the bathroom wall, and repair a leak in the shower. He said he had a late afternoon appointment up the coast, wanted the work done while he was out. Mavity was going to do the refrigerator while Pearl Ann took care of the repairs."

"And did you see his car, before you left for the Blackburns'?"

"I wouldn't have; he keeps it in the garage. I thought he was gone. I . . ."

"What?"

"I think he must have been gone. Or—or already dead. Pearl Ann had the windows open, and he would never have allowed that."

"You didn't see his car when you came back from the Blackburn place?"

"No. Isn't it in the garage?"

"There's a black Mercedes convertible parked down the street. We passed it, coming up. I've sent Brennan to check the registration and to check the garage."

Officer Ray came out of the master suite to say that the towel rod had been reset and that there was fresh caulking around the bottom of the shower and between some of the tile. Soon Lieutenant Brennan returned. The garage was empty. He had run the plates on the black Mercedes parked down the street. It belonged to Jergen. Harper returned his attention to Charlie.

"What time did you get back from the Blackburns'? Were the two women still here?"

"Around six-thirty. They were both gone. I came up to close the windows, and he—I found him."

"You realize I have to consider you a suspect, Charlie, along with Mavity and Pearl Ann."

"That's your job," she said quietly.

"Was anyone else in the building when you left? Clyde or any other workers?"

"No, just Mavity and Pearl Ann. Clyde hadn't planned to come up. He had a busy schedule at the shop."

"Do you have an address for Pearl Ann?"

"It's that old brick office building down on Valley, across from the mission."

"The Davidson Building?"

"Yes. She rents a room above those pokey little offices. But she'll be on her way to San Francisco by now; she planned to spend the weekend."

"How long have you known about her weekend plans?"

"For weeks. She was really excited—she grew up somewhere on the east coast and she's never seen San Francisco."

"How long has she been in Molena Point? How long has she lived at the Davidson Building?"

"Four months, more or less—to both questions. Said she moved in there the day after she arrived."

"She picked a great place to settle."

"She's very frugal with money. I think she doesn't have much."

"How long has she worked for you?"

"The whole four months."

"Married?"

"No, she's single. And she's a good worker."

"What kind of car?"

"She doesn't have a car—she walks to work."

"What brought her to the west coast? Where does she come from?"

"Arkansas maybe, or Tennessee, I'm not sure. She told me she wanted to get as far away from her overbearing family as she could."

"How old is she?"

"Twenty-seven."

Harper made some notes. "Did you and Mavity talk about the sheaf of statements we found in Dora Sleuder's luggage? Did she give you any idea why Dora might have them?"

"We didn't talk, no." She looked at him questioningly.

"Did Mavity keep a gun?"

"No. She's afraid of guns." She looked at Harper, frowning. "But that—that terrible wound . . . Mavity couldn't . . . A gun couldn't cause that?"

"So far as you know, she did not have a gun?"

"Well, she might. She told me once that her husband kept a gun, that after he died she was afraid to touch it. She asked Greeley to lock it away for her in a strongbox at the back of her closet. She said her husband had always kept a strongbox, a little cash laid by at home in case of some emergency."

Beneath the credenza, the cats tried to follow Harper's line of thought. Was he guessing that Jergen's throat could have been torn *after* a bullet entered and killed him, perhaps to confuse the police?

The cats remained hidden until Harper had sealed Jergen's apartment and Brennan had secured the stairs with crime scene tape. When everyone had gone, Dulcie leaped to the desk.

Though the officers hadn't touched the computer, Captain Harper had called the FBI in San Francisco, arranging for a computer specialist to examine the files. The file on the screen said BARNER TAX-FREE INCOME FUND and was in Winthrop Jergen's name.

"How much will the Bureau agent find," Dulcie said, "if he doesn't have Jergen's code? And, more important, if he doesn't have Pearl Ann's code?" She sat down beside the phone. Lifting a paw, she knocked the receiver off.

"Hold it," Joe said. "Harper's still down there. The police units are still out front—they must be searching the building."

"I'll call him when he gets back to the station." She lifted the receiver by its cord, biting gently, and used her paw to maneuver it back into the cradle. Turning, she sniffed at the computer. "The keyboard smells of Pearl Ann's perfume."

"Could be an old scent—she cleans around the desk."

"Cheap perfume doesn't last very long." She took another sniff and then leaped down, avoiding the bloodstained rug. Leaving the scene, the cats were soon following Max Harper through the lower apartments, padding along in the shadows beyond where lights had been switched on and well behind the photographer as he made bright strobe shots of the various footprints that had been left in the Sheetrock dust.

Too bad the department would have to labor to identify each set of prints, procuring shoes from everyone involved. Enough fuss to make a cat laugh, when Joe or Dulcie could have done the job in a second.

No amount of sweeping could eradicate the fine white Sheetrock dust that impregnated the plywood subfloor, and the cats, living close to the earth, knew intimately each set of prints left there: Charlie's and Clyde's jogging shoes, Pearl Ann's tennis shoes, the boot marks of the two hired carpenters, the prints of various subcontractors. Their quick identification could have been a great help to the police. *How unfair it is*, Dulcie thought, *that canine officers can gather evidence that would stand up in court, but a cat can't.*

A drug dog's sniffing out of evidence was accepted even if he didn't find the drug—he need only indicate to his handler that the drug had been there, and that was legitimate testimony. But similar intelligence, given by a feline volunteer, would be laughed at.

Just one more instance, Dulcie thought, *of prejudice in the workplace.*

Silently they watched the officers bag the workmen's trash, the drink cans and candy wrappers and wadded-up lunch sacks, and scraps of wallboard and lumber. They bagged, as well, Mavity's insulated lunch carrier and thermos, and Pearl Ann's duffle bag containing her dirty work clothes.

Pearl Ann would have changed clothes for her trip, leaving her duffle to take home on Monday. But Mavity's oversight was strange; Mavity never forgot that lunch bag.

Officer Wendell returned to tell Harper that Mavity was not at home, that there was no sign of her car and no answer when he pounded, and that her door was locked.

"I looked through the windows. The house was very neat, the bed made, three cups and saucers in the sink. I took a turn through the village but didn't see her VW."

Watching from behind a stack of crated plumbing fixtures, Dulcie licked her paw nervously. "*Was* Jergen stealing from Mavity? Could she have found out and been so angry that she killed him? Oh, I don't like to think that."

"Whoever thrust that ice tray divider into Jergen's throat, Dulcie, had to be bigger and stronger than Mavity."

"I don't know. She's pretty wiry."

"She might have shot him first."

"*I* don't think she shot him. I don't believe she would hurt anyone. And where was Pearl Ann? Had she already left when his killer entered the apartment?" She dropped her ears, frightened. "Was Mavity there alone? Did she see the killer?"

"Come on, they're leaving. Let's check the bathroom."

But the bathroom where Pearl Ann usually showered and changed was spotless. The shower was completely dry, not a drop of water.

Usually when Pearl Ann cleaned up, she left the shower floor wet, with Sheetrock dust or paint or plaster on the bathroom floor where she'd pulled off her work clothes.

"Maybe," Dulcie said, "she didn't want to pick up any dirt on her clean new clothes. Maybe she mopped up with paper towels, before she got dressed."

"But why would she dry the shower, too? And there are no paper towels in the bathroom trash basket." Nor did they remember the police taking any trash from the bathroom.

"And there's something else," Dulcie said. "Can't you smell it?"

"I do now," Joe said, sniffing at the shower and grimacing. Over the scent of soap and of Pearl Ann's jasmine perfume came a sharp, male odor. A man had used the shower, and recently. Even a careful wiping-up hadn't destroyed that aroma.

"So Pearl Ann had a man in the shower," Joe said. "So maybe she didn't go up to the city alone. Is that a crime?"

"Did you ever see her with a date? You've never seen anyone come by here to pick her up."

"She still could be seeing someone, or maybe living with someone—maybe wants to keep it quiet."

"Could one of the subcontractors have been here and used the shower?"

"There was no sub scheduled for today," Joe said. "Have you ever seen one of the subs use the shower?"

She switched her tail impatiently. "We have to call Harper—tell him there was a man in the shower and give him the codes for the computer. This could be the key to the whole puzzle."

"Before we make any calls and upset Harper, let's have a look at the Davidson Building—check out Pearl Ann's room."

"Don't you think Harper went over there to search? There'll be cops all over the place."

"He won't search without someone at home," Joe said. "You know how he is. Even if he gets a warrant, he won't go in until Pearl Ann gets back. Says it protects the evidence, saves a lot of fuss in court." His yellow eyes burned with challenge, his expression keen and predatory. "Come on, Dulcie, let's go toss Pearl Ann's place—we'll never have a better chance."

22

AS A BLUE-CLAD morgue attendant rolled the gurney bearing Winthrop Jergen's corpse into the cooler to await the coroner's knife, as Captain Max Harper sat at his desk in the Molena Point Police Station filling out his report on Jergen's death, and as Joe and Dulcie padded along the top of the fence behind the Davidson Building where Pearl Ann Jamison rented a room, along the lighted village streets Mavity's worried friends searched for her. Charlie, driving slowly past the crowded shops and cottages, stopped frequently to shine her flashlight among bushes and around porches, thinking she might find Mavity wandering confused and frightened. She kept picturing Mavity standing in the shadows of Jergen's hall watching some faceless assailant stab and stab him—then running, terrified.

She was aware of Wilma searching high above her up the dark hills; she caught frequent glimpses of Wilma's car lights winding back and forth along the narrow streets and the beam of her flashlight sweeping the houses and the open meadows.

But next time she glanced up, Wilma's lights had stopped—they were stationary, seemed to be somewhere above the apartment building.

Had she found Mavity?

But then the light swept slowly across the houses and grassy verges as if Wilma was walking the area, searching it again, though they had looked above the apartments earlier, thinking that Mavity might have run up there to escape Jergen's killer.

Wilma, leaving her car, moved among a tangle of gardens and slipped up driveways to shine her beam in through garage windows; she peered into cars parked on drives or in streets to see if they were empty, hoping no one saw her from some darkened house. She didn't need anyone calling the station, reporting a prowler. She couldn't stop thinking that Mavity, having witnessed Jergen's murder and able to identify the killer, had hidden up here.

Yet Mavity could have been struck down by the killer and dragged away, dumped anywhere—the far foothills, the bay . . .

Or had Mavity, driven by hurt and rage because Jergen cheated her, hefted that ridiculous weapon and flung herself at him with enough force to drive the blunt instrument into his soft flesh?

Before she left home, Wilma had examined an ice tray divider from her refrigerator, hefting it, trying to imagine killing with it.

She had put it down again and turned away sickened, appalled at her own lack of faith in her friend.

Earlier this evening as she walked the streets looking for Mavity, she had met Sue Marble closing up her Latin American Boutique, turning out the lights, dimming the window spots that shone across the display of native art. Sue hadn't seen Mavity for over a week. Wilma didn't stress the ungency of her search, didn't mention the murder.

Sue was full of friendly energy, her complexion rosy, her bobbed white hair gleaming. "I have something for you." She had unlocked her shop again and hurried inside, returning with two signed petitions in support of the library cat, her apple face alight with the accomplishment of having gotten fifty more signatures.

"Don't you tell Freda I did this. I'm supposed to be Freda's friend. She'd pitch a fit if she knew I was getting signatures. But I just can't agree with her about your little library cat. The way she's acting almost makes me want to drop her—except she's the only friend I have who likes to play Scrabble. I don't know why she's so down on cats.

"That black cat that visits me, he's such a handsome fellow. Comes right on in the shop, so regal." She laughed. "I'm a sucker for a friendly kitty. I thought at first he was a stray, but he was too sleek and well-fed. And then his master came in, that nice Greeley Urzey, and . . ."

"When was this?" Wilma asked.

"Oh, a couple of weeks ago." Sue colored slightly. "Greeley comes from Panama, so we had a nice visit. Would you believe we know some of the same people?" She pulled the door to, locking it. "I told him I'll be off on another buying trip, as soon as I can find an apartment and get moved."

"I didn't know you . . ."

"I can't stand the noise another minute, Wilma—that trumpet player next door practicing all the time and now a friend has moved in with him, and *he* plays the *drums*. Can you imagine the noise? The police can't be there every minute. And I can't bear the thought of swearing out a warrant—the idea of starting that kind of battle is just too much—I would really rather move. Dear me, is it urgent that you find Mavity? Is anything wrong? I could help you look."

"Nothing at all, of course not. Did you know that Clyde's apartments will be ready soon? He might be willing to hurry one up for you."

"Oh, yes, the girl who draws the wonderful cats—she's doing them up, isn't she? Charlie Getz? Well, of course, she's your niece. I remember seeing her van up there. Are the apartments nice?"

"Lovely big rooms," Wilma said, "and a wonderful view down over the village." She didn't mention that Winthrop Jergen's apartment might be for let soon. Sue would hear that on her own.

Tucking the petitions into her pocket, she thanked Sue and went on her way searching for Mavity.

The brick walls of the Davidson Building were black with grime, its closed windows caked with years of accumulated dirt. The plain, two-story building was constructed in the shape of a long U; a garbage-strewn alley separated its two parallel wings, closed at one end by the building itself, and at the other end by a board fence, atop which cats now crouched looking up at the impenetrable two floors rising above them.

No window was lighted on either floor to indicate human presence save, at the upper level, halfway down, one window reflecting a weak, greasy glow barely visible behind the dirty pane.

Padding along the top of the fence, the cats studied the metal fire escape that hung above them, folded against the bricks. They could see, just above it, a row of narrow, jutting bricks running the length of the building at the base of the upper windows, apparently a halfhearted attempt at architectural detail—otherwise, the structure was as plain as a prison. Nor was the little ledge much of a walkway, maybe wide enough for a broad-shouldered mouse.

They had already circled the building from the sidewalk. The front door was solidly locked, and there was no other way in. They had swung from the door's latch, pressing and pawing, but nothing gave. Now there was nothing left to try but the fire escape.

Crouching, Joe sprang high, grabbing the metal with his claws, fighting to gain purchase on the rusty steel. Dulcie followed him, and together they twisted and raked at the bars until they had pulled themselves up into the center of the folded tangle then onto the brick ledge above.

Precariously balancing, they pawed at the first window, but it was stuck or locked or nailed shut.

Padding around the corner on the thin ledge, they clung close to the long wall, leaning into the bricks, stopping at each dirty pane of glass. All the windows were stuck, and they couldn't see much through the grime. Most of the rooms looked empty. They made out the dim lines of an overstuffed chair, and in another room, when they had pawed dirt from the pane, a lone, unmade bed, its graying sheets wadded in a bundle on a stained mattress. The window halfway down the building where the thin light burned was caked with dirt as thick as garden soil. Dulcie pawed at it irritably.

"Lick the window."

"I'm not licking it. You lick it." She pressed her face against the glass. "And what's to see? A bunch of dusty boxes stacked up." She didn't like schlepping along the precarious ledge past blind windows where, behind the dirty film, anything could be observing them. She didn't like looking down at the dark alley, either, with its jagged cans and broken glass. Contrary to popular human opinion, a cat certainly could fall from high places—or could be pushed. She had the feeling they were being watched, that something was tracking their progress.

Slipping past the light they gained the corner and padded along the short, connecting wall. They had started up the other side when, across the way, the lighted window slid open.

Against the dull glow, a man stood silhouetted. His voice was grainy, thin.

"Come in, you two. Come on in here, if that's what you want." He shoved the window higher, and the light picked out his gnarled hands and wrinkled leather jacket. "Come on in—or go away and quit snooping." Reaching down, he fetched a cardboard box from somewhere beside his feet and fixed it under the raised window.

So this was where the old man was hiding. Had he been here ever since they saw him leaning over Dora and Ralph's bodies? They remained still, not sure whether to run from him, along the narrow ledge, or to go back and step inside.

"Come on, you cats. Get a move on." He leaned farther, peering across at them. "I know what you are. Do you think I wouldn't know?"

Joe glanced back at Dulcie, where she crouched behind him.

"Who you looking for?" Greeley said. "There ain't nobody here but me—and my friend." Slyly he glanced around to the shadowed crates behind him.

"Who you looking for?" he repeated. "Or are you just out for an evening's stroll, in this delightful portion of the village?"

"We weren't looking for you," Joe said coldly. Dulcie stared at him, shocked, and wanted to slap a paw over his mouth.

But why not speak? Obviously Azrael had told Greeley all about them—thank-you very much. And now from the shadows behind Greeley, a voice mumbled, and Greeley laughed harshly.

"Who you looking for, then, if not me?" Greeley said rudely.

There was another comment from behind him, and his eyes widened. "You cats looking for Pearl Ann? Is that it? You come looking for Pearl Ann Jamison?"

They hunched lower, crouching single file on the narrow ledge.

"You two don't want to mess with Pearl Ann. You don't know half about her. What you want with her?"

Joe glanced behind him at Dulcie. She would have to turn around and go first if they were to return the way they had come and approach Greeley.

She flattened her ears, shook her head. She didn't want to do that.

"Go on, Dulcie. Move it. We can't stay here all night."

She crouched, frozen.

He flipped around on the ledge, seeming to hang in midair, then crouched on the ledge facing her, waiting for her to turn back.

She hunched, staring at him, their noses inches apart, her green eyes huge and uncertain. He had seldom seen her afraid—fear was not her nature. Irritated, he tensed to spring over her along the thin protrusion.

She glared at him but at last she switched ends, flipping around precariously on the thin bricks, holding her breath as her three paws struck empty air then hit the bricks again, and she started back reluctantly toward Greeley. At every step she wanted to beat it out of there.

"Go on," Joe growled. "Hurry up."

She padded a trifle faster.

"Move it, Dulcie. What can he do to us?"

She could think of a number of things.

"Go *on.* Show a little spine."

That moved her. She gritted her teeth and headed fast for Greeley, racing along the bricks, her tail low, her ears plastered tight to her head.

As she reached the window the old man stepped aside, and she warily slipped beneath the raised glass, dropping to the floor and backing away from Greeley. Beside her Joe hit the floor with a heavy thud. Immediately Greeley slammed the window. They heard the lock slide home.

23

THE SMALL, crowded room was shut tight, the window bolted, the door securely closed. Around the cats towered cardboard cartons labeled Scotch, rum, bourbon, and vodka, either the supplies for a huge private party or perhaps the extra stock of a nearby liquor store. The room stunk of booze as if Greeley had been happily sampling the various brands. The only light was from a battery-operated lamp of the kind kept for emergency power outages. Anyone who had been through a California earthquake or considered such matters maintained a stock of battery-powered lamps, a radio, bottled water, and emergency food and medical supplies. The cats saw none of these other essentials, only enough booze to weather any quake, and the squat lamp, its light reflecting from the eyes of the black tomcat where he crouched atop the tallest stack of boxes glaring down at them: an ebony statue, the great *el primo gato*.

In the far corner an old, stained mattress lay nested between the cardboard cases, fitted out with a limp pillow ticked in gray stripes, and a wrinkled army blanket laced with moth holes. On a box beside the bed stood four cans of beans, with a can opener, a dirty paper plate, an open bag of chips, and a pair of dirty socks.

The opposite corner of the room served as a depository for trash and empty cans.

Greeley's shirt and pants were wrinkled and stained, and he smelled not only of rum but desperately in need of a bath.

"What you want, you cats? You didn't come to this dump sightseeing. Why you looking for Pearl Ann?"

But then the old man's face crumpled. "You didn't come to make condolences, either." He stared hard at them. "You saw her, didn't you. You saw her dead—*I* saw you looking!" He sat down on the mattress, eased a bottle of rum from under the blanket and upended it, taking a long pull. He was so pitiful that Dulcie wanted to pat his face with a soft paw.

"Ought to have swish 'n' swash," he said and took another swig. "But you need a coconut for that." He giggled at a joke the two cats didn't understand; they watched him, unblinking.

"What, for Christ's sake?" he shouted at them. "What you staring at?" He leaped up suddenly, lunging at them. Dulcie flipped away but Joe crouched snarling, ready to strike.

Greeley paused, uncertain.

"Pearl Ann Jamison," Joe hissed. "Where does she live? Which room?"

Greeley's laugh blasted the air, drowning them in the stink of rum. "I knew it. What you looking for *her* for?"

He sat unsteadily on a carton. "She rented the last empty room. All *I* could get was this storeroom."

He smirked at them, pleased. "Rental office let me have it cheap, when I tole 'em I was teetotal." And he belched and scratched his belly.

"So what do you want with her?" he said roughly. "You tell me what's your business with this Pearl Ann, maybe I'll show you which room."

For a moment, no one spoke; the three cats and the old man stared at each other, caught in a vacuum of silence. Then Greeley dug three paper cups from an open carton and set them in a row on the floor.

Pouring several inches of rum into each, he pushed two toward Joe and Dulcie. "Drink up, folks," he said, cheerfully lifting the bottle.

The biting smell of rum burned the cats' noses, made them back away. The old man stood up abruptly, catching himself against the cartons, and on tiptoe he reached to slide the third cup across the cartons to Azrael. Azrael turned his head and slitted his eyes against the fumes.

Greeley drained the bottle. And his face crumpled, tears streaking down.

"They were into something," he said softly. "Dora and Ralph. Playing cop maybe. Or maybe blackmail." He hiccuped and leaned against the cartons, scowling at the floor. He was silent for so long they thought he'd gone to sleep.

But suddenly he snatched up the battery light. "Well, come on!" He glared down at them, his red eyes watery. "I got a key to Pearl Ann's place, if that's what you're after."

His boozy laugh cracked. "*She* don't know I got it. Azrael fetched it. No trick at all for him to slip in through the transom. She thought she lost her key," he said, smirking. "She got another from the rent office. And what do they care?" He unbolted the door and led them down a narrow, dark hall that smelled of mice and human urine.

Padding warily after him along the dirty linoleum, Joe and Dulcie heard a loud thump behind them as Azrael hit the floor. They turned to see the black tom swagger out, taking up the rear like a guard walking behind two prisoners.

Pearl Ann's room was at the far end of the gloomy hall. Twisting a skeleton key in the lock, Greeley shoved the door open; when the cats hesitated, he laughed.

"Scared, huh? Scared I'll lock you in?" He slapped his knee, giggling, then crossed the room. Pounding on the window frame, he managed to loosen it. Lifting the bottom half, he propped it open with a dented metal wastebasket. "There, that suit you better?"

They padded into the close, sour-smelling room. In one corner stood an iron bed neatly made up with a worn chenille spread faded to the color of a grimy floor mop. The scarred dresser was of the waterfall era that had been popular in the forties, an incredibly ugly piece but one that had enjoyed a recent revival. Joe leaped to its top, onto a film of dust.

It appeared that Pearl Ann had not lived here alone. Before the mirror were two rows of toiletries, one for a man, one for a woman: hair spray and jasmine cologne on one side, can of shaving cream and bottle of shaving lotion on the other.

Two pairs of men's shoes stood in the open closet next to Pearl Ann's jogging shoes, all as neatly aligned as the shoes of soldiers placed for inspection. Above these hung a man's trousers and jeans and polo shirts and, in her half of the closet, four pastel jumpsuits of the kind that Pearl Ann favored for work, a skirt, and two blouses. In the tiny bathroom, which had no counter space but only a basin, the thin scent of shaving cream and aftershave was mixed with Pearl Ann's perfume. The man's odor was strongest around the bed. As the two cats inspected the room, Greeley stood leaning against the door frame with a strange little smile on his face, as if he were secretly amused. Azrael had remained in the hall, separating himself from their investigation with a barrier of disdain.

They had not told the black tom the results of their surveillance at Pander's restaurant, or who Dora and Ralph's host had been; they had not sought him out, to tell him, and Azrael had not come to them. Maybe, Joe thought, Azrael had gone to Pander's after all, had watched *them* watching Dora and Ralph. He didn't like to think that he had been so unaware, so blind to the dark tom's presence.

Now, searching for he knew not what, pawing open the drawers of the waterfall dresser, Joe found only a man's Jockey briefs and socks. No lady's panties or stockings or nighties—as if Pearl

Ann didn't have much, as if she'd taken what little she owned with her to San Francisco.

In the doorway, Greeley looked increasingly smug, harboring his amusing little secret. Joe, losing patience, leaped onto the dresser and fixed him with a hard stare.

"You can keep your own council if you choose, Greeley. Or you can trade it."

"What could a cat trade? What would a cat have that would interest old Greeley?"

Joe turned his back and began to wash.

"Well, what?" Greeley shouted.

"This is about your sister," he told Greeley.

"What about my sister?"

Joe looked back at him, remote and ungiving.

"What about her!" Greeley snapped.

"She's gone," Joe said. "She disappeared. You tell me about Pearl Ann—tell me what you're grinning about—and I'll tell you about Mavity."

"Gone where? What do you mean, gone?"

"The cops are looking for her."

"You're lying. Why would the cops . . . I don't believe you. Mavity wouldn't be into anything the cops care about. She's as straight as a fencepost. You cats are such liars."

"What do you know about Pearl Ann?"

"You, first. Can't trust a cat to keep a fair trade."

"She might be wanted for murder," Joe said shortly. "Or she might have been murdered. Murdered, while you wallowed here frying your brain in rum."

"You stupid cat—you think I believe what a cat says?"

"She vanished from Winthrop Jergen's apartment this afternoon." Joe looked at Greeley with distaste. "Jergen was found with his throat torn open. And Mavity has disappeared."

Greeley had turned very pale. "She wouldn't kill anyone. No matter what he did, she wouldn't kill him."

Joe stared at him.

Greeley looked back a long time, his glance flicking to Azrael, to Dulcie, to the window.

"Fair trade," Joe said. "Your turn."

Greeley picked up a straight chair from beside the dresser and set it beneath the overhead light.

"Pearl Ann Jamison," he said. "What a sweet little lady." Standing on the chair, he tipped the plastic light cover askew, reached inside, and drew out a thick envelope. Climbing down, he nearly toppled the chair, caught himself against the bed. Glancing out the door at Azrael, almost as if asking permission and receiving only a haughty look from the black cat, he tossed the packet on the chenille spread.

"My partner saw her hide this. He loves looking in windows. He's a regular voyeur." Withdrawing the contents of the envelope, he spread it across the chenille. Joe looked down from the dresser as Dulcie leaped up onto the bed. They studied with interest an airline ticket, a fistful of credit cards, and three driver's licenses.

The airline ticket was partially used, the stub indicating that the holder had traveled from Georgia to L.A., then L.A. to Molena Point. The date of arrival was about the time Pearl Ann had applied for a job with Charlie. The return portion didn't show any reservation. The ticket had been issued in the name of a Troy Hoke.

There was a Georgia driver's license and a Visa and social security cards for Troy Hoke, a second set for a Terrill John, a third set for William Skeel. The pictures were all of the same man: a thin, familiar face, long brown hair tied back in a ponytail. There was no ticket, and no license or charge card or ID for Pearl Ann; presumably she had her cards with her. Greeley leaned against the dresser, giggling.

Dulcie looked the cards over with widening eyes, her ears sharp forward, her tail twitching. Suddenly she leaped for the closet.

But Joe was ahead of her, sniffing at the lineup of shoes.

"All the same size," Joe said.

"And all the same stink," she replied. The cats looked at each other, their eyes dark with excitement.

Greeley began to laugh.

"You got it, you cats. You got it! You been looking for Pearl Ann Jamison." He guffawed, emitting rum-laced fumes, rocking back and forth.

"You got it. This Pearl Ann Jamison," Greeley shouted, spittling rum-laden spray, "this Pearl Ann fits them Jockey shorts just fine."

24

AT THREE A.M., Max Harper pulled into Sam's All Night Burger up on Highway One. He'd been looking for Mavity Flowers but, spotting Clyde's yellow '29 Chevy, he had wheeled in and parked beside it. He sat a moment admiring the car's gleaming finish and boxy, trim lines. Clyde had been working on this one for two years, and she was a beauty. Not many women had this much attention lavished on them—or turned out as elegant, either.

Clipping his phone to his belt beside his radio, he locked the unit and headed into the restaurant. Stopping at the counter to order cherry pie and coffee, he moved on back, where Damen sat hunched over a sandwich and coffee. Sliding into the booth, he picked up the menu out of habit. "Any luck?"

Clyde shook his head. He looked dead for sleep. "Not a sign of Mavity. And I haven't seen Wilma or Charlie for a while. If either one found her, they'd take her back to Wilma's. Her phone doesn't answer."

"I saw Wilma around midnight, up on Ridgeview. She had hoped Bernine would ride with her, said she guessed Bernine had gone out."

"Only Bernine Sage would party while her latest love interest lies cold in the morgue."

"He isn't her love interest anymore—he's no use to her now." Harper reached for a cigarette, tamped it, stuck it in his mouth unlit. "I wired Atlanta on this Warren Cumming. As Mavity said, charges against Cumming were dropped. His partner, Troy Hoke, was convicted, did a year for theft by fraud against Dora and Ralph Sleuder and five other victims. He's been out just over six months.

"Shortly after Hoke's trial, Cumming left the state. Gave a Florida forwarding address, a private postal box. Forfeited on the lease of his Atlanta apartment, closed his bank account, took the balance in cash."

"Big money?"

"Very small. I'm guessing he had larger accounts in other names and that the Florida move was a red herring."

Billie, the straw-blond night waitress, brought Harper's pie and coffee. She was sixtyish and smelled of stale cigarettes, her thin face dry and deeply lined. Setting the pie down, she spilled cherry juice on the table. Scowling, saying nothing, she wiped it up.

"What's with you?" Harper said.

"Fight with LeRoy," she said shortly. She looked hard at Harper. "What's with these guys? Does he have to mess around with that stupid motorcycle *all* the time?"

"Better than another woman," Harper told her.

"I don't know, Max. Perfume is easier to get out of the laundry than grease."

Harper tried to look sympathetic. When she'd gone, Clyde said, "Why doesn't she leave him?"

"Never will. She just likes bitching about him." But he looked distressed, too. Despite dealing with the dregs of the world, Harper never got used to people staying in a bad marriage. His own happy marriage had ended far too soon, when Millie died of cancer; he didn't have a lot of sympathy for people who put up with anything less than a completely wonderful union. To Max's way of thinking, it was better to be alone. He tasted his pie, ate half of it before he spoke again.

"After Hoke was released, he received several phone calls to his Atlanta apartment." He glanced up at Clyde. "All were placed from the Sleuders' phone. And a few days after the last call, he left the state. That was four months ago."

Clyde had stopped eating, was quiet.

"Shortly before the Sleuders flew out here on vacation, they placed several calls to a Molena Point pay phone a block from the Davidson Building.

"The way I see it, Dora Sleuder stumbled onto Cumming's whereabouts by chance. Try this: Dora makes a casual phone call to her aunt—evidently they talked once or twice a month, family stuff, keeping in touch. During the conversation, Mavity mentions her new investment counselor, brags about how well she's doing.

"She tells Dora how wonderful Jergen is and describes him—you know Mavity, going on about Jergen's youthful looks and silver hair. The description fits Cumming, and Dora starts asking questions."

Clyde nodded. "Like, how old is he? How does he dress and talk? How he furnishes his office, what kind of car he prefers . . ."

"Exactly. Now assume that Mavity's description was so much like Cumming that it got Dora and Ralph wondering, made them decide to check up on this Jergen."

"But . . ."

"They knew that Hoke was just out of prison—they'd kept track of him. And they knew he'd be burning to get at Cumming, for setting him up. Hoke did all the time for that scam. Cumming didn't do a lick.

"Dora and Ralph decide that this Jergen could be Warren Cumming, and they sick Hoke on him, encourage Hoke to come on out here and take a look."

"But how did they find Hoke? Through his parole officer?"

Harper nodded. "We have the parole officer's phone record, and we've talked with him. He remembers a woman calling him, said she was Hoke's niece, that Hoke had some things of her mother's that he'd put away before he went to prison, that she wanted to get them back. Parole officer wouldn't disclose any information, but he took her phone number, passed it on to Hoke—he's obliged to do that. Figures he'll watch developments. This officer keeps good records, the Sleuders' number was there in his logbook.

"So Hoke calls Dora, and she tells him about Winthrop Jergen. According to Hoke's phone bill, they talk for over an hour. The next day Hoke moves out of his apartment, leaves Altanta."

Harper slipped a photograph from his pocket, handed it across.

The man in the picture was thin and pale. Light brown hair, long and tied back. One low shoulder. A bony face, thin eyebrows.

Clyde stared. "The guy who hangs around the apartments. Mavity calls him 'the watcher.' This is Troy Hoke?"

"Yep. And we have Hoke's prints, from the Atlanta file." He mopped up cherry juice with a forkful of crust.

"Did they match the prints from the murder scene?"

"The only prints we got at the scene were for Jergen himself, and for Mavity and Charlie."

"You didn't get Pearl Ann's prints? They should be all over the place. She cleaned for him regularly, and she did the repairs. Except . . ." Clyde thought a minute. "Pearl Ann wears gloves. Has some allergy. Gloves to work on the Sheetrock, to clean, to paint."

"Charlie told me that. Rubber gloves or sometimes a soft leather pair."

Clyde nodded. "She takes them off several times a day, to put on some kind of prescription hand cream."

He looked intently at Harper. "Sounds like this will nail Hoke—but what about Mavity? It won't help us find Mavity." They were speaking softly. At three in the morning, the restaurant was nearly empty. Down at the far end of the counter two men in jeans and plaid shirts sat eating, intent on their fried eggs. In a booth near the door, an elderly couple was drinking coffee, each reading a section of a newspaper. At the counter near them, a striking blond was nibbling at a sandwich and sipping orange juice. As Harper signaled for a refill of coffee, his cellular phone buzzed. Picking it up, he started to speak, then went silent.

Watching him, Clyde thought the call was being transferred. The blond got up from the counter, wrapped her unfinished sandwich in a paper napkin, paid her check and left. Clyde watched through the window as she swung into a Chrysler van with the windows open and a huge white dog hanging his head out, watched her feeding the dog little bites of the sandwich. Across from him, Harper had stiffened.

Harper felt his blood go chill. The voice on the line was female, a smooth voice, a velvety, insinuating voice that made the hackles on his neck rise. He could never get used to hearing this woman. He didn't know her name, had never seen her, didn't know anything about her, but every time she called, the nerves in his stomach began to twitch.

"Captain Harper? Are you still there?"

He said nothing.

"Captain Harper, you have just sealed the scene of a murder up on Venta Street."

"Have I?"

"Your men didn't touch the computer. You left it on, and you have a Bureau man coming down early in the morning to check it out."

Harper remained silent. The pie in his stomach had turned sour. *No one* could know about the Bureau man except his own people and Charlie Getz. He tried to figure who, in his own department, would breach security, would pass along such information. The officers at the scene had been Brennan, Wendell, Ray, and Case. The two medics had left before he called the Bureau.

The caller was waiting for him to respond. He motioned for Clyde to listen. Clyde came around the table and sat down, shoving against Harper, jamming his ear to the phone.

"Captain Harper, there are two code words for the computer that your Bureau man will want. Jergen's code, to open his financial files, is *Cairo*.

"The second code word was used by Pearl Ann Jamison. It should open a set of files that Pearl Ann seems to have hidden from Jergen, on his own computer. That word is *Tiger.* I believe those are both Georgia towns; I looked them up on the map.

"In looking for suspects," the caller said softly, "you need to be looking for a man. Pearl Ann and he are . . ."

She gasped, Max heard a faint yelp of alarm and the line went dead.

Harper sat frozen, staring at the phone. Clyde exploded out of the booth like he was shot, threw a five-dollar bill on the table and fled out the door.

"Hold it," Harper shouted. "What the hell?" He stared after Clyde perplexed, watched the yellow roadster scorch out of the parking lot moving like a racing car and disappear down the hill toward the village.

He wanted to go after Clyde. Instead, he sat thinking about that soft voice.

You need to be looking for a man, Pearl Ann and he are . . . And then the gasp or yelp, a strange little sound, and then silence.

The two are *what?*

Working together? Pearl Ann and a man are working together? Involved? Involved in Jergen's death? Pearl Ann and who? Troy Hoke? And then that startled yelp, and Clyde taking off like his boots were on fire.

He motioned for more coffee, and dug in his pocket for some antacid. He didn't want to know where Clyde was headed. He didn't want to follow the yellow car. He didn't want to know who the caller was, with the soft and velvety voice.

25

IN THE DARKEST CORNER beneath Wilma's bed, Dulcie crouched, listening to the footsteps coming down the hall, ready to run if Bernine looked under and found her. At the first sound of someone approaching she had abandoned the phone and dived for the shadows, leaving Max Harper shouting through the receiver. If Bernine heard him and picked up the phone and started asking questions—and Harper started asking questions—all hell would break loose. There was no one else in the house, to have made the call.

But she daren't leap onto the bed again and try to hang up, there was no time, Bernine was nearly at the door . . .

She'd waited all night to make this call, waited for Bernine to get off the phone and now here she came when she should be in bed drifting off to sleep.

It had been nearly one A.M. when Dulcie slipped in through her cat door exhausted from listening for hours to drunken Greeley Urzey and breathing his stink of rum in Pearl Ann's pokey little room. They'd had to listen to him agonizing over Mavity and to his wild plans for finding her, which amounted to nothing, because by midnight he had drunk himself into a stupor. Azrael had looked intensely pleased that Mavity might have met with foul play, his amber eyes gleaming with malice. Pure hatred, Dulcie thought. The cat was filled with hate, that was his nature—loathing for anyone who didn't worship him.

Racing home, bolting in through her cat door, she'd realized that Wilma wasn't home; her car wasn't in the drive or in the open garage. She'd pictured Wilma still cruising the dark streets searching for Mavity, looking for Mavity's little VW.

Bernine's car was at the curb, but Bernine had gone out to dinner with a real estate broker. Dulcie hoped she was still out. But then, heading for the phone, she'd heard Bernine's voice.

Slipping through the dark dining room, she'd caught the scent of Bernine's perfume and seen her sitting at Wilma's desk talking on the phone. She'd listened for only a few minutes before she decided Bernine was making up with her estranged live-in. She slipped on into Wilma's bedroom, wishing they had two phone lines.

The curtains had not been drawn, and the faint light from the distant street lamp bathed the room in soft shadows. The bed was smoothly made. Leaping up onto the flowered, quilted spread, she had settled down to wait.

She'd waited for nearly two hours for Bernine to finish, had slipped periodically out into the hall to listen as the conversation swung from mushy love talk to angry argument to sweet words again in a sickening display of human indecision and female guile. Bernine had moved the phone to the couch, lay curled up on *her* patch of velvet, sweet-talking this bozo.

On the bed she'd dozed, waked to listen to Bernine going on and on, to see the light still burning in the living room and beneath the guest room door and feeling her stomach churn with impatience at the delay.

But then at last she heard Bernine leave the living room, head down the hall, and from the guest room she could hear little rustling sounds. Either Bernine was packing to leave or she was getting ready for bed.

Easing Wilma's bedroom door closed, catching it with her paw just before it latched, she'd leaped to the night table, nosing at the phone.

Her sensible self said, *Wait until Bernine's light goes out—don't do this while she's awake.*

But she'd waited too long. Her impatient self said, *She won't hear you. What are you afraid of? It's practically morning, let's get on with it.*

Lifting the headset by its cord, she had dropped it on the pillow, squinched up her paw and punched in Harper's number, cocking her head to the receiver. Joe was an old hand at this, but she still got nervous. The first time she'd dialed and heard a voice at the other end, she'd felt as weird as if she were communicating with someone on Mars.

When the dispatcher answered, she'd boldly asked for Max Harper.

"Captain Harper is not on duty. Lieutenant Brennan can help you."

"I have information to give to Captain Harper personally. About the Winthrop Jergen murder. Information that Harper must have before the Bureau agent arrives in the morning. I must give it to him now; I cannot call again."

It had taken some time for the dispatcher to switch the call to Harper's cellular phone, a degree of electronic sophistication that further awed Dulcie. The delay made her so edgy that her skin began to twitch, but at last Harper came on the line. She had tried to speak clearly, but she hadn't dared lift her voice above a whisper.

"Captain Harper, I have some information about Winthrop Jergen."

Harper didn't respond.

"Captain Harper? Are you still there?" He didn't answer, but she could hear him breathing. "Captain Harper, you have just sealed the scene of a murder up on Venta Street. Your men didn't touch the computer. You left it on, and you have a Bureau man coming down early in the morning to check it out."

Only silence and his ragged breathing. Her paws began to sweat. She wondered if Harper was nervous, too. This was so strange, the two of them linked not only by the wonder of electronics but by a far greater phenomenon, by a miracle that she hardly understood herself—and that Max Harper could never bring himself to believe. She imagined herself like those photographs where a cat's face is superimposed over a woman's face, becoming one, and she almost giggled.

"Captain Harper, there are two code words for the computer that your Bureau man will want. Jergen's code, to open his financial files, is *Cairo*.

"The second code word was used by Pearl Ann Jamison. It should open a set of files that Pearl Ann seems to have hidden from Jergen, on his own computer. That word is *Tiger*. I believe those are both Georgia towns . . ."

She was just starting to explain about Pearl Ann and Troy Hoke when she heard the footsteps; gasping a sharp mew, she leaped to the floor and under the bed. Above her Harper's angry voice had shouted, *"Hold it. What the hell?"*

Now as the bedroom door opened and the light flashed on, Dulcie's every muscle was tensed to sprint past Bernine's feet and down the hall to safety. Thank God the phone above her was silent—yet she'd heard no click as if Harper had hung up. She listened for those sharp beeps when the phone was left off the hook. She was so frightened that the sounds in the bedroom hardly registered: the hush of the closet door opening, someone rummaging among Wilma's clothes. All she could think was *If Bernine picks up the phone, what if he's still on the line? No one could have made that call, no one—there's no other human in the house. Only the cat crouched under the bed scared out of her kitty mind.* Shivering, she listened to the *whish* of garments from the closet.

Then she smelled Wilma's scent, Wilma's subtle bath powder.

Peering out from beneath the spread, she saw Wilma's bare feet as Wilma pulled on her slippers. Mewling with relief, she came out, curving around Wilma's ankles, purring so hard she trembled.

Wilma picked her up, stared into her face. "What?" she whispered, glancing toward the closed door. "What's the matter?"

"I thought—I thought you were Bernine," she breathed, snuggling against Wilma.

Only then did Wilma see the phone lying on the bed. She raised a disapproving eyebrow at Dulcie. "You didn't get my note?"

"What note? You left a note? Bernine . . ."

Wilma put her down on the bed, hung up the phone, and went down the hall. Dulcie heard her cross the kitchen and open the back door. She returned with a small, folded paper. "I left it tucked in the frame of your cat door, but only a little bit showing so Bernine wouldn't notice." As she moved to pull the bedroom door closed, Dulcie, peering down the hall, saw that Bernine's light had gone out. Had Bernine gone to sleep? Or was she standing just inside, straining to hear?

Wilma unfolded the paper and laid it on the bed.

Have gone to look for Mavity. Don't stay here alone. Go over to Joe's, now, where you'll be safe.

Dulcie looked at her intently. "Did you really think Bernine would . . ."

"I don't know what Bernine would do. But all night, while we looked for Mavity, I worried about you. Twice I swung by. When Bernine's light wasn't on, I felt easier. She must have gotten home very late."

"She came in about one. But she was on the phone for hours, talking to the guy she was living with. Weeping, shouting. Sweet-talking. What histrionics. Maybe she'll move out. You didn't find Mavity?"

"No." Wilma sat down on the bed, tired and drawn. "And when I think of Jergen's grisly death, I'm afraid for her. If Mavity saw the killer, her life isn't worth much." She looked at Dulcie a long time. "What is his death about? What's happening? Dulcie, what do you know about this?"

Dulcie looked back at her, panicked about what to do.

She had tried to tell Captain Harper, tonight, that Pearl Ann was Troy Hoke. Now, should she tell Wilma?

But what good? Wilma daren't tell Harper. He'd ask how she knew, and why she hadn't told him before. And if she said she'd just found out, he'd want to know *how* she learned Pearl Ann's secret on the same day of the murder. Wilma's sudden knowledge would implicate her in a way difficult to talk herself out of.

Wilma did not lie well to law enforcement, particularly to Max Harper. She was too truthful within her own profession. And if she attempted some hastily contrived excuse, Harper *would* be suspicious. Dulcie looked at her blankly, shrugged, and said nothing.

Wilma was turning down the bed, folding the quilted chintz back while Dulcie prowled across it, when a loud knocking from the back door startled them and they heard Clyde shouting.

Racing for the kitchen, Wilma jerked the door open. Behind her, Dulcie leaped to the breakfast table. Clyde rushed in, his voice loud with alarm. "Where is she? What hap . . . ?"

"Shhh," Wilma whispered, grabbing his arm. "*Don't wake Bernine.* What's wrong?"

Clyde's stubbled cheeks were dark and rough, his dark hair tangled. The underarms of his jogging suit were sweaty. When he saw Dulcie, he stopped shouting. Pulling out a chair, he sat down glaring at her, his face red with frustration. "You just about gave me heart failure. What the hell were you doing? What the hell happened here?"

Dulcie looked at him, puzzled.

"My God, Dulcie. When you called Harper—when you made that awful, frightened cry, I thought someone was killing you." He lowered his voice, glancing in the direction of the guest room. "That was bloodcurdling—that was the next thing to a yowl on the phone!"

"You were listening? Where were you?" Dulcie cocked her head. "And how did you know where I was?"

"Where else would you be? Except maybe my house. I came here first . . ." Clyde sighed. "You *mewed*, Dulcie—you almost *yowled* into the damned phone. Harper looked amazed, looked . . . I thought someone had snatched you up and was wringing your stupid cat neck." He glared hard at her. "These phone calls, Dulcie . . ."

"I didn't yowl. I didn't mew. I simply caught my breath. I thought," she said softly, "I thought I heard Bernine coming."

He simply looked at her.

"I thought she'd catch me with the phone. But then it wasn't Bernine, it was Wilma. What did Harper say?"

"He didn't *say* anything. *I* don't know what he said. I was out of there—came flying down here thinking you were being strangled. We were clear up at Sam's, on the highway. My God . . ."

Dulcie licked his hand. She was really very touched. "How could I know you were listening? I didn't mean to upset you."

"Why the hell wouldn't I be upset? And can you imagine what would happen if Harper heard you really *meow?* With all the questions he already has about you two, don't you think he'd just about go crazy? Questions I can't answer for him, Dulcie. Questions I wouldn't dare answer."

Clyde put his head in his hands. "Sometimes, Dulcie, between you and Joe, I can't handle this stuff."

She patted his hand with a soft paw. He looked so distressed that she didn't know whether to feel sorry for him or roll over laughing.

But still, she thought, Clyde handled most situations very well. From the moment Joe discovered he was endowed with human speech, that he could carry on a conversation in the English language and read the written word, Clyde had weathered Joe's—and her own—unusual lifestyle with a minimum of emotional chaos. He had indulged in very few out-of-control shouting spells. He had exhibited no mind-numbing bouts of terror that she knew of. He had even paid Joe's deli bills without undue grousing.

He had even put up with Joe's reading the front page first in the mornings and demanding anchovies for breakfast. Not until this morning, she thought, had he really lost it.

She patted his hand again and rubbed her whiskers against his knuckles. "You shouldn't get so worked up—it's bad for human blood pressure. You can see that I'm all right. It was just a simple phone call."

"*A* simple *phone call? Simple?* You should have seen Harper's face." Clyde sighed deeply. "You don't seem to realize, Dulcie, how this stuff upsets Harper."

Wilma rose from the table. Turning away, she took the milk from the refrigerator and busied herself making cocoa.

"Every time you and Joe meddle," Clyde said, "every time you phone Harper with some wild tip, he gets suspicious all over again. And he starts making skewered remarks, laying the whole damned thing in my lap."

"What whole damned thing?" Dulcie said softly, trying to keep her temper.

"He starts hinting that he wants answers. But he's too upset to come right out with the real question. And that isn't like Harper. He's the most direct guy I know. But this . . . Dulcie, this stuff is just too much."

She stared sweetly into Clyde's face. "Why is helping him solve a crime a *whole damned thing*, as you put it? Why is catching a murderer, to say nothing of boosting the department's statistics and impressing the mayor and the city council with Harper's absolutely perfect, hundred percent record . . ."

"Can it, Dulcie. I've heard all that. You're beginning to sound just like Joe. Going on and on with this ego-driven . . ."

"Oh, you can be rude!" She was so angry she raised her armored paw, facing him boldly, waiting for an apology.

She would not, several months ago, have dared such behavior with Clyde. When she first discovered her ability to speak, she had felt so shy she'd even been embarrassed to speak to Wilma.

Even when she and Joe began to discover the history and mythology of their lost race, to know that they were not alone, that there were others like them—and even though Clyde and Wilma read the research, too—it had taken all her courage to act natural and carry on a normal conversation. It had been months before she would speak to Clyde.

Wilma poured the cocoa and poured Dulcie a bowl of warm milk. Clyde sat trying to calm his temper. "Dulcie, let me explain. Max Harper lives a life totally oriented to hard facts. His world is made up of cold, factual evidence and logically drawn conclusions based on that evidence."

"I know that." She did not want to hear a lecture.

"How do you think Harper feels when the evidence implies something that he *knows* is totally impossible? What is he supposed to do when no one in the world would believe what the evidence tells him?"

"But . . ."

"Tonight, when Harper's phone rang, the minute he heard your voice, he went white. If you'd seen him . . ."

"But it was only a voice on the phone. He didn't . . ."

"Your voice—the snitch's voice—has him traumatized. This mysterious female voice that he links with all the past incidents . . . Oh, hell," Clyde said. "I don't need to explain this to you. You know what he suspects. You know you make him crazy."

Dulcie felt incredibly hurt. "The tips Joe and I have given him have solved three murders," she said quietly.

Wilma sat down at the table, cradling her cup of cocoa.

Clyde said, "Every crime where you and Joe have meddled, Harper has found cat hairs tainting the evidence—and sometimes pawprints. *Pawprints, Dulcie!* Your marks are all over the damned evidence. Do you think this doesn't upset him? And now, tonight, you yowl into the damned telephone."

"I didn't *yowl.*"

"*You* know the way he looks at you and Joe. *Joe* tells you the kind of stuff Harper says to me. How would you like it if Max Harper ended up in the funny farm—because of you two?"

"There is no way Max Harper is going to end up in a mental hospital. Talk about overdramatizing. Half of Harper's comments are just putting you on. And he only talks that way after a few beers."

Wilma refilled Clyde's cocoa cup and tried to turn the conversation. "You didn't find any trace of Mavity?"

Clyde shook his head.

"We'll start early in the morning," she said. "We can canvas the shops that were closed last night, see if anyone saw her."

"The whole department will be doing that. Mavity is a prime suspect." He reached to stroke Dulcie, wanting to make amends.

Reluctantly Dulcie allowed him to pet her. She couldn't believe that Max Harper would really suspect Mavity of killing Jergen. If he did suspect Mavity, he needed to know about Pearl Ann. She rose and moved away from Clyde, stood looking at him and Wilma until she had their full attention, until Clyde stopped glowering and waited for her to speak.

"Mavity isn't guilty," she told them. "I was trying to tell Harper that, on the phone."

"How do you know that?" Wilma said softly.

"Pearl Ann Jamison is the one Harper wants. I was *trying* to *tell* him that."

They both stared at her.

"Pearl Ann Jamison," Dulcie said, "is a guy in drag. I believe that he's the killer."

Clyde burst out laughing. "Come on, Dulcie. Just because Pearl Ann's strong, and a good carpenter, doesn't mean she's a guy. You . . ."

"Are you saying I don't know what I'm talking about?"

"Of course not. I just think you and Joe . . . Joe's never mentioned this. What would make you think . . ."

"I know the difference between male and female," she said tartly. "Which is more than you and Wilma seem to have figured out. When you get past the Jasmine perfume, Pearl Ann smells like a man. Without the perfume, we'd have known at once."

"She *smells* different? You're basing this wild accusation on a *smell?*"

"Of course he smells different. Testosterone, Clyde. He smells totally male. It's not my fault that humans are so—challenged when it comes to the olfactory skills."

Wilma watched the two of them solemnly.

"Pearl Ann smells like a man," Dulcie repeated. "Half the clothes in her closet belong to a man. The IDs hidden in her room—driver's licenses and credit cards, are for several different men."

Clyde sighed.

"One ID is in the name of Troy Hoke. He was . . ."

That brought Clyde up short. "Where did you hear that name?"

"I just told you. Pearl Ann has an ID for Troy Hoke. If you don't believe me or Joe, then ask Greeley—Greeley knows all about Pearl Ann. *He* let us into her room in the Davidson Building. *He* showed us the driver's licenses and credit cards hidden in the light fixture. He told us where Hoke parks the car he drives, that none of you have seen. An eight-year-old gray Chrysler."

They were both gawking at her, two looks of amazement that quite pleased her.

"That's where Greeley's been all this time," she said patiently. "Camping in a storeroom at the Davidson Building."

"Why didn't you tell us this before?" Wilma said. "It's not like you to keep something . . ."

This was really too much. "I just did tell you," she hissed angrily. Clyde's skeptical questions were one thing, she was used to Clyde's argumentative attitude. But for Wilma to question her—that hurt. "We just found out tonight," she said shortly and turned her back on Wilma, leaped off the table, and trotted away to the living room. If they didn't want to believe her, that was their problem. She'd call Harper back at once and tell him about Troy Hoke.

Leaping to the desk, she had just taken the phone cord in her teeth when the instrument shrilled, sending her careening off again.

The phone rang three times before Wilma ran in and

snatched it from the cradle. She listened, didn't speak. She patted the desk for Dulcie to jump up, but Dulcie turned away.

"What hospital?" Wilma said.

On the floor, Dulcie stopped washing.

"How bad is she?" Wilma said softly. "Can we see her?" And in a moment she hung up the phone and hurried away to dress and find her keys.

26

MAVITY'S hospital room at Salinas Medical was guarded by a thin, young deputy who had been on duty most of the night. His chin was stubbled with pale whiskers, and his uniform was wrinkled. Sitting on a straight-backed chair just outside Mavity's half-open door, he was enjoying an order of waffles and bacon served in a plastic carton. A Styrofoam cup of coffee sat on the floor beside his chair. He was present not only to assure that the suspect did not escape—a most unlikely event, considering Mavity's condition—but to bar intruders and protect the old woman in case she was not Jergen's killer but was a witness to his death.

Mavity's room was not much larger than a closet. The steel furniture was old and scarred, but the white sheets and blanket were snowy fresh. She slept fitfully, her breathing labored, her left hand affixed to an IV tube, her right hand clutching the blanket. A white bandage covered most of her head, as if she were wearing the pristine headgear of some exotic eastern cult. She had been in the hospital since one A.M., when she was transferred there by ambulance from an alley in Salinas where she had been found lying unconscious near her wrecked VW. She had not been able to tell the police or the nurses her name or where she lived. The Salinas police got that information from the registration of her wrecked car. They had notified the Molena Point PD only after an alert was faxed to them that a woman of Mavity's description was missing and was wanted for questioning in last evening's murder.

Salinas Medical was an hour's drive from Molena Point, lying inland where the weather was drier and warmer. The hospital complex consisted of half a dozen Spanish-style buildings surrounded by a circular drive. It was a training facility for medical staff and a bulwark of specialized medical services for the area, including an excellent cardiac unit and a long-term-care wing for patients in need of intensive nursing. Wilma, Clyde, and Charlie arrived at Salinas Medical at five-thirty A.M.

When Wilma had received Max Harper's phone call at four that morning, she and Clyde left her house in her car, making two stops, the first to drop Dulcie off at Clyde's place, an arrangement about which Dulcie was not happy. The last Wilma saw of the little cat, Dulcie was sulking alone on Clyde's steps, her ears down, her head hanging, looking as abandoned as she could possibly manage.

Wilma knew that the instant she drove away Dulcie would bolt inside to Joe, pacing and lashing her tail, complaining about the indignities a cat was subjected to by uncaring humans.

"They won't let you into the hospital," Wilma had told her. "And I don't want you alone here with Bernine."

"I could go in a shopping bag. They'd think I was extra clothes or homemade cookies. Don't you think *I* care about Mavity? Don't you think *I* care that that man might have killed her?"

"Or that *she* might have killed Jergen?"

"Nonsense. *You* know she didn't. I would fit in that canvas book tote. You could just . . ."

"Hospital security checks all parcels. They won't let you in. They'd throw you out in the street."

"But . . ."

"Stay with Joe," Wilma had snapped, and had unceremoniously tossed Dulcie into the car where she hunched miserably on the front seat.

The second stop had been to pick up Charlie, who was waiting in front of her building before the antique shop, sucking on a mug of coffee and snuggled in a fleece-lined denim jacket. She slid into the front seat between Clyde and Wilma, frowning with worry over Mavity.

"Has she remembered her name? Does she know what happened to her?"

"We haven't talked to the hospital," Wilma said. "All I know is what Harper told me when he called, that she was confused and groggy."

"Was she alone in the car?"

Clyde put his arm around her. "As far as we know, she was. They found the VW smashed against a lamppost, outside a pawnshop in the old part of town. Not a likely place for her to be in the middle of the night."

As they sped east on the nearly empty freeway, the dawn air was damp and cool through the open windows, helping to wake them. On either side of the road, the thickly wooded hills rose dark and solid against the dawn sky. Soon they were inland between flat fields, the crops laid out in long green rows, the dawn air smelling of onions. When they arrived at Salinas Medical, Mavity was asleep, an IV tube snaking up her arm to a slowly seeping bottle. In the corner of the room on a hard wooden chair, Max Harper dozed, his long legs splayed out before him. He came fully awake as they entered.

"I've been here about an hour," he replied to Wilma's questioning look. "Haven't gotten much out of her—she's pretty confused."

Clyde went out to the nursing station to get some chairs, and Charlie went to find the coffee machine, returning with four large cups of steaming brew that tasted like rusted metal.

"She has a cerebral contusion," Harper said. "A lot of swelling. They had a shunt in for a while, to relieve the pressure, to drain off some of the fluid. And she's had trouble breathing. They thought she'd have to have a tracheotomy, but the breathing has eased off. She's irritable and her memory's dicy, but that's to be expected. Not much luck trying to recall yesterday afternoon. And when she can't put it together, she gets angry. They're waking her every two hours." He sipped his coffee. He looked like he could use a smoke.

Wilma smoothed Mavity's blanket. "Were there any witnesses to the wreck?"

Harper shook his head. "None that we've found. We don't know yet whether another car was involved or if she simply ran off the street into the lamppost."

Mavity woke just after six and lay scowling at them, confused and bleary. Her wrinkled little face seemed very small surrounded by the thick white bandage and snowy bedding. When Wilma spoke to her, she did not respond. She frowned at Charlie's wild red hair and glared angrily at Harper. But soon something began to clear. She grew restless, and she reached up her hand to Wilma, trying to change position, kicking out of the blanket with one white, thin leg.

Wilma looked a question at Harper, and he nodded. She sat down on the edge of the bed, helping Mavity to get settled, holding her hand. "You had a little accident. You're in Salinas Medical. We came over to be with you."

Mavity scowled. Wilma smiled back. "Do you remember cleaning for Mr. Jergen yesterday afternoon?"

Mavity looked at her blankly.

"Mavity?"

"If it was his day, I cleaned for him," she snapped. "Why wouldn't I?" She looked around the room, puzzled. "I was fixing supper for Greeley—sauerkraut and hot dogs." She reached to touch her bandage and the IV tube swung, startling her. She tried to snatch it, but Wilma held her hand. "Leave it, Mavity. It will make you feel better."

Mavity sighed. "We had a terrible argument, Dora and Ralph and me. And the hardware store—I was in the hardware store just a minute ago. I don't understand. How did I get in a hospital?"

"You hit your head," Wilma told her.

Mavity went quiet. "Someone said I wrecked my car." She gave Wilma an angry glare. "I've never in my life had a wreck. I would remember if I wrecked my little car."

"When did you make sauerkraut for Greeley?"

"I—I don't know," she said crossly, as if Wilma was being very rude with her questions.

"When did you and Dora and Ralph argue?" Wilma persisted.

But Mavity turned over, jerking the blankets higher and nearly dislodging the IV, and soon she dropped into sleep. They sat in a tight little group waiting for her to wake.

When she did wake, she jerked up suddenly, trying to sit up. "Caulking," she told Wilma. "Caulking for the shower. Did I buy the caulking? Pearl Ann is waiting for it."

Wilma straightened the bedding and smoothed the sheet. "Pearl Ann sent you to buy caulking? When was this?"

But already she had forgotten. Again she scowled at Wilma, puzzled and disoriented, not remembering anything in its proper order. Perhaps not remembering, at all, Winthrop Jergen's ugly death?

27

IF WILMA GETZ hadn't spent thirty years working with federal criminals, Max Harper would not have placed Mavity Flowers in her custody. Two days after Mavity entered Salinas Medical, she was released to Wilma's care. Wilma drove her home, tucked her up in her own bed and moved a cot into the room for herself. Her official duties, besides helping Mavity, were a perfect excuse to evict Bernine Sage from the guest room, to make room for the twenty-four-hour police guard that Max Harper had assigned. The county attorney agreed that Mavity's care by an old friend might ease her fears and help her remember the circumstances of Winthrop Jergen's death; the case was growing in breadth as law enforcement agencies began to uncover links between Jergen/Cumming, Troy Hoke, and several unsolved crimes in Tennessee and Alabama.

No one knew how much of Mavity's memory loss was due to the cerebral contusion and how much resulted from the shock of what she had witnessed. Under Wilma's gentle questioning, she was beginning to recall more details, to put together the scattered scenes.

But Dulcie's information about Troy Hoke alias Pearl Ann

Jamison, which Dulcie passed on to Max Harper during an early-morning phone call, had been—so far as Dulcie and Joe could surmise—totally ignored. Harper felt certain that Troy Hoke had come here to Molena Point to find Warren Cumming; he'd told Clyde that much. So why did he ignore their important and dearly gathered information that Pearl Ann *was* Troy Hoke?

Mavity could remember returning from the hardware store with Pearl Ann's caulking. She could remember crossing the patio and hearing angry shouts from Jergen's apartment. "Two men shouting, and thuds," she had told Wilma. "Then seems like I was at the top of the stairs standing in the open door." But always, at this point, she went silent. "I don't remember any more. I can't remember."

"Did you see the other man?" Wilma would ask. "Did you know him?"

"I can't remember. When I think about it I feel scared and sort of sick."

Now Wilma glanced out toward the living room where the police guard sat reading the paper. "You were standing in the doorway," she said gently, "and the two men were shouting. And then . . . ?"

"A red neon sign, that's what I remember next. Red light shining in my face. It was night. I could hear people talking and cars passing."

"And nothing in between?"

"No. Nothing."

"The red neon—you were walking somewhere?"

"I was in my car. The lights—the lights hurt. I had to close my eyes."

"In your own car?"

"In the back, with the mops and buckets." Mavity looked at her, puzzled, her short gray hair a tangle of kinks, her face drawn into lines of bewilderment. "Why would I be in the back of my own car? I was lying on my extra pair of work shoes. The lights hurt my eyes. Then someone pulling me, dragging me. It was dark. Then a real bright light, and a nurse. I'm in that hospital bed, and my head hurting so bad. I couldn't hear nothing but the pounding in my head."

Wilma was careful not to prompt Mavity. She wanted her to remember the alley where the Salinas Police had found her and to remember wrecking her car, without being led by her suggestions.

"Greeley . . ." Mavity said, "I have to get home—Greeley's waiting. Dora and Ralph . . .They'll be worried. They won't know where I am. I left the meat thawing on the sink, and that cat will . . ."

"The meat's all right—they put the meat away. And they're not worried, they know where you are," Wilma lied. But maybe Dora and Ralph did know, from wherever they were beyond the pale. Who was she to say?

Mavity dozed again, her hand relaxed across Dulcie's shoulder where the cat lay curled on the quilt against her. But then in sleep Mavity's hand went rigid and she woke startled. "I have to get up. They won't know . . ."

"It's all right, Mavity," Wilma reassured her. "Everything's taken care of. Greeley will be along later."

"But Dora and . . ."

Suddenly Mavity stopped speaking.

Her eyes widened. She raised up in bed, staring at Wilma, then her face crumpled. "They're dead," she whispered. She looked terrified. "Dora and Ralph are dead."

Wilma sat down on the bed beside her, put her arm around Mavity. They sat quietly until Mavity said, "Greeley—I need Greeley." She looked nakedly at Wilma. "Is he all right?"

"Greeley's just fine, I promise." *Rolling drunk*, Wilma thought. *But he's all in one piece.*

"I need him." Mavity looked at her helplessly. "How can I ever tell him? Tell him that Dora's gone?"

"He'll be here soon. You won't need to tell him. Greeley knows about Dora. He knows about Dora and Ralph, and he's taking it very well. He'll be along soon, to be with you."

The police had picked Greeley up at the Davidson Building

and had held him until he sobered up enough for questioning regarding Dora and Ralph's deaths. When they released him, Max Harper said, he went directly back to the Davidson Building—to the companionship of several more cases of rum. Wilma had no intention of bringing him to see Mavity until he was sober and had cleaned himself up. Dulcie said he smelled like a drunk possum, and Harper said much the same.

The police now knew that Dora and Ralph had died of a drug overdose. The forensics report made it clear that, in Harper's words, Dora and Ralph Sleuder were loaded with enough morphine to put down a pair of cart horses.

"The coroner thinks they ingested the drug during dinner. They'd had a big meal, steak, potatoes, salad with French dressing, chocolate pie and coffee," Max had told them. "We don't know yet who they had dinner with, or where. That was the night after they met for dinner with Bernine."

Harper had learned about the dinner at Pander's from his mysterious informant during the same phone call in which she identified Pearl Ann as Troy Hoke. Checking with Pander's, Harper had learned that the threesome arrived at seven-thirty and were seated at a table on the terrace. Their waiter remembered what each of the three guests had ordered for dinner, what they had had to drink, what time they departed, and that Bernine paid the bill by credit card.

The doctors had said Mavity might be bad-tempered until her contusion healed, and she was. The four-inch gash in the back of her head was not the result of the car accident; she had been hit on the head from behind several hours before her car was wrecked—very likely she had been knocked out, loaded into the backseat of the VW, driven to Salinas, and her car deliberately wrecked against the lamppost where it was found. Harper had no intention of allowing Mavity to sustain another attack. Besides the twenty-four-hour guard, patrol units were all over the area.

Now, entering Wilma's pastel bedroom, Max Harper's uniform and solemn, leathery face contrasted in an interesting way with the feminine room, with the flowered chintz and white wicker furniture, putting Wilma in mind of a weathered soldier wandering among the petunias. As she poured coffee for him from the tray on Mavity's bed table, Mavity sat against the pillows, pleased at being fussed over, at being the center of attention. The facts she gave Max, as he questioned her, were the same she had given Wilma. Slowly the jigsaw pieces of her memory were slipping into place.

On the bed beside Mavity, Dulcie lay pretending to sleep as she fitted together Mavity's scenario with what she and Joe already knew.

Winthrop Jergen had left his apartment at about two, telling Mavity and Pearl Ann that he had an appointment up the coast. Charlie arrived at three and left again a few minutes later, headed for the Blackburn house. Pearl Ann was already upstairs in his rooms repairing the towel rack. As Charlie left, Mavity carried her cleaning things up to his apartment.

"When I came in, Pearl Ann said she was nearly out of shower caulking—that good, plastic kind that she likes. She said if I'd go down to the village for some, she'd start on the refrigerator for me, put the ice trays and shelves in a dishpan to soak. She don't mind working up there when Mr. Jergen's not home . . ." Mavity jerked her hand, sloshing coffee on the white sheet.

Grabbing a handful of tissues, she tried to mop up the spill. "I can't get used to it—that he's dead. His throat—the blood . . ."

Wilma took Mavity's cup and wiped the sheets. She handed her more tissues, wiped off the cup, and poured fresh coffee for her. Dulcie rose up from her nest of blankets to rub against Mavity's cheek. Mavity put her arm around the little cat and drew her close.

"Driving back up from the village, I passed Mr. Jergen's car parked three blocks from the apartments, and I thought that was strange. He'd said he was going up the coast. Oh, it was his car, I'd know that Mercedes anywhere, with its two antennas and those fancy hubcaps.

"Well, I thought he must have met his client there and taken their car. Though that did seem odd, that he would park three blocks away. Or maybe he'd had car trouble. I never heard of a Mercedes having car trouble, but I guess they can.

"I parked and hurried in through the patio because Pearl Ann would be waiting for the caulking. Mr. Jergen's windows were open, and I heard him and another man shouting at each other, real angry. It was a strange voice but—something about it seemed familiar.

"And then I heard banging and thuds like furniture being knocked over, and then a gasp. Then silence.

"I ran up the stairs, but I was scared. I was ready to run down again. I listened but I couldn't hear nothing, so I pushed open the door."

She stared into her coffee cup as if seeing a replay of Jergen's murder. When she looked up at Harper, her voice was hardly a whisper.

"He was on the floor. Lying on the floor beside his desk. The blood . . . And Pearl Ann—Pearl Ann kneeling over him stabbing and stabbing . . . Swinging her arm and stabbing into his throat with that terrible ice tray thing."

Mavity sat hugging herself. "I backed away real quiet, out the door. Pulled it closed, praying she didn't hear me, that she hadn't seen me.

"I didn't know where the other man was. I kept looking around for him. I felt weak as jelly. I took off my shoes so she wouldn't hear me going down the steps. I ran down in my socks, to my car. I never stopped for nothing. Kept seeing Pearl Ann kneeling over him stabbing and stabbing . . .

"I dug my keys out of my purse. I was trying to jam the key in the door . . ."

She looked up at Harper. "That's all I remember. Then the red neon sign at night glaring in my eyes, and I was in the backseat lying on my shoes, my face against a dirty shoe. There was a McDonald's wrapper on the floor—it smelled of mustard.

"And then being dragged or something, that's all fuzzy and

dark. Then I was in bed in that hospital and you were there, Captain Harper, sitting slumped in the chair." Mavity pulled the quilt up, careful not to disturb Dulcie.

"When you first entered the apartment," Harper said, "before you went out again for the caulking, do you remember anything strange, at that time, anything out of order in the room?"

"No. The room was neat, the way he keeps it. His desk was clean and neat, nothing on it except a few files lying in a neat pile on the blotter. Well, I guess you could say that was unusual. Mr. Jergen always put everything away, always left his desk with nothing but the blotter and the pens, the regular desk things, no papers."

She frowned. "There's one other thing. I'd forgot. I'm sure his computer was off when I first came in. But when I got back with the caulking and saw—saw . . . Pearl Ann . . . I think the computer was on."

Mavity hugged herself. "He shouldn't have been there at all. He had an appointment up the coast. Maybe he forgot to do something at the computer. Maybe he came back to do that."

She looked hard at Harper. "Why did she kill him? Why did this happen?"

"Besides the files and the computer," Harper said, "was there anything else out of order?"

"Not that I noticed. Seemed the same as always, neat, everything in order. Pearl Ann had started working in the bathroom, but she stopped to get the refrigerator started. The kitchen was neat and clean, the way he always left it."

Harper made some notes and rose. There was a tight, hard look about him. Wilma walked him to the door, where he paused, gave her a hug. "You look tired. She'll get through this, Wilma. If we can pick up Hoke, Mavity should be clear, I think we'll have enough to take him to the grand jury."

"And if you don't find Hoke?"

"Let's wait to see what happens."

Wilma leaned against him, very thankful for Max Harper. She would hate to face this, to try to help Mavity, without Max there to go the extra mile.

He stood looking down at her. "I didn't tell you this. Some of the blood on Mavity's white uniform was Jergen's."

She only looked at him, frightened again suddenly.

"The report came in this morning. But from the way the blood was smeared, the lab thinks it was wiped on, possibly by the murder weapon."

"It wasn't spattered or pooled on."

"Exactly. And we're not sure, yet, that the ice tray divider *was* the murder weapon."

He didn't move out the open door, just kept looking at her. "It would strengthen our case considerably, if I knew who our informant was. If I knew who the woman was, who tipped us about Hoke. It might make the case, if she were to testify against Hoke."

"I'm sure it would," Wilma said. "Maybe she'll come forward. Let's hope so." She hated this, hated lying to him.

"She never has. She's helped us on three cases but has never identified herself, never offered to testify." He continued to watch her. "Same voice, same woman."

Wilma widened her eyes. "You think it's me, Max? Are you saying I'm your mysterious informant?"

"No," Harper said. "I don't think that." He looked at Wilma for a long time, then turned away, heading for his car. Wilma moved to the window, watching the patrol unit slide away into the village, thinking what a tangled web had drawn them all in—and, for Harper, what a cat's cradle of leads and unanswerable questions.

28

GREELEY URZEY'S sour, boozy smell filled Wilma's car thicker than steam in a sauna. Despite the fact that she drove with all the windows down, the stink of secondhand rum and stale sweat made her want to boot the old man out and let him walk to her house—except, of course, he wouldn't. He'd head back for that hovel among his cases of 90 proof.

She *could* have stopped by Mavity's cottage and insisted that he take a bath and change his reeking clothes, but she hadn't wanted to take the time. Mavity was so anxious to see him; Wilma hadn't even waited, as she'd promised herself, for the old man to sober up.

But even as rum-sodden as Greeley was, he seemed genuinely worried about Mavity. He sat leaning forward, staring hard through the windshield as if to hurry the car faster—and clutching the black cat in his lap.

She had to smile at the way he'd slipped the cat in. After the police officer let her into the Davidson Building and saw her safely downstairs again with Greeley in tow, she'd waited alone in the dirty hall for Greeley to go back upstairs and fetch his jacket. She didn't think he'd run out on her—there was no other entry, just the second floor windows. She'd watched, amused, when he returned clutching not only the jacket but the black cat nestled down in the wadded-up leather as if the animal might not be noticed.

Drunk and argumentative, he'd insisted on bringing the beast despite the fact, as she'd pointed out, that Mavity disliked Azrael, and that it was Mavity's comfort they were concerned about here.

Now as she drove across the village, the cat sat possessively on Greeley's lap, a huge black presence which, unlike most cats, made no move to leap out the four open windows. "He'll do as I tell him," Greeley had promised drunkenly, "or he'll know what for."

Well, maybe the cat wasn't as bad as Mavity claimed. Certainly it was a handsome animal; admiring him, Wilma reached gently to stroke his broad black head—and drew her hand back at the blaze of rage that flamed in his slitted orange eyes.

So much for making friends. The animal was as unsocialized as its master.

The cat watched her narrowly as she parked in her drive and killed the engine, its gaze strangely calculating—as eerie as Poe's "The Black Cat" with its chilling stare. *The figure of a gigantic cat . . . I could not rid myself of the phantasm of the cat . . . a large and beautiful animal, entirely black, and sagacious to an astonishing degree . . .*

As she herded Greeley toward her kitchen door, escorting the drunken, smelly old man into her clean house, she felt like she was bringing home a parolee just released from the drunk tank—except that Greeley smelled worse. The instant she opened the door, the cat leaped inside, brushing boldly past their legs with none of the wariness most cats exhibited upon entering unfamiliar rooms.

Immediately he scented Dulcie's cat door and flew at it, sniffing and growling, and before she could stop him he turned his backside and drenched the little door with his testosterone-heavy stink, applying liberally the mark of male dominance and possession.

Shouting, she slapped at him with her purse—and jerked her hand away as he sprang at her, his swift claws raking her arm, leaving long red welts oozing drops of blood.

"You make that cat behave, Greeley. Or you'll put it outside."

Greeley shrugged and offered a helpless grin. Wilma found some peroxide in the emergency cupboard, poured some on a paper towel, and scrubbed the wounds, thinking of rare tropical infections and blood parasites. Snatching a spray bottle from the sink, she poured ammonia into it, to mix with the water. "He claws me again or sprays again, Greeley, he gets a shot of this in the face. He won't like it."

The cat glared. Greeley looked back grinning, amused that she would threaten his tomcat. Giggling, he headed for the dining room, stumbling unsteadily past her.

Before the cat could leap after him, Wilma slid through the door and slammed it in the beast's face.

Making sure the latch clicked, that the door was securely shut, she guided Greeley down the hall toward her bedroom. Ushering him in, she wondered if his boozy, sweaty smell would cling in the room forever. Down the hall behind her, she heard the kitchen door click open.

The cat came swaggering out of the kitchen, giving her a stare as sharp as a stabbing knife and pushed past her into the bedroom.

Mavity was asleep. Greeley leaned over his sister and delivered a peckish kiss, surely scratching stubble across her soft skin. Mavity woke, stared up at him vaguely, and drew away, grimacing at his smell.

Unperturbed, Greeley sat down on the bed beside her, taking her hands in his with a gentleness that surprised Wilma.

"Dora's gone," Greeley slurred. "My little girl's gone. And Ralph gone, and that man you set such store by." Glancing to where the cat was sniffing around the dresser, Greeley whispered, "Death sucked them in. Sucked them all in. Death—death before the moon is full." Strange words for the drunken little man. Leaning down, he put his arms around Mavity, holding her close.

The cat watched, seeming almost amused. And as brother and sister comforted each other, the beast began to prowl, nosing into every inch of the bedroom, turning occasionally to observe

Wilma, his huge topaz eyes as evil, she thought, as twin glimpses into hell.

Annoyed at her own fear, she went to make some coffee.

But, hurrying down the hall, she could feel the tomcat watching her. And when she glanced back, its eyes on her glowed so intently she turned away, shaken.

What was this beast?

Dulcie hadn't told her the nature of this animal.

Fixing a tray with coffee and sugar and cream and some pound cake, she returned quickly. The cat was not in sight. She set the tray on the night table and checked under the dresser and bed, then went to search the house. She didn't like to think of that creature alone with Dulcie.

She didn't find the animal. When she returned to the bedroom, Greeley was crying drunkenly, the tears rolling down his stubbled cheeks.

". . . feeding those chickens when she was only a little girl, and helping her mama to plant the garden—my little girl . . . And that old goose used to chase her! Oh, how she would run," Greeley blubbered. "I killed that goose, killed it . . . But now—I couldn't kill whoever hurt her, couldn't save my little girl. So cold—so cold there in all them lilies . . ."

As Greeley doubled over, weeping, the black cat reappeared and leaped onto the bed. Mavity paled and shrank away from it, looked as if she'd like to hit it. Wilma watched, shocked, as it began to stalk Mavity—and thought of the times Mavity had complained about the beast's dirty habits. Surely, there was no love between them. But now the animal looked dangerous. As he crouched to leap, Wilma grabbed him, tossed him to the floor. The black cat landed heavily and jumped at once to the foot of the bed where it began pawing Greeley's jacket that lay crumpled on the blanket.

Clawing at the wrinkled leather, he slid his paw into a pocket, and with a quick twist, dragged out a black-feathered carcass. Taking this in his mouth, his ears back, his head low, he began to stalk Mavity. She jerked away, gasping, as Wilma snatched the blood-streaked bird.

But it wasn't a bird. The thing was hard under her fingers, not soft and limp like a dead bird. She turned it over, looking.

It was a small wooden man, the black feathers wrapped around him like a cloak and tied with red cord. His face was painted with blood red lines like a primitive warrior. His hair felt like real human hair, the side locks stiff with dried red mud, as if he were made up for some primitive ritual.

"Voodoo doll," Mavity whispered, staring at the six-inch man then at Greeley. "You showed me those, in that shop. Where did you get that? Why would you bring that horrible thing here?"

"Only a plaything," Greeley said, patting Mavity's hand. "*I* didn't bring it. The cat—the cat likes a plaything. The cat found it . . ." He reached up to take the carving from Wilma.

She held it away. "Why did you bring this?"

"*I* didn't bring it! The cat brought it. Damn cat—always dragging in something."

"The *cat* put it in your pocket?"

Greeley shrugged. "He digs in my pockets." He grinned sheepishly. "He likes that Latin American shop. I expect it smells like home."

"I'll take it in the kitchen."

The black cat hadn't taken his eyes from the doll. But now he turned from it, fixed his gaze on Mavity, and crept up the bed again, toward her.

"Get him away!"

Grabbing the cat, Wilma drew back a bloodied hand. "Greeley, get the beast out of here."

"Get down!" Greeley scolded. "Get off the bed!" The cat hissed at him but leaped to the floor.

"And stay off," Greeley added ineffectually.

Wilma turned away, carrying the doll, but the tomcat leaped, grabbing for its grisly toy. She swung it at the cat's head until the beast ran. Mavity hadn't exaggerated—the creature gave her more than chills. When she turned to look back, the cat was not behind her and the hall was empty.

She laid the carving on the kitchen table. More than its ugliness bothered her. It seemed to hold around itself a deep oppression. As she stood studying the doll she glimpsed a shadow behind her, slipping along the floor.

She spun as the cat crouched to leap—whether at her or to snatch the doll she'd never know: At the same instant, an explosion of tabby fur hit him, knocking him sideways.

Dulcie was all over him, slashing and clawing. The black cat fought violently in a tangle of raking claws—but he fought only briefly before breaking away, and careened out through Dulcie's cat door, the empty door slapping behind him.

As quick as that, he was gone. Dulcie leaped to the table, looking twice her normal size, and began to lick blood from her claws. Gently Wilma stroked her.

"What a nasty beast. Are you hurt? Where did he hurt you?"

Dulcie spit out a mouthful of fur. "I'm fine. A few scratches. They'll clean right up." Her gaze fixed on the black-feathered doll. "Voodoo," she hissed. "Did Greeley bring this? That old, disgusting drunk . . . Or did Azrael carry it here?" She glared at Wilma, laying back her ears. "Why did you let Greeley bring that cat here—and with *this?*"

"I didn't know. I was trying to keep Greeley happy. I didn't want him making a scene, so I let him bring the cat. I didn't see this thing. And the cat seemed tame enough, seemed just an ordinary cat."

She looked hard at Dulcie. "But he isn't, is he?"

Dulcie studied Wilma a long time. "No," she said softly, "he's no ordinary cat. But he's not like us, either. He's not like Joe Grey—he's horrid." With an angry swipe, she knocked the feathered man to the floor.

"Azrael believes in these voodoo things," she said, hissing. "He believes in dark magic—he said it was a fine way to get back at those who mistreat you.

"I expect he wanted," Dulcie said softly, "to make Mavity

sicker—just because Mavity doesn't like him, because she complained about his manners."

She fixed her green gaze on Wilma. "Why else would he bring this terrible idol, if not to torment Mavity and frighten her—or try some wild spell on her? Can that stuff work?" she said, shivering, staring down at the black doll lying like a hunk of tar on the blue linoleum. Wilma snatched up the feathered figure and hurried down the hall. Following, Dulcie watched Wilma shove the ugly little idol in Greeley's face.

"What is this about, Greeley? What did you mean to do?"

"It's only a native doll," Greeley said, laughing. "Indian kid's playtoy. The cat brought it."

"Voodoo doll," Wilma replied.

"*Voodoo?*" He looked at her as if she wasn't bright and choked out a rum-laden laugh. "Child's toy. That Ms. Sue Marble, she's got all kinds of stuff—them Guatamala blankets, all that Panama clutter. Nothing of any use, all that artsy stuff. Even them little gold people aren't worth nothing—not the real thing, not the real gold. Gold birds. Gold lizards. Sue showed me." But suddenly his face colored and he looked embarrassed, his eyes shifting away.

"You must have gotten very friendly," Wilma said, amused, forgetting her anger.

"That nice little woman," Greeley said defensively, "wouldn't have nothing costly." He was blushing; he wouldn't look at her. She had to smile at his discomfiture, at his strange embarrassment.

Was he romancing Sue Marble? But why embarrassment? His distress puzzled her, made her uneasy.

Romancing Sue for her money?

Oh, that would be too bad.

Dropping the doll in the wastebasket, she carried the basket out to the kitchen to empty it with the trash, all the time pondering over Greeley—and keeping her ear cocked for the thump of Dulcie's cat door, for the stealthy return of Greeley's nasty little friend.

29

WALKING BACK the cat," Max Harper told Charlie as he popped open a can of beer, "means to lay out the evidence and work backward—reconstruct the crime." The five friends sat around a wrought-iron table in the landscaped patio of the freshly painted apartment building. Moonlight brightened the flower beds, which were softly lit by indirect lamps hidden behind the tall banks of Nile lilies that Wilma had planted as background for lower masses of textured ground cover. The brick paving had been pressure-washed, and it gleamed dull and rich, lending to the patio garden a quiet elegance. The new wrought-iron furniture in a heavy ivy pattern—umbrella table, lounge chairs, and chaises—completed the sense of comfort. Harper looked curiously at Charlie. "Where did you hear that phrase, to walk back the cat?"

"I'm not sure. Something I read, I suppose."

Wilma said, "Isn't that a CIA term?"

"I read that in a romance-mystery," Mavity offered. "That's the way it was used, when the CIA was wrapping up a case." The little woman seemed completely recovered. Her memory had returned fully—she had recalled clearly the events surrounding Winthrop Jergen's murder and, once she came to grips with the truth about

Jergen, she had been stoic and sensible, her idolization of the financier had turned to anger but then to a quiet resolve. Now she had put all her faith in Max Harper, to recover her savings.

But the fact that Dora and Ralph had come to Molena Point not only to trap Cumming but to keep Mavity from losing her money had hurt Mavity deeply—that Dora had died trying to help her.

Mavity was dressed, tonight, not in her usual worn white uniform but in a new, teal blue pants suit, a bargain that Wilma had found for her. The color became her, and the change of wardrobe, along with her returned health, seemed perhaps the mark of a new beginning.

Of the little group, only Max Harper, stretching out his long, Levi-clad legs and sipping his beer, seemed aware of Charlie's unease. He watched the young woman with interest. She was strung tight, seemed unable to keep her bony hands still, sat smoothing and smoothing her cotton skirt. As he considered the possible cause of her distress, and as he went over in his mind the last details of the Sleuder and Jergen case, while paying attention to the conversation around him, he was aware, as well, of the two cats crouched on the brick paving near the table—uncomfortably aware.

The two animals seemed totally preoccupied with eating fish and chips from a paper plate, yet they were so alert, ears following every voice, the tips of their tails twitching and pausing as if they were attending closely to every word. When he'd mentioned "walk back the cat," both cats' ears had swiveled toward him, and Dulcie's tail had jerked once, violently, before she stilled it.

He knew his preoccupation with the cats was paranoid—it was these crazy ideas about cats that made him question his own mental condition. Of course the two animals had simply responded to the word *cat,* they were familiar with the word from hearing it in relation to their own comfort. *Time to feed the cat. Have to let the cat out.* A simple Pavlovian reaction common to all animals.

Yet he watched them intently.

His gut feeling was that their quick attention was far more than conditioned response.

The cats didn't glance up at him. They seemed totally unaware of his intense scrutiny, as unheeding as any beast.

Except that beasts were not unheeding.

A dog or horse, if you stared at him, would generally look back at you. To stare at an animal was to threaten, and so of course it would look back. One of the rules in dealing with a vicious dog was never to stare at him. And cats hated to be watched. Certainly, with the cats' wide peripheral vision, these two were perfectly aware of his interest—yet they never glanced his way. Seemed deliberately to ignore him.

No one at the table noticed his preoccupation. Charlie and Clyde, Wilma and Mavity were deep into rehashing the reception they had just left.

They had come up directly from the library party, to enjoy a take-out supper in the newly completed patio and to continue the celebration—an affiar that had left Harper irritated yet greatly amused. A reception for a cat. A bash in honor of Wilma's library cat. That had to be a first—in Molena Point, and maybe for any public library.

The party, besides honoring Dulcie, had quietly celebrated as well the departure of Freda Brackett. The ex–head librarian had left Molena Point two days earlier, headed for L.A. and a higher paying position in a library which, presumably, would never tolerate a resident cat. A library, Harper thought, that certainly didn't embody the wit or originality—or enthusiasm—to be found in their own village institution.

He didn't much care for cats. But Molena Point's impassioned rally to save Dulcie's position—gaining the wholehearted support of almost the entire village—had been contagious even to a hard-assed old cop.

Dulcie ate her fish and chips slowly, half of her attention uncomfortably aware of Harper's scrutiny, the other half lost in the wonders of her reception. She had held court on a library reading table where she had secretly spent so many happy hours, had sat atop the table like royalty on a peach-toned silk cushion given to her by the Aronson Gallery. And as she was fawned over—as Joe admired her from atop the book stacks—Danny McCoy from the Molena Point *Gazette* had taken dozens of pictures: Dulcie with her guests, Dulcie with members of the city council and with the mayor, with all her good friends.

Danny had brought the local TV camera crew, too, so that highlights of the event would appear on the eleven o'clock news. Young Dillon Thurwell had cut the cake, which George Jolly himself had baked and decorated with a dark tabby cat standing over an open book, a rendering far more meaningful than Mr. Jolly or most of those present would ever imagine. Perhaps best of all, Charlie had donated a portrait of her to hang in the library's main reading room, above a scrapbook that would contain all forty signed petitions and any forthcoming press clippings.

Not even the famous Morris, who must have press people available at the twitch of a whisker, could have been more honored. She felt as pampered as an Egyptian cat-priestess presiding over the temples of Ur—she was filled to her ears with well-being and goodwill, so happy she could not stop purring.

Not only had the party turned her dizzy with pleasure, not only was Freda Brackett forever departed from Molena Point, but Troy Hoke was in jail for Jergen's murder and for the attempted murder of Mavity. And soon, if Max Harper was successful, Mavity would have her stolen money.

Life, Dulcie thought, was good.

Licking her whiskers, she listened with interest as Max Harper walked back the cat, lining up the events that had put Hoke behind bars awaiting trial for the murder of Warren Cumming.

Hoke had not been indicted for the murder of Dora and Ralph Sleuder. That crime, Harper speculated (and the cats agreed), would turn out to have been committed by Cumming himself—but Warren Cumming alias Winthrop Jergen need no longer worry about earthly punishment. If he was to face atonement, it would be meted out by a far more vigorous authority than the local courts.

A plastic bag containing morphine had been found in Jergen's apartment, taped inside the computer monitor, affixed to the plastic case.

"It's possible," Harper said, "that Hoke killed the Sleuders, and taped the drug there after he killed Jergen, to tie the Sleuders' murder to him. But so far we have no evidence of that, no prints, no trace of Hoke on the bag or inside the computer."

"But what about Bernine?" Charlie said. "Bernine had dinner with Dora and Ralph."

"That was the night before," Harper reminded her. "The night Dora and Ralph received the lethal dose, they had dinner at Lupe's Steaks, down on Shoreline—one of the private booths. Not likely they would know about those on their own. And despite Jergen's entry through the back door . . ." Harper laughed. ". . . wearing that pitiful football blazer and cap, one of the waiters knew him."

Harper shook his head. "The man might have been creative with the numbers, but he didn't know much about disguise.

"And Bernine Sage has an excellent alibi for the night of the Sleuders' deaths. She was out with a member of the city council. She was," he said, winking at Wilma, "trying to work a deal to destroy the petitions the committee had collected for Dulcie."

"The library cat petitions?" Wilma laughed. "That was pretty silly. Didn't she know we'd have done them over again?"

In the shadows, the cats smiled, but at once they shuttered their eyes again, as if dozing.

Their private opinion was that though Bernine had an alibi for the night the Sleuders were killed, she had been instrumental in their deaths. If she had not pumped the Sleuders for information, then reported to Jergen that the couple meant to blow the whistle on him, Jergen/Cumming would likely not have bothered to kill them.

"I can't believe," Charlie said, "that I worked with Pearl Ann for three months and didn't guess she was a man. That makes me feel really stupid."

"None of us guessed," Clyde said. "Hoke put together a good act. I swear he walked like a woman—guys notice that stuff. And that soft voice—really sexy."

They all stared at him. Clyde shrugged. Charlie patted his hand.

"A guy in drag," Harper said, "slight of build, thin arms, slim hands—a skilled forger and a top-flight computer hacker."

Hoke, dressed as Pearl Ann, had been picked up in Seattle carrying eight hundred thousand dollars in cash, sewn into the lining of his powder blue skirt and blazer—money he had transferred from Jergen's accounts to his own accounts in two dozen different names in nine San Francisco banks. It had taken him some time to draw out the money in various forms—cash, bank drafts, cashier's checks, which he laundered as he traveled from San Francisco to Seattle, where he was picked up. The police had found no witness that Pearl Ann had boarded the San Francisco bus in Molena Point. But they located the car Hoke had rented in Salinas, under the name of William Skeel, after deliberately wrecking Mavity's VW and dumping Mavity in the alley beside the pawnshop.

"It looks," Harper said, "as if Jergen had come to suspect Pearl Ann's identity. As if, the day he died, he had set Hoke up.

"He told everyone he was going up the coast, then doubled back hoping to catch Hoke red-handed copying his files. He parked a few blocks away and slipped into the apartment while Hoke/Pearl Ann was working. The hard files he'd left on his desk were bait—three files of accounts newly opened, with large deposits. All with bogus addresses and names that, so far, we've not been able to trace."

Harper sipped his beer. "Hoke comes up to do the repairs, opens those hard copy files with three new accounts, all with large sums deposited, and he can't wait to get into the computer. Sends Mavity on an errand, uses Jergen's code, intending to get the new deposit numbers and transfer the money. We're guessing that he was about ready to skip, perhaps another few days and he meant to pull out for good.

"But then Jergen walks in on him at the computer. They fight, Hoke stabs him with a screwdriver . . ." Harper looked around at his audience. "Yes, we found the real murder weapon," he said gruffly. "Jergen was near death when Hoke stabbed him with the ice tray divider—maybe to lay suspicion on Mavity, to confuse forensics. Or maybe out of rage, simply to tear at Jergen. This is all conjecture, now, but it's how I piece it together.

"He hears a noise, realizes Mavity has returned, maybe hears her running down the stairs. Goes after her, snatches up one of those loose bricks that were lying along the edge of the patio." He glanced at Mavity. "And he bops you, Mavity, as you're trying to get in the car.

"After he loads you in the backseat, he realizes he has the bloody screwdriver. Maybe he'd shoved it in his pocket. He buries it down the hill, with the brick.

"He may have moved the VW then, to get it out of sight. He cleans up and changes clothes, then heads out. Takes his bloody jumpsuit and shoes with him—all we found in the duffle he left was a clean, unused jumpsuit. We may never find the bloody clothes. They're probably in the bottom of some Dumpster or already dozed into a landfill—the Salinas PD checked the Dumpsters in that whole area around where Hoke wrecked Mavity's car.

"It's still dark when he dumps Mavity into the alley by her car and leaves her. He walks to the nearest car rental office, waits until eight when it opens. Gets a car and heads north. He's left his own car in the storage garage a block from the Davidson Building where he kept it—registered in one of his other names.

"We'd like to find the bloody clothes, but even without them we have plenty to take him to court. The money trail alone is a beauty."

The FBI computer expert who had come down from San Francisco to trace Cumming's computer transactions had followed Hoke's transfers from Jergen's accounts, using the code words supplied by Harper's anonymous informer. The Bureau had put out inter-office descriptions of Hoke and of Pearl Ann. Two Bureau agents picked him up at the Seattle airport, in his blue skirt and blazer, when he turned in an Avis rental in the name of Patsy Arlie. He was wearing a curly auburn wig.

"But the strangest part," Harper continued, watching the little group, "is my finding the screwdriver the way I did, the day after Jergen was killed."

He had discovered it the next morning when he came down the stairs from Jergen's apartment after meeting with the Bureau agent. He had been late getting back from Salinas Medical that morning; the agent, using a key supplied by Clyde, was already at work at Jergen's computer. The weapon was not on the steps when he went up to the apartment, nor did Harper see it when he arrived.

But when they came down, it was lying in plain sight on the steps, flecked with dirt and grass seed.

"When we started looking for where it might have been buried—worked down the hill where the grass was bent and broken and found the loose dirt—and dug there, we found the brick, too. The dirt and grass matched the debris on the screwdriver, and of course the traces of blood on it were Jergen's.

"It had been wiped hastily, but there were two partial prints, both Hoke's. Whoever found the weapon," Harper said, "saved the court considerable time and money, and certainly helped to strengthen our case."

He knew he should be fully satisfied with the case against Hoke—they had plenty to hang the man—but this business of the screwdriver, of evidence turning up in that peculiar way, gave him heartburn. This was getting to be a pattern, and one he didn't live with easily.

No cop liked this mysterious stuff, even when the evidence led to a conviction. Unexplainable scenarios were for artists, for fiction writers, for those who dealt in flights of fancy. Not for law enforcement who wanted only hard facts.

* * *

The cats, having finished their fish and chips, lay stretched out on the bricks sleepily licking their paws, staring past Harper but watching with their wide vision Harper's frequent glances in their direction. Dulcie, washing diligently, carefully hid her amused smile. Joe, rolling over away from the police captain, twitched his whiskers in a silent cat laugh.

The morning after the murder, just moments after Wilma deposited an angry Dulcie at Clyde's house and Wilma and Clyde and Charlie headed for Salinas Medical, Joe and Dulcie had bolted out his cat door and doubled-timed up the hills to the apartments, where they settled down to wait for the FBI investigator. How often did one have a chance to observe a Bureau specialist at work?

Crouching in Jergen's kitchen, they had watched the thin Bureau agent deftly scrolling through Jergen's files using the code words *Cairo* and *Tiger* that Dulcie had given to Harper, tracing each money transaction that Hoke/Pearl Ann had hidden. Only when they heard the crackle of a police radio, and a car door slam, did they slip back down between the walls, trotting into the patio in time to see Harper going up the stairs.

Leaving the patio, wandering down the hill to hunt, they had caught Pearl Ann's jasmine scent and followed it with interest through the tall grass. The trail was fresh, maybe a few hours old, the grass still sharp-scented where it had been trampled.

Where they found the earth disturbed, Pearl Ann's scent was strong. Digging into the loose soil, they had pawed out the screwdriver, then the brick. The brick smelled of human blood. They recognized the screwdriver as Pearl Ann's, a long Phillips with a deep nick in the black plastic handle. Gripping the dirt-crusted handle carefully in his teeth, Joe had carried the weapon up the hill and halfway up the stairs, where he laid it on a step in plain sight. They figured, as thorough as Harper was, he'd search for where it had been buried and discover the brick, as well.

But as for the village burglaries committed by Greeley and

Azrael, those crimes were another matter. Joe and Dulcie had given Harper no clue.

Maybe Greeley would confess and return the stolen money. If not, the cats still had plenty of time to nail him—Greeley and Mavity would be leaving early in the morning to take the bodies of Dora and Ralph home to Georgia. The funeral had been arranged through the Sleuders' pastor. Dora and Ralph had been active in their church and would be buried in the church plot they had purchased years before.

Mavity and Greeley would remain in Georgia long enough to sell the Sleuders' home and belongings, reserving whatever mementos they cared to keep. Whatever moneys of the Sleuders' might be recovered from Warren Cumming's hidden accounts would be divided between brother and sister. The moneys proven to be Mavity's would of course come to her, once the FBI accountants finished tracing each of Jergen's individual account transactions and Hoke's transfers.

The cats watched Charlie take the lid off a plastic cup of hot tea, handing it to Mavity. "Will Greeley be taking his cat with you on the plane? It seems . . ."

"Oh, no," Mavity said. "He doesn't need to take it. He'll come back with me when we're finished in Georgia—he can get the cat then. He's flying on one of them elderly coupons, so his fare's all the same even if he goes home through Molena Point. And a very nice lady, that Ms. Marble who has the South American shop, she's going to keep the cat. Why, she was thrilled. Seems she's very taken with the beast."

Dulcie and Joe exchanged a look.

"I didn't think," Charlie said, "that your brother knew anyone in the village."

"Greeley went in there because the cat kept going in, made itself right at home. They got to know each other, being as they've both lived in Latin America. It's nice Greeley has found a friend here. Well, she does keep those awful voodoo things . . ."

Mavity stirred sugar into her tea. "I'm sorry Greeley wouldn't come with us tonight. Said he just wanted to walk through the village, enjoy the shops one more time. I've never known Greeley to be so taken with a place."

The cats, imagining Greeley gazing casually into one of the village's exclusive shops while Azrael slipped down through its skylight, rose quickly and, feigning a stretch and a yawn, they beat it out of the patio and across the street, heading fast down the hill.

Watching them, Charlie rose, too, and slipped away.

Standing under the arch, she saw them disappear down the slope, watched their invisible trail shivering the grass as they hurried unseen toward the village.

They had certainly left suddenly.

But they were cats. Cats were filled with sudden whims.

Except, she didn't think their hasty departure was any whim.

From somewhere below she heard faint voices. The girl's laugh sounded exactly like the female voice she'd heard the night she watched Joe and Dulcie on the rooftops.

She shook her head, annoyed at her wild imaginings. Molena Point was a small village, one was bound to hear familiar voices—probably from one of the houses below her.

But she felt chilled, light-headed.

Hugging herself to steady her shaken nerves, she was gripped by an insight that, until this moment, she would not have let herself consider.

An insane thought.

But she knew it wasn't insane.

A footstep scuffed behind her, and Clyde stepped out from the shadows. He put his arm around her, stood hugging her close, the two of them looking down the hills. After a moment, she turned in the moonlight to look squarely at him.

She wanted to say, *I've suspected for a long time.* She wanted to say, *I know about the cats. I didn't know how to think about such a thing.*

But what if she was wrong?

Leaning her head against his shoulder, she felt giddy, disconnected. She recalled the night she'd walked home from dinner and saw Joe and Dulcie racing across the roofs so beautiful and free—the night she heard those same voices.

And suddenly she began to laugh. She collapsed against Clyde laughing, tears streaming. What if she was right, what if it was true? She couldn't stop laughing, he had to shake her to make her stop. Holding her shoulders, he looked down at her intently. He said nothing.

After a while, as they stood gazing down the empty hill, he said, "Were you really jealous of Bernine?"

"Who told you that?"

"A friend." He took her face in his hands. "So foolish—Bernine Sage is all glitz. There's nothing there, nothing real. She's nothing like you. What's to be jealous of?" He kissed her, standing on the moonlit hill, and whispered against her neck, "My friend tells me I'm not romantic enough—that it takes more than a few car repairs to an old VW van to please a lady."

Charlie smiled and kissed him back. It was a long time later when she said, "Doesn't your friend know how to mind her own business?"

"Oh, meddling is her business. That's how she gets her kicks." He held her tight.

Down the hills, not as far away as Charlie and Clyde imagined, the cats stood rearing among the tall grass, looking up the hill and watching the couple's hugging silhouette, and they smiled. Humans—so simple. So predictable.

Then Joe dropped down to all fours. "So what will it be? We find Greeley and blow the whistle on those two thieves—and maybe open a real can of worms for Harper? Or we find them, try to talk them out of this one last burglary?"

"Or we let it go?" Dulcie offered. "Let this hand play without us?" She went silent, thinking of dark Azrael: Satan metamorphosed. Beast of evil.

Portender of death? Was he really that—really a voodoo cat? A bearer of dark, twisted fate?

"When we charged out of the patio just now," Joe said, "hot to nail Greeley—that was a paw-jerk reaction." He waited to see the effect of his words, his eyes huge and dark in the moonlight.

She said, "I don't think we can stop them. Why would Greeley listen to us? And if we call the station . . ."

If Greeley was arrested and went to jail, and Azrael stayed on with Sue Marble, they might never see the last of his criminal proclivity, of his cruel nature.

She studied the village rooftops, the moonlit mosaic of shops and chimneys and oaks, so rich and peaceful. And she thought of Azrael moving in with Ms. Marble and all her voodoo trappings, and she wondered. *Was* there, unknown to Sue, evil power among those idols? A wickedness that Azrael could manipulate?

Joe said, "Greeley's all that Mavity has. It would break her heart to see him arrested."

"Maybe they'll go back to the jungle," she said, "if we let them go. If we don't interfere. Maybe they'll go where they belong—back to the jungle's dark ways."

Joe considered this. "Maybe," he said, and twitched a whisker. "And good riddance to *el gato diablo*." He looked down at Dulcie, and winked. And where moonlight washed the tall grass, their silhouettes twined together: one silhouette, purring.